Constitutional Law
Cases and Other Problems

LITTLE, BROWN AND COMPANY

Law Book Division

Editorial Advisory Board

A. James Casner, CHAIRMAN
Austin Wakeman Scott Professor of Law, Harvard University

Francis A. Allen
Edson R. Sunderland Professor of Law, University of Michigan

Clark Byse
Byrne Professor of Administrative Law, Harvard University

Thomas Ehrlich
*Professor of Law, Stanford University (on leave),
President, Legal Services Corporation*

Geoffrey C. Hazard, Jr.
John A. Garver Professor of Law, Yale University

Frank C. Newman
*Jackson H. Ralston Professor of International Law,
University of California at Berkeley*

Willis L. M. Reese
Charles Evans Hughes Professor of Law and Director, Parker School of Foreign and Comparative Law, Columbia University

Bernard Wolfman
Fessenden Professor of Law, Harvard University

Constitutional Law *Fourth Edition*
Cases and Other Problems

Paul A. Freund
Arthur E. Sutherland
Mark DeWolfe Howe
Ernest J. Brown

Little, Brown and Company *Boston and Toronto 1977*

Copyright © 1952, 1961 by Paul A. Freund, Arthur E. Sutherland, Mark DeWolfe Howe, and Ernest J. Brown.
Copyright © 1967 by Paul A. Freund, Arthur E. Sutherland, Mary M. Howe, Executrix of the Estate of Mark DeWolfe Howe, and Ernest J. Brown.
Copyright © 1977 by Paul A. Freund, Mary K. Sutherland, Mary M. Howe, Executrix of the Estate of Mark DeWolfe Howe, and Ernest J. Brown.
All rights reserved. No part of this book may be reproduced in any form or by any electronic or mechanical means including information storage and retrieval systems without permission in writing from the publisher, except by a reviewer who may quote brief passages in a review.

Library of Congress Catalog Card No. 76-54026

Fourth Edition

Second Printing

*Published simultaneously in Canada
by Little, Brown & Company (Canada) Limited*

PRINTED IN THE UNITED STATES OF AMERICA

Summary of Contents

Preface, xxiii
Preface to First Edition, xxv
Acknowledgments, xxix
Members of the Supreme Court of the United States, xxxi
Biographical Notes on Supreme Court Justices, xxxv
The Constitution of the United States, li

Part One. JUDICIAL REVIEW, 1

Chapter One. Historic Basis, 3
Chapter Two. Present Statutory Basis, 37
Chapter Three. Judicial Review in Operation, 49

Part Two. PROBLEMS OF FEDERALISM, 147

Chapter Four. Basic Issues of Federalism, 149
Chapter Five. National and State Power: The Early Struggle Toward Standards, 155
Chapter Six. Powers over Transportation, 207
Chapter Seven. National Power over the Economy, 225
Chapter Eight. The States in a Federal Union, 339
Chapter Nine. Methods of Cooperation and Accommodation, 603
Chapter Ten. Intergovernmental Immunities, 621
Chapter Eleven. Distribution of National Powers, 649
Chapter Twelve. The Constitution Overseas, 709

Part Three. SAFEGUARDS OF LIBERTY AND PROPERTY, 727

Chapter Thirteen. Acquisition and Deprivation of Nationality and Citizenship, 729
Chapter Fourteen. Privileges and Immunities, Equality, and Civil Rights, 753
Chapter Fifteen. Constitutional Requirements of Fair Procedure, 993

Chapter Sixteen. Constitutional Safeguards of Substantive Rights, 1077
Chapter Seventeen. Retroactivity, 1387

Table of Cases, 1403
Index, 1413

Contents

Preface, xxiii
Preface to First Edition, xxv
Acknowledgments, xxix
Members of the Supreme Court of the United States, xxxi
Biographical Notes on Supreme Court Justices, xxxv
The Constitution of the United States, li

Part One. JUDICIAL REVIEW, 1

Chapter One. HISTORIC BASIS, 3

    Marbury v. Madison, 3
    Eakin v. Raub, 10
    Cooper v. Aaron, 13
    Jefferson, Letter to Mrs. John Adams, 13
    Madison, Report on the Virginia Resolutions, 14
    Jackson, Veto of Bank Bill, 14
    Lincoln, First Inaugural Address, 15
    Curtis, Argument on Behalf of President Johnson in Impeachment Proceedings, 15
    Note: Foundations of Judicial Review, 16
    Note: Acts of Congress Held Unconstitutional, 18
    Martin v. Hunter's Lessee, 20
    House Report No. 43, 21st Cong., 2d Sess. (1831), 26
    Fletcher v. Peck, 28
    Note: Federal Common Law, 33
    Note: The Uses and Standards of Judicial Review, 33

Chapter Two. PRESENT STATUTORY BASIS, 37

    United States Code, Title 28 (Excerpts), 37
    Note: Jurisdiction of the Federal Courts in Constitutional Cases, 40

Note: Supreme Court Review of State Court Decisions: The Adequate State Ground Doctrine, 41
Henry v. Mississippi, 44
Note: The Aftermath of Henry v. Mississippi, 47

Chapter Three. JUDICIAL REVIEW IN OPERATION, 49
A. Introduction: Limitations on Judicial Power, 49
   Muskrat v. United States, 49
   United States v. Johnson, 54
   Baker v. Carr, 56
B. Justiciability: The Nature of the Question Presented, 71
   Powell v. McCormack, 71
   United States v. Sisson, 80
   Note, 84
   Note: "Political" Questions, 84
   Note: Mootness and Prematurity, 85
C. Standing: The Nature of the Complainant's Interest, 87
   Oral Argument in Ashwander v. Tennessee Valley Authority, 87
   Ashwander v. Tennessee Valley Authority, 91
   Freund, The Supreme Court of the United States, 99
   Massachusetts v. Mellon; Frothingham v. Mellon, 103
   Note: Standing of States to Sue in Federal Court, 107
   Doremus v. Board of Education, 108
   Flast v. Cohen, 111
   Note: Standing, 118
   Adler v. Board of Education, 122
   Note: Sovereign Immunity and Constitutional Litigation, 128
D. Further Issues in the Operation of Judicial Review, 132
   Status of District of Columbia Minimum Wage Law (Opinion of the Attorney General), 132
   Note: Effect of an Unconstitutional Statute and Prospective Overruling, 133
   Note: Methods and Materials of Constitutional Decision, 134
E. The Power of Congress to Limit the Jurisdiction of the Federal Courts, 136
   Sheldon v. Sill, 136
   Note: Legislation Governing Jurisdiction, 137
   Ex parte McCardle, 141
   Note: The Appellate Jurisdiction of the Supreme Court, 142

Part Two. PROBLEMS OF FEDERALISM, 147

Chapter Four. BASIC ISSUES OF FEDERALISM, 149
Dicey, Law of the Constitution, 149
Laski, The Obsolescence of Federalism, 150
Pound, Law and Federal Government, 151
Acton, Freedom in Antiquity, 151
Wechsler, The Political Safeguards of Federalism, 151
Freund, Foundations and Development of American Federalism, 153

Chapter Five. **NATIONAL AND STATE POWER: THE EARLY STRUGGLE TOWARD STANDARDS, 155**
    McCulloch v. Maryland, 155
    Note, 162
    Livingston v. Van Ingen, 163
    Gibbons v. Ogden, 164
    Note, 174
    Willson v. Black Bird Creek Marsh Co., 174
    Note, 175
    Cooley v. Board of Wardens of the Port of Philadelphia, 175
    Pennsylvania v. Wheeling & Belmont Bridge Co. (13 How. 518), 178
    Pennsylvania v. Wheeling & Belmont Bridge Co. (18 How. 421), 184
    Brown v. Maryland, 185
    Woodruff v. Parham, 188
    Brown v. Houston, 191
    Michelin Tire Corp. v. Wages, 192
    Leisy v. Hardin, 197
    Note: Developments in the Original-Package Doctrine, 200
    In re Rahrer, 200
    McDermott v. Wisconsin, 202

Chapter Six. **POWERS OVER TRANSPORTATION, 207**
    The Daniel Ball, 207
    Note, 209
    Wabash, St. Louis & Pacific Ry. v. Illinois, 210
    Minnesota Rate Cases, 213
    Houston, East & West Texas Ry. v. United States (The Shreveport Case), 214
    Note, 217
    Richard Olney, Attorney General, Memorandum Concerning the Pullman Strike, 1894, 218
    In re Debs, 220

Chapter Seven. **NATIONAL POWER OVER THE ECONOMY, 225**
  A. Trade, Production, and Employment, 225
    United States v. E. C. Knight Co., 225
    Addyston Pipe & Steel Co. v. United States, 227
    Northern Securities Co. v. United States, 227
    Swift & Co. v. United States, 228
    Stafford v. Wallace, 228
    Note, 229
    Lottery Case (Champion v. Ames), 230
    Hammer v. Dagenhart, 233
    Child Labor Tax Case (Bailey v. Drexel Furniture Co.), 237
    Note: Motives in Tax Legislation, 240
    Schechter Poultry Corp. v. United States, 242
    Note, 242
    Carter v. Carter Coal Co., 243
    Note, 252

United States v. Butler, 253
Note: Aftermath of the Butler Case, 259
Note: The Constitutional Crisis and the Court Reorganization Plan of 1937, 260
Steward Machine Co. v. Davis, 262
Note, 272
NLRB v. Jones & Laughlin Steel Corp., 273
United States v. Darby, 281
Oklahoma Press Publishing Co. v. Walling, 286
United States v. Five Gambling Devices, 286
National League of Cities v. Usery, 286
Note, 293
Wickard v. Filburn, 293
Note: Expansion of the Commerce Power and Problems of Statutory Coverage, 297
Note: Federal Price and Rent Control, 300
Heart of Atlanta Motel v. United States, 300
Katzenbach v. McClung, 304
Note: Daniel v. Paul, 308
Note: Commerce and Crime, 309
B. Money and Banking, 309
Note: Legal Tender Cases, 309
Norman v. Baltimore & Ohio R.R., 310
Perry v. United States, 317
Goldenweiser, American Monetary Policy, 322
Note, 324
Hopkins Federal Savings & Loan Assn. v. Cleary, 324
Note, 326
C. Water Resources and Government Property, 326
Ashwander v. Tennessee Valley Authority, 326
Note: Federal Development of Water Resources, 331
Note: Admiralty Jurisdiction, 334
D. Economic Regulation Under the War Powers, 334
Chastleton Corp. v. Sinclair, 334
Woods v. Miller Co., 336

Chapter Eight. **THE STATES IN A FEDERAL UNION, 339**
A. Movement of Persons, 339
Articles of Confederation, Article IV, 339
Crandall v. Nevada, 339
Edwards v. California, 341
Note, 345
Shapiro v. Thompson, 346
Note: State Durational Residency Requirements After Shapiro v. Thompson, 351
B. Protection of the Local Economy and Welfare, 352
1. State Restrictions on Marketing of Extrastate Goods, 352
Welton v. Missouri, 352

Robbins v. Shelby County Taxing District, 354
Wagner v. City of Covington, 357
Best & Co. v. Maxwell, 358
Note, 358
Memphis Steam Laundry Cleaner, Inc. v. Stone, 359
Note, 361
Minnesota v. Barber, 362
Brimmer v. Rebman, 365
Reymann Brewing Co. v. Brister, 365
Mintz v. Baldwin, 366
Taylor, Burtis, and Waugh, Barriers to Internal Trade in Farm Products, 367
Dean Milk Co. v. City of Madison, 367
Gallagher v. Lynn, 372
Breard v. Alexandria, 373
State Board v. Young's Market Co., 378
Department of Revenue v. James B. Beam Distilling Co., 380
Baldwin v. G. A. F. Seelig, Inc., 381
Henneford v. Silas Mason Co., 385

2. State Restrictions on Access to Local Products or Raw Materials, 388
   Milk Control Board v. Eisenberg Farm Products, 388
   Note, 390
   Pennsylvania v. West Virginia, 390
   Geer v. Connecticut, 396
   Hudson Water Co. v. McCarter, 397
   Sligh v. Kirkwood, 397
   Foster-Fountain Packing Co. v. Haydel, 398
   Clason v. Indiana, 400
   Note, 400
   Hood & Sons, Inc. v. Du Mond, 401

3. State Regulation of Interstate Transportation and Sales, 407
   Buck v. Kuykendall, 407
   Bradley v. Public Utilities Commission, 408
   Mayor of Vidalia v. McNeely, 410
   Wabash, St. Louis & Pacific Ry. v. Illinois, 411
   Note, 411
   Note: Regulation of Natural Gas, 411
   South Carolina State Highway Dept. v. Barnwell Bros., 412
   Southern Pacific Co. v. Arizona, 418
   Bibb v. Navajo Freight Lines, 426
   Hall v. De Cuir, 427
   Morgan v. Virginia, 429
   Bob-Lo Excursion Co. v. Michigan, 432
   McCarroll v. Dixie Greyhound Lines, 434
   Duckworth v. Arkansas, 438

4. Jurisdiction to Regulate, 441
   Osborn v. Ozlin, 441
   State Board of Insurance v. Todd Shipyards Corp., 444
   Connecticut Mutual Life Ins. Co. v. Moore, 448

xii **Contents**

        Note, 451
        Western Union Tel. Co. v. Pennsylvania, 451
        Note, 455
   C. Effects of Federal Action, 456
        New York Central R.R. v. Winfield, 457
        Maurer v. Hamilton, 465
        Castle v. Hayes Freight Lines, Inc., 467
        Huron Portland Cement Co. v. Detroit, 468
        Pennsylvania v. Nelson, 473
        Note: Federal Preemption, 478
   D. State Taxation, 479
     1. State Fixed-Fee License Taxes, 482
        Robbins v. Shelby County Taxing District, 482
        Browning v. Waycross, 482
        York Manufacturing Co. v. Colley, 485
        Note, 487
     2. Admeasured License or Franchise Taxes, 489
        Maine v. Grand Trunk Ry., 489
        Horn Silver Mining Co. v. New York, 492
        Western Union Telegraph Co. v. Kansas, 493
        Note: Unconstitutional Conditions, 497
        Ford Motor Co. v. Beauchamp, 497
     3. Property Taxes, 499
        Pullman's Palace Car Co. v. Pennsylvania, 499
        Union Tank Line Co. v. Wright, 503
        Note: State Jurisdiction to Tax Property, 504
        Standard Oil Co. v. Peck, 506
        Braniff Airways, Inc. v. Nebraska State Bd. of Equalization and Assessment, 508
        Central R.R. v. Pennsylvania, 513
        Note, 518
        Minnesota v. Blasius, 519
        Empresa Siderurgica v. County of Merced, 522
        Joy Oil Co., Ltd. v. State Tax Commission, 522
     4. Taxes on Transportation, 523
        Case of the State Freight Tax, 523
        State Tax on Railway Gross Receipts, 525
        Note, 528
        Illinois Central R.R. v. Minnesota, 528
        Note: State Taxation of Fuel Used in Interstate Commerce, 531
        Joseph v. Carter & Weekes Stevedoring Co., 531
        Railway Express Agency v. Virginia, 534
     5. Other Specific Excise Taxes, 538
        Heisler v. Thomas Colliery Co., 538
        Note, 540
        Western Live Stock v. Bureau of Revenue, 540
     6. Net Income Taxes, 544
        Crew Levick Co. v. Pennsylvania, 544
        United States Glue Co. v. Town of Oak Creek, 545

Contents xiii

    Atlantic Coast Line R.R. v. Daughton, 548
    Underwood Typewriter Co. v. Chamberlain, 549
    Note, 551
    Spector Motor Service, Inc. v. O'Connor, 552
    Northwestern States Portland Cement Co. v. Minnesota, 555
    Public Law No. 86-272, 560
    Note: State Jurisdiction to Tax Income and Estates, 562
 7. Sales, Use, and Gross Receipts Taxes, and Responsibility for the Collection Thereof, 564
    Banker Bros. Co. v. Pennsylvania, 564
    Henneford v. Silas Mason Co., 565
    McGoldrick v. Berwind-White Coal Mining Co., 565
    Note, 572
    Nelson v. Sears, Roebuck & Co., 572
    McLeod v. Dilworth Co., 574
    General Trading Co. v. State Tax Commission, 576
    International Harvester Co. v. Department of Treasury, 578
    Freeman v. Hewit, 583
    Note, 587
    French Versus German Steel, 587
    Norton Co. v. Department of Revenue, 588
    Note, 591
    Scripto, Inc. v. Carson, 591
    General Motors Corp. v. Washington, 593
    Note: Use Tax on Mail-Order Business, 601
    Note, 602

Chapter Nine. **METHODS OF COOPERATION AND ACCOMMODATION, 603**
    Clark Distilling Co. v. Western Maryland Ry., 603
    Note: Cooperation by "Adoption" of Laws, 606
    Steward Machine Co. v. Davis, 607
    Note: Fiscal Cooperation, 607
    West Virginia v. Sims, 608
    Note: Cooperation in Adjudication, 612
    Testa v. Katt, 613
    Note, 615
    Radio Station WOW v. Johnson, 616

Chapter Ten. **INTERGOVERNMENTAL IMMUNITIES, 621**
 A. Taxation, 621
    McCulloch v. Maryland, 621
    Collector v. Day, 621
    Note: Tides in the Doctrine of Tax Immunity, 623
    James v. Dravo Contracting Co., 623
    Note: Taxation of Government Contractors, 629
    Helvering v. Gerhardt, 630
    Note, 634
    City of Detroit v. Murray Corp., 635

xiv   Contents

        New York v. United States, 637
        Note: Taxation of Government Bonds, 641
  B. Non-Tax Immunities, 643
        Ohio v. Thomas, 643
        Johnson v. Maryland, 644
        James Stewart & Co. v. Sadrakula, 645
        Note: "Reciprocity" of Immunities, 647

Chapter Eleven. **DISTRIBUTION OF NATIONAL POWERS, 649**
  A. Separation of Powers, 649
    1. The General Doctrine, 649
        Madison, The Federalist No. 47, 650
        Frankfurter & Landis, Power of Congress over Procedure in Criminal Contempts in "Inferior" Federal Courts — A Study in Separation of Powers, 652
        Myers v. United States (Brandeis dissent), 653
    2. Separation of Congressional and Executive Powers, 653
        Note: The Delegation Doctrine, 653
        Note: Congressional Participation in Executive Functions, 658
        Youngstown Sheet & Tube Co. v. Sawyer, 659
        Note: The Steel Seizure Case, 668
    3. Some Areas of Dispute Between Congress and the Executive, 668
      a. The Pardoning Power, 668
      b. Control of Executive Personnel, 669
      c. Impoundment of Funds and the Pocket Veto, 671
        Note: Impoundment, 671
        Note: The Pocket Veto, 672
  B. The Autonomy of the Executive and Legislative Branches, 673
    1. Immunity from Liability, 673
        Barr v. Matteo, 673
    2. The Legislative Branch, 677
      a. Control of Membership, 677
      b. Bills of Attainder and Ex Post Facto Laws, 677
      c. The Contempt Power, 677
        Note: Congressional Power to Punish Contempts, 677
    3. The Executive Branch: Executive Privilege, 679
        United States v. Nixon, 679
        Note: Judicial versus Legislative Inquiry, 690
  C. International Relations, 690
        Note: Origins and Development of the Treaty Power, 690
        Note: Effect of Self-executing Treaties on State Law, 692
        Note: The Treaty Power and Constitutional Guarantees, 693
        Note: The Effect, on a Treaty, of a Subsequent Act of Congress, 694
        Missouri v. Holland, 695
        United States v. Curtiss-Wright Export Corp., 697
        United States v. Pink, 700
        Note: Proposed Constitutional Amendments to Restrict International Agreements, 705
        Note: Power of the President to Commit Military Forces to Action, 706

Chapter Twelve. **THE CONSTITUTION OVERSEAS, 709**
    In re Ross, 709
    Note, 711
    Downes v. Bidwell, 712
    Note: Incorporation of Territory, 714
    Best v. United States, 714
    In re Yamashita, 715
    Hirota v. MacArthur, 716
    Johnson v. Eisentrager, 719
    Note, 725

Part Three. **SAFEGUARDS OF LIBERTY AND PROPERTY, 727**

Chapter Thirteen. **ACQUISITION AND DEPRIVATION OF NATIONALITY AND CITIZENSHIP, 729**
  A. Acquisition of Nationality and Citizenship, 728
    Dred Scott v. Sandford, 728
    United States v. Wong Kim Ark, 734
    Hammerstein v. Lyne, 738
    Cook v. Tait, 738
    Note: Problems of Naturalization, 738
  B. Voluntary Renunciation of Nationality, 739
    Jefferson, Letter to Gallatin (1806), 739
    Note: What Constitutes Voluntary Renunciation, 740
    Afroyim v. Rusk, 741
    Rogers v. Bellei, 742
  C. Revocation of Naturalization, 743
    Note, 743
  D. Deportation, 746
    Harisiades v. Shaughnessy, 746
    Note: Developments in Deportation and Passport Matters, 749

Chapter Fourteen. **PRIVILEGES AND IMMUNITIES, EQUALITY, AND CIVIL RIGHTS, 753**
  A. Historical Note, 753
  B. Citizenship in a Federal Union, 754
    Corfield v. Coryell, 754
    Note, 755
    Crandall v. Nevada, 757
  C. Slavery and Federalism, 757
    Prigg v. Pennsylvania, 757
    Note, 759
    Problem Case (Kentucky v. Dennison), 760
    Dred Scott v. Sanford, 760
  D. Civil War Amendments and Civil Rights Statutes: The Search for Standards, 760
    Slaughter-House Cases, 763
    United States v. Hall, 771

xvi Contents

    Note, 772
    United States v. Cruikshank, 772
    Ex parte Virginia, 774
    Note, 777
    Civil Rights Cases, 777
  E. Secured Rights and State Action, 788
    Logan v. United States, 788
    Report on the Bisbee Deportations (1917), 790
    Note, 793
    Brewer v. Hoxie School District No. 46, 793
    Marsh v. Alabama, 797
    Lloyd Corp. v. Tanner, 801
    Note: Picketing at Shopping Centers, 807
    Shelley v. Kraemer, 808
    Note: Scope of Shelley v. Kraemer, 813
    Black v. Cutter Laboratories, 813
    Jones v. Alfred H. Mayer Co., 814
    Note: Implications of Jones v. Mayer, 822
    Burton v. Wilmington Parking Authority, 823
    Note: Economic Regulation and "State Action", 828
    Evans v. Newton, 832
    Note:Failure of Discriminatory Trust, 835
    Note: Government Assistance to Private Segregated Institutions, 835
    Reitman v. Mulkey, 837
    Note: The UCC and State Action, 840
    Note: Sequels to Reitman v. Mulkey, 841
  F. Liability under the Civil Rights Statutes, 841
    Screws v. United States, 841
    Williams v. United States, 850
    United States v. Guest, 851
    Note: Scope of Guest Case, 857
    Hague v. CIO, 857
    Note: The Uses of Section 1983, 859
    Note: Official and Sovereign Immunity, 862
    Griffin v. Breckenridge, 864
    Note: Section 1985(3), 866
    Bivens v. Six Unknown Named Agents of Federal Bureau of Narcotics, 867
    Note: Implying Liability for Unconstitutional Federal Action, 869
  G. Equal Protection of the Laws, 869
   1. Historical Themes, 869
    Yick Wo v. Hopkins, 869
    Note, 871
    Note: Equal Protection as a Limit on Administrative Discretion, 872
    Skinner v. Oklahoma, 872
    Note: Severability and Equal Protection, 876
    Kotch v. Board of River Port Pilot Commrs., 876
    Goesaert v. Cleary, 877
    Railway Express Agency v. New York, 879

Contents   xvii

2. Racial Discrimination, 881
   Plessy v. Ferguson, 881
   Missouri ex rel. Gaines v. Canada, 884
   Sweatt v. Painter, 885
   McLaurin v. Oklahoma State Regents, 886
   Brown v. Board of Education (1954), 887
   Bolling v. Sharpe, 890
   Brown v. Board of Education (1955), 891
   Note: The Aftermath of Brown, 892
   Griffin v. Prince Edward County School Board, 893
   Note: Further Developments in Southern School Desegregation, 897
   Note: Desegregation of Schools in the North, 899
   Washington v. Davis, 901
3. Congressional Enforcement and Reverse Discrimination, 902
   Katzenbach v. Morgan, 902
   Note: "Reverse Discrimination", 906
4. Suspect Classifications and Fundamental Rights, 907
   Griffin v. Illinois, 907
   Note: Indigence and Inequality, 909
   Shapiro v. Thompson, 912
   Dandridge v. Williams, 912
   Note: "Two-Tier" Equal Protection, 914
   San Antonio Indep. School Dist. v. Rodriguez, 916
   Note: Municipal Services and Equal Protection, 922
   In re Griffiths, 923
   Note: Aliens and Equal Protection, 926
   Note: Other Suspect Classifications: Illegitimacy, 926
   Frontiero v. Richardson, 930
   Note: Classification Based on Sex, 934
   Note: Discrimination by Age and by Social Grouping, 938
5. Alternative Approaches: "Irrebuttable Presumptions", 939
   U.S. Dept. of Agriculture v. Murry, 939
   Note: Questioning the "Irrebuttable Presumption" Doctrine, 941
   Weinberger v. Salfi, 942

H. The Suffrage, 943
   Ex parte Yarbrough, 943
   United States v. Classic, 945
   United States v. Saylor, 948
   Smith v. Allwright, 948
   Note, 953
   Gomillion v. Lightfoot, 953
   Baker v. Carr, 956
   The Cases of the State Legislatures, 956
   Alabama: Reynolds v. Sims, 956
   Colorado: Lucas v. Forty-fourth General Assembly, 962
   Note: The Unit Count and Contingency Elections, 970
   Note: Developments in Reapportionment, 971
   South Carolina v. Katzenbach, 974

xviii   Contents

　　　　　　Note: Section 5 of the Voting Rights Act, 980
　　　　　　Harper v. Virginia Board of Elections, 981
　　　　　　Note: Property Qualifications for Voting in Special-Purpose Units of Government, 984
　　　　　　Note: Restrictions on Ballot Access, 985
　　　　　　Oregon v. Mitchell, 987

Chapter Fifteen. CONSTITUTIONAL REQUIREMENTS OF FAIR PROCEDURE, 993

A. The Bill of Rights and the Meaning of Procedural Due Process, 993
　　　Note: Due Process in Substance and Procedure (Adamson v. California), 993
　　　Rochin v. California, 999
　　　Note: Poe v. Ullman, 1004
B. Applications of Due Process in a Federal System, 1006
　1. Freedom from Unreasonable Searches and Seizures, 1006
　　　Wolf v. Colorado, 1006
　　　Mapp v. Ohio, 1008
　　　United States v. Calandra, 1010
　2. Freedom from Compulsory Self-Incrimination, 1012
　　　Malloy v. Hogan, 1012
　　　Lefkowtiz v. Turley, 1015
　　　Note: Compelled Testimony and the Fifth Amendment, 1017
　3. Right to the Assistance of Counsel, 1018
　　　Gideon v. Wainwright, 1018
　　　Note: Right to Counsel, 1020
　　　Escobedo v. Illinois, 1021
　　　Miranda v. Arizona, 1024
　　　Johnson and Cassidy v. New Jersey, 1032
　　　Note: Retreat from Miranda, 1034
　4. Right to Jury Trial, 1035
　　　Duncan v. Louisiana, 1035
　　　Apodaca v. Oregon, 1038
　　　Note: Identity of State and Federal Rights, 1040
C. Procedural Due Process in Noncriminal Settings, 1041
　　　Board of Regents v. Roth, 1041
　　　Note: "Liberty" and "Property" under Due Process, 1044
　　　Note: What Process Is Due?, 1046
D. The Constitution and Military Tribunals, 1048
　　　Ex parte Merryman, 1048
　　　Ex parte Milligan, 1050
　　　Ex parte Quirin, 1054
　　　Duncan v. Kahanamoku, 1061
　　　Reid v. Covert, 1069
　　　Note: Trials of Servicemen in the Courts of the Nation Overseas in Which They Are Stationed, 1073
　　　Note: Military Trials of Dependents of Servicemen Stationed Overseas for Noncapital Crimes, and Military Trials of Civil Employees of the Armed Forces Stationed Overseas in Peacetime, 1073

Note: The Function of Civilian Courts in Review of Military Convictions, 1074
Note: "Miranda Rules" and Military Justice, 1075

Chapter Sixteen. CONSTITUTIONAL SAFEGUARDS OF SUBSTANTIVE RIGHTS, 1077

A. Property: Its Regulation and Its Taking, 1077
  1. Regulations of Business Activity, 1077
      Introductory Note, 1077
      Note: Corporations as "Persons", 1078
      Munn v. Illinois, 1078
      Note, 1082
      Holden v. Hardy, 1083
      Lochner v. New York, 1083
      Note, 1088
      Nebbia v. New York, 1089
      West Coast Hotel Co. v. Parrish, 1091
      Note, 1094
  2. "Taking" and Compensation, 1095
      Introductory Note, 1095
      Miller v. Schoene, 1095
      United States v. Causby, 1097
      United States v. Central Eureka Mining Co., 1100
      Note, 1102
      United States v. Fuller, 1103
  3. Zoning, 1105
      Village of Euclid v. Ambler Realty Co., 1105
      Village of Belle Terre v. Boraas, 1109
      Note: Developments in Zoning, 1111
B. The New "Liberty", 1112
      Griswold v. Connecticut, 1112
      Note, 1119
      Roe v. Wade, 1119
      Note: Reaction to Roe, 1125
      Note: The Developing Right of Privacy, 1126
C. Freedom of Speech and Association, 1130
  1. The Search for Standards, 1130
      Introductory Note, 1130
      Schenck v. United States, 1131
      Abrams v. United States, 1133
      Gitlow v. New York, 1134
      Note: The Learned Hand Alternative to the Clear and Present Danger Test, 1137
      Masses Pub. Co. v. Patten, 1137
      Whitney v. California, 1140
      Freund, The Great Disorder of Speech, 1144
      Near v. Minnesota, 1146
      New York Times Co. v. United States; United States v. Washington Post Co., 1149

Note: Marchetti v. United States, 1157
2. "Outdoors" Speech, 1158
   a. "Subversive" Advocacy, 1158
      Chafee, Free Speech in the United States, 1158
      Dennis v. United States, 1162
      Yates v. United States, 1170
      Note, 1172
      Brandenburg v. Ohio, 1173
      Note: Developments under the Brandenburg Test, 1175
   b. The Public Forum, 1175
      Thornhill v. Alabama, 1175
      Note, 1179
      Cantwell v. Connecticut, 1179
      Note: The Licensing of the Use of the Public Forum, 1183
      Kovacs v. Cooper, 1184
      Public Utilities Comm. v. Pollack, 1189
      Feiner v. New York, 1189
      Note, 1192
      Cox v. Louisiana, 1192
      Adderly v. Florida, 1199
      Note: The "Public Forum", 1203
      Police Dept. of Chicago v. Mosley, 1203
      Note, 1205
   c. Symbolic Speech, 1205
      United States v. O'Brien, 1205
      Tinker v. Des Moines Indep. Community School Dist., 1207
      Note: Flag Desecration, 1209
3. Defamation and Invasion of Privacy, 1210
      Beauharnais v. Illinois, 1210
      Note, 1215
      New York Times Co. v. Sullivan, 1215
      Note: Developments in Defamation, 1222
      Gertz v. Robert Welch, Inc., 1223
      Note, 1228
      Note: Invasion of Privacy and the First Amendment, 1228
4. Freedom of Association, 1230
      New York ex rel. Bryant v. Zimmerman, 1230
      De Jonge v. Oregon, 1232
      NAACP v. Alabama, 1235
      Note, 1239
      International Assn. of Machinists v. Street, 1239
      NAACP v. Button, 1241
      Note: Constitutional Status of Certain Associations, 1246
5. Access to and by the Media, 1247
   a. Access to the Media, 1247
      Red Lion Broadcasting Co. v. FCC, 1247
      Note: The Newspaper Analogy, 1251
   b. Political and Commercial Advertising, 1252
      Note: Political Advertising, 1252

Bigelow v. Virginia, 1254
Note: Commercial Advertising, 1257
  c. Access by the Media, 1257
Note: A Claimed Right of Access to Information, 1257
Note: The Freedom of Information Act, 1259
6. Political Campaigns, 1260
United Public Workers v. Mitchell, 1260
Note, 1264
Buckley v. Valeo, 1265
Note, 1283
7. Obscenity, 1283
Joseph Burstyn, Inc. v. Wilson, 1283
Kingsley Intl. Pictures Corp. v. Regents of New York, 1284
Roth v. United States; Alberts v. California, 1285
Note, 1290
Freedman v. Maryland, 1291
"Memoirs" v. Massachusetts, 1291
Ginzburg v. United States, 1293
Ginsberg v. New York, 1295
Note: Developments in Obscenity, 1298
Miller v. California, 1300
Paris Adult Theatre I v. Slaton, 1302
Note: Developments under Miller, 1304
8. Freedom of the Press and Criminal Justice, 1305
Sheppard v. Maxwell, 1305
Note: Free Press and Fair Trial, 1308
Branzburg v. Hayes, 1310
Note, 1314
9. Requirements of Disclosure and Disclaimer, 1315
  a. Legislative Investigation, 1315
Historical Note, 1315
Barenblatt v. United States, 1317
Gibson v. Florida Legislative Investigation Comm., 1322
Tenney v. Brandhove, 1325
Note: Developments in Legislative Immunity, 1330
  b. Loyalty Oaths and Related Tests, 1330
United States v. Lovett, 1330
Garner v. Board of Public Works, 1334
Flemming v. Nestor, 1337
United States v. Brown, 1338
Note: United States v. Robel, 1339
Keyishian v. Board of Regents, 1339
Note: Loyalty Oaths and Inquiries, 1343
D. Religion, 1344
Cantwell v. Connecticut, 1345
West Virginia State Board of Education v. Barnette, 1345
Everson v. Board of Education, 1350
Note, 1358
Zorach v. Clauson, 1359

Note, 1363
Note: Sunday Closing Laws, 1363
Sherbert v. Verner, 1367
Note: Developments in Religious Exemptions, 1370
School District of Abington v. Schempp; Murray v. Curlett, 1370
Note: Reactions and References, 1375
DeSpain v. DeKalb County Community School District, 1375
Epperson v. Arkansas, 1376
Note, 1380
Lemon v. Kurtzman; Early v. DiCenso, 1380
Note: Further Issues in Public Aid to Church-Related Schools, 1385

Chapter Seventeen. RETROACTIVITY, 1387
Introductory Note, 1387
Home Building & Loan Assn. v. Blaisdell, 1387
Note: Results of Blaisdell, 1393
Norman v. Baltimore & Ohio R.R., 1393
Perry v. United States, 1393
Faitoute Iron & Steel Co. v. City of Asbury Park, 1394
Addison v. Huron Stevedoring Corp., 1395
Note: Retroactive and Prospective Judicial Decisions, 1400

Table of Cases, 1403
Index, 1413

Preface

The general structure of the casebook has been retained in this fourth edition, but a number of significant changes have been made. A chapter on separation of powers has been added; the materials on equal protection and on freedom of speech and press have been cast in a more analytical framework; the issues of justiciability and standing, whose demise proved to be premature, have been fleshed out; and annotations and queries have been expanded throughout.

This expansion, together with the inclusion of recent decisions, has obviously required some countervailing compression, the more so in order to accommodate the materials in one volume. Partly this has been accomplished through changes in format, partly through a more rigorous editing of opinions, and partly through a substantial reduction in the coverage of the guarantees of criminal procedure. The latter topic, which is dealt with in courses on criminal law, has been retained insofar as it raises problems of federalism.

This edition, like its predecessors, is intended to give the instructor some latitude in coverage and arrangement. Judicial opinions remain the central focus. For the most part, cases are reproduced with sufficient fullness to give the reasoning and flavor of the opinions. The editorial notes and questions, it is hoped, will be facilitative and not coercive in setting directions of thought for the reader and the instructor. To be more specific: the philosophical premises of constitutional law and of judicial review in its various contexts are undergoing thoughtful and imaginative study. To perceive relationships of this deeper kind between superficially disparate phenomena, to seek the universal in the particular, is the special genius of the creative mind. It is hoped that the copious materials in this volume, concerned as they are with some basic issues of authority and autonomy, will stimulate, without unduly confining, this kind of reflection. In the house of scholars, too, there are many mansions.

In preparing this edition I have had the valuable assistance of Lawrence D. Bragg III, Peter Kirby, and William L. Pardee.

P.A.F.

Preface to First Edition

To prepare a casebook in constitutional law is, of course, an impossible task. No single volume could provide the materials requisite for an understanding of the subject; for such an understanding embraces a knowledge of our constitutional development, a critical judgment on problems of statecraft, and the faculty of legislative resourcefulness in planning within the constitutional framework. What Chief Justice Hughes said of Mr. Justice Brandeis — that he was master of both telescope and microscope — could describe the aim of legal education generally, but surely in special measure it marks the objective of a study of constitutional law. All of this was expressed by James Bradley Thayer in the Preface to his pioneering casebook in this subject: "For, while this is a body of *law*, — of law in a strict sense, as distinguished from constitutional history, politics, or literature, since it deals with the principles and rules which courts apply in deciding litigated cases; and while, therefore, it is an exact and technical subject; yet it has that quality which Phillipps, the writer on Evidence, alluded to when he said, in speaking of the State Trials, that 'The study of the law is ennobled by an alliance with history.' The study of Constitutional Law is allied not merely with history, but with statecraft, and with the political problems of our great and complex national life."

In speaking of the prepared mind of a judge in constitutional issues, Learned Hand described by implication the task of teacher and student: "I venture to believe that it is as important to a judge called upon to pass on a question of constitutional law, to have at least a bowing acquaintance with Acton and Maitland, with Thucydides, Gibbon and Carlyle, with Homer, Dante, Shakespeare and Milton, with Machiavelli, Montaigne and Rabelais, with Plato, Bacon, Hume and Kant, as with the books which have been specifically written on the subject. For in such matters everything turns upon the spirit in which he approaches the questions before him. The words he must construe are empty vessels into which he can pour nearly anything he will. Men do not gather figs of thistles, nor supple institutions from judges whose outlook is limited by parish or class. They must be aware that there are before them more than verbal problems; more than final solutions cast in generalizations of universal applicability. They must be aware of the changing social tensions in every society which make it an organism; which demand new schemata of adaptation; which will disrupt it, if rigidly confined."[a] If a casebook is a pathetically inadequate source of this essential wisdom, there may be reassurance for its compilers in the reflec-

---

[a] L. Hand, Sources of Tolerance, 79 U. of Pa. L. Rev. 1, 12 (1930), reprinted in The Spirit of Liberty 66, 81 (Dilliard ed. 1952).

tion that neither teacher nor student comes to the study of constitutional law devoid of relevant learning and outlook, and that neither of them will be content to be *homo unius libri*.

In the selection and editing of materials certain modest, yet we think important, aims have been kept in view. Noteworthy decisions of the Supreme Court on constitutional law are not merely data, they are events — legal, political, and (though here opinions will vary) literary. We have tried to preserve the flavor of the cases as cases, through full statements of facts and procedures, and as Great Debates, through generous reprintings of opinions, whether of the Court or of brethren in disagreement. We have tried, as a related object, to provide as full a gallery as possible of the members of the Court, through representative opinions. Exercising restraint lest discussion be robbed of spontaneity, we have sought nevertheless to frame provocative questions for reflection. Obviously certain offsetting economies have had to be made. Several topics have been omitted, which are treated in courses such as Procedure, Administrative Law, and Conflict of Laws. Among these topics are Jurisdiction of Courts, Separation and Delegation of Powers, and Full Faith and Credit. Moreover, on occasion the device has been used of printing only the facts of a case as reported; this practice has been employed particularly in the sections on state powers in the federal system, where in special degree the complexity of factual variations gives meaning and challenge to general principles, and where the judgments are often more significant than the talk. Further economy has been achieved by forbearing to compose footnotes dangling with cumulative citations, and annotations jangling with small change of constitutional law.

The resultant of the pressures of inclusion and exclusion is confessedly a large casebook. In this respect, at least, the present work resembles two pioneering predecessors, for Thayer's casebook in 1895 comprised 2400 pages and Hall's, in 1913, 1400 pages, followed by a supplement of 400 pages in 1926. In the succeeding period neither the subject nor the flow of opinion-writing has shrunk perceptibly. Those who use this book will cope with the problem of length in one or more ways: by omission or selective treatment of certain topics, as for example those relating to criminal procedure, which may be dealt with in Criminal Law; by regarding certain cases as background for others which are singled out for closer discussion; and by varying the pace to fit the nature of the material. In a subject as many-faceted as constitutional law it has seemed desirable to allow for differing interests and emphases.

The organization of the materials is largely self-explanatory. The four major Parts represent the large clusters of problems that face a constitutional lawyer today. Within these groupings we have tried to avoid an arrangement by clauses of the Constitution, preferring a more pragmatic organization. It will be seen that the fundamental arrangement is topical rather than historical. We have thought that, on balance, the topical arrangement is advisable on the score of interest and relevance for the professional student. The presentation of the subject primarily as a series of problems rather than of episodes should facilitate the development of what was earlier called the legislative faculty. Above all, the topical arrangement reflects a conviction that present-day students (doubtless differing from their predecessors of a generation ago) have greater need to be reminded that constitutional issues may yield to objective analysis and resolution than to be reinforced in the impression that the subject is an undisciplined expression of personalities. Of course neither the topical nor the historical element has exclusive title to validity, and both must find a place in presenting the subject. Ideally, perhaps, the course should be taught twice to each group of students, once historically and once topically — in emulation of the progressive-school teacher who boasted that she had taught American history twice, once in sand and once in clay. Ours has been something of a compromise: while the basic arrangement is by topics or problems, the early struggles with each of these are presented historically, as germinal forces. At a number of points we have tried to provide a focus by presenting statutes, actual or proposed, for scrutiny in the light of the materials studied.

To acknowledge that we owe a special intellectual debt to Thomas Reed Powell is simply to say that we are teachers of constitutional law. The references to his writings throughout this book are testimony to his influence; we would simply record here with gratitude the more intimate illumination of his teaching and friendship.

In the preparation of the manuscript we have enjoyed the careful and devoted assistance of Miss Jean Ryan, Mrs. Gloria W. Zoll, Mrs. Anne B. Jay, Miss Elizabeth June Roberts, and Mrs. Florence Littlefield.

THE EDITORS

Harvard Law School
May, 1954

Acknowledgments

Grateful acknowledgment is made to the following publishers for permission to reprint excerpts from the sources indicated: The New American Library, Inc.: Freund, The Supreme Court of the United States (1961); University of Chicago Press: Federalism and the New Nations of Africa (Currie ed. 1964); The New Republic: Laski, The Obsolescence of Federalism (May 3, 1939); McGraw-Hill Co.: Goldenweiser, American Monetary Policy (1951); Columbia Law Review: Wechsler, The Court and the Constitution, 65 Colum. L. Rev. 1005 (1965); The Economist: French versus German Steel (May 2, 1953); Harvard University Press: Wechsler, Principles, Politics, and Fundamental Law (1961); Chafee, Free Speech in the United States (1941).

P.A.F.

Harvard Law School
April, 1977

Members of the Supreme Court of the United States

Dates of Service and Source of Appointments

Chief Justices

John Jay (1789-1795)	Washington
John Rutledge (1795)	Washington
Oliver Ellsworth (1796-1800)	Washington
John Marshall (1801-1835)	Adams, John
Roger B. Taney (1836-1864)	Jackson
Salmon P. Chase (1864-1873)	Lincoln
Morrison R. Waite (1874-1888)	Grant
Melville W. Fuller (1888-1910)	Cleveland
Edward D. White (1910-1921)	Taft
William H. Taft (1921-1930)	Harding
Charles E. Hughes (1930-1941)	Hoover
Harlan F. Stone (1941-1946)	Roosevelt, F. D.
Fred M. Vinson (1946-1953)	Truman
Earl Warren (1953-1969)	Eisenhower
Warren E. Burger (1969-)	Nixon

Associate Justices

John Rutledge (1789-1791)	Washington
William Cushing (1789-1810)	Washington
James Wilson (1789-1798)	Washington
John Blair (1789-1796)	Washington
James Iredell (1790-1799)	Washington
Thomas Johnson (1791-1793)	Washington
William Paterson (1793-1806)	Washington
Samuel Chase (1796-1811)	Washington
Bushrod Washington (1798-1829)	Adams, John
Alfred Moore (1799-1804)	Adams, John

xxxii Members of the Supreme Court

William Johnson (1804-1834)	Jefferson
Brockholst Livingston (1806-1823)	Jefferson
Thomas Todd (1807-1826)	Jefferson
Gabriel Duval (1811-1835)	Madison
Joseph Story (1811-1845)	Madison
Smith Thompson (1823-1843)	Monroe
Robert Trimble (1826-1828)	Adams, J. Q.
John McLean (1829-1861)	Jackson
Henry Baldwin (1830-1844)	Jackson
James M. Wayne (1835-1867)	Jackson
Philip P. Barbour (1836-1841)	Jackson
John Catron (1837-1865)	Van Buren
John McKinley (1837-1852)	Van Buren
Peter V. Daniel (1841-1860)	Van Buren
Samuel Nelson (1845-1872)	Tyler
Levi Woodbury (1845-1851)	Polk
Robert C. Grier (1846-1870)	Polk
Benjamin R. Curtis (1851-1857)	Fillmore
John A. Campbell (1853-1861)	Pierce
Nathan Clifford (1858-1881)	Buchanan
Noah H. Swayne (1862-1881)	Lincoln
Samuel F. Miller (1862-1890)	Lincoln
David Davis (1862-1877)	Lincoln
Stephen J. Field (1863-1897)	Lincoln
William Strong (1870-1880)	Grant
Joseph P. Bradley (1870-1892)	Grant
Ward Hunt (1872-1882)	Grant
John M. Harlan (1877-1911)	Hayes
William B. Woods (1880-1887)	Hayes
Stanley Matthews (1881-1889)	Garfield
Horace Gray (1881-1902)	Arthur
Samuel Blatchford (1882-1893)	Arthur
Lucius Q. C. Lamar (1888-1893)	Cleveland
David J. Brewer (1889-1910)	Harrison
Henry B. Brown (1890-1906)	Harrison
George Shiras (1892-1903)	Harrison
Howell E. Jackson (1893-1895)	Harrison
Edward D. White (1894-1910)	Cleveland
Rufus W. Peckham (1895-1909)	Cleveland
Joseph McKenna (1898-1925)	McKinley
Oliver W. Holmes (1902-1932)	Roosevelt, T.
William R. Day (1903-1922)	Roosevelt, T.
William H. Moody (1906-1910)	Roosevelt, T.
Horace H. Lurton (1909-1914)	Taft
Charles E. Hughes (1910-1916)	Taft
Willis Van Devanter (1910-1937)	Taft
Joseph R. Lamar (1910-1916)	Taft
Mahlon Pitney (1912-1922)	Taft
James C. McReynolds (1914-1941)	Wilson
Louis D. Brandeis (1916-1939)	Wilson
John H. Clarke (1916-1922)	Wilson
George Sutherland (1922-1938)	Harding
Pierce Butler (1922-1939)	Harding

Members of the Supreme Court   xxxiii

Edward T. Sanford (1923-1930)	Harding
Harlan F. Stone (1925-1941)	Coolidge
Owen J. Roberts (1930-1945)	Hoover
Benjamin N. Cardozo (1932-1938)	Hoover
Hugo L. Black (1937-1971)	Roosevelt, F. D.
Stanley F. Reed (1938-1957)	Roosevelt, F. D.
Felix Frankfurter (1939-1962)	Roosevelt, F. D.
William O. Douglas (1939-1975)	Roosevelt, F. D.
Frank Murphy (1940-1949)	Roosevelt, F. D.
James F. Byrnes (1941-1942)	Roosevelt, F. D.
Robert H. Jackson (1941-1954)	Roosevelt, F. D.
Wiley B. Rutledge (1943-1949)	Roosevelt, F. D.
Harold H. Burton (1945-1958)	Truman
Tom C. Clark (1949-1967)	Truman
Sherman Minton (1949-1956)	Truman
John M. Harlan (1955-1971)	Eisenhower
William J. Brennan (1956-)	Eisenhower
Charles J. Whittaker (1957-1962)	Eisenhower
Potter Stewart (1958-	Eisenhower
Byron R. White (1962-)	Kennedy
Arthur J. Goldberg (1962-1965)	Kennedy
Abe Fortas (1965-1969)	Johnson
Thurgood Marshall (1967-)	Johnson
Harry A. Blackmun (1970-)	Nixon
Lewis F. Powell, Jr. (1971-)	Nixon
William H. Rehnquist (1971-)	Nixon
John Paul Stevens (1975-)	Ford

Biographical Notes on Supreme Court Justices

The materials in this casebook consist principally of opinions delivered by members of the Supreme Court of the United States. These opinions express not only the conclusions of the Court but the beliefs of its members. It seemed, therefore, that students should be given the opportunity, within the covers of this book, to see individual Justices with a perspective which is not easily achieved through scattered glimpses of their minds. In these biographical notes, accordingly, the Editors have sought to indicate the personal qualities which certain Justices possessed and to put opinions which are included in the casebook into the larger context which other opinions provide. By no means all the Justices whose opinions are reprinted appear in the notes. Those on whom biographical notes are presented have been selected for inclusion partly for the frequency with which their opinions appear in the casebook, and partly for the special importance which they have in the history of the Court. No Justice now living has been included.

Where opinions are mentioned in these notes, those which are not followed by a citation are printed or excerpted in the text and may be located by reference to the Table of Cases.

Hugo L. Black (1886-1971). On the rejection of President Roosevelt's Court plan in 1937, Justice Van Devanter retired, giving the President his first opportunity to appoint a member of the Supreme Court. He chose then-Senator Black of Alabama, who had been identified with the progressive wing of his party and was a supporter of the plan to enlarge the Court. The propensity of a majority of the "old" Court to read their own social and economic views into the Constitution was abhorrent to Hugo Black, as it was to Felix Frankfurter. But while Frankfurter's antidote for judicial excesses was the strict observance of jurisdictional and procedural limits on judicial power, and deference to legislative judgment, Black's response was that the Court should confine itself to the literal enforcement of constitutional guarantees, but within the confines of that literalism should exercise intensive review of legislative and administrative action.

Thus while Justice Black was commonly described by admirers and critics alike as an "activist" judge, he disavowed that characterization. He believed that literally unqualified guarantees, such as freedom of speech and press, must be taken as absolutes, without ifs, buts, or whereases (Beauharnais v. Illinois) (dissent). Faithful to his philosophy, where the terms of the Constitution contained no guarantee, as in the case of privacy, he protested against the judicial creation of such a right (Griswold v. Connecticut) (dissent). He had a Benthamist repugnance for "natural law," save as its precepts were enshrined in the Bill of Rights. Although he repudiated the idea that the meaning of the Constitution changed, he could be resourceful in interpretation, as when he found congressional malapportionment to be violative of the provision that the House of Representatives shall be elected by "the people." (Wesberry v. Sanders.) And the absolutism of his view of the First Amendment was made viable by an acknowledgment that there might be regulation of the time, place, and manner of speech, as distinguished from its content (Adderley v. Florida).

A devoted Jeffersonian, his firm and coherent philosophy, his sharp intelligence, and his powers of argumentation and exposition, made him one of the most influential figures in the history of the Court.

Joseph P. Bradley *(1813-1892).* The Court to which Mr. Justice Bradley came, on Grant's nomination in 1870, was sorely in need of those qualities which the new appointee possessed. Familiar, as a New Jersey practitioner, with railroad and corporate affairs, he was a lawyer of extensive learning whose balanced intelligence brought experience and logic into effective partnership. His judgments were not predetermined by political or economic theory, or by past professional associations. They were the response of a vigorous mind to the pressing needs of an expansive society. The precision of his literary style bespoke the quality of his intelligence. Insofar as national authority over the interstate movement of goods was concerned, he accepted the necessity of Congressional power (Baltimore & Ohio R.R. v. Maryland, 21 Wall. 456 (1875)). Recognizing that this necessity might curtail the authority of the states (Brown v. Houston; Coe v. Errol) and restrict the local taxing power (Robbins v. Shelby County Taxing District), he saw that the facts of economic and political history had made it clear that "in the matter of interstate commerce the United States are but one country." In his interpretations of the Civil War amendments Bradley sought to preserve some vitality in their provisions and, showing greater foresight than his colleague Field, found in the flexibility of the due process clause the source of that vitality (dissent in the Slaughter-House Cases). He was fearful, however, that judicial exuberance might make the clause a repressive barrier to state power (concurrence in Munn v. Illinois). See Fairman, What Makes a Great Justice? Mr. Justice Bradley and the Supreme Court, 1870-1892, 30 B.U.L. Rev. 49 (1950).

Louis Dembitz Brandeis *(1856-1941).* A native Kentuckian, Brandeis practiced law for forty years in Boston, where in addition to a highly successful conventional practice he undertook the representation of interests which had not generally enjoyed such formidable advocacy — the interests of consumers, investors, insurance policyholders, and workingmen. His nomination to the Court by Wilson in 1916 encountered desperate opposition, including a protest by seven ex-presidents of the American Bar Association. They might have recognized then, as they came to acknowledge later, that redoubtable as he was in advocacy, Brandeis's mind was essentially detached and constructive, his temperament singularly judicial. As a lawyer he had pressed on his employer clients the merits of the union shop and regularized employment, he had urged upon labor unions the unpopular cause of "scientific management," and he had disappointed the partisans of railroad shippers by giving partial approval, as special counsel for the ICC, to a claim by the carriers for an increase in freight rates. Despite — or perhaps because of — his immersion in large affairs at the bar, he believed profoundly that the span of human understanding is very limited; that judgment is at best fallible; and that mastery of the facts is a precondition of any reliable decision. These beliefs gave coherence to his judicial work and underlie his philosophy in such diverse areas of constitutional law as justiciability, federalism, civil liberties, and social legislation.

That even judicial judgment is fallible and ought not to be invoked where the facts cannot be adequately explored and resolved is the theme of his dissent in Pennsylvania v. West Virginia. Jurisdictional and procedural limitations were to be observed even when the Court was prepared to render an agreeable decision on the merits, as in Ashwander v. TVA, and even in a case involving civil liberties, as in Whitney v. California. Distrust of large abstractions and imposed uniformities made him sympathetic to the claims of local experimentation, whether challenged under the commerce clause (see New York Central R.R. v. Winfield) or under the due process clause (see, e.g., New State Ice Co. v. Liebmann, 285 U.S. 262, 310-311, where he said in dissent: "The discoveries in physical science, the triumphs in invention, attest the value of the process of trial and error. In large measure, these advances have been due to experimentation. . . . There must be power in the States and the Nation to remould, through experimentation, our economic practices and institutions to meet changing social and economic needs"). He was ready, nevertheless, to brand as an error of constitutional dimensions legislation which penalized expression without a showing of proximate danger (see the Whitney case) or which imposed local commercial restraints on the multistate market (see Buck v. Kuykendall).

The major opinions of Brandeis are massive and close-textured. They are frequently marked by a prophetic quality and by a moral and didactic note. Though he was writing of law-enforcement agencies in a case of wiretapping, his conception of the role of government would embrace judges as well: "Our Government is the potent, the omnipresent teacher. For good or for ill, it teaches the whole people by its example." Olmstead v. United States, 277 U.S. 438, 485.

David J. Brewer (*1837-1910*). "[I]f the Almighty should come and say to me that I *must* enter the kingdom of heaven, there is something in my Anglo-Saxon spirit which would stiffen my spinal column until it was like an iron ramrod, and force from my lips the reply 'I won't.'" These words spoken by Mr. Justice Brewer to the Virginia Bar Association in 1906 were reinforced by the opinions which he delivered on the Supreme Court of Kansas, the United States Circuit Court, and on the Supreme Court between 1889 and 1910. His dominant concern with the rights of the individual and his inordinate regard for the wisdom of courts led him, in opposing Munn v. Illinois, to state that "the paternal theory of government is to me odious" (Budd v. New York, 143 U.S. 517, 551 (1892); Reagan v. Farmers' Loan & Trust Co., 154 U.S. 362 (1894)), to condemn a graduated tax (dissent in Knowlton v. Moore, 178 U.S. 41, 110 (1900)), and to join the majority in the Lochner case. His opinion in the Debs case permitted an extraordinary exercise of judicial power, but in his judgment served to protect individuals and the nation from the coercive power of combinations (see his address "The Nation's Safeguard," 16 Proc. N.Y. State Bar Assn. 37 (1893)). Though he was fearful of the centralization of power, he eagerly applied the rule of Swift v. Tyson, 16 Pet. 1 (1842), to extend the authority of federal courts (Baltimore & Ohio R.R. v. Baugh, 149 U.S. 368 (1893)). While he rejoiced that the law of God prescribed that "the wealth of the community will be in the hands of a few," he was nonetheless willing to make the Sherman Act a relatively effective instrument for the control of bigness (concurring opinion in Northern Securities v. United States, 193 U.S. 197, 360 (1904)) and appreciated the economic realities of corporate wealth (Adams Express Co. v. Ohio State Auditor). In his dissenting opinion in Fong Yue Ting v. United States, 149 U.S. 698, 732 (1893), he sought with passion to protect the unpopular Chinese from American tyranny. His exaggerated sense of judicial competence (see his address "The Nation's Safeguard" supra) served the cause of personal liberty (dissenting opinions in United States v. Sing Tuck, 194 U.S. 161, 170 (1904), and United States v. Ju Toy, 198 U.S. 253, 264 (1904)). His convictions were in most matters similar to those of his uncle, Mr. Justice Field, but his more equable temper gave greater balance to his judgment.

Benjamin Robbins Curtis (*1809-1874*). Appointed to the Court from the Boston bar by President Fillmore in 1851, Curtis resigned his seat after six years. His greatest contribution to the development of constitutional doctrine was his formulation of what might be called the Rule in Cooley's Case (Cooley v. Board of Port Wardens). In a Court of eight, divided between those who thought that the mere grant of regulatory power to Congress excluded state regulation (e.g., McLean and Wayne, JJ.) and those who considered that state regulations were valid in the absence of Congressional action (e.g., Taney, C.J., and Daniel, J.), there seemed small chance that a formula acceptable to a majority could be discovered (see chart in Swisher, Rogert B. Taney 400 (1935)). Mr. Justice Curtis in the Cooley case discovered such a formula and in that action set the direction of commerce clause adjudication for close to one hundred years. His resignation followed his dissent in the Dred Scott case and dramatically reflected the tensions by which the Court and the nation were divided on the eve of the Civil War. Curtis's later career was principally devoted to private practice, but he appeared effectively on the public scene when he was counsel to President Johnson in the impeachment proceedings (infra page 15).

Stephen J. Field (1816-1899). When Lincoln in 1863 appointed the brother of David Dudley and Cyrus W. Field to the newly established tenth seat on the Court, he chose a Democrat who had made himself the dominant figure on the Supreme Court of California. Though it has often been supposed that party affiliations and political ambitions of Justice Field contributed to the enthusiasm with which he defended the rights of Southerners against Republican radicalism (Ex parte Garland; dissents in Miller v. United States, 11 Wall. 268, 314 (1870), and Ex parte Virginia), there were a number of occasions on which he willingly incurred political hostility in the defense of the oppressed (Hoh Ah Kow v. Nunan, 5 Sawyer 552 (1879), In re Quong Wu, 13 F. 229 (1882), but compare Barbier v. Connolly, 113 U.S. 27 (1885)). This concern for individual rights suggests that when he somewhat clumsily pressed the Thirteenth and Fourteenth Amendments into the service of property (dissents in the Slaughter-House Cases and Stone v. Wisconsin, 94 U.S. 181, 183 (1876)), he was not sanctifying private wealth but condemning public power. His fear of national authority led him, in dissent in Baltimore & Ohio R.R. v. Baugh, 149 U.S. 368, 390 (1893), to demand the virtual repudiation of Swift v. Tyson, 16 Pet. 1 (1842). At the time of Field's reluctant retirement from the Court in 1897, his efforts to provide constitutional security for business enterprise through the Fourteenth Amendment had been largely unsuccessful, but they were destined in another form, fashioned by Mr. Justice Peckham (Allgeyer v. Louisiana; Lochner v. New York) and supported by Field's energetic nephew, Mr. Justice Brewer, to enjoy triumphant successes for more than thirty years. The most dramatic incident in the life of Mr. Justice Field brought about the death of Mr. Justice Terry of the Supreme Court of California and left its mark on constitutional law (In re Neagle, 135 U.S. 1 (1890)). Would the dissenting individualism of Mr. Justice Field, one wonders, have supported the radicalism of his niece Anita Whitney (Whitney v. California)? For a study of Field's conservatism, see McCloskey, American Conservatism in the Age of Enterprise, c. 4 (1951).

Felix Frankfurter (1882-1965) came to the Court after a quarter century of teaching interspersed with Government service. His preoccupation had been procedure in the large sense, the law viewed as providing a rational process and structure for containing conflicts and fostering capacities in an open society. His teaching and pre-judicial writing were notable contributions to administrative law, the relations between federal and state courts, the labor injunction, and judicial review of legislation; his method was historical and philosophical, deeply influenced by the admonitions of Holmes and Brandeis against undue interposition by judges in the name of the Constitution in opposition to the law-making organs of government. On the Court these concerns continued and these cautionary principles persisted.

Frankfurter's judicial philosophy was tested in ways more searching than those that had typically confronted Holmes and Brandeis. Faced with the question of whether judicial self-restraint should give way, and the presumption of legislative validity be abandoned, when the challenge came in the form of freedom of speech, press, or assembly, Frankfurther refused to grant a mechanical "preferred position" to one set of guarantees and thereby, as he saw it, denigrate others (Kovacs v. Cooper). In the review of state legislation he saw no viable alternative to a particularistic judgment through the due process and equal protection clauses (Rochin v. California), again eschewing a mechanical "incorporation" of the Bill of Rights into the Fourteenth Amendment. His approach carried him as far as any of his colleagues in the application of these guarantees against racial discrimination (Cooper v. Aaron; Terry v. Adams) and governmental support of religion (Everson v. Board of Education; McCollum v. Board of Education), but in recognizing legitimate public concerns that set limits to the claims of freedom of speech, press, and association — concerns, for example, for public order, for the untrammeled administration of justice and for the vitality of labor unions — he was in disagreement with the prevailing view (Beauharnais v. Illinois; Bridges v. California; cf. Maryland v. Baltimore Radio Show; International Assn. of Machinists v. Street). His particularistic judgments were reflected as well in controversies pitting local interests of welfare against the claims of the national common market (Hood v. DuMond).

However history may judge the resolution of these issues, it cannot fail to look to his opinions for a deeply felt and articulate philosophy of the role of the Court in a constitutional democracy (West Virginia State Bd. of Education v. Barnette; Baker v. Carr).

Melville Weston Fuller *(1833-1910)*. Brought up with the odd inheritance of a Maine Democrat, Fuller had his professional career in Chicago, where his many-sided practice made him a considerable figure at the bar. He was appointed Chief Justice by Cleveland in 1888 and exerted a large influence on the Court more through his gentle tact and administrative competence as Chief than by unusual powers as a Justice. His constitutional inclinations were those of the political and professional world in which he had led his mature life; "he inclined toward strict construction of all governmental powers as against the political liberty and economic initiative of the citizen, and of federal powers as against the rights of the states" (7 Dictionary of American Biography 61 (1931)). His general tendency to prefer local authority over national did not blind him to the values in an economy unobstructed by barriers of provincial morality (Leisy v. Hardin; dissent in Hennington v. Georgia, 163 U.S. 299, 318 (1896)). That he stood firmly by the view that before the Sixteenth Amendment the federal income tax was unconstitutional has not surprised those who find in class bias a sufficient explanation for all decisions which they disapprove (see Myers, History of the Supreme Court (1912) passim), but such critics are less apt to notice that Fuller was, in certain circumstances at least, as willing to protect the oppressed as to safeguard the prosperous (dissent in Fong Yue Ting v. United States, 149 U.S. 698, 761 (1893)). His laissez-faire inclinations, however, were strong and revealed themselves in his hostility to extensions of the regulatory power of Congress (United States v. E. C. Knight Co., 156 U.S. 1 (1895); dissent in the Lottery Case).

John Marshall Harlan *(1833-1911)*. Of Southern ancestry, Harlan, "the Kentucky giant," recruited and commanded a regiment of Kentucky volunteers in the Union forces. Resigning his commission in 1863, he quickly became a leading figure at the Kentucky bar and a major force in Republican politics. In the period of reconstruction he moved from the position of a conservative to that of a radical Republican, and having supported Rutherford B. Hayes was named to the Supreme Court in 1877. Sitting on the Court until his death in 1911, he earned the reputation of a forceful dissenter, yet also could fairly be described by Mr. Justice Brewer as a man who "goes to bed every night with one hand on the Constitution and the other on the Bible, and so sleeps the sweet sleep of justice and righteousness." The consequence of such sleep was shown in Hennington v. Georgia, 163 U.S. 299 (1896), where the Court in an opinion by Harlan sustained a state statute which forbade the movement of freight trains on the Sabbath. The ruling conviction of Mr. Justice Harlan was that the Court had spun around the Constitution and Congressional statutes a web of subtleties which were destroying the vigor of government (dissent in Pollock v. Farmers' Loan & Trust Co., 157 U.S. 429, 652 (1895)). It was this conviction which led him to insist that the Civil War amendments and supplementary statutes were being emasculated by refinements (dissents in the Civil Rights Cases and Plessy v. Ferguson); that the "rule of reason" in antitrust cases was illegitimate judicial legislation (dissent in Standard Oil Co. v. United States, 221 U.S. 1, 82 (1911)), and that the powers of the Interstate Commerce Commission were being destroyed by an abuse of judicial power (ICC v. Alabama Midland Ry., 168 U.S. 144, 176 (1897); Harriman v. ICC, 211 U.S. 407 (1908)). These views, tending to an extension of federal authority, were coupled with an insistence that the police powers of the states must be preserved (Plumley v. Massachusetts, 155 U.S. 461 (1894); dissent in Bowman v. Chicago & N.W. Ry., 125 U.S. 465, 509 (1888)). Originally a vigorous defender of Munn v. Illinois, he came, with time, to insist that the courts had a responsibility to supervise rate regulation, and wrote the opinion in Smyth v. Ames. Describing Harlan's capacities, Holmes said that "he had a powerful vise the jaws of which couldn't be got nearer than two inches to each other." More picturesquely he described him as "the last of the tobacco-spitting judges." See Farrelly, Justice Harlan's Dissent in the Pollock Case, 24 S. Cal. L. Rev. 175 (1951); Waite, How Eccentric Was Mr. Justice Harlan? 37 Minn. L. Rev. 173 (1953); Watt and Orlikoff, The Coming Vindication of Mr. Justice Harlan, 44 Ill. L. Rev. 13 (1949).

John Marshall Harlan (*1899-1971*). The grandson of the first Justice Harlan was appointed to the Court by President Eisenhower after serving one year on the Court of Appeals for the Second Circuit. He had read law as a Rhodes scholar at Oxford and had enjoyed an active practice in New York, both as private practitioner and earlier as an assistant United States attorney, and had earned the deep respect of the bench and bar. His philosophy, however, had not been made explicit before coming to the Court. There he established himself as a firm exponent of federalism, prepared to allow the states somewhat greater latitude under the Fourteenth Amendment than is given to the federal government under the Bill of Rights — a position akin to that of Justice Holmes and Justice Jackson. He set himself against the current of what Justice Frankfurter called judicial freewheeling and was never reconciled, for example, to the use of the equal protection clause to supervise classifications for the suffrage, regarding such intervention as both unhistorical and unwise (Oregon v. Mitchell). In writing of Justice Black, with whom he often disagreed but with whom there was a warm and admiring relationship, he revealed his own standards at least as truly as his subject's: "He rejects the open-ended notion that the Court sits to do good in every circumstance where good is needed. . . . He considers himself to be a judge of cases, not of 'causes'. . . ." (81 Harv. L. Rev. 1 (1967)).

Beyond the positions he took on specific issues, his notable contribution to the work of the Court was the painstaking and transparent candor with which he analyzed a case, exposing its difficulties and setting forth dispassionately the elements of decision. In cases where he wrote a separate opinion, students and lawyers have commonly turned to it at the outset for an understanding of the problem.

Oliver Wendell Holmes (*1841-1935*). Perhaps the day will come when lawyers and students of government will lose interest in the figure of Mr. Justice Holmes. Some of his qualities have already passed beyond our reach. The aura of his father's reputation, in which — somewhat resentfully — he came to maturity, has dissipated with the years. That the Justice survived three wounds in the Civil War, today has the dimensions of a simple fact rather than those of a miracle. The impressive qualities of his person and of his talk are already nearly forgotten — despite the photographs, the anecdotes, and the letters. There were elements in his grandeur, however, which are likely to survive. It seems clear that fashions in taste will never be wholly unresponsive to his literary style. Lawyers will doubtless complain in the future, as they have in the past, that an opinion of Holmes's concealed unanswered difficulties beneath its shining surface. Generations which find skepticism an unsatisfactory answer to their hopes will always ask what sustenance was offered in his doubts. They will, however, always respect the mind which was willing to interpret questions of law as questions of philosophy.

The distinction which Holmes had achieved before he came to the Court in 1902, on Theodore Roosevelt's nomination, was not characteristic of that of other nominees. For twenty years he had sat on the Supreme Judicial Court of Massachusetts, and behind that period lay a professional career which was more that of a productive scholar than that of a successful practitioner. In 1902 it seemed unlikely that a judge at the age of sixty-two would for many years play a leading role in constitutional history. Yet Holmes did not retire until he was ninety, having for thirty unexpected years brought his special brand of skeptical vivacity to the Court's deliberations. This contribution was labeled "liberalism" by those who assume that conservatism is necessarily infected by fear. In fact it bespoke a conservative confidence that the nation's commitment to democracy was final and that in the long run — grueling as the run might be — the test of an individual's logic was the nation's experience. There was much truth in the statement that Holmes was fortunate in the fact that he survived into his own generation. He did not, however, live long enough to see the full fruition of his constitutional faith. Perhaps that faith, which has recently been recognized, is destined for repudiation, but it is at least a significant part of constitutional history.

Charles Evans Hughes (1862-1948). From practice at the New York bar, Hughes first came to public prominence in 1905 as the penetrating counsel for the state commission investigating insurance. Thereafter he became Governor of New York, resigning the office at the close of his second term in 1910 to accept Taft's appointment as an Associate Justice of the Supreme Court. For the next six years his capacity to organize and comprehend complex masses of fact and his willingness to acknowledge the necessities of national power were revealed in such opinions as those in the Minnesota Rate Cases and the Shreveport Case. His concern for the rights of minorities, which some had not expected in a Justice with his background, was indicated in Bailey v. Alabama, 219 U.S. 219 (1911). In 1916 he resigned from the Court when nominated as the Republican candidate for the Presidency. After his defeat he returned to a notably successful practice in New York, which was interrupted between 1921 and 1924 while he was Secretary of State in the Harding and Coolidge cabinets. In 1930 he was appointed by President Hoover to succeed Taft as Chief Justice. In 1941 he retired.

The judgment of history as to Hughes will turn principally upon its estimate of his second term of judicial service, and it is likely that his administrative role as presiding officer of the Court during that decade of tension will receive as much attention as his judicial opinions. There will surely be no question that his great intellectual capacities were so fortified by moral strength as to produce exceptional qualities of leadership (see Frankfurter, "The Administrative Side" of Chief Justice Hughes, 63 Harv. L. Rev. 1 (1949), and McElwain, The Business of the Supreme Court as Conducted by Chief Justice Hughes, 63 id. 5 (1949)). The part which he played as Chief and as Justice in the constitutional revolution of the late thirties (see infra page 260) will doubtless be discussed for many years to come (see Mason, Charles Evans Hughes: An Appeal to the Bar of History, 6 Vand. L. Rev. 1 (1952)), and none will question its historic importance. Though it is undeniable that the political and economic instincts of Hughes were closer to those of Mr. Justice Sutherland than to those of Mr. Justice Brandeis, his concern that the unorthodox should be protected in their heresies was revealed not only when he was a leader of the conservative bar but when he sat in judgment (see his eloquent dissent in United States v. Macintosh, 283 U.S. 605, 627 (1931), and his opinion in Near v. Minnesota). It has been said with great truth that Hughes "had a powerful rather than an exploratory mind" (Chafee, Charles Evans Hughes, 93 Proc. Am. Phil. Soc. 267, 279 (1949)). Does that suggest, perhaps, that he made a greater Chief Justice than would any of his associates?

Robert Houghwout Jackson *(1892-1954)*. When Robert Jackson was five years old, his family moved from Warren County, Pennsylvania, to Chautauqua County, New York, where he attended public schools, attended the Albany Law School for a year, and read law in a law office. Later he described himself as "the last relic of that method likely to find a niche on the Supreme Court." Leaving a congenial and diversified practice for Washington in 1934, he served successively as chief counsel of the Bureau of Internal Revenue, assistant attorney general for tax and later for antitrust litigation, solicitor general, and attorney general. Advocacy was his special delight; he had the barrister's gifts, and Justice Brandeis remarked that "Bob Jackson should be made Solicitor General for life." President Roosevelt had other ideas, and Jackson was confirmed as Associate Justice on October 6, 1941, filling the vacancy caused by the elevation of Justice Stone to the Chief Justiceship. On the Court his flair for the swordplay of words and wit was by no means wholly suppressed.

On constitutional issues his early upbringing and experience had left an impress, and not irrelevantly so, for his life was in the authentic American tradition. No Justice on the modern Court has been more solicitous than he for the freedom of interstate movement of persons and goods (Edwards v. California; Duckworth v. Arkansas). In applying the guarantees of the First Amendment, he endeavored to draw a bright line between control of beliefs on the one hand (West Virginia Board of Education v. Barnette; American Communications Assn. v. Douds; United States v. Ballard, 322 U.S. 78) and of aggressive speech or action on the other (Kunz v. New York; Dennis v. United States). This dichotomy, not always easy to maintain, appears to have been reinforced in Justice Jackson's thought by his experience as chief American prosecutor at the war crimes trials in Nuremberg. Emphasizing the responsibilities of local government for the maintenance of order, he would have accorded greater latitude to them than to the federal government in devising methods of accommodating public speech and public order (Beauharnais v. Illinois). See the memorial essays in 8 Stan. L. Rev. No. 1 (1955).

William Johnson *(1771-1834)*. Johnson, of South Carolina, was appointed to the Court by Jefferson in 1804 in the hope that his Republicanism might limit the successes which Federalist judges had achieved for judicial supremacy and for nationalism. To the extent that Johnson insisted on his responsibility to express his own opinion, whether in dissent from or in concurrence with that of Marshall, he amply fulfilled Jefferson's hope. He also proved himself faithful to Republican principle in his hostility to the expansive exercise of judicial power, as when he asserted that the federal courts had no jurisdiction to punish common law offenses (United States v. Hudson, 7 Cranch 32 (1812)) and opposed the extension of the admiralty jurisdiction (concurring opinion in Ramsay v. Allegre, 12 Wheat. 611, 614 (1827)). Yet there were many issues on which his independent intelligence disappointed Jeffersonian expectations. His respect for legislative judgment led him to recognize congressional powers which the expanding orthodoxies of localism would not tolerate (Elkison v. DeLiesseline, F. Cas. No. 4366 (1823); see Morgan, Justice William Johnson on the Treaty-Making Power, 22 Geo. Wash. L. Rev. 187 (1953)); his concurrence in Gibbons v. Ogden carried him farther toward nationalism than Marshall felt called upon to go, and he went as far as Story in his recognition of the congressional power to deal with bankruptcy (Morgan, Mr. Justice William Johnson and the Constitution, 57 Harv. L. Rev. 328 (1944)). He was unwilling to expand judicial power through a broad construction of the contracts clause (concurring opinion in Ogden v. Saunders, 12 Wheat. 213, 281 (1827)), but took the surprising position that the ex post facto clause applied to all retrospective laws, civil as well as criminal (note in 2 Pet. 681). Opposing, at the end of his life, the drift of his native state toward nullification, he would have preferred a constitution in which the power to invalidate state laws on federal grounds was vested in the Senate, yet under the Constitution as it was written, he recognized that the Court must on occasion condemn state legislation (Morgan, supra, 57 Harv. L. Rev. 328, 359-360).

John Marshall (1755-1835). Though Virginian Federalists seemed in the eyes of their New England allies to be "little better than half-way Jacobins" (Miller, Crisis in Freedom 184 (1951)), John Adams showed much political wisdom when he selected Marshall as Chief Justice in 1801. His nominee had revealed his political faith and his capacity when he had served as envoy to Paris, as Congressman, and as Secretary of State in Adams's cabinet. The heritage of Federalism, threatened by impending Republican victories, might best be preserved if the Chief Justice of the United States, with "lax, lounging manners," came from Virginia. Some Yankee Federalists would never forget that Marshall had opposed the Alien and Sedition Acts, but Adams may well have felt that commitments on that dying issue would be largely irrelevant to the nation's problems in the foreseeable future. When Holmes doubted whether "Marshall's work proved more than a strong intellect, a good style, personal ascendancy in his court, courage, justice and the convictions of his party," he also reminded us that "there fell to Marshall perhaps the greatest place that ever was filled by a judge" (Holmes, Speeches 90 (1913)). In that reminder he emphasized the fact that at the time Marshall became Chief Justice the human qualities and political principles which were his were those the country needed if it was to become a nation. Those qualities and those principles left their indelible impressions on American constitutional history.

Perhaps it is not oversimplifying the story of Marshall's Court to say that it is remembered for four principal achievements. First, it established the doctrine that the Court is competent to declare congressional legislation unconstitutional (Marbury v. Madison). Second, it determined that the Supreme Court could condemn state action which impaired the national authority and interest (Gibbons v. Ogden). Third, the Court recognized the existence of implied powers in the national government (McCulloch v. Maryland). Fourth, it held that the individual could appeal to the federal courts for the protection of his property from arbitrary state action (Fletcher v. Peck). If Marshall exercised judicial power with marked exuberance, it should not be forgotten that it was also the nation's power which he extended. Without that extension would Lincoln's name survive? See J. B. Thayer, John Marshall (1901).

James Clark McReynolds (1862-1946). When Woodrow Wilson appointed his Attorney General to the Court in 1914, the public knew the appointee as a Tennessee lawyer who, under both Roosevelt and Wilson, had shown himself to be a vigorous trust-buster. The dislike of uncontrolled power which inspired that vigor led him on the Court to become one of its most strict constructionists. Search through his opinions as one may, it is impossible to discover that the events of political and economic history modified his constitutional convictions; they merely confirmed his early forebodings. When the Gold Clause Cases were decided (Norman v. Baltimore & Ohio R.R.; Perry v. United States), he was understood to have pronounced that "this is Nero at his worst," and he admitted the pronouncement that "Shame and humiliation are on us now. Moral and financial chaos may confidently be expected." (334 U.S. at xi.) In his dissenting opinions he showed how firmly he stood committed to his own dictum that "an amorphous dummy unspotted by human emotion [is not] a becoming receptacle for judicial power" (dissent in Berger v. United States, 255 U.S. 22, 43 (1921)). He was the Court's spokesman in Southern Pacific Co. v. Jensen, 244 U.S. 205 (1917), the decision which prompted Holmes to protest that "the common law is not a brooding omnipresence in the sky," and which has been the fertile mother of litigation and perplexity (see Note, The Tangled Seine, 57 Yale L.J.

243 (1947)). His genial Chief, Taft, suggested the difficulties which his colleagues must have found in such an ill-tempered and ill-mannered colleague when he said that McReynolds "has a continual grouch" and "seems to delight in making others uncomfortable" (2 Pringle, The Life and Times of William Howard Taft 971 (1939)). Yet Holmes described him as "a kindly man" (1 Holmes-Laski Letters 555 (1953)). His name was not included among the signatories of the Court's letter of regret and affection when Brandeis announced his retirement (306 U.S. at v-vi). There was a stiff-necked fortitude in his convictions, and when he retired in 1941, no one charged that he had made concessions to expediency.

Samuel Freeman Miller *(1816-1890).* Miller's formal education and his first years of professional life were in medicine. An increasing interest in political questions led him into law. In 1847 he was admitted to the Kentucky bar, but moved to Iowa three years later and there pursued his new profession with conspicuous success. In 1862, on Lincoln's nomination, he was appointed to the Court. His systematic and vigorous intelligence quickly made itself felt and for twenty-eight years gave bright color to the achievements of the Court — no less bright than those contributed by his colorful associates, Bradley, Field, and Harlan. His economic inclinations favored agrarian radicalism (see his dissent in Woodson v. Murdock, 22 Wall. 351, 374 (1874)), and his political views favored broad national authority (see his dissent in Hepburn v. Griswold, 8 Wall. 603, 626 (1870), and his opinions in Wabash, St. Louis & Pacific Ry. v. Illinois, and Crandall v. Nevada). This last generalization will seem inaccurate, perhaps, to those who read the Slaughter-House Cases as a defense of localism and its peculiar institutions. If, however, one reads Mr. Justice Miller's opinion as an effort to set limits to the scope of judicial review, the generalization may be justified. It should not be forgotten that he wrote the Court's opinion in Ex parte Yarbrough. When personal rights were threatened by abusive processes, Mr. Justice Miller spoke with indignation. He wrote the Court's opinion in Kilbourn v. Thompson and added this comment in a letter to a friend: "I think the public has been much abused, the time of legislative bodies uselessly consumed and rights of the citizen ruthlessly invaded under the now familiar pretext of legislative investigation and that it is time that it was understood that courts and grand juries are the only inquisitions into crime in this country. I do not recognize the doctrine that Congress is *the grand inquest* of the nation, nor that it can by the name of a report slander the citizen so as to protect the newspaper which publishes such slander." (Quoted in Fairman, Mr. Justice Miller and the Supreme Court, 1862-1890, 334 (1939)). Even when personal rights were involved, however, he insisted that the presumption of constitutionality should affect the Court's judgment (dissents in Cummings v. Missouri and Ex parte Garland). All in all, Mr. Justice Miller stands as one of the giants in the Court's history.

William H. Moody *(1853-1917).* In his brief four years on the Court (1906-1910), Mr. Justice Moody made the unusual qualities of his mind an important part of the Court's history. In the five years which preceded his appointment he had served in Congress and had been Secretary of the Navy and Attorney General in Theodore Roosevelt's cabinet. These years of public service had followed upon a notably successful career at the Massachusetts bar. The sparse precision of his literary style reflected his careful intelligence. The two opinions on which his high reputation is principally based were his dissent in the Employers' Liability Cases, 207 U.S. 463, 504 (1908), in which he answered the resounding platitudes of Mr. Justice White with a telling assertion of congressional power to control the liability of interstate carriers to their employees, and his opinion for the majority in Twining v. New Jersey, in which he examined the consequences which the Fourteenth Amendment had had on American federalism. Though many persons, when he was appointed, had feared that his loyalty to Roosevelt would infect his judgment, at the time of his retirement he had secured the firm respect of his associates and of the bar.

Rufus Wheeler Peckham (*1838-1909*). The son of a judge of the New York Court of Appeals, Peckham was educated at the Albany Boys' Academy and is said to have had some additional education in Philadelphia. He traveled in Europe with his family, but had no college or university experience. He probably read law in an Albany, New York, office, and practiced there for nearly twenty years. He was District Attorney of Albany County and later corporation counsel of the city, was elected a justice of the New York Supreme Court, and in 1886 became a judge of the New York Court of Appeals. In 1895, President Cleveland nominated him for the United States Supreme Court. Senator Hill of New York, who had successfully opposed the confirmation of Wheeler Peckham, Judge Peckham's brother, nominated for the Supreme Court the preceding year, made no opposition to Rufus, though like his brother he had been somewhat independent politically. He took his seat on January 6, 1896.

Mr. Justice Peckham will probably be longest remembered for his prevailing opinion in Lochner v. New York. Holding unconstitutional a statute requiring a sixty-hour week limit for work by bakery employees, he wrote: "it may be true that the trade of baker does not appear to be as healthy as some other trades, and is also vastly more healthy than still others . . . It is unfortunately true that labor, even in any department, may possibly carry with it the seeds of unhealthiness. But are we all, at that account, at the mercy of legislative majorities?" In 1908 he wrote for the Court in Ex parte Young, 209 U.S. 123, upholding a federal court injunction against a state attorney general despite the Eleventh Amendment. He wrote the Court's opinion in Addyston Pipe & Steel Co. v. United States, 175 U.S. 211 (1899), upholding the application of the commerce power to restrict private agreements which impede commerce among the states. He wrote for the Court in Maxwell v. Dow, 176 U.S. 581 (1900), upholding a state conviction of robbery by trial before an eight-man jury, rejecting an argument that the Fourteenth Amendment incorporates the entire Bill of Rights. It is perhaps notable that from some of his best-known opinions — Maxwell v. Dow, Lochner v. New York, and Ex parte Young — Mr. Justice Harlan dissented vigorously. Peckham dissented without opinion (as did Brewer) from the majority in Holden v. Hardy, 169 U.S. 366 (1898), upholding an eight-hour day in a mine and ore reduction plant. Mr. Justice Peckham died in 1909 at his country home near Albany, New York. He was upright, conservative, and suspicious of the judgment of the multitude. It was of Peckham's opinion in Lochner that Holmes wrote in dissent, "This case is decided upon an economic theory which a large part of the country does not entertain. . . . The Fourteenth Amendment does not enact Mr. Herbert Spencer's Social Statics."

Harlan Fiske Stone (*1872-1946*). In 1924, when Stone became Attorney General in the Coolidge cabinet, he was known to the academic world as a lawyer of considerable learning who had been dean and professor at the Law School of Columbia University. He was known to the bar as a successful New York practitioner. A year later, when Coolidge nominated him to the Court, Western progressives saw the selection as responsive to the wishes of the bankers, and condemned the choice because Stone had "breathed the mephitic air of the Department of Justice." He was, however, quickly confirmed and after a few years showed that the avenues of his mind did not run parallel to Wall Street. In 1941, on President Roosevelt's nomination, he became Chief Justice and held the office until his death in 1946. The period of his judicial career made him the colleague of the unreconstructed conservatives — Butler, Sutherland, Van Devanter, and McReynolds — and of their successors on the reconstructed Court — Black, Douglas, Murphy, and Rutledge. By 1930, Stone had made it clear that his constitutional inclinations coincided essentially with those of Holmes and Brandeis, and his part in history was that of carrying those convictions of dissent into their age of acceptance. To say that is not to assert that Mr. Justice Stone merely carried the torch of others. Questions which Holmes and Brandeis had decided but not asked he faced (see his dissent in Minersville School

District v. Gobitis, 310 U.S. 586, 601 (1940), and the most famous footnote in constitutional history, footnote 4 in United States v. Carolene Products, 304 U.S. 144, 152-153 (1938)). Throughout his judicial career he endeavored to look beyond those formulas which offered the indecisive comforts of familiarity to considerations of a more conclusive sort (see, e.g., dissents in Di Santo v. Pennsylvania, 273 U.S. 34, 43 (1927), the Western Live Stock case, and McGoldrick v. Berwind-White Coal Co.). Field and Holmes may have known "the subtle rapture of a postponed power," but Stone knew the rapture without the subtlety of prolonged postponement, for in his lifetime, doctrine which he had supported in dissent was promulgated as law. Though Stone knew the satisfaction of becoming Chief Justice, one suspects that his name will be remembered more for his role as Associate Justice than for his achievements as Chief. See Wechsler, Stone and the Constitution, 46 Colum. L. Rev. 764 (1946).

Joseph Story (*1779-1845*). In the Federalist community of Boston, Story's early Republican inclinations made him a somewhat suspect character, but his great capacities gave Madison ample justification in 1811 for naming him, at the age of thirty-two, to the Supreme Court. It quickly became apparent, as Jefferson had suspected, that Story's nationalism would displace his early Republican sympathies, and he soon was an active partner with Marshall in establishing not only the finality of the Court's constitutional authority (Martin v. Hunter's Lessee) but also the supremacy, as against the states, of congressional powers (Prigg v. Pennsylvania, 16 Pet. 539 (1842)). Almost invariably in agreement with Marshall, he possessed, more than did his Chief, the equipment of a scholar, and it is commonly believed that when Marshall needed the scaffolding of scholarship to support his judgment, Story would provide it. As Circuit Justice he had "absorbed jurisdiction as a sponge took up water," and it was said that "if a bucket of water were brought into his court with a corn cob floating in it, he would at once extend the admiralty jurisdiction of the United States over it." (Note, 37 Am. L. Rev. 911, 916 (1903).) As prolific writer and as law teacher he played a part in the development of American law, even of a body of national law, no less important then that which he played as judge. After Marshall's death in 1835, Story continued on the Court for another ten years, seeking to preserve as constitutional law Marshall's conception of the Constitution. "I am the last of the old race of judges," he wrote in 1837, and as such saw the impending shift of emphasis from Marshall's to Taney's as a constitutional revolution. The Charles River Bridge decision found him in agonized dissent against what he believed to be the repudiation of the Dartmouth College Case, yet in most other matters the revolution which he had feared slightly disappointed him in its mildness. He was able during the regime of Taney to persuade a majority to nationalize commercial law (Swift v. Tyson, 16 Pet. 1 (1842)), and he rejoiced in the ingenuity by which Taney made it possible for corporate enterprise to extend across the nation (Bank of Augusta v. Earle, 13 Pet. 519 (1839)).

George Sutherland (*1862-1942*). A year of law study under Cooley at the University of Michigan gave doctrinal justification for the lesson which adversity, temperament, and hard work had already taught Sutherland in his Utah boyhood — that the individual's survival and success are his responsibility, not that of his government. Practice and politics in Utah brought him to the United States Senate where, between 1905 and 1917, he was recognized as an authority on constitutional questions. His occasional support of progressive causes did not significantly tarnish his growing reputation as a rugged Republican conservative. His defeat in 1917 led him to a Washington practice and the presidency of the American Bar Association. As close advisor to Warren G. Harding, he earned his nomination to the Supreme Court in 1922, where he sat as an Associate Justice until 1938 and became the dominant figure among the conservative Justices. The political storms which buffeted the Court in the concluding years of Mr. Justice Sutherland's career on the bench did not soften his conviction that the Constitution had enacted Spencer's Social

Statics, and to the end he stood in resolute defense of the constitutional order which the Court in fulfillment of Field's hopes had established in the first thirty years of the twentieth century (see, e.g., Carter v. Carter Coal Co.). The best example of his strong qualities is probably to be found in his dissent in Home Building & Loan Assn. v. Blaisdell; the inflexibility of his convictions is nowhere better revealed than in his opinion for the Court in the Adkins case, invalidating a minimum wage law for women. His tolerance of zoning (Euclid case) was perhaps based on the conviction that control of building would enhance the value of property (See Paschal, Mr. Justice Sutherland 242, 243 (1951)), but his respect for the individual led him to enforce vigorously constitutional guarantees of fair trials (Berger v. United States, 295 U.S. 78 (1935); Powell v. Alabama). It has been suggested that his understanding of economics was limited (Powell, Book Review, 65 Harv. L. Rev. 894, 896). The one area in which he gladly recognized extensive federal power was the field of international affairs (United States v. Curtiss-Wright; United States v. Belmont, 301 U.S. 324 (1937)). See also John Frank, Book Review, 61 Yale L.J. 598 (1952); Mason, The Conservative World of Mr. Justice Sutherland, 32 Am. Pol. Sci. Rev. 443 (1928).

William Howard Taft *(1857-1930)*. When the former President became Chief Justice, on Harding's nomination in 1921, the deepest ambition of the nominee was fulfilled. The variety of public offices which Taft had already occupied included the Solicitor-Generalship under President Benjamin Harrison and a judgeship in the Sixth Circuit from 1892 to 1900. What he brought to the Supreme Court was not simply the inherent conservatism that had marked his political career, but a strong conviction that each branch of the national government must be permitted to exercise a broad authority without interruption from the others or from the state governments. Insofar as congressional authority was concerned, this produced from the Chief Justice such opinions as those in Stafford v. Wallace, Dayton-Goose Creek Ry. v. United States, 263 U.S. 456 (1924), and Railroad Commission of Wisconsin v. Chicago, Burlington & Quincy R.R., 257 U.S. 563 (1922) — decisions which, it was later argued, had legalized the New Deal. As far as presidential prerogatives were concerned, the Chief Justice gave them protection in Myers v. United States, 272 U.S. 52 (1926), Ex parte Grossman, 267 U.S. 87 (1925), and Hampton & Co. v. United States, 276 U.S. 394 (1928). Taft revealed his belief that the federal courts should enjoy an effective independence, not only by his general willingness to allow an expansive interpretation of due process (Truax v. Corrigan, 257 U.S. 312 (1921)), but also by his deep and productive concern that those courts should control their own affairs with independent competence (Terral v. Burke Construction Co., 257 U.S. 529 (1922)). In furtherance of that end he took the lead in establishing the Annual Conference of Senior Circuit Judges, and, through the Judges Bill of 1925, in giving the Supreme Court a high degree of control over its own appellate jurisdiction (see Frankfurter and Landis, The Business of the Supreme Court, cc. 6, 7 (1927)). His interest in the institutional dignity of the Court was reflected, perhaps unfortunately, in his successful efforts to secure a law authorizing the construction of the Supreme Court building. Within the Court his interest was revealed in his general disapproval of dissenting opinions. On occasion, however, he felt called upon to express his disagreement with the majority, as in his notable dissent from Mr. Justice Sutherland's opinion in Adkins v. Children's Hospital, 261 U.S. 525, 562 (1923). It is surely no fault in a Chief Justice that he be "amiable and comfortable" (1 Holmes-Laski Letters 423 (1953)), and a nation which in the 1920's believed that it possessed those qualities could not but love Taft.

Roger Brooke Taney *(1777-1864)*. When Andrew Jackson in 1836 chose his faithful Attorney General and Secretary of the Treasury as Marshall's successor, it seemed clear to the Whigs that the Constitution, as Marshall had shaped it, would be molded to serve the ends of Jacksonian radicalism. Had it not been for the tragedy of Dred Scott, the legend that Taney's strength was that of a second-rate Maryland politician would never have taken root in American history, for the distorting shadow of that unhappy decision would not have fallen over the realities of his judicial career. In that decision he violated the principle to which he was otherwise dedicated — the principle that judicial power should be exercised with cautious humility (see Acheson, Roger Brooke Taney: Note upon Judicial Self-restraint (1936)). Between the extreme nationalism of Mr. Justice McLean (Passenger Cases, 7 How. 283, 392 (1849)) and the exaggerated localism of Mr. Justice Daniel (dissent in the License Cases, 5 How. 504, 611 (1847)), Taney followed a middle course which qualified but did not repudiate the nationalism of Marshall's Court (he concurred in the majority opinion in the Cooley case). Had Taney shared Daniel's agrarian bias he would not have allowed corporations to nationalize their activities (Bank of Augusta v. Earle, 13 Pet. 519 (1839); compare Daniel, J., dissenting in Marshall v. Baltimore & Ohio R.R., 16 How. 314, 338 (1853)). Had he fulfilled Story's worst fears he would not have condemned state moratory legislation (Bronson v. Kinzie, 1 How. 311 (1843)); yet had he been wholly true to Marshall's faith he would not have permitted evasion of the doctrine of the Dartmouth College Case in Charles River Bridge v. Warren Bridge Co. Contemporary opinion saw Ex parte Merryman as the expression of Southern defiance of presidential authority, but later generations have come to see it as a notably courageous defense of individual liberty. In considering the judicial career of Taney it should never be forgotten that the Court over which he presided was made up of judges who were passionately involved in the crisis of their times. As a consequence the Justices overlooked the institutional significance of the Court in their desire to clarify the idiosyncrasies of their own integrity. Even John Marshall might have lost command of such a Court.

Willis Van Devanter *(1859-1941)*. Lawyers need an occasional reminder that the history of the law as well as that of the nation is reflected in the Court's decisions. There have, in other words, been judges whose greatness lay not in their statesmanship but in their professional competence. Mr. Justice Van Devanter was such a judge. His thorough conservatism necessarily played a part in political history, for he sat on the Court from 1911 to 1937. His largest contribution to the Court's history, however, was not in his "votes" on constitutional issues but in his contribution to its functioning as a court of law and equity. It was due largely to his energetic interest that the Court's jurisdiction, in 1925, was redefined and largely subjected to its own control. He came to the Court from Wyoming after seven years on the Circuit Court of Appeals, and, knowing himself, aimed "to be a Judge and not a litterateur" (John W. Davis, in 316 U.S. at xxv). He was fully equipped with a lawyer's understanding of federal jurisdiction, a frontiersman's knowledge of Indian affairs, and a native hostility to governmental regulation. His associates in Washington made the fullest use of his special competence, and evidently found his shrewd precision of extraordinary value in conference (316 U.S. at xi-xii). He has accurately been described as "master of formulas that decided cases without creating precedents" (McCormack, A Law Clerk's Recollections, 46 Colum. L. Rev. 710, 711 (1946)). Voting invariably with those Justices who feared an extension of governmental authority, he never allowed the passion of personal emotion or political philosophy to infect the expression of his views. The lawyer's art — or at least the lawyer's skill — was shown in its most admirable form in his opinions in McGrain v. Daugherty and New York Central v. Winfield. His dissenting opinion in Herndon v. Lowry, 301 U.S. 242, 264 (1937), was perhaps a prophecy of things to come. In that respect it was not characteristic (compare Indian Motocycle Co. v. United States, 283 U.S. 570 (1931)).

Morrison R. Waite *(1816-1888)*. Elevated to the Chief-Justiceship in 1874 by Grant, from relative obscurity as a successful Republican practitioner in Ohio, Waite held the office until his death in 1888. The flatness of his style and a lawyer's fear of generalization made him a less dramatic figure than his three immediate predecessors, Marshall, Taney, and Chase. His dominant concern, in an era of legislative activity, was that the Court should exercise its power to review legislation with scrupulous caution. This principle, rather than a liking for the welfare state, led him to sustain the Granger legislation in Munn v. Illinois; to qualify if not largely to undermine the principles of the Dartmouth College Case (Spring Valley Water Works v. Schottler, 110 U.S. 347 (1884); Railroad Commission Cases, 116 U.S. 307 (1886)), and to make the Eleventh Amendment an effective safeguard of state power (Louisiana v. Jumel, 107 U.S. 711 (1882); Antoni v. Greenhow, 107 U.S. 769 (1882)). It led him also to sustain congressional regulations of commerce which more fearful colleagues saw as precursors of communism (Pensacola Telegraph Co. v. Western Union Telegraph Co., 96 U.S. 1 (1877)). At times conflicting with his basic respect for congressional judgment was a strong desire to preserve the power of the states — a desire which led him vigorously to apply the principles of the Slaughter-House Cases against radical reconstruction (United States v. Cruikshank, 92 U.S. 543 (1875); Minor v. Happerstett, 21 Wall. 162 (1874)). For a sharp criticism of Waite's "communistic" tendencies see Pomeroy, The Supreme Court and State Repudiation — The Virginia and Louisiana Cases, 17 Am. L. Rev. 684 (1883). A more balanced appraisal of his qualities is found in Frankfurter, The Commerce Clause under Marshall, Taney and Waite 74 et seq. (1937).

Earl Warren *(1891-1974)*. Appointed Chief Justice in 1953 by President Eisenhower, Earl Warren early succeeded in the difficult task of marshalling the Court for a unanimous decision in Brown v. Board of Education. While many observers would view this as his single greatest achievement, he himself regarded the reapportionment decisions as more fundamental. Be that as it may, the Court over which he presided brought about greater movement in constitutional law than in any period since Marshall's.

Whether this movement was a recrudescence of the judicial activism of the 1920s and early 1930s, except on the left rather than the right, and hence equally undemocratic, can be and is debated. Certain differences, however, apart from the subjective desirability of the results, can be pointed out — differences that are relevant to the principles of democratic government. First, by and large, the laws and practices condemned by the Court under Warren were of an older vintage — malapportionment, discriminations against minorities — and so may have reflected less surely the considered contemporary will. Secondly, and perhaps of more significance, the Court under Warren, by and large, dealt with matters of procedure and participation — civil and criminal procedural guarantees, official bias, interests of speech, assembly, association and suffrage — which are more appropriately the subject of judicial concern than, say, such products of the legislative process as laws regulating prices, wages, and production.

If this is a valid line of distinction, it must be acknowledged that it is a line difficult to hold in practice: the momentum of expansive judicial review may prove hard to cabin. Still, the effort to judge judicial review in terms of the theory of representative democracy seems preferable to the undifferentiating praise or censure to which Chief Justice Warren has been subjected. Whatever the fate of particular decisions of that period, the main directions taken seem destined to endure, as did those of the Marshall Court.

Edward Douglass White *(1845-1921)*. After serving in the Confederate forces White became a successful practitioner and important political figure in Louisiana. Between 1891 and 1894 he was in the United States Senate and was then named to the Court by Cleveland. In 1910 Taft, disregarding party considerations, made him Chief Justice. When White died, Taft, who was then his successor as Chief Justice, paid him tribute, and in doing so made clear the fact that White's fundamental commitment was to nationalism (257 U.S. at xxiv-xxix). This commitment led him to recognize an extensive congressional power over commerce (Clark Distilling case) and over elections of federal officers (concurring opinion in Newberry v. United States, 265 U.S. 232, 262 (1921)), and to sustain the Adamson Law, which established maximum hours for railroad workers (Wilson v. New, 243 U.S. 332 (1917)). His unpredictable positions on due process (he dissented in Lochner v. New York, yet did the same in Bunting v. Oregon, 243 U.S. 426 (1916), and Block v. Hirsh, 256 U.S. 135 (1921)) gave some support, perhaps, to Holmes's suspicion that White was "built rather for a politician than a judge" (1 Holmes-Laski Letters 294 (1953)). He had the satisfaction, and Harlan the indignant grief, of seeing a majority of the Court accept the "rule of reason" in the Antitrust Cases (Standard Oil Co. v. United States, 221 U.S. 1 (1911)), a formula which he had suggested in dissent (United States v. Trans-Missouri Freight Assn., 166 U.S. 190 (1897)).

What impresses later generations in White's opinions is less their substance than their extraordinary form. He moved portentously across the thinnest ice, confident that a lifeline of adverbs — "inevitably," "irresistibly," "clearly," and "necessarily" — was supporting him in his progress. His classic rejoinder — "To state the proposition is to refute it" (Employers' Liability Cases, 207 U.S. 463, 502 (1908)) — possessed a simplicity which was not characteristic of his style. More representative of his manner of expression was his reflection in Guinn v. United States, 238 U.S. 347, 366 (1915): "Of course, rigorous as is this rule and imperative as is the duty not to violate it, it does not mean that it applies in a case where it expressly appears that a contrary conclusion must be reached if the plain letter and necessary intendment of the provision under consideration so compels, or where such a result is rendered necessary because to follow the contrary course would give rise to such an extreme and anomalous situation as would cause it to be impossible to conclude that it could have been, upon any hypothesis whatever, within the mind of the law-making power." The quality of his rhetoric is well illustrated in his tribute to Mr. Justice Lamar (241 U.S. at xvi). See Davis, Edward Douglass White, 7 A.B.A.J. 376 (1921).

The Constitution of the United States

We the People of the United States, in Order to form a more perfect Union, establish Justice, insure domestic Tranquility, provide for the common defence, promote the general Welfare, and secure the Blessings of Liberty to ourselves and our Posterity, do ordain and establish this Constitution for the United States of America.

ARTICLE I

Section 1. All legislative Powers herein granted shall be vested in a Congress of the United States, which shall consist of a Senate and House of Representatives.

Section 2. The House of Representatives shall be composed of Members chosen every second Year by the People of the several States, and the Electors in each State shall have the Qualifications requisite for Electors of the most numerous Branch of the State Legislature.

No Person shall be a Representative who shall not have attained to the Age of twenty-five Years, and been seven Years a Citizen of the United States, and who shall not, when elected, be an Inhabitant of that State in which he shall be chosen.

Representatives and direct Taxes shall be apportioned among the several States which may be included within this Union, according to their respective Numbers, which shall be determined by adding to the whole Number of free Persons, including those bound to Service for a Term of Years, and excluding Indians not taxed, three fifths of all other Persons. The actual Enumeration shall be made within three Years after the first Meeting of the Congress of the United States, and within every subsequent Term of ten Years, in such Manner as they shall by Law direct. The number of Representatives shall not exceed one for every thirty Thousand, but each State shall have at Least one Representative; and until such enumeration shall be made, the State of New Hampshire shall be entitled to chuse three, Massachusetts eight, Rhode-Island and Providence Plantations one, Connecticut five, New-York six, New Jersey four, Pennsylvania eight, Delaware one, Maryland six, Virginia ten, North Carolina five, South Carolina five, and Georgia three.

When vacancies happen in the Representation from any State, the Executive Authority thereof shall issue Writs of Election to fill such Vacancies.

The House of Representatives shall chuse their Speaker and other Officers; and shall have the sole power of Impeachment.

Section 3. The Senate of the United States shall be composed of two Senators from each State, chosen by the Legislature thereof, for six Years; and each Senator shall have one Vote.

Immediately after they shall be assembled in Consequence of the first Election, they shall be divided as equally as may be into three Classes. The Seats of the Senators of the first Class shall be vacated at the Expiration of the Second Year, of the second Class at the Expiration of the fourth Year, and of the third Class at the Expiration of the sixth Year, so that one third may be chosen every second Year; and if Vacancies happen by Resignation, or otherwise, during the Recess of the Legislature of any State, the Executive thereof may make temporary Appointments until the next Meeting of the Legislature, which shall then fill such Vacancies.

No Person shall be a Senator who shall not have attained to the Age of thirty Years, and been nine Years a Citizen of the United States, and who shall not, when elected, be an Inhabitant of that State for which he shall be chosen.

The Vice President of the United States shall be President of the Senate, but shall have no Vote, unless they be equally divided.

The Senate shall chuse their other Officers, and also a President pro tempore, in the absence of the Vice President, or when he shall exercise the Office of President of the United States.

The Senate shall have the sole Power to try all Impeachments. When sitting for that Purpose, they shall be on Oath or Affirmation. When the President of the United States is tried, the Chief Justice shall preside: And no Person shall be convicted without the Concurrence of two thirds of the Members present.

Judgment in Cases of Impeachment shall not extend further than to removal from Office, and disqualification to hold and enjoy any Office of honor, Trust, or Profit under the United States: but the Party convicted shall nevertheless be liable and subject to Indictment, Trial, Judgment, and Punishment, according to Law.

Section 4. The Times, Places and Manner of holding Elections for Senators and Representatives shall be prescribed in each State by the Legislature thereof; but the Congress may at any time by Law make or alter such Regulations, except as to the Places of chusing Senators.

The Congress shall assemble at least once in every Year, and such Meeting shall be on the first Monday in December unless they shall by Law appoint a different Day.

Section 5. Each House shall be the Judge of the Elections, Returns, and Qualifications of its own Members, and a Majority of each shall constitute a Quorum to do Business; but a smaller Number may adjourn from day to day, and may be authorized to compel the Attendance of absent Members, in such Manner, and under such Penalties as each House may provide.

Each House may determine the Rules of its Proceedings, punish its Members for disorderly Behavior, and, with the Concurrence of two thirds, expel a Member.

Each House shall keep a Journal of its Proceedings, and from time to time publish the same, excepting such Parts as may in their Judgment require Secrecy; and the Yeas and Nays of the Members of either House on any question shall, at the Desire of one fifth of those Present, be entered on the Journal.

Neither House, during the Session of Congress, shall, without the Consent of the other, adjourn for more than three days, nor to any other Place than that in which the two Houses shall be sitting.

Section 6. The Senators and Representatives shall receive a Compensation for their Services, to be ascertained by Law, and paid out of the Treasury of the United States. They shall in all Cases, except Treason, Felony and Breach of the Peace, be privileged from Arrest during their Attendance at the Session of their respective Houses, and in going to and returning from the same; and for any Speech or Debate in either House, they shall not be questioned in any other Place.

No Senator or Representative shall, during the Time for which he was elected, be appointed to any civil Office under the Authority of the United States, which shall have been created, or the Emoluments whereof shall have been encreased during such time; and no Person holding any Office under the United States, shall be a Member of either House during his Continuance in Office.

Section 7. All Bills for raising Revenue shall originate in the House of Representatives; but the Senate may propose to concur with Amendments as on other Bills.

Every Bill which shall have passed the House of Representatives and the Senate, shall, before it become a Law, be presented to the President of the United States; if he approve he shall sign it, but if not he shall return it, with his Objections to that House in which it shall have originated, who shall enter the Objections at large on their Journal, and proceed to reconsider it. If after such Reconsideration two thirds of that House shall agree to pass the Bill, it shall be sent, together with the Objections, to the other House, by which it shall likewise be reconsidered, and if approved by two thirds of that House, it shall become a Law. But in all such Cases the Votes of both Houses shall be determined by Yeas and Nays, and the Names of the Persons voting for and against the Bill shall be entered on the Journal of each House respectively. If any Bill shall not be returned by the President within ten Days (Sundays excepted) after it shall have been presented to him, the Same shall be a Law, in like Manner as if he had signed it, unless the Congress by their Adjournment prevent its Return, in which Case it shall not be a Law.

Every Order, Resolution, or Vote to which the Concurrence of the Senate and House of Representatives may be necessary (except on a question of Adjournment) shall be presented to the President of the United States; and before the Same shall take Effect, shall be approved by him, or being disapproved by him, shall be repassed by two thirds of the Senate and House of Representatives, according to the Rules and Limitations prescribed in the Case of a Bill.

Section 8. The Congress shall have Power To lay and collect Taxes, Duties, Imposts and Excises, to pay the Debts and provide for the common Defence and general Welfare of the United States; but all Duties, Imposts and Excises shall be uniform throughout the United States;

To borrow money on the credit of the United States;

To regulate Commerce with foreign Nations, and among the several States, and with the Indian Tribes;

To establish an uniform Rule of Naturalization, and uniform Laws on the subject of Bankruptcy throughout the United States;

To coin Money, regulate the Value thereof, and of foreign Coin, and fix the Standard of Weights and Measures;

To provide for the Punishment of counterfeiting the Securities and current Coin of the United States;

To Establish Post Offices and post Roads;

To promote the Progress of Science and useful Arts, by securing for limited Times to Authors and Inventors the exclusive Right to their respective Writings and Discoveries;

To constitute Tribunals inferior to the supreme Court;

To define and punish Piracies and Felonies committed on the high Seas, and Offenses against the Law of Nations;

To declare War, grant Letters of Marque and Reprisal, and make Rules concerning Captures on Land and Water;

To raise and support Armies, but no Appropriation of Money to that Use shall be for a longer Term than two Years;

To provide and maintain a Navy;

To make Rules for the Government and Regulation of the land and naval Forces;

To provide for calling forth the Militia to execute the Laws of the Union, suppress Insurrections and repel Invasions;

To provide for organizing, arming, and disciplining the Militia, and for governing such Part of them as may be employed in the Service of the United States, reserving to the States respectively, the Appointment of the Officers, and the Authority of training the Militia according to the discipline prescribed by Congress;

To exercise exclusive Legislation in all Cases whatsoever, over such District (not exceeding ten Miles square) as may, by Cession of particular States, and the acceptance of Congress, become the Seat of the Government of the United States, and to exercise like Authority over all Places purchased by the Consent of the Legislature of the State in which the Same shall be, for the Erection of Forts, Magazines, Arsenals, dock-Yards, and other needful Buildings; — And

To make all Laws which shall be necessary and proper for carrying into Execution the foregoing Powers, and all other Powers vested by this Constitution in the Government of the United States, or in any Department or Officer thereof.

Section 9. The Migration or Importation of Such Persons as any of the States now existing shall think proper to admit, shall not be prohibited by the Congress prior to the Year one thousand eight hundred and eight, but a tax or duty may be imposed on such Importation, not exceeding ten dollars for each Person.

The privilege of the Writ of Habeas Corpus shall not be suspended, unless when in Cases of Rebellion or Invasion the public Safety may require it.

No Bill of Attainder or ex post facto Law shall be passed.

No capitation, or other direct, Tax shall be laid, unless in Proportion to the Census or Enumeration herein before directed to be taken.

No Tax or Duty shall be laid on Articles exported from any State.

No preference shall be given by any Regulation of Commerce or Revenue to the Ports of one State over those of another: nor shall Vessels bound to, or from, one State be obliged to enter, clear, or pay Duties in another.

No money shall be drawn from the Treasury, but in Consequence of Appropriations made by Law; and a regular Statement and Account of the Receipts and Expenditures of all public Money shall be published from time to time.

No Title of Nobility shall be granted by the United States: And no Person holding any Office of Profit or Trust under them, shall, without the Consent of the Congress, accept of any present, Emolument, Office, or Title, of any kind whatever, from any King, Prince, or foreign State.

Section 10. No State shall enter into any Treaty, Alliance, or Confederation; grant Letters of Marque and Reprisal; coin Money; emit Bills of Credit; make any Thing but gold and silver Coin a Tender in Payment of Debts; pass any Bill of Attainder, ex post facto Law, or Law impairing the Obligation of Contracts, or grant any Title of Nobility.

No State shall, without the Consent of the Congress, lay any Imposts or Duties on Imports or Exports, except what may be absolutely necessary for executing its inspection Laws: and the net Produce of all Duties and Imposts, laid by any State on Imports or Exports, shall be for the Use of the Treasury of the United States; and all such Laws shall be subject to the Revision and Control of the Congress.

No State shall, without the Consent of Congress, lay any duty of Tonnage, keep Troops, or Ships of War in time of Peace, enter into any Agreement or Compact with another State, or with a foreign Power, or engage in War, unless actually invaded, or in such imminent Danger as will not admit of delay.

ARTICLE II

Section 1. The executive Power shall be vested in a President of the United States of America. He shall hold his Office during the Term of four Years, and, together with the Vice-President, chosen for the same Term, be elected, as follows:

Each State shall appoint, in such Manner as the Legislature thereof may direct, a

Number of Electors, equal to the whole Number of Senators and Representatives to which the State may be entitled in the Congress: but no Senator or Representative, or Person holding an Office of Trust or Profit under the United States, shall be appointed an Elector.

The Electors shall meet in their respective States, and vote by Ballot for two persons, of whom one at least shall not be an Inhabitant of the same State with themselves. And they shall make a List of all the Persons voted for, and of the Number of Votes for each; which List they shall sign and certify, and transmit sealed to the Seat of the Government of the United States, directed to the President of the Senate. The President of the Senate shall, in the Presence of the Senate and House of Representatives, open all the Certificates, and the Votes shall then be counted. The Person having the greatest Number of Votes shall be the President, if such Number be a Majority of the whole Number of Electors appointed; and if there be more than one who have such Majority, and have an equal Number of Votes, then the House of Representatives shall immediately chuse by Ballot one of them for President; and if no Person have a Majority, then from the five highest on the List the said House shall in like Manner chuse the President. But in chusing the President, the Votes shall be taken by States, the Representation from each State having one Vote; A quorum for this Purpose shall consist of a Member or Members from two thirds of the States, and a Majority of all the States shall be necessary to a Choice. In every Case, after the Choice of the President, the Person having the greatest Number of Votes of the Electors shall be the Vice President. But if there should remain two or more who have equal Votes, the Senate shall chuse from them by Ballot the Vice President.

The Congress may determine the Time of chusing the Electors, and the Day on which they shall give their Votes; which Day shall be the same throughout the United States.

No person except a natural born Citizen, or a Citizen of the United States, at the time of the Adoption of this Constitution, shall be eligible to the Office of President; neither shall any Person be eligible to that Office who shall not have attained to the Age of thirty-five Years, and been fourteen Years a Resident within the United States.

In case of the removal of the President from Office, or of his Death, Resignation, or Inability to discharge the Powers and Duties of the said Office, the same shall devolve on the Vice President, and the Congress may by Law provide for the Case of Removal, Death, Resignation or Inability, both of the President and Vice President, declaring what Officer shall then act as President, and such Officer shall act accordingly, until the Disability be removed, or a President shall be elected.

The President shall, at stated Times, receive for his Services, a Compensation, which shall neither be encreased nor diminished during the Period for which he shall have been elected, and he shall not receive within that Period any other Emolument from the United States, or any of them.

Before he enter on the Execution of his Office, he shall take the following Oath or Affirmation: — "I do solemnly swear (or affirm) that I will faithfully execute the Office of President of the United States, and will to the best of my Ability, preserve, protect and defend the Constitution of the United States."

Section 2. The President shall be Commander in Chief of the Army and Navy of the United States, and the Militia of the several States, when called into the actual Service of the United States; he may require the Opinion, in writing, of the principal Officer in each of the executive Departments, upon any subject relating to the Duties of their respective Offices, and he shall have Power to grant Reprieves and Pardons for Offenses against the United States, except in Cases of Impeachment.

He shall have Power, by and with the Advice and Consent of the Senate, to make Treaties, provided two thirds of the Senators present concur; and he shall nominate, and by and with the Advice and Consent of the Senate, shall appoint Ambassadors, other public Ministers and Consuls, Judges of the supreme Court, and all other Officers of the United States, whose Appointments are not herein otherwise provided for, and which shall be established by Law; but the Congress may by Law vest the Appointment of such inferior Officers, as they think proper, in the President alone, in the Courts of Law, or in the Heads of Departments.

The President shall have Power to fill up all Vacancies that may happen during the Recess of the Senate, by granting Commissions which shall expire at the End of their next Session.

Section 3. He shall from time to time give to the Congress Information of the State of the Union, and recommend to their Consideration such Measures as he shall judge necessary and expedient; he may, on extraordinary Occasions, convene both Houses, or either of them, and in Case of Disagreement between them, with Respect to the Time of Adjournment, he may adjourn them to such Time as he shall think proper; he shall receive Ambassadors and other public Ministers; he shall take Care that the Laws be faithfully executed, and shall Commission all the Officers of the United States.

Section 4. The President, Vice President and all civil Officers of the United States, shall be removed from Office on Impeachment for, and Conviction of, Treason, Bribery, or other high Crimes and Misdemeanors.

ARTICLE III

Section 1. The judicial Power of the United States, shall be vested in one supreme Court, and in such inferior Courts as the Congress may from time to time ordain and establish. The Judges, both of the Supreme and inferior Courts, shall hold their Offices during good Behaviour, and shall, at stated Times, receive for their Services a Compensation which shall not be diminished during their Continuance in Office.

Section 2. The judicial Power shall extend to all Cases, in Law and Equity, arising under this Constitution, the Laws of the United States, and Treaties made, or which shall be made, under their authority; — to all Cases affecting Ambassadors, other public Ministers and Consuls; — to all Cases of admiralty and maritime Jurisdiction; — to Controversies to which the United States shall be a Party; — to Controversies between two or more States; — between a State and Citizens of another State; — between Citizens of different States; — between Citizens of the same State claiming Lands under Grants of different States, and between a State, or the Citizens thereof, and foreign States, Citizens or Subjects.

In all Cases affecting Ambassadors, other public Ministers and Consuls, and those in which a State shall be Party, the supreme Court shall have original Jurisdiction. In all the other Cases before mentioned, the supreme Court shall have appellate Jurisdiction, both as to Law and Fact, with such Exceptions, and under such Regulations as the Congress shall make.

The trial of all Crimes, except in Cases of Impeachment, shall be by Jury; and such Trial shall be held in the State where the said Crimes shall have been committed; but when not committed within any State, the Trial shall be at such Place or Places as the Congress may by Law have directed.

Section 3. Treason against the United States, shall consist only in levying War against them, or, in adhering to their Enemies, giving them Aid and Comfort. No Person shall be convicted of Treason unless on the Testimony of Two Witnesses to the same overt Act, or on Confession in open Court.

The Congress shall have power to declare the Punishment of Treason, but no Attainder of Treason shall work Corruption of Blood, or Forfeiture except during the Life of the Person attainted.

ARTICLE IV

Section 1. Full Faith and Credit shall be given in each State to the public Acts, Records, and judicial Proceedings of every other State. And the Congress may by general

Laws prescribe the Manner in which such Acts, Records and Proceedings shall be proved, and the Effect thereof.

Section 2. The Citizens of each State shall be entitled to all Privileges and Immunities of Citizens in the several States.

A Person charged in any State with Treason, Felony, or other Crime, who shall flee from Justice, and be found in another State, shall on demand of the executive Authority of the State from which he fled, be delivered up, to be removed to the State having Jurisdiction of the Crime.

No Person held to Service or Labour in one State, under the Laws thereof, escaping into another, shall, in Consequence of any Law or Regulation therein, be discharged from such Service or Labour, but shall be delivered up on Claim of the Party to whom such Service or Labour may be due.

Section 3. New States may be admitted by the Congress into this Union; but no new State shall be formed or erected within the Jurisdiction of any other State; nor any State be formed by the Junction of two or more States, or parts of States, without the Consent of the Legislatures of the States concerned as well as of the Congress.

The Congress shall have Power to dispose of and make all needful Rules and Regulations respecting the Territory or other Property belonging to the United States; and nothing in this Constitution shall be so construed as to Prejudice any Claims of the United States, or of any particular State.

Section 4. The United States shall guarantee to every State in this Union a Republican Form of Government, and shall protect each of them against Invasion; and on Application of the Legislature, or of the Executive (when the Legislature cannot be convened) against domestic Violence.

ARTICLE V

The Congress, whenever two thirds of both Houses shall deem it necessary, shall propose Amendments to this Constitution, or, on the Application of the Legislatures of two thirds of the several States, shall call a Convention for proposing Amendments, which, in either Case, shall be valid to all Intents and Purposes, as part of this Constitution, when ratified by the Legislatures of three fourths of the several States, or by Conventions in three fourths thereof, as the one or the other Mode of Ratification may be proposed by the Congress; Provided that no Amendment which may be made prior to the Year One thousand eight hundred and eight shall in any Manner affect the first and fourth Clauses in the Ninth Section of the first Article; and that no State, without its Consent, shall be deprived of its equal Suffrage in the Senate.

ARTICLE VI

All Debts contracted and Engagements entered into, before the Adoption of this Constitution shall be as valid against the United States under this Constitution, as under the Confederation.

This Constitution, and the Laws of the United States which shall be made in Pursuance thereof; and all Treaties made, or which shall be made, under the Authority of the United States, shall be the supreme Law of the Land; and the Judges in every State shall be bound thereby, any Thing in the Constitution or Laws of any State to the Contrary notwithstanding.

The Senators and Representatives before mentioned, and the Members of the several State Legislatures, and all executive and judicial Officers, both of the United States and of the several States, shall be bound by Oath or Affirmation, to support this Constitution; but no religious Test shall ever be required as a Qualification to any Office or public Trust under the United States.

ARTICLE VII

The Ratification of the Conventions of nine States shall be sufficient for the Establishment of this Constitution between the States so ratifying the Same.
Articles in Addition to, and Amendment of, the Constitution of the United States of America, Proposed by Congress and Ratified by the Several States, Pursuant to the Fifth Article of the Original Constitution

AMENDMENT I

Congress shall make no law respecting an establishment of religion, or prohibiting the free exercise thereof; or abridging the freedom of speech, or of the press; or the right of the people peaceably to assemble, and to petition the Government for a redress of grievances.

AMENDMENT II

A well regulated Militia, being necessary to the security of a free State, the right of the people to keep and bear Arms, shall not be infringed.

AMENDMENT III

No Soldier shall, in time of peace be quartered in any house, without the consent of the Owner, nor in time of war, but in a manner to be prescribed by law.

AMENDMENT IV

The right of the people to be secure in their persons, houses, papers, and effects, against unreasonable searches and seizures, shall not be violated, and no Warrants shall issue, but upon probable cause, supported by Oath or affirmation, and particularly describing the place to be searched, and the persons or things to be seized.

AMENDMENT V

No person shall be held to answer for a capital, or otherwise infamous crime, unless on a presentment or indictment of a Grand Jury, except in cases arising in the land or naval forces, or in the Militia, when in actual service in time of War or public danger; nor shall any person be subject for the same offence to be twice put in jeopardy of life or limb; nor shall be compelled in any criminal case to be a witness against himself, nor be deprived of life, liberty, or property, without due process of law; nor shall private property be taken for public use, without just compensation.

AMENDMENT VI

In all criminal prosecutions, the accused shall enjoy the right to a speedy and public trial, by an impartial jury of the State and district wherein the crime shall have been committed, which district shall have been previously ascertained by law, and to be informed of the nature and cause of the accusation; to be confronted with the witnesses against him; to have compulsory process for obtaining witnesses in his favor, and to have the Assistance of Counsel for his defence.

AMENDMENT VII

In suits at common law, where the value in controversy shall exceed twenty dollars, the right of trial by jury shall be preserved, and no fact tried by jury, shall be otherwise reexamined in any Court of the United States, than according to the rules of the common law.

AMENDMENT VIII

Excessive bail shall not be required, nor excessive fines imposed, nor cruel and unusual punishments inflicted.

AMENDMENT IX

The enumeration in the Constitution, of certain rights, shall not be construed to deny or disparage others retained by the people.

AMENDMENT X

The powers not delegated to the United States by the Constitution, nor prohibited by it to the States, are reserved to the States respectively, or to the people.

AMENDMENT XI [1798]

The Judicial power of the United States shall not be construed to extend to any suit in law or equity, commenced or prosecuted against one of the United States by Citizens of another State, or by Citizens or Subjects of any Foreign State.

AMENDMENT XII [1804]

The electors shall meet in their respective states and vote by ballot for President and Vice-President, one of whom, at least, shall not be an inhabitant of the same state with themselves; they shall name in their ballots the person voted for as President, and in distinct ballots the person voted for as Vice-President, and they shall make distinct lists of all persons voted for as President, and of all persons voted for as Vice-President, and of the number of votes for each, which lists they shall sign and certify, and transmit sealed to the seat of the government of the United States, directed to the President of the Senate; — The President of the Senate shall, in presence of the Senate and House of Representatives, open all the certificates and the votes shall then be counted; — The person having the greatest number of votes for President, shall be the President, if such number be a majority of the whole number of Electors appointed; and if no person have such majority, then from the persons having the highest numbers not exceeding three on the list of those voted for as President, the House of Representatives shall choose immediately, by ballot, the President. But in choosing the President, the votes shall be taken by states, the representation from each state having one vote; a quorum for this purpose shall consist of a member or members from two-thirds of the states, and a majority of all the states shall be necessary to a choice. And if the House of Representatives shall not choose a President whenever the right of choice shall devolve upon them, before the fourth day of March next following, then the Vice-President shall act as President, as in the case of the death or other constitutional disability of the President. — The person having the greatest number of votes as Vice-President, shall be the Vice-President, if such number be a majority of the whole number of Electors appointed, and if no person have a majority, then from the two highest numbers on the list, the Senate shall choose the Vice-President; a quorum for the purpose shall consist of two-thirds of the whole number of Senators, and a majority of the whole number shall be necessary to a choice. But no person constitutionally ineligible to the office of President shall be eligible to that of Vice-President of the United States.

AMENDMENT XIII [1865]

Section 1. Neither slavery nor involuntary servitude, except as a punishment for crime whereof the party shall have been duly convicted, shall exist within the United States, or any place subject to their jurisdiction.

Section 2. Congress shall have power to enforce this article by appropriate legislation.

AMENDMENT XIV [1868]

Section 1. All persons born or naturalized in the United States, and subject to the jurisdiction thereof, are citizens of the United States and of the State wherein they reside. No State shall make or enforce any law which shall abridge the privileges or immunities of citizens of the United States; nor shall any State deprive any person of life, liberty, or property, without due process of law; nor deny to any person within its jurisdiction the equal protection of the laws.

Section 2. Representatives shall be apportioned among the Several States according to their respective numbers, counting the whole number of persons in each State, excluding Indians not taxed. But when the right to vote at any election for the choice of electors for President and Vice President of the United States, Representatives in Congress, the Executive and Judicial officers of a State, or the members of the Legislature thereof, is denied to any of the male inhabitants of such State, being twenty-one years of age, and citizens of the United States, or in any way abridged, except for participation in rebellion, or other crime, the basis of representation therein shall be reduced in the proportion which the number of such male citizens shall bear to the whole number of male citizens twenty-one years of age in such State.

Section 3. No person shall be a Senator or Representative in Congress, or elector of President and Vice President, or hold any office, civil or military, under the United States, or under any State, who, having previously taken an oath, as a member of Congress, or as an officer of the United States, or as a member of any State legislature, or as an executive or judicial officer of any State, to support the Constitution of the United States, shall have engaged in insurrection or rebellion against the same, or given aid or comfort to the enemies thereof. But Congress may by a vote of two-thirds of each House, remove such disability.

Section 4. The validity of the public debt of the United States, authorized by law, including debts incurred for payment of pensions and bounties for services in suppressing insurrection or rebellion, shall not be questioned. But neither the United States nor any State shall assume or pay any debt or obligation incurred in aid of insurrection or rebellion against the United States, or any claim for the loss or emancipation of any slave; but all such debts, obligations and claims shall be held illegal and void.

Section 5. The Congress shall have power to enforce, by appropriate legislation, the provisions of this article.

AMENDMENT XV [1870]

Section 1. The right of citizens of the United States to vote shall not be denied or abridged by the United States or by any State on account of race, color, or previous condition of servitude —

Section 2. The Congress shall have power to enforce this article by appropriate legislation.

AMENDMENT XVI [1913]

The Congress shall have power to lay and collect taxes on incomes, from whatever source derived, without apportionment among the several States, and without regard to any census or enumeration.

AMENDMENT XVII [1913]

The Senate of the United States shall be composed of two Senators from each State, elected by the people thereof, for six years; and each Senator shall have one vote. The electors in each State shall have the qualifications requisite for electors of the most numerous branch of the State legislatures.

When vacancies happen in the representation of any State in the Senate, the executive authority of such State shall issue writs of election to fill such vacancies: *Provided*, That the legislature of any State may empower the executive thereof to make temporary appointments until the people fill the vacancies by election as the legislature may direct.

This amendment shall not be so construed as to affect the election or term of any Senator chosen before it becomes valid as part of the Constitution.

AMENDMENT XVIII [1919]

Section 1. After one year from the ratification of this article the manufacture, sale, or transportation of intoxicating liquors within, the importation thereof into, or the exportation thereof from the United States and all territory subject to the jurisdiction thereof for beverage purposes is hereby prohibited.

Section 2. The Congress and the several States shall have concurrent power to enforce this article by appropriate legislation.

Section 3. This article shall be inoperative unless it shall have been ratified as an amendment to the Constitution by the legislatures of the several States, as provided in the Constitution, within seven years from the date of the submission hereof to the States by the Congress.

AMENDMENT XIX [1920]

The right of citizens of the United States to vote shall not be denied or abridged by the United States or by any State on account of sex.

Congress shall have power to enforce this article by appropriate legislation.

AMENDMENT XX [1933]

Section 1. The terms of the President and Vice President shall end at noon on the 20th day of January, and the terms of Senators and Representatives at noon on the 3d day of January, of the years in which such terms would have ended if this article had not been ratified; and the terms of their successors shall then begin.

Section 2. The Congress shall assemble at least once in every year, and such meeting shall begin at noon on the 3d day of January, unless they shall by law appoint a different day.

Section 3. If, at the time fixed for the beginning of the term of the President, the President elect shall have died, the Vice President elect shall become President. If a President shall not have been chosen before the time fixed for the beginning of his term, or if the President elect shall have failed to qualify, then the Vice President elect shall act as President until a President shall have qualified; and the Congress may by law provide for the case wherein neither a President elect nor a Vice President elect shall have qualified, declaring who shall then act as President, or the manner in which one who is to act shall be selected, and such person shall act accordingly until a President or Vice President shall have qualified.

Section 4. The Congress may by law provide for the case of the death of any of the persons from whom the House of Representatives may choose a President whenever the right of choice shall have devolved upon them, and for the case of the death of any of the persons from whom the Senate may choose a Vice President whenever the right of choice shall have devolved upon them.

Section 5. Sections 1 and 2 shall take effect on the 15th day of October following the ratification of this article.

Section 6. This article shall be inoperative unless it shall have been ratified as an amendment to the Constitution by the legislatures of three-fourths of the several States within seven years from the date of its submission.

AMENDMENT XXI [1933]

Section 1. The eighteenth article of amendment to the Constitution of the United States is hereby repealed.

Section 2. The transportation or importation into any State, Territory, or possession of the United States for delivery or use therein of intoxicating liquors, in violation of the laws thereof, is hereby prohibited.

Section 3. This article shall be inoperative unless it shall have been ratified as an amendment to the Constitution by conventions in the several States, as provided in the Constitution, within seven years from the date of the submission hereof to the States by the Congress.

AMENDMENT XXII [1951]

Section 1. No person shall be elected to the office of the President more than twice, and no person who has held the office of President, or acted as President, for more than two years of a term to which some other person was elected President shall be elected to the office of the President more than once. But this Article shall not apply to any person holding the office of President when this article was proposed by the Congress, and shall not prevent any person who may be holding the office of President, or acting as President, during the term within which this Article becomes operative from holding the office of President or acting as President during the remainder of such term.

Section 2. This article shall be inoperative unless it shall have been ratified as an amendment to the Constitution by the legislatures of three-fourths of the several States within seven years from the date of its submission to the States by the Congress.

AMENDMENT XXIII [1961]

Section 1. The District constituting the seat of Government of the United States shall appoint in such manner as the Congress may direct:

A number of electors of President and Vice President equal to the whole number of Senators and Representatives in Congress to which the District would be entitled if it were a State, but in no event more than the least populous State; they shall be in addition to those appointed by the States, but they shall be considered, for the purposes of the election of President and Vice President, to be electors appointed by a State; and they shall meet in the District and perform such duties as provided by the twelfth article of amendment.

Section 2. The Congress shall have power to enforce this article by appropriate legislation.

AMENDMENT XXIV [1964]

Section 1. The right of citizens of the United States to vote in any primary or other election for President or Vice President, for electors for President or Vice President, or for Senator or Representative in Congress, shall not be abridged by the United States or any State by reason of failure to pay any poll tax or other tax.

Section 2. The Congress shall have power to enforce this article by appropriate legislation.

AMENDMENT XXV [1967]

Section 1. In case of the removal of the President from office or of his death or resignation, the Vice President shall become President.

Section 2. Whenever there is a vacancy in the office of the Vice President, the President shall nominate a Vice President who shall take office upon confirmation by a majority vote of both Houses of Congress.

Section 3. Whenever the President transmits to the President pro tempore of the Senate and the Speaker of the House of Representatives his written declaration that he is unable to discharge the powers and duties of his office, and until he transmits to them a written declaration to the contrary, such powers and duties shall be discharged by the Vice President as Acting President.

Section 4. Whenever the Vice President and a majority of either the principal officers of the executive departments or of such other body as Congress may by law provide, transmit to the President pro tempore of the Senate and the Speaker of the House of Representatives their written declaration that the President is unable to discharge the powers and duties of his office, the Vice President shall immediately assume the powers and duties of the office as Acting President.

Thereafter, when the President transmits to the President pro tempore of the Senate and the Speaker of the House of Representatives his written declaration that no inability exists, he shall resume the powers and duties of his office unless the Vice President and a majority of either the principal officers of the executive department or of such other body as Congress may by law provide, transmit within four days to the President pro tempore of the Senate and the Speaker of the House of Representatives their written declaration that the President is unable to discharge the powers and duties of his office. Thereupon Congress shall decide the issue, assembling within forty-eight hours for that purpose if not in session. If the Congress, within twenty-one days after receipt of the latter written declaration, or, if Congress is not in session, within twenty-one days after Congress is required to assemble, determines by two-thirds vote of both Houses that the President is unable to discharge the powers and duties of his office, the Vice President shall continue to discharge the same as Acting President; otherwise, the President shall resume the powers and duties of his office.

AMENDMENT XXVI [1971]

Section 1. The right of citizens of the United States, who are eighteen years of age or older, to vote shall not be denied or abridged by the United States or by any State on account of age.

Section 2. The Congress shall have power to enforce this article by appropriate legislation.

Throughout the book the numbered footnotes are reproduced from the text quoted, without change of number. Lettered footnotes, with consecutive lettering in each chapter, have been inserted by the Editors.

Judicial Review *Part One*

Chapter One Historic Basis

Marbury v. Madison *1 Cranch 137, 2 L. Ed. 60 (1803)*

[MARSHALL, C.J., delivered the opinion of the Court.]
　At the last term on the affidavits then read and filed with the clerk, a rule was granted in this case, requiring the secretary of state to show cause why a mandamus should not issue, directing him to deliver to William Marbury his commission as a justice of the peace for the county of Washington, in the District of Columbia.
　No cause has been shown, and the present motion is for a mandamus. The peculiar delicacy of this case, the novelty of some of its circumstances, and the real difficulty attending the points which occur in it, require a complete exposition of the principles on which the opinion to be given by the court is founded.
　These principles have been, on the side of the applicant, very ably argued at the bar. In rendering the opinion of the court, there will be some departure in form, though not in substance, from the points stated in that argument.
　In the order in which the court has viewed this subject, the following questions have been considered and decided.
　1st. Has the applicant a right to the commission he demands?
　2d. If he has a right, and that right has been violated, do the laws of his country afford him a remedy?
　3d. If they do afford him a remedy, is it a mandamus issuing from this court?
　The first object of inquiry is,
　1st. Has the applicant a right to the commission he demands?
　His right originates in an act of congress passed in February, 1801, concerning the District of Columbia.
　After dividing the district into two counties, the 11th section of this law enacts, "that there shall be appointed in and for each of the said counties, such number of discreet persons to be justices of the peace as the president of the United States shall, from time to time, think expedient, to continue in office for five years."
　It appears, from the affidavits, that in compliance with this law, a commission for William Marbury, as a justice of the peace for the county of Washington, was signed by John Adams, then President of the United States; after which the seal of the United States

Chapter One. Historic Basis

was affixed to it; but the commission has never reached the person for whom it was made out.

In order to determine whether he is entitled to this commission, it becomes necessary to inquire whether he has been appointed to the office. For if he has been appointed, the law continues him in office for five years, and he is entitled to the possession of those evidences of office, which, being completed, became his property.

The 2d section of the 2d article of the constitution declares, that "the president shall nominate, and, by and with the advice and consent of the senate, shall appoint, ambassadors, other public ministers and consuls, and all other officers of the United States, whose appointments are not otherwise provided for."

The 3d section declares, that "he shall commission all the officers of the United States."

An act of congress directs the secretary of state to keep the seal of the United States, "to make out and record, and affix the said seal to all civil commissions to officers of the United States, to be appointed by the president, by and with the consent of the senate, or by the president alone; provided, that the said seal shall not be affixed to any commission before the same shall have been signed by the President of the United States." . . .

The last act to be done by the President is the signature of the commission. He has then acted on the advice and consent of the senate to his own nomination. The time for deliberation has then passed. He has decided. His judgment, on the advice and consent of the senate concurring with his nomination, has been made, and the officer is appointed. . . .

It is, therefore, decidedly the opinion of the court, that when a commission has been signed by the President, the appointment is made; and that the commission is complete when the seal of the United States has been affixed to it by the Secretary of State.

Where an officer is removable at the will of the executive, the circumstance which completes his appointment is of no concern; because the act is at any time revocable; and the commission may be arrested, if still in the office. But when the officer is not removable at the will of the executive, the appointment is not revocable, and cannot be annulled. It has conferred legal rights which cannot be resumed.

The discretion of the executive is to be exercised until the appointment has been made. But having once made the appointment, his power over the office is terminated in all cases, where by law the officer is not removable by him. The right to the office is then in the person appointed, and he has the absolute, unconditional power of accepting or rejecting it. . . .

To withhold his commission, therefore, is an act deemed by the court not warranted by law, but violative of a vested legal right.

This brings us to the second inquiry; which is,

2d. If he has a right, and that right has been violated, do the laws of this country afford him a remedy?

The very essence of civil liberty certainly consists in the right of every individual to claim the protection of the laws, whenever he receives an injury. One of the first duties of government is to afford that protection. In Great Britain the king himself is sued in the respectful form of a petition, and he never fails to comply with the judgment of his court. . . .

The government of the United States has been emphatically termed a government of laws, and not of men. It will certainly cease to deserve this high appellation, if the laws furnish no remedy for the violation of a vested legal right.

If this obloquy is to be cast on the jurisprudence of our country, it must arise from the peculiar character of the case. . . .

It follows, then, that the question, whether the legality of an act of the head of a department be examinable in a court of justice or not, must always depend on the nature of that act. . . .

By the constitution of the United States, the President is invested with certain important political powers, in the exercise of which he is to use his own discretion, and is accountable only to his country in his political character and to his own conscience. To aid him in the performance of these duties, he is authorized to appoint certain officers, who act by his authority, and in conformity with his orders.

In such cases, their acts are his acts; and whatever opinion may be entertained of the manner in which executive discretion may be used, still there exists, and can exist, no power to control that discretion. The subjects are political. They respect the nation, not individual rights, and being intrusted to the executive, the decision of the executive is conclusive. The application of this remark will be perceived by adverting to the act of congress for establishing the department of foreign affairs. This officer, as his duties were prescribed by that act, is to conform precisely to the will of the President. He is the mere organ by whom that will is communicated. The acts of such an officer, as an officer, can never be examinable by the courts.

But when the legislature proceeds to impose on that officer other duties; when he is directed peremptorily to perform certain acts; when the rights of individuals are dependent on the performance of those acts; he is so far the officer of the law; is amenable to the laws for his conduct; and cannot at his discretion sport away the vested rights of others.

The conclusion from this reasoning is, that where the heads of departments are the political or confidential agents of the executive, merely to execute the will of the President, or rather to act in cases in which the executive possesses a constitutional or legal discretion, nothing can be more perfectly clear than that their acts are only politically examinable. But where a specific duty is assigned by law, and individual rights depend upon the performance of that duty, it seems equally clear that the individual who considers himself injured, has a right to resort to the laws of his country for a remedy. . . .

It remains to be inquired whether,

3d. He is entitled to the remedy for which he applies. This depends on,

1st. The nature of the writ applied for; and,

2d. The power of this court.

1st. The nature of the writ. . . .

This writ, if awarded, would be directed to an officer of government, and its mandate to him would be, to use the words of Blackstone, "to do a particular thing therein specified, which appertains to his office and duty, and which the court has previously determined, or at least supposes, to be consonant to right and justice." Or, in the words of Lord Mansfield, the applicant, in this case, has a right to execute an office of public concern, and is kept out of possession of that right.

These circumstances certainly concur in this case.

Still, to render the mandamus a proper remedy, the officer to whom it is to be directed, must be one to whom, on legal principles, such writ may be directed; and the person applying for it must be without any other specific and legal remedy.

1st. With respect to the officer to whom it would be directed. The initimate political relation subsisting between the President of the United States and the heads of departments, necessarily renders any legal investigation of the acts of one of those high officers peculiarly irksome, as well as delicate; and excites some hesitation with respect to the propriety of entering into such investigation. Impressions are often received without much reflection or examination, and it is not wonderful that in such a case as this the assertion, by an individual, of his legal claims in a court of justice, to which claims it is the duty of that court to attend, should at first view be considered by some, as an attempt to intrude into the cabinet, and to intermeddle with the prerogatives of the executive.

It is scarcely necessary for the court to disclaim all pretentions to such jurisdiction. An extravagance, so absurd and excessive, could not have been entertained for a moment. The province of the court is, solely, to decide on the rights of individuals, not to inquire how the executive, or executive officers, perform duties in which they have a discretion.

Questions in their nature political, or which are, by the constitution and laws, submitted to the executive, can never be made in this court.

But, if this be not such a question; if, so far from being an intrusion into the secrets of the cabinet, it respects a paper which, according to law, is upon record, and to a copy of which the law gives a right, on the payment of ten cents; if it be no intermeddling with a subject over which the executive can be considered as having exercised any control; what is there in the exalted station of the officer, which shall bar a citizen from asserting, in a court of justice, his legal rights, or shall forbid a court to listen to the claim, or to issue a mandamus directing the performance of a duty, not depending on executive discretion, but on particular acts of congress, and the general principles of law?

If one of the heads of departments commits any illegal act, under colour of his office, by which an individual sustains an injury, it cannot be pretended that his office alone exempts him from being sued in the ordinary mode of proceeding, and being compelled to obey the judgment of the law. How, then, can his office exempt him from this particular mode of deciding on the legality of his conduct if the case be such a case as would, were any other individual the party complained of, authorize the process? . . .

. . . [W]here he is directed by law to do a certain act affecting the absolute rights of individuals, in the performance of which he is not placed under the particular direction of the president, and the performance of which the president cannot lawfully forbid, and therefore is never presumed to have forbidden; as for example to record a commission, or a patent for land, which has received all the legal solemnities; or to give a copy of such record; in such cases, it is not perceived on what ground the courts of the country are further excused from the duty of giving judgment that right be done to an injured individual, than if the same services were to be performed by a person not the head of a department. . . .

This, then, is a plain case for a mandamus, either to deliver the commission, or a copy of it from the record; and it only remains to be inquired,

Whether it can issue from this court.

The act to establish the judicial courts of the United States authorizes the Supreme Court "to issue writs of mandamus in cases warranted by the principles and usages of law, to any courts appointed, or persons holding office, under the authority of the United States."[a]

The Secretary of State, being a person holding an office under the authority of the United States, is precisely within the letter of the description, and if this court is not authorized to issue a writ of mandamus to such an officer, it must be because the law is unconstitutional, and therefore absolutely incapable of conferring the authority, and assigning the duties which its words purport to confer and assign.

The constitution vests the whole judicial power of the United States in one Supreme Court, and such inferior courts as congress shall, from time to time, ordain and establish. This power is expressly extended to all cases arising under the laws of the United States; and, consequently, in some form, may be exercised over the present case; because the right claimed is given by a law of the United States.

---

[a] Section 13 of the Judiciary Act of 1789 provided: "*And it be further enacted*, That the Supreme Court shall have exclusive jurisdiction of all controversies of a civil nature, where a state is a party, except between a state and its citizens; and except also between a state and citizens of other states, or aliens, in which latter case it shall have original but not exclusive jurisdiction. And shall have exclusively all such jurisdiction of suits or proceedings against ambassadors, or other public ministers, or their domestics, or domestic servants, as a court of law can have or exercise consistently with the law of nations; and original, but not exclusive jurisdiction of all suits brought by ambassadors, or other public ministers, or in which a consul, or vice consul, shall be a party. And the trial of issues in fact in the Supreme Court, in all actions at law against citizens of the United States, shall be by jury. The Supreme Court shall also have appellate jurisdiction from the circuit courts and courts of the several states, in the cases herein after specially provided for; and shall have power to issue writs of prohibition to the district courts, when proceeding as courts of admiralty and maritime jurisdiction, and writs of *mandamus*, in cases warranted by the principles and usages of law, to any courts appointed, or persons holding office, under the authority of the United States." — Ed.

In the distribution of this power it is declared that "the Supreme Court shall have original jurisdiction in all cases affecting ambassadors, other public ministers and consuls, and those in which a state shall be a party. In all other cases, the Supreme Court shall have appellate jurisdiction."

It has been insisted, at the bar, that as the original grant of jurisdiction, to the Supreme and inferior courts, is general, and the clause, assigning original jurisdiction to the Supreme Court, contains no negative or restrictive words, the power remains to the legislature, to assign original jurisdiction to that court in other cases than those specified in the article which has been recited; provided those cases belong to the judicial power of the United States.

If it had been intended to leave it in the discretion of the legislature to apportion the judicial power between the Supreme and inferior courts according to the will of that body, it would certainly have been useless to have proceeded further than to have defined the judicial power, and the tribunals in which it should be vested. The subsequent part of the section is mere surplusage, is entirely without meaning, if such is to be the construction. If congress remains at liberty to give this court appellate jurisdiction, where the constitution has declared their jurisdiction shall be original; and original jurisdiction where the constitution has declared it shall be appellate; the distribution of jurisdiction, made in the constitution, is form without substance.

Affirmative words are often, in their operation, negative of other objects than those affirmed; and in this case, a negative or exclusive sense must be given to them, or they have no operation at all.

It cannot be presumed that any clause in the constitution is intended to be without effect; and, therefore, such a construction is inadmissible, unless the words require it.

If the solicitude of the convention, respecting our peace with foreign powers, induced a provision that the Supreme Court should take original jurisdiction in cases which might be supposed to affect them; yet the clause would have proceeded no further than to provide for such cases, if no further restriction on the powers of congress had been intended. That they should have appellate jurisdiction in all other cases, with such exceptions as congress might make, is no restriction; unless the words be deemed exclusive of original jurisdiction. . . .

To enable this court, then, to issue a mandamus, it must be shown to be an exercise of appellate jurisdiction, or to be necessary to enable them to exercise appellate jurisdiction.

It has been stated at the bar that the appellate jurisdiction may be exercised in a variety of forms, and that if it be the will of the legislature that a mandamus should be used for that purpose, that will must be obeyed. This is true, yet the jurisdiction must be appellate, not original.

It is the essential criterion of appellate jurisdiction, that it revises and corrects the proceedings in a cause already instituted, and does not create that cause. Although, therefore, a mandamus may be directed to courts, yet to issue such a writ to an officer for the delivery of a paper, is in effect the same as to sustain an original action for that paper, and, therefore, seems not to belong to appellate but to original jurisdiction. Neither is it necessary in such a case as this, to enable the court to exercise its appellate jurisdiction.

The authority, therefore, given to the Supreme Court, by the act establishing the judicial courts of the United States, to issue writs of mandamus to public officers, appears not to be warranted by the constitution; and it becomes necessary to inquire whether a jurisdiction so conferred can be exercised.

The question, whether an act, repugnant to the constitution, can become the law of the land, is a question deeply interesting to the United States; but, happily, not of an intricacy proportioned to its interest. It seems only necessary to recognize certain principles, supposed to have been long and well established, to decide it.

That the people have an original right to establish, for their future government, such principles, as, in their opinion, shall most conduce to their own happiness is the basis on which the whole American fabric has been erected. The exercise of this original right is a very great exertion; nor can it, nor ought it, to be frequently repeated. The principles, therefore, so established, are deemed fundamental. And as the authority from which they proceed is supreme, and can seldom act, they are designed to be permanent.

This original and supreme will organizes the government, and assigns to different departments their respective powers. It may either stop here, or establish certain limits not to be transcended by those departments.

The government of the United States is of the latter description. The powers of the legislature are defined and limited; and that those limits may not be mistaken, or forgotten, the constitution is written. To what purpose are powers limited, and to what purpose is that limitation committed to writing, if these limits may, at any time, be passed by those intended to be restrained? The distinction between a government with limited and unlimited powers is abolished, if those limits do not confine the persons on whom they are imposed, and if acts prohibited and acts allowed, are of equal obligation. It is a proposition too plain to be contested, that the constitution controls any legislative act repugnant to it; or, that the legislature may alter the constitution by an ordinary act.

Between these alternatives there is no middle ground. The constitution is either a superior paramount law, unchangeable by ordinary means, or it is on a level with ordinary legislative acts, and, like other acts, is alterable when the legislature shall please to alter it.

If the former part of the alternative be true, then a legislative act contrary to the constitution is not law: if the latter part be true, then written constitutions are absurd attempts, on the part of the people, to limit a power in its own nature illimitable.

Certainly all those who have framed written constitutions contemplate them as forming the fundamental and paramount law of the nation, and, consequently, the theory of every such government must be, that an act of the legislature, repugnant to the constitution, is void.

This theory is essentially attached to a written constitution, and is, consequently, to be considered, by this court, as one of the fundamental principles of our society. It is not therefore to be lost sight of in the further consideration of this subject.

If an act of the legislature, repugnant to the constitution, is void, does it, notwithstanding its invalidity, bind the courts, and oblige them to give it effect? Or, in other words, though it be not law, does it constitute a rule as operative as if it was a law? This would be to overthrow in fact what was established in theory; and would seem, at first view, an absurdity too gross to be insisted on. It shall, however, receive a more attentive consideration.

It is emphatically the province and duty of the judicial department to say what the law is. Those who apply the rule to particular cases, must of necessity expound and interpret that rule. If two laws conflict with each other, the courts must decide on the operation of each.

So if a law be in opposition to the constitution; if both the law and the constitution apply to a particular case, so that the court must either decide that case conformably to the law, disregarding the constitution; or conformably to the constitution, disregarding the law; the court must determine which of these conflicting rules governs the case. This is of the very essence of judicial duty.

If, then, the courts are to regard the constitution, and the constitution is superior to any ordinary act of the legislature, the constitution, and not such ordinary act, must govern the case to which they both apply.

Those, then, who controvert the principle that the constitution is to be considered, in court, as a paramount law, are reduced to the necessity of maintaining that courts must close their eyes on the constitution, and see only the law.

This doctrine would subvert the very foundation of all written constitutions. It would declare that an act which, according to the principles and theory of our government, is entirely void, is yet, in practice, completely obligatory. It would declare that if the legislature shall do what is expressly forbidden, such act, notwithstanding the express prohibition, is in reality effectual. It would be giving to the legislature a practical and real omnipotence, with the same breath which professes to restrict their powers within narrow limits. It is prescribing limits, and declaring that those limits may be passed at pleasure.

That it thus reduces to nothing what we have deemed the greatest improvement on political institutions, a written constitution, would of itself be sufficient, in America, where written constitutions have been viewed with so much reverence, for rejecting the construction. But the peculiar expressions of the constitution of the United States furnish additional arguments in favour of its rejection.

The judicial power of the United States is extended to all cases arising under the constitution.

Could it be the intention of those who gave this power, to say that in using it the constitution should not be looked into? That a case arising under the constitution should be decided without examining the instrument under which it arises?

This is too extravagant to be maintained.

In some cases, then, the constitution must be looked into by the judges. And if they can open it at all, what part of it are they forbidden to read or to obey?

There are many other parts of the constitution which serve to illustrate this subject.

It is declared that "no tax or duty shall be laid on articles exported from any state." Suppose a duty on the export of cotton, of tobacco, or of flour; and a suit instituted to recover it. Ought judgment to be rendered in such a case? Ought the judges to close their eyes on the constitution, and only see the law?

The constitution declares "that no bill of attainder or ex post facto law shall be passed."

If, however, such a bill should be passed, and a person should be prosecuted under it; must the court condemn to death those victims whom the constitution endeavors to preserve?

"No person," says the constitution, "shall be convicted of treason unless on the testimony of two witnesses to the same overt act, or on confession in open court."

Here the language of the constitution is addressed especially to the courts. It prescribes, directly for them, a rule of evidence not to be departed from. If the legislature should change that rule, and declare one witness, or a confession out of court, sufficient for conviction, must the constitutional principle yield to the legislative act?

From these, and many other selections which might be made, it is apparent, that the framers of the constitution contemplated that instrument as a rule for the government of courts, as well as of the legislature.

Why otherwise does it direct the judges to take an oath to support it? This oath certainly applies in an especial manner, to their conduct in their official character. How immoral to impose it on them, if they were to be used as the instruments, and the knowing instruments, for violating what they swear to support! . . .

It is also not entirely unworthy of observation, that in declaring what shall be the supreme law of the land, the constitution itself is first mentioned; and not the laws of the United States generally, but those only which shall be made in pursuance of the constitution, have that rank.

Thus, the particular phraseology of the constitution of the United States confirms and strengthens the principle, supposed to be essential to all written constitutions, that a law repugnant to the constitution is void; and that courts, as well as other departments, are bound by that instrument.

The rule must be discharged.[b]

[b] The several questions answered by the Chief Justice have been the subject of consideration in later cases:

1. *Completeness of an appointment on signing the commission.* See United States v. Le Baron, 19 How. 73 (1856) (effect of President's death); cf. United States v. Smith, 286 U.S. 6, 47 (1932): "The Executive Department has not always treated an appointment as complete upon the mere signing of a commission."

2. *Presidential power of removal.* Parsons v. United States, 167 U.S. 324 (1897) (effect of stated term of office); Myers v. United States, 272 U.S. 52 (1926) (removal of postmaster); Humphrey v. United States, 295 U.S.

Chapter One. Historic Basis

Eakin v. Raub 12 S. & R. 330 (Pa. 1825)

[Plaintiffs brought ejectment and defendants pleaded the statute of limitations, as amended. The amendment would have barred the plaintiffs immediately unless a prior saving clause for persons abroad was carried into the amendment. A majority of the court held that the saving clause was retained; Gibson, J., was of a contrary opinion and was obliged to consider the argument that if the amendment interposed an immediate bar it was unconstitutional. Only those portions of the opinions dealing with the latter issue are here printed.]

TILGHMAN, C.J. . . . Some doubts were thrown out by the counsel for the plaintiffs, whether, under the construction contended for by the counsel for the defendants, the supplementary act in question would not be contrary to the constitution of the United States and the state of Pennsylvania; and whether, in such case, this court should not declare it to be void. But, as I do not adopt the construction alluded to, no constitutional question can arise. At the same time, it may be expected, that I should express my opinion, as to what would be the duty of the court, if a case should be brought before them, in which they were clearly of opinion, that an act of assembly was made in violation of the constitution of the state or of the United States. I shall not enter into an argument on that point, as it is not brought before us, for judgment. It will be sufficient to say, that I adhere to the opinion which I have frequently expressed, that when a judge is convinced, beyond doubt, that an act has been passed in violation of the constitution, he is bound to declare it void, by his oath, by his duty to the party who has brought the cause before him, and to the people, the only source of legitimate power, who, when they formed the constitution of the state, expressly declared that certain things *"were excepted out of the general powers of government, and should for ever remain inviolate."* The people declared, also, on their adoption of the constitution of the United States, "that it should be the supreme law of the land, and that the judges in every state should be bound thereby, any thing in the constitution or laws of any state to the contrary notwithstanding." Upon this subject I have never entertained but one opinion, which has been strengthened by reflection, and fortified by the concurring sentiments of the Supreme Court of the United States, as well as of lawyers, judges, and statesmen of the highest standing in all parts of the United States of America. Nevertheless, the utmost deference is due to the opinion of the legislature, — so great, indeed, that a judge would be unpardonable, who, in a doubtful case should declare a law to be void. Let this suffice for the present occasion. Should a case arise, in which I shall think myself bound to decide against the validity of an act of assembly, I shall be prepared to give my reasons. . . .

GIBSON, J. . . . But it is said, that without it [the saving clause], the latter act would be unconstitutional; and, instead of controverting this, I will avail myself of it to express an opinion which I have deliberately formed, on the abstract right of the judiciary to declare an unconstitutional act of the legislature void.

It seems to me there is a plain difference, hitherto unnoticed, between acts that are repugnant to the constitution of the particular state, and acts that are repugnant to the constitution of the United States; my opinion being, that the judiciary is bound to execute the

---

602 (1935) (removal of Federal Trade Commissioner); Wiener v. United States, 357 U.S. 349 (1958) (removal of member of War Claims Commission); cf. McAllister v. United States, 141 U.S. 174 (1891) (suspension of territorial judge).

3. *Mandamus against a head of a department.* Kendall v. United States, 12 Pet. 524 (1838).

4. *Exclusiveness of Supreme Court's original jurisidction under Article III.* Cf. Ames v. Kansas, 111 U.S. 449 (1884) (suit by a state against citizen of another state); Bors v. Preston, 111 U.S. 252 (1884) (suit against foreign consul); Massachusetts v. Missouri, 308 U.S. 1 (1939) (suit by a state against citizens of another state); Ohio v. Wyandotte Chemicals Corp., 401 U.S. 493 (1971) (same).

Could Marbury have maintained his suit in another court?

See generally Van Alstyne, A Critical Guide to Marbury v. Madison, 1969 Duke L.J. 1. — ED.

former, but not the latter. I shall hereafter attempt to explain this difference, by pointing out the particular provisions in the constitution of the United States on which it depends. I am aware, that a right to declare all unconstitutional acts void, without distinction as to either constitution, is generally held as a professional dogma; but, I apprehend, rather as a matter of faith than of reason. I admit that I once embraced the same doctrine, but without examination, and I shall therefore state the arguments that impelled me to abandon it, with great respect for those by whom it is still maintained. But I may premise, that it is not a little remarkable, that although the right in question has all along been claimed by the judiciary, no judge has ventured to discuss it, except Chief Justice Marshall, (in Marbury v. Madison, 1 Cranch, 176), and if the argument of a jurist so distinguished for the strength of his ratiocinative powers be found inconclusive, it may fairly be set down to the weakness of the position which he attempts to defend. . . .

The constitution of Pennsylvania contains no express grant of political powers to the judiciary. But, to establish a grant by implication, the constitution is said to be a law of superior obligation; and, consequently, that if it were to come into collision with an act of the legislature, the latter would have to give way. This is conceded. But it is a fallacy, to suppose that they can come into collision *before the judiciary*. . . .

The constitution and the *right* of the legislature to pass the act, may be in collision. But is that a legitimate subject for judicial determination? If it be, the judiciary must be a peculiar organ, to revise the proceedings of the legislature, and to correct its mistakes; and in what part of the constitution are we to look for this proud pre-eminence? Viewing the matter in the opposite direction, what would be thought of an act of assembly in which it should be declared that the Supreme Court had, in a particular case, put a wrong construction on the constitution of the United States, and that the judgment should therefore be reversed? It would doubtless be thought a usurpation of judicial power. But it is by no means clear, that to declare a law void which has been enacted according to the forms prescribed in the constitution, is not a usurpation of legislative power. It is an act of sovereignty; and sovereignty and legislative power are said by Sir William Blackstone to be convertible terms. It is the business of the judiciary to interpret the laws, not scan the authority of the lawgiver; and without the latter, it cannot take cognizance of a collision between a law and the constitution. So that to affirm that the judiciary has a right to judge of the existence of such collision, is to take for granted the very thing to be proved. And, that a very cogent argument may be made in this way, I am not disposed to deny; for no conclusions are so strong as those that are drawn from the *petitio principii*.

But it has been said to be emphatically the business of the judiciary, to ascertain and pronounce what the law is; and that this necessarily involves a consideration of the constitution. It does so: but how far? If the judiciary will inquire into any thing beside the form of enactment, where shall it stop? There must be some point of limitation to such an inquiry; for no one will pretend, that a judge would be justifiable in calling for the election returns, or scrutinizing the qualifications of those who composed the legislature.

. . . But what I want more immediately to press on the attention, is the necessity of yielding to the acts of the legislature the same respect that is claimed for the acts of the judiciary. Repugnance to the constitution is not always self evident; for questions involving the consideration of its existence, require for their solution the most vigorous exertion of the higher faculties of the mind, and conflicts will be inevitable, if any branch is to apply the constitution after its own fashion to the acts of all the others. I take it, then, the legislature is entitled to all the deference that is due to the judiciary; that its acts are in no case to be treated as ipso facto void, except where they would produce a revolution in the government; and that, to avoid them, requires the act of some tribunal competent under the constitution, (if any such there be,) to pass on their validity. All that remains, therefore, is to inquire whether the judiciary or the people are that tribunal.

Now, as the judiciary is not expressly constituted for that purpose, it must derive whatever authority of the sort it may possess, from the reasonableness and fitness of the thing.

12　Chapter One.　Historic Basis

But, in theory, all the organs of the government are of equal capacity; or, if not equal, each must be supposed to have superior capacity only for those things which peculiarly belong to it; and, as legislation peculiarly involves the consideration of those limitations which are put on the law-making power, and the interpretation of the laws when made, involves only the construction of the laws themselves, it follows that the construction of the constitution in this particular belongs to the legislature, which ought therefore to be taken to have superior capacity to judge of the constitutionality of its own acts. But suppose all to be of equal capacity in every respect, why should one exercise a controlling power over the rest? That the judiciary is of superior rank, has never been pretended, although it has been said to be co-ordinate. It is not easy, however, to comprehend how the power which gives law to all the rest, can be of no more than equal rank with one which receives it, and is answerable to the former for the observance of its statutes. . . . Both the executive, strictly as such, and the judiciary are subordinate; and an act of superior power exercised by an inferior ought, one would think, to rest on something more solid than implication. . . .

But it has been said, that this construction would deprive the citizen of the advantages which are peculiar to a written constitution, by at once declaring the power of the legislature, in practice, to be illimitable. I ask, what are those advantages? The principles of a written constitution are more fixed and certain, and more apparent to the apprehension of the people, than principles which depend on tradition and the vague comprehension of the individuals who compose the nation, and who cannot all be expected to receive the same impressions or entertain the same notions on any given subject. But there is no magic or inherent power in parchment and ink, to command respect and protect principles from violation. In the business of government, a recurrence to first principles answers the end of an observation at sea with a view to correct the dead reckoning; and, for this purpose, a written constitution is an instrument of inestimable value. It is of inestimable value, also, in rendering its principles familiar to the mass of the people; for, after all, there is no effectual guard against legislative usurpation but public opinion, the force of which, in this country, is inconceivably great. . . . Once let public opinion be so corrupt as to sanction every misconstruction of the constitution and abuse of power which the temptation of the moment may dictate, and the party which may happen to be predominant, will laugh at the puny efforts of a dependent power to arrest it in its course.

. . . It might, perhaps, have been better to vest the power in the judiciary; as it might be expected that its habits of deliberation, and the aid derived from the arguments of counsel, would more frequently lead to accurate conclusions. On the other hand, the judiciary is not infallible; and an error by it would admit of no remedy but a more distinct expression of the public will, through the extraordinary medium of a convention; whereas, an error by the legislature admits of a remedy by an exertion of the same will, in the ordinary exercise of the right of suffrage, — a mode better calculated to attain the end, without popular excitement. It may be said, the people would probably not notice an error of their representatives. But they would as probably do so, as notice an error of the judiciary; and, beside, it is a *postulate* in the theory of our government, and the very basis of the superstructure, that the people are wise, virtuous, and competent to manage their own affairs: . . .

But in regard to an act of assembly, which is found to be in collision with the constitution, laws, or treaties of the United States, I take the duty of the judiciary to be exactly the reverse. By becoming parties to the federal constitution, the states have agreed to several limitations of their individual sovereignty, to enforce which, it was thought to be absolutely necessary to prevent them from giving effect to laws in violation of those limitations, through the instrumentality of their own judges. Accordingly, it is declared in the fifth article and second section [sic] of the federal constitution, that "This constitution, and the laws of the United States which shall be made in pursuance thereof, and all treaties made, or which shall be made under the authority of the United States, shall be the *supreme* law of the land; and the *judges* in every *state* shall be bound thereby: any thing in the *laws* or *constitution* of any *state* to the contrary notwithstanding." . . .ᶜ

COOPER v. AARON, 358 U.S. 1, 18, 78 S. Ct. 1401, 3 L. Ed. 2d 5 (1958): "Article VI of the Constitution makes the Constitution the 'supreme Law of the Land.' In 1803, Chief Justice Marshall, speaking for a unanimous Court, referring to the Constitution as 'the fundamental and paramount law of the nation,' declared in the notable case of Marbury v. Madison, 1 Cranch 137, 177, that 'It is emphatically the province and duty of the judicial department to say what the law is.' This decision declared the basic principle that the federal judiciary is supreme in the exposition of the law of the Constitution, and that principle has ever since been respected by this Court and the Country as a permanent and indispensable feature of our constitutional system. It follows that the interpretation of the Fourteenth Amendment enunciated by this Court in the Brown case is the supreme law of the land, and Art. VI of the Constitution makes it of binding effect on the States 'any Thing in the Constitution or Laws of any State to the Contrary notwithstanding.' Every state legislator and executive and judicial officer is solemnly committed by oath taken pursuant to Art. VI, cl. 3, 'to support this Constitution.' Chief Justice Taney, speaking for a unanimous Court in 1859, said that this requirement reflected the framers' 'anxiety to preserve it [the Constitution] in full force, in all its powers, and to guard against resistance to or evasion of its authority, on the part of a State. . . .' Ableman v. Booth, 21 How. 506, 524.

"No state legislator or executive or judicial officer can war against the Constitution without violating his undertaking to support it. Chief Justice Marshall spoke for a unanimous Court in saying that: 'If the legislatures of the several states may, at will, annul the judgments of the courts of the United States, and destroy the rights acquired under those judgments, the constitution itself becomes a solemn mockery. . . .' United States v. Peters, 5 Cranch 115, 136. A Governor who asserts a power to nullify a federal court order is similarly restrained. If he had such power, said Chief Justice Hughes, in 1932, also for a unanimous Court, 'it is manifest that the fiat of a state Governor, and not the Constitution of the United States, would be the supreme law of the land; that the restrictions of the Federal Constitution upon the exercise of state power would be but impotent phrases. . . .' Sterling v. Constantin, 287 U.S. 378, 397-398."

Consider the foregoing statement in the light of the following expressions relating to notable historic episodes. Do any of these expressions give support to refusals by state officials to be guided by decisions of the Supreme Court in the field, for example, of desegregation?

THOMAS JEFFERSON, Letter to Mrs. John Adams, September 11, 1804, in 8 Works 310-311n (1897): "You seem to think it devolved on the judges to decide on the validity of the sedition law. But nothing in the Constitution has given them a right to decide for the Executive, more than to the Executive to decide for them. Both magistracies are equally independent in the sphere of action assigned to them. The judges, believing the law constitutional, had a right to pass a sentence of fine and imprisonment; because that power was placed in their hands by the Constitution. But the Executive, believing the law to be unconstitutional, was bound to remit the execution of it; because that power has been confided to him by the Constitution. That instrument meant that its co-ordinate branches should be checks on each other. But the opinion which gives to the judges the right to decide what laws are constitutional, and what not, not only for themselves in their own

---

ᶜ Chief Justice Gibson said of this opinion, in 1845: "I have changed that opinion for two reasons. The late convention [to draft a constitution for Pennsylvania], by their silence, sanctioned the pretensions of the courts to deal freely with the Acts of the Legislature; and from experience of the necessity of the case." Norris v. Clymer, 2 Pa. 277, 281. — ED.

14 Chapter One. Historic Basis

sphere of action, but for the Legislature & Executive also, in their spheres, would make the judiciary a despotic branch. Nor does the opinion of the unconstitutionality, & consequent nullity of that law, remove all restraint from the overwhelming torrent of slander, which is confounding all vice and virtue, all truth & falsehood, in the U.S. The power to do that is fully possessed by the several State Legislatures. It was reserved to them, & was denied to the General Government, by the Constitution, according to our construction of it."

JAMES MADISON, Report on the Virginia Resolutions (1800), in 4 Elliot, Debates on the Federal Constitution 549-550 (1836): "But it is objected, that the judicial authority is to be regarded as the sole expositor of the Constitution in the last resort; and it may be asked for what reason the declaration by the General Assembly, supposing it to be theoretically true, could be required at the present day, and in so solemn a manner.

"On this objection it might be observed, first, that there may be instances of usurped power, which the forms of the Constitution would never draw within the control of the judicial department; secondly, that, if the decision of the judiciary be raised above the authority of the sovereign parties to the Constitution, the decisions of the other departments, not carried by the forms of the Constitution before the judiciary, must be equally authoritative and final with the decisions of that department. But the proper answer to the objection is, that the resolution of the General Assembly relates to those great and extraordinary cases, in which all the forms of the Constitution may prove ineffectual against infractions dangerous to the essential rights of the parties to it. The resolution supposes that dangerous powers, not delegated, may not only be usurped and executed by the other departments, but that the judicial department, also, may exercise or sanction dangerous powers beyond the grant of the constitution; and, consequently, that the ultimate right of the parties to the Constitution, to judge whether the compact has been dangerously violated, must extend to violations by one delegated authority as well as by another — by the judiciary as well as by the executive, or the legislature.

"However true, therefore, it may be, that the judicial department is, in all questions submitted to it by the forms of the Constitution, to decide in the last resort, this resort must necessarily be deemed the last in relation to the authorities of the other departments of the government; not in relation to the rights of the parties to the constitutional compact, from which the judicial, as well as the other departments, hold their delegated trusts. On any other hypothesis, the delegation of judicial power would annul the authority delegating it; and the concurrence of this department with the others in usurped powers, might subvert forever, and beyond the possible reach of any rightful remedy, the very Constitution which all were instituted to preserve."

ANDREW JACKSON, Veto of Bank Bill, July 10, 1832, in 2 Richardson, Messages and Papers of the Presidents 576, 581-582 (1896): "It is maintained by the advocates of the bank that its constitutionality in all its features ought to be considered as settled by the precedent and by the decision of the Supreme Court. To this conclusion I can not assent. Mere precedent is a dangerous source of authority, and should not be regarded as deciding questions of constitutional power except where the acquiescence of the people and the States can be considered as well settled. . . .

"If the opinion of the Supreme Court covered the whole ground of this act, it ought not to control the coordinate authorities of this Government. The Congress, the Executive, and the Court must each for itself be guided by its own opinion of the Constitution. Each public officer who takes an oath to support the Constitution swears that he will support it as he understands it, and not as it is understood by others. It is as much the duty of the House of Representatives, of the Senate, and of the President to decide upon the constitutionality of any bill or resolution which may be presented to them for passage or approval as it is of the supreme judges when it may be brought before them for judicial decision.

The opinion of the judges has no more authority over Congress than the opinion of Congress has over the judges, and on that point the President is independent of both. The authority of the Supreme Court must not, therefore, be permitted to control the Congress or the Executive when acting in their legislative capacities, but to have only such influence as the force of their reasoning may deserve."

ABRAHAM LINCOLN, First Inaugural Address, March 4, 1861, in 6 Richardson, Messages and Papers of the Presidents 5, 9-10 (1897): "I do not forget the position assumed by some that constitutional questions are to be decided by the Supreme Court, nor do I deny that such decisions must be binding in any case upon the parties to a suit as to the object of that suit, while they are also entitled to very high respect and consideration in all parallel cases by all other departments of the Government. And while it is obviously possible that such decision may be erroneous in any given case, still the evil effect following it, being limited to that particular case, with the chance that it may be overruled and never become a precedent for other cases, can better be borne than could the evils of a different practice. At the same time, the candid citizen must confess that if the policy of the Government upon vital questions affecting the whole people is to be irrevocably fixed by decisions of the Supreme Court, the instant they are made in ordinary litigation between parties in personal actions the people will have ceased to be their own rulers, having to that extent practically resigned their Government into the hands of that eminent tribunal. Nor is there in this view any assault upon the court or the judges. It is a duty from which they may not shrink to decide cases properly brought before them, and it is no fault of theirs if others seek to turn their decisions to political purposes."

BENJAMIN R. CURTIS, Argument on Behalf of President Johnson in Impeachment Proceedings, in Cong. Globe (Supp.), 40th Cong., 2d Sess. 126-127 (1868). [Among the Articles of Impeachment against President Johnson was one in which it was charged that he had committed an impeachable offense in refusing, on the ground that the statute was unconstitutional, to comply with the provisions of the Tenure of Office Act of 1867, which he had vetoed and which had been passed over his veto. 6 Richardson, Messages 492 (1897). The act provided that civil officers, including members of the cabinet, could not be removed by the President except with the consent of the Senate. Johnson, when he acted in defiance of the act, stated that he did so in the conscientious belief that the act was unconstitutional and in the belief that the question would ultimately be reviewed by the Supreme Court of the United States. Benjamin Robbins Curtis, former Associate Justice of the Supreme Court, one of the counsel for President Johnson in the impeachment proceedings, dealt with the article of impeachment summarized above in his opening argument for the defense.]

"I am aware that it is asserted to be the civil and moral duty of all men to obey those laws which have been passed through all the forms of legislation until they shall have been decreed by judicial authority not to be binding; but this is too broad a statement of the civil and moral duty incumbent either upon private citizens or public officers. If this is the measure of duty there never could be a judicial decision that a law is unconstitutional, inasmuch as it is only by disregarding a law that any question can be raised judicially under it. I submit to Senators that not only is there no such rule of civil or moral duty, but that it may be and has been a high and patriotic duty of a citizen to raise a question whether a law is within the Constitution of the country. Will any man question the patriotism or the propriety of John Hampden's act when he brought the question whether 'ship money' was within the Constitution of England before the courts of England? Not only is there no such rule incumbent upon private citizens which forbids them to raise such questions, but, let me repeat, there may be, as there not unfrequently have been, instances in which the highest patriotism and the purest civil and moral duty require it to be done. Let me ask any one of you, if you were a trustee for the rights of third persons, and those rights of third persons, which they could not defend themselves by reason, perhaps, of sex or age, should be attacked by an unconstitutional law, should you not deem it to be your sacred duty to resist it and have the question tried? And if a private trustee may be subject to such a duty, and impelled by it to such action, how is it possible to maintain that he who is a trustee for the people of powers confided to him for their protection, for their security, for their benefit, may not in that character of trustee defend what has thus been confided to him?

"Do not let me be misunderstood on this subject. I am not intending to advance upon or occupy any extreme ground, because no such extreme ground has been advanced upon or occupied by the President of the United States. He is to take care that the laws are faithfully executed. When a law has been passed through the forms of legislation, either with his assent or without his assent, it is his duty to see that that law is faithfully executed so long as nothing is required of him but ministerial action. He is not to erect himself into a judicial court and decide that the law is unconstitutional, and that therefore he will not execute it; for, if that were done, manifestly there never could be a judicial decision. He would not only veto a law, but he would refuse all action under the law after it had been passed, and thus prevent any judicial decision from being made. He asserts no such power. He has no such idea of his duty. His idea of his duty is that if a law is passed over his veto which he believes to be unconstitutional, and that law affects the interests of third persons, those whose interests are affected must take care of them, vindicate them, raise questions concerning them, if they should be so advised. If such a law affects the general and public interests of the people the people must take care at the polls that it is remedied in a constitutional way.

"But when, Senators, a question arises whether a particular law has cut off a power confided to him by the people through the Constitution, and he alone can raise that question, and he alone can cause a judicial decision to come between the two branches of the Government to say which of them is right, and after due deliberation, with the advice of those who are his proper advisers, he settles down firmly upon the opinion that such is the character of the law, it remains to be decided by you whether there is any violation of his duty when he takes the needful steps to raise that question and have it peacefully decided.

"Where shall the line be drawn? Suppose a law should provide that the President of the United States should not make a treaty with England or with any other country? It would be a plain infraction of his constitutional power, and if an occasion arose when such a treaty was in his judgment expedient and necessary it would be his duty to make it; and the fact that it should be declared to be a high misdemeanor if he made it would no more relieve him from the responsibility of acting through the fear of that law than he would be relieved of that responsibility by a bribe not to act."

NOTE Foundations of Judicial Review

Whether judicial review of legislation was a usurpation has been the subject of an immense controversial literature. Recent discussions are Hand, The Bill of Rights (1958), and Wechsler, Toward Neutral Principles of Constitutional Law, 73 Harv. L. Rev. 1 (1959).

Historical support for the practice has been found in several sources:

(a) The understanding of the Framers of the Constitution. See Beard, The Supreme Court and the Constitution (1912) (an analysis of the views of the members of the Convention); cf. The Federalist, Nos. 78 and 80 (Hamilton). Compare Corwin, Court over Constitution, c. 1 (1938); Corwin, The Doctrine of Judicial Review (1914); Corwin, The Establishment of Judicial Review, 9 Mich. L. Rev. 102, 283 (1910, 1911); Warren, Congress, the Constitution, and the Supreme Court (1925).

(b) The practice of the Privy Council in reviewing colonial legislation. See Thayer, Origin and Scope of the American Doctrine of Constitutional Law, 7 Harv. L. Rev. 129 (1893), reprinted in Thayer, Legal Essays 1 (1908); McGovney, The British Origin of Judicial Review of Legislation, 93 U. Pa. L. Rev. 1 (1944); J. H. Smith, Appeals to the Privy Council from the American Plantations (1950); Steamer, The Legal and Political Genesis of the Supreme Court, 77 Pol. Sci. Q. 546 (1962).

(c) The practice in the states prior to, and immediately following, the adoption of the Constitution. See Haines, The American Doctrine of Judicial Supremacy, c. 5 (2d ed. 1932). One of the most striking of the instances adduced is Trevett v. Weeden, decided by the Superior Court of Rhode Island in 1786, reprinted from a pamphlet in 1 Thayer, Cases on Constitutional Law 73 (1895); and see Coxe, Judicial Power and Unconstitutional Legislation 245 (1893). In that case the judges refused to take jurisdiction of an information brought against the defendant for rejecting paper bills of the state in payment for goods sold. The act authorizing the information dispensed with jury trials in such cases, and the defendant pleaded the unconstitutionality of the act. After the dismissal the judges were summoned before the state legislature to give their reasons for adjudging an act of the legislature unconstitutional. Three judges appeared and spoke earnestly of the independence of the judiciary. On a question being put for a vote, whether the Assembly was satisfied with the reasons given by the judges in support of their judgment, it was determined in the negative. A motion was made for dismissing the judges from office, but on the advice of the attorney general and others that removal could be had only by impeachment or other regular process, the legislature was content to discharge the judges from further attendance before that body. See generally G. Wood, Origins of the American Republic (1970); J. Goebel, Antecedents and Beginnings to 1801 (1 Oliver Wendell Holmes Devise History of the Supreme Court) Chs. 2, 3 (1971).

(d) The influence of Coke's statement in Dr. Bonham's Case, 8 Rep 118a: "It appeareth in our books, that in many cases the common law will controul Acts of Parliament and adjudge them to be uterly void; for where an Act of Parliament is against common right and reason or repugnant or impossible to be performed, the common law will controul it and adjudge it to be void." See Corwin, The "Higher Law" Background of American Constitutional Law, 42 Harv. L. Rev. 149, 365 (1928, 1929), Plucknett, Bonham's Case and Judicial Review, 40 id. 30 (1926); Thorne, Dr. Bonham's Case, 54 L.Q. Rev. 543 (1938).

A sharp attack on the force of these precedents is contained in 1 Boudin, Government by Judiciary (1932).

Discussions of the subject have not always discriminated between the power of judicial review and its finality, or between review of national and of state legislation. On the latter question a celebrated remark of Mr. Justice Holmes may be quoted: "I do not think the United States would come to an end if we lost our power to declare an act of Congress void. I do think the Union would be imperiled if we could not make that declaration as to the laws of the several states." Holmes, Law and the Court, in Collected Legal Papers 295-296 (1920).

Is judicial review essential in a federal system? In Switzerland the acts of the national legislature may be set aside by popular referendum but not by the courts. See generally Wheare, Federal Government, c. 4 (2d ed. 1951). On judicial review abroad, see Cappelletti and Adams, Judicial Review: European Antecedents and Adaptations, 79 Harv. L. Rev. 1207 (1966); Radin, The Judicial Review of Statutes in Continental Europe, 41 W. Va. L.Q. 112 (1935); Jaffin, New World Constitutional Harmony, 42 Colum. L. Rev. 523 (1942); Baeck, Postwar Judicial Review of Legislative Acts: Austria, 26 Tul. L. Rev. 70 (1951); Deener, Judicial Review in Modern Constitutional Systems, 46 Am. Pol. Sci. Rev. 1079 (1952); McWhinney, Judicial Review in the English-Speaking World (2d ed. 1960). For recent developments, see von Mehren, The New German Constitutional Court, 1 Am. J. Comp. L. 70 (1952); Soulier, La Délibération du Comité Constitutionnel du 18 Juin 1948, 65 Rev. de Droit Public 195 (1949); Rupp, Judicial

Review in the Federal Republic of Germany, 9 Am. J. Comp. L. 29 (1959); Eder, Judicial Review in Latin America, 21 Ohio St. L.J. 570 (1960); Rupp, Some Remarks on Judicial Self-Restraint, 21 Ohio St. L.J. 503 (1960); McWhinney, Constitutionalism in Germany and the Federal Constitutional Court (1962); Leibholz, Politics and Law [Germany] (Leyden, 1965); Maki, Court and Constitution in Japan (1964); Griswold, The Demise of the High Court of Parliament in South Africa, 66 Harv. L. Rev. 864 (1953); Livingston, Court and Parliament in South Africa, 10 Parliamentary Affairs 434 (1957).

NOTE Acts of Congress Held Unconstitutional

Justices of the Supreme Court, sitting on circuit, held unconstitutional a provision of an act of 1792 requiring circuit courts to pass upon the claims of invalid pensioners, these determinations to be subject to review by the Secretary of War and Congress. Hayburn's Case, 2 Dall. 409 (1792). See also Yale Todd's Case, decided by the Supreme Court in 1794, reported for the first time as a footnote to United States v. Ferreira, 13 How. 40, 52n. (1852), construing the act of 1792 not to authorize the circuit judges to sit as commissioners in the pension cases.

Following Marbury v. Madison the next case holding an Act of Congress invalid was Dred Scott v. Sandford, 19 How. 393 (1857).

In 1958 Chief Justice Warren observed that "In some 81 instances since this Court was established it has determined that congressional action exceeded the bounds of the Constitution." Trop v. Dulles, 356 U.S. 86, 104 (1958). For a collection of such instances down to 1936, see 80 Cong. Rec. 9251-9254 (1936).

Since 1937 the Court has held federal statutes unconstitutional in the following decisions:

Tot v. United States, 319 U.S. 463 (1943), creating a presumption that, where an ex-convict is in possession of a firearm, he received, shipped, or transported it in interstate commerce;

United States v. Lovett, 328 U.S. 303 (1946), prohibiting payment of any federal salary to three named persons, save for jury duty or military service;

United States v. Cardiff, 344 U.S. 174 (1952), penalizing, in self-contradictory terms, one who refuses to allow a federal officer to inspect a food factory;

Bolling v. Sharpe, 347 U.S. 497 (1954), providing for separate schools for Negro and white children in the District of Columbia;

United States ex rel. Toth v. Quarles, 350 U.S. 11 (1955), subjecting a former serviceman to trial by court-martial, after his discharge, for offenses committed while in service;

Reid v. Covert (Kinsella v. Kreuger), 354 U.S. 1 (1957), providing for trial by court-martial of dependents of servicemen, stationed overseas, for capital crimes. In 1960 the Supreme Court extended this holding to include dependents charged with noncapital crimes, Kinsella v. United States ex rel. Singleton, 361 U.S. 234 (1960); and civilian employees charged with capital or noncapital offenses, Grisham v. Hagan, 361 U.S. 278 (1960); McElroy v. United States ex rel. Guagliardo, 361 U.S. 281 (1960); Wilson v. Bohlender, 361 U.S. 281 (1960);

Trop v. Dulles, 356 U.S. 86 (1958), depriving of United States nationality one convicted by court-martial or wartime desertion, and dismissed or dishonorably discharged from the armed forces;

Kennedy v. Mendoza-Martinez, 372 U.S. 144 (1963), depriving of citizenship any person remaining outside the United States in time of war or national emergency for the purpose of avoiding military service;

Schneider v. Rusk, 377 U.S. 163 (1964), depriving of nationality any naturalized person who resides continuously for three years in the country of his origin or former nationality;

Chapter One. Historic Basis 19

Aptheker v. Secretary of State, 378 U.S. 500 (1964), forbidding the issuance of passports to members of organizations required to register under the Internal Security Act;

Lamont v. Postmaster General, 381 U.S. 301 (1965), requiring the Post Office Department to detain and destroy unsealed mail from abroad determined to be political propaganda, unless the addressee indicated his desire to receive it;

United States v. Brown, 381 U.S. 437 (1965), making it a crime for a member of the Communist party to serve as an officer or employee of a labor union;

Albertson v. Subversive Activities Control Board, 382 U.S. 70 (1965), holding that the requirements of §§8(a) and (c) of the Subversive Activities Control Act of 1950 with respect to individual's registering and filing registration statements conflicted with the privilege against self-incrimination;

United States v. Romano, 382 U.S. 136 (1955), holding that the provisions of 26 U.S.C. §5601(b)(1) authorizing an inference of possession from evidence of presence at the site of an illegal still violated the Due Process clause of the Fifth Amendment;

Afroyim v. Rusk, 387 U.S. 253 (1967), overruling Perez v. Brownell, 356 U.S. 44 (1958), and holding unconstitutional the provision of §401(e) of the Nationality Act of 1940 for loss of citizenship by virtue of having voted in a foreign political election;

United States v. Robel, 389 U.S. 258 (1967), holding invalid by reason of its overbreadth §5(a)(1)(D) of the Subversive Activities Control Act of 1950 making it unlawful for members of Communist-action organizations under final orders to register "to engage in any employment in any defense facility";

Marchetti v. United States, 390 U.S. 39 (1968), holding violative of the privilege against self-incrimination provisions with respect to the occupational tax on wagering imposed by 26 U.S.C. §4411 and the requirement of registration imposed by 26 U.S.C. §4412; Grosso v. United States, 390 U.S. 62 (1968), reaching a similar conclusion with respect to provisions regarding the excise tax on wagering imposed by 26 U.S.C. §4401; Haynes v. United States, 390 U.S. 85 (1968), reaching a similar conclusion with respect to the provisions of 26 U.S.C. §§5841 and 5851 regarding the registration of firearms and the possession of unregistered firearms;

United States v. Jackson, 390 U.S. 570 (1968), holding unconstitutional the provision of 18 U.S.C. §1201(a), the Federal Kidnaping Act, authorizing capital punishment upon recommendation of a jury; Pope v. United States, 392 U.S. 651 (1968), holding similarly with regard to a similar provision of the Federal Bank Robbery Act, 18 U.S.C. §2113(e);

Shapiro v. Thompson (Washington v. Legrant), 394 U.S. 618 (1969), holding unconstitutional the provision of §3-203 of the District of Columbia Code requiring a year's residence in the District before the award of public assistance to a needy individual;

Leary v. United States, 395 U.S. 6 (1969), holding violative of the privilege against self-incrimination certain provisions of the Marijuana Tax Act, 26 U.S.C. §§4741 et seq., and also holding unconstitutional the provision of 21 U.S.C. §176a, the Narcotic Drugs Import and Export Act, that possession of marijuana shall create a presumption of knowledge of its illegal importation;

O'Callahan v. Parker, 395 U.S. 258 (1969), holding unconstitutional the provisions of the Articles of War, 10 U.S.C. §§801 et seq., authorizing military trials of members of the Armed Forces charged with nonservice-connected crimes.

See also Schacht v. United States, 398 U.S. 58 (1970), holding that a condition imposed by 10 U.S.C. §772(f) permitting an actor in a theatrical or motion-picture production to wear the uniform of any branch of the armed services "if the portrayal does not tend to discredit that armed force" violated the First Amendment;

Oregon v. Mitchell, 400 U.S. 112 (1970), holding §302 of the Voting Rights Act Amendments of 1970 which purported to set the minimum voting age at 18 for both federal and state elections to be an unconstitutional interference with state authority to regulate state and local elections;

Blount v. Rizzi, 400 U.S. 410 (1971), holding that provisions of the Postal Reorganization Act, 39 U.S.C. §§4006, 4007, which empowered the Postmaster General to refuse use of the mails for the distribution of obscene matter violated the First Amendment because they lacked adequate safeguards against undue inhibition of protected expression;

Tilton v. Richardson, 403 U.S. 672 (1971), holding that a provision of the Higher Education Facilities Act of 1963, 20 U.S.C. §754(b)(2), which prohibited institutions receiving federal construction funds from using facilities constructed therewith for religious purposes for a 20-year period but did not prohibit such use thereafter was an establishment of religion in violation of the First Amendment;

Department of Agriculture v. Murry, 413 U.S. 508 (1973), invalidating §5(b) of the Food Stamp Act of 1964, as amended, which disqualified households containing a person over 18 years old who was claimed as a dependent child for federal income tax purposes by a taxpayer who was not a member of an eligible household as not a rational measure of a household's need and therefore in violation of Fifth Amendment due process;

Department of Agriculture v. Moreno, 413 U.S. 528 (1973), holding that §3(e) of the Food Stamp Act of 1964, as amended, restricting eligibility for food stamp benefits to households of related individuals was an irrational classification invalid under Fifth Amendment due process;

Frontiero v. Richardson, 411 U.S. 677 (1973), holding that provisions of the Career Compensation Act of 1949 and the Dependents' Medical Care Act of 1956 which provided that although the wife of a serviceman qualifies automatically for dependent benefits, the husband of a servicewoman must be shown to depend on her for more than one half of his support violated the due process clause of the Fifth Amendment;

Jimenez v. Weinberger, 417 U.S. 628 (1974), holding that a provision of the Social Security Act, 42 U.S.C. §416(h)(3)(B), denying benefits to certain illegitimate children born after the onset of a parent's disability violated the Fifth Amendment;

Weinberger v. Wiesenfeld, 420 U.S. 636 (1975), holding that a provision of the Social Security Act, 42 U.S.C. 402(g), which provides benefits to widows with minor children but not to similarly situated widowers, violated the Fifth Amendment.

In Buckley v. Valeo, 424 U.S. 1 (1976), the Court held that §§608(e), 608(c), and 608(f) of the Federal Election Campaign Act of 1971, Pub. L. No. 92-225, 86 Stat. 3 (1971), as amended, Pub. L. No. 93-443, 88 Stat. 1263 (1974), which variously limit individual or group expenditures on behalf of a clearly identified candidate and by a candidate (out of his personal or family funds), his campaign, or a political party on his behalf, unconstitutionally burdened freedom of speech; and that §437 of the act, which establishes a Federal Election Commission comprising eight members of whom a majority are to be appointed by Congress, and having extensive rule-making and adjudicative powers, violated the principle of separation of powers in that it enables Congress effectively to exercise executive power by controlling appointments.

In National League of Cities v. Usery, 426 U.S. 833 (1976), the Court held that the Fair Labor Standards Act, 29 U.S.C. §201 et seq., exceeds Congress's power under the commerce clause, insofar as the act, in §§203(d), 203(s)(5), and 203(x), sets minimum wages and maximum hours for state and municipal employees engaged in carrying out traditional governmental functions.

Martin v. Hunter's Lessee *1 Wheat. 304, 4 L. Ed. 97 (1816)*

[Lord Fairfax, a citizen and inhabitant of Virginia, who held title to the so-called Northern Neck of that State, devised it in 1781 to Denny Martin (who then took the name Fairfax), a citizen and resident of Great Britain. In 1789 the Commonwealth of Virginia, purporting to act pursuant to a state forfeiture law of 1785, issued a patent covering the land to David Hunter and his heirs. Denny Fairfax died between 1796 and 1803, leaving as his heir a nephew, Thomas Martin, a citizen of Virginia. Hunter's lessee brought an action of [ejectment in the state court. The Fairfax heirs asserted rights under treaties of 1783 and 1794 with Great Britain. The Virginia Court of Appeals decided in favor of the plaintiff. 1 Munf. 218. On writ of error the Supreme Court of the United States reversed, holding that Virginia had not perfected title to the land prior to the patent to Hunter, and that the treaty of 1794 confirmed the title remaining in Fairfax. Fairfax's Devisee v. Hunter's Lessee, 7 Cranch 603 (1813). The mandate of the Supreme Court (see 4 Munf. 3) stated: "You therefore are hereby commanded that such proceedings be had in said cause, as according to right and justice, and the laws of the United States, and agreeably to said judgment and instructions of said Supreme Court ought to be had, the said writ of error notwithstanding." The Virginia Court of Appeals, presided over by Judge Spencer Roane, refused to obey the mandate.]

STORY, J., delivered the opinion of the court:

This is a writ of error from the Court of Appeals of Virginia, founded upon the refusal of that court to obey the mandate of this court, requiring the judgment rendered in this very cause, at February term, 1813, to be carried into due execution. The following is the judgment of the Court of Appeals rendered on the mandate: "The court is unanimously of opinion that the appellate power of the Supreme Court of the United States does not extend to this court, under a sound construction of the constitution of the United States; that so much of the 25th section of the act of Congress to establish the judicial courts of the United States, as extends the appellate jurisdiction of the Supreme Court to this court, is not in pursuance of the constitution of the United States; that the writ of error, in this cause, was improvidently allowed under the authority of that act; that the proceedings thereon in the Supreme Court were, coram non judice, in relation to this court, and that obedience to its mandate be declined by the court."

The questions involved in this judgment are of great importance and delicacy. Perhaps it is not too much to affirm that, upon their right decision, rest some of the most solid principles which have hitherto been supposed to sustain and protect the constitution itself. The great respectability, too, of the court whose decisions we are called upon to review, and the entire deference which we entertain for the learning and ability of that court, add much to the difficulty of the task which has so unwelcomely fallen upon us. It is, however, a source of consolation that we have had the assistance of most able and learned arguments to aid our inquiries; and that the opinion which is now to be pronounced has been weighed with every solicitude to come to a correct result, and matured after solemn deliberation.

Before proceeding to the principal questions, it may not be unfit to dispose of some preliminary considerations which have grown out of the arguments at the bar. . . .

The constitution unavoidably deals in general language. It did not suit the purposes of the people, in framing this great charter of our liberties, to provide for minute specifications of its powers, or to declare the means by which those powers should be carried into execution. It was foreseen that this would be a perilous and difficult, if not an impracticable, task. The instrument was not intended to provide merely for the exigencies of a few years, but was to endure through a long lapse of ages, the events of which were locked up in the inscrutable purposes of Providence. . . .

The third article of the constitution is that which must principally attract our attention. . . .

Let this article be carefully weighed and considered. The language of the article throughout is manifestly designed to be mandatory upon the legislature. . . . The object of the constitution was to establish three great departments of government; the legislative, the executive and the judicial departments. The first was to pass laws, the second to approve and execute them, and the third to expound and enforce them. Without the latter it would be impossible to carry into effect some of the express provisions of the constitution. How, otherwise, could crimes against the United States be tried and punished? How could causes between two states be heard and determined? The judicial power must, therefore, be vested in some court, by Congress; and to suppose that it was not an obligation binding on them, but might, at their pleasure, be omitted or declined, is to suppose that, under the sanction of the constitution they might defeat the constitution itself; a construction which would lead to such a result cannot be sound. . . .

If, then, it is the duty of Congress to vest the judicial power of the United States, it is a duty to vest the *whole judicial power.* The language, if imperative as to one part, is imperative as to all. If it were otherwise, this anomaly would exist, that Congress might successively refuse to vest the jurisdiction in any one class of cases enumerated in the constitution, and thereby defeat the jurisdiction as to all; for the constitution has not singled out any class on which Congress are bound to act in preference to others.

The next consideration is as to the courts in which the judicial power shall be vested. It is manifest that a supreme court must be established; but whether it be equally obligatory to establish inferior courts is a question of some difficulty. If Congress may lawfully omit to establish inferior courts, it might follow that in some of the enumerated cases the judicial power could nowhere exist. . . .

But, even admitting that the language of the constitution is not mandatory, and that Congress may constitutionally omit to vest the judicial power in courts of the United States, it cannot be denied that when it is vested it may be exercised to the utmost constitutional extent.

This leads us to the consideration of the great question as to the nature and extent of the appellate jurisdiction of the United States. . . .

As, then, by the terms of the constitution, the appellate jurisdiction is not limited as to the Supreme Court, and as to this court it may be exercised in all other cases than those of which it has original cognizance, what is there to restrain its exercise over state tribunals in the enumerated cases? The appellate power is not limited by the terms of the third article to any particular courts. The words are, "the judicial power (which includes appellate power) shall extend to all cases," etc., and "in all other cases before mentioned the Supreme Court shall have appellate jurisdiction." It is the case, then, and not the court, that gives the jurisdiction. . . .

But it is plain that the framers of the constitution did contemplate that cases within the judicial cognizance of the United States not only might but would arise in the state courts, in the exercise of their ordinary jurisdiction. With this view the sixth article declares, that "this constitution, and the laws of the United States which shall be made in pursuance thereof, and all treaties made, or which shall be made, under the authority of the United States, shall be the supreme law of the land, and the judges in every state shall be bound thereby, anything in the constitution or laws of any state to the contrary notwithstanding." It is obvious that this obligation is imperative upon the state judges in their official, and not merely in their private, capacities. From the very nature of their judicial duties they would be called upon to pronounce the law applicable to the case in judgment. They were not to decide merely according to the laws or constitution of the state, but according to the constitution, laws and treaties of the United States — "the supreme law of the land."

A moment's consideration will show us the necessity and propriety of this provision in cases where the jurisdiction of the state courts is unquestionable. . . . Suppose an indictment for a crime in a state court, and the defendant should allege in his defense that the crime was created by an ex post facto act of the state, must not the state court, in the exercise of a jurisdiction which has already rightfully attached, have a right to pronounce on the validity and sufficiency of the defense? . . .

It must, therefore, be conceded that the constitution not only contemplated, but meant to provide for cases within the scope of the judicial power of the United States, which might yet depend before state tribunals. It was foreseen that in the exercise of their ordinary jurisdiction, state courts would incidentally take cognizance of cases arising under the constitution, the laws and treaties of the United States. Yet to all these cases the judicial power, by the very terms of the constitution, is to extend. It cannot extend by original jurisdiction if that was already rightfully and exclusively attached in the state courts, which (as has been already shown) may occur; it must, therefore, extend by appellate jurisdiction, or not at all. It would seem to follow that the appellate power of the United States must, in such cases, extend to state tribunals; and if in such cases, there is no reason why it should not equally attach upon all others within the purview of the constitution. . . .

Nor can such a right be deemed to impair the independence of state judges. It is assuming the very ground in controversy to assert that they possess an absolute independence of the United States. In respect to the powers granted to the United States, they are not independent; they are expressly bound to obedience by the letter of the constitution; and if they should unintentionally transcend their authority, or misconstrue the constitution, there is no more reason for giving their judgments an absolute and irresistible force than for giving it to the acts of the other co-ordinate departments of state sovereignty.

The argument urged from the possibility of the abuse of the revising power is equally unsatisfactory. It is always a doubtful course to argue against the use or existence of a power, from the possibility of its abuse. . . . From the very nature of things, the absolute right of decision, in the last resort, must rest somewhere — wherever it may be vested it is susceptible of abuse. In all questions of jurisdiction the inferior, or appellate court, must pronounce the final judgment; and common sense, as well as legal reasoning, has conferred it upon the latter. . . .

It is further argued that no great public mischief can result from a construction which shall limit the appellate power of the United States to cases in their own courts; first, because state judges are bound by an oath to support the constitution of the United States, and must be presumed to be men of learning and integrity; and, secondly, because Congress must have an unquestionable right to remove all cases within the scope of the judicial power from the state courts to the courts of the United States, at any time before final judgment, though not after final judgment. As to the first reason — admitting that the judges of the state courts are, and always will be, of as much learning, integrity, and wisdom, as those of the courts of the United States (which we very cheerfully admit), it does not aid the argument. . . . The constitution has presumed (whether rightly or wrongly we do not inquire) that state attachments, state prejudices, state jealousies, and state interests, might sometimes obstruct, or control, or be supposed to obstruct or control, the regular administration of justice. Hence, in controversies between states; between citizens of different states; between citizens claiming grants under different states; between a state and its citizens, or foreigners, and between citizens and foreigners, it enables the parties, under the authority of Congress, to have the controversies heard, tried, and determined before the national tribunals. No other reason than that which has been stated can be assigned, why some, at least, of those cases should not have been left to the cognizance of the state courts. In respect to the other enumerated cases — the cases arising under the constitution, laws, and treaties of the United States, cases affecting ambassadors and other public ministers, and cases of admiralty and maritime jurisdiction — reasons of a higher and more extensive nature, touching the safety, peace, and sovereignty of the nation, might well justify a grant of exclusive jurisdiction.

This is not all. A motive of another kind, perfectly compatible with the most sincere respect for state tribunals, might induce the grant of appellate power over their decisions. That motive is the importance, and even necessity of uniformity of decisions throughout the whole United States, upon all subjects within the purview of the constitution. Judges of equal learning and integrity, in different states, might differently interpret a statute, or a treaty of the United States, or even the constitution itself. If there were no revising authority to control these jarring and discordant judgments, and harmonize them into uniformity, the laws, the treaties, and the constitution of the United States would be different in different states, and might, perhaps, never have precisely the same construction, obligation, or efficacy, in any two states. . . .

There is an additional consideration, which is entitled to great weight. The constitution of the United States was designed for the common and equal benefit of all the people of the United States. The judicial power was granted for the same benign and salutary purposes. It was not to be exercised exclusively for the benefit of parties who might be plaintiffs, and would elect the national forum, but also for the protection of defendants who might be entitled to try their rights, or assert their privileges, before the same forum. Yet, if the construction contended for be correct, it will follow, that as the plaintiff may always elect the state court, the defendant may be deprived of all the security which the constitution intended in aid of his rights. Such a state of things can in no respect be considered as giving equal rights. To obviate this difficulty, we are referred to the power which it is admitted Congress possess to remove suits from state courts to the national courts; and this forms the second ground upon which the argument we are considering has been attempted to be sustained.

This power of removal is not to be found in express terms in any part of the constitution; if it be given, it is only given by implication, as a power necessary and proper to carry into effect some express power. The power of removal is certainly not, in strictness of language an exercise of original jurisdiction; it presupposes an exercise of original jurisdiction to have attached elsewhere. . . . If, then, the right of removal be included in the appellate jurisdiction, it is only because it is one mode of exercising that power, and as Congress is not limited by the constitution to any particular mode, or time of exercising it, it may authorize a removal either before or after judgment. The time, the process, and the manner, must be subject to its absolute legislative control. . . .

The remedy, too, of removal of suits would be utterly inadequate to the purposes of the constitution, if it could act only on the parties, and not upon the state courts. In respect to criminal prosecutions, the difficulty seems admitted to be insurmountable; and in respect to civil suits, there would, in many cases, be rights without corresponding remedies. If state courts should deny the constitutionality of the authority to remove suits from their cognizance, in what manner could they be compelled to relinquish the jurisdiction? In respect to criminal cases, there would at once be an end of all control, and the state decisions would be paramount to the constitution; and though in civil suits the courts of the United States might act upon the parties, yet the state courts might act in the same way; and this conflict of jurisdictions would not only jeopardize private rights, but bring into imminent peril the public interests.

On the whole, the court are of opinion that the appellate power of the United States does extend to cases pending in the state courts; and that the 25th section of the judiciary act, which authorizes the exercise of this jurisdiction in the specified cases, by a writ of error, is supported by the letter and spirit of the constitution. We find no clause in that instrument which limits this power; and we dare not interpose a limitation where the people have not been disposed to create one. . . .

The next question which has been argued is, whether the case at bar be within the purview of the 25th section of the judiciary act, so that this court may rightfully sustain the present writ of error. This section, stripped of passages unimportant in this inquiry, enacts, in substance, that a final judgment or decree in any suit in the highest court of law or equity of a state, where is drawn in question the validity of a treaty or statute of, or an authority exercised under, the United States, and the decision is against their validity; or where is drawn in question the validity of a statute of, or an authority exercised under, any state, on the ground of their being repugnant to the constitution, treaties, or laws, of the United States, and the decision is in favor of such their validity; or of the construction, or of a treaty or statute of, or commission held under, the United States, and the decision is against the title, right, privilege, or exemption, specially set up or claimed by either party under such clause of the said constitution, treaty, statute, or commission, may be reexamined and reversed or affirmed in the Supreme Court of the United States, upon a writ of error, in the same manner, and under the same regulations, and the writ shall have the same effect, as if the judgment or decree complained of has been rendered or passed in a circuit court, and the proceeding upon the reversal shall also be the same, except that the Supreme Court, instead of remanding the cause for a final decision, as before provided, may, at their discretion, if the cause shall have been once remanded before, proceed to a final decision of the same, and award execution. But no other error shall be assigned or regarded as a ground of reversal than such as appears on the face of the record, and immediately respects the before-mentioned question of validity or construction of the said constitution, treaties, statutes, commissions, or authorities in dispute. . . .

The objection urged at the bar is, that this court cannot inquire into the title, but simply into the correctness of the construction put upon the treaty by the Court of Appeals; and that their judgment is not re-examinable here, unless it appear on the face of the record that some construction was put upon the treaty. If, therefore, that court might have decided the case upon the invalidity of the title (and, non constat, that they did not), independent of the treaty, there is an end of the appellate jurisdiction of this court. In support of this objection much stress is laid upon the last clause of the section, which declares that no other cause shall be regarded as a ground of reversal than such as appears on the face of the record and immediately respects the construction of the treaty, etc., in dispute.

If this be the true construction of the section, it will be wholly inadequate for the purposes which it professes to have in view, and may be evaded at pleasure. . . . How, indeed, can it be possible to decide whether a title be within the protection of a treaty, until it is ascertained what that title is, and whether it have a legal validity? . . . One of the questions is as to the construction of a treaty upon a title specially set up by a party, and every error that immediately respects that question must, of course, be within the cognizance of the court. The title set up in this case is apparent upon the face of the record, and immediately respects the decision of that question; any error, therefore, in respect to that title must be re-examinable, or the case could never be presented to the court. . . .

We have not thought it incumbent on us to give any opinion upon the question, whether this court have authority to issue a writ of mandamus to the Court of Appeals to enforce the former judgments, as we do not think it necessarily involved in the decision of this cause.

It is the opinion of the whole court that the judgment of the Court of Appeals of Virginia, rendered on the mandate in this cause, be reversed, and the judgment of the District Court, held at Winchester, be, and the same is hereby affirmed.

JOHNSON, J. It will be observed in this case, that the court disavows all intention to decide on the right to issue compulsory process to the state courts; thus leaving us, in my opinion, where the constitution and laws place us — supreme over persons and cases as far as our judicial powers extend, but not asserting any compulsory control over the state tribunals.

In this view I acquiesce in their opinion, but not altogether in the reasoning, or opinion, of my brother who delivered it. Few minds are accustomed to the same habit of thinking, and our conclusions are most satisfactory to ourselves when arrived at in our own way.

I have another reason for expressing my opinion on this occasion. I view this question as one of the most momentous importance; as one which may affect, in its consequences, the permanence of the American Union. It presents an instance of collision between the judicial powers of the Union, and one of the greatest states in the Union, on a point the most delicate and difficult to be adjusted. . . .

In the case before us, the collision has been, on our part, wholly unsolicited. The exercise of this appellate jurisdiction over the state decisions has long been acquiesced in, and when the writ of error, in this case, was allowed by the president of the Court of Appeals of Virginia, we were sanctioned in supposing that we were to meet with the same acquiescence there. Had that court refused to grant the writ in the first instance, or had the question of jurisdiction, or on the mode of exercising jurisdiction, been made here originally, we should have been put on our guard, and might have so modeled the process of the court as to strip it of the offensive form of a mandate. In this case it might have been brought down to what probably the 25th section of the judiciary act meant it should be, to wit, an alternative judgment, either that the state court may finally proceed, at its option, to carry into effect the judgment of this court, or, if it declined doing so, that then this court would proceed itself to execute it. . . .

Does the judicial power of the United States extend to the revision of decisions of state courts, in cases arising under treaties? But, in order to generalize the question, and present it in the true form in which it presents itself in this case, we will inquire whether the constitution sanctions the exercise of a revising power over the decisions of state tribunals in those cases to which the judicial power of the United States extends.

And here it appears to me that the great difficulty is on the other side. That the real doubt is, whether the state tribunals can constitutionally exercise jurisdiction in any of the cases to which the judicial power of the United States extends. . . .

But I will assume the construction as a sound one, that the cession of power to the general government means no more than that they may assume the exercise of it whenever they think it advisable. It is clear that Congress have hitherto acted under that impression, and my own opinion is in favor of its correctness. But does it not then follow that the jurisdiction of the state court, within the range ceded to the general government, is permitted, and may be withdrawn whenever Congress think proper to do so? As it is a principle that every one may renounce a right introduced for his benefit, we will admit that as Congress have not assumed such jurisdiction, the state courts may, constitutionally, exercise jurisdiction in such cases. Yet, surely, the general power to withdraw the exercise of it includes in it the right to modify, limit, and restrain that exercise. . . .

Judgment affirmed.[d]

HOUSE REPORT No. 43, 21st Cong., 2d Sess. (1831): *"The Committee on the Judiciary, to which was referred a resolution instructing that committee to inquire into the expediency of repealing or modifying the twenty-fifth section of an act entitled 'An act to establish the judicial courts of the United States,' passed on the 4th September, 1789, report:*

"That the committee, profoundly impressed with the importance of the matter referred to their consideration, have bestowed upon it that deliberation it so eminently required; and the investigation has resulted in a solemn conviction, that the twenty-fifth section of an act of Congress, entitled 'An act to establish the judicial courts of the United States,'

---

[d] In Cohens v. Virginia, 6 Wheat. 264 (1821), the Court reviewed the validity of a state statute in a criminal case. Of this decision Judge Roane of Virginia said: "A most monstrous and unexampled decision. . . . It can only be accounted for from that love of power which all history informs us infects and corrupts all who possess it, and from which even the upright and eminent Judges are not exempt. . . ." 1 Warren, The Supreme Court in United States History 555-556 (1926).

On the bitter controversies over Supreme Court review of state decisions, see Warren, Legislative and Judicial Attacks on the Supreme Court of the United States, 47 Am. L. Rev. 1, 161 (1913); Dodd, Chief Justice Marshall and Virginia, 1813-1822, 12 Am. Hist. Rev. 776 (1907); Note, Judge Spencer Roane of Virginia: Champion of States' Rights — Foe of John Marshall, 66 Harv. L. Rev. 1242 (1953); Note, Interposition v. Judicial Power, 1 Race Rel. L. Rep. 465 (1956); McKay, With All Deliberate Speed: A Study of School Desegregation, 31 N.Y.U.L. Rev. 991 (1956); Freund, Storm over the American Supreme Court, 21 Mod. L. Rev. 345 (1958).

That the centrifugal forces were not confined to the South is made clear by Mr. Justice Story's exposure to the disaffection in New England over the War of 1812 and the embargo. "It was the Federalist lawbreakers and traitors of New England who produced the decision in Martin v. Hunter's Lessee, and not the pressure of Marshall's influence." 1 Warren, The Supreme Court in United States History 453 (1926). The relation is epitomized in the fact that the Virginia court delayed the announcement of a decision in this case for a year and a half in order not to strengthen the forces responsible for the Hartford Convention of 1814. See Warren, id. at 447; Note, supra, 66 Harv. L. Rev. 1242, 1250.

Mr. Justice Story was less successful in a cognate position that the federal courts may exercise a common law criminal jurisdiction in aid of national legislative policy; this position was repudiated by the Supreme Court. United States v. Coolidge, 1 Wheat. 415 (1816). — ED.

passed on the 4th September, 1789, is unconstitutional, and ought to be repealed. . . .

". . . The question is not a new one. In the great political contest in 1798 and 1799, this very question made a distinction, and marked the line of division between the two parties that then divided the country. The federal party, who were then in power, asserted that the federal court (which had just then declared and enforced as constitutional the alien and sedition laws) was the tribunal of last resort established by the constitution, to judge of and determine questions of controversy between the departments of the Federal Government, and between the Federal Government and the States. The republican or State rights party of that day, on the contrary, denied that the judicial department of the Federal Government, or all the departments of that Government conjointly, were empowered to decide finally and authoritatively, in questions of sovereignty, *controversies* between a State and the Federal Government, and asserted and insisted that there was no common tribunal established by the constitution for such a purpose, and that, consequently, each party had the right to judge of and determine the extent of its own rights and powers. The avowed political creed of that party was, that the Union was the result of a compact between the people of the several States, in their sovereign and corporate capacities and characters of separate and independent societies or States, and not as one entire people forming one nation. That these were the opinions and principles of the republican party of that day, is abundantly proven by Mr. Jefferson, Mr. Madison, and many other able constitutional lawyers.

". . . As it is now a matter of unquestioned history, that Mr. Jefferson penned the memorable resolutions commonly called the Kentucky resolutions, and that Mr. Madison wrote the Virginia report, the committee feel entitled to quote them as authority upon questions of constitutional law.

"*Kentucky Resolutions, passed November 10th, 1798.*

" '*Resolved*, That the several States composing the United States of America are not united on the principle of unlimited submission to their general government; but that, by compact, under the style and title of a constitution for the United States, and of amendments thereto, they constituted a general government for special purposes, delegated to that government certain definite powers, reserving, each State to itself, the residuary mass of right to their own self government; and that, whensoever the general government assumes undelegated powers, its acts are unauthoritative, void, and of no force; that to this compact each State acceded as a State, and is an integral party; that this government, created by this compact, was not made the exclusive or final judge of the extent of the powers delegated to itself, since that would have made its discretion, and not the constitution, the measure of its powers; but that, as in all other cases of compact among parties having no common judge, each party has an equal right to judge for itself, as well of infractions as of the mode and measure of redress.' . . .

"The committee are aware, that, since the able and unanswerable arguments on the twenty-fifth section in the Supreme Court of Virginia, the advocates of federal power have assumed the position that the right of appeal is claimed for the federal court on the ground that the *case* arises under the laws, treaties, and Constitution of the United States, and not on the ground that the State tribunal is an inferior one, from which a writ of error would lie. The natural result of this will be, that, if the position be true, it will prove too much. If the *nature* of the *case* be the only ground of jurisdiction, will it not authorize the Supreme Court to issue a citation or writ of error to a court of England or France, on the pretext that some one of the questions arose under a treaty of the United States? A judicial tribunal of one of those places is not more independent of the federal court than is a State court, if the character of the case be the only criterion or authority for federal jurisdiction. . . ."[e]

[e] James Madison, in a letter of April 1, 1833, set down his views on the movement to strip the Supreme Court of appellate jurisdiction over state decisions: "The jurisdiction claimed for the Federal Judiciary is truly the only

Chapter One. Historic Basis

Fletcher v. Peck 6 Cranch 87, 3 L. Ed. 162 (1810)

Error to the Circuit Court of the United States for the District of Massachusetts, in an action of covenant brought by Fletcher against Peck. . . .

The plaintiff sued out his writ of error. . . .

MARSHALL, Ch. J., delivered the opinion of the court as follows:

The pleadings being now amended, this cause comes on again to be heard on sundry demurrers, and on a special verdict.

The suit was instituted on several covenants contained in a deed made by John Peck, the defendant in error, conveying to Robert Fletcher, the plaintiff in error, certain lands which were part of a large purchase made by James Gunn and others, in the year 1795, from the state of Georgia, the contract for which was made in the form of a bill passed by the legislature of that state.

The first count in the declaration set forth a breach in the second covenant contained in the deed. The covenant is, "that the Legislature of the State of Georgia, at the time of passing the Act of Sale aforesaid, had good right to sell and dispose of the same in manner pointed out by the said Act." The breach assigned is, that the legislature had no power to sell.

The plea in bar sets forth the Constitution of the State of Georgia, and avers that the lands sold by the defendant to the plaintiff, were within that State. It then sets forth the granting Act, and avers the power of the legislature to sell and dispose of the premises as pointed out by the Act.

To this plea the plaintiff below demurred, and the defendant joined in demurrer.

That the Legislature of Georgia, unless restrained by its own Constitution, possesses the power of disposing of the unappropriated lands within its own limits, in such manner as its own judgment shall dictate, is a proposition not controverted. The only question, then, presented by this demurrer, for the consideration of the court, is this, did the then Constitution of the State of Georgia prohibit the legislature to dispose of the lands, which were the subject of this contract, in the manner stipulated by the contract?

The question, whether a law be void for its repugnancy to the Constitution, is, at all times, a question of much delicacy, which ought seldom, if ever, to be decided in the affirmative, in a doubtful case. The court, when impelled by duty to render such a judgment, would be unworthy of its station, could it be unmindful of the solemn obligations which that station imposes. But it is not on slight implication and vague conjecture that the legislature is to be pronounced to have transcended its powers, and its Acts to be considered as void. The opposition between the Constitution and the law should be such that the judge feels a clear and strong conviction of their incompatibility with each other.

In this case the court can perceive no such opposition. In the Constitution of Georgia,

---

defensive armor of the Federal Government, or rather for the Constitution and laws of the United States. Strip it of that armor, and the door is wide open for nullification, anarchy and convulsion, unless twenty-four States, independent of the whole and of each other, should exhibit the miracle of a voluntary and unanimous performance of every injunction of the parchment compact." Quoted in 1 Warren, The Supreme Court in United States History 740 (1926).

Chief Justice Marshall, in the same period, confided his apprehensions to Mr. Justice Story, in a letter of September 22, 1832: "If the prospects of our country inspire you with gloom, how do you think a man must be affected who partakes of all your opinions and whose geographical position enables him to see a great deal that is concealed from you? I yield slowly and reluctantly to the conviction that our Constitution cannot last. I had supposed that North of the Potomack a firm and solid government competent to the security of rational liberty might be preserved. Even that now seems doubtful. The case of the South seems to me to be desperate. Our opinions are incompatible with a united government even among ourselves. The Union has been prolonged thus far by miracles. I fear they cannot continue." Id. at 769.

The vigorous reaction of President Jackson, after his reelection in 1832, to the centrifugal forces then at work, notably his sponsorship of the Force Bill, which conferred on the federal courts protective jurisdiction on behalf of federal officers, helped to stave off the destiny feared by Marshall. Id. at 774-778. — ED.

adopted in the year 1789, the court can perceive no restriction on the legislative power, which inhibits the passage of the Act of 1795. They cannot say that, in passing that Act, the legislature has transcended its powers, and violated the Constitution.

In overruling the demurrer, therefore, to the first plea, the Circuit Court committed no error.

The 3d covenant is, that all the title which the state of Georgia ever had in the premises had been legally conveyed to John Peck, the grantor.

The second count assigns, in substance, as a breach of this covenant, that the original grantees from the state of Georgia promised and assured divers members of the legislature, then sitting in general assembly, that if the said members would assent to, and vote for, the passing of the act, and if the said bill should pass, such members should have a share of, and be interested in, all the lands purchased from the said state by virtue of such law. And that divers of the said members, to whom the said promises were made, were unduly influenced thereby, and, under such influence, did vote for the passing of the said bill; by reason whereof the said law was a nullity, etc., and so the title of the state of Georgia did not pass to the said Peck, etc.

The plea to this count, after protesting that the promises it alleges were not made, avers, that until after the purchase made from the original grantees by James Greenleaf, under whom the said Peck claims, neither the said James Greenleaf, nor the said Peck, nor any of the mesne vendors between the said Greenleaf and Peck, had any notice or knowledge that any such promises or assurances were made by the said original grantees, or either of them, to any of the members of the legislature of the state of Georgia.

To this plea the plaintiff demurred generally, and the defendant joined in the demurrer.

That corruption should find its way into the governments of our infant republics, and contaminate the very source of legislation, or that impure motives should contribute to the passage of a law, or the formation of a legislative contract, are circumstances most deeply to be deplored. How far a court of justice would, in any case, be competent, on proceedings instituted by the state itself, to vacate a contract thus formed, and to annul rights acquired, under that contract, by third persons having no notice of the improper means by which it was obtained, is a question which the court would approach with much circumspection. . . . Must it be direct corruption, or would interest or undue influence of any kind be sufficient? Must the vitiating cause operate on a majority, or on what number of the members? Would the act be null, whatever might be the wish of the nation, or would its obligation or nullity depend upon the public sentiment? . . .

This solemn question cannot be brought thus collaterally and incidentally before the court. It would be indecent in the extreme, upon a private contract between two individuals, to enter into an inquiry respecting the corruption of the sovereign power of a state. If the title be plainly deduced from a legislative act, which the legislature might constitutionally pass, if the act be clothed with all the requisite forms of a law, a court, sitting as a court of law, cannot sustain a suit brought by one individual against another founded on the allegation that the act is a nullity, in consequence of the impure motives which influenced certain members of the legislature which passed the law.

The Circuit Court, therefore, did right in overruling this demurrer.

The 4th covenant in the deed is, that the title to the premises has been in no way, constitutionally or legally, impaired by virtue of any subsequent act of any subsequent legislature of the state of Georgia.

The third count recites the undue means practiced on certain members of the legislature, as stated in the second count, and then alleges that, in consequence of these practices, and of other causes, a subsequent legislature passed an act annulling and rescinding the law under which the conveyance to the original grantees was made, declaring that conveyance void, and asserting the title of the state to the lands it contained. The count proceeds to recite at large, this rescinding act, and concludes with averring that, by reason

30 Chapter One. Historic Basis

of this act the title of the said Peck in the premises was constitutionally and legally impaired, and rendered null and void.

After protesting, as before, that no such promises were made as stated in this count, the defendant again pleads that himself and the first purchaser under the original grantees, and all intermediate holders of the property, were purchasers without notice.

To this plea there is a demurrer and joinder.

The importance and the difficulty of the questions, presented by these pleadings, are deeply felt by the court.

The lands in controversy vested absolutely in James Gunn and others, the original grantees, by the conveyance of the governor, made in pursuance of an act of assembly to which the legislature was fully competent. Being thus in full possession of the legal estate, they, for a valuable consideration, conveyed portions of the land to those who were willing to purchase. If the original transaction was infected with fraud, these purchasers did not participate in it, and had no notice of it. They were innocent. Yet the legislature of Georgia has involved them in the fate of the first parties to the transaction, and, if the act be valid, has annihilated their rights also.

The legislature of Georgia was a party to this transaction; and for a party to pronounce its own deed invalid, whatever cause may be assigned for its invalidity, must be considered as a mere act of power which must find its vindication in a train of reasoning not often heard in courts of justice. . . .

If the legislature felt itself absolved from those rules of property which are common to all the citizens of the United States, and from those principles of equity which are acknowledged in all our courts, its act is to be supported by its power alone, and the same power may devest any other individual of his lands, if it shall be the will of the legislature so to exert it.

It is not intended to speak with disrespect of the legislature of Georgia, or of its acts. Far from it. The question is a general question and is treated as one. For although such powerful objections to a legislative grant, as are alleged against this, may not again exist, yet the principle, on which alone this rescinding act is to be supported, may be applied to every case to which it shall be the will of any legislature to apply it. . . .

The principle asserted is, that one legislature is competent to repeal any act which a former legislature was competent to pass; and that one legislature cannot abridge the powers of a succeeding legislature.

The correctness of this principle, so far as respects general legislation, can never be controverted. But, if an act be done under a law, a succeeding legislature cannot undo it. The past cannot be recalled by the most absolute power. Conveyances have been made; those conveyances have vested legal estates, and, if those estates may be seized by the sovereign authority, still, that they originally vested is a fact, and cannot cease to be a fact.

When, then, a law is in its nature a contract, when absolute rights have vested under that contract; a repeal of the law cannot devest those rights; and the act of annulling them, if legitimate, is rendered so by a power applicable to the case of every individual in the community.

It may well be doubted whether the nature of society and of government does not prescribe some limits to the legislative power; and, if any be prescribed, where are they to be found, if the property of an individual, fairly and honestly acquired, may be seized without compensation? . . .

The validity of this rescinding act, then, might well be doubted, were Georgia a single sovereign power. But Georgia cannot be viewed as a single, unconnected, sovereign power, on whose legislature no other restrictions are imposed than may be found in its own constitution. She is a part of a large empire; she is a member of the American Union; and that Union has a constitution the supremacy of which all acknowledge, and which imposes limits to the legislatures of the several states, which none claim a right to pass. The constitution of the United States declares that no state shall pass any bill of attainder, ex post facto law or law impairing the obligation of contracts.

Does the case now under consideration come within this prohibitory section of the constitution?

In considering this very interesting question, we immediately ask ourselves what is a contract? Is a grant a contract?

A contract is a compact between two or more parties, and is either executory or executed. An executory contract is one in which a party binds himself to do, or not to do, a particular thing; such was the law under which the conveyance was made by the governor. A contract executed is one in which the object of contract is performed; and this, says Blackstone, differs in nothing from a grant. The contract between Georgia and the purchasers was executed by the grant. A contract executed, as well as one which is executory, contains obligations binding on the parties. A grant, in its own nature, amounts to an extinguishment of the right of the grantor, and implies a contract not to re-assert that right. A party is, therefore, always estopped by his own grant.

Since, then, in fact, a grant is a contract executed, the obligation of which still continues, and since the constitution uses the general term contract, without distinguishing between those which are executory and those which are executed, it must be construed to comprehend the latter as well as the former. . . .

If, under a fair construction of the constitution, grants are comprehended under the term contracts, is a grant from the state excluded from the operation of the provision? Is the clause to be considered as inhibiting the state from impairing the obligation of contracts between two individuals, but as excluding from that inhibition contracts made with itself?

The words themselves contain no such distinction. They are general, and are applicable to contracts of every description. If contracts made with the state are to be exempted from their operation, the exception must arise from the character of the contracting party, not from the words which are employed.

Whatever respect might have been felt for the state sovereignties, it is not to be disguised that the framers of the constitution viewed, with some apprehension, the violent acts which might grow out of the feelings of the moment; and that the people of the United States, in adopting that instrument, have manifested a determination to shield themselves and their property from the effects of those sudden and strong passions to which men are exposed. The restrictions on the legislative power of the states are obviously founded in this sentiment; and the constitution of the United States contains what may be deemed a bill of rights for the people of each state.

No state shall pass any bill of attainder, ex post facto law, or law impairing the obligation of contracts.

A bill of attainder may affect the life of an individual, or may confiscate his property, or may do both.

In this form the power of the legislature over the lives and fortunes of individuals is expressly restrained. What motive, then, for implying, in words which import a general prohibition to impair the obligation of contracts, an exception in favor of the right to impair the obligation of those contracts into which the state may enter? . . .

It is, then, the unanimous opinion of the court, that, in this case, the estate having passed into the hands of a purchaser for a valuable consideration, without notice, the state of Georgia was restrained, either by general principles, which are common to our free institutions, or by the particular provisions of the constitution of the United States, from passing a law whereby the estate of the plaintiff in the premises so purchased could be constitutionally and legally impaired and rendered null and void. . . .

Judgment affirmed with costs.

JOHNSON, J. In this case I entertain, on two points, an opinion different from that which has been delivered by the court.

I do not hesitate to declare that a state does not possess the power of revoking its own grants. But I do it on a general principle, on the reason and nature of things: a principle which will impose laws even on the Deity.

A contrary opinion can only be maintained upon the ground that no existing legislature can abridge the powers of those which will succeed it. To a certain extent this is certainly correct; but the distinction lies between power and interest, the right of jurisdiction and the right of soil. . . .

As to the idea, that the grant of a legislature may be void because the legislature are corrupt, it appears to me to be subject to insuperable difficulties. The acts of the supreme power of a country must be considered pure for the same reason that all sovereign acts must be considered just; because there is no power that can declare them otherwise. The absurdity in this case would have been strikingly perceived, could the party who passed the act of cession have got again into power, and declared themselves pure, and the intermediate legislature corrupt. . . .

I have thrown out these ideas that I may have it distinctly understood that my opinion on this point is not founded on the provision in the constitution of the United States, relative to laws impairing the obligation of contracts. . . .

There can be no solid objection to adopting the technical definition of the word "contract," given by Blackstone. The etymology, the classical signification, and the civil law idea of the word, will all support it. But the difficulty arises on the word "obligation," which certainly imports an existing moral or physical necessity. Now, a grant or conveyance by no means necessarily implies the continuance of an obligation beyond the moment of executing it. It is most generally but the consummation of a contract, is functus officio the moment it is executed, and continues afterwards to be nothing more than the evidence that a certain act was done.

I enter with great hesitation upon this question, because it involves a subject of the greatest delicacy and much difficulty. The states and the United States are continually legislating on the subject of contracts, prescribing the mode of authentication, the time within which suits shall be prosecuted for them, in many cases affecting existing contracts by the laws which they pass, and declaring them to cease or lose their effect for want of compliance, in the parties, with such statutory provisions. All these acts appear to be within the most correct limits of legislative powers, and most beneficially exercised, and certainly could not have been intended to be affected by this constitutional provision; yet where to draw the line, or how to define or limit the words, "obligation of contracts," will be found a subject of extreme difficulty.

To give it the general effect of a restriction of the state powers in favor of private rights, is certainly going very far beyond the obvious and necessary import of the words, and would operate to restrict the states in the exercise of that right which every community must exercise, of possessing itself of the property of the individual, when necessary for public uses; a right which a magnanimous and just government will never exercise without amply indemnifying the individual, and which perhaps amounts to nothing more than a power to oblige him to sell and convey, when the public necessities require it. . . .

I have been very unwilling to proceed to the decision of this cause at all. It appears to me to bear strong evidence, upon the face of it, of being a mere feigned case. It is our duty to decide on the rights but not on the speculations of parties. My confidence, however, in the respectable gentlemen who have been engaged for the parties, has induced me to abandon my scruples, in the belief that they would never consent to impose a mere feigned case upon this court.[f]

---

[f] For the history of this far-reaching land controversy see Magrath, Yazoo (1966). See also Burke, The Cherokee Cases, 21 Stan. L. Rev. 500 (1969). — ED.

NOTE Federal Common Law

Parallel to the development of Supreme Court review of constitutional questions was the exercise by the lower federal courts in their diversity of citizenship jurisdiction of power to decide, independently of state decisions, questions of "general common law," including commercial law and the law of torts. Swift v. Tyson, 16 Pet. 1 (1842), per Story, J. For a psychological explanation of Mr. Justice Story's position see Gray, The Nature and Sources of the Law 253 (2d ed. 1921). The overruling of Swift v. Tyson in Erie R.R. v. Tompkins, 304 U.S. 64 (1938), marked an important shift in federal-state relationships. See, e.g., Dobie, Seven Implications of Swift v. Tyson, 16 Va. L. Rev. 225 (1930); Shulman, The Demise of Swift v. Tyson, 47 Yale L.J. 1336 (1938); Jackson, The Rise and Fall of Swift v. Tyson, 24 A.B.A.J. 609 (1938); and, for a polemic French view of the "Balkanization" of American law caused by the abandonment of Story's position, see Lambert and Xirau, L'Ancêtre Américain du Droit Comparé — la Doctrine du Juge Story (1947).

See also Friendly, In Praise of Erie — and of the New Federal Common Law, 39 N.Y.U.L. Rev. 383 (1964), tracing the development of a uniform judge-made law through decisions making effective federal statutory law; Note, The Federal Common Law, 82 Harv. L. Rev. 1512 (1969).

Fostering the growth of diversity jurisdiction was the steadily evolved doctrine of the citizenship of corporations for this jurisdictional purpose. See McGovney, A Supreme Court Fiction: Corporations in the Diverse Citizenship Jurisdiction of the Federal Courts, 56 Harv. L. Rev. 853, 1019, 1225 (1945). By Act of July 25, 1958, 72 Stat. 415, 28 U.S.C. §1332(c), for purposes of diversity jurisdiction a corporation is "deemed a citizen of any State by which it has been incorporated and of the State where it has its principal place of business."

NOTE The Uses and Standards of Judicial Review

Since the power of judicial review of the acts of state and federal government is an accomplished fact, debate has centered on the proper functions and standards of its exercise. Twice in this century these questions have come to a climax within and without the Supreme Court: first in the early New Deal period, when state and federal social welfare legislation was freely invalidated by the Court; then during the 1950s and 1960s, when the Bill of Rights was given extensive application to "constitutionalize" many areas of legislative and administrative decisionmaking.

Discussion of these issues has too often been opportunistic, turning on whether at a given time the political-legislative climate or the judicial climate seems the more salubrious for the disputant. Politically conservative spokesmen applauded the nay-saying role of the Supreme Court in the early twentieth century but assailed the Court's active role after mid-century; and conversely for politically liberal critics. As observed in Leonard Levy (ed.), Judicial Review and the Supreme Court 1 (1967), "Much of the literature on the Supreme Court reflects the principle of the gored ox."

The functions and standards of judicial review can, however, be discussed on a higher level of principle. Should judges be regarded as the "conscience" of the country? Should they, in any event, serve as the special guardians of our constitutional order, and the special expounders of our constitutional philosophy? Since many constitutional questions require giving content to deliberately vague and perhaps open-ended terms, and since decisions of unconstitutionality require for correction, generally speaking, a constitutional amendment, is it consistent with democratic principles, and is it sensible, that judges, appointed from one profession and for life, exercise so free and decisive a voice in the shaping of social policy?

General principles, Justice Holmes remarked, do not decide concrete cases. Still, a judge's outlook on the institution of judicial review may, when other considerations are nicely balanced, determine the direction of his ultimate leap which is the decision of a case. That outlook may determine whether to exercise discretion to grant appellate review, whether to recognize a legally protected interest on the part of the complainant, whether to essay a broad or narrow decision, and whether to uphold or disapprove a legislative or administrative act. Consider the tenor of the "general propositions" in the following statements:

Warren, C.J., in Reynolds v. Sims, 377 U.S. 533, 566 (1964): "We are told that the matter of apportioning representation in a state legislature is a complex and many-faceted one. We are advised that States can rationally consider factors other than population in apportioning legislative representation. We are admonished not to restrict the power of the States to impose differing views as to political philosophy on their citizens. We are cautioned about the dangers of entering into political thickets and mathematical quagmires. Our answer is this: a denial of constitutionally protected rights demands judicial protection; our oath and our office require no less of us."

Frankfurter, J., concurring in Youngstown Sheet and Tube Co. v. Sawyer, 343 U.S. 579, 594 (1952): "The Framers, however, did not make the judiciary the overseer of our government. They were familiar with the revisory functions entrusted to judges in a few of the States and refused to lodge such powers in this Court. . . . Rigorous adherence to the narrow scope of the judicial function is especially demanded in controversies that arouse appeals to the Constitution. The attitude with which this Court must approach its duty when confronted with such issues is precisely the opposite of that normally manifested by the general public. So-called constitutional questions seem to exercise a mesmeric influence over the popular mind. This eagerness to settle — preferably forever — a specific problem on the basis of the broadest possible constitutional pronouncements may not unfairly be called one of our minor national traits. An English observer of our scene has acutely described it: 'At the first sound of a new argument over the United States Constitution and its interpretation the hearts of Americans leap with a fearful joy. The blood stirs powerfully in their veins and a new lustre brightens their eyes. Like King Harry's men before Harfleur, they stand like greyhounds in the slips, straining upon the start.' The Economist, May 10, 1952, p. 370."

Stone, J., dissenting in United States v. Butler, 297 U.S. 1, 78-79 (1936): "The power of courts to declare a statute unconstitutional is subject to two guiding principles of decision which ought never to be absent from judicial consciousness. One is that courts are concerned only with the power to enact statutes, not with their wisdom. The other is that while unconstitutional exercise of power by the executive and legislative branches of the government is subject to judicial restraint, the only check upon our own exercise of power is our own sense of self-restraint. For the removal of unwise laws from the statute books appeal lies not to the courts but to the ballot and to the processes of democratic government." Id. at 87: "The suggestion that it must now be curtailed by judicial fiat because it may be abused by unwise use hardly rises to the dignity of argument. So may judicial power be abused. . . . 'It must be remembered that legislators are the ultimate guardians of the liberties and welfare of the people in quite as great a degree as the courts.' Justice Holmes, in Missouri, Kansas & Texas Ry. Co. v. May, 194 U.S. 267, 270. . . ."

Should the readiness of courts to exercise judicial review, and the intensity of such review, be governed by uniform standards, whatever the nature of the case? If the standards should vary, according to what factors? — whether the constitutional guarantee is plain? whether the issue involves the scope of national or of state power? whether a provision of the Bill of Rights is involved? whether, if so, the provision safeguards "property" rights or "personal" rights? whether the right asserted is "fundamental"?

This set of questions is involved, implicitly or explicitly, in most of the materials throughout this casebook. Warrantable answers to these questions will depend on a study of the theory and practice of judicial review as reflected in the cases themselves.

In the immense literature on the subject, reference may be made to several recent writings: from the point of view of "judicial self-restraint," L. Hand, The Bill of Rights (1958); A. Bickel, The Least Dangerous Branch: The Supreme Court at the Bar of Politics (1962); A. Bickel, The Supreme Court and the Idea of Progress (1970); from the side of judicial "activism," C. Black, The People and the Court: Judicial Review in a Democracy (1960); J.S. Wright, Professor Bickel, the Scholarly Tradition, and the Supreme Court, 84 Harv. L. Rev. 769 (1971). Compare A. Cox, The Role of the Supreme Court in American Government (1976).

Chapter Two Present Statutory Basis

United States Code, Title 28

§ 1251. ORIGINAL JURISDICTION

(a) The Supreme Court shall have original and exclusive jurisdiction of:
(1) All controversies between two or more States;
(2) All actions or proceedings against ambassadors or other public ministers of foreign states or their domestics or domestic servants, not inconsistent with the law of nations.
(b) The Supreme Court shall have original but not exclusive jurisdiction of:
(1) All actions or proceedings brought by ambassadors or other public ministers of foreign states or to which consuls or vice consuls of foreign states are parties;
(2) All controversies between the United States and a State;
(3) All actions or proceedings by a State against the citizens of another State or against aliens.

§ 1252. DIRECT APPEALS FROM DECISION INVALIDATING ACTS OF CONGRESS

Any party may appeal to the Supreme Court from an interlocutory or final judgment, decree or order of any court of the United States, the United States District Court for the District of the Canal Zone, the District Court of Guam, and the District Court of the Virgin Islands and any court of record of Puerto Rico, holding an Act of Congress unconstitutional in any civil action, suit, or proceeding to which the United States or any of its agencies, or any officer or employee thereof, as such officer or employee, is a party.

A party who has received notice of appeal under this section shall take any subsequent appeal or cross appeal to the Supreme Court. All appeals or cross appeals taken to other courts prior to such notice shall be treated as taken directly to the Supreme Court.

§ 1253. DIRECT APPEALS FROM DECISIONS OF THREE-JUDGE COURTS

Except as otherwise provided by law, any party may appeal to the Supreme Court from an order granting or denying, after notice and hearing, an interlocutory or permanent injunction in any civil action, suit or proceeding required by any Act of Congress to be heard and determined by a district court of three judges.

Chapter Two. Present Statutory Basis

§ 1254. COURTS OF APPEALS; CERTIORARI; APPEAL; CERTIFIED QUESTIONS

Cases in the courts of appeals may be reviewed by the Supreme Court by the following methods:

(1) By writ of certiorari granted upon the petition of any party to any civil or criminal case, before or after rendition of judgment or decree;

(2) By appeal by a party relying on a State statute held by a court of appeals to be invalid as repugnant to the Constitution, treaties or laws of the United States, but such appeal shall preclude review by writ of certiorari at the instance of such appellant, and review on appeal shall be restricted to the Federal questions presented;

(3) By certification at any time by a court of appeals of any question of law in any civil or criminal case as to which instructions are desired, and upon such certification the Supreme Court may give binding instructions or require the entire record to be sent up for decision of the entire matter in controversy.

§ 1255. COURT OF CLAIMS; CERTIORARI; CERTIFIED QUESTIONS

Cases in the Court of Claims may be reviewed by the Supreme Court by the following methods:

(1) By writ of certiorari granted on petition of the United States or the claimant;

(2) By certification of any question of law by the Court of Claims in any case as to which instructions are desired, and upon such certification the Supreme Court may give binding instructions on such question.

§ 1256. COURT OF CUSTOMS AND PATENT APPEALS; CERTIORARI

Cases in the Court of Customs and Patent Appeals may be reviewed by the Supreme Court by writ of certiorari.

§ 1257. STATE COURTS; APPEALS; CERTIORARI

Final judgments or decrees rendered by the highest court of a State in which a decision could be had, may be reviewed by the Supreme Court as follows:

(1) By appeal, where is drawn in question the validity of a treaty or statute of the United States and the decision is against its validity.

(2) By appeal, where is drawn in question the validity of a statute of any state on the ground of its being repugnant to the Constitution, treaties or laws of the United States, and the decision is in favor of its validity.

(3) By writ of certiorari, where the validity of a treaty or statute of the United States is drawn in question or where the validity of a State statute is drawn in question on the ground of its being repugnant to the Constitution, treaties or laws of the United States, or where any title, right, privilege or immunity is specially set up or claimed under the Constitution, treaties or statutes of, or commission held or authority exercised under, the United States.

For the purposes of this section, the term "highest court of a State" includes the District of Columbia Court of Appeals.

§ 2281. INJUNCTION AGAINST ENFORCEMENT OF STATE STATUTE; THREE-JUDGE COURT REQUIRED [REPEALED, AUGUST 12, 1976]

An interlocutory or permanent injunction restraining the enforcement, operation or execution of any State statute by restraining the action of any officer of such State in the enforcement or execution of such statute or of an order made by an administrative board or commission acting under State statutes, shall not be granted by any district court or judge thereof upon the ground of the unconstitutionality of such statute unless the application therefor is heard and determined by a district court of three judges under section 2284 of this title.

§2282. INJUNCTION AGAINST ENFORCEMENT OF FEDERAL STATUTE; THREE-JUDGE COURT REQUIRED [REPEALED, AUGUST 12, 1976]

An interlocutory or permanent injunction restraining the enforcement, operation or execution of any Act of Congress for repugnance to the Constitution of the United States shall not be granted by any district court or judge thereof unless the application therefor is heard and determined by a district court of three judges under section 2284 of this title.

§2283. STAY OF STATE COURT PROCEEDINGS

A court of the United States may not grant an injunction to stay proceedings in a State court except as expressly authorized by Act of Congress, or where necessary in aid of its jurisdiction, or to protect or effectuate its judgments.

§2284. THREE-JUDGE COURT; WHEN REQUIRED; COMPOSITION; PROCEDURE

"(a) A district court of three judges shall be convened when otherwise required by Act of Congress, or when an action is filed challenging the constitutionality of the apportionment of congressional districts or the apportionment of any statewide legislative body.

(b) In any action required to be heard and determined by a district court of three judges under subsection (a) of this section, the composition and procedure of the court shall be as follows:

(1) Upon the filing of a request for three judges, the judge to whom the request is presented shall, unless he determines that three judges are not required, immediately notify the chief judge of the circuit, who shall designate two other judges, at least one of whom shall be a circuit judge. The judges so designated, and the judge to whom the request was presented, shall serve as members of the court to hear and determine the action or proceeding.

(2) If the action is against a State, or officer or agency thereof, at least five days' notice of hearing of the action shall be given by registered or certified mail to the Governor and attorney general of the State. The hearing shall be given precedence and held at the earliest practicable day.

(3) A single judge may conduct all proceedings except the trial, and enter all orders permitted by the rules of civil procedure except as provided in this subsection. He may grant a temporary restraining order on a specific finding, based on evidence submitted, that specified irreparable damage will result if the order is not granted, which order, unless previously revoked by the district judge, shall remain in force only until the hearing and determination by the district court of three judges of an application for a preliminary injunction. A single judge shall not appoint a master, or order a reference, or hear and determine any application for a preliminary or permanent injunction or motion to vacate such an injunction, or enter judgment on the merits. Any action of a single judge may be reviewed by the full court at any time before final judgment."

§2403. INTERVENTION BY UNITED STATES; CONSTITUTIONAL QUESTION

In any action, suit or proceeding in a court of the United States to which the United States or any agency, officer or employee thereof is not a party, wherein the constitutionality of any Act of Congress affecting the public interest is drawn in question, the court shall certify such fact to the Attorney General, and shall permit the United States to intervene for presentation of evidence, if evidence is otherwise admissible in the case, and for argument on the question of constitutionality. The United States shall, subject to the applicable provisions of law, have all the rights of a party and be subject to all liabilities of a party as to court costs to the extent necessary for a proper presentation of the facts and law relating to the question of constitutionality.[a]

NOTE Jurisdiction of the Federal Courts in Constitutional Cases

1. Certain historical facts are relevant to an understanding of constitutional litigation. Not until 1875 were the lower federal courts given general federal-question jurisdiction (that is, over all cases arising under the laws or Constitution of the United States), either originally or by removal from state courts. Of course, as in Fletcher v. Peck, page 28 supra, constitutional issues might arise in the federal courts in diversity-of-citizenship cases. But the state courts were the principal tribunals for the trial of federal-question cases until the Judiciary Act of 1875 conferred original and removal jurisdiction on the lower federal courts in this class of cases. A concise account of the evolution of federal jurisdiction is given in Frankfurter, Distribution of Judicial Power Between United States and State Courts, 13 Cornell L.Q. 499 (1928).

Before 1875 and for thirty-nine years thereafter the review of state decisions by the Supreme Court was confined to those which *denied* a claim of federal right. Thus a state court was the court of last resort for constitutional issues if it invalidated a state statute, thereby sustaining a claim founded on the Constitution. The theory, of course, was that parties needed protection in the Supreme Court only when a state court indulged a natural predilection to sustain state action or overturn federal action. The anomalous double standard thus created was dramatized for the public by the action of the New York Court of Appeals in holding unconstitutional the state workman's compensation law — a decision insulated from Supreme Court review. Ives v. South Buffalo Ry., 201 N.Y. 271 (1911). Agitation for enlarged jurisdiction in the Supreme Court bore fruit in 1914, with the establishment of review by certiorari in addition to that by writ of error. 38 Stat. 790. See Frankfurter, The Business of the Supreme Court, 39 Harv. L. Rev. 1046, 1047-1057 (1926).

There is irony in the fact that the Ives decision, which precipitated the jurisdictional change, had held the state law invalid under both the New York and federal constitutions. For the significance of this, see the following Note. Theodore Roosevelt, who pressed for the jurisdictional change after the Ives decision, campaigned also for the recall (by popular referendum) of state decisions holding state statutes unconstitutional; and the proposals were combined in the Progressive Party platform in 1912. See 19 Works of Theodore Roosevelt 185 et seq. (1925).

2. The criterion "arising under" the laws or Constitution of the United States is the foundation in Article III for the jurisdiction of both the lower federal courts and the Supreme Court. In interpreting the Judiciary Acts, however, the Court has given narrower scope to the jurisdiction of the lower federal courts in this regard. In Louisville & Nashville R.R. v. Mottley, 211 U.S. 149 (1908), a passenger sued a carrier in a federal court to compel performance of an agreement for free transportation, which had been entered into in settlement of a claim for personal injuries; the passenger alleged that an Act of Congress invalidating free passes was invalid. The carrier demurred. The Court held that the case did not arise under the laws or Constitution of the United States, and ordered the suit dismissed. Thereafter the passenger sued in a state court, and on appeal the highest court of the state held the statute invalid. On writ of error the Supreme Court took

---

[a] The Rules of the Supreme Court, which set forth, inter alia, the procedures on filing petitions for certiorari and appeals and the considerations governing the grant or denial of certiorari, may be found in 28 U.S.C.A. — ED.

jurisdiction and reversed on the merits. Louisville & Nashville R.R. v. Mottley, 219 U.S. 467 (1911). See Chadbourn and Levin, Original Jurisdiction of Federal Questions, 90 U. Pa. L. Rev. 639 (1942). If the federal claim must be part of the plaintiff's case for purposes of original jurisdiction in the federal courts, is it sound to allow the defendant to remove a federal-question case brought in a state court? The statutes allow such removal, although in diversity cases only a nonresident defendant is authorized to remove. See Wechsler, Federal Jurisdiction and the Revision of the Judicial Code, 13 Law & Contemp. Prob. 216, 233 (1948).

NOTE Supreme Court Review of State Court Decisions: The Adequate State Ground Doctrine

What questions are reviewable in the Supreme Court on review of a state court decision? Here the appellate jurisdiction of the Supreme Court is narrower than the original (or removal) jurisdiction of the lower federal courts. Only the federal questions are open in the Supreme Court on review of a state court. Murdock v. Memphis, 20 Wall. 590 (1875). Could the Court be given power to review all the questions in a case from a state court? See Curtis, Jurisdiction of the Courts of the United States 56-58 (1880); Hart, The Relations Between State and Federal Law, 54 Colum. L. Rev. 489, 499-506 (1954).

Certain important corollaries follow from this limitation. If the state court decision rests on two grounds — e.g., that the state statute of limitations has run and that in any event the plaintiff's claim of unconstitutionality of a state statute is without merit — why is there no basis for review in the Supreme Court? The usual phrase in dismissing appeals for this reason is that "the decision of the state court rests on an independent non-federal ground adequate to support it." Note that such a dismissal requires an affirmative response to two questions: "(1) Is the state court judgment *based* upon a non-federal ground? (2) Is that non-federal ground *adequate* to support the state court judgment?" Stern & Gressman, Supreme Court Practice 132 (4th ed. 1969).

The first question raises difficult problems only when both federal and nonfederal questions were presented, but the state court issued no opinion, or an ambiguous opinion, in rendering its judgment. Although the availability of an adequate state ground ordinarily creates a presumption that it was the basis of the state court decision, the Supreme Court has in several instances remanded the case to the state court for clarification or has postponed decision to enable the parties to seek a certificate from the state court stating the precise basis of the judgment. See Herb v. Pitcairn, 324 U.S. 117 (1945); Minnesota v. National Tea Co., 309 U.S. 551 (1940); Stern & Gressman, supra, at 133-138; Note, Supreme Court Treatment of State Court Cases Exhibiting Ambiguous Grounds of Decision, 62 Colum. L. Rev. 822 (1962).

The second question involves determination whether the state ground "is adequate to support the judgment of the federal question." Stern & Gressman, supra, at 138. The Supreme Court must consider whether the state ground is "broad enough, without reference to the federal question, to sustain the . . . judgment"; "independent of the federal question"; and "tenable, [not] 'so certainly unfounded that it properly may be regarded as essentially arbitrary, or a mere device to prevent a review of the decision upon the federal question.' Enterprise Irrig. Dist. v. Farmers' Mut. Canal Co., [243 U.S. 157, 164 (1917)]." Stern & Gressman, supra, at 138-139.

Consider the applicability of this standard to the following classes of state decisions: (a) holding a state law invalid under the due process clause of both the state and federal constitutions; (b) holding that a prior state decision of a federal question is res judicata; (c) holding that the federal question cannot now be considered because the prior decision on remand from the state supreme court in the same case is the "law of the case"; (d) holding that no valid contract was in force and therefore a state law did not violate the obligation of contract clause; (e) holding that a confession was not coerced and therefore the conviction did not violate the due process clause; (f) holding that under state practice the action should have been brought at law instead of in equity and hence the federal claims of the plaintiff cannot be considered, notwithstanding the fact that prior decisions allowed equitable actions and the statute of limitations has run at law; (g) holding that a constitutional question raised for the first time in a petition for rehearing comes too late to be considered.[b]

An anguishing situation is presented where state procedural rules operate to bar consideration of a serious substantive federal claim. In Patterson v. Alabama, 294 U.S. 600 (1935) (the Scottsboro case), and Williams v. Georgia, 349 U.S. 375 (1955), petitioners had been convicted of capital offenses by juries from which blacks had been unconstitutionally excluded. But in each case the state supreme court had refused to consider the federal claim on the ground that it had not been timely raised. In each case the Supreme Court remanded for reconsideration. In Patterson, the Court noted that in a companion case involving a codefendant, it was reversing the decision of the Alabama supreme court, which had reached the federal claim and upheld the jury selection procedure. Norris v. Alabama, 294 U.S. 587 (1935). The Court continued, "The state court decided the constitutional question against Norris, and it was manifestly with that conclusion in mind that the court approached the decision in the case of Patterson and struck his bill of exceptions. We are not satisfied that the court would have dealt with the case in the same way if it had determined the constitutional question as we have determined it. . . ." On remand, the Alabama supreme court ordered a new trial, and Patterson was again convicted and sentenced to 75 years' imprisonment.

In Williams, the Court remanded on its finding that the decision to enforce the state procedural rule was a matter of discretion in the state courts. It invited the Georgia supreme court to reconsider in light of the state's admission before the U.S. Supreme Court that the jury selection had been unconstitutional: "Fair regard for the principles which the Georgia courts have enforced in numerous cases and for the constitutional commands binding on all courts compels us to reject the assumption that the courts of Georgia would allow this man to go to his death as the result of a conviction secured from a jury which the State admits was unconstitutionally impaneled."

On remand, the Georgia supreme court entered the following opinion, Williams v. State, 211 Ga. 763, 88 S.E.2d 376 (1955): " 'The powers not delegated to the United States by the Constitution, nor prohibited by it to the States, are reserved to the States respectively, or to the people.' Constitution of the United States, 10th Amendment; Code § 1-810. Even though executives and legislators, not being constitutional lawyers, might often overstep the foregoing unambiguous constitutional prohibition of Federal invasion of state jurisdiction, there can never be an acceptable excuse for judicial failure to strictly observe it. This court bows to the Supreme Court on all Federal questions of law, but we will not supinely surrender sovereign powers of this State. In this case the opinion of the majority of that court recognizes that this court decided the case according to established rules of law, and that no Federal jurisdiction existed which would authorize that court to render a judgment either affirming or reversing the judgment of this court, which are the only judgments by that court that this court can constitutionally recognize.

"The Supreme Court undertakes to remand the case for further consideration, and in its opinion has pointed to Georgia law vesting in the trial judge discretion in ruling upon an extraordinary motion for new trial, and apparently concluded therefrom that this court should reverse the trial court because that discretion was not exercised in the way the Supreme Court would have exercised it. We know and respect the universally recognized rule that the exercise of discretion never authorizes a violation or defiance of law. In this

---

[b] Compare Brinkerhoff-Faris Co. v. Hill, 281 U.S. 673 (1930), with Herndon v. Georgia, 295 U.S. 441 (1935). See also Patterson v. Alabama, 294 U.S. 600 (1935); NAACP v. Alabama, 357 U.S. 449 (1958).

case, as pointed out by us, that law is that the question sought to be raised must be raised before trial and not otherwise.

"Not in recognition of any jurisdiction of the Supreme Court to influence or in any manner to interfere with the functioning of this court on strictly State questions, but solely for the purpose of completing the record of this court in a case that was first decided by us in 1953, and to avoid further delay, we state that our opinion in Williams v. State, 210 Ga. 665 (82 S.E. 2d 217), is supported by sound and unchallenged law, conforms with the State and Federal Constitutions, and stands as the judgment of all seven of the Justices of this Court."

Williams' petition for writ of certiorari was denied. 350 U.S. 950 (1956).

Was the Georgia court correct in saying that its decision to apply the procedural rule involved "strictly State questions"? See Sullivan v. Little Hunting Park, Inc., 396 U.S. 229 (1969), where the Court took jurisdiction on writ of certiorari despite the holding of the Supreme Court of Appeals of Virginia that because of petitioner's failure to comply with a rule of that court regarding presentation of the transcript of the trial court proceedings, that court lacked jurisdiction to review the dismissal of petitioner's action under the Civil Rights Acts, 42 U.S.C. §§ 1981, 1982. Writing for the Court, Justice Douglas held that the transcript rule was more properly deemed discretionary than jurisdictional, and could not serve as a procedural state ground adequate to bar Supreme Court review.[e]

In light of the "supervening event" of the state's admitting the unconstitutionality of its jury selection procedures, could the Williams Court have held that the procedural rule was no longer — if it had ever been — an adequate state ground for upholding the conviction? See Comment, Supreme Court Treatment of State Procedural Grounds Relied on in State Courts to Preclude Decision of Federal Questions, 61 Colum. L. Rev. 255, 272-275 (1961). And consider the following statement by Justice Frankfurter, dissenting in Daniels v. Allen, 344 U.S. 443, 557-558 (1953): "We were given to understand on the argument that if petitioners' lawyer had mailed his 'statement of case on appeal' on the 60th day and the prosecutor's office had received it on the 61st day the law of North Carolina would clearly have been complied with, but because he delivered it by hand on the 61st day all opportunities for appeal, both in the North Carolina courts and in the federal courts, are cut off although the North Carolina courts had discretion to hear this appeal. For me it is important to emphasize the fact that North Carolina does not have a fixed period for taking an appeal. The decisive question is whether a refusal to exercise a discretion which the Legislature of North Carolina has vested in its judges is an act so arbitrary and so cruel in its operation, considering that life is at stake, that in the circumstances of this case it constitutes a denial of due process in its rudimentary procedural aspect."

See also Michel v. Louisiana, 350 U.S. 91 (1955); Hill, The Inadequate State Ground, 65 Colum. L. Rev. 943, 984-985, 996-1000 (1965).

Compare the problem in the setting of federal habeas corpus. In Fay v. Noia, 372 U.S. 391 (1963), the Court held that on petition for habeas corpus brought in federal district court to challenge imprisonment following a state criminal conviction, failure properly to have raised a federal constitutional claim does not bar its consideration on petition for habeas corpus unless the failure is shown to have constituted knowing and intelligent waiver of a federal right and a "deliberate bypass [of] the orderly procedure of the state courts." Writing for the Court, Justice Brennan distinguished the powers of the federal courts to review state convictions in a de novo and collateral proceeding under the writ of habeas corpus from those of the Supreme Court in appellate review of state court proceed-

---

[e] See Justice Harlan's dissent, 396 U.S. at 242-247, arguing that a discretionary judgment on a state ground is not in itself inadequate but that the procedural ground failed in any event because the invocation of this rule by the Virginia court "was in my view based on a standard of reasonableness much stricter than that which could have been fairly extracted from the earlier Virginia cases applying the rule." Citing NAACP v. Alabama, supra.

ings. The adequate state ground doctrine, said Justice Brennan, "is a function of the limitations of *appellate* review." Compare, however, Francis v. Henderson, 425 U.S. 536 (1976).

Henry v. Mississippi 379 U.S. 443, 85 S. Ct. 564, 13 L. Ed. 2d 408 (1965)

MR. JUSTICE BRENNAN delivered the opinion of the Court.

Petitioner was convicted of disturbing the peace, by indecent proposals to and offensive contact with an 18-year-old hitchhiker to whom he is said to have given a ride in his car. The trial judge charged the jury that "you cannot find the defendant guilty on the unsupported and uncorroborated testimony of the complainant alone." The petitioner's federal claim derives from the admission of a police officer's testimony, introduced to corroborate the hitchhiker's testimony. The Mississippi Supreme Court held that the officer's testimony was improperly admitted as the fruit of "an unlawful search and was in violation of § 23, Miss. Constitution 1890." 154 So. 2d 289, 294. The tainted evidence tended to substantiate the hitchhiker's testimony by showing its accuracy in a detail which could have been seen only by one inside the car. In particular, it showed that the right-hand ashtray of the car in which the incident took place was full of Dentyne chewing gum wrappers, and that the cigarette lighter did not function. The police officer testified that after petitioner's arrest he had returned to the petitioner's home and obtained the permission of petitioner's wife to look in petitioner's car. The wife provided the officer with the keys, with which the officer opened the car. He testified that he tried the lighter and it would not work, and also that the ashtray "was filled with red dentyne chewing gum wrappers."

The Mississippi Supreme Court first filed an opinion which reversed petitioner's conviction and remanded for a new trial. The court held that the wife's consent to the search of the car did not waive petitioner's constitutional rights, and noted that the "[t]estimony of the State's witness . . . is, in effect, uncorroborated without the evidence disclosed by the inspection of defendant's automobile." 154 So. 2d, at 296 (advance sheet). Acting in the belief that petitioner had been represented by nonresident counsel unfamiliar with local procedure, the court reversed despite petitioner's failure to comply with the Mississippi requirement that an objection to illegal evidence be made at the time it is introduced. The court noted that petitioner had moved for a directed verdict at the close of the State's case, assigning as one ground the use of illegally obtained evidence; it did not mention petitioner's renewal of his motion at the close of all evidence.

After the first opinion was handed down, the State filed a Suggestion of Error, pointing out that petitioner was in fact represented at his trial by competent local counsel, as well as by out-of-state lawyers. Thereupon the Mississippi Supreme Court withdrew its first opinion and filed a new opinion in support of a judgment affirming petitioner's conviction. The new opinion is identical with the first save for the result, the statement that petitioner had local counsel, and the discussion of the effect of failure for whatever reason to make timely objection to the evidence. "In such circumstances, even if honest mistakes of counsel in respect to policy or strategy or otherwise occur, they are binding upon the client as part of the hazards of courtroom battle." 154 So. 2d, at 296 (bound volume). Moreover, the court reasoned, petitioner's cross-examination of the State's witness before the initial motion for directed verdict, and introduction of other evidence of the car's interior appearance afterward, "cured" the original error and estopped petitioner from complaining of the tainted evidence. We granted certiorari, 376 U.S. 904. We vacate the judgment of conviction and remand for a hearing on the question whether the petitioner is to be deemed to have knowingly waived decision of his federal claim when timely objection was not made to the admission of the illegally seized evidence.

It is, of course, a familiar principle that this Court will decline to review state court judgments which rest on independent and adequate state grounds, even where those judgments also decide federal questions. The principle applies not only in cases involving state substantive grounds, Murdock v. City of Memphis, 20 Wall. 590, but also in cases involving state procedural grounds. Compare Herb. v. Pitcairn, 324 U.S. 117, 125-126, with Davis v. Wechsler, 263 U.S. 22. But it is important to distinguish between state substantive grounds and state procedural grounds. Where the ground involved is substantive, the determination of the federal question cannot affect the disposition if the state court decision on the state law question is allowed to stand. Under the view taken in Murdock of the statutes conferring appellate jurisdiction on this Court, we have no power to revise judgments on questions of state law. Thus, the adequate nonfederal ground doctrine is necessary to avoid advisory opinions.

These justifications have no application where the state ground is purely procedural. A procedural default which is held to bar challenge to a conviction in state courts, even on federal constitutional grounds, prevents implementation of the federal right. Accordingly, we have consistently held that the question of when and how defaults in compliance with state procedural rules can preclude our consideration of a federal question is itself a federal question. Cf. Lovell v. City of Griffin, 303 U.S. 444, 450. As Mr. Justice Holmes said:

"When as here there is a plain assertion of federal rights in the lower court, local rules as to how far it shall be reviewed on appeal do not necessarily prevail. . . . Whether the right was denied or not given due recognition by the [state court] . . . is a question as to which the plaintiffs are entitled to invoke our judgment." Love v. Griffith, 266 U.S. 32, 33-34.

Only last Term, we reaffirmed this principle, holding that a state appellate court's refusal, on the ground of mootness, to consider a federal claim, did not preclude our independent determination of the question of mootness; that is itself a question of federal law which this Court must ultimately decide. Liner v. Jafco, Inc., 375 U.S. 301. These cases settle the proposition that a litigant's procedural defaults in state proceedings do not prevent vindication of his federal rights unless the State's insistence on compliance with its procedural rule serves a legitimate state interest. If it does not, the state procedural rule ought not be permitted to bar vindication of important federal rights.[1]

The Mississippi rule requiring contemporaneous objection to the introduction of illegal evidence clearly does serve a legitimate state interest. By immediately apprising the trial judge of the objection, counsel gives the court the opportunity to conduct the trial without using the tainted evidence. If the objection is well taken the fruits of the illegal search may be excluded from jury consideration, and a reversal and new trial avoided. But on the record before us it appears that this purpose of the contemporaneous-objection rule may have been substantially served by petitioner's motion at the close of the State's evidence asking for a directed verdict because of the erroneous admission of the officer's testimony. For at this stage the trial judge could have called for elaboration of the search and seizure argument and, if persuaded, could have stricken the tainted testimony or have taken other appropriate corrective action. For example, if there was sufficient competent evidence without this testimony to go to the jury, the motion for a directed verdict might have been denied, and the case submitted to the jury with a properly worded appropriate cautionary instruction. In these circumstances, the delay until the close of the State's case in presenting the objection cannot be said to have frustrated the State's interest in avoiding delay and waste of time in the disposition of the case. If this is so, and enforcement of the rule here would serve no substantial state interest, then settled principles would preclude treating the state ground as adequate; giving effect to the contemporaneous-objection rule for its own sake "would be to force resort to an arid ritual of meaningless form." Staub v. City of Baxley, 355 U.S. 313, 320; see also Wright v. Georgia, 373 U.S. 284, 289-291.[2]

[1] This will not lead inevitably to a plethora of attacks on the application of state procedural rules; where the state rule is a reasonable one and clearly announced to defendant and counsel, application of the waiver doctrine will yield the same result as that of the adequate nonfederal ground doctrine in the vast majority of cases.

[2] We do not rely on the principle that our review is not precluded when the state court has failed to exercise discretion to disregard the procedural default. See Williams v. Georgia, 349 U.S. 375. We read the second Mis-

We have no reason, however, to decide that question now or to express any view on the merits of petitioner's substantial constitutional claim. For even assuming that the making of the objection on the motion for a directed verdict satisfied the state interest served by the contemporaneous-objection rule, the record suggests a possibility that petitioner's counsel deliberately bypassed the opportunity to make timely objection in the state court, and thus that the petitioner should be deemed to have forfeited his state court remedies. . . .

Of course, in so remanding we neither hold nor even remotely imply that the State must forgo insistence on its procedural requirements if it finds no waiver. Such a finding would only mean that petitioner could have a federal court apply settled principles to test the effectiveness of the procedural default to foreclose consideration of his constitutional claim. If it finds the procedural default ineffective, the federal court will itself decide the merits of his federal claim, at least so long as the state court does not wish to do so. By permitting the Mississippi courts to make an initial determination of waiver, we serve the causes of efficient administration of criminal justice, and of harmonious federal-state judicial relations. Such a disposition may make unnecessary the processing of the case through federal courts already laboring under congested dockets,[3] or it may make unnecessary the relitigation in a federal forum of certain issues. See Townsend v. Sain, 372 U.S. 293, 312-319. The Court is not blind to the fact that the federal habeas corpus jurisdiction has been a source of irritation between the federal and state judiciaries. It has been suggested that this friction might be ameliorated if the States would look upon our decisions in Fay v. Noia [372 U.S. 391], and Townsend v. Sain, supra, as affording them an opportunity to provide state procedures, direct or collateral, for a full airing of federal claims. That prospect is better served by a remand than by relegating petitioner to his federal habeas remedy. Therefore, the judgment is vacated and the case is remanded to the Mississippi Supreme Court for further proceedings not inconsistent with this opinion.

MR. JUSTICE HARLAN, with whom MR. JUSTICE CLARK and MR. JUSTICE STEWART join, dissenting.

Flying banners of federalism, the Court's opinion actually raises storm signals of a most disquieting nature. While purporting to recognize the traditional principle that an adequate procedural, as well as substantive, state ground of decision bars direct review here of any federal claim asserted in the state litigation, the Court, unless I wholly misconceive what is lurking in today's opinion, portends a severe dilution, if not complete abolition, of the concept of "adequacy" as pertaining to state procedural grounds.

In making these preliminary observations I do not believe I am seeing ghosts. For I cannot account for the remand of this case in the face of what is a demonstrably adequate state procedural ground of decision by the Mississippi Supreme Court except as an early step toward extending in one way or another the doctrine of Fay v. Noia, 372 U.S. 391, to direct review. In that case, decided only two Terms ago, the Court turned its back on history (see dissenting opinion of this writer, at 448 et seq.), and did away with the adequate state ground doctrine in federal habeas corpus proceedings.

Believing that any step toward extending Noia to direct review should be flushed out and challenged at its earliest appearance in an opinion of this Court, I respectfully dissent. [The remainder of the opinion is omitted, as is a dissenting opinion of BLACK, J.]

---

sissippi Supreme Court opinion as holding that there is no such discretion where it appears that petitioner was represented by competent local counsel familiar with local procedure.

[3] Habeas corpus petitions filed by state prisoners in federal district courts increased from 1,903 to 3,531, or 85.5%, from the 1963 to the 1964 fiscal year. Annual Report of the Director, Administrative Office of the United States Courts, p. 46 (1964); our own Miscellaneous Docket, where cases of state prisoners are primarily listed, continues to show substantial increases. The number has increased from 878 for the 1956 Term to 1,532 for the 1963 Term.

NOTE The Aftermath of Henry v. Mississippi

On remand, the Mississippi Supreme Court directed a state trial judge to conduct a hearing into whether Henry had knowingly waived his right to object to the evidence and, on the record of this hearing, found that he had. 198 So. 2d 213 (1967). On the basis of this finding the prosecution brought a motion before the United States Supreme Court to reinstate the judgment of conviction. The Court denied this motion, citing the lack of "any new final judgment" by the state court. 388 U.S. 901 (1967). The Mississippi court reinstated the judgment, 202 So. 2d 40 (1967), and the Supreme Court denied Henry's petition for writ of certiorari "without prejudice to the bringing of a proceeding for relief in federal habeas corpus." 392 U.S. 931 (1968). On Henry's petition for such relief, the district court found that the failure of his lawyers to object to the evidence at the time it was introduced was "based upon a misconception of state law" and therefore could not "constitute a knowing and conscious waiver of a federal constitutionally protected right," and ordered Henry released. Henry v. Williams, 299 F. Supp. 36 (N.D. Miss. 1969).

The significance of the Court's dicta in Henry v. Mississippi is uncertain. See the analysis of subsequent decisions in Bator, Mishkin, Shapiro, and Wechsler, Hart & Wechsler's The Federal Courts and the Federal System 557-562 (2d ed. 1973). The authors note:

". . . When the Henry opinion was first announced, it was generally viewed as portending major change in the adequate non-federal ground rule, though it was far from clear what the change would be. Decisions in the years following have done little to clarify Henry or reinforce its authority. Most appear to have ignored it, even when it would have been relevant.

"Some opinions failed to cite Henry, though it would have supported the decision. . . .

"Others, also without citation of Henry, found state grounds adequate where Henry might have suggested the opposite. . . .

"Two opinions which cited Henry did little more to delineate its scope or authority. . . ."

See Monger v. Florida, 405 U.S. 958 (1972), denying writ of certiorari to review an obscenity conviction where the state supreme court had dismissed an appeal as untimely. The Court noted that the state decision apparently rested on an adequate state ground; but in the view of three dissenters the procedural rule in question served no substantial state interest.

In Walker v. Birmingham, 388 U.S. 307 (1967), defendants were convicted of contempt for having participated in a civil rights march despite a state court order enjoining the march. At trial, the state court refused to consider the constitutionality of the injunction. The Supreme Court affirmed, refusing to hold that application of the "firmly established" rule that restraining orders must be challenged by court action rather than by violation was an inadequate state ground. The Court noted that this rule was "consistent with the law followed in the federal courts." Can a state decision resting on a procedural rule that is adhered to in the federal courts ever be an inadequate state ground?

Inroads on the adequate procedural state ground rule appear to have been made in recent decisions construing the requirement under 28 U.S.C. §1257 that the federal question has been sufficiently and properly raised in the state court proceedings. See Cardinale v. Louisiana, 394 U.S. 437 (1969); Chambers v. Mississippi, 410 U.S. 284 (1973); Bator et al., supra, 531-538; Stern & Gressman, supra, 116-131.

For fuller discussion of the issues presented by the adequate state ground rule and §1257, see Bator et al., supra, 439-663; Stern & Gressman, supra, 116-146; Note, The Untenable Non-Federal Ground in the Supreme Court, 74 Harv. L. Rev. 1375 (1961).

State court evasion of the mandate of the Supreme Court. Closely related to the foregoing questions is the problem, foreshadowed in Martin v. Hunter's Lessee, page 20 supra, of evasion by a state court of the mandate of the Supreme Court. See Radio Station WOW v. Johnson, 326 U.S. 120 (1945), 59 Harv. L. Rev. 132 (1945), printed infra page 616. The Supreme Court can effect execution of its judgment through its own marshal. Tyler v. Magwire, 17 Wall. 253 (1873). See Note on Enforcement of the Mandate, in Bator, Mishkin, Shapiro, and Wechsler, Hart & Wechsler's The Federal Courts and the Federal System 458 (1973); Note, Evasion of Supreme Court Mandates in Cases Remanded to State Courts Since 1941, 67 Harv. L. Rev. 1251 (1954). See also the protracted (1949-1958) Hawkins litigation concerning the admission of a Negro student to the University of Florida law school, reported in part, Florida ex rel. Hawkins v. Board of Control, 350 U.S. 413 (1956); 93 So. 2d 354 (Fla. 1957); cert. denied without prejudice to petitioner seeking relief in United States District Court, 355 U.S. 839 (1957); 253 F.2d 752 (5th Cir. 1958); 162 F. Supp. 851 (N.D. Fla. 1958). The history of the litigation is given in 3 Race Rel. L. Rep. 657 (1958). See also Deen v. Hickman, 358 U.S. 57 (1958).

Chapter Three Judicial Review in Operation

Section A. INTRODUCTION: LIMITATIONS ON JUDICIAL POWER

Muskrat v. United States *219 U.S. 346, 31 S. Ct. 250, 55 L. Ed. 246 (1911)*

MR. JUSTICE DAY delivered the opinion of the court.

These cases arise under an act of Congress undertaking to confer jurisdiction upon the Court of Claims, and upon this court on appeal, to determine the validity of certain acts of Congress hereinafter referred to.

Case No. 330 was brought by David Muskrat and J. Henry Dick in their own behalf and in behalf of others in a like situation to determine the constitutional validity of the act of Congress of April 26, 1906, c. 1876, 34 Stat. 137, as amended by the act of June 21, 1906, c. 3504, 34 Stat. 325 et seq., and to have the same declared invalid in so far as the same undertook to increase the number of persons entitled to share in the final distribution of lands and funds of the Cherokees beyond those enrolled on September 1, 1902, in accordance with the act of Congress passed July 1, 1902, c. 1375, 32 Stat. 716-720-721. The acts subsequent to that of July 1, 1902, have the effect to increase the number of persons entitled to participate in the division of the Cherokee lands and funds, by permitting the enrollment of children who were minors living on March 4, 1906, whose parents had theretofore been enrolled as members of the Cherokee tribe or had applications pending for that purpose.

Case No. 331 was brought by Brown and Gritts on their own behalf and on behalf of other Cherokee citizens having a like interest in the property allotted under the act of July 1, 1902, c. 1368, 32 Stat. 710. Under this act, Brown and Gritts received allotments. The subsequent act of March 11, 1904, c. 505, 33 Stat. 65, empowered the Secretary of the Interior to grant rights of way for pipe lines over lands allotted to Indians under certain regulations. Another act, that of April 26, 1906, c. 1876, 34 Stat. 137, purported to extend to a period of twenty-five years the time within which full-blooded Indians of the Cherokee, Choctaw, Chickasaw, Creek and Seminole tribes were forbidden to alienate, sell, dispose of or encumber certain of their lands.

50   Chapter Three.   Judicial Review in Operation

The object of the petition of Brown and Gritts was to have the subsequent legislation of 1904 and 1906 declared to be unconstitutional and void, and to have the lands allotted to them under the original act of July 1, 1902, adjudged to be theirs free from restraints upon the rights to sell and convey the same. From this statement it is apparent that the purpose of the proceedings instituted in the Court of Claims and now appealed to this court is to restrain the enforcement of such legislation subsequent to the act of July 1, 1902, upon the ground that the same is unconstitutional and void. The Court of Claims sustained the validity of the acts and dismissed the petitions. 44 C. Cls. 137, 283.

These proceedings were begun under the supposed authority of an act of Congress passed March 1, 1907 (a part of the Indian appropriation bill), c. 2285, 34 Stat. 1015, 1028. As that legislation is important in this connection so much of the act as authorized the beginning of these suits is here inserted in full:

"That William Brown and Levi B. Gritts, on their own behalf and on behalf of all other Cherokee citizens, having like interests in the property allotted under the act of July first, nineteen hundred and two, entitled 'An act to provide for the allotment of lands of the Cherokee Nation, for the disposition of townsites therein, and for other purposes,' and David Muskrat and J. Henry Dick, on their own behalf, and on behalf of all Cherokee citizens enrolled as such for allotment as of September first, nineteen hundred and two, be and they are hereby, authorized and empowered to institute their suits in the Court of Claims to determine the validity of any acts of Congress passed since the said act of July first, nineteen hundred and two, in so far as said acts, or any of them, attempt to increase or extend the restrictions upon alienation, encumbrance, or the right to lease the allotments of lands of Cherokee citizens, or to increase the number of persons entitled to share in the final distribution of lands and funds of the Cherokees beyond those enrolled for allotment as of September first, nineteen hundred and two, and provided for in the said act of July first, nineteen hundred and two.

"And jurisdiction is hereby conferred upon the Court of Claims, with the right of appeal, by either party, to the Supreme Court of the United States, to hear, determine, and adjudicate each of said suits.

"The suits brought hereunder shall be brought on or before September first, nineteen hundred and seven, against the United States as a party defendant, and, for the speedy disposition of the questions involved, preference shall be given to the same by said courts, and by the Attorney General, who is hereby charged with the defense of said suits.

"Upon the rendition of final judgment by the Court of Claims or the Supreme Court of the United States denying the validity of any portion of the said acts authorized to be brought into question, in either or both of said cases, the Court of Claims shall determine the amount to be paid the attorneys employed by the above-named parties in the prosecution thereof for services and expenses, and shall render judgment therefor, which shall be paid out of the funds in the United States Treasury belonging to the beneficiaries under the said act of July first, nineteen hundred and two."

This act is the authority for the maintenance of these two suits.

The first question in these cases, as in others, involves the jurisdiction of this court to entertain the proceeding, and that depends upon whether the jurisdiction conferred is within the power of Congress, having in view the limitations of the judicial power as established by the Constitution of the United States.

[The Court quoted Sections 1 and 2 of Article III of the Constitution.]

It will serve to elucidate the nature and extent of the judicial power thus conferred by the Constitution to note certain instances in which this court has had occasion to examine and define the same. As early as 1792, an act of Congress, March 23, 1792, c. 11, 1 Stat. 243, was brought to the attention of this court, which undertook to provide for the settlement of claims of widows and orphans barred by the limitations theretofore established regulating claims to invalid pensions. The act was not construed by this court, but came under consideration before the then Chief Justice and another Justice of this court and the

District Judge, and their conclusions are given in the margin of the report of Hayburn's Case, 2 Dall. 409. The act undertook to devolve upon the Circuit Court of the United States the duty of examining proofs, of determining what amount of the monthly pay would be equivalent to the disability ascertained, and to certify the same to the Secretary of War, who was to place the names of the applicants on the pension list of the United States in conformity thereto, unless he had cause to suspect imposition or mistake, in which event he might withhold the name of the applicant and report the same to Congress.

In the note to the report of the case in 2 Dall. it appeared that Chief Justice Jay, Mr. Justice Cushing and District Judge Duane unanimously agreed:

"That by the Constitution of the United States, the government thereof is divided into three distinct and independent branches, and that it is the duty of each to abstain from, and to oppose, encroachments on either.

"That neither the legislative nor the executive branches can constitutionally assign to the judicial any duties but such as are properly judicial, and to be performed in a judicial manner.

"That the duties assigned to the Circuit Courts, by this act, are not of that description, and that the act itself does not appear to contemplate them as such; inasmuch as it subjects the decisions of these courts, made pursuant to those duties, first to the consideration and suspension of the Secretary of War, and then to the revision of the legislature; whereas by the Constitution, neither the Secretary of War, nor any other executive officer, nor even the legislature, are authorized to sit as a court of errors on the judicial acts or opinions of this court."

A further history of the case — and of another brought under the same act but unreported — will be found in United States v. Ferreira, 13 How. 40, in which the opinion of the court was by the Chief Justice, and the note by him on page 52 was inserted by order of the court. Concluding that note it was said:

"In the early days of the Government, the right of Congress to give original jurisdiction to the Supreme Court, in cases not enumerated in the Constitution, was maintained by many jurists, and seems to have been entertained by the learned judges who decided Todd's case. But discussion and more mature examination has settled the question otherwise; and it has long been the established doctrine, and we believe now assented to by all who have examined the subject, that the original jurisdiction of this court is confined to the cases specified in the Constitution, and that Congress cannot enlarge it. In all other cases its power must be appellate."

In the Ferreira case this court determined the effect of proceedings under an act of Congress, authorizing the District Judge of the United States for the Northern District of Florida to receive and adjudicate claims for losses for which this Government was responsible under the treaty of 1819 between the United States and Spain; decisions in favor of claimants, together with evidence given in connection therewith, to be reported to the Secretary of the Treasury, who, being satisfied that the same were just and equitable and within the treaty, was to pay the amount thereof. It was held that an award of the District Judge under that act was not the judgment of a court and did not afford a basis of appeal to this court.

In 1793, by direction of the President, Secretary of State Jefferson addressed to the Justices of the Supreme Court a communication soliciting their views upon the question whether their advice to the executive would be available in the solution of important questions of the construction of treaties, laws of nations and laws of the land, which the Secretary said were often presented under circumstances which "do not give a cognizance of them to the tribunals of the country." The answer to the question was postponed until the subsequent sitting of the Supreme Court, when Chief Justice Jay and his associates answered to President Washington that in consideration of the lines of separation drawn by the Constitution between the three departments of government, and being judges of a court of last resort, afforded strong arguments against the propriety of extrajudicially deciding the questions alluded to, and expressing the view that the power given by the Constitution to the President of calling on heads of departments for opinions "seems to have been purposely, as well as expressly, united to the executive departments." Correspondence & Public Papers of John Jay, vol. 3, p. 486.

The subject underwent a complete examination in the case of Gordon v. United States, reported in an appendix to 117 U.S. 697, in which the opinion of Mr. Chief Justice Taney, prepared by him and placed in the hands of the clerk, is published in full. It is said to have been his last judicial utterance, and the whole subject of the nature and extent of the judicial power conferred by the Constitution is treated with great learning and fulness. In that case an act of Congress was held invalid which undertook to confer jurisdiction upon the Court of Claims and thence by appeal to this court, the judgment, however, not to be paid until an appropriation had been estimated therefor by the Secretary of the Treasury; and, as was said by the Chief Justice, the result was that neither court could enforce its judgment by any process, and whether it was to be paid or not depended on the future action of the Secretary of the Treasury and of Congress. . . .

. . . "Judicial power," says Mr. Justice Miller in his work on the Constitution, "is the power of a court to decide and pronounce a judgment and carry it into effect between persons and parties who bring a case before it for decision." Miller on the Constitution, 314.

As we have already seen by the express terms of the Constitution, the exercise of the judicial power is limited to "cases" and "controversies." Beyond this it does not extend, and unless it is asserted in a case or controversy within the meaning of the Constitution, the power to exercise it is nowhere conferred.

What, then, does the Constitution mean in conferring this judicial power with the right to determine "cases" and "controversies"? A "case" was defined by Mr. Chief Justice Marshall as early as the leading case of Marbury v. Madison, 1 Cranch, 137, to be a suit instituted according to the regular course of judicial procedure. And what more, if anything, is meant in the use of the term "controversy"? That question was dealt with by Mr. Justice Field, at the circuit, in the case of In re Pacific Railway Commission, 32 Fed. Rep. 241, 255. Of these terms that learned Justice said:

"The judicial article of the Constitution mentions cases and controversies. The term 'controversies,' if distinguishable at all from 'cases,' is so in that it is less comprehensive than the latter, and includes only suits of a civil nature. Chisholm v. Georgia, 2 Dall. 431, 432; 1 Tuck. Bl. Comm. App. 420, 421. By cases and controversies are intended the claims of litigants brought before the courts for determination by such regular proceedings as are established by law or custom for the protection or enforcement of rights, or the prevention, redress, or punishment of wrongs. Whenever the claim of a party under the Constitution, laws, or treaties of the United States takes such a form that the judicial power is capable of acting upon it, then it has become a case. The term implies the existence of present or possible adverse parties whose contentions are submitted to the court for adjudication."

The power being thus limited to require an application of the judicial power to cases and controversies, is the act which undertook to authorize the present suits to determine the constitutional validity of certain legislation within the constitutional authority of the court? This inquiry in the case before us includes the broader question, When may this court, in the exercise of the judicial power, pass upon the constitutional validity of an act of Congress? That question has been settled from the early history of the court, the leading case on the subject being Marbury v. Madison, supra.

In that case Chief Justice Marshall, who spoke for the court, was careful to point out that the right to declare an act of Congress unconstitutional could only be exercised when a proper case between opposing parties was submitted for judicial determination; that there was no general veto power in the court upon the legislation of Congress; and that the authority to declare an act unconstitutional sprung from the requirement that the court, in administering the law and pronouncing judgment between the parties to a case, and choosing between the requirements of the fundamental law established by the people and embodied in the Constitution and an act of the agents of the people, acting under authority of the Constitution, should enforce the Constitution as the supreme law of the land. . . .

See also in this connection Chicago & Grand Trunk Railway Company v. Wellman, 143 U.S. 339. On page 345 of the opinion in that case the result of the previous decisions of this court was summarized in these apposite words by Mr. Justice Brewer, who spoke for the court:

"Whenever, in pursuance of an honest and actual antagonistic assertion of rights by one individual against another, there is presented a question involving the validity of any act of any legislature, State or Federal, and the decision necessarily rests on the competency of the legislature to so enact, the court must, in the exercise of its solemn duties, determine whether the act be constitutional or not; but such an exercise of power is the ultimate and supreme function of courts. It is legitimate only in the last resort, and as a necessity in the determination of real, earnest and vital controversy between individuals. It never was the thought that, by means of a friendly suit, a party beaten in the legislature could transfer to the courts an inquiry as to the constitutionality of the legislative act."

Applying the principles thus long settled by the decisions of this court to the act of Congress undertaking to confer jurisdiction in this case, we find that William Brown and Levi B. Gritts, on their own behalf and on behalf of all other Cherokee citizens having like interest in the property allotted under the act of July 1, 1902, and David Muskrat and J. Henry Dick, for themselves and representatives of all Cherokee citizens enrolled as such for allotment as of September 1, 1902, are authorized and empowered to institute suits in the Court of Claims to determine the validity of acts of Congress passed since the act of July 1, 1902, in so far as the same attempt to increase or extend the restrictions upon alienation, encumbrance, or the right to lease the allotments of lands of Cherokee citizens, or to increase the number of persons entitled to share in the final distribution of lands and funds of the Cherokees beyond those enrolled for allotment as of September 1, 1902, and provided for in the said act of July 1, 1902.

The jurisdiction was given for that purpose first to the Court of Claims and then upon appeal to this court. That is, the object and purpose of the suit is wholly comprised in the determination of the constitutional validity of certain acts of Congress; and furthermore, in the last paragraph of the section, should a judgment be rendered in the Court of Claims or this court, denying the constitutional validity of such acts, then the amount of compensation to be paid to attorneys employed for the purpose of testing the constitutionality of the law is to be paid out of funds in the Treasury of the United States belonging to the beneficiaries, the act having previously provided that the United States should be made a party and the Attorney General be charged with the defense of the suits.

It is therefore evident that there is neither more nor less in this procedure than an attempt to provide for a judicial determination, final in this court, of the constitutional validity of an act of Congress. Is such a determination within the judicial power conferred by the Constitution, as the same has been interpreted and defined in the authoritative decisions to which we have referred? We think it is not. That judicial power, as we have seen, is the right to determine actual controversies arising between adverse litigants, duly instituted in courts of proper jurisdiction. The right to declare a law unconstitutional arises because an act of Congress relied upon by one or the other of such parties in determining their rights is in conflict with the fundamental law. The exercise of this, the most important and delicate duty of this court, is not given to it as a body with revisory power over the action of Congress, but because the rights of the litigants in justiciable controversies require the court to choose between the fundamental law and a law purporting to be enacted within constitutional authority, but in fact beyond the power delegated to the legislative branch of the Government. This attempt to obtain a judicial declaration of the validity of the act of Congress is not presented in a "case" or "controversy," to which, under the Constitution of the United States, the judicial power alone extends. It is true the United States is made a defendant to this action, but it has no interest adverse to the claimants. The object is not to assert a property right as against the Government, or to demand compensation for alleged wrongs because of action upon its part. The whole purpose of the law is to determine the constitutional validity of this class of legislation, in a suit not arising between parties concerning a property right necessarily involved in the decision in question, but in a proceeding against the Government in its sovereign capacity, and concerning which the only judgment required is to settle the doubtful character of the legislation in question. Such judgment will not conclude private parties, when actual litigation brings to the court the question of the constitutionality of such legislation. In a legal sense the judgment could not be executed, and amounts in fact to no more than an expression of opinion upon the validity of the acts in question. Confining the jurisdiction of this court within the limitations conferred by the Constitution, which the court has hitherto been careful to observe, and whose boundaries it has refused to transcend, we think the Congress, in the act of March 1, 1907, exceeded the limitations of legislative authority, so far as it required of this court action not judicial in its nature within the meaning of the Constitution.

Nor can it make any difference that the petitioners had brought suits in the Supreme Court of the District of Columbia to enjoin the Secretary of the Interior from carrying into effect the legislation subsequent to the act of July 1, 1902, which suits were pending when the jurisdictional act here involved was passed. The latter act must depend upon its own terms and be judged by the authority which it undertakes to confer. If such actions as are here attempted, to determine the validity of legislation, are sustained, the result will be that this court, instead of keeping within the limits of judicial power and deciding cases or controversies arising between opposing parties, as the Constitution intended it should, will be required to give opinions in the nature of advice concerning legislative action, a function never conferred upon it by the Constitution, and against the exercise of which this court has steadily set its face from the beginning.

The questions involved in this proceeding as to the validity of the legislation may arise in suits between individuals, and when they do and are properly brought before this court for consideration they, of course, must be determined in the exercise of its judicial functions. For the reasons we have stated, we are constrained to hold that these actions present no justiciable controversy within the authority of the court, acting within the limitations of the Constitution under which it was created. As Congress, in passing this act as a part of the plan involved, evidently intended to provide a review of the judgment of the Court of Claims in this court, as the constitutionality of important legislation is concerned, we think the act cannot be held to intend to confer jurisdiction on that court separately considered. Connolly v. Union Sewer Pipe Co., 184 U.S. 540, 565; Employers' Liability Cases, 207 U.S. 463.

The judgments will be reversed and the cases remanded to the Court of Claims, with directions to dismiss the petitions for want of jurisdiction.[a]

United States v. Johnson 319 U.S. 302, 63 S. Ct. 1075, 87 L. Ed. 1413 (1943)

PER CURIAM.

One Roach, a tenant of residential property belonging to appellee, brought this suit in the district court alleging that the property was within a "defense rental area" established

---

[a] In the following year the Supreme Court reviewed the decision in the District of Columbia case, referred to in the opinion, and upheld the legislation affecting enrollment. Gritts v. Fisher, 224 U.S. 640 (1912).

The Court of Claims in 1953 was by statute "declared to be a court established under article III of the Constitution." 28 U.S.C. §171. See Glidden v. Zdanok, 370 U.S. 530 (1962). — ED.

by the Price Administrator pursuant to §§ 2(b) and 302(d) of the Emergency Price Control Act of 1942, 56 Stat. 23; that the Administrator had promulgated Maximum Rent Regulation No. 8 for the area; and that the rent paid by Roach and collected by appellee was in excess of the maximum fixed by the regulation. The complaint demanded judgment for treble damages and reasonable attorney's fees, as prescribed by § 205(e) of the Act. The United States, intervening pursuant to 28 U.S.C. § 401, filed a brief in support of the constitutionality of the Act, which appellee had challenged by motion to dismiss. The district court dismissed the complaint on the ground — as appears from its opinion (48 F. Supp. 833) and judgment — that the Act and the promulgation of the regulation under it were unconstitutional because Congress by the Act had unconstitutionally delegated legislative power to the Administrator.

Before entry of the order dismissing the complaint, the Government moved to reopen the case on the ground that it was collusive and did not involve a real case or controversy. This motion was denied. The Government brings the case here on appeal under § 2 of the Act of August 24, 1937, 50 Stat. 752, 28 U.S.C. § 349a, and assigns as error both the ruling of the district court on the constitutionality of the Act, and its refusal to reopen and dismiss the case as collusive.

The appeal of the plaintiff Roach to this Court was also allowed by the district court and is now pending. But this appeal has not been docketed here because of his neglect to comply with the Rules of this Court. As the record is now before us on the Government's appeal, we have directed that the two appeals be consolidated and heard as one case. We accordingly find it unnecessary to consider the question which we requested counsel to discuss, "whether any case or controversy exists reviewable in this Court, in the absence of an appeal by the party plaintiff in the district court."

The affidavit of the plaintiff, submitted by the Government on its motion to dismiss the suit as collusive, shows without contradiction that he brought the present proceeding in a fictitious name; that it was instituted as a "friendly suit" at appellee's request; that the plaintiff did not employ, pay, or even meet, the attorney who appeared of record in his behalf; that he had no knowledge who paid the $15 filing fee in the district court, but was assured by appellee that as plaintiff he would incur no expense in bringing the suit; that he did not read the complaint which was filed in his name as plaintiff; that in his conferences with the appellee and appellee's attorney of record, nothing was said concerning treble damages and he had no knowledge of the amount of the judgment prayed until he read of it in a local newspaper.

Appellee's counter-affidavit did not deny these allegations. It admitted that appellee's attorney had undertaken to procure an attorney to represent the plaintiff and had assured the plaintiff that his presence in court during the trial of the cause would not be necessary. It appears from the district court's opinion that no brief was filed on the plaintiff's behalf in that court.

The Government does not contend that, as a result of this cooperation of the two original parties to the litigation, any false or fictitious state of facts was submitted to the court. But it does insist that the affidavits disclose the absence of a genuine adversary issue between the parties, without which a court may not safely proceed to judgment, especially when it assumes the grave responsibility of passing upon the constitutional validity of legislative action. Even in a litigation where only private rights are involved, the judgment will not be allowed to stand where one of the parties has dominated the conduct of the suit by payment of the fees of both. Gardner v. Goodyear Dental Vulcanite Co., 131 U.S. Appendix, ciii.

Here an important public interest is at stake — the validity of an Act of Congress having far-reaching effects on the public welfare in one of the most critical periods in the history of the country. That interest has been adjudicated in a proceeding in which the plaintiff has had no active participation, over which he has exercised no control, and the expense of which he has not borne. He has been only nominally represented by counsel who was selected by appellee's counsel and whom he has never seen. Such a suit is collusive because it is not in any real sense adversary. It does not assume the "honest and actual antagonistic assertion of rights" to be adjudicated — a safeguard essential to the integrity of the judicial process, and one which we have held to be indispensable to adjudication of constitutional questions by this Court. Chicago & Grand Trunk Ry. Co. v. Wellman, 143 U.S. 339, 345; and see Lord v. Veazie, 8 How. 251; Cleveland v. Chamberlain, 1 Black 419; Bartemeyer v. Iowa, 18 Wall. 129, 134-35; Atherton Mills v. Johnston, 259 U.S. 13, 15. Whenever in the course of litigation such a defect in the proceedings is brought to the court's attention, it may set aside any adjudication thus procured and dismiss the cause without entering judgment on the merits. It is the court's duty to do so where, as here, the public interest has been placed at hazard by the amenities of parties to a suit conducted under the domination of only one of them. The district court should have granted the Government's motion to dismiss the suit as collusive. We accordingly vacate the judgment below with instructions to the district court to dismiss the cause on that ground alone. Under the statute, 28 U.S.C. §401, the Government is liable for costs which may be taxed as in a suit between private litigants; costs in this Court will be taxed against appellee.

Baker v. Carr 369 U.S. 186, 86 S. Ct. 691, 7 L. Ed. 2d 633 (1962)

MR. JUSTICE BRENNAN delivered the opinion of the Court.

This civil action was brought under 42 U.S.C. §§ 1983 and 1988 to redress the alleged deprivation of federal constitutional rights. The complaint, alleging that by means of a 1901 statute of Tennessee apportioning the members of the General Assembly among the State's 95 counties, "these plaintiffs and others similarly situated, are denied the equal protection of the laws accorded them by the Fourteenth Amendment to the Constitution of the United States by virtue of the debasement of their votes," was dismissed by a three-judge court convened under 28 U.S.C. §2281 in the Middle District of Tennessee. The court held that it lacked jurisdiction of the subject matter and also that no claim was stated upon which relief could be granted. 179 F. Supp. 824. We noted probable jurisdiction of the appeal. 364 U.S. 898. We hold that the dismissal was error, and remand the cause to the District Court for trial and further proceedings consistent with this opinion.

The General Assembly of Tennessee consists of the Senate with 33 members and the House of Representatives with 99 members. The Tennessee Constitution provides in Art. II as follows:

"Sec. 3. Legislative authority — Term of office. — The Legislative authority of this State shall be vested in a General Assembly, which shall consist of a Senate and House of Representatives, both dependent on the people; who shall hold their offices for two years from the day of the general election.

"Sec. 4. Census. — An enumeration of the qualified voters, and an apportionment of the Representatives in the General Assembly, shall be made in the year one thousand eight hundred and seventy-one, and within every subsequent term of ten years.

"Sec. 5. Apportionment of representatives. — The number of Representatives shall, at the several periods of making the enumeration, be apportioned among the several counties or districts, according to the number of qualified voters in each; and shall not exceed seventy-five, until the population of the State shall be one million and a half, and shall never exceed ninety-nine; provided, that any county having two-thirds of the ratio shall be entitled to one member.

"Sec. 6. Apportionment of senators. — The number of Senators shall, at the several periods of making the enumeration, be apportioned among the several counties or districts according to the number of qualified electors in each, and shall not exceed one-third the number of representatives. In apportioning the Senators among the different counties, the fraction that may be lost by any county or counties, in the apportionment of members to

Section A. Introduction

the House of Representatives, shall be made up to such county or counties in the Senate, as near as may be practicable. When a district is composed of two or more counties, they shall be adjoining; and no county shall be divided in forming a district."

Thus, Tennessee's standard for allocating legislative representation among her counties is the total number of qualified voters resident in the respective counties, subject only to minor qualifications. Decennial reapportionment in compliance with the constitutional scheme was affected by the General Assembly each decade from 1871 to 1901. The 1871 apportionment was preceded by an 1870 statute requiring an enumeration. The 1881 apportionment involved three statutes, the first authorizing an enumeration, the second enlarging the Senate from 25 to 33 members and the House from 75 to 99 members, and the third apportioning the membership of both Houses. In 1891 there were both an enumeration and an apportionment. In 1901 the General Assembly abandoned separate enumeration in favor of reliance upon the Federal Census and passed the Apportionment Act here in controversy. In the more than 60 years since that action, all proposals in both Houses of the General Assembly for reapportionment have failed to pass.

Between 1901 and 1961, Tennessee has experienced substantial growth and redistribution of her population. In 1901 the population was 2,020,616, of whom 487,380 were eligible to vote. The 1960 Federal Census reports the State's population at 3,567,089, of whom 2,092,891 are eligible to vote. The relative standings of the counties in terms of qualified voters have changed significantly. It is primarily the continued application of the 1901 Apportionment Act to this shifted and enlarged voting population which gives rise to the present controversy.

Indeed, the complaint alleges that the 1901 statute, even as of the time of its passage, "made no apportionment of Representatives and Senators in accordance with the constitutional formula . . . , but instead arbitrarily and capriciously apportioned representatives in the Senate and House without reference . . . to any logical or reasonable formula whatever." It is further alleged that "because of the population changes since 1900, and the failure of the Legislature to reapportion itself since 1901," the 1901 statute became "unconstitutional and obsolete." Appellants also argue that, because of the composition of the legislature effected by the 1901 Apportionment Act, redress in the form of a state constitutional amendment to change the entire mechanisms for reapportioning, or any other change short of that, is difficult or impossible.[14] The complaint concludes that "these plaintiffs and others similarly situated, are denied the equal protection of the laws accorded them by the Fourteenth Amendment to the Constitution of the United States by virtue of the debasement of their votes." They seek a declaration that the 1901 statute is unconstitutional and an injunction restraining the appellees from acting to conduct any further elections under it. They also pray that unless and until the General Assembly enacts a valid reapportionment, the District Court should either decree a reapportionment by mathematical application of the Tennessee constitutional formulae to the most recent Federal Census figures, or direct the appellees to conduct legislative elections, primary and general, at large. They also pray for such other and further relief as may be appropriate.

---

[14] The appellants claim that no General Assembly constituted according to the 1901 Act will submit reapportionment proposals either to the people or to a Constitutional Convention. There is no provision for popular initiative in Tennessee. Amendments proposed in the Senate or House must first be approved by a majority of all members of each House and again by two-thirds of the members in the General Assembly next chosen. The proposals are then submitted to the people at the next general election in which a Governor is to be chosen. Alternatively, the legislature may submit to the people at any general election the question of calling a convention to consider specified proposals. Such as are adopted at a convention do not, however, become effective unless approved by a majority of the qualified voters voting separately on each proposed change or amendment at an election fixed by the convention. Conventions shall not be held oftener than once in six years. Tenn. Const., Art. XI, §3 . . .

Chapter Three. Judicial Review in Operation

I. THE DISTRICT COURT'S OPINION AND ORDER OF DISMISSAL

Because we deal with this case on appeal from an order of dismissal granted on appellees' motions, precise identification of the issues presently confronting us demands clear exposition of the grounds upon which the District Court rested in dismissing the case. The dismissal order recited that the court sustained the appellee's grounds "(1) that the Court lacks jurisdiction of the subject matter, and (2) that the complaint fails to state a claim upon which relief can be granted. . . ." . . .

In light of the District Court's treatment of the case, we hold today only (a) that the court possessed jurisdiction of the subject matter; (b) that a justiciable cause of action is stated upon which appellants would be entitled to appropriate relief; and (c) because appellees raise the issue before this Court, that the appellants have standing to challenge the Tennessee apportionment statutes. Beyond noting that we have no cause at this stage to doubt the District Court will be able to fashion relief if violations of constitutional rights are found, it is improper now to consider what remedy would be most appropriate if appellants prevail at the trial.

II. JURISDICTION OF THE SUBJECT MATTER

The District Court was uncertain whether our cases withholding federal judicial relief rested upon a lack of federal jurisdiction or upon the inappropriateness of the subject matter for judicial consideration—what we have designated "nonjusticiability." The distinction between the two grounds is significant. In the instance of nonjusticiability, consideration of the cause is not wholly and immediately foreclosed; rather, the Court's inquiry necessarily proceeds to the point of deciding whether the duty asserted can be judicially identified and its breach judicially determined, and whether protection for the right asserted can be judicially molded. In the instance of lack of jurisdiction the cause either does not "arise under" the Federal Constitution, laws or treaties (or fall within one of the other enumerated categories of Art. III, §2), or is not a "case or controversy" within the meaning of that section; or the cause is not one described by any jurisdictional statute. Our conclusion, . . . infra, that this cause presents no nonjusticiable "political question" settles the only possible doubt that it is a case or controversy. Under the present heading of "Jurisdiction of the Subject Matter" we hold only that the matter set forth in the complaint does arise under the Constitution and is within 28 U.S.C. §1343. . . .

An unbroken line of our precedents sustains the federal courts' jurisdiction of the subject matter of federal constitutional claims of this nature. The first cases involved the redistricting of States for the purpose of electing Representatives to the Federal Congress. When the Ohio Supreme Court sustained Ohio legislation against an attack for repugnancy to Art. I, §4, of the Federal Constitution, we affirmed on the merits and expressly refused to dismiss for want of jurisdiction "In view . . . of the subject-matter of the controversy and the Federal characteristics which inhere in it. . . ." Ohio ex rel. Davis v. Hildebrant, 241 U.S. 565, 570. When the Minnesota Supreme Court affirmed the dismissal of a suit to enjoin the Secretary of State of Minnesota from acting under Minnesota redistricting legislation, we reviewed the constitutional merits of the legislation and reversed the State Supreme Court. Smiley v. Holm, 285 U.S. 380. And see companion cases from the New York Court of Appeals and the Missouri Supreme Court, Koenig v. Flynn, 285 U.S. 375; Carroll v. Becker, 285 U.S. 380. When a three-judge District Court, exercising jurisdiction under the predecessor of 28 U.S.C. §1343(3), permanently enjoined officers of the State of Mississippi from conducting an election of Representatives under a Mississippi redistricting act, we reviewed the federal questions on the merits and reversed the District Court. Wood v. Broom, 287 U.S. 1, reversing 1 F. Supp. 134. A similar decree of a District Court, exercising jurisdiction under the same statute, concerning a Kentucky redistricting act, was reviewed and the decree reversed. Mahan v. Hume, 287 U.S. 575, reversing 1 F. Supp. 142.

Section A. **Introduction** 59

The appellees refer to Colegrove v. Green, 328 U.S. 549, as authority that the District Court lacked jurisdiction of the subject matter. Appellees misconceive the holding of that case. The holding was precisely contrary to their reading of it. Seven members of the Court participated in the decision. Unlike many other cases in this field which have assumed without discussion that there was jurisdiction, all three opinions filed in Colegrove discussed the question. Two of the opinions expressing the views of four of the Justices, a majority, flatly held that there was jurisdiction of the subject matter. Mr. Justice Black joined by Mr. Justice Douglas and Mr. Justice Murphy stated: "It is my judgment that the District Court had jurisdiction . . . ," citing the predecessor of 28 U.S.C. § 1343(3), and Bell v. Hood [327 U.S. 678]. 328 U.S., at 568. Mr. Justice Rutledge, writing separately, expressed agreement with this conclusion. 328 U.S., at 564, 565, n.2. Indeed, it is even questionable that the opinion of Mr. Justice Frankfurter, joined by Justices Reed and Burton, doubted jurisdiction of the subject matter. Such doubt would have been inconsistent with the professed willingness to turn the decision on either the majority or concurring views in Wood v. Broom, supra. 328 U.S., at 551. . . .

Two cases decided with opinions after Colegrove likewise plainly imply that the subject matter of this suit is within District Court jurisdiction [discussing McDougall v. Green, 335 U.S. 281, and South v. Peters, 339 U.S. 276].

We hold that the District Court has jurisdiction of the subject matter of the federal constitutional claim asserted in the complaint.

III. STANDING

A federal court cannot "pronounce any statute, either of a State or of the United States, void, because irreconcilable with the Constitution, except as it is called upon to adjudge the legal rights of litigants in actual controversies." Liverpool Steamship Co. v. Commissioners of Emigration, 113 U.S. 33, 39. Have the appellants alleged such a personal stake in the outcome of the controversy as to assure that concrete adverseness which sharpens the presentation of issues upon which the court so largely depends for illumination of difficult constitutional questions? This is the gist of the question of standing. It is, of course, a question of federal law.

The complaint was filed by residents of Davidson, Hamilton, Knox, Montgomery, and Shelby Counties. Each is a person allegedly qualified to vote for members of the General Assembly representing his county. These appellants sued "on their own behalf and on behalf of all qualified voters of their respective counties, and further, on behalf of all voters of the State of Tennessee who are similarly situated. . . ." The appellees are the Tennessee Secretary of State, Attorney General, Coordinator of Elections, and members of the State Board of Elections; the members of the State Board are sued in their own right and also as representatives of the County Election Commissioners whom they appoint. . . .

These appellants seek relief in order to protect or vindicate an interest of their own, and of those similarly situated. Their constitutional claim is, in substance, that the 1901 statute constitutes arbitrary and capricious state action, offensive to the Fourteenth Amendment in its irrational disregard of the standard of apportionment prescribed by the State's Constitution or of any standard, effecting a gross disproportion of representation to voting population. The injury which appellants assert is that this classification disfavors the voters in the counties in which they reside, placing them in a position of constitutionally unjustifiable inequality vis-à-vis voters in irrationally favored counties. A citizen's right to a vote free of arbitrary impairment by state action has been judicially recognized as a right secured by the Constitution, when such impairment resulted from dilution by a false tally, cf. United States v. Classic, 313 U.S. 299; or by a refusal to count votes from arbitrarily selected precincts, cf. United States v. Mosley, 238 U.S. 383, or by a stuffing of the ballot box, cf. Ex parte Siebold, 100 U.S. 371; United States v. Saylor, 322 U.S. 385.

Chapter Three. Judicial Review in Operation

It would not be necessary to decide whether appellants' allegations of impairment of their votes by the 1901 apportionment will, ultimately, entitle them to any relief, in order to hold that they have standing to seek it. If such impairment does produce a legally cognizable injury, they are among those who have sustained it. They are asserting "a plain, direct and adequate interest in maintaining the effectiveness of their votes," Coleman v. Miller, 307 U.S. at 438, not merely a claim of "the right, possessed by every citizen, to require that the Government be administered according to law . . . ," Fairchild v. Hughes, 258 U.S., 126, 129; compare Leser v. Garnett, 258 U.S. 130. They are entitled to a hearing and to the District Court's decision on their claims. "The very essence of civil liberty certainly consists in the right of every individual to claim the protection of the laws, whenever he receives an injury." Marbury v. Madison, 1 Cranch 137, 163.

IV. JUSTICIABILITY

In holding that the subject matter of this suit was not justiciable, the District Court relied on Colegrove v. Green, supra, and subsequent per curiam cases. . . . We hold that this challenge to an apportionment presents no nonjusticiable "political question." The cited cases do not hold the contrary.

Of course, the mere fact that the suit seeks protection of a political right does not mean it presents a political question. Such an objection "is little more than a play upon words." Nixon v. Herndon, 273 U.S. 536, 540. Rather, it is argued that apportionment cases, whatever the actual wording of the complaint, can involve no federal constitutional right except one resting on the guaranty of a republican form of government, and that complaints based on that clause have been held to present political questions which are nonjusticiable.

We hold that the claim pleaded here neither rests upon nor implicates the Guaranty Clause and that its justiciability is therefore not foreclosed by our decisions of cases involving that clause. . . .

Our discussion, even at the price of extending this opinion, requires review of a number of political question cases, in order to expose the attributes of the doctrine — attributes which, in various settings, diverge, combine, appear, and disappear in seeming disorderliness. Since that review is undertaken solely to demonstrate that neither singly nor collectively do these cases support a conclusion that this apportionment case is nonjusticiable, we of course do not explore their implications in other contexts. That review reveals that in the Guaranty Clause cases and in the other "political question" cases, it is the relationship between the judiciary and the coordinate branches of the Federal Government, and not the federal judiciary's relationship to the States, which gives rise to the "political question." [The opinion reviews decisions in the areas of foreign relations, the dates of duration of war, the formal validity of legislative enactments, and the status of Indians as a tribe.]

It is apparent that several formulations which vary slightly according to the settings in which the questions arise may describe a political question, although each has one or more elements which identify it as essentially a function of the separation of powers. Prominent on the surface of any case held to involve a political question is found a textually demonstrable constitutional commitment of the issue to a coordinate political department; or a lack of judicially discoverable and manageable standards for resolving it; or the impossibility of deciding without an initial policy determination of a kind clearly for nonjudicial discretion; or the impossibility of a court's undertaking independent resolution without expressing lack of the respect due coordinate branches of government; or an unusual need for unquestioning adherence to a political decision already made; or the potentiality of embarrassment from multifarious pronouncements by various departments on one question. . . .

But it is argued that this case shares the characteristics of decisions that constitute a category not yet considered, cases concerning the Constitution's guaranty, in Art. IV, §4, of a republican form of government. A conclusion as to whether the case at bar does present a political question cannot be confidently reached until we have considered those cases with special care. We shall discover that Guaranty Clause claims involve those elements which define a "political question," and for that reason and no other, they are nonjusticiable. In particular, we shall discover that the nonjusticiability of such claims has nothing to do with their touching upon matters of state governmental organization.

Republican form of government: Luther v. Borden, 7 How. 1, though in form simply an action for damages for trespass was, as Daniel Webster said in opening the argument for the defense, "an unusual case." The defendants, admitting an otherwise tortious breaking and entering, sought to justify their action on the ground that they were agents of the established lawful government of Rhode Island, which State was then under martial law to defend itself from active insurrection; that the plaintiff was engaged in that insurrection; and that they entered under orders to arrest the plaintiff. The case arose "out of the unfortunate political differences which agitated the people of Rhode Island in 1841 and 1842," 7 How., at 34, and which had resulted in a situation wherein two groups laid competing claims to recognition as the lawful government. The plaintiff's right to recover depended upon which of the two groups was entitled to such recognition; but the lower court's refusal to receive evidence or hear argument on that issue, its charge to the jury that the earlier established or "charter" government was lawful, and the verdict for the defendants, were affirmed upon appeal to this Court.

Chief Justice Taney's opinion for the Court reasoned as follows: (1) If a court were to hold the defendants' acts unjustified because the charter government had no legal existence during the period in question, it would follow that all of that government's actions — laws enacted, taxes collected, salaries paid, accounts settled, sentences passed — were of no effect; and that "the officers who carried their decisions into operation [were] answerable as trespassers, if not in some cases as criminals." There was, of course, no room for application of any doctrine of de facto status to uphold prior acts of an officer not authorized de jure, for such would have defeated the plaintiff's very action. A decision for the plaintiff would inevitably have produced some significant measure of chaos, a consequence to be avoided if it could be done without abnegation of the judicial duty to uphold the Constitution.

(2) No state court had recognized as a judicial responsibility settlement of the issue of the locus of state governmental authority. Indeed, the courts of Rhode Island had in several cases held that "it rested with the political power to decide whether the charter government had been displaced or not," and that that department had acknowledged no change.

(3) Since "[t]he question relates, altogether, to the constitution and laws of [the] . . . State," the courts of the United States had to follow the state courts' decisions unless there was a federal constitutional ground for overturning them.

(4) No provision of the constitution could be or had been invoked for this purpose except Art. IV, §4, the Guaranty Clause. Having already noted the absence of standards whereby the choice between governments could be made by a court acting independently, Chief Justice Taney now found further textual and practical reasons for concluding that, if any department of the United States was empowered by the Guaranty Clause to resolve the issue, it was not the judiciary: . . .

Clearly, several factors were thought by the Court in Luther to make the question there "political": the commitment to the other branches of the decision as to which is the lawful state government; the unambiguous action by the President, in recognizing the charter government as the lawful authority; the need for finality in the executive's decision; and the lack of criteria by which a court could determine which form of government was republican. . . .

We come, finally, to the ultimate inquiry whether our precedents as to what constitutes

62 Chapter Three. Judicial Review in Operation

a nonjusticiable "political question" bring the case before us under the umbrella of that doctrine. A natural beginning is to note whether any of the common characteristics which we have been able to identify and label descriptively are present. We find none: The question here is the consistency of state action with the Federal Constitution. We have no question decided, or to be decided, by a political branch of government coequal with this Court. Nor do we risk embarrassment of our government abroad, or grave disturbance at home if we take issue with Tennessee as to the constitutionality of her action here challenged. Nor need the appellants, in order to succeed in this action, ask the Court to enter upon policy determinations for which judicially manageable standards are lacking. Judicial standards under the Equal Protection Clause are well developed and familiar, and it has been open to courts since the enactment of the Fourteenth Amendment to determine, if on the particular facts they must, that a discrimination reflects *no* policy, but simply arbitrary and capricious action. . . .

. . . And only last Term, in Gomillion v. Lightfoot, 364 U.S. 339, we applied the Fifteenth Amendment to strike down a redrafting of municipal boundaries which effected a discriminatory impairment of voting rights, in the face of what a majority of the Court of Appeals thought to be a sweeping commitment to state legislatures of the power to draw and redraw such boundaries.

. . . [I]n Kidd v. McCanless, 200 Tenn. 273, 292 S.W.2d 40, the Supreme Court of Tennessee held that it could not invalidate the very statute at issue in the case at bar, but its holding rested on its state law of remedies, i.e., the state view of de facto officers, and not on any view that the norm for legislative apportionment in Tennessee is not numbers of qualified voters resident in the several counties. Of course this Court was there precluded by the adequate state ground, and in dismissing the appeal, 352 U.S. 920, we cited Anderson [v. Jordan, 343 U.S. 912], as well as Colegrove. Nor does the Tennessee court's decision in that case bear upon this, for just as in Smith v. Holm, 220 Minn. 486, 19 N.W.2d 914, and Magraw v. Donovan, 163 F. Supp. 184, 177 F. Supp. 803, a state court's inability to grant relief does not bar a federal court's assuming jurisdiction to inquire into alleged deprivation of federal constitutional rights. . . .

We conclude that the complaint's allegations of a denial of equal protection present a justiciable constitutional cause of action upon which appellants are entitled to a trial and a decision. The right asserted is within the reach of judicial protection under the Fourteenth Amendment.

The judgment of the District Court is reversed and the cause is remanded for further proceedings consistent with this opinion.

Reversed and remanded.

MR. JUSTICE WHITTAKER did not participate in the decision of this case. . . .

MR. JUSTICE CLARK, concurring.

One emerging from the rash of opinions with their accompanying clashing of views may well find himself suffering a mental blindness. The Court holds that the appellants have alleged a cause of action. However, it refuses to award relief here — although the facts are undisputed — and fails to give the District Court any guidance whatever. One dissenting opinion, bursting with words that go through so much and conclude with so little, contemns the majority action as "a massive repudiation of the experience of our whole past." Another describes the complaint as merely asserting conclusory allegations that Tennessee's apportionment is "incorrect," "arbitrary," "obsolete," and "unconstitutional." I believe it can be shown that this case is distinguishable from earlier cases dealing with the distribution of political power by a State, that a patent violation of the Equal Protection Clause of the United States Constitution has been shown, and that an appropriate remedy may be formulated. . . .

The controlling facts cannot be disputed. It appears from the record that 37% of the voters of Tennessee elect 20 of the 33 Senators while 40% of the voters elect 63 of the 99 members of the House. But this might not on its face be an "invidious discrimination,"

Williamson v. Lee Optical of Oklahoma, 348 U.S. 483, 489 (1955), for a "statutory discrimination will not be set aside if any state of facts reasonably may be conceived to justify it." McGowan v. Maryland, 366 U.S. 420, 426 (1961).

It is true that the apportionment policy incorporated in Tennessee's Constitution, i.e., state-wide numerical equality of representation with certain minor qualifications, is a rational one. On a county-by-county comparison a districting plan based thereon naturally will have disparities in representation due to the qualifications. But this to my mind does not raise constitutional problems, for the overall policy is reasonable. However, the root of the trouble is not in Tennessee's Constitution, for admittedly its policy has not been followed. The discrimination lies in the action of Tennessee's Assembly in allocating legislative seats to counties or districts created by it. . . .

No one — except the dissenters advocating the Harlan "adjusted 'total representation' " formula — contends that mathematical equality among voters is required by the Equal Protection Clause. But certainly there must be some rational design to a State's districting. The discrimination here does not fit any pattern — as I have said, it is but a crazy quilt. . . .

III

Although I find the Tennessee apportionment statute offends the Equal Protection Clause, I would not consider intervention by this Court into so delicate a field if there were any other relief available to the people of Tennessee. But the majority of the people of Tennessee have no "practical opportunities for exerting their political weight at the polls" to correct the existing "invidious discrimination." Tennessee has no initiative and referendum. I have searched diligently for other "practical opportunities" present under the law. I find none other than through the federal courts. . . .

IV

Finally, we must consider if there are any appropriate modes of effective judicial relief. The federal courts are of course not forums for political debate, nor should they resolve themselves into state constitutional conventions or legislative assemblies. Nor should their jurisdiction be exercised in the hope that such a declaration as is made today may have the direct effect of bringing on legislative action and relieving the courts of the problem of fashioning relief. To my mind this would be nothing less than blackjacking the Assembly into reapportioning the State. If judicial competence were lacking to fashion an effective decree, I would dismiss this appeal. However, like the Solicitor General of the United States, I see no such difficulty in the position of this case. One plan might be to start with the existing assembly districts, consolidate some of them, and award the seats thus released to those counties suffering the most egregious discrimination. Other possibilities are present and might be more effective. But the plan here suggested would at least release the strangle hold now on the Assembly and permit it to redistrict itself. . . .

As John Rutledge (later Chief Justice) said 175 years ago in the course of the Constitutional Convention, a chief function of the Court is to secure the national rights. Its decision today supports the proposition for which our forebears fought and many died, namely, that to be fully conformable to the principle of right, the form of government must be representative. That is the keystone upon which our government was founded and lacking which no republic can survive. It is well for this Court to practice self-restraint and discipline in constitutional adjudication, but never in its history have those principles received sanction where the national rights of so many have been so clearly infringed for so long a time. National respect for the courts is more enhanced through the forthright enforcement of those rights rather than by rendering them nugatory through the interposition of subterfuges. In my view the ultimate decision today is in the greatest tradition of this Court. . . .

Mr. Justice Frankfurter, whom Mr. Justice Harlan joins, dissenting.

The Court today reverses a uniform course of decision established by a dozen cases, including one by which the very claim now sustained was unanimously rejected only five years ago. The impressive body of rulings thus cast aside reflected the equally uniform course of our political history regarding the relationship between population and legislative representation — a wholly different matter from denial of the franchise to individuals because of race, color, religion or sex. Such a massive repudiation of the experience of our whole past in asserting destructively novel judicial power demands a detailed analysis of the role of this Court in our constitutional scheme. Disregard of inherent limits in the effective exercise of the Court's "judicial Power" not only presages the futility of judicial intervention in the essentially political conflict of forces by which the relation between population and representation has time out of mind been and now is determined. It may well impair the Court's position as the ultimate organ of "the supreme Law of the Land" in that vast range of legal problems, often strongly entangled in popular feeling, on which this Court must pronounce. The Court's authority — possessed of neither the purse nor the sword — ultimately rests on sustained public confidence in its moral sanction. Such feeling must be nourished by the Court's complete detachment, in fact and in appearance, from political entanglements and by abstention from injecting itself into the clash of political forces in political settlements.

A hypothetical claim resting on abstract assumptions is now for the first time made the basis for affording illusory relief for a particular evil even though it foreshadows deeper and more pervasive difficulties in consequence. The claim is hypothetical and the assumptions are abstract because the Court does not vouchsafe the lower courts — state and federal — guidelines for formulating specific, definite, wholly unprecedented remedies for the inevitable litigations that today's umbrageous disposition is bound to stimulate in connection with politically motivated reapportionments in so many States. In such a setting, to promulgate jurisdiction in the abstract is meaningless. It is as devoid of reality as "a brooding omnipresence in the sky," for it conveys no intimation what relief, if any, a District Court is capable of affording that would not invite legislatures to play ducks and drakes with the judiciary. For this Court to direct the District Court to enforce a claim to which the Court has over the years consistently found itself required to deny legal enforcement and at the same time to find it necessary to withhold any guidance to the lower court how to enforce this turnabout, new legal claim, manifests an odd — indeed an esoteric — conception of judicial propriety. One of the Court's supporting opinions, as elucidated by commentary, unwittingly affords a disheartening preview of the mathematical quagmire (apart from divers judicially inappropriate and elusive determinants) into which this Court today catapults the lower courts of the country without so much as adumbrating the basis for a legal calculus as a means of extrication. Even assuming the indispensable intellectual disinterestedness on the part of judges in such matters, they do not have accepted legal standards or criteria or even reliable analogies to draw upon for making judicial judgments. To charge courts with the task of accommodating the incommensurable factors of policy that underlie these mathematical puzzles is to attribute, however flatteringly, omnicompetence to judges. The Framers of the Constitution persistently rejected a proposal that embodied this assumption and Thomas Jefferson never entertained it.

Recent legislation, creating a district appropriately described as "an atrocity of ingenuity," is not unique. Considering the gross inequality among legislative electoral units within almost every State, the Court naturally shrinks from asserting that in districting at least substantial equality is a constitutional requirement enforceable by courts. Room continues to be allowed for weighting. This of course implies that geography, economics, urban-rural conflict, and all the other non-legal factors which have throughout our history entered into political districting are to some extent not to be ruled out in the undefined vista now opened up by review in the federal courts of state reapportionments. To some extent — aye, there's the rub. In effect, today's decision empowers the courts of the country to devise what should constitute the proper composition of the legislatures of the fifty States. If state courts should for one reason or another find themselves unable to discharge this task, the duty of doing so is put on the federal courts or on this Court, if State views do not satisfy this Court's notion of what is proper districting.

We were soothingly told at the bar of this Court that we need not worry about the kind of remedy a court could effectively fashion once the abstract constitutional right to have courts pass on a state-wide system of electoral districting is recognized as a matter of judicial rhetoric, because legislatures would heed the Court's admonition. This is not only a euphoric hope. It implies a sorry confession of judicial impotence in place of frank acknowledgment that there is not under our Constitution a judicial remedy for every political mischief, for every undesirable exercise of legislative power. The Framers carefully and with deliberate forethought refused so to enthrone the judiciary. In this situation, as in others of like nature, appeal for relief does not belong here. Appeal must be to an informed, civically militant electorate. In a democratic society like ours, relief must come through an aroused popular conscience that sears the conscience of the people's representatives. In any event there is nothing judicially more unseemly nor more self-defeating than for this Court to make in terrorem pronouncements, to indulge in merely empty rhetoric, sounding a word of promise to the ear, sure to be disappointing to the hope. . . .

The Colegrove doctrine, in the form in which repeated decisions have settled it, was not an innovation. It represents long judicial thought and experience. From its earliest opinions this Court has consistently recognized a class of controversies which do not lend themselves to judicial standards and judicial remedies. To classify the various instances as "political questions" is rather a form of stating this conclusion than revealing of analysis. Some of the cases so labelled have no relevance here. But from others emerge unifying considerations that are compelling.

1. The cases concerning war or foreign affairs, for example, are usually explained by the necessity of the country's speaking with one voice in such matters. While this concern alone undoubtedly accounts for many of the decisions, others do not fit the pattern. It would hardly embarrass the conduct of war were this Court to determine, in connection with private transactions between litigants, the date upon which war is to be deemed terminated. But the Court has refused to do so. . . . And even for the purpose of determining the extent of congressional regulatory power over the tribes and dependent communities of Indians, it is ordinarily for Congress, not the Court, to determine whether or not a particular Indian group retains the characteristics constitutionally requisite to confer the power. E.g., United States v. Holliday, 3 Wall. 407; Tiger v. Western Investment Co., 221 U.S. 286; United States v. Sandoval, 231 U.S. 28. A controlling factor in such cases is that, decision respecting these kinds of complex matters of policy being traditionally committed not to courts but to the political agencies of government for determination by criteria of political expediency, there exists no standard ascertainable by settled judicial experience or process by reference to which a political decision affecting the question at issue between the parties can be judged. Where the question arises in the course of a litigation involving primarily the adjudication of other issues between the litigants, the Court accepts as a basis for adjudication the political departments' decision of it. But where its determination is the sole function to be served by the exercise of the judicial power, the Court will not entertain the action. See Chicago & Southern Air Lines, Inc. v. Waterman S. S. Corp., 333 U.S. 103. The dominant consideration is "the lack of satisfactory criteria for a judicial determination . . ." Mr. Chief Justice Hughes, for the Court, in Coleman v. Miller, 307 U.S. 433, 454-455. . . .

66   Chapter Three.   Judicial Review in Operation

2. The Court has been particularly unwilling to intervene in matters concerning the structure and organization of the political institutions of the States. The abstention from judicial entry into such areas has been greater even than that which marks the Court's ordinary approach to issues of state power challenged under broad federal guarantees. "We should be very reluctant to decide that we had jurisdiction in such a case, and thus in an action of this nature to supervise and review the political administration of a state government by its own officials and through its own courts. The jurisdiction of this court would only exist in case there had been . . . such a plain and substantial departure from the fundamental principles upon which our government is based that it could with truth and propriety be said that if the judgment were suffered to remain, the party aggrieved would be deprived of his life, liberty or property in violation of the provisions of the Federal Constitution." Wilson v. North Carolina, 169 U.S. 586, 596. . . .

Where, however, state law has made particular federal questions determinative of relations within the structure of state government, not in challenge of it, the Court has resolved such narrow, legally defined questions in proper proceedings. See Boyd v. Nebraska ex rel. Thayer, 143 U.S. 135. In such instances there is no conflict between state policy and the exercise of federal judicial power. This distinction explains the decisions in Smiley v. Holm, 285 U.S. 355; Koenig v. Flynn, 285 U.S. 375; and Carroll v. Becker, 285 U.S. 380, in which the Court released state constitutional provisions prescribing local law-making procedures from misconceived restriction of superior federal requirements. Adjudication of the federal claim involved in those cases was not one demanding the accommodation of conflicting interests for which no readily accessible judicial standards could be found. See McPherson v. Blacker, 146 U.S. 1, in which, in a case coming here on writ of error from the judgment of a state court which had entertained it on the merits, the Court treated as justiciable the claim that a State could not constitutionally select its presidential electors by districts, but held that Art. II, §1, cl. 2, of the Constitution left the mode of choosing electors in the absolute discretion of the States. Cf. Pope v. Williams, 193 U.S. 621; Breedlove v. Suttles, 302 U.S. 277. To read with literalness the abstracted jurisdictional discussion in the McPherson opinion reveals the danger of conceptions of "justiciability" derived from talk and not from the effective decision in a case. In probing beneath the surface of cases in which the Court has declined to interfere with the actions of political organs of government, of decisive significance is whether in each situation the ultimate decision has been to intervene or not to intervene. Compare the reliance in South v. Peters, 339 U.S. 276, on MacDougall v. Green, 335 U.S. 281, and the "jurisdictional" form of the opinion in Wilson v. North Carolina, 169 U.S. 586, 596, supra.

3. The cases involving Negro disfranchisement are no exception to the principle of avoiding federal judicial intervention into matters of state government in the absence of an explicit and clear constitutional imperative. For here the controlling command of Supreme Law is plain and unequivocal. An end of discrimination against the Negro was the compelling motive of the Civil War Amendments. The Fifteenth expresses this in terms, and it is no less true of the Equal Protection Clause of the Fourteenth. Slaughter-House Cases, 16 Wall. 36, 67-72; Strauder v. West Virginia, 100 U.S. 303, 306-307; Nixon v. Herndon, 273 U.S 536, 541. Thus the Court, in cases involving discrimination against the Negro's right to vote, has recognized not only the action at law for damages, but, in appropriate circumstances, the extraordinary remedy of declaratory or injunctive relief. Schnell v. Davis, 336 U.S. 933; Terry v. Adams, 345 U.S. 461. Injunctions in these cases, it should be noted, would not have restrained state-wide general elections. Compare Giles v. Harris, 189 U.S. 475.

4. The Court has refused to exercise its jurisdiction to pass on "abstract questions of political power, of sovereignty, of government." Massachusetts v. Mellon, 262 U.S. 447, 485. See Texas v. Interstate Commerce Commission, 258 U.S. 158, 162; New Jersey v. Sargent, 269 U.S. 328, 337. The "political question" doctrine, in this aspect, reflects the policies underlying the requirement of "standing": that the litigant who would challenge

official action must claim infringement of an interest particular and personal to himself, as distinguished from a cause of dissatisfaction with the general frame and functioning of government — a complaint that the political institutions are awry. . . . The crux of the matter is that courts are not fit instruments of decision where what is essentially at stake is the composition of those large contests of policy traditionally fought out in non-judicial forums, by which governments and the actions of governments are made and unmade. . . . Thus, where the Cherokee Nation sought by an original motion to restrain the State of Georgia from the enforcement of laws which assimilated Cherokee territory to the State's counties, abrogated Cherokee law, and abolished Cherokee government, the Court held that such a claim was not judicially cognizable. Cherokee Nation v. Georgia, 5 Pet. 1. And in Georgia v. Stanton, 6 Wall. 50, the Court dismissed for want of jurisdiction a bill by the State of Georgia seeking to enjoin enforcement of the Reconstruction Acts on the ground that the command by military districts which they established extinguished existing state government and replaced it with a form of government unauthorized by the Constitution: . . .

5. The influence of these converging considerations — the caution not to undertake decision where standards meet for judicial judgment are lacking, the reluctance to interfere with matters of state government in the absence of an unquestionable and effectively enforceable mandate, the unwillingness to make courts arbiters of the broad issues of political organization historically committed to other institutions and for whose adjustment the judicial process is ill-adapted — has been decisive of the settled line of cases, reaching back more than a century, which holds that Art. IV, §4, of the Constitution, guaranteeing to the States "a Republican Form of Government," is not enforceable through the courts. . . .

The starting point of the doctrine applied in these cases is, of course, Luther v. Borden, 7 How. 1. The case arose out of the Dorr Rebellion in Rhode Island in 1841-1842. Rhode Island, at the time of the separation from England, had not adopted a new constitution but had continued, in its existence as an independent State, under its original royal Charter, with certain statutory alterations. This frame of government provided no means for amendment of the fundamental law; the right of suffrage was to be prescribed by legislation, which limited it to freeholders. In the 1830's, largely because of the growth of towns in which there developed a propertied class whose means were not represented by freehold estates, dissatisfaction arose with the suffrage qualifications of the charter government. In addition, population shifts had caused a dated apportionment of seats in the lower house to yield substantial numerical inequality of political influence, even among qualified voters. The towns felt themselves underrepresented, and agitation began for electoral reform. When the charter government failed to respond, popular meetings of those who favored the broader suffrage were held and delegates elected to a convention which met and drafted a state constitution. This constitution provided for universal manhood suffrage (with certain qualifications); and it was to be adopted by vote of the people at elections at which a similarly expansive franchise obtained. This new scheme of government was ratified at the polls and declared effective by convention, but the government elected and organized under it, with Dorr at its head, never came to power. The charter government denied the validity of the convention, the constitution and its government and, after an insignificant skirmish, routed Dorr and his followers. It meanwhile provided for the calling of its own convention, which drafted a constitution that went peacefully into effect in 1843.

Luther v. Borden was a trespass action brought by one of Dorr's supporters in a United States Circuit Court to recover damages for the breaking and entering of his house. The defendants justified under military orders pursuant to martial law declared by the charter government, and plaintiff, by his reply, joined issue on the legality of the charter government subsequent to the adoption of the Dorr constitution. Evidence offered by the plaintiff tending to establish that the Dorr government was the rightful government of Rhode

Island was rejected by the Circuit Court; the court charged the jury that the charter government was lawful; and on a verdict for defendants, plaintiff brought a writ of error to this Court.

The Court, through Mr. Chief Justice Taney, affirmed. After noting that the issue of the charter government's legality had been resolved in that government's favor by the state courts of Rhode Island — that the state courts, deeming the matter a political one unfit for judicial determination, had declined to entertain attacks upon the existence and authority of the charter government — the Chief Justice held that the courts of the United States must follow those of the State in this regard. Id., at 39-40. It was recognized that the compulsion to follow state law would not apply in a federal court in the face of a superior command found in the Federal Constitution, ibid., but no such command was found. The Constitution, the Court said — referring to the Guarantee Clause of the Fourth Article — ". . . as far as it has provided for an emergency of this kind, and authorized the general government to interfere in the domestic concerns of a State, has treated the subject as political in its nature, and placed the power in the hands of that department." . . .

In determining this issue non-justiciable, the Court was sensitive to the same considerations to which its later decisions have given the varied applications already discussed. It adverted to the delicacy of judicial intervention into the very structure of government. It acknowledged that tradition had long entrusted questions of this nature to nonjudicial processes, and that judicial processes were unsuited to their decision. The absence of guiding standards for judgment was critical, for the question whether the Dorr constitution had been rightfully adopted depended, in part, upon the extent of the franchise to be recognized — the very point of contention over which rebellion had been fought. . . .

The present case involves all of the elements that have made the Guarantee Clause cases non-justiciable. It is, in effect, a Guarantee Clause claim masquerading under a different label. But it cannot make the case more fit for judicial action that appellants invoke the Fourteenth Amendment rather than Art. IV, §4, where, in fact, the gist of their complaint is the same — unless it can be found that the Fourteenth Amendment speaks with greater particularity to their situation. . . .

. . . In invoking the Equal Protection Clause, they assert that the distortion of representative government complained of is produced by systematic discrimination against them, by way of "a debasement of their votes. . . ." Does this characterization, with due regard for the facts from which it is derived, add anything to appellants' case?

At first blush, this charge of discrimination based on legislative underrepresentation is given the appearance of a more private, less impersonal claim, than the assertion that the frame of government is askew. Appellants appear as representatives of a class that is prejudiced as a class, in contradistinction to the polity in its entirety. However, the discrimination relied on is the deprivation of what appellants conceive to be their proportionate share of political influence. This, of course, is the practical effect of any allocation of power within the institutions of government. Hardly any distribution of political authority that could be assailed as rendering government nonrepublican would fail similarly to operate to the prejudice of some groups, and to the advantage of others, within the body politic. It would be ingenuous not to see, or consciously blind to deny, that the real battle over the initiative and referendum, or over a delegation of power to local rather than statewide authority, is the battle between forces whose influence is disparate among the various organs of government to whom power may be given. No shift of power but works a corresponding shift in political influence among the groups composing a society.

What, then, is this question of legislative apportionment? Appellants invoke the right to vote and to have their votes counted. But they are permitted to vote and their votes are counted. They go to polls, they cast their ballots, they send their representatives to the state councils. Their complaint is simply that the representatives are not sufficiently numerous or powerful — in short, that Tennessee has adopted a basis of representation with which they are dissatisfied. Talk of "debasement" or "dilution" is circular talk. One cannot speak of "debasement" or "dilution" of the value of a vote until there is first defined a standard of reference as to what a vote should be worth. What is actually asked of the Court in this case is to choose among competing bases of representation — ultimately, really, among competing theories of political philosophy — in order to establish an appropriate frame of government for the State of Tennessee and thereby for all the States of the Union.

In such a matter, abstract analogies which ignore the facts of history deal in unrealities; they betray reason. This is not a case in which a State has, through a device however oblique and sophisticated, denied Negroes or Jews or redheaded persons a vote, or given them only a third or a sixth of a vote. That was Gomillion v. Lightfoot, 364 U.S. 339. What Tennessee illustrates is an old and still widespread method of representation — representation by local geographical division, only in part respective of population — in preference to others, others, forsooth, more appealing. Appellants contest this choice and seek to make this Court the arbiter of the disagreement. They would make the Equal Protection Clause the charter of adjudication, asserting that the equality which it guarantees comports, if not the assurance of equal weight to every voter's vote, at least the basic conception that representation ought to be proportionate to population, a standard by reference to which the reasonableness of apportionment plans may be judged.

To find such a political conception legally enforceable in the broad and unspecific guarantee of equal protection is to rewrite the Constitution. . . .

The notion that representation proportioned to the geographic spread of population is so universally accepted as a necessary element of equality between man and man that it must be taken to be the standard of a political equality preserved by the Fourteenth Amendment — that it is, in appellants' words "the basic principle of representative government" — is, to put it bluntly, not true. However desirable and however desired by some among the great political thinkers and framers of our government, it has never been generally practiced, today or in the past. It was not the English system, it was not the colonial system, it was not the system chosen for the national government by the Constitution, it was not the system exclusively or even predominantly practiced by the States at the time of adoption of the Fourteenth Amendment, it is not predominantly practiced by the States today. Unless judges, the judges of this Court, are to make their private views of political wisdom the measure of the Constitution — views which in all honesty cannot but give the appearance, if not reflect the reality, of involvement with the business of partisan politics so inescapably a part of apportionment controversies — the Fourteenth Amendment, "itself a historical product," Jackman v. Rosenbaum Co., 260 U.S. 22, 31, provides no guide for judicial oversight of the representation problem. . . . [The opinion analyzes the bases of electoral representation found historically in Great Britain, in the American colonies and the Union, in the states at the time of the adoption of the Fourteenth Amendment and the states later admitted, and in contemporary practice.]

The stark fact is that if among the numerous widely varying principles and practices that control state legislative apportionment today there is any generally prevailing feature, that feature is geographic inequality in relation to the population standard. Examples could be endlessly multiplied. In New Jersey, counties of thirty-five thousand and of more than nine hundred and five thousand inhabitants respectively each have a single senator. Representative districts in Minnesota range from 7,290 inhabitants to 107,246 inhabitants. Ratios of senatorial representation in California vary as much as two hundred and ninety-seven to one. In Oklahoma, the range is ten to one for House constituencies and roughly sixteen to one for Senate constituencies. Colebrook, Connecticut — population 592 — elects two House representatives; Hartford — population 177,397 — also elects two. The first, third and fifth of these examples are the products of constitutional provi-

Chapter Three. Judicial Review in Operation

sions which subordinate population to regional considerations in apportionment; the second is the result of legislative inaction; the fourth derives from both constitutional and legislative sources. A survey made in 1955, in sum, reveals that less than thirty percent of the population inhabit districts sufficient to elect a House majority in thirteen States and a Senate majority in nineteen States. These figures show more than individual variations from a generally accepted standard of electoral equality. They show that there is not — as there has never been — a standard by which the place of equality as a factor in apportionment can be measured.

Manifestly, the Equal Protection Clause supplies no clearer guide for judicial examination of apportionment methods than would the Guarantee Clause itself. Apportionment, by its character, is a subject of extraordinary complexity, involving — even after the fundamental theoretical issues concerning what is to be represented in a representative legislature have been fought out or compromised — considerations of geography, demography, electoral convenience, economic and social cohesions or divergencies among particular local groups, communications, the practical effects of political institutions like the lobby and the city machine, ancient traditions and ties of settled usage, respect for proven incumbents of long experience and senior status, mathematical mechanics, censuses compiling relevant data, and a host of others. Legislative responses throughout the country to the reapportionment demands of the 1960 Census have glaringly confirmed that these are not factors that lend themselves to evaluations of a nature that are the staple of judicial determinations or for which judges are equipped to adjudicate by legal training or experience or native wit. And this is the more so true because in every strand of this complicated, intricate web of values meet the contending forces of partisan politics. The practical significance of apportionment is that the next election results may differ because of it. Apportionment battles are overwhelmingly party or intraparty contests. It will add a virulent source of friction and tension in federal-state relations to embroil the federal judiciary in them. . . .

. . . In all of the apportionment cases which have come before the Court, a consideration which has been weighty in determining their nonjusticiability has been the difficulty or impossibility of devising effective judicial remedies in this class of case. An injunction restraining a general election unless the legislature reapportions would paralyze the critical centers of a State's political system and threaten political dislocation whose consequences are not foreseeable. A declaration devoid of implied compulsion of injunctive or other relief would be an idle threat. Surely a Federal District Court could not itself remap the State: the same complexities which impede effective judicial review of apportionment a fortiori make impossible a court's consideration of these imponderables as an original matter. And the choice of elections at large as opposed to elections by district, however unequal the districts, is a matter of sweeping political judgment having enormous political implications, the nature and reach of which are certainly beyond the informed understanding of, and capacity for appraisal by, courts.

In Tennessee, moreover, the McCanless case has closed off several among even these unsatisfactory and dangerous modes of relief. . . . And it cannot be doubted that the striking down of the statute here challenged on equal protection grounds, no less than on grounds of failure to reapportion decenially, would deprive the State of all valid apportionment legislation and — under the ruling in McCanless — deprive the State of an effective law-based legislative branch. Just such considerations, among others here present, were determinative in Luther v. Borden and the Oregon initiative cases.

Although the District Court had jurisdiction in the very restricted sense of power to determine whether it could adjudicate the claim, the case is of that class of political controversy which, by the nature of its subject, is unfit for federal judicial action. The judgment of the District Court, in dismissing the complaint for failure to state a claim on which relief can be granted, should therefore be affirmed. . . .

[A concurring opinion by Mr. Justice Douglas and a dissenting opinion by Mr. Justice Harlan are omitted.][b]

Section B. JUSTICIABILITY: THE NATURE OF THE QUESTION PRESENTED

Powell v. McCormack 395 U.S. 486, 89 S. Ct. 1944, 23 L. Ed. 2d 491 (1969)

MR. CHIEF JUSTICE WARREN delivered the opinion of the Court. In November 1966, Petitioner Adam Clayton Powell, Jr., was duly elected from the 18th Congressional District of New York to serve in the United States House of Representatives for the 90th Congress. However, pursuant to a House resolution, he was not permitted to take his seat. Powell (and some of the voters of his district) then filed suit in Federal District Court, claiming that the House could exclude him only if it found he failed to meet the standing requirements of age, citizenship, and residence contained in Art. I, §2, of the Constitution — requirements the House specifically found Powell met — and thus had excluded him unconstitutionally. The District Court dismissed petitioners' complaint "for want of jurisdiction of the subject matter." The Court of Appeals affirmed the dismissal, although on somewhat different grounds, each judge filing a separate opinion. We have determined that it was error to dismiss the complaint and that Petitioner Powell is entitled to a declaratory judgment that he was unlawfully excluded from the 90th Congress.

I. FACTS

During the 89th Congress, a Special Subcommittee on Contracts of the Committee on House Administration conducted an investigation into the expenditures of the Committee on Education and Labor, of which Petitioner Adam Clayton Powell, Jr., was chairman. The Special Subcommittee issued a report concluding that Powell and certain staff employees had deceived the House authorities as to travel expenses. The report also indicated there was strong evidence that certain illegal salary payments had been made to Powell's wife at his direction. See H.R. Rep. No. 2349, 89th Cong., 2d Sess., 6-7 (1966). No formal action was taken during the 89th Congress. However, prior to the organization of the 90th Congress, the Democrat members-elect met in caucus and voted to remove Powell as chairman of the Committee on Education and Labor. See H.R. Rep. No. 27, 90th Cong., 1st Sess. 1-2 (1967).

When the 90th Congress met to organize in January 1967, Powell was asked to step aside while the oath was administered to the other members-elect. Following the administration of the oath to the remaining members, the House discussed the procedure to be followed in determining whether Powell was eligible to take his seat. After some debate, by a vote of 364 to 64 the House adopted House Resolution 1, which provided that the Speaker appoint a Select Committee to determine Powell's eligibility. 113 Cong. Rec. 16 (daily ed. Jan. 10, 1967). Although the resolution prohibited Powell from taking his seat

---

[b] See Neal, Baker v. Carr; Politics in Search of Law, 1962 Sup. Ct. Rev. 252; Lewis, Legislative Apportionment and the Federal Courts, 71 Harv. L. Rev. 1057 (1958); Symposium, 72 Yale L.J. 46 (1962); McCloskey, The Reapportionment Case, 76 Harv. L. Rev. 54 (1962); Jewell, ed., The Politics of Reapportionment (1962); Symposium, 63 Mich. L. Rev. 209 (1964). — ED.

72   Chapter Three.   Judicial Review in Operation

until the House acted on the Select Committee's report, it did provide that he should receive all the pay and allowances due a member during the period.

The Select Committee, composed of nine lawyer-members, issued an invitation to Powell to testify before the Committee. The invitation letter stated that the scope of the testimony and investigation would include Powell's qualifications as to age, citizenship, and residency; his involvement in a civil suit (in which he had been held in contempt); and "[m]atters of . . . alleged official misconduct since January 3, 1961." See Hearings on H.R. Res. No. 1 before Select Committee Pursuant to H.R. Res. No. 1, 90th Cong., 1st Sess., 5 (1967) (hereinafter Hearings). Powell appeared at the Committee hearing held on February 8, 1967. After the Committee denied in part Powell's request that certain adversary-type procedures be followed, Powell testified. He would, however, give information relating only to his age, citizenship, and residency; upon the advice of counsel, he refused to answer other questions.

On February 10, 1967, the Select Committee issued another invitation to Powell. In the letter, the Select Committee informed Powell that its responsibility under the House Resolution extended to determining not only whether he met the standing qualifications of Art. I, §2, but also to "inquire into the question of whether you should be punished or expelled pursuant to the powers granted . . . the House under article I, section 5, . . . of the Constitution . . ." Powell did not appear at the next hearing, held February 14, 1967. However, his attorney was present, and he informed the Committee that Powell would not testify about matters other than his eligibility under the standing qualifications of Art. I, §5 . . .

The Committee held one further hearing at which neither Powell nor his attorneys were present. Then, on February 23, 1967, the Committee issued its report, finding that Powell met the standing qualifications of Art. I, §2. H.R. Rep. No. 27, 90th Cong., 1st Sess., 31 (1967). However, the Committee further reported that Powell had asserted an unwarranted privilege and immunity from the processes of the courts of New York; that he had wrongfully diverted House funds for the use of others and himself; and that he had made false reports on expenditures of foreign currency to the Committee on House Administration. Id., at 31-32. The Committee recommended that Powell be sworn and seated as a member of the 90th Congress but that he be censured by the House, fined $40,000 and be deprived of his seniority. Id., at 33.

The report was presented to the House on March 1, 1967, and the House debated the Select Committee's proposed resolution. At the conclusion of the debate, by a vote of 222 to 202 the House rejected a motion to bring the resolution to a vote. An amendment to the resolution was then offered; it called for the exclusion of Powell and a declaration that his seat was vacant. The Speaker ruled that a majority vote of the House would be sufficient to pass the resolution if it were so amended. 113 Cong. Rec. 1942 (daily ed. March 1, 1967). After further debate, the amendment was adopted by a vote of 248 to 176. Then the House adopted by a vote of 307 to 116 House Resolution No. 278 in its amended form, thereby excluding Powell and directing that the Speaker notify the Governor of New York that the seat was vacant.

Powell and 13 voters of the 18th Congressional District of New York subsequently instituted this suit in the United States District Court for the District of Columbia. Five members of the House of Representatives were named as defendants individually and "as representatives of a class of citizens who are presently serving . . . as members of the House of Representatives." John W. McCormack was named in his official capacity as Speaker, and the Clerk of the House of Representatives, the Sergeant-at-Arms and the Doorkeeper were named individually and in their official capacities. The Complaint alleged that House Resolution No. 278 violated the Constitution, specifically Art. I, §2, cl. 1, because the resolution was inconsistent with the mandate that the members of the House shall be elected by the people of each State, and Art. I, §2, cl. 2, which, petitioners alleged, sets forth the exclusive qualifications for membership. The Complaint further alleged that the Clerk of the House threatened to refuse to perform the service for Powell to which a duly-elected Congressman is entitled, that the Sergeant-at-Arms refused to pay Powell his salary, and that the Doorkeeper threatened to deny Powell admission to the House Chamber.

Petitioners asked that a three-judge court be convened. Further, they requested the District Court grant a permanent injunction restraining respondents from executing the House Resolution, and enjoining the Speaker from refusing to administer the oath, the Clerk from refusing to perform the duties due a Representative, the Sergeant-at-Arms from refusing to pay Powell his salary and the Doorkeeper from refusing to admit Powell to the Chamber. The complaint also requested a declaratory judgment that Powell's exclusion was unconstitutional.

The District Court granted respondents' motion to dismiss the complaint "for want of jurisdiction of the subject matter." Powell v. McCormack, 266 F. Supp. 354 (D.C.D.C. 1967). The Court of Appeals for the District of Columbia Circuit affirmed on somewhat different grounds, with each judge filing a separate opinion. Powell v. McCormack, 129 U.S. App. D.C. 344, 395 F.2d 577 (C.A.D.C. Cir. 1968). We granted certiorari. 393 U.S. 949 (1968). While the case was pending on our docket, the 90th Congress officially terminated and the 91st Congress was seated. In November 1968, Powell had again been elected as the representative of the 18th Congressional District of New York, and he was seated by the 91st Congress. The resolution seating Powell also fined him $25,000. See H.R. Res. No. 2, 91st Cong., 1st Sess., 115 Cong. Rec. 21 (daily ed., January 3, 1969). Respondents then filed a suggestion of mootness. We postponed further consideration of this suggestion to a hearing on the merits. 393 U.S. 1060 (1969).

Respondents press upon us a variety of arguments to support the court below; they will be considered in the following order. (1) Events occurring subsequent to the grant of certiorari have rendered this litigation moot. (2) The Speech or Debate Clause of the Constitution, Art. I, §6, insulates respondents' action from judicial review. (3) The decision to exclude Petitioner Powell is supported by the power granted to the House of Representatives to expel a member. (4) This Court lacks subject matter jurisdiction over petitioners' action. (5) Even if subject matter jurisdiction is present, this litigation is not justiciable either under the general criteria established by this Court or because a political question is involved.

II. MOOTNESS

After certiorari was granted, respondents filed a memorandum suggesting that two events which occurred subsequent to our grant of certiorari require that the case be dismissed as moot. On January 3, 1969, the House of Representatives of the 90th Congress officially terminated, and Petitioner Powell was seated as a member of the 91st Congress. 115 Cong. Rec. 22 (daily ed., January 3, 1969). Respondents insist that the gravamen of petitioners' complaint was the failure of the 90th Congress to seat Petitioner Powell and that, since the House of Representatives is not a continuing body and Powell has now been seated, his claims are moot. Petitioners counter that three issues remain unresolved and thus this litigation presents a "case or controversy" within the meaning of Art. III: (1) whether Powell was unconstitutionally deprived of his seniority by his exclusion from the 90th Congress; (2) whether the resolution of the 91st Congress imposing as "punishment" a $25,000 fine is a continuation of respondents' allegedly unconstitutional exclusion, see H.R. Res. No. 2, 91st Cong., 1st Sess., 115 Cong. Rec. 21 (daily ed., January 3, 1969); and (3) whether Powell is entitled to salary withheld after his exclusion from the 90th Congress. We conclude that Powell's claim for back salary remains viable even though he has been seated in the 91st Congress and thus find it unnecessary to determine whether the other issues have become moot. . . .

. . . Despite Powell's obvious and continuing interest in his withheld salary, respondents insist that Alejandrino v. Quezon, 271 U.S. 528 (1926), leaves us no choice but to dismiss this litigation as moot. Alejandrino, a duly appointed Senator of the Philippine Islands, was suspended for one year by a resolution of the Philippine Senate and deprived of all "prerogatives, privileges and emoluments" for the period of his suspension. The Supreme Court of the Philippines refused to enjoin the suspension. By the time the case reached this Court, the suspension had expired and the Court dismissed as moot Alejandrino's request that the suspension be enjoined. Then, sua sponte, the Court considered whether the possibility that Alejandrino was entitled to back salary required it "to retain the case for the purpose of determining whether he [Alejandrino] may not have a mandamus for this purpose." Id., at 533. Characterizing the issue of Alejandrino's salary as a "mere incident" to his claim that the suspension was improper, the Court noted that he had not briefed the salary issue and that his request for mandamus did not set out with sufficient clarity the official or set of officials against whom the mandamus should issue. Id., at 533-534. The Court therefore refused to treat the salary claim and dismissed the entire action as moot.

Respondents believe that Powell's salary claim is also a "mere incident" to his insistence that he was unconstitutionally excluded so that we should likewise dismiss this entire action as moot. This argument fails to grasp that the reason for the dismissal in Alejandrino was not that Alejandrino's deprivation of salary was insufficiently substantial to prevent the case from becoming moot, but rather that his failure to plead sufficient facts to establish his mandamus claim made it impossible for any court to resolve the mandamus request. By contrast, petitioners' complaint names the official responsible for the payment of congressional salaries and asks for both mandamus and an injunction against that official.

Furthermore, even if respondents are correct that Powell's averments as to injunctive relief are not sufficiently definite, it does not follow that this litigation must be dismissed as moot. Petitioner Powell has not been paid his salary by virtue of an allegedly unconstitutional House resolution. That claim is still unresolved and hotly contested by clearly adverse parties. Declaratory relief has been requested, a form of relief not available when Alejandrino was decided. A court may grant declaratory relief even though it chooses not to issue an injunction or mandamus. See United Public Workers v. Mitchell, supra, at 93; cf. United States v. California, 332 U.S. 19, 25-26 (1947). A declaratory judgment can then be used as a predicate to further relief, including an injunction. . . .

. . . Alejandrino stands only for the proposition that, where one claim has become moot and the pleadings are insufficient to determine whether the plaintiff is entitled to another remedy, the action should be dismissed as moot. There is no suggestion that Powell's averments as to declaratory relief are insufficient and his allegedly unconstitutional deprivation of salary remains unresolved. . . .

Finally, respondents seem to argue that Powell's proper action to recover salary is a suit in the Court of Claims, so that, having brought the wrong action, a dismissal for mootness is appropriate. The short answer to this argument is that it confuses mootness with whether Powell has established a right to recover against the Sergeant-at-Arms, a question which is inappropriate to treat at this stage of the litigation.

III. SPEECH OR DEBATE CLAUSE

Respondents assert that the Speech or Debate Clause of the Constitution, Art. I, §6, is an absolute bar to petitioners' action. This Court has on four prior occasions — Dombrowski v. Eastland, 387 U.S. 82 (1967); United States v. Johnson, 383 U.S. 169 (1966); Tenney v. Brandhove, 341 U.S. 367 (1951); and Kilbourn v. Thompson, 103 U.S. 168 (1880) — been called upon to determine if allegedly unconstitutional action taken by legislators or legislative employees is insulated from judicial review by the Speech or Debate Clause. Both parties insist that their respective positions find support in these cases and tender for decision three distinct issues: (1) whether respondents in participating in the exclusion of Petitioner Powell were "acting in the sphere of legitimate legislative activity," Tenney v. Brandhove, supra, at 376; (2) assuming that respondents were so acting, does the fact that petitioners seek neither damages from any of the respondents nor a criminal prosecution lift the bar of the clause; and (3) even if this action may not be maintained against a Congressman, may those respondents who are merely employees of the House plead the bar of the clause. We find it necessary to treat only the last of these issues. . . .

The Court first articulated in Kilbourn and followed in Dombrowski v. Eastland[23] the doctrine that, although an action against a Congressman may be barred by the Speech or Debate Clause, legislative employees who participated in the unconstitutional activity are responsible for their acts. . . .

That House employees are acting pursuant to express orders of the House does not bar judicial review of the constitutionality of the underlying legislative decision. Kilbourn decisively settles this question, since the Sergeant-at-Arms was held liable for false imprisonment even though he did nothing more than execute the House resolution that Kilbourn be arrested and imprisoned. . . . Freedom of legislative activity and the purposes of the Speech or Debate Clause are fully protected if legislators are relieved of the burden of defending themselves. . . .

IV. EXCLUSION OR EXPULSION

The resolution excluding Petitioner Powell was adopted by a vote in excess of two-thirds of the 434 Members of Congress — 307 to 116. 113 Cong. Rec. 1956-1957 (daily ed. March 1, 1967). Article I, § 5, grants the House authority to expel a member "with the Concurrence of two thirds." Respondents assert that the House may expel a member for any reason whatsoever and that, since a two-thirds vote was obtained, the procedure by which Powell was denied his seat in the 90th Congress should be regarded as an expulsion not an exclusion. . . .

. . . The Speaker ruled that the House was voting to exclude Powell, and we will not speculate what the result might have been if Powell had been seated and expulsion proceedings subsequently instituted.

Nor is the distinction between exclusion and expulsion merely one of form. The misconduct for which Powell was charged occurred prior to the convening of the 90th Congress. On several occasions the House has debated whether a member can be expelled for actions taken during a prior Congress and the House's own manual of procedure applicable in the 90th Congress states that "both Houses have distrusted their power to punish in such cases." . . .

V. SUBJECT MATTER JURISDICTION

. . . Respondents . . . contend that this is not a case "arising under" the Constitution within the meaning of Article III. They emphasize that Art. I, § 5, assigns to each house of Congress the power to judge the elections and qualifications of its own members and to punish its members for disorderly behavior. Respondents also note that under Art. I, § 3, the Senate has the "sole power" to try all impeachments. Respondents argue that these delegations (to "judge," to "punish," and to "try") to the Legislative Branch are explicit grants of "judicial power" to the Congress and constitute specific exceptions to the general mandate of Article III that the "judicial power" shall be vested in the federal courts. Thus,

---

[23] In Dombrowski $500,000 in damages was sought against a Senator and the chief counsel of a Senate Subcommittee chaired by that Senator. Record, pp. 10-11. We affirmed the grant of summary judgment as to the Senator but reversed as to subcommittee counsel.

respondents maintain, the "power conferred on the courts by Article III does not authorize this Court to do anything more than declare its lack of jurisdiction to proceed."

We reject this contention. . . . It has long been held that a suit "arises under" the Constitution if petitioners' claims "will be sustained if the Constitution . . . [is] given one construction and will be defeated if it [is] given another." Bell v. Hood, 327 U.S. 678, 685 (1946). . . . Thus, this case clearly is one "arising under" the Constitution as the Court has interpreted that phrase. Any bar to federal courts reviewing the judgments made by the House or Senate in excluding a member arises from the allocation of powers between the two branches of the Federal Government (a question of justiciability), and not from the petitioners' failure to state a claim based on federal law.

Respondents next contend that the Court of Appeals erred in ruling that petitioners' suit is "authorized by a jurisdictional statute," i.e., 28 U.S.C. § 1331(a) (1964 ed.). Section 1331(a) provides that district courts shall have jurisdiction in "all civil actions wherein the matter in controversy . . . arises under the Constitution. . . ."

Respondents claim that the passage of the Force Act in 1870 lends support to their interpretation of the intended scope of § 1331. The Force Act gives the district courts jurisdiction over "any civil action to recover possession of any office . . . wherein it appears the sole question . . . arises out of the denial of the right to vote . . . on account of race, color or previous condition of servitude." However, the Act specifically excludes suits concerning the office of Congressman. Respondents maintain that this exclusion demonstrates Congress' intention to prohibit federal courts from entertaining suits regarding the seating of Congressmen. . . .

. . . The Force Act is limited to election challenges where a denial of the right to vote in violation of the Fifteenth Amendment is alleged. See 28 U.S.C. § 1344 (1964 ed.). Further, the Act was passed five years before the original version of § 1331 was enacted. While it might be inferred that Congress intended to give each House the exclusive power to decide congressional election challenges, there is absolutely no indication that the passage of this Act evidences an intention to impose other restrictions on the broad grant of jurisdiction in § 1331.

VI. JUSTICIABILITY

Having concluded that the Court of Appeals correctly ruled that the District Court had jurisdiction over the subject matter, we turn to the question whether the case is justiciable. Two determinations must be made in this regard. First, we must decide whether the claim presented and the relief sought are of the type which admit of judicial resolution. Second, we must determine whether the structure of the Federal Government renders the issue presented a "political question" — that is, a question which is not justiciable in federal court because of the separation of powers provided by the Constitution.

A. *General Considerations*

. . . Respondents . . . maintain . . . that this case is not justiciable because, they assert, it is impossible for a federal court to "mold effective relief for resolving this case." Respondents emphasize that petitioners asked for coercive relief against the officers of the House, and, they contend, federal courts cannot issue mandamus or injunctions compelling officers or employees of the House to perform specific official acts. Respondents rely primarily on the Speech or Debate Clause to support this contention.

We need express no opinion about the appropriateness of coercive relief in this case, for petitioners sought a declaratory judgment, a form of relief the District Court could have issued. . . .

B. *Political Question Doctrine*

1. *Textually Demonstrable Constitutional Commitment.*
. . . In Baker v. Carr, [369 U.S. 186], we noted that political questions are not jus-

ticiable primarily because of the separation of powers within the Federal Government. After reviewing our decisions in this area, we concluded that on the surface of any case held to involve a political question was at least one of the following formulations:

". . . [A] textually demonstrable constitutional commitment of the issue to a coordinate political department; or a lack of judicially discoverable and manageable standards for resolving it; or the impossibility of deciding without an initial policy determination of a kind clearly for nonjudicial discretion; or the impossibility of a court's undertaking independent resolution without expressing lack of the respect due coordinate branches of government; or an unusual need for unquestioning adherence to a political decision already made; or the potentiality of embarrassment from multifarious pronouncements by various departments on one question." Id., at 217.

Respondents' first contention is that this case presents a political question because under Art. I, §5, there has been a "textually demonstrable constitutional commitment" to the House of the "adjudicatory power" to determine Powell's qualifications. . . .

If examination of §5 disclosed that the Constitution gives the House judicially unreviewable power to set qualifications for membership and to judge whether prospective members meet those qualifications, further review of the House determination might well be barred by the political question doctrine. On the other hand, if the Constitution gives the House power to judge only whether elected members possess the three standing qualifications set forth in the Constitution, further consideration would be necessary to determine whether any of the other formulations of the political question doctrine are "inextricable from the case at bar."[42] Baker v. Carr, supra, at 217. . . .

In order to determine the scope of any "textual commitment" under Art. I, §5, we necessarily must determine the meaning of the phrase to "judge the qualifications of its members." . . . Our examination of the relevant historical materials leads us to the conclusion that petitioners are correct and that the Constitution leaves the House without authority to exclude any person, duly elected by his constituents, who meets all the requirements for membership expressly prescribed in the Constitution.

a. The Pre-Convention Precedents.

Since our rejection of respondents' interpretation of §5 results in significant measure from a disagreement with their historical analysis, we must consider the relevant historical antecedents in considerable detail. As do respondents, we begin with the English and colonial precedents.

[The Court examined 16th and 17th century precedents, finding them to be instances of expulsion. In 1712 the Commons excluded Robert Walpole, but he had been expelled earlier in the same term of Parliament. In 1782 the Commons resolved the long and bitter struggle over the claim of John Wilkes to be seated. Re-elected three times after his expulsion in 1764, he was refused a seat each time; but in 1782 the House voted to expunge its prior resolutions as "subversive of the Rights of the Whole Body of Electors of this Kingdom."]

Wilkes' struggle and his ultimate victory had a significant impact in the American colonies. His advocacy of libertarian causes and his pursuit of the right to be seated in Parliament became a cause célèbre for the colonists. "[T]he cry of 'Wilkes and Liberty' echoed loudly across the Atlantic Ocean as wide publicity was given to every step of Wilkes's public career in the colonial press. . . . The reaction in America took on significant proportions. Colonials tended to identify their cause with that of Wilkes. They saw him as a popular hero and a martyr to the struggle for liberty. . . . They named towns, counties, and even children in his honour." 11 L. Gipson, [The British Empire Before the American Revolution], at 222. It is within this historical context that we must examine the Convention debates in 1787, just five years after Wilkes' final victory.

---

[42] Consistent with this interpretation, federal courts might still be barred by the political question doctrine from reviewing the House's factual determination that a member did not meet one of the standing qualifications. This is an issue not presented in this case and we express no view as to its resolution.

Chapter Three. Judicial Review in Operation

b. *Convention Debates*.

. . . The Convention opened in late May 1787. By the end of July, the delegates adopted, with a minimum of debate, age requirements for membership in both the Senate and the House. The Convention then appointed a Committee of Detail to draft a constitution incorporating these and other resolutions adopted during the preceding months. . . .

The Committee reported in early August, proposing no change in the age requirement; however, it did recommend adding citizenship and residency requirements for membership. After first debating what the precise requirements should be, on August 8, 1787, the delegates unanimously adopted the three qualifications embodied in Art. I, §2. Id., at 213.

On August 10, the Convention considered the Committee of Detail's proposal that the "Legislature of the United States shall have the authority to establish such uniform qualifications of the members of each House, with regard to property, as to the said Legislature shall seem expedient." Id., at 179. The debate on this proposal discloses much about the views of the Framers on the issue of qualifications. For example, James Madison urged its rejection, stating that the proposal would vest ". . . an improper & dangerous power in the Legislature. The qualifications of electors and elected were fundamental articles in a Republican Govt. and ought to be fixed by the Constitution. If the Legislature could regulate those of either, it can by degrees subvert the Constitution. A Republic may be converted into an aristocracy or oligarchy as well by limiting the number capable of being elected, as the number authorized to elect. . . . It was a power also, which might be made subservient to the views of one faction agst. another. Qualifications founded on artificial distinctions may be devised, by the stronger in order to keep out partisans of a [weaker] faction." Id., at 249-250.

Significantly, Madison's argument was not aimed at the imposition of a property qualification as such, but rather at the delegation to the Congress of the discretionary power to establish any qualifications. The parallel between Madison's arguments and those made in Wilkes' behalf is striking.

. . . Shortly thereafter, the Convention rejected both Go[u]vern[eu]r Morris' motion and the Committee's proposal. Later the same day, the Convention adopted without debate the provision authorizing each House "to be the judge of the . . . qualifications of its own members." Id., at 254.

One other decision made the same day is very important to determining the meaning of Art. I, §5. When the delegates reached the Committee of Detail's proposal to empower each House to expel its members, Madison "observed that the right of expulsion . . . was too important to be exercised by a bare majority of a quorum: and in emergencies one faction might be dangerously abused." Id., at 254. He therefore moved that "with the concurrence of two-thirds" be inserted. With the exception of one State, whose delegation was divided, the motion was unanimously approved without debate, although Gouverneur Morris noted his opposition. The importance of this decision cannot be overemphasized. None of the parties to this suit disputes that prior to 1787 the legislative powers to judge qualifications and to expel were exercised by a majority vote. Indeed, without exception, the English and colonial antecedents to Art. I, §5, cl. 1 and 2, support this conclusion. Thus, the Convention's decision to increase the vote required to expel, because that power was "too important to be exercised by a bare majority," while at the same time not similarly restricting the power to judge qualifications, is compelling evidence that they considered the latter already limited by the standing qualifications previously adopted. . . .

Petitioners also argue that the post-Convention debates over the Constitution's ratification support their interpretation of §5. For example, they emphasize Hamilton's reply to the antifederalist charge that the new Constitution favored the wealthy and well-born:

"The truth is that there is no method of securing to the rich the preference apprehended but by prescribing qualifications of property either for those who may elect or be elected. But this forms no part of the power to be conferred upon the national government. Its authority would be expressly restricted to the regulation of the *times*, the *places*, the *manner* of elections. *The qualifications of the persons who may choose or be chosen, as has been remarked upon other occasions, are defined and fixed in the Constitution, and are unalterable by the legislature.*" The Federalist 371 (Mentor ed.). (Emphasis added in part.) . . .

c. *Post-Ratification.*

As clear as these statements appear, respondents dismiss them as "general statements . . . directed to other issues." They suggest that far more relevant is Congress' own understanding of its power to judge qualifications as manifested in post-ratification exclusion cases. Unquestionably, both the House and the Senate have excluded members-elect for reasons other than their failure to meet the Constitution's standing qualifications. For almost the first 100 years of its existence, however, Congress strictly limited its power to judge the qualfications of its members to those enumerated in the Constitution. . . .

The abandonment of such restraint, however, was among the casualties of the general upheaval produced in war's wake. In 1868, the House voted for the first time in its history to exclude a member-elect. It refused to seat two duly elected representatives for giving aid and comfort to the Confederacy. See 1 Hinds §§449-451. "This change was produced by the North's bitter enmity toward those who failed to support the Union cause during the war, and was effected by the Radical Republican domination of Congress. It was a shift brought by the naked urgency of power and was given little doctrinal support." Comment, Legislative Exclusion: Julian Bond and Adam Clayton Powell, 35 U. Chi. L. Rev. 151, 157 (1967). From that time until the present, congressional practice has been erratic; and on the few occasions when a member-elect was excluded although he met all the qualifications set forth in the Constitution, there were frequently vigorous dissents. Even the annotations to the official manual of procedure for the 90th Congress manifests doubt as to the House's power to exclude a member-elect who has met the constitutionally prescribed qualifications. See Rules of the House of Representatives, H.R. Doc. No. 529, 89th Cong., 2d Sess., §12, at 7-8 (1967).

Had these congressional exclusion precedents been more consistent, their precedential value still would be quite limited. See Note, the Power of a House of Congress to Judge the Qualifications of its Members, 81 Harv. L. Rev. 673, 679 (1968). That an unconstitutional action has been taken before surely does not render that same action any less unconstitutional at a later date. Particularly in view of the Congress' own doubts in those few cases where it did exclude members-elect, we are not inclined to give its precedents controlling weight. . . .

d. *Conclusion.*

Had the intent of the Framers emerged from these materials with less clarity, we would nevertheless have been compelled to resolve any ambiguity in favor of a narrow construction of the scope of Congress' power to exclude members-elect. A fundamental principle of our representative democracy is, in Hamilton's words, "that the people should choose whom they please to govern them." 2 Elliot's Debates 257. As Madison pointed out at the Convention, this principle is undermined as much by limiting whom the people can select as by limiting the franchise itself. In apparent agreement with this basic philosophy, the Convention adopted his suggestion limiting the power to expel. To allow essentially that same power to be exercised under the guise of judging qualifications, would be to ignore Madison's warning, borne out in the Wilkes case and some of Congress' own post-Civil War exclusion cases, against "vesting an improper & dangerous power in the Legislature." 2 Farrand 249. Moreover, it would effectively nullify the Convention's decision to require a two-thirds vote for expulsion. Unquestionably, Congress has an interest in preserving its institutional integrity, but in most cases that interest can be sufficiently safeguarded by the exercise of its power to punish its members for disorderly behavior and, in extreme cases, to expel a member with the concurrence of two-thirds. In short, both the intention of the Framers, to the extent it can be determined, and an examination of the basic principles of our democratic system persuade us that the Constitution does not vest in the Congress a discretionary power to deny membership by a majority vote. . . .

2. *Other Considerations.*

Respondents' alternate contention is that the case presents a political question because judicial resolution of petitioners' claim would produce a "potentially embarrassing confrontation between coordinate branches" of the Federal Government. But, as our interpretation of Art. I, §5, discloses, a determination of Petitioner Powell's right to sit would require no more than an interpretation of the Constitution. Such a determination falls within the traditional role accorded courts to interpret the law, and does not involve a "lack of respect due [a] coordinate branch of government," nor does it involve an "initial policy determination of a kind clearly for nonjudicial discretion." Baker v. Carr, supra, at 217. Our system of government requires that federal courts on occasion interpret the Constitution in a manner at variance with the construction given the document by another branch. The alleged conflict[86] that such an adjudication may cause cannot justify the courts' avoiding their constitutional responsibility. See United States v. Brown, 381 U.S. 437, 462 (1965); Youngstown Sheet and Tube Co. v. Sawyer, 343 U.S. 579, 613-614 (1952) (Frankfurter, J., concurring); Myers v. United States, 272 U.S. 52, 293 (1926) (Brandeis, J., dissenting).

. . . Finally, a judicial resolution of petitioner's claim will not result in "multifarious pronouncements by various departments on one question." For, as we noted in Baker v. Carr, supra, at 211, it is the responsibility of this Court to act as the ultimate interpreter of the Constitution. Marbury v. Madison, 1 Cranch 137 (1803). Thus, we conclude that petitioners' claim is not barred by the political question doctrine, and having determined that the claim is otherwise generally justiciable, we hold that the case is justiciable.

VII. CONCLUSION

. . . Petitioners seek additional forms of equitable relief, including mandamus for the release of Petitioner Powell's back pay. The propriety of such remedies, however, is more appropriately considered in the first instance by the courts below. Therefore, as to Respondents McCormack, Albert, Ford, Celler, and Moore, the judgment of the Court of Appeals for the District of Columbia Circuit is affirmed. As to Respondents Jennings, Johnson, and Miller, the judgment of the Court of Appeals for the District of Columbia Circuit is reversed and the case is remanded to the United States District Court for the District of Columbia with instructions to enter a declaratory judgment and for further proceedings consistent with this opinion.

It is so ordered.

[A concurring opinion was delivered by MR. JUSTICE DOUGLAS and a dissenting opinion by MR. JUSTICE STEWART. The latter maintained that the case was moot, since its essential purpose had been achieved with the seating of petitioner; and that the incidental claim for back salary could be litigated more appropriately in the Court of Claims, "in a vastly different and more conventional form."]

United States v. Sisson 294 F. Supp. 511 (D. Mass. 1968)

WYZANSKI, CHIEF JUDGE. The grand jury indicted Sisson for wilfully refusing to perform a duty required under the Military Selective Service Act of 1967, U.S.C. Title 50 App. §451 et seq., in that he refused to comply with an order of his draft board to submit to induction into the armed forces of the United States.

---

[86] In fact, the Court has noted that it is an "inadmissible suggestion" that action might be taken in disregard of a judicial determination. McPherson v. Blacker, 146 U.S. 1, 24 (1892).

He has moved to dismiss the indictment principally upon the ground that the draft act as applied to him violates the Constitution. He contends that there is under the Constitution of the United States no authority to conscript him to serve in a war not declared by Congress.

Intertwined are the issues as to whether Sisson has a standing to raise the question he poses and whether, indeed, it is authorized by the Constitution or contrary to its terms for him to be ordered to serve under the draft act at this time.

Two years ago those issues, while not squarely presented, were at least involved indirectly in the sentence I imposed upon Phillips, defendant in United States v. Phillips, Cr. 66-178-W. He claimed that the war in Vietnam was not duly authorized and that he could not be compelled to serve in it. In sentencing him I pointed out that he was unable to tell whether his service would involve any duties in Vietnam. So far as appeared, he might spend his total military service in the United States or in some foreign place other than Vietnam. I implied, without definitely so ruling, that under the then existing circumstances he had no standing to question the military actions in Vietnam or to avoid induction on the ground that he might be involved in such actions.

Two major changes have occurred since the sentencing of Phillips.

First, it appears incontrovertibly that draft calls, that is, the number of persons summoned for military service under the Act, if not directly determined by military demands in Vietnam, are so closely correlated as to be unmistakably inter-dependent. Thus, the risk of being drafted, which each individual like Sisson sustains, is seriously magnified by the Vietnam war. This risk is different from the one which the individual taxpayer sustains by an increase in his taxes due to the swollen appropriations evoked by military demands in Vietnam. One reason is that the very person of the conscript is affected so that his whole life is altered. He is not merely inconvenienced by a fringe detriment to his pocketbook. What is perhaps even more significant is that Selective Draft Law Cases, 245 U.S. 366, decided in 1917 that a person drafted for military duty does have a standing to raise at least some issues with respect to the constitutionality of draft legislation. See particularly p. 389, 38 S. Ct. 159. Thus there is a difference from the dicta in Flast v. Cohen, 392 U.S. 83, which suggest that a person required to pay a federal income tax has no standing to challenge an act appropriating money to be spent in connection with Vietnam.

The other difference between the situation today and that two years ago is that previously it was plausible to suppose that one drafted under the Act could, subsequent to his induction and at the very point when he was in peril of being transferred to Vietnam, raise the issue as to whether he personally could constitutionally be required to serve in that war. In recent years, repeated opposition by the executive and military branches of the Government of the United States has led courts in a virtually unanimous series of opinions to conclude that a soldier cannot raise in a civilian court, or indeed in a military court, the issue as to the constitutionality of his proposed transfer to Vietnam. Those cases may not represent the view which the Supreme Court of the United States will ultimately take. But it is indisputable that today there is no clear right of a soldier once he is in the armed forces to get a judicial ruling on the right of the Army to require him to serve in Vietnam. It follows that if there is to be a presently effective judicial review it must come at the point of induction and not later.

Faced with a defendant who has standing to raise the issue, this Court must inquire as to whether an order requiring service in the armed forces with a strong probability of ultimate service in Vietnam violates any provision of the United States Constitution so as to entitle the person so ordered to disregard the induction order. Put thus, the issue is somewhat deceptive. The court has a procedural, as well as a substantive, problem. It must decide whether the question sought to be raised is in that category of political questions which are not within a court's jurisdiction and, if the issue falls within the court's jurisdiction, whether, as a matter of substance the defendant is right in his contention that the order is repugnant to the Constitution. Again, while those two aspects are technically separate, they are so close as often to overlap.

82 Chapter Three. Judicial Review in Operation

Four different types of cases may be noticed.

(1) A person may be required to give military service in connection with a war declared by Congress. Selective Draft Law Cases, supra.

(2) A person may be required to give military service in order to be ready to serve in a war that might later be declared by Congress. Hamilton v. Regents of University of California, 293 U.S. 245, 260; United States v. O'Brien, 391 U.S. 367, 377.

(3) There is no Supreme Court case deciding whether a person who has been conscripted in time of peace may be required during his service to respond to an order to fight abroad pursuant to a direction of the President either as Chief Executive or as Commander-in-Chief, wholly unsupported by any Congressional authority but evoked by an emergency. It is important to note that the third hypothetical case is not the present case. The third case, for which, as shown in the June 1968 Harvard Law Review Note on Congress, The President, and The Power to Commit Forces to Combat, 81 Harv. L. Rev. 1771, there are many Caribbean and other precedents, has as its central characteristic that the President has to act quickly and in an emergency assigns to battle in foreign areas men in the armed forces whether they are volunteers or conscriptees.

Without in any way deciding the point, it may be assumed that to meet the emergency the President need not wait for an Act of Congress and need not segregate those who were conscripted from others who volunteered. Indeed, one may further assume, for the sake of argument, that if the power rests upon emergency and the necessities thereby created, it is within the judicial power to scrutinize the length of time that the emergency may be permitted to serve as a constitutional rationalization for the action. See for possibly comparable cases Justice Holmes's opinion in Chastleton Corp. v. Sinclair, 264 U.S. 543, his opinion in Moyer v. Peabody, 212 U.S. 78, and Chief Justice Hughes's opinion in Sterling v. Constantin, 287 U.S. 378.

Making such assumptions does not imply that the assumptions are correct. Caution is invited by Ex parte Milligan, 71 U.S. (4 Wall.) 2 (holding invalid Presidential emergency action, see particularly p. 108) and The Steel Seizure case, Youngstown Sheet & Tube Co. v. Sawyer, 343 U.S. 579, in President Truman's Administration (holding that executive action in an emergency even when closely connected with a foreign war was unconstitutional, perhaps partly because it seemed to circumvent a specific statute).

Moreover, as already observed, assumptions with respect to this third type of case are made merely for argument's sake, but do not purport to resolve authoritatively the highly debatable problem whether the issues as to whether emergency creates, or, as Home Bldg. & Loan Ass'n v. Blaisdell, 290 U.S. 398, phrases it, furnishes the occasion for the exercise of power and if so, and whether the emergency may last indefinitely, raise the sort of political questions not appropriate for judicial determination.

(4) The fourth case is the instant controversy before this Court. It presents the question whether a conscript can secure from a court a determination that a war carried on for a long time without a declaration of war but as a result of combined legislative and executive action is a war in which, against his will, he can be required to serve.

A central characteristic of this fourth case, that is the case at bar, is that there has been no declaration of war. But it is an equally central characteristic that in the military steps, including the drafting and assigning of soldiers, the President has not acted alone.

Congress in 1967 extended the Selective Service Act, Pub. L. No. 90-40, 81 Stat. 100. Congress acted with full knowledge that persons called for duty under the Act had been, and are likely to be, sent to Vietnam. Indeed, in 1965 Congress had amended the same Act with the hardly concealed object of punishing persons who tore up their draft cards out of protest at the Vietnam war. See United States v. O'Brien, 391 U.S. 367.

Moreover, Congress has again and again appropriated money for the draft act, for the Vietnam war, and for cognate activities. Congress has also enacted what is called the Tonkin Gulf Resolution, which some have viewed as advance authorization for the expansion of the Vietnam war.

What the court thus faces is a situation in which there has been joint action by the President and Congress, even if the joint action has not taken the form of a declaration of war.

The absence of the formal declaration of war is not to be regarded as a trivial omission. A declaration of war has more than ritualistic or symbolic significance. What something is called has much to do with how authorities act and also with how those subject to authority respond. . . .

But the fact that a declaration of war is a far more important act than an appropriation act or than an extension of a Selective Service Act does not go the whole way to show that in every situation of foreign military action, a declaration of war is a necessary prerequisite to conscription for that military engagement.

We are reminded by McCulloch v. Maryland, 17 U.S. (4 Wheat.) 316, and its progeny, that the national government has powers beyond those clearly stipulated in the Constitution. That the Constitution expresses one way of achieving a result does not inevitably carry a negative pregnant. Other ways may be employed by Congress as necessary and proper. Indeed, the implied powers may be not only Congressional but sometimes Presidential. In re Debs, 158 U.S. 564. And this implication may be most justifiable in foreign affairs. United States v. Curtiss-Wright Export Corp., 299 U.S. 304. What may be involved in the present case is a choice between a limited undeclared war approved by the President and Congress and an unlimited declaration of war through an Act of Congress. The two choices may find support in different, related, but not inconsistent Constitutional powers.

If the national government does have two or more choices there are readily imagined reasons not to elect to exercise the expressly granted power to declare war.

A declaration of war expresses in the most formidable and unlimited terms a belligerent posture against an enemy. In Vietnam it is at least plausibly contended by some in authority that our troops are not engaged in fighting any enemy of the United States but are participating in the defense of what is said to be one country from the aggression of what is said to be another country. It is inappropriate for this court in any way to intimate whether South Vietnam and North Vietnam are separate countries, or whether there is a civil war, or whether there is a failure on the part of the people in Vietnam and elsewhere to abide by agreements made in Geneva. It is sufficient to say that the present situation is one in which the State Department and the other branches of the executive treat our action in Vietnam as though it were different from an unlimited war against an enemy.

Moreover, in the Vietnam situation a declaration of war would produce consequences which no court can fully anticipate. A declaration of war affects treaties of the United States, obligations of the United States under international organizations, and many public and private arrangements. A determination not to declare war is more than an avoidance of a domestic constitutional procedure. It has international implications of vast dimensions. Indeed, it is said that since 1945 no country has declared war on any other country. Whether this is true or not, it shows that not only in the United States but generally, there is a reluctance to take a step which symbolically and practically entails multiple unforeseeable consequences.

From the foregoing this Court concludes that the distinction between a declaration of war and a cooperative action by the legislative and executive with respect to military activities in foreign countries is the very essence of what is meant by a political question. It involves just the sort of evidence, policy considerations, and constitutional principles which elude the normal processes of the judiciary and which are far more suitable for determination by coordinate branches of the government. It is not an act of abdication when a court says that political questions of this sort are not within its jurisdiction. It is a recognition that the tools with which a court can work, the data which it can fairly appraise, the conclusions which it can reach as a basis for entering judgments, have limits.

Because defendant Sisson seeks an adjudication of what is a political question, his motion to dismiss the indictment is denied.

NOTE

Five years later Judge Wyzanski, in an opinion joined by Chief Judge Bazelon, again dismissed an action seeking to test the constitutionality of United States military involvement in Southeast Asia. Mitchell v. Laird, 488 F.2d 611 (D.C. Cir. 1973) (sitting by designation). In that case the court rejected, 2 to 1, defendants' contention that military appropriations and other legislation had constituted congressional ratification of the Executive decision to commit troops. But the political question doctrine still barred judicial determination of the merits. The court reasoned that regardless of the legality of United States involvement in the first instance, the war had already begun when President Nixon took office in 1969. Legality therefore turned on whether the President's actions were within his responsibility as Commander-in-Chief to bring the war to an end as quickly as possible consistent with the interests of the United States or had gone beyond that by aggressive prosecution of the war. On this matter, the court found itself incompetent to judge:

"A court cannot procure the relevant evidence: some is in the hands of foreign governments, some is privileged. Even if the necessary facts were to be laid before it, a court would not substitute its judgment for that of the President, who has an unusually wide measure of discretion in this area, and who should not be judicially condemned except in a case of clear abuse amounting to bad faith. Otherwise a court would be ignoring the delicacies of diplomatic negotiation, the inevitable bargaining for the best solution of an international conflict, and the scope which in foreign affairs must be allowed to the President if this country is to play a responsible role in the council of the nations."

See also Holtzman v. Schlesinger, 484 F.2d 1307, 1308-1312 (2d Cir. 1973), cert. denied, 416 U.S. 936 (1974).

NOTE "Political" Questions

1. Questions held to be "political" and nonjusticiable include the issue whether the initiative and referendum are consistent with a "republican" form of government, Pacific States Tel. Co. v. Oregon, 223 U.S. 118 (1912); whether an enrolled Act of Congress conforms to the bill as passed by the two Houses, Field v. Clark, 143 U.S. 649 (1892); whether the statutory standards governing the grant or denial of applications to engage in overseas air transportation were followed in a decision of the Civil Aeronautics Board reviewed by the President, Chicago & Southern Air Lines v. Waterman S.S. Corp., 333 U.S. 103 (1948); whether a vessel is immune from suit as one owned by a foreign sovereign, when the State Department so certifies, Ex parte Peru, 318 U.S. 578 (1943); and whether a proposed amendment to the Constitution is still open to ratification by a state, Coleman v. Miller, 307 U.S. 433 (1939).

In the last-cited case two questions were chiefly considered: whether Kansas, having previously rejected the child labor amendment, was free to ratify it, and whether the amendment was no longer pending owing to the lapse of thirteen years between submission by Congress and the purported ratification. The action was brought by members of the legislature who had voted against ratification, to restrain the officers of the legislature from signing the resolution and delivering it to the Governor. The Kansas Supreme Court denied relief. The United States Supreme Court granted certiorari. The Court's opinion, by Chief Justice Hughes, held that ultimate authority over these problems rests with Congress, in its control over the promulgation of an amendment by the Secretary of State. Is this a satisfactory resolution of problems relating to the amending process? Did the plaintiffs have standing to raise the question or to apply for certiorari? Justices Frankfurter, Roberts, Black, and Douglas thought not.

A third question raised in Coleman v. Miller was whether the Lieutenant Governor had authority to cast the deciding vote in favor of ratification in the state senate. "Whether this contention presents a justiciable controversy, or a question which is political in its nature and hence not reviewable, is a question upon which the Court is equally divided and therefore the Court expresses no opinion upon that point." 307 U.S. at 447.

What, then, are the characteristics that mark certain questions as "political"?

See Dodd, Judicially Non-enforcible Provisions of Constitutions, 80 U. Pa. L. Rev. 54 (1931); Finkelstein, Judicial Self-limitation, 37 Harv. L. Rev. 338 (1924); Weston, Political Questions, 38 id. 296 (1925); Finkelstein, Further Notes on Judicial Self-limitation, 39 id. 221 (1925); Post, The Supreme Court and Political Questions (1936); Frank, Political Questions, in Supreme Court and Supreme Law 36 (Cahn ed. 1954); Symposium, Policy-Making in a Democracy: The Role of the United States Supreme Court, 6 J. Pub. L. 275 (1957); Sawer, Political Questions, 15 U. Toronto L.J. 49 (1963); Scharpf, Judicial Review and the Political Question, 75 Yale L.J. 517 (1966).

Should the judiciary enter delegate-seating disputes at national political conventions? O'Brien v. Brown, 409 U.S. 1 (1972), and Keane v. National Democratic Party, ibid., both arose out of the Credentials Committee's recommendations to the 1972 Democratic Convention that certain delegates originally certified as members of the California and Illinois delegations be replaced. The district court dismissed both complaints as nonjusticiable, but the U.S. Court of Appeals for the District of Columbia Circuit, while affirming the Illinois result, reversed in the California case. Presented with petitions for writs of certiorari and stays, the Supreme Court refused to take immediate action upon the writs because the novel questions involved could not be satisfactorily decided in the three days until the full convention, and it granted the stays. While not reaching the merits of the cases, the Court did express "grave doubts" about the action of the court of appeals in the California proceedings. See Note, The Supreme Court, 1971 Term, 85 Harv. L. Rev. 50, 218-234 (1972). See generally Chambers & Rotunda, Reform of Presidential Nominating Conventions, 56 Va. L. Rev. 179 (1970); Note, Bode v. National Democratic Party: Apportionment of Delegates to National Political Conventions, 85 Harv. L. Rev. 1460 (1972); Comment, Constitutional Reform of State Delegate Selection to National Political Party Conventions, 64 Nw. U.L. Rev. 915 (1970); Comment, The Presidential Nomination: Equal Protection at the Grass Roots, 42 S. Cal. L. Rev. 169 (1969); Comment, One Man, One Vote and Selection of Delegates to National Nominating Conventions, 37 U. Chi. L. Rev. 536 (1960); Note, Constitutional Safeguards in the Selection of Delegates to Presidential Nominating Conventions, 78 Yale L.J. 1228 (1969).

In Cousins v. Wigoda, 419 U.S. 477 (1975), the Court overturned an Illinois state court order enjoining one of two rival slates of delegates from Chicago to the 1972 Democratic National Convention from participating as delegates at that convention. The Court held that the order interfered with defendant's First Amendment rights of political association and with the Convention's interest in passing on the credentials of prospective delegates. The Court emphasized the national constituency and elective nature of the Convention and the disorder that would result if each state were allowed to establish and pass on the qualifications of delegates. Justice Powell, concurring in part, argued that although the state could not compel the Convention to seat certain delegates, it could exercise the negative power of enjoining prospective delegates from participation.

NOTE Mootness and Prematurity

In Pierce v. Society of Sisters, 268 U.S. 510 (1925), decided by the Supreme Court on June 1, 1925, the statute was to take effect in September 1926. On the need for a showing of "most exceptional circumstances" in order to enjoin threatened state criminal prosecution in a federal court, see, e.g., Beal v. Missouri Pac. R.R., 312 U.S. 45 (1941). What would constitute such circumstances? Why is this requirement imposed? Compare Dombrowski v. Pfister, 380 U.S. 479 (1965); Cameron v. Johnson, 381 U.S. 741 (1965).

Chapter Three. Judicial Review in Operation

Constitutional challenges may come too late as well as too early. In St. Pierre v. United States, 319 U.S. 41 (1943), petitioner had been sentenced to five months' imprisonment for contempt of court in refusing, on the ground of self-incrimination, to answer a question before the grand jury. Bail was denied, and he entered upon service of the sentence and appealed to the court of appeals, which affirmed the conviction; before certiorari was granted the sentence expired. The Supreme Court held that the case was moot and dismissed the writ of certiorari.

In Fiswick v. United States, 329 U.S. 211 (1946), the petitioner had similarly completed his sentence pending certiorari; but he was an alien, subject to deportation if convicted of a crime involving moral turpitude and ineligible for naturalization if not a person of good moral character. Compare United States v. Morgan, 346 U.S. 502 (1954) (challenge to first conviction after sentence as second offender); Pollard v. United States, 352 U.S. 354 (1957) (possibility of collateral legal consequences); Wetzel v. Ohio, 371 U.S. 62 (1962) (death of defendant-appellant).

In Montgomery Ward & Co. v. United States, 326 U.S. 690 (1945), the Court held moot the case brought by the government to compel compliance with its order seizing the company's properties, where the properties were restored to the company pending action on a petition for certiorari. Should the fact that questions of compensation might turn on the legality of the seizure have moved the Court to decide the latter issue? In Alejandrino v. Quezon, 271 U.S. 528 (1926), the Court held moot a mandamus proceeding involving the right of the Philippine Senate to suspend a member for a term, where the term had expired, notwithstanding the fact that a question would remain concerning the right to salary during the period of suspension. But cf. Powell v. McCormack, p. 71 supra.

In Sibron v. New York, 392 U.S. 40 (1968), the Court severely qualified St. Pierre v. United States, supra. Noting the "vital importance of keeping open avenues of judicial review of deprivations of constitutional right," the Court held that Sibron's appeal was not mooted by completion of his sentence. The "mere possibility" of collateral legal consequences, such as the use of the conviction as evidence of character in future proceedings, was sufficient to overcome mootness. See Ginsberg v. New York, 390 U.S. 629 (1968) (possibility that Commissioner of Buildings might "in his discretion" revoke defendant's luncheonette license for single criminal conviction held sufficient).

In civil cases, too, the likelihood of continuing collateral effects on the parties has been held to prevent mootness. In Carroll v. President & Commissioners, 393 U.S. 175 (1968), petitioners sought to challenge a ten-day ex parte restraining order forbidding them to hold political rallies. Although the ten-day period had long expired before the case reached the Supreme Court, the Court held that mootness was avoided because "it appears that the decision of the Maryland Court of Appeals [upholding the issuance of the restraining order] continues to play a substantial role in the response of officials to [petitioners'] activities." See Super Tire Engineering Co. v. McCorkle, 416 U.S. 115 (1974) (challenge to state policy of providing welfare assistance to striking workers held not moot even though strike had ended, because of policy's continuing effect on bargaining positions of employer and employees).

A similar justification for ignoring technical mootness is that a controversy may be "capable of repetition, yet evading review." Southern Pacific Terminal Co. v. ICC, 219 U.S. 498, 514-515 (1911). Where this is the case, the Court has allowed an individual plaintiff to continue to press his claim "as a member of the class of people affected" by the statute or action complained of. Dunn v. Blumstein, 405 U.S. 330, 333 n.2 (1972). In Dunn an election occurred before an aspiring voter could obtain review of residency requirements which barred him from the franchise. Although plaintiff would meet residency requirements as to future elections, the Court held that the case was not moot. Similarly, when the gestation period of a pregnant woman challenging an anti-abortion statute had ended before Supreme Court review could be secured, the Court nevertheless reached the merits of the controversy. Roe v. Wade, 410 U.S. 113 (1973).

These exceptions to the mootness doctrine were held not to apply in DeFunis v. Odegaard, 416 U.S. 312 (1974). There, an aspiring law student who had been denied admission to the University of Washington Law School challenged his rejection on the ground that the school's admissions policies discriminated against persons who were not members of certain racial or ethnic minorities. The school had subsequently admitted DeFunis on the order of the trial court, and DeFunis had only about three months until graduation when his case was argued in the Supreme Court. On the school's statement that DeFunis would be allowed to finish the term regardless of the Supreme Court's decision on the merits, the Court held that the case was moot. In a per curiam opinion the Court dismissed as "speculative contingencies" the possibility that DeFunis might be unable to complete the degree requirements by the end of the current term. The Court further noted that DeFunis had cast his complaint as an individual and not as a class action; and therefore that DeFunis' entire purpose in bringing his action was satisfied by the school's allowing him to graduate. The Court distinguished Southern Pacific on the grounds that DeFunis himself was no longer threatened by the school's admissions policies and that, since the Washington state courts had passed on the merits, Supreme Court review of similar cases arising in that state would be expedited. Thus, mere continuing public interest in the resolution of the underlying issues in a case is insufficient to prevent mootness. Compare Ihrke v. Northern States Power Co., 459 F. 2d 566 (8th Cir.), vacated and remanded with instructions to dismiss as moot, 409 U.S. 815 (1972) (mootness of challenge to utility termination procedures).

See generally Singer, Justiciability and Recent Supreme Court Cases, 21 Ala. L. Rev. 229 (1969); Diamond, Federal Jurisdiction to Decide Moot Cases, 94 U. Pa. L. Rev. 125 (1946); Note, The Mootness Doctrine in the Supreme Court, 88 Harv. L. Rev. 373 (1974); Note, Mootness on Appeal in the Supreme Court, 83 Harv. L. Rev. 1672 (1970); Note, Cases Moot on Appeal: A Limit on the Judicial Power, 103 U. Pa. L. Rev. 772 (1955); Stern & Gressman, Supreme Court Practice ch. 18 (4th ed. 1969).

Section C. STANDING: THE NATURE OF THE COMPLAINANT'S INTEREST

Oral Argument in Ashwander v. Tennessee Valley Authority[c]

COUNSEL. May it please the Court, this controversy challenges the validity of the effort of the Tennessee Valley Authority to commit the Government of the United States to a permanent commercial utility business. The characteristics of that Authority may be described by stating that they are permanent in type; they would be frozen, as shown by the record in this case, by contracts to endure, according to their terms, for 20, 30, and possibly 50 years, but by their inherent nature they are permanent in character, for the reason that when once the service has been introduced within any area, under the circumstances shown in the record, the civilian population would be dependent upon them, and both the findings of the Court and the admissions of the individual defendants, the proof in the record, indicate clearly that there would be no practical withdrawal, even if at the end of

---

[c] The excerpts are taken from an unofficial transcript. At that time there was no official reporter for oral arguments in the Court. The facts of the case are stated in the opinion printed following this excerpt from the argument. As will appear more fully, the plaintiffs, preferred stockholders of the Alabama Power Company, brought suit against the corporation and the TVA to enjoin the carrying out of a contract for the sale of certain transmission lines to the TVA and a division of business territory in Alabama, and to secure a declaration that the plan and program of the TVA for the sale of electric power was unconstitutional. — ED.

Chapter Three. Judicial Review in Operation

the time of the actionable contracts the Congress of the United States should conceive it to be in the interest of the public to discontinue the arrangement. [Page 1] . . .

THE CHIEF JUSTICE. Would you mind telling us at once what this suit is, who brought it, and against whom?

COUNSEL. I am just approaching that at this time.

THE CHIEF JUSTICE. And what the issue is? [Page 2] . . .

THE CHIEF JUSTICE. It would greatly help me . . . if you would refer us to the Authority itself. What was the Tennessee Valley Authority, what was the act of Congress under which it was constructed, and what was claimed to be the basis for the contract which you assail — so that we can see precisely what it is you challenge in this case.

COUNSEL. Yes, your Honor.

THE CHIEF JUSTICE. Apart from these more general considerations as to ultimate objects and purposes, what is the precise object of this challenge?

COUNSEL. Perhaps it would be best served if I should outline the functions under the act under which the Tennessee Valley Authority exists.

MR. JUSTICE BRANDEIS. At the proper time I hope you will tell us why this proceeding is brought by these stockholders. I presume the corporation is organized under the laws of Alabama, and I wish you would tell us whether you are alleging any lack of power under the Alabama law, and under the charter of the Authority, to do the things of which you are complaining, and why a stockholder, and not the power company, is suing, and what the authority of the power company is under the law of Alabama. [Page 8] . . .

MR. JUSTICE BRANDEIS. You are going to come back, I assume, to the status of these stockholders — why they have a right to complain? [Page 17] . . .

MR. JUSTICE BRANDEIS. These stockholders are preferred stockholders, as I understand, all of them, are they not?

COUNSEL. Yes, your Honor.

MR. JUSTICE BRANDEIS. They are preferred stockholders?

COUNSEL. There was no other stock outstanding except that held by the Commonwealth and Southern. They held all the common stock.

MR. JUSTICE BRANDEIS. Being preferred stockholders, I suppose the amount of their interest is just as limited as the amount of interest of a bondholder would be limited. They have not the position of an ordinary common stockholder, who has the opportunity of very great profit which may ultimately come from an industry. Anything that illegally interferes may be a basis under certain circumstances of an appeal by a common stockholder. But a preferred stockholder has a very limited status. Under the ordinary rules of equity, even if all other conditions be complied with, you have to show that these preferred stockholders, who have a limited interest like a bond interest in a corporation, are going to be injured by what has been done. Will you call my attention to the statement in the bill and the findings of fact which show the character, the nature and the extent of the injury?

COUNSEL. The bill avers it.

MR. JUSTICE BRANDEIS. Just give me the reference to it.

COUNSEL. It will take us just a moment, your Honor, to find it. [Page 34] . . .

MR. JUSTICE BRANDEIS. If it is not convenient now, will you later give the averments which show that, and find the corresponding findings which show that these preferred stockholders would be irreparably injured?

COUNSEL. It can be done in one moment without reference to the averment.

MR. JUSTICE BRANDEIS. I do not want to interrupt your argument, but I should like to have the reference.

COUNSEL. I earnestly hope you will interrupt me with questions of that character, or of any other character.

If the ratio of 60 per cent of the value be applied as the standard, which is accepted by

Section C. **Standing** 89

the Tennessee Valley Authority to make payment for these properties, were applied to the properties of the Alabama Power Company —
  Mr. Justice Brandeis. I want the findings on that, not the argument. I want the findings of the court on that question of injury.
  Counsel. The court in fact refused to hear testimony as to valuations, because —
  Mr. Justice Brandeis. I am not talking of that. You have to show, in a bill in equity, that rights which you possess are threatened with irreparable injury. You may have complied with everything else, but you have to show that. What I want are the allegations on which you rely and the findings of the court on the subject.
  Counsel. We rely, if your Honor please, upon the findings that first of all the company could not stand competitive duplication, and it meant the junking of its property, the complete loss of its property, and the loss to the stockholders of their entire investment.
  Mr. Justice Brandeis. You certainly do not mean that that is true in regard to this particular property which is the subject matter of the controversy?
  Counsel. No. The averment here is that that is about 60 per cent of the bare bones replacement value, without any value for a going concern, or for attached customers or for a going business.
  Mr. Justice Brandeis. At the appropriate time that is most convenient to you I hope you will show me the references.
  Counsel. If your Honor will permit me to proceed, I shall be glad to do that; but it does take some time.
  Mr. Justice Brandeis. After you get opportunity to get the papers together.
  Counsel. Whether the court felt it was necessary to make that finding as to the preferred stockholders or not, I do not think it did, but it made findings as to the injury to the company itself. I say that in answer to your Honor's question so far as the stockholders are concerned.
  Mr. Justice McReynolds. Are your clients all the preferred stockholders, or what proportion of them?
  Counsel. At the outset they represented, of course, a small minority, but the proof shows that at the time of the hearing in this cause, without any particular effort to invite their concurrence, 1800 stockholders had authorized their names to be signed.
  Mr. Justice McReynolds. Owning how much stock?
  Counsel. Owning an aggregate, I think, of three or four million dollars' worth of the thirty million dollars' worth of stock.
  Mr. Justice McReynolds. Your allegation was that if this thing went on that entire stock would be wiped out?
  Counsel. Absolutely. It would not pay the bonds.
  Mr. Justice McReynolds. Very well.
  Counsel. The trustee for the bondholders came in and asserted that it would not pay the bonds if this situation proceeded, and as trustee it invited the instructions of the court.
  Mr. Justice Brandeis. You will show me the findings of the court at some later time?
  Counsel. I shall be delighted to. [Pages 35-37] . . .
  Counsel. The theory of the District Court, if your Honor please, was that there was an affirmative breach of duty by yielding to an unconstitutional program and becoming participant in that program by transferring these properties under a contract which on its face excluded the idea of the utility properties being operated for anything but nongovernmental competitive purposes in competition in State domain.
  Mr. Justice Brandeis. That is treating the merits of the case. I am still struggling with the initial position as to whether you have a right to complain, and that depends upon your status in the first place. You have called our attention to certain things, and next as to whether there is danger or irreparable injury. I suppose the ordinary rules of equity apply, which require that you must prove irreparable injury.

90   Chapter Three.   Judicial Review in Operation

COUNSEL. Yes, your Honor.

MR. JUSTICE BRANDEIS. I merely want you at the proper time to give me the findings on that subject of injury to you.

COUNSEL. The Court made no finding other than as to the fact that the program was illegal.

MR. JUSTICE BRANDEIS. Many a program may be illegal, and a common stockholder might object because there might be great possibility of injury to him, but when you are dealing with a person who has only a very limited interest, the situation may be entirely different; at least, it seems to me that it may be entirely different, and I should like to know what the findings are on that subject.

COUNSEL. I think the District Court went upon the theory that as a stockholder, if the corporation were yielding to and particpating in an illegal program, it had the right, irrespective of any financial gain, to call for a termination of that arrangement.

MR. JUSTICE BRANDEIS. Would a bondholder have a right simply because the corporation did something?

COUNSEL. No, I should not say that point-blank, because I think a bondholder's relationship and the responsibility to stockholders are entirely different things.

MR. JUSTICE BRANDEIS. That may or may not be a different matter. However, that is a question of law. Can you refer me to any case in which a preferred stockholder has been allowed to maintain a suit of this character? There are cases mentioned in the briefs, but those which I have examined are all cases of common stockholders.

COUNSEL. I have no decision in mind. I can only refer your Honor to the Central Transportation Company case.

MR. JUSTICE BRANDEIS. If you have any case or cases in which relief of this character has been granted to preferred stockholders, I should like to have a reference to them.

COUNSEL. We will be glad to ascertain as to that, your Honor. [Pages 38-40] . . . [The Court adjourned, and on the following day co-counsel continued the argument.]

COUNSEL. If the Court please, I think my friend the learned Solicitor General has somewhat misconceived the nature of this case, and in so doing has erected a man of straw and vigorously belabored it. His suggestion is that the sole question in this case is the power to erect dams upon the Tennessee River in aid of navigation and for the purpose of flood control. That is not the basis of this suit. There is nothing in the bill whatever that seeks to enjoin the Government either from maintaining or developing any one of the one hundred forty-nine potential dams which the War Department has found to be available on the Tennessee River.

MR. JUSTICE BRANDEIS. . . . before entering upon your argument, will you permit me to ask whether since yesterday you have found any case in which a preferred stockholder was permitted to bring a suit of this character?

COUNSEL. We have the cases, but I have not given personal attention to that. I may say, however, although it is interrupting a thought I was trying to express, that I cannot see in this matter any distinction between a common and a preferred stockholder. They are both owners of the property. If there be any distinction, it is in favor of the preferred stockholder, because he has generally a prior lien, or at least he has a preferred claim, in the liquidation of the assets. However, I will leave that to my colleague.

MR. JUSTICE BRANDEIS. I may just ask this further question, as to whether you can call our attention to any evidence or statement in the record or the bill of complaint as to the irreparable damage, other than that which [counsel] gave us specifically after the recess yesterday.

COUNSEL. I shall come to that, and I am going to argue to the Court, and I think with reason, that it is not merely a question of irreparable damage to these preferred stockholders; it is a question of the absolute destruction of the Alabama Power Company, and I shall prove that from the contract itself. I want first to develop the thought with which I had started, however. [Pages 129-130] . . .

Ashwander v. Tennessee Valley Authority 297 U.S. 288, 56 S. Ct. 46, 80 L. Ed. 688 (1936)

MR. CHIEF JUSTICE HUGHES delivered the opinion of the Court.

On January 4, 1934, the Tennessee Valley Authority, an agency of the Federal Government, entered into a contract with the Alabama Power Company, providing (1) for the purchase by the Authority from the Power Company of certain transmission lines, substations, and auxiliary properties for $1,000,000, (2) for the purchase by the Authority from the Power Company of certain real property for $150,000, (3) for an interchange of hydroelectric energy, and in addition for the sale by the Authority to the Power Company of its "surplus power," on stated terms, and (4) for mutual restrictions as to the areas to be served in the sale of power. The contract was amended and supplemented in minor particulars on February 13 and May 24, 1934.

The Alabama Power Company is a corporation organized under the laws of Alabama and is engaged in the generation of electric energy and its distribution generally throughout that State, its lines reaching 66 counties. The transmission lines to be purchased by the Authority extend from Wilson Dam, at the Muscle Shoals plant owned by the United States on the Tennessee River in northern Alabama, into seven counties in that State, within a radius of about 50 miles. These lines serve a population of approximately 190,000, including about 10,000 individual customers, or about one-tenth of the total number served directly by the Power Company. The real property to be acquired by the Authority (apart from the transmission lines above mentioned and related properties) is adjacent to the area known as the "Joe Wheeler dam site," upon which the Authority is constructing the Wheeler Dam.

The contract of January 4, 1934, also provided for cooperation between the Alabama Power Company and the Electric Home and Farm Authority, Inc., a subsidiary of the Tennessee Valley Authority, to promote the sale of electrical appliances, and to that end the Power Company, on May 21, 1934, entered into an agency contract with the Electric Home and Farm Authority, Inc. It is not necessary to detail or discuss the proceedings in relation to that transaction, as it is understood that the latter corporation has been dissolved.

There was a further agreement on August 9, 1934, by which the Alabama Power Company gave an option to the Tennessee Valley Authority to acquire urban distribution systems which had been retained by the Power Company in municipalities within the area served by the transmission lines above mentioned. It appears that this option has not been exercised and that the agreement has been terminated.

Plaintiffs are holders of preferred stock of the Alabama Power Company. Conceiving the contract with the Tennessee Valley Authority to be injurious to the corporate interests and also invalid, because beyond the constitutional power of the Federal Government, they submitted their protest to the board of directors of the Power Company and demanded that steps should be taken to have the contract annulled. The board refused, and the Commonwealth & Southern Corporation, the holder of all the common stock of the Power Company, declined to call a meeting of the stockholders to take action. As the protest was unavailing, plaintiffs brought this suit to have the invalidity of the contract determined and its performance enjoined. Going beyond that particular challenge, and setting forth the pronouncements, policies and programs of the Authority, plaintiffs sought a decree restraining these activities as repugnant to the Constitution, and also asked a general declaratory decree with respect to the rights of the Authority in various relations.

The defendants, including the Authority and its directors, the Power Company and its mortgage trustee, and the municipalities within the described area, filed answers and the case was heard upon evidence. The District Court made elaborate findings and entered a final decree annulling the contract of January 4, 1934, and enjoining the transfer of the

92 Chapter Three. Judicial Review in Operation

transmission lines and auxiliary properties. The court also enjoined the defendant municipalities from making or performing any contracts with the Authority for the purchase of power, and from accepting or expending any funds received from the Authority or the Public Works Administration for the purpose of constructing a public distribution system to distribute power which the Authority supplied. The court gave no consideration to plaintiff's request for a general declaratory decree.

The Authority, its directors, and the city of Florence appealed from the decree and the case was severed as to the other defendants. Plaintiffs took a cross appeal.

The Circuit Court of Appeals limited its discussion to the precise issue with respect to the effect and validity of the contract of January 4, 1934. The District Court had found that the electric energy required for the territory served by the transmission lines to be purchased under that contract is available at Wilson Dam without the necessity for any interconnection with any other dam or power plant. The Circuit Court of Appeals accordingly considered the constitutional authority for the construction of Wilson Dam and for the disposition of the electric energy there created. In the view that the Wilson Dam had been constructed in the exercise of the war and commerce powers of the Congress and that the electric energy there available was the property of the United States and subject to its disposition, the Circuit Court of Appeals decided that the decree of the District Court was erroneous and should be reversed. The court also held that plaintiffs should take nothing by their cross appeal. 78 F.(2d) 578. On plaintiffs' application we granted writs of certiorari, 296 U.S. 562.

First. The right of plaintiffs to bring this suit. Plaintiffs sue in the right of the Alabama Power Company. They sought unsuccessfully to have that right asserted by the Power Company itself, and upon showing their demand and its refusal they complied with the applicable rule. While their stock holdings are small, they have a real interest and there is no question that the suit was brought in good faith. If otherwise entitled, they should not be denied the relief which would be accorded to one who owned more shares.

Plaintiffs did not simply challenge the contract of January 4, 1934, as improvidently made, — as an unwise exercise of the discretion vested in the board of directors. They challenged the contract both as injurious to the interests of the corporation and as an illegal transaction, — violating the fundamental law. In seeking to prevent the carrying out of the contract, the suit was directed not only against the Power Company but against the Authority and its directors upon the ground that the latter, under color of the statute, were acting beyond the powers which the Congress could validly confer. In such a case it is not necessary for stockholders — when their corporation refuses to take suitable measures for its protection — to show that the managing board or trustees have acted with fraudulent intent or under legal duress. To entitle the complainants to equitable relief, in the absence of an adequate legal remedy, it is enough for them to show the breach of trust or duty involved in the injurious and illegal action. Nor is it necessary to show that the transaction was ultra vires the corporation. The illegality may be found in the lack of lawful authority on the part of those with whom the corporation is attempting to deal. Thus, the breach of duty may consist in yielding, without appropriate resistance, to governmental demands which are without warrant of law or are in violation of constitutional restrictions. The right of stockholders to seek equitable relief has been recognized when the managing board or trustees of the corporation have refused to take legal measures to resist the collection of taxes or other exactions alleged to be unconstitutional (Dodge v. Woolsey, 18 How. 331, 339, 340, 345; Pollock v. Farmers' Loan & Trust Company, 157 U.S. 429, 433, 553, 554; Brushaber v. Union Pacific R.R. Co., 240 U.S. 1, 10); or because of the failure to assert the rights and franchises of the corporation against an unwarranted interference through legislative or administrative action (Greenwood v. Freight Company, 105 U.S. 13, 15, 16; Cotting v. Kansas City Stockyards Co., 183 U.S. 79, 114). The remedy has been accorded to stockholders of public service corporations with respect to rates alleged to be confiscatory (Smith v. Ames, 169 U.S. 466, 469, 517; Ex parte Young,

209 U.S. 123, 129, 130, 143). The fact that the directors in the exercise of their judgment, either because they were disinclined to undertake a burdensome litigation or for other reasons which they regarded as substantial, resolved to comply with the legislative or administrative demands, has not been deemed an adequate ground for denying to the stockholders an opportunity to contest the validity of the governmental requirements to which the directors were submitting. [Citations omitted.]

In Smith v. Kansas City Title Company, 255 U.S. 180, a shareholder of the Title Company sought to enjoin the directors from investing its funds in the bonds of Federal Land Banks and Joint Stock Land Banks upon the ground that the Act of Congress authorizing the creation of these banks and the issue of bonds was unconstitutional, and hence that the bonds were not legal securities in which the corporate funds could lawfully be invested. The proposed investment was not large, — only $10,000 in each of the classes of bonds described. Id., pp. 195, 196. And it appeared that the directors of the Title Company maintained that the Federal Farm Loan Act was constitutional and that the bonds were "valid and desirable investments." Id., p. 201. But neither the conceded fact as to the judgment of the directors nor the small amount to be invested, — shown by the averments of the complaint — availed to defeat the jurisdiction of the court to decide the question as to the validity of the Act and of the bonds which it authorized. The Court held that the validity of the Act was directly drawn in question and that the shareholder was entitled to maintain the suit. . . . A close examination of these decisions leads inevitably to the conclusion that they should either be followed or be frankly overruled. We think that they should be followed, and that the opportunity to resort to equity, in the absence of an adequate legal remedy, in order to prevent illegal transactions by those in control of corporate properties, should not be curtailed because of reluctance to decide constitutional questions.

We find no distinctions which would justify us in refusing to entertain the present controversy. It is urged that plaintiffs hold preferred shares and that, for the present purpose, they are virtually in the position of bondholders. The rights of bondholders, in case of injury to their interests through unconstitutional demands upon, or transactions with, their corporate debtor, are not before us. Compare Reagan v. Farmers' Loan & Trust Co., 154 U.S. 362, 367, 368. . . .

It is said that here, instead of parting with money, as in the case of illegal or unconstitutional taxes or exactions, the Power Company is to receive a substantial consideration under the contract in suit. But the Power Company is to part with transmission lines which supply a large area, and plaintiffs allege that the consideration is inadequate and that the transaction entails a disruption of services and a loss of business and franchises. If, as plaintiffs contend, those purporting to act as a governmental agency had no constitutional authority to make the agreement, its execution would leave the Power Company with doubtful remedy, either against the governmental agency which might not be able, or against the Government which might not be willing to respond to a demand for the restoration of conditions as they now exist. In what circumstances and with what result such an effort at restoration might be made is unpredictable. If, as was decided in Smith v. Kansas City Title Company, supra, stockholders had the right to sue to test the validity of a proposed investment in the bonds of land banks, we can see no reason for denying to these plaintiffs a similar resort to equity in order to challenge, on the ground of unconstitutionality, a contract involving such a dislocation and misapplication of corporate property as are charged in the instant case.

The Government urges that the Power Company is estopped to question the validity of the Act creating the Tennessee Valley Authority and hence that the stockholders, suing in the right of the corporation, cannot maintain this suit. It is said that the Power Company, in 1925, installed its own transformers and connections at Wilson Dam and has ever since purchased large quantities of electric energy there generated, and that the Power Company continued its purchases after the passage of the Act of 1933 constituting the Authority. The principle is invoked that one who accepts the benefit of a statute cannot be heard to question its constitutionality. Great Falls Manufacturing Co. v. Attorney General, 124 U.S. 581; Wall v. Parrot Silver & Copper Co., 244 U.S. 407; St. Louis Company v. Prendergast Company, 260 U.S. 469. We think that the principle is not applicable here. The prior purchase of power in the circumstances disclosed may have a bearing upon the question before us, but it is by no means controlling. The contract in suit manifestly has a broader range and we find nothing in the earlier transactions which preclude the contention that this contract goes beyond the constitutional power of the Authority. . . .

We think that plaintiffs have made a sufficient showing to entitle them to bring suit and that a constitutional question is properly presented and should be decided.

Second. The scope of the issue. We agree with the Circuit Court of Appeals that the question to be determined is limited to the validity of the contract of January 4, 1934. The pronouncements, policies and program of the Tennessee Valley Authority and its directors, their motives and desires, did not give rise to a justiciable controversy save as they had fruition in action of a definite and concrete character constituting an actual or threatened interference with the rights of the persons complaining. The judicial power does not extend to the determination of abstract questions. Muskrat v. United States, 219 U.S. 346, 361; Liberty Warehouse Company v. Grannis, 273 U.S. 70, 74; Willing v. Chicago Auditorium, 277 U.S. 274, 289; Nashville, Chattanooga & St. Louis Rwy. Co. v. Wallace, 288 U.S. 249, 262, 264. It was for this reason that the Court dismissed the bill of the State of New Jersey which sought to obtain a judicial declaration that in certain features the Federal Water Power Act exceeded the authority of the Congress and encroached upon that of the State. New Jersey v. Sargent, 269 U.S. 328. For the same reason, the State of New York, in her suit against the State of Illinois, failed in her effort to obtain a decision of abstract questions as to the possible effect of the diversion of water from Lake Michigan upon hypothetical water power developments in the indefinite future. New York v. Illinois, 274 U.S. 488. At the last term the Court held, in dismissing the bill of the United States against the State of West Virginia, that general allegations that the State challenged the claim of the United States that the rivers in question were navigable, and asserted a right superior to that of the United States to license their use for power production, raised an issue "too vague and ill-defined to admit of judicial determination." United States v. West Virginia, 295 U.S. 463, 474. Claims based merely upon "assumed potential invasions" of rights are not enough to warrant judicial intervention. Arizona v. California, 283 U.S. 423, 462.

The Act of June 14, 1934, providing for declaratory judgments, does not attempt to change the essential requisites for the exercise of judicial power. By its terms, it applies to "cases of actual controversy," a phrase which must be taken to connote a controversy of a justiciable nature, thus excluding an advisory decree upon a hypothetical state of facts. See Nashville, Chattanooga & St. Louis Rwy. Co. v. Wallace, supra. While plaintiffs, as stockholders, might insist that the board of directors should take appropriate legal measures to extricate the corporation from particular transactions and agreements alleged to be invalid, plaintiffs had no right to demand that the directors should start a litigation to obtain a general declaration of the unconstitutionality of the Tennessee Valley Authority Act in all its bearings or a decision of abstract questions as to the right of the Authority and of the Alabama Power Company in possible contingencies.

Examining the present record, we find no ground for a demand by plaintiffs except as it related to the contracts between the Authority and the Alabama Power Company. And as the contract of May 21, 1934, with the Electric Home and Farm Authority, Inc., and that of August 9, 1934, for an option to the Authority to acquire urban distribution systems, are understood to be inoperative, the only remaining questions that plaintiffs are entitled to raise concern the contract of January 4, 1934, providing for the purchase of transmission lines and the disposition of power.

There is a further limitation upon our inquiry. As it appears that the transmission lines in question run from the Wilson Dam and that the electric energy generated at that dam is more than sufficient to supply all the requirements of the contract, the questions that are properly before us relate to the constitutional authority for the construction of the Wilson Dam and for the disposition, as provided in the contract, of the electric energy there generated.

[The Court's discussion of the substantive issues is printed infra p. 326.]

MR. JUSTICE BRANDEIS, concurring. "Considerations of propriety, as well as long-established practice, demand that we refrain from passing upon the constitutionality of an act of Congress unless obliged to do so in the proper performance of our judicial function, when the question is raised by a party whose interests entitle him to raise it." Blair v. United States, 250 U.S. 273, 279.

I do not disagree with the conclusion on the constitutional question announced by the Chief Justice; but, in my opinion, the judgment of the Circuit Court of Appeals should be affirmed without passing upon it. The Government has insisted throughout the litigation that the plaintiffs have no standing to challenge the validity of the legislation. This objection to the maintenance of the suit is not overcome by presenting the claim in the form of a bill in equity and complying with formal prerequisites required by Equity Rule 27. The obstacle is not procedural. It inheres in the substantive law, in well settled rules of equity, and in the practice in cases involving the constitutionality of legislation. Upon the findings made by the District Court, it should have dismissed the bill.

From these it appears: The Alabama Power Company, a corporation of that State with transmission lines located there, has outstanding large issues of bonds, preferred stock, and common stock. Its officers agreed, with the approval of the board of directors, to sell to the Tennessee Valley Authority a part of these lines and incidental property. The management thought that the transaction was in the interest of the company. It acted in the exercise of its business judgment with the utmost good faith. There was no showing of fraud, oppression, or gross negligence. There was no showing of legal duress. There was no showing that the management believed that to sell to the Tennessee Valley Authority was in excess of the Company's corporate powers, or that it was illegal because entered into for a forbidden purpose.

Nor is there any basis in law for the assertion that the contract was ultra vires the Company. Under the law of Alabama, a public utility corporation may ordinarily sell a part of its transmission lines and incidental property to another such corporation if the approval of the Public Service Commission is obtained. The contract provided for securing such approval. Moreover, before the motion to dissolve the restraining order was denied, and before the hearing on the merits was concluded, the Legislature, by Act No. 1, approved January 24, 1935, and effective immediately, provided that a utility of the State may sell all or any of its property to the Tennessee Valley Authority without the approval of the Public Service Commission or of any other state agency.

First. The substantive law. The plaintiffs who object own about one-three hundred and fortieth of the preferred stock. They claimed at the hearing to represent about one-ninth of the preferred stock; that is, less than one forty-fifth in amount of all the securities outstanding. Their rights are not enlarged because the Tennessee Valley Authority entered into the transaction pursuant to an act of Congress. The fact that the bill calls for an enquiry into the legality of the transaction does not overcome the obstacle that ordinarily stockholders have no standing to interfere with the management. Mere belief that corporate action, taken or contemplated, is illegal gives the stockholder no greater right to interfere than is possessed by any other citizen. Stockholders are not guardians of the public. The function of guarding the public against acts deemed illegal rests with the public officials.

Within recognized limits, stockholders may invoke the judicial remedy to enjoin acts of the management which threaten their property interest. But they cannot secure the aid of a court to correct what appear to them to be mistakes of judgment on the part of the of-

96 Chapter Three. Judicial Review in Operation

ficers. Courts may not interfere with the management of the corporation, unless there is bad faith, disregard of the relative rights of its members, or other action seriously threatening their property rights. This rule applies whether the mistake is due to error of fact or of law, or merely to bad business judgment. It applies, among other things, where the mistake alleged is the refusal to assert a seemingly clear cause of action, or the compromise of it. United Copper Securities Co. v. Amalgamated Copper Co., 244 U.S 261, 263-264. If a stockholder could compel the officers to enforce every legal right, courts, instead of chosen officers, would be the arbiters of the corporation's fate. . . .

Second. The equity practice. Even where property rights of stockholders are alleged to be violated by the management, stockholders seeking an injunction must bear the burden of showing danger of irreparable injury, as do others who seek that equitable relief. In the case at bar the burden of making such proof was a peculiarly heavy one. The plaintiffs, being preferred stockholders, have but a limited interest in the enterprise, resembling, in this respect, that of a bondholder in contradistinction to that of a common stockholder. Acts may be innocuous to the preferred which conceivably might injure common stockholders. There was no finding that the property interests of the plaintiffs were imperiled by the transaction in question; and the record is barren of evidence on which any such finding could have been made.

Third. The practice in constitutional cases. The fact that it would be convenient for the parties and the public to have promptly decided whether the legislation assailed is valid, cannot justify a departure from these settled rules of corporate law and established principles of equity practice. On the contrary, the fact that such is the nature of the enquiry proposed should deepen the reluctance of courts to entertain the stockholder's suit. "It must be evident to any one that the power to declare a legislative enactment void is one which the judge, conscious of the fallibility of the human judgment, will shrink from exercising in any case where he can conscientiously and with due regard to duty and official oath decline the responsibility." — 1 Cooley, Constitutional Limitations (8th ed.), p. 332.

The Court has frequently called attention to the "great gravity and delicacy" of its function in passing upon the validity of an act of Congress; and has restricted exercise of this function by rigid insistence that the jurisdiction of federal courts is limited to actual cases and controversies; and that they have no power to give advisory opinions. On this ground it has in recent years ordered the dismissal of several suits challenging the constitutionality of important acts of Congress. In Texas v. Interstate Commerce Commission, 258 U.S. 158, 162, the validity of Titles III and IV of the Transportation Act of 1920. In New Jersey v. Sargent, 269 U.S. 328, the validity of parts of the Federal Water Power Act. In Arizona v. California, 283 U.S. 423, the validity of the Boulder Canyon Project Act. Compare United States v. West Virginia, 295 U.S. 463, involving the Federal Water Power Act and Liberty Warehouse Co. v. Grannis, 273 U.S. 70, where this Court affirmed the dismissal of a suit to test the validity of a Kentucky statute concerning the sale of tobacco; also Massachusetts State Grange v. Benton, 272 U.S. 525.

The Court developed, for its own governance in the cases confessedly within its jurisdiction a series of rules under which it has avoided passing upon a large part of all the constitutional questions pressed upon it for decision. They are:

'1.' The Court will not pass upon the constitutionality of legislation in a friendly, non-adversary, proceeding, declining because to decide such questions "is legitimate only in the last resort, and as a necessity in the determination of real, earnest and vital controversy between individuals. It never was the thought that, by means of a friendly suit, a party beaten in the legislature could transfer to the courts an inquiry as to the constitutionality of the legislative act." Chicago & Grand Trunk Ry. v. Wellman, 143 U.S. 339, 345. Compare Lord v. Veazie, 8 How. 251; Atherton Mills v. Johnston, 259 U.S. 13, 15.

'2.' The Court will not "anticipate a question of constitutional law in advance of the necessity of deciding it." Steamship Co. v. Emigration Commissioners, 113 U.S. 33, 39;

Abrams v. Van Schaick, 293 U.S. 188; Wilshire Oil Co. v. United States, 295 U.S. 100. "It is not the habit of the court to decide questions of a constitutional nature unless absolutely necessary to a decision of the case." Burton v. United States, 196 U.S. 283, 295.

3. The Court will not "formulate a rule of constitutional law broader than is required by the precise facts to which it is to be applied." Steamship Co. v. Emigration Commissioners, supra. Compare Hammond v. Schappi Bus Line, Inc., 275 U.S. 164, 169-172.

4. The Court will not pass upon a constitutional question although properly presented by the record, if there is also present some other ground upon which the case may be disposed of. This rule has found most varied application. Thus, if a case can be decided on either of two grounds, one involving a constitutional question, the other a question of statutory construction or general law, the Court will decide only the latter. Siler v. Louisville & Nashville R.R., 213 U.S. 175, 191; Light v. United States, 220 U.S. 523, 538. Appeals from the highest court of a state challenging its decision of a question under the Federal Constitution are frequently dismissed because the judgment can be sustained on an independent state ground. Berea College v. Kentucky, 211 U.S. 45, 53.

5. The Court will not pass upon the validity of a statute upon complaint of one who fails to show that he is injured by its operation. Tyler v. Judges, etc., 179 U.S. 405; Hendrick v. Maryland, 235 U.S. 610, 621. Among the many applications of this rule, none is more striking than the denial of the right of challenge to one who lacks a personal or property right. Thus, the challenge by a public official interested only in the performance of his official duty will not be entertained. Columbus & Greenville Ry. v. Miller, 283 U.S. 96, 99-100. In Fairchild v. Hughes, 258 U.S. 126, the Court affirmed the dismissal of a suit brought by a citizen who sought to have the Nineteenth Amendment declared unconstitutional. In Massachusetts v. Mellon, 262 U.S. 447, the challenge of the federal Maternity Act was not entertained although made by the Commonwealth on behalf of all its citizens.

6. The Court will not pass upon the constitutionality of a statute at the instance of one who has availed himself of its benefits. Great Falls Mfg. Co. v. Attorney General, 124 U.S. 581; Wall. v. Parrot Silver & Copper Co., 244 U.S. 407, 411-412; St. Louis Malleable Casting Co. v. Prendergast Construction Co., 260 U.S. 469.

7. "When the validity of an act of the Congress is drawn in question, and even if a serious doubt of constitutionality is raised, it is a cardinal principle that this Court will first ascertain whether a construction of the statute is fairly possible by which the question may be avoided." Crowell v. Benson, 285 U.S. 22, 62.

Fourth. I am aware that, on several occasions, this Court passed upon important constitutional questions which were presented in stockholders' suits bearing a superficial resemblance to that now before us. But in none of those cases was the question presented under circumstances similar to those at bar. In none, were the plaintiffs preferred stockholders. In some, the Court dealt largely with questions of federal jurisdiction and collusion. In most, the propriety of considering the constitutional question was not challenged by any party. In most, the statute challenged imposed a burden upon the corporation and penalties for failure to discharge it; whereas the Tennessee Valley Authority Act imposed no obligation upon the Alabama Power Company, and under the contract it received a valuable consideration. Among other things, the Authority agreed not to sell outside the area covered by the contract, and thus preserved the corporation against possible serious competition. The effect of this agreement was equivalent to a compromise of a doubtful cause of action. Certainly, the alleged invalidity of the Tennessee Valley Authority Act was not a matter so clear as to make compromise illegitimate. These circumstances present features differentiating the case at bar from all the cases in which stockholders have been held entitled to have this Court pass upon the constitutionality of a statute which the directors had refused to challenge. The cases commonly cited are these: [Discussion of several cases is omitted.]

Pollock v. Farmers' Loan & Trust Co., 157 U.S. 429, 553-554, was a suit brought by a

98 Chapter Three. Judicial Review in Operation

common stockholder to enjoin a breach of trust by paying voluntarily a tax which was said to be illegal. The stockholder's substantive right to object was not challenged. The question raised was that of equity jurisdiction. The allegation of threatened irreparable damage to the corporation and to the plaintiff was admitted. The Court said: "The objection of adequate remedy at law was not raised below, nor is it now raised by appellees, if it could be entertained at all at this stage of the proceedings; and, so far as it was within the power of the government to do so, the question of jurisdiction, for the purposes of the case, was explicitly waived on the argument. . . . Under these circumstances, we should not be justified in declining to proceed to judgment upon the merits." The jurisdictional issue discussed in the dissent (157 U.S. at 608-612) was the effect of R.S. §3224. . . .

Smith v. Kansas City Title & Trust Co., 255 U.S. 180, 199-202, was a suit brought by a common stockholder to enjoin investment by the company in bonds issued under the Federal Farm Loan Act. Neither the parties, nor the government which filed briefs as amicus, made any objection to the jurisdiction. But as both parties were citizens of Missouri, the Court raised, and considered fully, the question whether there was federal jurisdiction under §24 of the Judicial Code. It was on this question that Mr. Justice Holmes and Mr. Justice McReynolds dissented. The Court held that there was federal jurisdiction; and upon averments of the bill, assumed to be adequate, sustained the right of the stockholder to invoke the equitable remedy on the authority of the Brushaber and Pollock cases. . . .

If, or in so far as, any of the cases discussed may be deemed authority for sustaining this bill, they should now be disapproved. This Court, while recognizing the soundness of the rule of stare decisis where appropriate, has not hesitated to overrule earlier decisions shown, upon fuller consideration, to be erroneous.[11] Our present keener appreciation of the wisdom of limiting our decisions rigidly to questions essential to the disposition of the case before the court is evidenced by United States v. Hastings, 296 U.S. 188, decided at this term. There, we overruled United States v. Stevenson, 215 U.S. 190, 195, long a controlling authority on the Criminal Appeals Act.

Fifth. If the Company ever had a right to challenge the transaction with the Tennessee Valley Authority, its right had been lost by estoppel before this suit was begun; and as it is the Company's right which plaintiffs seek to enforce, they also are necessarily estopped. The Tennessee Valley Authority Act became a law on May 18, 1933. Between that date and January, 1934, the Company and its associates purchased approximately 230,000,000 kwh electric energy at Wilson Dam. Under the contract of January 4, 1934, which is here assailed, continued purchase of Wilson Dam power was provided for and made; and the Authority has acted in other matters in reliance on the contract. In May, 1934, the Company applied to the Alabama Public Service Commission for approval of the transfers provided for in the contract; and on June 1, 1934, the Commission made in general terms its finding that the proposed sale of the properties was consistent with the public interest. Moreover, the plaintiffs in their own right are estopped by their long inaction. Although widespread publicity was given to the negotiations for the contract and to these later proceedings, the plaintiffs made no protest until August 7, 1934; and did not begin this suit until more than eight months after the execution of the contract. Others — certain ice and coal companies who thought they would suffer as competitors — appeared before the Commission in opposition to the action of the Authority; and apparently they are now contributing to the expenses of this litigation.

Sixth. Even where by the substantive law stockholders have a standing to challenge the

---

[11] A notable recent example is Humphrey's Executor v. United States, 295 U.S. 602, which limited (p. 626 et seq.) Myers v. United States, 272 U.S. 52, disapproving important statements in the opinion. For lists of decisions of this Court later overruled, see Burnet v. Coronado Oil & Gas Co., 285 U.S. 393, 406-409; Malcolm Sharp, Movement in Supreme Court Adjudication — A study of Modified and Overruled Decisions, 46 Harv. L. Rev. 361, 593, 795. [See also Douglas, Stare Decisis, 49 Colum. L. Rev. 735 (1949) (containing a table of 30 overruling cases in the period 1937-1949). — Ed.]

validity of legislation under which the management of a corporation is acting, courts should, in the exercise of their discretion, refuse an injunction unless the alleged invalidity is clear. This would seem to follow as a corollary of the long established presumption in favor of the constitutionality of a statute.

Mr. Justice Iredell said, as early as 1798, in Calder v. Bull, 3 Dall. 386, 399: "If any act of Congress, or of the Legislature of a state, violates those constitutional provisions, it is unquestionably void; though, I admit, that as the authority to declare it void is of a delicate and awful nature, the Court will never resort to that authority, but in a clear and urgent case."

Mr. Chief Justice Marshall said, in Dartmouth College v. Woodward, 4 Wheat. 518, 625: "On more than one occasion, this Court has expressed the cautious circumspection with which it approaches the consideration of such questions; and has declared, that, in no doubtful case, would it pronounce a legislative act to be contrary to the constitution." . . .

Mr. Chief Justice Waite said in the Sinking-Fund Cases, 99 U.S. 700, 718: "This declaration [that an Act of Congress is unconstitutional] should never be made except in a clear case. Every possible presumption is in favor of the validity of a statute, and this continues until the contrary is shown beyond a rational doubt. One branch of the government cannot encroach on the domain of another without danger. The safety of our institutions depends in no small degree on a strict observance of this salutary rule."

The challenge of the power of the Tennessee Valley Authority rests wholly upon the claim that the act of Congress which authorized the contract is unconstitutional. As the opinions of this Court and of the circuit Court of Appeals show, that claim was not a matter "beyond peradventure clear." The challenge of the validity of the Act is made on an application for an injunction — a proceeding in which the court is required to exercise its judicial discretion. In proceedings for a mandamus, where, also, the remedy is granted not as a matter of right but in the exercise of a sound judicial discretion, Duncan Townsite Co. v. Lane, 245 U.S. 308, 311-312, courts decline to enter upon the enquiry when there is a serious doubt as to the existence of the right or duty sought to be enforced. As was said in United States v. Interstate Commerce Commission, 294 U.S. 50, 63: "Where the matter is not beyond peradventure clear we have invariably refused the writ [of mandamus], even though the question were one of law as to the extent of the statutory power of administrative officer or body." A fortiori this rule should have been applied here where the power challenged is that of Congress under the Constitution.

Mr. Justice Stone, Mr. Justice Roberts, and Mr. Justice Cardozo join in this opinion.

Mr. Justice McReynolds.

Considering the consistent rulings of this court through many years, it is not difficult for me to conclude that petitioners have presented a justiciable controversy which we must decide. In Smith v. Kansas City Title Co., 255 U.S. 180, the grounds for jurisdiction were far less substantial than those here disclosed. We may not with propriety avoid disagreeable duties by lightly forsaking long respected precedents and established practice. . . .

Freund, The Supreme Court of the United States *154-155, 156-161, 163-164 (1961)*

The long-drawn-out litigation over the TVA was a clash of two views of constitutional warfare. The power companies endeavored to attack what they described as the whole "plan and program" of the TVA, as revealed in speeches, official studies and promotional literature, dealing with the development of a great river system and electrification of the Valley. One of these documents to which the power companies were fond of pointing bore the lyrical title "There'll be Shouting in the Valley." The TVA, on the other hand, insisted that all that was in issue in the case was the lawfulness of certain hydroelectric structures already completed and the sale of power under contracts already in existence or definitely contemplated. The first case was in form a stockholders' suit by preferred stockholders against the Alabama Power Company and the TVA to enjoin the performance of a contract which the company had made with the Authority. [A discussion of the Ashwander case is omitted.]

This was, of course, only the preliminary skirmish, though it seemed to lay the groundwork for upholding the dams constructed under TVA auspices, with their generators and transmission lines. The strategy and counter-strategy became more subtle. The power companies now made sure that they would have a case presenting the TVA program in its broadest scope. They brought together nineteen companies, serving the southeastern United States, in a huge omnibus suit challenging all phases of the TVA power activities. This suit took a curious course before it was finally decided in the Supreme Court. As a matter of fact it started out not as one suit but as two identical ones. One was filed in the federal court for nothern Alabama and the other in a state court in Tennessee. They were identical bills of complaint and were filed on the same day. This maneuver reflected uncertainty regarding venue. The TVA statute provides that the legal residence of the TVA is at Muscle Shoals, Alabama. Doubtless counsel for the power companies feared that suit would have to be brought in Alabama, or at least that a suit elsewhere would run the risk of eventual dismissal on venue or jurisdictional grounds. Nevertheless, the power companies were anxious to try a forum other than Alabama and the Fifth Circuit, where the Court of Appeals had ruled adversely to them in the stockholders' case. Their plan evidently was to retain the Alabama suit simply as an anchor to windward while actively pursuing the Tennessee suit. The TVA met these tactics by attempting to bring on the Alabama suit for a prompt hearing on a motion to dismiss the bill of complaint, while filing an answer and moving slowly in the Tennessee case.

At this juncture the power companies decided to dismiss the Alabama suit voluntarily rather than risk its becoming the test case, and so they staked everything on the Tennessee proceeding, trusting that it would not be dismissed for lack of jurisdiction. They had very adroitly brought it in a state court in Tennessee, thus forcing the TVA to take the initiative in removing it to a federal court. By removing it, the TVA was barred from objecting in the federal court that the venue of the action was not properly laid in Tennessee. The TVA had one counter-move, which was ingenious but inadequate. Though objection to venue was lost by removal, lack of "jurisdiction" of the state court could still be set up, for the jurisdiction of a federal court on removal is derivative. The TVA argued that under Tennessee law an action against a public agency could be brought only in the courts of the agency's legal headquarters, which would be Alabama in this case. Had this argument been effective, the companies, which had deliberately instituted the case in the state rather than federal court in order to force a waiver of venue, would have been hoist by their own petard. Unfortunately for the cause of poetic justice, but I daresay properly, the Tennessee law was held not to support the TVA's argument *in extremis*.

The result of all these maneuvers was that the case was finally established in a federal court in Tennessee before a single judge. He granted a sweeping preliminary injunction against TVA; the TVA appealed to the circuit court of appeals. That court reversed the preliminary injunction and sent the case back for trial. [90 F.2d 885 (6th Cir. 1937).] Meanwhile, however, Congress and the President had been wrestling with the so-called reorganization of the federal judiciary, less politely known as the court-packing plan. That plan, of course, never became law, but out of it grew the Judiciary Act of 1937, which contained a provision that a three-judge court must be called when an injunction is sought against the enforcement of a federal statute on constitutional grounds. By the time the TVA case was remanded to the trial court, the provision was in force, and hence the district court judge who granted the injunction now found himself flanked by two associates. After a lengthy trial, the three-judge court ruled in favor of the TVA, with some adverse findings by the judge who had first sat in the case. [21 F. Supp. 947 (E.D. Tenn. 1938).]

It is always tempting to look back on history and speculate on what would have happened to the face of the world if Cleopatra's nose had been half an inch longer or if the Germans had kept their right flank stronger in the drive on Paris in 1914. If the power companies had not asked for a preliminary injunction, there would have been no basis for an intermediate appeal and the case might have been tried before the single judge and decided finally by him in favor of the power companies with appropriate findings before the three-judge-court provision was enacted into law. At any rate, the companies were defeated in the three-judge court and appealed to the Supreme Court. The TVA maintained throughout the case that the power companies had no standing to object to competition, whether the TVA, in the abstract, was or was not constitutional. In the Supreme Court it was this defense which prevailed. [306 U.S. 118 (1939).] Thus technically the Supreme Court did not give us a decision on the validity of the entire TVA power program. Yet I cannot help believing that the detailed findings of the three-judge court in support of the validity of the TVA as a coordinated navigation, flood control and hydroelectric project made it more comfortable for the Supreme Court to dismiss the power companies' case on what might appear to be somewhat technical grounds.

The TVA litigation is not the only illustration of jockeying for position in constitutional lawsuits. An even more vivid instance occurred in the holding-company litigation. The interests opposed to the Holding Company Act were anxious to secure as early as possible a sweeping decision declaring the whole scheme of regulation unconstitutional. They were on the alert for a case which would lend itself to this purpose. The government, on the other hand, and in particular the Securities and Exchange Commission which had the responsibility of administering the act, were anxious to confine the first case under the act to the question of the duty of utilities to register with the Commission. The other provisions of the act — the so-called control provisions, relating to issuance of securities, acquisition of property, intercorporate loans, simplification of holding company structure, and the like — would thus be left for decision as cases should arise in the course of action taken by the SEC against particular companies. The SEC, moreover, was anxious that the first case should involve a relatively large and representative system, so that the practices which led to the enactment of the statute could be fully and fairly presented.

The utilities believed that they had found a case suitable in all respects for their purposes in the bankruptcy proceedings involving a relatively small holding company in the Maryland federal court. One possibility of a quick and broad decision, without the hindrance of having the government as a party to the suit (for this was prior to the 1937 act), was simply that the trustee in bankruptcy might ask the court for instructions regarding the validity of the act in order to direct the trustee whether or not to comply. In a similar case in the Delaware federal court, Judge Nields refused to give such instructions, stating that it was an attempt to secure a decision striking down an act of Congress in the absence of those who were responsible for administering it. Such a course, he said, would violate accepted canons of judicial procedure. [In re Central West Pub. Serv. Co., 13 F. Supp. 239 (D. Del. 1935).] To be sure, such constitutional decisions had frequently been given in the absence of government representation; but here there was the special factor that the case did not seem to contain the safeguards of an adversary proceeding.

In the Maryland case, counsel were more careful. They took pains to see that there would be adverse claims made in the bankruptcy proceedings with respect to the validity of the statute. One bondholder, a corporation owning $150,000 in first lien bonds of the debtor, took the position that its interest would best be served by an outright liquidation of the company. It maintained that the Holding Company Act would require a liquidation because no reorganization of the system would be possible under the simplification provisions of the statute. Consequently, its counsel was in the position of arguing for the validity of the statute. The opposing side was taken in an intervening petition by another creditor who owned $2500 in bonds of the debtor. He agreed that the Holding Company Act would require liquidation and prevent reorganization; but he alleged that he desired a reorganization. His interest, therefore, was in having the statute declared unconstitutional.

At this juncture the Securities and Exchange Commission, through its counsel, came on the scene and urged the district court not to pass on the constitutional questions in this proceeding. They argued that such a decision would be premature since the time for registration had not yet arrived and the Commission had taken no action regarding the company; that the facts concerning this holding-company system were not adequately disclosed in the agreed statement; that counsel on both sides had joined in construing the Holding Company Act as preventing reorganization, a doubtful construction which the Commission should have an opportunity to consider in administrative proceedings relating to this company; and, finally, that it did not appear that the interests of the respective creditors were genuinely adverse. The circumstances surrounding the intervention of the creditor holding $2500 in bonds and attacking the validity of the statute were disclosed when he was subpoenaed and examined by counsel for the SEC. It turned out that he was a dentist who had bought the securities through a local brokerage office, and his broker had asked him to sign the document which constituted the intervening petition. The circumstances are best revealed in his testimony: [The testimony is omitted.]

The district court refused to dismiss or delay the proceedings and rendered a decision declaring the entire statute unconstitutional. [In re American States Pub. Serv. Co., 12 F. Supp. 667 (D. Md. 1935).] This decision was affirmed by the circuit court of appeals. [81 F.2d 721 (4th Cir. 1936).] Both sides, that is, the two creditors, joined in asking the Supreme Court to take the case on certiorari in order that a prompt decision could be had. At this point government counsel made a last effort to prevent this case from being the vehicle for a decision on the validity of the act. The government filed a memorandum in the Supreme Court as a friend of the court urging the inappropriateness of the case and asking that certiorari be denied. The Supreme Court denied certiorari. [Burco v. Whitworth, 297 U.S. 724 (1936).] Thus the campaign to make this the test case finally failed.

Meanwhile the government was besieged with dozens of injunction suits scattered over the country brought by utility companies to restrain the enforcement of the act prior to the date for registration. In order to hold these cases in abeyance, the government took defensive action. All government officers who might have had authority to take steps toward the enforcement of the act were instructed to do nothing pending a decision by the Supreme Court in a test case. The Postmaster General so instructed local postmasters with respect to their power over the mails; the Attorney General so instructed United States attorneys with respect to their power to commence criminal proceedings; and the SEC itself disclaimed any intention to enforce the statute until a test of the registration provisions could be had. In order to encourage the companies to register and to contest specific applications of the act later if they were so inclined, the Commission announced that registration would not waive any constitutional objections that might subsequently be raised, and that if any court should hold that registration was a waiver, the registration should be considered to be rescinded. The most serious of the injunction suits were those in the District of Columbia, where jurisdiction could be had over the members of the Commission. In these suits, the Attorney General took the unusual course of appearing in the district court and himself arguing for a stay order until a case which meanwhile was brought in the federal court in New York could be decided. The New York case was planned by the SEC as the test case; it involved Electric Bond & Share Company and was a proceeding to compel it to register, with the company filing a cross-bill asking that the act as a whole and its various control provisions in particular be declared unconstitutional. The District of Columbia court granted a stay in the cases pending before it, and, with some modification of its terms, the stay order was approved by the Supreme Court. [Landis v. North American Co., 299 U.S. 248 (1936).] So at last the way was cleared for the test case which in due course wound its way from the district court in New York through the circuit court of appeals and to the Supreme Court, and which resulted in a decision upholding the registration provisions of the act and declining to pass on the so-called control provisions. [Electric Bond & Share Co. v. SEC, 303 U.S. 419 (1938).]

Both here and in the TVA cases, the basic contest was over the scope of the issues. If the government could keep the case within a relatively narrow compass, it could confidently expect success. The opposition staked its chances on opening up the statutes to the widest possible attack before the government had a chance to settle down to the task of administering them. The fate of the statutes may well have turned on *how* the constitutional questions were presented. . . .

Massachusetts v. Mellon; Frothingham v. Mellon 262 U.S. 447, 43 S. Ct. 597, 67 L. Ed. 1078 (1923)

Mr. Justice Sutherland delivered the opinion of the court:

These cases were argued and will be considered and disposed of together. The first is an original suit in this court. The other was brought in the supreme court of the District of Columbia. That court dismissed the bill and its decree was affirmed by the district court of appeals. Thereupon the case was brought here by appeal. Both cases challenge the constitutionality of the Act of November 23, 1921, commonly called the Maternity Act. Briefly, it provides for an initial appropriation and thereafter annual appropriations for a period of five years, to be apportioned among such of the several states as shall accept and comply with its provisions, for the purpose of co-operating with them to reduce maternal and infant mortality and protect the health of mothers and infants. It creates a bureau to administer the act in co-operation with state agencies, which are required to make such reports concerning their operations and expenditures as may be prescribed by the Federal bureau. Whenever that bureau shall determine that funds have not been properly expended in respect of any state, payments may be withheld.

It is asserted that these appropriations are for purposes not national, but local to the states, and, together with numerous similar appropriations, constitute an effective means of inducing the states to yield a portion of their sovereign rights. It is further alleged that the burden of the appropriations provided by this act and similar legislation falls unequally upon the several states, and rests largely upon the industrial states, such as Massachusetts; that the act is a usurpation of power not granted to Congress by the Constitution — an attempted exercise of the power of local self-government reserved to the states by the 10th Amendment; and that the defendants are proceeding to carry the act into operation. In the Massachusetts Case it is alleged that the plaintiff's rights and powers as a sovereign state and the rights of its citizens have been invaded and usurped by these expenditures and acts; and that, although the state has not accepted the act, its constitutional rights are infringed by the passage thereof and the imposition upon the state of an illegal and unconstitutional option either to yield to the Federal government a part of its reserved rights or lose the share which it would otherwise be entitled to receive of the moneys appropriated. In the Frothingham Case plaintiff alleges that the effect of the statute will be to take her property, under the guise of taxation, without due process of law.

We have reached the conclusion that the cases must be disposed of for want of jurisdiction, without considering the merits of the constitutional questions.

In the first case, the state of Massachusetts presents no justiciable controversy either in its own behalf or as the representative of its citizens. The appellant in the second suit has no such interest in the subject-matter, nor is any such injury inflicted or threatened, as will enable her to sue.

First. The state of Massachusetts in its own behalf, in effect, complains that the act in question invades the local concerns of the state, and is a usurpation of power; viz., the power of local self-government reserved to the states.

Probably it would be sufficient to point out that the powers of the state are not invaded, since the statute imposes no obligation, but simply extends an option which the state is free to accept or reject. But we do not rest here. Under article 3, §2, of the Constitution, the judicial power of this court extends "to controversies . . . between a state and citizens of another state," and the court has original jurisdiction "in all cases . . . in which a state shall be a party." The effect of this is not to confer jurisdiction upon the court merely because a state is a party, but only where it is a party to a proceeding of judicial cognizance. Proceedings not of a justiciable character are outside the contemplation of the constitutional grant. In Wisconsin v. Pelican Ins. Co., 127 U.S. 265, 289, Mr. Justice Gray, speaking for the court said:

"As to 'controversies between a state and citizens of another state.' The object of vesting in the courts of the United States jurisdiction of suits by one state against the citizens of another was to enable such controversies to be determined by a national tribunal, and thereby to avoid the partiality, or suspicion of partiality, which might exist if the plaintiff state were compelled to resort to the courts of the state of which the defendants were citizens. Federalist, No. 80; Chief Justice Jay, in Chisholm v. Georgia, 2 Dall. 419, 475; Story, Const. §§ 1638, 1682. The grant is of 'judicial power,' and was not intended to confer upon the courts of the United States jurisdiction of a suit or prosecution by the one state, of such a nature that it could not, on the settled principles of public and international law, be entertained by the judiciary of the other state at all."

That was an action brought by the state of Wisconsin to enforce a judgment of one of its own courts for a penalty against a resident of another state, and, in pursuance of the doctrine announced by the language just quoted, this court declined to assume jurisdiction upon the ground that the courts of no country will execute the penal laws of another.

In an earlier case it was held that a proceeding by mandamus by one state to compel the governor of another to surrender a fugitive from justice was not within the powers of the judicial department, since the duty of the governor in the premises was in the nature of a moral rather than a legal obligation. Kentucky v. Dennison, 24 How. 66, 109. In New Hampshire v. Louisiana, New York v. Louisiana, 108 U.S. 76, this court declined to take jurisdiction of actions to enforce payment of the bonds of another state for the benefit of the assignors, citizens of the plaintiff states. In Georgia v. Stanton, 6 Wall. 50, 75, and kindred cases, to which we shall presently refer, jurisdiction was denied in respect of questions of a political or governmental character. On the other hand, jurisdiction was maintained in Texas v. White, 7 Wall. 700, . . . because proprietary rights were involved; in Georgia v. Tennessee Copper Co., 206 U.S. 230, 237, because the right of dominion of the state over the air and soil within its domain was affected; in Missouri v. Holland, 252 U.S. 416, because, as asserted, there was an invasion, by acts done and threatened, of the quasi sovereign right of the state to regulate the taking of wild game within its borders; and, in other cases, because boundaries were in dispute. It is not necessary to cite additional cases. The foregoing, for present purposes, sufficiently indicate the jurisdictional line of demarcation.

What, then, is the nature of the right of the state here asserted, and how is it affected by this statute? Reduced to its simplest terms, it is alleged that the statute constitutes an attempt to legislate outside the powers granted to Congress by the Constitution, and within the field of local powers exclusively reserved to the states. Nothing is added to the force or effect of this assertion by the further incidental allegations that the ulterior purpose of Congress thereby was to induce the states to yield a portion of their sovereign rights; that the burden of the appropriations falls unequally upon the several states; and that there is imposed upon the states an illegal and unconstitutional option either to yield to the Federal government a part of their reserved rights, or lose their share of the moneys appropriated. But what burden is imposed upon the states, unequally or otherwise? Certainly there is none, unless it be the burden of taxation, and that falls upon their inhabitants, who are within the taxing power of Congress as well as that of the states where they reside. Nor does the statute require the states to do or to yield anything. If Congress enacted it with the ulterior purpose of tempting them to yield, that purpose may be effectively frustrated by the simple expedient of not yielding.

In the last analysis, the complaint of the plaintiff state is brought to the naked contention that Congress has usurped the reserved powers of the several states by the mere enactment of the statute, though nothing has been done and nothing is to be done without their consent; and it is plain that that question, as it is thus presented, is political, and not judicial, in character, and therefore is not a matter which admits of the exercise of the judicial power.

In Georgia v. Stanton, supra, this court held that a bill to enjoin the Secretary of War and other officers from carrying into execution certain acts of Congress, which it was asserted would annul and abolish the existing state government and establish another and different one in its place, called for a judgment upon a political question, and presented no case within the jurisdiction of the court. . . .

It follows that in so far as the case depends upon the assertion of a right on the part of the state to sue in its own behalf we are without jurisdiction. In that aspect of the case we are called upon to adjudicate, not rights of persons or property, not rights of dominion over physical domain, not quasi sovereign rights actually invaded or threatened, but abstract questions of political power, of sovereignty, of government. . . . If an alleged attempt by congressional action to annul and abolish an existing state government, "with all its constitutional powers and privileges," presents no justiciable issue, as was ruled in Georgia v. Stanton, supra, no reason can be suggested why it should be otherwise where the attempt goes no farther, as it is here alleged, than to propose to share with the state the field of state power.

We come next to consider whether the suit may be maintained by the state as the representative of its citizens. To this the answer is not doubtful. We need not go so far as to say that a state may never intervene by suit to protect its citizens against any form of enforcement of unconstitutional acts of Congress, but we are clear that the right to do so does not arise here. Ordinarily, at least, the only way in which a state may afford protection to its citizens in such cases is through the enforcement of its own criminal statutes, where that is appropriate, or by opening its courts to the injured persons for the maintenance of civil suits or actions. But the citizens of Massachusetts are also citizens of the United States. It cannot be conceded that a state, as parens patriae, may institute judicial proceedings to protect citizens of the United States from the operation of the statutes thereof. While the state, under some circumstances, may sue in that capacity for the protection of its citizens (Missouri v. Illinois, 180 U.S. 208, 241), it is no part of its duty or power to enforce their rights in respect of their relations with the Federal government. In that field it is the United States, and not the state, which represents them as parens patriae, when such representation becomes appropriate; and to the former, and not to the latter, they must look for such protective measures as flow from that status.

Second. The attack upon the statute in the Frothingham Case is, generally, the same, but this plaintiff alleges, in addition, that she is a taxpayer of the United States; and her contention, though not clear, seems to be that the effect of the appropriations complained of will be to increase the burden of future taxation and thereby take her property without due process of law. The right of a taxpayer to enjoin the execution of a Federal appropriation act, on the ground that it is invalid and will result in taxation for illegal purposes, has never been passed upon by this court. In cases where it was presented, the question has either been allowed to pass sub silentio, or the determination of it expressly withheld. [Citations omitted.] The case last cited came here from the court of appeals of the District of Columbia, and that court sustained the right of the plaintiff to sue by treating the case as one directed against the District of Columbia, and therefore subject to the rule frequently stated by this court, that resident taxpayers may sue to enjoin an illegal use of the moneys of a municipal corporation. Roberts v. Bradfield, 12 App. D.C. 453, 459, 460. The interest of a taxpayer of a municipality in the application of its moneys is direct and immediate, and the remedy by injunction to prevent their misuse is not inappropriate. It is upheld by a large number of state cases and is the rule of this court. Crampton v. Zabriskie, 101 U.S. 601, 609. Nevertheless, there are decisions to the contrary. See, for example, Miller v. Grandy, 13 Mich. 540, 550. The reasons which support the extension of the equitable remedy to a single taxpayer in such cases are based upon the peculiar relation of the corporate taxpayer to the corporation, which is not without some resemblance to that subsisting between stockholder and private corporation. 4 Dill. Mun. Corp. 5th ed. §§ 1580 et seq. But the relation of a taxpayer of the United States to the Federal government is very different. His interest in the moneys of the Treasury — partly realized from taxation and partly from other sources — is shared with millions of others; is comparatively minute and indeterminable; and the effect upon future taxation of any payment out of the funds so remote, fluctuating, and uncertain that no basis is afforded for an appeal to the preventive powers of a court of equity.

The administration of any statute likely to produce additional taxation to be imposed upon a vast number of taxpayers, the extent of whose several liability is indefinite and constantly changing, is essentially a matter of public, and not of individual, concern. If one taxpayer may champion and litigate such a cause, then every other taxpayer may do the same, not only in respect to the statute here under review, but also in respect of every other appropriation act and statute whose administration requires the outlay of public money, and whose validity may be questioned. The bare suggestion of such a result, with its attendant inconveniences, goes far to sustain the conclusion which we have reached, that a suit of this character cannot be maintained. It is of much significance that no precedent sustaining the right to maintain suits like this has been called to our attention, although, since the formation of the government, as an examination of the acts of Congress will disclose, a large number of statutes appropriating or involving the expenditure of moneys for non-Federal purposes have been enacted and carried into effect.

The functions of government under our system are apportioned. To the legislative department has been committed the duty of making laws; to the executive the duty of executing them; and to the judiciary, the duty of interpreting and applying them in cases properly brought before the courts. The general rule is that neither department may invade the province of the other, and neither may control, direct, or restrain the action of the other. We are not now speaking of the merely ministerial duties of officials. Gaines v. Thompson, 7 Wall. 347. We have no power per se to review and annul acts of Congress on the ground that they are unconstitutional. That question may be considered only when the justification for some direct injury suffered or threatened, presenting a justiciable issue, is made to rest upon such an act. Then the power exercised is that of ascertaining and declaring the law applicable to the controversy. It amounts to little more than the negative power to disregard an unconstitutional enactment, which otherwise would stand in the way of the enforcement of a legal right. The party who invokes the power must be able to show not only that the statute is invalid, but that he has sustained or is immediately in danger of sustaining some direct injury as the result of its enforcement, and not merely that he suffers in some indefinite way in common with people generally. If a case for preventive relief be presented, the court enjoins, in effect, not the execution of the statute, but the acts of the official, the statute notwithstanding. Here the parties plaintiff have no such case. Looking through forms of words to the substance of their complaint, it is merely that officials of the executive department of the government are executing and will execute an act of Congress asserted to be unconstitutional; and this we are asked to prevent. To do so would be not to decide a judicial controversy, but to assume a position of authority over the governmental acts of another and co-equal department, — an authority which plainly we do not possess.

No. 24, Original dismissed.

No. 962 affirmed.

NOTE Standing of States to Sue in Federal Court

What is a justiciable interest of a state? Massachusetts v. Mellon was distinguished in Oklahoma v. United States Civil Service Commission, 330 U.S. 127 (1947). There, the federal Civil Service Commission had determined that an employee of the State had violated provisions of the Hatch Act prohibiting political activity by employees of state agencies receiving federal funds. Pursuant to the act, the commission had determined that the agency discharge the employee or become ineligible to receive federal funds. See 5 U.S.C. §§1501-1508. Oklahoma brought suit challenging the commission's determination and attacking the constitutionality of the Hatch Act. The Court held that the state had standing to bring this attack. It noted that the act provided that any party aggrieved by an order of the commission could seek review thereof in federal court and that, on such review, the courts had the power "to examine the constitutionality of the statute by virtue of which the [commission's] order was entered."

Suits to resolve boundary disputes are perhaps the clearest example of the state's justiciable interest as a sovereign; see cases collected in North Dakota v. Minnesota, 263 U.S. 583 (1924). A state has standing to assert its power to tax, to enforce its contracts, and to protect its public works, its quasi-public institutions, or its interest as a proprietor. Texas v. Florida, 306 U.S. 398 (1939) (taxation); Kentucky v. Indiana, 281 U.S. 163 (1930) (contract between highway commissions for the building of a bridge); Pennsylvania v. Wheeling & Belmont Bridge Co., 13 How. 518 (1852) (revenues from public works); Hopkins Federal Savings & Loan Assn. v. Cleary, 296 U.S. 315 (1935) (state corporations being converted into federal ones); Alabama v. Arizona, 291 U.S. 286 (1934) (to enjoin enforcement of statutes of defendant states prohibiting sale of prison-made goods). A state also can maintain suit when its position is indistinguishable from that of a private person. Georgia v. Evans, 316 U.S. 159 (1942) (state as buyer of asphalt held a "person" within the federal antitrust provision for treble damage suits).

The more difficult questions lie in determining when to acknowledge the state in the role of "parens patriae." Clearly, no pecuniary interest is required. Kansas v. Colorado, 185 U.S. 125, 141-142 (1902). In Pennsylvania v. West Virginia, 262 U.S. 553 (1924), the Court gave standing to sue to protect a supply of natural gas for the state's schools and also for its private consumers. See pp. 390-396 infra. The state has a cognizable interest in keeping its domain free from public nuisances generated beyond its borders, and in preserving the natural flow of interstate rivers which touch or enter it. Georgia v. Tennessee Copper Co., 206 U.S. 230, 237 (1907) (noxious fumes); New York v. New Jersey, 256 U.S. 296 (1921) (sewage in New York harbor); North Dakota v. Minnesota, 263 U.S. 365 (1923) (to enjoin artificial drainage into an interstate river).

In Ohio v. Wyandotte Chemicals Corp., 401 U.S. 493 (1971), the Court denied leave to the state to file an original complaint against corporations of other states to abate an alleged nuisance caused by the dumping of mercury into tributaries of Lake Erie. Jursdiction was declined because of the availability of the state courts to decide the questions of state law and the complex factual issues involved. Douglas, J., dissented.

See also Illinois v. City of Milwaukee, 406 U.S. 91 (1972), and Washington v. General Motors Corp., 406 U.S. 109 (1972). Compare Vermont v. New York, 406 U.S. 186 (1972), which was not sent back to the lower courts.

Does the "parens patriae" role include protecting the state's economy against allegedly unlawful business practices? The state of Georgia complained of a conspiracy among railroads to fix freight rates so as "to deny to many of Georgia's products equal access with

108   *Chapter Three.*   **Judicial Review in Operation**

those of other states to the national market; . . . to hold the Georgia economy in a state of arrested development." Has Georgia standing as parens patriae? Georgia v. Pennsylvania R. Co., 324 U.S 439 (1945); compare Oklahoma v. Atchison, T. & S.F.R., 220 U.S. 277 (1911). Should a state be allowed to attack federal administrative action which affects its economy, or is that precluded by the principle of Massachusetts v. Mellon? Reliance upon that case and upon Florida v. Mellon barred Minnesota from challenging, as representative of its milk industry, a federal milk marketing order. State ex rel. Lord v. Benson, 274 F.2d 764 (D.C. Cir. 1960). Compare New York v. United States, 331 U.S. 284 (1947).

Where a state is also the defendant, the Eleventh Amendment may dictate limitations on the standing of the plaintiff state to assert rights as parens patriae. Compare the Tennessee Copper Co. case with North Dakota v. Minnesota, both supra. In the former, Mr. Justice Holmes said that it was "a suit by a State for an injury to it in its capacity of *quasi*-sovereign. In that capacity the State has an interest independent of and behind the titles of its citizens, in all the earth and air within its domain." 206 U.S. at 237. But in the latter, Chief Justice Taft held that although the state had standing to seek an injunction to protect "as parens patriae . . . the general comfort, health, or property rights of its inhabitants," the Eleventh Amendment took away its power to seek damages for injury already done. 263 U.S. at 375, 376. The Eleventh Amendment has precluded suit by a state as mere assignee of the bonds of another state, since the bonds were actually owned by the plaintiff state's citizens; but South Dakota was allowed to sue North Carolina as donee of a handful of North Carolina bonds, although the donation was motivated by the belief that South Dakota's suit would benefit the private holders of the bulk of the bonds. New Hampshire v. Louisiana, 108 U.S. 76 (1883); South Dakota v. North Carolina, 192 U.S. 286 (1904).

See generally Barnes, Suits Between States in the Supreme Court, 7 Vand. L. Rev. 494 (1954); Note, The Original Jurisdiction of the United States Supreme Court, 11 Stan. L. Rev. 665 (1959) (with an appendix listing all cases in which there was at least one opinion); Note, Original Jurisdiction of the U.S. Supreme Court over Cases to Which a State Is a Party, 39 Harv. L. Rev. 1084 (1926).

Before international tribunals, ordinarily only a nation can be a party. E.g., Statute, P.C.I.J. art 34(1). In a few instances nations have conferred upon individuals the right of direct access to international bodies. 1 Oppenheim, International Law 638 n.3 (8th ed. 1955); an interesting example is the Council of Europe's Convention for the Protection of Human Rights & Fundamental Freedoms, art. 25, signed at Rome Nov. 4, 1950, Gt. Brit. T.S., No. 71 (1953).

Doremus v. Board of Education   342 U.S. 429, 72 S. Ct. 394, 96 L. Ed. 475 (1952)

MR. JUSTICE JACKSON delivered the opinion of the Court.

This action for a declaratory judgment on a question of federal constitutional law was prosecuted in the state courts of New Jersey. It sought to declare invalid a statute of that State which provides for the reading, without comment, of five verses of the Old Testament at the opening of each public-school day. N.J. Rev. Stat., 1937, 18:14-77, N.J.S.A. No issue was raised under the State Constitution, but the Act was claimed to violate the clause of the First Amendment to the Federal Constitution prohibiting establishment of religion.

No trial was held and we have no findings of fact, but the trial court denied relief on the merits on the basis of the pleadings and a pretrial conference, of which the record contains meager notes. The Supreme Court of New Jersey, on appeal, rendered its opinion that the Act does not violate the Federal Constitution, in spite of jurisdictional doubts which it pointed out but condoned as follows: "No one is before us asserting that his religious practices have been interfered with or that his right to worship in accordance with the dictates of his conscience has been suppressed. No religious sect is a party to the cause. No representative of, or spokesman for, a religious body has attacked the statute here or below. One of the plaintiffs is 'a citizen and taxpayer'; the only interest he asserts is just that and in those words, set forth in the complaint and not followed by specification or proof. It is conceded that he is a citizen and a taxpayer, but it is not charged and it is neither conceded nor proved that the brief interruption in the day's schooling caused by compliance with the statute adds cost to the school expenses or varies by more than an incomputable scintilla the economy of the day's work. The other plaintiff, in addition to being a citizen and a taxpayer, has a daughter, aged seventeen, who is a student of the school. Those facts are asserted, but, as in the case of the co-plaintiff, no violated rights are urged. It is not charged that the practice required by the statute conflicts with the convictions of either mother or daughter. Apparently the sole purpose and the only function of plaintiffs is that they shall assume the role of actors so that there may be a suit which will invoke a court ruling upon the constitutionality of the statute. Respondents urge that under the circumstances the question is moot as to the plaintiffs-appellants and that our declaratory judgment statute may not properly be used in justification of such a proceeding. Cf. New Jersey Turnpike Authority v. Parsons, 3 N.J. 235; Commonwealth of Massachusetts v. Mellon (1923), 262 U.S. 447, at page 488. The point has substance but we have nevertheless concluded to dispose of the appeal on its merits." 1950, 5 N.J. 435, 439.

Upon appeal to this Court, we considered appellants' jurisdictional statement but, instead of noting probable jurisdiction, ordered that "further consideration of the jurisdiction of this Court and of the motion to dismiss or affirm is postponed to the hearing of the case on the merits." On further study, the doubts thus indicated ripen into a conviction that we should dismiss the appeal without reaching the constitutional question.

The view of the facts taken by the court below, though it is entitled to respect, does not bind us and we may make an independent examination of the record. Doing so, we find nothing more substantial in support of jurisdiction than did the court below. Appellants, apparently seeking to bring themselves within Illinois ex rel. McCollum v. Board of Education of School Dist. No. 71, 333 U.S. 203, assert a challenge to the Act in two capacities — one as parent of a child subject to it, and both as taxpayers burdened because of its requirements.

In support of the parent-and-school child relationship, the complaint alleged that appellant Klein was parent of a seventeen-year-old pupil in Hawthorne High School, where Bible reading was practiced pursuant to the Act. That is all. There is no assertion that she was injured or even offended thereby or that she was compelled to accept, approve or confess agreement with any dogma or creed or even to listen when the Scriptures were read. On the contrary, there was a pretrial stipulation that any student, at his own or his parents' request, could be excused during Bible reading and that in this case no such excuse was asked. However, it was agreed upon argument here that this child had graduated from the public schools before this appeal was taken to this Court. Obviously no decision we could render now would protect any rights she may once have had, and this Court does not sit to decide arguments after events have put them to rest. United States v. Alaska Steamship Co., 253 U.S. 113, 116.

The complaint is similarly niggardly of facts to support a taxpayer's grievance. Doremus is alleged to be a citizen and taxpayer of the State of New Jersey and of the Township of Rutherford, but any relation of that Township to the litigation is not disclosed to one not familiar with local geography. Klein is set out as a citizen and taxpayer of the Borough of Hawthorne in the State of New Jersey, and it is alleged that Hawthorne has a high school supported by public funds. In this school the Bible is read, according to statute. There is no allegation that this activity is supported by any separate tax or paid for from any particular appropriation or that it adds any sum whatever to the cost of conducting the school. No

110   Chapter Three.   Judicial Review in Operation

information is given as to what kind of taxes are paid by appellants and there is no averment that the Bible reading increases any tax they do pay or that as taxpayers they are, will, or possibly can be out of pocket because of it.

The State raised the defense that appellants showed no standing to maintain the action but, on pretrial conference, perhaps with premonitions of success, waived it and acquiesced in a determination of the federal constitutional question. Whether such facts amount to a justiciable case or controversy is decisive of our jurisdiction.

This Court has held that the interests of a taxpayer in the moneys of the federal treasury are too indeterminable, remote, uncertain and indirect to furnish a basis for an appeal to the preventive powers of the Court over their manner of expenditure. Alabama Power Co. v. Ickes, 302 U.S. 464, 478-479; Commonwealth of Massachusetts v. Mellon, 262 U.S. 447, 486 et seq. The latter case recognized, however, that "The interest of a taxpayer of a municipality in the application of its moneys is direct and immediate and the remedy by injunction to prevent their misuse is not inappropriate." 262 U.S. at page 486. Indeed, a number of states provide for it by statute or decisional law and such causes have been entertained in federal courts. Crampton v. Zabriskie, 101 U.S. 601, 609. See Commonwealth of Massachusetts v. Mellon, supra, 262 U.S. at page 486. Without disparaging the availability of the remedy by taxpayer's action to restrain unconstitutional acts which result in direct pecuniary injury, we reiterate what the Court said of a federal statute as equally true when a state Act is assailed: "The party who invokes the power must be able to show, not only that the statute is invalid, but that he has sustained or is immediately in danger of sustaining some direct injury as a result of its enforcement, and not merely that he suffers in some indefinite way in common with people generally." Commonwealth of Massachusetts v. Mellon, supra, 262 U.S. at page 488.

It is true that this Court found a justiciable controversy in Everson v. Board of Education, 330 U.S. 1. But Everson showed a measurable appropriation or disbursement of school-district funds occasioned solely by the activities complained of. This complaint does not.

We do not undertake to say that a state court may not render an opinion on a federal constitutional question even under such circumstances that it can be regarded only as advisory. But, because our own jurisdiction is cast in terms of "case or controversy," we cannot accept as the basis for review, nor as the basis for conclusive disposition of an issue of federal law without review, any procedure which does not constitute such.

The taxpayer's action can meet this test, but only when it is a good-faith pocketbook action. It is apparent that the grievance which it is sought to litigate here is not a direct dollars-and-cents injury but is a religious difference. If appellants established the requisite special injury necessary to a taxpayer's case or controversy, it would not matter that his dominant inducement to action was more religious than mercenary. It is not a question of motivation but of possession of the requisite financial interest that is, or is threatened to be, injured by the unconstitutional conduct. We find no such direct and particular financial interest here. If the Act may give rise to a legal case or controversy on some behalf, the appellants cannot obtain a decision from this Court by a feigned issue of taxation.

The motion to dismiss the appeal is granted.

Mr. Justice Douglas, with whom Mr. Justice Reed and Mr. Justice Burton concur, dissenting.

I think this case deserves a decision on the merits. There is no group more interested in the operation and management of the public schools than the taxpayers who support them and the parents whose children attend them. Certainly a suit by all the taxpayers to enjoin a practice authorized by the school board would be a suit by vital parties in interest. They would not be able to show, any more than the two present taxpayers have done, that the reading of the Bible adds to the taxes they pay. But if they were right in their contentions on the merits, they would establish that their public schools were being deflected from the educational program for which the taxes were raised. That seems to me to be an adequate interest for the maintenance of this suit by all the taxpayers. If all can do it, there is no apparent reason why less than all may not, the interest being the same. In the present case the issues are not feigned; the suit is not collusive; the mismanagement of the school system that is alleged is clear and plain.

If this were a suit to enjoin a federal law, it could not be maintained by reason of Commonwealth of Massachusetts v. Mellon, 262 U.S. 447, 486. But New Jersey can fashion her own rules governing the institution of suits in her courts. If she wants to give these taxpayers the status to sue (by analogy to the right of shareholders to enjoin ultra vires acts of their corporation) I see nothing in the Constitution to prevent it. . . .

Flast v. Cohen 392 U.S. 83, 88, S. Ct. 1942, 20 L. Ed. 2d 947 (1968)

Mr. Chief Justice Warren delivered the opinion of the Court.

In Frothingham v. Mellon, 262 U.S. 447 (1923), this Court ruled that a federal taxpayer is without standing to challenge the constitutionality of a federal statute. That ruling has stood for 45 years as an impenetrable barrier to suits against Acts of Congress brought by individuals who can assert only the interest of federal taxpayers. In this case, we must decide whether the Frothingham barrier should be lowered when a taxpayer attacks a federal statute on the ground that it violates the Establishment and Free Exercise Clauses of the First Amendment.

Appellants filed suit in the United States District Court for the Southern District of New York to enjoin the allegedly unconstitutional expenditure of federal funds under Titles I and II of the Elementary and Secondary Education Act of 1965, 79 Stat. 27, 20 U.S.C. §§241a et seq., 821 et seq. (1964 ed., Supp. II). The complaint alleged that the seven appellants had as a common attribute that "each pay income taxes of the United States," and it is clear from the complaint that the appellants were resting their standing to maintain the action solely on their status as federal taxpayers. The appellees, who are charged by Congress with administering the Elementary and Secondary Education Act of 1965, were sued in their official capacities.

The gravamen of the appellants' complaints was that federal funds appropriated under the Act were being used to finance instruction in reading, arithmetic, and other subjects in religious schools, and to purchase textbooks and other instructional materials for use in such schools. Such expenditures were alleged to be in contravention of the Establishment and Free Exercise Clauses of the First Amendment. Appellants' constitutional attack focused on the statutory criteria which state and local authorities must meet to be eligible for federal grants under the Act. . . . The specific criterion . . . attacked by the appellants is the requirement ". . . that, to the extent consistent with the number of educationally deprived children in the school district of the local educational agency who are enrolled in private elementary and secondary schools, such agency has made provision for including special educational services and arrangements (such as dual enrollment, educational radio and television, and mobile educational services and equipment) in which such children can participate . . ." 20 U.S.C. §241e(a)(2).

Under §206 of the Act, 20 U.S.C. §241f, the Commissioner of Education is given broad powers to supervise a State's participation in Title I programs and grants. Title II of the Act establishes a program of federal grants for the acquisition of school library resources, textbooks, and other printed and published instructional materials "for the use of children and teachers in public and private elementary and secondary schools." 20 U.S.C. §821. A State wishing to participate in the program must submit a plan to the Commissioner for approval, and the plan must ". . . provide assurance that to the extent consistent with law such library resources, textbooks, and other instructional materials will be provided on an equitable basis for the use of children and teachers in private elementary and secondary schools in the State. . . ." 20 U.S.C. §823(a)(3)(B).

While disclaiming any intent to challenge as unconstitutional all programs under Title I of the Act, the complaint alleges that federal funds have been disbursed under the Act, "with the consent and approval of the [appellees]," and that such funds have been used and will continue to be used to finance "instruction in reading, arithmetic and other subjects and for guidance in religious and sectarian schools" and "the purchase of textbooks and instructional and library materials for use in religious and sectarian schools." Such expenditures of federal tax funds, appellants alleged, violate the First Amendment because "they constitute a law respecting an establishment of religion" and because "they prohibit the free exercise of religion on the part of the [appellants] . . . by reason of the fact that they constitute compulsory taxation for religious purposes." The complaint asked for a declaration that the appellees' actions in approving the expenditure of federal funds for the alleged purposes were not authorized by the Act or, in the alternative, that if appellees' actions are deemed within the authority and intent of the Act, "the Act is to that extent unconstitutional and void." The complaint also prayed for an injunction to enjoin appellees from approving any expenditure of federal funds for the allegedly unconstitutional purposes. The complaint further requested that a three-judge court be convened as provided in 28 U.S.C. §§2282, 2284.

The Government moved to dismiss the complaint on the ground that appellants lacked standing to maintain the action. District Judge Frankel, who considered the motion, recognized that Frothingham v. Mellon, supra, provided "powerful" support for the Government's position, but he ruled that the standing question was of sufficient substance to warrant the convening of a three-judge court to decide the question. 267 F. Supp. 351 (1967). The three-judge court received briefs and heard arguments limited to the standing question, and the court ruled on the authority of Frothingham that appellants lacked standing. Judge Frankel dissented. 271 F. Supp. 1 (1967). From the dismissal of their complaint on that ground, appellants appealed directly to this Court, 28 U.S.C. §1253, and we noted probable jurisdiction. 389 U.S. 895 (1967). For reasons explained at length below, we hold that appellants do have standing as federal taxpayers to maintain this action, and the judgment below must be reversed.

I

[Discussion of the convening of a three-judge District Court, and of jurisdiction to review the decision of that Court by direct appeal, is omitted.]

II

. . . Although the barrier Frothingham erected against federal taxpayer suits has never been breached, the decision has been the source of some confusion and the object of considerable criticism. The confusion has developed as commentators have tried to determine whether Frothingham establishes a constitutional bar to taxpayer suits or whether the Court was simply imposing a rule of self-restraint which was not constitutionally compelled. The conflicting viewpoints are reflected in the arguments made to this Court by the parties in this case. The Government has pressed upon us the view that Frothingham announced a constitutional rule, compelled by the Article III limitations on federal court jurisdiction and grounded in considerations of the doctrine of separation of powers. Appellants, however, insist that Frothingham expressed no more than a policy of judicial self-restraint which can be disregarded when compelling reasons for assuming jurisdiction over a taxpayer's suit exist. The opinion delivered in Frothingham can be read to support either position. The concluding sentence of the opinion states that, to take jurisdiction of the taxpayer's suit, "would be not to decide a judicial controversy, but to assume a position of authority over the governmental acts of another and co-equal department, an authority which plainly we do not possess." 262 U.S., at 489. Yet the concrete reasons given for denying standing to a federal taxpayer suggest that the Court's holding rests on something less than a constitutional foundation. For example, the Court conceded that standing had previously been conferred on municipal taxpayers to sue in that capacity. However, the Court viewed the interest of a federal taxpayer in total federal tax revenues as "comparatively minute and indeterminable" when measured against a municipal taxpayer's interest in a smaller city treasury. Id., at 486-487. This suggests that the petitioner in Frothingham was denied standing not because she was a taxpayer but because her tax bill was not large enough. In addition, the Court spoke of the "attendant inconveniences" of entertaining that taxpayer's suit because it might open the door of federal courts to countless such suits "in respect of every other appropriation act and statute whose administration requires the outlay of public money, and whose validity may be questioned." Id., at 487. Such a statement suggests pure policy considerations.

To the extent that Frothingham has been viewed as resting on policy considerations, it has been criticized as depending on assumptions not consistent with modern conditions. For example, some commentators have pointed out that a number of corporate taxpayers today have a federal tax liability running into hundreds of millions of dollars, and such taxpayers have a far greater monetary stake in the Federal Treasury than they do in any municipal treasury. To some degree, the fear expressed in Frothingham that allowing one taxpayer to sue would inundate the federal courts with countless similar suits has been mitigated by the ready availability of the devices of class actions and joinder under the Federal Rules of Civil Procedure, adopted subsequent to the decision in Frothingham. Whatever the merits of the current debate over Frothingham, its very existence suggests that we should undertake a fresh examination of the limitations upon standing to sue in a federal court and the application of those limitations to taxpayer suits.

III

. . . Embodied in the words "cases" and "controversies" are two complementary but somewhat different limitations. In part those words limit the business of federal courts to questions presented in an adversary context and in a form historically viewed as capable of resolution through the judicial process. And in part those words define the role assigned to the judiciary in a tripartite allocation of power to assure that the federal courts will not intrude into areas committed to the other branches of government. Justiciability is the term of art employed to give expression to this dual limitation placed upon federal courts by the case-and-controversy doctrine.

Justiciability is itself a concept of uncertain meaning and scope. Its reach is illustrated by the various grounds upon which questions sought to be adjudicated in federal courts have been held not to be justiciable. Thus, no justiciable controversy is presented when the parties seek adjudication of only a political question, when the parties are asking for an advisory opinion, when the question sought to be adjudicated has been mooted by subsequent developments, and when there is no standing to maintain the action. Yet it remains true that "[j]usticiability is . . . not a legal concept with a fixed content or susceptible of scientific verification. Its utilization is the resultant of many subtle pressures. . . ." Poe v. Ullman, 367 U.S. 497, 508 (1961).

Part of the difficulty in giving precise meaning and form to the concept of justiciability stems from the uncertain historical antecedents of the case-and-controversy doctrine. For example, Mr. Justice Frankfurter twice suggested that historical meaning could be imparted to the concepts of justiciability and case and controversy by reference to the practices of the courts of Westminster when the Constitution was adopted. Joint Anti-Fascist Committee v. McGrath, 341 U.S. 123, 150 (1951) (concurring opinion); Coleman v.

Miller, 307 U.S. 433, 460 (1939) (separate opinion). However, the power of English judges to deliver advisory opinions was well-established at the time the Constitution was drafted. 3 K. Davis, Administrative Law Treatise 127-128 (1958). And it is quite clear that "the oldest and most consistent thread in the federal law of justiciability is that the federal courts will not give advisory opinions." C. Wright, Federal Courts 34 (1963). Thus, the implicit policies embodied in Article III, and not history alone, impose the rule against advisory opinions on federal courts. When the federal judicial power is invoked to pass upon the validity of actions by the Legislative and Executive Branches of the Government, the rule against advisory opinions implements the separation of powers prescribed by the Constitution and confines federal courts to the role assigned them by Article III. See Muskrat v. United States, 219 U.S. 346 (1911); 3 H. Johnston, Correspondence and Public Papers of John Jay 486–489 (1891) (correspondence between Secretary of State Jefferson and Chief Justice Jay). However, the rule against advisory opinions also recognizes that such suits often "are not pressed before the Court with that clear concreteness provided when a question emerges precisely framed and necessary for decision from a clash of adversary argument exploring every aspect of a multifaced situation embracing conflicting and demanding interests." United States v. Fruehauf, 365 U.S. 146, 157 (1961). Consequently, the Article III prohibition against advisory opinions reflects the complementary constitutional considerations expressed by the justiciability doctrine: Federal judicial power is limited to those disputes which confine federal courts to a role consistent with a system of separated powers and which are traditionally thought to be capable of resolution through the judicial process. . . .

Standing is an aspect of justiciability and, as such, the problem of standing is surrounded by the same complexities and vagaries that inhere in justiciability. Standing has been called one of "the most amorphous [concepts] in the entire domain of public law." Some of the complexities peculiar to standing problems result because standing "serves, on occasion, as a shorthand expression for all the various elements of justiciability." In addition, there are at work in the standing doctrine the many subtle pressures which tend to cause policy considerations to blend into constitutional limitations.

Despite the complexities and uncertainties, some meaningful form can be given to the jurisdictional limitations placed on federal court power by the concept of standing. The fundamental aspect of standing is that it focuses on the party seeking to get his complaint before a federal court and not on the issues he wishes to have adjudicated. The "gist of the question of standing" is whether the party seeking relief has "alleged such a personal stake in the outcome of the controversy as to assure that concrete adverseness which sharpens the presentation of issues upon which the court so largely depends for illumination of difficult constitutional questions." Baker v. Carr, 369 U.S. 186, 204 (1962). In other words, when standing is placed in issue in a case, the question is whether the person whose standing is challenged is a proper party to request an adjudication of a particular issue and not whether the issue itself is justiciable. Thus, a party may have standing in a particular case, but the federal court may nevertheless decline to pass on the merits of the case because, for example, it presents a political question. A proper party is demanded so that federal courts will not be asked to decide "ill-defined controversies over constitutional issues," United Public Workers v. Mitchell, 330 U.S. 75, 90 (1947), or a case which is of "a hypothetical or abstract character," Aetna Life Insurance Co. v. Haworth, 300 U.S. 227, 240 (1937). So stated, the standing requirement is closely related to, although more general than, the rule that federal courts will not entertain friendly suits, Chicago & Grand Trunk R. Co. v. Wellman, [143 U.S. 339], or those which are feigned or collusive in nature, United States v. Johnson, 319 U.S. 302 (1943); Lord v. Veazie, 8 How. 251 (1850).

When the emphasis in the standing problem is placed on whether the person invoking a federal court's jurisdiction is a proper party to maintain the action, the weakness of the Government's argument in this case becomes apparent. . . . Thus, in terms of Article III limitations on federal court jurisdiction, the question of standing is related only to whether the dispute sought to be adjudicated will be presented in an adversary context and in a form historically viewed as capable of judicial resolution. It is for that reason that the emphasis in standing problems is on whether the party invoking federal court jurisdiction has "a personal stake in the outcome of the controversy," Baker v. Carr, supra, at 204, and whether the dispute touches upon "the legal relations of parties having adverse legal interests." Aetna Life Insurance Co. v. Haworth, supra, at 240-241. A taxpayer may or may not have the requisite personal stake in the outcome, depending upon the circumstances of the particular case. Therefore, we find no absolute bar in Article III to suits by federal taxpayers challenging allegedly unconstitutional federal taxing and spending programs. There remains, however, the problem of determining the circumstances under which a federal taxpayer will be deemed to have the personal stake and interest that imparts the necessary concrete adverseness to such litigation so that standing can be conferred on the taxpayer qua taxpayer consistent with the constitutional limitations of Article III.

IV

The various rules of standing applied by federal courts have not been developed in the abstract. Rather, they have been fashioned with specific reference to the status asserted by the party whose standing is challenged and to the type of question he wishes to have adjudicated. We have noted that, in deciding the question of standing, it is not relevant that the substantive issues in the litigation might be nonjusticiable. However, our decisions establish that, in ruling on standing, it is both appropriate and necessary to look to the substantive issues for another purpose, namely, to determine whether there is a logical nexus between the status asserted and the claim sought to be adjudicated. For example, standing requirements will vary in First Amendment religion cases depending upon whether the party raises an Establishment Clause claim or a claim under the Free Exercise Clause. See McGowan v. Maryland, 366 U.S. 420, 429-430 (1961). Such inquiries into the nexus between the status asserted by the litigant and the claim he presents are essential to assure that he is a proper and appropriate party to invoke federal judicial power. Thus, our point of reference in this case is the standing of individuals who assert only the status of federal taxpayers and who challenge the constitutionality of a federal spending program. Whether such individuals have standing to maintain that form of action turns on whether they can demonstrate the necessary stake as taxpayers in the outcome of the litigation to satisfy Article III requirements.

The nexus demanded of federal taxpayers has two aspects to it. First, the taxpayer must establish a logical link between that status and the type of legislative enactment attacked. Thus, a taxpayer will be a proper party to allege the unconstitutionality only of exercises of congressional power under the taxing and spending clause of Art. I, §8, of the Constitution. It will not be sufficient to allege an incidental expenditure of tax funds in the administration of an essentially regulatory statute. This requirement is consistent with the limitation imposed upon state taxpayer standing in federal courts in Doremus v. Board of Education, 342 U.S. 429 (1952). Secondly the taxpayer must establish a nexus between that status and the precise nature of the constitutional infringement alleged. Under this requirement, the taxpayer must show that the challenged enactment exceeds specific constitutional limitations imposed upon the exercise of the congressional taxing and spending power and not simply that the enactment is generally beyond the powers delegated to Congress by Art I, §8. When both nexuses are established, the litigant will have shown a taxpayer's stake in the outcome of the controversy and will be a proper and appropriate party to invoke a federal court's jurisdiction.

The taxpayer-appellants in this case have satisfied both nexuses to support their claim of standing under the test we announce today. Their constitutional challenge is made to an exercise by Congress of its power under Art. I, §8, to spend for the general welfare, and the challenged program involves a substantial expenditure of federal tax funds. In addition, appellants have alleged that the challenged expenditures violate the Establishment and Free Exercise Clauses of the First Amendment. Our history vividly illustrates that one of the specific evils feared by those who drafted the Establishment Clause and fought for its adoption was that the taxing and spending power would be used to favor one religion over another or to support religion in general. . . .

The allegations of the taxpayer in Frothingham v. Mellon, supra, were quite different from those made in this case, and the result in Frothingham is consistent with the test of taxpayer standing announced today. The taxpayer in Frothingham attacked a federal spending program and she, therefore, established the first nexus required. However, she lacked standing because her constitutional attack was not based on an allegation that Congress, in enacting the Maternity Act of 1921, has breached a specific limitation upon its taxing and spending power. The taxpayer in Frothingham alleged essentially that Congress, by enacting the challenged statute, had exceeded the general powers delegated to it by Art. I, §8, and that Congress had thereby invaded the legislative province reserved to the States by the Tenth Amendment. . . . In essence, Mrs. Frothingham was attempting to assert the States' interest in their legislative prerogatives and not a federal taxpayer's interest in being free of taxing and spending in contravention of specific constitutional limitations imposed upon Congress' taxing and spending power.

We have noted that the Establishment Clause of the First Amendment does specifically limit the taxing and spending power conferred by Art. I, §8. Whether the Constitution contains other specific limitations can be determined only in the context of future cases. . . .

While we express no view at all on the merits of appellants' claims in this case, their complaint contains sufficient allegations under the criteria we have outlined to give them standing to invoke a federal court's jurisdiction for an adjudication on the merits.

Reversed.

[Concurring opinions of JUSTICES DOUGLAS, STEWART, and FORTAS are omitted.]

MR. JUSTICE HARLAN, dissenting. The problems presented by this case are narrow and relatively abstract, but the principles by which they must be resolved involve nothing less than the proper functioning of the federal courts, and so run to the roots of our constitutional system. The nub of my view is that the end result of Frothingham v. Mellon, 262 U.S. 447, was correct, even though, like others, I do not subscribe to all of its reasoning and premises. Although I therefore agree with certain of the conclusions reached today by the Court, I cannot accept the standing doctrine that it substitutes for Frothingham, for it seems to me that this new doctrine rests on premises that do not withstand analysis. Accordingly, I repectfully dissent. . . .

As I understand it, the Court's position is that it is unnecessary to decide in what circumstances public actions should be permitted, for it is possible to identify situations in which taxpayers who contest the constitutionality of federal expenditures assert "personal" rights and interests, identical in principle to those asserted by Hohfeldian plaintiffs.[5] This position, if supportable, would of course avoid many of the difficulties of this case; indeed, if the Court is correct, its extended exploration of the subtleties of Article III is entirely unnecessary. But, for reasons that follow, I believe that the Court's position is untenable.

The Court's analysis consists principally of the observation that the requirements of standing are met if a taxpayer has the "requisite personal stake in the outcome" of his suit.

---

[5] The phrase is Professor Jaffe's, adopted, of course, from W. Hohfeld, Fundamental Legal Conceptions (1923). I have here employed the phrases "Hohfeldian" and "non-Hohfeldian" plaintiffs to mark the distinction between the personal and proprietary interests of the traditional plaintiff, and the representative and public interests of the plaintiff in a public action. I am aware that we are confronted here by a spectrum of interests of varying intensities, but the distinction is sufficiently accurate, and convenient, to warrant its use at least for purposes of discussion. [Text originally at footnote 5 has been deleted and footnote repositioned. — ED.]

. . . This does not, of course, resolve the standing problem; it merely restates it. The Court implements this standard with the declaration that taxpayers will be "deemed" to have the necessary personal interest if their suits satisfy two criteria: *first*, the challenged expenditure must form part of a federal spending program, and not merely be "incidental" to a regulatory program; and *second*, the constitutional provision under which the plaintiff claims must be a "specific limitation" upon Congress' spending powers. The difficulties with these criteria are many and severe, but it is enough for the moment to emphasize that they are not in any sense a measurement of any plaintiff's interest in the outcome of any suit. As even a cursory examination of the criteria will show, the Court's standard for the determination of standing and its criteria for the satisfaction of that standard are entirely unrelated. . . .

. . . The intensity of a plaintiff's interest in a suit is not measured, even obliquely, by the fact that the constitutional provision under which he claims is, or is not, a "specific limitation" upon Congress' spending powers. Thus, among the claims in Frothingham was the assertion that the Maternity Act, 42 Stat. 224, deprived the petitioner of property without due process of law. The Court has evidently concluded that this claim did not confer standing because the Due Process Clause of the Fifth Amendment is not a specific limitation upon the spending powers. Disregarding for the moment the formidable obscurity of the Court's categories, how can it be said that Mrs. Frothingham's interests in her suit were, as a consequence of her choice of a constitutional claim, necessarily less intense than those, for example, of the present appellants? I am quite unable to understand how, if a taxpayer believes that a given public expenditure is unconstitutional, and if he seeks to vindicate that belief in a federal court, his interest in the suit can be said necessarily to vary according to the constitutional provision under which he states his claim. . . .

. . . The difficulty, with which the Court never comes to grips, is that taxpayers' suits under the Establishment Clause are not in these circumstances meaningfully different from other public actions. If this case involved a tax specifically designed for the support of religion, as was the Virginia tax opposed by Madison in his Memorial and Remonstrance, I would agree that taxpayers have rights under the religious clauses of the First Amendment that would permit them standing to challenge the tax's validity in the federal courts. But this is not such a case, and appellants challenge an expenditure, not a tax. . . .

It seems to me clear that public actions, whatever the constitutional provisions on which they are premised, may involve important hazards for the continued effectiveness of the federal judiciary. Although I believe such actions to be within the jurisdiction conferred upon the federal courts by Article III of the Constitution, there surely can be little doubt that they strain the judicial function and press to the limit judicial authority. There is every reason to fear that unrestricted public actions might well alter the allocation of authority among the three branches of the Federal Government. It is not, I submit, enough to say that the present members of the Court would not seize these opportunities for abuse, for such actions would, even without conscious abuse, go far toward the final transformation of this Court into the Council of Revision which, despite Madison's support, was rejected by the Constitutional Convention. I do not doubt that there must be "some effectual power in the government to restrain or correct the infractions" of the Constitution's several commands, but neither can I suppose that such power resides only in the federal courts. We must as judges recall that, as Mr. Justice Holmes wisely observed, the other branches of the Government "are ultimate guardians of the liberties and welfare of the people in quite as great a degree as the courts." Missouri, Kansas & Texas R. Co. v. May, 194 U.S. 267, 270. The powers of the federal judiciary will be adequate for the great burdens placed upon them only if they are employed prudently, with recognition of the strengths as well as the hazards that go with our kind of representative government. . . .

. . . This Court has previously held that individual litigants have standing to represent the public interest, despite their lack of economic or other personal interests, if Congress has appropriately authorized such suits. See especially Oklahoma v. Civil Service Comm'n., 330 U.S. 127, 137-139. Compare Perkins v. Lukens Steel Co., 310 U.S. 113, 125-127. I would adhere to that principle. . . .

NOTE Standing

1. *Standing to challenge the actions of government agencies.* Does a *competitor* have standing to enjoin government competition? In Tennessee Electric Power Co. v. TVA, 306 U.S. 118 (1939), the nineteen electric utility companies that sued to enjoin the sale of power by the Authority were held not entitled to raise the issue of constitutionality. The competition, the Court held, was damnum absque injuria. The "right invaded" must be "a legal right, — one of property, one arising out of contract, one protected against tortious invasion, or one founded on a statute which confers a privilege." 306 U.S. at 137-138. Earlier the Court had reached a similar result in a suit by utility companies to enjoin as unconstitutional the making of loans and grants by the Public Works Administration to municipalities for the construction of competing electric systems. Alabama Power Co. v. Ickes, 302 U.S. 464 (1938).

If the nineteen-company suit had been decided prior to the Ashwander case, would the stockholders' standing have been stronger or weaker?

Does a *consumer* have standing to attack a minimum price order? In City of Atlanta v. Ickes, 308 U.S. 517 (1939), in a per curiam opinion, the Court held that the city, as a consumer, could not attack an order setting a minimum price for coal. But compare Associated Industries v. Ickes, 134 F.2d 694 (2d Cir. 1943), remanded as moot, 320 U.S. 707 (1943), where the court of appeals held that an association of consumers was a "party aggrieved" under the review provisions of the Bituminous Coal Act. See Davis, Administrative Law 705-708 (1951).

Standing to challenge the actions of government agencies has been considerably broadened by recent decisions interpreting the Administrative Procedure Act. Under §10 of the act, 5 U.S.C. §702 (1970), "A person suffering legal wrong because of agency action, or adversely affected or aggrieved by agency action within the meaning of a relevant statute, is entitled to judicial review thereof." In Association of Data Processing Service Organizations v. Camp, 397 U.S. 150 (1970), sellers of data processing services sought to challenge a ruling by the Comptroller of the Currency permitting national banks to sell data processing services to other banks and to bank customers. Plaintiffs relied on §10 of the A.P.A. and on §4 of the Bank Service Corporation Act of 1962, 12 U.S.C. §1864, which provides: "No bank service corporation may engage in any activity other than the performance of bank services of banks." Reversing both the district court and court of appeals, the Supreme Court, per Justice Douglas, held that plaintiffs had standing to bring their action. The Court prescribed a three-part text: (1) to satisfy the Article III requirement of a case or controversy plaintiff need allege only that "the challenged action has caused him injury in fact, economic or otherwise," and not that it has harmed his statutory or contractual "legal interests"; (2) plaintiff must be "arguably . . . within the zone of interests protected by" the substantive statutory provision involved, here §4 of the Bank Service Corporation Act; and (3) there must be no evidence that Congress affirmatively sought to preclude the judicial review sought by plaintiff. See also Barlow v. Collins, 397 U.S. 159 (1970).

The requirements of the "injury in fact" test have been considered in two more recent Supreme Court decisions. In Sierra Club v. Morton, 405 U.S. 727 (1972), the Court held that a complaint filed by an environmentalist organization challenging United States Forest Service decisions on the use of Mineral King Valley in Sequoia National Forest failed to allege "injury in fact." The Court acknowledged that harm to "aesthetic and environmental well-being" could constitute sufficient injury; but, through Justice Stewart, standing was not established where the plaintiff failed to allege "that it or its members would be affected in any of their activities or pastimes" by development of a ski resort at Mineral King. Without such an allegation of particular harm, the Court continued, plaintiff's "longstanding concern with and expertise in" environmental matters was insufficient to qualify it to bring a challenge to the Forest Service decision even in the name of the "public interest."

In United States v. Students Challenging Regulatory Agency Procedures (SCRAP), 412 U.S. 669 (1973), an environmental group sought to challenge an Interstate Commerce Commission decision to allow an increase in railroad freight rates. The plaintiff alleged that the rate increase would lead to decreased use of recyclable goods, thus promoting mining and other extractive activities to procure raw materials and accumulation of waste materials in the environment. SCRAP alleged that its members were being forced by the Commission decision to pay more for finished products and to suffer in the use of natural resources in the Washington area which would be subjected to increased pollution as the result of the order. The Court held that these allegations were sufficient to give standing. They met the test of alleging "perceptible harm," whose truth could be tested at trial or on motion for summary judgment.

In Simon v. Eastern Kentucky Welfare Rights Organization, 426 U.S. 26 (1976), the Court may have retreated from the liberalized position on standing exemplified in SCRAP, supra. Plaintiffs, indigent individuals (and their organizations) who had been denied hospital services, sued under the Administrative Procedure Act to set aside a revenue ruling that relaxed the criteria for charitable status of hospitals. No longer must a hospital provide services for indigents to its maximum financial capacity; it would suffice to provide emergency-room treatment. On the pleadings, which alleged that hospitals were "encouraged" by the new regulation to constrict their services for the poor, the Court held that insufficient causal connection was alleged, for purposes of Article III jurisdiction, between plaintiffs' damage and the actions of defendant revenue officials. Should the case have been treated in the special context of tax litigation, where the plaintiff, not a comparable taxpayer, asserts standing to complain of the tax treatment given to another? See the critique in 90 Harv. L. Rev. 205 (1976).

See also Trafficante v. Metropolitan Life Ins. Co., 409 U.S. 205 (1972); Scott, Standing in the Supreme Court — A Functional Analysis, 86 Harv. L. Rev. 645 (1973); Lewis, Constitutional Rights and the Misuse of "Standing," 14 Stan. L. Rev. 433 (1962); Sadler, Standing to Assert Jus Tertii in the Supreme Court, 71 Yale L.J. 599 (1962); Note, The Supreme Court and Standing to Sue, 34 N.Y.U.L. Rev. 141 (1959); Jaffe, Standing to Secure Judicial Review: Private Actions, 75 Harv. L. Rev. 255 (1961); Davis, The Liberalized Law of Standing, 37 U. Chi. L. Rev. 450 (1970).

2. *Citizen and taxpayer standing after Flast v. Cohen.* In companion decisions delivered by Chief Justice Burger, the Court limited the scope of taxpayer standing at issue in Flast. In Schlesinger v. Reservists Committee to Stop the War, 418 U.S. 208 (1974), plaintiffs sought declaratory and injunctive relief against the Department of Defense for enrolling members of Congress as reserve officers. Plaintiffs claimed this practice was in violation of the Ineligibility and Incompatibility Clauses, art. I, §6, which provide:

"No Senator or Representative shall, during the Time for which he was elected, be appointed to any civil Office under the Authority of the United States, which shall have been created, or the Emoluments whereof shall have been encreased during such time; and no Person holding any Office under the United States, shall be a Member of either House during his Continuance in Office."

The Court held that plaintiffs had failed to establish standing, whether as citizens or as taxpayers. The Court noted that as citizens plaintiffs shared with all others only an "abstract" interest in the observance of the Incompatibility Clause, and that allegations of specific harm resulting from nonobservance were "nothing more than a matter of speculation." As taxpayers, the Court went on, plaintiffs had failed to show the "nexus" required under Flast between the challenged government action and the exercise of the taxing and spending power.

In United States v. Richardson, 418 U.S. 166 (1974), plaintiff brought suit as a federal taxpayer claiming that §8 of the Central Intelligence Agency Act, 50 U.S.C. 403j(b), exempting the Agency from public reporting of expenditures, violated Article I, §9, cl. 7, which provides:

"No Money shall be drawn from the Treasury, but in Consequence of Appropriations made by Law; and a regular Statement and Account of the Receipts and Expenditures of all public Money shall be published from time to time."

In an opinion delivered by Chief Justice Burger the Court held that plaintiff had failed to establish taxpayer standing under Flast, as his challenge was not to an exercise of the taxing and spending clause, art. I, §8. To plaintiff's claim that he had nonetheless alleged injury in fact of another sort, stemming from the inability of citizens to "intelligently follow the actions of Congress or the Executive" with respect to the Agency, the Court replied that this alleged only an "undifferentiated" interest rather than a "particular concrete injury."

See Note, The Supreme Court, 1973 Term, 88 Harv. L. Rev. 41, 236-243 (1974).

3. *Standing to assert the rights of third parties*. It is commonly said that one who attacks a statute as unconstitutional must show that *as applied to him* the statute is invalid. But despite a general rule that "[o]rdinarily, one may not claim standing in this Court to vindicate the constitutional rights of some third party," Barrows v. Jackson, 346 U.S. 249, 255 (1953), the Supreme Court has recognized such standing in a variety of situations.

In Thornhill v. Alabama, 310 U.S. 88 (1940), the Court held that a person charged with violation of a statute which on its face implicates First Amendment liberties may challenge the statute as impermissibly vague or overbroad as to other persons, regardless of the constitutionality of its application in his own case. The Court reasoned that the "chilling effect" of an overbroad statute on protected First Amendment activities justifies its evaluation in terms of hypothetical as well as actual applications. See Gooding v. Wilson, 405 U.S. 518 (1972); Coates v. City of Cincinnati, 402 U.S. 611 (1971); Note, The First Amendment Overbreadth Doctrine, 83 Harv. L. Rev. 844 (1970). For application of the general rule where First Amendment values are not involved, see United States v. National Dairy Corp., 372 U.S. 29 (1963); United States v. Raines, 362 U.S. 17 (1960).

In recent decisions, however, the Court has signaled a retreat from a broad reading of Thornhill. In Broadrick v. Oklahoma, 413 U.S. 601 (1973), the Court held that as an exception to the general rule against third-party standing, the Thornhill doctrine becomes severely attenuated as the implicated First Amendment activity moves from speech to conduct and as the danger to protected activity becomes less "substantial." The Court therefore rejected an overbreadth attack on a statute restricting political activity by state employees. Similarly, in Parker v. Levy, 417 U.S. 733 (1974), the Court rejected an overbreadth attack on provisions of the Uniform Code of Military Justice on the grounds that the military context justified a narrower reading of First Amendment protections and that the particular conduct of the defendant was clearly within the permissible scope of the Military Code provisions.

Standing to assert the constitutional rights of third parties has been recognized in other circumstances. In Barrows v. Jackson, supra, a party to a racially restrictive covenant who had sold her property to a black was sued for damages by the other parties to the covenant. The Court held that although enforcement of the covenant against the defendant imperiled none of her own constitutional rights, she had standing to assert the rights of black purchasers. The Court noted that defendant herself had a substantial pecuniary interest in the case, that the rights of black purchasers would be much interfered with, or "diluted," if sellers were exposed to damage claims, and that "it would be difficult if not impossible for the persons whose rights are asserted to present their grievance before any court."

A special relationship between the asserter and the third party has frequently been held to support a finding of third-party standing. In NAACP v. Alabama ex rel. Patterson, 357 U.S. 449 (1958), an organization challenging an order to disclose its membership lists was held entitled to assert the First Amendment interests of its members. In Eisenstadt v. Baird, 405 U.S. 438 (1972), and Griswold v. Connecticut, 381 U.S. 479 (1965), the Court held that a distributor of contraceptives, an official of the Planned Parenthood League, and a physician had standing to assert third-party rights of access to contraceptive devices. Compare Tileston v. Ullman, 318 U.S. 44 (1943).

In Buchanan v. Warley, 245 U.S. 60 (1917), the Court sustained an appeal by a white person who challenged, under the Equal Protection Clause, a section of a city ordinance making it illegal for a Negro to occupy a residence on a block predominantly inhabited by white persons. The appellant had contracted to sell his property to the appellee, a Negro, on condition that the latter would have a legal right to occupy it, and the suit was brought by the appellant for specific performance.

Compare the problem of Truax v. Raich, 239 U.S. 33 (1915), sustaining the standing in the federal courts of an alien employee to enjoin the enforcement of an Arizona statute making it illegal for employers to employ aliens as more than 20 percent of their workers; the plaintiff had been notified of his discharge by his employer owing to fear of the statutory penalties. See also Pierce v. Society of Sisters, 268 U.S. 510 (1925), upholding a suit by a parochial school to enjoin the enforcement of an Oregon statute making it a misdemeanor for parents to fail to send their children to a public school.

See also Sedler, Standing to Assert Constitutional Jus Tertii in the Supreme Court, 71 Yale L.J. 599 (1962); Note, Standing to Assert Constitutional Jus Tertii, 88 Harv. L. Rev. 423 (1974).

4. May a *public officer* assert the unconstitutionality of a statute, e.g., in a mandamus proceeding against him as a tax assessor to enforce a statutory exemption which the assessor has disregarded on the ground of invalidity? See Note, Public Officer's Right to Question the Constitutionality of a Statute in Mandamus Proceedings, 42 Harv. L. Rev. 1071 (1929). If a state court allows the defense to be raised and holds the exemption valid under the federal Constitution, may the assessor obtain review on certiorari? Compare Myers v. United States, 272 U.S. 52 (1926), and Humphrey's Executor v. United States, 295 U.S. 602 (1935), actions by removed officials to recover salary, in which the United States maintained that certain statutory limitations on the President's removal power were unconstitutional.

The courts have held in several cases that members of Congress have standing to challenge the legality of certain actions taken by the executive branch. See Kennedy v. Sampson, 511 F.2d 430 (D.C. Cir. 1974) (pocket veto of legislation); Mitchell v. Laird, 488 F.2d 611 (D.C. Cir. 1973) (military involvement in Southeast Asia); Holtzman v. Schlesinger, 361 F. Supp. 544 (E.D.N.Y.), rev'd on other grounds, 484 F.2d 1307 (2d Cir. 1973), cert. denied, 416 U.S. 936 (1974) (same).

5. *How may the issues be raised?* The problem of the complainant's interest shades into the problem of procedures for raising constitutional issues.

Stockholders' suits must reckon with the decision in Norman v. Consolidated Edison Co., 89 F.2d 619 (2d Cir. 1937), holding that such a suit would not lie to enjoin the payment by the corporation of social security taxes, since the corporation had an adequate remedy at law. Contrast Pollock v. Farmers' Loan and Trust Co., 157 U.S. 429, 554 (1895). The statutory prohibition of suits to enjoin the collection of federal taxes is, of course, lurking in these cases. Internal Revenue Code § 3653(a).

On declaratory judgments see, in addition to the Ashwander case, Electric Bond and Share Co. v. SEC, 303 U.S. 419, 443 (1938). The hostility of Mr. Justice Brandeis to the declaratory judgment procedure was reflected in Willing v. Chicago Auditorium Assn., 277 U.S. 274 (1928), holding that a suit in a federal court by a lessee to determine its right under the lease to tear down a building and erect a new one was not a case or controversy within Article III of the Constitution. The Federal Declaratory Judgments Act was enacted six years later. It has been said (with what justification?) that Mr. Justice Brandeis was a liberal in constitutional questions but a conservative in matters of procedure. For some of the considerations involved see Note, Declaratory Relief in the Supreme Court, 45 Harv. L. Rev. 1089 (1932); Note, Declaratory Judgments, 1941-49, 62 id. 787, 867-874 (1949); Note, Applicability of Limitations on the Use of the Injunction in Constitutional Litigation to the Federal Declaratory Judgment, 35 Calif. L. Rev. 252 (1947); Public Service Commission v. Wycoff Co., 344 U.S. 237 (1952).

Suits by shippers against carriers for a mandatory injunction compelling the transportation of goods, where a statute forbids such carriage, and the carrier is in the position of defending the statute, have frequently been the vehicle for constitutional decisions. E.g., Bowman v. Chicago & N.W. Ry., 125 U.S. 465 (1888); Clark Distilling Co. v. Western Maryland Ry., 242 U.S. 311 (1917); Kentucky Whip & Collar Co. v. Illinois Central R.R., 299 U.S. 334 (1937); cf. Moor v. Texas & N.O.R.R., 297 U.S. 101 (1936). Compare also the cases of actions on contracts, e.g., Fletcher v. Peck, page 28 supra, and Buchanan v. Warley, page 121 supra.

If an action between private parties does not meet the standards of adverse interest required for a constitutional challenge, is the defect cured by the intervention of the government? See United States v. Johnson, 319 U.S. 302 (1943), supra page 54.

Adler v. Board of Education 342 U.S. 485, 72 S. Ct. 380, 96 L. Ed. 295 (1952)

MR. JUSTICE MINTON delivered the opinion of the Court.

Appellants brought a declaratory judgment action in the Supreme Court of New York, Kings County, praying that § 12-a of the Civil Service Law, McK. Consol. Laws, c. 7, as implemented by the so-called Feinberg Law,[2] be declared unconstitutional, and that action by the Board of Education of the City of New York thereunder be enjoined. On motion for judgment on the pleadings, the court held that subdivision (c) of § 12-a, the Feinberg Law, and the Rules of the State Board of Regents promulgated thereunder violated the Due Process Clause of the Fourteenth Amendment, and issued an injunction. Lederman v. Board of Education, 196 Misc. 873. The Appellate Division of the Supreme Court reversed, 276 App. Div. 527, and the Court of Appeals affirmed the judgment of the Appellate Division, Thompson v. Wallin, 301 N.Y. 476. The appellants come here by appeal under 28 U.S.C. § 1257.

Section 12-a of the Civil Service Law, hereafter referred to as § 12-a, is set forth in the margin.[3] To implement this law, the Feinberg Law was passed, adding a new section,

[2] N.Y. Laws 1949, c. 360.

[3] "§ 12-a. Ineligibility

"No person shall be appointed to any office or position in the service of the state or of any civil division or city thereof, nor shall any person presently employed in any such office or position be continued in such employment, nor shall any person be employed in the public service as superintendents, principals or teachers in a public school or academy or in a state normal school or college, or any other state educational institution who:
(a) By word of mouth or writing wilfully and deliberately advocates, advises or teaches the doctrine that the government of the United States or of any state or of any political subdivision thereof should be overthrown or overturned by force, violence or any unlawful means; or

"(b) Prints, publishes, edits, issues or sells, any book, paper, document or written or printed matter in any form containing or advocating, advising or teaching the doctrine that the government of the United States or of any state or of any political subdivision thereof should be overthrown by force, violence, or any unlawful means, and who advocates, advises, teaches, or embraces the duty, necessity or propriety of adopting the doctrine contained therein;

"(c) Organizes or helps to organize or becomes a member of any society or group of persons which teaches or advocates that the government of the United States or of any state or of any political subdivision thereof shall be overthrown by force or violence, or by any unlawful means;

"(d) A person dismissed or declared ineligible may within four months of such dismissal or declaration of in-

§ 3022, to the Education Law of the State of New York, McK. Consol. Laws, c. 16, which section here pertinent is set forth in the margin.[4] . . .

The preamble of the Feinberg Law, § 1, makes elaborate findings that members of subversive groups, particularly of the Communist Party and its affiliated organizations, have been infiltrating into public employment in the public schools of the State; that this has occurred and continues notwithstanding the existence of protective statutes designed to prevent the appointment to or retention in employment in public office, and particularly in the public schools, of members of any organizations which teach or advocate that the government of the United States or of any state or political subdivision thereof shall be overthrown by force or violence or by any other unlawful means. As a result, propaganda can be disseminated among the children by those who teach them and to whom they look for guidance, authority, and leadership. The Legislature further found that the members of such groups use their positions to advocate and teach their doctrines, and are frequently bound by oath, agreement, pledge, or understanding to follow, advocate and teach a prescribed party line or group dogma or doctrine without regard to truth or free inquiry. This propaganda, the Legislature declared, is sufficiently subtle to escape detection in the classroom; thus, the menace of such infiltration into the classroom is difficult to measure. Finally, to protect the children from such influence, it was thought essential that the laws prohibiting members of such groups, such as the Communist Party or its affiliated organizations, from obtaining or retaining employment in the public schools be rigorously enforced. It is the purpose of the Feinberg Law to provide for the disqualification and removal of superintendents of schools, teachers, and employees in the public schools in any city or school district of the State who advocate the overthrow of the Government by unlawful means or who are members of organizations which have a like purpose.

Section 3022 of the Education Law, added by the Feinberg Law, provides that the Board of Regents, which has charge of the public school system in the State of New York, shall, after full notice and hearing, make a listing of organizations which it finds advocate, advise, teach, or embrace the doctrine that the government should be overthrown by force or violence or any other unlawful means, and that such listing may be amended and revised from time to time.

It will be observed that the listings are made only after full notice and hearing. In addi-

---

eligibility be entitled to petition for an order to show cause signed by a justice of the supreme court, why a hearing on such charges should not be had. Until the final judgment on said hearing is entered, the order to show cause shall stay the effect of any order of dismissal or ineligibility based on the provisions of this section. The hearing shall consist of the taking of testimony in open court with opportunity for cross-examination. The burden of sustaining the validity of the order of dismissal or ineligibility by a fair preponderance of the credible evidence shall be upon the person making such dismissal or order of ineligibility."

[4] "§ 3022. Elimination of subversive persons from the public school system

"1. The board of regents shall adopt, promulgate, and enforce rules and regulations for the disqualification or removal of superintendents of schools, teachers or employees in the public schools in any city or school district of the state who violate the provisions of section three thousand twenty-one of this article or who are ineligible for appointment to or retention in any office or position in such public schools on any of the grounds set forth in section twelve-a of the civil service law and shall provide therein appropriate methods and procedure for the enforcement of such sections of this article and the civil service law.

"2. The board of regents shall, after inquiry, and after such notice and hearing as may be appropriate, make a listing of organizations which it finds to be subversive in that they advocate, advise, teach or embrace the doctrine that the government of the United States or of any state or of any political subdivision thereof shall be overthrown or overturned by force, violence or any unlawful means, or that they advocate, advise, teach or embrace, the duty, necessity or propriety of adopting any such doctrine, as set forth in section twelve-a of the civil service law. Such listings may be amended and revised from time to time. The board, in making such inquiry, may utilize any similar listings or designations promulgated by any federal agency or authority authorized by federal law, regulation or executive order, and for the purposes of such inquiry, the board may request and receive from such federal agencies or authorities any supporting material or evidence that may be made available to it. The board of regents shall provide in the rules and regulations required by subdivision one hereof that membership in any such organization included in such listing made by it shall constitute prima facie evidence of disqualification for appointment to or retention in any office or position in the public schools of the state."

tion, the Court of Appeals construed the statute in conjunction with Article 78 of the New York Civil Practice Act, Gilbert-Bliss' N.Y. Civ. Prac., Vol. 6B, so as to provide listed organizations a right of review.

The Board of Regents is further authorized to provide in rules and regulations, and has so provided, that membership in any listed organization, after notice and hearing, "shall constitute prima facie evidence for disqualification for appointment to or retention in any office or position in the school system"; but before one who is an employee or seeks employment is severed from or denied employment, he likewise must be given a full hearing with the privilege of being represented by counsel and the right to judicial review. It is §12-a of the Civil Service Law, as implemented by the Feinberg Law as above indicated, that is under attack here.

It is first argued that the Feinberg Law and the rules promulgated thereunder constitute an abridgment of speech and assembly of persons employed or seeking employment in the public schools of the State of New York.

It is clear that such persons have the right under our law to assemble, speak, think and believe as they will. American Communications Ass'n v. Douds, 339 U.S. 382. It is equally clear that they have no right to work for the State in the school system on their own terms. United Public Workers v. Mitchell, 330 U.S. 75. They may work for the school system upon the reasonable terms laid down by the proper authorities of New York. If they do not choose to work on such terms, they are at liberty to retain their beliefs and associations and go elsewhere. Has the State thus deprived them of any right to free speech or assembly? We think not. . . .

It is next argued by appellants that the provision in §3022 directing the Board of Regents to provide in rules and regulations that membership in any organization listed by the Board after notice and hearing, with provision for review in accordance with the statute, shall constitute prima facie evidence of disqualification, denies due process, because the fact found bears no relation to the fact presumed. In other words, from the fact found that the organization was one that advocated the overthrow of government by unlawful means and that the person employed or to be employed was a member of the organization and knew of its purpose,[8] to presume that such member is disqualified for employment is so unreasonable as to be a denial of due process of law. We do not agree.

"The law of evidence is full of presumptions either of fact or law. The former are, of course, disputable, and the strength of any inference of one fact from proof of another depends upon the generality of the experience upon which it is founded. . . .

"Legislation providing that proof of one fact shall constitute prima facie evidence of the main fact in issue is but to enact a rule of evidence, and quite within the general power of government. Statutes, national and state, dealing with such methods of proof in both civil and criminal cases, abound, and the decisions upholding them are numerous." Mobile, J. & K.C.R. Co. v. Turnipseed, 219 U.S. 35 at page 42.

Membership in a listed organization found to be within the statute and known by the member to be within the statute is a legislative finding that the member by his membership supports the thing the organization stands for, namely, the overthrow of government by unlawful means. We cannot say that such a finding is contrary to fact or that "generality of experience" points to a different conclusion. Disqualification follows therefore as a reasonable presumption from such membership and support. Nor is there here a problem of procedural due process. The presumption is not conclusive but arises only in a hearing where the person against whom it may arise has full opportunity to rebut it. . . .

Where, as here, the relation between the fact found and the presumption is clear and direct and is not conclusive, the requirements of due process are satisfied. . . .

---

[8] In the proceedings below, both the Appellate Division of the Supreme Court and the Court of Appeals construed the statute to require such knowledge. Lederman v. Board of Education, 276 App. Div. 527, 530; Thompson v. Wallin, 301 N.Y. 476, 494.

We find no constitutional infirmity in §12-a of the Civil Service Law of New York or in the Feinberg Law which implemented it, and the judgment is affirmed.

Affirmed.

Mr. Justice Frankfurter, dissenting. . . .

A New York enactment of 1949 precipitated this litigation. But that legislation is tied to prior statutes. By a law of 1917 "treasonable or seditious" utterances or acts barred employment in the public schools. New York Education Law, §3021. In 1939 a further enactment disqualified from the civil service and the educational system anyone who advocates the overthrow of government by force, violence or any unlawful means, or publishes material advocating such overthrow or organizes or joins any society advocating such doctrine. New York Civil Service Law, §12-a. This states with sufficient accuracy the provisions of this Law, which also included detailed provisions for the hearing and review of charges.

During the thirty-two years and ten years, respectively, that these laws have stood on the books, no proceedings, so far as appears, have been taken under them. In 1949 the Legislature passed a new act, familiarly known as the Feinberg Law, designed to reinforce the prior legislation. The Law begins with a legislative finding, based on "common report" of widespread infiltration by "members of subversive groups, and particularly of the communist party and certain of its affiliated organizations," into the educational system of the State and the evils attendant upon that infiltration. It takes note of existing laws and exhorts the authorities to greater endeavor of enforcement. The State Board of Regents, in which are lodged extensive powers over New York's educational system, was charged by the Feinberg Law with these duties:

(1) to promulgate rules and regulations for the more stringent enforcement of existing law;

(2) to list "after inquiry and after such notice and hearing as may be appropriate" those organizations membership in which is proscribed by subsection (c) of §12-a of the Civil Service law;

(3) to provide in its rules and regulations that membership in a listed organization shall be prima facie evidence of disqualification under §12-a;

(4) to report specially and in detail to the legislature each year on measures taken for the enforcement of these laws.

Accordingly, the Board of Regents adopted Rules for ferreting out violations of §3021 or §12-a. An elaborate machinery was designed for annual reports on each employee with a view to discovering evidence of violations of these sections and to assuring appropriate action on such discovery. The Board also announced its intention to publish the required list of proscribed organizations and defined the significance of an employee's membership therein in proceedings for his dismissal. These Rules by the Board of Regents were published with an accompanying Memorandum by the Commissioner of Education. . . .

It thus appears that we are asked to review a complicated statutory scheme prohibiting those who engage in the kind of speech or conduct that is proscribed from holding positions in the public school system. The scheme is aligned with a complex system of enforcement by administrative investigation, reporting and listing of proscribed organizations. All this must further be related to the general procedures under the New York law for hearing and reviewing charges of misconduct against educational employees, modified as those procedures may be by the Feinberg Law and the Regents' Rules.

This intricate machinery has not yet been set in motion. Enforcement has been in abeyance since the present suit, among others, was brought to enjoin the Board of Education from taking steps or spending funds under the statutes and Rules on the theory that these transgressed various limitations which the United States Constitution places on the power of the States. The case comes here on the bare bones of the Feinberg Law only partly given flesh by the Regents' Rules. It was decided wholly on pleadings: a complaint, identifying the plaintiffs and their interests, setting out the offending statutes and Rules, and concluding in a more or less argumentative fashion that these provisions violate numerous constitutional rights of the various plaintiffs; an answer, denying that the impact of the statute is unconstitutional and that the plaintiffs have any interest to support the suit. . . .

About forty plaintiffs brought the action initially; the trial court dismissed as to all but eight. 196 Misc. at page 877. The others were found without standing to sue under New York law. The eight who are here as appellants alleged that they were municipal taxpayers and were empowered, by virtue of N.Y. Gen. Municipal Law § 51, McK. Consol. Laws, c. 24 to bring suit against municipal agencies to enjoin waste of funds. New York is free to determine how the views of its courts on matters of constitutionality are to be invoked. But its action cannot of course confer jurisdiction on this Court, limited as that is by the settled construction of Article III of the Constitution. We cannot entertain, as we again recognize this very day, a constitutional claim at the instance of one whose interest has no material significance and is undifferentiated from the mass of his fellow citizens. Doremus v. Board of Education, 342 U.S. 429. This is not a "pocketbook action." As taxpayers these plaintiffs cannot possibly be affected one way or the other by any disposition of this case, and they make no such claim. It may well be that the authorities will, if left free, divert funds and effort from other purposes for the enforcement of the provisions under review, though how much leads to the merest conjecture. But the total expenditure, certainly the new expenditure, necessary to implement the Act and Rules may well be de minimis. . . .

This ends the matter for plaintiffs Krieger and Newman. But six of the plaintiffs advanced grounds other than that of taxpayers in bringing this action. Two are parents of children in New York City schools. Four are teachers in these schools. On the basis of the record before us these claims, too, are insufficient, in view of our controlling adjudications, to support the jurisdiction of this Court.

The trial court found the interests of the plaintiffs as parents inconsequential. Lederman v. Board of Education, 196 Misc., at page 875. I agree. Parents may dislike to have children educated in a school system where teachers feel restrained by unconstitutional limitations on their freedom. But it is like catching butterflies without a net to try to find a legal interest, indispensable for our jurisdiction, in a parent's desire to have his child educated in schools free from such restrictions. The hurt to parents' sensibilities is too tenuous or the inroad upon rightful claims to public education too argumentative to serve as the earthy stuff required for a legal right judicially enforceable. The claim does not approach in immediacy or directness or solidity that which our whole process of constitutional adjudication has deemed a necessary condition to the Court's settlement of constitutional issues. . . .

This leaves only the teachers, Adler, George and Mark Friedlander and Spencer. The question whether their interest as teachers was sufficient to give them standing to sue was thought by the trial court to be conclusively settled by our decision in United Public Workers v. Mitchell, 330 U.S. 75. I see no escape from the controlling relevance of the Mitchell case. There individual government employees sought to enjoin the provisions of the Hatch Act forbidding government employees to take active part in politics. The complaint contained detailed recitals of the desire, intent and specific steps short of violation on the part of plaintiffs to engage in the prohibited activities. See 330 U.S. at pages 87-88, note 18. There as here the law was attacked as violating constitutional guaranties of freedom of speech. We found jurisdiction wanting to decide the issue except as to one plaintiff whose conduct had already violated the applicable standards.

The allegations in the present action fall short of those found insufficient in the Mitchell case. These teachers do not allege that they have engaged in proscribed conduct or that they have any intention to do so. They do not suggest that they have been, or are, deterred from supporting causes or from joining organizations for fear of the Feinberg Law's interdict, except to say generally that the system complained of will have this effect on teachers as a group. They do not assert that they are threatened with action under the law, or that steps are imminent whereby they would incur the hazard of punishment for conduct innocent at the time, or under standards too vague to satisfy due process of law. They merely allege that the statutes and Rules permit such action against some teachers. Since we rightly refused in the Mitchell case to hear government employees whose conduct was much more intimately affected by the law there attacked than are the claims of plaintiffs here, this suit is wanting in the necessary basis for our review.

This case proves anew the wisdom of rigorous adherence to the prerequisites for pronouncement by this Court on matters of constitutional law. The absence in these plaintiffs of the immediacy and solidity of interest necessary to support jurisdiction is reflected in the atmosphere of abstraction and ambiguity in which the constitutional issues are presented. The broad, generalized claims urged at the bar touch the deepest interests of a democratic society: its right to self-preservation and ample scope for the individual's freedom, especially the teacher's freedom of thought, inquiry and expression. No problem of a free society is probably more difficult than the reconciliation or accommodation of these too often conflicting interests. The judicial role in this process of accommodation is necessarily very limited and must be carefully circumscribed. To that end the Court, in its long history, has developed "a series of rules" carefully formulated by Mr. Justice Brandeis, "under which it has avoided passing upon a large part of all the constitutional questions pressed upon it for decision." Ashwander v. Tennessee Valley Authority, 297 U.S. 288, 346. . . .

. . . [W]e are without enlightenment, for example, on the nature of the reporting system described by the Rules. This may be a vital matter, affecting not the special circumstances of a particular case but coloring the whole scheme. For it may well be of constitutional significance whether the reporting system contemplates merely the notation as to each teacher that no evidence of disqualification has turned up, if such be the case, or whether it demands systematic and continuous surveillance and investigation of evidence. The difference cannot be meaningless, it may even be decisive, if our function is to balance the restrictions on freedom of utterance and of association against the evil to be suppressed. . . .

This statement of reasons for declining jurisdiction sounds technical, perhaps, but the principles concerned are not so. Rare departures from them are regrettable chapters in the Court's history, and in well-known instances they caused great public misfortune.

MR. JUSTICE DOUGLAS, with whom MR. JUSTICE BLACK concurs, dissenting. . . .

The present law proceeds on a principle repugnant to our society — guilt by association. A teacher is disqualified because of her membership in an organization found to be "subversive." The finding as to the "subversive" character of the organization is made in a proceeding to which the teacher is not a party and in which it is not clear that she may even be heard. To be sure she may have a hearing when charges of disloyalty are leveled against her. But in that hearing the finding as to the "subversive" character of the organization apparently may not be reopened in order to allow her to show the truth of the matter. . . .

The very threat of such a procedure is certain to raise havoc with academic freedom. Youthful indiscretions, mistaken causes, misguided enthusiasms — all long forgotten — become the ghosts of a harrowing present. Any organization committed to a liberal cause, any group organized to revolt against an hysterical trend, any committee launched to sponsor an unpopular program becomes suspect. These are the organizations into which Communists often infiltrate. Their presence infects the whole, even though the project was not conceived in sin. A teacher caught in that mesh is almost certain to stand condemned. Fearing condemnation, she will tend to shrink from any association that stirs controversy. In that manner freedom of expression will be stifled. . . .

What happens under this law is typical of what happens in a police state. Teachers are under constant surveillance; their pasts are combed for signs of disloyalty; their utterances are watched for clues to dangerous thoughts. A pall is cast over the classrooms. There can be no real academic freedom in that environment. Where suspicion fills the air and holds scholars in line for fear of their jobs, there can be no exercise of the free intellect. Supineness and dogmatism take the place of inquiry. . . .

This, I think, is what happens when a censor looks over a teacher's shoulder. This system of spying and surveillance with its accompanying reports and trials cannot go hand in hand with academic freedom. It produces standardized thought, not the pursuit of truth. Yet it was the pursuit of truth which the First Amendment was designed to protect. A system which directly or inevitably has that effect is alien to our system and should be struck down. Its survival is a real threat to our way of life. We need be bold and adventuresome in our thinking to survive. A school system producing students trained as robots threatens to rob a generation of the versatility that has been perhaps our greatest distinction. The Framers knew the danger of dogmatism; they also knew the strength that comes when the mind is free, when ideas may be pursued wherever they lead. We forget these teachings of the First Amendment when we sustain this law.

Of course the school systems of the country need not become cells for Communist activities; and the classrooms need not become forums for propagandizing the Marxist creed. But the guilt of the teacher should turn on overt acts. So long as she is a law abiding citizen, so long as her performance within the public school system meets professional standards, her private life, her political philosophy, her social creed should not be the cause of reprisals against her.

[A separate dissenting opinion of MR. JUSTICE BLACK is omitted.][d]

NOTE Sovereign Immunity and Constitutional Litigation

1. From the beginning a dilemma has been recognized between the doctrine of sovereign immunity and the central principle of constitutional limitations on official power. The working out of an accommodation has been described in Note, Sovereign Immunity in Suits to Enjoin the Enforcement of Unconstitutional Legislation, 50 Harv. L. Rev. 956, 957-958 (1937), as follows:

"Whatever the origin of the doctrine of sovereign immunity, the accepted rationalization of its continued existence is that 'there can be no legal right as against the authority that makes the law on which the right depends.' [Holmes, J., in Kawananakoa v. Polyblank, 205 U.S. 349, 353 (1907).] The immunity of the United States from suit in the federal courts was early recognized by the Supreme Court but the adoption of the Eleventh Amendment was required to force recognition of a comparable immunity of the states. The impetus for the passage of this amendment was furnished by the agitation resulting from the decision in Chisholm v. Georgia [2 Dall. 419 (1793)] that the federal courts had jurisdiction to compel a state to pay its debts to citizens of other states and of foreign nations. For a long period the Court, under the guiding hand of Marshall, prevented the amendment from having any effect other than that of prohibiting the enforcement of such contract obligations of the states, by the holding in Osborn v. Bank of the United States [9 Wheat. 738 (1824)] that the Court would not look beyond the record in determining whether the state was a party to the suit. This position, however, was gradually weakened in cases where the interest of the state was too obvious to be ignored. In suits against a governor in his representative capacity; to enjoin an officer from not carrying out a state contract; and to enforce rights against state property, the Court began to bar actions which were nominally against individuals. This development resulted

---

[d] See Davis, Standing, Ripeness and Civil Liberties: A Critique of Adler v. Board of Education, 38 A.B.A.J. 924 (1952); Bernard, Avoidance of Constitutional Issues in the United States Supreme Court: Liberties of the First Amendment, 50 Mich. L. Rev. 261 (1951).

On the merits, the Feinberg law was later held unconstitutional for undue vagueness. Keyishian v. Board of Regents of New York, 385 U.S. 589 (1967), infra p. 1339 — ED.

finally in a clearcut reversal of principle in In re Ayers [123 U.S. 443 (1887)] by the ruling that whenever the state is the real party in interest and the record defendant is merely a nominal party the suit is against the state and within the prohibition of the amendment. The amendment was thus held to be merely declaratory of the common law, passed to overrule the erroneous decision in Chisholm v. Georgia and to give to the states an immunity equal to that of the federal government.

"This extension of immunity, however, did not lead the Court to deny jurisdiction to the federal courts in all cases involving the restraint of official action. Previous decisions involving actual or threatened trespasses by state and federal officers were relied upon for the distinction between suits to enforce rights against the state and those to restrain invasions of interests by individuals claiming to act under a legislative authority which could afford no protection because contrary to constitutional limitations. Since an action to recover property wrongfully taken or withheld, or for compensation therefor, can be maintained against an agent without joining the principal as a party, a suit to restrain such a threatened invasion could be entertained as a suit solely against the officer as agent and not one against the state as principal. The pressure for further judicial restraint of state action, however, forced the Court gradually to move away from this logically unimpeachable position into more dangerous ground. Thus the principle of In re Ayers, that a bill to enjoin the bringing of suits on behalf of the state by officers of the state in their representative capacity is in fact a suit against the state where no individual wrong is involved, was impliedly repudiated while avowedly followed by the line of cases involving restraints of unreasonable utility regulations."

The accommodation is generally symbolized as the doctrine of Ex parte Young, 209 U.S. 123 (1908). That case upheld the conviction of a state attorney general for contempt in disobeying an injunctive order of a federal court restraining him from enforcing certain utility commission rate orders alleged to be unconstitutional; his disobedience consisted in commencing proceedings against a railroad in a state court to compel observance of the rate orders. The Court reasoned that when a state officer acts under an unconstitutional state law, his action must be considered "without the authority of and one which does not affect the State in its sovereign or governmental capacity. It is simply an illegal act upon the part of a state official in attempting by the use of the name of the State to enforce a legislative enactment which is void because unconstitutional. . . . [T]he officer [thus] comes into conflict with the superior authority of [the federal] Constitution, and he is in that case stripped of his official or representative character and is subjected in his person to the consequences of his individual conduct. The State has no power to impart to him any immunity from responsibility to the supreme authority of the United States."

In Scheuer v. Rhodes, 416 U.S. 232 (1974), plaintiffs charged that the defendant state officers had acted beyond or in abuse of their statutory authority in a manner violative of federal rights in deploying troops of the Ohio National Guard on the campus of Kent State University. The Court unanimously held that the defendants could not assert the immunity of the state under the Eleventh Amendment. Does this result necessarily follow from the rationale of Ex parte Young? Or might a distinction be made between actions pursuant to an unconstitutional, and therefore void, statute and actions which are themselves unconstitutional but done pursuant to a state officer's interpretation of an admittedly constitutional state statute?

At least two logical problems are raised by the doctrine of Ex parte Young: (a) If the suit is against the officer in his individual capacity, how can his conduct amount to state or federal action within the scope of the Fourteenth or Fifth Amendment? (b) If the official character of the conduct comes in only by way of justification, and the invalidity of the statutory authority by way of reply to such justification, how can the case be said to "arise under" the Constitution within the meaning of the provisions of the Judicial Code conferring jurisdiction on the federal district courts?

Similar difficulties may arise in actions against state or municipal officers under § 1 of the Civil Rights Act of 1871, 42 U.S.C. §1983, which proscribes deprivation of federal rights by "any person" acting "under color of" state law but not by governmental units. See Note: The Uses of Section 1983, page 859 infra. See generally the cases and materials on official immunity, page 862 infra.

2. *Fiscal consequences of an equitable decree against state officers.* The Eleventh Amendment has been held to bar the awarding of damages against state officials where the real effect of the suit will be to impose liability on the state treasury. See, e.g., Ford Motor Co. v. Department of Treasury, 323 U.S. 459 (1945) (suit against Indiana state tax collectors for refund of taxes paid under protest). The amendment does not, however, bar injunctive relief which will in all practical certainty have the effect of requiring additional disbursements from the state treasury. These doctrines were discussed in Edelman v. Jordan, 415 U.S. 651 (1971). There, the Court reversed, 5 to 4, a district court order that the State of Illinois retroactively pay benefits wrongfully withheld from applicants to federal-state programs of Aid to the Aged, Blind and Disabled (AABD) established under the Social Security Act, 42 U.S.C. §1381 et seq. Writing for the Court, Justice Rehnquist held that federal jurisdiction to grant such relief was barred by the Eleventh Amendment. The Court noted that, like an award of damages against the state, the district court order would require immediate disbursement of funds from the state treasury. On this basis, it distinguished cases upholding prospective injunctive relief which was likely to have fiscal consequences. The Court stated: "[T]he rule has evolved that a suit by private parties seeking to impose a liability which must be paid from public funds in the state treasury is barred by the Eleventh Amendment. Great Northern Life Insurance Co. v. Reed [322 U.S. 47 (1944)]; Kennecott Copper Corp. v. State Tax Comm'n, 327 U.S. 573 (1946). . . .

". . . [T]he District Court's decree which petitioner challenges on Eleventh Amendment grounds . . . requires payment of state funds, not as a necessary consequence of compliance in the future with a substantive federal-question determination, but as a form of compensation to those whose applications were processed on the slower time schedule at a time when petitioner was under no court-imposed obligation to conform to a different standard. While the Court of Appeals described this retroactive award of monetary relief as a form of 'equitable restitution,' it is in practical effect indistinguishable in many aspects from an award of damages against the State."

Suppose that state welfare administrators in Massachusetts and New Hampshire, both of which are within the First Federal Judicial Circuit, follow identical procedures with regard to hearings before termination of welfare benefits. The Massachusetts procedures are challenged in federal district court in that state and held unconstitutional. The district court decision is affirmed by the Court of Appeals for the First Circuit. If the State of New Hampshire fails to amend its welfare procedures to conform with the ruling of the First Circuit, might it be amenable to suit not only for injunctive relief but also for payment of damages retroactive to the date of the First Circuit decision?

3. *The immunity of the sovereign can be waived.* Does a state statute providing that suits may be brought for the recovery of taxes "in the court having jurisdiction thereof, and they shall have precedence therein" constitute consent to be sued in a federal court? Great Northern Ins. Co. v. Read, 322 U.S. 47 (1944), held that it did not; Mr. Justice Frankfurter delivered a dissenting opinion, reflecting a philosophy of sovereign accountability which found expression later in his dissenting opinion in Larson v. Domestic & Foreign Commerce Corp., 337 U.S. 682 (1949), and earlier in Keifer v. RFC, 306 U.S. 381 (1939).

May a state or the United States be subjected to a counterclaim in the absence of consent to be sued? United States v. Shaw, 309 U.S. 495 (1940). See Note, Governmental Immunity from Counterclaims, 50 Colum. L. Rev. 505 (1950); 73 Harv. L. Rev. 602 (1960).

4. To what extent does participation in the federal union by itself require state amena-

bility to suit? Suits brought against a state by another state or by the United States may be entertained without consent, as "a necessary feature of the formation of a more perfect Union." See Monaco v. Mississippi, 292 U.S. 313, 329 (1934). But a state may not be thus sued by a foreign state. Ibid. Nor may the United States, without its consent, be sued by a state of the Union. Kansas v. United States, 204 U.S. 331 (1907).

In Edelman v. Jordan, supra, the Court further held that Illinois had not by its participation in the AABD program waived Eleventh Amendment immunity or "constructively consented" to suit in federal court. In dissent, Justice Brennan stated his view that on joining the federal Union the states surrendered their sovereign immunity "at least insofar as the States granted Congress specifically enumerated powers," under which the Social Security Act was enacted. " '[B]ecause of its surrender, no immunity exists that can be the subject of a Congressional declaration or a voluntary waiver,' " quoting Employees v. Department of Public Welfare, 411 U.S. 279, 300 (1973) (Brennan, J., dissenting).

Justice Marshall offered a narrower position: that although federal regulation, such as the Fair Labor Standards Act involved in Employees v. Department of Public Welfare, supra, might not by itself require a finding that the states have surrendered their immunity, state voluntary acceptance of federal benefits under the terms of a federal aid program presents a different situation. Despite the absence of any express requirement of waiver of state immunity in the Social Security Act, Justice Marshall would have held that effectuation of the purposes of the act logically required and justified a finding of such waiver.

Would it be constitutional if Congress were to require, as a condition to receipt of federal matching funds under the Social Security Act, that the states completely waive their Eleventh Amendment immunity to suit in the federal courts? Is Justice Marshall's position distinguishable? Cf. Note, Unconstitutional Conditions, 73 Harv. L. Rev. 1595 (1960). See page 497 infra.

For comment on Edelman see Note, The Supreme Court, 1973 Term, 88 Harv. L. Rev. 41, 243-251 (1974).

See generally Bator, Mishkin, Shapiro and Wechsler, Hart & Wechsler's The Federal Courts and the Federal System 251-258, 926-957 (2d ed. 1973); McCormack, Federalism and Section 1983 (pts. 1, 2), 60 Va. L. Rev. 1, 250 (1974); Comment, Implied Waiver of a State's Eleventh Amendment Immunity, 1974 Duke L.J. 925; Note, Attorneys' Fees and the Eleventh Amendment, 88 Harv. L. Rev. 1875 (1975).

5. Are subdivisions of the state entitled to immunity? Counties and municipalities are not deemed to partake of the immunity of a state. Lincoln County v. Luning, 135 U.S. 529 (1890); N. M. Patterson & Sons v. Chicago, 176 F. Supp. 323 (N.D. Ill. 1959). Whether suits against other state-created bodies are barred depends on their relationship to the state, in particular their capacity to obligate the state treasury. Compare Murray v. Wilson Distilling Co., 213 U.S. 151 (1909), with State Highway Commission v. Utah Construction Co., 278 U.S. 194 (1929). See Note, The Applicability of Sovereign Immunity to Independent Public Authorities, 74 Harv. L. Rev. 714 (1961).

6. The Tucker Act gives to the district courts, concurrently with the Court of Claims, jurisdiction over claims not exceeding $10,000 in amount (larger claims being confined to the Court of Claims), which are "founded either upon the Constitution, or any Act of Congress, or any regulation of an executive department, or upon any express or implied contract with the United States, or for liquidated or unliquidated damages in cases not sounding in tort." 28 U.S.C. §1346(a).

The Tort Claims Act of 1948, 28 U.S.C. §§1346(b), 2671 et seq., subjecting the United States to suit for tort claims, contains a number of exceptions from its coverage, including "any claim based upon an act or omission of an employee of the Government, exercising due care, in the execution of a statute or regulation, whether or not such statute or regulation be valid, or based upon the exercise or performance or the failure to exercise or perform a discretionary function or duty on the part of a federal agency or an employee of the Government, whether or not the discretion involved be abused." 28 U.S.C. § 2680(a). See Gellhorn and Schenck, Tort Actions Against the Federal Government, 47 Colum. L. Rev. 722 (1947); Note, The Discretionary Function Exception of the Federal Tort Claims Act, 66 Harv. L. Rev. 488 (1953); James, The Federal Tort Claims Act and the "Discretionary Function" Exception, 10 U. Fla. L. Rev. 184 (1957); Symposium, 24 Fed. B.J. 133 (1964), 26 id. 1 (1966); Dalehite v. United States, 346 U.S. 15 (1953); cf. Indian Towing Co. v. United States, 350 U.S. 61 (1955); Rayonier v. United States, 352 U.S. 315 (1956); United States v. Muniz, 374 U.S. 150 (1963) (prisoner's suit).

7. For comparative studies of sovereign immunity and responsibility see Street, Governmental Liability (1953); Governmental Tort Liability (Symposium), 9 Law & Contemp. Prob. 179 (1942); Governmental Tort Liability (Symposium), 29 N.Y.U.L. Rev. 1321 (1954).

Section D. FURTHER ISSUES IN THE OPERATION OF JUDICIAL REVIEW

Status of District of Columbia Minimum Wage Law
39 Ops. Atty. Gen. 22 (1937)

April 3, 1937

THE PRESIDENT.

MY DEAR MR. PRESIDENT: In answer to your request of April 2, 1937, for my opinion respecting the present status of the District of Columbia minimum-wage law, in view of the recent decision of the Supreme Court in the case of West Coast Hotel Co. v. Parrish, 300 U.S. 379, overruling the case of Adkins v. Children's Hospital, 261 U.S. 525, I have the honor to advise you as follows:

The District of Columbia minimum-wage law was approved and became effective on September 18, 1918 (c. 174, 40 Stat. 960). The act provided for its administration by a Minimum Wage Board to be appointed by the Commissioners of the District of Columbia. It further provided for the organization of the Board and defined its powers and duties. The Board appointed under the statute, acting in pursuance thereof, issued its order prohibiting the employment in the District of Columbia of women or minor girls in certain industries at less than a prescribed wage per month. The Children's Hospital sought to enjoin the Board from enforcing its order against the hospital. An injunction issued was sustained by the Supreme Court in the case of Adkins v. Children's Hospital, decided April 9, 1923, on the ground that the statute was unconstitutional. The effect of this decision was to suspend the further enforcement of the act.

In the case of West Coast Hotel Co. v. Parrish, supra, the Supreme Court said "Our conclusion is that the case of Adkins v. Children's Hospital, supra, should be, and it is, overruled."

The decisions are practically in accord in holding that the courts have no power to repeal or abolish a statute, and that notwithstanding a decision holding it unconstitutional a statute continues to remain on the statute books; and that if a statute be declared unconstitutional and the decision so declaring it be subsequently overruled the statute will then be held valid from the date it became effective. [Citations omitted.]

It is, therefore, my opinion that the District of Columbia minimum-wage law is now a valid act of the Congress and may be administered in accordance with its terms.

Respectfully,
HOMER CUMMINGS

NOTE Effect of an Unconstitutional Statute and Prospective Overruling

1. What is the effect of a decision that a law is unconstitutional? In Norton v. Shelby County, 114 U.S. 425, 442 (1886), holding unenforceable bonds issued by a board of commissioners created under an invalid statute, Mr. Justice Field said: "An unconstitutional act is not a law; it confers no rights; it imposes no duties; it affords no protection; it creates no office; it is, in legal contemplation, as inoperative as though it had never been passed."

Compare the statement of Chief Justice Hughes in Chicot County Drainage District v. Baxter State Bank, 308 U.S. 371, 374 (1940), holding that an unappealed decision applying the Municipal Bankruptcy Act was res judicata despite the subsequent decision of the Supreme Court in another case that the act was unconstitutional:

"The courts below have proceeded on the theory that the Act of Congress, having been found to be unconstitutional, was not a law; that it was inoperative, conferring no rights and imposing no duties, and hence affording no basis for the challenged decree. Norton v. Shelby County, 118 U.S. 425, 442; Chicago, I. & L. Ry. Co. v. Hackett, 228 U.S. 559, 566. It is quite clear, however, that such broad statements as to the effect of a determination of unconstitutionality must be taken with qualifications. The actual existence of a statute, prior to such a determination, is an operative fact and may have consequences which cannot justly be ignored. The past cannot always be erased by a new judicial declaration. The effect of the subsequent ruling as to invalidity may have to be considered in various aspects, — with respect to particular relations, individual and corporate, and particular conduct, private and official. Questions of rights claimed to have become vested, of status, of prior determinations deemed to have finality and acted upon accordingly, of public policy in the light of the nature both of the statute and of its previous application, demand examination. These questions are among the most difficult of those which have engaged the attention of courts, state and federal, and it is manifest from numerous decisions that an all-inclusive statement of a principle of absolute retroactive invalidity cannot be justitifed."[3]

2. May a court, in order to cushion the effects of a holding of unconstitutionality, limit its decision on invalidity to the future? Cf. Great Northern Ry. v. Sunburst Oil & Refg. Co., 287 U.S. 358 (1932), per Cardozo, J.; Warring v. Colpoys, 122 F.2d 642 (D.C. Cir. 1941), per Vinson, J.; Frank, J., dissenting, in Commissioner v. Hall's Estate, 153 F.2d 172, 174 (2d Cir. 1946); Frankfurter, J., concurring, in Griffin v. Illinois, 351 U.S. 12, 20 (1956); Note, Prospective Operation of Decisions Holding Statutes Unconstitutional or Overruling a Precedent, 60 Harv. L. Rev. 437 (1947); Levy, Realist Jurisprudence and Prospective Overruling, 109 U. Pa. L. Rev. 1 (1960).

What considerations should induce a court to apply a new principle prospectively only? And what is meant by "prospectively"? These questions were involved in the following cases: Linkletter v. Walker, 381 U.S. 618 (1965), held that Mapp v. Ohio, 367 U.S. 643 (1961), ruling that evidence obtained in violation of the search and seizure guarantee is inadmissible in a state court, would not be applied in cases where the judgment had become final, and time for direct review had expired, before the date of the Mapp decision. Tehan v. Shott, 382 U.S. 406 (1966), held similarly with respect to Griffin v. California, 380 U.S. 609 (1965), ruling unconstitutional a court's comment on the defendant's election not to take the stand in a criminal case. On the other hand, decisions requiring counsel to be appointed for an indigent defendant and forbidding a confession to reach the jury for an initial determination of its voluntariness have been rendered on review of habeas corpus proceedings. Gideon v. Wainwright, 372 U.S. 335 (1963); Jack-

---

[3] See Field, "The Effect of an Unconstitutional Statute," 42 Yale Law Journal 779; 45 Yale Law Journal 1533; 48 Harvard Law Review 1271; 25 Virginia Law Review 210.

son v. Denno, 378 U.S. 368 (1964). The application of new principles regarding confessions obtained without advising the prisoner of his right to counsel, or awaiting his opportunity to consult counsel, has been treated in still another way. After reversing on this ground, the Court held that these decisions would be applied "prospectively" only, and so declined to review numerous similar cases pending on direct review of convictions. Johnson and Cassidy v. New Jersey, 384 U.S. 719 (1966), refusing to apply Miranda v. Arizona, 384 U.S. 436 (1966).

See Mishkin, The High Court, the Great Writ, and the Due Process of Time and Law, 79 Harv. L. Rev. 56 (1965); for a critique of the Johnson and Cassidy case, supra, see 80 Harv. L. Rev. 91, 135-141 (1966).

NOTE Methods and Materials of Constitutional Decision

1. *The role of the constitutional text and of history.* How is the "meaning" of a constitutional provision to be ascertained? Of what significance are the records of the proceedings in the Convention of 1787 and the ratifying conventions? Of what significance is general history, either before or after the adoption of the Constitution? Compare the following statements: Holmes, J., in Missouri v. Holland, 252 U.S. 416, 433 (1920), on the scope of the treaty power: ". . . When we are dealing with words that also are a constituent act, like the Constitution of the United States, we must realize that they have called into life a being the development of which could not have been foreseen completely by the most gifted of its begetters. It was enough for them to realize or to hope that they had created an organism; it has taken a century and has cost their successors much sweat and blood to prove that they created a nation. The case before us must be considered in the light of our whole experience and not merely in that of what was said a hundred years ago." Stone, J., in McNally v. Hill, 293 U.S. 131, 136 (1934): "The statute does not define the term habeas corpus. To ascertain its meaning and the appropriate use of the writ in the federal courts, resort must be had to the common law, from which the term was drawn, and to the decisions of this Court interpreting and applying the common law principles which define its use when authorized by the statute. . . . Its use was defined and regulated by the Habeas Corpus Act of 1679, 31 Car. II, c. 2. This legislation and the decisions of the English courts interpreting it have been accepted by this Court as authoritative guides in defining the principles which control the use of the writ in the federal courts." See Wofford, The Blinding Light: The Uses of History in Constitutional Interpretation, 31 U. of Chi. L. Rev. 502 (1964); C. Miller, The Supreme Court and the Uses of History (1969).

2. *The role of precedent.* Compare the following statements: Taney, C.J., dissenting, in the Passenger Cases, 7 How. 283, 470 (1849): "I . . . am quite willing that it be regarded hereafter as the law of this court, that its opinion upon the construction of the Constitution is always open to discussion when it is supposed to have been founded in error, and that its judicial authority should hereafter depend altogether on the force of the reasoning by which it is supported." Brandeis, J., dissenting, in Burnet v. Coronado Oil & Gas Co., 285 U.S. 393, 406-408 (1932): "Stare decisis is usually the wise policy, because in most matters it is more important that the applicable rule of law be settled than that it be settled right. . . . This is commonly true even where the error is a matter of serious concern, provided correction can be had by legislation. But in cases involving the Federal Constitution, where correction through legislative action is practically impossible, this Court has often overruled its earlier decisions. The Court bows to the lessons of experience and the force of better reasoning, recognizing that the process of trial and error, so fruitful in the physical sciences, is appropriate also in the judicial function." Roberts, J., dissenting, in Smith v. Allwright, 321 U.S. 649, 669 (1944): "The reason for my concern is that the instant decision, overruling that announced about nine years ago, tends to bring adjudications of this tribunal into the same class as a restricted railroad

ticket, good for this day and train only." For collections of decisions overruled by the Supreme Court see the opinion of Brandeis, J., supra; Sharp, Movement in Supreme Court Adjudication, 46 Harv. L. Rev. 361, 593, 795 (1933); Douglas, Stare Decisis, 49 Colum. L. Rev. 735 (1949) (containing a table of 30 overruling cases in the period 1937-1949).

3. *The presumption of constitutionality.* An early expression of this presumption is contained in Marshall's opinion in Fletcher v. Peck, supra page 28. What are the bases for such a presumption? What is its operative effect? "The meaning and effect of it," said James Bradley Thayer, "are shortly and very strikingly intimated by a remark of Judge Cooley, to the effect that one who is a member of a legislature may vote against a measure as being, in his judgment, unconstitutional; and, being subsequently placed on the bench, when this measure, having been passed by the legislature in spite of his opposition, comes before him judicially, may there find it his duty, although he has in no degree changed his opinion, to declare it constitutional." The Origin and Scope of the American Doctrine of Constitutional Law, 7 Harv. L. Rev. 129, 144 (1893), reprinted in Thayer, Legal Essays 1, 22 (1908). Compare the action of Chief Justice Chase in asserting the unconstitutionality of the Legal Tender Acts although as Secretary of the Treasury he had supported their enactment. Legal Tender Cases, 12 Wall. 457, 576 (1871) (dissenting). Suppose that members of the legislature vote for a measure despite constitutional doubts, preferring that the question be resolved by the courts. Should the presumption of constitutionality be affected? Compare Thayer, supra, at 146. Should the presumption operate equally in cases of national and of state legislation; in cases of regulation of economic and of political activities?

4. *The significance of facts and the mode of proving them.* A close relationship between the presumption of constitutionality and the burden of proof in constitutional litigation can be drawn. See, e.g., the statement of Brandeis, J., in O'Gorman & Young v. Hartford Fire Ins. Co., 282 U.S. 251, 257-258 (1931), sustaining a state law regulating insurance agents' commissions: "As underlying questions of fact may condition the constitutionality of legislation of this character, the presumption of constitutionality must prevail in the absence of some factual foundation of record for overthrowing the statute." To what extent may these "underlying questions of fact" be explored dehors the record, as through presentation in an appellate brief? On the possibilities and limitations of the "Brandeis brief," so called from the brief submitted by him as counsel for the state in the Oregon hours-of-labor-for-women case, Muller v. Oregon, 208 U.S. 412 (1908), see Freund, The Supreme Court of the United States 120, 150-154 (1967). The presentation of "constitutional facts" as evidence in the trial court raises problems of its own. See Biklé, Judicial Determination of Questions of Fact Affecting the Constitutional Validity of Legislative Action, 38 Harv. L. Rev. 6 (1924); Davis, An Approach to Problems of Evidence in the Administrative Process, 45 id. 364, 402-410 (1942); Note, The Presentation of Facts Underlying the Constitutionality of Statutes, 49 id. 631 (1936); Note, Social and Economic Facts — Appraisal of Suggested Techniques for Presenting Them to the Courts, 61 id. 692 (1948); Note, Social Psychological Data, Legislative Fact and Constitutional Law, 29 Geo. Wash. L. Rev. 136 (1960); Karst, Legislative Facts in Constitutional Litigation, 1 Sup. Ct. Rev. 75 (1960); Kadish, Methodology and Criteria in Due Process Adjudication, 66 Yale L.J. 319 (1957). For Canadian and Australian practice, see Laskin, Canadian Constitutional Law 162-170, 184-187 (2d ed. 1960); Holmes, Evidence in Constitutional Cases, 23 Aust. L.J. 235 (1949); Commonwealth Freighters Ltd. v. Sneddon, 32 Austl. L.J. Rep. 410 (1959).

The significance of underlying facts is exhibited most clearly when a court which has previously held a law constitutional is not satisfied that the basis for its validity still exists. See, e.g., Chastleton Corp. v. Sinclair, 264 U.S. 543 (1924).

5. On the various topics suggested by this Note, see Supreme Court and Supreme Law (Cahn ed. 1954) (symposium).

Section E. THE POWER OF CONGRESS TO LIMIT THE JURISDICTION OF THE FEDERAL COURTS

Sheldon v. Sill 8 How. 441, 12 L. Ed. 1147 (1850)

Mr. Justice Grier delivered the opinion of the Court.

The only question which it will be necessary to notice in this case is, whether the Circuit Court had jurisdiction.

Sill, the complainant below, a citizen of New York, filed his bill in the Circuit Court of the United States for Michigan, against Sheldon, claiming to recover the amount of a bond and mortgage, which had been assigned him by Hastings, the President of the Bank of Michigan.

Sheldon, in his answer, among other things, pleaded that "the bond and mortgage in controversy, having been originally given by a citizen of Michigan to another citizen of the same State, and the complainant being assignee of them, the Circuit Court had no jurisdiction."

The eleventh section of the Judiciary Act, which defines the jurisdiction of the Circuit Courts, restrains them from taking "cognizance of any suit to recover the contents of any promissory note or other chose in action, in favor of an assignee, unless a suit might have been prosecuted in such court to recover the contents, if no assignment had been made, except in cases of foreign bills of exchange."

The third article of the Constitution declares that "the judicial power of the United States shall be vested in one Supreme Court, and such inferior courts as the Congress may, from time to time, ordain and establish." The second section of the same article enumerates the cases and controversies of which the judicial power shall have cognizance, and, among others, it specifies "controversies between citizens of different States."

It has been alleged, that this restriction of the Judiciary Act, with regard to assignees of choses in action, is in conflict with this provision of the Constitution, and therefore void.

It must be admitted, that if the Constitution had ordained and established the inferior courts, and distributed to them their respective powers, they could not be restricted or divested by Congress. But as it has made no such distribution, one of two consequences must result, — either that each inferior court created by Congress must exercise all the judicial powers not given to the Supreme Court, or that Congress, having the power to establish the courts, must define their respective jurisdictions. The first of these inferences has never been asserted, and could not be defended with any show of reason, and if not, the latter would seem to follow as a necessary consequence. And it would seem to follow, also, that, having a right to prescribe, Congress may withhold from any court of its creation jurisdiction of any of the enumerated controversies. Courts created by statute can have no jurisdiction but such as the statute confers. No one of them can assert a just claim to jurisdiction exclusively conferred on another, or withheld from all.

The Constitution has defined the limits of the judicial power of the United States, but has not prescribed how much of it shall be exercised by the Circuit Court; consequently, the statute which does prescribe the limits of their jurisdiction, cannot be in conflict with the Constitution, unless it confers powers not enumerated therein.

Such has been the doctrine held by this court since its first establishment. To enumerate all the cases in which it has been either directly advanced or tacitly assumed would be tedious and unnecessary.

In the case of Turner v. Bank of North America, 4 Dall. 10, it was contended, as in this case, that, as it was a controversy between citizens of different States, the Constitution gave the plaintiff a right to sue in the Circuit Court, notwithstanding he was an assignee within the restriction of the eleventh section of the Judiciary Act. But the court said, — "The political truth is, that the disposal of the judicial power (except in a few specified instances) belongs to Congress; and Congress is not bound to enlarge the jurisdiction of the Federal courts to every subject, in every form which the Constitution might warrant." This decision was made in 1799; since that time, the same doctrine has been frequently asserted by this court, as may be seen in McIntire v. Wood, 7 Cranch, 506; Kendall v. United States, 12 Peters, 616; Cary v. Curtis, 3 Howard, 245.

The only remaining inquiry is, whether the complainant in this case is the assignee of a "chose in action," within the meaning of the statute. . . .

The complainant in this case is the purchaser and assignee of a sum of money, a debt, a chose in action, not of a tract of land. He seeks to recover by this action a debt assigned to him. He is therefore the "assignee of a chose in action," within the letter and spirit of the act of Congress under consideration, and cannot support this action in the Circuit Court of the United States, where his assignor could not.

The judgment of the Circuit Court must therefore be reversed, for want of jurisdiction.

NOTE Legislation Governing Jurisdiction

1. A contrasting view on the obligation of Congress under Article III to create, and vest full federal jurisdiction in, lower federal courts was aired by Justice Story in Martin v. Hunter's Lessee, 1 Wheat. 304 (1816). See pages 21–24 supra. Story did not contend, however, that Article III is self-executing in this respect, or that it confers a constitutional right to litigate enumerated cases and controversies in federal court. For, only two years after Martin v. Hunter's Lessee, sitting as Circuit Justice, Story reluctantly dismissed an Article III dispute not within the Judiciary Act. White v. Fenner, 29 F. Cas. 1015 (No. 17,547) (C.C.D.R.I. 1818).

Story's views, which have been described as a product of his "militant federalism," have never gained currency. Appendix by Felix Frankfurter to H.R. Rep. No. 669, 72d Cong., 1st Sess. (1932). Nor, despite its considerable expansion of federal jurisdiction since 1850, has Congress ever extended the jurisdiction of the lower federal courts to the limits of Article III. For the history of the development of the federal court system and its jurisdiction, see 1 Moore's Federal Practice ¶¶0.1 to 0.3, 0.60, 0.71 (2d ed. 1974).

2. What limits are there, if any, to congressional power to restrict the jurisdiction of the lower federal courts? Cf. United States v. Klein, infra page 145.

(a) *The Norris-LaGuardia Act.* The Norris-LaGuardia Act of March 29, 1932, 29 U.S.C. §§101-115 (1970), was designed to counteract antilabor rulings by the federal courts by restricting their power to issue injunctions in cases growing out of labor disputes. The act denied the lower federal courts "jurisdiction" to issue orders enforcing "yellow dog" contracts, §103, or enjoining organizing or strike activities, §104; and injunction even of unlawful acts was forbidden unless plaintiff had met stringent versions of the equitable doctrines of irreparable injury and clean hands. §§107-108. The measure was enacted in the face of unfavorable precedent. In Truax v. Corrigan, 257 U.S. 312 (1921), the Court had held an Arizona statute limiting employers' remedies in labor disputes to violate due process insofar as it immunized striking employees from normal criminal penalties for picketing their employer's place of business and to violate equal protection insofar as it denied the availability of an injunction against strikers but not against others. But in Lauf v. E. G. Shinner & Co., 303 U.S. 323 (1938), the Norris-LaGuardia Act was upheld. The Court dismissed any constitutional objections in one sentence: "There can be no question of the power of Congress thus to define and limit the jurisdiction of the inferior federal courts of the United States." And see Brotherhood of Railroad Trainmen v.

138   Chapter Three.   Judicial Review in Operation

Toledo, Peoria & Western R.R., 321 U.S. 50 (1944), upholding the requirement of §108 that a plaintiff-employer make "every reasonable effort" to settle the labor dispute before being allowed to seek an injunction against violence or threats of violence to its property and operations.

Would it be satisfactory to distinguish Truax as involving an attempt to restrict the powers of state courts, which are courts of general jurisdiction? Cf. Hart, The Power of Congress to Limit the Jurisdiction of the Federal Courts: An Exercise in Dialectic, 66 Harv. L. Rev. 1362, 1401-1402 (1953).

Of what relevance are precedents holding that the due process clauses invalidated state and federal statutes which had attempted to outlaw "yellow dog" contracts by forbidding employers to fire employees for joining a union? See Coppage v. Kansas, 236 U.S. 1 (1915); Adair v. United States, 208 U.S. 161 (1908). Assuming that these decisions were still vital in 1938, do they reach to a mere denial of a federal remedy effected by the act's limitation of the jurisdiction of the lower federal courts? See H.R. Rep. No. 669, 72d Cong., 2d Sess. (1932); Frankfurter and Greene, The Labor Injunction 210-211 (1936); Frankfurter, Congressional Power over the Labor Injunction, 31 Colum. L. Rev. 385 (1931).

See also Note on Statutory Limitations upon Injunctions against State Officials, in Bator, Mishkin, Shapiro and Wechsler, Hart & Wechsler's The Federal Courts and the Federal System 965-979 (2d ed. 1973).

(b) *The Portal-to-Portal Litigation.* In §7 of the Fair Labor Standards Act of 1938, 29 U.S.C. §§201-219, Congress required that employees be paid time and one-half for overtime work, computed on a workweek of 40 to 44 hours. In a series of decisions construing §7 the Court held that working time included certain employee activity, such as walking from the punch clock to the workbench, which had not previously been regarded as compensable absent express provision in the labor contract. See, e.g., Anderson v. Mt. Clemens Pottery Co., 328 U.S. 680 (1946). Within six months after these decisions, over 1900 actions were filed in federal courts claiming over $5 billion in back pay and penalties. To erase these unexpected liabilities, Congress passed the Portal-to-Portal Act of 1947, 29 U.S.C. §§251-62, which both redefined the activities covered by the F.L.S.A. as excluding those added by the Court and purported to strip all courts, federal and state, of jurisdiction to enforce alleged liabilities for overtime pay based on any activity not expressly covered by the act.

The Supreme Court has never passed on the constitutionality of the Portal-to-Portal Act, but it has been upheld by all of the lower federal courts that have considered it. Most have refused, however, to accept the act as a limitation on their jurisdiction without having first satisfied themselves that the underlying liabilities were validly extinguished by the substantive portions of the act. Thus, in Battaglia v. General Motors Corp., 169 F.2d 254 (2d Cir.), cert. denied, 335 U.S. 887 (1948), the court stated:

"A few of the district court decisions sustaining [the act] have done so on the ground that since jurisdiction of federal courts other than the Supreme Court is conferred by Congress, it may at the will of Congress be taken away in whole or in part. . . . [T]hese district court decisions would, in effect, sustain [the jurisdictional limitation] regardless of whether [the substantive provisions] were valid. We think, however, that the exercise by Congress of its control over jurisdiction is subject to compliance with at least the requirements of the Fifth Amendment. That is to say, while Congress has the undoubted power to give, withhold, and restrict the jurisdiction of [the lower federal] courts . . . , it must not so exercise that power as to deprive any person of life, liberty, or property without due process of law or to take private property without just compensation. . . ."

Compare the following excerpt from Professor Hart's Exercise in Dialectic, 66 Harv. L. Rev. at 1371-1372:

"Q. . . . The bald truth is, isn't it, that the power to regulate jurisdiction is actually a power to regulate rights — rights to judicial process, whatever those are, and substantive rights generally? Why, that *must* be so. What can a court do if Congress says it has no jurisdiction, or only a restricted jurisdiction? It's helpless — helpless even to consider the validity of the limitation, let alone to do anything about it if it's invalid.

"A. Why, what monstrous illogic! To build up a mere power to regulate jurisdiction into a power to affect rights having nothing to do with jurisdiction! And into a power to do it in contradiction to all the other terms of the very document which confers the power to regulate jurisdiction!

"Q. Will you please explain what's wrong with the logic?

"A. What's wrong, for one thing, is that it violates a necessary postulate of constitutional government — that a court must always be available to pass on claims of constitutional right to judicial process, and to provide such process if the claim is sustained."

(c) *The Emergency Price Control Act.* Is the due process limitation enunciated in Battaglia avoided where *any* judicial forum is provided an aggrieved party? In the Emergency Price Control Act of 1942, 56 Stat. 23, which was designed to facilitate the administration of economic controls during World War II, Congress provided that the validity of price orders could be reviewed only by a federal Emergency Court of Appeals, with Supreme Court review, and that the Emergency Court could not enjoin enforcement of a contested order preliminarily but only after final determination of the merits. Other federal, and state, courts were forbidden either to issue injunctions against enforcement of price orders or to consider the defense of invalidity in enforcement actions brought by the government. (The act was amended in 1944 to require stays of enforcement suits when a defendant's challenge was pending before the Emergency Court. Stabilization Extension Act of June 30, 1944, 56 Stat. 632.)

In Lockerty v. Phillips, 319 U.S. 182 (1943), the Court upheld dismissal of a suit brought in a federal district court to enjoin criminal prosecutions for alleged violations of price orders. The Court based its holding on the narrow ground of congressional power to restrict the jurisdiction of the lower federal courts and declined to consider the due process adequacy of the act's limitations on jurisdiction to pass on the validity of price orders. The Court noted, however, that Congress could have deprived all inferior federal courts of jurisdiction if state courts had remained open: "Article III left Congress free to establish inferior federal courts or not as it thought appropriate. It could have declined to create any such courts, leaving suitors to the remedies afforded by state courts, with such appellate review by this Court as Congress might prescribe. The Congressional power to ordain and establish inferior courts includes the power of investing them with jurisdiction either limited, concurrent, or exclusive, and of withholding jurisdiction from them in the exact degree and character which to Congress may seem proper for the public good."

See Note on the Obligation of State Courts to Enforce Federal Law, in Bator et al., Hart & Wechsler, supra, at 434; Hart, The Relations Between State and Federal Law, 54 Colum. L. Rev. 489 (1954); Hill, Constitutional Remedies, 69 Colum. L. Rev. 1109 (1969); Note, State Remedies for Federally-Created Rights, 57 Minn. L. Rev. 815 (1963).

The constitutionality of the Emergency Price Control Act's removal of the issue of validity of orders from enforcement actions was squarely presented in Yakus v. United States, 321 U.S. 414 (1944). There the Court upheld a criminal conviction under the act. The Court construed the act to allow consideration of the constitutionality of the jurisdictional scheme set out by the act and then upheld it. The Court said that petitioners failed to show that the requirement that price orders be challenged only in the Emergency Court had denied them "a reasonable opportunity to be heard and present evidence." See also Bowles v. Willingham, 321 U.S. 489 (1944), rejecting a similar challenge to a civil enforcement decree.

(d) *The Selective Service Cases.* In Falbo v. United States, 320 U.S. 549 (1944), the Court upheld the conviction of a registrant for failure to report for induction despite the refusal of the court below to consider the registrant's claim that his draft board had erroneously and arbitrarily denied his application for exemption as a "regular or duly ordained" minister. The Court found that the Selective Training and Service Act of 1940, 54 Stat. 885, in order to assure the efficiency of the draft process, denied access to judicial review until after a registrant had reported for duty and been accepted by the armed forces or alternative service organization. The order to report, and thus a criminal prosecution for failure to do so, was "no more than an intermediate step" at which judicial review of a registrant's classification need not be available.

Falbo was qualified two years later in Estep v. United States, 327 U.S. 114 (1946), in which the Court overturned a conviction for refusal to submit to induction after the registrant had obeyed an order to report and had been accepted by the military. Distinguishing Falbo on the ground that in that case the registrant had failed to exhaust all administrative remedies, the Court held that although the courts were not authorized to conduct customary review of the correctness of the draft board's classification, petitioners were entitled to raise the issue whether the board's action was "so contrary to its granted authority as to exceed its jurisdiction."

Similar issues arose during the Vietnam war. In Wolff v. Selective Service Board No. 16, 372 F.2d 817 (2d Cir. 1967), the court rejected the prevailing view, dating from Estep, that draft board classifications could be challenged only as a defense to a criminal prosecution for failure to submit to induction or on writ of habeas corpus. The court held that where registrants had been deprived of student deferments and reclassified as I-A delinquents following their participation in an antiwar demonstration, the threat to the exercise of First Amendment rights required the court to take jurisdiction of a suit to enjoin further disciplinary action by the board and order the reinstatement of petitioners' deferments.

In response to Wolff, Congress enacted § 10(b)(3) of the Military Selective Service Act of 1967, 50 U.S.C. App. §460, which provided: "No judicial review shall be made of the classification or processing of any registrant . . . except as a defense to a criminal prosecution instituted . . . after the registrant has responded either affirmatively or negatively to an order to report for induction . . . *Provided,* That such review shall go to the question of the jurisdiction herein reserved to local boards . . . only when there is no basis in fact for the classification assigned to such registrant. . . ."

Nonetheless, in Oestereich v. Selective Service System Local Board No. 11, 393 U.S. 233 (1968), the Court reversed the dismissal of a suit for the same relief sought in Wolff which was brought by a registrant who had been deprived of his exempt classification as a student preparing for the ministry and reclassified I-A after he had returned his draft card in protest against United States involvement in Vietnam. Writing for the majority, Justice Douglas argued that as petitioner was clearly within the exempt category and as there was no indication in the selective service statutes that Congress had intended to authorize local boards to revoke statutory exemptions by means of delinquency classifications, the board's action in this case was "a clear departure . . . from its statutory mandate." He then held that § 10(b)(3) had not been intended to preclude preinduction review "in cases of this type." See the concurring opinion of Justice Harlan and the dissent by Justice Stewart, which Justices Brennan and White joined. See also Breen v. Selective Service Board No. 16, 396 U.S. 460 (1970), applying Oestereich to deprivation of a statutory deferment.

On the same day the Court reversed, per curiam, an order by a district court granting a preliminary injunction to a registrant who had been classified I-A after the board had rejected his application for exemption as a conscientious objector. Clark v. Gabriel, 393 U.S. 256 (1968). Petitioner's claim was merely that the board's classification had been erroneous. The Court held that the injunction was barred by § 10(b)(3) and that the registrant's opportunity to challenge the classification by writ of habeas corpus after induction or as a defense to prosecution for refusal to submit to induction satisfied the requirements of due process. Justice Douglas, concurring, distinguished Oestereich, saying "in my view it takes the extreme case where the Board can be said to flout the law . . . to warrant preinduction review of its actions."

In Boyd v. Clark, 393 U.S. 316 (1969), and Fein v. Selective Service System Local

Board No. 7, 405 U.S. 365 (1972), the Court held that § 10(b)(3) barred equal protection and due process challenges directed at the selective service statute on its face.

For further analysis of § 10(b)(3), see Petersen v. Clark, 285 F. Supp. 700 (N.D. Cal. 1968) (Zirpoli, J.) (holding § 10(b)(3) unconstitutional as violative of due process), rev'd per curiam on the basis of Clark v. Gabriel, supra, 411 F.2d 1217 (9th Cir. 1969); Donahue, The Supreme Court vs. Section 10(b)(3) of the Selective Service Act: A Study in Ducking Constitutional Issues, 17 U.C.L.A.L. Rev. 908 (1970).

Ex parte McCardle 7 Wall. 506, 19 L. Ed. 264 (1869)

[McCardle, editor of the Vicksburg Times, was arrested and held for trial before a military tribunal for publication of "incendiary and libellous" editorials critical of Reconstruction and of Union military commanders and urging that readers boycott federally sponsored elections. Military trial for persons accused of "impeding reconstruction" had been authorized by the Reconstruction Act of March 2, 1867, 14 Stat. 428. Before trial, McCardle petitioned for writ of habeas corpus in federal circuit court, arguing that the authorization of military trial for civilians was unconstitutional. The writ was denied, and McCardle appealed. Jurisdiction was based on the Act of February 5, 1867, 14 Stat. 385, which authorized issuance of the writ by lower federal courts and appeal from their decision to the Supreme Court.

This appeal raised much apprehension among Republican congressmen that Reconstruction would be endangered should the Court invalidate the military trial provision. After argument but before conference or decision of the case, Congress passed over President Johnson's veto the Act of March 27, 1868, 15 Stat. 44, which provided "that so much of the Act of February 5, 1867 . . . as authorized an appeal from the judgment of the Circuit Court to the Supreme Court of the United States, or the exercise of any such jurisdiction by said Supreme Court, on appeals which have been, or may hereafter be taken, be, and the same is, hereby repealed."

. . . The attention of the court was directed to this statute at the last term, but counsel having expressed a desire to be heard in argument upon its effect, and the Chief Justice being detained from his place here, by his duties in the Court of Impeachment, the cause was continued under advisement. Argument was now heard upon the effect of the repealing act. . . .

THE CHIEF JUSTICE delivered the opinion of the court.

The first question necessarily is that of jurisdiction; for, if the act of March, 1868, takes away the jurisdiction defined by the act of February, 1867, it is useless, if not improper, to enter into any discussion of other questions.

It is quite true, as was argued by the counsel for the petitioner, that the appellate jurisdiction of this court is not derived from acts of Congress. It is, strictly speaking, conferred by the Constitution. But it is conferred "with such exceptions and under such regulations as Congress shall make."

It is unnecessary to consider whether, if Congress had made no exceptions and no regulations, this court might not have exercised general appellate jurisdiction under rules prescribed by itself. For among the earliest acts of the first Congress, at its first session, was the act of September 24th, 1789, to establish the judicial courts of the United States. That act provided for the organization of this court, and prescribed regulations for the exercise of its jurisdiction.

The source of that jurisdiction, and the limitations of it by the Constitution and by statute, have been on several occasions subjects of consideration here. In the case of Durousseau v. The United States,* particularly, the whole matter was carefully examined, and

---

* 6 Cranch, 312; Wiscart v. Dauchy, 3 Dallas, 321.

the court held, that while "the appellate powers of this court are not given by the judicial act, but are given by the Constitution," they are, nevertheless, "limited and regulated by that act, and by such other acts as have been passed on the subject." The court said, further, that the judicial act was an exercise of the power given by the Constitution to Congress "of making exceptions to the appellate jurisdiction of the Supreme Court." "They have described affirmatively," said the court, "its jurisdiction, and this affirmative description has been understood to imply a negation of the exercise of such appellate power as is not comprehended within it."

The principle that the affirmation of appellate jurisdiction implies the negation of all such jurisdiction not affirmed having been thus established, it was an almost necessary consequence that acts of Congress, providing for the exercise of jurisdiction, should come to be spoken of as acts granting jurisdiction, and not as acts making exceptions to the constitutional grant of it.

The exception to appellate jurisdiction in the case before us, however, is not an inference from the affirmation of other appellate jurisdiction. It is made in terms. The provision of the act of 1867, affirming the appellate jurisdiction of this court in cases of habeas corpus is expressly repealed. It is hardly possible to imagine a plainer instance of positive exception.

We are not at liberty to inquire into the motives of the legislature. We can only examine into its power under the Constitution; and the power to make exceptions to the appellate jurisdiction of this court is given by express words.

What, then, is the effect of the repealing act upon the case before us? We cannot doubt as to this. Without jurisdiction the court cannot proceed at all in any cause. Jurisdiction is power to declare the law, and when it ceases to exist, the only function remaining to the court is that of announcing the fact and dismissing the cause. And this is not less clear upon authority than upon principle. . . .

. . .[T]he general rule, supported by the best elementary writers, is, that "when an act of the legislature is repealed, it must be considered, except as to transactions past and closed, as if it never existed." . . .

It is quite clear, therefore, that this court cannot proceed to pronounce judgment in this case, for it has no longer jurisdiction of the appeal; and judicial duty is not less fitly performed by declining ungranted jurisdiction than in exercising firmly that which the Constitution and the laws confer.

Counsel seem to have supposed, if effect be given to the repealing act in question, that the whole appellate power of the court, in cases of habeas corpus, is denied. But this is an error. The act of 1868 does not except from that jurisdiction any cases but appeals from Circuit Courts under the act of 1867. It does not affect the jurisdiction which was previously exercised.*

The appeal of the petitioner in this case must be

Dismissed for want of jurisdiction.

NOTE The Appellate Jurisdiction of the Supreme Court

1. Did McCardle deprive the petitioner of every avenue to Supreme Court review? Later in 1869 another Mississippi civilian detained for military trial petitioned the Court to review the circuit court's denial of habeas corpus by means of an original writ of certiorari. Noting its dictum at the end of McCardle, a unanimous Court issued the writ, construing the 1868 repealer to apply only to the appeal procedures set out in the 1867 act and not to the certiorari procedure in the Judiciary Act of 1789. Ex parte Yerger, 8 Wall. 85 (1869). Although Reconstruction was by this time almost complete, Republican congressmen

---

* Ex parte McCardle, 6 Wallace, 324.

sought to avoid a decision on the merits by introducing a bill that would have further restricted the Court's jurisdiction. But before the bill was enacted, the case was mooted by the government's voluntary agreement to release the petitioner to civilian authorities. For a historical account of these cases, see C. Fairman, Reconstruction and Reunion, 1864-88, Part I, chs. X, XII (1971). (6 Oliver Wendell Holmes Devise History of the Supreme Court of the United States.)

2. Did the McCardle Court properly interpret the "exceptions and regulations" clause? Several legal historians have argued that the Framers intended this language to authorize only minor, mainly procedural limitations. Thus, Raoul Berger has argued that the clause was intended mainly as a check on the power of the Court to review questions of fact as well as of law. Berger, Congress v. The Supreme Court chs. I, IX (1969). And in an account of the Constitutional Convention, Julius Goebel, Jr., noted that "in contemporary state practice, regulation had been confined largely to such details as setting appealable minima or periods of limitation, and 'exceptions' of certain proceedings where [writs of] neither error nor certiorari had been traditionally available." Goebel, Antecedents and Beginnings to 1801, at 240 (1971). (1 Oliver Wendell Holmes Devise History of the Supreme Court of the United States.) Is McCardle necessarily inconsistent with these interpretations? See also Merry, Scope of the Supreme Court's Appellate Jurisdiction: Historical Basis, 47 Minn. L. Rev. 53 (1962); Ratner, Congressional Power over the Appellate Jurisdiction of the Supreme Court, 109 U. Pa. L. Rev. 157 (1960).

3. The vulnerability of the Court to congressional restrictions on its appellate jurisdiction, as well as to other attacks, such as the "Court-packing plan" of 1937, led to the proposal by the New York City Bar Association of a series of constitutional amendments designed to insulate the Court. These proposals included fixing the number of Justices at nine and amending Article III, §2 to grant the Court appellate jurisdiction "in all cases arising under the Constitution of the United States, both as to law and fact, with such exceptions and under such regulations as *it* shall make." 34 A.B.A.J. 1072 (1948) (emphasis added). This proposal was endorsed by former Justice Owen J. Roberts, Now Is the Time: Fortifying the Supreme Court's Independence, 35 A.B.A.J. 1 (1949). For other views see Falk, In Time of Peace Prepare for War, 1 Record of N.Y.C.B.A. 245 (1946); Grinnell, Proposed Amendments to the Constitution: A Reply to Former Justice Roberts, 35 A.B.A.J. 648 (1949); Tweed, Provisions of the Constitution concerning the Supreme Court, 31 B.U.L. Rev. 1 (1951).

4. *Congressional attempts to limit the appellate jurisdiction of the Supreme Court.* That "resistance to the Court has been a persistent strain in American life" is evidenced by the introduction in Congress between 1821 and 1883 of at least ten bills seeking to deprive the Court of appellate jurisdiction in whole or in part. Freund, Storm over the American Supreme Court, 21 Modern L. Rev. 345, 346 (1958). See Warren, Legislative and Judicial Attacks upon the Supreme Court of the United States, 47 Am. L. Rev. 1 (1913). In response to controversial decisions of the Warren Court, attempts to limit the Court's jurisdiction mushroomed. Between 1953 and 1968, over 60 bills were introduced seeking to limit the jurisdiction of the federal courts, though none was adopted. See Bator et al., Hart & Wechsler, supra, at 360.

In 1957 Senator William Jenner (R. Ind.), ired by Court decisions regarding control of alleged subversives, introduced S. 2646, 85th Cong., 2d Sess. (1958). This bill would have divested the Court of jurisdiction to review any case involving the validity of (1) congressional investigative procedures, (2) any federal loyalty-security program, (3) state programs to control intrastate subversion, (4) public or private school programs to control subversive activities by teachers, and (5) state regulation of the admission of persons to the practice of law. The bill was favorably reported, although with only subsection (5) remaining. S. Rep. No. 1586, 85th Cong., 2d Sess. (1958). By a vote of 49 to 41, the Senate rejected the bill in the closing days of the 1958 Session. 104 Cong. Rec. 18687 (1958).

See W. Murphy, Congress and the Court: A Case Study in the American Political Pro-

144 Chapter Three. Judicial Review in Operation

cess (1962); C. Pritchett, Congress Versus the Supreme Court, 1957–1960 (1961); Elliot, Court-Curbing Proposals in Congress, 33 Notre Dame Law. 597 (1958); McKay, Court, Congress, and Reapportionment, 63 Mich. L. Rev. 255 (1964); Nagel, Court-Curbing Periods in American History, 18 Vand. L. Rev. 925 (1965); Note, Removal of Supreme Court Jurisdiction: A Weapon Against Obscenity?, 1969 Duke L.J. 291, Note, The Nixon Busing Bills and Congressional Power; 81 Yale L.J. 1542 (1972).

5. *Would McCardle be followed today?* In a dissenting opinion joined by Justice Black, Justice Douglas remarked that "[t]here is a serious question whether the McCardle case could command a majority view today." Glidden Co. v. Zdanok, 370 U.S. 530, 605 n.11 (1962). Consider the following statements by Professor Wechsler and Professor Hart:

". . . Congress has the power by enactment of a statute to strike at what it deems judicial excess by delimitations of the jurisdiction of the lower courts and of the Supreme Court's appellate jurisdiction. . . .

". . . I see no basis for [the view that the 'exceptions' clause has a narrow meaning, not including cases of constitutional dimension] and think it antithetical to the plan of the Constitution for the courts — which was quite simply that the Congress would decide from time to time how far the federal judicial institution should be used within the limits of the federal judicial power; or, stated differently, how far judicial jurisdiction should be left to the state courts, bound as they are by the Constitution as 'the supreme Law of the Land. . . .' Federal courts, including the Supreme Court, do not pass on constitutional questions because there is a special function vested in them to enforce the Constitution or police the other agencies of government. They do so rather for the reason that they must decide a litigated issue that is otherwise within their jurisdiction and in doing so must give effect to the supreme law of the land. That is, at least, what Marbury v. Madison was all about. . . ." Wechsler, The Courts and the Constitution, 65 Colum. L. Rev. 1001, 1005-1006 (1965).[e]

"Q. If you think an 'exception' implies some residuum of jurisdiction, Congress could meet that test by excluding everything but patent cases. This is so absurd, and it is so impossible to lay down any measure of a necessary reservation, that it seems to me the language of the Constitution must be taken as vesting plenary control in Congress.

"A. It's not impossible for me to lay down a measure. The measure is simply that the exceptions must not be such as will destroy the essential role of the Supreme Court in the constitutional plan. McCardle, you will remember, meets that test. The circuit courts of the United States were still open in habeas corpus. And the Supreme Court itself could

---

[e] Professor Wechsler continued: "The difficulty with legislative withdrawal of jurisdiction is not one of constitutional dimension, though, I should add that when I speak of withdrawal, I mean, of course, complete elimination of cognizance of cases of the kind. Congress could not, for example, employ federal courts as organs of enforcement and preclude them from attending to the Constitution in arriving at decision of the cause. There are, however, practical objections to complete withdrawal that are of immense importance and are often overlooked.

"To begin with, government cannot be run without the use of the courts for the enforcement of coercive sanctions and within large areas it will be thought that federal tribunals are essential to administer federal law. Within that area, the opportunity for litigating constitutional defenses is built in and cannot be foreclosed. The same necessity for federal tribunals will be felt in many situations that do not involve proceedings for enforcement. . . . The withdrawal of such jurisdiction would impinge adversely on so many varied interests that its durability can be assumed. Beyond this, if the jurisdiction of the Supreme Court alone is withdrawn in a given field, as happened in McCardle, issues are left to final resolution in the lower courts, which may, of course, reach contrary results in different sections of the country. If, in addition, all federal jurisdiction is withdrawn, the resolution is perforce left to the courts of fifty states, with even greater probability of contrariety in their decisions. How long would you expect such inconsistency in the interpretation of the law of the United States to be regarded as a tolerable situation? There is, moreover, still another difficulty. The lower courts or the state courts would still be faced with the decisions of the Supreme Court as precedents — decisions which that Court would now be quite unable to reverse or modify or even to explain. The jurisdictional withdrawal thus might work to freeze the very doctrines that had prompted its enactment, placing an intolerable moral burden on the lower courts." 65 Colum. L. Rev. at 1006.

Section E. Congressional Power 145

still entertain petitions for the writ which were filed with it in the first instance." Hart, Exercise in Dialectic, 66 Harv. L. Rev. at 1364–1365.[f]

See also Van Alstyne, A Critical Guide to Ex Parte McCardle, 15 Ariz. L. Rev. 229 (1973).

6. *United States v. Klein.* The Civil War enemy property acts authorized recovery in the Court of Claims by owners who had "never given any aid or comfort to the present rebellion." Act of March 3, 1863, 12 Stat. 820. In United States v. Padelford, 9 Wall. 531 (1870), the Supreme Court held that a presidential pardon brought a claimant within those entitled to recover. In United States v. Klein, 13 Wall. 128 (1872), the administrator of the estate of a deceased owner of property seized and sold by government agents recovered the proceeds in the Court of Claims under a pardon reciting previous disloyalty. While a government appeal was pending before the Court, Congress passed a law providing that no pardon could be admitted as evidence of eligibility to recover in the Court of Claims, that the Supreme Court should have no jurisdiction to review the loyalty determinations of the Court of Claims, and that a pardon reciting previous disloyalty should be taken as conclusive proof of ineligibility. Act of July 12, 1870, 16 Stat. 235. Noting that the act was also an unconstitutional interference with the power of the President to grant pardons, the Court held it an unconstitutional attempt to "prescribe rules for decision to the Judiciary Department":

"The substance of this enactment is that an acceptance of a pardon, without disclaimer, shall be conclusive evidence of the acts pardoned, but shall be null and void as evidence of the rights conferred by it, both in the Court of Claims and in this court on appeal. . . .

"Undoubtedly the legislature has complete control over the organization and existence of [the Court of Claims] and may confer or withhold the right of appeal from its decisions. And if this act did nothing more, it would be our duty to give it effect. If it simply denied the right of appeal in a particular class of cases, there could be no doubt that it must be regarded as an exercise of the power of Congress to make 'such exceptions from the appellate jurisdiction' as should seem to it expedient.

"But the language of the proviso shows plainly that it does not intend to withhold appellate jurisdiction except as a means to an end. Its great and controlling purpose is to deny to pardons granted by the President the effect which the court had adjudged them to have. . . .

"It is evident . . . that the denial of jurisdiction to this court, as well as to the Court of Claims, is founded solely on the application of a rule of decision, in causes pending, prescribed by Congress. The court has jurisdiction of the cause to a given point; but when it ascertains that a certain state of things exists, its jurisdiction is to cease and it is required to dismiss the cause for want of jurisdiction.

"It seems to us that this is not an exercise of the acknowledged power of Congress to make exceptions and prescribe regulations to the appellate power. . . .

". . . [W]e do not at all question what was decided in the case of Pennsylvania v. Wheeling Bridge Company.[*] In that case, after a decree in this court that the bridge, in the then state of the law, was a nuisance and must be abated as such, Congress passed an act legalizing the structure and making it a post-road; and the court, on a motion for process to enforce the decree, held that the bridge had ceased to be a nuisance by the exercise of the constitutional powers of Congress, and denied the motion. No arbitrary rule of decision was prescribed in that case, but the court was left to apply its ordinary rules to the

---

[f] Is Professor Wechsler right to conclude that removal of the Supreme Court's appellate jurisdiction of state court decisions would not, in Professor Hart's phrase, "destroy the essential role of the Supreme Court in the constitutional plan"? Consider the statement by Justice Holmes, quoted on page 17 supra.

[*] 18 Howard, 429.

146   Chapter Three.   Judicial Review in Operation

new circumstances created by the act. In the case before us no new circumstances have been created by the legislation. But the court is forbidden to give the effect to evidence which, in its own judgment, such evidence should have, and is directed to give it an effect precisely contrary.

"We must think that Congress has inadvertently passed the limit which separates the legislative from the judicial power."

How clearly defined is this limit? Compare Michaelson v. United States, 266 U.S. 42 (1924), upholding provisions of the Clayton Act, 18 U.S.C. §§402, 3691, that persons accused of criminal contempt for violation of federal court orders should have the option of demanding trial by jury.

Could Congress validly provide, by virtue of Article III, that in school desegregation cases the remedy of forced busing not be employed, or that it be employed only as a last resort?

Problems of Federalism

Part Two

Chapter Four Basic Issues of Federalism

The experience of the United States under a federal system is of interest not only for its own sake but as background for experiments now in the making that look toward federation on a regional or global scale.

What are the values conserved by a federal structure? Does federalism involve an undue degree of friction and present needless obstacles to human enterprise? Does federalism serve rather as a device whereby important problems are put beyond the reach of effective public control? What resources are available for mitigating these difficulties? These questions are suggested in the excerpts that immediately follow. The materials in this Part of the casebook, as well as certain of those in Part III, should provide some basis for answering these large questions.

Dicey, Law of the Constitution *171-180 (9th ed. 1939)*

Federal government means weak government. . . . Federalism tends to produce conservatism. . . . Federalism, lastly, means legalism — the predominance of the judiciary in the constitution — the prevalence of a spirit of legality among the people. . . .

That a federal system again can flourish only among communities imbued with a legal spirit and trained to reverence the law is as certain as can be any conclusion of political speculation. Federalism substitutes litigation for legislation, and none but a law-fearing people will be inclined to regard the decision of a suit as equivalent to the enactment of a law. The main reason why the United States has carried out the federal system with unequalled success is that the people of the Union are more thoroughly imbued with legal ideas than any other existing nation. Constitutional questions arising out of either the constitutions of the separate States or the articles of the federal constitution are of daily occurrence and constantly occupy the courts. Hence the citizens become a people of constitutionalists, and matters which excite the strongest popular feeling, as, for instance, the right of Chinese to settle in the country, are determined by the judicial Bench, and the decision of the Bench is acquiesced in by the people. This acquiescence or submission is due to the Americans inheriting the legal notions of the common law, i.e. of the "most legal system of law" (if the expression may be allowed) in the world. . . .

Laski, The Obsolescence of Federalism 98 New Republic 367 (May 3, 1939)

No one can travel the length and breadth of the United States without the conviction of its inexpugnable variety. East and West, South and North, its regions are real and different, and each has problems real and different too. The temptation is profound to insist that here, if ever, is the classic place for a federal experiment. . . . The large unit, as in Lamennais' phrase, would result in apoplexy at the center and anemia at the extremities. Imposed solutions from a distant Washington, blind, as it must be blind, to the subtle minutiae of local realities, cannot solve the ultimate problems that are in dispute. A creative America must be a federal America. The wider the powers exercised from Washington, the more ineffective will be the capacity for creative administration. Regional wisdom is the clue to the American future. The power to govern must go where that regional wisdom resides. So restrained, men learn by the exercise of responsibility the art of progress. They convince themselves by experiment from below. To fasten a uniformity that is not in nature upon an America destined to variety is to destroy the prospect of an ultimate salvation.

This kind of argument is familiar in a hundred forms. I believe that, more than any other philosophic pattern, it is responsible for the malaise of American democracy. My plea here is for the recognition that the federal form of state is unsuitable to the stage of economic and social development that America has reached. I infer from this postulate two conclusions: first, that the present division of powers, however liberal be the Supreme Court in its technique of interpretation, is inadequate to the needs America confronts; and, second, that any revision of those powers is one which must place in Washington, and Washington only, the power to amend that revision as circumstances change. I infer, in a word, that the epoch of federalism is over, and that only a decentralized system can effectively confront the problems of a new time. . . .

I do not think this argument is invalidated by the rise of coöperation between the federal government and the states, or between groups of states. That use has been carefully investigated in detail by Professor Jane Clark in an admirable and exhaustive monograph ("The Rise of a New Federalism," 1938). When all is made that can be made of the pattern she there reveals, I think it is true to say that, compared to the dimension of the problem, it amounts to very little. And set in the background of the urgent problems of time, it is, I think, clear from her account that in no fundamental matters will the pressure of political interests (behind which can be seen at every turn the hand of giant capitalism) permit the necessary uniformities to be attained by consent within the next fifty years. Not even the resiliency of American democracy can afford to wait so long. Professor Clark demonstrates admirably the inescapable interest of the federal government in a hundred subjects at every turn of which it encounters the power of the states; but she also demonstrates that the problems of dual occupancy of the same ground hinder at every turn the creative solution of the problems involved unless we conceive of those solutions in tems of geological time. . . .

Nor would the problem be met if, instead of the states, America were divided, as writers like Professor Howard Odum suggest, into regions more correspondent with the economic realities of the situation. If America were to consist of seven or nine regions, instead of forty-eight states, that would still leave unsolved the main issues if they operated upon the basis of the present division of powers, and if their consent were necessary to any fundamental change in that division. Once again, it must be emphasized that the unity which giant capitalism postulates in the economic sphere postulates a corresponding unity in the conference of political powers upon the federal government. There is no other way, up to a required minimum, in which the questions of taxation, labor relations and conditions, conservation, public utilities (in the widest sense), to take examples only, can be met. . . .

Pound, Law and Federal Government *Federalism as a Democratic Process 23 (Rutgers University 1942)*

No domain of continental extent has been ruled otherwise than as an autocracy or as a federal state. Confederacies have fallen apart. Consolidations of independent states, unless in a limited domain, have developed into autocracies. In antiquity the consolidation achieved by Alexander and the almost world-wide consolidation achieved by the Romans resulted in autocratically ruled empires. In the modern world the German-Roman empire of the Middle Ages fell apart. It was neither autocratic nor federal. The British commonwealth of nations has fallen apart politically. Russia has only changed its type of autocrat. But the United States and Canada and Australia show us what we may well call continental domains held together politically, sometimes under great stress, by a federal polity. . . .

Acton, Freedom in Antiquity (1877) *The History of Freedom and Other Essays 20 (1907)*

The Federal check was as familiar to the ancients as the Constitutional. For the type of all their Republics was the government of a city by its own inhabitants meeting in the public place. An administration embracing many cities was known to them only in the form of the oppression which Sparta exercised over the Messenians, Athens over her Confederates, and Rome over Italy. The resources which, in modern times, enabled a great people to govern itself through a single centre did not exist. Equality could be preserved only by Federalism; and it occurs more often amongst them than in the modern world. If the distribution of power among the several parts of the State is the most efficient restraint on monarchy, the distribution of power among several States is the best check on democracy. By multiplying centres of government and discussion it promotes the diffusion of political knowledge and the maintenance of healthy and independent opinion. It is the protectorate of minorities, and the consecration of self-government.

Wechsler, The Political Safeguards of Federalism *Principles, Politics, and Fundamental Law 77-82 (1961)*

Federalist considerations thus play an important part even in the selection of the President, although a lesser part than many of the framers must have contemplated. A presidential candidacy must be pointed towards the states of largest population in so far as they are doubtful. It must balance this direction by attention to the other elements of the full coalition that is looked to for an electoral majority. Both major parties have a strong incentive to absorb protest movements of such sectional significance that their development in strength would throw elections to the House. Both must give some attention to the organized minorities that may approach balance-of-power status in important states, without, however, making promises that will outrun the tolerance of other necessary elements of their required strength. Both parties recognize that they must appeal to some total combination of allegiance, choice, or interest that will yield sufficient nation-wide support to win elections and make possible effective government.

The most important element of party competition in this framework is the similarity of the appeal that each must make. This is a constant affront to those who seek purity of ideology in politics; it is the clue, however, to the success of our politics in the elimination of extremists — and to the tolerance and basic unity that is essential if our system is to work.

The President must be, as I have said above, the main repository of "national spirit" in the central government. But both the mode of his selection and the future of his party require that he also be responsive to local values that have large support within the states. And since his programs must, in any case, achieve support in Congress — in so far as they involve new action — he must surmount the greater local sensitivity of Congress before anything is done.

If this analysis is correct, the national political process in the United States — and especially the role of the states in the composition and selection of the central government — is intrinsically well adapted to retarding or restraining new intrusions by the center on the domain of the states. Far from a national authority that is expansionist by nature, the inherent tendency in our system is precisely the reverse, necessitating the widest support before intrusive measures of importance can receive significant consideration, reacting readily to opposition grounded in resistance within the states. Nor is this tendency effectively denied by pointing to the size or scope of the existing national establishment. However useful it may be to explore possible contractions in specific areas, such evidence points mainly to the magnitude of unavoidable responsibility under the circumstances of our time.

It is in light of this inherent tendency, reflected most importantly in Congress, that the governmental power distribution clauses of the Constitution gain their largest meaning as an instrument for the protection of the states. Those clauses, as is well known, have served far more to qualify or stop intrusive legislative measures in the Congress than to invalidate enacted legislation in the Supreme Court.

This does not differ from the expectation of the framers quite as markedly as might be thought. For the containment of the national authority Madison did not emphasize the function of the Court; he pointed to the composition of the Congress and to the political processes. . . .

The prime function envisaged for judicial review — in relation to federalism — was the maintenance of national supremacy against nullification or usurpation by the individual states, the national government having no part in their composition or their councils. This is made clear by the fact that reliance on the courts was substituted, apparently on Jefferson's suggestion, for the earlier proposal to give Congress a veto of state enactments deemed to trespass on the national domain. And except for the brief interlude that ended with the crisis of the thirties, it is mainly in the realm of such policing of the states that the Supreme Court has in fact participated in determining the balances of federalism.[1] This is not to say that the Court can decline to measure national enactments by the Constitution when it is called upon to face the question in the course of ordinary litigation; the supremacy clause governs there as well. It is rather to say that the Court is on weakest ground when it opposes its interpretation of the Constitution to that of Congress in the interest of the states, whose representatives control the legislative process and, by hypothesis, have broadly acquiesced in sanctioning the challenged Act of Congress.

Federal intervention as against the states is thus primarily a matter for congressional determination in our system as it stands. So too, moreover, is the question whether state enactments shall be stricken down as an infringement on the national authority. For while the Court has an important function in this area, as I have noted, the crucial point is that its judgments here are subject to reversal by Congress, which can consent to action by the states that otherwise would be invalidated. The familiar illustrations in commerce

---

[1] Of the great controversies with respect to national power before the Civil War, only the Bank and slavery within the territories were carried to the Court and its participation with respect to slavery was probably its greatest failure. The question of internal improvements, for example, which raised the most acute problem of constitutional construction, was fought out politically and in Congress. After the War only the Civil Rights Cases and income tax decisions were important in setting limits on national power — until the Child Labor Case and the New Deal decisions. The recasting of constitutional positions since the crisis acknowledges much broader power in the Congress — as against the states — than it is likely soon or ever to employ.

and in state taxation of federal instrumentalities do not by any means exhaust the field. The Court makes the decisive judgment only when — and to the extent that — Congress has not laid down the resolving rule.[2]

To perceive that it is Congress rather than the Court that on the whole is vested with the ultimate authority for managing our federalism is not, of course, to depreciate the role played by the Court, subordinate though it may be. It is no accident that Congress has been slow to exercise its managerial authority, remitting to the Court so much of what it could determine by a legislative rule. The difficulties of reaching agreement on such matters, not to speak of drafting problems of immense complexity, lend obvious attractiveness to the ad hoc judicial method of adjustment. Whether Congress could contribute more effectively to the solution of these problems is a challenging and open question. The legislative possibilities within this area of our polity have hardly been explored.

Freund, Foundations and Development of American Federalism
Federalism and the New Nations of Africa 160-162 (Currie ed. 1964)

If we turn to the Federalist papers, particularly those of Madison, we are given a rationale of liberty as a function of federalism itself. Addressing himself to the problem of "factions," not least the faction of a despotic majority — a problem on which a reading of Hume illuminated the evidence of experience — Madison contrived to make size and space an ally of republicanism.[1] Geography, the source of so much domestic conflict, could be enlisted in the service of a free society. By enlarging the area of representative government, interests become more diverse, an enduring majority less possible, shifting coalitions the pattern of government. Combined with the indirect election of the President, the separation of powers, and the division of functions in a federation, the diffusion of interests would provide a "double security." The emergence of factions in the form of national political parties soon came to transform the presidential electoral system and much else; but by a saving paradox the parties themselves became the sheltering arenas of shifting coalitions.

The federal structure evolved by the framers was not the system proposed by Hamilton in his eloquent speech early in the Convention: a president elected for life, and a national legislature which would appoint governors for the several states who would have a veto power over state legislation . . . Nonetheless the Constitution embodies principles that were in advance, as Professor B. F. Wright has pointed out, of any federal experience theretofore undertaken anywhere: election of the House by popular vote, not by state legislatures; representation according to population; the taxing power of the central government enforceable against individuals; a system of separate federal courts.[2]

If in its origins American federalism revealed traces of Newtonian mechanics, its development has been more characteristically Darwinian. As good a way as any to describe it would be to adopt that wonderful phrase in one of E. M. Forster's novels: a "creative mess."

---

[2] The judicial function in relation to federalism thus differs markedly from that performed in the application of those constitutional restraints on Congress or the states that are designed to safeguard individuals. In this latter area of the constitutional protection of the individual against the government, both federal and state, subordination of the Court to Congress would defeat the purpose of judicial mediation. For this is where the political processes cannot be relied upon to introduce their own correctives — except to the limited extent that individuals or small minorities may find a champion in some important faction. See Stone, J., in United States v. Carolene Products Co., 304 U.S. 144, 152-53 n.4 (1938); Mr. Justice Stone and the Constitution, . . . at pp. 129-130.

[1] See D. Adair, "That Politics May Be Reduced to a Science": David Hume, James Madison, and the Tenth Federalist, 20 Huntington Library Quarterly, XX, No. 4 (1956-57).

[2] B. F. Wright, Consensus and Continuity, 1776-1787 (1958).

The system has functioned badly when a single issue has hardened and sharpened sectional claims beyond the stage of compromise and accommodation, when the diversity and multiplicity of interests caught up at the center have ceased to be significant or strong enough to blunt the fixed swordpoint of contention. When in 1812 the west and south united to bring on a futile and unnecessary war with Britain, the northeast came close to secession. When in 1860 the Republicans elected Lincoln by carrying every free state and none of the others, the sectional division was so hardened and the prospects for the southern position so foreboding that secession was the desperate response.

If we grant that a multiplicity of interests is the clue to a liberal national government, at least in a domain of continental extent, is it a corollary that a federal structure is a necessary or helpful feature of the system? . . . Has not the menace of village or state-house tyrants been far more real than that of a national dictator? Moreover, given the mobility of society, racial minorities and the political splinter groups have not owed their recognition, on the whole, to territorial representation. Is not federalism, then, at worst a hindrance, at best an irrelevance, in the maintenance of an open society? Is not Lord Acton's fulsome tribute to federalism, that it is "the protectorate of minorities, and the consecration of self-government," at least inapt for the American experience? Again the answer is not self-evident. For it is a fallacy to set the national government over against the states without recognizing the distinctive political structure of the national government itself. Once more the character of American federalism cannot be separated from the character of its political parties. These national parties are locally based; their supreme aim is to capture the Presidency; and to do this, given the electoral system with a state's block of electoral votes counted as a unit, the great prizes are the closely contested, populous industrial states, where racial or other minority groups may hold the balance of power. Not territorial representation but the federal structure of American parties is the nexus between federalism and the recognition of group interests.

Chapter Five National and State Power: The Early Struggle Toward Standards

McCulloch v. Maryland *4 Wheat. 316, 4 L. Ed. 579 (1819)*

[An action was brought in a county court of Baltimore on behalf of Maryland against McCulloch, cashier of the Baltimore branch of the Bank of the United States, to recover penalties under a state statute for nonpayment by the bank of taxes on the issuance of bank notes.

The statute read as follows:

"An act to impose a tax on all banks or branches thereof in the state of Maryland, not chartered by the legislature.

"Be it enacted by the General Assembly of Maryland, That if any bank has established or shall, without authority from the state first had and obtained, establish any branch, office of discount and deposit, or office of pay and receipt, in any part of this state, it shall not be lawful for the said branch, office of discount and deposit, or office of pay and receipt, to issue notes in any manner, of any other denomination than five, ten, twenty, fifty, one hundred, five hundred and one thousand dollars, and no note shall be issued except upon stamped paper of the following denominations; that is to say, every five dollar note shall be upon a stamp of ten cents; every ten dollar note upon a stamp of twenty cents; every twenty dollar note upon a stamp of thirty cents; every fifty dollar note upon a stamp of fifty cents; every one hundred dollar note upon a stamp of one dollar; every five hundred dollar note upon a stamp of ten dollars; and every thousand dollar note upon a stamp of twenty dollars; which paper shall be furnished by the treasurer of the Western Shore, under the direction of the governor and council, to be paid for upon delivery. Provided always, That any institution of the above description may relieve itself from the operation of the provisions aforesaid, by paying annually, in advance, to the treasurer of the Western Shore, for the use of the state, the sum of fifteen thousand dollars.

"And be it enacted, That the president, cashier, each of the directors and officers of every institution established, or to be established as aforesaid, offending against the provisions aforesaid, shall forfeit a sum of five hundred dollars for each and every offense, . . ."

The Court of Appeals affirmed a judgment for the plaintiff.]

MARSHALL, C.J., delivered the opinion of the court:

In the case now to be determined, the defendant, a sovereign state, denies the obligation of a law enacted by the legislature of the Union, and the plaintiff, on his part, contests the validity of an act which has been passed by the legislature of that state. The constitution of our country, in its most interesting and vital parts, is to be considered; the conflicting powers of the government of the Union and of its members, as marked in that constitution, are to be discussed; and an opinion given, which may essentially influence the great operations of the government. No tribunal can approach such a question without a deep sense of its importance, and of the awful responsibility involved in its decision. But it must be decided peacefully, or remain a source of hostile legislation, perhaps of hostility of a still more serious nature; and if it is to be so decided, by this tribunal alone can the decision be made. On the Supreme Court of the United States has the constitution of our country devolved this important duty.

The first question made in the cause is, has Congress power to incorporate a bank?

It has been truly said that this can scarcely be considered as an open question, entirely unprejudiced by the former proceedings of the nation respecting it. The principle now contested was introduced at a very early period of our history, has been recognized by many successive legislatures, and has been acted upon by the judicial department, in cases of peculiar delicacy, as a law of undoubted obligation.

It will not be denied that a bold and daring usurpation might be resisted, after an acquiescence still longer and more complete than this. But it is conceived that a doubtful question, one on which human reason may pause, and the human judgment be suspended, in the decision of which the great principles of liberty are not concerned, but the respective powers of those who are equally the representatives of the people, are to be adjusted; if not put at rest by the practice of the government, ought to receive a considerable impression from that practice. An exposition of the constitution, deliberately established by legislative acts, on the faith of which an immense property has been advanced, ought not to be lightly disregarded.

The power now contested was exercised by the first Congress elected under the present constitution. The bill for incorporating the bank of the United States did not steal upon an unsuspecting legislature, and pass unobserved. Its principle was completely understood, and was opposed with equal zeal and ability. After being resisted, first in the fair and open field of debate, and afterwards in the executive cabinet, with as much persevering talent as any measure has ever experienced, and being supported by arguments which convinced minds as pure and as intelligent as this country can boast, it became a law. The original act was permitted to expire; but a short experience of the embarrassments to which the refusal to revive it exposed the government, convinced those who were most prejudiced against the measure of its necessity and induced the passage of the present law. It would require no ordinary share of intrepidity to assert that a measure adopted under these circumstances was a bold and plain usurpation, to which the constitution gave no countenance. . . .

The government of the Union, then (whatever may be the influence of this fact on the case), is, emphatically, and truly, a government of the people. In form and in substance it emanates from them. Its powers are granted by them and are to be exercised directly on them, and for their benefit.

This government is acknowledged by all to be one of enumerated powers. The principle, that it can exercise only the powers granted to it, would seem too apparent to have required to be enforced by all those arguments which its enlightened friends, while it was depending before the people, found it necessary to urge. That principle is now universally admitted. But the question respecting the extent of the powers actually granted, is perpetually arising, and will probably continue to arise, as long as our system shall exist.

If any one proposition could command the universal assent of mankind, we might expect it would be this: that the government of the Union, though limited in its powers, is supreme within its sphere of action. This would seem to result necessarily from its nature.

It is the government of all; its powers are delegated by all; it represents all, and acts for all. Though any one state may be willing to control its operations, no state is willing to allow others to control them. The nation, on those subjects on which it can act, must necessarily bind its component parts. But this question is not left to mere reason: the people have, in express terms, decided it, by saying "this Constitution, and the laws of the United States, which shall be made in pursuance thereof," "shall be the supreme law of the land," and by requiring that the members of the state legislatures, and the officers of the executive and judicial departments of the states, shall take the oath of fidelity to it.

The government of the United States, then, though limited in its powers, is supreme; and its laws, when made in pursuance of the Constitution, form the supreme law of the land, "anything in the Constitution or laws of any State, to the contrary notwithstanding."

Among the enumerated powers, we do not find that of establishing a bank or creating a corporation. But there is no phrase in the instrument which, like the articles of confederation, excludes incidental or implied powers; and which requires that everything granted shall be expressly and minutely described. Even the 10th amendment, which was framed for the purpose of quieting the excessive jealousies which had been excited, omits the word "expressly," and declares only that the powers "not delegated to the United States, nor prohibited to the states, are reserved to the states or to the people"; thus leaving the question, whether the particular power which may become the subject of contest has been delegated to the one government, or prohibited to the other, to depend on a fair construction of the whole instrument. The men who drew and adopted this amendment had experienced the embarrassments resulting from the insertion of this word in the articles of confederation, and probably omitted it to avoid those embarrassments. A constitution, to contain an accurate detail of all the subdivisions of which its great powers will admit, and of all the means by which they may be carried into execution, would partake of a prolixity of a legal code, and could scarcely be embraced by the human mind. It would probably never be understood by the public. Its nature, therefore, requires, that only its great outlines should be marked, its important objects designated, and the minor ingredients which compose those objects be deduced from the nature of the objects themselves. . . . In considering this question, then, we must never forget that it is a *constitution* we are expounding.

Although, among the enumerated powers of government, we do not find the word "bank" or "incorporation," we find the great powers to lay and collect taxes; to borrow money; to regulate commerce; to declare and conduct a war; and to raise and support armies and navies. The sword and the purse, all the external relations, and no inconsiderable portion of the industry of the nation, are entrusted to its government. It can never be pretended that these vast powers draw after them others of inferior importance, merely because they are inferior. Such an idea can never be advanced. But it may with great reason be contended, that a government, entrusted with such ample powers, on the due execution of which the happiness and prosperity of the nation so vitally depends, must also be entrusted with ample means for their execution. The power being given, it is the interest of the nation to facilitate its execution. It can never be their interest, and cannot be presumed to have been their intention, to clog and embarrass its execution by withholding the most appropriate means. Throughout this vast republic, from the St. Croix to the Gulf of Mexico, from the Atlantic to the Pacific, revenue is to be collected and expended, armies are to be marched and supported. The exigencies of the nation may require that the treasure raised in the north should be transported to the south, that raised in the east conveyed to the west, or that this order should be reversed. Is that construction of the constitution to be preferred which would render these operations difficult, hazardous, and expensive? Can we adopt that construction (unless the words imperiously require it) which would impute to the framers of that instrument, when granting these powers for the public good, the intention of impeding their exercise by withholding a choice of means? If, indeed, such be the mandate of the constitution, we have only to obey; but that instrument does not profess to enumerate the means by which the powers it confers may be executed; nor does it prohibit the creation of a corporation, if the existence of such a being be essential to the beneficial exercise of those powers. It is, then, the subject of fair inquiry, how far such means may be employed. . . .

The creation of a corporation, it is said, appertains to sovereignty. This is admitted. But to what portion of sovereignty does it appertain? Does it belong to one more than to another? . . . The power of creating a corporation, though appertaining to sovereignty, is not, like the power of making war, or levying taxes, or of regulating commerce, a great substantive and independent power, which cannot be implied as incidental to other powers, or used as a means of executing them. It is never the end for which other powers are exercised, but a means by which other objects are accomplished. No contributions are made to charity for the sake of an incorporation, but a corporation is created to administer the charity; no seminary of learning is instituted in order to be incorporated, but the corporate character is conferred to subserve the purposes of education. No city was ever built with the sole object of being incorporated, but is incorporated as affording the best means of being well governed. The power of creating a corporation is never used for its own sake, but for the purpose of effecting something else. No sufficient reason is, therefore, perceived, why it may not pass as incidental to those powers which are expressly given, if it be a direct mode of executing them.

But the constitution of the United States has not left the right of Congress to employ the necessary means for the execution of the powers conferred on the government to general reasoning. To its enumeration of powers is added that of making "all laws which shall be necessary and proper, for carrying into execution the foregoing powers, and all other powers vested by this constitution, in the government of the United States, or in any department thereof."

The counsel for the State of Maryland have urged various arguments, to prove that this clause, though in terms a grant of power, is not so in effect; but is really restrictive of the general right, which might otherwise be implied, of selecting means for executing the enumerated powers. . . .

But the argument on which most reliance is placed, is drawn from the peculiar language of this clause. Congress is not empowered by it to make all laws, which may have relation to the powers conferred on the government, but such only as may be "necessary and proper" for carrying them into execution. The word "necessary" is considered as controlling the whole sentence, and as limiting the right to pass laws for the execution of the granted powers, to such as are indispensable, and without which the power would be nugatory. That it excludes the choice of means, and leaves to Congress, in each case, that only which is most direct and simple.

Is it true that this is the sense in which the word "necessary" is always used? Does it always import an absolute physical necessity, so strong that one thing, to which another may be termed necessary, cannot exist without that other? We think it does not. If reference be had to its use, in the common affairs of the world, or in approved authors, we find that it frequently imports no more than that one thing is convenient, or useful, or essential to another. To employ the means necessary to an end, is generally understood as employing any means calculated to produce the end, and not as being confined to those single means, without which the end would be entirely unattainable. . . . A thing may be necessary, very necessary, absolutely or indispensably necessary. To no mind would the same idea be conveyed by these several phrases. This comment on the word is well illustrated by the passage cited at the bar, from the 10th section of the 1st article of the constitution. It is, we think, impossible to compare the sentence which prohibits a state from laying imposts or duties on imports or exports, except that may be "absolutely necessary for executing its inspection laws," with that which authorizes Congress "to make all laws which shall be necessary and proper for carrying into execution" the powers of the general government, without feeling a conviction that the convention understood itself to change materially the meaning of the word "necessary," by prefixing the word "absolutely." This word, then, like others, is used in various senses; and, in its construction, the subject, the context, the intention of the person using them, are all to be taken into view.

. . . This provision is made in a constitution intended to endure for ages to come, and, consequently, to be adapted to the various crises of human affairs. To have prescribed the means by which government should, in all future time, execute its powers, would have been to change, entirely, the character of the instrument, and give it the properties of a legal code. It would have been an unwise attempt to provide, by immutable rules, for exigencies which, if foreseen at all, must have been seen dimly, and which can be best provided for as they occur. To have declared that the best means shall not be used, but those alone without which the power given would be nugatory, would have been to deprive the legislature of the capacity to avail itself of experience, to exercise its reason, and to accommodate its legislation to circumstances. . . .

Take, for example, the power "to establish post-offices and post-roads." This power is executed by the single act of making the establishment. But, from this has been inferred the power and duty of carrying the mail along the post-road, from one post-office to another. And, from this implied power, has again been inferred the right to punish those who steal letters from the post-office, or rob the mail. It may be said, with some plausibility, that the right to carry the mail, and to punish those who rob it, is not indispensably necessary to the establishment of a post-office and post-road. This right is indeed essential to the beneficial exercise of the power, but not indispensably necessary to its existence. So, of the punishment of the crimes of stealing or falsifying a record or process of a court of the United States, or of perjury in such court. To punish these offenses is certainly conducive to the due administration of justice. But courts may exist, and may decide the causes brought before them, though such crimes escape punishment. . . .

The result of the most careful and attentive consideration bestowed upon this clause is, that if it does not enlarge, it cannot be construed to restrain the powers of Congress, or to impair the right of the legislature to exercise its best judgment in the selection of measures to carry into execution the constitutional powers of the government. If no other motive for its insertion can be suggested, a sufficient one is found in the desire to remove all doubts respecting the right to legislate on that vast mass of incidental powers which must be involved in the constitution, if that instrument be not a splendid bauble.

We admit, as all must admit, that the powers of the government are limited, and that its limits are not to be transcended. But we think the sound construction of the constitution must allow to the national legislature that discretion, with respect to the means by which the powers it confers are to be carried into execution, which will enable that body to perform the high duties assigned to it, in the manner most beneficial to the people. Let the end be legitimate, let it be within the scope of the constitution, and all means which are appropriate, which are plainly adapted to that end, which are not prohibited, but consist with the letter and spirit of the constitution, are constitutional. . . .

If a corporation may be employed indiscriminately with other means to carry into execution the powers of the government, no particular reason can be assigned for excluding the use of a bank, if required for its fiscal operations. To use one, must be within the discretion of Congress, if it be an appropriate mode of executing the powers of government. That it is a convenient, a useful, and essential instrument in the prosecution of its fiscal operations, is not now a subject of controversy. All those who have been concerned in the administration of our finances, have concurred in representing the importance and necessity; and so strongly have they been felt, that statesmen of the first class, whose previous opinions against it had been confirmed by every circumstance which can fix the human judgment, have yielded those opinions to the exigencies of the nation. . . .

But, were its necessity less apparent, none can deny its being an appropriate measure; and if it is, the degree of its necessity, as has been very justly observed, is to be discussed in another place. Should Congress, in the execution of its powers, adopt measures which are prohibited by the constitution; or should Congress, under the pretext of executing its powers, pass laws for the accomplishment of objects not entrusted to the government, it would become the painful duty of this tribunal, should a case requiring such a decision come before it, to say that such an act was not the law of the land. But where the law is not prohibited, and is really calculated to effect any of the objects entrusted to the government, to undertake here to inquire into the degree of its necessity, would be to pass the line which circumscribes the judicial department, and to tread on legislative ground. This court disclaims all pretensions to such a power. . . .

After the most deliberate consideration, it is the unanimous and decided opinion of this court that the act to incorporate the bank of the United States is a law made in pursuance of the constitution, and is a part of the supreme law of the land.

The branches, proceeding from the same stock, and being conducive to the complete accomplishment of the object, are equally constitutional. It would have been unwise to locate them in the charter, and it would be unnecessarily inconvenient to employ the legislative power in making those subordinate arrangements. The great duties of the bank are prescribed; those duties require branches; and the bank itself may, we think, be safely trusted with the selection of places where those branches shall be fixed; reserving always to the government the right to require that a branch shall be located where it may be deemed necessary.

It being the opinion of the court that the act incorporating the bank is constitutional, and that the power of establishing a branch in the state of Maryland might be properly exercised by the bank itself, we proceed to inquire:

2. Whether the state of Maryland may, without violating the constitution, tax that branch? . . .

All subjects over which the sovereign power of a state extends, are objects of taxation; but those over which it does not extend, are, upon the soundest principles, exempt from taxation. This proposition may almost be pronounced self-evident.

The sovereignty of a state extends to everything which exists by its own authority, or is introduced by its permission; but does it extend to those means which are employed by Congress to carry into execution — powers conferred on that body by the people of the United States? We think it demonstrable that it does not. Those powers are not given by the people of a single state. They are given by the people of the United States, to a government whose laws, made in pursuance of the constitution, are declared to be supreme. Consequently, the people of a single state cannot confer a sovereignty which will extend over them.

If we measure the power of taxation residing in a state by the extent of sovereignty which the people of a single state possess, and can confer on its government, we have an intelligible standard, applicable to every case to which the power may be applied. We have a principle which leaves the power of taxing the people and property of a state unimpaired; which leaves to a state the command of all its resources, and which places beyond its reach, all those powers which are conferred by the people of the United States on the government of the Union, and all those means which are given for the purpose of carrying those powers into execution. We have a principle which is safe for the states, and safe for the Union. We are relieved, as we ought to be, from clashing sovereignty; from interfering powers; from a repugnancy between a right in one government to pull down what there is an acknowledged right in another to build up; from the incompatibility of a right in one government to destroy what there is a right in another to preserve. We are not driven to the perplexing inquiry, so unfit for the judicial department, what degree of taxation is the legitimate use, and what degree may amount to the abuse of the power. . . .

That the power to tax involves the power to destroy; that the power to destroy may defeat and render useless the power to create; that there is a plain repugnance, in conferring on one government a power to control the constitutional measures of another, which other, with respect to those very measures, is declared to be supreme over that which exerts the control, are propositions not to be denied. But all inconsistencies are to be reconciled by the magic of the word confidence. Taxation, it is said, does not necessarily and unavoidably destroy. To carry it to the excess of destruction would be an abuse, to presume which, would banish that confidence which is essential to all government.

But is this a case of confidence? Would the people of any one state trust those of another with a power to control the most insignificant operations of their state government? We know they would not. Why, then, should we suppose that the people of any one state should be willing to trust those of another with a power to control the operations of a government to which they have confided the most important and most valuable interests? In the legislature of the Union alone, are all represented. The legislature of the Union alone, therefore, can be trusted by the people with the power of controlling measures which concern all, in the confidence that it will not be abused. This, then, is not a case of confidence, and we must consider it as it really is.

In the course of the argument, the "Federalist" has been quoted; and the opinions expressed by the authors of that work have been justly supposed to be entitled to great respect in expounding the Constitution. No tribute can be paid to them which exceeds their merit; but in applying their opinions to the cases which may arise in the progress of our government, a right to judge of their correctness must be retained; and, to understand the argument, we must examine the proposition it maintains, and the objections against which it is directed. The subject of those numbers, from which passages have been cited, is the unlimited power of taxation which is vested in the general government. The objection to this unlimited power, which the government seeks to remove, is stated with fulness and clearness. . . .

The objections to the Constitution which are noticed in these numbers, were to the undefined power of the government to tax, not the incidental privilege of exempting its own measures from state taxation. The consequences apprehended from this undefined power were, that it would absorb all the objects of taxation, "to the exclusion and destruction of the state governments." The arguments of the "Federalist" are intended to prove the fallacy of these apprehensions; not to prove that the government was incapable of executing any of its powers, without exposing the means it employed to the embarrassments of state taxation. Arguments urged against these objections, and these apprehensions, are to be understood as relating to the points they mean to prove. Had the authors of those excellent essays been asked, whether they contended for that construction of the Constitution, which would place within the reach of the states those measures which the government might adopt for the execution of its powers; no man, who has read their instructive pages, will hesitate to admit, that their answer must have been in the negative.

It has also been insisted, that, as the power of taxation in the general and state governments is acknowledged to be concurrent, every argument which would sustain the right of the general government to tax banks chartered by the states, will equally sustain the right of the states to tax banks chartered by the general government.

But the two cases are not on the same reason. The people of all the states have created the general government, and have conferred upon it the general power of taxation. The people of all the states, and the states themselves, are represented in Congress, and, by their representatives, exercise this power. When they tax the chartered institutions of the states, they tax their constituents; and these taxes must be uniform. But, when a state taxes the operations of the government of the United States, it acts upon institutions created, not by their own constituents, but by people over whom they claim no control. It acts upon the measures of a government created by others as well as themselves, for the benefit of others in common with themselves. The difference is that which always exists, and always must exist, between the action of the whole on a part, and the action of a part on the whole — between the laws of a government declared to be supreme, and those of a government which, when in opposition to those laws, is not supreme.

But if the full application of this argument could be admitted, it might bring into question the right of Congress to tax the state banks, and could not prove the right of the states to tax the Bank of the United States.

The court has bestowed on this subject its most deliberate consideration. The result is a conviction that the states have no power, by taxation or otherwise, to retard, impede, burden, or in any manner control the operations of the constitutional laws enacted by Congress to carry into execution the powers vested in the general government. This is, we think, the unavoidable consequence of that supremacy which the constitution has declared.

We are unanimously of opinion that the law passed by the legislature of Maryland, imposing a tax on the Bank of the United States, is unconstitutional and void.

This opinion does not deprive the states of any resources which they originally possessed. It does not extend to a tax paid by the real property of the bank, in common with the other real property within the state, nor to a tax imposed on the interest which the citizens of Maryland may hold in this institution, in common with other property of the same description throughout the state. But this is a tax on the operations of the bank, and is, consequently, a tax on the operation of an instrument employed by the government of the Union to carry its powers into execution. Such a tax must be unconstitutional.

NOTE

1. The Constitutional Convention defeated a motion by Madison to confer on Congress a power "to grant charters of incorporation where the interest of the United States might require and the legislative provisions of individual States may be incompetent." Documents Illustrative of the Formation of the Union 724 (Govt. Printing Office, 1927). Should this historical evidence have been taken into account in McCulloch v. Maryland? Should it have changed the result?

2. Before signing the bill incorporating the bank, on February 25, 1791, Washington procured written opinions on its constitutionality from Hamilton, Jefferson, and Randolph. The indebtedness of Marshall to Hamilton's opinion has often been noted. Jefferson's opinion was adverse, and Randolph submitted two opinions, one adverse, one ambiguous. Jefferson's view of "necessary and proper" may also be gauged from his comment in 1800 on a bill for federal incorporation of a copper mining enterprise in New Jersey: "Congress are authorized to defend the nation. Ships are necessary for defence; copper is necessary for ships; mines, necessary for copper; a company necessary to work the mines; and who can doubt this reasoning who has ever played at 'This is the House that Jack Built'?" 1 Warren, The Supreme Court in United States History 501 (1926).

3. An earlier, less comprehensive, treatment of the "necessary and proper" clause is to be found in United States v. Fisher, 2 Cranch 358 (1805), per Marshall, C.J., upholding an Act of Congress giving priority, in cases of insolvency, to debts due to the United States. The principle of McCulloch v. Maryland was held in First National Bank v. Fellows, 244 U.S. 416 (1917), to sustain a provision of the Federal Reserve Act of 1913 authorizing national banks to act as trustee, executor, administrator, or registrar of stocks and bonds. And in Smith v. Kansas City Title & Trust Co., 255 U.S. 180 (1921), the system of Federal Land Banks was upheld.

4. The problems of intergovernmental tax immunity are dealt with infra at pages 622-643.

5. For Marshall's extrajudicial (and anonymous) commentary, see G. Gunther, John Marshall's Defense of McCulloch v. Maryland (1969), also in 21 Stanf. L. Rev. 449 (1969).

Livingston v. Van Ingen 9 Johns. 507 (N.Y. 1812)

[By acts of the New York legislature, designed to encourage the development of navigation by steam, and requiring the grantees to produce proof of the practicability of such navigation on the Hudson, within two years, Livingston and Fulton were granted the exclusive right to employ steam vessels in the navigation of the waters within the jurisdiction of the state. They sued to enjoin Van Ingen and others from carrying passengers in a steamboat between New York and Albany. On appeal from a denial of the injunction the Court of Errors reversed. Seriatim opinions were delivered; only that of Chief Justice Kent is here printed.]

KENT, CH. J. The great point in this cause is, whether the several acts of the legislature which have been passed in favour of the appellants, are to be regarded as constitutional and binding.

This house, sitting in its judicial capacity as a court, has nothing to do with the policy or expediency of these laws. The only question here is, whether the legislature had authority to pass them. If we can satisfy ourselves upon this point, or, rather, unless we are fully persuaded that they are void, we are bound to obey them, and give them the requisite effect.

. . . The powers of the two governments are each supreme within their respective constitutional spheres. They may each operate with full effect upon different subjects, or they may, as in the case of taxation, operate upon different parts of the same object. The powers of the two governments cannot indeed be supreme over each other, for that would involve a contradiction. When those powers, therefore, come directly in contact, as when they are aimed at each other, or at one indivisible object, the power of the state is subordinate, and must yield. . . . We have, then, nothing to do, in the ordinary course of legislation, with the possible contingency of a collision, nor are we to embarrass ourselves in the anticipation of theoretical difficulties, than which nothing could, in general, be more fallacious. Such a doctrine would be constantly taxing our sagacity, to see whether the law might not contravene some future regulation of commerce, or some moneyed or some military operation of the United States. Our most simple municipal provisions would be enacted with diffidence, for fear we might involve ourselves, our citizens and our consciences in some case of usurpation. Fortunately, for the peace and happiness of this country, we have a plainer path to follow. We do not handle a work of such hazardous consequence. We are not always walking *per ignes suppositos cineri doloso.* Our safe rule of construction and of action is this, that if any given power was originally vested in this state, if it has not been exclusively ceded to congress, or if the exercise of it has not been prohibited to the states, we may then go on in the exercise of the power until it comes practically in collision with the actual exercise of some congressional power. When that happens to be the case, the state authority will so far be controlled, but it will still be good in all those respects in which it does not absolutely contravene the provision of the paramount law. . . .

As to the power to regulate commerce.

This power is not, in express terms, exclusive, and the only prohibition upon the states is, that they shall not enter into any treaty or compact with each other, or with a foreign power, nor lay any duty on tonnage, or on imports or exports, except what may be necessary for executing their inspection laws. Upon the principles above laid down, the states are under no other constitutional restriction, and are, consequently, left in possession of a vast field of commercial regulation; all the internal comerce of the state by land and water remains entirely, and I may say exclusively, within the scope of its original sovereignty. The congressional power relates to external not to internal commerce, and it is confined to the *regulation* of that commerce. To what extent these regulations may be carried, it is not our present duty to inquire. The limits of this power seem not to be susceptible of precise definition. It may be difficult to draw an exact line between those regulations which relate to external and those which relate to internal commerce, for every regulation of the one will, directly or indirectly, affect the other. To avoid doubts, embarrassment and contention on this complicated question, the general rule of interpretation which has been mentioned, is extremely salutary. It removes all difficulty, by its simplicity and certainty. The states are under no other restrictions than those expressly specified in the constitution, and such regulations as the national government may, by treaty, and by laws, from time to time, prescribe. Subject to these restrictions, I contend, that the states are at liberty to make their own commercial regulations. There can be no other safe or practicable rule of conduct, and this, as I have already shown, is the true constitutional rule arising from the nature of our federal system. This does away all colour for the suggestion that the steam-boat grant is illegal and void under this clause in the constitution. It comes not within any prohibition upon the states, and it interferes with no existing regulation. Whenever the case shall arise of an exercise of power by congress which shall be directly repugnant and destructive to the use and enjoyment of the appellants' grant, it would fall under this cognisance of the federal courts, and they would, of course, take care that the laws of the union are duly supported. I must confess, however, that I can hardly conceive of such a case, because I do not, at present, perceive any power which congress can lawfully carry to that extent. But when there is no existing regulation which interferes with the grant, nor any pretence of a constitutional interdict, it would be most extraordinary for us to adjudge it void, on the mere contingency of a collision with some future exercise of congressional power. Such a doctrine is a monstrous heresy. It would go, in a great degree, to annihilate the legislative power of the states. May not the legislature declare that no bank paper shall circulate, or be given or received in payment, but what originates from some incorporated bank of our own, or that none shall circulate under the nominal value of one dollar? But suppose congress should institute a national bank, with authority to issue and circulate throughout the union, bank notes, as well below as above that nominal value: This would so far control the state law, but it would remain valid and binding, except as to the paper of the national bank. The state law would be absolute, until the appearance of the national bank, and then it would have a qualified effect, and be good pro tanto. So, again, the legislature may declare that it shall be unlawful to vend lottery tickets, unless they be tickets of lotteries authorized by a law of this state, and who will question the validity of the provision? But suppose congress should deem it expedient to establish a national lottery, and should authorize persons in each state to vend the tickets, this would so far control the state prohibition, and leave it in full force as to all other lotteries. The possibility that a national bank, or a national lottery, might be instituted, would be a very strange reason for holding the state laws to be absolutely null and void. It strikes me to be an equally inadmissible proposition, that the state is devested of a capacity to grant an exclusive privilege of navigating a steam-boat, within its own waters, merely because we can imagine that congress, in the plenary exercise of its power to regulate commerce, may make some regulation inconsistent with the exercise of this privilege. When such a case arises, it will provide for itself; and there is, fortunately, a paramount power in the supreme court of the United States to guard against the mischiefs of collision. . . .

Gibbons v. Ogden 9 Wheat. 1, 6 L. Ed. 23 (1824)

[Ogden received an assignment of the right of Livingston and Fulton granted by acts of the New York legislature (considered in Livingston v. Van Ingen, page 163 supra) for the exclusive navigation of the waters of New York with boats moved by fire or steam, for a term of years which had not expired. Gibbons operated two steamboats between New York and Elizabethtown, New Jersey, in violation of the terms of the New York legislative acts; these boats were enrolled and licensed to be employed in the coasting trade under an

Act of Congress of 1793. The New York chancery court granted an injunction on behalf of Ogden against Gibbons, which was affirmed on appeal, Chancellor Kent writing the opinion holding the New York acts constitutional. 4 Johns. Ch. 150 (1819).]

Mr. Chief Justice Marshall delivered the opinion of the Court, and after stating the case, proceeded as follows:

The appellant contends that this decree is erroneous, because the laws which purport to give the exclusive privileges it sustains, are repugnant to the constitution and laws of the United States.

They are said to be repugnant:

1st. To that clause in the constitution which authorizes Congress to regulate commerce.

2d. To that which authorizes Congress to promote the progress of science and useful arts.

The state of New York maintains the constitutionality of these laws; and their legislature, their Council of Revision, and their judges have repeatedly concurred in this opinion. It is supported by great names — by names which have all the titles to consideration that virtue, intelligence, and office, can bestow. No tribunal can approach the decision of this question, without feeling a just and real respect for that opinion which is sustained by such authority; but it is the province of this Court, while it respects, not to bow to it implicitly; and the judges must exercise, in the examination of the subject, that understanding which Providence has bestowed upon them, with that independence which the people of the United States expect from this department of the government. . . .

The words are: "Congress shall have power to regulate commerce with foreign nations, and among the several states, and with the Indian tribes."

The subject to be regulated is commerce; and our constitution being, as was aptly said at the bar, one of enumeration, and not of definition, to ascertain the extent of the power it becomes necessary to settle the meaning of the word. The counsel for the appellee would limit it to traffic, to buying and selling, or the interchange of commodities, and do not admit that it comprehends navigation. This would restrict a general term, applicable to many objects, to one of its significations. Commerce, undoubtedly, is traffic, but it is something more; it is intercourse. It describes the commercial intercourse between nations, and parts of nations, in all its branches, and is regulated by prescribing rules for carrying on that intercourse. The mind can scarcely conceive a system for regulating commerce between nations, which shall exclude all laws concerning navigation, which shall be silent on the admission of the vessels of the one nation into the ports of the other, and be confined to prescribing rules for the conduct of individuals, in the actual employment of buying and selling, or of barter.

If commerce does not include navigation, the government of the Union has no direct power over that subject, and can make no law prescribing what shall constitute American vessels, or requiring that they shall be navigated by American seamen. Yet this power has been exercised from the commencement of the government, has been exercised with the consent of all, and has been understood by all to be a commercial regulation. All America understands, and has uniformly understood, the word "commerce" to comprehend navigation. It was so understood, and must have been so understood, when the constitution was framed. The power over commerce, including navigation, was one of the primary objects for which the people of America adopted their government, and must have been contemplated in forming it. The convention must have used the word in that sense; because all have understood it in that sense, and the attempt to restrict it comes too late.

If the opinion that "commerce" as the word is used in the constitution, comprehends navigation also, requires any additional confirmation, that additional confirmation is, we think, furnished by the words of the instrument itself.

It is a rule of construction, acknowledged by all, that the exceptions from a power mark its extent; for it would be absurd, as well as useless, to except from a granted power, that which was not granted — that which the words of the grant could not comprehend. . . .

The 9th section of the 1st article declares that "no preference shall be given, by any regulation of commerce or revenue, to the ports of one state over those of another." This clause cannot be understood as applicable to those laws only which are passed for the purposes of revenue, because it is expressly applied to commercial regulations; and the most obvious preference which can be given to one port over another, in regulating commerce, relates to navigation. But the subsequent part of the sentence is still more explicit. It is, "nor shall vessels bound to or from one state, be obliged to enter, clear, or pay duties, in another." These words have a direct reference to navigation.

The universally acknowledged power of the government to impose embargoes, must also be considered as showing that all America is united in that construction which comprehends navigation in the word commerce. . . .

When Congress imposed that embargo, which, for a time, engaged the attention of every man in the United States, the avowed object of the law was the protection of commerce, and the avoiding of war. By its friends and its enemies it was treated as a commercial, not as a war measure. The persevering earnestness and zeal with which it was opposed, in a part of our country which supposed its interests to be vitally affected by the act, cannot be forgotten. A want of acuteness in discovering objections to a measure to which they felt the most deep-rooted hostility, will not be imputed to those who were arrayed in opposition to this. Yet they never suspected that navigation was no branch of trade, and was, therefore, not comprehended in the power to regulate commerce. They did, indeed, contest the constitutionality of the act, but on a principle which admits the construction for which the appellant contends. They denied that the particular law in question was made in pursuance of the constitution, not because the power could not act directly on vessels, but because a perpetual embargo was the annihilation, and not the regulation of commerce. . . .

The word used in the constitution, then, comprehends, and has been always understood to comprehend, navigation within its meaning; and a power to regulate navigation is as expressly granted as if that term had been added to the word "commerce."

To what commerce does this power extend? The constitution informs us, to commerce "with foreign nations, and among the several states, and with the Indian tribes."

It has, we believe, been universally admitted that these words comprehend every species of commercial intercourse between the United States and foreign nations. No sort of trade can be carried on between this country and any other, to which this power does not extend. It has been truly said, that commerce, as the word is used in the constitution, is a unit, every part of which is indicated by the term.

If this be the admitted meaning of the word, in its application to foreign nations, it must carry the same meaning throughout the sentence, and remain a unit, unless there be some plain intelligible cause which alters it.

The subject to which the power is next applied, is to commerce "among the several states." The word "among" means intermingled with. A thing which is among others, is intermingled with them. Commerce among the states cannot stop at the external boundary line of each state, but may be introduced into the interior.

It is not intended to say that these words comprehend that commerce which is completely internal, which is carried on between man and man in a state, or between different parts of the same state, and which does not extend to or affect other states. Such a power would be inconvenient, and is certainly unnecessary.

Comprehensive as the word "among" is, it may very properly be restricted to the commerce which concerns more states than one. . . . The genius and character of the whole government seem to be, that its action is to be applied to all the external concerns of the nation, and to those internal concerns which affect the states generally; but not to those which are completely within a particular state, which do not affect other states, and with which it is not necessary to interfere, for the purpose of executing some of the general powers of the government. The completely internal commerce of a state, then, may be considered as reserved for the state itself. . . .

. . . Commerce among the states must, of necessity, be commerce with the states. In the regulation of trade with the Indian tribes, the action of the law, especially when the constitution was made, was chiefly within a state. The power of Congress, then, whatever it may be, must be exercised within the territorial jurisdiction of the several states. . . .

We are now arrived at the inquiry, What is this power?

It is the power to regulate; that is, to prescribe the rule by which commerce is to be governed. This power, like all others vested in Congress, is complete in itself, may be exercised to its utmost extent, and acknowledges no limitations, other than are prescribed in the constitution. These are expressed in plain terms, and do not affect the questions which arise in this case, or which have been discussed at the bar. If, as has always been understood, the sovereignty of Congress, though limited to specified objects, is plenary as to those objects, the power over commerce with foreign nations, and among the several States, is vested in Congress as absolutely as it would be in a single government, having in its constitution the same restrictions on the exercise of the power as are found in the constitution of the United States. The wisdom and the discretion of Congress, their identity with the people, and the influence which their constituents possess at election, are, in this, as in many other instances, as that, for example, of declaring war, the sole restraints on which they have relied, to secure them from its abuse. They are the restraints on which the people must often rely solely, in all representative governments. . . .

But it has been urged with great earnestness, that although the power of Congress to regulate commerce with foreign nations, and among the several states, be co-extensive with the subject itself, and have no other limits than are prescribed in the constitution, yet the states may severally exercise the same power within their respective jurisdictions. In support of this argument, it is said that they possessed it as an inseparable attribute of sovereignty, before the formation of the constitution, and still retain it, except so far as they have surrendered it by that instrument; that this principle results from the nature of the government, and is secured by the tenth amendment; that an affirmative grant of power is not exclusive, unless in its own nature it be such that the continued exercise of it by the former possessor is inconsistent with the grant, and that this is not of that description. . . .

The grant of the power to lay and collect taxes is, like the power to regulate commerce, made in general terms, and has never been understood to interfere with the exercise of the same power by the states; and hence has been drawn an argument which has been applied to the question under consideration. But the two grants are not, it is conceived, similar in their terms or their nature. Although many of the powers formerly exercised by the states, are transferred to the government of the Union, yet the state governments remain, and constitute a most important part of our system. The power of taxation is indispensable to their existence, and is a power which, in its own nature, is capable of residing in, and being exercised by, different authorities at the same time. We are accustomed to see it placed, for different purposes, in different hands. Taxation is the simple operation of taking small portions from a perpetually accumulating mass, susceptible of almost infinite division; and a power in one to take what is necessary for certain purposes, is not, in its nature, incompatible with a power in another to take what is necessary for other purposes. Congress is authorized to lay and collect taxes, etc., to pay the debts, and provide for the common defense and general welfare of the United States. This does not interfere with the power of the states to tax for the support of their own governments; nor is the exercise of that power by the states an exercise of any portion of the power that is granted to the United States. In imposing taxes for state purposes, they are not doing what Congress is empowered to do. Congress is not empowered to tax for those purposes which are within the exclusive province of the states. When, then, each government exercises the power of taxation, neither is exercising the power of the other. But, when a state proceeds to regulate commerce with foreign nations, or among the several states, it is exercising the very power that is granted to Congress, and is doing the very thing which Congress is authorized to do. There is no analogy, then, between the power of taxation and the power of regulating commerce.

In discussing the question, whether this power is still in the states, in the case under consideration, we may dismiss from it the inquiry, whether it is surrendered by the mere grant to Congress, or is retained until Congress shall exercise the power. We may dismiss that inquiry, because it has been exercised, and the regulations which Congress deemed it proper to make, are now in full operation. The sole question is, can a state regulate commerce with foreign nations and among the states, while Congress is regulating it?

The counsel for the respondent answer this question in the affirmative, and rely very much on the restrictions in the tenth section, as supporting their opinion. They say, very truly, that limitations of a power furnish a strong argument in favor of the existence of that power, and that the section which prohibits the states from laying duties on imports or exports, proves that this power might have been exercised, had it not been expressly forbidden; and, consequently, that any other commercial regulation, not expressly forbidden, to which the original power of the state is competent, may still be made.

That this restriction shows the opinion of the convention, that a state might impose duties on exports and imports, if not expressly forbidden, will be conceded; but that it follows as a consequence, from this concession, that a state may regulate commerce, with foreign nations and among the states, cannot be admitted.

We must first determine whether the act of laying "duties or imposts on imports or exports" is considered in the constitution as a branch of the taxing power, or of the power to regulate commerce. We think it very clear that it is considered as a branch of the taxing power. . . .

. . . It is true, that duties may often be, and in fact often are, imposed on tonnage, with a view to the regulation of commerce; but they may be also imposed with a view to revenue; and it was, therefore, a prudent precaution to prohibit the states from exercising this power. The idea that the same measure might, according to circumstances, be arranged with different classes of power, was no novelty to the framers of our constitution. . . .

These restrictions, then, are on the taxing power, not on that to regulate commerce; and presuppose the existence of that which they restrain, not of that which they do not purport to restrain.

But the inspection laws are said to be regulations of commerce, and are certainly recognized in the constitution, as being passed in the exercise of a power remaining with the states.

That inspection laws may have a remote and considerable influence on commerce, will not be denied; but that a power to regulate commerce is the source from which the right to pass them is derived, cannot be admitted. The object of inspection laws is to improve the quality of articles produced by the labor of the country; to fit them for exportation; or, it may be, for domestic use. They act upon the subject before it becomes an article of foreign commerce, or of commerce among the states and prepare it for that purpose. They form a portion of that immense mass of legislation which embraces everything within the territory of a state not surrendered to the general government; all which can be most advantageously exercised by the states themselves. Inspection laws, quarantine laws, health laws of every description, as well as laws for regulating the internal commerce of a state, and those which respect turnpike-roads, ferries, etc., are component parts of this mass.

. . . If Congress license vessels to sail from one port to another, in the same state, the act is supposed to be, necessarily, incidental to the power expressly granted to Congress, and implies no claim of a direct power to regulate the purely internal commerce of a state, or to act directly on its system of police. So, if a state, in passing laws on subjects acknowledged to be within its control, and with a view to those subjects, shall adopt a measure of the same character with one which Congress may adopt, it does not derive its authority from the particular power which has been granted, but from some other, which remains with the state, and may be executed by the same means. All experience shows that the same measures, or measures scarcely distinguishable from each other, may flow from distinct powers; but this does not prove that the powers themselves are identical. Although the means used in their execution may sometimes approach each other so nearly as to be confounded, there are other situations in which they are sufficiently distinct to establish their individuality. . . .

The acts of Congress, passed in 1796 and 1799, empowering and directing the officers of the general government to conform to, and assist in the execution of the quarantine and health laws of a state, proceed, it is said, upon the idea that these laws are constitutional. It is undoubtedly true that they do proceed upon that idea; and the constitutionality of such laws has never, so far as we are informed, been denied. But they do not imply an acknowledgment that a state may rightfully regulate commerce with foreign nations, or among the states; for they do not imply that such laws are an exercise of that power, or enacted with a view to it. On the contrary, they are treated as quarantine and health laws, are so denominated in the acts of Congress, and are considered as flowing from the acknowledged power of a state, to provide for the health of its citizens. But, as it was apparent that some of the provisions made for this purpose, and in virtue of this power, might interfere with, and be affected by the laws of the United States, made for the regulation of commerce, Congress, in that spirit of harmony and conciliation which ought always to characterize the conduct of governments standing in the relation which that of the Union and those of the states bear to each other, has directed its officers to aid in the execution of these laws; and has, in some measure, adapted its own legislation to this object, by making provisions in aid of those of the states. But in making these provisions, the opinion is unequivocally manifested, that Congress may control the state laws, so far as it may be necessary to control them, for the regulation of commerce. . . .

It has been said that the act of August 7th, 1789, acknowledges a concurrent power in the states to regulate the conduct of pilots, and hence is inferred an admission of their concurrent right with Congress to regulate commerce with foreign nations, and amongst the states. But this inference is not, we think, justified by the fact.

Although Congress cannot enable a state to legislate, Congress may adopt the provisions of a state on any subject. When the government of the Union was brought into existence, it found a system for the regulation of its pilots in full force in every state. The act which has been mentioned, adopts this system, and gives it the same validity as if its provisions had been specially made by Congress. But the act, it may be said, is prospective also, and the adoption of laws to be made in future, presupposes the right in the maker to legislate on the subject.

The act unquestionably manifests an intention to leave this subject entirely to the states, until Congress should think proper to interpose; but the very enactment of such a law indicates an opinion that it was necessary; that the existing system would not be applicable to the new state of things, unless expressly applied to it by Congress. But this section is confined to pilots within the "bays, inlets, rivers, harbors, and ports of the United States," which are, of course, in whole or in part, also within the limits of some particular state. The acknowledged power of a state to regulate its police, its domestic trade, and to govern its own citizens, may enable it to legislate on this subject to a considerable extent; and the adoption of its system by Congress, and the application of it to the whole subject of commerce, does not seem to the court to imply a right in the states so to apply it of their own authority. But the adoption of the state system being temporary, being only "until further legislative provision shall be made by Congress," shows, conclusively, an opinion that Congress could control the whole subject, and might adopt the system of the states, or provide one of its own. . . .

It has been contended by the counsel for the appellant, that, as the word "to regulate" implies in its nature, full power over the thing to be regulated, it excludes, necessarily, the action of all others that would perform the same operation on the same thing. That regulation is designed for the entire result, applying to those parts which remain as they were, as well as to those which are altered. It produces a uniform whole, which is as much disturbed and deranged by changing what the regulating power designs to leave untouched, as that on which it has operated.

There is great force in this argument, and the court is not satisfied that it has been refuted.

Since, however, in exercising the power of regulating their own purely internal affairs, whether of trading or police, the states may sometimes enact laws, the validity of which depends on their interfering with, and being contrary to, an act of Congress passed in pursuance of the constitution, the court will enter upon the inquiry, whether the laws of New York, as expounded by the highest tribunal of that state, have, in their application to this case, come into collision with an act of Congress, and deprived a citizen of a right to which that act entitles him. Should this collision exist, it will be immaterial whether those laws were passed in virtue of a concurrent power "to regulate commerce with foreign nations and among the several states," or in virtue of a power to regulate their domestic trade and police. In one case and the other, the acts of New York must yield to the law of Congress; and the decision sustaining the privilege they confer, against a right given by a law of the Union, must be erroneous. . . .

. . . The nullity of any act, inconsistent with the constitution, is produced by the declaration that the constitution is the supreme law. The appropriate application of that part of the clause which confers the same supremacy on laws and treaties, is to such acts of the state legislatures as do not transcend their powers, but, though enacted in the execution of acknowledged state powers, interfere with, or are contrary to, the laws of Congress, made in pursuance of the constitution, or some treaty made under the authority of the United States. In every such case, the act of Congress, or the treaty, is supreme; and the law of the state, though enacted in the exercise of powers not controverted, must yield to it. . . .

But we will proceed briefly to notice those sections [of the Act of Congress] which bear more directly on the subject.

The first section declares that vessels enrolled by virtue of a previous law, and certain other vessels enrolled as described in that act, and having a license in force, as is by the act required, "and no others, shall be deemed ships or vessels of the United States, entitled to the privileges of ships or vessels employed in the coasting trade."

This section seems to the court to contain a positive enactment, that the vessels it describes shall be entitled to the privileges of ships or vessels employed in the coasting trade. Those privileges cannot be separated from the trade, and cannot be enjoyed, unless the trade may be prosecuted. The grant of the privilege is an idle, empty form, conveying nothing, unless it convey the right to which the privilege is attached, and in the exercise of which its whole value consists. To construe these words otherwise than as entitling the ships or vessels described, to carry on the coasting trade, would be, we think, to disregard the apparent intent of the act.

The fourth section directs the proper officer to grant to a vessel qualified to receive it, "a license for carrying on the coasting trade"; and prescribes its form. After reciting the compliance of the applicant with the previous requisites of the law, the operative words of the instrument are, "license is hereby granted for the said steamboat, Bellona, to be employed in carrying on the coasting trade for one year from the date hereof, and no longer." . . .

The word "license" means permission, or authority; and a license to do any particular thing is a permission or authority to do that thing; and if granted by a person having power to grant it, transfers to the grantee the right to do whatever it purports to authorize. It certainly transfers to him all the right which the grantor can transfer, to do what is within the terms of the license. . . .

Notwithstanding the decided language of the license, it has also been maintained that it gives no right to trade; and that its sole purpose is to confer the American character.

The answer given to this argument, that the American character is conferred by the enrollment, and not by the license, is, we think, founded too clearly in the words of the law to require the support of any additional observations. The enrollment of vessels designed for the coasting trade, corresponds precisely with the registration of vessels designed for the foreign trade, and requires every circumstance which can constitute the American character. The license can be granted only to vessels already enrolled, if they be of the burden of twenty tons and upwards; and requires no circumstance essential to the American character. The object of the license, then, cannot be to ascertain the character of the vessel, but to do what it professes to do; that is, to give permission to a vessel already proved by her enrollment to be American, to carry on the coasting trade.

But, if the license be a permit to carry on the coasting trade, the respondent denies that these boats were engaged in that trade, or that the decree under consideration has restrained them from prosecuting it. The boats of the appellant were, we are told, employed in the transportation of passengers; and this is no part of that commerce which Congress may regulate.

If, as our whole course of legislation on this subject shows, the power of Congress has been universally understood in America to comprehend navigation, it is a very persuasive, if not a conclusive argument, to prove that the construction is correct; and, if it be correct, no clear distinction is perceived between the power to regulate vessels employed in transporting men for hire, and property for hire. The subject is transferred to Congress, and no exception to the grant can be admitted which is not proved by the words or the nature of the thing. A coasting vessel employed in the transportation of passengers, is as much a portion of the American marine as one employed in the transportation of a cargo; and no reason is perceived why such vessel should be withdrawn from the regulating power of that government, which has been thought best fitted for the purpose generally. . . .

As this decides the cause, it is unnecessary to enter in an examination of that part of the constitution which empowers Congress to promote the progress of science and the useful arts. . . .

Powerful and ingenious minds, taking, as postulates, that the powers expressly granted to the government of the Union are to be contracted, by construction, into the narrowest possible compass, and that the original powers of the States are retained, if any possible construction will retain them, may, by a course of well digested, but refined metaphysical reasoning, founded on these premises, explain away the constitution of our country, and leave it a magnificent structure indeed, to look at, but totally unfit for use. They may so entangle and perplex the understanding, as to obscure principles which were before thought quite plain, and induce doubts where, if the mind were to pursue its own course, none would be perceived. In such a case, it is peculiarly necessary to recur to safe and fundamental principles to sustain those principles, and, when sustained, to make them the tests of the arguments to be examined.

[The decree of the New York court was reversed and the bill for an injunction ordered to be dismissed.]

MR. JUSTICE JOHNSON. The judgment entered by the court in this cause has my entire approbation; but having adopted my conclusions on views of the subject materially different from those of my brethren, I feel it incumbent on me to exhibit those views. I have, also, another inducement. In questions of great importance and great delicacy, I feel my duty to the public best discharged by an effort to maintain my opinions in my own way.

In attempts to construe the constitution, I have never found much benefit resulting from the inquiry, whether the whole, or any part of it, is to be construed strictly, or literally. The simple, classical, precise, yet comprehensive language in which it is couched, leaves, at most, but very little latitude for construction; and when its intent and meaning is discovered, nothing remains but to execute the will of those who made it, in the best manner to effect the purposes intended. [A discussion of commercial rivalries of the states prior to the adoption of the Constitution is omitted.]

The history of the times will, therefore, sustain the opinion, that the grant of power over commerce, if intended to be commensurate with the evils existing, and the purpose of remedying those evils, could be only commensurate with the power of the states over the subject. And this opinion is supported by a very remarkable evidence of the general understanding of the whole American people, when the grant was made. There was not a state in the Union, in which there did not, at that time, exist a variety of commercial regulations; concerning which it is too much to suppose, that the whole ground covered by those regulations was immediately assumed by actual legislation, under the authority of the Union. But where was the existing statute on this subject, that a state attempted to execute? or by what state was it ever thought necessary to repeal those statutes? By common consent, those laws dropped lifeless from their statute books, for want of the sustaining power that had been relinquished to congress. . . .

It is impossible, with the views which I entertained of the principle on which the commercial privileges of the people of the United States, among themselves, rests, to concur in the view which this court takes of the effect of the coasting license in this cause. I do not regard it as the foundation of the right set up in behalf of the appellant. If there was any one object riding over every other in the adoption of the constitution, it was to keep the commercial intercourse among the states free from all invidious and partial restraints. And I cannot overcome the conviction, that if the licensing act was repealed to-morrow, the rights of the appellant to a reversal of the decision complained of, would be as strong as it is under this license. One-half the doubts in life arise from the defects of language, and if this instrument had been called an exemption instead of a license, it would have given a better idea of its character. Licensing acts, in fact, in legislation, are universally restraining acts; as, for example, acts licensing gaming houses, retailers of spirituous liquors, etc. The act, in this instance, is distinctly of that character, and forms part of an extensive system, the object of which is to encourage American shipping, and place them on an equal footing with the shipping of other nations. Almost every commercial nation reserves to its own subjects a monopoly of its coasting trade; and a countervailing privilege in favor of American shipping is contemplated, in the whole legislation of the United States on this subject. It is not to give the vessel an American character, that the license is granted; that effect has been correctly attributed to the act of her enrollment. But it is to confer on her American privileges, as contradistinguished from foreign; and to preserve the government from fraud by foreigners, in surreptitiously intruding themselves into the American commercial marine, as well as frauds upon the revenue in the trade coastwise, that this whole system is projected. Many duties and formalities are necessarily imposed upon the American foreign commerce, which would be burdensome in the active coasting trade of the states, and can be dispensed with. A higher rate of tonnage also is imposed, and this license entitles the vessels that take it, to those exemptions, but to nothing more. . . . I consider the license, therefore, as nothing more than what it purports to be, according to the 1st section of this act, conferring on the licensed vessel certain privileges in the trade, not conferred on other vessels; but the abstract right of commercial intercourse, stripped of those privileges, is common to all. . . .

But the principal objections to these opinions arise, 1st. From the unavoidable action of some of the municipal powers of the states, upon commercial subjects. 2d. From passages in the constitution which are supposed to imply a concurrent power in the states in regulating commerce.

It is no objection to the existence of distinct, substantive powers, that, in their application, they bear upon the same subject. The same bale of goods, the same cask of provisions, or the same ship, that may be the subject of commercial regulation, may also be the vehicle of disease. And the health laws that require them to be stopped and ventilated, are no more intended as regulations on commerce than the laws which permit their importation are intended to inoculate the community with disease. Their different purposes mark the distinction between the powers brought into action; and while frankly exercised, they can produce no serious collision. As to laws affecting ferries, turnpike roads, and other subjects of the same class, so far from meriting the epithet of commercial regulations, they are, in fact, commercial facilities, for which, by the consent of mankind, a compensation is paid, upon the same principle that the whole commercial world submit to pay light-money to the Danes. Inspection laws are of a more equivocal nature, and it is obvious that the constitution has viewed that subject with much solicitude. But so far from sustaining an inference in favor of the power of the states over commerce, I cannot but think that the guarded provisions of the 10th section, on this subject, furnish a strong argument against that inference. It was obvious that inspection laws must combine municipal with commercial regulations; and, while the power over the subject is yielded to the states, for obvious reasons, an absolute control is given over state legislation on the subject, as far as that legislation may be exercised, so as to affect the commerce of the country. The inferences, to be correctly drawn, from this whole article, appear to me to be altogether in favor of the exclusive grants to Congress of power over commerce, and the reverse of that which the appellee contends for. . . .

But instances have been insisted on, with much confidence, in argument, in which, by municipal laws, particular regulations respecting their cargoes have been imposed upon shipping in the ports of the United States; and one, in which forfeiture was made the penalty of disobedience.

Until such laws have been tested by exceptions to their constitutionality, the argument certainly wants much of the force attributed to it; but admitting their constitutionality, they present only the familiar case of punishment inflicted by both governments upon the same individual. He who robs the mail, may also steal the horse that carries it, and would, unquestionably, be subject to punishment, at the same time, under the laws of the state in which the crime is committed, and under those of the United States. And these punishments may interfere, and one render it impossible to inflict the other, and yet the two governments would be acting under powers that have no claim to identity.

It would be in vain to deny the possibility of a clashing and collision between the measures of the two governments. The line cannot be drawn with sufficient distinctness between the municipal powers of the one and the commercial powers of the other. In some points they meet and blend so as scarcely to admit of separation. Hitherto the only remedy has been applied which the case admits of — that of a frank and candid co-operation for the general good. Witness the laws of Congress requiring its officers to respect the inspection laws of the states, and to aid in enforcing their health laws; that which surrenders to the states the superintendence of pilotage, and the many laws passed to permit a tonnage duty to be levied for the use of their ports. Other instances could be cited, abundantly to prove that collision must be sought to be produced; and when it does arise, the question must be decided how far the powers of Congress are adequate to put it down. . . .[a]

---

[a] See Abel, The Commerce Clause in the Constitutional Convention and in Contemporary Comment, 25 Minn. L. Rev. 432 (1941); compare Crosskey, Politics and the Constitution, cc. 4-5 (1953).

The New York licensees had been given exclusive rights of steam navigation by Louisiana, while in New Jersey, Connecticut, and Ohio retaliatory statutes had been passed forbidding vessels under the New York license to navigate the waters of those states. Other persons were given exclusive rights in Massachusetts, New Hampshire, Vermont, and Georgia. See 1 Warren, The Supreme Court in United States History 598 (1926). For a report of the huzzas which greeted the decision, and the prompt increase in the number of steamboats plying from New York, see id. at 615.

On Justice Johnson's position, see his opinion on circuit in the DeLesseline case, 8 Fed. Cas. 493 (1823) (South Carolina law prohibiting free Negro seamen from coming ashore while in port). — ED.

NOTE

May Congress prohibit the following activities: the carrying of intoxicating liquor on the person, from one state to another, for personal consumption, United States v. Hill, 248 U.S. 420 (1919); interfering with federal officials who, pursuant to statutory duty, are engaged in the disinfecting of cattle which range across a state line, Thornton v. United States, 271 U.S. 414 (1926); the counterfeiting of bills of lading purporting to represent interstate shipments by rail, United States v. Ferger, 250 U.S. 199 (1919); the "seeding" of clouds to produce rain? What relevance, if any, does the meaning of "commerce among the several states" have to the solution of these questions?

Willson v. Black Bird Creek Marsh Co. 2 Pet. 245, 7 L. Ed. 412 (1829)

[The plaintiff company, pursuant to an act of the Delaware legislature, erected a dam in Black Bird Creek, by which navigation was obstructed. The defendants, owners of the sloop *Sally*, enrolled and licensed under federal law, broke and injured the dam in order to remove the obstruction. Damages were recovered by the company in a Delaware court, and the judgment was affirmed by the Court of Appeals.]

MR. CHIEF JUSTICE MARSHALL delivered the opinion of the court: . . .

The jurisdiction of the court being established, the more doubtful question is to be considered, whether the Act incorporating the Black Bird Creek Marsh Company is repugnant to the Constitution, so far as it authorizes a dam across the creek. The plea states the creek to be navigable, in the nature of a highway, through which the tide ebbs and flows.

The Act of Assembly by which the plaintiffs were authorized to construct their dam, shows plainly that this is one of those many creeks, passing through a deep, level marsh adjoining the Delaware, up which the tide flows for some distance. The value of the property on its banks must be enhanced by excluding the water from the marsh, and the health of the inhabitants probably improved. Measures calculated to produce these objects, provided they do not come into collision with the powers of the general government, are undoubtedly within those which are reserved to the States. But the measure authorized by this Act stops a navigable creek, and must be supposed to abridge the rights of those who have been accustomed to use it. But this abridgment, unless it comes in conflict with the Constitution or a law of the United States, is an affair between the government of Delaware and its citizens, of which this court can take no cognizance.

The counsel for the plaintiffs in error insist that it comes in conflict with the power of the United States "to regulate commerce with foreign nations and among the several States."

If Congress had passed any Act which bore upon the case; any Act in execution of the power to regulate commerce, the object of which was to control State legislation over those small navigable creeks into which the tide flows, and which abound throughout the lower country of the Middle and Southern States, we should feel not much difficulty in saying that a State law coming in conflict with such Act would be void. But Congress has passed no such Act. The repugnancy of the law of Delaware to the Constitution is placed entirely on its repugnancy to the power to regulate commerce with foreign nations and among the several States; a power which has not been so exercised as to affect the question.

We do not think that the Act empowering the Black Bird Creek Marsh Company to place a dam across the creek, can, under all the circumstances of the case, be considered as repugnant to the power to regulate commerce in its dormant state, or as being in conflict with any law passed on the subject.

There is no error, and the judgment is affirmed.

NOTE

The validity of state laws affecting foreign or interstate commerce was a subject of recurring and fundamental division among the members of the Court. The disagreement revolved about the question whether the commerce power was or was not "exclusive," and if it was, whether a particular state law was a "regulation of commerce" or an exercise of the state's "police power."

In Mayor of New York v. Miln, 11 Pet. 102 (1837), the Court sustained a provision of a New York statute requiring the masters of incoming vessels to report the names, place of birth, age, legal settlement, and occupation of every passenger landing in New York. Mr. Justice Story, dissenting, stated (p. 161) that his views "had the entire concurrence, upon the same grounds, of that great constitutional jurist, the late Mr. Chief Justice Marshall. Having heard the former arguments, his deliberate opinion was that the act of New York was unconstitutional; and that the present case fell directly within the principles established in the case of Gibbons v. Ogden. . . ."

In the License Cases, 5 How. 504 (1847), the Court sustained state laws requiring licenses for the sale of liquor, even though brought in from other states or foreign countries. Six opinions were delivered, concurring in the result.

In the Passenger Cases, 7 How. 283 (1849), the Court held invalid state laws imposing taxes on alien passengers arriving from foreign countries. The cases occupy 290 pages in the reports, and the headnote reads: "Inasmuch as there was no opinion of the court, as a court, the reporter refers the reader to the opinions of the judges for an explanation of the statutes and the points in which they conflicted with the Constitution and laws of the United States." Taney, C.J., and Daniel, Nelson, and Woodbury, J.J., dissented.

Cooley v. Board of Wardens of the Port of Philadelphia
12 How. 299, 13 L. Ed. 996 (1851)

MR. JUSTICE CURTIS delivered the opinion of the court:

These cases are brought here by writs of error to the Supreme Court of the Commonwealth of Pennsylvania.

They are actions to recover half pilotage fees under the 29th section of the Act of the Legislature of Pennsylvania, passed on the second day of March, 1803. The plaintiff in error alleges that the highest court of the State has decided against a right claimed by him under the Constitution of the United States. That right is to be exempted from the payment of the sums of money demanded, pursuant to the State law above referred to, because that law contravenes several provisions of the Constitution of the United States.

The particular section of the State law drawn in question is as follows:

"That every ship or vessel arriving from or bound to any foreign port or place, and every ship or vessel of the burden of seventy-five tons or more, sailing from or bound to any port not within the River Delaware, shall be obliged to receive a pilot. And it shall be the duty of the master of every such ship or vessel, within thirty-six hours next after the arrival of such ship or vessel at the City of Philadelphia, to make report to the master warden of the name of such ship or vessel, her draught of water, and the name of the pilot who shall have conducted her to the port. And when any such vessel shall be outward bound, the master of such vessel shall make known to the wardens the name of such vessel, and of the pilot who is to conduct her to the capes, and her draught of water at that time. And it shall be the duty of the wardens to enter every such vessel in a book to be by them kept for that purpose, without fee or reward. And if the master of any ship or vessel shall neglect to make such report, he shall forfeit and pay the sum of sixty dollars. And if the master of any such ship or vessel shall refuse or neglect to take a pilot, the master, owner or consignee of such vessel shall forfeit and pay to the warden aforesaid, a sum equal to the half pilotage of such ship or vessel, to the use of the Society for the Relief, etc., to be recovered as pilotage in the manner hereinafter directed: Provided always, that where it shall appear to the warden that, in case of an inward bound vessel, a pilot did not offer before she had reached Reedy Island; or, in case of an outward-bound vessel, that a pilot could not be obtained for twenty-four hours after such vessel was ready to depart, the penalty aforesaid, for not having a pilot, shall not be incurred." It constitutes one section of "An Act to Establish a Board of Wardens for the Port of Philadelphia, and for the Regulation of Pilots and Pilotages, etc.," and the scope of the Act is in conformity with the title to regulate the whole subject of the pilotage of that port.

[The Court rejected contentions that the law was invalid as a duty on imports, exports, or tonnage, or constituted a preference to a port.]

It remains to consider the objection, that it is repugnant to the third clause of the eighth section of the first article. "The Congress shall have power to regulate commerce with foreign nations and among the several States, and with the Indian tribes."

That the power to regulate commerce includes the regulation of navigation, we consider settled. And when we look to the nature of the service performed by pilots, to the relations which that service and its compensations bear to navigation between the several States, and between the ports of the United States, and foreign countries, we are brought to the conclusion, that the regulation of the qualifications of pilots, of the modes and times of offering and rendering their services, of the responsibilities which shall rest upon them, of the powers they shall possess, of the compensation they may demand, and of the penalties by which their rights and duties may be enforced, do constitute regulations of navigation, and consequently of commerce, within the just meaning of this clause of the Constitution. . . .

The Act of 1789, 1 Stat. at Large, 54, already referred to, contains a clear legislative exposition of the Constitution by the first Congress, to the effect that the power to regulate pilots was conferred on Congress by the Constitution; as does also the Act of March the 2d, 1837, . . . The weight to be allowed to this contemporaneous construction, and the practice of Congress under it, has, in another connection, been adverted to. And a majority of the court are of opinion that a regulation of pilots is a regulation of commerce, within the grant to Congress of the commercial power, contained in the third clause of the eighth section of the first article of the Constitution.

It becomes necessary, therefore, to consider whether this law of Pennsylvania, being a regulation of commerce, is valid.

The Act of Congress of the 7th of August, 1789, sec. 4, is as follows:

"That all pilots in the bays, inlets, rivers, harbors, and ports of the United States, shall continue to be regulated in conformity with the existing laws of the States, respectively, wherein such pilots may be, or with such laws as the States may respectively hereafter enact for the purpose, until further legislative provision shall be made by Congress."

If the law of Pennsylvania, now in question, had been in existence at the date of this Act of Congress, we might hold it to have been adopted by Congress, and thus made a law of the United States, and so valid. Because this Act does, in effect, give the force of an Act of Congress, to the then existing state laws on this subject, so long as they should continue unrepealed by the State which enacted them.

But the law on which these actions are founded was not enacted till 1803. What effect, then, can be attributed to so much of the Act of 1789 as declares that pilots shall continue to be regulated in conformity "with such laws as the States may respectively hereafter enact for the purpose, until further legislative provision shall be made by Congress"?

If the States were devested of the power to legislate on this subject by the grant of the commercial power to Congress, it is plain this Act could not confer upon them power thus to legislate. If the Constitution excluded the States from making any law regulating commerce certainly Congress cannot regrant, or in any manner reconvey to the States that power. And yet this Act of 1789 gives its sanction only to laws enacted by the States. This necessarily implies a constitutional power to legislate; for only a rule created by the sovereign power of a state acting in its legislative capacity, can be deemed a law, enacted by a state; and if the State has so limited its sovereign power that it no longer extends to a particular subject, manifestly it cannot, in any proper sense, be said to enact laws thereon. Entertaining these views we are brought directly and unavoidably to the consideration of the question, whether the grant of the commercial power to Congress, did per se deprive the States of all power to regulate pilots. This question has never been decided by this court, nor, in our judgment, has any case depending upon all the considerations which must govern this one, come before this court. The grant of commercial power to Congress does not contain any terms which expressly exclude the States from exercising an authority over its subject matter. If they are excluded it must be because the nature of the power, thus granted to Congress, requires that a similar authority should not exist in the States. If it were conceded on the one side, that the nature of this power, like that to legislate for the District of Columbia, is absolutely and totally repugnant to the existence or similar power in the States, probably no one would deny that the grant of the power to Congress, as effectually and perfectly excludes the States from all future legislation on the subject, as if express words had been used to exclude them. And on the other hand, if it were admitted that the existence of this power in Congress, like the power of taxation, is compatible with the existence of a similar power in the States, then it would be in conformity with the contemporary exposition of the Constitution (Federalist, No. 32), and with the judicial construction, given from time to time by this court, after the most deliberate consideration, to hold that the mere grant of such a power to Congress, did not imply a prohibition on the States to exercise the same power: that it is not the mere existence of such a power, but its exercise by Congress, which may be incompatible with the exercise of the same power by the States, and that the States may legislate in the absence of congressional regulations. Sturges v. Crowninshield, 4 Wheat. 193; Moore v. Houston, 5 Wheat. 1; Willson v. Black Bird Creek Marsh Co., 2 Peters, 251.

The diversities of opinion, therefore, which have existed on this subject, have arisen from the different views taken of the nature of this power. But when the nature of a power like this is spoken of, when it is said that the nature of the power requires that it should be exercised exclusively by Congress, it must be intended to refer to the subjects of that power, and to say they are of such a nature as to require exclusive legislation by Congress. Now, the power to regulate commerce, embraces a vast field, containing not only many, but exceedingly various subjects, quite unlike in their nature; some imperatively demanding a single uniform rule, operating equally on the commerce of the United States in every port; and some, like the subject now in question, as imperatively demanding that diversity, which alone can meet the local necessities of navigation.

Either absolutely to affirm, or deny, that the nature of this power requires exclusive legislation by Congress, is to lose sight of the nature of the subjects of this power, and to assert concerning all of them, what is really applicable but to a part. Whatever subjects of this power are in their nature national, or admit only of one uniform system, or plan of regulation, may justly be said to be of such a nature as to require exclusive legislation by Congress. That this cannot be affirmed of laws for the regulation of pilots and pilotage is plain. The Act of 1789 contains a clear and authoritative declaration by the first Congress, that the nature of this subject is such, that until Congress should find it necessary to exert its power, it should be left to the legislation of the States; that it is local and not national; that it is likely to be the best provided for, not by one system, or plan of regulations, but by as many as the legislative discretion of the several States should deem applicable to the local peculiarities of the ports within their limits.

Viewed in this light, so much of this Act of 1789 as declares that pilots shall continue to be regulated "by such laws as the States may respectively hereafter enact for that purpose," instead of being held to be inoperative, as an attempt to confer on the States a power to legislate, of which the Constitution had deprived them, is allowed an appropriate and important signification. It manifests the understanding of Congress, at the outset of the government, that the nature of this subject is not such as to require its exclusive legislation. The practice of the States, and of the national government, has been in conformity with this declaration, from the origin of the national government to this time; and the nature of the subject, when examined, is such as to leave no doubt of the superior fitness and propriety, not to say the absolute necessity, of different systems of regulation, drawn from local knowledge and experience, and conformed to local wants. How, then, can we say, that by the mere grant of power to regulate commerce, the States are deprived of all the power to legislate on this subject, because from the nature of the power the legislation of Congress must be exclusive. . . .

It is the opinion of a majority of the court that the mere grant to Congress of the power to regulate commerce, did not deprive the States of power to regulate pilots, and that although Congress has legislated on this subject, its legislation manifests an intention, with a single exception, not to regulate this subject, but to leave its regulation to the several States. To these precise questions, which are all we are called on to decide, this opinion must be understood to be confined. It does not extend to the question what other subjects, under the commercial power, are within the exclusive control of Congress, or may be regulated by the States in the absence of all congressional legislation; nor to the general question how far any regulation of a subject by Congress may be deemed to operate as an exclusion of all legislation by the States upon the same subject. We decide the precise questions before us, upon what we deem sound principles, applicable to this particular subject in the state in which the legislation of Congress has left it. We go no farther. . . .

[Judgments affirmed.]

[Mr. Justice McLean delivered a dissenting opinion. After quoting from the opinion of Chief Justice Marshall in Gibbons v. Ogden in relation to pilotage laws, he said: "Congress adopted the pilot-laws of the states, because it was well understood, that they could have no force, as regulations of foreign commerce or of commerce among the states, if not so adopted. By their adoption they were made acts of Congress, and ever since they have been so considered and enforced. . . . From this race of legislation between Congress and the states, and between the states, if this principle be maintained, will arise a conflict similar to that which existed before the adoption of the Constitution. The states favorably situated, as Louisiana, may levy a contribution upon the commerce of other states which shall be sufficient to meet the expenditures of the states. . . ."

Mr. Justice Daniel delivered an opinion concurring in the result. He said: "The power and the practice of enacting pilot-laws, which has been exercised by the states from the very origin of their existence, although it is one in some degree connected with commercial intercourse, does not come essentially and regularly within that power of commercial regulation vested by the Constitution in Congress, and which by the Constitution must, when exercised by Congress, be enforced with perfect equality, and without any kind of discrimination, local or otherwise in its application."]

Pennsylvania v. Wheeling & Belmont Bridge Co. 13 How. 518, 14 L. Ed. 249 (1852)

[The State of Pennsylvania by original bill in equity in the Supreme Court of the United States asked an injunction against the building of the defendant's bridge, and, by supplemental bill, sought an abatement of the completed bridge as a public nuisance. The bridge had been constructed with the authorization of the Virginia legislature. After the filing of the bill in equity in the Supreme Court, the Virginia legislature passed a supplementary and explanatory act declaring that the bridge was of "lawful height" and had been built "in conforming with" the initial authorization. Act of Jan. 11, 1850, c. 169. The bill alleged that the bridge would so obstruct the navigation of the river as to cut off and direct trade from the public works of Pennsylvania, and diminish the tolls and revenue of the state.]

MR. JUSTICE MCLEAN delivered the opinion of the court. . . .

[I]t is objected, if not as a matter going to the jurisdiction, as fatal to any further action in the case, that there are no statutory provisions to guide the court, either by the State of Virginia, or by Congress. It is said that there is no common law of the Union on which the procedure can be founded; that the common law of Virginia is subject to its legislative action, and that the bridge, having been constructed under its authority, it can in no sense be considered a nuisance. That whatever shall be done within the limits of a State, is subject to its laws, written or unwritten, unless it be a violation of the Constitution, or of some act of Congress.

It is admitted that the federal courts have no jurisdiction of common-law offences, and that there is no abstract pervading principle of the common law of the Union under which we can take jurisdiction. And it is admitted, that the case under consideration, is subject to the same rules of action as if the suit had been commenced in the Circuit Court for the District of Virginia.

In the second section of the third article of the Constitution it is declared, "the judicial power shall extend to all cases, in law and equity, arising under this Constitution, the laws of the United States, and treaties made, or which shall be made under their authority."

Chancery jurisdiction is conferred on the courts of the United States with the limitation "that suits in equity shall not be sustained in either of the courts of the United States, in any case where plain, adequate, and complete remedy may be had at law." The rules of the High Court of Chancery of England have been adopted by the courts of the United States. And there is no other limitation to the exercise of a chancery jurisdiction by these courts, except the value of the matter in controversy, the residence or character of the parties, or a claim which arises under a law of the United States, and which has been decided against in a State court.

In exercising this jurisdiction, the courts of the Union are not limited by the chancery system adopted by any State, and they exercise their functions in a State where no court of chancery has been established. The usages of the High Court of Chancery in England, whenever the jurisdiction is exercised, govern the proceedings. This may be said to be the common law of chancery, and since the organization of the government, it has been observed. . . .

An indictment at common law could not be sustained in the federal courts by the United States, against the bridge as a nuisance, as no such procedure has been authorized by Congress. But a proceeding, on the ground of a private and an irreparable injury, may be sustained against it by an individual or a corporation. Such a proceeding is common to the federal courts, and also to the courts of the State. The injury makes the obstruction a private nuisance to the injured party; and the doctrine of nuisance applies to the case where the jurisdiction is made out, the same as in a public prosecution. If the obstruction be unlawful, and the injury irreparable, by a suit at common law, the injured party may claim the extraordinary protection of a court of chancery. . . .

The act of Virginia, under which the bridge was built, with scrupulous care, guarded the rights of navigation. In the 19th section, it is declared "That, if the said bridge shall be so constructed as to injure the navigation of the said river, the said bridge shall be treated as a public nuisance, and shall be liable to abatement, upon the same principles and in the same manner that other public nuisances are." And, in the act of the 19th of March, 1847, to revive the first act, it is declared, in the 14th section, "that if the bridge shall be so erected as to obstruct the navigation of the Ohio River, in the usual manner, by such steamboats and other crafts as are now commonly accustomed to navigate the same, when the river shall be as high as the highest floods hereinbefore known, then, unless, upon such obstruction being found to exist, such obstruction shall be immediately removed or remedied, the said last-mentioned bridge may be treated as a public nuisance, and abated accordingly."

This is a full recognition of the public right on this great highway, and the grant to the Bridge Company was made subject to that right.

It is objected that there is no act of Congress prohibiting obstructions on the Ohio River, and that until there shall be such a regulation, a State, in the construction of bridges, has a right to exercise its own discretion on the subject.

Congress have not declared in terms that a State, by the construction of bridges, or otherwise, shall not obstruct the navigation of the Ohio, but they have regulated navigation upon it, as before remarked, by licensing vessels, establishing ports of entry, imposing duties upon masters and other officers of boats, and inflicting severe penalties for neglect of those duties, by which damage to life or property has resulted. And they have expressly sanctioned the compact made by Virginia with Kentucky, at the time of its admission into the Union, "that the use and navigation of the River Ohio, so far as the territory of the proposed State, or the territory that shall remain within the limits of this Commonwealth lies thereon, shall be free and common to the citizens of the United States." Now, an obstructed navigation cannot be said to be free. It was, no doubt, in view of this compact, that in the charter for the bridge, it was required to be so elevated, as not, at the greatest height of the water, to obstruct navigation. Any individual may abate a public nuisance. 5 Bac. Ab. 797; 2 Roll. Ab. 144, 145; 9 Co. 54; Hawk. P.C. 75, sect. 12.

This compact, by the sanction of Congress, has become a law of the Union. What further legislation can be desired for judicial action? In the case of Green et al. v. Biddle (8 Wheat. 1,) this court held that a law of the State of Kentucky, which was in violation of this compact between Virginia and Kentucky, was void; and they say this court has authority to declare a State law unconstitutional, upon the ground of its impairing the obligation of a compact between different States of the Union.

The case of Willson v. The Blackbird Creek Marsh Company, (2 Peters, 250,) is different in principle from the case before us. A dam was built over a creek to drain a marsh, required by the unhealthiness it produced. It was a small creek, made navigable by the flowing of the tide. The Chief Justice said it was a matter of doubt, whether the small creeks, which the tide makes navigable a short distance, are within the general commercial regulation, and that in such cases of doubt, it would be better for the court to follow the lead of Congress. Congress have led in regulating commerce on the Ohio, which brings the case within the rule above laid down. The facts of the two cases, therefore, instead of being alike, are altogether different.

No State law can hinder or obstruct the free use of a license granted under an act of Congress. Nor can any State violate the compact, sanctioned as it has been, by obstructing the navigation of the river. More than this is not necessary to give a civil remedy for an injury done by an obstruction. Congress might punish such an act criminally, but until they shall so provide, an indictment will not lie in the courts of the United States for an obstruction which is a public nuisance. But a public nuisance is also a private nuisance, where a special and an irremediable mischief is done to an individual. [The Court then examined the evidence and determined that the bridge did seriously obstruct navigation.]

For the reasons and facts stated, we think that the bridge obstructs the navigation of the Ohio, and that the State of Pennsylvania has been, and will be, injured in her public works, in such manner as not only to authorize the bringing of this suit, but to entitle her to the relief prayed. . . .

[The Court decreed that the bridge be elevated so that its lowest parts be not less than 111 feet from the low-water mark, or that it be abated.]

Mr. Chief Justice Taney dissenting.

As this is a case of much importance to the parties and the public, and I do not concur in the judgment of the court, it is my duty to express my opinion. I shall do so as briefly as I can.

The first question to be decided is, whether this bridge is a public nuisance or not, which this court has a right to abate. . . .

In examining this question, it must be borne in mind that, although the suit is brought in this court, the law of the case and the rights of the parties are the same as if it had been brought in the Circuit Court of Virginia, in which the bridge is situated. Pennsylvania, as a State, has the right to sue in this court. But a suit here merely changes the forum, and does not change the law of the case or the rights of the parties. And if, in the Circuit Court of the United States, sitting in Virginia, this bridge could not be adjudged a nuisance, and abated as such, neither can it be done in this court. The State, in this controversy, has the same rights as an individual, and nothing more. And the court is bound to administer to the State here the same law that would be administered to an individual suitor, suing for a like cause, in a Circuit Court of the United States, sitting in the State where the bridge is erected.

Assuming, then, that it does obstruct a public navigable river, and would, at common law, be a public nuisance, I proceed to inquire whether this court is authorized to declare it to be such, and order it to be abated.

The Ohio being a public navigable stream, Congress have undoubtedly the power to regulate commerce upon it. They have the right to prohibit obstructions to its navigation; to declare any such obstruction a public nuisance; to direct the mode of proceeding in the courts of the United States to remove it; and to punish anyone who may erect or maintain it; or it may declare what degree or description of obstruction shall be a public nuisance: as, for example, the height of a bridge over the river, or the distance to which a wharf may be extended into its navigable waters.

But this power has not been exercised. There is no law of the United States declaring an obstruction on the Ohio or any other navigable river, to be a public nuisance, and directing it to be abated as such. Nor is there any act of Congress regulating the height of bridges over the river. We can derive no jurisdiction, therefore, upon this subject, from any law of the United States, and if we exercise it we must derive our authority from some other source.

But we cannot derive it from the common law. For it has been settled, since the beginning of this government, that the courts of the United States as such, have no common-law jurisdiction, civil or criminal, unless conferred upon them by act of Congress. It is true that the courts of the United States, when sitting in a State, administer the common law, where it has been adopted by the State. But it is administered as the law of the State, under the authority and direction of the act of Congress, which makes the laws of the State the rule of decision in a court of the United States, when sitting in the State, provided such laws are not contrary to the Constitution, laws, or treaties, of the United States. We cannot, under the rule of decision thus prescribed, adjudge this bridge to be a nuisance, although it may obstruct the navigation of the river, unless it is a nuisance by the common law, as adopted in Virginia and modified by its statutes. But this bridge was built under the authority of a statute of the State. The structure, in its present form, has been sanctioned by the legislature. It is therefore no offence against the laws of the State; and a Circuit Court of the United States, sitting in the State and governed by its laws, when not in conflict with the Constitution or laws of the United States, or treaties, could not order it to be abated as a public nuisance; and this court has no higher power over this subject, either at law or in equity, nor any other rule to guide it, than a Circuit Court sitting in Virginia. And as the bridge is not a nuisance by the laws of that State, and there is no act of Congress making the obstruction of a public river an offence against the United States, and we have no common law to which the court may resort for jurisdiction, I do not understand by what law, or under what authority, this court can adjudge it to be a public nuisance and proceed to abate it, either upon a proceeding in chancery or by a process at law. . . .

The bridge in question is entirely within the territory of Virginia. Prior to the adoption of the Constitution of the United States, she had an unquestionable right to authorize its erection. She still possesses the same control over the river, subject to the power of Congress, so far as concerns the regulation of commerce. The United States and Virginia are the only sovereignties which can exercise any power over the river where the bridge is erected. Virginia has authorized it, and Congress have acquiesced in it. Congress have made no regulation declaring such a structure unlawful, or authorizing any judicial proceeding against it. If Congress, to whom the power is granted to regulate commerce, have acquiesced, how can the court, to whom the power is not granted, undertake to regulate it, and declare this bridge an unlawful obstruction, and the law of Virginia unconstitutional and void? With all my respect for my brethren, I think it is an error, and I had almost said, a grave one.

If it should be said that the compact between Virginia and Kentucky makes the river free independently of the Constitution, the answer is obvious. The compact does not deprive Virginia of the power to regulate the police of the river, or to authorize bridges or piers, or other structures in it. Such a compact between States has always been construed to mean nothing more than that the river shall be as free to the citizens or subjects for which the other party contracts, as it is to the citizens or subjects of the State in which it is situated. But if this compact or any compact should be construed to prohibit the erection of the bridge, the proceeding should be to enforce the observance of the compact. If erected in violation of a compact, it is still not a nuisance, because there is no law prohibiting it. It would be a breach of contract by the State, and the remedy in a very different mode of proceeding. . . .

The complainant, however, insists that the law of the United States for enrolling and licensing coasting vessels, gives to the vessel so enrolled and licensed, the right to navigate the river free from obstructions: that this law, therefore, by necessary implication, forbids the erection of the bridge which obstructs the navigation; and, consequently, defines the rights of the parties. And if a vessel is obstructed, the law is violated, and the injured party entitled to his remedy, and have the obstruction removed. The case of Gibbons v. Ogden is relied on to support this proposition. . . .

There was no question in that case as to the authority of a court of the United States to declare an obstruction in a river, which a State had authorized, to be a public nuisance, and treat it as an offense against the United States. The waters in question were navigable, and free from impediments of that description; and the boats of the parties who claimed the exclusive privilege were daily passing over them. The only question in the case was, whether all vessels, enrolled and licensed by Congress, had not the right to pass over the same waters as freely as the vessels of the monopolists. The court said they had; that they had an equal right with the complainant to use the navigable waters of New York. But the court do not say that an obstruction placed in the water, which renders navigation inconvenient or hazardous, is a violation of the act for licensing and enrolling coasting vessels, or in conflict with it; nor do they say that this act of Congress confers on the court the power to adjudge it a nuisance, and order it to be abated. There was no such question before the court. It was not in the case, nor was the attention of the court in any way called to it by the argument.

Now, in this case, Virginia has passed no law giving exclusive privileges to navigate the Ohio River through her territory. If the bridge is an obstruction, her own citizens, engaged in the navigation of the Ohio, are equally disabled from passing as the citizens of any other State. The question, therefore, on which this case must turn, did not arise in Gibbons v. Ogden. But it did arise, and was expressly decided in the case of Willson v. The Blackbird Creek Marsh Company, 2 Pet. 245. It was the point in the case. . . .

Indeed, apart from any decisions on the subject, I cannot perceive how the mere grant of power to the legislative department of the government to regulate commerce, can give to the judicial branch the power to declare what shall, and what shall not, be regarded as an unlawful obstruction; how high a bridge must be above the stream, and how far a wharf

Chapter Five. **National and State Power** 183

may be extended into the water, when we have no regulation of Congress to guide us. Nor do I see how we can order a bridge or a wharf to be removed, unless it is in violation of some law which we are authorized to administer. In taking jurisdiction, as the law now stands, we must exercise a broad and undefinable discretion, without any certain and safe rule to guide us. And such a discretion, when men of science differ, when we are to consider the amount and value of trade, and the number of travellers on and across the stream, the interests of communities and States sometimes supposed to be conflicting, and the proper height and form of steamboat chimneys, such a discretion appears to me much more appropriately to belong to the Legislature than to the Judiciary. . . .

Neither can the jurisdiction of a court of chancery be supported upon the ground that the injury is immediate and irreparable, or that any serious embarrassments lie in the way of an action at law. The injury, after two years' experience, has not been found serious enough to lessen the navigation and commerce of the river. On the contrary, they have been continually increasing since this bridge was built. And if it be an injury for which the party is entitled to a remedy, he has a plain and adequate remedy at law; and, therefore, upon general principles of equity, and more especially under the express provisions of the act of 1789, he has no right to come into chancery for relief. And if an action at law were brought by the State in the Circuit Court of the United States, sitting in Virginia, the proceeding at law would be as free from embarrassment and difficulty as any action at law for any injury for which the law gives a remedy. And there is no reason to suppose that the respondents are not able to answer to any amount of damage, which, upon the evidence in this case, the State of Pennsylvania might recover against them. . . .

But Pennsylvania has the right to sue in this court, or in the Circuit Court, at her election. She has the same right to sue here in an action at law as she has to file her bill in equity. And in an action at law brought here by the State of Georgia v. Brailsford et al. (3 Dal. 1,) the case was tried by a jury in the same manner as if the suit had been brought in the Circuit Court. And the jury, brought here to try this case, would be altogether free from suspicion of bias or prejudice. . . .

Indeed this case, in my view of it, pushes the jurisdiction of chancery further than has heretofore been done in England or in this country. . . .

So far I have considered the case upon the assumption that the bridge, upon common-law principles, might, upon the evidence, be determined to be a nuisance. And, admitting that to be the case, I think, for the reasons above stated, that in the absence of any legislation upon the subject by Congress, this proceeding cannot be maintained. I shall, therefore, very briefly express my opinion on the evidence.

I am by no means prepared to say, that this bridge would be a public nuisance even at common law. The evidence of the degree in which it obstructs navigation is exceedingly voluminous, and it is impossible to go fully into an examination of its comparative weight, in a manner that would do justice to the subject, without making this opinion itself a volume. . . . A structure which promotes the convenience of the public, cannot be a nuisance to it. And the public, whose interests are to be looked to in this case, is not the public of any particular town or district or country, or State or States, but the great public of the whole Union. Taking this view of the question, and looking to the testimony as set forth in the record, and more especially to that unerring test, *experience*, which the lapse of time has afforded, I am convinced that the detriment and inconvenience to the commerce and travel on the river, is small and occasional only, while the advantages which the public derives from the passage over, are great and constant. And if the courts of the United States had common-law jurisdiction, and the question was legally before us to determine whether this bridge was a public nuisance or not, I am of opinion that it is not; and that the advantages which the great body of the people of the United States reap from it, outweigh the disadvantages and inconvenience sustained by the commerce and navigation of the river.

Moreover, the jurisdiction exercised in this case, is new and without precedent in this court. Bridges have been erected over many navigable rivers, and built so near the water, that vessels can pass only through a draw. Such bridges are unquestionably obstructions, and impede navigation. For where the vessels are propelled by sails, and the wind is unfavorable, they are often detained not only for hours, but for days. The courts of the United States have never exercised jurisdiction over any of these obstructions, nor declared them to be nuisances. I should be unwilling, in a case like this, to exercise this high and delicate power without precedents to support me in analogous cases. The demolition of this bridge would occasion a heavy loss to the parties, and much inconvenience to a large portion of the community. The United States are not parties to this proceeding, and the particular injury sustained by the complainant is exceedingly small. And it is solely for the protection of her small, remote, contingent, and speculative interest in tolls, that this bridge is pulled down. For it must be remembered that although we see in the testimony that injuries are alleged to have been suffered by others, yet the State of Pennsylvania is the only party to this proceeding, the only one who appears in this court as complainant, and her particular loss is the only ground on which jurisdiction is claimed, and the only injury which the court is called on to redress; or has a right to consider in this proceeding.

The testimony, too, is conflicting; men of eminence and skill, and well qualified to speak on the subject, differing widely in their testimony. And I am the more unwilling to assume this questionable jurisdiction, because the legislative department of the general government has undoubted power over the whole subject, and may regulate the height of bridges over the Ohio, and of the chimneys of steamboats when passing under them, and may, while it guards the rights of navigation in the stream, at the same time protect the rights of passage and travel over it. That department of the government has better means, too, of obtaining information, than the narrow scope of judicial proceedings can afford. It may adopt regulations by which courts of justice may be guided in an inquiry like this with some degree of certainty, instead of leaving them to the undefined discretion which must now be exercised in every case that may be brought before us, without being able to lay down any certain rule, by which this discretion may be limited. It is too near the confines of legislation; and I think the court ought not to assume it.

Entertaining this opinion, I must, with all the respect I feel for the judgment of my brethren, with whom it is my misfortune to differ, enter my dissent.

[A dissenting opinion of Mr. Justice Daniel is omitted.][b]

PENNSYLVANIA v. WHEELING & BELMONT BRIDGE CO., 18 How. 421, 15 L. Ed. 435 (1856). In an opinion by Nelson, J. (McLean, Grier, and Wayne, JJ., dissenting), the Court sustained as a valid regulation of commerce an Act of Congress adopted on August 31, 1852, declaring that the Wheeling Bridge was a lawful structure in its present position and elevation and declaring it to be a post road, and authorizing the company to maintain the bridge at its present site and elevation. On congressional change of constitutional decisions see Note, 63 Harv. L. Rev. 861 (1950).

---

[b] Was a constitutional question presented in this case?

A contemporary document points out that the suit was brought in furtherance of the interest of Pittsburgh to the detriment of Philadelphia, and speaks of "chronic envy and cultivated malice," and "insane assault upon a neighbour's bridge." The Wheeling Bridge Suit: A Notice of Its History and Objects: Addressed to the Legislature of Pennsylvania 13 (Philadelphia, 1852). Would this intrastate conflict have any bearing on the legal issues in the case?

The decision was distinguished in Willamette Bridge Co. v. Hatch, 125 U.S. 1 (1888).

Modern federal authority over structures in navigable streams derives from the Dam Act of 1890, 26 Stat. 426. — Ed.

Brown v. Maryland 12 Wheat. 419, 6 L. Ed. 678 (1827)

Mr. Chief Justice Marshall delivered the opinion of the court:
　This is a writ of error to a judgment rendered in the Court of Appeals of Maryland, affirming a judgment of the City Court of Baltimore, on an indictment found in that court against the plaintiffs in error, for violating an act of the legislature of Maryland. The indictment was founded on the second section of that act, which is in these words: "And be it enacted, that all importers of foreign articles or commodities, of dry goods, wares, or merchandise, by bale or package, . . . and other persons selling the same by wholesale, bale or package, hogshead, barrel, or tierce, shall, before they are authorized to sell, take out a license, as by the original act is directed, for which they shall pay fifty dollars; and in case of neglect or refusal to take out such license, shall be subject to the same penalties and forfeitures as are prescribed by the original act to which this is a supplement." The indictment charges the plaintiffs in error with having imported and sold one package of foreign dry goods without having license to do so. A judgment was rendered against them on demurrer for the penalty which the act prescribes for the offense; and that judgment is now before this court.
　The cause depends entirely on the question, whether the legislature of a state can constitutionally require the importer of foreign articles to take out a license from the state, before he shall be permitted to sell a bale or package so imported.
　It has been truly said, that the presumption is in favor of every legislative act, and that the whole burthen of proof lies on him who denies its constitutionality. The plaintiffs in error take the burthen upon themselves, and insist that the act under consideration is repugnant to two provisions in the constitution of the United States:
　1. To that which declares that "no state shall, without the consent of Congress, lay any imposts, or duties on imports or exports, except what may be absolutely necessary for executing its inspection laws."
　2. To that which declares that Congress shall have power "to regulate commerce with foreign nations, and among the several states, and with the Indian tribes."
　1. The first inquiry is into the extent of the prohibition upon states "to lay any imposts or duties on imports or exports." The counsel for the state of Maryland would confine this prohibition to the laws imposing duties on the act of importation or exportation. The counsel for the plaintiffs in error give them a much wider scope.
　In performing the delicate and important duty of construing clauses in the constitution of our country, which involve conflicting powers of the government of the Union, and of the respective states, it is proper to take a view of the literal meaning of the words to be expounded, of their connection with other words, and of the general objects to be accomplished by the prohibitory clause, or by the grant of power. . . .
　. . . What, then, are "imports"? The lexicons inform us, they are "things imported." If we appeal to usage for the meaning of the word, we shall receive the same answer. They are the articles themselves which are brought into the country. "A duty on imports," then, is not merely a duty on the act of importation, but it is a duty on the thing imported. It is not, taken in its literal sense, confined to a duty levied while the article is entering the country, but extends to a duty levied after it has entered the country. The succeeding words of the sentence which limit the prohibition, show the extent in which it was understood. The limitation is, "except what may be absolutely necessary for executing its inspection laws." Now, the inspection laws, so far as they act upon articles for exportation, are generally executed on land, before the article is put on board the vessel; so far as they act upon importations, they are generally executed upon articles which are landed. The tax or duty of inspection, then, is a tax which is frequently, if not always, paid for service performed on land, while the article is in the bosom of the country. Yet this tax is an exception to the prohibition on the states to lay duties on imports or exports. The excep-

tion was made because the tax would otherwise have been within the prohibition. . . .

If we quit this narrow view of the subject, and passing from the literal interpretation of the words, look to the objects of the prohibition, we find no reason for withdrawing the act under consideration from its operation.

From the vast inequality between the different states of the confederacy, as to commercial advantages, few subjects were viewed with deeper interest, or excited more irritation, than the manner in which the several states exercised, or seemed disposed to exercise, the power of laying duties on imports. From motives which were deemed sufficient by the statesmen of that day, the general power of taxation, indispensably necessary as it was, and jealous as the states were of any encroachment on it, was so far abridged as to forbid them to touch imports or exports, with the single exception which has been noticed. Why are they restrained from imposing these duties? Plainly because, in the general opinion, the interest of all would be best promoted by placing that whole subject under the control of Congress. Whether the prohibition to "lay imposts, or duties on imports or exports," proceeded from an apprehension that the power might be so exercised as to disturb that equality among the states which was generally advantageous, or that harmony between them which it was desirable to preserve, or to maintain unimpaired our commercial connections with foreign nations, or to confer this source of revenue on the government of the Union, or whatever other motive might have induced the prohibition, it is plain that the object would be as completely defeated by a power to tax the article in the hands of the importer the instant it was landed as by a power to tax it while entering the port. . . . No goods would be imported if none could be sold. . . . It is obvious that the same power which imposes a light duty can impose a very heavy one, one which amounts to a prohibition. Questions of power do not depend on the degree to which it may be exercised. If it may be exercised at all, it must be exercised at the will of those in whose hands it is placed.

. . . Conceding, to the full extent which is required, that every state would, in its legislation on this subject, provide judiciously for its own interest, it cannot be conceded that each would respect the interest of others. A duty on imports is a tax on the article, which is paid by the consumer. The great importing states would thus levy a tax on the non-importing states, which would not be less a tax because their interest would afford ample security against its ever being so heavy as to expel commerce from their ports.

This would necessarily produce countervailing measures on the part of those states whose situation was less favorable to importation. For this, among other reasons, the whole power of laying duties on imports was, with a single and slight exception, taken from the states. . . .

The counsel for the state of Maryland insist, with great reason, that if the words of the prohibition be taken in their utmost latitude, they will abridge the power of taxation, which all admit to be essential to the states, to an extent which have never yet been suspected, and will deprive them of resources which are necessary to supply revenue, and which they have heretofore been admitted to possess. These words must therefore be construed with some limitation; and, if this be admitted, they insist, that entering the country is the point of time when the prohibition ceases, and the power of the state to tax commences. . . .

. . . The power, and the restriction on it, though quite distinguishable when they do not approach each other, may yet, like the intervening colors between white and black, approach so nearly as to perplex the understanding, as colors perplex the vision in marking the distinction between them. Yet the distinction exists, and must be marked as the cases arise. Till they do arise, it might be premature to state any rule as being universal in its application. It is sufficient for the present to say, generally, that when the importer has so acted upon the thing imported, that it has become incorporated and mixed up with the mass of property in the country, it has, perhaps, lost its distinctive character as an import, and has become subject to the taxing power of the State; but while remaining the property of the importer, in his warehouse, in the original form or package in which it was imported, a tax upon it is too plainly a duty on imports to escape the prohibition in the constitution.

The counsel for the plaintiffs in error contend that the importer purchases, by payment of the duty to the United States, a right to dispose of his merchandise, as well as to bring it into the country; and certainly the argument is supported by strong reason, as well as by the practice of nations, including our own.

The objective of importation is sale; it constitutes the motive for paying the duties; and if the United States possesses the power of conferring the right to sell, as the consideration for which the duty is paid, every principle of fair dealing requires that they should be understood to confer it. . . .

The counsel for the defendant in error have endeavored to illustrate their proposition, that the constitutional prohibition ceases the instant the goods enter the country, by an array of the consequences which they suppose must follow the denial of it. If the importer acquires the right to sell by the payment of duties, he may, they say, exert that right when, where, and as he pleases, and the state cannot regulate it. He may sell by retail, at auction, or as an itinerant peddler. He may introduce articles, as gunpowder, which endangers a city, into the midst of its population; he may introduce articles which endanger the public health, and the power of self-preservation is denied. An importer may bring in goods, as plate, for his own use, and thus retain much valuable property exempt from taxation.

These objections to the principle, if well founded, would certainly be entitled to serious consideration. But we think they will be found, on examination, not to belong necessarily to the principle, and, consequently, not to prove that it may not be resorted to with safety, as a criterion by which to measure the extent of the prohibition.

This indictment is against the importer, for selling a package of dry goods in the form in which it was imported, without a license. This state of things is changed if he sells them, or otherwise mixes them with the general property of the state, by breaking up his packages, and travelling with them as an itinerant peddler. In the first case, the tax intercepts the import, as an import, in its way to become incorporated with the general mass of property, and denies it the privilege of becoming so incorporated until it shall have contributed to the revenue of the state. It denies to the importer the right of using the privilege which he has purchased from the United States, until he shall have also purchased it from the state. In the last cases, the tax finds the article already incorporated with the mass of property by the act of the importer. He has used the privilege he had purchased, and has himself mixed them up with the common mass, and the law may treat them as it finds them. The same observations apply to plate, or other furniture used by the importer. . . .

But if it should be proved that a duty on the article itself would be repugnant to the constitution, it is still argued that this is not a tax upon the article, but on the person. The state, it is said, may tax occupations, and this is nothing more.

It is impossible to conceal from ourselves that this is varying the form, without varying the substance. It is treating a prohibition which is general, as if it were confined to a particular mode of doing the forbidden thing. All must perceive that a tax on the sale of an article, imported only for sale, is a tax on the article itself. It is true, the state may tax occupations generally, but this tax must be paid by those who employ the individual, or is a tax on his business. The lawyer, the physician, or the mechanic, must either charge more on the article in which he deals, or the thing itself is taxed through his person. This the state has a right to do, because no constitutional prohibition extends to it. So, a tax on the occupation of an importer is, in like manner, a tax on importation. It must add to the price of the article, and be paid by the consumer, or by the importer himself, in like manner as a direct duty on the article itself would be made. This the state has not a right to do, because it is prohibited by the constitution. . . .

2. Is it also repugnant to that clause in the constitution which empowers "Congress to regulate commerce with foreign nations, and among the several states, and with the Indian tribes"? . . .

. . . Sale is the object of importation, and is an essential ingredient of that intercourse, of which importation constitutes a part. It is as essential an ingredient, as indispensable to the existence of the entire thing, then, as importation itself. It must be considered as a component part of the power to regulate commerce. Congress has a right, not only to authorize importation, but to authorize the importer to sell.

If this be admitted — and we think it cannot be denied — what can be the meaning of an act of Congress which authorizes importation, and offers the privilege for sale at a fixed price to every person who chooses to become a purchaser? How is it to be construed, if an intent to deal honestly and fairly, an intent as wise as it is moral, is to enter into the construction? What can be the use of the contract? what does the importer purchase, if he does not purchase the privilege to sell? . . .

If the principles we have stated be correct, the result to which they conduct us cannot be mistaken. Any penalty inflicted on the importer for selling the article in his character of importer, must be in opposition to the act of Congress which authorizes importation. Any charge on the introduction and incorporation of the articles into and with the mass of property in the country, must be hostile to the power given to Congress to regulate commerce, since an essential part of that regulation, and principal object of it, is to prescribe the regular means for accomplishing that introduction and incorporation. . . .

. . . It results, necessarily, from this principle, that the taxing power of the states must have some limits. It cannot reach and restrain the action of the national government within its proper sphere. It cannot reach the administration of justice in the courts of the Union, or the collection of the taxes of the United States, or restrain the operation of any law which Congress may constitutionally pass. It cannot interfere with any regulation of commerce. If the states may tax all persons and property found on their territory, what shall restrain them from taxing goods in their transit through the state from one port to another, for the purpose of reexportation? The laws of trade authorize this operation, and general convenience requires it. Or what should restrain a state from taxing any article passing through it from one state to another, for the purpose of traffic? or from taxing the transportation of articles passing from the state itself to another state, for commercial purposes? These cases are all within the sovereign power of taxation, but would obviously derange the measures of Congress to regulate commerce, and affect materially the purpose for which that power was given. . . .

It may be proper to add, that we suppose the principles laid down in this case, to apply equally to importations from a sister state. We do not mean to give any opinion on a tax discriminating between foreign and domestic articles.

We think there is error in the judgment of the Court of Appeals of the State of Maryland, in affirming the judgment of the Baltimore City Court, because the act of the legislature of Maryland, imposing the penalty for which the said judgment is rendered, is repugnant to the constitution of the United States, and, consequently, void. The judgment is to be reversed, and the cause remanded to that court, with instructions to enter judgment in favor of the appellants.

[The dissenting opinion of Mr. Justice Thompson is omitted.]

Woodruff v. Parham 8 Wall. 123, 19 L. Ed. 382 (1869)

In error to the Supreme Court of Alabama. This action was brought in the Circuit Court of Mobile County, Alabama, to recover for an alleged wrongful taking of goods upon the collection of a certain tax. . . .

Mr. Justice Miller delivered the opinion of the court:

The charter of Mobile authorizes that City to impose a tax for municipal purposes on real and personal estate, auction sales and sales of merchandise, capital employed in business and income within the City. The plaintiff in error having sold as auctioneer and commission merchant, a large amount of goods for others, and also on his own account, claims that as to such goods as were brought into the State of Alabama from other States of the Union, and sold by him at wholesale in the original and unbroken packages, he is not liable to the tax which the ordinances of the City imposed upon all sales of merchandise.

The case was heard in the courts of the State of Alabama upon an agreed statement of facts, and that statement fully raises the question whether merchandise brought from other States and sold, under the circumstances stated, comes within the prohibition of the Federal Constitution, that no State shall, without the consent of Congress, levy any imposts or duties on imports or exports. And it is claimed that it also brings the case within the principles laid down by this court in Brown v. Md., 12 Wheat. 419.

That decision has been recognized for over forty years as governing the action of this court in the same class of cases, and its reasoning has been often cited and received with approbation in others to which it was applicable. We do not now propose to question its authority or to depart from its principles.

The tax of the State of Maryland, which was the subject of controversy in that case, was limited by its terms to importers of foreign articles or commodities, and the proposition that we are now to consider is whether the provision of the Constitution to which we have referred extends, in its true meaning and intent, to articles brought from one State of the Union into another. . . .

The words "impost," "imports" and "exports" are frequently used in the Constitution. They have a necessary correlation, and when we have a clear idea of what either word means in any particular connection in which it may be found, we have one of the most satisfactory tests of its definition in other parts of the same instrument.

In the case of Brown v. Maryland, the word "imports," as used in the clause now under consideration, is defined, both on the authority of the lexicons and of usage, to be articles brought into the country; and impost is there said to be a duty, custom, or tax levied on articles brought into the country. In the ordinary use of these terms at this day, no one would, for a moment, think of them as having relation to any other articles than those brought from a country foreign to the United States, and at the time the case of Brown v. Maryland was decided — namely: in 1827 — it is reasonable to suppose that the general usage was the same, and that in defining imports as articles brought into the country, the Chief Justice used the word "country" as a synonym for United States.

But the word is susceptible of being applied to articles introduced from one State into another, and we must inquire if it was so used by the framers of the Constitution. . . .

[The Court concluded, from the terminology of the Constitution, that reference to goods imported from one state to another by use of the word "imports" was "altogether improbable."]

If we turn for a moment from the consideration of the language of the Constitution to the history of its formation and adoption, we shall find additional reason to conclude that the words imports and imposts were used with exclusive reference to articles imported from foreign countries. . . .

Its very first grant of power to the new government about to be established, was to lay and collect imposts or duties on foreign goods imported into the country, and among its restraints upon the States was the corresponding one that they should lay no duties on imports or exports. It seems, however, from Mr. Madison's account of the debates, that while the necessity of vesting in Congress the power to levy duties on foreign goods was generally conceded, the right of the States to do so likewise was not given up without discussion, and was finally yielded with the qualification . . . that the States might lay such duties with the assent of Congress. Mr. Madison moved that the words "nor lay imposts or duties on imports" be placed in that class of prohibitions which were absolute, instead of those which were dependent on the consent of Congress. His reason was that the States interested in this power (meaning those who had good seaports) by which they could tax the imports of their neighbors passing through their markets, were a majority, and could gain the consent of Congress to the injury of New Jersey, North Carolina, and other nonimporting States. But his motion failed. . . .

Gov. Ellsworth, in opening the debate of the Connecticut Convention on the adoption of the Constitution, says: "Our being tributary to our sister States, is in consequence of the want of a Federal system. The State of New York raises £60,000 or £80,000 in a year by impost. Connecticut consumes about one third of the goods upon which this impost is laid and, consequently, pays one third of this sum to New York. If we import by the medium of Massachusetts, she has an impost, and to her we pay tribute." 2 Elliot, Debates, 192. . . .

Whether we look, then, to the terms of the clause of the Constitution in question, or to its relation to other parts of that instrument, or to the history of its formation and adoption, or to the comments of the eminent men who took part in those transactions, we are forced to the conclusion that no intention existed to prohibit, by this clause, the right of one State to tax articles brought into it from another. If we examine for a moment the results of an opposite doctrine, we shall be well satisfied with the wisdom of the Constitution as thus construed.

The merchant of Chicago who buys his goods in New York and sells at wholesale in the original packages, may have his millions employed in trade for half a lifetime and escape all state, county and city taxes; for all that he is worth is invested in goods which he claims to be protected as imports from New York. Neither the State nor the city which protects his life and property can make him contribute a dollar to support its government, improve its thoroughfares or educate its children. The merchant in a town in Massachusetts, who deals only in wholesale, if he purchase his goods in New York, is exempt from taxation. If his neighbor purchase in Boston, he must pay all the tax which Massachusetts levies with equal justice on the property of all the citizens.

These cases are merely mentioned as illustrations. But it is obvious that if articles brought from one State into another are exempt from taxation, even under the limited circumstances laid down in the case of Brown v. Maryland, the grossest injustice must prevail, and equality of public burdens in all our large cities is impossible. . . .

The case of Brown v. Maryland, as we have already said, arose out of a statute of that State, taxing, by way of discrimination, importers who sold, by wholesale, foreign goods.

Chief Justice Marshall, in delivering the opinion of the court, distinctly bases the invalidity of the statute, (1) On the clause of the Constitution which forbids a State to levy imposts or duties on imports; and (2) That which confers on Congress the power to regulate commerce with foreign nations, among the States, with the Indian tribes.

The casual remark, therefore, made in the close of the opinion, "that we suppose the principles laid down in this case to apply equally to importations from a sister State," can only be received as an intimation of what they might decide if the case ever came before them, for no such case was then to be decided. It is not, therefore, a judicial decision of the question, even if the remark was intended to apply to the first of the grounds on which that decision was placed.

But the opinion in that case discussed, as we have said, under two distinct heads, the two clauses of the Constitution which he supposed to be violated by the Maryland Statute, and the remark above quoted follows immediately the discussion of the second proposition, or the applicability of the commerce clause to that case.

If the court then meant to say that a tax levied on goods from a sister State which was not levied on goods of a similar character produced within the State, would be in conflict with the clause of the Contitution giving Congress the right "to regulate commerce among the States," as much as the tax on foreign goods, then under consideration, was in conflict with the authority "to regulate commerce with foreign nations," we agree with the proposition. . . .

The case before us is a simple tax on sales of merchandise, imposed alike upon all sales made in Mobile, whether the sales be made by a citizen of Alabama or of another State, and whether the goods sold are the produce of that State or some other. There is no attempt to discriminate injuriously against the products of other States or the rights of their citizens, and the case is not, therefore, an attempt to fetter commerce among the States, or to deprive the citizens of other States of any privilege or immunity possessed by citizens of Alabama. But a law having such operation would, in our opinion, be an infringement of the provisions of the Constitution which relate to those subjects and, therefore, void. There is also, in addition to the restraints which those provisions impose by their own force on the States, the unquestioned power of Congress, under the authority to regulate commerce among the States, to interpose, by the exercise of this power, in such a manner as to prevent the State from any oppressive interference with the free interchange of commodities by the citizens of one State with those of another.

Judgment affirmed.

MR. JUSTICE NELSON, dissenting. . . . In looking at this clause [Article I, § 10, Clause 3], it will be seen that there is nothing in its terms of connection that affords the slightest indication that it was intended to be confined to the prohibition of a tax upon foreign imports. . . . The same clause also provides: "No State shall, without the consent of Congress, lay any duty of tonnage," etc. Does this also relate to tonnage employed in foreign trade? If so, then it will be competent hereafter for the States to levy a tax upon the tonnage of vessels employed in carrying on commerce among the States, including the tonnage employed in the coasting trade. . . .

[A]t the time the delegates assembled in 1787 to form the Constitution, they represented States that for all substantial purposes of government were foreign and independent, and especially so in respect to all commercial relations among them, or with foreign countries. Looking at this condition of things, . . . is it reasonable or consistent with proper rules of construction to suppose, in the absence of any indication from the words of this clause prohibiting the tax on imports or exports, the members used the terms with exclusive reference to foreign countries — that is, countries foreign to the States — and not in reference to the States themselves? We again ask: if this distinction was intended, why was not the clause so framed as to indicate it on its face, and not left to mere conjecture and speculation? . . .

[If only discrimination is prohibited,] New York and Pennsylvania could lay a tax upon all sales of cotton, tobacco or rice within these States, which would be a tax without any discrimination; and yet would be, in fact, in its operation and effect, exclusively upon these Southern products. So in respect to the wheat, flour, pork, beef, butter and cheese, when shipped to [the] Southern States. Each State not producing the article sold, the general tax would not affect their people. . . .

Brown v. Houston *114 U.S. 622, 5 S. Ct. 1091, 29 L. Ed. 257 (1885)*

[Suit to restrain the defendant tax collector from collecting, by seizure and sale, the Louisiana personal property tax assessed upon cargoes of coal brought from Pittsburgh to New Orleans by flatboat, remaining afloat in the original condition and package, for sale by the flatboat load, at the time the tax was assessed.]

MR. JUSTICE BRADLEY delivered the opinion of the court: . . .

As to the character and mode of the assessment, little need be added. . . . It was not a tax imposed upon the coal as a foreign product, or as the product of another State than Louisiana, nor a tax imposed by reason of the coal being imported or brought into

Louisiana, nor a tax imposed whilst it was in a state of transit through that State to some other place of destination. It was imposed after the coal had arrived at its destination and was put up for sale. The coal had come to its place of rest, for final disposal or use, and was a commodity in the market of New Orleans. It might continue in that condition for a year or two years, or only for a day. It had become a part of the general mass of property in the State, and as such it was taxed for the current year (1880), as all other property in the City of New Orleans was taxed. Under the law, it could not be taxed again until the following year. It was subjected to no discrimination in favor of goods which were the product of Louisiana, or goods which were the property of citizens of Louisiana. It was treated in exactly the same manner as such goods were treated. . . .

We do not mean to say that if a tax collector should be stationed at every ferry and railroad depot in the City of New York, charged with the duty of collecting a tax on every wagonload, or carload of produce and merchandise brought into the city, that it would not be a regulation of and restraint upon interstate commerce, so far as the tax should be imposed on articles brought from other States. We think it would be, and that it would be an encroachment upon the exclusive powers of Congress. It would be very different from the tax laid on auction sales of all property indiscriminately, as in the case of Woodruff v. Parham [8 Wall. 123], which had no relation to the movement of goods from one State to another. It would be very different from a tax laid, as in the present case, on property which had reached its destination, and had become part of the general mass of property of the city, and which was only taxed as a part of that general mass in common with all other property in the city, and in precisely the same manner. . . .

Judgment [for defendant] affirmed.

Michelin Tire Corp. v. Wages 423 U.S. 276, 96 S. Ct. 535, 46 L. Ed. 2d 495 (1976)

MR. JUSTICE BRENNAN delivered the opinion of the Court.

Respondents, the Tax Commissioner and Tax Assessors of Gwinnett County, Ga., assessed ad valorem property taxes against tires and tubes imported by petitioner from France and Nova Scotia that were included on the assessment dates in an inventory maintained at its wholesale distribution warehouse in the county. Petitioner brought this action for declaratory and injunctive relief in the Superior Court of Gwinnett County, alleging that with the exception of certain passenger tubes that had been removed from the original shipping cartons, the ad valorem property taxes assessed against its inventory of imported tires and tubes were prohibited by Art. I, § 10, cl. 2, of the Constitution, which provides in pertinent part that "No State shall, without the consent of Congress, lay any Imposts or Duties on Imports or Exports, except what may be absolutely necessary for executing its Inspection Laws. . . ." After trial, the Superior Court granted the requested declaratory and injunctive relief. On appeal, the Supreme Court of Georgia affirmed in part and reversed in part, agreeing that the tubes in the corrugated shipping cartons were immune from ad valorem taxation, but holding that the tires had lost their status as imports and become subject to such taxation because they had been mingled with other tires imported in bulk, sorted, and arranged for sale. Wages v. Michelin Tire Corp., 233 Ga. 712, 214 S.E.2d 349 (1975). We granted petitioner's petition for certiorari, 422 U.S. 1040 (1975). The only question presented is whether the Georgia Supreme Court was correct in holding that the tires were subject to the ad valorem property tax. We affirm without addressing the question whether the Georgia Supreme Court was correct in holding that the tires had lost their status as imports. We hold that, in any event, Georgia's assessment of a nondiscriminatory ad valorem property tax against the imported tires is not within the constitutional prohibition against laying "any Imposts or Duties on Imports . . ." and that insofar as Low v. Austin, 13 Wall. 29 (1871) is to the contrary, that decision is overruled.

I

Petitioner, a New York corporation qualified to do business in Georgia, operates as an importer and wholesale distributor in the United States of automobile and truck tires and tubes manufactured in France and Nova Scotia by Michelin Tires, Ltd. The business is operated from distribution warehouses in various parts of the country. Distribution and sale of tires and tubes from the Gwinnett County warehouse is limited to the 250-300 franchised dealers with whom petitioner does all of its business in six southeastern States. Some 25% of the tires and tubes are manufactured in and imported from Nova Scotia, and are brought to the United States in tractor-driven over-the-road trailers packed and sealed at the Nova Scotia factory. The remaining 75% of the imported tires and tubes are brought to the United States by sea from France and Nova Scotia in sea vans packed and sealed at the foreign factories. Sea vans are essentially over-the-road trailers from which the wheels are removed before being loaded aboard ship. Upon arrival of the ship at the United States port of entry, the vans are unloaded, the wheels are replaced, and the vans are tractor-hauled to petitioner's distribution warehouse after clearing customs upon payment of a 4% import duty.

The imported tires, each of which has its own serial number, are packed in bulk into the trailers and vans, without otherwise being packaged or bundled. They lose their identity as a unit, however, when unloaded from the trailers and vans at the distribution warehouse. When unloaded they are sorted by size and style, without segregation by place of manufacture, stacked on wooden pallets each bearing four stacks of five tires of the same size and style, and stored in pallet stacks of three pallets each. This is the only processing required or performed to ready the tires for sale and delivery to the franchised dealers.

Sales of tires and tubes from the Gwinnett County distribution warehouse to the franchised dealers average 4,000-5,000 pounds per sale. Orders are filled without regard to the shipments in which the tires and tubes arrived in the United States or the place of their manufacture. Delivery to the franchised dealers is by common carrier or customer pickup.

II

. . . Low v. Austin, supra, is the leading decision of this Court holding that the States are prohibited by the Import-Export Clause from imposing a nondiscriminatory ad valorem property tax on imported goods until they lose their character as imports and become incorporated into the mass of property in the State. The Court there reviewed a decision of the California Supreme Court that had sustained the constitutionality of California's nondiscriminatory ad valorem tax on the ground that the Import-Export Clause only prohibited taxes upon the character of the goods as imports and therefore did not prohibit nondiscriminatory taxes upon the goods as property. See 13 Wall., at 30-31. This Court reversed on its reading of the seminal opinion construing the Import-Export Clause, Brown v. Maryland, 12 Wheat. 419 (1827), as holding that "Whilst retaining their character as imports, a tax upon them, in any shape, is within the constitutional prohibition." 13 Wall., at 34.

Scholarly analysis has been uniformly critical of Low v. Austin. It is true that Chief Justice Marshall, speaking for the Court in Brown v. Maryland, 12 Wheat., at 442, said that ". . . while [the thing imported remains] the property of the importer, in his warehouse, in the original form or package in which it was imported, a tax upon it is too plainly a duty on imports to escape the prohibition in the constitution." Commentators have uniformly agreed that Low v. Austin misread this dictum in holding that the Court in Brown included nondiscriminatory ad valorem property taxes among prohibited "imposts" or "duties," for the contrary conclusion is plainly to be inferred from consideration of the specific abuses which led the Framers to include the Import-Export Clause in the Constitution. See, e.g., Powell, State Taxation of Imports — When Does an Import Cease to Be an Import?, 58 Harv. L. Rev. 858 (1945); The Supreme Court, 1958 Term, 73 Harv. L. Rev. 126, 176 (1959); Early & Weitzman, A Century of Dissent: The Immunity of Goods Imported for Resale From Nondiscriminatory State Personal Property Taxes, 7 S.W.U.L. Rev. 247 (1975); Dakin, The Protective Cloak of the Export-Import Clause: Immunity for the Goods or Immunity for the Process?, 19 La. L. Rev. 747 (1959).

Our independent study persuades us that a nondiscriminatory ad valorem property tax is not the type of state exaction which the Framers of the Constitution or the Court in Brown had in mind as being an "impost" or "duty" and that Low v. Austin's reliance upon the Brown dictum to reach the contrary conclusion was misplaced.

III

One of the major defects of the Articles of Confederation, and a compelling reason for the calling of the Constitutional Convention of 1787, was the fact that the Articles essentially left the individual States free to burden commerce both among themselves and with foreign countries very much as they pleased. Before 1787 it was commonplace for seaboard States to derive revenue to defray the costs of state and local governments by imposing taxes on imported goods destined for customers in inland States. At the same time, there was no secure source of revenue for the central government. James Madison, in his Preface to Debates in the Convention of 1787, 3 M. Farrand, The Records of the Federal Convention of 1787, at 542 (1911), provides a graphic description of the situation: "The other source of dissatisfaction was the peculiar situation of some of the States, which having no convenient ports for foreign commerce, were subject to be taxed by their neighbors, thro whose ports, their commerce was carried on. New Jersey, placed between Phila. & N. York, was likened to a Cask tapped at both ends: and N. Carolina between Virga. & S. Carolina to a patient bleeding at both Arms. The Articles of Confederation provided no remedy for the complaint: which produced a strong protest on the part of N. Jersey; and never ceased to be a source of dissatisfaction & discord, until the new Constitution, superseded the old." . . .

The Framers of the Constitution thus sought to alleviate three main concerns by committing sole power to lay imposts and duties on imports in the Federal Government, with no concurrent state power: the Federal Government must speak with one voice when regulating commercial relations with foreign governments, and tariffs, which might affect foreign relations, could not be implemented by the States consistently with that exclusive power; import revenues were to be the major source of revenue of the Federal Government and should not be diverted to the States; and harmony among the States might be disturbed unless seaboard States, with their crucial ports of entry, were prohibited from levying taxes on citizens of other States by taxing goods merely flowing through their ports to the inland States not situated as favorably geographically.

Nothing in the history of the Import-Export Clause even remotely suggests that a nondiscriminatory ad valorem property tax which is also imposed on imported goods that are no longer in import transit was the type of exaction that was regarded as objectionable by the Framers of the Constitution. For such an exaction, unlike discriminatory state taxation against imported goods as imports, was not regarded as an impediment that severely hampered commerce or constituted a form of tribute by seaboard States to the disadvantage of the interior States.

It is obvious that such nondiscriminatory property taxation can have no impact whatsoever on the Federal Government's exclusive regulation of foreign commerce, probably the most important purpose of the clause's prohibition. By definition, such a tax does not fall on imports as such because of their place of origin. It cannot be used to create special protective tariffs or particular preferences for certain domestic goods, and it cannot be applied selectively to encourage or discourage any importation in a manner inconsistent with federal regulation. . . .

Nor will such taxation deprive the Federal Government of the exclusive right to all revenues from imposts and duties on imports and exports, since that right by definition only extends to revenues from exactions of a particular category; if nondiscriminatory ad valorem taxation is not in that category, it deprives the Federal Government of nothing to which it is entitled. . . .

Finally, nondiscriminatory ad valorem property taxes do not interfere with the free flow of imported goods among the States, as did the exactions by States under the Articles of Confederation directed solely at imported goods. Indeed, importers of goods destined for inland States can easily avoid even those taxes in today's world. Modern transportation methods such as air freight and containerized packaging, and the development of railroads and the Nation's internal waterways, enable importation directly into the inland States. Petitioner, for example, operates other distribution centers from wholesale warehouses in inland States. Actually, a quarter of the tires distributed from petitioner's Georgia warehouse are imported interstate directly from Canada. To be sure, allowance of nondiscriminatory ad valorem property taxation may increase the cost of goods purchased by "inland" consumers. But as already noted, such taxation is the quid pro quo for benefits actually conferred by the taxing State. There is no reason why local taxpayers should subsidize the services used by the importer; ultimate consumers should pay for such services as police and fire protection accorded the goods just as much as they should pay transportation costs associated with those goods. An evil to be prevented by the Import-Export Clause was the levying of taxes which could only be imposed because of the peculiar geographical situation of certain States that enabled them to single out goods destined for other States. In effect, the clause was fashioned to prevent the imposition of exactions which were no more than transit fees on the privilege of moving through a State. A nondiscriminatory ad valorem property tax obviously stands on a different footing, and to the extent there is any conflict whatsoever with this purpose of the clause, it may be secured merely by prohibiting the assessment of even nondiscriminatory property taxes on goods which are merely in transit through the State when the tax is assessed.

Admittedly, the wording of the prohibition of the Import-Export Clause does not in terms except nondiscriminatory taxes with some impact on imports or exports. But just as clearly, the clause is not written in terms of a broad prohibition of every "tax." The prohibition is only against States laying "imposts or duties" on "imports." By contrast, Congress is empowered to "lay and collect Taxes, Duties, Imposts, and Excises," which plainly lends support to a reading of the Import-Export Clause as not prohibiting every exaction or "tax" which falls in some measure on imported goods. . . .

IV

The Court in Low v. Austin nevertheless expanded the prohibition of the clause to include nondiscriminatory ad valorem property taxes, and did so with no analysis, but with only the statement that Brown v. Maryland had marked the line "where the power of Congress over the goods imported ends, and that of the State begins, with as much precision as the subject admits." 13 Wall., at 32. But the opinion in Brown v. Maryland cannot properly be read to propose such a broad definition of "imposts" or "duties." . . .

The Court stated that there were two situations in which the prohibition would not apply. One was the case of a state tax levied after the imported goods had lost their status as imports. The Court devised an evidentiary tool, the "original package" test, for use in making that determination. The formula was: "It is sufficient for the present to say, generally, that when the importer has so acted upon the thing imported, that it has become incorporated and mixed up with the mass of property in the country, it has, perhaps, lost its distinctive character as an import, and has become subject to the taxing power of the State; but while remaining the property of the importer, in his warehouse, in the original form or package in which it was imported, a tax upon it is too plainly a duty on imports to escape the prohibition in the constitution." 12 Wheat., at 441-442. "It is a matter of hornbook knowledge that the original package statement of Justice Marshall was an illustration, rather than a formula, and that its application is evidentiary, and not substantive. . . ." Galveston v. Mexican Petroleum Corp., 15 F.2d 208 (S.D. Tex. 1926).

The other was the situation of particular significance to our decision of this case, that is, when the particular state exaction is not a prohibited "impost" or "duty.". . . The characteristic of the prohibited levy, the Court said later in the opinion — illustrated by the Maryland license tax — was that ". . . the tax intercepts the import, *as an import*, in its way to become incorporated with the general mass of property, and denies it the privilege of becoming so incorporated until it shall have contributed to the revenue of the State." Id., at 443 (emphasis supplied). The Court illustrated the kinds of state exactions that in its view fell without the prohibition as examples of neutral and nondiscriminatory taxation: a tax on itinerant peddlers, a service charge for the use of a public auctioneer, a property tax on plate or furniture personally used by the importer. These could not be considered within the constitutional prohibition because they were imposed without regard to the origin of the goods taxed. Id., at 443, 444. In contrast, the Maryland exaction in question was a license fee which singled out imports, and therefore was prohibited because "the tax intercepts the import, *as an import*, in its way to become incorporated with the general mass of property." Id., at 443. (Emphasis supplied.)

Thus, it is clear that the Court's view in Brown was that merely because certain actions taken by the importer on his imported goods would so mingle them with the common property within the State so as to "lose their distinctive character as imports" and render them subject to the taxing power of the State, did not mean that in the absence of such action, no exaction could be imposed on the goods. Rather, the Court clearly implied that the prohibition would not apply to a state tax that treated imported goods in their original packages no differently from the "common mass of property in the country"; that is, treated it in a manner that did not depend on the foreign origins of the goods. . . .

Despite the language and objectives of the Import-Export Clause, and despite the limited nature of the holding in Brown v. Maryland, the Court in Low v. Austin ignored the warning that the boundary between the power of States to tax persons and property within their jurisdictions and the limitations on the power of the States to impose imposts or duties with respect to "imports" was a subtle and difficult line which must be drawn as the cases arise. Low v. Austin also ignored the cautionary remark that, for those reasons, it "might be premature to state any rule as being universal in its application." 12 Wheat., at 441. Although it was "sufficient" in the context of Maryland's license tax on the right to sell imported goods to note that a tax imposed directly on imported goods which have not been acted upon in any way would clearly fall within the constitutional prohibition, that observation did not apply, as the foregoing analysis indicates, to a state tax which treated those same goods without regard to the fact of their foreign origin. . . .

It follows from the foregoing that Low v. Austin was wrongly decided. That decision therefore must be, and is, overruled.

V

Petitioner's tires in this case were no longer in transit. They were stored in a distribution warehouse from which petitioner operated a wholesale operation, taking orders from franchised dealers and filling them from a constantly replenished inventory. The warehouse was operated no differently than would be a distribution warehouse utilized by a wholesaler dealing solely in domestic goods, and we therefore hold that the nondiscriminatory property tax levied on petitioner's inventory of imported tires was not interdicted by the Import-Export Clause of the Constitution. The judgment of the Supreme Court of Georgia is accordingly

Affirmed.

MR. JUSTICE STEVENS took no part in the consideration or decision of this case.

MR. JUSTICE WHITE, concurring in the judgment.

Being of the view that the goods involved here had lost their character as imports and that subjecting them to ad valorem taxation was consistent with the Constitution as interpreted by prior cases, including Low v. Austin, 13 Wall. 29 (1871), I would affirm the judgment. There is little reason and no necessity at this time to overrule Low v. Austin. None of the parties has challenged that case here, and the issue of its overruling has not been briefed or argued.

Leisy v. Hardin 135 U.S. 100, 10 S. Ct. 681, 34 L. Ed. 128 (1890)

[The plaintiffs, who were brewers in Peoria, Illinois, shipped sealed kegs and cases of beer to their agent in Keokuk, Iowa, for sale there. Statutes of Iowa prohibited the sale, keeping for sale, or manufacture for sale of any intoxicating liquor, except for medicinal, chemical, or sacramental purposes. Acting under these statutes, the defendant, marshal of Keokuk, seized a number of the kegs and cases. The plaintiffs brought an action of replevin. The Supreme Court of Iowa reversed a judgment for the plaintiffs.]

MR. CHIEF JUSTICE FULLER delivered the opinion of the court:

The power vested in Congress "to regulate commerce with foreign nations, and among the several States, and with the Indian tribes," is the power to prescribe the rule by which that commerce is to be governed, and is a power complete in itself, acknowledging no limitations other than those prescribed in the Constitution. It is co-extensive with the subject on which it acts and cannot be stopped at the external boundary of a State, but must enter its interior and must be capable of authorizing the disposition of those articles which it introduces, so that they may become mingled with the common mass of property within the territory entered. Gibbons v. Ogden, 9 Wheat. 1; Brown v. Maryland, 12 Wheat. 419.

And while, by virtue of its jurisdiction over persons and property within its limits, a State may provide for the security of the lives, limbs, health and comfort of persons and the protection of property so situated, yet a subject matter which has been confided exclusively to Congress by the Constitution is not within the jurisdiction of the police power of the State, unless placed there by congressional action. Henderson v. Mayor of New York, 92 U.S. 259; Railroad Co. v. Husen, 95 U.S. 465; Walling v. Michigan, 116 U.S. 466; Robbins v. Shelby Taxing District, 120 U.S. 489. The power to regulate commerce among the States is a unit, but if particular subjects within its operation do not require the application of a general or uniform system, the States may legislate in regard to them with a view to local needs and circumstances, until Congress otherwise directs; but the power thus exercised by the States is not identical in its extent with the power to regulate commerce among the States. The power to pass laws in respect to internal commerce, inspection laws, quarantine laws, health laws and laws in relation to bridges, ferries and highways, belongs to the class of powers pertaining to locality, essential to local intercommunication, to the progress and development of local prosperity and to the protection, the safety and the welfare of society, originally necessarily belonging to, and upon the adoption of the Constitution reserved by, the States, except so far as falling within the scope of a power confided to the general government. Where the subject matter requires a uniform system as between the States, the power controlling it is vested exclusively in

Congress, and cannot be encroached upon by the States; but where, in relation to the subject matter, different rules may be suitable for different localities, the States may exercise powers which, though they may be said to partake of the nature of the power granted to the general government, are strictly not such, but are simply local powers, which have full operation until or unless circumscribed by the action of Congress in effectuation of the general power. Cooley v. Port Wardens of Philadelphia, 12 How. 299. . . .

Whenever, however, a particular power of the general government is one which must necessarily be exercised by it, and Congress remains silent, this is not only not a concession that the powers reserved by the States may be exerted as if the specific power had not been elsewhere reposed, but, on the contrary, the only legitimate conclusion is that the general government intended that power should not be affirmatively exercised, and the action of the States cannot be permitted to effect that which would be incompatible with such intention. Hence, inasmuch as interstate commerce, consisting in the transportation, purchase, sale and exchange of commodities, is national in its character, and must be governed by a uniform system, so long as Congress does not pass any law to regulate it, or allowing the States so to do, it thereby indicates its will that such commerce shall be free and untrammelled. County of Mobile v. Kimball, 102 U.S. 691; Brown v. Houston, 114 U.S. 622, 631; Wabash, St. Louis &c. Railway v. Illinois, 118 U.S. 557; Robbins v. Shelby Taxing District, 120 U.S. 489, 493.

That ardent spirits, distilled liquors, ale and beer are subjects of exchange, barter and traffic like any other commodity in which a right of traffic exists, and are so recognized by the usages of the commercial world, the laws of Congress and the decisions of courts, is not denied. Being thus articles of commerce, can a State, in the absence of legislation on the part of Congress, prohibit their importation from abroad or from a sister State? or when imported prohibit their sale by the importer? If the importation cannot be prohibited without the consent of Congress, when does property imported from abroad, or from a sister State, so become part of the common mass of property within a State as to be subject to its unimpeded control?

[The Court discussed Brown v. Maryland and the License Cases.]

But conceding the weight properly to be ascribed to the judicial utterances of this eminent jurist [Chief Justice Taney], we are constrained to say that the distinction between subjects in respect of which there can be of necessity only one system or plan of regulation for the whole country, and subjects local in their nature, and, so far as relating to commerce, mere aids rather than regulations, does not appear to us to have been sufficiently recognized by him in arriving at the conclusions announced. That distinction has been settled by repeated decisions of this court, and can no longer be regarded as open to re-examination. After all, it amounts to no more than drawing the line between the exercise of power over commerce with foreign nations and among the States and the exercise of power over purely local commerce and local concerns.

The authority of Peirce v. New Hampshire, in so far as it rests on the view that the law of New Hampshire was valid because Congress had made no regulation on the subject, must be regarded as having been distinctly overthrown by the numerous cases hereinafter referred to. . . .

The plaintiffs in error are citizens of Illinois, are not pharmacists, and have no permit, but import into Iowa beer which they sell in original packages, as described. Under our decision in Bowman v. Chicago & N.W.R. Co. [125 U.S. 465], they had the right to import this beer into that State, and in the view which we have expressed they had the right to sell it, by which act alone it would become mingled in the common mass of property within the State. Up to that point of time, we hold that, in the absence of congressional permission to do so, the State had no power to interfere by seizure, or any other action, in prohibition of importation and sale by the foreign non-resident importer. Whatever our individual views may be as to the deleterious or dangerous qualities of particular articles, we cannot hold that any articles which Congress recognizes as subjects of interstate commerce are not such, or that whatever are thus recognized can be controlled by state laws amounting to regulations, while they retain that character; although, at the same time, if directly dangerous in themselves, the State may take appropriate measures to guard against injury before it obtains complete jurisdiction over them. To concede to a State the power to exclude, directly or indirectly, articles so situated, without congressional permission, is to concede to a majority of the people of a State, represented in the State Legislature, the power to regulate commercial intercourse between the States, by determining what shall be its subjects, when that power was distinctly granted to be exercised by the people of the United States, represented in Congress, and its possession by the latter was considered essential to that more perfect union which the Constitution was adopted to create. Undoubtedly there is difficulty in drawing the line between the municipal powers of the one government and the commercial powers of the other, but when that line is determined, in the particular instance, accommodation to it, without serious inconvenience, may readily be found, to use the language of Mr. Justice Johnson, in Gibbons v. Ogden, 9 Wheat. 1, 238, in "a frank and candid co-operation for the general good."

The legislation in question is to the extent indicated repugnant to the third clause of section 8 of Art. I of the Constitution of the United States, and therefore the judgment of the Supreme Court of Iowa is reversed and the cause remanded for further proceedings not inconsistent with this opinion.

MR. JUSTICE GRAY, with whom concurred MR. JUSTICE HARLAN and MR. JUSTICE BREWER, dissenting:

[A lengthy discussion of precedents is omitted.]

It only remains to sum up the reasons which have satisfied us that the judgment of the Supreme Court of Iowa in the case at bar should be affirmed.

The protection of the safety, the health, the morals, the good order and the general welfare of the people is the chief end of government. Salus populi suprema lex. The police power is inherent in the States, reserved to them by the Constitution, and necessary to their existence as organized governments. The Constitution of the United States and the laws made in pursuance thereof being the supreme law of the land, all statutes of a State must, of course, give way, so far as they are repugnant to the National Constitution and laws. But an intention is not lightly to be imputed to the framers of the Constitution, or to the Congress of the United States, to subordinate the protection of the safety, health and morals of the people to the promotion of trade and commerce. . . .

The statutes in question were enacted by the State of Iowa in the exercise of its undoubted power to protect its inhabitants against the evils, physical, moral and social, attending the free use of intoxicating liquors. They are not aimed at interstate commerce; they have no relation to the movement of goods from one State to another, but operate only on intoxicating liquors within the territorial limits of the State; they include all such liquors without discrimination, and do not even mention where they are made or whence they come. They affect commerce much more remotely and indirectly than laws of a State (the validity of which is unquestioned), authorizing the erection of bridges and dams across navigable waters within its limits, which wholly obstruct the course of commerce and navigation; or than quarantine laws, which operate directly upon all ships and merchandise coming into the ports of the State.

If the statutes of a State, restricting or prohibiting the sale of intoxicating liquors within its territory, are to be held inoperative and void as applied to liquors sent or brought from another State and sold by the importer in what are called "original packages," the consequence must be that an inhabitant of any State may, under the pretext of interstate commerce, and without license or supervision of any public authority, carry or send into, and sell in, any or all of the other States of the Union intoxicating liquors of whatever description, in cases or kegs, or even in single bottles or flasks, despite any legislation of those States on the subject, and although his own State should be the only one which had not enacted similar laws. It would require positive and explicit legislation on the part of Congress to convince us that it contemplated or intended such a result. . . .

The silence and inaction of Congress upon the subject, during the long period since the decision in the License Cases, appear to us to require the inference that Congress intended that the law should remain as thereby declared by this Court, rather than to warrant the presumption that Congress intended that commerce among the States should be free from the indirect effect of such an exercise of the police power for the public safety, as had been adjudged by that decision to be within the constitutional authority of the States.

For these reasons we are compelled to dissent from the opinion and judgment of the majority of the court.

NOTE Developments in the Original-Package Doctrine

The decision in Leisy v. Hardin has not been without subsequently developed limitations. It was followed in Schollenberger v. Pennsylvania, 171 U.S. 1 (1898), where the Court held that a Pennsylvania statute prohibiting the sale of oleomargarine could not be applied to the first sale of uncolored Rhode Island oleomargarine ("a proper subject of commerce") in its original package, and in Collins v. New Hampshire, 171 U.S. 30 (1898), which similarly limited the application of a New Hampshire statute prohibiting the sale of oleomargarine unless colored pink. (Peckham, J.: "It might equally as well provide that it should be colored blue or red or black . . . or give out a most offensive smell.") But even as applied to first sales in the original package, the Court has upheld state statutes prohibiting the sale of oleomargarine colored yellow ("customers are deluded . . . a fraud upon the general public"), Plumley v. Massachusetts, 155 U.S. 461 (1894); artificially colored coffee beans imported from abroad ("adulterated and fraudulently deceptive"), Crossman v. Lurman, 192 U.S. 189 (1904); stock food without label describing the contents, Savage v. Jones, 225 U.S. 501 (1912); meat misbranded as kosher, Hygrade Provision Co. v. Sherman, 266 U.S. 497 (1925). Moreover, the Court has indicated that a package must have certain minimum dimensions to qualify for the protection afforded the first sale in an original package. In Austin v. Tennessee, 179 U.S. 343 (1900), the defendant had been convicted and fined for violating a Tennessee statute prohibiting the sale of cigarettes. The defense was that the sales complained of were first sales in the original packages purchased from the North Carolina manufacturer, each containing ten cigarettes. The Court, after holding that tobacco, and — until proved otherwise — cigarettes, were legitimate articles of commerce, held (four Justices dissenting) that since the sales were of packages appropriate in size for the retail trade, and smaller than those traditionally used in manufacturers' shipments to wholesalers, the judgment should be affirmed.

The foregoing are instances of state power, in certain circumstances, to prohibit sales of out-of-state goods in the original packages. The original-package criterion is qualified also from the opposite direction: a state may not, in certain circumstances, condition the sale of out-of-state goods even after removal from the original package. See Baldwin v. Seelig, 294 U.S. 511 (1935), page 381 infra.

In re Rahrer 140 U.S. 545, 11 S. Ct. 865, 35 L. Ed. 572 (1891)

[Rahrer was arrested for violation of a statute of Kansas prohibiting the sale of intoxicating liquor, in that he sold a certain keg and bottle which had been shipped to him by the distiller in Missouri. On the day before the sale Congress had enacted the Wilson Act of 1890, 26 Stat. 313, which provided: "That all . . . intoxicating liquors . . . transported into any State or Territory or remaining therein for use, consumption, sale or storage therein, shall upon arrival in such State or Territory be subject to the operation and effect of the laws of such State or Territory enacted in the exercise of its police powers, to the same extent and in the same manner as though such liquids or liquors had been produced in such State or Territory, and shall not be exempt therefrom by reason of being introduced therein in original packages or otherwise."

Rahrer sought habeas corpus in a federal court and was discharged; the respondent sheriff appealed.]

MR. CHIEF JUSTICE FULLER delivered the opinion of the Court. . . .

The power of Congress to regulate commerce among the several States, when the subjects of that power are national in their nature, is also exclusive. The Constitution does not provide that interstate commerce shall be free, but, by the grant of this exclusive power to regulate it, it was left free except as Congress might impose restraint. Therefore, it has been determined that the failure of Congress to exercise this exclusive power in any case is an expression of its will that the subject shall be free from restrictions or impositions upon it by the several States. Robbins v. Shelby County Taxing Dist., 120 U.S. 489. And if a law passed by a State in the exercise of its acknowledged powers comes into conflict with that will, the Congress and the State cannot occupy the position of equal opposing sovereignties, because the Constitution declares its supremacy and that of the laws passed in pursuance thereof. Gibbons v. Ogden, 9 Wheat. 210. That which is not supreme must yield to that which is supreme. Brown v. Maryland, 12 Wheat. 448. . . .

The laws of Iowa under consideration in Bowman v. Chicago & N.W.R. Co., 125 U.S. 465, and Leisy v. Hardin, 135 U.S. 100, were enacted in the exercise of the police power of the State, and not at all as regulations of commerce with foreign nations and among the States, but as they inhibited the receipt of an imported commodity, or its disposition before it had ceased to become an article of trade between one State and another, or another country and this, they amounted in effect to a regulation of such commerce. Hence, it was held that inasmuch as interstate commerce, consisting in the transportation, purchase, sale and exchange of commodities, is national in its character and must be governed by a uniform system, so long as Congress did not pass any law to regulate it specifically, or in such way as to allow the laws of the State to operate upon it, Congress thereby indicated its will that such commerce should be free and untrammeled, and therefore that the laws of Iowa, referred to, were inoperative, in so far as they amounted to regulations of foreign or interstate commerce, in inhibiting the reception of such articles within the State, or their sale upon arrival, in the form in which they were imported there from a foreign country or another State. It followed, as a corollary, that when Congress acted at all, the result of its action must be to operate as a restraint upon that perfect freedom which its silence insured.

Congress has now spoken, and declared that imported liquors or liquids shall, upon arrival in a State, fall within the category of domestic articles of a similar nature. Is the law open to constitutional objection? . . .

It does not admit of argument that Congress can neither delegate its own powers nor enlarge those of a State. This being so, it is urged that the Act of Congress cannot be sustained as a regulation of commerce, because the Constitution, in the matter of interstate commerce, operates *ex proprio vigore* as a restraint upon the power of Congress to so regulate it as to bring any of its subjects within the grasp of the police power of the State. In other words, it is earnestly contended that the Constitution guarantees freedom of commerce among the States in all things, and that not only may intoxicating liquors be imported from one State into another, without being subject to regulation under the laws of the latter, but that Congress is powerless to obviate that result.

Thus the grant to the general government of a power designed to prevent embarrassing restrictions upon interstate commerce by any State would be made to forbid any restraint whatever. We do not concur in this view. In surrendering their own power over external commerce the States did not secure absolute freedom in such commerce, but only the protection from encroachment afforded by confiding its regulation exclusively to Congress.

By the adoption of the Constitution the ability of the several States to act upon the matter solely in accordance with their own will was extinguished, and the legislative will of the general government substituted. No affirmative guaranty was thereby given to any State of the right to demand as between it and the others what it could not have obtained before; while the object was undoubtedly sought to be attained of preventing commercial regulations partial in their character or contrary to the common interests. And the magnificent growth and prosperity of the country attest the success which has attended the accomplishment of that object. But this furnishes no support to the position that Congress could not, in the exercise of the discretion reposed in it, concluding that the common interests did not require entire freedom in the traffic in ardent spirits, enact the law in question. In so doing Congress has not attempted to delegate the power to regulate commerce, or to exercise any power reserved to the States, or to grant a power not possessed by the States, or to adopt state laws. It has taken its own course and made its own regulation, applying to these subjects of interstate commerce one common rule, whose uniformity is not affected by variations in state laws in dealing with such property.

The principle upon which Local Option Laws, so called, have been sustained is, that while the Legislature cannot delegate its power to make a law, it can make a law which leaves it to municipalities or the people to determine some fact or state of things, upon which the action of the law may depend; but we do not rest the validity of the Act of Congress on this analogy. The power over interstate commerce is too vital to the integrity of the nation to be qualified by any refinement of reasoning. The power to regulate is solely in the general government, and it is an essential part of that regulation to prescribe the regular means for accomplishing the introduction and incorporation of articles into and with the mass of property in the country or State. . . .

The decree is reversed, and the cause remanded for further proceedings in conformity with this opinion.

Mr. Justice Harlan, Mr. Justice Gray and Mr. Justice Brewer concurred in the judgment of reversal but not in all the reasoning of the opinion of the court.

McDermott v. Wisconsin *228 U.S. 115, 33 S. Ct. 431, 57 L. Ed. 754 (1913)*

Mr. Justice Day delivered the opinion of the Court.

The plaintiffs in error, George McDermott and T. H. Grady, were severally convicted in the Circuit Court of Dane County, in the State of Wisconsin, upon complaints made against them by an Assistant Dairy and Food Commissioner of that State for the violation of a statute of Wisconsin relating to the sale of certain articles and for the protection of the public health. The convictions were affirmed by the decision of the Supreme Court of Wisconsin. 143 Wisconsin 18.

The complaint against McDermott charged that on March 2, 1908, at Oregon, in Dane County, he "did unlawfully have in his possession with intent to sell, and did offer and expose for sale and did sell, a certain article, product, compound and mixture composed of more than seventy-five per cent. glucose and less than twenty-five per cent. of cane syrup, said cane syrup being then and there mixed with said glucose, and that the can containing said compound and mixture was then and there unlawfully branded and labeled 'Karo Corn Syrup' and was then and there further unlawfully branded and labeled '10% Cane Syrup, 90% Corn Syrup,' contrary to the statute in such case made and provided." As to Grady, the complaint was similar to that against McDermott except that the label designated the mixture as "Karo Corn Syrup with Cane Flavor," and added "Corn Syrup, 85%." The statute of Wisconsin for the violation of which plaintiffs in error were convicted is found in Laws of Wisconsin for 1907, §4601 at page 646, being chapter 557, and the pertinent parts of it are as follows:

"Section 1. . . . No person, . . . by himself . . . or agent . . . shall sell, offer or expose for sale or have in his possession with intent to sell any syrup, maple syrup, sugarcane syrup, sugar syrup, refiners' syrup, sorghum syrup or molasses, mixed with glucose, unless the barrel, cask, keg, can, pail or other original container, containing the same be distinctly branded or labeled so as to plainly show the true name of each and all of the ingredients composing such mixture, as follows: . . .

"Third. In case such mixture shall contain glucose in a proportion exceeding 75 per cent. by weight, it shall be labeled and sold as 'Glucose flavored with Sugar-cane Syrup,' . . . 'Glucose flavored with Refiners' Syrup' . . . as the case may be. The labels . . . shall bear the name and address of the manufacturer or dealer. . . . In all mixtures in which glucose is used in the proportion of more than 75 per cent. by weight, the name of the syrup or molasses which is mixed with the glucose for flavoring purposes and the words showing that said syrup or molasses is used as a flavoring, as provided in this section, shall be printed on the label of each container of such mixture. . . . The mixtures or syrups designated in this section shall have no other designation or brand than herein required that represents or is the name of any article which contains a saccharin substance; . . . nor shall any of the aforesaid glucose, syrups, molasses or mixtures contain any substance injurious to health, nor any other article or substance otherwise prohibited by law in articles of food."

The facts are that the plaintiffs in error were retail merchants in Oregon, Dane County, Wisconsin; that before the filing of the complaints against them each had bought for himself for resale as such merchant from wholesale grocers in Chicago and had received by rail from that city twelve half gallon tin cans or pails of the article designated in the complaints, each shipment being made in wooden boxes containing the cans, and that when the goods were received at their stores the respective plaintiffs in error took the cans from the boxes, placed them on the shelves for sale at retail, and destroyed the boxes in which the goods were shipped to them, as was customary in such cases. From their nature, the articles thus canned and offered to be sold, instead of being labeled as they were, if labeled in accordance with the state law, would have been branded with the words "Glucose flavored with Refiners' Syrup," and, as the statute provides that the mixtures or syrups offered for sale shall have upon them no designation or brand which represents or contains the name of a saccharin substance other than that required by the state law, the labels upon the cans must be removed, if the state authority is recognized.

Plaintiffs in error contend that the cans were labeled in accordance with the Food and Drugs Act passed by Congress, June 30, 1906, 34 Stat. 768, c. 3915. . . . And it is insisted that the Federal Food and Drugs Act passed under the authority of the Constitution has taken possession of this field of regulation and that the state act is a wrongful interference with the exclusive power of Congress over interstate commerce, in which, it appears, the goods in question were shipped. The case presents among other questions, the constitutional question whether the state act in permitting the sale of this article only when labeled according to the state law is open to the objection just indicated. . . .

The Food and Drugs Act was passed by Congress, under its authority to exclude from interstate commerce impure and adulterated food and drugs and to prevent the facilities of such commerce being used to enable such articles to be transported throughout the country from their place of manufacture to the people who consume and use them, and it is in the light of the purpose and of the power exerted in its passage by Congress that this act must be considered and construed. Hipolite Egg Co. v. United States [220 U.S. 45].

Section 2 of the act provides that "the introduction into any State or Territory or the District of Columbia from any other State or Territory or the District of Columbia . . . of any article of food or drugs which is adulterated or misbranded, within the meaning of this Act, is hereby prohibited; and any person who shall ship or deliver for shipment from any State or Territory or the District of Columbia to any other State or Territory or the District of Columbia . . . any such article so adulterated or misbranded within the meaning of this Act, . . . shall be guilty of a misdemeanor, and for such offense be fined," etc. The article of food or drugs, the shipment or delivery for shipment in interstate commerce of which is prohibited and punished, is such as is *adulterated or misbranded within the meaning of the act*. What it is to adulterate or misbrand food or drugs within the meaning of the act requires a consideration of its other provisions, wherein such adulteration or misbranding is defined. . . .

That the word "package" or its equivalent expression, as used by Congress in sections 7 and 8 in defining what shall constitute adulteration and what shall constitute misbranding within the meaning of the act, clearly refers to the immediate container of the article which is intended for consumption by the public, there can be no question. . . . Limiting the requirements of the act as to adulteration and misbranding simply to the outside wrapping or box containing the packages intended to be purchased by the consumer, so that the importer, by removing and destroying such covering, could prevent the operation of the law on the imported article yet unsold, would render the act nugatory and its provisions wholly inadequate to accomplish the purposes for which it was passed. . . .

While these regulations are within the power of Congress, it by no means follows that the State is not permitted to make regulations, with a view to the protection of its people against fraud or imposition by impure food or drugs. This subject was fully considered by this court in Savage v. Jones, 225 U.S. 501, in which the power of the State to make regulations concerning the same subject matter, reasonable in their terms and not in conflict with the acts of Congress, was recognized and stated, and certain regulations of the State of Indiana were held not to be inconsistent with the Food and Drugs Act of Congress. While this is true, it is equally well settled that the State may not, under the guise of exercising its police power or otherwise, impose burdens upon or discriminate against interstate commerce, nor may it enact legislation in conflict with the statutes of Congress passed for the regulation of the subject, and if it does, to the extent that the state law interferes with or frustrates the operation of the acts of Congress, its provisions must yield to the superior Federal power given to Congress by the Constitution. . . .

Having in view the interpretation we have given the Food and Drugs Act and applying the doctrine just stated to the instant cases, how does the matter stand? When delivered for shipment and when received through the channels of interstate commerce the cans in question bore brands or labels which were supposed to comply with the requirements of the act of Congress. . . .

To require the removal or destruction before the goods are sold of the evidence which Congress has, by the Food and Drugs Act, as we shall see, provided may be examined to determine the compliance or noncompliance with the regulations of the Federal law, is beyond the power of the State. The Wisconsin act which permits the sale of articles subject to the regulations of interstate commerce only upon condition that they contain the exclusive labels required by the statute is an act in excess of its legitimate power.

It is insisted, however, that, since at the time when the state act undertook to regulate the branding of these goods, namely, when in the possession of the plaintiffs in error and held upon their shelves for sale, the cans had been removed from the boxes in which they were shipped in the jurisdiction of Congress, and their regulation was exclusively a matter for state legislation. This assertion is based upon the original-package doctrine as it is said to have been laid down in the former decisions of this court. . . .

That doctrine has been many times applied in the decisions of this court in defining the line of demarcation which shall separate the Federal from the state authority involved in dealing with property. And where it has been found necessary to decide the boundary of Federal authority it has been generally held that, where goods prepared and packed for shipment in interstate commerce are transported in such commerce and delivered to the consignee and the package by him separated into its component parts, the power of Federal regulation has ceased and that of the State may be asserted. In the view, however, which we take of this case it is unnecessary to enter upon any extended consideration of the nature and scope of the principles involved in determining what is an original package. For, as we have said, keeping within its Constitutional limitations of authority, Congress may determine for itself the character of the means necessary to make its purpose effectual in preventing the shipment in interstate commerce of articles of a harmful character, and to this end may provide the means of inspection, examination and seizure necessary to enforce the prohibitions of the act, and when § 2 has been violated the Federal authority, in enforcing either § 2 or § 10, may follow the adulterated or misbranded article at least to the shelf of the importer. . . .

The doctrine of original packages had its origin in the opinion of Chief Justice Marshall in Brown v. Maryland. . . . It was intended to protect the importer in the right to sell the imported goods which was the real object and purpose of importation. To determine the time when an article passes out of interstate into state jurisdiction for the purpose of taxation is entirely different from deciding when an article which has violated a Federal prohibition becomes immune. The doctrine was not intended to limit the right of Congress, now asserted, to keep the channels of interstate commerce free from the carriage of injurious or fraudulently branded articles and to choose appropriate means to that end. The legislative means provided in the Federal law for its own enforcement may not be thwarted by state legislation having a direct effect to impair the effectual exercise of such means.

For the reasons stated, the statute of Wisconsin, in forbidding all labels other than the one it prescribed, is invalid, and it follows that the judgments of the state court affirming the convictions of the plaintiffs in error for selling the articles in question without the exclusive brand required by the State, must be

Reversed, and the cases are remanded to the state court for further proceedings not inconsistent with this opinion.[c]

[c] Compare Corn Products Co. v. Eddy, 249 U.S. 427 (1919) (additional labeling requirements imposed by state law).

On the issues raised by this chapter, see Dowling, Interstate Commerce and State Power, 27 Va. L. Rev. 1 (1940); Dowling, Interstate Commerce and State Power — Revised Version, 47 Colum. L. Rev. 547 (1947); Sholley, Negative Implications of the Commerce Clause, 3 U. Chi. L. Rev. 556 (1936). Problems of state power are explored in detail in Chapter 8. — ED.

Chapter Six Powers over Transportation

The Daniel Ball 10 Wall. 557, 19 L. Ed. 999 (1871)

[Federal statutes (5 Stat. 304; 10 Stat. 61) required the licensing of steam vessels carrying merchandise or passengers on the navigable waters of the United States, and prior inspection and certification of those carrying passengers. A penalty of $500 was provided for operation without the required license or certification.]

MR. JUSTICE FIELD delivered the opinion of the court: . . .

In March, 1868, The Daniel Ball, a vessel propelled by steam, of one hundred and twenty-three tons burden, was engaged in navigating Grand River, in the State of Michigan, between the cities of Grand Rapids and Grand Haven, and in the transportation of merchandise and passengers between those places, without having been inspected or licensed under the laws of the United States; and to recover the penalty provided for want of such inspection and license, the present libel was filed. . . .

It was admitted by stipulation of the parties that the steamer was employed in the navigation of Grand River between the cities of Grand Rapids and Grand Haven, and in the transportation of merchandise and passengers between those places; that she was not enrolled and licensed for the coasting trade; that some of the goods she shipped at Grand Rapids and carried to Grand Haven were destined and marked for places in other States than Michigan; and that some of the goods which she shipped at Grand Haven came from other States and were destined for places within that State.

It was also admitted that the steamer was so constructed as to draw only two feet of water, and was incapable of navigating the waters of Lake Michigan; that she was a common carrier between the cities named, but did not run in connection with nor in continuation of any line of steamers or vessels on the lake, or any line of railway in the State, although there were various lines of steamers and other vessels running from places in other States to Grand Haven, carrying merchandise, and a line of railway was running from Detroit, which touched at both the cities named.

The district court dismissed the libel. The circuit court reversed this decision, and gave a decree for the penalty demanded. . . .

Two questions are presented in this case for our determination.

First: whether the steamer was at the time designated in the libel engaged in transporting merchandise and passengers on a navigable water of the United States within the meaning of the Acts of Congress; and,

Second: whether those Acts are applicable to a steamer engaged as a common carrier between places in the same State, when a portion of the merchandise transported by her is destined to places in other States, or comes from places without the State, she not running in connection with or in continuation of any line of steamers or other vessels, or any railway line leading to or from another State.

Upon the first of these questions we entertain no doubt. The doctrine of the common law as to the navigability of waters has no application in this country. Here the ebb and flow of the tide do not constitute the usual test, as in England, or any test at all as to the navigability of waters. There no waters are navigable in fact, or at least to any considerable extent, which are not subject to the tide, and from this circumstance tide-water and navigable water there signify substantially the same thing. But in this country the case is widely different. Some of our rivers are as navigable for many hundreds of miles above as they are below the limits of tide-water, and some of them are navigable for great distances by large vessels, which are not even affected by the tide at any point during their entire length. Genesee Chief, 12 How. 457; The Hine v. Trevor, 4 Wall. 555. A different test must, therefore, be applied to determine the navigability of our rivers, and that is found in their navigable capacity. Those rivers must be regarded as public navigable rivers in law which are navigable in fact. And they are navigable in fact when they are used, or are susceptible of being used, in their ordinary condition, as highways for commerce, over which trade and travel are or may be conducted in the customary modes of trade and travel on water. And they constitute navigable waters of the United States within the meaning of the Acts of Congress, in contradistinction from the navigable waters of the States, when they form in their ordinary condition by themselves, or by uniting with other waters, a continued highway over which commerce is or may be carried on with other States or foreign countries in the customary modes in which such commerce is conducted by water.

If we apply this test to Grand River, the conclusion follows that it must be regarded as navigable water of the United States. From the conceded facts in the case the stream is capable of bearing a steamer of one hundred and twenty-three tons burden, laden with merchandise and passengers, as far as Grand Rapids, a distance of forty miles from its mouth in Lake Michigan. And by its junction with the lake it forms a continued highway for commerce, both with other States and with foreign countries, and is thus brought under the direct control of Congress in the exercise of its commercial power.

That power authorizes all appropriate legislation for the protection or advancement of either interstate or foreign commerce, and for that purpose such legislation as will insure the convenient and safe navigation of all the navigable waters of the United States, whether that legislation consists in requiring the removal of obstructions to their use, in prescribing the form and size of the vessels employed upon them, or in subjecting the vessels to inspection and license, in order to insure their proper construction and equipment. "The power to regulate commerce," this court said in Gilman v. Phila., 3 Wall. 724, "comprehends the control for that purpose, and to the extent necessary, of all navigable waters of the United States which are accessible from a State other than those in which they lie. For this purpose they are the public property of the Nation, and subject to all the requisite legislation of Congress."

But it is contended that the steamer, Daniel Ball, was only engaged in the internal commerce of the State of Michigan, and was not, therefore, required to be inspected or licensed, even if it be conceded that Grand River is a navigable water of the United States; and this brings us to the consideration of the second question presented.

There is, undoubtedly an internal commerce which is subject to the control of the States. The power delegated to Congress is limited to commerce "among the several States," with foreign nations, and with the Indian tribes. This limitation necessarily excludes from federal control all commerce not thus designated and, of course, that commerce which is carried on entirely within the limits of a State, and does not extend to or affect other States. Gibbons v. Ogden, 9 Wheat, 194. In this case it is admitted that the steamer was engaged in shipping and transporting, down Grand River, goods destined and marked for other States than Michigan, and in receiving and transporting up the river goods brought within the State from without its limits; but inasmuch as her agency in the transportation was entirely within the limits of the State, and she did not run in connection with, or in continuation of, any line of vessels or railway leading to other States, it is contended that she was engaged entirely in domestic commerce. But this conclusion does not follow. So far as she was employed in transporting goods destined for other States, or goods brought from without the limits of Michigan and destined to places within the State, she was engaged in commerce between the States, and however limited that commerce may have been, she was, so far as it went, subject to the legislation of Congress. She was employed as an instrument of that commerce; for whenever a commodity has begun to move as an article of trade from one State to another, commerce in that commodity between the States has commenced. The fact that several different and independent agencies are employed in transporting the commodity, some acting entirely in one State, and some acting through two or more States, does in no respect affect the character of the transaction. To the extent in which each agency acts in that transportation, it is subject to the regulation of Congress.

It is said that if the position here asserted be sustained, there is no such thing as the domestic trade of a State; that Congress may take the entire control of the commerce of the country, and extend its regulations to the railroads within a State on which grain or fruit is transported to a distant market.

We answer that the present case relates to transportation on the navigable waters of the United States, and we are not called upon to express an opinion upon the power of Congress over interstate commerce when carried on by land transportation. And we answer further, that we are unable to draw any clear and distinct line between the authority of Congress to regulate an agency employed in commerce between the States, when that agency extends through two or more States, and when it is confined in its action entirely within the limits of a single State. If its authority does not extend to an agency in such commerce when that agency is confined within the limits of a State, its entire authority over interstate commerce may be defeated. Several agencies combining, each taking up the commodity transported at the boundary line at one end of a State, and leaving it at the boundary line at the other end, the federal jurisdiction would be entirely ousted, and the constitutional provision would become a dead letter.

We perceive no error in the record, and the decree of the Circuit Court must be affirmed.

NOTE

Bradley, J., in Railroad Co. v. Maryland, 21 Wall. 456, 470-471 (1874), dealt thus with the historic differences between water and land transportation: "Commerce on land between the different States is so strikingly dissimilar, in many respects, from commerce on water, that it is often difficult to regard them in the same aspect in reference to the respective constitutional powers and duties of the State and Federal governments. No doubt commerce by water was principally in the minds of those who framed and adopted the Constitution, although both its language and spirit embrace commerce by land as well. Maritime transportation requires no artificial roadway. Nature has prepared to hand that portion of the instrumentality employed. The navigable waters of the earth are recognized public highways of trade and intercourse. No franchise is needed to enable the navigator to use them. Again, the vehicles of commerce by water being instruments of intercommunication with other nations, the regulation of them is assumed by the National legislature. So that State interference with transportation by water, and especially by sea, is at once clearly marked and distinctly discernible. But it is different with transportation by land. This, when the Constitution was adopted, was entirely performed on common roads, and the vehicles drawn by animal power. No one at that day imagined that the roads and bridges of the country (except when the latter crossed navigable streams) were not entirely subject, both as to their construction, repair, and management, to State regulation and control. They were all made either by the States or under their authority. The power of the State to impose or authorize such tolls, as it saw fit, was unquestioned. No one then supposed that the wagons of the country, which were the vehicles of this commerce, or the horses by which they were drawn, were subject to National regulation. The movement of persons and merchandise, so long as it was as free to one person as to another, to the citizens of other States as to the citizens of the State in which it was performed, was not regarded as unconstitutionally restricted and trammelled by tolls exacted on bridges or turnpikes, whether belonging to the State or to private persons. And when, in process of time, canals were constructed, no amount of tolls which was exacted thereon by the State or the companies that owned them, was ever regarded as an infringement of the Constitution. When constructed by the State itself, they might be the source of revenues largely exceeding the outlay without exciting even the question of constitutionality. So when, by the improvements and discoveries of mechanical science, railroads came to be built and furnished with all the apparatus of rapid and all-absorbing transportation, no one imagined that the State, if itself owner of the work, might not exact any amount whatever of toll or fare or freight, or authorize its citizens or corporations, if owners, to do the same."

In Davis v. United States, 185 F.2d 938 (9th Cir. 1950), the Federal Motor Boat Act was held applicable to a boat on Lake Tahoe, which is intersected by the California-Nevada boundary, but which has no outlet to the sea.

The Colorado River was held to be a navigable stream in Arizona v. California, 283 U.S. 423 (1931), despite allegations in the complaint, to which a motion to dismiss was interposed, that it was nonnavigable. The Court said (pp. 453-454): "We know judicially, from the evidence of history, that a large part of the Colorado River south of Black Canyon was formerly navigable, and that the main obstacles to navigation have been the accumulations of silt coming from the upper reaches of the river system, and the irregularities in the flow due to periods of low water. Commercial disuse resulting from changed geographical conditions and a Congressional failure to deal with them, does not amount to an abandonment of a navigable river or prohibit future exertion of federal control." See also United States v. Appalachian Electric Power Co., 311 U.S. 377 (1940).

The authority of the United States over water resources, and its admiralty jurisdiction, are dealt with more fully infra at pages 326-334.

Wabash, St. Louis & Pacific Ry. v. Illinois 118 U.S. 557, S. Ct. 4, 30 L. Ed. 244 (1886)

MR. JUSTICE MILLER delivered the opinion of the court:

This is a writ of error to the Supreme Court of Illinois. It was argued here at the last term of this court.

The case was tried in the court of original jurisdiction on an agreed statement of facts. This agreement is short and is here inserted in full:

"For the purposes of the trial of said cause, and to save the making of proof therein, it is hereby agreed on the part of the defendant that the allegations in the first count of the declaration are true, except that part of said count which avers that the same proportionate discrimination was made in the transportation of said property — oil cake and corn — in the State of Illinois, that was made between Peoria and the City of New York, and Gilman and New York City; which averment is not admitted because defendant claims that it is an inference from the fact that the rates charged in each case of said transportation of oil cake and corn were through rates; but it is admitted that said averment is a proper one."

The first count in the declaration, which is referred to in this memorandum of agreement, charged that the Wabash, St. Louis and Pacific Railway Company had, in violation of a Statute of the State of Illinois, been guilty of an unjust discrimination in its rates or charges of toll and compensation for the transportation of freight. The specific allegation is that the Railroad Company charged Elder & McKinney for transporting twenty-six thousand pounds of goods and chattels from Peoria, in the State of Illinois, to New York City, the sum of $39, being at the rate of fifteen cents per hundred pounds for said carload; and that on the same day it agreed to carry and transport for Isaac Bailey and F. O. Swannell another carload of goods and chattels from Gilman, in the State of Illinois, to said City of New York, for which it charged the sum of $65, being at the rate of twenty-five cents per hundred pounds. And it is alleged that the carload transported for Elder & McKinney was carried eighty-six miles further in the State of Illinois than the other carload of the same weight. This freight being of the same class in both instances, and carried over the same road, except as to the difference in the distance, it is obvious that a discrimination against Bailey & Swannell was made in the charges against them as compared with those against Elder & McKinney; and this is true whether we regard the charge for the whole distance from the terminal points in Illinois to New York City or the proportionate charge for the haul within the State of Illinois.

The language of the statute which is supposed to be violated by this transaction is to be found in chapter 114 of the Revised Statutes of Illinois, section 126. It is there enacted that if any railroad corporation shall charge, collect, or receive for the transportation of any passenger or freight of any description upon its railroad, for any distance within the State, the same or a greater amount of toll or compensation than is at the same time charged, collected, or received for the transportation in the same direction of any passenger or like quantity of freight of the same class over a greater distance of the same road, all such discriminating rates, charges, collections, or receipts, whether made directly or by means of rebate, drawback, or other shift or evasion, shall be deemed and taken against any such railroad corporation as prima facie evidence of unjust discrimination prohibited by the provisions of this Act. The statute further provides a penalty of not over $5,000 for that offense, and also that the party aggrieved shall have a right to recover three times the amount of damages sustained, with costs and attorneys' fees. [Judgment was rendered against the railroad.]

. . . The Supreme Court of Illinois, in the case now before us, conceding that each of these contracts was in itself a unit, and that the pay received by the Illinois Railroad Company was the compensation for the entire transportation from the point of departure in the State of Illinois to the City of New York, holds that while the Statute of Illinois is inoperative upon that part of the contract which has reference to the transportation outside of the State, it is binding and effectual as to so much of the transportation as was within the limits of the State of Illinois; People v. Wabash, St.L. & P.R.R. Co., 104 Ill. 476; and undertaking for itself to apportion the rates charged over the whole route, decides that the contract and the receipt of the money for so much of it as was performed within the State of Illinois violate the statute of the State on that subject.

If the Illinois Statute could be construed to apply exclusively to contracts for a carriage which begins and ends within the State, disconnected from a continuous transportation through or into other States, there does not seem to be any difficulty in holding it to be valid. For instance, a contract might be made to carry goods for a certain price from Cairo to Chicago, or from Chicago to Alton. The charges for these might be within the competency of the Illinois Legislature to regulate. . . . [The Court considered a number of prior decisions.]

These extracts show that the question of the right of the State to regulate the rates of fares and tolls on railroads, and how far that right was affected by the commerce clause of the Constitution of the United States, was presented to the court in those cases. And it must be admitted that, in a general way, the court treated the cases then before it as belonging to that class of regulations of commerce which, like pilotage, bridging navigable rivers, and many others, could be acted upon by the States, in the absence of any legislation by Congress on the same subject. . . .

It is not the railroads themselves that are regulated by this act of the Illinois Legislature so much as the charge for transportation, and, in language just cited, if each one of the States through whose territories these goods are transported can fix its own rules for prices, for modes of transit, for times and modes of delivery, and all the other incidents of transportation to which the word "regulation" can be applied, it is readily seen that the embarrassments upon interstate transportation, as an element of interstate commerce, might be too oppressive to be submitted to. "It was," in the language of the court cited above, "to meet just such a case that the commerce clause of the Constitution was adopted."

It cannot be too strongly insisted upon that the right of continuous transportation from one end of the country to the other is essential in modern times to that freedom of commerce from the restraints which the State might choose to impose upon it, that the commerce clause was intended to secure. This clause, giving to Congress the power to regulate commerce among the States and with foreign nations, as this court has said before, was among the most important of the subjects which prompted the formation of the Constitution. Cook v. Pennsylvania, 97 U.S. 566, 574; Brown v. Maryland, 12 Wheat. 419, 446. And it would be a very feeble and almost useless provision, but poorly adapted to secure the entire freedom of commerce among the States which was deemed essential to a more perfect union by the Framers of the Constitution, if, at every stage of the transportation of goods and chattels through the country, the State within whose limits a part of this transportation must be done could impose regulations concerning the price, compensation, or taxation, or any other restrictive regulation interfering with and seriously embarrassing this commerce. . . .

. . . The owner of corn, the principal product of the country, desiring to transport it from Peoria, in Illinois, to New York, finds a Railroad Company willing to do this at the rate of fifteen cents per hundred pounds for a carload, but is compelled to pay at the rate of twenty-five cents per hundred pounds, because the Railroad Company has received from a person residing at Gilman twenty-five cents per hundred pounds for the transportation of a carload of the same class of freight over the same line of road from Gilman to New York. This is the result of the Statute of Illinois, in its endeavor to prevent unjust discrimination, as construed by the Supreme Court of that State. The effect of it is, that whatever may be the rate of transportation per mile charged by the Railroad Company from Gilman to Sheldon, a distance of twenty-three miles, in which the loading and the unloading of the freight is the largest expense incurred by the Railroad Company, the same rate per mile must be charged from Peoria to the City of New York.

The obvious injustice of such a rule as this, which railroad companies are by heavy penalties compelled to conform to, in regard to commerce among the States, when applied to transportation which includes Illinois in a long line of carriage through several States, shows the value of the constitutional provision which confides the power of regulating interstate commerce to the Congress of the United States, whose enlarged view of the interests of all the States, and of the railroads concerned, better fits it to establish just and equitable rules.

. . . That this species of regulation is one which must be, if established at all, of a general and national character, and cannot be safely and wisely remitted to local rules and local regulations, we think is clear from what has already been said. And if it be a regulation of commerce, as we think we have demonstrated it is, and as the Illinois Court concedes it to be, it must be of that national character, and the regulation can only appropriately exist by general rules and principles, which demand that it should be done by the Congress of the United States under the commerce clause of the Constitution.

The judgment of the Supreme Court of Illinois is therefore reversed, and the case remanded to that court for further proceedings in conformity with this opinion.[a]

[The dissenting opinion of MR. JUSTICE BRADLEY, in which CHIEF JUSTICE WAITE and MR. JUSTICE GRAY joined, ended with the following passage: "The inconveniences which it has been supposed in argument would follow from the execution of the laws of Illinois, we think have been greatly exaggerated. But if it should be found to present any real difficulty in the modes of transacting business on through lines, it is always in the power of Congress to make such reasonable regulations as the interests of interstate commerce may demand, without denuding the States of their just powers over their own roads and their own corporations."]

MINNESOTA RATE CASES, 230 U.S. 352, 33 S. Ct. 729, 57 L. Ed. 1511 (1913). Stockholders of three railroads brought suit in the Federal Circuit (now District) Court for Minnesota to restrain the enforcement of orders of the Minnesota Railroad Commission prescribing maximum charges for passengers and freight. The defendants were the companies, the state attorney general, the members of the state commission, and certain shippers. The orders related solely to rates for traffic between points within the state, and brought these rates below the level of interstate rates with which they had previously been maintained on a parity. The plaintiffs contended, inter alia, that the state order resulted in discrimination against interstate commerce in marketing areas served from both within and without the state, and so was unconstitutional.

The jurisdiction of the federal court was sustained in Ex parte Young, 209 U.S. 123 (1908), supra page 129. Thereafter the circuit court held the orders invalid and issued an injunction. In the Supreme Court the railroad commissioners of eight states filed a brief as amici curiae, urging reversal of the decision. A 900-page brief for the plaintiff-appellees was filed by Pierce Butler, later appointed to the Court. Because of the complexity and importance of the case the Court was unable to reach a decision at its conference after argument, and the matter was assigned to Mr. Justice Hughes to work out a satisfactory solution. See 1 Pusey, Charles Evans Hughes 304 (1951).

The opinion of the Court, per Hughes, J., rejected the view of the lower court. It was held that the orders were neither repugnant to the commerce clause nor in violation of the Interstate Commerce Act. On the latter issue, the opinion referred to the proviso in §1 of the act that "the provisions of this act shall not apply to the transportation of passengers or property, wholly within one state, and not shipped to or from a foreign country, from or to any state or territory as aforesaid." The Court stated: "If the situation has become such, by reason of the interblending of the interstate and intrastate operations of interstate carriers, that adequate regulation of their interstate rates cannot be maintained without imposing requirements with respect to their intrastate rates which substantially affect the former, it is for Congress to determine, within the limits of its constitutional authority over interstate commerce and its instruments the measure of the regulation it should supply."

---

[a] In 1887, Congress enacted the Interstate Commerce Act. Mr. Justice Miller observed, in correspondence, that the Wabash decision "is said [to have] contributed very much to passage of the Interstate Commerce bill, a subject in regard to which I have been a pioneer, and an authority, ever since the opinion in the Clinton Bridge Case, Woolworth 150." Fairman, Mr. Justice Miller and the Supreme Court 314 n.31 (1939).

The Wabash case was an episode in the Granger movement, which stimulated legislation that from a constitutional standpoint presented chiefly due process problems. The most celebrated of the so-called Granger cases was Munn v. Illinois, 94 U.S. 113 (1877). See Fairman, The So-called Granger Cases, Lord Hale, and Justice Bradley, 5 Stan. L. Rev. 587 (1953). — ED.

Houston, East & West Texas Ry. v. United States
(The Shreveport Case) 234 U.S. 342, 34 S. Ct. 833, 58 L. Ed. 1341 (1914)

MR. JUSTICE HUGHES delivered the opinion of the court:
These suits were brought in the commerce court by the Houston, East & West Texas Railway Company and the Houston & Shreveport Railroad Company, and by the Texas & Pacific Railway Company, respectively, to set aside an order of the Interstate Commerce Commission, dated March 11, 1912, upon the ground that it exceeded the Commission's authority. Other railroad companies intervened in support of the petitions, and the Interstate Commerce Commission and the Railroad Commission of Louisiana intervened in opposition. The petitions were dismissed. 205 Fed. 380, 391.

The order of the Interstate Commerce Commission was made in a proceeding initiated in March, 1911, by the Railroad Commission of Louisiana. The complaint was that the appellants, and other interstate carriers, maintained unreasonable rates from Shreveport, Louisiana, to various points in Texas, and, further, that these carriers, in the adjustment of rates over their respective lines, unjustly discriminated in favor of traffic within the state of Texas, and against similar traffic between Louisiana and Texas. The carriers filed answers; numerous pleas of intervention by shippers and commercial bodies were allowed; testimony was taken and arguments were heard.

The gravamen of the complaint, said the Interstate Commerce Commission, was that the carriers made rates out of Dallas and other Texas points into eastern Texas which were much lower than those which they extended into Texas from Shreveport. The situation may be briefly described: Shreveport, Louisiana, is about 40 miles from the Texas state line, and 231 miles from Houston, Texas, on the line of the Houston, East & West Texas and Houston & Shreveport Companies (which are affiliated in interest); it is 189 miles from Dallas, Texas, on the line of the Texas & Pacific. Shreveport competes with both cities for the trade of the intervening territory. The rates on these lines from Dallas and Houston, respectively, eastward to intermediate points in Texas, were much less, according to distance, than from Shreveport westward to the same points. It is undisputed that the difference was substantial, and injuriously affected the commerce of Shreveport. It appeared, for example, that a rate of 60 cents carried first-class traffic a distance of 160 miles to the eastward from Dallas, while the same rate would carry the same class of traffic only 55 miles into Texas from Shreveport. The first-class rate from Houston to Lufkin, Texas, 118.2 miles, was 50 cents per 100 pounds, while the rate from Shreveport to the same point, 112.5 miles, was 69 cents. . . . These instances of differences in rates are merely illustrative; they serve to indicate the character of the rate adjustment.

The Interstate Commerce Commission found that the interstate class rates out of Shreveport to named Texas points were unreasonable, and it established maximum class rates for this traffic. These rates, we understand, were substantially the same as the class rates fixed by the Railroad Commission of Texas, and charged by the carriers, for transportation for similar distances in that state. . . .

. . . There are, it appears, commodity rates fixed by the Railroad Commission of Texas for intrastate hauls, which are substantially less than the class, or standard, rates prescribed by that Commission; and thus the commodity rates charged by the carriers from Dallas and Houston eastward to Texas points are less than the rates which they demand for the transportation of the same articles for like distances from Shreveport into Texas. The present controversy relates to these commodity rates.

[The order of the ICC provided that the railroad "shall cease and desist from charging higher rates upon any commodity from Shreveport into Texas than are contemporaneously charged for the carriage of such commodity from Dallas (or Houston) toward Shreveport for an equal distance. It will be the duty of the carriers under such order to duly and justly equalize the terms and conditions upon which they will extend transportation to traffic of a similar character moving into Texas from Shreveport with that moving wholly within Texas." 23 I.C.C. Rep. 31, 47.]

The point of the objection to the order is that, as the discrimination found by the Commission to be unjust arises out of the relation of intrastate rates, maintained under state authority, to interstate rates that have been upheld as reasonable, its correction was beyond the Commission's power. Manifestly the order might be complied with, and the discrimination avoided, either by reducing the interstate rates from Shreveport to the level of the competing intrastate rates, or by raising these intrastate rates to the level of the interstate rates, or by such reduction in the one case and increase in the other as would result in equality. But it is urged that, so far as the interstate rates were sustained by the Commission as reasonable, the Commission was without authority to compel their reduction in order to equalize them with the lower intrastate rates. The holding of the commerce court was that the order relieved the appellants from further obligation to observe the intrastate rates, and that they were at liberty to comply with the Commission's requirements by increasing these rates sufficiently to remove the forbidden discrimination. The invalidity of the order in this aspect is challenged upon two grounds:

(1) That Congress is impotent to control the intrastate charges of an interstate carrier even to the extent necessary to prevent injurious discrimination against interstate traffic; and

(2) That, if it be assumed that Congress has this power, still it has not been exercised, and hence the action of the Commission exceeded the limits of the authority which has been conferred upon it.

First. [A discussion of authorities, including those under the Federal Safety Appliance Acts, is omitted.]

While these decisions sustaining the Federal power relate to measures adopted in the interest of the safety of persons and property, they illustrate the principle that Congress, in the exercise of its paramount power, may prevent the common instrumentalities of interstate and intrastate commercial intercourse from being used in their intrastate operations to the injury of interstate commerce. This is not to say that Congress possesses the authority to regulate the internal commerce of a state, as such, but that it does possess the power to foster and protect interstate commerce, and to take all measures necessary or appropriate to that end, although intrastate transactions of interstate carriers may thereby be controlled.

This principle is applicable here. We find no reason to doubt that Congress is entitled to keep the highways of interstate communication open to interstate traffic upon fair and equal terms. That an unjust discrimination in the rates of a common carrier, by which one person or locality is unduly favored as against another under substantially similar conditions of traffic, constitutes an evil, is undeniable; and where this evil consists in the action of an interstate carrier in unreasonably discriminating against interstate traffic over its line, the authority of Congress to prevent it is equally clear. It is immaterial, so far as the protecting power of Congress is concerned, that the discrimination arises from intrastate rates as compared with interstate rates. . . .

It is to be noted — as the government has well said in its argument in support of the Commission's order — that the power to deal with the relation between the two kinds of rates, as a relation, lies exclusively with Congress. It is manifest that the state cannot fix the relation of the carrier's interstate and intrastate charges without directly interfering with the former, unless it simply follows the standard set by Federal authority. This question was presented with respect to the long and short haul provision of the Kentucky Constitution, adopted in 1891, which the court had before it in Louisville & N.R. Co. v. Eubank, 184 U.S. 27. The state court had construed this provision as embracing a long haul, from a place outside to one within the state, and a shorter haul on the same line and in the same direction between points within the state. This court held that, so construed, the provision was invalid as being a regulation of interstate commerce because "it linked the interstate rate to the rate for the shorter haul, and thus the interstate charge was directly controlled by the state law." See 230 U.S. pp. 428, 429. It is for Congress to supply the needed correction where the relation between intrastate and interstate rates presents the evil to be corrected, and this it may do completely, by reason of its control over the interstate carrier in all matters having such a close and substantial relation to interstate commerce that it is necessary or appropriate to exercise the control for the effective government of that commerce.

It is also clear that, in removing the injurious discriminations against interstate traffic arising from the relation of intrastate to interstate rates, Congress is not bound to reduce the latter below what it may deem to be a proper standard, fair to the carrier and to the public. Otherwise, it could prevent the injury to interstate commerce only by the sacrifice of its judgment as to interstate rates. Congress is entitled to maintain its own standard as to these rates, and to forbid any discriminatory action by interstate carriers which will obstruct the freedom of movement of interstate traffic over their lines in accordance with the terms it establishes. . . .

Second. The remaining question is with regard to the scope of the power which Congress has granted to the Commission.

Section 3 of the act to regulate commerce provides (24 Stat. at L. 379, 380, chap. 104):

"Sec. 3. That it shall be unlawful for any common carrier subject to the provisions of this act to make or give any undue or unreasonable preference or advantage to any particular person, company, firm, corporation, or locality, or any particular description of traffic, in any respect whatsoever, or to subject any particular person, company, firm, corporation, or locality, or any particular description of traffic, to any undue or unreasonable prejudice or disadvantage in any respect whatsoever."

This language is certainly sweeping enough to embrace all the discriminations of the sort described which it was within the power of Congress to condemn. There is no exception or qualification with respect to an unreasonable discrimination against interstate traffic produced by the relation of intrastate to interstate rates as maintained by the carrier. It is apparent from the legislative history of the act that the evil of discrimination was the principal thing aimed at, and there is no basis for the contention that Congress intended to exempt any discriminatory action or practice of interstate carriers affecting interstate commerce which it had authority to reach. The purpose of the measure was thus emphatically stated in the elaborate report of the Senate Committee on Interstate Commerce which accompanied it: "The provisions of the bill are based upon the theory that the paramount evil chargeable against the operation of the transportation system of the United States as now conducted is unjust discrimination between persons, places, commodities, or particular descriptions of traffic. The underlying purpose and aim of the measure is the prevention of these discriminations" (Senate Report No. 46, 49th Cong. 1st Sess. p. 215).

The opposing argument rests upon the proviso in the 1st section of the act which, in its original form, was as follows: "Provided, however, that the provisions of this act shall not apply to the transportation of passengers or property, or to the receiving, delivering, storage, or handling of property, wholly within one state, and not shipped to or from a foreign country from or to any state or territory as aforesaid." When the act was amended so as to confer upon the Commission the authority to prescribe maximum interstate rates, this proviso was re-enacted; and when the act was extended to include telegraph, telephone, and cable companies engaged in interstate business, an additional clause was inserted so as to exclude intrastate messages. [Citations omitted.]

Congress thus defined the scope of its regulation, and provided that it was not to extend to purely intrastate traffic. It did not undertake to authorize the Commission to prescribe intrastate rates, and thus to establish a unified control by the exercise of the rate-making power over both descriptions of traffic. Undoubtedly — in the absence of a finding by the Commission of unjust discrimination — intrastate rates were left to be fixed by the carrier, and subject to the authority of the states, or of the agencies created by the states. This was the question recently decided by this court in the Minnesota Rate Cases (Simpson v. Shepard), 230 U.S. 352. . . .

Here, the Commission expressly found that unjust discrimination existed under substantially similar conditions of transportation, and the inquiry is whether the Commission had power to correct it. We are of the opinion that the limitation of the proviso in § 1 does not apply to a case of this sort. The Commission was dealing with the relation of rates injuriously affecting, through an unreasonable discrimination, traffic that was interstate. The question was thus not simply one of transportation that was "wholly within one state." . . . It is urged that the practical construction of the statute has been the other way. But, in assailing the order, the appellants ask us to override the construction which has been given to the statute by the authority charged with its execution, and it cannot be said that the earlier action of the Commission was of such a controlling character as to preclude it from giving effect to the law. The Commission, having before it a plain case of unreasonable discrimination on the part of interstate carriers against interstate trade, carefully examined the question of its authority, and decided that it had the power to make this remedial order. The commerce court sustained the authority of the Commission, and it is clear that we should not reverse the decree unless the law has been misapplied. This we cannot say; on the contrary, we are convinced that the authority of the Commission was adequate. . . .

Affirmed.

MR. JUSTICE LURTON and MR. JUSTICE PITNEY dissent.

NOTE

1. In Railroad Commission of Wisconsin v. Chicago, B. & Q.R.R., 257 U.S. 563 (1922), the Court sustained an order of the ICC requiring a general increase in intrastate fares in Wisconsin to the level of interstate fares of the carriers, despite a state statute fixing a lower maximum. The order was supportable not as an elimination of unjust discrimination against persons or localities in interstate commerce, but as a means of carrying out the power under the Transportation Act, 1920, to remove "unjust discrimination against interstate commerce," in the light of the policy of that act "to maintain an adequate railway service for the people of the United States." But the burden of the intrastate rates on the carrier's revenues and the anticipated effects of the rate order on the revenues must be made the subject of express findings by the ICC. Compare Florida v. United States, 282 U.S. 194 (1931), with Florida v. United States, 292 U.S. 1 (1934). See also Colorado v. United States, 271 U.S. 153 (1926), involving the power of the ICC to authorize abandonment of an intrastate branch line of an interstate carrier; and Dayton–Goose Creek Ry. v. United States, 263 U.S. 456, 485 (1924), involving the "recapture" clause of the Transportation Act, 1920, as applied to excess income from intrastate as well as interstate traffic. Compare Palmer v. Massachusetts, 308 U.S. 79 (1939) (partial discontinuance of local service).

2. The Safety Appliance Acts are applicable to "all trains, locomotives, tenders, cars, and similar vehicles used on any railroad engaged in interstate commerce." May the acts be validly applied to operations of cars used for intrastate traffic by a carrier engaged also in interstate commerce? Southern Ry. v. United States, 222 U.S. 20 (1911).

3. The Federal Employers' Liability Act of 1906 imposed liability on "every common carrier engaged in trade or commerce . . . between the several states" to "any of its employes," in cases of injury caused by the carrier's negligence or defective equipment. In the Employers' Liability Cases, 207 U.S. 463 (1908), in actions by the personal representatives of firemen on locomotives engaged in interstate commerce, the Court held the act too broad in its coverage to be supportable under the Commerce Clause, and denied recovery. Justices Moody, Harlan, McKenna, and Holmes dissented.

The Federal Employers' Liability Act of 1908 imposed liability on "every common carrier by railroad while engaging in commerce between any of the several states" to "any person suffering injury while he is employed by such carrier in such commerce"; the basis of liability was similar to that in the 1906 act. In Second Employers' Liability Cases, 223 U.S. 1 (1912), the Court sustained the act, holding that where the victim was engaged in interstate commerce it is immaterial that the negligent employee may not have been so engaged. The Court also upheld the abrogation of the fellow-servant defense, the alteration of the defenses of contributory negligence and assumption of risk, and the compulsion on state courts of general jurisdiction to entertain actions under the federal act.

The problems of coverage raised by the Act of 1908 are vividly described in Schoene and Watson, Workmen's Compensation on Interstate Railways, 47 Harv. L. Rev. 389 (1934), where it is said (pp. 399-400): "By that time [1916] the Court was becoming oriented in the multifarious activities that make up railroading and had decided that a yard clerk who was struck while crossing the yard to meet an interstate train to check the car numbers and seals was engaged in interstate commerce; that the same was true of an employee who was struck while crossing the tracks to his boardinghouse after oiling and inspecting an engine preparatory to an interstate run; that no such close connection could be found for one who was killed while moving intrastate freight across the city preparatory to moving interstate freight; that a switchman on an engine used in interstate commerce was engaged in such commerce; that the same could be said of a brakeman who was on an intrastate car for the purpose of cutting it out in order that an interstate train might proceed; that mining coal in the railroad's mine for it to use in interstate commerce was not a part of the commerce; that the contrary was true of distributing the cars of an interstate train to make room for another interstate train, and also of making a trial run to test an engine for use in interstate commerce, and of taking an engine to another state for repairs; but that the question of interstate commerce was properly left to the jury when an employee was injured while switching 'empties' preparatory to switching coal cars that had come from outside the state. The Court, in Shanks v. Delaware, L. & W.R.R. [239 U.S. 556 (1916)], was then able to state what has since been referred to as the 'rule in the Shanks case': 'the true test is . . . was the employe at the time of the injury engaged in interstate transportation or in work so closely related to it as to be practically a part of it.' "

Consider the necessity and utility of this form of statutory drafting. Compare the questions of coverage under the Fair Labor Standards Act, page 293 infra.

The Federal Employers' Liability Act was amended in 1939 to allow recovery by "any employee of a carrier, any part of whose duties as such employee shall be in furtherance of interstate or foreign commerce; or shall, in any way directly or closely and substantially, affect such commerce. . . ." 53 Stat. 1404 (1939), 45 U.S.C. §51. See Reed v. Pennsylvania R.R., 351 U.S. 501 (1956) (act applicable to clerical employee, injured in her office, whose duties consisted of filing tracings of equipment from which blueprints were made).

4. The acquisition by a railroad of control of another carrier is subject to the approval of the ICC. New York Central Securities Corp. v. United States, 287 U.S. 12 (1932).

Richard Olney, Attorney General, Memorandum Concerning the Pullman Strike, 1894 *James, Richard Olney*
201-207 (1923)

The attention of the Department of Justice was first called to the [Chicago strike] by representations from the Post-Office Department that the passage of the mails in various parts of the country was seriously obstructed. As a result, orders to the United States Marshals were sent to the designated places directing them to see that the regular passage of the mails was not interfered with, and to that end to use such force of special deputy marshals as might be required. Chicago was the center of the disturbance, but in a few days all the principal Western cities were involved. It soon became evident that the movement engineered by Mr. Debs was on an extraordinary scale and of a most threatening character, and might have to be met and dealt with by the Army of the United States. The Department of Justice, in order to be prepared for the exigency, took measures to put itself in the position which had induced the President to authorize the use of troops as against the Coxey movement. That is to say, the Department of Justice instructed the District Attorney at Chicago, and afterwards other District Attorneys, to file bills in equity enjoining certain persons by name and all other persons cooperating with them from any interference with the mails or with interstate commerce — the bills being filed both on general grounds and under the express provisions of what is known as the Sherman Anti-Trust Law. The first bill was filed in Chicago in the name of the Attorney-General, by the District Attorney, Milchrist, ancillary bills being also filed at the same time by the various railroad corporations. The Attorney-General's bill was very comprehensive and was so drawn as to inhibit all interference with any interstate commerce railroads running into Chicago. The bills as filed called for interlocutory injunctions and, upon being presented to the court, such injunctions were issued. They were not, however, at first respected. Although Arnoled, the United States Marshal, had under his command at one time as many as three thousand special deputies, the field of operations of the strikers was very large, and he was generally outnumbered by the mob at any points where disturbances were going on. Though the injunctions were printed and pasted all over the city and were read wherever a gathering of strikers seemed to be meditating violence, no appreciable effect was produced. The marshal was hooted and his assistants overpowered, and though a few persons were taken in custody, the strike rather increased than abated in force.

In this situation of things, applications for the use of the United States troops were frequent, from the marshals, from lawyers, and from eminent citizens of Chicago. The President, however, deemed it best to follow strictly the precedent made in the Coxey case and not to move until satisfied that he must do so by proof that could not be resisted. In anticipation of such proof being furnished, however, the troops at Fort Sheridan were kept under arms, and a train ready to bring them to the city of Chicago was kept there with the locomotive fired up. Finally, Judge Grosscup, judge of the United States District Court, Mr. Milchrist, the United States District Attorney, and Mr. Walker, who had been retained specially in the business on behalf of the United States, joined the United States Marshal in a telegram to the Department stating that the writs and processes of the court could not be executed by the marshal and any force of deputies that he could collect, and asking for the immediate appearance on the scene of the United States troops. The President thereupon gave the order and the troops then at Fort Sheridan went by rail to the city of Chicago. . . .

The importance of the military demonstration in Chicago by the troops of the United States was, of course, very great. Yet it was the common opinion at the time — an opinion confirmed by the explicit declaration of Debs himself — that the action of the United States Courts enjoining the proceedings of Debs and his followers, and resulting so far as Debs himself was concerned in committing him to jail for contempt, really broke the back of the movement. It put the strikers in the wrong — in the position of rioters wantonly defying the law.

The President might have used the United States troops to prevent interference with the mails and with interstate commerce on his own initiative — without waiting for action by the courts and without justifying the proceeding as taken to enforce judicial decrees. But, as already intimated, it is doubtful — at least seemed doubtful to me at the time — whether the President could be induced to move except in support of the judicial tribunals. In the next place, assuming there was time enough to set the judiciary in motion, as it turned out that there was, it was unquestionably better to await its movements and make them the basis of Executive action. The injunctions were issued ex parte — and justifiably in view of the exigency and the irreparable character of the mischief going on and threatened. But, though issued ex parte, they were not final; the question of their legality and propriety was open and could have been raised at any moment by Debs or any parties enjoined by a simple motion in court for the dissolution of the injunctions. As law-abiding citizens — citizens who meant to respect the law — they were bound to take that course — and it always seemed to me unaccountable they were not advised so to do. In fact, they pursued exactly the opposite and a wholly indefensible course — Debs in particular proceeding after the injunctions as before and proclaiming at public meetings his intent to disregard the injunctions and urging his followers to do so likewise. He thus put himself hopelessly in the wrong. . . .

It probably should have been before stated — as one feature of the situation which to the Washington authorities seemed to make the use of United States troops at Chicago imperative — that both the Governor of the State (Altgeld) and the Mayor of the city (Hopkins) were known to be in sympathy with the strikers — so far at least that the Governor held himself aloof from the scene and made no effort to repress the disorders going on at the chief city of his State, while the Mayor, besides taking no active measures to prevent the violent and lawless interference with the running of interstate and mail trains and the lawless destruction of railroad property, even went so far as to openly wear the distinctive badge of the rioters. Both Altgeld and Hopkins were Democrats — largely by their efforts Illinois had been carried for Cleveland and the Democracy in 1892 — and some of the President's advisers, of whom Colonel Lamont was one, very much doubted the expediency of any action antagonizing or discrediting the Democratic Governor and Mayor. The President saw the point as clearly as any one, but never for a moment wavered in his determination to do what he believed to be his constitutional duty. . . .[b]

In re Debs 158 U.S. 564, 15 S. Ct. 900, 39 L. Ed. 1092 (1895)

[The United States brought a suit in a federal court in Illinois against Debs and other officers of the American Railway Union, to enjoin them from interfering in any manner with the business of twenty-two railroads engaged in the carriage of goods and passengers in interstate commerce and in the transportation of the mails. The bill alleged acts of intimidation and violence, and a conspiracy, in aid of the strike of the employees of the Pullman Company. An injunction was issued ex parte, the defendants were attached on an information charging violation of the injunction, and after a hearing they were sentenced to terms of three to six months for contempt. 64 F. 724. They applied to the Supreme Court for habeas corpus.]

MR. JUSTICE BREWER, after stating the case, delivered the opinion of the court.

The case presented by the bill is this: The United States, finding that the interstate transportation of persons and property, as well as the carriage of the mails, is forcibly obstructed, and that a combination and conspiracy exists to subject the control of such transportation to the will of the conspirators, applied to one of their courts, sitting as a court of equity, for an injunction to restrain such obstruction and prevent carrying into effect such conspiracy. Two questions of importance are presented: First. Are the relations of the general government to interstate commerce and the transportation of the mails such as authorize a direct interference to prevent a forcible obstruction thereof? Second. If authority ex-

---

[b] In the case of Coxey's march, "Federal intervention usually resulted from the fact that many of the western railroads were in the hands of receivers appointed by the United States courts." Rich, The Presidents and Civil Disorders 88 (1941). For an account of the intervention in the Pullman strike, see id. at 91-109. — ED.

ists, as authority in governmental affairs implies both power and duty, has a court of equity jurisdiction to issue an injunction in aid of the performance of such duty. . . .

Congress has exercised the power granted in respect to interstate commerce in a variety of legislative acts. . . .

Under the power vested in Congress to establish post offices and post roads, Congress has, by a mass of legislation, established the great post office system of the country, with all its detail of organization, its machinery for the transaction of business, defining what shall be carried and what not, and the prices of carriage, and also prescribing penalties for all offences against it.

Obviously these powers given to the national government over interstate commerce and in respect to the transportation of the mails were not dormant and unused. Congress had taken hold of these two matters, and by various and specific acts had assumed and exercised the powers given to it, and was in the full discharge of its duty to regulate interstate commerce and carry the mails. The validity of such exercise and the exclusiveness of its control had been again and again presented to this court for consideration. It is curious to note the fact that in a large proportion of the cases in respect to interstate commerce brought to this court the question presented was of the validity of state legislation in its bearings upon interstate commerce, and the uniform course of decision has been to declare that it is not within the competency of a State to legislate in such a manner as to obstruct interstate commerce. If a State with its recognized powers of sovereignty is impotent to obstruct interstate commerce, can it be that any mere voluntary association of individuals within the limits of that State has a power which the State itself does not possess?

As, under the Constitution, power over interstate commerce and the transportation of the mails is vested in the national government, and Congress by virtue of such grant has assumed actual and direct control, it follows that the national government may prevent any unlawful and forcible interference therewith. But how shall this be accomplished? Doubtless, it is within the competency of Congress to prescribe by legislation that any interference with these matters shall be offences against the United States, and prosecuted and punished by indictment in the proper courts. But is that the only remedy? Have the vast interests of the nation in interstate commerce, and in the transportation of the mails, no other protection than lies in the possible punishment of those who interfere with it? To ask the question is to answer it. . . .

. . . The entire strength of the nation may be used to enforce in any part of the land the full and free exercise of all national powers and the security of all rights entrusted by the Constitution to its care. The strong arm of the national government may be put forth to brush away all obstructions to the freedom of interstate commerce or the transportation of the mails. If the emergency arises, the army of the Nation, and all its militia, are at the service of the Nation to compel obedience to its laws.

But passing to the second question, is there no other alternative than the use of force on the part of the executive authorities whenever obstructions arise to the freedom of interstate commerce or the transportation of the mails? Is the army the only instrument by which rights of the public can be enforced and the peace of the nation preserved? Grant that any public nuisance may be forcibly abated either at the instance of the authorities, or by any individual suffering private damage therefrom, the existence of this right of forcible abatement is not inconsistent with nor does it destroy the right of appeal in an orderly way to the courts for a judicial determination, and an exercise of their powers by writ of injunction and otherwise to accomplish the same result. . . .

Neither can it be doubted that the government has such an interest in the subject-matter as enables it to appear as party plaintiff in this suit. It is said that equity only interferes for the protection of property, and that the government has no property interest. A sufficient reply is that the United States have a property in the mails, the protection of which was one of the purposes of this bill. . . .

Chapter Six. Powers over Transportation

We do not care to place our decision upon this ground alone. Every government, entrusted, by the very terms of its being, with powers and duties to be exercised and discharged for the general welfare, has a right to apply to its own courts for any proper assistance in the exercise of the one and the discharge of the other, and it is no sufficient answer to its appeal to one of those courts that it has no pecuniary interest in the matter. The obligations which it is under to promote the interest of all, and to prevent the wrongdoing of one resulting in injury to the general welfare, is often of itself sufficient to give it a standing in court. . . .

Again, it is objected that it is outside of the jurisdiction of a court of equity to enjoin the commission of crimes. This, as a general proposition, is unquestioned. A chancellor has no criminal jurisdiction. Something more than the threatened commission of an offence against the laws of the land is necessary to call into exercise the injunctive powers of the court. There must be some interferences, actual or threatened, with property or rights of a pecuniary nature, but when such interferences appear the jurisdiction of a court of equity arises, and is not destroyed by the fact that they are accompanied by or are themselves violations of the criminal law. . . .

Further, it is said by counsel in their brief:

"No case can be cited where such a bill in behalf of the sovereign has been entertained against riot and mob violence, though occurring on the highway. It is not such fitful and temporary obstruction that constitutes a nuisance. The strong hand of executive power is required to deal with such lawless demonstrations.

"The courts should stand aloof from them and not invade executive prerogative, nor even at the behest or request of the executive travel out of the beaten path of well-settled judicial authority. A mob cannot be suppressed by injunction; nor can its leaders be tried, convicted, and sentenced in equity.

"It is too great a strain upon the judicial branch of the government to impose this essentially executive and military power upon courts of chancery."

We do not perceive that this argument questions the jurisdiction of the court, but only the expediency of the action of the government in applying for its process. . . . But does not counsel's argument imply too much? Is it to be assumed that these defendants were conducting a rebellion or inaugurating a revolution, and that they and their associates were thus placing themselves beyond the reach of the civil process of the courts? We find in the opinion of the Circuit Court a quotation from the testimony given by one of the defendants before the United States Strike Commission, which is sufficient answer to this suggestion:

"As soon as the employes found that we were arrested, and taken from the scene of action, they became demoralized, and that ended the strike. It was not the soldiers that ended the strike. It was not the old brotherhoods that ended the strike. It was simply the United States courts that ended the strike. Our men were in a position that never would have been shaken under any circumstances, if we had been permitted to remain upon the field among them. Once we were taken from the scene of action, and restrained from sending telegrams or issuing orders or answering questions, then the minions of the corporations would be put to work. . . . Our headquarters were temporarily demoralized and abandoned, and we could not answer any messages. The men went back to work, and the ranks were broken, and the strike was broken up, . . . not by the army, and not by any other power, but simply and solely by the action of the United States courts in restraining us from discharging our duties as officers and representatives of our employes." . . .

We enter into no examination of the [Sherman Antitrust] act of July 2, 1890, c. 647, 26 Stat. 209, upon which the Circuit Court relied mainly to sustain its jurisdiction. It must not be understood from this that we dissent from the conclusions of that court in reference to the scope of the act, but simply that we prefer to rest our judgment on the broader ground which has been discussed in this opinion, believing it of importance that the principles underlying it should be fully stated and affirmed.

The petition for a writ of habeas corpus is
Denied.[c]

[c] See Brewer, The Nation's Safeguard, 16 Rep. N.Y. St. Bar Assn. 37 (1893); Brewer, Government by Injunction, 15 Nat. Corp. Rep. 848 (1898). For a critique of the decision see Dunbar, Government by Injunction, 52 L.Q. Rev. 347 (1897). Cf. Simpson, Fifty Years of American Equity, 50 Harv. L. Rev. 171, 193-199 (1936). Compare Chance v. Lambeth, 186 F.2d 879 (4th Cir. 1951), cert. denied, 341 U.S. 941 (1951), 198 F.2d 549 (1952), cert. denied, 344 U.S. 877 (1952). — ED.

Chapter Seven National Power over the Economy

Section A. TRADE, PRODUCTION, AND EMPLOYMENT

United States v. E. C. Knight Co. 156 U.S. 1, 15 S. Ct. 249, 39 L. Ed. 325 (1895)

[The United States brought a bill under the Sherman Antitrust Act of 1890 against the American Sugar Refining Company and other sugar refining companies to cancel certain agreements whereby, it was alleged, the defendants had conspired to, and did, monopolize the manufacture and sale of refined sugar in the United States. The trial court found that American had produced about 65 percent of the sugar refined in this country, and the other defendants about 33 percent; that American purchased the stock of the shareholders in the other defendants; and that subsequently about 90 percent of the sugar refined and sold in this country was the product of the refineries controlled by American. The court held that a violation of the Sherman Act was not established and dismissed the bill. The circuit court of appeals affirmed. The Sherman Act prohibits any person from monopolizing or attempting or conspiring to monopolize "any part of the trade or commerce among the several States, or with foreign nations," as well as every contract, combination, or conspiracy in restraint of such commerce.]

MR. CHIEF JUSTICE FULLER delivered the opinion of the court: . . .

The fundamental question is whether conceding that the existence of a monopoly in manufacture is established by the evidence, that monopoly can be directly suppressed under the Act of Congress in the mode attempted by this bill.

It cannot be denied that the power of a state to protect the lives, health, and property of its citizens, and to preserve good order and the public morals, "the power to govern men and things within the limits of its dominion," is a power originally and always belonging to the states, not surrendered by them to the general government, nor directly restrained by the Constitution of the United States, and essentially exclusive. The relief of the citizens of each state from the burden of monopoly and the evils resulting from the restraint of trade among such citizens was left with the states to deal with, and this court has recognized their possession of that power even to the extent of holding that an employment of business carried on by private individuals, when it becomes a matter of such public interest and importance as to create a common charge or burden upon the citizen; in other words, when it becomes a practical monopoly, to which the citizen is compelled to resort and by means of which a tribute can be exacted from the community, is subject to regulation by state legislative power. On the other hand, the power of Congress to regulate commerce among the several states is also exclusive. . . .

It is vital that the independence of the commercial power and of the police power, and the delimitation between them, however sometimes perplexing, should always be recognized and observed, for while the one furnishes the strongest bond of union, the other is essential to the preservation of the autonomy of the states as required by our dual form of government; and acknowledged evils, however grave and urgent they may appear to be, had better be borne, than the risk be run, in the effort to suppress them, of more serious consequences by resort to expedients of even doubtful constitutionality.

It will be perceived how far-reaching the proposition is that the power of dealing with a monopoly directly may be exercised by the general government whenever interstate or international commerce may be ultimately affected. The regulation of commerce applies to the subjects of commerce and not to matters of internal police. Contracts to buy, sell, or exchange goods to be transported among the several states, the transportation and its instrumentalities, and articles bought, sold, or exchanged for the purpose of such transit among the states, or put in the way of transit, may be regulated, but this is because they form part of interstate trade or commerce. The fact that an article is manufactured for export to another state does not of itself make it an article of interstate commerce, and the intent of the manufacturer does not determine the time when the article or product passes from the control of the state and belongs to commerce. This was so ruled in Coe v. Erroll, 116 U.S. 517, in which the question before the court was whether certain logs cut at a place in New Hampshire and hauled to a river town for the purpose of transportation to the state of Maine were liable to be taxed like other property in the state of New Hampshire. . . .

And again, in Kidd v. Pearson, 128 U.S. 1, 20, 24, where the question was discussed whether the right of a state to enact a statute prohibiting within its limits the manufacture of intoxicating liquors, except for certain purposes, could be overthrown by the fact that the manufacturer intended to export the liquors when made, it was held that the intent of the manufacturer did not determine the time when the article or product passed from the control of the state and belonged to commerce, and that, therefore, the statute, in omitting to except from its operation the manufacture of intoxicating liquors within the limits of the state for export, did not constitute an unauthorized interference with the right of Congress to regulate commerce. . . .

In Gibbons v. Ogden, Brown v. Maryland, and other cases often cited, the state laws, which were held inoperative, were instances of direct interference with, or regulations of, interstate or international commerce; yet in Kidd v. Pearson the refusal of a state to allow articles to be manufactured within her borders even for export was held not to directly affect external commerce, and state legislation which, in a great variety of ways, affected interstate commerce and persons engaged in it, has been frequently sustained because the interference was not direct. . . .

. . . It is true that the bill alleged that the products of these refineries were sold and distributed among the several states, and that all the companies were engaged in trade or commerce with the several states and with foreign nations; but this was no more than to say that trade and commerce served manufacture to fulfill its function. Sugar was refined for sale, and sales were probably made at Philadelphia for consumption, and undoubtedly for resale by the first purchasers throughout Pennsylvania and other states, and refined sugar was also forwarded by the companies to other states for sale. Nevertheless it does not follow that an attempt to monopolize, or the actual monopoly of, the manufacture was an attempt, whether executory or consummated, to monopolize commerce, even though, in order to dispose of the product, the instrumentality of commerce was necessarily invoked. There was nothing in the proofs to indicate any intention to put a restraint upon trade or commerce, and the fact, as we have seen, that trade or commerce might be indirectly affected was not enough to entitle complainants to a decree. The subject-matter of the sale was shares of manufacturing stock, and the relief sought was the surrender of property which had already passed and the suppression of the alleged monopoly in manufacture by the restoration of the status quo before the transfers, yet the Act of Congress only authorized the circuit courts to proceed by way of preventing and restraining violations of the Act in respect of contracts, combinations, or conspiracies in restraint of interstate or international trade or commerce. . . .

Decree affirmed.

[The dissenting opinion of Mr. Justice Harlan is omitted.]

ADDYSTON PIPE & STEEL CO. v. UNITED STATES, 175 U.S. 211 (1899). The United States brought suit under the Antitrust Act against six corporations engaged in the manufacture, sale, and transportation of iron pipe. The defendants had entered into an agreement dividing sales territory, arranging for noncompetitive bidding, and requiring "bonuses" on sales to be allotted among the companies. The trial court dismissed the bill; the court of appeals reversed, in an opinion by Circuit Judge Taft (as he then was). 85 F. 271 (6th Cir. 1898). The Supreme Court unanimously affirmed the court of appeals, except that the decree was ordered to exclude any combination in regard to contracts for "the delivery of pipe in the same State where some of the defendants resided and carried on their business" (p. 247). The Court said (pp. 240-241): "While no particular contract regarding the furnishing of pipe and the price for which it should be furnished was in the contemplation of the parties to the combination at the time of its formation, yet it was their intention, as it was the purpose of the combination, to directly and by means of such combination increase the price for which all contracts for the delivery of pipe within the territory above described should be made, and the latter result was to be achieved by abolishing all competition between the parties to the combination. The direct and immediate result of the combination was therefore necessarily a restraint upon interstate commerce in respect of articles manufactured by any of the parties to it to be transported beyond the State in which they were made. The defendants by reason of this combination and agreement could only send their goods out of the State in which they were manufactured for sale and delivery in another State, upon the terms and pursuant to the provisions of such combination. As pertinently asked by the court below, was not this a direct restraint upon interstate commerce in those goods?"

NORTHERN SECURITIES CO. v. UNITED STATES, 193 U.S. 197 (1904). The United States brought suit under the Antitrust Act against the Northern Securities Company, the Northern Pacific Railway Company, the Great Northern Railway Company, and certain individuals, to set aside the acquisition by the Northern Securities Company of controlling stock interests in the two railways which operate parallel lines. An earlier arrangement, whereby the Great Northern was to acquire a controlling stock interest in the Northern Pacific, exchange traffic, and divide earnings, was defeated under Minnesota law in a stockholder's suit. Pearsall v. Great Northern Ry., 161 U.S. 646 (1896). In the present suit the Supreme Court affirmed a decree for the United States. Chief Justice Fuller and Justices White, Peckham, and Holmes dissented.

The dissenting opinion of Mr. Justice Holmes, dealing with the scope of the Sherman Act, contains the following statement (pp. 402-403): "Finally, the statute must be construed in such a way as not merely to save its constitutionality but, so far as is consistent with a fair interpretation, not to raise grave doubts on that score. I assume for the purposes of discussion, although it would be a great and serious step to take, that in some case that seemed to it to need heroic measures, Congress might regulate not only commerce, but intruments of commerce or contracts the bearing of which upon commerce would be only indirect. But it is clear that the mere fact of an indirect effect upon commerce not shown to be certain and very great, would not justify such a law. The point decided in United States v. E. C. Knight Co., 156 U.S. 1, 17, was that 'the fact that trade or commerce might be indirectly affected was not enough to entitle complainants to a decree.' Commerce depends upon population, but Congress could not, on that ground, undertake to regulate marriage and divorce. If the act before us is to be carried out according to what seems to me the logic of the argument for the Government, which I do not believe that it will be, I can see no part of the conduct of life with which on similar principles Congress might not interfere."

SWIFT & CO. v. UNITED STATES, 196 U.S. 375 (1905). The United States sued for an injunction under the Sherman Act, alleging a combination of a dominant proportion of the dealers in fresh meat throughout the United States not to bid against each other in the livestock markets of the different states, to bid up prices for a few days in order to induce cattlemen to send their stock to the stockyards, to fix prices at which they will sell, and to that end to restrict shipments of meat when necessary. In affirming a decree sustaining the bill on motion to dismiss, the Court said, per Holmes, J. (pp. 398-399):

"[C]ommerce among the States is not a technical legal conception, but a practical one, drawn from the course of business. When cattle are sent for sale from a place in one State, with the expectation that they will end their transit, after purchase, in another, and when in effect they do so, with only the interruption necessary to find a purchaser at the stock yards, and when this is a typical, constantly recurring course, the current thus existing is a current of commerce among the States, and the purchase of the cattle is a part and incident of such commerce. . . . It should be added that the cattle in the stock yard are not at rest even to the extent that was held sufficient to warrant taxation in American Steel & Wire Co. v. Speed, 192 U.S. 500. But it may be that the question of taxation does not depend upon whether the article taxed may or may not be said to be in the course of commerce between the States, but depends upon whether the tax so far affects that commerce as to amount to a regulation of it."

STAFFORD v. WALLACE, 258 U.S. 495 (1922). The Packers and Stockyards Act of 1921 brought under the administrative control of the Secretary of Agriculture the practices and charges of stockyard owners, dealers, packers, and commission men at the large stockyards of the country. In affirming a decision sustaining the act, in a suit to enjoin its enforcement, the Court said, per Taft, C.J. (pp. 516, 518-519):

"The stockyards are but a throat through which the current flows, and the transactions which occur therein are only incident to this current from the West to the East, and from one State to another. Such transactions can not be separated from the movement to which they contribute and necessarily take on its character. . . . The application of the commerce clause of the Constitution in the Swift Case was the result of the natural development of interstate commerce under modern conditions. It was the inevitable recognition of the great central fact that such streams of commerce from one part of the country to another which are ever flowing are in their very essence the commerce among the States and with foreign nations which historically it was one of the chief purposes of the Constitution to bring under national protection and control. This court declined to defeat this purpose in respect of such a stream and take it out of complete national regulation by a nice and technical inquiry into the noninterstate character of some of its necessary incidents and facilities when considered alone and without reference to their association with the movement of which they were an essential but subordinate part."

Section A. **Trade, Production, and Employment** 229

NOTE

1. In both the Knight and Northern Securities cases the companies were represented by John G. Johnson of the Philadelphia bar, who twice declined a nomination to the Supreme Court, and of whom Chief Justice White is reported to have said: "When I first became a member of the court, Johnson was constantly before us, and we all thought of him as by far the most powerful advocate of his day. But when later Johnson argued the great anti-trust cases, which in fact gave him his great national reputation, all the justices felt that he was not at his best because he had lived into an economic era which he could not understand." Winkelman, John G. Johnson 244 (1942). See also Twiss, Lawyers and the Constitution 206-213 (1942).

2. The Supreme Court first applied the Sherman Act to a labor organization in Loewe v. Lawlor, 208 U.S. 274 (1908), involving an attempt by a national labor union to force all manufacturers of fur hats to organize their workers, through a boycott against the purchase of products of nonunion manufacturers shipped in interstate commerce. Other labor boycotts and refusals to work on products in the hands of the purchaser were likewise held to be within the act. Duplex Printing Press Co. v. Deering, 254 U.S. 443 (1921); Bedford Cut Stone Co. v. Journeymen Stone Cutters' Assn., 274 U.S. 37 (1927). A strike to unionize a mine that shipped its product in interstate commerce was held not covered by the act in United Mine Workers v. Coronado Coal Co., 259 U.S. 344 (1922). But in Coronado Coal Co. v. United Mine Workers, 268 U.S 295 (1925) (Second Coronado Case), where on a trial upon amended pleadings it appeared that the purpose of the union's acts was to stop the production of nonunion coal and prevent its shipment to other states where by competition it would tend to reduce prices and wages in unionized mines, the act was held applicable. That the distinction rested on the scope of the act and not on the constitutional power of Congress was asserted in Apex Hosiery Co. v. Leader, 310 U.S. 469, 509 (1940), which by construing the act to be directed against control of commercial markets took many union activities outside its scope. A similar trend was established from another direction in United States v. Hutcheson, 312 U.S. 219 (1941), extending the immunities conferred by the Clayton and Norris-La Guardia Acts upon certain peaceful labor activities to criminal prosecution under the Sherman Act. The Labor Management Relations Act, however, prohibits a number of "unfair" union practices.

3. May the Sherman Act be applied to major league baseball? The Court held not in Federal Baseball Club v. National League, 259 U.S. 200 (1922). Mr. Justice Holmes, for the Court, said (p. 209): "As it is put by the defendants, personal effort, not related to production, is not a subject of commerce. That which in its consummation is not commerce does not become commerce among the States because the transportation that we have mentioned takes place. To repeat the illustrations given by the Court below, a firm of lawyers sending out a member to argue a case, or the Chautauqua lecture bureau sending out lecturers, does not engage in such commerce because the lawyer or lecturer goes to another State." But cf. Gardella v. Chandler, 172 F.2d 402 (2d Cir. 1949), noted in 62 Harv. L. Rev. 1240 (1949).

In Toolson v. New York Yankees, 346 U.S. 356 (1953), the Court again held that the agreements among major league baseball clubs concerning employment of players are not subject to the antitrust laws. The following is the per curiam opinion:

"In Federal Baseball Club of Baltimore v. National League of Professional Baseball Clubs, 259 U.S. 200, this Court held that the business of providing public baseball games for profit between clubs of professional baseball players was not within the scope of the federal antitrust laws. Congress has had the ruling under consideration but has not seen fit to bring such business under these laws by legislation having prospective effect. The business has thus been left for thirty years to develop, on the understanding that it was not subject to existing antitrust legislation. The present cases ask us to overrule the prior decision and, with retrospective effect, hold the legislation applicable. We think that if there are evils in this field which now warrant application to it of the antitrust laws it should be by legislation. Without re-examination of the underlying issues, the judgments below are affirmed on the authority of Federal Baseball Club of Baltimore v. National League of Professional Baseball Clubs, supra, so far as that decision determines that Congress had no intention of including the business of baseball within the scope of the federal antitrust laws." Justices Burton and Reed dissented with an opinion by the former.

Professional boxing and football, however, have been held covered by the Sherman Act. United States v. International Boxing Club, 348 U.S. 236 (1955); Radovich v. National Football League, 352 U.S. 445 (1957). For decisions applying the Sherman Act to other professional sports, see Haywood v. National Basketball Assn., 401 U.S. 1204 (1971) (Douglas, Circuit Justice); Deesen v. Professional Golfers' Assn., 358 F.2d 165 (9th Cir.), cert. denied, 385 U.S. 846 (1966); Philadelphia World Hockey Club, Inc. v. Philadelphia Hockey Club, Inc., 351 F. Supp. 457 (E.D. Pa. 1972). Nonetheless, in Flood v. Kuhn, 407 U.S. 258 (1972), the Court reaffirmed the exemption for professional baseball, largely on the reasoning of Toolson. The Court also rejected petitioner's claim that the reserve clause placed him in peonage and involuntary servitude in violation of the Thirteenth Amendment.

For an argument that application vel non of the antitrust laws made little practical difference, see Jacobs & Winter, Antitrust Principles and Collective Bargaining by Athletes: Of Superstars in Peonage, 81 Yale L.J. 1 (1971). See generally collections of articles on sports and the law in 38 Law & Contemp. Prob. 1-171 (1973) and N.Y.L.F. 815-933 (1973).

In 1869 the Supreme Court held that Virginia could validly regulate insurance companies doing business there; objection under the commerce clause was dismissed on the ground that "issuing a policy of insurance is not a transaction of commerce." Paul v. Virginia, 8 Wall. 168, 183. This proposition was repeatedly adhered to in sustaining state laws regulating or taxing insurance companies. E.g., New York Life Ins. Co. v. Deer Lodge County, 231 U.S. 495 (1913). The applicability of the federal antitrust laws to insurance company practices was raised directly in United States v. South-Eastern Underwriters, 322 U.S. 533 (1944), infra page 299. See also Goldfarb v. Virginia State Bar, 421 U.S. 773 (1975), unanimously holding that minimum fee schedules set by bar associations violate the antitrust laws.

Lottery Case (Champion v. Ames) 188 U.S. 321, 23 S. Ct. 321, 47 L. ed. 492 (1903)

[The appellant was arrested and held in the Northern District of Illinois for removal to a federal court in Texas, where he had been indicted for conspiracy to violate the Federal Lottery Act of 1895, which penalized the importation, mailing, or interstate carriage of lottery tickets. The indictment charged that appellant had shipped a box, containing tickets for a Paraguayan lottery, from Texas to California by means of an express company. In the Northern District of Illinois he applied for a writ of habeas corpus, alleging the invalidity of the Act of 1895 as applied. The writ was dismissed by the circuit court.]

MR. JUSTICE HARLAN delivered the opinion of the Court: . . .

It was said in argument that lottery tickets are not of any real or substantial value in themselves, and therefore are not subjects of commerce. If that were conceded to be the only legal test as to what are to be deemed subjects of the commerce that may be regulated by Congress, we cannot accept as accurate the broad statement that such tickets are of no value. Upon their face they showed that the lottery company offered a large capital prize, to be paid to the holder of the ticket winning the prize at the drawing advertised to be held at Asuncion, Paraguay. Money was placed on deposit in different banks in the United

States to be applied by the agents representing the lottery company to the prompt payment of prizes. These tickets were the subject of traffic; they could have been sold; and the holder was assured that the company would pay to him the amount of the prize drawn. . . .

We are of opinion that lottery tickets are subjects of traffic, and therefore are subjects of commerce, and the regulation of the carriage of such tickets from state to state, at least by independent carriers, is a regulation of commerce among the several states.

But it is said that the statute in question does not regulate the carrying of lottery tickets from state to state, but by punishing those who cause them to be so carried Congress in effect prohibits such carrying; that in respect of the carrying from one state to another of articles or things that are, in fact, or according to usage in business, the subjects of commerce, the authority given Congress was not to *prohibit*, but only to *regulate*. This view was earnestly pressed at the bar by learned counsel, and must be examined. . . .

We have said that the carrying from state to state of lottery tickets constitutes interstate commerce, and that the regulation of such commerce is within the power of Congress under the Constitution. Are we prepared to say that a provision which is, in effect, a *prohibition* of the carriage of such articles from state to state is not a fit or appropriate mode for the *regulation* of that particular kind of commerce? If lottery traffic, *carried on through interstate commerce,* is a matter of which Congress may take cognizance and over which its power may be exerted, can it be possible that it must tolerate the traffic, and simply regulate the manner in which it may be carried on? Or may not Congress, for the protection of the people of all the states, and under the power to regulate interstate commerce, devise such means, within the scope of the Constitution, and not prohibited by it, as will drive that traffic out of commerce among the states?

In determining whether regulation may not under some circumstances properly take the form or have the effect of prohibition, the nature of the interstate traffic which it was sought by the act of May 2d, 1895, to suppress cannot be overlooked. . . . In other cases we have adjudged that authority given by legislative enactment to carry on a lottery, although based upon a consideration in money, was not protected by the contract clause of the Constitution; this, for the reason that no state may bargain away its power to protect the public morals, nor excuse its failure to perform a public duty by saying that it had agreed, by legislative enactment, not to do so. Stone v. Mississippi, 101 U.S. 814; Douglas v. Kentucky, 168 U.S. 488.

If a state, when considering legislation for the suppression of lotteries within its own limits, may properly take into view the evils that inhere in the raising of money, in that mode, why may not Congress, invested with the power to regulate commerce among the several states, provide that such commerce shall not be polluted by the carrying of lottery tickets from one state to another? . . .

It is said, however, that if, in order to suppress lotteries carried on through interstate commerce, Congress may exclude lottery tickets from such commerce, that principle leads necessarily to the conclusion that Congress may arbitrarily exclude from commerce among the states any article, commodity, or thing, of whatever kind or nature, or however useful or valuable, which it may choose, no matter with what motive, to declare shall not be carried from one state to another. It will be time enough to consider the constitutionality of such legislation when we must do so. The present case does not require the court to declare the full extent of the power that Congress may exercise in the regulation of commerce among the states. We may, however, repeat, in this connection, what the court has heretofore said, that the power of Congress to regulate commerce among the states, although plenary, cannot be deemed arbitrary, since it is subject to such limitations or restrictions as are prescribed by the Constitution. This power, therefore, may not be exercised so as to infringe rights secured or protected by that instrument. It would not be difficult to imagine legislation that would be justly liable to such an objection as that stated, and be hostile to the objects for the accomplishment of which Congress was invested with the general power to regulate commerce among the several states. But, as often said, the possible abuse of a power is not an argument against its existence. There is probably no governmental power that may not be exerted to the injury of the public. If what is done by Congress is manifestly in excess of the powers granted to it, then upon the courts will rest the duty of adjudging that its action is neither legal nor binding upon the people. But if what Congress does is within the limits of its power, and is simply unwise or injurious, the remedy is that suggested by Chief Justice Marshall in Gibbons v. Ogden, when he said: "The wisdom and the discretion of Congress, their identity with the people, and the influence which their constituents possess at elections, are, in this, as in many other instances, as that, for example, of declaring war, the sole restraints on which they have relied, to secure them from its abuse. They are the restraints on which the people must often rely solely, in all representative governments." . . .

The judgment is affirmed.

MR. CHIEF JUSTICE FULLER, with whom concur MR. JUSTICE BREWER, MR. JUSTICE SHIRAS, and MR. JUSTICE PECKHAM, dissenting: . . .

The ground on which prior acts forbidding the transmission of lottery matter by the mails was sustained, was that the power vested in Congress to establish postoffices and post roads embraced the regulation of the entire postal system of the country, and that under that power Congress might designate what might be carried in the mails and what excluded. Re Rapier, 143 U.S. 110; Ex parte Jackson, 96 U.S. 727. . . .

[T]his act cannot be brought within the power to regulate commerce among the several states, unless lottery tickets are articles of commerce, and therefore, when carried across state lines, of interstate commerce; or unless the power to regulate interstate commerce includes the absolute and exclusive power to prohibit the transportation of anything or anybody from one state to another. . . .

Is the carriage of lottery tickets from one state to another commercial intercourse?

The lottery ticket purports to create contractual relations, and to furnish the means of enforcing a contract right.

This is true of insurance policies, and both are contingent in their nature. Yet this court has held that the issuing of fire, marine, and life insurance policies, in one state, and sending them to another, to be there delivered to the insured on payment of premium, is not interstate commerce. Paul v. Virginia, 8 Wall. 168; Hooper v. California, 155 U.S. 648; New York L. Ins. Co. v. Cravens, 178 U.S. 399. . . .

If a lottery ticket is not an article of commerce, how can it become so when placed in an envelope or box or other covering, and transported by an express company? To say that the mere carrying of an article which is not an article of commerce in and of itself nevertheless becomes such the moment it is to be transported from one state to another, is to transform a noncommercial article into a commercial one simply because it is transported. I cannot conceive that any such result can properly follow.

It would be to say that everything is an article of commerce the moment it is taken to be transported from place to place, and of interstate commerce if from state to state.

An invitation to dine, or to take a drive, or a note of introduction, all become articles of commerce under the ruling in this case, by being deposited with an express company for transportation. This in effect breaks down all the differences between that which is, and that which is not, an article of commerce, and the necessary consequence is to take from the states all jurisdiction over the subject so far as interstate communication is concerned. It is a long step in the direction of wiping out all traces of state lines, and the creation of a centralized government. . . .

It is argued that the power to regulate commerce among the several states is the same as the power to regulate commerce with foreign nations, and with the Indian tribes. But is its scope the same?

As in effect before observed, the power to regulate commerce with foreign nations and the power to regulate interstate commerce, are to be taken diverso intuitu, for the latter was intended to secure equality and freedom in commercial intercourse as between the states, not to permit the creation of impediments to such intercourse; while the former clothed Congress with that power over international commerce, pertaining to a sovereign nation in its intercourse with foreign nations, and subject, generally speaking, to no implied or reserved power in the states. The laws which would be necessary and proper in the one case would not be necessary or proper in the other. . . .

Thus it is seen that the right of passage of persons and property from one state to another cannot be prohibited by Congress. But that does not challenge the legislative power of a sovereign nation to exclude foreign persons or commodities, or place an embargo, perhaps not permanent, upon foreign ships or manufactures.

The power to prohibit the transportation of diseased animals and infected goods over railroads or on steamboats is an entirely different thing, for they would be in themselves injurious to the transaction of interstate commerce, and, moreover, are essentially commercial in their nature. And the exclusion of diseased persons rests on different ground, for nobody would pretend that persons could be kept off the trains because they were going from one state to another to engage in the lottery business. However enticing that business may be, we do not understand these pieces of paper themselves can communicate bad principles by contact. . . .

I regard this decision as inconsistent with the views of the framers of the Constitution, and of Marshall, its great expounder. Our form of government may remain notwithstanding legislation or decision, but, as long ago observed, it is with governments, as with religions: the form may survive the substance of the faith. . . .

Hammer v. Dagenhart *247 U.S. 251, 38 S. Ct. 529, 62 L. Ed. 1101 (1918)*

MR. JUSTICE DAY delivered the opinion of the court:

A bill was filed in the United States district court for the western district of North Carolina by a father in his own behalf and as next friend of his two minor sons, one under the age of fourteen years and the other between the ages of fourteen and sixteen years, employees in a cotton mill at Charlotte, North Carolina, to enjoin the enforcement of the act of Congress intended to prevent interstate commerce in the products of child labor. 39 Stat. at L. 675, chap. 432.

The district court held the act unconstitutional and entered a decree enjoining its enforcement. This appeal brings the case here. The 1st section of the act is in the margin.[1] . . .

The power essential to the passage of this act, the government contends, is found in the commerce clause of the Constitution, which authorizes Congress to regulate commerce with foreign nations and among the states.

In Gibbons v. Ogden, 9 Wheat. 1, Chief Justice Marshall, speaking for this court, and defining the extent and nature of the commerce power, said: "It is the power to regulate, — that is, to prescribe the rule by which commerce is to be governed." In other words, the power is one to control the means by which commerce is carried on, which is directly the contrary of the assumed right to forbid commerce from moving and thus de-

---

[1] That no producer, manufacturer, or dealer shall ship or deliver for shipment in interstate or foreign commerce any article or commodity the product of any mine or quarry, situated in the United States, in which within thirty days prior to the time of the removal of such product therefrom children under the age of sixteen years have been employed or permitted to work, or any article or commodity the product of any mill, cannery, workshop, factory, or manufacturing establishment, situated in the United States, in which within thirty days prior to the removal of such product therefrom children under the age of fourteen years have been employed or permitted to work, or children between the ages of fourteen years and sixteen years have been employed or permitted to work more than eight hours in any day, or more than six days in any week, or after the hour of 7 o'clock postmeridian, or before the hour of 6 o'clock antemeridian.

stroy it as to particular commodities. But it is insisted that adjudged cases in this court establish the doctrine that the power to regulate given to Congress incidentally includes the authority to prohibit the movement of ordinary commodities, and therefore that the subject is not open for discussion. The cases demonstrate the contrary. They rest upon the character of the particular subjects dealt with and the fact that the scope of governmental authority, state or national, possessed over them, is such that the authority to prohibit is, as to them, but the exertion of the power to regulate.

The first of these cases is Champion v. Ames, 188 U.S. 321, the so-called Lottery Case, in which it was held that Congress might pass a law having the effect to keep the channels of commerce free from use in the transportation of tickets used in the promotion of lottery schemes. In Hipolite Egg Co. v. United States, 220 U.S. 45, this court sustained the power of Congress to pass the Pure Food and Drug Act, which prohibited the introduction into the states by means of interstate commerce of impure foods and drugs. In Hoke v. United States, 227 U.S. 308, this court sustained the constitutionality of the so-called "White Slave Traffic Act," whereby transportation of a woman in interstate commerce for the purpose of prostitution was forbidden. In that case we said, having reference to the authority of Congress, under the regulatory power, to protect the channels of interstate commerce:

"If the facility of interstate transportation can be taken away from the demoralization of lotteries, the debasement of obscene literature, the contagion of diseased cattle or persons, the impurity of food and drugs, the like facility can be taken away from the systematic enticement to and the enslavement in prostitution and debauchery of women, and, more insistently, of girls."

In Caminetti v. United States, 242 U.S. 470, we held that Congress might prohibit the transportation of women in interstate commerce for the purposes of debauchery and kindred purposes.[a] In Clark Distilling Co. v. Western Maryland R. Co., 242 U.S. 311, the power of Congress over the transportation of intoxicating liquors was sustained. . . .

And concluding the discussion which sustained the authority of the government to prohibit the transportation of liquor in interstate commerce, the court said:

"The exceptional nature of the subject here regulated is the basis upon which the exceptional power exerted must rest, and affords no ground for any fear that such power may be constitutionally extended to things which it may not, consistently with the guaranties of the Constitution, embrace."

In each of these instances the use of interstate transportation was necessary to the accomplishment of harmful results. In other words, although the power over interstate transportation was to regulate, that could only be accomplished by prohibiting the use of the facilities of interstate commerce to effect the evil intended.

This element is wanting in the present case. The thing intended to be accomplished by this statute is the denial of the facilities of interstate commerce to those manufacturers in the states who employ children within the prohibited ages. The act in its effect does not regulate transportation among the states, but aims to standardize the ages at which children may be employed in mining and manufacturing within the states. The goods shipped are of themselves harmless. The act permits them to be freely shipped after thirty days from the time of their removal from the factory. When offered for shipment, and before transportation begins, the labor of their production is over, and the mere fact that they were intended for interstate commerce transportation does not make their production subject to Federal control under the commerce power. . . .

Over interstate transportation, or its incidents, the regulatory power of Congress is ample, but the production of articles intended for interstate commerce is a matter of local regulation. . . . If it were otherwise, all manufacture intended for interstate shipment would be brought under Federal control to the practical exclusion of the authority of the

---

[a] On the "White Slave" Case see 50 Cong. Rec. 2874-2906, 3006-3023 (1913). — ED.

Section A. Trade, Production, and Employment 235

states, — a result certainly not contemplated by the framers of the Constitution when they vested in Congress the authority to regulate commerce among the states. Kidd v. Pearson, 128 U.S. 1, 21.

It is further contended that the authority of Congress may be exerted to control interstate commerce in the shipment of child-made goods because of the effect of the circulation of such goods in other states where the evil of this class of labor has been recognized by local legislation, and the right to thus employ child labor has been more rigorously restrained than in the state of production. In other words, that the unfair competition thus engendered may be controlled by closing the channels of interstate commerce to manufacturers in those states where the local laws do not meet what Congress deems to be the more just standard of other states.

There is no power vested in Congress to require the states to exercise their police power so as to prevent possible unfair competition. Many causes may co-operate to give one state, by reason of local laws or conditions, an economic advantage over others. The commerce clause was not intended to give to Congress a general authority to equalize such conditions. In some of the states laws have been passed fixing minimum wages for women; in others, the local law regulates the hours of labor of women in various employments. Business done in such states may be at an economic disadvantage when compared with states which have no such regulations; surely, this fact does not give Congress the power to deny transportation in interstate commerce to those who carry on business where the hours of labor and the rate of compensation for women have not been fixed by a standard in use in other states and approved by Congress.

The grant of power to Congress over the subject of interstate commerce was to enable it to regulate such commerce, and not to give it authority to control the states in their exercise of the police power over local trade and manufacture. . . .

In our view the necessary effect of this act is, by means of a prohibition against the movement in interstate commerce of ordinary commercial commodities, to regulate the hours of labor of children in factories and mines within the states, — a purely state authority. Thus the act in a twofold sense is repugnant to the Constitution. It not only transcends the authority delegated to Congress over commerce, but also exerts a power as to a purely local matter to which the Federal authority does not extend. The far-reaching result of upholding the act cannot be more plainly indicated than by pointing out that if Congress can thus regulate matters intrusted to local authority by prohibition of the movement of commodities in interstate commerce, all freedom of commerce will be at an end, and the power of the states over local matters may be eliminated, and thus our system of government be practically destroyed.

For these reasons we hold that this law exceeds the constitutional authority of Congress. It follows that the decree of the District Court must be affirmed.

Mr. Justice Holmes, dissenting: . . .

The first step in my argument is to make plain what no one is likely to dispute, — that the statute in question is within the power expressly given to Congress if considered only as to its immediate effects, and that if invalid it is so only on some collateral ground. The statute confines itself to prohibiting the carriage of certain goods in interstate or foreign commerce. Congress is given power to regulate such commerce in unqualified terms. It would not be argued to-day that the power to regulate does not include the power to prohibit. Regulation means the prohibition of something, and when interstate commerce is the matter to be regulated I cannot doubt that the regulations may prohibit any part of such commerce that Congress sees fit to forbid. At all events it is established by the Lottery Case and others that have followed it that a law is not beyond the regulative power of Congress merely because it prohibits certain transportation out and out. Champion v. Ames, 188 U.S. 321, 355, 359 et seq. . . .

The question, then, is narrowed to whether the exercise of its otherwise constitutional power by Congress can be pronounced unconstitutional because of its possible reaction upon the conduct of the states in a matter upon which I have admitted that they are free from direct control. I should have thought that that matter had been disposed of so fully as to leave no room for doubt. I should have thought that the most conspicuous decisions of this court had made it clear that the power to regulate commerce and other constitutional powers could not be cut down or qualified by the fact that it might interfere with the carrying out of the domestic policy of any state.

The manufacture of oleomargarine is as much a matter of state regulation as the manufacture of cotton cloth. Congress levied a tax upon the compound when colored so as to resemble butter that was so great as obviously to prohibit the manufacture and sale. In a very elaborate discussion the present Chief Justice excluded any inquiry into the purpose of an act which, apart from that purpose, was within the power of Congress. McCray v. United States, 195 U.S. 27. . . . Fifty years ago a tax on state banks, the obvious purpose and actual effect of which was to drive them, or at least their circulation, out of existence, was sustained, although the result was one that Congress had no constitutional power to require. The court made short work of the argument as to the purpose of the act. "The judicial cannot prescribe to the legislative departments of the government limitations upon the exercise of its acknowledged powers." Veazie Bank v. Fenno, 8 Wall. 533. So it well might have been argued that the corporation tax was intended, under the guise of a revenue measure, to secure a control not otherwise belonging to Congress, but the tax was sustained, and the objection, so far as noticed, was disposed of by citing McCray v. United States; Flint v. Stone Tracy Co., 220 U.S. 107. And to come to cases upon interstate commerce, notwithstanding United States v. E. C. Knight Co., 156 U.S. 1, the Sherman Act has been made an instrument for the breaking up of combinations in restraint of trade and monopolies, using the power to regulate commerce as a foothold, but not proceeding because that commerce was the end actually in mind. The objection that the control of the states over production was interfered with was urged again and again, but always in vain. [Citations omitted.]

The Pure Food and Drug Act which was sustained in Hipolite Egg Co. v. United States . . . with the intimation that "no trade can be carried on between the states to which it [the power of Congress to regulate commerce] does not extend," 57, applies not merely to articles that the changing opinions of the time condemn as intrinsically harmful, but to others innocent in themselves, simply on the ground that the order for them was induced by a preliminary fraud. Weeks v. United States, 245 U.S. 618. It does not matter whether the supposed evil precedes or follows the transportation. It is enough that, in the opinion of Congress, the transportation encourages the evil. I may add that in the cases on the so-called White Slave Act it was established that the means adopted by Congress as convenient to the exercise of its power might have the character of police regulations. Hoke v. United States, 227 U.S. 308, 323; Caminetti v. United States, 242 U.S. 470, 492. . . .

The notion that prohibition is any less prohibition when applied to things now thought evil I do not understand. But if there is any matter upon which civilized countries have agreed, — far more unanimously than they have with regard to intoxicants and some other matters over which this country is now emotionally aroused, — it is the evil of premature and excessive child labor. I should have thought that if we were to introduce our own moral conceptions where, in my opinion, they do not belong, this was preeminently a case for upholding the exercise of all powers by the United States.

But I had thought that the propriety of the exercise of a power admitted to exist in some cases was for the consideration of Congress alone, and that this court always had disavowed the right to intrude its judgment upon questions of policy or morals. It is not for this court to pronounce when prohibition is necessary to regulation if it ever may be necessary, — to say that it is permissible as against strong drink, but not as against the product of ruined lives.

The act does not meddle with anything belonging to the states. They may regulate their internal affairs and their domestic commerce as they like. But when they seek to send their products across the state line they are no longer within their rights. If there were no Constitution and no Congress their power to cross the line would depend upon their neighbors. Under the Constitution such commerce belongs not to the states, but to Congress to regulate. It may carry out its views of public policy whatever indirect effect they may have upon the activities of the states. Instead of being encountered by a prohibitive tariff at her boundaries, the state encounters the public policy of the United States which it is for Congress to express. The public policy of the United States is shaped with a view to the benefit of the nation as a whole. If, as has been the case within the memory of men still living, a state should take a different view of the propriety of sustaining a lottery from that which generally prevails, I cannot believe that the fact would require a different decision from that reached in Champion v. Ames. Yet in that case it would be said with quite as much force as in this that Congress was attempting to intermeddle with the state's domestic affairs. The national welfare as understood by Congress may require a different attitude within its sphere from that of some self-seeking state. It seems to me entirely constitutional for Congress to enforce its understanding by all the means at its command.

MR. JUSTICE MCKENNA, MR. JUSTICE BRANDEIS, and MR. JUSTICE CLARKE concur in this opinion.

Child Labor Tax Case (Bailey v. Drexel Furniture Co.)
259 U.S. 20, 42 S. Ct. 449, 66 L. Ed. 817 (1922)

MR. CHIEF JUSTICE TAFT delivered the opinion of the court:

This case presents the question of the constitutional validity of the Child Labor Tax Law. The plaintiff below, the Drexel Furniture Company, is engaged in the manufacture of furniture in the western district of North Carolina. On September 20, 1921, it received a notice from Bailey, United States collector of internal revenue for the district, that it had been assessed $6,312.79 for having during the taxable year 1919, employed and permitted to work in its factory a boy under fourteen years of age, thus incurring the tax of 10 per cent on its net profits for that year. The company paid the tax under protest, and, after rejection of its claim for a refund, brought this suit. On demurrer to an amended complaint, judgment was entered for the company against the collector for the full amount with interest. The writ of error is prosecuted by the collector direct from the district court under §238 of the Judicial Code.

The Child Labor Tax Law is Title No. 12 of an act entitled, "An Act to Provide Revenue and for Other Purposes," approved February 24, 1919, 40 Stat. at L. 1057, 1138. The heading of the title is "Tax on Employment of Child Labor." It begins with §1200 and includes eight sections. Section 1200 is as follows:

"Sec. 1200. That every person (other than a bona fide boys' or girls' canning club recognized by the Agricultural Department of a state and of the United States) operating (a) any mine or quarry situated in the United States in which children under the age of sixteen years have been employed or permitted to work during any portion of the taxable year; or (b) any mill, cannery, workshop, factory, or manufacturing establishment situated in the United States in which children under the age of fourteen years have been employed or permitted to work, or children between the ages of fourteen and sixteen have been employed or permitted to work more than eight hours in any day or more than six days in any week, or after the hour of seven o'clock postmeridian, or before the hour of six o'clock antemeridian, during any portion of the taxable year, shall pay for each taxable year, in addition to all other taxes imposed by law, an excise tax equivalent to 10 per centum of the entire net profits received or accrued for such year from the sale or disposition of the product of such mine, quarry, mill, cannery, workshop, factory, or manufacturing establishment."

Section 1203 relieves from liability to the tax anyone who employs a child, believing him to be of proper age, relying on a certificate to this effect issued by persons prescribed by a board consisting of the Secretary of the Treasury, the Commissioner of Internal Revenue, and the Secretary of Labor, or issued by state authorities. The section also provides in ¶(b) that "the tax imposed by this title shall not be imposed in the case of any person who proves to the satisfaction of the Secretary that the only employment or permission to work which but for this section would subject him to the tax, has been of a child employed or permitted to work under a mistake of fact as to the age of such child and without intention to evade the tax."

Section 1206 gives authority to the Commissioner of Internal Revenue or any other person authorized by him, "to enter and inspect at any time any mine, quarry, mill, cannery, workshop, factory or manufacturing establishment." The Secretary of Labor, or any person whom he authorizes, is given like authority in order to comply with a request of the Commissioner to make such inspection and report the same. Any person who refuses entry or obstructs inspection is made subject to fine or imprisonment or both.

. . . We must construe the law and interpret the intent and meaning of Congress from the language of the act. The words are to be given their ordinary meaning unless the context shows that they are differently used. Does this law impose a tax with only that incidental restraint and regulation which a tax must inevitably involve? Or does it regulate by the use of the so-called tax as a penalty? If a tax, it is clearly an excise. If it were an excise on a commodity or other thing of value we might not be permitted, under previous decisions of this court, to infer, solely from its heavy burden, that the act intends a prohibition instead of a tax. But this act is more. It provides a heavy exaction for a departure from a detailed and specified course of conduct in business. That course of business is that employers shall employ in mines and quarries, children of an age greater than sixteen years; in mills and factories, children of an age greater than fourteen years; and shall prevent children of less than sixteen years in mills and factories from working more than eight hours a day or six days in the week. If an employer departs from this prescribed course of business, he is to pay to the government one tenth of his entire net income in the business for a full year. The amount is not to be proportioned in any degree to the extent or frequency of the departures, but is to be paid by the employer in full measure whether he employs five hundred children for a year, or employs only one for a day. Moreover, if he does not know the child is within the named age limit, he is not to pay; that is to say, it is only where he knowingly departs from the prescribed course that payment is to be exacted. Scienters are associated with penalties, not with taxes. The employer's factory is to be subject to inspection at any time not only by the taxing officers of the Treasury, the Department normally charged with the collection of taxes, but also by the Secretary of Labor and his subordinates, whose normal function is the advancement and protection of the welfare of the workers. In the light of these features of the act, a court must be blind not to see that the so-called tax is imposed to stop the employment of children within the age limits prescribed. Its prohibitory and regulatory effect and purpose are palpable. All others can see and understand this. How can we properly shut our minds to it? . . .

. . . Grant the validity of this law, and all that Congress would need to do hereafter, in seeking to take over to its control any one of the great number of subjects of public interest, jurisdiction of which the states have never parted with, and which are reserved to them by the 10th Amendment, would be to enact a detailed measure of complete regulation of the subject and enforce it by a so-called tax upon departures from it. To give such magic to the word "tax" would be to break down all constitutional limitation of the powers of Congress and completely wipe out the sovereignty of the states. . . .

The case before us cannot be distinguished from that of Hammer v. Dagenhart, 247 U.S. 251. . . .

But it is pressed upon us that this court has gone so far in sustaining taxing measures the effect and tendency of which was to accomplish purposes not directly within congressional power that we are bound by authority to maintain this law.

Section A. Trade, Production, and Employment 239

The first of these is Veazie Bank v. Fenno, 8 Wall. 533. In that case, the validity of a law which increased a tax on the circulating notes of persons and state banks from 1 per centum to 10 per centum was in question. The main question was whether this was a direct tax, to be apportioned among the several states "according to their respective numbers." This was answered in the negative. The second objection was stated by the court:

"It is insisted, however, that the tax in the case before us is excessive, and so excessive as to indicate a purpose on the part of Congress to destroy the franchise of the bank, and is, therefore, beyond the constitutional power of Congress."

To this the court answered:

"The first answer to this is that the judicial cannot prescribe to the legislative departments of the government limitations upon the exercise of its acknowledged powers. The power to tax may be exercised oppressively upon persons, but the responsibility of the legislature is not to the courts, but to the people by whom its members are elected. So if a particular tax bears heavily upon a corporation, or a class of corporations, it cannot, for that reason only, be pronounced contrary to the Constitution."

It will be observed that the sole objection to the tax here was its excessive character. Nothing else appeared on the face of the act. It was an increase of a tax admittedly legal to a higher rate, and that was all. There were no elaborate specifications on the face of the act, as here, indicating the purpose to regulate matters of state concern and jurisdiction through an exaction so applied as to give it the qualities of a penalty for violation of law rather than a tax. . . .

But more than this, what was charged to be the object of the excessive tax was within the congressional authority, as appears from the second answer which the court gave to the objection. After having pointed out the legitimate means taken by Congress to secure a national medium or currency, the court said (p. 549):

"Having thus, in the exercise of undisputed constitutional powers, undertaken to provide a currency for the whole country, it cannot be questioned that Congress may, constitutionally, secure the benefit of it to the people by appropriate legislation. . . ."

The next case is that of McCray v. United States, 195 U.S. 27. That, like the Veazie Bank Case, was the increase of an excise tax upon a subject properly taxable, in which the taxpayers claimed that the tax had become invalid because the increase was excessive. It was a tax on oleomargarine, a substitute for butter. The tax on the white oleomargarine was one quarter of a cent a pound, and on the yellow oleomargarine was first 2 cents and was then by the act in question increased to 10 cents per pound. This court held that the discretion of Congress in the exercise of its constitutional powers to levy excise taxes could not be controlled or limited by the courts because the latter might deem the incidence of the tax oppressive or even destructive. . . . In neither of these cases did the law objected to show on its face, as does the law before us, the detailed specifications of a regulation of a state concern and business with a heavy exaction to promote the efficacy of such regulation.

The third case is that of Flint v. Stone Tracy Co., 220 U.S. 107. It involved the validity of an excise tax levied on the doing of business by all corporations, joint stock companies, associations organized for profit having a capital stock represented by shares, and insurance companies, and measured the excise by the net income of the corporations. There was not in that case the slightest doubt that the tax was a tax, and a tax for revenue; but it was attacked on the ground that such a tax could be made excessive, and thus used by Congress to destroy the existence of state corporations. To this, this court gave the same answer as in the Veazie Bank and McCray Cases. It is not so strong an authority for the government's contention as they are.

The fourth case is United States v. Doremus, 249 U.S. 86. That involved the validity of the Narcotic Drug Act (December 17, 1914, 38 Stat. at L. 785), which imposed a special tax on the manufacture, importation, and sale or gift of opium or coca leaves or their compounds or derivatives. It required every person subject to the special tax to register with the collector of internal revenue his name and place of business, and forbade him to sell except upon the written order of the person to whom the sale was made, on a form prescribed by the Commissioner of Internal Revenue. The vendor was required to keep the order for two years, and the purchaser to keep a duplicate for the same time, and all were to be subject to official inspection. Similar requirements were made as to sales upon prescriptions of a physician, and as to the dispensing of such drugs directly to a patient by a physician. The validity of a special tax in the nature of an excise tax on the manufacture, importation, and sale of such drugs was, of course, unquestioned. The provisions for subjecting the sale and distribution of the drugs to official supervision and inspection were held to have a reasonable relation to the enforcement of the tax, and were therefore held valid.

The court said that the act could not be declared invalid just because another motive than taxation, not shown on the face of the act, might have contributed to its passage. This case does not militate against the conclusion we have reached in respect to the law before us. The court, there, made manifest its view that the provisions of the so-called taxing act must be naturally and reasonably adapted to the collection of the tax, and not solely to the achievement of some other purpose plainly within state power.

For the reasons given, we must hold the Child Labor Tax Law invalid, and the judgment of the District Court is affirmed.[b]

MR. JUSTICE CLARKE dissents.

NOTE Motives in Tax Legislation

1. For an Australian predecessor of the Child Labor Tax Case, see King v. Barger, 6 C.L.R. 41 (1908) (Isaacs and Higgins, JJ., dissenting).

2. On "motives" in federal tax legislation, compare the following cases:

Veazie Bank v. Fenno, 8 Wheat. 533 (1869). An act of 1866 imposed a tax of 10 percent on the amount of any notes of state banks paid out for circulation. The tax was sustained.

McCray v. United States, 195 U.S. 27 (1904). The Oleomargarine Tax Act imposed a tax of one quarter of a cent per pound on the manufacture and sale of oleomargarine not artificially colored to resemble yellow butter, and a tax of 10 cents per pound in respect of oleomargarine so colored. The tax was sustained.

United States v. Constantine, 296 U.S. 287 (1935). The Revenue Act of 1926 imposed, in addition to a $25 excise tax on retail liquor dealers, a special excise tax of $1000 on such dealers when they carry on the business contrary to state or municipal law. After the repeal of the Eighteenth Amendment the special excise was held unconstitutional. Mr. Justice Cardozo, joined by Justices Brandeis and Stone, dissented, insisting that no inquiry into motives should have been made, and stating (p. 299): "Thus the process of psychoanalysis has spread to unaccustomed fields."

Sonzinsky v. United States, 300 U.S. 506 (1937). The Firearms Act of 1934 imposed an excise tax of $200 on dealers in "firearms," defined to mean sawed-off shotguns, machine guns, and mufflers and silencers for these. The tax was sustained.

United States v. Sanchez, 340 U.S. 42 (1950). The Marihuana Tax Act embodies a plan of taxation described as follows (p. 43): "In enacting the Marihuana Tax Act, the Congress had two objectives: 'First, the development of a plan of taxation which will raise revenue and at the same time render extremely difficult the acquisition of marihuana by persons who desire it for illicit uses and, second, the development of an adequate means of publicizing dealings in marihuana in order to tax and control the traffic effectively.' S.

---

[b] For internal evidence that at one stage the Court may have been prepared to sustain the child labor tax, see Bickel, The Unpublished Opinions of Mr. Justice Brandeis, c. 1 (1957). — ED.

Rep. No. 900, 75th Cong., 1st Sess. 3. To the same effect, see H.R. Rep. No. 792, 75th Cong., 1st Sess. 2.

"Pursuant to these objectives, §3230 of the Code imposes a special tax ranging from $1 to $24 on 'every person who imports, manufactures, produces, compounds, sells, deals in, dispenses, prescribes, administers, or gives away marihuana.' For purposes of administration, §3231 requires such persons to register at the time of the payment of the tax with the Collector of the District in which their businesses are located. The Code then makes it unlawful — with certain exceptions not pertinent here — for any person to transfer marihuana except in pursuance of a written order of the transferee on a blank form issued by the Secretary of the Treasury, §2591. Section 2590 requires the transferee at the time he applies for the order form to pay a tax on such transfer of $1 per ounce or fraction thereof if he has paid the special tax and registered, §2590(a)(1), or $100 per ounce or fraction thereof if he has not paid the special tax and registered. §2590(a)(2). The transferor is also made liable for the tax so imposed, in the event the transfer is made without an order form and without the payment of the tax by the transferee. §2590(b). Defendants in this case are transferors."

The tax was sustained. Cf. also United States v. Doremus, 249 U.S. 86 (1919), and Nigro v. United States, 276 U.S. 332 (1928) (taxes on narcotics).

United States v. Kahriger, 345 U.S. 22 (1953). The Internal Revenue Code imposes a 10 percent tax on wagers payable to persons engaged in the business of accepting such wagers, and exempts wagers placed with a pari-mutuel enterprise licensed under state law. The tax was sustained.

Kahriger was pro tanto overruled in Marchetti v. United States, 390 U.S. 39 (1968), and Grosso v. United States, 390 U.S. 62 (1968). There, the Court reversed convictions for failure to register and to pay occupational and excise taxes under the gambling provisions of the Internal Revenue Code, 26 U.S.C. §§4401 et seq., on the ground that the requirements of the statute violated the Fifth Amendment privilege against self-incrimination.

3. In Hill v. Wallace, 259 U.S. 44 (1922), decided the same day as the Child Labor Tax Case, the Court held invalid the Future Trading Act of 1921, imposing a tax of 20 cents per bushel on sales of grain for future delivery, except sales on boards of trade designated as contract markets by the Secretary of Agriculture on fulfillment by such boards of certain conditions and requirements set forth in the act. Thereafter Congress enacted the Grain Futures Act of 1922, placing grain boards of trade under federal regulation; the act contained recitals, based on legislative hearings, concerning the effect of speculation and manipulation on prices of, and interstate commerce in, grain and by-products. The act, as applied to the Chicago Board of Trade, was sustained in Chicago Board of Trade v. Olsen, 262 U.S. 1 (1923).

4. For a converse shift, from a regulation of commerce held invalid to a taxing measure held valid, compare Railroad Retirement Bd. v. Alton R.R., 295 U.S. 330 (1935), with California v. Anglim, 129 F.2d 455 (9th Cir. 1942), cert. denied, 317 U.S. 669 (1942). The former case held the Railroad Retirement Act unconstitutional on the ground that compulsory retirement pensions for railroad employees had no sufficient relation to economy or efficiency of the transportation system. Chief Justice Hughes, joined by Justices Brandeis, Stone, and Cardozo, dissented, stating, inter alia (pp. 381-382): "The power of Congress to pass a compensation act to govern interstate carriers and their employees engaged in interstate commerce does not seem to be questioned. . . . A thorough examination of the question of constitutional authority to adopt such a compulsory measure was made some years ago by a commission constituted under a Joint Resolution of Congress of which Senator Sutherland (now Mr. Justice Sutherland) was chairman. 36 Stat. 884. Its elaborate and unanimous report, transmitted to Congress by President Taft with his complete approval, considered the constitutional question in all aspects, upheld the congressional power, and proposed its exercise. Sen. Doc. No. 338, 62d Cong. 2d

sess. . . . The effort to dispose of the analogy serves only to make it the more impressive." See Powell, Commerce, Pensions, and Codes, 49 Harv. L. Rev. 1, 193 (1935). The Carriers' Taxing Act, sustained in the Anglim case, supra, imposed a tax on carriers; a separate statute authorized appropriations from the general funds in the Treasury for retirement benefits for railroad employees.

5. On the relevance of legislative motive generally, see Ely, Legislative and Administrative Motivation in Constitutional Law, 79 Yale L.J. 1205 (1970); Brest, Palmer v. Thompson: An Approach to the Problem of Unconstitutional Legislative Motive, 1971 S. Ct. Rev. 95. See pages 872, 901-902 infra on the relevance of "motive" in racial discrimination under the equal protection clause.

SCHECHTER POULTRY CORP. v. UNITED STATES, 295 U.S. 495, 55 S. Ct. 837, 79 L. Ed. 1570 (1935). The defendants were convicted for violations of the Live Poultry Code, promulgated by the President under the National Industrial Recovery Act of 1933. They were engaged in the business of slaughtering and wholesale distribution of poultry in New York City, buying the poultry from commission men at a market or at railroad terminals and selling, usually within twenty-four hours, to dealers who resold to consumers. Ninety-six percent of the live poultry marketed in New York City comes from other states. The provisions of the Code in question fixed maximum hours and minimum wages for employees, and established certain trade practices, in particular a requirement for "straight killings" requiring slaughterers to accept the "run of any coop" as purchased. The court of appeals sustained the convictions for violation of the "straight killing" provisions but reversed on the counts involving wages and hours. The defendants and the government petitioned for certiorari, which was granted on April 15, 1935. The act was to expire, unless renewed, on June 16, 1935.

The Supreme Court reversed the convictions on all counts, holding the act invalid both for excessive delegation of power to the President and for exceeding, as applied, the power under the Commerce Clause. Chief Justice Hughes, for the Court, distinguished cases under the antitrust acts on the basis of "direct and indirect effects" on interstate commerce. The antitrust acts had been successfully applied to the same enterprise — wholesale slaughterers of live poultry in New York — in Local 167 v. United States, 291 U.S. 293 (1934), involving a conspiracy among marketmen, teamsters, and slaughterers to increase prices, accompanied by boycotts and intimidation of recalcitrant members of these groups.

NOTE

On the same day that the Schechter case was decided, May 27, 1935, the Court announced two other unanimous decisions which caused the day to become known in Administration circles as Black Monday. See Jackson, The Struggle for Judicial Supremacy 106 (1941). Humphrey's Executor v. United States, 295 U.S. 602, held that the President was without power under the Federal Trade Commission Act to remove a commissioner on the ground that his views were uncongenial to the President. Louisville Joint Stock Land Bank v. Radford, 295 U.S. 555, held that the Frazier-Lemke Act, in its provisions for the relief of debtor farmers under the bankruptcy law, was repugnant to the Fifth Amendment.

Following the Schechter case, proposals for constitutional amendment were discussed. One such proposal, which had been introduced by Senator Costigan, provided:

"Section 1: The Congress shall have power to regulate hours and conditions of labor and to establish minimum wages in any employment and to regulate production, industry, business, trade and commerce to prevent unfair methods and practices therein.

"Section 2: The Due-process-of-law clauses of the Fifth and Fourteenth Amendments shall be construed to impose no limitation upon legislation by the Congress or by the several States with respect to any of the subjects referred to in Section 1, except as to the methods or procedure for the enforcement of such legislation.

"Section 3: Nothing in this article shall be construed to impair the regulatory power of the several States with respect to any of the subjects referred to in Section 1, except to the extent that the exercise of such powers by a State is in conflict with legislation enacted by the Congress pursuant to this article." 79 Cong. Rec. 104 (1935); see New York Times, May 30, 1935, p. 11. Other proposals were directed to procedures: that Congress might by two-thirds vote overcome an adverse decision on the validity of an Act of Congress; and that more than a simple majority of the Court be required to hold a law unconstitutional.

An intimate account of the constitutional litigation of this period is given in Stern, The Commerce Clause and the National Economy, 1933-1946, 59 Harv. L. Rev. 645, 883 (1946), and in Jackson, The Struggle for Judicial Supremacy (1941).

Carter v. Carter Coal Co. 298 U.S. 238, 56 S. Ct. 855, 80 L. Ed. 1160 (1936)

[A stockholder's suit was brought by Carter against the company of which he was president, to enjoin it from accepting a code formulated under the Bituminous Coal Conservation Act of 1935, and from paying the tax imposed by the act. The collector of internal revenue was joined as a defendant.

The act imposed an excise tax on the sale or other disposal of bituminous coal, in the amount of 15 percent of the sale price at the mine, or of the fair market value in the case of captive coal. But a drawback or credit of 90 percent of the tax was authorized in respect of producers who accepted a code to be formulated by the Bituminous Coal Commission, with the aid of district boards. The code was to establish (a) minimum prices for various mines and areas; (b) maximum hours of labor, whenever such maximum hours were agreed upon by producers of two-thirds the national tonnage and representatives of more than half the mine workers; (c) minimum wages for members in a given district, whenever such minimum wages were agreed upon by producers of two-thirds of the tonnage in that district and representatives of a majority of the workers in that district.

The suit was brought in the District Court for the District of Columbia on August 31, 1935, the day following the approval of the act by the President. Extensive testimony and exhibits were introduced on the effects of price-cutting and wage-cutting in the industry. (Sixty-seven pages of the government's brief in the Supreme Court were devoted to a presentation of this material, together with data drawn from congressional investigations of the industry extending over twenty years.) The district court on December 10, 1935, dismissed the bill, with findings based on the government's evidence. Appeal was taken on December 10 to the court of appeals, and petition for certiorari (joined in by the government) was filed in the Supreme Court and granted on December 23.]

MR. JUSTICE SUTHERLAND delivered the opinion of the Court. . . .

The questions involved will be considered under the following heads:

1. The right of stockholders to maintain suits of this character.
2. Whether the suits were prematurely brought.
3. Whether the exaction of 15 per centum on the sale price of coal at the mine is a tax or a penalty.
4. The purposes of the act as set forth in §1, and the authority vested in Congress by the Constitution to effectuate them.
5. Whether the labor provisions of the act can be upheld as an exercise of the power to regulate interstate commerce.
6. Whether subdivision (g) of Part III. of the Code, is an unlawful delegation of power.
7. The constitutionality of the price-fixing provisions, and the question of severabil-

ity — that is to say, whether, if either the group of labor provisions or the group of price-fixing provisions be found constitutionally invalid, the other can stand as separable.

First. . . .

Without repeating the long averments of the several bills, we are of opinion that the suits were properly brought and were maintainable in a court of equity. The right of stockholders to bring such suits under the circumstances disclosed is settled by the recent decision of this court in Ashwander v. Tennessee Valley Authority, 297 U.S. 288, and requires no further discussion.

Second. That the suits were not prematurely brought also is clear. Section 2 of the act is mandatory in its requirement that the commission be appointed by the President. The provisions of §4 that the code be formulated and promulgated are equally mandatory. The so-called tax of 15% is definitely imposed, and its exaction certain to ensue. [The Court discussed several precedents, including Pierce v. Society of Sisters, 268 U.S. 510.]

Third. The so-called excise tax of 15 per centum on the sale price of coal at the mine, or, in the case of captive coal the fair market value, with its drawback allowance of 13½%, is clearly not a tax but a penalty. The exaction applies to all bituminous coal produced, whether it be sold, transported or consumed in interstate commerce, or transactions in respect of it be confined wholly to the limits of the state. It also applies to "captive coal" — that is to say, coal produced for the sole use of the producer.

It is very clear that the "excise tax" is not imposed for revenue but exacted as a penalty to compel compliance with the regulatory provisions of the act. The whole purpose of the exaction is to coerce what is called an agreement — which, of course, it is not, for it lacks the essential element of consent. One who does a thing in order to avoid a monetary penalty does not agree; he yields to compulsion precisely the same as though he did so to avoid a term in jail.

. . . That the "tax" is in fact a penalty is not seriously in dispute. The position of the government, as we understand it, is that the validity of the exaction does not rest upon the taxing power but upon the power of Congress to regulate interstate commerce; and that if the act in respect of the labor and price-fixing provisions be not upheld, the "tax" must fall with them. With that position we agree and confine our consideration accordingly.

Fourth. Certain recitals contained in the act plainly suggest that its makers were of opinion that its constitutionality could be sustained under some general federal power, thought to exist, apart from the specific grants of the Constitution. The fallacy of that view will be apparent when we recall fundamental principles which, although hitherto often expressed in varying forms of words, will bear repetition whenever their accuracy seems to be challenged. The recitals to which we refer are contained in §1 (which is simply a preamble to the act), and, among others, are to the effect that the distribution of bituminous coal is of national interest, affecting the health and comfort of the people and the general welfare of the nation; that this circumstance, together with the necessity of maintaining just and rational relations between the public, owners, producers, and employees, and the right of the public to constant and adequate supplies at reasonable prices, require regulation of the industry as the act provides. The affirmations — and the further ones that the production and distribution of such coal "directly affect interstate commerce," because of which and of the waste of the national coal resources and other circumstances, the regulation is necessary for the protection of such commerce — do not constitute an exertion of the *will* of Congress which is legislation, but a recital of considerations which in the *opinion* of that body existed and justified the expression of its will in the present act. Nevertheless, this preamble may not be disregarded. On the contrary it is important, because it makes clear, except for the pure assumption that the conditions described "directly" affect interstate commerce, that the powers which Congress undertook to exercise are not specific but of the most general character — namely, to protect the general public interest and the health and comfort of the people, to conserve privately-owned coal, maintain just relations between producers and employees and others, and promote the general welfare,

Section A. Trade, Production, and Employment

by controlling nation-wide production and distribution of coal. These, it may be conceded, are objects of great worth; but are they ends, the attainment of which has been committed by the Constitution to the federal government? This is a vital question; for nothing is more certain than that beneficent aims, however great or well directed, can never serve in lieu of constitutional power. . . .

The proposition, often advanced and as often discredited, that the power of the federal government inherently extends to purposes affecting the nation as a whole with which the states severally cannot deal or cannot adequately deal, and the related notion that Congress, entirely apart from those powers delegated by the Constitution, may enact laws to promote the general welfare, have never been accepted but always definitely rejected by this court. . . . In the Framers' Convention, the proposal to confer a general power akin to that just discussed was included in Mr. Randolph's resolutions, the sixth of which, among other things, declared that the National Legislature ought to enjoy the legislative rights vested in Congress by the Confederation, and "moreover to legislate in all cases to which the separate States are incompetent, or in which the harmony of the United States may be interrupted by the exercise of individual Legislation." The convention, however, declined to confer upon Congress power in such general terms; instead of which it carefully limited the powers which it thought wise to entrust to Congress by specifying them, thereby denying all others not granted expressly or by necessary implication. . . .

There are many subjects in respect of which the several states have not legislated in harmony with one another, and in which their varying laws and the failure of some of them to act at all have resulted in injurious confusion and embarrassment. [Citation omitted.] The state laws with respect to marriage and divorce present a case in point; and the great necessity of national legislation on that subject has been from time to time vigorously urged. Other pertinent examples are laws with respect to negotiable instruments, desertion and non-support, certain phases of state taxation, and others which we do not pause to mention. In many of these fields of legislation, the necessity of bringing the applicable rules of law into general harmonious relation has been so great that a Commission on Uniform State Laws, composed of commissioners from every state in the Union, has for many years been industriously and successfully working to that end by preparing and securing the passage by the several states of uniform laws. If there be an easier and constitutional way to these desirable results through congressional action, it thus far has escaped discovery. . . .

We have set forth, perhaps at unnecessary length [four pages omitted], the foregoing principles because it seemed necessary to do so in order to demonstrate that the general purposes which the act recites, and which, therefore, unless the recitals be disregarded, Congress undertook to achieve, are beyond the power of Congress except so far, and only so far, as they may be realized by an exercise of some specific power granted by the Constitution. Proceeding by a process of elimination, which it is not necessary to follow in detail, we shall find no grant of power which authorizes Congress to legislate in respect of these general purposes unless it be found in the commerce clause — and this we now consider.

Fifth. Since the validity of the act depends upon whether it is a regulation of interstate commerce, the nature and extent of the power conferred upon Congress by the commerce clause becomes the determinative question in this branch of the case. . . .

Chief Justice Fuller, speaking for this court in United States v. E. C. Knight Co., 156 U.S. 1, 12, 13, said:

"Doubtless the power to control the manufacture of a given thing involves in a certain sense the control of its disposition, but this is a secondary and not the primary sense; and although the exercise of that power may result in bringing the operation of commerce into play, it does not control it, and affects it only incidentally and indirectly. Commerce succeeds to manufacture, and is not a part of it. . . ."

. . . The employment of men, the fixing of their wages, hours of labor and working conditions, the bargaining in respect of these things — whether carried on separately or collectively — each and all constitute intercourse for the purposes of production, not of trade. The latter is a thing apart from the relation of employer and employee, which in all producing occupations is purely local in character. Extraction of coal from the mine is the aim and the completed result of local activities. Commerce in the coal mined is not brought into being by force of these activities, but by negotiations, agreements, and circumstances entirely apart from production. Mining brings the subject matter of commerce into existence. Commerce disposes of it.

A consideration of the foregoing, and of many cases which might be added to those already cited, renders inescapable the conclusion that the effect of the labor provisions of the act, including those in respect of minimum wages, wage agreements, collective bargaining, and the Labor Board and its powers, primarily falls upon production and not upon commerce; and confirms the further resulting conclusion that production is a purely local activity. It follows that none of these essential antecedents of production constitutes a transaction in or forms any part of interstate commerce. . . .

Certain decisions of this court, superficially considered, seem to lend support to the defense of the act now under review. But upon examination, they will be seen to be inapposite. Thus, Coronado Coal Co. v. United Mine Workers, 268 U.S. 295, 310, and kindred cases, involved conspiracies to restrain interstate commerce in violation of the Anti-trust laws. The acts of the persons involved were local in character; but the intent was to restrain interstate commerce, and the means employed were calculated to carry that intent into effect. Interstate commerce was the direct object of attack; and the restraint of such commerce was the necessary consequence of the acts and the immediate end in view. Bedford Cut Stone Co. v. Journeymen Stone Cutters' Assn., 274 U.S. 37, 46. The applicable law was concerned not with the character of the acts or of the means employed, which might be in and of themselves purely local, but with the intent and direct operation of those acts and means upon interstate commerce. "The mere reduction in the supply of an article," this court said in the Coronado Coal Co. Case, supra (268 U.S. 310), "to be shipped in interstate commerce by the illegal or tortious prevention of its manufacture or production is ordinarily an indirect and remote obstruction to that commerce. But when the intent of those unlawfully preventing the manufacture or production is shown to be to restrain or control the supply entering and moving in interstate commerce, or the price of it in interstate markets, their action is a direct violation of the Anti-Trust Act."

Another group of cases, of which Swift & Co. v. United States, 196 U.S. 375, is an example, rest upon the circumstances that the acts in question constituted direct interferences with the "flow" of commerce among the states. In the Swift & Co. Case, livestock was consigned and delivered to stockyards — not as a place of final destination, but, as the court said in Stafford v. Wallace, 258 U.S. 495, 516, "a throat through which the current flows." The sales which ensued merely changed the private interest in the subject of the current without interfering with its continuity. Industrial Assn. v. United States, 268 U.S. 64, 79. It was nowhere suggested in these cases that the interstate commerce power extended to the growth or production of the things which, after production, entered the flow. If the court had held that the raising of the cattle, which were involved in the Swift & Co. Case, including the wages paid to and working conditions of the herders and others employed in the business, could be regulated by Congress, that decision and decisions holding similarly would be in point; for it is that situation, and not the one with which the court actually dealt, which here concerns us. . . .

But § 1 (the preamble) of the act now under review declares that all production and distribution of bituminous coal "bear upon and directly affect its interstate commerce;" and that regulation thereof is imperative for the protection of such commerce. The contention of the government is that the labor provisions of the act may be sustained in that view.

That the production of every commodity intended for interstate sale and transportation has some effect upon interstate commerce may be, if it has not already been, freely granted; and we are brought to the final and decisive inquiry, whether here that effect is

Section A. Trade, Production, and Employment

direct, as the "preamble" recites, or indirect. The distinction is not formal, but substantial in the highest degree, as we pointed out in the Schechter Case [295 U.S. 495], pp. 546 et seq. . . .

Whether the effect of a given activity or condition is direct or indirect is not always easy to determine. The word "direct" implies that the activity or condition invoked or blamed shall operate proximately — not mediately, remotely, or collaterally — to produce the effect. It connotes the absence of an efficient intervening agency or condition. And the extent of the effect bears no logical relation to its character. The distinction between a direct and an indirect effect turns, not upon the magnitude of either the cause or the effect, but entirely upon the manner in which the effect has been brought about. If the production by one man of a single ton of coal intended for interstate sale and shipment, and actually so sold and shipped, affects interstate commerce indirectly, the effect does not become direct by multiplying the tonnage, or increasing the number of men employed, or adding to the expense or complexities of the business, or by all combined. It is quite true that rules of law are sometimes qualified by considerations of degree, as the government argues. But the matter of degree has no bearing upon the question here, since that question is not — What is the *extent* of the local activity or condition, or the *extent* of the effect produced upon interstate commerce? but — What is the *relation* between the activity or condition and the effect?

Much stress is put upon the evils which come from the struggle between employers and employees over the matter of wages, working conditions, the right of collective bargaining, etc., and the resulting strikes, curtailment and irregularity of production and effect on prices; and it is insisted that interstate commerce is *greatly* affected thereby. But, in addition to what has just been said, the conclusive answer is that the evils are all local evils over which the federal government has no legislative control. The relation of employer and employee is a local relation. At common law, it is one of the domestic relations. The wages are paid for the doing of local work. Working conditions are obviously local conditions. The employees are not engaged in or about commerce, but exclusively in producing a commodity. And the controversies and evils, which it is the object of the act to regulate and minimize, are local controversies and evils affecting local work undertaken to accomplish that local result. Such effect as they may have upon commerce, however extensive it may be, is secondary and indirect. An increase in the greatness of the effect adds to its importance. It does not alter its character. . . .

Sixth. That the act, whatever it may be in form, in fact is compulsory clearly appears. We have already discussed §3, which imposes the excise tax as a penalty to compel "acceptance" of the code. Section 14 provides that the United States shall purchase no bituminous coal produced at any mine where the producer has not complied with the provisions of the code; and that each contract made by the United States shall contain a provision that the contractor will buy no bituminous coal to use on, or in the carrying out of, such contract unless the producer be a member of the code, as certified by the coal commission. In the light of these provisions we come to a consideration of subdivision (g) of Part III. of §4, dealing with "Labor Relations."

That subdivision delegates the power to fix maximum hours of labor to a part of the producers and the miners — namely, "the producers of more than two-thirds of the annual national tonnage production for the preceding calendar year" and "more than one-half of the mine workers employed;" and to producers of more than two-thirds of the district annual tonnage during the preceding calendar year and a majority of the miners, there is delegated the power to fix minimum wages for the district or group of districts. The effect, in respect of wages and hours, is to subject the dissentient minority, either of producers or miners or both, to the will of the stated majority, since, by refusing to submit, the minority at once incurs the hazard of enforcement of the drastic compulsory provisions of the act to which we have referred. To "accept," in these circumstances, is not to exercise a choice, but to surrender to force.

The power conferred upon the majority is, in effect, the power to regulate the affairs of an unwilling minority. This is legislative delegation in its most obnoxious form; for it is not even delegation to an official or an official body, presumptively disinterested, but to private persons whose interests may be and often are adverse to the interests of others in the same business. . . . Some coal producers favor the code; others oppose it; and the record clearly indicates that this diversity of view arises from their conflicting and even antagonistic interests. The difference between producing coal and regulating its production is, of course, fundamental. The former is a private activity; the latter is necessarily a governmental function, since, in the very nature of things, one person may not be entrusted with the power to regulate the business of another, and especially of a competitor. And a statute which attempts to confer such power undertakes an intolerable and unconstitutional interference with personal liberty and private property. The delegation is so clearly arbitrary, and so clearly a denial of rights safeguarded by the due process clause of the Fifth Amendment, that it is unnecessary to do more than refer to decisions of this court which foreclose the question. A. L. A. Schechter Poultry Corp. v. United States, 295 U.S. at p. 537; Eubank v. Richmond, 226 U.S. 137, 143; Washington ex rel. Seattle Title Trust Co. v. Roberge, 278 U.S. 116, 121, 122.

Seventh. Finally, we are brought to the price-fixing provisions of the code. The necessity of considering the question of their constitutionality will depend upon whether they are separable from the labor provisions so that they can stand independently. Section 15 of the act provides:

"If any provision of this Act, or the application thereof to any person or circumstances, is held invalid, the remainder of the Act and the application of such provisions to other persons or circumstances shall not be affected thereby."

In the absence of such a provision, the presumption is that the legislature intends an act to be effective as an entirety — that is to say, the rule is against the mutilation of a statute; and if any provision be unconstitutional, the presumption is that the remaining provisions fall with it. The effect of the statute is to reverse this presumption in favor of inseparability, and create the opposite one of separability. . . . But under either rule, the determination, in the end, is reached by applying the same test — namely, What was the intent of the lawmakers?

Under the statutory rule, the presumption must be overcome by considerations which establish "the clear probability that the invalid part being eliminated the legislature would not have been satisfied with what remains," Williams v. Standard Oil Co., 278 U.S. 235, 241 et seq.; or, as stated in Utah Power & L. Co. v. Pfost, 286 U.S. 165, 184, 185, "the clear probability that the legislature would not have been satisfied with the statute unless it had included the invalid part." . . . The presumption in favor of separability does not authorize the court to give the statute "an effect altogether different from that sought by the measure viewed as a whole." Railroad Retirement Bd. v. Alton R. Co., 295 U.S. 330, 362.

. . . Perhaps a fair approach to a solution of the problem is to suppose that while the bill was pending in Congress a motion to strike out the labor provisions had prevailed, and to inquire whether, in that event, the statutes should be so construed as to justify the conclusion that Congress, notwithstanding, probably would not have passed the price-fixing provisions of the code. . . .

. . . The interdependence of wages and prices is manifest. Approximately two-thirds of the cost of producing a ton of coal is represented by wages. Fair prices necessarily depend upon the cost of production; and since wages constitute so large a proportion of the cost, prices cannot be fixed with any proper relation to cost without taking into consideration this major element. If one of them becomes uncertain, uncertainty with respect to the other necessarily ensues. . . .

. . . The conclusion is unavoidable that the price-fixing provisions of the code are so related to and dependent upon the labor provisions as conditions, considerations or compensations, as to make it clearly probable that the latter being held bad, the former would not have been passed. The fall of the latter therefore, carries down with it the former. [Citations omitted.]

The price-fixing provisions of the code are thus disposed of without coming to the question of their constitutionality; but neither this disposition of the matter, nor anything we have said, is to be taken as indicating that the court is of opinion that these provisions, if separately enacted, could be sustained. . . .

Separate opinion of Mr. Justice Hughes.

I agree that the stockholders were entitled to bring their suits; that, in view of the question whether any part of the Act could be sustained, the suits were not premature; that the so-called tax is not a real tax, but a penalty; that the constitutional power of the Federal Government to impose this penalty must rest upon the commerce clause, as the Government concedes; that production — in this case mining — which precedes commerce, is not itself commerce; and that the power to regulate commerce among the several States is not a power to regulate industry within the State. . . .

I also agree that subdivision (g) of Part III. of the prescribed Code is invalid upon three counts: (1) It attempts a broad delegation of legislative power to fix hours and wages without standards or limitation. The Government invokes the analogy of legislation which becomes effective on the happening of a specified event, and says that in this case the event is the agreement of a certain proportion of producers and employees, whereupon the other producers and employees become subject to legal obligations accordingly. I think that the argument is unsound and is pressed to the point where the principle would be entirely destroyed. It would remove all restrictions upon the delegation of legislative power, as the making of laws could thus be referred to any designated officials or private persons whose orders or agreements would be treated as "events," with the result that they would be invested with the force of law having penal sanctions. (2) The provision permits a group of producers and employees, according to their own views of expediency, to make rules as to hours and wages for other producers and employees who were not parties to the agreement. Such a provision, apart from the mere question of the delegation of legislative power, is not in accord with the requirement of due process of law which under the Fifth Amendment dominates the regulations which Congress may impose. (3) The provision goes beyond any proper measure of protection of interstate commerce and attempts a broad regulation of industry within the State.

But that is not the whole case. The Act also provides for the regulation of the prices of bituminous coal sold in interstate commerce and prohibits unfair methods of competition in interstate commerce. Undoubtedly transactions in carrying on interstate commerce are subject to the federal power to regulate that commerce and the control of charges and the protection of fair competition in that commerce are familiar illustrations of the exercise of the power, as the Interstate Commerce Act, the Packers and Stockyards Act, and the Anti-Trust Acts abundantly show. The Court has repeatedly stated that the power to regulate interstate commerce among the several States is supreme and plenary. Minnesota Rate Cases (Simpson v. Shepard), 230 U.S. 352, 398. It is "complete in itself, and may be exercised to its utmost extent, and acknowledges no limitations other than are prescribed in the Constitution." Gibbons v. Ogden, 9 Wheat. 1, 196. We are not at liberty to deny to the Congress, with respect to interstate commerce, a power commensurate with that enjoyed by the States in the regulation of their internal commerce. See Nebbia v. New York, 291 U.S. 502. . . .

In the legislation before us, Congress has set up elaborate machinery for the fixing of prices of bituminous coal sold in interstate commerce. That provision is attacked in limine. Prices have not yet been fixed. If fixed, they may not be contested. If contested, the Act provides for review of the administrative ruling. If in fixing prices, due process is violated by arbitrary, capricious or confiscatory action, judicial remedy is available. If an attempt is made to fix prices for sales in intrastate commerce, that attempt will also be subject to attack by appropriate action. In that relation it should be noted that in the Carter cases, the court below found that substantially all the coal mined by the Carter Coal Company is sold f.o.b. mines and is transported into States other than those in which it is produced for the purpose of filling orders obtained from purchasers in such States. Such transactions are in interstate commerce. Savage v. Jones, 225 U.S. 501, 520. The court below also found that "the interstate distribution and sale and the intrastate distribution and sale" of the coal are so "intimately and inextricably connected" that "the regulation of interstate transactions of distribution and sale cannot be accomplished effectively without discrimination against interstate commerce unless transactions of intrastate distribution and sale be regulated." Substantially the same situation is disclosed in the Kentucky cases. In that relation, the Government invokes the analogy of transportation rates. Shreveport Case (Houston, E. & W.T.R. Co. v. United States), 234 U.S. 342; Railroad Commission v. Chicago, B. & Q.R. Co., 257 U.S. 563. The question will be the subject of consideration when it arises in any particular application of the Act.

Upon what ground, then, can it be said that this plan for the regulation of transactions in interstate commerce in coal is beyond the constitutional power of Congress? The Court reaches that conclusion in the view that the invalidity of the labor provisions requires us to condemn the Act in its entirety. I am unable to concur in that opinion. I think that the express provisions of the Act preclude such a finding of inseparability. . . .

I do not think that the question of separability should be determined by trying to imagine what Congress would have done if certain provisions found to be invalid were excised. That, if taken broadly, would lead us into a realm of pure speculation. Who can tell amid the host of divisive influences playing upon the legislative body what its reaction would have been to a particular excision required by a finding of invalidity? The question does not call for speculation of that sort but rather for an inquiry whether the provisions are inseparable by virtue of inherent character. That is, when Congress states that the provisions of the Act are not inseparable and that the invalidity of any provision shall not affect others, we should not hold that the provisions are inseparable unless their nature, by reason of an inextricable tie, demands that conclusion.

. . . Thus we are brought, as I have said, to the question whether, despite this purpose of Congress, we must treat the marketing provisions and the labor provisions as inextricably tied together because of their nature. I find no such tie. The labor provisions are themselves separated and placed in a separate part (Part III.) of the Code. It seems quite clear that the validity of the entire Act cannot depend upon the provisions as to hours and wages in paragraph (g) of Part III. For what was contemplated by that paragraph is manifestly independent of the other machinery of the Act, as it cannot become effective unless the specified proportion of producers and employees reach an agreement as to particular wages and hours. And the provision for collective bargaining in paragraphs (a) and (b) of Part III. is apparently made separable from the Code itself by §9 of the Act, providing, in substance, that the employees of all producers shall have the right of collective bargaining even when producers do not accept or maintain the Code.

The marketing provisions (Part II.) of the Code naturally form a separate category. The interdependence of wages and prices is no clearer in the coal business than in transportation. But the broad regulation of rates in order to stabilize transportation conditions has not carried with it the necessity of fixing wages. . . . Congress evidently desired stabilization through both the provisions relating to marketing and those relating to labor, but the setting up of the two sorts of requirements did not make the one dependent upon the validity of the other. It is apparent that they are not so interwoven that they cannot have separate operation and effect. The marketing provisions in relation to interstate commerce can be carried out as provided in Part II. without regard to the labor provisions contained in Part III. That fact, in the light of the congressional declaration of separability, should be considered of controlling importance.

In this view, the Act, and the Code for which it provides, may be sustained in relation

Section A. Trade, Production, and Employment

to the provisions for marketing in interstate commerce, and the decisions of the courts below, so far as they accomplish that result, should be affirmed.

Mr. Justice Cardozo (dissenting in Nos. 636, 649 and 650, and in No. 651 concurring in the result):

My conclusions compendiously stated are these:

(a) Part II. of the statute sets up a valid system of price-fixing as applied to transactions in interstate commerce and to those in intrastate commerce where interstate commerce is directly or intimately affected. The prevailing opinion holds nothing to the contrary.

(b) Part II., with its system of price-fixing, is separable from Part III. which contains the provisions as to labor considered and condemned in the opinion of the court.

(c) Part II. being valid, the complainants are under a duty to come in under the code, and are subject to a penalty if they persist in a refusal.

(d) The suits are premature in so far as they seek a judicial declaration as to the validity or invalidity of the regulations in respect of labor embodied in Part III. No opinion is expressed either directly or by implication as to those aspects of the case. It will be time enough to consider them when there is the threat or even the possibility of imminent enforcement. If that time shall arrive, protection will be given by clear provisions of the statute (§ 3) against any adverse inference flowing from delay or acquiescence.

(e) The suits are not premature to the extent that they are intended to avert a present wrong, though the wrong upon analysis will be found to be unreal. . . .

First: I am satisfied that the Act is within the power of the central government in so far as it provides for minimum and maximum prices upon sales of bituminous coal in the transactions of interstate commerce and in those of intrastate commerce where interstate commerce is directly or intimately affected. . . .

Regulation of prices being an exercise of the commerce power in respect of interstate transactions, the question remains whether it comes within that power as applied to intrastate sales where interstate prices are directly or intimately affected. Mining and agriculture and manufacture are not interstate commerce considered by themselves, yet their relation to that commerce may be such that for the protection of the one there is need to regulate the other. A. L. A. Schechter Poultry Corp. v. United States, 295 U.S. 495, 544-546. Sometimes it is said that the relation must be "direct" to bring that power into play. In many circumstances such a description will be sufficiently precise to meet the needs of the occasion. But a great principle of constitutional law is not susceptible of comprehensive statement in an adjective. The underlying thought is merely this, that "the law is not indifferent to considerations of degree." A. L. A. Schechter Poultry Corp. v. United States, supra, concurring opinion, p. 554. It cannot be indifferent to them without an expansion of the commerce clause that would absorb or imperil the reserved powers of the states. At times, as in the case cited, the waves of causation will have radiated so far that their undulatory motion, if discernible at all, will be too faint or obscure, too broken by cross-currents, to be heeded by the law. In such circumstances the holding is not directed at prices or wages considered in the abstract, but at prices or wages in particular conditions. The relation may be tenuous or the opposite according to the facts. Always the setting of the facts is to be viewed if one would know the closeness of the tie. Perhaps, if one group of adjectives is to be chosen in preference to another, "intimate" and "remote" will be found to be as good as any. At all events, "direct" and "indirect," even if accepted as sufficient, must not be read too narrowly. Cf. Stone, J., in Di Santo v. Pennsylvania, 273 U.S. 34, 44. A survey of the cases shows that the words have been interpreted with suppleness of adaptation and flexibility of meaning. The power is as broad as the need that evokes it. . . .

What has been said in this regard is said with added certitude when complainants' business is considered in the light of the statistics exhibited in the several records. In No. 636, the Carter Case, the complainant has admitted that "substantially all" (over 97½%) of the sales of the Carter Company are made in interstate commerce. In No. 649 the percentages of intrastate sales are, for one of the complaining companies, twenty-five per cent, for another one per cent, and for most of the others two per cent or four. The Carter Company has its mines in West Virginia; the mines of the other companies are located in Kentucky. In each of those states, moreover, coal from other regions is purchased in large quantities, and is thus brought into competition with the coal locally produced. Plainly, it is impossible to say either from the statute itself or from any figures laid before us that interstate sales will not be prejudicially affected in West Virginia and Kentucky if intrastate prices are maintained on a lower level. If it be assumed for present purposes that there are other states or regions where the effect may be different, the complainants are not the champions of any rights except their own. . . .

Second: The next inquiry must be whether Part I. of the statute which creates the administrative agencies, and Part II. which has to do in the main with the price-fixing machinery, as well as preliminary sections levying a tax or penalty, are separable from Part III. which deals with labor relations in the industry, with the result that what is earlier would stand if what is later were to fall. [Mr. Justice Cardozo concluded that the separability clause should be given effect.]

. . . The failure to agree upon a wage scale or upon maximum hours of daily or weekly labor may make the statutory scheme abortive in the very phases and aspects that the court has chosen to condemn. What the code will provide as to wages and hours of labor, or whether it will provide anything, is still in the domain of prophecy. The opinion of the court begins at the wrong end. To adopt a homely form of words, the complainants have been crying before they are really hurt.

My vote is for affirmance.

I am authorized to state that MR. JUSTICE BRANDEIS and MR. JUSTICE STONE join in this opinion.

NOTE

1. Congress in 1937 reenacted in substance the price and marketing provisions of the Bituminous Coal Act, and these were sustained in Sunshine Anthracite Coal Co. v. Adkins, 310 U.S. 381 (1940).

2. On the problem of delegation of power to a portion of an industry, compare the opinion of Mr. Justice Sutherland in Old Dearborn Distributing Co. v. Seagram-Distillers Corp., 299 U.S. 183 (1936), upholding the Illinois Fair Trade Act, which penalizes dealers who knowingly sell trademarked articles below a price stipulated in a contract between the producer and other dealers. See Jaffe, Law Making by Private Groups, 51 Harv. L. Rev. 201 (1937).

3. Prior to the passage of the Coal Act, President Roosevelt sent to the chairman of the House subcommittee considering the bill a letter urging approval, the last sentence of which became celebrated in political discussion. The concluding portion of the letter reads as follows:

"Admitting that mining coal, considered separately and apart from its distribution in the plan of interstate commerce, is an intrastate transaction, the constitutionality of the provisions based on the commerce clause of the Constitution depends upon the final conclusion as to whether production conditions directly affect, promote or obstruct interstate commerce in the commodity.

"Manifestly, no one is in a position to give assurance that the proposed act will withstand constitutional tests, for the simple fact that you can get not ten but a thousand differing legal opinions on the subject. But the situation is so urgent and the benefits of the legislation so evident that all doubts should be resolved in favor of the bill, leaving to the courts, in an orderly fashion, the ultimate question of constitutionality. . . . I hope your committee will not permit doubts as to constitutionality, however reasonable, to block the suggested legislation." 4 Public Papers and Addresses of Franklin D. Roosevelt 297 (1938).

United States v. Butler 297 U.S. 1, 56 S. Ct. 312, 80 L. Ed. 477 (1936)

MR. JUSTICE ROBERTS delivered the opinion of the Court.

In this case we must determine whether certain provisions of the Agricultural Adjustment Act, 1933, conflict with the federal Constitution.

Title I of the statute is captioned "Agricultural Adjustment." Section 1 recites that an economic emergency has arisen, due to disparity between the prices of agricultural and other commodities, with consequent destruction of farmers' purchasing power and breakdown in orderly exchange, which, in turn, have affected transactions in agricultural commodities with a national public interest and burdened and obstructed the normal currents of commerce, calling for the enactment of legislation.

Section 2 declares it to be the policy of Congress:

"To establish and maintain such balance between the production and consumption of agricultural commodities, and such marketing conditions therefor, as will re-establish prices to farmers at a level that will give agricultural commodities a purchasing power with respect to articles that farmers buy, equivalent to the purchasing power of agricultural commodities in the base period."

The base period, in the case of cotton, and all other commodities except tobacco, is designated as that between August, 1909, and July, 1914. . . .

Section 8 provides, amongst other things, that "In order to effectuate the declared policy," the Secretary of Agriculture shall have power

"(1) To provide for reduction in the acreage or reduction in the production for market, or both, of any basic agricultural commodity, through agreements with producers or by other voluntary methods, and to provide for rental or benefit payments in connection therewith or upon that part of the production of any basic agricultural commodity required for domestic consumption, in such amounts as the Secretary deems fair and reasonable, to be paid out of any moneys available for such payments. . . ."

It will be observed that the Secretary is not required, but is permitted, if, in his uncontrolled judgment, the policy of the act will so be promoted, to make agreements with individual farmers for a reduction of acreage or production upon such terms as he may think fair and reasonable.

Section 9(a) enacts:

"To obtain revenue for extraordinary expenses incurred by reason of the national economic emergency, there shall be levied processing taxes as hereinafter provided. When the Secretary of Agriculture determines that rental or benefit payments are to be made with respect to any basic agricultural commodity, he shall proclaim such determination, and a processing tax shall be in effect with respect to such commodity from the beginning of the marketing year therefor next following the date of such proclamation. The processing tax shall be levied, assessed, and collected upon the first domestic processing of the commodity, whether of domestic product or imported, and shall be paid by the processor. . . ."

The Secretary may from time to time, if he finds it necessary for the effectuation of the policy of the act, readjust the amount of the exaction to meet the requirements of subsection (b). The tax is to terminate at the end of any marketing year if the rental or benefit payments are discontinued by the Secretary with the expiration of that year.

Section 9(b) fixes the tax "at such rate as equals the difference between the current average farm price for the commodity and the fair exchange value," with power in the Secretary, after investigation, notice, and hearing, to readjust the tax so as to prevent the accumulation of surplus stocks and depression of farm prices. . . .

Section 12(a) appropriates $100,000,000 "to be available to the Secretary of Agriculture for administrative expenses under this title and for rental and benefit payments . . ."; and § 12(b) appropriates the proceeds derived from all taxes imposed under the act "to be available to the Secretary of Agriculture for expansion of markets and removal of surplus agricultural products . . . administrative expenses, rental and benefit payments, and refunds on taxes.". . .

On July 14, 1933, the Secretary of Agriculture, with the approval of the President, proclaimed that he had determined rental and benefit payments should be made with respect to cotton; that the marketing year for that commodity was to begin August 1, 1933; and calculated and fixed the rates of processing and floor taxes on cotton in accordance with the terms of the act.

The United States presented a claim to the respondents as receivers of the Hoosac Mills Corporation for processing and floor taxes on cotton levied under §§ 9 and 16 of the act. The receivers recommended that the claim be disallowed. The District Court found the taxes valid and ordered them paid. Upon appeal the Circuit Court of Appeals reversed the order. . . .

First. At the outset the United States contends that the respondents have no standing to question the validity of the tax. . . . It is said that what the respondents are endeavoring to do is to challenge the intended use of the money pursuant to Congressional appropriation when, by confession, that money will have become the property of the Government and the taxpayer will no longer have any interest in it. Massachusetts v. Mellon, 262 U.S. 447, is claimed to foreclose litigation by the respondents or other taxpayers, as such, looking to restraint of the expenditure of government funds. That case might be an authority in the petitioners' favor if we were here concerned merely with a suit by a taxpayer to restrain the expenditure of the public moneys. . . . But here the respondents who are called upon to pay moneys as taxes, resist the exaction as a step in an unauthorized plan. This circumstance clearly distinguishes the case. The Government in substance and effect asks us to separate the Agricultural Adjustment Act into two statutes, the one levying an excise on processors of certain commodities, the other appropriating the public moneys independently of the first. Passing the novel suggestion that two statutes enacted as parts of a single scheme should be tested as if they were distinct and unrelated, we think the legislation now before us is not susceptible of such separation and treatment. . . .

The tax plays an indispensable part in the plan of regulation. As stated by the Agricultural Adjustment Administrator, it is "the heart of the law"; a means of "accomplishing one or both of two things intended to help farmers attain parity prices and purchasing power." . . .

It is inaccurate and misleading to speak of the exaction from processors prescribed by the challenged act as a tax, or to say that as a tax it is subject to no infirmity. A tax, in general understanding of the term, and as used in the Constitution, signifies an exaction for the support of the Government. The word has never been thought to connote the expropriation of money from one group for the benefit of another. We may concede that the latter sort of imposition is constitutional when imposed to effectuate regulation of a matter in which both groups are interested and in respect of which there is a power of legislative regulation. But manifestly no justification for it can be found unless as an integral part of such regulation. The exaction cannot be wrested out of its setting, denominated an excise for raising revenue and legalized by ignoring its purpose as a mere instrumentality for bringing about a desired end. To do this would be to shut our eyes to what all others than we can see and understand. Child Labor Tax Case (Bailey v. Drexel Furniture Co.), 259 U.S. 20, 37.

We conclude that the act is one regulating agricultural production; that the tax is a mere incident of such regulation and that the respondents have standing to challenge the legality of the exaction. . . .

Second. The Government asserts that even if the respondents may question the propriety of the appropriation embodied in the statute their attack must fail because Article 1, § 8 of the Constitution authorizes the contemplated expenditure of the funds raised by the tax. This contention presents the great and the controlling question in the case. We approach its decision with a sense of our grave responsibility to render judgment in accordance with the principles established for the governance of all three branches of the Government.

There should be no misunderstanding as to the function of this court in such a case. It is sometimes said that the court assumes a power to overrule or control the action of the people's representatives. This is a misconception. . . . When an act of Congress is appropriately challenged in the courts as not conforming to the constitutional mandate the judicial branch of the Government has only one duty, — to lay the article of the Constitution which is invoked beside the statute which is challenged and to decide whether the latter squares with the former. All the court does, or can do, is to announce its considered judgment upon the question. The only power it has, if such it may be called, is the power of judgment. This court neither approves nor condemns any legislative policy. Its delicate and difficult office is to ascertain and declare whether the legislation is in accordance with, or in contravention of, the provisions of the Constitution; and, having done that, its duty ends.

. . . Despite a reference in its first section to a burden upon, and an obstruction of the normal currents of commerce, the act under review does not purport to regulate transactions in interstate or foreign[10] commerce. Its stated purpose is the control of agricultural production, a purely local activity, in an effort to raise the prices paid the farmer. Indeed, the Government does not attempt to uphold the validity of the act on the basis of the commerce clause, which, for the purpose of the present case, may be put aside as irrelevant.

The clause thought to authorize the legislation, — the first, — confers upon the Congress power "to lay and collect Taxes, Duties, Imposts and Excises, to pay the Debts and provide for the common Defence and general Welfare of the United States. . . ." It is not contended that this provision grants power to regulate agricultural production upon the theory that such legislation would promote the general welfare. The Government concedes that the phrase to "provide for the general welfare" qualifies the power "to lay and collect taxes." The view that the clause grants power to provide for the general welfare, independently of the taxing power, has never been authoritatively accepted. Mr. Justice Story points out that if it were adopted "it is obvious that under color of the generality of the words, to 'provide for the common defence and general welfare,' the government of the United States is, in reality, a government of general and unlimited powers, notwithstanding the subsequent enumeration of specific powers." The true construction undoubtedly is that the only thing granted is the power to tax for the purpose of providing funds for payment of the nation's debts and making provision for the general welfare.

Nevertheless the Government asserts that warrant is found in this clause for the adoption of the Agricultural Adjustment Act. The argument is that congress may appropriate and authorize the spending of moneys for the "general welfare"; that the phrase should be liberally construed to cover anything conducive to national welfare; that decision as to what will promote such welfare rests with Congress alone, and the courts may not review its determination; and finally that the appropriation under attack was in fact for the general welfare of the United States. . . .

Since the foundation of the nation sharp differences of opinion have persisted as to the true interpretation of the phrase. Madison asserted it amounted to no more than a reference to the other powers enumerated in the subsequent clauses of the same section; that, as the United States is a government of limited and enumerated powers, the grant of power to tax and spend for the general national welfare must be confined to the enumerated legislative fields committed to the Congress. In this view the phrase is mere tautology, for taxation and appropriation are or may be necessary incidents of the exercise

---

[10] The enactment of protective tariff laws has its basis in the power to regulate foreign commerce. See University of Illinois v. United States, 289 U.S. 48, 58.

of any of the enumerated legislative powers. Hamilton, on the other hand, maintained the clause confers a power separate and distinct from those later enumerated, is not restricted in meaning by the grant of them, and Congress consequently has a substantive power to tax and to appropriate, limited only by the requirement that it shall be exercised to provide for the general welfare of the United States. Each contention has had the support of those whose views are entitled to weight. This court has noticed the question, but has never found it necessary to decide which is the true construction. Mr. Justice Story, in his Commentaries, espouses the Hamiltonian position. We shall not review the writings of public men and commentators or discuss the legislative practice. Study of all these leads us to conclude that the reading advocated by Mr. Justice Story is the correct one. While, therefore, the power to tax is not unlimited, its confines are set in the clause which confers it, and not in those of §8 which bestow and define the legislative powers of the Congress. It results that the power of Congress to authorize expenditure of public moneys for public purposes is not limited by the direct grants of legislative power found in the Constitution.

But the adoption of the broader construction leaves the power to spend subject to limitations. . . .

That the qualifying phrase must be given effect all advocates of broad construction admit. Hamilton, in his well known Report on Manufactures, states that the purpose must be "general, and not local." Monroe, an advocate of Hamilton's doctrine, wrote: "Have Congress a right to raise and appropriate the money to any and to every purpose according to their will and pleasure? They certainly have not." Story says that if the tax be not proposed for the common defence or general welfare, but for other objects wholly extraneous, it would be wholly indefensible upon constitutional principles. And he makes it clear that the powers of taxation and appropriation extend only to matters of national, as distinguished from local, welfare. . . .

We are not now required to ascertain the scope of the phrase "general welfare of the United States" or to determine whether an appropriation in aid of agriculture falls within it. Wholly apart from that question, another principle embedded in our Constitution prohibits the enforcement of the Agricultural Adjustment Act. The act invades the reserved rights of the states. It is a statutory plan to regulate and control agricultural production, a matter beyond the powers delegated to the federal government. The tax, the appropriation of the funds raised, and the direction for their disbursement, are but parts of the plan. They are but means to an unconstitutional end.

From the accepted doctrine that the United States is a government of delegated powers, it follows that those not expressly granted, or reasonably to be implied from such as are conferred, are reserved to the states or to the people. To forestall any suggestion to the contrary, the Tenth Amendment was adopted. . . .

[The Court discussed the Child Labor Tax Case (Bailey v. Drexel Furniture Co.), 259 U.S. 20, and United States v. Constantine, 296 U.S. 287.] These decisions demonstrate that Congress could not, under the pretext of raising revenue, lay a tax on processors who refuse to pay a certain price for cotton and exempt those who agree so to do, with the purpose of benefiting producers.

Third. If the taxing power may not be used as the instrument to enforce a regulation of matters of state concern with respect to which the Congress has no authority to interfere, may it, as in the present case, be employed to raise the money necessary to purchase a compliance which the Congress is powerless to command? The Government asserts that whatever might be said against the validity of the plan, if compulsory, it is constitutionally sound because the end is accomplished by voluntary cooperation. There are two sufficient answers to the contention. The regulation is not in fact voluntary. The farmer, of course, may refuse to comply, but the price of such refusal is the loss of benefits. The amount offered is intended to be sufficient to exert pressure on him to agree to the proposed regulation. The power to confer or withhold unlimited benefits is the power to coerce or destroy.

Section A. Trade, Production, and Employment

If the cotton grower elects not to accept the benefits, he will receive less for his crops; those who receive payments will be able to undersell him. The result may well be financial ruin. The coercive purpose and intent of the statute is not obscured by the fact that it has not been perfectly successful. It is pointed out that, because there still remained a minority whom the rental and benefit payments were insufficient to induce to surrender their independence of action, the Congress has gone further and, in the Bankhead Cotton Act, used the taxing power in a more directly minatory fashion to compel submission. This progression only serves more fully to expose the coercive purpose of the so-called tax imposed by the present act. It is clear that the Department of Agriculture has properly described the plan as one to keep a non-cooperating minority in line. This is coercion by economic pressure. The asserted power of choice is illusory. . . .

But if the plan were one for purely voluntary cooperation it would stand no better so far as federal power is concerned. At best it is a scheme for purchasing with federal funds submission to federal regulation of a subject reserved to the states.

. . . An appropriation to be expended by the United States under contracts calling for a violation of a state law clearly would offend the Constitution. Is a statute less objectionable which authorizes expenditure of federal moneys to induce action in a field in which the United States has no power to intermeddle? The Congress cannot invade state jurisdiction to compel individual action; no more can it purchase such action. . . .

We are not here concerned with a conditional appropriation of money, nor with a provision that if certain conditions are not complied with the appropriation shall no longer be available. By the Agricultural Adjustment Act the amount of the tax is appropriated to be expended only in payment under contracts whereby the parties bind themselves to regulation by the federal government. There is an obvious difference between a statute stating the conditions upon which moneys shall be expended and one effective only upon assumption of a contractual obligation to submit to a regulation which otherwise could not be enforced. Many examples pointing the distinction might be cited. We are referred to appropriations in aid of education, and it is said that no one has doubted the power of Congress to stipulate the sort of education for which money shall be expended. But an appropriation to an educational institution which by its terms is to become available only if the beneficiary enters into a contract to teach doctrines subversive of the Constitution is clearly bad. An affirmance of the authority of Congress so to condition the expenditure of an appropriation would tend to nullify all constitutional limitations upon legislative power.

But it is said that there is a wide difference in another respect, between compulsory regulation of the local affairs of a state's citizens and the mere making of a contract relating to their conduct; that, if any state objects, it may declare the contract void and thus prevent those under the state's jurisdiction from complying with its terms. The argument is plainly fallacious. The United States can make the contract only if the federal power to tax and to appropriate reaches the subject matter of the contract. If this does reach the subject matter, its exertion cannot be displaced by state action. . . .

. . . It does not help to declare that local conditions throughout the nation have created a situation of national concern; for this is but to say that whenever there is a widespread similarity of local conditions, Congress may ignore constitutional limitations upon its own powers and usurp those reserved to the states. If, in lieu of compulsory regulation of subjects within the states' reserved jurisdiction, which is prohibited, the Congress could invoke the taxing and spending power as a means to accomplish the same end, clause 1 of §8 of Article I would become the instrument for total subversion of the governmental powers reserved to the individual states.

If the act before us is a proper exercise of the federal taxing power, evidently the regulation of all industry throughout the United States may be accomplished by similar exercises of the same power. It would be possible to exact money from one branch of an industry and pay it to another branch in every field of activity which lies within the province of the states. The mere threat of such a procedure might well induce the surrender of rights and the compliance with federal regulation as the price of continuance in business. A few instances will illustrate the thought. . . .

Suppose that there are too many garment workers in the large cities; that this results in dislocation of the economic balance. Upon the principle contended for an excise might be laid on the manufacture of all garments manufactured and the proceeds paid to those manufacturers who agree to remove their plants to cities having not more than a hundred thousand population. Thus, through the asserted power of taxation, the federal government, against the will of individual states, might completely redistribute the industrial population. . . .

Hamilton himself, the leading advocate of broad interpretation of the power to tax and to appropriate for the general welfare, never suggested that any power granted by the Constitution could be used for the destruction of local self-government in the states. Story countenances no such doctrine. It seems never to have occurred to them, or to those who have agreed with them, that the general welfare of the United States (which has aptly been termed "an indestructible Union, composed of indestructible States,") might be served by obliterating the constituent members of the Union.

But to this fatal conclusion the doctrine contended for would inevitably lead. And its sole premise is that, though the makers of the Constitution, in erecting the federal government, intended sedulously to limit and define its powers, so as to reserve to the states and the people sovereign power, to be wielded by the states and their citizens and not to be invaded by the United States, they nevertheless by a single clause gave power to the Congress to tear down the barriers, to invade the states' jurisdiction, and to become a parliament of the whole people, subject to no restrictions save such as are self-imposed. The argument when seen in its true character and in the light of its inevitable results must be rejected. . . .

The judgment is affirmed.

MR. JUSTICE STONE, dissenting.

I think the judgment should be reversed. . . .

The Constitution requires that public funds shall be spent for a defined purpose, the promotion of the general welfare. Their expenditure usually involves payment on terms which will insure use by the selected recipients within the limits of the constitutional purpose. Expenditures would fail of their purpose and thus lose their constitutional sanction if the terms of payment were not such that by their influence on the action of the recipients the permitted end would be attained. The power of Congress to spend is inseparable from persuasion to action over which Congress has no legislative control. Congress may not command that the science of agriculture be taught in state universities. But if it would aid the teaching of that science by grants to state institutions, it is appropriate, if not necessary, that the grant be on the condition, incorporated in the Morrill Act, 12 Stat. at L. 503, chap. 130, 26 Stat. at L. 417, chap. 841, that it be used for the intended purpose. Similarly it would seem to be compliance with the Constitution, not violation of it, for the government to take and the university to give a contract that the grant would be so used. It makes no difference that there is a promise to do an act which the condition is calculated to induce. Condition and promise are alike valid since both are in furtherance of the national purpose for which the money is appropriated. . . .

That the governmental power of the purse is a great one is not now for the first time announced. Every student of the history of government and economics is aware of its magnitude and of its existence in every civilized government. Both were well understood by the framers of the Constitution when they sanctioned the grant of the spending power to the federal government, and both were recognized by Hamilton and Story, whose views of the spending power as standing on a parity with the other powers specifically granted, have hitherto been generally accepted.

The suggestion that it must now be curtailed by judicial fiat because it may be abused by unwise use hardly rises to the dignity of argument. So may judicial power be abused. . . . The power to tax and spend is not without constitutional restraints. One restriction is that the purpose must be truly national. Another is that it may not be used to coerce action left to state control. Another is the conscience and patriotism of Congress and the Executive. "It must be remembered that legislators are the ultimate guardians of the liberties and welfare of the people in quite as great a degree as the courts." Justice Holmes, in Missouri, K. & T.R. Co. v. May, 194 U.S. 267, 270.

A tortured construction of the Constitution is not to be justified by recourse to extreme examples of reckless congressional spending which might occur if courts could not prevent — expenditures which, even if they could be thought to effect any national purpose, would be possible only by action of a legislature lost to all sense of public responsibility. Such suppositions are addressed to the mind accustomed to believe that it is the business of courts to sit in judgment on the wisdom of legislative action. Courts are not the only agency of government that must be assumed to have capacity to govern. Congress and the courts both unhappily may falter or be mistaken in the performance of their constitutional duty. But interpretation of our great charter of government which proceeds on any assumption that the responsibility for the preservation of our institutions is the exclusive concern of any one of the three branches of government, or that it alone can save them from destruction, is far more likely, in the long run, "to obliterate the constituent members" of "an indestructible union of indestructible states" than the frank recognition that language, even of a constitution, may mean what it says: that the power to tax and spend includes the power to relieve a nation-wide economic maladjustment by conditional gifts of money.

MR. JUSTICE BRANDEIS and MR. JUSTICE CARDOZO join in this opinion.[c]

NOTE Aftermath of the Butler Case

The decision in the Butler case not only undermined the Administration's farm program; it left in its wake problems of unjust enrichment as well. Many processors had doubtless passed the economic burden of the tax on to their customers or back to the producers, in the form of price adjustments. These processors fell into two groups: those who had paid the tax and were now entitled to refunds from the government, and those who had not paid the tax, under the protection of injunctions.

Injunctions had been issued to restrain collection of the processing tax in 1600 cases, and denied in only 166, despite the statutory prohibition on injunctions to restrain the collection of federal taxes (R.S. §3224, now I.R.C. §3653(a)). See S. Doc. No. 42, 75th Cong., 1st Sess. (1937). The invalidity of the Child Labor Tax had been held not to justify injunctive relief. Bailey v. George, 259 U.S. 16 (1922). But one week after the Butler decision the Court ordered that processing taxes which had been impounded by the district court be returned to the taxpayers. Rickert Rice Mills v. Fontenot, 297 U.S. 110 (1936).

Congress enacted two remedial measures: (a) a requirement that the taxpayer show he had borne the burden of the processing tax, as a condition of refund; (b) a "windfall profits" tax of 90 per cent of a processor's income attributable to injunctive protection against collection of the tax, where the processor had not borne the burden of the tax. See Anniston Mfg. Co. v. Davis, 301 U.S. 337 (1937). On the device of a windfall tax, compare United States v. Hudson, 299 U.S. 498 (1937), sustaining a tax on profits from dealings in silver futures, made retroactive for thirty-five days; the purpose was to thwart market speculation while a bill to increase government purchases of silver was pending.

[c] See Hart, Processing Taxes and Protective Tariffs, 49 Harv. L. Rev. 610 (1936), an imaginary judicial opinion holding the protective tariff unconstitutional on the basis of the Butler case. — ED.

260   Chapter Seven. National Power over the Economy

Does this decision have any relevance to the problem of the Child Labor Tax Case (Bailey v. Drexel)?

NOTE The Constitutional Crisis and the Court Reorganization Plan of 1937

1. *The background.* The Roosevelt Administration saw in the constitutional decisions of 1933-1937 a barrier to its program for economic recovery. The President and his advisers, moreover, were persuaded that the obstacle did not inhere in the Constitution but was the handiwork of Justices who were out of sympathy with both the program and the best traditions of constitutional decision.

The Court had held the following legislation invalid: (a) Section 9(c) of the National Industrial Recovery Act, authorizing the President to prohibit the interstate shipment of oil produced in excess of state-fixed quotas, Panama Refining Co. v. Ryan, 293 U.S. 389 (1935) (Cardozo, J., dissenting); (b) Railway Pension Act, Railroad Retirement Board v. Alton R.R., 295 U.S. 330 (1935) (Hughes, C.J., Brandeis, Stone, and Cardozo, JJ., dissenting); (c) Farm Mortgage Act, Louisville Joint Stock Land Bank v. Radford, 295 U.S. 555 (1935); (d) National Industrial Recovery Act, Schechter Poultry Corp. v. United States, 295 U.S. 495 (1935); (e) Agricultural Adjustment Act, United States v. Butler, 297 U.S. 1 (1936) (Stone, Brandeis, and Cardozo, JJ., dissenting); (f) Bituminous Coal Act, Carter v. Carter Coal Co., 298 U.S. 238 (1936) (Hughes, C.J., Brandeis, Stone, and Cardozo, JJ., dissenting); (g) Municipal Bankruptcy Act, Ashton v. Cameron County District, 298 U.S. 513 (1936) (Cardozo, J., Hughes, C.J., Stone and Brandeis, JJ., dissenting); (h) New York minimum wage law for women, Morehead v. Tipaldo, 298 U.S. 587 (1936) (Hughes, C.J., Stone, Brandeis, and Cardozo, JJ., dissenting). In addition, only by an equally divided Court (Stone, J., not participating), a New York decision holding the state unemployment compensation law valid had been affirmed. Associated Industries v. Department of Labor, 299 U.S. 515 (1936).

The Court had held the following legislation valid: (a) Gold Clause Resolution and related acts, Norman v. Baltimore & Ohio R.R., 294 U.S. 240 (1935) (McReynolds, Van Devanter, Sutherland, and Butler, JJ., dissenting); (b) TVA Act as applied to Wilson Dam, Ashwander v. TVA, 297 U.S. 288 (1936) (McReynolds, J., dissenting); (c) Minnesota mortgage moratorium, Home Bldg. & Loan Assn. v. Blaisdell, 290 U.S. 398 (1934) (Sutherland, Van Devanter, McReynolds, and Butler, JJ., dissenting); (d) New York minimum price law for milk, Nebbia v. New York, 291 U.S. 502 (1934) (McReynolds, Van Devanter, Sutherland, and Butler, JJ., dissenting).

Early in 1937 there remained for decision the validity of the National Labor Relations Act, the old-age pensions and unemployment compensation provisions of the Social Security Act, the TVA Act in its full scope, and the Public Utility Holding Company Act, to name the most important measures.

2. *The plan.* On February 5, 1937, the President addressed to Congress a message containing a plan for reorganization of the judiciary. H.R. Doc. No. 142, 75th Cong., 1st Sess. The heart of the proposal was a provision for the appointment of additional judges in all federal courts where there are incumbent judges of retirement age who do not choose to retire or resign. This was coupled with an extension of retirement privileges to Supreme Court Justices (who theretofore, unlike lower court judges, had only the option of resignation with its attendant risk of termination of compensation). The maximum size of the Supreme Court was to be fixed at fifteen members.

The plan was chosen by the President from a number of proposals submitted, at the President's direction, by Attorney General Cummings. There is good reason to believe that the plan had special attractiveness for the President because a similar proposal, limited to the lower federal courts, had been urged by Attorney General McReynolds in

1913, and repeated in 1914, 1915, and 1916. Cf. Cummings and McFarland, Federal Justice 531 (1937); and see the President's message, cited supra.

The launching of the plan thus met only obliquely the impasse between Administration and Court. This indirection, focusing on the age of judges and their asserted inefficiency, had unfortunate consequences for the Administration. An atmosphere of unreality was created; friends of Mr. Justice Brandeis and the late Mr. Justice Holmes were alienated; and an opportunity was given for a letter to be obtained by Senator Wheeler from Chief Justice Hughes, signed also by Justices Van Devanter and Brandeis as the senior Associate Justices, describing the dispatch with which the Court's business was conducted and the inefficiencies that would result from an increase in membership. The proponents of the plan could not long avoid the central controversy. On March 9, 1937, the President delivered a radio address in which he quoted from dissenting opinions in several of the recent cases which had invalidated legislation; his attack became a frontal one: "When I commenced to review the situation with the problem squarely before me, I came by a process of elimination to the conclusion that short of amendments the only method which was clearly constitutional, and would at the same time carry out other much needed reforms, was to infuse new blood into all our Courts. We must have men worthy and equipped to carry out impartial justice. But, at the same time, we must have Judges who will bring to the Courts a present-day sense of the Constitution — Judges who will retain in the Courts the judicial functions of a court, and reject the legislative powers which the Courts have today assumed."

After extensive hearings, the bills embodying the President's proposal failed of passage. Hearings Before Senate Committee on Judiciary on S. 1392, 75th Cong., 1st Sess. (1937); S. Rep. No. 711, 75th Cong., 1st Sess. (1937) (adverse report); 81 Cong. Rec. 7375-7381 (1937) (bill recommitted); see also H.R. 7765, 75th Cong., 1st Sess. (1937); 81 Cong. Rec. 6869 (1937) (referred to committee).

The background of the plan, together with its sequels in judicial decisions, is described in Jackson, The Struggle for Judicial Supremacy (1941) (including, in an appendix, the President's message to Congress and his radio address of March 9, 1937). The behind-the-scenes maneuvers are recounted in Alsop and Catledge, 168 Days (1938). Chief Justice Hughes's role is told in 2 Pusey, Charles Evans Hughes 749-765 (1951), and in Mason, Brandeis 626-627 (1946). See also Mason, Harlan Fiske Stone and FDR's Court Plan, 61 Yale L.J. 791 (1952); Leuchtenberg, The Origins of Franklin D. Roosevelt's "Court-Packing" Plan, 1966 Sup. Ct. Rev. 347; Freund, Charles Evans Hughes as Chief Justice, 81 Harv. L. Rev. 4 (1967).

3. *The legislative sequel: The Judiciary Act of 1937.* Although the core of the measure was lost, certain reforms in judicial organization and procedure were effected by Congress.

Retirement privileges were extended to Supreme Court Justices. Act of March 1, 1937, c. 21, 50 Stat. 24. On June 2, 1937, Mr. Justice Van Devanter retired under this act, and was succeeded by Mr. Justice Black.

Three major changes were incorporated in the Judiciary Act of 1937. Act of August 24, 1937, c. 754, 50 Stat. 751. Each change was a response to a need deemed exigent. (a) Section 1 required notice to, and authorized intervention by, the Attorney General in any case involving the constitutionality of an Act of Congress affecting the public interest in which the United States was not a party. Cf. In re American States Public Service Co., 12 F. Supp. 667 (D. Md. 1935), aff'd sub nom. Burco v. Whitworth, 81 F.2d 721 (4th Cir. 1936), cert. denied, 297 U.S. 724 (1936) (challenge to validity of Holding Company Act in proceeding for instructions under Bankruptcy Act); the circumstances are described at page 101 supra. In a number of cases, moreover, municipalities had been enjoined from accepting federal PWA loans, on constitutional grounds, without the participation of a federal officer in the suit. See S. Doc. No. 27, 75th Cong., 1st Sess. 27 (1937).

(b) Section 2 authorized direct appeal to the Supreme Court from a decision of a district court holding an Act of Congress unconstitutional. This section extended a device which had been in effect for dismissals of indictments on constitutional grounds under the Criminal Appeals Act of 1907. It bears a close relation to §3, discussed in the next paragraph.

(c) Section 3 required a three-judge district court to be convened when an injunction was sought against enforcement of an Act of Congress on grounds of unconstitutionality; and a direct appeal to the Supreme Court from the district court's decision was provided. This extended to federal statutes a procedural safeguard afforded to state statutes under the Act of March 4, 1913, c. 160, 37 Stat. 1013, amended by Act of Feb. 13, 1925, c. 229, 43 Stat. 938. The multitude of injunctions against federal activities in 1935-1937 had led to a request by the Senate for information from the agencies affected. The replies are contained in a series of Senate Documents, 75th Cong., 1st Sess.: Nos. 25 (WPA); 26 (Railroad Retirement Board); 27 (PWA); 28 (Social Security Board); 29 (NLRB); 30 (Power Commission); 31 (FCC); 32 (Veterans' Administration); 33 (FTC); 37 (Interior Dept.); 38 (Agriculture Dept.); 39 (Commerce Dept.); 42 (Justice and Treasury Depts.); 43 (SEC); 44 (TVA). The PWA reported 59 injunctions in cases where the administrator was a party, and 20 where he was not. For the strategy of the SEC in avoiding more than 40 injunction suits by stays pending the outcome of a test case, see Landis v. North American Co., 299 U.S. 248 (1936); Electric Bond & Share Co. v. SEC, 303 U.S. 419 (1938); and pages 102-103 supra. After the sweeping preliminary injunction granted by Judge Gore in Tennessee Elec. Power Co. v. TVA, 21 F. Supp. 947 (M.D. Tenn. 1936), was reversed on appeal, 90 F.2d 885 (6th Cir. 1937), the TVA case was tried before a three-judge court under the 1937 act.

The legislative history of the 1937 act, and the circumstances which engendered it, are discussed in Frankfurter and Fisher, The Business of the Supreme Court at the October Terms, 1935 and 1936, 51 Harv. L. Rev. 577, 610-619 (1938).

Steward Machine Co. v. Davis 301 U.S. 548, 57 S. Ct. 883, 81 L. Ed. 1279 (1937)

MR. JUSTICE CARDOZO delivered the opinion of the Court.

The validity of the tax imposed by the Social Security Act on employers of eight or more is here to be determined.

Petitioner, an Alabama corporation, paid a tax in accordance with the statute, filed a claim for refund with the Commissioner of Internal Revenue, and sued to recover the payment ($46.14), asserting a conflict between the statute and the Constitution of the United States. Upon demurrer the District Court gave judgment for the defendant dismissing the complaint, and the Circuit Court of Appeals for the Fifth Circuit affirmed. 89 F.(2d) 207. . . .

The Social Security Act (Act of August 14, 1935, c. 531, 49 Stat. 620, 42 U.S.C., c. 7 (Supp.)) is divided into seven separate titles, of which only Titles IX and III are so related to this case as to stand in need of summary.

The caption of Title IX is "Tax on Employers of Eight or More." Every employer (with stated exceptions) is to pay for each calendar year "an excise tax, with respect to having individuals in his employ," the tax to be measured by prescribed percentages of the total wages payable by the employer during the calendar year with respect to such employment. §901. One is not, however, an "employer" within the meaning of the act unless he employs eight persons or more. §907(a). There are also other limitations of minor importance. . . . The proceeds, when collected, go into the Treasury of the United States like internal-revenue collections generally. §905(a). They are not earmarked in any way. In certain circumstances, however, credits are allowable. §902. If the taxpayer has made contributions to an unemployment fund under a state law, he may credit such contributions against the federal tax, provided, however, that the total credit allowed to any taxpayer shall not exceed 90 per centum of the tax against which it is credited, and provided also that the state law shall have been certified to the Secretary of the Treasury by the Social Security Board as satisfying certain minimum criteria. §902. The provisions of §903 defining those criteria are stated in the margin.[1] Some of the conditions thus attached to the allowance of a credit are designed to give assurance that the state unemployment compensation law shall be one in substance as well as name. Others are designed to give assurance that the contributions shall be protected against loss after payment to the state. To this last end there are provisions that before a state law shall have the approval of the Board it must direct that the contributions to the state fund be paid over immediately to the Secretary of the Treasury to the credit of the "Unemployment Trust Fund." . . . For the moment it is enough to say that the Fund is to be held by the Secretary of the Treasury, who is to invest in government securities any portion not required in his judgment to meet current withdrawals. He is authorized and directed to pay out of the Fund to any competent state agency such sums as it may duly requisition from the amount standing to its credit. §904(f).

Title III, which is also challenged as invalid, has the caption "Grants to States for Unemployment Compensation Administration." Under this title, certain sums of money are "authorized to be appropriated" for the purpose of assisting the states in the administration of their unemployment compensation laws, the maximum for the fiscal year ending June 30, 1936 to be $4,000,000, and $49,000,000 for each fiscal year thereafter. §301. No present appropriation is made to the extent of a single dollar. All that the title does is to authorize future appropriations. Actually only $2,250,000 of the $4,000,000 authorized was appropriated for 1936 (Act of Feb. 11, 1936, c. 49, 49 Stat. 1109, 1113) and only $29,000,000 of the $49,000,000 authorized for the following year. Act of June 22, 1936, c. 689, 49 Stat. 1597, 1605. The appropriations when made were not specifically out of the proceeds of the employment tax, but out of any moneys in the Treasury. Other sections of the title prescribe the method by which the payments are to be made to the state (§302) and also certain conditions to be established to the satisfaction of the Social Security Board before certifying the propriety of a payment to the Secretary of the

---

[1] Sec. 903. (a) The Social Security Board shall approve any State law submitted to it, within thirty days of such submission which it finds provides that —

(1) All compensation is to be paid through public employment offices in the State or such other agencies as the Board may approve;

(2) No compensation shall be payable with respect to any day of unemployment occurring within two years after the first day of the first period with respect to which contributions are required;

(3) All money received in the employment fund shall immediately upon such receipt be paid over to the Secretary of the Treasury to the credit of the Unemployment Trust Fund established by Section 904;

(4) All money withdrawn from the Unemployment Trust Fund by the State agency shall be used solely in the payment of compensation, exclusive of expenses of administration;

(5) Compensation shall not be denied in such State to any otherwise eligible individual for refusing to accept new work under any of the following conditions: (A) If the position offered is vacant due directly to a strike, lockout, or other labor dispute; (B) if the wages, hours, or other conditions of the work offered are substantially less favorable to the individual than those prevailing for similar work in the locality; (C) if as a condition of being employed the individual would be required to join a company union or to resign from or refrain from joining any bona fide labor organization;

(6) All the rights, privileges, or immunities conferred by such law or by acts done pursuant thereto shall exist subject to the power of the legislature to amend or repeal such law at any time.

The Board shall, upon approving such law, notify the Governor of the State of its approval.

(b) On December 31 in each taxable year the Board shall certify to the Secretary of the Treasury each State whose law it has previously approved, except that it shall not certify any State which, after reasonable notice and opportunity for hearing to the State agency, the Board finds has changed its law so that it no longer contains the provisions specified in subsection (a) or has with respect to such taxable year failed to comply substantially with any such provision.

(c) If, at any time during the taxable year, the Board has reason to believe that a State whose law it has previously approved, may not be certified under subsection (b), it shall promptly so notify the Governor of such State.

Treasury. §303. They are designed to give assurance to the Federal Government that the moneys granted by it will not be expended for purposes alien to the grant, and will be used in the administration of genuine unemployment compensation laws.

The assault on the statute proceeds on an extended front. Its assailants take the ground that the tax is not an excise; that it is not uniform throughout the United States as excises are required to be; that its exceptions are so many and arbitrary as to violate the Fifth Amendment; that its purpose was not revenue, but an unlawful invasion of the reserved powers of the states; and that the states in submitting to it have yielded to coercion and have abandoned governmental functions which they are not permitted to surrender.

The objections will be considered seriatim with such further explanation as may be necessary to make their meaning clear.

First. The tax, which is described in the statute as an excise, is laid with uniformity throughout the United States as a duty, an impost or an excise upon the relation of employment.

1. We are told that the relation of employment is one so essential to the pursuit of happiness that it may not be burdened with a tax. Appeal is made to history. From the precedents of colonial days we are supplied with illustrations of excises common in the colonies. They are said to have been bound up with the enjoyment of particular commodities. Appeal is also made to principle or the analysis of concepts. An excise, we are told, imports a tax upon a privilege; employment, it is said, is a right, not a privilege, from which it follows that employment is not subject to an excise. Neither the one appeal nor the other leads to the desired goal. . . .

2. The tax being an excise, its imposition must conform to the canon of uniformity. There has been no departure from this requirement. According to the settled doctrine the uniformity exacted is geographical, not intrinsic. [Citations omitted.] "The rule of liability shall be the same in all parts of the United States." Florida v. Mellon, 273, U.S. 12, 17.

Second. The excise is not invalid under the provisions of the Fifth Amendment by force of its exemptions.

The statute does not apply, as we have seen, to employers of less than eight. It does not apply to agricultural labor, or domestic service in a private home or to some other classes of less importance. Petitioner contends that the effect of these restrictions is an arbitrary discrimination vitiating the tax.

The Fifth Amendment unlike the Fourteenth has no equal protection clause. [Citations omitted.] But even the states, though subject to such a clause, are not confined to a formula of rigid uniformity in framing measures of taxation. . . .

The classifications and exemptions directed by the statute now in controversy have support in considerations of policy and practical convenience that cannot be condemned as arbitrary. The classifications and exemptions would therefore be upheld if they had been adopted by a state and the provisions of the Fourteenth Amendment were invoked to annul them. This is held in two cases passed upon today in which precisely the same provisions were the subject of attack, the provisions being contained in the Unemployment Compensation Law of the State of Alabama. Carmichael v. Southern Coal & Coke Co., and Carmichael v. Gulf States Paper Corp. [301 U.S.], 495. . . . The act of Congress is therefore valid, so far at least as its system of exemptions is concerned, and this though we assume that discrimination, if gross enough, is equivalent to confiscation and subject under the Fifth Amendment to challenge and annulment.

Third. The excise is not void as involving the coercion of the States in contravention of the Tenth Amendment or of restrictions implicit in our federal form of government.

The proceeds of the excise when collected are paid into the Treasury at Washington, and thereafter are subject to appropriation like public moneys generally. Cincinnati Soap Co. v. United States [301 U.S.], 308. No presumption can be indulged that they will be misapplied or wasted.[8] Even if they were collected in the hope or expectation that some other and collateral good would be furthered as an incident, that without more would not make the act invalid. Sonzinsky v. United States, 300 U.S. 506. This indeed is hardly questioned. The case for the petitioner is built on the contention that here an ulterior aim is wrought into the very structure of the act, and what is even more important that the aim is not only ulterior, but essentially unlawful. In particular, the 90 per cent credit is relied upon as supporting that conclusion. But before the statute succumbs to an assault upon these lines, two propositions must be made out by the assailant. Cincinnati Soap Co. v. United States, supra. There must be a showing in the first place that separated from the credit the revenue provisions are incapable of standing by themselves. There must be a showing in the second place that the tax and the credit in combination are weapons of coercion, destroying or impairing the autonomy of the states. The truth of each proposition being essential to the success of the assault, we pass for convenience to a consideration of the second, without pausing to inquire whether there has been a demonstration of the first.

To draw the line intelligently between duress and inducement there is need to remind ourselves of facts as to the problem of unemployment that are now matters of common knowledge. West Coast Hotel Co. v. Parrish, 300 U.S. 379. The relevant statistics are gathered in the brief of counsel for the Government. Of the many available figures a few only will be mentioned. During the years 1929 to 1936, when the country was passing through a cyclical depression, the number of the unemployed mounted to unprecedented heights. Often the average was more than 10 million; at times a peak was attained of 16 million or more. Disaster to the breadwinner meant disaster to dependents. Accordingly the roll of the unemployed, itself formidable enough, was only a partial roll of the destitute or needy. The fact developed quickly that the states were unable to give the requisite relief. The problem had become national in area and dimensions. There was need of help from the nation if the people were not to starve. It is too late today for the argument to be heard with tolerance that in a crisis so extreme the use of the moneys of the nation to relieve the unemployed and their dependents is a use for any purpose narrower than the promotion of the general welfare. Cf. United States v. Butler, 297 U.S. 1, 65, 66, Helvering v. Davis, decided herewith [301 U.S.], p. 619. The nation responded to the call of the distressed. Between January 1, 1933 and July 1, 1936, the states (according to statistics submitted by the Government) incurred obligations of $689,291,802 for emergency relief; local subdivisions an additional $775,675,366. In the same period the obligations for emergency relief incurred by the national government were $2,929,307,125, or twice the obligations of states and local agencies combined. According to the President's budget message for the fiscal year 1938, the national government expended for public works and unemployment relief for the three fiscal years 1934, 1935, and 1936, the stupendous total of $8,681,000,000. The parens patriae has many reasons — fiscal and economic as well as social and moral — for planning to mitigate disasters that bring these burdens in their train.

In the presence of this urgent need for some remedial expedient, the question is to be answered whether the expedient adopted has overlept the bounds of power. The assailants of the statute say that its dominant end and aim is to drive the state legislatures under the whip of economic pressure into the enactment of unemployment compensation laws at the bidding of the central government. Supporters of the statute say that its operation is not constraint, but the creation of a larger freedom, the states and the nation joining in a

[8] The total estimate receipts without taking into account the 90 per cent deduction, range from $225,000,000 in the first year to over $900,000,000 seven years later. Even if the maximum credits are available to taxpayers in all states, the maximum estimated receipts from Title IX will range between $22,000,000, at one extreme, to $90,000,000 at the other. If some of the states hold out in their unwillingness to pass statutes of their own, the receipts will be still larger.

coöperative endeavor to avert a common evil. Before Congress acted, unemployment compensation insurance was still, for the most part, a project and no more. Wisconsin was the pioneer. Her statute was adopted in 1931. At times bills for such insurance were introduced elsewhere, but they did not reach the stage of law. In 1935, four states (California, Massachusetts, New Hampshire and New York) passed unemployment laws on the eve of the adoption of the Social Security Act, and two others did likewise after the federal act and later in the year. The statutes differed to some extent in type, but were directed to a common end. In 1936, twenty-eight other states fell in line, and eight more the present year. But if states had been holding back before the passage of the federal law, inaction was not owing, for the most part, to the lack of sympathetic interest. Many held back through alarm lest, in laying such a toll upon their industries, they would place themselves in a position of economic disadvantage as compared with neighbors or competitors. See House Report, No. 615, 74th Congress, 1st session, p. 8; Senate Report, No. 628, 74th Congress 1st session, p. 11.[9] Two consequences ensued. One was that the freedom of a state to contribute its fair share to the solution of a national problem was paralyzed by fear. The other was that in so far as there was failure by the states to contribute relief according to the measure of their capacity, a disproportionate burden, and a mountainous one, was laid upon the resources of the Government of the nation.

The Social Security Act is an attempt to find a method by which all these public agencies may work together to a common end. Every dollar of the new taxes will continue in all likelihood to be used and needed by the nation as long as states are unwilling, whether through timidity or for other motives, to do what can be done at home. At least the inference is permissible that Congress so believed, though retaining undiminished freedom to spend the money as it pleased. On the other hand fulfillment of the home duty will be lightened and encouraged by crediting the taxpayer upon his account with the Treasury of the nation to the extent that his contributions under the laws of the locality have simplified or diminished the problem of relief and the probable demand upon the resources of the fisc. Duplicated taxes, or burdens that approach them, are recognized hardships that government, state or national, may properly avoid. Henneford v. Silas Mason Co. [300 U.S. 577]; Kidd v. Alabama, 188 U.S. 730, 732; Watson v. State Comptroller, 254 U.S. 122, 125. If Congress believed that the general welfare would better be promoted by relief through local units than by the system then in vogue, the coöperating localities ought not in all fairness to pay a second time.

Who then is coerced through the operation of this statute? Not the taxpayer. He pays in fulfilment of the mandate of the local legislature. Not the state. Even now she does not offer a suggestion that in passing the unemployment law she was affected by duress. See Carmichael v. Southern Coal & Coke Co., and Carmichael v. Gulf States Paper Corp., supra. For all that appears she is satisfied with her choice, and would be sorely disappointed if it were now to be annulled. The difficulty with the petitioner's contention is that it confuses motive with coercion. "Every tax is in some measure regulatory. To some extent it interposes an economic impediment to the activity taxed as compared with others not taxed." Sonzinsky v. United States, supra. In like manner every rebate from a tax when conditioned upon conduct is in some measure a temptation. But to hold that motive or temptation is equivalent to coercion is to plunge the law in endless difficulties. The outcome of such a doctrine is the acceptance of a philosophical determinism by which

---

[9] The attitude of Massachusetts is significant. Her act became a law August 12, 1935, two days before the federal act. Even so, she prescribed that its provisions should not become operative unless the federal bill became a law, or unless eleven of the following states (Alabama, Connecticut, Delaware, Georgia, Illinois, Indiana, Iowa, Maine, Maryland, Michigan, Minnesota, Missouri, New Hampshire, New Jersey, New York, North Carolina, Ohio, Rhode Island, South Carolina, Tennessee, Vermont) should impose on their employers burdens substantially equivalent. Acts of 1935, c. 479, p. 655. Her fear of competition is thus forcefully attested. See also California Laws, 1935, c. 352, Art. I, §2; Idaho Laws, 1936 (Third Extra Session), c. 12, §26; Mississippi Laws, 1936, c. 176, §2-a.

Section A. Trade, Production, and Employment

choice becomes impossible. Till now the law has been guided by a robust common sense which assumes the freedom of the will as a working hypothesis in the solution of its problems. The wisdom of the hypothesis has illustration in this case. . . .

In ruling as we do, we leave many questions open. We do not say that a tax is valid, when imposed by act of Congress, if it is laid upon the condition that a state may escape its operation through the adoption of a statute unrelated in subject matter to activities fairly within the scope of national policy and power. No such question is before us. In the tender of this credit Congress does not intrude upon fields foreign to its function. The purpose of its intervention, as we have shown, is to safeguard its own treasury and as an incident to that protection to place the states upon a footing of equal opportunity. Drains upon its own resources are to be checked; obstructions to the freedom of the states are to be leveled. It is one thing to impose a tax dependent upon the conduct of the taxpayers, or of the state in which they live, where the conduct to be stimulated or discouraged is unrelated to the fiscal need subserved by the tax in its normal operation, or to any other end legitimately national. The Child Labor Tax Case, 259 U.S. 20, and Hill v. Wallace, 259 U.S. 44, were decided in the belief that the statutes there condemned were exposed to that reproach. Cf. United States v. Constantine, 296 U.S. 287. It is quite another thing to say that a tax will be abated upon the doing of an act that will satisfy the fiscal need, the tax and the alternative being approximate equivalents. In such circumstances, if in no others, inducement or persuasion does not go beyond the bounds of power. We do not fix the outermost line. Enough for present purposes that wherever the line may be, this statute is within it. Definition more precise must abide the wisdom of the future.

Florida v. Mellon, 273 U.S. 12, supplies us with a precedent, if precedent be needed. What was in controversy there was §301 of the Revenue Act of 1926, which imposes a tax upon the transfer of a decedent's estate, while at the same time permitting a credit, not exceeding 80 per cent, for "the amount of any estate, inheritance, legacy, or succession taxes actually paid to any State or Territory." Florida challenged that provision as unlawful. Florida had no inheritance taxes and alleged that under its constitution it could not levy any. 273 U.S. 12, 15. Indeed, by abolishing inheritance taxes, it had hoped to induce wealthy persons to become its citizens. See 67 Cong. Rec., Part 1, pp. 735, 752. It argued at our bar that "the Estate Tax provision was not passed for the purpose of raising federal revenue" (273 U.S. 12, 14), but rather "to coerce States into adopting estate or inheritance tax laws." 273 U.S. 12, 13. In fact, as a result of the 80 per cent credit, material changes of such laws were made in 36 states. In the face of that attack we upheld the act as valid. Cf. Massachusetts v. Mellon, 262 U.S. 447, 482; also Act of August 5, 1861, c. 45, 12 Stat. 292; Act of May 13, 1862, c. 66, 12 Stat. 384.

United States v. Butler, supra, is cited by petitioner as a decision to the contrary. There a tax was imposed on processors of farm products, the proceeds to be paid to farmers who would reduce their acreage and crops under agreements with the Secretary of Agriculture, the plan of the act being to increase the prices of certain farm products by decreasing the quantities produced. The court held (1) that the so-called tax was not a true one (pp. 56, 61), the proceeds being earmarked for the benefit of farmers complying with the prescribed conditions, (2) that there was an attempt to regulate production without the consent of the state in which production was affected, and (3) that the payments to farmers were coupled with coercive contracts (p. 73), unlawful in their aim and oppressive in their consequences. The decision was by a divided court, a minority taking the view that the objections were untenable. None of them is applicable to the situation here developed.

(a) The proceeds of the tax in controversy are not earmarked for a special group.

(b) The unemployment compensation law which is a condition of the credit has had the approval of the state and could not be a law without it.

(c) The condition is not linked to an irrevocable agreement, for the state at its pleasure may repeal its unemployment law, §903(a)(6), terminate the credit, and place itself where it was before the credit was accepted.

(d) The condition is not directed to the attainment of an unlawful end, but to an end, the relief of unemployment, for which nation and state may lawfully coöperate.

Fourth. The statute does not call for a surrender by the states of powers essential to their quasi-sovereign existence.

Argument to the contrary has its source in two sections of the act. One section (903) defines the minimum criteria to which a state compensation system is required to conform if it is to be accepted by the Board as the basis for a credit. The other section (904) rounds out the requirement with complementary rights and duties. Not all the criteria or their incidents are challenged as unlawful. We will speak of them first generally, and then more specifically in so far as they are questioned.

A credit to taxpayers for payments made to a State under a state unemployment law will be manifestly futile in the absence of some assurance that the law leading to the credit is in truth what it professes to be. An unemployment law framed in such a way that the unemployed who look to it will be deprived of reasonable protection is one in name and nothing more. What is basic and essential may be assured by suitable conditions. The terms embodied in these sections are directed to that end. A wide range of judgment is given to the several states as to the particular type of statute to be spread upon their books. For anything to the contrary in the provisions of this act they may use the pooled unemployment form, which is in effect with variations in Alabama, California, Michigan, New York, and elsewhere. They may establish a system of merit ratings applicable at once or to go into effect later on the basis of subsequent experience. Cf. §§ 909, 910. They may provide for employee contributions as in Alabama and California, or put the entire burden upon the employer as in New York. They may choose a system of unemployment reserve accounts by which an employer is permitted after his reserve has accumulated to contribute at a reduced rate or even not at all. This is the system which had its origin in Wisconsin. What they may not do, if they would earn the credit, is to depart from those standards which in the judgment of Congress are to be ranked as fundamental. . . . In the event that some particular condition shall be found to be too uncertain to be capable of enforcement, it may be severed from the others, and what is left will still be valid.

We are to keep in mind steadily that the conditions to be approved by the Board as the basis for a credit are not provisions of a contract, but terms of a statute, which may be altered or repealed. § 903(a)(6). The state does not bind itself to keep the law in force. It does not even bind itself that the moneys paid into the federal fund will be kept there indefinitely or for any stated time. On the contrary, the Secretary of the Treasury will honor a requisition for the whole or any part of the deposit in the fund whenever one is made by the appropriate officials. The only consequence of the repeal or excessive amendment of the statute, or the expenditure of the money, when requisitioned, for other than compensation uses or administrative expenses, is that approval of the law will end, and with it the allowance of a credit, upon notice to the state agency and an opportunity for hearing. § 903(b)(c).

These basic considerations are in truth a solvent of the problem. Subjected to their test, the several objections on the score of abdication are found to be unreal. . . .

Finally and chiefly, abdication is supposed to follow from § 904 of the statute and the parts of § 903 that are complementary thereto. § 903 (a)(3). By these the Secretary of the Treasury is authorized and directed to receive and hold in the Unemployment Trust Fund all moneys deposited therein by a state agency for a state unemployment fund and to invest in obligations of the United States such portion of the Fund as is not in his judgment required to meet current withdrawals. We are told that Alabama in consenting to that deposit has renounced the plenitude of power inherent in her statehood. . . .

There are very good reasons of fiscal and governmental policy why a State should be willing to make the Secretary of the Treasury the custodian of the fund. His possession of the moneys and his control of investments will be an assurance of stability and safety in times of stress and strain. A report of the Ways and Means Committee of the House of

Representatives, quoted in the margin, develops the situation clearly.[13] Nor is there risk of loss or waste. The credit of the Treasury is at all times back of the deposit, with the result that the right of withdrawal will be unaffected by the fate of any intermediate investments, just as if a checking account in the usual form had been opened in a bank.

The inference of abdication thus dissolves in thinnest air when the deposit is conceived of as dependent upon a statutory consent, and not upon a contract effective to create a duty. By this we do not intimate that the conclusion would be different if a contract were discovered. Even sovereigns may contract without derogating from their sovereignty. Perry v. United States, 294 U.S. 330, 353; 1 Oppenheim, International Law, 4th ed., §§493, 494; Hall, International Law, 8th ed., §107; 2 Hyde, International Law, §489. The states are at liberty, upon obtaining the consent of Congress, to make agreements with one another. Constitution, Art. 1, §10, par. 3. Poole v. Fleeger, 11 Pet. 185, 209; Rhode Island v. Massachusetts, 12 Pet. 657, 725. We find no room for doubt that they may do the like with Congress if the essence of their statehood is maintained without impairment. Alabama is seeking and obtaining a credit of many millions in favor of her citizens out of the Treasury of the nation. Nowhere in our scheme of government — in the limitations express or implied of our federal constitution — do we find that she is prohibited from assenting to conditions that will assure a fair and just requital for benefits received. But we will not labor the point further. An unreal prohibition directed to an unreal agreement will not vitiate an act of Congress, and cause it to collapse in ruin.

Fifth. Title III of the act is separable from Title IX, and its validity is not at issue.

The essential provisions of that title have been stated in the opinion. As already pointed out, the title does not appropriate a dollar of the public moneys. It does no more than authorize appropriations to be made in the future for the purpose of assisting states in the administration of their laws, if Congress shall decide that appropriations are desirable. The title might be expunged, and Title IX would stand intact. Without a severability clause we should still be led to that conclusion. The presence of such a clause (§1103) makes the conclusion even clearer. Williams v. Standard Oil Co., 278 U.S. 235, 242; Utah Power & Light Co. v. Pfost, 286 U.S. 165, 184; Carter v. Carter Coal Co., 298 U.S. 238, 312.

The judgment is
Affirmed.[d]

Separate opinion of MR. JUSTICE MCREYNOLDS.

That portion of the Social Security legislation here under consideration, I think, exceeds the power granted to Congress. It unduly interferes with the orderly government of the State by her own people and otherwise offends the Federal Constitution.

In Texas v. White, 7 Wall. 700, 725 (1869), a cause of momentous importance, this Court, through Chief Justice Chase, declared —

---

[13] "This last provision will not only afford maximum safety for these funds but is very essential to insure that they will operate to promote the stability of business rather than the reverse. Unemployment reserve funds have the peculiarity that the demands upon them fluctuate considerably, being heaviest when business slackens. If, in such times, the securities in which these funds are invested are thrown upon the market for liquidation, the net effect is likely to be increased deflation. Such a result is avoided in this bill through the provision that all reserve funds are to be held by the United States Treasury, to be invested and liquidated by the Secretary of the Treasury in a manner calculated to promote business stability. When business conditions are such that investment in securities purchased on the open market is unwise, the Secretary of the Treasury may issue special nonnegotiable obligations exclusively to the unemployment trust fund. When a reverse situation exists and heavy drains are made upon the fund for payment of unemployment benefits, the Treasury does not have to dispose of the securities belonging to the fund in open market but may assume them itself. With such a method of handling the reserve funds, it is believed that this bill will solve the problem often raised in discussions of unemployment compensation, regarding the possibility of transferring purchasing power from boom periods to depression periods. It will in fact operate to sustain purchasing power at the onset of a depression without having any counteracting deflationary tendencies." House Report, No. 615, 74th Congress, 1st session, p. 9.

[d] An interesting account of the drafting of the Social Security bill is given in Eliot, The Social Security Bill 25 Years After, 206 Atlantic Monthly 72 (Aug. 1960). — ED.

"... The Constitution, in all its provisions, looks to an indestructible Union, composed of indestructible States."

The doctrine thus announced and often repeated, I had supposed was firmly established. Apparently the States remained really free to exercise governmental powers, not delegated or prohibited, without interference by the Federal Government through threats of punitive measures or offers of seductive favors. Unfortunately, the decision just announced opens the way for practical annihilation of this theory; and no cloud of words or ostentatious parade of irrelevant statistics should be permitted to obscure that fact.

The invalidity, also the destructive tendency, of legislation like the Act before us were forcefully pointed out by President Franklin Pierce in a veto message sent to the Senate May 3, 1854.[1] He was a scholarly lawyer of distinction and enjoyed the advice and counsel of a rarely able Attorney General — Caleb Cushing of Massachusetts. This message considers with unusual lucidity points here specially important. I venture to set out pertinent portions of it which must appeal to all who continue to respect both the letter and spirit of our great charter.

To the Senate of the United States:

"The bill entitled 'An Act making a grant of public lands to the several States for the benefit of indigent insane persons,' which was presented to me on the 27th ultimo, has been maturely considered, and is returned to the Senate, the House in which it orginated, with a statement of the objections which have required me to withhold from it my approval. . . .

"It can not be questioned that if Congress has power to make provision for the indigent insane without the limits of this District it has the same power to provide for the indigent who are not insane, and thus to transfer to the Federal Government the charge of all the poor in all the States. It has the same power to provide hospitals and other local establishments for the care and cure of every species of human infirmity, and thus to assume all that duty of either public philanthropy or public necessity to the dependent, the orphan, the sick, or the needy which is now discharged by the States themselves or by corporate institutions or private endowments existing under the legislation of the States. The whole field of public beneficence is thrown open to the care and culture of the Federal Government. Generous impulses no longer encounter the limitations and control of our imperious fundamental law; for however worthy may be the present object in itself, it is only one of a class. . . .

"In my judgment you can not by tributes to humanity make any adequate compensation for the wrong you would inflict by removing the sources of power and political action from those who are to be thereby affected. If the time shall ever arrive when, for an object appealing, however strongly, to our sympathies, the dignity of the States shall bow to the dictation of Congress by conforming their legislation thereto, when the power and majesty and honor of those who created shall become subordinate to the thing of their creation, I but feebly utter my apprehensions when I express my firm conviction that we shall see 'the beginning of the end.' . . ."

No defense is offered for the legislation under review upon the basis of emergency. The hypothesis is that hereafter it will continuously benefit unemployed members of a class. Forever, so far as we can see, the States are expected to function under federal direction concerning an internal matter. By the sanction of this adventure, the door is open for progressive inauguration of others of like kind under which it can hardly be expected that the States will retain genuine independence of action. And without independent States a Federal Union as contemplated by the Constitution becomes impossible. . . .

Ordinarily, I must think, a denial that the challenged action of Congress and what has

---

[1] "Messages and Papers of the President" by James D. Richardson, Vol. V, pp. 247-256.

been done under it amount to coercion and impair freedom of government by the people of the State would be regarded as contrary to practical experience. Unquestionably our federate plan of government confronts an enlarged peril.

Separate opinion of Mr. Justice Sutherland.

With most of what is said in the opinion just handed down, I concur. . . .

But the question with which I have difficulty is whether the administrative provisions of the act invade the governmental administrative powers of the several states reserved by the Tenth Amendment. . . .

I do not, of course, doubt the power of the state to select and utilize a depository for the safekeeping of its funds; but it is quite another thing to agree with the selected depository that the funds shall be withdrawn for certain stipulated purposes, and for no other. Nor do I doubt the authority of the federal government and a state government to coöperate to a common end, provided each of them is authorized to reach it. . . .

But this is not the situation with which we are called upon to deal in the present case. For here, the state *must* deposit the proceeds of its taxation in the federal treasury, upon terms which make the deposit suspiciously like a forced loan to be repaid only in accordance with restrictions imposed by federal law. Title IX, §§ 903(a)(3), 904(a), (b), (e). All moneys withdrawn from this fund must be used exclusively for the payment of compensation. § 903(a)(4). And this compensation is to be paid through public employment offices in the state or such other agencies as a *federal board may approve*. § 909(a)(1). The act, it is true, recognizes [§ 903(a)(6)] the power of the legislature to amend or repeal its compensation law at any time. But there is nothing in the act, as I read it, which justifies the conclusion that the state may, in that event, unconditionally withdraw its funds from the federal treasury. Section 903(b) provides that the board shall certify in each taxable year to the Secretary of the Treasury each state whose law has been approved. But the board is forbidden to certify any state which the board finds has so changed its law that it no longer contains the provisions specified in subsection (a), "or has with respect to such taxable year failed to comply substantially with any such provision." The federal government, therefore, in the person of its agent, the board, sits not only as a perpetual overseer, interpreter and censor of state legislation on the subject, but, as lord paramount, to determine whether the state is faithfully executing its own law — as though the state were a dependency under pupilage and not to be trusted. The foregoing, taken in connection with the provisions that money withdrawn can be used only in payment of compensation and that it must be paid through an agency approved by the federal board, leaves it, to say the least, highly uncertain whether the right of the state to withdraw any part of its own funds exists, under the act, otherwise than upon these various statutory conditions. It is true also that subsection (f) of § 904 authorizes the Secretary of the Treasury to pay to any state agency "such amount as it may duly requisition, not exceeding the amount standing to the account of such State agency at the time of such payment." But it is to be observed that the payment is to be made to the state *agency*, and only such amount as that agency may *duly* requisition. It is hard to find in this provision any extension of the right of the state to withdraw its funds except in the manner and for the specific purpose prescribed by the act.

By these various provisions of the act, the federal agencies are authorized to supervise and hamper the administrative powers of the state to a degree which not only does not comport with the dignity of a quasi-sovereign state — a matter with which we are not judicially concerned — but which denies to it that supremacy and freedom from external interference in respect of its affairs which the Constitution contemplates — a matter of very definite judicial concern. . . .

If we are to survive as the United *States*, the balance between the powers of the nation and those of the states must be maintained. There is grave danger in permitting it to dip in either direction, danger — if there were no other — in the precedent thereby set for further departures from the equipoise. The threat implicit in the present encroachment upon the administrative functions of the states is that greater encroachments, and encroachments upon other functions, will follow.

For the foregoing reasons, I think the judgment below should be reversed.

Mr. Justice Van Devanter joins in this opinion.

Mr. Justice Butler, dissenting.

I think that the objections to the challenged enactment expressed in the separate opinions of Mr. Justice McReynolds and Mr. Justice Sutherland are well taken. I am also of opinion that, in principle and as applied to bring about and to gain control over state unemployment compensation, the statutory scheme is repugnant to the Tenth Amendment: "The powers not delegated to the United States by the Constitution, nor prohibited by it to the States, are reserved to the States respectively, or to the people." The Constitution grants to the United States no power to pay unemployed persons or to require the States to enact laws or to raise or disburse money for that purpose. The provisions in question, if not amounting to coercion in a legal sense, are manifestly designed and intended directly to affect state action in the respects specified. And, if valid as so employed, this "tax and credit" device may be made effective to enable federal authorities to induce, if not indeed to compel, state enactments for any purpose within the realm of state power, and generally to control state administration of state laws. . . .

When the federal Act was passed Wisconsin was the only State paying unemployment compensation. Though her plan then in force is by students of the subject generally deemed the best yet devised, she found it necessary to change her law in order to secure federal approval. In the absence of that, Wisconsin employers subject to the federal tax would not have been allowed any deduction on account of their contribution to the state fund. Any State would be moved to conform to federal requirements, not utterly objectionable, in order to save its taxpayers from the federal tax imposed in addition to the contributions under state laws.

Federal agencies prepared and took draft bills to state legislatures to enable and induce them to pass laws providing for unemployment compensation in accordance with federal requirements, and thus to obtain relief for the employers from the impending federal exaction. Obviously the Act creates the peril of federal tax not to raise revenue but to persuade. Of course, each State was free to reject any measure so proposed. But, if it failed to adopt a plan acceptable to federal authority, the full burden of the federal tax would be exacted. And, as federal demands similarly conditioned may be increased from time to time as Congress shall determine, possible federal pressure in that field is without limit. Already at least 43 States, yielding to the inducement resulting immediately from the application of the federal tax and credit device, have provided for unemployment compensation in form to merit approval of the Social Security Board. Presumably the remaining States will comply whenever convenient for their legislatures to pass the necessary laws.

The terms of the measure make it clear that the tax and credit device was intended to enable federal officers virtually to control the exertion of powers of the States in a field in which they alone have jurisdiction and from which the United States is by the Constitution excluded.

I am of opinion that the judgment of the Circuit Court of Appeals should be reversed.

NOTE

1. In Helvering v. Davis, 301 U.S. 619 (1937), decided the same day, the Court sustained Title II of the Social Security Act, providing for the payment of old-age benefits, in a stockholders' suit to enjoin the payment of taxes under Title VIII. Justices McReynolds and Butler dissented. The Court chose not to decide whether Title VIII, imposing a tax on employers and employees, was separable from Title II, stating (p. 645): "Title II being

valid, there is no occasion to inquire whether title VIII would have to fall if title II were set at naught. The argument for the respondent is that the provisions of the two titles dovetail in such a way as to justify the conclusion that Congress would have been unwilling to pass one without the other. The argument for petitioners is that the tax moneys are not earmarked, and that Congress is at liberty to spend them as it will. The usual separability clause is embodied in the act. Section 1103. We find it unnecessary to make a choice between the arguments, and so leave the question open."

2. On the problems of fiscal policy involved in the financing of social security and the investment of the reserve funds, see Modlin, The Old-Age Reserve Account and Its Economic Implications, 3 Law & Contemp. Prob. 221 (1936); Harris, Economics of Social Security, c. 5 (1941); Hansen, Full Recovery or Stagnation, c. 8 (1938); Hansen, Economic Policy and Full Employment 124-128 (1947); Witte, Social Security, in Harris, ed., Saving American Capitalism, c. 26 (1948); Merriam, Social Security Financing (Fed. Sec. Agency 1952).

3. In Canada and Australia, provision for federal unemployment and old-age payments has been thought to require constitutional amendment.

The British North America Act (1867) confers on the Dominion Parliament power to legislate "for the peace, order and good government of Canada" in "matters not coming within the classes of subjects by this Act assigned exclusively to the legislatures of the provinces," and specifically, inter alia, without regard to the powers exclusively conferred on the provinces, to legislate in matters of "the raising of money by any mode or system of taxation." §91(3). The provincial legislatures are given power to legislate in relation, inter alia, to "property and civil rights in the province." A Dominion act establishing a plan of unemployment compensation by taxation of employers and employees was held invalid in Attorney-General for Canada v. Attorney-General for Ontario, [1937] A.C. 355, aff'g [1936] S.C.R. (Can.) 427. In 1940 there was adopted a constitutional amendment authorizing Dominion unemployment insurance, and in 1951 an amendment authorizing Dominion old-age pensions.

The Australian Constitution confers on the Commonwealth Parliament power to legislate "for the peace, order and good government of the Commonwealth with respect to . . . taxation" (§51(ii)), and provides: "All revenues or moneys raised or received by the Executive Government of the Commonwealth shall form one Consolidated Revenue Fund, to be appropriated for the purposes of the Commonwealth in the manner and subject to the charges and liabilities imposed by this Constitution." §81. In the Pharmaceutical Benefits Case, 71 C.L.R. 237 (1946), the High Court held invalid a Commonwealth law covering out of public funds the cost of medicines prescribed by a physician on an approved form and supplied by an approved pharmaceutical chemist. A constitutional amendment was adopted the same year, granting power to the Commonwealth to legislate in respect of "maternity allowances, widows' pensions, child endowment, unemployment, pharmaceutical, sickness and hospital benefits, medical and dental services (but not so as to authorize any form of civil conscription), benefits to students and family allowances."

NLRB v. Jones & Laughlin Steel Corp. 301 U.S. 1, 57 S. Ct. 615, 81 L. Ed. 893 (1937)

Mr. Chief Justice Hughes delivered the opinion of the Court.

In a proceeding under the National Labor Relations Act of 1935, the National Labor Relations Board found that the respondent, Jones & Laughlin Steel Corporation, had violated the Act by engaging in unfair labor practices affecting commerce. The proceeding was instituted by the Beaver Valley Lodge No. 200, affiliated with the Amalgamated Association of Iron, Steel and Tin Workers of America, a labor organization. The unfair labor practices charged were that the corporation was discriminating against members of the union with regard to hire and tenure of employment, and was coercing and intimidating its employees in order to interfere with their self-organization. The discriminatory and coercive action alleged was the discharge of certain employees.

The National Labor Relations Board, sustaining the charge, ordered the corporation to cease and desist from such discrimination and coercion, to offer reinstatement to ten of the employees named, to make good their losses in pay, and to post for thirty days notices that the corporation would not discharge or discriminate against members, or those desiring to become members, of the labor union. As the corporation failed to comply, the Board petitioned the Circuit Court of Appeals to enforce the order. The court denied the petition, holding that the order lay beyond the range of federal power. 83 F.(2d)998. We granted certiorari.

The scheme of the National Labor Relations Act — which is too long to be quoted in full — may be briefly stated. The first section sets forth findings with respect to the injury to commerce resulting from the denial by employers of the right of employees to organize and from the refusal of employers to accept the procedure of collective bargaining. There follows a declaration that it is the policy of the United States to eliminate these causes of obstruction to the free flow of commerce. The Act then defines the terms it uses, including the terms "commerce" and "affecting commerce." §2. It creates the National Labor Relations Board and prescribes its organization. §§3-6. It sets forth the right of employees to self-organization and to bargain collectively through representatives of their own choosing. §7. It defines "unfair labor practices." §8. It lays down rules as to the representation of employees for the purpose of collective bargaining. §9. The Board is empowered to prevent the described unfair labor practices affecting commerce and the Act prescribes the procedure to that end. The Board is authorized to petition designated courts to secure the enforcement of its order. The findings of the Board as to the facts, if supported by evidence, are to be conclusive. If either party on application to the court shows that additional evidence is material and that there were reasonable grounds for the failure to adduce such evidence in the hearings before the Board, the court may order the additional evidence to be taken. Any person aggrieved by a final order of the Board may obtain a review in the designated courts with the same procedure as in the case of an application by the Board for the enforcement of its order. §10. The Board has broad powers of investigation. §11. Interference with members of the Board or its agents in the performance of their duties is punishable by fine and imprisonment. §12. Nothing in the Act is to be construed to interfere with the right to strike. §13. There is a separability clause to the effect that if any provision of the Act or its application to any person or circumstances shall be held invalid, the remainder of the Act or its application to other persons or circumstances shall not be affected. §15. The particular provisions which are involved in the instant case will be considered more in detail in the course of the discussion. . . .

The facts as to the nature and scope of the business of the Jones & Laughlin Steel Corporation have been found by the Labor Board and, so far as they are essential to the determination of this controversy, they are not in dispute. The Labor Board has found: The corporation is organized under the laws of Pennsylvania and has its principal office at Pittsburgh. It is engaged in the business of manufacturing iron and steel in plants situated in Pittsburgh and nearby Aliquippa, Pennsylvania. It manufactures and distributes a widely diversified line of steel and pig iron, being the fourth largest producer of steel in the United States. With its subsidiaries — nineteen in number — it is a completely integrated enterprise, owning and operating ore, coal and limestone properties, lake and river transportation facilities and terminal railroads located at its manufacturing plants. It owns or controls mines in Michigan and Minnesota. It operates four ore steamships on the Great Lakes, used in the transportation of ore to its factories. It owns coal mines in Pennsylvania. It operates towboats and steam barges used in carrying coal to its factories. It owns limestone properties in various places in Pennsylvania and West Virginia. It owns the Monongahela connecting railroad which connects the plants of the Pittsburgh works and forms an interconnection with the Pennsylvania, New York Central and Baltimore and Ohio Railroad systems. It owns the Aliquippa and Southern Railroad Company which connects the Aliquippa works with the Pittsburgh and Lake Erie, part of the New York Central system. Much of its product is shipped to its warehouses in Chicago, Detroit, Cincinnati and Memphis, — to the last two places by means of its own barges and transportation equipment. In Long Island City, New York, and in New Orleans it operates structural steel fabricating shops in connection with the warehousing of semi-finished materials sent from its works. Through one of its wholly-owned subsidiaries it owns, leases and operates stores, warehouses and yards for the distribution of equipment and supplies for drilling and operating oil and gas mills and for pipe lines, refineries and pumping stations. It has sales offices in twenty cities in the United States and a wholly-owned subsidiary which is devoted exclusively to distributing its product in Canada. Approximately 75 per cent of its products is shipped out of Pennsylvania.

Summarizing these operations, the Labor Board concluded that the works in Pittsburgh and Aliquippa "might be likened to the heart of a self-contained, highly integrated body. They draw in the raw materials from Michigan, Minnesota, West Virginia, Pennsylvania in part through arteries and by means controlled by the respondent; they transform the materials and then pump them out to all parts of the nation through the vast mechanism which the respondent has elaborated." . . .

Practically all the factual evidence in the case, except that which dealt with the nature of respondent's business, concerned its relations with the employees in the Aliquippa plant whose discharge was the subject of the complaint. These employees were active leaders in the labor union. Several were officers and others were leaders of particular groups. Two of the employees were motor inspectors; one was a tractor driver; three were crane operators; one was a washer in the coke plant; and three were laborers. Three other employees were mentioned in the complaint but it was withdrawn as to one of them and no evidence was heard on the action taken with respect to the other two. . . .

First. The scope of the Act. — The Act is challenged in its entirety as an attempt to regulate all industry, thus invading the reserved powers of the States over their local concerns. It is asserted that the references in the Act to interstate and foreign commerce are colorable at best; that the Act is not a true regulation of such commerce or of matters which directly affect it but on the contrary has the fundamental object of placing under the compulsory supervision of the Federal government all industrial labor relations within the nation. The argument seeks support in the broad words of the preamble (section one) and in the sweep of the provisions of the Act, and it is further insisted that its legislative history shows an essential universal purpose in the light of which its scope cannot be limited by either construction or by the application of the separability clause.

If this conception of terms, intent and consequent inseparability were sound, the Act would necessarily fall by reason of the limitation upon the Federal power which inheres in the constitutional grant, as well as because of the explicit reservation of the Tenth Amendment. A. L. A. Schechter Poultry Corp. v. United States, 295 U.S. 495, 549, 550, 554. The authority of the Federal government may not be pushed to such an extreme as to destroy the distinction, which the commerce clause itself establishes, between commerce "among the several States" and the internal concerns of a State. That distinction between what is national and what is local in the activities of commerce is vital to the maintenance of our Federal system. Ibid.

But we are not at liberty to deny effect to specific provisions, which Congress has constitutional power to enact, by superimposing upon them inferences from general legislative declarations of an ambiguous character, even if found in the same statute. The cardinal principle of statutory construction is to save and not to destroy. We have repeatedly held that as between two possible interpretations of a statute, by one of which it would be unconstitutional and by the other valid, our plain duty is to adopt that which will save the act. Even to avoid a serious doubt the rule is the same. [Citation omitted.]

We think it clear that the National Labor Relations Act may be construed so as to operate within the sphere of constitutional authority. The jurisdiction conferred upon the Board, and invoked in this instance, is found in §10(a), which provides:

"Sec. 10(a). The Board is empowered, as hereinafter provided, to prevent any persons from engaging in any unfair labor practice (listed in §8) affecting commerce."

The critical words of this provision, prescribing the limits of the Board's authority in dealing with the labor practices, are "affecting commerce." The Act specifically defines the "commerce" to which it refers (§2(6)):

"The term 'commerce' means trade, traffic, commerce, transportation, or communication among the several States, or between the District of Columbia or any Territory of the United States and any State or other Territory, or between any foreign country and any State, Territory, or the District of Columbia, or within the District of Columbia or any Territory, or between points in the same State but through any other State or any Territory or the District of Columbia or any foreign country."

. . . The Act also defines the term "affecting commerce" (§2(7)):

"The term 'affecting commerce' means in commerce, or burdening or obstructing commerce or the free flow of commerce, or having led or tending to lead to a labor dispute burdening or obstructing commerce or the free flow of commerce."

. . . It is a familiar principle that acts which directly burden or obstruct interstate or foreign commerce, or its free flow, are within the reach of the congressional power. Acts having that effect are not rendered immune because they grow out of labor disputes. [Citations omitted.] It is the effect upon commerce, not the source of the injury, which is the criterion. Second Employers' Liability Cases (Mondou v. New York, N.H. & H.R. Co.), 223 U.S. 1, 51. Whether or not particular action does affect commerce in such a close and intimate fashion as to be subject to Federal control, and hence to lie within the authority conferred upon the Board, is left by the statute to be determined as individual cases arise. We are thus to inquire whether in the instant case the constitutional boundary has been passed.

Second. The unfair labor practices in question. — The unfair labor practices found by the Board are those defined in §8, subdivision (1) and (3). These provide:

"Sec. 8. It shall be an unfair labor practice for an employer —

"(1) To interfere with, restrain, or coerce employees in the exercise of the rights guaranteed in §7."

"(3) By discrimination in regard to hire or tenure of employment or any term or condition of employment to encourage or discourage membership in any labor organization. . . ."

Section 8, subdivision (1), refers to §7, which is as follows:

"Sec. 7. Employees shall have the right to self-organization, to form, join, or assist labor organizations, to bargain collectively through representatives of their own choosing, and to engage in concerted activities, for the purpose of collective bargaining or other mutual aid or protection."

Thus, in its present application, the statute goes no further than to safeguard the right of employees to self-organization and to select representatives of their own choosing for collective bargaining or other mutual protection without restraint or coercion by their employer.

That is a fundamental right. Employees have as clear a right to organize and select their representatives for lawful purposes as the respondent has to organize its business and select its own officers and agents. Discrimination and coercion to prevent the free exercise of the right of employees to self-organization and representation is a proper subject for condemnation by competent legislative authority. Long ago we stated the reason for labor organizations. We said that they were organized out of the necessities of the situation; that a single employee was helpless in dealing with an employer; that he was dependent ordinarily on his daily wage for the maintenance of himself and family; that if the employer refused to pay him the wages that he thought fair, he was nevertheless unable to leave the employ and resist arbitrary and unfair treatment; that union was essential to give laborers opportunity to deal on an equality with their employer. American Steel Foundries v. Tri-City Central Trades Council, 257 U.S. 184, 209. We reiterated these views when we had under consideration the Railway Labor Act of 1926. Fully recognizing the legality of collective action on the part of employees in order to safeguard their proper interests, we said that Congress was not required to ignore this right but could safeguard it. Congress could seek to make appropriate collective action of employees an instrument of peace rather than of strife. We said that such collective action would be a mockery if representation were made futile by interference with freedom of choice. Hence the prohibition by Congress of interference with the selection of representatives for the purpose of negotiation and conference between employers and employees, "instead of being an invasion of the constitutional right of either, was based on the recognition of the rights of both." Texas & N.O.R. Co. v. Brotherhood of R. & S.S. Clerks, 281 U.S. 548. We have reasserted the same principle in sustaining the application of the Railway Labor Act as amended in 1934. Virginian R. Co. v. System Federation, R.E.D., 300 U.S. 515.

Third. The application of the Act to employees engaged in production. — The principle involved. — Respondent says that whatever may be said of employees engaged in interstate commerce, the industrial relations and activities in the manufacturing department of respondent's enterprise are not subject to Federal regulation. The argument rests upon the proposition that manufacturing in itself is not commerce. [Citations omitted.]

The Government distinguishes these cases. The various parts of respondent's enterprise are described as interdependent and as thus involving "a great movement of iron ore, coal and limestone along well-defined paths to the steel mills, thence through them, and thence in the form of steel products into the consuming centers of the country — a definite and well-understood course of business." It is urged that these activities constitute a "stream" or "flow" of commerce, of which the Aliquippa manufacturing plant is the focal point, and that industrial strife at that point would cripple the entire movement. Reference is made to our decision sustaining the Packers and Stockyards Act. Stafford v. Wallace, 258 U.S. 495. The Court found that the stockyards were but a "throat" through which the current of commerce flowed and the transactions which there occurred could not be separated from that movement. . . . Applying the doctrine of Stafford v. Wallace, supra, the Court sustained the Grain Futures Act of 1922 with respect to transactions on the Chicago Board of Trade, although these transactions were "not in and of themselves interstate commerce." Congress had found that they had become "a constantly recurring burden and obstruction to that commerce." Board of Trade v. Olsen, 262 U.S. 1, 32; compare Hill v. Wallace, 259 U.S. 44, 69. See also Tagg Bros. & Moorhead v. United States, 280 U.S. 420.

Respondent contends that the instant case presents material distinctions. . . . The finished products which emerge "are to a large extent manufactured without reference to pre-existing orders and contracts and are entirely different from the raw materials which enter at the other end." . . .

We do not find it necessary to determine whether these features of defendant's business dispose of the asserted analogy to the "stream of commerce" cases. The instances in which that metaphor has been used are but particular, and not exclusive, illustrations of the protective power which the Government invokes in support of the present Act. The congressional authority to protect interstate commerce from burdens and obstructions is not limited to transactions which can be deemed to be an essential part of a "flow" of interstate or foreign commerce. Burdens and obstructions may be due to injurious action springing from other sources. The fundamental principle is that the power to regulate commerce is the power to enact "all appropriate legislation" for "its protection and advancement" (The Daniel Ball, 10 Wall. 557, 564); to adopt measures "to promote its growth and insure its safety" (Mobile County v. Kimball, 102 U.S. 691, 696, 697); "to foster, protect, control and restrain." Second Employers' Liability Cases (Mondou v. New York, N.H. & H.R.

278   Chapter Seven. National Power over the Economy

Co.) supra (223 U.S. 47). See Texas & N.O.R. Co. v. Brotherhood of R. & S.S. Clerks, 281 U.S. 548. That power is plenary and may be exerted to protect interstate commerce "no matter what the source of the dangers which threaten it." Second Employers' Liability Cases, p. 51; A. L. A. Schechter Poultry Corp. v. United States, 295 U.S. 495. Although activities may be intrastate in character when separately considered, if they have such a close and substantial relation to interstate commerce that their control is essential or appropriate to protect that commerce from burdens and obstructions, Congress cannot be denied the power to exercise that control. A. L. A. Schechter Poultry Corp. v. United States, supra. Undoubtedly the scope of this power must be considered in the light of our dual system of government and may not be extended so as to embrace effects upon interstate commerce so indirect and remote that to embrace them, in view of our complex society, would effectually obliterate the distinction between what is national and what is local and create a completely centralized government. Id. The question is necessarily one of degree. . . .

That intrastate activities, by reason of close and intimate relation to interstate commerce, may fall within Federal Control is demonstrated in the case of carriers who are engaged in both interstate and intrastate transportation. There Federal control has been found essential to secure the freedom of interstate traffic from interference or unjust discrimination and to promote the efficiency of the interstate service. . . . It is said that this exercise of Federal power has relation to the maintenance of adequate instrumentalities of interstate commerce. But the agency is not superior to the commerce which uses it. The protective power extends to the former because it exists as to the latter.

The close and intimate effect which brings the subject within the reach of Federal power may be due to activities in relation to productive industry although the industry when separately viewed is local. This has been abundantly illustrated in the application of the Federal Anti-Trust Act. . . .

Upon the same principle, the Anti-Trust Act has been applied to the conduct of employees engaged in production. Loewe v. Lawlor, 208 U.S. 274; United Mine Workers v. Coronado Coal Co., 259 U.S. 344; Bedford Cut Stone Co. v. Journeymen Stone Cutters' Asso., 274 U.S. 37. . . . The decisions dealing with the question of that application illustrate both the principle and its limitation. Thus, in the first Coronado Coal Co. Case, the Court held that mining was not interstate commerce, that the power of Congress did not extend to its regulation as such, and that it had not been shown that the activities there involved — a local strike — brought them within the provisions of the Anti-Trust Act, notwithstanding the broad terms of that statute. . . . But in the first Coronado Case the Court also said that "if Congress deems certain recurring practices, though not really part of interstate commerce, likely to obstruct, restrain or burden it, it has the power to subject them to national supervision and restraint." 259 U.S. p. 408. And in the second Coronado Coal Co. Case the Court ruled that while the mere reduction in the supply of an article to be shipped in interstate commerce by the illegal or tortious prevention of its manufacture or production is ordinarily an indirect and remote obstruction to that commerce, nevertheless when the "intent of those unlawfully preventing the manufacture or production is shown to be to restrain or control the supply entering and moving in interstate commerce, or the price of it in interstate markets, their action is a direct violation of the Anti-Trust Act." 268 U.S. p. 310. And the existence of that intent may be a necessary inference from proof of the direct and substantial effect produced by the employees' conduct. Industrial Asso. v. United States, 268 U.S. p. 81. What was absent from the evidence in the first Coronado Coal Co. Case appeared in the second and the Act was accordingly applied to the mining employees.

It is thus apparent that the fact that the employees here concerned were engaged in production is not determinative. The question remains as to the effect upon interstate commerce of the labor practice involved. In the A. L. A. Schechter Poultry Corp. Case,

Section A. Trade, Production, and Employment

295 U.S. 495, we found that the effect there was so remote as to be beyond the Federal power. To find "immediacy or directness" there was to find it "almost everywhere," a result inconsistent with the maintenance of our Federal system. In the Carter Case, 298 U.S. 238, the Court was of the opinion that the provisions of the statute relating to production were invalid upon several grounds, — that there was improper delegation of legislative power, and that the requirements not only went beyond any sustainable measure of protection of interstate commerce but were also inconsistent with due process. These cases are not controlling here.

Fourth. Effects of the unfair labor practice in respondent's enterprise. — Giving full weight to respondent's contention with respect to a break in the complete continuity of the "stream of commerce" by reason of respondent's manufacturing operations, the fact remains that the stoppage of those operations by industrial strife would have a most serious effect upon interstate commerce. In view of respondent's far-flung activities, it is idle to say that the effect would be indirect or remote. It is obvious that it would be immediate and might be catastrophic. We are asked to shut our eyes to the plainest facts of our national life and to deal with the question of direct and indirect effects in an intellectual vacuum. Because there may be but indirect and remote effects upon interstate commerce in connection with a host of local enterprises throughout the country, it does not follow that other industrial activities do not have such a close and intimate relation to interstate commerce as to make the presence of industrial strife a matter of the most urgent national concern. When industries organize themselves on a national scale, making their relation to interstate commerce the dominant factor in their activities, how can it be maintained that their industrial labor relations constitute a forbidden field into which Congress may not enter when it is necessary to protect interstate commerce from the paralyzing consequences of industrial war? We have often said that interstate commerce itself is a practical conception. It is equally true that interferences with that commerce must be appraised by a judgment that does not ignore actual experience.

Experience has abundantly demonstrated that the recognition of the right of employees to self-organization and to have representatives of their own choosing for the purpose of collective bargaining is often an essential condition of industrial peace. . . .

These questions have frequently engaged the attention of Congress and have been the subject of many inquiries.[8] The steel industry is one of the great basic industries of the United States, with ramifying activities affecting interstate commerce at every point. The Government aptly refers to the steel strike of 1919-1920 with its far-reaching consequences. The fact that there appears to have been no major disturbance in that industry in the more recent period did not dispose of the possibilities of future and like dangers to interstate commerce which Congress was entitled to foresee and to exercise its protective power to forestall. It is not necessary again to detail the facts as to respondent's enterprise. Instead of being beyond the pale, we think that it presents in a most striking way the close and intimate relation which a manufacturing industry may have to interstate commerce and we have no doubt that Congress had constitutional authority to safeguard the right of respondent's employees to self-organization and freedom in the choice of representatives for collective bargaining.

Fifth. The means which the Act employs. — Questions under the due process clause and other constitutional restrictions. — Respondent asserts its right to conduct its business in an orderly manner without being subjected to arbitrary restraints. What we have said points to the fallacy in the argument. Employees have their correlative right to orga-

---

[8] See, for example, Final Report of the Industrial Commission (1902), vol. 19, p. 844; Report of the Anthracite Coal Strike Commission (1902), Sen. Doc. No. 6, 58th Cong., spec. sess.; Final Report of Commission on Industrial Relations (1916), Sen. Doc. No. 415, 64th Cong., 1st sess., vol. 1; National War Labor Board, Principles and Rules of Procedure (1919), p. 4; Bureau of Labor Statistics, Bulletin No. 287 (1921), pp. 52-64; History of the Shipbuilding Labor Adjustment Board, U.S. Bureau of Labor Statistics, Bulletin No. 283.

nize for the purpose of securing the redress of grievances and to promote agreements with employers relating to rates of pay and conditions of work. Texas & N.O.R. Co. v. Brotherhood of R. & S.S. Clerks, 281 U.S. 548; Virginian R. Co. v. System Federation, R.E.D., 300 U.S. 515. Restraint for the purpose of preventing an unjust interference with that right cannot be considered arbitrary or capricious. . . .

. . . The Act does not interfere with the normal exercise of the right of the employer to select its employees or to discharge them. The employer may not, under cover of that right, intimidate or coerce its employees with respect to their self-organization and representation, and, on the other hand, the Board is not entitled to make its authority a pretext for interference with the right of discharge when that right is exercised for other reasons than such intimidation and coercion. The true purpose is the subject of investigation with full opportunity to show the facts. It would seem that when employers freely recognize the right of their employees to their own organizations and their unrestricted right of representation there will be much less occasion for controversy in respect to the free and appropriate exercise of the right of selection and discharge.

The Act has been criticised as one-sided in its application; that it subjects the employer to supervision and restraint and leaves untouched the abuses for which employees may be responsible; that it fails to provide a more comprehensive plan, — with better assurances of fairness to both sides and with increased chances of success in bringing about, if not compelling, equitable solutions of industrial disputes affecting interstate commerce. But we are dealing with the power of Congress, not with a particular policy, or with the extent to which policy should go. We have frequently said that the legislative authority, exerted within its proper field, need not embrace all the evils within its reach. The Constitution does not forbid "cautious advance, step by step," in dealing with the evils which are exhibited in activities within the range of legislative power. . . .

Respondent complains that the Board not only ordered reinstatement but directed the payment of wages for the time lost by the discharge, less amounts earned by the employee during that period. This part of the order was also authorized by the Act. §10(c). It is argued that the requirement is equivalent to a money judgment and hence contravenes the Seventh Amendment with respect to trial by jury. The Seventh Amendment provides that "In suits at common law, where the value in controversy shall exceed twenty dollars, the right of trial by jury shall be preserved." The Amendment thus preserves the right which existed under the common law when the Amendment was adopted. . . . It does not apply where the proceeding is not in the nature of a suit at common law. Guthrie Nat. Bank v. Guthrie, 173 U.S. 528, 537.

The instant case is not a suit at common law or in the nature of such a suit. The proceeding is one unknown to the common law. It is a statutory proceeding. Reinstatement of the employee and payment for time lost are requirements imposed for violation of the statute and are remedies appropriate to its enforcement. The contention under the Seventh Amendment is without merit.

Our conclusion is that the order of the Board was within its competency and that the Act is valid as here applied. The judgment of the Circuit Court of Appeals is reversed and the cause is remanded for further proceedings in conformity with this opinion.

Reversed.

[Two companion cases were decided on the authority of the principal case: NLRB v. Fruehauf Trailer Co., 301 U.S. 49, and NLRB v. Friedman-Harry Marks Clothing Co., 301 U.S. 58. The former involved the largest manufacturer of commercial trailers in the country, with distributors and dealers in the principal cities. The latter involved a clothing manufacturer in Richmond, Virginia, which purchased over 99 percent of its cloth outside the state, and sold over 82 percent of its finished garments to customers outside the state.

A lengthy dissenting opinion, covering the three cases, was delivered by MR. JUSTICE MCREYNOLDS, in which JUSTICES VAN DEVANTER, SUTHERLAND, and BUTLER joined. In the course of the opinion the following statement appears: "It is gravely stated that experience teaches that if an employer discourages membership in 'any organization of any kind' 'in which employees participate, and which exists for the purpose in whole or in part of dealing with employers concerning grievances, labor disputes, wages, rates of pay, hours of employment or conditions of work,' discontent may follow and this in turn may lead to a strike, and as the outcome of the strike there may be a block in the stream of interstate commerce. Therefore Congress may inhibit the discharge! Whatever effect any cause of discontent may ultimately have upon commerce is far too indirect to justify Congressional regulation. Almost anything — marriage, birth, death — may in some fashion affect commerce."]

United States v. Darby 312 U.S. 100, 61 S. Ct. 451, 85 L. Ed. 609 (1941)

MR. JUSTICE STONE delivered the opinion of the Court:

The two principal questions raised by the record in this case are, *first*, whether Congress has constitutional power to prohibit the shipment in interstate commerce of lumber manufactured by employees whose wages are less than a prescribed minimum or whose weekly hours of labor at that wage are greater than a prescribed maximum, and, *second*, whether it has power to prohibit the employment of workmen in the production of goods "for interstate commerce" at other than prescribed wages and hours. A subsidiary question is whether in connection with such prohibitions Congress can require the employer subject to them to keep records showing the hours worked each day and week by each of his employees including those engaged "in the production and manufacture of goods to wit, lumber, for 'interstate commerce.' "

Appellee demurred to an indictment found in the district court for southern Georgia charging him with violation of §15(a)(1), (2) and (5) of the Fair Labor Standards Act of 1938, 52 Stat. 1060, chap. 676. The district court sustained the demurrer and quashed the indictment and the case comes here on direct appeal under §238 of the Judicial Code as amended, which authorizes an appeal to this Court when the judgment sustaining the demurrer "is based upon the invalidity or construction of the statute upon which the indictment is founded."

The Fair Labor Standards Act set up a comprehensive legislative scheme for preventing the shipment in interstate commerce of certain products and commodities produced in the United States under labor conditions as respects wages and hours which fail to conform to standards set up by the Act. Its purpose, as we judicially know from the declaration of policy in §2(a) of the Act, and the reports of Congressional committees proposing the legislation, . . . is to exclude from interstate commerce goods produced for the commerce and to prevent their production for interstate commerce, under conditions detrimental to the maintenance of the minimum standards of living necessary for health and general well-being; and to prevent the use of interstate commerce as the means of competition in the distribution of goods so produced, and as the means of spreading and perpetuating such substandard labor conditions among the workers of the several states. The Act also sets up an administrative procedure whereby those standards may from time to time be modified generally as to industries subject to the Act or within an industry in accordance with specified standards, by an administrator acting in collaboration with "Industry Committees" appointed by him. . . .

The indictment charges that appellee is engaged, in the state of Georgia, in the business of acquiring raw materials, which he manufactures into finished lumber with the intent, when manufactured, to ship it in interstate commerce to customers outside the state, and that he does in fact so ship a large part of the lumber so produced. There are numerous counts charging appellee with the shipment in interstate commerce from Georgia to points outside the state of lumber in the production of which, for interstate commerce, appellee has employed workmen at less than the prescribed minimum wage or more than the prescribed maximum hours without payment to them of any wage for overtime. Other counts charge the employment by appellee of workmen in the production of lumber for interstate commerce at wages at less than 25 cents an hour or for more than the maximum hours per week without payment to them of the prescribed overtime wage. . . .

The demurrer, so far as now relevant to the appeal, challenged the validity of the Fair Labor Standards Act under the Commerce Clause and the Fifth and Tenth Amendments. The district court quashed the indictment in its entirety upon the broad grounds that the Act, which it interpreted as a regulation of manufacture within the states, is unconstitutional. . . .

. . . The appeal statute limits our jurisdiction on this appeal to a review of the determination of the district court so far only as it is based on the validity or construction of the statute. United States v. Borden Co., 308 U.S. 188, 193-195, and cases cited. Hence we accept the district court's interpretation of the indictment and confine our decision to the validity and construction of the statute.

The prohibition of shipment of the proscribed goods in interstate commerce. Section 15(a)(1) prohibits, and the indictment charges, the shipment in interstate commerce, of goods produced for interstate commerce by employees whose wages and hours of employment do not conform to the requirements of the Act. Since this section is not violated unless the commodity shipped has been produced under labor conditions prohibited by §6 and §7, the only question arising under the commerce clause with respect to such shipments is whether Congress has the constitutional power to prohibit them.

While manufacture is not of itself interstate commerce the shipment of manufactured goods interstate is such commerce and the prohibition of such shipment by Congress is indubitably a regulation of the commerce. The power to regulate commerce is the power "to prescribe the rule by which commerce is governed." Gibbons v. Ogden, 9 Wheat. 1, 196. It extends not only to those regulations which aid, foster and protect the commerce, but embraces those which prohibit it. Reid v. Colorado, 187 U.S. 137; Lottery Case (Champion v. Ames), 188 U.S. 321; [additional citations omitted]. It is conceded that the power of Congress to prohibit transportation in interstate commerce includes noxious articles, . . . stolen articles, . . . kidnapped persons, . . . and articles such as intoxicating liquor or convict-made goods, traffic in which is forbidden or restricted by the laws of the state of destination. Kentucky Whip & Collar Co. v. Illinois C. R. Co., 299 U.S. 34.

But it is said that the present prohibition falls within the scope of none of these categories; that while the prohibition is nominally a regulation of the commerce its motive or purpose is regulation of wages and hours of persons engaged in manufacture, the control of which has been reserved to the states and upon which Georgia and some of the states of destination have placed no restriction; that the effect of the present statute is not to exclude the prescribed articles from interstate commerce in aid of state regulation as in Kentucky Whip & Collar Co. v. Illinois C.R. Co. supra, but instead, under the guise of a regulation of interstate commerce, it undertakes to regulate wages and hours within the state contrary to the policy of the state which has elected to leave them unregulated.

. . . Congress, following its own conception of public policy concerning the restrictions which may appropriately be imposed on interstate commerce, is free to exclude from the commerce articles whose use in the states for which they are destined it may conceive to be injurious to the public health, morals or welfare, even though the state has not sought to regulate their use. Reid v. Colorado, 187 U.S. 137; Lottery Case (Champion v. Ames), 188 U.S. 321; Hipolite Egg Co. v. United States, 220 U.S. 45, and Hoke v. United States, 227 U.S. 308.

Such regulation is not a forbidden invasion of state power merely because either its motive or its consequence is to restrict the use of articles of commerce within the states of destination and is not prohibited unless by other constitutional provisions. It is no objection to the assertion of the power to regulate interstate commerce that its exercise is attended by

Section A. Trade, Production, and Employment

the same incidents which attend the exercise of the police power of the states. Seven Cases v. United States, 239 U.S. 510, 514; Hamilton v. Kentucky Distilleries & Warehouse Co., 251 U.S. 146, 156; United States v. Carolene Products Co., 304 U.S. 144, 147; United States v. Appalachian Electric Power Co., 311 U.S. 377. . . .

. . . Whatever their motive and purpose, regulations of commerce which do not infringe some constitutional prohibition are within the plenary power conferred on Congress by the Commerce Clause. Subject only to that limitation, presently to be considered, we conclude that the prohibition of the shipment interstate of goods produced under the forbidden substandard labor conditions is within the constitutional authority of Congress.

In the more than a century which has elapsed since the decision of Gibbons v. Ogden, these principles of constitutional interpretation have been so long and repeatedly recognized by this Court as applicable to the Commerce Clause, that there would be little occasion for repeating them now were it not for the decision of this Court twenty-two years ago in Hammer v. Dagenhart, 247 U.S. 251. In that case it was held by a bare majority of the Court over the powerful and now classic dissent of Mr. Justice Holmes setting forth the fundamental issues involved, that Congress was without power to exclude the products of child labor from interstate commerce. The reasoning and conclusion of the Court's opinion there cannot be reconciled with the conclusion which we have reached, that the power of Congress under the Commerce Clause is plenary to exclude any article from interstate commerce subject only to the specific prohibitions of the Constitution.

Hammer v. Dagenhart has not been followed. The distinction on which the decision was rested that Congressional power to prohibit interstate commerce is limited to articles which in themselves have some harmful or deleterious property — a distinction which was novel when made and unsupported by any provision of the Constitution — has long since been abandoned. Brooks v. United States, 267 U.S. 432; Kentucky Whip & Collar Co. v. Illinois C.R. Co., 299 U.S. 334; Electric Bond & Share Co. v. Securities & Exch. Commission, 303 U.S. 419; Mulford v. Smith, 307 U.S. 38. The thesis of the opinion that the motive of the prohibition or its effect to control in some measure the use or production within the states of the article thus excluded from the commerce can operate to deprive the regulation of its constitutional authority has long since ceased to have force. [Citations omitted.] And finally we have declared "The authority of the federal government over interstate commerce does not differ in extent or character from that retained by the states over intrastate commerce." United States v. Rock Royal Co-operative, 307 U.S. 533, 569.

The conclusion is inescapable that Hammer v. Dagenhart was a departure from the principles which have prevailed in the interpretation of the commerce clause both before and since the decision and that such vitality, as a precedent, as it then had has long since been exhausted. It should be and now is overruled.

Validity of the wage and hour requirements. Section 15(a)(2), and §§6 and 7, require employers to conform to the wage and hour provisions with respect to all employees engaged in the production of goods for interstate commerce. As appellee's employees are not alleged to be "engaged in interstate commerce" the validity of the prohibition turns on the question whether the employment, under other than the prescribed labor standards, of employees engaged in the production of goods for interstate commerce is so related to the commerce and so affects it as to be within the reach of the power of Congress to regulate it.

To answer this question we must at the outset determine whether the particular acts charged in the counts which are laid under §15(a)(2) as they were construed below, constitute "production for commerce" within the meaning of the statute. As the Government seeks to apply the statute in the indictment, and as the court below construed the phrase "produced for interstate commerce," it embraces at least the case where an employer engaged, as is appellee, in the manufacture and shipment of goods in filling orders of extrastate customers, manufactures his product with the intent or expectation that according to the normal course of his business all or some part of it will be selected for shipment to those customers.

Without attempting to define the precise limits of the phrase, we think the acts alleged in the indictment are within the sweep of the statute. . . .

The recognized need of drafting a workable statute and the well known circumstances in which it was to be applied are persuasive of the conclusion, which the legislative history supports, . . . that the "production for commerce" intended includes at least production of goods, which, at the time of production, the employer, according to the normal course of his business, intends or expects to move in interstate commerce although, through the exigencies of the business, all of the goods may not thereafter actually enter interstate commerce.

There remains the question whether such restriction on the production of goods for commerce is a permissible exercise of the commerce power. . . .

While this Court has many times found state regulation of interstate commerce, when uniformity of its regulation is of national concern, to be incompatible with the Commerce Clause even though Congress has not legislated on the subject, the Court has never implied such restraint on state control over matters intrastate not deemed to be regulations of interstate commerce or its instrumentalities even though they affect the commerce. Minnesota Rate Cases (Simpson v. Shepard), 230 U.S. 352, 398 et seq., and cases cited. . . .

But it does not follow that Congress may not by appropriate legislation regulate intrastate activities where they have a substantial effect on interstate commerce. See Santa Cruz Fruit Packing Co. v. National Labor Relations Bd., 303 U.S. 453, 466. A recent example is the National Labor Relations Act. . . . But long before the adoption of the National Labor Relations Act this Court had many times held that the power of Congress to regulate interstate commerce extends to the regulation through legislative action of activities intrastate which have a substantial effect on the commerce or the exercise of the Congressional power over it.

In such legislation Congress has sometimes left it to the courts to determine whether the intrastate activities have the prohibited effect on the commerce, as in the Sherman Act. It has sometimes left it to an administrative board or agency to determine whether the activities sought to be regulated or prohibited have such effect, as in the case of the Interstate Commerce Act, and the National Labor Relations Act, or whether they come within the statutory definition of the prohibited Act as in the Federal Trade Commission Act. And sometimes Congress itself has said that a particular activity affects the commerce as it did in the present act, the Safety Appliance Act and the Railway Labor Act. In passing on the validity of legislation of the class last mentioned the only function of courts is to determine whether the particular activity regulated or prohibited is within the reach of the federal power. [Citations omitted.]

Congress, having by the present Act adopted the policy of excluding from interstate commerce all goods produced for the commerce which do not conform to the specified labor standards, it may choose the means reasonably adapted to the attainment of the permitted end, even though they involve control of intrastate activities. Such legislation has often been sustained with respect to powers, other than the commerce power granted to the national government, when the means chosen, although not themselves within the granted power, were nevertheless deemed appropriate aids to the accomplishment of some purpose within an admitted power of the national government. [Citations omitted.] A familiar like exercise of power is the regulation of intrastate transactions which are so commingled with or related to interstate commerce that all must be regulated if the interstate commerce is to be effectively controlled. [Citations omitted.] Similarly Congress may require inspection and preventive treatment of all cattle in a disease-infected area in order to prevent shipment in interstate commerce of some of the cattle without the treatment. Thornton v. United States, 271 U.S. 414. It may prohibit the removal, at destination, of labels required by the Pure Food & Drugs Act to be affixed to articles transported in interstate commerce. McDermott v. Wisconsin, 228 U.S. 115. And we have recently held that Congress in the exercise of its power to require inspection and grading of tobacco shipped in interstate commerce may compel such inspection and grading of all tobacco sold at local auction rooms from which a substantial part but not all of the tobacco sold is shipped in interstate commerce. Currin v. Wallace, 306 U.S. 11, and see to the like effect United States v. Rock Royal Co-operative, 307 U.S. 568, note 37.

We think also that § 15(a)(2), now under consideration, is sustainable independently of § 15(a)(1), which prohibits shipment or transportation of the proscribed goods. As we have said the evils aimed at by the Act are the spread of substandard labor conditions through the use of facilities of interstate commerce for competition by the goods so produced with those produced under the prescribed or better labor conditions; and the consequent dislocation of the commerce itself caused by the impairment or destruction of local businesses by competition made effective through interstate commerce. The Act is thus directed at the suppression of a method or kind of competition in interstate commerce which it has in effect condemned as "unfair," as the Clayton Act has condemned other "unfair methods of competition" made effective through interstate commerce. See George Van Camp & Sons Co. v. American Can Co., 278 U.S. 245; Federal Trade Commission v. R. F. Keppel & Bro., 291 U.S. 304.

The Sherman Act and the National Labor Relations Act are familiar examples of the exertion of the commerce power to prohibit or control activities wholly intrastate because of their effect on interstate commerce. . . .

Congress, to attain its objective in the suppression of nation-wide competition in interstate commerce by goods produced under substandard labor conditions, has made no distinction as to the volume or amount of shipments in the commerce or of production for commerce by any particular shipper or producer. It recognized that in present day industry, competition by a small part may affect the whole and that the total effect of the competition of many small producers may be great. See H. Rept. No. 2182, 75th Cong. 1st Sess. p. 7. The legislation aimed at a whole embraces all its parts. Cf. National Labor Relations Bd. v. Fainblatt, 306 U.S. 606.

So far as Carter v. Carter Coal Co., 298 U.S. 238, is inconsistent with this conclusion, its doctrine is limited in principle by the decisions under the Sherman Act and the National Labor Relations Act, which we have cited and which we follow. [Citations omitted.]

Our conclusion is unaffected by the Tenth Amendment which provides: "The powers not delegated to the United States by the Constitution nor prohibited by it to the states are reserved to the states respectively or to the people." The amendment states but a truism that all is retained which has not been surrendered. There is nothing in the history of its adoption to suggest that it was more than declaratory of the relationship between the national and state governments as it had been established by the Constitution before the amendment or that its purpose was other than to allay fears that the new national government might seek to exercise powers not granted, and that the states might not be able to exercise fully their reserved powers. [Citations omitted.]

From the beginning and for many years the amendment has been construed as not depriving the national government of authority to resort to all means for the exercise of a granted power which are appropriate and plainly adapted to the permitted end. [Citations omitted.] Whatever doubts may have arisen of the soundness of that conclusion, they have been put at rest by the decisions under the Sherman Act and the National Labor Relations Act which we have cited. See also Ashwander v. Tennessee Valley Authority, 297 U.S. 288, 330, 331; Wright v. Union Cent. L. Ins. Co., 304 U.S. 502, 516. . . .

[A discussion of due process is omitted.]

Reversed.

OKLAHOMA PRESS PUBLISHING CO. v. WALLING, 327 U.S. 186, 66 S. Ct. 494, 90 L. Ed. 614 (1946). The Administrator of the Fair Labor Standards Act brought suit in a federal district court for enforcement of subpoenas duces tecum issued by him for the production of certain records to determine whether the company was violating the act. The company contended that the question of coverage under the act should be determined before enforcement of the subpoenas. In rejecting this contention, the Court said (p. 205 n.32): "The power is not limited to inquiring concerning matters which Congress may regulate otherwise than by requiring the production of information, at any rate when it is made to appear that some phase of the activity is in commerce or affects it. See United States v. New York Central R. Co., 272 U.S. 457, 464, and authorities cited; Federal Trade Commission v. Claire Furnace Co., 274 U.S. 160. Nor must the 'jurisdictional' line be drawn in such cases before the information is called for."

UNITED STATES v. FIVE GAMBLING DEVICES, 346 U.S. 441, 74 S. Ct. 190, 98 L. Ed. 179 (1953). An Act of January 2, 1951, 64 Stat. 1134, makes it unlawful knowingly to transport in interstate commerce any gambling device, except to a state which by law has exempted itself from the provisions of the act. In addition, the act provides that "every manufacturer of and dealer in gambling devices shall file with the Attorney General an inventory and record of all sales and deliveries of gambling devices. . . ." Indictments and libel for forfeiture were filed in respect of unreported sales and deliveries of slot machines. There was no allegation that the defendants sold or moved gambling devices in interstate commerce. The Court held that the indictments and libel should be dismissed. An opinion by Justices Jackson, Frankfurter, and Minton refused to give the reporting provision its literal meaning because of the serious constitutional questions which would be raised, stating: ". . . we must assume that the implications and limitations of our federal system constitute a major premise of all congressional legislation, though not repeatedly recited therein." Justices Black and Douglas, completing the majority, concurred in the result but on a different ground, the vagueness of a certain feature of the reporting requirement. Mr. Justice Clark, joined by Chief Justice Warren and Justices Reed and Burton, delivered a dissenting opinion, stating: "The question has not been previously decided because the legislative scheme utilized has not been heretofore attempted. But its novelty should not suggest its unconstitutionality." See further the Note on Expansion of the Commerce Power and Problems of Statutory Coverage, page 297 infra.

National League of Cities v. Usery 426 U.S. 833, 96 S. Ct. 2465, 49 L. Ed. 2d 245 (1976)

MR. JUSTICE REHNQUIST delivered the opinion for the Court. . . .

The original Fair Labor Standards Act passed in 1938 specifically excluded the States and their political subdivisions from its coverage. In 1974, however, Congress enacted the most recent of a series of broadening amendments to the Act. By these amendments Congress has extended the minimum wage and maximum hour provisions to almost all public employees employed by the States and by their various political subdivisions. Appellants in these cases include individual cities and States, the National League of Cities, and the National Governors' Conference; they brought an action in the District Court for the District of Columbia which challenged the validity of the 1974 amendments. They asserted in effect that when Congress sought to apply the Fair Labor Standards Act provisions virtually across the board to employees of state and municipal governments it "infringed a constitutional prohibition" running in favor of the States *as States*. The gist of their complaint was not that the conditions of employment of such public employees were beyond the scope of the commerce power had those employees been employed in the private sector, but that the established constitutional doctrine of intergovernmental immunity consistently recognized in a long series of our cases affirmatively prevented the exercise of this authority in the manner which Congress chose in the 1974 Amendments.

I

In a series of amendments beginning in 1961 Congress began to extend the provisions of the Fair Labor Standards Act to some types of public employees. The 1961 amendment to the Act extended its coverage to persons who were employed in "enterprises" engaged in commerce or in the production of goods for commerce. And in 1966, with the amendment of the definition of employers under the Act, the exemption heretofore extended to the States and their political subdivisions was removed with respect to employees of state hospitals, institutions, and schools. We nevertheless sustained the validity of the combined effect of these two amendments in Maryland v. Wirtz, 392 U.S. 183 (1968).

In 1974, Congress again broadened the coverage of the Act. The definition of "employer" in the Act now specifically "includes a public agency," 29 U.S.C. §203(d). . . . By its 1974 amendments, then, Congress has now entirely removed the exemption previously afforded States and their political subdivisions, substituting only the Act's general exemption for executive, administrative, or professional personnel, 29 U.S.C. §213(a)(1), which is supplemented by provisions excluding from the Act's coverage those individuals holding public elective office or serving such an officeholder in one of several specific capacities. . . .

Challenging these 1974 amendments in the District Court, appellants sought both declaratory and injunctive relief against the amendments' application to them, and a three-judge court was accordingly convened pursuant to 28 U.S.C. §2282. That court, after hearing argument on the law from the parties, granted appellee Secretary of Labor's motion to dismiss the complaint for failure to state a claim upon which relief might be granted. . . .

We noted probable jurisdiction in order to consider the important questions recognized by the District Court. 420 U.S. 906 (1975). We agree with the District Court that the appellants' contentions are substantial. Indeed upon full consideration of the question we have decided that the "far-reaching implications" of Wirtz, should be overruled, and that the judgment of the District Court must be reversed.

II

. . . Congressional enactments which may be fully within the grant of legislative authority contained in the Commerce Clause may nonetheless be invalid because found to offend against the right to trial by jury contained in the Sixth Amendment, United States v. Jackson, 390 U.S. 570 (1968), or the Due Process Clause of the Fifth Amendment, Leary v. United States, 395 U.S. 6 (1969). Appellants' essential contention is that the 1974 amendments to the Act, while undoubtedly within the scope of the Commerce Clause, encounter a similar constitutional barrier because they are to be applied directly to the States and subdivisions of States as employers.

This Court has never doubted that there are limits upon the power of Congress to override state sovereignty, even when exercising its otherwise plenary powers to tax or to regulate commerce which are conferred by Art. I of the Constitution. . . .

In New York v. United States, 326 U.S. 572 (1946), Chief Justice Stone, speaking for four Members of an eight-Member Court in rejecting the proposition that Congress could impose taxes on the States so long as it did so in a nondiscriminatory manner, observed: "A State may, like a private individual, own real property and receive income. But in view of our former decisions we could hardly say that a general nondiscriminatory real estate tax (apportioned), or an income tax laid upon citizens and States alike could be constitutionally applied to the State's capitol, its State-house, its public school houses, public parks, or its revenues from taxes or school lands, even though all real property and all income of the citizen is taxed." 326 U.S., at 587-588. . . .

One undoubted attribute of state sovereignty is the States' power to determine the wages which shall be paid to those whom they employ in order to carry out their governmental functions, what hours those persons will work, and what compensation will be provided where these employees may be called upon to work overtime. The question we must resolve in this case, then, is whether these determinations are "functions essential to separate and independent existence," Coyle v. Smith, [221 U.S. 559] at 580, quoting from Lane County v. Oregon, [7 Wall.] at 76, so that Congress may not abrogate the States' otherwise plenary authority to make them.

In their complaint appellants advanced estimates of substantial costs which will be imposed upon them by the 1974 amendments. Since the District Court dismissed their complaint, we take its well-pleaded allegations as true, although it appears from appellee's submissions in the District Court and in this Court that resolution of the factual disputes as to the effect of the amendments is not critical to our disposition of the case.

Judged solely in terms of increased costs in dollars, these allegations show a significant impact on the functioning of the governmental bodies involved. The Metropolitan Government of Nashville and Davidson County, Tenn., for example, asserted that the Act will increase its costs of providing essential police and fire protection, without any increase in service or in current salary levels, by $938,000 per year. Cape Girardeau, Mo., estimated that its annual budget for fire protection may have to be increased by anywhere from $250,000 to $400,000 over the current figure of $350,000. The State of Arizona alleged that the annual additional expenditures which will be required if it is to continue to provide essential state services may total $2½ million dollars. The State of California, which must devote significant portions of its budget to fire suppression endeavors, estimated that application of the Act to its employment practices will necessitate an increase in its budget of between $8 million and $16 million.

Increased costs are not, of course, the only adverse effects which compliance with the Act will visit upon state and local governments, and in turn upon the citizens who depend upon those governments. In its complaint in intervention, for example, California asserted that it could not comply with the overtime costs (approximately $750,000 per year) which the Act required to be paid to California Highway Patrol cadets during their academy training program. California reported that it had thus been forced to reduce its academy training program from 2,080 hours to only 960 hours, a compromise undoubtedly of substantial importance to those whose safety and welfare may depend upon the preparedness of the California Highway Patrol. . . .

Quite apart from the substantial costs imposed upon the States and their political subdivisions, the Act displaces state policies regarding the manner in which they will structure delivery of those governmental services which their citizens require. The Act, speaking directly to the States qua States, requires that they shall pay all but an extremely limited minority of their employees the minimum wage rates currently chosen by Congress. It may well be that as a matter of economic policy it would be desirable that States, just as private employers, comply with these minimum wage requirements. But it cannot be gainsaid that the federal requirement directly supplants the considered policy choices of the States' elected officials and administrators as to how they wish to structure pay scales in state employment. The State might wish to employ persons with little or no training, or those who wish to work on a casual basis, or those who for some other reason do not possess minimum employment requirements, and pay them less than the federally prescribed minimum wage. It may wish to offer part time or summer employment to teenagers at a figure less than the minimum wage, and if unable to do so may decline to offer such employment at all. But the Act would forbid such choices by the States. . . .

The degree to which the FLSA amendments would interfere with traditional aspects of state sovereignty can be seen even more clearly upon examining the overtime requirements of the Act. . . .

Our examination of the effect of the 1974 amendments, as sought to be extended to the States and their political subdivisions, satisfies us that both the minimum wage and the maximum hour provisions will impermissibly interfere with the integral governmental functions of these bodies. . . . This exercise of congressional authority does not comport with the federal system of government embodied in the Constitution. We hold that insofar as the challenged amendments operate to directly displace the States' freedom to structure integral operations in areas of traditional governmental functions, they are not within the authority granted Congress by Art. I, §8, cl. 3.

III

One final matter requires our attention. Appellee has vigorously urged that we cannot, consistently with the Court's decisions in Wirtz, supra, and Fry [v. United States, 421 U.S. 542 (1975)], rule against him here. It is important to examine this contention so that it will be clear what we hold today, and what we do not.

With regard to Fry, we disagree with appellee. There the Court held that the Economic Stabilization Act of 1970 was constitutional as applied to temporarily freeze the wages of state and local government employees. . . . The Court recognized that the Economic Stabilization Act was "an emergency measure to counter severe inflation that threatened the national economy." 421 U.S., at 548.

We think our holding today quite consistent with Fry. . . .

With respect to the Court's decision in Wirtz, we reach a different conclusion. Both appellee and the District Court thought that decision required rejection of appellants' claims. Appellants, in turn, advance several arguments by which they seek to distinguish the facts before the Court in Wirtz from those presented by the 1974 amendments to the Act. There are undoubtedly factual distinctions between the two situations, but in view of the conclusions expressed earlier in this opinion we do not believe the reasoning in Wirtz may any longer be regarded as authoritative. . . .

. . . Congress may not exercise [the commerce] power so as to force directly upon the States its choices as to how essential decisions regarding the conduct of integral governmental functions are to be made. We agree that such assertions of power, if unchecked, would indeed, as Mr. Justice Douglas cautioned in his dissent in Wirtz, allow "the National Government [to] devour the essentials of state sovereignty," 392 U.S., at 205, and would therefore transgress the bounds of the authority granted Congress under the Commerce Clause. While there are obvious differences between the schools and hospitals involved in Wirtz, and the fire and police departments affected here, each provides an integral portion of those governmental services which the States and their political subdivisions have traditionally afforded their citizens. We are therefore persuaded that Wirtz must be overruled.

The judgment of the District Court is accordingly reversed and the case is remanded for further proceedings consistent with this opinion.

So ordered.

Mr. Justice Blackmun, concurring.

The Court's opinion and the dissents indicate the importance and significance of this case as it bears upon the relationship between the Federal Government and our States. Although I am not untroubled by certain possible implications of the Court's opinion — some of them suggested by the dissents — I do not read the opinion so despairingly as does my Brother Brennan. In my view, the result with respect to the statute under challenge here is necessarily correct. I may misinterpret the Court's opinion, but it seems to me that it adopts a balancing approach, and does not outlaw federal power in areas such as environmental protection, where the federal interest is demonstrably greater and where state facility compliance with imposed federal standards would be essential. . . . With this understanding on my part of the Court's opinion, I join it.

Mr. Justice Brennan, with whom Mr. Justice White and Mr. Justice Marshall join, dissenting.

The Court concedes, as of course it must, that Congress enacted the 1974 amendments pursuant to its exclusive power under Art. I, §8, cl. 3, of the Constitution "To regulate Commerce . . . among the several States." It must therefore be surprising that my Brethren should choose this Bicentennial year of our independence to repudiate principles governing judicial interpretation of our Constitution settled since the time of Chief Justice John Marshall, discarding his postulate that the Constitution contemplates that restraints upon exercise by Congress of its plenary commerce power lie in the political process and not in the judicial process. For 152 years ago Chief Justice Marshall enunciated that principle to which, until today, his successors on this Court have been faithful.

"[T]he power over commerce . . . is vested in Congress as absolutely as it would be in a single government, having in its constitution the same restrictions on the exercise of the power as are found in the constitution of the United States. *The wisdom and the discretion of Congress, their identity with the people, and the influence which their constituents possess at elections, are . . . the sole restraints on which they have relied, to secure them from its abuse. They are the restraints on which the people must often rely solely, in all representative governments.*" Gibbons v. Ogden, 9 Wheat. 1, 197 (1824) (emphasis added). . . .

My Brethren purport to find support for their novel state sovereignty doctrine in the concurring opinion of Chief Justice Stone in New York v. United States, 326 U.S. 572, 586 (1946). That reliance is plainly misplaced. That case presented the question whether the Constitution either required immunity of New York State's mineral water business from federal taxation or denied to the Federal Government power to lay the tax. The Court sustained the federal tax. Chief Justice Stone observed in his concurring opinion that "a federal tax which is not discriminatory as to the subject matter may nevertheless so affect the State merely because it is a State that is being taxed, as to interfere unduly with the State's performance of its sovereign functions of government." Id., at 587. But the Chief Justice was addressing not the question of a state sovereignty restraint upon the exercise of the commerce power, but rather the principle of implied immunity of the States and Federal Government from taxation by the other: "The counterpart of such undue interference has been recognized since Marshall's day as the implied immunity of each of the dual sovereignties of our constitutional system from taxation by the other." Ibid.

In contrast, the apposite decision that Term to the question whether the Constitution implies a state sovereignty restraint upon congressional exercise of the commerce power is Case v. Bowles, 327 U.S. 92 (1946). The question there was whether the Emergency Price Control Act could apply to the sale by the State of Washington to timber growing on lands granted by Congress to the State for the purport of common schools. The State contended that "there is a doctrine implied in the Federal Constitution that 'the two governments, national and state, are each to exercise its powers so as not to interfere with the free and full exercise of the powers of the other' . . . [and] that the Act cannot be applied to this sale because it was 'for the purpose of gaining revenue to carry out an essential governmental function — the education of its citizens.' " Id., at 101. The Court emphatically rejected that argument, in an opinion joined by Chief Justice Stone, reasoning:

"Since the Emergency Price Control Act has been sustained as a congressional exercise of the war power, the [State's] argument is that the extent of that power as applied to state functions depends on whether these are 'essential' to the state government. The use of the same criterion in measuring the constitutional power of Congress to tax has proved to be unworkable, and we reject it as a guide in the field here involved. Cf. United States v. California, supra, 297 U.S. at 183-185." 327 U.S., at 101.

The footnote to this statement rejected the suggested dichotomy between essential and nonessential state governmental functions as having "proved to be unworkable" by referring to "the several opinions in New York v. United States, 326 U.S. 572." 327 U.S., at 101 n.7. Even more significant for our purposes is the Court's citation of United States v. California, a case concerned with Congress' power to regulate commerce, as supporting the rejection of the State's contention that state sovereignty is a limitation on Congress' war power. California directly presented the question whether any state sovereignty restraint precluded application of the Federal Safety Appliance Act to a state-owned and operated railroad. The State argued "that as the state is operating the railroad without profit, for the purpose of facilitating the commerce of the port, and is using the net proceeds of operation for harbor improvement . . . it is engaged in performing a public function in its sovereign capacity and for that reason cannot constitutionally be subjected to the provisions of the federal Act." 297 U.S., at 183. Mr. Justice Stone rejected the contention in an opinion for a unanimous Court. . . .

Today's repudiation of this unbroken line of precedents that firmly reject my Brethren's ill-conceived abstraction can only be regarded as a transparent cover for invalidating a congressional judgment with which they disagree. The only analysis even remotely resembling that adopted today is found in a line of opinions dealing with the Commerce Clause and the Tenth Amendment that ultimately provoked a constitutional crisis for the Court in the 1930's. E.g., Carter v. Carter Coal Co., 298 U.S. 238 (1936); United States v. Butler, 297 U.S. 1 (1936); Hammer v. Dagenhart, 247 U.S. 251 (1918). See Stern, The Commerce Clause and the National Economy, 1933-1946, 59 Harv. L. Rev. 645 (1946). We tend to forget that the Court invalidated legislation during the Great Depression, not solely under the Due Process Clause, but also and primarily under the Commerce Clause and the Tenth Amendment. It may have been the eventual abandonment of that overly restrictive construction of the commerce power that spelled defeat for the Courtpacking plan, and preserved the integrity of this institution, id., at 682, see, e.g., United States v. Darby, [312 U.S. 100 (1941)]; Mulford v. Smith, 307 U.S. 38 (1939); NLRB v. Jones & Laughlin Steel Corp., 301 U.S. 1 (1937), but my Brethren today are transparently trying to cut back on that recognition of the scope of the commerce power. My Brethren's approach to this case is not far different from the dissenting opinions in the cases that averted the crisis. See, e.g., Mulford v. Smith, 307 U.S., at 51 (Butler, J., dissenting); NLRB v. Jones & Laughlin Steel Corp., 301 U.S., at 76 (McReynolds, J., dissenting).

That no precedent justifies today's result is particularly clear from the awkward extension of the doctrine of state immunity from federal taxation — an immunity conclusively distinguished by Mr. Justice Stone in California, and an immunity that is "narrowly limited" because "the people of all the states have created the national government and are represented in Congress," Helvering v. Gerhardt, 304 U.S. 405, 416 (1938) (Stone, J.) — to fashion a judicially enforceable restraint on Congress' exercise of the commerce power that the Court has time and again rejected as having no place in our constitutional jurisprudence. "[W]here [Congress] keeps within its sphere and violates no express constitutional limitation it has been the rule of this Court, going back almost to the founding days of the Republic, not to interfere." Katzenbach v. McClung, supra, at 305.

. . . I cannot recall another instance in the Court's history when the reasoning of so many decisions covering so long a span of time has been discarded roughshod. That this is done without any justification not already often advanced and consistently rejected, clearly renders today's decision an ipse dixit reflecting nothing but displeasure with a congressional judgment. . . .

My Brethren do more than turn aside longstanding constitutional jurisprudence that emphatically rejects today's conclusion. More alarming is the startling restructuring of our federal system, and the role they create therein for the federal judiciary. This Court is simply not at liberty to erect a mirror of its own conception of a desirable governmental structure. If the 1974 amendments have any "vice," ante, at 15, my Brother Stevens is surely right that it represents "merely . . . a policy issue which has been firmly resolved by the branches of government having power to decide such questions." . . . It bears repeating "that effective restraints on . . . exercise [of the Commerce power] must proceed from political rather than from judicial processes." Wickard v. Filburn, supra, at 120.

It is unacceptable that the judicial process should be thought superior to the political process in this area. Under the Constitution the judiciary has no role to play beyond finding that Congress has not made an unreasonable legislative judgment respecting what is "commerce." My Brother Blackmun suggests that controlling judicial supervision of the relationship between the States and our National Government by use of a balancing approach diminishes the ominous implications of today's decision. Such an approach, however, is a thinly veiled rationalization for judicial supervision of a policy judgment that our system of government reserves to Congress.

Judicial restraint in this area merely recognizes that the political branches of our Government are structured to protect the interests of the States, as well as the Nation as a whole, and that the States are fully able to protect their own interests in the premises. . . . Judicial redistribution of powers granted the National Government by the terms of the Constitution violates the fundamental tenet of our federalism that the extent of federal intervention into the States' affairs in the exercise of delegated powers shall be determined by the States' exercise of political power through their representatives in Congress. See Wechsler, The Political Safeguards of Federalism: The Role of the States in the Composition and Selection of the National Government, 54 Col. L. Rev. 543 (1954). . . .

We are left then with a catastrophic judicial body blow at Congress' power under the Commerce Clause. Even if Congress may nevertheless accomplish its objectives — for example by conditioning grants of federal funds upon compliance with federal minimum wage and overtime standards, cf. Oklahoma v. United States Civil Service Comm'n, 330 U.S. 127, 144 (1947) — there is an ominous portent of disruption of our constitutional structure implicit in today's mischievous decision. I dissent.

MR. JUSTICE STEVENS, dissenting.

The Court holds that the Federal Government may not interfere with a sovereign state's inherent right to pay a substandard wage to the janitor at the state capitol. The principle on which the holding rests is difficult to perceive.

The Federal Government may, I believe, require the State to act impartially when it hires or fires the janitor, to withhold taxes from his pay check, to observe safety regulations when he is performing his job, to forbid him from burning too much soft coal in the capitol furnace, from dumping untreated refuse in an adjacent waterway, from overloading a state-owned garbage truck or from driving either the truck or the governor's limousine over 55 miles an hour. Even though these and many other activities of the capitol janitor are activities of the state qua state, I have no doubt that they are subject to federal regulation.

I agree that it is unwise for the Federal Government to exercise its power in the ways described in the Court's opinion. . . .

My disagreement with the wisdom of this legislation may not, of course, affect my judgment with respect to its validity. On this issue there is no dissent from the proposition that the Federal Government's power over the labor market is adequate to embrace these employees. Since I am unable to identify a limitation on that federal power that would not also invalidate federal regulation of state activities that I consider unquestionably permissible, I am persuaded that this statute is valid. Accordingly, with respect and a great deal of sympathy for the views expressed by the Court, I dissent from its constitutional holding.

NOTE

1. The Fair Labor Standards Act, like the Federal Employers' Liability Act, has given rise to numerous questions of statutory coverage. It has been held applicable to employees of a newspaper having an out-of-state circulation of 45 copies, or 0.5 percent of its total sales. Mabee v. White Plains Pub. Co., 327 U.S. 178 (1946); and to maintenance workers in an office building owned and principally tenanted by a company which elsewhere manufactured products for interstate commerce, Borden Co. v. Borella, 325 U.S. 679 (1945). But it was held not applicable to maintenance employees of an independent office building occupied by various tenants, some of which were in the business of producing goods for interstate commerce. 10 East Street Bldg., Inc. v. Callus, 325 U.S. 578 (1945).

2. The evolution of national power over commerce, and its relation to state power, are well illustrated in cases dealing with agriculture, and in particular the milk industry.

As part of a plan to aid milk producers, New York set minimum prices on the retail sales of milk. This was upheld, over due process objections, as applied to local sales by a grocery, in Nebbia v. New York, 291 U.S. 502 (1934), infra page 1089. New York also imposed minimum price requirements on purchases from milk producers, and in order to protect local producers from the competition of unregulated sales by out-of-state producers in the New York market, New York forbade the sale within the state of milk purchased outside at less than the prices set under New York law. This application of the law was held invalid in Baldwin v. Seelig, 294 U.S. 511 (1935), infra page 381.

Under the Federal Agricultural Marketing Agreement Act of 1937 certain marketing areas for milk were designated by the Secretary of Agriculture, who prescribed minimum prices to be paid to producers of milk delivered to a handler for sale in a particular marketing area. As applied to the New York City marketing area, the Secretary prescribed minimum prices to producers for milk not regulated by the state authorities; the federal and state officials held joint hearings and cooperated in the issuance of orders. Two thirds of the milk produced for the New York area moves in interstate commerce. The federal price order for New York was challenged and sustained in United States v. Rock Royal Cooperative, 307 U.S. 533 (1939). For the Chicago marketing area, about 60 percent of the milk is produced in Illinois. The Secretary applied a price order to handlers who both bought and sold milk wholly in Illinois. This application was sustained in United States v. Wrightwood Dairy Co., 315 U.S. 110 (1942).

Wickard v. Filburn 317 U.S. 111, 63 S. Ct. 82, 87 L. Ed. 122 (1942)

MR. JUSTICE JACKSON delivered the opinion of the Court:

The appellee filed his complaint against the Secretary of Agriculture of the United States, three members of the County Agricultural Conservation Committee for Montgomery County, Ohio, and a member of the State Agricultural Conservation Committee for Ohio. He sought to enjoin enforcement against himself of the marketing penalty imposed by the amendment of May 26, 1941, to the Agricultural Adjustment Act of [February 16] 1938, upon that part of his 1941 wheat crop which was available for marketing in excess of the marketing quota established for his farm. He also sought a declaratory judgment that the wheat marketing quota provisions of the Act as amended and applicable to him were unconstitutional because not sustainable under the Commerce Clause or consistent with the Due Process Clause of the Fifth Amendment.

The Secretary moved to dismiss the action against him for improper venue but later waived his objection and filed an answer. The other appellants moved to dismiss on the ground that they had no power or authority to enforce the wheat marketing quota provisions of the Act, and after their motion was denied they answered reserving exceptions to the ruling on their motion to dismiss. The case was submitted for decision on the pleadings and upon a stipulation of facts.

The appellee for many years past has owned and operated a small farm in Montgomery County, Ohio, maintaining a herd of dairy cattle, selling milk, raising poultry, and selling poultry and eggs. It has been his practice to raise a small acreage of winter wheat, sown in the Fall and harvested in the following July; to sell a portion of the crop; to feed part to poultry and livestock on the farm, some of which is sold; to use some in making flour for home consumption; and to keep the rest for the following seeding. The intended disposition of the crop here involved has not been expressly stated.

In July of 1940, pursuant to the Agricultural Adjustment Act of 1938, as then amended, there were established for the appellee's 1941 crop a wheat acreage allotment of 11.1 acres and a normal yield of 20.1 bushels of wheat an acre. He was given notice of such allotment in July of 1940 before the Fall planting of his 1941 crop of wheat, and again in July of 1941, before it was harvested. He sowed, however, 23 acres, and harvested from his 11.9 acres of excess acreage 239 bushels, which under the terms of the Act as amended on May 26, 1941, constituted farm marketing excess, subject to a penalty of 49 cents a bushel, or $117.11 in all. The appellee has not paid the penalty and he has not postponed or avoided it by storing the excess under regulations of the Secretary of Agriculture, or by delivering it up to the Secretary. The Committee, therefore, refused him a marketing card, which was, under the terms of Regulations promulgated by the Secretary, necessary to protect a buyer from liability to the penalty and upon its protecting lien.

The general scheme of the Agricultural Adjustment Act of 1938 as related to wheat is to control the volume moving in interstate and foreign commerce in order to avoid surpluses and shortages and the consequent abnormally low or high wheat prices and obstructions to commerce. Within prescribed limits and by prescribed standards the Secretary of Agriculture is directed to ascertain and proclaim each year a national acreage allotment for the next crop of wheat, which is then apportioned to the states and their counties, and is eventually broken up into allotments for individual farms. Loans and payments to wheat farmers are authorized in stated circumstances.

The Act provides further that whenever it appears that the total supply of wheat as of the beginning of any marketing year, beginning July 1, will exceed a normal year's domestic consumption and export by more than 35 per cent, the Secretary shall so proclaim not later than May 15 prior to the beginning of such marketing year; and that during the marketing year a compulsory national marketing quota shall be in effect with respect to the marketing of wheat. Between the issuance of the proclamation and June 10, the Secretary must, however, conduct a referendum of farmers who will be subject to the quota to determine whether they favor or oppose it; and if more than one third of the farmers voting in the referendum do oppose, the Secretary must prior to the effective date of the quota by proclamation suspend its operation.

On May 19, 1941, the Secretary of Agriculture made a radio address to the wheat farmers of the United States in which he advocated approval of the quotas and called attention to the pendency of the amendment of May 26, 1941, which had at the time been sent by Congress to the White House, and pointed out its provision for an increase in the loans on wheat to 85 per cent of parity. He made no mention of the fact that it also increased the penalty from 15 cents a bushel to one half of the parity loan rate of about 98 cents, but stated that "Because of the uncertain world situation, we deliberately planted several million extra acres of wheat. . . . . Farmers should not be penalized because they have provided insurance against shortages of food."

Pursuant to the Act, the referendum of wheat growers was held on May 31, 1941. According to the required published statement of the Secretary of Agriculture, 81 per cent of those voting favored the marketing quota, with 19 per cent opposed.

The court below held, with one judge dissenting, that the speech of the Secretary invalidated the referendum; and that the amendment of May 26, 1941, "in so far as it increased the penalty for the farm marketing excess over the fifteen cents per bushel prevailing at the time of planting and subjected the entire crop to a lien for the payment thereof," should not be applied to the appellee because as so applied it was retroactive and in violation of the Fifth Amendment; and, alternatively, because the equities of the case so required. 43 F. Supp. 1017. Its judgment permanently enjoined appellants from collecting a marketing penalty of more than 15 cents a bushel on the farm marketing excess of appellee's 1941 wheat crop, from subjecting appellee's entire 1941 crop to a lien for the payment of the penalty, and from collecting a 15-cent penalty except in accordance with the provisions of §339 of the Act as that section stood prior to the amendment of May 26, 1941.[10] The Secretary and his co-defendants have appealed.

I

The holding of the court below that the Secretary's speech invalidated the referendum is manifest error. Read as a whole and in the context of world events that constituted his principal theme, the penalties of which he spoke were more likely those in the form of ruinously low prices resulting from the excess supply rather than the penalties prescribed in the Act. But under any interpretation the speech cannot be given the effect of invalidating the referendum. . . .

II

It is urged that under the Commerce Clause of the Constitution, Article 1, §8, clause 3, Congress does not possess the power it has in this instance sought to exercise. The question would merit little consideration since our decision in United States v. Darby, 312 U.S. 100, sustaining the federal power to regulate production of goods for commerce except for the fact that this Act extends federal regulation to production not intended in any part for commerce but wholly for consumption on the farm. The Act includes a definition of "market" and its derivatives so that as related to wheat in addition to its conventional meaning it also means to dispose of "by feeding (in any form) to poultry or livestock which, or the products of which, are sold, bartered, or exchanged, or to be so disposed of." Hence, marketing quotas not only embrace all that may be sold without penalty but also what may be consumed on the premises. Wheat produced on excess acreage is designated as "available for marketing" as so defined and the penalty is imposed thereon. Penalties do not depend upon whether any part of the wheat either within or without the quota is sold or intended to be sold. The sum of this is that the Federal Government fixes a quota including all that the farmer may harvest for sale or for his own farm needs, and declares that wheat produced on excess acreage may neither be disposed of nor used except upon payment of the penalty or except it is stored as required by the Act or delivered to the Secretary of Agriculture. . . .

The Government's concern lest the Act be held to be a regulation of production or consumption rather than of marketing is attributable to a few dicta and decisions of this Court which might be understood to lay it down that activities such as "production," "manufacturing," and "mining" are strictly "local" and, except in special circumstances which are not present here, cannot be regulated under the commerce power because their effects upon interstate commerce are, as matter of law, only "indirect." . . . We believe that a review of the course of decision under the Commerce Clause will make plain, however, that questions of the power of Congress are not to be decided by reference to any formula which would give controlling force to nomenclature such as "production" and "indirect"

---

[10] 7 U.S.C.A. §1339. This imposed a penalty of 15¢ per bushel upon wheat marketed in excess of the farm marketing quota while such quota was in effect. . . .

296   Chapter Seven.   **National Power over the Economy**

and foreclose consideration of the actual effects of the activity in question upon interstate commerce. . . .

The parties have stipulated a summary of the economics of the wheat industry. Commerce among the states in wheat is large and important. Although wheat is raised in every state but one, production in most states is not equal to consumption. Sixteen states on average have had a surplus of wheat above their own requirements for feed, seed, and food. Thirty-two states and the District of Columbia, where production has been below consumption, have looked to these surplus-producing states for their supply as well as for wheat for export and carry-over.

The wheat industry has been a problem industry for some years. Largely as a result of increased foreign production and import restrictions, annual exports of wheat and flour from the United States during the ten-year period ending in 1940 averaged less than 10 per cent of total production, while during the 1920's they averaged more than 25 per cent. The decline in the export trade has left a large surplus in production which in connection with an abnormally large supply of wheat and other grains in recent years caused congestion in a number of markets; tied up railroad cars; and caused elevators in some instances to turn away grains, and railroads to institute embargoes to prevent further congestion.

Many countries, both importing and exporting, have sought to modify the impact of the world market conditions on their own economy. Importing countries have taken measures to stimulate production and self-sufficiency. The four large exporting countries of Argentina, Australia, Canada, and the United States have all undertaken various programs for the relief of growers. Such measures have been designed in part at least to protect the domestic price received by producers. Such plans have generally evolved towards control by the central government.[27]

In the absence of regulation the price of wheat in the United States would be much affected by world conditions. During 1941 producers who cooperated with the Agricultural Adjustment program received an average price on the farm of about $1.16 a bushel as compared with the world market price of 40 cents a bushel.

Differences in farming conditions, however, make these benefits mean different things to different wheat growers. There are several large areas of specialization in wheat, and the concentration in this crop reaches 27 per cent of the crop land, and the average harvest runs as high as 155 acres. Except for some use of wheat as stock feed and for seed, the practice is to sell the crop for cash. Wheat from such areas constitutes the bulk of the interstate commerce therein.

On the other hand, in some New England states less than one per cent of the crop land is devoted to wheat, and the average harvest is less than five acres per farm. In 1940 the average percentage of the total wheat production that was sold in each state as measured by value ranged from 29 per cent thereof in Wisconsin to 90 per cent in Washington. Except in regions of large-scale production, wheat is usually grown in rotation with other crops; for a nurse crop for grass seeding; and as a cover crop to prevent soil erosion and

---

[27] It is interesting to note that all of these have federated systems of government, not of course without important differences. In all of them wheat regulation is by the national government. In Argentina wheat may be purchased only from the national Grain Board. A condition of sale to the Board, which buys at pegged prices, is the producer's agreement to become subject to restrictions on planting. See Nolan, Argentine Grain Price Guaranty, Foreign Agriculture (Office of Foreign Agricultural Relations, Department of Agriculture) May, 1942, pp. 185, 202. The Australian system of regulation includes the licensing of growers, who may not sow more than the amount licensed, and who may be compelled to cut part of their crops for hay if a heavy crop is in prospect. See Wright, Australian Wheat Stabilization, Foreign Agriculture (Office of Foreign Agricultural Relations, Department of Agriculture) September, 1942, pp. 329, 336. The Canadian Wheat Board has wide control over the marketing of wheat by the individual producer. 4 Geo. VI, chap. 25, § 5. Canadian wheat has also been the subject of numerous Orders in Council. E.g., 6 Proclamations and Orders in Council (1942) 183, which gives the Wheat Board full control of sale, delivery, milling and disposition by any person or individual. See also Wheat Acreage Reduction Act, 1942, 6 Geo. VI, chap. 10.

leaching. Some is sold, some kept for seed, and a percentage of the total production much larger than in areas of specialization is consumed on the farm and grown for such purpose. Such farmers, while growing some wheat, may even find the balance of their interest on the consumer's side.

The effect of consumption of home-grown wheat on interstate commerce is due to the fact that it constitutes the most variable factor in the disappearance of the wheat crop. Consumption on the farm where grown appears to vary in an amount greater than 20 per cent of average production. The total amount of wheat consumed as food varies but relatively little, and use as seed is relatively constant.

The maintenance by government regulation of a price for wheat undoubtedly can be accomplished as effectively by sustaining or increasing the demand as by limiting the supply. The effect of the statute before us is to restrict the amount which may be produced for market and the extent as well to which one may forestall resort to the market by producing to meet his own needs. That appellee's own contribution to the demand for wheat may be trivial by itself is not enough to remove him from the scope of federal regulation where, as here, his contribution, taken together with that of many others similarly situated, is far from trivial. National Labor Relations Bd. v. Fainblatt, 306 U.S. 601, 606 et seq.; United States v. Darby, supra (312 U.S. at 123).

It is well established by decisions of this Court that the power to regulate commerce includes the power to regulate the prices at which commodities in that commerce are dealt in and practices affecting such prices. One of the primary purposes of the Act in question was to increase the market price of wheat and to that end to limit the volume thereof that could affect the market. It can hardly be denied that a factor of such volume and variability as home-consumed wheat would have a substantial influence on price and market conditions. This may arise because being in marketable condition such wheat overhangs the market and if induced by rising prices tends to flow into the market and check price increases. But if we assume that it is never marketed, it supplies a need of the man who grew it which would otherwise be reflected by purchases in the open market. Home-grown wheat in this sense competes with wheat in commerce. The stimulation of commerce is a use of the regulatory function quite as definitely as prohibitions or restrictions thereon. This record leaves us in no doubt that Congress may properly have considered that wheat consumed on the farm where grown if wholly outside the scheme of regulation would have a substantial effect in defeating and obstructing its purpose to stimulate trade therein at increased prices.

It is said, however, that this Act, forcing some farmers into the market to buy what they could provide for themselves, is an unfair promotion of the markets and prices of specializing wheat growers. It is of the essence of regulation that it lays a restraining hand on the self-interest of the regulated and that advantages from the regulation commonly fall to others. The conflicts of economic interest between the regulated and those who advantage by it are wisely left under our system to resolution by the Congress under its more flexible and responsible legislative process. Such conflicts rarely lend themselves to judicial determination. And with the wisdom, workability, or fairness, of the plan of regulation we have nothing to do. . . .

[A discussion of due process is omitted.]

Reversed.

NOTE Expansion of the Commerce Power and Problems of Statutory Coverage

1. In setting individual farm quotas for tobacco, Congress required that actual past marketing figures be used. Penalties attached only to marketing in excess of quotas. The regulation was sustained in Mulford v. Smith, 307 U.S. 38 (1939). Originally, under the Agri-

298   Chapter Seven.   **National Power over the Economy**

cultural Adjustment Act of 1938, a similar plan was applicable to wheat. The reasons for the change, effected in 1941 amendments, were explained by the government in its brief on reargument in Wickard v. Filburn, supra. Quotas based on individual past marketing were not, to be sure, attempted for each of the 1.5 million farms producing wheat; the lack of records of individual marketing would have made the plan unworkable. The alternative originally adopted for wheat was the fixing of a national marketing percentage of the total acreage allotment, based on past overall experience in the relation of marketing to production, and the application of this percentage to each acreage allotment, as a marketing quota. The difficulties asserted were the problem of policing and the inequities among individual farms. The farmer who would normally use on the farm at least the average national proportion of a crop so utilized, or who could do so, would not be required to reduce his marketing, while the farmer who was not in a position to use wheat for feed would bear the burden of the reduction in the marketing quota. It is evident, moreover, that this original plan tended to depress the market for commercial feeds and seed.

Thus the amended plan, considered in the light of its background, suggests two issues. (a) May administrative difficulties justify extension of control beyond interstate commerce? For example, may all cattle in infected areas be subjected to federal inspection and dipping? Thornton v. United States, 271 U.S. 414 (1926). May all unfit meat found in a plant be destroyed, before it is known whether it is to move out of the state? Cf. United States v. Lewis, 235 U.S. 282 (1914). (b) May Congress, in regulating interstate commerce, adopt a policy in favor of one segment of an industry or one competing group at the expense of another? Cf. Carolene Products Co. v. United States, 323 U.S. 18 (1944), involving the Filled Milk Act, which prohibits the interstate shipment of milk to which has been added any fat or oil other than milk fat, so that the product is in semblance or imitation of milk. On what ground should the validity of the statute be rested?

2. Wickard v. Filburn may reflect the current crest of the commerce power in the state of origin. In the state of destination, perhaps the crest is United States v. Sullivan, 332 U.S. 689 (1948), applying the Food, Drug, and Cosmetic Act to a retail druggist who sold, without the required labeling, sulfa tablets which he had removed from a properly labeled bulk container of the tablets bought from a local wholesaler, who in turn had bought the container of tablets from an out-of-state supplier. Or the peak may have been reached in the Oleomargarine Act of 1950, 64 Stat. 20, 21 U.S.C. §347, which provides: "Colored oleomargarine or colored margarine which is sold in the same State or Territory in which it is produced shall be subject in the same manner and to the same extent to the provisions of this Act as if it had been introduced in interstate commerce. . . . No person shall serve colored oleomargarine or colored margarine at a public eating place, whether or not any charge is made therefor, unless (1) each separate serving bears or is accompanied by labeling identifying it as oleomargarine or margarine, or (2) each separate serving thereof is triangular in shape. . . . For the purpose of this section colored oleomargarine or colored margarine is oleomargarine or margarine having a tint or shade containing more than one and six tenths degrees of yellow, or of yellow and red collectively, but with an excess of yellow over red, measured in terms of Lovibond tintometer scale or its equivalent."

Mr. Justice Jackson has said, in a case applying the Sherman Act to a group of manufacturers contracting for work on clothing for jobbers who would ship them interstate: "If it is interstate commerce that feels the pinch, it does not matter how local the operation which applies the squeeze." United States v. Women's Sportswear Mfrs. Assn., 336 U.S. 460, 464 (1949).

In Lorain Journal Co. v. United States, 342 U.S. 143 (1951), the Sherman Act was applied to a newspaper in Lorain, Ohio, having a daily circulation of over 20,000 copies, 165 of which were sent out of Ohio. The newspaper had no competition until 1948, when a small radio station, capable of being heard in certain surrounding counties, began to operate. The newspaper refused to accept advertising from any local advertiser who used the radio station. On what reasoning could the Sherman Act be held applicable, under the commerce clause?

3. The tides of decision concerning federal power under the commerce clause are traced in Roberts, The Court and the Constitution, c. 2 (1951); Stern, That Commerce Which Concerns More States Than One, 47 Harv. L. Rev. 335 (1934); Stern, The Commerce Clause and the National Economy, 1933-1946, 59 id. 645, 883 (1946); Stern, The Problems of Yesteryear — Commerce and Due Process, 4 Vand. L. Rev. 446 (1951); Levi, An Introduction to Legal Reasoning, 15 U. Chi. L. Rev. 501, 541-574 (1948).

4. With the expansion of the concept of constitutional power under the commerce clause, problems have arisen in the interpretation of statutes enacted in an era of more restrictive constitutional standards. Insofar as the statutory language is general, should it be regarded as open-ended, calculated to reach whatever it constitutionally can? The issue was acute when the Sherman Act was made the basis for a prosecution of fire insurance companies. The Court was unanimous in the view that the business could constitutionally be brought under federal regulation, despite repeated early assertions that "insurance is not commerce." But only by a 4 to 3 decision was it held that the Sherman Act of 1890 could be made to apply. United States v. South-Eastern Underwriters, 322 U.S. 533 (1944). Areas other than interstate commerce are beset with similar problems in the wake of changes in constitutional decision. Compare, e.g., Helvering v. Griffiths, 318 U.S. 371 (1943) (taxation of stock dividends as income); Girouard v. United States, 328 U.S. 61 (1946) (naturalization of conscientious objector); The Eagle, 8 Wall. 15 (1868) (admiralty jurisdiction); Burnet v. Brooks, 288 U.S. 378 (1933) (taxation of bonds and deposits kept in this country by nonresident aliens); cf. FPC v. East Ohio Gas Co., 338 U.S. 464 (1950) (prior regulatory gap filled by Natural Gas Act). See Lyon, Old Statutes and New Constitution, 44 Colum. L. Rev. 599 (1944).

5. Related problems of interpretation and draftsmanship turn on the statutory formula for describing coverage: from trademarks "used in commerce," defined to mean "all commerce which may lawfully be regulated by Congress," in the Lanham Act, 60 Stat. 427 (1946), 15 U.S.C. §1051, 1127, to "unfair methods of competition in commerce," defined as "commerce among the several states or with foreign nations . . ." in the Federal Trade Commission Act. See FTC v. Bunte Bros., 312 U.S. 349 (1941). Considerations of both range and precision may determine the appropriate form of drafting. How, for example, should coverage be defined in a bill for federal enactment of the Uniform Commercial Code? See Braucher, Federal Enactment of the Uniform Commercial Code, 16 Law & Contemp. Prob. 100 (1951), collecting a variety of statutory formulas for coverage under the commerce power.

In Gulf Oil Corp. v. Copp Paving Co., 419 U.S. 186 (1974), the Court considered the application of the "in commerce" language of the Robinson-Patman and Clayton Acts to activities of manufacturers of asphaltic concrete used for surfacing highways and sold entirely intrastate. Writing for the Court, Justice Powell distinguished the language of §1 of the Sherman Act, which makes reference to conduct "in restraint of trade or commerce among the several States, or with foreign nations." Whereas this language was interpreted to indicate Congress' intention to reach to the limits of its powers under the commerce clause, the "in commerce" language of the Clayton and Robinson-Patman Acts was held to require that the discriminatory practices alleged under these Acts not merely affect interstate commerce but occur directly in interstate transactions by the defendants. The Court thus rejected plaintiff's argument that the use of asphaltic concrete on interstate highway systems established the applicability of the Clayton and Robinson-Patman Acts. Justices Douglas and Brennan dissented.

May Congress require state officers to aid in administering a federal regulatory plan, such as environmental protection? Is the constitutional power doubtful enough to caution a narrow reading of the statute in this regard? See District of Columbia v. Train, 521 F.2d

971 (D.C. Cir. 1975); Note, 29 Vand. L. Rev. 276 (1976); Note, The Clear Air Amendments of 1970: Can Congress Compel State Cooperation in Achieving National Environmental Standards?, 11 Harv. Civ. Rights-Civ. Lib. L. Rev. 701 (1976).

NOTE Federal Price and Rent Control

The Emergency Price Control Act of 1942 empowered a Price Administrator to set maximum prices for wholesale and retail transactions, as a curb on wartime inflation. The prices were to be "generally fair and equitable" for the industry. This was interpreted by the Administrator to mean that prices must afford an industry as a whole (though not every firm therein) earnings equivalent to those in a prewar base period, and must cover out-of-pocket costs of the particular commodity whose price was in question. The act embodied a number of procedural stringencies. Any objection to a price regulation must be taken within 60 days of its issuance; the objection must be in the form of a protest filed with the Administrator; judicial review of regulations was confined to a special Emergency Court of Appeals, whose decisions were in turn reviewable on certiorari in the Supreme Court. No stay of a price order could be granted before final decision.

In Yakus v. United States, 321 U.S. 414 (1944), a small beef-slaughtering enterprise was prosecuted for violation of price regulations. Pursuant to the procedural provisions of the statute, the trial court refused to permit the defendant to challenge the fairness of the regulation, and protest to the Administrator would have been out of time. Conviction was upheld, over a dissent based on procedural due process grounds. See generally The Emergency Price Control Act, 9 Law & Contemp. Prob. 1 (1942) (symposium); Nathanson and Hyman, Judicial Review of Price Control: The Battle of the Meat Regulations, 42 Ill. L. Rev. 584 (1947).

Rent control provisions of the act were upheld in Bowles v. Willingham, 321 U.S. 503 (1944).

Heart of Atlanta Motel v. United States 379 U.S. 241, 85 S. Ct. 348, 13 L. Ed. 2d 258 (1964)

Mr. Justice Clark delivered the opinion of the Court.

This is a declaratory judgment action, 28 U.S.C. §2201 and §2202, attacking the constitutionality of Title II of the Civil Rights Act of 1964, 78 Stat. 241. In addition to declaratory relief the complaint sought an injunction restraining the enforcement of the Act and damages against respondents based on allegedly resulting injury in the event compliance was required. Appellees counterclaimed for enforcement under §206(a) of the Act and asked for a three-judge district court under §206(b). A three-judge court, empaneled under §206(b) as well as 28 U.S.C. §2282, sustained the validity of the Act and issued a permanent injunction on appellee's counterclaim restraining appellants from continuing to violate the Act which remains in effect on order of Mr. Justice Black, 85 Sup. Ct. 1. We affirm the judgment.

1. THE FACTUAL BACKGROUND AND CONTENTIONS OF THE PARTIES

The case comes here on admissions and stipulated facts. Appellant owns and operates the Heart of Atlanta Motel, which has 216 rooms available to transient guests. The motel is located on Courtland Street, two blocks from downtown Peachtree Street. It is readily accessible to interstate highways 75 and 85 and state highways 23 and 41. Appellant solicits patronage from outside the State of Georgia through various national advertising media, including magazines of national circulation; it maintains over 50 billboards and highway signs within the State, soliciting patronage for the motel; it accepts convention trade from outside Georgia and approximately 75% of its registered guests are from out of State. Prior to passage of the Act the motel had followed a practice of refusing to rent rooms to Negroes, and it alleged that it intended to continue to do so. In an effort to perpetuate that policy this suit was filed.

The appellant contends that Congress in passing this Act exceeded its power to regulate commerce under Art. I, §8, cl. 3, of the Constitution of the United States; that the Act violates the Fifth Amendment because appellant is deprived of the right to choose its customers and operate its business as it wishes, resulting in a taking of its liberty and property without due process of law and a taking of its property without just compensation; and, finally, that by requiring appellant to rent available rooms to Negroes against its will, Congress is subjecting it to involuntary servitude in contravention of the Thirteenth Amendment.

The appellees counter that the unavailability to Negroes of adequate accommodations interferes significantly with interstate travel, and that Congress, under the Commerce Clause, has power to remove such obstructions and restraints; that the Fifth Amendment does not forbid reasonable regulation and that consequential damage does not constitute a "taking" within the meaning of that amendment; that the Thirteenth Amendment claim fails because it is entirely frivolous to say that an amendment directed to the abolition of human bondage and the removal of widespread disabilities associated with slavery places discrimination in public accommodations beyond the reach of both federal and state law.

At the trial the appellant offered no evidence, submitting the case on the pleadings, admissions and stipulation of facts; however, appellees proved the refusal of the motel to accept Negro transients after the passage of the Act. The District Court sustained the constitutionality of the sections of the Act under attack (§§ 201(a), (b)(1) and (c)(1)) and issued a permanent injunction on the counterclaim of the appellees. It restrained the appellant from "refusing to accept Negroes as guests in the motel by reason of their race or color" and from "making any distinction whatever upon the basis of race or color in the availability of the goods, services, facilities, privileges, advantages or accommodations offered or made available to guests of the motel, or to the general public, within or upon any of the premises of the Heart of Atlanta Motel, Inc."

2. THE HISTORY OF THE ACT [OMITTED]

3. TITLE II OF THE ACT

This Title is divided into seven sections beginning with §201(a) which provides that:

"All persons shall be entitled to the full and equal enjoyment of the goods, services, facilities, privileges, advantages, and accommodations of any place of public accommodation, as defined in this section, without discrimination or segregation on the ground of race, color, religion, or national origin."

There are listed in §201(b) four classes of business establishments, each of which "serves the public" and "is a place of public accommodation" within the meaning of §201(a) "if its operations affect commerce, or if discrimination or segregation by it is supported by State action." The covered establishments are:

(1) any inn, hotel, motel, or other establishment which provides lodging to transient guests, other than an establishment located within a building which contains not more than five rooms for rent or hire and which is actually occupied by the proprietor of such establishment as his residence;

(2) any restaurant, cafeteria . . . [not here involved];

(3) any motion picture house . . . [not here involved];

(4) any establishment . . . which is physically located within the premises of any establishment otherwise covered by this subsection, or . . . within the premises of which is physically located any such covered establishment . . . [not here involved].

Section 201(c) defines the phrase "affect commerce" as applied to the above establishments. It first declares that "any inn, hotel, motel, or other establishment which provides lodging to transient guests" affects commerce per se. Restaurants, cafeterias, etc., in the second class affect commerce only if they serve or offer to serve interstate travelers or if a substantial portion of the food which they serve or products which they sell have "moved in commerce." Motion picture houses and other places listed in class three affect commerce if they customarily present films, performances, etc., "which move in commerce." And the establishments listed in class four affect commerce if they are within, or include within their own premises, an establishment "the operations of which affect commerce." Private clubs are excepted under certain conditions. See §201(e).

Section 201(d) declares that "discrimination or segregation" is supported by state action when carried on under color of any law, statute, ordinance, regulation or any custom or usage required or enforced by officials of the State or any of its subdivisions. . . .

4. APPLICATION OF TITLE II TO HEART OF ATLANTA MOTEL

It is admitted that the operation of the motel brings it within the provisions of §201(a) of the Act and that appellant refused to provide lodging for transient Negroes because of their race or color and that it intends to continue that policy unless restrained.

The sole question posed is, therefore, the constitutionality of the Civil Rights Act of 1964 as applied to these facts. The legislative history of the Act indicates that Congress based the Act on §5 and the Equal Protection Clause of the Fourteenth Amendment as well as its power to regulate interstate commerce under Art. I, §8, cl. 3 of the Constitution.

The Senate Commerce Committee made it quite clear that the fundamental object of Title II was to vindicate "the deprivation of personal dignity that surely accompanies denials of equal access to public establishments." At the same time, however, it noted that such an objective has been and could be readily achieved "by congressional action based on the commerce power of the Constitution." S. Rep. No. 872, at 16-17. Our study of the legislative record, made in the light of prior cases, has brought us to the conclusion that Congress possessed ample power in this regard, and we have therefore not considered the other grounds relied upon. This is not to say that the remaining authority upon which it acted was not adequate, a question upon which we do not pass, but merely that since the commerce power is sufficient for our decision here we have considered it alone. Nor is §201(d) or §202, having to do with state action, involved here and we do not pass upon those sections.

5. THE CIVIL RIGHTS CASES, 109 U.S. 3 (1883), AND THEIR APPLICATION

In light of our ground for decision, it might be well at the outset to discuss the Civil Rights Cases, supra, which declared provisions of the Civil Rights Act of 1875 unconstitutional. 18 Stat. 335, 336. We think that decision inapposite, and without precedential value in determining the constitutionality of the present Act. Unlike Title II of the present legislation, the 1875 Act broadly proscribed discrimination in "inns, public conveyances on land or water, theaters, and other public places of amusement," without limiting the categories of affected businesses to those impinging upon interstate commerce. In contrast, the applicability of Title II is carefully limited to enterprises having a direct and substantial relation to the interstate flow of goods and people, except where state action is involved. Further, the fact that certain kinds of businesses may not in 1875 have been sufficiently involved in interstate commerce to warrant bringing them within the ambit of the commerce power is not necessarily dispositive of the same question today. Our populace had not reached its present mobility, nor were facilities, goods and services circulating as readily in interstate commerce as they are today. Although the principles which we apply today are those first formulated by Chief Justice Marshall in Gibbons v. Ogden, 9 Wheat.

1 (1824), the conditions of transportation and commerce have changed dramatically, and we must apply those principles to the present state of commerce. The sheer increase in volume of interstate traffic alone would give discriminatory practices which inhibit travel a far larger impact upon the nation's commerce than such practices had in the economy of another day. Finally, there is language in the Civil Rights Cases which indicates that the Court did not fully consider whether the 1875 Act could be sustained as an exercise of the commerce power. . . .

6. THE BASIS OF CONGRESSIONAL ACTION

While the Act as adopted carried no congressional findings, the record of its passage through each house is replete with evidence of the burdens that discrimination by race or color places upon interstate commerce. . . . This testimony included the fact that our people have become increasingly mobile with millions of all races traveling from State to State; that Negroes in particular have been the subject of discrimination in transient accommodations, having to travel great distances to secure the same; that often they have been unable to obtain accommodations and have had to call upon friends to put them up overnight, S. Rep. No. 872, at 14-22; and that these conditions had become so acute as to require the listing of available lodging for Negroes in a special guidebook which was itself "dramatic testimony of the difficulties" Negroes encounter in travel, Senate Commerce Hearings, at 692-694. These exclusionary practices were found to be nationwide, the Under Secretary of Commerce testifying that there is "no question that this discrimination in the North still exists to a large degree" and in the West and Midwest as well. Senate Commerce Hearings, at 735, 744. This testimony indicated a qualitative as well as quantitative effect on interstate travel by Negroes. The former was the obvious impairment of the Negro traveler's pleasure and convenience that resulted when he continually was uncertain of finding lodging. As for the latter, there was evidence that this uncertainty stemming from racial discrimination had the effect of discouraging travel on the part of a substantial portion of the Negro community. Senate Commerce Hearings, at 744. This was the conclusion not only of the Under Secretary of Commerce but also of the Administrator of the Federal Aviation Agency, who wrote the Chairman of the Senate Commerce Committee that it was his "belief that air commerce is adversely affected by the denial to a substantial segment of the traveling public of adequate and desegregated public accommodations." Senate Commerce Hearings, at 12-13. We shall not burden this opinion with further details since the voluminous testimony presents overwhelming evidence that discrimination by hotels and motels impeded interstate travel.

7. THE POWER OF CONGRESS OVER INTERSTATE TRAVEL

The power of Congress to deal with these obstructions depends on the meaning of the Commerce Clause. Its meaning was first enunciated 140 years ago by the great Chief Justice John Marshall in Gibbons v. Ogden, 9 Wheat. 1 (1824), in these words: [quotation omitted]. In short, the determinative test of the exercise of power by the Congress under the Commerce Clause is simply whether the activity sought to be regulated is "commerce which concerns more than one State" and has a real and substantial relation to the national interest. Let us now turn to this facet of the problem.

That the "intercourse" of which the Chief Justice spoke included the movement of persons through more States than one was settled as early as 1849, in the Passenger Cases, 7 How. 283, where Mr. Justice McLean stated: "That the transportation of passengers is a part of commerce is not now an open question." At 401. Again in 1913 Mr. Justice McKenna, speaking for the Court, said: "Commerce among the States, as we have said, consists of intercourse and traffic between their citizens, and includes the transportation of persons and property." Hoke v. United States, 227 U.S. 308, 320. . . .

The same interest in protecting interstate commerce which led Congress to deal with segregation in interstate carriers and the white slave traffic has prompted it to extend the exercise of its power to gambling, Lottery Case, 188 U.S. 321 (1903); to criminal enterprises, Brooks v. United States, 267 U.S. 432 (1925); to deceptive practices in the sale of products, Federal Trade Comm'n v. Mandel Bros., Inc., 359 U.S. 385 (1959); to fraudulent security transactions, Securities & Exchange Comm'n v. Ralston Purina Co., 346 U.S. 119 (1935); to misbranding of drugs, Weeks v. United States, 245 U.S. 618 (1918); to wages and hours, United States v. Darby, 312 U.S. 100 (1941); to members of labor unions, Labor Board v. Jones & Laughlin Steel Corp., 301 U.S. 1 (1937); to crop control, Wickard v. Filburn, 317 U.S. 111 (1942); to discrimination against shippers, United States v. Baltimore & Ohio R. Co., 333 U.S. 169 (1948); to the protection of small business from injurious price cutting, Moore v. Mead's Fine Bread Co., 348 U.S. 115 (1954); to resale price maintenance, Hudson Distributors, Inc. v. Eli Lilly & Co., 377 U.S. 386 (1964); Schwegmann v. Calvert Distillers Corp., 341 U.S. 384 (1951); to professional football, Radovich v. National Football League, 352 U.S. 445 (1957); and to racial discrimination by owners and managers of terminal restaurants, Boynton v. Virginia, 364 U.S. 454 (1960).

That Congress was legislating against moral wrongs in many of these areas rendered its enactments no less valid. In framing Title II of this Act Congress was also dealing with what it considered a moral problem. But that fact does not detract from the overwhelming evidence of the disruptive effect that racial discrimination has had on commercial intercourse. . . .

It is said that the operation of the motel here is of a purely local character. But, assuming this to be true, "if it is interstate commerce that feels the pinch, it does not matter how local the operation that applies the squeeze." United States v. Women's Sportswear Mfrs. Assn., 336 U.S. 460, 464 (1949). . . .

[The Court then considered and rejected arguments based on the Fifth and Thirteenth Amendments. Concurring opinions were delivered by JUSTICES BLACK, DOUGLAS, and GOLDBERG.]

Katzenbach v. McClung 379 U.S. 294, 85 S. Ct. 377,
13 L. Ed. 2d 290 (1964)

MR. JUSTICE CLARK delivered the opinion of the Court.

This case was argued with No. 515, Heart of Atlanta Motel v. United States. . . . This complaint for injunctive relief against appellants attacks the constitutionality of the Act as applied to a restaurant. The case was heard by a three-judge United States District Court and an injunction was issued restraining appellants from enforcing the Act against the restaurant. 233 F. Supp. 815. On direct appeal, 28 U.S.C. §§ 1252, 1253 (1958 ed.), we noted probable jurisdiction. 379 U.S. 802. We now reverse the judgment.

1. THE MOTION TO DISMISS

The appellants moved in the District Court to dismiss the complaint for want of equity jurisdiction and that claim is pressed here. The grounds are that the Act authorizes only preventive relief; that there has been no threat of enforcement against the appellees and that they have alleged no irreparable injury. It is true that ordinarily equity will not interfere in such cases. However, we may and do consider this complaint as an application for a declaratory judgment under 28 U.S.C. §§ 2201 and 2202 (1958 ed.). In this case, of course, direct appeal to this Court would still lie under 28 U.S.C. § 1252 (1958 ed.). But even though Rule 57 of the Federal Rules of Civil Procedure permits declaratory relief although another adequate remedy exists, it should not be granted where a special statutory proceeding has been provided. See Notes on Rule 57 of Advisory Committee on Rules, 28

U.S.C. App. 5178 (1958 ed.). Title II provides for such a statutory proceeding for the determination of rights and duties arising thereunder, §§ 204-207, and courts should, therefore, ordinarily refrain from exercising their jurisdiction in such cases.

The present case, however, is in a unique position. The interference with governmental action has occurred and the constitutional question is before us in the companion case of Heart of Atlanta Motel as well as in this case. It is important that a decision on the constitutionality of the Act as applied in these cases be announced as quickly as possible. For these reasons, we have concluded, with the above caveat, that the denial of discretionary relief is not required here.

2. THE FACTS

Ollie's Barbecue is a family-owned restaurant in Birmingham, Alabama, specializing in barbecued meats and homemade pies, with a seating capacity of 220 customers. It is located on a state highway, 11 blocks from an interstate one, and a somewhat greater distance from railroad and bus stations. The restaurant caters to a family and white-collar trade with a take-out service for Negroes. It employs 36 persons, two-thirds of whom are Negroes.

In the 12 months preceding the passage of the Act, the restaurant purchased locally approximately $150,000 worth of food, $69,683 or 46% of which was meat that it bought from a local supplier who had procured it from outside the State. The District Court expressly found that a substantial portion of the food served in the restaurant had moved in interstate commerce. The restaurant has refused to serve Negroes in its dining accommodations since its original opening in 1927, and since July 2, 1964, it has been operating in violation of the Act. The court below concluded that if it were required to serve Negroes it would lose a substantial amount of business. . . .

As to the Commerce Clause, the court found that it was "an express grant of power to Congress to regulate interstate commerce, which consists of the movement of persons, goods or information from one state to another"; and it found that the clause was also a grant of power "to regulate intrastate activities, but only to the extent that action on its part is necessary or appropriate to the effective execution of its expressly granted power to regulate interstate commerce." There must be, it said, a close and substantial relation between local activities and interstate commerce which requires control of the former in the protection of the latter. The court concluded, however, that the Congress, rather than finding facts sufficient to meet this rule, had legislated a conclusive presumption that a restaurant affects interstate commerce if it serves or offers to serve interstate travelers or if a substantial portion of the food which it serves has moved in commerce. This, the court held, it could not do because there was no demonstrable connection between food purchased in interstate commerce and sold in a restaurant and the conclusion of Congress that discrimination in the restaurant would affect that commerce. . . .

3. THE ACT AS APPLIED

. . . Sections 201(b)(2) and (c) place any "restaurant . . . principally engaged in selling food for consumption on the premises" under the Act "if . . . it serves or offers to serve interstate travelers or a substantial portion of the food which it serves . . . has moved in commerce."

Ollie's Barbecue admits that it is covered by these provisions of the Act. The Government makes no contention that the discrimination at the restaurant was supported by the State of Alabama. There is no claim that interstate travelers frequented the restaurant. The sole question, therefore, narrows down to whether Title II, as applied to a restaurant annually receiving about $70,000 worth of food which has moved in commerce, is a valid exercise of the power of Congress. The Government has contended that Congress had ample basis upon which to find that racial discrimination at restaurants which receive from out of state a substantial portion of the food served does, in fact, impose commercial burdens of national magnitude upon interstate commerce. The appellees' major argument is directed to this premise. They urge that no such basis existed. It is to that question that we now turn.

4. THE CONGRESSIONAL HEARINGS

As we noted in Heart of Atlanta Motel both Houses of Congress conducted prolonged hearings on the Act. And, as we said there, while no formal findings were made, which of course are not necessary, it is well that we make mention of the testimony at these hearings the better to understand the problem before Congress and determine whether the Act is a reasonable and appropriate means toward its solution. The record is replete with testimony of the burdens placed on interstate commerce by racial discrimination in restaurants. A comparison of per capita spending by Negroes in restaurants, theaters, and like establishments indicates less spending, after discounting income differences, in areas where discrimination is widely practiced. This condition, which was especially aggravated in the South, was attributed in the testimony of the Under Secretary of Commerce to racial segregation. See Hearings before the Senate Committee on Commerce on S. 1732, 88th Cong., 1st Sess., 695. This diminutive spending springing from a refusal to serve Negroes and their total loss as customers has, regardless of the absence of direct evidence, a close connection to interstate commerce. The fewer customers a restaurant enjoys the less food it sells and consequently the less it buys. S. Rep. No. 872, 88th Cong., 2d Sess., at 19; Senate Commerce Committee Hearings, at 207. In addition, the Attorney General testified that this type of discrimination imposed "an artificial restriction on the market" and interfered with the flow of merchandise. Id., at 18-19; also, on this point, see testimony of Senator Magnuson, 110 Cong. Rec. 7402-7403. In addition, there were many references to discriminatory situations causing wide unrest and having a depressant effect on general business conditions in the respective communities. See, e.g., Senate Commerce Committee Hearings, at 623-630, 695-700, 1384-1385.

Moreover there was an impressive array of testimony that discrimination in restaurants had a direct and highly restrictive effect upon interstate travel by Negroes. This resulted, it was said, because discriminatory practices prevent Negroes from buying prepared food served on the premises while on a trip, except in isolated and unkempt restaurants and under most unsatisfactory and often unpleasant conditions. This obviously discourages travel and obstructs interstate commerce for one can hardly travel without eating. Likewise, it was said, that discrimination deterred professional, as well as skilled, people from moving into areas where such practices occurred and thereby caused industry to be reluctant to establish there. S. Rep. No. 872, supra, at 18-19.

We believe that this testimony afforded ample basis for the conclusion that established restaurants in such areas sold less interstate goods because of the discrimination, that interstate travel was obstructed directly by it, that business in general suffered and that many new businesses refrained from establishing there as a result of it. Hence the District Court was in error in concluding that there was no connection between discrimination and the movement of interstate commerce. The court's conclusion that such a connection is outside "common experience" flies in the face of stubborn fact.

It goes without saying that, viewed in isolation, the volume of food purchased by Ollie's Barbecue from sources supplied from out of state was insignificant when compared with the total foodstuffs moving in commerce. But, as our late Brother Jackson said for the Court in Wickard v. Filburn, 317 U.S. 111 (1942): "That appellee's own contribution to the demand for wheat may be trivial by itself is not enough to remove him from the scope of federal regulation where, as here, his contribution, taken together with that of many others similarly situated, is far from trivial." At 127-128.

We noted in Heart of Atlanta Motel that a number of witnesses attested to the fact that racial discrimination was not merely a state or regional problem but was one of nationwide scope. Against this background, we must conclude that while the focus of the legislation was on the individual restaurant's relation to interstate commerce, Congress appropriately considered the importance of that connection with the knowledge that the discrimination was but "representative of many others throughout the country, the total incidence of which if left unchecked may well become far-reaching in its harm to commerce." Polish Alliance v. Labor Board, 322 U.S. 643, 648 (1944).

With this situation spreading as the record shows, Congress was not required to await the total dislocation of commerce. As was said in Consolidated Edison Co. v. Labor Board, 305 U.S. 197 (1938): "But it cannot be maintained that the exertion of federal power must await the disruption of that commerce. Congress was entitled to provide reasonable preventive measures and that was the object of the National Labor Relations Act." At 222.

5. THE POWER OF CONGRESS TO REGULATE LOCAL ACTIVITIES

. . . Much is said about a restaurant business being local but "even if appellee's activity be local and though it may not be regarded as commerce, it may still, whatever its nature, be reached by Congress if it exerts a substantial economic effect on interstate commerce. . . ." Wickard v. Filburn, supra, at 125. The activities that are beyond the reach of Congress are "those which are completely within a particular State, which do not affect other States, and with which it is not necessary to interfere, for the purpose of executing some of the general powers of the government." Gibbons v. Ogden, 9 Wheat. 1, 195 (1824). This rule is as good today as it was when Chief Justice Marshall laid it down almost a century and a half ago. . . .

The appellees contend that Congress has arbitrarily created a conclusive presumption that all restaurants meeting the criteria set out in the Act "affect commerce." Stated another way, they object to the omission of a provision for a case-by-case determination — judicial or administrative — that racial discrimination in a particular restaurant affects commerce.

But Congress' action in framing this Act was not unprecedented. In United States v. Darby, 312 U.S. 100 (1941), this Court held constitutional the Fair Labor Standards Act of 1938. . . . The appellees in that case argued, as do the appellees here, that the Act was invalid because it included no provision for an independent inquiry regarding the effect on commerce of substandard wages in a particular business. (Brief for appellees, pp. 76-77, United States v. Darby, 312 U.S. 100.) But the Court rejected the argument, observing that: "[S]ometimes Congress itself has said that a particular activity affects the commerce, as it did in the present Act, the Safety Appliance Act and the Railway Labor Act. In passing on the validity of legislation of the class last mentioned the only function of courts is to determine whether the particular activity regulated or prohibited is within the reach of the federal power." At 120-121.

Here, as there, Congress has determined for itself that refusals of service to Negroes have imposed burdens both upon the interstate flow of food and upon the movement of products generally. Of course, the mere fact that Congress has said when particular activity shall be deemed to affect commerce does not preclude further examination by this Court. But where we find that the legislators, in light of the facts and testimony before them, have a rational basis for finding a chosen regulatory scheme necessary to the protection of commerce, our investigation is at an end. The only remaining question — one answered in the affirmative by the court below — is whether the particular restaurant either serves or offers to serve interstate travelers or serves food a substantial portion of which has moved in interstate commerce.

The appellees urge that Congress, in passing the Fair Labor Standards Act and the National Labor Relations Act, made specific findings which were embodied in those statutes.

Here, of course, Congress has included no formal findings. But their absence is not fatal to the validity of the statute, see United States v. Carolene Products Co., 304 U.S. 144, 152 (1938), for the evidence presented at the hearings fully indicated the nature and effect of the burdens on commerce which Congress meant to alleviate.

Confronted as we are with the facts laid before Congress, we must conclude that it has a rational basis for finding that racial discrimination in restaurants had a direct and adverse effect on the free flow of interstate commerce. Insofar as the sections of the Act here relevant are concerned, §§ 201(b)(2) and (c), Congress prohibited discrimination only in those establishments having a close tie to interstate commerce, i.e., those, like the McClungs', serving food that has come from out of the State. We think in so doing that Congress acted well within its power to protect and foster commerce in extending the coverage of Title II only to those restaurants offering to serve interstate travelers or serving food, a substantial portion of which has moved in interstate commerce.

The absence of direct evidence connecting discriminatory restaurant service with the flow of interstate food, a factor on which the appellees place much reliance, is not, given the evidence as to the effect of such practices on other aspects of commerce, a crucial matter.

The power of Congress in this field is broad and sweeping; where it keeps within its sphere and violates no express constitutional limitation it has been the rule of this Court, going back almost to the founding days of the Republic, not to interfere. The Civil Rights Act of 1964, as here applied, we find to be plainly appropriate in the resolution of what the Congress found to be a national commercial problem of the first magnitude. We find it in no violation of any express limitations of the Constitution and we therefore declare it valid.

The judgment is therefore
Reversed.

NOTE Daniel v. Paul

In Daniel v. Paul, 395 U.S. 298 (1969), the Court held that § 201 of Title II of the 1964 Civil Rights Act applied to the Lake Nixon Club, a recreational facility near Little Rock, Arkansas, described as "a 232-acre amusement area with swimming, boating, sun bathing, picnicking, miniature golf, dancing facilities, and a snack bar." The Court first rejected the club's attempt to style itself as an exempt private club under § 201(e) of the act by charging "a 25-cent 'membership' fee." The Court then set forth two theories under which the club could be held a "place of public accommodation" whose operations "affect commerce" within the meaning of §§ 201(b) and (c). First, the club's snack bar fit within the act as a restaurant offering to serve interstate travellers, as indicated by club advertising in local newspapers and radio spots, and serving food which was moved in interstate commerce, as indicated by the likely ingredients of soft drinks and hotdog buns. Once the snack bar qualified under the act, the other facilities were brought in by §§ 201(b)(4) and (c)(4) as located on the same premises as a facility covered by the act. Alternatively, the Court held that the recreational facilities were independently covered by §§ 201(b)(3) and (c)(3) as a "place of entertainment." The requisite independent effect on commerce was found in the presence of paddle boats and a juke box manufactured outside of Arkansas.

Justice Black dissented, concluding: "While it is the duty of courts to enforce this important Act, we are not called on to hold nor should we hold subject to that Act this country people's recreation center, lying in what may be, so far as we know, a little 'sleepy hollow' between Arkansas hills miles away from any interstate highway. This would be stretching the Commerce Clause so as to give the Federal Government complete control over every little remote country place of recreation in every nook and cranny of every precinct and county in every one of the 50 States. This goes too far for me."

NOTE Commerce and Crime

In Perez v. United States, 402 U.S. 146 (1971), a provision of the Federal Consumer Protection Act was sustained under the Commerce Clause. The provision penalized "loan sharking" activities, i.e., unlawfully using extortionate means in collecting and attempting to collect an extension of credit. Answering the argument that the activities were local in nature, the Court deemed adequate the findings of Congress to support the conclusion that loan sharking substantially supports organized interstate crime. Justice Stewart dissented.

Compare the position taken by the Court in United States v. Bass, 404 U.S. 336 (1971). Respondent was convicted of possessing firearms in violation of Title VII of the Omnibus Crime Control and Safe Streets Act of 1968, 18 U.S.C. App. §1202(a), which makes it a crime for a convicted felon to "receive, possess, or transport in commerce or affecting commerce . . . any firearm." On appeal to the circuit court respondent challenged the government's failure to allege that the weapons involved had been possessed "in commerce or affecting commerce." The government argued that, properly construed, the phrase applied only to transportation and not to possession. After discussing inconclusive arguments based on grammar and legislative history, the court of appeals reversed the conviction on the ground that "serious doubts" as to the constitutionality of the statute as interpreted by the government compelled it to adopt respondent's narrower reading. 434 F.2d 1296 (2d Cir. 1970). On certiorari the Supreme Court affirmed. After stating that the narrower construction was supported by general rules regarding the interpretation of criminal statutes, Justice Marshall, writing for the Court, continued:

"There is a second principle supporting today's result: unless Congress conveys its purpose clearly, it will not be taken to have significantly changed the federal-state balance. Congress has traditionally been reluctant to define as a federal crime conduct readily denounced as criminal by the States. . . . [W]e will not be quick to assume that Congress has meant to effect a significant change in the sensitive relation between federal and state criminal jurisdiction." (Footnotes omitted.) The Court did not, however, in terms endorse the doubts on the constitutionality of the statute as read by the government. Justice Blackmun, joined by Chief Justice Burger, dissented. See also United States v. Enmons, 410 U.S. 396 (1973), holding that the Hobbs Act, 18 U.S.C. §1951, which makes it a federal crime to obstruct interstate commerce by robbery or extortion, does not reach to the use of violence by labor union members pursuing legitimate union objectives.

See Stern, The Commerce Clause Revisited — The Federalization of Intrastate Crime, 15 Ariz. L. Rev. 271 (1973).

Section B. MONEY AND BANKING

NOTE Legal Tender Cases

The Legal Tender Acts, passed during the Civil War, made United States notes (greenbacks) legal tender for debts, public and private, with certain exceptions. The validity of the acts as applied to antecedent debts was challenged in Hepburn v. Griswold, 8 Wall. 603 (1869). The Court was then composed of only eight Justices, owing to the legislation which had been enacted to curb the appointing power of President Johnson. The decision was 5 to 3 against the validity of the acts as applied; Chief Justice Chase, who was Secretary of the Treasury when the legislation was passed (see page 135 supra) wrote the opinion, with Justices Miller, Swayne, and Davis dissenting. A private memorandum left by the dissenting Justices describes the tension within the Court and an evidently successful effort at the conference on the case "to convince an aged and infirm member of the court [Mr. Justice Grier] that he had not understood the question on which he voted," converting an equal division into a majority for holding the acts invalid. See Ratner, Was the Supreme Court Packed by President Grant, 50 Pol. Sci. Q. 343 (1935); Fairman, Mr. Justice Miller and the Supreme Court, c. 7 (1939). On the day the decision was announced, President Grant nominated to the Court William Strong and Joseph P. Bradley, to fill the vacancy caused by the resignation of Mr. Justice Grier and to restore the membership of the Court to nine. On the question whether Grant "packed" the Court, see Ratner, supra, and Fairman, Mr. Justice Bradley's Appointment to the Supreme Court and the Legal Tender Cases, 54 Harv. L. Rev. 977, 1128 (1941).

After further internal struggles in the Court over the hearing of arguments in additional legal tender cases (see 2 Warren, The Supreme Court in United States History 522 (1926)), Hepburn v. Griswold was overruled in Legal Tender Cases, 12 Wall. 457 (1871), in an opinion by Mr. Justice Strong, with a dissenting opinion by Chief Justice Chase and the three other surviving members of the former majority. See C. Fairman, Reconstruction and Reunion, Part One, 1864-88, c. 14 (1971).

The question of the application of the Legal Tender Acts to debts expressly payable in gold coin was not involved in the foregoing cases but was decided in Bronson v. Rodes, 7 Wall. 229 (1868), construing the acts as not applying to such obligations. Thus not only was a dual system of money put into effect, paper money frequently circulating at a discount from gold, but a dual system of monetary dollar claims was continued.

Norman v. Baltimore & Ohio R.R. *294 U.S. 240, 55 S. Ct. 407, 79 L. Ed. 885 (1935)*

Mr. Chief Justice Hughes delivered the opinion of the Court.

These cases present the question of the validity of the Joint Resolution of the Congress, of June 5, 1933, with respect to the "gold clauses" of private contracts for the payment of money. 48 Stat. at L. 112.

This Resolution . . . declares that "every provision contained in or made with respect to any obligation which purports to give the obligee a right to require payment in gold or a particular kind in coin or currency, or in an amount in money of the United States measured thereby" is "against public policy." Such provisions in obligations thereafter incurred are prohibited. The Resolution provides that "Every obligation, heretofore or hereafter incurred, whether or not any such provision is contained therein or made with respect thereto, shall be discharged upon payment, dollar for dollar, in any coin or currency which at the time of payment is legal tender for public and private debts."

In No. 270, the suit was brought upon a coupon of a bond made by the Baltimore and Ohio Railroad Company under date of February 1, 1930, for the payment of $1,000 on February 1, 1960, and interest from date at the rate of 4½ per cent. per annum, payable semi-annually. The bond provided that the payment of principal and interest "will be made . . . in gold coin of the United States of America of or equal to the standard of weight and fineness existing on February 1, 1930." The coupon in suit, for $22.50, was payable on February 1, 1934. The complaint alleged that on February 1, 1930, the standard weight and fineness of a gold dollar of the United States as a unit of value "was fixed to consist of twenty-five and eight-tenths grains of gold, nine-tenths fine," pursuant to the Act of Congress of March 14, 1900; and that by the Act of Congress known as the "Gold Reserve Act of 1934," and by the order of the President under that Act, the standard unit of value of a gold dollar of the United States "was fixed to consist of fifteen and five-twenty-firsts grains of gold, nine-tenths fine," from and after January 31, 1934. On presentation of the coupon, defendant refused to pay the amount in gold, or the equivalent of gold in legal tender of the United States which was alleged to be, on February 1,

Section B. Money and Banking

1934, according to the standard of weight and fineness existing on February 1, 1930, the sum of $38.10, and plaintiff demanded judgment for that amount.

Defendant answered that by Acts of Congress, and, in particular, by the Joint Resolution of June 5, 1933, defendant had been prevented from making payment in gold coin "or otherwise than dollar for dollar, in coin or currency of the United States (other than gold coin and gold certificates)" which at the time of payment constituted legal tender. Plaintiff, challenging the validity of the Joint Resolution under the Fifth and Tenth Amendments, and Article I, § 1, of the Constitution of the United States, moved to strike the defense. The motion was denied. Judgment was entered for plaintiff for $22.50, the face of the coupon, and was affirmed upon appeal. The Court of Appeals of the State considered the federal question and decided that the Joint Resolution was valid. 265 N.Y. 37. This Court granted a writ of certiorari, October 8, 1934. . . .

The Joint Resolution of June 5, 1933, was one of a series of measures relating to the currency. . . . On March 6, 1933, the President, stating that there had been "heavy and unwarranted withdrawals of gold and currency from our banking institutions for the purpose of hoarding" and "extensive speculative activity abroad in foreign exchange" which had resulted "in severe drains on the Nation's stocks of gold," and reciting the authority conferred by § 5(b) of the Act of October 6, 1917, declared "a bank holiday" until March 9, 1933. On the same date, the Secretary of the Treasury, with the President's approval, issued instructions to the Treasurer of the United States to make payments in gold in any form only under license issued by the Secretary.

On March 9, 1933, the Congress passed the Emergency Banking Act. All orders issued by the President or the Secretary of the Treasury since March 4, 1933, under the authority conferred by § 5(b) of the Act of October 6, 1917, were confirmed. That section was amended so as to provide that during any period of national emergency declared by the President, he might "investigate, regulate or prohibit," by means of licenses or otherwise, "any transactions in foreign exchange, transfers of credit between or payments by banking institutions as defined by the President, and export, hoarding, melting, or ear-marking of gold or silver coin or bullion or currency, by any person within the United States or any place subject to the jurisdiction thereof." The Act also amended § 11 of the Federal Reserve Act so as to authorize the Secretary of the Treasury to require all persons to deliver to the Treasurer of the United States "any or all gold coin, gold bullion, and gold certificates" owned by them, and that the Secretary should pay therefor "an equivalent amount of any other form of coin or currency coined or issued under the laws of the United States." By Executive Order of March 10, 1933, the President authorized banks to be reopened, as stated, but prohibited the removal from the United States, or any place subject to its jurisdiction, of "any gold coin, bullion, or gold certificates, except in accordance with regulations prescribed by or under license issued by the Secretary of the Treasury." By further Executive Order of April 5, 1933, forbidding hoarding, all persons were required to deliver, on or before May 1, 1933, to stated banks "all gold coin, gold bullion and gold certificates," with certain exceptions, the holder to receive "an equivalent amount of any other form of coin or currency coined or issued under the laws of the United States." Another Order of April 20, 1933, contained further requirements with respect to the acquisition and export of gold and to transactions in foreign exchange.

By § 43 of the Agricultural Adjustment Act of May 12, 1933, it was provided that the President should have authority, upon the making of prescribed findings and in the circumstances stated, "to fix the weight of the gold dollar in grains nine-tenths fine and also to fix the weight of the silver dollar in grains nine-tenths fine at a definite fixed ratio in relation to the gold dollar at such amounts as he finds necessary from his investigation to stabilize domestic prices or to protect the foreign commerce against the adverse effect of depreciated foreign currencies," and it was further provided that the "gold dollar, the weight of which is so fixed, shall be the standard unit of value," and that "all forms of money shall be maintained at a parity with this standard," but that "in no event shall the weight of the gold dollar be fixed so as to reduce its present weight by more than 50 per centum."

Then followed the Joint Resolution of June 5, 1933. There were further Executive Orders . . . and orders of the Secretary of the Treasury, approved by the President, on December 28, 1933, and January 15, 1934, for the delivery of gold coin, gold bullion and gold certificates to the United States Treasury.

On January 30, 1934, the Congress passed the "Gold Reserve Act of 1934" which, by §13, ratified and confirmed all the actions, regulations and orders taken or made by the President and the Secretary of the Treasury under the Act of March 9, 1933, or under §43 of the Act of May 12, 1933, and, by §12, with respect to the authority of the President to fix the weight of the gold dollar, provided that it should not be fixed "in any event at more than 60 per centum of its present weight." On January 31, 1934, the President issued his proclamation declaring that he fixed "the weight of the gold dollar to be $15^5/_{21}$ grains nine-tenths fine," from and after that date.

We have not attempted to summarize all the provisions of these measures. We are not concerned with their wisdom. The question before the Court is one of power, not of policy. And that question touches the validity of these measures at but a single point, that is, in relation to the Joint Resolution denying effect to "gold clauses" in existing contracts. The Resolution must, however, be considered in its legislative setting and in the light of other measures in pari materia.

First. The interpretation of the gold clauses in suit. [The Court discussed the interpretation advanced by the obligor, that the bonds were "gold coin" obligations, and the interpretation advanced by the creditors, that the bonds were "gold value" obligations.]

We are of the opinion that the gold clauses now before us were not contracts for payment in gold coin as a commodity, or in bullion, but were contracts for the payment of money. The bonds were severally for the payment of one thousand dollars. We also think that, fairly construed, these clauses were intended to afford a definite standard or measure of value, and thus to protect against a depreciation of the currency and against the discharge of the obligation by a payment of lesser value than that prescribed. When these contracts were made they were not repugnant to any action of the Congress. In order to determine whether effect may now be given to the intention of the parties in the face of the action taken by the Congress, or the contracts may be satisfied by the payment dollar for dollar, in legal tender, as the Congress has now prescribed, it is necessary to consider (1) the power of the Congress to establish a monetary system and the necessary implications of that power; (2) the power of the Congress to invalidate the provisions of existing contracts which interfere with the exercise of its constitutional authority; and (3) whether the clauses in question do constitute such an interference as to bring them within the range of that power.

Second. The power of the Congress to establish a monetary system. It is unnecessary to review the historic controversy as to the extent of this power, or again to go over the ground traversed by the Court in reaching the conclusion that the Congress may make treasury notes legal tender in payment of debts previously contracted, as well as of those subsequently contracted, whether that authority be exercised in course of war or in time of peace. Legal Tender Cases (Knox v. Lee), 12 Wall. 457; Legal Tender Case (Juilliard v. Greenman), 110 U.S. 421. We need only consider certain postulates upon which that conclusion rested.

The Constitution grants to the Congress power "To coin money, regulate the value thereof, and of foreign coin." Art. 1, §8, ¶5. But the Court in the legal tender cases did not derive from that express grant alone the full authority of the Congress in relation to the currency. The Court found the source of that authority in all the related powers conferred upon the Congress and appropriate to achieve "the great objects for which the government was framed," — "a national government, with sovereign powers." M'Culloch v. Maryland, 4 Wheat. 316, 404-407; Legal Tender Cases (Knox v. Lee) supra (12 Wall. 532,

536); Legal Tender Case (Juilliard v. Greenman) supra (110 U.S. 438). The broad and comprehensive national authority over the subjects of revenue, finance and currency is derived from the aggregate of the powers granted to the Congress, embracing the powers to lay and collect taxes, to borrow money, to regulate commerce with foreign nations and among the several States, to coin money, regulate the value thereof, and of foreign coin, and fix the standards of weights and measures, and the added express power "to make all laws which shall be necessary and proper for carrying into execution" the other enumerated powers. Legal Tender Case (Juilliard v. Greenman) supra (110 U.S. 439, 440). . . .

Moreover, by virtue of this national power, there attach to the ownership of gold and silver those limitations which public policy may require by reason of their quality as legal tender and as a medium of exchange. Ling Su Fan v. United States, 218 U.S. 302, 310. Those limitations arise from the fact that the law "gives to such coinage a value which does not attach as a mere consequence of intrinsic value." Their quality as legal tender is attributed by the law, aside from their bullion value. Hence the power to coin money includes the power to forbid mutilation, melting and exportation of gold and silver coin, — "to prevent its outflow from the country of its origin." Id. p. 311.

Dealing with the specific question as to the effect of the legal tender acts upon contracts made before their passage, that is, those for the payment of money generally, the Court, in the legal tender cases, recognized the possible consequences of such enactments in frustrating the expected performance of contracts, — in rendering them "fruitless or partially fruitless." The Court pointed out that the exercise of the powers of Congress may affect "apparent obligations" of contracts in many ways. The Congress may pass bankruptcy acts. The Congress may declare war, or, even in peace, pass non-intercourse acts, or direct an embargo, which may operate seriously upon existing contracts. And the Court reasoned that if the legal tender acts "were justly chargeable with impairing contract obligations, they would not, for that reason, be forbidden, unless a different rule is to be applied to them from that which has hitherto prevailed in the construction of other powers granted by the fundamental law." The conclusion was that contracts must be understood as having been made in reference to the possible exercise of the rightful authority of the Government, and that no obligation of a contract "can extend to the defeat" of that authority. Legal Tender Cases (Knox v. Lee) supra (12 Wall. pp. 549-551).

On similar grounds, the Court dismissed the contention under the Fifth Amendment forbidding the taking of private property for public use without just compensation or the deprivation of it without due process of law. That provision, said the Court, referred only to a direct appropriation. A new tariff, an embargo, or a war, might bring upon individuals great losses; might, indeed, render valuable property almost valueless, — might destroy the worth of contracts. "But whoever supposed," asked the Court, "that, because of this, a tariff could not be changed or a non-intercourse act, or embargo be enacted, or a war be declared." The Court referred to the Act of June 28, 1834, by which a new regulation of the weight and value of gold coin was adopted, and about six per cent. was taken from the weight of each dollar. The effect of the measure was that all creditors were subjected to a corresponding loss, as the debts then due "became solvable with six per cent. less gold than was required to pay them before." But it had never been imagined that there was a taking of private property without compensation or without due process of law. The harshness of such legislation, or the hardship it may cause, afforded no reason for considering it to be unconstitutional. Id. pp. 551, 552.

The question of the validity of the Joint Resolution of June 5, 1933, must be determined in the light of these settled principles.

Third. *The power of the Congress to invalidate the provisions of existing contracts which interfere with the exercise of its constitutional authority.* The instant cases involve contracts between private parties, but the question necessarily relates as well to the contracts or obligations of States and municipalities, or of their political subdivisions, that is, to such engagements as are within the reach of the applicable national power. The Government's own contracts — the obligations of the United States — are in a distinct category and demand separate consideration. See Perry v. United States, 294 U.S. 330.

The contention is that the power of the Congress, broadly sustained by the decisions we have cited in relation to private contracts for the payment of money generally, does not extend to the striking down of express contracts for gold payments. The acts before the Court in the legal tender cases, as we have seen, were not deemed to go so far. Those acts left in circulation two kinds of money, both lawful and available, and contracts for payments in gold, one of these kinds, were not disturbed. The Court did not decide that the Congress did not have the constitutional power to invalidate existing contracts of that sort, if they stood in the way of the execution of the policy of the Congress in relation to the currency. Mr. Justice Bradley, in his concurring opinion, expressed the view that the Congress had that power and had exercised it. Legal Tender Cases (Knox v. Lee) supra (12 Wall. 566, 567). And, upon that ground, he dissented from the opinion of the Court in Trebilcock v. Wilson (12 Wall. 699), as to the validity of contracts for payment *"in specie."* It is significant that Mr. Justice Bradley, referring to this difference of opinion in the legal tender cases, remarked (in his concurring opinion) that "of course" the difference arose "from the different construction given to the legal tender acts." "I do not understand," he said, "the majority of the court to decide that an act so drawn as to embrace, in terms, contracts payable in specie, would not be constitutional. Such a decision would completely nullify the power claimed for the government. For it would be very easy, by the use of one or two additional words, to make all contracts payable in specie."

Here, the Congress has enacted an express interdiction. The argument against it does not rest upon the mere fact that the legislation may cause hardship or loss. Creditors who have not stipulated for gold payments may suffer equal hardship or loss with creditors who have so stipulated. The former, admittedly, have no constitutional grievance. And, while the latter may not suffer more, the point is pressed that their express stipulations for gold payments constitute property, and that creditors who have not such stipulations are without that property right. And the contestants urge that the Congress is seeking not to regulate the currency, but to regulate contracts, and thus has stepped beyond the power conferred.

This argument is in the teeth of another established principle. Contracts, however express, cannot fetter the constitutional authority of the Congress. Contracts may create rights of property, but when contracts deal with a subject matter which lies within the control of the Congress, they have a congenital infirmity. Parties cannot remove their transactions from the reach of dominant constitutional power by making contracts about them. See Hudson Water Co. v. McCarter, 209 U.S. 349, 357.

This principle has familiar illustration in the exercise of the power to regulate commerce. If shippers and carriers stipulate for specified rates, although the rates may be lawful when the contracts are made, if Congress through the Interstate Commerce Commission exercises its authority and prescribes different rates, the latter control and override inconsistent stipulations in contracts previously made. This is so, even if the contract be a charter granted by a State and limiting rates, or a contract between municipalities and carriers. [Citations omitted.]

In Addyston Pipe & Steel Co. v. United States, 175 U.S. 211, 229, 230, the Court raised the pertinent question — if certain kinds of private contracts directly limit or restrain, and hence regulate interstate commerce, why should not the power of Congress reach such contracts equally with legislation of a State to the same effect? "What sound reason," said the Court, "can be given why Congress should have the power to interfere in the case of the State, and yet have none in the case of the individual? . . ."

Applying that principle, the Court held that a contract, valid when made (in 1871) for the giving of a free pass by an interstate carrier, in consideration of a release of a claim for damages, could not be enforced after the Congress had passed the Act of June 29, 1906. . . . Louisville & N.R. Co. v. Mottley, 219 U.S. 467. . . .

The principle is not limited to the incidental effect of the exercise by the Congress of its constitutional authority. There is no constitutional ground for denying to the Congress the power expressly to prohibit and invalidate contracts although previously made, and valid when made, when they interfere with the carrying out of the policy it is free to adopt. The exercise of this power is illustrated by the provision of § 5 of the Employers' Liability Act of 1908 relating to any contract the purpose of which was to enable a common carrier to exempt itself from the liability which the Act created. Such a stipulation the Act explicitly declared to be void. In the Second Employers' Liability Cases, 223 U.S. 1, 52, the Court decided that as the Congress possessed the power to impose the liability, it also possessed the power "to insure its efficacy by prohibiting any contract, rule, regulation or device in evasion of it." And this prohibition the Court has held to be applicable to contracts made before the Act was passed. Philadelphia, B. & W.R. Co. v. Schubert, 224 U.S. 603. . . .

The same reasoning applies to the constitutional authority of the Congress to regulate the currency and to establish the monetary system of the country. If the gold clauses now before us interfere with the policy of the Congress in the exercise of that authority they cannot stand.

Fourth. The effect of the gold clauses in suit in relation to the monetary policy adopted by the Congress. Despite the wide range of the discussion at the bar and the earnestness with which the arguments against the validity of the Joint Resolution have been pressed, these contentions necessarily are brought, under the dominant principles to which we have referred, to a single and narrow point. That point is whether the gold clauses do constitute an actual interference with the monetary policy of the Congress in the light of its broad power to determine that policy. Whether they may be deemed to be such an interference depends upon an appraisement of economic conditions and upon determinations of questions of fact. With respect to those conditions and determinations, the Congress is entitled to its own judgment. We may inquire whether its action is arbitrary or capricious, that is, whether it has reasonable relation to a legitimate end. If it is an appropriate means to such an end, the decision of the Congress as to the degree of the necessity for the adoption of that means, is final. [Citations omitted.]

The Committee on Banking and Currency of the House of Representatives stated in its report recommending favorable action upon the Joint Resolution (H.R. Rep. No. 169, 73d Cong., 1st Sess.):

"The occasion for the declaration in the resolution that the gold clauses are contrary to public policy arises out of the experiences of the present emergency. These gold clauses render ineffective the power of the Government to create a currency and determine the value thereof. If the gold clause applied to a very limited number of contracts and security issues, it would be a matter of no particular consequence, but in this country virtually all obligations, almost as a matter of routine, contain the gold clause. In the light of this situation two phenomena which have developed during the present emergency make the enforcement of the gold clauses incompatible with the public interest. The first is the tendency which has developed internally to hoard gold; the second is the tendency for capital to leave the country. Under these circumstances no currency system, whether based upon gold or upon any other foundation, can meet the requirements of a situation in which many billions of dollars of securities are expressed in a particular form of the circulating medium, particularly when it is the medium upon which the entire credit and currency structure rests."

And the Joint Resolution itself recites the determination of the Congress in these words:

"Whereas the existing emergency has disclosed that provisions of obligations which purport to give the obligee a right to require payment in gold or a particular kind of coin or currency of the United States, or in an amount in money of the United States measured thereby, obstruct the power of the Congress to regulate the value of the money of the United States, and are inconsistent with the declared policy of the Congress to maintain at all times the equal power of every dollar, coined or issued by the United States, in the markets and in the payment of debts."

Can we say that this determination is so destitute of basis that the interdiction of the gold clauses must be deemed to be without any reasonable relation to the monetary policy adopted by the Congress?

. . . The estimates submitted at the bar indicate that when the Joint Resolution was adopted there were outstanding seventy-five billion dollars or more of such obligations, the annual interest charges on which probably amounted to between three and four billion dollars. It is apparent that if these promises were to be taken literally, as calling for actual payment in gold coin, they would be directly opposed to the policy of Congress, as they would be calculated to increase the demand for gold, to encourage hoarding, and to stimulate attempts at exportation of gold coin. . . .

But, if the clauses are treated as "gold value" clauses, that is, as intended to set up a measure or standard of value if gold coin is not available, we think they are still hostile to the policy of the Congress and hence subject to prohibition. It is true that when the Joint Resolution was adopted on June 5, 1933, while gold coin had largely been withdrawn from circulation and the Treasury had declared that "gold is not now paid, nor is it available for payment, upon public or private debts," the dollar had not yet been devalued. But devaluation was in prospect and a uniform currency was intended. Section 43 of the Act of May 12, 1933, provided that the President should have authority, on certain conditions, to fix the weight of the gold dollar as stated, and that its weight as so fixed should be "the standard unit of value" with which all forms of money should be maintained "at a parity." The weight of the gold dollar was not to be reduced by more than 50 per centum. The Gold Reserve Act of 1934 provided that the President should not fix the weight of the gold dollar at more than 60 per cent. of its present weight. The order of the President of January 31, 1934, fixed the weight of the gold dollar at $15^5/_{21}$ grains nine-tenths fine as against the former standard $25^8/_{10}$ grains nine-tenths fine. If the gold clauses interfered with the congressional policy and hence could be invalidated, there appears to be no constitutional objection to that action by the Congress in anticipation of the determination of the value of the currency. And the questions now before us must be determined in the light of that action.

The devaluation of the dollar placed the domestic economy upon a new basis. In the currency as thus provided, States and municipalities must receive their taxes; railroads, their rates and fares; public utilities, their charges for services. The income out of which they must meet their obligations is determined by the new standard. Yet, according to the contentions before us, while that income is thus controlled by law, their indebtedness on their "gold bonds" must be met by an amount of currency determined by the former gold standard. Their receipts, in this view, would be fixed on one basis; their interest charges, and the principal of their obligations, on another. It is common knowledge that the bonds issued by these obligors have generally contained gold clauses, and presumably they account for a large part of the outstanding obligations of that sort. It is also common knowledge that a similar situation exists with respect to numerous industrial corporations that have issued their "gold bonds" and must now receive payments for their products in the existing currency. It requires no acute analysis or profound economic inquiry to disclose the dislocation of the domestic economy which would be caused by such a disparity of conditions in which, it is insisted, those debtors under gold clauses should be required to pay one dollar and sixty-nine cents in currency while respectively receiving their taxes, rates, charges and prices on the basis of one dollar of that currency.

We are not concerned with consequences, in the sense that consequences, however serious, may excuse an invasion of constitutional right. We are concerned with the constitutional power of the Congress over the monetary system of the country and its attempted frustration. Exercising that power, the Congress has undertaken to establish a uniform currency, and parity between kinds of currency, and to make that currency, dollar for dollar, legal tender for the payment of debts. In the light of abundant experience, the Congress was entitled to choose such a uniform monetary system, and to reject a dual system, with respect to all obligations within the range of the exercise of its constitutional authority. The contention that these gold clauses are valid contracts and cannot be struck down proceeds upon the assumption that private parties, and States and municipalities, may make and enforce contracts which may limit that authority. Dismissing that untenable assumption, the facts must be faced. We think that it is clearly shown that these clauses interfere with the exertion of the power granted to the Congress and certainly it is not established that the Congress arbitrarily or capriciously decided that such an interference existed.

The judgment and decree, severally under review, are affirmed.

MR. JUSTICE MCREYNOLDS, MR. JUSTICE VAN DEVANTER, MR. JUSTICE SUTHERLAND, and MR. JUSTICE BUTLER dissent. [The dissenting opinion is appended to Perry v. United States, immediately following, to which it was also directed.]

Perry v. United States *294 U.S. 330, 55 S. Ct. 432, 79 L. Ed. 912 (1935)*

MR. CHIEF JUSTICE HUGHES delivered the opinion of the Court.

The certificate from the Court of Claims shows the following facts:

Plaintiff brought suit as the owner of an obligation of the United States for $10,000, known as "Fourth Liberty Loan 4¼% Gold Bond of 1933-1938." This bond was issued pursuant to the Act of September 24, 1917, as amended, and Treasury Department circular No. 121 dated September 28, 1918. The bond provided: "The principal and interest hereof are payable in United States gold coin of the present standard of value.". . .

The Court of Claims has certified the following questions:

"1. Is the claimant, being the holder and owner of a Fourth Liberty Loan 4¼% bond of the United States, of the principal amount of $10,000, issued in 1918, which was payable on and after April 15, 1934, and which bond contained a clause that the principal is 'payable in United States gold coin of the present standard of value,' entitled to receive from the United States an amount in legal tender currency in excess of the face amount of the bond?

"2. Is the United States, as obligor in a Fourth Liberty Loan 4¼% gold bond, Series of 1933-1938, as stated in Question One liable to respond in damages in a suit in the Court of Claims on such bond as an express contract, by reason of the change in or impossibility of performance in accordance with the tenor thereof, due to the provisions of Public Resolution No. 10, 73rd Congress, abrogating the gold clause in all obligations?"

First. The import of the obligation. The bond in suit differs from an obligation of private parties, or of States or municipalities, whose contracts are necessarily made in subjection to the dominant power of the Congress. Norman v. Baltimore & O.R. Co., 294 U.S. 240. The bond now before us is an obligation of the United States. The terms of the bond are explicit. . . .

This obligation must be fairly construed. The *"present* standard of value" stood in contradistinction to a *lower* standard of value. The promise obviously was intended to afford protection against loss. That protection was sought to be secured by setting up a standard or measure of the Government's obligation. We think that the reasonable import of the promise is that it was intended to assure one who lent his money to the Government and took its bond that he would not suffer loss through depreciation in the medium of payment. . . .

Second. The binding quality of the obligation. The question is necessarily presented whether the Joint Resolution of June 5, 1933 is a valid enactment so far as it applies to the obligations of the United States. . . . This enactment was expressly extended to obligations of the United States and provisions for payment in gold, "contained in any law authorizing obligations to be issued by or under authority of the United States," were repealed.

There is no question as to the power of the Congress to regulate the value of money, that is, to establish a monetary system and thus to determine the currency of the country. The question is whether the Congress can use that power so as to invalidate the terms of the obligations which the Government has theretofore issued in the exercise of the power to borrow money on the credit of the United States. In attempted justification of the Joint Resolution in relation to the outstanding bonds of the United States, the Government argues that "earlier Congresses could not validly restrict the 73rd Congress from exercising its constitutional powers to regulate the value of money, borrow money, or regulate foreign and interstate commerce"; and, from this premise, the Government seems to deduce the proposition that when, with adequate authority, the Government borrows money and pledges the credit of the United States, it is free to ignore that pledge and alter the terms of its obligation in case a later Congress finds their fulfillment inconvenient. The Government's contention thus raises a question of far greater importance than the particular claim of the plaintiff. On that reasoning, if the terms of the Government's bond as to the standard of payment can be repudiated, it inevitably follows that the obligation as to the amount to be paid may also be repudiated. The contention necessarily imports that the Congress can disregard the obligations of the Government at its discretion and that, when the Government borrows money, the credit of the United States is an illusory pledge.

We do not so read the Constitution. There is a clear distinction between the power of the Congress to control or interdict the contracts of private parties when they interfere with the exercise of its constitutional authority, and the power of the Congress to alter or repudiate the substance of its own engagements when it has borrowed money under the authority which the Constitution confers. In authorizing the Congress to borrow money, the Constitution empowers the Congress to fix the amount to be borrowed and the terms of payment. By virtue of the power to borrow money "*on the credit of the United States,*" the Congress is authorized to pledge that credit as an assurance of payment as stipulated, — as the highest assurance the Government can give, its plighted faith. To say that the Congress may withdraw or ignore that pledge is to assume that the Constitution contemplates a vain promise, a pledge having no other sanction than the pleasure and convenience of the pledgor. This Court has given no sanction to such a conception of the obligations of our Government.

The binding quality of the obligations of the Government was considered in the Sinking Fund Cases, 99 U.S. 700, 718, 719. The question before the Court in those cases was whether certain action was warranted by a reservation to the Congress of the right to amend the charter of a railroad company. While the particular action was sustained under this right of amendment, the Court took occasion to state emphatically the obligatory character of the contracts of the United States. The Court said: "The United States are as much bound by their contracts as are individuals. If they repudiate their obligations, it is as much repudiation, with all the wrong and reproach that term implies, as it would be if the repudiator had been a State or a municipality or a citizen."

When the United States, with constitutional authority, makes contracts, it has rights and incurs responsibilities similar to those of individuals who are parties to such instruments. There is no difference, said the Court in United States v. Bank of the Metropolis, 15 Pet. 377, 392, except that the United States cannot be sued without its consent. [Citations omitted.] In Lynch v. United States, 292 U.S. 571, 580, with respect to an attempted abrogation by the Act of March 20, 1933, of certain outstanding war risk insurance policies, which were contracts of the United States, the Court quoted with approval the statement in the Sinking Fund Cases, 99 U.S. 700, supra, and said: "Punctilious fulfillment of contractual obligations is essential to the maintenance of the credit of public as well as private debtors. No doubt there was in March, 1933, great need of economy. In the administration of all government business economy had become urgent because of lessened revenues and the heavy obligations to be issued in the hope of relieving widespread distress. Congress was free to reduce gratuities deemed excessive. But Congress was without power to reduce expenditures by abrogating contractual obligations of the United States. To abrogate contracts, in the attempt to lessen government expenditure, would be not the practice of economy, but an act of repudiation."

The argument in favor of the Joint Resolution, as applied to government bonds, is in substance that the Government cannot by contract restrict the exercise of a sovereign power. But the right to make binding obligations is a competence attaching to sovereignty.[4] . . . The powers conferred upon the Congress are harmonious. The Constitution gives to the Congress the power to borrow money on the credit of the United States, an unqualified power, a power vital to the Government — upon which in an extremity its very life may depend. The binding quality of the promise of the United States is of the essence of the credit which is so pledged. Having this power to authorize the issue of definite obligations for the payment of money borrowed, the Congress has not been vested with authority to alter or destroy those obligations. The fact that the United States may not be sued without its consent is a matter of procedure which does not affect the legal and binding character of its contracts. While the Congress is under no duty to provide remedies through the courts, the contractual obligation still exists and, despite infirmities of procedure, remains binding upon the conscience of the sovereign. Lynch v. United States, supra (292 U.S. 571).

The Fourteenth Amendment, in its fourth section, explicitly declares: "The validity of the public debt of the United States, authorized by law, . . . shall not be questioned." While this provision was undoubtedly inspired by the desire to put beyond question the obligations of the Government issued during the Civil War, its language indicates a broader connotation. We regard it as confirmatory of a fundamental principle which applies as well to the government bonds in question, and to others duly authorized by the Congress, as to those issued before the Amendment was adopted. Nor can we perceive any reason for not considering the expression "the *validity* of the public debt" as embracing whatever concerns the integrity of the public obligations.

We conclude that the Joint Resolution of June 5, 1933, in so far as it attempted to override the obligation created by the bond in suit, went beyond the congressional power.

Third. The question of damages. In this view of the binding quality of the Government's obligations, we come to the question as to the plaintiff's right to recover damages. That is a distinct question. Because the Government is not at liberty to alter or repudiate its obligations, it does not follow that the claim advanced by the plaintiff should be sustained. The action is for breach of contract. As a remedy for breach, plaintiff can recover no more than the loss he has suffered and of which he may rightfully complain. He is not entitled to be enriched. Plaintiff seeks judgment for $16,931.25, in present legal tender currency, on his bond for $10,000. The question is whether he has shown damage to that extent, or any actual damage, as the Court of Claims has no authority to entertain an action for nominal damages. [Citations omitted.]

Plaintiff computes his claim for $16,931.25 by taking the weight of the gold dollar as fixed by the President's proclamation of January 31, 1934, . . . that is, at $15^{5}/_{21}$ grains nine-tenths fine, as compared with the weight fixed by the Act of March 14, 1900, or 25.8 grains nine-tenths fine. But the change in the weight of the gold dollar did not necessarily

---

[4] Oppenheim, International Law, 4th ed., vol. 1, §§493, 494. This is recognized in the field of international engagements. Although there may be no judicial procedure by which such contracts may be enforced in the absence of the consent of the sovereign to be sued, the engagement validity made by a sovereign state is not without legal force, as readily appears if the jurisdiction to entertain a controversy with respect to the performance of the engagement is conferred upon an international tribunal. Hall, International Law, 8th ed., §107; Oppenheim, loc. cit.; Hyde, International Law, vol. 2, §489.

cause loss to the plaintiff of the amount claimed. The question of actual loss cannot fairly be determined without considering the economic situation at the time the Government offered to pay him the $10,000, the face of his bond, in legal tender currency. The case is not the same as if gold coin had remained in circulation. . . . Before the change in the weight of the gold dollar in 1934, gold coin had been withdrawn from circulation. The Congress had authorized the prohibition of the exportation of gold coin and the placing of restrictions upon transactions in foreign exchange. . . . That action the Congress was entitled to take by virtue of its authority to deal with gold coin as a medium of exchange. And the restraint thus imposed upon holders of gold coin was incident to the limitations which inhered in their ownership of that coin and gave them no right of action. Ling Su Fan v. United States, 218 U.S. 302, 310, 311. . . . The same reasoning is applicable to the imposition of restraints upon transactions in foreign exchange. We cannot say, in view of the conditions that existed, that the Congress having this power exercised it arbitrarily or capriciously. And the holder of an obligation, or bond, of the United States, payable in gold coin of the former standard, so far as the restraint upon the right to export gold coin or to engage in transactions in foreign exchange is concerned, was in no better case than the holder of gold coin itself.

In considering what damages, if any, the plaintiff has sustained by the alleged breach of his bond, it is hence inadmissible to assume that he was entitled to obtain gold coin for recourse to foreign markets or for dealings in foreign exchange or for other purposes contrary to the control over gold coin which the Congress had the power to exert, and had exerted, in its monetary regulation. Plaintiff's damages could not be assessed without regard to the internal economy of the country at the time the alleged breach occurred. The discontinuance of gold payments and the establishment of legal tender currency on a standard unit of value with which "all forms of money" of the United States were to be "maintained at a parity," had a controlling influence upon the domestic economy. It was adjusted to the new basis. A free domestic market for gold was non-existent.

Plaintiff demands the "equivalent" in currency of the gold coin promised. But "equivalent" cannot mean more than the amount of money which the promised gold coin would be worth to the bondholder for the purposes for which it could legally be used. That equivalence or worth could not properly be ascertained save in the light of the domestic and restricted market which the Congress had lawfully established. In the domestic transactions to which the plaintiff was limited, in the absence of special license, determination of the value of the gold coin would necessarily have regard to its use as legal tender and as a medium of exchange under a single monetary system with an established parity of all currency and coins. And in view of the control of export and foreign exchange, and the restricted domestic use, the question of value, in relation to transactions legally available to the plaintiff, would require a consideration of the purchasing power of the dollars which the plaintiff could have received. Plaintiff has not shown, or attempted to show, that in relation to buying power he has sustained any loss whatever. On the contrary, in view of the adjustment of the internal economy to the single measure of value as established by the legislation of the Congress, and the universal availability and use throughout the country of the legal tender currency in meeting all engagements, the payment to the plaintiff of the amount which he demands would appear to constitute not a recoupment of loss in any proper sense but an unjustified enrichment.

Plaintiff seeks to make his case solely upon the theory that by reason of the change in the weight of the dollar he is entitled to one dollar and sixty-nine cents in the present currency for every dollar promised by the bond, regardless of any actual loss he has suffered with respect to any transaction in which his dollars may be used. We think that position is untenable.

In the view that the facts alleged by the petition fail to show a cause of action for actual damages, the first question submitted by the Court of Claims is answered in the negative. It is not necessary to answer the second question.

Question No. 1 is answered "No."

Mr. Justice Stone (concurring in part):

I agree that the answer to the first question is "No," but I think our opinion should be confined to answering that question and that it should essay an answer to no other.

I do not doubt that the gold clause in the Government bonds, like that in the private contracts just considered, calls for the payment of value in money, measured by a stated number of gold dollars of the standard defined in the clause, Feist v. Société Intercommunale Belge d'Electricité, [1934] A.C. 161, 170-173; Serbian & Brazilian Bond Cases, P.C.I.J., series A., Nos. 20-21, pp. 32-34, 109-119. In the absence of any further exertion of governmental power, that obligation plainly could not be satisfied by payment of the same number of dollars, either specie or paper, measured by a gold dollar of lesser weight, regardless of their purchasing power or the state of our internal economy at the due date.

I do not understand the Government to contend that it is any the less bound by the obligation than a private individual would be, or that it is free to disregard it except in the exercise of the constitutional power "to coin money" and "regulate the value thereof." In any case, there is before us no question of default apart from the regulation by Congress of the use of gold as currency.

While the Government's refusal to make the stipulated payment is a measure taken in the exercise of that power, this does not disguise the fact that its action is to that extent a repudiation of its undertaking. As much as I deplore this refusal to fulfill the solemn promise of bonds of the United States, I cannot escape the conclusion, announced for the Court, that in the situation now presented, the Government, through the exercise of its sovereign power to regulate the value of money, has rendered itself immune from liability for its action. To that extent it has relieved itself of the obligation of its domestic bonds, precisely as it has relieved the obligors of private bonds in No. 270, Norman v. Baltimore & O.R. Co. . . .

Moreover, if the gold clause be viewed as a gold value contract, as it is in Norman v. Baltimore & O.R. Co. supra, it is to be noted that the Government has not prohibited the free use by the bondholder of the paper money equivalent of the gold clause obligation; it is the prohibition, by the Joint Resolution of Congress, of payment of the increased number of depreciated dollars required to make up the full equivalent, which alone bars recovery. In that case it would seem to be implicit in our decision that the prohibition, at least in the present situation, is itself a constitutional exercise of the power to regulate the value of money.

I therefore do not join in so much of the opinion as may be taken to suggest that the exercise of the sovereign power to borrow money on credit, which does not override the sovereign immunity from suit, may nevertheless preclude or impede the exercise of another sovereign power, to regulate the value of money; or to suggest that although there is and can be no present cause of action upon the repudiated gold clause, its obligation is nevertheless, in some manner and to some extent, not stated, superior to the power to regulate the currency which we now hold to be superior to the obligation of the bonds.

Mr. Justice McReynolds, dissenting:

Mr. Justice Van Devanter, Mr. Justice Sutherland, Mr. Justice Butler and I conclude that, if given effect, the enactments here challenged will bring about confiscation of property rights and repudiation of national obligations. Acquiescence in the decisions just announced is impossible; the circumstances demand statement of our views. "To let oneself slide down the easy slope offered by the course of events and to dull one's mind against the extent of the danger, . . . that is precisely to fail in one's obligation of responsibility."

Just men regard repudiation and spoliation of citizens by their sovereign with abhorrence; but we are asked to affirm that the Constitution has granted power to accomplish both. No definite delegation of such a power exists; and we cannot believe the farseeing framers, who labored with hope of establishing justice and securing the blessings of liberty, intended that the expected government should have authority to annihilate its own obligations and destroy the very rights which they were endeavoring to protect. Not only is there no permission for such actions; they are inhibited. And no plenitude of words can conform them to our charter. . . .

The fundamental problem now presented is whether recent statutes passed by Congress in respect of money and credits, were designed to attain a legitimate end. Or whether, under the guise of pursuing a monetary policy, Congress really has inaugurated a plan primarily designed to destroy private obligations, repudiate national debts and drive into the Treasury all gold within the country in exchange for inconvertible promises to pay, of much less value.

Considering all the circumstances, we must conclude they show that the plan disclosed is of the latter description and its enforcement would deprive the parties before us of their rights under the Constitution. Consequently the Court should do what it can to afford adequate relief. . . .

This Resolution was not appropriate for carrying into effect any power entrusted to Congress. The gold clauses in no substantial way interfered with the power of coining money or regulating its value or providing an uniform currency. Their existence, as with many other circumstances, might have circumscribed the effect of the intended depreciation and disclosed the unwisdom of it. But they did not prevent the exercise of any granted power. They were not inconsistent with any policy theretofore declared. To assert the contrary is not enough. The Court must be able to see the appropriateness of the thing done before it can be permitted to destroy lawful agreements. . . .

Congress has power to coin money but this cannot be exercised without the possession of metal. Can Congress authorize appropriation, without compensation, of the necessary gold? Congress has power to regulate commerce, to establish post roads, &c. Some approved plan may involve the use or destruction of A's land or a private way. May Congress authorize the appropriation or destruction of these things without adequate payment? Of course not. The limitations prescribed by the Constitution restrict the exercise of all power. . . .

These [Government] bonds are held by men and women in many parts of the world; they have relied upon our honor. Thousands of our own citizens of every degree not doubting the good faith of their sovereign have purchased them. It will not be easy for this multitude to appraise the form of words which establishes that they have suffered no appreciable damage; but perhaps no more difficult for them than for us. And their difficulty will not be assuaged when they reflect that ready calculation of the exact loss suffered by the Philippine government moved Congress to satisfy it by appropriating, in June 1934, $23,862,750.78 to be paid out of the Treasury of the United States. . . .

Under the challenged statutes it is said the United States have realized profits amounting to $2,800,000,000. But this assumes that gain may be generated by legislative fiat. To such counterfeit profits there would be no limit; with each new debasement of the dollar they would expand. Two billions might be ballooned indefinitely — to twenty, thirty, or what you will.

Loss of reputation for honorable dealing will bring us unending humiliation; the impending legal and moral chaos is appalling.

GOLDENWEISER, American Monetary Policy 13-16 (1951): "In the early part of 1933, under the influence of severe depression and the administration's distrust of prevailing professional opinion, a policy was adopted based on the belief that commodity prices can be regulated at will by changes in the gold content of currencies. An uncritical study of long-term trends and a mystical belief in their inevitability underlay the theory. It may be stated in simple terms. If a certain physical amount of gold is called one dollar and will buy one bushel of wheat, all that is necessary to double the price of wheat expressed in dollars is to call the same amount of gold two dollars instead of one. Thus the wheat grower would get twice as many dollars for his wheat, though the equivalent of the same amount of gold, and, since debts were expressed in dollars rather than in gold, he would be able to discharge his debts by selling one-half as much wheat as would have been necessary before. This conception is easily understood by the general public as well as by statesmen. To raise the dollar price of commodities, all you need to do is to reduce the amount of gold in the dollar, Q.E.D.

"The difficulty with this conception is that it has little relation to modern reality. The seller of goods is not desirous of obtaining gold but wishes to have dollars with which to buy other goods and services, or to pay debts. If one leaves aside international relationships, the direct link between the gold content of the dollar and prices was weakened when the economy ceased to depend on gold coin or bullion as its principal means of payment. Today, when most payments are made in paper money and to an even greater extent by check, there is no direct or immediate relationship between the number of grains of gold in the dollar and the prices that are paid for goods. What is used in the market to bid for goods is the dollar, not gold. The amount of gold that can be obtained for the dollar, the legal gold content of the dollar, is not an important factor in market transactions. It has no direct bearing on the domestic price the owner of a commodity can receive for it.

"Though there are no direct and immediate relationships, certain indirect relationships exist. They operate through foreign exchanges, and through the effect the price of gold has on the amount of gold production and on the reserve position of the treasury and the central bank. If the gold content of the dollar is cut in two, while the gold content of sterling, for example, remains unchanged, a pound sterling will buy twice as many dollars as it did before. This enables British buyers without spending more sterling to buy twice as much American wheat and cotton at the old dollar price as they did before. Consequently the international competitive situation will be changed by a change in the price of gold and, so long as other countries do not alter the gold content of their currencies, one of two developments is bound to follow: either the dollar price of export wheat and cotton will increase or the world price of these commodities will decline. Which of these developments or what combination of the two will follow and what effect this will have on imports and exports will depend on numerous economic circumstances which determine the competitive condition of the commodities in world markets. There is no assurance that the price of certain export commodities will increase in proportion to the increased price of gold but a tendency toward such a rise will operate. Ordinarily this would result in encouraging exports by the country which had devalued, and discouraging imports by that country. This situation in turn is likely to result in other countries taking protective measures which can nullify the effects of the devaluation. These countering protective moves are the more likely if devaluation in the first instance is by a large country whose sales and purchases in the international market are an important part of world trade. Under certain conditions of world supply and demand, devaluation by an important supplier may bring a decline in the price of the commodities in terms of foreign currencies, with little or no change in their domestic price. . . .

"Gold revaluation has another result, namely, a windfall profit to a treasury or a central bank, depending on who holds the gold and to whom the increment is awarded. This windfall profit may become an inflationary force. In the United States the revaluation of gold in 1934 from $20 to $35 an ounce gave the Treasury a dollar profit of $2.8 billion. These dollars, however, were not used in an inflationary way. Two billion was turned over to the Stabilization Fund where the bulk of it was kept inactive; subsequently, a part of this fund was used in setting up the International Monetary Fund. Most of the remainder was used indirectly to retire national bank notes which had been issued prior to the establishment of the Federal Reserve System; it was a substitution of one form of currency for another without adding to the total volume of money. Amateurish and naïve as the government's policy was in regard to changes in gold value, it handled the resultant windfall profit in a workmanlike manner."

NOTE

1. Might the bondholders in the private-bond cases have succeeded by arguing that the Joint Resolution was inseparable?
2. What further steps were open to the holders of government gold-clause bonds? Cf. Ogden v. Morgenthau, 302 U.S. 702 (1937), a mandamus suit to compel the payment of gold. What obstacles lay in the path of this suit? For other actions by bondholders see Smyth v. United States, 302 U.S. 329 (1937); Perry v. United States, 87 Ct. Cl. 182, cert. denied, 305 U.S. 624 (1938).
3. What further steps were open to the Government to protect its position in relation to public gold-clause bonds?
4. If we should accept the statement of Dr. Goldenweiser, supra, did the success of the government in the Perry case rest on the failure of the monetary program?
5. Could Congress outlaw escalator clauses in contracts, geared to a commodity price index or cost-of-living standard?

Hopkins Federal Savings & Loan Assn. v. Cleary 296 U.S. 315, 56 S. Ct. 235, 80 L. Ed. 251 (1935)

MR. JUSTICE CARDOZO delivered the opinion of the Court.

The controversy in each of these causes is one as to the meaning and validity of an Act of Congress whereby building and loan associations organized under the laws of a state may be converted into Federal Savings & Loan Associations upon the vote of a majority of the shareholders present at a meeting legally convened.

In number 55, an original suit was brought in the Supreme Court of Wisconsin by the respondents, constituting the Banking Commission of that state, against the Hopkins Federal Savings & Loan Association, formerly the Hopkins Street Building & Loan Association, its officers and directors. The complaint prayed for a decree annulling the proceedings whereby the state association had attempted to convert itself into a federal one, and compelling the directors and officers to continue the business in accordance with Wisconsin law or else to wind it up. The state court granted the decree upon grounds to be considered later. 217 Wis. 179, 257 N.W. 684. . . .

The petitioners insist that without the consent of Wisconsin the transmutation from a state into a federal association has become possible now by virtue of an Act of Congress. The Act relied upon for that purpose is § 5 of the Home Owners' Loan Act of 1933. . . . Subdivision (i), the one that concerns us specially, permits state associations to be converted into federal ones. As amended in April, 1934, its provisions are as follows:

"(i) Any member of a Federal Home Loan Bank may convert itself into a Federal Savings and Loan Association under this Act upon a vote of 51 per centum or more of the votes cast at a legal meeting called to consider such action; but such conversion shall be subject to such rules and regulations as the Board may prescribe, and thereafter the converted association shall be entitled to all the benefits of this section and shall be subject to examination and regulation to the same extent as other associations incorporated pursuant to this Act." . . .

First: Congress did not mean that the conversion from state associations into federal ones should be conditioned upon the consent of the state or compliance with its laws. . . .

Second: The Home Owners' Loan Act, to the extent that it permits the conversion of state associations into federal ones in contravention of the laws of the place of their creation, is an unconstitutional encroachment upon the reserved powers of the states. United States Constitution, Amendment Ten.

If § 5(i) may be upheld when state laws are inconsistent, any savings bank or insurance company as well as any building and loan association may be converted into a savings and loan association with a charter from the central government, provided only that 51 per cent of the shares represented at a meeting vote approval of the change. Indeed, as counsel for the petitioners insisted at our bar, the power of transformation, if it is adequate in such conditions, is not confined to building and loan associations or savings banks or insurance companies or to members of the Home Loan Bank, except by the adventitious features of this particular enactment. It extends in that view to moneyed corporations generally and even to other corporations if Congress chooses to convert them into creatures of the federal government. Compulsion, by hypothesis, being lawful, the percentage of assenting shares voted in an instance or exacted by a given statute assumes the aspect of an accident. Fifty-one per cent is the minimum required here. Another act may reduce the minimum to ten percent or even one, or dispense with approval altogether. If non-assenting shareholders or creditors were parties to these suits, the question would be urgent whether property interests may be so transformed consistently with the restraints of the Fifth Amendment. . . .

For the purposes of these cases we find it needless to consider whether Congress has the power to create building and loan associations and thereupon to invest them with corporate capacity. As to that we do not indicate an opinion either one way or the other. The critical question here is something very different. The critical question is whether along with such a power there goes the power also to put an end to corporations created by the states and turn them into different corporations created by the nation. . . .

We are not concerned at this time with the applicable rule in situations where the central government is at liberty (as it is under the commerce clause when such a purpose is disclosed) to exercise a power that is exclusive as well as paramount. [Citations omitted.] That is not the situation here. No one would say with reference to the business conducted by these petitioners that Congress could prohibit the formation or continuance of such associations by the states, whatever may be its power to charter them itself. So also we are not concerned with the rule to be applied where the business of an association under charter from a state is conducted in such a way as to be a menace or obstruction to the legitimate activities of its federal competitors. Cf. Northern Securities Co. v. United States, 193 U.S. 197, 344-346; Houston, E & W.T.R. Co. v. United States, 234 U.S. 342, 351; New York v. United States, 257 U.S. 591, 600, 601. For anything here shown, the two classes of associations, federal and state, may continue to dwell together in harmony and order. A concession of this possibility is indeed implicit in the statute, for conversion is not mandatory, but dependent upon the choice of a majority of the voters. . . . The destruction of associations established by a state is not an exercise of power reasonably necessary for the maintenance by the central government of other associations created by itself in furtherance of kindred ends.[6]

Given the encroachment, the standing of the state to seek redress as suitor is not to be gainsaid, unless protest without action is the only method of resistance. Analogy combines with reason in telling us that this is not the law. By writs of quo warranto as well as through other remedial devices the state has been accustomed to keep its juristic creatures within the limits of the charters that define the purpose of their being. . . . In its capacity of quasi-sovereign, the state repulses an assault upon the quasi-public institutions that are

---

[6] The court has upheld the validity of a statute whereby national banks are given the same power as state banks to act as executors or administrators, to the end that the two classes of banks may compete on equal terms. First Nat. Bank v. Fellows, 244 U.S. 416. This is far from a holding that the function of acting as executors and administrators may be withdrawn from the state banks and lodged by the Congress in the national banks alone.

the product and embodiment of its statutes and its policy. Finding them about to deviate from the law of their creation, it met by the excuse that everything done or purposed is permitted by an Act of Congress. The excuse is inadequate unless the power to give absolution for overstepping such restrictions has been surrendered by the state to the Government at Washington.

The standing of Wisconsin to resist a trespass on its powers is confirmed if we view the subject from another angle of approach. In the creation of corporations of this quasi-public order and in keeping them thereafter within the limits of their charters, the state is parens patriae, acting in a spirit of benevolence for the welfare of its citizens. Shareholders and creditors have assumed a relation to the business in the belief that the assets will be protected by all the power of the government against use for other ends than those stated in the charter. Aside from the direct interest of the state in the preservation of agencies established for the common good, there is thus the duty of the parens patriae to keep faith with those who have put their trust in the parental power. . . .

The ruling in Massachusetts v. Mellon, 262 U.S. 447, is nothing to the contrary, though it is made a cornerstone of the argument in favor of the statute. There the state of Massachusetts attempted to enjoin the enforcement of an Act of Congress appropriating money to be used in cooperation with the states to reduce maternal and infant mortality. The ruling was that it was no part of the duty or power of a state to enforce the rights of its citizens in respect of their relations to the Federal Government. Cf. Florida v. Mellon, 273 U.S. 12. Here, on the contrary, the state becomes a suitor to protect the interests of its citizens against the unlawful acts of corporations created by the state itself. . . .

Confining ourselves now to the precise and narrow question presented upon the records here before us, we hold that the conversion of petitioners from state into federal associations is of no effect when voted against the protest of Wisconsin. Beyond that we do not go. No question is here as to the scope of the war power or of the power of eminent domain or of the power to regulate transactions affecting interstate or foreign commerce. The effect of these, if they have any, upon the powers reserved by the Constitution to the states or to the people will be considered when the need arises.

The judgments are affirmed.

NOTE

Could Congress require all banks to take out federal charters and come under the National Banking Act? Cf. Veazie Bank v. Fenno, 8 Wall. 533 (1869), supra page 240. See Wyatt, Constitutionality of Legislation Providing for a Uniform Commercial Banking System for the United States, 19 Fed. Res. Bull. 166 (1933).

Section C. WATER RESOURCES AND GOVERNMENT PROPERTY

Ashwander v. Tennessee Valley Authority 297 U.S. 288, 56 S. Ct. 466, 80 L. Ed. 688 (1936)

[The first part of the opinion is printed at page 91 supra.]

MR. CHIEF JUSTICE HUGHES delivered the opinion of the Court:

Third. The constitutional authority for the construction of the Wilson Dam. The

Congress may not, "under the pretext of executing its powers, pass laws for the accomplishment of objects not entrusted to the government." Chief Justice Marshall, in McCulloch v. Maryland, 4 Wheat. 316, 423; Linder v. United States, 268 U.S. 15, 17. The Government's argument recognizes this essential limitation. The Government's contention is that the Wilson Dam was constructed, and the power plant connected with it was installed, in the exercise by the Congress of its war and commerce powers, that is, for the purposes of national defense and the improvement of navigation.

Wilson Dam is described as a concrete monolith one hundred feet high and almost a mile long, containing two locks for navigation and eight installed generators. Construction was begun in 1917 and completed in 1926. Authority for its construction is found in section 124 of the National Defense Act of June 3, 1916. . . .

We may take judicial notice of the international situation at the time the Act of 1916 was passed, and it cannot be successfully disputed that the Wilson Dam and its auxiliary plants, including the hydro-electric power plant, are, and were intended to be, adapted to the purposes of national defense. While the District Court found that there is no intention to use the nitrate plants or the hydro-electric units installed at Wilson Dam for the production of war materials in time of peace, "the maintenance of said properties in operating condition and the assurance of an abundant supply of electric energy in the event of war, constitute national defense assets." This finding has ample support.

The Act of 1916 also had in view "improvements to navigation." Commerce includes navigation. "All America understands, and has uniformly understood," said Chief Justice Marshall in Gibbons v. Ogden, 9 Wheat. 1, 190, "the word 'commerce,' to comprehend navigation." The power to regulate interstate commerce embraces the power to keep the navigable rivers of the United States free from obstructions to navigation and to remove such obstructions when they exist. "For these purposes," said the Court in Gilman v. Philadelphia, 3 Wall. 713, 725, "Congress possesses all the powers which existed in the States before the adoption of the national Constitution, and which have always existed in the Parliament in England." See, also, Philadelphia Company v. Stimson, 223 U.S. 605, 634.

The Tennessee River is a navigable stream, although there are obstructions at various points because of shoals, reefs and rapids. The improvement of navigation on this river has been a matter of national concern for over a century. Recommendation that provision be made for navigation around Muscle Shoals was made by the Secretary of War, John C. Calhoun, in his report transmitted to the Congress by President Monroe in 1824, and, from 1852, the Congress has repeatedly authorized projects to develop navigation on that and other portions of the river, both by open channel improvements and by canalization. The Wilson Dam project, adopted in 1918, gave a nine foot slack water development, for fifteen miles above Florence, over the Muscle Shoals rapids and, as the District Court found, "flooded out the then existing canal and locks which were inadequate." The District Court also found that a "high dam of this type was the only feasible means of eliminating this most serious obstruction to navigation." By the Act of 1930, after a protracted study by the Corps of Engineers of the United States Army, the Congress adopted a project for a permanent improvement of the main stream "for a navigable depth of nine feet."

While, in its present condition, the Tennessee River is not adequately improved for commercial navigation, and traffic is small, we are not at liberty to conclude either that the river is not susceptible of development as an important waterway, or that Congress has not undertaken that development, or that the construction of the Wilson Dam was not an appropriate means to accomplish a legitimate end.

The Wilson Dam and its power plant must be taken to have been constructed in the exercise of the constitutional functions of the Federal Government.

Fourth. The constitutional authority to dispose of electric energy generated at the Wilson Dam. The Government acquired full title to the dam site, with all riparian rights.

328 Chapter Seven. National Power over the Economy

The power of falling water was an inevitable incident of the construction of the dam. That water power came into the exclusive control of the Federal Government. The mechanical energy was convertible into electric energy, and the water power, the right to convert it into electric energy, and the electric energy thus produced, constitute property belonging to the United States. See Green Bay Canal Company v. Pattern Paper Company, 172 U.S. 58, 80; United States v. Chandler-Dunbar Company, 229 U.S. 53, 72, 73; Utah Power & Light Co. v. Pfost, 286 U.S. 165, 170.

Authority to dispose of property constitutionally acquired by the United States is expressly granted to the Congress by section 3 of Article IV of the Constitution. This section provides:

"The Congress shall have Power to dispose of and make all needful Rules and Regulations respecting the Territory or other Property belonging to the United States; and nothing in this Constitution shall be so construed as to Prejudice any Claims of the United States, or of any particular State."

To the extent that the power of disposition is thus expressly conferred, it is manifest that the Tenth Amendment is not applicable. And the Ninth Amendment (which petitioners also invoke) in insuring the maintenance of the rights retained by the people does not withdraw the rights which are expressly granted to the Federal Government. The question is as to the scope of the grant and whether there are inherent limitations which render invalid the disposition of property with which we are now concerned.

The occasion for the grant was the obvious necessity of making provision for the government of the vast territory acquired by the United States. The power to govern and to dispose of that territory was deemed to be indispensable to the purposes of the cessions made by the States. And yet it was a matter of grave concern because of the fear that "the sale and disposal" might become "a source of such immense revenue to the national government, as to make it independent of and formidable to the people." Story on the Constitution, secs. 1325, 1326. The grant was made in broad terms, and the power of regulation and disposition was not confined to territory, but extended to "other property belonging to the United States," so that the power may be applied, as Story says, "to the due regulation of all other personal and real property rightfully belonging to the United States." And so, he adds, "it has been constantly understood and acted upon." Id.

This power of disposal was early construed to embrace leases, thus enabling the Government to derive profit through royalties. The question arose with respect to a government lease of lead mines on public lands, under the Act of March 3, 1807. The contention was advanced that "disposal is not letting or leasing"; that Congress had no power "to give or authorize leases" and "to obtain profits from the working of the mines." The Court overruled the contention, saying: "The disposal must be left to the discretion of Congress. And there can be no apprehensions of any enroachments upon state rights, by the creation of a numerous tenantry within their borders, as has been so strenuously urged in the argument." United States v. Gratiot, 14 Pet. 526, 533, 538. The policy, early adopted and steadily pursued, of segregating mineral lands from other public lands and providing for leases, pointed to the recognition both of the full power of disposal and of the necessity of suitably adapting the methods of disposal to different sorts of property. The policy received particular emphasis following the discovery of gold in California in 1848. For example, an Act of 1866, dealing with grants to Nevada, declared that "in all cases lands valuable for mines of gold, silver, quicksilver, or copper shall be reserved from sale." And Congress from the outset adopted a similar practice in reserving salt springs. Morton v. Nebraska, 21 Wall. 660, 667; Montello Salt Company v. Utah, 221 U.S. 452. It was in the light of this historic policy that the Court held that the school grant to Utah by the Enabling Act of 1894 was not intended to embrace land known to be valuable for coal. United States v. Sweet, 245 U.S. 563, 572. See, also, as to the reservation and leases of oil lands, Pan American Company v. United States, 273 U.S. 456, 487.

But when Congress thus reserved mineral lands for special disposal, can it be doubted that Congress could have provided for mining directly by its own agents, instead of giving that right to lessees on the payment of royalties? Upon what ground could it be said that the Government could not mine its own gold, silver, coal, lead, or phosphates in the public domain, and dispose of them as property belonging to the United States? That it could dispose of its land but not of what the land contained? It would seem to be clear that under the same power of disposition which enabled the Government to lease and obtain profit from sales by its lessees, it could mine and obtain profit from its own sales.

The question is whether a more limited power of disposal should be applied to the water power, convertible into electric energy, and to the electric energy thus produced at the Wilson Dam constructed by the Government in the exercise of its constitutional functions. If so, it must be by reason either of (1) the nature of the particular property, or (2) the character of the "surplus" disposed of, or (3) the manner of disposition.

(1) That the water power and the electric energy generated at the dam are susceptible of disposition as property belonging to the United States is well established. . . .

In United States v. Chandler-Dunbar Company, 229 U.S. 53, the United States had condemned land in Michigan, lying between the St. Marys River and the ship canal strip of the Government, in order to improve navigation. The riparian owner, under revocable permits from the Secretary of War, had placed in the rapids "the necessary dams, dykes and forebays for the purpose of controlling the current and using its power for commercial purposes." Id., p. 68. The Act of March 3, 1909, authorizing the improvement, had revoked the permit. We said that the Government "had dominion over the water power of the rapids and falls" and could not be required to pay "any hypothetical additional value to a riparian owner who had no right to appropriate the current to his own commercial use." Id., p. 76. The Act of 1909 also authorized the Secretary of War to lease "any excess of water power which results from the conservation of the flow of the river, and the works which the Government may construct." "If the primary purpose is legitimate," said the Court, "we can see no sound objection to leasing any excess of power over the needs of the Government. The practice is not unusual in respect to similar public works constructed by state governments." . . .

(2) The argument is stressed that, assuming that electric energy generated at the dam belongs to the United States, the Congress has authority to dispose of this energy only to the extent that it is a surplus necessarily created in the course of making munitions of war or operating the works for navigation purposes; that is, that the remainder of the available energy must be lost or go to waste. We find nothing in the Constitution which imposes such a limitation. It is not to be deduced from the mere fact that the electric energy is only potentially available until the generators are operated. The Government has no less right to the energy thus available by letting the water course over its turbines than it has to use the appropriate processes to reduce to possession other property within its control, as, for example, oil which it may recover from a pool beneath its lands, and which is reduced to possession by boring oil wells and otherwise might escape its grasp. See Ohio Oil Company v. Indiana, 177 U.S. 190, 208. And it would hardly be contended that, when the Government reserves coal on its lands, it can mine the coal and dispose of it only for the purpose of heating public buildings or for other governmental operations. Or, if the Government owns a silver mine, that it can obtain the silver only for the purpose of storage or coinage. Or that when the Government extracts the oil it has reserved, it has no constitutional power to sell it. Our decisions recognize no such restriction. United States v. Gratiot, supra; Kansas v. Colorado, 206 U.S. 46, 88, 89; Light v. United States, 220 U.S. 523, 536, 537; Ruddy v. Rossi, 248 U.S. 104, 106. The United States owns the coal, or the silver, or the lead, or the oil, it obtains from its lands, and it lies in the discretion of the Congress, acting in the public interest, to determine of how much of the property it shall dispose.

We think that the same principle is applicable to electric energy. The argument pressed upon us leads to absurd consequences in the denial, despite the broad terms of the constitutional provision, of a power of disposal which the public interest may imperatively require. Suppose, for example, that in the erection of a dam for the improvement of navigation, it became necessary to destroy a dam and power plant which had previously been erected by a private corporation engaged in the generation and distribution of energy which supplied the needs of neighboring communities and business enterprises. Would anyone say that, because the United States had built its own dam and plant in the exercise of its constitutional functions, and had complete ownership and dominion over both, no power could be supplied to the communities and enterprises dependent on it, not because of any unwillingness of the Congress to supply it, or of any overriding governmental need, but because there was no constitutional authority to furnish the supply? Or that, with abundant power available, which must otherwise be wasted, the supply to the communities and enterprises whose very life may be at stake must be limited to the slender amount of surplus unavoidably involved in the operation of the navigation works, because the Constitution does not permit any more energy to be generated and distributed? . . .

The decisions which petitioners cite give no support to their contention. Pollard v. Hagan, 3 How. 212; Shively v. Bowlby, 152 U.S. 1, and Port of Seattle v. Oregon-Washington Railway Co., 255 U.S. 56, dealt with the title of the States to tidelands and the soil under navigable waters within their borders. See Borax Consolidated v. Los Angeles, 296 U.S. 10, 15. Those cases did not concern the dominant authority of the Federal Government in the interest of navigation to erect dams and avail itself of the incidental water power. . . .

(3) We come then to the question as to the validity of the method which has been adopted in disposing of the surplus energy generated at the Wilson Dam. The constitutional provision is silent as to the method of disposing of property belonging to the United States. That method, of course, must be an appropriate means of disposition according to the nature of the property, it must be one adopted in the public interest as distinguished from private or personal ends, and we may assume that it must be consistent with the foundation principles of our dual system of government and must not be contrived to govern the concerns reserved to the States. See Kansas v. Colorado, supra. In this instance, the method of disposal embraces the sale of surplus energy by the Tennessee Valley Authority to the Alabama Power Company, the interchange of energy between the Authority and the Power Company, and the purchase by the Authority from the Power Company of certain transmission lines.

As to the mere sale of surplus energy, nothing need be added to what we have said as to the constitutional authority to dispose. The Government could lease or sell and fix the terms. Sales of surplus energy to the Power Company by the Authority continued a practice begun by the Government several years before. The contemplated interchange of energy is a form of disposition and presents no questions which are essentially different from those that are pertinent to sales.

The transmission lines which the Authority undertakes to purchase from the Power Company lead from the Wilson Dam to a large area within about fifty miles of the dam. These lines provide the means of distributing the electric energy, generated at the dam, to a large population. They furnish a method of reaching a market. The alternative method is to sell the surplus energy at the dam, and the market there appears to be limited to one purchaser, the Alabama Power Company, and its affiliated interests. We know of no constitutional ground upon which the Federal Government can be denied the right to seek a wider market. We suppose that in the early days of mining in the West, if the Government had undertaken to operate a silver mine on its domain, it could have acquired the mules or horses and equipment to carry its silver to market. And the transmission lines for electric energy are but a facility for conveying to market that particular sort of property, and the acquisition of these lines raises no different constitutional question, unless in some way there is an invasion of the rights reserved to the State or to the people. We find no basis for concluding that the limited undertaking with the Alabama Power Company amounts to such an invasion. Certainly, the Alabama Power Company has no constitutional right to insist that it shall be the sole purchaser of the energy generated at the Wilson Dam; that the energy shall be sold to it or go to waste.

We limit our decision to the case before us, as we have defined it. The argument is earnestly presented that the Government by virtue of its ownership of the dam and power plant could not establish a steel mill and make and sell steel products, or a factory to manufacture clothing or shoes for the public, and thus attempt to make its ownership of energy, generated at its dam, a means of carrying on competitive commercial enterprises and thus drawing to the Federal Government the conduct and management of business having no relation to the purposes for which the Federal Government was established. The picture is eloquently drawn but we deem it to be irrelevant to the issue here. The Government is not using the water power at the Wilson Dam to establish any industry or business. It is not using the energy generated at the dam to manufacture commodities of any sort for the public. The Government is disposing of the energy itself which simply is the mechanical energy, incidental to falling water at the dam, converted into the electric energy which is susceptible of transmission. The question here is simply as to the acquisition of the transmission lines as a facility for the disposal of that energy. And the Government rightly conceded at the bar, in substance, that it was without constitutional authority to acquire or dispose of such energy except as it comes into being in the operation of works constructed in the exercise of some power delegated to the United States. As we have said, these transmission lines lead directly from the dam, which has been lawfully constructed, and the question of the constitutional right of the Government to acquire or operate local or urban distribution systems is not involved. We express no opinion as to the validity of such an effort, as to the status of any other dam or power development in the Tennessee Valley, whether connected with or apart from the Wilson Dam, or as to the validity of the Tennessee Valley Authority Act or of the claims made in the pronouncements and program of the Authority apart from the questions we have discussed in relation to the particular provisions of the contract of January 4, 1934, affecting the Alabama Power Company.

The decree of the Circuit Court of Appeals is affirmed.

Affirmed.

[Mr. Justice McReynolds delivered a dissenting opinion, which concluded: "I think the trial court reached the correct conclusion and that its decree should be approved. If under the thin mask of disposing of property the United States can enter the business of generating, transmitting and selling power as, when and wherever some board may specify, with the definite design to accomplish ends wholly beyond the sphere marked out for them by the Constitution, an easy way has been found for breaking down the limitations heretofore supposed to guarantee protection against aggression."]

NOTE Federal Development of Water Resources

1. In the sequel to the Ashwander case the power companies were held to have no standing to enjoin competition by the TVA. Tennessee Electric Power Co. v. TVA, 306 U.S. 118 (1939), page 101 supra. The three-judge district court, however, heard extensive engineering testimony and made detailed findings. The TVA project involves a series of high dams, with power installations, on both the Tennessee and its tributaries. The companies attempted to show that the maintenance of a nine-foot channel on the Tennessee, together with flood control on that river, could have been achieved much more cheaply by the construction of a series of low dams on the main stream and storage dams on the tributaries — a combination of structures creating no power potential. The court accepted the evidence on behalf of TVA to the effect that in design and coordinated operation the TVA system produced power consistently with the achievement of superior flood

332   Chapter Seven.   National Power over the Economy

control on both the Tennessee and lower Mississippi and the maintenance of a nine-foot channel. 21 F. Supp. 947 (1938).

On the problem of formulas for allocating costs among the navigation, flood control, and power functions of the dams, see Report of Joint Committee Investigating the T.V.A. 153-161 (1939). See Twentieth Century Fund, Electric Power and Government Policy, c. 10 (1948), for a comprehensive study of TVA operations and their significance for private utility systems.

Compare Arizona v. California, 283 U.S. 423 (1931), in which Arizona sought to enjoin the carrying out of the interstate compact relating to Boulder (now Hoover) Dam. The Court took judicial notice that the Colorado River is navigable, despite averments to the contrary in both the compact and bill of complaint, admitted on motion to dismiss. The dam contained no locks, but the Court sustained the project as one "not unrelated to navigation." There, however, the government leased emplacements at the dam for power purposes to public and private wholesale distributors having their own transmission lines.

2. When the federal government undertakes a waterways project, for what items of damage to riparian owners must compensation be paid? It is often said that the United States has an "easement" in navigable waters for the improvement of navigable capacity. This statement describes the conclusion that certain losses caused by such improvements are noncompensable.

The United States may, to promote navigation, raise the level of a navigable stream to the mean high-water mark without payment for losses caused by flooding, loss of access to the stream, loss of power head at a hydroelectric plant on the stream, or loss of potential power thereon. See United States v. Chandler-Dunbar Co., 229 U.S. 53 (1913), discussed in the Ashwander case. Permanent flooding of the upland, however, i.e., above mean high-water mark, is compensable. Compare the flooding of an embankment rising above such mark but built up from low-water mark in the bed of the stream. United States v. Chicago, M. & St. P. Ry., 312 U.S. 592 (1941).

Suppose that a federal navigation dam on a navigable stream raises the level of a nonnavigable tributary. Is the loss of power head on the tributary compensable? United States v. Cress, 243 U.S. 316 (1917); compare United States v. Willow River Power Co., 324 U.S. 499 (1945), where the claimant's power dam was situated at the junction of a nonnavigable and a navigable stream, and the tailrace discharged the water from the turbines into the navigable stream. Should compensation be due to a riparian owner on a non-navigable tributary for permanent undergound seepage and blockage caused by a federal dam downstream on a navigable river? United States v. Kansas City Life Ins. Co., 339 U.S. 799 (1950); see Note, The Supreme Court, 1949 Term, 64 Harv. L. Rev. 114, 138-139 (1950). Compare United States v. Gerlach Live Stock Co., 339 U.S. 725 (1950), where the government was held liable to riparian owners on a navigable stream for loss of benefits theretofore derived from periodic inundations of their land, owing to a navigation and reclamation project; the project was regarded as undertaken under the Reclamation Act, and that act was interpreted to require compensation.

3. Under the Federal Power Act the Power Commission may license private or publicly owned utilities to construct and operate hydroelectric projects on navigable waters. Questions, statutory and constitutional, have arisen over the authority of a licensee to act in contravention of state law. First Iowa Hydro-Electric Cooperative v. Federal Power Commission, 328 U.S. 152 (1946); Tacoma v. Taxpayers of Tacoma, 357 U.S. 320 (1958); Ivanhoe Irrigation District v. McCracken, 357 U.S. 275 (1958).

4. For a conflict of jurisdiction between the Power Commission and the Secretary of the Interior, reflecting a difference on the issue of public versus private construction, see United States v. Federal Power Commission, 345 U.S. 153 (1953).

5. On the resale-rate provisions in contracts between TVA and municipalities, see TVA v. Lenoir City, 72 F. Supp. 457 (E.D. Tenn. 1947). The contract set maximum rates and required the city to devote the revenues from its system first to the payment of

certain charges and then either to the retirement of bonds which had financed the acquisition of the system or to a reduction in rates. The city attempted to pledge the revenues as security for payments on a new bond issue, and an ordinance required the city to charge rates sufficient to meet such payments. The TVA sued for an injunction. What constitutional questions were involved?

Compare the provisions in contracts between the Bureau of Reclamation and water users, whereby irrigable lands in excess of 160 acres under single ownership may not receive water until the excess is agreed to be sold at prices not exceeding the maximum set by the Interior Department. Cf. United States v. Hanson, 167 F. 881 (9th Cir. 1909); Oregon & Calif. R.R. v. United States, 238 U.S. 393 (1915).

6. Does the United States own the waters on the public domain? In Nebraska v. Wyoming, 325 U.S. 589 (1945), involving apportionment of waters in the North Platte River, a nonnavigable stream, among Nebraska, Wyoming, and Colorado, the United States intervened, claiming ownership of all the unappropriated waters in the river. The claim was left undecided as being largely academic, in view of the provisions of the Reclamation Act, which directed the Secretary of the Interior to proceed in conformity with state laws in appropriating water for irrigation purposes, and the practice of making appropriation thereunder for the use of the landowners. 325 U.S. at 611-616. See also Kansas v. Colorado, 206 U.S. 46 (1907). Cf. Winters v. United States, 207 U.S. 564 (1908).

7. The United States, rather than California, was held to have dominion over the resources of the soil under the marginal sea adjoining that state. United States v. California, 332 U.S. 19 (1947). California maintained that it was entitled, by virtue of the conventional "equal footing" clause in the act admitting it to the Union, to the rights enjoyed by the original states, and that those states owned the waters and subsoil in the three-mile belt beyond low-water mark. The Court concluded that such ownership had not been established at the time of the Constitution, and that the interests of sovereignty favored national dominion. In the subsequent case involving Texas, the state insisted that its status was different: Whereas California had been a federal territory prior to admission and was claiming rights by implication, Texas had been a sovereign republic, with dominion over the marginal sea which it had never surrendered by implication. The Court, however, by a kind of reverse English on the "equal footing" clause, held that Texas was in no better case than California and the original states. United States v. Texas, 339 U.S. 707 (1950).

In United States v. Maine, 420 U.S. 515 (1975), the Court followed United States v. California and United States v. Texas in rejecting the claims of Atlantic seaboard states that colonial charters had granted them sovereignty over the marginal sea beyond the three-mile limit. See Morris, The Forging of the Union Reconsidered: A Historical Refutation of State Sovereignty over Seabeds, 74 Colum. L. Rev. 1056 (1974).

The Submerged Lands Act of 1953, 67 Stat. 29, vested in the states the ownership of lands beneath the marginal sea adjacent to the respective states. The Supreme Court citing decisions under the property clause of the Constitution, denied leave to file complaints challenging the statute. Alabama v. Texas, and Rhode Island v. Louisiana, 347 U.S. 272 (1954). Subsequently the Court held that the act does not grant Louisiana, Mississippi, or Alabama any rights beyond three geographic miles, but does grant to Texas and Florida rights in the Gulf of Mexico extending for three marine leagues opposite the coast. United States v. Louisiana, 363 U.S. 1 (1960).

8. On the entire subject of this section, see Report of President's Water Resources Policy Commission, Water Resources Law (1950); compare Johnson, Federal and State Control of Natural Resources, 4 Vand. L. Rev. 739 (1951). On the question whether licensees under the Federal Power Act must pay compensation to owners of water rights under state law, see Niagara-Mohawk Power Corp. v. FPC, 347 U.S. 239 (1954). See Schwartz, Niagara-Mohawk v. FPC: Have Private Water Rights Been Destroyed by the Federal Power Act? 102 U. Pa. L. Rev. 31 (1953). On federal and state control over the natural gas industry see note, page 411 infra.

NOTE Admiralty Jurisdiction

1. *Subject matter:* In DeLovio v. Boit, 2 Gall. 389 (1815), Mr. Justice Story, on Circuit, held that the admiralty jurisdiction of federal courts was not confined, as it was in England, to events occurring on tidewater, but that transactions which were maritime in character, such as contracts of marine insurance made on land, were within the admiralty jurisdiction of the federal courts sitting in admiralty. This doctrine, which was finally accepted by the Supreme Court in New England Mutual Ins. Co. v. Dunham, 11 Wall. 1 (1870), gave the federal courts an extensive authority to develop a body of commercial law for the nation.

2. *Geographical extent:* In Genesee Chief v. Fitzhugh, 12 How. 443 (1851), in an opinion by Taney, C.J., the Court decided that the admiralty jurisdiction extended to the waters of the Great Lakes, which, though not tidal, were public navigable waters "on which commerce is carried on between different states or nations." In The Hine, 4 Wall. 555 (1866), Mr. Justice Miller substituted for Taney's phrase, "public navigable water," the phrase "navigable water of the United States," and since that time it has been settled doctrine that the admiralty jurisdiction as defined in Article III extends to all waterways, natural or artificial, which are navigable in fact and which are used as highways of interstate or foreign commerce, and that such waters are to be described as "navigable waters of the United States." See, e.g., The Daniel Ball, supra page 207, The Robert W. Parsons, 191 U.S. 17 (1903).

3. *Congressional power:* Article III in its terms grants no power to Congress to enact or amend the maritime law enforced by courts of admiralty. The Court on many occasions, however, has found that Congress possesses an authority over the maritime law which is to be traced to Article III, §2, and which is not derived from the commerce clause. See, e.g., In re Garnett, 141 U.S. 1 (1890); Panama Railroad Co. v. Johnson, 264 U.S. 375 (1924); United States v. Flores, 289 U.S. 137 (1933); The Thomas Barlum, 293 U.S. 21 (1934). Justification for the congressional power to alter and amend the maritime law has also been found in the Necessary and Proper Clause. Southern Pacific Co. v. Jensen, 244 U.S. 205 (1917). This congressional power to deal with the maritime law on navigable waters of the United States must be distinguished from the power of the United States to control and improve its waters which are capable of use as interstate highways. With respect to that power, the Court has held that it "arises from the commerce clause of the Constitution." United States v. Appalachian Electric Power Co., 311 U.S. 377, 404 (1940). The Court in that case further stated that a waterway "otherwise suitable for navigation, is not barred from that classification merely because artificial aids must make the highway suitable for use before commercial navigation may be undertaken. . . . [T]he limits are necessarily a matter of degree. There must be a balance between cost and need at a time when the improvement would be useful." 311 U.S. at 407-408.

See Note, From Judicial Grant to Legislative Power: The Admiralty Clause in the Nineteenth Century, 67 Harv. L. Rev. 1214 (1954).

Section D. ECONOMIC REGULATION UNDER THE WAR POWERS

Chastleton Corp. v. Sinclair 264 U.S. 543, 44 S. Ct. 405, 68 L. Ed. 841 (1924)

MR. JUSTICE HOLMES delivered the opinion of the court:

This is a bill in equity, brought to restrain the enforcement of an order of the Rent

Section D. Economic Regulation under the War Powers 335

Commission of the District of Columbia, cutting down the rents for apartments in the Chastleton apartment house, in this city. The defendants are the Rent Commission and the tenants of the building. The order was passed on August 7, 1922, and purports to fix the reasonable rates from the preceding 1st of March. The bill seems to have been filed on October 27, 1922, and seeks relief on several grounds. The first and most important is that the emergency that justified interference with ordinarily existing private rights in 1919 had come to an end in 1922, and no longer could be applied consistently with the 5th Amendment of the Constitution. . . . On motion the bill was dismissed by the courts below, the court of appeals, in view of Block v. Hirsh, 256 U.S. 135, leaving it for this court to say whether conditions had so far changed as to affect the constitutional applicability of the law. . . . [W]e feel bound to consider the constitutional question that the bill seeks to raise. . . .

The original Act of October 22, 1919, chap. 80, title 2, 41 Stat. at L. 297, Fed. Stat. Anno. Supp. 1919, p. 49, considered in Block v. Hirsh, was limited to expire in two years. §122. The Act of August 24, 1921, chap. 91, 42 Stat. at L. 200, Fed. Stat. Anno. Supp. 1921, p. 51, purported to continue it in force, with some amendments, until May 22, 1922. On that day a new act declared that the emergency described in the original title 2 still existed, re-enacted with further amendments the amended Act of 1919, and provided that it was continued until May 22, 1924. Act of May 22, 1922, chap. 197, 42 Stat. at L. 543.

We repeat what was stated in Block v. Hirsh, 256 U.S. 135, 154, as to the respect due to a declaration of this kind by the legislature so far as it relates to present facts. But, even as to them, a court is not at liberty to shut its eyes to an obvious mistake, when the validity of the law depends upon the truth of what is declared. 256 U.S. 154. Chas. Wolff Packing Co. v. Court of Industrial Relations, 262 U.S. 522, 536. And still more obviously, so far as this declaration looks to the future, it can be no more than prophecy, and is liable to be controlled by events. A law depending upon the existence of an emergency or other certain state of facts to uphold it may cease to operate if the emergency ceases or the facts change, even though valid when passed. Perrin v. United States, 232 U.S. 478, 486, 487; Missouri v. Chicago, B. & Q.R. Co., 241 U.S. 533, 539, 540. In Newton v. Consolidated Gas Co., 258 U.S. 165, a statutory rate that had been sustained for earlier years in Wilcox v. Consolidated Gas Co., 212 U.S. 19, was held confiscatory for 1918 and 1919.

The order, although retrospective, was passed some time after the latest statute, and long after the original act would have expired. In our opinion it is open to inquire whether the exigency still existed upon which the continued operation of the law depended. It is a matter of public knowledge that the government has considerably diminished its demand for employees that was one of the great causes of the sudden afflux of people to Washington, and that other causes have lost at least much of their power. It is conceivable that, as is shown in an affidavit attached to the bill, extensive activity in building has added to the ease of finding an abode. If about all that remains of war conditions is the increased cost of living, that is not, in itself, a justification of the act. Without going beyond the limits of judicial knowledge, we can say at least that the plaintiffs' allegations cannot be declared offhand to be unmaintainable, and that it is not impossible that a full development of the facts will show them to be true. In that case the operation of the statute would be at an end.

We need not inquire how far this court might go in deciding the question for itself, on the principles explained in Prentis v. Atlantic Coast Line Co., 211 U.S. 210, 227. See Gardner v. Collector (Gardner v. Barney) 6 Wall. 499; South Ottawa v. Perkins, 94 U.S. 260; Jones v. United States, 137 U.S. 202; Travis v. Yale & T. Mfg. Co., 252 U.S. 60, 80. These cases show that the court may ascertain as it sees fit any fact that is merely a ground for laying down a rule of law, and if the question were only whether the statute is in force to-day, upon the facts that we judicially know, we should be compelled to say that the law has ceased to operate. Here, however, it is material to know the condition of Washington at different dates in the past. Obviously, the facts should be accurately ascertained and carefully weighed, and this can be done more conveniently in the supreme court of the District than here. The evidence should be preserved, so that, if necessary, it can be considered by this court.

Judgment reversed.

MR. JUSTICE BRANDEIS, concurring in part:

So far as concerns the Chastleton Corporation and Hahn, I agree that the decree should be reversed. [The opinion of Mr. Justice Brandeis stated that the rent order in question was void as to Chastleton Corporation and Hahn, because a statutory notice was not given them. As a nonconstitutional ground would dispose of the case, the constitutional question, he wrote, should not be decided.][e]

Woods v. Miller Co. 333 U.S. 138, 68 S. Ct. 421, 92 L. Ed. 596 (1948)

MR. JUSTICE DOUGLAS delivered the opinion of the Court.

The case is here on a direct appeal, Act of Aug. 24, 1937, 50 Stat. 751, 752, c. 754, 28 U.S.C. §349(a), from a judgment of the District Court holding unconstitutional Title II of the Housing and Rent Act of [June 30] 1947. Pub. Law, 129, 80th Cong., 1st Sess., 5 U.S.C. §1001.

The Act became effective on July 1, 1947, and the following day the appellee demanded of its tenants increases of 40% and 60% for rental accommodations in the Cleveland Defense-Rental Area, an admitted violation of the Act and regulations adopted pursuant thereto. Appellant thereupon instituted this proceeding under §206(b) of the Act to enjoin the violations. A preliminary injunction issued. After a hearing it was dissolved and a permanent injunction denied.

The District Court was of the view that the authority of Congress to regulate rents by virtue of the war power (see Bowles v. Willingham, 321 U.S. 503) ended with the Presidential Proclamation terminating hostilities on December 31, 1946, since that proclamation inaugurated "peace-in-fact" though it did not mark termination of the war. It also concluded that, even if the war power continues, Congress did not act under it because it did not say so, and only if Congress says so, or enacts provisions so implying, can it be held that Congress intended to exercise such power. That Congress did not so intend, said the District Court, follows from the provision that the Housing Expediter can end controls in any area without regard to the official termination of the war, and from the fact that the preceding federal rent control laws (which were concededly exercises of the war power) were neither amended nor extended. The District Court expressed the further view that rent control is not within the war power because "the emergency created by housing shortage came into existence long before the war." It held that the Act "lacks in uniformity of application and distinctly constitutes a delegation of legislative power not within the grant of Congress" because of the authorization to the Housing Expediter to lift controls in any area before the Act's expiration. It also held that the Act in effect provides "low rentals for certain groups without taking the property or compensating the owner in any way." See 74 F. Supp. 546.

---

[e] For state rent control and tenancy legislation in a state, after World War I, see Marcus Brown Holding Co. v. Feldman, 256 U.S. 170 (1921). The effect on constitutional powers of economic emergencies, as distinguished from those of a military character, is discussed in Home Building and Loan Assn. v. Blaisdell, 290 U.S. 398 (1934), page 2155 infra. See also Rossiter, Constitutional Dictatorship, c. 19, The New Deal and the Great Depression (1948). In East New York Savings Bank v. Hahn, 326 U.S. 230 (1945), the Supreme Court upheld a renewal (with some modifications) in 1943 of New York mortgage moratorium legislation originally passed to cope with the economic crisis of the early 1930's, even though inflationary rather than depression conditions now obtained. Mr. Justice Frankfurter concluded the opinion of the Court, "It only remains to say that in Chastleton v. Sinclair, 264 U.S. 543, which was strongly pressed on us, the Court dealt with quite a different situation. The differentiating factors are too glaring to require exposition." — ED.

We conclude, in the first place, that the war power sustains this legislation. The Court said in Hamilton v. Kentucky Distilleries & Warehouse Co., 251 U.S. 146, 161, that the war power includes the power "to remedy the evils which have arisen from its rise and progress" and continues for the duration of that emergency. Whatever may be the consequences when war is officially terminated,[5] the war power does not necessarily end with the cessation of hostilities. We recently held that it is adequate to support the preservation of rights created by wartime legislation. Fleming v. Mohawk Wrecking & Lumber Co., 331 U.S. 111. But it has a broader sweep. In Hamilton v. Kentucky Distilleries & Warehouse Co., supra, and Jacob Ruppert, Inc. v. Caffey, 251 U.S. 264, prohibition laws which were enacted after the Armistice in World War I were sustained as exercises of the war power because they conserved manpower and increased efficiency of production in the critical days during the period of demobilization, and helped to husband the supply of grains and cereals depleted by the war effort. Those cases followed the reasoning of Stewart v. Kahn (Stewart v. Bloom) 11 Wall. 493, which held that Congress had the power to toll the statute of limitations of the States during the period when the process of their courts was not available to litigants due to the conditions obtaining in the Civil War.

The constitutional validity of the present legislation follows a fortiori from those cases. The legislative history of the present Act makes abundantly clear that there has not yet been eliminated the deficit in housing which in considerable measure was caused by the heavy demobilization of veterans and by the cessation or reduction in residential construction during the period of hostilities due to the allocation of building materials to military projects. Since the war effort contributed heavily to that deficit, Congress has the power even after the cessation of hostilities to act to control the forces that a short supply of the needed article created. If that were not true, the Necessary and Proper Clause, Art. 1, §8, cl. 18, would be drastically limited in its application to the several war powers. The Court has declined to follow that course in the past. . . . We decline to take it today. The result would be paralyzing. It would render Congress powerless to remedy conditions the creation of which necessarily followed from the mobilization of men and materials for successful prosecution of the war. So to read the Constitution would be to make it self-defeating.

We recognize the force of the argument that the effects of war under modern conditions may be felt in the economy for years and years, and that if the war power can be used in days of peace to treat all the wounds which war inflicts on our society, it may not only swallow up all other powers of Congress but largely obliterate the Ninth and the Tenth Amendments as well. There are no such implications in today's decision. We deal here with the consequences of a housing deficit greatly intensified during the period of hostilities by the war effort. Any power, of course, can be abused. But we cannot assume that Congress is not alert to its constitutional responsibilities. And the question whether the war power has been properly employed in cases such as this is open to judicial inquiry. Hamilton v. Kentucky Distilleries & Warehouse Co., 251 U.S. 146, and Jacob Ruppert, Inc. v. Caffey, 251 U.S. 264, both supra.

The question of the constitutionality of action taken by Congress does not depend on recitals of the power which it undertakes to exercise. Here it is plain from the legislative history that Congress was invoking its war power to cope with a current condition of which the war was a direct and immediate cause. Its judgment on that score is entitled to the respect granted like legislation enacted pursuant to the police power. See Block v. Hirsh, 256 U.S. 135; Marcus Brown Holding Co. v. Feldman, 256 U.S. 170; Chastleton Corp. v. Sinclair, 264 U.S. 543.

Under the present Act the Housing Expediter is authorized to remove the rent controls in any defense-rental area if in his judgment the need no longer exists by reason of new construction or satisfaction of demand in other ways. The powers thus delegated are far

---

[5] See Commercial Trust Co. v. Miller, 262 U.S. 51, 57.

less extensive than those sustained in Bowles v. Willingham, supra (321 U.S. pp. 512-515). Nor is there here a grant of unbridled administrative discretion. The standards prescribed pass muster under our decisions. See Bowles v. Willingham, supra (321 U.S. pp. 514-516), and cases cited. . . .

The fact that the property regulated suffers a decrease in value is no more fatal to the exercise of the war power (Bowles v. Willingham, supra (321 U.S. pp. 517, 518)) than it is where the police power is invoked to the same end. See Block v. Hirsh, 256 U.S. 135, supra.

Reversed.

MR. JUSTICE FRANKFURTER concurs in this opinion because it decides no more than was decided in Hamilton v. Kentucky Distilleries & Warehouse Co., 251 U.S. 146, and Jacob Ruppert, Inc. v. Caffey, 251 U.S. 264, and merely applies those decisions to the situation now before the Court.

MR. JUSTICE JACKSON, concurring.

I agree with the result in this case, but the arguments that have been addressed to us lead me to utter more explicit misgivings about war powers than the Court has done. The Government asserts no constitutional basis for this legislation other than this vague, undefined and undefinable "war power."

No one will question that this power is the most dangerous one to free government in the whole catalogue of powers. It usually is invoked in haste and excitement when calm legislative consideration of constitutional limitation is difficult. It is executed in a time of patriotic fervor that makes moderation unpopular. And, worst of all, it is interpreted by the Judges under the influence of the same passions and pressures. Always, as in this case, the Government urges hasty decision to forestall some emergency or serve some purpose and pleads that paralysis will result if its claims to power are denied or their confirmation delayed.

Particularly when the war power is invoked to do things to the liberties of people, or to their property or economy that only indirectly affect conduct of the war and do not relate to the management of the war itself, the constitutional basis should be scrutinized with care.

I think we can hardly deny that the war power is as valid a ground for federal rent control now as it has been at any time. We still are technically in a state of war. I would not be willing to hold that war powers may be indefinitely prolonged merely by keeping legally alive a state of war that had in fact ended. I cannot accept the argument that war powers last as long as the effects and consequences of war for if so they are permanent — as permanent as the war debts. But I find no reason to conclude that we could find fairly that the present state of war is merely technical. We have armies abroad exercising our war power and have made no peace terms with our allies not to mention our principal enemies. I think the conclusion that the war power has been applicable during the lifetime of this legislation is unavoidable.

Chapter Eight The States in a Federal Union

Section A. MOVEMENT OF PERSONS

ARTICLES OF CONFEDERATION: "Article IV. The better to secure and perpetuate mutual friendship and intercourse among the people of the different states in this union, the free inhabitants in each of these states, paupers, vagabonds and fugitives from justice excepted, shall be entitled to all privileges and immunities of free citizens in the several states; and the people of each state shall have free ingress and egress to and from any other state, and shall enjoy therein all the privileges of trade and commerce, subject to the same duties, impositions and restrictions as the inhabitants thereof respectively, provided that such restriction shall not extend so far as to prevent the removal of property imported into any state, to any other state, of which the Owner is an inhabitant; provided also that no imposition, duties or restrictions shall be laid by any state, on the property of the united states, or either of them. . . ."

Crandall v. Nevada 6 Wall. 35, 18 L. Ed. 745 (1868)

Error to the Supreme Court of Nevada [which had denied an application for a writ of habeas corpus after plaintiff in error had been committed for disobeying an order to make reports required by statute].

In 1865, the legislature of Nevada enacted that "there shall be levied and collected a capitation tax of one dollar upon every person leaving the State by any railroad, stage coach, or other vehicle engaged or employed in the business of transporting passengers for hire," . . . For the purpose of collecting the tax, another section required from persons engaged in such business, or their agents, a report every month . . . of the number of persons so transported, and the payment of the tax. . . .

With the statute in existence, Crandall, who was the agent of a stage company engaged in carrying passengers through the State of Nevada, was arrested for refusing to report the number of passengers that had been carried by the coaches of his company, and for refusing to pay the tax of one dollar imposed on each passenger by the law of that State. . . .

Mr. Justice Miller delivered the opinion of the court.

The question for the first time presented to the court by this record is one of importance. The proposition to be considered is the right of a State to levy a tax upon persons residing in the State who may wish to get out of it, and upon persons not residing in it who may have occasion to pass through it. . . .

In the argument of the counsel for the defendant in error, and in the opinion of the Supreme Court of Nevada . . . it is assumed that this question must be decided by an exclusive reference to two provisions of the Constitution, namely: that which forbids any State, without the consent of Congress, to lay any imposts or duties on imports or exports, and that which confers on Congress the power to regulate commerce with foreign nations and among the several States. . . .

But we do not concede that the question before us is to be determined by the two clauses of the Constitution which we have been examining.

The people of these United States constitute one nation. They have a government in which all of them are deeply interested. This government has necessarily a capital established by law, where its principal operations are conducted. Here sits its legislature, composed of senators and representatives, from the States and from the people of the States. Here resides the President, directing through thousands of agents, the execution of the laws over all this vast country. Here is the seat of the supreme judicial power of the nation, to which all its citizens have a right to resort to claim justice at its hands. Here are the great executive departments, administering the offices of the mails, of the public lands, of the collection and distribution of the public revenues, and of our foreign relations. These are all established and conducted under the admitted powers of the Federal government. That government has a right to call to this point any or all of its citizens to aid in its service, as members of the Congress, of the courts, of the executive departments, and to fill all its other offices; and this right cannot be made to depend upon the pleasure of a State over whose territory they must pass to reach the point where these services must be rendered. The government, also, has its offices of secondary importance in all other parts of the country. On the sea-coasts and on the rivers it has its ports of entry. In the interior it has its land offices, its revenue offices, and its sub-treasuries. In all these it demands the services of its citizens, and is entitled to bring them to those points from all quarters of the nation, and no power can exist in a State to obstruct this right that would not enable it to defeat the purposes for which the government was established.

The Federal power has a right to declare and prosecute wars, and, as a necessary incident, to raise and transport troops through and over the territory of any State of the Union.

If this right is dependent in any sense, however limited, upon the pleasure of a State, the government itself may be overthrown by an obstruction to its exercise. Much the largest part of the transportation of troops during the late rebellion was by railroads, and largely through States whose people were hostile to the Union. If the tax levied by Nevada on railroad passengers had been the law of Tennessee, enlarged to meet the wishes of her people, the treasury of the United States could not have paid the tax necessary to enable its armies to pass through her territory.

But if the government has these rights on her own account, the citizen also has correlative rights. He has the right to come to the seat of government to assert any claim he may have upon that government, or to transact any business he may have with it. To seek its protection, to share its offices, to engage in administering its functions. He has a right to free access to its sea-ports, through which all the operations of foreign trade and commerce are conducted, to the sub-treasuries, the land offices, the revenue offices, and the courts of justice in the several States, and this right is in its nature independent of the will of any State over whose soil he must pass in the exercise of it. . . .

MR. JUSTICE CLIFFORD. I agree that the State law in question is unconstitutional and void, but I am not able to concur in the principal reasons assigned in the opinion of the court in support of that conclusion. On the contrary, I hold that the act of the State legislature is inconsistent with the power conferred upon Congress to regulate commerce among the several States, and I think the judgment of the court should have been placed exclusively upon that ground. Strong doubts are entertained by me whether Congress possesses the power to levy any such tax, but whether so or not, I am clear that the State legislature cannot impose any such burden upon commerce among the several States. Such commerce is secured against such legislation in the States by the Constitution, irrespective of any Congressional action.

THE CHIEF JUSTICE also dissents, and concurs in the views I have expressed.

Judgment reversed . . . with directions to discharge the plaintiff in error from custody.[a]

Edwards v. California 314 U.S. 160, 62 S. Ct. 164, 86 L. Ed. 119 (1941)

MR. JUSTICE BYRNES delivered the opinion of the Court:

The facts of this case are simple and are not disputed. Appellant is a citizen of the United States and a resident of California. In December, 1939, he left his home in Marysville, California, for Spur, Texas, with the intention of bringing back to Marysville his wife's brother, Frank Duncan, a citizen of the United States and a resident of Texas. When he arrived in Texas, appellant learned that Duncan had last been employed by the Works Progress Administration. Appellant thus became aware of the fact that Duncan was an indigent person and he continued to be aware of it throughout the period involved in this case. The two men agreed that appellant should transport Duncan from Texas to Marysville in appellant's automobile. Accordingly, they left Spur on January 1, 1940, entered California by way of Arizona on January 3, and reached Marysville on January 5. When he left Texas, Duncan had about $20. It had all been spent by the time he reached Marysville. He lived with appellant for about ten days until he obtained financial assistance from the Farm Security Administration. During the ten-day interval, he had no employment.

In Justice Court a complaint was filed against appellant under § 2615 of the Welfare and Institutions Code of California, which provides: "Every person, firm or corporation, or officer or agent thereof that brings or assists in bringing into the State any indigent person who is not a resident of the State, knowing him to be an indigent person, is guilty of a misdemeanor." On demurrer to the complaint, appellant urged that the section violated several provisions of the Federal Constitution. The demurrer was overruled, the cause was tried, appellant was convicted and sentenced to six months' imprisonment in the county jail, and sentence was suspended. . . .

Article 1, § 8, of the Constitution delegates to the Congress the authority to regulate interstate commerce. And it is settled beyond question that the transportation of persons is "commerce," within the meaning of that provision. It is nevertheless true that the States are not wholly precluded from exercising their police power in matters of local concern even though they may thereby affect interstate commerce. California v. Thompson, 313 U.S. 109, 113. The issue presented in this case, therefore, is whether the prohibition embodied in § 2615 against the "bringing" or transportation of indigent persons into California is within the police power of that State. We think that it is not, and hold that it is an unconstitutional barrier to interstate commerce.

The grave and perplexing social and economic dislocation which this statute reflects is a

---

[a] Crandall v. Nevada was distinguished in Evansville-Vanderburgh Airport Authority District v. Delta Airlines, Inc., 405 U.S. 707 (1972), which upheld a head tax on emplaning passengers where the amounts collected do not exceed the costs of maintaining the airport, and the tax is collected from both interstate and intrastate passengers. Justice Douglas dissented in defense of the citizen's right to travel. — ED.

matter of common knowledge and concern. We are not unmindful of it. We appreciate that the spectacle of large segments of our population constantly on the move has given rise to urgent demands upon the ingenuity of government. Both the brief of the Attorney General of California and that of the Chairman of the Select Committee of the House of Representatives of the United States as amicus curiae have sharpened this appreciation. The State asserts that the huge influx of migrants into California in recent years has resulted in problems of health, morals, and especially finance, the proportions of which are staggering. It is not for us to say that this is not true. We have repeatedly and recently affirmed, and we now reaffirm, that we do not conceive it our function to pass upon "the wisdom, need, or appropriateness" of the legislative efforts of the States to solve such difficulties. See Olsen v. Nebraska, 313 U.S. 236, 246.

But this does not mean that there are no boundaries to the permissible area of State legislative activity. There are. And none is more certain than the prohibition against attempts on the part of any single State to isolate itself from difficulties common to all of them by restraining the transportation of persons and property across its borders. It is frequently the case that a State might gain a momentary respite from the pressure of events by the simple expedient of shutting its gates to the outside world. But, in the words of Mr. Justice Cardozo: "The Constitution was framed under the dominion of a political philosophy less parochial in range. It was framed upon the theory that the peoples of the several States must sink or swim together, and that in the long run prosperity and salvation are in union and not division." Baldwin v. G. A. F. Seelig, Inc., 294 U.S. 511, 523.

It is difficult to conceive of a statute more squarely in conflict with this theory than the section challenged here. Its express purpose and inevitable effect is to prohibit the transportation of indigent persons across the California border. The burden upon interstate commerce is intended and immediate; it is the plain and sole function of the statute. Moreover, the indigent nonresidents who are the real victims of the statute are deprived of the opportunity to exert political pressure upon the California legislature in order to obtain a change in policy. South Carolina State Highway Dept. v. Barnwell Bros., 303 U.S. 177, 185, note 2. We think this statute must fail under any known test of the validity of State interference with interstate commerce.

It is urged, however, that the concept which underlies §2615 enjoys a firm basis in English and American history.[2] This is the notion that each community should care for its own indigent, that relief is solely the responsibility of local government. Of this it must first be said that we are not now called upon to determine anything other than the propriety of an attempt by a State to prohibit the transportation of indigent nonresidents into its territory. The nature and extent of its obligation to afford relief to newcomers is not here involved. We do, however, suggest that the theory of the Elizabethan poor laws no longer fits the facts. Recent years, and particularly the past decade, have been marked by a growing recognition that in an industrial society the task of providing assistance to the needy has ceased to be local in character. The duty to share the burden, if not wholly to assume it, has been recognized not only by State governments, but by the Federal government as well. The changed attitude is reflected in the Social Security laws under which the Federal and State governments cooperate for the care of the aged, the blind and dependent children. 42 U.S.C. §§301-1307, esp. §§301, 501, 601, 701, 721, 801, 1201. It is reflected in the works programs under which work is furnished the unemployed, with the States supplying approximately 25% and the Federal government approximately 75% of the cost. See, e.g., Joint Resolution of June 26, 1940, chap. 432, §1(d), 76th Cong., 3d Sess., 54 Stat. at L. 611, 613. It is further reflected in the Farm Security laws, under which the entire cost of the relief provisions is borne by the Federal government. Id. at §§2(a), 2(b), 2(d).

Indeed the record in this very case illustrates the inadequate basis in fact for the theory

---

[2] See Hirsch, H. M., Our Settlement Laws (N.Y. Dept. of Social Welfare, 1933), passim.

that relief is presently a local matter. Before leaving Texas, Duncan had received assistance from the Works Progress Administration. After arriving in California he was aided by the Farm Security Administration, which, as we have said, is wholly financed by the Federal government. This is not to say that our judgment would be different if Duncan had received relief from local agencies in Texas and California. Nor is it to suggest that the financial burden of assistance to indigent persons does not continue to fall heavily upon local and State governments. It is only to illustrate that in not inconsiderable measure the relief of the needy has become the common responsibility and concern of the whole nation.

What has been said with respect to financing relief is not without its bearing upon the regulation of the transportation of indigent persons. For the social phenomenon of large-scale interstate migration is as certainly a matter of national concern as the provision of assistance to those who have found a permanent or temporary abode. Moreover, and unlike the relief problem, this phenomenon does not admit of diverse treatment by the several States. The prohibition against transporting indigent nonresidents into one State is an open invitation to retaliatory measures, and the burdens upon the transportation of such persons become cumulative. . . . The scope of congressional power to deal with this problem we are not now called upon to decide.

There remains to be noticed only the contention that the limitation upon State power to interfere with the interstate transportation of persons is subject to an exception in the case of "paupers." It is true that support for this contention may be found in early decisions of this Court. In New York v. Miln, 11 Pet. 102, at 143, it was said that it is "as competent and as necessary for a State to provide precautionary measures against the moral pestilence of paupers, vagabonds, and possibly convicts, as it is to guard against the physical pestilence which may arise from unsound and infectious articles imported. . . ." This language has been casually repeated in numerous later cases up to the turn of the century. [Citations omitted.] In none of these cases, however, was the power of a State to exclude "paupers" actually involved.

Whether an able-bodied but unemployed person like Duncan is a "pauper" within the historical meaning of the term is open to considerable doubt. See 53 Harvard L. Rev. 1031, 1032. But assuming that the term is applicable to him and to persons similarly situated, we do not consider ourselves bound by the language referred to. New York v. Miln was decided in 1837. Whatever may have been the notion then prevailing, we do not think it will now be seriously contended that because a person is without employment and without funds he constitutes a "moral pestilence." Poverty and immorality are not synonymous.

We are of the opinion that §2615 is not a valid exercise of the police power of California, that it imposes an unconstitutional burden upon interstate commerce, and that the conviction under it cannot be sustained. In the view we have taken it is unnecessary to decide whether the section is repugnant to other provisions of the Constitution.

Reversed.

MR. JUSTICE DOUGLAS concurring:

I express no view on whether or not the statute here in question runs afoul of Art. 1, §8, of the Constitution granting to Congress the power "to regulate Commerce with foreign Nations, and among the several States." But I am of the opinion that the right of persons to move freely from State to State occupies a more protected position in our constitutional system than does the movement of cattle, fruit, steel and coal across state lines. While the opinion of the Court expresses no view on that issue, the right involved is so fundamental that I deem it appropriate to indicate the reach of the constitutional question which is present.

The right to move freely from State to State is an incident of *national* citizenship protected by the privileges and immunities clause of the Fourteenth Amendment against state interference, Mr. Justice Moody in Twining v. New Jersey, 211 U.S. 78, 97, stated,

"Privileges and immunities of citizens of the United States . . . are only such as arise out of the nature and essential character of the National Government, or are specifically granted or secured to all citizens or persons by the Constitution of the United States." And he went on to state that one of those rights of *national* citizenship was "the right to pass freely from State to State." Id., 211 U.S. p. 97. . . . It was so decided in 1868 by Crandall v. Nevada, 6 Wall. 35. . . .

The conclusion that the right of free movement is a right of *national* citizenship stands on firm historical ground. If a state tax on that movement, as in the Crandall Case, is invalid, a fortiori a state statute which obstructs or in substance prevents that movement must fall. That result necessarily follows unless perchance a State can curtail the right of free movement of those who are poor or destitute. But to allow such an exception to be engrafted on the rights of *national* citizenship would be to contravene every conception of national unity. It would also introduce a caste system utterly incompatible with the spirit of our system of government. It would permit those who were stigmatized by a State as indigents, paupers, or vagabonds to be relegated to an inferior class of citizenship. It would prevent a citizen because he was poor from seeking new horizons in other States. It might thus withhold from large segments of our people that mobility which is basic to any guarantee of freedom of opportunity. The result would be a substantial dilution of the rights of *national* citizenship, a serious impairment of the principles of equality. Since the state statute here challenged involves such consequences, it runs afoul of the privileges and immunities clause of the Fourteenth Amendment.

MR. JUSTICE BLACK and MR. JUSTICE MURPHY join in this opinion.

MR. JUSTICE JACKSON, concurring:

I concur in the result reached by the Court, and I agree that the grounds of its decision are permissible ones under applicable authorities. But the migrations of a human being, of whom it is charged that he possesses nothing that can be sold and has no wherewithal to buy, do not fit easily into my notions as to what is commerce. To hold that the measure of his rights is the commerce clause is likely to result eventually either in distorting the commercial law or in denaturing human rights. I turn, therefore, away from principles by which commerce is regulated to that clause of the Constitution by virtue of which Duncan is a citizen of the United States and which forbids any state to abridge his privileges or immunities as such.

This clause was adopted to make United States citizenship the dominant and paramount allegiance among us. The return which the law had long associated with allegiance was protection. The power of citizenship as a shield against oppression was widely known from the example of Paul's Roman citizenship, which sent the centurion scurrying to his higher-ups with the message: "Take heed what thou doest: for this man is a Roman." . . .

The right of the citizen to migrate from state to state which, I agree with Mr. Justice Douglas, is shown by our precedents to be one of national citizenship, is not, however, an unlimited one. In addition to being subject to all constitutional limitations imposed by the federal government, such citizen is subject to some control by state governments. He may not, if a fugitive from justice, claim freedom to migrate unmolested, nor may he endanger others by carrying contagion about. These causes, and perhaps others that do not occur to me now, warrant any public authority in stopping a man where it finds him and arresting his progress across a state line quite as much as from place to place within the state.

It is here that we meet the real crux of this case. Does "indigence" as defined by the application of the California statute constitute a basis for restricting the freedom of a citizen, as crime or contagion warrants its restriction? We should say now, and in no uncertain terms, that a man's mere property status, without more, cannot be used by a state to test, qualify, or limit his rights as a citizen of the United States. "Indigence" in itself is neither a source of rights nor a basis for denying them. The mere state of being without funds is a neutral fact — constitutionally an irrelevance, like race, creed, or color. I agree with what I understand to be the holding of the Court that cases which may indicate the contrary are overruled. . . .

I think California had no right to make the condition of Duncan's purse, with no evidence of violation by him of any law or social policy which caused it, the basis of excluding him or of punishing one who extended him aid. . . .

NOTE

1. See Roback, Legal Barriers to Interstate Migration, 28 Cornell L.Q. 286 and 483 (1943); Note, Depression Migrants and the States, 53 Harv. L. Rev. 1031 (1940). Decisions dealing with the scope of the privileges and immunities clauses in this context are discussed in Meyers, Federal Privileges and Immunities: Application to Ingress and Egress, 29 Cornell L.Q. 489 (1944). See also 55 Harv. L. Rev. 873 (1942). Compare the problem involved in Wheeler v. United States, 254 U.S. 281 (1920), described in the Report, infra pages 790-792.

2. Federal legislation concerning the movement of persons within the United States has prohibited (a) the transportation in interstate commerce of any woman or girl for the purpose of prostitution or other immoral purpose (18 U.S.C. §2421, upheld in Hoke v. United States, 227 U.S. 308 (1913), and Caminetti v. United States, 242 U.S. 470 (1917), and applied to transportation of plural wives by members of a polygamous sect in Cleveland v. United States, 329 U.S. 14 (1946)); (b) the transportation in interstate commerce of any person who has been unlawfully kidnaped and held for ransom or otherwise (18 U.S.C. §1201, applied in Robinson v. United States, 324 U.S. 282 (1945), and Gooch v. United States, 297 U.S. 124 (1936)); (c) the transportation of strikebreakers in interstate commerce (18 U.S.C. §1231); (d) moving or traveling in interstate commerce to avoid prosecution, or confinement after conviction, under local law, or to avoid giving testimony in criminal proceedings (18 U.S.C. §1073); (e) shanghaiing sailors onto vessels engaged in commerce among the several states or navigating any navigable water of the United States (18 U.S.C §2194); (f) travel in interstate commerce "in aid of racketeering enterprises" (18 U.S.C. §1952). See also Executive Order No. 9066, 7 Fed. Reg. 1407 (1942), and Act of March 21, 1942, 56 Stat. 173, involved in the so-called Japanese Relocation Cases, Hirabayashi v. United States, 320 U.S. 81 (1942), Korematsu v. United States, 323 U.S. 214 (1944), and Ex parte Endo, 323 U.S. 283 (1944).

3. Note the attempt to deal with the migrant dependent on a comprehensive basis by uniform state legislation in the Uniform Transfer of Dependents Act, 9A Uniform Laws Annotated (1935). Compare Adams County v. Burleigh County, 69 N.D. 780, 291 N.W. 281 (1940). See also Matter of Chirillo, 283 N.Y. 417, 28 N.E.2d 895 (1940), and Chirillo v. Lehman, 38 F. Supp. 65 (1940).

4. In Austin v. New Hampshire, 420 U.S. 656 (1975), the Supreme Court held that the New Hampshire Commuters Income Tax on nonresidents' earnings within the state violated the Privileges and Immunities Clause of Article IV. Under the challenged plan nonresidents' New Hampshire earnings over $2000 were taxed at 4 percent or at the income tax rate of the taxpayer's home state, whichever was less. New Hampshire imposed no tax, however, on the foreign or domestic earnings of New Hampshire residents. The state argued that since the nonresidents received a tax credit from their home states for taxes paid to New Hampshire, the challenged plan subjected them to no greater taxes than they would incur by working in their home states. The Court rejected this argument, holding that disparity in treatment of resident and nonresident taxpayers itself constituted a violation of the Privileges and Immunities Clause. The Court pointed also to the loss of income by neighboring states giving credits for the New Hampshire tax. Justice Blackmun dissented.

Shapiro v. Thompson 394 U.S. 618, 89 S. Ct. 1322, 22 L. Ed. 2d 600 (1969)

MR. JUSTICE BRENNAN delivered the opinion of the Court. These three appeals were restored to the calendar for reargument. 392 U.S. 920 (1968). Each is an appeal from a decision of a three-judge District Court holding unconstitutional a State or District of Columbia statutory provision which denies welfare assistance to residents of the State or District who have not resided within their jurisdictions for at least one year immediately preceding their applications for such assistance. We affirm the judgments of the District Courts in the three cases.

I

In No. 9, the Connecticut Welfare Department invoked §17-2d of the Connecticut General Statutes[2] to deny the application of appellee Vivian Marie Thompson for assistance under the program for Aid to Families with Dependent Children (AFDC). She was a 19-year-old unwed mother of one child and pregnant with her second child when she changed her residence in June 1966 from Dorchester, Massachusetts, to Hartford, Connecticut, to live with her mother, a Hartford resident. She moved to her own apartment in Hartford in August 1966, when her mother was no longer able to support her and her infant son. Because of her pregnancy, she was unable to work or enter a work training program. Her application for AFDC assistance, filed in August was denied in November solely on the ground that, as required by §17-2d, she had not lived in the State for a year before her application was filed. She brought this action in the District Court for the District of Connecticut where a three-judge court, one judge dissenting, declared §17-2d unconstitutional. 270 F. Supp. 331 (1967). The majority held that the waiting-period requirement is unconstitutional because it "has a chilling effect on the right to travel." Id., at 336. The majority also held that the provision was a violation of the Equal Protection Clause of the Fourteenth Amendment because the denial of relief to those resident in the State for less than a year is not based on any permissible purpose but is solely designed, as "Connecticut states quite frankly," "to protect its fisc by discouraging entry of those who come needing relief." Id., at 336-337. We noted probable jurisdiction. 389 U.S. 1032 (1968).

[The statements of facts in cases from The District of Columbia and Pennsylvania are omitted.]

II

. . . On reargument, appellees' central contention is that the statutory prohibition of benefits to residents of less than a year creates a classification which constitutes an invidious discrimination denying them equal protection of the laws.[6] We agree. The inter-

---

[2] Conn. Gen. Stat. Rev. §17-2d (1966), now §17-2c provides:
"When any person comes into this state without visible means of support for the immediate future and applies for aid to dependent children under chapter 301 or general assistance under part I of chapter 308 within one year from his arrival, such person shall be eligible only for temporary aid or care until arrangements are made for his return, provided ineligibility for aid to dependent children shall not continue beyond the maximum federal residence requirement."

An exception is made for those persons who come to Connecticut with a bona fide job offer or are self-supporting upon arrival in the State and for three months thereafter. 1 Conn. Welfare Manual, c. II, §219.1 [to] 219.2 (1966).

[6] This constitutional challenge cannot be answered by the argument that public assistance benefits are a "privilege" and not a "right." See Sherbert v. Verner, 374 U.S. 398, 404 (1963).

ests which appellants assert are promoted by the classification either may not constitutionally be promoted by government or are not compelling governmental interests.

III

Primarily, appellants justify the waiting-period requirement as a protective device to preserve the fiscal integrity of state public assistance programs. It is asserted that people who require welfare assistance during their first year of residence in a State are likely to become continuing burdens on state welfare programs. Therefore, the argument runs, if such people can be deterred from entering the jurisdiction by denying them welfare benefits during the first year, state programs to assist long-time residents will not be impaired by a substantial influx of indigent newcomers.[7]

There is weighty evidence that exclusion from the jurisdiction of the poor who need or may need relief was the specific objective of these provisions. In the Congress, sponsors of federal legislation to eliminate all residence requirements have been consistently opposed by representatives of state and local welfare agencies who have stressed the fears of the States that elimination of the requirements would result in a heavy influx of individuals into States providing the most generous benefits. . . . The sponsor of the Connecticut requirement said in its support: "I doubt that Connecticut can and should continue to allow unlimited migration into the State on the basis of offering instant money and permanent income to all who can make their way to the State regardless of their ability to contribute to the economy." . . .

We do not doubt that the one-year waiting period device is well suited to discourage the influx of poor families in need of assistance. . . . But the purpose of inhibiting migration by needy persons into the State is constitutionally impermissible.

This Court long ago recognized that the nature of our Federal Union and our constitutional concepts of personal liberty unite to require that all citizens be free to travel throughout the length and breadth of our land uninhibited by statutes, rules, or regulations which unreasonably burden or restrict this movement. That proposition was early stated by Chief Justice Taney in the Passenger Cases, 7 How. 283, 492 (1849):

"For all the great purposes for which the Federal government was formed, we are one people, with one common country. We are all citizens of the United States; and, as members of the same community, must have the right to pass and repass through every part of it without interruption, as freely as in our own States."

We have no occasion to ascribe the source of this right to travel interstate to a particular constitutional provision.[8] It suffices that as Mr. Justice Stewart said for the Court in United States v. Guest, 383 U.S. 745, 757-758 (1966):

"The constitutional right to travel from one State to another . . . occupies a position fundamental to the concept of our Federal Union. It is a right that has been firmly established and repeatedly recognized.

[7] The waiting-period requirement has its antecedents in laws prevalent in England and the American Colonies centuries ago which permitted the ejection of individuals and families if local authorities thought they might become public charges. . . .

[8] In Corfield v. Coryell, 6 F. Cas. 546, 552 (No. 3230) (C.C.E.D. Pa. 1823), Paul v. Virginia, 8 Wall. 168, 180 (1808), and Ward v. Maryland, 12 Wall. 418, 430 (1870), the right to travel interstate was grounded upon the Privileges and Immunities Clause of Art. IV, § 2. See also Slaughter-House Cases, 16 Wall. 36, 79 (1872); Twining v. New Jersey, 211 U.S. 78, 97 (1908). In Edwards v. California, 314 U.S. 160, 181, 183-185 (Douglas and Jackson, JJ. concurring), and Twining v. New Jersey, supra, reliance was placed on the Privileges and Immunities Clause of the Fourteenth Amendment. See also Crandall v. Nevada, 6 Wall. 35 (1868). In Edwards v. California, supra, and Passenger Cases, 7 How. 283 (1849), a Commerce Clause approach was employed.

See also Kent v. Dulles, 357 U.S. 116, 125 (1958); Aptheker v. Rusk, 378 U.S. 500, 505-506 (1964); Zenel v. Rusk, 381 U.S. 1, 14 (1966), where the freedom of Americans to travel outside the country was grounded upon the Due Process Clause of the Fifth Amendment.

"[The] right finds no explicit mention in the Constitution. The reason, it has been suggested, is that a right so elementary was conceived from the beginning to be a necessary concomitant of the stronger Union the Constitution created. In any event, freedom to travel throughout the United States has long been recognized as a basic right under the Constitution."

Thus, the purpose of deterring the in-migration of indigents cannot serve as justification for the classification created by the one-year waiting period, since that purpose is constitutionally impermissible. If a law has "no other purpose . . . than to chill the assertion of constitutional rights by penalizing those who choose to exercise them, then it [is] patently unconstitutional." United States v. Jackson, 390 U.S. 570, 581 (1968).

Alternatively, appellants argue that even if it is impermissible for a State to attempt to deter the entry of all indigents, the challenged classification may be justified as a permissible state attempt to discourage those indigents who would enter the State solely to obtain larger benefits. We observe first that none of the statutes before us is tailored to serve that objective. . . .

More fundamentally, a State may no more try to fence out those indigents who seek higher welfare benefits than it may try to fence out indigents generally. Implicit in any such distinction is the notion that indigents who enter a state with the hope of securing higher welfare benefits are somehow less deserving than indigents who do not take this consideration into account. But we do not perceive why a mother who is seeking to make a new life for herself and her children should be regarded as less deserving because she considers, among other factors, the level of a State's public assistance. Surely such a mother is no less deserving than a mother who moves into a particular State in order to take advantage of its better education facilities.

Appellants argue further that the challenged classification may be sustained as an attempt to distinguish between new and old residents on the basis of the greater contribution to the State in taxes than indigent residents who have recently arrived. If the argument is based on contributions made in the past by the long-term residents, . . . [a]ppellants' reasoning would logically permit the State to bar new residents from schools, parks, and libraries or deprive them of police and fire protection. Indeed it would permit the State to apportion all benefits and services according to the past tax contributions of its citizens. The Equal Protection Clause prohibits such an apportionment of state services.

We recognize that a State has a valid interest in preserving the fiscal integrity of its programs. It may legitimately attempt to limit its expenditures, whether for public assistance, public education, or any other program. But a State may not accomplish such a purpose by invidious distinctions between classes of its citizens. It could not, for example, reduce expenditures for education by barring indigent children from its schools. Similarly, in the cases before us, appellants must do more than show that denying welfare benefits to new residents saves money. The saving of welfare costs cannot be an independent ground for an invidious classification.

In sum, neither deterrence of indigents from migrating to the State nor limitation of welfare benefits to those regarded as contributing to the State is a constitutionally permissible state objective.

IV

Appellants next advance as justification certain administrative and related governmental objectives allegedly served by the waiting-period requirement. They argue that the requirement (1) facilitates the planning of the welfare budget; (2) provides an objective test of residency; (3) minimizes the opportunity for recipients fraudulently to receive payments from more than one jurisdiction; and (4) encourages early entry of new residents into the labor force.

At the outset, we reject appellants' argument that a mere showing of a rational relationship between the waiting period and these four admittedly permissible state objectives will suffice to justify the classification. . . . The waiting-period provision denies welfare benefits to otherwise eligible applicants solely because they have recently moved into the jurisdiction. But in moving from State to State or to the District of Columbia appellees were exercising a constitutional right, and any classification which serves to penalize the exercise of that right, unless shown to be necessary to promote a compelling governmental interest, is unconstitutional. . . .

The argument that the waiting-period requirement facilitates budget predictability is wholly unfounded. The records in all three cases are utterly devoid of evidence that either State or the District of Columbia in fact uses the one-year requirement as a means to predict the number of people who will require assistance in the budget year. None of the appellants takes a census of new residents or collects any other data that would reveal the number of newcomers in the State less than a year. . . .

The argument that the waiting period serves as an administratively efficient rule of thumb for determining residency similarly will not withstand scrutiny. The residence requirement and the one-year waiting-period requirement are distinct and independent prerequisites for assistance under these three statutes, and the facts relevant to the determination of each are directly examined by the welfare authorities. . . .

Similarly, there is no need for a State to use the one-year waiting period as a safeguard against fraudulent receipt of benefits; for less drastic means are available, and are employed, to minimize that hazard. Of course, a State has a valid interest in preventing fraud by any applicant, whether a newcomer or a long-time resident. It is not denied however that the investigations now conducted entail inquiries into facts relevant to that subject. In addition, cooperation among state welfare departments is common. The District of Columbia, for example, provides interim assistance to its former residents who have moved to a State which has a waiting period. As a matter of course, District officials send a letter to the welfare authorities in the recipient's new community "to request the information needed to continue assistance." A like procedure would be an effective safeguard against the hazard of double payments. Since double payments can be prevented by a letter or a telephone call, it is unreasonable to accomplish this objective by the blunderbuss method of denying assistance to all indigent newcomers for an entire year.

We conclude therefore that appellants in these cases do not use and have no need to use the one-year requirement for the governmental purposes suggested. Thus, even under traditional equal protection tests a classification of welfare applicants according to whether they have lived in the State for one year would seem irrational and unconstitutional. But, of course, the traditional criteria do not apply in these cases. Since the classification here touches on the fundamental right of interstate movement, its constitutionality must be judged by the stricter standard of whether it promotes a compelling state interest. Under this standard, the waiting period requirement clearly violates the Equal Protection Clause.[21]

V

Connecticut and Pennsylvania argue, however, that the constitutional challenge to the waiting period requirements must fail because Congress expressly approved the imposition of the requirement by the States as part of the jointly funded AFDC program.

---

[21] We imply no view of the validity of waiting period or residence requirements determining eligibility to vote, eligibility for tuition-free education, to obtain a license to practice a profession, to hunt or fish, and so forth. Such requirements may promote compelling state interests on the one hand, or, on the other, may not be penalties upon the exercise of the constitutional right of interstate travel.

Section 402(b) of the Social Security Act of 1935, as amended, 42 U.S.C. §602(b), provides that:

"The Secretary shall approve any [state assistance] plan which fulfills the conditions specified in subsection (a) of this section, except that he shall not approve any plan which imposes as a condition of eligibility for aid to families with dependent children, a residence requirement which denies aid with respect to any child residing in the State (1) who has resided in the State for one year immediately preceding the application for such aid, or (2) who was born within one year immediately preceding the application, if the parent or other relative with whom the child is living has resided in the State for one year immediately preceding the birth."

On its face, the statute does not approve, much less prescribe, a one-year requirement. It merely directs the Secretary of Health, Education, and Welfare not to disapprove plans submitted by the States because they include such a requirement. . . .

But even if we were to assume, arguendo, that Congress did approve the imposition of a one-year waiting period, it is the responsive *state* legislation which infringes constitutional rights. By itself §402(b) has absolutely no restrictive effect. It is therefore not that statute but only the state requirements which pose the constitutional question.

Finally, even if it could be argued that the constitutionality of §402(b) is somehow at issue here, it follows from what we have said that the provision, insofar as it permits the one-year waiting-period requirement, would be unconstitutional. Congress may not authorize the States to violate the Equal Protection Clause. Perhaps Congress could induce wider state participation in school construction if it authorized the use of joint funds for the building of segregated schools. But could it seriously be contended that Congress would be constitutionally justified in such authorization by the need to secure state cooperation? Congress is without power to enlist state cooperation in a joint federal-state program by legislation which authorizes the States to violate the Equal Protection Clause. . . .

VI

The waiting-period requirement in the District of Columbia Code involved in No. 33 is also unconstitutional even though it was adopted by Congress as an exercise of federal power. In terms of federal power, the discrimination created by the one-year requirement violates the Due Process Clause of the Fifth Amendment. "[W]hile the Fifth Amendment contains no equal protection clause, it does forbid discrimination that is 'so unjustifiable as to be violative of due process.'" Schneider v. Rusk, 377 U.S. 163, 168 (1964); Bolling v. Sharpe, 347 U.S. 497 (1954). . . .

Accordingly, the judgments in Nos. 9, 33, and 34 are

Affirmed.

[A concurring opinion was delivered by MR. JUSTICE STEWART. Dissenting opinions were delivered by CHIEF JUSTICE WARREN, in which MR. JUSTICE BLACK joined, and by MR. JUSTICE HARLAN. The CHIEF JUSTICE'S opinion states: "Although the Court dismisses §402(b) with the remark that Congress cannot authorize the States to violate equal protection, I believe that the dispositive issue is whether under its commerce power Congress can impose residence requirements.

". . . I am convinced that Congress does have power to enact residence requirements of reasonable duration or to authorize the States to do so and that it has exercised this power.

"The Court's decision reveals only the top of the iceberg. Lurking beneath are the multitude of situations in which States have imposed residence requirements including eligibility to vote, to engage in certain professions or occupations or to attend a state-supported university. Although the Court takes pains to avoid acknowledging the ramifications of its decision, its implications cannot be ignored. I dissent."

Mr. Justice Harlan's opinion concludes: "I consider it particularly unfortunate that this judicial roadblock to the powers of Congress in this field should occur at the very threshold of the current discussions regarding the 'federalizing' of these aspects of welfare relief."]

NOTE State Durational Residency Requirements After Shapiro v. Thompson

As suggested by footnote 21 of Justice Brennan's opinion, Shapiro v. Thompson does not require that every durational residency requirement that places any burden on interstate travel be supported by a compelling state interest. Rather, strict scrutiny has come to be limited to requirements deemed to "penalize" exercise of the travel right.

Thus, in Memorial Hospital v. Maricopa County, 415 U.S. 250 (1974), the Court struck down an Arizona statute restricting free nonemergency medical care to indigents who had been residents of the same county for the previous 12 months. In requiring the statute to meet the compelling-interest test, the Court said (footnotes omitted):

"Whatever the ultimate parameters of the Shapiro penalty analysis, it is at least clear that medical care is as much 'a basic necessity of life' to an indigent as welfare assistance. And, governmental privileges or benefits necessary to basic sustenance have often been viewed as being of greater constitutional significance than less essential forms of governmental entitlements."

Similarly, in Dunn v. Blumstein, 405 U.S. 330 (1972), the Court applied strict scrutiny to invalidate a Tennessee statute requiring one year of residence in the state and three months in the county before a citizen could register to vote. The Court emphasized the fundamental importance of the right to vote. The Court recognized, however, that some minimal durational requirement was a practical necessity:

"Fixing a constitutionally acceptable period is surely a matter of degree. It is sufficient to note here that 30 days appears to be an ample period of time for the State to complete whatever administrative tasks are necessary to prevent fraud — and a year, or three months, too much."

In Marston v. Lewis, 410 U.S. 679 (1973), and Burns v. Fortson, 410 U.S. 686 (1973), the Court upheld, 6 to 3, 50-day durational residency requirements for voting in elections other than presidential elections in Arizona and Georgia.

See also King v. New Rochelle Municipal Housing Authority, 442 F.2d 646 (2d Cir.), cert. denied, 404 U.S. 863 (1971), and Cole v. Housing Authority of City of Newport, 435 F.2d 807 (1st Cir. 1970), striking durational residency requirements of five and two years for admission to public housing projects.

In other contexts durational residency requirements have been upheld. In Vlandis v. Kline, 412 U.S. 441 (1973), the Court struck down as an irrebuttable presumption violative of the due process clause a Connecticut statute providing that students in the state university system who had not resided in the state during the 12 months prior to their application for admission were ineligible for lower "in-state" tuition rates at any time during their university career. The Court did not base its decision on infringement of the right to travel, however, and indeed suggested that "a reasonable durational residency requirement" might be employed as one test of bona fide residence for the purpose of allocating tuition rates. Compare Sturgis v. Washington, 368 F. Supp. 38 (W.D. Wash.) (three-judge court), aff'd mem., 414 U.S. 1057 (1973), and Starns v. Malkerson, 326 F. Supp. 234 (D. Minn. 1970) (three-judge court), aff'd mem., 401 U.S. 985 (1971), upholding one-year waiting periods for resident status for tuition purposes. See Note, The Supreme Court, 1972 Term, 87 Harv. L. Rev. 1, 67-75 (1973).

Durational residency requirements for candidates for state political office were upheld in

Sununu v. Stark, 383 F. Supp. 1287 (D.N.H. 1974) (three-judge court), aff'd mem., 420 U.S. 958 (1975) (seven-year residency requirement for state senatorial candidate), and in Chimento v. Stark, 353 F. Supp. 1211 (D.N.H.) (three-judge court), aff'd mem., 414 U.S. 802 (1973) (seven-year requirement for gubernatorial candidates). See Note, Developments in the Law — Elections, 88 Harv. L. Rev. 1111, 1225-1230 (1975).

For other decisions upholding durational residency requirements, see Sosna v. Iowa, 419 U.S. 393 (1975) (one-year residency requirement for filing divorce petition); Suffling v. Bondurant, 339 F. Supp. 257 (D.N.M.) (three-judge court), aff'd mem. sub nom. Rose v. Bondurant, 409 U.S. 1020 (1972) (six-month requirement for admission to the bar).

Section B. PROTECTION OF THE LOCAL ECONOMY AND WELFARE

1. State Restrictions on Marketing of Extrastate Goods

Welton v. Missouri 91 U.S. 275, 23 L. Ed. 347 (1876)

[Writ of error to the Supreme Court of Missouri. Plaintiff in error was convicted of dealing as a peddler without the license required by Missouri statute, and was fined fifty dollars. The judgment was affirmed by the state Supreme Court, 55 Mo. 288.]

MR. JUSTICE FIELD delivered the opinion of the court: . . .

The statute, under which the conviction was had, declares that whoever deals in the sale of goods, wares or merchandise, except books, charts, maps and stationery, which are not the growth, produce or manufacture of the State, by going from place to place to sell the same, shall be deemed a peddler; and then enacts that no person shall deal as a peddler without a license, and prescribes the rates of charge for the licenses, these varying according to the manner in which the business is conducted, whether by the party carrying the goods himself on foot, or by the use of beasts of burden, or by carts or other land carriage, or by boats or other river vessels. Penalties are imposed for dealing without the license prescribed. No license is required for selling in a similar way, by going from place to place in the State, goods which are the growth, product, or manufacture of the State.

The license charge exacted is sought to be maintained as a tax upon a calling. It was held to be such a tax by the Supreme Court of the State; a calling, says the court, which is limited to the sale of merchandise not the growth or product of the State.

The general power of the State to impose taxes in the way of licenses upon all pursuits and occupations within its limits is admitted, but, like all other powers, must be exercised in subordination to the requirements of the Federal Constitution. Where the business or occupation consists in the sale of goods, the license tax required for its pursuit is, in effect, a tax upon the goods themselves. If such a tax be within the power of the State to levy, it matters not whether it be raised directly from the goods, or indirectly from them through the license to the dealer; but, if such tax conflict with any power vested in Congress by the Constitution of the United States, it will not be any less invalid because enforced through the form of a personal license.

In the case of Brown v. Md., 12 Wheat. 425, 444, the question arose, whether an Act of the Legislature of Maryland, requiring importers of foreign goods to pay the State a license tax before selling them in the form and condition in which they were imported, was valid and constitutional. . . . Treating the exaction of the license tax from the importer as a tax on the goods imported, the court held that the Act of Maryland was in conflict with the Constitution; with the clause prohibiting a State, without the consent of Congress, from laying any impost or duty on imports or exports; and with the clause investing Congress with the power to regulate commerce with foreign nations.

So, in like manner, the license tax exacted by the State of Missouri from dealers in goods which are not the product or manufacture of the State, before they can be sold from place to place within the State, must be regarded as a tax upon such goods themselves; and the question presented is, whether legislation, thus discriminating against the products of other States in the conditions of their sale by a certain class of dealers, is valid under the Constitution of the United States. . . .

The power which insures uniformity of commercial regulation must cover the property which is transported as an article of commerce from hostile or interfering legislation, until it has mingled with and become a part of the general property of the country, and subjected like it to similar protection, and to no greater burdens. If, at any time before it has thus become incorporated into the mass of property of the State or nation, it can be subjected to any restrictions by state legislation, the object of investing the control in Congress may be entirely defeated. If Missouri can require a license tax for the sale by traveling dealers of goods which are the growth, product or manufacture of other States or countries, it may require such license tax as a condition of their sale from ordinary merchants, and the amount of the tax will be a matter resting exclusively in its discretion.

The power of the State to exact a license tax of any amount being admitted, no authority would remain in the United States or in this court to control its action, however unreasonable or oppressive. Imposts operating as an absolute exclusion of the goods would be possible, and all the evils of discriminating state legislation, favorable to the interests of one State and injurious to the interests of other States and countries, which existed previous to the adoption of the Constitution, might follow, and the experience of the last fifteen years shows would follow, from the action of some of the States.

There is a difficulty, it is true, in all cases of this character, in drawing the line precisely where the commercial power of Congress ends and the power of the State begins. A similar difficulty was felt by this court, in Brown v. Maryland in drawing the line of distinction between the restriction upon the power of the States to lay a duty on imports, and their acknowledged power to tax persons and property; but the court observed, that the two, though quite distinguishable when they do not approach each other, may yet, like the intervening colors between white and black approach so nearly as to perplex the understanding, as colors perplex the vision in marking the distinction between them; but that, as the distinction exists, it must be marked as the cases arose. And the court, after observing that it might be premature to state any rule as being universal in its application, held that when the importer had so acted upon the thing imported that it had become incorporated and mixed up with the mass of property in the country, it had lost its distinctive character as an import and become subject to the taxing power of the State; but that, while remaining the property of the importer in his warehouse in the original form and package in which it was imported, the tax upon it was plainly a duty on imports prohibited by the Constitution.

Following the guarded language of the court in that case, we observe here, as was observed there, that it would be premature to state any rule which would be universal in its application to determine when the commercial power of the Federal Government over a commodity has ceased, and the power of the State has commenced. It is sufficient to hold now that the commercial power continues until the commodity has ceased to be the subject of discriminating legislation by reason of its foreign character. That power protects it, even after it has entered the State, from any burdens imposed by reason of its foreign origin. The Act of Missouri encroaches upon this power in this respect and is, therefore, in our judgment, unconstitutional and void.

The fact that Congress has not seen fit to prescribe any specific rules to govern interstate commerce does not affect the question. Its inaction on this subject, when considered with reference to its legislation with respect to foreign commerce, is equivalent to a declaration that interstate commerce shall be free and untrammeled. As the main object of that commerce is the sale and exchange of commodities, the policy thus established would be defeated by discriminating legislation like that of Missouri. . . .

The judgment of the Supreme Court of the State of Missouri must be reversed. . . .

Robbins v. Shelby County Taxing District 120 U.S. 489, 7 S. Ct. 592, 30 L. Ed. 694 (1887)

MR. JUSTICE BRADLEY delivered the opinion of the court:

This case originated in the following manner: Sabine Robbins, the plaintiff in error, in February, 1884, was engaged at the City of Memphis, in the State of Tennessee, in soliciting the sale of goods for the firm of Rose, Robbins & Co., of Cincinnati, in the state of Ohio, dealers in paper, and other articles of stationery, and exhibited samples for the purpose of effecting such sales, — an employment usually denominated as that of a "drummer." There was in force at that time a Statute of Tennessee, relating to the subject of taxation in the taxing districts of the State, applicable, however, only to the Taxing District of Shelby County (formerly the City of Memphis), by which it was enacted, amongst other things, that "All drummers, and all persons not having a regular licensed house of business in the Taxing District, offering for sale or selling goods, wares, or merchandise therein, by sample, shall be required to pay to the county trustee the sum of ten dollars ($10) per week, or twenty-five dollars per month, for such privilege; and no license shall be issued for a longer period than three months." Act of 1881, chap. 96, § 16.

The business of selling by sample and nearly sixty other occupations had been by law declared to be privileges, and were taxed as such, and it was made a misdemeanor, punishable by a fine of not less than $5 nor more than $50, to exercise any of such occupations without having first paid the tax or obtained the license required therefor.

Under this law Robbins, who had not paid the tax nor taken a license, was prosecuted, convicted and sentenced to pay a fine of $10, together with the state and county tax, and costs; and on appeal to the Supreme Court of the State, the judgment was affirmed [13 Lea 303]. This writ of error is brought to review the judgment of the supreme court, on the ground that the law imposing the tax was repugnant to that clause of the Constitution of the United States which declares that Congress shall have power to regulate commerce among the several States. . . .

That is the question before us, and it is one of great importance to the people of the United States, both as it respects their business interests and their constitutional rights. It is presented in a nutshell, and does not, at this day, require for its solution any great elaboration of argument or review of authorities. Certain principles have been already established by the decisions of this court, which will conduct us to a satisfactory decision. Among those principles are the following: . . .

It is . . . an established principle, as already indicated, that the only way in which commerce between the States can be legitimately affected by state laws is when, by virtue of its police power, and its jurisdiction over persons and property within its limits, a State provides for the security of the lives, limbs, health and comfort of persons and the protection of property; or when it does those things which may otherwise incidentally affect commerce, such as the establishment and regulation of highways, canals, railroads, wharves, ferries and other commercial facilities; the passage of inspection laws to secure the due quality and measure of products and commodities; the passage of laws to regulate or restrict the sale of articles deemed injurious to the health or morals of the community; the imposition of taxes upon persons residing within the State or belonging to its population, and upon avocations and employments pursued therein, not directly connected with foreign or interstate commerce or with some other employment or business exercised under authority of the Constitution and laws of the United States; and the imposition of taxes upon all property within the State, mingled with and forming part of the great mass of property therein. But in making such internal regulations a State cannot impose taxes upon persons passing through the State, or coming into it merely for a temporary purpose, especially if connected with interstate or foreign commerce; nor can it impose such taxes upon property imported into the State from abroad, or from another State, and not yet become part of the common mass of property therein; and no discrimination can be made, by any such regulations, adversely to the persons or property of other States; and no regulations can be made directly affecting interstate commerce. Any taxation or regulation of the latter character would be an unauthorized interference with the power given to Congress over the subject. . . .

In a word, it may be said that in the matter of interstate commerce the United States are but one country, and are and must be subject to one system of regulations, and not to a multitude of systems. The doctrine of the freedom of that commerce, except as regulated by Congress, is so firmly established that it is unnecessary to enlarge further upon the subject.

In view of these fundamental principles, which are to govern our decision, we may approach the question submitted to us in the present case, and inquire whether it is competent for a State to levy a tax or impose any other restriction upon the citizens or inhabitants of other States, for selling or seeking to sell their goods in such State before they are introduced therein. Do not such restrictions affect the very foundation of interstate trade? How is a manufacturer, or a merchant, of one State, to sell his goods in another State, without, in some way, obtaining orders therefor? Must he be compelled to send them at a venture, without knowing whether there is any demand for them? This may, undoubtedly, be safely done with regard to some products for which there is always a market and a demand, or where the course of trade has established a general and unlimited demand. A raiser of farm produce in New Jersey or Connecticut, or a manufacturer of leather or wooden ware, may perhaps safely take his goods to the City of New York and be sure of finding a stable and reliable market for them. But there are hundreds, perhaps thousands, of articles which no person would think of exporting to another State without first procuring an order for them. It is true, a merchant or manufacturer in one State may erect or hire a warehouse or store in another State, in which to place his goods, and await the chances of being able to sell them. But this would require a warehouse or a store in every State with which he might desire to trade.

Surely, he cannot be compelled to take this inconvenient and expensive course. In certain branches of business, it may be adopted with advantage. Many manufacturers do open houses or places of business in other States than those in which they reside, and send their goods there to be kept on sale. But this is a matter of convenience, and not of compulsion, and would neither suit the convenience nor be within the ability of many others engaged in the same kind of business, and would be entirely unsuited to many branches of business. In these cases, then, what shall the merchant or manufacturer do, who wishes to sell his goods in other States? Must he sit still in his factory or warehouse, and wait for the people of those States to come to him? This would be a silly and ruinous proceeding.

The only other way, and the one, perhaps, which most extensively prevails, is to obtain orders from persons residing or doing business in those other States. But how is the merchant or manufacturer to secure such orders. If he may be taxed by such States for doing so, who shall limit the tax? It may amount to prohibition. To say that such a tax is not a burden upon interstate commerce is to speak at least unadvisedly and without due attention to the truth of things. . . .

To deny to the State the power to lay the tax, or require the license in question, will not, in any perceptible degree, diminish its resources or its just power of taxation. It is very true that if the goods when sold were in the State, and part of its general mass of property, they would be liable to taxation; but then brought into the State in consequence of the sale they will be equally liable; so that, in the end, the State will derive just as much revenue from them as if they were there before the sale. As soon as the goods are in the State and become part of its general mass of property, they will become liable to be taxed in the same manner as other property of similar character, as was distinctly held by this court in the case of Brown v. Houston, 114 U.S. 622. When goods are sent from one State to another for sale, or, in consequence of a sale, they become part of its general property, and amenable to its laws; provided that no discrimination be made against them *as* goods from another State, and that they be not taxed by reason of being brought from another State, but only taxed in the usual way as other goods are. Brown v. Houston, qua supra; Machine Co. v. Gage, 100 U.S. 676. But to tax the sale of such goods, or the offer to sell them, before they are brought into the State, is a very different thing, and seems to us clearly a tax on interstate commerce itself.

It is strongly urged, s if it were a material point in the case, that no discrimination is made between domestic and foreign drummers — those of Tennessee and those of other States; that all are taxed alike. But that does not meet the difficulty. Interstate commerce cannot be taxed at all, even though the same amount of tax should be laid on domestic commerce, or that which is carried on solely within the State. This was decided in the case of The State Freight Tax Cases [15 Wall. 232]. The negotiation of sales of goods which are in another State, for the purpose of introducing them into the State in which the negotiation is made, is interstate commerce. A New Orleans merchant cannot be taxed there for ordering goods from London or New York, because, in the one case, it is an act of foreign, and, in the other, of interstate commerce, both of which are subject to regulation by Congress alone.

It would not be difficult, however, to show that the tax authorized by the State of Tennessee in the present case is discriminative against the merchants and manufacturers of other States. They can only sell their goods in Memphis by the employment of drummers and by means of samples; whilst the merchants and manufacturers of Memphis, having regular licensed houses of business there, have no occasion for such agents; and if they had, they are not subject to any tax therefor. They are taxed for their licensed houses, it is true; but so, it is presumable, are the merchants and manufacturers of other States in the places where they reside; and the tax on drummers operates greatly to their disadvantage in comparison with the merchants and manufacturers of Memphis. And such was undoubtedly one of its objects. This kind of taxation is usually imposed at the instance and solicitation of domestic dealers, as a means of protecting them from foreign competition.

And in many cases there may be some reason in their desire for such protection. But this shows in a still stronger light the unconstitutionality of the tax. It shows that it not only operates as a restriction upon interstate commerce, but that it is intended to have that effect as one of its principal objects. And if a State can, in this way, impose restrictions upon interstate commerce for the benefit and protection of its own citizens, we are brought back to the condition of things which existed before the adoption of the Constitution, and which was one of the principal causes that led to it.

If the selling of goods by sample and the employment of drummers for that purpose, injuriously affect the local interest of the States, Congress, if applied to, will undoubtedly make such reasonable regulations as the case may demand. And Congress alone can do it; for it is obvious that such regulations should be based on a uniform system applicable to the whole country, and not left to the varied, discordant or retaliatory enactments of forty different States. The confusion into which the commerce of the country would be thrown by being subject to state legislation on this subject, would be but a repetition of the disorder which prevailed under the Articles of Confederation.

To say that the tax, if invalid as against drummers, from other States, operates as a discrimination against the drummers of Tennessee, against whom it is conceded to be valid, is no argument; because the State is not bound to tax its own drummers; and if it does so whilst having no power to tax those of other States, it acts of its own free will, and is itself the author of such discrimination. As before said, the State may tax its own internal commerce; but that does not give it any right to tax interstate commerce.

The judgment of the Supreme Court of Tennessee is reversed, and the plaintiff in error must be discharged.

Mr. Chief Justice Waite, dissenting:

I am unable to agree to this judgment. . . .

The license fee is demanded for the privilege of selling goods by sample within the Taxing District. The fee is exacted from all alike who do that kind of business, unless they have "a licensed house of business" in the District. There is no discrimination between citizens of the State and citizens of other States. The tax is upon the business, and this I have always understood to be lawful, whether the business was carried on by a citizen of the State under whose authority the exaction was made, or a citizen of another State, unless there was discrimination against citizens of other States. . . .

This case shows the need of such authority in the States. The Taxing District is situated on the western boundary of Tennessee. To get into another State it is only necessary to cross the Mississippi River to Arkansas. It may be said to be an historical fact that the charter of Memphis was abolished and the Taxing District established because of the oppressive debt of Memphis, and the records of this court furnish abundant evidence of the heavy taxation to which property and business within the limits of both the old corporation and the new have been for many years necessarily subjected. Merchants in Tennessee are by law required to pay taxes on the amount of their stocks on hand and a privilege tax besides. Under these circumstances it is easy to see that if a merchant from another State could carry on a business in the District by sending his agents there with samples of his goods to secure orders for deliveries from his stock at home, he would enjoy a privilege of exemption from taxation which the local merchant would not have unless in some form he could be subjected to taxation for what he did in the locality. The same would be true in respect to all inhabitants of the State who were sellers by sample in this District, but who had no place of business there. And so they, like citizens of other States, were required to pay for the privilege. Thus all were treated alike, whether they were citizens of Tennessee or of some other State, and under these circumstances I can see no constitutional objection to such a taxation of citizens of the other States for their business in the District. . . .

Mr. Justice Field and Mr. Justice Gray concur in this dissent.

WAGNER v. CITY OF COVINGTON, 251 U.S. 95, 40 S. Ct. 93, 64 L. Ed. 157 (1919). Pitney, J. : "This was an action brought by plaintiffs in error in a state court of Kentucky against the city of Covington, a municipal corporation of that state, to recover license fees theretofore paid by them under certain ordinances of the city for the conduct of their business in Covington, and to enjoin the enforcement against them of a later ordinance calling for further like payments. The several ordinances . . . required all persons carrying on certain specified businesses in the city to take out licenses and pay license fees; among others, the business of wholesale dealer in what are known as 'soft drinks.' Plaintiffs were and are manufacturers of such drinks, having their factory and bottling works in the city of Cincinnati, in the state of Ohio, on the opposite side of the Ohio river from Covington. They . . . carry on the business of selling in Covington soft drinks, the product of their manufacture, in the following manner: They have a list of retail dealers in Covington to whom they have been and are in the habit of making sales; two or three times a week a wagon or other vehicle owned by plaintiffs is loaded at the factory in Cincinnati and sent across the river to Covington, and calls upon the retail dealers mentioned, many of whom have been for years on plaintiffs' list and have purchased their goods under a general understanding that plaintiffs' vehicle would call occasionally and furnish them with such soft drinks as they might need or desire to purchase from plaintiffs; when a customer's place of business is reached by the vehicle the driver goes into the storeroom and either asks or looks to see what amount of drinks is needed or wanted; he then goes out to the vehicle and brings from it the necessary quantity, which he carries into the store and delivers to the customer; upon his trips to Covington he always carries sufficient drinks to meet the probable demands of the customers, based on past experience; but, with the exception of occasional small amounts carried for delivery in response to particular orders previously received at plaintiffs' place of business in Cincinnati, all sales in Covington are made from the vehicle by the driver in the manner mentioned. Sometimes the driver succeeds in selling there the entire supply thus carried upon the wagon, sometimes only a part thereof; or he may return after having made but a few sales, or none at all; in which event he carries the unsold supply back to plaintiffs' place of business in Cincinnati. . . ."

What decision? Why?[b]

BEST & CO. v. MAXWELL, 311 U.S. 454, 61 S. Ct. 334, 85 L. Ed. 275 (1940). Reed, J.: "Appellant, a New York retail merchandise establishment, rented a display room in a North Carolina hotel for several days during February, 1938, and took orders for goods corresponding to samples; it filled the orders by shipping direct to the customers from New York City. Before using the room appellant paid under protest the tax required by chapter 127, §121(e), of the North Carolina Laws of 1937, which levies an annual privilege tax of $250 on every person or corporation, not a regular retail merchant in the state, who displays samples in any hotel room rented or occupied temporarily for the purpose of securing retail orders. Appellant not being a regular retail merchant of North Carolina admittedly comes within the statute. Asserting, however, that the tax was unconstitutional, especially in view of the commerce clause, it brought this suit for a refund. . . ."

What decision? Why?

NOTE

A "long line of drummer cases" following Robbins v. Shelby County Taxing District, page 354 supra, also includes decisions involving the licensing of door-to-door salesmen selling, by sample, goods to be delivered from beyond the state. See Real Silk Hosiery Mills v. Portland, 268 U.S. 325 (1925), where the Court, citing the Robbins decision, enjoined the enforcement of a local ordinance requiring a $12.50 quarterly license fee and the deposit of a bond in the sum of $500 from every person going from place to place taking orders for goods for future delivery, and receiving payment or any deposit of money in advance. Compare DiSanto v. Pennsylvania, 273 U.S. 34 (1927), and California v. Thompson, 313 U.S. 109 (1941).

Nippert v. Richmond, 327 U.S. 416 (1946), was a prosecution for having engaged in the business of a solicitor in the city of Richmond, Virginia, without having previously procured the license required by local ordinance. The fee for such a license was a minimum of $50 annually. The appellant had been soliciting orders for garments to be shipped to Richmond purchasers by her employer in Washington, D.C. The city argued

---

[b] Cf. Dalton Adding Mach. Co. v. Virginia, 246 U.S. 498 (1918). See Hollander, Nineteenth Century Anti-Drummer Legislation in the United States, 38 Business History Rev. 479 (1964). — ED.

that an intervening decision with reference to sales taxes (McGoldrick v. Berwind-White Coal Mining Co., page 565 infra) required the overruling of the series of decisions extending from Robbins v. Shelby County through Real Silk v. Portland. Mr. Justice Rutledge, writing for the majority of the Court, pointed out that in the sales tax case the drummer cases had been differentiated because the license taxes there involved "in their practical operation worked discriminatorily against interstate commerce to impose upon it a burden, either in fact or by the very threat of its incidence, which they did not place upon the competing local business." He pointed out that the operations of the door-to-door salesman in a given city were typically "casual, spasmodic and irregular," and that appellant was shown to have operated in Richmond for only four days. In contrast with a sales tax, he stressed the fact that the license fee was exacted in advance of operations and bore no relation to the volume of business done, and emphasized the exclusionary effect of this upon the small and irregular operator moving from city to city. In reversing the judgment, he concluded: "The tax here in question inherently involves too many probabilities, and we think actualities, for exclusion of or discrimination against interstate commerce, in favor of local competing business, to be sustained in any application substantially similar to the present one. . . . Provincial interests and local political power are at their maximum weight in bringing about this type of legislation. With the forces behind it, this is the very kind of barrier the commerce clause was put in the fundamental law to guard against."

Justices Black, Douglas, and Murphy dissented. Mr. Justice Douglas, in his dissenting opinion, wrote: "It [the ordinance] treats a solicitor for a Virginia manufacturer exactly the same as it treats solicitors for manufacturers located in other states. . . . The problem, however, does not end there. . . . In the present case the tax on Nippert may or may not, in practical operation, work to the disadvantage of this interstate business. It would be one thing if Nippert's business took her from town to town throughout the State. But, so far as we know, Nippert may be a resident of Richmond working exclusively there, full or part time. In that event, we could not determine the issue of discrimination without knowing what taxes the retail merchants in Richmond must pay. If the facts were known, it might appear that the tax, now struck down, in fact resulted in parity of treatment between Nippert and her local competitors. The record does not enlighten us on any of these matters. I think that one who complains that a state tax, though not discriminatory on its face, discriminates against interstate commerce in its actual operation should be required to come forward with proof to sustain the charge. . . ."

Memphis Steam Laundry Cleaner, Inc. v. Stone 342 U.S. 389, 72 S. Ct. 424, 96 L. Ed. 436 (1952)

Mr. Chief Justice Vinson delivered the opinion of the Court.

The question before us is whether a Mississippi tax laid upon the privilege of soliciting business for a laundry not licensed in that State infringes the Commerce Clause.

Appellant operates a laundry and cleaning establishment in Memphis, Tennessee. In serving the area surrounding Memphis, appellant sends ten of its trucks into eight Mississippi counties where its drivers pick up, deliver and collect for laundry and cleaning and seek to acquire new customers. Appellee, who is Chairman of the State Tax Commission of the State of Mississippi, demanded that appellant pay $500 under the following provisions of the Mississippi "state-wide privilege tax law of 1944":

"Sec. 3. Every person desiring to engage in any business, or exercise any privilege hereafter specified shall first, before commencing same, apply for, pay for, and procure from the state tax commissioner or commissioner of insurance, a privilege license authorizing him to engage in the business or exercise the privilege specified therein, and the amount of tax shown in the following sections is hereby imposed for the privilege of engaging or continuing in the business set out therein.

"SEC. 45. Upon each person doing business as a transient vendor, or dealer, as defined in this section, and upon which a privilege tax is not specifically imposed by another section of this act, a tax for each county according to the following schedules: . . .

"(t) Upon each person soliciting business for a laundry not licensed in this state as such, in each county . . . $50.00 . . .

"(y) Provided however, that where any person subject to the payment of the tax imposed in this section, makes use of more than one vehicle in carrying on such business, the tax herein imposed shall be paid on each vehicle used in carrying on such business."

After paying the $500 tax as demanded to prevent arrest of its drivers and seizure of its ten trucks, appellant sued for refund in a state court, claiming that the Mississippi tax act was not applicable to its operations and that, if so applied, the tax would violate the Commerce Clause. Judgment was entered for appellant in the trial court but the Mississippi Supreme Court reversed, holding that appellant's drivers were "transient vendors or dealers" within the meaning of the statute and that application of the tax to appellant did not conflict with the Commerce Clause. The case is here on appeal. 28 U.S.C. (Supp. IV) § 1257(2).

In passing upon the validity of a state tax challenged under the Commerce Clause, we first look to the "operating incidence" of the tax. The Mississippi Act requires a "privilege license" and imposes a "privilege tax" upon appellant's employees "soliciting business." The Mississippi Supreme Court described the tax as follows:

". . . The tax involved here is not a tax on interstate commerce, but a tax on a person soliciting business for a laundry not licensed in this state, a local activity which applies to residents and non-residents alike."

The State may determine for itself the operating incidence of its tax. But it is for this Court to determine whether the tax, as construed by the highest court of the State, is or is not "a tax on interstate commerce."

It would appear from portions of the opinion of the court below that the tax is laid upon the privilege of soliciting interstate business on the theory that solicitation of customers for interstate commerce is a local activity subject to state taxation. However, the opinion below may also be read as construing the statutory term "soliciting" more broadly, thereby resting the tax upon appellant's activities apart from soliciting new customers in Mississippi, namely the pick up and delivery of laundry and cleaning on regular routes within the State. Each construction of the statute raises different considerations. But clarification of the operating incidence of the tax is not required for disposition of this case since we find that the tax violates the Commerce Clause under either reading of the statute.

I

In the long line of "drummer" cases, beginning with Robbins v. Shelby County Taxing District, 120 U.S. 489 (1887), this Court has held that a tax imposed upon the solicitation of interstate business is a tax upon interstate commerce itself. Whether or not solicitation of interstate business may be regarded as a local incident of interstate commerce, the Court has not permitted state taxation to carve out this incident from the integral economic process of interstate commerce. As the Court noted last term in a case involving door-to-door solicitation of interstate business, "Interstate commerce itself knocks on the local door."

If the Mississippi tax is imposed upon the privilege of soliciting interstate business, the tax stands on no better footing than a tax upon the privilege of doing interstate business. A tax so imposed cannot stand under the Commerce Clause. Spector Motor Service v. O'Connor, 340 U.S. 602, 608-609 (1951), and cases cited therein.

II

On the assumption that the tax is imposed upon appellant's Mississippi activities of picking up and delivering laundry and cleaning, the "peddler" cases are invoked in support of the tax. Under that line of decisions, this Court has sustained state taxation upon itinerant hawkers and peddlers on the ground that the local sale and delivery of goods is an essentially intrastate process whether a retailer operates from a fixed location or from a wagon. However, assuming for the purposes of this case that Mississippi imposes its $50 per truck tax only upon the privilege of conducting intrastate activities, the tax must be held invalid as one discriminating against interstate commerce.

The $50 per truck tax is applicable only to vehicles used by a person "soliciting business for a laundry *not licensed in this state as such*." (Emphasis supplied.) Laundries licensed in Mississippi pay a fixed fee to the municipality in which located, plus a tax of $8 per truck upon each truck used in other municipalities.[14] As a result, if appellant "solicits" business in a Mississippi municipality, it must pay a tax of $50 per truck while a competitor located in another Mississippi locality must pay a tax of only $8 per truck. The "peddler" cases are inapposite under such a showing of discrimination since they support state taxation only where no discrimination against interstate commerce appears either upon the face of the tax laws or in their practical operation.

To sum up, we hold that the tax before us infringes the Commerce Clause under either interpretation of the operating incidence of the tax. The Commerce Clause created the nation-wide area of free trade essential to this country's economic welfare by removing state lines as impediments to intercourse between the states. The tax imposed in this case made the Mississippi state line into a local obstruction to the flow of interstate commerce that cannot stand under the Commerce Clause.

Reversed.

MR. JUSTICE BLACK dissents.

NOTE

1. Is it significant that the "solicitation of interstate business" which the Court mentioned in Part I of its opinion was with respect to a service industry, i.e., the processing of goods originating in Mississippi, laundered or cleaned in Tennessee, and redelivered in Mississippi? Cf. Department of Treasury v. Ingram-Richardson Mfg. Co., 313 U.S. 252 (1941).

2. Clarksdale, Miss. (pop. 16,539 (1950 census) — a municipality of class 2), is roughly midway between Greenville, Miss. (pop. 29,936 (1950 census) — a municipality of class 1), and Memphis. The Court, in Part II of its opinion, appears to deal with this case as though it involved, for example, a truck from a Memphis laundry competing for business in Clarksdale with a truck from a Greenville laundry. The record, however, does not establish what, if any, competition the trucks from the Memphis laundry were meeting. Would it make a difference if a laundry truck from Memphis was competing only with a Clarksdale laundry in Clarksdale? Cf. Caskey Baking Co. v. Virginia, 313 U.S. 117 (1941). What if a single truck from the Memphis laundry solicited business in some Mississippi towns with only local laundry competition and in some where there was com-

---

[14] Laws of Mississippi, 1944, c. 137, §110, imposes the following tax:
Upon each person operating a laundry other than a hand laundry, as follows:

In municipalities of class 1	$120.00
In municipalities of class 2	80.00
In municipalities of classes 3 and 4	60.00
In municipalities of classes 5, 6, 7 and elsewhere in the county	32.00
Upon each truck or other vehicle for such laundry in a municipality other than where the laundry is located	8.00

petition with trucks from laundries located in other Mississippi towns? Should these and other possibilities have affected the Court's order, absent a clarification of the situation? Note the opinion below, 53 So.2d 89 (Miss. 1951). Compare West Point Wholesale Grocery Co. v. Opelika, 354 U.S. 390 (1957). Opelika, Alabama, imposed an annual privilege tax of $250 on any wholesale grocery firm delivering within the city from points outside (in or out of Alabama). Appellant, a Georgia company, solicited and delivered in Opelika. Local Opelika companies were taxed at a graduated rate on gross receipts; to reach a tax of $250 such a company would have to gross $280,000 in sales for the year. The tax on appellant was held invalid. Taking this case with the Memphis Laundry case, may it be said that the Commerce Clause requires a kind of most-favored-nation treatment for out-of-state enterprise?

3. In Dunbar-Stanley Studios, Inc. v. Alabama, 393 U.S. 537 (1969), the Court upheld a license tax imposed upon a "transient or traveling photographer" in the sum of $5 per week for each county, town, or city in which he plied his trade. Upon a photographer operating at "a fixed location" a license tax was imposed at an annual rate varying from $25 in large cities to $3 in communities of less than 1000 residents. The taxpayer had its principal office and processing plant in North Carolina. It sent photographers several times a year for periods of two to five days to take photographs in the units of a department-store chain operating in eight Alabama cities, as requested by the managers of the stores. Customers dealt with the management of the store at which a photograph was taken, and taxpayer was paid a percentage of the receipts. Exposed film was shipped to North Carolina for processing, and the finished photograph was shipped from there to the originating store for delivery to the customer.

Minnesota v. Barber   136 U.S. 313, 10 S. Ct. 862, 34 L. Ed. 455 (1890)

MR. JUSTICE HARLAN delivered the opinion of the court.

Henry E. Barber, the appellee, was convicted before a justice of the peace in Ramsey County, Minnesota, of the offense of having wrongfully and unlawfully offered and exposed for sale, and of having sold, for human food, one hundred pounds of fresh uncured beef, part of an animal slaughtered in the State of Illinois, but which had not been inspected in Minnesota, and "certified" before slaughter by an inspector appointed under the laws of the latter State. Having been committed to the common jail of the county pursuant to a judgment of imprisonment for the term of thirty days, he sued out a writ of habeas corpus. . . .

From the judgment discharging Barber the State has prosecuted the present appeal. Rev. Stat. §764; 23 Stat. 437, chap. 353. . . .

The Statute of Minnesota upon the validity of which the decision of the case depends is as follows:

"An Act for the Protection of the Public Health by Providing for Inspection before Slaughter of Cattle, Sheep and Swine Designed for Slaughter for Human Food. . . .

"SEC. 3. It shall be the duty of the inspectors appointed hereunder to inspect all cattle, sheep and swine slaughtered for human food within their respective jurisdictions within twenty-four hours before the slaughter of the same, and, if found healthy and in suitable condition to be slaughtered for human food, to give to the applicant a certificate in writing to that effect. If found unfit for food by reason of infectious disease, such inspectors shall order the immediate removal and destruction of such diseased animals, and no liability for damages shall accrue by reason of such action.

"SEC. 4. Any person who shall sell, expose or offer for sale for human food in this State any fresh beef, veal, mutton, lamb or pork whatsoever, which has not been taken from an animal inspected and certified before slaughter by the proper local inspector appointed

Section B. Protection of Local Economy and Welfare

hereunder, shall be deemed guilty of a misdemeanor, and upon conviction thereof shall be punished by a fine of not more than one hundred dollars, or by imprisonment not exceeding three months, for each offense. . . ."

The presumption that this Statute was enacted, in good faith, for the purpose expressed in the title, namely, to protect the health of the people of Minnesota, cannot control the final determination of the question whether it is not repugnant to the Constitution of the United States. There may be no purpose upon the part of a Legislature to violate the provisions of that instrument, and yet a statute enacted by it, under the forms of law, may by its necessary operation, be destructive of rights granted or secured by the Constitution. In such cases, the courts must sustain the supreme law of the land by declaring the Statute unconstitutional and void. . . .

Underlying the entire argument in behalf of the State is the proposition that it is impossible to tell, by an inspection of fresh beef, veal, mutton, lamb or pork, designed for human food, whether or not it came from animals that were diseased when slaughtered; that inspection on the hoof, within a very short time before animals are slaughtered, is the only mode by which their condition can be ascertained with certainty. And it is insisted, with great confidence, that of this fact the court must take judicial notice. If a fact, alleged to exist, and upon which the rights of parties depend, is within common experience and knowledge, it is one of which the courts will take judicial notice. [Citations omitted.] But we cannot assent to the suggestion that the fact alleged in this case to exist is of that class. It may be the opinion of some that the presence of disease in animals, at the time of their being slaughtered, cannot be determined by inspection of the meat taken from them; but we are not aware that such is the view universally, or even generally, entertained. But if, as alleged, the inspection of fresh beef, veal, mutton, lamb or pork will not necessarily show whether the animal from which it was taken was diseased when slaughtered, it would not follow that a statute like the one before us is within the constitutional power of the State to enact. On the contrary, the enactment of a similar statute by each one of the States composing the Union would result in the destruction of commerce among the several States, so far as such commerce is involved in the transportation from one part of the country to another of animal meats designed for human food, and entirely free from disease. A careful examination of the Minnesota Act will place this construction of it beyond question.

. . . As the inspection must take place within the twenty-four hours immediately before the slaughtering, the Act, by its necessary operation, excludes from the Minnesota market, practically, all fresh beef, veal, mutton, lamb or pork — in whatever form, and although entirely sound, healthy and fit for human food — taken from animals slaughtered in other States; and directly tends to restrict the slaughtering of animals, whose meat is to be sold in Minnesota for human food, to those engaged in such business in that State. This must be so, because the time, expense and labor of sending animals from points outside of Minnesota to points in that State to be there inspected, and bringing them back, after inspection, to be slaughtered at the place from which they were sent — the slaughtering to take place within twenty-four hours after inspection, else the certificate of inspection becomes of no value — will be so great as to amount to an absolute prohibition upon sales, in Minnesota, of meat from animals not slaughtered within its limits. When to this is added the fact that the Statute, by its necessary operation, prohibits the sale, in the State, of fresh beef, veal, mutton, lamb or pork, from animals that may have been inspected carefully and thoroughly in the State where they were slaughtered, and before they were slaughtered, no doubt can remain as to its effect upon commerce among the several States. It will not do to say — certainly no judicial tribunal can, with propriety, assume — that the people of Minnesota may not, with regard to their health, rely upon inspections in other States of animals there slaughtered for purposes of human food. If the object of the Statute had been to deny altogether to the citizens of other States the privilege of selling, within the limits of Minnesota, for human food, any fresh beef, veal, mutton, lamb or pork, from animals slaughtered outside of that State, and to compel the people of Minnesota, wishing to buy such meats, either to purchase those taken from animals inspected and slaughtered in the State, or to incur the cost of purchasing them, when desired for their own domestic use, at points beyond the State, that object is attained by the Act in question. Our duty to maintain the Constitution will not permit us to shut our eyes to these obvious and necessary results of the Minnesota Statute. If this legislation does not make such discrimination against the products and business of other States in favor of the products and business of Minnesota, as interferes with and burdens commerce among the several States, it would be difficult to enact legislation that would have that result. . . .

The learned counsel for the State relies with confidence upon Patterson v. Kentucky, 97 U.S. 501, as supporting the principles for which he contends. In that case we sustained the constitutionality of a Statute of Kentucky, forbidding the sale within that Commonwealth of oils or fluids used for illuminating purposes, and the product of coal, petroleum or other bituminous substances, that would ignite at less than a certain temperature. Having a patent from the United States for an improved burning oil, Patterson claimed the right, by virtue of his patent, to sell anywhere in the United States the oil described in it, without regard to the Inspection Laws of any State, enacted to protect the public safety. It was held that the Statute of Kentucky was a mere police regulation, embodying the deliberate judgment of that Commonwealth that burning fluids, the product of coal, petroleum or other bituminous substances, which would ignite or permanently burn at less than a prescribed temperature, are unsafe for illuminating purposes. . . . There is no real analogy between that case and the one before us. The Kentucky Statute prescribed no test of inspection which, in view of the nature of the property, was either unusual or unreasonable, or which by its necessary operation discriminated against any particular oil because of the locality of its production. If it had prescribed a mode of inspection to which citizens of other States, having oils designed for illuminating purposes, and which they desired to sell in the Kentucky market, could not have reasonably conformed, it would undoubtedly have been held to be an unauthorized burden upon interstate commerce. Looking at the nature of the property to which the Kentucky Statute had reference, there was no difficulty in the way of the patentee of the particular oil there in question submitting to the required local inspection.

But a law providing for the inspection of animals whose meats are designed for human food cannot be regarded as a rightful exertion of the police powers of the State, if the inspection prescribed is of such a character, or is burdened with such conditions, as will prevent altogether the introduction into the State of sound meats, the product of animals slaughtered in other States. It is one thing for a State to exclude from its limits cattle, sheep or swine, actually diseased, or meats that, by reason of their condition, or the condition of the animals from which they are taken, are unfit for human food, and punish all sales of such animals or of such meats within its limits. It is quite a different thing for a State to declare, as does Minnesota by the necessary operation of its Statute, that fresh beef, veal, mutton, lamb or pork — articles that are used in every part of this country to support human life — shall not be sold at all for human food within its limits, unless the animal from which such meats are taken is inspected in that State, or, as is practically said, unless the animal is slaughtered in that State.

One other suggestion by the counsel for the State deserves to be examined. It is that, so far as this Statute is concerned, the people of Minnesota can purchase in other States fresh beef, veal, mutton, lamb and pork, and bring such meats into Minnesota for their personal use. We do not perceive that this view strengthens the case for the State, for it ignores the right which the people of other States have in commerce between those States and the State of Minnesota. And it ignores the right of the people of Minnesota to bring into that State, for purposes of sale, sound and healthy meat, wherever such meat may have come into existence. But there is a consideration arising out of the suggestion just alluded to which militates somewhat against the theory that the Statute in question is a legitimate exertion of the police powers of the State for the protection of the public health. If every hotel-keeper, railroad or mining corporation, or contractor, in Minnesota, furnishing subsistence to large numbers of persons, and every private family in that State, that is so disposed, can, without violating this Statute, bring into the State from other States and use for their own purposes, fresh beef, veal, mutton, lamb and pork, taken from animals slaughtered outside of Minnesota which may not have been inspected at all, or not within twenty-four hours before being slaughtered, what becomes of the argument, pressed with so much earnestness, that the health of the people of that State requires that they be protected against the use of meats from animals not inspected in Minnesota within the twenty-four hours before being slaughtered? . . .

The judgment discharging the appellee from custody is affirmed.

BRIMMER v. REBMAN, 138 U.S. 78, 11 S. Ct. 213, 34 L. Ed. 862 (1891). Harlan, J.: "William Rebman was tried and convicted before a justice of the peace in Norfolk, Virginia . . . of the offence of having wrongfully, unlawfully, and knowingly sold and offered for sale 'eighteen pounds of fresh meat, to wit, fresh, uncured beef, the same being the property of Armour & Co., citizens of the State of Illinois, and a part of an animal that had been slaughtered in the County of Cook and State of Illinois, a distance of one hundred miles and over from the said city of Norfolk . . . , without having first applied to and had the said fresh meat inspected by the fresh meat inspectors of the said city of Norfolk . . . as required by the act of the General Assembly of Virginia.' . . . The sole question to be determined is whether the statute under which Rebman was arrested and tried is repugnant to the Constitution of the United States. The statute is as follows: 'Whereas it is believed that unwholesome meats are being offered for sale in this Commonwealth; therefore 1. Be it enacted . . . That it shall not be lawful to offer for sale, within the limits of this State, any fresh meats (beef, veal or mutton) which shall have been slaughtered one hundred miles or over from the place at which it is offered for sale, until and except it has been inspected and approved as hereinafter provided . . . 3. And for all fresh meat so inspected said inspector shall receive as his compensation one cent per pound, to be paid by the owner of the meat. 4. It shall be the duty of any and all persons, firms or corporations, before offering for sale in this State, fresh meats, which under the provisions of this act are required to be inspected, to apply to the fresh meat inspector of the county or city where the same is proposed to be sold and have said meat inspected. . . .'"

What decision? Why?[c]

REYMANN BREWING CO. v. BRISTER, 179 U.S. 445, 21 S. Ct. 201, 45 L. Ed. 269 (1900). Shiras, J.: "On January 13, 1898, the Reymann Brewing Company . . . filed a bill of complaint . . . against Harry Brister, treasurer of the county of Jefferson, State of Ohio, seeking to restrain and enjoin the said Brister from retaining the possession of certain personal property belonging to the brewing company, which he had seized in enforcement of certain laws of the State of Ohio, which provide for the collection of a tax known as the 'Dow tax.' The cause was submitted upon the bill, a general demurrer thereto, and a statement of facts agreed upon by the parties. The statement of facts was [in part] as follows:

" 'The Reymann Brewing Company . . . owns and operates a brewery at Wheeling, West Virginia, where it manufactures a beverage of malt and intoxicating liquor commonly known as beer. It packs said beer in wooden barrels . . . and also in glass bottles

---

[c] Cf. Hale v. Bimco Trading Co., 306 U.S. 375 (1939). And compare, e.g., Patapsco Guano Co. v. North Carolina Board of Agriculture, 171 U.S. 345 (1898). — Ed.

. . . in . . . cases. These barrels and cases are . . . shipped to Steubenville, in the county of Jefferson, State of Ohio, where they are received by Bert Meyer, who is employed by the Reymann Brewing Company in the capacity of soliciting agent, salesman and driver. . . . Said agent also makes sales of said packages at and delivers the same from the place where stored at Steubenville. . . .'

"The Ohio statute . . . known as the 'Dow law' provides: 'Sec. 1. That upon the business of trafficking in spirituous, vinous, malt or any intoxicating liquors, there shall be assessed, yearly and shall be paid into the county treasury, as hereinafter provided, by every person, corporation or copartnership engaged therein, and for each place where such business is carried on by or for such person, corporation or copartnership, the sum of three hundred and fifty dollars. . . . Sec. 8. The phrase "trafficking in intoxicating liquors," as used in this act, means the buying or procuring and selling of intoxicating liquors otherwise than upon prescription issued in good faith by reputable physicians in active practice, or for exclusively known mechanical, pharmaceutical or sacramental purposes, but such phrase does not include the manufacture of intoxicating liquors from the raw material, and the sale thereof, at the manufactory, by the manufacturer of the same in quantities of one gallon or more at any one time.' . . ."

What decision? Why?

Mintz v. Baldwin 289 U.S. 346, 53 S. Ct. 611, 77 L. Ed. 1245 (1933)

Appeal by plaintiffs from a decree of the District Court of the United States for the Northern District of New York dismissing a bill to enjoin the enforcement of an order by a state commissioner of agriculture imposing conditions on the importation of cattle into the state.

MR. JUSTICE BUTLER delivered the opinion of the Court.

Plaintiffs have a large and valuable business in the raising, and in the sale and transportation from Wisconsin to New York, of cattle for dairy and breeding purposes. Defendant, acting under state statutes, made and is enforcing an order to guard against Bang's disease, bovine infectious abortion. The order requires that the cattle imported into New York for such purposes and also the herds from which they come shall be certified to be free from that disease by the chief sanitary official of the State of origin and that each shipment be accompanied by such a certificate.

Plaintiffs shipped 20 head from Wisconsin for delivery to one Bartlett in New York. The animals were accompanied by a certificate which was sufficient as to them, but there was nothing to show the freedom from Bang's disease of the herd or herds from which they came. For that reason defendant refused to permit them to be delivered, and so plaintiffs were compelled to take them out of New York.

Plaintiffs brought this suit for a temporary and perpetual injunction to restrain enforcement of the order. Their claim, so far as here material, is that the order is repugnant to the commerce clause because in conflict with federal statutes relating to interstate transportation of livestock. . . . Their application for a temporary injunction was brought on for hearing before a specially constituted court. U.S.C. title 28, § 380. Defendant answered and, upon stipulation of the parties, plaintiffs' motion for interlocutory decree and defendant's motion to dismiss the complaint were submitted upon the pleadings, the affidavit of one of the plaintiffs, the affidavit of defendant and affidavits of others in his behalf. Temporary injunction was denied and the bill was dismissed. [2 F. Supp. 700.]

The court made special findings of fact which include the following: Bang's disease prevails throughout the United States and is one of the greatest limiting factors, both as to reproduction and milk yield. Undulant fever may be caused by the disease germs when introduced into the human body by drinking raw milk of an infected cow. The disease may generally be diagnosed about 60 days after infection though the time may be considerably longer. Two blood tests are customarily made to detect the disease but they may not disclose it in the incubative stage. A substantial percentage of cattle imported into New York under certificate that they have passed tests for the disease are shown to have been infected. There is a body of expert opinion that such cattle should only be admitted when certified to have come from a clean herd, and that by such a safeguard danger of infection would be greatly lessened. The disease is exceedingly infectious and the defendant concluded that in order to protect herd owners and milk consumers he should require a certificate not only that imported cattle showed no infection but that they come from herds free from disease. This resulted in the order. By reason of danger of infection from the disease, many States of the Union have imposed restrictions upon the admission of cattle. The Federal Department of Agriculture, November 15, 1932, by letter to defendant declared that the Department had issued no quarantine or regulations pertaining to Bang's disease and that its policy for the present is to leave the control with the various States.

The order is an inspection measure. Undoubtedly it was promulgated in good faith and is appropriate for the prevention of further spread of the disease among dairy cattle and to safeguard public health. It cannot be maintained therefore that the order so unnecessarily burdens interstate transportation as to contravene the commerce clause. Gibbons v. Ogden, 9 Wheat. 1, 203, 204; The Minnesota Rate Cases (Simpson v. Shepard) 230 U.S. 352, 402, 406; Reid v. Colorado, 187 U.S. 137, 151, 152; Hannibal & St. J.R. Co. v. Husen, 95 U.S. 465; Henderson v. New York (Henderson v. Wickham) 92 U.S. 259, 268. Unless limited by the exercise of federal authority under the commerce clause, the State has power to make and enforce the order. . . .

[The Court concluded that no federal statute gave overriding authorization to deliver the cattle in New York.]

Affirmed.

TAYLOR, BURTIS, and WAUGH, Barriers to Internal Trade in Farm Products 93 (U.S. Dept. of Agriculture, 1939): "At the annual meetings of the United States Live Stock Sanitary Association in 1932 and 1933 a regulation of the State of New York was criticized. It required dairy cattle being brought into the State to have passed tests of such severity that only a very small percentage of the dairy stock in the United States could have been expected to qualify. The purpose of the regulation was to make sure that all dairy cattle brought into the State would be free from Bang's disease. But at that time Bang's disease was widespread in the State and no steps were being taken to see that the incoming cattle were placed in clean herds. The regulation reduced the movement of dairy stock from Wisconsin to New York to from 5 to 10 per cent of the volume in the years just preceding. . . . It should perhaps be emphasized that examples of quarantines or embargoes that do not have a sound biological basis are rare. . . ." And see, as cited in the above, Melder, State and Local Barriers to Interstate Commerce in the United States 135, Table 18 (University of Maine Studies, 2d series, No. 43, 1937).

Dean Milk Co. v. City of Madison 340 U.S. 349, 71 S. Ct. 295, 95 L. Ed. 329 (1951)

MR. JUSTICE CLARK delivered the opinion of the Court.

This appeal challenges the constitutional validity of two sections of an ordinance of the City of Madison, Wisconsin, regulating the sale of milk and milk products within the municipality's jurisdiction. One section in issue makes it unlawful to sell any milk as pasteurized unless it has been processed and bottled at an approved pasteurization plant within a radius of five miles from the central square of Madison. Another section, which prohibits the sale of milk, or the importation, receipt or storage of milk for sale, in Madison unless from a source of supply possessing a permit issued after inspection by Madison officials, is attacked insofar as it expressly relieves municipal authorities from any duty to inspect farms located beyond twenty-five miles from the center of the city.

Appellant is an Illinois corporation engaged in distributing milk and milk products in Illinois and Wisconsin. It contended below as it does here that both the five-mile limit on pasteurization plants and the twenty-five-mile limit on sources of milk violate the Commerce Clause and the Fourteenth Amendment to the Federal Constitution. The Supreme Court of Wisconsin upheld the five-mile limit on pasteurization. As to the twenty-five-mile limitation the court ordered the complaint dismissed for want of a justiciable controversy. 257 Wis. 308, 43 N.W.2d 480 (1950). This appeal, contesting both rulings, invokes the jurisdiction of this Court under 28 U.S.C. §1257 (2).

The City of Madison is the county seat of Dane County. Within the county are some 5,600 dairy farms with total raw milk production in excess of 600,000,000 pounds annually and more than ten times the requirements of Madison. Aside from the milk supplied to Madison, fluid milk produced in the county moves in large quantities to Chicago and more distant consuming areas, and the remainder is used in making cheese, butter and other products. At the time of trial the Madison milkshed was not of "Grade A" standing by the standards recommended by the United States Public Health Service, and no milk labeled "Grade A" was distributed in Madison.

The area defined by the ordinance with respect to milk sources encompasses practically all of Dane County and includes some 500 farms which supply milk for Madison. Within the five-mile area for pasteurization are plants of five processors, only three of which are engaged in the general wholesale and retail trade in Madison. Inspection of these farms and plants is scheduled once every thirty days and is performed by two municipal inspectors, one of whom is full-time. The courts below found that the ordinance in question promotes convenient, economical and efficient plant inspection.

Appellant purchases and gathers milk from approximately 950 farms in northern Illinois and southern Wisconsin, none being within twenty-five miles of Madison. Its pasteurization plants are located at Chemung and Huntley, Illinois, about 65 and 85 miles respectively from Madison. Appellant was denied a license to sell its products within Madison solely because its pasteurization plants were more than five miles away.

It is conceded that the milk which appellant seeks to sell in Madison is supplied from farms and processed in plants licensed and inspected by public health authorities of Chicago, and is labeled "Grade A" under the Chicago ordinance which adopts the rating standards recommended by the United States Public Health Service. Both the Chicago and Madison ordinances, though not the sections of the latter here in issue, are largely patterned after the Model Milk Ordinance of the Public Health Service. However, Madison contends and we assume that in some particulars its ordinance is more rigorous than that of Chicago.

Upon these facts we find it necessary to determine only the issue raised under the Commerce Clause, for we agree with appellant that the ordinance imposes an undue burden on interstate commerce.

This is not an instance in which an enactment falls because of federal legislation which, as a proper exercise of paramount national power over commerce, excludes measures which might otherwise be within the police power of the states. See Currin v. Wallace, 306 U.S. 1, 12, 13 (1939). There is no pertinent national regulation by the Congress, and statutes enacted for the District of Columbia indicate that Congress has recognized the appropriateness of local regulation of the sale of fluid milk. D.C. Code, 1940, §§33-301 et seq. It is not contended, however, that Congress has authorized the regulation before us.

Nor can there be objection to the avowed purpose of this enactment. We assume that difficulties in sanitary regulation of milk and milk products originating in remote areas may present a situation in which "upon a consideration of all the relevant facts and circumstances it appears that the matter is one which may appropriately be regulated in the interest of the safety, health and well-being of local communities. . . ." [Citations omitted.] We also assume that since Congress has not spoken to the contrary, the subject matter of the ordinance lies within the sphere of state regulation even though interstate commerce may be affected. [Citations omitted.]

But this regulation, like the provision invalidated in Baldwin v. G. A. F. Seelig, Inc. [294 U.S. 511], in practical effect excludes from distribution in Madison wholesome milk produced and pasteurized in Illinois. "The importer . . . may keep his milk or drink it, but sell it he may not." Id. at 521. In thus erecting an economic barrier protecting a major local industry against competition from without the State, Madison plainly discriminates against interstate commerce. This it cannot do, even in the exercise of its unquestioned power to protect the health and safety of its people, if reasonable nondiscriminatory alternatives, adequate to conserve legitimate local interests, are available. Cf. . . . Minnesota v. Barber, 136 U.S. 313, 328 (1890). A different view, that the ordinance is valid simply because it professes to be a health measure, would mean that the Commerce Clause of itself imposes no limitations on state action other than those laid down by the Due Process Clause, save for the rare instance where a state artlessly discloses an avowed purpose to discriminate against interstate goods. Cf. H. P. Hood & Sons, Inc. v. Du Mond, 336 U.S. 525. Our issue then is whether the discrimination inherent in the Madison ordinance can be justified in view of the character of the local interests and the available methods of protecting them. Cf. Union Brokerage Co. v. Jensen, 322 U.S. 202, 211 (1944).

It appears that reasonable and adequate alternatives are available. If the City of Madison prefers to rely upon its own officials for inspection of distant milk sources, such inspection is readily open to it without hardship for it could charge the actual and reasonable cost of such inspection to the importing producers and processors. Cf. Sprout v. South Bend, 277 U.S. 163, 169 (1928); see Miller v. Williams, 12 F. Supp. 236, 242, 244 (D.C. Md. 1935). Moreover, appellee health commissioner of Madison testified that as proponent of the local milk ordinance he had submitted the provisions here in controversy and an alternative proposal based on §11 of the Model Milk Ordinance recommended by the United States Public Health Service. The model provision imposes no geographical limitation on location of milk sources and processing plants but excludes from the municipality milk not produced and pasteurized conformably to standards as high as those enforced by the receiving city.[5] In implementing such an ordinance, the importing city obtains milk ratings based on uniform standards and established by health authorities in the jurisdiction where production and processing occur. The receiving city may determine the extent of enforcement of sanitary standards in the exporting area by verifying the accuracy of safety ratings of specific plants or of the milkshed in the distant jurisdiction through the United States Public Health Service, which routinely and on request spot checks the local ratings. The Commissioner testified that Madison consumers "would be adequately safeguarded" under either proposal and that he had expressed no preference. The milk sanitarian of the Wisconsin State Board of Health testified that the State Health Department recommends the adoption of a provision based on the Model

---

[5] Section 11 of the United States Public Health Service Milk Ordinance as recommended in 1939 provides:
"Milk and milk products from points beyond the limits of routine inspection of the city of . . . . may not be sold in the city of . . . . or its police jurisdiction, unless produced and/or pasteurized under provisions equivalent to the requirements of this ordinance; provided that the health officer shall satisfy himself that the health officer having jurisdiction over the production and processing is properly enforcing such provisions."

The following comment on this section is contained in the Public Health Service Milk Code:
"It is suggested that the health officer approve of milk products from distant points without his inspection if they are produced and processed under regulations equivalent to those of this ordinance, and if the milk or milk products have been awarded by the State control agency a rating of 90 percent or more on the basis of the Public Health Service rating method." Federal Security Agency, Public Health Bulletin No. 220 (1939) 145.

Ordinance. Both officials agreed that a local health officer would be justified in relying upon the evaluation by the Public Health Service of enforcement conditions in remote producing areas.

To permit Madison to adopt a regulation not essential for the protection of local health interests and placing a discriminatory burden on interstate commerce would invite a multiplication of preferential trade areas destructive of the very purposes of the Commerce Clause. Under the circumstances here presented, the regulation must yield to the principle that "one state in its dealings with another may not place itself in a position of economic isolation." Baldwin v. G. A. F. Seelig, Inc., supra.

For these reasons we conclude that the judgment below sustaining the five-mile provision as to pasteurization must be reversed.

The Supreme Court of Wisconsin thought it unnecessary to pass upon the validity of the twenty-five-mile limitation, apparently in part for the reason that this issue was made academic by its decision upholding the five-mile section. In view of our conclusion as to the latter provision, a determination of appellant's contention as to the other section is now necessary. As to this issue, therefore, we vacate the judgment below and remand for further proceedings not inconsistent with the principles announced in this opinion.

It is so ordered.

MR. JUSTICE BLACK, with whom MR. JUSTICE DOUGLAS and MR. JUSTICE MINTON concur, dissenting.

Today's holding invalidates §7.21 of the Madison, Wisconsin ordinance on the following reasoning: (1) the section excludes wholesome milk coming from Illinois; (2) this imposes a discriminatory burden on interstate commerce; (3) such a burden cannot be imposed where, as here, there are reasonable, nondiscriminatory and adequate alternatives available. I disagree with the Court's premises, reasoning, and judgment.

(1) This ordinance does not exclude wholesome milk coming from Illinois or anywhere else. It does require that all milk sold in Madison must be pasteurized within five miles of the center of the city. But there was no finding in the state courts, nor evidence to justify a finding there or here, that appellant, Dean Milk Company, is unable to have its milk pasteurized within the defined geographical area. As a practical matter, so far as the record shows, Dean can easily comply with the ordinance whenever it wants to. Therefore, Dean's personal preference to pasteurize in Illinois, not the ordinance, keeps Dean's milk out of Madison.

(2) Characterization of §7.21 as a "discriminatory burden" on interstate commerce is merely a statement of the Court's result, which I think incorrect. The section does prohibit the sale of milk in Madison by interstate and intrastate producers who prefer to pasteurize over five miles distant from the city. But both state courts below found that §7.21 represents a good-faith attempt to safeguard public health by making adequate sanitation inspections possible. While we are not bound by these findings, I do not understand the Court to overturn them. Therefore, the fact that §7.21, like all health regulations, imposes some burden on trade, does not mean that it "discriminates" against interstate commerce.

(3) This health regulation should not be invalidated merely because the Court believes that alternative milk-inspection methods might insure the cleanliness and healthfulness of Dean's Illinois milk. I find it difficult to explain why the Court uses the "reasonable alternative" concept to protect trade when today it refuses to apply the same principle to protect freedom of speech. Feiner v. New York, 340 U.S. 315. For while the "reasonable alternative" concept has been invoked to protect First Amendment rights, e.g., Schneider v. Irvington, 308 U.S. 147, 162, it has not heretofore been considered an appropriate weapon for striking down local health laws. Since the days of Chief Justice Marshall, federal courts have left states and municipalities free to pass bona fide health regulations subject only "to the paramount authority of Congress if it decides to assume control. . . ."

Section B. Protection of Local Economy and Welfare 371

The Minnesota Rate Cases (Simpson v. Shepard) 230 U.S. 352, 406; Gibbons v. Ogden, 9 Wheat. 1, 203, 204; Mintz v. Baldwin, 289 U.S. 346, 349, 350; and see Baldwin v. G. A. F. Seelig, Inc., 294 U.S. 511, 524. This established judicial policy of refusing to invalidate genuine local health laws under the Commerce Clause has been approvingly noted even in our recent opinions measuring state regulation by stringent standards. See e.g., H. P. Hood & Sons, Inc. v. Du Mond, 336 U.S. 525, 531, 532. No case is cited, and I have found none, in which a bona fide health law was struck down on the ground that some other method of safeguarding health would be as good as, or better than, the one the Court was called on to review. In my view, to use this ground now elevates the right to traffic in commerce for profit above the power of the people to guard the purity of their daily diet of milk.

If, however, the principle announced today is to be followed, the Court should not strike down local health regulations unless satisfied beyond a reasonable doubt that the substitutes it proposes would not lower health standards. I do not think that the Court can so satisfy itself on the basis of its judicial knowledge. And the evidence in the record leads me to the conclusion that the substitute health measures suggested by the Court do not insure milk as safe as the Madison ordinance requires.

One of the Court's proposals is that Madison require milk processors to pay reasonable inspection fees at the milk supply "sources." Experience shows, however, that the fee method gives rise to prolonged litigation over the calculation and collection of the charges. E.g., Sprout v. South Bend, 277 U.S. 163; Capitol Greyhound Lines v. Brice, 339 U.S. 542. To throw local milk regulation into such a quagmire of uncertainty jeopardizes the admirable milk-inspection systems in force in many municipalities. Moreover, nothing in the record before us indicates that the fee system might not be as costly to Dean as having its milk pasteurized in Madison. Surely the Court is not resolving this question by drawing on its "judicial knowledge" to supply information as to comparative costs, convenience, or effectiveness.

The Court's second proposal is that Madison adopt §11 of the "Model Milk Ordinance." The state courts made no findings as to the relative merits of this inspection ordinance and the one chosen by Madison. The evidence indicates to me that enforcement of the Madison law would assure a more healthful quality of milk than that which is entitled to use the label of "Grade A" under the Model Ordinance. Indeed, the United States Board of Public Health, which drafted the Model Ordinance, suggests that the provisions are "minimum standards only." The Model Ordinance does not provide for continuous investigation of all pasteurization plants as does §7.21 of the Madison ordinance. Under §11, moreover, Madison would be required to depend on the Chicago inspection system since Dean's plants, and the farms supplying them with raw milk, are located in the Chicago milkshed. But there is direct and positive evidence in the record that milk produced under Chicago standards did not meet the Madison requirements.

Furthermore, the Model Ordinance would force the Madison health authorities to rely on "spot checks" by the United States Public Health Service to determine whether Chicago enforced its milk regulations. The evidence shows that these "spot checks" are based on random inspection of farms and pasteurization plants: the United States Public Health Service rates the ten thousand or more dairy farms in the Chicago milkshed by a sampling of no more than two hundred farms. The same sampling technique is employed to inspect pasteurization plants. There was evidence that neither the farms supplying Dean with milk nor Dean's pasteurization plants were necessarily inspected in the last "spot check" of the Chicago milkshed made two years before the present case was tried.

From what this record shows, and from what it fails to show, I do not think that either of the alternatives suggested by the Court would assure the people of Madison as pure a supply of milk as they receive under their own ordinance. On this record I would uphold the Madison law. At the very least, however, I would not invalidate it without giving the parties a chance to present evidence and get findings on the ultimate issues the Court thinks crucial — namely, the relative merits of the Madison ordinance and the alternatives suggested by the Court today.[d]

Gallagher v. Lynn [1937] A.C. 863

LORD ATKIN. My Lords, this is an appeal from an order of the Court of Appeal of Northern Ireland dismissing an appeal from the Recorder of Londonderry who on appeal affirmed a conviction of the appellant by the justices for the County of the City of Londonderry for selling milk in the city of Londonderry without a licence in contravention of s. I, sub-s. I(c), of the Milk and Milk Products Act (Northern Ireland), 1934. . . . The case involves a question as to the construction and validity of the . . . Act. . . . I need not set out verbatim the material provisions of the Act. They provide that a person shall not sell milk except under and in accordance with the Act . . . ; that a person shall not sell milk of Grade A, B or C (defined by the Act) unless he hold either a producer's or a distributor's licence . . . ; that the Ministry of Agriculture shall, on application made in the prescribed manner, grant to any person upon the prescribed conditions a licence and that the holder of a licence shall keep milk records . . . and permit the records to be inspected by an authorized officer. . . . The Act further provided that an authorized officer should have power to enter and inspect at any reasonable time any part of the land or possessions occupied by the holder of a licence in connection with his business and examine milk found there and take samples. . . . Regulations . . . provide . . . that the Minister before granting a producer's licence shall satisfy himself that the applicant's arrangements for dealing with the milk . . . are such as will enable him to comply with the Act and Regulations. . . .

The appellant is one of several farmers whose farms are situate in the county of Donegal outside the territory of Northern Ireland but within a few miles of the boundary. For a considerable time before 1934 they had been in the habit of selling their milk in the city of Londonderry, which appears to have been their natural market. In 1935 Mr. Alexander, a solicitor practising in Londonderry, having also a dairy farm in county Donegal, having asked for a producer's licence and being refused, applied for a mandamus to the Minister to grant him a licence. . . . The ground taken by the Minister and upheld by the Courts was that it was impossible to apply the Act to producers whose premises were outside Northern Ireland territory; and that such persons were not entitled to a licence under the Act. . . .

. . . [T]here remains the important issue as to the constitutional validity of this Act. This is attacked by reference to the terms of s. 4 of the Government of Ireland Act, 1920, of which the provisions relating to Northern Ireland remain in force. "Subject to the provisions of this Act . . . the Parliament of Northern Ireland shall . . . have power to make laws for the peace, order and good government of . . . Northern Ireland with the following limitations, namely that they shall not have power to make laws except in respect of matters exclusively relating to the portion of Ireland within their jurisdiction . . . and . . . they shall not have power to make laws in respect of the following matters in particular, namely . . . (7). Trade with any place out of the part of Ireland within their jurisdiction, except so far as trade may be affected by the exercise of the powers of taxation given to the said parliaments, or by regulations made for the sole purpose of preventing contagious disease, or by steps taken by means of inquiries or agencies out of the part of

---

[d] See Taylor, Burtis, and Waugh, Barriers to Internal Trade in Farm Products (U.S. Dept. of Agriculture, 1939), Dairy Products, pp. 5-16; Symposium, Governmental Marketing Barriers, 8 Law & Contemp. Prob. 207-414 (1941).
Cf. Florida Lime & Avocado Growers, Inc. v. Paul, 373 U.S. 132 (1963). — ED.

Ireland within their jurisdiction for the improvement of the trade of that part or for the protection of traders of that part from fraud." It is said that the provisions of the Milk Act interfere with, indeed, put an end to, the trade in milk between the farmers of Donegal and customers in Derry; and that therefore they offend against the express limitations imposed by s. 4, sub-s. 7. My Lords, the short answer to this is that this Milk Act is not a law "in respect of" trade; but is a law for the peace, order and good government of Northern Ireland "in respect of" precautions taken to secure the health of the inhabitants of Northern Ireland by protecting them from the dangers of an unregulated supply of milk. These questions affecting limitations on the legislative powers of subordinate parliaments or the distribution of powers between parliaments in a federal system are now familiar, and I do not propose to cite the whole range of authority which has largely arisen in discussion of the powers of Canadian Parliaments. It is well established that you are to look at the "true nature and character of the legislation": Russell v. The Queen (7 App. Cas. 839), "the pith and substance of the legislation." If, on the view of the statute as a whole, you find that the substance of the legislation is within the express powers, then it is not invalidated if incidentally it affects matters which are outside the authorized field. The legislation must not under the guise of dealing with one matter in fact encroach upon the forbidden field. Nor are you to look only at the object of the legislator. An Act may have a perfectly lawful object, e.g., to promote the health of the inhabitants, but may seek to achieve that object by invalid methods, e.g., a direct prohibition of any trade with a foreign country. In other words, you may certainly consider the clauses of an Act to see whether they are passed "in respect of" the forbidden subject. In the present case any suggestion of an indirect attack upon trade is disclaimed by the appellant. There could be no foundation for it. The true nature and character of the Act, its pith and substance, is that it is an Act to protect the health of the inhabitants of Northern Ireland; and in those circumstances, though it may incidentally affect trade with County Donegal, it is not passed "in respect of" trade, and is therefore not subject to attack on that ground. I am of opinion, therefore, that this appeal should be dismissed with costs.

LORD THANKERTON. My Lords, I agree with the opinion which has been expressed by my noble and learned friend Lord Atkin.

LORD MACMILLAN. My Lords, I also agree.

LORD WRIGHT. My Lords, I also concur.

LORD MAUGHAM. My Lords, I concur.

Appeal dismissed.

Breard v. Alexandria *341 U.S. 622, 71 S. Ct. 920, 95 L. Ed 1233 (1951)*

MR. JUSTICE REED delivered the opinion of the Court.

The appellant here, Jack H. Breard, a regional representative of Keystone Readers Service, Inc., a Pennsylvania corporation, was arrested while going from door to door in the City of Alexandria, Louisiana, soliciting subscriptions for nationally known magazines. The arrest was solely on the ground that he had violated an ordinance because he had not obtained the prior consent of the owners of the residences solicited. Breard, a resident of Texas, was in charge of a crew of solicitors who go from house to house in the various cities and towns in the area under Breard's management and solicit subscriptions for nationally known magazines and periodicals. . . . These solicitors spend only a few days in each city depending upon its size. Keystone sends a card from its home office to the new subscribers acknowledging receipt of the subscription and thereafter the periodical is forwarded to the subscriber by the publisher in interstate commerce through the mails.

The ordinance under which the arrest was made, so far as is here pertinent, reads as follows:

"Section 1. Be it ordained by the Council of the City of Alexandria, Louisiana, in legal session convened that the practice of going in and upon private residences in the City of Alexandria, Louisiana by solicitors, peddlers, hawkers, itinerant merchants or transient vendors of merchandise not having been requested or invited so to do by the owner or owners, occupant or occupants of said private residences for the purpose of soliciting orders for the sale of goods, wares and merchandise and/or disposing of and/or peddling or hawking the same is declared to be a nuisance and punishable as such nuisance as a misdemeanor."

It, or one of similar import, has been on the statute books of Alexandria for many years. It is stipulated that: "Such ordinance was enacted by the City Council, among other reasons, because some householders complained to those in authority that in some instances, for one reason or another, solicitors were undesirable or discourteous, and some householders complained that, whether a solicitor was courteous or not, they did not desire any uninvited intrusion into the privacy of their homes."

The protective purposes of the ordinance were underscored by the Supreme Court of Louisiana in its opinion. 217 La. 820, at 825-828, 47 So.2d 553, at 555.

At appellant's trial for violation of the ordinance there was a motion to quash on the ground that the ordinance violates the Due Process Clause of the Fourteenth Amendment to the Federal Constitution; that it violates the Federal Commerce Clause; and that it violates the guarantees of the First Amendment of freedom of speech and of the press, made applicable to the states by the Fourteenth Amendment to the Constitution of the United States. Appellant's motion to quash was overruled by the trial court and he was found guilty and sentenced to pay a $25 fine or serve 30 days in jail. The Supreme Court of Louisiana affirmed appellant's conviction and expressly rejected the federal constitutional objections. 217 La. 820, 47 So.2d 553. The case is here on appeal, 28 U.S.C. §1257; Jamison v. Texas, 318 U.S. 413.

All declare for liberty and proceed to disagree among themselves as to its true meaning. There is equal unanimity that opportunists, for private gain, cannot be permitted to arm themselves with an acceptable principle, such as that of a right to work, a privilege to engage in interstate commerce, or a free press, and proceed to use it as an iron standard to smooth their path by crushing the living rights of others to privacy and repose. This case calls for an adjustment of constitutional rights in the light of the particular living conditions of the time and place. Everyone cannot have his own way and each must yield something to the reasonable satisfaction of the needs of all.

It is true that the knocker on the front door is treated as an invitation or license to attempt an entry, justifying ingress to the home by solicitors, hawkers and peddlers for all kinds of salable articles. When such visitors are barred from premises by notice or order, however, subsequent trespasses have been punished. Door-to-door canvassing has flourished increasingly in recent years with the ready market furnished by the rapid concentration of housing. The infrequent and still welcome solicitor to the rural home became to some a recurring nuisance in town when the visits were multiplied. Unwanted knocks on the door by day or night are a nuisance or worse to peace and quiet. The local retail merchant, too, has not been unmindful of the effective competition furnished by house-to-house selling in many lines. As a matter of business fairness, it may be thought not really sporting to corner the quarry in his home and through his open door put pressure on the prospect to purchase. As the exigencies of trade are not ordinarily expected to have a higher rating constitutionally than the tranquillity of the fireside, responsible municipal officers have sought a way to curb the annoyances while preserving complete freedom for desirable visitors to the homes. The idea of barring classified salesmen from homes by means of notices posted by individual householders was rejected early as less practical than an ordinance regulating solicitors.

The Town of Green River, Wyoming, undertook in 1931 to remedy by ordinance the irritating incidents of house-to-house canvassing for sales. The substance of that ordi-

Section B. Protection of Local Economy and Welfare 375

nance, so far as here material, is the same as that of Alexandria, Louisiana.[5] The Green River ordinance was sustained by the Circuit Court of Appeals of the Tenth Circuit in 1933 against an attack by a nonresident corporation, a solicitor of orders, through a bill for an injunction to prohibit its enforcement, on the federal constitutional grounds of interference with interstate commerce, deprivation of property without due process of law, and denial of the equal protection of the laws. Green River v. Fuller Brush Co., 65 F.2d 112. No review of that decision was sought. An employee of the Brush Company challenged the same ordinance again in the courts of Wyoming in 1936 on a prosecution by the town for the misdemeanor of violating its terms. On this attack certain purely state grounds were relied upon, which we need not notice, and the charges of violation of the Federal Constitution were repeated. The ordinance was held valid by the Supreme Court of Wyoming. Green River v. Bunger, 50 Wyo. 52, 58 P.2d 456.

Due Process. — On appeal to this Court, appellant urged particularly the unconstitutionality under the Fourteenth Amendment Due Process Clause of such unreasonable restraints as the Green River ordinance placed on "the right to engage in one of the common occupations of life," . . . He also relied upon the alleged prohibition of interstate commerce under the guise of a police regulation.

Here this Court dismissed for want of a substantial federal question. 300 U.S. 638. . . . We hold that this ordinance is not invalid under the Due Process Clause of the Fourteenth Amendment.

Commerce Clause. — Appellant does not, of course, argue that the Commerce Clause forbids all local regulation of solicitation for interstate business.

"Under our constitutional system, there necessarily remains to the States, until Congress acts, a wide range for the permissible exercise of power appropriate to their territorial jurisdiction although interstate commerce may be affected. . . . States are thus enabled to deal with local exigencies and to exert in the absence of conflict with federal legislation an essential protective power."[16]

Such state power has long been recognized. Appellant argues that the ordinance violates the Commerce Clause "because the practical operation of the ordinance, as applied to appellant and others similarly situated, imposes an undue and discriminatory burden upon interstate commerce and in effect is tantamount to a prohibition of such commerce." The attempt to secure the householder's consent is said to be too costly and the results negligible. The extent of this interstate business, as stipulated, is large. . . .[18] It is urged that our recent cases of H. P. Hood & Sons v. Du Mond, 336 U.S. 525, and Dean Milk Co. v. Madison, 340 U.S. 349, demonstrate that this Court will not permit local interests to protect themselves against out-of-state competition by curtailing interstate business.[20]

It was partly because the regulation in Dean Milk Co. discriminated against interstate commerce that it was struck down. "In thus erecting an economic barrier protecting a

---

[5] The ordinance now under consideration, §3, does not apply to "the sale, or soliciting of orders for the sale of milk, dairy products, vegetables, poultry, eggs and other farm and garden produce. . . ." Appellant makes no point against the present ordinance on the ground of invalid classification.

[16] Kelly v. Washington, 302 U.S. 1, 9, 10.

[18] "The solicitation of subscriptions in the field regularly accounts for from 50% to 60% of the total annual subscription circulation of nationally-distributed magazines which submit verified circulation reports to the Audit Bureau of circulations. . . . During the period from 1925 to date, the average circulation per issue of such magazines attributable to field subscription solicitation, . . . has amounted to more than 30% of the total average annual circulation per issue. . . ." The total subscription value obtained by Keystone Readers Service, appellant's employer, in 1948 was $5,319,423.40. There is a national association of magazine publishers, a trade organization whose members publish some 400 nationally distributed magazines with a combined circulation of 140 million copies. This association sponsors and maintains a central registry plan to which agencies like Keystone, soliciting subscriptions, belong.

[20] So far as this argument seeks to blame the passage of the ordinance on local retailers, we disregard it. Such arguments should be presented to legislators, not to courts. Arizona v. California, 283 U.S. 423, 455.

major local industry against competition from without the State, Madison plainly discriminates against interstate commerce. This it cannot do, even in the exercise of its unquestioned power to protect the health and safety of its people, if reasonable nondiscriminatory alternatives, adequate to conserve legitimate local interests, are available." Id. 340 U.S. at 354. Nor does the clause as to alternatives apply to the Alexandria ordinance. Interstate commerce itself knocks on the local door. It is only by regulating that knock that the interests of the home may be protected by public as distinct from private action. . . .

We recognize the importance to publishers of our many periodicals of the house-to-house method of selling by solicitation. As a matter of constitutional law, however, they in their business operations are in no different position so far as the Commerce Clause is concerned than the sellers of other wares. Appellant, as their representative or in his own right as a door-to-door canvasser, is no more free to violate local regulations to protect privacy than are other solicitors. As we said above, the usual methods of seeking business are left open by the ordinance. That such methods do not produce as much business as house-to-house canvassing is, constitutionally, immaterial and a matter for adjustment at the local level in the absence of federal legislation. Cf. Prudential Ins. Co. v. Benjamin, 328 U.S. 408. Taxation that threatens interstate commerce with prohibition or discrimination is bad, Nippert v. Richmond, 327 U.S. 416, 434, but regulation that leaves out-of-state sellers on the same basis as local sellers cannot be invalid for that reason.

While taxation and licensing of hawking or peddling, defined as selling and delivering in the state, has long been thought to show no violation of the Commerce Clause, solicitation of orders with subsequent interstate shipment has been immune from such an exaction. These decisions have been explained by this Court as embodying a protection of commerce against discrimination made most apparent by fixed-sum licenses regardless of sales. Where the legislation is not an added financial burden upon sales in commerce or an exaction for the privilege of doing interstate commerce but a regulation of local matters, different considerations apply.

We think Alexandria's ordinance falls in the classification of regulation. The economic effects on interstate commerce in door-to-door soliciting cannot be gainsaid. To solicitors so engaged, ordinances such as this compel the development of a new technique of approach to prospects. Their local retail competitors gain advantages from the location of their stores and investments in their stock but the solicitor retains his flexibility of movement and freedom from heavy investment.

The general use of the Green River type ordinance shows its adaptation to the needs of the many communities that have enacted it. We are not willing even to appraise the suggestion, unsupported in the record, that such wide use springs predominantly from the selfish influence of local merchants.

Even before this Court's decision in Martin v. Struthers, 319 U.S. 141, holding invalid, when applied to a person distributing leaflets advertising a religious meeting, an ordinance of the City of Struthers, Ohio, forbidding the summoning of the occupants of a residence to the door, our less extreme cases had created comment. See Professor Zechariah Chafee, Free Speech in the United States (1942) 406.[27]

To the city council falls the duty of protecting its citizens against the practices deemed subversive of privacy and of quiet. A householder depends for protection on his city board rather than churlishly guarding his entrances with orders forbidding the entrance of solici-

[27] "House to house canvassing raises more serious problems. Of all the methods of spreading unpopular ideas, this seems the least entitled to extensive protection. The possibilities of persuasion are slight compared with the certainties of annoyance. Great as is the value of exposing citizens to novel views, home is one place where a man ought to be able to shut himself up in his own ideas if he desires. There he should be free not only from unreasonable searches and seizures but also from hearing uninvited strangers expound distasteful doctrines. A doorbell cannot be disregarded like a handbill. It takes several minutes to ascertain the purpose of a propagandist and at least several more to get rid of him. . . . Moreover, hospitable housewives dislike to leave a visitor on a windy

tors. A sign would have to be a small billboard to make the differentiations between the welcome and unwelcome that can be written in an ordinance once cheaply for all homes. . . . When there is a reasonable basis for legislation to protect the social, as distinguished from the economic, welfare of a community, it is not for this Court because of the Commerce Clause to deny the exercise locally of the sovereign power of Louisiana. Changing living conditions or variations in the experiences or habits of different communities may well call for different legislative regulations as to methods and manners of doing business. Powers of municipalities are subject to control by the states. Their judgment of local needs is made from a more intimate knowledge of local conditions than that of any other legislative body. We cannot say that this ordinance of Alexandria so burdens or impedes interstate commerce as to exceed the regulatory powers of that city.

First Amendment. — Finally we come to a point not heretofore urged in this Court as a ground for the invalidation of a Green River ordinance. This is that such an ordinance is an abridgment of freedom of speech and the press. Only the press or oral advocates of ideas could urge this point. It was not open to the solicitors for gadgets or brushes. . . . However, if as we have shown above, a city council may speak for the citizens on matters subject to the police power, we would have in the present prosecution the time-honored offense of trespass on private grounds after notice. . . .

Subscriptions may be made by anyone interested in receiving the magazines without the annoyances of house-to-house canvassing. We think those communities that have found these methods of sale obnoxious may control them by ordinance. It would be, it seems to us, a misuse of the great guarantees of free speech and free press to use those guarantees to force a community to admit the solicitors of publications to the home premises of its residents. We see no abridgment of the principles of the First Amendment in this ordinance.

Affirmed.

Mr. Chief Justice Vinson, with whom Mr. Justice Douglas joins, dissenting. . . .

In passing upon other ordinances affecting solicitors, this Court has not hesitated in noting the economic fact that "the 'real competitors' of [solicitors] are, among others, the local retail merchants." Nippert v. Richmond, supra, at 433, ... The Court acknowledges "effective competition" between solicitors and the local retail merchants, . . . but is deliberate in its refusal to appraise the practical effect of this ordinance as a deterrent to interstate commerce, ... I think it plain that a "blanket prohibition" upon appellant's solicitation discriminates against and unduly burdens interstate commerce in favoring local retail merchants. "Whether or not it was so intended, those are its necessary effects." Nippert v. Richmond, supra. The fact that this ordinance exempts solicitation by the essentially local purveyors of farm products shows that local economic interests are relieved of the burdensome effects of the ordinance. No one doubts that protection of the home is a proper subject of legislation, but that end can be served without prohibiting interstate commerce. Our prior decisions cannot be avoided by limiting their authority to the limited categories of tax and license. On the contrary, we must guard against state action which, "in any form or under any guise, directly burden[s] the prosecution of interstate business." . . . I cannot agree that this Court should defer to the City Council of Alexandria as though we had before us an act of Congress regulating commerce. . . . [T]his Court, and not the state legislature [or the city council], is under the commerce clause the final arbiter of the competing demands of state [or local] and national interests." Southern Pacific Co. v. Arizona, 325 U.S. 761, 769 (1945).

---

doorstep while he explains his errand, yet once he is inside the house robbery or worse may happen. So peddlers of ideas and salesmen of salvation in odd brands seem to call for regulation as much as the regular run of commercial canvassers. . . . Freedom of the home is as important as freedom of speech. I cannot help wondering whether the Justices of the Supreme Court are quite aware of the effect of organized front-door intrusions upon people who are not sheltered from zealots and impostors by a staff of servants or the locked entrance of an apartment house."

The Court relies upon Bunger v. Green River, 300 U.S. 638 (1937), where the conviction of a Fuller Brush man was sustained under an ordinance akin to the one before us. The order was entered without argument, without opinion. . . .

I would apply to this case the principles so recently announced in Dean Milk Co. v. Madison, 340 U.S. 349 (1951). In the course of its discussion of our Dean Milk decision, the Court remarks that in the instant case "Interstate commerce itself knocks on the local door." . . . As I read the prior decisions of this Court, that fact, far from justifying avoidance of Dean Milk, buttresses my conclusion that the ordinance cannot be applied to appellant consonant with the Commerce Clause.

MR. JUSTICE BLACK, with whom MR. JUSTICE DOUGLAS joins, dissenting: . . .

The constitutional sanctuary for the press must necessarily include liberty to publish and circulate. In view of our economic system, it must also include freedom to solicit paying subscribers. Of course homeowners can if they wish forbid newsboys, reporters or magazine solicitors to ring their doorbells. But when the homeowner himself has not done this, I believe that the First Amendment, interpreted with due regard for the freedoms it guarantees, bars laws like the present ordinance which punish persons who peacefully go from door to door as agents of the press.[1]

[In his volume We the Judges, Justice Douglas wrote of this decision (p. 236): "No more extreme case of a state legislating in the federal domain can be found in our books."]

State Board v. Young's Market Co. 299 U.S. 59, 57 S. Ct. 77, 81 L. Ed. 38 (1936)

MR. JUSTICE BRANDEIS delivered the opinion of the Court.

This suit, brought in the federal court for southern California, challenges the validity, under the Twenty-first Amendment of the Federal Constitution, of the provisions of a statute of that State, and of the regulations thereunder, which impose a license-fee of $500 for the privilege of importing beer to any place within its borders. The license does not confer the privilege of selling. Compare Premier-Pabst Sales Co. v. Grosscup, 298 U.S. 226.

The plaintiffs are domestic corporations and individual citizens of California who sue on behalf of themselves and of others similarly situated. Each is engaged in selling at wholesale at one or more places of business within the State beer imported from Missouri or Wisconsin; and has a wholesaler's license which entitles the holder to sell there to licensed dealers beer lawfully possessed, whether it be imported or is of domestic make. For that license the fee is $50. Each plaintiff has refused to apply for an importer's license, claiming that the requirement discriminates against wholesalers of imported beer; and that, hence, the statute violates both the commerce clause and the equal protection clause. The bill alleges that heavy penalties are exacted for importing, or having in possession, imported beer without having secured an importer's license; that unless enjoined defendants will enforce the statute; that enforcement would subject each of the plaintiffs to irreparable injury; and that the matter in controversy exceeds $3000.

The several state officials charged with the duty of enforcing the statute, were joined as defendants, and made return to an order to show cause. They assert that the challenged statutory provisions and regulations are valid because of the Twenty-first Amendment, ratified December 5, 1933, which provides, by §2:

"The transportation or importation into any State, Territory, or possession of the United States for delivery or use therein of intoxicating liquors, in violation of the laws thereof, is hereby prohibited."

---

[1] Of course I believe that the present ordinance could constitutionally be applied to a "merchant" who goes from door to door "selling pots." Compare Martin v. Struthers, 319 U.S. 141, 144, with Valentine v. Chrestensen, 316 U.S. 52.

Section B. Protection of Local Economy and Welfare

First. The main contention of the plaintiffs is that the exaction of the importer's license fee violates the commerce clause by discriminating against the wholesaler of imported beer. But there is no discrimination against them qua wholesalers. Everyone holding a wholesaler's license who is lawfully possessed of any beer, may sell it. The fee exacted for the privilege of selling, and the conditions under which a sale may be made, are the same whether the beer to be sold is imported or domestic or is both. The difference in position charged as a discrimination is not in the terms under which beer may be sold. It arises from the fact that no one may import beer without securing a license therefor. What the plaintiffs complain of is the refusal to let them import beer without paying for the privilege of importation. Prior to the Twenty-first Amendment it would obviously have been unconstitutional to have imposed any fee for that privilege. The imposition would have been void, not because it resulted in discrimination, but because the fee would be a direct burden on interstate commerce; and the commerce clause confers the right to import merchandise free into any state, except as Congress may otherwise provide. The exaction of a fee for the privilege of importation would not, before the Twenty-first Amendment, have been permissible even if the State had exacted an equal fee for the privilege of transporting domestic beer from its place of manufacture to the wholesaler's place of business. Compare Case of the State Freight Tax, 15 Wall. 232, 274, 277. Thus, the case does not present a question of discrimination prohibited by the commerce clause.

The Amendment which "prohibited" the "transportation or importation" of intoxicating liquors into any state "in violation of the laws thereof," abrogated the right to import free, so far as concerns intoxicating liquors. The words used are apt to confer upon the State the power to forbid all importations which do not comply with the conditions which it prescribes. The plaintiffs ask us to limit this broad command. They request us to construe the Amendment as saying, in effect: The State may prohibit the importation of intoxicating liquors provided it prohibits the manufacture and sale within its borders; but if it permits such manufacture and sale, it must let imported liquors compete with the domestic on equal terms. To say that, would involve not a construction of the Amendment, but a rewriting of it.

The plaintiffs argue that, despite the Amendment, a State may not regulate importations except for the purpose of protecting the public health, safety or morals; and that the importer's license fee was not imposed to that end. Surely the State may adopt a lesser degree of regulation than total prohibition. Can it be doubted that a State might establish a state monopoly of the manufacture and sale of beer, and either prohibit all competing importations, or discourage importations by confining them to a single consignee? Compare Slaughter-House Cases, 16 Wall. 36; Vance v. W. A. Vandercook Co. (No. 1), 170 U.S. 438, 447. There is no basis for holding that it may prohibit, or so limit, importation only if it establishes monopoly of the liquor trade. It might permit the manufacture and sale of beer, while prohibiting hard liquors absolutely. If it may permit the domestic manufacture of beer and exclude all made without the State, may it not, instead of absolute exclusion, subject the foreign article to a heavy importation fee? Moreover, in the light of history, we cannot say that the exaction of a high license fee for importation may not, like the imposition of the high license fees exacted for the privilege of selling at retail, serve as an aid in policing the liquor traffic. Compare Phillips v. Mobile, 208 U.S. 472, 479.

The plaintiffs argue that limitation of the broad language of the Twenty-first Amendment is sanctioned by its history; and by the decisions of this Court on the Wilson Act, the Webb-Kenyon Act and the Reed Amendment. As we think the language of the Amendment is clear, we do not discuss these matters. The plaintiffs insist that to sustain the exaction of the importer's license-fee would involve a declaration that the Amendment has, in respect to liquor, freed the States from all restrictions upon the police power to be found in other provisions of the Constitution. The question for decision requires no such generalization.

Second. The claim that the statutory provisions and the regulations are void under the equal protection clause may be briefly disposed of. A classification recognized by the

Twenty-first Amendment cannot be deemed forbidden by the Fourteenth. Moreover, the classification in taxation made by California rests on conditions requiring difference in treatment. Beer sold within the States comes from two sources. The brewer of the domestic article may be required to pay a license-fee for the privilege of manufacturing it; and under the California statute is obliged to pay $750 a year. Compare Brown-Forman Co. v. Kentucky, 217 U.S. 563. The brewer of the foreign article cannot be so taxed; only the importer can be reached. He is subjected to a license-fee of $500. Compare Kidd v. Alabama, 188 U.S. 730, 732.

Reversed.[e]

Mr. Justice Butler concurs in the result. . . .

Department of Revenue v. James B. Beam Distilling Co.
377 U.S. 341, 84 S. Ct. 1247, 12 L. Ed. 2d 362 (1964)

Mr. Justice Stewart delivered the opinion of the Court.

This case requires consideration of the relationship between the Export-Import Clause and the Twenty-first Amendment of the Constitution.

The respondent, a Kentucky producer of distilled spirits, is also the sole distributor in the United States of "Gilbey's Spey Royal" Scotch Whisky. This whisky is produced in Scotland and is shipped via the ports of Chicago or New Orleans directly to the respondent's bonded warehouses in Kentucky. It is subsequently sold by the respondent to customers in domestic markets throughout the United States.

A Kentucky law provides:

"No person shall ship or transport or cause to be shipped or transported into the state any distilled spirits from points without the state without first obtaining a permit from the department and paying a tax of ten cents on each proof gallon contained in the shipment." KRS 243.680(2)(a).

Under the authority of this statute the Kentucky Department of Revenue, petitioner, required the respondent to pay a tax of 10 cents on each proof gallon of whisky which it thus imported from Scotland. It is not disputed that, as stated by the Kentucky Court of Appeals, "the tax was collected while the whisky remained in unbroken packages in the hands of the original importer and prior to resale or use by the importer." The respondent filed a claim for refund of the taxes, upon the ground that their imposition violated the Import-Export Clause of the Constitution. The Kentucky Tax Commission and a Kentucky Circuit Court denied the claim, but on appeal the Kentucky Court of Appeals upheld it. 367 S.W.2d 267. We granted certiorari to consider the constitutional issue which the case presents. 375 U.S. 811.

The Kentucky Court of Appeals held that the tax in question, although an occupational or license tax in form, is a tax on imports in fact. "[T]he incidence of the tax is the act of transporting or shipping the distilled spirits under consideration into this state." 367 S.W.2d, at 270. The court further held that the tax cannot be characterized as an inspection measure, in view of the fact that neither the statute nor the regulations implementing it provide for any actual inspection. Concluding, therefore, that the tax falls squarely within the interdiction of the Export-Import Clause, the court held that this provision of the Constitution has not been repealed, insofar as intoxicants are concerned, by the Twenty-first Amendment. Accordingly, the court ruled that the respondent was entitled

---

[e] Cf. Indianapolis Brewing Co. v. Liquor Control Commission, 305 U.S. 391 (1939); Gordon v. Texas, 355 U.S. 369 (1958), aff'g 310 S.W.2d 328 (1956).

See Note, Economic Localism in State Alcoholic Beverage Laws — Experience Under the Twenty-first Amendment, 72 Harv. L. Rev. 1145 (1959). Cf. Seagram & Sons v. Hostetter, 384 U.S. 35 (1966). — Ed.

to a refund of the taxes it had paid. We agree with the Kentucky Court of Appeals and affirm the judgment before us. . . .

To sustain the tax which Kentucky has imposed in this case would require nothing short of squarely holding that the Twenty-first Amendment has completely repealed the Export-Import Clause so far as intoxicants are concerned. Nothing in the language of the Amendment nor in its history leads to such an extraordinary conclusion. This Court has never intimated such a view, and now that the claim for the first time is squarely presented, we expressly reject it.

We have no doubt that under the Twenty-first Amendment Kentucky could not only regulate, but could completely prohibit the importation of some intoxicants, or of all intoxicants, destined for distribution, use, or consumption within its borders. There can surely be no doubt, either, of Kentucky's plenary power to regulate and control, by taxation or otherwise, the distribution, use, or consumption of intoxicants within her territory after they have been imported. All we decide today is that, because of the explicit and precise words of the Export-Import Clause of the Constitution, Kentucky may not lay this impost on these imports from abroad.

Affirmed.[f]

MR. JUSTICE BRENNAN took no part in the decision in this case.

MR. JUSTICE BLACK, with whom MR. JUSTICE GOLDBERG joins, dissenting.

This case, like Hostetter v. Idlewild Bon Voyage Liquor Corp., also decided today, 377 U.S. 324, deprives the States of a large part of the power which I think the Twenty-first Amendment gives them to regulate the liquor business by taxation or otherwise. . . . Surely the Import-Export Clause is no more exalted and no more worthy to be excepted from the Twenty-first Amendment than are the Commerce and Equal Protection Clauses. . . . The Amendment, after all, does not talk about "foreign" liquors or "domestic" liquors; it simply speaks of "liquors" — all liquors whatever their origin. . . . A State may choose to have wine only, beer only, Scotch only, bourbon only, or none of these. As the Court said in State Board v. Young's Market Co., supra, 299 U.S. at 63, a State can "either prohibit all competing importation, or discourage importation by laying a heavy impost, or channelize desired importations. . . ." Although I was brought up to believe that Scotch whisky would need a tax preference to survive in competition with Kentucky bourbon, I never understood the Constitution to require a State to give such preference. (My dissenting Brother asks me to say that this statement does not necessarily represent his views on the respective merits of Scotch and bourbon.) . . .

I would uphold the Kentucky tax.

Baldwin v. G. A. F. Seelig, Inc. *294 U.S. 511, 55 S. Ct. 497, 79 L. Ed. 1032 (1935)*

MR. JUSTICE CARDOZO delivered the opinion of the Court.

Whether and to what extent the New York Milk Control Act (N.Y. Laws, 1933, chap. 158; Laws of 1934, chap. 126) may be applied against a dealer who has acquired title to the milk as the result of a transaction in interstate commerce is the question here to be determined.

G. A. F. Seelig, Inc. (appellee in No. 604 and appellant in No. 605) is engaged in business as a milk dealer in the city of New York. It buys its milk, including cream, in Fair Haven, Vermont, from the Seelig Creamery Corporation, which in turn buys from the producers on the neighboring farms. The milk is transported to New York by rail in forty-quart cans, the daily shipment amounting to about 200 cans of milk and 20 cans of cream. Upon arrival in New York about 90% is sold to customers in the original cans, the

---

[f] Cf. Hostetter v. Idlewild Bon Voyage Liquor Corp., 377 U.S. 324 (1964). — ED.

buyers being chiefly hotels, restaurants and stores. About 10% is bottled in New York, and sold to customers in bottles. By concession title passes from the Seelig Creamery to G. A. F. Seelig, Inc. at Fair Haven, Vermont. For convenience the one company will be referred to as the Creamery and the other as Seelig.

The New York Milk Control Act with the aid of regulations made thereunder has set up a system of minimum prices to be paid by dealers to producers. The validity of that system in its application to producers doing business in New York State has support in our decisions. Nebbia v. New York, 291 U.S. 502; Hegeman Farms Corp. v. Baldwin, 293 U.S. 163. Cf. Borden's Farm Products Co. v. Baldwin, 293 U.S. 194. From the farms of New York the inhabitants of the so-called Metropolitan Milk District, comprising the City of New York and certain neighboring communities, derive about 70% of the milk requisite for their use. To keep the system unimpaired by competition from afar, the Act has a provision whereby the protective prices are extended to that part of the supply (about 30%) which comes from other states. The substance of the provision is that, so far as such a prohibition is permitted by the Constitution, there shall be no sale within the state of milk bought outside unless the price paid to the producers was one that would be lawful upon a like transaction within the state. The statute, so far as pertinent, is quoted in the margin together with supplementary regulations by the Board of Milk Control.[1]

Seelig buys its milk from the Creamery in Vermont at prices lower than the minimum payable to producers in New York. The Commissioner of Farms and Markets refuses to license the transaction of its business unless it signs an agreement to conform to the New York statute and regulations in the sale of the imported product. This the applicant declines to do. Because of that refusal other public officers, parties to these appeals, announce a purpose to prosecute for trading without a license and to recover heavy penalties. This suit has been brought to restrain the enforcement of the Act in its application to the complainant, repugnancy being charged between its provisions when so applied and limitations imposed by the Constitution of the United States. United States Constitution, Art. 1, §8, clause 3; Fourteenth Amendment, §1. A District Court of three judges, organized in accordance with §266 of the Judicial Code, has granted a final decree restraining the enforcement of the Act in so far as sales are made by the complainant while the milk is in the cans or other original packages in which it was brought into New York, but refusing an injunction as to milk taken out of the cans for bottling, and thereafter sold in bottles. See opinion on application for interlocutory injunction: — 7 F. Supp. 776; and cf. 293 U.S. 522. The case is here on cross-appeals. U.S.C. title 28, §380.

First. An injunction was properly granted restraining the enforcement of the Act in its application to sales in the original packages.

New York has no power to project its legislation into Vermont by regulating the price to be paid in that state for milk acquired there. So much is not disputed. New York is equally without power to prohibit the introduction within her territory of milk of wholesome qual-

---

[1] Section 258(m)(4), Article 21-a, New York Agriculture & Markets Law, Laws 1934, chap. 126, formerly §312(g), Article 25, Laws 1933, chap. 158: "It is the intent of the legislature that the instant, whenever that may be, that the handling within the State by a milk dealer of milk produced outside of the state becomes a subject of regulation by the State, in the exercise of its police powers, the restrictions set forth in this article respecting such milk so produced shall apply and the powers conferred by this article shall attach. After any such milk so produced shall have come to rest within the State, any sale, within the State by a licensed milk dealer or a milk dealer required by this article to be licensed, of any such milk purchased from the producer at a price lower than that required to be paid for milk produced within the State purchased under similar conditions, shall be unlawful."

Order of New York Milk Control Board, July 1, 1933: "Any continuous and regular purchase or sale or delivery or receipt of milk passing to a milk dealer at any place and available for utilization as fluid milk and/or cream within New York State, followed by such utilization in one or more instances, where the price involved in such purchase or sale or delivery or receipt is less than the sum of the minimum price established to be paid to producers for such milk plus actual costs of transporting and handling and processing such milk to the place and to the condition involved in such purchase or sale or delivery or receipt, hereby is forbidden."

Section B. **Protection of Local Economy and Welfare** 383

ity acquired in Vermont, whether at high prices or at low ones. This again is not disputed. Accepting those postulates, New York asserts her power to outlaw milk so introduced by prohibiting its sale thereafter if the price that has been paid for it to the farmers of Vermont is less than would be owing in like circumstances to farmers in New York. The importer in that view may keep his milk or drink it, but sell it he may not.

Such a power, if exerted, will set a barrier to traffic between one state and another as effective as if customs duties, equal to the price differential, had been laid upon the thing transported. Imposts or duties upon commerce with other countries are placed, by an express prohibition of the Constitution, beyond the power of a state, "except what may be absolutely necessary for executing its inspection laws." Constitution, Art. I, §10, clause 2; Woodruff v. Parham, 8 Wall. 123. Imposts and duties upon interstate commerce are placed beyond the power of a state, without the mention of an exception, by the provision committing commerce of that order to the power of the Congress. Constitution, Art. I, §8, clause 3. "It is the established doctrine of this court that a state may not, in any form or under any guise, directly burden the prosecution of interstate business." [Citations omitted.] Nice distinctions have been made at times between direct and indirect burdens. They are irrelevant when the avowed purpose of the obstruction, as well as its necessary tendency, is to suppress or mitigate the consequences of competition between the states. Such an obstruction is direct by the very terms of the hypothesis. We are reminded in the opinion below that a chief occasion of the commerce clause was "the mutual jealousies and aggressions of the States, taking form in customs barriers and other economic retaliation." Farrand, Records of the Federal Convention, vol. II, p. 308; vol. III, pp. 478, 547, 548; the Federalist, No. XLII; Curtis, History of the Constitution, vol. 1, p. 502; Story on the Constitution, §259. If New York in order to promote the economic welfare of her farmers, may guard them against competition with the cheaper prices of Vermont, the door has been opened to rivalries and reprisals that were meant to be averted by subjecting commerce between the states to the power of the nation.

The argument is pressed upon us, however, that the end to be served by the Milk Control Act is something more than the economic welfare of the farmers or of any other class or classes. The end to be served is the maintenance of a regular and adequate supply of pure and wholesome milk, the supply being put in jeopardy when the farmers of the state are unable to earn a living income. Nebbia v. New York, 291 U.S. 502. Price security, we are told, is only a special form of sanitary security; the economic motive is secondary and subordinate; the state intervenes to make its inhabitants healthy, and not to make them rich. On that assumption we are asked to say that intervention will be upheld as a valid exercise by the state of its internal police power, though there is an incidental obstruction to commerce between one state and another. This would be to eat up the rule under the guise of an exception. Economic welfare is always related to health, for there can be no health if men are starving. Let such an exception be admitted, and all that a state will have to do in times of stress and strain is to say that its farmers and merchants and workmen must be protected against competition from without, lest they go upon the poor relief lists or perish altogether. To give entrance to that excuse would be to invite a speedy end of our national solidarity. The Constitution was framed under the dominion of a political philosophy less parochial in range. It was framed upon the theory that the peoples of the several states must sink or swim together, and that in the long run prosperity and salvation are in union and not division.

We have dwelt up to this point upon the argument of the state that economic security for farmers in the milkshed may be a means of assuring to consumers a steady supply of a food of prime necessity. There is, however, another argument which seeks to establish a relation between the well-being of the producer and the quality of the product. We are told that farmers who are underpaid will be tempted to save the expense of sanitary precautions. This temptation will affect the farmers outside New York as well as those within it. For that reason the exclusion of milk paid for in Vermont below the New York minimum will tend, it is said, to impose a higher standard of quality and thereby promote health. We think the argument will not avail to justify impediments to commerce between the states. There is neither evidence nor presumption that the same minimum prices established by order of the Board for producers in New York are necessary also for producers in Vermont. But apart from such defects of proof, the evils springing from uncared for cattle must be remedied by measures of repression more direct and certain than the creation of a parity of prices between New York and other states. Appropriate certificates may be exacted from farmers in Vermont and elsewhere (Mintz v. Baldwin, 289 U.S. 346; Reid v. Colorado, 187 U.S. 137); milk may be excluded if necessary safeguards have been omitted; but commerce between the states is burdened unduly when one state regulates by indirection the prices to be paid to producers in another, in the faith that augmentation of prices will lift up the level of economic welfare, and that this will stimulate the observance of sanitary requirements in the preparation of the product. The next step would be to condition importation upon proof of a satisfactory wage scale in factory or shop, or even upon proof of the profits of the business. Whatever relation there may be between earnings and sanitation is too remote and indirect to justify obstructions to the normal flow of commerce in its movement between states. [Citations omitted.] One state may not put pressure of that sort upon others to reform their economic standards. If farmers or manufacturers in Vermont are abandoning farms or factories, or are failing to maintain them properly, the legislature of Vermont and not that of New York must supply the fitting remedy.

Many cases from our reports are cited by counsel for the state. They do not touch the case at hand. The line of division between direct and indirect restraints of commerce involves in its marking a reference to considerations of degree. Even so, the borderland is wide between the restraints upheld as incidental and those attempted here. Subject to the paramount power of the Congress, a state may regulate the importation of unhealthy swine or cattle . . . or decayed or noxious foods. . . . Things such as these are not proper subjects of commerce, and there is no unreasonable interference when they are inspected and excluded. So a state may protect its inhabitants against the fraudulent substitution, by deceptive coloring or otherwise, of one article for another. . . . It may give protection to travelers against the dangers of overcrowded highways . . . and protection to its residents against unnecessary noises. . . . At times there are border cases, such as New York ex rel. Silz v. Hesterberg, 211 U.S. 31, where the decision in all likelihood was influenced, even if it is not wholly explained, by a recognition of the special and restricted nature of rights of property in game. Interference was there permitted with sale and importation, but interference for a close season and no longer, and in aid of a policy of conservation common to many states. . . . None of these statutes — inspection laws, game laws, laws intended to curb fraud or exterminate disease — approaches in drastic quality the statute here in controversy which would neutralize the economic consequences of free trade among the states.

Second. There was error in refusing an injunction to restrain the enforcement of the Act in its application to milk in bottles to be sold by the importer.

The test of the "original package," which came into our law with Brown v. Maryland, 12 Wheat. 419, is not inflexible and final for the transactions of interstate commerce, whatever may be its validity for commerce with other countries. Cf. Woodruff v. Parham, 8 Wall. 123; Anglo-Chilean Nitrate Sales Corp. v. Alabama, 288 U.S. 218, 226. There are purposes for which merchandise, transported from another state, will be treated as a part of the general mass of property at the state of destination though still in the original containers. This is so, for illustration, where merchandise so contained is subjected to a non-discriminatory property tax which it bears equally with other merchandise produced within the state. [Citations omitted.] There are other purposes for which the same merchandise will have the benefit of the protection appropriate to interstate commerce, though the original packages have been broken and the contents subdivided. "A state tax upon merchandise brought in from another State, or upon its sales, whether in original packages or not, after it has reached its destination and is in a state of rest, is lawful only when the tax is not discriminating in its incidence against the merchandise because of its origin in another State." . . . In brief, the test of the original package is not an ultimate principle. It is an illustration of a principle. Pennsylvania Gas Co. v. Public Serv. Commission, 225 N.Y. 397, 403. It marks a convenient boundary and one sufficiently precise save in exceptional conditions. What is ultimate is the principle that one state in its dealings with another may not place itself in a position of economic isolation. Formulas and catchwords are subordinate to this overmastering requirement. Neither the power to tax nor the police power may be used by the state of destination with the aim and effect of establishing an economic barrier against competition with the products of another state or the labor of its residents. Restrictions so contrived are an unreasonable clog upon the mobility of commerce. They set up what is equivalent to a rampart of customs duties designed to neutralize advantages belonging to the place of origin. They are thus hostile in conception as well as burdensome in result. The form of the packages in such circumstances is immaterial, whether they are original or broken. The importer must be free from imposts framed for the very purpose of suppressing competition from without and leading inescapably to the suppression so intended.

The statute here in controversy will not survive that test. A dealer in milk buys it in Vermont at prices there prevailing. He brings it to New York, and is told he may not sell it if he removes it from the can and pours it into bottles. He may not do this for the reason that milk in Vermont is cheaper than milk in New York at the regimented prices, and New York is moved by the desire to protect her inhabitants from the cut prices and other consequences of Vermont competition. To overcome that competition a common incident of ownership — the privilege of sale in convenient receptacles — is denied to one who has bought in interstate commerce. He may not sell on any terms to any one, whether the orders were given in advance or came to him thereafter. The decisions of this court as to the significance of the original package in interstate transactions were not meant to be a cover for retortion or suppression.

The distinction is clear between a statute so designed and statutes of the type considered in Leisy v. Hardin, 135 U.S. 100, to take one example out of many available. By the teaching of that decision intoxicating liquors are not subject to license or prohibition by the state of destination without congressional consent. They become subject, however, to such laws when the packages are broken. There is little, if any, analogy between restrictions of that type and those in controversy here. In licensing or prohibiting the sale of intoxicating liquors a state does not attempt to neutralize economic advantages belonging to the place of origin. What it does is no more than to apply its domestic policy, rooted in its conceptions of morality and order, to property which for such a purpose may fairly be deemed to have passed out of commerce and to be commingled in an absorbing mass. So also the analogy is remote between restrictions like the present ones upon the sale of imported milk and restrictions affecting sales in unsanitary sweat-shops. It is one thing for a state to exact adherence by an importer to fitting standards of sanitation before the products of the farm or factory may be sold in its markets. It is a very different thing to establish a wage scale or a scale of prices for use in other states, and to bar the sale of the products, whether in the original packages or in others, unless the scale has been observed.

The decree in No. 604 is affirmed, and that in No. 605 reversed, and the cause remanded for proceedings in accordance with this opinion.

Henneford v. Silas Mason Co. *300 U.S. 577, 57 S. Ct. 524, 81 L. Ed. 814 (1937)*

MR. JUSTICE CARDOZO delivered the opinion of the Court.

A statute of Washington taxing the use of chattels in that state is assailed in this suit as a violation of the commerce clause (Constitution of the United States, article I, §8) in so far

386 Chapter Eight. **The States in a Federal Union**

as the tax is applicable to chattels purchased in another state and used in Washington thereafter.

Plaintiffs (appellees in this court) are engaged either as contractors or as subcontractors in the construction of the Grand Coulée Dam on the Columbia River. In the performance of that work they have brought into the state of Washington machinery, materials and supplies, such as locomotives, cars, conveyors, pumps, and trestle steel, which were bought at retail in other states. The cost of all the articles with transportation expenses added was $921,189.34. Defendants, the Tax Commission of Washington (appellants in this court) gave notice that plaintiffs had become subject through the use of this property to a tax of $18,423.78, two per cent of the cost, and made demand for payment. A District Court of three judges, organized in accordance with §266 of the Judicial Code (28 U.S.C. §380), adjudged the statute void upon its face, and granted an interlocutory injunction, one judge dissenting. 15 F. Supp. 958. The case is here upon appeal. 28 U.S.C. §380.

Chapter 180 of the Laws of Washington for the year 1935, consisting of twenty titles, lays a multitude of excise taxes on occupations and activities. Only two of these taxes are important for the purposes of the case at hand, the "tax on retail sales," imposed by title III. and the "compensating tax," imposed by title IV. on the privilege of use. Title III. provides that after May 1, 1935, every retail sale in Washington, with a few enumerated exceptions, shall be subject to a tax of 2% of the selling price. Title IV. with the heading "compensating tax," provides (§§31, 35) that there shall be collected from every person in the state "a tax or excise for the privilege of using within this state any article of tangible personal property purchased subsequent to April 30, 1935," at the rate of 2% of the purchase price, including in such price the cost of transportation from the place where the article was purchased. If those provisions stood alone, they would mean that retail buyers within the state would have to pay a double tax, 2% upon the sale and 2% upon the use. Relief from such a burden is provided in another section (§32) which qualifies the use tax by allowing four exceptions. Only two of these exceptions (b and c) call for mention at this time.[2] Subdivision (b) provides that the use tax shall not be laid unless the property has been bought at retail. Subdivision (c) provides that the tax shall not apply to the "use of any article of tangible personal property the sale or use of which has already been subjected to a tax equal to or in excess of that imposed by this title whether under the laws of this state or of some other state of the United States." If the rate of such other tax is less than 2%, the exemption is not to be complete (§33), but in such circumstances the rate is to be measured by the difference.

The plan embodied in these provisions is neither hidden nor uncertain. A use tax is never payable where the user has acquired property by retail purchase in the state of Washington, except in the rare instances in which retail purchases in Washington are not subjected to a sales tax. On the other hand, a use tax is always payable where the user has acquired property by retail purchase in or from another state, unless he has paid a sales or use tax elsewhere before bringing it to Washington. The tax presupposes everywhere a retail purchase by the user before the time of use. If he has manufactured the chattel for himself, or has received it from the manufacturer as a legacy or gift, he is exempt from the use tax, whether title was acquired in Washington or elsewhere. The practical effect of a system thus conditioned is readily perceived. One of its effects must be that retail sellers in Washington will be helped to compete upon terms of equality with retail dealers in other states who are exempt from a sales tax or any corresponding burden. Another effect, or at least another tendency, must be to avoid the likelihood of a drain upon the revenues of the

---

[2] For greater certainty exceptions (a) and (d) are stated in this note:

"The provisions of this title shall not apply:

"(a) In respect to the use of any article of tangible personal property brought into the State of Washington by a non-resident thereof for his or her use or enjoyment while within the state;

"(d) In respect to the use of tangible personal property purchased during any calendar month, the total purchase price of which is less than twenty ($20.00) dollars."

Section B. Protection of Local Economy and Welfare

state, buyers being no longer tempted to place their orders in other states in the effort to escape payment of the tax on local sales. Do these consequences, which must have been foreseen, necessitate a holding that the tax upon the use is either a tax upon the operations of interstate commerce or a discrimination against such commerce, obstructing or burdening it unlawfully?

1. The tax is not upon the operations of interstate commerce, but upon the privilege of use after commerce is at an end.

Things acquired or transported in interstate commerce may be subjected to a property tax, non-discriminatory in its operation, when they have become part of the common mass of property within the state of destination. [Citations omitted.] This is so, indeed, though they are still in the original packages. . . . For like reasons they may be subjected, when once they are at rest, to a non-discriminatory tax upon use or enjoyment. . . . The privilege of use is only one attribute, among many, of the bundle of privileges that make up property or ownership. . . . A state is at liberty, if it pleases, to tax them all collectively, or to separate the faggots and lay the charge distributively. . . .

. . . A tax upon a use so closely connected with delivery as to be in substance a part thereof might be subject to the same objections that would be applicable to a tax upon the sale itself. If the rules are too drastic in that respect or others, the defect is unimportant in relation to this case. Here the machinery and other chattels subjected to the tax have had continuous use in Washington long after the time when delivery was over. The plaintiffs are not the champions of any rights except their own.

2. The tax upon the use after the property is at rest is not so measured or conditioned as to hamper the transactions of interstate commerce or discriminate against them.

Equality is the theme that runs through all the sections of the statute. There shall be a tax upon the use, but subject to an offset if another use or sales tax has been paid for the same thing. This is true where the offsetting tax became payable to Washington by reason of purchase or use within the state. It is true in exactly the same measure where the offsetting tax has been paid to another state by reason of use or purchase there. No one who uses property in Washington after buying it at retail is to be exempt from a tax upon the privilege of enjoyment except to the extent that he has paid a use or sales tax somewhere. Every one who has paid a use or sales tax anywhere, or, more accurately, in any state, is to that extent to be exempt from the payment of another tax in Washington.

When the account is made up, the stranger from afar is subject to no greater burdens as a consequence of ownership than the dweller within the gates. The one pays upon one activity or incident, and the other upon another, but the sum is the same when the reckoning is closed. Equality exists when the chattel subjected to the use tax is bought in another state and then carried into Washington. It exists when the imported chattel is shipped from the state of origin under an order received directly from the state of destination. In each situation the burden borne by the owner is balanced by an equal burden where the sale is strictly local. . . .

Baldwin v. G. A. F. Seelig, 294 U. S. 511, is invoked by appellees as decisive of the controversy, but the case is far apart from this one. . . . New York was attempting to project its legislation within the borders of another state by regulating the price to be paid in that state for milk acquired there. She said in effect to farmers in Vermont: Your milk cannot be sold by dealers to whom you ship it in New York unless you sell it to them in Vermont at a price determined here. What Washington is saying to sellers beyond her borders is something very different. In substance what she says is this: You may ship your goods in such amounts and at prices as you please, but the goods when used in Washington after the transit is completed, will share an equal burden with goods that have been purchased here.

We are told that a tax upon the use, even though not unlawful by force of its effects alone, is vitiated by the motives that led to its adoption. These motives cause it to be stigmatized as equivalent to a protective tariff. But motives alone will seldom, if ever, invalidate a tax that apart from its motives would be recognized as lawful. [Citations omitted.] Least of all will they be permitted to accomplish that result when equality and not preference is the end to be achieved. Catchwords and labels, such as the words "protective tariff," are subject to the dangers that lurk in metaphors and symbols, and must be watched with circumspection lest they put us off our guard. A tariff, whether protective or for revenue, burdens the very act of importation, and if laid by a state upon its commerce with another is equally unlawful whether protection or revenue is the motive back of it. But a tax upon use, or, what is equivalent for present purposes, a tax upon property after importation is over, is not a clog upon the process of importation at all, any more than a tax upon the income or profits of a business. The contention would be futile that Washington in laying an ownership tax would be doing a wrong to non-residents in allowing a credit for a sales tax already borne by the owner as a result of the same ownership. To contend this would be to deny that a state may develop its scheme of taxation in such a way as to rid its exactions of unnecessary oppression. In the statute in dispute such a scheme has been developed with sedulous regard for every interest affected. Yet a word of caution should be added here to avoid the chance of misconception. We have not meant to imply by anything said in this opinion that allowance of a credit for other taxes paid to Washington made it mandatory that there should be a like allowance for taxes paid to other states. A state, for many purposes, is to be reckoned as a self-contained unit, which may frame its own system of burdens and exemptions without heeding systems elsewhere. If there are limits to that power, there is no need to mark them now. It will be time enough to mark them when a taxpayer paying in the state of origin is compelled to pay again in the state of destination. This statute by its framework avoids that possibility. The offsetting allowance has been conceded, whether the concession was necessary or not, and thus the system has been divested of any semblance of inequality or prejudice. A taxing act is not invalid because its exceptions are more generous than the state would have been free to make them by exerting the full measure of her power. . . .

The interlocutory injunction was erroneously granted, and the decree must be reversed.

MR. JUSTICE MCREYNOLDS and MR. JUSTICE BUTLER dissent.[g]

2. State Restrictions on Access to Local Products or Raw Materials

Milk Control Board v. Eisenberg Farm Products 306 U.S. 346, 59 S. Ct. 528, 83 L. Ed. 752 (1939)

MR. JUSTICE ROBERTS delivered the opinion of the Court:

We are called upon to determine whether a local police regulation unconstitutionally regulates or burdens interstate commerce. Pennsylvania, by an Act of April 30, 1935, has declared the milk industry in that Commonwealth to be a business affected with a public interest. The statute defines a milk dealer as any person "who purchases or handles milk within the Commonwealth for sale, shipment, storage, processing or manufacture within or without the Commonwealth." It creates a Milk Control Board with authority to investigate, supervise, and regulate the industry and imposes penalties for violations of the law or of the Board's orders issued pursuant to the law, and requires a dealer to obtain a license by application to the Board. Licenses may be refused, suspended, or revoked for specified causes. A requisite of obtaining a license is that the dealer shall file with the Board a bond

---

[g] Cf. Polar Ice Cream & Creamery Co. v. Andrews, 375 U.S. 361 (1964).

For the valuation of goods for purposes of a use tax where the component materials are assembled out of state by the user-taxpayer, see Halliburton Oil Well Cementing Co. v. Reily, 373 U.S. 64 (1973). — ED.

Section B. Protection of Local Economy and Welfare

conditioned for prompt payment of all amounts due to producers for milk purchased by the licensee. The act empowers the Board to require the dealer to keep certain records and directs the Board, with the approval of the Governor, to "fix, by official order, the minimum prices to be paid by milk dealers to producers and others for milk." The Board may vary the price according to the production, use, form, grade or class of milk.

The petitioner, the Milk Control Board, filed its bill in a Common Pleas Court to restrain the appellee from continuing to do business without complying with the statute. The respondent by its answers sought to justify failure to comply on the ground that it was engaged in interstate commerce. After trial the court dismissed the bill. The Supreme Court of Pennsylvania affirmed the decree. [332 Pa. 34, 200 Atl. 854.]

The respondent, a Pennsylvania corporation, leases and operates a milk receiving plant in Elizabethville, Pennsylvania, at which it buys milk from approximately one hundred and seventy-five farmers in the neighborhood, who bring their milk to the plant in their own cans. There the milk is weighed and tested by the respondent and emptied into large receiving tanks in which it is cooled preparatory to shipment. This requires retention of the milk for less than twenty-four hours; it is not processed, and no change occurs in its constituent elements. The milk is then drawn from the cooling tanks into tank trucks operated by a contract carrier and transported into New York City for sale there by the respondent. The journey is continuous from Elizabethville to New York City. All milk purchased by the respondent at Elizabethville is shipped to and sold in New York. During the year 1934 approximately 4,500,000,000 pounds of milk were produced in Pennsylvania, of which approximately 470,000,000 pounds were shipped out of the state.

The respondent contends that the act, if construed to require it to obtain a license, to file a bond for the protection of producers, and to pay the farmers the prices prescribed by the Board, unconstitutionally regulates and burdens interstate commerce. The State Supreme Court has held that the statute is a valid police regulation. The petitioner concedes that the purchase, shipment into another state, and sale there of the milk in which the respondent deals is interstate commerce. The question for decision is whether, in the absence of federal regulation, the enforcement of the statute is prohibited by Article 1, §8 of the Constitution. We hold that it is not. . . .

The purpose of the statute under review obviously is to reach a domestic situation in the interest of the welfare of the producers and consumers of milk in Pennsylvania. Its provisions with respect to license, bond, and regulation of prices to be paid to producers are appropriate means to the ends in view. The question is whether the prescription of prices to be paid producers in the effort to accomplish these ends constitutes a prohibited burden on interstate commerce, or an incidental burden which is permissible until superseded by Congressional enactment. That question can be answered only by weighing the nature of the respondent's activities, and the propriety of local regulation of them, as disclosed by the record.

The respondent maintains a receiving station in Pennsylvania where it conducts the local business of buying milk. At that station the neighboring farmers deliver their milk. The activity affected by the regulation is essentially local in Pennsylvania. Upon the completion of that transaction the respondent engages in conserving and transporting its own property. The Commonwealth does not essay to regulate or to restrain the shipment of the respondent's milk into New York or to regulate its sale or the price at which respondent may sell it in New York. If dealers conducting receiving stations in various localities in Pennsylvania were free to ignore the requirements of the statute on the ground that all or a part of the milk they purchase is destined to another state the uniform operation of the statute locally would be crippled and might be impracticable. Only a small fraction of the milk produced by farmers in Pennsylvania is shipped out of the Commonwealth. There is, therefore, a comparatively large field remotely affecting and wholly unrelated to interstate commerce within which the statute operates. These considerations we think justify the conclusion that the effect of the law on interstate commerce is incidental and not forbidden by the Constitution, in the absence of regulation by Congress.

None of the decisions on which the court below and the respondent rely rules the instant case. DiSanto v. Pennsylvania, 273 U.S. 34, involved a state law directed solely at foreign commerce; Lemke v. Farmers' Grain Co., 258 U.S. 50, condemned a state statute affecting commerce, over ninety per cent. of which was interstate, and essaying to regulate the price of commodities sold within the state payable and receivable in the state of destination; Shafer v. Farmers' Grain Co., 268 U.S. 189, also dealt with a state law intended to regulate commerce almost wholly interstate in character. In Baldwin v. G. A. F. Seelig, 294 U.S. 511, this court condemned an enactment aimed solely at interstate commerce attempting to affect and regulate the price to be paid for milk in a sister state, and we indicated that the attempt amounted in effect to a tariff barrier set up against milk imported into the enacting state.

The decree must be reversed and the cause remanded for further proceedings not inconsistent with this opinion.

Reversed.

MR. JUSTICE MCREYNOLDS and MR. JUSTICE BUTLER are of opinion that the Supreme Court of Pennsylvania properly concluded that under former opinions of this Court the questioned regulations constituted a burden upon interstate commerce prohibited by the Federal Constitution.

NOTE

Dahnke-Walker Milling Co. v. Bondurant, 257 U.S. 282 (1921), was an action for damages for breach of contract to sell and deliver the defendant's wheat crop. The plaintiff was a Tennessee corporation operating a mill in that state, the defendant a farmer in Kentucky, where the contract in question was negotiated and made. By its terms, delivery of the wheat was to be on board the cars of a carrier in Hickman, Kentucky; the plaintiff intended to ship the wheat from there to its mill in Tennessee. The principal defense was that the plaintiff had not complied with the statutory conditions on which foreign corporations might do business in Kentucky. The Court reversed a judgment for the defendant, and held that the business done by the plaintiff in Kentucky, of which the transaction with the defendant was a specimen, was not such that Kentucky could condition or prohibit to foreign corporations.

Lemke v. Farmers' Grain Co., 258 U.S. 50 (1922), and Shafer v. Farmers' Grain Co., 268 U.S. 189 (1925), were suits by operators of grain elevators in North Dakota to enjoin the enforcement of North Dakota statutes variously regulating the grading, weighing, inspecting, or pricing of wheat when purchased by elevator operators from local producers. It was shown that only about 10 per cent of the wheat grown in North Dakota was consumed locally, and that the remainder was principally sold to local elevator operators who bought with the purpose of shipping and selling in terminal markets outside the state. The Court in each instance held that enforcement of the statute against such elevator operators should be enjoined.

For questions relevant to an economic analysis of the Commerce Clause problem where a state regulates the price of a locally produced commodity, see Note, page 411 infra.

Pennsylvania v. West Virginia 262 U.S. 553, 43 S. Ct. 658, 67 L. Ed. 1117 (1923)

MR. JUSTICE VAN DEVANTER delivered the opinion of the court:

These are suits, one by the commonwealth of Pennsylvania and the other by the state of

Section B. Protection of Local Economy and Welfare

Ohio, to enjoin the state of West Virginia from enforcing an act passed by her legislature (Acts 1919, chap. 71) which the complainants believe will largely curtail or cut off the supply of natural gas heretofore and now carried by pipe lines from West Virginia into their territory and there sold and used for fuel and lighting purposes. . . .

. . . The complainants challenge its validity on the ground that it directly interferes with interstate commerce and therefore contravenes the commerce clause of the Constitution of the United States, and they rest their right to relief on the grounds that to enforce the act will subject them to irreparable injury in respect of many of their public institutions and governmental agencies, which long have been and now are using this gas, and will subject them to further and incalculable injury in that (a) it will imperil the health and comfort of thousands of their people who use the gas in their homes and are largely dependent thereon, and (b) will halt or curtail many industries which seasonally use great quantities of the gas and wherein thousands of persons are employed and millions of taxable wealth are invested. . . .

In West Virginia the production of natural gas began as much as thirty years ago and for the last fourteen years has been greater than in any other state. The producing fields include thirty-two of her fifty-five counties. At first the gas was produced only in the course of oil operations, was regarded as a nuisance, and was permitted to waste into the air. But it soon came to be regarded as valuable for heating and lighting, and the economy and convenience attending its use made it a preferred fuel. Its use within the state became relatively general, but was far less than the production, so the producers turned to neighboring states, notably Pennsylvania and Ohio, for a further market.

. . . The effort to find a further market succeeded, and the gas came to be extensively carried into Pennsylvania as far as Pittsburgh, and into Ohio as far as Cleveland, Toledo, and Cincinnati. . . .

. . . [Pipe] lines long have been and now are supplying gas to the three states for use in their charitable, educational, and penal institutions, to their counties and municipalities for use in county, city, and school buildings, to local utilities serving particular communities, to the people generally in many cities and towns for use in their homes, places of business, and offices, and, in seasons when there is an adequate supply, to industrial plants for use in their operation. The predominant use is for fuel purposes, that for lighting being relatively small. All gas going into Pennsylvania and Ohio is carried and supplied under prior engagements respecting its disposal, — most of it under long-time contracts exacted or preferred by the purchasers or consumers. . . .

Latterly, during the colder months — from November 1 to May 1 — the combined needs of domestic and industrial consumers have been largely in excess of the production, and the pipe line companies generally have adopted and are pursuing the policy of preferring domestic consumers during those months. All the long-time contracts contain provisions admitting of such a preference. During other months, when there is little occasion for heating homes and offices, the needs of domestic consumers drop so materially that much gas may be and is supplied for industrial use without affecting the domestic use. But increased population, enlarged industry, — particularly in West Virginia, — and the advantages inhering in the gas as a fuel have finally resulted in a gross demand, which cannot be satisfied even in the summer months. The present actual consumption is all that the production will sustain. The pipe line companies cannot supply more gas in West Virginia without cutting down what they carry into Pennsylvania and Ohio; nor can they carry more into Pennsylvania and Ohio without cutting down what they supply in West Virginia. In short, the situation is such that to constrain the companies to supply more gas in any one of the three states necessarily will constrain them to supply less in the other two. . . .

The act whose enforcement is sought to be enjoined was passed by the legislature of West Virginia February 10, 1919, and went into effect May 11th following. These suits were brought eight days thereafter by direction of the legislatures of the complainant states, and by leave of this court. Interlocutory injunctions were prayed and granted at the outset and are still in force.

Three questions bearing on the propriety of entertaining the suits were raised soon after the suits were begun, and consideration of them was postponed to the final hearing.

The first question is whether the suits involve a justiciable controversy between states in the sense of the Judiciary Article of the Constitution. We are of opinion that they do and that every element of such a controversy is present.

Each suit presents a direct issue between two states as to whether one may withdraw a natural product, a common subject of commercial dealings, from an established current of commerce moving into the territory of the other. . . .

The attitude of the complainant states is not that of mere volunteers attempting to vindicate the freedom of interstate commerce or to redress purely private grievances. . . .

Each state uses large amounts of the gas in her several institutions and schools, — the greater part in the discharge of duties which are relatively imperative. A break or cessation in the supply will embarrass her greatly in the discharge of those duties and expose thousands of dependents and school children to serious discomfort, if not more. To substitute another form of fuel will involve very large public expenditures.

The private consumers in each state not only include most of the inhabitants of many urban communities, but constitute a substantial portion of the state's population. Their health, comfort, and welfare are seriously jeopardized by the threatened withdrawal of the gas from the interstate stream. This is a matter of grave public concern in which the state, as the representative of the public, has an interest apart from that of the individuals affected. It is not merely a remote or ethical interest, but one which is immediate and recognized by law.

In principle these views have full support in prior decisions, ... [Citations omitted.]

The second question is whether the suits were brought prematurely. They were brought a few days after the West Virginia act went into force. No order under it had been made by the public service commission, nor had it been tested in actual practice. But this does not prove that the suits were premature. Of course they were not so, if it otherwise appeared that the act certainly would operate as the complainant states apprehended it would. One does not have to await the consummation of threatened injury to obtain preventive relief. If the injury is certainly impending that is enough.

Turning to the act, we find that by its first section it lays on every pipe line company a positive duty — to the extent of its supply of gas produced in the state, whether produced by it or others — to satisfy the needs, whether for domestic, industrial, or other use, of all intending consumers, whether old or new, who are willing to pay for the gas and want it for use within the section of the state in which it is produced, in that through which it is transported, or in that wherein it is supplied to others. This is a substantive provision whose terms are both direct and certain, and to which immediate obedience is commanded. No order of the commission is required to give it precision or make it obligatory, and it leaves nothing to the discretion of those who are to enforce it. On the contrary, it prescribes a definite rule of conduct and in itself puts the rule in force. It imposes an unconditional and mandatory duty, as counsel for the state admit, and obviously is intended to enforce a preferred recognition and satisfaction of the needs of consumers within the state, present and prospective, regardless of the effect on the interstate stream or on consumers outside the state. . . .

The fourth section empowers the commission to entertain complaints by persons aggrieved or affected by any "violation" of the act and to require that the violation be discontinued and the act obeyed, subject to a right of review in the courts, and also provides means of compelling obedience to the act pending the proceedings before the commission and until the decision on review.

Other sections contain penal and remedial provisions designed to make those just described effective. . . . [One] in the sixth section subjects any company violating the act to an action for damages by anyone claiming to have been wronged by the violation.

We regard it as entirely clear that the act is intended to compel the retention within the state of whatever gas may be required to meet the local needs for all purposes, and that its procedural, penal, and remedial provisions are amply adequate to accomplish that result. And we think it equally clear from the allegations in the bills, now established by the evidence, that the situation when the suits were brought was such that the act directly and immediately would work a large curtailment of the volume of gas moving into the complainant states. Indeed, the conclusion is unavoidable that with the increasing demand in West Virginia, and the decreasing production, the act in a few years would work a practical cessation of the interstate stream.

It must be held, therefore, that the suits were not brought prematurely.

The third question is whether the requisite parties have been brought into the suits. It is objected that the pipe line companies have not been brought in. But there is nothing which makes their presence essential. . . .

We turn now to the principal issue, whether a state wherein natural gas is produced and is a recognized subject of commercial dealings may require that in its sale and disposal consumers in that state shall be accorded a preferred right of purchase over consumers in other states, when the requirement necessarily will operate to withdraw a large volume of the gas from an established interstate current whereby it is supplied in other states to consumers there. . . . The question is an important one; for what one state may do others may, and there are ten states from which natural gas is exported for consumption in other states. Besides, what may be done with one natural product may be done with others, and there are several states in which the earth yields products of great value which are carried into other states and there used. But, notwithstanding the importance of the question, its solution is not difficult. The controlling principles have been settled by many adjudications, — some so closely in point that the discussion here may be relatively brief. . . .

Natural gas is a lawful article of commerce, and its transmission from one state to another for sale and consumption in the latter is interstate commerce. A state law, whether of the state where the gas is produced or that where it is to be sold, which by its necessary operation prevents, obstructs, or burdens such transmission, is a regulation of interstate commerce, — a prohibited interference. [Citations omitted.] The West Virginia act is such a law. Its provisions and the conditions which must surround its operation are such that it necessarily and directly will compel the diversion to local consumers of a large and increasing part of the gas heretofore and now going to consumers in the complainant states, and therefore will work a serious interference with that commerce.

But it is urged that there are special considerations which take the act out of the general rule and sustain its validity, even though there be an interference. . . .

[One] consideration advanced to the same end is that the gas is a natural product of the state and has become a necessity therein, that the supply is waning and no longer sufficient to satisfy local needs and be used abroad, and that the act is therefore a legitimate measure of conservation in the interest of the people of the state. If the situation be as stated, it affords no ground for the assumption by the state of power to regulate interstate commerce, which is what the act attempts to do. That power is lodged elsewhere. A contention, in essence the same, was presented and considered in West v. Kansas Natural Gas Co., 221 U.S. 229, a case involving the validity of an Oklahoma statute designed to accomplish the retention of natural gas within the state. . . .

Referring to . . . a contention that the ruling principle of the statute was conservation of a needed natural resource, the court said:

"The results of the contention repel its acceptance. Gas, when reduced to possession, is a commodity; it belongs to the owner of the land, and, when reduced to possession, is his individual property subject to sale by him, and may be a subject of intrastate commerce and interstate commerce. The statute of Oklahoma recognizes it to be a subject of intrastate commerce, but seeks to prohibit it from being the subject of interstate commerce, and this is the purpose of its conservation. . . . If the states have such power a singular situation might result. Pennsylvania might keep its coal, the Northwest its timber, the mining states their minerals. And why may not the products of the field be brought within the principle? Thus enlarged, or without that enlargement, its influence on interstate commerce need not be pointed out. To what consequences does such power tend? If one state has it, all states have it; embargo may be retaliated by embargo, and commerce will be halted at state lines. And yet we have said that 'in matters of foreign and interstate commerce there are no state lines.' " . . .

Finally, it is urged that this court cannot prescribe and execute regulations respecting the apportionment and use of the gas among the three states, and therefore that the bills should be dismissed. The conclusion does not follow from the premise. The object of the suits is not to obtain decretal regulations, but to enjoin the enforcement of the West Virginia act on the ground that it is an unconstitutional enactment and its intended enforcement will subject the complainant states to injury of serious magnitude. On full consideration, we reach the conclusion that the act is unconstitutional. . . . In this situation the appropriate decree is one declaring the act invalid and enjoining its enforcement. . . . If there be need for regulating the interstate commerce involved, the regulation should be sought from the body in whom the power resides.

Decrees for complainants.

MR. JUSTICE HOLMES, dissenting:

The statute seeks to reach natural gas before it has begun to move in commerce of any kind. It addresses itself to gas thereafter to be collected and states to what uses it first must be applied. The gas is collected under and subject to the law, if valid, and at that moment it is not yet matter of commerce among the states. I think that the products of a state, until they are actually started to a point outside it, may be regulated by the state notwithstanding the commerce clause. . . .

. . . The right of the state so to regulate the use of natural gas as to prevent waste was sustained as against the 14th Amendment in Walls v. Midland Carbon Co., 254 U.S. 300, and I do not suppose that the plaintiffs would have fared any better had they invoked the commerce clause. . . . I am aware that there is some general language in West v. Kansas Natural Gas Co., 221 U.S. 229, 255, a decision that I thought wrong, implying that Pennsylvania might not keep its coal, or the Northwest its timber, etc. But I confess I do not see what is to hinder. Certainly if the owners of the mines or the forests saw fit not to export their products the Constitution would not make them do it. I see nothing in that instrument that would produce a different result if the state gave the owners motive for their conduct, as by offering a bonus. . . .

I agree substantially with my brothers McReynolds and Brandeis, but think that there is jurisdiction in such a sense as to justify a statement of my opinion upon the merits of the case. I think that the bill should be dismissed.

MR. JUSTICE McREYNOLDS, dissenting:

It seems to me quite clear that the record presents no justiciable controversy; certainly none within the original jurisdiction of this court. . . .

If West Virginia should prohibit the drilling of new gas wells, I hardly suppose complainants could demand an injunction here even if it were admitted that their supplies would be cut off. But why not, under the doctrine announced? Production has been permitted for years and appealing hardships would follow its cessation. And suppose West Virginia should repeal the charters of all her public service corporations now transporting gas, and thereby disable them, could we interfere upon the demands of another state who claimed that she would suffer? . . .

Concluding his opinion in Chisholm v. Georgia (1793), Mr. Justice Iredell exclaimed: "I pray to God that if the Attorney General's doctrine, as to the law, be established by the

Section B. Protection of Local Economy and Welfare

judgment of this court, all the good he predicts from it may take place, and none of the evils with which, I have the concern to say, it appears to me to be pregnant." A like prayer seems not inappropriate here and now.

MR. JUSTICE BRANDEIS, dissenting:

The statement made by Mr. Justice Holmes seems to me unanswerable. But, like Mr. Justice McReynolds, I think that there are reasons why the bills should be dismissed without passing upon the constitutional question presented. . . .

First. This court is without jurisdiction of the subject-matter.

The bills present neither a "case," nor a "controversy," within the meaning of the Federal Constitution. Marbury v. Madison, 1 Cranch. 137; Muskrat v. United States, 219 U.S. 346, 356, 359; Texas v. Interstate Commerce Commission, 258 U.S. 158. They are not proceedings "instituted according to the regular course of judicial procedure" to protect some right of property or personal right. They are, like McChord v. Louisiana & N.R. Co., 183 U.S. 483, 495, an attempt to enjoin, not executive action, but legislation. They are instituted frankly to secure from this court a general declaration that the West Virginia Act of February 17, 1919, is unconstitutional. Compare Giles v. Harris, 189 U.S. 475, 486. The well-settled rule that the court is without power to entertain such a proceeding applies equally, whether the party invoking its aid is a state or a private person. And the rule cannot be overcome by giving to pleadings the form of a bill in equity for an injunction. Compare Fairchild v. Hughes, 258 U.S. 126; Atherton Mills v. Johnston, 259 U.S. 13, 15; Texas v. Interstate Commerce Commission, supra.

. . . The mere enactment of the statute, obviously, does not constitute a threat to interrupt the flow of gas into the plaintiff states. The importation into Ohio and Pennsylvania is conducted, not by the state of West Virginia, but wholly by twelve privately owned public service corporations. If the importation ceases it will be, primarily at least, because of acts or omissions of these twelve corporations. Yet there is not even an allegation that these corporations threaten, or intend, to discontinue the importation; or that they will be compelled to do so unless the state of West Virginia is enjoined from enforcing the statute.

On the other hand, it clearly appears that, under the laws of West Virginia, there can be no present danger that any of these twelve corporations will be summarily prevented by that state from continuing in full volume the export of gas, or will be compelled to reduce it. The only restriction, if any, imposed by the Act of 1919 upon exportation of gas, is that which may result from the requirement that West Virginia public service corporations shall not, by means of export, disable themselves from performing their duties to consumers and to other distributing companies within the state. Before there can be, in a legal sense, danger that restriction will result, it must appear that one or more of the twelve exporting companies is disabling itself by such exportation, or is about to do so; and also that some state official is about to take effective action to prevent the exportation. But under the legislation of West Virginia many things would have to happen and much time must elapse before any of the exporting corporations would be under any legal duty to discontinue or lessen their exports, and still more time before it could actually be prevented from exporting gas. . . . The objection here is not, as in Georgia v. Tennessee Copper Co., 206 U.S. 230, 238, that those interested should be left to an action at law for redress of any injuries which may be suffered. It is that the "judicial stage" of the controversy had not been reached when these suits were begun; and, indeed, has not been since. See Prentis v. Atlantic Coast Line Co., 211 U.S. 210; 228; Bacon v. Rutland R. Co., 232 U.S. 134, 137.

Second. There is a fatal lack of necessary parties. It is only by failure of the twelve exporting companies to continue the exportation of gas that the plaintiffs and other consumers, or the distributing companies in Pennsylvania or Ohio, can be injured. Primarily, at least, it is the rights of these twelve corporations, if of anyone, which would be invaded by enforcing the statute; and rights of consumers and of distributing corporations of Pennsylvania and of Ohio are derivative merely. Whether the West Virginia corporations may furnish gas to the plaintiff states, and whether those corporations may be regulated as the statute attempts, are, at most, controversies between West Virginia and those corporations. They have not submitted their rights to adjudication in these suits. It is intimated that these corporations wish to have the act declared void. But we may not assume that such is their wish. Conceivably a decision holding the act valid might benefit them; since it might relieve them from improvident contracts with distributing companies in Pennsylvania and Ohio. Or it may be that some of the twelve corporations would be benefited and others injured by any decision made of the question presented. Unless the twelve corporations are legally represented either by the plaintiff or the defendant, they would not be bound by a decree in either of these suits. . . .

Third. But if all other obstacles could be overcome, this court, sitting as a court of equity, should dismiss the bills, because it would be unable to grant the only relief appropriate. This court, sitting in equity, clearly should not lend its aid to enable West Virginia public service corporations to discriminate against West Virginia consumers in the interest of Ohio and Pennsylvania consumers. Therefore, an appropriate decree should be framed so as to require each of the West Virginia corporations to treat West Virginia customers at least as well as it does those outside of the state, and the decree should not leave any West Virginia public service corporation free to export gas in disregard of the duty not to discriminate against the public in that state. But natural gas is produced also in Pennsylvania and Ohio; and the local production furnishes a large part of the supplies consumed in those states. Furthermore, West Virginia gas is exported also to Maryland, Indiana, and Kentucky; and in two of those states natural gas is produced in quantity. Clearly the court should, in no event, go further than to compel West Virginia to share its production equitably with other states now dependent upon it for a part of their gas supply. But in order to determine what is equitable (that is, what part of the West Virginia production that state might require its public service corporations to retain, and what part they should be free to export to other states) it would obviously be necessary to marshal the resources and the demands, or needs, of the six states, and to consider, in respect of each, both the conduct of the business therein and the circumstances attending its development. The factors necessary to be considered in determining what division of the West Virginia production would be fair, the conditions under which the determination would have to be made, and the character of the questions to be decided are such that this court would be obliged to refuse to undertake the task. For this reason, the bills should be dismissed, even if it were held both that rights legally represented by plaintiffs were in present danger of irreparable injury by wrongful acts of defendant and that there was not a fatal lack of necessary parties. . . .

Clearly, this court could not undertake such determinations. To make equitable distribution would be a task of such complexity and difficulty that even an interstate public service commission, with broad powers, perfected administrative machinery, ample resources, practical experience, and no other duties, might fail to perform it satisfactorily. As this court would be powerless to frame a decree and provide machinery by means of which such equitable distribution of the available supply could be effected, it should, according to settled practice, refuse to entertain the suits.[h]

GEER v. CONNECTICUT, 161 U.S. 519, 16 S. Ct. 600, 40 L. Ed. 793 (1896). White, J.: "The General Statutes of the State of Connecticut provide . . . (Sec. 2546 [Revision of 1888]): 'No person shall at any time kill any woodcock, ruffled grouse or quail for the purpose of conveying the same beyond the limits of this State; or shall transport or have in

[h] Cf. Justice Brandeis' dissenting opinion in International News Service v. Associated Press, 248 U.S. 215 (1918). — ED.

Section B. Protection of Local Economy and Welfare

possession, with intent to procure the transportation beyond said limits, any of such birds killed within this State . . .' [Section 2530 prohibited the killing of such birds between the first day of January and the first day of October.]

"An information was filed against the plaintiff in error in the police court of New London, Connecticut, charging him with, on the 19th day of October, 1889, unlawfully receiving and having in his possession, with . . . unlawful intent to procure the transportation beyond the limits of the State certain woodcock, ruffled grouse and quail killed within [the] State after the first day of October, 1889. The trial . . . resulted in the conviction of the defendant and the imposing of a fine upon him. . . . In the Supreme Court the conviction was affirmed. . . . To this judgment of affirmance this writ of error is prosecuted. . . ."

What decision? Why?

HUDSON WATER CO. v. McCARTER, 209 U.S. 349, 28 S. Ct. 529, 52 L. Ed. 828 (1908). Holmes, J.: "This is an information, alleging that the defendant (the plaintiff in error), under a contract with the City of Bayonne in New Jersey, has laid mains in that city for the purpose of carrying water to Staten Island in the State of New York. By other contracts it is to get the water from the Passaic River, at Little Falls, where the East Jersey Water Company has a large plant. . . . On May 11, 1905, the State of New Jersey, reciting the need of peserving the fresh water of the State for the health and prosperity of the citizens, enacted that 'It shall be unlawful for any person or corporation to transport or carry, through pipes, conduits, ditches or canals, the waters of any fresh water lake, pond, . . . river or stream of this State into any other State, for use therein.' By a second section a proceeding like the present was authorized, in order to enforce the act. . . . After the passage of this statute the defendant made a contract with the City of New York to furnish a supply of water adequate for the Borough of Richmond, and of not less than three million gallons a day. Thereupon this information was brought, praying that, pursuant to the above act and otherwise, the defendant might be enjoined from carrying the waters of the Passaic River out of the State. . . . The defendant sets up that the statute, if applicable to it, is contrary to the Constitution of the United States. . . . An injunction was issued by the Chancellor, 70 N.J. Eq. 525, the decree was affirmed by the Court of Errors and Appeals, 70 N.J. Eq. 695, and the case then was brought here. . . ."

What decision? Why?

SLIGH v. KIRKWOOD, 237 U.S. 52, 35 S. Ct. 501, 59 L. Ed. 835 (1915). Day, J.: "A statute of the State of Florida undertakes to make it unlawful for anyone to sell, offer for sale, or deliver for shipment, any citrus fruits which are immature or otherwise unfit for consumption.

"Plaintiff in error, S. J. Sligh, was charged by information containing three counts in the Criminal Court of Record in Orange County, Florida, with a violation of this statute. One of the counts charged that Sligh delivered to an agent of the Seaboard Air Line Railway Company . . . , for shipment to Winecoff & Adams, Birmingham, Alabama, one car of oranges, which were citrus fruits, then and there immature and unfit for consumption. Upon petition for writ of habeas corpus in the Circuit Court of Florida . . . , the court refused to order the release of Sligh, and remanded him to the custody of the Sheriff. Upon writ of error to the Supreme Court of Florida, that judgment was affirmed (65 Florida, 123), and the case is brought here . . ."

What decision? Why?

Foster-Fountain Packing Co. v. Haydel 278 U.S. 1, 49 S. Ct. 1, 73 L. Ed. 147 (1928)

MR. JUSTICE BUTLER delivered the opinion of the court:

Appellants, plaintiffs below, are engaged in the business of catching and canning shrimp for shipment and sale in interstate commerce. Appellees, defendants below, are public officers in Louisiana charged with the duty of enforcing Act No. 103, known as the "Shrimp Act," passed in July, 1926; . . . . Plaintiffs sued to enjoin enforcement of certain of its provisions on the ground, among others, that they violate the commerce clause of the Federal Constitution. The district judge granted a restraining order pending application for a temporary injunction. There was a hearing before the court, consisting of three judges, organized as required by § 266 of the Judicial Code, U.S.C. title 28, § 380; it set aside the restraining order and denied the injunction. Then the court allowed this appeal, found that the plaintiffs will sustain irreparable harm and damage, and stayed the enforcement of the act pending determination here. . . .

. . . The Foster Company and the Sea Food Company have a contract by which the former agrees to catch in Louisiana waters and deliver to the latter in Biloxi [Mississippi] a carload of raw shrimp per month during specified periods. The supply is intended for the interstate and foreign business of the Sea Food Company; and, if prevented from obtaining such shrimp, the business of that company will be destroyed and its plants will be of no value.

. . . Shrimp are taken by nets dragged by power boats, and are then put on large vessels and transported to Biloxi. To prepare the meat for canning, the heads and hulls are picked off; most of them are thrown into the water where they are consumed by scavengers of the sea. But some are made into "shrimp bran," which is used to a small extent in the manufacture of commercial fertilizer.

The act declares all shrimp and parts thereof in Louisiana waters to be the property of the state, and regulates their taking and reduction to private ownership. It grants the right to take, can, pack and dry shrimp to residents and also to corporations, domiciled or organized in the state, operating a canning or packing factory or drying platform therein. § 4. It is made unlawful to export from the state any shrimp from which the heads and hulls have not been removed. But, in order that all its inhabitants "may enjoy the state's natural food product," the act declares it lawful to ship unshelled shrimp to any point within the state. Whoever shall lawfully take shrimp from the waters is granted a qualified interest which may be sold within the state. And, when the tail meat is removed within the state, the taker or possessor has title and the right to sell and ship the same "beyond the limit[s] of the state, without restriction or reservation." It is declared unlawful to export from the state any raw shells or hulls and heads "as they are required to be manufactured into fertilizer or used for an element in chicken feed." But, when they have been "conserved for the purpose herein stated, the right of property therein theretofore existing in the state shall pass to the lawful taker or the possessor thereof." § 13. Penalties are prescribed for violations. § 19. . . .

At the hearing on their motion for a temporary injunction, plaintiffs presented affidavits which tend to show the facts following: By reason of favorable topographical, climatic, labor and other conditions, shrimp taken from the Louisiana marshes may be more conveniently and economically canned at Biloxi than in Louisiana near to the source of supply. The Biloxi plants have long constituted an important center of the industry, and they are largely dependent upon the Louisiana marshes for their supply. The enforcement of the act would injure or destroy the shrimp business of plaintiffs and the industry at Biloxi. About 95 percent of the shrimp obtained from the waters of Louisiana, when taken, is intended for consumption outside the state. Some shrimp bran is made from the hulls and heads in Louisiana; but all of it is shipped to Biloxi where it is used to make fer-

Section B. Protection of Local Economy and Welfare

tilizer. It is worth less than 1 per cent of the value of the shrimp. Not more than half the hulls and heads removed in Louisiana are used for any purpose. They have no market value, cannot be sold or given away, and often constitute a nuisance.

The facts alleged in the complaint, the details set forth in plaintiffs' affidavits and the provisions of the act to be restrained show that the conservation of hulls and heads is a feigned and not the real purpose. They support plaintiffs' contention that the purpose of the enactment is to prevent the interstate movement of raw shrimp from the Louisiana marshes to the plants at Biloxi in order through commercial necessity to bring about the removal of the packing and canning industries from Mississippi to Louisiana. The conditions imposed by the act upon the interstate movement of the meat and other products of shrimp are not intended and do not operate to conserve them for the use of the people of the state.

One challenging the validity of a state enactment on the ground that it is repugnant to the commerce clause is not necessarily bound by the legislative declarations of purpose. It is open to him to show that in their practical operation its provisions directly burden or destroy interstate commerce. Minnesota v. Barber, 136 U.S. 313, 319, ... In determining what is interstate commerce, courts look to practical considerations and the established course of business. [Citations omitted.] Interstate commerce includes more than transportation; it embraces all the component parts of commercial intercourse among states. And a state statute that operates directly to burden any of its essential elements is invalid. [Citations omitted.] A state is without power to prevent privately owned articles of trade from being shipped and sold in interstate commerce on the ground that they are required to satisfy local demands or because they are needed by the people of the state. Pennsylvania v. West Virginia, 262 U.S. 553, 596; West v. Kansas Natural Gas Co., 221 U.S. 229, 255. . . .

. . . As the representative of its people, the state might have retained the shrimp for consumption and use therein. But, in direct opposition to conservation for intrastate use, this enactment permits all parts of the shrimp to be shipped and sold outside the state. The purpose is not to retain the shrimp for the use of the people of Louisiana; it is to favor the canning of the meat and the manufacture of bran in Louisiana by withholding raw or unshelled shrimp from the Biloxi plants. But by permitting its shrimp to be taken and all the products thereof to be shipped and sold in interstate commerce, the state necessarily releases its hold, and, as to the shrimp so taken, definitely terminates its control. Clearly such authorization and the taking in pursuance thereof put an end to the trusts upon which the state is deemed to own or control the shrimp for the benefit of its people. And those taking the shrimp under the authority of the act necessarily thereby become entitled to the rights of private ownership and the protection of the commerce clause. They are not bound to comply with, or estopped from objecting to, the enforcement of, conditions that conflict with the Constitution of the United States. [Citations omitted.]

If the facts are substantially as claimed by plaintiffs, the practical operation and effect of the provisions complained of will be directly to obstruct and burden interstate commerce. [Citations omitted.] The affidavits give substantial and persuasive support to the facts alleged. And as, pending the trial and determination of the case, plaintiffs will suffer great and irremediable loss if the challenged provisions shall be enforced, their right to have a temporary injunction is plain. From the record it quite clearly appears that the lower court's refusal was an important exercise of judicial discretion.

Decree reversed.

Separate opinion of MR. JUSTICE McREYNOLDS:

I think the court below properly applied the correct doctrine and that the challenged decree should be affirmed. . . .

Manifestly, Louisiana has full power absolutely to forbid interstate shipments of shrimp taken within her territory. These crustaceans belong to her and she may appropriate them for the exclusive use and benefit of citizens. If the state should conclude that the best interest of her people requires all shrimp to be canned or manufactured therein before becoming part of interstate commerce, nothing in the Federal Constitution would prevent appropriate action to that end. This would not interfere with any right guaranteed to an outsider. How wild life may be utilized in order to advantage her own citizens is for the producing state to determine. To enlarge opportunity for employment is one way, and often the most effective way, to promote their welfare. . . .

Any profitable discussion of this controversy must take into consideration the marked distinction between game and property subject to absolute ownership. . . . A state may regulate the sale and transportation of wild things in ways not permissible where wheat is the subject-matter. . . .[1]

CLASON v. INDIANA, 306 U.S. 439, 59 S. Ct. 609, 83 L. Ed. 858 (1939). McReynolds, J.: "The Supreme Court of Indiana affirmed a judgment which convicted appellant of violating section eleven of the Animals Disposal Act approved March 12, 1937 (c. 278, Acts 1937) by transporting a dead horse over a highway of that State and into Illinois without license. Forbidden transportation is admitted; also that while license can be obtained under prescribed conditions for such transportation within the State it is prohibited for points outside.

"Section eleven is a part of a comprehensive statute which requires, and undertakes to regulate, the prompt disposition of large dead animals (not slaughtered for human food) under the general supervision of the State Veterinarian. The obvious purpose of the enactment is to prevent the spread of disease and the development of nuisances.

"The prescribed plan exacts that within twenty-four hours after death owners shall bury or burn such bodies on their premises, or there deliver them to the representative of a disposal plant licensed to do business within the State. It further directs that the body shall be promptly carried to such plant in a sanitary vehicle and speedily rendered innocuous. The conveyance must be thoroughly and promptly disinfected at the plant.

"The validity of the Statute was unsuccessfully challenged on the ground that it unduly discriminates against and burdens interstate commerce and thereby violates the Federal Constitution. . . ."

What decision? Why?

NOTE

1. The California Fish and Game Code prohibited, with exceptions not here relevant, the use of the edible parts of fish caught in or brought into the state in the manufacture of fish flour, fish meal (used for chicken feed), fertilizer, etc. In Bayside Fish Flour Co. v. Gentry, 297 U.S. 422 (1936), the petitioner manufactured such products from sardines caught on the high seas and brought to its plant in California, and then shipped these products in interstate and foreign commerce. It sought to enjoin the threatened enforcement of the statute against it. The Court upheld the statute, stating, with reference to a commerce clause challenge, that its direct operation was wholly local, and, answering a due process argument, that the statute served the permissible purpose of preventing waste and conserving for food the available fish supply. Compare Walls v. Midland Carbon Co., 254 U.S. 300 (1920), upholding a Wyoming statute prohibiting "wasteful and extravagant use of natural gas" in the manufacture of carbon black, and Champlin Refining Co. v. Corporation Commission, 286 U.S. 210 (1932), with Thompson v. Consolidated Gas Util. Corp., 300 U.S. 55 (1937). See Note, The Constitution and State Control of Natural Resources, 64 Harv. L. Rev. 642 (1951).

---

[1] Cf. Toomer v. Witsell, 334 U.S. 385 (1948); Alaska v. Arctic Maid, 366 U.S. 199 (1961). — ED.

Section B. **Protection of Local Economy and Welfare** 401

2. Most of the raisins consumed in the United States are produced in California, and over 90 percent of the raisins grown in California are ultimately shipped in interstate and foreign commerce after sale to local packers who process and pack them. The California Agricultural Prorate Act required producers to pool over two thirds of their 1940 crop for classification and marketing by a Program Committee; the remainder could be marketed by the producer through commercial channels of his choice. These controls were declared to be enacted to "conserve the agricultural wealth of the State" and to "prevent economic waste in marketing." In Parker v. Brown, 317 U.S. 341 (1943), the Court upheld the California statute against the challenge of a producer who wished to market his crop free of the controls imposed and sought an injunction against enforcement of the statute. To the claim that the statute and practices under it conflicted with the Sherman Act, the Court replied that that act did not restrain state action; to the claim that the statute conflicted with the commerce clause, the Court answered that (1) viewed mechanically, the statute controlled only local transactions, and (2) taking into account its ultimate impact upon interstate and foreign commerce, the local action was in accord with the price-parity policy of the Federal Agricultural Marketing Agreement Act of 1937, as was demonstrated by the fact that the Secretary of Agriculture had refrained from initiating a federal stabilization program with respect to raisins, and, as authorized by the federal statute, had assisted the financing of the state program by loans conditioned upon the adoption of the program.

3. Compare the series of decisions: James v. South Australia, 40 C.L.R. 1 (Australia 1927); James v. Cowan, [1932] A.C. 542 (P.C.), and James v. Commonwealth, [1936] A.C. 578 (P.C.). In the first two the High Court of Australia and the Privy Council, respectively, held invalid under §92 of the Commonwealth Constitution state legislation of South Australia imposing marketing quotas with respect to dried fruits. In the third the Privy Council also held invalid under §92 Commonwealth legislation of like character. See Freund, A Supreme Court in a Federation, 53 Colum L. Rev. 597, 608 (1953). Note Hartley v. Walsh, 57 C.L.R. 372 (Australia 1937), upholding the sanitary restrictions imposed by the Dried Fruits Act of 1928 of Victoria.

4. In Colgate v. Harvey, 296 U.S. 404 (1935), the Court held invalid, as in conflict with the privileges and immunities clause of the Fourteenth Amendment, the provisions of a Vermont income tax statute which applied generally to income from interest-bearing securities, but exempted interest on account of money loaned within the state at a rate of interest not exceeding 5 percent. This decision was overruled in Madden v. Kentucky, 309 U.S. 83 (1940), which upheld a Kentucky statute imposing on citizens of that state an annual tax on bank deposits at the rate of fifty cents per hundred dollars on deposits in banks outside the state and ten cents per hundred dollars on deposits in local banks.

Hood & Sons, Inc. v. Du Mond 336 U.S. 525, 69 S. Ct. 657, 93 L. Ed. 865 (1949)

[H. P. Hood & Sons, Inc., is a Massachusetts corporation distributing milk and milk products in the Boston area, among other places. Over 90 percent of the fluid milk sold there comes from states other than Massachusetts. Hood and a competitor have for some years been purchasing a part of the milk they supply to the Boston area at points in the counties of Rensselaer, Washington, and St. Lawrence, New York. Article 21 of the New York Agriculture and Markets Law forbids a dealer to buy milk from a producer unless licensed by the Commissioner of Agriculture and Markets. Hood, having three licensed receiving depots in the area described, at which it purchased milk from producers, sought a license for a fourth. Hood concededly met all other statutory requirements, but the Commissioner denied the requested additional license pursuant to provisions of §258-c, which require the Commissioner, before issuance, to be satisfied "that the issuance of a license will not tend to a destructive competition in a market already adequately served, and that the issuance of the license is in the public interest."]

MR. JUSTICE JACKSON delivered the opinion of the Court. . . .

Upon the hearing pursuant to the statute, milk dealers competing with Hood as buyers in the area opposed licensing the proposed Greenwich plant. They complained that Hood, by reason of conditions under which it sold in Boston, had competitive advantages under applicable federal milk orders, Boston health regulations, and OPA ceiling prices. There was also evidence of a temporary shortage of supply in the Troy, New York market during the fall and winter of 1945-46. The Commissioner was urged not to allow Hood to compete for additional supplies of milk or to take on producers then delivering to other dealers.

The Commissioner found that Hood, if licensed at Greenwich, would permit its present suppliers, at their option, to deliver at the new plant rather than the old ones and for a substantial number this would mean shorter hauls and savings in delivery costs. The new plant also would attract twenty to thirty producers, some of whose milk Hood anticipates will or may be diverted from other buyers. Other large milk distributors have plants within the general area and dealers serving Troy obtain milk in the locality. He found that Troy was inadequately supplied during the preceding short season.

In denying the application for expanded facilities, the Commissioner states his grounds as follows:

"If applicant is permitted to equip and operate another milk plant in this territory, and to take on producers now delivering to plants other than those which it operates, it will tend to reduce the volume of milk received at the plants which lose those producers, and will tend to increase the cost of handling milk in those plants.

"If applicant takes producers now delivering milk to local markets such as Troy, it will have a tendency to deprive such markets of a supply needed during the short season.

"There is no evidence that any producer is without a market for his milk. There is no evidence that any producers not now delivering milk to applicant would receive any higher price, were they to deliver their milk to applicant's proposed plant.

"The issuance of a license to applicant which would permit it to operate an additional plant, would tend to a destructive competition in a market already adequately served, and would not be in the public interest."

Denial of the license was sustained by the Court of Appeals over constitutional objections duly urged under the Commerce Clause and, because of the importance of the question involved, we brought the case here by certiorari.

Production and distribution of milk are so intimately related to public health and welfare that the need for regulation to protect those interests has long been recognized and is, from a constitutional standpoint, hardly controversial. Also, the economy of the industry is so eccentric that economic controls have been found at once necessary and difficult. These have evolved detailed, intricate and comprehensive regulations, including price-fixing. They have been much litigated but were generally sustained by this Court as within the powers of the State over its internal commerce as against the claim that they violated the Fourteenth Amendment. Nebbia v. New York, 291 U.S. 502; . . . . As the states extended their efforts to control various phases of export and import also, questions were raised as to limitations on state power under the Commerce Clause of the Constitution. . . .

The present controversy begins where the Eisenberg decision [306 U.S. 346] left off. New York's regulations, designed to assure producers a fair price and a responsible purchaser, and consumers a sanitary and modernly equipped handler, are not challenged here but have been complied with. It is only additional restrictions, imposed for the avowed purpose and with the practical effect of curtailing the volume of interstate commerce to aid local economic interests, that are in question here, and no such measures were attempted or such ends sought to be served in the Act before the Court in the Eisenberg case.

Our decision in a milk litigation most relevant to the present controversy deals with the converse of the present situation. Baldwin v. Seelig, 294 U.S. 511. In that case, New York placed conditions and limitations on the local sale of milk imported from Vermont designed in practical effect to exclude it, while here its order proposes to limit the local facilities for purchase of additional milk so as to withhold milk from export. The State agreed then, as now, that the Commerce Clause prohibits it from directly curtailing movement of milk into or out of the State. But in the earlier case, it contended that the same result could be accomplished by controlling delivery, bottling and sale after arrival, while here it says it can do so by curtailing facilities for its purchase and receipt before it is shipped out. In neither case is the measure supported by health or safety considerations but solely by protection of local economic interests, such as supply for local consumption and limitation of competition. This Court unanimously rejected the State's contention in the Seelig case and held that the Commerce Clause, even in the absence of congressional action, prohibits such regulations for such ends. . . .

[The] distinction between the power of the State to shelter its people from menaces to their health or safety and from fraud, even when those dangers emanate from interstate commerce, and its lack of power to retard, burden or constrict the flow of such commerce for their economic advantage, is one deeply rooted in both our history and our law.

When victory relieved the Colonies from the pressure for solidarity that war had exerted, a drift toward anarchy and commercial warfare between states began. ". . . each State would legislate according to its estimate of its own interests, the importance of its own products, and the local advantages or disadvantages of its position in a political or commercial view." This came "to threaten at once the peace and safety of the Union." Story, The Constitution, §§259, 260. See Fiske, The Critical Period of American History, 144; Warren, The Making of the Constitution, 567. The sole purpose for which Virginia initiated the movement which ultimately produced the Constitution was "to take into consideration the trade of the United States; to examine the relative situations and trade of the said States; to consider how far a uniform system in their commercial regulations may be necessary to their common interest and their permanent harmony" and for that purpose the General Assembly of Virginia in January of 1786 named commissioners and proposed their meeting with those from other states. Documents, Formation of the Union, H.R. Doc. No. 398, 12 H. Docs., 69th Cong., 1st Sess., p. 38.

The desire of the Forefathers to federalize regulations of foreign and interstate commerce stands in sharp contrast to their jealous preservation of the state's power over its internal affairs. No other federal power was so universally assumed to be necessary, no other state power was so readily relinquished. . . .

[The] principle that our economic unit is the Nation, which alone has the gamut of powers necessary to control of the economy, including the vital power of erecting customs barriers against foreign competition, has as its corollary that the states are not separable economic units. . . .

The material success that has come to inhabitants of the states which make up this federal free trade unit has been the most impressive in the history of commerce, but the established interdependence of the states only emphasizes the necessity of protecting interstate movements of goods against local burdens and repressions. We need only consider the consequences if each of the few states that produce copper, lead, high-grade iron ore, timber, cotton, oil or gas should decree that industries located in that state shall have priority. What fantastic rivalries and dislocations and reprisals would ensue if such practices were begun? Or suppose that the field of discrimination and retaliation be industry. May Michigan provide that automobiles cannot be taken out of that State until local dealers' demands are fully met? Would she not have every argument in the favor of such a statute that can be offered in support of New York's limiting sales of milk for out-of-state shipment to protect the economic interests of her competing dealers and local consumers? Could Ohio then pounce upon the rubber-tire industry, on which she has a substantial grip, to retaliate for Michigan's auto monopoly?

Our system, fostered by the Commerce Clause, is that every farmer and every craftsman shall be encouraged to produce by the certainty that he will have free access to every market in the Nation, that no home embargoes will withhold his exports, and no foreign state will by customs duties or regulations exclude them. Likewise, every consumer may look to the free competition from every producing area in the Nation to protect him from exploitation by any. Such was the vision of the Founders; such has been the doctrine of this Court which has given it reality.

The State, however, insists that denial of the license for a new plant does not restrict or obstruct interstate commerce, because petitioner has been licensed at its other plants without condition or limitation as to the quantities it may purchase. Hence, it is said, all that has been denied petitioner is a local convenience — that of being able to buy and receive at Greenwich quantities of milk it is free to buy at Eagle Bridge and Salem. It suggests that, by increased efficiency or enlarged capacity at its other plants, petitioner might sufficiently increase its supply through those facilities.

The weakness of this contention is that a buyer has to buy where there is a willing seller, and the peculiarities of the milk business necessitate location of a receiving and cooling station for nearby producers. The Commissioner has not made and there is nothing to persuade us that he could have made findings that petitioner can obtain such additional supplies through its existing facilities; indeed he found that "applicant has experienced some difficulty during the flush season because of the inability of the plant facilities to handle the milk by 9:00 a.m.," the time its receipt is required by Boston health authorities unless it is cooled by the farmer before delivery, and a substantial part of it is not.

But the argument also asks us to assume that the Commissioner's order will not operate in the way he found that it would as a reason for making it. He found that petitioner, at its new plant, would divert milk from the plants of some other large handlers in the vicinity, which plants "can handle more milk." This competition he did not approve. He also found it would tend to deprive local markets of needed supplies during the short season. In the face of affirmative findings that the proposed plant would increase petitioner's supply, we can hardly be asked to assume that denial of the license will not deny petitioner access to such added supplies. While the state power is applied in this case to limit expansion by a handler of milk who already has been allowed some purchasing facilities, the argument for doing so, if sustained, would be equally effective to exclude an entirely new foreign handler from coming into the State to purchase. . . .

Since the statute as applied violates the Commerce Clause and is not authorized by federal legislation pursuant to that Clause, it cannot stand. The judgment is reversed and the cause remanded for proceedings not inconsistent with this opinion.

It is so ordered.

MR. JUSTICE BLACK, dissenting.

In this case the Court sets up a new constitutional formula for invalidation of state laws regulating local phases of interstate commerce. I believe the New York law is invulnerable to constitutional attack under constitutional rules which the majority of this Court have long accepted. The new formula subjects state regulations of local business activities to greater constitutional hazards than they have ever had to meet before. The consequences of the new formula, as I understand it, will not merely leave a large area of local business activities free from state regulation. All local activities that fall within the scope of this new formula will be free from any regulatory control whatever. For it is inconceivable that Congress could pass uniform national legislation capable of adjustment and application to all the local phases of interstate activities that take place in the 48 states. See Robertson v. California, 328 U.S. 440, 449, 459-460. It is equally inconceivable that Congress would attempt to control such diverse local activities through a "swarm of statutes only locally applicable and utterly inconsistent." Kidd v. Pearson, 128 U.S. 1, 21.

First. New York has a comprehensive set of regulations to control the production, distribution and sale of milk. Their over-all purposes are two: (1) to promote health by maintaining an adequate supply and an orderly distribution of uncontaminated milk; (2) to promote the general welfare by saving farmer milk-producers from impoverishment and insolvency. The state legislature concluded that achievement of these goals demanded elimination of destructive competition among milk dealers. The legislature believed that while cutthroat competition among purchaser dealers temporarily raises the price of farmers' milk, the end result of the practice in New York had been economic distress for the farmers. After destructive dealer competition had driven financially weak dealers from the contest, the more opulent survivors had pushed producers' prices far below production costs. Nebbia v. New York, 291 U.S. 502, 515-516, gives a graphic description of the plight of these farmers prior to the enactment of these regulations and makes clear that the chief incentive for the regulations was the promotion of health and the general welfare by financial rehabilitation of the farmers. And despite due-process objections, the Nebbia case sustained the state's constitutional power to apply its law to New York dealers in order to promote the health, economic stability and general welfare of the state's people. . . .

Second. . . .

Had a dealer supplying New York customers applied for a license to operate a new plant, the commissioner would have been compelled under the Act to protect petitioner's plants supplying Boston consumers in the same manner that this order would have protected New York consumers. In protecting inter- or intra-state dealers from destructive competition which would endanger the milk farmers' price structure or the continued supply of healthful milk to the customers of existing dealers, the commissioner would be faithful to the Act's avowed purposes. The commerce clause should not be stretched to forbid New York's fair attempt to protect the healthful milk supply of consumers, even though some of the consumers in this case happen to live in Troy, New York. And unless this Court is willing to charge an unfairness to the commissioner that has not been charged by petitioner or shown by the evidence, the Court cannot attribute to the commissioner an invidious purpose to discriminate against petitioner's interstate business in order to benefit local intrastate competitors and their local consumers. Of course if this were a case involving such discrimination, relief could be obtained under the principles announced in Best & Co. v. Maxwell, 311 U.S. 454.

The language of this state Act is not discriminatory, the legislative history shows it was not so intended, and the commissioner has not administered it with a hostile eye. The Act must stand or fall on this basis notwithstanding the overtones of the Court's opinion. If petitioner and other interstate milk dealers are to be placed above and beyond this law, it must be done solely on this Court's new constitutional formula which bars a state from protecting itself against local destructive competitive practices so far as they are indulged in by dealers who ship their milk into other states. . . .

Sixth. The Court strongly relies on Baldwin v. Seelig, 294 U.S. 511. . . . New York's object was to save its farmers from competition with Vermont milk. And the Court saw the New York law as a discriminatory "barrier to traffic between one state and another as effective as if customs duties, equal to the price differential, had been laid upon the thing transported." Baldwin v. Seelig, supra, at 521. The effect of the law, therefore, was precisely the same as though in order to protect its farmers from competition with Vermont milk, New York had imposed substantially higher taxes on sellers of Vermont produced articles than it imposed on sellers of New York produced articles. Under many previous decisions of this Court such discriminations against interstate commerce were not permitted. See Best & Co. v. Maxwell, 311 U.S. 454.

Even though the Court regarded the Baldwin v. Seelig law as discriminatory, other considerations were added to weight the scales on the side of invalidation. Its impact on

Vermont economy and Vermont legislative power was weighed. To whatever extent it is desirable to reform the economic standards of Vermont, the "legislature of Vermont and not that of New York must supply the fitting remedy." Baldwin v. Seelig, supra, at 524. This is a due process concept. In emphasizing the due process objectionable phase of New York's law, the Court was well within the Cooley philosophy. Furthermore under the Cooley rule, aside from due process, a state's regulation that immediately bears upon nothing but activities wholly within its boundaries is far less vulnerable than one which casts burdens on activities within the boundaries of another state.

It was because New York attempted to project its law into Vermont that even its admitted health purpose was insufficient to outweigh Vermont's interest in controlling its own local affairs. Baldwin v. Seelig, supra, p. 524. Added to this was the Court's appraisal of the law as a plain discrimination against interstate commerce that would inescapably erect a barrier to suppress competitive sales of Vermont milk in New York, thus leading to retaliatory "rivalries and reprisals," at p. 522. Quite differently here New York has not attempted to regulate the price of milk in Massachusetts or the manner in which it will be distributed there; it has not attempted to put pressure on Massachusetts to reform its economic standards; its law is not hostile to interstate commerce in conception or operation; its purpose to conserve health and promote economic stability among New York producers is not stretched to the breaking point by an argument that New York cannot safely aid its own people's health unless permitted to trespass upon the power of Massachusetts to regulate local affairs in Massachusetts. Nor is this New York law, fairly administered as it has been, the kind that breeds "rivalries and reprisals." The circumstances and conditions that brought about invalidation of the law considered in the Baldwin case are too different from those here considered to rest today's holding on the Baldwin decision. . . .

The basic question here is not the greatness of the commerce clause concept, but whether all local phases of interstate business are to be judicially immunized from state laws against destructive competitive business practices such as those prohibited by New York's law. Of course, there remains the bare possibility Congress might attempt to federalize all such local business activities in the forty-eight states. While I have doubt about the wisdom of this New York law, I do not conceive it to be the function of this Court to revise that state's economic judgments. Any doubt I may have concerning the wisdom of New York's law is far less, however, than is my skepticism concerning the ability of the Federal Government to reach out and effectively regulate all the local business activities in the forty-eight states.

I would leave New York's law alone.

MR. JUSTICE MURPHY joins in this opinion.

MR. JUSTICE FRANKFURTER, with whom MR. JUSTICE RUTLEDGE joins, dissenting.

If the Court's opinion has meaning beyond deciding this case in isolation, its effect is to hold that no matter how important to the internal economy of a State may be the prevention of destructive competition, and no matter how unimportant the interstate commerce affected, a State cannot as a means of preventing such competition deny an applicant access to a market within the State if that applicant happens to intend the out-of-state shipment of the product that he buys. I feel constrained to dissent because I cannot agree in treating what is essentially a problem of striking a balance between competing interests as an exercise in absolutes. Nor does it seem to me that such a problem should be disposed of on a record from which we cannot tell what weights to put in which side of the scales. . . .

It is argued . . . that New York can have no interest in the restriction of competition great enough to warrant shutting its doors to one who would buy its products for shipment to another State. This must mean that the protection of health and the promotion of fair dealing are of a different order, somehow, than the prevention of destructive competition. But the fixing of prices was a main object of the regulation upheld in the Eisenberg case, and it is obvious that one of the most effective ways of maintaining a price structure is to control competition. . . . In view of the importance that we have hitherto found in regulation of the economy of agriculture, I cannot understand the justification for assigning, as a matter of law, so much higher a place to milk dealers' standards of bookkeeping than to the economic well-being of their industry. . . .

3. State Regulation of Interstate Transportation and Sales

Buck v. Kuykendall 267 U.S. 307, 45 S. Ct. 324, 69 L. Ed. 623 (1925)

MR. JUSTICE BRANDEIS delivered the opinion of the court:

This is an appeal, under §238 of the Judicial Code, from a final decree of the Federal court for western Washington, dismissing a bill brought to enjoin the enforcement of §4 of chapter 111 of the Laws of Washington, 1921. That section prohibits common carriers for hire from using the highways by auto vehicles between fixed termini or over regular routes, without having first obtained from the director of public works a certificate declaring that public convenience and necessity require such operation. . . . The main question for decision is whether the statute, so construed and applied, is consistent with the Federal Constitution. . . .

Buck, a citizen of Washington, wished to operate an auto stage line over the Pacific Highway between Seattle, Washington, and Portland, Oregon, as a common carrier for hire, exclusively for through interstate passengers and express. He obtained from Oregon the license prescribed by its laws. Having complied with the laws of Washington relating to motor vehicles, their owners and drivers (Carlsen v. Cooney, 123 Wash. 441, 212 Pac. 575), and alleging willingness to comply with all applicable regulations concerning common carriers, Buck applied there for the prescribed certificate of public convenience and necessity. It was refused. The ground of refusal was that, under the laws of the state, the certificate may not be granted for any territory which is already being adequately served by the holder of a certificate; and that, in addition to frequent steam railroad service, adequate transportation facilities between Seattle and Portland were already being provided by means of four connecting auto stage lines, all of which held such certificates from the state of Washington. Re Buck, P.U.R. 1923E, 737. To enjoin interference by its officials with the operation of the projected line, Buck brought this suit against Kuykendall, the director of public works. . . .

. . . It may be assumed that §4 of the state statute is consistent with the 14th Amendment; and also, that appropriate state regulations, adopted primarily to promote safety upon the highways and conservation in their use, are not obnoxious to the commerce clause, where the indirect burden imposed upon interstate commerce is not unreasonable. Compare Michigan Pub. Utilities Commission v. Duke, 266 U.S. 570. The provision here in question is of a different character. Its primary purpose is not regulation with a view of safety or to conservation of the highways, but the prohibition of competition. It determines not the manner of use, but the persons by whom the highways may be used. It prohibits such use to some persons while permitting it to others for the same purpose and in the same manner. Moreover, it determines whether the prohibition shall be applied by resort, through state officials, to a test which is peculiarly within the province of Federal action — the existence of adequate facilities for conducting interstate commerce. The vice of the legislation is dramatically exposed by the fact that the state of Oregon had issued its certificate, which may be deemed equivalent to a legislative declaration that, despite existing facilities, public convenience and necessity required the establishment by Buck of the auto stage line between Seattle and Portland. Thus, the provision of the Washington statute is a regulation, not of the use of its own highways, but of interstate commerce. Its effect upon such commerce is not merely to burden but to obstruct it. Such state action is forbidden by the commerce clause. It also defeats the purpose of

Congress expressed in the legislation giving Federal aid for the construction of interstate highways.

By motion to dismiss, filed in this court, the state makes the further contention that Buck is estopped from seeking relief against the provisions of §4. The argument is this: Buck's claim is not that the department's action is unconstitutional because arbitrary or unreasonable. It is that §4 is unconstitutional because use of the highways for interstate commerce is denied unless the prescribed certificate shall have been secured. Buck applied for a certificate. Thus he invoked the exercise of the power which he now assails. One who invokes the provisions of a law may not thereafter question its constitutionality. The argument is unsound. It is true that one cannot, in the same proceeding, both assail a statute and rely upon it. Hurley v. Commission of Fisheries, 257 U.S. 223, 225. Compare Wall v. Parrot Silver & Copper Co., 244 U.S. 407, 411. Nor can one who avails himself of the benefits conferred by a statute deny its validity. St. Louis Malleable Casting Co. v. George C. Prendergast Constr. Co., 260 U.S. 469, 472. But in the case at bar, Buck does not rely upon any provision of the statute assailed; and he has received no benefit under it. He was willing, if permitted to use the highways, to comply with all the laws relating to common carriers. But the permission sought was denied. The case presents no element of estoppel. Compare Arizona ex rel. Gaines v. Cooper Queen Consol. Min. Co., 233 U.S. 87.

Reversed.[j]

Mr. Justice McReynolds dissents . . .

Bradley v. Public Utilities Commission 289 U.S. 92, 53 S. Ct. 577, 77 L. Ed. 1053 (1933)

Mr. Justice Brandeis delivered the opinion of the Court.

Bradley applied to the Public Utilities Commission of Ohio for a certificate of public convenience and necessity to operate by motor as a common carrier of property over State Route No. 20, extending from Cleveland, Ohio, to the Ohio-Michigan line, with Flint, Michigan, as final destination. The New York Central Railroad and the Pennsylvania Railroad, opposing, moved that the application be dismissed on the grounds of the present congested condition of that highway. Upon a full hearing, the Commission found "that said State Route No. 20, at this time, is so badly congested by established motor vehicle operations, that the addition of the applicant's proposed service would create and maintain an excessive and undue hazard to the safety and security of the travelling public, and the property upon such highway." It therefore ordered: "That in the interest of preserving the public welfare, the application be, and hereby is, denied."

In a petition for a rehearing, which was also denied, Bradley urged, among other things, that denial of the application for the certificate on the ground stated violated rights guaranteed to the applicant by the commerce clause of the Federal Constitution and the equality clause of the Fourteenth Amendment. The same claims were asserted in a petition in error to the Supreme Court of the State; were there denied (125 Ohio State 381; 181 N.E. 668) upon the authority of Motor Transport Co. v. Public Utilities Co., 125 Ohio State 374; 181 N.E. 665; and are renewed here upon this appeal. We are of opinion that the claims are unfounded.

First. It is contended that the order of the Commission is void because it excludes Bradley from interstate commerce. The order does not in terms exclude him from operating interstate. The denial of the certificate excludes him merely from Route 20. In

---

[j] Cf. Hughes & Vale Proprietary Ltd. v. State of New South Wales, [1955] A.C. 241; see comment thereon, 68 Harv. L. Rev. 1457 (1955). See also Commissioner for Motor Transport v. Antill Ranger & Co. Proprietary Ltd., [1956] A.C. 527. — Ed.

Section B. Protection of Local Economy and Welfare 409

specifying the route, Bradley complied with the statutory requirement that an applicant for a certificate shall set forth "the complete route" over which he desires to operate. Ohio General Code, §614-90(c). But the statute confers upon an applicant the right to amend his application before or after hearing or action by the Commission. §614-91. And it authorizes him, after the certificate is refused, to "file a new application or supplement any former application, for the purpose of changing" the route. §614-93. No amendment of the application was made or new application filed. For aught that appears, some alternate or amended route was available on which there was no congestion. If no other feasible route existed and that fact was deemed relevant, the duty to prove it rested upon the applicant. It was not incumbent upon the Commission to offer a certificate over an alternate route.

Second. It is contended that an order denying to a common carrier by motor a certificate to engage in interstate transportation necessarily violates the Commerce Clause. The argument is that under the rule declared in Buck v. Kuykendall, 267 U.S. 307, and Bush & Sons Co. v. Maloy, 267 U.S. 317, an interstate carrier is entitled to a certificate as of right; and that hence the reason for the commission's refusal and its purpose are immaterial. In those cases, safety was doubtless promoted when the certificate was denied, because intensification of traffic was thereby prevented. See Stephenson v. Binford, 287 U.S. 251, 269-272. But there, promotion of safety was merely an incident of the denial. Its purpose was to prevent competition deemed undesirable. The test employed was the adequacy of existing transportation facilities; and since the transportation in question was interstate, denial of the certificate invaded the province of Congress. In the case at bar, the purpose of the denial was to promote safety; and the test employed was congestion of the highway. The effect of the denial upon interstate commerce was merely an incident.

Protection against accidents, as against crime, presents ordinarily a local problem. Regulation to ensure safety is an exercise of the police power. It is primarily a state function, whether the locus be private property or the public highways. Congress has not dealt with the subject. Hence, even where the motor cars are used exclusively in interstate commerce, a State may freely exact registration of the vehicle and an operator's license, Hendrick v. Maryland, 235 U.S. 610, 622; Clark v. Poor, 274 U.S. 554, 557; Sprout v. South Bend, 277 U.S. 163, 169; may require the appointment of an agent upon whom process can be served in an action arising out of operation of the vehicle within the State, Kane v. New Jersey, 242 U.S. 160; Hess v. Pawloski, 274 U.S. 352, 356; and may require carriers to file contracts providing adequate insurance for the payment of judgments recovered for certain injuries resulting from their operations. Continental Baking Co. v. Woodring, 286 U.S. 352, 365-366. Compare Packard v. Banton, 264 U.S. 140; Sprout v. South Bend, 277 U.S. 163, 171-172; Hodge Co. v. Cincinnati, 284 U.S. 335, 337. The State may exclude from the public highways vehicles engaged exclusively in interstate commerce, if of a size deemed dangerous to the public safety, Morris v. Duby, 274 U.S. 135, 144; Sproles v. Binford, 286 U.S. 374, 389-390. Safety may require that no additional vehicle be admitted to the highway. The Commerce Clause is not violated by denial of the certificate to the appellant, if upon adequate evidence denial is deemed necessary to promote the public safety. Compare Hammond v. Schappi Bus Line, 275 U.S. 164, 170-171.

Third. It is contended that the order is void under the Commerce Clause because the finding of congestion of Route 20 is unsupported by evidence. The argument is that the only evidence introduced on that issue consisted of two traffic counts, both in the single city of Fremont; that this evidence was insufficient because Route 20 extends for only 2.2 miles through Fremont, whereas the total length of the portion which would be traversed is about 100 miles; and that the evidence was conflicting. The evidence was adequate to support the finding. Moreover, no such objection is set forth in the statement as to jurisdiction filed pursuant to Rule 12.

Fourth. It is contended that the statute as applied to the plaintiff violates the equal protection clause of the Fourteenth Amendment. There is no suggestion that the plaintiff was treated less favorably than others who applied at the same time or thereafter for certificates as common carriers; nor is there any suggestion that the classification operates to favor intrastate over interstate carriers. One argument is that the statute discriminates unlawfully against common carriers in favor of shippers who operate their own trucks. In dealing with the problem of safety of the highways, as in other problems of motor transportation, the State may adopt measures which favor vehicles used solely in the business of their owners, as distinguished from those which are operated for hire by carriers who use the highways as their place of business. See Packard v. Banton, 264 U.S. 140, 144. Compare Bekins Van Lines v. Riley, 280 U.S. 80, 82; Continental Baking Co. v. Woodring, 286 U.S. 352, 373; Sproles v. Binford, 286 U.S. 374, 396. Another objection is that to deny certificates to subsequent applicants discriminates unlawfully in favor of carriers previously certificated. But classification based on priority of authorized operation has a natural and obvious relation to the purpose of the regulation. Conceivably, restriction of the volume of traffic might be secured by limiting the extent of each certificate-holder's use. But that would involve re-apportionment whenever a new applicant appeared. The guaranty of equal protection does not prevent the State from adopting the simple expedient of prohibiting operations by additional carriers. . . .

Affirmed.

MAYOR OF VIDALIA v. McNEELY, 274 U.S. 676, 47 S. Ct. 758, 71 L. Ed. 1292 (1927). Van Devanter, J.: "This is a suit to restrain the town of Vidalia, Louisiana, from unwarrantably interfering with the operation by the complainant of a public ferry from that town across the Mississippi River to Natchez, Mississippi. . . .

"The complainant, McNeely, is a citizen and resident of Mississippi and for more than 20 years has been operating a public ferry from Vidalia . . . to Natchez and from Natchez to Vidalia. He has three boats in the service and has floating steel docks and other equipment at both Vidalia and Natchez which he uses in making landings and in receiving and discharging passengers and freight. . . . At Vidalia his floating docks and landing equipment have been moored and maintained at and near the foot of Concordia street, which was designated by the town as the landing place for his ferry when he began operating it. The variation in the rise and fall of the river is about 55 feet, and a levee extends along the bank and across Concordia street. So it has been essential for him to construct and maintain a ramp or graduated approach from his docks to the intersection of the street and levee. While operating the ferry, he acquired and still holds the lots abutting on the river for several hundred feet on either side of Concordia street. Occasionally he has moved his docks and landing facilities to one side of the street or the other, but only in front of his own lots. . . .

"This suit was begun in October, 1924. Theretofore the complainant had been operating the ferry under licenses granted by Vidalia and Natchez, but these licenses had then terminated. Early in 1924 the town of Vidalia adopted an ordinance specially granting to the city of Natchez and its assigns a license. . . . The license so granted . . . was transferred . . . to the Royal Route Company. . . . Vidalia recognized the transfer and then adopted a further ordinance designating for such assignee the same landing place at the foot of Concordia street which it theretofore had designated for the complainant and which he was still using. This ordinance forbade any one other than such assignee to moor, tie, anchor or keep any craft or object . . . in the river within 150 feet of that landing place [and] imposed a substantial penalty for every violation of that provision. . . .

"The complainant . . . continued to operate his ferry, whereupon the town proceeded to arrest and punish him under the provisions just described. He then brought this suit. . . . The District Court . . . was . . . of opinion that the river bank, although belonging to the owner . . . is . . . subject to a servitude permitting its use for various public purposes including . . . a landing for ferry boats . . . and that . . . designation of land-

Section B. **Protection of Local Economy and Welfare** 411

ing places . . . is a matter ordinarily resting with local municipal authorities . . . [But the court] designated for the Royal Route Company 300 feet of the bank and water frontage beginning 10 feet north of the north line of Concordia street and extending thence upstream, and confined the complainant to the portion beginning 10 feet south of the south line of the street and extending thence downstream . . . [6 F.2d 19, 21].

"Both parties complain of the part of the decree designating the landing places to be used by the competing ferries. . . ."

What decision? Why?

Wabash, St. Louis & Pacific Ry. v. Illinois *118 U.S. 557, 7 S. Ct. 4, 30 L. Ed. 244 (1886)*

[For the opinion in this case see page 210 supra.]

NOTE

In the case of interstate ferries, may either of the terminal states regulate the rates charged? If so, which? What of rates for round-trip tickets? See Port Richmond and Bergen Point Ferry Co. v. Board of Chosen Freeholders, 234 U.S. 317 (1914), and New York Central & H.R.R.R. v. Board of Chosen Freeholders, 227 U.S. 248 (1913). Cf. Covington & Cincinnati Bridge Co. v. Kentucky, 154 U.S. 204 (1894).

NOTE Regulation of Natural Gas

1. For a graphic case study of some of the limitations, state and federal, upon rate regulation with respect to gas originating in one state and consumed in another, and of the interplay of the regulatory activities of the Federal Power Commission with local regulation, see Note, The East Ohio Gas Company Litigation, 64 Harv. L. Rev. 464 (1951). See also Powell, Physics and Law — Commerce in Gas and Electricity, 58 Harv. L. Rev. 1072 (1945). For legislative history of the Natural Gas Act, see H.R. Rep. No. 709, 75th Cong., 1st Sess., adopted in S. Rep. No. 1162, 75th Cong., 1st Sess. (1937).

2. Gas rates to distributors and to consumers are, of course, affected by the field or "wellhead" price charged the transporting company by the producer. May a state in which gas is produced regulate the price at which it may be sold at the wellhead to a pipeline company chiefly engaged in transporting and reselling gas to purchasers in other states? In Cities Service Gas Co. v. Peerless Oil & Gas Co., 340 U.S. 179 (1950), the Supreme Court upheld, as a "conservation" measure, minimum wellhead prices fixed by the Oklahoma Corporation Commission — prices which increased the previously existing price of gas purchased for interstate transportation and sale.

It will be recalled that in Milk Control Board v. Eisenberg Farm Products, 306 U.S. 346 (1939), page 388 supra, the Supreme Court stressed the fact that "Only a small fraction of the milk produced by farmers in Pennsylvania is shipped out of the Commonwealth." Compare the Farmers' Grain Co. cases, noted page 390 supra, and Parker v. Brown, noted page 401 supra. In the Cities Service case it was stated that "About 90 percent of Guymon-Hugoton's [the Oklahoma gas field there involved] production is ultimately consumed outside the State." Of what significance, if any, is the ratio of domestic as against extrastate consumption in the case of a commodity regulated as to producer's price? Is it significant whether the regulation establishes minimum or maximum prices? Is it significant whether the commodity is in surplus or in short supply? Whether there are alternative sources or alternative competing products? Whether there are other factors creating elasticity of demand? Cf. Heisler v. Thomas Colliery Co., 260 U.S. 245 (1922), page 538 infra.

3. In Phillips Petroleum Co., 10 F.P.C. 246 (1951), the Federal Power Commission, after reviewing the legislative history of the Natural Gas Act and referring to the Cities Service decision, supra, held that Phillips, an independent producer of gas selling in the field to interstate pipeline companies, was not a "natural-gas company" within the meaning of the act. The result was that the prices at which Phillips sold gas were not subject to regulation by the Commission. In Phillips Petroleum Co. v. Wisconsin, 347 U.S. 672 (1954), the Supreme Court (5 to 3) affirmed a judgment of the Court of Appeals for the District of Columbia (205 F.2d 706) reversing the order of the Federal Power Commission. One of the principal decisions relied upon in the Phillips case was Interstate Natural Gas Co. v. FPC, 331 U.S. 682 (1947), which, in its turn, had relied upon Jersey Central Power & Light Co. v. FPC, 319 U.S. 61 (1943), a decision under the Federal Power Act. Compare 16 U.S.C. §824(c) (Federal Power Act) with 15 U.S.C. §717a(7) (Natural Gas Act).

4. As the Supreme Court soon acknowledged (Natural Gas Pipeline Co. v. Panoma Corp., 349 U.S. 44 (1955); Cities Service Gas Co. v. State Corporation Commission, 355 U.S. 391 (1958)), the Phillips decision effectively overruled Cities Service Gas Co. v. Peerless Oil & Gas Co., supra. The decision also required the Federal Power Commission to formulate pricing policies in situations unlike those usually prevailing with respect to public utility rate regulation. See Wisconsin v. FPC, 373 U.S. 294 (1963). It has also brought within Commission control many other aspects of the relations between producers and interstate distributors of gas. See, e.g., United Gas Improvement Co. v. Continental Oil Co., 381 U.S. 392 (1965), and United Gas Pipe Line Co. v. FPC, 385 U.S. 83 (1966).

South Carolina State Highway Dept. v. Barnwell Bros.
303 U.S. 177, 58 S. Ct. 510, 82 L. Ed. 734 (1938)

MR. JUSTICE STONE delivered the opinion of the Court.

Act No. 259 of the General Assembly of South Carolina, of April 28, 1933, 38 Stat. at L. 340, prohibits use on the state highways of motor trucks and "semi-trailer motor trucks" whose width exceeds 90 inches, and whose weight including load exceeds 20,000 pounds. For purposes of the weight limitation §2 of the statute provides that a semi-trailer motor truck, which is a motor propelled truck with a trailer whose front end is designed to be attached to and supported by the truck, shall be considered a single unit. The principal question for decision is whether these prohibitions impose an unconstitutional burden upon interstate commerce.

Appellees include the original plaintiffs below, who are truckers and interstate shippers; the Interstate Commerce Commission; and certain others who were permitted to intervene as parties plaintiff. The suit was brought in the district court for eastern South Carolina against various state officials, to enjoin them from enforcing §§4 and 6 of the Act among others, on the ground that they have been superseded by the Federal Motor Carrier Act of 1935, c. 498, 49 Stat. 546; that they infringe the due process clause of the Fourteenth Amendment; and that they impose an unconstitutional burden on interstate commerce. Certain railroads interested in restricting the competition of interstate motor carriers were permitted to intervene as parties defendant.

The district court of three judges [17 F. Supp. 803], after hearing evidence, ruled that the challenged provisions of the statute have not been superseded by the Federal Motor Carrier Act, and adopted as its own the ruling of the state Supreme Court in State ex rel.

Section B. Protection of Local Economy and Welfare

Daniel v. John P. Nutt Co., 180 S.C. 19, 185 S.E. 25, that the challenged provisions, being an exercise of the state's power to regulate the use of its highways so as to protect them from injury and to insure their safe and economical use, do not violate the Fourteenth Amendment. But it held that the weight and width prohibitions place an unlawful burden on interstate motor traffic passing over specified highways of the state, which for the most part are of concrete or a concrete base surfaced with asphalt. It accordingly enjoined the enforcement of the weight provision against interstate motor carriers on the specified highways, and also the width limitation of 90 inches, except in the case of vehicles exceeding 96 inches in width. It exempted from the operation of the decree, bridges on those highways "not constructed with sufficient strength to support the heavy trucks of modern traffic or too narrow to accommodate such traffic safely," provided the state highway department should place at each end of the bridge proper notices warning that the use of the bridge is forbidden by trucks exceeding the weight or width limits and provided the proper authorities take the necessary steps to enforce the law against such use of the bridges. The case comes here on appeal under § 266 of the Judicial Code.

The trial court rested its decision that the statute unreasonably burdens interstate commerce, upon findings, not assailed here, that there is a large amount of motor truck traffic passing interstate in the southeastern part of the United States, which would normally pass over the highways of South Carolina, but which will be barred from the state by the challenged restrictions if enforced, and upon its conclusion that, when viewed in the light of their effect upon interstate commerce, these restrictions are unreasonable.

To reach this conclusion the court weighed conflicting evidence and made its own determinations as to the weight and width of motor trucks commonly used in interstate traffic and the capacity of the specified highways of the state to accommodate such traffic without injury to them or danger to their users. It found that interstate carriage by motor trucks has become a national industry; that from 85 to 90% of the motor trucks used in interstate transportation are 96 inches wide and of a gross weight, when loaded, of more than ten tons; that only four other states prescribe a gross load weight as low as 20,000 pounds; and that the American Association of State Highway Officials and the National Conference on Street and Highway Safety in the Department of Commerce have recommended for adoption weight and width limitations in which weight is limited to axle loads of 16,000 to 18,000 pounds and width is limited to 96 inches.

It found in detail that compliance with the weight and width limitations demanded by the South Carolina Act would seriously impede motor truck traffic passing to and through the state and increase its cost; that 2,417 miles of state highways, including most of those affected by the injunction, are of the standard construction of concrete or concrete base with asphalt surface, 7½ or 8 inches thick at the edges and 6 or 6½ inches thick at the center; that they are capable of sustaining without injury a wheel load of 8,000 to 9,000 pounds or an axle load of double those amounts, depending on whether the wheels are equipped with high pressure or low pressure pneumatic tires; that all but 100 miles of the specified highways are from 18 to 20 feet in width; that they constitute a connected system of highways which have been improved with the aid of federal money grants, as a part of a national system of highways; and that they constitute one of the best highway systems in the southeastern part of the United States.

It also found that the gross weight of vehicles is not a factor to be considered in the preservation of concrete highways, but that the appropriate factor to be considered is wheel or axle weight; that vehicles engaged in interstate commerce are so designed and the pressure of their weight is so distributed by their wheels and axles that gross loads of more than 20,000 pounds can be carried over concrete roads without damage to the surface; that a gross weight limitation of that amount, especially as applied to semi-trailer motor trucks, is unreasonable as a means of preserving the highways; that it has no reasonable relation to safety of the public using the highways; and that the width limitation of 90 inches is unreasonable when applied to standard concrete highways of the state, in view of the fact that all other states permit a width of 96 inches, which is the standard width of trucks engaged in interstate commerce.

In reaching these conclusions, and at the same time holding that the weight and width limitations do not infringe the Fourteenth Amendment, the court proceeded upon the assumption that the commerce clause imposes upon state regulations to secure the safe and economical use of highways a standard of reasonableness which is more exacting when applied to the interstate traffic than that required by the Fourteenth Amendment as to all traffic; that a standard of weight and width of motor vehicles which is an appropriate state regulation when applied to intrastate traffic may be prohibited because of its effect on interstate commerce, although the conditions attending the two classes of traffic with respect to safety and protection of the highways are the same.

South Carolina has built its highways and owns and maintains them. It has received from the federal government, in aid of its highway improvements, money grants which have been expended upon the highways to which the injunction applies. But appellees do not challenge the ruling of the district court that Congress has not undertaken to regulate the weight and size of motor vehicles in interstate motor traffic, and has left undisturbed whatever authority in that regard the states have retained under the Constitution.

While the constitutional grant to Congress of power to regulate interstate commerce has been held to operate of its own force to curtail state power in some measure,[2] it did not forestall all state action affecting interstate commerce. Ever since Willson v. Black Bird Creek Marsh Co., 2 Pet. 245, and Cooley v. Port Wardens, 12 How. 299, it has been recognized that there are matters of local concern, the regulation of which unavoidably involves some regulation of interstate commerce but which, because of their local character and their number and diversity, may never be fully dealt with by Congress. Notwithstanding the commerce clause, such regulation in the absence of Congressional action has for the most part been left to the states by the decisions of this Court, subject to the other applicable constitutional restraints.

The commerce clause, by its own force, prohibits discrimination against interstate commerce, whatever its form or method, and the decisions of this Court have recognized that there is scope for its like operation when state legislation nominally of local concern is in point of fact aimed at interstate commerce, or by its necessary operation is a means of gaining a local benefit by throwing the attendant burdens on those without the state. [Citations omitted.] It was to end these practices that the commerce clause was adopted. [Citations omitted.] The commerce clause has also been thought to set its own limitation upon state control of interstate rail carriers so as to preclude the subordination of the efficiency and convenience of interstate traffic to local service requirements.

But the present case affords no occasion for saying that the bare possession of power by Congress to regulate the interstate traffic forces the states to conform to standards which Congress might, but has not adopted, or curtails their power to take measures to insure the safety and conservation of their highways which may be applied to like traffic moving intrastate. Few subjects of state regulation are so peculiarly of local concern as is the use of state highways. There are few, local regulation of which is so inseparable from a substantial effect on interstate commerce. Unlike the railroads, local highways are built, owned and maintained by the state or its municipal subdivisions. The state has a primary and im-

---

[2] State regulations affecting interstate commerce, whose purpose or effect is to gain for those within the state an advantage at the expense of those without, or to burden those out of the state without any corresponding advantage to those within, have been thought to impinge upon the constitutional prohibition even though Congress has not acted....

Underlying the stated rule has been the thought, often expressed in judicial opinion, that when the regulation is of such a character that its burden falls principally upon those without the state, legislative action is not likely to be subjected to those political restraints which are normally exerted on legislation where it affects adversely some interests within the State....

Section B. Protection of Local Economy and Welfare 415

mediate concern in their safe and economical administration. The present regulations, or any others of like purpose, if they are to accomplish their end, must be applied alike to interstate and intrastate traffic both moving in large volume over the highways. The fact that they affect alike shippers in interstate and intrastate commerce in large number within as well as without the state is a safeguard against their abuse.

From the beginning it has been recognized that a state can, if it sees fit, build and maintain its own highways, canals and railroads and that in the absence of Congressional action their regulation is peculiarly within its competence, even though interstate commerce is materially affected. Minnesota Rate Cases (Simpson v. Shepard), 230 U.S. 352, 416. Congress not acting, state regulation of intrastate carriers has been upheld regardless of its effect upon interstate commerce. Id. With respect to the extent and nature of the local interests to be protected and the unavoidable effect upon interstate and intrastate commerce alike, regulations of the use of the highways are akin to local regulation of rivers, harbors, piers and docks, quarantine regulations, and game laws, which, Congress not acting, have been sustained even though they materially interfere with interstate commerce.

The nature of the authority of the state over its own highways has often been pointed out by this Court. It may not, under the guise of regulation, discriminate against interstate commerce. But "In the absence of national legislation especially covering the subject of interstate commerce, the state may rightly prescribe uniform regulations adapted to promote safety upon its highways and the conservation of their use applicable alike to vehicles moving in interstate commerce and those of its own citizens." Morris v. Duby, 274 U.S. 135, 143. This formulation has been repeatedly affirmed, . . . and never disapproved. This Court has often sustained the exercise of that power although it has burdened or impeded interstate commerce. It has upheld weight limitations lower than those presently imposed, applied alike to motor traffic moving interstate and intrastate. . . . Restrictions favoring passenger traffic over the carriage of interstate merchandise by truck have been similarly sustained, . . . as has the exaction of a reasonable fee for the use of the highways. . . .

In each of these cases regulation involves a burden on interstate commerce. But so long as the state action does not discriminate, the burden is one which the Constitution permits because it is an inseparable incident of the exercise of a legislative authority, which, under the Constitution, has been left to the states.

Congress, in the exercise of its plenary power to regulate interstate commerce, may determine whether the burdens imposed on it by state regulation, otherwise permissible, are too great, and may, by legislation designed to secure uniformity or in other respects to protect the national interest in the commerce, curtail to some extent the state's regulatory power. But that is a legislative, not a judicial function, to be performed in the light of the Congressional judgment of what is appropriate regulation of interstate commerce, and the extent to which, in that field, state power and local interests should be required to yield to the national authority and interest. In the absence of such legislation the judicial function, under the commerce clause as well as the Fourteenth Amendment, stops with the inquiry whether the state legislature in adopting regulations such as the present has acted within its province, and whether the means of regulation chosen are reasonably adapted to the end sought. [Citations omitted.]

Here the first inquiry has already been resolved by our decisions that a state may impose non-discriminatory restrictions with respect to the character of motor vehicles moving in interstate commerce as a safety measure and as a means of securing the economical use of its highways. In resolving the second, courts do not sit as legislatures, either state or national. They cannot act as Congress does when, after weighing all the conflicting interests, state and national, it determines when and how much the state regulatory power shall yield to the larger interests of a national commerce. And in reviewing a state highway regulation where Congress has not acted, a court is not called upon, as are state legislatures, to determine what, in its judgment, is the most suitable restriction to be applied of those that are possible, or to choose that one which in its opinion is best adapted to all the diverse interests affected. Parkersburg & O. River Transp. Co. v. Parkersburg, 107 U.S. 691, 695. When the action of a legislature is within the scope of its power, fairly debatable questions as to its reasonableness, wisdom and propriety are not for the determination of courts, but for the legislative body, on which rest the duty and responsibility of decision. [Citations omitted.] This is equally the case when the legislative power is one which may legitimately place an incidental burden on interstate commerce. It is not any the less a legislative power committed to the states because it affects interstate commerce, and courts are not any the more entitled, because interstate commerce is affected, to substitute their own for the legislative judgment. [Citations omitted.]

Since the adoption of one weight or width regulation rather than another, is a legislative not a judicial choice, its constitutionality is not to be determined by weighing in the judicial scales the merits of the legislative choice and rejecting it if the weight of evidence presented in court appears to favor a different standard. . . . Being a legislative judgment it is presumed to be supported by facts known to the legislature unless facts judicially known or proved preclude that possibility. Hence, in reviewing the present determination we examine the record, not to see whether the findings of the court below are supported by evidence, but to ascertain upon the whole record whether it is possible to say that the legislative choice is without rational basis. . . . Not only does the record fail to exclude that possibility, but it shows affirmatively that there is adequate support for the legislative judgment.

At the outset it should be noted that underlying much of the controversy is the relative merit of a gross weight limitation as against an axle or wheel weight limitation. While there is evidence that weight stresses on concrete roads are determined by wheel rather than gross load weights, other elements enter into choice of the type of weight limitation. There is testimony to show that the axle or wheel weight limitation is the more easily enforced through resort to weighing devices adapted to ascertaining readily the axle or wheel weight. But it appears that in practice the weight of truck loads is not evenly distributed over axles and wheels; that commonly the larger part of the load — sometimes as much as 70 to 80% — rests on the rear axle and that it is much easier for those who load trucks to make certain that they have complied with a gross load weight limitation than with an axle or wheel weight limitation. While the report of the National Conference on State and Highway Safety, on which the court below relied, suggested a wheel weight limitation of 8,000 or 9,000 pounds, it also suggested that a gross weight limitation might be adopted and should be subject to the recommended wheel limitation. But the conference declined to fix the amount of gross weight limitation, saying: "In view of the varying conditions of traffic, and lack of uniformity in highway construction in the several States, no uniform gross-weight limitations are here recommended for general adoption throughout the country." The choice of a weight limitation based on convenience of application and consequent lack of need for rigid supervisory enforcement is for the legislature, and we cannot say that its preference for the one over the other is in any sense arbitrary or unreasonable. The choice is not to be condemned because the legislature prefers a workable standard, less likely to be violated than another under which the violations will probably be increased but more easily detected. It is for the legislature to say whether the one test or the other will in practical operation better protect the highways from the risk of excessive loads.

If gross load weight is adopted as the test it is obvious that the permissible load must be somewhat lighter than if the axle or wheel weight test were applied. With the latter the gross weight of a loaded motor truck can never exceed twice the axle and four times the wheel limit. But the fact that the rear axle may and often does support as much as 70 or 80% of the gross load, with wheel weight in like proportion, requires that a gross load limit be fixed at considerably less than four times the permissible wheel limit.

There was testimony before the court to support its conclusion that the highways in

Section B. Protection of Local Economy and Welfare

question are capable of sustaining without injury a wheel load of 8,000 or 9,000 pounds, the difference depending upon the character of the tire in use, as against a wheel load of as much as 8,000 pounds, which would be possible under the statutory load limit of 20,000 pounds as applied to motor trucks, and approximates the axle limit in addition to the gross load limit recommended by the National Conference on Street and Highway Safety. Much of this testimony appears to have been based on theoretical strength of concrete highways laid under ideal conditions and none of it was based on an actual study of the highways of South Carolina or of the subgrade and other road building conditions which prevail there and which have a material bearing on the strength and durability of such highways. There is uncontradicted testimony that approximately 60% of the South Carolina standard paved highways in question were built without a longitudinal center joint which has since become standard practice, the portion of the concrete surface adjacent to the joint being strengthened by reinforcement or by increasing its thickness; and that owing to the distribution of the stresses on concrete roads when in use, those without a center joint have a tendency to develop irregular longitudinal cracks. As the concrete in the center of such roads is thinner than that at the edges, the result is that the highway is split into two irregular segments, each with a weak inner edge which, according to the expert testimony, is not capable of supporting indefinitely wheel loads in excess of 4,200 pounds.

There is little in the record to mark any controlling distinction between the application of the gross load weight limitation to the motor truck and to the semi-trailer motor truck. There is testimony which is applicable to both types of vehicle, that in case of accident the danger from the momentum of a colliding vehicle increases with gross load weight. The record is without convincing evidence of the actual distribution, in practice, of the gross load weight over the wheels and axles of the permissible types of semi-trailer motor trucks, but this does not enable us to say that the legislature was without substantial ground for concluding that the relative advantages of a gross load over a wheel weight limitation are substantially the same for the two types, or that it could not have concluded that they were so nearly alike for regulatory purposes as to justify the adoption of a single standard for both, as a matter of practical convenience. Even if the legislature were to accept appellees' assumption that net load weights are, in practice, evenly distributed over the wheels supporting the load of a permissible semi-trailer so that with the statutory gross load limit the load on the rear axle would be about 8,000 pounds it might, as we have seen, also conclude that the danger point would then have been reached in the case of some 1,200 miles of concrete state roads constructed without a center joint.

These considerations, with the presumption of constitutionality, afford adequate support for the weight limitation without reference to other items of the testimony tending to support it. Furthermore, South Carolina's own experience is not to be ignored. Before adoption of the limitation South Carolina had had experience with higher weight limits. In 1924 it had adopted a combined gross weight limit of 20,000 pounds for vehicles of four wheels or less, and an axle weight limit of 15,000 pounds. In 1930 it had adopted a combined gross weight limit of 12½ tons with a five ton axle weight limit for vehicles having more than two axles. Act No. 721, 33 Stat. 1182; Act No. 685, 36 Stat. 1192, 1193. In 1931 it appointed a commission to investigate motor transportation in the state, to recommend legislation, and to report in 1932. The present weight limitation was recommended by the commission after a full consideration of relevant data, including a report by the state engineer who had constructed the concrete highways of the state and who advised a somewhat lower limitation as necessary for their preservation. The fact that many states have adopted a different standard is not persuasive. The conditions under which highways must be built in the several states, their construction and the demands made upon them, are not uniform. The road building art, as the record shows, is far from having attained a scientific certainty and precision, and scientific precision is not the criterion for the exercise of the constitutional regulatory power of the states. Sproles v. Binford [286 U.S. 388]. The legislature, being free to exercise its own judgment, is not bound by that of other legislatures. It would hardly be contended that if all the states had adopted a single standard none, in the light of its own experience and in the exercise of its judgment upon all the complex elements which enter into the problem, could change it.

Only a word need be said as to the width limitation. While a large part of the highways in question are from 18 to 20 feet in width, approximately 100 miles are only 16 feet wide. On all the use of a 96 inch truck leaves but a narrow margin for passing. On the road 16 feet wide it leaves none. The 90 inch limitation has been in force in South Carolina since 1920 and the concrete highways which it has built appear to be adapted to vehicles of that width. The record shows without contradiction that the use of heavy loaded trucks on the highway tends to force other traffic off the concrete surface onto the shoulders of the road adjoining its edges and to increase repair costs materially. It appears also that as the width of trucks is increased it obstructs the view of the highway, causing much inconvenience and increased hazard in its use. It plainly cannot be said that the width of trucks used on the highways in South Carolina is unrelated to their safety and cost of maintenance, or that a 90 inch width limitation adopted to safeguard the highways of the State, is not within the range of the permissible legislative choice.

The regulatory measures taken by South Carolina are within its legislative power. They do not infringe the Fourteenth Amendment, and the resulting burden on interstate commerce is not forbidden.

Reversed.

Southern Pacific Co. v. Arizona 325 U.S. 761, 65 S. Ct. 1515, 89 L. Ed. 1915 (1945)

Mr. Chief Justice Stone delivered the opinion of the Court.

The Arizona Train Limit Law of May 16, 1912, Arizona Code Anno. 1939, §69-119, makes it unlawful for any person or corporation to operate within the state a railroad train of more than fourteen passenger or seventy freight cars, and authorizes the state to recover a money penalty for each violation of the Act. The questions for decision are whether Congress has, by legislative enactment, restricted the power of the states to regulate the length of interstate trains as a safety measure and, if not, whether the statute contravenes the commerce clause of the Federal Constitution.

In 1940 the State of Arizona brought suit in the Arizona Superior Court against appellant, the Southern Pacific Company, to recover the statutory penalties for operating within the state two interstate trains, one a passenger train of more than fourteen cars, and one a freight train of more than seventy cars. Appellant answered, admitting the train operations, but defended on the ground that the statute offends against the commerce clause and the due process clause of the Fourteenth Amendment and conflicts with federal legislation. After an extended trial, without a jury, the court made detailed findings of fact on the basis of which it gave judgment for the railroad company. The Supreme Court of Arizona reversed and directed judgment for the state. 61 Ariz. 66, 145 P.(2d) 530. The case comes here on appeal under §237(a) of the Judicial Code, appellant raising by its assignments of error the questions presented here for decision.

The Supreme Court left undisturbed the findings of the trial court and made no new findings. It held that the power of the state to regulate the length of interstate trains had not been restricted by Congressional action. It sustained the Act as a safety measure to reduce the number of accidents attributed to the operation of trains of more than the statutory maximum length, enacted by the state legislature in the exercise of its "police power." This power the court held extended to the regulation of the operations of interstate commerce in the interests of local health, safety and well-being. It thought that a state statute, enacted in the exercise of the police power, and bearing some reasonable

Section B. **Protection of Local Economy and Welfare** 419

relation to the health, safety and well-being of the people of the state, of which the state legislature is the judge, was not to be judicially overturned, notwithstanding its admittedly adverse effect on the operation of interstate trains.

Purporting to act under §1, ¶¶10-17 of the Interstate Commerce Act, 24 Stat. 379, as amended (49 U.S.C.A. §§1 et seq.), the Interstate Commerce Commission, as of September 15, 1942, promulgated as an emergency measure Service Order No. 85, 7 Fed. Reg. 7258, suspending the operation of state train limit laws for the duration of the war, and denied an application to set aside the order. Re Service Order No. 85, 256 Inters. Com. Rep. (F) 523. . . .

The Commission's order was not in effect in 1940 when the present suit was brought for violations of the state law in that year, and the Commission's order is inapplicable to the train operations here charged as violations. . . . We can hardly suppose that Congress, merely by conferring authority on the Commission to regulate car service in an "emergency," intended to restrict the exercise, otherwise lawful, of state power to regulate train lengths before the Commission finds an "emergency" to exist. . . .

The contention, faintly urged, that the provisions of the Safety Appliance Act, 45 U.S.C.A. §§1 and 9, providing for brakes on trains, and of §25 of Part I of the Interstate Commerce Act, 49 U.S.C.A. §26(b), permitting the Commission to order the installation of train stop and control devices, operate of their own force to exclude state regulation of train lengths, has even less support. Congress, although asked to do so, has declined to pass legislation specifically limiting trains to seventy cars. We are therefore brought to appellant's principal contention, that the state statute contravenes the commerce clause of the Federal Constitution.

Although the commerce clause conferred on the national government power to regulate commerce, its possession of the power does not exclude all state power of regulation. Ever since Willson v. Black Bird Creek Marsh Co., 2 Pet. 245, and Cooley v. Port Wardens, 12 How. 299, it has been recognized that, in the absence of conflicting legislation by Congress, there is a residuum of power in the state to make laws governing matters of local concern which nevertheless in some measure affect interstate commerce or even, to some extent, regulate it. [Citations omitted.] Thus the states may regulate matters which, because of their number and diversity, may never be adequately dealt with by Congress. . . . When the regulation of matters of local concern is local in character and effect, and its impact on the national commerce does not seriously interfere with its operation, and the consequent incentive to deal with them nationally is slight, such regulation has been generally held to be within state authority. South Carolina State Highway Dept. v. Barnwell Bros. [303 U.S. 177, 188] and cases cited; . . . .

But ever since Gibbons v. Ogden, 9 Wheat. 1, the states have not been deemed to have authority to impede substantially the free flow of commerce from state to state, or to regulate those phases of the national commerce which, because of the need of national uniformity, demand that their regulation, if any, be prescribed by a single authority. . . . Whether or not this long recognized distribution of power between the national and the state governments is predicated upon the implications of the commerce clause itself, . . . ; or upon the presumed intention of Congress, where Congress has not spoken, . . . the result is the same.

In the application of these principles some enactments may be found to be plainly within and others plainly without state power. But between these extremes lies the infinite variety of cases, in which regulation of local matters may also operate as a regulation of commerce, in which reconciliation of the conflicting claims of state and national power is to be attained only by some appraisal and accommodation of the competing demands of the state and national interests involved. [Citations omitted.] . . .

Congress has undoubted power to redefine the distribution of power over interstate commerce. It may either permit the states to regulate the commerce in a manner which would otherwise not be permissible, Re Rahrer [140 U.S. 561] . . . , or exclude state regulation even of matters of peculiarly local concern which nevertheless affect interstate commerce. [Citations omitted.]

But in general Congress has left it to the courts to formulate the rules thus interpreting the commerce clause in its application, doubtless because it has appreciated the destructive consequences to the commerce of the nation if their protection were withdrawn, . . . and has been aware that in their application state laws will not be invalidated without the support of relevant factual material which will "afford a sure basis" for an informed judgment. Terminal R. Asso. v. Brotherhood of R. Trainmen [318 U.S. 8]; Southern R. Co. v. King, 217 U.S. 524. Meanwhile, Congress has accommodated its legislation, as have the states, to these rules as an established feature of our constitutional system. There has thus been left to the states wide scope for the regulation of matters of local state concern, even though it in some measure affects the commerce, provided it does not materially restrict the free flow of commerce across state lines, or interfere with it in matters with respect to which uniformity of regulation is of predominant national concern.

Hence the matters for ultimate determination here are the nature and extent of the burden which the state regulation of interstate trains, adopted as a safety measure, imposes on interstate commerce, and whether the relative weights of the state and national interests involved are such as to make inapplicable the rule, generally observed, that the free flow of interstate commerce and its freedom from local restraints in matters requiring uniformity of regulation are interests safeguarded by the commerce clause from state interference.

While this Court is not bound by the findings of the state court, and may determine for itself the facts of a case upon which an asserted federal right depends, . . . the facts found by the state trial court showing the nature of the interstate commerce involved, and the effect upon it of the train limit law, are not seriously questioned. Its findings with respect to the need for and effect of the statute as a safety measure, although challenged in some particulars which we do not regard as material to our decision, are likewise supported by evidence. Taken together the findings supply an adequate basis for decision of the constitutional issue.

The findings show that the operation of long trains, that is trains of more than fourteen passenger and more than seventy freight cars, is standard practice over the main lines of the railroads of the United States, and that, if the length of trains is to be regulated at all, national uniformity in the regulation adopted, such as only Congress can prescribe, is practically indispensable to the operation of an efficient and economical national railway system. On many railroads passenger trains of more than fourteen cars and freight trains of more than seventy cars are operated, and on some systems freight trains are run ranging from one hundred and twenty-five to one hundred and sixty cars in length. Outside of Arizona, where the length of trains is not restricted, appellant runs a substantial proportion of long trains. In 1939 on its comparable route for through traffic through Utah and Nevada from 66 to 85% of its freight trains were over 70 cars in length and over 43% of its passenger trains included more than fourteen passenger cars.

In Arizona, approximately 93% of the freight traffic and 95% of the passenger traffic is interstate. Because of the Train Limit Law appellant is required to haul over 30% more trains in Arizona than would otherwise have been necessary. The record shows a definite relationship between operating costs and the length of trains, the increase in length resulting in a reduction of operating costs per car. The additional cost of operation of trains complying with the Train Limit Law in Arizona amounts for the two railroads traversing that state to about $1,000,000 a year. The reduction in train lengths also impedes efficient operation. More locomotives and more manpower are required; the necessary conversion and reconversion of train lengths at terminals and the delay caused by breaking up and remaking long trains upon entering and leaving the state in order to comply with the law, delays the traffic and diminishes its volume moved in a given time, especially when traffic is heavy. . . .

The unchallenged findings leave no doubt that the Arizona Train Limit Law imposes a serious burden on the interstate commerce conducted by appellant. It materially impedes the movement of appellant's interstate trains through that state and interposes a substantial obstruction to the national policy proclaimed by Congress, to promote adequate, economical and efficient railway transportation service. Interstate Commerce Act, preceding § 1, 54 Stat. 898, 899. Enforcement of the law in Arizona, while train lengths remain unregulated or are regulated by varying standards in other states, must inevitably result in an impairment of uniformity of efficient railroad operation because the railroads are subjected to regulation which is not uniform in its application. Compliance with a state statute limiting train lengths requires interstate trains of a length lawful in other states to be broken up and reconstituted as they enter each state according as it may impose varying limitations upon train lengths. The alternative is for the carrier to conform to the lowest train limit restriction of any of the states through which its trains pass, whose laws thus control the carriers' operations both within and without the regulating state. . . .

At present the seventy freight car laws are enforced only in Arizona and Oklahoma, with a fourteen car passenger car limit in Arizona. The record here shows that the enforcement of the Arizona statute results in freight trains being broken up and reformed at the California border and in New Mexico, some distance from the Arizona line. Frequently it is not feasible to operate a newly assembled train from the New Mexico yard nearest to Arizona, with the result that the Arizona limitation governs the flow of traffic as far east as El Paso, Texas. For similar reasons the Arizona law often controls the length of passenger trains all the way from Los Angeles to El Paso.

If one state may regulate train lengths, so may all the others, and they need not prescribe the same maximum limitation. The practical effect of such regulation is to control train operations beyond the boundaries of the state exacting it because of the necessity of breaking up and reassembling long trains at the nearest terminal points before entering and after leaving the regulating state. The serious impediment to the free flow of commerce by the local regulation of train lengths and the practical necessity that such regulation, if any, must be prescribed by a single body having a nation-wide authority are apparent.

The trial court found that the Arizona law had no reasonable relation to safety, and made train operation more dangerous. Examination of the evidence and the detailed findings makes it clear that this conclusion was rested on facts found which indicate that such increased danger of accident and personal injury as may result from the greater length of trains is more than offset by the increase in the number of accidents resulting from the larger number of trains when train lengths are reduced. In considering the effect of the statute as a safety measure, therefore, the factor of controlling significance for present purposes is not whether there is basis for the conclusion of the Arizona Supreme Court that the increase in length of trains beyond the statutory maximum has an adverse effect upon safety of operation. The decisive question is whether in the circumstances the total effect of the law as a safety measure in reducing accidents and casualties is so slight or problematical as not to outweigh the national interest in keeping interstate commerce free from interferences which seriously impede it and subject it to local regulation which does not have a uniform effect on the interstate train journey which it interrupts.

The principal source of danger of accident from increased length of trains is the resulting increase of "slack action" of the train. Slack action is the amount of free movement of one car before it transmits its motion to an adjoining coupled car. This free movement results from the fact that in railroad practice cars are loosely coupled, and the coupling is often combined with a shock-absorbing device, a "draft gear," which, under stress, substantially increases the free movement as the train is started or stopped. Loose coupling is necessary to enable the train to proceed freely around curves and is an aid in starting heavy trains, since the application of the locomotive power to the train operates on each car in the train successively, and the power is thus utilized to start only one car at a time.

The slack action between cars due to loose couplings varies from seven-eighths of an inch to one and one-eighth inches and, with the added free movement due to the use of draft gears, may be as high as six or seven inches between cars. The length of the train increases the slack since the slack action of a train is the total of the free movement between its several cars. The amount of slack action has some effect on the severity of the shock of train movements, and on freight trains sometimes results in injuries to operatives, which most frequently occur to occupants of the caboose. The amount and severity of slack action, however, are not wholly dependent upon the length of train, as they may be affected by the mode and conditions of operation as to grades, speed, and load. And accidents due to slack action also occur in the operation of short trains. On comparison of the number of slack action accidents in Arizona with those in Nevada, where the length of trains is now unregulated, the trial court found that with substantially the same amount of traffic in each state the number of accidents was relatively the same in long as in short train operations. While accidents from slack action do occur in the operation of passenger trains, it does not appear that they are more frequent or the resulting shocks more severe on long than on short passenger trains. Nor does it appear that slack action accidents occurring on passenger trains, whatever their length, are of sufficient severity to cause serious injury or damage.

As the trial court found, reduction of the length of trains also tends to increase the number of accidents because of the increase in the number of trains. The application of the Arizona law compelled appellant to operate 30.08%, or 4,304, more freight trains in 1938 than would otherwise have been necessary. And the record amply supports the trial court's conclusion that the frequency of accidents is closely related to the number of trains run. The number of accidents due to grade crossing collisions between trains and motor vehicles and pedestrians, and to collisions between trains, which are usually far more serious than those due to slack action, and accidents due to locomotive failures, in general vary with the number of trains. Increase in the number of trains results in more starts and stops, more "meets" and "passes," and more switching movements, all tending to increase the number of accidents not only to train operatives and other railroad employees, but to passengers and members of the public exposed to danger by train operations.

Railroad statistics introduced into the record tend to show that this is the result of the application of the Arizona Train Limit Law to appellant, both with respect to all railroad casualties within the state and those affecting only trainmen whom the train limit law is supposed to protect. The accident rate in Arizona is much higher than on comparable lines elsewhere, where there is no regulation of length of trains. The record lends support to the trial court's conclusion that the train length limitation increased rather than diminished the number of accidents. This is shown by comparison of appellant's operations in Arizona with those in Nevada, and by comparison of operations of appellant and of the Santa Fe Railroad in Arizona with those of the same roads in New Mexico and by like comparison between appellant's operations in Arizona and operations throughout the country. . . .

We think, as the trial court found, that the Arizona Train Limit Law, viewed as a safety measure, affords at most slight and dubious advantage, if any, over unregulated train lengths, because it results in an increase in the number of trains and train operations and the consequent increase in train accidents of a character generally more severe than those due to slack action. Its undoubted effect on the commerce is the regulation, without securing uniformity, of the length of trains operated in interstate commerce, which lack is itself a primary cause of preventing the free flow of commerce by delaying it and by substantially increasing its cost and impairing its efficiency. In these respects the case differs from those where a state, by regulatory measures affecting the commerce, has removed or reduced safety hazards without substantial interference with the interstate movement of trains. Such are measures abolishing the car stove, New York, N.H. & H.R. Co. v. New York, 165 U.S. 628; requiring locomotives to be supplied with electric headlights, Atlan-

Section B. Protection of Local Economy and Welfare 423

tic coast Line R. Co. v. Georgia, 234 U.S. 280; providing for full train crews, Chicago, R.I. & P.R. Co. v. Arkansas, 219 U.S. 453, . . . ; and for the equipment of freight trains with cabooses, Terminal R. Asso. v. Brotherhood of R. Trainmen, 318 U.S. 1.

The principle that, without controlling Congressional action, a state may not regulate interstate commerce so as substantially to affect its flow or deprive it of needed uniformity in its regulation is not to be avoided by "simply invoking the convenient apologetics of the police power," Kansas Southern R. Co. v. Kaw Valley Drainage Dist. [233 U.S. 75, 79]. . . .

Here we conclude that the state does go too far. Its regulation of train lengths, admittedly obstructive to interstate train operation, and having a seriously adverse effect on transportation efficiency and economy, passes beyond what is plainly essential for safety since it does not appear that it will lessen rather than increase the danger of accident. Its attempted regulation of the operation of interstate trains cannot establish nation-wide control such as is essential to the maintenance of an efficient transportation system, which Congress alone can prescribe. The state interest cannot be preserved at the expense of the national interest by an enactment which regulates interstate train lengths without securing such control, which is a matter of national concern. To this the interest of the state here asserted is subordinate.

Appellees especially rely on the full train crew cases, Chicago, R.I. & P.R. Co. v. Arkansas, 219 U.S. 453, . . . and also on South Carolina State Highway Dept. v. Barnwell Bros., 303 U.S. 177, as supporting the state's authority to regulate the length of interstate trains. While the full train crew laws undoubtedly placed an added financial burden on the railroads in order to serve a local interest, they did not obstruct interstate transportation or seriously impede it. They had no effects outside the state beyond those of picking up and setting down the extra employees at the state boundaries; they involved no wasted use of facilities or serious impairment of transportation efficiency, which are among the factors of controlling weight here. In sustaining those laws the Court considered the restriction a minimal burden on the commerce comparable to the law requiring the licensing of engineers as a safeguard against those of reckless and intemperate habits, sustained in Smith v. Alabama, 124 U.S. 465, or those afflicted with color blindness, upheld in Nashville C. & St. L.R. Co. v. Alabama, 128 U.S. 96 and other similar regulations. . . .

South Carolina State Highway Dept. v. Barnwell Bros., supra, was concerned with the power of the state to regulate the weight and width of motor cars passing interstate over its highways, a legislative field over which the state has a far more extensive control than over interstate railroads. . . .

The contrast between the present regulation and the full train crew laws in point of their effects on the commerce, and the like contrast with the highway safety regulations, in point of the nature of the subject of regulation and the state's interest in it, illustrate and emphasize the considerations which enter into a determination of the relative weights of state and national interests where state regulation affecting interstate commerce is attempted. Here examination of all the relevant factors makes it plain that the state interest is outweighed by the interest of the nation in an adequate, economical and efficient railway transportation service, which must prevail.

Reversed.

Mr. Justice Rutledge concurs in the result.

Mr. Justice Black, dissenting: . . .

For more than a quarter of a century, railroads and their employees have engaged in controversies over the relative virtues and dangers of long trains. Railroads have argued that they could carry goods and passengers cheaper in long trains than in short trains. They have also argued that while the danger of personal injury to their employees might in some respects be greater on account of the operation of long trains, this danger was more than offset by an increased number of accidents from other causes brought about by

424   *Chapter Eight.* **The States in a Federal Union**

the operation of a much larger number of short trains. These arguments have been, and are now, vigorously denied. While there are others, the chief causes assigned for the belief that long trains unnecessarily jeopardize the lives and limbs of railroad employees relate to "slack action." . . . The argument that "slack movements" are more dangerous in long trains than in short trains seems never to have been denied. The railroads have answered it by what is in effect a plea of confession and avoidance. They say that the added cost of running short trains places an unconstitutional burden on interstate commerce. Their second answer is that the operation of short trains requires the use of more separate train units; that a certain number of accidents resulting in injury are inherent in the operation of each unit, injuries which may be inflicted either on employees or on the public; consequently, they have asserted that it is not in the public interest to prohibit the operation of long trains.

In 1912, the year Arizona became a state, its legislature adopted and referred to the people several safety measures concerning the operation of railroads. . . . The third safety statute which the Arizona legislature submitted to the electorate, and which was adopted by it, is the train limitation statute now under consideration. By its enactment the legislature and the people adopted the viewpoint that long trains were more dangerous than short trains, and limited the operation of train units to 14 cars for passenger and 70 cars for freight. This same question was considered in other states, and some of them, over the vigorous protests of railroads, adopted laws similar to the Arizona statute.

This controversy between the railroads and their employees, which was nation-wide, was carried to Congress. Extensive hearings took place. . . . In 1937, the Senate Interstate Commerce Committee after its own exhaustive hearings unanimously recommended that trains be limited to 70 cars as a safety measure. . . . The Senate passed the bill but the House Committee failed to report it out.

During the hearings on that measure, frequent references were made to the Arizona statute. It is significant, however, that American railroads never once asked Congress to exercise its unquestioned power to enact uniform legislation on the subject, and thereby invalidate the Arizona law. That which for some unexplained reason they did not ask Congress to do when it had the very subject of train length limitations under consideration, they shortly thereafter asked an Arizona state court to do.

In the state court a rather extraordinary "trial" took place. Charged with violating the law, the railroad admitted the charge. It alleged that the law was unconstitutional, however, and sought a trial of facts on that issue. . . . Thus, the issue which the Court "tried" was not whether the railroad was guilty of violating the law, but whether the law was unconstitutional either because the legislature had been guilty of misjudging the facts concerning the degree of the danger of long trains, or because the 1912 conditions of danger no longer existed.

Before the state trial judge finally determined that the dangers found by the legislature in 1912 no longer existed, he heard evidence over a period of 5½ months which appears in about 3000 pages of the printed record before us. It then adopted findings of fact submitted to it by the railroad, which cover 148 printed pages, and conclusions of law which cover 5 pages. We can best understand the nature of this "trial" by analogizing the same procedure to a defendant charged with violating a state or national safety appliance act, where the defendant comes into court and admits violation of the act. In such cases, the ordinary procedure would be for the court to pass upon the constitutionality of the act, and either discharge or convict the defendant. The procedure here, however, would justify quite a different trial method. Under it, a defendant is permitted to offer voluminous evidence to show that a legislative body has erroneously resolved disputed facts in finding a danger great enough to justify the passage of the law. This new pattern of trial procedure makes it necessary for a judge to hear all the evidence offered as to why a legislature passed a law and to make findings of fact as to the validity of those reasons. If under today's ruling a court does make findings, as to a danger contrary to the findings of the legislature, and the evidence heard "lends support" to those findings, a court can then invalidate the law. In this respect, the Arizona County Court acted, and this Court today is acting, as a "super-legislature."[4]

Even if this method of invalidating legislative acts is a correct one, I still think that the "findings" of the state court do not authorize today's decision. That court did not find that there is no unusual danger from slack movements in long trains. It did decide on disputed evidence that the long train "slack movement" dangers were more than offset by prospective dangers as a result of running a larger number of short trains, since many people might be hurt at grade crossings. There was undoubtedly some evidence before the state court from which it could have reached such a conclusion. There was undoubtedly as much evidence before it which would have justified a different conclusion.

Under those circumstances, the determination of whether it is in the interest of society for the length of trains to be governmentally regulated is a matter of public policy. Someone must fix that policy — either the Congress, or the state, or the courts. A century and a half of constitutional history and government admonishes this Court to leave that choice to the elected legislative representatives of the people themselves, where it properly belongs both on democratic principles and the requirements of efficient government. . . .

We are not left in doubt as to why, as against the potential peril of injuries to employees, the Court tips the scales on the side of "uniformity." For the evil it finds in a lack of uniformity is that it (1) delays interstate commerce, (2) increases its cost and (3) impairs its efficiency. All three of these boil down to the same thing, and that is that running shorter trains would increase the cost of railroad operations. The "burden" on commerce reduces itself to mere cost because there was no finding, and no evidence to support a finding, that by the expenditure of sufficient sums of money, the railroads could not enable themselves to carry goods and passengers just as quickly and efficiently with short trains as with long trains. Thus the conclusion that a requirement for long trains will "burden interstate commerce" is a mere euphemism for the statement that a requirement for long trains will increase the cost of railroad operations.

In the report of the Senate Committee, . . . attention was called to the fact that in 1935, 6,351 railroad employees were injured while on duty, with a resulting loss of more than 200,000 working days, and that injuries to trainmen and enginemen increased more than 29% in 1936. Nevertheless, the Court's action in requiring that money costs outweigh human values is sought to be buttressed by a reference to the express policy of Congress to promote an "economical national railroad system." I cannot believe that if Congress had defined what it meant by "economical," it would have required money to be saved at the expense of the personal safety of railway employees. Its whole history for the past 25 years belies such an interpretation of its language. Judicial opinions rather than legislative enactments have tended to emphasize costs. . . .

. . . Representatives elected by the people to make their laws, rather than judges appointed to interpret those laws, can best determine the policies which govern the people. That at least is the basic principle on which our democratic society rests. I would affirm the judgment of the Supreme Court of Arizona.

MR. JUSTICE DOUGLAS, dissenting:

I have expressed my doubts whether the courts should intervene in situations like the

---

[4] The Court today invalidates the Arizona law in accordance with the identical "super-legislature" method (so designated by Justices Brandeis and Holmes) used by the majority to invalidate a Nebraska statute regulating the weights of loaves of bread. Jay Burns Baking Co. v. Bryan, 264 U.S. 504, 534. For here, as there, this Court has overruled a state legislature's finding that an evil existed, and that the state law would not impose an unconstitutional "burden" upon those regulated. . . .

That decision rested on the Due Process Clause while today's decision rests on the Commerce Clause. But that difference does not make inapplicable here the principles invoked by the dissenters in the Jay Burns Baking Co. Case. . . .

present and strike down state legislation on the grounds that it burdens interstate commerce. . . .

. . . If I sat as a member of the Interstate Commerce Commission or of a legislative committee to decide whether Arizona's train-limit law should be superseded by a federal regulation, the question would not be free from doubt for me. If we had before us the ruling of the Interstate Commerce Commission (Re Service Order No. 85, 256 Inters. Com. Rep. (F) 523, 534) that Arizona's train-limit law infringes, "the national interest in maintaining the free flow of commerce under the present emergency war conditions," I would accept its expert appraisal of the facts, assuming it had the authority to act. But that order is not before us. And the present case deals with a period of time which antedates the war emergency. . . . I am not persuaded that the evidence adduced by the railroads overcomes the presumption of validity to which this train-limit law is entitled. For the reasons stated by Mr. Justice Black, Arizona's train-limit law should stand as an allowable regulation enacted to protect the lives and limbs of the men who operate the trains.

BIBB v. NAVAJO FREIGHT LINES, 359 U.S. 520, 79 S. Ct. 962, 3 L. Ed. 2d 1003 (1959). Douglas, J.: "We are asked in this case to hold that an Illinois statute requiring the use of a certain type of rear fender mudguard on trucks and trailers operated on the highways of that State conflicts with the Commerce Clause of the Constitution. The statutory specification for this type of mudguard provides that the guard shall contour the rear wheel, with the inside surface being relatively parallel to the top 90 degrees of the rear 180 degrees of the whole surface. The surface of the guard must extend downward to within 10 inches from the ground when the truck is loaded to its maximum legal capacity. The guards must be wide enough to cover the width of the protected tire, must be installed not more than 6 inches from the tire surface when the vehicle is loaded to maximum capacity, and must have a lip or flange on its outer edge of not less than 2 inches.

"Appellees, interstate motor carriers holding certificates from the Interstate Commerce Commission, challenged the constitutionality of the Illinois Act. A specially constituted three-judge District Court concluded that it unduly and unreasonably burdened and obstructed interstate commerce, because it made the conventional or straight mudflap, which is legal in at least 45 States, illegal in Illinois, and because the statute, taken together with a Rule of the Arkansas Commerce Commission requiring straight mudflaps, rendered the use of the same motor vehicle equipment in both States impossible. The statute was declared to be violative of the Commerce Clause and appellants were enjoined from enforcing it. 159 F. Supp. 385. An appeal was taken and we noted probable jurisdiction. 358 U.S. 808. . . .

"Illinois introduced evidence seeking to establish that contour mudguards had a decided safety factor in that they prevented the throwing of debris into the faces of drivers of passing cars and into the windshields of a following vehicle. But the District Court in its opinion stated that it was 'conclusively shown that the contour mud flap possesses no advantages over the conventional or straight mud flap previously required in Illinois and presently required in most of the states' (159 F. Supp., at 388) and that 'there is rather convincing testimony that use of the contour flap creates hazards previously unknown to those using the highways.' Id., at 390. These hazards were found to be occasioned by the fact that this new type of mudguard tended to cause an accumulation of heat in the brake drum, thus decreasing the effectiveness of brakes, and by the fact that they were suceptible of being hit and bumped when the trucks were backed up and of falling off on the highway. . . ."

What decision? Why?[k]

---

[k] In Brotherhood of Locomotive Firemen & Enginemen v. Chicago, Rock Island & P.R. Co., 393 U.S. 129 (1968), the Court upheld Arkansas full-crew laws applicable to interstate railroads. The district court had held

Section B. **Protection of Local Economy and Welfare** 427

Hall v. De Cuir 95 U.S. 485, 24 L. Ed. 547 (1878)

MR. CHIEF JUSTICE WAITE delivered the opinion of the court:

By the Constitution of Louisiana (art. 13) it is provided that "All persons shall enjoy equal rights and privileges upon any conveyance of a public character." [A statute, approved February 23, 1869, implements this constitutional provision, and provides a right of action for damages, actual and exemplary, to one injured by violation.]

Benson (the defendant below) was the master and owner of . . . a steamboat enrolled and licensed under the laws of the United States for the coasting trade, and plying as a regular packet . . . between New Orleans, in the State of Louisiana, and Vicksburg, in the State of Mississippi, touching at the intermediate landings both within and without Louisiana, as occasion required. The defendant in error (plaintiff below), a person of color, took passage upon the boat, on her trip up the river from New Orleans, for Hermitage, a landing-place within Louisiana, and being refused accommodations, on account of her color, in the cabin specially set apart for white persons, brought this action . . . to recover damages for her mental and physical suffering on that account. Benson, by way of defense, insisted among other things, that the statute was inoperative and void as to him . . . because, as to his business, it was an attempt to "regulate commerce among the States" . . . The District Court of the parish held that the statute made it imperative upon Benson to admit Mrs. De Cuir to the privileges of the cabin for white persons, and that it was not a regulation of commerce among the States and, therefore, not void. After trial, judgment was given against Benson for $1,000; from which he appealed to the Supreme Court of the State where the rulings of the District Court were sustained [27 La. Ann. 1].

This decision of the Supreme Court is here for re-examination under section 709, R.S.

For the purposes of this case, we must treat the statute, as requiring those engaged in interstate commerce to give all persons traveling in Louisiana, upon the public conveyances employed in such business, equal rights and privileges in all parts of the conveyance, without distinction or discrimination on account of race or color. Such was the construction given to that Act in the courts below, and it is conclusive upon us as the construction of a state law by the state courts. It is with this provision of the statute alone that we have to deal. We have nothing whatever to do with it as a regulation of internal commerce, or as affecting anything else than commerce among the States.

There can be no doubt but that exclusive power has been conferred upon Congress in respect to the regulation of commerce among the several States. The difficulty has never been as to the existence of this power, but as to what is to be deemed an encroachment upon it; for, as has been often said, "Legislation may in a great variety of ways affect commerce and persons engaged in it without constituting a regulation of it within the meaning of the Constitution." [Citations omitted.] Thus, in Munn v. Illinois [94 U.S. 113], it was decided that a State might regulate the charges of public warehouses, and in R.R. Co. v. Iowa [94 U.S. 155], of railroads situate entirely within the State, even though those engaged in commerce among the States might sometimes use the warehouses or the railroads in the prosecution of their business. . . . By such statutes the States regulate, as a matter of domestic concern, the instruments of commerce situated wholly within their own jurisdiction, and over which they have exclusive governmental control except when employed in foreign or interstate commerce. As they can only be used in the State, their regulation for all purposes may properly be assumed by the State, until Congress acts in reference to their foreign or interstate relations. When Congress does act, the state laws are superseded only to the extent that they affect commerce outside the State as it comes

---

that as a result of economic and technical developments that had transpired since earlier decisions, including Chicago, Rock Island & P.R. Co. v. Arkansas, 219 U.S. 453 (1911), upholding this and similar statutes, they could no longer be justified as safety measures, and had held the Arkansas statute unconstitutional. — ED.

within the State. It has also been held that health and inspection laws may be passed by the States, ... The line which separates the powers of the States from this exclusive power of Congress is not always distinctly marked, and oftentimes it is not easy to determine on which side a particular case belongs. Judges not infrequently differ in their reasons for a decision in which they concur. Under such circumstances it would be a useless task to undertake to fix an arbitrary rule by which the line must in all cases be located. It is far better to leave a matter of such delicacy to be settled in each case upon a view of the particular rights involved.

But we think it may safely be said that state legislation which seeks to impose a direct burden upon interstate commerce, or to interfere directly with its freedom, does encroach upon the exclusive power of Congress. The statute now under consideration, in our opinion, occupies that position. It does not act upon the business through the local instruments to be employed after coming within the State, but directly upon the business as it comes into the State from without or goes out from within. While it purports only to control the carrier when engaged within the State, it must necessarily influence his conduct to some extent in the management of his business throughout his entire voyage. His disposition of passengers taken up and put down within the State, or taken up within to be carried without, cannot but affect, in a greater or less degree, those taken up without and brought within, and sometimes those taken up and put down without. A passenger in the cabin set apart for the use of whites without the State must, when the boat comes within, share the accommodations of that cabin with such colored persons as may come on board afterwards, if the law is enforced.

It was to meet just such a case that the commercial clause in the Constitution was adopted. The River Mississippi passes through or along the borders of ten different States, and its tributaries reach many more. The commerce upon these waters is immense, and its regulation clearly a matter of national concern. If each State was at liberty to regulate the conduct of carriers while within its jurisdiction, the confusion likely to follow could not but be productive of great inconvenience and unnecessary hardship. Each State could provide for its own passengers and regulate the transportation of its own freight, regardless of the interests of others. Nay more, it could prescribe rules by which the carrier must be governed within the State in respect to passengers and property brought from without. On one side of the river or its tributaries he might be required to observe one set of rules, and on the other another. Commerce cannot flourish in the midst of such embarrassments. No carrier of passengers can conduct his business with satisfaction to himself, or comfort to those employing him, if, on one side of a state line, his passengers, both white and colored, must be permitted to occupy the same cabin, and on the other be kept separate. Uniformity in the regulations by which he is to be governed from one end to the other of his route is a necessity in his business, and to secure it Congress, which is untrammeled by state lines, has been invested with the exclusive legislative power of determining what such regulations shall be. If this statute can be enforced against those engaged in interstate commerce, it may be as well against those engaged in foreign; and the master of a ship clearing from New Orleans for Liverpool, having passengers on board would be compelled to carry all, white or colored, in the same cabin during his passage down the river, or be subject to an action for damages, "exemplary as well as actual," by anyone who felt himself aggrieved because he had been excluded on account of his color.

This power of regulation may be exercised without legislation as well as with it. By refraining from action, Congress, in effect, adopts as its own regulations those which the common law or the civil law, where that prevails, has provided for the government of such business, and those which the States, in the regulation of their domestic concerns, have established affecting commerce, but not regulating it within the meaning of the Constitution. In fact, congressional legislation is only necessary to cure defects in existing laws, as they are discovered, and to adapt such laws to new developments of trade. As was said by Mr. Justice Field, speaking for the court in Welton v. Missouri, 91 U.S. 282,

"Inaction [by Congress] . . . is equivalent to a declaration that interstate commerce shall remain free and untrammeled." Applying that principle to the circumstances of this case, congressional inaction left Benson at liberty to adopt such reasonable rules and regulations for the disposition of passengers upon his boat, while pursuing her voyage within Louisiana or without, as seemed to him most for the interest of all concerned. The statute under which this suit is brought, as construed by the State Court, seeks to take away from him that power so long as he is within Louisiana; and while recognizing to the fullest extent the principle which sustains a statute, unless its unconstitutionality is clearly established, we think this statute, to the extent that it requires those engaged in the transportation of passengers among the States to carry colored passengers in Louisiana in the same cabin with whites, is unconstitutional and void. If the public good requires such legislation, it must come from Congress and not from the States. . . .

The judgment of the Supreme Court of Louisiana is reversed and the cause remanded, with instructions to reverse the judgment of the District Court, and direct such further proceedings in conformity with this opinion as may appear to be necessary.[1]

MR. JUSTICE CLIFFORD concurred in the judgment. . . .

Morgan v. Virginia 328 U.S. 373, 66 S. Ct. 1050, 90 L. Ed. 1317 (1946)

MR. JUSTICE REED delivered the opinion of the Court.

This appeal brings to this Court the question of the constitutionality of an act of Virginia, which requires all passenger motor vehicle carriers, both interstate and intrastate, to separate without discrimination the white and colored passengers in their motor buses so that contiguous seats will not be occupied by persons of different races at the same time. A violation of the requirement of separation by the carrier is a misdemeanor. The driver or other person in charge is directed and required to increase or decrease the space allotted to the respective races as may be necessary or proper and may require passengers to change their seats to comply with the allocation. The operator's failure to enforce the provisions is made a misdemeanor.

These regulations were applied to an interstate passenger, this appellant, on a motor vehicle then making an interstate run or trip. According to the statement of fact by the Supreme Court of Appeals of Virginia, appellant, who is a Negro, was traveling on a motor common carrier, operating under the above-mentioned statute, from Gloucester County, Virginia, through the District of Columbia, to Baltimore, Maryland, the destination of the bus. There were other passengers, both white and colored. On her refusal to accede to a request of the driver to move to a back seat, which was partly occupied by other colored passengers, so as to permit the seat that she vacated to be used by white passengers, a warrant was obtained and appellant was arrested, tried and convicted of a violation of §4097dd of the Virginia Code. [This section makes a bus passenger's refusal to obey such lawful directions of the driver a misdemeanor.] On a writ of error the conviction was affirmed by the Supreme Court of Appeals of Virginia. 184 Va. 24, 34 S.E.2d 491. . . .

The errors of the Court of Appeals that are assigned and relied upon by appellant are in form only two. The first is that the decision is repugnant to Clause 3, §8, Article 1 of the Constitution of the United States, and the second the holding that powers reserved to the states by the Tenth Amendment include the power to require an interstate motor passenger to occupy a seat restricted for the use of his race. Actually, the first question alone needs consideration for if the statute unlawfully burdens interstate commerce, the reserved powers of the state will not validate it.

---

[1] Hermitage, Mrs. De Cuir's destination, is in Pointe Coupee Parish, Louisiana. See 27 La. Ann. 1, 2 (1875). Cf. South Covington & Cincinnati R. Co. v. Kentucky, 252 U.S. 399 (1920). — ED.

We think, as the Court of Appeals apparently did, that the appellant is a proper person to challenge the validity of this statute as a burden on commerce. If it is an invalid burden, the conviction under it would fail. The statute affects appellant as well as the transportation company. Constitutional protection against burdens on commerce is for her benefit on a criminal trial for violation of the challenged statute. New York ex rel. Hatch v. Reardon, 204 U.S. 152, 160; Alabama State Federal of Labor v. McAdory, 325 U.S. 450, 463. . . .

This statute is attacked on the ground that it imposes undue burdens on interstate commerce. It is said by the Court of Appeals to have been passed in the exercise of the state's police power to avoid friction between the races. But this Court pointed out years ago "that a State cannot avoid the operation of this rule by simply invoking the convenient apologetics of the police power." Burdens upon commerce are those actions of a state which directly "impair the usefulness of its facilities for such traffic." That impairment, we think, may arise from other causes than costs or long delays. A burden may arise from a state statute which requires interstate passengers to order their movements on the vehicle in accordance with local rather than national requirements.

On appellant's journey, this statute required that she sit in designated seats in Virginia. Changes in seat designation might be made "at any time" during the journey when "necessary or proper for the comfort and convenience of passengers." This occurred in this instance. Upon such change of designation, the statute authorizes the operator of the vehicle to require, as he did here, "any passenger to change his or her seat as it may be necessary or proper." An interstate passenger must if necessary repeatedly shift seats while moving in Virginia to meet the seating requirements of the changing passenger group. On arrival at the District of Columbia line, the appellant would have had freedom to occupy any available seat and so to the end of her journey.

Interstate passengers traveling via motor buses between the north and south or the east and west may pass through Virginia on through lines in the day or in the night. The large buses approach the comfort of pullmans and have seats convenient for rest. On such interstate journeys the enforcement of the requirements for reseating would be disturbing.

Appellant's argument, properly we think, includes facts bearing on interstate motor transportation beyond those immediately involved in this journey under the Virginia statutory regulations. To appraise the weight of the burden of the Virginia statute on interstate commerce, related statutes of other states are important to show whether there are cumulative effects which may make local regulations impracticable. Eighteen states, it appears, prohibit racial separation on public carriers. Ten require separation on motor carriers. [Citation of statutes omitted.] Of these, Alabama applies specifically to interstate passengers with an exception for interstate passengers with through tickets from states without laws on separation of passengers. . . .

In states where separation of races is required in motor vehicles, a method of identification as white or colored must be employed. This may be done by definition. Any ascertainable Negro blood identifies a person as colored for purposes of separation in some states. [Citation of statutes omitted.] In the other states which require the separation of the races in motor carriers, apparently no definition generally applicable or made for the purposes of the statute is given. Court definition or further legislative enactments would be required to clarify the line between the races. Obviously there may be changes by legislation in the definition.

The interferences to interstate commerce which arise from state regulation of racial association on interstate vehicles has long been recognized. Such regulation hampers freedom of choice in selecting accommodations. The recent changes in transportation brought about by the coming of automobiles does not seem of great significance in the problem. People of all races travel today more extensively than in 1878 when this Court first passed upon state regulation of racial segregation in commerce. The factual situation set out in preceding paragraphs emphasizes the soundness of this Court's early conclusion in Hall v. De Cuir, 95 U.S. 485. . . .

In weighing the factors that enter into our conclusion as to whether this statute so burdens interstate commerce or so infringes the requirements of national uniformity as to be invalid, we are mindful of the fact that conditions vary between northern or western states such as Maine or Montana, with practically no colored population; industrial states such as Illinois, Ohio, New Jersey and Pennsylvania with a small, although appreciable, percentage of colored citizens; and the states of the deep south with percentages of from twenty-five to nearly fifty percent colored, all with varying densities of the white and colored races in certain localities. Local efforts to promote amicable relations in difficult areas by legislative segregation in interstate transportation emerge from the latter racial distribution. As no state law can reach beyond its own border nor bar transportation of passengers across its boundaries, diverse seating requirements for the races in interstate journeys result. As there is no federal act dealing with the separation of races in interstate transportation, we must decide the validity of this Virginia statute on the challenge that it interferes with commerce, as a matter of balance between the exercise of the local police power and the need for national uniformity in the regulations for interstate travel. It seems clear to us that seating arrangements for the different races in interstate motor travel require a single uniform rule to promote and protect national travel. Consequently, we hold the Virginia statute in controversy invalid.

Reversed.

MR. JUSTICE RUTLEDGE concurs in the result.

MR. JUSTICE BLACK concurring.

The Commerce Clause of the Constitution provides that "Congress shall have power . . . to regulate commerce . . . among the several States." I have believed, and still believe that this provision means that Congress can regulate commerce and that the courts cannot. But in a series of cases decided in recent years this Court over my protest has held that the Commerce Clause justifies this Court in nullifying state legislation which this Court concludes imposes an "undue burden" on interstate commerce. I think that whether state legislation imposes an "undue burden" on interstate commerce raises pure questions of policy, which the Constitution intended should be resolved by the Congress.

. . . I . . . still believe, that in these cases the Court was assuming the role of a "super-legislature" in determining matters of governmental policy.

But the Court, at least for the present, seems committed to this interpretation of the Commerce Clause. . . .

So long as the Court remains committed to the "undue burden on commerce formula," I must make decisions under it. . . . [That formula] requires the majority's decision. In view of the Court's present disposition to apply that formula, I acquiesce.

MR. JUSTICE FRANKFURTER, concurring.

My brother Burton has stated with great force reasons for not invalidating the Virginia statute. But for me Hall v. De Cuir, 95 U.S. 485, is controlling. Since it was decided nearly seventy years ago, that case on several occasions has been approvingly cited and has never been questioned. Chiefly for this reason I concur in the opinion of the Court. . . .

MR. JUSTICE BURTON, dissenting.

On the application of the interstate commerce clause of the Federal Constitution to this case, I find myself obliged to differ from the majority of the Court. I would sustain the Virginia statute against that clause. The issue is neither the desirability of the statute nor the constitutionality of racial segregation as such. The opinion of the Court does not claim that the Virginia statute, regulating seating arrangements for interstate passengers in motor vehicles, violates the Fourteenth Amendment or is in conflict with a federal statute. The Court holds this statute unconstitutional for but one reason. It holds that the burden imposed by the statute upon the nation's interest in interstate commerce so greatly outweighs the contribution made by the statute to the state's interest in its public welfare as to make it unconstitutional.

The undue burden upon interstate commerce thus relied upon by the Court is not complained of by the Federal Government, by any state, or by any carrier. This statute has been in effect since 1930. The carrier concerned is operating under regulations of its own which conform to the statute. The statute conforms to the policy adopted by Virginia as to steamboats (1900), electric or street cars and railroads (1902-1904). . . .

If the mere diversity between the Virginia statute and comparable statutes of other states is so serious as to render the Virginia statute invalid, it probably means that the comparable statutes of those other states, being diverse from it and from each other, are equally invalid. . . . In the absence of federal law, this may eliminate state regulation of racial separation in the seating of interstate passengers on motor vehicles and leave the regulation of the subject to the respective carriers.

The present decision will lead to the questioning of the validity of statutory regulation of the seating of intrastate passengers in the same motor vehicles with interstate passengers. . . .

The basic weakness in the appellant's case is the lack of facts and findings essential to demonstrate the existence of such a serious and major burden upon the national interest in interstate commerce as to outweigh whatever state or local benefits are attributable to the statute and which would be lost by its invalidation. . . . In weighing these competing demands, if this Court is to justify the invalidation of this statute, it must, first of all, be satisfied that the many years of experience of the state and the carrier that are reflected in this state law should be set aside. It represents the tested public policy of Virginia regularly enacted, long maintained and currently observed. The officially declared state interests, even when affecting interstate commerce, should not be laid aside summarily by this Court in the absence of Congressional action. It is only Congress that can supply affirmative national uniformity of action. . . .

The Court makes its own further assumption that the question of racial separation of interstate passengers in motor vehicle carriers requires national uniformity of treatment rather than diversity of treatment at this time. The inaction of Congress is an important indication that, in the opinion of Congress, this issue is better met without nationally uniform affirmative regulation than with it. Legislation raising the issue long has been, and is now, pending before Congress but has not reached the floor of either House. The fact that 18 states have prohibited in some degree racial separation in public carriers is important progress in the direction of uniformity. The fact, however, that 10 contiguous states in some degree require, by state law, some racial separation of passengers on motor carriers indicates a different appraisal by them of the needs and conditions in those areas than in others. The remaining 20 states have not gone equally far in either direction. This recital of existing legislative diversity is evidence against the validity of the assumption by this Court that there exists today a requirement of a single uniform national rule on the subject.

It is a fundamental concept of our Constitution that where conditions are diverse the solution of problems arising out of them may well come through the application of diversified treatment matching the diversified needs as determined by our local governments. Uniformity of treatment is appropriate where a substantial uniformity of conditions exists.

BOB-LO EXCURSION CO. v. MICHIGAN, 333 U.S. 28, 68 S. Ct. 358, 92 L. Ed. 455 (1948). Rutledge, J.: "Bois Blanc Island is part of the Province of Ontario, Canada. It lies just above the mouth of the Detroit River, some fifteen miles from Michigan's metropolis upstream. The island, known in Detroit by the corruption 'Bob-Lo,' has been characterized as that city's Coney Island.

---

[1] "A small fenced-off tract at one end is reserved for lighthouse purposes, and three small cottage lots. . . ."

Section B. Protection of Local Economy and Welfare

"Appellant owns almost all of Bois Blanc in fee.[1] For many years it has operated the island, during the summer seasons, as a place of diverse amusements for Detroit's varied population. Appellant also owns and operates two steamships for transporting its patrons of the island's attractions from Detroit to Bois Blanc and return. The vessels engage in no other business on these trips. No freight, mail or express is carried; the only passengers are the patrons bent on pleasure, who board ship at Detroit; they go on round-trip one-day-limit tickets which include the privilege of landing at Bois Blanc and going back by a later boat. No intermediate stops are made on these excursions. . . . The record indicates there are no established means of access from the Canadian shore to the island. There is no evidence of even surreptitious entry from the Canadian mainland. Appellant's vessels not only are the sole means of transportation to and from the island, but carry only its own patrons of Bois Blanc's recreational facilities. . . .

"In conducting this business of amusement and transportation, appellant long has followed the policy, by advertisement and otherwise, to invite and encourage all comers, except two classes. One is the disorderly; the other, colored people. From the latter exclusion this case arises.

"In June of 1945 Sarah Elizabeth Ray, the complaining witness, was employed by the Detroit Ordnance District. She and some forty other girls were also members of a class conducted at the Commerce High School under the auspices of the ordnance district. The class planned an excursion to Bois Blanc for June 21 under the district's sponsorship.

"On that morning thirteen girls with their teacher appeared at appellant's dock in Detroit to go on the outing. All were white except Miss Ray. Each girl paid eighty-five cents to one of the group, who purchased round-trip tickets and distributed them. The party then passed through the gate, each member giving in her ticket without question from the ticket taker. They then checked their coats, went to the upper decks and took chairs.

"Shortly afterward Devereaux, appellant's assistant general manager, and a steward named Fox appeared and stated that Miss Ray could not go along because she was colored. At first she remonstrated against the discrimination and refused to leave. But when it appeared she would be ejected forcibly, she said she would go. Devereaux and Fox then escorted her ashore, saying the company was a private concern and could exclude her if it wished. They took her to the ticket office and offered to return her fare. She refused to accept it, took their names, and left the company's premises. There is no suggestion that she or any member of her party was guilty of unbecoming conduct. Nor is there any dispute concerning the facts.

"This criminal prosecution followed in the Recorder's Court for Detroit, for violation of the Michigan civil rights act in the discrimination practiced against Miss Ray. Jury trial being formally waived, the court after hearing evidence and argument found appellant guilty as charged and sentenced it to pay a fine of $25. On appeal the Supreme Court of Michigan affirmed the judgment, holding the statute applicable to the circumstances presented by the case and valid in that application, as against the constitutional and other objections put forward. 317 Mich. 686, 27 N.W.2d 139. In due course probable jurisdiction was noted here. Judicial Code, §237(a).

"The Michigan Civil Rights Act, §146, enacts:

"'All persons within the jurisdiction of this state shall be entitled to full and equal accommodations, advantages, facilities and privileges of inns, hotels, restaurants, eating houses, barber shops, billiard parlors, stores, public conveyances on land and water, theaters, motion picture houses, public educational institutions, in elevators, on escalators, in all methods of air transportation and all other places of public accommodation, amusement, and recreation, where refreshments are or may hereafter be served, subject only to the conditions and limitations established by law and applicable alike, to all citizens and to all citizens alike, with uniform prices.'

"By §147, any owner, lessee, proprietor, agent or employee of any such place who directly or indirectly withholds any accommodation secured by §146, on account of race, creed or color, becomes guilty of a misdemeanor, punishable as the section states, and liable to a civil action for treble damages. . . ."[m]

What decision? Why?

McCarroll v. Dixie Greyhound Lines *309 U.S. 176, 60 S. Ct. 504, 84 L. Ed. 683 (1940)*

MR. JUSTICE McREYNOLDS delivered the opinion of the Court:

An Arkansas statute[1] prohibits entry into the State of any automobile or truck "carrying over twenty (20) gallons of gasoline in the gasoline tank of such automobile or truck or in auxiliary tanks of said trucks to be used as motor fuel in said truck or motor vehicles until the state tax thereon [six and one-half cents per gallon][2] has been paid."

Appellee, a Delaware corporation, operates passenger busses propelled by gasoline motors, from Memphis, Tennessee across Arkansas to St. Louis, Missouri, and in reverse. The route between these points approximates 342 miles — 3 in Tennessee, 78 in Arkansas, 261 in Missouri. Like busses ply between Memphis and points within and beyond Arkansas, and in reverse. It is only necessary now to consider the facts connected with operation of the Memphis-St. Louis line. They are typical.

Each bus consumes about one gallon of gasoline for every five miles traversed. Sixty-eight gallons are required for the journey from Memphis to St. Louis — under one in Tennessee, sixteen in Arkansas, fifty-one in Missouri. The practice is to place in the bus tank at Memphis the sixty-eight gallons of gasoline commonly required for the trip; also ten more to meet any emergency. Thus upon arrival at the Arkansas line the tank contains some seventy-seven gallons of which sixteen probably will be consumed within that State. As a condition precedent to entry there, appellant — revenue officer of the State — demands that each bus pay six and one-half cents upon every gallon of this gasoline above twenty, and threatens enforcement.

By a bill in the District Court, appellee unsuccessfully sought an injunction against this threatened action. The Circuit Court of Appeals Eighth Circuit took a different view.

. . . [I]t reversed the District Court and directed entry of a decree there enjoining appellant "from enforcing the challenged tax against it [the appellee] with respect to all gasoline in the fuel tanks of its interstate busses which is being carried through Arkansas for use in other states."

This action we approve.

The often announced rule is that while generally a state may not directly burden interstate commerce by taxation she may require all who use her roads to make reasonable compensation therefor. Hendrick v. Maryland, 235 U.S. 610, 622; Interstate Transit v. Lindsey [283 U.S. 183]; Bingaman v. Golden Eagle Western Lines, 297 U.S. 626, 628.

---

[m] The order of the Court's statement of facts has been changed slightly. — ED.

[1] Act 67 General Assembly Arkansas, approved March 2, 1933 —

Section 1. On and after the passage of this Act it shall be a violation of the law for any person, co-partnership or company to drive or cause to be driven into the State of Arkansas any automobile or truck carrying over twenty (20) gallons of gasoline in the gasoline tank of such automobile or truck or in auxiliary tanks of said trucks to be used as motor fuel in said truck or motor vehicles until the state tax thereon has been paid.

Section 2. Any person, co-partnership or company violating the provisions of this Act shall be deemed guilty of a misdemeanor and upon conviction thereof shall be fined in any sum not exceeding one hundred ($100) dollars. Each load carried into the state shall constitute a separate offense.

[2] Act 11 Extraordinary Sessions, Arkansas, approved February 12, 1934 —

Section 22. Paragraph (c) of §1 of Act No. 63 of the General Assembly, approved February 25, 1931, is amended to read as follows:

"(c) There is hereby levied a privilege or excise tax of six and one-half cents on each gallon of motor vehicle fuel as defined in this Act, sold or used in this State or purchased for sale or use in this State."

Section B. Protection of Local Economy and Welfare

Here, the revenue officer demanded payment of appellee on account of gasoline to be immediately transported over the roads of Arkansas for consumption beyond. If, considering all the circumstances, this imposition reasonably can be regarded as proper compensation for using the roads it is permissible. But the facts disclosed are incompatible with that view. A fair charge could have no reasonable relation to such gasoline. That could not be even roughly computed by considering only the contents of the tank. Moreover, we find no purpose to exact fair compensation only from all who make use of the highways. Twenty gallons of gasoline ordinarily will propel a bus across the State and if only that much is in the tank at the border no charge whatever is made. Evidently large use without compensation is permissible and easy to obtain.

The point here involved has been much discussed. Our opinions above referred to and others there cited define the applicable principles. The present controversy is within those approved by Interstate Transit v. Lindsey, supra. Neither Hicklin v. Coney, 290 U.S. 169, nor Bingaman v. Golden Eagle Western Lines, supra, relied upon by appellant's counsel, properly understood, sanctions a different view.

The challenged judgment must be affirmed.

MR. JUSTICE STONE, concurring.

THE CHIEF JUSTICE, MR. JUSTICE ROBERTS, MR. JUSTICE REED and I agree with MR. JUSTICE McREYNOLDS, but we think a word should be said of appellant's contention that the tax in its practical operation may be taken as a fair measure of respondent's use of the highways.

Since the subject taxed, gasoline introduced into the state in the tank of a vehicle, for use solely in propelling it in interstate commerce, is immune from state taxation except for a limited state purpose, the exaction of a reasonable charge for the use of its highways, it is not enough that the tax when collected is expended upon the state's highways. It must appear on the face of the statute or be demonstrable that the tax as laid is measured by or has some fair relationship to the use of the highways for which the charge is made. [Citations omitted.]

While the present tax, laid on gasoline in the tank in excess of twenty gallons, admittedly has no necessary or apparent relationship to any use of the highways intrastate, appellant argues that, as applied to the reserve gasoline in each of appellee's vehicles, the tax either is, or with a reduction of the reserves would be, substantially equivalent to a tax which the state could lay, but has not, on the gasoline consumed within the state. That could be true only in case the taxed gasoline, said to be reserved for the extrastate journey, were by chance or design of substantially the same amount as that consumed intrastate.

That the relationship between tax and highway use does not in fact exist as the business is now conducted, is demonstrated by appellant's showing that on all of appellee's routes, taken together, the taxed gasoline which is reserved for extrastate use is substantially more than that consumed on those routes within the state. In three the taxed reserve in excess of the twenty gallons exemption is substantially the same as the amount of the intrastate consumption. But on the fourth route the taxed reserve on busses moving in one direction is more than four times that consumed within the state. In the other it is approximately the same. With the three scheduled trips daily each way on the Memphis-St. Louis route, the excess of the gasoline taxed over that consumed in the state is more than 150 gallons per day. In no case does it appear that the amount of taxed gasoline has any relation to the size or weight of the vehicles.

It cannot be said that such a tax whose equivalence to a fair charge for the use of the highways, when not fortuitous, is attained only by appellee's abandonment of some of the commerce which is taxed, has any such fair relationship to the use of the highways by appellee as would serve to relieve the state from the constitutional prohibition against the taxation of property moving in interstate commerce. A tax so variable in its revenue production when compared with the taxpayer's intrastate movement cannot be thought to be "levied only as compensation for the use of the highways." Interstate Transit v. Lindsey, supra. Justification of the tax, as a compensation measure, by treating it as the equivalent of one which could be laid on gasoline consumed within the state must fail because the statute on its face and in its application discriminates against the commerce by measuring the tax by the consumption of gasoline moving and used in interstate commerce which occurs outside the state. [Citations omitted.]

It is no answer to the challenge to the levy to say that by altering the amount of the gasoline brought into the state for extrastate consumption appellee could so moderate the tax that it would bear a fair relation to the use of the highways within the state. In the circumstances of this case the state is without power to regulate the amount of gasoline carried interstate in appellee's tanks. It cannot be said, if that were material, that the amount carried is not appropriate for the interstate commerce in which appellee is engaged and it can hardly be supposed that the state could compel appellee to purchase there all the gasoline which it uses intrastate upon an interstate journey, because that would be a convenient means of laying and collecting a tax for the use of the highways. There are ways enough in which the state can take its lawful toll without any suppression of the commerce which it taxes. In laying an exaction as a means of collecting compensation for the use of its highways the state must tax the commerce as it is done, and not as it might be done if the state could control it. Appellant cannot justify an unlawful exaction by insisting that it would be lawful if the taxpayer were to relinquish some of the commerce which the Constitution protects from state interference.

Mr. Justice Black, Mr. Justice Frankfurter, and Mr. Justice Douglas, dissenting:

We take a different view. Measured by the oft-repeated judicial rule that every enactment of a legislature carries a presumption of constitutional validity, the Arkansas tax has not, in our opinion, been shown to be beyond all reasonable doubt in violation of the constitutional provisions that "Congress shall have power to . . . regulate commerce . . . among the States." "In case of real doubt, a law must be sustained." Mr. Justice Holmes in Interstate Consol. Street R. Co. v. Massachusetts, 207 U.S. 79, 88. Congress, sole constitutional legislative repository of power over that commerce, has enacted no regulation prohibiting Arkansas from levying a tax — on gasoline in excess of twenty gallons brought into the State — in return for the use of its highways. Gasoline taxes are widely utilized for building and maintaining public roads, and the proceeds of this Arkansas tax are pledged to that end. Arkansas can levy a gallonage tax on any gasoline withdrawn from storage within the State and placed in the tanks of this carrier's vehicles "notwithstanding that its ultimate function is to generate motive power for carrying on interstate commerce." Edelman v. Boeing Air Transport, 289 U.S. 249, 252. The present tax aims at carriers who would escape such taxation, unless we are to require Arkansas to shape its taxes to the circumstances of each carrier.

The cost entailed by the construction and maintenance of modern highways creates for the forty-eight States one of their largest financial problems. A major phase of this problem is the proper apportionment of the financial burden between those who use a State's highways for transportation within its borders and those who do so in the course of interstate transportation. Striking a fair balance involves incalculable variants and therefore is beset with perplexities. The making of these exacting adjustments is the business of legislation — that of state legislatures and of Congress. . . .

Arkansas' tax hits the big, heavy busses and trucks which, it is well established, entail most serious wear and tear upon roads. Had Arkansas expressly declared the challenged statute to be a means of working out a fair charge upon these heavy vehicles for cost and maintenance of the roads they travel in the State, the relationship between the means employed and these allowable ends — however crude and awkward — would have been rendered more explicit, but not made more evidently a matter of policy and administration, and therefore not for judicial determination. Certainly, the State had power to impose flat fees or taxes graduated according to gasoline used, horsepower, weight and ca-

Section B. **Protection of Local Economy and Welfare** 437

pacity or mileage, and yet those taxes would not measure with exact precision the taxpayers' use of Arkansas highways. It is not for us to measure the refinements of fiscal duties which a State may exact from these heavy motor vehicles.

This case again illustrates the wisdom of the Founders in placing interstate commerce under the protection of Congress. The present problem is not limited to Arkansas, but is of national moment. Maintenance of open channels of trade between the States was not only of paramount importance when our Constitution was framed; it remains today a complex problem calling for national vigilance and regulation.

Our disagreement with the opinions just announced does not arise from a belief that Federal action is unnecessary to bring about appropriate uniformity in regulations of interstate commerce. Indeed, state legislation recently before this Court indicates quite the contrary. For instance, we sustained the right of South Carolina — in the absence of congressional prohibition — to regulate the width and weight of interstate trucks using her highways, even though the unassailed findings showed that a substantial amount of interstate commerce would thereby be barred from the State. South Carolina State Highway Dept. v. Barnwell Bros. [303 U.S. 177]. We did not thereby approve the desirability of such state regulations. It is not for us to approve or disapprove. We did decide that "courts do not sit as legislatures, either state or national. They cannot act as Congress does when, after weighing all the conflicting interests, state and national, it determines when and how much the state regulatory power shall yield to the larger interests of national commerce." As both the Union and the States are more and more dependent upon the exercise of their taxing powers for carrying on government, it becomes more and more important that potential conflicts between state and national powers should not be found where Congress has not found them, unless conflict is established by demonstrable concreteness. See Hammond v. Schappi Bus Line, 275 U.S. 164.

Even under the principle enunciated by the majority — that Arkansas may not measure her tax by gasoline carried in appellee's tanks for use in other States — the challenged judgment should not stand.

Arkansas admittedly has power to tax appellee upon gasoline used within her borders, and need not, of course, extend to appellee any exemption for a reserve. The record discloses that appellee's busses travel 1188.8 miles each day over Arkansas highways. The trial judge found, and there is evidence to support the finding, that these busses use about one gallon of gasoline for every five miles traveled. Thus, appellee uses about 237.76 gallons of gasoline a day in Arkansas, upon which the tax of 6.5 cents per gallon used would amount to $15.45 a day.

Appellee's busses travel four different routes, two from Memphis through Arkansas to Missouri, and two from Memphis to cities in Arkansas. On the trips to Missouri the tax now exacted by Arkansas is greater than would be a tax on the gasoline actually used in Arkansas. But on the trips from Memphis into Arkansas and back, the tax exacted, because of the 20-gallon exemption, is less than would be a tax on the gasoline used in Arkansas.

As appellant points out in his brief, when all the routes are taken together, the daily tax which Arkansas would collect if appellee carried only enough gasoline to complete each trip would only amount to $13.00 — actually $2.45 less than a tax on gasoline consumed in Arkansas.

This amount — $2.45 — equals the present tax on 37 gallons of gasoline. Appellee's busses enter Arkansas 13 times each day. It follows that appellee may carry a reserve of almost three gallons on each trip and still pay no more than the tax which, as the majority assumes, Arkansas could constitutionally impose on the gasoline actually consumed on her own roads. There is nothing in the record to show that a greater reserve is necessary. An interstate carrier has no absolute right to fix the size and character of its equipment used in interstate commerce, in total disregard of the necessities of the enterprise and the requirements of States through which the carrier operates. Exactions by such States may well be designed to operate upon the quantity of gasoline reserves for considerations analogous to those which have called into being state regulations of the size, weight and number of the vehicles themselves. And a state tax which may induce a reduction in the amount of reserve previously carried is no more to be condemned on that sole ground alone than is a state law actually prohibiting vehicles above a certain size or weight. That this reduction may be attributable to a tax rather than to a regulatory measure expressly passed in the interests of public safety should not be controlling. Particularly is this so when the proceeds of the tax are utilized exclusively for highway purposes and the tax itself is directed to gasoline used, just as other equipment is used, in the course of interstate business and involves no manifestation of hostility to — or levy upon — gasoline carried as a commodity in interstate commerce. It is presumably safe to rely on appellee's self-interest to work out any schedules of refueling at its various storage facilities by changes in reserves carried. We cannot believe that appellee is able to attack the constitutionality of this tax on the ground that as to others it might operate differently and serve to burden the use of gasoline in other States. It is important to bear in mind that we are not passing upon a statute as such but upon the incidence of this statute in the single concrete situation presented by a specific objector on this specific record. The very fact that such niceties of calculation have to be indulged in as the concurring opinion finds necessary in order to establish the mischief of the statute, makes manifest the "real doubt" of any showing of unconstitutionality and indicates that a burden of calculation and speculation is assumed in the exercise of the judicial function which should be left to the legislatures of the States and the Congress.

Judicial control of national commerce — unlike legislative regulations — must from inherent limitations of the judicial process treat the subject by the hit-and-miss method of deciding single local controversies upon evidence and information limited by the narrow rules of litigation. Spasmodic and unrelated instances of litigation cannot afford an adequate basis for the creation of integrated national rules which alone can afford that full protection for interstate commerce intended by the Constitution. We would, therefore, leave the questions raised by the Arkansas tax for consideration of Congress in a nationwide survey of the constantly increasing barriers to trade among the States. Unconfined by "the narrow scope of judicial proceedings" Congress alone can, in the exercise of its plenary constitutional control over interstate commerce, not only consider whether such a tax as now under scrutiny is consistent with the best interests of our national economy, but can also on the basis of full exploration of the many aspects of a complicated problem devise a national policy fair alike to the States and our Union. Diverse and interacting state laws may well have created avoidable hardships. See, Comparative Charts of State Statutes Illustrating Barriers to Trade between States, Works Progress Administration, May, 1939; Proceedings, The National Conference on Interstate Trade Barriers, The Council of State Governments, 1939. But the remedy, if any is called for, we think is within the ample reach of Congress.

Duckworth v. Arkansas 314 U.S. 390, 62 S. Ct. 311, 86 L. Ed. 294 (1941)

MR. CHIEF JUSTICE STONE delivered the opinion of the Court:

Appellant was convicted and fined by an Arkansas court for transporting intoxicating liquor through the state without a permit as required by an Arkansas statute. The question for decision is whether this statutory requirement and its penal sanction unduly encroach upon the power over interstate commerce delegated to Congress. The Arkansas Supreme Court sustained the requirement of the permit as a local police regulation permissible under the commerce clause. 201 Ark. 1123, 148 S.W.(2d) 656. The case comes here on appeal under the provisions of § 237 (a) of the Judicial Code.

Section 14,177, Pope's 1937 Digest of Arkansas Statutes, § 5, Act 109 of 1935, under

Section B. **Protection of Local Economy and Welfare** 439

which appellant was convicted, makes it unlawful for any person to ship into the state any distilled spirits without first having obtained a permit from the state commissioner of revenue. The statute provides that the form of permit and the shipments into the state shall be governed by rules and regulations promulgated by the commissioner. Appellant was tried upon a stipulation of facts which tended to show that when arrested in Arkansas he was engaged in transporting by motor truck, without a permit, a load of distilled spirits from a point in Illinois to a point in Mississippi. The state court held that this violated § 14,177. At the time of the offense there were no regulations specifically applicable to transportation passing through the state, the regulations then in force being adapted to transportation for delivery within the state or from point to point within the state.

We have no occasion to decide whether the Arkansas statute, when applied to transportation passing through that state for delivery or use in another, derives support from the Twenty-first Amendment, which prohibits the "transportation or importation" of intoxicating liquors "into any state . . . for delivery or use therein" in violation of its laws, cf. United States v. Gudger, 249 U.S. 373. . . . For we are of the opinion that upon principles of constitutional interpretation consistently accepted and followed by this Court ever since the decisions in Willson v. Black Bird Creek Marsh Co., 2 Pet. 245, and Cooley v. Port Wardens, 12 How. 299, the commerce clause does not foreclose the Arkansas regulation with which we are now concerned. . . .

The Arkansas Supreme Court in this case has declared that under the statute appellant was entitled to a permit on application, which he does not appear to have made; that the permit requirement is in its nature an inspection measure for which only a nominal fee, necessary to defray the cost of issuing it and of police inspection and of necessary reports, is charged. It also said that any failure by the state commissioner to act reasonably and promptly in administering the law would be controlled by the courts through mandamus. In a later case, Hardin v. Spiers, 202 Ark. 804, 152 S.W.(2d) 1010, arising under regulations not in force at the time of appellant's conviction, the same court declared that the commissioner must exercise this power in a reasonable, not an arbitrary, manner.

. . . As we had occasion to point out at the last term of Court, there are many matters which are appropriate subjects of regulation in the interest of the safety, health and well-being of local communities which, because of their local character and their number and diversity and because of the practical difficulties involved, may never be adequately dealt with by Congress. Because of their local character also there is wide scope for local regulation without impairing the uniformity of control over the commerce in matters of national concern and without materially obstructing the free flow of commerce, which were the principal objects sought to be secured by the commerce clause. Such regulations, in the absence of supervening Congressional action, have for the most part been sustained by this Court, notwithstanding the commerce clause. See California v. Thompson, 313 U.S. 109, 113 et seq., and cases cited. . . .

While the subject matter of the present regulation, transportation of liquor, with its attendant dangers to the communities through which it passes, differs in many respects from those which we have mentioned, all are alike in their tendency, if unregulated, to affect the public interest adversely in varying ways depending on local conditions. The efforts at effective regulation, state and national, of intoxicating liquor, evidenced by the long course of litigation in this Court, have not left us unaware of the peculiar difficulties of controlling it or of its tendency to get out of legal bounds. The present requirement of a permit is not shown to be more than a means of establishing the identity of those who are to engage in the transportation, their route and point of destination, and affords opportunity for local officials to take appropriate measures to insure that the liquor is transported without diversion, in conformity to the permit. The permit device is not unlike state requirements of health certificates for animals or certificates of inspection for goods, which have been sustained here both as to transportation into a state, . . . and through it, Reid v. Colorado, 187 U.S. 137. . . . Where the power to regulate commerce for local protection exists, the states may adopt effective measures to accomplish the permitted end. The Arkansas statute does not conflict with any act of Congress. It does not forbid or preclude the transportation, or interfere with the free flow of commerce among the states beyond what is reasonably necessary to protect the local public interest in preventing unlawful distribution or use of liquor within the state. It does not violate the commerce clause. Cf. Ziffrin, Inc. v. Reeves, 308 U.S. 132.

What we have said is restricted to the statute as applied under the regulations in force at the time of petitioner's alleged offense. It will be time enough to deal with abuses of the permit system if and when they arise. Nor have we occasion to consider the state's authority to regulate other articles of commerce less susceptible to uses injurious to the communities through which they pass. Cf. Clark Distilling Co. v. Western Maryland R. Co., 242 U.S. 311, 332; Ziffrin, Inc. v. Reeves, supra.

Affirmed.

MR. JUSTICE JACKSON, concurring in result:

I agree that this Court should not relieve Duckworth of his conviction, but I would rest the decision on the constitutional provision applicable only to the transportation of liquor, and refrain from what I regard as an unwise extension of state power over interstate commerce.

I

. . . Duckworth now contends that it is our duty to assure him safe conduct as against the action of Arkansas, although his goal is to violate both the laws of Mississippi and the Federal Constitution. He asks us to hold that one provision of the Constitution guarantees him an opportunity to violate another. The law is not that tricky.

Whether one transporting liquor across Arkansas to a legal destination might not have some claim to federal protection, we do not need to consider. One who assails the constitutionality of a statute must stand on his own right to relief. Since this appellant had no rightful claim to constitutional protection for his trip, the whole purpose of which was to violate the Constitution which he invokes, we should leave him where we find him, and for this reason I concur in the judgment of this Court affirming the conviction.

II

If we yield to an urge to go beyond this rather narrow but adequate ground of decision, we should then consider whether this liquor controversy cannot properly be determined by guidance from the liquor clauses of the Constitution. . . . The people of the United States knew that liquor is a lawlessness unto itself. They determined that it should be governed by a specific and particular constitutional provision. They did not leave it to the courts to devise special distortions of the general rules as to interstate commerce to curb liquor's "tendency to get out of legal bounds." . . .

III

The opinion of the Court solves the present case through a construction of the interstate commerce power. It regards this liquor as a legitimate subject of a lawful commerce, and then, because of its special characteristics, approves this admittedly novel permit system and thus expands the power of the state to regulate such lawful commerce beyond anything this Court has yet approved.

The extent to which state legislation may be allowed to affect the conduct of interstate business in the absence of Congressional action on the subject has long been a vexatious problem. Recently the tendency has been to abandon the earlier limitations and to sustain more freely such state laws on the ground that Congress has power to supersede them with regulation of its own. It is a tempting escape from a difficult question to pass to Congress the responsibility for continued existence of local restraints and obstructions to national commerce. But these restraints are individually too petty, too diversified, and too local to get the attention of a Congress hard pressed with more urgent matters. The practical result is that in default of action by us they will go on suffocating and retarding and Balkanizing American commerce, trade and industry.

I differ basically with my brethren as to whether the inertia of government shall be on the side of restraint of commerce or on the side of freedom of commerce. The sluggishness of government, the multitude of matters that clamor for attention, and the relative ease with which men are persuaded to postpone troublesome decisions, all make inertia one of the most decisive powers in determining the course of our affairs and frequently gives to the established order of things a longevity and vitality much beyond its merits. Because that is so, I am reluctant to see any new local systems for restraining our national commerce get the prestige and power of established institutions. The Court's present opinion and tendency would allow the states to establish the restraints and let commerce struggle for Congressional action to make it free. This trend I am unwilling to further in any event beyond the plain requirements of existing cases.

If the reaction of this Court against what many of us have regarded as an excessive judicial interference with legislative action is to yield wholesome results, we must be cautious lest we merely rush to other extremes. The excessive use for insufficient reason of a judicially inflated due process clause to strike down states' laws regulating their own internal affairs, such as hours of labor in industry, minimum wage requirements, and standards for working conditions, is one thing. To invoke the interstate commerce clause to keep the many states from fastening their several concepts of local "well-being" onto the national commerce is a wholly different thing.

Our national free intercourse is never in danger of being suddenly stifled by dramatic and sweeping acts of restraint. That would produce its own antidote. Our danger, as the forefathers well knew, is from the aggregate strangling effect of a multiplicity of individually petty and diverse and local regulations. Each may serve some local purpose worthy enough by itself. Congress may very properly take into consideration local policies and dangers when it exercises its power under the commerce clause. But to let each locality conjure up its own dangers and be the judge of the remedial restraints to be clamped onto interstate trade inevitably retards our national economy and disintegrates our national society. It is the movement and exchange of goods that sustain living standards, both of him who produces and of him who consumes. This vital national interest in free commerce among the states must not be jeopardized.

I do not suppose the skies will fall if the Court does allow Arkansas to rig up this handy device for policing liquor on the ground that it is not forbidden by the commerce clause, but in doing so it adds another to the already too numerous and burdensome state restraints of national commerce and pursues a trend with which I would have no part.

4. Jurisdiction to Regulate

Osborn v. Ozlin 310 U.S. 53, 60 S. Ct. 758, 84 L. Ed. 1074 (1940)

MR. JUSTICE FRANKFURTER delivered the opinion of the Court:
Appellants have challenged the validity of a Virginia statute regulating the insurance of Virginia risks and have brought this suit to enjoin state officers from enforcing it. Its rele-

vant provisions, . . . forbid contracts of insurance or surety by companies authorized to do business within that Commonwealth "except through regularly constituted and registered resident agents or agencies of such companies." Acts of 1938, §4222, chap. 218. Such resident agents "shall be entitled to and shall receive the usual and customary commissions allowed on such contracts," and may not share more than half of this commission with a non-resident broker. §4226-a. Disobedience of these provisions (from which life, title and marine companies are exempted) may entail a fine or revocation of the corporate license in Virginia, or both. A district court of three judges, convened under §266 of the Judicial Code as amended, dismissed appellants' bill on the basis of elaborate findings of fact and conclusions of law, set forth in an opinion by Circuit Judge Soper. 29 F. Supp. 71. From this decree the case comes here on appeal under §238 of the Judicial Code as amended.

The bill was brought by foreign corporations authorized to do casualty and surety business in Virginia, and by some of their salaried employees. It is their claim that the statute deprives them of rights protected by the Fourteenth Amendment of the Constitution. The exact nature of these claims will appear more clearly in the setting of the illuminating findings below which may here be abbreviated.

The "production" of insurance — "production" being insurance jargon for obtaining business — is, in the main, carried on by two groups, agents and brokers. Though both are paid by commission, the different ways in which the two groups perform their functions have important practical consequences in the conduct of the insurance business, and hence in its regulation. The agent is tied to his company. But his ability to "produce" business depends upon the confidence of the community in him. He must therefore cultivate the good will and sense of dependence of his clients. He may finance the payment of premiums; he frequently assists in the filing and prosecution of claims; he acts as mediator between insurer and assured in the diverse situations which arise. The broker, on the other hand, is an independent middleman, not tied to a particular company. He meets more specially the needs of large customers, using their concentrated bargaining power to obtain the most favorable terms from competing companies. His activities, being largely confined to the big commercial centers, take place mostly outside Virginia.

A policy, whether "produced" by broker or agent, must be "serviced" — an insurance term for assistance rendered a customer in minimizing his risks. To this end the companies exert themselves directly, but the "producer" may render additional service. Only to a limited extent can risks be minimized at long range; local activity is essential. When the contract is "produced" by a non-resident broker the "servicing" function is normally performed by the company exclusively. When the "producer" is a resident agent, the case is ordinarily otherwise. For this, as well as for other reasons, it is obvious that non-resident brokers prefer to negotiate their contracts covering Virginia risks with companies authorized to do business in the Commonwealth.

These basic elements in the insurance business attain special significance in the case of enterprises operating not only in Virginia but in other states as well. For them the brokerage system offers the attractions of large-scale production. Through what is known as a master or "hotchpotch" policy, the assured may obtain a cheaper rate by pooling all his risks, whether in or out of Virginia. This wholesale insurance may furnish not only a reduced rate but a reduced commission to the customer. These are advantages which naturally draw the Virginia business of interstate enterprises away from local agents in Virginia to the great insurance centers.

In affecting the cost of these master policies, say the appellants, Virginia is intruding upon business transactions beyond its borders. Not only is a licensed company forbidden to write insurance except through a resident agent, but the agent cannot retain less than one-half of the customary commission allowed on such a contract for what may, so far as the requirements of the law are concerned, be no more than the perfunctory service of countersigning the policy.

But the question is not whether what Virginia has done will restrict appellants' freedom of action outside Virginia by subjecting the exercise of such freedom to financial burdens. The mere fact that state action may have repercussions beyond state lines is of no judicial significance so long as the action is not within that domain which the Constitution forbids. Alaska Packers Asso. v. Industrial Acci. Commission, 294 U.S. 532; Great Atlantic & P. Tea Co. v. Grosjean, 301 U.S. 412. Compare Equitable Life Assur. Soc. v. Pennsylvania, 238 U.S. 143. It is equally immaterial that such state action may run counter to the economic wisdom either of Adam Smith or of J. Maynard Keynes, or may be ultimately mischievous even from the point of view of avowed state policy. Our inquiry must be much narrower. It is whether Virginia has taken hold of a matter within her power, or has reached beyond her borders to regulate a subject which was none of her concern because the Constitution has placed control elsewhere. Compare Wallace v. Hines, 253 U.S. 66, 69.

Virginia has not sought to prohibit the making of contracts beyond her borders. She merely claims that her interest in the risks which these contracts are designed to prevent warrants the kind of control she has here imposed. This legislation is not to be judged by abstracting an isolated contract written in New York from the organic whole of the insurance business, the effect of that business on Virginia, and Virginia's regulation of it.

A network of legislation controls the surety and casualty business in Virginia. Insolvent companies may not engage in it. Virginia Code, §4180. Neither companies nor agents may give rebates. §4222-c. Rates for workmen's compensation, automobile liability and surety contracts are determined by its Corporation Commission. §§ 1887 (75), 4326-a-1, 4350-3. The difficulty of enforcing these regulations, so the District Court found, may be increased if policies covering Virginia risks are "produced" without participation by responsible local agents. Rebates evading local restriction may be granted under cover of business done outside the state. Contrariwise, if resident Virginia agents are made necessary conduits for insurance on Virginia risks now included in master policies, the state may have better means of acquiring accurate information for the effectuation of measures which it deems protective of its interests.

It is claimed that the requirement that not less than one-half of the customary commission be retained by the resident agent is a bald exaction for what may be no more than the perfunctory service of countersigning policies. The short answer to this is that the state may rely on this exaction as a mode of assuring the active use of resident agents for procuring and "servicing" policies covering Virginia risks. These functions, when adequately performed, benefit not only the company, the producer, and the assured. By minimizing the risks of casualty and loss, they redound in a pervasive way to the benefit of the community. At least Virginia may so have believed. And she may also have concluded that an agency system, such as this legislation was designed to promote, is better calculated to further these desirable ends than other modes of "production." When these beliefs are emphasized by legislation embodying similar notions of policy in a dozen states, it would savor of intolerance for us to suggest that a legislature could not constitutionally entertain the views which the legislation adopts. Compare Prudential Ins. Co. v. Cheek, 259 U.S. 530, 537.

The present case, therefore, is wholly unlike those instances in which a "so-called right is used as part of a scheme to accomplish a forbidden result." Fidelity & D. Co. v. Tafoya, 270 U.S. 426, 434. For it is clear that Virginia has a definable interest in the contracts she seeks to regulate and that what she has done is very different from the imposition of conditions upon appellants' privilege of engaging in local business which would bring within the orbit of state power matters unrelated to any local interests. It is not our province to measure the social advantage to Virginia of regulating the conduct of insurance companies within her borders insofar as it affects Virginia risks. Government has always had a special relation to insurance. The ways of safeguarding against the untoward manifestations of nature and other vicissitudes of life have long been withdrawn from the benefits and caprices of free competition. . . . In the light of all these exertions of state power it does not seem possible to doubt that the state could, if it chose, go into the insurance business, just as it can operate warehouses, flour mills, and other business ventures, Green v. Frazier, 253 U.S. 233, or might take "the whole business of banking under its control," Noble State Bank v. Haskell, 219 U.S. 104, 113. If the state, as to local risks, could thus pre-empt the field of insurance for itself, it may stay its intervention short of such a drastic step by insisting that its own residents shall have a share in devising and safeguarding protection against its local hazards. La Tourette v. McMaster, 248 U.S. 465. All these are questions of policy not for us to judge. . . .

In reaching this conclusion we have been duly mindful of the cases urged upon us by appellants. In Allgeyer v. Louisiana, 165 U.S. 578, apart from the doubts that have been cast upon the opinion in that case, the state attempted to penalize the making of contracts by its residents outside its borders with companies which had never subjected themselves to local control. Thus the statute was thought to be directed not at the regulation of insurance within the state, but at the making of contracts without. This was followed in St. Louis Cotton Compress Co. v. Arkansas, 260 U.S. 346; but see the refined distinctions drawn in Compania General de Tabacos v. Collector of Internal Revenue, 275 U.S. 87. In Fidelity & D. Co. v. Tafoya, 270 U.S. 426, the Court found that New Mexico had exceeded its power by forbidding "the payment of any emolument of any nature to any [nonresident] for the obtaining, placing or writing of any policy covering risks in New Mexico." The Court was of opinion that this statute went "beyond any legitimate interest of the State . . . ," 270 U.S. at 435, but carefully withheld its judgment as to the validity of a later New Mexico statute not unlike the Virginia law here under review.[7]

The decree must be affirmed.

MR. JUSTICE ROBERTS, dissenting:

I am unable to agree with the decision in this case. I think it sanctions an exertion of power by Virginia over transactions beyond her jurisdiction. . . .

The plain effort of Virginia is to compel a nonresident to pay a resident of Virginia for services which the latter does not in fact render and is not required to render. The principles underlying former decisions of this court are at war with the existence of any such asserted power.

THE CHIEF JUSTICE and MR. JUSTICE MCREYNOLDS join in this opinion.[n]

State Board of Insurance v. Todd Shipyards Corp. 370 U.S. 451, 82 S. Ct. 1380, 8 L. Ed. 2d 620 (1962)

MR. JUSTICE DOUGLAS delivered the opinion of the Court.

When we held in United States v. South-Eastern Underwriters Assn., 322 U.S. 533, that the modern business of insurance was "interstate commerce," we put it in a category which Congress could regulate and which, if our prior decisions controlled, could not in

---

[7] Hartford Acci. & Indem. Co. v. Delta & Pine Land Co., 292 U.S. 143, resting on Home Ins. Co. v. Dick, 281 U.S. 397, held that the terms of a contract validly made in Tennessee could not be subsequently enlarged by Mississippi as to a condition of "substantial importance" when suit was later brought on the policy in Mississippi, simply because "the interest insured was in Mississippi when the obligation to indemnify . . . matured, and it was . . . [the company's] duty to make payment there." 292 U.S. at 149. At the time the contract was entered into Mississippi had no interest in the risk covered. The Court felt that, even at the time of suit, "performance at most involved only the casual payment of money in Mississippi," 292 U.S. at 150, and that was an interest so subordinate to that of Tennessee that the latter was entitled to have the right of way. No question was thus involved touching the right of a state to regulate companies doing business within its borders as to contracts of insurance covering local risks.

[n] Cf. Clay v. Sun Insurance Office, Ltd., 377 U.S. 179 (1964). — ED.

some respects be regulated by the States, even in the absence of federal regulation. See Frankfurter, The Commerce Clause (1937); Rutledge, A Declaration of Legal Faith (1947).

Congress promptly passed the McCarran-Ferguson Act, 59 Stat. 33, 15 U.S.C. §1011, which provided that the regulation and taxation of insurance be left to the States, without restriction by reason of the Commerce Clause.[1] Subsequently, by force of the McCarran-Ferguson Act, we upheld the continued taxation and regulation by the States of interstate insurance transactions. Prudential Ins. Co. v. Benjamin, 328 U.S. 408.

Prior to the South-Eastern Underwriters decision, we had given broad scope to local regulation of the insurance business. Osborn v. Ozlin, 310 U.S. 53; Hoopeston Canning Co. v. Cullen, 318 U.S. 313. The Osborn case upheld a Virginia requirement that insurance companies authorized to do business in that State must write policies through resident agents. The Hoopeston case, while it involved the making of out-of-state insurance contracts, also involved servicing of policies in New York, the regulating State.

Here, unlike the Osborn and Hoopeston cases, the insurance companies carry on no activities within the State of Texas. Of course, the insured does business in Texas and the property insured is located there. It is earnestly argued that, unless the philosophy of the Osborn and Hoopeston decisions is to be restricted, the present Texas tax[2] on premiums paid out-of-state on out-of-state contracts should be sustained. We are urged to follow the approach of the Osborn and Hoopeston decisions, look to the aspects of the insurance transactions taken as a whole, and decide that there are sufficient contacts with Texas to justify this tax under the requirements of due process.

Were the Osborn and Hoopeston cases and the bare bones of the McCarran-Ferguson Act our only criteria for decision, we would have presented the question whether three prior decisions — Allgeyer v. Louisiana, 165 U.S. 578; St. Louis Cotton Compress Co. v. Arkansas, 260 U.S. 346; Connecticut General Life Ins. Co. v. Johnson, 303 U.S. 77 — have continuing vitality. The first two were distinguished in the Osborn (310 U.S., at 66-67) and Hoopeston (318 U.S., at 318-319) cases. The Allgeyer case held that Louisiana by reason of the Due Process Clause of the Fourteenth Amendment could not make it a misdemeanor to effect insurance on Louisiana risks with an insurance company not licensed to do business in Louisiana, where the insured through use of the mails contracted in New York for the policy. The St. Louis Cotton Compress case held invalid under the Due Process Clause an Arkansas tax on the premiums paid for a policy on Arkansas risks, made with an out-of-state company having no office or agents in Arkansas. The Connecticut General Life Insurance case held invalid under the Due Process Clause a California tax on premiums paid in Connecticut by one insurance company to another for reinsurance of life insurance policies written in California on California residents, even though both insurance companies were authorized to do business in California. The Court stated:

---

[1] 15 U.S.C. §1011 provides:

"Congress declares that the continued regulation and taxation by the several States of the business of insurance is in the public interest, and that silence on the part of the Congress shall not be construed to impose any barrier to the regulation or taxation of such business by the several States."

15 U.S.C. §1012 provides, so far as relevant here:

"(a) The business of insurance, and every person engaged therein, shall be subject to the laws of the several States which relate to the regulation or taxation of such business."

[2] 14 Vernon's Tex. Civ. Stat., 1652 (Cum. Supp. 1961), Art. 21.38, §2(e) provides:

"If any person, firm, association or corporation shall purchase from an insurer not licensed in the State of Texas a policy of insurance covering risks within this State in a manner other than through an insurance agent licensed as such under the laws of the State of Texas, such person, firm, association or corporation shall pay to the Board a tax of five per cent (5%) of the amount of the gross premiums paid by such insured for such insurance. Such tax shall be paid not later than thirty (30) days from the date on which such premium is paid to the unlicensed insurer."

"All that appellant did in effecting the reinsurance was done without the state and for its transaction no privilege or license by California was needful. The tax cannot be sustained either as laid on property, business done, or transactions carried on within the state, or as tax on a privilege granted by the state." 303 U.S., at 82.

The Texas Court of Civil Appeals, 340 S.W.2d 339, and the Texas Supreme Court, feeling bound by these decisions, held the tax on premiums unconstitutional, 162 Tex. 8, 343 S.W.2d 241. We granted certiorari, 368 U.S. 810.

The insurance transactions involved in the present litigation take place entirely outside Texas. The insurance, which is principally insurance against loss or liability arising from damage to property, is negotiated and paid for outside Texas. The policies are issued outside Texas. All losses arising under the policies are adjusted and paid outside Texas. The insurers are not licensed to do business in Texas, have no office or place of business in Texas, do not solicit business in Texas, have no agents in Texas, and do not investigate risks or claims in Texas.

The insured is not a domiciliary of Texas but a New York corporation doing business in Texas. Losses under the policies are payable not to Texas residents but to the insured at its principal office in New York City. The only connection between Texas and the insurance transactions is the fact that the property covered by the insurance is physically located in Texas.

We need not decide de novo whether the results (and the reasons given) in the Allgeyer, St. Louis Cotton Compress, and Connecticut General Life Insurance decisions are sound and acceptable. For we have in the history of the McCarran-Ferguson Act an explicit, unequivocal statement that the Act was so designed as not to displace those three decisions. The House Report stated:

"It is not the intention of Congress in the enactment of this legislation to clothe the States with any power to regulate or tax the business of insurance beyond that which they had been held to possess prior to the decision of the United States Supreme Court in the Southeastern Underwriters Association case. Briefly, your committee is of the opinion that we should provide for the continued regulation and taxation of insurance by the States, subject always, however, to the limitations set out in the controlling decisions of the United States Supreme Court, as, for instance, in Allgeyer v. Louisiana (165 U.S. 578), St. Louis Cotton Compress Co. v. Arkansas (260 U.S. 346), and Connecticut General Insurance Co. v. Johnson (303 U.S. 77), which hold, inter alia, that a State does not have power to tax contracts of insurance or reinsurance entered into outside its jurisdiction by individuals or corporations resident or domiciled therein covering risks within the State or to regulate such transactions in any way." H.R. Rep. No. 143, 79th Cong., 1st Sess., p. 3.

Senator McCarran, after reading the foregoing part of the House Report during the Senate debate, stated, ". . . we give to the States no more powers than those they previously had, and we take none from them." 91 Cong. Rec. 1442.

So, while Congress provided in 15 U.S.C. §1012(a) that the insurance business "shall be subject to the laws of the several States which relate to the regulation or taxation of such business," it indicated without ambiguity that such state "regulation or taxation" should be kept within the limits set by the Allgeyer, St. Louis Cotton Compress, and Connecticut General Life Insurance decisions.

The power of Congress to grant protection to interstate commerce against state regulation or taxation (Bethelehem Steel Co. v. State Board, 330 U.S. 767, 775-776; Rice v. Santa Fe Elevator Corp., 331 U.S. 218, 235-236) or to withhold it (In re Rahrer, 140 U.S. 545, 560 et seq.; Prudential Ins. Co. v. Benjamin, supra) is so complete that its ideas of policy should prevail.

Congress, of course, does not have the final say as to what constitutes due process under the Fourteenth Amendment. And while Congress has authority by §5 of that Amendment to enforce its provisions (Ex parte Virginia, 100 U.S. 339; Monroe v. Pape, 365 U.S.

167), the McCarran-Ferguson Act does not purport to do so. We have, of course, freedom to change our decisions on the constitutionality of laws. Smith v. Allwright, 321 U.S. 649, 665. But the policy announced by Congress in the McCarran-Ferguson Act was one on which the industry had reason to rely since 1897, when the Allgeyer decision was announced; and we are advised by an amicus brief how severe the impact would be on small insurance companies should the old rule be changed. When, therefore, Congress has posited a regime of state regulation on the continuing validity of specific prior decisions (see Federal Trade Comm'n v. Travelers Health Assn., 362 U.S. 293, 301-302), we should be loath to change them. . . .

In Toolson v. New York Yankees, Inc., 346 U.S. 356, 357, we refused to re-examine a prior decision holding baseball not to be covered by the antitrust laws, stating that "[t]he business has thus been left for thirty years to develop, on the understanding that it was not subject to existing antitrust legislation." In that case Congress had remained silent, not changing the law. Here Congress tailored the new regulations for the insurance business with specific reference to our prior decisions. Since these earlier decisions are part of the arch on which the new structure rests, we refrain from disturbing them lest we change the design that Congress fashioned.

Affirmed.

Mr. Justice Frankfurter took no part in the decision of this case.

Mr. Justice White took no part in the consideration or decision of this case.

Mr. Justice Black, dissenting.

In holding that the McCarran-Ferguson Act withdrew from the States the power to tax the ownership and use of insurance policies on property located within their borders merely because those policies were made by representatives of the insurer and the insured in another State, I think the Court places an unwarranted construction upon that Act which may seriously impair the capacity of Texas and other States to provide and enforce effective regulation of the insurance business. The Texas statute held invalid was enacted by the State Legislature in 1957 in order to protect the State's comprehensive supervision of insurance companies and their policies from being undercut by the practice of insuring Texas property with insurance companies not authorized to do business in that State. Prior to 1957, the whole cost of the Texas program had been placed upon those insurance companies which had subjected themselves to Texas regulation and taxation by qualifying to do business in the State. The 1957 statute was passed for the express purpose of equalizing that burden by placing a tax upon the purchasers of unregulated insurance roughly equal to that imposed directly upon regulated companies. In this way the State tried to protect its qualified and regulated companies from unfair competition by companies which could sell insurance on Texas property cheaper because they did not have to pay their part of the cost of the Texas insurance regulation program. The Court's construction of the McCarran-Ferguson Act bars Texas from providing this sort of protection to regulated companies. This holding seems to me to threaten the whole foundation of the Texas regulatory program for it plainly encourages Texas residents to insure their property with unregulated companies and discourages out-of-state companies from qualifying to do business in and subjecting themselves to regulation and taxation by the State of Texas.

I cannot believe that an Act which was basically designed to leave the power to regulate and tax insurance companies to the States was intended to have any such effect. . . . I think the McCarran-Ferguson Act left Texas with adequate power to place a tax on the ownership and use of insurance policies covering the vast properties owned and operated by this respondent in Texas, and I therefore dissent.º

º Cf. Prudential Insurance Co. v. Benjamin, 328 U.S. 408 (1946). — Ed.

Connecticut Mutual Life Ins. Co. v. Moore 333 U.S. 541, 68 S. Ct. 682, 92 L. Ed. 863 (1948)

MR. JUSTICE REED delivered the opinion of the Court.

We are asked in this suit to consider the validity of the New York Abandoned Property Law as applied to policies of insurance issued for delivery in New York on the lives of residents of New York by companies incorporated in states other than New York.

Article VII of the Abandoned Property Law, headed "Unclaimed Life Insurance Funds," was enacted in 1943. In 1944 the law was amended so as to cover insurance companies incorporated outside the state. Section 700 states that "any moneys held or owing" by life insurance companies in the following three classes of policies issued on the lives of residents of New York shall be deemed abandoned property: (1) matured endowment policies which have been unclaimed for seven years; (2) policies payable on death where the insured, if living, would have attained the limiting age under the mortality table on which the reserves are based (an age varying from 96 to 100), as to which no transaction has occurred for seven years; and (3) policies payable on death in which the insured has died and no claim by the person entitled thereto has been made for seven years. Other sections of Art. VII provide that insurance corporations doing business in New York shall make an annual report of abandoned property falling within the definitions of §700, the lists shall be advertised, and if the abandoned property advertised remains unclaimed, the amounts due and owing shall be paid to the state comptroller so as to be in the care and custody of the state. Art. VII, §703, Art. XIV, §1402; State Finance Law, §95. Upon payment to the state, the companies are discharged of any obligation, and any person subsequently setting up a claim must file a claim with the comptroller. A penalty of $100 a day is provided for failure to file the required report. Art. XIV, §1412.

The present suit was brought by nine insurance companies, incorporated in states other than New York, in the Supreme Court of New York for a declaration of the invalidity of the Abandoned Property Law of New York, as applied to the plaintiffs, and to enjoin the state comptroller and all other persons acting under state authority from taking any steps under the statute. The Supreme Court ruled that the Abandoned Property Law was void in so far as it applied to policies of life insurance issued for delivery outside of New York by foreign life insurance companies. As no appeal from this ruling was taken by the state, it is not before us. The Supreme Court reserved to the appellant insurance companies the right to assert the invalidity of the Abandoned Property Law or any application thereof in so far as such law or state action thereunder sought to deprive them of any defense against any claim under any life insurance policy. With the above exceptions, the Supreme Court upheld the life insurance sections of the Abandoned Property Law against appellants' attack. The Appellate Division affirmed and the Court of Appeals reversed the judgment of the Supreme Court in so far as it reserved to the companies further right to assert defense against claims under the policies. The Court of Appeals by its interpretation of the New York statute left open to the insurance companies all defenses except the statute of limitations, non-compliance with policy provisions calling for proof of death or of other designated contingency and failure to surrender a policy on making a claim. 297 N.Y. 1, 74 N.E.2d 24. With this modification, it affirmed the trial court's judgment. Appeal to this Court was perfected under §237(a) of the Judicial Code and probable jurisdiction noted on October 20, 1947.

In addition to objections under New York law, appellants raised in their complaint and have consistently maintained that the statute impairs the obligation of contract within the meaning of Art. I, §10, of the Constitution and deprives them of their property without due process of law under the Fourteenth Amendment. Their argument under the Contract Clause is that the statute transforms into a liquidated obligation an obligation which was previously only conditional. Their argument under the Due Process Clause is that New York has no power to sequester funds of these life insurance companies to meet the companies' obligations on insurance policies issued on New York residents for delivery in New York.

I. . . . We find no reason for invalidating the statutory plan under the Contract Clause.

II. Nor do we agree with appellants' argument that New York lacks constitutional power to take over unclaimed moneys due to its residents on policies issued for delivery in the state by life insurance corporations chartered outside the state. The appellants claim that only the state of incorporation could take these abandoned moneys. They say that only one state may take custody of a debt. The statutory reference to "any moneys held or owing" does not refer to any specific assets of an insurance company, but simply to the obligation of the life insurance company to pay. The problem of what another state than New York may do is not before us. That question is not passed upon. To prevail appellee need only show, as he does as to policies on residents issued for delivery in New York, that there may be abandoned moneys, over which New York has power, in the hands of appellants. The question is whether the State of New York has sufficient contacts with the transactions here in question to justify the exertion of the power to seize abandoned moneys due to its residents. Appellants urge that the following considerations should be determinative in choosing the state of incorporation as the state for conservation of abandoned indebtedness, if such moneys are to be taken from the possession of the corporation. It is pointed out that the present residence of missing policyholders is unknown; that with our shifting population residence is a changeable factor; that as the insured chose a foreign corporation as his insurer, his choice should be respected; that moneys should escheat to the sovereignty that guards them at the time of abandonment. As a practical matter, it is urged that restricting escheat or conservancy to the state of incorporation avoids conflicts of jurisdiction between states as to the location of abandoned property and simplifies the corporations' reports by limiting them to one state with one law. Attention is called to presently enacted statutes in Pennsylvania, New Jersey, and Massachusetts. None of these statutes apply to corporations chartered outside of the respective states. Furthermore, it is argued that the analogous bank deposit cases have upheld escheat or conservancy by the state of the bank's incorporation. Finally reliance is placed on the undisputed fact that the policies are payable at the out-of-state main offices of the corporations, the evidences of their intangible assets are there located and there claims must be made and other transactions carried on.

These are reasons which have no doubt been weighed in legislative consideration. We are here dealing with a matter of constitutional power. Power to demand the care and custody of the moneys due these beneficiaries is claimed by New York, under Art. VII of the Abandoned Property Law as construed by its courts, only where the policies were issued for delivery in New York upon the lives of persons then resident in New York. We sustain the constitutional validity of the provisions as thus interpreted with these exceptions. We do not pass upon the validity in instances where insured persons, after delivery, cease to be residents of New York or where the beneficiary is not a resident of New York at maturity of the policy. As interests of other possible parties not represented here may be affected by our conclusions and as no specific instances of those types appear in the record, we reserve any conclusion as to New York's power in such situations. . . .

. . . The Court of Appeals . . . said:

"For the core of the debtor obligations of the plaintiff companies was created through acts done in this State under the protection of its laws, and the ties thereby established between the companies and the State were without more sufficient to validate the jurisdiction here asserted by the Legislature."

We agree with this statement and hold that New York had power to take over these abandoned moneys in the hands of appellants.

The judgment of the Court of Appeals of New York is affirmed except as to issues specifically reserved.

MR. JUSTICE FRANKFURTER, dissenting.

450 Chapter Eight. The States in a Federal Union

My brother Jackson's opinion, with which I substantially agree, persuades me that we should decline to exercise jurisdiction in this case. The wise practice governing constitutional adjudication requires it. For this proceeding poses merely hypothetical questions, all of which are intertwined and concern interests not represented before us. Circumstances not more compelling, surely, than this record discloses led us in a series of recent cases to avoid borrowing trouble by declining to adjudicate premature constitutional issues. Alabama State Federation of Labor v. McAdory, 325 U.S. 450; United Public Workers of America v. Mitchell, 330 U.S. 75; Rescue Army v. Municipal Court, 331 U.S. 549.

In appearance this is a suit between a few insurance companies and the State of New York. But at the heart of the controversy are the conflicting claims of several States in a hotchpot of undifferentiated obligations. The proceeds of "abandoned" life insurance policies cannot, I assume, be seized as for escheat more than once. Since the rights and liabilities growing out of such policies are, to a vast extent, the results of a process that concerns two or more States, their interests may come into conflict when, in exigent search for revenue, they invoke the opportunities of escheat against unclaimed proceeds from insurance policies. I assume merely conflicting State interests and lay aside considerations that may be drawn from the decision in United States v. South-Eastern Underwriters Association, 322 U.S. 533. . . .

The way is open to secure a determination by this Court of the rights of the different States in the variant situations presented by abandoned obligations on matured insurance policies. It is precisely for the settlement of such controversies among the several States that the Constitution conferred original jurisdiction upon this Court. If Florida, Massachusetts, New York and Texas could bring here for determination their right to levy a death tax in respect to a particular succession, Texas v. Florida, 306 U.S. 398, even more fitting is it that the claims of various States to seize the matured obligation of abandoned insurance policies should be presented by those States at the bar of this Court and be adjudicated here after full reflection on all these claims. Of course the insurance companies have interests to protect and to present. But the essential problem is the legal adjustment of the conflicting interests of different States, because each may have some relation to transactions which give rise to funds that undoubtedly are subject to escheat. Until that is duly before us we should not peck at the problem in an abstract, hypothetical way.

The appeal should be dismissed.

MR. JUSTICE JACKSON, with whom MR. JUSTICE DOUGLAS joins, dissenting.

I find myself unable to join the Court in this case. I cannot agree that we may affirm the judgment below without facing, or by reserving our opinion upon, the constitutional question inherent in this statute by which New York would escheat unclaimed insurance proceeds not located either actually or constructively in New York and which are the property of a beneficiary who may never have been a resident or citizen of New York. . . .

Neither the Act nor the decision below contemplates that the right to escheat is based on residence of the owner of the proceeds at the time of escheat, or at any other time, but rather on these two facts: (1) that the policy was issued for delivery in New York, and (2) that the *insured* was then a resident of New York. Thus, the State claims power to escheat what is due a *beneficiary* solely because it was the residence of the *insured* when the policy was issued and irrespective of the nonresidence at that time and at all times of the beneficiary whose property it takes. Thus, the escheat of one man's property is based on another man's one-time residence in the state. Further, the seizure of today is based not even on the assured's residence at the time the policy matured, but on his residence at some prior date, which, in view of the long-term nature of insurance contracts, may have been many years ago.

The effect of the Court's affirmance of the judgment upholding this statute is that a residence by the insured in New York at the time a policy was "issued for delivery" there shows "sufficient contacts with the transaction" so that the State may escheat proceeds owned by a beneficiary who may never have lived in that State. Even in the abstract, I find the concept of "sufficient contacts with the transaction" too vague to be helpful in defining practical bounds of a state's jurisdiction or power to escheat. . . .

The weakness of the Court's test of sufficient contacts with the "transaction" is more fully revealed when we consider that by its application today other states are cut off from escheating the proceeds (unless the company is subject to multiple escheats), although by the same tests they have many more and much closer "contacts" with some part of the transaction. . . .

It seems to me that the constitutional doctrine we are applying here, if we are consistent in its application, leaves us in this dilemma: In sustaining the broad claims of New York, we either cut off similar and perhaps better rights of escheat by other states or we render insurance companies liable to two or more payments of their single liability. If we impale ourselves, and the state and insurance companies along with us, on either horn of this dilemma, I think the fault is in ourselves, not in our Constitution. . . .

While we may evade it for a time, the competition and conflict between states for "escheats" will force us to some lawyerlike definition of state power over this subject. It is naive beyond even requirements of the judicial office to assume that this lately manifest concern of the states over abandoned insurance proceeds reflects only solicitude for the unknown claimants. If it did, the states' claims might reconcile more easily. But escheat of these interests is a newly exploited, if not newly discovered, source of state revenue. Escheat, of course, is not to be denied on constitutional grounds merely because the motive of the states savors more of the publican than of the guardian. But it is relevant to the caution and precision we should use in sustaining one state's claim, lest we be foreclosing other better-founded ones.

. . . The Pennsylvania statute "escheats," as the Court says, only proceeds of policies issued by companies incorporated in Pennsylvania. But it escheats all of those regardless of residence of the insured or of where the policy was delivered. Its conflict with the law before us is patent and immediate. We cannot sustain New York's statute without, to the extent here indicated, striking down that of Pennsylvania, which is not a party here and whose claims have not been heard. . . .

For the reasons outlined herein, I should express disapproval of the declaratory judgment below, decline to certify the validity of this legislation at this time, and deal with this problem only as presented by concrete cases or controversies involving particular funds and facts. But if we are to render a decision in the abstract, I should say that New York by this statute overreaches its sister states by the tests I have set forth.

NOTE

See also Standard Oil Co. v. New Jersey, 341 U.S. 428 (1951), upholding (5 to 4) the application of the New Jersey Escheat Law to shares of stock and unclaimed dividends on shares of stock of a New Jersey corporation, standing on the records of the corporation in the names of nonresidents of New Jersey. For comment see Notes, 65 Harv. L. Rev. 1408 (1952), 35 Va. L. Rev. 336 (1949).

Western Union Tel. Co. v. Pennsylvania 368 U.S. 71, 82 S. Ct. 199, 7 L. Ed. 2d 139 (1961)

MR. JUSTICE BLACK delivered the opinion of the Court.

Pennsylvania law provides that "any real or personal property within or subject to the

452 Chapter Eight. **The States in a Federal Union**

control of this Commonwealth . . . shall escheat to the Commonwealth" whenever it "shall be without a rightful or lawful owner," "remain unclaimed for the period of seven successive years" or "the whereabouts of such owner . . . shall be and remain unknown for the period of seven successive years." These proceedings were begun under that law in a Pennsylvania state court to escheat certain obligations of the Western Union Telegraph Company — alleged to be "property within" Pennsylvania — to pay sums of money owing to various people who had left the monies unclaimed for more than seven years and whose whereabouts were unknown. The facts were stipulated.

Western Union is a corporation chartered under New York law with its principal place of business in that State. . . .

In the thousands of money order transactions carried on by the company, it sometimes happens that it can neither make payment to the payee nor make a refund to the sender. Similarly payees and senders who accept drafts as payment or refund sometimes fail to cash them. For this reason large sums of money due from Western Union for undelivered money orders and unpaid drafts accumulate over the years in the company's offices and bank accounts throughout the country. It is an accumulation of this kind that Pennsylvania seeks to escheat here — specifically, the amount of undisbursed money held by Western Union arising out of money orders bought in Pennsylvania offices to be transmitted to payees in Pennsylvania and other States, chiefly other States.

Western Union, while not claiming these monies for itself, challenged Pennsylvania's right to take ownership of them for itself. Among other grounds the company urged that a judgment of escheat for Pennsylvania in its courts would not protect the company from multiple liability either in Pennsylvania or in other States. Its argument in this respect was that senders of money orders and holders of drafts would not be bound by the Pennsylvania judgment because the service by publication did not, for two reasons, give the state court jurisdiction: (1) that under the doctrine of Pennoyer v. Neff, 95 U.S. 714, the presence of property, called a "res," within the State is a prerequisite for service by publication and that these obligations did not constitute such property within Pennsylvania, and (2) that the notice by publication given in this case did not give sufficient information or afford sufficient likelihood of actual notice to meet due process requirements. In addition, Western Union urged that there might be escheats claimed by other States which would not be bound by the Pennsylvania judgment because they were not and could not be made parties to this Pennsylvania proceeding. Western Union's apprehensions that other States might later escheat the same funds were buttressed by the Pennsylvania court's finding that New York had already seized and escheated a part of the very funds here claimed by Pennsylvania. With reference to this the Pennsylvania Court of Common Pleas said: "We take this opportunity of stating that we do not recognize New York's authority to escheat that money, but since it has been done we have no jurisdiction over this sum." 73 Dauphin County Rep. 160, 173. Both the Pennsylvania trial court and the State Supreme Court rejected the contentions of Western Union and declared the unclaimed obligations escheated. 73 Dauphin County Rep. 160; 74 Dauphin County Rep. 49; 400 Pa. 337, 162 A.2d 617. Since the record showed substantial questions as to the jurisdiction of the Pennsylvania courts over the individual owners of the unclaimed monies and as to the power of the State of Pennsylvania to enter a binding judgment that would protect Western Union against subsequent liability to other States, we noted probable jurisdiction. 365 U.S. 801.

We find it unnecessary to decide any of Western Union's contentions as to the adequacy of notice to and validity of service on the individual claimants by publication. For as we view these proceedings, there is a far more important question raised by this record — whether Pennsylvania had power at all to render a judgment of escheat which would bar New York or any other State from escheating this same property.

Pennsylvania does not claim and could not claim that the same debts or demands could be escheated by two States. See Standard Oil Co. v. New Jersey, 341 U.S. 428, 443. And our prior opinions have recognized that when a state court's jurisdiction purports to be based, as here, on the presence of property within the State, the holder of such property is deprived of due process of law if he is compelled to relinquish it without assurance that he will not be held liable again in another jurisdiction or in a suit brought by a claimant who is not bound by the first judgment. Anderson National Bank v. Luckett, 321 U.S. 233, 242-243; Security Savings Bank v. California, 263 U.S. 282, 286-290. Applying that principle, there can be no doubt that Western Union has been denied due process by the Pennsylvania judgment here unless the Pennsylvania courts had power to protect Western Union from any other claim, including the claim of the State of New York that these obligations are property "within" New York and are therefore subject to escheat under its laws. But New York was not a party to this proceeding and could not have been made a party, and, of course, New York's claims could not be cut off where New York was not heard as a party. Moreover, the potential multi-state claims to the "property" which is the subject of this escheat make it not unlikely that various States will claim in rem jurisdiction over it. Therefore, Western Union was not protected by the Pennsylvania judgment, for a state court judgment need not be given full faith and credit by other States as to parties or property not subject to the jurisdiction of the court that rendered it. Pennoyer v. Neff, 95 U.S. 714; Riley v. New York Trust Co., 315 U.S. 343.

It is true that, on the facts there presented, this Court said in Standard Oil Co. v. New Jersey, 341 U.S. 428, 433, that "The debts or demands . . . having been taken from the appellant company by a valid judgment of New Jersey, the same debts or demands against appellant [Standard Oil] cannot be taken by another state. The Full Faith and Credit Clause bars any such double escheat." But the Court went on to point out that "The claim of no other state to this property is before us and, of course, determination of any right of a claimant state against New Jersey for the property escheated by New Jersey must await presentation here." Here, unlike Standard Oil, there is in reality a controversy between States, possibly many of them, over the right to escheat part or all of these funds.

The claims of New York are particularly aggressive, not merely potential, but actual, active and persistent — best shown by the fact that New York has already escheated part of the very funds originally claimed by Pennsylvania. These claims of New York were presented to us in both the brief and oral argument of that State as amicus curiae. In presenting its claims New York also called our attention to the potential claims of other States for escheat based on their contacts with the separate phases of the multistate transactions out of which these unclaimed funds arose, including: the State of residence of the payee, the State of the sender, the State where the money order was delivered, and the State where the fiscal agent on which the money order was drawn is located. Arguments more than merely plausible can doubtless be made to support claims of all these and other States to escheat all or parts of all unclaimed funds held by Western Union. And the large area of the company's business makes it entirely possible that *every State* may now or later claim a right to participate in these funds. But even if, as seems unlikely, no other State will assert such a claim, the active controversy between New York and Pennsylvania is enough in itself to justify Western Union's contention that to require it to pay this money to Pennsylvania before New York has had its full day in court might force Western Union to pay a single debt more than once and thus take its property without due process of law.

Our Constitution has wisely provided a way in which controversies between States can be settled without subjecting individuals and companies affected by those controversies to a deprivation of their right to due process of law. Article III, §2 of the Constitution gives this Court original jurisdiction of cases in which a State is a party. The situation here is in all material respects like that which caused us to take jurisdiction in Texas v. Florida, 306 U.S. 398. There four States sought to collect death taxes out of an estate. The tax depended upon the domicile of the decedent, and this Court said that "By the law of each state a decedent can have only a single domicile for purposes of death taxes. . . ." Id., at 408. Thus, there was only one tax due to only one State. The estate was sufficient to pay the tax of any one State, but the total of the claims of the four States greatly exceeded the net value of the estate. For this reason, as we said, the risk of loss to the State of domicile was real and substantial, unless we exercised our jurisdiction. Under these circumstances we exercised our original jurisdiction to avoid "the risk of loss ensuing from the demands in separate suits of rival claimants to the same debt or legal duty." Id., at 405. The rival state claimants here, as in Texas v. Florida, can invoke our original jurisdiction.

While we have previously decided some escheat cases where it was apparent that rival state claims were in the offing, we have not in any of them closed the door to the exercise of our jurisdiction. In Connecticut Mutual Life Ins. Co. v. Moore, 333 U.S. 541, we sustained the power of New York to take custody as a conservator of unclaimed funds due persons insured by that company through policies issued for delivery in New York to persons then resident in New York. In doing so we rejected an argument that the State of domicile of the insurance companies involved alone had jurisdiction to escheat. But there we were careful to point out that "The problem of what another State than New York may do is not before us. That question is not passed upon." Id., at 548. Even though this reservation was made and New York only took custody of the funds, leaving the way clear for all claimants to bring action to recover them at any time, there were dissents urging that a way should be then found for the conflicting claims of States to be determined. Several years later a divided Court in Standard Oil Co. v. New Jersey, 341 U.S. 428, upheld the right of New Jersey to escheat certain unclaimed shares of stock and dividends due stockholders and employees of the Standard Oil Company. In that case New Jersey's jurisdiction to escheat was rested, at least in part, on the fact that Standard Oil was a domiciliary of that State. Again, however, the court justified its conclusion by saying as to claims of other States: "The claim of no other state to this property is before us and, of course, determination of any right of a claimant state against New Jersey for the property escheated by New Jersey must await presentation here." Id., at 443. Later New York sought leave to file an original action here against New Jersey, alleging a controversy between the two States over jurisdiction to take custody of monies arising out of unclaimed travelers checks, outstanding for more than 15 years, issued by American Express Company, a joint stock company organized under New York law with its principal office in New York. Answering, New Jersey pointed out that under New York's then controlling law it disclaimed any purpose to escheat property claimed for escheat by any other State. In this state of the New York law, we refused to take jurisdiction. 358 U.S. 924. By an act effective March 29, 1960, New York amended its law eliminating the disclaimer and now strongly asserts its claim to these funds under its new law.

The rapidly multiplying state escheat laws, originally applying only to land and other tangible things but recently moving into the elusive and wide-ranging field of intangible transactions have presented problems of great importance to the States and persons whose rights will be adversely affected by escheats. This makes it imperative that controversies between different States over their right to escheat intangibles be settled in a forum where all the States that want to do so can present their claims for consideration and final, authoritative determination. Our Court has jurisdiction to do that. Whether and under what circumstances we will exercise our jurisdiction to hear and decide these controversies ourselves in particular cases, and whether we might under some circumstances refer them to United States District Courts, we need not now determine. Cf. Massachusetts v. Missouri, 308 U.S. 1, 18-20. Nor need we, at this time, attempt to decide the difficult legal questions presented when many different States claim power to escheat intangibles involved in transactions taking place in part in many States. It will be time enough to consider those complicated problems when all interested States — along with all other claimants — can be afforded a full hearing and a final, authoritative determination. It is plain that Pennsylvania courts, with no power to bring other States before them, cannot give such hearings. They have not done so here; they have not attempted to do so. As a result, their judgments, which cannot, with the assurance that comes only from a full trial with all necessary parties present, protect Western Union from having to pay the same single obligation twice, cannot stand. When this situation developed, the Pennsylvania courts should have dismissed the case.

Accordingly, the judgment of the Supreme Court of Pennsylvania is reversed, and the cause is remanded to that Court for further proceedings not inconsistent with this opinion.

It is so ordered.

Memorandum of Mr. Justice Stewart.

The appellant is a New York corporation with its principal office in that State. The funds representing these unpaid money orders are located there. I think only New York has power to escheat the property involved in this case. For that reason, while disagreeing with the Court's opinion, which for me creates more problems than it solves, I join in the judgment of reversal.

NOTE

1. For comment upon Western Union Tel. Co. v. Pennsylvania, supra, see The Supreme Court, 1961 Term, 76 Harv. L. Rev. 54, 132-140 (1962).

In Texas v. New Jersey, 379 U.S. 674 (1965), Texas brought suit in the Supreme Court against New Jersey, Pennsylvania, and the Sun Oil Company to determine its right to escheat unclaimed debts of the company either evidenced on the books of its Texas offices or owing to persons whose last known address was in Texas. The Court decided that the debts are subject to escheat only by the state of the creditor's last known address, as shown on the books of the company. As to property owed to persons for whom no address was known, or whose last known address was in a state not providing for escheat, the state of corporate domicile may escheat, retaining the property unless and until a state with a superior interest establishes its claim.

How can the original jurisdiction of the Court be explained in this case? Compare Texas v. Florida, 306 U.S. 398 (1939).

2. Osborn v. Ozlin, page 441 supra, and the escheat cases suggest problems of the distribution of power which might, in the abstract, be termed problems of "jurisdiction to regulate," or, in the phrase of Mr. Justice Jackson in the article cited infra, "legislative jurisdiction." (The Todd Shipyards case would conventionally be classified under the related head, "jurisdiction to tax," but it bears an obvious relationship to Osborn v. Ozlin and suggests a function for congressional power in this area, and so is included here.) Such problems appear to be inherent in a federal system, particularly in one in which persons and business organizations are frequently active in several states. See Schoch, Conflict of Laws in a Federal State: The Experience of Switzerland, 55 Harv. L. Rev. 738 (1942). They have come to the fore with reference to insurance companies and associations. Compare with the cases above Order of Commercial Travelers v. Wolfe, 331 U.S. 586 (1947); State Farm Mutual Automobile Ins. Co. v. Duel, 324 U.S. 154 (1945); Hoopeston Canning Co. v. Cullen, 318 U.S. 313 (1943). But they are by no means confined to insurance operations, as the more recent escheat cases demonstrate. Among other fields nonuniform state laws concerning such matters as workmen's compensation and corporate dividends have been shown to present analogous problems. Traditionally, these have been thought of as falling within the subject matter of conflict of laws. The question has arisen to what extent these are either desirably or necessarily to be considered federal, or constitutional, questions. See Dodd, The Power of the Supreme Court to Review State Decisions in the Field of Conflict of Laws, 39 Harv. L. Rev. 533 (1926); Ross, Has the Conflict of Laws Become a Branch of Constitutional Law? 15 Minn. L. Rev. 161 (1931); Schoch, supra; and, more recently, Coleman, Corporate Dividends and the Conflict of Laws, 63 Harv. L. Rev. 433 (1950), particularly at 457-467. For a decision which presents

a cognate question largely in terms of bankruptcy law and conflict of laws, but which might have been thought to present constitutional questions, see Vanston Bondholders Protective Committee v. Green, 329 U.S. 156 (1946). The concurring opinion of Mr. Justice Frankfurter in that case should be compared with his opinion for the Court in Osborn v. Ozlin, supra.

Insofar as these problems have been recognized as constitutional questions, they are usually considered as arising under the due process clause of the Fourteenth Amendment, although the full faith and credit clause (Article IV, §1) has also been brought into play. Mr. Justice Jackson has suggested that the latter clause is capable of being given a more extended scope in a fashion which might afford federal guides in dealing with some of the problems suggested above. See Jackson, Full Faith and Credit — The Lawyer's Clause of the Constitution, 45 Colum. L. Rev. 1 (1945). Cf. Hanson v. Denckla, 357 U.S. 235 (1958); and see Scott, Hanson v. Denckla, 72 Harv. L. Rev. 695 (1959).

For a consideration of the territorial limitations upon a state's criminal jurisdiction, see Skiriotes v. Florida, 313 U.S. 69 (1941). Cf. Blackmer v. United States, 284 U.S. 421 (1932); United States v. Bowman, 260 U.S. 94 (1922). Cf. also Vermilya-Brown Co. v. Connell, 335 U.S. 377 (1948).

Section C. EFFECTS OF FEDERAL ACTION

The inference to be drawn from the inaction, or silence, of Congress in an area where it may act, or speak, is not a subject on which judgments have invariably been unanimous. In Gibbons v. Ogden, page 164 supra, it will be recalled, Chief Justice Marshall, though perhaps more intent upon the silence of the Constitution, appeared to anticipate the problem when he observed, "It has been contended . . . [t]hat regulation is designed for the entire result, applying to those parts which remain as they were, as well as to those which are altered. It produces a uniform whole, which is as much disturbed and deranged by changing what the regulating power desires to leave untouched, as that on which it has operated. There is great force in this argument, and the court is not satisfied that it has been refuted." To a later Chief Justice, in Leisy v. Hardin, page 197 supra, the silence was imperative. But silence speaks in different voices at different times and to different hearers. To Mr. Justice Burton, dissenting in Morgan v. Virginia, page 429 supra — to cite only one example — the soft tones of silence were those of acquiescence: "The inaction of Congress is an important indication that, in the opinion of Congress, this issue is better met without nationally uniform affirmative regulation than with it." This subject has been touched, as have many others, by the wit and insight of Thomas Reed Powell. See Powell, The Still Small Voice of the Commerce Clause, Proc. Nat. Tax Assn., 1937 (1938), 337, 338-339, reprinted in 3 Selected Essays on Constitutional Law 931 (1938). See also Biklé, The Silence of Congress, 41 Harv. L. Rev. 200 (1927), reprinted in id. 911 (1938).

Suppose Congress speaks, but only a little. The subsequent silence may be the more eloquent, but is rarely the more explicit. Has all been said? Or may the states join in, to supplement if not to contradict? Attention to the subject, to the speaking, and to the overtones of speech in an attempt to supply an answer has previously been indicated in cases where the answer to this problem seemed easy, e.g., Southern Pacific Co. v. Arizona, page 418 supra. It is not always so. See Note, "Occupation of the Field" in Commerce Clause Cases, 1936-1946: Ten Years of Federalism, 60 Harv. L. Rev. 262 (1946); Note, The Preemption Doctrine: Shifting Perspectives on Federalism and the Burger Court, 75 Colum. L. Rev. 623 (1975). In the following cases it was not.

New York Central R.R. v. Winfield 244 U.S. 147, 37 S. Ct. 546, 61 L. Ed. 1045 (1917)

MR. JUSTICE VAN DEVANTER delivered the opinion of the court:

While in the service of a railroad company in the state of New York, James Winfield sustained a personal injury whereby he lost the use of an eye. At that time the railroad company was engaging in interstate commerce as a common carrier and Winfield was employed by it in such commerce. The injury was not due to any fault or negligence of the carrier, or of any of its officers, agents, or employees, but arose out of one of the ordinary risks of the work in which Winfield was engaged. He was a section laborer assisting in the repair of the carrier's main track, and while tamping cross ties struck a pebble which chanced to rebound and hit his eye. Following the injury he sought compensation therefor from the carrier under the Workmen's Compensation Law of the State and an award was made to him by the state Commission, one member dissenting. The carrier appealed and the award was affirmed by the Appellate Division of the Supreme Court, two judges dissenting, 168 App. Div. 351, and also by the Court of Appeals, 216 N.Y. 284. Before the Commission and in the state courts the carrier insisted that its liability or obligation and the employee's right were governed exclusively by the Employers' Liability Act of Congress, c. 149, 35 Stat. 65; c. 143, 36 Stat. 291, and therefore that no award could be made under the law of the state. That insistence is renewed here.

It is settled that under the commerce clause of the Constitution Congress may regulate the obligation of common carriers and the rights of their employees arising out of injuries sustained by the latter where both are engaged in interstate commerce; and it also is settled that when Congress acts upon the subject all state laws covering the same field are necessarily superseded by reason of the supremacy of the national authority. Congress acted upon the subject in passing the Employers' Liability Act, and the extent to which that act covers the field is the point in controversy. By one side it is said that the act, although regulating the liability or obligation of the carrier and the right of the employee where the injury results in whole or in part from negligence attributable to the carrier, does not cover injuries occurring without such negligence, and therefore leaves that class of injuries to be dealt with by state laws; and by the other side it is said that the act covers both classes of injuries and is exclusive as to both. The state decisions upon the point are conflicting. The New York court in the present case and the New Jersey court in Winfield v. Erie R. Co., 88 N.J.L. 619, hold that the act relates only to injuries resulting from negligence, while the California court in Smith v. Industrial Acci. Commission, 26 Cal. App. 560, and the Illinois court in Staley v. Illinois C.R. Co., 268 Ill. 356, hold that it has a broader scope and makes negligence a test, — not of the applicability of the act, but of the carrier's duty or obligation to respond pecuniarily for the injury.

In our opinion the latter view is right and the other wrong. Whether and in what circumstances railroad companies engaging in interstate commerce shall be required to compensate their employees in such commerce for injuries sustained therein are matters in which the nation as a whole is interested, and there are weighty considerations why the controlling law should be uniform and not change at every state line. Baltimore & O.R. Co. v. Baugh 149 U.S. 368, 378, 379. It was largely in recognition of this that the Employers' Liability Act was enacted by Congress. Second Employers' Liability Cases, 223 U.S. 1, 51. It was drafted and passed shortly following a message from the President advocating an adequate national law covering all such injuries, and leaving to the action of the several states only the injuries occurring in intrastate employment. Cong. Rec., 60th Cong., 1st Sess., 1347. And the reports of the congressional committees having the bill in charge disclose, without any uncertainty, that it was intended to be very comprehensive, to withdraw all injuries to railroad employees in interstate commerce from the operation of varying state laws, and to apply to them a national law having a uniform operation throughout all the states. House Report No. 1386 and Senate Report No. 460, 60th Cong., 1st Sess. Thus, in the House Report it is said: "It [the bill] is intended in its scope to cover all commerce to which the regulative power of Congress extends. . . . By this bill it is hoped to fix a uniform rule of liability throughout the Union with reference to the liability of common carriers to their employees. . . . A Federal statute of this character will supplant the numerous state statutes on the subject so far as they relate to interstate commerce. It will create uniformity throughout the Union, and the legal status of such employer's liability for personal injuries, instead of being subject to numerous rules, will be fixed by one rule in all the states."

True, the act does not require the carrier to respond for injuries occurring where it is not chargeable with negligence, but this is because Congress, in its discretion, acted upon the principle that compensation should be exacted from the carrier where, and only where, the injury results from negligence imputable to it. Every part of the act conforms to this principle, and no part points to any purpose to leave the states free to require compensation where the act withholds it. By declaring in §1 that the carrier shall be liable in damages for any injury to the employee "resulting in whole or in part from the negligence of any of the officers, agents, or employees of such carrier, or by reason of any defect or insufficiency, due to its negligence, in its cars, engines, appliances, machinery, track," etc., the act plainly shows, as was expressly held in Seaboard Air Line R. Co. v. Horton, 233 U.S. 492, 501, that it was the intention of Congress to make negligence the basis of the employee's right to damages, and to exclude responsibility of the carrier to the employee for an injury not resulting from its negligence or that of its officers, agents, or other employees. The same principle is seen also in §3, which requires that where the carrier and the employee are both negligent, the recovery shall be diminished in proportion to the employee's contribution to the total negligence; and in §4, which regards injuries arising from risks assumed by the employee as among those for which the carrier should not be made to respond. The committee reports upon the bill show that this principle was adopted deliberately, notwithstanding there were those within and without the committees who looked with greater favor upon a different principle which puts negligence out of view and regards the employee as entitled to compensation wherever the injury is an incident of the service in which he is employed. A few years after the passage of the act a legislative commission drafted and the Committees on the Judiciary in the two Houses of Congress favorably reported a bill substituting the latter principle for the other, Senate Report No. 553, 62d Cong., 2d Sess., House Report No. 1441, 62d Cong., 3d Sess., but that bill did not become a law.

That the act is comprehensive and also exclusive is distinctly recognized in repeated decisions of this court. Thus, in Missouri, K. & T.R. Co. v. Wulf, 226 U.S. 570, 576, and other cases, it is pointed out that the subject which the act covers is "the responsibility of interstate carriers by railroad to their employees injured in such commerce"; in Michigan C.R. Co. v. Vreeland, 227 U.S. 59, 66, 67, it is said that "we may not piece out this act of Congress by resorting to the local statutes of the state of procedure or that of the injury"; that by it "Congress has undertaken to cover the subject of the liability of railroad companies to their employees injured while engaged in interstate commerce," and that it is "paramount and exclusive"; in North Carolina R. Co. v. Zachary, 232 U.S. 248, 256, it is held that where it appears that the injury occurred while the carrier was engaged and the employee employed in interstate commerce, the Federal act governs to the exclusion of the state law; in Seaboard Air Line R. Co. v. Horton, supra, pp. 501, 503, it is said not only that Congress intended "to exclude responsibility of the carrier to its employees" in the absence of negligence, but that it is not conceivable that Congress "intended to permit the legislatures of the several states to determine the effect of contributory negligence and assumption of risk, by enacting statutes for the safety of employees, since this would in effect relegate to state control two of the essential factors that determine the responsibility of the employer"; and in Wabash R. Co. v. Haynes, 234 U.S. 86, 89, it is said: "Had the injury occurred in interstate commerce, as was alleged, the Federal act undoubtedly would have been controlling, and a recovery could not have been had under the common or statute law of the state; in other words, the Federal act would have been exclusive in its operation, not merely cumulative [citing cases]. On the other hand, if the injury occurred outside of interstate commerce, the Federal act was without application and the law of the state was controlling." . . .

Only by disturbing the uniformity which the act is designed to secure and by departing from the principle which it is intended to enforce can the several states require such carriers to compensate their employees for injuries in interstate commerce occurring without negligence. But no state is at liberty thus to interfere with the operation of a law of Congress. As before indicated, it is a mistake to suppose that injuries occurring without negligence are not reached or affected by the act, for, as is said in Prigg v. Pennsylvania, 16 Pet. 539, 617, "if Congress have a constitutional power to regulate a particular subject, and they do actually regulate it in a given manner, and in a certain form, it cannot be that the state legislatures have a right to interfere; and, as it were, by way of complement to the legislation of Congress, to prescribe additional regulations, and what they may deem auxiliary provisions for the same purpose. In such a case, the legislation of Congress, in what it does prescribe, manifestly indicates that it does not intend that there shall be any further legislation to act upon the subject-matter. Its silence as to what it does not do is as expressive of what its intention is as the direct provisions made by it." Thus the act is as comprehensive of injuries occurring without negligence, as to which class it impliedly excludes liability, as it is of those as to which it imposes liability. In other words, it is a regulation of the carriers' duty or obligation as to both. And the reasons which operate to prevent the states from dispensing with compensation where the act requires it equally prevent them from requiring compensation where the act withholds or excludes it.

It follows that, in the present case, the award under the state law cannot be sustained.
Judgment reversed.

MR. JUSTICE BRANDEIS, dissenting:

I dissent from the opinion of the court; and the importance of the question involved induces me to state the reasons.

By the Employers' Liability Act of April 22, 1908, Congress provided, in substance, that railroads engaged in interstate commerce shall be liable in damages for their negligence resulting in injury or death of employees while so engaged. The majority of the court now holds that by so doing Congress manifested its will to cover the whole field of compensation or relief for injuries suffered by railroad employees engaged in interstate commerce; or, at least, the whole field of obligation of carriers relating thereto; and that it thereby withdrew the subject wholly from the domain of state action. In other words, the majority of the court declares that Congress, by passing the Employers' Liability Act, prohibited states from including within the protection of their general Workmen's Compensation Laws employees who, *without fault on the railroad's part*, are injured or killed while engaged in interstate commerce; although Congress itself offered them no protection. That Congress *could* have done this is clear. The question presented is: Has Congress done so? Has Congress so willed?

The Workmen's Compensation Law of New York here in question has been declared by this court to be among those which "bear so close a relation to the protection of the lives and safety of those concerned that they properly may be regarded as coming within the category of police regulations." New York C.R. Co. v. White, 243 U.S. 188, 207. And this court has definitely formulated the rules which should govern in determining when a Federal statute regulating commerce will be held to supersede state legislation in the exercise of the police power. These rules are:

1. "In conferring upon Congress the regulation of commerce, it was never intended to cut the states off from legislating on all subjects relating to the health, life, and safety of their citizens, though the legislation might indirectly affect the commerce of the country." Sherlock v. Alling, 93 U.S. 99, 103.

2. "If the purpose of the act cannot otherwise be accomplished, — if its operation

460   Chapter Eight.   **The States in a Federal Union**

within its chosen field else must be frustrated and its provisions be refused their natural effect, — the state law must yield to regulation of Congress within the sphere of its delegated power. . . .

"But the intent to supersede the exercise by the state of its police power as to matters not covered by the Federal legislation is not to be inferred from the mere fact that Congress has seen fit to circumscribe its regulation and to occupy a limited field. In other words, such intent is not to be implied unless the act of Congress, fairly interpreted, is in actual conflict with the law of the state." Savage v. Jones, 225 U.S. 501, 533.

3. "The question must, of course, be determined with reference to the settled rule that a statute enacted in execution of a reserved power of the state is not to be regarded as inconsistent with an act of Congress passed in the execution of a clear power, under the Constitution, unless the repugnance or conflict is so direct and positive that the two acts cannot be reconciled or stand together." Missouri, K. & T.R. Co. v. Haber, 169 U.S. 613, 623.

Guided by these rules and the cases in which they have been applied[4] we endeavor to determine whether Congress, in enacting the Employers' Liability Act, intended to pre-

---

[4] The following cases show that Congress, in legislating upon a particular subject of interstate commerce, will not be held to have inhibited by implication the exercise by the states of their reserved police power, unless such state action would actually frustrate or impair the intended operation of the Federal legislation.

1. In Sligh v. Kirkwood, 237 U.S. 52, 62, it was held that the Federal Food and Drugs Act, dealing, among other things, with shipment in interstate commerce of fruit in filthy, decomposed, or putrid condition, did not prevent a state from penalizing the shipment of citrus fruits "which are immature or otherwise unfit for consumption."

2. In Atlantic Coast Line R. Co. v. Georgia, 234 U.S. 280, 293, it was held that Congress did not, by the passage of the Federal Safety Appliance Acts, dealing with the equipment of locomotives, as well as cars, and the Act to Regulate Commerce, preclude the state from legislating concerning locomotive headlights, as to which Congress had not specifically acted.

3. In Missouri, K. & T.R. Co. v. Harris, 234 U.S. 412, 420, it was held that the Carmack Amendment, regulating the carrier's liability for loss of interstate shipments, did not prevent a state from providing for the allowance of a moderate attorney's fee in a statute applicable both in the case of interstate and intrastate shipments.

4. In Savage v. Jones, 225 U.S. 501, 529, it was held that the passage by Congress of the Food and Drugs Act of 1906, which, among other things, prohibited misbranding, did not prevent the states from regulating the sale and requiring to be affixed a statement of ingredients and minimum percentage of fat and proteins.

5. In Missouri P.R. Co. v. Larabee Flour Mills Co., 211 U.S. 612, 623, it was held that Congress, by granting, in the Act to Regulate Commerce, power to the Interstate Commerce Commission to compel equal switching service on cars destined to interstate commerce, did not, in the absence of the exercise by the Commission of its power, prohibit states from legislating on the subject.

6. In Asbell v. Kansas, 209 U.S. 251, 257, it was held that Congress, in providing that a certificate of inspection issued by the National Bureau of Animal Industry should entitle cattle to be shipped into any state without further inspection, did not prevent a state from penalizing the importation of cattle which had not been inspected either by the Federal Bureau or by designated state officials.

7. In Crossman v. Lurman, 192 U.S. 189, 199, it was held that the Act of Congress of August 30, 1890, prohibiting importation into the United States of adulterated and unwholesome food, did not prevent the states from legislating for the prevention of the sale of articles of food so adulterated, as come within valid prohibitions in their statutes.

8. In Reid v. Colorado, 187 U.S. 137, 149, it was held that Congress, by making it an offense under the Animal Industry Act for anyone to send from state to state cattle known to be affected with communicable disease, did not prevent the states from penalizing the importation of cattle without inspection by designated state officials.

9. In Missouri, K. & T.R. Co. v. Haber, 169 U.S. 613, 623, it was held that the Federal Animal Industry Act, making it a misdemeanor for any person or corporation to transport cattle known to be affected with contagious disease, did not prevent a state from imposing a civil liability for damages sustained by owners of domestic cattle by reason of the importation of such diseased cattle.

10. In Smith v. Alabama, 124 U.S. 465, 482, it was held that Congress did not, by the passage of the Act to Regulate Commerce, prohibit the states from enacting laws requiring persons to undergo examination before being permitted to act as locomotive engineers.

11. In Sherlock v. Alling, 93 U.S. 99, it was held that Congress did not, by the passage of many laws regulating navigation, with a view to safety, and providing for liability in certain cases, prohibit the application to an accident in navigable waters of a state of a statute providing for liability for wrongful death. . . .

vent states from entering the specific field of compensation for injuries to employees arising *without fault on the railroad's part*, for which Congress made no provision.

To ascertain the intent we must look, of course, first at what Congress has said; then at the action it has taken, or omitted to take. We look at the words of the statute to see whether Congress has used any which in terms express that will. We inquire whether, without the use of explicit words, that will is expressed in specific action taken. For Congress must be presumed to have intended the necessary consequences of its action. And if we find that its will is not expressed, or is not clearly expressed, either in words or by specific action, we should look at the circumstances under which the Employers' Liability Act was passed; look, on the one hand, at its origin, scope, and purpose; and, on the other, at the nature, methods, and means of state Workmen's Compensation Laws. If the will is not clearly expressed in words, we must consider all these in order to determine what Congress intended.

First: As to words used: The act contains no words expressing a will by Congress to cover the whole field of compensation or relief for injuries received by or for death of such employees while engaged in interstate commerce; or the whole field of carriers' obligations in relation thereto. The language of that act, so far as it indicates anything in this respect, points to just the contrary. For its title is: "An Act Relative to the Liability of Common Carriers by Railroad in Certain Cases."

Second: As to specific action taken: The power exercised by Congress is not such that, when exercised, it *necessarily* excludes the state action here under consideration. It would obviously have been possible for Congress to provide in terms, that wherever such injuries or death result from the railroad's negligence, the remedy should be sought by action for damages; and wherever injury or death results from causes other than the railroad's negligence, compensation may be sought under the Workmen's Compensation Laws of the states. Between the Federal and the state law there would be no conflict whatsoever. They would, on the contrary, be complementary.

Third: As to origin, purpose, and scope of the Employers' Liability Act and the nature, methods, and means of state Workmen's Compensation Laws: The facts are of common knowledge. Do they manifest that, by entering upon one section of the field of indemnity or relief for injuries or death suffered by employees engaged in interstate commerce, Congress purposed to occupy the whole field?

(A) THE ORIGIN OF THE FEDERAL EMPLOYERS' LIABILITY ACT

By the common law as administered in the several states, the employee, like every other member of the community, was expected to bear the risks necessarily attendant upon life and work, subject only to the right to be indemnified for any loss inflicted by wrongdoers. The employer, like every other member of the community, was in theory liable to all others for loss resulting from his wrongs; the scope of his liability for wrongs being amplified by the doctrine of respondeat superior. This legal liability, which, in theory, applied between employer and employee as well as between others, came, in course of time, to be seriously impaired in practice. The protection it provided employees seemed to wane as the need for it grew. Three defenses — the doctrines of fellow servant's negligence, of assumption of risk, and of contributory negligence, rose and flourished. When applied to huge organizations and hazardous occupations, as in railroading, they practically abolished the liability of employers to employees; and in so doing they worked great hardship and apparent injustice. The wrongs suffered were flagrant; the demand for redress insistent; and the efforts to secure remedial legislation widespread. But the opponents were alert, potent, and securely intrenched. The evils of the fellow servant rule as applied to railroads were recognized as early as 1856, when Georgia passed the first law abolishing the defense. Between the passage of that act and the passage of the first Federal Employers' Liability Act, fifty years elapsed. In those fifty years only four more states had wholly abolished the defense of fellow servant's negligence. Furthermore, in only one state had a statute been passed making recovery possible where the employee had been guilty of contributory negligence. Meanwhile, the number of accidents to railroad employees had become appalling. In the year 1905-06 the number killed while on duty was 3,807, and the number injured 55,524. The promoters of remedial action, unable to overcome the efficient opposition presented in the legislatures of the several states, sought and secured the powerful support of the President. Congress was appealed to and used its power over interstate commerce to afford relief. The promotion of safety was, of course, referred to in the committee's report as justifying congressional action; but the moving cause for the Federal Employers' Liability Act was not the desire to promote safety or to secure uniformity, as in standardizing equipment by the Safety Appliance Acts.[9] There was, in the nature of things, no more reason for providing a Federal remedy for negligent injury to employees, than there would have been for providing such a remedy for negligent injury to passengers or to other members of the public. The Federal Employers' Liability Act was, in a sense, emergency legislation. The circumstances attending its passage were such as to preclude the belief that thereby Congress intended to deny to the states the power to provide for compensation or relief for injuries not covered by it.

(B) THE SCOPE OF THE FEDERAL EMPLOYERS' LIABILITY ACT

(1) The act leaves uncovered a large part of the injuries which result from the railroads' negligence. The decision of this court in the first Employers' Liability Cases, 207 U.S. 463, had declared that Congress lacked power to legislate in respect to any injuries occurring otherwise than to employees *engaged* in interstate commerce. Later decisions disclose how large a part of the injuries resulting from the railroads' negligence are thus excluded from the operation of the Federal law. For the act was held to apply only to those *directly* engaged in interstate commerce. This excludes not only those engaged in intrastate commerce, but also the many who — while engaged on work *for* interstate commerce, as in repairing engines or cars — are not directly engaged *in* it. Likewise it excludes employees who, though habitually engaged directly in interstate commerce, *happen* to be injured or killed through the railroads' negligence, while performing some work in intrastate commerce.

(2) The act leaves uncovered all of the injuries which result *otherwise* than from the railroads' negligence, though occurring when the employee is engaged directly in interstate commerce.

The scope of the act is so narrow as to preclude the belief that thereby Congress in-

---

[9] The following facts are significant as showing that employers' liability was not deemed a factor in safety to employees or the public, or a matter in which uniformity was desirable, or as otherwise presenting a railroad problem:

(1) The Annual Reports of the Interstate Commerce Commission to Congress for the eleven years ending December, 1908, deal each year at large with accidents, casualties to employees, and promotion of safety. These reports contain numerous recommendations for legislation concerning safety appliances, hours of labor, block signals, train control, inspection, and accident reporting; but no recommendation or even mention of employers' liability.

(2) The National Convention of Railroad Commissioners, an association comprising the commissioners of the several states, is formed for the purpose of discussing and aiding in the solution of American railroad problems. Likewise, in its reports for eleven years ending October, 1908, no reference has been found, either in the annual president's address, or in the report of the committee on legislation, or in the discussions, to the subject of employers' liability; or any mention of the passage by Congress of the two Employers' Liability Acts, or of the decision of this court on the first act.

The absence of such reference is particularly noteworthy in the legislative report for the year 1908, pp. 218-233, which is devoted to a consideration of harmonious or uniform legislation. It contains a résumé of the legislation in Congress recommended and supported by the National Convention of Railroad Commissioners during a period of nineteen years and attendances at congressional hearings on safety appliances, block signal, and hours of labor legislation.

tended to deny to the states the power to provide compensation or relief for injuries not covered by it.

(C) THE PURPOSE OF THE EMPLOYERS' LIABILITY ACT

The facts showing the origin and scope of the act discussed above indicate also its purpose. It was to end the denial of the right to damages for injuries due to the railroads' negligence — a right denied under judicial decisions through the interposition of the defenses of fellow servant, assumption of risk, and contributory negligence. It was not the purpose of the act to deny to the states the power to grant *the wholly new right* to protection or relief in the case of injuries suffered otherwise than through fault of the railroads.

The Federal Employers' Liability Act was, in no respect, a departure from the individualistic basis of right and of liability. It was, on the contrary, an attempt to enforce truly and impartially the old conception of justice as between individuals. The common-law liability for fault was to be restored by removing the abuses which prevented its full and just operation. The liability of the employer under the Federal act, as at common law, is merely a penalty for wrongdoing. The remedy assured to the employee is merely a more efficient means of making the wrongdoer indemnify him whom he has wronged. This limited purpose of the Employers' Liability Act precludes the belief that Congress intended thereby to deny to the states the power to provide compensation or relief for injuries not covered by the act.

(D) THE NATURE OF WORKMEN'S COMPENSATION ACTS

In the effort to remove abuses, a study had been made of facts, and of the world's experience in dealing with industrial accidents. That study uncovered as fiction many an assumption upon which American judges and lawyers had rested comfortably. The conviction became widespread that our individualistic conception of rights and liability no longer furnished an adequate basis for dealing with accidents in industry. It was seen that no system of indemnity dependent upon fault on the employers' part could meet the situation, even if the law were perfected and its administration made exemplary. For, in probably a majority of cases of injury, there was no assignable fault; and in many more it must be impossible of proof. It was urged: Attention should be directed, not to the employer's fault, but to the employee's misfortune. Compensation should be general, not sporadic; certain, not conjectural; speedy, not delayed; definite as to amount and time of payment; and so distributed over long periods as to insure actual protection against lost or lessened earning capacity. To a system making such provision, and not to wasteful litigation, dependent for success upon the coincidence of fault and the ability to prove it, society, as well as the individual employee and his dependents, must look for adequate protection. Society needs such a protection as much as the individual; because ultimately society must bear the burden, financial and otherwise, of the heavy losses which accidents entail. And since accidents are a natural, and in part an inevitable, concomitant of industry as now practiced, society, which is served thereby, should in some way provide the protection. To attain this end, co-operative methods must be pursued; some form of insurance — that is, some form of taxation. Such was the contention which has generally prevailed. Thus, out of the attempt to enforce individual justice grew the attempt to do social justice. But when Congress passed the Employers' Liability Act of April 22, 1908, these truths had gained little recognition in the United States. Not one of the thirty-seven states or territories which now have Workmen's Compensation Laws had introduced the system. Yet the conception and value of compensation laws was not unknown to Congress. It then had under consideration the first Compensation Law for Federal Employees which was enacted in the following month (Act of May 30, 1908, 35 Stat. 556). The need of its speedy passage had been called to the attention of Congress by the President in the same special message which uged the passage of this Employers' Liability Act.

Can it be contended that Congress, by simply passing the Employers' Liability Act, prohibited the states from providing in *any* way for the maintenance of such employees (and their dependents) for whose injuries a railroad, innocent of all fault, could not be called upon to make indemnity under that act? It is the state which is both primarily and ultimately concerned with the care of the injured and of those dependent upon him, even though the accident may occur while the employee is engaged directly in interstate commerce. Upon the state falls the financial burden of dependency, if provision be not otherwise made. Upon the state falls directly the far heavier burden of the demoralization of its citizenry and of the social unrest which attend destitution and the denial of opportunity. Upon the state also rests, under our dual system of government, the duty owed to the individual, to avert misery and promote happiness so far as possible. Surely we may not impute to Congress the will to deny to the states the power to perform either this duty to humanity or their fundamental duty of self-preservation. And if the states are left free to provide compensation, what is there in the Employers' Liability Act to show an intent on the part of Congress to deny to them the power to make the provision by raising the necessary contributions, in the first instance, through employers?

(E) METHODS AND MEANS OF WORKMEN'S COMPENSATION LAWS

The principle underlying Workmen's Compensation Laws is the same in all the states. The methods and means by which that principle is carried out vary materially. The principle is that of insurance, the premiums to which are contributed by employers generally. How the insurance fund shall be raised and administered; what the scale of compensation or relief shall be; how the contributing groups of employers shall be formed; whether or not a state fund shall be created; whether the individual employer shall be permitted to become a self-insurer; whether he shall be permitted to deal directly with the employee in making settlement of the compensation to be awarded; on all these questions the laws of the several states do and properly may differ radically.

What methods and means the state shall adopt in order to provide compensation for injuries to citizens or residents where Congress has left it free to legislate rests (subject to constitutional limitations) wholly within the judgment of the state. It might conclude, in view of the hazard involved, that no one should engage in the occupation of railroading without providing against the financial consequences of accidents through contributing an adequate amount to an accident insurance fund. It might conclude that it was wise to make itself the necessary contributions to such a fund, out of moneys raised from general taxation. Or it might conclude, as the state of Washington did, that the fairest and wisest form of taxation for the purpose was to impose upon the employer directly the duty of making the required contributions — relying upon the laws of trade to effect, through the medium of transportation charges, an equitable distribution of the burden. The method last suggested is pursued in substance also by the state of New York. In its essence the laws of the states are the same in this respect, as is shown in Mountain Timber Co. v. Washington, 243 U.S. 219. It is misleading to speak of the new obligation of the employer to contribute to compensation for injuries to workmen as an increase of the "employer's liability." It is not a liability for a violation of a duty. It is a direct — a primary — obligation in the nature of a tax. And the right of the employee is as free from any suggestion of wrong done to him as the new right granted by Mothers' Pension Laws.

(F) FEDERAL AND STATE LEGISLATION ARE NOT IN CONFLICT

The practical difficulty of determining in a particular case, according to presence or absence of railroad fault, whether indemnity is to be sought under the Federal Employers' Liability Act or under a state compensation law, affords, of course, no reason for imputing to Congress the will to deny to the states power to afford relief through such a system. The difficulty and uncertainty is, at worst, no greater than that which now exists in so many cases where it is necessary to determine whether the employee was, at the time of the accident, engaged in interstate or intrastate commerce. Expedients for minimizing inherent difficulties will doubtless be found by experience. All the difficulties may conceivably be overcome in practice. Or they may prove so great as to lead Congress to repeal the Federal Employers' Liability Act and leave to the states (which alone can deal comprehensively with it), the whole subject of indemnity and compensation for injuries to employees, whether engaged in interstate or intrastate commerce, and whether such injuries arise from negligence or without fault of the employer.

We are admonished also by weighty consideration not to impute to Congress the will to deny to the states this power. The subject of compensation for accidents in industry is one peculiarly appropriate for state legislation. There must, necessarily, be great diversity in the conditions of living and in the needs of the injured and of his dependents, according to whether they reside in one or the other of our states and territories, so widely extended. In a large majority of instances they reside in the state in which the accident occurs. Though the principle that compensation should be made, or relief given, is of universal application, the great diversity of conditions in the different sections of the United States may, in a wise application of the principle, call for differences between states in the amount and method of compensation, the periods in which payment shall be made, and the methods and means by which the funds shall be raised and distributed. The field of compensation for injuries appears to be one in which uniformity is *not* desirable, or at least not essential to the public welfare.

The contention that Congress has, by legislating on one branch of a subject relative to interstate commerce, pre-empted the whole field, has been made often in this court; and, as the cases above cited show, has been repeatedly rejected in cases where the will of Congress to leave the balance of the field open to state action was far less clear than under the circumstances here considered. Tested by those decisions and by the rules which this court has framed for its guidance, I am of opinion, as was said in Atlantic Coast Line R. Co. v. Georgia, 234 U.S. 280, 294, that "the intent to supersede the exercise of the state police power with respect to this subject cannot be inferred from the restricted action which thus far has been taken." The field covered by Congress was a limited field of the carrier's liability for negligence, not the whole field of the carrier's obligation arising from accidents. I find no justification for imputing to Congress the will to deny to a large class of persons engaged in a necessarily hazardous occupation and otherwise unprovided for, the protection afforded by beneficent statutes enacted in the long-deferred performance of an insistent duty and in a field peculiarly appropriate for state action.

MR. JUSTICE CLARKE concurs in this dissent.[p]

MAURER v. HAMILTON, 309 U.S. 598, 60 S. Ct. 726, 84 L. Ed. 969 (1940). Stone, J.: "The question for decision is whether a statute of Pennsylvania prohibiting the operation over its highways of any motor vehicle carrying any other vehicle over the head of the operator of such carrier vehicle, is superseded by the rules and regulations promulgated by the Interstate Commerce Commission under the Motor Carrier Act of 1935, 49 Stat. 543, 49 U.S.C. §§301-327, applicable to common and contract carriers in interstate commerce.

"Appellants, co-partners engaged as common carriers in the business of transporting in interstate commerce new automobiles upon motor trucks specially constructed for that purpose, brought this suit in the Pennsylvania state courts to enjoin appellees, state of-

---

[p] Cf. South Buffalo Ry. v. Ahern, 344 U.S. 367 (1953), sustaining an award under the New York Compensation Law where both the railroad and the employee joined in invoking it. Justice Douglas dissented, stating (p. 374): "I would join four in overruling the Winfield cases. But they are still the law, and their holdings are in my view quite inconsistent with what the Court now does." — ED.

466   Chapter Eight.   **The States in a Federal Union**

ficers, from enforcing against appellants § 1033(c) of the Pennsylvania Vehicle Code, effective June 29, 1937, 75 P.S. §642, which prohibits the operation on the highways of the state of any vehicle carrying any other vehicle 'above the cab of the carrier vehicle or over the head of the operator of such carrier vehicle.' Two other like suits brought by motor carriers engaged in like transportation interstate were consolidated with the present suit.

"After a hearing in which there was extensive evidence tending to show that the transportation by appellants over the state highways of cars placed above the cab of the transporting vehicle is unsafe to the driver and to the public, the trial court found that the location of motor vehicles over the cab of the carrier rendered its operation dangerous on the curves and grades of the Pennsylvania highways. It found that such location of the carried car above the driver raises the center of gravity of the loaded car above that which is normal in trucking operations, places excessive weight on the front axles and tires, obscures the vision of the driver of the carrier car, with the results that it increases the difficulty of steering the loaded car, adversely affects braking, particularly on curves, and affects the balance of the loaded car so as to make its use on the highways dangerous.

"It also found that in case of collision or loss of control the overhead car has a tendency to fly off the cab, in consequence of which, in numerous cases, serious injury had resulted to the operator of the truck or to the colliding car and its occupants, or both, and that the height of the overhead car and its interference with the driver's vision causes him to drive on the wrong side of the road in order to avoid overhead obstructions. The court concluded that the state statute was a safety regulation of motorcars using the highways of the state and that, as applied to appellants, it infringed neither the commerce clause of the Federal Constitution nor the due process clause of the Fourteenth Amendment, and gave judgment dismissing the complaint. On appeal the Supreme Court of Pennsylvania confirmed the findings of the trial court and affirmed the decree. 336 Pa. 17, 7 A.(2d) 466. The case comes here on appeal under §237 of the Judicial Code, as amended. 28 U.S.C. §344.

"Before the present suit was brought, the Interstate Commerce Commission, purporting to act under the Motor Carrier Act, had promulgated regulations effective July 1, 1936, with respect to 'safety of operation and equipment' of common and contract motor carriers in interstate commerce, subject to the Act. These regulations contained no provisions specifically applicable to cars carried over the cab of the carrier vehicle. On March 11, 1939, while the present case was pending before the Supreme Court of Pennsylvania, the Interstate Commerce Commission, in Car Over Cab Operations, 12 M.C.C. 127, issued its report of an investigation of the practice of the car over cab method of transportation of motor vehicles, in which it announced its conclusion that

" 'The record discloses no testimony whatsoever to show that the operation of motor vehicles, used in transporting new automobiles, and which are so constructed that one of the automobiles being transported extends in whole or in part over the cab, is unsafe. On the contrary, the evidence is clear that the average number of accidents in which vehicles of this type are involved is less than the country's average for all trucks. We find no reasons of record why the operations of such vehicles should be forbidden. The safety regulations heretofore prescribed by us, of course, apply to these as well as other vehicles operated by common and contract carriers in interstate or foreign commerce. The operations of vehicles so equipped are therefore permitted by the existing regulations, and there is no need for change.' (p. 132.)

"The Supreme Court of Pennsylvania took judicial notice of this action of the Commission, but concluded that the authority of the state to enact §1033(c) of the Vehicle Code was unimpaired by federal action. . . .

". . . The declared policy of the [Motor Carrier Act of 1935], §202(a), is to preserve and foster the economic and commercial advantages of an efficient transportation system. . . . Section 204(a), provides:

" 'It shall be the duty of the Commission — (1) to regulate common carriers by motor vehicle as provided in this part, and to that end the Commission may establish reasonable requirements with respect to continuous and adequate service, transportation of baggage and express, uniform systems of accounts, records, and reports, preservation of records, qualifications and maximum hours of service of employees, and safety of operation and equipment.'

"Subdivision (2) imposes a like duty upon the Commission to regulate 'contract carriers.' Subdivision (3) imposes the duty

" 'To establish for private carriers of property by motor vehicle, if need therefor is found, reasonable requirements to promote safety of operation, and to that end prescribe qualifications and maximum hours of service of employees, and standards of equipment.'

"Section 225 provides:

" 'The Commission is hereby authorized to investigate and report on the need for Federal regulation of the size and weight of motor vehicles and combinations of motor vehicles and of the qualifications and maximum hours of service of employees of all motor carriers and private carriers of property by motor vehicle. . . . ' "

What decision? Why?

Castle v. Hayes Freight Lines, Inc. 348 U.S. 61, 75 S. Ct. 191, 99 L. Ed. 68 (1954)

MR. JUSTICE BLACK delivered the opinion of the Court.

This case raises important questions concerning the power of states to bar interstate motor carriers from use of state roads as punishment for repeated violations of state highway regulations. The respondent Hayes Freight Lines, Inc. is such a carrier transporting goods to and from many points in Illinois and seven other states. This extensive interstate business is done under a certificate of convenience and necessity issued by the Interstate Commerce Commission under authority of the Federal Motor Carrier Act. Hayes also does an intrastate carrier business in Illinois under a certificate issued by state authorities. Illinois has a statute which limits the weight of freight that can be carried in commercial trucks over Illinois highways; the same statute also provides for a balanced distribution of freight loads in relation to the truck's axles. Repeated violations of these provisions by trucks of a carrier are made punishable by total suspension of the carrier's right to use Illinois state highways for periods of ninety days and one year.[4] This action was brought in a state court to restrain Illinois officials from prosecuting Hayes as a repeated violator. The State Supreme Court held that the punishment of suspension provided by the state statute could not be imposed on the interstate operations of the respondent Hayes. Such a state suspension of interstate transportation, it was decided, would conflict with the Federal Motor Carrier Act which is the supreme law of the land.[5] We granted the State's petition for certiorari. 347 U.S. 1009.

Congress in the Motor Carrier Act adopted a comprehensive plan for regulating the carriage of goods by motor truck in interstate commerce. The federal plan of control was so all-embracing that former power of states over interstate motor carriers was greatly reduced. No power at all was left in states to determine what carriers could or could not operate in interstate commerce. Exclusive power of the Federal Government to make this determination is shown by §306 of 49 U.S.C. which describes the conditions under

---

[4] Ill. Rev. Stat., 1953, c. 95½, §229b. This section provides for a 90-day suspension upon a finding of 10 or more violations. If thereafter the same carrier is found to have been guilty of 10 or more later violations the suspension is for one year.

[5] 2 Ill. 2d 58, 117 N.E.2d 106. But the State Supreme Court held that Hayes' intrastate operations could be suspended. Hayes appealed to this Court. We dismissed for want of a substantial federal question. 374 U.S. 994.

which the Interstate Commerce Commission can issue certificates of convenience and necessity. And §312 of the same title provides that all certificates, permits or licenses issued by the Commission "shall remain in effect until suspended or terminated as herein provided." But in order to provide stability for operating rights of carriers, Congress placed within very narrow limits the Commission's power to suspend or revoke an outstanding certificate. No certificate is to be revoked, suspended or changed until after a hearing and a finding that a carrier has willfully failed to comply with the provisions of the Motor Carrier Act or with regulations promulgated under it. Under these circumstances, it would be odd if a state could take action amounting to a suspension or revocation of an interstate carrier's commission-granted right to operate. Cf. Hill v. Florida, 325 U.S. 538. It cannot be doubted that suspension of this common carrier's right to use Illinois highways is the equivalent of a partial suspension of its federally granted certificate. The highways of Illinois are not only used by Hayes to transport interstate goods to and from that State but are also used as connecting links to points in other states which the Commission has authorized Hayes to serve. Consequently if the ninety-day or the one-year suspension should become effective, the carriage of interstate goods into Illinois and other states would be seriously disrupted.

That Illinois seeks to punish Hayes for violations of its road regulations does not justify this disruption of federally authorized activities. A state's regulation of weight and distribution of loads carried in interstate trucks does not itself conflict with the Federal Act. The reason for this as pointed out in Maurer v. Hamilton, 309 U.S. 598, is that the Federal Act has a provision designed to leave states free to regulate the sizes and weights of motor vehicles. But it would stretch this statutory provision too much to say that it also allowed states to revoke or suspend the right of interstate motor carriers for violation of state highway regulations.

It is urged that without power to impose punishment by suspension states will be without appropriate remedies to enforce their laws against recalcitrant motor carriers. We are not persuaded, however, that the conventional forms of punishment are inadequate to protect states from overweighted or improperly loaded motor trucks. Moreover, a Commission regulation requires motor carriers to abide by valid state highway regulations. And as previously pointed out, the Commission can revoke in whole or in part certificates of motor carriers which willfully refuse to comply with any lawful regulation of the Commission. If, therefore, motor carriers persistently and repeatedly violate the laws of a state, we know of no reason why the Commission may not protect the state's interest, either on the Commission's own initiative or on complaint of the state.

We agree with the Supreme Court of Illinois that the right of this carrier to use Illinois highways for interstate transportation of goods cannot be suspended by Illinois.

Affirmed.[q]

Huron Portland Cement Co. v. Detroit *362 U.S. 440, 80 S. Ct. 813, 4 L. Ed. 2d 852 (1960)*

Mr. Justice Stewart delivered the opinion of the Court.

This appeal from a judgment of the Supreme Court of Michigan draws in question the constitutional validity of certain provisions of Detroit's Smoke Abatement Code as applied to ships owned by appellant and operated in interstate commerce.

The appellant is a Michigan corporation, engaged in the manufacture and sale of cement. It maintains a fleet of five vessels which it uses to transport cement from its mill in Alpena, Michigan, to distributing plants located in various states bordering the Great

---

[q] See Note, Motor Vehicle Size and Weight Statutes: Enforcement Against Carriers in Interstate Commerce, 45 Va. L. Rev. 106 (1959). Cf. Service Storage & Transfer Co. v. Virginia, 359 U.S. 171 (1959). — Ed.

Section C. **Effects of Federal Action** 469

Lakes. Two of the ships, the S.S. *Crapo* and the S.S. *Boardman*, are equipped with hand-fired Scotch marine boilers. While these vessels are docked for loading and unloading it is necessary, in order to operate deck machinery. to keep the boilers fired and to clean the fires periodically. When the fires are cleaned, the ship's boiler stacks emit smoke which in density and duration exceeds the maximum standards allowable under the Detroit Smoke Abatement Code. Structural alterations would be required in order to insure compliance with the Code.

Criminal proceedings were instituted in the Detroit Recorder's Court against the appellant and its agents for violations of the city law during periods when the vessels were docked at the Port of Detroit. The appellant brought an action in the State Circuit Court to enjoin the city from further prosecuting the pending litigation in the Recorder's Court, and from otherwise enforcing the smoke ordinance against its vessels, "except where the emission of smoke is caused by the improper firing or the improper use of the equipment upon said vessels." The Circuit Court refused to grant relief, and the Supreme Court of Michigan affirmed, 355 Mich. 227, 93 N.W.2d 888. . . .

In support of the claim that the ordinance cannot constitutionally be applied to appellant's ships, two basic arguments are advanced. First, it is asserted that since the vessels and their equipment, including their boilers, have been inspected, approved and licensed to operate in interstate commerce in accordance with a comprehensive system of regulation enacted by Congress, the City of Detroit may not legislate in such a way as, in effect, to impose additional or inconsistent standards. Secondly, the argument is made that even if Congress has not expressly pre-empted the field, the municipal ordinance "materially affects interstate commerce in matters where uniformity is necessary." We have concluded that neither of these contentions can prevail, and that the Federal Constitution does not prohibit application to the appellant's vessels of the criminal provisions of the Detroit ordinance.

The ordinance was enacted for the manifest purpose of promoting the health and welfare of the city's inhabitants. Legislation designed to free from pollution the very air that people breathe clearly falls within the exercise of even the most traditional concept of what is compendiously known as the police power. In the exercise of that power, the states and their instrumentalities may act, in many areas of interstate commerce and maritime activities, concurrently with the federal government. [Citations omitted.]

The basic limitations upon local legislative power in this area are clear enough. The controlling principles have been reiterated over the years in a host of this Court's decisions. Evenhanded local regulation to effectuate a legitimate local public interest is valid unless pre-empted by federal action, . . . [citations omitted] . . . or unduly burdensome on maritime activities or interstate commerce, Minnesota v. Barber, 136 U.S. 313; Morgan v. Virginia, 328 U.S. 373; Bibb v. Navajo Freight Lines, 359 U.S. 520.

In determining whether state regulation has been pre-empted by federal action, "the intent to supersede the exercise by the State of its police power as to matters not covered by the Federal legislation is not to be inferred from the mere fact that Congress has seen fit to circumscribe its regulation and to occupy a limited field. In other words, such intent is not to be implied unless the act of Congress fairly interpreted is in actual conflict with the law of the State." Savage v. Jones, 225 U.S. 501, 533. . . .

In determining whether the state has imposed an undue burden on interstate commerce, it must be borne in mind that the Constitution when "conferring upon Congress the regulation of commerce, . . . never intended to cut the States off from legislating on all subjects relating to the health, life, and safety of their citizens, though the legislation might indirectly affect the commerce of the country. Legislation, in a great variety of ways, may affect commerce and persons engaged in it without constituting a regulation of it, within the meaning of the Constitution." Sherlock v. Alling, 93 U.S. 99, 103; . . . . But a state may not impose a burden which materially affects interstate commerce in an area where uniformity of regulation is necessary. Hall v. De Cuir, 95 U.S. 485; . . . .

Although verbal generalizations do not of their own motion decide concrete cases, it is nevertheless within the framework of these basic principles that the issues in the present case must be determined.

I

For many years Congress has maintained an extensive and comprehensive set of controls over ships and shipping. Federal inspection of steam vessels was first required in 1838, 5 Stat. 304, and the requirement has been continued ever since. 5 Stat. 626; 10 Stat. 61; 14 Stat. 227; 16 Stat. 440; 22 Stat. 346; 28 Stat. 699; 32 Stat. 34; 34 Stat. 68; 60 Stat. 1097; 73 Stat. 475. Steam vessels which carry passengers must pass inspection annually, 46 U.S.C. §391(a), and those which do not, every two years. 46 U.S.C. §391(b). Failure to meet the standards invoked by law results in revocation of the inspection certificate, or refusal to issue a new one, 46 U.S.C. §391(d). It is unlawful for a vessel to operate without such a certificate. 46 U.S.C. §390c(a).

These inspections are broad in nature, covering "the boilers, unfired pressure vessels, and appurtenances thereof, also the propelling and auxiliary machinery, electrical apparatus and equipment, of all vessels subject to inspection . . ." 46 U.S.C. §392(b). The law provides that "No boiler . . . shall be allowed to be used if constructed in whole or in part of defective material or which because of its form, design, workmanship, age, use, or for any other reason is unsafe." 46 U.S.C. §392(c).

As is apparent on the face of the legislation, however, the purpose of the federal inspection statutes is to insure the seagoing safety of vessels subject to inspection. Thus 46 U.S.C. §392(c) makes clear that inspection of boilers and related equipment is for the purpose of seeing to it that the equipment "may be safely employed in the service proposed." The safety of passengers, 46 U.S.C. §391(a), and of the crew, 46 U.S.C. §391(b), is the criterion. The thrust of the federal inspection laws is clearly limited to affording protection from the perils of maritime navigation. Cf. Ace Waterways v. Fleming, 98 F. Supp. 666. See also Steamship Co. v. Joliffe, 2 Wall. 450.

By contrast, the sole aim of the Detroit ordinance is the elimination of air pollution to protect the health and enhance the cleanliness of the local community. Congress recently recognized the importance and legitimacy of such a purpose, when in 1955 it provided: "[I]n recognition of the dangers to the public health and welfare, injury to agricultural crops and livestock, damage to and deterioration of property, and hazards to air and ground transportation, from air pollution, it is hereby declared to be the policy of Congress to preserve and protect the primary responsibilities and rights of the States and local governments in controlling air pollution, to support and aid technical research to devise and develop methods of abating such pollution, and to provide Federal technical services and financial aid to State and local government air pollution control agencies and other public or private agencies and institutions in the formulation and execution of their air pollution abatement research programs." 69 Stat. 322; 42 U.S.C. §1857.

Congressional recognition that the problem of air pollution is peculiarly a matter of state and local concern is manifest in this legislation. Such recognition is underlined in the Senate Committee Report: "The committee recognizes that it is the primary responsibility of State and local governments to prevent air pollution. The bill does not propose any exercise of police power by the Federal Government and no provision in it invades the sovereignty of States, counties or cities." S. Rep. No. 389, 84th Cong., 1st Sess. 3.

We conclude that there is no overlap between the scope of the federal ship inspection laws and that of the municipal ordinance here involved. For this reason we cannot find that the federal inspection legislation has pre-empted local action. To hold otherwise would be to ignore the teaching of this Court's decisions which enjoin seeking out conflicts between state and federal regulation where none clearly exists. Savage v. Jones, 225 U.S. 501; Welch Co. v. New Hampshire, 306 U.S. 79; Maurer v. Hamilton, 309 U.S. 598.

An additional argument is advanced, however, based not upon the mere existence of the federal inspection standards, but upon the fact that the appellant's vessels were actually licensed, 46 U.S.C. §263, and enrolled, 46 U.S.C. §§259-260, by the national government. It is asserted that the vessels have thus been given a dominant federal right to the use of the navigable waters of the United States, free from the local impediment that would be imposed by the Detroit ordinance.

The scope of the privilege granted by the federal licensing scheme has been well delineated. A state may not exclude from its waters a ship operating under a federal license. Gibbons v. Ogden, 9 Wheat. 1. A state may not require a local occupation license, in addition to that federally granted, as a condition precedent to the use of its waters. Moran v. New Orleans, 112 U.S. 69. While an enrolled and licensed vessel may be required to share the costs of benefits it enjoys, Huse v. Glover, 119 U.S. 543, and to pay fair taxes imposed by its domicile, Transportation Co. v. Wheeling, 99 U.S. 273, it cannot be subjected to local license imposts exacted for the use of a navigable waterway, Harman v. Chicago, 147 U.S. 396. See also Sinnot v. Davenport, 22 How. 227.

The mere possession of a federal license, however, does not immunize a ship from the operation of the normal incidents of local police power, not constituting a direct regulation of commerce. Thus, a federally licensed vessel is not, as such, exempt from local pilotage laws, Cooley v. Board of Wardens of Port of Philadelphia, 12. How 299, or local quarantine laws, Morgan's Steamship Co. v. Louisiana Board of Health, 118 U.S. 455, or local safety inspections, Kelly v. Washington, 302 U.S. 1, or the local regulation of wharves and docks, Packet Co. v. Catlettsburg, 105 U.S. 559. Indeed this Court has gone so far as to hold that a State, in the exercise of its police power, may actually seize and pronounce the forfeiture of a vessel "licensed for the coasting trade, under the laws of the United States, while engaged in that trade." Smith v. Maryland, 18 How. 71, 74. The present case obviously does not even approach such an extreme, for the Detroit ordinance requires no more than compliance with an orderly and reasonable scheme of community regulation. The ordinance does not exclude a licensed vessel from the Port of Detroit, nor does it destroy the right of free passage. We cannot hold that the local regulation so burdens the federal license as to be constitutionally invalid.

II

The claim that the Detroit ordinance, quite apart from the effect of federal legislation, imposes as to the appellant's ships an undue burden on interstate commerce needs no extended discussion. State regulation, based on the police power, which does not discriminate against interstate commerce or operate to disrupt its required uniformity, may constitutionally stand. . . .

It has not been suggested that the local ordinance, applicable alike to "any person, firm or corporation" within the city, discriminates against interstate commerce. It is a regulation of general application, designed to better the health and welfare of the community. And while the appellant argues that other local governments might impose differing requirements as to air pollution, it has pointed to none. The record contains nothing to suggest the existence of any such competing or conflicting local regulations. Cf. Bibb v. Navajo Freight Lines, 359 U.S. 520. We conclude that no impermissible burden on commerce has been shown.

The judgment is affirmed.

MR. JUSTICE DOUGLAS, with whom MR. JUSTICE FRANKFURTER concurs, dissenting.

The Court treats this controversy as if it were merely an inspection case with the City of Detroit supplementing a federal inspection system as the State of Washington did in Kelly v. Washington, 302 U.S. 1. There a state inspection system touched matters "which the federal laws and regulations" left "untouched." Id., at 13. This is not that type of case. Nor is this the rare case where state law adopts the standards and requirements of federal law and is allowed to exact a permit in addition to the one demanded by federal law. California v. Zook, 336 U.S. 725, 735. Here we have a criminal prosecution against a shipowner and officers of two of its vessels for using the very equipment on these vessels which the Federal Government says may be used. At stake are a possible fine of $100 on the owner and both a fine and a 30-day jail sentence on the officers.

Appellant has a federal certificate for each of its vessels. . . . The one issued on March 21, 1956, by the United States Coast Guard for S.S. S. T. Crapo is typical. The certificate states "The said vessel is permitted to be navigated for one year on the Great Lakes." The certificate specifies the boilers which are and may be used — "Main Boilers Number 3, Year built 1927, Mfr. Manitowoc Boiler Wks." It also specifies the fuel which is used and is to be used in those boilers — "Fuel coal."

Appellant, operating the vessel in waters at the Detroit dock, is about to be fined criminally for using the precise equipment covered by the federal certificate because, it is said, the use of that equipment will violate a smoke ordinance of the City of Detroit.

The federal statutes give the Coast Guard the power to inspect "the boilers" of freight vessels every two years, and provide that when the Coast Guard approves the vessel and her equipment throughout, a certificate to that effect shall be made.

The requirements of the Detroit smoke ordinance are squarely in conflict with the federal statute. Section 2.2A of the ordinance prohibits the emission of the kind of smoke which cannot at all times be prevented by vessels equipped with hand-fired Scotch marine boilers such as appellant's vessels use. Section 2.16 of the ordinance makes it unlawful to use any furnace or other combustion equipment or device in the city without a certificate of operation which issues only after inspection. . . . [Statement of procedure set forth in ordinance omitted.]

Thus it is plain that the ordinance requires not only the inspection and approval of equipment which has been inspected and approved by the Coast Guard but also the sealing of equipment, even though it has been approved by the Coast Guard. Under the Detroit ordinance a certificate of operation would not issue for a hand-fired Scotch marine boiler, even though it has been approved by the Coast Guard. In other words, this equipment approved and licensed by the federal government for use on navigable waters cannot pass muster under local law.

If local law required federally licensed vessels to observe local speed laws, obey local traffic regulations, or dock at certain times or under prescribed conditions, we would have local laws not at war with the federal license, but complementary to it. In Kelly v. Washington, supra, at 14-15, the Court marked precisely that distinction. While it allowed state inspection of hull and machinery of tugs over and above that required by federal statutes, it noted that state rules which changed the federal standards "for the structure and equipment of vessels" would meet a different fate. . . .

Here the Coast Guard would be entitled to insist on different equipment. But it has not done so. The boats of appellant, therefore, have credentials good for any port; and I would not allow this local smoke ordinance to work in derogation of them. The fact that the Federal Government in certifying equipment applies standards of safety for seagoing vessels, while Detroit applies standards of air pollution seems immaterial. Federal preemption occurs when the boilers and fuel to be used in the vessels are specified in the certificate. No state authority can, in my view, change those specifications. Yet that is in effect what is allowed here.

. . . Yet whether fine or imprisonment is considered, the effect on the federal certificate will be crippling. However the issue in the present case is stated it comes down to making criminal in the Port of Detroit the use of a certificate issued under paramount federal law. Mintz v. Baldwin, 289 U.S. 346, upheld the requirement of a state inspection certificate where a federal certificate might have been, but was not, issued. Cf. California

v. Thompson, 313 U.S. 109, 112. Never before, I believe, have we recognized the right of local law to make the use of an unquestionably legal federal license a criminal offense.

What we do today is in disregard of the doctrine long accepted and succinctly stated in the 1851 Term in Pennsylvania v. Wheeling & Belmont Bridge Co., 13 How. 518, 566, "No State law can hinder or obstruct the free use of a license granted under an act of Congress." The confusion and burden arising from the imposition by one State of requirements for equipment which the Federal Government has approved was emphasized in Kelly v. Washington. . . . The requirements of Detroit may be too lax for another port. Cf. People v. Cunard White Star, Ltd., 280 N.Y. 413, 21 N.E.2d 489. The variety of requirements for equipment which the States may provide in order to meet their air pollution needs underlines the importance of letting the Coast Guard license serve as authority for the vessel to use, in all our ports, the equipment which it certifies.

Pennsylvania v. Nelson 350 U.S. 497, 76 S. Ct. 477, 100 L. Ed. 640 (1956)

MR. CHIEF JUSTICE WARREN delivered the opinion of the Court.

The respondent Steve Nelson, an acknowledged member of the Communist Party, was convicted in the Court of Quarter Sessions of Allegheny County, Pennsylvania, of a violation of the Pennsylvania Sedition Act and sentenced to imprisonment for twenty years and to a fine of $10,000 and to costs of prosecution in the sum of $13,000. . . . The Supreme Court of Pennsylvania, . . . decided the case on the narrow issue of supersession of the state law by the Federal Smith Act.[3] In its opinion, the court stated:

"And, while the Pennsylvania statute proscribes sedition against either the Government of the United States or the Government of Pennsylvania, it is only alleged sedition against the United States with which the instant case is concerned. Out of all the voluminous testimony, we have not found, nor has anyone pointed to, a single word indicating a seditious act or even utterance directed against the Government of Pennsylvania."

The precise holding of the court, and all that is before us for review, is that the Smith Act of 1940, as amended in 1948,[6] which prohibits the knowing advocacy of the overthrow of the Government of the United States by force and violence, supersedes the enforceability of the Pennsylvania Sedition Act which proscribes the same conduct.

Many State Attorneys General and the Solicitor General of the United States appeared as amici curiae for petitioner, and several briefs were filed on behalf of the respondent. Because of the important question of federal-state relationship involved, we granted certiorari. 348 U.S. 814.

It should be said at the outset that the decision in this case does not affect the right of States to enforce their sedition laws at times when the Federal Government has not occupied the field and is not protecting the entire country from seditious conduct. The distinction between the two situations was clearly recognized by the court below. Nor does it limit the jurisdiction of the States where the Constitution and Congress have specifically given them concurrent jurisdiction, as was done under the Eighteenth Amendment and the Volstead Act. United States v. Lanza, 260 U.S. 377. Neither does it limit the right of the State to protect itself at any time against sabotage or attempted violence of all kinds. Nor does it prevent the State from prosecuting where the same act constitutes both a federal offense and a state offense under the police power, as was done in Fox v. Ohio, 5 How. 410, and Gilbert v. Minnesota, 254 U.S. 325, relied upon by petitioner as authority herein. In neither of those cases did the state statute impinge on federal jurisdiction. In the Fox case, the federal offense was counterfeiting. The state offense was defrauding the person to whom the spurious money was passed. In the Gilbert case this Court, in

---
[3] 377 Pa. 58, 104 A.2d 133.
[6] 18 U.S.C. §2385. . . .

upholding the enforcement of a state statute, proscribing conduct which would "interfere with or discourage the enlistment of men in the military or naval forces of the United States or of the State of Minnesota," treated it not as an act relating to "the raising of armies for the national defense, nor to rules and regulations for the government of those under arms [a constitutionally exclusive federal power]. It [was] simply a local police measure. . . ."

Where, as in the instant case, Congress has not stated specifically whether a federal statute has occupied a field in which the States are otherwise free to legislate, different criteria have furnished touchstones for decision. Thus,

"[t]his Court, in considering the validity of state laws in the light of . . . federal laws touching the same subject, has made use of the following expressions: conflicting; contrary to; occupying the field; repugnance; difference; irreconcilability; inconsistency; violation; curtailment; and interference. But none of these expressions provide an infallible constitutional test or an exclusive constitutional yardstick. In the final analysis, there can be no one crystal clear distinctly marked formula." Hines v. Davidowitz, 312 U.S. 52, 67.

And see Rice v. Santa Fe Elevator Corp., 331 U.S. 218, 230-231. In this case, we think that each of several tests of supersession is met.

First, "[t]he scheme of federal regulation [is] so pervasive as to make reasonable the inference that Congress left no room for the States to supplement it." Rice v. Santa Fe Elevator Corp., 331 U.S., at 230. The Congress determined in 1940 that it was necessary for it to re-enter the field of antisubversive legislation, which had been abandoned by it in 1921. In that year, it enacted the Smith Act which proscribes advocacy of the overthrow of any government — federal, state or local — by force and violence and organization of and knowing membership in a group which so advocates. Conspiracy to commit any of these acts is punishable under the general criminal conspiracy provisions in 18 U.S.C. §371. The Internal Security Act of 1950 is aimed more directly at Communist organizations. It distinguishes between "Communist-action organizations" and "Communist-front organizations," requiring such organizations to register and to file annual reports with the Attorney General giving complete details as to their officers and funds. Members of Communist-action organizations who have not been registered by their organization must register as individuals. Failure to register in accordance with the requirements of Sections 786-787 is punishable by a fine of not more than $10,000 for an offending organization and by a fine of not more than $10,000 or imprisonment for not more than five years or both for an individual offender — each day of failure to register constituting a separate offense. And the Act imposes certain sanctions upon both "action" and "front" organizations and their members. The Communist Control Act of 1954 declares "that the Communist Party of the United States, although purportedly a political party, is in fact an instrumentality of a conspiracy to overthrow the Government of the United States" and that "its role as the agency of a hostile foreign power renders its existence a clear present and continuing danger to the security of the United States." It also contains a legislative finding that the Communist Party is a "Communist-action organization" within the meaning of the Internal Security Act of 1950 and provides that "knowing" members of the Communist Party are "subject to all the provisions and penalties" of that Act. It furthermore sets up a new classification of "Communist-infiltrated organizations" and provides for the imposition of sanctions against them.

We examine these Acts only to determine the congressional plan. Looking to all of them in the aggregate, the conclusion is inescapable that Congress has intended to occupy the field of sedition. Taken as a whole, they evince a congressional plan which makes it reasonable to determine that no room has been left for the States to supplement it. Therefore, a state sedition statute is superseded regardless of whether it purports to supplement the federal law. As was said by Mr. Justice Holmes in Charleston & Western Carolina R. Co. v. Varnville Furniture Co., 237 U.S. 597, 604: "When Congress has taken the particular subject-matter in hand coincidence is as ineffective as opposition, and a state law is not to be declared a help because it attempts to go farther than Congress has seen fit to go."[r]

Second, the federal statutes "touch a field in which the federal interest is so dominant that the federal system [must] be assumed to preclude enforcement of state laws on the same subject." Rice v. Santa Fe Elevator Corp., 331 U.S., at 230, citing Hines v. Davidowitz, supra. Congress has devised an all-embracing program for resistance to the various forms of totalitarian aggression. Our external defenses have been strengthened, and a plan to protect against internal subversion has been made by it. It has appropriated vast sums, not only for our own protection, but also to strengthen freedom throughout the world. It has charged the Federal Bureau of Investigation and the Central Intelligence Agency with responsibility for intelligence concerning Communist seditious activities against our Government, and has denominated such activities as part of a world conspiracy. It accordingly proscribed sedition against all government in the nation — national, state and local. Congress declared that these steps were taken "to provide for the common defense, to preserve the sovereignty of the United States as an independent nation, and to guarantee to each State a republican form of government. . . ." Congress having thus treated seditious conduct as a matter of vital national concern, it is in no sense a local enforcement problem. As was said in the court below:

"Sedition against the United States is not a *local* offense. It is a crime against the *Nation*. As such, it should be prosecuted and punished in the Federal courts where this defendant has in fact been prosecuted and convicted and is now under sentence. It is not only important but vital that such prosecutions should be exclusively within the control of the Federal Government. . . ."

Third, enforcement of state sedition acts presents a serious danger of conflict with the administration of the federal program. Since 1939, in order to avoid a hampering of uniform enforcement of its program by sporadic local prosecutions, the Federal Government has urged local authorities not to intervene in such matters, but to turn over to the federal authorities immediately and unevaluated all information concerning subversive activities. The President made such a request on September 6, 1939, when he placed the Federal Bureau of Investigation in charge of investigation in this field:

"The Attorney General has been requested by me to instruct the Federal Bureau of Investigation of the Department of Justice to take charge of investigative work in matters relating to espionage, sabotage, and violations of the neutrality regulations.

"This task must be conducted in a comprehensive and effective manner on a national basis, and all information must be carefully sifted out and correlated in order to avoid confusion and irresponsibility.

"To this end I request all police officers, sheriffs, and all other law enforcement officers in the United States promptly to turn over to the nearest representative of the Federal Bureau of Investigation any information obtained by them relating to espionage, counterespionage, sabotage, subversive activities and violations of the neutrality laws."

And in addressing the Federal-State Conference on Law Enforcement Problems of National Defense, held on August 5 and 6, 1940, only a few weeks after the passage of the Smith Act, the Director of the Federal Bureau of Investigation said:

"The fact must not be overlooked that meeting the spy, the saboteur and the subverter is a problem that must be handled on a nation-wide basis. An isolated incident in the middle west may be of little significance, but when fitted into a national pattern of similar incidents, it may lead to an important revelation of subversive activity. It is for this reason that the President requested all of our citizens and law enforcing agencies to report directly to the Federal Bureau of Investigation any complaints or information dealing with espionage, sabotage or subversive activities. In such matters, time is of the essence. It is unfor-

---

[r] Cf. California v. Zook, 336 U.S. 725 (1949). — Ed.

tunate that in a few States efforts have been made by individuals not fully acquainted with the far-flung ramifications of this problem to interject superstructures of agencies between local law enforcement and the FBI to sift what might be vital information, thus delaying its immediate reference to the FBI. This cannot be, if our internal security is to be best served. This is no time for red tape or amateur handling of such vital matters. There must be a direct and free flow of contact between the local law enforcement agencies and the FBI. The job of meeting the spy or saboteur is one for experienced men of law enforcement."

Moreover, the Pennsylvania Statute presents a peculiar danger of interference with the federal program. For, as the court below observed:

"Unlike the Smith Act, which can be administered only by federal officers acting in their official capacities, indictment for sedition under the Pennsylvania statute can be initiated upon an information made by a private individual. The opportunity thus present for the indulgence of personal spite and hatred or for furthering some selfish advantage or ambition need only be mentioned to be appreciated. . . ."

In his brief, the Solicitor General states that forty-two States plus Alaska and Hawaii have statutes which in some form prohibit advocacy of the violent overthrow of established government. These statutes are entitled anti-sedition statutes, criminal anarchy laws, criminal syndicalist laws, etc. Although all of them are primarily directed against the overthrow of the United States Government, they are in no sense uniform. And our attention has not been called to any case where the prosecution has been successfully directed against an attempt to destroy state or local government. . . .

Since we find that Congress has occupied the field to the exclusion of parallel state legislation, that the dominant interest of the Federal Government precludes state intervention, and that administration of state Acts would conflict with the operation of the federal plan, we are convinced that the decision of the Supreme Court of Pennsylvania is unassailable.

We are not unmindful of the risk of compounding punishments which would be created by finding concurrent state power. In our view of the case, we do not reach the question whether double or multiple punishment for the same overt acts directed against the United States has constitutional sanction. Without compelling indication to the contrary, we will not assume that Congress intended to permit the possibility of double punishment. Cf. Houston v. Moore, 5 Wheat. 1, 31, 75; Jerome v. United States, 318 U.S. 101, 105.

The judgment of the Supreme Court of Pennsylvania is

Affirmed. . . .

Mr. Justice Reed, with whom Mr. Justice Burton and Mr. Justice Minton join, dissenting. . . .

First, the Court relies upon the pervasiveness of the antisubversive legislation embodied in the Smith Act of 1940, 18 U.S.C. §2385, the Internal Security Act of 1950, 64 Stat. 987, and the Communist Control Act of 1954, 68 Stat. 775. It asserts that these Acts in the aggregate mean that Congress has occupied the "field of sedition" to the exclusion of the States. The "occupation of the field" argument has been developed by this Court for the Commerce Clause and legislation thereunder to prevent partitioning of this country by locally erected trade barriers. In those cases this Court has ruled that state legislation is superseded when it conflicts with the comprehensive regulatory scheme and purpose of a federal plan. Cloverleaf Butter Co. v. Patterson, 315 U.S. 148. . . .

But the federal sedition laws are distinct criminal statutes that punish willful advocacy of the use of force against "the government of the United States or the government of any State." These criminal laws proscribe certain local activity without creating any statutory or administrative regulation. There is, consequently, no question as to whether some general congressional regulatory scheme might be upset by a coinciding state plan. In these circumstances the conflict should be clear and direct before this Court reads a congressional intent to void state legislation into the federal sedition acts. . . .

Moreover, it is quite apparent that since 1940 Congress has been keenly aware of the magnitude of existing state legislation proscribing sedition. It may be validly assumed that in these circumstances this Court should not void state legislation without a clear mandate from Congress.

We cannot agree that the federal criminal sanctions against sedition directed at the United States are of such a pervasive character as to indicate an intention to void state action.

Secondly, the Court states that the federal sedition statutes touch a field "in which the federal interest is so dominant" they must preclude state laws on the same subject. This concept is suggested in a comment on Hines v. Davidowitz, 312 U.S. 52, in the Rice case, at 230. The Court in Davidowitz ruled that federal statutes compelling alien registration preclude enforcement of state statutes requiring alien registration. We read Davidowitz to teach nothing more than that, when the Congress provided a single nationwide integrated system of regulation so complete as that for aliens' registration (with fingerprinting, a scheduling of activities, and continuous information as to their residence), the Act bore so directly on our foreign relations as to make it evident that Congress intended only one uniform national alien registration system.

We look upon the Smith Act as a provision for controlling incitements to overthrow by force and violence the Nation, or any State, or any political subdivision of either. Such an exercise of federal police power carries, we think, no such dominancy over similar state powers as might be attributed to continuing federal regulations concerning foreign affairs or coinage, for example. In the responsibility of national and local governments to protect themselves against sedition, there is no "dominant interest." . . .

Thirdly, the Court finds ground for abrogating Pennsylvania's antisedition statute because, in the Court's view, the State's administration of the Act may hamper the enforcement of the federal law. Quotations are inserted from statements of President Roosevelt and Mr. Hoover, the Director of the Federal Bureau of Investigation, to support the Court's position. But a reading of the quotations leads us to conclude that their purpose was to gain prompt knowledge of evidence of subversive activities so that the federal agency could be fully advised. We find no suggestion from any official source that state officials should be less alert to ferret out or punish subversion. The Court's attitude as to interference seems to us quite contrary to that of the Legislative and Executive Departments. Congress was advised of the existing state sedition legislation when the Smith Act was enacted and has been kept current with its spread. No declaration of exclusiveness followed. In this very case the Executive appears by brief of the Department of Justice, amicus curiae. The brief summarizes this point:

"The administration of the various state laws has not, in the course of the fifteen years that the federal and state sedition laws have existed side by side, in fact interfered with, embarrassed, or impeded the enforcement of the Smith Act. The significance of this absence of conflict in administration or enforcement of the federal and state sedition laws will be appreciated when it is realized that this period has included the stress of wartime security requirements and the federal investigation and prosecution under the Smith Act of the principal national and regional Communist leaders." Id., at 30-31.

Mere fear by courts of possible difficulties does not seem to us in these circumstances a valid reason for ousting a State from exercise of its police power. Those are matters for legislative determination.

Finally, and this one point seems in and of itself decisive, there is an independent reason for reversing the Pennsylvania Supreme Court. The Smith Act appears in Title 18 of the United States Code, which Title codifies the federal criminal laws. Section 3231 of that Title provides:

"Nothing in this title shall be held to take away or impair the jurisdiction of the courts of the several States under the laws thereof." That declaration springs from the federal character of our Nation. It recognizes the fact that maintenance of order and fairness rests primarily with the States. The section was first enacted in 1825 and has appeared successively in the federal criminal laws since that time. This Court has interpreted the section to mean that States may provide concurrent legislation in the absence of explicit congressional intent to the contrary. Sexton v. California, 189 U.S. 319, 324-325. The majority's position in this case cannot be reconciled with that clear authorization of Congress. . . ."[s]

NOTE Federal Preemption

1. A number of bills were introduced into the Congress as responses to the Nelson decision. None achieved enactment into law. Perhaps typical was H.R. 486, Jan 7, 1959: "Section 1. No Act of Congress shall be construed as indicating an intent on the part of Congress to occupy the field in which such Act operates, to the exclusion of all State laws on the same subject matter, unless such Act contains an express provision to that effect. No Act of Congress shall be construed as invalidating a provision of State law which would be valid in the absence of such Act unless there is a direct and positive conflict between an express provision of such Act and such provision of State law so that the two cannot be reconciled or consistently stand together. . . ." Cf. Note, State Control of Subversion: A Problem in Federalism, 66 Harv. L. Rev. 327 (1952).

2. The intricate interrelationships of federal and state labor legislation have resulted in extensive litigation, numerous Supreme Court decisions, a certain amount of amendatory legislation, and a growing legal literature. Many of the problems are canvassed, and much of the literature is referred to, in Michelman, State Power to Govern Concerted Employee Activities, 74 Harv. L. Rev. 641 (1961); Meltzer, The Supreme Court, Congress, and State Jurisdiction over Labor Relations, 59 Colum. L. Rev. 6, 269 (1959).

For the impact of federal labor legislation upon an eligibility provision of the Florida Unemployment Compensation Law, see Nash v. Industrial Commission, 389 U.S. 235 (1967).

3. For decisions involving the interaction of federal and state statutes and regulations in other areas, see: Kesler v. Department of Public Safety, 369 U.S. 153 (1962), involving Utah's Motor Vehicle Safety Responsibility Act and the federal Bankruptcy Act; Free v. Bland, 369 U.S. 663 (1962), involving Treasury Regulations with respect to the terms of issuance and transfer of United States Savings Bonds, and the Texas community property law; Campbell v. Hussey, 368 U.S. 297 (1961), and Florida Lime & Avocado Growers, Inc. v. Paul, 373 U.S. 132 (1963), involving state and federal controls of agricultural products; Sperry v. Florida ex rel. Florida Bar, 373 U.S. 379 (1963), and Keller v. Wisconsin ex rel. State Bar of Wisconsin, 374 U.S. 102 (1963), both involving state control of the practice of law and authorization to act in a representative capacity before or in respect of federal administrative agencies; see further with respect to the Keller case, 21 Wis. 2d 100 (1963), cert. denied, 377 U.S. 964 (1964). United States v. Yazell, 382 U.S. 341 (1966), involving state law of coverture and a contract with a federal agency.

For the effect of federal primacy in foreign affairs and international relations upon a state's escheat law, see Zschernig v. Miller, 389 U.S. 429 (1968).

A provision of the Arizona Motor Vehicle Safety Responsibility Act providing that a judgment arising out of an automobile accident should survive a discharge in bankruptcy was held invalid under the supremacy clause in Perez v. Campbell, 402 U.S. 637 (1971). Kesler v. Department of Public Safety, 369 U.S. 153 (1962), was discredited and distinguished. Justices Blackmun, Harlan and Stewart, and Chief Justice Burger, dissented.

On the preemptive effect of federal patent legislation, compare Sears, Roebuck & Co. v. Stiffel Co., 376 U.S. 225 (1964), holding that state unfair competition laws cannot be used to prohibit copying of an unpatentable article, with Kewanee Oil Co. v. Bicron

---

[s] Cf. Uphaus v. Wyman, 360 U.S. 72 (1959). — Ed.

Corp., 416 U.S. 740 (1974), holding that state trade secrets laws are not preempted by federal patent legislation.

In City of Burbank v. Lockheed Air Terminal, Inc., 411 U.S. 624 (1973), the Court struck down a city ordinance making it unlawful for jet aircraft to take off from the city airport between the hours of 11 P.M. and 7 A.M. The Court found preemption because of the pervasive nature of federal regulation in the area, which reflected the need for a uniform and exclusive system of federal regulation occasioned by the interdependence of safety, efficiency, and noise considerations.

Compare Askew v. American Waterways Operators, Inc., 411 U.S. 325 (1973), sustaining a Florida statute imposing no-fault liability on waterfront oil-handling facilities and ships entering or leaving such facilities for any oil-spill damage to the state, including clean-up costs, or private persons against a preemption challenge based on the federal Water Quality Act, which is concerned only with the recovery of federal clean-up costs and which expressly presupposes a coordinated federal-state effort to deal with coastal oil pollution.

4. When a state statute is held to be overridden, displaced, or otherwise rendered inoperative by virtue of federal legislation, it is often, though perhaps inexactly, said that the state statute has been held to be "unconstitutional." In Swift & Co., Inc. v. Wickham, 382 U.S. 111 (1965), overruling Kesler v. Department of Public Safety, supra, on this point, it was held that in an action in a United States District Court to enjoin the enforcement of a state statute on the ground that it was overridden by a federal statute, the provisions of 28 U.S.C. §2281, which required a three-judge court for the issuance of an injunction on the ground of unconstitutionality, are not applicable. See The Supreme Court, 1965 Term, 80 Harv. L. Rev. 91, 217-220 (1966).

Section D. STATE TAXATION

This section considers the extent to which the states in the federal Union are or are not autonomous in their taxing legislation. The limitations which are imposed on state action in this area spring principally from two sources: (1) the commerce clause, giving sanction to the idea of a national market and to the idea that state legislation, taxing as well as regulatory, should be held unconstitutional if it creates an impediment to access to that market which is deemed inappropriate or excessive; and (2) the due process clause of the Fourteenth Amendment, under which ideas of the restraints, territorial and otherwise, deemed appropriate to the component units of a federal system are given sanction as jurisdictional limitations imposed upon the states. In some instances one source of limitation is and can be clearly differentiated from the other; in other instances the task of differentiation is not undertaken by the judges, and may be one of considerable difficulty. In still other instances the student may come to believe that the sources or reasons for limitation have been confused.

Unfortunately for the sake of brevity, consideration of state taxes in order to determine or test standards of appropriateness within the federal system cannot be a unitary task. Taxes differ greatly. They differ, among other ways, in operation, in economic and political impact (both immediate and ultimate), and in tempo of recurrence. One of the products of these differences is that they differ also in the ease with which, when imposed by a state, they may be fitted into a federal system, and in the strains and frictions they impose upon such a system. In other words, different taxes produce different constitutional problems. If this is true, it is likely that wise and appropriate solutions will also differ. "Apportionment," for example, may be a helpful device in dealing with some property tax and some net income tax problems, while being, perhaps, of more limited usefulness in dealing with sales taxes.

In any event, in considering the constitutional problems created by state taxation, it seems necessary first to analyze the manner in which the particular tax operates. There may be underlying similarities or unities which careful analysis will disclose, but the past warns against a too ready equating of one tax with another. The opinion in Pollock v. Farmers Loan & Trust Co., 157 U.S. 429 (1895), turned on the equating of a tax on property with a tax on the income from property. That questionable identity asserted, the Court proceeded to a decision which required a constitutional amendment for its overturn. And in Brown v. Maryland, supra page 185, the decision, wise and almost inevitable as it now seems, was reached through an opinion which appears to have been one of Chief Justice Marshall's less happy efforts. It is interesting to speculate on what might have been the course of constitutional doctrine and decision had the Chief Justice not discussed a discriminatory license tax in terms more appropriate to property taxation. Had he not done so, the "original package" doctrine might not have emerged to embarrass the Court in Woodruff v. Parham, supra page 188. If not faced by that doctrine, Mr. Justice Miller and the Court might there have reached the same result without the historically questionable limitation on the import-export clause which Woodruff v. Parham imposed. And had that clause been preserved for what was probably its intended function, the student may like to speculate on the possible opinions and decisions in a number of more recent cases, particularly in the field of sales and use taxes. He will of course note, in some of the cases to follow, the distinction which one or more Justices have drawn between cases where the now-restricted import-export clause operates and those where only the commerce clause comes into play.

Because different types of taxes (classification presents its own problems) produce different constitutional questions and perhaps different answers, it has seemed wise to group the cases which are here considered not by doctrinal pronouncement but by the general type of tax involved. Accordingly this section is divided into seven subsections dealing with: (1) fixed-fee license taxes; (2) admeasured license or franchise taxes; (3) property taxes; (4) taxes on transportation; (5) other specific excise taxes; (6) net income taxes; (7) sales, use, and gross receipts taxes. A few words about each group may not be inappropriate at this point.

1. *Fixed-fee license taxes.* It is arguable that these cases should not be considered tax cases at all. (Indeed the York Manufacturing Co. case clearly is not, and Robbins and similar cases have previously been considered with regulatory legislation). They are cases where a state has forbidden doing business within its borders unless a license has first been obtained and a stated fee paid therefor. The early cases were prosecutions for doing business without the required license. Perhaps because of this the Court has usually treated such cases as presenting the simple issue of the state's power to exclude. It has not differentiated in this area between forbidding and conditioning, nor has it been willing to look upon the license fee as an obligation to contribute to the cost of government, without reference to the power to exclude. Certainly these decisions do not mean that successful litigants are exempt from other taxes. This perhaps rigid insistence upon the basic form and architecture of the structure which gives access to the national market has found worthy defense. See Henderson, The Position of Foreign Corporations in American Constitutional Law, c. 7 (1918).

2. *Admeasured license or franchise taxes.* Here, as in subsection 1, the state exacts a tax or fee for the privilege of doing business or for the privilege of doing business in corporate form. But here, in most instances, there is no doubt that the state can exact some fee or tax for a privilege it could withdraw, i.e., doing a local business. Here the problem is usually the amount of fee or tax, which is not a fixed sum, but is measured by property, income, receipts, or the like. Naturally, in terms of dollars, a tax or fee measured by prop-

erty is likely to be similar in amount to a tax at the same rate on property — and so with taxes on income and taxes measured by income. But the subject-measure dichotomy has its own history, and in not every case is the terminology merely an alternative styling of the same dollar burden.

The cases in this subsection constitute only an introduction to, and a sampling of the employment of, the subject-measure dichotomy. It may be observed as it recurs in subsequent sections, at times ignored and at other times dealt with explicitly.

3. *Property taxes.* These cases present problems arising from the imposition, by states or subdivisions thereof, of what is usually an annually recurrent tax on (a) carriers' moving equipment, and (b) moving goods. It may be of interest to note that at times the commerce clause has been invoked, and at other times the due process clause of the Fourteenth Amendment, to fulfill what may be the same function. It may be of interest to determine which is the more appropriate.

In earlier editions of this book, there were also presented cases involving the allocation of value of other non-moving property, tangible and intangible, in multi-state enterprises. Considerations of space have required their elimination, but the student may wish to refer to the following cases for a sampling of the problems: Adams Express Co. v. Ohio State Auditor, 166 U.S. 185 (1897); Fargo v. Hart, 193 U.S. 490 (1904) (with which compare Pittsburgh, C.C. & St. L. Ry. v. Backus, 154 U.S. 421 (1894)); Nashville, C. & St. L. Ry. v. Browning, 310 U.S. 362 (1940) (with which compare Louisville & N.R. Co. v. Public Service Commission, 249 F. Supp. 894 (1966)); Cream of Wheat Co. v. County of Grand Forks, 253 U.S. 325 (1920); Wheeling Steel Corp. v. Fox, 298 U.S. 193 (1936); Wheeling Steel Corp. v. Glander, 337 U.S. 562 (1949).

4. *Taxes on transportation.* These cases involve taxes on the transportation of goods or passengers, or taxes on the receipts from such transportation, or generally imposed gross receipts taxes insofar as they apply to receipts from transportation. As is the case with the problems in subsection 7, the problems are of substantial economic (and perhaps fiscal) importance. They are also, in both instances, difficult and persistent. It may seem strange that this should be so, for the taxes are, for the most part, relatively uncomplex transaction taxes. Yet difficulty persists. It will probably continue to exist (unless disposed of by federal legislation) at least as long as the Court fails even to attempt to articulate the standards by which it judges such taxes. For most of the opinions in both areas are essentially inarticulate. (Not many of the Justices summon history and geography as did Mr. Justice Miller in his dissent in the State Tax on Railway Gross Receipts case.) The frequently used phrases communicate little meaning; "direct burden" has often been derided, and is not precisely descriptive in the absence of a known constitutional geometry. If we substituted "inappropriate" for "direct" it would more frankly disclose itself as a word of judgment, not measure, with the standards employed still inarticulate or undisclosed. "Interstate commerce must pay its way" only restates a problem; the answer is still concealed within a silent determination. Other concepts or ideas, "cumulative burdens" and "apportionment," for example, have been advanced as panacean tests or solutions, but the undifferentiating enthusiasm of their more devoted adherents has neither called for, nor encouraged, functionally critical evaluations.

5. *Other specific excise taxes.* This subsection presents a sampling of problems arising from excises on specific activities or with respect to specific goods.

6. *Net income taxes.* At least three fourths of the states impose some form of tax on or measured by net income. Constitutional challenges have most frequently been addressed to jurisdiction to tax and to the highly variant methods of allocating or apportioning the income of multi-state enterprises. If few of these challenges have been successful, that is not necessarily an indication that the financial, and ultimately economic, problems are not significant.

A word is probably in order to explain why the first case in the subsection on net income taxes is Crew Levick Co. v. Pennsylvania, 245 U.S. 292, a case dealing not with a net income tax but with a tax on gross receipts of wholesalers. The purpose is neither to mystify nor to confuse, but to indicate, by comparison with the United States Glue case that follows, the differing effects that the Court attributed to gross receipts and to net income taxes.

7. *Sales, use, and gross receipts taxes, and responsibility for the collection thereof.* Sales and use taxes, and, to a lesser extent, gross receipts taxes, now constitute a major element in the tax structures of most of the states. Responsibility for collection is usually, by statute, imposed upon the seller. Most of the constitutional problems have arisen with respect to what may be compendiously termed the interstate sale. The problems were long discussed in terms of the commerce clause. More recently, judicial opinions have been cast in terms of jurisdiction, as a function of the due process clause of the Fourteenth Amendment. This is particularly true insofar as the problems concern the responsibility of an extra-state seller to collect and remit a use tax. Comment upon the method of decision has been made above, in paragraph 4, taxes on transportation.

Responsive to Title II of Public Law 86-272, 73 Stat. 555 (1959), infra page 560, as amended, 75 Stat. 41 (1961), a Special Subcommittee of the House Judiciary Committee made an extensive study of the operation of state income taxes, sales and use taxes, capital stock taxes, and gross receipts taxes, and their impact upon manufacturing and mercantile enterprises engaged in interstate commerce. The Report of the Special Subcommittee on State Taxation of Interstate Commerce of the Committee on the Judiciary of the House of Representatives was made in four volumes in 1964 and 1965, appearing as H.R. Rep. No. 1480, 88th Cong., 2d Sess. (1964), and H.R. Rep. Nos. 565 and 952, 89th Cong., 1st Sess. (1965). Volume 4 (H.R. Rep. No. 952) sets forth the recommendations of the subcommittee for legislative action. A bill, H.R. 11798 (1965), embodying those recommendations was filed. After hearings which extended through the first four months of 1966, a revised bill, H.R. 16491 (1966), was favorably reported by the House Judiciary Committee, H.R. Rep. No. 2013, 89th Cong., 2d Sess., too late for action at that session.

1. State Fixed-Fee License Taxes

Robbins v. Shelby County Taxing District *120 U.S. 489, 7 S. Ct. 592, 30 L. Ed. 694 (1887)*

[For the opinion in this case see page 354 supra.]

Browning v. Waycross *233 U.S. 16, 34 S. Ct. 578, 58 L. Ed. 828 (1914)*

MR. CHIEF JUSTICE WHITE delivered the opinion of the court.

The plaintiff in error was charged in a municipal court with violating an ordinance which imposed an annual occupation tax of $25 upon "lightning rod agents or dealers engaged in putting up or erecting lightning rods within the corporate limits" of the City of Waycross. Although admitting that he had carried on the business he pleaded not guilty and defended upon the ground that he had done so as the agent of a St. Louis corporation on whose behalf he had solicited orders for the sale of lightning rods; had received the rods when shipped on such orders from St. Louis and had erected them for the corporation, the price paid for the rods to the corporation including the duty to erect them without further charge. This, it was asserted, constituted the carrying on of interstate commerce

Section D. **State Taxation** 483

which the city could not tax without violating the Constitution of the United States. Although the facts alleged were established without dispute, there was a conviction and sentence and the same result followed from a trial de novo in the Superior Court of Ware County where the case was carried by certiorari. On error to the Court of Appeals that judgment was affirmed, the court stating its reasons for doing so in a careful and discriminating opinion reviewing and adversely passing upon the defense under the Constitution of the United States (11 Ga. App. 46). From that judgment this writ of error is prosecuted because of the constitutional question and because under the law of Georgia the Court of Appeals had final authority to conclude the issue.

The general principles by which it has been so frequently determined that a State may not burden by taxation or otherwise the taking of orders in one State for goods to be shipped from another or the shipment of such goods in the channels of interstate commerce up to and including the consummation by delivery of the goods at the point of shipment have been so often stated as to cause them to be elementary and as to now require nothing but a mere outline of the principle. The sole question, therefore, here is whether carrying on the business of erecting lightning rods in the State under the conditions established, was interstate commerce beyond the power of the State to regulate or directly burden. The solution of the inquiry will, we think, be most readily reached by briefly reviewing a few of the more recently decided cases which are relied upon to establish that although the interstate transit of the lightning rods had terminated and they had been delivered at the point of destination to the agent of the seller, the business of subsequently attaching them to the houses, for which they were intended, constituted the carrying on of interstate commerce. The cases relied on are Caldwell v. North Carolina, 187 U.S. 622; Rearick v. Pennsylvania, 203 U.S. 507, and Dozier v. Alabama, 218 U.S. 124.

Caldwell v. North Carolina concerned the validity of an ordinance of the village of Greensboro, imposing a tax upon the business of selling or delivering picture frames, photographs, etc. The question was whether Caldwell, the agent of an Illinois corporation, was liable for this tax because in Greensboro he had taken from a railroad freight office certain packages of frames and pictures which were awaiting delivery and which had been shipped to Greensboro by the selling corporation to its own order for the purpose of filling orders previously obtained by its agents in North Carolina. After the packages of frames and pictures were received by Caldwell, in a room in a hotel, the pictures and frames were fitted together and were delivered to those who had ordered them. The assertion that there was liability for the tax was based on the contention that the act of Caldwell in receiving the pictures and frames and bringing them together was not under the protection of the commerce clause, but was the transaction of local business after the termination of interstate commerce, especially because the pictures and frames had been shipped from Chicago in separate packages and, because the pictures and frames were incomplete on their arrival, and were made complete in the State by the union accomplished after the end of their movement in interstate commerce. Both of these propositions were decided to be unsound and it was adjudged that as both the pictures and frames had been ordered from another State and their shipment was the fulfillment of an interstate commerce transaction, the mere fact that they were shipped in separate packages and brought together at the termination of the transit, did not amount to the transaction of business within North Carolina which the State could tax without placing a direct burden upon interstate commerce. In Rearick v. Pennsylvania, where the right to levy a tax was decided not to exist because to sustain it would be a direct burden upon interstate commerce, the only question was whether the form in which certain shipments of goods were made from Ohio into Pennsylvania to fill orders was of such a character as to cause the act of the agent of the shipper, who opened the packages for the purpose of distributing the goods to those for whom they were intended, to amount to the carrying on of business in the State of Pennsylvania. Dozier v. Alabama in substance concerned the principles applied in the two previous cases with the modification that it was there held that because there was no binding obligation on a purchaser to accept the frame which was to accompany a picture ordered from another State and transmitted through interstate commerce, did not take the case out of the previous ruling.

It is evident that these cases when rightly considered, instead of sustaining, serve to refute, the claim of protection under the interstate commerce clause which is here relied upon since the cases were concerned only with merchandise which had moved in interstate commerce and where the transactions which it was asserted amounted to the doing of local business consisted only of acts concerning interstate commerce goods, dissociated from any attempt to connect them with or make them a part in the State of property which had not and could not have been the subject of interstate commerce. Thus, in Caldwell v. North Carolina, the court laid emphasis upon the fact that the shipment of the pictures in interstate commerce in one package and the frames in another was not essential but accidental for the two could have been united at the point of shipment before interstate commerce began as well as be brought together after delivery at the point of destination. And this was also the condition in the Rearick Case. Indeed, it is apparent in all three cases that there was not the slightest purpose to enlarge the scope of interstate commerce so as to cause it to embrace acts and transactions theretofore confessedly local, but simply to prevent the recognized local limitations from being used to put the conceded interstate commerce power in a strait-jacket so as to destroy the possibilities of its being adapted to meet mere changes in the form by which business of an inherently interstate commerce character could be carried on.

We are of the opinion that the court below was right in holding that the business of erecting lightning rods under the circumstances disclosed, was within the regulating power of the State and not the subject of interstate commerce for the following reasons: (a) Because the affixing of lightning rods to houses was the carrying on of a business of a strictly local character, peculiarly within the exclusive control of state authority. (b) Because, besides, such business was wholly separate from interstate commerce, involved no question of the delivery of property shipped in interstate commerce or of the right to complete an interstate commerce transaction, but concerned merely the doing of a local act after interstate commerce had completely terminated. It is true, that it was shown that the contract under which the rods were shipped bound the seller, at his own expense, to attach the rods to the houses of the persons who ordered rods, but it was not within the power of the parties by the form of their contract to convert what was exclusively a local business, subject to state control, into an interstate commerce business protected by the commerce clause. It is manifest that if the right here asserted were recognized or the power to accomplish by contract what is here claimed, were to be upheld, all lines of demarcation between National and state authority would become obliterated, since it would necessarily follow that every kind or form of material shipped from one State to the other and intended to be used after delivery in the construction of buildings or in the making of improvements in any form would or could be made interstate commerce.

Of course we are not called upon here to consider how far interstate commerce might be held to continue to apply to an article shipped from one State to another, after delivery and up to and including the time when the article was put together or made operative in the place of destination in a case where because of some intrinsic and peculiar quality or inherent complexity of the article, the making of such agreement was essential to the accomplishment of the interstate transaction. In saying this we are not unmindful of the fact that some suggestion is here made that the putting up of the lightning rods after delivery by the agent of the seller was so vital and so essential as to render it impossible to contract without an agreement to that effect, a suggestion however which we deem it unnecessary to do more than mention in order to refute it.

Affirmed.

York Manufacturing Co. v. Colley 247 U.S. 21, 38 S. Ct. 430, 62 L. Ed. 963 (1918)

MR. CHIEF JUSTICE WHITE delivered the opinion of the court:

The York Manufacturing Company, a Pennsylvania corporation, sued for the amount due upon a contract for the purchase of ice manufacturing machinery and to foreclose a lien upon the same. By answer the defendants alleged that the plaintiff was a foreign corporation, that it maintained an office and transacted business in Texas without having obtained a permit therefor, and was hence, under Texas statutes, not authorized to prosecute the suit in the courts of the state, and a dismissal was prayed. In reply the plaintiff averred that the contract sued on was interstate commerce and that the state statute, if held to apply, was repugnant to the commerce clause of the Constitution of the United States. At the trial it was shown without dispute that the contract covered an ice plant guaranteed to produce 3 tons of ice a day, consisting of gas compression pumps, a compressor, ammonia condensers, freezing tank and cans, evaporating coals, a brine agitator, and other machinery and accessories, including apparatus for utilizing exhaust steam for making distilled water for filling the ice cans. These parts of machinery, it was provided, were to be shipped from Pennsylvania to the point of delivery in Texas, and were there to be erected and connected. This work, it was stipulated, was to be done under the supervision of an engineer to be sent by the York Manufacturing Company for whose services a fixed per diem charge of $6 was to be paid by the purchasers, and who should have the assistance of mechanics furnished by the purchasers, the supervision to include not only the erection but the submitting of the machinery to a practical test in operation before the obligation to finally receive it would arise. It was, moreover, undisputed that these provisions were carried out; that about three weeks were consumed in erecting the machinery and about a week in practically testing it, when, after a demonstration of its successful operation, it was accepted by the purchasers.

The trial court, not doubting that the contract of sale was interstate commerce, nevertheless concluding that the stipulation as to supervision by an engineer to be sent by the seller was intrastate commerce and wholly separable from the interstate transaction, held that the seller, by carrying out that provision, had engaged in local business in the state, and as the permit required by the state statutes had not been secured, gave effect to the statutes and dismissed the suit. The case is here to review the action of the court below sustaining such conclusion, its judgment being that of the court of last resort of the state, in consequence of the refusal of the supreme court of the state to allow a writ of error. . . .

But we are of opinion this decision was erroneous, whether it be examined from the point of view of what was assumed to be the controlling effect of the ruling in the Waycross Case, or whether it be tested by the elementary doctrines as to what constitutes interstate commerce. In the first place the Waycross Case concerned merely the right of the city of Waycross to collect a charge against a person who was carrying on a business of erecting lightning rods as the agent of one who had sold the rods in another state and shipped them to Waycross under an agreement, after their arrival, to erect them. The case turned exclusively upon the nature and character of the business of erecting lightning rods and the relevant or appropriate relation to interstate commerce of a stipulation in an interstate contract of sale of such rods, providing for their erection when delivery under the sale was made. As it was determined that the business of erecting lightning rods bore no relevant or appropriate relation to the contract made for the sale of such rods, it was decided that the contract for the erection of the rods did not lose its local character simply because it was made a part of an interstate commerce contract for the sale of the rods any more than would a contract for materials with which to build a house cause the building of the house to be a transaction of interstate commerce, and not local business. But the broad distinction which is established by the statement just made between what was decided in the Waycross Case and the question here presented does not rest alone upon the implication resulting from what was under consideration in that case, but, moreover, expressly results from the fact that in the Waycross Case, through abundance of precaution, attention was directed to the fact that the ruling there made was not controlling as to a case where the service to be done in a state as the result of an interstate commerce sale was essentially connected with the subject-matter of the sale; that is, might be made to appropriately inhere in the duty of performance. 233 U. S. 23.

As, in the second place, since the ruling in M'Culloch v. Maryland, 4 Wheat. 316, there has been no doubt that the interstate commerce power embraced that which is relevant or reasonably appropriate to the power granted, so also from such doctrine there can be no doubt that the right to make an interstate commerce contract includes in its very terms the right to incorporate into such contract provisions which are relevant and appropriate to the contract made. The only possible question open, therefore, is, Was the particular provision of the contract for the service of an engineer to assemble and erect the machinery in question at the point of destination and to practically test its efficiency before complete delivery relevant and appropriate to the interstate sale of the machinery? When the controversy is thus brought in last analysis to this issue there would seem to be no room for any but an affirmative answer. Generically this must be unless it can be said that an agreement to direct the assembling and supervision of machinery whose intrinsic value largely depends upon its being united and made operative as a whole is not appropriate to its sale. The consequence of such a ruling, if made in this case, would be particularly emphasized by a consideration of the functions of the machinery composing the plant which was sold, of its complexity, of the necessity of its aggregation and unison with mechanical skill and precision in order that the result of the contract of sale — the ice plant purchased — might come into existence. In its essential principle, therefore, the case is governed by Caldwell v. North Carolina, 187 U. S. 622; Rearick v. Pennsylvania, 203 U. S. 507; and Dozier v. Alabama, 218 U. S. 124. In fact, those cases were relied upon in the Waycross Case as supporting the contention that a mere agreement for the erection of lightning rods in a contract made concerning the shipment of such rods in interstate commerce caused the act of erection to be itself interstate commerce. But the basis upon which the cases were held to be not apposite, that is the local characteristic of the work of putting up lightning rods, not only demonstrates beyond doubt the mistake concerning the ruling as to the Waycross Case which was below committed, but serves unerringly to establish the soundness of the distinction by which the particular question before us is brought within the reach of interstate commerce.

Of course we are concerned only with the case before us; that is, with a contract inherently relating to and intrinsically dealing with the thing sold, — the machinery and all its parts constituting the ice plant. This view must be borne in mind in order to make it clear that what is here said does not concern the subject passed on in General R. Signal Co. v. Virginia, 246 U. S. 500, since in that case the work required to be done by the contract over and above its inherent and intrinsic relation to the subject-matter of the interstate commerce contract involved the performance of duties over which the state had a right to exercise control because of their inherent intrastate character. In fact, the case last referred to, when looked at from a broad point of view, is but an illustration of the principle applied in the Waycross Case to the effect that that which was inherently intrastate did not lose its essential nature because it formed part of an interstate commerce contract to which it had no necessary relation. And this truth by a negative pregnant states the obverse view that that which is intrinsically interstate and immediately and inherently connected with interstate commerce is entitled to the protection of the Constitution of the United States resulting from that relation.

It follows, therefore, that the judgment must be and it is reversed and the case remanded to the court below for further proceedings not inconsistent with this opinion. And it is so ordered.

Mr. Justice Pitney dissents.

NOTE

1. In General Railway Signal Co. v. Virginia, 246 U.S. 500 (1918), referred to in the opinion above and decided only a month earlier, the Court had upheld an order of the Virginia Corporation Commission imposing a fine upon the signal company for doing business in the state without obtaining prior authorization. The company was a New York corporation with a factory at Rochester, N.Y. It manufactured railway signal equipment which it sold and installed. It agreed to furnish materials, supplies, equipment, and labor, to install signals and apparatus along fifty-eight miles of Southern Railway track in Virginia, and to turn over to the railway as a finished job the completed signals system. It was for engaging in this installation operation without state authorization that the fine was imposed. Compare Kansas City Structural Steel Co. v. Arkansas, 269 U.S. 148 (1925).

A similar issue concerning the power to require fixed-fee licenses has been frequently litigated in state courts by a photographic enterprise with headquarters in Tennessee and photographers operating in other states. See, e.g., Olan Mills, Inc. v. Barre, 123 Vt. 478 (1963); Olan Mills, Inc. v. Opelika, 207 F. Supp. 332 (1962); Haden v. Olan Mills, Inc., 273 Ala. 129, 135 So. 2d 388 (1961); Olan Mills, Inc. v. Town of Kingstree, 236 S.C. 535, 115 S.E.2d 52 (1960); Olan Mills, Inc. v. City of Tallahassee, 100 So. 2d 164 (Fla. 1958), cert. denied, 359 U.S. 924 (1959); Commonwealth v. Olan Mills, Inc., 196 Va. 898, 86 S.E.2d 27 (1955); Olan Mills, Inc. v. City of Cape Girardeau, 364 Mo. 1089, 272 S.W.2d 244 (1954); Graves v. State, 258 Ala. 359, 62 So. 2d 446 (1953); State v. Mobley, 234 N.C. 55, 66 S.E.2d 12 (1951).

Compare Dunbar-Stanley Studios, Inc. v. Alabama, 393 U.S. 537 (1969), with these decisions in state courts involving Olan Mills, Inc. See Note, page 362 supra.

2. In the York Manufacturing Co. case, the Court deals with the matter in the context of prior decisions as though the statute (Tex. Rev. Stat. 1911, art. 1314) required the payment of a fee in order to obtain a permit to do business in the state. As a matter of fact, the statute required only that any foreign corporation desiring to transact business in the state file with the Secretary of State a copy of its articles of incorporation, an affidavit concerning its capitalization, and an affidavit that it was not acting in restraint of trade; thereupon the Secretary was directed to issue the required permit. In Union Brokerage Co. v. Jensen, 322 U.S. 202 (1944), the Court, while purporting not to pass upon Minnesota's taxing power, upheld a Minnesota licensing statute insofar as it denied access to Minnesota courts to a foreign corporation transacting business in the state unless it (1) had filed a certificate giving certain information about its origin, activities, and officers and appointing an agent upon whom process might be served and (2) had paid a fee characterized by the Supreme Court as "no larger in amount than is reasonably required to defray the expense of administering the regulations." The brokerage company's business activity in Minnesota was that of a federally licensed and regulated customhouse broker. The trial court found, and the Supreme Court accepted the finding, that such activity "aids in the collection of customs duties and facilitates the free flow of commerce between a foreign country and the United States"; the Supreme Court appears to have proceeded upon the assumption that the company was therefore engaged solely in foreign commerce. For treatment of a similar problem, compare Eli Lilly & Co. v. Sav-On Drugs, Inc., 366 U.S. 276 (1961).

3. The Port of Mobile, Alabama, required telegraph companies operating in the city to have a license, obtainable by payment of a fee of $225, and made operating without a license a misdemeanor. The local agent of the Western Union Telegraph Company was prosecuted for operating without a license, and was fined $5. In a suit to recover the

amount of the fine it appeared that the telegraph company transmitted messages to and from points within Alabama, as well as to and from points outside the state. The Supreme Court gave judgment against the Port of Mobile, saying, ". . . it is argued that a portion of the telegraph company's business is internal to the State of Alabama, and therefore taxable by the State. But that fact does not remove the difficulty. The tax affects the whole business without discrimination. . . ." Leloup v. Port of Mobile, 127 U.S. 640 (1888). The result was that as against an enterprise engaged in both local and interstate business, the licensing statute could be enforced only if it was explicit in requiring a license for doing local business. The instruction in draftsmanship which this forced upon state and municipal legislators at times resulted in somewhat Pyrrhic victories for taxpayers. Allen v. Pullman's Palace Car Co., 191 U.S. 171 (1903), dealt with a series of Tennessee licensing statutes. The first, requiring a license fee of $50 for each sleeping car run or used on railroads in Tennessee, was held ineffective when it was shown that each car was used at least in part in interstate commerce. The second, requiring a $500 license fee from sleeping car companies doing business in the state, on each car, was ineffective for the same reason. A later statute, however, was completely explicit, and it was upheld. It imposed a tax on "Sleeping car companies . . . for one or more passengers taken up at one point in this state and delivered at another point in this state, and transported wholly within the state, per annum, $3,000." The Court thought it of no controlling significance that the local business constituted but a small proportion of the entire business of the company within the state.

The rigors of explicit draftsmanship which the so-called Leloup rule imposed were subject to relaxation in cases reaching the Supreme Court from the state courts if the latter would impute to the legislature enacting an apparently undifferentiating licensing statute, a purpose to exact the license fee only with respect to local business. In Raley & Bros. v. Richardson, 264 U.S. 157 (1924), the Supreme Court observed that "The state courts, by whose construction we are bound, held that the statute did not apply to interstate business; and we consider it as though it so provided in terms."

In Sprout v. South Bend, 277 U.S. 163 (1928), and in Cooney v. Mountain States Tel. & Tel. Co., 294 U.S. 384 (1935), the Court followed the Leloup decision in holding ineffective undifferentiating licensing requirements as applied, in the first case, to a bus operator operating both locally and interstate, and in the second, to each telephone instrument where it was shown that each instrument was available for, and probably used in, interstate and foreign communication as well as for local calls. In the former case, Mr. Justice Brandeis summed up the doctrinal position as follows: "A state may, by appropriate legislation, require payment of an occupation tax from one engaged in both intrastate and interstate commerce. . . . And it may delegate a part of that power to a municipality. . . . But in order that the fee or tax shall be valid, it must appear that it is imposed solely on account of the intrastate business; that the amount exacted is not increased because of the interstate business done; that one engaged exclusively in interstate commerce would not be subject to the imposition; and that the person taxed could discontinue the intrastate business without withdrawing also from the interstate business. . . ." The requirement last stated that a person be able to discontinue the intrastate business without withdrawing from the interstate, appears to have arisen when a common carrier engaged in interstate business asserted that the state imposed upon it a legal compulsion to carry local passengers, and then sought to use the local business as a basis for the exaction of a license fee. See Pullman Co. v. Adams, 189 U.S. 420 (1903), and Allen v. Pullman's Palace Car Co., supra. In Pacific Tel. & Tel. Co. v. State Tax Commission, 297 U.S. 403 (1936), the Court considered, as a basis for resisting a license tax on doing a local business, a claim that it was not economically feasible to engage in the interstate operation without engaging in the local business as well. It appears to have found that the claim was not effectively proven; it does not appear to have rejected the premise that this was a relevant consideration.

The Leloup doctrine appears to have been at least departed from, and perhaps tacitly overruled, in two Supreme Court decisions. To put at least the first of those in its proper setting, it should be pointed out that the Court has long upheld the authority of a state to exact a registration or license fee from the operators of motor vehicles using its highways, and this even though the operator and vehicle were engaged exclusively in interstate commerce. Hendrick v. Maryland, 235 U.S. 610 (1915); Clark v. Poor, 274 U.S. 554 (1927). Since such a charge against an interstate operator is sustained as compensation for use of the highways, the Court has held that it will not be upheld against such an operator if it is shown to have no reasonable relation to the privilege of using the highways. Interstate Transit, Inc. v. Lindsay, 283 U.S. 183 (1931); McCarroll v. Dixie Greyhound Lines, supra page 434. But the Court has been tolerant in finding such a reasonable relation; perhaps the most notable example is Capitol Greyhound Lines v. Brice, 339 U.S. 542 (1950), where the Court upheld, as against an operator of large buses traversing some nine miles of Maryland highways on a fixed route between Washington and Cincinnati, a tax or fee based upon the fair market value of each vehicle. Mr. Justice Frankfurter, in a dissenting opinion, collects and analyzes the earlier decisions.

In Bode v. Barrett, 344 U.S. 583 (1953), a group of truck operators, some of whom operated partly in interstate commerce, sought to enjoin enforcement of a 1951 amendment to the Illinois Motor Vehicle Act, asserting, among other things, that the license fee was unreasonably high and bore no fair relation to the use of the highways. In denying relief, Mr. Justice Douglas, for the majority of the Court, wrote in part: "The main emphasis of the argument is on the Commerce Clause. . . . We do not stop to analyze the evidence tendered by appellants. For we do not reach the issue in this case. It is true that some of the appellants are interstate carriers. But it is also true that each of the interstate carriers does an intrastate business as well. . . . No showing has been made by any of the appellants that the tax bears no reasonable relation to the use he makes of the highways in his intrastate oprations." In dissenting from this disposition of the case Justices Frankfurter and Jackson protested that the decision marked a departure from Leloup v. Port of Mobile, supra.

In Chicago v. Willett Co., 344 U.S. 574 (1953), decided on the same day as Bode v. Barrett, the Court, in an opinion by Mr. Justice Frankfurter for the majority, upheld a Chicago license tax on carters, applied to a truck operator transporting goods both within Chicago and in interstate commerce. The opinion appears to have relied in part on the opinion of the Supreme Court of Illinois, apparently interpreted as having stated that the tax was solely on intracity trucking. The opinion of the Supreme Court of Illinois (409 Ill. 480, 101 N.E.2d 205) appears by no means explicit to that effect. Mr. Justice Douglas, citing Sprout v. South Bend, supra, dissented on the ground that "The interstate business, by increasing the number of trucks operated by respondent, therefore increases the amount of the tax." For comment on these decisions see Note, The Supreme Court, 1952 Term, 67 Harv. L. Rev. 91, 125-128 (1953).

2. Admeasured License or Franchise Taxes

Maine v. Grand Trunk Ry. *142 U.S. 217, 12 S. Ct. 121, 35 L. Ed. 994 (1891)*

The defendant is a corporation created under the laws of Canada, and has its principal place of business at Montreal, in that province. Its railroad in Maine was constructed by the Atlantic and St. Lawrence Railroad Company, under a charter from that State, which authorized it to construct and operate a railroad from the city of Portland to the boundary line of the State; and, with the permission of New Hampshire and Vermont, it constructed a railroad from that city to Island Pond, in Vermont, a distance of 149½ miles, of which 82½ miles are within the State of Maine. In March, 1853, that company leased its rights and privileges to the defendant, the Grand Trunk Railway Company, which had obtained legislative permission to take the same; and since then it has operated that road and used its franchises.

A statute of Maine, passed in 1881, enacted that every corporation, person, or association, operating a railroad in the State, should pay to the state treasurer, for the use of the State, "an annual excise tax for the privilege of exercising its franchises" in the State, and it provided that the amount of such tax should be ascertained as follows: "The amount of the gross transportation receipts, as returned to the railroad commissioners for the year ending on the thirtieth of September next preceding the levying of such tax, shall be divided by the number of miles of railroad operated to ascertain the average gross receipts per mile; when such average receipts per mile shall not exceed twenty-two hundred and fifty dollars, the tax shall be equal to one quarter of one per centum of the gross transportation receipts; when the average receipts per mile exceed twenty-two hundred and fifty dollars, and do not exceed three thousand dollars, the tax shall be equal to one half of one per centum of the gross receipts; and so on increasing the rate of the tax one quarter of one per centum for each additional seven hundred and fifty dollars of average gross receipts per mile or fractional part thereof, *provided*, the rate shall in no event exceed three and one quarter per centum. When a railroad lies partly within and partly without this State, or is operated as a part of a line or system extending beyond this State, the tax shall be equal to the same proportion of the gross receipts in this State, as herein provided, and its amount determined as follows: the gross transportation receipts of such railroad, line, or system, as the case may be, over its whole extent. within and without the State, shall be divided by the total number of miles operated, to obtain the average gross receipts per mile, and the gross receipts in this State shall be taken to be the average gross receipts per mile, multiplied by the number of miles operated within this State." . . .

MR. JUSTICE FIELD, after stating the case, delivered the opinion of the court:

The tax, for the collection of which this action is brought, is an excise tax upon the defendant corporation for the privilege of exercising its franchises within the State of Maine. It is so declared in the statute which imposes it; and that a tax of this character is within the power of the State to levy there can be no question. . . . The privilege of exercising the franchises of a corporation within a State is generally one of value, and often of great value, and the subject of earnest contention. It is natural, therefore, that the corporation should be made to bear some proportion of the burdens of government. As the granting of the privilege rests entirely in the discretion of the State, whether the corporation be of domestic or foreign origin, it may be conferred upon such conditions, pecuniary or otherwise, as the State in its judgment may deem most conducive to its interests or policy. It may require the payment into its treasury, each year, of a specific sum, or may apportion the amount exacted according to the value of the business permitted, as disclosed by its gains or receipts of the present or past years. The character of the tax, or its validity, is not determined by the mode adopted in fixing its amount for any specific period or the times of its payment. The whole field of inquiry into the extent of revenue from sources at the command of the corporation, is open to the consideration of the State in determining what may be justly exacted for the privilege. The rule of apportioning the charge to the receipts of the business would seem to be eminently reasonable and likely to produce the most satisfactory results, both to the State and the corporation taxed.

The court below held that the imposition of the taxes was a regulation of commerce, interstate and foreign, and therefore in conflict with the exclusive power of Congress in that respect; and on that ground alone it ordered judgment for the defendant. This ruling was founded upon the assumption that a reference by the statute to the transportation receipts and to a certain percentage of the same in determining the amount of the excise tax, was in effect the imposition of the tax upon such receipts, and therefore an interference with interstate and foreign commerce. But a resort to those receipts was simply to ascertain the value of the business done by the corporation, and thus obtain a guide to a reasonable conclusion as to the amount of the excise tax which should be levied; and we are unable to perceive in that resort any interference with transportation, domestic or foreign, over the road of the railroad company, or any regulation of commerce which consists in such transportation. If the amount ascertained were specifically imposed as the tax, no objection to its validity would be pretended. And if the inquiry of the State as to the value of the privilege were limited to receipts of certain past years instead of the year in which the tax is collected, it is conceded that the validity of the tax would not be affected; and if not, we do not see how a reference to the results of any other year could affect its character. There is no levy by the statute on the receipts themselves, either in form or fact; they constitute, as said above, simply the means of ascertaining the value of the privilege conferred. . . .

The case of Philadelphia & S.S.S. Co. v. Pennsylvania, 122 U.S. 326, in no way conflicts with this decision. That was the case of a tax, in terms, upon the gross receipts of a steamship company, incorporated under the laws of the State, derived from the transportation of persons and property between different states and to and from foreign countries. Such tax was held, without any dissent, to be a regulation of interstate and foreign commerce, and, therefore, invalid. We do not question the correctness of that decision, nor do the views we hold in this case in any way qualify or impair them.

It follows, from what we have said, that the judgment of the court below must be reversed and the cause remanded, with directions to enter judgment in favor of the State for the amount of the taxes demanded; and it is so ordered.

MR. JUSTICE BRADLEY, dissenting:

JUSTICES HARLAN, LAMAR, BROWN and myself, dissent from the judgment of the court in this case. We do so both on principle and authority. On principle because, whilst the purpose of the law professes to be to lay a tax upon the foreign company for the privilege of exercising its franchise in the State of Maine, the mode of doing this is unconstitutional. The mode adopted is the laying of a tax on the gross receipts of the company, and these receipts, of course, include receipts for interstate and international transportation between other States and Maine, and between Canada and the United States, Now, if after the previous legislation which has been adopted with regard to admitting the company to carry on business within the State, the Legislature has still the right to tax it for the exercise of its franchises, it should do so in a constitutional manner, and not (as it has done) by a tax on the receipts derived from interstate and international transportation. . . .

. . . The tax, it is true, is called a tax on a franchise. It is so called, but what is it in fact? It is a tax on the receipts of the company derived from international transportation.

This court and some of the state courts have gone a great length in sustaining various forms of taxes upon corporations. The train of reasoning upon which it is founded may be questionable. A corporation, according to this class of decisions, may be taxed several times over. It may be taxed for its charter, for its franchises, for the privilege of carrying on its business. It may be taxed on its capital, and it may be taxed on its property. Each of these taxations may be carried to the full amount of the property of the company. I do not know that jealousy of corporate institutions could be carried much further. This court held that the taxation of the capital stock of the Western Union Telegraph Company in Massachusetts, graduated according to the mileage of lines in that State compared with the lines in all the states, was nothing but a taxation upon the property of the company; yet it was in terms a tax upon its capital stock, and might as well have been a tax upon its gross receipts. By the present decision it is held that taxation may be imposed upon the gross receipts of the company for the exercise of its franchise within the State, if graduated according to the number of miles that the road runs in the State. Then it comes to this: A State may tax a railroad company upon its gross receipts, in proportion to the number of miles run within the State, as a tax on its property; and may also lay a tax upon these same gross receipts in proportion to the same number of miles for the privilege of exercising its franchise in the State. I do not know what else it may not tax the gross receipts for. If the interstate commerce of the country is not, or will not be, handicapped by this course of decision, I do not understand the ordinary principles which govern human conduct.

We dissent from the opinion of the court.

Horn Silver Mining Co. v. New York   143 U.S. 305, 12 S. Ct. 403, 36 L. Ed. 164 (1892)

Mr. Justice Field delivered the opinion of the court:

The defendant below, the plaintiff in error here, the Horn Silver Mining Company, is a corporation created under the laws of the Territory of Utah. The present action is brought by the People of the State of New York, upon the allegation that it was doing business within the State in 1881 and 1882, to recover certain taxes alleged to be chargeable on its "corporate franchise or business" for those years and the penalty prescribed for their non-payment in each year.

By the Act of the Legislature of New York, approved May 26, 1881, amending a previous Act providing for levying taxes for the use of the State upon certain corporations, joint-stock companies, and associations, it was declared that every corporation, joint-stock company, or association then or thereafter incorporated or organized under any law of the State, or of any other State or country, and doing business in the State, with certain specified exceptions not important in this case, should be subject to a tax "upon its corporate franchise or business," to be computed in a mode specified, which was by a certain percentage upon its capital stock measured by the dividend on the par value of that stock, or, where there were no dividends, or its dividends were less than a certain percentage upon the par value of the capital stock, then according to a certain percentage upon the actual value of the capital stock during the year. . . .

The defendant answered the various allegations of the complaint, denying them so far as they charge liability to the people of New York, and setting up that it had been at all times a manufacturing corporation organized and existing under the laws of Utah; that it had never exercised any franchises or powers under the laws of New York; that its capital stock of ten millions of dollars was issued in payment for real estate in Utah and Illinois, which consists entirely of mining property and improvements thereon, and a refinery; that during the years ending November 1st, 1881 and 1882, it carried on in the State of New York the business of manufacturing bars of silver from Utah and Illinois into standard bars; that said business constituted but a small portion of its entire business, and was the only business carried on in the State of New York, except its financial business and correspondence; that its capital stock was only partially employed in New York; and that it paid taxes both in Utah and in Illinois. . . .

Upon the findings of the referee judgment was entered in the supreme court of the State for the amount reported, and the case, being taken to the Court of Appeals, was there affirmed. Being then remitted to the supreme court and entered there, the case was brought, on a writ of error, to this court. . . .

The granting of the rights and privileges which constitute the franchises of a corporation being a matter resting entirely within the control of the Legislature, to be exercised in its good pleasure, it may be accompanied with any such conditions as the Legislature may deem most suitable to the public interests and policy. It may impose as a condition of the grant as well as, also, of its continued exercise, the payment of a specific sum to the State each year, or a portion of the profits or gross receipts of the corporation, and may prescribe such mode in which the sum shall be ascertained as may be deemed convenient and just. There is no constitutional inhibition against the Legislature adopting any mode to arrive at the sum which it will exact as a condition of the creation of the corporation or of its continued existence. There can be, therefore, no possible objection to the validity of the tax prescribed by the statute of New York, so far as it relates to its own corporations. Nor can there be any greater objection to a similar tax upon a foreign corporation doing business by its permission within the State. As to a foreign corporation — and all corporations in states other than the State of its creation are deemed to be foreign corporations — it can claim a right to do business in another State to any extent, only subject to the conditions imposed by its laws.

As said in Paul v. Virginia, 8 Wall. 168, 181, "the recognition of its existence even by other states, and the enforcement of its contracts made therein, depend purely upon the comity of those states, a comity which is never extended where the existence of the corporation or the exercise of its powers is prejudicial to their interests or repugnant to their policy. Having no absolute right of recognition in other states, but depending for such recognition and the enforcement of its contracts upon their assent, it follows, as a matter of course, that such assent may be granted upon such terms and conditions as those states may think proper to impose. They may exclude the foreign corporation entirely; they may restrict its business to particular localities, or they may exact such security for the performance of its contracts with their citizens as in their judgment will best promote the public interest. The whole matter rests in their discretion."

This doctrine has been so frequently declared by this court that it must be deemed no longer a matter of discussion, if any question can ever be considered at rest.

Only two exceptions or qualifications have been attached to it in all the numerous adjudications in which the subject has been considered, since the judgment of this court was announced more than a half century ago in Bank of Augusta v. Earle, 13 Pet. 519. One of these qualifications is that the State cannot exclude from its limits a corporation engaged in interstate or foreign commerce, established by the decision in Pensacola Teleg. Co. v. Western U. Teleg. Co., 96 U.S. 1, 12. The other limitation on the power of the State is, where the corporation is in the employ of the general government, an obvious exception, first stated, we think by the late Mr. Justice Bradley in Stockton v. Baltimore & N.Y.R. Co., 32 Fed. Rep. 9, 14. . . .

Having the absolute power of excluding the foreign corporation the State may, of course, impose such conditions upon permitting the corporation to do business within its limits as it may judge expedient; and it may make the grant or privilege dependent upon the payment of a specific license tax, or a sum proportioned to the amount of its capital. . . .

Judgment affirmed.

MR. JUSTICE HARLAN dissented.

Western Union Telegraph Co. v. Kansas 216 U.S. 1, 30 S. Ct. 190, 54 L. Ed. 355 (1910)

This action was brought by the state of Kansas in one of its courts against the Western Union Telegraph Company, a New York corporation, to obtain a decree ousting and restraining that corporation from doing, in Kansas, any telegraphic business that was wholly internal to that state, and not pursuant to some arrangement or to meet its contracts with, or obligations to, the government of the United States. Upon . . . a demurrer to the answer, a final decree was rendered, prohibiting and enjoining the telegraph company from transacting intrastate business in Kansas as a corporation, the decree, however, not to affect the company's duties to or contracts with the United States. From that decree the present writ of error was prosecuted.

The state contends that the decree is in exact conformity with certain provisions of the Kansas statutes . . . Those provisions, . . . known as the Bush act [contain] . . . these important sections: "Each corporation which has received authority from the charter board to organize shall, before filing its charter with the secretary of state, as provided by law, pay to the state treasurer of Kansas, *for the benefit of the permanent school fund*, a charter fee *of ¹/₁₀ of 1 per cent of its authorized capital*, upon the first $100,000 *of its capital stock, or any part thereof*; and upon the next $400,000, or any part thereof, ¹/₂₀ *of 1 per cent*; and for each million or major part thereof over and above the sum of $500,000, $200. . . . All the provisions of this act, including the payment of the fees herein provided, shall apply to *foreign* corporations *seeking to do business in this state*, . . ."

The company refused to pay the fee thus required, and continued, as before, to do telegraph business of all kinds in Kansas. Thereupon the present action was brought, the sole ground of complaint being that, in consequence of the failure of the telegraph company to pay the charter fee of $20,100, it was without authority to continue doing any *intra*state or local business in Kansas. . . .

MR. JUSTICE HARLAN, after making the above statement, delivered the opinion of the court: . . .

The contentions of the company, to which particular attention will be directed, are, in substance, that the requirement that it pay, for the benefit of the permanent school fund of the state, *a given per cent of its authorized capital*, wherever and however employed, as a *condition* of its right to continue to do domestic business in Kansas, is a regulation which, by its necessary operation directly burdens or embarrasses interstate commerce, and therefore is illegal under the commerce clause of the Constitution; further, that such a requirement involves the taxation not only of the company's interstate business everywhere, but equally the property employed by it beyond the limits of the state, — a thing which could not be done consistently with the due process of law enjoined by the 14th Amendment. . . .

Looking, then, at the natural and reasonable effect of the statute, disregarding mere forms of expression, it is clear that the making of the payment by the telegraph company, as a charter fee, of a given per cent *of its authorized capital*, representing, as that capital clearly does, *all* of its business and property, both within and *outside of the state*, a *condition* of its right to do local business in Kansas, is, in its essence, not simply a tax for the privilege of doing local business in the state, but a burden and tax on the company's interstate business and on its property located or used outside of the state. The express words of the statute leave no doubt as to what is the *basis* on which the fee specified in the state statute rests. That fee, plainly, is not based on such of the company's capital stock as is represented in its local business and property in Kansas. The requirement is a given per cent of the company's authorized capital; that is, all its capital, wherever or however employed, whether in the United States or in foreign countries, and whatever may be the extent of its lines in Kansas as compared with its lines outside of that state. What part of the fee exacted is to be attributed to the company's domestic business in Kansas and what part to interstate business, the state has not chosen to ascertain and declare in the statute. It strikes at the company's entire business, wherever conducted, and its property, wherever located, and, in terms, makes it a *condition* of the telegraph company's right to transact purely local business in Kansas that it shall contribute, for the benefit of the state school fund, a given per cent of its whole authorized capital, representing all of its property and all its business and interests everywhere. . . .

But it is said to be well settled that a state, in the exercise of its reserved powers, may prescribe the *terms* on which a foreign corporation, whatever the nature of its business, may enter and do business within its limits.

It is true that, in many cases, the *general* rule has been laid down that a state may, if it chooses to do so, exclude foreign corporations from its limits, or impose such terms and conditions on their doing business in the state as, in its judgment, may be consistent with the interests of the people. But those were cases in which the particular foreign corporation before the court was engaged in ordinary business, and not directly or regularly in interstate or foreign commerce. . . .

Whatever may be the extent of the state's authority over intrastate business, was it competent for the state to require that the telegraph company, — which surely had the right to enter and remain in the state for interstate business, — as a *condition* of its right to continue doing domestic business in Kansas, should pay, in the form of a fee, a specified per cent of its capital stock representing the interests, property, and operations of the company not only in Kansas, but throughout the United States and foreign countries? Is such a regulation consistent with the power of Congress to regulate commerce among the states, or with rights growing out of such commerce, and secured by the Constitution of the United States? Can the state, in this way, relieve its own treasury from the burden of supporting its public schools, and put that burden, in whole or in part, upon the interstate business and property of foreign corporations? Can such a regulation be deemed constitutional any more than one requiring the company, as a condition of its doing intrastate business, that it should surrender its right, for instance, to invoke the protection of the Constitution when it is proposed to deprive it of its property without due process of law, or to deny it the equal protection of the laws? . . . If a domestic corporation engaged in the business of soliciting orders for goods manufactured, sold, and delivered in a state should, in addition, solicit orders for goods manufactured in and to be brought from another state for delivery, could the former state make it a *condition* of the right to engage in local business within its limits that the corporation pay a given per cent of *all* fees or commissions received by it in its business, interstate and domestic? There can be but one answer to this question, namely, that such a condition would operate as a direct burden on interstate commerce, and therefore would be unconstitutional and void. Consistently with the Constitution no court could, by any form of decree, recognize or give effect to or enforce such a condition.

We repeat that the statutory requirement that the telegraph company shall, as a condition of its right to engage in local business in Kansas, first pay into the state school fund a given per cent of its authorized capital, representing all its business and property everywhere, is a burden on the company's interstate commerce and its privilege to engage in that commerce, in that it makes both such commerce, as conducted by the company, and its property outside of the state, contribute to the support of the state's schools. Such is the necessary effect of the statute, and that result cannot be avoided or concealed by calling the exaction of such a per cent of its capital stock a "fee" for the privilege of doing local business. To hold otherwise, is to allow form to control substance. It is easy to be seen that if every State should pass a statute similar to that enacted by Kansas not only the freedom of interstate commerce would be destroyed, the decisions of this court nullified and the business of the country thrown into confusion, but each State would continue to meet its own local expenses not only by exactions that directly burdened such commerce, but by taxation upon property situated beyond its limits. We cannot fail to recognize the intimate connection which, at this day, exists between the interstate business done by interstate companies and the local business which, for the convenience of the people, must be done or can generally be better and more economically done by such interstate companies rather than by domestic companies organized to conduct only local business. . . .

We need not stop to discuss at length the specific question whether the state can, by any regulation, make the property of the company, outside of Kansas, contribute directly to the support of its schools; such being the effect of the requirement that it pay into the state treasury, for the benefit of the state school fund, a given per cent of all its capital stock as a condition of its doing local business in Kansas. It is firmly established that, consistently with the due-process clause of the Constitution of the United States, a state cannot tax property located or existing permanently beyond its limits. . . .

. . . The right of the telegraph company to continue the transaction of local business in Kansas could not be made to depend upon its submission to a condition prescribed by that state, which was hostile both to the letter and spirit of the Constitution. The company was not bound, under any circumstances, to surrender its constitutional exemption from state taxation, direct or indirect, in respect of its interstate business and its property outside of the state, any more than it would have been bound to surrender any other right secured by the national Constitution. . . .

The judgment of the Supreme Court of Kansas is reversed and the cause remanded for such proceedings as may be consistent with this opinion.

Reversed.

MR. JUSTICE WHITE, concurring:

It is shown that the telegraph company, many years ago, went into the state of Kansas, constructed its lines, established its offices, etc., and has since been engaged in business, both interstate and local. It is not disputed that there was no law in the state forbidding the company from doing as it did. . . . In other words, this case involves determining, not how far a state may arbitrarily exclude, but to what extent, after allowing a corporation to come in and acquire property, a state may take its property within the state without compensation, upon the theory that the corporation is not in the state, and has no property right therein which is not subject to confiscation. The difference between the premise upon which the proposition contended for rests and the situation here presented seems to me self-evident. . . .

Resting, as I do, my concurrence in the decree in this case upon the grounds just previously stated, it becomes unnecessary for me to say anything concerning the wider ground upon which the opinion of the court proceeds, but I do not wish to be understood as dissenting in any respect from the fundamental principle which the opinion of the court embodies and applies.

MR. JUSTICE HOLMES, dissenting:

I think that the judgment of the supreme court of Kansas was right, and it will not take me long to give my reasons. I assume that a state cannot tax a corporation on commerce carried on by it with another state, or on property outside the jurisdiction of the taxing state, and I assume further that, for that reason, a tax on or measured by the value of the total stock of a corporation like the Western Union Telegraph Company is void. But I also assume that it is not intended to deny or overrule what has been regarded as unquestionable since Bank of Augusta v. Earle, 13 Pet. 439, that, as to foreign corporations seeking to do business wholly within a state, that state is the master, and may prohibit or tax such business at will. . . .

Now what has Kansas done? She has not undertaken to tax the Western Union. She has not attempted to impose an absolute liability for a single dollar. She simply has said to the company that, if it wants to do local business, it must pay a certain sum of money, just as Mississippi said to the Pullman Company that, if it wanted to carry on local traffic, it must pay a certain sum. It does not matter if the sum is extravagant. Even in the law the whole generally includes its parts. If the state may prohibit, it may prohibit with the privilege of avoiding the prohibition in a certain way. . . .

What I have said shows, I think, the fallacy involved in talking about unconstitutional conditions. Of course, if the condition was the making of a contract contrary to the policy of the Constitution of the United States, the contract would be void. That was all that was decided in Southern P. Co. v. Denton, 146 U.S. 202. But it does not follow that, if keeping the contract was made a condition of staying in the state, the condition would be void. I confess my inability to understand how a condition can be unconstitutional when attached to a matter over which a state has absolute arbitrary power. This court was equally unable to understand it in Horn Silver Min. Co. v. New York, 143 U.S. 305, 315, ...

THE CHIEF JUSTICE and MR. JUSTICE McKENNA concur in this dissent.

The late MR. JUSTICE PECKHAM took part in the consideration of the case and agreed with the minority.

NOTE Unconstitutional Conditions

1. The decision in Western Union Tel. Co. v. Kansas, supra, was followed two weeks later in Pullman Co. v. Kansas, 216 U.S. 56 (1910), and one month later, with reference to a similar Arkansas statute, in Ludwig v. Western Union Tel. Co., 216 U.S. 146 (1910). In International Paper Co. v. Massachusetts, 246 U.S. 135 (1918), a unanimous Court, on the authority of the above cases, held invalid a Massachusetts statute imposing upon foreign corporations a franchise tax measured by entire authorized capital stock, when applied to a New York corporation with less than 2 percent of its assets in Massachusetts. Compare Hump Hairpin Manufacturing Co. v. Emmerson, 258 U.S. 290 (1922); Air-Way Electric Appliance Corp. v. Day, 266 U.S. 71 (1924); New York v. Latrobe, 279 U.S. 421 (1929).

2. In Terral v. Burke Construction Co., 257 U.S. 529 (1922), the Court held unconstitutional an Arkansas statute which provided for the revocation of a corporation's authority to do business in the state if the corporation removed to the federal courts any suit brought against it in the state courts, or instituted any suit against a citizen of the state in the federal courts. The corporation was a foreign corporation doing business in Arkansas. Its allegation that it was engaged in interstate commerce was denied, and the case was considered on the undenied allegations. On the doctrine of "unconstitutional conditions" see Henderson, The Position of Foreign Corporations in American Constitutional Law 132-147 (1918); Merrill, Unconstitutional Conditions, 77 U. Pa. L. Rev. 879 (1929); Hale, Unconstitutional Conditions and Constitutional Rights, 35 Colum. L. Rev. 321 (1935); Note, Unconstitutional Conditions, 73 Harv. L. Rev. 1595 (1960).

3. In Atlantic Refining Co. v. Virginia, 302 U.S. 22 (1937), the Court unanimously upheld a Virginia statute imposing upon foreign corporations seeking authority to do intrastate business an "entrance fee" graduated according to the corporation's authorized capital stock. The Court (Brandeis, J.) differentiated Western Union v. Kansas and similar decisions by stating that in those cases "The exaction, although called in some of those cases a filing fee, was in each case strictly a tax; for it was imposed after the admittance of the corporation into the State. In the case at bar the situation is different." Suppose the entrance, or admission, fee gives authority to enter and transact business only for a year, or other limited period. Can it be differentiated, as above, only if the statute makes it clear that it is nonrecurrent? Is there any other difference between authority to enter and stay only a limited period and the ordinary annual franchise tax? Cf. Lincoln Life Ins. Co. v. Read, 325 U.S. 673 (1945). And see Note, 51 Harv. L. Rev. 508 (1938).

4. Railway Express Agency, Inc. v. Virginia, 282 U.S. 440 (1931), upheld a Virginia constitutional provision forbidding any foreign corporation to carry on intrastate business as a public service company. See Note, Compulsory Incorporation and the Power to Tax, 44 Harv. L. Rev. 1111 (1931).

5. Are all constitutional "rights" to be treated alike in applying the doctrine of unconstitutional conditions? Consider conditions attached to federal grants to the states; see page 131 supra. May the federal government grant a license for a hydroelectric plant on a navigable river on condition that the government may take the plant after a certain number of years at less than what would be "just compensation"? May a court grant a motion to advance the trial of a case on condition that the moving party waive a jury trial?

Ford Motor Co. v. Beauchamp 308 U.S. 331, 60 S. Ct. 273, 84 L. Ed. 304 (1939)

MR. JUSTICE REED delivered the opinion of the Court:

The question for determination in this proceeding is the validity, as applied to this petitioner, of a statute of the State of Texas levying an annual franchise tax on all corporations chartered or authorized to do business in Texas, measured by a graduated charge upon such proportion of the outstanding capital stock, surplus and undivided profits of the corporation, plus its long term obligations, as the gross receipts of its Texas business bear to the total gross receipts from its entire business.

The Court of Appeals affirmed the judgment of the District Court, upholding the validity of the tax. On account of an alleged probable conflict with the principles underlying certain decisions of this Court certiorari was granted. The applicable provisions of the statute appear below.[3]

. . . This suit was instituted [to recover the tax paid under protest] in the District Court of the United States, Western District, Austin Division, against the state officials authorized to be made defendants. Defendants joined in a demurrer on the ground that no cause of action was set out in the petition.

Petitioner owns and operates a large manufactory of motor vehicles in Michigan and assembly plants in Texas. No parts for the automobiles produced by petitioner are manufactured at any point within Texas. The manufactured parts are shipped to petitioner's assembly plants in Texas and are there assembled. The assembled vehicles are sold in intrastate commerce to various dealers who in turn sell the vehicles to the public. A relatively small number of completed vehicles are shipped into Texas and later sold in intrastate commerce along with large quantities of motor parts and accessories. Without undertaking to be precise, the gross receipts from business done in Texas for the year in question amounted to approximately $34,000,000. Petitioner's total gross receipts were about $888,000,000. The ratio of Texas receipts to total receipts was 3.85+ per cent. Petitioner's total taxable capital was $600,000,000+. The value of all assets located in Texas was somewhat over $3,000,000, while the value of the capital allocated to Texas as a base for taxation by the statutory formula would be in excess of $23,000,000.

For the taxable year beginning May 1, 1936, a franchise tax was tendered Texas in the sum of $1,224, computed on the actual net book value of all of petitioner's assets in Texas. On demand and under protest an additional franchise tax and penalty was paid in the sum of $7,529, based on the allocation to Texas of capital as calculated by the statutory formula. This suit was brought to recover the alleged unlawful exaction.

This exaction, petitioner pleads, is calculated from a formula that results in the levy of a tax on assets used in petitioner's interstate business in violation of Article 1, §8, of the Constitution. It is further alleged that the tax operates to deprive petitioner of its property without due process of law in violation of the Fourteenth Amendment because it must pay a tax on property neither located nor used within the State of Texas and on activities beyond the borders of Texas.

The statute calls the excise a franchise tax. It is obviously payment for the privilege of carrying on business in Texas. There is no question but that the State has the power to make a charge against domestic or foreign corporations for the opportunity to transact this intrastate business. The exploitation by foreign corporations of intrastate opportunities under the protection and encouragement of local government offers a basis for taxation as unrestricted as that for domestic corporations. In laying a local privilege tax, the state sovereignty may place a charge upon that privilege for the protection afforded. When that charge, as here, is based upon the proportion of the capital employed in Texas, calculated

[3] "Article 7084. Amount of Tax. — (A) Except as herein provided, every domestic and foreign corporation heretofore or hereafter chartered or authorized to do business in Texas, shall, . . . each year, pay . . . a franchise tax . . . , based upon that proportion of the outstanding capital stock, surplus and undivided profits, plus the amount of outstanding bonds, notes and debentures, other than those maturing in less than a year from date of issue, as the gross receipts from its business done in Texas bears to the total gross receipts of the corporation from its entire business, which tax shall be computed at the following rates for each One Thousand Dollars ($1,000.00) or fractional part thereof; One Dollar ($1.00) to One Million Dollars ($1,000,000.00), sixty cents (60¢) . . ."

by the percentage of sales which are within the state, no provision of the Federal Constitution is violated.

The motor vehicles for the marketing of which the privilege is used are concededly sold in intrastate commerce. The tax here levied is not for the privilege of engaging in any transaction across state lines or activity carried on in another state. . . .

In a unitary enterprise, property outside the state, when correlated in use with property within the state, necessarily affects the worth of the privilege within the state. Financial power inherent in the possession of assets may be applied, with flexibility, at whatever point within or without the state the managers of the business may determine. For this reason it is held that an entrance fee may be properly measured by capital wherever located. The weight, in determining the value of the intrastate privilege, given the property beyond the state boundaries is but a recognition of the very real effect its existence has upon the value of the privilege granted within the taxing state. This was recognized by this Court in Atlantic & Pacific Tea Co. v. Grosjean [12] where an occupation or license tax on chain stores was graduated "on the number of stores or mercantile establishments" included under the same management "whether operated in this State or not." We said: "The law rates the privilege enjoyed in Louisiana according to the nature and extent of that privilege in the light of the advantages, the capacity, and the competitive ability of the chain's stores in Lousiana considered not by themselves, as if they constituted the whole organization, but in their setting as integral parts of a much larger organization."[13] This same rule applies here. James v. Dravo Contracting Co.[14] contains nothing contrary to this view. The statute under consideration there levied a privilege tax "equal to two per cent of the gross income of the business." In so far as it was upon receipts in other states for work done in other states, it was conceded to be outside of the taxing power of the statute.

Affirmed.[t]

MR. JUSTICE MCREYNOLDS is of opinion that the judgment complained of should be reversed.

MR. JUSTICE BLACK and MR. JUSTICE DOUGLAS concur in the result.

3. Property Taxes

Pullman's Palace Car Co. v. Pennsylvania 141 U.S. 18, 11 S. Ct. 876, 35 L. Ed. 613 (1891)

MR. JUSTICE GRAY delivered the opinion of the court.

This was an action brought by the State of Pennsylvania against Pullman's Palace Car Company, a corporation of Illinois, in the Court of Common Pleas of the county of Dauphin in the State of Pennsylvania, to recover the amount of a tax settled by the auditor general and approved by the treasurer of that State, for the years 1870 to 1880 inclusive, on the defendant's capital stock, taking as the basis of assessment such proportion of its capital stock as the number of miles of railroad over which cars were run by the defendant in Pennsylvania bore to the whole number of miles in this and other States over which its cars were run.

---

[12] 301 U.S. 412, 424, 425.
[13] 301 U.S. 425.
[14] 302 U.S. 134, 139.
[t] Cf. Powell, The Current Current of the Commerce Clause and State Taxation, Proc. Nat. Tax Assn. 1940 (1940) 274, 275, 310-312. See also International Harvester Co. v. Evatt, 329 U.S. 416 (1947).

The cases in the foregoing section deal with the problem of a good subject for the tax and a bad measure; compare the problem of a bad subject and a good measure, pages 552-555 infra. — ED.

All these taxes were levied under successive statutes of Pennsylvania, imposing taxes on capital stock of corporations, incorporated by the laws of Pennsylvania or of any other State, and doing business in Pennsylvania, computed on a certain percentage of dividends made or declared. . . .

A trial by jury was waived, and the case submitted to the decision of the court, which found the following facts: "The defendant is a corporation of the State of Illinois, having its principal office in Chicago. Its business was, during all the time for which tax is charged, to furnish sleeping coaches and parlor and dining-room cars to the various railroad companies with which it contracted on the following terms: The defendant furnished the coaches and cars, and the railroad companies attached and made them part of their trains, no charge being made by either party against the other. The railroad companies collected the usual fare from passengers who travelled in their coaches and cars, and the defendant collected a separate charge for the use of the seats, sleeping berths and other conveniences. Business has been carried on continuously by the defendant in this way in Pennsylvania since February 17, 1870, and it has had about one hundred coaches and cars engaged in this way in the State during that time. The cars used in this State have, during all the time for which tax is charged, been running into, through and out of this State."

Upon these facts the court held "that the proportion of the capital stock of the defendant invested and used in Pennsylvania is taxable under these acts; and that the amount of the tax may be properly ascertained by taking as a basis the proportion which the number of miles operated by the defendant in this State bears to the whole number of miles operated by it, without regard to the question where any particular car or cars were used"; and therefore gave judgment for the State.

That judgment was affirmed, upon writ of error, by the Supreme Court of the State. . . .

Upon this writ of error, whether this tax was in accordance with the law of Pennsylvania is a question on which the decision of the highest court of the State is conclusive. The only question of which this court has jurisdiction is whether the tax was in violation of the clause of the Constitution of the United States granting to Congress the power to regulate commerce among the several States. The plaintiff in error contends that its cars could be taxed only in the State of Illinois, in which it was incorporated and had its principal place of business.

No general principles of law are better settled, or more fundamental, than that the legislative power of every State extends to all property within its borders, and that only so far as the comity of that State allows can such property be affected by the law of any other State. The old rule, expressed in the maxim *mobilia sequuntur personam,* by which personal property was regarded as subject to the law of the owner's domicil, grew up in the Middle Ages, when movable property consisted chiefly of gold and jewels, which could be easily carried by the owner from place to place, or secreted in spots known only to himself. In modern times, since the great increase in amount and variety of personal property, not immediately connected with the person of the owner, that rule has yielded more and more to the lex situs, the law of the place where the property is kept and used. Green v. Van Buskirk, 5 Wall. 307, and 7 Wall. 139; . . . Story on Conflict of Laws, § 550; Wharton on Conflict of Laws, §§ 297-311. As observed by Mr. Justice Story, in his commentaries just cited, "although movables are for many purposes to be deemed to have no situs, except that of the domicil of the owner, yet this being but a legal fiction, it yields, whenever it is necessary for the purpose of justice that the actual situs of the thing should be examined. A nation within whose territory any personal property is actually situate has an entire dominion over it while therein, in point of sovereignty and jurisdiction, as it has over immovable property situate there."

For the purposes of taxation, as has been repeatedly affirmed by this court, personal property may be separated from its owner; and he may be taxed, on its account, at the place where it is, although not the place of his own domicil, and even if he is not a citizen or a resident of the State which imposes the tax. Lane County v. Oregon, 7 Wall. 71, 77. . . .

It is equally well settled that there is nothing in the Constitution or laws of the United States which prevents a State from taxing personal property within its jurisdiction. Delaware Railroad Tax, 18 Wall. 206, 232. . . .

Ships or vessels, indeed, engaged in interstate or foreign commerce upon the high seas, or other waters which are a common highway, and having their home port, at which they are registered under the laws of the United States, at the domicil of their owners in one State, are not subject to taxation in another State at whose ports they incidentally and temporarily touch for the purpose of delivering or receiving passengers or freight. But that is because they are not, in any proper sense, abiding within its limits, and have no continuous presence or actual situs within its jurisdiction, and, therefore, can be taxed only at their legal situs, their home port and the domicil of their owners. Hays v. Pacific Mail Steamship Co., 17 How. 596. . . .

Between ships and vessels, having their situs fixed by act of Congress, and their course over navigable waters, and touching land only incidentally and temporarily; and cars or vehicles of any kind, having no situs so fixed, and traversing the land only, the distinction is obvious. . . .

The tax now in question is not a license tax or a privilege tax; it is not a tax on business or occupation; it is not a tax on, or because of, the transportation, or the right of transit, of persons or property through the State to other States or countries. The tax is imposed equally on corporations doing business within the State, whether domestic or foreign, and whether engaged in interstate commerce or not. The tax on the capital of the corporation, on account of its property within the State, is, in substance and effect, a tax on that property. Gloucester Ferry Co. v. Pennsylvania, 114 U.S. 196, 209. . . . This is not only admitted, but insisted on, by the plaintiff in error.

The cars of this company within the State of Pennsylvania are employed in interstate commerce; but their being so employed does not exempt them from taxation by the State; and the State has not taxed them because of their being so employed, but because of their being within its territory and jurisdiction. The cars were continuously and permanently employed in going to and fro upon certain routes of travel. If they had never passed beyond the limits of Pennsylvania, it could not be doubted that the State could tax them, like other property, within its borders, notwithstanding they were employed in interstate commerce. The fact that, instead of stopping at the state boundary, they cross that boundary in going out and coming back, cannot affect the power of the State to levy a tax upon them. The State, having the right, for the purposes of taxation, to tax any personal property found within its jurisdiction, without regard to the place of the owner's domicil, could tax the specific cars which at a given moment were within its borders. The route over which the cars travel extending beyond the limits of the State, particular cars may not remain within the State; but the company has at all times substantially the same number of cars within the State, and continuously and constantly uses there a portion of its property; and it is distinctly found, as matter of fact, that the company continuously, throughout the periods for which these taxes were levied, carried on business in Pennsylvania, and had about one hundred cars within the State.

The mode which the State of Pennsylvania adopted, to ascertain the proportion of the company's property upon which it should be taxed in that State, was by taking as a basis of assessment such proportion of the capital stock of the company as the number of miles over which it ran cars within the State bore to the whole number of miles, in that and other States, over which its cars were run. This was a just and equitable method of assessment; and, if it were adopted by all the States through which these cars ran, the company would be assessed upon the whole value of its capital stock, and no more.

The validity of this mode of apportioning such a tax is sustained by several decisions of this court, in cases which came up from the Circuit Courts of the United States, and in which, therefore, the jurisdiction of this court extended to the determination of the whole case, and was not limited, as upon writs of error to the state courts, to questions under the Constitution and laws of the United States. . . .

For these reasons, and upon these authorities, the court is of opinion that the tax in question is constitutional and valid. The result of holding otherwise would be that, if all the States should concur in abandoning the legal fiction that personal property has its situs at the owner's domicil, and in adopting the system of taxing it at the place at which it is used and by whose laws it is protected, property employed in any business requiring continuous and constant movement from one State to another would escape taxation altogether.

Judgment affirmed.

MR. JUSTICE BRADLEY, with whom concurred MR. JUSTICE FIELD and MR. JUSTICE HARLAN, dissenting.

I dissent from the judgment of the court in this case, and will state briefly my reasons. I concede that all property, personal as well as real, within a State, and belonging there, may be taxed by the State. Of that there can be no doubt. But where property does not belong in the State another question arises. It is the question of the jurisdiction of the State over the property. . . .

But, when personal property is permanently located within a State for the purpose of ordinary use or sale, then, indeed, it is subject to the laws of the State and to the burdens of taxation; as well when owned by persons residing out of the State, as when owned by persons residing in the State. It has then acquired a situs in the State where it is found. . . .

Of course I do not mean to say that either railroad cars or ships are to be free from taxation, but I do say that they are not taxable by those States in which they are only transiently present in the transaction of their commercial operations. A British ship coming to the harbor of New York from Liverpool ever so regularly and spending half its time (when not on the ocean) in that harbor, cannot be taxed by the State of New York (harbor, pilotage and quarantine dues not being taxes). So New York ships plying regularly to the port of New Orleans, so that one of the line may be always lying at the latter port, cannot be taxed by the State of Louisiana. . . . No more can a train of cars belonging in Pennsylvania, and running regularly from Philadelphia to New York, or to Chicago, be taxed by the State of New York, in the one case, or by Illinois, in the other. If it may lawfully be taxed by these States, it may lawfully be taxed by all the intermediate States, New Jersey, Ohio and Indiana. And then we should have back again all the confusion and competition and state jealousies which existed before the adoption of the Constitution, and for putting an end to which the Constitution was adopted.

In the opinion of the court it is suggested that if all the States should adopt as equitable a rule of proportioning the taxes on the Pullman Company as that adopted by Pennsylvania, a just system of taxation of the whole capital stock of the company would result. Yes, if — ! But Illinois may tax the company on its whole capital stock. Where would be the equity then? This, however, is a consideration that cannot be compared with the question as to the power to tax at all, — as to the relative power of the State and general governments over the regulation of internal commerce, — as to the right of the States to resume those powers which have been vested in the government of the United States. . . .

. . . The same difficulty as to the method of determining value exists in the present case which existed in [Western Union Telegraph Co. v. Massachusetts, 125 U.S. 530]; but the more serious difficulty lies in the question of the situs of the property, and the consequent jurisdiction of the State of Pennsylvania to tax it. It is not fast property; it does not consist of real estate; it does not attach itself to the land; it is movable and engaged in interstate commerce, not in Pennsylvania alone, but in that and other States, and the question is, how can such property be taxed by a State to which it does not belong? It is in-

Section D. State Taxation

directly, but virtually, taxing the passengers, many of them carried from New York to Chicago, or from Chicago to New York, and most of them from one State to another. It is clearly a burden on interstate commerce. The opinion of the court is based on the idea that the cars are taxable in Pennsylvania because a certain number continuously abide there. But how can they be said to abide there when they only stop at Philadelphia and other stations to take on passengers? And it is all the same whether they cross the State entirely, or run into or out of other States with a terminus in Pennsylvania. . . .

UNION TANK LINE CO. v. WRIGHT, 249 U.S. 275, 39 S. Ct. 276, 63 L. Ed. 602 (1919). McReynolds, J.: "This cause requires us to consider the power of a State to lay and collect taxes upon instrumentalities of interstate commerce which move both within and without its jurisdiction.

"Union Tank Line — plaintiff in error — an equipment company incorporated in New Jersey which has never carried on business or had an office in Georgia, owns twelve thousand tank cars suitable for transporting oil over railroads and rents them to shippers at agreed rates, based on size and capacity. The roads over which they move also pay therefor stipulated compensation. Under definite contract certain of these cars were furnished to the Standard Oil Company of Kentucky and all of those which came into Georgia were being operated by the Oil Company under such agreement. They were not permanently within that State but passed 'in and out.'

"March 16, 1914, the Tank Line made the following tax return to the Comptroller General for 1913 —

Name of company	Union Tank Line
Value of real estate owned by company in or out of Georgia	None
Number of miles of R.R. lines in Georgia over which . . . cars are run	6976.5
Total value of . . . cars and . . . other personal property [in Georgia and elsewhere]	$10,518,333.16
Value franchise [in Georgia]	No franchise
Total number of miles R.R. lines over which . . . cars are run [in Georgia and elsewhere]	251,999
Total value of property taxable in Georgia	$47,310.00
Union Tank Line Company had an average of 57 tank cars in Georgia during 1913 which at a value of $830 per car equals	$47,310.00

"Defendant in error expressly admitted that the average number of cars in Georgia during 1913 was fifty-seven, the value of each being $830 — total $47,310; that the owner had paid into the state treasury as taxes the full amount required on such valuation and during that year had no other property in the State. Acting upon information contained in return above quoted, the Comptroller General assessed the Tank Line's property for 1913 at $291,196, its franchise at $27,685; and demanded payment. In explanation of this action he wrote to it as follows:

" 'As to the return filed, you have furnished the data desired, but have made an error in the application of same. After giving the mileage for the Company everywhere and for Georgia, you then go ahead and assign 57 tank cars for this State and value them at $830 each, making the total for Georgia $47,310. This is an incorrect method. If you were to be allowed to merely assign so many cars to the State for taxation there would be no need for the mileage figures to be furnished. The valuation to be assigned to Georgia must be in the same proportion to the valuation for the entire company, as the mileage in Georgia bears to the entire mileage everywhere. . . . Or to work it out by percentage instead of proportion: 6,976.5 the Georgia mileage, is 2.76846 per cent. of 251,999, the entire mileage. Georgia is therefore entitled to 2.76846 per cent. of the entire valuation. This per cent. of $10,518,333 is $291,195.84, or the same sum arrived at by proportion, if we call the 84 cents an even dollar. . . . A franchise value should also be returned. And whatever the valuation you place on the franchise for the entire country, 2.76846 per cent. of same must be assigned to Georgia. Thus, if you should value your franchise at $1,000,000, the franchise value to be asigned to Georgia would be $27,685.

" 'The valuation for Georgia was determined by taking 2.76846 per cent. of the valuation you gave for the entire company, exclusive of franchise. The 2.76846 per cent. is the ratio the Georgia mileage bears to the entire mileage, as explained in a previous letter. The franchise value was obtained by placing your franchise for the entire country at an even million dollars and giving Georgia 2.76846 per cent. thereof.'

"Thereupon, plaintiff in error instituted this proceeding in Fulton County Superior Court alleging invalidity of the assessment, that to enforce the tax would violate the Fourteenth Amendment, and asked appropriate relief. The cause was tried upon pleadings and agreed statement of facts. Among other things, the parties stipulated:

" 'On April 7, 1914, when the defendant entered an assessment in his office of property and franchise of the plaintiff as shown hereinbefore, he had no other information for any of the years 1907 to 1914 inclusive than was contained in the said return filed by the plaintiff on March 16, 1914, and embraced in this statement and which was refused by the defendant, and did not know what cars defendant had had in Georgia during any of said named years nor did he ascertain the value of such cars, but his action was taken on such information hereinbefore shown; and that the assessment so entered by the defendant in his office against the plaintiff's property during said period for each of said years embraces the valuation of about three hundred cars in excess of what the plaintiff actually had in the State of Georgia, during said years of the approximate value of $250,000.00 each year; and that the true value of a tank car is about eight hundred and thirty ($830.00) dollars per car.

" 'That for the year 1914 the assessment entered against plaintiff by defendant covered the value of at least three hundred and fifty cars in excess of the number of cars plaintiff actually had in the State of Georgia for the time said tax was assessed.

" 'That defendant in entering said assessment never understood to ascertain the actual property of plaintiff's located in the State of Georgia during the said years or to assess its property . . . otherwise than by simply ascertaining the percentage of its entire property shown by the ratio of the railroad traversed by its equipment in Georgia and the railroad mileage traversed by its equipment everywhere as shown by its said return filed on March 16, 1914.'

"The trial court adjudged the assessment good as to both franchise and physical property. The Supreme Court held no taxable franchise existed, but that the physical property had been assessed as required by statutes not in conflict with either state or Federal Constitution. 143 Georgia, 765, 769, 771, 773; 146 Georgia, 489. . . ."

What decision? Why?

NOTE State Jurisdiction to Tax Property

1. The Supreme Court has consistently upheld state property taxes upon the rolling stock of railroads, if a permissible apportionment was made. In American Refrigerator Transit Co. v. Hall, 174 U.S. 70 (1899), the company was an Illinois corporation. Its cars frequently moved into and out of Colorado. It was stipulated that during the year for which the tax was imposed, the average number of cars in Colorado was forty. A tax upon the value of forty cars was upheld. Similarly in Union Refrigerator Transit Co. v. Lynch, 177 U.S. 149 (1900), a tax on the value of the average number of cars in Utah was upheld. Union Refrigerator Transit Company was a Kentucky corporation. It owned over

2000 refrigerator cars which it rented to shippers, who used them throughout the country. Kentucky sought to impose a property tax upon the value of all the cars. The Court held that Kentucky was limited to taxing the average number of cars found in Kentucky. Union Refrigerator Transit Co. v. Kentucky, 199 U.S. 194 (1905). However, in New York ex rel. New York Central R.R. v. Miller, 202 U.S. 584 (1906), the Court upheld New York's imposition of a franchise tax upon a domestic corporation computed on the amount of its capital stock employed within the state, and here including the value of all cars owned by the railroad company, though it was clear that many of them were frequently and for extended periods operating not only outside the state but on other lines of railroad. This decision might have been based upon considerations peculiar to franchise taxes upon domestic corporations. However, Mr. Justice Holmes, for the Court, wrote in terms of the property tax decisions. He disposed of Union Refrigerator Transit Co. v. Kentucky, supra, with the remark, "It is true that it has been decided that property, even of a domestic corporation, cannot be taxed if it is permanently out of the State," and added, "In the present case, however, it does not appear that any specific cars or any average of cars was so continuously in any other State as to be taxable there." In Johnson Oil Co. v. Oklahoma, 290 U.S. 158 (1933), Oklahoma sought to impose a property tax upon the value of all of the tank cars owned by the oil company, an Illinois corporation. The company's principal refinery was in Oklahoma, and the cars were principally used to transport petroleum products from that refinery to points throughout the country. They were infrequently used in connection with an oil plant owned by the company in Illinois. They made an average of 1½ round trips from and to Oklahoma every thirty days and were usually at the refinery for reloading from one to ten days. In limiting Oklahoma's tax to an apportioned valuation, Chief Justice Hughes indicated that while it could not be doubted that the cars had a situs for taxation outside Illinois, this did not mean that the situs of the entire fleet was at the refinery in Oklahoma. "The jurisdiction of Oklahoma to tax property of this description must be determined on a basis which is consistent with the like jurisdiction of other States."

In Norfolk & Western Ry. v. State Tax Commission, 390 U.S. 317 (1968), the Court held invalid an assessment of railroad rolling stock on a proportional track mileage basis where the valuation was about twice the amount that had been arrived at on a separate in-state valuation.

2. With respect to ships and barges, the suggestion in the opinion in Hays v. Pacific Mail Steamship Co., 17 How. 596 (1855), that the port of registration or enrollment might be the situs for taxation was not borne out. In St. Louis v. Wiggins Ferry Co., 11 Wall. 423 (1871); Morgan v. Parham, 16 Wall. 471 (1873); and Ayer & L. Tie Co. v. Kentucky, 202 U.S. 409 (1906), the city or state of enrollment was not allowed to impose a property tax on ships or barges, even though they spent some appreciable time there. In each case it was stated that such craft could be taxed only by the state of domicile of the owner. And in Southern Pac. Co. v. Kentucky, 222 U.S. 63 (1911), a Kentucky property tax upon twenty vessels owned by a Kentucky corporation and registered in New York was upheld, though the vessels operated regularly between New York, New Orleans, Galveston, and Havana. The exception to property taxation by the state of domicile of the owner appeared in Old Dominion S.S Co. v. Virginia, 198 U.S. 299 (1905), where a vessel owned by a New York corporation and registered in New York was held subject to a property tax imposed by Virginia, since it operated solely in Virginia.

3. Northwest Airlines, Inc. v. Minnesota, 322 U.S. 292 (1944), presented to the Supreme Court its first case involving property taxes upon airplanes. The Court (5 to 4) upheld Minnesota's imposition of a property tax based upon the value of the entire fleet of airplanes owned by Northwest Airlines, Inc., a Minnesota corporation operating a commercial airline through a number of states, with its principal operating and maintenance bases in Minnesota and with St. Paul registered as its home port in accordance with the provisions of the federal Civil Aeronautics Act. There was no single opinion for the ma-

jority of the Court. Mr. Justice Frankfurter, writing for himself and two others, stressed the combination of factors centering on Minnesota, and cited Mr. Justice Holmes's opinion in New York ex rel. New York Central R.R. v. Miller, supra, as controlling. Mr. Justice Black concurred in the result, but would not foreclose the taxing rights of other states. Mr. Justice Jackson concurred in the result, but on the assumption that it indicated other states could not tax; he suggested that the "home port" concept advanced in Hays v. Pacific Mail Steamship Co., supra, should be controlling in the case of airplanes. Chief Justice Stone wrote a lengthy dissenting opinion, concurred in by Justices Roberts, Reed, and Rutledge.

4. All of the above is reviewed in Powell, Northwest Airlines v. Minnesota: State Taxation of Airplanes, 57 Harv. L. Rev. 1097 (1944). See also Multiple Taxation of Air Commerce, H.R. Doc. No. 141, 79th Cong., 1st Sess. (1945), particularly pp. 43-60, 84.

5. In 1945 the Legislature of Minnesota enacted Chapter 418 of the Laws of 1945, providing for the taxation of the "flight property" of airlines operating within the state on an apportioned basis. The apportionment factors employed in the Minnesota legislation were somewhat different from those in a proposed uniform statute set forth in Report of the Committee on Taxation of Airlines, Revenue Administration — 1947 (Nat. Assn. of Tax Administrators) 49.

Standard Oil Co. v. Peck 342 U.S. 382, 72 S. Ct. 309, 96 L. Ed. 427 (1952)

MR. JUSTICE DOUGLAS delivered the opinion of the Court.

Appellant, an Ohio corporation, owns boats and barges which it employs for the transportation of oil along the Mississippi and Ohio Rivers. The vessels neither pick up oil nor discharge it in Ohio. The main terminals are in Tennessee, Indiana, Kentucky, and Louisiana. The maximum river mileage traversed by the boats and barges on any trip through waters bordering Ohio was 17½ miles. These 17½ miles were in the section of the Ohio River which had to be traversed to reach Bromley, Kentucky. While this stretch of water bordered Ohio, it was not necessarily within Ohio. The vessels were registered in Cincinnati, Ohio, but only stopped in Ohio for occasional fuel or repairs. These stops were made at Cincinnati; but none of them involved loading or unloading cargo.

The Tax Commissioner of Ohio, acting under §§ 5325 and 5328 of the Ohio General Code, levied an ad valorem personal property tax on all of these vessels. The Board of Tax Appeals affirmed (with an exception not material here), and the Supreme Court of Ohio sustained the Board, 155 Ohio St. 61, 98 N.E.2d 8, over the objection that the tax violated the Due Process Clause of the Fourteenth Amendment. The case is here on appeal 28 U.S.C. § 1257 (2).

Under the earlier view governing the taxability of vessels moving in the inland waters (St. Louis v. Ferry Co., 11 Wall. 423; Ayer & Lord Tie Co. v. Kentucky, 202 U.S. 409; cf. Old Dominion S.S. Co. v. Virginia, 198 U.S. 299) Ohio, the state of the domicile, would have a strong claim to the whole of the tax that has been levied. But the rationale of those cases was rejected in Ott v. Mississipi Barge Line Co., 336 U.S. 169, where we held that vessels moving in interstate operations along the inland waters were taxable by the same standards as those which Pullman's Car Co. v. Pennsylvania, 141 U.S. 18, first applied to railroad cars in interstate commerce. The formula approved was one which fairly apportioned the tax to the commerce carried on within the state. In that way we placed inland water transportation on the same constitutional footing as other interstate enterprises.

The Ott case involved a tax by Louisiana on vessels of a foreign corporation operating in Louisiana waters. Louisiana sought to tax only that portion of the value of the vessels represented by the ratio between the total number of miles in Louisiana and the total number of miles in the entire operation. The present case is sought to be distinguished on the ground that Ohio is the domiciliary state and therefore may tax the whole value even though the boats and barges operate outside Ohio. New York Central R. Co. v. Miller, 202 U. S. 584, sustained a tax by the domiciliary state on all the rolling stock of a railroad. But in that case it did not appear that "any specific cars or any average of cars" was so continuously in another state as to be taxable there. P. 597. Northwest Airlines, Inc. v. Minnesota, 322 U. S. 292, allowed the domiciliary state to tax the entire fleet of airplanes operating interstate; but in that case, as in the Miller case, it was not shown that "a defined part of the domiciliary corpus" had acquired a taxable situs elsewhere. P. 295. Those cases, though exceptional on their facts, illustrate the reach of the taxing power of the state of the domicile as contrasted to that of the other states. But they have no application here since most, if not all, of the barges and boats which Ohio has taxed were almost continuously outside Ohio during the taxable year. No one vessel may have been continuously in another state during the taxable year. But we do know that most, if not all, of them were operating in other waters and therefore under Ott v. Mississippi Barge Line Co., supra, could be taxed by the several states on an apportionment basis. The rule which permits taxation by two or more states on an apportionment basis precludes taxation of all of the property by the state of the domicile. See Union Transit Co. v. Kentucky, 199 U. S. 194. Otherwise there would be multiple taxation of interstate operations and the tax would have no relation to the opportunities, benefits, or protection which the taxing state gives those operations.

Reversed.

Mr. Justice Black dissents.

Mr. Justice Minton, dissenting.

I assume for the purposes of this dissent that none of the vessels in question were within Ohio during the tax year, and that they were taxed to their full value by Ohio. The record shows that the vessels were all registered in Cincinnati, Ohio, as the home port, and that Ohio is the domicile of the owner. Ohio claims the right to tax these vessels because they have not acquired a tax situs elsewhere than their home port and domicile. . . .

The record in this case is silent as to whether any proportion of the vessels were in any one state for the whole of a taxable year. The record does show that no other state collected taxes on the vessels for the years in question or any other year. Until this case, it has not been the law that the state of the owner's domicile is prohibited from taxing under such circumstances.

Southern Pacific Co. v. Kentucky, supra, is a case in point. There the owner of the vessels was a Kentucky corporation which operated between various coastal ports. None of the vessels were ever near Kentucky, but Kentucky was allowed to tax them because it was the state of the owner's domicile. The vessels were in and out of other states' ports, just as the instant vessels were in and out of other states' ports; but the mere possibility that some other state might attempt to levy an apportioned tax on the vessels was not permitted to destroy Kentucky's power to tax. The crucial fact was that the vessels were not shown to have acquired a tax situs elsewhere.

As recently as 1944 this Court would seem to have added vitality to the doctrine which should govern this case. Minnesota had taxed an airline on the full value of its airplanes, including those used in interstate commerce. Mr. Justice Frankfurter, announcing the judgment of the Court upholding the tax, stated:

"The fact that Northwest paid personal property taxes for the year 1939 upon 'some proportion of its full value' of its airplane fleet in some other States does not abridge the power of taxation of Minnesota as the home State of the fleet in the circumstances of the present case. The taxability of any part of this fleet by any other State than Minnesota, in view of the taxability of the entire fleet by that State, is not now before us. It . . . is not shown here that a defined part of the domiciliary corpus has acquired a permanent location, i.e., a taxing situs, elsewhere." Northwest Airlines v. Minnesota, 322 U.S. 292, 295.

The fear of "double taxation" was much more real in that case than in the instant case; yet the Minnesota tax was sustained because there was no showing that a taxing situs *had* been acquired elsewhere. The question of what some other state might do is no more before the Court in this case than it was in the Northwest case.

The majority today seeks to distinguish the earlier cases by magnifying the relevance of the continuous absence of the vessels from the domiciliary state. But the operative fact of the earlier cases was the absence or presence of another taxing situs. Where no other taxing situs was shown to exist, the state of the domicile was permitted to tax, irrespective of the amount of time the vessels were present in that state. Southern Pacific Co. v. Kentucky, supra.

As it is admittedly not shown on that record that these vessels have acquired a tax situs elsewhere, Ohio should be permitted to tax them as the state of the owner's domicile. I would affirm.[u]

Braniff Airways, Inc. v. Nebraska State Bd. of Equalization and Assessment 347 U.S. 590, 74 S. Ct. 757, 98 L. Ed. 967 (1954)

MR. JUSTICE REED delivered the opinion of the Court.

The question presented by this appeal from the Supreme Court of Nebraska is whether the Constitution bars the State of Nebraska from levying an apportioned ad valorem tax on the flight equipment of appellant, an interstate air carrier. Appellant is not incorporated in Nebraska and does not have its principal place of business or home port registered under the Civil Aeronautics Act, 52 Stat. 973, 977, 49 U.S.C. §§401-705, in that state. Such flight equipment is employed as a part of a system of interstate air commerce operating over fixed routes and landing on and departing from airports within Nebraska on regular schedules. Appellant does not challenge the reasonableness of the apportionment prescribed by the taxing statute or the application of such apportionment to its property. It contends only that its flight equipment used in interstate commerce is immune from taxation by Nebraska because without situs in that state and because regulation of air navigation by the Federal Government precludes such state taxation.

This petition for a declaratory judgment of the invalidity of §§77-1244 to 77-1250 of the state tax statute and an injunction against the collection of taxes assessed under such provisions for previous years was filed as an original action in the court below by Mid-Continent Airlines, Inc., and tried upon stipulated facts. Subsequent to filing, but before the decision, Mid-Continent and appellant were merged on August 1, 1952, and appellant was substituted as the party plaintiff. Mid-Continent had been incorporated in Delaware with its corporate place of business in Wilmington in that state, and Braniff is incorporated in Oklahoma and has its corporate place of business in Oklahoma City. Pursuant to the merger Mid-Continent's main executive offices were moved from Kansas City, Missouri, and merged with appellant's in Dallas, Texas. The number of regularly scheduled stops in Nebraska, fourteen per day at Omaha and four at Lincoln, was not affected by the merger.

The home port registered with the Civil Aeronautics Authority and the overhaul base for the aircraft in question is the Minneapolis-St. Paul Airport, Minnesota. All of the aircraft not undergoing overhaul fly regular schedules upon a circuit ranging from Minot, North Dakota, to New Orleans, Louisiana, with stops in fourteen states including Minnesota, Nebraska and Oklahoma. No stops were made in Delaware. The Nebraska stops

---

[u] Cf. Ott v. Mississippi Barge Line Co., 336 U.S. 169 (1949); see comment thereon, when decided by the Court of Appeals for the Fifth Circuit, 61 Harv. L. Rev. 1464 (1948). — ED.

Section D. **State Taxation** 509

are of short duration since utilized only for the discharge and loading of passengers, mail, express, and freight, and sometimes for refueling. Appellant neither owns nor maintains facilities for repairing, reconditioning, or storing its flight equipment in Nebraska, but rents depot space and hires other services as required. The Supreme Court of Nebraska made no distinction as to taxability between those years when no flights were made into the state of domicile (Delaware) and those when flights did enter the state of new domicile (Oklahoma).

It is stipulated that the tax in question is assessed only against regularly scheduled air carriers and is not applied to carriers who operate only intermittently in the state. The statute defines "flight equipment" as "aircraft fully equipped for flight," and provides that "any tax upon or measured by the value of flight equipment of air carriers incorporated or doing business in this state shall be assessed and collected by the Tax Commissioner." A formula is prescribed for arriving at the proportion of a carrier's flight equipment to be allocated to the state.[4]

The statute uses the allocation formula of the "proposed uniform statute to provide for an equitable method of state taxation of air carriers" adopted by the Council of State Governments upon the recommendation of the National Association of Tax Administrators in 1947. Use of a uniform allocation formula to apportion air-carrier taxes among the states follows the recommendation of the Civil Aeronautics Board in its report to Congress.[6] The Nebraska statute provides for reports, levy, and rate of tax by state average.

Required reports filed by Mid-Continent for 1950 show that about 9% of its revenue and 11½% of the total system tonnage originated in Nebraska and about 9% of its total stops were made in that state. From these figures, using the statutory formula, the Tax Commissioner arrived at a valuation of $118,901, allocable to Nebraska, resulting in a tax of $4,280.44. Since Mid-Continent filed no return for 1951 the same valuation was used and an increased rate resulted in assessment of $4,518.29. The Supreme Court of Nebraska held the statute not violative of the Commerce Clause and dismissed appellant's petition.

[The Court rejected an argument by the taxpayer based upon the terms of the federal Civil Aeronautics Act.]

Nor has appellant demonstrated that the Commerce Clause otherwise bars this tax as a burden on interstate commerce. We have frequently reiterated that the Commerce Clause does not immunize interstate instrumentalities from all state taxation, but that such commerce may be required to pay a nondiscriminatory share of the tax burden. And appellant does not allege that this Nebraska statute discriminates against it nor, as noted above, does it challenge the reasonableness of the apportionment prescribed by the statute.

The argument upon which appellant depends ultimately, however, is that its aircraft

---

[4] . . . This section provides that "The proportion of flight equipment allocated to this state for purposes of taxation shall be the arithmetical average of the following three ratios: (1) The ratio which the aircraft arrivals and departures within this state scheduled by such air carrier during the preceding calendar year bears to the total aircraft arrivals and departures within and without this state scheduled by such carrier during the same period; *Provided*, that in the case of nonscheduled operations all arrivals and departures shall be substituted for scheduled arrivals and departures; (2) the ratio which the revenue tons handled by such air carrier at airports within this state during the preceding calendar year bears to the total revenue tons handled by such carrier at airports within and without this state during the same period; and (3) the ratio which such air carrier's originating revenue within this state for the preceding calendar year bears to the total originating revenue of such carrier within and without this state for the same period."

[6] Multiple Taxation of Air Commerce, H.R. Doc. No. 141, 79th Cong., 1st Sess. Recommendations by various interested groups as to the proper method of apportionment are included in that report and its appendices. See also Arditto, State and Local Taxation of Scheduled Local Airlines, 16 J. Air L. & Com. 162; Kassell, Interstate Cooperation and Airlines, 25 Taxes 302. Mr. Bulwinkle introduced bills in accordance with the recommendation of the C.A.B. report that the National Government should prescribe the method of state taxation of air carriers. The bills adopted the Council formula utilized by Nebraska. Neither was enacted. H.R. 3446, 79th Cong., 1st Sess.; H.R. 1241, 80th Cong., 1st Sess.

never "attained a taxable situs within Nebraska" from which it argues that the Nebraska tax imposes a burden on interstate commerce. In relying upon the Commerce Clause on this issue and in not specifically claiming protection under the Due Process Clause of the Fourteenth Amendment, appellant names the wrong constitutional clause to support its position. While the question of whether a commodity en route to market is sufficiently settled in a state for purpose of subjection to a property tax has been determined by this Court as a Commerce Clause question, the bare question whether an instrumentality of commerce has tax situs in a state for the purpose of subjection to a property tax is one of due process. However, appellant timely raised and preserved its contention that its property was not taxable because such property had attained no taxable situs in Nebraska. Though inexplicit, we consider the due process issue within the clear intendment of such contention and hold such issue sufficiently presented. . . .

Appellant relies upon cases involving ocean-going vessels to support its contention that its aircraft attained no tax situs in Nebraska. See, e.g., Hays v. Pacific Mail S.S. Co., 17 How. 596; Morgan v. Parham, 16 Wall. 471; Southern Pacific Co. v. Kentucky, 222 U.S. 63. The first two cases were efforts to tax the entire value of the ships as other local property, without apportionment, when they were used to plow the open seas. The last case holds the state of corporate domicile has power to tax vessels that are not taxable elsewhere. A closer analogy exists between planes flying interstate and boats that ply the inland waters. We perceive no logical basis for distinguishing the constitutional power to impose a tax on such aircraft from the power to impose taxes on river boats. Ott v. Mississippi Valley Barge Line Co., 336 U.S. 169; Standard Oil Co. v. Peck, 342 U.S. 382. The limitation imposed by the Due Process Clause upon state power to impose taxes upon such instrumentalities was succinctly stated in the Ott case: "So far as due process is concerned the only question is whether the tax in practical operation has related to opportunities, benefits, or protection conferred or afforded by the taxing State." 363 U.S. at 174. . . .

Thus the situs issue devolves into the question of whether eighteen stops per day by appellant's aircraft is sufficient contact with Nebraska to sustain that state's power to levy an apportioned ad valorem tax on such aircraft. We think such regular contact is sufficient to establish Nebraska's power to tax even though the same aircraft do not land every day and even though none of the aircraft is continuously within the state. "The basis of the jurisdiction is the habitual employment of the property within the State." Appellant rents its ground facilities and pays for fuel it purchases in Nebraska. This leaves it in the position of other carriers such as rails, boats and motors that pay for the use of local facilities so as to have the opportunity to exploit the commerce, traffic, and trade that originates in or reaches Nebraska. Approximately one-tenth of appellant's revenue is produced by the pickup and discharge of Nebraska freight and passengers. Nebraska certainly affords protection during such stops and these regular landings are clearly a benefit to appellant.

Nor do we think that Nebraska's power to levy this tax was affected by the merger of Mid-Continent with Braniff. Since "the rule which permits taxation by two or more states on an apportionment basis precludes taxation of all of the property by the state of the domicile," Standard Oil Co. v. Peck, supra, at 384, we deem it immaterial that before the merger Mid-Continent was domiciled in Delaware, a state through which its planes did not fly, and after the merger Braniff is domiciled in Oklahoma, a state through which these aircraft make regular flights.

Appellant urges that Northwest Airlines v. Minnesota, 322 U.S. 292, precludes this tax unless that case is to be overruled. In that case Minnesota, as the domicile of the air carrier and its "home port," was permitted to tax the entire value of the fleet ad valorem although it ranged by fixed routes through eight states. While no one view mustered a majority of this Court, it seems fair to say that without the position stated in the Conclusion and Judgment which announced the decision of this Court, the result would have been the reverse. That position was that it was not shown "that a defined part of the domiciliary

Section D. State Taxation

corpus has acquired a permanent location, i.e., a taxable situs, elsewhere." P. 295. That opinion recognized the "doctrine of tax apportionment for instrumentalities engaged in interstate commerce," p. 297, but held it inapplicable because no "property (or a portion of fungible units) is permanently situated in a State other than the domiciliary State." P. 298. When Standard Oil Co. v. Peck, 342 U.S. 382, 384, was here, the Court interpreted the Northwest Airlines case to permit states other than those of the corporate domicile to tax boats in interstate commerce on the apportionment basis in accordance with their use in the taxing state. We adhere to that interpretation.

Affirmed.

MR. JUSTICE BLACK concurs in the result.

MR. JUSTICE JACKSON dissents for the reasons stated in his concurring opinion in Northwest Airlines v. Minnesota, 322 U.S. 292, 320.

MR. JUSTICE DOUGLAS, concurring.

Braniff Airways, in challenging the power of Nebraska to lay this ad valorem tax, claims only that its planes have no taxable situs in the State. It does not claim that no fraction of the aircraft, on an apportioned basis, is permanently in the State. Nor does it attack this apportionment formula.

My understanding of our decisions is that the power to lay an ad valorem tax turns on the permanency of the property in the State. All the property may be there or only a fraction of it. Property in transit, whether a plane discharging passengers or an automobile refueling, is not subject to an ad valorem tax. Property in transit may move so regularly and so continuously that part of it is always in the State. Then the fraction, but no more, may be taxed ad valorem.

I mention these elemental points to reserve explicitly the validity of the apportionment formula that serves as the basis of this ad valorem tax. The formula used presents substantial questions. What might be an adequate formula for a gross receipts tax might be inadequate for an ad valorem tax. Moreover, when we are faced with a due process question, we have a problem we may not delegate to Congress.

I do not think the Court takes a position contrary to what I have said. But there are passages in the opinion which blur the constitutional issues as they are blurred and confused in the interesting report of the Civil Aeronautics Board, H.R. Doc. No. 141, 79th Cong., 1st Sess., entitled Multiple Taxation of Air Commerce. Hence I have joined in the judgment of the Court but not in the opinion.

MR. JUSTICE FRANKFURTER, dissenting.

One of the most treacherous tendencies in legal reasoning is the transfer of generalizations developed for one set of situations to seemingly analogous, yet essentially very different, situations. The doctrines evolved in adjusting rights as between the States to tax property bearing some relation to a number of States, and the taxing power of the States as against the freedom from State interferences secured by the Commerce Clause, bear, of course, a practical relation to what it is that is taxed. It took a considerable time to make this adjustment in regard to taxation of railroad property and railroad income — to decide when the States are wholly excluded from levying certain taxes, when an ad valorem tax may be levied on railroad property reasonably deemed to be permanently in a given State, and on what basis income from interstate railroad business may fairly be apportioned among different States. Even as to railroads, nice distinctions had to be made and the making of them has not been concluded.

It stands to reason that the drastic differences between slow-moving trains and the birdlike flight of airplanes would be reflected in the law's response to the claims of the different States and the limitations of the Commerce Clause upon those claims. The differences in result and the conflict even among those who agreed in result in Northwest Airlines v. Minnesota, 322 U.S. 292, demonstrate not the contrariness or caprice of different minds but the inherent perplexities of the law's adjustment to such novel problems as the exercise of the taxing power over commercial aviation in a federal system. The problems canvassed in that case were unprecedented, and perhaps the most important thing that was there decided was the refusal of the Court to apply to air transportation the doctrines that had been enunciated with regard to land and water transportation.

The plain intimation of the case — that these novel problems, affecting the taxing power of the States and the Nation, call for the comprehensive powers of legislation possessed by Congress — found response in a resolution of Congress directing the Civil Aeronautics Board to develop the "means for eliminating and avoiding, as far as practicable, multiple taxation of persons engaged in air commerce . . . which has the effect of unduly burdening or unduly impeding the development of air commerce." 58 Stat. 723. The inquiry thus set afoot produced an illuminating report. See H.R. Doc. No. 141, 79th Cong., 1st Sess., which analyzed the difficulties and also made concrete proposals. The gist of these proposals was that Congress make an apportionment of taxes among the States over which air carriers fly, based upon relevant factors and in appropriate ratios. The basis of taxation by Nebraska, here under review, substantially reflects the factors which the Civil Aeronautics Board recommended to the Congress. It is one thing, however, for the individual States to determine what factors should be taken into account and how they should be weighted. It is quite another for Congress to devise, as the Civil Aeronautics Board recommended it should, a scheme of apportionment binding on all the States. Until that time, Nebraska may rely on one scheme of apportionment; other States on other schemes. And each State may, from time to time, modify the relevant factors.

The exercise of the taxing power by one of the States by means of a formula, based on such criteria as tonnage, revenue, and arrivals and departures, may, in isolation, impose no unfair burden on commerce. And the adoption by all the States of such a basis for taxation, which only congressional action could ensure, would not offend the Commerce Clause. It is the diverse and fluctuating exercise of power by the various States, even where based on concededly relevant factors, which imposes an undue burden on interstate commerce.

The complexity of the proposals of the Board's Report — the items to be taken into account, the balance to be struck among them, the problem of giving the States their due without unfairly burdening an industry of vital national import — indicates how ill-adapted the judicial process is, as against the choices open to Congress, for dealing with these problems and how warily this Court should move within the limits of its own inescapable duty to act. The protection of interstate commerce against the burden of multiple taxation ought not to be left to litigation growing out of changes in the methods of taxation. . . .

This Court has held that a State may levy an ad valorem tax on the basis of a showing that the total time spent in a State by different units of a carrier's property is such that a certain proportion of that property may be said to have a permanent location in that State. Such a doctrine of apportionment, as the basis of property taxation, was adopted by this Court in Pullman's Car Co. v. Pennsylvania, 141 U.S. 18, with relation to railroad cars; and in Ott v. Mississippi Barge Line Co., 336 U.S. 169, with relation to barges. But boats and railroad cars which spend hours and days at a time in a State have a closeness and duration of relationship to that State obviously not true of planes which make brief stopovers for a few minutes.

The appealing phrase that "interstate business must pay its way" can be invoked only when we know what the "way" is for which interstate business must pay. Of course, the appellant must pay for the use of airports and other services it enjoys in Nebraska. It must pay a tax on all its property permanently located in Nebraska. Like everyone else it must pay a gasoline tax. In fact it pays approximately $22,000 a year for the use of the airport, $14,000 a year in gasoline taxes, and appropriate property taxes on office equipment, trucks and other items permanently in Nebraska.

But only those who have a sufficiently substantial relation to Nebraska that they may fairly be said to partake of the benefits, though impalpable and unspecific, it gives as an ordered society, may be taxed because they partake of those benefits. And even then, of course, an undue burden must not be cast on commerce. Not unless Nebraska can show that appellant has airplanes that have a substantially permanent presence in Nebraska can Nebraska exert its taxing power on their presence. I do not believe that planes which pause for a few moments can be made the basis for the exercise of such power. If Nebraska can tax without such a tie, every other State through which the planes fly or in which they alight for a few minutes can tax. Surely this is an obvious inroad upon the Commerce Clause and as such barred by the Constitution.

It cannot be said that for airplanes, flying regularly scheduled flights, to alight, stop over for a short time and then take off is so tenuously related to Nebraska that it would deny due process for that State to seize on these short stopovers as the basis of an ad valorem tax. But the incidence of a tax may offend the Commerce Clause, even though it may satisfy the Due Process Clause.

I am not unaware that there is an air of imprecision about what I have written. Such is the intention. Until Congress acts, the vital thing for the Court in this new and subtle field is to focus on the process of interstate commerce and protect it from inroads of taxation by a State beyond "opportunities which it has given, . . . protection which it has afforded, . . . benefits which it has conferred by the fact of being an orderly, civilized society." Wisconsin v. J. C. Penney Co., 311 U.S. 435, 444.[v]

Central R.R. v. Pennsylvania 370 U.S. 607, 82 S. Ct. 1297, 8 L. Ed. 2d 720 (1962)

MR. JUSTICE HARLAN delivered the opinion of the Court.

In this case we must decide whether the Commonwealth of Pennsylvania may, consistently with the Commerce Clause and the Due Process and Equal Protection Clauses of the Fourteenth Amendment to the Constitution of the United States, impose an annual property tax on the total value of freight cars owned by the appellant, a Pennsylvania corporation, despite the fact that a considerable number of such cars spend a substantial portion of the tax year on the lines of other railroads located outside the State. The Supreme Court of Pennsylvania upheld the application of the State's Capital Stock Tax, Purdon's Pa. Stat. Ann., 1949, Tit. 72, §§1871, 1901, to the full value of all appellant's freight cars. 403 Pa. 419, 169 A.2d 878. . . .

We take the facts pertinent to decision from a stipulation submitted by the parties to the trial court. The appellant is a Pennsylvania corporation authorized to operate a railroad only within the State. It has not been licensed to do business elsewhere. The company's track runs from the anthracite coal region in Pennsylvania to the Pennsylvania-New Jersey border, at Easton, where it connects with the lines of the Central Railroad Company of New Jersey (hereinafter CNJ), a New Jersey corporation which owns all the outstanding shares of appellant's stock.

In 1951, the year for which the tax was assessed, the appellant owned 3,074 freight cars which were put to use in ordinary transport operations in three ways: (1) by the appellant on its own tracks; (2) by CNJ on that company's tracks in New Jersey; (3) by other unaffiliated railroads on their own lines in various parts of the country. CNJ's use of appellant's cars was pursuant to operating agreements under which CNJ was obliged to pay a daily rental equal to the then-effective rate prescribed by the Association of American

---

[v] Cf. Flying Tiger Line, Inc. v. County of Los Angeles, 51 Cal. 2d 314, 333 P.2d 323 (1958), cert. denied, 359 U.S. 1001 (1959). See Comments, 72 Harv. L. Rev. 1584 (1959), 43 Minn. L. Rev. 1015 (1959), 11 Stan. L. Rev. 518 (1959).

Cf. also Scandinavian Airlines System, Inc. v. County of Los Angeles, 56 Cal. 2d 11, 363 P.2d 25 (1961), cert. denied, 368 U.S. 899 (1961). — ED.

Railroads. In order to facilitate interstate transportation by the interchange of equipment among carriers, as prescribed by 49 U.S.C. §1, pars. (4), (10), (12), the members of the Association, including the appellant, had entered into a separate "Car Service and Per Diem Agreement" under which each subscriber was authorized to use on its own lines the available freight cars of other subscribers at the established per diem rental. Consequently during 1951 many of the appellant's freight cars were also used by other railroads on lines outside Pennsylvania.

Appellant contended in the state courts, as it does here, that in computing its Pennsylvania capital stock tax, which is measured by the value of such property as is not exempt from taxation . . . , it was constitutionally entitled to deduct from the value of its taxable assets a proportional share reflecting the time spent by its freight cars outside Pennsylvania. In support of this claim appellant offered a statistical summary of the use of its freight cars during 1951, seeking to prove that a daily average of more than 1,659 of its 3,074 cars were located on the lines of railroads (including CNJ) which owned no track in Pennsylvania.[2]

It also claimed that a daily average of approximately 1,056 other cars had been used by railroads having lines both within and without Pennsylvania. As to such cars, appellant sought to allocate to Pennsylvania only such portions of their value as the combined ratio of road miles of each user-railroad's tracks within Pennsylvania bore to its total road mileage throughout the United States.[3]

These claims were disallowed by the Pennsylvania Board of Finance and Revenue, by the Court of Common Pleas of Dauphin County, and by the Supreme Court of Pennsylvania. The state courts relied primarily on this Court's decision in New York Central R. Co. v. Miller, 202 U.S. 584, which upheld the constitutionality of a domiciliary State's ad valorem property tax levied upon the full value of a railroad's rolling stock, albeit "some considerable proportion of the [railroad's] . . . cars always . . . [was] absent from the State." Id., at 595.

I

Since Miller this Court has decided numerous cases touching on the intricate problems of accommodating, under the Due Process and Commerce Clauses, the taxing powers of domiciliary and other States with respect to the instrumentalities of interstate commerce. None of these decisions has weakened the pivotal holding in Miller — that a railroad or other taxpayer owning rolling stock cannot avoid the imposition of its domicile's property tax on the full value of its assets merely by proving that some determinable fraction of its property was absent from the State for part of the tax year. This Court has consistently held that the State of domicile retains jurisdiction to tax tangible personal property which has "not acquired an actual situs elsewhere." Johnson Oil Refining Co. v. Oklahoma, 290 U.S. 158, 161.

This is because a State casts no forbidden burden upon interstate commerce by subjecting its own corporations, though they be engaged in interstate transport, to nondiscriminatory property taxes. It is only "multiple taxation of interstate operations," Standard Oil Co. v. Peck, 342 U.S. 382, 385, that offends the Commerce Clause. And obviously multiple taxation is possible only if there exists some jurisdiction, in addition

---

[2] If appellant's entire fleet of cars (3,074) is multiplied by the number of days in the year 1951 (365), the total number of "car days" comes to 1,122,010. Appellant's schedules show that 605,678 "car days" were spent on railroads which owned no track in Pennsylvania. If this latter number is divided by 365, the quotient (1,659) represents the average number of cars located on such railroads on any one day during 1951.

[3] For example, appellant computes 91,899 "car days" as having been spent on the lines of the New York Central Railroad. Since 7.36% of that railroad's track mileage is within Pennsylvania, appellant allocates 6,764 "car days," a proportional share, to Pennsylvania.

to the domicile of the taxpayer, which may constitutionally impose an ad valorem tax.

Nor does the Due Process Clause confine the domiciliary State's taxing power to such proportion of the value of the property being taxed as is equal to the fraction of the tax year which the property spends within the State's borders. Union Refrigerator Transit Co. v. Kentucky, 199 U.S. 194, held only that the Due Process Clause prohibited ad valorem taxation by the owner's domicile of tangible personal property *permanently* located in some other State. Northwest Airlines, Inc. v. Minnesota, 322 U.S. 292, reaffirmed the principle established by earlier cases that tangible property for which *no* tax situs has been established elsewhere may be taxed to its full value by the owner's domicile. See New York Central R. Co. v. Miller, supra; Southern Pacific Co. v. Kentucky, 222 U.S. 63, 69; Johnson Oil Refining Co. v. Oklahoma, supra. If such property has had insufficient contact with States other than the owner's domicile to render any one of these jurisdictions a "tax situs," it is surely appropriate to presume that the domicile is the only State affording the "opportunities, benefits, or protection" which due process demands as a prerequisite for taxation. See Ott v. Mississippi Valley Barge Line Co., 336 U.S. 169, 174.

Accordingly, the burden is on the taxpayer who contends that some portion of its total assets are beyond the reach of the taxing power of its domicile to prove that the same property may be similarly taxed in another jurisdiction. Cf. Dixie Ohio Express Co. v. State Revenue Comm'n, 306 U.S. 72.

The controlling question here is, therefore, the same as it was in Standard Oil Co. v. Peck, 342 U.S. 382, where the decision whether a state property tax might constitutionally be imposed on the full value of a domiciliary's moving assets turned on whether " 'a defined part of the domiciliary corpus' " — there consisting of boats and barges traveling along inland waters — "could be taxed by the several states on an apportionment basis," 342 U.S., at 384.

Since the burden of proving an exemption is on the taxpayer who claims it, we must consider whether the stipulated facts show that some determinable portion of the value of the appellant's freight cars had acquired a tax situs in a jurisdiction other than Pennsylvania.

II

With respect to the freight cars that had been used on the lines of CNJ during the taxable year, the stipulation establishes that they "were run on fixed routes and regular schedules . . . over the lines of CNJ . . . in New Jersey." Their habitual employment within the jurisdiction in this manner would assuredly support New Jersey's imposition of an *apportioned* ad valorem tax on the value of the appellant's fleet of freight cars. Consequently, the daily average of freight cars located on the CNJ lines in the 1951 tax year, 158 in number, could not constitutionally be included in the computation of this Pennsylvania tax. In this respect, the Pennsylvania Supreme Court's decision . . . cannot be accepted.

III

We conclude, however, that on the record before us Pennsylvania was constitutionally permitted to tax, at full value, the remainder of appellant's fleet of freight cars, including those used by other railroads under the Car Service and Per Diem Agreement of the Association of American Railroads. These were, in the language of the stipulation, "regularly, habitually and/or continuously employed" in this manner, but they did not run "on fixed routes and regular schedules" as did the cars used by CNJ.

Since the domiciliary State is precluded from imposing an ad valorem tax on any property to the extent that it *could* be taxed by another State, not merely on such property as *is* subjected to tax elsewhere, the validity of Pennsylvania's tax must be determined by considering whether the facts in the record disclose a possible tax situs in some other jurisdiction. Had the record shown that appellant's cars traveled through other States along fixed and regular routes, even if it were silent with respect to the length of time spent in each nondomiciliary State, it would doubtless follow that the States through which the regular traffic flowed could impose a property tax measured by some fair apportioning formula. Cf. Braniff Airways, Inc. v. Nebraska Board of Equalization, 347 U.S. 590. And this would render unconstitutional any domiciliary ad valorem tax at full value on property that could thus be taxed elsewhere. Standard Oil Co. v. Peck, supra, at 384.

Alternatively a nondomiciliary tax situs may be acquired even if the rolling stock does not follow prescribed routes and schedules in its course through the nondomiciliary State. In American Refrigerator Transit Co. v. Hall, 174 U.S. 70, this Court sustained the constitutionality of a Colorado property tax on a stipulated average number of railroad cars that had been located within the territorial limits of Colorado during the tax year, although it was agreed by the parties that the cars "never were run in said State in fixed numbers nor at regular times, nor as a regular part of particular trains." Id., at 72. Habitual employment within the State of a substantial number of cars, albeit on irregular routes, may constitute sufficient contact to establish a tax situs permitting taxation of the average number of cars so engaged.

On the record before us, however, we find no evidence, except as to the CNJ cars, of either regular routes through *particular* nondomiciliary States or habitual presence, though on irregular missions, in *particular* nondomiciliary States. It is not disputed that many of the railroads listed as owning no track within Pennsylvania do have lines in more than one State, but there is no way of knowing which, if any, of these States may have acquired taxing jurisdiction over some of appellant's freight cars. And even with respect to railroads whose lines do not extend beyond the borders of a single State, it cannot be determined whether their use of appellant's cars was habitual or merely sporadic. It must be obvious that the fraction of a railroad's lines located within Pennsylvania is wholly unilluminating as to the consistency with which that railroad used appellant's cars in some other state.

In short, except as to freight cars traveling on the lines of the CNJ, this record shows only that a determinable number of appellant's cars were employed outside the Commonwealth of Pennsylvania during the relevant tax year. But as this leaves at large the possibility of their having a nondomiciliary tax situs elsewhere, that showing does not suffice under our cases to exclude Pennsylvania from taxing such cars to their full value. Neither Union Refrigerator Transit Co. v. Kentucky, supra, nor Standard Oil Co. v. Peck, supra, is properly read to the contrary. In the former, the case was remanded for further proceedings "not inconsistent" with the Court's opinion that the cars in question, "so far as they were [permanently] located and employed in other States," were not subject to the taxing power of the domiciliary State. 199 U.S., at 211. In the latter, the existence of a tax situs in one or more nondomiciliary States sufficiently appeared from the record. . . . To accept the proposition that a mere general showing of continuous use of movable property outside the domiciliary State is sufficient to exclude the taxing power of that State with respect to it, would surely result in an unsound rule; in instances where it was ultimately found that a tax situs existed in no other State such property would escape this kind of taxation entirely.

As we have shown there is nothing to the contrary in Standard Oil Co. v. Peck. . . . And neither the Braniff nor Ott case points to a different conclusion. In Braniff the airplanes held subject to nondomiciliary taxation were shown by the record to have flown on fixed and regular routes. 347 U.S., at 600-601. In Ott the Court was careful to point out that "the statute 'was intended to cover *and actually covers here*, an average portion of property permanently within the State — and by permanently is meant throughout the taxing year.' " 366 U.S., at 175. (Emphasis added.) In the case before us it is impossible to tell, except as to cars on the lines of the CNJ, what the average number of cars was annually in any given State. . . .

Accordingly, we conclude that with respect to all cars other than those employed by CNJ on its lines in New Jersey the appellant has failed to sustain its burden of proving that a tax situs had been acquired elsewhere. The exemption was properly disallowed in this regard.

The judgment of the Supreme Court of Pennsylvania is vacated and the case is remanded for further proceedings not inconsistent with this opinion.

It is so ordered.

MR. JUSTICE FRANKFURTER took no part in the decision of this case.

MR. JUSTICE WHITE took no part in the consideration or decision of this case.

MR. JUSTICE BLACK, concurring.

In holding that one State's property tax may be invalidated in part because excessive under the Commerce Clause upon the showing of a risk that some other State could impose a tax on part of the value of the same property, the Court is following principles announced in prior decisions of this Court from which I dissented. While my views expressed in those cases remain unchanged, the necessity of this Court's deciding cases requires me to make decisions under the constitutional doctrine there declared so long as the Court remains committed to it. Where a party seeks to invoke that doctrine, as here, I wholly agree with the Court that the burden of showing that there is a risk of multiple taxation should rest upon the party challenging the constitutionality of a state tax. I also agree with the Court that the railroad in this case has failed to show a risk of multiple taxation with reference to any cars other than the average number that are in New Jersey on any given day. It is for the foregoing reasons that I concur in the Court's judgment and its opinion insofar as it rests on the Commerce Clause.

Since I think partial invalidation of the tax as to the average number of cars in New Jersey on any given day in the taxable year is fully supported by the Commerce Clause as this Court has interpreted it, I would have been content not to discuss the due process question at all. But since the Court does rest in part on due process, I find it necessary to express my doubts about the use of the Due Process Clause to strike down state tax laws. The modern use of due process to invalidate state taxes rests on two doctrines: (1) that a State is without "jurisdiction to tax" property beyond its boundaries, and (2) that multiple taxation of the same property by different States is prohibited. Nothing in the language or the history of the Fourteenth Amendment, however, indicates any intention to establish either of these two doctrines concerning the power of States to tax. In fact neither of these doctrines originated in the Due Process Clause at all, but were first declared by this Court long before the Fourteenth Amendment with its Due Process Clause was adopted in 1868.[3] And in the first case striking down a state tax for lack of jurisdiction to tax after the passage of that Amendment neither the Amendment nor its Due Process Clause nor any other constitutional provision was even mentioned; the Court simply struck down the state tax saying that to sustain it would be "giving effect to the acts of the legislature of Pennsylvania upon property and interests lying beyond her jurisdiction."[4] These cases and others that followed for many years after the adoption of the Amendment rested either on the Commerce Clause or on no constitutional provision at all. In fact not a single state tax was struck down by this Court as a violation of the Due Process Clause until 1903[6] — 35 years after the adoption of the Amendment — and then wholly without any historical or

---

[3] Hays v. Pacific Mail Steamship Co., 17 How. 596 (1854). See also The Apollon, 9 Wheat. 362, 370 (1824); Braniff Airways, Inc. v. Nebraska State Board of Equalization, 347 U.S. 590, 599 n. 18.

[4] Railroad Co. v. Jackson, 7 Wall. 262, 268 (1869).

[6] Louisville & Jeffersonville Ferry Co. v. Kentucky, 188 U.S. 385.

518   Chapter Eight.   The States in a Federal Union

other reasons to show why the cryptic words of the Due Process Clause justified the invalidation of otherwise lawful state taxes. Nor did the Court reveal its reasons for giving due process this meaning in the next case.[7] Finally, in the third case applying the Due Process Clause to strike down a state tax, the Court's complete lack of explanation led Mr. Justice Holmes to say:

"It seems to me that the result reached by the court probably is a desirable one, but I hardly understand how it can be deduced from the Fourteenth Amendment, and as the Chief Justice feels the same difficulty, I think it proper to say that my doubt has not been removed." [199 U.S. 194, 211.]

The Court has ever since used the Due Process Clause to strike down state laws by finding in it substantially the same protection for interstate commerce as it has found in the Commerce Clause. But there is no reference to commerce in the Fourteenth Amendment and the Court has still never adequately explained just what the basis for its constitutional doctrine is. Because of this I have long entertained many of the same doubts that Mr. Justice Holmes expressed as to the use of this flexible and expansive interpretation of due process to invalidate state tax laws, but since the Court's holding here adequately rests on the presently prevailing interpretation of the Commerce Clause, I do not find this to be an appropriate occasion to suggest reconsideration of the applicability of the Due Process Clause to state tax laws.

MR. JUSTICE DOUGLAS, with whom THE CHIEF JUSTICE and MR. JUSTICE STEWART join, dissenting in part.

The stipulations of fact in this case show that an average of 158 freight cars (of the value of $525,765.71) run on fixed routes and regular schedules over railroad lines outside of Pennsylvania. The Court properly holds that they are beyond the constitutional reach of Pennsylvania.

The stipulations of fact also show that an average of 2189.30 freight cars (of the value of $7,282,773) run regularly, habitually, and continuously on the lines of other railroads outside of Pennsylvania, though not on fixed schedules. The Pennsylvania tax on these cars is sustained on the authority of New York Central R. Co. v. Miller, 202 U.S. 584; and if that case is still intact the Court is correct in denying the exemption claimed.

With all deference we cannot, however, allow Pennsylvania to lay this tax and adhere to our recent decisions. . . .

As a result of the Ott, Peck and Braniff cases the average of 2189.30 freight cars that run regularly, habitually, and continuously on lines of other railroads outside Pennsylvania could be taxed by other States, even though no State can identify the precise cars within its borders and even though the complement of cars is constantly changing. Since that average of freight cars is regularly, habitually, and continuously outside Pennsylvania, those cars are taxable elsewhere and thus beyond Pennsylvania's reach. The fact that we do not know the average annual number of cars in any given State does not help Pennsylvania's case. Whatever the average in any one State, the total outside Pennsylvania and taxable elsewhere is known and definite. Since that is true, we sanction double taxation when we sustain this tax. We would not allow it in the case of any other interstate business; and, as I read the Constitution, no exception is made that puts the railroad business at a disadvantage.[w]

NOTE

One important class of transportation equipment is conspicuously missing from these cases: trucks and buses. The reason presumably is that taxes on motor vehicles usually

---

[7] Delaware, Lackawanna & Western R. Co. v. Pennsylvania, 198 U.S. 341 (1905).

[w] For comment see The Supreme Court, 1961 Term, 76 Harv. L. Rev. 54, 154-159 (1962). — ED.

wear the garb of fees for the use of highways. See Capitol Greyhound Lines v. Brice, 339 U.S. 542 (1950), noted supra page 489.

Minnesota v. Blasius 290 U.S. 1, 54 S. Ct. 34, 78 L. Ed. 131 (1933)

Mr. Chief Justice Hughes delivered the opinion of the Court.

Respondent, George Blasius, is a trader in livestock at the St. Paul Union Stockyards in South St. Paul, Minnesota. On May 1, 1929, he owned and had in his possession in these yards eleven head of cattle which were assessed for taxation as his personal property, under the general tax law of the State. In this action, brought to collect the tax, Blasius defended upon the ground that the cattle were in course of interstate commerce, and a part of that commerce, and were not subject to state taxation. The Supreme Court of the State, overruling the decision of the trial court, sustained this defense, and this Court granted certiorari. 187 Minn. 420; 245 N.W. 612; 289 U.S. 717.

The material facts, as found by the trial court, are these: At the St. Paul Union Stockyards, thousands of head of livestock arrive daily by railroad and truck and are promptly sold and moved. The livestock comes from the State of Minnesota and other States throughout the northwest. The class of livestock which Blasius buys on the market are those that go immediately thereafter into the hands of feeders or growers within and without the State of Minnesota and principally beyond the borders of that State. He has not dealt in livestock for immediate slaughter. Thus, it was the practice of Blasius to go upon the market at the stockyards and buy livestock to meet the requirements of his trade, and in the regular course of his business practically all cattle purchased by him were sold and shipped to non-residents of the State, although selling and shipping to residents of the State did sometimes occur.

The eleven head of cattle in question came to the yards from some point outside the State of Minnesota; they had been consigned to commission firms for sale at the South St. Paul market; the consignors "had no intent to transport said cattle to any other place than South St. Paul, nor did they have any intent that such cattle should be transported to any particular place after their sale"; they were bought by Blasius from the commission merchants on April 30, 1929, and on May 1, 1929, the tax date, they were owned by him and "had not been entered with any carrier for shipment to any point," but were being offered for sale on the market; seven of the eleven head were sold on that day to a non-resident purchaser and were immediately shipped by the purchaser to points outside the State of Minnesota; the remaining four head were similarly sold and shipped on the following day. After his purchase Blasius placed the cattle in pens leased by him from the stockyards company; he paid for their feed and water up to the time of resale.

The court found that Blasius was not "subject to any discrimination in favor of cattle solely the product of the State of Minnesota"; that the assessment was made at the regular time and in the usual manner for taxation of personal property within the State; that the transportation of the cattle ceased after purchase from the commission men; that the cattle were not held by Blasius for the purpose of promoting their safe or convenient transit but were purchased and held by him because he desired to make a profit at their resale; that they were held at his pleasure and that he would sell to anyone, resident or non-resident, who was the highest bidder; that Blasius did not buy the cattle for the purpose of export or shipment to another State; and that after their purchase by him, and until he resold, the cattle were "at absolute and complete rest in the yards at South St. Paul" and "were a part of the general mass of cattle in the State and locally owned." The Court also found that the cattle were "handled by the defendant as a part of the chain of title from the original producer thereof to the final consumer thereof," and that such handling was "a necessary factor in the center of chain of commerce from West to the East and South."

The dealings at the South St. Paul stockyards including the transactions of Blasius, as described in these findings, manifestly were so related to a current of commerce among the States as to be subject to the power of regulation vested in the Congress. Applying the cardinal principle that interstate commerce as contemplated by the Constitution "is not a technical legal conception, but a practical one, drawn from the course of business," this Court said, in Swift & Co. v. United States, 196 U.S. 375, 398, 399: "When cattle are sent for sale from a place in one State, with the expectation that they will end their transit, after purchase, in another, and when in effect they do so, with only the interruption necessary to find a purchaser at the stockyards, and when this is a typical, constantly recurring course, the current thus existing is a current of commerce among the States, and the purchase of the cattle is a part and incident of such commerce." In that case, the question was as to the reach of the federal power through the prohibitions of the Anti-Trust Act of July 2, 1890 (26 Stat. 209), and these were held to apply to an attempt to monopolize commerce among the States by "a combination of independent dealers to restrict the competition of their agents when purchasing stock for them in the stockyards." On the same fundamental principle, the Court sustained the Packers and Stockyards Act of 1921 (42 Stat. 159) providing for the supervision by federal authority of the business of commission men and livestock dealers in the great stockyards of the country. Stafford v. Wallace, 258 U.S. 495. It was in deference to these decisions that the state court denied validity to the tax here assailed. 187 Minn., p. 426.

But because there is a flow of interstate commerce which is subject to the regulating power of the Congress, it does not necessarily follow that, in the absence of a conflict with the exercise of that power, a State may not lay a non-discriminatory tax upon property which, although connected with that flow as a general course of business, has come to rest and has acquired a situs within the State. . . .

The States may not impose direct burdens upon interstate commerce, that is, they may not regulate or restrain that which from its nature should be under the control of the one authority and be free from restriction save as it is governed in the manner that the national legislature constitutionally ordains. This limittion applies to the exertion of the State's taxing power as well as to any other interference by the State with the essential freedom of interstate commerce. Thus, the States cannot tax interstate commerce, either by laying the tax upon the business which constitutes such commerce or the privilege of engaging in it, or upon the receipts, as such, derived from it. Similarly, the States may not tax property in transit in interstate commerce. But, by reason of a break in the transit, the property may come to rest within a State and become subject to the power of the State to impose a non-discriminatory property tax. Such an exertion of state power belongs to that class of cases in which, by virtue of the nature and importance of local concerns, the State may act until Congress, if it has paramount authority over the subject, substitutes its own regulation. The "crucial question," in determining whether the State's taxing power may thus be exerted, is that of "continuity of transit." Carson Petroleum Co. v. Vial, 279 U.S. 95, 101.

If the interstate movement had not begun, the mere fact that such a movement is contemplated does not withdraw the property from the State's power to tax it. Coe v. Errol, 116 U.S. 517; Diamond Match Co. v. Ontonagon, 188 U.S. 82. If the interstate movement has begun, it may be regarded as continuing, so as to maintain the immunity of the property from state taxation, despite temporary interruptions due to the necessities of the journey or for the purpose of safety and convenience in the course of the movement. Coe v. Errol, supra; Kelley v. Rhoads, 188 U.S. 1: Champlain Co. v. Brattleboro, 260 U.S. 366. Formalities, such as the forms of billing, and mere changes in the method of transportation do not affect the continuity of the transit. The question is always one of substance, and in each case it is necessary to consider the particular occasion or purpose of the interruption during which the tax is sought to be levied. Champlain Co. v. Brattleboro, supra; Southern Pacific Terminal Co. v. Interstate Commerce Comm'n, 219 U.S. 498; Texas & N.O.R. Co. v. Sabine Tram Co., 227 U.S. 111; Carson Petroleum Co. v. Vial, supra. The mere power of the owner to divert the shipment already started does not take it out of interstate commerce if it appears "that the journey has already begun in good faith and temporary interruption of the passage is reasonable and in furtherance of the intended tranportation." Hughes Bros. Co. v. Minnesota, 272 U.S. 469, 476.

Where property has come to rest within a State, being held there at the pleasure of the owner, for disposal or use, so that he may dispose of it either within the State, or for shipment elsewhere, as his interest dictates, it is deemed to be a part of the general mass of property within the State and is thus subject to its taxing power. In Brown v. Houston, 114 U.S. 622, coal mined in Pennsylvania and sent by water to New Orleans to be sold there in the open market, was held to have "come to its place of rest, for final disposal or use," and to be "a commodity in the market of New Orleans," and thus to be subject to taxation under the general laws of the State; although the property might, after arrival, be sold from the vessel on which the transportation was made for the purpose of shipment to a foreign port. As the Court said in Champlain Co. v. Brattleboro, supra, the coal in Brown v. Houston "was being held for sale to anyone who might wish to buy." A similar case is Pittsburgh & Southern Coal Co. v. Bates, 156 U.S. 577. In General Oil Co. v. Crain, 209 U.S. 211, the company conducted an oil business at Memphis where it gathered oil from the North and maintained an establishment for its distribution. Part of the oil was deposited in a tank, appropriately marked for distribution in smaller vessels in order to fill orders for oil already sold in Arkansas, Louisiana and Mississippi. The Court held that the first shipment had ended, that the storage of the oil at Memphis for division and distribution to various points was "for the business purposes and profit of the company"; and that the tank at Memphis had thus become a depot in its oil business for preparing the oil for another interstate journey. This decision followed the principle announced in American Steel & Wire Co. v. Speed, 192 U.S. 500. See Champlain Co. v. Brattleboro, supra; Atlantic Coast Line R. Co. v. Standard Oil Co., 275 U.S. 257, 270; Carson Petroleum Co. v. Vial, supra.

In Bacon v. Illinois [227 U.S. 504], Bacon, the owner of the grain and the taxpayer, had bought it in the South and had secured the right from the railroads transporting it to remove it to his private grain elevator for the purpose of inspecting, weighing, grading, mixing, etc. He had power to change its ownership, consignee or destination, or to restore the grain, after the processes above mentioned, to the carrier to be delivered at destination in another State according to his original intention. The Court held that, whatever his intention, the grain was at rest within his complete power of disposition, and was taxable; that "it was not being actually transported and it was not held by carriers for transportation"; that the purpose of the withdrawal from the carriers "did not alter the fact that it had ceased to be transported and had been placed in his hands"; that he had "the privilege of continuing the transportation under the shipping contracts, but of this he might avail himself or not as he chose. He might sell the grain in Illinois or forward it as he saw fit." What he had done was to establish a "local facility in Chicago for his own benefit; and while, through its employment, the grain was there at rest, there was no reason why it should not be included with his other property within the State in an assessment for taxation which was made in the usual way without discrimination." In Champlain Co. v. Brattleboro, supra, the court thus restated the point of the Bacon case: "His storing of the grain was not to facilitate interstate shipment of the grain, or save it from the danger of the journey." "He made his warehouse a depot for its preparation for further shipment and sale. He had thus suspended the interstate commerce journey and brought the grain within the taxable jurisdiction of the State." See, also, Susquehanna Coal Co. v. South Amboy, 228 U.S. 665, 669, and Nashville, C. & St. L. R. Co. v. Wallace, 288 U.S. 249, 266.

The case of Blasius is a stronger one for the state tax than that of Bacon. Here the original shipment was not suspended; it was ended. That shipment was to the South St. Paul stockyards for sale on that market. That transportation had ceased, and the cattle were sold on that market to Blasius, who became absolute owner and was free to deal with them as he liked. He could sell the cattle within the State or for shipment outside the State. He placed them in pens and cared for them awaiting such disposition as he might see fit to make for his own profit. The tax was assessed on the regular tax day while Blasius thus owned and possessed them. The cattle were not held by him for the purpose of promoting their safe or convenient transit. They were not in transit. Their situs was in Minnesota where they had come to rest. There was no federal right to immunity from the tax.

Judgment reversed. [x]

EMPRESA SIDERURGICA v. COUNTY OF MERCED, 337 U.S. 154, 69 S. Ct. 995, 93 L. Ed. 1276 (1949). Douglas, J.: "There was a cement plant in Merced County, California, which was sold to petitioner — a corporation of Colombia — for export to South America. An export license was obtained and a letter of credit in favor of the seller deposited here. Title passed and possession was taken for the purchaser. A company, which was a common carrier, was employed to do the dismantling and packaging for shipment. As the dismantling proceeded, shipments were labeled with appellant's name as consignee and delivered to a rail carrier.

"Respondent, acting under a California statute, levied a personal property tax on the property for the tax year 1945-1946. The tax date was March 5, 1945. On that date 12 per cent of the plant had been shipped out of the county. That portion was relieved of the tax. The balance was taxed. That included the 10 per cent which had been dismantled and crated or prepared for shipment, 34 per cent which had been dismantled but not crated or prepared for shipment, and 44 per cent which had not been dismantled. But before the end of January, 1946, all the property had been shipped by rail to a port and was en route to South America by ocean carrier.

". . . Appellant claimed that this tax was . . . unconstitutional. It paid the tax under protest and brought this suit to recover it. The trial court . . . granted judgment for appellant. The Supreme Court of California reversed. 32 Cal. 2d 68, 194 P.2d 527. The case is here on appeal . . ."

What decision? Why?

JOY OIL CO., LTD. v. STATE TAX COMMISSION, 337 U.S. 286, 69 S. Ct. 1075, 93 L. Ed. 1366 (1949). Frankfurter, J.: "On December 29, 1945, petitioner Joy Oil Company, Ltd., a Canadian corporation, purchased 1,500,000 gallons of gasoline from Mid-West Refineries, Inc., of Grand Rapids, Michigan. The bills of lading issued by the railroad to which the gasoline was delivered were marked 'For Export to Canada,' but the gasoline was consigned to petitioner at Detroit. In order to secure the benefits of lower export freight rates and exemption from the federal transportaion and manufacturers' excise taxes, petitioner furnished Mid-West Refineries and the railroad prescribed forms certifying that the gasoline was purchased for export. Rail shipments were begun in January and completed in February of 1946. As the gasoline reached Detroit it was accumulated in storage tanks leased by petitioner at Dearborn.

"On April 1, 1947, the city of Dearborn assessed an ad valorem property tax on the gasoline, all of which, except 50,000 gallons, shipped to Canada by truck over the Ambassador Bridge, had then been in the Dearborn tanks for fifteen months. Shipment by truck was halted by a federal regulation prohibiting the transportation of inflammables over any

---

[x] Cf. Independent Warehouses v. Scheele, 331 U.S. 70 (1947); see Powell, Taxation of Things in Transit, 7 Va. L. Rev. 167, 245, 429, 497 (1920-1921). — Ed.

international bridge, and petitioner apparently chose not to ship the gasoline by rail across the Detroit River. In July of 1947 petitioner began to ship it to Canada by water; the last tanker load departed on August 22, 1947. Petitioner explains the delay as due to inability to obtain shipping space at any earlier date.

"Petitioner resisted payment of the tax. . . . The Tax Commission of Michigan sustained Dearborn's assessment of the tax, and the Supreme Court of Michigan affirmed. 321 Mich. 335, 32 N.W.2d 472. We granted certiorari. . . ."

What decision? Why?

4. Taxes on Transportation

Case of the State Freight Tax 15 Wall. 232, 21 L. Ed. 146 (1873)

MR. JUSTICE STRONG delivered the opinion of the court:

This is a writ of error to the supreme court of Pennsylvania, and we are called upon to review a judgment of that court, affirming the validity of a statute of the state, which the plaintiffs in error alleged to be repugnant to the Federal Constitution.

The statute was enacted on the 25th of August, 1864, and was entitled "An Act to Provide Additional Revenues for the Use of the Commonwealth." Its first section enacted "that the president, . . . or other financial officer of every railroad company, steamboat company, canal company, . . . shall, within thirty days after the first days of January, April, July, and October of every year . . . pay to the state treasurer for the use of the commonwealth, on each two thousand pounds of freight so carried, tax at the following rates: 'First, on the product of mines' (and other articles), 'two cents'; 'second, on another class of articles, three cents'; and 'on a third class, five cents.' " The section further enacted that "when the same freight shall be carried over different, but continuous lines, such freight shall be chargeable with tax as if it had been carried but upon one line, and the whole tax shall be paid by such one of said companies as the state treasurer may select and notify thereof . . . but in no case shall tax be twice charged on the same freight carried in or over the same line . . . provided, . . . every corporation, company or individual of any other state holding and enjoying any franchises, property or privileges whatever in this state, by virtue of the laws thereof, shall . . . pay for the freight carried over, through and upon that portion of their lines within this state, as if the whole of their respective lines were within this state."

It is the validity of this statute which is now asssailed, and the case we have before us presents the question whether, so far as it imposes a tax upon freight taken up within the state and carried out of it, or taken up outside the state and delivered within it; or, in different words, upon all freight other than that taken up and delivered within the state, it is not repugnant to the provision of the Constitution of the United States which ordained:

"That Congress shall have power to regulate commerce with foreign nations and among the several states," or in conflict with the provision that "no state shall, without the consent of Congress, lay any imposts or duties on imports or exports, except what may be absolutely necessary for executing its inspection laws." . . .

Before proceeding, however, to a consideration of the direct question whether the statute is in direct conflict with any provision of the Constitution of the United States, it is necessary to have a clear apprehension of the subject and the nature of the tax imposed by it. . . .

Upon what, then, is the tax imposed by the act of August 25, 1864, to be considered as laid? Where does the substantial burden rest? Very plainly it was not intended to be, nor is it in fact, a tax upon the franchise of the carrying companies, or upon their property, or upon their business measured by the number of tons of freight carried. On the contrary, it is expressly laid upon the freight carried. . . . And this tax is not proportioned to the business done in transportation. It is the same whether the freight be moved one mile or three hundred. If freight be put upon a road and carried at all, tax is to be paid upon it, the amount of the tax being determined by the character of the freight. [The opinion summarizes various provisions of the statute.] In view of these provisions of the statute, it is impossible to escape from the conviction that the burden of the tax rests upon the freight transported, or upon the consignor or consignee of the freight (imposed because the freight is transported), and that the company authorized to collect the tax and required to pay it into the state treasury is, in effect, only a tax gatherer. . . .

Then, why is not a tax upon freight transported from state to state a regulation of interstate transportation and, therefore, a regulation of commerce among the states? Is it not prescribing a rule for the transporter, by which he is to be controlled in bringing the subjects of commerce into the state, and in taking them out? The present case is the best possible illustration. The legislature of Pennsylvania has, in effect, declared that every ton of freight taken up within the state and carried out, or taken up in other states and brought within her limits shall pay a specified tax. The payment of that tax is a condition, upon which is made dependent the prosecution of this branch of commerce. And as there is no limit to the rate of taxation she may impose, if she can tax at all, it is obvious the condition may be made so onerous that an interchange of commodities with other states would be rendered impossible. The same power that may impose a tax of two cents per ton upon coal carried out of the state, may impose one of $5. Such an imposition, whether large or small, is a restraint of the privilege or right to have the subjects of commerce pass freely from one state to another without being obstructed by the intervention of state lines. It would hardly be maintained, we think, that had the state established customhouses on her borders, wherever a railroad or canal comes to the state line, and demanded at these houses a duty for allowing merchandise to enter or to leave the state upon one of those railroads or canals, such an imposition would not have been a regulation of commerce with her sister states. Yet it is difficult to see any substantial difference between the supposed case and the one we have in hand. The goods of no citizen of New York, New Jersey, Ohio, or of any other state, may be placed upon a canal, railroad, or steamboat within the state for transportation any distance, either into or out of the state, without being subjected to the burden. Nor can it make any difference that the legislative purpose was to raise money for the support of the state government, and not to regulate transportation. It is not the purpose of the law, but its effect, which we are now considering. Nor is it at all material that the tax is levied upon all freight, as well that which is wholly internal as that embarked in interstate trade. We are not, at this moment, inquiring further than whether taxing goods carried because they are carried, is a regulation of carriage. The state may tax its internal commerce; but if an act to tax interstate or foreign commerce is unconstitutional, it is not cured by including in its provisions subjects within the domain of the state. . . .

If, then, this is a tax upon freight carried between states, and a tax because of its transportation, and if such a tax is in effect a regulation of interstate commerce, the conclusion seems to be inevitable that it is in conflict with the Constitution of the United States. It is not necessary to the present case to go at large into the much-debated question whether the power given to Congress by the Constitution to regulate commerce among the states is exclusive. . . . However this may be, the rule has been asserted with great clearness, that whenever the subjects over which a power to regulate commerce is asserted are in their nature national, or admit of one uniform system or plan of regulation, they may justly be said to be of such a nature as to require exclusive legislation by Congress. Cooley v. Port Wardens, 12 How. 299; Gilman v. Philadelphia [3 Wall. 713]; Crandall v. The State of

Nevada, 6 Wall. 42. Surely transportation of passengers or merchandise through a state, or from one state to another, is of this nature. It is of national importance that over that subject there should be but one regulating power, for if one state can directly tax persons or property passing through it, or tax them indirectly by levying a tax upon their transportation, every other may, and thus commercial intercourse between states remote from each other may be destroyed. The produce of western states may thus be effectually excluded from eastern markets, for though it might bear the imposition of a single tax, it would be crushed under the load of many. It was to guard against the possibility of such commercial embarrassments, no doubt, that the power of regulating commerce among the states was conferred upon the Federal government. . . .

The conclusion of the whole is that, in our opinion, the act of the legislature of Pennsylvania of Aug. 25, 1864, so far as it applies to articles carried through the state, or articles taken up in the state and carried out of it, or articles taken up without the state and brought into it, is unconstitutional and void.

Judgment reversed, and the record is remitted for further proceedings in accordance with this opinion.

MR. JUSTICE SWAYNE, dissenting:

I dissent from the opinion just read. In my judgment, the tax is imposed upon *the business* of those required to pay it. The tonnage is only the mode of ascertaining the extent of the business. That no discrimination is made between freight carried wholly within the state, and that brought into or carried through or out of it, sets this, as I think, in a clear light, and is conclusive on the subject.

I am authorized to say that MR. JUSTICE DAVIS unites with me in this dissent.

State Tax on Railway Gross Receipts 15 Wall. 284, 21 L. Ed. 164 (1873)

MR. JUSTICE STRONG delivered the opinion of the court:

By an act of the legislature of Pennsylvania, passed on the 23d day of February, 1866, entitled "An Act to Amend the Revenue Laws of the Commonwealth," a tax was imposed upon the gross receipts of certain companies. The 2d section is as follows: "In addition to the taxes now provided by law, every railroad, canal and transportation company incorporated under the laws of this commonwealth, and not liable to the tax upon income under existing laws, shall pay to the commonwealth a tax of three fourths of one per centum upon the gross receipts of said company. The said tax shall be paid semi-annually, upon the first days of July and January, commencing on the first day of July, 1866; and for the purpose of ascertaining the amount of the same, it shall be the duty of the treasurer, or other proper officer of said company, to transmit to the auditor general a statement under oath or affirmation, of the amount of gross receipts of said company during the preceding six months. . . ."

. . . It was claimed in the state courts that the act is unconstitutional so far as it taxes that portion of the gross receipts of companies which are derived from transportation from the state to another state, or into the state from another, and the supreme court of the state having decided adversely to the claim, the case has been brought here for review.

We have recently decided in another case between these parties, that freight transported from state to state is not subject to state taxation, because thus transported. Such a burden we regard as an invasion of the domain of Federal power, a regulation of interstate commerce, which Congress only can make. If, then, a tax upon the gross receipts of a railroad, or a canal company, derived in part from the carriage of goods from one state to another is to be regarded as a tax upon interstate transportation, the question before us is already decided. . . .

Is, then, the tax, imposed by the act of February 23, 1866, a tax upon freight transported into or out of the state, or upon the owner of freight, for the right of thus transporting it? Certainly it is not directly. Very manifestly it is a tax upon the railroad company, measured in amount by the extent of its business, or the degree to which its franchise is exercised. That its ultimate effect may be to increase the cost of transportation must be admitted. So it must be admitted that a tax upon any article of personal property that may become a subject of commerce, or upon any instrument of commerce, affects commerce itself. If the tax be upon the instrument, such as a stage coach, a railroad car, or a canal, or steamboat, its tendency is to increase the cost of transportation. Still it is not a tax upon transportation, or upon commerce, and it has never been seriously doubted that such a tax may be laid. A tax upon landlords as such affects rents, and generally increases them, but it would be a misnomer to call it a tax upon tenants. A tax upon the occupation of a physician or an attorney, measured by the income of his profession, or upon a banker, graduated according to the amount of his discounts or deposits, will hardly be claimed to be a tax on his patients, clients, or customers, though the burden ultimately falls upon them. It is not their money which is taken by the government. The law exacts nothing from them. But when, as in the other case between these parties, a company is made an instrument by the laws to collect the tax from transporters, when the statute plainly contemplates that the contribution is to come from them, it may properly be said they are the persons charged. Such is not this case. The tax is laid upon the gross receipts of the company; laid upon a fund which has become the property of the company, mingled with its other property, and possibly expended in improvements or put out at interest. The statute does not look beyond the corporation to those who may have contributed to its treasury. The tax is not levied and, indeed, such a tax cannot be, until the expiration of each half year, and until the money received for freights, and from other sources of income, has actually come into the company's hands. Then it has lost its distinctive character as freight earned, by having become incorporated into the general mass of the company's property. While it must be conceded that a tax upon interstate transportation is invalid, there seems to be no stronger reason for denying the power of the state to tax the fruits of such transportation after they have become intermingled with the general property of the carrier, than there is for denying her power to tax goods which have been imported, after their original packages have been broken, and after they have been mixed with the mass of personal property in the country. That such a tax is not unwarranted is plain. . . .

There is another view of this case to which brief reference may be made. It is not to be questioned that the states may tax the franchises of companies created by them, and that the tax may be proportioned either to the value of a franchise granted, or to the extent of its exercise; nor is it deniable that gross receipts may be a measure of proximate value, or, if not, at least of the extent of enjoyment. If the tax be, in fact, laid upon the companies, adopting such a measure imposes no greater burden upon any freight or business from which the receipts come than would an equal tax laid upon a direct valuation of the franchise. In both cases, the necessity of higher charges to meet the exaction is the same.

Influenced by these considerations, we hold that the act of the legislature of the state imposing a tax upon the plaintiffs in error equal to three quarters of one per cent of their gross receipts, is not invalid because in conflict with the power of Congress to regulate commerce among the states. And under the decision made in Woodruff v. Parham, 8 Wall. 123, it is not invalid because it lays an impost or duty on imports or exports.

The judgment of the Supreme Court is, therefore, affirmed.

MR. JUSTICE MILLER, dissenting:

The principles announced in the case of the tax on the ton of freight, and the argument by which those principles are supported, meet my full approval. They lie at the foundation of our present Federal Constitution. The burdens which states, possessed of safe and commodious harbors, imposed by way of taxes called imposts upon the transit of merchandise through those ports to their destination for consumption in other states, were the cause as much as any one class of grievances of the formation of that Constitution; and the

Section D. State Taxation

reluctance of the little state of Rhode Island to give up the tax which she thus levied on the commerce of her sister states through the harbor of Newport, then the largest importing place in the Union, was the reason that she refused for nearly two years to ratify that instrument.

The clauses of the Constitution which forbid the states to levy duties on imports, and which gave to Congress the right to regulate commerce, were designed to remedy that evil, and have always been supposed to be sufficient for that purpose. The one is the complement of the other and something more. The first forbids the states to levy the tax on goods imported from abroad. The second places the entire control of commerce, with the exception of such as may be begun and completed within a single state, under the control of Congress. That commerce which is carried on with foreigners, or with the Indian tribes, or between citizens of different states, is under the jurisdiction of the general government.

The opinion which affirms the tax of so much per ton on freight carried from one state to another to be a tax upon transportation, and therefore a regulation of the commerce among the several states, forbidden by the Constitution, receives the approbation of all the members of this court except two. And it is there declared that any tax upon the freight so transported, or upon the carrier on account of such transportation, is within the prohibition.

Is the tax in the present case also within the evil intended to be remedied by the commerce clause of the Constitution?

It seems to me that to hold that the tax on freight is within it, and that on gross receipts arising from such transportation is not, is "to keep the word of promise to the ear and break it to the hope." If the state of Pennsylvania, availing herself of her central position across the great line of necessary commercial intercourse between the east and the west, and of the fact that all the ways of land and water carriage must go through her territory, is determined to support her government and pay off her debt by a tax on this commerce, it is of small moment that we say she cannot tax the goods so transported, but may tax every dollar paid for such transportation. Her tax by the ton being declared void, she has only to effect her purpose by increasing correspondingly her tax on gross receipts. In either event the tax is one for the privilege of transportation within her borders; in either case the tax is one on transportation. . . .

The tax does not depend on the profits of the companies. It is the same whether the profits or the losses preponderate in a given year. A road may do a large carrying trade at a loss, but the state says, nevertheless, "for every dollar that you receive for transportation I claim one cent or half a cent."

It is conceded that railroads may be taxed as other corporations are taxed on their capital stock, on their property, real and personal, and in any other way that does not impose necessarily a burden on transportation between one state and another. But a railroad or canal company differs from corporations for banking, insurance, or manufacturing purposes in this: that while their business is only remotely or incidentally connected with commerce, the business of roads and canals, namely, transportation of persons and property, is itself commerce. So much of said commerce as is exclusively within the state is subject to its regulations by taxation or otherwise, but that which carries goods from or to another state is exempted by the Constitution from its control.

I lay down the broad proposition that by no device or evasion, by no form of statutory words, can a state compel citizens of other states to pay to it a tax, contribution, or toll, for the privilege of having their goods transported through that state by the ordinary channels of commerce. And that this was the purpose of the framers of our Constitution I have no doubt; and I have just as little doubt that the full recognition of this principle is essential to the harmonious future of this country now, as it was then. The internal commerce of that day was of small importance, and the foreign was considered as of great consequence. But both were placed beyond the power of the states to control. The interstate commerce today far exceeds in value that which is foreign, and it is of immense importance that it should not be shackled by restrictions imposed by any state in order to place on others the burden of supporting its own government, as was done in the days of the helpless Confederation.

I think the tax on gross receipts is a violation of the Federal Constitution and, therefore, void.

I am authorized to say that MR. JUSTICE FIELD and MR. JUSTICE HUNT concur in this dissent.

NOTE

In Philadelphia and Southern Steamship Co. v. Pennsylvania, 122 U.S. 326 (1887), a unanimous Court appears to have repudiated the reasoning of the majority in the case of the State Tax on Railway Gross Receipts, supra. A Pennsylvania statute imposed a tax upon the gross receipts of every railroad, steamship company, etc., doing business in the state. The taxpayer resisted imposition of the tax upon gross receipts "derived from freight and passage money between the ports of Philadelphia and Savannah, and in foreign trade from New Orleans, and a small amount for charter parties in the like trade." Bradley, J., for the Court wrote: "If, then, the commerce carried on by the plaintiff in error in this case could not be constitutionally taxed by the state, could the fares and freights received for transportation in carrying on that commerce be constitutionally taxed? If the state may not tax the transportation, may it, nevertheless, tax the fares and freights received therefor? Where is the difference? Looking at the substance of things, and not at mere forms, it is very difficult to see any difference. The one thing seems to be tantamount to the other. It would seem to be rather metaphysics than plain logic for the state officials to say to the company: 'We will not tax you for the transportation you perform, but we will tax you for what you get for performing it.' Such a position can hardly be said to be based on a sound method of reasoning." The opinion then reviewed the two grounds upon which decision in the earlier case was based, and concluded "[T]he first ground . . . is not tenable. . . . We do not think [the second] can be affirmed in the present case." The tax, as there applied, was held unconstitutional.

Illinois Central R.R. v. Minnesota 309 U.S. 157, 60 S. Ct. 419, 84 L. Ed. 670 (1940)

MR. JUSTICE DOUGLAS delivered the opinion of the Court:

Minnesota imposes on every railroad company owning or operating lines within its borders a five per cent tax on gross earnings derived from its operation within the state. This tax, payable in lieu of all other taxes, has been sustained by this Court, in various applications, as a property tax.[2] In this case, which is here on appeal (28 U.S.C. §344(a)) from a judgment of the Supreme Court of Minnesota (205 Minn. 1, 621, 284 N.W. 360, 286 N.W. 359), appellant contends that the statute as construed and applied to it violates the Fourteenth Amendment and the commerce clause of the federal Constitution.

Appellant, an Illinois railroad corporation, owns no lines in Minnesota but operates leased lines with 30.15 miles of trackage in that state. It owns or operates about 5,000 miles in other states. The item of gross earnings which the state seeks here to tax arises out of debits and credits for exchange of freight cars which appellant makes with other railroads, the using road being charged $1 per day per car. During the years here involved

---

[2] Great Northern R. Co. v. Minnesota, 278 U.S. 503; Cudahy Packing Co. v. Minnesota, 246 U.S. 450; United States Exp. Co. v. Minnesota, 223 U.S. 335.

appellant had credits in its favor for such use of its cars by other roads operating in Minnesota of $17,427,862; and debits owing such roads of $14,924,508, leaving a net credit balance in favor of appellant of $2,503,353. These debits and credits represented use of cars in other states as well as in Minnesota. In absence of adequate and accurate records their use was apportioned to Minnesota pursuant to the following formula:

Each reporting road was charged with such percentage of the credit balance owing from each using railroad as was determined by ascertaining the ratio of each using railroad's Minnesota revenue freight car miles to its system car miles.

Each reporting road was given credit for such percentage of the debit balance owing each other road as was determined by ascertaining the ratio of the reporting railroad's Minnesota revenue freight car miles to its system car miles.

The credit and debit balances were computed and apportioned annually; and the net credits were then ascertained, to which the statutory tax of 5 per cent was applied.

Thus for the year 1922 appellant had credit balances of $691,433.97 owing from 13 other roads. Their Minnesota revenue freight car miles varied from 2.3% to 100% of their system car miles, making Minnesota's proportion of the credit balances $95,359.49. For the same year appellant had debit balances from freight car hire owing to 8 other roads of $215,863.05. Appellant's Minnesota revenue freight car miles were only .11% of its system car miles for that year. Hence, it was permitted to deduct only .11% of $215,863.05 or $237.43, leaving $95,122.06 to which the tax was applicable. On similar computations for each of the following seven years the tax for which the state brought suit totalled $26,414.59.

Appellant's contention under the Fourteenth Amendment is that the statute as applied in the foregoing formula denies it equal protection of the law and due process. We do not think that contention is tenable.

First as to the credit balances. These represent payments to appellant for use of its freight cars by other roads which operate in Minnesota. Minnesota does not seek to reach all of those receipts. As the statute reaches only revenues derived from operations in the state, the formula effects an apportionment. Certainly the ratio of Minnesota revenue freight car miles to system car miles is consistent with the statutory scheme of ascertaining what payments represent use in Minnesota. That the apportionment may not result in mathematical exactitude is certainly not a constitutional defect.[4] Rough approximation rather than precision is, as a practical matter, the norm in any such tax system.[5]

Second as to the debit balances. As we have said, appellant is not taxed on all of its credit balances but only on that portion which accrues as a result of the use of its cars by others in Minnesota. Hence it is not permitted under the formula to deduct all of its debit balances but only the portion thereof which it pays others for the use of their cars in Minnesota. Certainly if appellant receives $50,000 from one road for use of appellant's cars in Minnesota and pays another road $50,000 for appellant's use of that road's cars outside of Minnesota, it cannot realistically be said that no part of the $50,000 received by appellant has a Minnesota origin. On the contrary, the whole $50,000 paid appellant derives from use of its cars in Minnesota. For Minnesota then to lay a tax on the whole amount (as it does under this formula) is to exercise a jurisdiction which constitutionally is hers. Similarly to permit under the formula a deduction of only those debit balances owing by virtue of the use by appellant in Minnesota of cars of other roads results in determining a net credit balance for its Minnesota activity of renting out and borrowing freight cars. To hold that that net cannot constitutionally be taxed by Minnesota but must be reduced by the amount of payments made by appellant for its use of cars in other states would be to deprive Minnesota of her jurisdiction over property within her borders. For as appellant's cars move over tracks of other roads in Minnesota and as cars of other roads move over its

[4] Cf. Rowley v. Chicago & N.W.R. Co. 293 U.S. 102, 109.
[5] Cf. Dane v. Jackson, 256 U.S. 589, 598, 599.

tracks in Minnesota, certain credits and debits accrue. To say that the resultant net credit balance does not derive wholly from operations within Minnesota is to deny the fact.

But the nub of appellant's objection seems to rest on the equal protection clause of the Fourteenth Amendment. Most of its contentions come back to the point that it has only 30 odd miles of tracks in the state. On this phase, appellant makes two points. First, as compared with other roads having extensive mileage in Minnesota, it is permitted to deduct only a small fraction (between .1% and .13%) of its debit balances. Second, it is penalized for having nominal trackage in Minnesota, for roads with no trackage in the state pay no tax on these items though they may have substantial revenues from rentals of cars for use in Minnesota.

We have in substance already dealt with the first of these contentions. All roads operating in Minnesota are taxed on precisely the same, not on different bases. So far as the present incidence of the statute is concerned, the tax is laid on the net credit balances from the business of renting and borrowing cars used in Minnesota. The fact that appellant receives a larger net than others from its Minneosta activity of renting and borrowing cars and hence must pay a larger tax does not mean that Minnesota has overstepped her constitutional bounds. Appellant is not singled out for special treatment. It is not taxed on one formula; the others, on another. They are all taxed pursuant to the same formula; and the formula is adapted to ascertainment of value of property situated in Minnesota. And appellant's contention that the tax is discriminatory because it has only 30 miles of track yet must pay a tax while others with hundreds of miles may pay none, is beside the point. The business taxed is not adequately measured by trackage alone. Though appellant has but few miles of track in the state, nevertheless its cars are constantly moving over other lines in Minnesota. That produces revenue. A tax on that revenue certainly bears a close relationship to appellant's property in the state which no computation based on trackage can alter.

As to appellant's second objection under this head, little need be said. Companies not owning or operating roads within the state are not reached by this tax statute; roads that do, are. That certainly is not discrimination in the constitutional sense. Appellant has subjected itself to the jurisdiction of Minnesota. Those doing likewise are similarly treated by the state, as are domestic companies engaged in that business. The fact that that entails burdens is a part of the price for enjoyment of the privileges which Minnesota extends.

Appellant makes some point of double taxation. But the flaw in that argument is exposed by the familiar doctrine, aptly phrased by Mr. Justice Holmes, that the "Fourteenth Amendment no more forbids double taxation than it does doubling the amount of a tax; short of confiscation or proceedings unconstitutional on other grounds." [9]

Appellant's constitutional objection based on the commerce clause has been adequately answered in the prior decisions of this Court sustaining other taxes levied under this statute.[10] The right of a state to tax property, although it is used in interstate commerce, is well settled. And certainly if such tax has a fair relation to the property employed in the state (as this tax clearly does) it cannot be said to run afoul of the prohibition against state taxation on interstate commerce. As Chief Justice Fuller once said on that point, "by whatever name the exaction may be called, if it amounts to no more than the ordinary tax upon property or a just equivalent therefor, ascertained by reference thereto, it is not open to attack as inconsistent with the Constitution." [11] . . .

In conclusion, appellant contends that the Supreme Court of Minnesota erred in holding that the credits here taxed are "gross earnings" within the meaning of the statute. But on such matters of construction we defer to the state court's interpretation.

Affirmed.

---

[9] Ft. Smith Lumber Co. v. Arkansas, 251 U.S. 532, 533.
[10] . . . supra, note 2.
[11] Postal Teleg. Cable Co. v. Adams, 155 U.S. 697.

NOTE State Taxation of Fuel Used in Interstate Commerce

Another approach to the problem of apportionment of state taxing powers over interstate activities has been developed with regard to state taxation of fuel used in interstate commerce. In Helson v. Kentucky, 279 U.S. 245 (1929), the Court struck down a state tax on gasoline purchased outside the state but consumed within its limits by a commercial ferry line. Helson was distinguished in Edelman v. Boeing Air Transport, Inc., 289 U.S. 249 (1933). There, the Court upheld a state use tax on fuel imported from outside the state by an air transport company for use in its own planes. The Court reasoned that the taxable event was transfer of the fuel from storage to the airplane fuel tanks, a process completed before use of the fuel in interstate commerce. Edelman was followed in United Air Lines, Inc. v. Mahin, 410 U.S. 623 (1973). In reaffirming Edelman, Justice Blackmun wrote, in an opinion joined by five justices:

"The line drawn between an impermissible tax on mere consumption of fuel, as in Helson, and a permissible tax on storage of fuel before loading, as in Edelman and Nashville [, Chattanooga, & St. Louis R. Co. v. Wallace, 288 U.S. 249 (1933)], continues to serve rational purposes. Retaining the line at this point minimizes the danger of double taxation and yet provides a source of revenue having a relation to the event taxed. Double taxation is minimized because the fuel cannot be taxed by States through which it is transported, under Michigan-Wisconsin Pipe Line Co. v. Calvert, 347 U.S. 157 (1954), nor by the State in which it is merely consumed, under Helson. A fair result is achieved because a State in which preloading storage facilities are maintained is likely to provide substantial services to those facilities, including police protection and the maintenance of public access roads."

Joseph v. Carter & Weekes Stevedoring Co. 330 U.S. 422, 67 S. Ct. 815, 91 L. Ed. 993 (1947)

MR. JUSTICE REED delivered the opinion of the Court.

These two writs of certiorari bring before this Court contentions in regard to the application to the respective respondents, Carter & Weekes Stevedoring Company and John T. Clark & Son, of New York City, of the general business tax laws covering, when both cases are considered, the years 1937 to 1941 inclusive. The character of the taxes in issue will appear from a section, set out below, of a local law imposing the tax for 1939 and 1940.[2] The respective taxpayers are liable also for the general income and ad valorem taxes of the State and City of New York. Both respondents are corporations engaged in the business of general stevedoring. For these cases, the business of respondents may be considered as consisting only of taking freight from a convenient place on the pier or lighter wholly within the territorial limits of New York City and storing it properly for safety and for handling in or on the outgoing vessel alongside, or of similarly unloading a vessel on its arrival. The vessels moved in interstate or foreign commerce, without a call at any other port of New York. We do not find it necessary to consider separately interstate and foreign commerce. The Commerce Clause covers both.

Through statutory proceedings unnecessary to particularize, the Comptroller of the City of New York determined that the respondents were liable for percentage taxes upon

---

[2] Local Laws of the City of New York (1940), No. 78:

"§ R41-2.0. Imposition of tax. a. For the privilege of carrying on or exercising for gain or profit within the city any trade, business, profession, vocation or commercial activity other than a financial business, or of making sales to persons within such city, . . . every person shall pay an excise tax which shall be equal to one-tenth of one percentum upon all receipts received in and/or allocable to the city from such profession, vocation, trade, business or commercial activity exercised or carried on by him during the calendar year in which such period shall commence. . . ."

the entire gross receipts from the above activities for the years in question under the provisions of the respective local laws to which reference has been made. Review of these determinations was had by respondents in the Supreme Court of New York, Appellate Division. The determinations of the Comptroller were annulled on the authority of Puget Sound Stevedoring Co. v. State Tax Commission, 302 U.S. 90, 269 App. Div. 685, 54 N.Y.S.2d 380, 383. These orders were affirmed by the Court of Appeals, 294 N.Y. 906, 908, 63 N.E.2d 112 . . . .

Petitioners recognize the force of the Puget Sound Case as a precedent. Their argument is that subsequent holdings of this Court have indicated that the reasons which underlay the decision are no longer controlling in judicial examination of the constitutionality of state taxation of the gross proceeds derived from commerce, subject to federal regulation. They cite, among others, these later decisions: Western Live Stock v. Bureau of Revenue, 303 U.S. 250; Southern P. Co. v. Gallagher, 306 U.S. 167; McGoldrick v. Berwind-White Coal Min. Co., 309 U.S. 33; Department of Treasury v. Wood Preserving Corp., 313 U.S. 62.

In the Puget Sound Case a state tax on gross receipts, indistinguishable from that laid by New York City in this case, was held invalid as applied to stevedoring activities exactly like those with which we are here concerned. The Puget Sound opinion pointed out, 302 U.S. pp. 92 et seq., that transportation by water is impossible without loading and unloading. Those incidents to transportation occupy the same relation to that commerce whether performed by the crew or by stevedore, contracting independently to handle the cargo. The movement of cargo off and on the ship is substantially a continuation of the transportation. Cf. Baltimore & O.S.W.R. Co. v. Burtch, 263 U.S. 540. . . .

We do not think that a tax on gross income from stevedoring, obviously a "continuation of the transportation," is a tax apportioned to income derived from activities within the taxing state. The transportation in commerce, at the least, begins with loading and ends with unloading. Loading and unloading has effect on transportation outside the taxing state because those activities are not only preliminary to but are an essential part of the safety and convenience of the transportation itself.

When we come to weigh the burden or interference of this tax on the gross receipts from interstate commerce, the purposes of that portion of the Commerce Clause — the freeing of business from unneighborly regulations that inhibit the intercourse which supplies reciprocal wants by commerce — is a significant factor for consideration. An interpretation of the text to leave the states free to tax commerce until Congress intervened would have permitted intolerable discriminations. Nippert v. Richmond, 327 U.S. 416, and cases collected in notes 13, 14, 15 and 16. . . .

A power in a state to tax interstate commerce or its gross proceeds, unhampered by the Commerce Clause, would permit a multiple burden upon that commerce. This has been noted as ground for their invalidation. Western Live Stock v. Bureau of Revenue, 303 U.S. 250, 255. The selection of an intrastate incident as the taxable event actually carries a similar threat to the commerce but, where the taxable event is considered sufficiently disjoined from the commerce, it is thought to be a permissible state levy. This result generally is reached because the local incident selected is one that is essentially local and is not repeated in each taxing unit. In the present case, the threat of a multiple burden, except in the few instances in the record of interstate, in distinction to foreign, commerce, is absent. The multiple burden on interstate transportation from taxation of the gross receipts from stevedoring arises from the possibility of a similar tax for unloading. The actual effect on the cost of carrying on the commerce does not differ from that imposed by any other tax exaction — ad valorem, net income or excise. Cf. Western Live Stock v. Bureau of Revenue, supra. We need consider only whether or not the loading and unloading is distinct enough from the commerce to permit the tax on the gross.

On precedent, the Puget Sound Case is controlling. . . . We come now face to face with the problem of overruling or approving the case.

Since Puget Sound there has been full consideration of how far a state may go in taxing intrastate incidents closely related in time and movement to the interstate commerce. . . . The 2% excise tax levied by New Mexico on the gross receipts of publishers from advertising, upheld in Western Live Stock, was found to be an exaction for carrying on a local business. The Gallagher Case turns expressly on our conclusion that a use tax is validly levied on an intrastate event, "separate and apart from interstate commerce," p. 176, and the Wood Preserving Case reached a similar result by reason of the fact that the taxpayer sold and delivered its ties intrastate before transportation began, 313 U.S. at 67. This is likewise true of American Mfg. Co. v. St. Louis, 250 U.S. 459, as explained in the Storen Case. When we examine the Berwind-White tax on the purchasers of tangible personal property for consumption, there is the same reliance upon the local character of the sale . . . .

Though all of these cases were closely related to transportation in commerce both in time and movement, it will be noted that in each there can be distinguished a definite separation between the taxable event and the commerce itself. We have no reason to doubt the soundness of their conclusions.

Stevedoring is more a part of the commerce than any of the instances to which reference has just been made. Although state laws do not discriminate against interstate commerce or in actuality or by possibility subject it to the cumulative burden of multiple levies, those laws may be unconstitutional because they burden or interfere with commerce. See Southern P. Co. v. Arizona, 325 U.S. 761, 767. Stevedoring, we conclude, is essentially a part of the commerce itself and therefore a tax upon its gross receipts or upon the privilege of conducting the business of stevedoring for interstate and foreign commerce, measured by those gross receipts, is invalid. We reaffirm the rule of Puget Sound Stevedoring Company. "What makes the tax invalid is the fact that there is interference by a State with the freedom of interstate commerce." Freeman v. Hewit [329 U.S. 256]. Such a rule may in practice prohibit a tax that adds no more to the cost of commerce than a permissible use or sales tax. What lifts the rule from formalism is that it is a recognition of the effects of state legislation and its actual or probable consequences. Not only does it follow a line of precedents outlawing taxes on the commerce itself but it has reason to support it in the likelihood that such legislation will flourish more luxuriantly where the most revenue will come from foreign or interstate commerce. Thus in port cities and transportation or handling centers, without discrimination against out-state as compared with local business, larger proportions of necessary revenue could be obtained from the flow of commerce. The avoidance of such a local toll on the passage of commerce through a locality was one of the reasons for the adoption of the Commerce Clause.

Affirmed.

Mr. Justice Black dissents.

Mr. Justice Douglas, with whom Mr. Justice Rutledge concurs, dissenting in part.

First. I think the tax is valid insofar as it reaches the gross receipts from loading and unloading vessels engaged in interstate commerce. . . .

The tax in [Philadelphia & S. Mail S.S. Co. v. Pennsylvania, 122 U.S. 326] was a tax on the gross receipts from fares and freight for the transportation of persons and goods in interstate and foreign commerce. It was unapportioned. . . .

The distinction between an apportioned gross receipts tax and a tax on all the gross receipts of an interstate business, such as was involved in Philadelphia & S. Mail S.S. Co. v. Pennsylvania . . . was explained in Western Live Stock v. Bureau of Revenue, 303 U.S. 250, 256, which was decided in 1938. The Court stated that the latter type of tax could be imposed or added to "with equal right by every state which the commerce touches, merely because interstate commerce is being done, so that without the protection of the commerce clause it would bear cumulative burdens not imposed on local commerce." . . .

Second. I think the tax is unconstitutional insofar as it reaches the gross receipts from loading and unloading vessels engaged in foreign commerce. Such a tax is repugnant to Article 1, §10, Clause 2 of the Constitution which provides that "No State shall, without the Consent of the Congress, lay any Imposts or Duties on Imports or Exports, except what may be absolutely necessary for executing its inspection Laws. . . ."

Loading and unloading are a part of "the exporting process" which the Import-Export Clause protects from state taxation. See Thames & M.M. Ins. Co. v. United States, 237 U.S. 19, 27. Activity which is a "step in exportation" has that immunity. A. G. Spalding & Bros. v. Edwards, 262 U.S. 66, 68. As the Court says, loading and unloading cargo are "a continuation of the transportation." Indeed, the commencement of exportation would occur no later. See Richfield Oil Corp. v. State Bd. of Equalization, 329 U.S. 69. And the gross receipts tax is an impost on an export within the meaning of the Clause, since the incident "which gave rise to the accrual of the tax was a step in the export process." Richfield Oil Corp. v. State Bd. of Equalization, supra.

As we pointed out in that case, the Commerce Clause and the Import-Export Clause "though complementary, serve different ends." 329 U.S. p. 76. Since the Commerce Clause does not expressly forbid any tax, the Court has been free to balance local and national interests. Taxes designed to make interstate commerce bear a fair share of the cost of local government from which it receives benefits have been upheld; taxes which discriminate against interstate commerce, which impose a levy for the privilege of doing it, or which place an undue burden on it have been invalidated. But the Import-Export Clause is written in terms which admit of no exception but the single one it contains. Accordingly a state tax might survive the tests of validity under the Commerce Clause and fail to survive the Import-Export Clause. For me the present tax is a good example.

MR. JUSTICE MURPHY joins in this dissent except as to the second part, as to which he is of the opinion that the tax in relation to the gross receipts from loading and unloading vessels engaged in foreign commerce is constitutional.[y]

Railway Express Agency v. Virginia *358 U.S. 434, 79 S. Ct. 411, 3 L. Ed. 2d 450 (1959)*

MR. JUSTICE CLARK delivered the opinion of the Court.

Once again the effort of the Commonwealth of Virginia to levy a tax against express agencies is before us for decision. Nearly five years ago this Court struck down as a "privilege tax" violative of the Commerce Clause of the Federal Constitution its tax statute under which was laid an assessment on appellant's "privilege of doing business" in Virginia. Railway Express Agency v. Virginia, 347 U.S. 359 (1954). Subsequently the Virginia General Assembly enacted the Act here involved levying a "franchise tax" on express companies, measured by gross receipts from operations within Virginia, in lieu of all other property taxes on intangibles and rolling stock. In due course an assessment against appellant was made thereunder for 1956. Both the State Corporation Commission, which has jurisdiction of such levies in Virginia, and the Commonwealth's highest court have upheld the validity of the new law as well as the assessment made thereunder, Railway Express Agency v. Virginia, 199 Va. 589, 100 S.E.2d 785. Appellant levels a dual attack, the first being that the statute is a "privilege tax" and like the former one violates the Commerce Clause; or, secondly, that in any event the assessment under it is calculated in such a manner as to deprive appellant of its property without due process of law in violation of the Fourteenth Amendment. . . . We believe that Virginia has eliminated the Commerce Clause objections sustained against its former tax law. While

---

[y] Cf. Canton R.R. v. Rogan, 340 U.S. 511 (1951), aff'g 195 Md. 206, 73A.2d 12 (1950); Central Greyhound Lines v. Mealey, 334 U.S. 653 (1948); Lockhart, Gross Receipts Taxes on Interstate Transportation and Communication, 57 Harv. L. Rev. 40 (1943). — ED.

the tax is in lieu of other property taxes which Virginia can legally assess and should be their just equivalent in amount, Postal Telegraph Cable Co. v. Adams, 155 U.S. 688, 696 (1895), we will not inquire into the exactitudes of the formula where appellant has not shown it to be so baseless as to violate due process. Nashville, C. & St. L.R. v. Browning, 310 U.S. 362 (1940). The failure of the appellant to furnish, in its return, certain necessary information showing its gross receipts allocated to Virginia, called for under the statute and requested by the Commonwealth, has left the correct amount unobtainable by the latter except by some method of approximation and places the burden on appellant to come forward with affirmative evidence of extraterritorial assessment.

BACKGROUND AND ACTIVITY OF APPELLANT IN VIRGINIA

Since the opinion in the former appeal . . . relates the factual details concerning appellant's operations in Virginia, we believe it sufficient to say here that it is a Delaware corporation, owned by 68 of the railroads of the United States. It is engaged in both an interstate and intrastate express business throughout the Nation, save in Virginia, where a constitutional provision bars foreign corporations from possessing or exercising any of the powers or functions of public service corporations. There it operates a wholly owned subsidiary, a Virginia corporation, which carries on its intrastate functions within the Commonwealth. Appellant's Virginia business is thus of an exclusively interstate nature. Through exclusive contract arrangements with 177 of the railroads of the Nation appellant is the sole operator of express facilities on their lines, including Virginia. It pays therefor all of its net income, thus achieving one of the stated purposes of the agreement — that appellant ". . . shall have no net taxable income." In turn, appellant's Virginia subsidiary pays all of its net income over to it for the privilege of exercising appellant's exclusive contracts in intrastate business in the Commonwealth. Appellant owns property within Virginia, its return filed with the Commonwealth for tax purposes showing $120,110.70 in cash in deposit; automotive equipment and trucks $262,719.63; real estate of the value of $32,850; and office equipment listed at $42,884.83.

VIRGINIA'S GENERAL TAXING SYSTEM

The Commonwealth has a comprehensive tax structure covering public service corporations. It empowers local governments to levy ad valorem taxes on the "dead" value of all real property and tangible personal property, except rolling stock, located within their respective jurisdictions. This leaves free for state purposes taxes on rolling stock, money and other intangibles, and the "live" or "going-concern" value of the business in Virginia. We are concerned only with the state tax which is levied on the franchises of express companies. It provides in pertinent part that "[e]ach express company . . . shall . . . pay to the State a franchise tax which shall be in lieu of taxes upon all of its other intangible property and in lieu of property taxes on its rolling stock."

The franchise tax is measured by "the gross receipts derived from operations within" Virginia which is deemed "to be all receipts on business beginning and ending within this State and all receipts derived from the transportation within this State of express transported through, into, or out of this State."

The State Corporation Commission is directed, after notice, to assess the franchise tax on the basis of a report to be filed by the company involved or, in case of its failure to file such report, the Commission is to base the assessment "upon the best and most reliable information that it can procure."

THE ISSUES UNDER THE STATUTE

First, let us clear away the dead underbrush of the old law. The new tax is not denominated a license tax laid on the "privilege of doing business in Virginia"; nor is it "in addition to the property tax" levied against appellant, nor a condition precedent to its engaging in interstate commerce in the Commonwealth. The General Assembly has made crystal-clear that the tax is now a franchise tax laid on the intangible property of appellant, and is levied "in lieu of taxes upon all of its other intangible property and . . . rolling stock." The measure of the tax is on gross receipts, fairly apportioned, and, as to appellant, is laid only on those "derived from the transportation within this State of express transported through, into, or out of this State."

Appellant concedes that the Commerce Clause does not prohibit the States from levying a tax on property owned by a concern doing an interstate business. It agrees that it has rolling stock and money in the Commonwealth, as well as intangibles, including its exclusive express privileges with the railroads. It readily admits that the latter agreements are "valuable contract rights" and contribute a principal element to the "going concern value" of its business in the Commonwealth. Subsuming that a valid tax levy might be levied on such intangibles, it argues, however, that the incidence of the tax is on appellant's privilege to carry on an exclusively interstate business in Virginia rather than on intangible property. Our sole question under the Commerce Clause is whether the tax in practical operation is on property or on privilege.

The due process issue is entangled with appellant's failure to file, in its report, data covering its gross receipts allocated to Virginia. Failing to do this the State Corporation Commission used a formula which in effect ascribed to Virginia the proportion of such receipts as the mileage of carriers within Virginia bore to the total national mileage of the same lines. Appellant contends that the assessment made in this manner is violative of due process and that the resulting amount of tax levied was confiscatory.

In any event, appellant argues, the "in lieu" provisions of the law, as applied to it, are invalid. Admitting that it had cash, intangibles and rolling stock that were subject to a state tax but which suffered none because of the "in lieu" provisions of this law, it contends that the tax assessed under the latter was no just equivalent of the "in lieu" taxes but was greatly in excess thereof and violative of due process.

VALIDITY OF THE LAW UNDER THE COMMERCE CLAUSE

As we have pointed out, the statute levies a franchise tax in lieu of all taxes on "*other* intangible property" and rolling stock. (Emphasis added.) This leaves no room for doubt that the General Assembly intended to levy a tax upon appellant's intangibles. Moreover, supporting this interpretation, both the State Commission and the Supreme Court of Appeals have construed it as a tax on appellant's intangible property and "going concern" value. This trinity of agreement by three state agencies, though not conclusive, has great weight in our determination of the natural and reasonable effect of the statute. [Citations omitted.] This is not to say that a legislature may effect a validation of a tax, otherwise unconstitutional, by merely changing its descriptive words. Lawrence v. State Tax Commission, 286 U.S. 276, 280 (1932); Galveston, H. & San Antonio R. Co. v. Texas, 210 U.S. 217, 227 (1908). One must comprehend, however, the difference between the use of magic words or labels validating an otherwise invalid tax and their use to disable an otherwise constitutional levy. The latter this Court has said may sometimes be done. Railway Express Agency v. Virginia, supra, at 364; Spector Motor Service v. O'Connor [340 U.S. 602], at 607; McLeod v. Dilworth Co., 322 U.S. 327, 330 (1944).

Appellant buttresses its argument with reasoning that a tax on "going concern" value just cannot be measured by fairly apportioned gross receipts. While it may be true that gross receipts are not the best measure, it is too late now to question its constitutionality. Illinois Cent. R. Co. v. Minnesota, 309 U.S. 157 (1940); Great Northern R. Co. v. Minnesota, 278 U.S. 503 (1929); Pullman Co. v. Richardson, 261 U.S. 330 (1923); Cudahy Packing Co. v. Minnesota, 246 U.S. 450 (1918); United States Express Co. v. Minnesota, 223 U.S. 335 (1912); Wisconsin & M.R. Co. v. Powers, 191 U.S. 379 (1903). These decisions are still in good standing on our books. Even on the former appeal this Court used the following language:

Section D. State Taxation

"Of course, we have held, and it is but common sense to hold, that a physical asset may fluctuate in value according to the income it can be made to produce. A live horse is worth more than a dead one, though the physical object may be the same, and a smooth-going automobile is worth more than an unassembled collection of all its parts. The physical facilities used in carrying on a prosperous business are worth more than the same assets in bankruptcy liquidation or on sale by the sheriff. No one denies the right of the State, when assessing tangible property, to use any fair formula which will give effect to the intangible factors which influence real values. Adams Express Co. v. Ohio State Auditor, 166 U.S. 185. But Virginia has not done this." 347 U.S. at 364.

We feel that Virginia has now done just that. . . .

Nor is there any substance to the contention that since Virginia could not prohibit appellant from engaging in its exclusively interstate business, it therefore may not tax "good will" or "going concern" value which is built up thereby. . . .

VALIDITY OF THE TAX UNDER THE DUE PROCESS CLAUSE

In view of the fact that appellant failed to file the required information as to its gross receipts, thus placing an almost insurmountable burden on the Commonwealth to ascertain them, it is necessary that appellant make an affirmative showing that the mileage method used by Virginia is so palpably unreasonable that it violates due process. This it has failed to do. Appellant rests its argument not on facts and figures covering its actual gross income in Virginia but on comparative statistics based on tangible assets. It points out that during the taxable year the value of its tangible assets in Virginia ($475,065) was only 0.6% of its total assets ($79,700,426), while the amount of gross receipts apportioned to Virginia by the State Corporation Commission was 1.7% ($6,499,519) of its total gross receipts ($387,241,764). . . .

There is nothing in the record even to indicate that the tangible assets that appellant carries in its own name in Virginia did not actually generate the amount of gross receipts attributed to it by the State Corporation Commission. In this connection, we note that 1.9% of appellant's total contract mileage was located there. Even where taxpayers have attempted to show through evidence, as this appellant has not, that a given apportionment formula effected an appropriation of more than that to which the State was entitled, this Court has required " 'clear and cogent evidence' that it results in extraterritorial values being taxed." . . .

Appellant's final argument is to the effect that the tax in question, in the amount of $139,739.66, is "no just equivalent" of the tax "in lieu of which" it was levied, and therefore violates the Due Process Clause. This argument is based upon a false premise which can be quickly disposed of. Appellant states that under Virginia's system of segregation of property for state and local taxation the only property which the Commonwealth had the power to tax was cash on hand and on deposit and appellant's rolling stock, which, under the old rates, would have yielded a tax of $679.77. Appellant is clearly in error. As we read the Virginia statutes, and as they were construed below, the Commonwealth (as contrasted with the local) government also had the power to tax the "going concern" value of *all* of appellant's Virginia property, as well as its other intangible property rights such as its valuable express privileges. Thus, the new tax is not only in lieu of the previous tax on rolling stock and cash on hand, but also reaches intangible rights of great value which since Railway Express, supra, had escaped taxation altogether.

It follows from what we have said that the tax is valid, and the judgment below is therefore

Affirmed.

MR. JUSTICE FRANKFURTER concurs in the result.

MR. JUSTICE HARLAN, concurring.

I share the reservation of Mr. Justice Brennan as to the propriety of considering the tax described in the opinion of the Court as a property tax. I find myself unable, however, to distinguish in any constitutional sense the "in lieu" tax here involved from similar levies the validity of which has been sustained as applied to interstate enterprises in the line of cases cited in the Court's opinion, and therefore join the opinion.

MR. JUSTICE BRENNAN, concurring.

While I join the opinion and judgment of the Court, I must admit to some reservations whether the tax at bar can fairly be thought of as a property tax. The discussion of the Court in this case's predecessor, Railway Express Agency, Inc., v. Virginia, 347 U.S. 359, 364-367, cast serious doubt on the propriety of viewing Virginia's former tax as a property tax, and I share that doubt. The only modification in the mathematical demonstration of the prior decision necessitated by the revision of the tax statute is brought about by the new statute's provision that the tax is in lieu of other taxes on the appellant's intangible property and rolling stock. In practical effect, this means that payment of this $139,739.66 tax is "in lieu" of a $1/5\%$ tax on $120,110.70 of cash, amounting to $240.22; a tax, amounting to $427.56, on the value, apportioned to the State, of the appellant's refrigerator cars; and a 2½% tax on its trucks, valued at $262,719, amounting to $6,567.98. These taxes, in lieu of which the $139,739.66 tax at bar is payable, aggregate $7,235.76. It seems to me doubtful whether this makes a significant alteration in the demonstration the Court made on the prior appeal with respect to the status as a property tax of the gross receipts tax on express companies. While the tax may be a rough equivalent of some sort of property tax that Virginia might conceivably levy on express companies, I do not see that it has been made clear that it bears any equivalence to any sort of property tax that she in fact levies on other sorts of businesses or has in fact previously levied on express companies. Cf. Pullman Co. v. Richardson, 261 U.S. 330, 339. On the other hand, I cannot deny that this Court has, in decisions cited by the Court's opinion, frequently admitted gross receipts taxes to the characterization of "property taxes" in situations where their equivalence with any actual property tax was somewhat tenuous. See, e.g., Illinois Central R. Co. v. Minnesota, 309 U.S. 157.

To me, the more realistic way of viewing the tax and evaluating its constitutional validity is to take it as what it is in substance, a levy on gross receipts fairly apportionable to the taxing State. . . .

[MR. JUSTICE WHITTAKER, with whom MR. JUSTICE STEWART joined, dissented.]

5. Other Specific Excise Taxes

Heisler v. Thomas Colliery Co. 260 U.S. 245, 43 S. Ct. 83, 67 L. Ed. 237 (1922)

MR. JUSTICE MCKENNA delivered the opinion of the court: . . .

In 1921 the commonwealth [of Pennsylvania] passed the act here involved. It provided that from and after its passage each ton of anthracite coal mined, "washed, or screened, or otherwise prepared for market" in the commonwealth, should be "subject to a tax of 1½ per cent of the value thereof when prepared for market." It was provided that the tax should be assessed at the time when the coal has been subjected to the indicated preparation "and is ready for shipment or market."

Plaintiff in error, alleging himself to be a stockholder of the Thomas Colliery Company, brought this suit to have the act adjudged and decreed to be unconstitutional and void, and to enjoin that company and its directors from complying with the act, and to enjoin defendant in error, Samuel L. Lewis, auditor general of the commonwealth, and the defendant in error, Charles A. Snyder, treasurer of the commonwealth, from enforcing the act. . . .

Anthracite coal . . . is asserted to be found in only nine counties in the state, and practically nowhere else in the United States. The fact, it is further said, gives the state a monopoly of it, and that a tax upon it is levying a tribute upon the consumption of other states, and nine of them have appeared by their attorneys gneral to assail it as illegal, and denounce it as an attempt to regulate interstate commerce. In emphasis of the contention, the governor of the state is quoted as urging the tax because of that effect. The fact, tribute upon the consumers of the coal in other states, is pronounced inevitable, as, it is the assertion, 80 percent of the total production is shipped to other states, and that this constitutes its "major 'market.' " And the dependency upon Pennsylvania is represented as impossible of evasion or relief. Anthracite coal, is the assertion, has become a prime necessity of those states, "particularly for domestic purposes," and even "municipal laws and ordinances have been passed, forbidding the use of other coal for heating purposes." . . .

The contention that the tax is a regulation of interstate commerce seems to be based somewhat upon the declaration of the governor of the state of its effect upon consumers in other states. We are unable to discern in the fact any materiality or pertinency, nor in the fact that Pennsylvania has a monopoly (if we may use the word) of the coal. Whether any statute or action of a state impinges upon interstate commerce depends upon the statute or action, not upon what is said about it or the motive which impelled it; and a tax upon articles in one state that are destined for use in another state cannot be called a regulation of interstate commerce, whether imposed in the certainty of a return from a monopoly existing, or in the doubt and chances because of competition. The action of the state, as a regulation of interstate commerce, does not depend upon the degree of interferemce; it is illegal in any degree.

We may, therefore, disregard the adventitious considerations referred to and their confusion, and, by doing so, we can estimate the contention made. It is that the products of a state that have, or are destined to have, a market in other states, are subjects of interstate commerce, though they have not moved from the place of their production or preparation.

The reach and consequences of the contention repel its acceptance. If the possibility, or indeed, certainty, of exportation of a product or article from a state, determines it to be in interstate commerce before the commencement of its movement from the state, it would seem to follow that it is in such commerce from the instant of its growth or production; and in the case of coals, as they lie in the ground. The result would be curious. It would nationalize all industries; it would nationalize and withdraw from state jurisdiction and deliver to Federal commercial control the fruits of California and the South, the wheat of the West and its meats, the cotton of the South, the shoes of Massachusetts, and the woolen industries of other states, at the very inception of their production or growth; that is, the fruits unpicked, the cotton and wheat ungathered, hides and flesh of cattle yet "on the hoof," wool yet unshorn, and coal yet unmined, because they are, in varying percentages, destined for and surely to be exported to states other than those of their production.

However, we need not proceed further in speculation and argument. Ingenuity and imagination have been exercised heretofore upon a like contention. There is temptation to it in the relation of the states to the Federal government, being yet superior to the states in instances, or rather having spheres of action exclusive of them. The instances cannot in all cases be precisely defined. And the uncertainty attracts disputes, and is availed of to assert or suppose collisions which in fact do not exist. There is illustration in the cases. In Coe v. Errol, 116 U.S. 517, the precise contention here made was passed upon and rejected. It involved the taxing power of a state, and the property subject to it (timber cut in its forests) was intended for exportation, and had progressed nearer to exportation than the coal in the present case. . . .

Other cases have decided the same and afford illustrations of it. [Citations omitted.]

The effect of these cases is attempted to be evaded by the assertion that the statute, in imposing the tax when the coal " 'is ready for shipment or market,' is a plain and intentional fraud upon the commerce clause." We cannot accept the accusation as justified, or that the situation of the coal can be changed by it, and as moving in interstate commerce when it is plainly not so moving. The coal, therefore, is too definitely situated to be misunderstood, and the cases cited to establish a different character and subjection need not be reviewed.

Decree affirmed.[z]

NOTE

In Michigan-Wisconsin Pipe Line Co. v. Calvert, 347 U.S. 157 (1954), the Court held unconstitutional a Texas tax on the occupation of "gathering gas," measured by the entire volume of gas "taken," as applied to natural gas pipeline companies purchasing gas exclusively for transportation to and sale in other states. The gas was purchased at the outlet from a gasoline plant, where certain components of natural gas had been removed. The Court said that the problem was "whether here the State has delayed the incidence of the tax beyond the step where production and processing have ceased and transmission in interstate commerce has begun." It concluded: "Here it is perhaps sufficient that the privilege taxed, namely the taking of the gas, is not so separate and distinct from interstate transportation as to support the tax."

Western Live Stock v. Bureau of Revenue 303 U.S. 250, 58 S. Ct. 546, 82 L. Ed. 823 (1938)

Mr. Justice Stone delivered the opinion of the Court.

Section 201, chap, 7, of the New Mexico Special Session Laws of 1934, levies a privilege tax upon the gross receipts of those engaged in certain specified businesses. Subdivision I imposes a tax of 2% of amounts received from the sale of advertising space by one engaged in the business of publishing newspapers or magazines. The question for decision is whether the tax laid under this statute on appellants, who sell without the state, to advertisers there, space in a journal which they publish in New Mexico and circulate to subcribers within and without the state, imposes an unconstitutional burden on interstate commerce.

Appellants brought the present suit in the state district court to recover the tax, which they had paid under protest, as exacted in violation of the commerce clause of the Federal Constitution. The trial court overruled a demurrer to the complaint and gave judgment for appellants, which the Supreme Court reversed. 41 N.M. 141, 65 P.(2d) 863. Appellants refusing to plead further, the district court gave judgment for the appellees, which the Supreme Court affirmed. 41 N.M. 288, 67 P.(2d) 505. The case comes here on appeal from the second judgment under §237 of the Judicial Code, 28 U.S.C. §344.

Appellants publish a monthly livestock trade journal which they wholly prepare, edit, and publish within the state of New Mexico, where their only office and place of business is located. The journal has a circulation in New Mexico and other states, being distributed to paid subscribers through the mails or by other means of transportation. It carries advertisements, some of which are obtained from advertisers in other states through appellants' solicitation there. Where such contracts are entered into, payment is made by remittances to appellants sent interstate; and the contracts contemplate and provide for the interstate shipment by the advertisers to appellants of advertising cuts, mats, information

---

[z] Cf. Utah Power & Light Co. v. Pfost, 286 U.S. 165 (1932); Hope Natural Gas Co. v. Hall, 274 U.S. 284 (1927). See also, and compare, American Mfg. Co. v. St. Louis, 250 U.S. 459 (1919).

See comment on "Resource Profiteers" in 75 Harv. L. Rev. 953, 970-971 (1962). — Ed.

Section D. State Taxation

and copy. Payment is due after the printing of such advertisements in the journal and its ultimate circulation and distribution, which is alleged to be in New Mexico and other states.

Appellants insist here, as they did in the state courts, that the sums earned under the advertising contracts are immune from the tax because the contracts are entered into by transactions across state lines and result in the like transmission of advertising materials by advertisers to appellants, and also because performance involves the mailing or other distribution of appellants' magazines to points without the state.

That the mere formation of a contract between persons in different states is not within the protection of the commerce clause, at least in the absence of Congressional action, unless the performance is within its protection, is a proposition no longer open to question. Paul v. Virginia, 8 Wall. 168, ... Hence it is unnecessary to consider the impact of the tax upon the advertising contracts except as it affects their performance, presently to be discussed. Nor is taxation of a local business or occupation which is separate and distinct from the transportation and intercourse which is interstate commerce forbidden merely because in the ordinary course such transportation or intercourse is induced or occasioned by the business. Williams v. Fears, 179 U.S. 270, ... Here the tax which is laid on the compensation received under the contract, is not forbidden either because the contract, apart from its performance, is within the protection of the commerce clause, or because as an incident preliminary to printing and publishing the advertisements the advertisers send cuts, copy and the like to appellants.

We turn to the other and more vexed question, whether the tax is invalid because the performance of the contract, for which the compensation is paid, involves to some extent the distribution, interstate, of some copies of the magazine containing the advertisements. We lay to one side the fact that appellants do not allege specifically that the contract stipulates that the advertisements shall be sent to subscribers out of the state, or is so framed that the compensation would not be earned if subscribers outside the state should cancel their subscriptions. We assume the point in appellants' favor and address ourselves to their argument that the present tax infringes the commerce clause because it is measured by gross receipts which are to some extent augmented by appellants' maintenance of an interstate circulation of their magazine.

It was not the purpose of the commerce clause to relieve those engaged in interstate commerce from their just share of state tax burden even though it increases the cost of doing the business. "Even interstate business must pay its way," Postal Teleg.-Cable Co. v. Richmond, 249 U.S. 252, 259; Ficklen v. Taxing Dist., 145 U.S. 1, 24, . . . and the bare fact that one is carrying on interstate commerce does not relieve him from many forms of state taxation which add to the cost of his business. He is subject to a property tax on the instruments employed in the commerce, Western U. Teleg. Co. v. Atty. Gen. 125 U.S. 530, . . . and if the property devoted to interstate transportation is used both within and without the state a tax fairly apportioned to its use within the state will be sustained. Pullman's Palace Car Co. v. Pennsylvania, 141 U.S. 18, ... Net earnings from interstate commerce are subject to income tax, United States Glue Co. v. Oak Creek, 247 U. 321, and if the commerce is carried on by a corporation a franchise tax may be imposed, measured by the net income from business done within the state, including such portion of the income derived from interstate commerce as may be justly attributable to business done within the state by a fair method of apportionment. Underwood Typewriter Co. v. Chamberlain, 254 U.S. 113, . . .

All of these taxes in one way or another add to the expense of carrying on interstate commerce, and in that sense burden it; but they are not for that reason prohibited. On the other hand, local taxes, measured by gross receipts from interstate commerce, have often been pronounced unconstitutional. The vice characteristic of those which have been held invalid is that they have placed on the commerce burdens of such a nature as to be capable, in point of substance, of being imposed . . . Philadelphia & S. Mail S.S. Co. v.

Pennsylvania, 122 U.S. 326; Galveston, H. & S.A.R. Co. v. Texas, 210 U.S. 217 . . . or added to (Crew Levick Co. v. Pennsylvania, 245 U.S. 292; Fisher's Blend Station v. Tax Commission, 297 U.S. 650) with equal right by every state which the commerce touches, merely because interstate commerce is being done, so that without the protection of the commerce clause it would bear cumulative burdens not imposed on local commerce. See Philadelphia & S. Mail S.S. Co. v. Pennsylvania, supra; State Freight Tax Case, 15 Wall. 232, 280; Bradley, J., dissenting in Maine v. Grand Trunk R. Co., 142 U.S. 217, 235, . . . The multiplication of state taxes measured by the gross receipts from interstate transactions would spell the destruction of interstate commerce and renew the barriers to interstate trade which it was the object of the commerce clause to remove. Baldwin v. G. A. F. Seelig, 294 U.S. 511, 523.

It is for these reasons that a state may not lay a tax measured by the amount of merchandise carried in interstate commerce, State Freight Tax Case, 15 Wall. 232, supra, or upon the freight earned by its carriage. Fargo v. Michigan (Fargo v. Stevens), 121 U.S. 230; Philadelphia & S. Mail S.S. Co. v. Pennsylvania, 122 U.S. 326, restricting the effect of State Tax on R. Gross Receipts, 15 Wall. 284, with which compare Miller, J., dissenting in that case at p. 297. Taxation measured by gross receipts from interstate commerce has been sustained when fairly apportioned to the commerce carried on within the taxing state, Wisconsin & M.R. Co. v. Powers, 191 U.S. 379; Maine v. Grand Trunk R. Co., 142 U.S. 217, . . . and in other cases has been rejected only because the apportionment was found to be inadequate or unfair. Fargo v. Michigan (Fargo v. Stevens), supra; . . . Whether the tax was sustained as a fair means of measuring a local privilege or franchise, as in Maine v. Grand Trunk R. Co., 142 U.S. 217; Ficklen v. Taxing Dist., 145 U.S. 1, supra; American Mfg. Co. v. St. Louis, 250 U.S. 459, or as a method of arriving at the fair measure of a tax substituted for local property taxes, Cudahy Packing Co. v. Minnesota, 246 U.S. 450; United States Exp. Co. v. Minnesota, 223 U.S. 335, . . . it is a practical way of laying upon the commerce its share of the local tax burden without subjecting it to multiple taxation not borne by local commerce and to which it would be subject if gross receipts, unapportioned, could be made the measure of a tax laid in every state where the commerce is carried on. . . .

In the present case the tax is, in form and substance, an excise conditioned on the carrying on of a local business, that of providing and selling advertising space in a published journal, which is sold to and paid for by subscribers, some of whom receive it in interstate commerce. The price at which the advertising is sold is made the measure of the tax. This Court has sustained a similar tax said to be on the privilege of manufacturing, measured by the total gross receipts from sales of the manufactured goods both intrastate and interstate. American Mfg. Co. v. St. Louis, supra. The actual sales prices which measured the tax were taken to be no more than the measure of the value of the goods manufactured, and so an appropriate measure of the value of the privilege, the taxation of which was deferred until the goods were sold. Ficklen v. Taxing Dist., 145 U.S. 1, sustained a license tax measured by a percentage of the gross annual commissions received by brokers engaged in negotiating sales within for sellers without the state.

Viewed only as authority, American Mfg. Co. v. St. Louis, supra, would seem decisive of the present case. But we think the tax assailed here finds support in reason, and in the practical needs of a taxing system which, under constitutional limitations, must accommodate itself to the double demand that interstate business shall pay its way, and that at the same time it shall not be burdened with cumulative exactions which are not similarly laid on local business.

As we have said, the carrying on of a local business may be made the condition of state taxation, if it is distinct from interstate commerce, and the business of preparing, printing and publishing magazine advertising is peculiarly local and distinct from its circulation whether or not that circulation be interstate commerce. Cf. Puget Sound Stevedoring Co. v. Tax Commission, 302 U.S. 90. No one would doubt that the tax on the privilege would be valid if it were measured by the amount of advertising space sold. Utah Power & L. Co. v. Pfost, 286 U.S. 165, . . . Selling price, taken as a measure of value whose accuracy appellants do not challenge, is for all practical purposes a convenient means of arriving at an equitable measure of the burden which may be imposed on an admittedly taxable subject matter. Unlike the measure of the tax sustained in American Mfg. Co. v. St. Louis, 250 U.S. 459, supra, it does not embrace the purchase price (here the magazine subscription price) of the articles shipped in interstate commerce. So far as the advertising rates reflect a value attributable to the maintenance of a circulation of the magazine interstate, we think the burden on the interstate business is too remote and too attenuated to call for a rigidly logical application of the doctrine that gross receipts from interstate commerce may not be made the measure of a tax. Experience has taught that the opposing demands that the commerce shall bear its share of local taxation, and that it shall not, on the other hand, be subjected to multiple tax burdens merely because it is interstate commerce, are not capable of reconciliation by resort to the syllogism. Practical rather than logical distinctions must be sought. . . . Recognizing that not every local law that affects commerce is a regulation of it in a constitutional sense, this Court has held that local taxes may be laid on property used in the commerce; that its value for taxation may include the augmentation attributable to the commerce in which it is employed; and, finally, that the equivalent of that value may be computed by a measure related to gross receipts when a tax of the latter is substituted for a tax of the former. . . .

Here it is perhaps enough that the privilege taxed is of a type which has been regarded as so separate and distinct from interstate transportation as to admit of different treatment for purposes of taxation, Utah Power & L. Co. v. Pfost, 286 U.S. 165 . . . and that the value of the privilege is fairly measured by the receipts. The tax is not invalid because the value is enhanced by appellants' circulation of their journal interstate any more than property taxes on railroads are invalid because property value is increased by the circumstance that the railroads do an interstate business.

But there is an added reason why we think the tax is not subject to the objection which has been leveled at taxes laid upon gross receipts derived from interstate communication or transportation of goods. So far as the value contributed to appellants' New Mexico business by circulation of the magazine interstate is taxed, it cannot again be taxed elsewhere any more than the value of railroad property taxed locally. The tax is not one which in form or substance can be repeated by other states in such manner as to lay an added burden on the interstate distribution of the magazine. As already noted, receipts from subscriptions are not included in the measure of the tax. It is not measured by the extent of the circulation of the magazine interstate. All the events upon which the tax is conditioned — the preparation, printing and publication of the advertising matter, and the receipt of the sums paid for it — occur in New Mexico and not elsewhere. All are beyond any control and taxing power which, without the commerce clause, those states could exert through its dominion over the distribution of the magazine or its subscribers. The dangers which may ensue from the imposition of a tax measured by gross receipts derived directly from interstate commerce are absent.

In this and other ways the case differs from Fisher's Blend Station v. State Tax Commission, 297 U.S. 650, on which appellants rely. There the exaction was a privilege tax laid upon the occupation of broadcasting, which the Court held was itself interstate communication, comparable to that carried on by the telegraph and the telephone, and was measured by the gross receipts derived from that commerce. If broadcasting could be taxed, so also could reception. Station WBT v. Poulnot (D.C.) 46 F.(2d) 671. In that event a cumulative tax burden would be imposed on interstate communication such as might ensue if gross receipts from interstate transportation could be taxed. This was the vice of the tax of a percentage of the gross receipts from goods sold by a wholesaler in interstate commerce, held invalid in Crew Levick Co. v. Pennsylvania, 245 U.S. 292. In form and in substance the tax was thought not to be one for the privilege of doing a local business separable from interstate commerce. Cf. American Mfg. Co. v. St. Louis, supra. In none of these respects is the present tax objectionable.

Affirmed.

MR. JUSTICE MCREYNOLDS and MR. JUSTICE BUTLER are of opinion that the judgment should be reversed.

6. Net Income Taxes

Crew Levick Co. v. Pennsylvania 245 U.S. 292, 38 S. Ct. 126, 62 L. Ed. 295 (1917)

MR. JUSTICE PITNEY delivered the opinion of the court.

The State of Pennsylvania, by an Act of May 2, 1899, P.L., p. 184, imposes an annual mercantile license tax of three dollars upon each wholesale vender of or dealer in goods, wares, and merchandise, and "one-half mill additional on each dollar of the whole volume, gross, of business transacted annually," and like taxes at another rate upon retail venders, and at still another upon venders at an exchange or board of trade. In the year 1913 plaintiff in error sold and delivered at wholesale, from a warehouse located in that State, merchandise to the value of about $47,000 to purchasers within the State, and merchandise to the value of about $430,000 to customers in foreign countries: the latter sales usually having been negotiated by agents abroad who took orders and transmitted them to plaintiff in error at its office in the State of Pennsylvania, subject to its approval, while in some cases orders were sent direct by the customers in foreign countries to plaintiff in error; and the goods thus ordered, upon the acceptance of the orders, having been shipped direct by plaintiff in error from its warehouse in Pennsylvania to its customers in the foreign countries. Under the Act of 1899 a mercantile license tax was imposed upon plaintiff in error, based upon the amount of its gross annual receipts. Plaintiff in error protested against the assessment of so much of the tax as was based upon the gross receipts from merchandise shipped to foreign countries. The Court of Common Pleas of Philadelphia and, upon appeal, the Supreme Court of the State (256 Pa. St. 508) sustained the tax, overruling the contention that it amounted to a regulation of foreign commerce and also was an impost or duty on exports levied without the consent of Congress, contrary to §§ 8 and 10 of Art. I of the Constitution of the United States.

Whether there was error in the disposition of the federal question is the only subject with which we have to deal. . . .

We are constrained to hold that the answer must be in the affirmative. No question is made as to the validity of the small fixed tax of $3 imposed upon wholesale venders doing business within the State in both internal and foreign commerce; but the additional imposition of a percentage upon each dollar of the gross transactions in foreign commerce seems to us to be, by its necessary effect, a tax upon such commerce, and therefore a regulation of it; and, for the same reason, to be in effect an impost or duty upon exports. This view is so clearly supported by numerous previous decisions of this court that it is necessary to do little more than refer to a few of the most pertinent. Case of the State Freight Tax, 15 Wall. 232, 276-277; Robbins v. Shelby County Taxing District, 120 U.S. 489. . . .

Most of these cases related to interstate commerce, but there is no difference between this and foreign commerce, so far as the present question is concerned.

The principal reliance of the Commonwealth is upon Ficklen v. Shelby County Taxing District, 145 U.S. 1. Undoubtedly that case is near the border line; but we think its authority would have to be stretched in order to sustain such a tax as here in question.

Consistently with due regard for the constitutional provisions, we are unable thus to extend it. In that case the complaining parties were established in business within the taxing district as general merchandise brokers, and had taken out general and unrestricted licenses to do business of all kinds, both internal and interstate. As it happened, one of them (Ficklen), during the year in question did an interstate business exclusively, and the other (Cooper & Co.) did a business nine-tenths of which was interstate. And the court, by Mr. Chief Justice Fuller, said (p. 21): "Where a resident citizen engages in general business subject to a particular tax, the fact that the business done chances to consist, for the time being, wholly or partially in negotiating sales between resident and non-resident merchants, of goods situated in another State, does not necessarily involve the taxation of interstate commerce, forbidden by the Constitution"; and again (p. 24): "What position they [the plaintiffs in error] would have occupied if they had not undertaken to do a general commission business, and had taken out no licenses therefor, but had simply transacted business for non-resident principals, is an entirely different question, which does not arise upon this record." Besides, the tax imposed in the Ficklen Case was not directly upon the business itself or upon the volume thereof, but upon the amount of commissions earned by the brokers, which, although probably corresponding with the volume of the transactions, was not necessarily proportionate thereto. For these and other reasons the case has been deemed exceptional. . . .

The tax now under consideration . . . bears no semblance of a property tax, or a franchise tax in the proper sense; nor is it an occupation tax except as it is imposed upon the very carrying on of the business of exporting merchandise. It operates to lay a direct burden upon every transaction in commerce by withholding, for the use of the State, a part of every dollar received in such transactions. That it applies to internal as well as to foreign commerce cannot save it; for, as was said in Case of the State Freight Tax, 15 Wall. 343, 277, "The State may tax its internal commerce, but if an act to tax interstate or foreign commerce is unconstitutional, it is not cured by including in its provisions subjects within the domain of the State." That portion of the tax which is measured by the receipts from foreign commerce necessarily varies in proportion to the volume of that commerce, and hence is a direct burden upon it.

So obvious is the distinction between this tax and those that were sustained in Maine v. Grand Trunk Ry. Co., 142 U.S. 217; U.S. Express Co. v. Minnesota, 223 U.S. 335, 347; Baltic Mining Co. v. Massachusetts, 231 U.S. 68, 87; Kansas City &c. Ry. Co. v. Kansas, 240 U.S. 227, 232, 235; and some other cases of the same class, that no time need be spent upon it.

The judgment under review must be reversed.[aa]

United States Glue Co. v. Town of Oak Creek 247 U.S. 321, 38 S. Ct. 499, 62 L. Ed. 1135 (1918)

Mr. Justice Pitney delivered the opinion of the court:

The judgment brought up by this writ of error was entered by the circuit court of Milwaukee county upon the mandate of the supreme court of the state of Wisconsin, issued on reversal of a previous judgment of the circuit court in an action brought by plaintiff in error to recover the sum of $2,835.38, paid under protest as part of a tax assessed and levied by the taxing authorities of the state upon plaintiff's income for the year 1911, under chap. 658, Wisconsin Laws 1911. The supreme court overruled plaintiff's contention that the portion of the tax that was in controversy, having been imposed upon income derived by plaintiff from interstate commerce, amounted to a burden upon that commerce, contravening the commerce clause of §8 of article 1 of the Constitution of the

---

[aa] Cf. Spalding & Bros. v. Edwards, 262 U.S. 66 (1923). — Ed.

United States. 161 Wis. 211, 153 N.W. 241. And this is the sole question presented for our consideration.

The act, which was passed under the authority of an amendment to the state Constitution (Income Tax Cases, 148 Wis. 456, 134 N.W. 673, 135 N.W. 164), imposes a tax upon incomes received during the year ending December 31, 1911, and annually thereafter; defines the term "income" as including (a) rent of real estate; (b) interest derived from money loaned or invested in notes, mortgages, bonds, or other evidences of debt: (c) wages, salaries, and the like; (d) dividends or profits derived from stock, or from the purchase and sale of property acquired within three years previous, or from any business whatever; (e) royalties derived from the possession or use of franchise or legalized privileges; and (f) all other income derived from any source, except such as is exempted. There is a provision: "That any person engaged in business within and without the state shall, with respect to income other than that derived from rentals, stocks, bonds, securities or evidences of indebtedness, be taxed only upon that proportion of such income as is derived from business transacted and property located within the state," which is to be determined in a particular manner specified in §1770b, as far as applicable.

Corporations are allowed to make certain deductions from gross income, including amounts paid for personal services of officers and employees and other ordinary expenses paid out of income in the maintenance and operation of business and property, including a reasonable allowance for depreciation, losses not compensated for by insurance or otherwise, taxes, etc. These need not be further mentioned, beyond saying that the intent and necessary effect of the act is to tax not gross receipts, but net income; that from the stipulated facts it appears that the tax in question was imposed upon plaintiff's net income; and that this is in accord with the construction of the act adopted by the supreme court of the state in this and other cases. State ex rel. Manitowoc Gas Co. v. Wisconsin Tax Commission, 161 Wis. 111, 116, 152 N.W. 848; . . .

In order to determine what part of the income of a corporation engaged in business within and without the state (other than that derived from rentals, stocks, bonds, securities, etc.) is to be taxed as derived from business transacted and property located within the state, reference is had to a formula prescribed by another statute (Wis. Stat. §1770b, subsec. 7, ¶ [e]) for apportioning the capital stock of foreign corporations, under which the gross business in dollars of the corporation in the state, added to the value in dollars of its property in the state, is made the numerator of a fraction of which the denominator consists of the total gross business in dollars of the corporation both within and without the state, added to the value in dollars of its property within and without the state. The resulting fraction is taken by the income tax law, as representing the proportion of the income which is deemed to be derived from business transacted and property located within the state. This formula was applied in apportioning plaintiff's net "business income" for the year 1911, and upon the portion thus attributed to the state, plus the income from rentals, stocks, bonds, etc., the tax in question was levied.

Plaintiff was and is a corporation organized under the laws of the state of Wisconsin, having its principal office and place of business in the town of Oak Creek, where it conducted an extensive manufacturing plant, selling its products throughout the state and in other states and foreign countries. Its net "business income" in the year 1911, exclusive of that derived from rentals, stocks, bonds, etc., and after making the deductions allowed by the act, amounted to about $124,000, derived from the following sources: (a) About $16,000 from goods sold to customers within the state and delivered from its factory; (b) about $65,000 from goods sold to customers outside of the state and delivered from its factory; (c) about $31,000 from goods sold to customers outside of the state, the sales having been made and goods shipped from plaintiff's branches in other states, and the goods having been manufactured at plaintiff's factory and shipped before sale to said branches; (d) about $7,000 from goods sold to customers outside of the state, the sales having been made and goods shipped from plaintiff's branches without the state, these goods having been purchased by plaintiff outside of the state and shipped to plaintiff's factory in the state, and thence shipped before sale from the factory to the branches; (e) about $5,000 from goods sold outside of the state, the sales having been made and goods shipped from said branches, and the goods having been purchased by plaintiff outside of the state and shipped from the points of purchase to the branches without coming into the state of Wisconsin.

No contention was made as to the taxability of the income designated in item (a). Plaintiff's contention that items (d) and (e) were not taxable because not derived from property located or business transacted within the state was upheld by the state courts. Thus the controversy is narrowed to the contention, overruled by the supreme court, that items (b) and (c) were not taxable because derived from interstate commerce.

Stated concisely, the question is whether a state, in levying a general income tax upon the gains and profits of a domestic corporation, may include in the computation the net income derived from transactions in interstate commerce without contravening the commerce clause of the Constitution of the United States.

It is settled that a state may not directly burden interstate commerce, either by taxation or otherwise. But a tax that only indirectly affects the profits or returns from such commerce is not within the rule. . . .

Yet it is obvious that taxes imposed upon property or franchises employed in interstate commerce must be paid from the net returns of such commerce, and diminish them in the same sense that they are diminished by a tax imposed upon the net returns themselves.

The distinction between direct and indirect burdens, with particular reference to a comparison between a tax upon the gross returns of carriers in interstate commerce and a general income tax imposed upon all inhabitants, incidentally affecting carriers engaged in such commerce, was the subject of consideration in Philadelphia & S. Mail S.S. Co. v. Pennsylvania, 122 U.S. 326, 345, where the court, by Mr. Justice Bradley, said: "The corporate franchises, the property, the business, the income of corporations created by a state, may undoubtedly be taxed by the state; but in imposing such taxes care should be taken not to interfere with or hamper, directly or by indirection, interstate or foreign commerce, or any other matter exclusively within the jurisdiction of the Federal government." Many previous cases were referred to.

The correct line of distinction is so well illustrated in two cases decided at the present term that we hardly need go further. In Crew Levick Co. v. Pennsylvania, 245 U.S. 292, we held that a state tax upon the business of selling goods in foreign commerce, measured by a certain percentage of the gross transactions in such commerce, was by its necessary effect a tax upon the commerce, and at the same time a duty upon exports, contrary to §§8 and 10 of article 1 of the Constitution, since it operated to lay a direct burden upon every transaction by withholding for the use of the state a part of every dollar received. On the other hand, in Peck & Co. v. Lowe (decided May 20th last) 247 U.S. 165, we held that the Income Tax of October 3, 1913, chap. 16, §II, 38 Stat. 166, 172, when carried into effect by imposing an assessment upon the entire net income of a corporation, approximately three fourths of which was derived from the export of goods to foreign countries, did not amount to laying a tax or duty on articles exported within the meaning of art. 1, §9, cl. 5 of the Constitution. The distinction between a direct and an indirect burden by way of tax or duty was developed, and it was shown that an income tax laid generally on net incomes, not on income from exportation because of its source, or in the way of discrimination, but just as it was laid on other income, and affecting only the net receipts from exportation after all expenses were paid and losses adjusted and the recipient of the income was free to use it as he chose, was only an indirect burden.

The difference in effect between a tax measured by gross receipts and one measured by net income, recognized by our decisions, is manifest and substantial, and it affords a convenient and workable basis of distinction between a direct and immediate burden upon the business affected and a charge that is only indirect and incidental. A tax upon gross

548   Chapter Eight.   The States in a Federal Union

receipts affects each transaction in proportion to its magnitude, and irrespective of whether it is profitable or otherwise. Conceivably it may be sufficient to make the difference between profit and loss, or to so diminish the profit as to impede or discourage the conduct of the commerce. A tax upon the net profits has not the same deterrent effect, since it does not arise at all unless a gain is shown over and above expenses and losses, and the tax cannot be heavy unless the profits are large. Such a tax, when imposed upon net incomes from whatever source arising, is but a method of distributing the cost of government, like a tax upon property, or upon franchises treated as property; and if there be no discrimination against interstate commerce, either in the admeasurement of the tax or in the means adopted for enforcing it, it constitutes one of the ordinary and general burdens of government, from which persons and corporations otherwise subject to the jurisdiction of the states are not exempted by the Federal Constitution because they happen to be engaged in commerce among the states.

And so we hold that the Wisconsin Income Tax Law, as applied to the plaintiff in the case before us, cannot be deemed to be so direct a burden upon plaintiff's interstate business as to amount to an unconstitutional interference with or regulation of commerce among the states. It was measured not by the gross receipts, but by the net proceeds from this part of plaintiff's business, along with a like imposition upon its income derived from other sources, and in the same way that other corporations doing business within the state are taxed upon that proportion of their income derived from business transacted and property located within the state, whatever the nature of their business.

Judgment affirmed.

MR. CHIEF JUSTICE WHITE concurs in the result.

ATLANTIC COAST LINE R.R. v. DAUGHTON, 262 U.S. 413, 43 S. Ct. 620, 67 L. Ed. 1051 (1923). Brandeis, J.: "The Constitution of North Carolina . . . authorizes the General Assembly to tax incomes at a rate not exceeding six per cent. The Income Tax Act of March 8, 1921 . . . laid upon corporations a tax equal to three per cent of the entire net income as therein defined and upon individuals a progressive tax not exceeding that percentage. For the purpose of ascertaining the taxable income the statute divides taxpayers into three classes — individuals, ordinary corporations and public service corporations (including railroads). The statute, in terms, taxes only net income. For railroads and other public service corporations required to keep accounts according to the method established by the Interstate Commerce Commission, it makes those accounts the basis for determining the 'net operating income' (§ 202 as amended); and it directs that, in order to ascertain the 'net income,' there shall be deductible from the net operating income (a) uncollectible revenue; (b) taxes for the income year, other than income taxes, and war profits and excess profits taxes; (c) amounts paid for car hire. Whether the statute is unconstitutional, because it fails to include among the deductions from income allowed public service corporations the capital charges, including other rentals paid, is the main question for decision.

"The first year's tax under the act was payable in 1922, with respect to the net income received during the calendar year 1921. To enjoin its enforcement these four corporations brought suit in the federal court for the Eastern District of North Carolina against the Commissioner of Revenue and others. Each plaintiff owns and operates a line of railroad within the State, and is an interstate carrier. Each assails the statute on the grounds that it violates the commerce clause, the Fourteenth Amendment and the state constitution . . .

". . . To appreciate the objections urged . . . it is necessary to show the incidence of the tax. This may be done by examining how the assessment of $13,133.09 made upon the Seaboard Air Line, and here assailed, was calculated.

". . . The results of operations within the State calculated according to the statute were these:

Section D. **State Taxation** 549

Operating revenues	$8,457,328.52	
Operating expenses	7,308,823.29	
Net operating income		$1,148,505.23

From the net operating income were deducted:

Uncollectible revenue	$ 6,342.31	
Taxes paid	410,043.38	
Car hire	294,350.02	
Additional deductions		$710,735.71
Net taxable income		$437,769.52

Tax on $437,769.52 at 3 per cent. $13,133.09

". . . The Seaboard insists that it had no net income taxable in North Carolina; but, on the contrary, a loss . . ." [The Seaboard's computation was as follows: To the statutory net income of $437,769.52 it adds nonoperating income, not taken into account under the statute, of $539,643.30. The chief items in this amount were dividend income ($113,350.45), income (interest) from securities ($111,039.37), and rents received ($306,410.57). This gives a total of $977,412.82. From this it deducts $1,231,703.04, items not allowed as deductions under the statute, giving a net loss or deficit of over $250,000. The chief items which it would deduct, and which were not allowed as deductions by the statute, were interest on funded debt ($1,179,252.20), interest on unfunded debt ($43,823.64), and rent paid ($71,095.07).]

What decision? Why?

Underwood Typewriter Co. v. Chamberlain 254 U.S. 113, 41 S. Ct. 45, 65 L. Ed. 165 (1920)

MR. JUSTICE BRANDEIS delivered the opinion of the court:

This action was brought by the Underwood Typewriter Company, a Delaware corporation, in the superior court for the county of Hartford, Connecticut, to recover the amount of a tax assessed upon it by the latter state, and paid under protest. The company contended that, as applied to it, the taxing act violated rights guaranteed by the Federal Constitution. The constitutional questions involved were reserved by that court for consideration and advice by the supreme court of errors. The answers to these questions being favorable to the state (94 Conn. 47, 108 Atl. 154), judgment was entered by the superior court, confirming the validity of the tax. The case comes here on writ of error to that court.

Connecticut established in 1915 a comprehensive system of taxation applicable alike to all foreign and domestic corporations carrying on business within the state. This system prescribes practically the only method by which such corporations are taxed, other than the general property tax to which all property located within the state, whether the owner be a resident or a nonresident, an individual or a corporation, is subject. The act divides business corporations into four classes, and the several classes are taxed by somewhat different methods. The fourth class, "miscellaneous corporations," includes, among others, manufacturing and trading companies, and with these alone are we concerned here. Upon their net income earned during the preceding year from business carried on within the state a tax of 2 per cent is imposed annually. The amount of the net income is ascertained by reference to the income upon which the corporation is required to pay a tax to the United States. If the company carries on business also outside the state of Connecticut, the proportion of its net income earned from business carried on within the state is ascertained by apportionment in the following manner: The corporation is required to state in its annual return to the tax commissioner from what general source its profits are principally derived. If the company's net profits are derived principally from ownership, sale, or rental of real property, or from the sale or use of tangible personal property, the tax is imposed on such proportion of the whole net income as the fair cash value of the real and the tangible personal property within the state bears to the fair cash value of all the real and tangible personal property of the company. . . .

The Underwood Typewriter Company is engaged in the business of manufacturing typewriters and kindred articles; in selling its product and also certain accessories and supplies which it purchases; and in repairing and renting such machines. Its main office is in New York City. All its manufacturing is done in Connecticut. It has branch offices in other states for the sale, lease, and repair of machines and the sale of supplies; and it has one such branch office in Connecticut. All articles made by it — and some which it purchases — are stored in Connecticut until shipped direct to the branch offices, purchasers, or lessees. In its return to the tax commissioner of Connecticut, made in 1916, under the above law, the company declared that its net profits during the preceding year had been derived principally from tangible personal property; that these profits amounted to $1,336,586.13; that the fair cash value of the real estate and tangible personal property in Connecticut was $2,977,827.67, and the fair cash value of the real estate and tangible personal property outside that state was $3,343,155.11. The proportion of the real estate and tangible personal property within the state was thus 47 per cent. The tax commissioner apportioned that percentage of the net profits, namely, $629,668.50, as having been earned from the business done within the state, and assessed thereon a tax of $12,593.37, being at the rate of 2 per cent. The company, having paid the tax under protest, brought this action in the superior court for the county of Hartford, to recover the whole amount.

First. It is contended that the tax burdens interstate commerce, and hence is void under §8 of article 1 of the Federal Constitution. Payment of the tax is not made a condition precedent to the right of the corporation to carry on business, including interstate business. Its enforcement is left to the ordinary means of collecting taxes. St. Louis Southwestern R. Co. v. Arkansas, 235 U.S. 350, 364, . . . The statute is, therefore, not open to the objection that it compels the company to pay for the privileges of engaging in interstate commerce. A tax is not obnoxious to the commerce clause merely because imposed upon property used in interstate commerce, even if it takes the form of a tax for the privilege of exercising its franchise within the state. Postal Teleg. Cable Co. v. Adams, 155 U.S. 688, 695. This tax is based upon the net profits earned within the state. That a tax measured by net profits is valid, although these profits may have been derived in part, or indeed mainly, from interstate commerce, is settled. United States Glue Co. v. Oak Creek, 247 U.S. 321, . . . Whether it be deemed a property tax or a franchise tax, it is not obnoxious to the commerce clause.

Second. It is contended that the tax violates the 14th Amendment because, directly or indirectly, it is imposed on income arising from business conducted beyond the boundaries of the state. In considering this objection, we may lay on one side the question whether this is an excise tax purporting to be measured by the income accruing from business within the state, or a direct tax upon that income; for "the argument upon analysis resolves itself into a mere question of definitions, and has no legitimate bearing upon any question raised under the Federal Constitution." Shaffer v. Carter, 252 U.S. 37, 55. In support of its objection that business outside the state is taxed, plaintiff rests solely upon the showing that, of its net profits, $1,293,643.95 was received in other states and $42,942.18 in Connecticut; while, under the method of apportionment of net income required by the statute, 47 per cent of its net income is attributable to operations in Connecticut. But this showing wholly fails to sustain the objection. The profits of the corporation were largely earned by a series of transactions beginning with manufacture in Connecticut, and ending with sale in other states. In this it was typical of a large part of the manufacturing business conducted in the state. The legislature, in attempting to put upon this business its fair share of the burden of taxation, was faced with the impossibility of allocating specifically the profits earned by the processes conducted within its borders. It therefore adopted a method of apportionment which, for all that appears in this record, reached, and was meant to reach, only the profits earned within the state. "The plaintiff's argument on this branch of the case," as stated by the supreme court of errors, "carries the burden of showing that 47 per cent of its net income is not reasonably attributable, for purposes of taxation, to the manufacture of products from the sale of which 80 per cent of its gross earnings was derived after paying manufacturing costs." 94 Conn. 47, 108 Atl. 159. The corporation has not even attempted to show this; and, for aught that appears, the percentage of net profits earned in Connecticut may have been much larger than 47 per cent. There is, consequently, nothing in this record to show that the method of apportionment adopted by the state was inherently arbitrary, or that its application to this corporation produced an unreasonable result.

We have no occasion to consider whether the rule prescribed, if applied under different conditions, might be obnoxious to the Constitution. Adams Exp. Co. v. Ohio State Auditor, 166 U.S. 185, 122. Nor need we consider the contention made on behalf of the state, that the statute is necessarily valid, because the prescribed rule of apportionment is not rigid, and provision is made for rectifying, by proceedings in the superior court, any injustice resulting from its application. . . .

Affirmed.

NOTE

1. For other decisions involving apportionment formulas or allocation methods as applied to net income used as a measure of a franchise tax, see Butler Bros. v. McColgan, 315 U.S. 501 (1942); Norfolk & Western Ry. v. North Carolina, 297 U.S. 682 (1936); Hans Rees' Sons, Inc. v. North Carolina, 283 U.S. 123 (1931); Bass, Ratcliff & Gretton v. State Tax Commission, 266 U.S. 271 (1924). See also Lynn, The Uniform Division of Income for Tax Purposes Act Re-examined, 46 Va. L. Rev. 1257 (1960); Silverstein, Problems of Apportionment in Taxation of Multistate Business, 4 Tax L. Rev. 207 (1949); Magill, Allocation of Income by Corporate Contract, 44 Harv. L. Rev. 935 (1931).

2. Report of the Special Commission on Taxation (Massachusetts), Part V, The Taxation of Business and Manufacturing Corporations (1952), at p. 39: "The problem of a suitable allocation formula for general business income has produced much controversy in tax circles. It is unlikely that any single formula will prove entirely acceptable to every one concerned. The Commission has made a detailed investigation of the allocation formulas used by many of the other States. These include a three-factor formula in which 'manufacturing costs' are substituted for the pay-roll factor; two-factor formulas with such combinations as property and sales, or property and manufacturing costs; and even a one-factor formula consisting of the sales factor alone. Some States apply a different formula to mercantile and manufacturing business. One State, New Jersey, arbitrarily allocates to New Jersey 50 per cent of each sale where the goods are shipped across the state line in either direction.

"As a result of its investigations the Commission is satisfied that no other State has developed a formula that is so demonstrably superior to the Massachusetts formula that a change should be recommended . . ."

3. Report, supra, p. 31: "In so far as the income measure is concerned, it is probable that Massachusetts could levy a non-discriminatory tax on the entire net income of a domestic corporation and yet stay clear of federal constitutional objections. Where the

legal domicile of a corporation is outside the State an apportionment is required so that the tax may be related only to activities carried on within the State. Apart from constitutional considerations, however, sound tax policy supports a fair allocation of corporate income derived from business within and without the State for both domestic and foreign corporations."

4. See the entire Report, above, not only for a description of the complex taxing system of one state, but also for a careful appraisal of its operation and of proposed changes and reforms.

5. See also, and compare, Report on State Taxation of Interstate Commerce, H.R. Rep. No. 1480, 88th Cong., 2d Sess., particularly ch. 7, pp. 153-249 (1964), and Recommendations, H.R. Rep. No. 952, 89th Cong., 1st Sess., pp. 1135-1136, 1139-1164 (1965).

6. In addition to the payment of a net income tax on that part of income attributable to Wisconsin, that state required corporations doing business therein to deduct and withhold from dividends what was termed a privilege dividend tax, i.e., a tax on that part of dividends declared attributable to earnings from Wisconsin, even though paid from central offices located outside Wisconsin and to stockholders in other states. The tax was upheld in Wisconsin v. J. C. Penney Co., 311 U.S. 435 (1940), the Court reasoning that it amounted to an additional and deferred tax on corporate income attributable to Wisconsin. This equating of taxes produced not only a rejoinder from the Supreme Court of Wisconsin that the tax was not on the income of the corporation, but also problems concerning federal income tax deductions and the effect of the tax on the rights of preferred stockholders. See International Harvester Co. v. Wisconsin Dept. of Taxation, 322 U.S. 435 (1944); Wisconsin Gas & Electric Co. v. United States, 322 U.S. 526 (1944).

For a description of a French tax statute somewhat similar to that of Wisconsin and of American attempts by treaty to limit its impact upon American corporations operating in France, see Carroll, Will Franco-American Tax Treaty Aid Business with France? 23 Taxes 228 (1945).

Spector Motor Service, Inc. v. O'Connor 340 U.S. 602, 71 S. Ct. 508, 95 L. Ed. 573 (1951)

MR. JUSTICE BURTON delivered the opinion of the Court.

This proceeding attacks, under the Commerce Clause of the Constitution of the United States, the validity of a state tax imposed upon the franchise of a foreign corporation for the privilege of doing business within the State when (1) the business consists solely of interstate commerce, and (2) the tax is computed at a nondiscriminatory rate on that part of the corporation's net income which is reasonably attributable to its business activities within the State. For the reasons hereinafter stated, we hold this application of the tax invalid.

Petitioner, Spector Motor Service, Inc., is a Missouri corporation engaged exclusively in interstate trucking. It instituted this action in 1942 in the United States District Court for the District of Connecticut against the Tax Commissioner of that State. It sought to enjoin collection of assessments and penalties totaling $7,795.50, which had been levied against it, for various periods between June 1, 1935, and December 31, 1940, under the Connecticut Corporation Business Tax Act of 1935 and amendments thereto. It asked also for a declaratory judgment as to its liability, if any, under that Act. It claimed that the tax imposed by the Act did not apply to it and that, if it did, such application violated both the Connecticut Constitution and the Commerce and Due Process Clauses of the United States Constitution. . . .

The vital issue which remains is whether the application of the tax to petitioner violates the Commerce Clause of the Federal Constitution. We come to that issue now with the benefit of a statement from the state court of final jurisdiction showing exatly what it is that the State has sought to tax. The all-important "operating incidence" of the tax is thus made clear. After full consideration and with knowledge that its statement would be made the basis of determining the validity of the application of the tax under the Commerce Clause, that court said:

"The tax is then a tax or excise upon the franchise of corporations for the privilege of carrying on or doing business in the state, whether they be domestic or foreign. Staley Works v. Hackett, 122 Conn. 547, 551, 190 A. 743. Net earnings are used merely for the purpose of determining the amount to be paid by each corporation, a measure which, by the application of the rate charged, was intended to impose upon each corporation a share of the general tax burden as nearly as possible equivalent to that borne by other wealth in the state. As regards a corporation doing business both within and without the state, the intention was, by the use of a rather complicated formula, to measure the tax by determining as fairly as possible the proportionate amount of its business done in this state. There is no ground upon which the tax can be said to rest upon the use of highways by motor trucks. . . ." 135 Conn. at 56, 57, 61 A.2d at 98, 99.

The incidence of the tax is upon no intrastate commerce activities because there are none. Petitioner is engaged only in interstate transportation. . . . It has not been authorized by the State of Connecticut to do intrastate trucking and does not engage in it. See Terminal Taxicab Co. v. Kutz, 241 U.S. 252, 253, 254. . . .

The tax does not discriminate between interstate and intrastate commerce. Neither the amount of the tax nor its computation need be considered by us in view of our disposition of the case. The objection to its validity does not rest on a claim that it places an unduly heavy burden on interstate commerce in return for protection given by the State. The tax is not levied as compensation for the use of highways or collected in lieu of an ad valorem property tax. Those bases of taxation have been disclaimed by the highest court of the taxing State. It is not a fee for an inspection or a tax on sales or use. It is a "tax or excise" placed unequivocally upon the corporation's franchise for the privilege of carrying on exclusively interstate transportation in the State. It serves no purpose for the State Tax Commissioner to suggest that, if there were some intrastate commerce involved or if an appropriate tax were imposed as compensation for petitioner's use of the highways, the same sum of money as is at issue here might be collected lawfully from petitioner. Even though the financial burden on interstate commerce might be the same, the question whether a state may validly make interstate commerce pay its way depends first of all upon the constitutional channel through which it attempts to do so. Freeman v. Hewit, 329 U.S. 249; McLeod v. J. E. Dilworth Co. 322 U.S. 327.

Taxing power is inherent in sovereign states, yet the states of the United States have divided their taxing power between the Federal Government and themselves. They delegated to the United States the exclusive power to tax the privilege to engage in interstate commerce when they gave Congress the power "To regulate Commerce with foreign Nations, and among the several States. . . ." U.S. Const. Art. 1, §8, cl. 3. While the reach of the reserved taxing power of a state is great, the constitutional separation of the federal and state powers makes it essential that no state be permitted to exercise, without authority from Congress, those functions which it has delegated exclusively to Congress. Another example of this basic separation of powers is the inability of the states to tax the agencies through which the United States exercises its sovereign powers. See M'Culloch v. Maryland, 4 Wheat. 316, 425-537; Brown v. Maryland, 12 Wheat. 419, 445-449; Mayo v. United States, 319 U.S. 441. . . .

This Court heretofore has struck down, under the Commerce Clause, state taxes upon the privilege of carrying on a business that was *exclusively* interstate in character. The constitutional infirmity of such a tax persists no matter how fairly it is apportioned to business done within the state. Alpha Portland Cement Co. v. Massachusetts, 268 U.S. 203 (measured by percentages of "corporate excess" and net income); Ozark Pipe Line Corp.

v. Monier, 266 U.S. 555 (measured by percentage of capital stock and surplus). See Interstate Oil Pipe Line Co. v. Stone, 337 U.S. 662, 669 et seq. (dissenting opinion which discusses the issue on the assumption that the activities were in interstate commerce); Joseph v. Carter & Weekes Stevedoring Co., 330 U.S. 422; Freeman v. Hewit, 329 U.S. 249, supra.

Our conclusion is not in conflict with the principle that, where a taxpayer is engaged both in intrastate and interstate commerce, a state may tax the privilege of carrying on intrastate business and, within reasonable limits, may compute the amount of the charge by applying the tax rate to a fair proportion of the taxpayer's business done within the state, including both interstate and intrastate. Interstate Oil Pipe Line Co. v. Stone, 337 U.S. 662, supra; International Harvester Co. v. Evatt, 329 U.S. 416; Atlantic Lumber Co. v. Commissioner of Corporations & Taxation, 298 U.S. 553. The same is true where the taxpayer's business activity is local in nature, such as the transportation of passengers between points within the same state, although including interstate travel, Central Greyhound Lines v. Mealey, 334 U.S. 653, or the publication of a newspaper, Western Live Stock v. Bureau of Revenue, 303 U.S. 250. See also Memphis Gas Co. v. Stone, 335 U.S. 80.

In this field there is not only reason but long-established precedent for keeping the federal privilege of carrying on exclusively interstate commerce free from state taxation. To do so gives lateral support to one of the cornerstones of our constitutional law — M'Culloch v. Maryland, 4 Wheat. 316.

The judgment of the Court of Appeals, which reversed that of the District Court, is accordingly

Reversed.

MR. JUSTICE CLARK, with whom MR. JUSTICE BLACK and MR. JUSTICE DOUGLAS join, dissenting.

The Court assumes, and I think it has been clearly demonstrated, that the tax under challenge is nondiscriminatory, fairly apportioned and not an undue burden on interstate commerce. Hence, if an appellant had been engaged in an iota of activity which the Court would be willing to call "intrastate," Connecticut could have applied its tax to the company's interstate business in the precise form which it now seeks to employ — a tax on the privilege of doing business in Connecticut measured by the entire net income attributable to the State, even though derived from interstate commerce.

But solely because Spector engages in what the Court calls "exclusively interstate" business, a different standard is applied. The Court does not ask whether the State is merely asking interstate commerce to pay its way, or whether the State in fact provides protection and services for which such commerce may fairly be charged. Nor is the Court concerned whether the tax puts interstate business at a competitive disadvantage or is likely to do so. Instead, the tax is declared invalid simply because the State has verbally characterized it as a levy on the privilege of doing business within its borders. The Court concedes, or at least appears to concede, that if the Connecticut legislature or highest court had described the tax as one for the use of highways or in lieu of an ad valorem property tax, Spector would have had to pay the same amount, calculated in the same way, as is sought to be collected here. In acknowledging this, the Court's own opinion totally refutes its protestation that the standard employed to strike down Connecticut's tax is more than a matter of labels. Spector remains free — as it has since the tax law was adopted in 1935 — from paying any share of the State's expenses, and its tax-free status continues until Connecticut renames or reshuffles its tax.

Neither such a standard nor such a result persuades me. . . . In the not too distant past, this seemed to be quite clear. In Memphis Natural Gas Co. v. Beeler, 315 U.S. 649 (1942), a tax was upheld as being reasonably attributable to intrastate activities. But Chief Justice Stone, speaking for a unanimous Court, went further to state:

"In any case, even if taxpayer's business were wholly interstate commerce, a nondiscriminatory tax by Tennessee upon the net income of a foreign corporation having a commercial domicile there, . . . or upon net income derived from within the state, . . . is not prohibited by the commerce clause. . . ." Id. 315 U.S. at 656.

In light of the apparent need for clearing up the tangled underbrush of past cases, it appears that this view was delivered advisedly. Nor do I understand it to have been upset by Freeman v. Hewit, 329 U.S. 249 (1946), or Joseph v. Carter & Weeks Stevedoring Co., 330 U.S. 422 (1947). The former involved a gross-receipts tax capable of duplication by another state; the latter involved a gross-receipts tax rather than a net-income tax; and the opinion in each case was written by a member of the Court who joined in the Beeler decision.

But in any event, I would confine those decisions to their "special facts." Freeman v. Hewit, supra. The Connecticut tax meets every practical test of fairness and propriety enunciated in cases upholding privilege taxes on corporations doing a mixed intrastate and interstate business. These cases should govern here, for there is no apparent difference between an "exclusively interstate" business and a "mixed" business which would warrant different constitutional regard. There is nothing spiritual about interstate commerce. It is rarely devoid of significant contacts with the several states. . . .

It has taken eight years and eight courts to bring this battered litigation to an end. The taxes involved go back thirteen years. It is therefore no answer to Connecticut and some thirty other states who have similar tax measures that they can now collect the same revenues by enacting laws more felicitously drafted. Because of its failure to use the right tag, Connecticut cannot collect from Spector for the years 1937 to date, and it and other states may well have past collections taken away and turned into taxpayer bonanzas by suits for refund which come within the respective statutes of limitations.[bb] . . .

Northwestern States Portland Cement Co. v. Minnesota
358 U.S. 450, 79 S. Ct. 357, 3 L. Ed. 2d 421 (1959)

MR. JUSTICE CLARK delivered the opinion of the Court.

These cases concern the constitutionality of state net income tax laws levying taxes on that portion of a foreign corporation's net income earned from and fairly apportioned to business activities within the taxing State when those activities are exclusively in furtherance of interstate commerce. No question is raised in either case as to the reasonableness of the apportionment of net income under the State's formulas nor to the amount of the final assessment made. The Minnesota tax was upheld by its Supreme Court, 250 Minn. 32, 84 N.W.2d 373, while the Supreme Court of Georgia invalidated its statute as being violative of "both the commerce and due process clauses of the Federal Constitution. . . ." 213 Ga. 713, 101 S.E.2d 197. The importance of the question in the field of state taxation is indicated by the fact that thirty-five States impose direct net income taxes on corporations. . . . It is contended that each of the state statutes, as applied, violates both the Due Process and the Commerce Clauses of the United States Constitution. We conclude that net income from the interstate operations of a foreign corporation may be subjected to state taxation provided the levy is not discriminatory and is properly apportioned to local activities within the taxing State forming sufficient nexus to support the same.

[bb] Cf. Memphis Natural Gas Co. v. Stone, 335 U.S. (1948).
In Colonial Pipeline Co. v. Traigle, 421 U.S. 100 (1975), the Court sustained a franchise tax levied by Louisiana, on the privilege of engaging in business in corporate form, upon a Delaware corporation whose business in Louisiana was solely interstate. Spector was distinguished. Does Spector have any continuing vitality? See Complete Auto Transit v. Brady, — U.S. — (1977). — ED.

556   Chapter Eight.   The States in a Federal Union

NO. 12 — NORTHWESTERN STATES PORTLAND CEMENT CO.
V. STATE OF MINNESOTA

This is an appeal from judgments of Minnesota's courts upholding the assessment by the State of income taxes for the years 1933 through 1948 against appellant, an Iowa corporation engaged in the manufacture and sale of cement at its plant in Mason City, Iowa, some forty miles from the Minnesota border. The tax was levied under §290.03 of the Minnesota statutes, which imposes an annual tax upon the taxable net income of residents and nonresidents alike. One of four classes taxed by the statute is that of "domestic and foreign corporations whose business within this state during the taxable year consists exclusively of foreign commerce, interstate commerce, or both." Minnesota has utilized three ratios in determining the portion of net income taxable under its law. The first is that of the taxpayer's sales assignable to Minnesota during the year to its total sales during that period made everywhere; the second, that of the taxpayer's total tangible property in Minnesota for the year to its total tangible property used in the business that year wherever situated. The third is the taxpayer's total payroll in Minnesota for the year to its total payroll for its entire business in the like period. As we have noted, appellant takes no issue with the fairness of this formula nor of the accuracy of its application here.

Appellant's activities in Minnesota consisted of a regular and systematic course of solicitation of orders for the sale of its products, each order being subject to acceptance, filling and delivery by it from its plant at Mason City. It sold only to eligible dealers, who were lumber and building material supply houses, contractors and ready-mix companies. . . . Forty-eight percent of appellant's entire sales were made in this manner to such dealers in Minnesota. For efficient handling of its activity in that State, appellant maintained in Minneapolis a leased sales office equipped with its own furniture and fixtures and under the supervision of an employee-salesman known as "district manager." Two salesmen, including this district manager, and a secretary occupied this three-room office. Two additional salesmen used it as a clearing house. . . . . Appellant maintained no bank account in Minnesota, owned no real estate there, and warehoused no merchandise in the State. . . . Orders received by the salesmen or at the Minneapolis office were transmitted daily to appellant in Mason City, were approved there, and acknowledged directly to the purchaser with copies to the salesman.

In addition to the solicitation of approved dealers, appellant's salesmen also contacted potential customers and users of cement products, such as builders, contractors, architects, and state, as well as local government purchasing agents. Orders were solicited and received from them, on special forms furnished by appellant, directed to an approved local dealer who in turn would fill them by placing a like order with appellant. Through this system appellant's salesmen would in effect secure orders for local dealers which in turn were filled by appellant in the usual manner. Salesmen would also receive and transmit claims against appellant for loss or damage in any shipments made by it, informing the company of the nature thereof and requesting instructions concerning the same.

No income tax returns were filed with the State by the appellant. The assessments sued upon, aggregating some $102,000, with penalties and interest, were made by the Commissioner of Taxation on the basis of information available to him.

NO. 33 — T. V. WILLIAMS, COMMISSIONER
V. STOCKHAM VALVES & FITTINGS, INC.

The respondent here is a Delaware Corporation with its principal office and plant in Birmingham, Alabama. It manufactures and sells valves and pipe fittings through established local wholesalers and jobbers who handle products other than respondent's. . . . However, the corporation maintained no warehouse or storage facilities in Georgia. It did maintain a sales-service office in Atlanta, which served five States. This office was headquarters for one salesman who devoted about one-third of his time to solicitation of orders in Georgia. . . . Respondent's salesman carried on the usual sales activities, including regular solicitation, receipt and forwarding of orders to the Birmingham office and the promotion of business and good will for respondent. Orders were taken by him, as well as the sales-service office, subject to approval of the home office and were shipped from Birmingham direct to the customer on an "f.o.b. warehouse" basis. Other than office equipment, supplies, advertising literature and the like, respondent had no property in Georgia, deposited no funds there and stored no merchandise in the State.

Georgia levies a tax on net incomes "received by every corporation, foreign or domestic, owning property or doing business in the state." The Act defines the latter as including "any activities or transactions" carried on within the State "for the purpose of financial profit or gain" regardless of its connection with interstate commerce. To apportion net income, the Act applies a three-factor ratio based on inventory, wages and gross receipts. Under the Act the State Revenue Commissioner assessed and collected a total of $1,478.31 from respondent for the taxable years 1952, 1954 and 1955, and after claims for refunds were denied the respondent filed this suit to recover such payments. It bases its rights to recover squarely upon the constitutionality of Georgia's Act under the Commerce and the Due Process Clauses of the Constitution of the United States.

That there is a "need for clearing up the tangled underbrush of past cases" with reference to the taxing power of the States is a concomitant to the negative approach resulting from a case-by-case resolution of "the extremely limited restrictions that the Constitution places upon the states. . . ." Wisconsin v. J. C. Penney Co., 311 U.S. 435, 445 (1940). Commerce between the States having grown up like Topsy, the Congress meanwhile not having undertaken to regulate taxation of it, and the States having understandably persisted in their efforts to get some return for the substantial benefits they have afforded it, there is little wonder that there has been no end of cases testing out state tax levies. The resulting judicial application of constitutional principles to specific state statutes leaves much room for controversy and confusion and little in the way of precise guides to the States in the exercise of their indispensable power of taxation. This Court alone has handed down some three hundred full-dress opinions spread through slightly more than that number of our reports. As was said in Miller Bros. Co. v. Maryland, 347 U.S. 340, 344 (1954), the decisions have been "not always clear . . . consistent or reconcilable. A few have been specifically overruled, while others no longer fully represent the present state of the law." From the quagmire there emerge, however, some firm peaks of decision which remain unquestioned. . . .

[I]t has been established since 1918 that a net income tax on revenues derived from interstate commerce does not offend constitutional limitations upon state interference with such commerce. The decision of William E. Peck & Co. v. Lowe, 247 U.S. 165, pointed the way. . . . The first case in this Court applying the doctrine to interstate commerce was that of United States Glue Co. v. Oak Creek, 247 U.S. 321 (1918). . . . This landmark case and those usually cited as upholding the doctrine there announced [citations omitted] dealt with corporations which were domestic to the taxing State. . . . or which had "established a commercial domicile" there. . . .

But that the presence of such a circumstance is not controlling is shown by the cases of Bass, Ratcliff & Gretton, Ltd. v. State Tax Comm., 266 U.S. 271 (1924), and Norfolk & W. R. Co. v. North Carolina, 297 U.S. 682 (1936). In neither of these cases was the taxpayer a domiciliary of the taxing State, incorporated or with its principal place of business there, though each carried on substantial local activities. . . . These cases stand for the doctrine that the entire net income of a corporation, generated by interstate as well as intrastate activities, may be fairly apportioned among the States for tax purposes by formulas utilizing in-state aspects of interstate affairs. In fact, in Bass, Ratcliff & Gretton the operations in the taxing State were conducted at a loss, and still the Court allowed part of the overall net profit of the corporation to be attributed to the State. A reading of the statute in Norfolk & W. R. Co. reveals further that one facet of the apportionment formula was specifically designed to attribute a portion of the interstate hauls to the taxing State.

Any doubt as to the validity of our position here was entirely dispelled . . . in a unanimous per curiam in West Pub. Co. v. McColgan, 328 U.S. 823 . . . The case involved the validity of California's tax on the apportioned net income of West Publishing Company, whose business was exclusively interstate. See 27 Cal. 2d 705, 166 P.2d 861. While the statement of the facts in that opinion recites that "The employees were given space in the offices of attorneys in return for the use of plaintiff's books stored in such offices, it is significant to note that West had not qualified to do business in California and the State's statute itself declared that the tax was levied on income derived from interstate commerce within the State, as well as any arising intrastate. The opinion was not grounded on the triviality that office space was given West's solicitors by attorneys in exchange for the chanceful use of what books they may have had on hand for their sales activities. Rather, it recognized that the income taxed arose from a purely interstate operation. . . .

We believe that the rationale of these cases, involving income levies by States, controls the issues here. The taxes are not regulations in any sense of that term. Admittedly they do not discriminate against or subject either corporation to an undue burden. . . .

While the economic wisdom of state net income taxes is one of state policy not for our decision, one of the "realities" raised by the parties is the possibility of a multiple burden resulting from the exactions in question. The answer is that none is shown to exist here. This is not an unapportioned tax which by its very nature makes interstate commerce bear more than its fair share. . . . Logically it is impossible, when the tax is fairly apportioned, to have the same income taxed twice. In practical operation, however, apportionment formulas being what they are, the possibility of the contrary is not foreclosed, especially by levies in domiciliary States. But that question is not before us. . . .

It is also contended that Spector Motor Service, Inc. v. O'Connor, 340 U.S. 602 (1951), requires a contrary result. But there it was repeatedly emphasized that the tax was "imposed upon the franchise of a foreign corporation for the privilege of doing business within the State. . . ." Thus, it was invalid under a long line of precedents, some of which we have mentioned. . . .

Nor will the argument that the exactions contravene the Due Process Clause bear scrutiny. The taxes imposed are levied only on that portion of the taxpayer's net income which arises from its activities within the taxing State. . . . It strains reality to say, in terms of our decisions, that each of the corporations here was not sufficiently involved in local events to forge "some definite link, some minimum connection" sufficient to satisfy due process requirements. . . . The record is without conflict that both corporations engage in substantial income-producing activity in the taxing States. In fact in No. 12 almost half of the corporation's income is derived from the taxing State's sales which are shown to be promoted by vigorous and continuous sales campaigns run through a central office located in the State. While in No. 33 the percent of sales is not available, the course of conduct was largely identical. . . .

No. 12 — Affirmed.
No. 33 — Reversed.

Mr. Justice Harlan, concurring.

In joining the opinion of the Court, I deem it appropriate to make some further comments as to the issues in these cases because of the strongly held contrary views manifested in the dissenting opinions of Mr. Justice Frankfurter and Mr. Justice Whittaker. I preface what follows by saying that in my view the past decisions of this Court clearly point to, if indeed they do not compel, the sustaining of these two state taxing measures. . . .

I think it no more a "regulation of," "burden on," or "interference with" interstate commerce to permit a State within whose borders a foreign corporation engages *solely* in activities in aid of that commerce to tax the net income derived therefrom on a properly apportioned basis than to permit the same State to impose a nondiscriminatory net income tax of general application on a corporation engaging in *both* interstate and intrastate commerce therein and to take into account income from both categories. Cf. William E. Peck & Co. v. Lowe, 247 U.S. 165. In each case the amount of the tax will increase as the profitability of the interstate business done increases. This Court has consistently upheld state net income taxes of general application so applied as to reach that portion of the profits of interstate business enterprises fairly allocable to activities within the State's borders. We do no more today.

MR. JUSTICE WHITTAKER, with whom MR. JUSTICE FRANKFURTER and MR. JUSTICE STEWART join, dissenting.

I respectfully dissent. My disagreement with the Court is over what I think are constitutional fundamentals. I think that the Commerce Clause of the Constitution, Art. 1, § 8, cl. 3, as consistently interpreted by this Court until today, precludes the States from laying taxes directly on, and thereby regulating, "exclusively interstate commerce." But the Court's decision today holds that the States may do so. . . .

MR. JUSTICE FRANKFURTER, dissenting.

By way of emphasizing my agreement with my brother Whittaker, I add a few observations.

The Court sustains the taxing power of the States in these two cases essentially on the basis of precedents. For me, the result of today's decisions is to break new ground. I say this because among all the hundreds of cases dealing with the power of the States to tax commerce, there is not a single decision adjudicating the precise situation now before us. Concretely, we have never decided that a State may tax a corporation when that tax is on income related to the State by virtue of activities within it when such activities are exclusively part of the process of doing interstate commerce. . . .

The case that argumentatively comes the closest to the situation now before the Court is West Publishing Co. v. McColgan, 328 U.S. 823. But in that case too, as the opinion of the California Supreme Court which we there summarily sustained clearly set forth, 27 Cal. 2d 705, 166 P.2d 861, the West Publishing Company did not merely complete in California the business which began in Minnesota. It employed permanent workers who engaged in business activities localized in California, activities which were apart from and in addition to the purely interstate sale of law books. These activities were more than an essential part of the process of interstate commerce; they were, in legal shorthand, local California activities constituting intrastate business. . . .

Accordingly, today's decision cannot rest on the basis of adjudicated precedents. This does not bar the making of a new precedent. The history of the Commerce Clause is the history of judicial evolution. It is one thing, however, to recognize the taxing power of the States in relation to purely interstate activities and quite another thing to say that that power has already been established by the decisions of this Court. If new ground is to be broken, the ground must be justified and not treated as though it were old ground.

I do not think we should take this new step. My objection is the policy that underlies the Commerce Clause, namely, whatever disadvantages may accrue to the separate States from making of the United States a free-trade territory are far outweighed by the advantages not only to the United States as a Nation, but to the component States. I am assuming, of course, that today's decision will stimulate, if indeed it does not compel, every State of the Union, which has not already done so, to devise a formula of apportionment to tax the income of enterprises carrying on exclusively interstate commerce. As a result, interstate commerce will be burdened not hypothetically but practically, and we have been admonished again and again that taxation is a practical matter.

I think that interstate commerce will be not merely argumentatively but actively burdened for two reasons:

First. It will not, I believe, be gainsaid that there are thousands of relatively small or moderate size corporations doing exclusively interstate business spread over several States. To subject these corporations to a separate income tax in each of these States means that they will have to keep books, make returns, store records, and engage legal counsel, all to meet the divers and variegated tax laws of forty-nine States, with their different times for filing returns, different tax structures, different modes for determining "net income," and, different, often conflicting, formulas of apportionment. This will involve large increases in bookkeeping, accounting, and legal paraphernalia to meet these new demands. The cost of such a far-flung scheme for complying with the taxing requirements of the different States may well exceed the burden of the taxes themselves, especially in the case of small companies doing a small volume of business in several States.[2]

Second. The extensive litigation in this Court which has challenged formulas of apportionment in the case of railroad and express companies — challenges addressed to the natural temptation of the States to absorb more than their fair share of interstate revenue — will be multiplied many times when such formulas are applied to the infinitely larger number of other businesses which are engaged in exclusively interstate commerce. . . .

The question is not whether a fair share of the profits derived from the carrying on of exclusively interstate commerce should contribute to the cost of the state governments. The question is whether the answer to this problem rests with this Court or with Congress. . . .

At best, this Court can only act negatively; it can determine whether a specific state tax is imposed in violation of the Commerce Clause. Such decisions must necessarily depend on the application of rough and ready legal concepts. We cannot make a detailed inquiry into the incidence of diverse economic burdens in order to determine the extent to which such burdens conflict with the necessities of national economic life. Neither can we devise appropriate standards for dividing up national revenue on the basis of more or less abstract principles of constitutional law, which cannot be responsive to the subtleties of the interrelated economies of Nation and State.

The problem calls for solution by devising a congressional policy. Congress alone can provide for a full and thorough canvassing of the multitudinous and intricate factors which compose the problem of the taxing freedom of the States and the needed limits on such state taxing power. Congressional committees can make studies and give the claims of the individual States adequate hearing before the ultimate legislative formulation of policy is made by the representatives of all the States. The solution to these problems ought not to rest on the self-serving determination of the States of what they are entitled to out of the Nation's resources. Congress alone can formulate policies founded upon economic realities, perhaps to be applied to the myriad situations involved by a properly constituted and duly informed administrative agency.[cc]

Public Law No. 86-272 *73 Stat. 555 (1959)*

An Act relating to the power of the States to impose net income taxes on income derived from interstate commerce, and authorizing studies by congressional committees of matters pertaining thereto.

---

[2] For a detailed exposition of the manifold difficulties in complying with the diverse and complex taxing systems of the States, see Cohen, State Tax Allocations and Formulas which Affect Management Operating Decisions, 1 Jour. Taxation, No. 2 (July 1954), p. 2.

[cc] Cf. Brown-Forman Distillers Corp. v. Collector of Revenue, 234 La. 651, 101 So. 2d 70 (1958), appeal dismissed and cert. denied, 359 U.S. 28 (1959). — Ed.

TITLE I — IMPOSITION OF MINIMUM STANDARD

SEC. 101. (a) No State, or political subdivision thereof, shall have power to impose, for any taxable year ending after the date of the enactment of this Act, a net income tax on the income derived within such State by any person from interstate commerce if the only business activities within such State by or on behalf of such person during such taxable year are either, or both, of the following:

(1) the solicitation of orders by such person, or his representative, in such State for sales of tangible personal property, which orders are sent outside the State for approval or rejection, and, if approved, are filled by shipment or delivery from a point outside the State; and

(2) the solicitation of orders by such person, or his representative, in such State in the name of or for the benefit of a prospective customer of such person, if orders by such customer to such person to enable such customer to fill orders resulting from such solicitation are orders described in paragraph (1).

(b) The provisions of subsection (a) shall not apply to the imposition of a net income tax by any State, or political subdivision thereof, with respect to —

(1) any corporation which is incorporated under the laws of such State;

(2) any individual who, under the laws of such State, is domiciled in, or a resident of, such State.

(c) For purposes of subsection (a), a person shall not be considered to have engaged in business activities within a State during any taxable year merely by reason of sales in such State, or the solicitation of orders for sales in such State, of tangible personal property on behalf of such person by one or more independent contractors, or by reason of the maintenance of an office in such State by one or more independent contractors whose activities on behalf of such person in such State consist solely of making sales, or soliciting orders for sales, of tangible personal property.

(d) For purposes of this section —

(1) the term "independent contractor" means a commission agent, broker, or other independent contractor who is engaged in selling, or soliciting orders for the sale of, tangible personal property for more than one principal and who holds himself out as such in the regular course of his business activities; and

(2) the term "representative" does not include an independent contractor.

SEC. 102. (a) No State, or political subdivision thereof, shall have power to assess, after the date of the enactment of this Act, any net income tax which was imposed by such State or political subdivision, as the case may be, for any taxable year ending on or before such date, on the income derived within such State by any person from interstate commerce, if the imposition of such tax for a taxable year ending after such date is prohibited by section 101.

(b) The provisions of subsection (a) shall not be construed —

(1) to invalidate the collection, on or before the date of the enactment of this Act, of any net income tax imposed for a taxable year ending on or before such date, or

(2) to prohibit the collection, after the date of the enactment of this Act, of any net income tax which was assessed on or before such date for a taxable year ending on or before such date.

SEC. 103. For purposes of this title, the term "net income tax" means any tax imposed on, or measured by, net income.

SEC. 104. If any provision of this title or the application of such provision to any person or circumstance is held invalid, the remainder of this title or the application of such provision to persons or circumstances other than those to which it is held invalid, shall not be affected thereby.

562   Chapter Eight. **The States in a Federal Union**

TITLE II — STUDY AND REPORT BY CONGRESSIONAL COMMITTEES

SEC. 201. The Committee on the Judiciary of the House of Representatives and the Committee on Finance of the United States Senate, acting separately or jointly, or both, or any duly authorized subcommittees thereof, shall make full and complete studies of all matters pertaining to the taxation by the States of income derived within the States from the conduct of business activities which are exclusively in furtherance of interstate commerce or which are a part of interstate commerce, for the purpose of recommending to the Congress proposed legislation providing uniform standards to be observed by the States in imposing income taxes on income so derived.

SEC. 302. The Committees shall report to their respective Houses the results of such studies together with their proposals for legislation on or before July 1, 1962.[dd]

NOTE State Jurisdiction to Tax Income and Estates

1. State income taxes have also presented explicit questions of jurisdiction, usually deemed to be controlled by the due process clause of the Fourteenth Amendment. These relate principally to the power of a state to impose upon nonresidents a tax upon income asserted to have its source in the state, and to the power of a state to impose upon residents a tax upon income asserted to have its source in other states. The principal Supreme Court decisions are: (1) Shaffer v. Carter, 252 U.S. 37 (1920), upholding the imposition of the Oklahoma net income tax upon over $1,500,000 of income of a resident of Illinois derived from the ownership and operation of a number of oil and gas leases covering property in Oklahoma, and the ownership in fee and operation of oil-producing property in Oklahoma. (2) Maguire v. Trefry, 253 U.S. 12 (1920), upholding the imposition of the Massachusetts income tax upon income of a resident of Massachusetts derived from a testamentary trust created under the will of a decedent who had resided in Pennsylvania; the trustee was a trust company located in Pennsylvania, the trust was administered under the laws of Pennsylvania, and the securities making up the corpus of the trust were held in Pennsylvania. (3) Lawrence v. State Tax Commission, 286 U.S. 276 (1932), upholding the imposition of the Mississippi income tax upon income of a resident of Mississippi arising from the construction by him of public highways in the state of Tennessee; the Court also rejected a claim that in exempting domestic corporations from a tax on income derived from activities outside the state, the state denied the taxpayer the equal protection of the laws guaranteed by the Fourteenth Amendment. (4) New York ex rel. Whitney v. Graves, 299 U.S. 366 (1937), upholding New York's imposition of income tax upon the profit realized by a resident of Massachusetts in the sale of a "right" to a fractional interest in a seat on the New York Stock Exchange, and this though the taxpayer did business in Boston and not in New York, and had a seat on the Exchange principally because it enabled him to have New York members of the Exchange execute orders at 40 percent of the commissions charged to nonmembers. (5) New York ex rel. Cohn v. Graves, 300 U.S. 308 (1937), upholding the imposition of the New York income tax upon income of a resident of New York derived from rents of land located outside the state and from interest on bonds physically outside the state and secured by mortgage on lands outside the state.

Suppose T, a resident of Massachusetts, sells stock in a Delaware corporation to another resident of Massachusetts at a profit. May Delaware impose an income tax upon the profit from the sale? (Cf., with respect to state inheritance taxes, State Tax Commission of Utah v. Aldrich, 315 U.S. 174 (1942). Is there a significant difference between income

[dd] For an analysis of this statute, see Note, State Taxation of Interstate Commerce: Pub. L. No. 86-272, 46 Va. L. Rev. 297 (1960). For comment on the Northwest Portland Cement Co. decision, on Pub. L. No. 86-272, and on related matters, see A Symposium on State Taxation of Interstate Commerce, 46 Va. L. Rev. 1051 et seq. (1960). — ED.

Section D. State Taxation

and inheritance taxes in such a case?) Suppose the sale were executed on the New York Stock Exchange and the purchaser were a resident of New Jersey with an office for the conduct of an investment business in Pennsylvania. How many, and which, states could tax the profit on the sale?

2. The Report of the Special Subcommittee on State Taxation of Interstate Commerce, made in response to Title II of Public Law No. 86-272, supra, considers in detail the difficulties and costs of enforcement of and compliance with the provisions of state income tax statutes where there is the minimal permissible basis for jurisdiction. See H.R. Rep. No. 1480, 88th Cong., 2d Sess., particularly chapters 6, 9, 10, 11, 13, 14, 15, and 18. Recommendations for a uniform jurisdictional rule with respect to manufacturing and mercantile enterprises are made in H.R. Rep. No. 952, 89th Cong., 1st Sess., pp. 1156-1158 (1965).

3. As the reference to State Tax Commission v. Aldrich, above, suggests, jurisdictional problems have frequently arisen with respect to state inheritance or estate taxes. Upon death, it has been characteristic for the state of domicile of the decedent to impose a comprehensive estate or inheritance tax upon his net estate. It appears to be accepted now that real estate, if located elsewhere, and tangible personal property having acquired a situs of some permanence in a state other than the state of domicile, can be subjected to, or included in the measure of, such a tax only by the state where located. Frick v. Pennsylvania, 268 U.S. 473 (1925); Treichler v. Wisconsin, 338 U.S. 251 (1949). But note Bittker, The Taxation of Out-of-State Tangible Property, 56 Yale L.J. 640 (1947). The persistent difficulty has arisen chiefly with respect to securities and other intangible property — bonds, for example, which may be (1) owned by a decedent domiciled in State A, (2) physically located in State B, (3) the obligation of a debtor residing in State C, (4) perhaps secured by mortgage on property in State D. Shares of stock may present contacts with a similar multiplicity of jurisdictions, and the intervention of trusts and powers of appointment may increase the number of states possibly interested.

The law with respect to these problems appears to have passed through three distinct phases. The first phase, decisions of which Blackstone v. Miller, 188 U.S. 189 (1903), Wheeler v. Sohmer, 233 U.S. 434 (1914), and Bullen v. Wisconsin, 240 U.S. 625 (1916), might be considered exemplars, permitted the domiciliary state to include all of such intangibles in the taxable estate and found no constitutional objection if other states having some appreciable connection with transferred property also imposed an inheritance or estate tax with respect to such property. The second phase was made up of a brief series of decisions beginning with Farmers Loan & Trust Co. v. Minnesota, 280 U.S. 204 (1930), and extending through First National Bank v. Maine, 284 U.S. 312 (1932). In those cases the Court overruled some of the earlier decisions and, by jurisdictional limitations held to be imposed by the Fourteenth Amendment, sharply limited the multiple incidence of death taxes on intangibles. The third phase is marked by more recent decisions in which the Court has abandoned the jurisdictional limitations imposed by the decisions of the early 1930s, has explicitly overruled First National Bank v. Maine, and "restore[d] these intangibles to the constitutional status which they occupied up to a few years ago." Curry v. McCanless, 307 U.S. 357 (1939); State Tax Commission of Utah v. Aldrich, 316 U.S. 174 (1942). The majority opinion of Mr. Justice Stone in the former case and the dissenting opinion of Mr. Justice Jackson in the latter perhaps give the divergent points of view their most comprehensive judicial statements. Does the opinion of Mr. Justice Stone deal more relevantly with the powers of sovereign states than with the problem of states in a federal system? Or is the problem one to be dealt with by agencies other than the courts? Cf. Faught, Reciprocity in State Taxation as the Next Step in Empirical Legislation, 92 U. Pa. L. Rev. 258 (1944).

Extensive materials concerning these problems are collected in Hellerstein, State and Local Taxation 496-538 (3d ed. 1969).

7. Sales, Use, and Gross Receipts Taxes, and Responsibility for the Collection Thereof

Banker Brothers Co. v. Pennsylvania 222 U.S. 210, 32 S. Ct. 38, 56 L. Ed. 168 (1911)

MR. JUSTICE LAMAR delivered the opinion of the court.

The Banker Brothers Company, a corporation doing business in Pittsburgh, was charged, as retail vendors, with a tax of 1 per cent on $351,000 on sales of automobiles to persons in Pennsylvania under a statute of that State. It denied liability on the ground that the sales were interstate transactions. A decision of that point involves the question as to whether Banker Brothers Company acted as principal or as agent of a New York manufacturer.

It appears that the George N. Pierce Company was engaged in the business of manufacturing automobiles in Buffalo, and in 1905 made a contract by which it agreed "to build for and sell automobiles to Banker Brothers Company at twenty per cent less than list price. Deliveries to be f.o.b. Buffalo as soon as practicable after order for deliveries are received. Payments to be made in cash."

The Banker Brothers Company kept no machines in stock except those used for demonstration, and were allowed to sell only within a restricted territory on terms stipulated by the manufacturer. The purchaser of the machine was to pay at least ten per cent when he signed a printed form addressed to Banker Brothers Company requesting it "to enter my order for ———— motor car, for which I agree to pay the list price f.o.b. factory, as follows: $———— upon signing this order, and the balance upon delivery of the car to me."

The name of the Pierce Company did not appear anywhere on this printed form furnished by it, but when the Banker Brothers Company accepted the order it remitted the cash to the Pierce Company. If the latter accepted the order, it agreed thereupon to make the automobile and ship it, drawing on Banker Brothers Company for the balance of the list price, less twenty per cent, with bill of lading attached. The Banker Brothers Company, on paying the draft, took up the bill of lading, received from the carrier an automobile which though shipped in interstate commerce had become at rest in the State of Pennsylvania. Banker Brothers Company had the title and delivered it to the buyer on his paying the balance of the purchase money. Compare Dozier v. Alabama, 218 U.S. 124. The written contract was silent on the subject, but it was stipulated that the Pierce Company warranted the machine direct to the purchaser.

It is contended that Banker Brothers Company were agents and the Pierce Company an undisclosed principal. It is urged that the sale was an interstate transaction between the manufacturer and the purchaser, with Banker Brothers Company merely acting as an agent which looked after the delivery of the machine and collected the purchase price.

This is one of the common cases in which parties find it to their interest to occupy the position of vendor and vendee for some purposes under a contract containing terms which, for the purpose of restricting sales and securing payment, come near to creating the relation of principal and agent. But as between Banker Brothers Company and the Pittsburgh purchaser, there can be no doubt that it occupied the position of vendor. As such it was bound by its contract to him and under the duty of paying to the State a tax on the sale.

The name of the Pierce Company was not mentioned in the order signed by the purchaser. Had there been a breach of its terms he would have had a cause of action against the Banker Brothers Company, with whom alone he dealt. If he had failed to complete the purchase the Pierce Company would have no right to sue him on the contract. The fact that he was liable for the freight by virtue of the agreement to "pay the list price f.o.b. factory" did not convert it into a sale by the manufacturer at the factory; neither was that result accomplished because, with the machine, Banker Brothers Company also delivered to the buyer in Pittsburgh a warranty from the manufacturer direct.

These were mere incidents of the intrastate contract of sale between Banker Brothers Company and the purchaser in Pittsburgh, who was not concerned with the question as to how the machine was acquired by his vendor, or whether that company bought it from another dealer in the same city or from the manufacturer in New York. The contract was made in Pennsylvania, and was there to be performed by the delivery of the automobile and the payment of the balance of the purchase price. See American Steel & Wire Co. v. Speed, 192 U.S. 500; American Express v. Iowa, 196 U.S. 133, 146. The court properly held it was not an interstate transaction, but taxable under the laws of Pennsylvania.

Affirmed.[ee]

Henneford v. Silas Mason Co. 300 U.S. 577, 57 S. Ct. 524, 81 L. Ed. 814 (1937)

[For the opinion in this case see page 385 supra.][ff]

McGoldrick v. Berwind-White Coal Mining Co. 309 U.S. 33, 60 S. Ct. 388, 84 L. Ed. 565 (1940)

MR. JUSTICE STONE delivered the opinion of the Court:

The question for decision is whether the New York City tax laid upon sales of goods for consumption, as applied to respondent, infringes the commerce clause of the Federal Constitution.

Upon certiorari to review a determination by the Comptroller of the City of New York that respondent was subject to New York City sales tax in the sum of $176,703, the Appellate Division of the New York Supreme Court held that the taxing statute as applied to respondent does so infringe, 255 App. Div. 961. . . . The New York Court of Appeals affirmed without opinion, 281 N.Y. 610, 22 N.E.(2d) 173, . . . We granted certiorari December 4, 1939 [308 U.S. 546], the question presented being of public importance, upon a petition which challenged the decision of the state court as not in accord with applicable decisions of this Court in Banker Bros. v. Pennsylvania, 222 U.S. 210; Wiloil Corp. v. Pennsylvania, 294 U.S. 169. . . .

Pursuant to [statutory] authority the municipal assembly of the City of New York adopted Local Law No. 24 of 1934 (published as Local Law No. 25), since annually renewed, which laid a tax upon purchasers for consumption of tangible personal property generally (except foods and drugs furnished on prescription), of utility services in supplying gas, electricity, telephone service, etc., and of meals consumed in restaurants. By §2 the tax was fixed at "two percentum upon the amount of the receipts from every sale in the City of New York," "sale" being defined by §1(e) as "any transfer of title or possession, or both . . . in any manner or by any means whatsoever for a consideration or any agreement therefor." Another clause of §2 commands that the tax "shall be paid by the purchaser to the vendor for and on account of the City of New York." By the same clause the vendor, who is authorized to collect the tax, is required to charge it to the purchaser, separately from the sales price; and is made liable, as an insurer, for its payment to the

---

[ee] The assumptions underlying this decision are indicated more explicitly in Sonneborn Bros. v. Cureton, 262 U.S. 506, particularly at 515 (1923).
Cf. Wiloil Corp. v. Pennsylvania, 294 U.S. 169 (1935). — ED.
[ff] Cf. Gregg Dyeing Co. v. Query, 286 U.S. 472 (1932). — ED.

city. . . . Purchases for resale are exempt from the tax, and a purchaser who pays the tax and later resells is entitled to a refund.

The ultimate burden of the tax, both in form and in substance, is thus laid upon the buyer, for consumption, of tangible personal property, and measured by the sales price. Only in event that the seller fails to pay over to the city the tax collected or to charge and collect it as the statute requires, is the burden cast on him. It is conditioned upon events occurring within the state, either transfer of title or possession of the purchased property, or an agreement within the state, "consummated" there, for the transfer of title, or possession. The duty of collecting the tax and paying it over to the Comptroller is imposed on the seller in addition to the duty imposed upon the buyer to pay the tax to the Comptroller when not so collected. . . .

Respondent, a Pennsylvania corporation, is engaged in the production of coal of specified grades, said to possess unique qualities, from its mines within that state and in selling it to consumers and dealers. It maintains a sales office in New York City and sells annually to its customers, 1,500,000 tons of its product, of which approximately 1,300,000 tons are delivered by respondent to some twenty public utility and steamship companies. The coal moves by rail from mine to dock in Jersey City, thence in most instances by barge to the point of delivery. All the sales contracts with the New York customers in question were entered into in New York City, . . . call for delivery of the coal by respondent by barge, alongside the purchasers' plants or steamships. In many instances the price of the coal was stated to be subject to any increase or decrease of mining costs including wages, and of railroad rates between the mines and the Jersey City terminal to which the coal was to be shipped. All the deliveries, with the exceptions already noted, were made within New York City, and all such are concededly subject to the tax except insofar as it infringes the commerce clause. . . .

But it was not the purpose of the commerce clause to relieve those engaged in interstate commerce of their just share of state tax burdens, merely because an incidental or consequential effect of the tax is an increase in the cost of doing the business, Western Live Stock v. Bureau of Revenue, 303 U.S. 250, 254. Not all state taxation is to be condemned because, in some manner, it has an effect upon commerce between the states, and there are many forms of tax whose burdens, when distributed through the play of economic forces, affect interstate commerce, which nevertheless fall short of the regulation of the commerce which the Constitution leaves to Congress. A tax may be levied on net income wholly derived from interstate commerce. Non-discriminatory taxation of the instrumentalities of interstate commerce is not prohibited. The like taxation of property, shipped interstate, before its movement begins, or after it ends, is not a forbidden regulation. An excise for the warehousing of merchandise preparatory to its interstate shipment or upon its use, or withdrawal for use, by the consignee after the interstate journey has ended is not precluded. Nor is taxation of a local business or occupation which is separate and distinct from the transportation or intercourse which is interstate commerce, forbidden merely because in the ordinary course such transportation or intercourse is induced or occasioned by such business, or is prerequisite to it. Western Live Stock v. Bureau of Revenue, supra, and cases cited.

In few of these cases could it be said with assurance that the local tax does not in some measure affect the commerce or increase the cost of doing it. But in them as in other instances of constitutional interpretation so as to insure the harmonious operation of powers reserved to the states with those conferred upon the national government, courts are called upon to reconcile competing constitutional demands, that commerce between the states shall not be unduly impeded by state action, and that the power to lay taxes for the support of state government shall not be unduly curtailed. See Woodruff v. Parham, 8 Wall. 123, 131, . . .

Certain types of tax may, if permitted at all, so readily be made the instrument of impeding or destroying interstate commerce as plainly to call for their condemnation as forbidden regulations. Such are the taxes . . . which are aimed at or discriminate against the commerce or impose a levy for the privilege of doing it, or tax interstate transportation or communication or their gross earnings, or levy an exaction on merchandise in the course of its interstate journey. Each imposes a burden which intrastate commerce does not bear, and merely because interstate commerce is being done places it at a disadvantage in comparison with intrastate business or property in circumstances such that if the asserted power to tax were sustained, the states would be left free to exert it to the detriment of the national commerce.

The present tax as applied to respondent is without the possibility of such consequences. Equality is its theme, cf. Henneford v. Silas Mason Co., 300 U.S. 577, 583. It does not aim at or discriminate against interstate commerce. It is laid upon every purchaser, within the state, of goods for consumption, regardless of whether they have been transported in interstate commerce. Its only relation to the commerce arises from the fact that immediately preceding transfer of possession to the purchaser within the state, which is the taxable event regardless of the time and place of passing title, the merchandise has been transported in interstate commerce and brought to its journey's end. Such a tax has no different effect upon interstate commerce than a tax on the "use" of property which has just been moved in interstate commerce sustained in Monamotor Oil Co. v. Johnson, 292 U.S. 86; Henneford v. Silas Mason Co., 300 U.S. 577, . . . or the tax on storage or withdrawal for use by the consignee of gasoline, similarly sustained in Gregg Dyeing Co. v. Query, 286 U.S. 472, . . . or the familiar property tax on goods by the state of destination at the conclusion of their interstate journey. Brown v. Houston, 114 U.S. 622, . . .

If, as guides to decision we look to the purpose of the commerce clause to protect interstate commerce from discriminatory or destructive state action, and at the same time to the purpose of the state taxing power under which interstate commerce admittedly must bear its fair share of state tax burdens, and to the necessity of judicial reconciliation of these competing demands, we can find no adequate ground for saying that the present tax is a regulation which, in the absence of congressional action, the commerce clause forbids. This Court has uniformly sustained a tax imposed by the state of the buyer upon a sale of goods, in several instances in the "original package," effected by delivery to the purchaser upon arrival at destination after an interstate journey, both when the local seller has purchased the goods extra-state for the purpose of resale, Woodruff v. Parham, 8 Wall. 123, . . . and when the extra-state seller has shipped them into the taxing state for sale there. Hinson v. Lott, 8 Wall. 148, . . . It has likewise sustained a fixed-sum license tax imposed on the agent of the interstate seller for the privilege of selling merchandise brought into the taxing state for the purpose of sale. . . . Wagner v. Covington, 251 U.S. 95.

The only challenge made to these controlling authorities is by reference to unconstitutional "burdens" on interstate commerce made in general statements which are inapplicable here because they are torn from their setting in judicial opinions and speak of state regulations or taxes of a different kind laid in different circumstances from those with which we are now concerned. See for example, Galveston, H. & S.A.R. Co. v. Texas, 210 U.S. 217; Cooney v. Mountain States Teleph. & Teleg. Co., 294 U.S. 384; Fisher's Blend Station v. Tax Commission, 297 U.S. 650. Others will presently be discussed. But unless we are now to reject the plain teaching of this line of sales tax decisions, extending back for more than seventy years from Graybar Electric Co. v. Curry, 308 U.S. 513, decided this term, to Woodruff v. Parham, 8 Wall. 123, supra, the present tax must be upheld. As we have seen, the ruling of these decisions does not rest on precedent alone. It has the support of reason and of due regard for the just balance between national and state power. In sustaining these taxes on sales emphasis was placed on the circumstances that they were not so laid, measured or conditioned as to afford a means of obstruction to the commerce or of discrimination against it, and that the extension of the immunity of the commerce clause contended for would be at the expense of state taxing power by withholding from taxation property and transactions within the state without the gain of any needed protection to interstate commerce. [Citations omitted.]

Apart from these more fundamental considerations which we think are of controlling force in the application of the commerce clause, we can find no adequate basis for distinguishing the present tax laid on the sale or purchase of goods upon their arrival at destination at the end of an interstate journey from the tax which may be laid in like fashion on the property itself. That the latter is a permissible tax has long been established by an unwavering line of authority. [Citations omitted.] As we have often pointed out, there is no distinction in this relationship between a tax on property, the sum of all the rights and powers incident to ownership, and the taxation of the exercise of some of its constituent elements. Nashville, C. & St.L. R. Co. v. Wallace [288 U.S. 267]. . . . If coal situated as that in the present case, was, before its delivery, subject to a state property tax, see Brown v. Houston, 114 U.S. 622, . . . transfer of possession of the coal upon a sale is equally taxable, see Wiloil Corp. v. Pennsylvania, supra, just as was the storage or use of the property in similar circumstances held taxable in Nashville, C. & St.L. R. Co. v. Wallace, 288 U.S. 249, . . .

Respondent, pointing to the course of its business and to its contracts which contemplate the shipment of the coal interstate upon orders of the New York customers, insists that a distinction is to be taken between a tax laid on sales made, without previous contract, after the merchandise has crossed the state boundary, and sales, the contracts for which when made contemplate or require the transportation of merchandise interstate to the taxing state. Only the sales in the state of destination in the latter class of cases, it is said, are protected from taxation by the commerce clause, a qualification which respondent concedes is a salutary limitation upon the reach of the clause since its use is thus precluded as a means of avoiding state taxation of merchandise transported to the state in advance of the purchase order or contract of sale.

But we think this distinction is without the support of reason or authority. A very large part, if not most of the merchandise sold in New York City, is shipped interstate to that market. In the case of products like cotton, citrus fruits and coal, not to mention many others which are consumed there in vast quantities, all have crossed the state line to seek a market, whether in fulfilment of a contract or not. That is equally the case with other goods sent from without the state to the New York market, whether they are brought into competition with like goods produced within the state or not. We are unable to say that the present tax, laid generally upon all sales to consumers within the state, subjects the commerce involved where the goods sold are brought from other states, to any greater burden or affects it more, in any economic or practical way, whether the purchase order or contract precedes or follows the interstate shipment. Since the tax applies only if a sale is made, and in either case the object of interstate shipment is a sale at destination, the deterrent effect of the tax would seem to be the same on both. Restriction of the scope of the commerce clause so as to prevent recourse to it as a means of curtailing state taxing power seems as salutary in the one case as in the other.

True, the distinction has the support of a statement obiter in Sonneborn Bros. v. Cureton [262 U.S. 515], and seems to have been tacitly recognized in Ware & Leland v. Mobile County, 209 U.S. 405, 412, and Banker Bros. Co. v. Pennsylvania, 222 U.S. 210, supra, although in each case a tax on the sale of goods brought into the state for sale was upheld. But we have sustained the tax where the course of business and the agreement for sale plainly contemplated the shipment interstate in fulfilment of the contract. Wiloil Corp. v. Pennsylvania, supra; Graybar Electric Co. v. Curry, supra. In the same circumstances the Court has upheld a property tax on the merchandise transported, . . . upon its use, . . . and upon its storage; . . . Taxation of property or the exercise of a power over it immediately preceding its previously contemplated shipment interstate has been similarly sustained. . . . For reasons already indicated all such taxes upon property or the exercise of the powers of ownership stand in no different relation to interstate commerce and have no different effect upon it than has the present sales tax upon goods whose shipment interstate into the taxing state was contemplated when the contract was entered into.

It is also urged that the conclusion which we reach is inconsistent with the long line of decisions of this Court following Robbins v. Taxing Dist., 120 U.S. 489, which have held invalid, license taxes to the extent that they have sought to tax the occupation of soliciting orders for the purchase of goods to be shipped into the taxing state. In some instances the tax appeared to be aimed at suppression or placing at a disadvantage this type of business when brought into competition with competing intrastate sales. . . . In all, the statute, in its practical operation, was capable of use, through increase in the tax, and in fact operated to some extent to place the merchant thus doing business interstate at a disadvantage in competition with untaxed sales at retail stores within the state. While a state, in some circumstances, may by taxation suppress or curtail one type of intrastate business to the advantage of another type of competing business which is left untaxed, see Puget Sound Power & L. Co. v. Seattle, 291 U.S. 619, 625, and cases cited, it does not follow that interstate commerce may be similarly affected by the practical operation of a state taxing statute. Compare Hammond Packing Co. v. Montana, 233 U.S. 331, . . . It is enough for present purposes that the rule of Robbins v. Taxing Dist., 120 U.S. 489, supra, has been narrowly limited to fixed-sum license taxes imposed on the business of soliciting orders for the purchase of goods to be shipped interstate . . . and that the actual and potential effect on the commerce of such a tax is wholly wanting in the present case.

Finally it is said that the vice of the present tax is that it is measured by the gross receipts from interstate commerce and thus in effect reaches for taxation the commerce carried on both within and without the taxing state. J. D. Adams Mfg. Co. v. Storen, 304 U.S. 307, . . . It is true that a state tax upon the operations of interstate commerce measured either by its volume or the gross receipts derived from it has been held to infringe the commerce clause, because the tax if sustained would exact tribute for the commerce carried on beyond the boundaries of the taxing state, and would leave each state through which the commerce passes free to subject it to a like burden not borne by intrastate commerce. . . .

In J. D. Adams Mfg. Co. v. Storen, supra, a tax on gross receipts, so far as laid by the state of the seller upon the receipts from sales of goods manufactured in the taxing state and sold in other states, was held invalid because there the court found the receipts derived from activities in interstate commerce, as distinguished from the receipts from activities wholly intrastate, were included in the measure of the tax, the sales price, without segregation or apportionment. It was pointed out, . . . that had the tax been conditioned upon the exercise of the taxpayer's franchise or its privilege of manufacturing in the taxing state, it would have been sustained, despite its incidental effect on interstate commerce since the taxpayer's local activities or privileges were sufficient to support such a tax, and that it could fairly be measured by the sales price of the goods. . . .

The rationale of the J. D. Adams Mfg. Co. case does not call for condemnation of the present tax. Here the tax is conditioned upon a local activity, delivery of goods within the state upon their purchase for consumption. It is an activity which, apart from its effect on the commerce, is subject to the state taxing power. The effect of the tax, even though measured by the sales price, as has been shown, neither discriminates against nor obstructs interstate commerce more than numerous other state taxes which have repeatedly been sustained as involving no prohibited regulation of interstate commerce. . . .

Reversed.

Mr. Chief Justice Hughes, dissenting:

The pressure of mounting outlays has led the States to seek new sources of revenue, and we have gone far in sustaining state power to tax property and transactions subject to their jurisdiction despite incidental or indirect effects upon interstate commerce. But hitherto we have also maintained the principle that the States cannot lay a direct tax upon that commerce. In the instant case, the Court of Appeals of New York has decided unanimously that the tax as here applied is such a tax and goes beyond the limit of state power. 281 N.Y. 610, 22 N.E.(2d) 173. . . . I think that the judgment should be affirmed. . . .

In confiding to Congress the power to regulate interstate commerce, the aim was to provide a free national market, — to pull down and prevent the re-erection of state barriers to the free intercourse between the people of the States. That free intercourse was deemed, and has proved, to be essential to our national economy. It should not be impaired. . . .

. . . And, but a year ago, in Gwin, White & Prince v. Henneford, 305 U.S. 434-436, 438, we held invalid a state tax measured by the gross receipts from the business of marketing fruit shipped in interstate commerce from the State of production to places in other States where the sales and deliveries were made and the proceeds collected. If the question now before us is controlled by precedent, the result would seem to be clear.

In relation to the present transaction, it would hardly be contended that New York could tax the transportation of the coal from Pennsylvania to New York or a contract for that transportation. But the movement of the coal from the one State to the other was definitely required by the contracts of sale and these sales must be regarded as an essential part of the commercial intercourse contemplated by the commerce clause. Gibbons v. Ogden, 9 Wheat. 1, 188. The tax on the gross receipts of the seller from these sales was manifestly an imposition upon the sales themselves. Whether the tax be small or large, it is plainly to the extent of it a burden upon interstate commerce; and as it is imposed immediately upon the gross receipts from that commerce, it is a direct burden. And, as we have often said, where what is taxed is subject to the jurisdiction of the State, the size of the tax lies within the discretion of the State, and not of this Court. . . .

How then can the laying of such a burden upon interstate commerce by justified? It is urged that there is a taxable event within the State. That event is said to be the delivery of the coal. But how can that event be deemed to be taxable by the State? The delivery is but the necessary performance of the contract of sale. Like the shipment from the mines, it is an integral part of the interstate transaction. It is said that title to the coal passes to the purchaser on delivery. But the place where the title passes has not been regarded as the test of the interstate character of a sale. We have frequently decided that where a commodity is mined or manufactured in one State and in pursuance of contracts of sale is delivered for transportation to purchasers in another State, the mere fact that the sale is f.o.b. cars in the seller's State and the purchaser pays the freight does not make the sale other than interstate. And when, as here, the buyer in an interstate sale takes delivery in his own State, that delivery in completion of the sale is as properly immune from state taxation as is the transportation to the purchaser's dock or vessel. Moreover, even if it were possible to sustain a state tax by reason of such delivery within the State, there would still be no ground for sustaining a tax upon the whole of the interstate transaction of which the delivery is only a part, as in the case of a tax upon the entire gross receipts.

Petitioner strongly insists that in substance the tax here should be regarded as the same as a *use* tax the validity of which this Court has sustained. Henneford v. Silas Mason Co., 300 U.S. 577, . . . But in the Henneford Case, Mr. Justice Cardozo, in speaking for the Court, was most careful to show that the use tax was upheld because it was imposed after interstate commerce had come to an end. In making this distinction, the Court clearly recognized that a tax imposed directly upon interstate commerce would be beyond the State's power, and the tax was sustained as one upon property which had come to rest within the State and like other property was subject to its jurisdiction. . . .

The ground most strongly asserted for sustaining the tax in the present case is that it is non-discriminatory. Undoubtedly a state tax may be bad because it is so laid as to involve a hostile discrimination against interstate commerce. But does it follow that a State may lay a direct tax upon interstate commerce because it is free to tax its own commerce in a similar way? Thus, a State may tax intrastate transportation, but it may not tax interstate transportation. The State may tax intrastate sales, but can the State tax interstate sales in order to promote its local business? It would seem to be extraordinary if a State could escape the restriction against direct impositions upon interstate commerce by first laying exactions upon its own trade and then insisting that in order to make its local policy completely effective it must be allowed to lay similar exactions upon interstate trade. That would apparently afford a simple method for extending state power into what has hitherto been regarded as a forbidden field. . . .

So, while recognizing that a tax discriminating against interstate commerce is necessarily invalid, it has long been held by this Court in the interest of the constitutional freedom of that commerce that a direct tax upon it is not saved because the same or a similar tax is laid also upon intrastate commerce. . . .

We have directed attention to a vice in imposing direct taxes upon interstate commerce in that such taxes might be imposed with equal right by every State which the commerce touches. . . . But petitioner has insisted that in the present case there is no danger of multiple taxation in that New York puts its tax upon an event which cannot occur in any other State. Of course the delivery of the coal in New York is an event which cannot occur in another State. Just as New York cannot tax the shipment of coal from the mines in Pennsylvania or the transshipment of the coal in New Jersey, so neither Pennsylvania nor New Jersey can tax the delivery in New York. Petitioner's argument misses the point as to the danger of multiple taxation in relation to interstate commerce. The shipment, the transshipment and the delivery of the coal are but parts of a unitary interstate transaction. They are integral parts of an interstate sale. If, because of the delivery in New York, that State can tax the gross receipts from the sale, why cannot Pennsylvania by reason of the shipment of the coal in that State tax the gross receipts there? That would not be difficult, as the seller is a Pennsylvania corporation and in fact in many, if not in most, instances, the purchase price of the goods shipped to New York is there received. The point is not that the delivery in New York is an event which cannot be taxed by other States, but that the authority of New York to impose a tax on that delivery cannot properly be recognized without also recognizing the authority of other States to tax the parts of the interstate transaction which take place within their borders. If New York can tax the delivery, Pennsylvania can tax the shipment and New Jersey the transshipment. And the latter States, respectively, would be as much entitled to tax the gross receipts from the sales as would New York. Even if it were assumed that the gross receipts from the interstate sales could be apportioned so that each State could tax such portion of the receipts as could be deemed to relate to the part of the transaction within its territory, still this would not help New York here, as there has been no attempt at apportionment. The taxation of the gross receipts in New York, on any appropriate view of what pertains to the interstate sales, would seem clearly to involve the danger of multiple taxation to which we have adverted in recent decisions.

Doubtless much can be said as to the desirability of a comprehensive system of taxation through the cooperation of the Union and the States so as to avoid the differentiations which beset the application of the commerce clause and thus to protect both state and national governments by a just and general scheme for raising revenues. However important such a policy may be, it is not a matter for this Court. We have the duty of maintaining the immunity of interstate commerce as contemplated by the Constitution. That immunity still remains an essential buttress of the Union, and a free national market, so far as it can be preserved without violence to state power over the subjects within state jurisdiction, is not less now than heretofore a vital concern of the national economy.

The tax as here applied is open to the same objection as a tariff upon the entrance of the coal into the State of New York, or a state tax upon the privilege of doing an interstate business, and in my view it cannot be sustained without abandoning principles long established and a host of precedents soundly based.

Mr. Justice McReynolds and Mr. Justice Roberts join in this opinion.

NOTE

1. See companion cases reported as McGoldrick v. Felt & Tarrant Manufacturing Co., 309 U.S. 70 (1940).

2. For comments on the above and related cases see Powell, New Light on Gross Receipts Taxes, 53 Harv. L. Rev. 909 (1940); Lockhart, State Tax Barriers to Interstate Trade, id. at 1253.

Nelson v. Sears, Roebuck & Co. 312 U.S. 359, 61 S. Ct. 586, 85 L. Ed. 888 (1941)

MR. JUSTICE DOUGLAS delivered the opinion of the Court:

This case involves the constitutionality of the Iowa Use Tax (Iowa Code 1939, §§6943.102-6943.125) as applied to respondent's mail order business conducted directly between customers in Iowa and respondent's mail order houses located outside Iowa. The Supreme Court of Iowa, in a five to four decision, held for respondent on that issue. 228 Iowa 1273, 292 N.W. 130. We granted certiorari because of the importance of the constitutional question presented. Judicial Code §237(b), 28 U.S.C. §344(b).

The Iowa Use Tax is complementary to the Iowa Retail Sales Tax. Iowa Code 1939, §§6943.074, et seq. It is a tax on the use in Iowa of tangible personal property at the rate of two per cent of the purchase price. "Use," so far as material here, is defined as "the exercise by any person of any right or power over tangible personal property incident to the ownership of that property." §6943.102. While the tax is imposed on "every person using such property within the state until such tax has been paid" (§6943.103), it is further provided (§6943.109) that every "retailer maintaining a place of business in this state and making sales of tangible personal property for use in this state . . . shall at the time of making such sales, whether within or without the state, collect the tax imposed by this act from the purchaser. . . ." By §6943.112 the tax constitutes a "debt owed by the retailer" to the state. And if the retailer fails to collect the tax, etc., his retailer's permit (§6943.084) may be revoked; and in case of a foreign corporation, its permit to do business in the state as well. §6943.122.

Respondent is a New York corporation authorized since 1928 to do business in Iowa. It has various retail stores there. It pays the tax on sales made at those stores. It also pays the tax on orders placed at those stores, though shipment is made direct to the purchaser from one of respondent's out of state branches. But it has refused to collect the tax on mail orders sent by Iowa purchasers to its out of state branches and filled by direct shipments through the mails or a common carrier from those branches to the purchasers. On threat of petitioners to revoke respondent's permit because of such refusal, respondent brought this suit for an injunction, alleging, inter alia, that the Act as applied violates §8 of Article 1 of the Constitution and the Fourteenth Amendment.

The Iowa Supreme Court held that if respondent had limited its activities to a mail order business of the kind here involved, it would not be doing business in Iowa; that, although technically the tax may be on the purchaser, it must be collected when the sale is made, at which time the property is outside the state; that these sales are separate and distinct from respondent's activities in Iowa. It therefore concluded that the tax as applied was unconstitutional since Iowa has no power to regulate respondent's activities outside the state or to regulate such activities as a condition to respondent's right to continue to do business in the state.

In passing on the constitutionality of a tax law "we are concerned only with its practical operation, not its definition or the precise form of descriptive words which may be applied to it." Lawrence v. State Tax Commission, 286 U.S. 276, 280, . . . The fact that under Iowa law the sale is made outside of the state does not mean that the power of Iowa "has nothing on which to operate." Wisconsin v. J. C. Penney Co. [311 U.S. 435]. The purchaser is in Iowa and the tax is upon use in Iowa. The validity of such a tax, so far as the purchaser is concerned, "has been withdrawn from the arena of debate." Henneford v. Silas Mason Co., 300 U.S. 577, 583. . . . It is one of the well-known functions of the integrated use and sales tax to remove the buyers' temptation "to place their orders in other states in the effort to escape payment of the tax on local sales." Henneford v. Silas Mason Co. supra. As pointed out in that case, the fact that the buyer employs agencies of interstate commerce in order to effectuate his purchase is not material, since the tax is "upon the privilege of use after commerce is at an end." . . . Use in Iowa is what is taxed regardless of the time and place of passing title and regardless of the time the tax is required to be paid. Cf. McGoldrick v. Berwind-White Co., 309 U.S. 33, 49.

So the nub of the present controversy centers on the use of respondent as the collection agent for Iowa. The imposition of such a duty, however, was held not to be an unconstitutional burden on a foreign corporation in Monamotor Oil Co. v. Johnson, 292 U.S. 86, and Felt & T. Mfg. Co. v. Gallagher, 306 U.S. 62. But respondent insists that those cases involved local activity by the foreign corporation as a result of which property was sold to its local customers, while in the instant case there is no local activity by respondent which generates or which relates to the mail orders here involved. Yet these orders are still a part of respondent's Iowa business. The fact that respondent could not be reached for the tax if it were not qualified to do business in Iowa would merely be a result of the "impotence of state power." Wisconsin v. J. C. Penny Co., 311 U.S. 435. Since Iowa has extended to it that privilege, Iowa can exact this burden as a price of enjoying the full benefits flowing from its Iowa business. Cf. Wisconsin v. J. C. Penny Co. supra. Respondent cannot avoid that burden though its business is departmentalized. Whatever may be the inspiration for these mail orders, however they may be filled, Iowa may rightly assume that they are not unrelated to respondent's course of business in Iowa. They are nonetheless a part of that business though none of respondent's agents in Iowa actually solicited or placed them. Hence to include them in the global amount of benefits which respondent is receiving from Iowa business is to conform to business facts.

Nor is the mode of enforcing the tax on the privileges of these Iowa transactions any discrimination against interstate commerce. As we have seen, the use tax and the sales tax are complementary. Sales made wholly within Iowa carry the same burden as these mail order sales. A tax or other burden obviously does not discriminate against interstate commerce where "equality is its theme." Henneford v. Silas Mason Co. supra . . .

Respondent, however, insists that the duty of tax collection placed on it constitutes a regulation of and substantial burden upon interstate commerce and results in an impairment of the free flow of such commerce. It points to the fact that in its mail order business it is in competition with out of state mail order houses which need not and do not collect the tax on their Iowa sales. But those other concerns are not doing business in the state as foreign corporations. Hence, unlike respondent, they are not receiving benefits from Iowa for which it has the power to exact a price. Respondent further stresses the cost to it of making these collections and its probable loss as a result of its inability to collect the tax on all sales. But cost and inconvenience inhered in the same duty imposed on the foreign corporations in the Monamotor Oil Co. and Felt & T. Mfg. Co. cases. And so far as assumed losses on tax collections are concerned, respondent is in no position to found a constitutional right on the practical opportunities for tax avoidance which its method of doing business affords Iowa residents, or to claim a constitutional immunity because it may elect to deliver the goods before the tax is paid.

Prohibited discriminatory burdens on interstate commerce are not to be determined by abstractions. Particular facts of specific cases determine whether a given tax prohibitively discriminates against interstate commerce. Hence a review of prior adjudications based on widely disparate facts, howsoever embedded in general propositions, does not facilitate an answer to the present problem.

The judgment is reversed and the cause is remanded to the Iowa Supreme Court for proceedings not inconsistent with this opinion.

Reversed.

MR. JUSTICE STONE took no part in the consideration or disposition of this case.

MR. JUSTICE ROBERTS [with whom Chief Justice Hughes concurred], dissenting:

I think that the judgment should be affirmed. . . .

McLeod v. Dilworth Co. 322 U.S. 327, 64 S. Ct. 1023, 88 L. Ed. 1304 (1944)

MR. JUSTICE FRANKFURTER delivered the opinion of the Court:

We are asked to reverse a decision of the Supreme Court of Arkansas holding that the Commerce Clause precludes liability for the sales tax of that State upon the transactions to be set forth.

We take the descriptions of these transactions from the opinion under review. Respondents are Tennessee corporations with home offices and places of business in Memphis where they sell machinery and mill supplies. They are not qualified to do business in Arkansas and have neither sales office, branch plant nor any other place of business in that State. Orders for goods come to Tennessee through solicitation in Arkansas by traveling salesmen domiciled in Tennessee, by mail or telephone. But no matter how an order is placed it requires acceptance by the Memphis office, and on approval the goods are shipped from Tennessee. Title passes upon delivery to the carrier in Memphis, and collection of the sales price is not made in Arkansas. In short, we are here concerned with sales made by Tennessee vendors that are consummated in Tennessee for the delivery of goods in Arkansas. . . .

We agree with the Arkansas Supreme Court that the Berwind-White Case presented a situation different from this case and that this case is on the other side of the line which marks off the limits of state power. A boundary line is none the worse for being narrow. Once it is recognized, as it long has been by this Court, that federal and state taxation do not move within wholly different orbits, that there are points of intersection between the powers of the two governments, and that there are transactions of what colloquially may be deemed a single process across state lines which may yet be taxed by the State of their occurrence, "nice distinctions are to be expected," Galveston, J. & S.A.R. Co. v. Texas, 210 U.S. 217, 225. The differentiations made by the court below between this case and the Berwind-White Case are relevant and controlling. "The distinguishing point between the Berwind-White Coal Case and the cases at bar, is that in the Berwind-White Coal Case the corporation maintained its sales office in New York City, took its contracts in New York City and made actual delivery in New York City. . . ." 205 Ark. at 786, 171 S.W.(2d) 65. This, according to practical notions of what constitutes a sale which is reflected by what the law deems a sale, constituted a sale in New York and accordingly we sustained a retail sales tax by New York. Here, as the Arkansas Supreme court continued, "the offices are maintained in Tennessee, the sale is made in Tennessee, and the delivery is consummated either in Tennessee or in interstate commerce with no interruption from Tennessee until delivery to the consignee essential to complete the interstate journey." Because the relevant factors in the two cases decided together with the Berwind-White Case were the same as those in Berwind-White, the decision in that case controlled the two other cases. "In both cases the tax was imposed on all the sales of merchandise for which orders were taken within the city and possession of which was transferred to the purchaser there. Decision in both is controlled by our decision in the Berwind-White Coal Min. Co. Case." McColdrick v. Felt & T. Mfg. Co., 309 U.S. 70, 77. In Berwind-White the Pennsylvania seller completed his sales in New York; in this case the Tennessee seller was through selling in Tennessee. We would have to destroy both business and legal notions to deny that under these circumstances the sale — the transfer of ownership — was made in Tennessee. For Arkansas to impose a tax on such transaction would be to project its powers beyond its boundaries and to tax an interstate transaction.

It is suggested, however, that Arkansas could have levied a tax of the same amount on the use of these goods in Arkansas by the Arkansas buyers, and that such a use would not exceed the limits upon state power derived from the United States Constitution. Whatever might be the fate of such a tax were it before us, the not too short answer is that Arkansas has chosen not to impose such a use tax, as its Supreme Court so emphatically found. A sales tax and a use tax in many instances may bring about the same result. But they are different in conception, are assessments upon different transactions, and in the interlacings of the two legislative authorities within our federation may have to justify themselves on different constitutional grounds. A sales tax is a tax on the freedom of purchase — a freedom which wartime restrictions serve to emphasize. A use tax is a tax on the enjoyment of that which was purchased. In view of the differences in the basis of these two taxes and the differences in the relation of the taxing state to them, a tax on an interstate sale like the one before us and unlike the tax on the enjoyment of the goods sold, involves an assumption of power by a State which the Commerce Clause was meant to end. The very purpose of the Commerce Clause was to create an area of free trade among the several States. That clause vested the power of taxing a transaction forming an unbroken process of interstate commerce in the Congress, not in the States.

The difference in substance between a sales and a use tax was adverted to in the leading case sustaining a tax on the use after a sale had spent its interstate character: "A tax upon a use so closely connected with delivery as to be in substance a part thereof might be subject to the same objections that would be applicable to a tax upon the sale itself." Henneford v. Silas Mason Co., 300 U.S. 577, 583. Thus we are not dealing with matters of nomenclature even though they be matters of nicety. . . . Though sales and use taxes may secure the same revenues and serve complementary purposes, they are, as we have indicated, taxes on different transactions and for different opportunities afforded by a State. . . .

Judgment affirmed.

Mr. Justice Douglas, with whom Mr. Justice Black and Mr. Justice Murphy concur, dissenting:

The present decision marks a retreat from the philosophy of the Berwind-White Coal Min. Co.'s Case, 309 U.S. 33. It draws a distinction between the use tax (Felt & T. Mfg. Co. v. Gallagher, 306 U.S. 62) and the sales tax which on the facts of this case seems irrelevant to the power of Arkansas to tax. And it is squarely opposed to McGoldrick v. Felt & T. Mfg. Co., 309 U.S. 70, which should be overruled if the present decision goes down. . . .

In McGoldrick v. Felt & T. Mfg. Co. we allowed New York City to collect its sales tax on sales which Felt & Tarrant made to New York purchasers under substantially the same course of dealing as obtained in case of the California use tax. Moreover, there were other transactions in McGoldrick v. Felt & T. Mfg. Co. which were even closer to the sales in the present case. I refer to the sales to New York City buyers by a Massachusetts corporation (Du Grenier, Inc.) which was not authorized to do business in New York and which had no employee there. Another company, Stewart & McGuire, Inc., acted as its exclusive agent and solicited orders in New York City. The orders were forwarded to Massachusetts where they were accepted. Shipments were made by rail or truck (F.O.B. Haverhill, Mass.) to the purchaser in New York City, who paid the freight. Yet we allowed New York City to collect its sales tax on those transactions.

If the federal Constitution does not prohibit New York City from levying its sales tax on the proceeds of those interstate transactions or California from exacting its use tax on the final stage of an interstate movement of goods, I fail to see why Arkansas should be prohibited from collecting the present tax.

576   Chapter Eight.   The States in a Federal Union

It is not enough to say that the use tax and the sales tax are different. A use tax may of course have a wider range of application than a sales tax. Henneford v. Silas Mason Co., 300 U.S. 577. But a use tax and a sales tax applied at the very end of an interstate transaction have precisely the same economic incidence. Their effect on interstate commerce is identical. We stated as much in the Berwind-White Case where, in speaking of the sales tax, we said: "It does not aim at or discriminate against interstate commerce. It is laid upon every purchaser, within the state, of goods for consumption, regardless of whether they have been transported in interstate commerce. Its only relation to the commerce arises from the fact that immediately preceding transfer of possession to the purchaser within the state, which is the taxable event regardless of the time and place of passing title, the merchandise has been transported in interstate commerce and brought to its journey's end. Such a tax has no different effect upon interstate commerce than a tax on the 'use' of property which has just been moved in interstate commerce," citing use tax cases including Henneford v. Silas Mason Co. and Felt & T. Mfg. Co. v. Gallagher.

The sales tax and the use tax are, to be sure, taxes on different phases of the interstate transaction. We may agree that the use tax is a tax "on the enjoyment of that which was purchased." But realistically the sales tax is a tax on the receipt of that which was purchased. For as we said in the excerpt from the Berwind-White Case quoted above, it is the "transfer of possession to the purchaser within the state" which is the "taxable event regardless of the time and place of passing title." And McGoldrick v. Felt & T. Mfg. Co. makes plain that the transfer of possession need not be by the seller, for in that case, as in the present one, deliveries were made by common carriers which accepted the goods F.O.B. at points outside the State. In terms of state power, receipt of goods within the State of the buyer is as adequate a basis for the exercise of the taxing power as use within the State. And there should be no difference in result under the Commerce Clause where, as here, the practical impact on the interstate transaction is the same.

It is no answer to say that the Arkansas sales tax may not be imposed because the out-of-state seller was "through selling" when the tax was incurred. That was likewise true of both the use tax cases, including General Trading Co. v. State Tax Commission, decided this day, and the sales tax decision in McGoldrick v. Felt & T. Mfg. Co. The question is whether there is a phase of the interstate transaction on which the State of the buyer can lay hold without placing interstate commerce at a disadvantage. There is no showing that Tennessee was exacting from these vendors a tax on these same transactions or that Arkansas discriminated against them. I can see no warrant for an interpretation of the Commerce Clause which puts local industry at a competitive disadvantage with interstate business. If there is a taxable event within the State of the buyer, I would make the result under the Commerce Clause turn on practical considerations and business realities rather than on dialectics. If that is not done, I think we should retreat from the view that interstate commerce should carry its fair share of the costs of government in the localities where it finds its markets and adopt the views expressed in the dissent in the Berwind-White Case.

MR. JUSTICE RUTLEDGE also dissents in a separate opinion. . . .

General Trading Co. v. State Tax Commission 322 U.S. 355, 64 S. Ct. 1028, 88 L. Ed. 1309 (1944)

MR. JUSTICE FRANKFURTER delivered the opinion of the Court:
The State Tax Commission of Iowa brought this suit under the authority of the Iowa Use Tax Law which was recently here in Nelson v. Sears, R. & Co., 312 U.S. 359, and Nelson v. Montgomery Ward & Co., 312 U.S. 373. The question now presented is, in short, whether Iowa may collect, in the circumstances of this case, such a use tax from General Trading Company, a Minnesota corporation, on the basis of property bought

Section D. **State Taxation** 577

from Trading Company and sent by it from Minnesota to purchasers in Iowa for use and enjoyment there.

By the Iowa Use Tax Law a tax is "imposed on the use in this state of tangible personal property purchased . . . for use in this state at the rate of two percent of the purchase price of such property. Said tax is . . . imposed upon every person using such property within this state until such tax has been paid directly to the county treasurer, to a retailer, or to the commission. . . ." Iowa Code 1939, §6943.103. The use of property the sale of which is subject to Iowa's sales tax is exempted from the use tax (§6943.104 (1)), but the sales tax can be laid only on sales at retail within the State. §6943.075. The use tax constitutes a debt owed by the retailer to the State. §6943.112. But "Every retailer maintaining a place of business" in Iowa must collect this tax from the purchaser (§6943.109), and may not advertise that he will himself absorb the tax. §6943.111. Finally an offsetting credit (see Henneford v. Silas Mason Co., 300 U.S. 577, 584, 586, 587) if another use or sales tax has been paid for the same thing elsewhere is allowed, and if the tax "imposed in such other state is two percent or more, then no tax shall be due on such articles." §6943.125.

A judgment in favor of the Tax Commission by one of the lower courts was affirmed by the Supreme Court of Iowa, 233 Iowa 877, 10 N.W.(2d) 659. The application by that Court of its local laws and the facts on which it founded its judgment are of course controlling here. From these it appears that General Trading Company had never qualified to do business as a foreign corporation in Iowa nor does it maintain there any office, branch or warehouse. The property on which the use tax was laid was sent to Iowa as a result of orders solicited by traveling salesmen sent into Iowa from their Minnesota headquarters. The orders were always subject to acceptance in Minnesota whence the goods were shipped into Iowa by common carriers or the post. Upon these facts and its holding that Trading Company was a "retailer maintaining a place of business in this state" within the meaning of the Iowa statute, the Iowa Supreme Court held that Iowa had not exceeded its powers in the imposition of this use tax on Iowa purchasers, and that collection could validly be made through the Trading Company.

We brought the case here, 320 U.S. 731, to meet the claim that there was need for further precision regarding the scope of our previous rulings on the power of States to levy use taxes. In view, however, of the clear understanding by the court below that the facts we have summarized bring the transaction within the taxing power of Iowa, there is little need for elaboration. We agree with the Iowa Supreme Court that Felt & T. Mfg. Co. v. Gallagher, 306 U.S. 62; Nelson v. Sears, R. & Co., 312 U.S. 359; and Nelson v. Montgomery Ward & Co., 312 U.S. 373, supra, are controlling. The Gallagher Case is indistinguishable — certainly nothing can turn on the more elaborate arrangements for soliciting orders for an intricate machine for shipment from without a State as in the Gallagher Case, compared with the apparently simpler needs for soliciting business in this case. And the fact that in the Sears, R. & Co. and Montgomery Ward & Co. cases the interstate vendor also had retail stores in Iowa, whose sales were appropriately subjected to the sales tax, is constitutionally irrelevant to the right of Iowa sustained in those cases to exact a use tax from purchasers on mail order goods forwarded into Iowa from without the State. All these differentiations are without constitutional significance. Of course, no State can tax the privilege of doing interstate business. See Western Live Stock v. Bureau, 303 U.S. 250. That is within the protection of the Commerce Clause and subject to the power of Congress. On the other hand, the mere fact that property is used for interstate commerce or has come into an owner's possession as a result of interstate commerce does not diminish the protection which he may draw from a State to the upkeep of which he may be asked to bear his fair share. But a fair share precludes legislation obviously hostile or practically discriminatory toward interstate commerce. See Best & Co. v. Maxwell, 311 U.S. 454.

None of these infirmities affects the tax in this case any more than it did in the other cases with which it forms a group. The tax is what it professes to be — a non-discriminatory excise laid on all personal property consumed in Iowa. The property is enjoyed by an Iowa resident partly because the opportunity is given by Iowa to enjoy the property no matter whence acquired. The exaction is made against the ultimate consumer — the Iowa resident who is paying taxes to sustain his own state government. To make the distributor the tax collector for the State is a familiar and sanctioned device. Monamotor Oil Co. v. Johnson, 292 U.S. 86, 93, 94; Felt & T. Mfg. Co. v. Gallagher, 306 U.S. 62.

Affirmed.

Mr. Justice Rutledge concurs in a separate opinion. . . .

Mr. Justice Jackson dissenting:

This decision authorizes in my opinion an unwarranted extension of the power of a state to subject persons to its taxing power who are not within its jurisdiction and have not in any manner submitted themselves to it. The General Trading Company is, in the language of the opinion, made "the tax collector for the State." We have heretofore held, and I think properly, that the state may make tax collectors of those who come in and do business within its jurisdiction, for thereby they submit themselves to its power. Such was the situation in both Monamotor Oil Co. v. Johnson, 292 U.S. 86, and Felt & T. Mfg. Co. v. Gallagher, 306 U.S. 62. These are the only authorities cited by the Court on this point, and they clearly are not precedents to support this decision.

In this case, as the opinion points out, the General Trading Company never qualified in Iowa and has no office, branch, warehouse, or general agent in the State. From Minnesota it ships goods ordered from salesmen by purchasers in Iowa. Orders are accepted only in Minnesota. The transaction of sale is not taxed and, being clearly interstate commerce, is not taxable. McLeod v. J. E. Dilworth Co., No. 311, decided today. So we are holding that a state has power to make a tax collector of one whom it has no power to tax. Certainly no state has a constitutional warrant for making a tax collector of one as the price of the privilege of doing interstate commerce. He does not get the right from the state, and the state cannot qualify it. I can imagine no principle of states' rights or state comity which can justify what is done here. Nor does the practice seem conducive to good order in the federal system. The power of Iowa to enforce collection in other states is certainly very limited and the effort to do so on any wide scale is unlikely either to be systematically pursued or successfully executed.

I recognize the pressure to uphold all manner of efforts to collect tax moneys. But this decision, by which one may not ship goods from anywhere in the United States to a purchaser in Iowa without becoming a non-resident tax collector, exceeds everything so far done by this Court. In my opinion the statute is an effort to exert extraterritorial control beyond any which a state could exert if there were no Constitution at all. I can think of nothing in or out of the Constitution which warrants this effort to reach beyond the State's own border to make out-of-state merchants tax collectors because they engage in interstate commerce with the State's citizens.

Mr. Justice Roberts joins in this opinion.

International Harvester Co. v. Department of Treasury
322 U.S. 340, 64 S. Ct. 1019, 88 L. Ed. 1313 (1944)

Mr. Justice Douglas delivered the opinion of the Court:

This case raises questions concerning the constitutionality of the Indiana Gross Income Tax Act of 1933 (Laws 1933, p. 388, Burns's Ind. Stat. Anno. §64-2601) as construed and applied to certain business transactions of appellant companies. The suit was brought by appellants to recover gross income taxes paid to Indiana during the years 1935 and 1936. The Indiana Supreme Court sustained objections to the imposition of the tax on certain sales but allowed the tax to be imposed on other types of transactions. 221 Ind. 416, 47

N.E.(2d) 150. The correctness of the latter ruling is challenged by the appeal which brings the case here. Judicial Code §237, 28 U.S.C. §344(a); 28 U.S.C. §861(a).

Appellants are corporations authorized to do business in Indiana but incorporated under the laws of other States. They manufacture farm implements and motor trucks and sell those articles both at wholesale and retail. During the period here in question they maintained manufacturing plants at Richmond and Fort Wayne, Indiana and selling branches at Indianapolis, Terre Haute, Fort Wayne, and Evansville, Indiana. They also had manufcturing plants and sales branches in adjoining States and elsewhere. Each branch had an assigned territory. In some instances parts of Indiana were within the exclusive jurisdiction of branch offices which were located outside the State. The transactions which Indiana says may be taxed without infringement of the Federal Constitution are described by the Indiana Supreme Court as follows:

"Class C: Sales by branches located outside Indiana to dealers and users residing in Indiana. The orders were solicited in Indiana and the customers took delivery to themselves at the factories in Indiana to save time and expense of shipping.

"Class D: Sales by branches located in Indiana to dealers and users residing outside of Indiana, in which the customers came to Indiana and accepted delivery to themselves in this state.

"Class E: Sales by branches located in Indiana to dealers and users residing in Indiana, in which the goods were shipped from points outside Indiana to customers in Indiana, pursuant to contracts so providing." . . .

[The Court, Mr. Justice Jackson dissenting and Mr. Justice Roberts taking no part in consideration or decision of the case, affirmed the judgment of the Supreme Court of Indiana. Compare Department of Treasury v. Wood Preserving Corp., 313 U.S. 62 (1941), another decision involving the application of the Indiana Gross Income Tax Act.][gg]

MR. JUSTICE RUTLEDGE concurring in Nos. 441 [General Trading Co. v. State Tax Commission] and 355 [International Harvester Co. v. Department of Treasury], and dissenting in No. 311 [McLeod v. Dilworth Co.].

These three cases present in various applications the question of the power of a state to tax transactions having a close connection with interstate commerce. . . .

I

For constitutional purposes, I see no difference but one of words and possibly one of the scope of coverage between the Arkansas tax in No. 311 and the Iowa tax in No. 441. This is true whether the issue is one of due process or one of undue burden on interstate commerce. Each tax is imposed by the consuming state. On the records here, each has a due process connection with the transaction in that fact and in the regular, continuous solicitation there. Neither lays a greater burden on the interstate business involved than it does on wholly intrastate business of the same sort. Neither segregates the interstate transaction for separate or special treatment. In each instance therefore interstate and intrastate business reach these markets on identical terms, so far as the effects of the state taxes are concerned. . . .

II

The Court's different treatment of the two taxes does not result from any substantial difference in the facts under which they are levied or the effects they may have on interstate

---
[gg] See also Adams Mfg. Co. v. Storen, 304 U.S. 307 (1938), an earlier decision involving the same Indiana statute. Cf. Gwin, White & Prince, Inc. v. Henneford, 305 U.S. 434 (1939).
And cf. Richfield Oil Corp. v. State Board of Equalization, 329 U.S. 69 (1946). — ED.

trade. It arises rather from applying different constitutional provisions to the substantially identical taxes, in the one case to invalidate that of Arkansas, in the other to sustain that of Iowa. Due process destroys the former. Absence of undue burden upon interstate commerce sustains the latter.

. . . The cases are not different in the burden the two taxes place upon the interstate transactions. Nor in my opinion are they different in the existence of due process to sustain the taxes.

"Due process" and "commerce clause" conceptions are not always sharply separable in dealing with these problems. Cf. e.g., Western U. Teleg. Co. v. Kansas, 216 U.S. 1. To some extent they overlap. If there is a want of due process to sustain the tax, by that fact alone any burden the tax imposes on the commerce among the states becomes "undue." But, though overlapping, the two conceptions are not identical. There may be more than sufficient factual connections, with economic and legal effects, between the transaction and the taxing state to sustain the tax as against due process objections. Yet it may fall because of its burdening effect upon the commerce. And, although the two notions cannot always be separated, clarity of consideration and of decision would be promoted if the two issues are approached, where they are presented, at least tentatively as if they were separate and distinct, not intermingled ones.

Thus, in the case from Arkansas no more than in that from Iowa should there be difficulty in finding due process connections with the taxing state sufficient to sustain the tax. As in the Iowa case, the goods are sold and shipped to Arkansas buyers. Arkansas is the consuming state, the market these goods seek and find. They find it by virtue of a continuous course of solicitation there by the Tennessee seller. The old notion that "mere solicitation" is not "doing business" when it is regular, continuous and persistent is fast losing its force. In the General Trading Co. Case it loses force altogether, for the Iowa statute defines this process in terms as "a retailer maintaining a place of business in this state." The Iowa Supreme Court sustains the definition and this Court gives effect to its decision in upholding the tax. Fiction the definition may be; but it is fiction with substance because, for every relevant constitutional consideration affecting taxation of transactions, regular, continuous, persistent solicitation has the same economic, and should have the same legal, consequences as does maintainaing an office for soliciting and even contracting purposes or maintaining a place of business, where the goods actually are shipped into the state from without for delivery to the particular buyer. There is no difference between the Iowa and the Arkansas situations in this respect. Both involve continuous, regular, and not intermittent or casual courses of solicitation. Both involve the shipment of goods from without to a buyer within a state. Both involve taxation by the state of the market. And if these substantial connections are sufficient to underpin the tax with due process in the one case, they are also in the other.

That is true, if labels are not to control, unless something which happens or may happen outside the taxing state operates in the one case to defeat the jurisdiction, but does not defeat it in the other.

As I read the Court's opinion, though it does not explicitly so state, the Arkansas tax falls because Tennessee could tax the transaction and, as between the two states, has exclusive power to do so. This is because "the sale — the transfer of ownership — was made in Tennessee," Arkansas' relation to the transaction is constitutionally different from that of New York in the Berwind-White Case, though both are the state of the market, because the Berwind-White Company "maintained its sales office in New York City, took its contracts in New York City and made actual delivery in New York City." This "constituted a sale in New York and accordingly we sustained a retail sales tax by New York." So here the company's "offices are maintained in Tennessee, the sale is made in Tennessee, and the delivery is consummated either in Tennessee or in interstate commerce. . . ." The inevitable conclusion, it seems to me, is that the Court is deciding not only that Arkansas cannot tax the transaction, but that Tennessee can tax it and is the only state which can do so. To put the matter shortly, Arkansas cannot levy the tax because Tennessee can levy it. Hence "for Arkansas to impose a tax on such transaction would be to project its powers beyond its boundaries and to tax an interstate transaction."

This statement of the matter appears to be a composite of due process and commerce clause ideas. If so, it is hard to see why the same considerations do not nullify Iowa's power to levy her tax in the identical circumstances and vest exclusive jurisdiction in Minnesota to tax these transactions. . . . Unless the sheer difference in the terms "sale" and "use," and whatever difference these might make as a matter of legislative selection of the transactions which are to bear the tax, are to control upon the existence of the power to tax, the result should be the same in both cases.

Merely as a matter of due process, it is hard to see why any of the four states cannot tax the transactions these cases involve. Each has substantial relations and connections with the transaction, the state of market not less in either case than the state of origin. It "sounds better" for the state of origin to call its tax a "sales tax" and the state of market to name its tax a "use tax." But in the Berwind-White Case the latter's "sales tax" was sustained, where it is true more of the incidents of sale conjoined with the location of the place of market than do in either No. 311 or No. 441. If this is the distinguishing factor, as it might be for selecting one of the two connected jurisdictions for exclusive taxing power, it is not one which applies to either of these transactions. The identity is not between the Dilworth Case and Berwind-White. It is rather between Dilworth and General Trading with Berwind-White differing from both. And, so far as due process alone is concerned, it should make no difference whether the tax in the one case is laid by Arkansas or Tennessee and in the other by Iowa or Minnesota. Each state has a sufficiently substantial and close connection with the transaction, whether by virtue of tax benefits conferred in general police protection and otherwise or on account of ideas of territorial sovereignty concerning occurrence of "taxable incidents" within its borders, to furnish the due process foundation necessary to sustain the exercise of its taxing power. Whether it exerts this by selecting for "impingement" of the tax some feature or incident of the transaction which it denominates "sale" or "use" is both illusory and unimportant in any bearing upon its constitutional authority as a matter of due process. If this has any substantive effect, it is merely one of legislative intent in selecting the transactions to bear the tax and thus fixing the scope of its coverage, not one of constitutional power. "Use" may cover more transactions with which a state has due process connections than "sale." But whenever sale occurs and is taxed the tax bears equally, in final incidence of burden, upon the use which follows immediately upon it.

The great difficulty in allocating taxing power as a matter of due process between the state of origin and the state of market arises from the fact that each state, considered without reference to the other, always has a sufficiently substantial relation in fact and in tax benefit conferred to the interstate transaction to sustain an exertion of its taxing power, a fact not always recognized. And from this failure, as well as from the terms in which statutes not directed specifically to reaching these transactions are cast, comes the search for some "taxable incident taking place within the state's boundaries" as a hook for hanging constitutionality under due process ideas. "Taxable incident" there must be. But to take what is in essence and totality an interstate transaction between a state of origin and one of market and hang the taxing power of either state upon some segmented incident of the whole and declare that this does or does not "tax an interstate transaction" is to do two things. It is first to ignore that any tax hung on such an incident is levied on an interstate transaction. For the part cannot be separated from the whole. It is also to ignore the fact that each state, whether of origin or of market, has by that one fact alone a relation to the whole transaction so substantial as to nullify any due process prohibition. Whether the tax is levied on the "sale" or on the "use," by the one state or by the other, it is in fact and effect a tax levied on an interstate transaction. Nothing in due process requirements prohibits either state to levy either sort of tax on such transactions. That Tennessee therefore may tax this transaction by a sales tax does not, in any proper conception of due process, deprive Arkansas of the same power.

III

When, however, the issue is turned from due process to the prohibitive effect of the commerce clause, more substantial considerations arise from the fact that both the state of origin and that of market exert or may exert their taxing powers upon the interstate transaction. The long history of this problem boils down in general statement to the formula that the states, by virtue of the force of the commerce clause, may not unduly burden interstate commerce. This resolves itself into various corollary formulations. . . .

In these interstate transactions cases involving taxation by the state of origin or that of market, the trouble arises, under the commerce clause, not from any danger that either tax taken alone, whether characterized as "sales" or "use" tax, will put interstate trade at a disadvantage which will burden unduly its competition with the local trade. So long as only one tax is applied and at the same rate as to wholly local transactions, no unduly discriminatory clog actually attaches to the interstate transaction of business.

The real danger arises most obviously when both states levy the tax. Thus, if in the instant cases it were shown that, on the one hand, Arkansas and Iowa actually were applying a "use" tax and Tennessee and Minnesota a "sales" tax, so that in each case the interstate transaction were taxed at both ends, the heavier cumulative burden thus borne by the interstate business in comparison with the local trade in either state would be obvious. If in each case the state of origin were shown to impose a sales tax of three per cent and the state of market a use tax of the same amount, interstate transactions between the two obviously would bear double the local tax burden borne by local trade in each state. This is a difference of substance, not merely one of names, relevant to the problem created by the commerce clause, though not to that of "jurisdiction" under due process conceptions. And the difference would be no less substantial if the taxes levied by both the state of origin and that of market were called "sales" taxes or if, indeed, both were called "use taxes."

The Iowa tax in No. 441 avoids this problem by allowing credit for any sales tax shown to be levied upon the transaction whether in Iowa or elsewhere. Clearly therefore that tax cannot in fact put the interstate transaction at a tax disadvantage with local trade done in Iowa or elsewhere.

However, the Arkansas tax in No. 311 provides for no such credit. But in that case there is no showing that Tennessee actually imposes any tax upon the transaction. If there is a burden or clog on commerce, therefore, it arises from the fact that Tennessee has power constitutionally to impose a tax, may exercise it, and when this occurs the cumulative effect of both taxes will be discriminatorily burdensome, though neither tax singles out the transaction or bears upon it more heavily than upon the local trade to which it applies. In short, the risk of multiple taxation creates the unconstitutional burden which actual taxation by both states would impose in fact.

In my opinion this is the real question and the only one presented in No. 311. And in my judgment it is determined the wrong way, not on commerce clause grounds but upon an unsustainable application of the due process prohibition.

Where the cumulative effect of two taxes, by whatever name called, one imposed by the state of origin, the other by the state of market, actually bears in practical effect upon such an interstate transaction, there is no escape under the doctrine of undue burden from one of two possible alternatives. Either one tax must fall or, what is the same thing, be required to give way to the other by allowing credit as the Iowa tax does, or there must be apportionment. Either solution presents an awkward alternative. But one or the other must be accepted unless that doctrine is to be discarded and one of two extreme positions taken, namely, that neither state can tax the interstate transaction or that both may do so until Congress intervenes to give its solution for the problem. It is too late to accept the former extreme, too early even if it were clearly desirable or permissible to follow the latter.

As between apportionment and requiring one tax to fall or allow credit, the latter perhaps would be the preferable solution. And in my opinion it is the one which the Court in effect, though not in specific statement, adopts. That the decision is cast more largely in terms of due process than in those of the commerce clause does not nullify that effect.

If in this case it were necessary to choose between the state of origin and that of market for the exercise of exclusive power to tax, or for requiring allowance of credit in order to avoid the cumulative burden, in my opinion the choice should lie in favor of the state of market rather than the state of origin. The former is the state where the goods must come in competition with those sold locally. It is the one where the burden of the tax necessarily will fall equally on both classes of trade. To choose the tax of the state of origin presents at least some possibilities that the burden it imposes on its local trade, with which the interstate traffic does not compete, at any rate directly, will be heavier than that placed by the consuming state on its local business of the same character. If therefore choice has to be made, wiether as a matter of exclusive power to tax or as one of allowing credit, it should be in favor of the state of market or consumption as the one most certain to place the same tax load on both the interstate and competing local business. Hence, if the risk of taxation by both states may be said to have the same constitutional consequences, under the commerce clause, as taxation in actuality by both, the Arkansas tax, rather than the power of Tennessee to tax, should stand.

It may be that the mere risk of double taxation would not have the same consequences, given always of course a sufficient due process connections with the taxing states, that actual double taxation has, or may have, for application of the commerce clause prohibition. Risk of course is not irrelevant to burden or to the clogging effect the rule against undue burden is intended to prevent. But in these situations it may be doubted, on entirely practical grounds, that the mere risk Tennessee may apply its taxing power to these transactions will have any substantial effect in restraining the commerce such as the actual application of that power would have. In any event, whether or not the choice must be made now or, as I think, has been made, it should go in favor of Arkansas, not Tennessee. . . .

Accordingly, I concur in the decisions in Nos. 441 and 355, but dissent from the decision in No. 311.[hh]

Freeman v. Hewit 329 U.S. 249, 67 S. Ct. 274, 91 L. Ed. 265 (1946)

MR. JUSTICE FRANKFURTER delivered the opinion of the Court.

This case presents another phase of the Indiana Gross Income Tax Act of 1933, which has been before this Court in a series of cases beginning with J. D. Adams Mfg. Co. v. Storen, 304 U.S. 307. . . .

Appellant's predecessor, domiciled in Indiana, was trustee of an estate created by the will of a decedent domiciled in Indiana at the time of his death. During 1940, the trustee instructed his Indiana broker to arrange for the sale at stated prices of securities forming part of the trust estate. Through the broker's New York correspondents the securities were offered for sale on the New York Stock Exchange. When a purchaser was found, the New York broker notified the Indiana broker who in turn informed the trustee, and the latter brought the securities to his broker for mailing to New York. Upon their delivery to the

---

[hh] See Powell, Sales and Use Taxes: Collection from Absentee Vendors, 57 Harv. L. Rev. 1086 (1944); see also Note, Enforcing State Consumption Taxes on Out-of-State Purchases, 65 id. at 301 (1952). — ED.

purchasers, the New York brokers received the purchase price, which, after deducting expenses and commission, they transmitted to the Indiana broker. The latter delivered the proceeds less his commission to the trustee. On the gross receipts of these sales, amounting to $65,214.20, Indiana, under the Act of 1933, imposed a tax of 1%. Having paid the tax under protest, the trustee brought this suit for its recovery. The Supreme Court of Indiana, reversing a court of first instance, sustained the tax on the ground that the situs of the securities was in Indiana. 221 Ind. 675, 51 N.E.2d 6. The case is here on appeal under §237 (a) of the Judicial Code, 28 U.S.C. 344 (a), and has had the consideration which two arguments afford. . . .

This history of this problem is spread over hundreds of volumes of our Reports. To attempt to harmonize all that has been said in the past would neither clarify what has gone before nor guide the future. Suffice it to say that especially in this field opinions must be read in the setting of the particular cases and as the product of preoccupation with their special facts.

Our starting point is clear. In two recent cases we applied the principle that the Commerce Clause was not merely an authorization to Congress to enact laws for the protection and encouragement of commerce among the States, but by its own force created an area of trade free from interference by the States. In short, the Commerce Clause even without implementing legislation by Congress is a limitation upon the power of the States. Southern P. Co. v. Arizona, 325 U.S. 761; Morgan v. Virginia, 328 U.S. 373. In so deciding we reaffirmed, upon fullest consideration, the course of adjudication unbroken through the Nation's history. This limitation on State power, as the Morgan Case so well illustrates, does not merely forbid a State to single out interstate commerce for hostile action. A State is also precluded from taking any action which may fairly be deemed to have the effect of impeding the free flow of trade between States. It is immaterial that local commerce is subjected to a similar encumbrance. It may commend itself to a State to encourage a pastoral instead of an industrial society. That is its concern and its privilege. But to compare a State's treatment of its local trade with the exertion of its authority against commerce in the national domain is to compare incomparables.

These principles of limitation on State power apply to all State policy no matter what State interest gives rise to its legislation. . . . A police regulation of local aspects of interstate commerce is a power often essential to a State in safeguarding vital local interests. At least until Congress chooses to enact a nation-wide rule, the power will not be denied to the State. [Citations omitted.] State taxation falling on interstate commerce, on the other hand, can only be justified as designed to make such commerce bear a fair share of the cost of the local government whose protection it enjoys. But revenue serves as well no matter what its source. To deny to a State a particular source of income because it taxes the very process of interstate commerce does not impose a crippling limitation on a State's ability to carry on its local function. Moreover, the burden on interstate commerce involved in a direct tax upon it is inherently greater, certainly less uncertain in its consequences, than results from the usual police regulations. The power to tax is a dominant power over commerce. Because the greater or more threatening burden of a direct tax on commerce is coupled with the lesser need to a State of a particular source of revenue, attempts at such taxation have always been more carefully scrutinized and more consistently resisted than police power regulations of aspects of such commerce. The task of scrutinizing is a task of drawing lines. This is the historic duty of the Court so long as Congress does not undertake to make specific arrangements between the national government and the States in regard to revenues from interstate commerce. See Act of July 3, 1944, 58 Stat. 723; H. Doc. 141, 79th Cong., 1st Sess., "Multiple Taxation of Air Commerce"; and compare 54 Stat. 1059, 4 U.S.C. §§13 et seq. (permission to States to extend taxing power to Federal areas). Considerations of proximity and degree are here, as so often in the law, decisive.

It has been suggested that such a tax is valid when a similar tax is placed on local trade, and a specious appearance of fairness is sought to be imparted by the argument that interstate commerce should not be favored at the expense of local trade. So to argue is to disregard the life of the Commerce Clause. Of course a State is not required to give active advantage to interstate trade. But it cannot aim to control that trade even though it desires to control its own. It cannot justify what amounts to a levy upon the very process of commerce across State lines by pointing to a similar hobble on its local trade. It is true that the existence of a tax on its local commerce detracts from the deterrent effect of a tax on interstate commerce to the extent that it removes the temptation to sell the goods locally. But the fact of such a tax, in any event, puts impediments upon the currents of commerce across the State line, while the aim of the Commerce Clause was precisely to prevent States from exacting toll from those engaged in national commerce. The Commerce Clause does not involve an exercise in the logic of empty categories. It operates within the framework of our federal scheme and with due regard to the national experience reflected by the decisions of this Court, even though the terms in which these decisions have been cast may have varied. Language alters, and there is a fashion in judicial writing as in other things.

This case, like J. D. Adams Mfg. Co. v. Storen, supra, involves a tax imposed by the State of the seller on the proceeds of interstate sales. To extract a fair tithe from interstate commerce for the local protection afforded to it, a seller State need not impose the kind of tax which Indiana here levied. As a practical matter, it can make such commerce pay its way, as the phrase runs, apart from taxing the very sale. Thus, it can tax local manufacture even if the products are destined for other States. For some purposes, manufacture and the shipment of its products beyond a State may be looked upon as an integral transaction. But when accommodation must be made between state and national interests, manufacture within a State, though destined for shipment outside, is not a seamless web so as to prevent a State from giving the manufacturing part detached relevance for purposes of local taxation. American Mfg. Co. v. St. Louis, 250 U.S 459, . . . It can impose license taxes on domestic and foreign corporations who would do business in the State, Cheney Bros. Co. v. Massachusetts, 246 U.S. 147, . . . though it cannot, even under the guise of such excises, "hamper" interstate commerce. Western U. Teleg. Co. v. Kansas, 216 U.S. 1, . . . Henderson, The Position of Foreign Corporations in American Constitutional Law (1918) 118-123, 128-131. It can tax the privilege of residence in the State and measure the privilege by net income, including that derived from interstate commerce. United States Glue Co. v. Oak Creek, 247 U.S. 321, . . . And where, as in this case, the commodities subsequently sold interstate are securities, they can be reached by a property tax by the State of domicil of the owner. Virginia v. Imperial Coal Sales Co., 293 U.S. 15, 19, . . .

These illustrative instances show that a seller State has various means of obtaining legitimate contribution to the cost of its government, without imposing a direct tax on interstate sales. While these permitted taxes may, in an ultimate sense, come out of interstate commerce, they are not, as would be a tax on gross receipts, a direct imposition on that very freedom of commerical flow which for more than a hundred and fifty years has been the ward of the Commerce Clause.

It is suggested, however, that the validity of a gross sales tax should depend on whether another State has also sought to impose its burden on the transactions. If another State has taxed the same interstate transaction, the burdensome consequences to interstate trade are undeniable. But that, for the time being, only one State has taxed is irrelevant to the kind of freedom of trade which the Commerce Clause generated. The immunities implicit in the Commerce Clause and the potential taxing power of a State can hardly be made to depend, in the world of practical affairs, on the shifting incidence of the varying tax laws of the various States at a particular moment. Courts are not possessed of instruments of determination so delicate as to enable them to weigh the various factors in a complicated economic setting which, as to an isolated application of a State tax, might mitigate the obvious burden generally created by a direct tax on commerce. Nor is there any warrant in the constitutional principles heretofore applied by this Court to support the notion that a State may be allowed one single-tax-worth of direct interference with the free flow of commerce. An exaction by a State from interstate commerce falls not because of a proven increase in the cost of the product. What makes the tax invalid is the fact that there is interference by a State with the freedom of interstate commerce. Such a tax by the seller State alone must be adjudged burdensome in the context of the circumstances in which the tax takes effect. Trade being a sensitive plant, a direct tax upon it to some extent at least deters trade even if its effect is not precisely calculable. Many States, for instance, impose taxes on the consumption of goods, and such taxes have been sustained regardless of the extra-State origin of the goods, or whether a tax on their sale had been imposed by the seller State. Such potential taxation by consumer States is but one factor pointing to the deterrent effect on commerce by a superimposed gross receipts tax.

It has been urged that the force of the decision in the Adams Case has been sapped by McGoldrick v. Berwind-White Co., 309 U.S. 33. The decision in McGoldrick v. Berwind-White was found not to impinge upon "the rationale of the Adams Mfg. Co. Case," and the tax was sustained because it was "conditioned upon a local activity, delivery of goods within the State upon their purchase for consumption." 309 U.S. at 58. Compare McLeod v. J. E. Dilworth Co., 322 U.S. 327. Taxes which have the same effect as consumption taxes are properly differentiated from a direct imposition on interstate commerce, such as was before the Court in the Adams Case and is now before us. The tax on the sale itself cannot be differentiated from a direct unapportioned tax on gross receipts which has been definitely held beyond the State taxing power ever since Fargo v. Michigan, 121 U.S. 230, and Philadelphia & S. Mail S.S. Co. v. Pennsylvania, 122 U.S. 326, . . . For not even an "internal regulation" by a State will be allowed if it directly affects interstate commerce. Robbins v. Taxing Dist., 120 U.S. 489, 494.

Nor is American Mfg. Co. v. St. Louis, 250 U.S. 459, or International Harvester Co. v. Department of Treasury, 322 U.S. 340, any justification for the present tax. The American Mfg. Co. Case involved an imposition by St. Louis of a license fee upon the conduct of manufacturing within that city. It has long been settled that a State can levy such an occupation tax graduated according to the volume of manufacture. In that case, to lighten the manufacturer's burden, the imposition of the occupation tax was made contingent upon the actual sale of the goods locally manufactured. Sales in St. Louis of goods made elsewhere were not taken into account in measuring the license fee. That tax, then, unlike this, was not in fact a tax on gross receipts. Cf. Cornell v. Coyne, 192 U.S. 418. And, if words are to correspond to things, the tax now here is not "a tax on the transfer of property" within the State, which was the basis for sustaining the tax in International Harvester Co. v. Department of Treasury, supra.

There remains only the claim that an interstate sale of intangibles differs from an interstate sale of tangibles in respects material to the issue in this case. It was by this distinction that the Supreme Court of Indiana sought to escape the authority of J. D. Adams Mfg. Co. v. Storen, supra. Latin tags like mobilia sequuntur personam often do service for legal analysis, but they ought not to confound constitutional issues. What Mr. Justice Holmes said about that phrase is relevant here. "It is a fiction, the historical origin of which is familiar to scholars, and it is this fiction that gives whatever meaning it has to the saying mobilia sequuntur personam. But being a fiction it is not allowed to obscure the facts, when the facts become important." Blackstone v. Miller, 188 U.S. 189, 204. Of course this is an interstate sale. And constitutionally it is commerce no less and no different because the subject was pieces of paper worth $65,214.20, rather than machines.

Reversed.

Mr. Justice Black dissents.

Mr. Justice Rutledge, concurring.

This is a case in which the grounding of the decision is more important than the decision itself. Whether the Court now intends simply to qualify or to repudiate entirely, except in result, J. D. Adams Mfg. Co. v. Storen 304 U.S. 307, I am unable to determine from its opinion. But that one or the other consequence is intended seems obvious from its refusal to rest the present decision squarely on that case, together with the wholly different foundation on which it now relies. In either event, the matter is important and calls for discussion. . . .

[Mr. Justice Rutledge's opinion, concurring in the result, developed somewhat more fully the ideas expressed in the latter part of his opinion dissenting in McLeod v. Dilworth Co. and concurring in General Trading Co. v. State Tax Commission, supra.]

Mr. Justice Douglas, with whom Mr. Justice Murphy concurs, dissenting. . . .

The present tax is not aimed at interstate commerce and does not discriminate against it. It is not imposed as a levy for the privilege of doing it. It is not a tax on interstate transportation or communication. It is not an exaction on property in its interstate journey. It is not a tax on interstate selling. The tax is on the proceeds of the sales less the brokerage commissions and therefore does not reach the revenues from the only interstate activities involved in these transactions. It is therefore essentially no different, so far as the Commerce Clause is concerned, from a tax by Indiana on the proceeds of the sale of a farm or other property in New York where the mails are used to authorize it, to transmit the deed, and to receive the proceeds.

I would adhere to the philosophy of our recent cases and affirm the judgment below.

NOTE

1. See Powell, More Ado About Gross Receipts Taxes, 60 Harv. L. Rev. 501, 710 (1947).

2. For a careful analysis of the position of Mr. Justice Rutledge in the above cases and others arising under the commerce clause, see Abel, The Commerce Power: An Instrument of Federalism, 35 Iowa L. Rev. 625 (1950), 25 Ind. L. Rev. 498 (1950), from a symposium on Mr. Justice Rutledge printed in both periodicals.

3. In Professor Abel's article, referred to above, appears the following footnote (n. 187, 35 Iowa L. Rev. 658, 25 Ind. L. Rev. 527-528): "In discussing Freeman v. Hewit with him, I questioned the preference for the state of market and suggested the superior interests of the state of origin, on the various grounds that its resources of materials and labor were incorporated in the commodity and often depleted to the extent of the transfer, that the tendency of the preference was to a further colonialization of producing regions of the country for the benefit of those already favored historically by previous accumulation of capital (to an appreciable extent as a result of the Court's own prior decisions), and that the tax resources of the producing states were on balance apt to be more limited in quantity and variety than those of states of market. His answer was that the problem merited further consideration but that the preference expressed did not represent a holding and that the Court had not had the benefit of argument as to which state should be given the green light, a matter which could be definitely decided when it should be presented for decision." Do you agree with Professor Abel's suggestions? Compare the item from the Economist, below. May considerations other than those suggested by Professor Abel lead one to agree with his conclusion?

4. Is there a jurisdictional problem in Freeman v. Hewit as well as a commerce problem? Cf. New York ex rel. Hatch v. Reardon, 204 U.S. 152 (1907).

FRENCH VERSUS GERMAN STEEL, 167 Economist 312 (May 2, 1953): "The European Coal-Steel Community had to postpone the opening of its common market for steel from April 10th to May 1st in order to give officials time to straighten out the problem of taxation. Tax systems vary widely throughout the six countries and some producers felt that the disparity would give their competitors an unfair advantage. A commission of experts, headed by Professor Tinbergen, was appointed to sort out the intricacies and to recommend some arrangement which, short of revising the entire fiscal systems of the Community, would ensure fair competitive conditions. Its final recommendations have raised a storm of protest from the German steel producers.

"Briefly, the commission proposed that French steel sold to Germany, for example, should be divested of all French indirect taxes at the frontier and should bear only the indirect taxes imposed by the receiving country, in this case Germany. It would thus compete with German steel in the German home market solely on the basis of differences in costs of production and transport. The Germans had opted for the reverse solution — that French steel should carry its own high domestic tax wherever it went in the Community.

"To the Germans the commission's proposal seems outrageously unfair. German indirect taxes are comparatively low and insofar as industry is concerned the German government raises its revenue by relatively high rates of direct taxation. This is completely contrary to the French fiscal system, where indirect taxes are high and direct taxation low. The upshot is that French steel exporters will pay little to their government from any profits they make on steel sold to Germany, while German exporters will not only have to bear high French indirect taxes but will also have to pass on a big share of their profits to the German government in the form of direct taxes.

"At first glance, the case presented by the Germans seems to be a fairly strong one. But the commission's report puts a finger on the weaknesses. The argument that high direct taxes in any country can destroy the profitability of a country's export trade is a hoary and, in the main, very muddled one; the commission dismisses it with the somewhat debonair argument that it is the function of rates of exchange to offset any discrepancies between nations in the burden of direct taxation. As for differences in the rate of indirect taxation, the report, in a very concise table, shows that if its proposal is adopted, these variations will in no way harm Germany's competitive position. The report rejects the solution advocated by Germany simply because it would entail a radical alteration of all six fiscal systems.

"In fact, these technical arguments disguise what is probably for the Germans the heart of the matter — the fact that since last summer, French steel producers have kept their prices low, largely in response to M. Pinay's pleas to save the franc. The Germans, on the other hand, have allowed their prices to rise sharply in order to build up substantial profits for ploughing back into their steel industry. Therefore, at the prices currently prevailing in the two countries, and given the commission's proposed solution, French steel would undercut German steel in the German market. The prize for producers in both countries is the south German market, where the Ruhr now has a slight advantage because of a special rebate it grants to users there and because of a German monopoly selling arrangement in the area; under the treaty both of these practices must go.

"The Germans are so exercised about the affair that they now threaten to manipulate their taxes in such a way as to protect their steel industry, unless French steel prices are raised or unless the commission's proposal is modified."[ii]

Norton Co. v. Department of Revenue 340 U.S. 534, 71 S. Ct. 377, 95 L. Ed. 517 (1951)

MR. JUSTICE JACKSON delivered the opinion of the Court.

Petitioner, a Massachusetts corporation, manufactures and sells abrasive machines and supplies. Under consent from the State of Illinois to do business therein, it operates a branch office and warehouse in Chicago from which it makes local sales at retail. These

---

[ii] Cf. Mendershausen, First Tests of the Schuman Plan, 35 Rev. Econ. & Stat. 269, 278-282 (1953). — ED.

Section D. **State Taxation** 589

sales admittedly subject it to an Illinois Occupation Tax "upon persons engaged in the business of selling tangible personal property at retail in this State." The base for computation of the tax is gross receipts.

Not all of petitioner's sales to Illinois customers are over-the-counter, but the State has collected, under protest, the tax on the entire gross income of this company from sales to its inhabitants. The statute specifically exempts "business in interstate commerce" as required by the Constitution, and the question is whether the State has exceeded the constitutional range of its taxing power by taxing all of petitioner's Illinois derived income.

In Worcester, Massachusetts, petitioner manufactures some 225,000 items, 18,000 of which it usually carries in stock. There are its general management, accounting, and credit offices, where it accepts or rejects all direct mail orders and orders forwarded by its Chicago office. If an order calls for specially built machines, it is there studied and accepted or rejected. Orders are filled by shipment f.o.b. Worcester either directly to the customer or via the Chicago office.

The Chicago place of business performs several functions. It carries an inventory of about 3,000 most frequently purchased items. From these it serves cash customers and those whose credit the home office has approved, by consummating direct sales. Income from these sales petitioner admits to be constitutionally taxable. But this office also performs useful functions for other classes of customers. For those of no established credit, those who order items not in local stock, and those who want special equipment, it receives their order and forwards it to the home office for action there. For many of these Illinois customers it also acts as an intermediary to reduce freight charges. Worcester packages and marks each customer's goods but accumulates them until a carload lot can be consigned to the Chicago office. Chicago breaks the carload and reconsigns the separate orders in their original package to customers. The Chicago office thus intervenes between vendor and Illinois vendees and performs service helpful to petitioner's competition for that trade in all Illinois sales except when the buyer orders directly from Worcester, and the goods are shipped from there directly to the buyer.

The Illinois Supreme Court recognized that it was dealing with interstate commerce. It reiterated its former holdings "that there could be no tax on solicitation of orders only" in the State. But no solicitors work the territory out of either the home office or the Chicago branch, although petitioner will supply engineering and technical advice. The Illinois court held that the presence of petitioner's local retail outlet, in the circumstances of this case, was sufficient to attribute all income derived from Illinois sales to that outlet and render it all taxable.

Where a corporation chooses to stay at home in all respects except to send abroad advertising or drummers to solicit orders which are sent directly to the home office for acceptance, filling, and delivery back to the buyer, it is obvious that the state of the buyer has no local grip on the seller. Unless some local incident occurs sufficient to bring the transaction within its taxing power, the vendor is not taxable. McLeod v. J. E. Dilworth Co., 322 U.S. 327. Of course, a state imposing a sales or use tax can more easily meet this burden, because the impact of those taxes is on the local buyer or user. Cases involving them are not controlling here, for this tax falls on the vendor.

But when, as here, the corporation has gone into the State to do local business by state permission and has submitted itself to the taxing power of the State, it can avoid taxation on some Illinois sales only by showing that particular transactions are dissociated from the local business and interstate in nature. The general rule, applicable here, is that a taxpayer claiming immunity from a tax has the burden of establishing his exemption.

This burden is never met merely by showing a fair difference of opinion which as an original matter might be decided differently. This corporation, by submitting itself to the taxing power of Illinois, likewise submitted itself to its judicial power to construe and apply its taxing statute insofar as it keeps within constitutional bounds. Of course, in constitutional cases, we have power to examine the whole record to arrive at an independent judgment as to whether constitutional rights have been invaded, but that does not mean that we will re-examine, as a court of first instance, findings of fact supported by substantial evidence.

This corporation has so mingled taxable business with that which it contends is not taxable that it requires administrative and judicial judgment to separate the two. We conclude that, in the light of all the evidence, the judgment attributing to the Chicago branch income from all sales that utilized it either in receiving the order or distributing the goods was within the realm of permissible judgment. Petitioner has not established that such services as were rendered by the Chicago office were not decisive factors in establishing and holding this market. On this record, no other source of the customer relationship is shown.

This corporation could have approached the Illinois market through solicitors only and it would have been entitled to the immunity of interstate commerce as set out in the Dilworth Case. But, from a competitive point of view, that system has disadvantages. The trade may view the seller as remote and inaccessible. He cannot be reached with process of local courts for breach of contract, or for service if the goods are defective or in need of replacement. Petitioner elected to localize itself in the Illinois market with the advantages of a retail outlet in the State, to keep close to the trade, to supply locally many items and take orders for others, and to reduce freight costs to local consumers. Although the concern does not, by engaging in business within the State, lose its right to do interstate business with tax immunity, Cooney v. Mountain States Tel. & Tel. Co., 294 U.S. 384, it cannot channel business through a local outlet to gain the advantage of a local business and also hold the immunities of an interstate business.

The only items that are so clearly interstate in character that the State could not reasonably attribute its proceeds to the local business are orders sent directly to Worcester by the customer and shipped directly to the customer from Worcester. Income from those we think was not subject to this tax. [Compare Nelson v. Sears, Roebuck & Co., page 572 supra.]

The judgment below is vacated and the cause remanded for further proceedings not inconsistent herewith.

It is so ordered.

[Mr. Justice Reed dissented in part.]

Mr. Justice Reed concurs with the Court's opinion and judgment except as it permits Illinois to use as a base for the tax computation petitioner's sales, consummated in Massachusetts by the acceptance of orders forwarded to petitioner there by its Illinois branch office, filled in Massachusetts, and shipped from Massachusetts directly, and not by transhipment through the Illinois branch, to the buyer. . . .

. . . I can see no difference, constitutionally, between solicitation by salesmen in a branch office or on the road. Such sales, consummated by direct shipment to Illinois buyers from out of state are interstate business and free of the tax Illinois has levied. So far as the Supreme Court of Illinois holds those transactions taxable, it should be reversed.

Mr. Justice Clark, dissenting in part.

I believe the respondent reasonably attributed all of the proceeds of petitioner's sales in Illinois to the company's local activities. I therefore agree with the Illinois Supreme Court that under the circumstances shipments sent directly to Illinois customers on orders sent directly to Worcester were subject to the tax.

As the Court points out, petitioner can avoid taxation on its direct sales only "by showing that . . . [they] are dissociated from the local business and [are] interstate in nature. The general rule, applicable here, is that a taxpayer claiming immunity from a tax has the burden of establishing his exemption." Petitioner has failed to meet this burden. In fact Illinois has shown that petitioner's Chicago office is its only source of customer relationship in Illinois; that the Chicago office provides the sole means through which petitioner can be reached with process by Illinois courts in the event a customer is aggrieved; that the local office affords service to machines after sale, as well as replacement of machines which are defective; that it stands ready to receive complaints and to offer engineering and technical advice; and that these multitudinous activities give to petitioner a local character which is most helpful in all its Illinois operations. Surely the Court's conclusion, that "Petitioner has not established that such services as were rendered by the Chicago office were not decisive factors in establishing and holding this market," applies with equal validity to the direct sales.

In maintaining a local establishment of such magnitude, petitioner has adopted the label of a hometown merchant. After it has received the manifold advantages of that label, we should not give our sanction to its claim made at taxpaying time that with respect to direct sales it is only an itinerant drummer. For the foregoing and other reasons which need not be stated, I would affirm in its entirety the judgment below.

MR. JUSTICE BLACK and MR. JUSTICE DOUGLAS join in this opinion.

NOTE

In Miller Bros. Co. v. Maryland, 347 U.S. 340 (1954), the Court (5 to 4) held that a Maryland statute imposing a use tax, and requiring that vendors collect it, could not be applied to require a Delaware corporation operating a store in Delaware to collect the tax with respect to goods sold to residents of Maryland who came to the store and made purchases. The Delaware store's regular newspaper and radio advertising reached Maryland, as well as Delaware, customers. Some of the items purchased were taken with them by the Maryland purchasers, others were delivered in Maryland by common carrier, and others by the seller's trucks. Maryland had seized one of these trucks in its attempt to enforce the statutory obligation to collect the tax. The Court, without dealing with possible interstate commerce aspects of the case, held that Maryland had no jurisdiction to impose the statutory obligation upon the seller.

Scripto, Inc. v. Carson 362 U.S. 207, 80 S. Ct. 619, 4 L. Ed. 2d 660 (1960)

MR. JUSTICE CLARK delivered the opinion of the Court.

Florida, by statute, requires appellant, a Georgia corporation, to be responsible for the collection of a use tax on certain mechanical writing instruments which appellant sells and ships from its place of business in Atlanta to residents of Florida for use and enjoyment there. Upon Scripto's failure to collect the tax, the appellee Comptroller levied a use tax liability of $5,150.66 against it. Appellant then brought this suit to test the validity of the imposition, contending that the requirement of Florida's statute places a burden on interstate commerce and violates the Due Process Clause of the Fourteenth Amendment to the Constitution. It claimed, in effect, that the nature of its operations in Florida does not form a sufficient nexus to subject it to the statute's exactions. Both the trial court and the Supreme Court of Florida held that appellant does have sufficient jurisdictional contacts in Florida and, therefore, must register as a dealer under the statute and collect and remit to the State the use tax imposed on its aforesaid sales. 105 So.2d 775. We noted probable jurisdiction. 361 U.S. 806. We agree with the result reached by Florida's courts.

Appellant operates in Atlanta an advertising specialty division trading under the name of Adgif Company. Through it, appellant is engaged in the business of selling mechanical writing instruments which are adapted to advertising purposes by the placing of printed material thereon. In its Adgif operation, appellant does not (1) own, lease, or maintain any office, distributing house, warehouse or other place of business in Florida, or (2) have any regular employee or agent there. Nor does it own or maintain any bank account or stock of merchandise in the State. Orders for its products are solicited by advertising specialty brokers or, as the Supreme Court of Florida called them, wholesalers or jobbers, who are residents of Florida. At the time of suit, there were 10 such brokers — each having a written contract and a specific territory. The somewhat detailed contract provides, inter alia, that all compensation is to be on a commission basis on the sales made, provided they are accepted by appellant; repeat orders, even if not solicited, also carry a commission if the salesman has not become inactive through failure to secure acceptable orders during the previous 60 days. The contract specifically provides that it is the intention of the parties "to create the relationship . . . of independent contractor." Each order is to be signed by the solicitor as a "salesman"; however, he has no authority to make collections or incur debts involving appellant. Each salesman is furnished catalogs, samples, and advertising material, and is actively engaged in Florida as a representative "of Scripto for the purpose of attracting, soliciting and obtaining Florida customers" for its mechanical advertising specialties. Orders for such products are sent by these salesmen directly to the Atlanta office for acceptance or refusal. If accepted, the sale is consummated there and the salesman is paid his commission directly. No money passes between the purchaser and the salesman — although the latter does occasionally accept a check payable to the appellant, in which event he is required to forward it to appellant with the order.

As construed by Florida's highest court, the impost levied by the statute is a tax "on the privilege of using personal property . . . which has come to rest . . . and has become a part of the mass of property" within the State. 105 So.2d, at 781. It is not a sales tax, but "was developed as a device to complement [such a tax] in order to prevent evasion . . . by the completion of purchases in a non-taxing state and shipment by interstate commerce into a taxing forum." Id., at 779. The tax is collectible from "dealers" and is to be added to the purchase price of the merchandise "as far as practicable." In the event that a dealer fails to collect the tax he himself is liable for its payment. The statute has the customary use tax provisions "against duplication of the tax, an allowance to the dealer for making the collection, and a reciprocal credit arrangement which credits against the Florida tax any amount up to the amount of the Florida tax which might have been paid to another state." Id., at 782. Florida held appellant to be a dealer under its statute. "The application by that Court of its local laws and the facts on which it founded its judgment are of course controlling here." General Trading Co. v. State Tax Comm'n, 322 U.S. 335, 337 (1944).

The question remaining is whether Florida, in the light of appellant's operations there, may collect the State's use tax from it on the basis of property bought from appellant and shipped from its home office to purchasers in Florida for use there.

Florida has well stated the course of this Court's decisions governing such levies, and we need but drive home its clear understanding. There must be, as our Brother Jackson stated in Miller Bros. Co. v. Maryland, 347 U.S. 340, 344-345 (1954). "Some definite link, some minimum connection, between a state and the person, property or transaction it seeks to tax." We believe that such a nexus is present here. First, the tax is a nondiscriminatory exaction levied for the use and enjoyment of property which has been purchased by Florida residents and which has actually entered into and become a part of the mass of property in that State. The burden of the tax is placed on the ultimate purchaser in Florida and it is he who enjoys the use of the property, regardless of its sources. We note that the appellant is charged with no tax — save when, as here, he fails or refuses to collect it from the Florida customer. Next, as Florida points out, appellant has 10 wholesalers, jobbers, or "salesmen" conducting continuous local solicitation in Florida and forwarding the resulting orders from that State to Atlanta for shipment of the ordered goods. The only incidence of this sales transaction that is nonlocal is the acceptance of the order. True, the "salesmen" are not regular employees of appellant devoting full time to its service, but we conclude that such a fine distinction is without constitutional significance. The formal shift in the contractual tagging of the salesman as "independent" neither results in changing his local function of solicitation nor bears upon its effectiveness in securing a substantial flow of goods into Florida. This is evidenced by the amount assessed against appellant on the statute's 3% basis over a period of but four years. To permit such formal "contractual shifts" to make a constitutional difference would open the gates to a stampede of tax avoidance. See Thomas Reed Powell, Sales and Use Taxes: Collection from Absentee Vendors, 57 Harv. L. Rev. 1086, 1090. Moreover, we cannot see, from a constitutional standpoint, "that it was important that the agent worked for several principals." Chief Judge Learned Hand, in Bomze v. Nardis Sportswear, 165 F.2d 33, 36. The test is simply the nature and extent of the activities of the appellant in Florida. In short, we conclude that this case is controlled by General Trading Co., supra. . . .

Nor do we believe that Florida's requirement that appellant be its tax collector on such orders from its residents changes the situation. As was pointed out in General Trading Co., this is "a familiar and sanctioned device." Ibid. Moreover, we note that Florida reimburses appellant for its service in this regard.

Appellant earnestly contends that Miller Bros. Co. v. Maryland, supra, is to the contrary. We think not. Miller had no solicitors in Maryland; there was no "exploitation of the consumer market"; no regular, systematic displaying of its products by catalogs, samples or the like. But, on the contrary, the goods on which Maryland sought to force Miller to collect its tax were sold to residents of Maryland when personally present at Miller's store in Delaware. True, there was an "occasional" delivery of such purchases by Miller into Maryland, and it did occasionally mail notices of special sales to former customers; but Marylanders went to Delaware to make purchases — Miller did not go to Maryland for sales. Moreover, it was impossible for Miller to determine that goods sold for cash to a customer over the counter at its store in Delaware were to be used and enjoyed in Maryland. This led the Court to conclude that Miller would be made "more vulnerable to liability for another's tax than to a tax on itself." 347 U.S., at 346. In view of these considerations, we conclude that the "minimum connections" not present in Miller are more than sufficient here.

The judgment is therefore
Affirmed.

MR. JUSTICE FRANKFURTER, deeming this case to be nearer to General Trading Co. v. State Tax Commission, 322 U.S. 335, than it is to Miller Bros. Co. v. Maryland, 347 U.S. 340, concurs in the result.

MR. JUSTICE WHITTAKER, believing that Florida's action denies to appellant due process of law and also directly burdens interstate commerce as held in Miller Bros. Co. v. Maryland, 347 U.S. 340, and in McLeod v. Dilworth Co., 322 U.S. 327, and adhering to his views expressed in Northwestern Cement Co. v. Minnesota, 358 U.S. 450, 457, would reverse the judgment.

General Motors Corp. v. Washington 377 U.S. 436, 84 S. Ct. 1564, 12 L. Ed. 2d 430 (1964)

MR. JUSTICE CLARK delivered the opinion of the Court.

This appeal tests the constitutional validity, under the Commerce and Due Process Clauses, of Washington's tax imposed upon the privilege of engaging in business activities with the State. The tax is measured by the appellant's gross wholesale sales of motor vehicles, parts and accessories delivered in the State. Appellant claims that the tax is levied on unapportioned gross receipts from such sales and is, therefore, a tax on the privilege of engaging in interstate commerce; is inherently discriminatory; results in the imposition of a multiple tax burden; and is a deprivation of property without due process of law. The Washington Superior Court held that the presence of a branch office in Seattle rendered some of the Chevrolet transactions subject to tax, but, as to the remainder, held that the application of the statute would be repugnant to the Commerce and the Due Process Clauses of the United States Constitution. On appeal, the Supreme Court of Washington reversed the latter finding, holding that all of the appellant's transactions were subject to the tax on the ground that the tax bore a reasonable relation to the appellant's activities within the State. 60 Wash. 2d 862, 376 P.2d 843. Probable jurisdiction was noted. 374 U.S. 824. We have concluded that the tax is levied on the incidents of a substantial local business in Washington and is constitutionally valid and, therefore, affirm the judgment.

I

We start with the proposition that "[i]t was not the purpose of the commerce clause to relieve those engaged in interstate commerce from their just share of state tax burden even though it increases the cost of doing the business." Western Live Stock v. Bureau of Revenue, 303 U.S. 250, 254 (1938). "Even interstate business must pay its way," Postal Telegraph-Cable Co. v. Richmond, 249 U.S. 252, 259 (1919), as is evidenced by numerous opinions of this Court . . . [listing numerous decisions sustaining state taxes].

However, local taxes measured by gross receipts from interstate commerce have not always fared as well. Because every State has equal rights when taxing the commerce it touches, there exists the danger that such taxes can impose cumulative burdens upon interstate transactions which are not presented to local commerce. Cf. Michigan-Wisconsin Pipe Line Co. v. Calvert, 347 U.S. 157, 170 (1954); Philadelphia and Southern S.S. Co. v. Pennsylvania, 122 U.S. 326, 346 (1887). Such burdens would destroy interstate commerce and encourage the re-erection of those trade barriers which made the Commerce Clause necessary. Cf. Baldwin v. G. A. F. Seelig, Inc., 294 U.S. 511, 521-522 (1935). And in this connection, we have specifically held that interstate commerce cannot be subjected to the burden of "multiple taxation." Michigan-Wisconsin Pipe Line Co. v. Calvert, supra, at 170. Nevertheless, as we have seen, it is well established that taxation measured by gross receipts is constitutionally proper if it is fairly apportioned.

A careful analysis of the cases in this field teaches that the validity of the tax rests upon whether the State is exacting a constitutionally fair demand for that aspect of interstate commerce to which it bears a special relation. For our purposes the decisive issue turns on the operating incidence of the tax. In other words, the question is whether the State has exerted its power in proper proportion to appellant's activities within the State and to appellant's consequent enjoyment of the opportunities and protections which the State has afforded. Where, as in the instant case, the taxing State is not the domiciliary State, we look to the taxpayer's business activities within the State, i.e., the local incidents, to determine if the gross receipts from sales therein may be fairly related to those activities. . . .

Here it is admitted that General Motors has entered the State and engaged in activities therein. In fact, General Motors voluntarily pays considerable taxes on its Washington operations but contests the validity of the tax levy on four of its Divisions, Chevrolet, Pontiac, Oldsmobile and General Motors Parts. Under these circumstances appellant has the burden of showing that the operations of these Divisions in the State are "dissociated from the local business and interstate in nature. The general rule, applicable here, is that a taxpayer claiming immunity from a tax has the burden of establishing his exemption." Norton Co. v. Department of Revenue, 340 U.S. 534, 537 (1951). . . .

II

1. GENERAL MOTORS' CORPORATE ORGANIZATION AND SALES OPERATION

General Motors is a Delaware corporation which was engaged in business in Washington during the period of time involved in this case, January 1, 1949, through June 30,

1953. Chevrolet, Pontiac, Oldsmobile and General Motors Parts are divisions of General Motors, but they operate substantially independently of each other. The corporation manufactures automobiles, trucks and other merchandise which are sold to dealers in Washington. However, all of these articles are manufacturered in other States. In order to carry on the sale, in Washington, of the products of Chevrolet, Pontiac, Oldsmobile and General Motors Parts, the corporation maintains an organization of employees in each of these divisions on a national, regional and district level. During the taxing period in question, the State of Washington was located in the western region of the corporation's national organization and each division, except General Motors Parts, maintained a zone office at Portland, Oregon. These zone offices serviced General Motor's operations in Oregon, Washington, Idaho, portions of Montana and Wyoming and all of the then Territory of Alaska. Chevrolet Division also maintained a branch office at Seattle which was under the jurisdiction of the Portland zone office and which rendered special service to all except the nine southern counties of Washington, which were still serviced by the Portland office. The zone offices of each division were broken down into geographical district offices and it is in these districts that the dealers, to whom the corporation sold its products for re-sale, were selected and located. The orders for these products were sent by the dealers to the zone office located at Portland. They were accepted or rejected there or at the factory and the sales were completed by shipments f.o.b. the factories.

2. PERSONNEL RESIDING WITHIN THE STATE AND THEIR ACTIVITIES

The sales organizations of the Chevrolet, Pontiac and Oldsmobile Divisions were similar in most respects. The zone manager was located in Portland and had charge of the sales operation. His job was "to secure and maintain a quality dealer organization . . . to administer and promote programs, plans and procedures that will cause that dealer organization to give . . . the best possible business representation in this area." R. 76. The district managers lived within the State of Washington and their jobs were "the maintenance of a quality organization — dealer organization — and the follow-through and administration of programs, plans and procedures within their district, that will help to develop the dealer organization, for the best possible financial and sales results." R. 109. While he had no office within the State, the district manager operated from his home where he received mail and telephone calls and otherwise carried on the corporation's business. He called upon each dealer in his district on an average of at least once a month, and often saw the larger dealers weekly. A district manager had from 12 to 30 dealers under his supervision and functioned as the zone manager's direct contact with these dealers, acting "in a supervisory or advisory capacity to see that they have the proper sales organization and to acquaint them with the Divisional sales policies and promotional and training plans to improve the selling ability of the sales organization." R. 246. In this connection, the district manager also assisted in the organization and training of the dealer's sales force. At appropriate times he distributed promotional material and advised on used car inventory control.

It was also the duty of the district manager to discuss and work out with the dealer the 30-, 60- and 90-day projection of orders of estimated needs which the dealer or the district manager then filed with the zone manager. . . .

In addition to the district manager, each of the Chevrolet, Pontiac and Oldsmobile Divisions also maintained service representatives who called on the dealers with regularity, assisting the service department in any troubles it experienced with General Motors products. These representatives also checked the adequacy of the service department inventory to make certain that the dealer's agreement was being complied with and to ensure the best possible service to customers. It was also their duty to note the appearance of the dealer's place of business and, where needed, to require rehabilitation, improved cleanliness or any other repairs necessary to achieve an attractive sales and service facility.

At the dealer's request, or on direction from his zone superior, the service representative also conducted service clinics at the dealer's place of business, for the purpose of teaching the dealer and his service personnel the proper techniques necessary to the operation of an efficient service department. The service representative also gave assistance to the dealer with the more difficult customer complaints, some of which were registered with the dealer, but others of which were registered with the corporation.

During the tax period involved here the Chevrolet, Oldsmobile and Pontiac Division had an average of about 20 employees resident or principally employed in Washington. General Motors Parts Division employed about 20 more.

The Chevrolet Division's branch office at Seattle consisted of one man and his secretary. That office performed the function of getting better service for Washington dealers on orders of Chevrolet Division products. The branch office had no jurisdiction over sales or over other Chevrolet personnel in the State. Since January 1, 1954, Chevrolet Division has maintained a zone office in Seattle and has paid the tax without dispute.

3. OUT-OF-STATE PERSONNEL, PERFORMING IN-STATE ACTIVITIES

The zone manager, who directed all zone activities, visited with each Washington dealer on the average of once each 60 days, the larger ones, each month. About one-half of these visits were staged at the dealer's place of business and the others were at Portland. The zone business management manager was the efficiency expert for the zone and supervised the capital structure and financing of the Washington dealers. The zone parts and service manager held responsibility for the adequacy of the Washington dealer services to customers. He worked through the local Washington service representative, but also made personal visits to Washington dealers and conducted schools for the promotion of good service policies. The zone used car manager (for the Chevrolet Division only) assisted Washington dealers in the disposition of used cars through appropriate display and reconditioning.

4. ACTIVITIES OF GENERAL MOTORS PARTS DIVISION

During the period of this tax, the General Motors Parts Division warehoused, sold and shipped parts and accessories to Washington dealers for Chevrolet, Pontiac and Oldsmobile vehicles. It maintained warehouses in Portland and Seattle. No personnel of this division visited the dealers, but all of the Chevrolet, Pontiac and Oldsmobile dealers in Washington obtained their parts and accessories from these warehouses. Items carried by the Seattle warehouse were shipped from it, and those warehoused at Portland were shipped from there. The Seattle warehouse, which carried the items most often called for in Washington, employed from 20 to 28 people during the taxing period. The Portland warehouse carried the less-frequently needed parts. The tax on the orders filled at the Seattle warehouse was paid but the tax on the Portland shipments is being protested.

III

"[I]t is beyond dispute," we said in Northwestern States Portland Cement Co. v. Minnesota, 358 U.S. [450] at 458, "that a State may not lay a tax on the 'privilege' of engaging in interstate commerce." But that is not this case. To so contend here is to overlook a long line of cases of this Court holding that an in-state activity may be a sufficient local incident upon which a tax may be based. . . . We place little weight on the fact that these divisions had no formal offices in the State, since in actuality the homes of these officials were used as corporate offices. Despite their label as "homes" they served the corporation just as effectively as "offices." In addition, the corporation had a Chevrolet branch office and a General Motors Parts Division warehouse in Seattle.

Thus, in the bundle of corporate activity, which is the test here, we see General Motors activity so enmeshed in local connections that it voluntarily paid taxes on various of its operations but insists that it was not liable on others. Since General Motors elected to enter the State in this fashion, we cannot say that the Supreme Court of Washington erred in holding that these local incidents were sufficient to form the basis for the levy of a tax that would not run contrary to the Constitution. Norton Co. v. Department of Revenue, supra.

IV

The tax that Washington levied is measured by the wholesale sales of the respective General Motors Divisions in the State. It is unapportioned and, as we have pointed out, is, therefore, suspect. We must determine whether it is so closely related to the local activities of the corporation as to form "some definite link, some minimum connection, between a state and the person, property or transaction it seeks to tax." Miller Bros. Co. v. Maryland, 347 U.S. 340, 344-345 (1954). On the basis of the facts found by the State court we are not prepared to say that its conclusion was constitutionally impermissible. Norton Co. v. Department of Revenue, supra, 340 U.S. at 538. Here, just as in Norton, the corporation so mingled its taxable business with that which it claims nontaxable that we can only "conclude that, in the light of all the evidence, the judgment attributing . . . [the corporation's Washington sales to its local activity] was within the realm of permissible judgment. Petitioner has not established that such services as were rendered . . . [through in-state activity] were not decisive factors in establishing and holding this market." Ibid. Although mere entry into a State does not take from a corporation the right to continue to do an interstate business with tax immunity, it does not follow that the corporation can channel its operations through such a maze of local connections as does General Motors, and take advantage of its gain on domesticity, and still maintain that same degree of immunity.

V

A more difficult question might arise from appellant's claim of multiple taxation. Gwin, White & Prince, Inc., v. Henneford, 305 U.S. 434, 440 (1939). General Motors claims that some of its products taxed by Washington are manufactured in St. Louis where a license tax, measured by sales before shipment, is levied. See American Mfg. Co. v. St. Louis, 250 U.S. 459 (1919). It is also urged that General Motors' Oregon-based activity which concerns Washington sales might afford sufficient incidents for a similar tax by Oregon. The Court touched upon the problem of multiple taxation in Northwest Airlines v. Minnesota, 322 U.S. at 295, but laid it to one side as "not now before us." Thereafter, in Northwestern States Portland Cement Co. v. Minnesota, supra, 358 U.S. at 463, we held that "[i]n this type of case the taxpayers must show that the formula places a burden upon interstate commerce in a constitutional sense." Appellant has not done this. It has not demonstrated what definite burden, in a constitutional sense, the St. Louis tax places on the identical interstate shipments by which Washington measures its tax. Cf. International Harvester Co. v. Evatt, 329 U.S. 416, 421-423 (1947). And further, it has not been shown that Oregon levies any tax on appellant's activity bearing on Washington sales. In such cases we have refrained from passing on the question of "multiple taxation," e.g., Northwestern States Portland Cement Co. v. Minnesota, supra, and we adhere to that position.

Affirmed.

Mr. Justice Brennan, dissenting. . . .

The Court recognizes that "taxation measured by gross receipts is constitutionally proper if it is fairly apportioned," . . . In concluding that the tax in this case includes a fair apportionment, however, the Court relies upon the fact that Washington has sufficient contacts with the sale to satisfy the Norton standard, which was formulated to meet the quite different problem of defining the requirements of the Due Process Clause. See Part IV, supra. Our prior decisions clearly indicate that a quite different scheme of apportionment is required. Of course, when a sale may be localized completely in one State, then there is no danger of multiple taxation, and, as in the case of a retail sales tax, the State may use as its tax base the total gross receipts arising within its borders. See McGoldrick v. Berwind-White Coal Mining Co., 309 U.S. 33. But far more common in our complex economy is the kind of sale presented in this case, which exhibits significant contacts with more than one State. In such a situation, it is the commercial activity within the State, and not the sales volume, which determines the State's power to tax, and by which the tax must be apportioned. While the ratio of in-state out-of-state sales is often taken into account as one factor among others in apportioning a firm's total net income, see, e.g., the description of the "Massachusetts Formula" in Note, 75 Harv. L. Rev. 953, 1011 (1962), it nevertheless remains true that if commercial activity in more than one State results in a sale in one of them, that State may not claim as all its own the gross receipts to which the activity within its borders has contributed only a part. Such a tax must be apportioned to reflect the business activity within the taxing State. Cf. my concurring opinion in Railway Express Agency v. Virginia, 358 U.S. 434, 446. Since the Washington tax on wholesales is, by its very terms, applied to the "gross proceeds of sales" of those "engaging within this state in the business of making sales at wholesale," 82 Rev. Code Wash. §82.04.270, it cannot be sustained under the standards required by the Commerce Clause.

Mr. Justice Goldberg, with whom Mr. Justice Stewart and Mr. Justice White join, dissenting.

The issue presented is whether the Commerce Clause permits a State to assess an unapportioned gross receipts tax on the interstate wholesale sales of automobiles delivered to dealers for resale in that State. In upholding the tax involved in this case, the Court states as a general proposition that "taxation measured by gross receipts [from interstate sales] is constitutionally proper if it is fairly apportioned." . . . The Court concludes from this that the validity of Washington's wholesale sales tax may be determined by asking " 'the simple but controlling question [of] whether the state has given anything for which it can ask return.' " Ibid. This elusively simple test and its application to this case represent an important departure from a fundamental purpose of the Commerce Clause and from an established principle which had heretofore provided guidance in an area otherwise fraught with complexities and inconsistencies. . . .

. . . This decision departs from Norton Co. v. Department of Revenue, 340 U.S. 534, and adopts a test there rejected. . . . [The opinion summarizes the facts and decision in the Norton case.]

Although the opinion of the Court seems to imply that there still is some threshold requirement of in-state activity which must be found to exist before a "fairly apportioned" tax may be imposed on interstate sales, it is difficult to conceive of a state gross receipts tax on interstate commerce which could not be sustained under the rationale adopted today. Every interstate sale invariably involves some local incidents — some "in-state" activity. It is difficult, for example, to distinguish between the in-state activities of the representatives here involved and the in-state activities of solicitors or traveling salesmen — activities which the Court has held are insufficient to constitute a basis for imposing a tax on interstate sales. McLeod v. J. E. Dilworth Co., 322 U.S. 327; cf. Real Silk Hosiery Mills v. City of Portland, 268 U.S. 325; Robbins v. Shelby County Taxing District, 120 U.S. 489. Surely the distinction cannot rest on the fact that the solicitors or salesmen make hotels or motels their "offices" whereas in the present case the sales representatives made their homes their "offices." In this regard, the Norton decision rested solidly on the fact that the taxpayer had a branch office and warehouse making intrastate retail sales.

The opinion of the Court goes beyond a consideration of whether there has been in-state activity of appropriate character to satisfy a threshold requirement for imposing a tax on interstate sales. The Court asserts as a general principle that the validity of a tax on interstate commerce "rests upon whether the State is exacting a constitutionally fair demand for that aspect of interstate commerce to which it bears a special relation." . . . What is "fair"? How are we to determine whether a State has exerted its power in "proper proportion to appellant's activities within the State"? Ibid. See Developments — Federal Limitations on State Taxation of Interstate Business. 75 Harv. L. Rev. 953, 957 (1962). I submit, with due respect for the complexity of the problem, that the formulation suggested by the Court is unworkable. Constitutional adjudication under the Commerce Clause would find little guidance in a concept of state interstate sales taxation tested and limited by the tax's "fair" proportion or degree. The attempt to determine the "fairness" of an interstate sales tax of a given percentage imposed on given activities in one State would be almost as unseemly as an attempt to determine whether that same tax was "fairly" apportioned in light of taxes levied on the same transaction by other States. The infinite variety of factual configurations would readily frustrate the usual process of clarification through judicial inclusion and exclusion. The only coherent pattern that could develop would, in reality, ultimately be based on a wholly permissive attitude toward state taxation of interstate-commerce.

The dilemma inhering in the Court's formulation is revealed by its treatment of the "more difficult," but inextricably related, question arising from the alleged multiple taxation. The Court would avoid the basic question by saying that appellant "has not demonstrated what definite burden, in a constitutional sense, the St. Louis tax places on the identical interstate shipments. . . . And further, it has not been shown that Oregon levies any tax on appellant's activity bearing on Washington sales." . . . These problems are engendered by the rule applied here and cannot be evaded. For if it is "fair" to subject the interstate sales to the Washington wholesale sales tax because of the activities of the sales representatives in Washington, then it would seem equally "fair" for Oregon, which is the site of the office directing and consummating these sales, to tax the same gross sales receipts. Moreover, it would seem "fairer" for California, Michigan or Missouri — States in which automobiles are manufactured, assembled or delivered — to impose a tax measured by, and effectively bearing upon, the same gross sales receipts. See Note, 38 Wash. L. Rev. 277, 281 (1963). Presumably, if there is to be a limitation on the taxing power of each of these States, that limitation surely cannot be on a first-come-first-tax basis. Alternatively, if diverse local incidents can afford bases for multistate taxation of the same interstate sale, then the Court is left to determine, out of some hypothetical maximum taxable amount, which proportion is "fair" for each of the States having a sufficient "in-state" contact with the interstate transaction.

The burden on interstate commerce and the dangers of multiple taxation are made apparent by considering Washington's tax provisions. The Washington provision here involved — the "tax on wholesalers" — provides that every person "engaging within this state in the business of making sales at wholesale" shall pay a tax on such business "equal to the gross proceeds of sales of such business multiplied by the rate of one-quarter of one per cent." Rev. Code Wash. 82.04.270(e); Wash. Laws 1949, c. 228, § 1(e). In the same chapter Washington imposes a "tax on manufacturers" which similarly provides that every person "engaging within this state in business as a manufacturer" shall pay a tax on such business "equal to the value of the products . . . manufactured, multiplied by the rate of one-quarter of one per cent." Rev. Code Wash. 82.04.240(b); Wash. Laws 1949, c. 228 § 1(b). Then in a provision entitled "Persons taxable on multiple activities" the statute endeavors to insure that local Washington products will not be subjected both to the "tax on manufacturers" and to the "tax on wholesalers." Rev. Code Wash. 82.04.440; Wash.

Laws 1949, c. 228, §2-A. Prior to its amendment in 1950 the exemptive terms of this "multiple activities" provision were designed so that a Washington manufacturer-wholesaler would pay the manufacturing tax and be exempt from the wholesale tax. This provision, on its face, discriminated against interstate wholesale sales to Washington purchasers for it exempted the intrastate sales of locally made products while taxing the competing sales of interstate sellers. In 1950, however, the "multiple activities" provision was amended, reversing the tax and the exemption, so that a Washington manufacturer-wholesaler should first be subjected to the wholesale tax and then, to the extent that he is taxed thereunder, exempted from the manufacturing tax. Rev. Code Wash. 82.04.440; Wash. Laws 1950 (special session), c. 5, §2. See McDonnell & McDonnell v. State, 62 Wash. 2d 553, 557, 383 P.2d 905, 908. This amended provision would seem to have essentially the same economic effect on interstate sales but has the advantage of appearing non-discriminatory.

Even under the amended "multiple activities" exemption, however, an out-of-state firm manufacturing goods in a State having the same taxation provisions as does Washington would be subjected to two taxes on interstate sales to Washington customers. The firm would pay the producing State a local manufacturing tax measured by sales receipts and would also pay Washington a tax on wholesale sales to Washington residents. Under such taxation programs, if an out-of-state manufacturer competes with a Washington manufacturer, the out-of-state manufacturer may be seriously disadvantaged by the duplicative taxation. Even if the out-of-state firm has no Washington competitors, the imposition of interstate sales taxes, which add to cost of producing, may diminish the demand for the product in Washington and thus affect the allocation of resources in the national economy. Moreover, the threat of duplicative taxation, even where there is no competitor manufacturing in the consuming State, may compel the out-of-state producer to relocate his manufacturing operations to avoid multiple taxation. Thus taxes such as the one upheld today may discourage the development of multistate business operations and the most advantageous distribution of our national resources; the economic effect inhibits the realization of a free and open economy unencumbered by local tariffs and protective devices. As the Court said in McLeod v. J. E. Dilworth Co., 322 U.S., at 330-331: "The very purpose of the Commerce Clause was to create an area of free trade among the several States. That clause vested the power of taxing a transaction forming an unbroken process of interstate commerce in the Congress, not in the States."

It may be urged that the Washington tax should be upheld because it taxes in a non-discriminatory fashion all wholesale sales, intrastate and interstate, to Washington purchasers. The Commerce Clause, however, was designed, as Mr. Justice Jackson said in H. P. Hood & Sons, Inc., v. Du Mond, 336 U.S. 525, 538, to create a "federal free trade unit" — a common national market among the States; and the Constitution thereby precludes a State from defending a tax on interstate sales on the ground that the State taxes intrastate sales generally. Nondiscrimination alone is no basis for burdening the flow of interstate commerce. The Commerce Clause "does not merely forbid a State to single out interstate commerce for hostile action. A State is also precluded from taking any action which may fairly be deemed to have the effect of impeding the free flow of trade between States. It is immaterial that local commerce is subjected to a similar encumbrance." Freeman v. Hewit, 329 U.S., at 252. A State therefore should not be enabled to put out-of-state producers and merchants at a disadvantage by imposing a tax to "equalize" their costs with those of local businessmen who would otherwise suffer a competitive disadvantage because of the State's own taxation scheme. The disadvantage stemming from the wholesale sales tax was created by the State itself and therefore the fact that the State simultaneously imposes the same tax on interstate transactions should not obscure the fact that interstate commerce is burdened in order to protect the local market.

In my view the rules set forth in Norton Co. v. Department of Revenue, supra, reflect an attempt to adhere to the basic purposes of the Commerce Clause. Therefore, in dealing with unapportioned taxes on interstate sales, I would adhere to the Norton rules instead of departing from them by adopting a standard of "fairness." I would hold that a manufacturer or wholesaler making interstate sales is not subject to a state gross receipts tax merely because those sales were solicited or processed by agents living or traveling in the taxing State. As Norton recognized, a different rule may be applied to the taxation of sales substatially connected with an office or warehouse making intrastate sales. The test adopted by the Court today, if followed logically in future cases, would seem to mean that States will be permitted to tax wholly interstate sales by any company selling through local agents or traveling salesmen. Such a rule may leave only mail-order houses free from state taxes on interstate sales. With full sympathy for the revenue needs of States, I believe there are other legitimate means of raising state revenues without undermining the common national market created by the Commerce Clause. I therefore respectfully dissent.

NOTE Use Tax on Mail-Order Business

In National Bellas Hess, Inc. v. Department of Revenue, 386 U.S. 753 (1967), the Court held invalid an attempt to make an out-of-state mail order company a collecting agent for taxes on the purchase of goods by local residents solely through the medium of catalogs, where the company had no facilities or agents in the taxing state. The facts of the case were thus stated in Department of Revenue v. National Bellas Hess, Inc., 34 Ill. 2d 164, 214 N. E. 2d 755 (1966) (House, J.): ". . . Defendant is a national mail-order company. It issues annually two main catalogues . . . and it also issues during the year a number of intermediate smaller 'sale books' or 'flyers.' The catalogue contains approximately 4000 different items of merchandise for retail sale, and it is mailed to the company's own list of customers. This list, which contained 5,000,000 names when the company acquired it in 1932, is kept current with active and recent customers. The 'flyers,' which are less costly to distribute, are mailed to a less restricted list of customers or potential customers. They are occasionally mailed in bulk addressed to 'occupant' or inclosed in the parcels sent to customers in filling orders from a prior 'flyer' or catalogue.

"The company's only plant is located in North Kansas City, Missouri, and all of its mail-order activities occur there, except for purchasing, which is done initially by a wholly owned subsidiary in New York. All of the catalogues and 'flyers' are mailed from North Kansas City; orders from customers are received and accepted there; the goods are mailed or shipped by common carrier from there; and payment by the customer is mailed there.

"The company is a Delaware corporation and is qualified to do business only in Delaware and Missouri. It does not maintain in Illinois any office, distribution house, sales house, warehouse or any other place of business; it does not have in Illinois any agent, salesman, canvasser, solicitor or other type of representative to sell or take orders, to deliver merchandise, to accept payments, or to service merchandise it sells; it does not own any tangible property, real or personal, in Illinois; it has no telephone listing in Illinois and it has not advertised its merchandise for sale in newspapers, on billboards, or by radio or television in Illinois.

"Section 3 of the Use Tax Act, which became effective in July, 1955, imposes a tax 'upon the privilege of using in this State tangible personal property purchased at retail . . . from a retailer.' It also provides that the tax '. . . shall be collected from the purchaser by a retailer maintaining a place of business in this State . . .' (Ill. Rev. Stat. 1961, chap. 120, par. 439.3). . . . Section 2 of the act, which defines various terms used in the act, was amended effective July 17, 1961, (the commencement date of the assessment here in question) by adding a new paragraph to the definition of a 'retailer maintaining a place of business in this State.' The new paragraph, referred to as the 'catalogue amendment,' defines a 'retailer maintaining a place of business in this State' as any re-

602   Chapter Eight.   The States in a Federal Union

tailer 'Engaging in soliciting orders within this State from users by means of catalogues or other advertising, whether such orders are received or accepted within or without this State.' Ill. Rev. Stat. 1963, chap. 120, par. 439.2.

"The Use Tax Act was also amended in July, 1961, by adding a new section, section 12a, which provides for substituted service of process on a nonresident falling within the definition of 'retailer maintaining a place of business in this State'. . . ."

NOTE

1. See Report of the Special Subcommittee on State Taxation of Interstate Commerce, H.R. Rep. No. 565, 89th Cong., 1st Sess. (1965), for the report on sales and use taxes, and on gross receipts taxes. Recommendations for legislation are set forth in H.R. Rep. No. 952, 89th Cong., 1st Sess., pp. 1136-1138 and 1173-1196 (1965). Note that different legislative treatment is recommended with respect to sales and use taxes, on the one hand, and gross receipts taxes, on the other.

2. Many of the problems considered in this chapter are discussed in Developments in the Law — Federal Limitations on State Taxation of Interstate Business, 75 Harv. L. Rev. 953 (1962). See also Brown, The Open Economy: Justice Frankfurter and the Position of the Judiciary, 67 Yale L.J. 219 (1957).

3. See also, for discussion of these problems, Barrett, "Substance" vs. "Form" in the Application of the Commerce Clause to State Taxation, 101 U. Pa. L. Rev. 740 (1953), and Barrett, State Taxation of Interstate Commerce, 4 Vand. L. Rev. 496 (1951). Cf. Hellerstein and Hennefeld, State Taxation in a National Economy, 54 Harv. L. Rev. 949 (1941). Note earlier recommendations in Federal, State and Local Government Fiscal Relations, S. Doc. No. 69, 78th Cong., 1st Sess. (1943). For related materials, see Groves, Viewpoints on Public Finance (1947). See also Hartman, State Taxation of Interstate Commerce (1953).

Chapter Nine Methods of Cooperation and Accommodation

This chapter is concerned with devices for maintaining a middle ground between national control and individual state control. Working arrangements to that end may exist between states or between the national Government and the states. These arrangements may operate on the legislative, administrative, or judicial level. Do any of the devices canvassed here offer suggestions for rendering more tractable in a federal system such unruly problems as these: migratory divorce; "tramp" corporations; migrant labor and migrant paupers; mail-order insurance; rain-making; environmental protection?

Clark Distilling Co. v. Western Maryland Ry. 242 U.S. 311, 37 S. Ct. 180, 61 L. Ed. 326 (1917)

[The plaintiff company sued the carrier in a federal district court to compel it to transport intoxicating liquors from Maryland to customers in West Virginia, who had ordered the liquor for their personal use. The state of West Virginia intervened. A statute of West Virginia forbade the manufacture or sale of intoxicating liquors; there was dispute as to the application of the statute to sales for personal use. The trial court held that the Webb-Kenyon Act, enacted by Congress in 1913, forbade the shipments and that it was constitutional. The state statute was amended while the case was pending in the Supreme Court, to provide that "no common carrier . . . shall bring or carry into this state, or carry from one place to another within the state, intoxicating liquors for another, even when intended for personal use; . . ."]

CHIEF JUSTICE WHITE delivered the opinion of the Court. . . .
Omitting words irrelevant to the subject now under consideration, the title and text of the Webb-Kenyon Act are as follows:
"An Act Divesting Intoxicating Liquors of Their Interstate Character in Certain Cases.
". . . That the shipment or transportation, in any manner or by any means whatsoever, of any spirituous, vinous, malted, fermented, or other intoxicating liquor of any kind, from one state, territory, or district of the United States, . . . into any other state, territory, or district of the United States, . . . which said spirituous, vinous, malted, fermented, or other intoxicating liquor is intended, by any person interested therein, to be

received, possessed, sold, or in any manner used, either in the original package or otherwise, in violation of any law of such state, territory, or district of the United States . . . is hereby prohibited."

As the state law forbade the shipment into or transportation of liquor in the state, whether from inside or out, and all receipt and possession of liquor so transported, without regard to the use to which the liquor was to be put, and as the Webb-Kenyon Act prohibited the transportation in interstate commerce of all liquor "intended to be received, possessed, sold or in any manner used, either in the original package or otherwise, in violation of any law of such state," there would seem to be no room for doubt that the prohibitions of the state law were made applicable by the Webb-Kenyon Law. If that law was valid, therefore, the state law was not repugnant to the commerce clause.

Did Congress have power to enact the Webb-Kenyon Law?

We are not unmindful that opinions adverse to the power of Congress to enact the law were formed and expressed in other departments of the government. Opinion of the Attorney General, 30 Ops. Atty. Gen. 88; Veto Message of the President, 49 Cong. Rec. 4291. We are additionally conscious, therefore, of the responsibility of determining these issues and of their serious character.

It is not in the slightest degree disputed that if Congress had prohibited the shipment of all intoxicants in the channels of interstate commerce, and therefore had prevented all movement between the several states, such action would have been lawful, because within the power to regulate which the Constitution conferred. Lottery Case (Champion v. Ames) 188 U.S. 321; Hoke v. United States, 227 U.S. 308. The issue, therefore, is not one of an absence of authority to accomplish in substance a more extended result than that brought about by the Webb-Kenyon Law, but of a want of power to reach the result accomplished because of the method resorted to for that purpose. This is certain since the sole claim is that the act was not within the power given to Congress to regulate because it submitted liquors to the control of the states by subjecting interstate commerce in such liquors to present and future state prohibitions, and hence, in the nature of things, was wanting in uniformity. Let us test the contentions by reason and authority. . . .

The argument as to delegation to the states rests upon a mere misconception. It is true the regulation which the Webb-Kenyon Act contains permits state prohibitions to apply to movements of liquor from one state into another, but the will which causes the prohibitions to be applicable is that of Congress, since the application of state prohibitions would cease the instant the act of Congress ceased to apply. In fact, the contention previously made, that the prohibitions of the state law were not applicable to the extent that they were broader than the Webb-Kenyon Act, is in direct conflict with the proposition as to delegation now made.

So far as uniformity is concerned, there is no question that the act uniformly applies to the conditions which call its provisions into play, — that its provisions apply to all the states, — so that the question really is a complaint as to the want of uniform existence of things to which the act applies, and not to an absence of uniformity in the act itself. But, aside from this, it is obvious that the argument seeks to engraft upon the Constitution a restriction not found in it; that is, that the power to regulate conferred upon Congress obtains subject to the requirement that regulations enacted shall be uniform throughout the United States. . . .

It is settled, says the argument, that interstate commerce is divided into two great classes, one embracing subjects which do not exact uniformity, and which, although subject to the regulation of Congress, are, in the absence of such regulation, subject to the control of the several states (Cooley v. Port Wardens, 12 How. 299), and the other embracing subjects which do require uniformity, and which, in the absence of regulation by Congress, remain free from all state control (Leisy v. Hardin, 135 U.S. 100). As to the first, it is said, Congress may, when regulating, to the extent it deems wise to do so, permit state legislation enacted or to be enacted to govern, because to do so would only be to do that which would exist if nothing had been done by Congress. As to the second class, the argument is, that in adopting regulations Congress is wholly without power to provide for the application of state power to any degree whatever, because, in the absence of the exertion by Congress of power to regulate, the subject-matter would have been free from state control; and because, besides, the recognition of state power under such circumstances would be to bring about a want of uniformity. But granting the accuracy of the two classifications which the proposition states, the limitation upon the power of Congress to regulate which is deduced from the classifications finds no support in the authority relied upon to sustain it. Let us see if this is not the case by examining the authority relied upon. . . .

. . . As we have already pointed out, the very regulation made by Congress in enacting the Wilson Law to minimize the evil resulting from violating prohibitions of state law by sending liquor through interstate commerce into a state, and selling it in violation of such law, was to divest such shipments of their interstate commerce character and to strip them of the right to be sold in the original package free from state authority which otherwise would have obtained. And that Congress had the right to enact this legislation making existing and future state prohibitions applicable was the express result of the decided cases to which we have referred, beginning with Re Rahrer, 140 U.S. 545. As the power to regulate which was manifested in the Wilson Act, and that which was exerted in enacting the Webb-Kenyon Law, are essentially identical, the one being but a larger degree of exertion of the identical power which was brought into play in the other, we are unable to understand upon what principle we could hold that the one was not a regulation without holding that the other had the same infirmity, — a result which, as we have previously said, would reverse Leisy v. Hardin and overthrow the many adjudications of this court sustaining the Wilson Act.

These considerations dispose of the contention, but we do not stop with stating them, but recur again to the reason of things for the purpose of pointing out the fundamental error upon which the contention rests. It is this: the mistaken assumption that the accidental considerations which cause a subject, on the one hand, to come under state control in the absence of congressional regulation, and other subjects, on the contrary, to be free from state control until Congress has acted, are the essential criteria by which to test the question of the power of Congress to regulate and the mode in which the exertion of that power may be manifested. The two things are widely different, since the right to regulate and its scope and the mode of exertion must depend upon the power possessed by Congress over the subject regulated. Following the unerring path pointed out by that great principle we can see no reason for saying that although Congress, in view of the nature and character of intoxicants, had a power to forbid their movement in interstate commerce, it had not the authority to so deal with the subject as to establish a regulation (which is what was done by the Webb-Kenyon Law) making it impossible for one state to violate the prohibitions of the laws of another through the channels of interstate commerce. Indeed, we can see no escape from the conclusion that if we accepted the proposition urged, we would be obliged to announce the contradiction in terms that because Congress had exerted a regulation lesser in power than it was authorized to exert, therefore its action was void for excess of power. Or, in other words, stating the necessary result of the argument from a concrete consideration of the particular subject here involved, that because Congress, in adopting a regulation, had considered the nature and character of our dual system of government, state and nation, and instead of absolutely prohibiting, had so conformed its regulation as to produce cooperation between the local and national forces of government to the end of preserving the rights of all, it had thereby transcended the complete and perfect power of regulation conferred by the Constitution. And it is well again to point out that this abnormal result to which the argument leads concerns a subject as to which both state and nation, in their respective spheres of authority, possessed the supremest authority before the action of Congress which is complained of; and hence

606 Chapter Nine. Methods of Cooperation and Accommodation

the argument virtually comes to the assertion that, in some undisclosed way, by the exertion of congressional authority, power possessed has evaporated. . . .
Affirmed.
MR. JUSTICE MCREYNOLDS concurs in the result.
MR. JUSTICE HOLMES and MR. JUSTICE VAN DEVANTER dissent.

NOTE Cooperation by "Adoption" of Laws

1. For a critical comment by Mr. Justice Holmes see 1 Holmes-Laski Letters 54 (Howe ed. 1953).
See Powell, The Validity of State Legislation Under the Webb-Kenyon Law, 2 So. L.Q. 112 (1917), reprinted in 3 Selected Essays on Constitutional Law 880 (1938).

2. The pattern of the Wilson and Webb-Kenyon Acts was followed in the regulation of the sale of convict-made goods. Whitfield v. Ohio, 297 U.S. 431 (1936) (Hawes-Cooper Act); Kentucky Whip & Collar Co. v. Illinois Cent. R.R., 299 U.S. 334 (1937) (Ashurst-Sumners Act).

Federal prohibition of shipment out of, rather than into, a state, in implementation of the state's policy, is the device used for petroleum products. The Connally Act of 1935, 49 Stat. 30, 15 U.S.C. §715, prohibits the interstate transportation of "contraband oil," defined as oil produced or withdrawn from storage in excess of a state-fixed quota. See Griswold v. President of the U.S., 82 F.2d 922 (5th Cir. 1936).

Insurance is also the subject of cooperative legislation. After the decision in United States v. South-Eastern Underwriters Assn., 322 U.S. 533 (1944), Congress enacted the McCarran Act, 59 Stat. 33, 15 U.S.C. §1011-1015, which declared that the business of insurance shall be subject to the laws of the several states relating to the regulation or taxation of such business. South Carolina had imposed on foreign insurance companies a tax of 3 percent of the premiums received from business done in South Carolina; no similar tax was required of South Carolina corporations. After the McCarran Act, was the tax valid? Prudential Ins. Co. v. Benjamin, 328 U.S. 408 (1946). Would it have been valid prior to the McCarran Act? Was it necessary to consider whether that act did, or could, authorize state taxes discriminatory against interstate commerce? See Note, Congressional Consent to Discriminatory State Legislation, 45 Colum. L. Rev. 927 (1945).

A related form of cooperation is illustrated by the so-called Jenkins Act of Oct. 19, 1949, 63 Stat. 884, 15 U.S.C. Supp. §§375-377, requiring that those who ship cigarettes in interstate commerce to purchasers in states imposing a sales or use tax furnish invoices of such shipments to the respective state tax administrators. Consumer Mail Order Assn. of America v. McGrath, 94 F. Supp. 705 (D.D.C. 1950), aff'd per curiam, 340 U.S. 925 (1951).

In regulating the conduct of elections for federal offices after the Civil War, Congress made it a federal offense to violate state election laws. See Ex parte Siebold, 100 U.S. 371 (1879).

Contrast the judicial treatment of congressional efforts at cooperation in the maritime field. After it was held in Southern Pac. Co. v. Jensen, 244 U.S. 205 (1917), that state workmen's compensation laws could not be applied to maritime injuries, Congress enacted legislation to permit such laws to be applied. This legislation was held unconstitutional. Knickerbocker Ice Co. v. Stewart, 253 U.S. 149 (1920); Washington v. Dawson & Co., 264 U.S. 219 (1924). For a critical discussion see Morrison, Workmen's Compensation and the Maritime Law, 38 Yale L.J. 472 (1929). Thereafter Congress enacted the Longshoremen's and Harbor Workers' Act of 1927, which provided compensation "if recovery for the disability or death through workmen's compensation proceedings may not validly be provided by state law." 33 U.S.C. §§901 et seq. The statutory boundaries are thus coincident with the constitutional ones and are inevitably hazy; but the Court has somewhat alleviated the difficulties by recognizing a "twilight zone" in which, apparently, presumptive validity will attach to the taking of jurisdiction by either the state or the federal administrative authorities. Davis v. Department of Labor, 317 U.S. 249 (1942). Compare Moore's Case, 323 Mass. 162, 80 N.E. 2d 478 (1948), aff'd, 335 U.S. 874 (1948); Baskin v. Industrial Accident Commission, 89 Cal. App. 2d 632, 201 P. 2d 549 (1949), vacated and remanded, 338 U.S. 854 (1949).

3. The problem of criminal jurisdiction over offenses committed on lands under the exclusive or concurrent jurisdiction of the federal government has been resolved by the Assimilative Crimes Act, 18 U.S.C. §13. That act adopts the criminal law of the state in which the place is situated, in cases where no act of Congress makes the conduct punishable. Until 1948 the statute adopted only those state laws which were in force at the date of the federal statute, and the date was moved forward by periodic reenactments of the federal statute. The revision of 1948 deliberately omitted any specification of a date, and thus, according to the Reviser's Note, "will authorize the Federal courts to apply the same measuring stick to such offenses as is applied in the adjoining State and will make unnecessary periodic pro forma amendments of this section to keep abreast of changes of local laws." The statute was upheld in United States v. Sharpnack, 355 U.S. 286 (1958), Justices Douglas and Black dissenting. The opinion contains a résumé of federal laws "adopting" or dependent upon the provisions of state law.

Similar problems arise under state constitutions when a state legislature seeks to adopt existing or prospective federal legislation. Cf. Opinion of the Justices, 239 Mass. 606 (1921); Darwegar v. Staats, 267 N.Y. 290 (1935); Kauper, Validity of State Recovery Acts Adopting Federal Codes, 33 Mich. L. Rev. 597 (1935); Note, 34 Colum. L. Rev. 1077 (1934).

4. On the entire subject of cooperative legislation, see the symposium in 23 Iowa L. Rev. 455-650 (1938).

For comparable problems in Canada, see Ballem, Delegation by the Dominion Parliament to a Provincial Board, 30 Can. B. Rev. 1050 (1952).

Steward Machine Co. v. Davis *301 U.S. 548, 57 S. Ct. 883, 81 L. Ed. 1279 (1937)*

[For the opinion in this case see page 262 supra.]

NOTE Fiscal Cooperation

The problem of meeting the financial needs of a region with the resources available is a thorny one in most federations. A major cooperative device to meet the problem is the grant-in-aid, conditional or unconditional. See Williams, Grants-in-Aid Under Public Works Administration (1939); Key, The Administration of Federal Grants to States (1937); Maxwell, The Fiscal Impact of Federalism in the United States, c. 17 (1946); MacDonald, Federal Aid to the States: 1940 Model, 34 Am. Pol. Sci. Rev. 489 (1940); Foley, Recent Developments in Federal-Municipal Relationships, 86 U. Pa. L. Rev. 485 (1938); Duke Power Co. v. Greenwood County, 91 F. 2d 665 (4th Cir. 1937), aff'd on ground of lack of standing of complainants, 302 U.S. 485 (1938).

See generally Maxwell, Financing State and Local Governments (1965); Heller, New Dimensions of Political Economy, c. 3 (1966); Grodzins, The American System (1966).

The structure of a federal system may be profoundly affected by federal grants. Australia and Canada are cases in point. See Wheare, Federal Government 114-125 (3d ed. 1953).

In Australia, the Commonwealth levies a high income tax and offers grants to each state that refrains from imposing an income tax of its own. The arrangement, upheld in

South Australia v. Commonwealth, 65 C.L.R. 373 (1942), has produced a kind of collective bargaining between representatives of the states and of the Commonwealth for yearly allotments of federal funds. A little-used provision of the Australian Constitution (§ 51(xxxvii) authorizes any state or states to refer a matter otherwise within state power to the national legislature, whose action will then be effective within the assenting states. It has been suggested that the device of the conditional grant could provide leverage upon the states to induce them to utilize references more extensively. Anderson, Reference of Powers by the States to the Commonwealth. 2 Ann. L. Rev. 1 (1951). See also Bailey, Fifty Years of the Australian Constitution, 25 Austl. L.J. 314, 323-325 (1951). In addition to the arrangement for taxation and grants, Australia employs a collaborative device for governmental borrowing, whereby a Federal Loan Council, composed of representatives of the states and the national government, sets limits on the borrowing to be done on behalf of each by the Commonwealth, which has sole power to borrow. The arrangement was formalized by a constitutional amendment in 1929 (§ 105A). On the question of whether the spending power of the Commonwealth extends to purposes beyond the enumerated powers, see Victoria v. Commonwealth, 50 Austl. L.J. 157 (1976).

In Canada, various provinces (not including Ontario and Quebec) have entered into agreements with the Dominion whereby in return for federal grants they undertake not to levy specified taxes. See Dominion-Provincial Taxation Agreement Act, 1942, c. 13; Dominion-Provincial Tax Rental Agreements Act, 1947, c. 58; Buck, Financing Canadian Government, cc. 9-10 (1949); Eggleston, The Road to Nationhood (1946); Scott, Centralization and Decentralization in Canadian Federalism, 29 Can. B. Rev. 1095, 1120 (1951).

See also Brown, Some Aspects of Federal-State Financial Relations (Australia), in Federalism: An Australian Jubilee Study 49 (Sawer ed. 1952); Mackintosh, Federal Finance (Canada), id. at 80.

West Virginia v. Sims 341 U.S. 22, 71 S. Ct. 557, 95 L. Ed. 713 (1951)

MR. JUSTICE FRANKFURTER delivered the opinion of the Court.

After extended negotiations eight States entered into a Compact to control pollution in the Ohio River system. See Ohio River Valley Water Sanitation Compact, 54 Stat. 752, ch. 581, 33 U.S.C. § 567a, note. Illinois, Indiana, Kentucky, New York, Ohio, Pennsylvania, Virginia and West Virginia recognized that they were faced with one of the problems of government that are defined by natural rather than political boundaries. Accordingly, they pledged themselves to cooperate in maintaining waters in the Ohio River basin in a sanitary condition through the administrative mechanism of the Ohio River Valley Water Sanitation Commission, consisting of three members from each State and three representing the United States.

The heart of the Compact is Article VI. This provides that sewage discharged into boundary streams or streams flowing from one State into another "shall be so treated, within a time reasonable for the construction of the necessary works, as to provide for substantially complete removal of settleable solids, and the removal of not less than forty-five per cent (45%) of the total suspended solids; provided that, in order to protect the public health or to preserve the waters for other legitimate purposes, . . . in specific instances such higher degree of treatment shall be used as may be determined to be necessary by the Commission after investigation, due notice and hearing." Industrial wastes are to be treated "to such degree as may be determined to be necessary by the Commission after investigation, due notice and hearing." . . .

Article IX provides that the Commission may, after notice and hearing, issue orders for compliance enforceable in the State and federal courts. It further provides: "No such order shall go into effect unless and until it receives the assent of at least a majority of the commissioners from each of not less than a majority of the signatory States; and no such order upon a municipality, corporation, person or entity in any State shall go into effect unless and until it receives the assent of not less than a majority of the Commissioners from such State."

By Article X the States also agree "to appropriate for the salaries, office and other administrative expenses, their proper proportion of the annual budget as determined by the Commission and approved by the Governors of the signatory States. . . ."

The present controversy arose because of conflicting views between officials of West Virginia regarding the responsibility of West Virginia under the Compact.

The Legislature of that State ratified and approved the Compact on March 11, 1939. W. Va. Acts 1939, ch. 38. Congress gave its consent on July 11, 1940, 54 Stat. 752, ch. 581, and upon adoption by all the signatory States the Compact was formally executed by the Governor of West Virginia on June 30, 1948. At its 1949 session the West Virginia Legislature appropriated $12,250 as the State's contribution to the expenses of the Commission for the fiscal year beginning July 1, 1949. W. Va. Acts 1949, ch. 9, Item 93. Respondent Sims, the auditor of the State, refused to issue a warrant upon its treasury for payment of this appropriation. To compel him to issue it, the West Virginia Commissioners to the Compact Commission and the members of the West Virginia State Water Commission instituted this original mandamus proceeding in the Supreme Court of Appeals of West Virginia. The court denied relief on the merits, 134 W. Va. 278, 58 S.E.2d 766, and we brought the case here, 340 U.S. 807, because questions of obviously important public interest are raised.

The West Virginia court found that the "sole question" before it was the validity of the Act of 1939 approving West Virginia's adherence to the Compact. It found that Act invalid in that (1) the Compact was deemed to delegate West Virginia's police power to other States and to the Federal Government, and (2) it was deemed to bind future legislatures to make appropriations for the continued activities of the Sanitation Commission and thus to violate Art. 10, §4 of the West Virginia Constitution.

Briefs filed on behalf of the United States and other States, as amici, invite the Court to consider far reaching issues relating to the Compact Clause of the United States Constitution. Art. I, §10, cl. 3. The United States urges that the Compact be so read as to allow any signatory State to withdraw from its obligations at any time. Pennsylvania, Ohio, Indiana, Illinois, Kentucky and New York contend that the Compact Clause precludes any State from limiting its power to enter into a compact to which Congress has consented. We must not be tempted by these inviting vistas. We need not go beyond the issues on which the West Virginia court found the Compact not binding on that State. That these are issues which give this Court jurisdiction to review the State court proceeding, 28 U.S.C. §1257, needs no discussion after Delaware River Joint Toll Bridge Comm'n. v. Colburn, 310 U.S. 419, 427.

Control of pollution in interstate streams might, on occasion, be an appropriate subject for national legislation. Compare Oklahoma ex rel. Phillips v. Guy F. Atkinson Co., 313 U.S. 508. But, with prescience, the Framers left the States free to settle regional controversies in diverse ways. Solution of the problem underlying this case may be attempted directly by the affected States through contentious litigation before this Court. Missouri v. Illinois, 180 U.S. 208, 200 U.S. 496; New York v. New Jersey, 256 U.S. 296. Adjudication here of conflicting State interests affecting stream pollution does not rest upon the law of a particular State. This Court decides such controversies according to "principles it must have power to declare." Missouri v. Illinois, supra (200 U.S. at 519). But the delicacy of interstate relationships and the inherent limitations upon this Court's ability to deal with multifarious local problems have naturally led to exacting standards of judicial intervention and have inhibited the formulation of a code for dealing with such controversies. As Mr. Justice Holmes put it: "Before this court ought to intervene the case should be of serious magnitude, clearly and fully proved, and the principle to be applied should be one which the court is prepared deliberately to maintain against all considerations on the other side." Missouri v. Illinois, supra (200 U.S. at 521).

Indeed, so awkward and unsatisfactory is the available litigious solution for these problems that this Court deemed it appropriate to emphasize the practical constitutional alternative provided by the Compact Clause. Experience led us to suggest that a problem such as that involved here is "more likely to be wisely solved by cooperative study and by conference and mutual concession on the part of representatives of the States so vitally interested in it than by proceedings in any court however constituted." New York v. New Jersey, supra (256 U.S. at 313). The suggestion has had fruitful response.

The growing interdependence of regional interests, calling for regional adjustments, has brought extensive use of compacts. A compact is more than a supple device for dealing with interests confined within a region. That it is also a means of safeguarding the national interest is well illustrated in the Compact now under review. Not only was congressional consent required, as for all compacts; direct participation by the Federal Government was provided in the President's appointment of three members of the Compact Commission. Art. IV; Art. XI, §3.

But a compact is after all a legal document. Though the circumstances of its drafting are likely to assure great care and deliberation, all avoidance of disputes as to scope and meaning is not within human gift. Just as this Court has power to settle disputes between States where there is no compact, it must have final power to pass upon the meaning and validity of compacts. It requires no elaborate argument to reject the suggestion that an agreement solemnly entered into between States by those who alone have political authority to speak for a State can be unilaterally nullified, or given final meaning by an organ of one of the contracting States. A State cannot be its own ultimate judge in a controversy with a sister State. To determine the nature and scope of obligations as between States, whether they arise through the legislative means of compact or the "federal common law" governing interstate controversies (Hinderlider v. La Plata River & C. Creek Ditch Co., 304 U.S. 92, 110), is the function and duty of the Supreme Court of the Nation. Of course every deference will be shown to what the highest court of a State deems to be the law and policy of its State, particularly when recondite or unique features of local law are urged. Deference is one thing; submission to a State's own determination of whether it has undertaken an obligation, what that obligation is, and whether it conflicts with a disability of the State to undertake it is quite another.

The Supreme Court of Appeals of the State of West Virginia is, for exclusively State purposes, the ultimate tribunal in construing the meaning of her Constitution. Two prior decisions of this Court make clear, however, that we are free to examine determinations of law by State courts in the limited field where a compact brings in issue the rights of other States and the United States.

Kentucky v. Indiana, 281 U.S. 163, dealt with a compact to build a bridge across the Ohio River. In an original action brought before this Court, Indiana defended on the ground that she should not be compelled to perform until the Indiana courts decided, in a pending case, whether her officials had been authorized to enter into the compact. Mr. Chief Justice Hughes, speaking for a unanimous Court, dismissed the argument: "Where the States themselves are before this Court for the determination of a controversy between them, neither can determine their rights inter sese, and this Court must pass upon every question essential to such a determination, although local legislation and questions of state authorization may be involved. Virginia v. West Virginia, 11 Wall. 39, 56; 220 U.S. 1, 28. A decision in the present instance by the state court would not determine the controversy here." 281 U.S. at 176, 177.

In reaching this conclusion the Chief Justice could hardly avoid analogizing the situation to that where a question is raised whether a State has impaired the obligation of a contract. "It has frequently been held that when a question is suitably raised whether the law of a State has impaired the obligation of a contract, in violation of the constitutional provision, this Court must determine for itself whether a contract exists, what are its obligations, and whether they have been impaired by the legislation of the State. While this Court always examines with appropriate respect the decisions of state courts bearing upon such questions, such decisions do not detract from the responsibility of this Court in reaching its own conclusions as to the contract, its obligations and impairment, for otherwise the constitutional guaranty could not properly be enforced. Larson v. South Dakota, 278 U.S. 429, 433, and cases there cited." 281 U.S. at 176. And see Indiana ex rel. Anderson v. Brand, 303 U.S. 95, 100.

Hinderlider v. La Plata River & C. Creek Ditch Co., 304 U.S. 92, is the second of these cases. It also makes clear, if authority be needed, that the fact the compact questions reach us on a writ of certiorari rather than by way of an original action brought by a State does not affect the power of this Court. In the Hinderlider Case, an action was brought in the Colorado courts to enjoin performance of a compact between Colorado and New Mexico concerning water rights in the La Plata River. The State court held that the compact was invalid because it affected appropriation rights guaranteed by the Colorado State Constitution. 101 Colo. 73; see also 93 Colo. 128. Mr. Justice Brandeis, likewise speaking for a unanimous Court, held that the relative claims of New Mexico and Colorado citizens could be determined by compact and reversed the decision of the State court.

The issue in the Hinderlider Case was whether the Colorado legislature had authority, under the State constitution, to enter into a compact which affected the water rights of her citizens. The issue before us is whether the West Virginia legislature had authority, under her constitution, to enter into a compact which involves delegation of power to an interstate agency and an agreement to appropriate funds for the administrative expenses of the agency.

That a legislature may delegate to an administrative body the power to make rules and decide particular cases is one of the axioms of modern government. The West Virginia court does not challenge the general proposition but objects to the delegation here involved because it is to a body outside the State and because its legislature may not be free, at any time, to withdraw the power delegated. We are not here concerned, and so need not deal, with specific language in a State constitution requiring that the State settle its problems with other States without delegating power to an interstate agency. What is involved is the conventional grant of legislative power. We find nothing in that to indicate that West Virginia may not solve a problem such as the control of river pollution by compact and by the delegation, if such it be, necessary to effectuate such solution by compact. If this Court, in the exercise of its original jurisdiction, were to enter a decree requiring West Virginia to abate pollution of interstate streams, that decree would bind the State. The West Virginia Legislature would have no part in determining the State's obligation. The State Legislature could not alter it; it could not disregard it, as West Virginia on another occasion so creditably recognized.[a] The obligation would be fixed by this Court on the basis of a master's report. Here, the State has bound itself to control pollution by the more effective means of an agreement with other States. The Compact involves a reasonable and carefully limited delegation of power to an interstate agency. Nothing in its Constitution suggests that, in dealing with the problem dealt with by the Compact, West Virginia must wait for the answer to be dictated by this Court after harassing and unsatisfactory litigation. . . .

The State court also held that the Compact is in conflict with Art. 10, §4, of the State Constitution and for that reason is not binding on West Virginia. This section provides:

"No debt shall be contracted by this State, except to meet casual deficits in the revenue, to redeem a previous liability of the State, to suppress insurrection, repel invasion or defend the State in time of war; but the payment of any liability other than that for the or-

---

[a] Virginia v. West Virginia, 246 U.S. 565 (1918). See Powell, Coercing a State to Pay a Judgment: Virginia v. West Virginia, 17 Mich. L. Rev. 1 (1918). — Ed.

dinary expenses of the State, shall be equally distributed over a period of at least twenty years."

The Compact was evidently drawn with great care to meet the problem of debt limitation in light of this section and similar restrictive provisions in the constitutions of other States. Although, under Art. X of the Compact, the States agree to appropriate funds for administrative expenses the annual budget must be approved by the Governors of the signatory States. In addition, Article V provides: "The Commission shall not incur any obligations of any kind prior to the making of appropriations adequate to meet the same; nor shall the Commission pledge the credit of any of the signatory States, except by and with the authority of the legislature thereof." In view of these provisions, we conclude that the obligation of the State under the Compact is not in conflict with Art. 10, §4 of the State constitution.

Reversed and remanded.

MR. JUSTICE BLACK concurs in the result.

MR. JUSTICE REED, concurring.

I concur in the judgment of the court but disagree with the assertion of power by this Court to interpret the meaning of the West Virginia Constitution. This Court must accept the State court's interpretation of its own Constitution unless it is prepared to say that the interpretation is a palpable evasion to avoid a federal rule.

There is no problem concerning the binding effect upon this Court of state court interpretation of state law under the Compact Clause such as there is under the clause against impairing the Obligation of Contracts. Under the latter clause, this Court, in order to determine whether the subsequent state law, constitutional or statutory, impairs the federal prohibition against impairment of contracts, has asserted power to construe for itself the disputed agreement, to decide whether it is a contract, and to interpret the subsequent state statute to decide whether it impairs that contract. Even then we accept state court conclusions unless "manifestly wrong." . . .

Under the Compact Clause, however, the federal questions are the execution, validity and meaning of federally approved state compacts. The interpretation of the meaning of the compact controls over a state's application of its own law through the Supremacy Clause and not by any implied federal power to construe state law. . . .

MR. JUSTICE JACKSON, concurring. . . .

Estoppel is not often to be invoked against a government. But West Virginia assumed a contractual obligation with equals by permission of another government that is sovereign in the field. After Congress and sister States had been induced to alter their positions and bind themselves to terms of a covenant, West Virginia should be estopped from repudiating her act. For this reason, I consider that whatever interpretation she may put on the generalities of her Constitution, she is bound by the Compact, and on that basis I concur in the judgment.

NOTE Cooperation in Adjudication

On the history and utility of interstate compacts, see Frankfurter and Landis, The Compact Clause of the Constitution, 34 Yale L.J. 691 (1925); Zimmerman and Wendell, The Interstate Compact Since 1925 (1951); Thursby, Interstate Cooperation: A Study of the Interstate Compact (1953). See also Smith, The Proposed Development Authority Compact for New England, 66 Pol. Sci. Q. 37 (1951). On the West Virginia case, see Abel, Ohio Valley Panorama, 54 W. Va. L.Q. 186 (1952).

On the role of Congress, see Note, Congress and the Port of New York Authority, 70 Yale L.J. 812 (1961); United States v. Tobin, 195 F. Supp. 588 (D.C. Cir. 1961), rev'd, 306 F.2d 750 (D.C. Cir. 1962), cert. denied, 371 U.S. 902 (1962).

What are the practical differences, if any, between compacts and reciprocal state legislation?

Many statutes sponsored by the Commissioners on Uniform State Laws are directed to cooperation among the states. See, e.g., Act to Secure the Attendance of Witnesses from Without a State in Criminal Proceedings, 9 U.L.A. 37; Criminal Extradition Act, id. 169; Divorce Recognition Act, id. 364; Enforcement of Foreign Judgments Act, id. 376; Foreign Depositions Act, 9A U.L.A. 39; Interstate Arbitration of Death Taxes Act, id. 163; Interstate Compromise of Death Taxes Act, id. 172; Proof of Statutes Act, id. 245; Reciprocal Transfer Tax Act, id. 258; Transfer of Dependents Act, id. 270; Unauthorized Insurers Act, id. 347.

The Criminal Extradition Act, supra, provides for surrender of accused persons even though they were not in the demanding state at the time of the commission of the crime and have not fled therefrom. Is this provision constitutional? See People ex rel. Faulds v. Herberich, 93 N.Y.S.2d 272 (1949), 276 App. Div. 852 (1949), aff'd, 301 N.Y. 614 (1950); English v. Matowitz, 148 Ohio St. 39 (1947).

The Act to Secure the Attendance of Witnesses, supra, was sustained in New York v. O'Neill, 359 U.S. 1 (1959), Justices Douglas and Black dissenting. The dissent relied on a "right to free ingress and egress" as a privilege of national citizenship.

Testa v. Katt 330 U.S. 386, 67 S. Ct. 810, 91 L. Ed. 967 (1947)

MR. JUSTICE BLACK delivered the opinion of the Court.

Section 205(e) of the Emergency Price Control Act provides that a buyer of goods above the prescribed ceiling price may sue the seller "in any court of competent jurisdiction" for not more than three times the amount of the overcharge plus costs and a reasonable attorney's fee. Section 205(c) provides that federal district courts shall have jurisdiction of such suits "concurrently with State and Territorial courts." Such a suit under §205(e) must be brought "in the district or county in which the defendant resides or has a place of business. . . ."

The respondent was in the automobile business in Providence, Providence County, Rhode Island. In 1944 he sold an automobile to petitioner Testa, who also resides in Providence, for $1100, $210 above the ceiling price. The petitioner later filed this suit against respondent in the State District Court in Providence. Recovery was sought under §205(e). The court awarded a judgment of treble damages and costs to petitioner. On appeal to the State Superior Court, where the trial was de novo, the petitioner was again awarded judgment, but only for the amount of the overcharge plus attorney's fees. Pending appeal from this judgment, the Price Administrator was allowed to intervene. On appeal, the State Supreme Court reversed, 71 R.I. 472, 47 A.2d 312. It interpreted §205(e) to be "a penal statute in the international sense." It held that an action for violation of §205(e) could not be maintained in the courts of that State. The State Supreme Court rested its holding on its earlier decision in Robinson v. Norato, 71 R.I. 256 (1945) in which it had reasoned that: A state need not enforce the penal laws of a government which is foreign in the international sense; §205(e) is treated by Rhode Island as penal in that sense; the United States is "foreign" to the State in the "private international" as distinguished from "public international" sense; hence Rhode Island courts, though their jurisdiction is adequate to enforce similar Rhode Island "penal" statutes, need not enforce §205(e). Whether state courts may decline to enforce federal laws on these grounds is a question of great importance. For this reason, and because the Rhode Island Supreme Court's holding was alleged to conflict with this Court's previous holding in Second Employers' Liability Cases (Mondou v. New York, N.H. & H.R. Co.) 223 U.S. 1, we granted certiorari. 329 U.S. 703.

For the purposes of this case, we assume, without deciding, that §205(e) is a penal statute in the "public international," "private international," or any other sense. So far as the question of whether the Rhode Island courts properly declined to try this action, it makes no difference into which of these categories the Rhode Island court chose to place the statute which Congress has passed. For we cannot accept the basic premise on which the Rhode Island Supreme Court held that it has no more obligation to enforce a valid penal law of the United States than it has to enforce a penal law of another state or a foreign country. Such a broad assumption flies in the face of the fact that the States of the Union constitute a nation. It disregards the purpose and effect of Article VI of the Constitution which provides: "This Constitution, and the Laws of the United States which shall be made in Pursuance thereof; and all Treaties made, or which shall be made, under the authority of the United States, shall be the supreme Law of the Land; and the Judges in every State shall be bound thereby, any Thing in the Constitution or Laws of any State to the Contrary notwithstanding."

It cannot be assumed, the supremacy clause considered, that the responsibilities of a state to enforce the laws of a sister state are identical with its responsibilities to enforce federal laws. Such an assumption represents an erroneous evaluation of the statutes of Congress and the prior decisions of this Court in their historic setting. Those decisions establish that state courts do not bear the same relation to the United States that they do to foreign countries. The first Congress that convened after the Constitution was adopted conferred jurisdiction upon the state courts to enforce important federal civil laws,[4] and succeeding Congresses conferred on the states jurisdiction over federal crimes and actions for penalties and forfeitures.[5]

Enforcement of federal laws by state courts did not go unchallenged. Violent public controversies existed throughout the first part of the Nineteenth Century until the 1860's concerning the extent of the constitutional supremacy of the Federal Government. During that period there were instances in which this Court and state courts broadly questioned the power and duty of state courts to exercise their jurisdiction to enforce United States civil and penal statutes or the power of the Federal Government to require them to do so. But after the fundamental issues over the extent of federal supremacy had been resolved by war, this Court took occasion in 1876 to review the phase of the controversy concerning the relationship of state courts to the Federal Government. Claflin v. Houseman, 93 U.S. 130. The opinion of a unanimous court in that case was strongly buttressed by historic references and persuasive reasoning. It repudiated the assumption that federal laws can be considered by the states as though they were laws emanating from a foreign sovereign. Its teaching is that the Constitution and the laws passed pursuant to it are the supreme laws of the land, binding alike upon states, courts, and the people, "anything in the Constitution or Laws of any State to the contrary notwithstanding." It asserted that the obligation of states to enforce these federal laws is not lessened by reason of the form in which they are cast or the remedy which they provide. And the Court stated that "if an act of Congress gives a penalty to a party aggrieved, without specifying a remedy for its enforcement, there is no reason why it should not be enforced, if not provided otherwise by some act of Congress, by a proper action in a state court." Id. 93 U.S. at 137. And see United States v. Bank of New York & T. Co., 296 U.S. 463, 479.

The Claflin opinion thus answered most of the arguments theretofore advanced against the power and duty of state courts to enforce federal penal laws. And since that decision, the remaining areas of doubt have been steadily narrowed. There have been statements in cases concerned with the obligation of states to give full faith and credit to the proceedings of sister states which suggested a theory contrary to that pronounced in the Claflin opin-

---

[4] Judiciary Act of 1789, 1 Stat. 73, 77, c. 20 (suits by aliens for torts committed in violation of federal laws and treaties; suits by the United States).

[5] 1 Stat. 376, 378, c. 48 (June 5, 1794) (fines, forfeitures and penalties for violation of the License Tax on Wines and Spirits); 1 Stat. 373, 375, c. 45 (June 5, 1794) (the Carriage Tax Act); 1 Stat. 452, c. 13 (penalty for purchasing guns from Indians); 1 Stat. 733, 740, c. 43 (March 2, 1799) (criminal and civil actions for violation of the postal laws). See Warren, Federal Criminal Laws and the State Courts, 38 Harv. L. Rev. 545; Barnett, The Delegation of Federal Jurisdiction to State Courts, 3 Selected Essays on Constitutional Law 1202 (1938).

ion. But when in Second Employers' Liability Cases (Mondou v. New York, N.H. & H.R. Co.) 223 U.S. 1, this Court was presented with a case testing the power and duty of states to enforce federal laws, it found the solution in the broad principles announced in the Claflin opinion. . . .

So here, the fact that Rhode Island has an established policy against enforcement by its courts of statutes of other states and the United States which it deems penal, cannot be accepted as a "valid excuse." Cf. Douglas v. New York, N.H. & H.R. Co., 279 U.S. 377, 388. For the policy of the federal Act is the prevailing policy in every state. . . .

The Rhode Island court in its Robinson decision on which it relies, cites cases of this Court which have held that states are not required by the full faith and credit clause of the Constitution to enforce judgments of the courts of other states based on claims arising out of penal statutes. But those holdings have no relevance here, for this case raises no full faith and credit question. Nor need we consider in this case prior decisions to the effect that federal courts are not required to enforce state penal laws. Compare Wisconsin v. Pelican Ins. Co., 127 U.S. 265, with Massachusetts v. Missouri, 308 U.S. 1, 20. For whatever consideration they may be entitled to in the field in which they are relevant, those decisions did not bring before us our instant problem of the effect of the supremacy clause on the relation of federal laws to state courts. Our question concerns only the right of a state to deny enforcement to claims growing out of a valid federal law.

It is conceded that this same type of claim arising under Rhode Island law would be enforced by that State's courts. Its courts have enforced claims for double damages growing out of the Fair Labor Standards Act. Thus the Rhode Island courts have jurisdiction adequate and appropriate under established local law to adjudicate this action. Under these circumstances the state courts are not free to refuse enforcement of petitioners' claim. See McKnett v. St. Louis & S.F.R. Co., 292 U.S. 230; and compare Herb v. Pitcairn, 324 U.S. 117; 323 U.S. 77. The case is reversed and the cause is remanded for proceedings not inconsistent with this opinion.

Reversed.

NOTE

1. Compare the refusal of a state to entertain actions for wrongful death under the law of another state, held invalid under the full faith and credit clause in Hughes v. Fetter, 341 U.S. 609 (1951). Is the result different where the forum would take the case if service of process could not be had on the defendant in the state where the injury occurred? First Natl. Bank v. United Air Lines, 342 U.S. 396 (1952).

On the potentialities of the full faith and credit clause, see Mr. Justice Jackson's address, Full Faith and Credit: The Lawyer's Clause of the Constitution, 45 Colum. L. Rev. 1 (1946), cited supra page 456; cf. Freund, Chief Justice Stone and the Conflict of Laws, 59 Harv. L. Rev. 1210, 1225-1236 (1946). The subject is dealt with at length in Conflict of Laws. Here it may be useful to distinguish three sets of problems for which the clause may be employed as an instrument for a more effective federal system: (a) recognition of sister-state judgments; (b) access to courts on out-of-state causes of action; (c) compulsory effect to the statutes of a sister state. Should these constitutional problems be approached differently, and if so why?

2. Could the federal government require state officers to assist in enforcing federal laws? Cf. Prigg v. Pennsylvania, 16 Pet. 539 (1842) (Fugitive Slave Law); Kentucky v. Dennison, 24 How. 66 (1860) (interstate rendition); see Holcombe, The States as Agents of the Nation, 1 Sw. Pol. Sci. Q. 307 (1921), reprinted in 3 Selected Essays on Constitutional Law 1187 (1938); Field, States Versus Nation and the Supreme Court, 28 Am. Pol. Sci. Rev. 241 (1934). For the problem in the environmental field, see pp. 299-300 supra.

3. May a state criminal case ever be removed to a federal court? Congress has provided for such removal in certain prosecutions of federal officials; the procedure was upheld in Tennessee v. Davis, 100 U.S. 257 (1879). See also Maryland v. Soper, 270 U.S. 9, 36 (1926). The present provision for removal by federal officers is 28 U.S.C. §1442(a).

Under 28 U.S.C. §1443, criminal or civil action may be removed where brought against "any person who is denied or cannot enforce in the courts of such State a right under any law providing for the equal civil rights of citizens of the United States. . . ." For a construction of the section, see Georgia v. Rachel, 384 U.S. 780 (1966); cf. Greenwood v. Peacock, 384 U.S. 808 (1966).

Habeas corpus in a federal court is made available to one in custody for an act done in pursuance of a law of the United States, or of an order of a federal court or judge. 28 U.S.C. §2241(c)(2). What are the practical differences between the remedies of removal and habeas corpus in this situation?

In re Neagle, 135 U.S. 1 (1890), applied the habeas corpus provision at the instance of Mr. Justice Field's official bodyguard, who in the line of duty fatally shot Judge Terry of California and was held by the state authorities for murder. The melodramatic background of the Field-Terry feud is given in Swisher, Stephen J. Field, c. 13 (1930).

4. Cooperation on the administrative level may take many forms, including informal advice, joint boards, and employment of common personnel. See the full discussion in Clark, The New Federalism (1938); also, Kauper, Utilization of State Commissioners in the Administration of the Federal Motor Carrier Act, 34 Mich. L. Rev. 58 (1935); Lindahl, Cooperation Between the Interstate Commerce Commission and the State Commissions in Railroad Regulation, 33 id. 338 (1935). For an example of voluntary assistance, see Federal Power Commission v. Hope Natural Gas Co., 320 U.S. 591, 618 (1944), where the FPC made findings regarding the lawfulness of past rates which the company had charged its interstate customers. These findings were made on the complaint of the city of Cleveland, in aid of state regulation, even though the FPC has no power to make reparation orders.

Radio Station WOW v. Johnson 326 U.S. 120, 65 S. Ct. 1475, 89 L. Ed. 2092 (1945)

MR. JUSTICE FRANKFURTER delivered the opinion of the Court:

This case concerns the relation of the Federal Communications Act, 48 Stat. 1064, c. 651, 47 U.S.C. §§151 et seq., to the power of a State to adjudicate conflicting claims to the property used by a licensed radio station. At the outset, however, our right to review the decision below is seriously challenged.

The facts relevant to the jurisdictional problem as well as to the main issues are these, summarized as briefly as accuracy permits. Petitioner, Woodmen of the World Life Insurance Society, a fraternal benefit association of Nebraska, owns radio station WOW. The Society leased this station for fifteen years to petitioner, Radio Station WOW, Inc., a Nebraska corporation formed to operate the station as lessee. After the Society and the lessee had jointly applied to the Federal Communications Commission for consent to transfer the station license, Johnson, the respondent, a member of the Society, filed this suit to have the lease and the assignment of the license set aside for fraud. While this suit was pending, the Federal Communications Commission consented to assignment of the license, and the Society transferred both the station properties and the license to the lessee. Thereafter the Society answered that "the Federal Communications Commission . . . has and concedes that it has no jurisdiction over the subject matter of plaintiff's action, except jurisdiction to determine the transfer of the license to operate said radio station, which jurisdiction after full and complete showing and notwithstanding objections filed thereto, was exercised in the approval of the transfer of said license to the defendant

Radio Station WOW, Inc. and further order to the Society to execute and perform the provisions of said lease by virtue of which the possession of said lease property has now been delivered to the lessee, all as more particularly herein found." Respondent's reply admitted "that the Federal Communications Commission has and concedes that it has no jurisdiction over the subject matter of plaintiff's action except jurisdiction to determine the transfer of the license to operate said radio station." The trial court found no fraud and dismissed the suit.

The Supreme Court of Nebraska, three Judges dissenting, reversed and entered judgment for respondent, directing that the lease and license be set aside and that the original position of the parties be restored as nearly as possible. 144 Neb. 406. The judgment further ordered that an accounting be had of the operation of the station by the lessee since it came into its possession and that the income less operating expenses be returned to the Society. On motions for rehearing, the petitioners asserted that only the Federal Communications Commission and the Federal courts had jurisdiction over the subject matter, not the Nebraska courts. These motions were denied in an opinion in which the Nebraska Supreme Court stated, "We conclude at the outset that the power to license a radio station, or to transfer, assign or annul such a license, is within the exclusive jurisdiction of the Federal Communcations Commission. . . . The effect of our former opinion was to vacate the lease of the radio station and to order a return of the property to its former status, the question of the Federal license being a question solely for the Federal Communications Commission. Our former opinion should be so construed." The claim that the Nebraska courts had no jurisdiction over the subject matter of the action was thus dealt with: "The fact that the property involved was used in a licensed business was an incident to the suit only. The answer of the defendants, heretofore quoted, squarely contradicts the position they now endeavor to assume. Their position is unsound on its merits and, in addition thereto, it was eliminated from the case by the pleadings they filed in their own behalf." 144 Neb. 432. Because of the importance of the contention that the State court's decision had invaded the domain of the Federal Communications Commission, we granted certiorari.

. . . The court below decreed the transfer of property used as a radio station. It conceded that it had no jurisdiction over the transfer of the license under which WOW was operating. That is a matter which Congress has put in the keeping of the Federal Communications Commission. Petitioners claim that the court's decree in effect involves an exercise of the very authority which the court disavowed. This presents a Federal question which was duly made below, and we must consider it.

But it is not open to us to consider independently the claim that the Federal Communications Act has withdrawn from the State court jurisdiction over the physical properties of the station and given it to the Federal Communications Commission. The Society's answer admitted that this controversy was outside the jurisdiction of the Commission except as it related to the transfer of the license, and respondent joined in this view. Only after the Nebraska Supreme Court's original opinion did petitioners, by motions to dismiss the suit and for rehearing, claim that the Nebraska courts were wholly without jurisdiction over the controversy. In its opinion on rehearing the Nebraska Supreme Court rejected this claim as "contrary to the pleadings filed" in the trial court, and also denied it on its merits. "The answer of the defendants, heretofore quoted," that court wrote, "squarely contradicts the position they now endeavor to assume. Their position is unsound on its merits and, in addition thereto, it was eliminated from the case by the pleadings they filed in their own behalf." Questions first presented to the highest State court on a petition for rehearing come too late for consideration here, unless the State Court exerted its jurisdiction in such a way that the case could have been brought here had the questions been raised prior to the original disposition. [Citations omitted.] Here the Nebraska Supreme Court held that the Federal question had dropped out as a matter of pleading and also denied its merits.

This brings the situation clearly within the settled rule whereby this Court will not review a State court decision resting on an adequate and independent non-Federal ground even though the State court may have also summoned to its support an erroneous view of Federal law. . . .

The Federal question that remains is whether, although the Nebraska court clearly recognized that the power to vacate a license and to authorize its transfer lies exclusively with the Federal Communications Commission, its decree in effect is inconsistent with such recognition. This is urged on two grounds. It is asserted that the Nebraska Supreme Court, by ordering the transfer of the licensed facilities from Radio Station WOW, Inc. to the Society although not having power to direct the transfer of the license, severed the licensed facilities from the license and therefore nullified the license. Secondly, it is urged that by ordering the parties "to do all things necessary" to secure a return of the license to the defrauded Society, the State court invaded the Commission's function.

The judgment, following the original opinion, ordered that "the transfer of the license to operate the station be vacated and set aside." On rehearing, the court made it quite plain that it was within the exclusive jurisdiction of the Communications Commission to vacate radio licenses and declared that its former opinion should be so construed. While it did not formally modify its judgment, it is reasonable to assume that the view which it unambiguously rejected in its opinion it did not mean to assert through its judgment. . . .

In any event, we think the court went outside its bounds when it ordered the parties "to do all things necessary" to secure a return of the license. Plainly that requires the Society to ask the Commission for a retransfer of the license to it and requires WOW not to oppose such transfer. The United States, in a brief field at our request, suggests that this provision of the decree would probably also disqualify WOW from "applying for a new license to operate a radio station in Omaha on the same frequency, should it become equipped to do so." To be sure, the Communications Commission's power of granting, revoking and transferring licenses involves proper application of those criteria that determine "public convenience, interest, or necessity." Section 307(a), 48 Stat. 1064, 1083, c. 651, 47 U.S.C. §307(a). But insofar as the Nebraska decree orders the parties "to do all things necessary" to secure the return of the license, it hampers the freedom of the Society not to continue in broadcasting and to restrict itself, as it properly may, to its insurance business. Equally does it prevent WOW from opposing a return to the Society, or, as the United States suggests, from seeking another license of its own. These are restrictions not merely upon the private rights of parties as to whom a State court may make appropriate findings of fraud. They are restrictions upon the licensing system which Congress established. It disregards practicalities to deny that, by controlling the conduct of parties before the Communications Commission, the court below reached beyond the immediate controversy and into matters that do not belong to it.

The most troublesome question raised by this case remains. While the decree of the State court concerning the transfer of the leasehold is, in view of the pleadings, not here as an independent question, due consideration of the Federal question relating to the transfer of the license makes it proper to consider the bearing of a decree ordering an immediate transfer of the leasehold upon the status of the radio license. A proper regard for the implications of the policy that permeates the Communications Act makes disposition of licensed facilities prior to action by the Communications Commission a subsidary issue to the license question. We have no doubt of the power of the Nebraska court to adjudicate, and conclusively, the claim of fraud in the transfer of the station by the Society to WOW and upon finding fraud to direct a reconveyance of the lease to the Society. And this, even though the property consists of licensed facilities and the Society chooses not to apply for retransfer of the radio license to it, or the Commission, upon such application, refuses the retransfer. The result may well be the termination of a broadcasting station. The Communications Act does not explicitly deal with this problem, and we find nothing in its interstices that dislodges the power of the States to deal with fraud merely because licensed facilities are involved. The "public interest" with which the Commission is charged is that involved in granting licenses. Safeguarding of that interest can hardly imply that the interest of States in enforcing their laws against fraud have been nullified insofar as licensed facilities may be the instruments of fraud.

On the other hand, if the State's power over fraud can be effectively respected while at the same time reasonable opportunity is afforded for the protection of that public interest which led to the granting of a license, the principle of fair accommodation between State and Federal authority, where the powers of the two intersect, should be observed. Severance of the licensed facilities from the license so precipitously that the Federal Communications Commission is deprived of the opportunity of enabling the two to be kept together needlessly disables the Commission from protecting the public interest committed to its charge. This presents a practical and not a hypothetical situation. To carry out abruptly a State decree separating licensed facilities from the license deprives the public of those advantages of broadcasting which presumably led the Commission to grant a license. To be sure, such a license is merely a permit to serve the public and not a duty to do so. Therefore, as we have concluded, the State has not been deprived by Federal legislation of the practical power to terminate the broadcasting service by a proper adjudication separating the physical property from the license. We think that State power is amply respected if it is qualified merely to the extent of requiring it to withhold execution of that portion of its decree requiring retransfer of the physical properties until steps are ordered to be taken, with all deliberate speed, to enable the Commission to deal with new applications in connection with the station. Of course, the question of fraud adjudicated by the State court will no longer be open insofar as it bears upon the reliability as licensee of any of the parties.

New situations call for new adaptation of judicial remedies. We have had occasion to limit the conceded jurisdiction of the Federal courts in order to give State courts opportunity to pass authoritatively on State issues involved in Federal litigation. See, e.g., Spector Motor Service v. McLaughlin, 323 U.S. 101. It will give full play both to the powers that belong to the States and to those that are entrusted to the Federal Communications Commission, where the two are intertwined as they are here, to enforce the accommodation we have formulated.

Accordingly, the judgment is reversed and the cause remanded for further proceedings not inconsistent with this opinion.

MR. JUSTICE DOUGLAS concurs in the result.

MR. JUSTICE ROBERTS is of the opinion that the judgment should be affirmed.

MR. JUSTICE BLACK took no part in the consideration or decision of this case.

MR. JUSTICE JACKSON, dissenting: [Opinion omitted.] [b]

---

[b] On remand, the Supreme Court of Nebraska repudiated the direction to withhold execution of its decree. 146 Neb. 429, 19 N.W.2d 853 (1945). Compare pages 47-48 supra on evasion of a Supreme Court mandate.
— ED.

Chapter Ten Intergovernmental Immunities

Section A. TAXATION

McCulloch v. Maryland 4 Wheat. 316, 4 L. Ed. 579 (1819)

[For the opinion in this case see page 155 supra.][a]

Collector v. Day 11 Wall. 113, 20 L. Ed. 122 (1871)

MR. JUSTICE NELSON delivered the opinion of the court:
This is a writ of error to the circuit court of the United States for the district of Massachusetts.

Day, the plaintiff in the court below and defendant in error, brought a suit against Buffington, collector of the internal revenue, to recover back $61.51 and interest, assessed upon his salary in the years 1866 and 1867, as judge of the court of probate and insolvency for the county of Barnstable, state of Massachusetts, paid under protest. The salary is fixed by law, and payable out of the treasury of the state. The case was submitted to the court below on an agreed statement of acts, and upon which judgment was rendered for the plaintiff. It is now here for re-examination. It presents the question, whether or not it is competent for Congress, under the Constitution of the United States, to impose a tax upon the salary of a judicial officer of a state.

In the case of Dobbins v. Erie Co., 16 Pet. 435, it was decided that it was not competent for the legislature of a state to levy a tax upon the salary or emoluments of an officer of the United States. The decision was placed mainly upon the ground that the officer was a means or instrumentality employed for carrying into effect some of the legitimate powers of the government, which could not be interfered with by taxation or otherwise by the states, and that the salary or compensation for the service of the officer was inseparably

---

[a] For the scope and operation of a federal statute with respect to state taxation of national banks, see First Agricultural Natl. Bank v. State Tax Commission, 392 U.S. 339 (1968). Compare Note, The Supreme Court, 1967 Term, 82 Harv. L. Rev. 63, 284 (1968). — ED.

connected with the office; that if the officer, as such, was exempt, the salary assigned for his support or maintenance while holding the office, was also, for like reasons, equally exempt. . . .

The general government, and the states, although both exist within the same territorial limits, are separable and distinct sovereignties, acting separately and independently of each other, within their respective spheres. The former, in its appropriate sphere, is supreme; but the states within the limits of their powers not granted; or, in the language of the 10th Amendment, "reserved," are as independent of the general government as that government within its sphere is independent of the states. . . . Such being the separate and independent condition of the states in our complex system, as recognized by the Constitution, and the existence of which is so indispensable, that, without them, the general government itself would disappear from the family of nations, it would seem to follow, as a reasonable, if not a necessary consequence, that the means and instrumentalities employed for carrying on the operations of their governments for preserving their existence, and fulfilling the high and responsible duties assigned to them in the Constitution, should be left free and unimpaired; should not be liable to be crippled, much less defeated by the taxing power of another government, which power acknowledges no limits but the will of the legislative body imposing the tax. And, more especially, those means and instrumentalities which are the creation of their sovereign and reserved rights, one of which is the establishment of the judicial department, and the appointment of officers to administer their laws. Without this power, and the exercise of it, we risk nothing in saying that no one of the states, under the form of government guaranteed by the Constitution could long preserve its existence. . . .

The supremacy of the general government, therefore, so much relied on in the argument of the counsel for the plaintiff in error, in respect to the question before us, cannot be maintained. The two governments are upon an equality, and the question is whether the power "to lay and collect taxes" enables the general government to tax the salary of a judicial officer of the state, which officer is a means or instrumentality employed to carry into execution one of its most important functions, the administration of the laws, and which concerns the exercise of a right reserved to the states. . . .

But we are referred to The Veazie Bk. v. Fenno, 8 Wall. 533, in support of this power of taxation. That case furnishes a strong illustration of the position taken by the Chief Justice in McCulloch v. Md. [4 Wheat. 316], namely, "that the power to tax involves the power to destroy."

The power involved was one which had been exercised by the states since the foundation of the government and had been, after the lapse of three quarters of a century, annihilated from excessive taxation by the general government, just as the judicial office in the present case might be, if subject, at all, to taxation by that government. But notwithstanding the sanction of this taxation by a majority of the court, it is conceded, in the opinion, that "the reserved rights of the states, such as the right to pass laws; to give effect to laws through executive action; to administer justice through the courts, and to employ all necessary agencies for legitimate purposes of state government, are not proper subjects of the taxing power of Congress." This concession covers the case before us, and adds the authority of this court in support of the doctrine which we have endeavored to maintain.

The judgment of the court below is affirmed.

MR. JUSTICE BRADLEY, dissenting:

I dissent from the opinion of the court in this case, because it seems to me that the general government has the same power of taxing the income of officers of the state governments as it has of taxing that of its own officers. It is the common government of all alike; and every citizen is presumed to trust his own government in the matter of taxation. No man ceases to be a citizen of the United States by being an officer under the state government. I cannot accede to the doctrine that the general government is to be regarded as in any sense foreign or antagonistic to the state governments, their officers, or people; nor can I agree that a presumption can be admitted that the general government will act in a manner hostile to the existence or functions of the state governments, which are constituent parts of the system or body politic forming the basis on which the general government is founded. The taxation by the state governments of the instruments employed by the general government in the exercise of its powers is a very different thing. Such taxation involves an interference with the powers of a government in which other states and their citizens are equally interested with the state which imposes the taxation. In my judgment, the limitation of the power of taxation in the general government, which the present decision establishes, will be found very difficult to control. Where are we to stop in enumerating the functions of the state governments which will be interfered with by Federal taxation? If a state incorporates a railroad to carry out its purposes of internal improvement, or a bank to aid its financial arrangements, reserving, perhaps, a percentage on the stock or profits, for the supply of its own treasury, will the bonds or stock of such an institution be free from Federal taxation? How can we now tell what the effect of this decision will be? I cannot but regard it as founded on a fallacy, and that it will lead to mischievous consequences. I am as much opposed as anyone can be to any interference by the general government with the just powers of the state governments. But no concession of any of the just powers of the general government can easily be recalled. I, therefore, consider it my duty to at least record my dissent when such concession appears to be made. An extended discussion of the subject would answer no useful purpose.

NOTE Tides in the Doctrine of Tax Immunity

The doctrine of immunity was applied at an early date to a property tax assessed on government bonds, Weston v. Charleston, 2 Pet. 449 (1829), and subsequently to an income tax on the interest therefrom, Pollock v. Farmers' Loan & Trust Co., 157 U.S. 429, 563-584, 601-604, 652; 158 U.S. 601, 618 (1895).

During the first third of this century the doctrine went through a highly expansive phase. Among the taxes held invalid were the following: sales tax on articles sold to the government, Panhandle Oil Co. v. Mississippi, 277 U.S. 218 (1928); Indian Motocycle Co. v. United States, 283 U.S. 570 (1931); income tax on earnings from patents and copyrights, Long v. Rockwood, 277 U.S. 142 (1928); income tax on income derived by lessees of public lands, Gillespie v. Oklahoma, 257 U.S. 501 (1922); Burnet v. Coronado Oil & Gas Co., 285 U.S. 393 (1932).

At the same time, a number of inroads or qualifications on the doctrine were established. Among the taxes held valid were the following: corporate franchise tax measured by income including that from government bonds, Flint v. Stone-Tracy Co., 220 U.S. 107 (1911); inheritance or estate tax measured in part by government bonds, Plummer v. Coler, 178 U.S. 115 (1900); Greiner v. Llewellyn, 258 U.S. 384 (1922); income tax on capital gain on resale of government bonds, Willcuts v. Bunn, 282 U.S. 216 (1931); income tax on net income of contractors with the government, Metcalf v. Mitchell, 269 U.S. 514 (1926).

The contemporary phase of the problem begins with James v. Dravo Contracting Co., infra. See generally Powell, The Waning of Intergovernmental Tax Immunities, 58 Harv. L. Rev. 633 (1945), and The Remnant of Intergovernmental Tax Immunities, id. at 757 (1945); Roberts, The Court and the Constitution, c. 1 (1951).

James v. Dravo Contracting Co. 302 U.S. 134, 58 S. Ct. 208, 82 L. Ed. 155 (1937)

Mr. Chief Justice Hughes delivered the opinion of the Court.

This case presents the question of the constitutional validity of a tax imposed by the

State of West Virginia upon the gross receipts of respondent under contracts with the United States.

Respondent, The Dravo Contracting Company, is a Pennsylvania corporation engaged in the general contracting business, with its principal office and plant at Pittsburgh in that State, and is admitted to do business in the State of West Virginia. In the years 1932 and 1933, respondent entered into four contracts with the United States for the construction of locks and dams in the Kanawha River and locks in the Ohio River, both navigable streams. The State Tax Commissioner assessed respondent for the years 1933 and 1934 in the sum of $135,761.51 (taxes and penalties) upon the gross amounts received from the United States under these contracts.

Respondent brought suit in the District Court of the United States for the Southern District of West Virginia to restrain the collection of the tax. The case was heard by three judges (28 U.S.C. §380) and upon findings the court entered a final decree granting a permanent injunction. 16 F. Supp. 527. The case comes here on appeal.

The statute is known as the Gross Sales and Income Tax Law. Code of West Virginia, 1931, chap. 11, Art. 3, amended effective May 27, 1933. Acts of 1933, chap. 33. It provides for "annual privilege taxes" on account of "business and other activities." The clause in question here is as follows:

"Upon every person engaging or continuing within this State in the business of contracting, the tax shall be equal to two per cent. of the gross income of the business."

The tax was in addition to other state taxes upon respondent, to wit, the license tax on foreign corporations (Code of West Virginia, chap. 11, Art. 12, §§69, 71) and ad valorem taxes upon real and personal property of the contractor within the State.

The questions presented are (1) whether the State had territorial jurisdiction to impose the tax, and (2) whether the tax was invalid as laying a burden upon the operations of the Federal Government.

After hearing we directed reargument and requested the Attorney General of the United States to present the views of the Government upon the two questions above stated. Reargument has been had and the Government has been heard.

First. — As to territorial jurisdiction. — Unless the activities which are the subject of the tax were carried on within the territorial limits of West Virginia, the State had no jurisdiction to impose the tax. [Citations omitted.] The question has two aspects (1) as to work alleged to have been done outside the exterior limits of West Virginia and (2) as to work done within those limits but (a) in the bed of the rivers, (b) on property acquired by the Federal Government on the banks of the rivers, and (c) on property leased by respondent and used for the accommodation of its equipment.

1. A large part of respondent's work was performed at its plant at Pittsburgh. . . .

It is clear that West Virginia had no jurisdiction to lay a tax upon respondent with respect to this work done in Pennsylvania. As to the material and equipment there fabricated, the business and activities of respondent in West Virginia consisted of the installation at the respective sites within that State and an apportionment would in any event be necessary to limit the tax accordingly. Hans Rees' Sons v. North Carolina, 283 U.S. 123.

2. As to work done within the exterior limits of West Virginia, the question is whether the United States has acquired exclusive jurisdiction over the respective sites. Wherever the United States has such jurisdiction the State would have no authority to lay the tax. Surplus Trading Co. v. Cook, 281 U.S. 647.

(a) As to the beds of the Kanawha and Ohio rivers. The present question is not one of the paramount authority of the Federal Government to have the work performed for purposes within the federal province [citations omitted], or whether the tax lays a burden upon governmental operations; it is simply one of territorial jursidiction.

The title to the beds of the rivers was in the State. . . . No transfer of that title appears. The Solicitor General conceded in his argument at bar that the State of West Virginia retained its territorial jurisdiction over the river beds and we are of the opinion that this is the correct view.

(b) As to lands acquired by the United States by purchase or condemnation for the purposes of the improvements. Lands were thus acquired on the banks of the rivers from individual owners and the United States obtained title in fee simple. Respondent contends that by virtue of Article 1, §8, Clause 17, of the Federal Constitution the United States acquired exclusive jurisdiction.

Clause 17 provides that Congress shall have power "to exercise exclusive legislation" over "all places purchased by the consent of the legislature of the State in which the same shall be, for the erection of forts, magazines, arsenals, dockyards, and other needful buildings." "Exclusive legislation" is consistent only with exclusive jurisdiction. Surplus Trading Co. v. Cook, supra (281 U.S. 652). As we said in that case, it is not unusual for the United States to own within a State lands which are set apart and used for public purposes. Such ownership and use without more do not withdraw the lands from the jurisdiction of the State. The lands "remain part of her territory and within the operation of her laws, save that the latter cannot affect the title of the United States or embarrass it in using the lands or interfere with its right of disposal." Id., p. 650. Clause 17 governs those cases where the United States acquires lands with the consent of the legislature of the State for the purposes there described. If lands are otherwise acquired, and jurisdiction is ceded by the State to the United States, the terms of the cession, to the extent that they may lawfully be prescribed, that is, consistently with the carrying out of the purpose of the acquisition, determine the extent of the federal jurisdiction. [Citations omitted.]

Are the locks and dams in the instant case "needful buildings" within the purview of Clause 17? The State contends that they are not. If the clause were construed according to the rule of ejusdem generis, it could be plausibly contended that "needful buildings" are those of the same sort as forts, magazines, arsenals and dock-yards, that is, structures for military purposes. And it may be that the thought of such "strongholds" was uppermost in the minds of the framers. 5 Elliot, Debates, pp. 130, 440, 511; cf. 2 Story, Const. §1224. But such a narrow construction has been found not to be absolutely required and to be unsupported by sound reason in view of the nature and functions of the national government which the Constitution established. . . .

The legislature of West Virginia by general statute had given its consent to the acquisition by the United States, but questions are presented as to the construction and effect of the consent. The provision is found in §3 of chapter 1, article 1, of the Code of West Virginia of 1931. . . . The third paragraph cedes to the United States "concurrent jurisdiction with this State in and over any land so acquired . . . for all purposes." . . .

The third paragraph of §3 carefully defines the jurisdiction ceded by the State and there is no permissible construction which would ignore this definite expression of intention in considering the effect upon jurisdiction of the consent given by the first paragraph.

But it is urged that if the paragraph be construed as seeking to qualify the consent of the State, it must be treated as inoperative. That is, that the State cannot qualify its consent, which must be taken as carrying with it exclusive jurisdiction by virtue of Clause 17. . . .

It is not questioned that the State may refuse its consent and retain jurisdiction consistent with the governmental purposes for which the property was acquired. The right of eminent domain inheres in the Federal Government by virtue of its sovereignty and thus it may, regardless of the wishes either of the owners or of the States, acquire the lands which it needs within their borders. Kohl v. United States, 91 U.S. 367, 371, 372. In that event, as in cases of acquisition by purchase without consent of the State, jurisdiction is dependent upon cession by the State and the State may qualify its cession by reservations not inconsistent with the governmental uses. [Citations omitted.] The result to the Federal Government is the same whether consent is refused and cession is qualified by a reservation of concurrent jurisdiction, or consent to the acquisition is granted with a like qualification. As the Solicitor General has pointed out, a transfer of legislative jurisdiction carries with it not only benefits but obligations, and it may be highly desirable, in the interest both of the national government and of the State, that the latter should not be entirely ousted of its jurisdiction. The possible importance of reserving to the State jurisdiction for local purposes which involve no interference with the performance of governmental functions is becoming more and more clear as the activities of the Government expand and large areas within the States are acquired. There appears to be no reason why the United States should be compelled to accept exclusive jurisdiction or the State be compelled to grant it in giving its consent to purchases.

Normally, where governmental consent is essential, the consent may be granted upon terms appropriate to the subject and transgressing no constitutional limitation. Thus, as a State may not be sued without its consent and "permission is altogether voluntary" it follows "that it may prescribe the terms and conditions on which it consents to be sued." Beers v. Arkansas, 20 How. 527, 529; Smith v. Reeves, 178 U.S. 436, 441, 442. Treaties of the United States are to be made with the advice and consent of the Senate, but it is familiar practice for the Senate to accompany the exercise of this authority with reservations. 2 Hyde, International Law, §519. The Constitution provides that no State without the consent of Congress shall enter into a compact with another State. It can hardly be doubted that in giving consent Congress may impose conditions. See Arizona v. California, 292 U.S. 341, 345.

. . . In the present case the reservation by West Virginia of concurrent jurisdiction did not operate to deprive the United States of the enjoyment of the property for the purposes for which it was acquired, and we are of the opinion that the reservation was applicable and effective.

(c) As to property leased by respondent and used for the accommodation of its equipment. There can be no question as to the jurisdiction of the State over this area.

We conclude that, so far as territorial jurisdiction is concerned, the State had authority to lay the tax with respect to the respondent's activities carried on at the respective dam sites.

Second. — Is the tax invalid upon the ground that it lays a direct burden upon the Federal Government? The Solicitor General speaking for the Government supports the contention of the State that the tax is valid. Respondent urges the contrary.

The tax is not laid upon the Government, its property or officers. Dobbins v. Erie County, 16 Pet. 435, 449, 450.

The tax is not laid upon an instrumentality of the Government. [Citations omitted.]

The tax is not laid upon the contract of the Government. [Citations omitted.] The application of the principle which denies validity to such a tax has required the observing of close distinctions in order to maintain the essential freedom of government in performing its functions, without unduly limiting the taxing power which is equally essential to both nation and state under our dual system. In Weston v. Charleston, 2 Pet. 449, and Pollock v. Farmers' Loan & T. Co., 157 U.S. 429, taxes on interest from government securities were held to be laid on the government's contract — upon the power to borrow money — and hence were invalid. But we held in Willcuts v. Bunn, 282 U.S. 216, that the immunity from taxation does not extend to the profits derived by their owners upon the sale of government bonds. We said (id., p. 225): "The power to tax is no less essential than the power to borrow money, and, in preserving the latter it is not necessary to cripple the former by extending the constitutional exemption of taxation to those subjects which fall within the general application of non-discriminatory laws, and where no direct burden is laid upon the governmental instrumentality, and there is only a remote, if any, influence upon the exercise of the functions of government." Many illustrations were given. . . .

In Panhandle Oil Co. v. Mississippi, 277 U.S. 218, and Indian Motocycle Co. v. United States, 283 U.S. 570, the taxes were held to be invalid as laid on the sales to the respective governments, the one being a state tax on a sale to the United States, and the other a federal tax on the sale to a municipal corporation of Massachusetts. A similar result was reached in Graves v. Texas Co., 298 U.S. 393. These cases have been distinguished and must be deemed to be limited to their particular facts. . . .

In Alward v. Johnson, 282 U.S. 509, 514, the Court sustained a state tax upon the gross receipts of an independent contractor carrying the mails. The taxpayer operated an automotive stage line. Two-thirds of his gross receipts, upon the whole of which he was taxed, were derived from carriage of United States mails and the remainder from carriage of passengers and freight. The Court found that the property used in earning these receipts was devoted chiefly to carrying the mails and that without his contract with the Government the stage line could not be operated profitably. In upholding the tax upon his gross receipts we distinguished Panhandle Oil Co. v. Mississippi, 277 U.S. 218, saying: "There was no tax upon the contract for such carriage; the burden laid upon the property employed affected operations of the Federal Government only remotely. . . . The facts in Panhandle Oil Co. v. Mississippi, 277 U.S. 218, and New Jersey Bell Teleph. Co. v. State Bd. of Taxes & Assessments, 280 U.S. 338 were held to establish direct interference with or burden upon the exercise of a Federal right. The principles there applied are not controlling here."

. . . There is no ineluctable logic which makes the doctrine of immunity with respect to government bonds applicable to the earnings of an independent contractor rendering services to the Government. That doctrine recognizes the direct effect of a tax which "would operate on the power to borrow before it is exercised" (Pollock v. Farmers' Loan & T. Co., 157 U.S. 429) and which would directly affect the government's obligation as a continuing security. Vital considerations are there involved respecting the permanent relations of the Government to investors in its securities and its ability to maintain is credit — considerations which are not found in connection with contracts made from time to time for the services of independent contractors. And in dealing with the question of the taxability of such contractors upon the fruits of their work, we are not bound to consider or decide how far immunity from taxation is to be deemed essential to the protection of government in relation to its purchases of commodities or whether the doctrine announced in the cases of that character which we have cited deserves revision or restriction.

The question of the taxability of a contractor upon the fruits of his services is closely analogous to that of the taxability of the property of the contractor which is used in performing the services. His earnings flow from his work; his property is employed in securing them. In both cases, the taxes increase the cost of the work and diminish his profits. Many years ago the Court recognized and enforced the distinction between a tax laid directly upon a government contract or an instrumentality of the United States and a tax upon the property employed by an agent or contractor in performing services for the United States. "Taxation of the agency is taxation of the means; taxation of the property of the agent is not always, or generally, taxation of the means." Thomson v. Union P.R. Co., 9 Wall. 579, 591. . . .

The question of immunity from taxation of the earnings of an independent contractor under a government contract arose in Metcalf v. Mitchell, 269 U.S. 514. The services were rendered to a political subdivision of a State and the contractor's earnings were held to be subject to the federal income tax. That was a pivotal decision, for we had to meet the question whether the earnings of the contractor stood upon the same footing as interest upon government securities or the income of an instrumentality of government. It is true that the tax was laid upon net income. But if the tax upon the earnings of the contractor had been regarded as imposing a direct burden upon a governmental agency, the fact that the tax was laid upon net income would not save it under the doctrine of Gillespie v. Oklahoma, 257 U.S. 501. And if the doctrine of the immunity of interest upon government bonds had been deemed to apply, the tax would have been equally bad whether the tax was upon net or gross income. The ruling in Pollock v. Farmers' Loan & T. Co., 157 U.S. 429, related to net income. The uniform ruling in such a case has been that the interest upon government securities cannot be included in gross income for the purpose of an income tax computed upon net income. The pith of the decision in the case of Metcalf is that government bonds and contracts for the services of an independent contractor are not upon the same footing. The decision was a definite refusal to extend the doctrine of cases relating to government securities, and to the instrumentalities of government, to earnings under contracts for labor.

The reasoning upon which that decision was based is controlling here. We recognized that in a broad sense "the burden of federal taxation necessarily sets an economic limit to the practical operation of the taxing power of the States and vice versa." "Taxation by either the state or the federal government affects in some measure the cost of operation of the other." As "neither government may destroy the other, or control in any substantial manner the exercise of its powers," we said that the limitation upon the taxing power of each, so far as it affects the other, "must receive a practical construction which permits both to function with the minimum of interference each with the other; and that limitation cannot be so varied or extended as seriously to impair either the taxing power of the government imposing the tax . . . or the appropriate exercise of the functions of the government affected by it." Metcalf v. Mitchell, supra (269 U.S. 523, 524). . . .

While the Metcalf Case was one of a federal tax, the reasoning and the practical criterion it adopts are clearly applicable to the case of a state tax upon earnings under a contract with the Federal Government.

As we have observed, the fact that the tax in the present case is laid upon the gross receipts, instead of net earnings, is not a controlling distinction. Respondent invokes our decisions in the field of interstate commerce, where a tax upon the gross income of the taxpayer derived from interstate commerce has long been held to be an unconstitutional burden. [Citations omitted.]

But the difference is plain. Persons have a constitutional right to engage in interstate commerce free from burdens imposed by a state tax upon the business which constitutes such commerce or the privilege of engaging in it or the receipts as such derived from it. Minnesota Rate Cases (Simpson v. Shepard) 230 U.S. 352, 400. Interstate commerce is not an abstraction; it connotes the transactions of those engaged in it and they enjoy the described immunity in their own right. Here, respondent's activities at the dam sites are local and not in interstate commerce. Respondent has no constitutional right to immunity from non-discriminatory local taxation and the mere fact that the tax in question burdens respondent is no defense. The defense is that the tax burdens the Government and respondent's right is at best a derivative one. He asserts an immunity which, if it exists, pertains to the Government and which the Government disclaims.

In Alward v. Johnson, 282 U.S. 509, as already noted, the tax was upon gross receipts and these were derived from a contract for carrying the mails, but the tax was upheld. It there appeared that the tax was in lieu of taxes upon the property and had been treated by the state court as a property tax. But if the tax as actually laid upon the gross receipts placed a direct burden upon the Federal Government so as to interfere with the performance of its functions, it could not be saved because it was in lieu of a tax upon property or was so characterized. . . .

The contention ultimately rests upon the point that the tax increases the cost to the Government of the service rendered by the taxpayer. But this is not necessarily so. The contractor, taking into consideration the state of the competitive market for the service, may be willing to bear the tax and absorb it in his estimated profit rather than lose the contract. In the present case, it is stipulated that respondent's estimated costs of the respective works, and the bids based thereon, did not include, and there was not included in the contract price paid to respondent, any specified item to cover the gross receipts tax, although respondent knew of the West Virginia act imposing it, and respondent's estimates of cost did include "compensation and liability insurance, construction bond and property taxes."

But if it be assumed that the gross receipts tax may increase the cost to the Government, that fact would not invalidate the tax. With respect to that effect, a tax on the contractor's gross receipts would not differ from a tax on the contractor's property and equipment necessarily used in the performance of the contract. Concededly, such a tax may validly be laid. . . .

There is the further suggestion that if the present tax of two percent. is upheld, the State may lay a tax of twenty per cent. or fifty per cent. or even more, and make it difficult or impossible for the Government to obtain the service it needs. The argument ignores the power of Congress to protect the performance of the functions of the national government and to prevent interference therewith through any attempted state action. In Thomson v. Union P.R. Co., 9 Wall. 579, the Court pointedly referred to the authority of Congress to prevent such an interference through the use of the taxing power of the State. "It cannot," said the Court, "be so used, indeed, as to defeat or hinder the operations of the National government; but it will be safe to conclude, in general, in reference to persons and State corporations employed in government service, that when Congress has not interposed to protect their property from State taxation, such taxation is not obnoxious to that objection." See Van Allen v. Assessors (Churchill v. Utica) 3 Wall. 573, 585; Fidelity & D. Co. v. Pennsylvania, 240 U.S. 319.

We hold that the West Virginia tax so far as it is laid upon the gross receipts of respondent derived from its activities within the borders of the State does not interfere in any substantial way with the performance of federal functions and is a valid exaction. The decree of the District Court is reversed and the cause is remanded for further proceedings in conformity with this opinion.

Reversed.

MR. JUSTICE ROBERTS, dissenting.

I regret that I am unable to concur in the Court's opinion. I should not set forth my views in detail were I not convinced the decision runs counter to the settled rule that a state may not, by taxation, burden or impede the United States in the exercise of its delegated powers. The judgment seems to me to overrule, sub silentio, a century of precedents, and to leave the application of the rule uncertain and unpredictable. [The remainder of the opinion is omitted. Justices McReynolds, Sutherland, and Butler joined in the dissent.]

NOTE Taxation of Government Contractors

It is noteworthy that in the preceding case the Department of Justice argued successfully for the taxability of the government's own contractor. This was the beginning of a campaign to overturn the doctrine of reciprocal tax immunity as applied to private persons having relationships with a state or the United States, whether as contractors, employees, lessees, or in similar status. Pressure from budget-conscious departments, however, faced with wartime cost-plus contracts that placed the economic burden of state sales and gross receipts taxes on the government, caused the Department of Justice to argue in Alabama v. King & Boozer, 314 U.S. 1 (1941), that a contractor under a cost-plus contract was immune from a state sales tax on the purchase of building materials to be incorporated into a government project. Mr. Justice Roberts observed that in this case "the Government repented its generosity." See United States v. County of Allegheny, 322 U.S. 174, 193 (1944) (dissent). But the tide of recession from immunity was not to be stemmed; and in the King & Boozer case the contractor was held taxable.

Two courses were open to the government to restore immunity for contractors. First, Congress could expressly so provide, as suggested near the close of the opinion in the Dravo case. The Atomic Energy Act of 1946 provides, in §9(b): "The Commission, and the property, activities, and income of the Commission, are hereby expressly exempted from taxation in any manner or form by any State, county, municipality, or any subdivision thereof." In view of the general understanding that the Commission would operate projects through independent contractors, the statute was held to exempt from a state sales and use tax the purchase of goods by the contractors managing the plants and town at Oak Ridge, Tennessee. Carson v. Roane-Anderson Co., 342 U.S. 232 (1952); see also Pittman v. HOLC, 308 U.S. 21 (1939). Second, in the absence of a congressional exemption provision, the department involved could convert the contractor into a purchasing agent, by contractual arrangement. If this is done, it has been held that a state sales tax may not be collected from the "agent" of the United States on purchase of materials for the government project. Kern-Limerick v. Scurlock, 347 U.S. 110 (1954). Does the state have a way of avoiding the effect of this decision?

Helvering v. Gerhardt 304 U.S. 405, 58 S. Ct. 969, 82 L. Ed. 1427 (1938)

MR. JUSTICE STONE delivered the opinion of the Court.

The question for decision is whether the imposition of a Federal income tax for the calendar years 1932 and 1933 on salaries received by respondents, as employees of the Port of New York Authority, places an unconstitutional burden on the State of New York and New Jersey.

The Port Authority is a bi-state corporation, created by compact between New York and New Jersey, . . . approved by the Congress of the United States by Joint Resolution of August 23, 1921, chap. 77, 42 Stat. at L. 174. The compact authorized the Authority to acquire and operate "any terminal or transportation facility" within a specified district embracing the Port of New York and lying partially within each state. It directed the Authority to recommend a comprehensive plan for improving the port and facilitating its use, by the construction and operation of bridges, tunnels, terminals and other facilities. The Authority made such a recommendation in its report of December, 1921, adopted by the two states in 1922. . . .

In conformity to the plan, and pursuant to further legislation of the two states, the Authority has constructed . . . interstate vehicular bridges all passing over waters of the harbor or adjacent to it. It has also constructed the Holland Tunnel and the Lincoln Tunnel, interstate vehicular tunnels passing under the Hudson River. These enterprises were financed in large part by funds advanced by the two states and by the Port Authority's issue and sale of its bonds. . . .

The respondents, during the taxable years in question, were respectively a construction engineer and two assistant general managers, employed by the Authority at annual salaries ranging between $8,000 and $15,000. . . . The several respondents having failed to return their respective salaries as income for the taxable years in question, the commissioner determined deficiencies against them. The Board of Tax Appeals found that the Port Authority was engaged in the performance of a public function for the states of New York and New Jersey, and ruled that the compensation received by the Authority's employees was exempt from Federal income tax. The Court of Appeals for the Second Circuit 9 F.(2d) 999, affirmed without opinion on the authority of Brush v. Commissioner of Internal Revenue (C.C.A.2d) 85 F.(2d) 32, reversed in 300 U.S. 352; Commissioner of Internal Revenue v. Ten Eyck (C.C.A.2d) 76 F.(2d) 515, and New York ex rel. Rogers v. Graves, 299 U.S. 401. . . .

The Constitution contains no express limitation on the power of either a state or the national government to tax the other, or its instrumentalities. The doctrine that there is an implied limitation stems from M'Culloch v. Maryland, 4 Wheat. 316, . . . It was held that Congress, having power to establish a bank by laws which, when enacted under the Constitution, are supreme, also had power to protect the bank by striking down state action impeding its operations; and it was thought that the state tax in question was so inconsistent with Congress's constitutional action in establishing the bank as to compel the conclusion that Congress intended to forbid application of the tax to the Federal bank notes.[1] Cf. Osborn v. Bank of United States, 9 Wheat. 738, 865-868.

In sustaining the immunity from state taxation, the opinion of the Court, by Chief Justice Marshall, recognized a clear distinction between the extent of the power of a state to tax national banks and that of the national government to tax state instrumentalities. He was careful to point out not only that the taxing power of the national government is supreme, by reason of the constitutional grant, but that in laying a Federal tax on state instrumentalities the people of the states, acting through their representatives, are laying a tax on their own institutions and consequently are subject to political restraints which can be counted on to prevent abuse. State taxation of national instrumentalities is subject to no such restraint, for the people outside the state have no representatives who participate in the legislation; and in a real sense, as to them, the taxation is without representation. The exercise of the national taxing power is thus subject to a safeguard which does not operate when a state undertakes to tax a national instrumentality.

It was perhaps enough to have supported the conclusion that the tax was invalid, that it was aimed specifically at national banks and thus operated to discriminate against the exercise by the Congress of a national power. Such discrimination was later recognized to be in itself a sufficient ground for holding invalid any form of state taxation adversely affecting the use or enjoyment of Federal instrumentalities. Miller v. Milwaukee, 272 U.S. 713; cf. Pacific Co. v. Johnson, 285 U.S. 480, 493. But later cases have declared that Federal instrumentalities are similarly immune from non-discriminatory state taxation — from the taxation of obligations of the United States as an interference with the borrowing power; Weston v. Charleston, 2 Pet. 449, and from a tax on "offices" levied upon the office of a captain of a revenue cutter. Dobbins v. Erie County, 16 Pet. 435.

That the taxing power of the Federal government is nevertheless subject to an implied restriction when applied to state instrumentalities was first decided in Collector v. Day, 11 Wall. 113, where the salary of a state officer, a probate judge, was held to be immune from Federal income tax. . . . It is enough for present purposes that the state immunity from the national taxing power, when recognized in Collector v. Day, was narrowly limited to a state judicial officer engaged in the performance of a function which pertained to state governments at the time the Constitution was adopted, without which no state "could long preserve its existence."

There are cogent reasons why any constitutional restriction upon the taxing power granted to Congress, so far as it can be properly raised by implication, should be narrowly limited. One, as was pointed out by Chief Justice Marshall in M'Culloch v. Maryland, supra, and Weston v. Charleston, supra (2 Pet. 465, 466), is that the people of all the states have created the national government and are represented in Congress. Through that representation they exercise the national taxing power. The very fact that when they are exercising it they are taxing themselves, serves to guard against its abuse through the possibility of resort to the usual processes of political action which provides a readier and more adaptable means than any which courts can afford, for securing accommodation of the competing demands for national revenue, on the one hand, and for reasonable scope for the independence of state action, on the other.

---

[1] It follows that in considering the immunity of federal instrumentalities from state taxation two factors may be of importance which are lacking in the case of a claimed immunity of state instrumentalities from federal taxation. Since the acts of Congress within its constitutional power are supreme, the validity of state taxation of federal instrumentalities must depend (a) on the power of Congress to create the instrumentality and (b) its intent to protect it from state taxation. Congress may curtail an immunity which might otherwise be implied, Van Allen v. Assessors (Churchill v. Utica) 3 Wall. 573, or enlarge it beyond the point where, Congress being silent, the Court would set its limits. Bank of New York v. New York County, 7 Wall. 26, 30, 31; see Thomson v. Union P.R. Co., 9 Wall. 759, 588, 590; Shaw v. Gibson-Zahniser Oil Corp., 276 U.S. 575, 581, and cases cited; James v. Dravo Contracting Co., 302 U.S. 134, 161.

The analysis is comparable where the question is whether federal corporate instrumentalities are immune from state judicial process. Federal Land Bank v. Priddy, 295 U.S. 229, 234, 235.

632 Chapter Ten. Intergovernmental Immunities

Another reason rests upon the fact that any allowance of a tax immunity for the protection of state sovereignty is at the expense of the sovereign power of the nation to tax. Enlargement of the one involves diminution of the other. When enlargement proceeds beyond the necessity of protecting the state, the burden of the immunity is thrown upon the national government with benefit only to a privileged class of taxpayers. See Metcalf v. Mitchell, 269 U.S. 514; cf. Thomson v. Union P.R. Co., 9 Wall. 579, 588, 590. With the steady expansion of the activity of state governments into new fields they have undertaken the performance of functions not known to the states when the Constitution was adopted, and have taken over the management of business enterprises once conducted exclusively by private individuals subject to the national taxing power. In a complex economic society tax burdens laid upon those who directly or indirectly have dealings with the states, tend, to some extent not capable of precise measurement, to be passed on economically and thus to burden the state government itself. But if every Federal tax which is laid on some new form of state activity, or whose economic burden reaches in some measure the state or those who serve it, were to be set aside as an infringement of state sovereignty, it is evident that a restriction upon national power, devised only as a shield to protect the states from curtailment of the essential operations of government which they have exercised from the beginning, would become a ready means for striking down the taxing power of the nation. See South Carolina v. United States, 199 U.S. 437, 454, 455. Once impaired by the recognition of a state immunity found to be excessive, restoration of that power is not likely to be secured through the action of state legislatures; for they are without the inducements to act which have often persuaded Congress to waive immunities thought to be excessive. . . .

In a period marked by a constant expansion of government activities and the steady multiplication of the complexities of taxing systems, it is perhaps too much to expect that the judicial pronouncements marking the boundaries of state immunity should present a completely logical pattern. But they disclose no purposeful departure from, and indeed definitely establish, two guiding principles of limitation for holding the tax immunity of state instrumentalities to its proper function. The one, dependent upon the nature of the function being performed by the state or in its behalf, excludes from the immunity activities thought not to be essential to the preservation of state governments even though the tax be collected from the state treasury. The state itself was taxed for the privilege of carrying on the liquor business in South Carolina v. United States, 199 U.S. 437, and in Ohio v. Helvering, 292 U.S. 360; and a tax on the income of a state officer engaged in the management of a state-owned corporation operating a street railroad was sustained in Helvering v. Powers, 293 U.S. 214, because it was thought that the functions discouraged by these taxes were not indispensable to the maintenance of a state government. The other principle, exemplified by those cases where the tax laid upon individuals affects the state only as the burden is passed on to it by the taxpayer, forbids recognition of the immunity when the burden on the state is so speculative and uncertain that if allowed it would restrict the Federal taxing power without affording any corresponding tangible protection to the state government; even though the function be thought important enough to demand immunity from a tax upon the state itself, it is not necessarily protected from a tax which well may be substantially or entirely absorbed by private persons. Metcalf v. Mitchell, 269 U.S. 514; Willcuts v. Bunn, 282 U.S. 216.

With these controlling principles in mind we turn to their application in the circumstances of the present case. The challenged taxes . . . are upon the net income of respondents, derived from their employment in common occupations not shown to be different in their methods or duties from those of similar employees in private industry. . . . A non-discriminatory tax laid on their net income, in common with that of all other members of the community, could by no reasonable probability be considered to preclude the performance of the function which New York and New Jersey have undertaken, or to obstruct it more than like private enterprises are obstructed by our taxing system. Even though, to some unascertainable extent, the tax deprives the states of the advantage of paying less than the standard rate for the services which they engage, it does not curtail any of those functions which have been thought hitherto to be essential to their continued existence as states. At most it may be said to increase somewhat the cost of the state governments because, in an interdependent economic society, the taxation of income tends to raise (to some extent which economists are not able to measure, see Indian Motocycle Co. v. United States, supra (283 U.S. p. 581, footnote 1)) the price of labor and materials. The effect of the immunity if allowed would be to relieve respondents of their duty of financial support to the national government, in order to secure to the state a theoretical advantage so speculative in its character and measurement as to be unsubstantial. A tax immunity devised for protection of the states as governmental entities cannot be pressed so far. . . .

. . . In Brush v. Commissioner of Internal Revenue (C.C.A.2d) 85 F.(2d) 32, affirmed in 300 U.S. 352, the applicable treasury regulation upon which the Government relied exempted from income tax the compensation of "state officers and employees" for "services rendered in connection with the exercise of an essential governmental function of the State." The sole contention of the Government was that the maintenance of the New York City water supply system was not an essential governmental function of the state. The Government did not attack the regulation. No contention was made by it or considered or decided by the Court that the burden of the tax on the state was so indirect or conjectural as to be but an incident of the coexistence of the two governments, and therefore not within the constitutional immunity. If determination of that point was implicit in the decision it must be limited by what is now decided.

The pertinent provisions of the regulation applicable in the Brush Case were continued in Regulations 77, Article 643, under the 1932 Revenue Act until January 7, 1938, when they were amended to provide that "Compensation received for services rendered to a State is to be included in gross income unless the person receives such compensation from the state as an officer or employee thereof and such compensation is immune from taxation under the Constitution of the United States." The applicable provisions of § 116 of the 1932 Act do not authorize the exclusion from gross income of the salaries of employees of a state or a state-owned corporation. If the regulation be deemed to embrace the employees of a state-owned corporation such as the Port Authority, it was unauthorized by the statute. But we think it plain that employees of the Port Authority are not employees of the state or a political subdivision of it within the meaning of the regulations as originally promulgated — an additional reason why the regulation, even before the 1938 amendment, was ineffectual to exempt the salaries here involved. . . .

Expressing no opinion whether a Federal tax may be imposed upon the Port Authority itself with respect to its receipt of income or its other activities, we decide only that the present tax neither precludes nor threatens unreasonably to obstruct any function essential to the continued existence of the state government. . . .

Reversed.

Mr. Justice Cardozo and Mr. Justice Reed took no part in the consideration or decision of this case.

Mr. Justice Black, concurring.

I agree that this cause should be reversed for the reasons expressed in that part of the opinion just read pointing out that: respondents, though employees of the New York Port Authority, are citizens of the United States; the tax levied upon their incomes from the Authority is the same as that paid by other citizens receiving equal net incomes; and payment of this non-discriminatory income tax by respondents cannot impair or defeat in whole or in part the governmental operations of the State of New York. A citizen who receives his income from a State, owes the same obligation to the United States as other citizens who draw their salaries from private sources or the United States and pay Federal income taxes.

634   *Chapter Ten.* **Intergovernmental Immunities**

While I believe these reasons, without more, are adequate to support the tax, I find it difficult to reconcile this result with the principle announced in Collector v. Day, 11 Wall. 113, and later decisions applying that principle. This leads me to the conclusion that we should review and reexamine the rule based upon Collector v. Day. That course would logically require the entire subject of intergovernmental tax immunity to be reviewed in the light of the effect of the Sixteenth Amendment authorizing Congress to levy a tax on incomes from "whatever source derived"; and, in that event, the decisions interpreting the Amendment would also be reexamined. . . .

The present controversy illustrates the necessity for further reexamination. New York created the Port Authority with power to engage in activities which that State believed to be essential. Yet, under this test, New York's determination is not final until reviewed in a tax litigation between the government and a single citizen.

Conceptions of "essential governmental functions" vary with individual philosophies. Some believe that "essential governmental functions" include ownership and operation of water plants, power and transportation systems, etc. Others deny that such ownership and operation could ever be "essential governmental functions" on the ground that such functions "could be carried on by private enterprise." A Federal income tax levied against the manager of the state-operated elevated railway company of Boston was sustained even though this manager was a public officer appointed by the Governor of Massachusetts "with the advice and consent of the council."[3] On the other hand, the Federal government was denied — although with strong dissent — the right to collect an income tax from the chief engineer in charge of New York City's municipally owned water supply.[4] An implied constitutional distinction which taxes income of an officer of a state-operated transportation system and exempts income of the manager of a municipal water works system manifests the uncertainty created by the "essential" and "non-essential" test.

There is not, and there cannot be, any unchanging line of demarcation between essential and non-essential governmental functions. Many governmental functions of today have at some time in the past been non-governmental. The genius of our government provides that, within the sphere of constitutional action, the people — acting not through the courts but through their elected legislative representatives — have the power to determine as conditions demand, what services and functions the public welfare requires.

Surely, the Constitution contains no imperative mandate that public employees — or others — drawing equal salaries (income) should be divided into taxpaying and non-taxpaying groups. Ordinarily such a result is discrimination. Uniform taxation upon those equally able to bear their fair shares of the burdens of government is the objective of every just government. The language of the Sixteenth Amendment empowering Congress to "collect taxes on incomes from whatever source derived" — given its most obvious meaning — is broad enough to accomplish this purpose.

[Mr. Justice Butler delivered a dissenting opinion, in which Mr. Justice McReynolds joined.]

NOTE

In a petition for rehearing the state asked that the decision be given prospective effect only. The Solicitor General conceded the Court's power so to limit its decision. Cf. page 133 supra. But he maintained that this was not a suitable case for such action. Why not?

On March 27, 1939, the Court sustained the application of the New York income tax to the salary of an attorney employed by the Federal Home Owners' Loan Corporation. Collector v. Day was "overruled so far as [it] recognize[d] an implied constitutional im-

---

[3] Helvering v. Powers, 293 U.S. 214, 222, 223.
[4] Brush v. Commissioner of Internal Revenue, 300 U.S. 352; cf. Metcalf v. Mitchell, 269 U.S. 514.

munity from income taxation of the salaries of officers or employees of the national or a state government or their instrumentalities." Graves v. O'Keefe, 306 U.S. 466, 486 (1939).

On April 12, 1939, Congress enacted the Public Salaries Taxing Act, 53 Stat. 574, which forbade an assessment on compensation of state and municipal employees for prior tax years, but the exemption was made inapplicable to employees of a state or subdivision that taxed the compensation of federal employees in respect to prior tax years.

City of Detroit v. Murray Corp. 355 U.S. 489, 78 S. Ct. 485, 2 L. Ed. 2d 441 (1958)

MR. JUSTICE BLACK delivered the opinion of the Court.

This is the third in a series of cases from the State of Michigan decided today involving a claim of constitutional tax immunity.[b]

In 1952 Murray Corporation was acting as a subcontractor under a prime contract for the manufacture of airplane parts between two other private companies and the United States. From time to time Murray received partial payments from the two prime contractors as it performed its obligations under the subcontract. By agreement, title to all parts, materials and work in process acquired by Murray in performance of the subcontract vested in the United States upon any such partial payment, even though Murray retained possession.

On January 1, 1952, the City of Detroit and the County of Wayne, Michigan, each assessed a tax against Murray which in part was based on the value of materials and work in process in its possession to which the United States held legal title under the title-vesting provisions of the subcontract. Murray paid this part of each tax under protest and then sued in a Federal District Court for a refund from the city and county. It contended that full title to the property was in the United States and that the taxes infringed the Federal Government's immunity from state taxation to the extent they were based on such property. The Government intervened on Murray's behalf. On motion for summary judgment the District Court entered judgment for Murray and the Court of Appeals for the Sixth Circuit affirmed. 234 F.2d 380. From this decision the city and county both appealed and petitioned for certiorari. We granted certiorari and postponed the question of jurisdiction on appeal to the hearing on the merits. 352 U.S. 960, 963. The appeal was proper. 28 U.S.C. 1254(2).

We believe that this case is also controlled by the principles expressed in our opinions in Nos. 26 and 37, [see note b, infra], and that the taxes challenged here do not violate the Constitution. These taxes were not levied directly against the United States or its property. To the contrary they were imposed on Murray, a private corporation, and there was no effort to hold the United States or its property accountable. In fact Michigan expressly exempts from taxation all public property belonging to the United States, 6 Mich. Stat. Ann., 1950, 7.7, and those taxes were assessed from the beginning "subject to prior rights of the Federal Government." Cf. S.R.A. v. Minnesota, 327 U.S. 558, 559, 561; City of New Brunswick v. United States, 276 U.S. 547.

The taxes imposed on Murray were styled a personal property tax by the Michigan stat-

---

[b] The two companion cases were United States v. Detroit, 355 U.S. 466 (1958), and United States v. Muskegon, 355 U.S. 484 (1958). In each the Court sustained a Michigan statute which provided that whenever tax-exempt property is leased or otherwise made available to a business user, he is taxable as though he were the owner. In the first case a federally owned plant was leased to Borg-Warner for commercial production; in the second, government facilities were made available to Continental Motors to fulfill contracts with the army. The Court regarded the tax as on the privilege of use rather than on the property.

The three cases are discussed in 72 Harv. L. Rev. 157 (1958). — ED.

utes and it relies upon this to support its contention that they were actually laid against government property. However in passing on the constitutionality of a state tax "we are concerned only with its practical operation, not its definition or the precise form of descriptive words which may be applied to it." Lawrence v. State Tax Commission, 286 U.S. 276, 280. Consequently in determining whether these taxes violate the Government's constitutional immunity we must look through form and behind labels to substance. This is at least as true to uphold a state tax as to strike one down. Cf. Wisconsin v. J. C. Penney Co., 311 U.S. 435, 443-445; Capitol Greyhound Lines v. Brice, 339 U.S. 542. Due regard for the State's power to tax requires no less. As applied — and of course that is the way they must be judged — the taxes involved here imposed a levy on a private party possessing government property which it was using or processing in the course of its own business. It is not disputed that Michigan law authorizes the taxation of the party in possession under such circumstances. Cf. Detroit Shipbuilding Co. v. Detroit, 228 Mich. 145, 199 N.W. 645; City of Detroit v. Gray, 314 Mich. 516, 22 N.W.2d 771. In their practical operation and effect the taxes in question are identical to those which we upheld in Nos. 26 and 37 on persons using exempt real property. We see no essential difference so far as constitutional tax immunity is concerned between taxing a person for using property he possesses and taxing him for possessing property he uses when in both instances he uses the property for his own private ends. Nor have we been pointed to anything else which would bar a State from taxing possession in such circumstances. Cf. Carstairs v. Cochran, 193 U.S. 10. Lawful possession of property is a valuable right when the possessor can use it for his own personal benefit. . . .

There is no claim that the challenged taxes discriminate against persons holding government property. To the contrary the tax is a general tax which applies and has been applied throughout the State. If anything the economic burden on the United States is more remote and less certain than in other cases where this Court has upheld taxes on private parties. Of course the Government will eventually feel the financial burden of at least some of the tax but the only principle in this area which has heretofore been clearly settled is that the imposition of an increased financial burden on the Government does not by itself invalidate a state tax. . . .

In all important particulars the taxes imposed here are very similar to that upheld in Esso Standard Oil Co. v. Evans, 345 U.S. 495, on the storage of gasoline for the United States. A tax on storage is not intrinsically different from a tax on possession, at least where in both instances the private party is holding the property for his own gain. The tax in Esso was measured by the quantity of government gasoline stored while the taxes here are measured by the value of government property possessed but such technical distinction is of no significance in determining whether the Constitution bars this tax and is completely unrelated to any rational basis for governmental tax immunity.

We find nothing in the Constitution which compels us to strike down these states taxes. There was no discrimination against the Federal Government, its property or those with whom it does business. There was no crippling obstruction of any of the Government's functions, no sinister effort to hamstring its power, not even the slightest interference with its property. Cf. M'Culloch v. Maryland, 4 Wheat. 316. In such circumstances the Congress is the proper agency, as we pointed out in United States v. City of Detroit, to make the difficult policy decisions necessarily involved in determining whether and to what extent private parties who do business with the Government should be given immunity from states taxes.

The judgment of the Court of Appeals is reversed and the cause is remanded for further proceedings not inconsistent with this opinion.

Opinion of MR. JUSTICE FRANKFURTER. . . .

I cannot believe that the Court would outright reject the doctrine of constitutional immunity from taxation of the Government and its property. I cannot believe that the Court is prepared frankly to jettison what has been part of our constitutional system for almost

150 years. But it does not save the principle to disregard it in practice. And it disregards it in practice to argue from the right of a State to levy an excise tax against a contractor for the enjoyment of property that gives him an economic advantage because it is otherwise immune from taxation, to the right of a State professedly and directly to lay an ad valorem property tax on what is indubitably government property. . . .

The danger of hindrance of the Federal Government in the use of its property, resulting in erosion of the fundamental command of the Supremacy Clause, is at its greatest when the State may, through regulation or taxation, move directly against the activities of the Government. Scarcely less is the danger when the subject of a tax, that at which the State has consciously and purposefully aimed in attaching the consequence of taxability, is the property of the Federal Government. It is not only that the likelihood of local legislation deliberately or unwittingly discriminatory against government property either by its terms or application may be enhanced. Even a nondiscriminatory tax, if it is expressly laid on government property, is more likely to result in interference with the effective use of that property, whether because of an ill-advised attempt by the tax collector to levy on the property itself or because it is sought to hold the Government or its officers to account for the tax, even if ultimately the endeavor may fail. The defense of sovereign immunity to a suit against government officers for the tax, or a suit to assert title to or recover property erroneously levied upon to satisfy a tax, may in practice be an inadequate substitute for the clear assertion of federal interest at the threshold.

The fact that a tax on a third party for the privilege of using government property may itself have an indirect impeding effect is no reason against a rule designed to avoid the more direct and obvious evil. Because a constitutional doctrine is not pushed to the logical extremities of its policy is no argument against maintaining it as far as it has historically extended. From the beginning a broad cloak of immunity for government property has been thought the best way to allay the danger of state encroachment on the national interest, and the character of our federal system and the relations between the Nation and the States have not in this regard so changed that the principle has become outmoded.

[Justices Harlan, Whittaker and Burton also dissented.] [c]

New York v. United States 326 U.S. 572, 66 S. Ct. 310, 90 L. Ed. 326 (1946)

MR. JUSTICE FRANKFURTER announced the judgment of the Court and delivered an opinion in which MR. JUSTICE RUTLEDGE joined.

Section 615(a)(5) of the 1932 Revenue Act . . . imposed a tax on mineral waters. The United States brought this suit to recover taxes assessed against the State of New York on the sale of mineral waters taken from Saratoga Springs, New York. The State claims immunity from this tax on the ground that "in the bottling and sale of the said waters the defendant State of New York was engaged in the exercise of a usual, traditional and essential government function." The claim was rejected by the District Court and judgment went for the United States, 48 F. Supp. 15. The judgment was affirmed by the Circuit Court of Appeals for the Second Circuit. 140 F.2d 608. The strong urging of New York for further clarification of the amenability of States to the taxing power of the United States led us to grant certiorari. 322 U.S. 724. After the case was argued at the 1944 Term, reargument was ordered.

On the basis of authority the case is quickly disposed of. When States sought to control the liquor traffic by going into the liquor business, they were denied immunity from federal taxes upon the liquor business. South Carolina v. United States, 199 U.S. 437; Ohio

[c] Compare Phillips Chemical Co. v. Dumas School District, 361 U.S. 376 (1960); Moses Lake Homes v. Grant County, 365 U.S. 744 (1961). — ED.

v. Helvering, 292 U.S. 360. And in rejecting a claim of immunity from federal taxation when Massachusetts took over the street railways of Boston, this Court a decade ago said: "We see no reason for putting the operation of a street railway [by a state] in a different category from the sale of liquors." Helvering v. Powers, 293 U.S. 214, 227. We certainly see no reason for putting soft drinks in a different constitutional category from hard drinks. See also Allen v. University System, 304 U.S. 439.

One of the greatest sources of strength of our law is that it adjudicates concrete cases and does not pronounce principles in the abstract. But there comes a time when even the process of empiric adjudication calls for a more rational disposition than that the immediate case is not different from preceding cases. The argument pressed by New York and the forty-five other States who, as amici curiae, have joined her deserves an answer. . . .

. . . the fear that one government may cripple or obstruct the operations of the other early led to the assumption that there was a reciprocal immunity of the instrumentalities of each from taxation by the other. It was assumed that there was an equivalence in the implications of taxation by a State of the governmental activities of the National Government and the taxation by the National Government of State instrumentalities. This assumed equivalence was nourished by the phrase of Chief Justice Marshall that "the power to tax involves the power to destroy." M'Culloch v. Maryland, 4 Wheat. 316, 431. To be sure, it was uttered in connection with a tax of Maryland which plainly discriminated against the use by the United States of the Bank of the United States as one of its instruments. What he said may not have been irrelevant in its setting. But Chief Justice Marshall spoke at a time when social complexities did not so clearly reveal as now the practical limitations of a rhetorical absolute. See Holmes, J., in Long v. Rockwood, 277 U.S. 142, 148, and in Panhandle Oil Co. v. Mississippi, 277 U.S. 218, 223. The phrase was seized upon as the basis of a broad doctrine of intergovernmental immunity, while at the same time an expansive scope was given to what were deemed to be "instrumentalities of government" for purposes of tax immunity. As a result, immunity was until recently accorded to all officers of one government from taxation by the other, and it was further assumed that the economic burden of a tax on any interest derived from a government imposes a burden on that government so as to involve an interference by the taxing government with the functioning of the other government. . . .

. . . When this Court for the first time relieved State officers from a nondiscriminatory Congressional tax, not because of anything said in the Constitution but because of the supposed implications of our federal system, Mr. Justice Bradley pointed out the invalidity of the notion of reciprocal intergovernmental immunity. The considerations bearing upon taxation by the States of activities or agencies of the federal government are not correlative with the considerations bearing upon federal taxation of State agencies or activities. . . . [Quoting the dissenting opinion in Collector v. Day, 11 Wall. 113, 128.] Since then we have moved away from the theoretical assumption that the National Government is burdened if its functionaries, like other citizens, pay for the upkeep of their State governments, and we have denied the implied constitutional immunity of federal officials from State taxes. [Citations omitted.] . . .

When this Court came to sustain the federal taxing power upon a transportation system operated by a State, it did so in ways familiar in developing the law from precedent to precedent. It edged away from reliance on a sharp distinction between the "governmental" and the "trading" activities of a State, by denying immunity from federal taxation to a State when it "is undertaking a business enterprise of a sort that is normally within the reach of the federal taxing power and is distinct from the usual governmental functions that are immune from federal taxation in order to safeguard the necessary independence of the State." Helvering v. Powers, supra (293 U.S. at 227). But this likewise does not furnish a satisfactory guide for dealing with such a practical problem as the constitutional power of the United States over State activities. To rest the federal taxing power on what is "normally" conducted by private enterprise in contradiction to the "usual" governmental functions is too shifting a basis for determining constitutional power and too entangled in expediency to serve as a dependable legal criterion. The essential nature of the problem cannot be hidden by an attempt to separate manifestations of indivisible governmental powers. See Wambaugh, Present Scope of Government (1897) 20 A.B.A. Rep. 307, Frankfurter, The Public and its Government (1930). . . .

In the older cases, the emphasis was on immunity from taxation. The whole tendency of recent cases reveals a shift in emphasis to that of limitation upon immunity. They also indicate an awareness of the limited rôle of courts in assessing the relative weight of the factors upon which immunity is based. Any implied limitation upon the supremacy of the federal power to levy a tax like that now before us, in the absence of discrimination against State activities, brings fiscal and political factors into play. The problem cannot escape issues that do not lend themselves to judgment by criteria and methods of reasoning that are within the professional training and special competence of judges. Indeed the claim of implied immunity by States from federal taxation raises questions not wholly unlike provisions of the Constitution, such as that of Art. 4, §4, guaranteeing States a republican form of government, see Pacific States Teleph. & Teleg. Co. v. Oregon, 223 U.S. 118, which this Court has deemed not within its duty to adjudicate.

We have already held that by engaging in the railroad business a State cannot withdraw the railroad from the power of the federal government to regulate commerce. United States v. California, 297 U.S. 175. See also University of Illinois v. United States, 289 U.S. 48. Surely the power of Congress to lay taxes has impliedly no less a reach than the power of Congress to regulate commerce. There are, of course, State activities and State-owned property that partake of uniqueness from the point of view of intergovernmental relations. These inherently constitute a class by themselves. Only a State can own a State-house; only a State can get income by taxing. These could not be included for purposes of federal taxation in any abstract category of taxpayers without taxing the State as a State. But so long as Congress generally taps a source of revenue by whomsoever earned and not uniquely capable of being earned only by a State, the Constitution of the United States does not forbid it merely because its incidence falls also on a State. . . . After all, the representatives of all the States, having, as the appearance of the Attorneys General of forty-six States at the bar of this Court shows, common interests, alone can pass such a taxing measure and they alone in their wisdom can grant or withhold immunity from federal taxation of such State activities.

The process of Constitutional adjudication does not thrive on conjuring up horrible possibilities that never happen in the real world and devising doctrines sufficiently comprehensive in detail to cover the remotest contingency. Nor need we go beyond what is required for a reasoned disposition of the kind of controversy now before the Court. The restriction upon States not to make laws that discriminate against interstate commerce is a vital constitutional principle, even though "discrimination" is not a code of specifics but a continuous process of application. So we decide enough when we reject limitations upon the taxing power of Congress derived from such untenable criteria as "proprietary" against "governmental" activities of the States, or historically sanctioned activities of Government, or activities conducted merely for profit,[5] and find no restriction upon Congress to include the States in levying a tax exacted equally from private persons upon the same subject matter.

Judgment affirmed.

Mr. Justice Jackson took no part in the consideration or decision of this case.

---

[5] Attempts along similar lines to solve kindred problems arising under the Canadian and Australian Constitutions have also proved a barren process. See Australia Constitution Act, 1900, §114, in Edgerton, Federations and Unions in the British Empire (2d ed. 1924) 225; Pond, Intergovernmental Immunity: A Comparative Study of the Federal System (1941) 26 Iowa L. Rev. 272; Kennedy & Wells, The Law of the Taxing Power in Canada (1931) 35-37. . . .

640 Chapter Ten. Intergovernmental Immunities

[The concurring opinion of MR. JUSTICE RUTLEDGE is omitted.]

MR. CHIEF JUSTICE STONE concurring.

MR. JUSTICE REED, MR. JUSTICE MURPHY, MR. JUSTICE BURTON and I concur in the result. We are of the opinion that the tax here involved should be sustained and the judgment below affirmed.

In view of our decisions in South Carolina v. United States, 199 U.S. 437; Ohio v. Helvering, 292 U.S. 360; Helvering v. Powers, 293 U.S. 214, and Allen v. University System, 304 U.S. 439, we would find it difficult not to sustain the tax in this case, even though we regard as untenable the distinction between "governmental" and "proprietary" interests on which those cases rest to some extent. But we are not prepared to say that the national government may constitutionally lay a non-discriminatory tax on every class of property and activities of States and individuals alike. . . .

A State may, like a private individual, own real property and receive income. But in view of our former decisions we could hardly say that a general non-discriminatory real estate tax (apportioned), or an income tax laid upon citizens and States alike could be constitutionally applied to the State's capitol, its State-house, its public school houses, public parks, or its revenues from taxes or school land, even though all real property and all income of the citizen is taxed. If it be said that private citizens do not own State-houses or public school buildings or receive tax revenues, it may equally be said that private citizens do not conduct a State-owned liquor business or derive revenue from a State-owned athletic field. . . .

It is enough for present purposes that the immunity of the State from federal taxation would, in this case, accomplish a withdrawal from the taxing power of the nation [of] a subject of taxation of a nature which has been traditionally within that power from the beginning. Its exercise now, by a non-discriminatory tax, does not curtail the business of the state government more than it does the like business of the citizen. It gives merely an accustomed and reasonable scope to the federal taxing power. Such a withdrawal from a non-discriminatory federal tax, and one which does not bear on the State any differently than on the citizen, is itself an impairment of the taxing power of the national government, and the activity taxed is such that its taxation does not unduly impair the State's functions of government. . . . The national taxing power would be unduly curtailed if the State, by extending its activities, could withdraw from it subjects of taxation traditionally within it. . . .

MR. JUSTICE DOUGLAS, with whom MR. JUSTICE BLACK concurs, dissenting.

I

If South Carolina v. United States, 199 U.S. 437, is to stand, the present judgment would have to be affirmed. . . .

I do not believe South Carolina v. United States states the correct rule. A State's project is as much a legitimate governmental activity whether it is traditional, or akin to private enterprise, or conducted for profit. Cf. Helvering v. Gerhardt, 304 U.S. 405, 426, 427. A State may deem it as essential to its economy that it own and operate a railroad, a mill, or an irrigation system as it does to own and operate bridges, street lights, or a sewage disposal plant. What might have been viewed in an earlier day as an improvident or even dangerous extension of state activities may today be deemed indispensable. . . .

III

. . . A tax is a powerful, regulatory instrument. . . . Many state activities are in marginal enterprises where private capital refuses to venture. Add to the cost of these projects a federal tax and the social program may be destroyed before it can be launched. In any case, the repercussions of such a fundamental change on the credit of the States and on their programs to take care of the needy and to build for the future would be considerable. To say the present tax will be sustained because it does not impair the State's functions of government is to conclude either that the sale by the State of its mineral water is not a function of government or that the present tax is so slight as to be no burden. The former obviously is not true. The latter overlooks the fact that the power to tax lightly is the power to tax severely. The power to tax is indeed one of the most effective forms of regulation. And no more powerful instrument for centralization of government could be devised. For with the federal government immune and the States subject to tax, the economic ability of the federal government to expand its activities at the expense of the States is at once apparent. That is the result whether the rule of South Carolina v. United States be perpetuated or a new rule of discrimination be adopted.

The notion that the sovereign position of the States must find its protection in the will of a transient majority of Congress is foreign to and a negation of our constitutional system. There will often be vital regional interests represented by no majority in Congress. The Constitution was designed to keep the balance between the States and the nation outside the field of legislative controversy. . . .

IV

Those who agreed with South Carolina v. United States had the fear that an expanding program of state activity would dry up sources of federal revenues and thus cripple the national government. 199 U.S. pp. 454, 455. That was in 1905. That fear is expressed again today when we have the federal income tax, from which employees of the States may not claim exemption on constitutional grounds. Helvering v. Gerhardt, 304 U.S. 405. The fear of depriving the national government of revenue if the tax immunity of the States is sustained has no more place in the present decision than the spectre of socialism, the fear of which, said Holmes "was translated into doctrines that had no proper place in the Constitution or the common law."[5]

There is no showing whatsoever that an expanding field of state activity even faintly promises to cripple the federal government in its search for needed revenues. If the truth were known, I suspect it would show that the activity of the States in the fields of housing, public power and the like have increased the level of income of the people and have raised the standards of marginal or sub-marginal groups. Such conditions affect favorably, not adversely, the tax potential of the federal government.

NOTE Taxation of Government Bonds

1. In the light of the developments in the sphere of tax immunity, may Congress tax the interest on bonds issued by states and their subdivisions? The issue has been forestalled by the specific provision in the Revenue Acts exempting from gross income "interest upon the obligations of a State, Territory, or any political subdivision thereof." The Treasury sought to secure a constitutional ruling by assessing a tax in respect of interest on bonds issued by the Port of New York Authority. The tax court and the court of appeals held, with a dissent in each court, that the bonds were covered by the statutory exemption. Commissioner v. Shamberg's Estate, 144 F.2d 998 (2d Cir. 1944), aff'g 3 T.C. 131 (1944). The Supreme Court denied certiorari, 323 U.S. 792 (1945).

A study made by the Department of Justice in 1938 maintained that state bond interest

[5] Holmes, Collected Legal Papers, 1921, p. 295.

was constitutionally taxable, both within the doctrine of immunity and by reason of the Sixteenth Amendment. Taxation of Government Bondholders and Employees (Dept. of Justice, 1938), reviewed in 52 Harv. L. Rev. 180 (1938).

In considering the taxability of income from government bonds, note that such interest may be included in the measure of a corporate franchise tax measured by net income, Flint v. Stone-Tracy Co., 222 U.S. 107 (1911), and of an inheritance tax, Plummer v. Coler, 178 U.S. 115 (1900); cf. Snyder v. Bettman, 190 U.S. 249 (1903) (upholding federal inheritance tax applied to bequest to a state). Note also that the profit on a resale of government bonds may be reached by an income tax. Willcuts v. Bunn, 282 U.S. 216 (1931).

On the relevance of the Sixteenth Amendment, attention may be drawn to the message of Governor Hughes recommending rejection of the amendment in submitting it to the New York legislature, on the ground that the words "if taken in their natural sense, would include not only incomes from ordinary real or personal property, but also incomes derived from State and municipal securities." Special Message from the Governor, N.Y. Senate, No. 3 (1910). Senator Root took a contrary position. 43 Cong. Rec. 2539 (1910). In Evans v. Gore, 253 U.S. 245 (1920), Mr. Justice Holmes, dissenting from the judgment holding the salary of a federal judge immune from taxation under Article III, relied in part on the Sixteenth Amendment. The decision itself was discredited in O'Malley v. Woodrough, 307 U.S. 277 (1939), but without reference to the Sixteenth Amendment.

2. May a state tax the bonds issued by another state? Cf. Tax Court v. Bonaparte, 104 U.S. 592 (1881).

3. What are the economic considerations for and against the immunity of interest on government bonds? See the materials in Surrey and Warren, Federal Income Taxation 175-202 (1960); also Simons, Personal Income Taxation 170-183 (1938), reprinted in Groves, Viewpoints on Public Finance 471-478 (1947).

What special problems, legal and economic, are presented by the existence of outstanding tax-exempt state and federal securities, and how might these bondholders be treated if a policy of reciprocal taxation were undertaken? See Fitch, Taxing Municipal Bond Income 81-112 (1950) (with bibliography).

4. Assuming that outright taxation of bond income would not be valid, are there permissible methods of mitigating the effects of the immunity? Consider the possibilities and limitations suggested by the cases that follow.

(a) Maxwell v. Bugbee, 250 U.S. 525 (1919). A New Jersey statute imposed inheritance taxes on the estates of nonresidents by computing a tax at progressive rates as if all the property were in New Jersey and taking such portion of that amount as the property in the state bore to the total property of the decedent. The statute was sustained.

(b) Miller v. Milwaukee, 272 U.S. 713 (1927). A Wisconsin income tax statute exempted income in the form of dividends received from corporations whose income was taxed; where only part of the corporation's income was taxed, only a corresponding part of the dividend could be exempted. The taxpayer received dividends from a corporation part of whose earnings was attributable to interest on United States bonds. The Court held that the taxpayer was entitled to an exemption without abatement for the immune source of the dividends. Mr. Justice Brandeis, with whom Mr. Justice Stone joined, concurred specially on the ground that a stipulation, asserting that the dividends were in part directly declared from interest accruing from United States bonds, brought the tax within the provision of the Act of Congress that the interest shall be exempt from state income taxation.

(c) National Life Ins. Co. v. United States, 277 U.S. 508 (1928). Congress imposed a tax on interest, dividends, and rent received by life insurance companies, with a deduction, inter alia, for interest derived from tax-exempt securities and a deduction of 4 percent of the company's legal reserve diminished by the amount of tax-exempt interest received. The Court held invalid the abatement of the deduction for reserves. Justices

Holmes, Brandeis, and Stone dissented. Compare United States v. Atlas Life Ins. Co., 381 U.S. 233 (1965).

(d) Missouri Life Ins. Co. v. Gehner, 281 U.S. 313 (1930). A Missouri statute which taxed the net assets of insurance companies directed that from the value of the personal property there should be deducted the amount of the legal reserve, unpaid policy claims, and United States bonds, provided, however, that the reserve and unpaid claims were to be reduced by the proportion that the value of the United States bonds bore to total assets. The Court held invalid the abatement of the deduction. Justices Holmes, Stone, and Brandeis dissented. Cf. New Jersey Realty Title Ins. Co. v. Division of Tax Appeals, 338 U.S. 665 (1950); 64 Harv. L. Rev. 134-135 (1950). See Wurzel, Tax-Exempt Interest of Life Insurance Companies: A Study in "Discriminatory" Taxation, 70 Yale L.J. 15 (1960).

(e) Denman v. Slayton, 282 U.S. 514 (1931). In the federal income tax Congress provided a deduction for interest paid, but disallowed the deduction where the interest was paid on indebtedness incurred to purchase securities upon which interest was exempt from the income tax. This provision was sustained.

5. The distinction between a property tax on the bonds and a franchise tax measured by their value has been maintained. Society for Savings v. Bowers, 349 U.S. 143 (1955); Werner Machine Co. v. Director of Taxation, 350 U.S. 492 (1956).

Section B. NON-TAX IMMUNITIES

Ohio v. Thomas 173 U.S. 276, 19 S. Ct. 453, 43 L. Ed. 699 (1899)

[An Ohio statute of 1894 required every restaurant or eating house that served oleomargarine to display a placard not less than ten by fourteen inches in size containing the words "oleomargarine sold and used here," and also prohibited the serving of oleomargarine as or for butter when butter was asked for or purported to be furnished. Appellee was the manager of the Central Branch of the National Home for Disabled Volunteer Soldiers, and had not complied with the statute. Upon being convicted and sentenced to pay a fine of fifty dollars he applied to a federal circuit court for a writ of habeas corpus. From a judgment discharging the appellee, affirmed by the circuit court of appeals, the state appealed.]

Mr. Justice Peckham, after stating the facts, delivered the opinion of the court: . . .

The persons entitled to the benefits of the home are "officers and soldiers who served in the late war for the suppression of the rebellion," and also other soldiers and sailors. The inmates are subject to the rules and articles of war, the same as if they were in the army. Rev. Stat. §§4832, 4835.

Under the statutes above cited, in which it is provided that the board of managers shall furnish to the Secretary of War, in each year, estimates, in detail, for the support of the home for the succeeding fiscal year, it would naturally be the duty of the governor of each home, in order to enable the board of managers to perform their own duty, to report to the board the same kind of detailed estimates that the board is by law directed to report to the Secretary of War, and which are to be included by the Secretary in the estimates for his department. At all events, the duty is laid upon the board of managers, by the very terms of the statute, to make these estimates in detail. It is admitted in the record that the oleomargarine complained about herein was served and furnished by the appellee as food and as part of the rations furnished the inmates under the appropriations made by Congress for the support of such inmates. . . .

... The appropriation does not precede the detailed estimates, but is made subsequently and is presumably enacted with reference thereto. Congress has therefore in effect provided oleomargarine as part of the rations for the inmates of the home. It is given them in the mess room of the institution and under the rules and regulations for feeding them there. In making provision for so feeding the inmates, the governor, under the direction of the board of managers and with the assent and approval of Congress, is engaged in the internal administration of a Federal institution, and we think a state legislature has no constitutional power to interfere with such management as is provided by Congress. . . .

Some of the same authorities also show that this is one of the cases where it is proper to issue a writ of habeas corpus from the Federal court, instead of awaiting the slow process of a writ of error from this court to the highest court of the state where a decision could be had. One of the grounds for making such a case as this an exception to the general rule laid down in Ex parte Royall, 117 U.S. 241, Whitten v. Tomlinson, 160 U.S. 231, and Baker v. Grice, 169 U.S. 284, consists in the fact that the Federal officer proceeded against in the courts of the state may, upon conviction, be imprisoned as a means of enforcing the sentence of a fine, and thus the operations of the Federal government might in the meantime be obstructed. This is such a case. . . .

For the reasons herein given we think the order of the Circuit Court of Appeals, affirming the Circuit Court, was right, and it must be affirmed.

Johnson v. Maryland 254 U.S. 51, 41 S. Ct. 16, 65 L. Ed. 126 (1920)

MR. JUSTICE HOLMES delivered the opinion of the court:

The plaintiff in error was an employee of the Post Office Department of the United States, and, while driving a government motor truck in the transportation of mail over a post road from Mt. Airy, Maryland, to Washington, was arrested in Maryland, and was tried, convicted, and fined for so driving without having obtained a license from the state. He saved his constitutional rights by motion to quash, by special pleas, which were overruled upon demurrer, and by motion in arrest of judgment. The facts were admitted, and the naked question is whether the state has power to require such an employee to obtain a license by submitting to an examination concerning his competence and paying $3, before performing his official duty in obedience to superior command. . . .

Of course, an employee of the United States does not secure a general immunity from state law while acting in the course of his employment. That was decided long ago by Mr. Justice Washington in United States v. Hart, Pet. C.C. 390, Fed. Cas. No. 15,316; 5 Ops. Atty. Gen. 554. It very well may be that, when the United States has not spoken, the subjection to local law would extend to general rules that might affect incidentally the mode of carrying out the employment, — as, for instance, a statute or ordinance regulating the mode of turning at the corners of streets. Com. v. Closson, 229 Mass. 329. This might stand on much the same footing as liability under the common law of a state to a person injured by the driver's negligence. But even the most unquestionable and most universally applicable of state laws, such as those concerning murder will not be allowed to control the conduct of a marshal of the United States, acting under and in pursuance of the laws of the United States. Re Neagle, 135 U.S. 1.

It seems to us that the immunity of the instruments of the United States from state control in the performance of their duties extends to a requirement that they desist from performance until they satisfy a state officer, upon examination, that they are competent for a necessary part of them, and pay a fee for permission to go on. Such a requirement does not merely touch the government servants remotely by a general rule of conduct; it lays hold of them in their specific attempt to obey orders, and requires qualifications in addition to those that the government has pronounced sufficient. It is the duty of the Department to employ persons competent for their work, and that duty it must be presumed has been performed. Keim v. United States, 177 U.S. 290, 293.

Judgment reversed.[d]

MR. JUSTICE PITNEY and MR. JUSTICE MCREYNOLDS dissent.

James Stewart & Co. v. Sadrakula 309 U.S. 94, 60 S. Ct. 431, 84 L. Ed. 596 (1940)

MR. JUSTICE REED delivered the opinion of the Court:

This is an appeal from a final judgment of the Supreme Court of New York awarding damages for accidental death. . . .

The issue of law involved is whether an existing provision of a state statute requiring the protection of places of work in the manner specified in the statute remains effective as a statute of the United States applicable to the particular parcel after the federal government acquires exclusive jurisdiction of a parcel of realty on which work is being done.

The decedent, an employee of a rigging company, a sub-contractor engaged in the construction of the New York post office, fell from an unplanked tier of steel beams down a bay and was killed. In an action of tort against the general contractor, his administratrix narrowed the scope of the charges of negligence until violation of the quoted sub-section of the Labor Law only was alleged. The trial court found that the proximate cause of the accident was the negligent failure to plank the beams as required by the statute. The Appellate Division affirmed on the ground that the Labor Law provision continued effective over the post-office site after the transfer of sovereignty, and the Court of Appeals, by an order of remittitur (280 N.Y. 730) also affirmed on the same ground with a statement that in its affirmance it necessarily passed upon the validity and applicability of §241(4) of the Labor Law under Article 1, §8 of the Constitution. . . .

If the quoted provision of the Labor Law is operative even though exclusive jurisdiction had already vested in the United States, it is unnecessary to determine whether exclusive jurisdiction had actually passed to the United States. The state courts assumed that federal sovereignty was complete through consent by the state and we make the same assumption. Does the acceptance of sovereignty by the United States have the effect of displacing this sub-section of the New York Labor Law? We think it did not. The sub-section continues as a part of the laws of the federal territory.

It is now settled that the jurisdiction acquired from a state by the United States whether by consent to the purchase or by cession may be qualified in accordance with agreements reached by the respective governments. The Constitution does not command that every vestige of the laws of the former sovereignty must vanish. On the contrary its language has long been interpreted so as to permit the continuance until abrogated of those rules existing at the time of the surrender of sovereignty which govern the rights of the occupants of the territory transferred. This assures that no area however small will be left without a developed legal system for private rights. In Chicago, R.I. & P.R. Co. v. McGlinn, 114 U.S. 542, a Kansas statute relating to recovery against a railroad for the injury to livestock on its right of way existed at the time of the cession to the United States of exclusive jurisdiction over Fort Leavenworth Military Reservation. It was held that the statute was carried over into the law covering the Reservation. Conversely, in Arlington Hotel Co. v. Fant, 278 U.S. 439, an Arkansas statute relieving innkeepers, passed after cession of Hot Springs Reservation, was held unavailing as a defense to a Reservation innkeeper's common-law liability in accordance with Arkansas law before the cession. Such holdings assimilate the laws of the federal territory, where the Congress has not legislated otherwise, to the laws of the surrounding state.

[d] Cf. Leslie Miller, Inc. v. Arkansas, 352 U.S. 187 (1956). — ED.

The Congress has recognized in certain instances the desirability of such similarity between the municipal laws of the state and those of the federal parcel. Since only the law in effect at the time of the transfer of jurisdiction continues in force, future statutes of the state are not a part of the body of laws in the ceded area. Congressional action is necessary to keep it current. Consequently as defects become apparent legislation is enacted covering certain phases. This occurred as to rights of action for accidental death by negligence or wrongful act. After this statute was held inapplicable to claims under state workmen's compensation acts further legislation undertook to extend the provisions of those acts to the places under federal sovereignty. With growing frequency the federal government leaves largely unimpaired the civil and criminal authority of the state over national reservations or properties. While exclusive federal jurisdiction attaches, state courts are without power to punish for crimes committed on federal property. This has made necessary the legislation which gives federal courts jurisdiction over these crimes. The tendency toward a uniformity between the federal and surrounding state territory has caused a series of congressional acts adopting the state criminal laws. Through these concessions our dual system of government works co-operatively towards harmonious adjustment.

It is urged that the provisions of the Labor Law contain numerous administrative and other provisions which cannot be relevant to the federal territory. The Labor Law does have a number of articles. Obviously much of their language is directed at situations that cannot arise in the territory. With the domestication in the excised area of the entire applicable body of state municipal law much of the state law must necessarily be inappropriate. Some sections authorize quasi-judicial proceedings or administrative action and may well have no validity in the federal area. It is not a question here of the exercise of state administrative authority in federal territory. We do not agree, however, that because the Labor Law is not applicable as a whole, it follows that none of its sections are. We have held in Collins v. Yosemite Park & C. Co. [304 U.S. 518] that the sections of a California statute which levied excises on sales of liquor in Yosemite National Park were enforceable in the Park, while sections of the same statute providing regulation of the Park liquor traffic through licenses were unenforceable.

But the authority of state laws or their administration may not interfere with the carrying out of a national purpose. Where enforcement of the state law would handicap efforts to carry out the plans of the United States, the state enactment must, of course, give way.

May it be said that the continued application of §241(4) of the Labor Law will interfere with the construction of the building upon this site? . . . In answer to the argument that a similar increased cost from taxation would "make it difficult or impossible" for the government to obtain the service it needs, we said in James v. Dravo Contracting Co. [302 U.S. 134] that such a contention "ignores the power of Congress to protect the performance of the functions of the National Government and to prevent interference therewith through any attempted state action." Such a safety requirement is akin to the safety provisions of Maryland law which in Baltimore & A.R. Co. v. Lichtenberg[23] were held applicable to trucks of an independent contractor transporting government employees under a contract with the United States.

Finally the point is made that a provision requiring boarding over of open steel tiers is a direct interference with the government. This is said to follow from the fact that the contract for the construction of the post office is an instrumentality of the federal government. As a corollary to this argument, error is assigned to the refusal of the trial court to admit in evidence a clause of the contract between the United States and the appellant reading, "State or Municipal Building Regulations do not apply to work inside the Government's lot lines." While, of course, in a sense the contract is the means by which the United States secures the construction of its post office, certainly the contractor in this independent operation does not share any governmental immunity. Nor do we think there was

---

[23] 176 Md. 383, appeal dismissed for want of a substantial federal question, sub nom. United States v. Baltimore & A.R. Co. No. 78, October Term, 1939, decided December 18, 1939 [308 U.S. 525].

error in refusing to admit the clause of the contract as to building regulations. The quoted sentence is in a section of the contract relating to "licenses, permits, etc." We are of the opinion that it is intended to relieve the contractor from provisions as to types of material, fire hazards and the like, which are covered by the New York City Building Code.

Such a safety regulation as §241(4) of the New York Labor Law provides is effective in the federal area, until such time as the Congress may otherwise provide.

Affirmed.[e]

NOTE "Reciprocity" of Immunities

1. In the tax cases there has been much talk of reciprocity of governmental immunity. What part has this criterion played in the nontax aspects of the problem of immunity?

(a) *Regulatory measures.* Compare United States v. California, 297 U.S. 175 (1936), upholding the application of the Federal Safety Appliance Acts to the state-owned California Belt Railroad, with Ohio v. Thomas and Johnson v. Maryland, supra pages 643 and 644. But cf. National League of Cities v. Usery, page 286 supra. In Mayo v. United States, 319 U.S. 436 (1943), a state inspection fee was held invalid as applied to fertilizer shipped into Florida by the United States for distribution pursuant to the Federal Soil Conservation Act. May a customs duty be levied on goods imported by a State? In Board of Trustees of University of Illinois v. United States, 289 U.S. 48 (1933), sustaining the duty, the Court treated the tariff as a regulation of foreign commerce, although in Hampton & Co. v. United States, 276 U.S. 394 (1928), the flexible tariff was upheld as an exercise of the taxing power.

(b) *Eminent domain.* Compare Utah Power & Light Co. v. United States, 243 U.S. 389, 405 (1917), denying state power of eminent domain over federal lands, with Oklahoma v. Atkinson Co., 313 U.S. 508 (1941), sustaining federal condemnation of state-owned lands.

(c) *Habeas corpus.* Compare In re Neagle, 135 U.S. 1 (1890), supra page 616, with Ableman v. Booth, 21 How. 506 (1858), denying power in a state court to discharge a prisoner held in federal custody for violation of the Fugitive Slave Law.

(d) *Mandamus.* Compare Riggs v. Johnson County, 6 Wall. 166 (1868), ordering county officers to levy a tax to satisfy a federal judgment, with McClung v. Silliman, 6 Wheat. 598 (1821), denying power in a state court to issue mandamus to a federal officer.[f]

---

[e] See Report of Interdepartmental Committee for Study of Jurisdiction Over Federal Areas Within the States (Two Parts, Govt. Ptg. Office, 1956, 1957). — ED.

[f] Riggs v. Johnson County was one incident in the running battle between federal and state courts in the mid-nineteenth century over the enforcement of municipal bonds which had been issued in exchange for stock in the expanding railroad systems. The classic symbol of the whole episode is Gelpcke v. Dubuque, 1 Wall. 175 (1864), holding that a federal court should apply the decisional law of the state as of the time the bonds were issued, and not the supervening decisions which would render the bonds unenforceable. The theoretical and practical relation of Gelpcke v. Dubuque to the doctrine of Swift v. Tyson makes an interesting study in the mainsprings of the judicial process. See the criticisms by Holmes, J., dissenting, in Kuhn v. Fairmount Coal Co., 215 U.S. 349, 371 (1910); cf. Thayer, The Case of Gelpcke v. Dubuque, 4 Harv. L. Rev. 311 (1891); Rand, Swift v. Tyson Versus Gelpcke v. Dubuque, 8 id. at 328 (1895); Gray, Nature and Sources of the Law 251 et seq. (2d ed. 1931). At all events, federal courts found themselves ordering local officials to do what a state court had forbidden them to do, and punishing failure to comply.

To all this Mr. Justice Miller made vigorous and repeated protests. Dissenting in Butz v. Muscatine, 8 Wall. 575, 587 (1869), he said: "These frequent dissents in this class of subjects are as distasteful to me as they can be to any one else. But when I am compelled, as I was last spring, by the decision of this court, to enter an order to commit to jail at one time over a hundred of the best citizens of Iowa, for obeying as they thought their oath of office required them to do, an injunction issued by a competent court of their own State, founded, as these gentlemen conscientiously believed, on the true interpretation of their own statute, an injunction which, in my own private judgment, they were legally bound to obey, I must be excused if, when sitting here, I give expression to convictions which my duty compels me to disregard in the circuit court."

The story is vividly told in Fairman, Mr. Justice Miller, c. 9 (1939). — ED.

(e) *Injunctions against officers.* Compare Ex parte Young, 209 U.S. 123 (1908), upholding, in contempt proceedings, a federal injunction against a state attorney general restraining him from enforcing railroad rates deemed confiscatory, with Brooks v. Dewar, 313 U.S. 354 (1941), reserving the question whether a state court may enjoin federal officers.

(f) *Suits between sovereigns.* Compare United States v. California, 297 U.S. 175 (1936), supra paragraph (a), and United States v. California, 332 U.S. 19 (1947), sustaining jurisdiction in the district court and the Supreme Court, respectively, with Louisiana v. McAdoo, 234 U.S. 637 (1914), denying jurisdiction over suits brought by a state against the United States without the latter's consent.

2. Is reciprocity in tax immunity a standard more appropriate for legislative than for judicial application? Congress has frequently consented to the local taxation of federally owned real estate, and has also authorized contributions from the revenues of federal agencies to states and counties in lieu of taxes. See H.R. Doc. No. 216, 78th Cong., 1st Sess. (1943) (Federal Contributions to States and Local Governmental Units with Respect to Federally Owned Real Estate). In authorizing agreements for payments in lieu of taxes on federal slum-clearance and low-cost housing projects, Congress provided: "Such sums shall be . . . based upon the cost of public or municipal services to be supplied for the benefit of such project or the persons residing on or occupying such premises, but taking into consideration the benefits to be derived by such State or subdivision from such projects." 49 Stat. 2026.

The TVA is authorized to pay to the states a percentage of its gross revenues. How should such payments be allocated? See Lilienthal, TVA: Democracy on the March 159 (1944); Ramsmeirer, The Tennessee Valley Authority 72-76 (1942); Prichett, The Tennessee Valley Authority 111-115 (1943); Durisch and Macon, Payments in Lieu of Taxes by the Tennessee Valley Authority, 3 J. Pol. 318 (1941); Edelman, Public Ownership and Tax Replacement by the TVA, 35 Am. Pol. Sci. Rev. 727 (1941). For a comparison by TVA of estimated savings to consumers with losses in property and business taxes, see Electric Power and Government Policy 632 (Twentieth Century Fund, 1948).

Chapter Eleven Distribution of National Powers

Section A. SEPARATION OF POWERS

1. The General Doctrine

Political philosophers with whom the framers were familiar considered it essential that all the powers of government not be concentrated in the same hands. John Locke insisted that the representatives elected to the legislature could not pass their constituents' trust to others by delegating their lawmaking powers and should not be offered the temptations inherent in being allowed to enforce the laws themselves. Second Treatise of Government (An Essay Concerning the True Origin, Extent and End of Civil Government) §§141, 143 (Gough 3d ed. 1966). The importance of separation of powers to maintenance of political freedoms was put most plainly by Montesquieu:

"The political liberty of the subject is a tranquillity of mind arising from the opinion each person has of his safety. In order to have this liberty, it is requisite the government be so constituted as one man need not be afraid of another.

"When the legislative and executive powers are united in the same person, or in the same body of magistrates, there can be no liberty; because apprehensions may arise, lest the same monarch or senate should enact tyrannical laws, to execute them in a tyrannical manner.

"Again, there is no liberty, if the judiciary power be not separated from the legislative and executive. Were it joined with the legislative, the life and liberty of the subject would be exposed to arbitrary control; for the judge would then be the legislator. Were it joined to the executive power, the judge might behave with violence and oppression.

"There would be an end of everything, were the same man or the same body, whether of the nobles or of the people, to exercise those three powers, that of enacting laws, that of executing the public resolutions, and of trying the causes of individuals." The Spirit of the Laws 151-152 (Nugent trans. 1949).

Madison, The Federalist No. 47 *Cooke ed. 1961*

. . . One of the principal objections inculcated by the more respectable adversaries to the constitution, is its supposed violation of the political maxim, that the legislative, executive and judiciary departments ought to be separate and distinct. In the structure of the federal government, no regard, it is said, seems to have been paid to this essential precaution in favor of liberty. The several departments of power are distributed and blended in such a manner, as at once to destroy all symmetry and beauty of form; and to expose some of the essential parts of the edifice to the danger of being crushed by the disproportionate weight of other parts.

No political truth is certainly of greater intrinsic value or is stamped with the authority of more enlightened patrons of liberty than that on which the objection is founded. The accumulation of all powers legislative, executive and judiciary in the same hands, whether of one, a few or many, and whether hereditary, self appointed, or elective, may justly be pronounced the very definition of tyranny. Were the federal constitution therefore really chargeable with this accumulation of power or with a mixture of powers having a dangerous tendency to such an accumulation, no further arguments would be necessary to inspire a universal reprobation of the system. I persuade myself however, that it will be made apparent to every one, that the charge cannot be supported, and that the maxim on which it relies, has been totally misconceived and misapplied. In order to form correct ideas on this important subject, it will be proper to investigate the sense, in which the preservation of liberty requires, that the three great departments of power should be separate and distinct.

The oracle who is always consulted and cited on this subject, is the celebrated Montesquieu. If he be not the author of this invaluable precept in the science of politics, he has the merit at least of displaying, and recommending it most effectually to the attention of mankind. Let us endeavour in the first place to ascertain his meaning on this point.

The British constitution was to Montesquieu, what Homer has been to the didactic writers on epic poetry. As the latter have considered the work of the immortal Bard, as the perfect model from which the principles and rules of the epic art were to be drawn, and by which all similar works were to be judged; so this great political critic appears to have viewed the constitution of England, as the standard, or to use his own expression, as the mirrour of political liberty; and to have delivered in the form of elementary truths, the several characteristic principles of that particular system. That we may be sure then not to mistake his meaning in this case, let us recur to the source from which the maxim was drawn.

On the slightest view of the British constitution we must perceive, that the legislative, executive and judiciary departments are by no means totally separate and distinct from each other. The executive magistrate forms an integral part of the legislative authority. He alone has the prerogative of making treaties with foreign sovereigns, which when made have, under certain limitations, the force of legislative acts. All the members of the judiciary department are appointed by him; can be removed by him on the address of the two Houses of Parliament, and form, when he pleases to consult them, one of his constitutional councils. One branch of the legislative department forms also, a great constitutional council to the executive chief; as on another hand, it is the sole depositary of judicial power in cases of impeachment, and is invested with the supreme appellate jurisdiction, in all other cases. The judges again are so far connected with the legislative department, as often to attend and participate in its deliberations, though not admitted to a legislative vote.

From these facts by which Montesquieu was guided it may clearly be inferred, that in saying "there can be no liberty where the legislative and executive powers are united in the same person, or body of magistrates," or "if the power of judging be not separated from the legislative and executive powers," he did not mean that these departments ought to have no *partial agency* in, or no *controul* over the acts of each other. His meaning, as his own words import, and still more conclusively as illustrated by the example in his eye, can amount to no more than this, that where the *whole* power of one department is exercised by the same hands which possess the *whole* power of another department, the fundamental principles of a free constitution, are subverted. This would have been the case in the constitution examined by him, if the King who is the sole executive magistrate, had possessed also the compleat legislative power, or the supreme administration of justice; or if the entire legislative body, had possessed the supreme judiciary, or the supreme executive authority. This however is not among the vices of that constitution. . . .

The reasons on which Montesquieu grounds his maxim are a further demonstration of his meaning. . . .

If we look into the constitutions of the several states we find that notwithstanding the emphatical, and in some instances, the unqualified terms in which this axiom has been laid down, there is not a single instance in which the several departments of power have been kept absolutely separate and distinct. New-Hampshire, whose constitution was the last formed, seems to have been fully aware of the impossibility and inexpediency of avoiding any mixture whatever of these departments; and has qualified the doctrine by declaring "that the legislative, executive and judiciary powers ought to be kept as separate from, and independent of each other *as the nature of a free government will admit; or as is consistent with that chain of connection, that binds the whole fabric of the constitution in one indissoluble bond of unity and amity.*" Her constitution accordingly mixes these departments in several respects. The senate which is a branch of the legislative department is also a judicial tribunal for the trial of empeachments. The president who is the head of the executive department, is the presiding member also of the senate; and besides an equal vote in all cases, has a casting vote in case of a tie. The executive head is himself eventually elective every year by the legislative department; and his council is every year chosen by and from the members of the same department. Several of the officers of state are also appointed by the legislature. And the members of the judiciary department are appointed by the executive department.

The constitution of Massachusetts has observed a sufficient though less pointed caution in expressing this fundamental article of liberty. It declares "that the legislative department shall never exercise the executive and judicial powers, or either of them: The executive shall never exercise the legislative and judicial powers, or either of them: The judicial shall never exercise the legislative and executive powers, or either of them." This declaration corresponds precisely with the doctrine of Montesquieu as it has been explained, and is not in a single point violated by the plan of the Convention. It goes no farther than to prohibit any one of the entire departments from exercising the powers of another department. In the very constitution to which it is prefixed, a partial mixture of powers has been admitted. The Executive Magistrate has a qualified negative on the Legislative body; and the Senate, which is a part of the Legislature, is a court of impeachment for members both of the executive and judiciary departments. The members of the judiciary department again are appointable by the executive department, and removeable by the same authority, on the address of the two legislative branches. Lastly, a number of the officers of government are annually appointed by the legislative department. As the appointment to offices, particularly executive offices, is in its nature an executive function, the compilers of the Constitution have in this last point at least, violated the rule established by themselves. . . .

In citing these cases in which the legislative, executive and judiciary departments, have not been kept totally separate and distinct, I wish not to be regarded as an advocate for the particular organizations of the several state governments. I am fully aware that among the many excellent principles which they exemplify, they carry strong marks of the haste, and still stronger of the inexperience, under which they were framed. It is but too obvious that in some instances, the fundamental principle under consideration has been violated by too great a mixture, and even an actual consolidation of the different powers; and that in no instance has a competent provision been made for maintaining in practice the separation delineated on paper. What I have wished to evince is, that the charge brought against the proposed constitution, of violating a sacred maxim of free government, is warranted neither by the real meaning annexed to that maxim by its author; nor by the sense in which it has hitherto been understood in America. . . .

Frankfurter and Landis, Power of Congress over Procedure in Criminal Contempts in "Inferior" Federal Courts — A Study in Separation of Powers 37 Harv. L. Rev. 1010 (1924)

At the bottom of our problem lies the doctrine of the separation of powers. That doctrine embodies cautions against tyranny in government through undue concentration of power. The environment of the Constitution, the debates at Philadelphia, the writings in support of the adoption of the Constitution, unite in proof that the true meaning which lies behind "the separation of powers" is fear of the absorption of one of the three branches of government by another. As a principle of statesmanship the practical demands of government preclude its doctrinaire application. The latitude with which the doctrine must be observed in a work-a-day world was steadily insisted upon by those shrewd men of the world who framed the Constitution and by the statesman who became the great Chief Justice. A distinguished student of comparative constitutional law, one of Montesquieu's countrymen, has summed up the significance of his doctrine:

"The separation of powers is merely a formula, and formulas are not working principles of government. Montesquieu had chiefly aimed to indicate by his formula the aspirations of his times and country. He could not and did not wish to propose a definite and permanent solution of all the questions brought up by the government of men and their long-felt longings for fairness and justice."

In a word, we are dealing with what Sir Henry Maine, following Madison, calls a "political doctrine," and not a technical rule of law. Nor has it been treated by the Supreme Court as a technical legal doctrine. From the beginning that Court has refused to draw abstract, analytical lines of separation and has recognized necessary areas of interaction. Duties have been cast on courts as to which Congress itself might have legislated; matters have been withdrawn from courts and vested in the executive; laws have been sustained which are contingent upon executive judgment on highly complicated factors, instead of insisting on self-defining legislation; even though "the distinction between amnesty and pardon is of no practical importance" the specific power of the President to grant pardons does not invalidate congressional acts of amnesty, nor does the President's power to pardon offenses preclude Congress from giving the Secretary of the Treasury the authority to remit fines and forfeitures. Even more significant than the decisions themselves are the considerations which induced them, and the insistence on an abstract doctrine of separation of powers which they rejected. "The necessities of the case," "to stop the wheels of government," "practical exposition," are the variations in the *motif* of the decisions. The dominant note is respect for the action of that branch of the government upon which is cast the primary responsibility for adjusting public affairs. The accommodations among the three branches of the government are not automatic. They are undefined, and in the very nature of things could not have been defined, by the Constitution. To speak of *lines* of demarcation is to use an inapt figure. There are vast stretches of ambiguous territory. Certainly in the first instance Congress must mark metes and bounds. Therefore the courts will not judge what is fundamentally a political problem by technical considerations. On the contrary, the Supreme Court has consistently sustained congressional discretion when moving in the general legislative field not bound by specific limitations, even though the particular field may border on territory dominantly in control of another department of the government.

Myers v. United States 272 U.S. 52 (1926)

BRANDEIS, J., dissenting.

The separation of the powers of government did not make each branch completely autonomous. It left each, in some measure, dependent upon the others, as it left to each power to exercise, in some respects, functions in their nature executive, legislative and judicial. Obviously the President cannot secure full execution of the laws, if Congress denies to him adequate means of doing so. Full execution may be defeated because Congress declines to create offices indispensable for that purpose. Or, because Congress, having created the office, declines to make the indispensable appropriation. Or, because Congress, having both created the office and made the appropriation, prevents, by restrictions which it imposes, the appointment of officials who in quality and character are indispensable to the efficient execution of the law. If, in any such way, adequate means are denied to the President, the fault will lie with Congress. The President performs his full constitutional duty, if, with the means and instruments provided by Congress and within the limitations prescribed by it, he uses his best endeavors to secure the faithful execution of the laws enacted. Compare Kendall v. United States, 12 Pet. 524, 613, 626.

Checks and balances were established in order that this should be "a government of laws and not of men." As White said in the House, in 1789, an uncontrollable power of removal in the Chief Executive "is a doctrine not to be learned in American governments." Such power had been denied in Colonial Charters, and even under Proprietary Grants and Royal Commissions. It had been denied in the thirteen States before the framing of the Federal Constitution. The doctrine of the separation of powers was adopted by the Convention of 1787, not to promote efficiency but to preclude the exercise of arbitrary power. The purpose was, not to avoid friction, but, by means of the inevitable friction incident to the distribution of the governmental powers among three departments, to save the people from autocracy. In order to prevent arbitrary executive action, the Constitution provided in terms that presidential appointments be made with the consent of the Senate, unless Congress should otherwise provide; and this clause was construed by Alexander Hamilton in The Federalist, No. 77, as requiring like consent to removals. Limiting further executive prerogatives customary in monarchies, the Constitution empowered Congress to vest the appointment of inferior officers, "as they think proper, in the President alone, in the Courts of Law, or in the Heads of Departments." Nothing in support of the claim of uncontrollable power can be inferred from the silence of the Convention of 1787 on the subject of removal. For the outstanding fact remains that every specific proposal to confer such uncontrollable power upon the President was rejected. In America, as in England, the conviction prevailed then that the people must look to representative assemblies for the protection of their liberties. And protection of the individual, even if he be an official, from the arbitrary or capricious exercise of power was then believed to be an essential of free government.

2. Separation of Congressional and Executive Powers

NOTE The Delegation Doctrine

A corollary of the separation of powers doctrine is the rule, attributed to Bracton, "Delegata potestas non potest delegari" — "Delegated power may not be delegated." Most commonly, the rule is employed to mean that a legislature, which has received from the people the power to make laws, may not surrender this power to another body, most commonly the executive. The difficulty is that the legislature may often lack the time or expertise to develop each legislative program in detail, particularly in the area of government regulation of economic matters, and many questions are left to be resolved by the executive officers who administer the program. The Supreme Court has, by and large, taken a practical, lenient view of Bracton's rule. In Field v. Clark, 143 U.S. 649 (1892), the Court upheld provisions of the Tariff Act of 1890 authorizing the President to suspend free importation of certain goods from any country on his determination that that country was placing import duties on United States products which "he may deem to be reciprocally unequal and unreasonable." Writing for the Court, Justice Harlan stated: "[When the President] ascertained the fact that duties and exactions, reciprocally unequal and unreasonable, were imposed upon the . . . products of the United States . . . , it became his duty to issue a proclamation declaring the suspension . . . which Congress had determined should occur. . . . Legislative power was exercised when Congress declared that the suspension should take effect upon a named contingency. What the President was required to do was simply in execution of the Act of Congress. It was not the making of law. He was the mere agent of the law making department to ascertain and declare the event upon which its expressed will was to take effect. . . ."

Over the next forty years, the Court elaborated the circumstances in which rulemaking power may be delegated to the executive. In United States v. Grimaud, 220 U.S. 506 (1911), the Court upheld a criminal conviction for violation of a regulation promulgated by the Secretary of Agriculture which required persons to secure permits to graze their animals on federal forest reserves. The power to make rules and regulations "to ensure the objects of such reservations; namely, to regulate their occupancy and use, and to preserve the forests thereon from destruction," had been delegated to the Secretary in the Act of February 1, 1905, 33 Stat. 628. The Court affirmed that "when Congress ha[s] legislated and indicated its will, it [can] give to those who were to act under such general provisions 'power to fill up the details' by the establishment of administrative rules and regulations . . . ," quoting Wayman v. Southard, 10 Wheat. 42 (1825). Compare Buttfield v. Stranahan, 192 U.S. 470 (1904), where the Court upheld a delegation on its finding that Congress had "fix[ed] a primary standard, and devolved upon the Secretary . . . the mere executive duty to effectuate the legislative policy declared in the statute."

In subsequent cases the Court held that to determine whether Congress has given sufficient guidance to the executive, the Court may look not only to the language of the statute but also to settled practice, which may have given well-understood meaning to otherwise ambiguous words. See, e.g., Mahler v. Eby, 264 U.S. 32, 40 (1924).

In Hampton & Co. v. United States, 276 U.S. 394 (1928), Chief Justice Taft took another step towards flexible interpretation of the delegation doctrine in upholding the Flexible Tariff of 1922: "In determining what [a branch of government] may do in seeking assistance from another branch, the extent and character of that assistance must be fixed according to common sense and the inherent necessities of the governmental co-ordination.

"The field of Congress involves all and many varieties of legislative action, and Congress has found it frequently necessary to use officers of the Executive Branch, within defined limits, to secure the exact effect intended by its acts of legislation, by vesting discretion in such officers to make public regulations interpreting a statute and directing the details of its execution, even to the extent of providing for penalizing a breach of such regulations. . . .

"[O]ne of the great functions conferred on Congress by the Federal Constitution is the regulation of interstate commerce and rates to be exacted by interstate carriers for the passenger and merchandise traffic. The rates to be fixed are myriad. If Congress were to be required to fix every rate, it would be impossible to exercise the power at all. Therefore, common sense requires that in the fixing of such rates, Congress may provide a Commission, as it does, called the Interstate Commerce Commission, to fix those rates, after hearing evidence and argument concerning them from interested parties, all in accord with a general rule that Congress first lays down, that rates shall be just and reasonable considering the service given, and not discriminatory. . . .

". . . The same principle that permits Congress to exercise its rate-making power in interstate commerce, by declaring the rule which shall prevail in the legislative fixing of rates, and enables it to remit to a rate-making body created in accordance with its provisions the fixing of such rates, justifies a similar provision for the fixing of customs duties on imported merchandise. If Congress shall lay down by legislative act an intelligible principle to which the person or body authorized to fix such rates is directed to conform, such legislative action is not a forbidden delegation of legislative power. . . ."

By 1930 Bracton's rule seemed moribund, at least in its application to the federal government. The Supreme Court had recognized the powerful countervailing argument that in order to manage the tasks of regulation, Congress had to be free to leave broad questions to those who would administer the law; and the delegation doctrine had been reduced to requiring merely legislative prescription of an "intelligible principle" to which the administrators might refer. The doctrine had never been the basis of a Supreme Court decision invalidating an act of Congress; but less than a decade after the Court's decision in Hampton, Bracton's rule was revived to strike down the National Industrial Recovery Act of 1933.

Following a "Declaration of Policy," Title I of the act granted the President broad powers of economic regulation. The Declaration read: "A national emergency productive of widespread unemployment and disorganization of industry, which burdens interstate and foreign commerce, affects the public welfare, and undermines the standards of living of the American people, is hereby declared to exist. It is hereby declared to be the policy of Congress to remove obstructions to the free flow of interstate and foreign commerce which tend to diminish the amount thereof; and to provide for the general welfare by promoting the organization of industry for the purpose of cooperative action among trade groups, to induce and maintain united action of labor and management under adequate governmental sanctions and supervision, to eliminate unfair competitive practices, to promote the fullest possible utilization of the present productive capacity of industries, to avoid undue restriction of production (except as may be temporarily required), to increase the consumption of industrial and agricultural products by increasing purchasing power, to reduce and relieve unemployment, to improve standards of labor, and otherwise to rehabilitate industry and to conserve natural resources."

Title I of the act fell in two decisions. The first concerned only § 9(c), which authorized the President to prohibit interstate or foreign shipment of oil produced in excess of production ceilings set by the states and prescribed a fine or imprisonment for violation of a presidential order. In Panama Refining Co. v. Ryan, 293 U.S. 388 (1935), the Court invalidated § 9(c) as a grant of power to be used however the President saw fit, without the limitation of even an "intelligible principle." Writing for the Court, Chief Justice Hughes examined the Act "to see whether the Congress has declared a policy with respect to [whether out-of-state transportation of excess oil was to be prohibited]; whether the Congress has set up a standard for the President's action; whether the Congress has required any finding by the President in the exercise of the authority to enact the prohibition." He found none of these, either in § 9(c) or in the "Declaration of Policy." The latter was seen as nothing more than a "broad outline" of "numerous and diverse objectives" which in no way limited or controlled the use of the authority granted by § 9(c). The section's reference to state production ceilings "simply defin[ed] the subject of the prohibition which the President is authorized to enact, or not to enact, as he pleases." The Court concluded, after reviewing the major precedents: "Thus, in every case in which the question has been raised, the Court has recognized that there are limits of delegation which there is no constitutional authority to transcend. We think that §9(c) goes beyond those limits. As to the transportation in excess of state permission, the Congress has declared no policy, has established no standard, has laid down no rule. There is no requirement, no definition of circumstances and conditions in which the transportation is to be allowed or prohibited.

"If §9(c) were held valid, it would be idle to pretend that anything would be left of limitations upon the power of the Congress to delegate its law-making function. The reasoning of the many decisions we have reviewed would be made vacuous and their distinctions nugatory. Instead of performing its law-making function, the Congress could at will and as to such subjects as it chose transfer that function to the President or other officer or to an administrative body. The question is not of the importance of the particular statute before us, but of the constitutional processes of legislation which are an essential part of our system of government."

Justice Cardozo dissented. He found a clear relation between the President's order under §9(c) and policies set out in Congress' "Declaration of Policy," and he argued that the perception of such relationships was properly left to the Executive: "The ascertainment of [the need to act under §9(c)] at any time or place was a task too intricate and special to be performed by Congress itself through a general enactment in advance of the event. All that Congress could safely do was to declare the act to be done and the policies to be promoted, leaving to the delegate of its power the ascertainment of the shifting facts that would determine the relation between the doing of the act and the attainment of its stated ends."

Substantially the rest of Title I fell four months later in Schechter Poultry Corp. v. United States, 295 U.S. 495 (1935). Title I authorized the President, on application by a trade or industrial group or on his own initiative, to promulgate "Codes of Fair Competition," violation of which would be a misdemeanor punishable by fine. The Schechter case involved the "Live Poultry Code," which prescribed trade practices among dealers in live poultry in New York City. The code was far-reaching. It fixed minimum wages and maximum work weeks for employees. It required slaughterhouse operators, in proportion to their sales volume, to employ a minimum number of employees. It proscribed various "unfair methods of competition"; for example, the code prohibited the custom of allowing wholesale purchasers to select individual chickens — a practice which left wholesalers with an overstock of less desirable birds, which had to be sold off at reduced prices — and required that wholesaler-slaughterers sell by the coop, a practice known as "straight killing." The defendants, who operated wholesale slaughtering businesses, were convicted of violating the wage and hour provisions of the code and the requirement of straight killing; the court of appeals affirmed the convictions on the latter count.

On certiorari, the Supreme Court unanimously overturned the convictions. Chief Justice Hughes, writing for the Court, found these provisions of the act impermissible both as a delegation of legislative responsibility and as beyond the reach of congressional power under the commerce clause. At the threshold he rejected the government's contention "that the provision of the statute authorizing the adoption of codes must be viewed in the light of the grave national crisis with which Congress was confronted. Undoubtedly, the conditions to which power is addressed are always to be considered when the exercise of power is challenged. Extraordinary conditions may call for extraordinary remedies. But the argument necessarily stops short of an attempt to justify action which lies outside the sphere of constitutional authority. Extraordinary conditions do not create or enlarge constitutional power."

The Chief Justice then framed the question whether Congress had "overstepped" the limitations of the delegation doctrine: "whether Congress in authorizing 'codes of fair competition' has itself established the standards of legal obligation, thus performing its essential legislative function, or, by the failure to enact such standards, has attempted to transfer that function to others." Noting that the act's meaning of "fair competition"

Section A. Separation of Powers

could not be circumscribed by reference either to the common law or to the Federal Trade Commission Act, Chief Justice Hughes turned to Title I's "Declaration of Policy." The Declaration, he found, "clearly disclosed" the purpose of the Title "to authorize new and controlling prohibitions through codes of laws which would embrace what the formulators would propose, and what the President would approve, or prescribe, as wise and beneficent measures for the government of trades and industries in order to bring about their rehabilitation, correction and development according to the general declaration of policy in section one. Codes of laws of this sort are styled 'codes of fair competition.'"

He continued: ". . . Congress cannot delegate legislative power to the President to exercise an unfettered discretion to make whatever laws he thinks may be needed or advisable for the rehabilitation and expansion of trade or industry. See Panama Refining Co. v. Ryan, supra, and cases there reviewed.

". . . Section 3 of the Recovery Act is without precedent. It supplies no standards for any trade, industry or activity. It does not undertake to prescribe rules of conduct to be applied to particular states of fact determined by appropriate administrative procedure. Instead of prescribing rules of conduct, it authorizes the making of codes to prescribe them. For that legislative undertaking, §3 sets up no standards, aside from the statement of the general aims of rehabilitation, correction and expansion described in section one. In view of the scope of that broad declaration, and of the nature of the few restrictions that are imposed, the discretion of the President in approving or prescribing codes, and thus enacting laws for the government of trade and industry throughout the country, is virtually unfettered. We think that the code-making authority thus conferred is an unconstitutional delegation of legislative power."

Justice Cardozo concurred. He condemned the code authorization as a license to the President "to inquire into evils and upon discovery correct them" in the name of "fair competition." In the conception of the legislators and administrators of the Recovery Act, Justice Cardozo stated, "a code is not to be restricted to the elimination of business practices that would be characterized by general acceptance as oppressive or unfair. It is to include whatever ordinances may be desirable or helpful for the well-being or prosperity of the industry affected. In that view, the function of its adoption is not merely negative, but positive; the planning of improvements as well as the extirpation of abuses. What is fair, as thus conceived, is not something to be contrasted with what is unfair or fraudulent or tricky. The extension becomes as wide as the field of industrial regulation. If that conception shall prevail, anything that Congress may do within the limits of the commerce clause for the betterment of business may be done by the President upon the recommendation of a trade association by calling it a code. This is delegation running riot. No such plenitude of power is susceptible of transfer."

For the history of the development and implementation of the Recovery Act, see Schlesinger, The Coming of the New Deal (1958).

Since Schechter and Panama Refining, the Court has upheld a number of complex regulatory schemes and has barred none as an unconstitutional delegation of legislative power to executive officials. See, e.g., United States v. Rock Royal Co-op., Inc., 307 U.S. 533 (1939) (upholding the Agricultural Marketing Act of 1937, which authorized the Secretary of Agriculture to set "parity prices" for agricultural products); Yakus v. United States, 321 U.S. 414 (1944) (upholding the delegation of power to the Office of Price Administration to set "fair and equitable" maximum prices under the Emergency Price Control Act of 1942). See also Amalgamated Meat Cutters v. Connally, 337 F. Supp. 737 (D.D.C. 1971) (three-judge court) (upholding the President's power to set wages and prices under the Economic Stabilization Act of 1970). But cf. Carter v. Carter Coal Co., 298 U.S. 238 (1936) (delegation to private groups). For a history and analysis of the delegation doctrine, see Jaffe, Judicial Control of Administrative Action 28-86 (1965); Jaffe & Nathanson, Administrative Law: Cases and Materials 34-107 (4th ed. 1976).

In recent years the delegation doctrine has received attention as a possible means of controlling the increasing powers of the federal administrative agencies. On this issue, see Stewart, The Reform of American Administrative Law, 88 Harv. L. Rev. 1667 (1975).

While issues of delegation of power may appear to be political questions, from the standpoint of the persons regulated they may be viewed as questions of due process of law. This aspect is put in a strong light when the "delegation" is to another sovereign or to private groups. How do we justify, for example, making a tariff rate depend on a foreign country's rate, or the criminal law in a federal enclave depend on the law in the surrounding state? Here the doctrine of "independent legal significance" is useful: the other sovereign is not legislating for our national government; rather, its legislation, enacted under normal domestic safeguards, becomes a fact or circumstance relevant to our national regulatory policy.

Sometimes a similar rationale is available to justify "delegation" to a private group, as where the wages to be paid under a federal construction contract must conform to the prevailing wages in the area. But compare the instances where the contingency does not have independent legal significance, as where an agricultural program is to go into effect only upon a referendum of the farmers affected, Mulford v. Smith, 307 U.S. 38 (1939), or where an exclusive bargaining agent under the National Labor Relations Act is chosen by majority vote of the appropriate bargaining unit. Here the due-process aspect focuses attention on the appropriateness and fairness of the group for decision-making purposes.

Do these forms of delegation, and the criteria for judging them, cast a reflexive light on one form of legislative-executive conflict, namely, the so-called "one-house veto"? Under this statutory design, a rule promulgated by an administrative agency lies on the table in Congress for a specified period and becomes effective if, and only if, neither House disapproves it within that time. If this form of contingency lawmaking is valid, would it follow that one house could abrogate an administrative regulation already in force? Or that a regulation could be prevented from taking effect by the adverse action of a congressional committee, or a committee chairman?

NOTE Congressional Participation in Executive Functions

In Springer v. Philippine Islands, 277 U.S. 189 (1928), the Court held it a violation of the separation-of-powers provisions of the Philippine Organic Act for the Philippine legislature to place the power of voting stock in two corporations created by the legislature in a board composed of the Governor General, President of the Senate, and Speaker of the House. Writing for the Court, Justice Sutherland said:

"Legislative power, as distinguished from executive power, is the authority to make laws, but not to enforce them or appoint the agents charged with the duty of such enforcement. The latter are executive functions. . . .

"Not having the power of appointment, unless expressly granted or incidental to its powers, the legislature cannot engraft executive duties upon a legislative office, since that would be to usurp the power of appointment by indirection. . . ."

Justice Holmes, with whom Justice Brandeis joined, dissented, arguing that "the functions of the board . . . plainly are no part of the executive functions of the Government but rather fall into the indiscriminate residue of matters within legislative control."

Compare, with reference to the usurpation argument, President Franklin Roosevelt's argument that it was unconstitutional for Congress to provide in the Lend Lease Act that it should terminate in three years, or earlier on passage by both Houses of a concurrent resolution that the act was "no longer necessary to promote the defense of the United States." The President believed that exercise of this clause would constitute a repeal of the act, tantamount to the enactment of new legislation, without allowing him the opportunity to veto and require repassage by a two-thirds majority, as set out at Article I, §7 of the Constitution. See Jackson, A Presidential Legal Opinion, 66 Harv. L. Rev. 1353 (1953).

Compare the materials on presidential use of the "pocket veto" and impoundment of funds, infra pp. 671-673, which may present the converse situation — presidential attempts to scotch legislation without allowing Congress the opportunity to repass it by a conclusive two-thirds vote.

On the congressional practice of overseeing executive activities by use of concurrent resolutions and other methods, see Ginnane, The Control of Federal Administration by Congressional Resolutions and Committees, 66 Harv. L. Rev. 569 (1953).

In Buckley v. Valeo, 424 U.S. 1 (1976), the Court held invalid the method of appointment of members of the Federal Elections Commission. The statute vested the appointment of two members in the President, two in the president pro tempore of the Senate, and two in the speaker of the House. Insofar as the commission exercised enforcement powers to bring civil actions, to make rules, to disqualify candidates, and to enlarge convention expenditure limits, its members were acting as "officers of the United States" within the appointments clause of Article II, §2, and hence the vesting of appointing power in members of Congress violated that clause and the principle of separation of powers.

Youngstown Sheet and Tube Co. v. Sawyer 343 U.S. 579, 72 S. Ct. 863, 96 L. Ed. 1153 (1952)

MR. JUSTICE BLACK delivered the opinion of the Court.

We are asked to decide whether the President was acting within his constitutional power when he issued an order directing the Secretary of Commerce to take possession of and operate most of the Nation's steel mills. The mill owners argue that the President's order amounts to lawmaking, a legislative function which the Constitution has expressly confided to the Congress and not to the President. The Government's position is that the order was made on findings of the President that his action was necessary to avert a national catastrophe which would inevitably result from a stoppage of steel production, and that in meeting this grave emergency the President was acting within the aggregate of his constitutional powers as the Nation's Chief Executive and the Commander in Chief of the Armed Forces of the United States. The issue emerges here from the following series of events:

In the latter part of 1951, a dispute arose between the steel companies and their employees over terms and conditions that should be included in new collective bargaining agreements. Long-continued conferences failed to resolve the dispute. On December 18, 1951, the employees' representative, United Steelworkers of America, C.I.O., gave notice of an intention to strike when the existing bargaining agreements expired on December 31. The Federal Mediation and Conciliation Service then intervened in an effort to get labor and management to agree. This failing, the President on December 22, 1951, referred the dispute to the Federal Wage Stabilization Board to investigate and make recommendations for fair and equitable terms of settlement. This Board's report resulted in no settlement. On April 4, 1952, the Union gave notice of a nation-wide strike called to begin at 12:01 A.M. April 9. The indispensability of steel as a component of substantially all weapons and other war materials led the President to believe that the proposed work stoppage would immediately jeopardize our national defense and that governmental seizure of the steel mills was necessary in order to assure the continued availability of steel. Reciting these considerations for his action, the President, a few hours before the strike was to begin, issued Executive Order 10340. . . . The order directed the Secretary of Commerce to take possession of most of the steel mills and keep them running. The Secretary immediately issued his own possessory orders, calling upon the presidents of the various seized companies to serve as operating managers for the United States. They were directed to carry on their activities in accordance with regulations and directions of the

Secretary. The next morning the President sent a message to Congress reporting his action. Cong. Rec., April 9, 1952, p. 3962. Twelve days later he sent a second message. Cong. Rec., April 21, 1952, p. 4192. Congress has taken no action.

Obeying the Secretary's orders under protest, the companies brought proceedings against him in the District Court. Their complaints charged that the seizure was not authorized by an act of Congress or by any constitutional provisions. The District Court was asked to declare the orders of the President and the Secretary invalid and to issue preliminary and permanent injunctions restraining their enforcement. Opposing the motion for preliminary injunction, the United States asserted that a strike disrupting steel production for even a brief period would so endanger the well-being and safety of the Nation that the President had "inherent power" to do what he had done — power "supported by the Constitution, by historical precedent, and by court decisions." The Government also contended that in any event no preliminary injunction should be issued because the companies had made no showing that their available legal remedies were inadequate or that their injuries from seizure would be irreparable. Holding against the Government on all points, the District Court on April 30 issued a preliminary injunction restraining the Secretary from "continuing the seizure and possession of the plants . . . and from acting under the purported authority of Executive Order No. 10340." 103 F. Supp. 569. On the same day the Court of Appeals stayed the District Court's injunction. 197 F.2d 582. Deeming it best that the issues raised be promptly decided by this Court, we granted certiorari on May 3 and set the cause for argument on May 12. 343 U.S. 937.

Two crucial issues have developed: *First.* Should final determination of the constitutional validity of the President's order be made in this case which has proceeded no further than the preliminary injunction stage? *Second.* If so, is the seizure order within the constitutional power of the President? . . .

II

The President's power, if any, to issue the order must stem either from an act of Congress or from the Constitution itself. There is no statute that expressly authorizes the President to take possession of property as he did here. Nor is there any act of Congress to which our attention has been directed from which such a power can fairly be implied. Indeed, we do not understand the Government to rely on statutory authorization for this seizure. . . .

Moreover, the use of the seizure technique to solve labor disputes in order to prevent work stoppages was not only unauthorized by any congressional enactment; prior to this controversy, Congress had refused to adopt that method of settling labor disputes. When the Taft-Hartley Act was under consideration in 1947, Congress rejected an amendment which would have authorized such governmental seizures in cases of emergency. Apparently it was thought that the technique of seizure, like that of compulsory arbitration, would interfere with the process of collective bargaining. Consequently, the plan Congress adopted in that Act did not provide for seizure under any circumstances. Instead, the plan sought to bring about settlements by use of the customary devices of mediation, conciliation, investigation by boards of inquiry, and public reports. In some instances temporary injunctions were authorized to provide cooling-off periods. All this failing, unions were left free to strike after a secret vote by employees as to whether they wished to accept their employers' final settlement offer.

It is clear that if the President had authority to issue the order he did, it must be found in some provision of the Constitution. And it is not claimed that express constitutional language grants this power to the President. The contention is that presidential power should be implied from the aggregate of his powers under the Constitution. Particular reliance is placed on provisions in Article II which say that "The executive Power shall be vested in a President . . ."; that "he shall take Care that the Laws be faithfully executed";

and that he "shall be Commander in Chief of the Army and Navy of the United States."

The order cannot properly be sustained as an exercise of the President's military power as Commander in Chief of the Armed Forces. The Government attempts to do so by citing a number of cases upholding broad powers in military commanders engaged in day-to-day fighting in a theater of war. Such cases need not concern us here. Even though "theater of war" be an expanding concept, we cannot with faithfulness to our constitutional system hold that the Commander in Chief of the Armed Forces has the ultimate power as such to take possession of private property in order to keep labor disputes from stopping production. This is a job for the Nation's lawmakers, not for its military authorities.

Nor can the seizure order be sustained because of the several constitutional provisions that grant executive power to the President. In the framework of our Constitution, the President's power to see that the laws are faithfully executed refutes the idea that he is to be a lawmaker. The Constitution limits his functions in the lawmaking process to the recommending of laws he thinks wise and the vetoing of laws he thinks bad. And the Constitution is neither silent nor equivocal about who shall make laws which the President is to execute. The first section of the first article says that "All legislative Powers herein granted shall be vested in a Congress of the United States . . . ." After granting many powers to the Congress, Article I goes on to provide that Congress may "make all Laws which shall be necessary and proper for carrying into Execution the foregoing Powers, and all other Powers vested by this Constitution in the Government of the United States, or in any Department or Officer thereof."

The President's order does not direct that a congressional policy be executed in a manner prescribed by Congress — it directs that a presidential policy be executed in a manner prescribed by the President. The preamble of the order itself, like that of many statutes, sets out reasons why the President believes certain policies should be adopted, proclaims these policies as rules of conduct to be followed, and again, like a statute, authorizes a government official to promulgate additional rules and regulations consistent with the policy proclaimed and needed to carry that policy into execution. The power of Congress to adopt such public policies as those proclaimed by the order is beyond question. It can authorize the taking of private property for public use. It can make laws regulating the relationships between employers and employees, prescribing rules designed to settle labor disputes, and fixing wages and working conditions in certain fields of our economy. The Constitution does not subject this lawmaking power of Congress to presidential or military supervision or control.

It is said that other Presidents without congressional authority have taken possession of private business enterprises in order to settle labor disputes. But even if this be true, Congress has not thereby lost its exclusive constitutional authority to make laws necessary and proper to carry out the powers vested by the Constitution "in the Government of the United States, or any Department or Officer thereof."

The Founders of this Nation entrusted the lawmaking power to the Congress alone in both good and bad times. It would do no good to recall the historical events, the fears of power and the hopes for freedom that lay behind their choice. Such a review would but confirm our holding that this seizure order cannot stand.

The judgment of the District Court is
Affirmed.

MR. JUSTICE FRANKFURTER.

Although the considerations relevant to the legal enforcement of the principle of separation of powers seem to me more complicated and flexible than may appear from what Mr. Justice Black has written, I join his opinion because I thoroughly agree with the application of the principle to the circumstances of this case. Even though such differences in attitude toward this principle may be merely differences in emphasis and nuance, they can hardly be reflected by a single opinion for the Court. Individual expression of views in reaching a common result is therefore important. . . .

The question before the Court comes in this setting. Congress has frequently — at least 16 times since 1916 — specifically provided for executive seizure of production, transportation, communications, or storage facilities. In every case it has qualified this grant of power with limitations and safeguards. . . .

Congress in 1947 was again called upon to consider whether governmental seizure should be used to avoid serious industrial shutdowns. Congress decided against conferring such power generally and in advance, without special Congressional enactment to meet each particular need. Under the urgency of telephone and coal strikes in the winter of 1946, Congress addressed itself to the problems raised by "national emergency" strikes and lockouts. The termination of wartime seizure powers on December 31, 1946, brought these matters to the attention of Congress with vivid impact. A proposal that the President be given powers to seize plants to avert a shutdown where the "health or safety" of the Nation was endangered, was thoroughly canvassed by Congress and rejected. No room for doubt remains that the proponents as well as the opponents of the bill which became the Labor Management Relations Act of 1947 clearly understood that as a result of that legislation the only recourse for preventing a shutdown in any basic industry, after failure of mediation, was Congress. . . . The Senate Labor Committee, through its Chairman, explicitly reported to the Senate that a general grant of seizure powers had been considered and rejected in favor of reliance on ad hoc legislation, as a particular emergency might call for it. An amendment presented in the House providing that, where necessary "to preserve and protect the public health and security," the President might seize any industry in which there is an impending curtailment of production, was voted down after debate, by a vote of more than three to one. . . .

By the Labor Management Relations Act of 1947, Congress said to the President, "You may not seize. Please report to us and ask for seizure power if you think it is needed in a specific situation." This of course calls for a report on the unsuccessful efforts to reach a voluntary settlement, as a basis for discharge by Congress of its responsibility — which it has unequivocally reserved — to fashion further remedies than it provided. But it is now claimed that the President has seizure power by virtue of the Defense Production Act of 1950 and its Amendments. And the claim is based on the occurrence of new events — Korea and the need for stabilization, etc. — although it was well known that seizure power was withheld by the Act of 1947, and although the President, whose specific requests for other authority were in the main granted by Congress, never suggested that in view of the new events he needed the power of seizure which Congress in its judgment had decided to withhold from him. The utmost that the Korean conflict may imply is that it may have been desirable to have given the President further authority, a freer hand in these matters. Absence of authority in the President to deal with a crisis does not imply want of power in the Government. Conversely the fact that power exists in the Government does not vest it in the President. The need for new legislation does not enact it. Nor does it repeal or amend existing law. . . .

Apart from his vast share of responsibility for the conduct of our foreign relations, the embracing function of the President is that "he shall take Care that the Laws be faithfully executed. . . ." Art. II, §3. The nature of that authority has for me been comprehensively indicated by Mr. Justice Holmes. "The duty of the President to see that the laws be executed is a duty that does not go beyond the laws or require him to achieve more than Congress sees fit to leave within his power." Myers v. United States, 272 U.S. 52, 177. The powers of the President are not as particularized as are those of Congress. But unenumerated powers do not mean undefined powers. The separation of powers built into our Constitution gives essential content to undefined provisions in the frame of our government.

To be sure, the content of the three authorities of government is not to be derived from an abstract analysis. . . . Deeply embedded traditional ways of conducting government cannot supplant the Constitution or legislation, but they give meaning to the words of a text or supply them. It is an inadmissibly narrow conception of American constitutional law to confine it to the words of the Constitution and to disregard the gloss which life has written upon them. In short, a systematic, unbroken, executive practice, long pursued to the knowledge of the Congress and never before questioned, engaged in by Presidents who have also sworn to uphold the Constitution, making as it were such exercise of power part of the structure of our government, may be treated as a gloss on "executive Power" vested in the President by § 1 of Art. II.

Such was the case of United States v. Midwest Oil Co., 236 U.S. 459. The contrast between the circumstances of that case and this one helps to draw a clear line between authority not explicitly conferred yet authorized to be exercised by the President and the denial of such authority. In both instances it was the concern of Congress under express constitutional grant to make rules and regulations for the problems with which the President dealt. In the one case he was dealing with the protection of property belonging to the United States; in the other with the enforcement of the Commerce Clause and with raising and supporting armies and maintaining the Navy. In the Midwest Oil case, lands which Congress had opened for entry were, over a period of 80 years and in 252 instances, and by Presidents learned and unlearned in the law, temporarily withdrawn from entry so as to enable Congress to deal with such withdrawals. No remotely comparable practice can be vouched for executive seizure of property at a time when this country was not at war, in the only constitutional way in which it can be at war. . . .

Down to the World War II period, then, the record is barren of instances comparable to the one before us. Of twelve seizures by President Roosevelt prior to the enactment of the War Labor Disputes Act in June, 1943, three were sanctioned by existing law, and six others were effected after Congress, on December 8, 1941, had declared the existence of a state of war. In this case, reliance on the powers that flow from declared war has been commendably disclaimed by the Solicitor General. Thus the list of executive assertions of the power of seizure in circumstances comparable to the present reduces to three in the six-month period from June to December of 1941. We need not split hairs in comparing those actions to the one before us, though much might be said by way of differentiation. Without passing on their validity, as we are not called upon to do, it suffices to say that these three isolated instances do not add up, either in number, scope, duration or contemporaneous legal justification, to the kind of executive construction of the Constitution revealed in the Midwest Oil case. Nor do they come to us sanctioned by long-continued acquiescence of Congress giving decisive weight to a construction by the Executive of its powers.

A scheme of government like ours no doubt at times feels the lack of power to act with complete, all-embracing, swiftly moving authority. No doubt a government with distributed authority, subject to be challenged in the courts of law, at least long enough to consider and adjudicate the challenge, labors under restrictions from which other governments are free. It has not been our tradition to envy such governments. In any event our government was designed to have such restrictions. The price was deemed not too high in view of the safeguards which these restrictions afford. . . .

MR. JUSTICE JACKSON, concurring in the judgment and opinion of the Court. . . .

The actual art of governing under our Constitution does not and cannot conform to judicial definitions of the power of any of its branches based on isolated clauses or even single Articles torn from context. While the Constitution diffuses power the better to secure liberty, it also contemplates that practice will integrate the dispersed powers into a workable government. It enjoins upon its branches separateness but interdependence, autonomy but reciprocity. Presidential powers are not fixed but fluctuate, depending upon their disjunction or conjunction with those of Congress. We may well begin by a somewhat over-simplified grouping of practical situations in which a President may doubt, or others may challenge, his powers, and by distinguishing roughly the legal consequences of this factor of relativity.

1. When the President acts pursuant to an express or implied authorization of Congress, his authority is at its maximum, for it includes all that he possesses in his own right plus all that Congress can delegate. In these circumstances, and in these only, may he be said (for what it may be worth) to personify the federal sovereignty. If his act is held unconstitutional under these circumstances, it usually means that the Federal Government as an undivided whole lacks power. A seizure executed by the President pursuant to an Act of Congress would be supported by the strongest of presumptions and the widest latitude of judicial interpretation, and the burden of persuasion would rest heavily upon any who might attack it.

2. When the President acts in absence of either a congressional grant or denial of authority, he can only rely upon his own independent powers, but there is a zone of twilight in which he and Congress may have concurrent authority, or in which its distribution is uncertain. Therefore, congressional inertia, indifference or quiescence may sometimes, at least as a practical matter, enable, if not invite, measures on independent presidential responsibility. In this area, any actual test of power is likely to depend on the imperatives of events and contemporary imponderables rather than on abstract theories of law.

3. When the President takes measures incompatible with the expressed or implied will of Congress, his power is at its lowest ebb, for then he can rely only upon his own constitutional powers minus any constitutional powers of Congress over the matter. Courts can sustain exclusive presidential control in such a case only by disabling the Congress from acting upon the subject. Presidential claim to a power at once so conclusive and preclusive must be scrutinized with caution, for what is at stake is the equilibrium established by our constitutional system.

Into which of these classifications does this executive seizure of the steel industry fit? It is eliminated from the first by admission, for it is conceded that no congressional authorization exists for this seizure. . . .

Can it then be defended under flexible tests available to the second category? It seems clearly eliminated from that class because Congress has not left seizure of private property an open field but has covered it by three statutory policies inconsistent with this seizure. In cases where the purpose is to supply needs of the Government itself, two courses are provided: one, seizure of a plant which fails to comply with obligatory orders placed by the Government; another, condemnation of facilities, including temporary use under the power of eminent domain. The third is applicable where it is the general economy of the country that is to be protected rather than exclusive governmental interests. None of these were invoked. In choosing a different and inconsistent way of his own, the President cannot claim that it is necessitated or invited by failure of Congress to legislate upon the occasions, grounds and methods for seizure of industrial properties.

This leaves the current seizure to be justified only by the severe tests under the third grouping, where it can be supported only by any remainder of executive power after subtraction of such powers as Congress may have over the subject. In short, we can sustain the President only by holding that seizure of such strike-bound industries is within his domain and beyond control by Congress. Thus, this Court's first review of such seizures occurs under circumstances which leave presidential power most vulnerable to attack and in the least favorable of possible constitutional postures.

I did not suppose, and I am not persuaded, that history leaves it open to question, at least in the courts, that the executive branch, like the Federal Government as a whole, possesses only delegated powers. The purpose of the Constitution was not only to grant power, but to keep it from getting out of hand. However, because the President does not enjoy unmentioned powers does not mean that the mentioned ones should be narrowed by a niggardly construction. Some clauses could be made almost unworkable, as well as immutable, by refusal to indulge some latitude of interpretation for changing times. I have heretofore, and do now, give to the enumerated powers the scope and elasticity afforded by what seem to be reasonable, practical implications instead of the rigidity dictated by a doctrinaire textualism.

The Solicitor General seeks the power of seizure in three clauses of the Executive Article, the first reading, "The executive Power shall be vested in a President of the United States of America." Lest I be thought to exaggerate, I quote the interpretation which his brief puts upon it: "In our view, this clause constitutes a grant of all the executive powers of which the Government is capable." If that be true, it is difficult to see why the forefathers bothered to add several specific items, including some trifling ones.

The example of such unlimited executive power that must have most impressed the forefathers was the prerogative exercised by George III, and the description of its evils in the Declaration of Independence leads me to doubt that they were creating their new Executive in his image. Continental European examples were no more appealing. And if we seek instruction from our own times, we can match it only from the executive powers in those governments we disparagingly describe as totalitarian. I cannot accept the view that this clause is a grant in bulk of all conceivable executive power but regard it as an allocation to the presidential office of the generic powers thereafter stated.

The clause on which the Government next relies is that "The President shall be Commander in Chief of the Army and Navy of the United States. . . ." These cryptic words have given rise to some of the most persistent controversies in our constitutional history. Of course, they imply something more than an empty title. But just what authority goes with the name has plagued presidential advisers who would not waive or narrow it by nonassertion yet cannot say where it begins or ends. It undoubtedly puts the Nation's armed forces under presidential command. Hence, this loose appellation is sometimes advanced as support for any presidential action, internal or external, involving use of force, the idea being that it vests power to do anything, anywhere, that can be done with an army or navy. . . .

Assuming that we are in a war de facto, whether it is or is not a war de jure, does that empower the Commander in Chief to seize industries he thinks necessary to supply our army? The Constitution expressly places in Congress power "to raise and *support* Armies" and "to *provide* and *maintain* a Navy." (Emphasis supplied.) This certainly lays upon Congress primary responsibility for supplying the armed forces. Congress alone controls the raising of revenues and their appropriation and may determine in what manner and by what means they shall be spent for military and naval procurement. I suppose no one would doubt that Congress can take over war supply as a Government enterprise. On the other hand, if Congress sees fit to rely on free private enterprise collectively bargaining with free labor for support and maintenance of our armed forces, can the Executive, because of lawful disagreements incidental to that process, seize the facility for operation upon Government-imposed terms? . . .

The third clause in which the Solicitor General finds seizure powers is that "he shall take Care that the Laws be faithfully executed. . . ." That authority must be matched against words of the Fifth Amendment that "No person shall be . . . deprived of life, liberty or property, without due process of law. . . ." One gives a governmental authority that reaches so far as there is law, the other gives a private right that authority shall go no farther. These signify about all there is of the principle that ours is a government of laws, not of men, and that we submit ourselves to rulers only if under rules.

The Solicitor General lastly grounds support of the seizure upon nebulous, inherent powers never expressly granted but said to have accrued to the office from the customs and claims of preceding administrations. The plea is for a resulting power to deal with a crisis or an emergency according to the necessities of the case, the unarticulated assumption being that necessity knows no law.

Loose and irresponsible use of adjectives colors all nonlegal and much legal discussion of presidential powers. "Inherent" powers, "implied" powers, "incidental" powers, "plenary" powers, "war" powers and "emergency" powers are used, often interchangeably and without fixed or ascertainable meanings.

The vagueness and generality of the clauses that set forth presidential powers afford a plausible basis for pressures within and without an administration for presidential action beyond that supported by those whose responsibility it is to defend his actions in court. The claim of inherent and unrestricted presidential powers has long been a persuasive dialectical weapon in political controversy. While it is not surprising that counsel should grasp support from such unadjudicated claims of power, a judge cannot accept self-serving press statements of the attorney for one of the interested parties as authority in answering a constitutional question, even if the advocate was himself. But prudence has counseled that actual reliance on such nebulous claims stop short of provoking a judicial test. . . .

In view of the ease, expedition and safety with which Congress can grant and has granted large emergency powers, certainly ample to embrace this crisis, I am quite unimpressed with the argument that we should affirm possession of them without statute. Such power either has no beginning or it has no end. If it exists, it need submit to no legal restraint. I am not alarmed that it would plunge us straightway into dictatorship, but it is at least a step in that wrong direction.

As to whether there is imperative necessity for such powers, it is relevant to note the gap that exists between the President's paper powers and his real powers. The Constitution does not disclose the measure of the actual controls wielded by the modern presidential office. That instrument must be understood as an Eighteenth-Century sketch of a government hoped for, not as a blueprint of the Government that is. Vast accretions of federal power, eroded from that reserved by the States, have magnified the scope of presidential activity. . . .

Executive power has the advantage of concentration in a single head in whose choice the whole Nation has a part, making him the focus of public hopes and expectations. . . . By his prestige as head of state and his influence upon public opinion he exerts a leverage upon those who are supposed to check and balance his power which often cancels their effectiveness.

Moreover, rise of the party system has made a significant extraconstitutional supplement to real executive power. No appraisal of his necessities is realistic which overlooks that he heads a political system as well as a legal system. Party loyalties and interests, sometimes more binding than law, extend his effective control into branches of government other than his own and he often may win, as a political leader, what he cannot command under the Constitution. . . . I cannot be brought to believe that this country will suffer if the Court refuses further to aggrandize the presidential office, already so potent and so relatively immune from judicial review, at the expense of Congress.

But I have no illusion that any decision by this Court can keep power in the hands of Congress if it is not wise and timely in meeting its problems. A crisis that challenges the President equally, or perhaps primarily, challenges Congress. If not good law, there was worldly wisdom in the maxim attributed to Napoleon that "The tools belong to the man who can use them." We may say that power to legislate for emergencies belongs in the hands of Congress, but only Congress itself can prevent power from slipping through its fingers. . . .

MR. JUSTICE CLARK, concurring in the judgment of the Court.

One of this Court's first pronouncements upon the powers of the President under the Constitution was made by Mr. Chief Justice John Marshall some one hundred and fifty years ago. In Little v. Barreme,[1] he used this characteristically clear language in discussing the power of the President to instruct the seizure of the *Flying Fish*, a vessel bound from a French port: "It is by no means clear that the president of the United States whose high duty it is to 'take care that the laws be faithfully executed,' and who is commander in

---

[1] 2 Cranch 170 (1804).

Section A. Separation of Powers

chief of the armies and navies of the United States, might not, without any special authority for that purpose, in the then existing state of things, have empowered the officers commanding the armed vessels of the United States, to seize and send into port for adjudication, American vessels which were forfeited by being engaged in this illicit commerce. But when it is observed that [an act of Congress] gives a special authority to seize on the high seas, and limits that authority to the seizure of vessels bound or sailing *to* a French port, the legislature seem to have prescribed that the manner in which this law shall be carried into execution, was to exclude a seizure of any vessel *not* bound *to* a French port." Accordingly, a unanimous Court held that the President's instructions had been issued without authority and that they could not "legalize an act which without those instructions would have been a plain trespass." I know of no subsequent holding of this Court to the contrary.[3]

The limits of presidential power are obscure. . . . Some of our Presidents, such as Lincoln, "felt that measures otherwise unconstitutional might become lawful by becoming indispensable to the preservation of the Constitution through the preservation of the nation." Others, such as Theodore Roosevelt, thought the President to be capable, as a "steward" of the people, of exerting all power save that which is specifically prohibited by the Constitution or the Congress. In my view . . . the Constitution does grant to the President extensive authority in times of grave and imperative national emergency. In fact, to my thinking, such a grant may well be necessary to the very existence of the Constitution itself. As Lincoln aptly said, "[is] it possible to lose the nation and yet preserve the Constitution?"[a] In describing this authority I care not whether one calls it "residual," "inherent," "moral," "implied," "aggregate," "emergency," or otherwise. I am of the conviction that those who have had the gratifying experience of being the President's lawyer have used one or more of these adjectives only with the utmost of sincerity and the highest of purpose.

I conclude that where Congress has laid down specific procedures to deal with the type

---

[3] Decisions of this Court which have upheld the exercise of presidential power include the following: Prize Cases, 2 Black 635 (1863) (subsequent ratification of President's acts by Congress); In re Neagle, 135 U.S. 1 (1890) (protection of federal officials from personal violence while performing official duties); In re Debs, 158 U.S. 564 (1895) (injunction to prevent forcible obstruction of interstate commerce and the mails); United States v. Midwest Oil Co., 236 U.S. 459 (1915) (acquiescence by Congress in more than 250 instances of exercise of same power by various Presidents over period of 80 years); Myers v. United States, 272 U.S. 52 (1926) (control over subordinate officials in executive department) [but see Humphrey's Executor v. United States, 295 U.S. 602, 626-628 (1935)]; Hirabayashi v. United States, 320 U.S. 81 (1943), and Korematsu v. United States, 323 U.S. 214 (1944) (express congressional authorization); cf. United States v. Russell, 13 Wall 623 (1871) (imperative military necessity in area of combat during war); United States v. Curtiss-Wright Export Corp., 299 U.S. 304 (1936) (power to negotiate with foreign governments); United States v. United Mine Workers, 330 U.S. 258 (1947) (seizure under specific statutory authorization).

[a] President Lincoln was responding to the opinion of Chief Justice Taney, sitting as Circuit Justice, in Ex parte Merryman, 17 F. Cas. 144, No. 9,487 (C.C.D. Md. 1861), excerpted infra page 1048. There, Justice Taney held that under Article I, §9 only Congress was empowered to order suspension of the writ of habeas corpus. In a message to Congress on July 4, 1861, Lincoln replied that he had been compelled to suspend the writ to protect against Southern sympathizers. He said, ". . . the attention of the country has been called to the proposition that one who is sworn to 'take care that the laws be faithfully executed' should not himself be one to violate them. Of course some consideration was given to the questions of power and propriety before this matter was acted upon. The whole of the laws which were required to be executed were being resisted . . . in nearly one-third of the States. Must they be allowed to finally fail? Are all the laws but one to go unexecuted, and that Government itself go to pieces, lest that one be violated? . . ." Reprinted in Randall, Constitutional Problems Under Lincoln 122 (rev. ed. 1951). The Merryman case was mooted by his delivery to civilian authorities, and later Congress passed the Habeas Corpus Act of 1863, 12 Stat. 755, which authorized suspension of the writ by the President but empowered the courts to order release if the government later failed to secure an indictment against the prisoner. Civil liberties questions continued, nonetheless, to bring the judiciary into conflict with the other departments during the Civil War and during Reconstruction. Cf., for example, Ex parte McCardle, excerpted supra page 141. The history of the period is given in Randall, supra, and in Volumes 5 and 6 of the Oliver Wendell Holmes Devise History of the Supreme Court: Swisher, The Taney Period, 1836-64 (1974), and Fairman, Reconstruction and Reunion, 1864-88, Part One (1971). — ED.

of crisis confronting the President, he must follow those procedures in meeting the crisis; but that in the absence of such action by Congress, the President's independent power to act depends upon the gravity of the situation confronting the nation. I cannot sustain the seizure in question because here, as in Little v. Barreme, Congress had prescribed methods to be followed by the President in meeting the emergency at hand. . . .[b]

NOTE The Steel Seizure Case

The Steel Seizure Case, like the Tapes Case considered later in this chapter, received special accelerated treatment in the courts. From the seizure order on April 9, 1952, to announcement of the Court's decision on June 2, 1952, less than two months elapsed. On the day the Court announced its decision, the plants were returned to private control and the workers went out on strike. The strike continued until July 24, when settlement was finally reached. The history of the steel seizure, including selections from the lower court transcript and the briefs of the parties, is told in Alan F. Westin's The Anatomy of a Constitutional Law Case (1958). For a critique of the Court's reaching the constitutional issue in the procedural posture of the case, see Freund, The Year of the Steel Case, 66 Harv. L. Rev. 89 (1952).

3. Some Areas of Dispute Between Congress and the Executive

a. The Pardoning Power

Under Article II, §2 the President is empowered to "grant Reprieves and Pardons for Offences against the United States, except in Cases of Impeachment." This power has been broadly construed. In Ex parte Garland, 4 Wall. 333 (1867), the Court held that Congress could not by statute defeat the terms of a pardon issued a former Confederate senator by President Johnson. In 1862 Congress had passed a law prescribing that all United States officials, civil and military, take an oath that they had never participated in rebellion against the United States; in January 1865 this law was extended to apply to attorneys admitted to practice in federal courts. In July 1865 Garland received a "full pardon." On this basis, he petitioned the Court to be allowed to practice without having to take the oath. The Court held the statutory requirement invalid, both as an ex post facto law and as an unconstitutional attempt to restrict the President's pardoning power.

Compare United States v. Klein, 13 Wall. 128 (1872), excerpted supra pages 145-146 which held that a statute forbidding the introduction of a pardon as evidence of loyalty to the United States was invalid not only as an improper invasion of judicial prerogative but also as an unconstitutional restraint on the President's pardoning power.

Congressional amnesty and the pardoning power. In Brown v. Walker, 161 U.S. 591 (1896), in the course of upholding the Compulsory Testimony Act of 1893, 27 Stat. 443, which gave absolute immunity from prosecution to witnesses before the Interstate Commerce Commission in order to disarm claims of Fifth Amendment privilege not to testify, the Court made the following observations on the relationship between amnesty and pardon:

"The act of Congress in question securing to witnesses immunity from prosecution is virtually an act of general amnesty, and belongs to a class of legislation which is not uncommon either in England . . . or in this country. Although the Constitution vests in the President 'power to grant reprieves and pardons for offences against the United States,

---

[b] Concurring opinions by Justices Douglas and Burton, and a dissenting opinion by Chief Justice Vinson, with whom Justices Reed and Minton joined, are omitted. — ED.

except in cases of impeachment,' this power has never been held to take from Congress the power to pass acts of general amnesty, and is ordinarily exercised only in cases of individuals after conviction. . . .

"The distinction between amnesty and pardon is of no practical importance. It is said in Knote v. United States, 95 U.S. 149, 152 [153 (1877)], 'the Constitution does not use the word "amnesty," and, except that the term is generally applied where pardon is extended to whole classes or communities, instead of individuals, the distinction between them is one rather of philological interest than of legal importance.' "

Constitutional limitations on the pardoning power. The Knote case established one restriction on the pardoning power which derived from the separation of powers. It held that President Johnson's grant of pardon to Southern Civil War participants, though it purported to grant "restoration of all rights, privileges, and immunities," could not extend to restoration of property seized by the Union which had been sold and the proceeds paid into the United States Treasury. The Court reasoned that the Constitution gave Congress an exclusive right to authorize disbursements from the Treasury, which could not be abrogated by the terms of a presidential pardon.

See also Schick v. Reed, 419 U.S. 256 (1974), upholding a conditional pardon which commuted petitioner's sentence from death to life imprisonment without opportunity for future parole, despite the fact that the statutes authorizing sentences of imprisonment for the crime committed by the petitioner would have allowed opportunity for parole after he had served fifteen years of a life term.

b. Control of Executive Personnel

In Myers v. United States, 272 U.S. 52 (1926), the Court held unconstitutional a federal statute providing that certain postmasters could be removed by the President prior to the expiration of their four-year term only with the consent of the Senate. Quoting Madison's remarks in the First Congress, "If there is any point in which the separation of the Legislative and Executive powers ought to be maintained with great caution, it is that which relates to officers and offices," Chief Justice Taft, perhaps a stronger exponent of executive power as Chief Justice than as President, maintained that the power granted to Congress to approve appointments in Article II, §2 must be narrowly construed to prevent undue restriction of the President's power to control his subordinates. The Court recognized a distinction between close associates of the President and "inferior officers." As to the latter, the Court said, Congress might set procedures and standards to govern their removal from office before the expiration of their terms; but Congress still could not participate in the removal decision. Compare United States v. Perkins, 116 U.S. 483 (1886) (upholding statutory provision that military officers could not be dismissed from service during peacetime, except following court-martial).

Justices Holmes, Brandeis, and McReynolds dissented. Justice Holmes said, in part:

"The arguments drawn from the executive power of the President, and from his duty to appoint officers of the United States (when Congress does not vest the appointment elsewhere), to take care that the laws be faithfully executed, and to commission all officers of the United States, seem to me spider's webs inadequate to control the dominant facts.

"We have to deal with an office that owes its existence to Congress and that Congress may abolish tomorrow. Its duration and the pay attached to it while it lasts depend on Congress alone. Congress alone confers on the President the power to appoint to it and at any time may transfer the power to other hands. With such power over its own creation, I have no more trouble in believing that Congress has power to prescribe a term of life for it free from any interference than I have in the undoubted power of Congress to decree its end. I have equally little trouble in accepting its power to prolong the tenure of an incumbent until Congress or the Senate shall have assented to his removal. The duty of the Presi-

670   Chapter Eleven. Distribution of National Powers

dent to see that the laws be executed is a duty that does not go beyond the laws or require him to achieve more than Congress sees fit to leave within his power." See also the excerpt from Justice Brandeis' dissent, page 653 supra.

Myers has been limited in subsequent decisions. In Humphrey's Executor v. United States, 295 U.S. 602 (1935), the Court unanimously upheld the section of the Federal Trade Commission Act of 1914 which provided that commissioners should be appointed for seven-year terms and removed prior to the expiration of their terms only for "inefficiency, neglect of duty, or malfeasance in office." The Court squared this decision with Myers not by attempting to characterize a Federal Trade Commissioner as an "inferior officer" but by holding that Myers extended to members of the executive branch subordinate to the President, who — like a postmaster — are "restricted to the performance of executive functions" and "charged with no duty at all related to the legislative or judicial power." This reasoning could not reach, said the Court, to officers of a "quasi-legislative" independent agency. Similarly, in Wiener v. United States, 357 U.S. 349 (1958), the Court held that the President had acted beyond his power in removing without cause a member of the War Claims Commission. The commission had been established by Congress in 1948 to adjudicate claims of certain persons who had suffered personal or property damage at the hands of the enemy in World War II. Congress had made no provision for removal of commissioners, apparently intending the commission itself to be of such short duration that only one set of commissioners would be needed. Wiener and the other commissioners were removed by President Eisenhower on the sole ground that the President deemed it "in the national interest" that the commission proceed "with personnel of my own selection." The Court reasoned that Humphrey's Executor had drawn "a sharp line of cleavage between officials who were part of the Executive establishment and were thus removable by virtue of the President's constitutional powers, and those who are members of a body 'to exercise its judgment without the leave or hindrance of any other official or any department of the government,' 295 U.S., at 625-626, as to whom a power of removal exists only if Congress may fairly be said to have conferred it." As an "adjudicatory body," the War Crimes Commission, the Court held, fell not on the postmaster's but on the Federal Trade Commission's side of the constitutional fence.

Compare Nader v. Bork, 366 F. Supp. 104 (D.D.C. 1973). There, the Court held that the dismissal of Watergate Special Prosecutor Archibald Cox without cause and despite regulations providing that he might be discharged only for "extraordinary improprieties" was illegal. The court reasoned, first, that the Special Prosecutor was an inferior officer (within the meaning of Myers) who "served subject to Congressional rather than Presidential control," and second, that the executive was precluded from discharging officials except in accordance with its own regulations so long as those remained in force. See, e.g., Vitarelli v. Seaton, 359 U.S. 535 (1959).

Following the discharge of Cox, the regulations were amended to provide that his successor should be entitled to sue for release of any documents and tapes relating to Watergate held by the White House and should not be removed without congressional consultation. The regulation provided: ". . . the Special Prosecutor will have the greatest degree of independence that is consistent with the Attorney-General's statutory accountability for all matters falling within the jurisdiction of the Department of Justice. The Attorney General will not countermand or interfere with the Special Prosecutor's decisions or actions. The Special Prosecutor will determine whether and to what extent he will inform or consult with the Attorney General about the conduct of his duties and responsibilities. In accordance with assurances given by the President to the Attorney General that the President will not exercise his constitutional powers to effect the discharge of the Special Prosecutor or to limit the independence he is hereby given, the Special Prosecutor will not be removed from his duties except for extraordinary improprieties on his part and without the President's first consulting the Majority and Minority Leaders and Chairmen and ranking Minority Members of the Judiciary Committees of the Senate and House of

Representatives and ascertaining that their consensus is in accord with his proposed action." 38 Fed. Reg. 30739, as amended, id. 32805. In light of Myers and Springer, supra, is the last provision of these regulations enforceable?

In the Tapes Case, United States v. Nixon, infra, a threshold issue was whether the action by the Special Prosecutor to require production of documents held by his superior, the President, presented a "case or controversy" within the meaning of Article III. The Court rested its holding that it did on the argument that regulations are binding so long as they are in force. Thus, where the President and Attorney General had ceded to the Special Prosecutor the decision whether to seek the tapes, a normal superior-subordinate relationship did not obtain and the action should not be dismissed as a mere "intrabranch" dispute. This holding has raised questions with commentators who wonder whether the executive may thus force the courts to take jurisdiction of its internal disputes. See, e.g., The Supreme Court, 1973 Term, 88 Harv. L. Rev. 41, 50-61 (1974). The special situation presented by the Watergate investigation, involving the ambivalent position of President Nixon, would appear both to have justified the Court's assumption of jurisdiction in this case and to have left no unwieldy precedents for the future. See Freund, Foreword — On Presidential Privilege, 88 Harv. L. Rev. 13, 14-17 (1974). Compare the Court's assumption of jurisdiction over another class of "intrabranch" disputes — those between an executive department and an independent regulatory agency. See, e.g., United States v. ICC, 337 U.S. 426 (1949). As to the practices of the Department of Justice when it is asked to represent conflicting claims of two executive departments, see Stern, "Inconsistency" in Government Litigation, 64 Harv. L. Rev. 759 (1951).

c. Impoundment of Funds and the Pocket Veto

NOTE Impoundment

In Local 2677 v. Phillips, 358 F. Supp. 60 (D.D.C. 1973), the court held invalid the attempt by the Acting Director of the Office of Economic Opportunity to terminate certain programs of the agency for which funds had been appropriated by Congress. The Director acted in conformity with a budget message of the President, recommending the termination of OEO. The court's decision was based on a construction of the applicable appropriation statutes, which were held mandatory and binding on the executive.

As the foregoing case indicates, a major issue in impoundment cases has been whether the President has been authorized by statute to decline to spend funds. The executive has claimed such authority on the basis of statutes which set limits on federal spending and the federal debt, authorize reduced spending to take into account unforeseen economies or changing needs within a particular program, or leave program administrators with some amount of discretion over how much of the available funds will be spent. The first two sets of statutes have been surveyed and analyzed in Note, Impoundment of Funds, 86 Harv. L. Rev. 1505, 1516-1523 (1973). The third statutory claim has received the greatest consideration in the courts. Two decisions construed §§205 and 207 of the Water Pollution Control Act Amendments of 1972, 33 U.S.C. §§1285, 1287, which provide that the Environmental Protection Administrator "shall allot" federal grants for construction of sewage treatment plants in sums "not to exceed" certain amounts. In Train v. City of New York, 494 F.2d 1033 (D.C. Cir. 1973), the court, stating first that it could "find no way to harmonize the term 'shall allot' and the language concerning sums 'not to exceed,' " id. at 1039, made an extensive analysis of the legislative history of the amendments and on that basis concluded that Congress had intended to require the Administrator to allot all the sums available. In Train v. Campaign Clean Water, Inc., 489 F.2d 492 (4th Cir. 1973), the court took a different approach. It found that where the language concerning executive discretion was vague, the burden falls on the plaintiff to show that the Administrator's decision not to allot funds exceeded his grant of discretion.

The Supreme Court resolved the issue in Train v. City of New York, 420 U.S. 35 (1975), holding the threshold allotment provision of the act to be mandatory, whatever discretion might be retained to expend less than the maximum because of a lack of qualified applications.

In 1974 Congress passed the Impoundment Control Act, 31 U.S.C. §§1401-1417, designed to rationalize control over withholdings of available funds. The act distinguishes between "rescissions" and "deferrals" of "budget authority," that is, "authority provided by law to enter into obligations which will result in immediate or future outlays involving Government funds." A deferral is a postponement of spending, and a rescission represents a decision not to spend the available funds at any time. See Joint Conference Rep. No. 93-924, 93d Cong., 2d Sess. (1974). When the President decides to rescind budget authority, he is required to transmit to Congress a thorough explanatory statement; and unless both Houses within 45 days pass bills supporting the President's proposal, the rescission will be considered disallowed. In the case of deferrals, however, the President's proposals will be considered disallowed only *if* either House passes a resolution disapproving the deferral.

See Fisher, Funds Impounded by the President: The Constitutional Issue, 38 Geo. Wash. L. Rev. 124 (1969); Abascal and Kramer, Presidential Impoundment: Historical Genesis and Constitutional Framework, 62 Geo. L.J. 1549 (1974); Baade, Mandatory Appropriations of Public Funds: A Comparative Study, 60 Va. L. Rev. 393, 611 (1974); Stassen, Separation of Powers and the Uncommon Defense: The Case Against Impounding of Weapons Systems Appropriations, 57 Geo. L.J. 1159 (1969).

NOTE The Pocket Veto

Regarding executive assertions of independent constitutional authority to impound, consider the following statement: "An executive power to impound would give the President authority much more extensive than that implicit in an item veto. Where an Executive has an item veto, his determination that particular spending is unwise or unwarranted can be overriden by two-thirds of the legislature. Impoundment permits no override. Since the Constitution denies the Executive the item veto, a claim to the stronger power must be viewed with some skepticism." Note, Protecting the Fisc: Executive Impoundment and Congressional Power, 82 Yale L.J. 1636, 1638-1639 (1973).

Another device by which the executive has claimed to avoid Congress' authority to override a veto is use of the pocket veto provision of Article I, §7, which provides, in part:

"Every Bill which shall have passed the House of Representatives and the Senate, shall, before it become a Law, be presented to the President of the United States; If he approve he shall sign it, but if not he shall return it . . . . If any Bill shall not be returned by the President within ten Days (Sundays excepted) after it shall have been presented to him, the Same shall be a Law, in like manner as if he had signed it, *unless the Congress by their Adjournment prevent its return, in which case it shall not be a Law.*" (Italics added.)

The danger is that if Congress is in temporary recess, of perhaps only a few days, when the ten-day period expires, a President may be able to kill a piece of legislation without subjecting his decision to an overriding vote, by stating that he was prevented from returning the bill on the tenth day. The courts have taken a practical view of the pocket veto clause, however, and have sought to limit its application to situations where the President is in fact prevented from making a return. The Court has upheld the validity of a return to the Secretary of the Senate when the Senate was in a three-day recess. Wright v. United States, 302 U.S. 583, 592-593 (1937). Although the pocket veto provision applies when the tenth day falls after the adjournment of a Congress or of the first session of a Congress,

The Pocket Veto Cases, Okanogon Indian Tribe v. United States, 279 U.S. 655 (1929), it is apparently inapplicable to an intrasession recess of Congress where an agent of the House to which the bill is to be returned is available to receive it. See Kennedy v. Sampson, 511 F.2d 430 (D.C. Cir. 1974). And as Okanogon was decided with reference to the adjournment of the First Session of the 69th Congress on July 3, 1926 — not to meet again until the next year — one may question the continuing validity of that case now that Congress meets virtually year-round. Consider the remarks of Chief Justice Hughes in Wright:

"[W]hen there is a mere temporary recess . . . . there is no withholding of the bill from appropriate legislative record for weeks or perhaps months, no keeping of the bill in a state of suspended animation with no certain knowledge on the part of the public whether it was seasonably delivered, no causing of any undue delay in its reconsideration. When there is nothing but such a temporary recess the organization of the House and its appropriate officers continue to function without interruption, the bill is properly safeguarded for a very limited period of time and is promptly reported and may be reconsidered immediately after the short recess is over. . . .

"The constitutional provisions have two fundamental purposes: (1) that the President shall have suitable opportunity to consider the bills presented to him, and (2) that the Congress shall have suitable opportunity to consider his objections to bills and on such consideration to pass them over his veto provided there are the requisite votes. Edwards v. United States, 286 U.S. 482, 486 [1932] . . . . We should not adopt a construction which would frustrate either of these purposes."

Section B. THE AUTONOMY OF THE EXECUTIVE AND LEGISLATIVE BRANCHES

1. Immunity from Liability

Barr v. Matteo *360 U.S. 564, 79 S. Ct. 1335, 3 L. Ed. 2d 1434 (1959)*

MR. JUSTICE HARLAN announced the judgment of the Court, and delivered an opinion, in which MR. JUSTICE FRANKFURTER, MR. JUSTICE CLARK, and MR. JUSTICE WHITTAKER join.

We are called upon in this case to weigh in a particular context two considerations of high importance which now and again come into sharp conflict — on the one hand, the protection of the individual citizen against pecuniary damage caused by oppressive or malicious action on the part of officials of the Federal Government; and on the other, the protection of the public interest by shielding responsible governmental officers against the harassment and inevitable hazards of vindictive or ill-founded damage suits brought on account of action taken in the exercise of their official responsibilities.

This is a libel suit, brought in the District Court of the District of Columbia by respondents, former employees of the Office of Rent Stabilization. The alleged libel was contained in a press release issued by the office on February 5, 1953, at the direction of petitioner, then its Acting Director. The circumstances which gave rise to the issuance of the release follow.

In 1950 the statutory existence of the Office of Housing Expediter, the predecessor agency of the Office of Rent Stabilization, was about to expire. Respondent Madigan, then Deputy Director in charge of personnel and fiscal matters, and respondent Matteo, chief of the personnel branch, suggested to the Housing Expediter a plan designed to utilize some $2,600,000 of agency funds earmarked in the agency's appropriation for the fiscal year of 1950 exclusively for terminal-leave payments. The effect of the plan would have been to obviate the possibility that the agency might have to make large terminal-leave payments during the next fiscal year out of general agency funds, should the life of the agency be extended by Congress. In essence, the mechanics of the plan were that agency employees would be discharged, paid accrued annual leave out of the $2,600,000 earmarked for terminal-leave payments, rehired immediately as temporary employees, and restored to permanent status should the agency's life in fact be extended.

Petitioner, at the time General Manager of the agency, opposed respondents' plan on the ground that it violated the spirit of the Thomas Amendment, 64 Stat. 768,[2] and expressed his opposition to the Housing Expediter. The Expediter decided against general adoption of the plan, but at respondent Matteo's request gave permission for its use in connection with approximately fifty employees, including both respondents, on a voluntary basis.[3] Thereafter the life of the agency was in fact extended.

Some two and a half years later, on January 28, 1953, the Office of Rent Stabilization received a letter from Senator John J. Williams of Delaware, inquiring about the terminal-leave payments made under the plan in 1950. Respondent Madigan drafted a reply to the letter, which he did not attempt to bring to the attention of petitioner, and then prepared a reply which he sent to petitioner's office for his signature as Acting Director of the agency. Petitioner was out of the office, and a secretary signed the submitted letter, which was then delivered by Madigan to Senator Williams on the morning of February 3, 1953.

On February 4, 1953, Senator Williams delivered a speech on the floor of the Senate strongly criticizing the plan, stating that "to say the least it is an unjustifiable raid on the Federal Treasury, and heads of every agency in the Government who have condoned this practice should be called to task." The letter above referred to was ordered printed in the Congressional Record. Other Senators joined in the attack on the plan. Their comments were widely reported in the press on February 5, 1953, and petitioner, in his capacity as Acting Director of the agency, received a large number of inquiries from newspapers and other news media as to the agency's position on the matter.

On that day petitioner served upon respondents letters expressing his intention to suspend them from duty, and at the same time ordered issuance by the office of the press release which is the subject of this litigation, and the text of which appears in the margin.[5]

Respondents sued, charging that the press release, in itself and as coupled with the contemporaneous news reports of senatorial reaction to the plan, defamed them to their injury, and alleging that its publication and terms had been actuated by malice on the part of petitioner. Petitioner defended, inter alia, on the ground that the issuance of the press

---

[2] This statute, part of the General Appropriation Act of 1951, provided that:

"No part of the funds of, or available for expenditure by any corporation or agency included in this Act, including the government of the District of Columbia, shall be available to pay for annual leave accumulated by any civilian officer or employee during the calendar year 1950 and unused at the close of business on June 30, 1951. . . ."

[3] The General Accounting Office subsequently ruled that the payments were illegal, and respondents were required to return them. Respondent Madigan challenged this determination in the Court of Claims, which held that the plan was not in violation of law. Madigan v. United States, 142 Ct. Cl. 641.

[5] "William G. Barr, Acting Director of Rent Stabilization today served notice of suspension on the two officials of the agency who in June 1950 were responsible for the plan which allowed 53 of the agency's 2,681 employees to take their accumulated annual leave in cash.

"Mr. Barr's appointment as Acting Director becomes effective Monday, February 9, 1953, and the suspension of these employees will be his first act of duty. The employees are John J. Madigan, Deputy Director for Administration, and Linda Matteo, Director of Personnel.

" 'In June 1950,' Mr. Barr stated, 'my position in the agency was not one of authority which would have permitted me to stop the action. Furthermore, I did not know about it until it was almost completed.

" 'When I did learn that certain employees were receiving cash annual leave settlements and being returned to agency employment on a temporary basis, I specifically notified the employees under my supervision that if they

Section B. Executive and Legislative Branch Autonomy   675

release was protected by either a qualified or an absolute privilege. The trial court overruled these contentions, and instructed the jury to return a verdict for respondents if it found the release defamatory. The jury found for respondents.

Petitioner appealed, raising only the issue of absolute privilege. The judgment of the trial court was affirmed by the Court of Appeals, which held that "in explaining his decision [to suspend respondents] to the general public [petitioner] . . . went entirely outside his line of duty" and that thus the absolute privilege, assumed otherwise to be available, did not attach. 100 U.S. App. D.C. 319, 244 F.2d 767. We granted certiorari, vacated the Court of Appeals' judgment, and remanded the case "with directions to pass upon petitioner's claim of a qualified privilege." 355 U.S. 171, 173. On remand the Court of Appeals held that the press release was protected by a qualified privilege, but that there was evidence from which a jury could reasonably conclude that petitioner had acted maliciously, or had spoken with lack of reasonable grounds for believing that his statement was true, and that either conclusion would defeat the qualified privilege. Accordingly it remanded the case to the District Court for retrial. 103 U.S. App. D.C. 176, 256 F.2d 890. At this point petitioner again sought, and we again granted certiorari, 358 U.S. 917, to determine whether in the circumstances of this case petitioner's claim on absolute privilege should have stood as a bar to maintenance of the suit despite the allegations of malice made in the complaint.

The law of privilege as a defense by officers of government to civil damage suits for defamation and kindred torts has in large part been of judicial making, although the Constitution itself gives an absolute privilege to members of both Houses of Congress in respect to any speech, debate, vote, report, or action done in session.[6] This Court early held that judges of courts of superior or general authority are absolutely privileged as respects civil suits to recover for actions taken by them in the exercise of their judicial functions, irrespective of the motives with which those acts are alleged to have been performed, Bradley v. Fisher, 13 Wall. 335, and that a like immunity extends to other officers of government whose duties are related to the judicial process. Yaselli v. Goff, 12 F.2d 396, aff'd per curiam, 275 U.S. 503, involving a Special Assistant to the Attorney General. Nor has the privilege been confined to officers of the legislative and judicial branches of the Government and executive officers of the kind involved in Yaselli. In Spalding v. Vilas, 161 U.S. 483, petitioner brought suit against the Postmaster General, alleging that the latter had maliciously circulated widely among postmasters, past and present, information which he knew to be false and which was intended to deceive the postmasters to the detriment of the plaintiff. This Court sustained a plea by the Postmaster General of absolute privilege. . . .

The reasons for the recognition of the privilege have been often stated. It has been thought important that officials of government should be free to exercise their duties unembarrassed by the fear of damage suits in respect of acts done in the course of those duties — suits which would consume time and energies which would otherwise be devoted to governmental service and the threat of which might appreciably inhibit the fearless, vigorous, and effective administration of policies of government. The matter has been admirably expressed by Judge Learned Hand:

---

applied for such cash settlements I would demand their resignations and the record will show that my immediate employees complied with my request.

" 'While I was advised that the action was legal, I took the position that it violated the spirit of the Thomas Amendment and I violently opposed it. Monday, February 9th, when my appointment as Acting Director becomes effective, will be the first time my position in the agency has permitted me to take any action on this matter, and the suspension of these employees will be the first official act I shall take.'

"Mr. Barr also revealed that he has written to Senator Joseph McCarthy, Chairman of the Committee on Government Operations, and to Representative John Phillips, Chairman of the House Subcommittee on Independent Offices Appropriations, requesting an opportunity to be heard on the entire matter."

[6] U.S. Const., Art. I, §6. See Kilbourn v. Thompson, 103 U.S. 168.

"It does indeed go without saying that an official, who is in fact guilty of using his powers to vent his spleen upon others, or for any other personal motive not connected with the public good, should not escape liability for the injuries he may so cause; and, if it were possible in practice to confine such complaints to the guilty, it would be monstrous to deny recovery. The justification for doing so is that it is impossible to know whether the claim is well founded until the case has been tried, and that to submit all officials, the innocent as well as the guilty, to the burden of a trial and to the inevitable danger of its outcome, would dampen the ardor of all but the most resolute, or the most irresponsible, in the unflinching discharge of their duties. Again and again the public interest calls for action which may turn out to be founded on a mistake, in the face of which an official may later find himself hard put to it to satisfy a jury of his good faith. There must indeed be means of punishing public officers who have been truant to their duties; but that is quite another matter from exposing such as have been honestly mistaken to suit by anyone who has suffered from their errors. As is so often the case, the answer must be found in a balance between the evils inevitable in either alternative. In this instance it has been thought in the end better to leave unredressed the wrongs done by dishonest officers than to subject those who try to do their duty to the constant dread of retaliation. . . .

"The decisions have, indeed, always imposed as a limitation upon the immunity that the official's act must have been within the scope of his powers; and it can be argued that official powers, since they exist only for the public good, never cover occasions where the public good is not their aim, and hence that to exercise a power dishonestly is necessarily to overstep its bounds. A moment's reflection shows, however, that that cannot be the meaning of the limitation without defeating the whole doctrine. What is meant by saying that the officer must be acting within his power cannot be more than that the occasion must be such as would have justified the act, if he had been using his power for any of the purposes on whose account it was vested in him. . . ." Gregoire v. Biddle, 177 F.2d 579, 581.

. . . The privilege is not a badge or emolument of exalted office, but an expression of a policy designed to aid in the effective functioning of government. The complexities and magnitude of governmental activity have become so great that there must of necessity be a delegation and redelegation of authority as to many functions, and we cannot say that these functions become less important simply because they are exercised by officers of lower rank in the executive hierarchy.

To be sure, the occasions upon which the acts of the head of an executive department will be protected by the privilege are doubtless far broader than in the case of an officer with less sweeping functions. But that is because the higher the post, the broader the range of responsibilities and duties, and the wider the scope of discretion, it entails. It is not the title of his office but the duties with which the particular officer sought to be made to respond in damages is entrusted — the relation of the act complained of to "matters committed by law to his control or supervision," Spalding v. Vilas, supra, at 498 — which must provide the guide in delineating the scope of the rule which clothes the official acts of the executive officer with immunity from civil defamation suits.

Judged by these standards, we hold that petitioner's plea of absolute privilege in defense of the alleged libel published at his direction must be sustained. The question is a close one, but we cannot say that it was not an appropriate exercise of the discretion with which an executive officer of petitioner's rank is necessarily clothed to publish the press release here at issue in the circumstances disclosed by this record. . . .

We are told that we should forbear from sanctioning any such rule of absolute privilege lest it open the door to wholesale oppression and abuses on the part of unscrupulous government officials. It is perhaps enough to say that fears of this sort have not been realized within the wide area of government where a judicially formulated absolute privilege of broad scope has long existed. It seems to us wholly chimerical to suggest that what hangs in the balance here is the maintenance of high standards of conduct among those in the public service. To be sure, as with any rule of law which attempts to reconcile fundamentally antagonistic social policies, there may be occasional instances of actual injustice which will go unredressed, but we think that price a necessary one to pay for the greater good. And there are of course other sanctions than civil tort suits available to deter the executive official who may be prone to exercise his functions in an unworthy and irresponsible manner. We think that we should not be deterred from establishing the rule which we announce today by any such remote forebodings.

Reversed.

[A concurring opinion by JUSTICE BLACK, and dissenting opinions by the CHIEF JUSTICE and JUSTICES BRENNAN and STEWART, are omitted. For the judicial incorporation of principles of absolute or qualified immunity in the Civil Rights Act, see Note, page 862 infra. Can Barr v. Matteo stand in light of those principles?]

2. The Legislative Branch

a. Control of Membership

[See Powell v. McCormack, page 71 supra.]

b. Bills of Attainder and Ex Post Facto Laws

[See pages 1330-1339 infra.]

c. The Contempt Power

NOTE Congressional Power to Punish Contempts

Article I, §5 of the United States Constitution confers on each House of Congress power to punish contempts committed by its own members. On many occasions in the early history of the nation both the Senate and the House of Representatives took action against contemptuous nonmembers, thus indicating that congressional opinion did not consider that the affirmative grant of power over members implied a lack of power over nonmembers. (See 2 Hinds' Precedents of the House of Representatives 1046 et seq. (1907).) In 1800, for instance, William Duane, editor of the anti-Federalist newspaper, the Aurora, was summoned to the bar of the Senate, as was then the custom in all such matters, and charged with a breach of its privileges in having published a libel on the Senate. Thomas Jefferson in his Manual of Parliamentary Practice 18 (1873 ed.) wrote of the constitutional issue thus presented as follows:

"The editor of the Aurora having, in his paper of February 19, 1800, inserted some paragraphs defamatory of the Senate, and failed in his appearance was ordered to be committed. In debating the legality of this order it was insisted in support of it that every man, by the law of nature, and every body of men, possesses the right of self-defense; that all public functionaries are essentially invested with the powers of self-preservation; that they have an inherent right to do all acts necessary to keep themselves in a condition to discharge the trusts confided to them; that whenever authorities are given, the means of carrying them into execution are given by necessary implication; that thus we see the British Parliament exercise the right of punishing contempts; all the state legislatures exercise the same power, and every court does the same; that if we have it not, we sit at the mercy of every intruder who may enter our doors or gallery, and, by noise and tumult, render proceedings in business impracticable; that if our tranquility is to be perpetually disturbed

678 Chapter Eleven. Distribution of National Powers

by newspaper defamation, it will not be possible to exercise our functions with the requisite coolness and deliberation; and that we must therefore have a power to punish these disturbers of our peace and proceedings. To this it was answered that the Parliament and courts of England have cognizance of contempts by the express provisions of their law; that the State legislatures have equal authority because their powers are plenary; they represent their constituents completely, and possess all their powers, except such as their constitutions have expressly denied them; that the courts of the several states have the same powers by the laws of their States, and those of the Federal Government by the same State laws adopted in each State, by a law of Congress; that none of these bodies, therefore, derive those powers from natural or necessary right, but from express law; that Congress have no such natural or necessary power, nor any powers but such as are given them by the Constitution; that that has given them directly exemption from personal arrest, exemption from any question elsewhere for what is said in their House, and power over their own Members and proceedings; for these no further law is necessary, the Constitution being the law; that, moreover, by that article of the Constitution which authorizes them 'to make all laws necessary and proper for carrying into execution the powers vested by the Constitution in them,' they may provide by law for an undisturbed exercise of their functions, e.g., for the punishment of contempts, of affrays or tumult in their presence, etc., but, till the law be made, it does not exist, and does not exist from their own neglect; that, in the meantime, however, they are not unprotected, the ordinary magistrates and courts of law being open and competent to punish all unjustifiable disturbances or defamations, and even their own sergeant, who may appoint deputies ad libitum to aid him (3 Grey, 59, 147, 255), is equal to small disturbances; that in requiring a previous law, the Constitution had regard to the inviolability of the citizen, as well as of the Member; as, should one House, in the regular form of a bill, aim at too broad privileges without control, it may do it on the spur of the occasion, conceal the law in its own breast, and, after the fact committed, make its sentence both the law and the judgment on that fact; if the offense is to be kept undefined and to be declared only ex re nata, and according to the passions of the moment, and there be no limitation either in the manner or measure of the punishment, the condition of the citizen will be perilous indeed. Which of these doctrines will prevail time will decide."

Time, as Jefferson predicted, has made its decision, but not with perfect clarity. In Anderson v. Dunn, 6 Wheat. 206 (1821), the Court sustained the contention that each House possesses an inherent power, implied in the Constitution, to imprison nonmembers for obstructing the work of Congress. In an opinion by Justice Johnson the Court reasoned: "But if there is one maxim which necessarily rides over all others, in the practical application of government, it is, that the public functionaries must be left at liberty to exercise the powers which the people have intrusted to them. The interests and dignity of those who created them, require the exertion of the powers indispensable to the attainment of the ends of their creation." The Court stated that Congress' power to imprison a nonmember for contempt was limited to imprisonment only until Congress adjourned.

Although both Houses of Congress continued to assert that persons who interfered with the orderly conduct of congressional business, as by physical assaults on members or by bribery, were punishable by the offended House for contempt, Congress in 1857 altered the normal procedure as to persons who refused to give testimony demanded by a House by providing that recalcitrance was to be reported to the offended House, which would certify the fact of contempt to a United States Attorney for prosecution in the courts. This procedure still prevails, 2 U.S.C §§ 192, 194 (1970), though punishment by the offended House itself is still, apparently, an alternative. See Jurney v. MacCracken, 294 U.S. 125 (1935), and McGrain v. Daugherty, 273 U.S. 135 (1927), in which the Court refused to order the release of recalcitrant witnesses who had been taken into custody by the Sergeant-at-Arms of the Senate.

As an implied power, however, the contempt power has been limited to the punishment of actions which obstruct legitimate legislative activities. Thus the courts assumed an obligation to pass on two questions, whether the contemptuous action in fact obstructed congressional business and whether that business was a legitimate concern of Congress. The former inquiry was made in Marshall v. Gordon, 243 U.S. 541 (1917), in which the Court at last considered the issue presented in the matter of William Duane's alleged contempt. There, the Court held that publication of offensive and vexatious charges against the Congress could not be labeled contempt when the only effect of the assertions would be to arouse public opinion and to stir the indignation of members of Congress. The latter form of review was undertaken in Kilbourn v. Thompson, 103 U.S. 168 (1880), in which the Court held that plaintiff could maintain an action for damages against the Sergeant-at-Arms of the House of Representatives who had imprisoned plaintiff for 45 days for refusing to answer questions put to him by a House committee investigating a real estate pool managed by the recently bankrupt firm of Jay Cooke & Co. Writing for the Court, Justice Miller distinguished Anderson v. Dunn on the ground that in Kilbourn the investigators' questions clearly exceeded congressional authority: insofar as it was directed towards legislation regarding this particular bankruptcy, the investigation represented congressional infringement upon the domain of the judiciary and in any case "could result in no valid legislation on the subject to which the inquiry referred." The Court dismissed the action against members of Congress who had been named defendants on the ground that they were immune under the speech and debate clause. Since Kilbourn, and particularly during the 1950s, congressional attempts to punish recalcitrant witnesses, whether directly or by means of prosecution under 2 U.S.C. §§192, 194, have frequently been challenged on the ground that inquiry was beyond Congress' constitutional powers or beyond the resolution authorizing a committee or subcommittee investigation. These cases are treated at pages 1315 et seq. infra.

No clear guidelines have emerged concerning the procedural rights of persons accused of contempt of Congress. In Groppi v. Leslie, 404 U.S. 496 (1972), however, the Court unanimously held that a person accused of leading a demonstration onto the floor of the Wisconsin State Assembly was entitled to some notice and opportunity to be heard before being jailed for contempt. The Court indicated that a full trial would not be required and referred, apparently with approval, to the "customary practice in Congress . . . [of providing] the contemnor with an opportunity to appear before the bar of the House, or before a committee, and give answer to the misconduct charged against him." See also Watkins v. United States, 354 U.S. 178 (1957), holding that the due process clause requires that before a witness may be convicted of contempt of Congress for having failed to answer questions put by a congressional committee, the pertinency of the disputed questions to the matters under investigation by the committee must have been made clear to the witness.

3. The Executive Branch: Executive Privilege

United States v. Nixon 418 U.S. 683, 94 S. Ct. 3090, 41 L. Ed. 2d 1039 (1974)

MR. CHIEF JUSTICE BURGER delivered the opinion of the Court.

[This litigation] present[s] for review the denial of a motion, filed on behalf of the President of the United States, in the case of United States v. Mitchell at al. (D.C. Crim. No. 74-110), to quash a third-party subpoena duces tecum issued by the United States District Court for the District of Columbia, pursuant to Fed. Rule Crim. Proc. 17(c). The subpoena directed the President to produce certain tape recordings and documents relating to his conversations with aides and advisers. The court rejected the President's claims of absolute executive privilege, of lack of jurisdiction, and of failure to satisfy the requirements of Rule 17(c). The President appealed to the Court of Appeals. We granted the United States' petition for certiorari before judgment, and also the President's responsive cross petition for certiorari before judgment,[2] because of the public importance of the issues presented and the need for their prompt resolution. 417 U.S. 927 and 960 (1974).

On March 1, 1974, a grand jury of the United States District Court for the District of Columbia returned an indictment charging seven named individuals with various offenses, including conspiracy to defraud the United States and to obstruct justice. Although he was not designated as such in the indictment, the grand jury named the President, among others, as an unindicted coconspirator. On April 18, 1974, upon motion of the Special Prosecutor, see n.8, infra, a subpoena duces tecum was issued pursuant to Rule 17(c) to the President by the United States District Court and made returnable on May 2, 1974. This subpoena required the production, in advance of the September 9 trial date, of certain tapes, memoranda, papers, transcripts or other writings relating to certain precisely identified meetings between the President and others. The Special Prosecutor was able to fix the time, place and persons present at these discussions because the White House daily logs and appointment records had been delivered to him. On April 30, the President publicly released edited transcripts of 43 conversations; portions of 20 conversations subject to subpoena in the present case were included. On May 1, 1974, the President's counsel filed a "special appearance" and a motion to quash the subpoena, under Rule 17(c). This motion was accompanied by a formal claim of privilege. At a subsequent hearing, further motions to expunge the grand jury's action naming the President as an unindicted coconspirator and for protective orders against the disclosure of that information were filed or raised orally by counsel for the President.

On May 20, 1974, the District Court denied the motion to quash and the motions to expunge and for protective orders. 377 F. Supp. 1326 (1974). It further ordered "the President or any subordinate officer, official, or employee with custody or control of the documents or objects subpoenaed," id., at 1331 to deliver to the District Court, on or before May 31, 1974, the originals of all subpoenaed items, as well as an index and analysis of those items, together with tape copies of those portions of the subpoenaed recordings for which transcripts had been released to the public by the President on April 30. . . .

The District Court held that the judiciary, not the President, was the final arbiter of a claim of executive privilege. The court concluded that under the circumstances of this case the presumptive privilege was overcome by the Special Prosecutor's prima facie "demonstration of need sufficiently compelling to warrant judicial examination in chambers. . . ." 377 F. Supp., at 1330. The court held, finally, that the Special Prosecutor had satisfied the requirements of Rule 17(c). The District Court stayed its order pending appellate review on condition that review was sought before 4 P.M., May 24. The court further provided that matters filed under seal remain under seal when transmitted as part of the record.

On May 24, 1974, the President filed a timely notice of appeal from the District Court order, and the certified record from the District Court was docketed in the United States Court of Appeals for the District of Columbia Circuit. On the same day, the President also filed a petition for writ of mandamus in the Court of Appeals seeking review of the District Court order.

Later on May 24, the Special Prosecutor also filed, in this Court, a petition for a writ of

---

[2] The cross-petition in No. 73-1834 raised the issue whether the grand jury acted within its authority in naming the President as a coconspirator. Since we find resolution of this issue unnecessary to resolution of the question whether the claim of privilege is to prevail, the cross-petition for certiorari is dismissed as improvidently granted and the remander of this opinion is concerned with the issues raised in No. 73-1766. . . .

certiorari before judgment. On May 31, the petition was granted with an expedited briefing schedule, 417 U.S. 927 (1974). On June 6, the President filed, under seal, a cross-petition for writ of certiorari before judgment. This cross-petition was granted June 15, 1974, 417 U.S. 960 (1974), and the case was set for argument on July 8, 1974.

I

JURISDICTION

The threshold question presented is whether the May 20, 1974, order of the District Court was an appealable order and whether this case was properly "in," 28 U.S.C. §1254, the United States Court of Appeals when the petition for certiorari was filed in this Court. Court of Appeals jurisdiction under 28 U.S.C. §1291 encompasses only "final decision of the district courts." Since the appeal was timely filed and all other procedural requirements were met, the petition is properly before this Court for consideration if the District Court order was final. 28 U.S.C. §1254(1);28 U.S.C. §2101(e).

The finality requirement of 28 U.S.C. §1291 embodies a strong congressional policy against piecemeal reviews, and against obstructing or impeding an ongoing judicial proceeding by interlocutory appeals. . . . In applying this principle to an order denying a motion to quash and requiring the production of evidence pursuant to a subpoena duces tecum, it has been repeatedly held that the order is not final and hence not appealable. . . .

The requirement of submitting to contempt, however, is not without exception and in some instances the purposes underlying the finality rule require a different result. For example, in Perlman v. United States, 247 U.S. 7 950 (1918), a subpoena had been directed to a third party requesting certain exhibits; the appellant, who owned the exhibits, sought to raise a claim of privilege. The Court held an order compelling production was appealable because it was unlikely that the third party would risk a contempt citation in order to allow immediate review of the appellant's claim of privilege. Id., at 12-13. That case fell within the "limited class of cases where denial of immediate review would render impossible any review whatsoever of an individual's claims." United States v. Ryan, 402 U.S., at 533.

Here too the traditional contempt avenue to immediate appeal is peculiarly inappropriate due to the unique setting in which the question arises. To require a President of the United States to place himself in the posture of disobeying an order of a court merely to trigger the procedural mechanism for review of the ruling would be unseemly, and present an unnecessary occasion for constitutional confrontation between two branches of the Government. Similarly, a federal judge should not be placed in the posture of issuing a citation to a President simply in order to invoke review. The issue whether a President can be cited for contempt could itself engender protracted litigation, and would further delay both review on the merits of his claim of privilege and the ultimate termination of the underlying criminal action for which his evidence is sought. These considerations lead us to conclude that the order of the District Court was an appealable order. . . .

II

JUSTICIABILITY

In the District Court, the President's counsel argued that the court lacked jurisdiction to issue the subpoena because the matter was an intra-branch dispute between a subordinate and superior officer of the Executive Branch and hence not subject to judicial resolution. That argument has been renewed in this Court with emphasis on the contention that the dispute does not present a "case" or "controversy" which can be adjudicated in the federal courts. The President's counsel argues that the federal courts should not intrude into areas committed to the other branches of Government. He views the present dispute as essentially a "jurisdictional" dispute within the Executive Branch which he analogizes to a dispute between two congressional committees. Since the Executive Branch has exclusive authority and absolute discretion to decide whether to prosecute a case, Confiscation Cases, 7 Wall. 454 (1869), United States v. Cox, 342 F.2d 167, 171 (CA5), cert. denied, 381 U.S. 935 (1965), it is contended that a President's decision is final in determining what evidence is to be used in a given criminal case. Although his counsel concedes the President has delegated certain specific powers to the Special Prosecutor, he has not "waived nor delegated to the Special Prosecutor the President's duty to claim privilege as to all materials . . . which fall within the President's inherent authority to refuse to disclose to any executive officer." Brief for the President 47. The Special Prosecutor's demand for the items therefore presents, in the view of the President's counsel, a political question under Baker v. Carr, 369 U.S. 186 (1962), since it involves a "textually demonstrable" grant of power under Art. II.

The mere assertion of a claim of an "intra-branch dispute," without more, has never operated to defeat federal jurisdiction; justiciability does not depend on such a surface inquiry. In United States v. ICC, 337 U.S. 426 (1949), the Court observed, "courts must look behind names that symbolize the parties to determine whether a justiciable case or controversy is presented." Id., at 430. See also: Powell v. McCormack, 395 U.S. 486 (1969); ICC v. Jersey City, 322 U.S. 503 (1944); United States ex rel. Chapman v. FPC, 345 U.S. 153 (1953); Secretary of Agriculture v. United States, 347 U.S. 645 (1954); FMB v. Isbrandsten Co., 356 U.S. 481, 482 n. 2 (1958); United States v. Marine Bancorporation Corp., 418 U.S. 602 (1974), and United States v. Connecticut National Bank, 418 U.S. 656 (1974).

Our starting point is the nature of the proceeding for which the evidence is sought — here a pending criminal prosecution. It is a judicial proceeding in a federal court alleging violation of federal laws and is brought in the name of the United States as sovereign. Berger v. United States, 295 U.S. 78, 88 (1935). Under the authority of Art. II, §2, Congress has vested in the Attorney General the power to conduct the criminal litigation of the United States Government. 28 U.S.C. §516. It has also vested in him the power to appoint subordinate officers to assist him in the discharge of his duties. 28 U.S.C. §§509, 510, 515, 533. Acting pursuant to those statutes, the Attorney General has delegated the authority to represent the United States in these particular matters to a Special Prosecutor with unique authority and tenure.[8] The regulation gives the Special Prosecutor explicit power to contest the invocation of executive privilege in the process of seeking evidence

---

[8] The regulation issued by the Attorney General pursuant to his statutory authority, vests in the Special Prosecutor plenary authority to control the course of investigations and litigation related to "all offenses arising out of the 1972 Presidential Election for which the Special Prosecutor deems it necessary and appropriate to assume responsibility, allegations involving the President, members of the White House staff, or Presidential appointees, and any other matters which he consents to have assigned to him by the Attorney General." 38 Fed. Reg. 30739, as amended by 38 Fed. Reg. 32805. In particular, the Special Prosecutor was given full authority, inter alia, "to contest the assertion of 'Executive Privilege' . . . and handl[e] all aspects of any cases within his jurisdiction." Ibid. The regulations then go on to provide:

"In exercising this authority, the Special Prosecutor will have the greatest degree of independence that is consistent with the Attorney-General's statutory accountability for all matters falling within the jurisdiction of the Department of Justice. . . . In accordance with assurances given by the President to the Attorney General that the President will not exercise his Constitutional powers to effect the discharge of the Special Prosecutor or to limit the independence he is hereby given, the Special Prosecutor will not be removed from his duties except for extraordinary improprieties on his part and without the President's first consulting the Majority and Minority Leaders and Chairman and ranking Minority Members of the Judiciary Committees of the Senate and House of Representatives and ascertaining that their consensus is in accord with his proposed action."

deemed relevant to the performance of these specially delegated duties. 38 Fed. Reg. 30739.

So long as this regulation is extant it has the force of law. In Accardi v. Shaughnessy, 347 U.S. 260 (1953), regulations of the Attorney General delegated certain of his discretionary powers to the Board of Immigration Appeals and required that Board to exercise its own discretion on appeals in deportation cases. The Court held that so long as the Attorney General's regulations remained operative, he denied himself the authority to exercise the discretion delegated to the Board even though the original authority was his and he could reassert it by amending the regulations. . . .

Here, as in Accardi, it is theoretically possible for the Attorney General to amend or revoke the regulation defining the Special Prosecutor's authority. But he has not done so. So long as this regulation remains in force the Executive Branch is bound by it, and indeed the United States as the sovereign composed of the three branches is bound to respect and to enforce it. Moreover, the delegation of authority to the Special Prosecutor in this case is not an ordinary delegation by the Attorney General to a subordinate officer: with the authorization of the President, the Acting Attorney General provided in the regulation that the Special Prosecutor was not to be removed without the "consensus" of eight designated leaders of Congress. Note 8, supra.

The demands of and the resistance to the subpoena present an obvious controversy in the ordinary sense, but that alone is not sufficient to meet constitutional standards. In the constitutional sense, controversy means more than disagreement and conflict; rather it means the kind of controversy courts traditionally resolve. Here at issue is the production or nonproduction of specified evidence deemed by the Special Prosecutor to be relevant and admissible in a pending criminal case. It is sought by one official of the Government within the scope of his express authority; it is resisted by the Chief Executive on the ground of his duty to preserve the confidentiality of the communications of the President. Whatever the correct answer on the merits, these issues are "of a type which are traditionally justiciable." United States v. ICC, 337 U.S., at 430. The independent Special Prosecutor with his asserted need for the subpoenaed material in the underlying criminal prosecution is opposed by the President with his steadfast assertion of privilege against disclosure of the material. This setting assures there is "that concrete adverseness which sharpens the presentation of issues upon which the court so largely depends for illumination of difficult constitutional questions." Baker v. Carr, 369 U.S., at 204. Moreover, since the matter is one arising in the regular course of a federal criminal prosecution, it is within the traditional scope of Art. III power. Id., at 198.

In light of the uniqueness of the setting in which the conflict arises, the fact that both parties are officers of the Executive Branch cannot be viewed as a barrier to justiciability. It would be inconsistent with the applicable law and regulation, and the unique facts of this case to conclude other than that the Special Prosecutor has standing to bring this action and that a justiciable controversy is presented for decision.

III

RULE 17(C)

The subpoena duces tecum is challenged on the ground that the Special Prosecutor failed to satisfy the requirements of Fed. Rule Crim. Proc. 17(c) which governs the issuance of subpoenas duces tecum in federal criminal proceedings. If we sustained this challenge, there would be no occasion to reach the claim of privilege asserted with respect to the subpoenaed material. Thus we turn to the question whether the requirements of Rule 17(c) have been satisfied. . . .

Rule 17(c) provides:

"A subpoena may also command the person to whom it is directed to produce the books, papers, documents or other objects designated therein. The court on motion made promptly may quash or modify the subpoena if compliance would be unreasonable or oppressive. The court may direct that books, papers, documents or objects designated in the subpoena be produced before the court at a time prior to the trial or prior to the time when they are to be offered in evidence and may upon their production permit the books, papers, documents or objects or portions thereof to be inspected by the parties and their attorneys."

A subpoena for documents may be quashed if their production would be "unreasonable or oppressive," but not otherwise. The leading case in this Court interpreting this standard is Bowman Dairy Co. v. United States, 341 U.S. 214 (1950). This case recognized certain fundamental characteristics of the subpoena duces tecum in criminal cases: (1) it was not intended to provide a means of discovery for criminal cases. Id., at 220; (2) its chief innovation was to expedite the trial by providing a time and place *before* trial for the inspection of subpoenaed materials. Ibid. As both parties agree, cases decided in the wake of Bowman have generally followed Judge Weinfeld's formulation in United States v. Iozia, 13 F.R.D. 335, 338 (S.D.N.Y. 1952), as to the required showing. Under this test, in order to require production prior to trial, the moving party must show: (1) that the documents are evidentiary and relevant; (2) that they are not otherwise procurable reasonably in advance of trial by exercise of due diligence; (3) that the party cannot properly prepare for trial without such production and inspection in advance of trial and that the failure to obtain such inspection may tend unreasonably to delay the trial; (4) that the application is made in good faith and is not intended as a general "fishing expedition."

Against this background, the Special Prosecutor, in order to carry his burden, must clear three hurdles: (1) relevancy; (2) admissibility; (3) specificity. . . . With respect to many of the tapes, the Special Prosecutor offered the sworn testimony or statements of one or more of the participants in the conversations as to what was said at the time. As for the remainder of the tapes, the identity of the participants and the time and place of the conversations, taken in their total context, permit a rational inference that at least part of the conversations relate to the offenses charged in the indictment.

We also conclude there was a sufficient preliminary showing that each of the subpoenaed tapes contains evidence admissible with respect to the offenses charged in the indictment. The most cogent objection to the admissibility of the taped conversations here at issue is that they are a collection of out-of-court statements by declarants who will not be subject to cross-examination and that the statements are therefore inadmissible hearsay. Here, however, most of the tapes apparently contain conversations to which one or more of the defendants named in the indictment were party. The hearsay rule does not automatically bar all out-of-court statements by a defendant in a criminal case. Declarations by one defendant may also be admissible against other defendants upon a sufficient showing, by independent evidence, of a conspiracy among one or more other defendants and the declarant and if the declarations at issue were in furtherance of that conspiracy. The same is true of declarations of coconspirators who are not defendants in the case on trial. Dutton v. Evans, 400 U.S. 74, 81 (1970). Recorded conversations may also be admissible for the limited purpose of impeaching the credibility of any defendant who testifies or any other coconspirator who testifies. Generally, the need for evidence to impeach witnesses is insufficient to require its production in advance of trial. See, e.g., United States v. Carter, 15 F.R.D. 367, 371 (D.D.C. 1954). Here, however, there are other valid potential evidentiary uses for the same material and the analysis and possible transcription of the tapes may take a significant period of time. Accordingly, we cannot say that the District Court erred in authorizing the issuance of the subpoena duces tecum. . . .

IV

THE CLAIM OF PRIVILEGE

A

Having determined that the requirements of Rule 17(c) were satisfied, we turn to the claim that the subpoena should be quashed because it demands "confidential conversations between a President and his close advisors that it would be inconsistent with the public interest to produce." App. 48a. The first contention is a broad claim that the separation of powers doctrine precludes judicial review of a President's claim of privilege. The second contention is that if he does not prevail on the claim of absolute privilege, the court should hold as a matter of constitutional law that the privilege prevails over the subpoena duces tecum.

In the performance of assigned constitutional duties each branch of the Government must initially interpret the Constitution, and the interpretation of its powers by any branch is due great respect from the others. The President's counsel, as we have noted, reads the Constitution as providing an absolute privilege of confidentiality for all presidential communications. Many decisions of this Court, however, have unequivocally reaffirmed the holding of Marbury v. Madison, 1 Cranch 137 (1803), that "it is emphatically the province and duty of the judicial department to say what the law is." Id., at 177.

No holding of the Court has defined the scope of judicial power specifically relating to the enforcement of a subpoena for confidential presidential communications for use in a criminal prosecution, but other exercises of powers by the Executive Branch and the Legislative Branch have been found invalid as in conflict with the Constitution. Powell v. McCormack, supra; Youngstown, supra. . . .

Notwithstanding the deference each branch must accord the others, the "judicial power of the United States" vested in the federal courts by Art. III, § 1 of the Constitution can no more be shared with the Executive Branch than the Chief Executive, for example, can share with the Judiciary the veto power, or the Congress share with the Judiciary the power to override a presidential veto. Any other conclusion would be contrary to the basic concept of separation of powers and the checks and balances that flow from the scheme of a tripartite government. The Federalist, No. 47, p. 313 (C. F. Mittel ed. 1938). We therefore reaffirm that it is "emphatically the province and the duty" of this Court "to say what the law is" with respect to the claim of privilege presented in this case. Marbury v. Madison, supra, 1 Cranch at 177.

B

In support of his claim of absolute privilege, the President's counsel urges two grounds one of which is common to all governments and one of which is peculiar to our system of separation of powers. The first ground is the valid need for protection of communications between high government officials and those who advise and assist them in the performance of their manifold duties; the importance of this confidentiality is too plain to require further discussion. Human experience teaches that those who expect public dissemination of their remarks may well temper candor with a concern for appearances and for their own interests to the detriment of the decisionmaking process. Whatever the nature of the privilege of confidentiality of presidential communications in the exercise of Art. II powers the privilege can be said to derive from the supremacy of each branch within its own assigned area of constitutional duties. Certain powers and privileges flow from the nature of enumerated powers; the protection of the confidentiality of presidential communications has similar constitutional underpinnings.

The second ground asserted by the President's counsel in support of the claim of absolute privilege rests on the doctrine of separation of powers. Here it is argued that the independence of the Executive Branch within its own sphere, . . . insulates a president from a judicial subpoena in an ongoing criminal prosecution, and thereby protects confidential presidential communications.

However, neither the doctrine of separation of powers, nor the need for confidentiality of high level communications, without more, can sustain an absolute, unqualified presidential privilege of immunity from judicial process under all circumstances. The President's need for complete candor and objectivity from advisers calls for great deference from the courts. However, when the privilege depends solely on the broad, undifferentiated claim of public interest in the confidentiality of such conversations, a confrontation with other values arises. Absent a claim of need to protect military, diplomatic or sensitive national security secrets, we find it difficult to accept the argument that even the very important interest in confidentiality of presidential communications is significantly diminished by production of such material for in camera inspection with all the protection that a district court will be obliged to provide.

The impediment that an absolute, unqualified privilege would place in the way of the primary constitutional duty of the Judicial Branch to do justice in criminal prosecutions would plainly conflict with the function of the courts under Art. III. In designing the structure of our Government and dividing and allocating the sovereign power among three coequal branches, the Framers of the Constitution sought to provide a comprehensive system, but the separate powers were not intended to operate with absolute independence. . . . To read the Art. II powers of the President as providing an absolute privilege as against a subpoena essential to enforcement of criminal statutes on no more than a generalized claim of the public interest in confidentiality of nonmilitary and nondiplomatic discussions would upset the constitutional balance of "a workable government" and gravely impair the role of the courts under Art. III.

C

Since we conclude that the legitimate needs of the judicial process may outweigh presidential privilege, it is necessary to resolve those competing interests in a manner that preserves the essential functions of each branch. The right and indeed the duty to resolve that question does not free the judiciary from according high respect to the representations made on behalf of the President. United States v. Burr, 25 Fed. Cas. pp. 187, 190, 191-192 (No. 14,694) (1807).

The expectation of a President to the confidentiality of his conversations and correspondence, like the claim of confidentiality of judicial deliberations, for example, has all the values to which we accord deference for the privacy of all citizens and added to those values the necessity for protection of the public interest in candid, objective, and even blunt or harsh opinions in presidential decisionmaking. A President and those who assist him must be free to explore alternatives in the process of shaping policies and making decisions and to do so in a way many would be unwilling to express except privately. These are the considerations justifying a presumptive privilege for presidential communications. The privilege is fundamental to the operation of government and inextricably rooted in the separation of powers under the Constitution. In Nixon v. Sirica, 487 F.2d 700 (1973), the Court of Appeals held that such presidential communications are "presumptively privileged," id., at 717, and this position is accepted by both parties in the present litigation. We agree with Mr. Chief Justice Marshall's observation, therefore, that "in no case of this kind would a court be required to proceed against the President as against an ordinary individual." United States v. Burr, 25 Fed. Cas. pp. 187, 192 (No. 14,694) (C.C.D. Va. 1807).

But this presumptive privilege must be considered in light of our historic commitment to the rule of law. This is nowhere more profoundly manifest than in our view that "the twofold aim [of criminal justice] is that guilt shall not escape or innocence suffer." Berger

v. United States, 295 U.S. 78, 88 (1935). We have elected to employ an adversary system of criminal justice in which the parties contest all issues before a court of law. The need to develop all relevant facts in the adversary system is both fundamental and comprehensive. The ends of criminal justice would be defeated if judgments were to be founded on a partial or speculative presentation of the facts. The very integrity of the judicial system and public confidence in the system depend on full disclosure of all the facts, within the framework of the rules of evidence. To ensure that justice is done, it is imperative to the function of courts that compulsory process be available for the production of evidence needed either by the prosecution or by the defense.

Only recently the Court restated the ancient proposition of law, albeit in the context of a grand jury inquiry rather than a trial, " 'that the public . . . has a right to every man's evidence' except for those persons protected by a constitutional, common law, or statutory privilege, United States v. Bryan, 339 U.S. [323], at 331 (1949); Blackmer v. United States, 284 U.S. 421, 438. . . ." Branzburg v. United States, 408 U.S. 665, 688 (1973).

The privileges referred to by the Court are designed to protect weighty and legitimate competing interests. Thus, the Fifth Amendment to the Constitution provides that no man "shall be compelled in any criminal case to be a witness against himself." And, generally, an attorney or a priest may not be required to disclose what has been revealed in professional confidence. These and other interests are recognized in law by privileges against forced disclosure, established in the Constitution, by statute, or at common law. Whatever their origins, these exceptions to the demand for every man's evidence are not lightly created nor expansively construed, for they are in derogation of the search for truth.

In this case the President challenges a subpoena served on him as a third party requiring the production of materials for use in a criminal prosecution on the claim that he has a privilege against disclosure of confidential communications. He does not place his claim of privilege on the ground they are military or diplomatic secrets. As to these areas of Art. II duties the courts have traditionally shown the utmost deference to presidential responsibilities. In C. & S. Air Lines v. Waterman Steamship Corp., 333 U.S. 103, 111 (1948), dealing with presidential authority involving foreign policy considerations, the Court said:

"The President, both as Commander-in-Chief and as the Nation's organ for foreign affairs, has available intelligence services whose reports are not and ought not to be published to the world. It would be intolerable that courts, without the relevant information, should review and perhaps nullify actions of the Executive taken on information properly held secret." Id., at 111.

In United States v. Reynolds, 345 U.S. 1 (1952), dealing with a claimant's demand for evidence in a damage case against the Government the Court said:

"It may be possible to satisfy the court, from all the circumstances of the case, that there is a reasonable danger that compulsion of the evidence will expose military matters which, in the interest of national security, should not be divulged. When this is the case, the occasion for the privilege is appropriate, and the court should not jeopardize the security which the privilege is meant to protect in insisting upon an examination of the evidence, even by the judge alone, in chambers."

No case of the Court, however, has extended this high degree of deference to a President's generalized interest in confidentiality. Nowhere in the Constitution, as we have noted earlier, is there any explicit reference to a privilege of confidentiality, yet to the extent this interest relates to the effective discharge of a President's powers, it is constitutionally based.

The right to the production of all evidence at a criminal trial similarly has constitutional dimensions. The Sixth Amendment explicitly confers upon every defendant in a criminal trial the right "to be confronted with the witnesses against him" and "to have compulsory process for obtaining witnesses in his favor." Moreover, the Fifth Amendment also guarantees that no person shall be deprived of liberty without due process of law. It is the manifest duty of the courts to vindicate those guarantees and to accomplish that it is essential that all relevant and admissible evidence be produced.

In this case we must weigh the importance of the general privilege of confidentiality of presidential communications in performance of his responsibilities against the inroads of such a privilege on the fair administration of criminal justice.[19] The interest in preserving confidentiality is weighty indeed and entitled to great respect. However we cannot conclude that advisers will be moved to temper the candor of their remarks by the infrequent occasions of disclosure because of the possibility that such conversations will be called for in the context of a criminal prosecution.[20]

On the other hand, the allowance of the privilege to withhold evidence that is demonstrably relevant in a criminal trial would cut deeply into the guarantee of due process of law and gravely impair the basic function of the courts. A President's acknowledged need for confidentiality in the communications of his office is general in nature, whereas the constitutional need for production of relevant evidence in a criminal proceeding is specific and central to the fair adjudication of a particular criminal case in the administration of justice. Without access to specific facts a criminal prosecution may be totally frustrated. The President's broad interest in confidentiality of communications will not be vitiated by disclosure of a limited number of conversations preliminarily shown to have some bearing on the pending criminal cases.

We conclude that when the ground for asserting privilege as to subpoenaed materials sought for use in a criminal trial is based only on the generalized interest in confidentiality, it cannot prevail over the fundamental demands of due process of law in the fair administration of crminal justice. The generalized assertion of privilege must yield to the demonstrated, specific need for evidence in a pending criminal trial.

D

We have earlier determined that the District Court did not err in authorizing the issuance of the subpoena. If a President concludes that compliance with a subpoena would be injurious to the public interest he may properly, as was done here, invoke a claim of privilege on the return of the subpoena. Upon receiving a claim of privilege from the Chief Executive, it became the further duty of the District Court to treat the subpoenaed material as presumptively privileged and to require the Special Prosecutor to demonstrate that the presidential material was "essential to the justice of the [pending criminal] case." United States v. Burr, supra, 25 Fed. Cas., at 192. Here the District Court treated the material as presumptively privileged, proceeded to find that the Special Prosecutor had made a sufficient showing to rebut the presumption and ordered an in camera examination of the subpoenaed material. On the basis of our examination of the record we are unable to conclude that the District Court erred in ordering the inspection. Accordingly we

---

[19] We are not here concerned with the balance between the President's generalized interest in confidentiality and the need for relevant evidence in civil litigation, nor with that between the confidentiality interest and congressional demands for information, nor with the President's interest in preserving state secrets. We address only the conflict between the President's assertion of a generalized privilege of confidentiality against the constitutional need for relevant evidence in criminal trials.

[20] Mr. Justice Cardozo made this point in an analogous context. Speaking for a unanimous Court in Clark v. United States, 289 U.S. 1 (1933), he emphasized the importance of maintaining the secrecy of the deliberations of a petit jury in a criminal case. "Freedom of debate might be stifled and independence of thought checked if jurors were made to feel that their arguments and ballots were to be freely published in the world." Id., at 13. Nonetheless, the Court also recognized that isolated inroads on confidentiality designed to serve the paramount need of the criminal law would not vitiate the interests served by secrecy:

"A juror of integrity and reasonable firmness will not fear to speak his mind if the confidences of debate [are] barred to the ears of mere impertinence or malice. He will not expect to be shielded against the disclosure of his conduct in the event that there is evidence reflecting upon his honor. The chance that now and then there may be found some timid soul who will take counsel of his fears and give way to their repressive power is too remote and shadowy to shape the course of justice." Id., at 16.

affirm the order of the District Court that subpoenaed materials be transmitted to that court. We now turn to the important question of the District Court's responsibilities in conducting the in camera examination of presidential materials or communications delivered under the compulsion of the subpoena duces tecum.

E

Enforcement of the subpoena duces tecum was stayed pending this Court's resolution of the issues raised by the petitions for certiorari. Those issues now having been disposed of, the matter of implementation will rest with the District Court. "[T]he guard, furnished to [the President] to protect him from being harassed by vexatious and unnecessary subpoenas, is to be looked for in the conduct of the [district] court after the subpoenas have issued; not in any circumstance which is to precede their being issued." United States v. Burr, supra, at 34. Statements that meet the test of admissibility and relevance must be isolated; all other material must be excised. At this stage the District Court is not limited to representations of the Special Prosecutor as to the evidence sought by the subpoena; the material will be available to the District Court. It is elementary that in camera inspection of evidence is always a procedure calling for scrupulous protection against any release or publication of material not found by the court, at that stage, probably admissible in evidence and relevant to the issues of the trial for which it is sought. That being true of an ordinary situation, it is obvious that the District Court has a very heavy responsibility to see to it that presidential conversations, which are either not relevant or not admissible, are accorded that high degree of respect due the President of the United States. Mr. Chief Justice Marshall sitting as a trial judge in the Burr case, supra, was extraordinarily careful to point out that:

"[I]n no case of this kind would a court be required to proceed against the President as against an ordinary individual." United States v. Burr, 25 Fed. Cas. pp. 187, 192 (No. 14,694).

Marshall's statement cannot be read to mean in any sense that a President is above the law, but relates to the singularly unique role under Art. II of a President's communications and activities, related to the performance of duties under that Article. Moreover, a President's communications and activities encompass a vastly wider range of sensitive material than would be true of any "ordinary individual." It is therefore necessary [21] in the public interest to afford presidential confidentiality the greatest protection consistent with the fair administration of justice. The need for confidentiality even as to idle conversations with associates in which casual reference might be made concerning political leaders within the country or foreign statesmen is too obvious to call for further treatment. We have no doubt that the District Judge will at all times accord to presidential records that high degree of deference suggested in United States v. Burr, supra, and will discharge his responsibility to see to it that until released to the Special Prosecutor no in camera material is revealed to anyone. This burden applies with even greater force to excised material; once the decision is made to excise, the material is restored to its privileged status and should be returned under seal to its lawful custodian.

Since this matter came before the Court during the pendency of a criminal prosecution, and on representations that time is of the essence, the mandate shall issue forthwith.

Affirmed.

MR. JUSTICE REHNQUIST took no part in the consideration or decision of these cases.

---

[21] When the subpoenaed material is delivered to the District Judge in camera questions may arise as to the excising of parts and it lies within the discretion of that court to seek the aid of the Special Prosecutor and the President's counsel for in camera consideration of the validity of particular excisions, whether the basis of excision is relevancy or admissibility or under such cases as Reynolds, supra, or Waterman Steamship, supra.

NOTE Judicial versus Legislative Inquiry

In Senate Select Committee on Presidential Campaign Activities v. Nixon, 498 F.2d 725 (D.C. Cir. 1974) (en banc), the court of appeals refused to order the President to turn over tapes subpoenaed by the Select Committee. The court held that the committee had failed to establish sufficient need for the materials to overcome the executive's interest in confidentiality. The court argued that other investigative bodies, specifically the House Judiciary Committee considering the possible impeachment of the President, were serving the Select Committee's purpose of uncovering and publicizing executive wrongdoing; and that for the purposes of developing new campaign legislation, the Select Committee had not shown sufficient need for the particular details of the President's reelection campaign.

See Freund, The Supreme Court, 1973 Term — Foreword: On Presidential Privilege, 88 Harv. L. Rev. 13 (1974); Symposium: United States v. Nixon, 22 U.C.L.A.L. Rev. 4 (1974). See generally Berger, Executive Privilege: A Constitutional Myth (1974); Cox, Executive Privilege, 122 U. Pa. L. Rev. 1383 (1974); Dorsen & Shattuck, Executive Privilege, the Congress, and the Courts, 18 Ohio St. L.J. 1 (1974).

Section C. INTERNATIONAL RELATIONS

NOTE Origins and Development of the Treaty Power

From the moment of its difficult birth, the new United States felt essentially the same conflicts of interest that plague it today. It needed allies to help it face foreign hostility; it needed reconciliation with its enemies and a chance to earn a peaceful living; but at the same time its people feared alien influence in their internal affairs. The men of 1787 resented the assertion of foreign claims to lands within their borders. They resented the prospect that claims against American citizens, held by foreign creditors, subjects of an enemy nation, might survive a war in which Americans had succeeded. Localism, then as now, was more apparent in state legislatures than in the national government; a considerable body of state law imposed disabilities on alien inheritance of land;[c] and a Virginia statute of 1777 provided for the discharge, by payment to state officials, of debts owed to enemy aliens.[d]

The three treaties with France signed on February 6, 1778,[e] gave us a military ally and, among other limitations on local law, gave to the nationals of both countries a right of inheritance to "goods moveable and immovable." The loose federal structure of the United States at the time must have made somewhat doubtful the effect of this provision on lands in any states which restricted inheritance by aliens. The Congress ratified the three treaties on May 4, 1778, but Virginia separately ratified the first two the following year.[f] The power of the federal government to affect the interests of the states by treaties

---

[c] For New York, see Pratt, Present Alienage Disabilities Under New York State Law in Real Property, 12 Brooklyn L. Rev. 1, 15 (1942); for Pennsylvania, Lessee of Jackson v. Burns, 3 Binn. 75 (Pa. 1810); the situation in Virginia is explained in Martin v. Hunter's Lessee, 1 Wheat. 304 (1816). — ED.

[d] See Ware v. Hylton, 3 Dall. 199 (1796). — ED.

[e] 8 Stat. 6, 12 (1778); 17 Stat. 795 (1778); 2 Miller, Treaties and Other International Acts of the United States 3, 35, 45 (1932). — ED.

[f] 2 id. at 30. On June 17, 1779, Gerard, the French Minister, wrote from Philadelphia to the Count de Vergennes that the Virginia action had somewhat offended the Congress, as that body thought it contrary to its own prerogatives. See 4 Doniol, Histoire de la Participation de la France à l'Etablissement des Etats-Unis d'Amérique 155, 165, 167 (1886). — ED.

Section C. **International Relations** 691

was thus among the earliest problems of foreign relations that faced the United States.

The treaty with the Netherlands signed at The Hague on October 8, 1782,[g] provided for liberty of worship by the nationals of the respective countries in the other's territories and for reciprocal rights of inheritance — again affecting the internal laws of the states.

The Treaty of Peace of 1783, which ended the Revolutionary War,[h] attempted to provide satisfactorily for the solution of the problems of debts owed to British creditors, and of British claims to lands in the United States. The provision for debts was terse: "It is agreed that Creditors on either side, shall meet with no lawful Impediment to the Recovery of the full value in Sterling Money of all bona fide Debts heretofore contracted."[i]

Future confiscation of loyalist lands was forbidden.[j] Where lands had already been confiscated, more difficult questions appeared, as the claims of purchasers had now intervened. Instead of declaring invalid any titles so created, the treaty required the Congress to recommend to the several states provision for the restitution of confiscated British estates.

This hopeful exhortation proved insufficient. During the Constitutional Convention delegates repeatedly said that experience had shown a tendency in the states to violate the national treaties.[k] Madison's Preface speaks of disregard of the authority of the Confederation by violations of the existing treaties with France and Holland, and of the Treaty of Peace of 1783;[l] and when the supremacy clause was being formulated, Madison secured the addition of phraseology to express the intention that existing as well as future treaties be law in the several states and their courts.[m] And to quiet fears of New England lest a treaty hamper her fisheries, and of the West lest a treaty close the Mississippi, the two-thirds rule was adopted to give some degree of minority protection.[n]

In 1777 the state of Virginia had enacted a law much like a modern statute setting up an alien property custodian.[o] It provided in substance that any citizen of Virginia who owed money to a British subject might pay the debt to an officer of the state of Virginia and thereby obtain a discharge. On April 26, 1780, a Virginia business house called Hylton and Co. paid a portion of such a debt to the appropriate Virginia officer. After the adoption of the federal Constitution, the administrator of the British creditor sued Hylton and Co. in the Federal Circuit Court for Virginia upon their obligations, including that portion which Hylton thought had been discharged by payment to the Virginia public officer. In the circuit court Hylton successfully pleaded the payment as a discharge, and the disappointed creditor brought error in the Supreme Court of the United States. John Marshall (not yet a judge) argued for the Virginia debtor that nothing in the new Constitution revived the debt already paid under Virginia law, but the Supreme Court reversed the lower federal court and held that Hylton must pay over again, this time to the British creditor. Under the newly adopted Constitution, the treaty with England prevailed over the laws of Virginia.[p]

Other difficulties arose over land titles. Lord Fairfax was the owner of a great tract of land in what was known as the Northern Neck of Virginia. His title came from grants

---

[g] 8 Stat. 32 (1782); 2 Miller, op. cit. supra note e, at 59. The guarantee of freedom of worship was notable at a time when a number of the states still retained established churches. See Sutherland, Due Process and Disestablishment, 62 Harv. L. Rev. 1306, 1323 (1949). The Treaty with Sweden of 1783, 8 Stat. 60, 2 Miller, op. cit. supra note e, at 123, and that with Prussia of 1785, 8 Stat. 84, 2 Miller, op. cit. supra note e, at 162, also contained reciprocal guarantees of inheritance and of freedom of worship. — ED.

[h] 8 Stat. 54 (1782); 2 Miller, op. cit. supra note e, at 96. — ED.

[i] Art. 4 — ED.

[j] Art. 6. — ED.

[k] 1 Farrand, Records of the Federal Convention 164, 316 (rev. ed. 1937); 3 id. at 113. — ED.

[l] 3 id. at 548. — ED.

[m] 2 id. at 417. — ED.

[n] See Hearings Before Subcommittee No. 3 of the House Committee on the Judiciary on H. Jt. Res. 6, etc., 78th Cong., 2d Sess. (1944); for a discussion of sectional influence in the 1787 Convention, see Warren, The Mississippi River and the Treaty Clause of the Constitution, 2 Geo. Wash. L. Rev. 271 (1934). — ED.

[o] For the circumstances and litigation here discussed see Ware v. Hylton, 3 Dall. 199 (1796). — ED.

[p] The Supreme Court rejected an argument that a subject of Great Britain was in no position to rely on the

made to his predecessors by Charles II and James II. When Fairfax died in 1781, he devised 300,000 acres of this land to the Reverend Denny Martin, who was and remained a subject of George III. Virginia, pursuant to certain statutes providing for the escheat of lands owned by British subjects, granted the land on April 30, 1789, to a man named Hunter. In 1791, Hunter, claiming under Virginia, brought ejectment against Martin in the Virginia courts. In 1794, while the case was pending, the Jay treaty confirmed all royal land titles. The Court of Appeals of Virginia in 1810 nevertheless found in favor of the Virginia grantee, Hunter; but the disappointed British subject, Martin, brought error in the Supreme Court of the United States, which reversed and held that the treaty prevailed over the Virginia title. The state authorities, much irritated, refused to carry out the decision and it was necessary for Lord Fairfax's devisee to go back to the Supreme Court a second time before he could get his judgment enforced. For the circumstances and litigation here discussed see Fairfax's Devisee v. Hunter's Lessee, 7 Cranch 603 (1813), and Martin v. Hunter's Lessee, 1 Wheat. 304 (1816), page 20 supra. The litigation is reviewed in Note, 66 Harv. L. Rev. 1242 (1953).

The self-executing feature of treaties under Article VI of the United States Constitution was thus no matter of ill-considered whim. The draftsmen found it necessary, and the Supreme Court enforced it. The disadvantages of enabling the President and Senate to legislate for the entire nation were drawn to the attention of the Constitutional Convention, of the state ratifying conventions, and of the people of the nation. Their choice was made deliberately as one of the necessary adjustments between reserved state power and national policy — one of many such compromises essential to the creation of a federal nation.

NOTE Effect of Self-executing Treaties on State Law

The federal government has frequently undertaken international obligations which themselves change the local law of the states. Litigation concerning the effect of treaties has involved the right of an alien to engage in pawnbroking despite a local ordinance (Asakura v. Seattle, 265 U.S. 332 (1924)), and to pay no more inheritance tax than a national of the United States (Neilsen v. Johnson, 279 U.S. 47 (1929)). In Clarke v. Deckebach, 274 U.S. 392 (1927), an alien claimed, without success, that a treaty gave him a right to operate a poolroom in Cincinnati.

The United Nations Charter is a multilateral treaty containing certain language indicating that it is an objective of the signatories that all persons shall have fundamental freedoms without regard to race, sex, language, or religion. Preamble, Arts. 1, 2, 55, 56. For many years California had a statute barring from the ownership of real property an alien ineligible to citizenship. In Fujii v. State, 217 P.2d 481, rehearing denied, 218 P.2d 595 (1950), a California district court of appeal held that the United Nations Charter was predominant over the local law of California, and that Fujii, though a Japanese national ineligible to citizenship, was entitled to hold his land despite the alien land law. (It is worth noting that Japan was not a signatory to the charter.)

An appeal was taken to the Supreme Court of California, but in the meantime the opinion of the intermediate appellate court occasioned much comment in state legislatures, in Congress, and by scholars in the field of international law. Judge Hudson felt that it was based on a mistaken idea that these provisions were self-executing, and pointed out that there was venerable precedent in the United States for the construction of some

---

treaty because, in violation of it, British troops continued to garrison Detroit and Niagara, and supplied Indians with munitions to keep up hostilities.

Thomas Jefferson is said to have paid some debts once to the Virginia officer, and then, as a result of the principle established in Ware v. Hylton, over again to British creditors. Malone, Jefferson the Virginian 260 (1948). — ED.

treaties as non-self-executing, citing Foster v. Neilson, 2 Pet. 253 (1829). See Charter Provisions on Human Rights in American Law, 44 Am. J. Intl. L. 543 (1950). Professor Quincy Wright approved of the decision. See National Courts and Human Rights — The Fujii Case, 45 id. 62 (1951). The prospect of this charter as a self-executing treaty occasioned some alarm. Senator Bricker said in the Senate, "If the Fujii case should eventually be affirmed by the United States Supreme Court, or if the principle announced therein should be sustained, literally thousands of Federal and State laws will automatically become invalid. . . . Obviously something must be done to prevent treaties from having such far-reaching and unintended consequences." See 98 Cong. Rec. 925 (Feb. 7, 1952). The Colorado legislature urged the United States Senate to amend the Constitution to avoid the effects of the decision which, it found, disclosed a "peril to the very fundamentals of American law and liberty, and the entire theory of popular government, a peril which certainly the founding fathers never contemplated and which must be obviated at the earliest possible moment; . . ."

However, the California Supreme Court displaced the opinion of the district court of appeal, instead holding that the treaty provisions were not self-executing, and did not supersede the California land laws; the court held the land laws invalid under the Fourteenth Amendment. See Fujii v. California, 38 Cal. 2d 718, 242 P.2d 617 (1952).[q] See Fairman, Finis to Fujii, 46 Am. J. Intl. L. 682 (1952). Compare Kolovrat v. Oregon, 366 U.S. 187 (1961).

NOTE **The Treaty Power and Constitutional Guarantees**

The supremacy clause is unqualified in terms. It contains no provision limiting the predominance of treaties over the Constitution to such matters as merely alter the distribution of legislative power between the states and the federal government; there is no express exception leaving supreme over any treaties such constitutional limitations on governmental power as those controlling criminal trials in Article III. A reasonable argument can be made from the circumstances surrounding the adoption of the supremacy clause that original constitutional limitations intended for the protection of the citizen, for civil liberties, are entirely outside the reason for the supremacy clause, the desire to protect British claims to land and credits. The same argument applies with even greater force to the Bill of Rights and the post-Civil War amendments.

Mr. Justice Field, in a much quoted dictum, said in 1890:

". . . The treaty power, as expressed in the Constitution, is in terms unlimited except by those restraints which are found in that instrument against the action of the government[r] or of its departments, and those arising from the nature of the government itself and of that of the States. It would not be contended that it extends so far as to authorize what the Constitution forbids, or a change in the character of the government or in that of one of the States, or a cession of any portion of the territory of the latter, without its consent."[s]

President Coolidge and the Senate evidently thought that a treaty could prevail over at least one amendment. In 1924 the United States entered into a treaty with Great Britain which allowed British ships to bring intoxicating liquor under seal into waters of the United States[t] although the Supreme Court of the United States had held during the pre-

[q] See Schachter, The Charter and the Constitution: The Human Rights Provisions in American Law, 4 Vand. L. Rev. 643 (1951). — ED.

[r] The extent to which courts will undertake to review acts of the executive in the field of foreign policy is not clear. See Chicago & Southern Air Lines, Inc. v. Waterman S.S. Corp., 333 U.S. 103, 111 (1948). — ED.

[s] Geofroy v. Riggs, 133 U.S. 258, 267 (1890). See also Missouri v. Holland, 252 U.S. 416, 433 (1920); United States v. Minnesota, 270 U.S. 181, 207 et seq. (1926). — ED.

[t] 43 Stat. 1761 (1924). — ED.

ceding year that the Eighteenth Amendment prohibited such importation.[u] A sensible argument could be made that the prohibition amendment resembled more closely the commercial and real-property legislation which the supremacy clause was intended to affect than it resembled provisions of the Bill of Rights, and that the treaty of 1924 was valid while a treaty purporting to establish, say, press censorship would not be. In the only case[v] which challenged the 1924 treaty, however, the standing of the plaintiffs, who were a mariner, a secretary of an incorporated masters' and mates' association, and others interested in American shipping, which suffered by the competition of more attractive British ships, was held insufficient to sustain an adjudication on the validity of the treaty.

NOTE The Effect, on a Treaty, of a Subsequent Act of Congress

The federal Constitution is, of course, superior in its effect to any act of Congress. The question can occur whether a treaty, as internal law in the United States, may be modified by a federal statute subsequent to the treaty.

This came before the Supreme Court in the Chinese Exclusion Case (Chae Chan Ping v. United States), 130 U.S. 581 (1889). A treaty between the United States and the Emperor of China, dated July 28, 1868, provided that ". . . Chinese subjects visiting or residing in the United States shall enjoy the same privileges, immunities, and exemptions in respect to travel or residence as may there be enjoyed by the citizens of the most favored nation." A supplementary treaty of November 17, 1880, made similar provision as to "Chinese laborers who are now in the United States. . . ." An act of Congress of May 6, 1882, provided that Chinese laborers in the United States on the date of the supplementary treaty who wished to leave the United States and return might obtain from the collector of customs of the district from which the laborer was departing a certificate of identification. The statute continued, "The certificate herein provided for shall entitle the Chinese laborer to whom the same is issued to return to and re-enter the United States upon producing and delivering the same to the collector of customs at the district at which such Chinese laborer shall seek to re-enter."

Chae Chan Ping, a subject of the Emperor of China, a day laborer by occupation, who had lived in California from 1875 until 1887, went to China in that year for a visit, having in his possession a certificate duly issued to him by the San Francisco Collector of Customs under the Act of May 6, 1882, in terms entitling him to reenter the United States. He sailed from Hong Kong for San Francisco on his return journey on September 7, 1888. On October 1, 1888, while the ship was at sea, the President approved a new act of Congress providing:

"Be it enacted, by the Senate and House of Representatives of the United States of America in Congress assembled, That from and after the passage of this Act, it shall be unlawful for any Chinese laborer who shall at any time heretofore have been, or who may now or hereafter be, a resident within the United States, and who shall have departed, or shall depart, therefrom, and shall not have returned before the passage of this Act to return to, or remain in, the United States.

"Sec. 2. That no certificates of identity provided for in the fourth and fifth sections of the Act to which this is a supplement shall hereafter be issued; and every certificate heretofore issued in pursuance thereof is hereby declared void and of no effect, and the Chinese laborer claiming admission by virtue thereof shall not be permitted to enter the United States." 25 Stat. 504, c. 1064.

When Chae Chan Ping reached San Francisco on October 8, 1888, the collector of the

---

[u] Cunard S.S. Co. v. Mellon, 262 U.S. 100 (1923). — Ed.
[v] Milliken v. Stone, 16 F.2d 981 (2d Cir.), cert. denied, 274 U.S. 748 (1927). — Ed.

port refused him permission to land. The captain of his steamer detained him on board, and the Chinese sought release on habeas corpus. The United States Circuit Court for the Northern District of California held him not entitled to enter the United States and ordered him remanded to the custody of the master of the steamship. He appealed to the Supreme Court of the United States, which affirmed the judgment of the circuit court. Mr. Justice Field wrote in an opinion for the Supreme Court:

"To preserve its independence, and give security against foreign aggression and encroachment, is the highest duty of every nation, and to attain these ends nearly all other considerations are to be subordinated. It matters not in what form such aggression and encroachment come, whether from the foreign nation acting in its national character or from hordes of its people crowding in upon us. . . . Whatever license, therefore, Chinese laborers may have obtained previous to the Act of October 1, 1888, to return to the United States after their departure, is held at the will of the Government, revocable at any time, at its pleasure. Whether a proper consideration by our Government of its previous laws, or a proper respect for the nation whose subjects are affected by its action, ought to have qualified its inhibition and made it applicable only to persons departing from the country after the passage of the Act, are not questions for judicial determination. If there be any just ground of complaint on the part of China, it must be made to the political department of our Government, which is alone competent to act upon the subject. The rights and interests created by a treaty, which have become so vested that its expiration or abrogation will not destroy or impair them, are such as are connected with and lie in property capable of sale and transfer, or other disposition, not such as are personal and untransferable in their character." 130 U.S. at 606.

Unilateral repudiatory legislation by one nation, a party to a treaty, can govern the actions of that nation's officials; it cannot cancel the claims of the other party nation, any more than a resolution of the stockholders or directors of a private corporation can cancel its debts. The nation which repudiates its treaty obligations remains open to such reprisals or recourse to international tribunals as the offended nation may choose.

Missouri v. Holland 252 U.S. 416, 40 S. Ct. 382, 64 L. Ed. 641 (1920)

MR. JUSTICE HOLMES delivered the opinion of the court:

This is a bill in equity, brought by the state of Missouri to prevent a game warden of the United States from attempting to enforce the Migratory Bird Treaty Act of July 3, 1918, chap. 128, 40 Stat. at L. 755, and the regulations made by the Secretary of Agriculture in pursuance of the same. The ground of the bill is that the statute is an unconstitutional interference with the rights reserved to the states by the 10th Amendment, and that the acts of the defendant, done and threatened under that authority, invade the sovereign right of the state and contravene its will manifested in statutes. The state also alleges a pecuniary interest, as owner of the wild birds within its borders and otherwise, admitted by the government to be sufficient, but it is enough that the bill is a reasonable and proper means to assert the alleged quasi-sovereign rights of a state. Kansas v. Colorado, 185 U.S. 125, 142; Georgia v. Tennessee Copper Co., 206 U.S. 230, 237; Marshall Dental Mfg. Co. v. Iowa, 226 U.S. 460, 462. A motion to dismiss was sustained by the district court on the ground that the act of Congress is constitutional. . . .

On December 8, 1916, a treaty between the United States and Great Britain was proclaimed by the President. It recited that many species of birds in their annual migrations traversed many parts of the United States and of Canada, that they were of great value as a source of food and in destroying insects injurious to vegetation, but were in danger of extermination through lack of adequate protection. It therefore provided for specified close seasons and protection in other forms, and agreed that the two powers would take or propose to their lawmaking bodies the necessary measures for carrying the treaty out. 39 Stat. at L. 1702. The above-mentioned Act of July 3, 1918, entitled, "An Act to Give Effect to the Convention," prohibited the killing, capturing, or selling any of the migratory birds included in the terms of the treaty except as permitted by regulations compatible with those terms, to be made by the Secretary of Agriculture. Regulations were proclaimed on July 31, and October 25, 1918. 40 Stat. at L. 1812, 1863. It is unnecessary to go into any details, because, as we have said, the question raised is the general one whether the treaty and statute are void as an interference with the rights reserved to the states.

To answer this question it is not enough to refer to the 10th Amendment, reserving the powers not delegated to the United States, because by article 2, §2, the power to make treaties is delegated expressly, and by article 6, treaties made under the authority of the United States, along with the Constitution and laws of the United States, made in pursuance thereof, are declared the supreme law of the land. If the treaty is valid, there can be no dispute about the validity of the statute under article 1, §8, as a necessary and proper means to execute the powers of the government. The language of the Constitution as to the supremacy of treaties being general, the question before us is narrowed to an inquiry into the ground upon which the present supposed exception is placed.

It is said that a treaty cannot be valid if it infringes the Constitution; that there are limits, therefore, to the treaty-making power; and that one such limit is that what an act of Congress could not do unaided, in derogation of the powers reserved to the states, a treaty cannot do. An earlier act of Congress that attempted by itself, and not in pursuance of a treaty, to regulate the killing of migratory birds within the states, had been held bad in the district court. United States v. Shauver, 214 Fed. 154; United States v. McCullagh, 221 Fed. 288. Those decisions were supported by arguments that migratory birds were owned by the states in their sovereign capacity, for the benefit of their people, and that under cases like Geer v. Connecticut, 161 U.S. 519, this control was one that Congress had no power to displace. The same argument is supposed to apply now with equal force.

Whether the two cases cited were decided rightly or not, they cannot be accepted as a test of the treaty power. Acts of Congress are the supreme law of the land only when made in pursuance of the Constitution, while treaties are declared to be so when made under the authority of the United States. It is open to question whether the authority of the United States means more than the formal acts prescribed to make the convention. We do not mean to imply that there are no qualifications to the treaty-making power; but they must be ascertained in a different way. It is obvious that there may be matters of the sharpest exigency for the national well-being that an act of Congress could not deal with, but that a treaty followed by such an act could, and it is not lightly to be assumed that, in matters requiring national action, "a power which must belong to and somewhere reside in every civilized government" is not to be found. Andrews v. Andrews, 188 U.S. 14, 33. What was said in that case with regard to the powers of the states applies with equal force to the powers of the nation in cases where the states individually are incompetent to act. We are not yet discussing the particular case before us, but only are considering the validity of the test proposed. With regard to that, we may add that when we are dealing with words that also are a constituent act, like the Constitution of the United States, we must realize that they have called into life a being the development of which could not have been foreseen completely by the most gifted of its begetters. It was enough for them to realize or to hope that they had created an organism; it has taken a century and has cost their successors much sweat and blood to prove that they created a nation. The case before us must be considered in the light of our whole experience, and not merely in that of what was said a hundred years ago. The treaty in question does not contravene any prohibitory words to be found in the Constitution. The only question is whether it is forbidden by some invisible radiation from the general terms of the 10th Amendment. We must consider what this country has become in deciding what that amendment has reserved.

The state, as we have intimated, founds its claim of exclusive authority upon an assertion of title to migratory birds, — an assertion that is embodied in statute. No doubt it is true that, as between a state and its inhabitants, the state may regulate the killing and sale of such birds, but it does not follow that its authority is exclusive of paramount powers. To put the claim of the state upon title is to lean upon a slender reed. Wild birds are not in the possession of anyone; and possession is the beginning of ownership. The whole foundation of the state's rights is the presence within their jurisdiction of birds that yesterday had not arrived, to-morrow may be in another state, and in a week a thousand miles away. If we are to be accurate, we cannot put the case of the state upon higher ground than that the treaty deals with creatures that for the moment are within the state borders, that it must be carried out by officers of the United States within the same territory, and that, but for the treaty, the state would be free to regulate this subject itself.

As most of the laws of the United States are carried out within the states, and as many of them deal with matters which, in the silence of such laws, the state might regulate, such general grounds are not enough to support Missouri's claim. Valid treaties, of course, "are as binding within the territorial limits of the states as they are effective throughout the dominion of the United States." Baldwin v. Franks, 120 U.S. 678, 683. No doubt the great body of private relations usually falls within the control of the state, but a treaty may override its power. We do not have to invoke the later developments of constitutional law for this proposition; it was recognized as early as Hopkirk v. Bell, 3 Cranch, 454, with regard to statutes of limitation, and even earlier, as to confiscation, in Ware v. Hylton, 3 Dall. 199. It was assumed by Chief Justice Marshall with regard to the escheat of land to the state in Chirac v. Chirac, 2 Wheat. 259, 275; Hauenstein v. Lynham, 100 U.S. 483; Geofroy v. Riggs, 133 U.S. 258; Blythe v. Hinckley, 180 U.S. 333, 340. So, as to a limited jurisdiction of foreign consuls within a state. Wildenhus's Case (Mali v. Keeper of Common Jail) 120 U.S. 1. See Re Ross, 140 U.S. 453. Further illustration seems unnecessary, and it only remains to consider the application of established rules to the present case.

Here a national interest of very nearly the first magnitude is involved. It can be protected only by national action in concert with that of another power. The subject-matter is only transitorily within the state, and has no permanent habitat therein. But for the treaty and the statute, there soon might be no birds for any powers to deal with. We see nothing in the Constitution that compels the government to sit by while a food supply is cut off and the protectors of our forests and of our crops are destroyed. It is not sufficient to rely upon the states. The reliance is vain, and were it otherwise, the question is whether the United States is forbidden to act. We are of opinion that the treaty and statute must be upheld. Cary v. South Dakota, 250 U.S. 118.

Decree affirmed.

MR. JUSTICE VAN DEVANTER and MR. JUSTICE PITNEY dissent.

United States v. Curtiss-Wright Export Corp. 299 U.S. 304, 57 S. Ct. 216, 81 L. Ed. 255 (1936)

MR. JUSTICE SUTHERLAND delivered the opinion of the Court.

On January 27, 1936, an indictment was returned in the court below, the first count of which charges that appellees, beginning with the 29th day of May, 1934, conspired to sell in the United States certain arms of war, namely fifteen machine guns, to Bolivia, a country then engaged in armed conflict in the Chaco, in violation of the Joint Resolution of Congress approved May 28, 1934, and the provisions of a proclamation issued on the same day by the President of the United States pursuant to authority conferred by § 1 of the resolution. In pursuance of the conspiracy, the commission of certain overt acts was alleged, details of which need not be stated. The Joint Resolution (chap. 365, 48 Stat. at L. 811) follows:

"Resolved by the Senate and House of Representatives of the United States of America in Congress assembled, That if the President finds that the prohibition of the sale of arms and munitions of war in the United States to those countries now engaged in armed conflict in the Chaco may contribute to the reestablishment of peace between those countries, and if after consultation with the governments of other American Republics and with their cooperation, as well as that of such other governments as he may deem necessary, he makes proclamation to that effect, it shall be unlawful to sell, except under such limitations and exceptions as the President prescribes, any arms or munitions of war in any place in the United States to the countries now engaged in that armed conflict, or to any person, company, or association acting in the interest of either country, until otherwise ordered by the President or by Congress.

"Sec. 2. Whoever sells any arms or munitions of war in violation of section 1 shall, on conviction, be punished by a fine not exceeding $10,000 or by imprisonment not exceeding two years, or both." . . .

Appellees severally demurred to the first count of the indictment. . . . The points urged in support of the demurrers were, first, that the joint resolution effects an invalid delegation of legislative power to the Executive; . . .

The court below sustained the demurrers upon the first point, . . . 14 F. Supp. 230. The government appealed to this court under the provisions of the Criminal Appeals Act of March 2, 1907. . . .

Whether, if the Joint Resolution had related to internal affairs it would be open to the challenge that it constituted an unlawful delegation of legislative power to the Executive, we find it unnecessary to determine. The whole aim of the resolution is to affect a situation entirely external to the United States, and falling within the category of foreign affairs. The determination which we are called to make, therefore, is whether the Joint Resolution, as applied to that situation, is vulnerable to attack under the rule that forbids a delegation of the law-making power. In other words, assuming (but not deciding) that the challenged delegation, if it were confined to internal affairs, would be invalid, may it nevertheless be sustained on the ground that its exclusive aim is to afford a remedy for a hurtful condition within foreign territory?

It will contribute to the elucidation of the question if we first consider the differences between the powers of the Federal government in respect of foreign or external affairs and those in respect of domestic or internal affairs. That there are differences between them, and that these differences are fundamental, may not be doubted.

The two classes of powers are different, both in respect of their origin and their nature. The broad statement that the Federal government can exercise no powers except those specifically enumerated in the Constitution, and such implied powers as are necessary and proper to carry into effect the enumerated powers, is categorically true only in respect to our internal affairs. In that field, the primary purpose of the Constitution was to carve from the general mass of legislative powers *then possessed by the states* such portions as it was thought desirable to vest in the Federal government, leaving those not included in the enumeration still in the states. Carter v. Carter Coal Co., 298 U.S. 238, 294. That this doctrine applies only to powers which the states had, is self-evident. And since the states severally never possessed international powers, such powers could not have been carved from the mass of state powers but obviously were transmitted to the United States from some other source. During the colonial period, those powers were possessed exclusively by and were entirely under the control of the Crown. By the Declaration of Independence, "the Representatives of the United States of America" declared the United [not the several] Colonies to be free and independent states, and as such to have "full power to levy War, conclude Peace, contract Alliances, establish Commerce and to do all other Acts and Things which Independent States may of right do."

As a result of the separation from Great Britain by the colonies, acting as a unit, the powers of external sovereignty passed from the Crown not to the colonies severally, but to the colonies in their collective and corporate capacity as the United States of America. Even before the Declaration, the colonies were a unit in foreign affairs, acting through a common agency — namely the Continental Congress, composed of delegates from the thirteen colonies. That agency exercised the powers of war and peace, raised an army, created a navy, and finally adopted the Declaration of Independence. . . . The treaty of peace, made on September 3, 1783, was concluded between his Britannic Majesty and the "United States of America." 8 Stat. at L. — European Treaties — 80.

The Union existed before the Constitution, which was ordained and established among other things to form "a more perfect Union." Prior to that event, it is clear that the Union, declared by the Articles of Confederation to be "perpetual," was the sole possessor of external sovereignty, and in the Union it remained without change save in so far as the Constitution in express terms qualified its exercise. The Framers' Convention was called and exerted its powers upon the irrefutable postulate that though the states were several their people in respect of foreign affairs were one. . . .

It results that the investment of the Federal government with the powers of external sovereignty did not depend upon the affirmative grants of the Constitution. The powers to declare and wage war, to conclude peace, to make treaties, to maintain diplomatic relations with other sovereignties, if they had never been mentioned in the Constitution, would have vested in the Federal government as necessary concomitants of nationality. Neither the Constitution nor the laws passed in pursuance of it have any force in foreign territory unless in respect of our own citizens (see American Banana Co. v. United Fruit Co., 213 U.S. 347, 356); and operations of the nation in such territory must be governed by treaties, international understandings and compacts, and the principles of international law. As a member of the family of nations, the right and power of the United States in that field are equal to the right and power of the other members of the international family. Otherwise, the United States is not completely sovereign. The power to acquire territory by discovery and occupation (Jones v. United States, 137 U.S. 202, 212), the power to expel undesirable aliens (Fong Yue Ting v. United States, 149 U.S. 698, 705 et seq.), the power to make such international agreements as do not constitute treaties in the constitutional sense (S. Altman & Co. v. United States, 224 U.S. 583, 600, 601; Crandall, Treaties, Their Making and Enforcement, 2d ed. p. 102 and note 1), none of which is expressly affirmed by the Constitution, nevertheless exist as inherently inseparable from the conception of nationality. This the court recognized, and in each of the cases cited found the warrant for its conclusions not in the provisions of the Constitution, but in the law of nations. . . .

Not only, as we have shown, is the Federal power over external affairs in origin and essential character different from that over internal affairs, but participation in the exercise of the power is significantly limited. In this vast external realm, with its important, complicated, delicate and manifold problems, the President alone has the power to speak or listen as a representative of the nation. He *makes* treaties with the advice and consent of the Senate; but he alone negotiates. . . .

It is important to bear in mind that we are here dealing not alone with an authority vested in the President by an exertion of legislative power, but with such an authority plus the very delicate, plenary and exclusive power of the President as the sole organ of the Federal government in the field of international relations — a power which does not require as a basis for its exercise an act of Congress, but which, of course, like every other governmental power, must be exercised in subordination to the applicable provisions of the Constitution. It is quite apparent that if, in the maintenance of our international relations, embarrassment — perhaps serious embarrassment — is to be avoided and success for our aims achieved, congressional legislation which is to be made effective through negotiation and inquiry within the international field must often accord to the President a degree of discretion and freedom from statutory restriction which would not be admissible were domestic affairs alone involved. Moreover, he, not Congress, has the better opportunity of knowing the conditions which prevail in foreign countries, and especially is this true in time of war. He has his confidential sources of information. He has his agents in the form of diplomatic, consular and other officials. Secrecy in respect of information gathered by them may be highly necessary, and the premature disclosure of it productive of harmful results. Indeed, so clearly is this true that the first President refused to accede to a request to lay before the House of Representatives the instructions, correspondence and documents relating to the negotiation of the Jay Treaty — a refusal the wisdom of which was recognized by the House itself and has never since been doubted. . . .

The marked difference between foreign affairs and domestic affairs in this respect is recognized by both houses of Congress in the very form of their requisitions for information from the executive departments. In the case of every department except the Department of State, the resolution *directs* the official to furnish the information. In the case of the State Department, dealing with foreign affairs, the President is requested to furnish the information "if not incompatible with the public interest." A statement that to furnish the information is not compatible with the public interest rarely, if ever, is questioned.

When the President is to be authorized by legislation to act in respect of a matter intended to affect a situation in foreign territory, the legislator properly bears in mind the important consideration that the form of the President's action — or, indeed, whether he shall act at all — may well depend, among other things, upon the nature of the confidential information which he has or may thereafter receive, or upon the effect which his action may have upon our foreign relations. This consideration, in connection with what we have already said on the subject, discloses the unwisdom of requiring Congress in this field of governmental power to lay down narrowly definite standards by which the President is to be governed. . . .

The judgment of the court below must be reversed and the cause remanded for further proceedings in accordance with the foregoing opinion.

Reversed.

Mr. Justice McReynolds does not agree. He is of opinion that the court below reached the right conclusion and its judgment ought to be affirmed.

Mr. Justice Stone took no part in the consideration or decision of this case.

United States v. Pink 315 U.S. 203, 62 S. Ct. 552, 86 L. Ed. 796 (1942)

Mr. Justice Douglas delivered the opinion of the Court:

This action was brought by the United States to recover the assets of the New York branch of the First Russian Insurance Co. which remained in the hands of respondent after the payment of all domestic creditors. The material allegations of the complaint were in brief as follows:

The First Russian Insurance Co., organized under the laws of the former Empire of Russia, established a New York branch in 1907. It deposited with the Superintendent of Insurance, pursuant to the laws of New York, certain assets to secure payment of claims resulting from transactions of its New York branch. By certain laws, decrees, enactments and orders in 1918 and 1919 the Russian Government nationalized the business of insurance and all of the property, wherever situated, of all Russian insurance companies (including the First Russian Insurance Co.) and discharged and cancelled all the debts of such companies and the rights of all shareholders in all such property. The New York branch of the First Russian Insurance Co. continued to do business in New York until 1925. At that time respondent, pursuant to an order of the Supreme Court of New York, took possession of its assets for a determination and report upon the claims of the policyholders and creditors in the United States. Thereafter all claims of domestic creditors, i.e., all claims arising out of the business of the New York branch, were paid by respondent, leaving a balance in his hands of more than $1,000,000. In 1931 the New York Court of Appeals (255 N.Y. 415) directed respondent to dispose of that balance as follows:

Section C. International Relations

first, to pay claims of foreign creditors who had filed attachment prior to the commencement of the liquidation proceeding and also such claims as were filed prior to the entry of the order on remittitur of that court; and second, to pay any surplus to a quorum of the board of directors of the company. Pursuant to that mandate, respondent proceeded with the liquidation of the claims of the foreign creditors. Some payments were made, thereon. The major portion of the allowed claims, however, were not paid, a stay having been granted pending disposition of the claim of the United States. On November 16, 1933, the United States recognized the Union of Soviet Socialist Republics as the de jure Government of Russia and as an incident to that recognition accepted an assignment (known as the Litvinov Assignment) of certain claims. The Litvinov Assignment was in the form of a letter, dated November 16, 1933, to the President of the United States from Maxim Litvinov, People's Commissar for Foreign Affairs, reading as follows:

"Following our conversations I have the honor to inform you that the Government of the Union of Soviet Socialist Republics agrees that, preparatory to a final settlement of the claims and counterclaims between the Government of the Union of Soviet Socialist Republics and the United States of America and the claims of their nationals, the Government of the Union of Soviet Socialist Republics will not take any steps to enforce any decisions of courts or initiate any new litigations for the amounts admitted to be due or that may be found to be due it, as the successor of prior Governments of Russia, or otherwise, from American nationals, including corporations, companies, partnerships, or associations, and also the claim against the United States of the Russian Volunteer Fleet, now in litigation in the United States Court of Claims, and will not object to such amounts being assigned and does hereby release and assign all such amounts to the Government of the United States, the Government of the Union of Soviet Socialist Republics to be duly notified in each case of any amount realized by the Government of the United States from such release and assignment.

"The Government of the Union of Soviet Socialist Republics further agrees, preparatory to the settlement referred to above not to make any claims with respect to:

"(a) judgment rendered or that may be rendered by American courts in so far as they relate to property, or rights, or interests therein, in which the Union of Soviet Socialist Republics or its nationals may have had or may claim to have an interest; or,

"(b) acts done or settlements made by or with the Government of the United States, or public officials in the United States, or its nationals, relating to property, credits, or obligations of any Government of Russia or nationals thereof."

This was acknowledged by the President on the same date. The acknowledgment, after setting forth the terms of the assignment, concluded:

"I am glad to have these undertakings by your Government and I shall be pleased to notify your Government in each case of any amount realized by the Government of the United States from the release and assignment to it of the amounts admitted to be due, or that may be found to be due, the Government of the Union of Soviet Socialist Republics, and of the amount that may be found to be due on the claim of the Russian Volunteer Fleet."

On November 14, 1934, the United States brought an action in the federal District Court for the Southern District of New York, seeking to recover the assets in the hands of respondent. This Court held in United States v. Bank of New York & T. Co., 296 U.S. 463, that the well settled "principles governing the convenient and orderly administration of justice require that the jurisdiction of the state court should be respected" (p. 480); and that whatever might be "the effect of recognition" of the Russian Government, it did not terminate the state proceedings. p. 479. The United States was remitted to the state court for determination of its claim, no opinion being intimated on the merits. p. 481. The United States then moved for leave to intervene in the liquidation proceedings. Its motion was denied "without prejudice to the institution of the time-honored form of action." That order was affirmed on appeal.

Thereafter the present suit was instituted in the Supreme Court of New York. The de-

702   Chapter Eleven. **Distribution of National Powers**

fendants, other than respondent, were certain designated policyholders and other creditors who had presented in the liquidation proceedings claims against the corporation. The complaint prayed, inter alia, that the United States be adjudged to be the sole and exclusive owner entitled to immediate possession of the entire surplus fund in the hands of the respondent.

Respondent's answer denied the allegations of the complaint that title to the funds in question passed to the United States and that the Russian decrees had the effect claimed. It also set forth various affirmative defenses — that the order of distribution pursuant to the decree in 255 N.Y. 415, could not be affected by the Litvinov Assignment; that the Litvinov Assignment was unenforceable because it was conditioned upon a final settlement of claims and counterclaims which had not been accomplished; that under Russian law the nationalization decrees in question had no effect on property not factually taken into possession by the Russian Government prior to May 22, 1922; that the Russian decrees had no extraterritorial effect, according to Russian law; that if the decrees were given extraterritorial effect, they were confiscatory and their recognition would be unconstitutional and contrary to the public policy of the United States and of the State of New York: and that the United States under the Litvinov Assignment acted merely as a collection agency for the Russian Government and hence was foreclosed from asserting any title to the property in question.

The answer was filed in March 1938. On April, 1939, the New York Court of Appeals decided Moscow F. Ins. Co. v. Bank of New York & T. Co., 280 N.Y. 286. In May, 1939, respondent (but not the other defendants) moved pursuant to Rule 113 of the Rules of the New York Civil Practice Act and §476 of that Act for an order dismissing the complaint and awarding summary judgment in favor of respondent "on the ground . . ." that the facts in the Moscow F. Ins. Co. Case and the instant one, so far as material, were "parallel" and the Russian decrees the same; and that the Moscow F. Ins. Co. Case authoritatively settled the principles of law governing the instant one. . . . On June 29, 1939, the Supreme Court of New York granted the motion and dismissed the complaint "on the merits," citing only the Moscow F. Ins. Co. Case in support of its action. On September 2, 1939, a petition for certiorari in the Moscow F. Ins. Co. Case was filed in this Court. The judgment in that case was affirmed here by an equally divided Court. 309 U.S. 624. Subsequently the Appellate Division of the Supreme Court of New York affirmed, without opinion, the order of dismissal in the instant case. The Court of Appeals affirmed . . . (284 N.Y. 555) . . . .

We granted the petition for certiorari because of the nature and public importance of the questions raised. . . .

Second. The New York Court of Appeals held in the Moscow F. Ins. Co. Case that the Russian decrees in question had no extraterritorial effect. If that is true, it is decisive of the present controversy. For the United States acquired under the Litvinov Assignment only such rights as Russia had. Guaranty Trust Co. v. United States, 304 U.S. 126, 143. If the Russian decrees left the New York assets of the Russian insurance companies unaffected, then Russia had nothing here to assign. But that question of foreign law is not to be determined exclusively by the state court. The claim of the United States based on the Litvinov Assignment raises a federal question. United States v. Belmont, 301 U.S. 324. This Court will review or independently determine all questions on which a federal right is necessarily dependent. . . . Here title obtained under the Litvinov Assignment depends on a correct interpretation of Russian law. . . .

We hold that so far as its intended effect is concerned the Russian decree embraced the New York assets of the First Russian Insurance Co.

Third. The question of whether the decree should be given extraterritorial effect is of course a distinct matter. One primary issue raised in that connection is whether under our constitutional system New York law can be allowed to stand in the way.

The decision of the New York Court of Appeals in the Moscow F. Ins. Co. Case is unequivocal. It held that "under the law of this State such confiscatory decrees do not affect the property claimed here" (280 N.Y. 314); that the property of the New York branch acquired a "character of its own" which was "dependent" on the law of New York (p. 310); that no "rule of comity and no act of the United States government constrains this State to abandon any part of its control or to share it with a foreign State" (p. 310); . . .

. . . That power was denied New York in United States v. Belmont, 301 U.S. 324, supra. With one qualification to be noted, the Belmont Case is determinative of the present controversy.

That case involved the right of the United States under the Litvinov Assignment to recover from a custodian or stakeholder in New York funds which had been nationalized and appropriated by the Russian decrees. . . .

The holding in the Belmont Case is therefore determinative of the present controversy unless the stake of the foreign creditors in this liquidation proceeding and the provision which New York has provided for their protection call for a different result.

Fourth. The Belmont Case forecloses any relief to the Russian corporation. For this Court held in that case (301 U.S. at p. 332) ". . . our Constitution, laws, and policies have no extraterritorial operation, unless in respect of our own citizens. . . . What another country has done in the way of taking over property of its nationals, and especially of its corporations, is not a matter for judicial consideration here. Such nationals must look to their own government for any redress to which they may be entitled."

But it is urged that different considerations apply in case of the foreign creditors to whom the New York Court of Appeals (255 N.Y. 415) ordered distribution of these funds. The argument is that their rights in these funds have vested by virtue of the New York decree; that to deprive them of the property would violate the Fifth Amendment which extends its protection to aliens as well as to citizens; and that the Litvinov Assignment cannot deprive New York of its power to administer the balance of the fund in accordance with its laws for the benefit of these creditors.

At the outset it should be noted that, so far as appears, all creditors whose claims arose out of dealings with the New York branch have been paid. Thus we are not faced with the question whether New York's policy of protecting the so-called local creditors by giving them priority in the assets deposited with the State . . . should be recognized within the rule of Clark v. Williard, 294 U.S. 211 . . . or should yield to the Federal policy expressed in the international compact or agreement. Santovincenzo v. Egan, 284 U.S. 30, 40; United States v. Belmont, 301 U.S. 324. We intimate no opinion on that question. The contest here is between the United States and creditors of the Russian corporation who, we assume, are not citizens of this country and whose claims did not arise out of transactions with the New York branch. The United States is seeking to protect not only claims which it holds but also claims of its nationals. H. Rep. No. 865, 76th Cong., 1st Sess. Such claims did not arise out of transactions with this Russian corporation; they are, however, claims against Russia or its nationals. The existence of such claims and their non-payment had for years been one of the barriers to recognition of the Soviet regime by the Executive Department. . . . Congress tacitly recognized that policy. Acting in anticipation of the realization of funds under the Litvinov Assignment (H. Rep. No. 865, 76th Cong., 1st Sess.) it authorized the appointment of a Commissioner to determine the claims of American nationals against the Soviet Government. Joint Resolution of August 4, 1939, 53 Stat. at L. 1199, chap. 421.

If the President had the power to determine the policy which was to govern the question of recognition, then the Fifth Amendment does not stand in the way of giving full force and effect to the Litvinov Assignment. To be sure, aliens as well as citizens are entitled to the protection of the Fifth Amendment. Russian Volunteer Fleet v. United States, 282 U.S. 481. A State is not precluded, however, by the Fourteenth Amendment from according priority to local creditors as against creditors who are nationals of foreign countries and whose claims arose abroad. Disconto Gesellschaft v. Umbreit, 208 U.S. 570. By the same token, the Federal Government is not barred by the Fifth Amendment from securing for itself and our nationals priority against such creditors. And it matters not that the procedure adopted by the Federal Government is globular and involves a regrouping of assets. There is no Constitutional reason why this Government need act as the collection agent for nationals of other countries when it takes steps to protect itself or its own nationals on external debts. There is no reason why it may not through such devices as the Litvinov Assignment make itself and its nationals whole from assets here before it permits such assets to go abroad in satisfaction of claims of aliens made elsewhere and not incurred in connection with business conducted in this country. The fact that New York has marshaled the claims of the foreign creditors here involved and authorized their payment does not give them immunity from that general rule. . . .

. . . Unless such a power exists, the power of recognition might be thwarted or seriously diluted. No such obstacle can be placed in the way of rehabilitation of relations between this country and another nation, unless the historic conception of the powers and responsibilities of the President in the conduct of foreign affairs (see Moore, Treaties and Executive Agreements, 20 Pol. Sc. Q. 385, 403-417) is to be drastically revised. It was the judgment of the political department that full recognition of the Soviet Government required the settlement of all outstanding problems including the claims of our nationals. Recognition and the Litvinov Assignment were interdependent. We would usurp the executive function if we held that that decision was not final and conclusive in the courts.

"All constitutional acts of power, whether in the executive or in the judicial department, have as much legal validity and obligation as if they proceeded from the legislature. . . ." The Federalist, No. 64. A treaty is a "Law of the Land" under the supremacy clause (Art. 6, Cl. 2) of the Constitution. Such international compacts and agreements as the Litvinov Assignment have a similar dignity. United States v. Belmont, supra (301 U.S. p. 331). See Corwin, The President, Office & Powers (1940) pp. 228-240. . . .

Enforcement of New York's policy as formulated by the Moscow case would collide with and subtract from the Federal policy, whether it was premised on the absence of extraterritorial effect of the Russian decrees, the conception of the New York branch as a distinct juristic personality, or disapproval by New York of the Russian program of nationalization. . . . Thus the action of New York tends to restore some of the precise irritants which had long affected the relations between these two great nations and which the policy of recognition was designed to eliminate.

. . . Certainly the conditions for "enduring friendship" between the nations, which the policy of recognition in this instance was designed to effectuate, are not likely to flourish where contrary to national policy a lingering atmosphere of hostility is created by state action. . . .

. . . And the policies of the States become wholly irrelevant to judicial inquiry, when the United States, acting within its constitutional sphere, seeks enforcement of its foreign policy in the courts. For such reasons, Mr. Justice Sutherland stated in United States v. Belmont, supra (301 U.S. p. 331), "In respect of all international negotiations and compacts, and in respect of our foreign relations generally, state lines disappear. As to such purposes the State of New York does not exist."

We hold that the right to the funds or property in question became vested in the Soviet Government as the successor to the First Russian Insurance Co.; that this right has passed to the United States under the Litvinov Assignment; and that the United States is entitled to the property as against the corporation and the foreign creditors.

The judgment is reversed and the cause is remanded to the Supreme Court of New York for proceedings not inconsistent with this opinion.

Reversed.

MR. JUSTICE REED and MR. JUSTICE JACKSON did not participate in the consideration or decision of this case.

[A concurring opinion by MR. JUSTICE FRANKFURTER is omitted.]

Mr. Chief Justice Stone, dissenting:
I think the judgment should be affirmed. . . .
. . . The only questions before us are whether New York has constitutional authority to adopt its own rules of law defining rights in property located in the state, and if so whether that authority has been curtailed by the exercise of a superior federal power by recognition of the Soviet Government and acceptance of its assignment to the United States of claims against American nationals, including the New York property. . . .

It is plain that under New York law the claimants in this case, both creditors and those asserting rights of the insurance company, have enforcible rights with respect to the property located there which have been recognized though not created by the judgments of its courts. The conclusion is inescapable that had there been no assignment and this suit had been maintained by the Soviet Government subsequent to recognition, or by a private individual claiming under an assignment from it, the decision of the New York court would have presented no question reviewable here. . . .

We are not pointed to anything on the face of the documents or in the diplomatic correspondence which even suggests that the United States was to be placed in a better position with respect to the claim which it now asserts, than was the Soviet Government and nationals. . . .

. . . The only obligation to be found in the assignment and its acknowledgment by the President is that of the United States, already mentioned, to report the amounts collected. This can hardly be said to be an undertaking to strike down valid defenses to the assigned claims. Treaties, to say nothing of executive agreements and assignments which are mere transfers of rights, have hitherto been construed not to override state law or policy unless it is reasonably evident from their language that such was the intention. . . . The practical consequences of the present decision would seem to be, in every case of recognition of a foreign government, to foist upon the executive the responsibility for subordinating domestic to foreign law in conflicts cases, whether intended or not, unless such a purpose is affirmatively disclaimed. . . .

Mr. Justice Roberts joins in this opinion.

NOTE Proposed Constitutional Amendments to Restrict International Agreements

For expressions of apprehension at the extent of the treaty power, see Deutsch, The Treaty-Making Clause: A Decision for the People of America, 37 A.B.A.J. 659 (1951); Fleming, Danger to America: The Draft Covenant on Human Rights, 37 id. 739, 816 (1951); Ober, The Treaty-Making and Amending Powers: Do They Protect Our Fundamental Rights? 36 id. 715 (1950): Holman, Treaty Law-Making: A Blank Check for Writing a New Constitution, 36 id. 707 (1950); Hatch, The Treaty Power and the Constitution: The Case for Amendment, 40 id. 207 (1954).

For the view that such fears are unfounded and that amendment of the treaty clauses would be unwise, see Chafee, Amending the Constitution to Cripple Treaties, 12 La. L. Rev. 345 (1952); Perlman, On Amending the Treaty Power, 52 Colum. L. Rev. 825 (1952); Dean, The Bricker Amendment and Authority over Foreign Affairs, 32 Foreign Affairs 1 (1953); MacChesney, The Treaty Power and the Constitution: The Case Against Amendment, 40 A.B.A.J. 203 (1954); the texts of various proposals for amendment are summarized in Sutherland, Restricting the Treaty Power, 65 Harv. L. Rev. 1305 (1952), and The Bricker Amendment, Executive Agreements, and Imported Potatoes, 67 id. 281 (1953).

Control of executive agreements by prior acts of Congress. The Court of Appeals for the Fourth Circuit held that an act of Congress, if inconsistent with a subsequent executive agreement, invalidates the executive agreement. United States v. Guy W. Capps, Inc.,

204 F.2d 655 (4th Cir. 1953). Certiorari was granted, 346 U.S. 884 (1953). The Supreme Court affirmed the judgment on different grounds, declining to pass on the question of the validity of the executive agreement. 348 U.S. 296 (1955).

NOTE Power of the President to Commit Military Forces to Action

The constitutional grant of power to Congress to declare war may be satisfied otherwise than by a formal declaration, notably by congressional approval of presidential action already taken. In April 1861, shortly after the Confederate attack on Fort Sumter, President Lincoln ordered a blockade of Southern ports and seizure of any vessel attempting to run the blockade. Owners of four ships captured after the proclamation of blockade and before July 13, 1861, when Congress passed an act approving and authorizing the blockade, appealed from decrees of condemnation awarded by federal district courts. In a 5 to 4 decision the Supreme Court affirmed the decrees, except as to some particulars. The Prize Cases, 2 Black 635 (1863). A history of presidential commitments of troops is given in S. Rep. No. 797, 90th Cong. 1st sess. (1967) (Foreign Relations Committee). See also Note, Congress, the President, and the Power to Commit Forces to Combat, 81 Harv. L. Rev. 1771 (1968). On the original understanding, see Lofgren, War-Making Under the Constitution, 81 Yale L.J. 672 (1972); Berger, War-Making by the President, 121 U. Pa. L. Rev. 29 (1972); Reveley, Constitutional Allocation of War Powers Between President and Congress, 15 Va. J. Intl. L. 73 (1974); A. Sofaer, War, Foreign Affairs and Constitutional Power (1976).

The hostilities in Vietnam, carried on without a declaration of war, brought into sharp focus the question of the roles of Congress and the President. Challenges to the legality of the war were rejected by the First and Second Circuits, which inferred ratification from the Tonkin Gulf Resolution of 1964, 78 Stat. 384, and from "military appropriations or other war-implementing legislation." Orlando v. Laird, 443 F.2d 1039, 1043 (2d Cir.), cert. denied, 404 U.S. 869 (1971). See also DaCosta v. Laird, 448 F.2d 1368 (2d Cir. 1971), cert. denied, 405 U.S. 979 (1972); Massachusetts v. Laird, 451 F.2d 26 (1st Cir. 1971).

After the repeal of the Tonkin Gulf Resolution, 84 Stat. 2055 (1971), the issue of congressional ratification was given a starker aspect. In Mitchell v. Laird, 488 F.2d 611 (D.C. Cir. 1973), Judge Wyzanski (sitting by designation), writing for a 2 to 1 majority, stated that appropriation and other enabling acts could not be taken to constitute approval of the war: "A Congressman wholly opposed to the war's commencement and continuation might vote for the military appropriations and for the draft measures because he was unwilling to abandon without support men already fighting. An honorable, decent compassionate act of aiding those already in peril is no proof of consent to the actions that placed and continued them in that dangerous posture." Nevertheless, the court unanimously affirmed dismissal of the complaint, holding that the judiciary was in no position to determine whether the current executive actions were a continued prosecution of the war or were an effort to bring the war to an expeditious close "consistent with the safety of those fighting and with a profound concern for the durable interests of the nation — its defense, its honor, its morality." 488 F.2d at 616.

Military operations in Cambodia brought the constitutional issue into even sharper focus. Beginning in 1970, every military appropriation and authorization act withheld authority to use funds for military support of Cambodia, with the proviso that support could be given for "actions required to insure the safe and orderly withdrawal or disengagement of U.S. Forces from Southeast Asia, or to aid in the release of Americans held as prisoners of war." On July 1, 1973 two appropriation acts were signed by the President which prohibited support of combat activities in or over Vietnam or Cambodia after August 15,

1973. Suit was brought by members of Congress and military officers to enjoin combat operations in Cambodia and elsewhere in Indochina during the period between July 1 and August 15, 1973. District Judge Judd granted the application on the ground that congressional authorization was lacking. Holtzman v. Schlesinger, 361 F. Supp. 553 E.D.N.Y. 1973). On August 8 the court of appeals reversed, holding 2 to 1 that the case presented a nonjusticiable political question; the court could not determine whether the military actions furthered or hindered the goals of the legislative directives. 484 F.2d 1307 (2d Cir. 1973). After the August 15 effective date of the resolutions, the Supreme Court denied certiorari. 416 U.S. 936 (1974). For a contretemps between Justices Marshall and Douglas on the denial of an application to vacate an order of the court of appeals staying the district court's order, see 414 U.S. 1304, 1316 (1973). Justice Douglas stated: "Under the law as it is written the order of Mr. Justice Marshall of August 4, 1973, will in time be reversed by that Higher Court which invariably sits in judgment on the decisions of this Court." 414 U.S. at 1326.

An effort to codify the roles of the President and Congress in embarking on an undeclared war is embodied in the War Powers Resolution, which was enacted over the President's veto on November 7, 1973. Pub. L. No. 93-148, 87 Stat. 555. The resolution provides that in the absence of a declaration of war, if the President introduces armed forces into hostilities, he shall report within 48 hours to Congress, stating the circumstances and the constitutional authority for his action. Within 60 days of the report, the President shall terminate such use of armed forces unless Congress (1) has declared war or enacted specific authorization for such use, or (2) has extended by law the 60-day period, or (3) is physically unable to meet on account of an armed attack on the United States. The 60-day period may extend a further 30 days if the President certifies that the safety of our armed forces requires continued use of armed forces in the course of bringing about prompt removal of such forces. The War Powers Resolution also provides that whenever armed forces are engaged in hostilities outside the United States without a declaration of war or specific statutory authorization, such forces shall be removed if Congress so directs by concurrent resolution. The War Powers Resolution states: "Nothing in this resolution is intended to alter the constitutional authority of the Congress or the President, or the provisions of existing treaties."

Does the War Powers Resolution raise any serious constitutional problems? Does it enlarge or curtail the legitimate authority of the President, or strike a proper accommodation? For conflicting senatorial views, see Javits, Who Makes War: The President versus Congress (1973); Eagleton, War and Presidential Power: A Chronicle of Congressional Surrender (1974). See generally Van Alstyne, Congress, the President, and the Power to Declare War, 121 U. Pa. L. Rev. 1 (1972); Hearings on S. Res. No. 151, 90th Cong. 1st. sess. (1967); Rostow, Great Cases Make Bad Law: The War Powers Act, 50 Texas L. Rev. 833 (1972); Bickel, Congress, the President, and the Power to Wage War, 48 Chi.-Kent L. Rev. 131 (1971).

Chapter Twelve The Constitution Overseas

The great increase in the number of civilian and military officials of the United States on duty in all parts of the world makes relevant a consideration of the bearing of the Constitution on their duties. Does the Bill of Rights define the obligations of an American official toward American military personnel or civilians abroad? If the entire Constitution is not controlling under these circumstances, is a standard of due process in force? Has an American official a lower obligatory standard of conduct toward foreign nationals? Does it make a difference whether the United States official acts on leased American property abroad, or in territory occupied by American forces? What if the occupation is conducted jointly with other nations? If the Constitution defines the duties of American officials overseas, what agency of the government enforces it? The judiciary? Or the executive alone?

Compare Reid v. Covert, 354 U.S. 1 (1957), page 1069 infra, with Madsen v. Kinsella, 343 U.S. 341 (1952); and see Wilson v. Girard, 354 U.S. 524 (1957), Kinsella v. United States, McElroy v. Guagliardo, Wilson v. Bohlender, and Grisham v. Hagan, 361 U.S. 234, 281, 278 (1960).

In re Ross 140 U.S. 453, 11 S. Ct. 897, 35 L. Ed. 581 (1891)

The petitioner below, the appellant here, is imprisoned in the penitentiary at Albany in the State of New York. He was convicted on the 20th of May, 1880, in the American consular tribunal in Japan, of the crime of murder committed on board of an American ship in the Harbor of Yokohama in that empire, and sentenced to death.

On the 6th of August following his sentence was commuted by the President to imprisonment for life in the penitentiary at Albany, and to that place he was taken and there has ever since been confined. Nearly ten years afterwards, on the 19th of March, 1890, he applied to the Circuit Court of the United States for the Northern District of New York for a writ of habeas corpus for his discharge, alleging that his conviction, sentence and imprisonment were unlawful, and stating the causes thereof and the attendant circumstances. The writ was issued directed to the superintendent of the penitentiary, who made return that he held the petitioner under the warrant of the President. . . .

... The case was then heard by the circuit court, counsel appearing for the petitioner and the assistant United States attorney for the government. On the hearing, a copy of the record of the proceedings before the consular tribunal, and of the communications by the consul general to the State Department respecting them, on file in that Department, was given in evidence. No objection was made to its admissibility.

The facts of the case as thus disclosed, so far as they are deemed material to the decision of the question presented, are substantially as follows:

On the 9th of May, 1880, the appellant, John M. Ross, was one of the crew of the American ship "Bullion," then in the waters of Japan, and lying at anchor in the Harbor of Yokohama. On that day, on board of the ship, he assaulted Robert Kelly, its second mate, with a knife, inflicting in his neck a mortal wound, of which in a few minutes afterward he died on the deck of the ship. Ross was at once arrested by direction of the master of the vessel and placed in irons, and on the same day he was taken ashore and confined in jail at Yokohama. On the following day, May 10, the master filed with the American consul general at that place, Thomas B. Van Buren, a complaint against Ross, charging him with the murder of the mate. . . .

. . . The accused appeared with counsel before the consul general, and the complaint being read to him he presented an affidavit stating that he was a subject of Great Britain, a native of Prince Edward's Island, a dependency of the British Empire, and had never renounced the rights or liabilities of a British subject or been expatriated from his native allegiance or been naturalized in any other country. Upon this affidavit he contended that the court was without jurisdiction over him, by reason of his being a subject of Great Britain, and he prayed that he be discharged. His contention is termed in the record a demurrer to the complaint.

The court held that as the accused was a seaman on an American vessel, he was subject to its jurisdiction, and overruled the objection. The counsel of the accused then moved that the charge against him be dismissed, on the ground that he could not be held for the offense except upon the presentment or indictment of a grand jury, but this motion was also overruled.

Four associates were drawn, as required by statute and the consular regulations, to sit with the consul general on the trial of the accused, and being sworn to answer questions as to their eligibility, the accused stated that he had no questions to ask them on that subject. They were then sworn in to try the cause "in accordance with court regulations." A motion for a jury on the trial was also made and denied. The amended complaint was then substituted in place of the original, to which no objection was interposed, and to it the accused pleaded "not guilty," and asked for the names of the witnesses for the prosecution, which were furnished to him. The witnesses were then sworn and examined, and they established beyond all possible doubt the offense of murder charged against the accused, which was committed under circumstances of great atrocity. The court found him guilty of murder, and he was sentenced to suffer death in such manner and at such time and place as the United States minister should direct. . . .

The circuit court, after hearing argument of counsel and full consideration of the subject, made an order on January 21, 1891, denying the motion of the prisoner for this discharge, and remanding him to the penitentiary and the custody of its superintendent. 44 Fed. Rep. 185. From that order the case was brought here on appeal.

MR. JUSTICE FIELD, after stating the case, delivered the opinion of the court. . . .

The treaty-making power vested in our government extends to all proper subjects of negotiation with foreign governments. It can, equally with any of the former or present governments of Europe, make treaties providing for the exercise of judicial authority in other countries by its officers appointed to reside therein.

We do not understand that any question is made by counsel as to its power in this respect. His objection is to the legislation by which such treaties are carried out, contending that, so far as crimes of a felonious character are concerned, the same protection and guarantee against an undue accusation or an unfair trial, secured by the Constitution to citizens of the United States at home, should be enjoyed by them abroad. In none of the laws which have been passed by Congress to give effect to treaties of the kind has there been any attempt to require indictment by a grand jury before one can be called upon to answer for a public offense of that grade committed in those countries, or to secure a jury on the trial of the offense. Yet the laws on that subject have been passed without objection to their constitutionality. Indeed, objection on that ground was never raised in any quarter, so far as we are informed, until a recent period.

It is now, however, earnestly pressed by counsel for the petitioner, but we do not think it tenable. By the Constitution a government is ordained and established "for the United States of America," and not for countries outside of their limits. The guarantees it affords against accusation of capital or infamous crimes, except by indictment or presentment by a grand jury, and for an impartial trial by a jury when thus accused, apply only to citizens and others within the United States, or who are brought there for trial for alleged offenses committed elsewhere, and not to residents or temporary sojourners abroad. Cook v. United States, 138 U.S. 157, 181. The Constitution can have no operation in another country. . . . The framers of the Constitution, who were fully aware of the necessity of having judicial authority exercised by our consuls in non-Christian countries, if commercial intercourse was to be had with their people, never could have supposed that all the guarantees in the administration of the law upon criminals at home were to be transferred to such consular establishments, and applied before an American who had committed a felony there could be accused and tried. They must have known that such a requirement would defeat the main purpose of investing the consul with judicial authority. While, therefore, in one aspect the American accused of crime committed in those countries is deprived of the guarantees of the Constitution against unjust accusation and a partial trial, yet in another aspect he is the gainer, in being withdrawn from the procedure of their tribunals, often arbitrary and oppressive, and sometimes accompanied with extreme cruelty and torture. . . .

We turn now to the treaties between Japan and the United States. [The Court found that treaty provisions in force provided that Americans committing offenses in Japan should be tried by the American consul general or consul.]

We are satisfied that the true rule of construction in the present case was adopted by the Department of State in the correspondence with the English government, and that the action of the consular tribunal in taking the jurisdiction of the prisoner Ross, though an English subject, for the offense committed, was authorized. While he was an enlisted seaman on the American vessel, which floated the American flag, he was, within the meaning of the statute and the treaty, an American, under the protection and subject to the laws of the United States equally with the seaman who was native born. As an American seaman he could have demanded a trial before the consular court as a matter of right, and must therefore be held subject to it as a matter of obligation. . . .

Order affirmed.

NOTE

The occupation of Cuba by United States forces at the time of the Spanish-American War did not give an American postal embezzler under the occupation government a right of jury trial. Neely v. Henkel, 180 U.S. 109 (1901). Cf. Thompson v. Utah, 170 U.S. 343 (1898), for territories on the North American continent. Compare trial, by consent of American authorities, of an American soldier by a Japanese civil court. Wilson v. Girard, 354 U.S. 524 (1957).

Downes v. Bidwell 182 U.S. 244, 21 S. Ct. 770, 45 L. Ed. 1088 (1901)

MR. JUSTICE BROWN . . . announced the conclusion and judgment of the court.

This case involves the question whether merchandise brought into the port of New York from Porto Rico since the passage of the Foraker act is exempt from duty, notwithstanding the third section of that act, which requires the payment of "fifteen per centum of the duties which are required to be levied, collected and paid upon like articles of merchandise imported from foreign countries." . . .

. . . In the case of De Lima v. Bidwell, just decided, 182 U.S. 1, we held that, upon the ratification of the treaty of peace with Spain, Porto Rico ceased to be a foreign country, and became a territory of the United States, and that duties were no longer collectible upon merchandise brought from that island. We are now asked to hold that it became a part of the United States within that provision of the Constitution which declares that "all duties, imposts, and excises shall be uniform throughout the United States." Art. 1, Sec. 8. If Porto Rico be a part of the United States, the Foraker act imposing duties upon its products is unconstitutional, not only by reason of a violation of the uniformity clause, but because by section 9 "vessels bound to or from one State" cannot "be obliged to enter, clear, or pay duties in another."

The case also involves the broader question whether the revenue clauses of the Constitution extend of their own force to our newly acquired territories. The Constitution itself does not answer the question. Its solution must be found in the nature of the government created by that instrument, in the opinion of its contemporaries, in the practical construction put upon it by Congress, and in the decisions of this court. . . .

We suggest, without intending to decide, that there may be a distinction between certain natural rights enforced in the Constitution by prohibitions against interference with them, and what may be termed artificial or remedial rights, which are peculiar to our own system of jurisprudence. Of the former class are the rights to one's own religious opinion and to a public expression of them, or, as sometimes said, to worship God according to the dictates of one's own conscience; the right to personal liberty and individual property; to freedom of speech and of the press; to free access to courts of justice, to due process of law and to an equal protection of the laws; to immunities from unreasonable searches and seizures, as well as cruel and unusual punishments; and to such other immunities as are indispensable to a free government. Of the latter class are the rights to citizenship, to suffrage, Minor v. Happersett, 21 Wall. 162, and to the particular methods of procedure pointed out in the Constitution, which are peculiar to Anglo-Saxon jurisprudence, and some of which have already been held by the States to be unnecessary to the proper protection of individuals.

Whatever may be finally decided by the American people as to the *status* of these islands and their inhabitants — whether they shall be introduced into the sisterhood of States or be permitted to form independent governments — it does not follow that, in the meantime, awaiting that decision, the people are in the matter of personal rights unprotected by the provisions of our Constitution and subject to the merely arbitrary control of Congress. Even if regarded as aliens, they are entitled under the principles of the Constitution to be protected in life, liberty and property. This has been frequently held by this court in respect to the Chinese, even when aliens, not possessed of the political rights of citizens of the United States. Yick Wo v. Hopkins, 118 U.S. 356; Fong Yue Ting v. United States, 149 U.S. 698; Lem Moon Sing v. United States, 158 U.S. 538, 547; Wong Wing v. United States, 163 U.S. 228. We do not desire, however, to anticipate the difficulties which would naturally arise in this connection, but merely to disclaim any intention to hold that the inhabitants of these territories are subject to an unrestrained power on the part of Congress to deal with them upon the theory that they have no rights which it is bound to respect. . . .

Patriotic and intelligent men may differ widely as to the desirableness of this or that acquisition, but this is solely a political question. We can only consider this aspect of the case so far as to say that no construction of the Constitution should be adopted which would prevent Congress from considering each case upon its merits, unless the language of the instrument imperatively demand it. A false step at this time might be fatal to the development of what Chief Justice Marshall called the American Empire. Choice in some cases, the natural gravitation of small bodies towards large ones in others, the result of a successful war in still others, may bring about conditions which would render the annexation of distant possessions desirable. If those possessions are inhabited by alien races, differing from us in religion, customs, laws, methods of taxation and modes of thought, the administration of government and justice, according to Anglo-Saxon principles, may for a time be impossible; and the question at once arises whether large concessions ought not to be made for a time, that, ultimately, our own theories may be carried out, and the blessings of a free government under the Constitution extended to them. We decline to hold that there is anything in the Constitution to forbid such action.

We are therefore of opinion that the Island of Porto Rico is a territory appurtenant and belonging to the United States, but not a part of the United States within the revenue clauses of the Constitution; that the Foraker act is constitutional, so far as it imposes duties upon imports from such island, and that the plaintiff cannot recover back the duties exacted in this case.

The judgment of the Circuit Court is therefore
Affirmed.

MR. JUSTICE WHITE, with whom concurred MR. JUSTICE SHIRAS and MR. JUSTICE MCKENNA, uniting in the judgment of affirmance. . . .

MR. JUSTICE GRAY, concurring. . . .

So long as Congress has not incorporated the territory into the United States, neither military occupation nor cession by treaty makes the conquered territory domestic territory, in the sense of the revenue laws. But those laws concerning "foreign countries" remain applicable to the conquered territory until changed by Congress. Such was the unanimous opinion of this court, as declared by Chief Justice Taney, in Fleming v. Page, 9 How. 603, 617. . . .

MR. CHIEF JUSTICE FULLER, (with whom concurred MR. JUSTICE HARLAN, MR. JUSTICE BREWER and MR. JUSTICE PECKHAM), dissenting. . . .

MR. JUSTICE HARLAN, MR. JUSTICE BREWER, MR. JUSTICE PECKHAM and myself are unable to concur in the opinions and judgment of the court in this case. The majority widely differ in reasoning by which the conclusion is reached, although there seems to be concurrence in the view that Porto Rico belongs to the United States, but nevertheless, and notwithstanding the act of Congress, is not a part of the United States, subject to the provisions of the Constitution in respect of the levy of taxes, duties, imposts and excises. . . .

MR. JUSTICE HARLAN, dissenting.

I concur in the dissenting opinion of the CHIEF JUSTICE. The grounds upon which he and MR. JUSTICE BREWER and MR. JUSTICE PECKHAM regard the Foraker act as unconstitutional in the particulars involved in this action meet my entire approval. . . .

The wise men who framed the Constitution, and the patriotic people who adopted it, were unwilling to depend for their safety upon what, in the opinion referred to, is described as "certain principles of natural justice inherent in Anglo-Saxon character, which need no expression in constitutions or statutes to give them effect or to secure dependencies against legislation manifestly hostile to their real interests." They proceeded upon the theory — the wisdom of which experience has vindicated — that the only safe guaranty against governmental oppression was to withhold or restrict the power to oppress. They well remembered that Anglo-Saxons across the ocean had attempted, in defiance of law and justice, to trample upon the rights of Anglo-Saxons on this continent and had sought, by military force, to establish a government that could at will destroy the privileges that inhere in liberty. . . .

. . . The Constitution is supreme over every foot of territory, wherever situated, under the jurisdiction of the United States, and its full operation cannot be stayed by any branch of the Government in order to meet what some may suppose to be extraordinary emergencies. If the Constitution is in force in any territory, it is in force there for every purpose embraced by the objects for which the Government was ordained. . . .

NOTE Incorporation of Territory

For other problems of "incorporation" of newly acquired territory, see Hawaii v. Mankichi, 190 U.S. 197 (1903); Dorr v. United States, 195 U.S. 138 (1904); Balzac v. United States, 258 U.S. 298 (1922). See, for a discussion of the "Insular Cases" and "incorporation," 1 Willoughby, Constitutional Law, c. 31 (2d ed. 1929).

The Fifth Amendment has been held to extend to Puerto Rico ex proprio vigore. Arroyo v. Puerto Rico Trans. Authority, 164 F.2d 748 (1st Cir. 1947).

Best v. United States 184 F.2d 131 (1st Cir. 1950), cert. denied, 340 U.S. 939 (1951)

MAGRUDER, Chief Judge.

This is an appeal from a judgment sentencing Robert H. Best to life imprisonment and a fine of $10,000, upon a conviction by a jury on an indictment charging the crime of treason against the United States. The charge was predicated upon appellant's radio broadcasting activities within Germany and Austria during World War II, under the auspices of the German Radio Broadcasting Company, an agency of the German Government under the jurisdiction of the Ministry of Public Enlightenment and Propaganda. The case bears a close resemblance to Chandler v. United States, 1 Cir., 1948, 171 F.2d 921, certiorari denied, 1949, 336 U.S. 918, ...

There was little or no conflict in the testimony, certainly not in any important particular. On the evidence, the jury were warranted in finding the following:

. . . Toward the end of 1922, Best came to Vienna, which he liked very much. He settled down there, and from time to time did journalistic work. . . .

After the Nazis came to power in Germany, Best found much to admire in the Hitler regime. He became more and more fanatically anti-Jewish and anti-Communist. In the summer of 1941 he made overtures to be allowed to broadcast to America over the German radio, to warn against certain tendencies in the foreign policy of the Government of the United States; but no such arrangement was consummated at that time.

When the Japanese attack on Pearl Harbor brought the United States into the war, Best was promptly taken into custody in Vienna by the Gestapo and held in jail. A few days thereafter he was lodged in an internment camp in Bad Nauheim, Germany, ...

During his stay at Bad Nauheim, Best communicated with various German officials with reference to his desire to remain in Germany. He was given permission to travel to Berlin unaccompanied, and there he talked to one Rasche, an official of the Press Department of the Foreign Office, who particularly inquired whether Best was still interested in speaking over the German radio. . . .

In April, 1942, Best commenced his radio activities in Berlin. At the outset he served in a dual capacity, as a news editor and as a radio commentator.

His job as news editor was to take raw German news items which had been supplied to him, "translating them or writing them into English as he saw fit, and editing them for use in the news service." He also wrote the so-called Bell reports, which "covered the number of allied vessels sunk by German warships, and gave description of the circumstances and where it occurred." At the beginning of these broadcasts "bells were rung to indicate the number of ships sunk, and then there would follow a short commentary by Mr. Best." . . .

A search and seizure point, which was not presented in the Chandler case, deserves some comment. It concerns a search of Best's Vienna apartment without a judicial warrant by officers of the United States Army of Occupation some weeks after Best had been taken into custody, and seizure of certain documents found there. A motion to suppress made by appellant was the subject of an extensive hearing by the district judge, at which witnesses were heard and affidavits submitted. Judge Ford gave careful consideration to the facts and the law, in a memorandum which appears in 76 F. Supp. 857-865, and concluded, in the unprecedented situation before him, that the motion to suppress should be denied. We refer to this memorandum for a fuller statement of the facts.

For present purposes we assume, and we think it is probably so, that the protection of the Fourth Amendment extends to United States citizens in foreign countries under occupation by our armed forces. Cf. Eisentrager v. Forrestal, 1949, 84 App. D.C. 396, rev'd on other grounds sub nom. Johnson v. Eisentrager, 1950 [339 U.S. 763]. We do not regard In re Ross, 1891, 140 U.S. 453, at page 464, as holding anything to the contrary, notwithstanding the isolated statement therein: "The constitution can have no operation in another country." See Ex parte Bakelite Corp., 1929, 279 U.S. 438, 451. For example, suppose A, a citizen of the United States, goes to Germany to take employment in a civilian capacity under the High Commissioner. He is suspected of having previously transported stolen goods in interstate commerce, in violation of 18 U.S.C. §2314. Agents of the F.B.I., without any search warrant, break into A's dwelling in Germany, ransack the place, find and seize the alleged stolen goods. Upon a subsequent prosecution of A in the United States for that offense, it can hardly be doubted that the evidence so obtained would be excluded as the product of a search and seizure forbidden by the Fourth Amendment. And this would be so, even though no judicial officer had been authorized to issue a warrant for a search in occupied Germany. Obviously, Congress may not nullify the guarantees of the Fourth Amendment by the simple expedient of not empowering any judicial officer to act on an application for a warrant. If the search is one which would otherwise be unreasonable, and hence in violation of the Fourth Amendment, without the sanction of a search warrant, then in such a case, for lack of a warrant, no search could lawfully be made.

But the question now at issue is not necessarily concluded in appellant's favor upon the assumption that the United States Army officers who conducted the search were subject to the Fourth Amendment. In the recent case of United States v. Rabinowitz, 1950, 339 U.S. 56, the Supreme Court stated: "It is unreasonable searches that are prohibited by the Fourth Amendment. Carroll v. United States, 267 U.S. 132, 147. It was recognized by the framers of the Constitution that there were reasonable searches for which no warrant was required." . . . "Reasonableness is in the first instance for the District Court to determine." [The court concluded that in the circumstances the search was not unreasonable.]

The judgment of the District Court is affirmed.

GOODRICH, Circuit Judge, concurring.

I concur in the judgment, and in the opinion of the Court, except that I do not wish to intimate any opinion as to the extraterritorial application of the Fourth Amendment.[a]

In re YAMASHITA, 327 U.S. 1, 66 S. Ct. 340, 90 L. Ed. 499 (1946). General Yamashita was commander of the Japanese 14th Army Group in the Philippines. He became a prisoner of war on September 3, 1945, and was tried before a military commission of five officers of the United States Army on charges of violating the law of war by failing to control the members of his command, permitting them to commit atrocities against people of

---

[a] See, for a somewhat similar case, Gillars v. United States, 182 F.2d 962 (D.C. Cir. 1950). — ED.

the United States and of its allies and dependencies, particularly the Philippines. He was defended by appointed military counsel. On December 7, 1945, he was found guilty and sentenced to be hanged. His counsel then applied to the Supreme Court of the United States for leave to file a petition for habeas corpus and prohibition, and for certiorari to review an order of the Supreme Court of the Commonwealth of the Philippines denying a like application. The United States Supreme Court ordered oral argument, 326 U.S. 694. On February 4, 1946, after hearing counsel, it denied both applications. Chief Justice Stone, writing for the Court, found insufficient the petitioner's contentions that no military commission could lawfully try General Yamashita for violations of the laws of war after hostilities had ceased; that the charge preferred failed to state a violation of the laws of war; that the order governing the procedure of the commission, which permitted in evidence hearsay and opinion matter against the defendant, violated the Articles of War, the Geneva Convention (47 Stat. 2021), and the due process clause of the Fifth Amendment; and that the commission lacked jurisdiction because the United States had failed to give notice to Switzerland, the neutral power representing the interests of Japanese prisoners under Article 60 of the Geneva Convention (47 Stat. 2021, 2051). Justices Murphy and Rutledge wrote dissenting opinions. Mr. Justice Rutledge wrote: "The difference between the Court's view of this proceeding and my own comes down in the end to the view, on the one hand, that there is no law restrictive upon these proceedings other than whatever rules and regulations may be prescribed for their government by the executive authority or the military and, on the other hand, that the provisions of the Articles of War, of the Geneva Convention and the Fifth Amendment apply.

"I cannot accept the view that anywhere in our system resides or lurks a power so unrestrained to deal with any human being through any process of trial. What military agencies or authorities may do with our enemies in battle or invasion, apart from proceedings in the nature of trial and some semblance of judicial action, is beside the point. Nor has any human being heretofore been held to be wholly beyond elementary procedural protection by the Fifth Amendment. I cannot consent to even implied departure from that great absolute." For an account of the trial written by one of assigned counsel for the defendant, see Reel, The Case of General Yamashita (1949). The case is analyzed by Professor Fairman in The Supreme Court on Military Jurisdiction: Martial Rule in Hawaii and the Yamashita Case, 59 Harv. L. Rev. 833 (1946). The Yamashita case was followed in Homma v. Patterson, 327 U.S. 759 (1946), the Court handing down a brief memorandum, and Justices Murphy and Rutledge writing dissenting opinions.

Hirota v. MacArthur 338 U.S. 197, 69 S. Ct. 197, 93 L. Ed. 1902 (1948, 1949)

[The United States Supreme Court denied the petitions of Koki Hirota and others for leave to file petitions for writs of habeas corpus.]

PER CURIAM.

The petitioners, all residents and citizens of Japan, are being held in custody pursuant to the judgment of a military tribunal in Japan. Two of the petitioners have been sentenced to death, the others to terms of imprisonment. They filed motions in this Court for leave to file petitions for habeas corpus. We set all the motions for hearing on the question of our power to grant the relief prayed and that issue has now been fully presented and argued.

We are satisfied that the tribunal sentencing these petitioners is not a tribunal of the United States. The United States and other allied countries conquered and now occupy and control Japan. General Douglas MacArthur has been selected and is acting as the Supreme Commander for the Allied Powers. The military tribunal sentencing these petitioners has been set up by General MacArthur as the agent of the Allied Powers.

Under the foregoing circumstances the courts of the United States have no power or authority to review, to affirm, set aside or annul the judgments and sentences imposed on these petitioners and for this reason the motions for leave to file petitions for writs of habeas corpus are denied.

Mr. Justice Murphy dissents.

Mr. Justice Rutledge reserves decision and the announcement of his vote until a later time.

Mr. Justice Jackson took no part in the final decision on these motions.

Mr. Justice Douglas, concurring.

These cases present new, important and difficult problems.

Petitioners are citizens of Japan. They were all high officials of the Japanese Government or officers of the Japanese Army during World War II. They are held in custody pursuant to a judgment of the International Military Tribunal for the Far East. They were found guilty by that tribunal of various so-called war crimes against humanity.

Petitioners at the time of argument of these cases were confined in Tokyo, Japan, under the custody of respondent Walker, Commanding General of the United States Eighth Army, who held them pursuant to the orders of respondent MacArthur, Supreme Commander for the Allied Powers. Other respondents are the Chief of Staff of the United States Army, the Secretary of the Department of the Army, and the Secretary of Defense.

First. There is an important question of jurisdiction that lies at the threshold of these cases. Respondents contend that the Court is without power to issue a writ of habeas corpus in these cases. It is argued that the Court has no original jurisdiction as defined in Art. III, §2, Cl. 2 of the Constitution, since these are not cases affecting an ambassador, public minister, or consul; nor is a State a party. And it is urged that appellate jurisdiction is absent (1) because military commissions do not exercise judicial power within the meaning of Art. III, §2 of the Constitution and hence are not agencies whose judgments are subject to review by the Court; and (2) no court of the United States to which the potential appellate jurisdiction of this Court extends has jurisdiction over this case.

It is to the latter contention alone that consideration need be given. I think it is plain that a District Court of the United States does have jurisdiction to entertain petitions for habeas corpus to examine into the cause of the restraint of liberty of the petitioners.

The question now presented was expressly reserved in Ahrens v. Clark, 335 U.S. 188, 192, note 4. In that case aliens detained at Ellis Island sought to challenge by habeas corpus the legality of their detention in the District Court for the District of Columbia. It was argued that that court had jurisdiction because the Attorney General, who was responsible for their custody, was present there. We rejected that view, holding that it was the District Court where petitioners were confined that had jurisdiction to issue the writ. It is now argued that no District Court can act in these cases because if in one case their jurisdiction under the habeas corpus statute is limited to inquiries into the causes of restraints of liberty of those confined within the territorial jurisdictions of those courts, it is so limited in any other.

That result, however, does not follow. In Ahrens v. Clark, supra, we were dealing with the distribution of judicial power among the several District Courts. There was an explicit legislative history, indicating disapproval of a practice of moving prisoners from one district to another in order to grant them the hearings to which they are entitled. We held that the court at the place of confinement was the court to which application must be made. But it does not follow that, where that place is not within the territorial jurisdiction of any District Court, judicial power to issue the writ is rendered impotent.

. . . In Ahrens v. Clark, supra, denial of a remedy in one District Court was not a denial of a remedy in all of them. There was a District Court to which those petitioners could resort. But in these cases there is none if the jurisdiction of the District Court is in all respects restricted to cases of prisoners who are confined within their geographical boundaries.

Such a holding would have grave and alarming consequences. Today Japanese war lords appeal to the Court for application of American standards of justice. Tomorrow or next year an American citizen may stand condemned in Germany or Japan by a military court or commission. If no United States court can inquire into the lawfulness of his detention, the military have acquired, contrary to our traditions (see Ex parte Quirin, 317 U.S. 1; In re Yamashita, 327 U.S. 1), a new and alarming hold on us.

I cannot agree to such a grave and startling result. It has never been deemed essential that the prisoner in every case be within the territorial limits of the district where he seeks relief by way of habeas corpus. In Ex parte Endo, 323 U.S. 283, 304-306, a prisoner had been removed, pending an appeal, from the district where the petition had been filed. We held that the District Court might act if there was a respondent within reach of its process who had custody of the prisoner. The aim of the statute is the practical administration of justice. The allocation of jurisdiction among the District Courts, recognized in Ahrens v. Clark, is a problem of judicial administration, not a method of contracting the authority of the courts so as to delimit their power to issue the historic writ.

The place to try the issues of this case is in the district where there is a respondent who is responsible for the custody of petitioners. That district is obviously the District of Columbia. That result was reached by the Court of Appeals for the District of Columbia in Eisentrager v. Forrestal, 84 App. D.C. 396, 174 F.2d 961. It held, in the case of a German national confined in Germany in the custody of the United States Army, that the court having jurisdiction over those who have directive power over the jailer outside the United States could issue the writ. In my view that is the correct result. For we would have to conclude that the United States Generals who have custody of petitioners are bigger than our government to hold that the respondent-officials of the War Department have no control or command over them. That result would raise grave constitutional questions, as Eisentrager v. Forrestal, supra, suggests.

It is therefore clear to me that the District Court of the District of Columbia is the court to hear these motions. The appropriate course would be to remit the parties to it, reserving any further questions until the cases come here by certiorari. But the Court is unwilling to take that course, apparently because it deems the cases so pressing and the issues so unsubstantial that the motions should be summarily disposed of.

Second. The Court in denying leave to file states:

"We are satisfied that the tribunal sentencing these petitioners is not a tribunal of the United States. The United States and other allied countries conquered and now occupy and control Japan. General Douglas MacArthur has been selected and is acting as the Supreme Commander for the Allied Powers. The military tribunal sentencing these petitioners has been set up by General MacArthur as the agent of the Allied Powers.

"Under the foregoing circumstances the courts of the United States have no power or authority to review, to affirm, set aside or annul the judgments and sentences imposed on these petitioners . . ."

But that statement does not in my opinion adequately analyze the problem. The formula which it evolves to dispose of the cases is indeed potentially dangerous. It leaves practically no room for judicial scrutiny of this new type of military tribunal which is evolving. It leaves the power of those tribunals absolute. Prisoners held under its mandates may have appeal to the conscience or mercy of an executive; but they apparently have no appeal to law.

The fact that the tribunal has been set up by the Allied Powers should not of itself preclude our inquiry. Our inquiry is directed not to the conduct of the Allied Powers but to the conduct of our own officials. Our writ would run not to an official of an Allied Power but to our own official. We would want to know not what authority our Allies had to do what they did but what authority our officials had.

If an American General holds a prisoner, our process can reach him wherever he is. To that extent at least, the Constitution follows the flag. It is no defense for him to say that he acts for the Allied Powers. He is an American citizen who is performing functions for our government. . . .

These are increasingly important questions as collaboration among nations at the international level continues. They pose questions for which there is no precedent. But we sacrifice principle when we stop our inquiry once we ascertain that the tribunal is international.

I cannot believe that we would adhere to that formula if these petitioners were American citizens. I cannot believe we would adhere to it if this tribunal or some other tribunal were trying American citizens for offenses committed either before or during the occupation. In those cases we would, I feel, look beyond the character of the tribunal to the persons being tried and the offenses with which they were charged. We would ascertain whether, so far as American participation is concerned, there was authority to try the defendants for the precise crimes with which they are charged. That is what we should do here. . . .

[Mr. Justice Douglas then stated that the President's agreements with allied nations raised political, not justiciable questions.] Agreement with foreign nations for the punishment of war criminals . . . is a part of the prosecution of the war. It falls as clearly in the realm of political decisions as all other aspects of military alliances in furtherance of the common objective of victory. Cf. Georgia v. Stanton, 6 Wall. 50, 71. . . .

. . . Insofar as American participation is concerned, there is no constitutional objection to that action. For the capture and control of those who were responsible for the Pearl Harbor incident was a political question on which the President as Commander-in-Chief, and as spokesman for the nation in foreign affairs, had the final say.[b]

Johnson v. Eisentrager 339 U.S. 763, 70 S. Ct. 936, 94 L. Ed. 1255 (1950)

MR. JUSTICE JACKSON delivered the opinion of the Court.

The ultimate question in this case is one of jurisdiction of civil courts of the United States vis-à-vis military authorities in dealing with enemy aliens overseas. The issues come here in this way:

Twenty-one German nationals petitioned the District Court of the District of Columbia for writs of habeas corpus. They alleged that, prior to May 8, 1945, they were in service of German armed forces in China. They amended to allege that their employment there was by civilian agencies of the German Government. Their exact affiliation is disputed and, for our purposes, immaterial. On May 8, 1945, the German High Command executed an act of unconditional surrender, expressly obligating all forces under German control at once to cease active hostilities. These prisoners have been convicted of violating laws of war, by engaging in, permitting or ordering continued military activity against the United States after surrender of Germany and before surrender of Japan. Their hostile operations consisted principally of collecting and furnishing intelligence concerning American forces and their movements to the Japanese armed forces. They, with six others who were acquitted, were taken into custody by the United States Army after the Japanese surrender and were tried and convicted by a Military Commission constituted by our Commanding General at Nanking by delegation from the Commanding General, United States Forces, China Theatre, pursuant to authority specifically granted by the Joint Chiefs of Staff of the United States. The Commission sat in China, with express consent of the Chinese Government. The proceeding was conducted wholly under American auspices and involved no international participation. After conviction, the sentences were

---

[b] For a number of memoranda decisions in which the Supreme Court held that it had no jurisdiction to review judgments of military tribunals set up in Germany, see note 1 of Mr. Justice Jackson's memorandum in Hirota v. MacArthur, 335 U.S. 876 (1948). — ED.

duly reviewed and, with immaterial modification, approved by military reviewing authority.

The prisoners were repatriated to Germany to serve their sentences. Their immediate custodian is Commandant of Landsberg Prison, an American Army officer under the Commanding General, Third United States Army, and the Commanding General, European Command. He could not be reached by process from the District Court. Respondents named in the petition are Secretary of Defense, Secretary of the Army, Chief of Staff of the Army, and the Joint Chiefs of Staff of the United States.

The petition alleges, and respondents denied, that the jailer is subject to their direction. The Court of Appeals assumed, and we do likewise, that, while prisoners are in immediate physical custody of an officer or officers not parties to the proceeding, respondents named in the petition have lawful authority to effect their release.

The petition prays an order that the prisoners be produced before the District Court, that it may inquire into their confinement and order them discharged from such offenses and confinement. It is claimed that their trial, conviction and imprisonment violate Articles I and III of the Constitution, and the Fifth Amendment thereto, and other provisions of the Constitution and laws of the United States and provisions of the Geneva Convention governing treatment of prisoners of war.

A rule to show cause issued, to which the United States made return. Thereupon the petition was dismissed on authority of Ahrens v. Clark, 335 U.S. 188.

The Court of Appeals reversed and, reinstating the petition, remanded for further proceedings. 84 App. D.C. 396. It concluded that any person, including an enemy alien, deprived of his liberty anywhere under any purported authority of the United States is entitled to the writ if he can show that extension to his case of any constitutional rights or limitations would show his imprisonment illegal; that, although no statutory jurisdiction of such cases is given, courts must be held to possess it as part of the judicial power of the United States; that where deprivation of liberty by an official act occurs outside the territorial jurisdiction of any District Court, the petition will lie in the District Court which has territorial jurisdiction over officials who have directive power over the immediate jailer.

The obvious importance of these holdings to both judicial administration and military operations impelled us to grant certiorari. 338 U.S. 877. The case is before us only on issues of law. The writ of habeas corpus must be granted "unless it appears from the application" that the applicants are not entitled to it. 28 U.S.C. §2243.

We are cited to no instance where a court, in this or any other country where the writ is known, has issued it on behalf of an alien enemy who, at no relevant time and in no stage of his captivity, has been within its territorial jurisdiction. Nothing in the text of the Constitution extends such a right, nor does anything in our statutes. Absence of support from legislative or juridical sources is implicit in the statements of the court below that "The answers stem directly from fundamentals. They cannot be found by casual reference to statutes or cases." The breadth of the court's premises and solution requires us to consider questions basic to alien enemy and kindred litigation which for some years have been beating upon our doors.[1]

---

[1] From January 1948 to today, motions for leave to file petitions for habeas corpus in this Court, and applications treated by the Court as such, on behalf of over 200 German enemy aliens confined by American military authorities abroad were filed and denied. Brandt v. United States, and 13 companion cases, 333 U.S. 836; Re Eichel [one petition on behalf of three persons], 333 U.S. 865; Everett v. Truman [one petition on behalf of 74 persons], 334 U.S. 824; Re Krautwurst, and 11 companion cases, 334 U.S. 826; Re Ehlen and Re Girke, 334 U.S. 836; Re Gronwald, 334 U.S. 857; Re Stattmann, and 3 companion cases, 335 U.S. 805; Re Vetter, and 6 companion cases, 335 U.S. 841; Re Eckstein, 335 U.S. 851; Re Heim, 335 U.S. 856; Re Dammann, and 4 companion cases, 336 U.S. 922, 923; Re Muhlbauer, and 57 companion cases, covering at least 80 persons, 336 U.S. 964; Re Felsch, 337 U.S. 953; Re Buerger, 338 U.S. 884; Re Hans, 339 U.S. 976; Re Schmidt, 339 U.S. 976; Lammers v. United States, 339 U.S. 976. And see also Milch v. United States, 332 U.S. 789.

These cases and the variety of questions they raised are analyzed and discussed by Fairman, Some New Problems of the Constitution Following the Flag, 1 Stanford L. Rev. 587.

I

Modern American law has come a long way since the time when outbreak of war made every enemy national an outlaw, subject to both public and private slaughter, cruelty and plunder. But even by the most magnanimous view, our law does not abolish inherent distinctions recognized throughout the civilized world between citizens and aliens, nor between aliens of friendly and of enemy allegiance, nor between resident enemy aliens who have submitted themselves to our laws and nonresident enemy aliens who at all times have remained with, and adhered to, enemy governments.

With the citizen we are now little concerned, except to set his case apart as untouched by this decision and to take measure of the difference between his status and that of all categories of aliens. Citizenship as a head of jurisdiction and a ground of protection was old when Paul invoked it in his appeal to Caesar. The years have not destroyed nor diminished the importance of citizenship nor have they sapped the vitality of a citizen's claims upon his government for protection. . . .

The alien, to whom the United States has been traditionally hospitable, has been accorded a generous and ascending scale of rights as he increases his identity with our society. Mere lawful presence in the country creates an implied assurance of safe conduct and gives him certain rights; . . . .

But, in extending constitutional protections beyond the citizenry, the Court has been at pains to point out that it was the alien's presence within its territorial jurisdiction that gave the Judiciary power to act. In the pioneer case of Yick Wo v. Hopkins, the Court said of the Fourteenth Amendment, "These provisions are universal in their application, *to all persons within the territorial jurisdiction,* without regard to any differences of race, or color, or of nationality; . . ." (Italics supplied.) 118 U.S. 356, 369. . . .

II

The foregoing demonstrates how much further we must go if we are to invest these enemy aliens, resident, captured and imprisoned abroad, with standing to demand access to our courts.

We are here confronted with a decision whose basic premise is that these prisoners are entitled, as a constitutional right, to sue in some court of the United States for a writ of habeas corpus. To support that assumption we must hold that a prisoner of our military authorities is constitutionally entitled to the writ, even though he (a) is an enemy alien; (b) has never been or resided in the United States; (c) was captured outside of our territory and there held in military custody as a prisoner of war; (d) was tried and convicted by a Military Commission sitting outside the United States; (e) for offenses against laws of war committed outside the United States; (f) and is at all times imprisoned outside the United States.

We have pointed out that the privilege of litigation has been extended to aliens, whether friendly or enemy, only because permitting their presence in the country implied protection. No such basis can be invoked here, for these prisoners at no relevant time were within any territory over which the United States is sovereign and the scenes of their offense, their capture, their trial and their punishment were all beyond the territorial jurisdiction of any court of the United States.

Another reason for a limited opening of our courts to resident aliens is that among them are many of friendly personal disposition to whom the status of enemy is only one imputed by law. But these prisoners were actual enemies, active in the hostile service of an enemy power. There is no fiction about their enmity. Yet the decision below confers upon them a right to use our courts, free even of the limitation we have imposed upon resident alien enemies, to whom we deny any use of our courts that would hamper our war effort or aid the enemy.

A basic consideration in habeas corpus practice is that the prisoner will be produced before the court. This is the crux of the statutory scheme established by the Congress, indeed, it is inherent in the very term "habeas corpus." And though production of the prisoner may be dispensed with where it appears on the face of the application that no cause for granting the writ exists, Walker v. Johnston, 312 U.S. 275, 284, we have consistently adhered to and recognized the general rule. Ahrens v. Clark, 335 U.S. 188, 190, 191. To grant the writ to these prisoners might mean that our army must transport them across the seas for hearing. . . .

Moreover, we could expect no reciprocity for placing the litigation weapon in unrestrained enemy hands. The right of judicial refuge from military action, which it is proposed to bestow on the enemy, can purchase no equivalent for benefit of our citizen soldiers.

The prisoners rely, however, upon two decisions of this Court to get them over the threshold — Ex parte Quirin, 317 U.S. 1, and Re Yamashita, 327 U.S. 1. . . .

. . . After hearing all contentions they have seen fit to advance and considering every contention we can base on their application and the holdings below, we arrive at the same conclusion the Court reached in each of those cases, viz.: that no right to the writ of habeas corpus appears.

III

The Court of Appeals dispensed with all requirement of territorial jurisdiction based on place of residence, captivity, trial, offense, or confinement. It could not predicate relief upon any intraterritorial contact of these prisoners with our laws or institutions. Instead, it gave our Constitution an extraterritorial application to embrace our enemies in arms. Right to the writ, it reasoned, is a subsidiary procedural right that follows from possession of substantive constitutional rights. These prisoners, it considered, are invested with a right of personal liberty by our Constitution and therefore must have the right to the remedial writ. The court stated the steps in its own reasoning as follows: "*First.* The Fifth Amendment, by its terms, applies to 'any person.' *Second.* Action of Government officials in violation of the Constitution is void. This is the ultimate essence of the present controversy. *Third.* A basic and inherent function of the judicial branch of a government built upon a constitution is to set aside void action by government officials, and so to restrict executive action to the confines of the constitution. In our jurisprudence, no Government action which is void under the Constitution is exempt from judicial power. *Fourth.* The writ of habeas corpus is the established, time-honored process in our law for testing the authority of one who deprives another of his liberty, — 'the best and only sufficient defense of personal freedom.' . . ." 84 App. D.C. 396, 398, 399.

The doctrine that the term "any person" in the Fifth Amendment spreads its protection over alien enemies anywhere in the world engaged in hostilities against us, should be weighed in light of the full text of that Amendment: . . . .

When we analyze the claim prisoners are asserting and the court below sustained, it amounts to a right not to be tried at all for an offense against our armed forces. If the Fifth Amendment protects them from military trial, the Sixth Amendment as clearly prohibits their trial by civil courts. The latter requires in all criminal prosecutions that "the accused" be tried "by an impartial jury of the State and district wherein the crime shall have been committed, which district shall have been previously ascertained by law." And if the Fifth be held to embrace these prisoners because it uses the inclusive term "no person," the Sixth must, for it applies to all "accused." No suggestion is advanced by the court below or by prisoners of any constitutional method by which any violations of the laws of war endangering the United States forces could be reached or punished, if it were not by a Military Commission in the theatre where the offense was committed. . . .

If this Amendment invests enemy aliens in unlawful hostile action against us with immunity from military trial, it puts them in a more protected position than our own soldiers. . . .

The decision below would extend coverage of our Constitution to nonresident alien enemies denied to resident alien enemies. The latter are entitled only to judicial hearing to determine what the petition of these prisoners admits: that they are really alien enemies. When that appears, those resident here may be deprived of liberty by Executive action without hearing. Ludecke v. Watkins, 335 U.S. 160. While this is preventive rather than punitive detention, no reason is apparent why an alien enemy charged with having committed a crime should have greater immunities from Executive action than one who it is only feared might at some future time commit a hostile act.

If the Fifth Amendment confers its rights on all the world except Americans e aged in defending it, the same must be true of the companion civil-rights Amendments, for none of them is limited by its express terms, territorially or as to persons. Such a construction would mean that during military occupation irreconcilable enemy elements, guerrilla fighters, and "werewolves" could require the American Judiciary to assure them freedoms of speech, press, and assembly as in the First Amendment, right to bear arms as in the Second, security against "unreasonable" searches and seizures as in the Fourth, as well as rights to jury trial as in the Fifth and Sixth Amendments.

Such extraterritorial application of organic law would have been so significant an innovation in the practice of governments that, if intended or apprehended, it could scarcely have failed to excite contemporary comment. Not one word can be cited. No decision of this Court supports such a view. Cf. Downes v. Bidwell, 182 U.S. 244. None of the learned commentators on our Constitution has even hinted at it. The practice of every modern government is opposed to it.

We hold that the Constitution does not confer a right of personal security or an immunity from military trial and punishment upon an alien enemy engaged in the hostile service of a government at war with the United States.

IV

The Court of Appeals appears to have been of opinion that the petition shows some action by some official of the United States in excess of his authority which confers a private right to have it judicially voided. Its Second and Third propositions were that "action by Government officials in violation of the Constitution is void" and "a basic and inherent function of the judicial branch . . . is to set aside void action by government officials. . . ." For this reason it thought the writ could be granted. . . .

We are unable to find that the petition alleges any fact showing lack of jurisdiction in the military authorities to accuse, try and condemn these prisoners or that they acted in excess of their lawful powers.

V

. . . Since in the present application we find no basis for invoking federal judicial power in any district, we need not debate as to where, if the case were otherwise, the petition should be filed.

For reasons stated, the judgment of the Court of Appeals is reversed and the judgment of the District Court dismissing the petition is affirmed.

Reversed.

MR. JUSTICE BLACK, with whom MR. JUSTICE DOUGLAS and MR. JUSTICE BURTON concur, dissenting. . . .

This case tests the power of courts to exercise habeas corpus jurisdiction on behalf of aliens, imprisoned in Germany, under sentences imposed by the executive through military tribunals. The trial court held that, because the persons involved are imprisoned overseas, it had no territorial jurisdiction even to consider their petitions. The Court of Appeals reversed the District Court's dismissal on the ground that the judicial rather than the executive branch of government is vested with final authority to determine the legality of imprisonment for crime. 84 App. D.C. 396. This Court now affirms the District Court's dismissal. I agree with the Court of Appeals and need add little to the cogent reasons given for its decision. The broad reach of today's opinion, however, requires discussion. . . .

. . . The Court cannot, and despite its rhetoric on the point does not, deny that if they were imprisoned in the United States our courts would clearly have jurisdiction to hear their habeas corpus complaints. Does a prisoner's right to test legality of a sentence then depend on where the Government chooses to imprison him? Certainly, the Quirin and Yamashita opinions lend no support to that conclusion, for in upholding jurisdiction they place no reliance whatever on territorial location. The Court is fashioning wholly indefensible doctrine if it permits the executive branch, by deciding where its prisoners will be tried and imprisoned, to deprive all federal courts of their power to protect against a federal executive's illegal incarcerations.

If the opinion thus means, and it apparently does, that these petitioners are deprived of the privilege of habeas corpus solely because they were convicted and imprisoned overseas, the Court is adopting a broad and dangerous principle. The range of that principle is underlined by the argument of the Government brief that habeas corpus is not even available for American citizens convicted and imprisoned in Germany by American military tribunals. While the Court wisely disclaims any such necessary effect for its holding, rejection of the Government's argument is certainly made difficult by the logic of today's opinion. Conceivably a majority may hereafter find citizenship a sufficient substitute for territorial jurisdiction and thus permit courts to protect Americans from illegal sentences. But the Court's opinion inescapably denies courts power to afford the least bit of protection for any alien who is subject to our occupation government abroad, even if he is neither enemy nor belligerent and even after peace is officially declared.[3]

It would be fantastic to suggest that alien enemies could hail our military leaders into judicial tribunals to account for their day-to-day activities on the battlefront. Active fighting forces must be free to fight while hostilities are in progress. But that undisputable axiom has no bearing on this case or the general problem from which it arises.

When a foreign enemy surrenders, the situation changes markedly. If our country decides to occupy conquered territory either temporarily or permanently, it assumes the problem of deciding how the subjugated people will be ruled, what laws will govern, who will promulgate them, and what governmental agency of ours will see that they are properly administered. This responsibility immediately raises questions concerning the extent to which our domestic laws, constitutional and statutory, are transplanted abroad. Probably no one would suggest, and certainly I would not, that this nation either must or should attempt to apply every constitutional provision of the Bill of Rights in controlling temporarily occupied countries. But that does not mean that the Constitution is wholly inapplicable in foreign territories that we occupy and govern. See Downes v. Bidwell, 182 U.S. 244.

The question here involves a far narrower issue. Springing from recognition that our government is composed of three separate and independent branches, it is whether the judiciary has power in habeas corpus proceedings to test the legality of criminal sentences

---

[3] The Court indicates that not even today can a nonresident German or Japanese bring even a civil suit in American courts. With this restrictive philosophy compare Ex parte Kawato, 317 U.S. 69. See also McKenna v. Fisk, 1 How. 241, 249.

imposed by the executive through military tribunals in a country which we have occupied for years. The extent of such a judicial test of legality under charges like these, as we have already held in the Yamashita Case, is of most limited scope. We ask only whether the military tribunal was legally constituted and whether it had jurisdiction to impose punishment for the conduct charged. Such a limited habeas corpus review is the right of every citizen of the United States, civilian or soldier (unless the Court adopts the Government's argument that Americans imprisoned abroad have lost their right to habeas corpus). Any contention that a similarly limited use of habeas corpus for these prisoners would somehow give them a preferred position in the law cannot be taken seriously.

Though the scope of habeas corpus review of military tribunal sentences is narrow, I think it should not be denied to these petitioners and others like them. We control that part of Germany we occupy. These prisoners were convicted by our own military tribunals under our own Articles of War, years after hostilities had ceased. However illegal their sentences might be, they can expect no relief from German courts or any other branch of the German Government we permit to function. Only our own courts can inquire into the legality of their imprisonment. Perhaps, as some nations believe, there is merit in leaving the administration of criminal laws to executive and military agencies completely free from judicial scrutiny. Our Constitution has emphatically expressed a contrary policy.

As the Court points out, Paul was fortunate enough to be a Roman citizen when he was made the victim of prejudicial charges; that privileged status afforded him an appeal to Rome, with a right to meet his "accusers face to face." Acts 25:16. But other martyrized disciples were not so fortunate. Our Constitution has led people everywhere to hope and believe that wherever our laws control, all people, whether our citizens or not, would have an equal chance before the bar of criminal justice.

. . . Habeas corpus, as an instrument to protect against illegal imprisonment, is written into the Constitution. Its use by courts cannot in my judgment be constitutionally abridged by Executive or by Congress. I would hold that our courts can exercise it whenever any United States official illegally imprisons any person in any land we govern. Courts should not for any reason abdicate this, the loftiest power with which the Constitution has endowed them.

NOTE

For a review of authorities see Fairman, Some New Problems of the Constitution Following the Flag, 1 Stan. L. Rev. 587 (1949).

Removing a trial overseas. Toth was a civilian living in Pittsburgh, Pennsylvania. He was a former member of the armed forces of the United States and had served as such in Korea. He was arrested by military police in Pittsburgh and taken to Korea for trial by court-martial on a charge of having committed murder there while a member of the armed forces. A petition for habeas corpus was filed on his behalf in the United States District Court for the District of Columbia. What result? See United States ex rel. Toth v. Quarles, 350 U.S. 11 (1955).

Quaere: Could the Congress provide for holding terms of United States District Courts overseas, for the trial of dependents of the armed forces, and of civilian employees, thus affording the protections of Article III and the Fifth and Sixth Amendments and avoiding the problems presented by Reid v. Covert, 354 U.S. 1 (1957), page 1069 infra, and McElroy v. Guagliardo, 361 U.S. 281 (1960), discussed in a note, page 1074 infra. See Sutherland, The Constitution, the Civilian, and Military Justice, 36 St. John's L. Rev. 215 (1961). Compare the turning over of a soldier in the United States Army to the Japanese authorities for trial in a Japanese civil court on charges of a crime committed in Japan. Wilson v. Girard, 354 U.S. 524 (1957).

Chapter Twelve. The Constitution Overseas

An International Criminal Court? From time to time proposals have been made for the establishment of an International Criminal Court. See Pella, Towards an International Criminal Court, 44 Am. J. Intl. L. 37 (1905); Parker, An International Criminal Court: The Case for Its Adoption, 38 A.B.A.J. 641 (1952); Finch, An International Criminal Court: The Case Against Its Adoption, id. at 644 (1952).

Safeguards of Liberty and Property

Part Three

Chapter Thirteen

Acquisition and Deprivation of Nationality and Citizenship

Section A. ACQUISITION OF NATIONALITY AND CITIZENSHIP

Dred Scott v. Sandford 19 How. 393, 15 L. Ed. 691 (1857)

[Dred Scott, admittedly once a Negro slave but claiming now to be a citizen of Missouri, brought an action for trespass in the Circuit Court of the United States for the District of Missouri against John F. A. Sandford, a citizen of New York. The action was based on the theory that Dred Scott had become free when a former master took him into Illinois, and into the Territory of Louisiana north of the state of Missouri. In each of these areas slavery was forbidden — in Illinois by the state constitution, and in the Territory by the federal statute embodying the Missouri Compromise — the Act of March 6, 1820, 3 Stat. 545. Among other defenses to Scott's action, Sandford raised a question of federal jurisdiction, asserting that Scott was not a citizen of Missouri and had no standing in a federal court under the diversity provisions of Article III of the Constitution. In the circuit court, the plea to the jurisdiction failed, but the defendant won on the merits. Scott then brought his case to the Supreme Court by writ of error.]

TANEY, C.J., delivered the opinion of the court.[a] . . .

. . . [I]n the present instance, the plea in abatement is necessarily under consideration; and it becomes, therefore, our duty to decide whether the facts stated in the plea are or are

---

[a] The report of the case occupies 240 pages of 19 Howard. All nine Justices wrote opinions. Three (Wayne, Daniel, and Campbell), concurring with Chief Justice Taney, thought the case should be dismissed. One (Grier) concurred with the Chief Justice on the citizenship point, found the plaintiff not entitled to recover on the merits, and found the form of the disposition of the case of little importance. Two (Nelson and Catron) would affirm the judgment. Thus seven Justices held against Scott and his wife and children, whose status was also in issue. Two (McLean and Curtis) wrote for reversal. The extracts here printed concern only the citizenship point. Omitted are the discussions of the question whether the procedure below had foreclosed consideration in the Supreme Court of the citizenship point and the treatment of the highly controversial matter of the Fifth Amendment due process clause and the unconstitutionality of the Missouri Compromise. — ED.

not sufficient to show that the plaintiff is not entitled to sue as a citizen in a court of the United States.

This is certainly a very serious question, and one that now for the first time has been brought for decision before this court. But it is brought here by those who have a right to bring it, and it is our duty to meet it and decide it.

The question is simply this: can a negro, whose ancestors were imported into this country and sold as slaves, become a member of the political community formed and brought into existence by the Constitution of the United States, and as such become entitled to all rights, and privileges, and immunities, guaranteed by that instrument to the citizen. One of these rights is the privilege of suing in a court of the United States in the cases specified in the Constitution.

It will be observed, that the plea applies to that class of persons only whose ancestors were negroes of the African race, and imported into this country, and sold and held as slaves. The only matter in issue before the court, therefore, is, whether the descendants of such slaves, when they shall be emancipated, or who are born of parents who had become free before their birth, are citizens of a state, in the sense in which the word 'citizen' is used in the Constitution of the United States. . . .

We proceed to examine the case as presented by the pleadings.

The words "people of the United States" and "citizens" are synonymous terms, and mean the same thing. They both describe the political body, who, according to our republican institutions, form the sovereignty, and who hold the power and conduct the government through their representatives. They are what we familiarly call the "sovereign people," and every citizen is one of this people, and a constituent member of this sovereignty. The question before us is, whether the class of persons described in the plea in abatement compose a portion of this people, and are constituent members of this sovereignty. We think they are not, and that they are not included, and were not intended to be included, under the word "citizens" in the Constitution, and can, therefore, claim none of the rights and privileges which that instrument provides for and secures to citizens of the United States. On the contrary, they were at that time considered as a subordinate and inferior class of beings, who had been subjugated by the dominant race, and whether emancipated or not, yet remained subject to their authority, and had no rights or privileges but such as those who held the power and the government might choose to grant them.

It is not the province of the court to decide upon the justice or injustice, the policy or impolicy of these laws. The decision of that question belonged to the political or law-making power; to those who formed the sovereignty and framed the Constitution. The duty of the court is to interpret the instrument they have framed, with the best lights we can obtain on the subject, and to administer it as we find it, according to its true intent and meaning when it was adopted.

In discussing this question, we must not confound the rights of citizenship which a state may confer within its own limits, and the rights of citizenship as a member of the Union. It does not by any means follow, because he has all the rights and privileges of a citizen of a State, that he must be a citizen of the United States. He may have all the rights and privileges of the citizen of a State, and yet not be entitled to the rights and privileges of a citizen in any other State. For, previous to the adoption of the Constitution of the United States, every State had the undoubted right to confer on whomsoever it pleased the character of a citizen, and to endow him with all its rights. But this character, of course, was confined to the boundaries of the State, and gave him no rights or privileges in other States beyond those secured to him by the laws of nations and the comity of States. Nor have the several States surrendered the power of conferring these rights and privileges by adopting the Constitution of the United States. Each State may still confer them upon an alien, or any one it thinks proper, or upon any class or description of persons; yet he would not be a citizen in the sense in which that word is used in the Constitution of the United

States, nor entitled to sue as such in one of its courts, nor to the privileges and immunities of a citizen in the other States. The rights which he would acquire would be restricted to the State which gave them. The Constitution has conferred on Congress the right to establish an uniform rule of naturalization, and this right is evidently exclusive, and has always been held by this court to be so. Consequently, no State, since the adoption of the Constitution, can, by naturalizing an alien, invest him with the rights and privileges secured to a citizen of a State under the federal government, although, so far as the State alone was concerned, he would undoubtedly be entitled to the rights of a citizen, and clothed with all the rights and immunities which the Constitution and laws of the State attached to that character. . . .

The question then arises, whether the provisions of the Constitution, in relation to the personal rights and privileges to which the citizen of a State should be entitled, embraced the negro African race, at that time in this country, or who might afterwards be imported, who had then or should afterwards be made free in any State; and to put it in the power of a single State to make him a citizen of the United States, and endue him with the full rights of citizenship in every other State without their consent. Does the Constitution of the United States act upon him whenever he shall be made free under the laws of a State, and raised there to the rank of a citizen, and immediately clothe him with all the privileges of a citizen in every other State, and in its own courts?

The court think the affirmative of these propositions cannot be maintained. And if it cannot, the plaintiff in error could not be a citizen of the State of Missouri, within the meaning of the Constitution of the United States, and, consequently, was not entitled to sue in its courts. . . .

In the opinion of the court, the legislation and histories of the times, and the language used in the Declaration of Independence, show, that neither the class of persons who had been imported as slaves, nor their descendants, whether they had become free or not, were then acknowledged as a part of the people, nor intended to be included in the general words used in that memorable instrument.

It is difficult at this day to realize the state of public opinion in relation to that unfortunate race, which prevailed in the civilized and enlightened portions of the world at the time of the Declaration of Independence, and when the Constitution of the United States was framed and adopted. But the public history of every European nation displays it, in a manner too plain to be mistaken.

They had for more than a century before been regarded as beings of an inferior order; and altogether unfit to associate with the white race, either in social or political relations; and so far inferior, that they had no rights which the white man was bound to respect; and that the negro might justly and lawfully be reduced to slavery for his benefit. He was bought and sold, and treated as an ordinary article of merchandise and traffic, whenever a profit could be made by it. This opinion was at that time fixed and universal in the civilized portion of the white race. It was regarded as an axiom in morals as well as in politics, which no one thought of disputing, or supposed to be open to dispute; and men in every grade and position in society daily and habitually acted upon it in their private pursuits, as well as in matters of public concern, without doubting for a moment the correctness of this opinion.

And in no nation was this opinion more firmly fixed or more uniformly acted upon than by the English government and English people. They not only seized them on the coast of Africa, and sold them or held them in slavery for their own use; but they took them as ordinary articles of merchandise to every country where they could make a profit on them, and were far more extensively engaged in this commerce than any other nation in the world.

The opinion thus entertained and acted upon in England was naturally impressed upon the colonies they founded on this side of the Atlantic. And, accordingly, a negro of the African race was regarded by them as an article of property, and held, and bought and sold as such, in every one of the thirteen Colonies which united in the Declaration of Independence, and afterwards formed the Constitution of the United States. The slaves were more or less numerous in the different Colonies, as slave labor was found more or less profitable. But no one seems to have doubted the correctness of the prevailing opinion of the time.

[The Court then referred to Maryland and Massachusetts colonial legislation penalizing interracial marriages.]

We refer to these historical facts for the purpose of showing the fixed opinions concerning that race, upon which the statesmen of that day spoke and acted. It is necessary to do this, in order to determine whether the general terms used in the Constitution of the United States, as to the rights of man and the rights of the people, [were] intended to include them, or to give to them or their posterity the benefit of any of its provisions.

The language of the Declaration of Independence is equally conclusive.

It begins by declaring that, "when in the course of human events it becomes necessary for one people to dissolve the political bands which have connected them with another, and to assume among the powers of the earth the separate and equal station to which the laws of nature and nature's God entitle them, a decent respect for the opinions of mankind requires that they should declare the causes which impel them to the separation."

It then proceeds to say: "We hold these truths to be self-evident: that all men are created equal; that they are endowed by their Creator with certain inalienable rights; that among them is life, liberty, and pursuit of happiness; that to secure these rights, governments are instituted, deriving their just powers from the consent of the governed."

The general words above quoted would seem to embrace the whole human family, and if they were used in a similar instrument at this day, would be so understood. But it is too clear for dispute, that the enslaved African race were not intended to be included, and formed no part of the people who framed and adopted this Declaration; for if the language, as understood in that day, would embrace them, the conduct of the distinguished men who framed the Declaration of Independence would have been utterly and flagrantly inconsistent with the principles they asserted; and instead of the sympathy of mankind, to which they so confidently appealed, they would have deserved and received universal rebuke and reprobation.

Yet the men who framed this Declaration were great men — high in literary acquirements — high in their sense of honor, and incapable of asserting principles inconsistent with those on which they were acting. They perfectly understood the meaning of the language they used, and how it would be understood by others; and they knew that it would not, in any part of the civilized world, be supposed to embrace the negro race, which, by common consent, had been excluded from civilized governments and the family of nations, and doomed to slavery. They spoke and acted according to the then established doctrines and principles, and in the ordinary language of the day, and no one misunderstood them. The unhappy black race were separated from the white by indelible marks, and laws long before established, and were never thought of or spoken of except as property, and when the claims of the owners or the profit of the trader were supposed to need protection.

This state of public opinion had undergone no change when the Constitution was adopted, as is equally evident from its provisions and language. . . .

But there are two clauses in the Constitution which point directly and specifically to the negro race as a separate class of persons, and show clearly that they were not regarded as a portion of the people or citizens of the government then formed.

One of these clauses reserves to each of the thirteen States the right to import slaves until the year 1808, if it thinks proper. . . . And by the other provision the States pledge themselves to each other to maintain the right of property of the master, by delivering up to him any slave who may have escaped from his service, and be found within their respective territories. . . . And these two provisions show, conclusively, that neither the description of persons therein referred to, nor their descendants, were embraced in any of the other provisions of the Constitution; for certainly these two clauses were not intended to confer on them or their posterity the blessings of liberty, or any of the personal rights so carefully provided for the citizen. . . .

No one, we presume, supposes that any change in public opinion or feeling in relation to this unfortunate race, in the civilized nations of Europe or in this country, should induce the court to give to the words of the Constitution a more liberal construction in their favor than they were intended to bear when the instrument was framed and adopted. Such an argument would be altogether inadmissible in any tribunal called on to interpret it. If any of its provisions are deemed unjust, there is a mode prescribed in the instrument itself by which it may be amended; but while it remains unaltered, it must be construed now as it was understood at the time of its adoption. It is not only the same in words, but the same in meaning, and delegates the same powers to the government, and reserves and secures the same rights and privileges to the citizen; and as long as it continues to exist in its present form, it speaks not only in the same words, but with the same meaning and intent with which it spoke when it came from the hands of its framers, and was voted on and adopted by the people of the United States. Any other rule of construction would abrogate the judicial character of this court, and make it the mere reflex of the popular opinion or passion of the day. This court was not created by the Constitution for such purposes. Higher and graver trusts have been confided to it, and it must not falter in the path of duty. . . .

And upon a full and careful consideration of the subject, the court is of opinion that, upon the facts stated in the plea in abatement, Dred Scott was not a citizen of Missouri within the meaning of the Constitution of the United States, and not entitled as such to sue in its courts; and, consequently, that the Circuit Court had no jurisdiction of the case, and that the judgment on the plea in abatement is erroneous. . . .

Its judgment for the defendant must, consequently, be reversed, and a mandate issued directing the suit to be dismissed for want of jurisdiction.

[JUSTICES McLEAN and CURTIS dissented. MR. JUSTICE CURTIS summarized his view of the jurisdictional question as follows:] [b]

The conclusions at which I have arrived on this part of the case are:

First. That the free native-born citizens of each State are citizens of the United States.

Second. That as free colored persons born within some of the States are citizens of those States, such persons are also citizens of the United States.

Third. That every such citizen, residing in any State, has the right to sue and is liable to be sued in the federal courts, as a citizen of that State in which he resides.

Fourth. That as the plea to the jurisdiction in this case shows no facts, except that the plaintiff was of African descent, and his ancestors were sold as slaves, and as these facts are not inconsistent with his citizenship of the United States, and his residence in the State of Missouri, the plea to the jurisdiction was bad, and the judgment of the Circuit Court overruling it, was correct.

I dissent, therefore, from that part of the opinion of the majority of the court, in which it is held that a person of African descent cannot be a citizen of the United States; . . . .

---

[b] 19 How. at 588. See, for background material on the Dred Scott case, 2 Warren, The Supreme Court in United States History 279 (1926); Hopkins, Dred Scott's Case (1951); Swisher, The Taney Period (V Holmes Devise History of the Supreme Court) c. 24 (1974). The Scott family was manumitted in May 1857, a little over two months after the decision of the case. Dred Scott, by this time something of a celebrity, became a porter at a St. Louis hotel. See, for the circumstances of the manumission, and the subsequent history, of the family, Hopkins, id. at 176, 177. — ED.

United States v. Wong Kim Ark 169 U.S. 649, 18 S. Ct. 456, 42 L. Ed. 890 (1898)

Statement by Mr. Justice Gray:

This was a writ of habeas corpus issued October 2, 1898, by the district court of the United States for the northern district of California, to the collector of customs at the port of San Francisco, in behalf of Wong Kim Ark, who alleged that he was a citizen of the United States [and that the collector refused to permit him to land from a steamship].

At the hearing, the district attorney of the United States was permitted to intervene in behalf of the United States in opposition to the writ, and stated the grounds of his intervention in writing as follows: . . .

"That the said Wong Kim Ark is not entitled to land in the United States, or to be or remain therein, because he does not belong to any of the privileged classes enumerated in any of the acts of Congress, known as the Chinese exclusion acts, which would exempt him from the class or classes which are especially excluded from the United States by the provisions of the said acts. . . ."

The case was submitted to the decision of the court upon the following facts agreed by the parties:

"That the said Wong Kim Ark was born in the year of 1873, at No. 751 Sacramento Street, in the city and county of San Francisco, state of California, United States of America, and that his mother and father were persons of Chinese descent and subjects of the Emperor of China, and that said Wong Kim Ark was and is a laborer.

"That at the time of his said birth his mother and father were domiciled residents of the United States, ...

"That during all the time of their said residence in the United States as domiciled residents therein the said mother and father of said Wong Kim Ark were engaged in the prosecution of business and were never engaged in any diplomatic or official capacity under the Emperor of China. . . .

"That in the year 1890 the said Wong Kim Ark departed for China upon a temporary visit and with the intention of returning to the United States, and did return thereto on July 26, 1890, on the steamship Gaelic, and was permitted to enter the United States by the collector of customs upon the sole ground that he was a native born citizen of the United States.

"That after his said return the said Wong Kim Ark remained in the United States, claiming to be a citizen thereof, until the year 1894, when he again departed for China upon a temporary visit, and with the intention of returning to the United States, and did return thereto in the month of August, 1895, and applied to the collector of customs to be permitted to land; and that such application was denied upon the sole ground that said Wong Kim Ark was not a citizen of the United States.

"That said Wong Kim Ark has not, either by himself or his parents acting for him, ever renounced his allegiance to the United States, and that he has never done or committed any act or thing to exclude him therefrom."

The court ordered Wong Kim Ark to be discharged, upon the ground that he was a citizen of the United States. 71 Fed. Rep. 382. The United States appealed to this court.

Mr. Justice Gray delivered the opinion of the court: . . .

The question presented by the record is whether a child born in the United States, of parents of Chinese descent, who at the time of his birth are subjects of the Emperor of China, but have a permanent domicil and residence in the United States, and are there carrying on business, and are not employed in any diplomatic or official capacity under the Emperor of China, becomes at the time of his birth a citizen of the United States, by virtue of the first clause of the 14th Amendment of the Constitution: "All persons born or naturalized in the United States, and subject to the jurisdiction thereof, are citizens of the United States and of the state wherein they reside."

Section A. Acquisition of Nationality and Citizenship

I. . . . .

The Constitution nowhere defines the meaning of these words, ... In this, as in other respects, it must be interpreted in the light of the common law, the principles and history of which were familiarly known to the framers of the Constitution. . . .

II. The fundamental principle of the common law with regard to English nationality was birth within the allegiance, also called "ligealty," "obedience," "faith," or "power," of the King. The principle embraced all persons born within the King's allegiance and subject to his protection. . . .

It thus clearly appears that by the law of England for the last three centuries, beginning before the settlement of this country, and continuing to the present day, aliens, while residing in the dominions possessed by the Crown of England, were within the allegiance, the obedience, the faith or loyalty, the protection, the power, the jurisdiction, of the English sovereign; and therefore every child born in England of alien parents was a natural-born subject, unless the child of an ambassador or other diplomatic agent of a foreign state, or of an alien enemy in hostile occupation of the place where the child was born.

III. The same rule was in force in all the English colonies upon this continent down to the time of the Declaration of Independence, and in the United States afterwards, and continued to prevail under the Constitution as originally established.

In the early case of The Charming Betsy [Murray v. The Charming Betsy] (1804), it appears to have been assumed by this court that all persons born in the United States were citizens of the United States; Chief Justice Marshall saying: "Whether a person born within the United States, or becoming a citizen according to the established laws of the country, can devest himself absolutely of that character otherwise than in such manner as may be prescribed by law, is a question which it is not necessary at present to decide." 2 Cranch, 64, 119. . . .

IV. . . . .

Passing by questions once earnestly controverted, but finally put at rest by the 14th Amendment of the Constitution, it is beyond doubt that, before the enactment of the civil rights act of 1866, or the adoption of the constitutional amendment, all white persons, at least, born within the sovereignty of the United States, whether children of citizens or of foreigners, excepting only children of ambassadors or public ministers of a foreign government, were native born citizens of the United States.

V. In the forefront, both of the 14th Amendment of the Constitution, and of the civil rights act of 1866, the fundamental principle of citizenship by birth within the dominion was reaffirmed in the most explicit and comprehensive terms.

The civil rights act, passed at the first session of the Thirty-ninth Congress, began by enacting that "all persons born in the United States and not subject to any foreign power, excluding Indians not taxed, are hereby declared to be citizens of the United States; and such citizens, of every race and color, without regard to any previous condition of slavery or involuntary servitude, except as a punishment for crime whereof the party shall have been duly convicted, shall have the same right, in every state and territory in the United States, to make and enforce contracts, to sue, be parties, and give evidence, to inherit, purchase, lease, sell, hold, and convey real and personal property, and to full and equal benefit of all laws and proceedings for the security of person and property, as is enjoyed by white citizens, and shall be subject to like punishment, pains, and penalties, and to none other, any law, statute, ordinance, regulation, or custom to the contrary notwithstanding." Act of April 9, 1866 (14 Stat. at L. 27, chap. 31, §1).

The same Congress, shortly afterwards, evidently thinking it unwise, and perhaps unsafe, to leave so important a declaration of rights to depend upon an ordinary act of legislation, which might be repealed by any subsequent Congress, framed the 14th Amendment of the Constitution, and on June 16, 1866, by joint resolution proposed it to the legislatures of the several states; and on July 28, 1868, the Secretary of State issued a proclamation showing it to have been ratified by the legislatures of the requisite number of states. 14 Stat. at L. 358; 15 Stat. at L. 708.

736   Chapter Thirteen.   **Nationality and Citizenship**

The 1st section of the 14th Amendment of the Constitution begins with the words, "all persons born or naturalized in the United States, and subject to the jurisdiction thereof, are citizens of the United States and of the state wherein they reside." As appears upon the face of the Amendment, as well as from the history of the times, this was not intended to impose any new restrictions upon citizenship, or to prevent any persons from becoming citizens by the fact of birth within the United States, who would thereby have become citizens according to the law existing before its adoption. It is declaratory in form, and enabling and extending in effect. Its main purpose doubtless was, as has been often recognized by this court, to establish the citizenship of free negroes, which had been denied in the opinion delivered by Chief Justice Taney in Dred Scott v. Sandford (1857) 19 How. 393, and to put it beyond doubt that all blacks, as well as whites, born or naturalized within the jurisdiction of the United States, are citizens of the United States. The Slaughter-House Cases (1873) 16 Wall. 36, 73. . . .

The only adjudication that has been made by this court upon the meaning of the clause, "and subject to the jurisdiction thereof," in the leading provision of the 14th Amendment, is Elk v. Wilkins, 112 U.S. 94, in which it was decided that an Indian born a member of one of the Indian tribes within the United States, which still existed and was recognized as an Indian tribe by the United States, who had voluntarily separated himself from his tribe, and taken up his residence among the white citizens of a state, but who did not appear to have been naturalized, or taxed, or in any way recognized or treated as a citizen, either by the United States or by the state, was not a citizen of the United States, as a person born in the United States, "and subject to the jurisdiction thereof," within the meaning of the clause in question.

That decision was placed upon the grounds that the meaning of those words was, "not merely subject in some respect or degree to the jurisdiction of the United States, but completely subject to their political jurisdiction, and owing them direct and immediate allegiance;" that by the Constitution, as originally established, "Indians not taxed" were excluded from the persons according to whose numbers representatives in Congress and direct taxes were apportioned among the several states, and Congress was empowered to regulate commerce, not only "with foreign nations" and among the several states, but "with the Indian tribes;" that the Indian tribes, being within the territorial limits of the United States, were not, strictly speaking, foreign states but were alien nations, distinct political communities, the members of which owed immediate allegiance to their several tribes, and were not part of the people of the United States; . . . 112 U.S. 99-103.

Mr. Justice Harlan and Mr. Justice Woods, dissenting, were of opinion that the Indian in question, having severed himself from his tribe and become a bona fide resident of a state, had thereby become subject to the jurisdiction of the United States, within the meaning of the 14th Amendment; . . . .

The decision in Elk v. Wilkins concerned only members of the Indian tribes within the United States, and had no tendency to deny citizenship to children born in the United States of foreign parents of Caucasian, African, or Mongolian descent, not in the diplomatic service of a foreign country.[c]

The real object of the 14th Amendment of the Constitution, in qualifying the words,

---

[c] Section 301 of the Immigration and Nationality Act, June 27, 1952, Pub. L. No. 414, 82d Cong., 2d Sess., c. 477, 66 Stat. 235, 8 U.S.C. §1401, provides in part:

"(a) The following shall be nationals and citizens of the United States at birth:

"(1) a person born in the United States and subject to the jurisdiction thereof;

"(2) a person born in the United States to a member of an Indian, Eskimo, Aleutian, or other aboriginal tribe: *Provided*, That the granting of citizenship under this subsection shall not in any manner impair or otherwise affect the right of such person to tribal or other property; . . ." [Remainder of §1401 here omitted.]

Section 101(a)(38) [8 U.S.C. §1101(a)(38)]. "The term 'United States,' except as otherwise specifically herein provided, when used in a geographical sense, means the continental United States, Alaska, Hawaii, Puerto Rico, Guam, and the Virgin Islands of the United States." — ED.

"all persons born in the United States," by the addition, "and subject to the jurisdiction thereof," would appear to have been to exclude, by the fewest and fittest words (besides children of members of the Indian tribes, standing in a peculiar relation to the national government, unknown to the common law), the two classes of cases — children born of alien enemies in hostile occupation, and children of diplomatic representatives of a foreign state — both of which, as has already been shown by the law of England, and by our own law, from the time of the first settlement of the English colonies in America, had been recognized exceptions to the fundamental rule of citizenship by birth within the country. Calvin's Case, 7 Rep. 1, 18b; Cockburn, Nationality, 7; Dicey, Confl. Laws, 177; Inglis v. Sailor's Snug Harbor, 3 Pet. 99, 155; 2 Kent, Com. 39, 42. . . .

To hold that the 14th Amendment of the Constitution excludes from citizenship the children, born in the United States, of citizens or subjects of other countries, would be to deny citizenship to thousands of persons of English, Scotch, Irish, German, or other European parentage, who have always been considered and treated as citizens of the United States.

VI. Whatever considerations, in the absence of a controlling provision of the Constitution, might influence the legislative or the executive branch of the government to decline to admit persons of the Chinese race to the status of citizens of the United States, there are none that can constrain or permit the judiciary to refuse to give full effect to the peremptory and explicit language of the 14th Amendment, which declares and ordains that "all persons born or naturalized in the United States, and subject to the jurisdiction thereof, are citizens of the United States."

Chinese persons, born out of the United States, remaining subjects of the Emperor of China, and not having become citizens of the United States, are entitled to the protection of and owe allegiance to the United States so long as they are permitted by the United States to reside here; and are "subject to the jurisdiction thereof," in the same sense as all other aliens residing in the United States. Yick Wo v. Hopkins (1886) 118 U.S. 356. . . .

In Yick Wo v. Hopkins the decision was that an ordinance of the city of San Francisco, regulating a certain business, and which, as executed by the board of supervisors, made an arbitrary discrimination between natives of China, still subjects of the Emperor of China, but domiciled in the United States, and all other persons, was contrary to the 14th Amendment of the Constitution. . . .

The decision in Yick Wo v. Hopkins, indeed, did not directly pass upon the effect of these words in the 14th Amendment, but turned upon subsequent provisions of the same section. But, as already observed, it is impossible to attribute to the words, "subject to the jurisdiction thereof," that is to say, of the United States, at the beginning, a less comprehensive meaning than to the words "within its jurisdiction," that is, of the state, at the end of the same section; or to hold that persons, who are indisputably "within the jurisdiction" of the state, are not "subject to the jurisdiction" of the nation.

It necessarily follows that persons born in China, subjects of the Emperor of China, but domiciled in the United States, having been adjudged, in Yick Wo v. Hopkins, to be within the jurisdiction of the state, within the meaning of the concluding sentence, must be held to be subject to the jurisdiction of the United States, within the meaning of the first sentence of this section of the Constitution; and their children, "born in the United States," cannot be less "subject to the jurisdiction thereof." . . .

VII. Upon the facts agreed in this case, the American citizenship which Wong Kim Ark acquired by birth within the United States has not been lost or taken away by anything happening since his birth. No doubt he might himself, after coming of age, renounce this citizenship, and become a citizen of the country of his parents, or of any other country; for by our law, as solemnly declared by Congress, "the right of expatriation is a natural and inherent right of all people," and "any declaration, instruction, opinion, order, or decision of any officer of the United States which denies, restricts, impairs, or questions the right of expatriation, is declared inconsistent with the fundamental principles of the Republic." Rev. Stat. §1999, re-enacting act of July 27, 1868 (15 Stat. at L. 223, 224, chap. 249, §1). Whether any act of himself, or of his parents, during his minority, could have the same effect, is at least doubtful. But it would be out of place to pursue that inquiry; inasmuch as it is expressly agreed that his residence has always been in the United States, and not elsewhere; that each of his temporary visits to China, the one for some months when he was about seventeen years old, and the other something like a year about the time of his coming of age, was made with the intention of returning, and was followed by his actual return, to the United States; and "that said Wong Kim Ark has not, either by himself or his parents acting for him, ever renounced his allegiance to the United States, and that he has never done or committed any act or thing to exclude him therefrom."

The evident intention, and the necessary effect, of the submission of this case to the decision of the court upon the facts agreed by the parties, were to present for determination the single question, stated at the beginning of this opinion, namely, whether a child born in the United States, of parents of Chinese descent, who, at the time of his birth, are subjects of the Emperor of China, but have a permanent domicil and residence in the United States, and are there carrying on business, and are not employed in any diplomatic or official capacity under the Emperor of China, becomes at the time of his birth a citizen of the United States. For the reasons above stated, this court is of opinion that the question must be answered in the affirmative. Order affirmed.

MR. JUSTICE MCKENNA, not having been a member of the court when this case was argued, took no part in the decision.

MR. CHIEF JUSTICE FULLER, with whom concurred MR. JUSTICE HARLAN, dissenting: . . . .

HAMMERSTEIN v. LYNE, 200 F. 165 (W.D. Mo. 1912). Felice Lyne was born in Missouri. In 1907 she gave up her home in Kansas City, Missouri, and went with her mother to live in Paris, France, and began an operatic career. Later she moved to London, where she made her home thereafter. In 1912 she came to the United States on a temporary visit and contracted with Oscar Hammerstein, a well-known impresario, to place herself under his exclusive management for the season of 1912-1913, and to pay him one half of her receipts from musical performances. On October 7, 1912, Miss Lyne appeared in a musical production at Kansas City, Missouri, and received a substantial sum of money for her services. She did not pay Mr. Hammerstein his share of this sum, and he brought an action against her in the federal courts in Missouri for an accounting, and an injunction.

Assuming that Mr. Hammerstein duly made personal service on Miss Lyne in the state of Missouri, can he maintain his action in the federal court within the terms of Article III, §2, of the Federal Constitution?

COOK v. TAIT, Collector of Internal Revenue, 265 U.S. 47, 44 S. Ct. 444, 68 L. Ed. 895 (1924). George W. Cook, a citizen of the United States, moved to Mexico and made his home there. He acquired certain real and personal property located in Mexico from which he derived an income. A United States Collector of Internal Revenue made a demand on Mr. Cook for payment of an income tax on the income so derived. Mr. Cook paid the first installment of tax under protest and brought an action against the collector to recover the tax. Can the collector retain the money?

NOTE Problems of Naturalization

In Chirac v. Chirac, 2 Wheat. 259, 269 (1817), Marshall, C.J., wrote: "That the power of naturalization is exclusively in Congress does not seem to be, and certainly ought not to be controverted; . . . . ." In Holmgren v. United States, 217 U.S. 509 (1910), the Supreme Court upheld the delegation to state courts of the functions of naturalization under the federal legislation.

In United States v. Schwimmer, 279 U.S. 644 (1929), the Supreme Court of the United States held that a woman who stated in her application for naturalization that she would not be willing to take up arms in defense of the United States was ineligible for naturalization although no statute in terms called for such willingness. Mr. Justice Holmes, dissenting, wrote, "It is agreed that she is qualified for citizenship except so far as the views set forth in a statement of fact may show that the applicant is not attached to the principles of the Constitution of the United States. . . . She is an optimist and states in strong and, I do not doubt, sincere words belief that war will disappear and that the impending destiny of mankind is to unite in peaceful leagues. I do not share that optimism nor do I think that a philosophic view of the world would regard war as absurd. But most people who have known it regard it with horror, as a last resort, and, even if not yet ready for cosmopolitan efforts would welcome any practicable combinations that would increase the power on the side of peace. . . . Some of her answers might excite popular prejudice, but if there is any principle of the Constitution that more imperatively calls for attachment than any other, it is the principle of free thought — not free thought for those who agree with us but freedom for the thought that we hate. . . . I would suggest that the Quakers have done their share to make the country what it is, that many citizens agree with the applicant's belief, that I had not supposed hitherto that we regretted our inability to expel them because they believe more than some of us do in the teachings of the Sermon on the Mount."

In United States v. MacIntosh, 283 U.S. 605 (1931), United States v. Schwimmer was followed. MacIntosh was a member of the faculty of the Yale Divinity School who had, during the war of 1914-1918, voluntarily served as a chaplain with the Canadian Army, and then been in charge of an American YMCA hut in France. He was denied naturalization, because, in the course of the proceedings, he insisted on qualifying his oath of allegiance by reserving to his own opinion the determination whether any war was necessarily or morally justified, as a condition to his bearing arms in defense of the United States.

In Girouard v. United States, 328 U.S. 61 (1946), a conscientious objector who refused to bear arms was admitted to citizenship; the Schwimmer and MacIntosh cases and a similar case, United States v. Bland, 283 U.S. 636 (1931), were all overruled. The argument that the Congress, by enacting the Nationality Act of 1940 and reenacting the naturalization oath in its preexisting form, had adopted and reenacted the rule of the Schwimmer, MacIntosh, and Bland cases, was rejected by the majority of the Court. Mr. Justice Stone, who had dissented in the MacIntosh and Bland cases, dissented in the Girouard case on the ground that the Congress in the Nationality Act of 1940 had adopted and confirmed the previous construction given by the Court to the nationality act. Justices Reed and Frankfurter joined in the opinion of Mr. Justice Stone.

The present United States statutory provisions on nationality and naturalization are found in the Immigration and Nationality Act, June 27, 1952, Pub. L. No. 414, 82d Cong., 2d Sess., c. 477, 66 Stat. 166, 8 U.S.C. §§1101 et seq., as amended.

Section B. VOLUNTARY RENUNCIATION OF NATIONALITY

THOMAS JEFFERSON, President of the United States, Letter to Albert Gallatin, Secretary of the Treasury, June 26, 1806. 8 Ford, The Writings of Thomas Jefferson 458 (1897).

"The Attorney-General being absent, we must decide for ourselves the question raised by Colonel Newton's letter, whether Mr. Cooper can own a registered vessel? or, in other words, whether he is a citizen of the United States?

"I hold the right of expatriation to be inherent in every man by the laws of nature, and incapable of being rightfully taken from him even by the united will of every other person in the nation. If the laws have provided no particular mode by which the right of expatriation may be exercised, the individual may do it by any effectual and unequivocal act or declaration. The laws of Virginia have provided a mode; Mr. Cooper is said to have exercised his right solemnly and exactly according to that mode, and to have departed from the Commonwealth; whereupon the law declares that 'he shall thenceforth be deemed no citizen.' Returning afterwards he returns an alien, and must proceed to make himself a citizen if he desires it, as every other alien does. At present he can hold no lands, receive nor transmit any inheritance, nor enjoy any other right peculiar to a citizen.

"The general government has nothing to do with this question. Congress may by the Constitution 'establish an uniform rule of naturalization,' that is, by what rule an alien may become a citizen. But they cannot take from a citizen his natural right of divesting himself of the character of a citizen by expatriation."

NOTE What Constitutes Voluntary Renunciation

In 1868 Congress explicitly recognized that the "right of expatriation is a natural and inherent right of all people." 15 Stat. 223, R.S. §1999. It first began to define the acts by which citizens could be held to have renunciated their citizenship with the Expatriation Act of 1907. A later consolidation, §401 of the Nationality Act of 1940, 54 Stat. 1137, 1168, provided:

"A person who is a national of the United States, whether by birth or naturalization, shall lose his nationality by:

"(a) Obtaining naturalization in a foreign state . . . ; or

"(b) Taking an oath or making an affirmation or other formal declaration of allegiance to a foreign state; or

"(c) Entering, or serving in, the armed forces of a foreign state unless expressly authorized by the laws of the United States, if he has or acquires the nationality of such foreign state; or

"(d) Accepting, or performing the duties of, any office, post, or employment under the government of a foreign state or political subdivision thereof for which only nationals of such state are eligible; . . . ."

In Kawakita v. United States, 343 U.S. 717 (1952), the petitioner, a national of both the United States and Japan, sought to avoid a conviction of treason with the defense that he had voluntarily renounced his nationality. Because he had been born in this country of Japanese parents who were citizens of Japan, wrote Justice Douglas for the Court, "he was thus a citizen of the United States by birth (Amendment XIV, §1) and, by reason of Japanese law, a national of Japan." He traveled to Japan shortly before the war and registered as an alien with the Japanese police. He did not serve in the Japanese military during the war but instead finished his schooling and worked for private industry. In 1943, however, he did register in the Koseki, a family census register.

The Court in Kawakita sustained the finding that these actions, as a matter of law, did not amount to a renunciation of nationality under §401. Under the concept of dual nationality, his enrollment in the Koseki could be read simply as a reassertion of his Japanese nationality, and not necessarily as a rejection of his American citizenship. In addition, his work in industry did not amount to the performance of the duties of any "state" office. Because the issue had not been "squarely presented," the Court did not reach the question whether there were other methods, beyond those listed in §401, for a voluntary renunciation of nationality. He had been convicted of treasonous acts toward American prisoners of war; the Court rejected his claim that the crime of treason, Art. 3, §3, contained a territorial limitation. Justices Vinson, Black, and Burton dissented.

Section 401 of the 1940 Nationality Act, as amended in 1944, 58 Stat. 746, also provided for loss of citizenship by:

"(e) Voting in a political election in a foreign state or participating in an election or plebiscite to determine the sovereignty over foreign territory; or . . .

"(j) Departing from or remaining outside of the jurisdiction of the United States in time of war or during a period declared by the President to be a period of national emergency for the purpose of evading or avoiding training and service in the land or naval forces of the United States."

In Perez v. Brownell, 356 U.S. 46 (1958), the petitioner sued for a declaratory judgment that he was still a national even though he "had remained outside of the United States from November 1944 to July 1947 for the purpose of avoiding service in the armed forces of the United States and that he had voted in a 'political election' in Mexico in 1946." Justice Frankfurter, writing for the Court, upheld the constitutionality of §401(e) as an exercise of congressional power to deal with foreign affairs. The loss of citizenship, he agreed, was reasonably calculated to prevent the "embarrassment in the conduct of our foreign relations attributable to voting by American citizens in foreign political elections." In support of congressional power over citizenship, he relied, in part, upon the 1915 case of MacKenzie v. Hare, 239 U.S. 299. By a 1907 statute, since repealed, a native-born citizen and resident had become an alien when she married a subject of Great Britain. There as well, the Court sustained that Act under the foreign policy power to avoid "embarrassment." With §401(e) upheld in Perez, the Court found it unnecessary to consider §401(j).

Compare Trop v. Dulles, 356 U.S. 86 (1958), where the Court struck down, as cruel and unusual punishment, the loss of citizenship under §401(g) for a person who had been convicted by court-martial of wartime desertion and dishonorably discharged. For the current law on expatriation see Immigration and Nationality Act, June 27, 1952, Pub. L. No. 414, 82d Cong., 2d Sess., c. 477, tit. 3, c. 3 (Loss of Nationality), 66 Stat. 267, 8 U.S.C. §§1481-1489, as amended.

Afroyim v. Rusk *387 U.S. 253, 87 S. Ct. 1660, 18 L. Ed. 2d 757 (1967)*

MR. JUSTICE BLACK delivered the opinion of the Court.

Petitioner, born in Poland in 1893, immigrated to this country in 1912 and became a naturalized American citizen in 1926. He went to Israel in 1950, and in 1951 he voluntarily voted in an election for the Israeli Knesset, the legislative body of Israel. In 1960, when he applied for renewal of his United States passport, the Department of State refused to grant it on the sole ground that he had lost his American citizenship by virtue of §401(e) of the Nationality Act of 1940 which provides that a United States citizen shall "lose" his citizenship if he votes "in a political election in a foreign state.". . .

The fundamental issue before this Court here, as it was in Perez, is whether Congress can consistently with the Fourteenth Amendment enact a law stripping an American of his citizenship which he has never voluntarily renounced or given up. The majority in Perez held that Congress could do this because withdrawal of citizenship is "reasonably calculated to effect the end that is within the power of Congress to achieve." 356 U.S., at 60. That conclusion was reached by this chain of reasoning: Congress has an implied power to deal with foreign affairs as an indispensable attribute of sovereignty; this implied power, plus the Necessary and Proper Clause, empowers Congress to regulate voting by American citizens in foreign elections; involuntary expatriation is within the "ample scope" of "appropriate modes" Congress can adopt to effectuate its general regulatory power. Id., at 57-60. Then, upon summarily concluding that "there is nothing in the

... Fourteenth Amendment to warrant drawing from it a restriction upon the power otherwise possessed by Congress to withdraw citizenship," id., at 58, n.3, the majority specifically rejected the "notion that the power of Congress to terminate citizenship depends upon the citizen's assent," id., at 61.

First we reject the idea expressed in Perez that, aside from the Fourteenth Amendment, Congress has any general power, express or implied, to take away an American citizen's citizenship without his assent. This power cannot, as Perez indicated, be sustained as an implied attribute of sovereignty possessed by all nations. Other nations are governed by their own constitutions, if any, and we can draw no support from theirs. In our country the people are sovereign and the Government cannot sever its relationship to the people by taking away their citizenship. Our Constitution governs us and we must never forget that our Constitution limits the Government to those powers specifically granted or those that are necessary and proper to carry out the specifically granted ones. The Constitution, of course, grants Congress no express power to strip people of their citizenship, whether in the exercise of the implied power to regulate foreign affairs or in the exercise of any specifically granted power. . . .

[A]ny doubt as to whether prior to the passage of the Fourteenth Amendment Congress had the power to deprive a person against his will of citizenship once obtained should have been removed by the unequivocal terms of the Amendment itself. It provides its own constitutional rule in language calculated completely to control the status of citizenship: "All persons born or naturalized in the United States . . . are citizens of the United States. . . ." There is no indication in these words of a fleeting citizenship, good at the moment it is acquired but subject to destruction by the Government at any time. Rather the Amendment can most reasonably be read as defining a citizenship which a citizen keeps unless he voluntarily relinquishes it. Once acquired, this Fourteenth Amendment citizenship was not to be shifted, canceled, or diluted at the will of the Federal Government, the States, or any other governmental unit. . . .

To uphold Congress' power to take away a man's citizenship because he voted in a foreign election in violation of §401(e) would be equivalent to holding that Congress has the power to "abridge," "affect," "restrict the effect of," and "take . . . away" citizenship. Because the Fourteenth Amendment prevents Congress from doing any of these things, we agree with The Chief Justice's dissent in the Perez case that the Government is without power to rob a citizen of his citizenship under §401(e).[23] . . .

. . . We hold that the Fourteenth Amendment was designed to, and does, protect every citizen of this Nation against a congressional forcible destruction of his citizenship, whatever his creed, color, or race. Our holding does no more than to give to this citizen that which is his own, a constitutional right to remain a citizen in a free country unless he voluntarily relinquishes that citizenship.

Perez v. Brownell is overruled. The judgment is

Reversed.[d]

ROGERS v. BELLEI, 401 U.S. 815, 91 S. Ct. 1060, 28 L. Ed. 2d 499 (1971). "Section 301(a) of the [Immigration and Nationality Act], 8 U.S.C. §1401(a), defines those persons who "shall be nationals and citizens of the United States at birth." Paragraph (7) of §301(a) includes in that definition a person born abroad 'of parents one of whom is an alien, and the other a citizen of the United States' who has met specified conditions of residence in this country. Section 301(b), however, provides that one who is a citizen at birth under §301(a)(7) shall lose his citizenship unless, after age 14 and before age 28, he shall

---

[23] Of course, as The Chief Justice said in his dissent, 356 U.S., at 66, naturalization unlawfully procured can be set aside. See, e.g., Knauer v. United States, 328 U.S. 654; Baumgartner v. United States, 322 U.S. 665; Schneiderman v. United States, 320 U.S. 118.

[d] A dissenting opinion by Mr. Justice Harlan, in which Justices Clark, Stewart, and White joined, is omitted. — ED.

come to the United States and be physically present here continuously for at least five years. . . .

"The facts are stipulated:

"1. The appellee, Aldo Mario Bellei . . . , was born in Italy on December 22, 1939. He is now 31 years of age.

"2. The plaintiff's father has always been a citizen of Italy and never has acquired United States citizenship. The plaintiff's mother, however, was born in Philadelphia in 1915 and thus was a native-born United States citizen. . . .

"5. The plaintiff has come to the United States five different times. He was physically present here during the following periods:
April 27 to July 31, 1948
July 10 to October 5, 1951
June to October 1955
December 18, 1962 to February 13, 1963
May 26 to June 13, 1965. . . .

"7. The plaintiff was warned in writing by United States authorities of the impact of §301(b) when he was in this country in January 1963 and again in November of that year when he was in Italy. Sometime after February 11, 1964, he was orally advised by the American Embassy at Rome that he had lost his United States citizenship pursuant to §301(b). In November 1966 he was so notified in writing by the American Consul in Rome when the plaintiff requested another American passport."

Appellee challenges his loss of citizenship on grounds of the Fourteenth Amendment and of Fifth Amendment due process. What result and why?

Section C. REVOCATION OF NATURALIZATION

NOTE

Immigration and Nationality Act, June 27, 1952, as amended Sept. 3, 1954, 8 U.S.C.. §1451:

"SEC. 340. *Revocation of Naturalization.* (a) It shall be the duty of the United States attorneys for the respective districts, upon affidavit showing good cause therefor, to institute proceedings . . . for the purpose of revoking and setting aside the order admitting such person to citizenship and canceling the certificate of naturalization on the ground that such order and certificate of naturalization were procured by concealment of a material fact or by willful misrepresentation, and such revocation and setting aside of the order admitting such person to citizenship and such canceling of certificate of naturalization shall be effective as of the original date of the order and certificate, respectively: *Provided,* That refusal on the part of a naturalized citizen within a period of ten years following his naturalization to testify as a witness in any proceeding before a congressional committee concerning his subversive activities, in a case where such person has been convicted of contempt for such refusal, shall be held to constitute a ground for revocation of such person's naturalization under this subsection as having been procured by concealment of a material fact or by willful misrepresentation. . . .

"(b) The party to whom was granted the naturalization alleged to have been procured by concealment of a material fact or by willful misrepresentation shall, in any such proceedings under subsection (a) of this section, have sixty days' personal notice, . . .

"(c) If a person who shall have been naturalized after the effective date of this Act shall within five years next following such naturalization become a member of or affiliated with any organization, membership in or affiliation with which at the time of naturalization would have precluded such person from naturalization under the provisions of section 313, it shall be considered prima facie evidence that such person was not attached to the principles of the Constitution of the United States and was not well disposed to the good order and happiness of the United States at the time of naturalization, and, in the absence of countervailing evidence, it shall be sufficient in the proper proceeding to authorize the revocation and setting aside of the order admitting such person to citizenship and the cancellation of the certificate of naturalization as having been obtained by concealment of a material fact or by willful misrepresentation, . . .

"(d) If a person who shall have been naturalized shall, within five years after such naturalization, return to the country of his nativity, or go to any other foreign country, and take permanent residence therein, it shall be considered prima facie evidence of a lack of intention on the part of such person to reside permanently in the United States at the time of filing his petition for naturalization, and, in the absence of countervailing evidence, it shall be sufficient in the proper proceeding to authorize the revocation and setting aside of the order admitting such person to citizenship and the cancellation of the certificate of naturalization. . . .

"(e) The revocation and setting aside of the order admitting any person to citizenship and canceling his certificate of naturalization under the provisions of subsection (a) of section 338 of the Nationality Act of 1940 shall not, where such action takes place after the effective date of this chapter, result in the loss of citizenship or any right or privilege of citizenship which would have been derived by or been available to a wife or minor child of the naturalized person had such naturalization not been revoked: *Provided,* That this subsection shall not apply in any case in which the revocation and setting aside of the order was the result of actual fraud.

"(f) Any person who claims United States citizenship through the naturalization of a parent or spouse in whose case there is revocation and setting aside of the order admitting such parent or spouse to citizenship under the provisions of subsection (a) of this section on the ground that the order and certificate of naturalization were procured by concealment of a material fact or by willful misrepresentation shall be deemed to have lost and to lose his citizenship and any right or privilege of citizenship which he may have, now has, or may hereafter acquire under and by virtue of such naturalization of such parent or spouse, regardless of whether such person is residing within or without the United States at the time of the revocation and setting aside of the order admitting such parent or spouse to citizenship. Any person who claims United States citizenship through the naturalization of a parent or spouse in whose case there is a revocation and setting aside of the order admitting such parent or spouse to citizenship and the cancellation of the certificate of naturalization under the provisions of subsection (c) or (d) of this section, or under the provisions of section 329 (c) of this title on any ground other than that the order and certificate of naturalization were procured by concealment of a material fact or by willful misrepresentation, shall be deemed to have lost and to lose his citizenship and any right or privilege of citizenship which would have been enjoyed by such person had there not been a revocation and setting aside of the order admitting such parent or spouse to citizenship and the cancellation of the certificate of naturalization, unless such person is residing in the United States at the time of the revocation and setting aside of the order admitting such parent or spouse to citizenship and the cancellation of the certificate of naturalization." [The remainder of § 1451 is here omitted.]

In Baumgartner v. United States, 322 U.S. 665 (1944), the United States sued in 1942 to set aside a naturalization decree of 1932 and cancel a certificate of naturalization as then fraudulently obtained. The complaint charged that Baumgartner swore falsely when he declared on oath that he renounced his allegiance to the German Reich. The government showed that between 1927 and 1941 he made statements comparing Germany favorably to the United States, engaged in pro-Hitler activities and justified the German invasions of the late 1930s, and rejoiced when Dunkerque fell. He testified at his trial that his attitude toward the principles of the American Government were the same when he took his oath in 1932 as it had been ever since. The District Court for the Western District of Missouri set aside the naturalization, and the Eighth Circuit Court of Appeals affirmed. The Supreme Court reversed.

In Schneiderman v. United States, 320 U.S. 118 (1943), the government brought an action in 1939 to cancel Schneiderman's certificate of citizenship granted in 1927, on the ground of illegal procurement, in that when he was naturalized he had not fulfilled the statutory condition that during the preceding five years "he has behaved as a man . . . attached to the principles of the Constitution of the United States, and well disposed to the good order and happiness of the same." The complaint was predicated on Schneiderman's membership in and support of "the Workers (Communist) Party of America and the Young Workers (Communist) League of America" during that period. The United States District Court for the Northern District of California set aside the naturalization certificate as illegally procured; the Ninth Circuit Court of Appeals affirmed this judgment. The United States Supreme Court reversed the judgment below.[e]

In Knauer v. United States, 328 U.S. 654 (1946), the United States instituted proceedings in the United States District Court for the Eastern District of Wisconsin to cancel Knauer's certificate of naturalization, granted April 15, 1937, on the ground that it was fraudulently procured in that Knauer had fraudulently represented in his petition that he was attached to the principles of the Constitution, and that he had taken a false oath of allegiance. The district court found that Knauer had not been and was not attached to the principles of the Constitution and that he took a false oath of allegiance, and accordingly entered an order canceling his certificate and revoking the order admitting him to citizenship. The Circuit Court of Appeals for the Seventh Circuit affirmed. On certiorari the Supreme Court of the United States also affirmed. Mr. Justice Douglas wrote in the majority opinion:

[W]e are dealing in cases of this kind with questions of intent. Here it is whether Knauer swore falsely on April 13, 1937. Intent is a subjective state, illusory and difficult to establish in absence of voluntary confession. What may appear objectively to be false may still fall short of establishing an intentional misrepresentation which is necessary in order to prove that the oath was perjurious. And as Baumgartner v. United States [322 U.S. 665] indicates, utterances made in years subsequent to the oath are not readily to be charged against the state of mind existing when the oath was administered. 322 U.S. p. 675. Troubled times and the emotions of the hour may elicit expressions of sympathy for old acquaintances and relatives across the waters. . . .

"We have read with care the voluminous record in this case. . . . We conclude with the District Court and the Circuit Court of Appeals that there is solid, convincing evidence that Knauer before the date of his naturalization, at that time, and subsequently was a thorough-going Nazi and a faithful follower of Adolph Hitler. The conclusion is irresistible, therefore, that when he forswore allegiance to the German Reich he swore falsely. The character of the evidence, the veracity of the witnesses against Knauer as determined by the District Court, the corroboration of challenged evidence presented by the government, the consistent pattern of Knauer's conduct before and after naturalization convince us that the two lower courts were correct in their conclusions. The standard of

[e] On the Schneiderman case, Justice Frankfurter wrote of his conversation with Justice Murphy: "For, while it may not be true of us," I went on to say, "you know very well, Frank, that it is true of some of the members of the Court that the dominating consideration in this case is thought of Russia and Russia's share in this war. And because of that legal principles are going to be twisted all out of shape. And when we get the case of the Bundists next year there will be some fine somersaulting." From the Diaries of Felix Frankfurter 259 (J. Lash ed. 1975). — Ed.

proof, not satisfied in either the Schneiderman or Baumgartner Cases, is therefore plainly met here.

"We will review briefly what we, as well as the two lower courts, accept as the true version of the facts. . . ."

The majority opinion reviewed various statements which Knauer had made from 1931 through 1938 which indicated his attitude toward Germany. The Court also reviewed Knauer's activities with the German Winter Relief Fund in 1934 and 1935 and with the German-American Bund in 1936 to 1938. The majority of the Supreme Court here found convincing evidence that the two lower courts were correct in concluding that when Knauer was admitted to citizenship on April 13, 1937, he had obtained his naturalization by fraud. Justices Rutledge and Murphy dissented.

In Schneider v. Rusk, 377 U.S. 163 (1964), the Supreme Court passed on the case of Mrs. Angelika Schneider, by birth a German national, who had thereafter acquired derivative American nationality through her mother. In an action for a declaratory judgment, brought by Mrs. Schneider, the United States contended that §352(a)(1) of the Immigration and Nationality Act of 1952, which provided that a naturalized citizen loses his American nationality by having a continuous residence for three years in the territory of a foreign state of which he was formerly a national or in which the place of his birth is situated, had terminated Mrs. Schneider's American nationality. The Supreme Court held this provision unconstitutional under the Fifth Amendment due process clause. Mr. Justice Douglas wrote for the Court, "while the Fifth Amendment contains no equal protection clause, it does forbid discrimination that is 'so unjustifiable as to be violative of due process.' Bolling v. Sharpe, 347 U.S. 497, 499. A native-born citizen is free to reside abroad indefinitely without suffering loss of citizenship. The discrimination aimed at naturalized citizens drastically limits their rights to live and work abroad in a way that other citizens may. It creates indeed a second-class citizenship. . . ." Mr. Justice Clark dissented in an opinion joined by Justices Harlan and White. Mr. Justice Brennan took no part.

Section D. DEPORTATION

Harisiades v. Shaughnessy 342 U.S. 580, 72 Sup. Ct. 512, 96 L. Ed. 586 (1952)

MR. JUSTICE JACKSON delivered the opinion of the Court.

The ultimate question . . . is whether the United States constitutionally may deport a legally resident alien because of membership in the Communist Party which terminated before enactment of the Alien Registration Act of 1940.

Harisiades, a Greek national, accompanied his father to the United States in 1916, when thirteen years of age, and has resided here since. He has taken a wife and sired two children, all citizens. He joined the Communist Party in 1925, when it was known as the Workers Party, and served as an organizer, Branch Executive Committeeman, secretary of its Greek Bureau, and editor of its paper "Empros." The party discontinued his membership, along with that of other aliens, in 1939, but he has continued association with members. He was familiar with the principles and philosophy of the Communist Party and says he still believes in them. He disclaims personal belief in use of force and violence and asserts that the party favored their use only in defense. A warrant for his deportation because of his membership was issued in 1930 but was not served until 1946. The delay was due to inability to locate him because of his use of a number of aliases. After hearings, he was ordered deported on the grounds that after entry he had been a member of an organization which advocates overthrow of the Government by force and violence and distributes printed matter so advocating. He sought release by habeas corpus, which was denied by the District Court. The Court of Appeals for the Second Circuit affirmed. . . .

[The Court recited the facts in the cases involving Mascitti, a citizen of Italy, and Mrs. Coleman, a citizen of Russia.]

. . . Admittedly, each of these deportations is authorized and required by the letter, spirit and intention of the statute. But the Act is assailed on three grounds: (1) that it deprives the aliens of liberty without due process of law in violation of the Fifth Amendment; (2) that it abridges their freedoms of speech and assembly in contravention of the First Amendment; and, (3) that it is an ex post facto law which Congress is forbidden to pass by Art. 1, §9, cl. 3 of the Constitution.

We have in each case a finding, approved by the court below, that the Communist Party during the period of the alien's membership taught and advocated overthrow of the Government of the United States by force and violence. Those findings are not questioned here.

I

These aliens ask us to forbid their expulsion by a departure from the long-accepted application to such cases of the Fifth Amendment provision that no person shall be deprived of life, liberty or property without due process of law. Their basic contention is that admission for permanent residence confers a "vested right" on the alien, equal to that of the citizen, to remain within the country, and that the alien is entitled to constitutional protection in that matter to the same extent as the citizen. Their second line of defense is that if any power to deport domiciled aliens exists it is so dispersed that the judiciary must concur in the grounds for its exercise to the extent of finding them reasonable. The argument goes on to the contention that the grounds prescribed by the Act of 1940 bear no reasonable relation to protection of legitimate interests of the United States and concludes that the Act should be declared invalid. Admittedly these propositions are not founded in precedents of this Court.

For over thirty years each of these aliens has enjoyed such advantages as accrue from residence here without renouncing his foreign allegiance or formally acknowledging adherence to the Constitution he now invokes. . . . Each has been offered naturalization, with all of the rights and privileges of citizenship, conditioned only upon open and honest assumption of undivided allegiance to our government. But acceptance was and is not compulsory. Each has been permitted to prolong his original nationality indefinitely.

. . . The state of origin of each of these aliens could presently enter diplomatic remonstrance against these deportations if they were inconsistent with international law, the prevailing custom among nations or their own practices.

The alien retains immunities from burdens which the citizen must shoulder. . . . [C]ertain dispensations from conscription for any military service have been granted foreign nationals.[6] They can not, consistently with our international commitments, be compelled "to take part in the operations of war directed against their own country." In addition to such general immunities they may enjoy particular treaty privileges.

Under our law, the alien in several respects stands on an equal footing with citizens,[9]

---

[6] §2 of the Selective Draft Act of 1917, 40 Stat. 76, as amended, 50 U.S.C. Appx. §202; §3 of the Selective Training and Service Act of 1940, 54 Stat. 885, as amended, 50 U.S.C. Appx. §303; §4(a) of the Selective Service Act of 1948, 62 Stat. 604, as amended, 50 U.S.C. Appx. §454(a). Cf. Moser v. United States, 341 U.S. 41.

[9] This Court has held that the Constitution assures him a large measure of equal economic opportunity, Yick Wo v. Hopkins, 118 U.S. 356; Truax v. Raich, 239 U.S. 33; he may invoke the writ of habeas corpus to protect

but in others has never been conceded legal parity with the citizen.[10] Most importantly, to protract this ambiguous status within the country is not his right but is a matter of permission and tolerance. The Government's power to terminate its hospitality has been asserted and sustained by this Court since the question first arose.[11] . . .

This brings us to the alternative defense under the Due Process Clause — that, granting the power, it is so unreasonably and harshly exercised by this enactment that it should be held unconstitutional.

In historical context the Act before us stands out as an extreme application of the expulsion power. There is no denying that as world convulsions have driven us toward a closed society the expulsion power has been exercised with increasing severity, manifest in multiplication of grounds for deportation, in expanding the subject classes from illegal entrants to legal residents, and in greatly lengthening the period of residence after which one may be expelled. This is said to have reached a point where it is the duty of this Court to call a halt upon the political branches of the Government.

It is pertinent to observe that any policy toward aliens is vitally and intricately interwoven with contemporaneous policies in regard to the conduct of foreign relations, the war power, and the maintenance of a republican form of government. Such matters are so exclusively entrusted to the political branches of government as to be largely immune from judicial inquiry or interference.[16] . . .

Under the conditions which produced this Act can we declare that congressional alarm about a coalition of Communist power without and Communist conspiracy within the United States is either a fantasy or a pretense? This Act was approved by President Roosevelt June 28, 1940, when a world war was threatening to involve us, as soon it did. Communists in the United States were exerting every effort to defeat and delay our preparations. Certainly no responsible American would say that there were then or are now no possible grounds on which Congress might believe that Communists in our midst are inimical to our security. . . .

We hold that the Act is not invalid under the Due Process Clause. . . .

II

The First Amendment is invoked as a barrier against this enactment. The claim is that in joining an organization advocating overthrow of government by force and violence the alien has merely exercised freedoms of speech, press and assembly which that Amendment guarantees to him. . . .

---

his personal liberty, Nishimura Ekiu v. United States, 142 U.S. 651, 660; in criminal proceedings against him he must be accorded the protections of the Fifth and Sixth Amendments, Wong Wing v. United States, 163 U.S. 228; and, unless he is an enemy alien, his property cannot be taken without just compensation. Russian Volunteer Fleet v. United States, 282 U.S. 481.

[10] He cannot stand for election to many public offices. For instance, Art. 1, §2, cl. 2, §3, cl. 3 of the Constitution respectively require that candidates for election to the House of Representatives and Senate be citizens. See Borchard, Diplomatic Protection of Citizens Abroad 63. The states, to whom is entrusted the authority to set qualifications of voters, for most purposes require citizenship as a condition precedent to the voting franchise. The alien's right to travel temporarily outside the United States is subject to restrictions not applicable to citizens. 43 Stat. 158, as amended, 8 U.S.C. §210. If he is arrested on a charge of entering the country illegally, the burden is his to prove "his right to enter or remain" — no presumptions accrue in his favor by his presence here. 39 Stat. 889, as amended, 8 U.S.C. §155(a).

[11] Fong Yue Ting v. United States, 149 U.S. 698, 707, 711-714, 730 [other citations omitted].

[16] United States v. Curtiss-Wright Export Corp., 299 U.S. 304, 319-322; Chicago & Southern Air Lines, Inc. v. Waterman S.S. Corp., 333 U.S. 103, 111; U.S. Const., Art. 4, §4; Luther v. Borden, 7 How. 1, 42; Pacific States Tel. & Tel. Co. v. Oregon, 223 U.S. 118; Marshall v. Dye, 231 U.S. 250. In respect to the war power over even citizens, see Hirabayashi v. United States, 320 U.S. 81, 92; Korematsu v. United States, 323 U.S. 214, 217, 218. That English courts also refuse to review grounds for deportation orders appears from Rex v. Home Secretary: Ex parte Bressler, 27 Cox Cr. Cas. 655.

Our Constitution sought to leave no excuse for violent attack on the status quo by providing a legal alternative — attack by ballot. To arm all men for orderly change, the Constitution put in their hands a right to influence the electorate by press, speech and assembly. This means freedom to advocate or promote Communism by means of the ballot box, but it does not include the practice or incitement of violence.

. . . We think the First Amendment does not prevent the deportation of these aliens.

III

The remaining claim is that this Act conflicts with Art. 1, §9, of the Constitution forbidding ex post facto enactments. An impression of retroactivity results from reading as a new and isolated enactment what is actually a continuation of prior legislation.

During all the years since 1920 Congress has maintained a standing admonition to aliens, on pain of deportation, not to become members of any organization that advocates overthrow of the United States by force and violence, a category repeatedly held to include the Communist Party. These aliens violated that prohibition and incurred liability to deportation. They were not caught unawares by a change of law. There can be no contention that they were not adequately forewarned both that their conduct was prohibited and of its consequences. . . .

However, even if the Act were found to be retroactive, to strike it down would require us to overrule the construction of the ex post facto provision which has been followed by the Court from earliest times. It always has been considered that that which it forbids is penal legislation which imposes or increases criminal punishment for conduct lawful previous to its enactment. Deportation, however severe its consequences, has been consistently classified as a civil rather than a criminal procedure. . . .

We find none of the constitutional objections to the Act well founded. The judgments accordingly are

Affirmed.[f]

NOTE Developments in Deportation and Passport Matters

In 1954 the Supreme Court extended the rule of Harisiades.

"This brings us to petitioner's constitutional attack on the statute. Harisiades v. Shaughnessy, 342 U.S. 580, sustained the constitutionality of the Alien Registration Act of 1940. 54 Stat. 670. That Act made membership in an organization which advocates the overthrow of the Government of the United States by force or violence a ground for deportation, notwithstanding that membership in such organization had terminated before enactment of the statute. Under the 1940 Act, it was necessary to prove in each case, where membership in the Communist Party was made the basis of deportation, that the Party did, in fact, advocate the violent overthrow of the government. The Internal Security Act of 1950 dispensed with the need for such proof. . . .

"In this respect — the dispensation with proof of the character of the Communist Party — the present case goes beyond Harisiades. . . ."

The Court denied habeas corpus. Galvan v. Press, 347 U.S. 522, 529, 530.

A statute terminating Social Security Act benefits to an alien who is deported on the ground of past Communist party membership is not unconstitutional as denying due process, or as a bill of attainder or ex post facto law, or as punishing him without a judicial trial guaranteed by Article III and by the Sixth Amendment. Flemming v. Nestor, 363 U.S. 603 (1960).

[f] A concurring opinion of Justice Frankfurter and a dissenting opinion of Justice Douglas, in which Justice Black joined, are omitted. — ED.

750   Chapter Thirteen.   Nationality and Citizenship

If no other nation will accept an alien under deportation from the United States, he may face indefinite detention. This was the situation in Shaughnessy v. United States ex rel. Mezei, 345 U.S. 206 (1953). Some months after this decision, however, the Department of Justice granted Mezei a parole. New York Times, Aug. 10, 1954, p. 10, col. 2.

An alien seeking admission to the United States has no "right" to enter; the procedural devices by which the Congress or the immigration authorities determine the propriety of entry are not controlled by the due process requirements of the Fifth Amendment. Knauff v. Shaughnessy, 338 U.S. 537 (1950). The alien here concerned, the wife of an American veteran, who had sought admission in 1948 under the "War Brides Act" of December 28, 1945, 59 Stat. 659, c. 591, 8 U.S.C. §§232-236, and had been rejected on security grounds without a hearing, carried on a long and unsuccessful struggle to obtain a judicial reversal of the immigration authorities. See Knauff v. McGrath, 181 F.2d 839, 182 F.2d 1020 (2d Cir. 1950), cert. granted and cause remanded with directions to dismiss as moot, 340 U.S. 940 (1951). Legislation was introduced in the Congress on her behalf; but she finally obtained admission when the Board of Immigration Appeals, reversing its previous decision, recommended that she be allowed to enter, and the Attorney General, on November 2, 1951, gave his approval. See New York Times, Nov. 3, 1951, p. 1, col. 1. The questions raised in the Knauff litigation are treated in Note, Due Process in Proceedings to Exclude or Deport Aliens, 94 L. Ed. 329 (1950).

The Knauff case provoked this dissent from Justice Jackson: "Now this American citizen is told he cannot bring his wife to the United States, but he will not be told why. He must abandon his bride to live in his own country or forsake his country to live with his bride. . . . Security is like liberty in that many are the crimes committed in its name. The menace to the security of this country, be it great as it may, from this girl's admission is as nothing compared to the menace to free institutions inherent in procedures of this pattern." 338 U.S. at 550-551.

In Shaughnessy v. Pedreiro, 349 U.S. 48 (1955), the Supreme Court, under the Immigration and Nationality Act of 1952, gave Pedreiro, an alien under order of deportation, a remedy by judicial review of the action of the District Director of Immigration and Naturalization under the Administrative Procedure Act. The Court declined to follow Heikkila v. Barber, 345 U.S. 229 (1953), which arose under the Immigration Act of 1917.

Section 242D of the Immigration and Nationality Act of 1952, 8 U.S.C. §1252D, as amended, requires an alien against whom an order of deportation has been outstanding for more than six months to give to federal officers information under oath ". . . as to his nationality, circumstances, habits, associations, and activities, and such other information, whether or not related to the foregoing, as the Attorney General may deem fit and proper; . . . ." Willful failure to comply is made a crime. One Witkovich, such an alien, refused to answer questions concerning his attendance at Communist party meetings, his membership vel non in the Communist party, in the Slovene American National Council, in the United Committee of South Slavic Americans, and similar questions. The Supreme Court, in United States v. Witkovich, 353 U.S. 194 (1957), affirming a district court judgment, held that the statute authorized only questions reasonably calculated to keep the Attorney General advised concerning the alien's availability for departure.

In Aptheker v. Secretary of State, 378 U.S. 500 (1964), the Supreme Court held unconstitutional so much of §6 of the Subversive Activities Control Act of 1950 as provided, in pertinent part, that where an order of registration had become final against a Communist organization, it should be unlawful for any member, having knowledge of the final order, to apply for a U.S. passport or a renewal, or to use or attempt to use any such passport. Mr. Justice Goldberg wrote in the Court's opinion: "We hold, for the reasons stated below, that §6 of the Control Act too broadly and indiscriminately restricts the right to travel and thereby abridges the liberty guaranteed by the Fifth Amendment." Justices Clark and Harlan dissented; Mr. Justice White dissented in part.

In Zemel v. Rusk, 381 U.S. 1 (1965), the Supreme Court held that the Congress had authorized the Secretary of State to refuse to validate passports of United States citizens for travel to Cuba; and that exercise of that authority was constitutionally permissible, as supported by the "weightiest considerations of national security." Id. at 16. Justices Black, Douglas, and Goldberg dissented.

In Kleindienst v. Mandel, 408 U.S. 753 (1972), the Supreme Court rejected a challenge to the refusal of the Attorney General to exercise his statutory power to allow the admission of an alien otherwise ineligible under the Immigration and Nationality Act of 1952. Mandel, a Belgian national, was invited to participate in academic conferences in the United States but was denied a visa under §212(a) of the act, which includes Marxists among aliens ineligible to receive visas. Under §212(d), however, ineligible aliens could be admitted temporarily if the Department of State requested and the Attorney General approved a waiver of ineligibility. Such a request was made by the State Department but denied by the Attorney General. As grounds for the refusal, the Immigration and Naturalization Service stated that on an earlier visit to the United States Mandel had violated the terms of a waiver of ineligibility by failing to adhere to his stated itinerary and to confine his activities within the stated purposes of his trip. Suit to compel the Attorney General to grant a waiver was brought by several American scholars who claimed that the denial infringed their First Amendment right to hear and exchange views with Mandel. The Supreme Court rejected the constitutional claim as inapplicable to "plenary congressional power to make policies and rules for exclusion of aliens" and to delegation of this power to the Attorney General, at least where the Attorney General has exercised his authority "on the basis of a facially legitimate and bona fide reason." Justices Douglas, Brennan, and Marshall dissented.

Chapter Fourteen Privileges and Immunities, Equality, and Civil Rights

Section A. HISTORICAL NOTE

Under the Constitution as originally ratified, the principal safeguards of personal and property rights against national power were found in §9 of Article I. Section 10 of the same article set some limitations upon the powers of the states — e.g., that no state shall "pass any Bill of Attainder, ex post facto law, or Law impairing the Obligation of Contracts." Fears that liberty was insufficiently secured against the powers delegated to the national government led to the assurance that a Bill of Rights would be added to the Constitution. The consequence of this commitment was the submission of the first ten amendments to the states for their ratification. The process of ratification, commenced in 1789, was concluded in 1791.

The fact that in all but two of the first eight amendments (the First and the Seventh) the limitation on power was so phrased as to be grammatically applicable to the states led litigants from time to time to argue that the actions of states had violated the Bill of Rights. The Supreme Court, however, regularly rejected this argument. See, e.g., Barron v. Baltimore, 7 Pet. 243 (1833), in which a unanimous Court repudiated the contention that the provision in the Fifth Amendment that "private property [shall not] be taken for public use, without just compensation" set limits to the power of states. See also Permoli v. First Municipality of New Orleans, 3 How. 589 (1845). An occasional voice has been heard in protest against these holdings. It seems clear, however, that the Court which refused to treat the federal Bill of Rights as a schedule of limitations on state power was true to the intention of those who made it a part of the Constitution. See Fairman, The Supreme Court and the Constitutional Limitations on State Governmental Authority, 21 U. Chi. L. Rev. 40 (1953).

In Magill v. Brown, F. Cas. No. 8,952 (1833), Baldwin, J., hearing a diversity case on circuit, discussed what action the court should take if the enforcement of a rule of law of the state where the federal court sat would result in the establishment of religion or the denial of religious liberty. "Bound to decide on the laws of a state, as the courts of a state do, we must look to that which is supreme, as the only rule of our decision, where its language is plain; in its application to this case, it cannot be mistaken, nor can we overlook the first amendment to the constitution of the United States, which, in our opinion, wholly prohibits the action of the legislative or judicial power of the Union on the subject matter of a religious establishment, or any restraint on the free exercise of religion." Id. at 427. Cf. 1 Annals of Cong. 758 (1834).

So far as we know, Baldwin, J., concurred in Marshall's opinion in Barron v. Baltimore. If, sitting on circuit, he felt compelled to take no official action which would violate the provisions of the First Amendment, how could he justify participation in a decision of the Supreme Court which permitted private property to be taken for public use without compensation? Cf. Shelley v. Kraemer, page 808 infra.

Beyond the explicit limitations on state and national powers, the Justices were able, from time to time, to discover principles of political theory which set barriers to governmental action. See, e.g., Chase, J., in Calder v. Bull, 3 Dall. 386, 388 (1798); Story, J., in Terrett v. Taylor, 9 Cranch 43, 50 (1815); and Johnson, J., concurring in Fletcher v. Peck, page 28 supra.

Even before the adoption of the Fourteenth Amendment, one who enjoyed the status of citizen either of the United States or of a state of the Union (or of both) might feel entitled to claim that he was vested with certain rights, privileges, and immunities against governmental action. Until that amendment specified the persons who are citizens of the United States and of the several states, the courts and legal officers of the government were compelled to feel their way through general principles without the guidance of constitutional provisions.

Section B. CITIZENSHIP IN A FEDERAL UNION

Corfield v. Coryell 4 Wash. C.C. 371 (U.S. Cir. Ct., E.D. Pa., 1825)

[In an action of trespass the plaintiff, a citizen of Pennsylvania, charged that the defendant had seized the plaintiff's vessel, the *Hiram*, while she was dredging for oysters in the waters of New Jersey, and that the defendant thereafter had initiated judicial proceedings in a New Jersey court in which the plaintiff's vessel had been condemned and sold. The condemnation had occurred under a statute of New Jersey making it unlawful for nonresidents to gather oysters in New Jersey waters. At the trial of the plaintiff's action the jury returned a verdict in his favor, subject to the opinion of the court on the questions of law. Among other arguments the plaintiff urged that the New Jersey statute was void under that provision of Article IV of the United States Constitution, which states that "the Citizens of each State shall be entitled to all Privileges and Immunities of Citizens in the several States."]

WASHINGTON, J., delivered the opinion of the court. . . .

The inquiry is, what are the privileges and immunities of citizens in the several States? We feel no hesitation in confining these expressions to those privileges and immunities which are, in their nature, *fundamental*; which belong, of right, to the citizens of all free governments; and which have, at all times, been enjoyed by the citizens of the several States which compose this Union, from the time of their becoming free, independent, and sovereign. What these fundamental principles are, it would perhaps be more tedious than difficult to enumerate. They may, however, be all comprehended under the following general heads: protection by the government; the enjoyment of life and liberty, with the right to acquire and possess property of every kind, and to pursue and obtain happiness and safety; subject nevertheless to such restraints as the government may justly prescribe for the general good of the whole. The right of a citizen of one State to pass through, or to reside in any other State, for purposes of trade, agriculture, professional pursuits, or otherwise; to claim the benefit of the writ of habeas corpus; to institute and maintain actions of any kind in the courts of the State; to take, hold and dispose of property, either real or personal; and an exemption from higher taxes or impositions than are paid by the other citizens of the State; may be mentioned as some of the particular privileges and immunities of citizens, which are clearly embraced by the general description of privileges deemed to be fundamental; to which may be added, the elective franchise, as regulated and established by the laws or constitution of the State in which it is to be exercised. These, and many others which might be mentioned, are, strictly speaking, privileges and immunities, and the enjoyment of them by the citizens of each State, in every other State, was manifestly calculated (to use the expressions of the preamble of the corresponding provision in the old Articles of Confederation) "the better to secure and perpetuate mutual friendship and intercourse among the people of the different States of the Union."

But we cannot accede to the proposition which was insisted on by the counsel, that, under this provision of the Constitution, the citizens of the several States are permitted to participate in all the rights which belong exclusively to the citizens of any other particular State, merely upon the ground that they are enjoyed by those citizens; much less, that in regulating the use of the common property of the citizens of such State, the Legislature is bound to extend to the citizens of all the other States the same advantages as are secured to their own citizens.

A several fishery, either as the right to it respects running fish, or such as are stationary, such as oysters, clams, and the like, is as much the property of the individual to whom it belongs, as dry land, or land covered by water; and is equally protected by the laws of the State against the aggressions of others, whether citizens or strangers. Where those private rights do not exist to the exclusion of the common right, that of fishing belongs to all the citizens or subjects of the State. It is the property of all; to be enjoyed by them in subordination to the laws which regulate its use. They may be considered as tenants in common of this property; and they are so exclusively entitled to the use of it, that it cannot be enjoyed by others without the tacit consent, or the express permission of the sovereign who has the power to regulate its use. . . .

NOTE

Lynch v. Clarke, 1 Sandf. Ch. 583 (N.Y. 1844). By the common law of New York, aliens were precluded from inheriting land. The plaintiff was born in New York of alien parents temporarily sojourning there. Held, that under the common law of the United States the plaintiff was to be considered a citizen of the United States and therefore might take New York land by inheritance. At 641-642 the Court wrote as follows: "The provisions of the Constitution of the United States demonstrate that the right of citizenship, as distinguished from alienage, is a national right or condition, and does not pertain to the individual states. . . . The Constitution declares that the citizens of each state shall be entitled to all the privileges and immunities of citizens in the several states. (Article IVth, Sec. 2.) The effect of this clause in the first instance, was to bring within the fold of citizenship of the United States, and thus of each and every state, all who at the time of the Constitution, were by birth, adoption or any of their discordant laws of naturalization, citizens of any one of the thirteen states." Cf. 2 Story, Commentaries on the Constitution §1806 (2d ed. 1851): "The intention of this clause [Art. IV, §2] was to confer . . . if one may so say, a general citizenship. . . ." Rawle, A View of the Constitution of the United States 86 (2d ed. 1829): "The citizens of each state constituted the citizens of the United

States when the Constitution was adopted. The rights which appertained to them as citizens of those respective commonwealths, accompanied them in the formation of the great, compound commonwealth which ensued. They became citizens of the latter, without ceasing to be citizens of the former, and he who was subsequently born a citizen of a state, became at the moment of his birth a citizen of the United States. Therefore every person born within the United States, its territories or districts, whether the parents are citizens or aliens, is a natural born citizen in the sense of the Constitution [Art. II, § 1(5)], and entitled to all the rights and privileges appertaining to that capacity."

With some frequency the Attorneys General were called upon to define the concept of United States citizenship. In 1821, William Wirt advised the Secretary of the Treasury that "free persons of color" in Virginia were not citizens of the United States within the meaning of the federal statutes qualifying such citizens to command vessels. "I am of opinion," he wrote, "that the constitution, by the description of 'citizens of the United States' intended those only who enjoyed the full and equal privileges of white citizens in the State of their residence." 1 Op. Atty. Gen. 506, 507. Cf. Taney, C.J., in Dred Scott v. Sandford, page 729 supra. See also Swisher, Roger B. Taney 146-159 (1935). A contrary opinion of Edward Bates, Lincoln's Attorney General, was delivered to Salmon P. Chase, then Secretary of the Treasury, in November 1862, and was much relied upon four years later when the Civil Rights Act (page 761 infra) was under discussion in Congress. Excerpts from that opinion (10 Op. Atty. Gen. 382) follow:

"Who is a citizen? What constitutes a citizen of the United States? I have often been pained by the fruitless search in our law books and the records of our courts, for a clear and satisfactory definition of the phrase *citizen of the United States*. . . . Eighty years of practical enjoyment of citizenship, under the Constitution, have not sufficed to teach us either the exact meaning of the word, or the constituent elements of the thing we prize so highly. . . .

"In my opinion, the Constitution uses the word citizen only to express the political quality of the individual in his relations to the nation; to declare that he is a member of the body politic, and bound to it by the reciprocal obligation of allegiance on the one side and protection on the other. And I have no knowledge of any other kind of political citizenship, higher or lower, statal or national, or of any other sense in which the word has been used in the Constitution, or can be used properly in the laws of the United States. The phrase, 'a citizen of the United States,' without addition or qualification, means neither more nor less than a member of the nation. And all such are, politically and legally, equal — the child in the cradle and its father in the Senate, are equally citizens of the United States. And it needs no argument to prove that every citizen of a State is, necessarily, a citizen of the United States; and to me it is equally clear that every citizen of the United States is a citizen of the particular State in which he is domiciled. . . .

"Those who most indulge in the assumption that to constitute a citizen at all, the person must have all the privileges and immunities which any citizen can enjoy, rarely venture to specify precisely what they mean. Generally, I think, the inference is plain that they mean suffrage and eligibility; and, in that connection, I think I have already shown that suffrage and eligibility have no necessary connection with citizenship, and that the one may, and often does, exist without the other.

"Again, 'immunities' are enjoyed to a very large extent by free negroes in all the slaveholding States. They are generally exempted by law from the onerous duties of jurors in the courts, and militia men in the field; and these are immunities eagerly desired by many white men in all the States. . . .

"And now, upon the whole matter, I give it as my opinion that the *free man of color*, mentioned in your letter, if born in the United States, is a citizen of the United States; and, if otherwise qualified, is competent, according to the acts of Congress, to be master of a vessel engaged in the coasting trade."

Crandall v. Nevada 6 Wall. 35, 18 L. Ed. 744 (1868)

[For the opinion in this case see page 339 supra.]

Section C. SLAVERY AND FEDERALISM

Prigg v. Pennsylvania 16 Pet. 539, 10 L. Ed. 1060 (1842)

MR. JUSTICE STORY delivered the opinion of the Court.

This is a writ of error to the Supreme Court of Pennsylvania, brought under the 25th section of the judiciary act of 1789, ch. 20, for the purpose of revising the judgment of that Court, in a case involving the construction of the Constitution and laws of the United States.

The facts are briefly these: The plaintiff in error was indicted in the Court of Oyer and Terminer for York county, for having, with force and violence, taken and carried away from that county to the state of Maryland, a certain negro woman, named Margaret Morgan, with a design and intention of selling and disposing of, and keeping her as a slave or servant for life, contrary to a statute of Pennsylvania, passed on the 26th of March, 1826.

[The statute provided criminal penalties for any person who carried away any Negro from Pennsylvania into slavery. The jury found the plaintiff in error guilty of the crime charged. The Supreme Court of Pennsylvania affirmed the judgment and the plaintiff in error brought a writ of error to the Supreme Court.]

There are two clauses in the constitution upon the subject of fugitives, which stand in juxtaposition with each other, and have been thought mutually to illustrate each other. They are both contained in the second section of the fourth article, and are in the following words: "A person charged in any state with treason, felony, or other crime, who shall flee from justice, and be found in another state, shall, on demand of the executive authority of the state from which he fled, be delivered up, to be removed to the state having jurisdiction of the crime."

"No person held to service or labour in one state under the laws thereof, escaping into another, shall in consequence of any law or regulation therein, be discharged from such service or labour; but shall be delivered up, on claim of the party to whom such service or labour may be due."

The last clause is that, the true interpretation whereof is directly in judgment before us. Historically, it is well known, that the object of this clause was to secure to the citizens of the slaveholding states the complete right and title of ownership in their slaves, as property, in every state in the Union into which they might escape from the state where they were held in servitude. The full recognition of this right and title was indispensable to the security of this species of property in all the slaveholding states; and, indeed, was so vital to the preservation of their domestic interests and institutions, that it cannot be doubted that it constituted a fundamental article, without the adoption of which the Union could not have been formed. Its true design was to guard against the doctrines and principles prevalent in the non-slaveholding states, by preventing them from intermeddling with, or obstructing, or abolishing the rights of the owners of slaves. . . .

And this leads us to the consideration of the other part of the clause, which implies at once a guaranty and duty. It says, "But [the slave] shall be delivered up, on claim of the party to whom such service or labour may be due." Now, we think it exceedingly difficult, if not impracticable, to read this language and not to feel, that it contemplated some farther remedial redress than that, which might be administered at the hands of the owner himself. A claim is to be made. What is a claim? It is, in a just juridical sense, a demand of some matter as of right made by one person upon another, to do or to forbear to do some act or thing as a matter of duty. . . . [T]he natural, if not the necessary conclusion is, that the national government, in the absence of all positive provisions to the contrary, is bound, through its own proper departments, legislative, judicial, or executive, as the case may require, to carry into effect all the rights and duties imposed upon it by the Constitution. The remark of Mr. Madison, in the Federalist, (No. 43,) would seem in such cases to apply with peculiar force. "A right [says he] implies a remedy; and where else would the remedy be deposited, than where it is deposited by the Constitution?" meaning, as the context shows, in the government of the United States. . . .

Congress has taken this very view of the power and duty of the national government. As early as the year 1791, the attention of Congress was drawn to it, (as we shall hereafter more fully see,) in consequence of some practical difficulties arising under the other clause, respecting fugitives from justice escaping into other states. The result of their deliberations, was the passage of the act of the 12th of February, 1763, ch. 51, (7,) . . . [The Fugitive Slave Act allowed an owner of a fugitive slave to transport him out of the state if a federal or state judge certified the claim.]

The remaining question is, whether the power of legislation upon this subject is exclusive in the national government, or concurrent in the states, until it is exercised by Congress. In our opinion it is exclusive; and we shall now proceed briefly to state our reasons for that opinion. The doctrine stated by this Court, in Sturgis v. Crowninshield, 4 Wheat. Rep. 122, 193, contains the true, although not the sole rule of consideration, which is applicable to this particular subject. "Wherever," said Mr. Chief Justice Marshall, in delivering the opinion of the Court, "the terms in which a power is granted to Congress, or the nature of the power require that it should be exercised exclusively by Congress, the subject is as completely taken from the state legislatures, as if they had been forbidden to act." The nature of the power, and the true objects to be attained by it, are then as important to be weighed, in considering the question of its exclusiveness, as the words in which it is granted.

In the first place, it is material to state, (what has been already incidentally hinted at,) that the right to seize and retake fugitive slaves, and the duty to deliver them up, in whatever state of the Union they may be found, and of course the corresponding power in Congress to use the appropriate means to enforce the right and duty, derive their whole validity and obligation exclusively from the Constitution of the United States, and are there, for the first time, recognised and established in that peculiar character. Before the adoption of the Constitution, no state had any power whatsoever over the subject, except within its own territorial limits, and could not bind the sovereignty or the legislation of other states. Whenever the right was acknowledged or the duty enforced in any state, it was as a matter of comity and favour, and not as a matter of strict moral, political, or international obligation or duty. Under the Constitution it is recognised as an absolute, positive, right and duty, pervading the whole Union with an equal and supreme force, uncontrolled and uncontrollable by state sovereignty or state legislation. It is, therefore, in a just sense a new and positive right, independent of comity, confined to no territorial limits, and bounded by no state institutions or policy. The natural inference deducible from this consideration certainly is, in the absence of any positive delegation of power to the state legislatures, that it belongs to the legislative department of the national government, to which it owes its origin and establishment. . . .

In the next place, the nature of the provision and the objects to be attained by it, require that it should be controlled by one and the same will, and act uniformly by the same system of regulations throughout the Union. If, then, the states have a right, in the absence of legislation by Congress, to act upon the subject, each state is at liberty to prescribe just such regulations as suit its own policy, local convenience, and local feelings. The legislation of one state may not only be different from, but utterly repugnant to and incompatible with that of another. . . .

It is scarcely conceivable, that the slaveholding states would have been satisfied with leaving to the legislation of the non-slaveholding states, a power of regulation, in the absence of that of Congress, which would or might practically amount to a power to destroy the rights of the owner. If the argument, therefore, of a concurrent power in the states to act upon the subject-matter in the absence of legislation by Congress, be well founded; then, if Congress had never acted at all, or if the act of Congress should be repealed without providing a substitute, there would be a resulting authority in each of the states to regulate the whole subject at its pleasure, and to dole out its own remedial justice, or withhold it at its pleasure and according to its own views of policy and expediency. Surely such a state of things never could have been intended, under such a solemn guarantee of right and duty. On the other hand, construe the right of legislation as exclusive in Congress, and every evil, and every danger vanishes. The right and the duty are then co-extensive and uniform in remedy and operation throughout the whole Union. The owner has the same security, and the same remedial justice, and the same exemption from state regulation and control, through however many states he may pass with his fugitive slave in his possession, in transitu, to his own domicile. But, upon the other supposition, the moment he passes the state line, he becomes amenable to the laws of another sovereignty, whose regulations may greatly embarrass or delay the exercise of his rights, and even be repugnant to those of the state where he first arrested the fugitive. Consequences like these show, that the nature and objects of the provision imperiously require, that, to make it effectual, it should be construed to be exclusive of state authority. . . .

Upon these grounds, we are of opinion that the act of Pennsylvania upon which this indictment is founded, is unconstitutional and void. It purports to punish as a public offence against that state, the very act of seizing and removing a slave by his master, which the Constitution of the United States was designed to justify and uphold. The special verdict finds this fact, and the State Courts have rendered judgment against the plaintiff in error upon that verdict. The judgment must, therefore, be reversed, and the cause remanded to the Supreme Court of Pennsylvania, with directions to carry into effect the judgment of this Court rendered upon the special verdict in favour of the plaintiff in error.[a]

NOTE

Daniel Webster's reflections on the meaning of the constitutional clause with respect to rendition of fugitive laborers casts some light on the general problem of the applicability of the Constitution's provisions to "private" action.

"I have always thought that the Constitution addressed itself to the legislatures of the States or to the States themselves. It says that those persons escaping to other States 'shall be delivered up,' and I confess I have always been of the opinion that it was an injunction upon the States themselves.

"When it is said that a person escaping into another State, and coming within the jurisdiction of that State, shall be delivered up, it seems to me the import of the clause is, that the State itself, in obedience to the Constitution, shall cause him to be delivered up. That is my judgment. I have always entertained that opinion, and I entertain it now. But when the subject, some years ago, was before the Supreme Court of the United States, the majority of the judges held that the power to cause fugitives from service to be delivered up was a power to be exercised under the authority of this government. I do not know, on the

---

[a] Concurring opinions were delivered by Taney, C.J., and by Baldwin, Wayne, Daniel, and M'Lean, JJ. — Ed.

whole, that it may not have been a fortunate decision. My habit is to respect the result of judicial deliberations and the solemnity of judicial decisions. As it now stands, the business of seeing that these fugitives are delivered up resides in the power of Congress and the national judicature. . . ." Daniel Webster, Speech of 7th March, 1850, 6 Works 354.

As to whether Prigg had a "fortunate" impact, Carl Swisher has concluded: "Because while upholding the power of the federal government to provide for the return of fugitive slaves, it nullified the obligation and seemed to nullify the power of the states to aid in the process, it at once gave incentive to abolitionist activities and led the South to demand enactment of a Fugitive Slave Act which could be effectively administered without the aid of the states. Thereby it added to the furor of sectional conflict and the hysteria of competing parties." Swisher, The Taney Period, 1836-1864, 546 (1974) (V Holmes Devise History of the Supreme Court).

PROBLEM CASE

Kentucky v. Dennison, 24 How. 66 (1861): In original proceedings in the Supreme Court, the state of Kentucky sought a writ of mandamus to the Governor of Ohio commanding him to cause Willis Lago, a fugitive from justice, to be delivered up to be removed to Kentucky for trial on an indictment charging him with assisting a slave to escape. Governor Dennison had previously been requested to arrest and deliver Lago up to Kentucky's authorized representative, but he had refused to do so asserting that the crime for which Lago had been indicted was unknown to the laws of Ohio. The petition for mandamus was supported by authenticated copies of the Kentucky proceedings. Counsel for Kentucky urged that under the provisions of Article IV, §2, of the Constitution, supplemented by the Act of 1793 (1 Stat. 302), Governor Dennison was obliged to render the fugitive. The statutory provision in question stated that upon production of the authenticated documents by representatives of the demanding state "it shall be the duty of the executive authority of the state or territory to which such person shall have fled, to cause him or her to be arrested . . . and to cause the fugitive to be delivered to" the agent of the demanding state.

Should the writ of mandamus issue?

Dred Scott v. Sandford   19 How. 393, 15 L. Ed. 691 (1857)

[For the opinions in this case see page 729 supra.]

Section D.   CIVIL WAR AMENDMENTS AND CIVIL RIGHTS STATUTES: THE SEARCH FOR STANDARDS

The Thirteenth Amendment and the Civil Rights Act. The first great constitutional event after Appomattox was the adoption of the Thirteenth Amendment, which, on December 31, 1865, was certified by the Secretary of State to have become a part of the Constitution through ratification by the legislatures of twenty-seven states. Its adoption, however, contributed little if any doctrine in terms of which the great and continuing constitutional struggle between the President and the Republican Radicals in Congress might be re-

Section D. Civil War Amendments and Civil Rights Statutes 761

solved. That controversy turned upon the issue whether the President or Congress had authority to set the policies for Reconstruction and determine when and by what means the Southern states should be readmitted to the Union. Beneath that constitutional issue lay, of course, disagreement as to the desirable policy of Reconstruction. See McKitrick, Andrew Johnson and Reconstruction (1960).

Shortly after the adoption of the Thirteenth Amendment the Senate Judiciary Committee presented a Civil Rights Bill for enactment. The declared purpose of its sponsors was to make the Thirteenth Amendment effective in those Southern states which had recently adopted the so-called "Black Codes" and other police regulations designed to control the conduct of the Negro population.[b] As passed by the Congress on March 13, 1866, and as enacted on April 9 over President Johnson's veto, the Civil Rights Act (14 Stat. 27) contained the following provisions:

"Be it enacted, That all persons born in the United States and not subject to any foreign power, excluding Indians not taxed, are hereby declared to be citizens of the United States; and such citizens, of every race and color, without regard to any previous condition of slavery or involuntary servitude, except as a punishment for crime whereof the party shall have been duly convicted, shall have the same right, in every State and Territory in the United States, to make and enforce contracts, to sue, be parties, and give evidence, to inherit, purchase, lease, sell, hold, and convey real and personal property, and to full and equal benefit of all laws and proceedings for the security of person and property, as is enjoyed by white citizens, and shall be subject to like punishment, pains, and penalties, and to none other, any law, statute, ordinance, regulation, or custom, to the contrary notwithstanding.

"Sec. 2. And be it further enacted, That any person who, under color of any law, statute, ordinance, regulation, or custom, shall subject, or cause to be subjected, any inhabitant of any State or Territory to the deprivation of any right secured or protected by this act, or to different punishment, pains, or penalties on account of such person having at any time been held in a condition of slavery or involuntary servitude, except as a punishment for crime whereof the party shall have been duly convicted, or by reason of his color or race, than is prescribed for the punishment of white persons, shall be deemed guilty of a misdemeanor, and, on conviction, shall be punished by fine not exceeding one thousand dollars, or imprisonment not exceeding one year, or both, in the discretion of the court."

In a message on March 27th, President Johnson gave some of the following reasons for his veto of the Civil Rights Act (6 Richardson, Messages and Papers of the Presidents 405 (1897)): . . . .

"The first section of the bill also contains an enumeration of the rights to be enjoyed by these classes so made citizens 'in every State and Territory in the United States.' These rights are 'to make and enforce contracts; to sue, be parties, and give evidence; to inherit, purchase, lease, sell, hold, and convey real and personal property,' and to have 'full and equal benefit of all laws and proceedings for the security of person and property as is enjoyed by white citizens.' So, too, they are made subject to the same punishment, pains, and penalties in common with white citizens, and to none other. Thus a perfect equality of the white and colored races is attempted to be fixed by Federal law in every State of the Union over the vast field of State jurisdiction covered by these enumerated rights. In no one of these can any State ever exercise any power of discrimination between the different races. In the exercise of State policy over matters exclusively affecting the people of each State it has frequently been thought expedient to discriminate between the two races. By the statutes of some of the States, Northern as well as Southern, it is enacted, for instance,

---

[b] The Senate debates concerning the Civil Rights Act are in Cong. Globe, 39th Cong., 1st Sess. 474-481, 497-507, 522-530, 569-578; 594-607; the House debates, id. at 1115-1125, 1151-1162, 1262-1272; 1290-1296, 1366-1367 (1866). — Ed.

762 Chapter Fourteen. Privileges & Immunities; Equality; Civil Rights

that no white person shall intermarry with a negro or mulatto. Chancellor Kent says, speaking of the blacks, that —

" 'Marriages between them and the whites are forbidden in some of the States where slavery does not exist, and they are prohibited in all the slaveholding States; and when not absolutely contrary to law, they are revolting, and regarded as an offense against public decorum.'

"I do not say that this bill repeals State laws on the subject of marriage between the two races, for as the whites are forbidden to intermarry with the blacks, the blacks can only make such contracts as the whites themselves are allowed to make, and therefore can not under this bill enter into the marriage contract with the whites. I cite this discrimination, however, as an instance of the State policy as to discrimination, and to inquire whether if Congress can abrogate all State laws of discrimination between the two races in the matter of real estate, of suits, and of contracts generally Congress may not also repeal the State laws as to the contract of marriage between the two races. Hitherto every subject embraced in the enumeration of rights contained in this bill has been considered as exclusively belonging to the States. They all relate to the internal police and economy of the respective States. They are matters which in each State concern the domestic condition of its people, varying in each according to its own peculiar circumstances and the safety and well-being of its own citizens."

Congress adopted the Civil Rights Act over the President's veto after extensive debate in the Senate.[c] Senator Trumbull, for example, responded as follows to the President's criticism:[d]

"This bill in no manner interferes with the municipal regulations of any State which protects all alike in their rights of person and property. It could have no operation in Massachusetts, New York, Illinois or most of the States of the Union. How preposterous, then, to charge that unless some State can have and exercise the right to punish somebody, or to deny somebody a civil right on account of his color, its rights as a State will be destroyed. It is manifest that unless this bill can be passed, nothing can be done to protect the freedmen in their liberty and their rights."

The provision of the statute giving testimonial capacity to Negroes was held unconstitutional in Bowlin v. Commonwealth, 2 Bush (Ky.) 5 (1867).

The Supreme Court and congressional powers with respect to Reconstruction. Between 1867 and 1869 three serious attempts were made to have the Supreme Court of the United States determine that the congressional plans of Reconstruction, which had been adopted over the objections of the President, were unconstitutional. In each case it was found, on different grounds, that the Court lacked jurisdiction to consider the constitutional problems. The cases were Mississippi v. Johnson, 4 Wall. 475 (1867); Georgia v. Stanton, 6 Wall. 50 (1867); and Ex parte McCardle, 7 Wall. 506 (1869). The story of these cases is told in Fairman, Reconstruction and Reunion, 1864-1888, Part One, chs. VIII-X (1971) (VI Holmes Devise History of the Supreme Court). See also 2 Warren, The Supreme Court in United States History, c. 30 (1926).

The adoption of the Fourteenth Amendment. Of the considerable body of literature concerning the adoption of the Fourteenth Amendment, the most important works are Kendrick, The Journal of the Joint Committee of Fifteen on Reconstruction (1914); Flack, The Adoption of the Fourteenth Amendment (1908); Fairman, Does the Fourteenth Amendment Incorporate the Bill of Rights? The Original Understanding, 2 Stan. L. Rev. 5 (1949); James, The Framing of the Fourteenth Amendment (1956); Fairman, Reconstruction and Reunion, 1864-1888, Part One, c. XX (1971).

---

[c] Cong. Globe, 39th Cong., 1st Sess. (Senate) 1755-1761; 1775-1787; 1801-1809, app. 181-185; (House) 1832-1837, 1857-1861 (1866). — ED.
[d] Id. at 1761. — ED.

Section D. Civil War Amendments and Civil Rights Statutes 765

connection with the history of the times, which cannot fail to have an important bearing on any question of doubt concerning their true meaning. . . .

The institution of African slavery, as it existed in about half the states of the Union, and the contests pervading the public mind for many years, between those who desired its curtailment and ultimate extinction and those who desired additional safeguards for its security and perpetuation, culminated in the effort, on the part of most of the states in which slavery existed, to separate from the Federal government, and to resist its authority. This constituted the War of the Rebellion, and whatever auxiliary causes may have contributed to bring about this war, undoubtedly the overshadowing and efficient cause was African slavery.

In that struggle slavery, as a legalized social relation, perished. It perished as a necessity of the bitterness and force of the conflict. . . .

. . . Hence the 13th article of amendment of that instrument. Its two short sections seem hardly to admit of construction; so vigorous is their expression and so appropriate to the purpose we have indicated.

1. Neither slavery nor involuntary servitude, except as a punishment for crime, whereof the party shall have been duly convicted, shall exist within the United States or any place subject to their jurisdiction.

2. Congress shall have power to enforce this article by appropriate legislation. . . .

That a personal servitude was meant, is proved by the use of the word "involuntary," which can only apply to human beings. The exception of servitude as a punishment for crime gives an idea of the class of servitude that is meant. The word "servitude" is of larger meaning than "slavery," as the latter is popularly understood in this country, and the obvious purpose was to forbid all shades and conditions of African slavery. It was very well understood that in the form of apprenticeship for long terms, as it had been practised in the West India Islands, on the abolition of slavery by the English government, or by reducing the slaves to the condition of serfs attached to the plantation, the purpose of the article might have been evaded, if only the word "slavery" had been used. . . .

[T]o establish a clear and comprehensive definition of citizenship which should declare what should constitute citizenship of the United States and also citizenship of a state, the 1st clause of the 1st section [of the 14th article] was framed:

"All persons born or naturalized in the United States and subject to the jurisdiction thereof are citizens of the United States and of the state wherein they reside."

The first observation we have to make on this clause is that it puts at rest both the questions which we stated to have been the subject of differences of opinion. It declares that persons may be citizens of the United States without regard to their citizenship of a particular state, and it overturns the Dred Scott decision by making all persons born within the United States and subject to its jurisdiction citizens of the United States. That its main purpose was to establish the citizenship of the negro can admit of no doubt. The phrase "subject to its jurisdiction" was intended to exclude from its operation children of ministers, consuls and citizens or subjects of foreign states born within the United States.

The next observation is more important in view of the arguments of counsel in the present case. It is that the distinction between citizenship of the United States and citizenship of a state is clearly recognized and established. Not only may a man be a citizen of the United States without being a citizen of a state, but an important element is necessary to convert the former into the latter. He must reside within the state to make him a citizen of it, but it is only necessary that he should be born or naturalized in the United States to be a citizen of the Union.

It is quite clear, then, that there is a citizenship of the United States and a citizenship of a state, which are distinct from each other and which depend upon different characteristics or circumstances in the individual.

We think this distinction and its explicit recognition in this Amendment of great weight in this argument, because the next paragraph of this same section, which is the one mainly relied on by the plaintiffs in error, speaks only of privileges and immunities of citizens of the United States, and does not speak of those of citizens of the several states. The argument, however, in favor of the plaintiffs, rests wholly on the assumption that the citizenship is the same and the privileges and immunities guaranteed by the clause are the same. . . .

The first occurrence of the words "privileges and immunities" in our constitutional history is to be found in the fourth of the Articles of the old Confederation.

It declares "That, the better to secure and perpetuate mutual friendship and intercourse among the people of the different states in this Union, the free inhabitants of each of these states, paupers, vagabonds, and fugitives from justice excepted, shall be entitled to all the privileges and immunities of free citizens in the several states; and the people of each state shall have free ingress and regress to and from any other state, and shall enjoy therein all the privileges of trade and commerce, subject to the same duties, impositions, and restrictions as the inhabitants thereof respectively."

In the Constitution of the United States, which superseded the Articles of Confederation, the corresponding provision is found in section two of the 4th article, in the following words: The citizens of each state shall be entitled to all the privileges and immunities of citizens of the several states.

There can be but little question that the purpose of both these provisions is the same, and that the privileges and immunities intended are the same in each. In the article of the Confederation we have some of these specifically mentioned, and enough perhaps to give some general idea of the class of civil rights meant by the phrase.

Fortunately we are not without judicial construction of this clause of the Constitution. The first and the leading case on the subject is that of Corfield v. Coryell, decided by Mr. Justice Washington in the circuit court for the district of Pennsylvania in 1823. 4 Wash. C.C. 371.

"The inquiry," he says, "is, what are the privileges and immunities of citizens of the several states? We feel no hesitation in confining these expressions to those privileges and immunities which are fundamental; which belong of right to the citizens of all free governments, and which have at all times been enjoyed by citizens of the several states which compose this Union, from the time of their becoming free, independent, and sovereign. What these fundamental principles are, it would be more tedious than difficult to enumerate." "They may all, however, be comprehended under the following general heads: protection by the government, with the right to acquire and possess property of every kind, and to pursue and obtain happiness and safety, subject, nevertheless, to such restraints as the government may prescribe for the general good of the whole." . . .

In the case of Paul v. Virginia, 8 Wall. 180, the court, in expounding this clause of the Constitution, says that "the privileges and immunities secured to citizens of each state in the several states, by the provision in question, are those privileges and immunities which are common to the citizens in the latter states under their Constitution and laws by virtue of their being citizens."

The constitutional provision there alluded to did not create those rights, which it called privileges and immunities of citizens of the states. It threw around them in that clause no security for the citizen of the state in which they were claimed or exercised. Nor did it profess to control the power of the state governments over the rights of its own citizens.

Its sole purpose was to declare to the several states, that whatever those rights, as you grant or establish them to your own citizens, or as you limit or qualify, or impose restrictions on their exercise, the same, neither more nor less, shall be the measure of the rights of citizens of other states within your jurisdiction.

It would be the vainest show of learning to attempt to prove by citations of authority, that up to the adoption of the recent Amendments, no claim or pretense was set up that those rights depended on the Federal government for their existence or protection, beyond the very few express limitations which the Federal Constitution imposed upon the states — such, for instance, as the prohibition against ex post facto laws, bills of attainder, and laws impairing the obligation of contracts. But with the exception of these and a few other restrictions, the entire domain of the privileges and immunities of citizens of the states, as above defined, lay within the constitutional and legislative power of the states, and without that of the Federal government. Was it the purpose of the 14th Amendment, by the simple declaration that no state should make or enforce any law which shall abridge the privileges and immunities of citizens of the United States, to transfer the security and protection of all the civil rights which we have mentioned, from the states to the Federal government? And where it is declared that Congress shall have the power to enforce that article, was it intended to bring within the power of Congress the entire domain of civil rights heretofore belonging exclusively to the states?

All this and more must follow, if the proposition of the plaintiffs in error be sound. For not only are these rights subject to the control of Congress whenever in its discretion any of them are supposed to be abridged by state legislation, but that body may also pass laws in advance, limiting and restricting the exercise of legislative power by the states, in their most ordinary and usual functions, as in its judgment it may think proper on all such subjects. And still further, such a construction followed by the reversal of the judgments of the supreme court of Louisiana in these cases would constitute this court a perpetual censor upon all legislation of the states, on the civil rights of their own citizens, with authority to nullify such as it did not approve as consistent with those rights, as they existed at the time of the adoption of this Amendment. The argument, we admit, is not always the most conclusive which is drawn from the consequences urged against the adoption of a particular construction of an instrument. But when, as in the case before us, these consequences are so serious, so far-reaching and pervading, so great a departure from the structure and spirit of our institutions; when the effect is to fetter and degrade the state governments by subjecting them to the control of Congress, in the exercise of powers heretofore universally conceded to them of the most ordinary and fundamental character; when in fact it radically changes the whole theory of the relations of the state and Federal governments to each other and of both these governments to the people; the argument has a force that is irresistible, in the absence of language which expresses such a purpose too clearly to admit of doubt.

We are convinced that no such results were intended by the Congress which proposed these amendments, nor by the legislatures of the states, which ratified them.

Having shown that the privileges and immunities relied on in the argument are those which belong to citizens of the states as such, and that they are left to the state governments for security and protection, and not by this article placed under the special care of the Federal government, we may hold ourselves excused from defining the privileges and immunities of citizens of the United States which no state can abridge, until some case involving those privileges may make it necessary to do so.

But lest it should be said that no such privileges and immunities are to be found if those we have been considering are excluded, we venture to suggest some which owe their existence to the Federal government, its national character, its Constitution, or its laws.

One of these is well described in the case of Crandall v. Nevada, 6 Wall. 36. It is said to be the right of the citizen of this great country, protected by implied guaranties of its Constitution, "to come to the seat of government to assert any claim he may have upon that government, to transact any business he may have with it, to seek its protection, to share its offices, to engage in administering its functions. He has the right of free access to its seaports, through which all operations of foreign commerce are conducted, to the subtreasuries, land-offices, and courts of justice in the several states." And quoting from the language of Chief Justice Taney in another case, it is said "that, for all the great purposes for which the Federal government was established, we are one people with one common country; we are all citizens of the United States"; and it is as such citizens that their rights are supported in this court in Crandall v. Nevada.

Another privilege of a citizen of the United States is to demand the care and protection of the Federal government over his life, liberty, and property when on the high seas or within the jurisdiction of a foreign government. Of this there can be no doubt, nor that the right depends upon his character as a citizen of the United States. The right to peaceably assemble and petition for redress of grievances, the privilege of the writ of habeas corpus, are rights of the citizen guaranteed by the Federal Constitution. The right to use the navigable waters of the United States, however they may penetrate the territory of the several states, and all rights secured to our citizens by treaties with foreign nations, are dependent upon citizenship of the United States, and not citizenship of a state. One of these privileges is conferred by the very article under consideration. It is that a citizen of the United States can, of his own volition, become a citizen of any state of the Union by a bona fide residence therein, with the same rights as other citizens of that state. To these may be added the rights secured by the 13th and 15th articles of Amendment, and by the other clause of the Fourteenth, next to be considered.[f]

But it is useless to pursue this branch of the inquiry, since we are of opinion that the rights claimed by these plaintiffs in error, if they have any existence, are not privileges and immunities of citizens of the United States within the meaning of the clause of the 14th Amendment under consideration. . . .

The argument has not been much pressed in these cases that the defendant's charter deprives the plaintiffs of their property without due process of law, or that it denies to them the equal protection of the law. The first of these paragraphs has been in the Constitution since the adoption of the 5th Amendment, as a restraint upon the Federal power. It is also to be found in some form of expression in the constitutions of nearly all the states, as a restraint upon the power of the states. This law, then, has practically been the same as it now is during the existence of the government, except so far as the present Amendment may place the restraining power over the states in this matter in the hands of the Federal government.

We are not without judicial interpretation, therefore, both state and national, of the meaning of this clause. And it is sufficient to say that under no construction of that provision that we have ever seen, or any that we deem admissible, can the restraint imposed by the state of Louisiana upon the exercise of their trade by the butchers of New Orleans be held to be a deprivation of property within the meaning of that provision.

"Nor shall any state deny to any person within its jurisdiction the equal protection of the laws."

In the light of the history of these amendments, and the pervading purpose of them, which we have already discussed, it is not difficult to give a meaning to this clause. The existence of laws in the states where the newly emancipated negroes resided, which discriminated with gross injustice and hardship against them as a class, was the evil to be remedied by this clause, and by it such laws are forbidden.

If, however, the states did not conform their laws to its requirements, then by the 5th section of the article of amendment Congress was authorized to enforce it by suitable legislation. We doubt very much whether any action of a state not directed by way of discrimination against the negroes as a class, or on account of their race, will ever be held to come within the purview of this provision. It is so clearly a provision for that race and that emergency, that a strong case would be necessary for its application to any other. But as it is a state that is to be dealt with, and not alone the validity of its laws, we may safely leave that matter until Congress shall have exercised its power, or some case of state oppression, by denial of equal justice in its courts, shall have claimed a decision at our hands. We find no such case in the one before us, and we do not deem it necessary to go over the argument again, as it may have relation to this particular clause of the Amendment.

In the early history of the organization of the government, its statesmen seem to have divided on the line which should separate the powers of the national government from

---

[f] Cf. Bradley, J., in Live Stock Assn. v. Crescent City Co., 1 Abbott 388, 398, 15 F. Cas. 649, 652 (1870). See also Senator Frelinghuysen, Cong. Globe, 43d Cong., 1st Sess. 4087. — ED.

those of the state governments, and though this line has never been very well defined in public opinion, such a division has continued from that day to this.

The adoption of the first eleven amendments to the Constitution so soon after the original instrument was accepted shows a prevailing sense of danger at that time from the Federal power and it cannot be denied that such a jealousy continued to exist with many patriotic men until the breaking out of the late Civil War. It was then discovered that the true danger to the perpetuity of the Union was in the capacity of the state organizations to combine and concentrate all the powers of the state, and of contiguous states, for a determined resistance to the general government.

Unquestionably this has given great force to the argument, and added largely to the number of those who believe in the necessity of a strong national government.

But, however pervading this sentiment, and however it may have contributed to the adoption of the Amendments we have been considering, we do not see in those Amendments any purpose to destroy the main features of the general system. Under the pressure of all the excited feeling growing out of the war, our statesmen have still believed that the existence of the states with powers for domestic and local government, including the regulation of civil rights, the rights of person and of property, was essential to the perfect working of our complex form of government, though they have thought proper to impose additional limitations on the states, and to confer additional power on that of the nation.

But whatever fluctuations may be seen in the history of public opinion on this subject during the period of our national existence, we think it will be found that this court, so far as its functions required, has always held, with a steady and an even hand, the balance between state and Federal power, and we trust that such may continue to be the history of its relation to that subject so long as it shall have duties to perform which demand of it a construction of the Constitution, or of any of its parts.

The judgments of the Supreme Court of Louisiana in these cases are affirmed.

Mr. Justice Field, dissenting:

I am unable to agree with the majority of the court in these cases, and will proceed to state the reasons of my dissent from their judgment. . . .

The question presented is . . . one of the gravest importance, not merely to the parties here, but to the whole country. It is nothing less than the question whether the recent Amendments to the Federal Constitution protect the citizens of the United States against the deprivation of their common rights by state legislation. In my judgment the fourteenth Amendment does afford such protection, and was so intended by the Congress which framed and the states which adopted it. . . .

The first clause of this Amendment determines who are citizens of the United States, and how their citizenship is created. Before its enactment there was much diversity of opinion among jurists and statesmen whether there was any such citizenship independent of that of the state, and, if any existed, as to the manner in which it originated. With a great number the opinion prevailed that there was no such citizenship independent of the citizenship of the state. . . .

The first clause of the fourteenth Amendment changes this whole subject, and removes it from the region of discussion and doubt. It recognizes in express terms, if it does not create, citizens of the United States, and it makes their citizenship dependent upon the place of their birth, or the fact of their adoption, and not upon the Constitution or laws of any state or the condition of their ancestry. A citizen of a state is now only a citizen of the United States residing in that state. The fundamental rights, privileges, and immunities which belong to him as a free man and a free citizen, now belong to him as a citizen of the United States, and are not dependent upon his citizenship of any state. . . .

The terms "privileges and immunities" are not new in the Amendment; they were in the Constitution before the Amendment was adopted. They are found in the 2d section of the 4th article, which declares that "the citizens of each state shall be entitled to all privileges and immunities of citizens in the several states," and they have been the subject of frequent consideration in judicial decisions. In Corfield v. Coryell, 4 Wash. C.C. 380, Mr. Justice Washington said he had "no hesitation in confining these expressions to those privileges and immunities which were, in their nature, fundamental; which belong of right to citizens of all free governments, and which have at all times been enjoyed by the citizens of the several states which composed the Union, from the time of their becoming free, independent, and sovereign"; and in considering what those fundamental privileges were, he said that perhaps it would be more tedious than difficult to enumerate them, but that they might be "all comprehended under the following general heads: protection by the government; the enjoyment of life and liberty, with the right to acquire and possess property of every kind, and to pursue and obtain happiness and safety; subject, nevertheless, to such restraints as the government may justly prescribe for the general good of the whole." This appears to me to be a sound construction of the clause in question. The privileges and immunities designated are those which of right belong to the citizens of all free governments. Clearly among these must be placed the right to pursue a lawful employment in a lawful manner, without other restraint than such as equally affects all persons. In the discussions in Congress upon the passage of the civil rights act repeated reference was made to this language of Mr. Justice Washington. It was cited by Senator Trumbull with the observation that it enumerated the very rights belonging to a citizen of the United States set forth in the 1st section of the act, and with the statement that all persons born in the United States, being declared by the act citizens of the United States, would thenceforth be entitled to the rights of citizens, and that these were the great fundamental rights set forth in the act; and that they were set forth "as appertaining to every freeman." . . .

I am authorized by MR. CHIEF JUSTICE CHASE, MR. JUSTICE SWAYNE and MR. JUSTICE BRADLEY, to state that they concur with me in this dissenting opinion.

MR. JUSTICE BRADLEY, dissenting:

I concur in the opinion which has just been read by MR. JUSTICE FIELD, but desire to add a few observations for the purpose of more fully illustrating my views on the important question decided in these cases, and the special grounds on which they rest. . . .

In my view, a law which prohibits a large class of citizens from adopting a lawful employment, or from following a lawful employment previously adopted, does deprive them of liberty as well as property, without due process of law. Their right of choice is a portion of their liberty; their occupation is their property. Such a law also deprives those citizens of the equal protection of the laws, contrary to the last clause of the section. . . .

The mischief to be remedied was not merely slavery and its incidents and consequences; but that spirit of insubordination and disloyalty to the National government which had troubled the country for so many years in some of the States, and that intolerance of free speech and free discussion which often rendered life and property insecure, and led to much unequal legislation. The amendment was an attempt to give voice to the strong National yearning for that time and that condition of things, in which American citizenship should be a sure guarantee of safety, and in which every citizen of the United States might stand erect on every portion of its soil, in the full enjoyment of every right and privilege belonging to a freeman, without fear of violence or molestation.

In my opinion the judgment of the Supreme Court of Louisiana ought to be reversed.[g]

---

[g] A dissenting opinion by Swayne, J., is omitted. The dramatic and critical part which John A. Campbell of Alabama, former Associate Justice of the Supreme Court, played in arguing the Slaughter-House Cases and formulating the doctrine which Field and Bradley, JJ., utilized in their dissents is effectively told in Twiss, Lawyers and the Constitution, c. 3 (1942). It is, perhaps, significant that Campbell some years after the case was decided against him said that "it was probably best for the country that the case so turned out." Connor, John Archibald Campbell 231 (1920).

In Butchers' Union Slaughter-House Co. v. Crescent City Slaughter-House Co., 111 U.S. 746 (1883), the Court, in an opinion by Miller, J., with Field and Bradley, JJ., writing concurrent opinions, sustained the action of Louisiana repealing the statute which had created the monopoly involved in the Slaughter-House Cases. — ED.

United States v. Hall F. Cas. No. 15282 (C.C.E.D. Ala. 1871)

Woods, Circuit Judge. This is an indictment for a violation of the 6th section of the act of congress, approved May 31, 1870 [16 Stat. 140] entitled "An act to enforce the rights of citizens of the United States to vote in the several states of this Union, and for other purposes." It contains two counts. The first count in substance charges that the defendants did unlawfully and feloniously band and conspire together, with intent to injure, oppress, threaten and intimidate Charles Hays and others, naming them, citizens of the United States of America, with intent to prevent and hinder their free exercise and enjoyment of the right of freedom of speech, the same being a right and privilege granted and secured to them by the constitution of the United States. The second count charges in substance that the defendants did unlawfully and feloniously band and conspire together, with intent to injure, oppress, threaten and intimidate William Miller and others, naming them, good and lawful citizens of the United States, with intent to prevent and hinder their free exercise and enjoyment of the right and privilege to peaceably assemble, the same being a right and privilege granted and secured to them by the constitution of the United States. A demurrer is filed to this indictment based on the following grounds; (1) That the matters charged in said counts are not in violation of any right or privilege granted or secured by the constitution of the United States. (2) That they are not in violation of any provision of the act of congress, on which the indictment is based, or of any statute of the United States. (3) That each of said counts charges the commission of several and distinct offenses.

[As to some of the alleged sources of congressional authority, Judge Woods concluded:] We are of opinion, therefore, that under the original constitution and the first eight articles of amendment congress had not the power to protect by law the people of a state in the freedom of speech and of the press, in the free exercise of religion, or in the right peaceably to assemble. . . .

We have thus far considered this demurrer, and it seems to have been argued for the defense, without reference to the recent amendments to the constitution. As we are of opinion that the fourteenth amendment has a vital bearing upon the question raised, it is well that we should look to its provisions. It declares that "all persons, born or naturalized in the United States, and subject to the jurisdiction thereof, are citizens of the United States, and the state wherein they reside." By the original constitution citizenship in the United States was a consequence of citizenship in a state. By this clause this order of things is reversed. Citizenship in the United States is defined; it is made independent of citizenship in a state, and citizenship in a state is a result of citizenship in the United States. So that a person born or naturalized in the United States, and subject to its jurisdiction, is, without reference to state constitutions or laws, entitled to all the privileges and immunities secured by the constitution of the United States to citizens thereof. The amendment proceeds: "No state shall make or enforce any law which shall abridge the privileges and immunities of citizens of the United States." What are the privileges and immunities of citizens of the United States here referred to? They are undoubtedly those which may be denominated fundamental: which belong of right to the citizens of the several states which compose this Union from the time of their becoming free, independent and sovereign. Corfield v. Coryell [4 Wash. C.C. 371]: . . . Among these we are safe in including those which in the constitution are expressly secured to the people, either as against the action of the federal or state governments. Included in these are the right of freedom of speech, and the right peaceably to assemble.

To recur now to the first ground of demurrer: are these rights secured to the people by the constitution of the United States? We find that congress is forbidden to impair them by the first amendment, and the states are forbidden to impair them by the fourteenth amendment. Can they not, then, be said to be completely secured? They are expressly recognized, and both congress and the states are forbidden to abridge them. Before the fourteenth amendment, congress could not impair them, but the states might. Since the fourteenth amendment, the bulwarks about these rights have been strengthened, and now the states are positively inhibited from impairing or abridging them, and so far as the provisions of the organic law can secure them they are completely and absolutely secured. The next clause of the fourteenth amendment reads: "Nor shall any state deny to any person within its jurisdiction the equal protection of the laws." Then follows an express grant of power to the federal government: "Congress may enforce this provision by appropriate legislation." From these provisions it follows clearly, as it seems to us, that congress has the power, by appropriate legislation, to protect the fundamental rights of citizens of the United States against unfriendly or insufficient state legislation, for the fourteenth amendment not only prohibits the making or enforcing of laws which shall abridge the privileges of the citizen, but prohibits the states from denying to all persons within its jurisdiction the equal protection of the laws. Denying includes inaction as well as action, and denying the equal protection of the laws includes the omission to protect, as well as the omission to pass laws for protection. The citizen of the United States is entitled to the enforcement of the laws for the protection of his fundamental rights, as well as the enactment of such laws. Therefore, to guard against the invasion of the citizen's fundamental rights, and to insure their adequate protection, as well against state legislation as state inaction, or incompetency, the amendment gives congress the power to enforce its provisions by appropriate legislation. And as it would be unseemly for congress to interfere directly with state enactments, and as it cannot compel the activity of state officials, the only appropriate legislation it can make is that which will operate directly on offenders and offenses, and protect the rights which the amendment secures. The extent to which congress shall exercise this power must depend on its discretion in view of the circumstances of each case. If the exercise of it in any case should seem to interfere with the domestic affairs of a state, it must be remembered that it is for the purpose of protecting federal rights, and these must be protected even though it interferes with state laws or the administration of state laws. We think, therefore, that the right of freedom of speech, and the other rights enumerated in the first eight articles of amendment to the constitution of the United States are the privileges and immunities of citizens of the United States, that they are secured by the constitution, that congress has the power to protect them by appropriate legislation. We are further of opinion that the act on which this indictment is founded applies to cases of this kind, and that it is legislation appropriate to the end in view, namely, the protection of the fundamental rights of citizens of the United States. . . .

We are of opinion, also, that this indictment is sufficiently definite and certain. The law describes particularly the offense created by it, and the indictment follows the language of the law. Our conclusion is, therefore, that the demurrer to this indictment must be overruled.

NOTE

For correspondence between Judge (later Justice) Woods and Justice Bradley concerning the Hall case, see Magrath, Morrison R. Waite: The Triumph of Character 121 (1963). See also Graham, The Waite Court and the Fourteenth Amendment, 17 Vand. L. Rev. 525, 528 (1964).

UNITED STATES v. CRUIKSHANK, 1 Woods 308, F. Cas. No. 14,897 (C.C.D. La. 1874). "The judges not being agreed, Mr. Circuit Justice Bradley delivered the following opinion in favor of the motion, which was granted accordingly, and the case was certified to the supreme court:

"The indictment in this case is founded on the 6th and 7th sections of the act of congress approved May 31, 1870, entitled 'an act to enforce the rights of citizens of the

Section D. Civil War Amendments and Civil Rights Statutes

United States to vote in the several states of this Union, and for other purposes.' (16 Stat. 140.) It contains two distinct series of counts, in one of which the defendants are charged with having unlawfully and feloniously banded or conspired together to intimidate certain persons of African descent (specified by name), and thereby to hinder and prevent them in, and deprive them of, the free exercise and enjoyment of certain supposed constitutional rights and privileges, respectively specified in the several counts of the indictment, such as, in one count, the right peaceably to assemble themselves together; in another, the right to keep and bear arms; in a third, the right to be protected against deprivation of life, liberty and property without due process of law; in a fourth, the right to the full and equal benefit of the laws; in another, the right to vote, etc. The second series of counts charges murder in addition to, and whilst carrying out, the conspiracies charged. Three of the defendants, Cruikshank, Hadnot and Irwin, have been convicted of conspiracy under the first series of counts, which are founded on the sixth section of the act, and now move in arrest of judgment, on the ground that the act is unconstitutional, and that the indictment does not charge any crime under it.

"The main ground of objection is that the act is municipal in its character, operating directly on the conduct of individuals, and taking the place of ordinary state legislation; and that there is no constitutional authority for such an act, inasmuch as the state laws furnish adequate remedy for the alleged wrongs committed. . . .

"The XIIIth amendment declares that neither slavery nor involuntary servitude, except as a punishment for crime, shall exist within the United States or any place subject to its jurisdiction, and that congress shall have power to enforce this article by appropriate legislation.

"This is not merely a prohibition against the passage or enforcement of any law inflicting or establishing slavery or involuntary servitude, but it is a positive declaration that *slavery shall not exist*. It prohibits the thing. In the enforcement of this article, therefore, congress has to deal with the subject matter. If an amendment had been adopted that polygamy should not exist within the United States, and a similar power to enforce it had been given as in the case of slavery, congress would certainly have had the power to legislate for the suppression and punishment of polygamy. So, undoubtedly, by the XIIIth amendment congress has power to legislate for the entire eradication of slavery in the United States. . . .

"But this power does not authorize congress to pass laws for the punishment of ordinary crimes and offenses against persons of the colored race or any other race. That belongs to the state government alone. . . .

"To illustrate: if in a community or neighborhood composed principally of whites, a citizen of African descent, or of the Indian race, not within the exception of the amendment, should propose to lease and cultivate a farm, and a combination should be formed to expel him and prevent him from the accomplishment of his purpose on account of his race or color, it cannot be doubted that this would be a case within the power of congress to remedy and redress. It would be a case of interference with that person's exercise of his equal rights as a citizen because of his race. But if that person should be injured in his person or property by any wrong-doer for the mere felonious or wrongful purpose of malice, revenge, hatred, or gain, without any design to interfere with his rights of citizenship or equality before the laws, as being a person of a different race and color from the white race, it would be an ordinary crime, punishable by the state laws only.

"To constitute an offense, therefore, of which congress and the courts of the United States have a right to take cognizance under this amendment, there must be a design to injure a person, or deprive him of his equal right of enjoying the protection of the laws, by reason of his race, color, or previous condition of servitude. Otherwise it is a case exclusively within the jurisdiction of the state and its courts.

[Mr. Justice Bradley examined the counts of the indictment and held them all invalid. Among other failings in the indictment, he found that the counts did not allege that the defendants had "committed the acts complained of with a design to deprive the injured persons of their rights on account of their race, color or previous condition of servitude."]

"In my opinion the motion in arrest of judgment must be granted."[h]

Ex parte Virginia 100 U.S. 339, 25 L. Ed. 676 (1880)

MR. JUSTICE STRONG delivered the opinion of the court:

The petitioner, J. D. Coles, was arrested, and he is now held in custody under an indictment found against him in the District Court of the United States for the Western District of Virginia. The indictment charged that the said Coles, being a Judge of the County Court of Pittsylvania County of that State, and an officer charged by law with the selection of jurors to serve in the Circuit and County courts of said county in the year 1878, did then and there exclude and fail to select as grand and petit jurors certain citizens of said County of Pittsylvania, of African race and black color, said citizens possessing all other qualifications prescribed by law, and being by him the said J. D. Coles, excluded from the jury lists made out by him as such Judge, on account of their race, color and previous condition of servitude, and for no other reason, against the peace and dignity of the United States, and against the form of the Statute of the United States in such case made and provided. [F. Cas. No. 18259.] . . .

In the present case, the petitioner Coles is in custody under a bench-warrant directed by the District Court, and the averment is that the court had no jurisdiction of the indictment on which the warrant is founded. . . .

The indictment and bench-warrant, in virtue of which the petitioner Coles has been arrested and is held in custody, have their justification if any they have, in the Act of Congress of March 1, 1875, sec. 4, 18 Stat. at L., 336. That section enacts that "No citizen, possessing all other qualifications which are or may be prescribed by law shall be disqualified for service as grand or petit juror in any court of the United States, or of any State, on account of race, color or previous condition of servitude; and any officer or other person charged with any duty in the selection or summoning of jurors who shall exclude or fail to summon any citizen for the cause aforesaid, shall, on conviction thereof, be deemed guilty of a misdemeanor, and be fined not more than $5,000." The defendant has been indicted for the misdemeanor described in this Act, and it is not denied that he is now properly held in custody to answer the indictment, if the Act of Congress was warranted by the Constitution. The whole merits of the case are involved in the question, whether the Act was thus warranted.

The provisions of the Constitution that relate to this subject are found in the 13th and 14th Amendments. . . .

One great purpose of these Amendments was to raise the colored race from that condition of inferiority and servitude in which most of them had previously stood into perfect equality of civil rights with all other persons within the jurisdiction of the States. They were intended to take away all possibility of oppression by law because of race or color. They were intended to be, what they really are, limitations of the power of the States and enlargements of the power of Congress. They are, to some extent, declaratory of rights, and though in form prohibitions, they imply immunities, such as may be protected by congressional legislation. We had occasion in the Slaughter-House Cases, 16 Wall. 36, to express our opinion of their spirit and purpose, and to some extent of their meaning. We have again been called to consider them in the cases of Tenn. v. Davis [100 U.S. 257] and Strauder v. West Va., just decided [100 U.S. 303]. In this latter case we held that the 14th Amendment secures, among other civil rights, to colored men, when charged with criminal offenses against a State, an impartial jury trial by jurors indifferently selected or

[h] Affirmed, United States v. Cruikshank, 92 U.S. 542 (1876). — ED.

chosen without discrimination against such jurors because of their color. We held that immunity from any such discrimination is one of the equal rights of all persons, and that any withholding it by a State is a denial of the equal protection of the laws, within the meaning of the Amendment. We held that such an equal right to an impartial jury trial, and such an immunity from unfriendly discrimination, are placed by the Amendment under the protection of the General Government and guaranteed by it. We held, further, that this protection and this guarantee, as the 5th section of the Amendment expressly ordains, may be enforced by Congress by means of appropriate legislation. . . .

We have said the prohibitions of the 14th Amendment are addressed to the States. . . . They have reference to actions of the political body denominated a State, by whatever instruments or in whatever modes that action may be taken. A State acts by its legislative, its executive or its judicial authorities. It can act in no other way. The constitutional provision, therefore, must mean that no agency of the State, or of the officers or agents by whom its powers are exerted, shall deny to any person within its jurisdiction the equal protection of the laws. Whoever, by virtue of public position under a state government, deprives another of property, life or liberty without due process of law, or denies or takes away the equal protection of the laws, violates the constitutional inhibition; and as he acts in the name and for the State, and is clothed with the State's power, his act is that of the State. This must be so, or the constitutional prohibition has no meaning. Then the State has clothed one of its agents with power to annul or to evade it. . . .

It was insisted during the argument on behalf of the petitioner that Congress cannot punish a State judge for his official acts; and it was assumed that Judge Cole[s], in selecting the jury as he did, was performing a judicial act. This assumption cannot be admitted. Whether the act done by him was judicial or not is to be determined by its character, and not by the character of the agent. Whether he was a county judge or not is of no importance. The duty of selecting jurors might as well have been committed to a private person as to one holding the office of a judge. It often is given to county commissioners, or supervisors or assessors. In former times, the selection was made by the sheriff. In such cases, it surely is not a judicial act, in any such sense as is contended for here. It is merely a ministerial act, as much so as the act of a sheriff holding an execution, in determining upon what piece of property he will make a levy, or the act of a roadmaster in selecting laborers to work upon the roads. That the jurors are selected for a court makes no difference. So are court-criers, tipstaves, sheriffs, etc. Is their election or their appointment a judicial act?

But if the selection of jurors could be considered in any case a judicial act, can the act charged against the petitioner be considered such when he acted outside of his authority and in direct violation of the spirit of the state statute? That statute gave him no authority, when selecting jurors, from whom a panel might be drawn for a Circuit Court, to exclude all colored men merely because they were colored. Such an exclusion was not left within the limits of his discretion. It is idle, therefore, to say that the Act of Congress is unconstitutional because it inflicts penalties upon state judges for their judicial action. It does no such thing.

Upon the whole, as we are of opinion that the Act of Congress upon which the indictment against the petitioner was founded is constitutional, and that he is correctly held to answer it, and as, therefore, no object would be secured by issuing a writ of habeas corpus, the petitions are denied.

MR. JUSTICE FIELD, dissenting:

I dissent from the judgment of the court in this case, and from the reasons by which it is supported; and I will state the grounds of my dissent. . . .

The petitioner, J. D. Coles, is the Judge of the County Court of the County of Pittsylvania, in Virginia, and has held that office for some years. It is not pretended that, in the discharge of his judicial duties, he has ever selected as jurors persons who were not qualified to serve in that character, or who were not of sound judgment, or who were not free from legal exception. It is not even suggested in argument that he has not at all times faithfully obeyed the law of the State; yet he has been indicted in the District Court of the United States for the Western District of Virginia for having, on some undesignated day in the year 1878, excluded and failed to select as grand and petit jurors citizens of the county, on account of race, color and previous condition of servitude. The indictment does not state who those citizens were, or set forth any particulars of the offense, but charges it in the general words of a definition. . . .

The 13th and 14th Amendments are relied upon, as already stated, to support the legislation in question. . . .

I cannot think I am mistaken in saying that a change so radical in the relation between the federal and state authorities, as would justify legislation interfering with the independent action of the different departments of the state governments, in all matters over which the States retain jurisdiction, was never contemplated by the recent Amendments. . . . [The 13th Amendment] was intended to render everyone within the domain of the Republic a freeman, with the right to follow the ordinary pursuits of life without other restraints than such as are applied to all others, and to enjoy equally with them the earnings of his labor. But it confers no political rights; it leaves the States free, as before its adoption, to determine who shall hold their offices and participate in the administration of their laws. A similar prohibition of slavery and involuntary servitude was in the Constitution of several States previous to its adoption by the United States; and it was never held to confer any political rights. . . .

. . . In the consideration of questions growing out of those Amendments much confusion has arisen from a failure to distinguish between the civil and the political rights of citizens. Civil rights are absolute and personal. Political rights, on the other hand, are conditioned and dependent upon the discretion of the elective or appointing power, whether that be the People acting through the ballot, or one of the departments of their government. The civil rights of the individual are never to be withheld, and may be always judicially enforced. The political rights which he may enjoy, such as holding office and discharging a public trust, are qualified because their possession depends on his fitness, to be adjudged by those whom society has clothed with the elective authority. The 13th and 14th Amendments were designed to secure the civil rights of all persons, of every race, color and condition; but they left to the States to determine to whom the possession of political powers should be intrusted. This is manifest from the fact that when it was desired to confer political power upon the newly made citizens of the States, as was done by inhibiting the denial to them of the suffrage on account of race, color or previous condition of servitude, a new amendment was required.

. . . Those who regard the independence of the States in all their reserved powers — and this includes the independence of their Legislative, Judicial and Executive Departments — as essential to the successful maintenance of our form of government, cannot fail to view, with the gravest apprehension for the future, the indictment, in a court of the United States, of a judicial officer of a State for the manner in which he has discharged his duties under her laws, and of which she makes no complaint. The proceeding is a gross offense to the State; it is an attack upon her sovereignty, in matters over which she has never surrendered her jurisdiction. The doctrine which sustains it, carried to its logical results, would degrade and sink her to the level of a mere local municipal corporation; for if Congress can render an officer of a State criminally liable for the manner in which he discharges his duties under her laws, it can prescribe the nature and extent of the penalty to which he shall be subjected on conviction; it may imprison him for life, or punish him by removal from office. And if it can make the exclusion of persons from jury service on account of race or color a criminal offense, it can make their exclusion from office on that account also criminal; and, adopting the doctrine of the District Judge in this case, the failure to appoint them to office will be presumptive evidence of their exclusion on that ground. To such a result are we logically led. The legislation of Congress is founded, and is sustained by this court, as it seems to me, upon a theory as to what constitutes the equal protection of the laws, which is purely speculative, not warranted by any experience of the country, and not in accordance with the understanding of the people as to the meaning of those terms since the organization of the government.

I am authorized to say that Mr. Justice Clifford concurs with me in this opinion.

NOTE

Could the section of the federal statute sustained and enforced in Ex parte Virginia be enforced against a prosecuting attorney who, by peremptory challenge, excludes all Negroes from a criminal jury? See Swain v. Alabama, 380 U.S. 202 (1965).

Civil Rights Cases 109 U.S. 3, 3 S. Ct. 18, 27 L. Ed. 835 (1883)

These cases were all founded on the first and second sections of the Act of Congress, known as the Civil Rights Act, passed March 1st, 1875, entitled "An Act to protect all citizens in their civil and legal rights." 18 Stat. 335.[i] Two of the cases, those against Stanley and Nichols, were indictments for denying to persons of color the accommodations and privileges of an inn or hotel; two of them, those against Ryan and Singleton, were, one on information, the other an indictment, for denying to individuals the privileges and accommodations of a theatre, the information against Ryan being for refusing a colored person a seat in the dress circle of Maguire's theatre in San Francisco; and the indictment against Singleton was for denying to another person, whose color was not stated, the full enjoyment of the accommodations of the theatre known as the Grand Opera House in New York, "said denial not being made for any reasons by law applicable to citizens of every race and color, and regardless of any previous condition of servitude." The case of Robinson and wife against the Memphis & Charlston R.R. Company was an action brought in the Circuit Court of the United States for the Western District of Tennessee, to recover the penalty of five hundred dollars given by the second section of the act; and the gravamen was the refusal by the conductor of the railroad company to allow the wife to ride in the ladies' car, for the reason, as stated in one of the counts, that she was a person of African descent. The jury rendered a verdict for the defendants in this case upon the merits, under a charge of the court to which a bill of exceptions was taken by the plaintiffs. The case was tried on the assumption by both parties of the validity of the act of Congress; and the principal point made by the exceptions was, that the judge allowed evidence to go to the jury tending to show that the conductor had reason to suspect that the plaintiff, the

---

[i] "Sec. 1. That all persons within the jurisdiction of the United States shall be entitled to the full and equal enjoyment of the accommodations, advantages, facilities, and privileges of inns, public conveyances on land or water, theatres, and other places of public amusement; subject only to the conditions and limitations established by law, and applicable alike to citizens of every race and color, regardless of any previous condition of servitude.

"Sec. 2. That any person who shall violate the foregoing section by denying to any citizen, except for reasons by law applicable to citizens of every race and color, and regardless of any previous condition of servitude, the full enjoyment of any of the accommodations, advantages, facilities, or privileges in said section enumerated, or by aiding or inciting such denial, shall for every such offence forfeit and pay the sum of five hundred dollars to the person aggrieved thereby, to be recovered in an action of debt, with full costs; and shall also, for every such offence, be deemed guilty of a misdemeanor, and, upon conviction thereof, shall be fined not less than five hundred nor more than one thousand dollars, or shall be imprisoned not less than thirty days nor more than one year: *Provided,* That all persons may elect to sue for the penalty aforesaid, or to proceed under their rights at common law and by State statutes; and having so elected to proceed in the one mode or the other, their right to proceed in the other jurisdiction shall be barred. But this provision shall not apply to criminal proceedings, either under this act or the criminal law of any State: *And provided further,* That a judgment for the penalty in favor of the party aggrieved, or a judgment upon an indictment, shall be a bar to either prosecution respectively." — Ed.

wife, was an improper person, because she was in company with a young man whom he supposed to be a white man, and on that account inferred that there was some improper connection between them; and the judge charged the jury, in substance, that if this was the conductor's bona fide reason for excluding the woman from the car, they might take it into consideration on the question of the liability of the company. The case was brought here by writ of error at the suit of the plaintiffs. The cases of Stanley, Nichols, and Singleton, came up on certificates of division of opinion between the judges below as to the constitutionality of the first and second sections of the act referred to; and the case of Ryan, on a writ of error to the judgment of the Circuit Court for the District of California sustaining a demurrer to the information.

The Stanley, Ryan, Nichols, and Singleton cases were submitted together by the solicitor general at the last term of court, on the 7th day of November, 1882. There were no appearances and no briefs filed for the defendants.

The Robinson case was submitted on the briefs at the last term, on the 29th day of March, 1883.

MR. JUSTICE BRADLEY delivered the opinion of the court. . . .

It is obvious that the primary and important question in all the cases, is the constitutionality of the law; for if the law is unconstitutional, none of the prosecutions can stand. . . .

Are [§§ 1 and 2 of the Civil Rights Act] constitutional? The 1st section, which is the principal one, cannot be fairly understood without attending to the last clause, which qualifies the preceding part.

The essence of the law is, not to declare broadly that all persons shall be entitled to the full and equal enjoyment of the accommodations, advantages, facilities and privileges of inns, public conveyances and theatres; but that such enjoyment shall not be subject to any conditions applicable only to citizens of a particular race or color, or who had been in a previous condition of servitude. In other words: it is the purpose of the law to declare that, in the enjoyment of the accommodations and privileges of inns, public conveyances, theaters and other places of public amusement, no distinction shall be made between citizens of different race or color, or between those who have and those who have not been slaves. . . . The 2nd section makes it a penal offense in any person to deny to any citizen of any race or color, regardless of previous servitude, any of the accommodations or privileges mentioned in the 1st section.

Has Congress constitutional power to make such a law? Of course, no one will contend that the power to pass it was contained in the Constitution before the adoption of the last three Amendments. The power is sought, first, in the 14th Amendment, and the views and arguments of distinguished Senators, advanced whilst the law was under consideration, claiming authority to pass it by virtue of that Amendment, are the principal arguments adduced in favor of the power. We have carefully considered those arguments, as was due to the eminent ability of those who put them forward, and have felt, in all its force, the weight of authority which always invests a law that Congress deems itself competent to pass. But the responsibility of an independent judgment is now thrown upon this court; and we are bound to exercise it according to the best lights we have.

The 1st section of the 14th Amendment, which is the one relied on, after declaring who shall be citizens of the United States, and of the several States, is prohibitory in its character, and prohibitory upon the States. It declares that "No State shall make or enforce any law which shall abridge the privileges or immunities of citizens of the United States; nor shall any State deprive any person of life, liberty or property without due process of law; nor deny to any person within its jurisdiction the equal protection of the laws." It is state action of a particular character that is prohibited. Individual invasion of individual rights is not the subject-matter of the Amendment. It has a deeper and broader scope. It nullifies and makes void all state legislation, and state action of every kind, which impairs the privileges and immunities of citizens of the United States, or which injures them in life, liberty or property without due process of law, or which denies to any of them the equal protection of the laws. It not only does this, but, in order that the national will, thus declared, may not be a mere *brutum fulmen*, the last section of the Amendment invests Congress with power to enforce it by appropriate legislation. To enforce what? To enforce the prohibition. To adopt appropriate legislation for correcting the effects of such prohibited state laws and state Acts, and thus to render them effectually null, void and innocuous. This is the legislative power conferred upon Congress, and this is the whole of it. It does not invest Congress with power to legislate upon subjects which are within the domain of state legislation; but to provide modes of relief against state legislation or state action, of the kind referred to. It does not authorize Congress to create a code of municipal law for the regulation of private rights; but to provide modes of redress against the operation of state laws, and the action of state officers executive or judicial, when these are subversive of the fundamental rights specified in the Amendment. Positive rights and privileges are undoubtedly secured by the 14th Amendment; but they are secured by way of prohibition against state laws and state proceedings affecting those rights and privileges, and by power given to Congress to legislate for the purpose of carrying such prohibition into effect; and such legislation must, necessarily, be predicated upon such supposed state laws or state proceedings, and be directed to the correction of their operation and effect. . . .

And so in the present case, until some state law has been passed or some state action through its officers or agents has been taken, adverse to the rights of citizens sought to be protected by the 14th Amendment, no legislation of the United States under said Amendment, nor any proceeding under such legislation, can be called into activity; for the prohibitions of the Amendment are against state laws and acts done under state authority. Of course, legislation may and should be provided in advance to meet the exigency when it arises; but it should be adapted to the mischief and wrong which the Amendment was intended to provide against; and that is, state laws, or state action of some kind, adverse to the rights of the citizen secured by the Amendment. Such legislation cannot properly cover the whole domain of rights appertaining to life, liberty and property, defining them and providing for their vindication. That would be to establish a code of municipal law regulative of all private rights between man and man in society. It would be to make Congress take the place of the State Legislatures and to supersede them. It is absurd to affirm that, because the rights of life, liberty and property, which include all civil rights that men have, are, by the Amendment, sought to be protected against invasion on the part of the State without due process of law, Congress may, therefore, provide due process of law for their vindication in every case; and that, because the denial by a State to any persons, of the equal protection of the laws, is prohibited by the Amendment, therefore Congress may establish laws for their equal protection. In fine, the legislation which Congress is authorized to adopt in this behalf is not general legislation upon the rights of the citizen, but corrective legislation, that is, such as may be necessary and proper for counteracting such laws as the States may adopt or enforce, and which, by the Amendment, they are prohibited from making or enforcing, or such acts and proceedings as the States may commit or take, and which, by the Amendment, they are prohibited from committing or taking. It is not necessary for us to state, if we could, what legislation would be proper for Congress to adopt. It is sufficient for us to examine whether the law in question is of that character.

An inspection of the law shows that it makes no reference whatever to any supposed or apprehended violation of the 14th Amendment on the part of the States. It is not predicated on any such view. It proceeds ex directo to declare that certain acts committed by individuals shall be deemed offenses, and shall be prosecuted and punished by the proceedings in the courts of the United States. It does not profess to be corrective of any constitutional wrong committed by the States; it does not make its operation to depend upon any such wrong committed. It applies equally to cases arising in States which have the justest laws respecting the personal rights of citizens and whose authorities are ever ready to enforce such laws, as to those which arise in States that may have violated the prohibition of the Amendment. In other words, it steps into the domain of local jurisprudence, and lays down rules for the conduct of individuals in society towards each other, and imposes sanctions for the enforcement of those rules, without referring in any manner to any supposed action of the State or its authorities.

If this legislation is appropriate for enforcing the prohibitions of the Amendment, it is difficult to see where it is to stop. Why may not Congress with equal show of authority enact a code of laws for the enforcement and vindication of all rights of life, liberty and property? If it is supposable that the States may deprive persons of life, liberty and property without due process of law, and the Amendment itself does suppose this, why should not Congress proceed at once to prescribe due process of law for the protection of every one of these fundamental rights, in every possible case, as well as to prescribe equal privileges in inns, public conveyances and theaters? The truth is, that the implication of a power to legislate in this manner is based upon the assumption that if the States are forbidden to legislate or act in a particular way on a particular subject, and power is conferred upon Congress to enforce the prohibition, this gives Congress power to legislate generally upon that subject, and not merely power to provide modes of redress against such state legislation or action. The assumption is certainly unsound. It is repugnant to the 10th Amendment of the Constitution, which declares that powers not delegated to the United States by the Constitution, nor prohibited by it to the States, are reserved to the States respectively or to the people. . . .

In this connection it is proper to state that civil rights, such as are guaranteed by the Constitution against state aggression, cannot be impaired by the wrongful acts of individuals, unsupported by state authority in the shape of laws, customs or judicial or executive proceedings. The wrongful act of an individual, unsupported by any such authority, is simply a private wrong, or a crime of that individual; an invasion of the rights of the injured party, it is true, whether they affect his person, his property or his reputation; but if not sanctioned in some way by the State, or not done under state authority, his rights remain in full force, and may presumably be vindicated by resort to the laws of the State for redress. An individual cannot deprive a man of his right to vote, to hold property, to buy and to sell, to sue in the courts or to be a witness or a juror; he may, by force or fraud, interfere with the enjoyment of the right in a particular case; he may commit an assault against the person, or commit murder, or use ruffian violence at the polls, or slander the good name of a fellow citizen; but, unless protected in these wrongful acts by some shield of state law or state authority, he cannot destroy or injure the right; he will only render himself amenable to satisfaction or punishment; and amenable therefor to the laws of the State where the wrongful acts are committed. Hence, in all those cases where the Constitution seeks to protect the rights of the citizen against discriminative and unjust laws of the State by prohibiting such laws, it is not individual offenses, but abrogation and denial of rights, which it denounces, and for which it clothes the Congress with power to provide a remedy. This abrogation and denial of rights, for which the States alone were or could be responsible, was the great seminal and fundamental wrong which was intended to be remedied. And the remedy to be provided must necessarily be predicated upon that wrong. It must assume that in the cases provided for, the evil or wrong actually committed rests upon some state law or state authority for its excuse and perpetration. . . .

We have . . . discussed the validity of the law in reference to cases arising in the States only; and not in reference to cases arising in the Territories or the District of Columbia, which are subject to the plenary legislation of Congress in every branch of municipal regulation. Whether the law would be a valid one as applied to the Territories and the District, is not a question for consideration in the cases before us; they all being cases arising within the limits of States. And whether Congress, in the exercise of its power to regulate commerce amongst the several States, might or might not pass a law regulating rights in

Section D. Civil War Amendments and Civil Rights Statutes

public conveyances passing from one State to another, is also a question which is not now before us, as the sections in question are not conceived in any such view.[j]

But the power of Congress to adopt direct and primary, as distinguished from corrective, legislation on the subject in hand, is sought, in the second place, from the 13th Amendment, which abolishes slavery. . . .

This Amendment, as well as the 14th, is undoubtedly self-executing without any ancillary legislation, so far as its terms are applicable to any existing state of circumstances. By its own unaided force and effect, it abolished slavery and established universal freedom. Still, legislation may be necessary and proper to meet all the various cases and circumstances to be affected by it, and to prescribe proper modes of redress for its violation in letter or spirit. And such legislation may be primary and direct in its character; for the Amendment is not a mere prohibition of state laws establishing or upholding slavery, but an absolute declaration that slavery or involuntary servitude shall not exist in any part of the United States.

It is true, that slavery cannot exist without law, any more than property in lands and goods can exist without law; and, therefore, the 13th Amendment may be regarded as nullifying all state laws which establish or uphold slavery. But it has a reflex character also, establishing and decreeing universal civil and political freedom throughout the United States; and it is assumed that the power vested in Congress to enforce the article by appropriate legislation, clothes Congress with power to pass all laws necessary and proper for abolishing all badges and incidents of slavery in the United States; and upon this assumption it is claimed that this is sufficient authority for declaring by law that all persons shall have equal accommodations and privileges in all inns, public conveyances and places of public amusement; the argument being, that the denial of such equal accommodations and privileges is, in itself, a subjection to a species of servitude within the meaning of the Amendment. Conceding the major proposition to be true, that Congress has a right to enact all necessary and proper laws for the obliteration and prevention of slavery with all its badges and incidents, is the minor proposition also true, that the denial to any person of admission to the accommodations and privileges of an inn, a public conveyance or a theater, does subject that person to any form of servitude, or tend to fasten upon him any badge of slavery? If it does not, then power to pass the law is not found in the 13th Amendment. . . .

[I]s there any similarity between . . . servitudes [imposed by old law or old custom] and a denial by the owner of an inn, a public conveyance, or a theatre of its accommodations and privileges to an individual, even though the denial be founded on the race or color of that individual? Where does any slavery or servitude, or badge of either arise from such an act of denial? Whether it might not be a denial or a right which, if sanctioned by the state law, would be obnoxious to the prohibitions of the Fourteenth Amendment, is another question. But what has it to do with slavery?

It may be that, by the Black Code, as it was called, in the times when slavery prevailed, the proprietors of inns and public conveyances were forbidden to receive persons of the African race, because it might assist slaves to escape from the control of their masters.

---

[j] In the report of the Civil Rights Cases as it appears in 27 L. Ed. 835, 837-838, William M. Randolph, arguing for one of the appellants, had made the following argument: "Our case involves the rights of a citizen of one State travelling 'by a public conveyance by land' through another State for the purpose of reaching a place in a third State. We maintain that so far as the Act of Congress applies to such a case, the power to pass it is beyond question. Independently of the 'power to enforce by appropriate legislation' the 14th Amendment, there are, . . . at least two other clauses of the Constitution on either of which the Act may rest. The first is the power in Congress to regulate commerce . . . among the several states . . . ; and the other is the provision that 'The citizens of each State shall be entitled to all the privileges and immunities of citizens in the several States.' . . . These provisions, taken in connection with the grant of 'all legislative powers' to Congress (article 1, sec. 1) and the power 'To make all laws which shall be necessary and proper for carrying into execution the foregoing powers . . .' we submit, leave very little room for argument." — Ed.

This was merely a means of preventing such escapes, and was no part of the servitude itself. A law of that kind could not have any such object now, however justly it might be deemed an invasion of the party's legal right as a citizen, and amenable to the prohibitions of the 14th Amendment.

The long existence of African slavery in this country gave us very distinct notions of what it was, and what were its necessary incidents. Compulsory service of the slave for the benefit of the master, restraint of his movements except by the master's will, disability to hold property, to make contracts, to have a standing in court, to be a witness against a white person, and such like burdens and incapacities were the inseparable incidents of the institution. Severer punishments for crimes were imposed on the slave than on free persons guilty of the same offenses. Congress . . . by the Civil Rights Bill of 1866, passed in view of the 13th Amendment, before the 14th was adopted, undertook to wipe out these burdens and disabilities, the necessary incidents of slavery, constituting its substance and visible form; and to secure to all citizens of every race and color, and without regard to previous servitude, those fundamental rights which are the essence of civil freedom, namely: the same right to make and enforce contracts, to sue, be parties, give evidence, and to inherit, purchase, lease, sell and convey property, as is enjoyed by white citizens. Whether this legislation was fully authorized by the 13th Amendment alone, without the support which it afterwards received from the 14th Amendment, after the adoption of which it was reenacted with some additions, it is not necessary to inquire. It is referred to for the purpose of showing that at that time, in 1866, Congress did not assume, under the authority given by the 13th Amendment, to adjust what may be called the social rights of men and races in the community; but only to declare and vindicate those fundamental rights which appertain to the essence of citizenship, and the enjoyment or deprivation of which constitutes the essential distinction between freedom and slavery. . . .

The only question under the present head, therefore, is, whether the refusal to any persons of the accommodations of an inn or a public conveyance or a place of public amusement, by an individual and without any sanction or support from any state law or regulation, does inflict upon such persons any manner of servitude, or form of slavery, as those terms are understood in this country? Many wrongs may be obnoxious to the prohibitions of the 14th Amendment which are not, in any just sense, incidents or elements of slavery. Such, for example, would be the taking of private property without due process of law; or allowing persons who have committed certain crimes, horse stealing, for example, to be seized and hung by the *posse comitatus* without regular trial; or denying to any person or class of persons the right to pursue any peaceful avocations allowed to others. What is called "class legislation" would belong to this category, and would be obnoxious to the prohibitions of the 14th Amendment, but would not necessarily be so to the 13th, when not involving the idea of any subjection of one man to another. The 13th Amendment has respect, not to distinctions of race or class or color, but to slavery. The 14th Amendment extends its protection to races and classes, and prohibits any state legislation which has the effect of denying to any race or class or to any individual, the equal protection of the laws.

Now, conceding, for the sake of the argument, that the admission to an inn, a public conveyance or a place of public amusement, on equal terms with all other citizens, is the right of every man and all classes of men, is it any more than one of those rights which the States by the 14th Amendment are forbidden to deny to any person? And is the Constitution violated until the denial of the right has some state sanction or authority? Can the act of a mere individual, the owner of the inn, the public conveyance or place of amusement, refusing the accommodation, be justly regarded as imposing any badge of slavery or servitude upon the applicant, or only as inflicting an ordinary civil injury, properly cognizable by the laws of the State, and presumably subject to redress by those laws until the contrary appears?

After giving to these questions all the consideration which their importance demands,

Section D. Civil War Amendments and Civil Rights Statutes

we are forced to the conclusion that such an act of refusal has nothing to do with slavery or involuntary servitude, and that if it is violative of any right of the party, his redress is to be sought under the laws of the State; or if those laws are adverse to his rights and do not protect him, his remedy will be found in the corrective legislation which Congress has adopted, or may adopt, for counteracting the effect of state laws, or state action, prohibited by the 14th Amendment. It would be running the slavery argument into the ground, to make it apply to every act of discrimination which a person may see fit to make as to the guests he will entertain, or as to the people he will take into his coach or cab or car, or admit to his concert or theater, or deal with in other matters of intercourse or business. Innkeepers and public carriers, by the laws of all the States, so far as we are aware, are bound, to the extent of their facilities, to furnish proper accommodation to all unobjectionable persons who in good faith apply for them. If the laws themselves make any unjust discrimination, amenable to the prohibitions of the 14th Amendment, Congress has full power to afford a remedy, under that Amendment and in accordance with it.

When a man has emerged from slavery, and by the aid of beneficent legislation has shaken off the inseparable concomitants of that state, there must be some stage in the progress of his elevation when he takes the rank of a mere citizen, and ceases to be the special favorite of the laws, and when his rights, as a citizen or a man, are to be protected in the ordinary modes by which other men's rights are protected. There were thousands of free colored people in this country before the abolition of slavery, enjoying all the essential rights of life, liberty and property the same as white citizens; yet no one, at that time, thought that it was any invasion of their personal *status* as freemen because they were not admitted to all the privileges enjoyed by white citizens, or because they were subjected to discriminations in the enjoyment of accommodations in inns, public conveyances and places of amusement. Mere discriminations on account of race or color were not regarded as badges of slavery. If, since that time, the enjoyment of equal rights in all these respects has become established by constitutional enactment, it is not by force of the 13th Amendment, which merely abolishes slavery, but by force of the 14th and 15th Amendments.

On the whole we are of opinion, that no countenance of authority for the passage of the law in question can be found in either the 13th or 14th Amendment of the Constitution; and no other ground of authority for its passage being suggested, it must necessarily be declared void, at least so far as its operation in the several States is concerned. . . .

MR. JUSTICE HARLAN dissenting:

The opinion in these cases proceeds, it seems to me, upon grounds entirely too narrow and artificial. I cannot resist the conclusion that the substance and spirit of the recent Amendments of the Constitution have been sacrificed by a subtle and ingenious verbal criticism. "It is not the words of the law but the internal sense of it that makes the law; the letter of the law is the body; the sense and reason of the law is the soul." Constitutional provisions, adopted in the interest of liberty, and for the purpose of securing, through national legislation, if need be, rights inhering in a state of freedom, and belonging to American citizenship, have been so construed as to defeat the ends the people desired to accomplish, which they attempted to accomplish, and which they supposed they had accomplished by changes in their fundamental law. By this I do not mean that the determination of these cases should have been materially controlled by considerations of mere expediency or policy. I mean only, in this form, to express an earnest conviction that the court has departed from the familiar rule requiring, in the interpretation of constitutional provisions, that full effect be given to the intent with which they were adopted. . . .

The 13th Amendment, it is conceded, did something more than to prohibit slavery as an *institution*, resting upon distinctions of race, and upheld by positive law. My brethren admit that it established and decreed universal *civil freedom* throughout the United States. But did the freedom thus established involve nothing more than exemption from actual slavery? Was nothing more intended than to forbid one man from owning another as property? Was it the purpose of the Nation simply to destroy the institution, and then remit the race, theretofore held in bondage, to the several States for such protection, in their civil rights, necessarily growing out of freedom, as those States, in their discretion, might choose to provide? Were the States against whose protest the institution was destroyed, to be left free, so far as national interference was concerned, to make or allow discriminations against that race, as such, in the enjoyment of those fundamental rights which by universal concession, inhere in a state of freedom? . . .

That there are burdens and disabilities which constitute badges of slavery and servitude, and that the power to enforce by appropriate legislation the 13th Amendment may be exerted by legislation of a direct and primary character, for the eradication, not simply of the institution, but of its badges and incidents, are propositions which ought to be deemed indisputable. They lie at the foundation of the Civil Rights Act of 1866. Whether that Act was authorized by the 13th Amendment alone, without the support which it subsequently received from the 14th Amendment, after the adoption of which it was re-enacted with some additions, my brethren do not consider it necessary to inquire. But I submit, with all respect to them, that its constitutionality is conclusively shown by their opinion. They admit, as I have said, that the 13th Amendment established freedom; that there are burdens and disabilities, the necessary incidents of slavery, which constitute its substance and visible form; that Congress, by the Act of 1866, passed in view of the 13th Amendment, before the 14th was adopted, undertook to remove certain burdens and disabilities, the necessary incidents of slavery, and to secure to all citizens of every race and color, and without regard to previous servitude, those fundamental rights which are the essence of civil freedom, namely, the same right to make and enforce contracts, to sue, be parties, give evidence, and to inherit, purchase, lease, sell and convey property as is enjoyed by white citizens; that under the 13th Amendment, Congress has to do with slavery and its incidents; and that legislation, so far as necessary or proper to eradicate all forms and incidents of slavery and involuntary servitude, may be direct and primary, operating upon the acts of individuals, whether sanctioned by state legislation or not. These propositions being conceded, it is impossible, as it seems to me, to question the constitutional validity of the Civil Rights Act of 1866. I do not contend that the 13th Amendment invests Congress with authority, by legislation, to define and regulate the entire body of the civil rights which citizens enjoy, or may enjoy, in the several States. But I hold that since slavery, as the court has repeatedly declared, Slaughter-House Cases, 16 Wall. 36; Strauder v. W. Va., 100 U.S. 303, was the moving or principal cause of the adoption of that Amendment, and since that institution rested wholly upon the inferiority, as a race, of those held in bondage, their freedom necessarily involved immunity from, and protection against, all discrimination against them, because of their race, in respect of such civil rights as belong to freemen of other races. Congress, therefore, under its express power to enforce that Amendment, by appropriate legislation, may enact laws to protect that people against the deprivation, *because of their race*, of any civil rights granted to other freemen in the same State; and such legislation may be of a direct and primary character, operating upon States, their officers and agents and, also, upon, at least, such individuals and corporations as exercise public functions and wield power and authority under the State. . . .

It remains now to inquire: what are the legal rights of colored persons in respect of the accommodations, privileges and facilities of public conveyances, inns and places of public amusement? . . .

In many courts it has been held that, because of the public interest in such a corporation, the land of a railroad company cannot be levied on and sold under execution by a creditor. The sum of the adjudged cases is that a railroad corporation is a governmental agency, created primarily for public purposes, and subject to be controlled for the public benefit. Upon this ground the State, when unfettered by contract, may regulate, in its discretion, the rates of fares of passengers and freight. And upon this ground, too, the State may regulate the entire management of railroads in all matters affecting the convenience and safety of the public; as, for example, by regulating speed, compelling stops of prescribed length at stations, and prohibiting discriminations and favoritism. If the cor-

Section D. Civil War Amendments and Civil Rights Statutes 785

poration neglect or refuse to discharge its duties to the public, it may be coerced to do so by appropriate proceedings in the name or in behalf of the State. . . .

[Mr. Justice Harlan next urged that inns and places of public amusement, like railroads, fulfilled public or quasi-public functions.]

It remains now to consider these cases with reference to the power Congress has possessed since the adoption of the 14th Amendment. Much that has been said as to the power of Congress under the 13th Amendment is applicable to this branch of the discussion, and will not be repeated. . . .

The assumption that this Amendment consists wholly of prohibitions upon state laws and state proceedings in hostility to its provisions, is unauthorized by its language. The first clause of the 1st section — "All persons born or naturalized in the United States, and subject to the jurisdiction thereof, are citizens of the United States, and of the State wherein they reside" — is of a distinctly affirmative character. In its application to the colored race, previously liberated, it created and granted, as well citizenship of the United States, as citizenship of the State in which they respectively resided. It introduced all of that race, whose ancestors had been imported and sold as slaves, at once, into the political community known as the "People of the United States." They became, instantly, citizens of the United States, *and* of their respective States. Further, they were brought, by this supreme act of the Nation, within the direct operation of that provision of the Constitution which declares that "The citizens of each State shall be entitled to all privileges and immunities of citizens in the several States." Art. 4, sec. 2.

The citizenship thus acquired, by that race, in virtue of an affirmative grant from the Nation, may be protected, not alone by the judicial branch of the government, but by congressional legislation of a primary direct character; this, because the power of Congress is not restricted to the enforcement of prohibitions upon state laws or state action. It is, in terms distinct and positive, to enforce "the *provisions* of *this article*" of Amendment; not simply those of a prohibitive character, but the provisions — *all* of the provisions — affirmative and prohibitive, of the Amendment. It is, therefore, a grave misconception to suppose that the 5th section of the Amendment has reference exclusively to express prohibitions upon state laws or state action. If any right was created by that Amendment, the grant of power, through appropriate legislation, to enforce its provisions, authorizes Congress, by means of legislation, operating throughout the entire Union, to guard, secure and protect that right.

It is, therefore, an essential inquiry what, if any, right, privilege or immunity was given, by the Nation, to colored persons, when they were made citizens of the State in which they reside? Did the constitutional grant of state citizenship to that race, of its own force, invest them with any rights, privileges and immunities whatever? That they became entitled, upon the adoption of the 14th Amendment, "to all privileges and immunities of citizens in the several States," within the meaning of section 2 of article 4 of the Constitution, no one, I suppose, will for a moment question. What are the privileges and immunities to which, by that clause of the Constitution, they became entitled? To this it may be answered, generally, upon the authority of the adjudged cases, that they are those which are fundamental in citizenship in a free republican government, such as are "common to the citizens in the latter States under their constitutions and laws by virtue of their being citizens." Of that provision it has been said, with the approval of this court, that no other one in the Constitution has tended so strongly to constitute the citizens of the United States one people. Ward v. Maryland, 12 Wall. 418; Corfield v. Coryell, 4 Wash. C.C. 371; Paul v. Va., 8 Wall. 168; Slaughter-House Cases, 16 id. 36.

Although this court has wisely forborne any attempt, by a comprehensive definition, to indicate all of the privileges and immunities to which the citizen of a State is entitled, of right, when within the jurisdiction of other States, I hazard nothing, in view of former adjudications, in saying that no State can sustain her denial to colored citizens of other States, while within her limits, of privileges or immunities, fundamental in republican citizenship, upon the ground that she accords such privileges and immunities only to her white citizens and withholds them from her colored citizens. The colored citizens of other States, within the jurisdiction of that State, could claim, in virtue of section 2 of article 4 of the Constitution, every privilege and immunity which that State secures to her white citizens. Otherwise, it would be in the power of any State, by discriminating class legislation against its own citizens of a particular race or color, to withhold from citizens of other States, belonging to that proscribed race when within her limits, privileges and immunities of the character regarded by all courts as fundamental in citizenship; and that, too, when the constitutional guaranty is that the citizens of each State shall be entitled to "all privileges and immunities of citizens of the several States." No State may, by discrimination against a portion of its own citizens of a particular race, in respect of privileges and immunities fundamental in citizenship, impair the constitutional right of citizens of other States, of whatever race, to enjoy in that State all such privileges and immunities as are there accorded to her most favored citizens. A colored citizen of Ohio or Indiana, while in the jurisdiction of Tennessee, is entitled to enjoy any privilege or immunity, fundamental in citizenship, which is given to citizens of the white race in the latter State. It is not to be supposed that anyone will controvert this proposition.

But what was secured to colored citizens of the United States — as between them and their respective States — by the national grant to them of State citizenship? With what rights, privileges, or immunities did this grant invest them? There is one, if there be no other — exemption from race discrimination in respect of any civil right belonging to citizens of the white race in the same State. That, surely, is their constitutional privilege when within the jurisdiction of other States. And such must be their constitutional right, in their own State, unless the recent amendments be splendid baubles, thrown out to delude those who deserved fair and generous treatment at the hands of the nation. Citizenship in this country necessarily imports at least equality of civil rights among citizens of every race in the same State. . . .

This court has always given a broad and liberal construction to the Constitution, so as to enable Congress, by legislation, to enforce rights secured by that instrument. The legislation which Congress may enact, in execution of its power to enforce the provisions of this Amendment, is such as may be appropriate to protect the right granted. The word "appropriate" was undoubtedly used with reference to its meaning, as established by repeated decisions of this court. Under given circumstances, that which the court characterizes as corrective legislation might be deemed by Congress appropriate and entirely sufficient. Under other circumstances primary direct legislation may be required. But it is for Congress, not the judiciary, to say that legislation is appropriate; that is, best adapted to the end to be attained. The judiciary may not, with safety to our institutions, enter the domain of legislative discretion, and dictate the means which Congress shall employ in the exercise of its granted powers. That would be sheer usurpation of the functions of a coordinate department, which, if often repeated, and permanently acquiesced in, would work a radical change in our system of government. . . .

. . . If the grant to colored citizens of the United States of citizenship in their respective States, imports exemption from race discrimination, in their States, in respect of such civil rights as belong to citizenship, then, to hold that the Amendment remits that right to the States for their protection, primarily, and stays the hands of the Nation, until it is assailed by state laws or state proceedings, is to adjudge that the Amendment, so far from enlarging the powers of Congress — as we have heretofore said it did — not only curtails them, but reverses the policy which the General Government has pursued from its very organization. Such an interpretation of the Amendment is a denial to Congress of the power, by appropriate legislation, to enforce one of its provisions. In view of the circumstances under which the recent Amendments were incorporated into the Constitution, and especially in view of the peculiar character of the new rights they created and secured, it ought not to be presumed that the General Government has abdicated its authority, by national legislation, direct and primary in its character to guard and protect privileges and immunities secured by that instrument. Such an interpretation of the Constitution ought not to be accepted if it be possible to avoid it. Its acceptance would lead to this anomalous result: that whereas, prior to the Amendments, Congress, with the sanction of this court, passed the most stringent laws — operating directly and primarily upon States and their officers and agents, as well as upon individuals — in vindication of slavery and the right of the master, it may not now, by legislation of a like primary and direct character, guard, protect and secure the freedom established, and the most essential right of the citizenship granted, by the constitutional amendments. . . .

It does not seem to me that the fact that, by the second clause of the first section of the Fourteenth Amendment, the States are expressly prohibited from making or enforcing laws abridging the privileges and immunities of citizens of the United States, furnishes any sufficient reason for holding or maintaining that the amendment was intended to deny Congress the power, by general, primary, and direct legislation, of protecting citizens of the several States, being also citizens of the United States, against all discrimination, in respect of their rights as citizens, which is founded on race, color, or previous condition of servitude. . . .

It is said that any interpretation of the Fourteenth Amendment different from that adopted by the majority of the court, would imply that Congress has authority to enact a municipal code for all the States, covering every matter affecting the life, liberty, and property of the citizens of the several States. Not so. Prior to the adoption of that amendment the constitutions of the several States, without perhaps an exception, secured all *persons* against deprivations of life, liberty, or property, otherwise than by due process of law, and, in some form, recognized the right of all *persons* to the equal protection of the laws. Those rights, therefore, existed before that amendment was proposed or ratified, and were not created by it. . . . Exemption from race discrimination in respect of the civil rights which are fundamental in *citizenship* in a republican government, is, as we have seen, a new right created by the nation, with express power in Congress, by legislation, to enforce the constitutional provision from which it is derived. If, in some sense, such race discrimination is, within the letter of the last clause of the first section, a denial of that equal protection of the laws which is secured against State denial to all persons, whether citizens or not, it cannot be possible that a mere prohibition upon such State denial, or a prohibition upon State laws abridging the privileges and immunities of citizens of the United States, takes from the nation the power which it has uniformly exercised of protecting, by direct, primary legislation, those privileges and immunities which existed under the Constitution before the adoption of the Fourteenth Amendment, or have been created by that Amendment in behalf of those thereby made *citizens* of their respective States. . . .

In every material sense applicable to the practical enforcement of the 14th Amendment, railroad corporations, keepers of inns and managers of places of public amusement are agents or instrumentalities of the State, because they are charged with duties to the public, and are amenable, in respect of their duties and functions, to governmental regulation. It seems to me that, within the principle settled in Ex parte Virginia, a denial, by these instrumentalities of the State, to the citizen, because of his race, of that equality of civil rights secured to him by law, is a denial by the State, within the meaning of the 14th Amendment. If it be not, then that race is left, in respect of the civil rights in question, practically at the mercy of corporations and individuals wielding power under the States. . . .

The court, in its opinion, reserves the question whether Congress, in the exercise of its power to regulate commerce amongst the several States, might or might not pass a law regulating rights in public conveyances passing from one State to another. I beg to suggest that that precise question was substantially presented here in the only one of these cases relating to railroads — Robinson and Wife v. Memphis & Charleston Railroad Company. In that case it appears that Mrs. Robinson, a citizen of Mississippi, purchased a railroad ticket entitling her to be carried from Grand Junction, Tennessee, to Lynchburg,

Virginia. Might not the Act of 1875 be maintained in that case, as applicable at least to commerce between the States, notwithstanding it does not, upon its face, profess to have been passed in pursuance of the power of Congress to regulate commerce? Has it ever been held that the judiciary should overturn a statute, because the legislative department did not accurately recite therein the particular provision of the Constitution authorizing its enactment? We have often enforced municipal bonds in aid of railroad subscriptions, where they failed to recite the statute authorizing their issue, but recited one which did not sustain their validity. The inquiry in such cases has been: was there, in any statute, authority for the execution of the bonds? Upon this branch of the case, it may be remarked that the State of Louisiana, in 1869, passed a statute giving to passengers, without regard to race or color, equality of right in the accommodations of railroad and street cars, steamboats or other water crafts, stage-coaches, omnibuses or other vehicles. But in Hall v. De Cuir, 95 U.S. 487, that Act was pronounced unconstitutional so far as it related to commerce between the States, this court saying that "If the public good requires such legislation it must come from Congress, and not from the States." I suggest, that it may become a pertinent inquiry whether Congress may, in the exertion of its power to regulate commerce among the States, enforce among passengers on public conveyances, equality of right, without regard to race, color or previous condition of servitude, if it be true — which I do not admit — that such legislation would be an interference by government with the social rights of the people.

. . . Today, it is the colored race which is denied, by corporations and individuals wielding public authority, rights fundamental in their freedom and citizenship. At some future time, it may be that some other race will fall under the ban of race discrimination. If the constitutional Amendments be enforced, according to the intent with which, as I conceive, they were adopted, there cannot be in this Republic, any class of human beings in practical subjection to another class, with power in the latter to dole out to the former just such privileges as they may choose to grant. The supreme law of the land has decreed that no authority shall be exercised in this country upon the basis of discrimination, in respect of civil rights, against freemen and citizens because of their race, color or previous condition of servitude. To that decree — for the due enforcement of which, by appropriate legislation, Congress has been invested with express power — every one must bow, whatever may have been, or whatever now are, his individual views as to the wisdom or policy, either of the recent changes in the fundamental law, or of the legislation which has been enacted to give them effect.

For the reasons stated I feel constrained to withhold my assent to the opinion of the court.

Section E. SECURED RIGHTS AND STATE ACTION

Logan v. United States 144 U.S. 263, 12 S. Ct. 617, 36 L. Ed. 429 (1892)

[Six men, citizens of the United States, had been arrested by federal officers and were in the custody of a deputy United States marshal to answer a federal indictment charging them with larceny in Indian territory. While guarded en route to jail, a mob, in complicity with the guards, attacked the prisoners, killing two. The defendants, guards or attackers, were indicted under §§ 5508 and 5509 of the Revised Statutes (page 760 supra) in the District Court for the Northern District of Texas charged with a conspiracy to injure and oppress citizens of the United States in the free exercise of a right secured to them by the Constitution and laws of the United States, "to wit, the right to then and there be pro-

Section E. Secured Rights and State Action

tected by said deputy United States marshal, from the assault" of the defendants "and the right then and there to be held in the power, custody and control of said deputy United States marshal . . . and the further right, while in said custody, to be secure in their persons from bodily harm and injury and assaults and cruelties until they . . . had been discharged by due process of the laws of the United States. . . ." In the district court the defendants by appropriate motion challenged the indictment. The motion was overruled, the defendants excepted, were tried and convicted, and brought the case to the Supreme Court of the United States on writ of error.]

MR. JUSTICE GRAY . . . delivered the opinion of the court. . . .

The principal question in this case is whether the right of a citizen of the United States, in the custody of a United States marshal under a lawful commitment to answer for an offence against the United States, to be protected against lawless violence, is a right secured to him by the Constitution or laws of the United States, or whether it is a right which can be vindicated only under the laws of the several States. . . .

Among the powers which the Constitution expressly confers upon Congress is the power to make all laws necessary and proper for carrying into execution the powers specifically granted to it, and all other powers vested by the Constitution in the government of the United States, or in any department or officer thereof. In the exercise of this general power of legislation, Congress may use any means, appearing to it most eligible and appropriate, which are adapted to the end to be accomplished, and are consistent with the letter and the spirit of the Constitution. McCulloch v. Maryland, 4 Wheat. 316, 421; Julliard v. Greenman, 110 U.S. 421, 440, 441.

Although the Constitution contains no grant, general or specific, to Congress of the power to provide for the punishment of crimes, except piracies and felonies on the high seas, offences against the law of nations, treason, and counterfeiting the securities and current coin of the United States, no one doubts the power of Congress to provide for the punishment of all crimes and offences against the United States, whether committed within one of the States of the Union, or within territory over which Congress has plenary and exclusive jurisdiction.

To accomplish this end, Congress has the right to enact laws for the arrest and commitment of those accused of any such crime or offence, and for holding them in safe custody until indictment and trial; and persons arrested and held pursuant to such laws are in the exclusive custody of the United States, and are not subject to the judicial process or executive warrant of any State. Ableman v. Booth, 21 How. 506; Tarble's Case, 13 Wall. 397; Robb v. Connolly, 111 U.S. 624. The United States, having the absolute right to hold such prisoners, have an equal duty to protect them, while so held, against assault or injury from any quarter. The existence of that duty on the part of the government necessarily implies a corresponding right of the prisoners to be so protected; and this right of the prisoners is a right secured to them by the Constitution and laws of the United States. . . .

The prisoners were in the exclusive custody and control of the United States, under the protection of the United States, and in the peace of the United States. There was a co-extensive duty on the part of the United States to protect against lawless violence persons so within their custody, control, protection and peace; and a corresponding right of those persons, secured by the Constitution and laws of the United States, to be so protected by the United States. If the officers of the United States, charged with the performance of the duty, in behalf of the United States, of affording that protection and securing that right, neglected or violated their duty, the prisoners were not the less under the shield and panoply of the United States.

The cases heretofore decided by this court, and cited in behalf of the plaintiffs in error, are in no way inconsistent with these views, but, on the contrary, contain much to support them. The matter considered in each of those cases was whether the particular right there in question was secured by the Constitution of the United States, and was within the acts of Congress. But the question before us is so important, and the learned counsel for

790   Chapter Fourteen.   Privileges & Immunities; Equality; Civil Rights

the plaintiffs in error have so strongly relied on those cases, that it is fit to review them in detail. [The discussion of cases is omitted.]

The whole scope and effect of this series of decisions is that, while certain fundamental rights, recognized and declared, but not granted or created, in some of the Amendments to the Constitution, are thereby guaranteed only against violations or abridgment by the United States, or by the States, as the case may be, and cannot therefore be affirmatively enforced by Congress against unlawful acts or individuals; yet that every right, created by, arising under or dependent upon, the Constitution of the United States, may be protected and enforced by Congress by such means and in such manner as Congress, in the exercise of the correlative duty of protection, or of the legislative powers conferred upon it by the Constitution, may in its discretion deem most eligible and best adapted to attain the object.

Among the particular rights which this court, as we have seen, has adjudged to be secured, expressly or by implication, by the Constitution and laws of the United States, and to be within section 5508 of the Revised Statutes, providing for the punishment of conspiracies by individuals to oppress or injure citizens in the free exercise and enjoyment of rights so secured, are the political right of a voter to be protected from violence while exercising his right of suffrage under the laws of the United States; and the private right of a citizen, having made a homestead entry, to be protected from interference while remaining in the possession of the land for the time of occupancy which Congress has enacted shall entitle him to a patent.

In the case at bar, the right in question does not depend upon any of the Amendments to the Constitution, but arises out of the creation and establishment by the Constitution itself of a national government, paramount and supreme within its sphere of action. Any government which has power to indict, try and punish for crime, and to arrest the accused and hold them in safekeeping until trial, must have the power and the duty to protect against unlawful interference its prisoners so held, as well as its executive and judicial officers charged with keeping them and trying them. . . .

The United States are bound to protect against lawless violence all persons in their service or custody in the course of the administration of justice. This duty and the correlative right of protection are not limited to the magistrates and officers charged with expounding and executing the laws, but apply, with at least equal force, to those held in custody on accusation of crime, and deprived of all means of self-defence.

For these reasons, we are of opinion that the crime of which the plaintiffs in error were indicted and convicted was within the reach of the constitutional powers of Congress, and was covered by section 5508 of the Revised Statutes.[k] . . .

Report on the Bisbee Deportations Made by the President's Mediation Commission to the President of the United States
Department of Labor, Office of the Secretary, November 6, 1917

THE PRESIDENT:

The deportations on the 12th of July last, from the Warren district of Arizona, as well as the practices which followed such deportations, have deeply affected the opinions of laboring men, as well as the general public, throughout the country. . . .

. . . After hearing the representatives of the different elements involved in the deportation, both official and private, the President's Mediation Commission makes these findings:

1. A strike was called in the Warren district on June 26, 1917, to be effective the fol-

---

[k] Mr. Justice Lamar did not concur in the Court's interpretation of § 5508 of the Revised Statutes. — ED.

lowing day. While undoubtedly the men sincerely felt that several grievances called for rectification by the companies, having regard to the conditions in this district and the Government's need for its copper production, the grievances were not of such a nature as to have justified the strike. Here as elsewhere there was, however, no machinery for the adjustment of difficulties between the companies and the men which provided for the determination of alleged grievances by some authoritative disinterested tribunal in which both the companies and the men had confidence and before which they had an equal opportunity of urging their respective claims. . . .

2. Many of those who went out did not in fact believe in the justice of the strike, but supported it, as is common among workingmen, because of their general loyalty to the cause represented by the strikers and their refusal to be regarded in their own estimation, as well as in the minds of their fellow workers, as "scabs."

3. Shortly after the strike was called, the sheriff of the county, through the governor of Arizona, requested the aid of Federal troops. The request was based on the fact that the State militia had been drafted into the Federal service and the State therefore was without its normal militia protection. Gov. Campbell recommended to the Secretary of War that an immediate investigation of the situation at Bisbee be made by a Regular Army officer, in order to ascertain the need of troops. The governor's recommendation was followed, and an investigation of the situation in Bisbee was made by an experienced officer. Such investigation was made on June 30 and again on July 2, and after both investigations the officer reported that everything was peaceable and that troops were neither needed nor warranted under existing conditions.

4. That the conditions in Bisbee were in fact peaceful and free from any manifestations of disorder or violence is the testimony of reputable citizens as well as of officials of the city and county, who are in a position to report accurately and speak without bias.

5. Early on the morning of July 12 the sheriff and a large armed force presuming to act as deputies under the sheriff's authority, comprising about 2,000 men, rounded up 1,186 men in the Warren district, put them aboard a train, and carried them to Columbus, N. Mex. The authorities at Columbus refused to permit those in charge of the deportation to leave the men there, and the train carried them back to the desert town of Hermanas, N. Mex., a near-by station. The deportees were wholly without adequate supply of food and water and shelter for two days. At Hermanas the deported men were abandoned by the guards who had brought them, and they were left to shift for themselves. The situation was brought to the attention of the War Department, and on July 14 the deportees were escorted by troops to Columbus, N. Mex., where they were maintained by the Government until the middle of September.

6. According to an Army census of the deported men, 199 were native-born Americans, 468 were citizens, 472 were registered under the selective-draft law, and 433 were married. Of the foreign-born, over 20 nationalities were represented, including 141 British, 82 Serbians, and 179 Slavs. Germans and Austro-Hungarians (other than Slavs) were comparatively few.

7. The deportation was carried out under the sheriff of Cochise County. It was formally decided upon at a meeting of citizens on the night of July 11 participated in by the managers and other officials of the Copper Queen Consolidated Mining Co. (Phelps-Dodge Corporation, Copper Queen division) and the Calumet & Arizona Mining Co. Those who planned and directed the deportation purposely abstained from consulting about their plans either with the United States attorney in Arizona, or the law officers of the State or county, or their own legal advisers.

8. In order to carry the plans for the deportation into successful execution, the leaders in the enterprise utilized the local offices of the Bell Telephone Co. and exercised or attempted to exercise a censorship over parts of interstate connections of both the telephone and telegraph lines in order to prevent any knowledge of the deportation reaching the outside world.

9. The plan for the deportation and its execution are attributable to the belief in the minds of those who engineered it that violence was contemplated by the strikers and sympathizers with the strikers who had come into the district from without, that life and property would be insecure unless such deportation was undertaken, and that the State was without the necessary armed force to prevent such anticipated violence and to safeguard life and property within the district. This belief has no justification in the evidence in support of it presented by the parties who harbored it.

10. Neither such fear on the part of the leaders of the deportation as to anticipated violence nor evidence justifying such fear was ever communicated to the governor of the State of Arizona with a view to renewing the request for Federal troops, based upon changing conditions, nor were the Federal authorities in fact ever apprised that a change of conditions had taken place in the district from that found by the investigating Army officer to call for or warrant the interposition of Federal troops.

11. The deportation was wholly illegal and without authority in law, either State or Federal.

12. Following the deportation of the 12th, in the language of Gov. Campbell of Arizona, "the constitutional rights of citizens and others have been ignored by processes not provided by law, viz., by deputy sheriffs, who refused persons admittance into the district and the passing of judgment by a tribunal without legal jurisdiction resulting in further deportations." . . .

14. Among those who were deported from the district and who thereafter were arrested in seeking entrance into it were several who were registered under the selective-draft law and sought to return or remain in the district in order to discharge their legal duty of reporting for physical examination under the draft.

These findings of facts make certain recommendations by the President's Mediation Commission inevitable:

1. All illegal practices and the denial of rights safeguarded by the Constitution and statutes must at once cease. The right of unimpeded admittance into the Warren District of all who seek entrance into it in a lawful and peaceful manner must be respected. The right of all persons freely to move about in the Warren District or to continue to reside within it must be scrupulously observed except in so far as such right is restricted by the orderly process of the law. . . .

2. In so far as the deportation of July 12 and the events following constitute violations of the laws of Arizona, we join in the recommendation of Gov. Campbell that the responsible law officers of the State and county pursue appropriate remedies for the vindication of such laws.

3. In so far as the evidence before the commission indicates interference with the enforcement of the selective-draft law, the facts should be brought to the attention of the Attorney General of the United States. . . .

4. In so far as the evidence before the commission indicates an interference with interstate lines of communication, the facts should be submitted for appropriate attention by the Interstate Commerce Commission. . . .

5. In so far as deportation[s] such as we have set forth have not yet been made a Federal offense, it is our duty to report to the President the wisdom of recommending to the Congress that such occurrences hereafter be made criminal under the Federal law to the full extent of the constitutional authority of the Federal Government.

Respectfully submitted.

> The President's Mediation Commission,
> W. B. WILSON, *Chairman*.
> E. P. MARSH.
> JOHN H. WALKER.
> J. L. SPANGLER.

Felix Frankfurter,
Counsel to the Commission.

NOTE

Did the Bisbee offenses violate § 19 of the Criminal Code? See United States v. Wheeler, 254 U.S. 281 (1920); United States v. Guest, 383 U.S. 745, 757, infra page 851. See also Meyers, Federal Privileges and Immunities: Application to Ingress and Egress, 29 Cornell L.Q. 489 (1944).

If the offenses did not violate federal law in force in 1917, could such offenses constitutionally be punished by federal authority? Would it be relevant to the constitutional problem that none of the persons deported were citizens of states other than Arizona?

If any of the deportees had been aliens protected by international treaties to which the United States was a party, would the persons responsible for their deportation be guilty of a federal offense? See Baldwin v. Franks, 120 U.S. 678 (1887).

Brewer v. Hoxie School Dist. No. 46 238 F.2d 91 (8th Cir. 1956)

Before WOODROUGH, VOGEL and VAN OOSTERHOUT, Circuit Judges.

WOODROUGH, Circuit Judge.

Prior to 1955, the public schools in Hoxie School District No. 46 of Lawrence County, Arkansas, servicing about a thousand white students and twenty-four negroes, were operated in accord with the laws of the State prescribing segregation of the white and colored pupils, but on June 5, 1955, following the two decisions of the Supreme Court of the United States in Brown v. Board of Education of Topeka, 347 U.S. 483 and 349 U.S. 294, the school board of directors determined that as the Fourteenth Amendment to the United States Constitution, interpreted in those decisions, invalidated all state laws imposing segregated public education, the Board was required to desegregate the schools within their jurisdiction as soon as all administrative obstacles could be removed. The Board further determined that under Article VI, Clause 3 of the United States Constitution requiring state officers to bind themselves by oath to support the Constitution which by Article VI, Clause 2 is the supreme law of the land, they had the right and duty to change to a non-discriminatory system without awaiting repeal of the Arkansas segregation statutes.

On June 25, 1955, the Board determined that all legally cognizable obstacles to desegregation had been removed, and resolved to desegregate the schools within its jurisdiction, and on July 11, 1955, the schools were opened without segregation. Such operation of them was effective for several weeks with satisfactory reaction from pupils and the local community, but thereafter attempts to obstruct and prevent the operation of the schools on the integrated basis were systematically planned and set on foot, and the present action was brought by the School District, the members of the School Board and the School Superintendent in the federal district court in Arkansas to obtain restraining order and injunction against such obstruction.[1]

The defendants named in the complaint are individuals and organizations alleged to have entered into and carried on a conspiracy to obstruct the school board from securing the equal protection of the laws in the operation of the public schools to all persons within the district. It was alleged that defendants in furtherance of their conspiracy claimed and asserted that Arkansas laws required a continuation of segregation and that plaintiff's resolution to desegregate the schools was illegal. That defendants committed numerous acts of trespass upon the school property and acts of annoying, threatening, and intimidating the individual plaintiffs, and made inflammatory speeches at mass meetings condoning physical violence and calling for mass action in resistance to desegregation, and to the same end made threats to boycott the schools and to subject the members of the school board to

---

[1] Declaratory judgment was also prayed for but was not awarded and no issue is here preserved in respect to it.

endless, expensive litigation, and attempted by fear and persuasion to deter the children from attendance at schools of the district. The acts of defendants caused discontinuance of a school session, reduction of school attendance resulting in immediate loss of annual revenue to the school district, and restoration of segregation demanded by defendants would cost an immediate additional expenditure. That the matter in controversy exceeded, exclusive of interest and costs, the sum of $3,000, and that plaintiffs would suffer irreparable injury unless granted injunctive relief.

The plaintiffs asserted jurisdiction in the federal court under Title 28 U.S.C.A. Section 1331, and that the action arose under Article VI, Clauses 2 and 3 of the Constitution of the United States; the Fourteenth Amendment to the Constitution of the United States, and Article IV, Section 4 of the Constitution. Jurisdiction was also invoked pursuant to Title 28 U.S.C.A. Section 1343 with further allegation that the action also arose under Title 42 U.S.C.A. Sections 1983, 1985(2), and 1988, and under Title 18 U.S.C.A. Sections 241 and 242.

A temporary restraining order was issued by Judge Trimble, presiding in the district court, on presentation of the verified complaint supported by affidavits, and thereafter hearing was had on a motion by defendants to dismiss. Judge Trimble denied the motion and accompanied the ruling with written opinion, 135 F. Supp. 296. Thereafter, issues having been joined, plenary trial was had in the district court on the merits before Judge Reeves and judgment was rendered against the defendants and all persons acting in concert with them enjoining them from "interfering by acts of trespass, boycott or picketing with the free operation of schools within plaintiff's jurisdiction; from in any manner deterring the attendance at school of children within said school district and from in any manner threatening or intimidating the individual plaintiffs; from taking any acts of any kind whatsoever which seek to compel by force, intimidation, threats or violence a rescission of the orders heretofore made integrating the public schools of Hoxie."

The judgment was based on meticulously detailed and complete findings of fact which are reported along with the opinion of Judge Reeves at 137 F. Supp. 364.

All of the defendants in the action have joined in this appeal to obtain a reversal of the judgment. They do not assign any specified finding of fact of the trial court as clearly erroneous, though in their statement of the facts set forth in the brief, some differences from the findings are observed.

They contend for reversal that the federal court was without jurisdiction of the action; that the complaint failed to state facts sufficient to constitute a cause of action; that the evidence was insufficient; and that the injunction granted is violative of the First Amendment of the Constitution in that it abridges freedom of speech and denies the right peaceably to assemble and petition. . . .

Turning first to the question of federal jurisdiction, it is the position of the appellees that federal jurisdiction of the case exists under the general provision of the federal law, in that the complaint presents a civil action arising under the Constitution and laws of the United States wherein the amount in controversy exceeds $3,000 (28 U.S.C.A. Sec. 1331) and it arises under the Supremacy Clause of the Constitution implementing the Fourteenth Amendment, and the corollary or related constitutional provision imposing an oath or affirmation upon state officers to support the Constitution.

Appellees contend that as they are under a constitutional duty to support and obey the Fourteenth Amendment and to accord equal protection of the law in their operation of schools, they have a federal right to be free from wrongful interference with the performance of that duty. They say they rest their claim of a federal constitutional right squarely on the fundamental and pervasive provisions of the Constitution and statutes, and declare that the nubbin of their case against defendants in the federal court is the jurisdiction which stems from the Fourteenth Amendment in conjunction with the Supremacy Clause of the Constitution and the cause of action under Section 1331 to which they give rise. That the right of the members of the school board to be free from interference with their performance of a duty which the Constitution itself imposes on them derives directly from the Supremacy Clause and the related constitutional provision imposing upon the state officers the oath or affirmation to support the constitution and it is a federal right. The school board is attempting to obey and apply the federal law laid down by the Supreme Court in the Brown case and the defendants attempt and threaten to subvert and prevent it.

Both of the learned and experienced district judges who rendered decision in the case reached the conclusion that the complaint disclosed that federal jurisdiction existed under the provisions of the general law relied on as above stated, and we are in accord with that conclusion. . . .

PLAINTIFFS' FEDERAL RIGHT

The plaintiffs being bound by constitutionally imposed duty and their oaths of office to support the Fourteenth Amendment and to accord equal protection of the laws to all persons in their operation of the Hoxie schools must be deemed to have a right, which is a federal right, to be free from direct interference in the performance of that duty. In Brown v. Board of Education and the companion cases, supra, the Supreme Court held that segregated public education is a denial of the equal protection of the laws. A state granting public education must do so on an equal basis without racial distinction. Separation of the races in a public education system is discriminatory. In the field of public education, the doctrine of separate but equal has no place. Because of the wide applicability of the decision and the great variety of local conditions, the Court deferred formulation of the decrees in the Brown case, emphasizing merely that "We have now announced that such segregation is a denial of the equal protection of the laws." . . .

Plaintiffs are under a duty to obey the Constitution. Const. Art. VI, cl. 2. They are bound by oath or affirmation to support it and are mindful of their obligation. It follows as a necessary corollary that they have a federal right to be free from direct and deliberate interference with the performance of the constitutionally imposed duty. The right arises by necessary implication from the imposition of the duty as clearly as though it had been specifically stated in the Constitution. In many cases the implied rights which have been upheld by the courts have been of far less importance than the right against being interfered with in obeying the Constitution which is here involved. Included among such implied rights are the following: The right to be protected against violence while in the lawful custody of a federal officer (Logan v. United States, 144 U.S. 263, 294 — a right which the Court stated "does not depend upon any of the Amendments to the Constitution, but arises out of the creation and establishment of a national government, paramount and supreme within its sphere of action"); the right to inform a federal officer of a violation of the laws, In re Quarles, 158 U.S. 532, 536; see also Motes v. United States, 178 U.S. 458, 462-463; Nicholson v. United States, 79 F.2d 387 (C.A. 8); Hawkins v. State, 293 Fed. 586 (C.A. 5); the right of the people peaceably to assemble for the purpose of petitioning Congress for a redress of grievance or for anything else connected with the powers and duties of the national government (United States v. Cruikshank, 92 U.S. 542, which the Court held was implied by the very idea of a government, republican in form; see also Powe v. United States, 109 F.2d 147, 151 (C.A. 5), cert. den., 309 U.S. 679); the right to vote in federal elections, Ex parte Yarbrough, 110 U.S. 651; the right of a voter in a federal election to have his ballot counted fairly, United States v. Mosley, 238 U.S. 383; United States v. Classic, 313 U.S. 299; and United States v. Saylor, 322 U.S. 385; the right to furnish military supplies to the federal government for defense purposes, Anderson v. United States, 269 Fed. 65 (C.A. 9), cert. den., 255 U.S. 576; the right of a witness to be protected in giving testimony before a federal tribunal, Foss v. United States, 266 Fed. 881 (C.A. 9); the right to enforce a decree of a federal court by contempt proceedings, United States v. Lancaster, 44 Fed. 885, 44 Fed. 896 (C.C.W.D. Ga.); and the right to hold federal office, McDonald v. United States, 9 F.2d 506 (C.A. 8); see also

United States v. Patrick, 54 Fed. 338 (C.C.M.D. Tenn.). See, generally, United States v. Moore, 129 Fed. 630, 632-633 (C.C.N.D. Ala.).

Threatened abridgment of the rights which the courts held existed by implication in the Constitution actually supported criminal prosecutions in most of the foregoing cases, and not merely, as here, the relatively mild restraint of the injunctive process.

The existence of a constitutional duty presupposes a correlative Constitutional right in the person for whom the duty is to be exercised. Thus in Logan v. United States, 144 U.S. 263, the Supreme Court upheld what is now Title 18, United States Code, Section 241, as the basis for conviction of three men charged with mob violence against prisoners in the custody of a United States Marshal. The Court held that the prisoners, who were awaiting trial for an offense against the United States, had a federal right to be protected in their persons while in federal custody. The Court said (144 U.S., at 284) that the existence of a duty on the part of the government to protect its prisoners "implies a corresponding right of the prisoners to be so protected." Cf. U.S. v. Cruikshank, 25 Fed. Cas. 707, 709, No. 14,897, affirmed 92 U.S. 542. . . .

THE MERITS

The facts as found by the district court show that defendants acted as they did for the purpose of preventing the plaintiff board from continuing to operate desegregated schools. It was found by the court, for example, that defendants' conduct at the August 3, 1955, meeting "revealed a concert of action and a general agreement on their part to compel, by force and intimidation, a rescission of the order of the Board of Directors in integrating the races in the schools. . . . The words used, and the very nature of the speeches, would have and did have the effect, not only to encourage violence but to intimidate those who are charged with the responsibility of integrating the races. . . ." "Following the first mass meeting and in between and after the others, the defendants, both in meetings with members of the Board of Directors and the individual members thereof, and by telephone calls, and by threats to throw a picket line about the schools, and by acts of terrorism so far as the Superintendent of Schools was concerned, so intimidated the parents and patrons of the schools, as to force a suspension of school activities." These and other facts found by the court warranted, among others, the conclusions of law that "the defendants, having acted in concert for the common purpose of compelling a rescission of the integration order of the Board of Directors of Hoxie School District No. 46, were conspirators, and the acts of each conspirator were binding upon all the others." And "All the defendants in this case had joined in the common conspiracy, from which none of the defendants has to date withdrawn, for the express purpose of forcing the plaintiffs to return to segregation in the Hoxie schools. To effect this conspiracy the defendants have resorted to threats, violence, and intimidations against plaintiffs and those who uphold their actions. Defendants seek to prevent plaintiffs from exercising their civil right to secure equal protection of the laws to all citizens within the school district. Defendants have challenged the legality of the action of plaintiffs in establishing integrated schools."

The conduct of the defendants briefly described above was not in the nature of merely private tortious action; it was action directed to prevent the plaintiff school board members from carrying out their duty as state officials to put into effect a desegregation program in public schools. It was deliberately aimed at preventing the school board from affording to all children within the school district the equal protection of the laws. The findings that the conduct of the defendants caused damages and, unless restrained, would result in irreparable injury for which there was no adequate remedy at law were supported.

As to the First Amendment. The terms of the injunction that was issued in this case did not go beyond preventing a continuation of the acts defendants were engaging in and the kind of speech in which they indulged as fully set forth in the findings of the court appearing in 137 F. Supp. 364, 368 to 374. Those acts and that type of speech were calculated and intended, at the times and under the circumstances in which they were made, to incite disobedience of the law and the overthrow of law and order and to coerce, intimidate, and compel the school board to cease and desist from the performance of its sworn and lawful duty, and to engage in unlawful conduct. They present no legitimate issue of free speech or assembly. We think the injunction in the form in which it was issued is justified under the decisions of the Supreme Court in Cantwell v. Connecticut, 310 U.S. 296; Feiner v. New York, 340 U.S. 315; Giboney v. Empire Storage & Ice Co., 336 U.S. 490; Chaplinsky v. New Hampshire, 315 U.S. 568.

CIVIL RIGHTS ACTS

[The court found "additional support" for its jurisdiction and for the injunction in the provision of 42 U.S.C.A. for a damage suit by any person deprived of his equal protection rights. While not affording an independent basis for the injunction, the statute, the court agreed, suggested that relief here accorded with the "legislative purpose" of Congress.]

Plaintiffs also contended before Judge Reeves and repeat here that the identity of interest between the school board and the school children is sufficiently close so as to permit the school board to assert the rights of the school children under the Fourteenth Amendment in a federal equitable proceeding to restrain the illegal conduct. . . . The school board having the duty to afford the children the equal protection of the law has the correlative right, as has been pointed out, to protection in performance of its function. Its right is thus intimately identified with the right of the children themselves. The right does not arise solely from the interest of the parties concerned, but from the necessity of the government itself. (Cf. Ex parte Yarbrough, 110 U.S. 651, 662.) Though, generally speaking, the right to equal protection is a personal right of individuals, this is "only a rule of practice" (Barrows v. Jackson, 346 U.S. 249, 257) which will not be followed where the identity of interest between the party asserting the right and the party in whose favor the right directly exists is sufficiently close. . . .

As we have found no error in the judgment appealed from, it is in all respects affirmed.[1]

Marsh v. Alabama 326 U.S. 501, 66 S. Ct. 276, 90 L. Ed. 265 (1946)

MR. JUSTICE BLACK delivered the opinion of the Court.

In this case we are asked to decide whether a State, consistently with the First and Fourteenth Amendments, can impose criminal punishment on a person who undertakes to distribute religious literature on the premises of a company-owned town contrary to the wishes of the town's management. The town, a suburb of Mobile, Alabama, known as Chickasaw, is owned by the Gulf Shipbuilding Corporation. Except for that it has all the characteristics of any other American town. The property consists of residential buildings, streets, a system of sewers, a sewage disposal plant and a "business block" on which business places are situated. A deputy of the Mobile County Sheriff, paid by the company, serves as the town's policeman. Merchants and service establishments have rented the stores and business places on the business block and the United States uses one of the places as a post office from which six carriers deliver mail to the people of Chickasaw and the adjacent area. The town and the surrounding neighborhood, which cannot be distinguished from the Gulf property by anyone not familiar with the property lines, are thickly settled, and according to all indications the residents use the business block as their regular shopping center. To do so, they now, as they have for many years, make use of a company-owned paved street and sidewalk located alongside the store fronts in order to enter and leave the stores and the post office. Intersecting company-owned roads at each end of the business block lead into a four-lane public highway which runs parallel to the business

[1] See Case Note, 70 Harv. L. Rev. 1299 (1957); Note, Legal Sanctions to Enforce Desegregation in the Public Schools: The Contempt Power and the Civil Rights Act, 65 Yale L.J. 630 (1956). — ED.

block at a distance of thirty feet. There is nothing to stop highway traffic from coming onto the business block and upon arrival a traveler may make free use of the facilities available there. In short the town and its shopping district are accessible to and freely used by the public in general and there is nothing to distinguish them from any other town and shopping center except the fact that the title to the property belongs to a private corporation.

Appellant, a Jehovah's Witness, came onto the sidewalk we have just described, stood near the post office and undertook to distribute religious literature. In the stores the corporation had posted a notice which read as follows: "This Is Private Property, and Without Written Permission, No Street, or House Vendor, Agent or Solicitation of Any Kind Will Be Permitted." Appellant was warned that she could not distribute the literature without a permit and told that no permit would be issued to her. She protested that the company rule could not be constitutionally applied so as to prohibit her from distributing religious writings. When she was asked to leave the sidewalk and Chickasaw she declined. The deputy sheriff arrested her and she was charged in the state court with violating Title 14, §426 of the 1940 Alabama Code which makes it a crime to enter or remain on the premises of another after having been warned not to do so. Appellant contended that to construe the state statute as applicable to her activities would abridge her right to freedom of press and religion contrary to the First and Fourteenth Amendments to the Constitution. This contention was rejected and she was convicted. The Alabama Court of Appeals affirmed the conviction, holding that the statute as applied was constitutional because the title to the sidewalk was in the corporation and because the public use of the sidewalk had not been such as to give rise to a presumption under Alabama law of its irrevocable dedication to the public. 21 So.2d 558. The State Supreme Court denied certiorari, 246 Ala. 539, and the case is here on appeal under §237(a) of the Judicial Code, 28 U.S.C. §344(a).

Had the title to Chickasaw belonged not to a private but a municipal corporation and had appellant been arrested for violating a municipal ordinance rather than a ruling by those appointed by the corporation to manage a company town it would have been clear that appellant's conviction must be reversed. Under our decision in Lovell v. Griffin, 303 U.S. 444, . . . neither a state nor a municipality can completely bar the distribution of literature containing religious or political ideas on its streets, sidewalks and public places or make the right to distribute dependent on a flat license tax or permit to be issued by an official who could deny it at will. We have also held that an ordinance completely prohibiting the dissemination of ideas on the city streets cannot be justified on the ground that the municipality holds legal title to them. Jamison v. Texas, 318 U.S. 413. And we have recognized that the preservation of a free society is so far dependent upon the right of each individual citizen to receive such literature as he himself might desire that a municipality could not, without jeopardizing that vital individual freedom, prohibit door-to-door distribution of literature. Martin v. Struthers, 319 U.S. 141, 146, 147. From these decisions it is clear that had the people of Chickasaw owned all the homes, and all the stores, and all the streets, and all the sidewalks, all those owners together could not have set up a municipal government with sufficient power to pass an ordinance completely barring the distribution of religious literature. Our question then narrows down to this: Can those people who live in or come to Chickasaw be denied freedom of press and religion simply because a single company has legal title to all the town? For it is the state's contention that the mere fact that all the property interests in the town are held by a single company is enough to give that company power, enforceable by a state statute, to abridge these freedoms.

We do not agree that the corporation's property interests settle the question. The State urges in effect that the corporation's right to control the inhabitants of Chickasaw is coextensive with the right of a homeowner to regulate the conduct of his guests. We cannot accept that contention. Ownership does not always mean absolute dominion. The more an owner, for his advantage, opens up his property for use by the public in general, the more do his rights become circumscribed by the statutory and constitutional rights of those who

Section E. Secured Rights and State Action 799

use it. . . . Thus, the owners of privately held bridges, ferries, turnpikes and railroads may not operate them as freely as a farmer does his farm. Since these facilities are built and operated primarily to benefit the public and since their operation is essentially a public function, it is subject to state regulation. And, though the issue is not directly analogous to the one before us we do want to point out by way of illustration that such regulation may not result in an operation of these facilities, even by privately owned companies, which unconstitutionally interferes with and discriminates against interstate commerce. Port Richmond & B. P. Ferry Co. v. Hudson County [234 U.S. 317, 326]; cf. South Carolina State Highway Dept. v. Barnwell Bros., 303 U.S. 177. Had the corporation here owned the segment of the four-lane highway which runs parallel to the "business block" and operated the same under a State franchise, doubtless no one would have seriously contended that the corporation's property interest in the highway gave it power to obstruct through traffic or to discriminate against interstate commerce. . . . And even had there been no express franchise but mere acquiescence by the State in the corporation's use of its property as a segment of the four-lane highway, operation of all the highway, including the segment owned by the corporation, would still have been performance of a public function and discrimination would certainly have been illegal.[4]

We do not think it makes any significant constitutional difference as to the relationship between the rights of the owner and those of the public that here the State, instead of permitting the corporation to operate a highway, permitted it to use its property as a town, operate a "business block" in the town and a street and sidewalk on that business block. Cf. Barney v. Keokuk, 94 U.S. 324, 340. Whether a corporation or a municipality owns or possesses the town the public in either case has an identical interest in the functioning of the community in such manner that the channels of communication remain free. As we have heretofore stated, the town of Chickasaw does not function differently from any other town. The "business block" serves as the community shopping center and is freely accessible and open to the people in the area and those passing through. The managers appointed by the corporation cannot curtail the liberty of press and religion of these people consistently with the purposes of the Constitutional guarantees, and a state statute, as the one here involved, which enforces such action by criminally punishing those who attempt to distribute religious literature clearly violates the First and Fourteenth Amendments to the Constitution.

Many people in the United States live in company-owned towns. These people, just as residents of municipalities, are free citizens of their State and country. Just as all other citizens which affect the welfare of community and nation. To act as good citizens they must be informed. In order to enable them to be properly informed their information must be uncensored. There is no more reason for depriving these people of the liberties guaranteed by the First and Fourteenth Amendments than there is for curtailing these freedoms with respect to any other citizen.[6]

---

[4] And certainly the corporation can no more deprive people of freedom of press and religion than it can discriminate against commerce. In his dissenting opinion in Jones v. Opelika, 316 U.S. 584, 600, which later was adopted as the opinion of the Court, 319 U.S. 103, 104, Mr. Chief Justice Stone made the following pertinent statement: "Freedom of press and religion, explicitly guaranteed by the Constitution, must at least be entitled to the same freedom from burdensome taxation which it has been thought that the more general phraseology of the commerce clause has extended to interstate commerce. Whatever doubts may be entertained as to this Court's function to relieve, unaided by Congressional legislation, from burdensome taxation under the commerce clause, see Gwin, White & Prince v. Henneford, 305 U.S. 434, 441, 446-455; McCarroll v. Dixie Greyhound Lines, 309 U.S. 176, 184, 185, it cannot be thought that that function is wanting under the explicit guaranties of freedom of speech, press and religion." 316 U.S. at 610, 611.

[6] As to the suppression of civil liberties in company-towns and the need of those who live there for Constitutional protection, see the summary of facts aired before the Senate Committee on Education and Labor, Violations of Free Speech and Rights of Labor, Hearings pursuant to S. Res. 266 (74th Cong. 2d Sess. 1933) summarized in Bowden, Freedom for Wage Earners, Annals of The American Academy of Political and Social Science, Nov. 1938, p. 185; Z. Chafee, The Inquiring Mind (New York, 1928), pp. 173, 174; Pamphlet published in 1923 by the Bituminous Operators' Special Committee under the title The Company Town; U.S. Coal Commission, Report, 1925, Part III, p. 1331.

When we balance the Constitutional right of owners of property against those of the people to enjoy freedom of press and religion, as we must here, we remain mindful of the fact that the latter occupy a preferred position. As we have stated before, the right to exercise the liberties safeguarded by the First Amendment "lies at the foundation of free government by free men" and we must in all cases "weigh the circumstances and . . . appraise the . . . reasons . . . in support of the regulation . . . of the rights." Schneider v. Irvington, 308 U.S. 147, 161. In our view the circumstance that the property rights to the premises where the deprivation of liberty, here involved, took place, were held by others than the public, is not sufficient to justify the State's permitting a corporation to govern a community of citizens so as to restrict their fundamental liberties and the enforcement of such restraint by the application of a state statute. In so far as the State has attempted to impose criminal punishment on appellant for undertaking to distribute religious literature in a company town, its action cannot stand. The case is reversed and the cause remanded for further proceedings not inconsistent with this opinion.

Reversed and remanded.

MR. JUSTICE JACKSON took no part in the consideration or decision of this case.

MR. JUSTICE FRANKFURTER, concurring.

So long as the views which prevailed in Jones v. Opelika, 319 U.S. 103, in connection with 316 U.S. 584, 600; Murdock v. Pennsylvania, 319 U.S. 105; Martin v. Struthers, 319 U.S. 141, express the law of the Constitution, I am unable to find legal significance in the fact that a town in which the Constitutional freedoms of religion and speech are invoked happens to be company-owned. These decisions accorded the purveyors of ideas, religious or otherwise, "a preferred position," Murdock v. Pennsylvania, supra (319 U.S. at 115), even to the extent of relieving them from an unhampering and non-discriminatory duty of bearing their share of the cost of maintaining the peace and the other amenities of a civilized society. Constitutional privileges having such a reach ought not to depend upon a State court's notion of the extent of "dedication" of private property to public purposes. Local determinations of such technical matters govern controversies affecting property. But when decisions by State courts involving local matters are so interwoven with the decision of the question of Constitutional rights that one necessarily involves the other, State determination of local questions cannot control the Federal Constitutional right.

A company-owned town gives rise to a net-work of property relations. As to these, the judicial organ of a State has the final say. But a company-owned town is a town. In its community aspects it does not differ from other towns. These community aspects are decisive in adjusting the relations now before us, and more particularly in adjudicating the clash of freedoms which the Bill of Rights was designed to resolve — the freedom of the community to regulate its life and the freedom of the individual to exercise his religion and to disseminate his ideas. Title to property as defined by State law controls property relations; it cannot control issues of civil liberties which arise precisely because a company town is a town as well as a congeries of property relations. And similarly the technical distinctions on which a finding of "trespass" so often depends are too tenuous to control decision regarding the scope of the vital liberties guaranteed by the Constitution.

Accordingly, as I have already indicated, so long as the scope of the guarantees of the Due Process Clause of the Fourteenth Amendment by absorption of the First remains that which the Court gave to it in the series of cases in the October Term, 1942, the circumstances of the present case seem to me clearly to fall within it. And so I agree with the opinion of the Court, except that portion of it which relies on arguments drawn from the restrictions which the Commerce Clause imposes on State regulation of commerce. It does not seem to me to further constitutional analysis to seek help for the solution of the delicate problems arising under the First Amendment from the very different order of problems which the Commerce Clause presents. The latter involves an accommodation between National and State powers operating in the same field. Where the First Amendment applies, it is a denial of all governmental power in our Federal system.

Mr. Justice Reed dissenting. . . .

Both Federal and Alabama law permit, so far as we are aware, company towns. By that we mean an area occupied by numerous houses, connected by passways, fenced or not, as the owners may choose. These communities may be essential to furnish proper and convenient living conditions for employees on isolated operations in lumbering, mining, production of high explosives and large-scale farming. The restrictions imposed by the owners upon the occupants are sometimes galling to the employees and may appear unreasonable to outsiders. Unless they fall under the prohibition of some legal rule, however, they are a matter for adjustment between owner and licensee, or by appropriate legislation. Compare Western Turf Asso. v. Greenberg, 204 U.S. 359. . . .

Our constitution guarantees to every man the right to express his views in an orderly fashion. An essential element of "orderly" is that the man shall also have a right to use the place he chooses for his exposition. The rights of the owner, which the Constitution protects as well as the right of free speech, are not outweighed by the interests of the trespasser, even though he trespasses in behalf of religion or free speech. We cannot say that Jehovah's Witnesses can claim the privilege of a license, which has never been granted, to hold their meetings in other private places, merely because the owner has admitted the public to them for other limited purposes. Even though we have reached the point where this Court is required to force private owners to open their property for the practice there of religious activities or propaganda distasteful to the owner, because of the public interest in freedom of speech and religion, there is no need for the application of such a doctrine here. Apellant, as we have said, was free to engage in such practices on the public highways, without becoming a trespasser on the company's property.

The Chief Justice and Mr. Justice Burton join in this dissent.

Lloyd Corp. v. Tanner 407 U.S. 551, 92 S. Ct. 2219, 33 L. Ed. 2d 131 (1972)

Mr. Justice Powell delivered the opinion of the Court.

This case presents the question reserved by the Court in Amalgamated Food Employees Union v. Logan Valley Plaza, 391 U.S. 308 (1968), as to the right of a privately owned shopping center to prohibit the distribution of handbills on its property when the handbilling is unrelated to the shopping center's operations. Relying primarily on Marsh v. Alabama, 326 U.S. 501 (1946), and Logan Valley, the United States District Court for the District of Oregon sustained an asserted First Amendment right to distribute handbills in petitioner's shopping center, and issued a permanent injunction restraining petitioner from interfering with such right. 308 F. Supp. 128 (1970). The Court of Appeals for the Ninth Circuit affirmed, 446 F.2d 545 (1971). We granted certiorari to consider petitioner's contention that the decision below violates rights of private property protected by the Fifth and Fourteenth Amendments. 404 U.S. 1037 (1972).

Lloyd Corp., Ltd. (Lloyd), owns a large, modern retail shopping center in Portland, Oregon. Lloyd Center embraces altogether about 50 acres, including some 20 acres of open and covered parking facilities which accommodate more than 1,000 automobiles. It has a perimeter of almost one and one-half miles, bounded by four public streets. It is crossed in varying degrees by several other public streets, all of which have adjacent public sidewalks. Lloyd owns all land and buildings within the Center, except these public streets and sidewalks. There are some 60 commercial tenants, including small shops and several major department stores.

The Center embodies a relatively new concept in shopping center design. The stores are all located within a single large, multi-level building complex sometimes referred to as the "Mall." Within this complex, in addition to the stores, there are parking facilities, malls, private sidewalks, stairways, escalators, gardens, an auditorium, and a skating rink.

Some of the stores open directly on the outside public sidewalks, but most open on the interior privately owned malls. Some stores open on both. There are no public streets or public sidewalks within the building complex, which is enclosed and entirely covered except for the landscaped portions of some of the interior malls.

The distribution of the handbills occurred in the malls. . . .

The Center is open generally to the public, with a considerable effort being made to attract shoppers and prospective shoppers, and to create "customer motivation" as well as customer goodwill in the community. In this respect the Center pursues policies comparable to those of major stores and shopping centers across the country, although the Center affords superior facilities for these purposes. Groups and organizations are permitted, by invitation and advance arrangement, to use the auditorium and other facilities. Rent is charged for use of the auditorium except with respect to certain civic and charitable organizations, such as the Cancer Society and Boy and Girl Scouts. The Center also allows limited use of the malls by the American Legion to sell poppies for disabled veterans, and by the Salvation Army and Volunteers of America to solicit Christmas contributions. It has denied similar use to other civic and charitable organizations. Political use is also forbidden, except that presidential candidates of both parties have been allowed to speak in the auditorium.[3]

The Center had been in operation for some eight years when this litigation commenced. Throughout this period it had a policy, strictly enforced, against the distribution of handbills within the building complex and its malls. No exceptions were made with respect to handbilling, which was considered likely to annoy customers, to create litter, potentially to create disorders, and generally to be incompatible with the purpose of the Center and the atmosphere sought to be preserved.

On November 14, 1968, the respondents in this case distributed within the Center handbill invitations to a meeting of the "Resistance Community" to protest the draft and the Vietnam war. The distribution, made in several different places on the mall walkways by five young people, was quiet and orderly, and there was no littering. There was a complaint from one customer. Security guards informed the respondents that they were trespassing and would be arrested unless they stopped distributing the handbills within the Center. The guards suggested that respondents distribute their literature on the public streets and sidewalks adjacent to but outside of the Center complex. Respondents left the premises as requested "to avoid arrest" and continued the handbilling outside. Subsequently this suit was instituted in the District Court, seeking declaratory and injunctive relief.

I

The District Court, emphasizing that the Center "is open to the general public," found that it is "the functional equivalent of a public business district." 308 F. Supp., at 130. That court then held that Lloyd's "rule prohibiting the distribution of handbills within the Mall violates . . . First Amendment rights." 308 F. Supp., at 131. In a per curiam opinion, the Court of Appeals held that it was bound by the "factual determination" as to the character of the Center, and concluded that the decisions of this Court in Marsh v. Alabama, 326 U.S. 501 (1946), and Amalgamated Food Employees Union v. Logan Valley Plaza, 391 U.S. 308 (1968), compelled affirmance.[5] . . .

---

[3] The manager of the Center, explaining why presidential candidates were allowed to speak, said: "We do that for one reason and that is great public interest. It . . . brings a great many people to Lloyd Center who may shop before they leave." App. 51.

[5] The Court of Appeals also relied on Wolin v. Port of New York Authority, 392 F.2d 83 (CA2 1968).

Section E. Secured Rights and State Action

In Logan Valley the Court extended the rationale of Marsh to peaceful picketing of a store located in a large shopping center, known as Logan Valley Mall, near Altoona, Pennsylvania. Weis Markets, Inc. (Weis), an original tenant, had opened a supermarket in one of the larger stores and was employing a wholly nonunion staff. Within 10 days after Weis opened, members of Amalgamated Food Employees Union Local 590 (Union) began picketing Weis, carrying signs stating that it was a nonunion market and that its employees were not receiving union wages or other union benefits. The picketing, conducted by nonemployees, was carried out almost entirely in the parcel pickup area immediately adjacent to the store and on portions of the adjoining parking lot. The picketing was peaceful, with the number of pickets varying from four to 13.

Weis and Logan Valley Plaza, Inc., sought and obtained an injunction against this picketing. The injunction required that all picketing be confined to public areas outside the shopping center. On appeal the Pennsylvania Supreme Court affirmed the issuance of the injunction, and this Court granted certiorari. In framing the question, this Court stated:

"The case squarely presents . . . the question whether Pennsylvania's generally valid rule against trespass to private property can be applied in these circumstances to bar petitioners from the Weis and Logan premises." 391 U.S., at 315.

The Court noted that the answer would be clear "if the shopping center premises were not privately owned but instead constituted the business area of a municipality." . . .

The Court then considered Marsh v. Alabama, supra, and concluded that: "The shopping center here is clearly the functional equivalent of the business district of Chickasaw involved in Marsh." 391 U.S., at 318. But the Court was careful not to go further and say that for all purposes and uses the privately owned streets, sidewalks, and other areas of a shopping center are analogous to publicly owned facilities:

"All we decide here is that because the shopping center serves as the community business block 'and is freely accessible and open to the people in the area and those passing through,' Marsh v. Alabama, 326 U.S., at 508, the State may not delegate the power, through the use of its trespass laws, wholly to exclude those members of the public wishing to exercise their First Amendment rights on the premises in a manner and for a purpose generally consonant with the use to which the property is actually put." Id., at 319-320.

The Court noted that the scope of its holding was limited, and expressly reserved judgment on the type of issue presented in this case:

"The picketing carried on by petitioners was directed specifically at patrons of the Weis Market located within the shopping center and the message sought to be conveyed to the public concerned the manner in which that particular market was being operated. We are, therefore, not called upon to consider whether respondents' property rights could, consistently with the First Amendment, justify a bar on picketing which was not directly related in its purpose to the use to which the shopping center property was being put." Id., at 320 n.9.

The Court also took specific note of the facts that the Union's picketing was "directed solely at one establishment within the shopping center," id., at 321, and that the public berms and sidewalks were "from 350 to 500 feet away from the Weis store." Id., at 322. This distance made it difficult "to communicate [with] patrons of Weis" and "to limit [the] effect [of the picketing] to Weis only." Id., at 322, 323. Logan Valley was decided on the basis of this factual situation, and the facts in this case are significantly different.

II

The courts below considered the critical inquiry to be whether Lloyd Center was "the functional equivalent of a public business district." . . .

[But the] holding in Logan Valley was not dependent upon the suggestion that the privately owned streets and sidewalks of a business district or a shopping center are the equivalent, for First Amendment purposes, of municipally owned streets and sidewalks. No such expansive reading of the opinion of the Court is necessary or appropriate. The opinion was carefully phrased to limit its holding to the picketing involved, where the picketing was "directly related in its purpose to the use to which the shopping center property was being put," 391 U.S., at 320 n. 9, and where the store was located in the center of a large private enclave with the consequence that no other reasonable opportunities for the pickets to convey their message to their intended audience were available.

Neither of these elements is present in the case now before the Court.

A

The handbilling by respondents in the mall of Loyd Center had no relation to any purpose for which the center was built and being used. . . . There is no open-ended invitation to the public to use the Center for any and all purposes, however incompatible with the interests of both the stores and the shoppers whom they serve. . . .

B

A further fact, distinguishing the present case from Logan Valley, is that the Union pickets in that case would have been deprived of all reasonable opportunity to convey their message to patrons of the Weis store had they been denied access to the shopping center. The situation at Lloyd Center was notably different. The central building complex was surrounded by public sidewalks, totaling 66 linear blocks. All persons who enter or leave the private areas within the complex must cross public streets and sidewalks, either on foot or in automobiles. When moving to and from the privately owned parking lots, automobiles are required by law to come to a complete stop. Handbills may be distributed conveniently to pedestrians, and also to occupants of automobiles, from these public sidewalks and streets. Indeed, respondents moved to these public areas and continued distribution of their handbills after being requested to leave the interior malls. It would be an unwarranted infringement of property rights to require them to yield to the exercise of First Amendment rights under circumstances where adequate alternative avenues of communication exist. Such an accommodation would diminish property rights without significantly enhancing the asserted right of free speech. . . .

III

The basic issue in this case is whether respondents, in the exercise of asserted First Amendment rights, may distribute handbills on Lloyd's private property contrary to its wishes and contrary to a policy enforced against *all* handbilling. In addressing this issue, it must be remembered that the First and Fourteenth Amendments safeguard the rights of free speech and assembly by limitations on *state* action, not on action by the owner of private property used nondiscriminatorily for private purposes only. The Due Process Clauses of the Fifth and Fourteenth Amendments are also relevant to this case. They provide that "[n]o person shall . . . be deprived of life, liberty, or property, without due process of law." There is the further proscription in the Fifth Amendment against the taking of "private property . . . for public use, without just compensation."

Although accommodations between the values protected by these three Amendments are sometimes necessary, and the courts properly have shown a special solicitude for the guarantees of the First Amendment, this Court has never held that a trespasser or an uninvited guest may exercise general rights of free speech on property privately owned and used nondiscriminatorily for private purposes only. . . .

Nor does property lose its private character merely because the public is generally invited to use it for designated purposes. Few would argue that a free-standing store, with abutting parking space for customers, assumes significant public attributes merely because the public is invited to shop there. Nor is size alone the controlling factor. The essentially private character of a store and its privately owned abutting property does not change by virtue of being large or clustered with others stores in a modern shopping center. . . . [T]he Fifth and Fourteenth Amendment rights of private property owners, as well as the First Amendment rights of all citizens, must be respected and protected. The Framers of the Constitution certainly did not think these fundamental rights of a free society are incompatible with each other. There may be situations where accommodations between them, and the drawing of lines to assure due protection of both, are not easy. But on the facts presented in this case, the answer is clear.

We hold that there has been no such dedication of Lloyd's privately owned and operated shopping center to public use as to entitle respondents to exercise therein the asserted First Amendment rights. Accordingly, we reverse the judgment and remand the case to the Court of Appeals with directions to vacate the injunction.

It is so ordered.

MR. JUSTICE MARSHALL, with whom MR. JUSTICE DOUGLAS, MR. JUSTICE BRENNAN, and MR. JUSTICE STEWART join, dissenting.

. . . Today, this Court reverses the judgment of the Court of Appeals and attempts to distinguish this case from Logan Valley. In my view, the distinction that the Court sees between the cases does not exist. As I read the opinion of the Court, it is an attack not only on the rationale of Logan Valley, but also on this Court's longstanding decision in Marsh v. Alabama, 326 U.S. 501 (1946). Accordingly, I dissent.

I

. . . A. The question presented by this case is whether one of the incidents of petitioner's private ownership of the Lloyd Center is the power to exclude certain forms of speech from its property. In other words, we must decide whether ownership of the Center gives petitioner unfettered discretion to determine whether or not it will be used as a public forum. . . .

B. In the instant case the District Court found that "the Mall is the functional equivalent of a public business district" within the meaning of Marsh and Logan Valley. The Court of Appeals specifically affirmed this finding, and it is overwhelmingly supported by the record. . . .

In sum, the Lloyd Center is an integral part of the Portland community. From its inception, the city viewed it as a "business district" of the city and depended on it to supply much-needed employment opportunities. To insure the success of the Center, the city carefully integrated it into the pattern of streets already established and planned future development of streets around the Center. It is plain, therefore, that Lloyd Center is the equivalent of a public "business district" within the meaning of Marsh and Logan Valley. In fact, the Lloyd Center is much more analogous to the company town in Marsh than was the Logan Valley Plaza. . . .

II

. . . The First Amendment activity in both Logan Valley and the instant case was peaceful and nondisruptive; and both cases involve traditionally acceptable modes of speech. Why then should there be a different result here? The Court's answer is that the speech in this case was directed at topics of general interest — the Vietnam war and the draft — whereas the speech in Logan Valley was directed to the activities of a store in the shopping center, and that this factual difference is of constitutional dimensions. I cannot agree.

A. It is true that in Logan Valley we explicitly left open the question whether "property rights could, consistently with the First Amendment, justify a bar on picketing [or handbilling] which was not . . . directly related in its purpose to the use to which the shopping center property was being put." 391 U.S., at 320 n. 9. But, I believe that the Court errs in concluding that this issue must be faced in the instant case.

The District Court observed that Lloyd Center invites schools to hold football rallies, presidential candidates to give speeches, and service organizations to hold Veterans Day ceremonies on its premises. The court also observed that the Center permits the Salvation Army, the Volunteers of America, and the American Legion to solicit funds in the Mall. Thus, the court concluded that the Center was already open to First Amendment activities, and that respondents could not constitutionally be excluded from distributing leaflets solely because Lloyd Center was not enamored of the form or substance of their speech. The Court of Appeals affirmed, taking the position that it was not extending either Logan Valley or Marsh. In other words, the District Court found that Lloyd Center had deliberately chosen to open its private property to a broad range of expression and that having done so it could not constitutionally exclude respondents, and the Court of Appeals affirmed this finding. . . .

B. If respondents had distributed handbills complaining about one or more stores in Lloyd Center or about the Center itself, petitioner concedes that our decision in Logan Valley would insulate that conduct from proscription by the Center. I cannot see any logical reason to treat differently speech that is related to subjects other than the Center and its member stores.

We must remember that it is a balance that we are striking — a balance between the freedom to speak, a freedom that is given a preferred place in our hierarchy of values, and the freedom of a private property owner to control his property. When the competing interests are fairly weighed, the balance can only be struck in favor of speech. . . .

For many persons who do not have easy access to television, radio, the major newspapers, and the other forms of mass media, the only way they can express themselves to a broad range of citizens on issues of general public concern is to picket, or to handbill, or to utilize other free or relatively inexpensive means of communication. The only hope that these people have to be able to communicate effectively is to be permitted to speak in those areas in which most of their fellow citizens can be found. One such area is the business district of a city or town or its functional equivalent. And this is why respondents have a tremendous need to express themselves within Lloyd Center.

Petitioner's interests, on the other hand, pale in comparison. For example, petitioner urges that respondents' First Amendment activity would disturb the Center's customers. It is undisputed that some patrons will be disturbed by any First Amendment activity that goes on, regardless of its object. But, there is no evidence to indicate that speech directed to topics unrelated to the shopping center would be more likely to impair the motivation of customers to buy than speech directed to the uses to which the Center is put, which petitioner concedes is constitutionally protected under Logan Valley. On the contrary, common sense would indicate that speech that is critical of a shopping center or one or more of its stores is more likely to deter consumers from purchasing goods or services than speech on any other subject. Moreover, petitioner acknowledges that respondents have a constitutional right to "leaflet" on any subject on public streets and sidewalks within Lloyd Center. It is difficult for me to understand why leafletting in the Mall would be so much more disturbing to the Center's customers.

I also find patently frivolous petitioner's argument that if handbilling in the Mall is permitted, Lloyd Center would face inordinate difficulties in removing litter from its premises. . . .

In sum, the balance plainly must be struck in favor of speech. . . .

III

. . . As stated above, I believe that . . . there is no legitimate way of following Logan Valley and not applying it to this case. But, one may suspect from reading the opinion of the Court that it is Logan Valley itself that the Court finds bothersome. The vote in Logan Valley was 6-3, and that decision is only four years old. But, I am aware that the composition of this Court has radically changed in four years. The fact remains that Logan Valley is binding unless and until it is overruled. There is no valid distinction between that case and this one, and, therefore, the results in both cases should be the same. . . .

We noted in Logan Valley that the large-scale movement of this country's population from the cities to the suburbs has been accompanied by the growth of suburban shopping centers. In response to this phenomenon, cities like Portland are providing for large-scale shopping areas within the city. It is obvious that privately owned shopping areas could prove to be greatly advantageous to cities. They are totally self-sufficient, needing no financial support from local government; and if, as here, they truly are the functional equivalent of a public business area, the city reaps the advantages of having such an area without paying for them. Some of the advantages are an increased tax base, a drawing attraction for residents, and stimulus to further growth.

It would not be surprising in the future to see cities rely more and more on private businesses to perform functions once performed by governmental agencies. The advantage of reduced expenses and an increased tax base cannot be overstated. As governments rely on private enterprise, public property decreases in favor of privately owned property. It becomes harder and harder for citizens to find means to communicate with other citizens. Only the wealthy may find effective communication possible unless we adhere to Marsh v. Alabama and continue to hold that "[t]he more an owner, for his advantage, opens up his property for use by the public in general, the more do his rights become circumscribed by the statutory and constitutional rights of those who use it," 326 U.S., at 506.

When there are no effective means of communication, free speech is a mere shibboleth. I believe that the First Amendment requires it to be a reality. Accordingly, I would affirm the decision of the Court of Appeals.

NOTE Picketing at Shopping Centers

Compare Justice Powell's opinion for the Court in Erznoznik v. City of Jacksonville, 422 U.S. 205, 211, 215 (1975), invalidating a ban on the showing of nudity at a drive-in theater: "The Jacksonville ordinance discriminates among movies solely on the basis of content." He continues: " '[A]bove all else, the First Amendment means that government has no power to restrict expression because of its message, its ideas, its subject matter, or its content.' Police Dept. of Chicago v. Mosley, 408 U.S., at 95."

In Lenrich Associates v. Heyda, 504 P.2d 112 (Ore. Sup. Ct. 1972), the owner of a shopping center in Portland, Oregon, brought suit against members of the International Society of Krishna Consciousness to enjoin them from chanting, selling their magazines, and engaging in related activities on plaintiff's property. Attempting to distinguish Lloyd Corp. v. Tanner, defendants argued that they were afforded greater freedom of religion and expression under the Oregon Constitution than under the First and Fourteenth Amendments. A plurality of the Oregon Supreme Court held that, whether or not defendants' interpretation of this provision was correct, Lloyd Corp. v. Tanner would nonetheless compel decision in favor of the shopping center owner:

"The issue raised by plaintiff is whether its rights under the Constitution of the United States as the owner of private property are outweighed by defendants' First Amendment rights of free speech. If that is the question decided by Tanner we are bound by that decision and must apply it in this case. . . . Throughout Mr. Justice Powell's opinion are recurring statements making it clear that the court was engaged in weighing the First Amendment rights of the respondents against the Fifth and Fourteenth Amendment rights of private property owners. . . .

"The issue in this case, as in Tanner, is the extent to which plaintiff's rights as a property owner can be infringed in favor of the rights of the public to free speech and freedom of expression. In the absence of any significant factual differences the decision in Tanner is controlling. . . ."

Lenrich Associates is discussed in 86 Harv. L. Rev. 1592 (1973).

In a case involving the labor picketing of a store in a shopping center, Hudgens v. NLRB, 424 U.S. 507 (1976), the Court overruled Logan Valley, saying "the reasoning of the Court's opinion in Lloyd cannot be squared with the reasoning of the Court's opinion in Logan Valley."

Shelley v. Kraemer 334 U.S. 1, 68 S. Ct. 836, 92 L. Ed. 1161 (1948)

MR. CHIEF JUSTICE VINSON delivered the opinion of the Court. . . .

The first of these cases comes to this Court on certiorari to the Supreme Court of Missouri. On February 16, 1911, thirty out of a total of thirty-nine owners of property fronting both sides of Labadie Avenue between Taylor Avenue and Cora Avenue in the city of St. Louis, signed an agreement, which was subsequently recorded, providing in part:

". . . the said property is hereby restricted to the use and occupancy for the term of Fifty (50) years from this date, so that it shall be a condition all the time and whether recited and referred to as [sic] not in subsequent conveyances and shall attach to the land, as a condition precedent to the sale of the same, that hereafter no part of said property or any portion thereof shall be, for said term of Fifty years, occupied by any person not of the Caucasian race, it being intended hereby to restrict the use of said property for said period of time against the occupancy as owners or tenants of any portion of said property for resident or other purpose by people of the Negro or Mongolian Race."

The entire district described in the agreement included fifty-seven parcels of land. The thirty owners who signed the agreement held title to forty-seven parcels, including the particular parcel involved in this case. At the time the agreement was signed, five of the parcels in the district were owned by Negroes. One of those had been occupied by Negro families since 1882, nearly thirty years before the restrictive agreement was executed. The trial court found that owners of seven out of nine homes on the south side of Labadie Avenue, within the restricted district and "in the immediate vicinity" of the premises in question, had failed to sign the restrictive agreement in 1911. At the time this action was brought, four of the premises were occupied by Negroes, and had been so occupied for periods ranging from twenty-three to sixty-three years. A fifth parcel had been occupied by Negroes until a year before this suit was instituted.

On August 11, 1945, pursuant to a contract of sale, petitioners Shelley, who are Negroes, for valuable consideration received from one Fitzgerald a warranty deed to the parcel in question. The trial court found that petitioners had no actual knowledge of the restrictive agreement at the time of the purchase.

On October 9, 1945, respondents, as owners of other property subject to the terms of the restrictive covenant, brought suit in the Circuit Court of the city of St. Louis praying that petitioners Shelley be restrained from taking possession of the property and that judgment be entered divesting title out of petitioners Shelley and revesting title in the immediate grantor or in such other person as the court should direct. The trial court denied the requested relief on the ground that the restrictive agreement, upon which respondents based their action, had never become final and complete because it was the intention of the parties to that agreement that it was not to become effective until signed by all property owners in the district, and signatures of all the owners had never been obtained.

The Supreme Court of Missouri sitting en banc reversed and directed the trial court to grant the relief for which respondents had prayed. That court held the agreement effective and concluded that enforcement of its provisions violated no rights guaranteed to petitioners by the Federal Constitution.[2] At the time the court rendered its decision, petitioners were occupying the property in question. [The Court's description of the substantially identical issues presented in the companion case, Sipes v. McGhee, 316 Mich. 614, is omitted.]

Petitioners have placed primary reliance on their contentions, first raised in the state courts, that judicial enforcement of the restrictive agreements in these cases has violated rights guaranteed to petitioners by the Fourteenth Amendment of the Federal Constitution and Acts of Congress passed pursuant to that Amendment. Specifically, petitioners urge that they have been denied the equal protection of the laws, deprived of property without due process of law, and have been denied privileges and immunities of citizens of the United States. We pass to a consideration of those issues.

I

Whether the equal protection clause of the Fourteenth Amendment inhibits judicial enforcement by state courts of restrictive covenants based on race or color is a question which this Court has not heretofore been called upon to consider. Only two cases have been decided by this Court which in any way have involved the enforcement of such agreements. The first of these was the case of Corrigan v. Buckley, 271 U.S. 323. There, suit was brought in the courts of the District of Columbia to enjoin a threatened violation of certain restrictive covenants relating to lands situated in the city of Washington. Relief was granted, and the case was brought here on appeal. It is apparent that that case, which had originated in the federal courts and involved the enforcement of covenants on land located in the District of Columbia, could present no issues under the Fourteenth Amendment; for that Amendment by its terms applies only to the States. Nor was the question of the validity of court enforcement of the restrictive covenants under the Fifth Amendment properly before the Court, as the opinion of this Court specifically recognizes. The only constitutional issue which the appellants had raised in the lower courts, and hence the only constitutional issue before this Court on appeal, was the validity of the covenant agreements as such. This Court concluded that since the inhibitions of the constitutional provisions invoked, apply only to governmental action, as contrasted to action of private individuals, there was no showing that the covenants, which were simply agreements between private property owners, were invalid. Accordingly, the appeal was dismissed for want of a substantial question. . . .

The second of the cases involving racial restrictive covenants was Hansberry v. Lee, 311 U.S. 32. In that case, petitioners, white property owners, were enjoined by the state courts from violating the terms of a restrictive agreement. The state Supreme Court had held petitioners bound by an earlier judicial determination, in litigation in which petitioners were not parties, upholding the validity of the restrictive agreement, although, in fact, the agreement had not been signed by the number of owners necessary to make it effective under state law. This Court reversed the judgment of the state Supreme Court

---

[2] Kraemer v. Shelley, 355 Mo. 814, 198 S.W.2d 679 (1946).

upon the ground that petitioners had been denied due process of law in being held estopped to challenge the validity of the agreement on the theory, accepted by the state court, that the earlier litigation, in which petitioners did not participate, was in the nature of a class suit. In arriving at its result, this Court did not reach the issues presented by the cases now under consideration.

It is well, at the outset, to scrutinize the terms of the restrictive agreements involved in these cases. In the Missouri case, the covenant declares that no part of the affected property shall be "occupied by any person not of the Caucasian race, it being intended hereby to restrict the use of said property . . . against the occupancy as owners or tenants of any portion of said property for resident or other purpose by people of the Negro or Mongolian Race." Not only does the restriction seek to proscribe use and occupancy of the affected properties by members of the excluded class, but as construed by the Missouri courts, the agreement requires that title of any person who uses his property in violation of the restriction shall be divested. The restriction of the covenant in the Michigan case seeks to bar occupancy by persons of the excluded class. It provides that "This property shall not be used or occupied by any person or persons except those of the Caucasian race." . . .

It cannot be doubted that among the civil rights intended to be protected from discriminatory state action by the Fourteenth Amendment are the right to acquire, enjoy, own and dispose of property. . . . Thus, §1978 of the Revised Statutes, 8 U.S.C. §42, derived from §1 of the Civil Rights Act of 1866 which was enacted by Congress while the Fourteenth Amendment was also under consideration, provides:

"All citizens of the United States shall have the same right, in every State and Territory, as is enjoyed by white citizens thereof to inherit, purchase, lease, sell, hold, and convey real and personal property." This Court has given specific recognition to the same principle. Buchanan v. Warley, 245 U.S. 60.

It is likewise clear that restrictions on the right of occupancy of the sort sought to be created by the private agreements in these cases could not be squared with the requirements of the Fourteenth Amendment if imposed by state statute or local ordinance. We do not understand respondents to urge the contrary. In the case of Buchanan v. Warley, supra, a unanimous Court declared unconstitutional the provisions of a city ordinance which denied to colored persons the right to occupy houses in blocks in which the greater number of houses were occupied by white persons, and imposed similar restrictions on white persons with respect to blocks in which the greater number of houses were occupied by colored persons. During the course of the opinion in that case, this Court stated: "The Fourteenth Amendment and these statutes enacted in furtherance of its purpose operate to qualify and entitle a colored man to acquire property without state legislation discriminating against him solely because of color." . . .[10]

But the present cases, . . . do not involve action by state legislatures or city councils. Here the particular patterns of discrimination and the areas in which the restrictions are to operate, are determined, in the first instance, by the terms of agreements among private individuals. Participation of the State consists in the enforcement of the restrictions so defined. The crucial issue with which we are here confronted is whether this distinction removes these cases from the operation of the prohibitory provisions of the Fourteenth Amendment.

Since the decision of this Court in the Civil Rights Cases, 109 U.S. 3, the principle has become firmly embedded in our constitutional law that the action inhibited by the first section of the Fourteenth Amendment is only such action as may fairly be said to be that of the States. That Amendment erects no shield against merely private conduct, however discriminatory or wrongful.

We conclude, therefore, that the restrictive agreements standing alone cannot be regarded as violative of any rights guaranteed to petitioners by the Fourteenth Amend-

---

[10] Buchanan v. Warley, 245 U.S. 60, 79.

ment. So long as the purposes of those agreements are effectuated by voluntary adherence to their terms, it would appear clear that there has been no action by the State and the provisions of the Amendment have not been violated. Cf. Corrigan v. Buckley, supra.

But here there was more. These are cases in which the purposes of the agreements were secured only by judicial enforcement by state courts of the restrictive terms of the agreements. The respondents urge that judicial enforcement of private agreement does not amount to state action; or, in any event, the participation of the States is so attenuated in character as not to amount to state action within the meaning of the Fourteenth Amendment. Finally, it is suggested, even if the States in these cases may be deemed to have acted in the constitutional sense, their action did not deprive petitioners of rights guaranteed by the Fourteenth Amendment. We move to a consideration of these matters.

II

That the action of state courts and of judicial officers in their official capacities is to be regarded as action of the State within the meaning of the Fourteenth Amendment, is a proposition which has long been established by decisions of this Court. That principle was given expression in the earliest cases involving the construction of the terms of the Fourteenth Amendment. Thus, in Virginia v. Rives, 100 U.S. 313, 318, this Court stated: "It is doubtless true that a State may act through different agencies, — either by its legislative, its executive, or its judicial authorities; and the prohibitions of the amendment extend to all action of the State denying equal protection of the laws, whether it be action by one of these agencies or by another." . . .

Similar expressions, giving specific recognition to the fact that judicial action is to be regarded as action of the State for the purposes of the Fourteenth Amendment, are to be found in numerous cases which have been more recently decided. . . . In Brinkerhoff-Faris Trust & Sav. Co. v. Hill, 281 U.S. 673, 680, the Court, through Mr. Justice Brandeis, stated: "The federal guaranty of due process extends to state action through its judicial as well as through its legislative, executive or administrative branch of government." . . .

In numerous cases, this Court has reversed criminal convictions in state courts for failure of those courts to provide the essential ingredients of a fair hearing. Thus it has been held that convictions obtained in state courts under the domination of a mob are void. Moore v. Dempsey, 261 U.S. 86. And see Frank v. Mangum, 237 U.S. 309. Convictions obtained by coerced confessions, by the use of perjured testimony known by the prosecution to be such, or without the effective assistance of counsel, have also been held to be exertions of state authority in conflict with the fundamental rights protected by the Fourteenth Amendment.

But the examples of state judicial action which have been held by this Court to violate the Amendment's commands are not restricted to situations in which the judicial proceedings were found in some manner to be procedurally unfair. It has been recognized that the action of state courts in enforcing a substantive common-law rule formulated by those courts, may result in the denial of rights guaranteed by the Fourteenth Amendment, even though the judicial proceedings in such cases may have been in complete accord with the most rigorous conceptions of procedural due process. Thus, in American Federation of Labor v. Swing, 312 U.S. 321, enforcement by state courts of the common-law policy of the State, which resulted in the restraining of peaceful picketing, was held to be state action of the sort prohibited by the Amendment's guaranties of freedom of discussion. In Cantwell v. Connecticut, 310 U.S. 296, a conviction in a state court of the common-law crime of breach of the peace was, under the circumstances of the case, found to be a violation of the Amendment's commands relating to freedom of religion. In Bridges v. California, 314 U.S. 252, enforcement of the state's common-law rule relating to contempts by publication was held to be state action inconsistent with the prohibitions of the Fourteenth Amendment. . . .

We have no doubt that there has been state action in these cases in the full and complete sense of the phrase. The undisputed facts disclose that petitioners were willing purchasers of properties upon which they desired to establish homes. The owners of the properties were willing sellers; and contracts of sale were accordingly consummated. It is clear that but for the active intervention of the state courts, supported by the full panoply of state power, petitioners would have been free to occupy the properties in question without restraint.

These are not cases, as has been suggested, in which the States have merely abstained from action, leaving private individuals free to impose such discriminations as they see fit. Rather, these are cases in which the States have made available to such individuals the full coercive power of government to deny to petitioners, on the grounds of race or color, the enjoyment of property rights in premises which petitioners are willing and financially able to acquire and which the grantors are willing to sell. The difference between judicial enforcement and non-enforcement of the restrictive covenants is the difference to petitioners between being denied rights of property available to other members of the community and being accorded full enjoyment of those rights on an equal footing.

The enforcement of the restrictive agreements by the state courts in these cases was directed pursuant to the common-law policy of the States as formulated by those courts in earlier decisions. . . . We have noted that previous decisions of this Court have established the proposition that judicial action is not immunized from the operation of the Fourteenth Amendment simply because it is taken pursuant to the State's common-law policy.[24] Nor is the Amendment ineffective simply because the particular pattern of discrimination, which the State has enforced, was defined initially by the terms of a private agreement. State action, as that phrase is understood for the purposes of the Fourteenth Amendment, refers to exertions of state power in all forms. And when the effect of that action is to deny rights subject to the protection of the Fourteenth Amendment, it is the obligation of this Court to enforce the constitutional commands.

We hold that in granting judicial enforcement of the restrictive agreements in these cases, the States have denied petitioners the equal protection of the laws and that, therefore, the action of the state courts cannot stand. We have noted that freedom from discrimination by the States in the enjoyment of property rights was among the basic objectives sought to be effectuated by the framers of the Fourteenth Amendment. That such discrimination has occurred in these cases is clear. . . .

Respondents urge, however, that since the state courts stand ready to enforce restrictive covenants excluding white persons from the ownership or occupancy of property covered by such agreements, enforcement of covenants excluding colored persons may not be deemed a denial of equal protection of the laws to the colored persons who are thereby affected.[28] This contention does not bear scrutiny. The parties have directed our attention to no case in which a court, state or federal, has been called upon to enforce a covenant excluding members of the white majority from ownership or occupancy of real property on grounds of race or color. But there are more fundamental considerations. The rights created by the first section of the Fourteenth Amendment are, by its terms, guaranteed to the individual. The rights established are personal rights. It is, therefore, no answer to these petitioners to say that the courts may also be induced to deny white persons rights of ownership and occupancy on grounds of race or color. Equal protection of the laws is not achieved through indiscriminate imposition of inequalities. . . .

---

[24] Bridges v. California, 314 U.S. 252; American Federation of Labor v. Swing, 312 U.S. 321.

[28] It should be observed that the restrictions relating to residential occupancy contained in ordinances involved in the Buchanan Case, 245 U.S. 60, . . . and declared by this Court to be inconsistent with the requirements of the Fourteenth Amendment, applied equally to white persons and Negroes.

For the reasons stated, the judgment of the Supreme Court of Missouri and the judgment of the Supreme Court of Michigan must be reversed.

Reversed.

MR. JUSTICE REED, MR. JUSTICE JACKSON, and MR. JUSTICE RUTLEDGE took no part in the consideration or decision of these cases.

NOTE Scope of Shelley v. Kraemer

Does a state court's award of damages for breach of a racial restrictive covenant constitute a violation of the Fourteenth Amendment? If so, may the party who broke the contract protect himself from liability by setting up the rights of those against whom the covenant was directed? See Barrows v. Jackson, 346 U.S. 249 (1953).

In Rice v. Sioux City Memorial Park Cemetery, Inc., 348 U.S. 880 (1954), 349 id. 70 (1955), the widow of a Winnebago Indian brought suit in an Iowa state court for money damages to compensate her for mental suffering resulting from the defendant's alleged breach of contract to bury her husband's remains in a specified lot. The cemetery corporation relied on a Caucasion-race-only clause in the contract. The trial court dismissed the case; the Supreme Court of Iowa affirmed (245 Iowa 147, 60 N.W.2d 110). On certiorari the United States Supreme Court divided equally; the judgment of dismissal was therefore affirmed. On petition for rehearing before the full Court, attention was focused on an Iowa statute, enacted after the commencement of the litigation, which declared void such a clause as that in Mrs. Rice's contract. The United States Supreme Court vacated its previous order of affirmance, and dismissed the writ of certiorari as "improvidently granted."

Would the Fourteenth Amendment be violated if a state court should hold one spouse in contempt of court for his or her failure to carry out an antenuptial agreement with respect to the religious upbringing of the children of the marriage when that agreement was embodied in a judicial decree of separation? See Lynch v. Uhlenhopp, 248 Iowa 68, 76 N.W.2d 491; Hackett v. Hackett, 150 N.E.2d 431 (Ohio 1958), noted in 72 Harv. L. Rev. 372 (1958).

At the 1963 and 1964 Terms, the Supreme Court reviewed a series of state convictions of civil rights demonstrators who had unsuccessfully sought nondiscriminatory service at restaurants, lunch counters, and other places of public accommodation, and when such services were denied remained seated until removed by the police at the request of the proprietor. At neither Term was a conviction for the sit-in sustained, for in every case the Court was able to find a sufficient degree of official support of the discriminatory practice to bring it within the reach of the Fourteenth Amendment. The Court never, however, answered the much-discussed question whether the sanctioning of "private" choice by the processes of the criminal law was a violation of the Constitution. The cases are helpfully discussed in Lewis, The Sit-In Cases: Great Expectations, 1963 Sup. Ct. Rev. 101; Paulsen, The Sit-In Cases of 1964: "But Answer Came There None," 1964 id. 137. Between the two Terms of Court the Congress enacted the Civil Rights Act of 1964.

See also Gregory v. City of Chicago, 394 U.S. 111 (1969). Cf. Thompson v. City of Louisville, 362 U.S. 199 (1960).

BLACK v. CUTTER LABORATORIES, 351 U.S. 292, 76 S. Ct. 824, 100 L. Ed. 1188 (1956). Clark, J.: "In 1949 Mrs. Doris Walker was discharged from her job at Cutter Laboratories, a manufacturer of pharmaceutical and biological products, on the claimed grounds that she was an active member of the Communist Party. . . . Petitioner [union] sought reinstatement of Mrs. Walker before an Arbitration Board pursuant to a valid collective-bargaining agreement which authorized discharge for 'just cause' only. . . . [T]he Supreme Court of California construed the term 'just cause' to embrace membership in the Communist Party [and reversed an order for reinstatement issued by the Arbitration Board and confirmed by the lower courts]. Petitioners contend that the decision . . . below violate[s] principles embraced in the Equal Protection and Due Process Clauses of the Fourteenth Amendment. We granted certiorari."

What decision? Why?

Jones v. Alfred H. Mayer Co. 392 U.S. 409, 88 S. Ct. 2186, 20 L. Ed. 2d 1189 (1968)

MR. JUSTICE STEWART delivered the opinion of the Court. In this case we are called upon to determine the scope and the constitutionality of an Act of Congress, 42 U.S.C. § 1982, which provides that:

"All citizens of the United States shall have the same right, in every State and Territory, as is enjoyed by white citizens thereof to inherit, purchase, lease, sell, hold, and convey real and personal property."

On September 2, 1965, the petitioners filed a complaint in the District Court for the Eastern District of Missouri, alleging that the respondents had refused to sell them a home in the Paddock Woods community of St. Louis County for the sole reason that petitioner Joseph Lee Jones is a Negro. Relying in part upon § 1982, the petitioners sought injunctive and other relief. The District Court sustained the respondents' motion to dismiss the complaint, and the Court of Appeals for the Eighth Circuit affirmed, concluding that § 1982 applies only to state action and does not reach private refusals to sell. We granted certiorari to consider the questions thus presented. For the reasons that follow, we reverse the judgment of the Court of Appeals. We hold that § 1982 bars *all* racial discrimination, private as well as public, in the sale or rental of property, and that the statute, thus construed, is a valid exercise of the power of Congress to enforce the Thirteenth Amendment.[1]

At the outset, it is important to make clear precisely what this case does not involve. Whatever else it may be, 42 U.S.C. § 1982 is not a comprehensive open housing law. In sharp contrast to the Fair Housing Title (Title VIII) of the Civil Rights Act of 1968, Pub. L. 90-284, 82 Stat. 81, the statute in this case deals only with racial discrimination and does not address itself to discrimination on grounds of religion or national origin. It does not deal specifically with discrimination in the provision of services or facilities in connection with the sale or rental of a dwelling. It does not prohibit advertising or other representations that indicate discriminatory preferences. It does not refer explicitly to discrimination in financing arrangements or in the provision of brokerage services. It does not empower a federal administrative agency to assist aggrieved parties. It makes no provision for intervention by the Attorney General. And, although it can be enforced by injunction, it contains no provision expressly authorizing a federal court to order the payment of damages.

Thus, although § 1982 contains none of the exemptions that Congress included in the Civil Rights Act of 1968, it would be a serious mistake to suppose that § 1982 in any way diminishes the significance of the law recently enacted by Congress. Indeed, the Senate Subcommittee on Housing and Urban Affairs was informed in hearings held after the Court of Appeals had rendered its decision in this case that § 1982 might well be a "presently valid federal statutory ban against discrimination by private persons in the sale or lease of real property." The Subcommittee was told, however, that even if this Court should so construe § 1982, the existence of that statute would not "eliminate the need for

---

[1] Because we have concluded that the discrimination alleged in the petitioners' complaint violated a federal statute that Congress had the power to enact under the Thirteenth Amendment, we find it unnecessary to decide whether that discrimination also violated the Equal Protection Clause of the Fourteenth Amendment.

Section E. Secured Rights and State Action

congressional action" to spell out "responsibility on the part of the federal government to enforce the rights it protects." The point was made that, in light of the many difficulties confronted by private litigants seeking to enforce such rights on their own, "legislation is needed to establish federal machinery for enforcement of the rights guaranteed under Section 1982 of Title 42 even if the plaintiffs in Jones v. Alfred H. Mayer Company should prevail in the United States Supreme Court." . . .

This Court last had occasion to consider the scope of 42 U.S.C. §1982 in 1948, in Hurd v. Hodge, 334 U.S. 24. That case arose when property owners in the District of Columbia sought to enforce racially restrictive covenants against the Negro purchasers of several homes on their block. . . .

The basic source of the injury in Hurd was, of course, the action of private individuals — white citizens who had agreed to exclude Negroes from a residential area. But an arm of the Government — in that case, a federal court — had assisted in the enforcement of that agreement. Thus Hurd v. Hodge, supra, did not present the question whether *purely* private discrimination, unaided by any action on the part of government, would violate §1982 if its effect were to deny a citizen the right to rent or buy property solely because of his race or color. . . .

It is true that a dictum in Hurd said that §1982 was directed only toward "governmental action," 334 U.S., at 31, but neither Hurd nor any other case before or since has presented that precise issue for adjudication in this Court. Today we face that issue for the first time.

We begin with the language of the statute itself. In plain and unambiguous terms, §1982 grants to all citizens, without regard to race or color, "the same right" to purchase and lease property "as is enjoyed by white citizens." As the Court of Appeals in this case evidently recognized, that right can be impaired as effectively by "those who place property on the market" as by the State itself. . . . So long as a Negro citizen who wants to buy or rent a home can be turned away simply because he is not white, he cannot be said to enjoy "the *same* right . . . as is enjoyed by white citizens . . . to . . . purchase [and] lease . . . real and personal property." . . .

On its face, therefore, §1982 appears to prohibit *all* discrimination, against Negroes in the sale or rental of property — discrimination by private owners as well as discrimination by public authorities. Indeed, even the respondents seem to concede that, if §1982 "means what it says" — to use the words of the respondents' brief — then it must encompass every racially motivated refusal to sell or rent and cannot be confined to officially sanctioned segregation in housing. Stressing what they consider to be the revolutionary implications of so literal a reading of §1982, the respondents argue that Congress cannot possibly have intended any such result. Our examination of the relevant history, however, persuades us that Congress meant exactly what it said.

In its original form, 42 U.S.C. §1982 was part of §1 of the Civil Rights Act of 1866. That section was cast in sweeping terms:

"Be it enacted by the Senate and House of Representatives of the United States of America in Congress assembled, That all persons born in the United States and not subject to any foreign power, . . . are hereby declared to be citizens of the United States; and such citizens, of every race and color, without regard to any previous conditions of slavery or involuntary servitude, . . . shall have the same right, in every State and Territory in the United States, to make and enforce contracts, to sue, be parties, and give evidence, to inherit, purchase, lease, sell, hold, and convey real and personal property, and to full and equal benefit of all laws and proceedings for the security of person and property, as is enjoyed by white citizens, and shall be subject to like punishment, pains, and penalties, and to none other, any law, statute, ordinance, regulation, or custom, to the contrary notwithstanding."

The crucial language for our purposes was that which guaranteed all citizens "the same right, in every State and Territory in the United States, . . . to inherit, purchase, lease, sell, hold, and convey real and personal property . . . as is enjoyed by white citizens. . . ." To the Congress that passed the Civil Rights Act of 1866, it was clear that the right to do these things might be infringed not only by "State or local law" but also by "custom, or prejudice."[4] Thus, when Congress provided in §1 of the Civil Rights Act that the right to purchase and lease property was to be enjoyed equally throughout the United States by Negro and white citizens alike, it plainly meant to secure that right against interference from any source whatever, whether governmental or private.

Indeed, if §1 had been intended to grant nothing more than an immunity from *governmental* interference, then much of §2 would have made no sense at all.[5] For that section, which provided fines and prison terms for certain individuals who deprived others of rights "secured or protected" by §1, was carefully drafted to exempt private violations of §1 from the criminal sanctions it imposed.[6] There would, of course, have been no private violations to exempt if the only "right" granted by §1 had been a right to be free of discrimination by public officials. Hence the structure of the 1866 Act, as well as its language, points to the conclusion urged by the petitioners in this case — that §1 was meant to prohibit *all* racially motivated deprivations of the rights enumerated in the statute, although only those deprivations perpetrated "under color of law" were to be criminally punishable under §2.

In attempting to demonstrate the contrary, the respondents rely heavily upon the fact that the Congress which approved the 1866 statute wished to eradicate the recently enacted Black Codes — laws which had saddled Negroes with "onerous disabilities and burdens, and curtailed their rights . . . to such an extent that their freedom was of little value. . . ." Slaughter-House Cases, 16 Wall. 36, 70. The respondents suggest that the only evil Congress sought to eliminate was that of racially discriminatory laws in the former Confederate States. But the Civil Rights Act was drafted to apply throughout the country, and its language was far broader than would have been necessary to strike down discriminatory statutes.

That broad language, we are asked to believe, was a mere slip of the legislative pen. We disagree. For the same Congress that wanted to do away with the Black Codes *also* had before it an imposing body of evidence pointing to the mistreatment of Negroes by private individuals and unofficial groups, mistreatment unrelated to any hostile state legislation. . . . The congressional debates are replete with references to private injustices against Negroes — references to white employers who refused to pay their Negro workers, white

[4] Several weeks before the House began its debate on the Civil Rights Act of 1866, Congress had passed a bill (S. No. 60) to enlarge the powers of the Freedmen's Bureau (created by Act of March 3, 1865, c. 90, 13 Stat. 507) by extending military jurisdiction over certain areas in the South where, "in consequence of any State or local law, . . . *custom, or prejudice,* any of the civil rights . . . belonging to white persons (including the right . . . to inherit, purchase, lease, sell, hold, and convey real and personal property . . .) are refused or denied to negroes . . . on account of race, color, or any previous condition of slavery or involuntary servitude. . . ." See Cong. Globe, 39th Cong., 1st Sess., 129, 209. (Emphasis added.) Both Houses had passed S. No. 60 (see id., at 421, 688, 748, 775), and although the Senate had failed to override the President's veto (see id., at 915-916, 943) the bill was nonetheless significant for its recognition that the "right to purchase" was a right that could be "refused or denied" by "custom or prejudice" as well as by "State or local law." . . .

[5] Section 2 provided: "That any person who, *under color of any law, statute, ordinance, regulation, or custom,* shall subject, or cause to be subjected, any inhabitant of any State or Territory to the deprivation of any right secured or protected by this act, or to different punishment, pains, or penalties on account of such person having at any time been held in a condition of slavery or involuntary servitude, except as a punishment for crime whereof the party shall have been duly convicted, or by reason of his color or race, than is prescribed for the punishment of white persons, shall be deemed guilty of a misdemeanor, and, on conviction, shall be punished by fine not exceeding one thousand dollars, or imprisonment not exceeding one year, or both, in the discretion of the court." (Emphasis added.) For the evolution of this provision into 18 U.S.C. §242, see Screws v. United States, 325 U.S. 91, 98-99; United States v. Price, 383 U.S. 787, 804.

[6] . . . Congress might have thought it appropriate to confine criminal punishment to state officials, oath-bound to support the supreme federal law, while allowing only civil remedies — or perhaps only preventive relief — against private violators. Or Congress might have thought that States which did not authorize abridgment of the rights declared in §1 would themselves punish all who interfered with those rights without official

Section E. Secured Rights and State Action

planters who agreed among themselves not to hire freed slaves without the permission of their former masters, white citizens who assaulted Negroes or who combined to drive them out of their communities.

Indeed, one of the most comprehensive studies then before Congress stressed the prevalence of private hostility toward Negroes and the need to protect them from the resulting persecution and discrimination. The report noted the existence of laws virtually prohibiting Negroes from owning or renting property in certain towns, but described such laws as "mere isolated cases," representing "the local outcroppings of a spirit . . . found to prevail everywhere" — a spirit expressed, for example, by lawless acts of brutality directed against Negroes who traveled to areas where they were not wanted. The report concluded that, even if anti-Negro legislation were "repealed in all the States lately in rebellion," equal treatment for the Negro would not yet be secured. . . .

On January 5, 1866, Senator Trumbull introduced the bill he had in mind — the bill which later became the Civil Rights Act of 1866. He described its objectives in terms that belie any attempt to read it narrowly:

"Mr. President, I regard the bill to which the attention of the Senate is now called as the most important measure that has been under its consideration since the adoption of the constitutional amendment abolishing slavery. That amendment declared that all persons in the United States should be free. This measure is intended to give effect to that declaration and secure to all persons within the United States practical freedom. There is very little importance in the general declaration of abstract truths and principles unless they can be carried into effect, unless the persons who are to be affected by them have some means of availing themselves of their benefits."

Of course, Senator Trumbull's bill would, as he pointed out, "destroy all [the] discriminations" embodied in the Black Codes, but it would do more: It would affirmatively secure for all men, whatever their race or color, what the Senator called the "great fundamental rights": ". . . the right to acquire property, the right to go and come at pleasure, the right to enforce rights in the courts, to make contracts, and to inherit and dispose of property."

As to those basic civil rights, the Senator said, the bill would "break down *all* discrimination between black men and white men." . . . [Emphasis added throughout.]

In the House, as in the Senate, much was said about eliminating the infamous Black Codes. But, like the Senate, the House was moved by a larger objective — that of giving real content to the freedom guaranteed by the Thirteenth Amendment. Representative Thayer of Pennsylvania put it this way:

"[W]hen I voted for the amendment to abolish slavery . . . I did not suppose that I was offering . . . a mere paper guarantee. And when I voted for the second section of the amendment, I felt . . . certain that I had . . . given to Congress ability to protect . . . the rights which the first section gave. . . ."

"The bill which now engages the attention of the House has for its object to carry out and guaranty the reality of that great measure. It is to give to it practical effect and force. It is to prevent that great measure from remaining a dead letter upon the constitutional page of this country. . . . The events of the last four years . . . have changed [a] large class of people . . . from a condition of slavery to that of freedom. *The practical question now to be decided is whether they shall be in fact freemen. It is whether they shall have the benefit of this great charter of liberty* given to them by the American people." . . .

President Andrew Johnson vetoed the Act on March 27, and in the brief congressional debate that followed, his supporters characterized its reach in all-embracing terms. One

---

authority. See, e.g., Cong. Globe, 39th Cong., 1st Sess., 1758, 1785. Cf. Civil Rights Cases, 109 U.S. 3, 19, 24-25.

Whatever the reason, it was repeatedly stressed that the only violations "reached *and punished*" by the bill, see Cong. Globe, 39th Cong., 1st Sess., at 1294 (emphasis added), would be those "done under color of State authority."

stressed the fact that §1 would confer "the right . . . to purchase . . . real estate . . . without any qualification and without any restriction whatever. . . ." Another predicted, as a corollary, that the Act would preclude preferential treatment for white persons in the rental of hotel rooms and in the sale of church pews. Those observations elicited no reply. On April 6 the Senate, and on April 9 the House, overrode the President's veto by the requisite majorities, and the Civil Rights Act of 1866 became law.

In light of the concerns that led Congress to adopt it and the contents of the debates that preceded its passage, it is clear that the Act was designed to do just what its terms suggest: to prohibit all racial discrimination, whether or not under color of law, with respect to the rights enumerated therein — including the right to purchase or lease property.

Nor was the scope of the 1866 Act altered when it was re-enacted in 1870, some two years after the ratification of the Fourteenth Amendment. It is quite true that some members of Congress supported the Fourteenth Amendment "in order to eliminate doubt as to the constitutional validity of the Civil Rights Act as applied to the States." Hurd v. Hodge, 334 U.S. 24, 32-33. But it certainly does not follow that the adoption of the Fourteenth Amendment or the subsequent readoption of the Civil Rights Act were meant somewhat to limit its application to state action. The legislative history furnishes not the slightest factual basis for any such speculation, and the conditions prevailing in 1870 make it highly implausible. For by that time most, if not all, of the former Confederate States, then under the control of "reconstructed" legislatures, had formally repudiated racial discrimination, and the focus of congressional concern had clearly shifted from hostile statutes to the activities of groups like the Ku Klux Klan, operating wholly outside the law. . . .

The remaining question is whether Congress has power under the Constitution to do what §1982 purports to do: to prohibit all racial discrimination, private and public, in the sale and rental of property. Our starting point is the Thirteenth Amendment, for it was pursuant to that constitutional provision that Congress originally enacted what is now §1982. . . .

As its text reveals, the Thirteenth Amendment "is not a mere prohibition of State laws establishing or upholding slavery, but an absolute declaration that slavery or involuntary servitude shall not exist in any part of the United States." Civil Rights Cases, 109 U.S. 3, 20. It has never been doubted, therefore, "that the power vested in Congress to enforce the article by appropriate legislation," ibid., includes the power to enact laws "direct and primary, operating upon the acts of individuals, whether sanctioned by State legislation or not." Id., at 23.[7]

Thus, the fact that §1982 operates upon the unofficial acts of private individuals, whether or not sanctioned by state law, presents no constitutional problem. If Congress has power under the Thirteenth Amendment to eradicate conditions that prevent Negroes from buying and renting property because of their race or color, then no federal statute calculated to achieve that objective can be thought to exceed the constitutional power of Congress simply because it reaches beyond state action to regulate the conduct of private individuals. The constitutional question in this case, therefore, comes to this: Does the authority of Congress to enforce the Thirteenth Amendment "by appropriate legislation" include the power to eliminate all racial barriers to the acquisition of real and personal property? We think the answer to that question is plainly yes. . . .

. . . Surely Congress has the power under the Thirteenth Amendment rationally to determine what are the badges and the incidents of slavery, and the authority to translate that determination into effective legislation. Nor can we say that the determination Congress has made is an irrational one. For this Court recognized long ago that, whatever

---

[7] So it was, for example, that this Court unanimously upheld the power of Congress under the Thirteenth Amendment to make it a crime for one individual to compel another to work in order to discharge a debt. Clyatt v. United States, 197 U.S. 207.

Section E. Secured Rights and State Action

else they may have encompassed, the badges and incidents of slavery — its "burdens and disabilities" — included restraints upon "those fundamental rights which are the essence of civil freedom, namely, the same right . . . to inherit, purchase, lease, sell and convey property, as is enjoyed by white citizens." Civil Rights Cases, 109 U.S. 3, 22. Just as the Black Codes, enacted after the Civil War to restrict the free exercise of those rights, were substitutes for the slave system, so the exclusion of Negroes from white communities became a substitute for the Black Codes. And when racial discrimination herds men into ghettos and makes their ability to buy property turn on the color of their skin, then it too is a relic of slavery. . . .

. . . The judgment is
Reversed.

[A concurring opinion of MR. JUSTICE DOUGLAS is omitted.]

MR. JUSTICE HARLAN, whom MR. JUSTICE WHITE joins, dissenting. The decision in this case appears to me to be most ill-considered and ill-advised. . . .

I shall deal first with the Court's construction of §1982, which lies at the heart of its opinion. That construction is that the statute applies to purely private as well as to state-authorized discrimination.

The Court's opinion focuses upon the statute's legislative history, but it is worthy of note that the precedents in this Court are distinctly opposed to the Court's view of the statute.

[The opinion examines the Civil Rights Cases, Buckley v. Corrigan, and Hurd v. Hodge.] . . .

Like the Court, I begin analysis of §1982 by examining its language. . . . For me, there is an inherent ambiguity in the term "right," as used in §1982. The "right" referred to may either be a right to equal status under the law, in which case the statute operates only against state-sanctioned discrimination, or it may be an "absolute" right enforceable against private individuals. To me, the words of the statute, taken alone, suggest the former interpretation, not the latter. . . .

. . . It seems to me that . . . §1 of the Act (as well as §2, which is explicitly so limited) was intended to apply only to action taken pursuant to state or community authority, in the form of a "law, statute, ordinance, regulation, or custom." And with deference I suggest that the language of §2, taken alone, no more implies that §2 "was carefully drafted to exempt private violations of §1 from the criminal sanctions it imposed," see ante, at 425, than it does that §2 was carefully drafted to enforce all of the rights secured by §1.

The Court rests its opinion chiefly upon the legislative history of the Civil Rights Act of 1866. . . .

On January 5, Senator Trumbull introduced both the Freedmen's bill and the civil rights bill. The Freedmen's bill would have strengthened greatly the existing system by which agents of the Freedmen's Bureau exercised protective supervision over freedmen wherever they were present in large numbers. Inter alia, the Freedmen's bill would have permitted the President, acting through the Bureau, to extend "military protection and jurisdiction" over all cases in which persons in the former rebel States were "in consequence of any State or local law, ordinance, police or other regulation, custom, or prejudice, [denied or refused] any of the civil rights or immunities belonging to white persons, including the right . . . to inherit, purchase, lease, sell, hold and convey real and personal property, . . . on account of race. . . ." The next section of the Freedmen's bill provided that the agents of the Freedmen's Bureau might try and convict of a misdemeanor any person who deprived another of such rights on account of race and "under color of any State or local law, ordinance, police, or other regulation or custom. . . ." Thus, the Freedmen's bill, which was generally limited in its application to the Southern States and which was correspondingly more sweeping in its protection of the freedmen than the civil rights bill, defined both the rights secured and the denials of those rights which were criminally punishable in terms of acts done under the aegis of a State or locality. The only significant distinction was that denials which occurred "in consequence of a State or local . . . prejudice" would have entitled the victim to military protection but would not have been criminal. In the corresponding section of the companion and generally parallel civil rights bill, which was to be effective throughout the Nation, the reference to "prejudice" was omitted from the rights-defining section. This would seem to imply that the more widely applicable civil rights bill was meant to provide protection only against those discriminations which were legitimated by a state or community sanction sufficiently powerful to deserve the name "custom." . . .

The civil rights bill was debated intermittently in the Senate from January 12, 1866, until its eventual passage over the President's veto on April 6. In the course of the debates, Senator Trumbull, who was by far the leading spokesman for the bill, made a number of statements which can be taken only to mean that the bill was aimed at "state action" alone. For example, on January 29, 1866, Senator Trumbull began by citing a number of recently enacted Southern laws depriving men of rights named in the bill. He stated that "[t]he purpose of the bill under consideration is to destroy *all these discriminations*, and carry into effect the constitutional amendment." Later the same day, Senator Trumbull quoted § 2 of the bill in full, and said:

"This is the valuable section of the bill so far as protecting the rights of freedmen is concerned. . . . When it comes to be understood in all parts of the United States that *any person* who shall deprive another of *any right* . . . in consequence of his color or race will expose himself to fine and imprisonment, I think such acts will soon cease."

These words contain no hint that the "rights" protected by § 2 were intended to be any less broad than those secured by § 1. Of course, § 2 plainly extended only to "state action." That Senator Trumbull viewed §§ 1 and 2 as co-extensive appears even more clearly from his answer the following day when asked by Senator Cowan whether there was "not a provision [in the bill] by which State officers are to be punished?" Senator Trumbull replied: "Not State officers especially, but *everybody who violates the law. It is the intention to punish everybody who violates the law.*" [8]

On January 29, Senator Trumbull also uttered the first of several remarkably similar and wholly unambiguous statements which indicated that the bill was aimed only at "state action." He said:

"[This bill] may be assailed as drawing to the Federal Government powers that properly belong to 'States'; but I apprehend, rightly considered, it is not obnoxious to that objection. *It will have no operation in any State where the laws are equal, where all persons have the same civil rights without regard to color or race. It will have no operation in the State of Kentucky when her slave code and all her laws discriminating between persons on account of race or color shall be abolished.*" . . .

. . . On April 4, after the President's veto of the bill, Senator Trumbull . . . said:

"This bill in no manner interferes with the municipal regulations of any State which protects all alike in their rights of person and property. *It could have no operation in Massachusetts, New York, Illinois, or most of the States of the Union.*"

The remarks just quoted constitute the plainest possible statement that the civil rights

---

[8] Id., at 500. (Emphasis added.) The Civil Rights Cases, 109 U.S. 3, suggest how Senator Trumbull might have expected § 2 to affect persons other than "officers" in spite of its "under color" language, for it was there said in dictum that:

"The Civil Rights Bill . . . is analogous . . . to [a law] under the original Constitution, declaring that the validity of contracts should not be impaired, and that if *any person* bound by a contract should refuse to comply with it, *under color or pretence that it had been rendered void or invalid by a State law*, he should be liable to an action upon it in the courts of the United States, *with the addition of a penalty for setting up such an unjust and unconstitutional defence.*" 109 U.S., at 17. (Emphasis added.)

Section E. Secured Rights and State Action 821

bill was intended to apply only to state-sanctioned conduct and not to purely private actions. . . .

The Court puts forward in support of its construction an impressive number of quotations from and citations to the Senate debates. However, upon more circumspect analysis than the Court has chosen to give, virtually all of these appear to be either irrelevant or equally consistent with a "state action" interpretation. . . .

. . . Once it is recognized that the word "right" as used in the bill is ambiguous, then Senator Cowan's statement, ante, at 435, that the bill would confer "the right . . . to purchase . . . real estate . . . without any qualification" must inevitably share that ambiguity. The remarks of Senator Davis, ante, at 435, with respect to rental of hotel rooms and sale of church pews are, when viewed in context, even less helpful to the Court's thesis. For these comments were made immediately following Senator Davis' plaintive acknowledgment that "this measure proscribes all discriminations . . . that may be made . . . by any 'ordinance, regulation, or custom,' as well as by 'law or statute.' " Senator Davis then observed that ordinances, regulations, and customs presently conferred upon white persons the most comfortable accommodations in ships and steamboats, hotels, churches and railroad cars, and stated that "[t]he bill . . . declares all persons who enforce those distinctions to be criminals against the United States. . . ." Thus, Senator Davis not only tied these obnoxious effects of the bill to its "customs" provision but alleged that they were brought about by §2 as well as §1. There is little wonder that his remarks "elicited no reply," see ante, at 435, from the bill's supporters.

The House debates are even fuller of statements indicating that the civil right[s] bill was intended to reach only state-endorsed discrimination. Representative Wilson was the bill's sponsor in the House. On the very first day of House debate, March 1, Representative Wilson said in explaining the bill:

"[I]f the States, seeing that we have citizens of different races and colors, would but shut their eyes to these differences and legislate, so far at least as regards civil rights and immunities, as though all citizens were of one race or color, our troubles as a nation would be well-nigh over. . . . It will be observed that *the entire structure of this bill rests on the discrimination relative to civil rights and immunities made by the States* on 'account of race, color, or previous condition of slavery.' "

[A further, lengthy analysis of the debates is omitted.]

The foregoing analysis of the language, structure, and legislative history of the 1866 Civil Rights Act shows, I believe, that the Court's thesis that the Act was meant to extend to purely private action is open to the most serious doubt, if indeed it does not render that thesis wholly untenable. Another, albeit less tangible, consideration points in the same direction. Many of the legislators who took part in the congressional debates inevitably must have shared the individualistic ethic of their time, which emphasized personal freedom and embodied a distaste for governmental interference which was soon to culminate in the era of laissez-faire. It seems to me that most of these men would have regarded it as a great intrusion on individual liberty for the Government to take from a man the power to refuse for personal reasons to enter into a purely private transaction involving the disposition of property, albeit those personal reasons might reflect racial bias. It should be remembered that racial prejudice was not uncommon in 1866, even outside the South. Although Massachusetts had recently enacted the Nation's first law prohibiting racial discrimination in public accommodations, Negroes could not ride within Philadelphia streetcars or attend public schools with white children in New York City. Only five States accorded equal voting rights to Negroes, and it appears that Negroes were allowed to serve on juries only in Massachusetts. Residential segregation was the prevailing pattern almost everywhere in the North. There was no state "fair housing" laws in 1866, and it appears that none had ever been proposed. In this historical context, I cannot conceive that a bill thought to prohibit purely private discrimination not only in the sale or rental of housing but in *all* property transactions would not have received a great deal of criticism explicitly directed to this feature. The fact that the 1866 Act received no criticism of this kind is for me strong additional evidence that it was not regarded as extending so far. . . .

In holding that the Thirteenth Amendment is sufficient constitutional authority for § 1982 as interpreted, the Court also decides a question of great importance. . . .

The only apparent way of deciding this case without reaching those issues would be to hold that the petitioners are entitled to relief on the alternative ground advanced by them: that the respondents' conduct amounted to "state action" forbidden by the Fourteenth Amendment. However, that route is not without formidable obstacles of its own, for the opinion of the Court of Appeals makes it clear that this case differs substantially from any "state action" case previously decided by this Court. See 379 F.2d, at 40-45.

[The opinion concludes that, in view of the enactment of the Civil Rights Act of 1968, the constitutional issues should not be decided, and the writ of certiorari should be dismissed.]

NOTE Implications of Jones v. Mayer

The majority's interpretation of the legislative history of § 1981 is criticized in Fairman, Reconstruction and Reunion, 1864-88, Part One 1207-1259 (1971) (VI Holmes Devise History of the Supreme Court).

On the uses and consequences of Jones's interpretation of the Thirteenth Amendment, see Note, Federal Power to Regulate Private Discrimination: The Revival of the Enforcement Clauses of the Reconstruction Era Amendments, 74 Colum. L. Rev. 449 (1974); Note, The "New" Thirteenth Amendment: A Preliminary Analysis, 82 Harv. L. Rev. 1294 (1969); Comment, Jones v. Alfred H. Mayer Co. Extended to Private Education: Gonzales v. Fairfax-Brewster School, Inc., 122 U. Pa. L. Rev. 471 (1973).

In a sequel to Jones v. Alfred H. Mayer Co., the Court held in Sullivan v. Little Hunting Park, Inc., 396 U.S. 229 (1969), that damages as well as an injunction could be obtained for violation of 42 U.S.C § 1982. Moreover, the recovery was had by a white person, who had been expelled from membership in a residential park association because he had assigned part of his interest to a Negro.

Title 28 U.S.C. § 1981 provides, in part, that all persons shall have the same right to make contracts as white persons. In Runyon v. McCrary, 427 U.S. 160 (1976), the Court held that § 1981 prohibits private, commercially operated, nonsectarian schools from denying admission to applicants because they are black. Powell, J., concurring, stressed that the schools were not "private" in the sense that employment of a private tutor might be. Stevens, J., concurring, thought Jones v. Mayer wrongly decided as a matter of interpreting the 1866 act, but did not vote to overrule it because to do so would have "effects that would not have arisen from a correct decision in the first instance." (Id. at 190-192). White and Rehnquist, JJ., dissented, arguing that even if Jones v. Mayer is accepted for § 1982 cases (property transactions), § 1981 had a different legislative background, deriving mediately from the 1870 Civil Rights Act, enacted under the Fourteenth Amendment. The dissenters foresaw awkward problems for the courts: "As the associational or contractual relationships become more private, the pressures to hold § 1981 inapplicable to them will increase. Imaginative judicial construction of the word 'contract' is foreseeable; Thirteenth Amendment limitation on Congress' power to ban 'badges and incidents of slavery' may be discovered; the doctrine of the right to association may be bent to cover a given situation." (Id. at 213-214).

McDonald v. Santa Fe Transp. Co., 427 U.S. 273 (1976), held that disciplinary discharges of white employees while black employees committing the same offenses were retained violated both Title VII of the Civil Rights Act of 1964 and 42 U.S.C. § 1981. The Court did not discuss the constitutional basis for the application of either provision.

Burton v. Wilmington Parking Authority 365 U.S. 715, 81 S. Ct. 856, 6 L. Ed. 2d 45 (1961)

MR. JUSTICE CLARK delivered the opinion of the Court.

In this action for declaratory and injunctive relief it is admitted that the Eagle Coffee Shoppe, Inc., a restaurant located within an off-street automobile parking building in Wilmington, Delaware, has refused to serve appellant food or drink solely because he is a Negro. The parking building is owned and operated by the Wilmington Parking Authority, an agency of the State of Delaware, and the restaurant is the Authority's lessee. Appellant claims that such refusal abridges his rights under the Equal Protection Clause of the Fourteenth Amendment to the United States Constitution. The Supreme Court of Delaware has held that Eagle was acting in a "purely private capacity" under its lease; that its action was not that of the Authority and was not, therefore, state action within the contemplation of the prohibitions contained in that Amendment. It also held that under 24 Del. Code, § 1501,[1] Eagle was a restaurant, not an inn, and that as such it "is not required [under Delaware law] to serve any and all persons entering its place of business." [39 Del. Ch. 10], 157 A.2d 894 (1960). On appeal here from the judgment as having been based upon a statute construed unconstitutionally, we postponed consideration of the question of jurisdiction under 28 U.S.C. § 1257(2) to the hearing on the merits. 364 U.S. 810. We agree with the respondents that the appeal should be dismissed and accordingly the motion to dismiss is granted. However, since the action of Eagle in excluding appellant raises an important constitutional question, the papers whereon the appeal was taken are treated as a petition for a writ of certiorari, 28 U.S.C. § 2103, and the writ is granted. 28 U.S.C. § 1257(3). On the merits we have concluded that the exclusion of appellant under the circumstances shown to be present here was discriminatory state action in violation of the Equal Protection Clause of the Fourteenth Amendment.

The Authority was created by the City of Wilmington pursuant to Tit. 22, Del. Code, c. 5, §§ 501-515. It is "a public body corporate and politic, exercising public powers of the State as an agency thereof." § 504. Its statutory purpose is to provide adequate parking facilities for the convenience of the public and thereby relieve the "parking crisis, which threatens the welfare of the community. . . ." § 501(7), (8) and (9). To this end the Authority is granted wide powers including that of constructing or acquiring by lease, purchase or condemnation, lands and facilities, and that of leasing "portions of any of its garage buildings or structures for commercial use by the lessee, where, in the opinion of the Authority, such leasing is necessary and feasible for the financing and operation of such facilities." § 504(a). The Act provides that the rates and charges for its facilities must be reasonable and are to be determined exclusively by the Authority "for the purposes of providing for the payment of the expenses of the Authority, the construction, improvement, repair, maintenance, and operation of its facilities and properties, the payment of the principal of and interest on its obligations, and to fulfill the terms and provisions of any agreements made with the purchasers or holders of any such obligations or with the city." § 504(b)(8). The Authority has no power to pledge the credit of the State of Delaware but may issue its own revenue bonds which are tax exempt. Any and all property owned or used by the Authority is likewise exempt from state taxation.

The first project undertaken by the Authority was the erection of a parking facility on Ninth Street in downtown Wilmington. The tract consisted of four parcels, all of which were acquired by negotiated purchases from private owners. Three were paid for in cash,

---

[1] The statute provides that: "No keeper of an inn, tavern, hotel or restaurant or other place of public entertainment or refreshment of travelers, guests or customers shall be obliged, by law, to furnish entertainment or refreshment to persons whose reception or entertainment by him would be offensive to the major part of his customers and would injure his business. The term customers shall be taken to include all who have occasion for entertainment or refreshment."

borrowed from Equitable Security Trust Company, and the fourth, purchased from Diamond Ice and Coal Company, was paid for "partly in Revenue Bonds of the Authority and partly in cash [$934,000] donated by the City of Wilmington, pursuant to 22 Del. C., c. 5. . . . Subsequently the City of Wilmington gave the Authority $1,822,827.69 which sum the Authority applied to the redemption of the Revenue Bonds delivered to Diamond Ice & Coal Co. and to the repayment of the Equitable Security Trust Company loan."

Before it began actual construction of the facility, the Authority was advised by its retained experts that the anticipated revenue for the parking of cars and proceeds from sale of its bonds would not be sufficient to finance the construction costs of the facility. Moreover, the bonds were not expected to be marketable if payable solely out of parking revenues. To secure additional capital needed for its "debt-service" requirements, and thereby to make bond financing practicable, the Authority decided it was necessary to enter long-term leases with responsible tenants for commercial use of some of the space available in the projected "garage building." The public was invited to bid for these leases.

In April 1957 such a private lease, for 20 years and renewable for another 10 years, was made with Eagle Coffee Shoppe, Inc., for use as a "restaurant, dining room, banquet hall, cocktail lounge and bar and for no other use and purpose." The multi-level space of the building which was let to Eagle, although "within the exterior walls of the structure, has no marked public entrance leading from the parking portion of the facility into the restaurant proper . . . [whose main entrance] is located on Ninth Street." In its lease the Authority covenanted to complete construction expeditiously, including completion of "the decorative finishing of the leased premises and utilities therefor, without cost to Lessee," including necessary utility connections, toilets, hung acoustical tile and plaster ceilings; Vinyl asbestos, ceramic tile and concrete floors; connecting stairs and wrought iron railings; and wood-floored show windows. Eagle spent some $220,000 to make the space suitable for its operation and, to the extent such improvements were so attached to realty as to become part thereof, Eagle to the same extent enjoys the Authority's tax exemption.

The Authority further agreed to furnish heat for Eagle's premises, gas service for the boiler room, and to make, at its own expense, all necessary structural repairs, all repairs to exterior surfaces except store fronts and any repairs caused by lessee's own act or neglect. The Authority retained the right to place any directional signs on the exterior of the let space which would not interfere with or obscure Eagle's display signs. Agreeing to pay an annual rental of $28,700, Eagle covenanted to "occupy and use the leased premises in accordance with all applicable laws, statutes, ordinances and rules and regulations of any federal, state or municipal authority." Its lease, however, contains no requirement that its restaurant services be made available to the general public on a nondiscriminatory basis, in spite of the fact that the Authority has power to adopt rules and regulations respecting the use of its facilities except any as would impair the security of its bondholders. §511.

Other portions of the structure were leased to other tenants, including a bookstore, retail jeweler, and a food store. Upon completion of the building, the Authority located at appropriate places thereon official signs indicating the public character of the building, and flew from mastheads on the roof both the state and national flags.

In August 1958 appellant parked his car in the building and walked around to enter the restaurant by its front door on Ninth Street. Having entered and sought service, he was refused it. Thereafter he filed this declaratory judgment action in the Court of Chancery. On motions for summary judgment, based on the pleadings and affidavits, the Chancellor concluded, contrary to the contentions of respondents, that whether in fact the lease was a "device" or was executed in good faith, it would not "serve to insulate the public authority from the force and effect of the Fourteenth Amendment." 150 A.2d 197. He found it not necessary, therefore, to pass upon the rights of private restaurateurs under state common and statutory law, including 24 Del. Code §1501. The Supreme Court of Delaware reversed as we mentioned above, holding that Eagle "in the conduct of its business, is acting

Section E. Secured Rights and State Action 825

in a purely private capacity." It, therefore, denied appellant's claim under the Fourteenth Amendment. Upon reaching the application of state law, it held, contrary to appellant's assertion that Eagle maintained an inn, that Eagle's operation was "primarily a restaurant and thus subject to the provisions of 24 Del. C. §1501, which does not compel the operator of a restaurant to give service to all persons seeking such." Delaware's highest court has thus denied both the equal protection claims of the appellant as well as his state-law contention concerning the applicability of §1501.

On the jurisdictional question, we agree that the judgment of Delaware's court does not depend for its ultimate support upon a determination of the constitutional validity of a state statute, but rather upon the holding that on the facts Eagle's racially discriminatory action was exercised in "a purely private capacity" and that it was, therefore, beyond the prohibitive scope of the Fourteenth Amendment.

The Civil Rights Cases, 109 U.S. 3 (1883), "embedded in our constitutional law" the principle "that the action inhibited by the first section [equal protection clause] of the Fourteenth Amendment is only such action as may fairly be said to be that of the States. That Amendment erects no shield against merely private conduct, however discriminatory or wrongful." Chief Justice Vinson in Shelley v. Kraemer, 334 U.S. 1, 13 (1948). It was language in the opinion in the Civil Rights Cases, supra, that phrased the broad test of state responsibility under the Fourteenth Amendment, predicting its consequence upon "State action of every kind . . . which denies . . . the equal protection of the laws." At p. 11. And only two Terms ago, some 75 years later, the same concept of state responsibility was interpreted as necessarily following upon "state participation through any arrangement, management, funds or property." Cooper v. Aaron, 358 U.S. 1, 4 (1958). It is clear, as it always has been since the Civil Rights Cases, supra, that "individual invasion of individual rights is not the subject matter of the amendment," at p. 11, and that private conduct abridging individual rights does no violence to the Equal Protection Clause unless to some significant extent the State in any of its manifestations has been found to have become involved in it. Because the virtue of the right to equal protection of the laws could lie only in the breadth of its application, its constitutional assurance was reserved in terms whose imprecision was necessary if the right were to be enjoyed in the variety of individual-state relationships which the Amendment was designed to embrace. For the same reason, to fashion and apply a precise formula for recognition of state responsibility under the Equal Protection Clause is "an impossible task" which "this Court has never attempted." Kotch v. Pilot Comm'rs, 330 U.S. 552, 556. Only by sifting facts and weighing circumstances can the nonobvious involvement of the State in private conduct be attributed its true significance.

The trial court's disposal of the issues on summary judgment has resulted in a rather incomplete record, but the opinion of the Supreme Court as well as that of the Chancellor presents the facts in sufficient detail for us to determine the degree of state participation in Eagle's refusal to serve petitioner. In this connection the Delaware Supreme Court seems to have placed controlling emphasis on its conclusion, as to the accuracy of which there is no doubt, that only some 15% of the total cost of the facility was "advanced" from public funds; that the cost of the entire facility was allocated three-fifths to the space for commercial leasing and two-fifths to parking space; that anticipated revenue from parking was only some 30.5% of the total income, the balance of which was expected to be earned by the leasing; that the Authority had no original intent to place a restaurant in the building, it being only a happenstance resulting from the bidding; that Eagle expended considerable moneys on furnishings; that the restaurant's main and marked public entrance is on Ninth Street without any public entrance direct from the parking area; and that "the only connection Eagle has with the public facility . . . is the furnishing of the sum of $28,700 annually in the form of rent which is used by the Authority to defray a portion of the operating expense of an otherwise unprofitable enterprise." 157 A.2d 894, 901. While these factual considerations are indeed validly accountable aspects of the enterprise upon which the State has embarked, we cannot say that they lead inescapably to the conclusion that state action is not present. Their persuasiveness is diminished when evaluated in the context of other factors which must be acknowledged.

The land and building were publicly owned. As an entity, the building was dedicated to "public uses" in performance of the Authority's "essential governmental functions." 22 Del. Code, c. 5, §§ 501, 514. The costs of land acquisition, construction, and maintenance are defrayed entirely from donations by the City of Wilmington, from loans and revenue bonds and from the proceeds of rentals and parking services out of which the loans and bonds were payable. Assuming that the distinction would be significant, cf. Derrington v. Plummer, 240 F.2d 922, 925, the commercially leased areas were not surplus state property, but constituted a physically and financially integral and, indeed, indispensable part of the State's plan to operate its project as a self-sustaining unit. Upkeep and maintenance of the building, including necessary repairs, were responsibilities of the Authority and were payable out of public funds. It cannot be doubted that the peculiar relationship of the restaurant to the parking facility in which it is located confers on each an incidental variety of mutual benefits. Guests of the restaurant are afforded a convenient place to park their automobiles, even if they cannot enter the restaurant directly from the parking area. Similarly, its convenience for diners may well provide additional demand for the Authority's parking facilities. Should any improvements effected in the leasehold by Eagle become part of the realty, there is no possibility of increased taxes being passed on to it since the fee is held by a tax-exempt government agency. Neither can it be ignored, especially in view of Eagle's affirmative allegation that for it to serve Negroes would injure its business, that profits earned by discrimination not only contribute to, but are indispensable elements in the financial success of a governmental agency.

Addition of all these activities, obligations and responsibilities of the Authority, the benefits mutually conferred, together with the obvious fact that the restaurant is operated as an integral part of a public building devoted to a public parking service, indicates that degree of state participation and involvement in discriminatory action which it was the design of the Fourteenth Amendment to condemn. It is irony amounting to grave injustice that in one part of a single building, erected and maintained with public funds by an agency of the State to serve a public purpose, all persons have equal rights, while in another portion, also serving the public, a Negro is a second-class citizen, offensive because of his race, without rights and unentitled to service, but at the same time fully enjoys equal access to nearby restaurants in wholly privately owned buildings. As the Chancellor pointed out, in its lease with Eagle the Authority could have affirmatively required Eagle to discharge the responsibilities under the Fourteenth Amendment imposed upon the private enterprise as a consequence of state participation. But no State may effectively abdicate its responsibilities by either ignoring them or by merely failing to discharge them whatever the motive may be. It is of no consolation to an individual denied the equal protection of the laws that it was done in good faith. Certainly the conclusions drawn in similar cases by the various Courts of Appeals do not depend upon such a distinction. By its inaction, the Authority, and through it the State, has not only made itself a party to a refusal of service, but has elected to place its power, property and prestige behind the admitted discrimination. The State has so far insinuated itself into a position of interdependence with Eagle that it must be recognized as a joint participant in the challenged activity, which, on that account, cannot be considered to have been so "purely private" as to fall without the scope of the Fourteenth Amendment.

Because readily applicable formulae may not be fashioned, the conclusions drawn from the facts and circumstances of this record are by no means declared as universal truths on the basis of which every state leasing agreement is to be tested. Owing to the very "largeness" of the government, a multitude of relationships might appear to some to fall within the Amendment's embrace, but that, it must be remembered, can be determined only in the framework of the peculiar facts or circumstances present. Therefore respondents' prophecy of nigh universal application of a constitutional precept so peculiarly dependent for its invocation upon appropriate facts fails to take into account "Differences in circumstances [which] beget appropriate differences in law," Whitney v. Tax Comm'n, 309 U.S. 530, 542. Specifically defining the limits of our inquiry, what we hold today is that when a State leases public property in the manner and for the purposes shown to have been the case here, the proscriptions of the Fourteenth Amendment must be complied with by the lessee as certainly as though they were binding covenants written into the agreement itself.

The judgment of the Supreme Court of Delaware is reversed and the cause remanded for further proceedings consistent with this opinion.

Reversed and remanded.

MR. JUSTICE STEWART, concurring.

I agree that the judgment must be reversed, but I reach that conclusion by a route much more direct than the one traveled by the Court. In upholding Eagle's rights to deny service to the appellant solely because of his race, the Supreme Court of Delaware relied upon a statute of that State which permits the proprietor of a restaurant to refuse to serve "persons whose reception or entertainment by him would be offensive to the major part of his customers. . . ." There is no suggestion in the record that the appellant as an individual was such a person. The highest court of Delaware has thus construed this legislative enactment as authorizing discriminatory classification based exclusively on color. Such a law seems to me clearly violative of the Fourteenth Amendment. I think, therefore, that the appeal was properly taken, and that the statute, as authoritatively construed by the Supreme Court of Delaware, is constitutionally invalid.[m]

MR. JUSTICE HARLAN, whom MR. JUSTICE WHITTAKER joins, dissenting.

The Court's opinion, by a process of first undiscriminatingly throwing together various factual bits and pieces and then undermining the resulting structure by an equally vague disclaimer, seems to me to leave completely at sea just what it is in this record that satisfies the requirement of "state action."

I find it unnecessary, however, to inquire into the matter at this stage, for it seems to me apparent that before passing on the far-reaching constitutional questions that may, or may not, be lurking in this judgment, the case should first be sent back to the state court for clarification as to the precise basis of its decision. In deciding this case the Delaware Supreme Court, among other things, said:

"It [Eagle] acts as a restaurant keeper and, as such, is not required to serve any and all persons entering its place of business, any more than the operator of a bookstore, barber shop, or other retail business is required to sell its product to everyone. This is the common law, and the law of Delaware as restated in 24 Del. C., §1501 with respect to restaurant keepers. 10 Am. Jr., Civil Rights, §§21, 22; 52 Am. Jr., Theatres, §9; Williams v. Howard Johnson's Restaurant, 268 F.2d 845. We, accordingly, hold that the operation of its restaurant by Eagle does not fall within the scope of the prohibitions of the Fourteenth Amendment."

If in the context of this record this means, as my Brother STEWART suggests, that the Delaware court construed this state statute "as authorizing discriminatory classification based exclusively on color," I would certainly agree, without more, that the enactment is offensive to the Fourteenth Amendment. It would then be quite unnecessary to reach the much broader questions dealt with in the Court's opinion. If, on the other hand, the state court meant no more than that under the statute, as at common law, Eagle was free to serve only those whom it pleased, then, and only then, would the question of "state action" be presented in full-blown form.

I think that sound principles of constitutional adjudication dictate that we should first ascertain the exact basis of this state judgment, and for that purpose I would either remand the case to the Delaware Supreme Court, see Musser v. Utah, 333 U.S. 95; cf. Harrison

---

[m] A dissenting opinion by Mr. Justice Frankfurter is omitted. — ED.

v. N.A.A.C.P., 360 U.S. 167, or hold the case pending application to the state court for clarification. See Herb v. Pitcairn, 324 U.S. 117. It seems to me both unnecessary and unwise to reach issues of such broad constitutional significance as those now decided by the Court, before the necessity for deciding them has become apparent.

NOTE Economic Regulation and "State Action"

In Moose Lodge No. 107 v. Irvis, 407 U.S. 163 (1972), the Court held, 6 to 3, that "state action" sufficient to bring the Fourteenth Amendment to bear was not present where a private club refused service to a guest solely because of his race, notwithstanding the fact that the club held a liquor license from the state of Pennsylvania. Under state law not more than one liquor license could be granted for each 1500 inhabitants of a municipality; in this calculation club licenses were not included, but when the maximum quota was reached (as it had been here) no additional club, as well as retail, license could be issued. Writing for the Court, Justice Rehnquist stated:

"Here there is nothing approaching the symbiotic relationship between lessor and lessee that was present in Burton [v. Wilmington Parking Authority], where the private lessee obtained the benefit of locating in a building owned by the state-created parking authority, and the parking authority was enabled to carry out its primary public purpose of furnishing parking space by advantageously leasing portions of the building constructed for that purpose to commercial lessees such as the owner of the Eagle Restaurant. Unlike Burton, the Moose Lodge building is located on land owned by it, not by any public authority. Far from apparently holding itself out as a place of public accommodation, Moose Lodge quite ostentatiously proclaims the fact that it is not open to the public at large. (Fn. omitted.) Nor is it located and operated in such surroundings that although private in name, it discharges a function or performs a service that would otherwise in all likelihood be performed by the State. In short, while Eagle was a public restaurant in a public building, Moose Lodge is a private social club in a private building. . . .

"The District Court was at pains to point out in its opinion what it considered to be the 'pervasive' nature of the regulation of private clubs by the Pennsylvania Liquor Control Board. As that court noted, an applicant for a club license must make such physical alterations in its premises as the board may require, must file a list of the names and addresses of its members and employees, and must keep extensive financial records. The board is granted the right to inspect the licensed premises at any time when patrons, guests, or members are present.

"However detailed this type of regulation may be in some particulars, it cannot be said to in any way foster or encourage racial discrimination. Nor can it be said to make the State in any realistic sense a partner or even a joint venturer in the club's enterprise. The limited effort of the prohibition against obtaining additional club licenses when the maximum number of retail licenses allotted to a municipality has been issued, when considered together with the availability of liquor from hotel, restaurant, and retail licensees, falls far short of conferring upon club licensees a monopoly in the dispensing of liquor in any given municipality or in the State as a whole. We therefore hold that, with the exception hereafter noted, the operation of the regulatory scheme enforced by the Pennsylvania Liquor Control Board does not sufficiently implicate the State in the discriminatory guest policies of Moose Lodge to make the latter 'state action' within the ambit of the Equal Protection Clause of the Fourteenth Amendment."

The Court unanimously struck down a portion of the law that required licensees to adhere to their own by-laws, insofar as the latter provided for racial discrimination.

Justices Douglas and Brennan each filed dissents joined by Justice Marshall. Justice Douglas stated, in part:

". . . Liquor licenses in Pennsylvania, unlike driver's licenses, or marriage licenses, are not freely available to those who meet racially neutral qualifications. . . . What the majority neglects to say is that the quota for Harrisburg, where Moose Lodge No. 107 is located, has been full for many years. No more club licenses may be issued in that city.

"This state-enforced scarcity of licenses restricts the ability of blacks to obtain liquor, for liquor is commercially available *only* at private clubs for a significant portion of each week. Access by blacks to places that serve liquor is further limited by the fact that the state quota is filled. A group desiring to form a nondiscriminatory club which would serve blacks must purchase a license held by an existing club, which can exact a monopoly price for the transfer. The availability of such a license is speculative at best, however, for, as Moose Lodge itself concedes, without a liquor license a fraternal organization would be hard pressed to survive.

"Thus, the State of Pennsylvania is putting the weight of its liquor license, concededly a valued and important adjunct to a private club, behind racial discrimination."

Justice Brennan stated, in part:

". . . Liquor licensing laws are only incidentally revenue measures; they are primarily pervasive regulatory schemes under which the State dictates and continually supervises virtually every detail of the operation of the licensee's business. Very few, if any, other licensed businesses experience such complete state involvement. Yet the Court holds that such involvement does not constitute 'state action' making the Lodge's refusal to serve a guest liquor solely because of his race a violation of the Fourteenth Amendment. The vital flaw in the Court's reasoning is its complete disregard of the fundamental value underlying the 'state action' concept. That value is discussed in my separate opinion in Adickes v. Kress & Co., 398 U.S. 144, 190-191 (1970):

" 'The state-action doctrine reflects the profound judgment that denials of equal treatment, and particularly denials on account of race or color, are singularly grave when government has or shares responsibility for them. Government is the social organ to which all in our society look for the promotion of liberty, justice, fair and equal treatment, and the setting of worthy norms and goals for social conduct. Therefore something is uniquely amiss in a society where the government, the authoritative oracle of community values, involves itself in racial discrimination. Accordingly, . . . the cases that have come before us [in which] this Court has condemned significant state involvement in racial discrimination, however subtle and indirect it may have been and whatever form it may have taken[,] . . . represent vigilant fidelity to the constitutional principle that no State shall in any significant way lend its authority to the sordid business of racial discrimination.'

"Plainly, the State of Pennsylvania's liquor regulations intertwine the State with the operation of the Lodge bar in a 'significant way [and] lend [the State's] authority to the sordid business of racial discrimination.' "

Jones v. Alfred H. Mayer Co. was not discussed. However, the black guest had also brought a complaint before the Pennsylvania Human Rights Commission, and the commission issued an order enjoining Lodge No. 107 to cease and desist its practice of denying dining room and bar facilities to black guests on account of their race. The order was upheld in Commonwealth v. Loyal Order of Moose, Lodge No. 107, 448 Pa. 451, 294 A.2d 594, appeal dismissed for want of substantial federal question, 409 U.S. 1052 (1972). The Pennsylvania Supreme Court held that the club's practice of serving white nonmembers who were guests of members made it a "public accommodation" within the meaning of the state Human Rights Act.

1. Compare with the statements of Justices Rehnquist, Douglas, and Brennan the view of Judge Friendly expressed in Powe v. Miles, 407 F.2d 73 (2d Cir. 1968). There, students complained that they had been suspended from Alfred University, a private institution, in violation of the First and Fourteenth Amendments. They sought to establish state action through state regulation of education, the "public function" performed by the university, and state financial support of a contract college operated as a subunit of Alfred, the State College of Ceramics. As to those students who were enrolled in other subunits,

the court held there was no state action. On the effect of state regulation Judge Friendly stated:

"The contention that New York's regulation of educational standards in private schools, colleges and universities . . . makes their acts in curtailing protest and disciplining students the acts of the State . . . overlooks the essential point — that the state must be involved not simply with some activity of the institution alleged to have inflicted injury upon a plaintiff but with the activity that caused the injury. Putting the point another way, the state action, not the private action, must be the subject of complaint."

2. In varying contexts the Supreme Court recently has rejected claims that government economic regulation or licensing had the effect of extending Fifth or Fourteenth Amendment responsibilities to formerly private institutions. Consider the following cases:

a. In Columbia Broadcasting System, Inc. v. Democratic National Committee, 412 U.S. 94 (1973), Chief Justice Burger, writing for the Court, but joined in this part of his opinion only by Justices Stewart and Rehnquist, held that broadcasters' receipt of licenses from and regulation by the Federal Communications Commission did not constitute "governmental action" such that broadcasters might be compelled to support the expression of First Amendment rights by accepting paid political and editorial advertising. The Chief Justice emphasized the delicate relationship between the broadcasters and their regulators:

"In dealing with the broadcast media, as in other contexts, the line between private conduct and governmental action cannot be defined by reference to any general formula unrelated to particular exercises of governmental authority. When governmental action is alleged there must be cautious analysis of the quality and degree of Government relationship to the particular acts in question. . . .

"The regulatory scheme evolved slowly, but very early the licensee's role developed in terms of a 'public trustee' charged with the duty of fairly and impartially informing the listening and viewing public. In this structure the Commission acts in essense as an 'overseer,' but the initial and primary responsibility for fairness, balance, and objectivity rests with the licensee. This role of the Government as an 'overseer' and ultimate arbiter and guardian of the public interest and the role of the licensee as a journalistic 'free agent' call for a delicate balancing of competing interests. The maintenance of this balance for more than 40 years has called on both the regulators and the licensees to walk a 'tightrope' to preserve the First Amendment values written into the Radio Act and its successor, the Communications Act. . . .

"The licensee policy challenged in this case is intimately related to the journalistic role of a licensee for which it has been given initial and primary responsibility by Congress. . . .

"Moreover, the Commission has not fostered the licensee policy challenged here; it has simply declined to command particular action because it fell within the area of journalistic discretion. . . .

"Thus, it cannot be said that the Government is a 'partner' to the action of a broadcast licensee complained of here, nor is it engaged in a 'symbiotic relationship' with the licensee, profiting from the invidious discrimination of its proxy. Compare Moose Lodge No. 107 v. Irvis, 407 U.S. 163, 174-177 (1972), with Burton v. Wilmington Parking Authority, 365 U.S., at 723-724. The First Amendment does not reach acts of private parties in every instance where the Congress or the Commission has merely permitted or failed to prohibit such acts."

In concurring opinions, Justice Douglas agreed there was no governmental action, and Justices White, Blackmun, and Powell stated they found it unnecessary to consider the question because in their views the First Amendment would not in any event compel broadcasters to accept editorial advertising.

See Note, The Supreme Court, 1972 Term, 87 Harv. L. Rev. 1, 175-188 (1973).

Section E. Secured Rights and State Action

b. In Jackson v. Metropolitan Edison Co., 419 U.S. 345 (1974), the Court held, 6 to 3, that an electrical utility customer whose service had been terminated without notice or an opportunity to be heard was not entitled to protection under the due process clause of the Fourteenth Amendment. Metropolitan Edison was a privately owned utility incorporated in Pennsylvania and operating under a certificate of public convenience issued by the Pennsylvania Public Utilities Commission. Under a provision of the tariff filed by the utility with the commission, Metropolitan Edison reserved the right to terminate service on reasonable notice when a customer failed to pay his bills. Writing for the Court, Justice Rehnquist stated:

"Here the action complained of was taken by a utility company which is privately owned and operated, but which in many particulars of its business is subject to extensive state regulation. The mere fact that a business is subject to state regulation does not by itself convert its action into that of the State for purposes of the Fourteenth Amendment. Moose Lodge No. 107 v. Irvis, supra, at 176-177. . . . Nor does the fact that the regulation is extensive and detailed, as in the case of most public utilities, do so. Public Utilities Comm'n v. Pollak, 343 U.S. 351 . . . (1952). It may well be that acts of a heavily regulated utility with at least something of a governmentally protected monopoly will more readily be found to be 'state' acts than will the acts of an entity lacking these characteristics. But the inquiry must be whether there is a sufficiently close nexus between the State and the challenged action of the regulated entity so that the action of the latter may be fairly treated as that of the State itself. . . ." (Footnote omitted.)

The Court then discussed various possible indicia of state involvement, finding none sufficient. The Court questioned whether the state's issuance of a certificate of public convenience amounted to a grant of monopoly status to the utility and whether, in any event, sufficient connection existed between the utility's monopoly position and its termination policy. The Court further found that the utility's traditional status as a business "affected with a public interest" obligated to furnish an essential public service on a reasonably continuous basis fell short of a finding of state action under the "public function" rationale: the obligation to provide service rests on the utility, not the state itself. Finally, acceptance of the utility's tariff provision by the commission did not amount to specific authorization or endorsement of the utility's termination policy by the State of Pennsylvania. Justices Douglas, Brennan, and Marshall dissented, each in a separate opinion.

See Note, Fourteenth Amendment Due Process in Terminations of Utility Services for Nonpayment, 86 Harv. L. Rev. 1477 (1973).

3. Justice Brennan wrote in Adickes v. Kress & Co., 398 U.S. 144, 190 (1970) (concurring in part and dissenting in part): "The state-action doctrine reflects the profound judgment that denials of equal treatment, and particularly denials on account of race and color, are singularly grave when government has or shares responsibility for them." To what extent, as this observation suggests, should the nature of the deprivation alleged by the plaintiff play a role in the determination whether "state action" is present? Should the Court have found "state action" in Jackson, for example, if the claim involved racial discrimination? Judge Friendly, for one, has indicated a willingness to apply a variable standard in this area, Grafton v. Brooklyn Law School, 478 F.2d 1137, 1142 (1973).

See generally Berle, Constitutional Limitations on Corporate Activity — Protection of Personal Rights from Invasion Through Economic Power, 100 U. Pa. L. Rev. 933, 948-950 (1952); Wellington, The Constitution, The Labor Union, and "Governmental Action," 70 Yale L.J. 345 (1961). Cf. Lewis, The Meaning of State Action, 60 Colum. L. Rev. 1083, 1097 (1960), Selected Essays on Constitutional Law 915 (1963); Black, The Supreme Court, 1966 Term — Foreword: "State Action," Equal Protection, and California's Proposition 14, 81 Harv. L. Rev. 69 (1967); Note, State Action: Theories for Applying Constitutional Restrictions to Private Activity, 74 Colum. L. Rev. 656 (1974); Note, State Action and the Burger Court, 60 Va. L. Rev. 840 (1974).

Evans v. Newton 382 U.S. 296, 86 S. Ct. 486, 15 L. Ed. 2d 373 (1966)

MR. JUSTICE DOUGLAS delivered the opinion of the Court.

In 1911 United States Senator Augustus O. Bacon executed a will that devised to the Mayor and Council of the City of Macon, Georgia, a tract of land which, after the death of the Senator's wife and daughters, was to be used as "a park and pleasure ground" for white people only, the Senator stating in the will that while he had only the kindest feeling for the Negroes he was of the opinion that "in their social relations the two races (white and negro) should be forever separate." The will provided that the park should be under the control of a Board of Managers of seven persons, all of whom were to be white. The city kept the park segregated for some years but in time let Negroes use it, taking the position that the park was a public facility which it could not constitutionally manage and maintain on a segregated basis.

Thereupon, individual members of the Board of Managers of the park brought this suit in the state court against the City of Macon and trustees of certain residuary beneficiaries of Senator Bacon's estate, asking that the city be removed as trustee and that the court appoint new trustees, to whom title to the park would be transferred. The city answered, alleging it could not legally enforce racial segregation in the park. The other defendants admitted the allegation and requested that the city be removed as trustee.

Several Negro citizens of Macon intervened, alleging that the racial limitation was contrary to the laws and public policy of the United States, and asking that the court refuse to appoint private trustees. Thereafter the city resigned as trustee and amended its answer accordingly. Moreover, other heirs of Senator Bacon intervened and they and the defendants other than the city asked for reversion of the trust property to the Bacon estate in the event that the prayer of the petition were denied.

The Georgia court accepted the resignation of the city as trustee and appointed three individuals as new trustees, finding it unnecessary to pass on the other claims of the heirs. On appeal of the Negro intervenors, the Supreme Court of Georgia affirmed, holding that Senator Bacon had the right to give and bequeath his property to a limited class, that charitable trusts are subject to supervision of a court of equity, and that the power to appoint new trustees so that the purpose of the trust would not fail was clear. 220 Ga. 280. The case is here on a writ of certiorari. 380 U.S. 971.

There are two complementary principles to be reconciled in this case. One is the right of the individual to pick his own associates so as to express his preferences and dislikes, and to fashion his private life by joining such clubs and groups as he chooses. The other is the constitutional ban in the Equal Protection Clause of the Fourteenth Amendment against state-sponsored racial inequality, which of course bars a city from acting as trustee under a private will that serves the racial segregation cause. Com. of Pennsylvania v. Board of Directors of City Trusts, 353 U.S. 230. Conduct that is formally "private" may become so entwined with governmental policies or so impregnated with a governmental character as to become subject to the constitutional limitations placed upon state action. The action of a city in serving as trustee of property under a private will serving the segregated cause is an obvious example. See Com. of Pennsylvania v. Board of Directors of City Trusts, supra. A town may be privately owned and managed, but that does not necessarily allow the company to treat it as if it were wholly in the private sector. Thus we held in Marsh v. State of Alabama, 326 U.S. 501, that the exercise of constitutionally protected rights on the public streets of a company town could not be denied by the owner. A State is not justified, we said, in "permitting a corporation to govern a community of citizens so as to restrict their fundamental liberties. . . ." Id., at 509. . . . We have also held that where a State delegates an aspect of the elective process to private groups, they become subject to the same restraints as the State. Terry v. Adams, 345 U.S. 461. That is to say, when private individuals or groups are endowed by the State with powers or functions governmental in nature, they become agencies or instrumentalities of the State and subject to its constitutional limitations.

Yet generalizations do not decide concrete cases. "Only by sifting facts and weighing circumstances" (Burton v. Wilmington Parking Authority, 365 U.S. [715,] 722, can we determine whether the reach of the Fourteenth Amendment extends to a particular case. The range of government activities is broad and varied, and the fact that government has engaged in a particular activity does not necessarily mean that an individual entrepreneur or manager of the same kind of undertaking suffers the same constitutional inhibitions. While a State may not segregate public schools so as to exclude one or more religious groups, those sects may maintain their own parochial educational systems. Pierce v. Society of Sisters, 268 U.S. 510.

If a testator wanted to leave a school or center for the use of one race only and in no way implicated the State in the supervision, control, or management of that facility, we assume arguendo that no constitutional difficulty would be encountered.

This park, however, is in a different posture. For years it was an integral part of the City of Macon's activities. From the pleadings we assume it was swept, manicured, watered, patrolled, and maintained by the city as a public facility for whites only, as well as granted tax exemption under Ga. Code Ann. § 92-201. The momentum it acquired as a public facility is certainly not dissipated ipso facto by the appointment of "private" trustees. So far as this record shows, there has been no change in municipal maintenance and concern over this facility. Whether these public characteristics will in time be dissipated is wholly conjectural. If the municipality remains entwined in the management or control of the park, it remains subject to the restraints of the Fourteenth Amendment just as the private utility in Public Utilities Commission of District of Columbia v. Pollak, 343 U.S. 451, 462, remained subject to the Fifth Amendment because of the surveillance which federal agencies had over its affairs. We only hold that where the tradition of municipal control had become firmly established, we cannot take judicial notice that the mere substitution of trustees instantly transferred this park from the public to the private sector.

This conclusion is buttressed by the nature of the service rendered the community by a park. The service rendered even by a private park of this character is municipal in nature. It is open to every white person, there being no selective element other than race. Golf clubs, social centers, luncheon clubs, schools such as Tuskegee was at least in origin,[4] and other like organizations in the private sector are often racially oriented. A park on the other hand, is more like a fire department or police department that traditionally serves the community. Mass recreation through the use of parks is plainly in the public domain, Watson v. Memphis [373 U.S. 526 (1963)]; and state courts that aid private parties to perform that public function on a segregated basis implicate the State in conduct proscribed by the Fourteenth Amendment. Like the streets of the company town in Marsh v. State of Alabama, supra, the elective process of Terry v. Adams, supra, and the transit system of Public Utilities Commission of District of Columbia v. Pollak, supra, the predominant character and purpose of this park is municipal.

Under the circumstances of this case, we cannot but conclude that the public institution is subject to the command of the Fourteenth Amendment, regardless of who now has title under state law. We may fairly assume that had the Georgia courts been of the view that even in private hands the park may not be operated for the public on a segregated basis, the resignation would not have been approved and private trustees appointed. We put the matter that way because on this record we cannot say that the transfer of title per se disentangled the park from segregation under the municipal regime that long controlled it.

Since the judgment below gives effect to that purpose, it must be and is
Reversed.

MR. JUSTICE WHITE, concurring. . . .

---

[4] Ala. Laws 1880-1881, pp. 395-396; Ala. Laws, 1882-1883, pp. 392-393.

I would . . . hold that the racial condition in the trust may not be given effect by the new trustee because, in my view, it is incurably tainted by discriminatory state legislation validating such a condition under state law. The state legislation to which I refer is §§ 69-504 and 69-505 of the Georgia Code, which were adopted in 1905, just six years before Senator Bacon's will was executed. Sections 69-504 and 69-505 make lawful charitable trusts "dedicated in perpetuity to the public use as a park, pleasure ground, or for other public purpose" and provide that "the use of said park, pleasure ground, or other property so conveyed to said municipality may be limited to the white race only or to white women and children only, or to the colored race only, or to colored women and children only, or to any other race, or to the women and children of any other race only. . . ."

As this legislation does not compel a trust settlor to condition his grant upon use only by a racially designated class, the State cannot be said to have directly coerced private discrimination. Nevertheless, if the validity of the racial condition in Senator Bacon's trust would have been in doubt but for the 1905 statute and if the statute removed such doubt only for racial restrictions, leaving the validity of nonracial restrictions still in question, the absence of coercive language in the legislation would not prevent application of the Fourteenth Amendment. For such a statute would depart from a policy of strict neutrality in matters of private discrimination by enlisting the State's assistance only in aid of racial discrimination and would so involve the State in the private choice as to convert the infected private discrimination into state action subject to the Fourteenth Amendment.[n]

MR. JUSTICE HARLAN, whom MR. JUSTICE STEWART joins, dissenting.

This decision, in my opinion, is more the product of human impulses, which I fully share, than of solid constitutional thinking. It is made at the sacrifice of long-established and still wise procedural and substantive constitutional principle. I must respectfully dissent. . . .

The first ground for the majority's state action holding rests on nothing but an assumption and a conjecture. The assumption is that the city itself maintained Baconsfield in the past. The conjecture is that it will continue to be connected with the administration of the park in the future. . . .

Quite evidently uneasy with its first ground of decision, the majority advances another which ultimately emerges as the real holding. This ground derives from what is asserted to be the "public character" . . . of Baconsfield and the "municipal . . . nature" of its services . . . Here it is not suggested that Baconsfield will use public property or funds, be managed by the city, enjoy an exclusive franchise, or even operate under continuing supervision of a public regulatory agency. State action is inherent in the operation of Baconsfield quite independently of any such factors, so it seems to be said, because a privately operated park whose only criterion for exclusion is racial is within the "public domain." . . .

Except for one case which will be found to be a shaky precedent, the cases cited by the majority do not support this novel state action theory. Public Utilities Commission of District of Columbia v. Pollak, 343 U.S. 451, applied due process standards, limited like equal protection standards to instances involving state action, to certain action of a private citywide transit company. State action was explicitly premised on the close legal regulation of the company by the public utilities commission and the commission's approval of the particular action under attack. The conclusion might alternatively have rested on the near-exclusive legal monopoly enjoyed by the company, 343 U.S., at 454, n. 1, but in all events nothing was rested on any "public function" theory. . . .

More serious than the absence of any firm doctrinal support for this theory of state action are its potentialities for the future. Its failing as a principle of decision in the realm of Fourteenth Amendment concerns can be shown by comparing — among other examples

---

[n] A dissenting opinion by Mr. Justice Black is omitted. — ED.

that might be drawn from the still unfolding sweep of governmental functions — the "public function" of privately established schools with that of privately owned parks. . . .

While this process of analogy might be spun out to reach privately owned orphanages, libraries, garbage collection companies, detective agencies, and a host of other functions commonly regarded as nongovernmental though paralleling fields of governmental activity, the example of schools is, I think, sufficient to indicate the pervasive potentialities of this "public function" theory of state action. It substitutes for the comparatively clear and concrete tests of state action a catch-phrase approach as vague and amorphous as it is far-reaching. It dispenses with the sound and careful principles of past decisions in this realm. And it carries the seeds of transferring to federal authority vast areas of concerns whose regulation has wisely been left by the Constitution to the States.

NOTE Failure of Discriminatory Trust

In a sequel to the Evans case, Evans v. Abney, 396 U.S. 435 (1970), the Court sustained the Georgia court's holding that an integrated park was so inconsistent with the testator's wishes that it would be inappropriate to apply the doctrine of cy pres. Thus, the devise failed and the property reverted to the testator's heirs. Justices Douglas and Brennan dissented. Justice Marshall did not participate. Justice Brennan's dissent argued that a governmental body was implicated in the arrangement that prevented the park from being used as an integrated public facility, and that state responsibility was also established under Shelley v. Kraemer and Mulkey v. Reitman. For comment, see Note, 84 Harv. L. Rev. 54 (1970).

In Palmer v. Thompson, 403 U.S. 217 (1971), the Court, per Justice Black, held that the Fourteenth Amendment was not violated when Jackson, Mississippi, shut down its municipal swimming pools rather than desegregate them. Justices Douglas, White, Marshall, and Brennan dissented. Compare Griffin v. Prince Edward County, page 894 infra.

NOTE Government Assistance to Private Segregated Institutions

In Norwood v. Harrison, 413 U.S. 455 (1973), the Supreme Court unanimously overturned a three-judge district court decision upholding a Mississippi statute authorizing free distribution of textbooks to all primary and secondary school students in the state, including those attending private segregated academies. The loan program had been started in 1940, some time before segregation academies were established in reaction to desegregation of the public schools. Writing for the Court, Chief Justice Burger stated, in part:

"The District Court's holding . . . raises the question whether and on what terms a State may — as a matter of legislative policy — provide tangible assistance to students attending private schools. Appellants assert, not only that the private schools are in fact racially discriminatory, but also that aid to them in any form is in derogation of the State's obligation not to support discrimination in education.

"This Court has consistently affirmed decisions enjoining state tuition grants to students attending racially discriminatory private schools. A textbook lending program is not legally distinguishable from the forms of state assistance foreclosed by the prior cases. Free textbooks, like tuition grants directed to private school students, are a form of financial assistance inuring to the benefit of the private schools themselves. An inescapable educational cost for students in both public and private schools is the expense of providing all necessary learning materials. When, as here, that necessary expense is borne by the State, the economic consequence is to give aid to the enterprise; if the school engages in discriminatory practices the State by tangible aid in the form of textbooks thereby gives support to such discrimination. Racial discrimination in state-operated schools is barred by the Constitution and '[i]t is also axiomatic that a state may not induce, encourage or promote private persons to accomplish what it is constitutionally forbidden to accomplish.' Lee v. Macon County Board of Education, 267 F. Supp. 458, 475-476 (M.D. Ala. 1967).

"We do not suggest that a State violates its constitutional duty merely because it has provided *any* form of state service that benefits private schools said to be racially discriminatory. Textbooks are a basic educational tool and, like tuition grants, they are provided only in connection with schools; they are to be distinguished from generalized services government might provide to schools in common with others. Moreover, the textbooks provided to private school students by the State in this case are a form of assistance readily available from sources entirely independent of the State — unlike, for example, 'such necessities of life as electricity, water, and police and fire protection.' Moose Lodge No. 107 v. Irvis, 407 U.S. 163, 173 (1972). The State has neither an absolute nor operating monopoly on the procurement of school textbooks; anyone can purchase them on the open market.

"The District Court laid great stress on the absence of showing by appellants that 'any child enrolled in private school, if deprived of free textbooks, would withdraw from private school and subsequently enroll in the public schools.'. . . We do not agree with the District Court in its analysis of the legal consequences of this uncertainty, for the Constitution does not permit the State to aid discrimination even when there is no precise causal relationship between state aid to a private school and the continued well-being of that school. A State may not grant the type of tangible financial aid here involved if that aid has a significant tendency to facilitate, reinforce, and support private discrimination. '[D]ecisions on the constitutionality of state involvement in private discrimination do not turn on whether the state aid adds up to 51 percent or adds up to only 49 percent of the support of the segregated institution.' Poindexter v. Louisiana Financial Assistance Comm'n, 275 F. Supp. 833, 854 (E.D. La. 1967).

". . . We need not assume that the State's textbook aid to private schools has been motivated by other than a sincere interest in the educational welfare of all Mississippi children. But good intentions as to one valid objective do not serve to negate the State's involvement in violation of a constitutional duty. 'The existence of a permissible purpose cannot sustain an action that has an impermissible effect.' Wright v. Council of City of Emporia, 407 U.S. 451, 462 (1972). The Equal Protection Clause would be a sterile promise if state involvement in possible private activity could be shielded altogether from constitutional scrutiny simply because its ultimate end was not discrimination but some higher goal."

Compare Gilmore v. City of Montgomery, 417 U.S. 556 (1974). Plaintiffs challenged the city's practice of allowing use of public recreational facilities by private segregated school groups and by other nonschool groups with membership limited on the basis of race. At the poles of the issue, the Court was clear: the city could not allow exclusive use, even if temporary, of city recreational facilities to private segregated schools and their affiliate groups; however, mere attendance at such a school did not prevent the city from allowing an individual access to public recreational facilities. The more difficult question in the Court's view was nonexclusive use of such facilities by segregated groups. The Court remanded this issue for further consideration. Writing for the Court, Justice Blackmun stated:

". . . The questions to be resolved . . . rest upon careful identification of the different types of city facilities that are available and the various uses to which they might be put by private groups.

"... Under appropriate circumstances, the District Court might conclude, as it did in the instance of exclusive use by private schools, that access in common to city facilities by private school groups would indeed contravene the school desegregation order. . . .

"Relief would also be appropriate if a particular use constitutes a vestige of the type of state-sponsored racial segregation in public recreational facilities that was prohibited in the parks decree [issued earlier against the city] and likewise condemned in Watson v. Memphis, 373 U.S. 526 . . . (1963). . . .

"The problem of private group use is much more complex. The Court of Appeals relied on Moose Lodge No. 107 v. Irvis, 407 U.S. 163 . . . (1972), in concluding that the use of city facilities by private clubs did not reflect a 'symbiotic' relationship between government and those groups as to constitute state action. . . .

". . . Because the city makes city property available for use by private entities, this case is more like Burton [v. Wilmington Parking Authority, 365 U.S. 715 (1961)] than Moose Lodge. The question then is whether there is significant state involvement in the private discrimination alleged. . . . Traditional state monopolies, such as electricity, water, and police and fire protection — all generalized governmental services — do not by their mere provision constitute a showing of state involvement in invidious discrimination. . . . The same is true of a broad spectrum of municipal recreational facilities: parks, playgrounds, athletic facilities, amphitheaters, museums, zoos, and the like. Cf. Evans v. Newton [382 U.S. 296, 302 (1966)]. It follows, therefore, that the portion of the District Court's order prohibiting the mere use of such facilities by *any* segregated 'private group, club, or organization' is invalid because it was not predicated upon a proper finding of state action.

"If, however, the city or other government entity rations otherwise freely accessible recreational facilities, the case for state action will naturally be stronger than if the facilities are simply available to all comers without condition or reservation. . . ."

See also McGlotten v. Connally, 338 F. Supp. 448 (D.D.C. 1972) (three-judge court) (holding that tax exemptions granted under the Internal Revenue Code to segregated fraternal organizations violate the Fifth Amendment guarantee of equal protection); Green v. Connally, 330 F. Supp. 1150 (D.D.C.) (three-judge court), aff'd mem. sub nom. Coit v. Green, 404 U.S. 997 (1971) (interpreting Internal Revenue Code §§ 171, 501 not to include segregated private schools within tax exemption and deduction of contributions granted to charitable, educational organizations). See Bittker & Kaufman, Taxes and Civil Rights: "Constitutionalizing" the Internal Revenue Code, 82 Yale L.J. 51 (1972); Comment, Tax Incentives As State Action, 122 U. Pa. L. Rev. 414 (1973).

Reitman v. Mulkey 387 U.S. 369, 87 S. Ct. 1627, 18 L. Ed. 2d 830 (1967)

MR. JUSTICE WHITE delivered the opinion of the Court. The question here is whether Art. I, § 26, of the California Constitution denies "to any person . . . the equal protection of the laws" within the meaning of the Fourteenth Amendment of the Constitution of the United States. Section 26 of Art. I, an initiated measure submitted to the people as Proposition 14 in a statewide ballot in 1964, provides in part as follows:

"Neither the State nor any subdivision or agency thereof shall deny, limit or abridge, directly or indirectly, the right of any person, who is willing or desires to sell, lease or rent any part or all of his real property, to decline to sell, lease or rent such property to such person or persons as he, in his absolute discretion, chooses."

The real property covered by § 26 is limited to residential property and contains an exception for state-owned real estate.

The issue arose in two separate actions in the California courts, Mulkey v. Reitman and Prendergast v. Snyder. In Reitman, the Mulkeys, who are husband and wife and respondents here, sued under § 51 and § 52 of the California Civil Code [1] alleging that petitioners had refused to rent them an apartment solely on account of their race. An injunction and damages were demanded. Petitioners moved for summary judgment on the ground that §§ 51 and 52, insofar as they were the basis for the Mulkeys' action, had been rendered null and void by the adoption of Proposition 14 after the filing of the complaint. The trial court granted the motion and respondents took the case to the California Supreme Court.

In the Prendergast case, respondents, husband and wife, filed suit in December 1964 seeking to enjoin eviction from their apartment; respondents alleged that the eviction was motivated by racial prejudice and therefore would violate § 51 and § 52 of the Civil Code. Petitioner Snyder cross-complained for a judicial declaration that he was entitled to terminate the month-to-month tenancy even if his action was based on racial considerations. In denying petitioner's motion for summary judgment, the trial court found it unnecessary to consider the validity of Proposition 14 because it concluded that judicial enforcement of an eviction based on racial grounds would in any event violate the Equal Protection Clause of the United States Constitution. The cross-complaint was dismissed with prejudice and petitioner Snyder appealed to the California Supreme Court which considered the case along with Mulkey v. Reitman. That court, in reversing the Reitman case, held that Art. I, § 26, was invalid as denying the equal protection of the laws guaranteed by the Fourteenth Amendment. 64 Cal. 2d 529, 413 P.2d 825. For similar reasons, the court affirmed the judgment in the Prendergast case. 64 Cal. 2d 877, 413, P.2d 847. We granted certiorari because the cases involve an important issue arising under the Fourteenth Amendment. 385 U.S. 967.

We affirm the judgments of the California Supreme Court. We first turn to the opinion of that court in Reitman, which quite properly undertook to examine the constitutionality of § 26 in terms of its "immediate objective," its "ultimate effect" and its "historical context and the conditions existing prior to its enactment." . . . [The opinion reviews and summarizes the opinion of the Supreme Court of California.]

. . . The judgment of the California court was that § 26 unconstitutionally involves the State in racial discriminations and is therefore invalid under the Fourteenth Amendment.

There is no sound reason for rejecting this judgment. . . .

The California court could very reasonably conclude that § 26 would and did have wider impact than a mere repeal of existing statutes. Section 26 mentioned neither the Unruh nor Rumford Act in so many words. Instead, it announced the constitutional right of any person to decline to sell or lease his real property to anyone to whom he did not desire to sell or lease. Unruh and Rumford were thereby pro tanto repealed. But the section struck more deeply and more widely. Private discriminations in housing were now not only free from Rumford and Unruh but they also enjoyed a far different status than was true before the passage of those statutes. The right to discriminate, including the right to discriminate on racial grounds, was now embodied in the State's basic charter, immune from legislative, executive, or judicial regulation at any level of the state government. Those practicing racial discriminations need no longer rely solely on their personal choice. They could now invoke express constitutional authority, free from censure or interference of any kind from official sources. . . . [a]nd other legal entities, as well as their agents and representatives, could now discriminate with respect to their residential real

---

[1] Cal. Civ. Code §§ 51 and 52 provide in part as follows:

"All persons within the jurisdiction of this State are free and equal, and no matter what their race, color, religion, ancestry, or national origin are entitled to the full and equal accommodations, advantages, facilities, privileges, or services in all business establishments of every kind whatsoever. . . .

"Whoever denies, or who aids, or incites such denial, or whoever makes any discrimination, distinction or restriction on account of color, race, religion, ancestry, or national origin, contrary to the provisions of Section 51 of this code, is liable for each and every such offense for the actual damages, and two hundred fifty dollars ($250) in addition thereto, suffered by any person denied the rights provided in Section 51 of this code."

property, which is defined as any interest in real property of any kind or quality, "irrespective of how obtained or financed," and seemingly irrespective of the relationship of the State to such interests in real property. Only the State is excluded with respect to property owned by it.

This Court has never attempted the "impossible task" of formulating an infallible test for determining whether the State "in any of its manifestations" has become significantly involved in private discriminations. "Only by sifting facts and weighing circumstances" on a case-by-case basis can a "nonobvious involvement of the State in private conduct be attributed its true significance." Burton v. Wilmington Parking Authority, 365 U.S. 715, 722. Here the California court, armed as it was with the knowledge of the facts and circumstances concerning the passage and potential impact of § 26, and familiar with the milieu in which that provision would operate, has determined that the provision would involve the State in private racial discriminations to an unconstitutional degree. We accept this holding of the California court.

The assessment of § 26 by the California court is similar to what this Court has done in appraising state statutes or other official actions in other contexts. In McCabe v. Atchison, Topeka & Santa Fe R. Co., 235 U.S. 151, the Court dealt with a statute which, as construed by the Court, authorized carriers to provide cars for white persons but not for Negroes. Though dismissal of the complaint on a procedural ground was affirmed, the Court made it clear that such a statute was invalid under the Fourteenth Amendment because a carrier refusing equal service to Negroes would be "acting in the matter under the authority of a state law." This was nothing less than considering a permissive state statute as an authorization to discriminate and as sufficient state action to violate the Fourteenth Amendment in the context of that case. . . .

In Peterson v. City of Greenville, 373 U.S. 244, and in Robinson v. Florida, 378 U.S. 153, the Court dealt with state statutes or regulations requiring, at least in some respects, segregation in facilities and services in restaurants. These official provisions, although obviously unconstitutional and unenforceable, were deemed in themselves sufficient to disentitle the State to punish, as trespassers, Negroes who had been refused service in the restaurants. In neither case was any proof required that the restaurant owner had actually been influenced by the state statute or regulation. Finally in Lombard v. Louisiana, 373 U.S. 267, the Court interpreted public statements by New Orleans city officials as announcing that the city would not permit Negroes to seek desegregated service in restaurants. Because the statements were deemed to have as much coercive potential as the ordinance in the Peterson case, the Court treated the city as though it had actually adopted an ordinance forbidding desegregated service in public restaurants.

None of these cases squarely controls the case we now have before us. But they do illustrate the range of situations in which discriminatory state action has been identified. They do exemplify the necessity for a court to assess the potential impact of official action in determining whether the State has significantly involved itself with invidious discriminations. Here we are dealing with a provision which does not just repeal an existing law forbidding private racial discriminations. Section 26 was intended to authorize, and does authorize, racial discrimination in the housing market. The right to discriminate is now one of the basic policies of the State. The California Supreme Court believes that the section will significantly encourage and involve the State in private discriminations. We have been presented with no persuasive considerations indicating that these judgments should be overturned.

Affirmed.

[A concurring opinion by JUSTICE DOUGLAS is omitted.]

MR. JUSTICE HARLAN, whom MR. JUSTICE BLACK, MR. JUSTICE CLARK, and MR. JUSTICE STEWART join, dissenting. I consider that this decision, which cuts deeply into state political processes, is supported neither by anything "found" by the Supreme Court of California nor by any of our past cases decided under the Fourteenth Amendment. In my view today's holding, salutary as its result may appear at first blush, may in the long run actually serve to handicap progress in the extremely difficult field of racial concerns. I must respectfully dissent. . . .

In the case at hand California, acting through the initiative and referendum, has decided to remain "neutral" in the realm of private discrimination affecting the sale or rental of private residential property; in such transactions private owners are now free to act in a discriminatory manner previously forbidden to them. In short, all that has happened is that California has effected a pro tanto repeal of its prior statutes forbidding private discrimination. This runs no more afoul of the Fourteenth Amendment than would have California's failure to pass any such antidiscrimination statutes in the first instance. The fact that such repeal was also accompanied by a constitutional prohibition against future enactment of such laws by the California Legislature cannot well be thought to affect, from a federal constitutional standpoint, the validity of what California has done. The Fourteenth Amendment does not reach such state constitutional action any more than it does a simple legislative repeal of legislation forbidding private discrimination. . . .

The Court attempts to fit §26 within the coverage of the Equal Protection Clause by characterizing it as in effect an affirmative call to residents of California to discriminate. The main difficulty with this viewpoint is that it depends upon a characterization of §26 that cannot fairly be made. The provision is neutral on its face, and it is only by in effect asserting that this requirement of passive official neutrality is camouflage that the Court is able to reach its conclusion. . . .

A moment of thought will reveal the far-reaching possibilities of the Court's new doctrine, which I am sure the Court does not intend. Every act of private discrimination is either forbidden by state law or permitted by it. There can be little doubt that such permissiveness — whether by express constitutional or statutory provision, or implicit in the common law — to some extent "encourages" those who wish to discriminate to do so. Under this theory "state action" in the form of laws that do nothing more than passively permit private discrimination could be said to tinge all private discrimination with the taint of unconstitutional state encouragement. . . .

The lines that have been and must be drawn in this area, fraught as it is with human sensibilities and frailties of whatever race or creed, are difficult ones. The drawing of them requires understanding, patience, and compromise, and is best done by legislatures rather than by courts. . . . Here the electorate itself overwhelmingly wishes to overrule and check its own legislature on a matter left open by the Federal Constitution. By refusing to accept the decision of the people of California, and by contriving a new and ill-defined constitutional concept to allow federal judicial interference, I think the Court has taken to itself powers and responsibilities left elsewhere by the Constitution. . . .

NOTE **The UCC and State Action**

Section 9-503 of the Uniform Commercial Code provides that a secured party may use self-help to repossess collateral upon default. It does not require that the party holding the collateral be given prior notice of the repossession or afforded an opportunity to be heard. Is a contract between private parties drafted pursuant to this provision subject to the requirements of procedural due process? On this threshold question, Adams v. Engley, 338 F. Supp. 614 (S.D. Cal. 1972), relied upon Reitman in finding that the authorization of self-help repossession by the UCC makes that conduct state action. Such authorization, the court concluded, "induced" the secured party to include self-help repossession in the contract. This issue provoked a storm of litigation. Compare, e.g., Kirksey v. Theilig, 351 F. Supp. 727 (D. Colo. 1972). See Burke & Reber, State Action, Congressional Power and Creditors' Rights: An Essay on the Fourteenth Amendment, 47 S. Cal. L. Rev. 1 (Part III) (1973).

Reviewing courts, however, have not deemed UCC authorization to be sufficient state involvement. Unlike the change of the law in Reitman, the reversing court said in Adams v. Southern California First National Bank, 492 F.2d 324, 332 (9th Cir. 1973), the UCC did not reverse prior law, "but merely codified existing law for the most part." As another court noted, Shirley v. State National Bank of Connecticut, 493 F.2d 739, 742 n.2 (2d Cir. 1974): "The right of a holder of a conditional sales contract to exercise self-help repossession had general recognition at common law. [Citations omitted.] The remedy existed even absent a contractual provision granting the right."

The prior case law in some areas, however, in Mississippi, for example, James v. Pinnix, 495 F.2d 206 (5th Cir. 1974), did not allow self-help repossession without an express agreement. The UCC, in contrast, allows self-help repossession "unless otherwise agreed." Can Reitman still be distinguished here?

As a paradigm of statutory authorization as state action, consider International Assn. of Machinists v. Street, infra page 1239, where the Court assumed, virtually without discussion, that the First Amendment applied to a labor union that was permitted by federal law to enter a union shop agreement and was able, thereby, to compel all employees to pay dues. Suppose permission came from a state statute, or common law.

NOTE Sequels to Reitman v. Mulkey

In Hunter v. Erickson, 393 U.S. 385 (1969), the Court invalidated as a deprivation of equal protection an amendment to the city charter of Akron, Ohio, which prevented the city council "from implementing any ordinance dealing with racial, religious, or ancestral discrimination in housing without the approval [by referendum] of a majority of the voters of [the city]." The Court noted that its holding did not mean that "mere repeal of an existing ordinance violates the Fourteenth Amendment":

"By adding § 137 to its Charter the City of Akron, which unquestionably wields state power, not only suspended the operation of the existing ordinance forbidding housing discrimination, but required the approval of the electors before any future ordinance could take effect. . . . The Akron Charter obviously made it substantially more difficult to secure enactment of ordinances subject to § 137."

In James v. Valtierra, 402 U.S. 137 (1971), however, the Court sustained an article of the California Constitution that required approval at a local election for development of state low-rent housing. The state constitution did not require approval at a local election for other types of public housing. Justice Black for the Court argued that, unlike Hunter, the article here did not rest on racial distinctions and that, moreover, "the record here would not support any claim that a law seemingly neutral on its face is in fact aimed at a racial minority." Justices Blackmun and Brennan joined in a dissent by Justice Marshall. Justice Douglas did not participate.

Section F. LIABILITY UNDER THE CIVIL RIGHTS STATUTES

Screws v. United States 325 U.S. 91, 65 S. Ct. 1031, 89 L. Ed. 1495 (1945)

MR. JUSTICE DOUGLAS announced the judgment of the Court and delivered the following opinion, in which the CHIEF JUSTICE, MR. JUSTICE BLACK and MR. JUSTICE REED concur.

This case involves a shocking and revolting episode in law enforcement. Petitioner Screws was sheriff of Baker County, Georgia. He enlisted the assistance of petitioner Jones, a policeman, and petitioner Kelly, a special deputy, in arresting Robert Hall, a citizen of the United States and of Georgia. The arrest was made late at night at Hall's home on a warrant charging Hall with theft of a tire. Hall, a young negro about thirty years of age, was handcuffed and taken by car to the court house. As Hall alighted from the car at the court-house square, the three petitioners began beating him with their fists and with a solid-bar blackjack about eight inches long and weighing two pounds. They claimed Hall had reached for a gun and had used insulting language as he alighted from the car. But after Hall, still handcuffed, had been knocked to the ground they continued to beat him from fifteen to thirty minutes until he was unconscious. Hall was then dragged feet first through the court-house yard into the jail and thrown upon the floor dying. An ambulance was called and Hall was removed to a hospital where he died within the hour and without regaining consciousness. There was evidence that Screws held a grudge against Hall and had threatened to "get" him.

An indictment was returned against petitioners — one count charging a violation of §20 of the Criminal Code, 18 U.S.C. §52 and another charging a conspiracy to violate §20 contrary to §37 of the Criminal Code, 18 U.S.C. §88. Sec. 20 provides:

"Whoever, under color of any law, statute, ordinance, regulation, or custom, willfully subjects, or causes to be subjected, any inhabitant of any State, Territory, or District to the deprivation of any rights, privileges, or immunities secured or protected by the Constitution and laws of the United States, or to different punishments, pains, or penalties, on account of such inhabitant being an alien, or by reason of his color, or race, than are prescribed for the punishment of citizens, shall be fined not more than $1,000, or imprisoned not more than one year, or both." The indictment charged that petitioners, acting under color of the laws of Georgia, "willfully" caused Hall to be deprived of "rights, privileges, or immunities secured or protected" to him by the Fourteenth Amendment — the right not to be deprived of life without due process of law; the right to be tried, upon the charge on which he was arrested, by due process of law and if found guilty to be punished in accordance with the laws of Georgia; . . . A like charge was made in the conspiracy count.

The case was tried to a jury. The court charged the jury that due process of law gave one charged with a crime the right to be tried by a jury and sentenced by a court. On the question of intent it charged that ". . . if these defendants, without its being necessary to make the arrest effectual or necessary to their own personal protection, beat this man, assaulted him or killed him while he was under arrest, then they would be acting illegally under color of law, as stated by this statute, and would be depriving the prisoner of certain constitutional rights guaranteed to him by the Constitution of the United States and consented to by the State of Georgia."

The jury returned a verdict of guilty and a fine and imprisonment on each count was imposed. The Circuit Court of Appeals affirmed the judgment of conviction, one judge dissenting. 140 F.2d 662. The case is here on a petition for a writ of certiorari which we granted because of the importance in the administration of the criminal laws of the questions presented.

I

We are met at the outset with the claim that §20 is unconstitutional, insofar as it makes criminal acts in violation of the due process clause of the Fourteenth Amendment. The argument runs as follows: It is true that this Act as construed in United States v. Classic, 313 U.S. 299, 328, was upheld in its application to certain ballot box frauds committed by state officials. But in that case the constitutional rights protected were the rights to vote specifically guaranteed by Art. I, §2 and §4 of the Constitution. Here there is no ascertainable standard of guilt. There have been conflicting views in the Court as to the proper construction of the due process clause. The majority have quite consistently construed it

Section F. Liability under the Civil Rights Statutes 843

in broad general terms. Thus it was stated in Twining v. New Jersey, 211 U.S. 78, 101, that due process requires that "no change in ancient procedure can be made which disregards those fundamental principles, to be ascertained from time to time by judicial action, which have relation to process of law and protect the citizen in his private right, and guard him against the arbitrary action of government." . . .

It is said that the Act must be read as if it contained those broad and fluid definitions of due process and that if it is so read it provides no ascertainable standard of guilt. It is pointed out that in United States v. Cohen Grocery Co., 255 U.S. 81, 89, an Act of Congress was struck down, the enforcement of which would have been "the exact equivalent of an effort to carry out a statute which in terms merely penalized and punished all acts detrimental to the public interest when unjust and unreasonable in the estimation of the court and jury." In that case the act declared criminal was the making of "any unjust or unreasonble rate or charge in handling or dealing in or with any necessaries." 255 U.S. p. 86. The Act contained no definition of an "unjust or unreasonable rate" nor did it refer to any source where the measure of "unjust or unreasonable" could be ascertained. In the instant case the decisions of the courts are, to be sure, a source of reference for ascertaining the specific content of the concept of due process. But even so the Act would incorporate by reference a large body of changing and uncertain law. That law is not always reducible to specific rules, is expressible only in general terms, and turns many times on the facts of a particular case. Accordingly, it is argued that such a body of legal principles lacks the basic specificity necessary for criminal statutes under our system of government. Congress did not define what it desired to punish but referred the citizen to a comprehensive law library in order to ascertain what acts were prohibited. . . .

The serious character of that challenge to the constitutionality of the Act is emphasized if the customary standard of guilt for statutory crimes is taken. As we shall see, specific intent is at times required. Holmes, The Common Law, pp. 66 et seq. But the general rule was stated in Ellis v. United States, 206 U.S. 246, 257, as follows: "If a man intentionally adopts certain conduct in certain circumstances known to him, and that conduct is forbidden by the law under those circumstances, he intentionally breaks the law in the only sense in which the law ever considers intent." . . . Under that test a local law enforcement officer violates §20 and commits a federal offense for which he can be sent to the penitentiary if he does an act which some court later holds deprives a person of due process of law. And he is a criminal though his motive was pure and though his purpose was unrelated to the disregard of any constitutional guarantee. The treacherous ground on which state officials — police, prosecutors, legislators, and judges — would walk is indicated by the character and closeness of decisions of this Court interpreting the due process clause of the Fourteenth Amendment. A confession obtained by too long questioning (Ashcraft v. Tennessee, 322 U.S. 143); the enforcement of an ordinance requiring a license for the distribution of religious literature (Murdock v. Pennsylvania, 319 U.S. 105); the denial of the assistance of counsel in certain types of cases (Cf. Powell v. Alabama, 287 U.S. 45 with Betts v. Brady [316 U.S. 455]); the enforcement of certain types of anti-picketing statutes (Thornhill v. Alabama, 310 U.S. 88); the enforcement of state price control laws (Olsen v. Nebraska, 313 U.S. 236); the requirement that public school children salute the flag (Board of Education v. Barnette, 319 U.S. 624) — these are illustrative of the kind of state action [2] which might or might not be caught in the broad reaches of §20 dependent on the prevailing view of the Court as constituted when the case arose. Those who enforced local law today might not know for many months (and meanwhile could not find out) whether what they did deprived some one of due process of law. The enforcement of a criminal statute so construed would indeed cast law enforcement agencies loose at their own risk on a vast uncharted sea.

[2] See Cong. Globe, 41st Cong., 2d Sess., pp. 3807-3808, 3881. Flack, The Adoption of the Fourteenth nance, regulation, or custom." Comparable uncertainties will exist in the application of the due process clause of the Fifth Amendment.

If such a construction is not necessary, it should be avoided. This Court has consistently favored that interpretation of legislation which supports its constitutionality. Ashwander v. Tennessee Valley Authority, 297 U.S. 288, 348; Labor Board v. Jones & Laughlin Steel Corp., 301 U.S. 1, 30; Anniston Mfg. Co. v. Davis, 301 U.S. 337, 351-352. That reason is impelling here so that if at all possible § 20 may be allowed to serve its great purpose — the protection of the individual in his civil liberties.

Sec. 20 was enacted to enforce the Fourteenth Amendment.[3] It derives from § 2 of the Civil Rights Act of April 9, 1866. 14 Stat. 27. Senator Trumbull, chairman of the Senate Judiciary Committee which reported the bill, stated that its purpose was "to protect all persons in the United States in their civil rights, and furnish the means of their vindication." Cong. Globe, 39th Cong., 1st Sess., p. 211. In origin it was an antidiscrimination measure (as its language indicated), framed to protect Negroes in their newly won rights. See Flack, The Adoption of the Fourteenth Amendment (1908), p. 21. It was amended by § 17 of the Act of May 31, 1870, 16 Stat. 144, and made applicable to "any inhabitant of any State or Territory." The prohibition against the "deprivation of any rights, privileges, or immunities, secured or protected by the Constitution and laws of the United States" was introduced by the revisers in 1874. R.S. § 5510. Those words were taken over from § 1 of the Act of April 20, 1871, 17 Stat. 13 (the so-called Ku-Klux Act) which provided civil suits for redress of such wrongs. See Cong. Rec., 43d Cong., 1st Sess., p. 828. The 1874 revision was applicable to any person who under color of law, etc., "subjects, or causes to be subjected" any inhabitant to the deprivation of any rights, etc. The requirement for a "willful" violation was introduced by the draftsmen of the Criminal Code of 1909. Act of March 4, 1909, 35 Stat. 1092. And we are told "willfully" was added to § 20 in order to make the section "less severe." 43 Cong. Rec., 60th Cong., 2d Sess., p. 3599.

We hesitate to say that when Congress sought to enforce the Fourteenth Amendment in this fashion it did a vain thing. We hesitate to conclude that for 80 years this effort of Congress, renewed several times, to protect the important rights of the individual guaranteed by the Fourteenth Amendment has been an idle gesture. . . . Only if no construction can save the Act from this claim of unconstitutionality are we willing to reach that result. We do not reach it, for we are of the view that if § 20 is confined more narrowly than the lower courts confined it, it can be preserved as one of the sanctions to the great rights which the Fourteenth Amendment was designed to secure.

II

We recently pointed out that "willful" is a word "of many meanings, its construction often being influenced by its context." Spies v. United States, 317 U.S. 492, 497. At times, as the Court held in United States v. Murdock, 290 U.S. 389, 394, the word denotes an act which is intentional rather than accidental. And see United States v. Illinois Central R. Co., 303 U.S. 239. But "when used in a criminal statute it generally means an act done with a bad purpose." Id., p. 394. . . . In that event something more is required than the doing of the act proscribed by the statute. Cf. United States v. Balint, 258 U.S. 250. An evil motive to accomplish that which the statute condemns becomes a constituent element of the crime. Spurr v. United States [174 U.S. 728], p. 734; United States v. Murdock, supra, p. 395. And that issue must be submitted to the jury under appropriate instructions. United States v. Ragen, 314 U.S. 513, 524.

An analysis of the cases in which "willfully" has been held to connote more than an act

---

[3] See Cong. Globe, 41st Cong., 2d Sess., pp. 3807-3808, 3881. Flack, The Adoption of the Fourteenth Amendment (1908), pp. 19-54, 219, 223, 227; Hague v. C.I.O., 307 U.S. 496, 510.

Section F. Liability under the Civil Rights Statutes

which is voluntary or intentional would not prove helpful as each turns on its own peculiar facts. Those cases, however, make clear that if we construe "willfully" in §20 as connoting a purpose to deprive a person of a specific constitutional right, we would introduce no innovation. The Court, indeed, has recognized that the requirement of a specific intent to do a prohibited act may avoid those consequences to the accused which may otherwise render a vague or indefinite statute invalid. The constitutional vice in such a statute is the essential injustice to the accused of placing him on trial for an offense, the nature of which the statute does not define and hence of which it gives no warning. See United States v. Cohen Grocery Co., supra. But where the punishment imposed is only for an act knowingly done with the purpose of doing that which the statute prohibits, the accused cannot be said to suffer from lack of warning or knowledge that the act which he does is a violation of law. The requirement that the act must be willful or purposeful may not render certain, for all purposes, a statutory definition of the crime which is in some respects uncertain. But it does relieve the statute of the objection that it punishes without warning an offense of which the accused was unaware. That was pointed out by Mr. Justice Brandeis speaking for the Court in Omaechevarria v. Idaho, 246 U.S. 343. An Idaho statute made it a misdemeanor to graze sheep "upon any range usually occupied by any cattle grower." The argument was that the statute was void for indefiniteness because it failed to provide for the ascertainment of boundaries of a "range" or for determining what length of time was necessary to make a prior occupation a "usual" one. The Court ruled that "any danger to sheepmen which might otherwise arise from indefiniteness, is removed by §6314 of Revised Codes, which provides that: 'In every crime or public offense there must exist a union, or joint operation, of act and intent, or criminal negligence.'" Id., p. 348. A similar ruling was made in Hygrade Provision Co. v. Sherman, 266 U.S. 497. The charge was that a criminal statute which regulated the sale of "kosher" meat or products "sanctioned by the orthodox Hebrew religious requirements" was unconstitutional for want of any ascertainable standard of guilt. The Court speaking through Mr. Justice Sutherland stated, ". . . since the statutes require a specific intent to defraud in order to encounter their prohibitions, the hazard of prosecution which appellants fear loses whatever substantial foundation it might have in the absence of such a requirement." 266 U.S. pp. 502-503. . . .

Moreover, the history of §20 affords some support for that narrower construction. As we have seen, the word "willfully" was not added to the Act until 1909. Prior to that time it may be that Congress intended that he who deprived a person of any right protected by the Constitution should be liable without more. . . . But as we have seen, the word "willfully" was added to make the section "less severe." We think the inference is permissible that its severity was to be lessened by making it applicable only where the requisite bad purpose was present, thus requiring specific intent not only where discrimination is claimed but in other situations as well. We repeat that the presence of a bad purpose or evil intent alone may not be sufficient. We do say that a requirement of a specific intent to deprive a person of a federal right made definite by decision or other rule of law saves the Act from any charge of unconstitutionality on the grounds of vagueness.

Once the section is given that construction, we think that the claim that the section lacks an ascertainable standard of guilt must fail. The constitutional requirement that a criminal statute be definite serves a high function. It gives a person acting with reference to the statute fair warning that his conduct is within its prohibition. This requirement is met when a statute prohibits only "willful" acts in the sense we have explained. One who does act with such specific intent is aware that what he does is precisely that which the statute forbids. He is under no necessity of guessing whether the statute applies to him (see Connally v. General Construction Co., 269 U.S. 385) for he either knows or acts in reckless disregard of its prohibition of the deprivation of a defined constitutional or other federal right. See Gorin v. United States, 312 U.S. 19, 27-28. Nor is such an act beyond the understanding and comprehension of juries summoned to pass on them. The Act would then not become a trap for law enforcement agencies acting in good faith. . . .

It is said, however, that this construction of the Act will not save it from the infirmity of vagueness since neither a law enforcement official nor a trial judge can know with sufficient definiteness the range of rights that are constitutional. But that criticism is wide of the mark. For the specific intent required by the Act is an intent to deprive a person of a right which has been made specific either by the express terms of the Constitution or laws of the United States or by decisions interpreting them. Take the case of a local officer who persists in enforcing a type of ordinance which the Court has held invalid as violative of the guarantees of free speech or freedom of worship. Or a local official continues to select juries in a manner which flies in the teeth of decisions of the Court. If those acts are done willfully, how can the officer possibly claim that he had no fair warning that his acts were prohibited by the statute? He violates the statute not merely because he has a bad purpose but because he acts in defiance of announced rules of law. He who defies a decision interpreting the Constitution knows precisely what he is doing. If sane, he hardly may be heard to say that he knew not what he did. Of course, willful conduct cannot make definite that which is undefined. But willful violators of constitutional requirements, which have been defined, certainly are in no position to say that they had no adequate advance notice that they would be visited with punishment. When they act willfully in the sense in which we use the word, they act in open defiance or in reckless disregard of a constitutional requirement which has been made specific and definite. When they are convicted for so acting, they are not punished for violating an unknowable something.

The Act so construed has a narrower range in all its applications than if it were interpreted in the manner urged by the government. But the only other alternative, if we are to avoid grave constitutional questions, is to construe it as applicable only to those acts which are clearly marked by the specific provisions of the Constitution as deprivations of constitutional rights, privileges, or immunities, and which are knowingly done within the rule of Ellis v. United States, supra. But as we have said, that course would mean that all protection for violations of due process of law would drop out of the Act. We take the course which makes it possible to preserve the entire Act and save all parts of it from constitutional challenge. If Congress desires to give the Act wider scope, it may find ways of doing so. . . .

United States v. Classic, supra, met the test we suggest. In that case we were dealing merely with the validity of an indictment, not with instructions to the jury. The indictment was sufficient since it charged a willful failure and refusal of the defendant election officials to count the votes cast, by their alteration of the ballots and by their false certification of the number of votes cast for the respective candidates. 313 U.S. pp. 308-309. The right so to vote is guaranteed by Art. I, §2 and §4 of the Constitution. Such a charge is adequate since he who alters ballots or without legal justification destroys them would be acting willfully in the sense in which §20 uses the term. The fact that the defendants may not have been thinking in constitutional terms is not material where their aim was not to enforce local law but to deprive a citizen of a right and that right was protected by the Constitution. When they so act they at least act in reckless disregard of constitutional prohibitions or guarantees. Likewise, it is plain that basic to the concept of due process of law in a criminal case is a trial — a trial in a court of law, not a "trial by ordeal." Brown v. Mississippi, 297 U.S. 278, 285. It could hardly be doubted that they who "under color of any law, statute, ordinance, regulation, or custom" act with that evil motive violate §20. Those who decide to take the law into their own hands and act as prosecutor, jury, judge, and executioner plainly act to deprive a prisoner of the trial which due process of law guarantees him. And such a purpose need not be expressed; it may at times be reasonably inferred from all the circumstances attendant on the act. See Tot v. United States, 319 U.S. 463.

The difficulty here is that this question of intent was not submitted to the jury with the proper instructions. The court charged that petitioners acted illegally if they applied more force than was necessary to make the arrest effectual or to protect themselves from the prisoner's alleged assault. But in view of our construction of the word "willfully" the jury should have been further instructed that it was not sufficient that petitioners had a generally bad purpose. To convict it was necessary for them to find that petitioners had the purpose to deprive the prisoner of a constitutional right, e.g. the right to be tried by a court rather than by ordeal. And in determining whether that requisite bad purpose was present the jury would be entitled to consider all the attendant circumstances — the malice of petitioners, the weapons used in the assault, its character and duration, the provocation, if any, and the like.

It is true that no exception was taken to the trial court's charge. Normally we would under those circumstances not take note of the error. See Johnson v. United States, 318 U.S. 189, 200. But there are exceptions to that rule. United States v. Atkinson, 297 U.S. 157, 160; Clyatt v. United States, 197 U.S. 207, 221-222. And where the error is so fundamental as not to submit to the jury the essential ingredients of the only offense on which the conviction could rest, we think it is necessary to take note of it on our own motion. Even those guilty of the most heinous offenses are entitled to a fair trial. Whatever the degree of guilt, those charged with a federal crime are entitled to be tried by the standards of guilt which Congress has prescribed.

III

It is said, however, that petitioners did not act "under color of any law" within the meaning of §20 of the Criminal Code. We disagree. We are of the view that petitioners acted under "color" of law in making the arrest of Robert Hall and in assaulting him. They were officers of the law who made the arrest. . . .

[The Court cited Ex parte Virginia, among others, for the proposition that "under 'color' of law" means under 'pretense' of law."] Thus acts of officers in the ambit of their personal pursuits are plainly excluded. Acts of officers who undertake to perform their official duties are included whether they hew to the line of their authority or overstep it. If, as suggested, the statute was designed to embrace only action which the State in fact authorized, the words "under color of any law" were hardly apt words to express the idea. . . .

But beyond that is the problem of stare decisis. The construction given §20 in the Classic case formulated a rule of law which has become the basis of federal enforcement in this important field. The rule adopted in that case was formulated after mature consideration. It should be good for more than one day only. . . . We add only to the instability and uncertainty of the law if we revise the meaning of §20 to meet the exigencies of each case coming before us.

Since there must be a new trial, the judgment below is

Reversed.

Mr. Justice Rutledge, concurring in the result.

For the compelling reason stated at the end of this opinion I concur in reversing the judgment and remanding the cause for further proceedings. But for that reason, my views would require that my vote be cast to affirm the judgment, for the reasons stated by Mr. Justice Murphy and others I feel forced, in the peculiar situation, to state. . . .

[S]tatutory specificity has two purposes, to give due notice that an act has been made criminal before it is done and to inform one accused of the nature of the offense charged, so that he may adequately prepare and make his defense. More than this certainly the Constitution does not require. Cf. Amend. VI. All difficulty on the latter score vanishes, under §20, with the indictment's particularization of the rights infringed and the acts infringing them. If it is not sufficient in either respect, in these as in other cases the motion to quash or one for a bill of particulars is at the defendant's disposal. The decided cases demonstrate that accused persons have had little or no difficulty to ascertain the rights they have been charged with transgressing or the acts of transgression. So it was with the defendants in this case. They were not puzzled to know for what they were indicted, as their proof and their defense upon the law conclusively show. They simply misconceived that the victim had no federal rights and that what they had done was not a crime within the federal power to penalize. That kind of error relieves no one from penalty. . . .

Furthermore, the argument of vagueness, to warn men of their conduct, ignores the nature of the criminal act itself and the notice necessarily given from this. Section 20 strikes only at abuse of official functions by state officers. It does not reach out for crimes done by men in general. Not murder per se, but murder by state officers in the course of official conduct and done with the aid of state power, is outlawed. These facts, inherent in the crime, give all the warning constitutionally required. For one, so situated, who goes so far in misconduct can have no excuse of innocence or ignorance. . . .

Accordingly, I would affirm the judgment.

My convictions are as I have stated them. Were it possible for me to adhere to them in my vote, and for the Court at the same time to dispose of the cause, I would act accordingly. The Court, however, is divided in opinion. If each member accords his vote to his belief, the case cannot have disposition. Stalemate should not prevail for any reason, however compelling, in a criminal cause or, if avoidable, in any other. My views concerning appropriate disposition are more nearly in accord with those stated by MR. JUSTICE DOUGLAS, in which three other members of the Court concur, than they are with the views of my dissenting brethren who favor outright reversal. Accordingly, in order that disposition may be made of this case, my vote has been cast to reverse the decision of the Court of Appeals and remand the cause to the District Court for further proceedings in accordance with the disposition required by the opinion of MR. JUSTICE DOUGLAS.

MR. JUSTICE MURPHY, dissenting.

I dissent. Robert Hall, a Negro citizen, has been deprived not only of the right to be tried by a court rather than by ordeal. He has been deprived of the right to life itself. That right belonged to him not because he was a Negro or a member of any particular race or creed. That right was his because he was an American citizen, because he was a human being. As such, he was entitled to all the respect and fair treatment that befits the dignity of man, a dignity that is recognized and guaranteed by the Constitution. Yet not even the semblance of due process has been accorded him. He has been cruelly and unjustifiably beaten to death by local police officers acting under color of authority derived from the state. It is difficult to believe that such an obvious and necessary right is indefinitely guaranteed by the Constitution or is foreign to the knowledge of local police officers so as to cast any reasonable doubt on the conviction under § 20 of the Criminal Code of the perpetrators of this "shocking and revolting episode in law enforcement." . . .

It is an illusion to say that the real issue in this case is the alleged failure of § 20 fully to warn the state officials that their actions were illegal. The Constitution, § 20 and their own consciences told them that. They knew that they lacked any mandate or authority to take human life unnecessarily or without due process of law in the course of their duties. They knew that their excessive and abusive use of authority would only subvert the ends of justice. The significant question, rather, is whether law enforcement officers and those entrusted with authority shall be allowed to violate with impunity the clear constitutional rights of the inarticulate and the friendless. Too often unpopular minorities, such as Negroes, are unable to find effective refuge from the cruelties of bigoted and ruthless authority. States are undoubtedly capable of punishing their officers who commit such outrages. But where, as here, the states are unwilling for some reason to prosecute such crimes the federal government must step in unless constitutional guarantees are to become atrophied.

This necessary intervention, however, will be futile if courts disregard reality and misuse the principle that criminal statutes must be clear and definite. Here state officers have violated with reckless abandon a plain constitutional right of an American citizen. The two courts below have found and the record demonstrates that the trial was fair and the evidence of guilt clear. And §20 unmistakably outlaws such actions by state officers. We should therefore affirm the judgment.

MR. JUSTICE ROBERTS, MR. JUSTICE FRANKFURTER and MR. JUSTICE JACKSON, dissenting. . . .

Of course the petitioners are punishable. The only issue is whether Georgia alone has the power and duty to punish, or whether this patently local crime can be made the basis of a federal prosecution. The practical question is whether the States should be relieved from responsibility to bring their law officers to book for homicide, by allowing prosecutions in the federal courts for a relatively minor offense carrying a short sentence. The legal question is whether, for the purpose of accomplishing this relaxation of State responsibility, hitherto settled principles for the protection of civil liberties shall be bent and tortured. . . .

[Justice Roberts concluded that congressional power under §5 of the Fourteenth Amendment cannot reach a state officer whose behavior was neither authorized nor commanded by the state.[o] Moreover, the dissent argued, Congress did not mean, in any event, to apply the full extent of its power in §20.] . . .

This intrinsic vagueness of the terms of §20 surely cannot be removed by making the statute applicable only where the defendant has the "requisite bad purpose." Does that not amount to saying that the black heart of the defendant enables him to know what are the constitutional rights deprivation of which the statute forbids, although we as judges are not able to define their classes or their limits, or, at least, are not prepared to state what they are unless it be to say that §20 protects whatever rights the Constitution protects?

Under the construction proposed for §20, in order for a jury to convict, it would be necessary "to find that petitioners had the purpose to deprive the prisoner of a constitutional right, e.g., the right to be tried by a court rather than by ordeal." There is no question that Congress could provide for a penalty against deprivation by State officials "acting under color of any law" of "the right to be tried by a court rather than by ordeal." But we cannot restrict the problem raised by §20 to the validity of penalizing a deprivation of this specific constitutional right. We are dealing with the reach of the statute, for Congress has not particularized as the Court now particularizes. Such transforming interpolation is not interpretation. And that is recognized by the sentence just quoted, namely, that the jury in order to convict under §20 must find that an accused "had the purpose to deprive" another "of a constitutional right," giving *this* specific constitutional right as "e.g.," by way of illustration. Hence a judge would have to define to the jury what the constitutional rights are deprivation of which is prohibited by §20. If that is a legal question as to which the jury must take instruction from the court, at least the trial court must be possessed of the means of knowing with sufficient definiteness the range of "rights" that are "constitutional." The court can hardly be helped out in determining that legal question by leaving it to the jury to decide whether the act was "willfully" committed. . . .

It was settled early in our history that prosecutions in the federal courts could not be founded on any undefined body of so-called common law. United States v. Hudson, 7 Cranch 32; United States v. Gooding, 12 Wheat. 460. Federal prosecutions must be founded on delineation by Congress of what is made criminal. To base federal prosecutions on the shifting and indeterminate decisions of courts is to sanction prosecutions for crimes based on definitions made by courts. This is tantamount to creating a new body of federal criminal common law. . . .

---

[o] In a dissenting opinion in Monroe v. Pape, 365 U.S. 167 (1961), Mr. Justice Frankfurter urged once more that the concept of "color of law" in the Civil Rights statutes did not extend to conduct of public officers acting in violation of state law. The majority, however, held that a civil suit could be brought under §1983 of Title 42 against police officers who lawlessly deprived persons of their secured rights. — ED.

It is as novel as it is an inadmissible principle that a criminal statute of indefinite scope can be rendered definite by requiring that a person "willfully" commit what Congress has not defined but which, if Congress had defined, could constitutionally be outlawed. Of course Congress can prohibit the deprivation of enumerated constitutional rights. But if Congress makes it a crime to deprive another of any right protected by the Constitution — and that is what § 20 does — this Court cannot escape facing decisions as to what constitutional rights are covered by § 20 by saying that in any event, whatever they are, they must be taken away "willfully." It has not been explained how all the considerations of unconstitutional vagueness which are laid bare in the early part of the Court's opinion evaporate by suggesting that what is otherwise too vaguely defined must be "willfully" committed. . . .

This case does not involve denying adequate *power* to Congress. There is no difficulty in passing effective legislation for the protection of civil rights against improper State action. What we are concerned with here is something basic in a democratic society, namely, the avoidance of the injustice of prohibiting conduct in terms so vague as to make the understanding of what is proscribed a guess-work too difficult for confident judgment even for the judges of the highest Court in the land. . . .

WILLIAMS v. UNITED STATES, 341 U.S. 97, 71 S. Ct. 576, 95 L. Ed. 774 (1951). Douglas, J.: "The question in this case is whether a special police officer who in his official capacity subjects a person suspected of crime to force and violence in order to obtain a confession may be prosecuted under § 20 of the Criminal Code, 18 U.S.C. (1946 ed.) § 52, now 18 U.S.C. § 242.

"Section 20 provides in pertinent part:

" 'Whoever, under color of any law, statute, ordinance, regulation, or custom, willfully subjects, or causes to be subjected, any inhabitant of any State, Territory, or District to the deprivation of any rights, privileges, or immunities secured or protected by the Constitution and laws of the United States . . . shall be fined not more than $1,000 or imprisoned not more than one year, or both.'

"The facts are these: The Lindsley Lumber Co. suffered numerous thefts and hired petitioner, who operated a detective agency, to ascertain the identity of the thieves. Petitioner held a special police officer's card issued by the City of Miami, Florida, and had taken an oath and qualified as a special police officer. Petitioner and others over a period of three days took four men to a paint shack on the company's premises and used brutal methods to obtain a confession from each of them. A rubber hose, a pistol, a blunt instrument, a sash cord and other implements were used in the project. One man was forced to look at a bright light for fifteen minutes; when he was blinded, he was repeatedly hit with a rubber hose and a sash cord and finally knocked to the floor. Another was knocked from a chair and hit in the stomach again and again. He was put back in the chair and the procedure was repeated. One was backed against the wall and jammed in the chest with a club. Each was beaten, threatened, and unmercifully punished for several hours until he confessed. One Ford, a policeman, was sent by his superior to lend authority to the proceedings. And petitioner, who committed the assaults, went about flashing his badge.

"The indictment charged among other things that petitioner acting under color of law used force to make each victim confess to his guilt and implicate others, and that the victims were denied the right to be tried by due process of law and if found guilty to be sentenced and punished in accordance with the laws of the state. Petitioner was found guilty by a jury under instructions which conformed with the rulings of the Court in Screws v. United States, 325 U.S. 91. The Court of Appeals affirmed. 179 F.2d 656."

What decision? Why?

United States v. Guest 383 U.S. 745, 86 S. Ct. 1170, 16 L. Ed. 2d 239 (1966)

Mr. Justice Stewart delivered the opinion of the Court.

The six defendants in this case were indicted by a United States grand jury in the Middle District of Georgia for criminal conspiracy in violation of 18 U.S.C. §241. . . . In five numbered paragraphs, the indictment alleged a single conspiracy by the defendants to deprive Negro citizens of the free exercise and enjoyment of several specified rights secured by the Constitution and laws of the United States.[1] The defendants moved to dismiss the indictment on the ground that it did not charge an offense under the laws of the United States. The District Court sustained the motion and dismissed the indictment as to all defendants and all numbered paragraphs of the indictment. 246 F. Supp. 475.

The United States appealed directly to this Court under the Criminal Appeals Act, 18 U.S.C. §373. We postponed decision of the question of our jurisdiction to the hearing on the merits. 381 U.S. 932. It is now apparent that this Court does not have jurisdiction to decide one of the issues sought to be raised on this direct appeal. As to the other issues, however, our appellate jurisdiction is clear, and for the reasons that follow, we reverse the judgment of the District Court. As in United States v. Price, 383 U.S. 787, decided today, we deal here with issues of statutory construction, not with issues of constitutional power.

---

[1] The indictment, filed on October 16, 1964, was as follows:

"The Grand Jury charges:

"Commencing on or about January 1, 1964, and continuing to the date of this indictment, Herbert Guest, James Spergeon Lackey, Cecil William Myers, Denver Willis Phillips, Joseph Howard Sims, and George Hampton Turner, did, within the Middle District of Georgia, Athens Division, conspire together, with each other, and with other persons to the Grand Jury unknown, to injure, oppress, threaten, and intimidate Negro citizens of the United States in the vicinity of Athens, Georgia, in the free exercise and enjoyment by said Negro citizens of the following rights and privileges secured to them by the Constitution and the laws of the United States:

"1. The right to the full and equal enjoyment of the goods, services, facilities, privileges, advantages, and accommodations of motion picture theaters, restaurants, and other places of public accommodation;

"2. The right to the equal utilization, without discrimination upon the basis of race, of public facilities in the vicinity of Athens, Georgia, owned, operated or managed by or on behalf of the State of Georgia or any subdivision thereof;

"3. The right to the full and equal use on the same terms as white citizens of the public streets and highways in the vicinity of Athens, Georgia;

"4. The right to travel freely to and from the State of Georgia and to use highway facilities and other instrumentalities of interstate commerce within the State of Georgia;

"5. Other rights exercised and enjoyed by white citizens in the vicinity of Athens, Georgia.

"It was a part of the plan and purpose of the conspiracy that its objects be achieved by various means, including the following:

"1. By shooting Negroes;

"2. By beating Negroes;

"3. By killing Negroes;

"4. By damaging and destroying property of Negroes;

"5. By pursuing Negroes in automobiles and threatening them with guns;

"6. By making telephone calls to Negroes to threaten their lives, property, and persons, and by making such threats in person;

"7. By going in disguise on the highway and on the premises of other persons;

"8. By causing the arrest of Negroes by means of false reports that such Negroes had committed criminal acts; and

"9. By burning crosses at night in public view.

"All in violation of Section 241, Title 18, United States Code."

The only additional indication in the record concerning the factual details of the conduct with which the defendants were charged is the statement of the District Court that: "It is common knowledge that two of the defendants, Sims and Myers, have already been prosecuted in the Superior Court of Madison County, Georgia for the murder of Lemuel A. Penn and by a jury found not guilty." 246 F. Supp. 475, 487.

I

The first numbered paragraph of the indictment, reflecting a portion of the language of §201(a) of the Civil Rights Act of 1964, 42 U.S.C. §2000a(a) (1964 ed.), alleged that the petitioners conspired to injure, oppress, threaten, and intimidate Negro citizens in the free exercise and enjoyment of: "The right to the full and equal enjoyment of the goods, services, facilities, privileges, advantages, and accommodations of motion picture theaters, restaurants, and other places of public accommodation." The District Court held that this paragraph of the indictment failed to state an offense against rights secured by the Constitution or laws of the United States. The court found a fatal flaw in the failure of the paragraph to include an allegation that the acts of the defendants were motivated by racial discrimination, an allegation the court thought essential to charge an interference with rights secured by Title II of the Civil Rights Act of 1964. The court went on to say that, in any event, 18 U.S.C. §241 is not an available sanction to protect rights secured by that title because §207(b) of the 1964 Act, 42 U.S.C. §2000a-6(b) (1964 ed.), specifies that the remedies provided in Title II itself are to be the exclusive means of enforcing the rights the title secures.

A direct appeal to this Court is available to the United States under the Criminal Appeals Act, 18 U.S.C. §3731, from "a decision or judgment . . . dismissing any indictment . . . or any count thereof, where such decision or judgment is based upon the . . . construction of the statute upon which the indictment . . . is founded." In the present case, however, the District Court's judgment as to the first paragraph of the indictment was based, at least alternatively, upon its determination that this paragraph was defective as a matter of pleading. Settled principles of review under the Criminal Appeals Act therefore preclude our review of the District Court's judgment on this branch of the indictment. . . .

It is hardly necessary to add that our ruling as to the Court's lack of jurisdiction now to review this aspect of the case implies no opinion whatsoever as to the correctness either of the District Court's appraisal of this paragraph of the indictment as a matter of pleading or of the court's view of the preclusive effect of §207(b) of the Civil Rights Act of 1964.

II

The second numbered paragraph of the indictment alleged that the defendants conspired to injure, oppress, threaten, and intimidate Negro citizens of the United States in the free exercise and enjoyment of: "The right to the equal utilization, without discrimination upon the basis of race, of public facilities in the vicinity of Athens, Georgia, owned, operated, or managed by or on behalf of the State of Georgia or any subdivision thereof."

Correctly characterizing this paragraph as embracing rights protected by the Equal Protection Clause of the Fourteenth Amendment, the District Court held as a matter of statutory construction that 18 U.S.C. §241 does not encompass any Fourteenth Amendment rights, and further held as a matter of constitutional law that "any broader construction of §241 . . . would render it void for indefiniteness." 246 F. Supp., at 486. In so holding, the District Court was in error, as our opinion in United States v. Price, 383 U.S. 787, decided today, makes abundantly clear. . . .

Unlike the indictment in Price, however, the indictment in the present case names no person alleged to have acted in any way under the color of state law. The argument is therefore made that, since there exist no Equal Protection Clause rights against wholly private action, the judgment of the District Court on this branch of the case must be affirmed. On its face, the argument is unexceptionable. The Equal Protection Clause speaks to the State or to those acting under the color of its authority.

In this connection, we emphasize that §241 by its clear language incorporates no more than the Equal Protection Clause itself; the statute does not purport to give substantive, as opposed to remedial, implementation to any rights secured by that Clause. Since we therefore deal here only with the bare terms of the Equal Protection Clause itself, nothing said in this opinion goes to the question of what kinds of other and broader legislation Congress might constitutionally enact under §5 of the Fourteenth Amendment to implement that Clause or any other provision of the Amendment.

It is a commonplace that rights under the Equal Protection Clause itself arise only where there has been involvement of the State or of one acting under the color of its authority. The Equal Protection Clause "does not . . . add anything to the rights which one citizen has under the Constitution against another." United States v. Cruikshank, 92 U.S. 542, 554-555. . . .

This is not to say, however, that the involvement of the State need be either exclusive or direct. In a variety of situations the Court has found state action of a nature sufficient to create rights under the Equal Protection Clause even though the participation of the State was peripheral, or its action was only one of several co-operative forces leading to the constitutional violations. See, e.g., Shelley v. Kraemer, 334 U.S. 1; Pennsylvania v. Board of Trusts, 353 U.S. 230; Burton v. Wilmington Parking Authority, 365 U.S. 715; Peterson v. City of Greenville, 373 U.S. 244; Lombard v. Louisiana, 373 U.S. 267; Griffin v. Maryland, 378 U.S. 130; Robinson v. Florida, 378 U.S. 163; Evans v. Newton [382 U.S. 296 (1966)].

This case, however, requires no determination of the threshold level that state action must attain in order to create rights under the Equal Protection Clause. This is so because, contrary to the argument of the litigants, the indictment in fact contains an express allegation of state involvement sufficient at least to require the denial of a motion to dismiss. One of the means of accomplishing the object of the conspiracy, according to the indictment, was "By causing the arrest of Negroes by means of false reports that such Negroes had committed criminal acts." In Bell v. Maryland, 378 U.S. 226, three members of the Court expressed the view that a private businessman's invocation of state police and judicial action to carry out his own policy of racial discrimination was sufficient to create Equal Protection Clause rights in those against whom the racial discrimination was directed. Three other members of the Court strongly disagreed with that view, and three expressed no opinion on the question. The allegation of the extent of official involvement in the present case is not clear. It may charge no more than cooperative private and state action similar to that involved in Bell, but it may go considerably further. For example, the allegation is broad enough to cover a charge of active connivance by agents of the State in the making of the "false reports," or other conduct amounting to official discrimination clearly sufficient to constitute denial of rights protected by the Equal Protection Clause. Although it is possible that a bill of particulars, or the proofs if the case goes to trial, would disclose no cooperative action of that kind by officials of the State, the allegation is enough to prevent dismissal of this branch of the indictment.

III

The fourth numbered paragraph of the indictment alleged that the defendants conspired to injure, oppress, threaten and intimidate Negro citizens of the United States in the free exercise and enjoyment of: "The right to travel freely to and from the State of Georgia and to use highway facilities and other instrumentalities of interstate commerce within the State of Georgia."

The District Court was in error in dismissing the indictment as to this paragraph. The constitutional right to travel from one State to another, and necessarily to use the highways and other instrumentalities of interstate commerce in doing so, occupies a position fundamental to the concept of our Federal Union. It is a right that has been firmly established and repeatedly recognized. [Citations omitted.] . . .

This does not mean, of course, that every criminal conspiracy affecting an individual's right of free interstate passage is within the sanction of 18 U.S.C. §241. A specific intent to interfere with the federal right must be proved, and at a trial the defendants are entitled to a jury instruction phrased in those terms. Screws v. United States, 325 U.S. 91, 106-107. Thus, for example, a conspiracy to rob an interstate traveler would not, of itself, violate §241. But if the predominant purpose of the conspiracy is to impede or prevent the exercise of the right of interstate travel, or to oppress a person because of his exercise of that right, then, whether or not motivated by racial discrimination, the conspiracy becomes a proper object of the federal law under which the indictment in this case was brought. Accordingly, it was error to grant the motion to dismiss on this branch of the indictment.

For these reasons, the judgment of the District Court is reversed and the case is remanded to that court for further proceedings consistent with this opinion.

It is so ordered.

MR. JUSTICE CLARK, with whom MR. JUSTICE BLACK and MR. JUSTICE FORTAS join, concurring. . . .

The Court carves out of its opinion [in Part II] the question of the power of Congress, under §5 of the Fourteenth Amendment, to enact legislation implementing the Equal Protection Clause or any other provision of the Fourteenth Amendment. The Court's interpretation of the indictment clearly avoids the question whether Congress, by appropriate legislation, has the power to punish private conspiracies that interfere with Fourteenth Amendment rights, such as the right to utilize public facilities. My Brother Brennan, however, says that the Court's disposition constitutes an acceptance of appellees' aforesaid contention as to §241. Some of his language further suggests that the Court indicates sub silentio that Congress does not have the power to outlaw such conspiracies. Although the Court specifically rejects any such connotation, . . . it is, I believe, both appropriate and necessary under the circumstances here to say that there now can be no doubt that the specific language of §5 empowers the Congress to enact laws punishing all conspiracies — with or without state action — that interfere with Fourteenth Amendment rights.

MR. JUSTICE HARLAN, concurring in part and dissenting in part.

I join Parts I and II of the Court's opinion, but I cannot subscribe to Part III in its full sweep. To the extent that it is there held that 18 U.S.C. (1964 ed.) reaches conspiracies, embracing only the action of private persons, to obstruct or otherwise interfere with the right of citizens freely to engage in interstate travel, I am constrained to dissent. On the other hand, I agree that §241 does embrace state interference with such interstate travel, and I therefore consider that this aspect of the indictment is sustainable on the reasoning of Part II of the Court's opinion.

This right to travel must be found in the Constitution itself. This is so because §241 covers only conspiracies to interfere with any citizen in the "free exercise or enjoyment" of a right or privilege "secured to him by the Constitution or laws of the United States," and no "right to travel" can be found in §241 or in any other law of the United States. My disagreement with this phase of the Court's opinion lies in this: While past cases do indeed establish that there is a constitutional "right to travel" between States free from unreasonable *governmental* interference, today's decision is the first to hold that such movement is also protected against *private* interference, and, depending on the constitutional source of the right, I think it either unwise or impermissible so to read the Constitution. . . .

Although the right to travel . . . has respectable precedent to support its status as a privilege and immunity of national citizenship, it is important to note that those cases all dealt with the right of travel simply as affected by oppressive *state* action. Only one prior case in this Court, United States v. Wheeler, 254 U.S. 281, was argued precisely in terms of a right to free movement as against interference by private individuals. There the Government alleged a conspiracy under the predecessor of §241 against the perpetrators of the notorious Bisbee Deportations. The case was argued straightforwardly in terms of whether the right to free ingress and egress, admitted by both parties to be a right of national citizenship, was constitutionally guaranteed against private conspiracies. The Brief for the Defendants in Error, whose counsel was Charles Evans Hughes, later Chief Justice of the United States, gives as one of its main points: "So far as there is a right pertaining to Federal citizenship to have free ingress and egress with respect to the several States, the right is essentially one of protection against the action of the States themselves and of those acting under authority." Brief, at p. i. The Court, with one dissent, accepted this interpretation of the right of unrestricted interstate movement, observing that Crandall v. Nevada [6 Wall. 35], was inapplicable because, inter alia, it dealt with state action. 254 U.S., at 299. More recent cases discussing or applying the right to interstate travel have always been in the context of oppressive state action. See, e.g., Edwards v. California, 314 U.S. 160, and other cases discussed, infra. . . .

As a general proposition it seems to me very dubious that the Constitution was intended to create certain rights of private individuals as against other private individuals. The Constitutional Convention was called to establish a nation, not to reform the common law. Even the Bill of Rights, designed to protect personal liberties, was directed at rights against governmental authority, not other individuals. . . .

I would sustain this aspect of the indictment only on the premise that it sufficiently alleges state interference with interstate travel, and on no other ground.

MR. JUSTICE BRENNAN, with whom THE CHIEF JUSTICE and MR. JUSTICE DOUGLAS join, concurring in part and dissenting in part.

I join Part I of the Court's opinion. I reach the same result as the Court on that branch of the indictment discussed in Part III of its opinion but for other reasons. See footnote 3, infra. And I agree with so much of Part II . . . as construes 18 U.S.C. §241 to encompass conspiracies to injure, oppress, threaten or intimidate citizens in the free exercise or enjoyment of Fourteenth Amendment rights and holds that, as so construed, §241 is not void for indefiniteness. I do not agree, however, with the remainder of Part II . . . which holds, as I read the opinion, that a conspiracy to interfere with the exercise of the right to equal utilization of state facilities is not, within the meaning of §241, a conspiracy to interfere with the exercise of a "right . . . secured . . . by the Constitution" unless discriminatory conduct by state officers is involved in the alleged conspiracy.

I

. . . In my view, however, a right can be deemed "secured . . . by the Constitution or laws of the United States," within the meaning of §241, even though only governmental interferences with the exercise of the right are prohibited by the Constitution itself (or another federal law). The term "secured" means "created by, arising under or dependent upon," Logan v. United States, 144 U.S. 263, 293, rather than "fully protected." A right is "secured . . . by the Constitution" within the meaning of §241 if it emanates from the Constitution, if it finds its source in the Constitution. Section 241 must thus be viewed, in this context, as an exercise of congressional power to amplify prohibitions of the Constitution addressed, as is invariably the case, to government officers; contrary to the view of the Court, I think we are dealing here with a statute that seeks to implement the Constitution, not with the "bare terms" of the Constitution. . . .

. . . The Fourteenth Amendment commands the State to provide the members of all races with equal access to the public facilities it owns or manages, and the right of a citizen to use those facilities without discrimination on the basis of race is a basic corollary of this command. Cf. Brewer v. Hoxie School District No. 46, 238 F.2d 91 (C.A. 8th Cir. 1956). Whatever may be the status of the right to equal utilization of *privately owned fa-*

cilities, see generally Bell v. Maryland, 378 U.S. 226, it must be emphasized that we are here concerned with the right to equal utilization of *public facilities owned or operated by or on behalf of the State.* . . .

In reversing the District Court's dismissal of the second numbered paragraph, I would therefore hold that proof at the trial of the conspiracy charged to the defendants in that paragraph will establish a violation of §241 without regard to whether there are also proofs that state law enforcement officers actively connived in causing the arrests of Negroes by means of false reports.

II

My view as to the scope of §241 requires that I reach the question of constitutional power — whether §241 or legislation indubitably designed to punish entirely private conspiracies to interfere with the exercise of Fourteenth Amendment rights constitutes a permissible exercise of the power granted to Congress by §5 of the Fourteenth Amendment "to enforce, by appropriate legislation, the provision of" the Amendment.

A majority of the members of the Court express the view today that §5 empowers Congress to enact laws punishing *all* conspiracies to interfere with the exercise of Fourteenth Amendment rights, whether or not state officers or others acting under the color of state law are implicated in the conspiracy. Although the Fourteenth Amendment itself, according to established doctrine, "speaks to the State or to those acting under the color of its authority," legislation protecting rights created by that Amendment, such as the right to equal utilization of state facilities, need not be confined to punishing conspiracies in which state officers participate. Rather, §5 authorizes Congress to make laws that it concludes are reasonably necessary to protect a right created by and arising under that Amendment; and Congress is thus fully empowered to determine that punishment of private conspiracies interfering with the exercise of such a right is necessary to its full protection. It made that determination in enacting §241, see the Appendix in United States v. Price, ante, and, therefore §241 is constitutional legislation as applied to reach the private conspiracy alleged in the second numbered paragraph of the indictment. . . .

III

Section 241 is certainly not model legislation for punishing private conspiracies to interfere with the exercise of the right of equal utilization of state facilities. It deals in only general language "with Federal rights and with all Federal rights" and protects them "in the lump," United States v. Mosely, 238 U.S. 383, 387; it protects in most general terms "any right or privilege secured . . . by the Constitution or laws of the United States." Congress has left it to the courts to mark the bounds of those words, to determine on a case-by-case basis whether the right purportedly threatened is a federal right. That determination may occur after the conduct charged has taken place or it may not have been anticipated in prior decisions; "a penumbra of rights may be involved, which none can know until decision has been made and infraction may occur before it is had."[11] Reliance on such wording plainly brings §241 close to the danger line of being void for vagueness. But, as the Court holds, a stringent scienter requirement saves §241 from condemnation as a criminal statute failing to provide adequate notice of the proscribed conduct. The gravamen of the offense is conspiracy, and therefore, like a statute making certain conduct criminal only if it is done "willfully," §241 requires proof of a specific intent for conviction. We have construed §241 to require proof that the persons charged conspired to act in

---

[11] Mr. Justice Rutledge in Screws v. United States, 325 U.S. at 130.

defiance, or in reckless disregard, of an announced rule making the federal right specific and definite. United States v. Williams, 341 U.S. 70, 93-95 (opinion of Douglas, J.) (involving the predecessor to 18 U.S.C. §242). Since this case reaches us on the pleadings, there is no occasion to decide now whether the Government will be able on trial to sustain the burden of proving the requisite specific intent vis-à-vis the right to travel freely from State to State or the right to equal utilization of state facilities. Compare James v. United States, 366 U.S. 213, 221-222 (opinion of Warren, C.J.). In any event, we may well agree that the necessity to discharge that burden can imperil the effectiveness of §241 where, as is often the case, the pertinent constitutional right must be implied from a grant of congressional power or a prohibition upon the exercise of governmental power. But since the limitation on the statute's effectiveness derives from Congress' failure to define — with any measure of specificity — the rights encompassed, the remedy is for Congress to write a law without this defect. To paraphrase my Brother Douglas' observation in Screws v. United States, 325 U.S., at 105, addressed to a companion statute with the same shortcoming, if Congress desires to give the statute more definite scope, it may find ways of doing so.

NOTE Scope of Guest Case

For comment on the Guest case and the other "civil rights" cases of the 1965 Term, see Cox, Foreword: Constitutional Adjudication and the Promotion of Human Rights, 80 Harv. L. Rev. 91 (1966).

United States v. Johnson, 390 U.S. 563 (1968), was a prosecution under 18 U.S.C. §241 for conspiring to assault Negroes for exercising their rights to equality in public accommodations under §201 of the Civil Rights Act of 1964. Section 207(b) of that act makes the equitable remedies therein provided the exclusive means of enforcing rights based thereon. The Court held that while §207(b) would limit actions against proprietors and owners of facilities to equitable relief for refusal to serve Negroes, it did not prohibit criminal prosecution of others for conspiracy to assault for exercising rights under the act.

In 1968, Congress passed a new statute, Pub. L. No. 90-284, 82 Stat. 73, 18 U.S.C. §245, to specify the political and civil rights that would be protected by federal prosecution. The act proscribes all interferences, "whether or not acting under color of law," with the exercise of certain enumerated rights, such as voting, §245(b)(1)(A). And it applies as well to other private interferences taken against a person on account of his "race, color, religion or national origin" because of his exercise of certain other enumerated rights, such as equal access to public accomodations, §245(b)(2)(F). The Senate report noted that the act was passed, in part, to remedy the problem of vagueness demonstrated by Screws and to clear up the question in Guest about its full application to private action. S. Rep. No. 721, 90th Cong., 2d Sess. (1968), 1968 U.S. Code Cong. & Ad. News 1840-1841. Senator Ervin, in a separate dissent, charged that the majority's reliance on the §5 power of the Fourteenth Amendment to reach private action "is directly contrary to reason, law and the clear words of the amendment." Id. at 1857.

Hague v. CIO *307 U.S. 496, 59 S. Ct. 954, 83 L. Ed. 1423 (1939)*

Certiorari, 306 U.S. 624, to review a decree which modified and affirmed a decree of injunction, 25 F.2d 127, in a suit brought by individuals, unincorporated labor organizations, and a membership corporation, against officials of a municipality to restrain alleged violations of constitutional rights of free speech and assembly.

MR. JUSTICE BUTLER, presiding in the absence of the CHIEF JUSTICE and MR. JUSTICE MCREYNOLDS:

858   Chapter Fourteen.   Privileges & Immunities; Equality; Civil Rights

The judgment of the court in this case is that the decree is modified and as modified affirmed. MR. JUSTICE FRANKFURTER and MR. JUSTICE DOUGLAS took no part in the consideration or decision of the case. MR. JUSTICE ROBERTS has an opinion in which MR. JUSTICE BLACK, concurs, and MR. JUSTICE STONE an opinion in which MR. JUSTICE REED concurs. The CHIEF JUSTICE concurs in an opinion. MR. JUSTICE MCREYNOLDS and MR. JUSTICE BUTLER dissent for reasons stated in opinions by them respectively.

MR. JUSTICE ROBERTS delivered an opinion in which MR. JUSTICE BLACK concurred:

We granted certiorari as the case presents important questions in respect of the asserted privilege and immunity of citizens of the United States to advocate action pursuant to a federal statute, by distribution of printed matter and oral discussion in peaceable assembly; and the jurisdiction of federal courts of suits to restrain the abridgment of such privilege and immunity.

The respondents, individual citizens, unincorporated labor organizations composed of such citizens, and a membership corporation, brought suit in the United States District Court against the petitioners, the Mayor, the Director of Public Safety, and the Chief of Police of Jersey City, New Jersey, and the Board of Commissioners, the governing body of the city.

[The opinion next summarized the allegations. In substance, they asserted that acting under certain ordinances the appellants (defendants below) had denied the respondents the right to hold meetings in Jersey City on the ground that they were Communists or Communist organizations, and had prevented the respondents from remaining in the city, distributing leaflets and pamphlets, and from holding meetings to explain to workers the purposes of the National Labor Relations Act.]

After trial upon the merits the District Court entered findings of fact and conclusions of law and a decree in favor of respondents. . . .

The findings are that the petitioners, as officials, have adopted and enforced a deliberate policy of forbidding the respondents and their associates from communicating their views respecting the National Labor Relations Act to the citizens of New Jersey by holding meetings or assemblies in the open air and at public places; that there is no competent proof that the proposed speakers have ever spoken at an assembly where a breach of the peace occurred or at which any utterances were made which violated the canons of proper discussion or gave occasion for disorder consequent upon what was said; that there is no competent proof that the parks of Jersey City are dedicated to any general purpose other than the recreation of the public and that there is competent proof that the municipal authorities have granted permits to various persons other than the respondents to speak at meetings in the streets of the city. . . .

The Circuit Court of Appeals concurred in the findings of fact; held the District Court had jurisdiction under § 24(1) and (14) of the Judicial Code; modified the decree in respect of one of its provisions, and, as modified, affirmed it. . . .

The question now presented is whether freedom to disseminate information concerning the provisions of the National Labor Relations Act, to assemble peaceably for discussion of the Act, and of the opportunities and advantages offered by it, is a privilege or immunity of a citizen of the United States secured against state abridgment by § 1 of the Fourteenth Amendment. . . .

Although it has been held that the Fourteenth Amendment created no rights in citizens of the United States, but merely secured existing rights against state abridgment, it is clear that the right peaceably to assemble and to discuss these topics, and to communicate respecting them, whether orally or in writing, is a privilege inherent in citizenship of the United States which the Amendment protects. . . .

The National Labor Relations Act declares the policy of the United States to be to remove obstructions to commerce by encouraging collective bargaining, protecting full freedom of association and self-organization of workers, and, through their representatives, negotiating as to conditions of employment.

Citizenship of the United States would be little better than a name if it did not carry with it the right to discuss national legislation and the benefits, advantages, and opportunities to accrue to citizens therefrom. All of the respondents' proscribed activities had this single end and aim. The District Court had jurisdiction under § 24(14).

Natural persons, and they alone, are entitled to the privileges and immunities which § 1 of the Fourteenth Amendment secures for "citizens of the United States." Only the individual respondents may, therefore, maintain this suit. . . .

MR. JUSTICE STONE:

I do not doubt that the decree below, modified as has been proposed, is rightly affirmed, but I am unable to follow the path by which some of my brethren have attained that end, and I think the matter is of sufficient importance to merit discussion in some detail.

It has been explicitly and repeatedly affirmed by this Court, without a dissenting voice, that freedom of speech and of assembly for any lawful purpose are rights of personal liberty secured to all persons, without regard to citizenship, by the due process clause of the Fourteenth Amendment. [Citations omitted.] It has never been held that either is a privilege or immunity peculiar to citizenship of the United States, to which alone the privileges and immunities clause refers, Slaughter-House Cases, 16 Wall. 36; Duncan v. Missouri, 152 U.S. 377, 382; Twining v. New Jersey, 211 U.S. 78, 97; Maxwell v. Bugbee, 250 U.S. 525, 538; Hamilton v. Regents, 293 U.S. 245, 261, and neither can be brought within the protection of that clause without enlarging the category of privileges and immunities of United States citizenship as it has hitherto been defined. . . .

If it be the part of wisdom to avoid unnecessary decision of constitutional questions, it would seem to be equally so to avoid the unnecessary creation of novel constitutional doctrine, inadequately supported by the record, in order to attain an end easily and certainly reached by following the beaten paths of constitutional decision. . . .

The right conferred by the Act of 1871 to maintain a suit in equity in the federal courts to protect the suitor against a deprivation of rights or immunities secured by the Constitution, has been preserved, and that whenever the right or immunity is one of personal liberty, not dependent for its existence upon the infringement of property rights, there is jurisdiction in the district court under § 24(14) of the Judicial Code to entertain it without proof that the amount in controversy exceeds $3,000. As the right is secured to "any person" by the due process clause, and as the statute permits the suit to be brought by "any person" as well as by a citizen, it is certain that resort to the privileges and immunities clause would not support the decree which we now sustain and would involve constitutional experimentation as gratuitous as it is unwarranted. We cannot be sure that its consequences would not be unfortunate. . . .[p]

NOTE The Uses of Section 1983

Rarely used before 1960, § 1983 and its "jurisdictional counterpart," 28 U.S.C. § 1343(3), both of which derive from the Civil Rights Act of 1871, have supported a burgeoning growth in private civil rights actions filed in the federal district courts. The number of civil rights actions filed each year (exclusive of petitions filed by state prisoners) increased from 296 in 1960 to 3,985 in 1970, and to 8,443 in 1974. See Director, Administrative Office of the United States Courts, Annual Report (1975).

This increase has been aided by several Supreme Court decisions taking an expansive view of the uses of § 1983. In Lynch v. Household Finance Corp., 405 U.S. 538 (1972), the Court unanimously rejected the property-liberty distinction drawn by Justice Stone in

---

[p] A concurring opinion of Chief Justice Hughes on jurisdiction is omitted, as are dissenting opinions on the merits by McReynolds and Butler, JJ. — ED.

Hague and held that appellant's claim that summary pre-judicial garnishment of her savings account violated Fourteenth Amendment due process could be maintained under § 1343(3) and was not subject to the jurisdictional amount requirement of the general federal question jurisdiction statute, 28 U.S.C. § 1331.

Other obstacles to access to the federal forum have been held not to apply to § 1983/§ 1343(3) jurisdiction. A petitioner need not, for example, have exhausted state judicial or administrative remedies before seeking federal relief. Monroe v. Pape, 365 U.S. 167 (1961); Wilwording v. Swenson, 404 U.S. 249 (1971) (per curiam); Carter v. Stanton, 405 U.S. 669 (1972) (per curiam). In an important recent decision, however, the Court limited the impact of this exemption with respect to petitions brought by state prisoners. The Court held that a prisoner seeking immediate or accelerated release from confinement could petition a federal court only by writ of habeas corpus, 28 U.S.C. § 2241(c)(3), a precondition to which is exhaustion of all available state remedies. Preiser v. Rodriguez, 411 U.S. 475 (1973). See The Supreme Court, 1972 Term, 87 Harv. L. Rev. 1, 263-71 (1973).

In Mitchum v. Foster, the Court held that the Anti-Injunction Act, 28 U.S.C. § 2283, does not bar actions brought under § 1983 to enjoin pending state court proceedings. The Court went on to note, however, that principles of federal-state comity would in some cases require a federal court to abstain from hearing such actions. For application of abstention principles, see Huffman v. Pursue, Ltd., 420 U.S. 592 (1975); Younger v. Harris, 401 U.S. 37 (1971). See Bator, Mishkin, Shapiro, & Wechsler, Hart & Wechsler's The Federal Courts and the Federal System ch. 7, §3 (2d ed. 1973).

Two textual limitations on the reach of § 1983 — that liability extends only to "persons" acting "under color of" state law — have received somewhat expansive interpretations. "Every person" has been held not to include governmental entities, such as municipal corporations, in suits either for equitable relief or for damages. City of Kenosha v. Bruno, 412 U.S. 507 (1973); Monroe v. Pape, supra. But the force of these holdings is reduced by the possibility that claims for relief, although ultimately directed at a governmental entity, may be brought against appropriate individual officeholders. Compare Westberry v. Fisher, 309 F. Supp. 12 (D. Me. 1970), dismissing § 1983 damages claims against state officials where award would in fact "be payable out of the public funds of the State," with United Farmworkers of Florida Housing Project, Inc. v. City of Delray Beach, 493 F.2d 799 (5th Cir. 1974), allowing § 1983 claims for equitable relief against city officials although the relief "will surely be felt by the City." Alternatively, federal question jurisdiction in actions charging violation of Fourteenth Amendment rights by a city or state may be established under § 1331 if the jurisdictional amount requirement is met. See City of Kenosha v. Bruno, supra, at 516 (Brennan, J., concurring); cf. Bivens v. Six Unknown Named Agents of the Federal Bureau of Narcotics, 403 U.S. 388 (1971). Lurking behind these questions is that of the extent of state immunity to suit in federal court under the Eleventh Amendment. For useful discussions, see Rochester v. White, 503 F.2d 263 (3d Cir. 1974); The Supreme Court, 1972 Term, 87 Harv. L. Rev. 1, 252-263 (1973).

The "under color of" state law requirement of § 1983 has been interpreted as substantially coextensive with the "state action" limitation to the underlying substantive provisions of the Fourteenth Amendment. United States v. Price, 383 U.S. 787, 794 n.7 (1966); Ouzts v. Maryland National Ins. Co., 505 F.2d 547, 550 (9th Cir. 1974) (en banc). The meaning of "color of statute . . . custom, or usage" in 42 U.S.C. § 1983 was considered in Adickes v. Kress & Co., 398 U.S. 144 (1970). A white schoolteacher from New York took six black students to lunch at defendant's store in Hattiesburg, Mississippi. They were refused service on the ground that interracial dining was not allowed. A directed verdict for defendant was affirmed by the Second Circuit Court of Appeals. The Supreme Court reversed. Justice Harlan stated, as had the lower courts, that the plaintiff must prove discrimination with knowledge of and pursuant to a custom having the force

Section F. Liability under the Civil Rights Statutes

of law, but disagreed with the lower courts' position that state enforcement could be shown only by reference to a Mississippi criminal trespass statute. Other possible bases would be police toleration of violence, threats against sit-in demonstrators, or police harassment. Moreover, the relevant custom would not necessarily be the refusal to serve interracial groups, but might be any form of racial segregation in public dining. The Court, however, rejected the view that mere proof of customs of the people would suffice for recovery under the statute. Justices Brennan and Douglas dissented. Jones v. Mayer was not cited.

In Monroe v. Pape, supra, the Court held that § 1983 applied to the actions of state officers acting beyond their lawful authority. Petitioner filed a civil action for damages against Chicago police officers and the city of Chicago under § 1983 for an alleged unlawful invasion of his home and illegal search, seizure, and detention. Lower federal courts had dismissed the action against both the city and the police officers. Although the Supreme Court affirmed the dismissal as to the city, finding that a municipality was not a "person" within the meaning of the statute, it held that the complaint against the policemen stated a cause of action. The alleged police action constituted a deprivation of "rights, privileges, or immunities secured by the Constitution" by persons acting "under color of" state law. In dissent, Justice Frankfurter argued that action "in defiance of state law and which no settled state practice, no systematic pattern of official action or inaction, no 'custom, or usage, of any State,' insulates from adequate regulation by state authorities" was not encompassed by § 1983. Writing for the majority, Justice Douglas relied on the parallel construction of the "under color of" language of the analogous criminal provision of the Civil Rights Act, 18 U.S.C. § 242, in Classic v. United States, 313 U.S. 299 (1941), Screws v. United States, 325 U.S. 91 (1945), and Williams v. United States, 341 U.S. 97 (1951), finding state officers in violation of the statute although acting wholly without authority in state law.

Since § 1983, unlike § 242, establishes a civil remedy and does not require "willful" action, the "specific intent" requirement of Screws was held inapplicable.

Section 1983 "should be read against the background of tort liability that makes a man responsible for the natural consequences of his action." Although Monroe v. Pape thus appeared to authorize claims based on mere negligence, early judicial responses were not so expansive. Some courts required a reprehensible motive or "shocking abuse," see, e.g., Striker v. Pancher, 317 F.2d 780 (6th Cir. 1973); and many required at least gross negligence or recklessness, see, e.g., Jenkins v. Averett, 424 F.2d 1228 (4th Cir. 1970). The requirement of reprehensible motive has been rejected, however. See Puckett v. Cox, 456 F.2d 233 (6th Cir. 1972); Whirl v. Kern, 407 F.2d 781 (5th Cir.), cert. denied, 396 U.S. 901 (1969). But the courts are divided on whether mere negligence may be actionable under § 1983. Compare Carter v. Carlson, 447 F.2d 358 (D.C. Cir. 1971), rev'd on other grounds sub nom. District of Columbia v. Carter, 409 U.S. 418 (1973), with Church v. Hegstrom, 416 F.2d 449 (2d Cir. 1969). Cf. Williams v. Field, 416 F.2d 483 (9th Cir. 1969), cert. denied, 397 U.S. 1016 (1970) ("more than an isolated incident of negligen[ce]" must be involved to allege deprivation of equal protection under § 1983).

The primary uses of § 1983 have come in cases of violence and abuse in the administration of law and prisoner suits against prison officials, but its application has spread dramatically. Consider, as representative of the claims now being brought under § 1983, the list which Chief Judge Coffin compiled from cases filed with the First Circuit Court of Appeals during the 1969-1970 term:

" — Do indigent tenants have to post a bond for costs and disbursements to remove an eviction case to federal court?

" — Do low income tenants alleging that their landlord seeks to evict them for reporting building code violations state a cause of action under the Civil Rights Act?

" — Do tenants in a federally subsidized housing project have a right to a hearing on a proposed rent increase?

" — Must indigents pay the statutorily required filing fee to secure a discharge in bankruptcy?
" — Do welfare mothers have an unlimited right to demonstrate at welfare offices?
" — Must hot lunches be furnished at all of a city's schools if they are furnished at some?
" — Must surplus food be distributed to the poor in all communities if they are distributed in a few?
" — May a university dismantle an 'embarrassing' corridor art exhibit?
" — May a high school suspend a teacher for discussing a magazine article exploring current obscenities?
" — May a high school arbitrarily suspend a student for having long hair?
" — Does a prisoner committed to solitary confinement have any due process rights?
" — Under what circumstances does a person committed to a mental institution for observation have a Civil Rights action?" Coffin, Justice and Workability: *Un Essai*, 5 Suffolk U.L Rev. 567, 569-70 (1971).

These claims have led in turn to the assumption of unaccustomed responsibilities by the federal judges charged with framing and administering relief. In a watershed decision in 1971, black plaintiffs successfully invoked § 1983 to challenge racial discrimination in the allocation of municipal services such as street paving and lighting, surface water drainage, sewers, water mains, and fire hydrants. Hawkins v. Town of Shaw, 437 F.2d 1286 (5th Cir. 1971), adhered to on rehearing en banc, 461 F.2d 1171 (1972). The municipality was required to submit a plan to redress the disparities. See generally Fessler & Haar, Beyond the Wrong Side of the Tracks: Municipal Services in the Interstices of Procedure, 6 Harv. Civ. Rights-Civ. Lib. L. Rev. 441 (1971).

The rapid expansion of actions filed under § 1983 has spawned proposals for limitations. Echoing the dissent of Justice Frankfurter in Monroe v. Pape, one writer described the growth of § 1983 actions as the "development of a variety of federal common law without a corresponding compelling federal interest." Shapo, Constitutional Tort: Monroe v. Pape and the Frontiers Beyond, 60 Nw. U.L. Rev. 277 (1965). See Friendly, Federal Jurisdiction: A General View, ch. 4 (1973). See also Note, Limiting the Section 1983 Action in the Wake of Monroe v. Pape, 82 Harv. L. Rev. 1486 (1969), and a rejoinder, Chevigny, Section 1983 Jurisdiction: A Reply, 83 Harv. L. Rev. 1352 (1970).

NOTE Official and Sovereign Immunity

1. The liability of state officers for damages under § 1983 is limited by substantive doctrines of privilege and immunity. In Tenney v. Brandhove, 341 U.S. 367 (1951), and Pierson v. Ray, 386 U.S. 547 (1967), the Court recognized absolute immunity for state legislators and judges acting within their official jurisdictions. In Pierson, however, the Court declined to extend unqualified immunity to policemen, although they were allowed the traditional tort defense of good faith and probable cause. Without such a defense, reasoned the Court, the threat of § 1983 liability might impair law enforcement.

In Imbler v. Pachtman, 424 U.S. 409 (1976), the Court recognized an absolute immunity for a state prosecutor sued under § 1983 for the knowing use of perjured testimony in a criminal case. Should the rule be different if the claim is that the prosecutor suppressed exculpatory evidence? Three members of the Court thought so.

Standards on the scope of qualified immunity for state executive officials were treated in Scheuer v. Rhodes, 416 U.S. 232 (1974), and Wood v. Strickland, 420 U.S. 308 (1975). On behalf of the estates of persons killed during a disorder on the campus of Kent State University in Ohio, plaintiffs in Scheuer brought § 1983 actions for damages against the Governor and members of the Ohio National Guard. The Court unanimously rejected the Court of Appeals' recognition of an absolute "executive immunity" for the defendant officials. The Court did allow, however, for qualified immunity for executive officers "in varying scope, . . . the variation dependent upon the scope of discretion and responsibilities of the office and all the circumstances as they reasonably appear at the time of the action on which liability is sought to be based." On the application of this language to the case at hand, the Court remanded for further findings by the district court. In Wood, the Court considered a claim under §1983 that public school officials had deprived students of due process in suspending them for use and possession of alcohol at a school function. Plaintiffs sought an injunction and compensatory and punitive damages. Writing for the Court, Justice White described a qualified "good faith" immunity for the defendants:

"Liability for damages for every action which is found subsequently to have been violative of a student's constitutional rights and to have caused compensable injury would unfairly impose upon the school decisionmaker the burden of mistakes made in good faith in the course of exercising his discretion within the scope of his official duties. . . .

"The disagreement between the Court of Appeals and the District Court over the immunity standard in this case has been put in terms of an 'objective' versus a 'subjective' test of good faith. As we see it, the appropriate standard necessarily contains elements of both. The official must himself be acting sincerely and with a belief that he is doing right, but an act violating a student's constitutional rights can be no more justified by ignorance or disregard of settled, indisputable law on the part of one entrusted with supervision of students' daily lives than by the presence of actual malice. . . . Therefore, in the specific context of school discipline, we hold that a school board member is not immune from liability for damages under §1983 if he knew or reasonably should have known that the action he took within his sphere of official responsibility would violate the constitutional rights of the student affected, or if he took the action with the malicious intention to cause a deprivation of constitutional rights or other injury to the student. . . ."

Justice Powell, joined by the Chief Justice and Justices Blackmun and Rehnquist, dissented from this part of the Court's opinion on the ground that the scope of the immunity described by the Court gave public officials insufficient protection.

On the scope of congressional immunity under the speech and debate clause of Article I, §6, see Gravel v. United States, 408 U.S. 606 (1972) (criminal liability), Powell v. McCormack, page 71 supra (civil liability).

See generally Kates, Immunity of State Judges under the Federal Civil Rights Acts: Pierson v. Ray Reconsidered, 65 Nw. U.L. Rev. 615 (1970); Note, Liability of Judicial Officers Under Section 1983, 79 Yale L.J. 322 (1969).

2. *The reach of the Eleventh Amendment.* In Edelman v. Jordan, 415 U.S. 651 (1974), the Court reversed, 5 to 4, a district court order that the State of Illinois retroactively pay benefits wrongfully withheld from applicants to federal-state programs of Aid to the Aged, Blind and Disabled (AABD) established under the Social Security Act, 42 U.S.C. §§1381 et seq. Writing for the Court, Justice Rehnquist held that federal jurisdiction to grant such relief was barred by the Eleventh Amendment. The Court noted that, like an award of damages against the state, the district court order would require immediate disbursement of funds from the state treasury. On this basis, it distinguished cases upholding prospective injunctive relief which was likely to have fiscal consequences. See, e.g., Ex parte Young, 209 U.S. 123 (1908). The Court further held that Illinois had not by its participation in the AABD program waived Eleventh Amendment immunity or "constructively consented" to suit in federal court. For comment on Edelman see Note, The Supreme Court, 1973 Term, 88 Harv. L. Rev. 41, 243-251 (1974). On the power of Congress under the Fourteenth Amendment to override sovereign immunity of a state under the Eleventh, see National League of Cities v. Usery, page 286 supra.

In Scheuer v. Rhodes, supra, the Court rejected an attempt by defendant public officials to plead sovereign immunity and held that state officials charged with personal liability for deprivation of a federal right under color of law cannot take refuge in the sovereign immunity of the state or in the Eleventh Amendment.

See generally Bator, Mishkin, Shapiro & Wechsler, Hart & Wechsler's The Federal Courts and the Federal System 251-258, 926-957 (2d ed. 1973); McCormack, Federalism and Section 1983 (pts. 1, 2), 60 Va. L. Rev. 1, 250 (1974); Comment, Implied Waiver of a State's Eleventh Amendment Immunity, 1974 Duke L.J. 925; Note, Attorneys' Fees and the Eleventh Amendment, 88 Harv. L. Rev. 1875 (1975). See Note, supra p. 128.

Griffin v. Breckenridge 403 U.S. 88, 91 S. Ct. 1790, 29 L. Ed. 2d 338 (1971)

MR. JUSTICE STEWART delivered the opinion of the Court.

[In an action under 42 U.S.C. §1985(3) for damages, black citizens of Mississippi alleged a conspiracy by various white citizens to assault them while in travel upon interstate highways in order to deprive them of equal rights. In particular, petitioners alleged that respondents stopped them on a public highway, under the false belief that one of them was a civil rights worker, maliciously beat and threatened them, and thereby prevented them from the exercise of equal rights to speech, assembly, and movement, among others.]

The District Court dismissed the complaint for failure to state a cause of action, relying on the authority of this Court's opinion in Collins v. Hardyman, 341 U.S. 651, which in effect construed the above language of § 1985(3) as reaching only conspiracies under color of state law. The Court of Appeals for the Fifth Circuit affirmed the judgment of dismissal. . . .

I

Collins v. Hardyman was decided 20 years ago. The complaint in that case alleged that the plaintiffs were members of a political club that had scheduled a meeting to adopt a resolution opposing the Marshall Plan, and to send copies of the resolution to appropriate federal officials; that the defendants conspired to deprive the plaintiffs of their rights as citizens of the United States peaceably to assemble and to equal privileges and immunities under the laws of the United States; that, in furtherance of the conspiracy, the defendants proceeded to the meeting site and, by threats and violence, broke up the meeting, thus interfering with the right of the plaintiffs to petition the Government for the redress of grievances; and that the defendants did not interfere or conspire to interfere with the meetings of other political groups with whose opinions the defendants agreed. [The Court held in Collins that this complaint did not state a cause of action under § 1985(3) because of failure to allege action "under color of state law."] . . .

The Court was careful to make clear that it was deciding no constitutional question, but simply construing the language of the statute, or more precisely, determining the applicability of the statute to the facts alleged in the complaint. . . . Nonetheless, the Court made equally clear that the construction it gave to the statute was influenced by the constitutional problems that it thought would have otherwise been engendered. . . .

II

Whether or not Collins v. Hardyman was correctly decided on its own facts is a question with which we need not here be concerned. But it is clear, in the light of the evolution of decisional law in the years that have passed since that case was decided, that many of the constitutional problems there perceived simply do not exist. Little reason remains, therefore, not to accord to the words of the statute their apparent meaning. . . .

III

We turn, then, to an examination of the meaning of §1985(3). On their face, the words of the statute fully encompass the conduct of private persons. . . .

The approach of this Court to other Reconstruction civil rights statutes in the years since Collins has been to "accord [them] a sweep as broad as [their] language." United States v. Price, 383 U.S. 787, 801; Jones v. Alfred H. Mayer Co., 392 U.S. 409, 437. . . . There appear to be three possible forms for a state action limitation on §1985(3) — that there must be action under color of state law, that there must be interference with or influence upon state authorities, or that there must be a private conspiracy so massive and effective that it supplants those authorities and thus satisfies the state action requirement. The Congress that passed the Civil Rights Act of 1871, 17 Stat. 13, §2 of which is the parent of §1985(3), dealt with each of these three situations in explicit terms in other parts of the same Act. An element of the cause of action established by the first section, now 42 U.S.C. §1983, is that the deprivation complained of must have been inflicted under color of state law. To read any such requirement into §1985(3) would thus deprive that section of all independent effect. As for interference with state officials, §1985(3) itself contains another clause dealing explicitly with that situation.[7] And §3 of the 1871 Act provided for military action at the command of the President should massive private lawlessness render state authorities powerless to protect the federal rights of classes of citizens, such a situation being defined by the Act as constituting a state denial of equal protection. 17 Stat. 14. Given the existence of these three provisions, it is almost impossible to believe that Congress intended, in the dissimilar language of the portion of §1985(3) now before us, simply to duplicate the coverage of one or more of them.

[Justice Stewart also found that his reading of the reach of §1985(3) was supported by its legislative history.]

. . . The Constitutional shoals that would lie in the path of interpreting §1985(3) as a general federal tort law can be avoided by giving full effect to the congressional purpose — by requiring, as an element of the cause of action, the kind of invidiously discriminatory motivation stressed by the sponsors of the limiting amendment. See the remarks of Representatives Willard and Shellabarger, [Cong. Globe, 42d Cong., 1st Sess., App. 68-69, 188 (1871)], at 100. The language requiring intent to deprive of *equal* protection, or *equal* privileges and immunities, means that there must be some racial, or perhaps otherwise class-based, invidiously discriminatory animus behind the conspirators' action.[9] The conspiracy, in other words, must aim at a deprivation of the equal enjoyment of rights secured by the law to all.

IV

[The Court held that the complaint alleged all the necessary elements for a cause of action under §1985(3).] . . . Indeed, the conduct here alleged lies so close to the core of the coverage intended by Congress that it is hard to conceive of wholly private conduct that would come within the statute if this does not. We must, accordingly, consider whether Congress had constitutional power to enact a statute that imposes liability under federal law for the conduct alleged in this complaint.

---

[7] "If two or more persons in any State or Territory conspire or go in disguise on the highway or on the premises of another . . . for the purpose of preventing or hindering the constituted authorities of any State or Territory from giving or securing to all persons within such State or Territory the equal protection of the laws. . . ."

[9] We need not decide, given the facts of this case, whether a conspiracy motivated by invidiously discriminatory intent other than racial bias would be actionable under the portion of §1985(3) before us. Cf. Cong. Globe, 42d Cong., 1st Sess., 567 (1871) (remarks of Sen. Edmunds).

V

A

. . . By the Thirteenth Amendment, we committed ourselves as a Nation to the proposition that the former slaves and their descendants should be forever free. To keep that promise, "Congress has the power under the Thirteenth Amendment rationally to determine what are the badges and the incidents of slavery, and the authority to translate that determination into effective legislation." Jones v. Alfred H. Mayer Co., supra, at 440. We can only conclude that Congress was wholly within its powers under §2 of the Thirteenth Amendment in creating a statutory cause of action for Negro citizens who have been the victims of conspiratorial, racially discriminatory private action aimed at depriving them of the basic rights that the law secures to all free men.

B

Our cases have firmly established that the right of interstate travel is constitutionally protected, does not necessarily rest on the Fourteenth Amendment, and is assertable against private as well as governmental interference. [Citations omitted.] . . . That right, like other rights of national citizenship, is within the power of Congress to protect by appropriate legislation. [Citations omitted.] . . .

C

In identifying these two constitutional sources of congressional power, we do not imply the absence of any other. More specifically, the allegations of the complaint in this case have not required consideration of the scope of the power of Congress under §5 of the Fourteenth Amendment. By the same token, since the allegations of the complaint bring this cause of action so close to the constitutionally authorized core of the statute, there has been no occasion here to trace out its constitutionally permissible periphery.

The judgment is reversed, and the case is remanded to the United States District Court for the Southern District of Mississippi for further proceedings consistent with this opinion.

It is so ordered.

Mr. Justice Harlan, concurring.

I agree with the Court's opinion, except that I find it unnecessary to rely on the "right of interstate travel" as a premise for justifying federal jurisdiction under §1985(3). With that reservation, I join the opinion and judgment of the Court.

NOTE Section 1985(3)

Section 1985(3) emerges as the only federal remedy protecting civil rights generally against private racial discrimination. Other federal civil remedies which had been held applicable to private action had been focused upon a few specific rights, such as the right to purchase or rent property, 42 U.S.C. §1982, or the right of equal access to equal accommodations, §203 of the Civil Rights Act of 1964, 42 U.S.C 2000a-3 (1964). Left unclear, however, is the scope of the rights protected by §1985(3) and of the required "discriminatory animus."

As the Griffin Court construed the statute to protect black citizens from deprivation of equal enjoyment of a "legal right," §1985(3) may be purely remedial: that is, it could be invoked only to redress the deprivation of a pre-existing right created by state law. Yet the Griffin Court itself intimated that private discriminatory interference with First Amendment rights per se might be actionable under §1985(3). Since the First Amendment is directed only at government action, such a construction would create new substantive rights. The prevailing view has been that the scope of §1985(3) is more limited, and broader readings were rejected in Arnold v. Tiffany, 487 F.2d 216 (9th Cir. 1973), cert. denied, 415 U.S. 984 (1974) (dictum) (First Amendment right of association); Dombrowski v. Dowling, 459 F.2d 190 (7th Cir. 1972) (discriminatory denial of rental space); and Place v. Shepherd, 446 F.2d 1239 (6th Cir. 1971) (denial of private employment and infringement of First Amendment freedom of speech). However, in Action v. Gannon, 450 F.2d 1227 (8th Cir. 1971) (en banc), members of a predominantly white Roman Catholic parish sought to enjoin disruption of its services by two black organizations motivated by racial and economic considerations; and the court held that interference with the First Amendment rights of freedom of assembly and worship was subject to §1985(3). See also Hayes v. United States, 464 F.2d 1252 (5th Cir. 1972) (en banc), a criminal prosecution under 18 U.S.C. §241 for destruction of school buses, describing as "appealing and persuasive" the argument that §241 protects the right of black children to attend public schools.

If the broader interpretation of rights protected by §1985(3) is accepted, would the statute reach all private racial discrimination? Could such a statute pass constitutional muster under the Thirteenth Amendment? See Note, The "New" Thirteenth Amendment: A Preliminary Analysis, 82 Harv. L. Rev. 1294 (1969).

The requirement of racial or class-based discrimination has proved another stumbling block to plaintiffs invoking §1985(3). The courts have rejected several claims that defendants were motivated by "discriminatory animus" against novel classes. See Arnold v. Tiffany, supra (independent newspaper dealers); Bricker v. Crane, 468 F.2d 1228 (1st Cir. 1972), cert. denied, 410 U.S. 930 (1973) (certain physicians); Hughes v. Ranger Fuel Corp., 467 F.2d 6 (4th Cir. 1972) (environmentalists). Nonetheless, courts have not limited the required motivation to racial bias and have allowed maintenance of §1985(3) actions where defendants are alleged to have conspired to deprive plaintiffs of equal protection of the laws by mounting campaigns of harassment. See Phillips v. Trello, 502 F.2d 1000 (3d Cir. 1974) (en banc) (dictum); Azar v. Conley, 456 F.2d 1382 (6th Cir. 1972).

Could such a reading of the statute rest on the Thirteenth Amendment? In Action, supra, the court found the Thirteenth Amendment inapplicable but sustained the application of §1985(3) on the enforcement clause of the Fourteenth Amendment. Although the Supreme Court has never held that §5 of the Fourteenth Amendment enpowers Congress to reach private action, it will be remembered that six Justices in United States v. Guest, 383 U.S. 745 (1966), supported such power. See H. Flack, The Adoption of the Fourteenth Amendment (1908); R. H. Harris, The Quest for Equality (1960); Cox, Constitutional Adjudication and the Promotion of Human Rights, 80 Harv. L. Rev. 91 (1966); Avins, The Ku Klux Klan Act of 1871: Some Reflected Light on State Action and the Fourteenth Amendment, 11 St. Louis U.L.J. 331 (1967); Frank & Munro, The Original Understanding of "Equal Protection of the Laws," 50 Colum. L. Rev. 131 (1950); Note, Theories of Federalism and Civil Rights, 75 Yale L.J. 1007 (1966).

Bivens v. Six Unknown Named Agents of Federal Bureau of Narcotics 403 U.S. 388, 91 S. Ct. 1999, 29 L. Ed. 2d 619 (1971)

Mr. Justice Brennan delivered the opinion of the Court.

The Fourth Amendment provides that: "The right of the people to be secure in their persons, houses, papers, and effects, against unreasonable searches and seizures, shall not be violated. . . ." In *Bell v. Hood*, 327 U.S. 678 (1946), we reserved the question whether violation of that command by a federal agent acting under color of his authority gives rise to a cause of action for damages consequent upon his unconstitutional conduct. Today we hold that it does.

This case has its origin in an arrest and search carried out on the morning of November

26, 1965. Petitioner's complaint alleged that on that day respondents, agents of the Federal Bureau of Narcotics acting under claim of federal authority, entered his apartment and arrested him for alleged narcotics violations. The agents manacled petitioner in front of his wife and children, and threatened to arrest the entire family. They searched the apartment from stem to stern. Thereafter, petitioner was taken to the federal courthouse in Brooklyn, where he was interrogated, booked, and subjected to a visual strip search.

On July 7, 1967, petitioner brought suit in Federal District Court. In addition to the allegations above, his complaint asserted that the arrest and search were effected without a warrant, and that unreasonable force was employed in making the arrest; fairly read, it alleges as well that the arrest was made without probable cause. Petitioner claimed to have suffered great humiliation, embarrassment, and mental suffering as a result of the agents' unlawful conduct, and sought $15,000 damages from each of them. The District Court, on respondents' motion, dismissed the complaint on the ground, *inter alia*, that it failed to state a cause of action. 276 F. Supp. 12 (EDNY 1967). The Court of Appeals, one judge concurring specially, affirmed on that basis. 409 F. 2d 718 (CA2 1969). We granted certiorari. 399 U.S. 905 (1970). We reverse.

. . . In respondents' view, however, the rights that petitioner asserts — primarily rights of privacy — are creations of state and not of federal law. Accordingly, they argue, petitioner may obtain money damages to redress invasion of these rights only by an action in tort, under state law, in the state courts. In this scheme the Fourth Amendment would serve merely to limit the extent to which the agents could defend the state law tort suit by asserting that their actions were a valid exercise of federal power: if the agents were shown to have violated the Fourth Amendment, such a defense would be lost to them and they would stand before the state law merely as private individuals.

We think that respondents' thesis rests upon an unduly restrictive view of the Fourth Amendment's protection against unreasonable searches and seizures by federal agents, a view that has consistently been rejected by this Court. . . .

[T]he Fourth Amendment operates as a limitation upon the exercise of federal power regardless of whether the State in whose jurisdiction that power is exercised would prohibit or penalize the identical act if engaged in by a private citizen. It guarantees to citizens of the United States the absolute right to be free from unreasonable searches and seizures carried out by virtue of federal authority.

. . . Of course, the Fourth Amendment does not in so many words provide for its enforcement by an award of money damages for the consequences of its violation. But "it is . . . well settled that where legal rights have been invaded, and a federal statute provides for a general right to sue for such invasion, federal courts may use any available remedy to make good the wrong done." Bell v. Hood, 327 U.S., at 684 (footnote omitted). . . . [W]e have here no explicit congressional declaration that persons injured by a federal officer's violation of the Fourth Amendment may not recover money damages from the agents, but must instead be remitted to another remedy, equally effective in the view of Congress. The question is merely whether petitioner, if he can demonstrate an injury consequent upon the violation by federal agents of his Fourth Amendment rights, is entitled to redress his injury through a particular remedial mechanism normally available in the federal courts. Cf. J. I. Case Co. v. Borak, 377 U.S. 426, 433 (1964); Jacobs v. United States, 290 U.S. 13, 16 (1933). "The very essence of civil liberty certainly consists in the right of every individual to claim the protection of the laws, whenever he receives an injury." Marbury v. Madison, 1 Cranch 137, 163 (1803). Having concluded that petitioner's complaint states a cause of action under the Fourth Amendment . . . , we hold that petitioner is entitled to recover money damages for any injuries he has suffered as a result of the agents' violation of the Amendment.[q]

---

[q] Mr. Justice Harlan concurred in a separate opinion. Chief Justice Burger and Justices Black and Blackmun dissented, all in separate opinions. — ED.

NOTE Implying Liability for Unconstitutional Federal Action

To what extent does Bivens suggest that § 1983 is applicable to *federal* officers? Should every violation of constitutional rights by federal officers be actionable for damages? What standards should guide the Court in fashioning these compensatory remedies: history, purpose, practicality, legislative acquiescence? How analogous, for example, are the cases where the Court creates a damage remedy from a federal statute? See, e.g., J. I. Case Co. v. Borak, 377 U.S. 426 (1964) (cause of action for false statement in corporate proxy, in violation of federal securities law). See also Note, Implying Civil Remedies From Federal Regulatory Statutes, 77 Harv. L. Rev. 285 (1963). How analogous should be the Court's experience with § 1983 itself, e.g. on the scope of official immunity?

Chief Justice Burger objected in dissent that the Bivens Court "imping(ed) on the legislative and policy functions that the Constitution vests in Congress." 403 U.S. at 418. His observation may be true to the extent that, as Justice Harlan pointed out in concurrence, "the range of policy considerations we may take into account is at least as broad as the range of those a legislature would consider with respect to an express statutory authorization of a traditional remedy." 403 U.S. at 407. But to what extent, if at all, does the Bivens remedy preclude a congressional function? Could Congress, for example, abolish the damage remedy if it determined that the exclusionary rule adequately deterred Fourth Amendment violations? Or, more topically (see the Appendix to the Chief Justice's dissent in Bivens), could Congress abolish the exclusionary rule if it provided, or there exists, an alternative damage remedy? For a recent view that policies like the exclusionary rule of the Fourth Amendment or the "overbreadth" doctrine of the First Amendment, that serve to implement constitutional provisions, should be subject to congressional modification, see Monaghan, The Supreme Court, 1974 Term — Foreword: Constitutional Common Law, 89 Harv. L. Rev. 1 (1975). See also Lusky, By What Right? (1976).

See generally Dellinger, Of Rights and Remedies: The Constitution as a Sword, 85 Harv. L. Rev. 1532 (1972); Hill, Constitutional Remedies, 69 Colum. L. Rev. 1109 (1969); Katz, The Jurisprudence of Remedies: Constitutional Legality and the Law of Torts in Bell v. Hood, 117 U. Pa. L. Rev. 1 (1968); Shapo, Constitutional Tort: Monroe v. Pape and the Frontiers Beyond, 60 Nw. U. L. Rev. 277 (1965).

Section G. EQUAL PROTECTION OF THE LAWS

1. Historical Themes

Yick Wo v. Hopkins *118 U.S. 356, 6 S. Ct. 1064, 30 L. Ed. 220 (1886)*

[An ordinance of San Francisco made it unlawful for any person to maintain a laundry in a wooden building without securing a license from the Board of Supervisors. Yick Wo was convicted of violating the ordinance and committed to prison for nonpayment of the fine. Thereupon he applied for a writ of habeas corpus, which was denied him by the Supreme Court of California. Another Chinese, Wo Lee, had been convicted in similar circumstances. He applied to a Circuit Court of the United States for a writ of habeas corpus. Yick Wo's case reached the Supreme Court of the United States on writ of error and Wo Lee's on appeal. The following facts were admitted to be true: that the appellants were aliens of Chinese descent; that the fire wardens and the sanitary inspectors had inspected the laundries operated by the appellants and had approved them; that of the 320 laundries in San Francisco, 310 were constructed of wood and 240 were operated by Chinese aliens; that the applications for licenses filed by 200 Chinese laundrymen were denied and all applications, save one, filed by non-Chinese applicants had been granted.]

MR. JUSTICE MATTHEWS delivered the opinion of the court: . . .

The ordinance drawn in question in the present case . . . does not prescribe a rule and conditions, for the regulation of the use of property for laundry purposes, to which all similarly situated may conform. It allows without restriction the use for such purposes of buildings of brick or stone; but, as to wooden buildings, constituting nearly all those in previous use, it divides the owners or occupiers into two classes, not having respect to their personal character and qualifications for the business, nor the situation and nature and adaptation of the buildings themselves, but merely by an arbitrary line, on one side of which are those who are permitted to pursue their industry by the mere will and consent of the supervisors, and on the other those from whom that consent is withheld, at their mere will and pleasure. And both classes are alike only in this: that they are tenants at will, under the supervisors, of their means of living. The ordinance, therefore, also differs from the not unusual case, where discretion is lodged by law in public officers or bodies to grant or withhold licenses to keep taverns, or places for the sale of spirituous liquors, and the like, when one of the conditions is that the applicant shall be a fit person for the exercise of the privilege, because in such cases the fact of fitness is submitted to the judgment of the officer, and calls for the exercise of a discretion of a judicial nature.

The rights of the petitioners, as affected by the proceedings of which they complain, are not less because they are aliens and subjects of the Emperor of China. By the third article of the Treaty between this government and that of China, concluded November 17, 1880, 22 Stat. at L. 827, it is stipulated: "If Chinese laborers, or Chinese of any other class, now either permanently or temporarily residing in the territory of the United States, meet with ill treatment at the hands of any other persons, the Government of the United States will exert all its powers to devise measures for their protection, and to secure to them the same rights, privileges, immunities and exemptions as may be enjoyed by the citizens or subjects of the most favored nation, and to which they are entitled by treaty."

The Fourteenth Amendment to the Constitution is not confined to the protection of citizens. It says: "Nor shall any State deprive any person of life, liberty, or property without due process of law; nor deny to any person within its jurisdiction the equal protection of the laws." These provisions are universal in their application, to all persons within the territorial jurisdiction, without regard to any differences of race, of color, or of nationality; and the equal protection of the laws is a pledge of the protection of equal laws. . . .

It is contended on the part of the petitioners, that the ordinances for violations of which they are severally sentenced to imprisonment are void on their face, as being within the prohibitions of the Fourteenth Amendment, and, in the alternative, if not so, that they are void by reason of their administration operating unequally, so as to punish in the present petitioners what is permitted to others as lawful, without any distinction of circumstances; an unjust and illegal discrimination, it is claimed, which, though not made expressly, by the ordinances, is made possible by them.

When we consider the nature and the theory of our institutions of government, the principles upon which they are supposed to rest, and review the history of their development, we are constrained to conclude that they do not mean to leave room for the play and action of purely personal and arbitrary power. Sovereignty itself is, of course, not subject to law, for it is the author and source of law; but in our system, while sovereign powers are delegated to the agencies of government, sovereignty itself remains with the people, by whom and for whom all government exists and acts. And the law is the definition and limitation of power. It is, indeed, quite true, that there must always be lodged somewhere, and in some person or body, the authority of final decision; and, in many cases of mere administration the responsibility is purely political, no appeal lying except to the ultimate tribunal of the public judgment, exercised either in the pressure of opinion or by means of the suffrage. But the fundamental rights to life, liberty, and the pursuit of happiness, considered as individual possessions, are secured by those maxims of constitutional law which are the monuments showing the victorious progress of the race in securing to men the blessings of civlization under the reign of just and equal laws, so that, in the famous language of the Massachusetts Bill of Rights, the government of the Commonwealth "may be a government of laws and not of men." For, the very idea that one man may be compelled to hold his life, or the means of living, or any material right essential to the enjoyment of life, at the mere will of another, seems to be intolerable in any country where freedom prevails, as being the essence of slavery itself. . . .

. . . In the present cases, we are not obliged to reason from the probable to the actual and pass upon the validity of the ordinances complained of, as tried merely by the opportunities which their terms afford, of unequal and unjust discrimination in their administration. For the cases present the ordinances in actual operation, and the facts shown establish an administration directed so exclusively against a particular class of persons as to warrant and require the conclusion that whatever may have been the intent of the ordinances as adopted, they are applied by the public authorities charged with their administration, and thus representing the State itself, with a mind so unequal and oppressive as to amount to a practical denial by the State of that equal protection of the laws which is secured to the petitioners, as to all other persons, by the broad and benign provisions of the Fourteenth Amendment to the Constitution of the United States. Though the law itself be fair on its face and impartial in appearance, yet, if it is applied and administered by public authority with an evil eye and an unequal hand, so as practically to make unjust and illegal discriminations between persons in similar circumstances, material to their rights, the denial of equal justice is still within the prohibition of the Constitution. This principle of interpretation has been sanctioned by this court in Henderson v. Mayor, etc. of New York, 92 U.S. 259; Chy Luny v. Freeman, 92 U.S. 275; Ex parte Va., 100 U.S. 339; Neal v. Delaware, 103 U.S. 370, and Soon Hing v. Crowley [113 U.S. 703].

The present cases, as shown by the facts disclosed in the record, are within this class. It appears that both petitioners have complied with every requisite, deemed by the law or by the public officers charged with its administration necessary for the protection of neighboring property from fire, or as a precaution against injury to the public health. No reason whatever, except the will of the supervisors, is assigned why they should not be permitted to carry on, in the accustomed manner, their harmless and useful occupation, on which they depend for a livelihood. And while this consent of the supervisors is withheld from them and from two hundred others who have also petitioned, all of whom happened to be Chinese subjects, eighty others, not Chinese subjects, are permitted to carry on the same business under similar conditions. The fact of this discrimination is admitted. No reason for it is shown, and the conclusion cannot be resisted, that no reason for it exists except hostility to the race and nationality to which the petitioners belong, and which in the eye of the law is not justified. The discrimination is therefore illegal, and the public administration which enforces it is a denial of the equal protection of the laws and a violation of the Fourteenth Amendment of the Constitution. The imprisonment of the petitioners is therefore illegal, and they must be discharged.

To this end, the judgment of the Supreme Court of California in the case of Yick Wo, and that of the Circuit Court of the United States for the District of California in the case of Wo Lee, are severally reversed, and the cases remanded, each to the proper court, with directions to discharge the petitioners from custody and imprisonment.

NOTE

A Chinese, convicted of an offense punishable by a fine of $10 or, in default of payment of the fine, by imprisonment in the county jail for five days, on failure to pay the fine was imprisoned. A San Francisco ordinance, popularly known as the "queue ordinance," required that the hair on the head of every male prisoner sentenced to imprisonment in the county jail should, immediately upon the prisoner's arrival, "be cut or clipped to an uniform length of one inch from the scalp." Assuming that the Chinese prisoner's religion teaches that the deprivation of the queue brings disgrace in this world and misfortune and suffering after death, could the ordinance constitutionally be enforced against the prisoner? See Ho Ah Kow v. Nunan, 5 Sawyer 552, 12 F. Cas. 252 (No. 6546) (C.C.D. Cal. 1879).

NOTE Equal Protection as a Limit on Administrative Discretion

Yick Wo has traditionally stood for the proposition that the exercise of discretion in law enforcement may not be "deliberately based upon an unjustifiable standard such as race, religion, or other arbitrary classification." Oyler v. Boles, 368 U.S. 448, 456 (1962). What ought to be considered some other "arbitrary" standards for selectivity — in the decision to bring a criminal prosecution, for example?

Recent cases in the lower courts have suggested that the government may not single out someone for prosecution "on the basis of the exercise of protected First Amendment activity." United States v. Falk, 479 F.2d 616, 620 (7th Cir. 1973) (en banc) (vocal draft resister charged with nonpossession of draft card). See also Dixon v. District of Columbia, 394 F.2d 966 (D.C. Cir. 1968) (reinstatement of criminal charges due to complaint about police misconduct); United States v. Steele, 461 F.2d 1148 (9th Cir. 1972) (vocal census resister convicted of refusal to answer census). In addition to a showing of such an "evil eye" in the prosecutor's motive, the defendant must also establish the "unequal hand" of the prosecutor by a showing that others similarly situated have not been charged. United States v. Berrios, 501 F.2d 1207, 1211 (2d Cir. 1974).

At what point might the review of prosecutorial discretion under Yick Wo violate the "separation of powers"? For instance, when might discovery into the internal decision-making behind a prosecution intrude upon "executive privilege"? Compare the refusal to inquire into legislative motive, Palmer v. Thompson, 403 U.S. 217 (1971) (whether town closed pools, arguably, to avoid desegregation). See generally Ely, Legislative and Administrative Motivation in Constitutional Law, 79 Yale L.J. 1205 (1970).

On the other hand, review under Yick Wo could prompt what a commentator has hailed as "a fresh look at the tradition that prevents [the judiciary] from reviewing the prosecuting function." K. Davis, Discretionary Justice 211 (1969). Professor Davis continues: "The reasons for a judicial check of prosecutors' discretion are stronger than for such a check of other administrative discretion that is traditionally reviewable. Important interests are at stake. Abuses are common." (Italics omitted.) Id. at 211-212. Is Yick Wo an appropriate entering wedge?

See Note, The Right to Nondiscriminatory Enforcement of State Penal Laws, 61 Colum. L. Rev. 1103 (1961); Givelber, The Application of Equal Protection Principles to Selective Enforcement of the Criminal Law, 1973 U. Ill. L.F. 88; Comment, Curbing the Prosecutor's Discretion: United States v. Falk, 9 Harv. Civ. Rights-Civ. Lib. L. Rev. 372 (1974).

Skinner v. Oklahoma 316 U.S. 535, 62 S. Ct. 1110, 86 L. Ed. 1655 (1942)

MR. JUSTICE DOUGLAS delivered the opinion of the Court.

This case touches a sensitive and important area of human rights. Oklahoma deprives certain individuals of a right which is basic to the perpetuation of a race — the right to have offspring. Oklahoma has decreed the enforcement of its law against petitioner, overruling his claim that it violated the Fourteenth Amendment. Because that decision raised grave and substantial constitutional questions, we granted the petition for certiorari.

The statute involved is Oklahoma's Habitual Criminal Sterilization Act. Okla. Stat. Ann. Tit. 57, §§171, et seq.; L. 1935, pp. 94 et seq. That Act defines an "habitual criminal" as a person who, having been convicted two or more times for crimes "amounting to felonies involving moral turpitude," either in an Oklahoma court or in a court of any other State, is thereafter convicted of such a felony in Oklahoma and is sentenced to a term of imprisonment in an Oklahoma penal institution. §173. Machinery is provided for the institution by the Attorney General of a proceeding against such a person in the Oklahoma courts for a judgment that such person shall be rendered sexually sterile. §§176, 177. Notice, an opportunity to be heard, and the right to a jury trial are provided. §§177-181. The issues triable in such a proceeding are narrow and confined. If the court or jury finds that the defendant is an "habitual criminal" and that he "may be rendered sexually sterile without detriment to his or her general health," then the court "shall render judgment to the effect that said defendant be rendered sexually sterile" (§182) by the operation of vasectomy in case of a male, and of salpingectomy in case of a female. §174. Only one other provision of the Act is material here, and that is §195, which provides that "offenses arising out of the violation of the prohibitory laws, revenue acts, embezzlement, or political offenses, shall not come or be considered within the terms of this Act."

Petitioner was convicted in 1926 of the crime of stealing chickens, and was sentenced to the Oklahoma State Reformatory. In 1929 he was convicted of the crime of robbery with firearms, and was sentenced to the reformatory. In 1934 he was convicted again of robbery with firearms, and was sentenced to the penitentiary. He was confined there in 1935 when the Act was passed. In 1936 the Attorney General instituted proceedings against him. Petitioner in his answer challenged the Act as unconstitutional by reason of the Fourteenth Amendment. A jury trial was had. The court instructed the jury that the crimes of which petitioner had been convicted were felonies involving moral turpitude, and that the only question for the jury was whether the operation of vasectomy could be performed on petitioner without detriment to his general health. The jury found that it could be. A judgment directing that the operation of vasectomy be performed on petitioner was affirmed by the Supreme Court of Oklahoma by a five to four decision. 189 Okla. 235, 115 P.2d 123.

Several objections to the constitutionality of the Act have been pressed upon us. It is urged that the Act cannot be sustained as an exercise of the police power, in view of the state of scientific authorities respecting inheritability of criminal traits. It is argued that due process is lacking because, under this Act, unlike the Act upheld in Buck v. Bell, 274 U.S. 200, the defendant is given no opportunity to be heard on the issue as to whether he is the probable potential parent of socially undesirable offspring. . . . It is also suggested that the Act is penal in character and that the sterilization provided for is cruel and unusual punishment and violative of the Fourteenth Amendment. . . . We pass those points without intimating an opinion on them, for there is a feature of the Act which clearly condemns it. That is, its failure to meet the requirements of the equal protection clause of the Fourteenth Amendment.

We do not stop to point out all of the inequalities in this Act. A few examples will suffice. In Oklahoma, grand larceny is a felony. Okla. Stats. Ann. Tit. 21, §§1705, 5. Larceny is grand larceny when the property taken exceeds $20 in value. Id. §1704. Embezzlement is punishable "in the manner prescribed for feloniously stealing property of the value of that embezzled." Id. §1462. Hence, he who embezzles property worth more than $20 is guilty of a felony. A clerk who appropriates over $20 from his employer's till (id. §1456) and a stranger who steals the same amount are thus both guilty of felonies. If the latter repeats his act and is convicted three times, he may be sterilized. But the clerk is not subject to the pains and penalties of the Act no matter how large his embezzlements nor how frequent his convictions. A person who enters a chicken coop and steals chickens commits a felony (id. §1719); and he may be sterilized if he is thrice convicted. If, however, he is a bailee of the property and fraudulently appropriates it, he is an embezzler. Id. §1455. Hence, no matter how habitual his proclivities for embezzlement are and no matter how often his conviction, he may not be sterilized. Thus, the nature of two crimes is intrinsically the same and they are punishable in the same manner. . . .

It was stated in Buck v. Bell, supra, that the claim that state legislation violates the equal protection clause of the Fourteenth Amendment is "the usual last resort of constitutional arguments." 274 U.S. p. 208. Under our constitutional system the States in determining the reach and scope of particular legislation need not provide "abstract symmetry." Patsone v. Pennsylvania, 232 U.S. 138, 144. They may mark and set apart the classes and types of problems according to the needs and as dictated or suggested by experience. See Bryant v. Zimmerman, 278 U.S. 63, and cases cited. It was in that connection that Mr. Justice Holmes, speaking for the Court in Bain Peanut Co. v. Pinson, 282 U.S. 499, 501, stated, "We must remember that the machinery of government would not work if it were not allowed a little play in its joints." Only recently we reaffirmed the view that the equal protection clause does not prevent the legislature from recognizing "degrees of evil" (Truax v. Raich, 239 U.S. 33, 43) by our ruling in Tigner v. Texas, 310 U.S. 141, 147, that "the Constitution does not require things which are different in fact or opinion to be treated in law as though they were the same." And see Nashville, C. & St. L. Ry. v. Browning, 310 U.S. 362. Thus, if we had here only a question as to a State's classification of crimes, such as embezzlement or larceny, no substantial federal question would be raised. . . . For a State is not constrained in the exercise of its police power to ignore experience which marks a class of offenders or a family of offenses for special treatment. Nor is it prevented by the equal protection clause from confining "its restrictions to those classes of cases where the need is deemed to be clearest." Miller v. Wilson, 236 U.S. 373, 384. . . . As stated in Buck v. Bell, supra, p. 208, ". . . the law does all that is needed when it does all that it can, indicates a policy, applies it to all within the lines, and seeks to bring within the lines all similarly situated so far and so fast as its means allow."

But the instant legislation runs afoul of the equal protection clause, though we give Oklahoma that large deference which the rule of the foregoing cases requires. We are dealing here with legislation which involves one of the basic civil rights of man. Marriage and procreation are fundamental to the very existence and survival of the race. The power to sterilize if exercised, may have subtle, far-reaching and devastating effects. In evil or reckless hands it can cause races or types which are inimical to the dominant group to wither and disappear. There is no redemption for the individual whom the law touches. Any experiment which the State conducts is to his irreparable injury. He is forever deprived of a basic liberty. We mention these matters not to reexamine the scope of the police power of the States. We advert to them merely in emphasis of our view that strict scrutiny of the classification which a State makes in a sterilization law is essential, lest unwittingly, or otherwise, invidious discriminations are made against groups or types of individuals in violation of the constitutional guaranty of just and equal laws. The guaranty of "equal protection of the laws is a pledge of the protection of equal laws." Yick Wo v. Hopkins, 118 U.S. 356, 369. When the law lays an unequal hand on those who have committed intrinsically the same quality of offense and sterilizes one and not the other, it has made as invidious a discrimination as if it had selected a particular race or nationality for oppressive treatment. Yick Wo v. Hopkins, supra; Gaines v. Canada, 305 U.S. 337. Sterilization of those who have thrice committed grand larceny, with immunity for those who are embezzlers, is a clear, pointed, unmistakable discrimination. Oklahoma makes no attempt to say that he who commits larceny by trespass or trick or fraud has biologically inheritable traits which he who commits embezzlement lacks. Oklahoma's line between larceny by fraud and embezzlement is determined, as we have noted, "with reference to the time when the fraudulent intent to convert the property to the taker's own use" arises. Riley v. State, supra, 64 Okla. Cr. at p. 189. We have not the slightest basis for inferring that that line has any significance in eugenics, nor that the inheritability of criminal traits follows the neat legal distinctions which the law has marked between those two offenses. In terms of fines and imprisonment, the crimes of larceny and embezzlement rate the same under the Oklahoma code. Only when it comes to sterilization are the pains and penalties of the law different. The equal protection clause would indeed be a formula of empty words if such conspicuously artificial lines could be drawn. . . . In Buck v. Bell, supra, the Virginia statute was upheld though it applied only to feeble-minded persons in institutions of the State. But it was pointed out that "so far as the operations enable those who otherwise must be kept confined to be returned to the world, and thus open the asylum to others, the equality aimed at will be more nearly reached." 274 U.S. p. 208. Here there is no such saving feature. Embezzlers are forever free. Those who steal or take in other ways are not. If such a classification were permitted, the technical common law concept of a "trespass" (Bishop, Criminal Law, 9th Ed., vol. 1, §§ 566, 567) based on distinctions which are "very largely dependent upon history for explanation" (Holmes, The Common Law, p. 73) could readily become a rule of human genetics.

It is true that the Act has a broad severability clause. But we will not endeavor to determine whether its application would solve the equal protection difficulty. The Supreme Court of Oklahoma sustained the Act without reference to the severability clause. We have therefore a situation where the Act as construed and applied to petitioner is allowed to perpetuate the discrimination which we have found to be fatal. Whether the severability clause would be so applied as to remove this particular constitutional objection is a question which may be more appropriately left for adjudication by the Oklahoma court. Dorchy v. Kansas, 264 U.S. 286. That is reemphasized here by our uncertainty as to what excision, if any, would be made as a matter of Oklahoma law. Cf. Smith v. Cahoon, 283 U.S. 553. It is by no means clear whether, if an excision were made, this particular constitutional difficulty might be solved by enlarging on the one hand or contracting on the other (cf. Mr. Justice Brandeis dissenting, National Life Ins. Co. v. United States, 277 U.S. 508, 534-535) the class of criminals who might be sterilized.

Reversed.

MR. CHIEF JUSTICE STONE, concurring:

I concur in the result, but I am not persuaded that we are aided in reaching it by recourse to the equal protection clause.

If Oklahoma may resort generally to the sterilization of criminals on the assumption that their propensities are transmissible to future generations by inheritance, I seriously doubt that the equal protection clause requires it to apply the measure to all criminals in the first instance, or to none. See Rosenthal v. New York, 226 U.S. 260, 271; Keokee Coke Co. v. Taylor, 234 U.S. 224, 227; Patsone v. Pennsylvania, 232 U.S. 138, 144.

Moreover, if we must presume that the legislature knows — what science has been unable to ascertain — that the criminal tendencies of any class of habitual offenders are transmissible regardless of the varying mental characteristics of its individuals, I should suppose that we must likewise presume that the legislature, in its wisdom, knows that the criminal tendencies of some classes of offenders are more likely to be transmitted than those of others. And so I think the real question we have to consider is not one of equal protection, but whether the wholesale condemnation of a class to such an invasion of personal liberty, without opportunity to any individual to show that his is not the type of case which would justify resort to it, satisfies the demands of due process.

There are limits to the extent to which the presumption of constitutionality can be pressed, especially where the liberty of the person is concerned (see United States v. Carolene Products Co., 304 U.S. 144, 152, n.4) and where the presumption is resorted to only to dispense with a procedure which the ordinary dictates of prudence would seem to demand for the protection of the individual from arbitrary action. Although petitioner here was given a hearing to ascertain whether sterilization would be detrimental to his health, he was given none to discover whether his criminal tendencies are of an inheritable type. Undoubtedly a state may, after appropriate inquiry, constitutionally interfere with the personal liberty of the individual to prevent the transmission by inheritance of his socially injurious tendencies. Buck v. Bell, 274 U.S. 200. But until now we have not been called upon to say that it may do so without giving him a hearing and opportunity to challenge the existence as to him of the only facts which could justify so drastic a measure.

Science has found and the law has recognized that there are certain types of mental deficiency associated with delinquency which are inheritable. But the State does not contend — nor can there be any pretense — that either common knowledge or experience, or scientific investigation, has given assurance that the criminal tendencies of any class of habitual offenders are universally or even generally inheritable. In such circumstances, inquiry whether such is the fact in the case of any particular individual cannot rightly be dispensed with. Whether the procedure by which a statute carries its mandate into execution satisfies due process is a matter of judicial cognizance. A law which condemns, without hearing, all the individuals of a class to so harsh a measure as the present because some or even many merit condemnation, is lacking in the first principles of due process. Morrison v. California, 291 U.S. 82, 90, and cases cited; Taylor v. Georgia, 315 U.S. 25. And so, while the state may protect itself from the demonstrably inheritable tendencies of the individual which are injurious to society, the most elementary notions of due process would seem to require it to take appropriate steps to safeguard the liberty of the individual by affording him, before he is condemned to an irreparable injury in his person, some opportunity to show that he is without such inheritable tendencies. The state is called on to sacrifice no permissible end when it is required to reach its objective by a reasonable and just procedure adequate to safeguard rights of the individual which concededly the Constitution protects.[r]

NOTE Severability and Equal Protection

Similar to the problem of severability discussed by the Court in the Skinner case is the issue, presented with some frequency in equal protection cases, as to the scope of the judicial power through statutory construction to prevent an unconstitutional inequality. See, e.g., Yu Cong Eng v. Trinidad, 271 U.S. 500, 515-523 (1926); Connolly v. Union Sewer Pipe, 184 U.S. 540, 565 (1902); Louisville & Nashville R. Co. v. Public Service Commission, 249 F. Supp. 894 (M.D. Tenn. 1966).

If the limiting language of a taxing or regulatory statute produces an unconstitutional inequality between those subjected to and those exempted from the statute's force, should relief be afforded by discarding the limitation, and thus extending the statute's reach, or by condemning the entire enactment? See Morey v. Doud, 354 U.S. 457 (1957), and its sequelae, Thillens, Inc. v. Morey, 11 Ill. 2d 579, 144 N.E. 2d 735 (1957), 355 U.S. 606 (1958).

If a statute that discriminates between the sexes in the age of majority is held unconstitutional, which age is then effective? See Stanton v. Stanton, 421 U.S. 7 (1975). Must it be the age favorable to the person seeking relief?

KOTCH v. BOARD OF RIVER PORT PILOT COMMRS., 330 U.S. 552, 67 S. Ct. 910, 91 L. Ed. 1093 (1947). Mr. Justice Black delivered the opinion of the Court: "Louisiana statutes provide in general that all seagoing vessels moving between New Orleans and foreign ports must be navigated through the Mississippi River approaches to

---

[r] A concurring opinion of Mr. Justice Jackson is omitted. On sterilization see Williams, The Sanctity of Human Life and the Criminal Law 70-109 (1958); St. John-Stevas, Life, Death, and the Law 160-197 (1961). — ED.

the port of New Orleans and within it exclusively by pilots who are State officers. New State pilots are appointed by the governor only upon certification of a State Board of River Pilot Commissioners, themselves pilots. Only those who have served a six-month apprenticeship under incumbent pilots and who possess other specific qualifications may be certified to the governor by the board. Appellants here have had at least fifteen years experience in the river, the port, and elsewhere, as pilots of vessels whose pilotage was not governed by the State law in question. Although they possess all the statutory qualifications except that they have not served the requisite six months apprenticeship under Louisiana officer pilots, they have been denied appointment as State pilots. Seeking relief in a Louisiana state court they alleged that the incumbent pilots, having unfettered discretion under the law in the selection of apprentices, had selected, with occasional exception, only the relatives and friends of incumbents; that the selections were made by electing prospective apprentices into the pilots' association, which the pilots have formed by authority of State law; that since 'membership . . . has been closed . . . to all except those having the favor of the pilots' the result is that only their relatives and friends have and can become State pilots. The Supreme Court of Louisiana has held that the pilotage law so administered does not violate the equal protection clause of the Fourteenth Amendment, 209 La. 737. The case is here on appeal from that decision under 28 U.S.C. §344(a)."

What decision? Why?

Goesaert v. Cleary 335 U.S. 464, 69 S. Ct. 198, 93 L. Ed. 163 (1948)

Mr. Justice Frankfurter delivered the opinion of the Court.

As part of the Michigan system for controlling the sale of liquor, bartenders are required to be licensed in all cities having a population of 50,000 or more, but no female may be so licensed unless she be "the wife or daughter of the male owner" of a licensed liquor establishment. Section 9a of Act 133 of the Public Acts of Michigan, 1945, Mich. Stat. Ann. §18.990(1) (Cum. Supp. 1947). The case is here on direct appeal from an order of the District Court of three judges, convened under §266 of the old Judicial Code, now 28 U.S.C. §2284, denying an injunction to restrain the enforcement of the Michigan law. The claim, denied below, one judge dissenting, 74 F. Supp. 735, and renewed here, is that Michigan cannot forbid females generally from being barmaids and at the same time make an exception in favor of the wives and daughters of the owners of liquor establishments. Beguiling as the subject is, it need not detain us long. To ask whether or not the Equal Protection of the Laws Clause of the Fourteenth Amendment barred Michigan from making the classification the State has made between wives and daughters of nonowners, is one of those rare instances where to state the question is in effect to answer it.

We are, to be sure, dealing with a historic calling. We meet the alewife, sprightly and ribald, in Shakespeare, but centuries before him she played a role in the social life of England. See, e.g., Jusserand, English Wayfaring Life in the Middle Ages, 133, 134, 136-37 (1889). The Fourteenth Amendment did not tear history up by the roots, and the regulation of the liquor traffic is one of the oldest and most untrammeled of legislative powers. Michigan could, beyond question, forbid all women from working behind a bar. This is so despite the vast changes in the social and legal position of women. The fact that women may now have achieved the virtues that men have long claimed as their prerogatives and now indulge in vices that men have long practiced, does not preclude the States from drawing a sharp line between the sexes, certainly in such matters as the regulation of the liquor traffic. See the Twenty-First Amendment and Carter v. Virginia, 321 U.S. 131. The Constitution does not require legislatures to reflect sociological insight, or shifting social standards, any more than it requires them to keep abreast of the latest scientific standards.

While Michigan may deny to all women opportunities for bartending, Michigan cannot play favorites among women without rhyme or reason. The Constitution in enjoining the equal protection of the laws upon States precludes irrational discrimination as between persons or groups of persons in the incidence of a law. But the Constitution does not require situations "which are different in fact or opinion to be treated in law as though they were the same." Tigner v. Texas, 310 U.S. 141, 147. Since bartending by women may, in the allowable legislative judgment, give rise to moral and social problems against which it may devise preventive measures, the legislature need not go to the full length of prohibition if it believes that as to a defined group of females other factors are operating which either eliminate or reduce the moral and social problems otherwise calling for prohibition. Michigan evidently believes that the oversight assured through ownership of a bar by a barmaid's husband or father minimizes hazards that may confront a barmaid without such protecting oversight. This Court is certainly not in a position to gainsay such belief by the Michigan legislature. If it is entertainable, as we think it is, Michigan has not violated its duty to afford equal protection of its laws. We cannot cross-examine either actually or argumentatively the mind of Michigan legislators nor question their motives. Since the line they have drawn is not without a basis in reason, we cannot give ear to the suggestion that the real impulse behind this legislation was an unchivalrous desire of male bartenders to try to monopolize the calling.

It would be an idle parade of familiar learning to review the multitudinous cases in which the constitutional assurance of the equal protection of the laws has been applied. The generalities on this subject are not in dispute; their application turns peculiarly on the particular circumstances of a case. Thus, it would be a sterile inquiry to consider whether this case is nearer to the nepotic pilotage law of Louisiana, sustained in Kotch v. Pilot Commissioners, 330 U.S. 552, than it is to the Oklahoma sterilization law, which fell in Skinner v. Oklahoma, 316 U.S. 535. Suffice it to say that "A statute is not invalid under the Constitution because it might have gone farther than it did, or because it may not succeed in bringing about the result that it intends to produce." Roschen v. Ward, 279 U.S. 337, 339.

Nor is it unconstitutional for Michigan to withdraw from women the occupation of bartending because it allows women to serve as waitresses where liquor is dispensed. The District Court has sufficiently indicated the reasons that may have influenced the legislature in allowing women to be waitresses in a liquor establishment over which a man's ownership provides control. Nothing need be added to what was said below as to the other grounds on which the Michigan law was assailed.

Judgment affirmed.

MR. JUSTICE RUTLEDGE, with whom MR. JUSTICE DOUGLAS and MR. JUSTICE MURPHY join, dissenting.

While the equal protection clause does not require a legislature to achieve "abstract symmetry" or to classify with "mathematical nicety," that clause does require lawmakers to refrain from invidious distinctions of the sort drawn by the statute challenged in this case.

The statute arbitrarily discriminates between male and female owners of liquor establishments. A male owner, although he himself is always absent from his bar, may employ his wife and daughter as barmaids. A female owner may neither work as a barmaid herself nor employ her daughter in that position, even if a man is always present in the establishment to keep order. This inevitable result of the classification belies the assumption that the statute was motivated by a legislative solicitude for the moral and physical well-being of women who, but for the law, would be employed as barmaids. Since there could be no other conceivable justification for such discrimination against women owners of liquor establishments, the statute should be held invalid as a denial of equal protection.

Railway Express Agency v. New York 336 U.S. 106, 69 S. Ct. 463, 93 L. Ed. 533 (1949)

Mr. Justice Douglas delivered the opinion of the Court.

Section 124 of the Traffic Regulations of the City of New York promulgated by the Police Commissioner provides:

"No person shall operate, or cause to be operated, in or upon any street an advertising vehicle; provided that nothing herein contained shall prevent the putting of business notices upon business delivery vehicles, so long as such vehicles are engaged in the usual business or regular work of the owner and not used merely or mainly for advertising."

Appellant is engaged in a nation-wide express business. It operates about 1,900 trucks in New York City and sells the space on the exterior sides of these trucks for advertising. That advertising is for the most part unconnected with its own business.[2] It was convicted in the magistrate's court and fined. The judgment of conviction was sustained in the Court of Special Sessions. 188 Misc. 342. The Court of Appeals affirmed without opinion by a divided vote. 297 N.Y. 703. The case is here on appeal. Judicial Code §237(a), 28 U.S.C. §344(a), as amended.

The Court in Fifth Ave. Coach Co. v. New York, 221 U.S. 467, sustained the predecessor ordinance to the present regulation over the objection that it violated the due process and equal protection clauses of the Fourteenth Amendment. It is true that that was a municipal ordinance resting on the broad base of the police power, while the present regulation stands or falls merely as a traffic regulation. But we do not believe that distinction warrants a different result in the two cases.

The court of Special Sessions concluded that advertising on vehicles using the streets of New York City constitutes a distraction to vehicle drivers and to pedestrians alike and therefore affects the safety of the public in the use of the streets. We do not sit to weigh evidence on the due process issue in order to determine whether the regulation is sound or appropriate; nor is it our function to pass judgment on its wisdom. See Olsen v. Nebraska, 313 U.S. 236. We would be trespassing on one of the most intensely local and specialized of all municipal problems if we held that this regulation had no relation to the traffic problem of New York City. It is the judgment of the local authorities that it does have such a relation. And nothing has been advanced which shows that to be palpably false.

The question of equal protection of the laws is pressed more strenuously on us. It is pointed out that the regulation draws the line between advertisements of products sold by the owner of the truck and general advertisements. It is argued that unequal treatment on the basis of such a distinction is not justified by the aim and purpose of the regulation. It is said, for example, that one of appellant's trucks carrying the advertisement of a commercial house would not cause any greater distraction of pedestrians and vehicle drivers than if the commercial house carried the same advertisement on its own truck. Yet the regulation allows the latter to do what the former is forbidden from doing. It is therefore contended that the classification which the regulation makes has no relation to the traffic problem since a violation turns not on what kind of advertisements are carried on trucks but on whose trucks they are carried.

That, however, is a superficial way of analyzing the problem, even if we assume that it is premised on the correct construction of the regulation. The local authorities may well have concluded that those who advertise their own wares on their trucks do not present the same traffic problem in view of the nature or extent of the advertising which they use. It would take a degree of omniscience which we lack to say that such is not the case. If that

---

[2] The advertisements for which appellant was convicted consisted of posters from three by seven feet to four by ten feet portraying Camel Cigarettes, Ringling Brothers and Barnum & Bailey Circus, and radio station WOR. Drivers of appellant's trucks carrying advertisements of Prince Albert Smoking Tobacco and the United States Navy were also convicted.

judgment is correct, the advertising displays that are exempt have less incidence on traffic than those of appellants.

We cannot say that that judgment is not an allowable one. Yet if it is, the classification has relation to the purpose for which it is made and does not contain the kind of discrimination against which the Equal Protection Clause affords protection. It is by such practical considerations based on experience rather than by theoretical inconsistencies that the question of equal protection is to be answered. Patsone v. Pennsylvania, 232 U.S. 138, 144; Marcus Brown Holding Co. v. Feldman, 256 U.S. 170, 198-199; Metropolitan Casualty Ins. Co. v. Brownell, 294 U.S. 580, 585-586. And the fact that New York City sees fit to eliminate from traffic this kind of distraction but does not touch what may be even greater ones in a different category, such as the vivid displays on Times Square, is immaterial. It is no requirement of equal protection that all evils of the same genus be eradicated or none at all. Central Lumber Co. v. South Dakota, 226 U.S. 157, 160.

It is finally contended that the regulation is a burden on interstate commerce in violation of Art. 1, §8 of the Constitution. Many of these trucks are engaged in delivering goods in interstate commerce from New Jersey to New York. Where traffic control and the use of highways are involved and where there is no conflicting federal regulation, great leeway is allowed local authorities, even though the local regulation materially interferes with interstate commerce. The case in that posture is controlled by South Carolina State Highway Dept. v. Barnwell Bros., 303 U.S. 177, 187 et seq. And see Maurer v. Hamilton, 309 U.S. 598.

Affirmed.

MR. JUSTICE RUTLEDGE acquiesces in the Court's opinion and judgment, dubitante on the question of equal protection of the laws.

MR. JUSTICE JACKSON, concurring.

There are two clauses of the Fourteenth Amendment which this Court may invoke to invalidate ordinances by which municipal governments seek to solve their local problems. One says that no state shall "deprive any person of life, liberty, or property, without due process of law." The other declares that no state shall "deny to any person within its jurisdiction the equal protection of the laws."

My philosophy as to the relative readiness with which we should resort to these two clauses is almost diametrically opposed to the philosophy which prevails on this Court. While claims of denial of equal protection are frequently asserted, they are rarely sustained. But the Court frequently uses the due process clause to strike down measures taken by municipalities to deal with activities in their streets and public places which the local authorities consider as creating hazards, annoyances or discomforts to their inhabitants. And I have frequently dissented when I thought local power was improperly denied. See, for example, opinion in Douglas v. Jeannette and companion cases, 319 U.S. 157, 166; and dissents in Saia v. New York, 334 U.S. 558, 566; Prince v. Massachusetts, 321 U.S. 158, 176.

The burden should rest heavily upon one who would persuade us to use the due process clause to strike down a substantive law or ordinance. Even its provident use against municipal regulations frequently disables all government — state, municipal and federal — from dealing with the conduct in question because the requirement of due process is also applicable to State and Federal Governments. Invalidation of a statute or an ordinance on due process grounds leaves ungoverned and ungovernable conduct which many people find objectionable.

Invocation of the equal protection clause, on the other hand, does not disable any governmental body from dealing with the subject at hand. It merely means that the prohibition or regulation must have a broader impact. I regard it as a salutary doctrine that cities, states and the Federal Government must exercise their powers so as not to discriminate between their inhabitants except upon some reasonable differentiation fairly related to the object of regulation. This equality is not merely abstract justice. The framers of the Constitution knew, and we should not forget today, that there is no more effective practical guaranty against arbitrary and unreasonable government than to require that the principles of law which officials would impose upon a minority must be imposed generally. Conversely, nothing opens the door to arbitrary action so effectively as to allow those officials to pick and choose only a few to whom they will apply legislation and thus to escape the political retribution that might be visited upon them if larger numbers were affected. Courts can take no better measure to assure that laws will be just than to require that laws be equal in operation. . . .

[Justice Jackson noted that, in this case, "it is one thing to tolerate action from those who act on their own and it is another thing to permit the same action to be promoted for a price." For, he concluded, "it is not difficult to see that, in a day of extravagant advertising more or less subsidized by tax deduction, the rental of truck space could become an obnoxious enterprise."][s]

2. Racial Discrimination

Plessy v. Ferguson 163 U.S. 537, 16 S. Ct. 1138, 41 L. Ed. 256 (1896)

MR. JUSTICE BROWN delivered the opinion of the court:

This case turns upon the constitutionality of an act of the general assembly of the state of Louisiana, passed in 1890, providing for separate railway carriages for the white and colored races. Acts 1890, No. 111, p. 152.

The 1st section of the statute enacts "that all railway companies carrying passengers in their coaches in this state shall provide equal but separate accommodations for the white and colored races, by providing two or more passenger coaches for each passenger train, or by dividing the passenger coaches by a partition so as to secure separate accommodations: Provided, That this section shall not be construed to apply to street railroads. No person or persons shall be permitted to occupy seats in coaches other than the ones assigned to them, on account of the race they belong to.". . .

The information filed in the criminal district court charged in substance that Plessy, being a passenger between two stations within the state of Louisiana, was assigned by officers of the company to the coach used for the race to which he belonged, but he insisted upon going into a coach used by the race to which he did not belong. Neither in the information nor plea was his particular race or color averred.

The petition for the writ of prohibition averred that petitioner was seven-eighths Caucasian and one-eighth African blood; that the mixture of colored blood was not discernible in him, and that he was entitled to every right, privilege, and immunity secured to citizens of the United States of the white race; and that, upon such theory, he took possession of a vacant seat in a coach where passengers of the white race were accommodated, and was ordered by the conductor to vacate said coach and take a seat in another assigned to persons of the colored race, and having refused to comply with such demand he was forcibly ejected with the aid of a police officer, and imprisoned in the parish jail to answer a charge of having violated the above act.

The constitutionality of this act is attacked upon the ground that it conflicts both with the 13th Amendment of the Constitution, abolishing slavery, and the 14th Amendment, which prohibits certain restrictive legislation on the part of the states.

[The Court found that the Thirteenth Amendment was not violated.]

---

[s] For a fuller elaboration of the views of Justice Jackson on legislative classification, see his The Supreme Court in the American System of Government (1955) (The Godkin Lectures at Harvard University). — ED.

The proper construction of [the Fourteenth] amendment was first called to the attention of this court in the Slaughter-House Cases, 16 Wall. 36, which involved, however, not a question of race, but one of exclusive privileges. The case did not call for any expression of opinion as to the exact right it was intended to secure to the colored race, but it was said generally that its main purpose was to establish the citizenship of the negro; to give definitions of citizenship of the United States and of the states, and to protect from the hostile legislation of the states the privileges and immunities of citizens of the United States, as distinguished from those of citizens of the states.

The object of the amendment was undoubtedly to enforce the absolute equality of the two races before the law, but in the nature of things it could not have been intended to abolish distinctions based upon color, or to enforce social, as distinguished from political, equality, or a commingling of the two races upon terms unsatisfactory to either. Laws permitting, and even requiring their separation in places where they are liable to be brought into contact do not necessarily imply the inferiority of either race to the other, and have been generally, if not universally, recognized as within the competency of the state legislatures in the exercise of their police power. The most common instance of this is connected with the establishment of separate schools for white and colored children, which have been held to be a valid exercise of the legislative power even by courts of states where the political rights of the colored race have been longest and most earnestly enforced.

One of the earliest of these cases is that of Roberts v. Boston, 5 Cush. 198, in which the supreme judicial court of Massachusetts held that the general school committee of Boston had power to make provision for the instruction of colored children in separate schools established exclusively for them, and to prohibit their attendance upon the other schools. "The great principle," said Chief Justice Shaw, "advanced by the learned and eloquent advocate of the plaintiff is, that by the Constitution and laws of Massachusetts, all persons without distinction of age or sex, birth or color, origin or condition, are equal before the law. . . . But when this great principle comes to be applied to the actual and various conditions of persons in society, it will not warrant the assertion that men and women are legally clothed with the same civil and political powers, and that children and adults are legally to have the same functions and be subject to the same treatment; but only that the rights of all, as they are settled and regulated by law, are equally entitled to the paternal consideration and protection of the law for their maintenance and security." It was held that the powers of the committee extended to the establishment of separate schools for children of different ages, sexes, and colors, and that they might also establish special schools for poor and neglected children, who have become too old to attend the primary school, and yet have not acquired the rudiments of learning, to enable them to enter the ordinary schools. Similar laws have been enacted by Congress under its general power of legislation over the District of Columbia (D.C. Rev. Stat. §§ 281, 282, 283, 310, 319) as well as by the legislatures of many of the states, and have been generally, if not uniformly, sustained by the courts. [Citations omitted.]

So far, then, as a conflict with the 14th Amendment is concerned, the case reduces itself to the question whether the statute of Louisiana is a reasonable regulation, and with respect to this there must necessarily be a large discretion on the part of the legislature. In determining the question of reasonableness it is at liberty to act with reference to the established usages, customs, and traditions of the people, and with a view to the promotion of their comfort, and the preservation of the public peace and good order. Gauged by this standard, we cannot say that a law which authorizes or even requires the separation of the two races in public conveyances is unreasonable or more obnoxious to the 14th Amendment than the acts of Congress requiring separate schools for colored children in the District of Columbia, the constitutionality of which does not seem to have been questioned, or the corresponding acts of state legislatures.

We consider the underlying fallacy of the plaintiff's argument to consist in the assumption that the enforced separation of the two races stamps the colored race with a badge of inferiority. If this be so, it is not by reason of anything found in the act, but solely because the colored race chooses to put that construction upon it. The argument necessarily assumes that if, as has been more than once the case, and is not unlikely to be so again, the colored race should become the dominant power in the state legislature, and should enact a law in precisely similar terms, it would thereby relegate the white race to an inferior position. We imagine that the white race, at least, would not acquiesce in this assumption. The argument also assumes that social prejudices may be overcome by legislation, and that equal rights cannot be secured to the negro except by an enforced commingling of the two races. We cannot accept this proposition. If the two races are to meet on terms of social equality, it must be the result of natural affinities, a mutual appreciation of each other's merits and a voluntary consent of individuals. . . .

The judgment of the court below is, therefore, affirmed.

Mr. Justice Brewer did not hear the argument or participate in the decision of this case.

Mr. Justice Harlan dissenting. . . .

While there may be in Louisiana persons of different races who are not citizens of the United States, the words in the act, "white and colored races," necessarily include all citizens of the United States of both races residing in that state. So that we have before us a state enactment that compels, under penalties, the separation of the two races in railroad passenger coaches, and makes it a crime for a citizen of either race to enter a coach that has been assigned to citizens of the other race.

Thus the state regulates the use of a public highway by citizens of the United States solely upon the basis of race.

However apparent the injustice of such legislation may be, we have only to consider whether it is consistent with the Constitution of the United States. . . .

In respect of civil rights, common to all citizens, the Constitution of the United States does not, I think, permit any public authority to know the race of those entitled to be protected in the enjoyment of such rights. Every true man has pride of race, and under appropriate circumstances, when the rights of others, his equals before the law, are not to be affected, it is his privilege to express such pride and to take such action based upon it as to him seems proper. But I deny that any legislative body or judicial tribunal may have regard to the race of citizens when the civil rights of those citizens are involved. Indeed such legislation as that here in question is inconsistent, not only with that equality of rights which pertains to citizenship, national and state, but with the personal liberty enjoyed by every one within the United States. . . .

The white race deems itself to be the dominant race in this country. And so it is, in prestige, in achievements, in education, in wealth and in power. So, I doubt not, it will continue to be for all time, if it remains true to its great heritage and holds fast to the principles of constitutional liberty. But in view of the Constitution, in the eye of the law, there is in this country no superior, dominant, ruling class of citizens. There is no caste here. Our Constitution is color-blind, and neither knows nor tolerates classes among citizens. . . .

In my opinion, the judgment this day rendered will, in time, prove to be quite as pernicious as the decision made by this tribunal in the Dred Scott Case. It was adjudged in that case that the descendants of Africans who were imported into this country and sold as slaves were not included nor intended to be included under the word "citizens" in the Constitution, and could not claim any of the rights and privileges which that instrument provided for and secured to citizens of the United States; that at the time of the adoption of the Constitution they were "considered as a subordinate and inferior class of beings, who had been subjugated by the dominant race, and, whether emancipated or not, yet remained subject to their authority, and had no rights or privileges but such as those who held the power and the government might choose to grant them." 19 How. 393, 404. The recent amendments of the Constitution, it was supposed, had eradicated these principles from our institutions. But it seems that we have yet, in some of the states, a dominant race, a superior class of citizens, which assumes to regulate the enjoyment of civil rights, common to all citizens, upon the basis of race. The present decision, it may well be apprehended, will not only stimulate aggressions, more or less brutal and irritating, upon the admitted rights of colored citizens, but will encourage the belief that it is possible, by means of state enactments, to defeat the beneficent purposes which the people of the United States had in view when they adopted the recent amendments of the Constitution, by one of which the blacks of this country were made citizens of the United States and of the states in which they respectively reside and whose privileges and immunities, as citizens, the states are forbidden to abridge. Sixty millions of whites are in no danger from the presence here of eight millions of blacks. The destinies of the two races in this country are indissolubly linked together, and the interests of both require that the common government of all shall not permit the seeds of race hate to be planted under the sanction of law. What can more certainly arouse race hate, what more certainly create and perpetuate a feeling of distrust between these races, than state enactments which in fact proceed on the ground that colored citizens are so inferior and degraded that they cannot be allowed to sit in public coaches occupied by white citizens? That, as all will admit, is the real meaning of such legislation as was enacted in Louisiana. . . .

If evils will result from the commingling of the two races upon public highways established for the benefit of all, they will be infinitely less than those that will surely come from state legislation regulating the enjoyment of civil rights upon the basis of race. We boast of the freedom enjoyed by our people above all other peoples. But it is difficult to reconcile that boast with a state of the law which, practically, puts the brand of servitude and degradation upon a large class of our fellow citizens, our equals before the law. The thin disguise of "equal" accommodations for passengers in railroad coaches will not mislead anyone, or atone for the wrong this day done. . . .

For the reasons stated, I am constrained to withhold my assent from the opinion and judgment of the majority.[t]

MISSOURI ex rel. GAINES v. CANADA, 305 U.S. 337, 59 S. Ct. 232, 83 L. Ed. 208 (1938). The petitioner, a Negro citizen of Missouri, sought a writ of mandamus to compel the curators of the State University of Missouri to admit him to the Law School of the University. Admission to the school had been denied him solely on racial grounds, but, in accordance with the statutes of the state, the Board of Curators had offered to pay his tuition out of state funds at any of the qualified law schools in neighboring states. The Missouri courts had denied the petitioner the relief he sought. On certiorari the judgment of the Supreme Court of Missouri was reversed. Chief Justice Hughes, for a majority of the Court, wrote as follows: "The basic consideration is not as to what sort of opportunities other States provide, or whether they are as good as those in Missouri, but as to what opportunities Missouri itself furnishes to white students and denies to negroes solely upon the ground of color. The admissibility of laws separating the races in the enjoyment of privileges by the State rests wholly upon the equality of the privileges which the laws give to the separated groups within the State." 305 U.S. at 349.

---

[t]In Cumming v. Board of Education, 175 U.S. 528 (1899), Mr. Justice Harlan, for a unanimous Court, affirmed the denial of injunctive relief sought by the parents of Negro children of high-school age against the collection of taxes for the maintenance of a high school for white children, no public high school for Negroes being available. — ED.

Sweatt v. Painter 339 U.S. 629, 70 S. Ct. 848, 94 L. Ed. 1114 (1950)

MR. CHIEF JUSTICE VINSON delivered the opinion of the Court.

This case and McLaurin v. Oklahoma State Regents, post, . . . present different aspects of this general question: To what extent does the Equal Protection Clause of the Fourteenth Amendment limit the power of a state to distinguish between students of different races in professional and graduate education in a state university? Broader issues have been urged for our consideration, but we adhere to the principle of deciding constitutional questions only in the context of the particular case before the Court. We have frequently reiterated that this Court will decide constitutional questions only when necessary to the disposition of the case at hand, and that such decisions will be drawn as narrowly as possible. Rescue Army v. Municipal Court, 331 U.S. 549 (1947), and cases cited therein. Because of this traditional reluctance to extend constitutional interpretations to situations or facts which are not before the Court, much of the excellent research and detailed argument presented in these cases is unnecessary to their disposition.

In the instant case, petitioner filed an application for admission to the University of Texas Law School for the February, 1946 term. His application was rejected solely because he is a Negro. Petitioner thereupon brought this suit for mandamus against the appropriate school officials, respondents here, to compel his admission. At that time there was no law school in Texas which admitted Negroes.

The state trial court recognized that the action of the State in denying petitioner the opportunity to gain a legal education while granting it to others deprived him of the equal protection of the laws guaranteed by the Fourteenth Amendment. The court did not grant the relief requested, however, but continued the case for six months to allow the State to supply substantially equal facilities. At the expiration of the six months, in December, 1946, the court denied the writ on the showing that the authorized university officials had adopted an order calling for the opening of a law school for Negroes the following February. While petitioner's appeal was pending, such a school was made available, but petitioner refused to register therein. The Texas Court of Civil Appeals set aside the trial court's judgment and ordered the cause "remanded generally to the trial court for further proceedings without prejudice to the rights of any party to this suit."

On remand, a hearing was held on the issue of the equality of the educational facilities at the newly established school as compared with the University of Texas Law School. Finding that the new school offered petitioner "privileges, advantages, and opportunities for the study of law substantially equivalent to those offered by the State to white students at the University of Texas," the trial court denied mandamus. The Court of Civil Appeals affirmed. 210 S.W.2d 442 (1948). Petitioner's application for a writ of error was denied by the Texas Supreme Court. We granted certiorari, 338 U.S. 865 (1949), because of the manifest importance of the constitutional issues involved.

The University of Texas Law School, from which petitioner was excluded, was staffed by a faculty of sixteen full-time and three part-time professors, some of whom are nationally recognized authorities in their field. Its student body numbered 850. The library contained over 65,000 volumes. Among the other facilities available to the students were a law review, moot court facilities, scholarship funds, and Order of the Coif affiliation. The school's alumni occupy the most distinguished positions in the private practice of the law and in the public life of the State. It may properly be considered one of the nation's ranking law schools.

The law school for Negroes which was to have opened in February, 1947, would have had no independent faculty or library. The teaching was to be carried on by four members of the University of Texas Law School faculty, who were to maintain their offices at the University of Texas while teaching at both institutions. Few of the 10,000 volumes ordered for the library had arrived; nor was there any full-time librarian. The school lacked accreditation.

Since the trial of this case, respondents report the opening of a law school at the Texas University for Negroes. It is apparently on the road to full accreditation. It has a faculty of five full-time professors; a student body of 23; a library of some 16,500 volumes serviced by a full-time staff; a practice court and legal aid association; and one alumnus who has become a member of the Texas Bar.

Whether the University of Texas Law School is compared with the original or the new law school for Negroes, we cannot find substantial equality in the educational opportunities offered white and Negro law students by the State. In terms of number of the faculty, variety of courses and opportunity for specialization, size of the student body, scope of the library, availability of law review and similar activities, the University of Texas Law School is superior. What is more important, the University of Texas Law School possesses to a far greater degree those qualities which are incapable of objective measurement but which make for greatness in a law school. Such qualities, to name but a few, include reputation of the faculty, experience of the administration, position and influence of the alumni, standing in the community, traditions and prestige. It is difficult to believe that one who had a free choice between these law schools would consider the question close.

Moreover, although the law is a highly learned profession, we are well aware that it is an intensely practical one. The law school, the proving ground for legal learning and practice, cannot be effective in isolation from the individuals and institutions with which the law interacts. Few students and no one who has practiced law would choose to study in an academic vacuum, removed from the interplay of ideas and the exchange of views with which the law is concerned. The law school to which Texas is willing to admit petitioner excludes from its student body members of the racial groups which number 85% of the population of the State and include most of the lawyers, witnesses, jurors, judges and other officials with whom petitioner will inevitably be dealing when he becomes a member of the Texas Bar. With such a substantial and significant segment of society excluded, we cannot conclude that the education offered petitioner is substantially equal to that which he would receive if admitted to the University of Texas Law School. . . .

We hold that the Equal Protection Clause of the Fourteenth Amendment requires that petitioner be admitted to the University of Texas Law School. The judgment is reversed and the cause is remanded for proceedings not inconsistent with this opinion.

Reversed.

McLAURIN v. OKLAHOMA STATE REGENTS, 339 U.S. 637, 70 S. Ct. 851, 94 L. Ed. 1149 (1950). After its refusal to admit appellant, a Negro citizen of Oklahoma, was held unconstitutional by a federal court, the University of Oklahoma Graduate School proceeded to conduct his program of instruction "upon a segregated basis," as required by state statute. Thus, wrote Chief Justice Vinson, for a unanimous Court: "He is now assigned to a seat in the classroom in a row specified for colored students; he is assigned to a table in the library on the main floor; and he is permitted to eat at the same time in the cafeteria as other students, although here again he is assigned to a special table."

Even though these separations are said to be "in form merely nominal," the Court found that "they signify that the State, in administering the facilities it affords for professional and graduate study, sets McLaurin apart from the other students. The result is that appellant is handicapped in his pursuit of effective graduate instruction. Such restrictions impair and inhibit his ability to study, to engage in discussions and exchange views with other students, and, in general, to learn his profession."

The Court concluded that "the conditions under which this appellant is required to receive his education deprive him of his personal and present right to the equal protection of the laws. See Sweatt v. Painter, 339 U.S. 629. We hold that under these circumstances the Fourteenth Amendment precludes differences in treatment by the state based upon race. Appellant, having been admitted to a state-supported graduate school, must receive the same treatment at the hands of the state as students of other races."

Brown v. Board of Education; Briggs v. Elliott; Davis v. County School Board; Gebhart v. Belton 347 U.S. 483, 74 S. Ct. 686, 98 L. Ed. 873 (1954)

MR. CHIEF JUSTICE WARREN delivered the opinion of the Court.

These cases come to us from the States of Kansas, South Carolina, Virginia, and Delaware. They are premised on different facts and different local conditions, but a common legal question justifies their consideration together in this consolidated opinion.[1]

In each of the cases, minors of the Negro race, through their legal representatives, seek the aid of the courts in obtaining admission to the public schools of their community on a nonsegregated basis. In each instance, they had been denied admission to schools attended by white children under laws requiring or permitting segregation according to race. This segregation was alleged to deprive the plaintiffs of the equal protection of the

---

[1] In the Kansas case, Brown v. Board of Education, the plaintiffs are Negro children of elementary school age residing in Topeka. They brought this action in the United States District Court for the District of Kansas to enjoin enforcement of a Kansas statute which permits, but does not require, cities of more than 15,000 population to maintain separate school facilities for Negro and white students. Kan. Gen. Stat. §72-1724 (1949). Pursuant to that authority, the Topeka Board of Education elected to establish segregated elementary schools. Other public schools in the community, however, are operated on a nonsegregated basis. The three-judge District Court, convened under 28 U.S.C. §§2281 and 2284, found that segregation in public education has a detrimental effect upon Negro children, but denied relief on the ground that the Negro and white schools were substantially equal with respect to buildings, transportation, curricula, and educational qualifications of teachers. 98 F. Supp. 797. The case is here on direct appeal under 28 U.S.C. §1253.

In the South Carolina case, Briggs v. Elliott, the plaintiffs are Negro children of both elementary and high school age residing in Clarendon County. They brought this action in the United States District Court for the Eastern District of South Carolina to enjoin enforcement of provisions in the state constitution and statutory code which require the segregation of Negroes and whites in public schools. S.C. Const., Art. XI, §7; S.C. Code §5377 (1942). The three-judge District Court, convened under 28 U.S.C. §§2281 and 2284, denied the requested relief. The court found that the Negro schools were inferior to the white schools and ordered the defendants to begin immediately to equalize the facilities. But the court sustained the validity of the contested provisions and denied the plaintiffs admission to the white schools during the equalization program. 98 F. Supp. 529. This Court vacated the District Court's judgment and remanded the case for the purpose of obtaining the court's views on a report filed by the defendants concerning the progress made in the equalization program. 342 U.S. 350. On remand, the District Court found that substantial equality had been achieved except for buildings and that the defendants were proceeding to rectify this inequality as well. 103 F. Supp. 920. The case is again here on direct appeal under 28 U.S.C. §1253.

In the Virginia case, Davis v. County School Board, the plaintiffs are Negro children of high school age residing in Prince Edward County. They brought this action in the United States District Court for the Eastern District of Virginia to enjoin enforcement of provisions in the state constitution and statutory code which require the segregation of Negroes and whites in public schools. Va. Const., §140; Va. Code §22-221 (1950). The three-judge District Court, convened under 28 U.S.C. §§2281 and 2284, denied the requested relief. The court found the Negro school inferior in physical plant, curricula, and transportation, and ordered the defendants forthwith to provide substantially equal curricula and transportation and to "proceed with all reasonable diligence and dispatch to remove" the inequality in physical plant. But, as in the South Carolina case, the court sustained the validity of the contested provisions and denied the plaintiffs admission to the white schools during the equalization program. 103 F. Supp. 337. The case is here on direct appeal under 28 U.S.C. §1253.

In the Delaware case, Gebhart v. Belton, the plaintiffs are Negro children of both elementary and high school age residing in New Castle County. They brought this action in the Delaware Court of Chancery to enjoin enforcement of provisions in the state constitution and statutory code which require the segregation of Negroes and whites in public schools. Del. Const., Art. X, §2; Del. Rev. Code §2631 (1935). The Chancellor gave judgment for the plaintiffs and ordered their immediate admission to schools previously attended only by white children, on the ground that the Negro schools were inferior with respect to teacher training, pupil-teacher ratio, extra-curricular activities, physical plant, and time and distance involved in travel. 87 A.2d 862. The Chancellor also found that segregation itself results in an inferior education for Negro children (see note 10, infra), but did not rest his decision on that ground. Id. at 865. The Chancellor's decree was affirmed by the Supreme Court of Delaware, which intimated, however, that the defendants might be able to obtain a modification of the decree after equalization of the Negro and white schools had been accomplished. 91 A.2d 137, 152. The defendants, contending only that the Delaware courts had erred in ordering the immediate admission of the Negro plaintiffs to the white schools, applied to this Court for certiorari. The writ was granted, 344 U.S. 891. The plaintiffs, who were successful below, did not submit a cross-petition.

laws under the Fourteenth Amendment. In each of the cases other than the Delaware case, a three-judge federal district court denied relief to the plaintiffs on the so-called "separate but equal" doctrine announced by this Court in Plessy v. Ferguson, 163 U.S. 537. Under that doctrine, equality of treatment is accorded when the races are provided substantially equal facilities, even though these facilities be separate. In the Delaware case, the Supreme Court of Delaware adhered to that doctrine, but ordered that the plaintiffs be admitted to the white schools because of their superiority to the Negro schools.

The plaintiffs contend that segregated public schools are not "equal" and cannot be made "equal," and that hence they are deprived of the equal protection of the laws. Because of the obvious importance of the question presented, the Court took jurisdiction. Argument was heard in the 1952 Term, and reargument was heard this Term on certain questions propounded by the Court.

Reargument was largely devoted to the circumstances surrounding the adoption of the Fourteenth Amendment in 1868. It covered exhaustively consideration of the Amendment in Congress, ratification by the states, then existing practices in racial segregation, and the views of proponents and opponents of the Amendment. This discussion and our own investigation convince us that, although these sources cast some light, it is not enough to resolve the problem with which we are faced. At best, they are inconclusive. The most avid proponents of the post-War Amendments undoubtedly intended them to remove all legal distinctions among "all persons born or naturalized in the United States." Their opponents, just as certainly, were antagonistic to both the letter and the spirit of the Amendments and wished them to have the most limited effect. What others in Congress and the state legislatures had in mind cannot be determined with any degree of certainty.

An additional reason for the inconclusive nature of the Amendment's history, with respect to segregated schools, is the status of public education at that time. In the South, the movement toward free common schools, supported by general taxation, had not yet taken hold. Education of white children was largely in the hands of private groups. Education of Negroes was almost non-existent, and practically all of the race were illiterate. In fact, any education of Negroes was forbidden by law in some states. Today, in contrast, many Negroes have achieved outstanding success in the arts and sciences as well as in the business and professional world. It is true that public education had already advanced further in the North, but the effect of the Amendment on Northern States was generally ignored in the congressional debates. Even in the North, the conditions of public education did not approximate those existing today. The curriculum was usually rudimentary; ungraded schools were common in rural areas; the school term was but three months a year in many states; and compulsory school attendance was virtually unknown. As a consequence, it is not surprising that there should be so little in the history of the Fourteenth Amendment relating to its intended effect on public education.

In the first cases in this Court construing the Fourteenth Amendment, decided shortly after its adoption, the Court interpreted it as proscribing all state-imposed discriminations against the Negro race. The doctrine of "separate but equal" did not make its appearance in this Court until 1896 in the case of Plessy v. Ferguson, supra, involving not education but transportation. American courts have since labored with the doctrine for over half a century. In this Court, there have been six cases involving the "separate but equal" doctrine in the field of public education. In Cumming v. County Board of Education, 175 U.S. 528, and Gong Lum v. Rice, 275 U.S. 78, the validity of the doctrine itself was not challenged. In more recent cases, all on the graduate school level, inequality was found in that specific benefits enjoyed by white students were denied to Negro students of the same educational qualifications. Missouri ex rel. Gaines v. Canada, 305 U.S. 337; Sipuel v. Oklahoma, 332 U.S. 631; Sweatt v. Painter, 339 U.S. 629; McLaurin v. Oklahoma State Regents, 339 U.S. 637. In none of these cases was it necessary to reexamine the doctrine to grant relief to the Negro plaintiff. And in Sweatt v. Painter, supra, the Court expressly reserved decision on the question whether Plessy v. Ferguson should be held inapplicable to public education.

In the instant cases, that question is directly presented. Here, unlike Sweatt v. Painter, there are findings below that the Negro and white schools involved have been equalized, or are being equalized, with respect to buildings, curricula, qualifications and salaries of teachers, and other "tangible" factors. Our decision, therefore, cannot turn on merely a comparison of these tangible factors in the Negro and white schools involved in each of the cases. We must look instead to the effect of segregation itself on public education.

In approaching this problem, we cannot turn the clock back to 1868 when the Amendment was adopted, or even to 1896 when Plessy v. Ferguson was written. We must consider public education in the light of its full development and its present place in American life throughout the Nation. Only in this way can it be determined if segregation in public schools deprives these plaintiffs of the equal protection of the laws.

Today, education is perhaps the most important function of state and local governments. Compulsory school attendance laws and the great expenditures for education both demonstrate our recognition of the importance of education to our democratic society. It is required in the performance of our most basic public responsibilities, even service in the armed forces. It is the very foundation of good citizenship. Today it is a principal instrument in awakening the child to cultural values, in preparing him for later professional training, and in helping him to adjust normally to his environment. In these days, it is doubtful that any child may reasonably be expected to succeed in life if he is denied the opportunity of an education. Such an opportunity, where the state has undertaken to provide it, is a right which must be made available to all on equal terms.

We come then to the question presented: Does segregation of children in public schools solely on the basis of race, even though the physical facilities and other "tangible" factors may be equal, deprive the children of the minority group of equal educational opportunities? We believe that it does.

In Sweatt v. Painter, supra, in finding that a segregated law school for Negroes could not provide them equal educational opportunities, this Court relied in large part on "those qualities which are incapable of objective measurement but which make for greatness in a law school." In McLaurin v. Oklahoma State Regents, supra, the Court, in requiring that a Negro admitted to a white graduate school be treated like all other students, again resorted to intangible considerations: ". . . his ability to study, to engage in discussions and exchange views with other students, and, in general, to learn his profession." Such considerations apply with added force to children in grade and high schools. To separate them from others of similar age and qualifications solely because of their race generates a feeling of inferiority as to their status in the community that may affect their hearts and minds in a way unlikely ever to be undone. The effect of this separation on their educational opportunities was well stated by a finding in the Kansas case by a court which nevertheless felt compelled to rule against the Negro plaintiffs: "Segregation of white and colored children in public schools has a detrimental effect upon the colored children. The impact is greater when it has the sanction of the law; for the policy of separating the races is usually interpreted as denoting the inferiority of the Negro group. A sense of inferiority affects the motivation of a child to learn. Segregation with the sanction of law, therefore, has a tendency to retard the educational and mental development of Negro children and to deprive them of some of the benefits they would receive in a racially integrated school system." Whatever may have been the extent of psychological knowledge at the time of Plessy v. Ferguson, this finding is amply supported by modern authority.[11] Any language in Plessy v. Ferguson contrary to this finding is rejected.

---

[11] K. B. Clark, Effect of Prejudice and Discrimination on Personality Development (Midcentury White House Conference on Children and Youth, 1950); Witmer and Kotinsky, Personality in the Making (1952), c. VI; Deutscher and Chein, the Psychological Effects of Enforced Segregation: a Survey of Social Science Opinion, 26 J. Psychol. 259 (1948); Chein, What are the Psychological Effects of Segregation Under Conditions of Equal Facilities?, 3 Int. J. Opinion and Attitude Res. 229 (1949); Brameld, Educational Costs, in Discrimination and National Welfare (McIver ed., 1949), 44-48; Frazier, The Negro in the United States (1949), 674-681. And see generally Myrdal, An American Dilemma (1944).

We conclude that in the field of public education the doctrine of "separate but equal" has no place. Separate educational facilities are inherently unequal. Therefore, we hold that the plaintiffs and others similarly situated for whom the actions have been brought are, by reason of the segregation complained of, deprived of the equal protection of the laws guaranteed by the Fourteenth Amendment. This disposition makes unnecessary any discussion whether such segregation also violates the Due Process Clause of the Fourteenth Amendment.

Because these are class actions, because of the wide applicability of this decision, and because of the great variety of local conditions, the formulation of decrees in these cases presents problems of considerable complexity. On reargument, the consideration of appropriate relief was necessarily subordinated to the primary question — the constitutionality of segregation in public education. We have now announced that such segregation is a denial of the equal protection of the laws. In order that we may have the full assistance of the parties in formulating decrees, the cases will be restored to the docket, and the parties are requested to present further argument on Questions 4 and 5 previously propounded by the Court for the reargument this Term. The Attorney General of the United States is again invited to participate. The Attorneys General of the states requiring or permitting segregation in public education will also be permitted to appear as amici curiae upon request to do so by September 15, 1954, and submission of briefs by October 1, 1954.

It is so ordered.

Bolling v. Sharpe 347 U.S. 497, 74 S. Ct. 693, 98 L. Ed. 884 (1954)

MR. CHIEF JUSTICE WARREN delivered the opinion of the Court.

This case challenges the validity of segregation in the public schools of the District of Columbia. The petitioners, minors of the Negro race, allege that such segregation deprives them of due process of law under the Fifth Amendment. They were refused admission to a public school attended by white children solely because of their race. They sought the aid of the District Court for the District of Columbia in obtaining admission. That court dismissed their complaint. We granted a writ of certiorari before judgment in the Court of Appeals because of the importance of the constitutional question presented. 344 U.S. 873.

We have this day held that the Equal Protection Clause of the Fourteenth Amendment prohibits the states from maintaining racially segregated public schools. The legal problem in the District of Columbia is somewhat different, however. The Fifth Amendment, which is applicable in the District of Columbia, does not contain an equal protection clause as does the Fourteenth Amendment which applies only to the states. But the concepts of equal protection and due process, both stemming from our American ideal of fairness, are not mutually exclusive. The "equal protection of the laws" is a more explicit safeguard of prohibited unfairness than "due process of law," and therefore, we do not imply that the two are always interchangeable phrases. But, as this Court has recognized, discrimination may be so unjustifiable as to be violative of due process.

Classifications based solely upon race must be scrutinized with particular care, since they are contrary to our traditions and hence constitutionally suspect. As long ago as 1896, this Court declared the principle "that the Constitution of the United States, in its present form, forbids, so far as civil and political rights are concerned, discrimination by the General Government, or by the States, against any citizen because of his race." And in Buchanan v. Warley, 245 U.S. 60, the Court held that a statute which limited the right of a property owner to convey his property to a person of another race was, as an unreasonable discrimination, a denial of due process of law.

Although the Court has not assumed to define "liberty" with any great precision, that term is not confined to mere freedom from bodily restraint. Liberty under law extends to the full range of conduct which the individual is free to pursue, and it cannot be restricted except for a proper governmental objective. Segregation in public education is not reasonably related to any proper governmental objective, and thus it imposes on Negro children of the District of Columbia a burden that constitutes an arbitrary deprivation of their liberty in violation of the Due Process Clause.

In view of our decision that the Constitution prohibits the states from maintaining racially segregated public schools, it would be unthinkable that the same Constitution would impose a lesser duty on the Federal Government. We hold that racial segregation in the public schools of the District of Columbia is a denial of the due process of law guaranteed by the Fifth Amendment to the Constitution.

For the reasons set out in Brown v. Board of Education, this case will be restored to the docket for reargument on Questions 4 and 5 previously propounded by the Court. 345 U.S. 972.

It is so ordered.[u]

Brown v. Board of Education 349 U.S. 294, 75 S. Ct. 753, 99 L. Ed. 1083 (1955)

MR. CHIEF JUSTICE WARREN delivered the opinion of the Court.

These cases were decided on May 17, 1954. The opinions of that date, declaring the fundamental principle that racial discrimination in public education is unconstitutional, are incorporated herein by reference. All provisions of federal, state, or local law requiring or permitting such discrimination must yield to this principle. There remains for consideration the manner in which relief is to be accorded.

Because these cases arose under different local conditions and their disposition will involve a variety of local problems, we requested further argument on the question of relief.[2] In view of the nationwide importance of the decision, we invited the Attorney General of the United States and the Attorneys General of all states requiring or permitting racial discrimination in public education to present their views on that question. The parties, the United States, and the States of Florida, North Carolina, Arkansas, Oklahoma, Maryland, and Texas filed briefs and participated in the oral argument.

These presentations were informative and helpful to the Court in its consideration of the complexities arising from the transition to a system of public education freed of racial discrimination. The presentations also demonstrated that substantial steps to eliminate racial discrimination in public schools have already been taken, not only in some of the

---

[u] Concerning the intention of those who drafted and ratified the equal protection clause of the Fourteenth Amendment, see Bickel, The Original Understanding and the Segregation Decision, 69 Harv. L. Rev. 1 (1955). — ED.

[2] Further argument was requested on the following questions, 347 U.S. 483, 495-496, n.13, previously propounded by the Court:

"4. Assuming it is decided that segregation in public schools violates the Fourteenth Amendment,

"(a) would a decree necessarily follow providing that, within the limits set by normal geographic school districting, Negro children should forthwith be admitted to schools of their choice, or

"(b) may this Court in the exercise of its equity powers, permit an effective gradual adjustment to be brought about from existing segregated systems to a system not based on color distinctions?

"5. On the assumption on which questions 4(a) and (b) are based, and assuming further that this Court will exercise its equity powers to the end described in question 4(b),

"(a) should this Court formulate detailed decrees in these cases;

"(b) if so, what specific issues should the decrees reach;

"(c) should this Court appoint a special master to hear evidence with a view to recommending specific terms for such decrees;

"(d) should this Court remand to the courts of first instance with directions to frame decrees in these cases, and if so what general directions should the decrees of this Court include and what procedures should the courts of first instance follow in arriving at the specific terms of more detailed decrees?"

communities in which these cases arose, but in some of the states appearing as amici curiae, and in other states as well. Substantial progress has been made in the District of Columbia and in the communities in Kansas and Delaware involved in this litigation. The defendants in the cases coming to us from South Carolina and Virginia are awaiting the decision of this Court concerning relief.

Full implementation of these constitutional principles may require solution of varied local school problems. School authorities have the primary responsibility for elucidating, assessing, and solving these problems; courts will have to consider whether the action of school authorities constitutes good faith implementation of the governing constitutional principles. Because of their proximity to local conditions and the possible need for further hearings, the courts which originally heard these cases can best perform this judicial appraisal. Accordingly, we believe it appropriate to remand the cases to those courts.

In fashioning and effectuating the decrees, the courts will be guided by equitable principles. Traditionally, equity has been characterized by a practical flexibility in shaping its remedies and by a facility for adjusting and reconciling public and private needs. These cases call for the exercise of these traditional attributes of equity power. At stake is the personal interest of the plaintiffs in admission to public schools as soon as practicable on a nondiscriminatory basis. To effectuate this interest may call for elimination of a variety of obstacles in making the transition to school systems operated in accordance with the constitutional principles set forth in our May 17, 1954, decision. Courts of equity may properly take into account the public interest in the elimination of such obstacles in a systematic and effective manner. But it should go without saying that the vitality of these constitutional principles cannot be allowed to yield simply because of disagreement with them.

While giving weight to these public and private considerations, the courts will require that the defendants make a prompt and reasonable start toward full compliance with our May 17, 1954, ruling. Once such a start has been made, the courts may find that additional time is necessary to carry out the ruling in an effective manner. The burden rests upon the defendants to establish that such time is necessary in the public interest and is consistent with good faith compliance at the earliest practicable date. To that end, the courts may consider problems related to administration, arising from the physical condition of the school plant, the school transportation system, personnel, revision of school districts and attendance areas into compact units to achieve a system of determining admission to the public schools on a nonracial basis, and revision of local laws and regulations which may be necessary in solving the foregoing problems. They will also consider the adequacy of any plans the defendants may propose to meet these problems and to effectuate a transition to a racially nondiscriminatory school system. During this period of transition, the courts will retain jurisdiction of these cases.

The judgments below, except that in the Delaware case, are accordingly reversed and the cases are remanded to the District Courts to take such proceedings and enter such orders and decrees consistent with this opinion as are necessary and proper to admit to public schools on a racially nondiscriminatory basis with all deliberate speed the parties to these cases. The judgment in the Delaware case — ordering the immediate admission of the plaintiffs to schools previously attended only by white children — is affirmed on the basis of the principles stated in our May 17, 1954, opinion, but the case is remanded to the Supreme Court of Delaware for such further proceedings as that Court may deem necessary in light of this opinion.

It is so ordered.

NOTE The Aftermath of Brown

A vast literature of commendation and of condemnation, of praise and of criticism, followed in the wake of the School Segregation Cases. The most thoughtful questioning of the decisions is that of Professor Wechsler in his lecture, Toward Neutral Principles of Constitutional Law, 73 Harv. L. Rev. 1 (1959), reprinted in his Principles, Politics, and Fundamental Law 3 (1961). Comments responsive to Professor Wechsler's lecture were Pollak, Racial Discrimination and Judicial Integrity, 108 U. Pa. L. Rev. 1 (1959); Black, The Lawfulness of the Segregation Decisions, 69 Yale L.J. 421 (1960).

In Browder v. Gayle, 142 F. Supp. 707 (1956), two members of a three-judge court in the District of Alabama read the School Segregation Cases as repudiating the holding of Plessy v. Ferguson, and thus denied the validity of publicly enforced racial segregation of passengers in intrastate commerce. In Gayle v. Browder, 352 U.S. 903 (1956), the Supreme Court, in a per curiam opinion, affirmed the decision. The School Segregation Cases were also held to outlaw racial segregation on public bathing beaches, Dawson v. Mayor, 220 F.2d 386 (4th Cir. 1955), aff'd per curiam, 350 U.S. 877 (1955), and on municipal golf courses, Holmes v. City of Atlanta, 350 U.S. 897 (1955). In State Athletic Commission v. Dorsey, 359 U.S. 533 (1959), the Court affirmed a decision that a state statute forbidding the participation of whites and Negroes in the same athletic contests was unconstitutional. Why would Professor Wechsler have considered these per curiam decisions to be departures from "principled" decisionmaking? Wechsler, supra, at 22.

Actual implementation of the Brown decision often meant, in the words of one commentator, "all deliberation and no speed." Much of the delay owed to the adamant resistance that often developed. On March 11, 1956, for example, almost the entire Southern delegation joined in the Congressional Manifesto, a criticism of Brown that amounted to "a calculated declaration of political war against the Court's decision." Bickel, The Least Dangerous Branch 256 (1962).

Cooper v. Aaron, 358 U.S. 1, 4 (1958), subsequently involved a claim by the Governor and the Legislature of Arkansas that "they are not bound by our holding in Brown." On the day of a planned desegregation of a high school in Little Rock, units of the National Guard, dispatched under orders from Governor Faubus, prevented the black students from attending. Soon thereafter, a court order compelled the National Guard to withdraw; federal troops sent by President Eisenhower maintained order for the rest of the school year. Midway through that school year, the school board petitioned the district court for a delay in the plan of desegregation because, it contended, the "extreme public hostility" caused by the actions of the Governor and the Legislature would make sound education impossible. 358 U.S. at 12. The district court granted the delay but was reversed by the court of appeals. Under the time pressure of the beginning of a new academic year, the Supreme Court issued an order the day after oral argument which affirmed the reversal below. In a later opinion signed individually by each Justice, the Court announced that "law and order are not here to be preserved by depriving the Negro children of their constitutional rights." 358 U.S. at 16. The violence and the disorder which has been the "product of state action," the Court said, "can also be brought under control by state action." 358 U.S. at 16. See Cooper v. Aaron, supra page 13.

A detailed account of the Brown litigation, including the deliberations in the Supreme Court, is given in Kugler, Simple Justice (1976). Accounts of legal struggles in the federal courts over desegregation in the Southern schools are given in Peltason, Fifty-Eight Lonely Men (1961).

Griffin v. Prince Edward County School Board 377 U.S. 218, 84 S. Ct. 1226, 12 L. Ed. 2d 754 (1964)

MR. JUSTICE BLACK delivered the opinion of the Court.

This litigation began in 1951 when a group of Negro school children living in Prince Edward County, Virginia, filed a complaint in the United States District Court for the Eastern District of Virginia alleging that they had been denied admission to public schools attended by white children and charging that Virginia laws requiring such school segregation denied complainants equal protection of the laws in violation of the Fourteenth Amendment. On May 17, 1954, ten years ago, we held that Virginia segregation laws did deny equal protection. Brown v. Board of Education, 347 U.S. 483 (1954). On May 31, 1955, after reargument on the nature of relief, we remanded this case, along with others heard with it, to the District Courts to enter such orders as "necessary and proper to admit [complainants] to public schools on a racially nondiscriminatory basis with all deliberate speed. . . ." Brown v. Board of Education, 349 U.S. 294, 301 (1955).

Efforts to desegregate Prince Edward County's schools met with resistance. In 1956 Section 141 of the Virginia Constitution was amended to authorize the General Assembly and local governing bodies to appropriate funds to assist students to go to public or to nonsectarian private schools, in addition to those owned by the State or by the locality. The General Assembly met in special session and enacted legislation to close any public schools where white and colored children were enrolled together, to cut off state funds to such schools, to pay tuition grants to children in nonsectarian private schools, and to extend state retirement benefits to teachers in newly created private schools. The legislation closing mixed schools and cutting off state funds was later invalidated by the Supreme Court of Appeals of Virginia, which held that these laws violated the Virginia Constitution. Harrison v. Day, 200 Va. 439, 106 S.E.2d 636 (1959). In April 1959 the General Assembly abandoned "massive resistance" to desegregation and turned instead to what was called a "freedom of choice" program. The Assembly repealed the rest of the 1956 legislation, as well as a tuition grant law of January 1959, and enacted a new tuition grant program. At the same time the Assembly repealed Virginia's compulsory attendance laws and instead made school attendance a matter of local option.

In June 1959, the United States Court of Appeals for the Fourth Circuit directed the Federal District Court (1) to enjoin discriminatory practices in Prince Edward County schools, (2) to require the County School Board to take "immediate steps" toward admitting students without regard to race to the white high school "in the school term beginning September 1959," and (3) to require the Board to make plans for admissions to elementary schools without regard to race. Allen v. County School Board of Prince Edward County, 266 F.2d 507, 511 (C.A. 4th Cir. 1959). Having as early as 1956 resolved that they would not operate public schools "wherein white and colored children are taught together," the Supervisors of Prince Edward County refused to levy any school taxes for the 1959-1960 school year, explaining that they were "confronted with a Court decree which requires the admission of white and colored children to all the schools of the county without regard to race or color." As a result, the county's public schools did not reopen in the fall of 1959 and have remained closed ever since, although the public schools of every other county in Virginia have continued to operate under laws governing the State's public school system and to draw funds provided by the State for that purpose. A private group, the Prince Edward School Foundation, was formed to operate private schools for white children in Prince Edward County and, having built its own school plant, has been in operation ever since the closing of the public schools. An offer to set up private schools for colored children in the county was rejected, the Negroes of Prince Edward preferring to continue the legal battle for desegregated public schools, and colored children were without formal education from 1959 to 1963, when federal, state, and county authorities cooperated to have classes conducted for Negroes and whites in school buildings owned by the county. During the 1959-1960 school year the Foundation's schools for white children were supported entirely by private contributions, but in 1960 the General Assembly adopted a new tuition grant program making every child, regardless of race, eligible for tuition grants of $125 or $150 to attend a nonsectarian private school or a public school outside his locality, and also authorizing localities to provide their own grants. The Prince Edward Board of Supervisors then passed an ordinance providing tuition grants of $100, so that each child attending the Prince Edward School Foundation's schools received a total of $225 if in elementary school or $250 if in high school. In the 1960-1961 session the major source of financial support for the Foundation was in the indirect form of these state and county tuition grants, paid to children attending Foundation schools. At the same time, the County Board of Supervisors passed an ordinance allowing property tax credits up to 25% for contributions to any "nonprofit, nonsectarian private school" in the county.

In 1961 petitioners here filed a supplemental complaint, adding new parties and seeking to enjoin the respondents from refusing to operate an efficient system of public free schools in Prince Edward County and to enjoin payment of public funds to help support private schools which excluded students on account of race. The District Court, finding that "the end result of every action taken by that body [Board of Supervisors] was designed to preserve separation of the races in the schools of Prince Edward County," enjoined the county from paying tuition grants or giving tax credits so long as public schools remained closed. Allen v. County School Board of Prince Edward County, 198 F. Supp. 497, 503 (D.C.E.D. Va. 1961). At this time the District Court did not pass on whether the public schools of the county could be closed but abstained pending determination by the Virginia courts of whether the constitution and laws of Virginia required the public schools to be kept open. Later, however, without waiting for the Virginia courts to decide the question,[9] the District Court held that "the public schools of Prince Edward County may not be closed to avoid the effect of the law of the land as interpreted by the Supreme Court, while the Commonwealth of Virginia permits other public schools to remain open at the expense of the taxpayers." Allen v. County School Board of Prince Edward County, 207 F. Supp. 349, 355 (D.C.E.D. Va. 1962). Soon thereafter, a declaratory judgment suit was brought by the County Board of Supervisors and the County School Board in a Virginia Circuit Court. Having done this, these parties asked the Federal District Court to abstain from further proceedings until the suit in the state courts had run its course, but the District Court declined; it repeated its order that Prince Edward's public schools might not be closed to avoid desegregation while the other public schools in Virginia remained open. The Court of Appeals reversed, Judge Bell dissenting, holding that the District Court should have abstained to await state court determination of the validity of the tuition grants and the tax credits, as well as the validity of the closing of the public schools. Griffin v. Board of Supervisors of Prince Edward County, 322 F.2d 332 (C.A. 4th Cir. 1963). We granted certiorari, stating:

"In view of the long delay in the case since our decision in the Brown case and the importance of the questions presented, we grant certiorari and put the case down for argument March 30, 1964 on the merits, as we have done in other comparable situations without waiting for final action by the Court of Appeals." 375 U.S. 391, 392.

For reasons to be stated, we agree with the District Court that, under the circumstances here, closing the Prince Edward County Schools while public schools in all the other counties of Virginia were being maintained, denied the petitioners and the class of Negro students they represent, the equal protection of the laws guaranteed by the Fourteenth Amendment. . . .

II

In County School Board of Prince Edward County v. Griffin, 204 Va. 650, 133 S.E.2d 565 (1963), the Supreme Court of Appeals of Virginia upheld as valid under state law the

---

[9] The Supreme Court of Appeals of Virginia had, in a mandamus proceeding instituted by petitioners, held that the State Constitution and statutes did not impose upon the County Board of Supervisors any mandatory duty to levy taxes and appropriate money to support free public schools. Griffin v. Board of Supervisors of Prince Edward County, 203 Va. 321, 124 S.E.2d 227 (1962).

closing of the Prince Edward County public schools, the state and county tuition grants for children who attend private schools, and the county's tax concessions for those who make contributions to private schools. The same opinion also held that each county had "an option to operate or not to operate public schools." 204 Va., at 671, 133 S.E.2d, at 580. We accept this case as a definitive and authoritative holding of Virginia law, binding on us, but we cannot accept the Virginia Court's further holding, based largely on the Court of Appeals' opinion in this case, 322 F.2d 332, that closing the county's public schools under the circumstances of the case did not deny the colored school children of Prince Edward County equal protection of the laws guaranteed by the Federal Constitution.

Since 1959, all Virginia counties have had the benefits of public schools but one: Prince Edward. However, there is no rule that counties, as counties, must be treated alike; the Equal Protection Clause relates to equal protection of the laws "between persons as such rather than between areas." Salsburg v. Maryland, 346 U.S. 545, 551 (1954). Indeed, showing that different persons are treated differently is not enough, without more, to show a denial of equal protection. Kotch v. Board of River Port Pilot Comm'rs, 330 U.S. 552, 556 (1947). It is the circumstances of each case which govern. Skinner v. Oklahoma ex rel. Williamson, 316 U.S. 535, 539-540 (1942).

Virginia law, as here applied, unquestionably treats the school children of Prince Edward differently from the way it treats the school children of all other Virginia counties. Prince Edward children must go to a private school or none at all; all other Virginia children can go to public schools. Closing Prince Edward's schools bears more heavily on Negro children in Prince Edward County since white children there have accredited private schools which they can attend, while colored children until very recently have had no available private schools, and even the school they now attend is a temporary expedient. Apart from this expedient, the result is that Prince Edward County school children, if they go to school in their own county, must go to racially segregated schools which, although designated as private, are beneficiaries of county and state support.

A State, of course, has a wide discretion in deciding whether laws shall operate statewide or shall operate only in certain counties, the legislature "having in mind the needs and desires of each." Salsburg v. Maryland, supra, 346 U.S., at 552. A State may wish to suggest, as Maryland did in Salsburg, that there are reasons why one county ought not to be treated like another. 346 U.S., at 553-554. But the record in the present case could not be clearer that Prince Edward's public schools were closed and private schools operated in their place with state and county assistance, for one reason, and one reason only: to ensure, through measures taken by the county and the State, that white and colored children in Prince Edward County would not, under any circumstances, go to the same school. Whatever nonracial grounds might support a State's allowing a county to abandon public schools, the object must be a constitutional one, and grounds of race and opposition to desegregation do not qualify as constitutional. . . .

III

We come now to the question of the kind of decree necessary and appropriate to put an end to the racial discrimination practiced against these petitioners under authority of the Virginia laws. That relief needs to be quick and effective. The party defendants are the Board of Supervisors, School Board, Treasurer, and Division Superintendent of Schools of Prince Edward County, and the State Board of Education and the State Superintendent of Education. All of these have duties which relate directly or indirectly to the financing, supervision, or operation of the schools in Prince Edward County. The Board of Supervisors has the special responsibility to levy local taxes to operate public schools or to aid children attending the private schools now functioning there for white children. The District Court enjoined the county officials from paying county tuition grants or giving tax exemptions and from processing applications for state tuition grants so long as the county's public schools remained closed. We have no doubt of the power of the court to give this relief to enforce the discontinuance of the county's racially discriminatory practices. It has long been established that actions against a county can be maintained in United States courts in order to vindicate federally guaranteed rights. E.g., Lincoln County v. Luning, 133 U.S. 529 (1890); Kennecott Copper Corp. v. State Tax Comm'n, 327 U.S. 573, 579 (1946). The injunction against paying tuition grants and giving tax credits while public schools remain closed is appropriate and necessary since those grants and tax credits have been essential parts of the county's program, successful thus far, to deprive petitioners of the same advantages of a public school education enjoyed by children in every other part of Virginia. For the same reasons the District Court may, if necessary to prevent further racial discrimination, require the Supervisors to exercise the power that is theirs to levy taxes to raise funds adequate to reopen, operate, and maintain without racial discrimination a public school system in Prince Edward County like that operated in other counties in Virginia.

The District Court held that "the public schools of Prince Edward County may not be closed to avoid the effect of the law of the land as interpreted by the Supreme Court, while the Commonwealth of Virginia permits other public schools to remain open at the expense of the taxpayers." Allen v. County School Board of Prince Edward County, 207 F. Supp. 349, 355 (D.C.E.D. Va. 1962). At the same time the court gave notice that it would later consider an order to accomplish this purpose if the public schools were not reopened by September 7, 1962. That day has long passed, and the schools are still closed. On remand, therefore, the court may find it necessary to consider further such an order. An order of this kind is within the court's power if required to assure these petitioners that their constitutional rights will no longer be denied them. The time for mere "deliberate speed" has run out, and that phrase can no longer justify denying these Prince Edward County school children their constitutional rights to an education equal to that afforded by the public schools in the other parts of Virginia.

The judgment of the Court of Appeals is reversed, the judgment of the District Court is affirmed, and the cause is remanded to the District Court with directions to enter a decree which will guarantee that these petitioners will get the kind of education that is given in the State's public schools. And, if it becomes necessary to add new parties to accomplish this end, the District Court is free to do so.

It is so ordered.

MR. JUSTICE CLARK and MR. JUSTICE HARLAN disagree with the holding that the federal courts are empowered to order the reopening of the public schools in Prince Edward County, but otherwise join in the Court's opinion.

NOTE Further Developments in Southern School Desegregation

May a school board allow student placement to be determined by a "freedom of choice" plan which allows a pupil to choose his or her own public school? In Green v. County School Board, 391 U.S. 430, 437-438 (1968), the unanimous Court said that the duty upon the school board under Brown was "to take whatever steps might be necessary to convert to a unitary system in which racial discrimination would be eliminated root and branch." The Court noted that after three years of "freedom of choice" in this district, where "there is no residential segregation," 85 percent of the Negro children attend what used to be the Negro school under the dual system. Moreover, since no whites had enrolled there, it was still an all-Negro school. Where other methods such as "zoning" promised a speedier conversion to a unitary, nonracial system, the Court ruled that "freedom of choice" plans would be unacceptable, unless they too showed their effectiveness as tools of desegregation.

In Monroe v. Board of Commissioners, 391 U.S. 450 (1968), a school board under court order to desegregate a dual system provided a plan that assigned pupils on a geographical basis but that allowed a "free transfer" to other schools of their choice. The plan did not, however, supply bus transportation. The Court found the plan "inadequate" under the Green standards since such a considerable number of pupils of both races transferred according to the "old, established discriminatory pattern" that the system became resegregated.

In Swann v. Board of Education, 402 U.S. 1 (1971), the Court dealt comprehensively and unanimously, in an opinion by Burger, C.J., with practical problems of school desegregation. In the outcome, the Court sustained in all respects the decree of the district court.

The Court limited its opinion to the legal situation at bar, where segregation by law had prevailed and compliance with the Brown decision was laggard. "The failure of local authorities to meet their constitutional obligations aggravated the massive problem of converting from the state-enforced discrimination of racially separate school systems. . . . The objective today remains to eliminate from the public schools all vestiges of state-imposed segregation. . . . Once a right and a violation have been shown, the scope of a district court's equitable powers to remedy past wrongs is broad, for breadth and flexibility are inherent in equitable remedies."

The Court held inapplicable the limitation in Title IV, §2000c of the Civil Rights Act of 1964, providing that "desegregation shall not mean the assignment of students to public schools in order to overcome racial balance," and that federal courts are not empowered by the act to require transportation in order to achieve racial balance "or otherwise enlarge the existing power of the court to insure compliance with constitutional standards." The Court concluded that this provision did not deny to federal courts their normal equity powers to enforce a constitutional mandate, but that it applied only to cases of so-called de facto segregation.

On specific issues, the Court ruled:

1. Racial balances or quotas. Although the district court set as a goal a racial balance in the schools of 71-29 percent, reflecting school population, this was not to be taken as a literal command. Not every school need reflect the racial composition of the system as a whole, but awareness of such composition is a "useful starting point" to correct past violations.

2. One-race schools. While the existence of some virtually one-race schools is not of itself a constitutional violation, "the burden upon the school authorities will be to satisfy the court that their racial composition is not the result of present or past discriminatory action on their part. . . . An optional majority-to-minority transfer provision has long been recognized as a useful part of every desegregation plan."

3. Altering of attendance zones. The pairing or clustering of schools in noncontiguous zones "as an interim corrective measure . . . cannot be said to be beyond the broad remedial powers of a court."

4. Transportation of students. "The importance of bus transportation as a normal and accepted tool of education policy is readily discernible in this and the companion case. . . . An objection to transportation of students may have validity when the time or distance of travel is so great as to risk either the health of the children or significantly impinge on the educational process."

See also North Carolina State Board of Education v. Swann, 402 U.S. 43 (1971), striking down a state statute which absolutely prohibited student busing for racial reasons.

See generally Kaplan, Segregation, Litigation and the Schools, 58 Nw. U.L. Rev. 1, 157 (1963), 59 id. 121 (1964); Fiss, Racial Imbalance in the Public Schools: The Constitutional Concepts, 78 Harv. L. Rev. 564 (1965); Fiss, The Charlotte-Mecklenburg Case — Its Significance for Northern School Desegregation, 38 U. Chi. L. Rev. 697 (1971); May, Busing, Swann v. Charlotte-Mecklenburg, and the Future of Desegregation in the Fifth Circuit, 49 Texas L. Rev. 884 (1971).

NOTE Desegregation of Schools in the North

Keyes v. School District No. 1, Denver, 413 U.S. 189 (1973), raised the question of the applicability of prior decisions to a school system that had never been segregated by law but in which racially imbalanced neighborhood public schools exist. The district court found that in one area of Denver, Park Hill, segregation was promoted since 1960 by a deliberate policy of the school board, evidenced by gerrymandering of school zones, the excessive use of mobile classroom units, the location of a new school, and other measures. The district court refused to hold that racial imbalance in the "core-city" schools must therefore also be corrected, but did hold that the latter were educationally inferior and that compensatory education must be provided in an integrated environment. The court of appeals reversed the latter branch of the decree. The Supreme Court, per Brennan, J., modified the decree of the court of appeals, remanding the case to the district court for further proceedings. Justice Rehnquist dissented; Justice Powell dissented in part.

The majority ordered a remand to determine whether the school board pursued a deliberate segregative policy in the core-city area, under a legal presumption, from the finding as to Park Hill, that shifts the burden of proof to the school board. If the burden is not met, a decree of all-out desegregation in the core-city schools must be entered.

Justice Powell's partial dissent took issue on two points. First, he would "not perpetuate the de jure-de facto distinction," turning on "segregative intent." Instead, he would impose a broader duty on public school authorities, north and south, to maintain an "integrated" system, defined as one where the authorities had taken appropriate steps to integrate faculties and administration, to assure equality of facilities, instruction, and curricula, to draw attendance zones to promote integration, and to locate new schools and close old ones with the same objective; and where transportation of pupils is undertaken it must be done with integrative opportunities in mind. Second, Justice Powell would deemphasize transportation of pupils, especially in the lower grades, as a prescribed means of achieving desegregation. He wrote: "Neighborhood school systems, neutrally administered, reflect the deeply felt desire of citizens for a sense of community in their public education. . . . Many citizens sense today a decline in the intimacy of our institutions — home, church, and school — which has caused a concomitant decline in the unity and communal spirit of our people. I pass not judgment on this viewpoint, but I do believe that this Court should be wary of compelling in the name of constitutional law what may seem to many a dissolution in the traditional, more personal fabric of their public schools." Thus, he would respect the concept of the neighborhood school, subject to an optional majority-to-minority transfer system, and, of course, to the obligations summarized above that school authorities must satisfy in order to maintain a unitary, integrated system.

See Goodman, De Facto School Segregation: A Constitutional and Empirical Analysis, 60 Calif. L. Rev. 275 (1972); Comment, Keyes v. School District No. 1: Unlocking the Northern Schoolhouse Doors, 9 Harv. Civ. Rights-Civ. Lib. L. Rev. 124 (1974).

In Milliken v. Bradley, 418 U.S. 717 (1974), the Supreme Court reversed, 5 to 4, a district court order contemplating metropolitan busing as a means of remedying racial segregation in the Detroit school system. The court had found that the Detroit school board had created and perpetuated school segregation in that city in the course of drawing attendance zones and choosing sites for new school construction and by other means. The court further found that Michigan state officials were implicated in the intracity segregation both directly, by legislation interfering with the implementation of a voluntary city desegregation plan, and by approval of segregative actions of the Detroit school board, and vicariously, because of the local board's status as a state agency. In its attempt to frame relief, the district court had concluded that intracity segregation could not be remedied unless Detroit's suburban school systems were included in the desegregation plan. It consequently ordered development of a plan that would envisage busing of students between Detroit and 53 suburban school districts.

Writing for the Court, Chief Justice Burger stated: ". . . it is obvious from the scope of the inter-district remedy itself that absent a complete restructuring of the laws of Michigan relating to school districts the District Court will become first, a de facto 'legislative authority' to resolve these complex [operational problems involved in designing the remedial system], and then the 'school superintendent' for the entire area. This is a task which few, if any, judges are qualified to perform and one which would deprive the people of control of schools through their elected representatives.

"Of course, no state law is above the Constitution. School district lines and the present laws with respect to local control, are not sacrosanct and if they conflict with the Fourteenth Amendment federal courts have a duty to prescribe appropriate remedies. See, e.g., Wright v. Council of City of Emporia, 407 U.S. 451; United States v. Scotland Neck Board of Education, 407 U.S. 484 (state or local officials prevented from carving out a new school district from an existing district that was in process of dismantling a dual school system); cf. Haney v. County board of Education of Sevier County, 429 F.2d 364 (CA8 1969) (State contributed to segregation of races by drawing of school district lines); United States v. Texas, 321 F. Supp. 1043 (ED Tex. 1970), aff'd, 447 F.2d 441 (CA5 1971), cert. denied, sub nom. Edgar v. United States, 404 U.S. 1016 (one or more school districts created and maintained for one race). But our prior holdings have been confined to violations and remedies within a single school district. We therefore turn to address, for the first time, the validity of a remedy mandating cross-district or inter-district consolidation to remedy a condition of segregation found to exist in only one district.

"The controlling principle consistently expounded in our holdings is that the scope of the remedy is determined by the nature and extent of the constitutional violation. [Citing Swann, supra.] Before the boundaries of separate and autonomous school districts may be set aside by consolidating the separate units for remedial purposes or by imposing a cross-district remedy, it must first be shown that there has been a constitutional violation within one district that produces a significant segregative effect in another district. Specifically it must be shown that racially discriminatory acts of the state or local school districts, or of a single school district have been a substantial cause of inter-district segregation. Thus an inter-district remedy might be in order where the racially discriminatory acts of one or more school districts caused racial segregation in an adjacent district, or where district lines have been deliberately drawn on the basis of race. . . .

"The record before us, voluminous as it is, contains evidence of de jure segregated conditions only in the Detroit schools; indeed, that was the theory on which the litigation was initially based and on which the District Court took evidence. . . . With no showing of significant violation by the 53 outlying school districts and no evidence of any interdistrict violation or effect, the court went beyond the original theory of the case as framed by the pleadings and mandated a metropolitan area remedy. . . .

"In dissent Mr. Justice White and Mr. Justice Marshall undertake to demonstrate that agencies having statewide authority participated in maintaining the dual school system found to exist in Detroit. They are apparently of the view that once such participation is shown, the District Court should have a relatively free hand to reconstruct school districts outside of Detroit in fashioning relief. Our assumption, arguendo, . . . that state agencies did participate in the maintenance of the Detroit school system, should make it clear that it is not on this point that we part company. The difference between us arises instead from established doctrine laid down by our cases. Brown, supra; Green, supra; Swann, supra; Scotland Neck, supra; and Emporia, supra; each addressed the issue of constitutional wrong in terms of an established geographical and administrative school system populated by both Negro and White children. In such a context, terms such as 'unitary' and 'dual' school systems, and 'racially identifiable schools,' have meaning, and the necessary federal authority to remedy the constitutional wrong is firmly established. But the remedy is necessarily designed, as all remedies are, to restore the victims of discriminatory conduct to the position they would have occupied in the absence of such conduct. Disparate treatment of White and Negro students occurred within the Detroit school system, and not elsewhere, and on this record the remedy must be limited to that system. . . ."

In a dissenting opinion joined by Justices Douglas, Brennan, and White, Justice Marshall wrote: ". . . the District Court's decision to expand its desegregation decree beyond the geographical limits of the city of Detroit rested in large part on its conclusions (A) that the State of Michigan was ultimately responsible for curing the condition of segregation within the Detroit city schools, and (B) that a Detroit-only remedy would not accomplish this task. In my view, both of these conclusions are well supported by the facts of this case and by this Court's precedents. . . .

[Justice Marshall reviewed the evidence that "the State of Michigan, through state officers and state agencies, had engaged in purposeful acts which created or aggravated segregation in the Detroit schools."]

"What action, then, could the District Court require the State to take in order to cure Detroit's condition of segregation? Our prior cases have not minced words as to what steps responsible officials and agencies must take in order to remedy segregation in the public schools. Not only must distinctions on the basis of race be terminated for the future, but school officials are also 'clearly charged with the affirmative duty to take whatever steps might be necessary to convert to a unitary system in which racial discrimination would be eliminated root and branch.' Green v. County School Board, 391 U.S. 430, 437-438 (1968). . . .

"We held in Swann that where de jure segregation is shown, school authorities must make 'every effort to achieve the greatest possible degree of actual desegregation.' 402 U.S., at 26. This is the operative standard re-emphasized in Davis v. Board of School Commissioners, 402 U.S. 33, 37 (1971). If these words have any meaning at all, surely it is that school authorities must, to the extent possible, take all practicable steps to ensure that Negro and white children in fact go to school together. This is, in the final analysis, what desegregation of the public schools is all about.

"Because of the already high and rapidly increasing percentage of Negro students in the Detroit system, as well as the prospect of white flight, a Detroit-only plan simply has no hope of achieving actual desegregation. Under such a plan white and Negro students will continue to attend all-Negro schools. The very evil that Brown I was aimed at will not be cured, but will be perpetuated for the future. . . ."

See Calkins & Gordon, The Right to Choose an Integrated Education: Voluntary Regional Integrated Schools — A Partial Remedy for De Facto Segregation, 9 Harv. Civ. Rights-Civ. Lib. L. Rev. 171 (1974); Note, Segregative Intent and the Single Governmental Entity in School Desegregation, 1973 Duke L.J. 1111; The Supreme Court, 1973 Term, 88 Harv. L. Rev. 41, 61-71 (1974); Note, Consolidation for Desegregation: The Unresolved Issue of the Inevitable Sequel, 82 Yale L.J. 1681 (1973).

WASHINGTON v. DAVIS, 426 U.S. 229 (1976). Unsuccessful applicants for the District of Columbia police force brought suit for an injunction and declaratory judgment, attacking a reading test as racially discriminatory in violation of the Fifth Amendment and Title VII of the Civil Rights Act of 1964. In its impact the test, which was devised by the Civil Service Commission and administered throughout the federal service, resulted in the disqualification of a substantially greater proportion of black than of white applicants. The district court gave judgment for the defendant officials; the court of appeals reversed, relying on decisions under Title VII, notably Griggs v. Duke Power Co., 401 U.S. 424 (1971), and Albemarle Paper Co. v. Moody, 422 U.S. 405 (1974). The Supreme Court reversed, reinstating the decree of dismissal by the district court.

Justice White, for the majority, stressed that, on the constitutional issue, invidious discrimination must be purposeful, and that to show a racially differential impact is not sufficient in itself nor does it place a burden on the government to justify the standards employed by "the weightiest of considerations." The evidence of racially disadvantaged impact is, however, not irrelevant: "With a prima facie case made out, 'the burden of proof shifts to the State to rebut the presumption of unconstitutional action by showing that permissible racially neutral selection criteria and procedures have produced the monochromatic result.' Alexander v. Louisiana, 405 U.S. 625, 632 (1972). . . . A rule that a statute designed to serve neutral ends is nevertheless invalid, absent compelling justification, if in practice it benefits or burdens one race more than another would be far-reaching and would raise serious questions about, and perhaps invalidate, a whole range of tax, welfare, public service, regulatory, and licensing statutes that may be more burdensome to the poor and to the average black than to the more affluent white." The Court also sustained the test under Title VII, on the ground that it was correlated with results in the police training program, aside from its possible relationship to actual performance as a police officer. Justices Brennan and Marshall dissented.

See Austin Independent School Dist. v. United States, 97 S. Ct. 517 (1976) (per curiam), vacating and remanding a desegregation order premised on a finding that a neighborhood school assignment plan perpetuates residential segregation.

See Brest, Foreword: In Defense of the Antidiscrimination Principle, 90 Harv. L. Rev. 1 (1976); Goodman, De Facto School Segregation: Constitutional and Empirical Analysis, 60 Calif. L. Rev. 275 (1970).

3. Congressional Enforcement and Reverse Discrimination

Katzenbach v. Morgan 384 U.S. 641, 86 S. Ct. 1717, 16 L. Ed. 2d 828 (1966)

MR. JUSTICE BRENNAN delivered the opinion of the court.

These cases concern the constitutionality of §4(e) of the Voting Rights Act of 1965. That law, in the respects pertinent in these cases, provides that no person who has successfully completed the sixth primary grade in a public school in, or a private school accredited by, the Commonwealth of Puerto Rico in which the language of instruction was other than English shall be denied the right to vote in any election because of his inability to read or write English. Appellees, registered voters in New York City, brought this suit to challenge the constitutionality of §4(e) insofar as it pro tanto prohibits the enforcement of the election laws of New York requiring an ability to read and write English as a condition of voting. Under these laws many of the several hundred thousand New York City residents who have migrated there from the Commonwealth of Puerto Rico had previously been denied the right to vote, and appellees attack §4(e) insofar as it would enable many of these citizens to vote. Pursuant to §14(b) of the Voting Rights Act of 1965, appellees commenced this proceeding in the District Court for the District of Columbia

Section G. **Equal Protection of the Laws** 903

seeking a declaration that §4(e) is invalid and an injunction prohibiting appellants, the Attorney General of the United States and the New York City Board of Elections, from either enforcing or complying with §4(e). A three-judge district court was designated. . . . Upon cross motions for summary judgment, that court, one judge dissenting, granted the declaratory and injunctive relief appellees sought. The court held that in enacting §4(e) Congress exceeded the powers granted to it by the Constitution and therefore usurped powers reserved to the States by the Tenth Amendment. 247 F. Supp. 196. . . . We reverse. We hold that, in the application challenged in these cases, §4(e) is a proper exercise of the powers granted to Congress by §5 of the Fourteenth Amendment[5] and that by force of the Supremacy Clause, Article VI, the New York English literacy requirement cannot be enforced to the extent that it is inconsistent with §4(e).

Under the distribution of powers effected by the Constitution, the States establish qualifications for voting for state officers, and the qualifications established by the States for voting for members of the most numerous branch of the state legislature also determine who may vote for United States Representatives and Senators, Art I, §2; Seventeenth Amendment. . . . But, of course, the States have no power to grant or withhold the franchise on conditions that are forbidden by the Fourteenth Amendment, or any other provision of the Constitution. Such exercises of state power are no more immune to the limitations of the Fourteenth Amendment than any other state action. The Equal Protection Clause itself has been held to forbid some state laws that restrict the right to vote.

The Attorney General of the State of New York argues that an exercise of congressional power under §5 of the Fourteenth Amendment that prohibits the enforcement of a state law can only be sustained if the judicial branch determines that the state law is prohibited by the provisions of the Amendment that Congress sought to enforce. More specifically, he urges that §4(e) cannot be sustained as appropriate legislation to enforce the Equal Protection Clause unless the judiciary decides — even with the guidance of a congressional judgment — that the application of the English literacy requirement prohibited by §4(e) is forbidden by the Equal Protection Clause itself. We disagree. Neither the language nor history of §5 supports such a construction.[7] As was said with regard to §5 in Ex parte Virginia, 100 U.S. 339, 345, "It is the power of Congress which has been enlarged. Congress is authorized to *enforce* the prohibitions by appropriate legislation. Some legislation is contemplated to make the amendments fully effective." A construction of §5 that would require a judicial determination that the enforcement of the state law precluded by Congress violated the Amendment, as a condition of sustaining the congressional enactment, would depreciate both congressional resourcefulness and congressional responsibility for implementing the Amendment.[8] It would confine the legislative power in this context to the insignificant role of abrogating only those state laws that the judicial branch was prepared to adjudge unconstitutional, or of merely informing the judgment of the ju-

---

[5] "SECTION 5. The Congress shall have power to enforce, by appropriate legislation, the provisions of this article."

[7] For the historical evidence suggesting that the sponsors and supporters of the Amendment were primarily interested in augmenting the power of Congress, rather than the judiciary, see generally Frantz, Congressional Power to Enforce the Fourteenth Amendment Against Private Acts, 73 Yale LJ 1353, 1356-1357; Harris, The Quest for Equality, 33-56 (1960); tenBroek, The Antislavery Origins of the Fourteenth Amendment, 187-217 (1951).

[8] Senator Howard, in introducing the proposed Amendment to the Senate, described §5 as "a direct affirmative delegation of power to Congress," and added:

"It casts upon Congress the responsibility of seeing to it, for the future, that all the sections of the amendment are carried out in good faith, and that no State infringes the rights of persons or property. I look upon this clause as indispensable for the reason that it thus imposes upon Congress this power and this duty. It enables Congress, in case the States shall enact laws in conflict with the principles of the amendment, to correct that legislation by a formal congressional enactment." Cong. Globe, 39th Cong., 1st Sess., 2766, 2768 (1866).

This statement of §5's purpose was not questioned by anyone in the course of the debate. Flack, The Adoption of the Fourteenth Amendment 138 (1908).

diciary by particularizing the "majesty generalities" of §1 of the Amendment. See Fay v. New York, 332 U.S. 261, 282-284.

Thus our task in this case is not to determine whether the New York English literacy requirement as applied to deny the right to vote to a person who successfully completed the sixth grade in a Puerto Rican school violates the Equal Protection Clause. Accordingly, our decision in Lassiter v. Northampton Election Bd., 360 U.S. 45, sustaining the North Carolina English literacy requirement as not in all circumstances prohibited by the first sections of the Fourteenth and Fifteenth Amendments, is inapposite.... Lassiter did not present the question before us here: Without regard to whether the judiciary would find that the Equal Protection Clause itself nullifies New York's English literacy requirement as so applied, could Congress prohibit the enforcement of the state law by legislating under §5 of the Fourteenth Amendment? In answering this question, our task is limited to determining whether such legislation is, as required by §5, appropriate legislation to enforce the Equal Protection Clause.

By including §5 the draftsmen sought to grant to Congress, by a specific provision applicable to the Fourteenth Amendment, the same broad powers expressed in the Necessary and Proper Clause, Art I, §8, cl. 18. The classic formulation of the reach of those two powers was established by Chief Justice Marshall in M'Culloch v. Maryland, 4 Wheat 316, 421. . . .

Ex parte Virginia, 100 U.S., at 345-346, decided 12 years after the adoption of the Fourteenth Amendment, held that congressional power under §5 had this same broad scope. . . .

We therefore proceed to the consideration whether §4(e) is "appropriate legislation" to enforce the Equal Protection Clause, that is, under the M'Culloch v. Maryland standard, whether §4(e) may be regarded as an enactment to enforce the Equal Protection Clause, whether it is "plainly adapted to that end" and whether it is not prohibited by but is consistent with "the letter and spirit of the constitution." [10]

There can be no doubt that §4(e) may be regarded as an enactment to enforce the Equal Protection Clause. Congress explicitly declared that it enacted §4(e) "to secure the rights under the fourteenth amendment of persons educated in American-flag schools in which the predominant classroom language was other than English." The persons referred to include those who have migrated from the Commonwealth of Puerto Rico to New York and who have been denied the right to vote because of their inability to read and write English, and the Fourteenth Amendment rights referred to include those emanating from the Equal Protection Clause. More specifically, §4(e) may be viewed as a measure to secure for the Puerto Rican community residing in New York nondiscriminatory treatment by government — both in the imposition of voting qualifications and the provision or administration of governmental services, such as public schools, public housing and law enforcement.

Section 4(e) may be readily seen as "plainly adapted" to furthering these aims of the Equal Protection Clause. The practical effect of §4(e) is to prohibit New York from denying the right to vote to large segments of its Puerto Rican community. Congress has thus prohibited the State from denying to that community the right that is "preservative of all rights." Yick Wo v. Hopkins, 118 U.S. 356, 370. This enhanced political power will be helpful in gaining nondiscriminatory treatment in public services for the entire Puerto Rican community. Section 4(e) thereby enables the Puerto Rican minority better to ob-

---

[10] Contrary to the suggestion of the dissent, §5 does not grant Congress power to exercise discretion in the other direction and to enact "statutes so as in effect to dilute equal protection and due process decisions of this Court." We emphasize that Congress' power under §5 is limited to adopting measures to enforce the guarantees of the Amendment; §5 grants Congress no power to restrict, abrogate, or dilute these guarantees. Thus, for example, an enactment authorizing the States to establish racially segregated systems of education would not be — as required by §5 — a measure "to enforce" the Equal Protection Clause since that clause of its own force prohibits such state laws.

tain "perfect equality of civil rights and the equal protection of the laws." It was well within congressional authority to say that this need of the Puerto Rican minority for the vote warranted federal intrusion upon any state interests served by the English literacy requirement. It was for Congress, as the branch that made this judgment, to assess and weigh the various conflicting considerations — the risk or pervasiveness of the discrimination in governmental services, the effectiveness of eliminating the state restriction on the right to vote as a means of dealing with the evil, the adequacy or availability of alternative remedies, and the nature and significance of the state interests that would be affected by the nullification of the English literacy requirement as applied to residents who have successfully completed the sixth grade in a Puerto Rican school. It is not for us to review the congressional resolution of these factors. It is enough that we be able to perceive a basis upon which the Congress might resolve the conflict as it did. There plainly was such a basis to support §4(e) in the application in question in this case. Any contrary conclusion would require us to be blind to the realities familiar to the legislators.

The result is no different if we confine our inquiry to the question whether §4(e) was merely legislation aimed at the elimination of an invidious discrimination in establishing voter qualifications. We are told that New York's English literacy requirement originated in the desire to provide an incentive for non-English speaking immigrants to learn the English language and in order to assure the intelligent exercise of the franchise. Yet Congress might well have questioned, in light of the many exemptions provided,[13] and some evidence suggesting that prejudice played a prominent role in the enactment of the requirement, whether these were actually the interests being served. Congress might have also questioned whether denial of a right deemed so precious and fundamental in our society was a necessary or appropriate means of encouraging persons to learn English, or of furthering the goal of an intelligent exercise of the franchise. Finally, Congress might well have concluded that as a means of furthering the intelligent exercise of the franchise, an ability to read or understand Spanish is as effective as ability to read English for those to whom Spanish-language newspapers and Spanish-language radio and television programs are available to inform them of election issues and governmental affairs. Since Congress undertook to legislate so as to preclude the enforcement of the state law, and did so in the context of a general appraisal of literacy requirements for voting, see South Carolina v. Katzenbach, supra, to which it brought a specially informed legislative competence, it was Congress' prerogative to weigh these competing considerations. . . .

There remains the question whether the congressional remedies adopted in §4(e) constitute means which are not prohibited by, but are consistent "with the letter and spirit of the constitution." The only respect in which appellees contend that §4(e) fails in this regard is that the section itself works an invidious discrimination in violation of the Fifth Amendment by prohibiting the enforcement of the English literacy requirement only for those educated in American-flag schools (schools located within United States jurisdiction) in which the language of instruction was other than English, and not for those educated in schools beyond the territorial limits of the United States in which the language of instruction was also other than English. This is not a complaint that Congress, in enacting §4(e), has unconstitutionally denied or diluted anyone's right to vote but rather that Congress violated the Constitution by not extending the relief effected in §4(e) to those educated in non-American-flag schools. . . .

. . . [T]he distinction challenged by appellees is presented only as a limitation on a reform measure aimed at eliminating an existing barrier to the exercise of the franchise. Rather, in deciding the constitutional propriety of the limitations in such a reform measure we are guided by the familiar principles that a "statute is not invalid under the Constitution because it might have gone farther than it did," Roschen v. Ward, 279 U.S. 337,

---

[13] The principal exemption complained of is that for persons who had been eligible to vote before January 1, 1922.

339, that a legislature need not "strike at all evils at the same time," Semler v. Dental Examiners, 294 U.S. 608, 610, and that "reform may take one step at a time, addressing itself to the phase of the problem which seems most acute to the legislative mind," Williamson v. Lee Optical Co. 348 U.S. 483, 489.

Guided by these principles, we are satisfied that appellees' challenge to this limitation in §4(e) is without merit. In the context of the case before us, the congressional choice to limit the relief effected in §4(e) may, for example, reflect Congress' greater familiarity with the quality of instruction in American-flag schools, a recognition of the unique historic relationship between the Congress and the Commonwealth of Puerto Rico, an awareness of the Federal Government's acceptance of the desirability of the use of Spanish as the language of instruction in Commonwealth schools, and the fact that Congress has fostered policies encouraging migration from the Commonwealth to the States. We have no occasion to determine in this case whether such factors would justify a similar distinction embodied in a voting-qualification law that denied the franchise to persons educated in non-American-flag schools. We hold only that the limitation on relief effected in §4(e) does not constitute a forbidden discrimination since these factors might well have been the basis for the decision of Congress to go "no farther than it did."

We therefore conclude that §4(e), in the application challenged in this case, is appropriate legislation to enforce the Equal Protection Clause and that the judgment of the District Court must be and hereby is

Reversed.[v]

NOTE "Reverse Discrimination"

1. On the reach of civil rights legislation under § 5 of the Fourteenth Amendment, compare Oregon v. Mitchell, page 987 infra. See also Heart of Atlanta Motel v. United States, and accompanying materials, page 300 supra (congressional power under the commerce clause); Jones v. Alfred H. Mayer Co., page 814 supra (Thirteenth Amendment); South Carolina v. Katzenbach, page 974 infra (Fifteenth Amendment). See generally Cox, The Role of Congress in Constitutional Determinations, 40 U. Cin. L. Rev. 199 (1971).

2. What is the power of Congress under § 5, as interpreted in Morgan, to prescribe measures of "reverse discrimination," such as racial or sexual quotas in employment? Pursuant to Executive Order No. 11246, 30 Fed. Reg. 12319 (1965), as amended, Executive Order No. 11375, 32 Fed. Reg. 14303 (1967), the Office of Federal Contract Compliance of the Department of Labor has propounded regulations requiring that every substantial government contractor must develop "affirmative action" programs which "shall provide in detail for specific steps to guarantee equal employment opportunity keyed to the problems and needs of members of minority groups, including, when there are deficiencies, the development of specific goals and time-tables for the prompt achievement of full and equal employment opportunity." 41 C.F.R. §60-1.40(a) (1973). In Contractors Assn. of Eastern Pennsylvania v. Secretary of Labor, 442 F.2d 159 (3d Cir.), cert. denied, 404 U.S. 854 (1971), the court upheld the "Philadelphia Plan" promulgated under Executive Order No. 11246. Under the plan, the Department of Labor required that bidders on federal or federally funded construction contracts in the metropolitan Philadelphia area submit affirmative action programs setting quotas for minority employment in six skilled crafts. The court rejected plaintiffs' claim that the plan conflicted with §703(a) of Title VII of the Civil Rights Act of 1964, 42 U.S.C. §2000e-2(a), which provides: "It shall be an unlawful employment practice — (1) to fail or refuse to hire . . . any individual . . . because of such individual's race . . . or (2) to . . . classify his employees in any way which would deprive . . . any individual of employment opportu-

---

[v] A concurring opinion by Justice Douglas and dissent by Justice Harlan have been omitted. — ED.

nities . . . because of such individual's race. . . ." Citing Quarles v. Philip Morris, Inc., 279 F. Supp. 505 (E.D. Va. 1968), the court "rejected the contention that existing, nondiscriminatory seniority arrangements were so sanctified by Title VII that the effects of past discrimination in job assignments could not be overcome." For cases holding that the equity powers of the federal courts include the authority to order similar affirmative action to remedy past discrimination, see Rios v. Enterprise Assn. Steamfitters Local 638, 501 F.2d 622 (2d Cir. 1974); NAACP v. Allen, 493 F.2d 614 (5th Cir. 1974). See also Swann v. Board of Education, noted page 898 supra, on the use of racial quotas in framing decrees remedying school segregation.

3. In DeFunis v. Odegaard, 416 U.S. 312 (1974), noted page 87 supra, the Court vacated as moot an equal protection challenge to preferential minority admissions quotas at the University of Washington Law School. Although the adoption of this admissions policy by a state school was not traceable to the enforcement powers of Congress under §5, the court below upheld the school's classification of candidates by race as "not invidious" "where the purpose is to bring together, rather than separate, the races" and as justified by a compelling state interest in "promoting integration in public education." 82 Wash. 2d 11, 507 P.2d 1169 (1973) (en banc). See also the dissent of Justice Douglas from the Supreme Court opinion.

On the merits of the DeFunis case, consider this selection from the Brief of Anti-Defamation League as amicus curiae at 22: "Each of the cases cited by the Washington Supreme Court to justify the racial discrimination indulged by the law school here, e.g. Swann, supra . . . , tolerates the use of a racial standard by the state, but only to cure racial discrimination imposed by the party against whom the remedy is ordered. In this case, however, there is nothing in the record on which to base a finding of unequal treatment by race in the University of Washington, or, indeed, in the State of Washington." Compare the following from the Brief of the National Council of Jewish Women as amici curiae at 44: "In fact, this Court has already indicated very clearly that State and local bodies *do* have a broad and flexible power to seek equal opportunity through the use of remedial racial classifications. The Court has said that this power is much broader and more flexible than that of courts acting alone, as in . . . Swann." Should the power to employ "reverse" racial discrimination for remedial purposes be more broadly allowed for legislative and executive action than for judicial orders? Cf. Katzenbach v. Morgan, supra.

For decisions upholding other state remedial discrimination, see Kahn v. Shevin, noted page 936 infra (tax exemption for widows but not for widowers); Associated General Contractors of Massachusetts, Inc. v. Altshuler, 490 F.2d 9 (1st Cir. 1973), cert. denied, 416 U.S. 957 (1974) (contract provision similar to Philadelphia Plan). See generally Bickel, The Least Dangerous Branch: The Supreme Court at the Bar of Politics 56-65 (1962); Ely, The Constitutionality of Reverse Racial Discrimination, 41 U. Chi. L. Rev. 723 (1974).

4. Suspect Classifications and Fundamental Rights

Griffin v. Illinois 351 U.S. 12, 76 S. Ct. 585, 100 L. Ed. 891 (1956)

MR. JUSTICE BLACK announced the judgment of the Court and an opinion in which the CHIEF JUSTICE, MR. JUSTICE DOUGLAS, and MR. JUSTICE CLARK join.

Illinois law provides that "Writs of error in all criminal cases are writs of right and shall be issued of course." The question presented here is whether Illinois may, consistent with the Due Process and Equal Protection Clauses of the Fourteenth Amendment, administer this statute so as to deny adequate appellate review to the poor while granting such review to all others.

The petitioners Griffin and Crenshaw were tried together and convicted of armed robbery in the Criminal Court of Cook County, Illinois. Immediately after their conviction they filed a motion in the trial court asking that a certified copy of the entire record, including a stenographic transcript of the proceedings, be furnished them without cost. They alleged that they were "poor persons with no means of paying the necessary fees to acquire the Transcript and Court Records needed to prosecute an appeal. . . ." These allegations were not denied. Under Illinois Law in order to get full direct appellate review of alleged errors by a writ of error it is necessary for the defendant to furnish the appellate court with a bill of exceptions or report of proceedings at the trial certified by the trial judge. As Illinois concedes, it is sometimes impossible to prepare such bills of exceptions or reports without a stenographic transcript of the trial proceedings. Indigent defendants sentenced to death are provided with a free transcript at the expense of the county where convicted. In all other criminal cases defendants needing a transcript, whether indigent or not, must themselves buy it. The petitioners contended in their motion before the trial court that failure to provide them with the needed transcript would violate the Due Process and Equal Protection Clauses of the Fourteenth Amendment. The trial court denied the motion without a hearing.

. . . The Illinois Supreme Court affirmed the dismissal solely on the ground that the charges raised no substantial state or federal constitutional questions — the only kind of questions which may be raised in Post-Conviction proceedings. We granted certiorari. . . .

Counsel for Illinois concedes that the petitioners needed a transcript in order to get adequate appellate review of their alleged trial errors. There is no contention that petitioners were dilatory in their efforts to get appellate review, or that the Illinois Supreme Court denied review on the ground that the allegations of trial error were insufficient. We must therefore assume for purposes of this decision that errors were committed in the trial which would merit reversal, but that the petitioners could not get appellate review of those errors solely because they were too poor to buy a stenographic transcript. Counsel for Illinois denies that this violates either the Due Process or the Equal Protection Clause, but states that if it does, the Illinois Post-Conviction statute entitles petitioners to a free transcript. The sole question for us to decide, therefore, is whether due process or equal protection has been violated. . . .

Surely no one would contend that either a State or the Federal Government could constitutionally provide that defendants unable to pay court costs in advance should be denied the right to plead not guilty or to defend themselves in court. Such a law would make the constitutional promise of a fair trial a worthless thing. Notice, the right to be heard, and the right to counsel would under such circumstances be meaningless promises to the poor. In criminal trials a State can no more discriminate on account of poverty than on account of religion, race, or color. Plainly the ability to pay costs in advance bears no rational relationship to a defendant's guilt or innocence and could not be used as an excuse to deprive a defendant of a fair trial. Indeed, a provision in the Constitution of Illinois of 1818 provided that every person in Illinois "ought to obtain right and justice freely, and without being obliged to purchase it, completely and without denial, promptly and without delay, conformably to the laws."

There is no meaningful distinction between a rule which would deny the poor the right to defend themselves in a trial court and one which effectively denies the poor an adequate appellate review accorded to all who have money enough to pay the costs in advance. It is true that a State is not required by the Federal Constitution to provide appellate courts or a right to appellate review at all. See, e.g., McKane v. Durston, 153 U.S. 684, 687-688. But that is not to say that a State that does grant appellate review can do so in a way that discriminates against some convicted defendants on account of their poverty.

Appellate review has now become an integral part of the Illinois trial system for finally adjudicating the guilt or innocence of a defendant. Consequently at all stages of the proceedings the Due Process and Equal Protection Clauses protect persons like petitioners from invidious discriminations. See Cole v. Arkansas, 333 U.S. 196, 201; Dowd v. United States, 340 U.S. 206, 208; Cochran v. Kansas, 316 U.S. 255, 257; Frank v. Mangum, 237 U.S. 309, 327.

All of the States now provide some method of appeal from criminal convictions, recognizing the importance of appellate review to a correct adjudication of guilt or innocence. Statistics show that a substantial proportion of criminal convictions are reversed by state appellate courts. Thus to deny adequate review to the poor means that many of them may lose their life, liberty or property because of unjust convictions which appellate courts would set aside. Many States have recognized this and provided aid for convicted defendants who have a right to appeal and need a transcript but are unable to pay for it. A few have not. Such a denial is a misfit in a country dedicated to affording equal justice to all and special privileges to none in the administration of its criminal law. There can be no equal justice where the kind of trial a man gets depends on the amount of money he has. Destitute defendants must be afforded as adequate appellate review as defendants who have money enough to buy transcripts.

The Illinois Supreme Court denied these petitioners relief under the Post-Conviction Act because of its holding that no constitutional rights were violated. In view of our holding to the contrary the State Supreme Court may decide that petitioners are now entitled to a transcript, as the State's brief suggests. See Ill. Rev. Stat. 1955, ch. 37 § 163f. Cf. Dowd v. United States, 340 U.S., at 209, 210. We do not hold, however, that Illinois must purchase a stenographer's transcript in every case where a defendant cannot buy it. The Supreme Court may find other means of affording adequate and effective appellate review to indigent defendants. For example, it may be that bystanders' bills of exceptions or other methods of reporting trial proceedings could be used in some cases. The Illinois Supreme Court appears to have broad power to promulgate rules of procedure and appellate practice. We are confident that the State will provide corrective rules to meet the problem which this case lays bare.

The judgment of the Supreme Court of Illinois is vacated and the cause is remanded to that court for further action not inconsistent with the foregoing paragraph. MR. JUSTICE FRANKFURTER joins in this disposition of the case.

Vacated and remanded.[w]

NOTE Indigence and Inequality

Variations on the problem of the Griffin case were considered in Lane v. Brown, 372 U.S. 477 (1963); Draper v. Washington, 372 U.S. 487 (1963); Douglas v. California, 372 U.S. 353 (1963). The cases are discussed in 77 Harv. L. Rev. 105 (1963). See Fahringer, Equal Protection and The Indigent Defendant: Griffin and Its Progeny, 16 Stan. L. Rev. 394 (1964). See also Rinaldi v. Yeager, 384 U.S. 305 (1966).

1. Adequate representation of the indigent criminal defendant: the right to a transcript. In Mayer v. City of Chicago, 404 U.S. 189 (1971), the Court extended Griffin to require that even where the offense charged is not a felony or is punishable only with a fine, the state must under the Fourteenth Amendment provide an indigent defendant with a transcript sufficient for effective appellate review. If the defendant's grounds for appeal make

---

[w] A concurring opinion of Justice Frankfurter and a separate dissent of Justice Harlan are omitted. A dissenting opinion by Justices Burton and Minton, joined by Justices Reed and Harlan, is also omitted. The case is discussed at length in Comment, 25 U. Chi. L. Rev. 143 (1957). With respect to Illinois's response to the decision see People v. Berman, 19 Ill. 2d 579 (1960). — ED.

out a colorable need for a complete transcript, the state has the burden of showing that anything less is sufficient.

In Britt v. North Carolina, 404 U.S. 226 (1971), the Court held that the state was not required to furnish an indigent defendant with a transcript of his first trial for murder, which ended in a hung jury, where the state showed that the court reporter from the first trial could have been put on the stand in the second trial. Justices Douglas and Brennan dissented.

See Gardner v. California, 393 U.S. 367 (1969), requiring that the state provide an indigent prisoner with a transcript of lower court proceedings denying writ of habeas corpus for use in connection with a new petition to higher state courts.

See also Comment, The Indigent's Right to a Transcript of Record, 20 Kansas L. Rev. 745 (1972).

2. State recoupment of the cost of an indigent's defense. In Fuller v. Oregon, 417 U.S. 40 (1974), the Court upheld a court order revoking petitioner's probation for failure to reimburse the state for the fees of an attorney and an investigator whose services had been provided by the state because petitioner was indigent at the time of his trial. The order was issued under a statute providing for recoupment of defense costs from a convicted defendant for whom payment would no longer impose manifest hardship. Justices Marshall and Brennan dissented. See James v. Strange, 407 U.S. 128 (1972), holding that a state recoupment statute may not deprive a defendant of protections accorded other judgment debtors.

See Note, Charging Costs of Prosecution to the Defendant, 59 Geo. L.J. 991 (1971); Comment, Reimbursement of Defense Costs as a Condition of Probation for Indigents, 67 Mich. L. Rev. 1404 (1969).

3. In Schilb v. Kuebel, 404 U.S. 357 (1971), the Court rejected an equal protection challenge to Illinois bail bond provisions. The statute authorized release of arrested persons pending trial in three ways: personal recognizance; execution of a bail bond secured by deposit of cash or property equal to the full amount of bail, all of which would be returned on performance of the bond conditions; or execution of a bail bond, with a deposit of 10 percent of the full amount of bail, all but 10 percent of which (amounting to 1 percent of the full bail) is returned on performance of the bond conditions. Appellant, who had been released under the third alternative and incurred a charge of $7.50, argued that the statute impermissibly discriminated against persons unable to post security equal to the full amount of bail. The Court upheld the statute as rational, noting that it had been enacted to replace an "odorous" professional bail bondsman system, that the failure to place direct charges on the other two alternatives could be justified by the state's lack of expenses with respect to the recognizance alternative and option to make use of the security in the second alternative, and that there was no evidence that state judges limited personal recognizance so as to discriminate against the poor. Justices Douglas, Stewart, and Brennan dissented.

4. Fines and indigent defendants. In Tate v. Short, 401 U.S. 395 (1971), the Court held invalid under the equal protection clause a provision of Texas law authorizing imprisonment of a convicted defendant unable to pay the fine imposed for his offense, even though the offense was not itself punishable by imprisonment. Writing for the Court, Justice Brennan stated that the statutory ceiling on punishment may not be exceeded because of indigency and noted that other methods of collecting fines, as through installment payments, might be available. He added: "our holding today does not suggest any constitutional infirmity in imprisonment of a defendant with the means to pay a fine who refuses or neglects to do so. Nor is our decision to be understood as precluding imprisonment as an enforcement method when alternative means are unsuccessful despite the defendant's reasonable efforts to satisfy the fines by those means; the determination of the constitutionality of imprisonment in that circumstance must await the presentation of a concrete case." Compare Williams v. Illinois, 399 U.S. 235 (1970), holding that a crimi-

nal defendant unable to pay a fine or court costs in a lump sum could not be incarcerated if his consequent aggregate jail time would exceed the maximum prison term specified for the underlying crime. See The Supreme Court, 1969 Term, 84 Harv. L. Rev. 1, 46-54 (1970).

5. Indigents as litigants in civil cases. In Boddie v. Connecticut, 401 U.S. 371 (1971), welfare recipients who were plaintiffs in divorce proceedings brought a class action challenging the requirement that they pay court fees and costs of service of process. Writing for the Court, Justice Harlan held the requirement invalid under the due process clause, in view of the state's monopoly of the means of dissolving a marriage and its consequent obligation to afford a meaningful opportunity to be heard. Justices Douglas and Brennan, concurring, would have rested the decision on the equal protection clause, treating wealth as a suspect classification. Justice Black dissented, distinguishing the rights of criminal defendants and stating: "Neither due process nor equal protection permits state laws to be invalidated on any such nonconstitutional standard as a judge's personal view of fairness."

Boddie was distinguished in United States v. Kras, 409 U.S. 434 (1973), upholding a $50 bankruptcy filing fee. Writing for the Court, Justice Blackmun distinguished Boddie on the two grounds that marriage, unlike discharge in bankruptcy, was a fundamental interest and that whereas judicial relief offered the only effective means of dissolving marriage, a debtor might make extrajudicial settlements with his creditors. Justices Douglas, Brennan, Stewart and Marshall dissented. See The Supreme Court, 1972 Term, 87 Harv. L. Rev. 1, 57-67 (1973). Compare Ortwein v. Schwab, 410 U.S. 656 (1973) (per curiam), in which the Court refused, 5 to 4, to extend Boddie to require waiver of filing fees for indigents attempting to appeal decisions of state administrative tribunals reducing or terminating public assistance.

In Lindsey v. Normet, 405 U.S. 56 (1972), the Court divided over equal protection and due process challenges to Oregon's forcible entry and wrongful detainer (FED) statute, which provided for speedy determination of a landlord's action for possession. Tenants attacked the statute's requirements (1) that trial take place not later than six days after service of the landlord's complaint, unless the tenant post security for accruing rent, (2) that issues at trial be limited to the tenant's default, excluding affirmative defenses, and (3) that tenant may appeal only on posting a bond equal to twice the amount of rent expected to accrue during the pendency of the appeal, the entire bond to be forfeited if the lower court decision is affirmed. Writing for the Court, Justice White held that the double-bond requirement for appeal constituted an "arbitrary and irrational" denial of equal protection discriminating against a particular class of civil appellants, and especially the indigent members of that class. The Court upheld, however, the early-trial provision and limitation of defenses as rationally related to the State goal of assuring "prompt as well as peaceful resolution of disputes over the right to possession of real property."

Justice Douglas concurred as to the double-bond provision but dissented to the rest of the decision. He argued that the early-trial provision and limitation of triable issues violated the due process clause:

"For slum tenants — not to mention the middle class — this kind of summary procedure usually will mean in actuality no opportunity to be heard. Finding a lawyer in two days, acquainting him with the facts, and getting necessary witnesses make the theoretical opportunity to be heard and interpose a defense a promise of empty words. It is, indeed, a meaningless notice and opportunity to defend. The trial is likely to be held in the presence of only the judge and the landlord and the landlord's attorney. . . .

"The Court . . . implies that to find for appellants in this case, we would have to hold, as a matter of constitutional law, that a lease is required to be interpreted as an ordinary contract. But . . . Oregon has already adopted the modern, contractual view of leasehold analysis. The issue that confronts the Court is not whether such a view is constitutionally compelled, but whether, once Oregon has gone this far as a matter of state law, the requirements of due process permit a restriction of contract-type defenses in an FED action. . . .

"Normally a State may bifurcate trials, deciding, say, the right to possession in one suit and the right to damages in another. See Bianchi v. Morales, 262 U.S. 170; American Surety Co. v. Baldwin, 287 U.S. 156.

"But where the right is so fundamental as the tenant's claim to his home, the requirements of due process should be more embracing. In the setting of modern urban life, the home, even though it be in the slums, is where man's roots are. To put him into the street when the slum landlord, not the slum tenant, is the real culprit deprives the tenant of a fundamental right without any real opportunity to defend. . . ."

See Note, Poverty and Equal Access to the Courts, 20 Stan. L. Rev. 766 (1968).

6. Wealth discrimination in other contexts. See Harper v. Virginia Board of Elections, page 912 infra, and accompanying materials (restrictions on voting and candidacy for public office); James v. Valtierra, page 841 supra (discrimination against low-rent housing). See generally Michelman, The Supreme Court, 1968 Term — Foreword: On Protecting the Poor through the Fourteenth Amendment, 83 Harv. L. Rev. 7 (1969); Bendich, Privacy, Poverty, and the Court, 54 Calif. L. Rev. 407 (1966).

Shapiro v. Thompson *394 U.S. 618, 89 S. Ct. 1322, 22 L. Ed. 2d 600 (1969)*

[For the opinion in this case see page 346 supra.]

Dandridge v. Williams *397 U.S. 471, 90 S. Ct. 1153, 25 L. Ed. 2d 491 (1970)*

MR. JUSTICE STEWART delivered the opinion of the Court. . . .

The operation of the Maryland welfare system is not complex. By statute the State participates in the AFDC program. It computes the standard of need for each eligible family based on the number of children in the family and the circumstances under which the family lives. In general, the standard of need increases with each additional person in the household, but the increments become proportionately smaller. The regulation here in issue imposes upon the grant that any single family may receive an upper limit of $250 per month in certain counties including Baltimore City, and of $240 per month elsewhere in the State. The appellees all have large families, so that their standards of need as computed by the State substantially exceed the maximum grants that they actually receive under the regulation. The appellees urged in the District Court that the maximum grant limitation operates to discriminate against them merely because of the size of their families, in violation of the Equal Protection Clause of the Fourteenth Amendment. . . . Maryland says that its maximum grant regulation is wholly free of any invidiously discriminatory purpose or effect, and that the regulation is rationally supportable on at least four entirely valid grounds. The regulation can be clearly justified, Maryland argues, in terms of legitimate state interests in encouraging gainful employment, in maintaining an equitable balance in economic status as between welfare families and those supported by a wage-earner, in providing incentives for family planning, and in allocating available public funds in such a way as fully to meet the needs of the largest possible number of families. The District Court, while apparently recognizing the validity of at least some of these state concerns, nonetheless held that the regulation "is invalid on its face for overreaching," 297 F. Supp., at 468 — that it violates the Equal Protection Clause "[b]ecause it cuts too broad a swath on an indiscriminate basis as applied to the entire group of AFDC eligibles to which it purports to apply. . . ." 297 F. Supp., at 469.

If this were a case involving government action claimed to violate the First Amendment

Section G. **Equal Protection of the Laws** 913

guarantee of free speech, a finding of "over-reaching" would be significant and might be crucial. For when otherwise valid governmental regulation sweeps so broadly as to impinge upon activity protected by the First Amendment, its very overbreadth may make it unconstitutional. See, e.g., Shelton v. Tucker, 364 U.S. 479. But the concept of "over-reaching" has no place in this case. For here we deal with state regulation in the social and economic field, not affecting freedoms guaranteed by the Bill of Rights, and claimed to violate the Fourteenth Amendment only because the regulation results in some disparity in grants of welfare payments to the largest AFDC families.[16] For this Court to approve the invalidation of state economic or social regulation as "overreaching" would be far too reminiscent of an era when the Court thought the Fourteenth Amendment gave it power to strike down state laws "because they may be unwise, improvident, or out of harmony with a particular school of thought." Williamson v. Lee Optical Co., 348 U.S. 483, 488. That era long ago passed into history. Ferguson v. Skrupa, 372 U.S. 726.

In the area of economics and social welfare, a State does not violate the Equal Protection Clause merely because the classifications made by its laws are imperfect. If the classification has some "reasonable basis," it does not offend the Constitution simply because the classification "is not made with mathematical nicety or because in practice it results in some inequality." Lindsley v. Natural Carbonic Gas Co., 220 U.S. 61, 78. "The problems of government are practical ones and may justify, if they do not require, rough accommodations — illogical, it may be, and unscientific." Metropolis Theatre Co. v. City of Chicago, 228 U.S. 61, 69-70. "A statutory discrimination will not be set aside if any state of facts reasonably may be conceived to justify it." McGowan v. Maryland, 366 U.S. 420, 426.

To be sure, the cases cited, and many others enunciating this fundamental standard under the Equal Protection Clause, have in the main involved state regulation of business or industry. The administration of public welfare assistance, by contrast, involves the most basic economic needs of impoverished human beings. We recognize the dramatically real factual difference between the cited cases and this one, but we can find no basis for applying a different constitutional standard.[17] See Snell v. Wyman, 281 F. Supp. 853, aff'd, 393 U.S. 323. It is a standard that has consistently been applied to state legislation restricting the availability of employment opportunities. Goesaert v. Cleary, 335 U.S. 464; Kotch v. Board of River Port Pilot Comm'rs., 330 U.S. 552. See also Flemming v. Nestor, 363 U.S. 603. And it is a standard that is true to the principle that the Fourteenth Amendment gives the federal courts no power to impose upon the States their views of wise economic or social policy.

Under this long-established meaning of the Equal Protection Clause, it is clear that the Maryland maximum grant regulation is constitutionally valid. We need not explore all the reasons that the State advances in justification of the regulation. It is enough that a solid foundation for the regulation can be found in the State's legitimate interest in encouraging employment and in avoiding discrimination between welfare families and the families of the working poor. By combining a limit on the recipient's grant with permission to retain money earned, without reduction in the amount of the grant, Maryland provides an incentive to seek gainful employment. And by keying the maximum family AFDC grants to the minimum wage a steadily employed head of a household receives, the State maintains some semblance of an equitable balance between families on welfare and those supported by an employed breadwinner.[19]

We do not decide today that the Maryland regulation is wise, that it best fulfills the rele-

[16] Cf. Shapiro v. Thompson, 394 U.S. 618, where, by contrast, the Court found state interference with the constitutionally protected freedom of interstate travel.
[17] It is important to note that there is no contention that the Maryland regulation is infected with a racially discriminatory purpose or effect such as to make it inherently suspect. Cf. McLaughlin v. Florida, 379 U.S. 184.
[19] The present federal minimum wage is $52-$64 per 40-hour week, 29 U.S.C. §206 (1964 ed., Supp. IV). The Maryland minimum wage is $46-$52 per week, Md. Code Ann., Art. 100, §83.

vant social and economic objectives that Maryland might ideally espouse, or that a more just and humane system could not be devised. Conflicting claims of morality and intelligence are raised by opponents and proponents of almost every measure, certainly including the one before us. But the intractable economic, social, and even philosophical problems presented by public welfare assistance programs are not the business of this Court. The Constitution may impose certain procedural safeguards upon systems of welfare administration, Goldberg v. Kelly, [397 U.S. 254]. But the Constitution does not empower this Court to second-guess state officials charged with the difficult responsibility of allocating limited public welfare funds among the myriad of potential recipients. Cf. Steward Mach. Co. v. Davis, 301 U.S. 548, 584-585; Helvering v. Davis, 301 U.S. 619, 644.

[JUSTICES DOUGLAS, MARSHALL, and BRENNAN dissented.]

NOTE "Two-Tier" Equal Protection

The two-tiered standard of review applied in certain equal protection cases may trace its lineage to footnote 4 of United States v. Carolene Products Co., 304 U.S. 144 (1938). There, in the course of sustaining against a due-process challenge a federal statute which excluded "filled milk," a wholesome product containing a substitute for butterfat, from interstate commerce, Justice Stone delimited and applied the traditional, or permissive, standard of review: "[R]egulatory legislation affecting ordinary commercial transactions is not to be pronounced unconstitutional unless in the light of the facts made known or generally assumed it is of such a character as to preclude the assumption that it rests upon some rational basis within the knowledge and experience of the legislators." To this statement Justice Stone affixed his celebrated footnote: "There may be narrower scope for operation of the presumption of constitutionality when legislation appears on its face to be within a specific prohibition of the Constitution, such as those of the first ten amendments, which are deemed equally specific when held to be embraced within the Fourteenth.

"It is unnecessary to consider now whether legislation which restricts those political processes which can ordinarily be expected to bring about repeal of undesirable legislation, is to be subjected to more exacting judicial scrutiny under the general prohibitions of the Fourteenth Amendment than are most other types of legislation.

"Nor need we inquire whether similar considerations enter into the review of statutes directed at particular religious, or national, or racial minorities: whether prejudice against discrete and insular minorities may be a special condition, which tends seriously to curtail the operation of those political processes ordinarily to be relied upon to protect minorities, and which may call for a correspondingly more searching judicial inquiry." (Citations omitted.)

Although the influence of footnote 4 was occasionally visible in subsequent years, see, e.g., Skinner v. Oklahoma, page 872 supra, it remained for the Warren Court to institutionalize the principle that where legislation impinged upon a "fundamental interest" or employed a "suspect classification," it had to be supported by a "compelling state interest" rather than mere "rationality" to pass muster under the equal protection clause. See Cox, The Supreme Court, 1965 Term — Foreword: Constitutional Adjudication and the Promotion of Human Rights, 80 Harv. L. Rev. 91 (1966); Tussman & tenBroek, The Equal Protection of the Laws, 37 Calif. L. Rev. 341 (1949); Note, Developments in the Law — Equal Protection, 82 Harv. L. Rev. 1065 (1969).

The result, two-tier equal protection analysis, was a categorical approach to challenged legislation. If a statute was found to involve a "fundamental interest" or a "suspect classification," it would almost invariably be found to lack "compelling" justification. A rare exception is Korematsu v. United States, 323 U.S. 214 (1944), upholding the forced evacuation of Japanese-Americans from designated areas on the West Coast. On the other hand, if neither prerequisite of strict scrutiny was present, the test of "mere rationality" was applied and the statute was again almost invariably sustained. For an exception see Morey v. Doud, 354 U.S. 457 (1957), invalidating an Illinois statute which exempted money orders of the American Express Co. from a requirement that any firm selling or issuing money orders in that state must secure a license and submit to state regulation. New Orleans v. Dukes, 427 U.S. 297 (1976), brought into question an ordinance which exempted from its prohibition of pushcart vending in the French Quarter vendors who had operated there for at least eight years. The classification, challenged by a vendor who had operated there for two years, was sustained under a test of "rationality." Morey v. Doud was overruled, leaving no decision in recent years that invalidated an economic regulation on equal-protection grounds.

The two-tier analysis functioned well in the polar cases: statutes impinging upon clear constitutional rights or discriminating on the basis of race or nationality, and simple economic regulation. Outside these areas, the analysis showed strain. The categorical scheme for applying strict or permissive scrutiny, in Professor Cox's words, "appear[ed] to rest upon two largely subjective judgments, perhaps coupled with a sense of how fast a change the community desires. One element is the relative invidiousness of the particular differentiation, such as between men of different race, farmer and city-dweller, rich and poor, literate and illiterate, or men and women. The second element is the relative importance of the subject with respect to which equality is sought, such as the vote, the defense of a criminal prosecution, or civil litigation. But although one can identify the critical elements, the opinions seem notably unsuccessful in elaborating a rational standard, or even points of reference, by which to judge what differentiations are permitted and when equality is required." Cox, supra, at 95. Moreover, the inflexibility of the two-tier test, once the statute had been pigeonholed as suspect or not, was seen to bind the Court to an unnatural formalism subordinating careful judgment to an elusive quest for objectivity. Compare the experience with the ill-fated two-tier classification for determining the validity of laws regulating rates and prices: whether the business was "affected with a public interest" or was not. See Nebbia v. New York, 291 U.S. 502 (1934), abandoning the test.

In the 1970s, debate over the two-tier test took place on two fronts. The first was over the proper delineation of fundamental interests and suspect classifications. Were the former limited to the express guarantees of the Bill of Rights? Or did they extend to rights implied by our federal union, such as that of interstate travel? Or did the demarcation of fundamental rights extend to interests that are themselves very important, such as housing or welfare, or that, in addition, like education, serve as pivotal preconditions for the effective exercise of constitutional rights and duties? As to suspect classifications, did they include discrimination against groups other than races or ethnic minorities, such as aliens, women, indigents, or illegitimates? If so, what would be the standards for determining for which groups "heightened judicial solicitude is appropriate"? Graham v. Richardson, 403 U.S. 365, 372 (1971).

The second debate involved whether, and how, to adopt a more variable standard of review of the state's interest in the classification. In an article reviewing the 1971 Term, Professor Gunther wrote: "In seven of the fifteen basic equal protection decisions, the Court upheld the constitutional claim or remanded it for consideration without mentioning the 'strict scrutiny' formula. Moreover, with only one exception, these cases found bite in the equal protection clause after explicitly voicing the traditionally toothless minimal scrutiny standard." Professor Gunther concluded that these cases showed the Court moving toward an intermediate test of "strict rationality," involving a close examination of the relationship between a statute and its purported ends but not a demand that the statute be supported by a compelling justification. Gunther, The Supreme Court, 1971 Term — Foreword: in Search of Evolving Doctrine on a Changing Court: A Model for a Newer

Equal Protection, 86 Harv. L. Rev. 1 (1972). How would the test of means-end relationship be applied where the legislative classification involves an exemption, or a purpose diluting the principal purpose of the law, as in Railway Express Co. v. New York, page 879 supra?

With a "middle tier" of review, the Court might be able to rank interests more flexibly but it would have to rank them nonetheless. For a recent recommendation as to how to order the different meanings of equality, see Wilkinson, The Supreme Court, The Equal Protection Clause, and the Three Faces Of Constitutional Equality, 61 Va. L. Rev. 945 (1975). Strictness of review, he argued, should depend, in descending order, on whether the classification affects "equality of participation within the political process," "equality of competitive opportunity," or "economic and material inequality." Such an analysis, he contended, is based upon "a search for those values which can validly be said to be protectable by the judiciary" in a democratic society. He defended, for example, the minimal rationality review of Dandridge, supra, because, "in voiding public welfare classifications, courts engage in what is indisputably the most basic of all legislative functions — from whom and to whom to raise and distribute revenue." See also Freund, The Judicial Process in Civil Liberties Cases, 1975 U. Ill. L.F. 493, 494.

Compare Justice Stevens' concurring opinion in Craig v. Boren, 97 S. Ct. 451 (1976), striking down a statute which permitted sales of 3.2 percent beer to females, but not to males, between the ages of 18 and 21: "There is only one Equal Protection Clause. It does not direct the courts to apply one standard of review in some cases and a different standard in other cases. Whatever criticism may be levelled at a judicial opinion implying that there are at least three such standards applies with equal force to a double standard. I am inclined to believe that what has become known as the two-tiered analysis of equal protection claims does not describe a completely logical method of deciding cases, but rather is a method the Court has employed to explain decisions that actually apply a single standard in a reasonably consistent fashion. I also suspect that a careful explanation of the reasons motivating particular decisions may contribute more to an identification of that standard than an attempt to articulate it in all-encompassing terms. . . ."

San Antonio Indep. School Dist. v. Rodriguez 411 U.S. 1, 93 S. Ct. 1278, 36 L. Ed. 2d 16 (1973)

MR. JUSTICE POWELL delivered the opinion of the Court. This suit attacking the Texas system of financing public education was initiated by Mexican-American parents whose children attend the elementary and secondary schools in the Edgewood Independent School District, an urban school district in San Antonio, Texas. They brought a class action on behalf of school children throughout the State who are members of minority groups or who are poor and reside in school districts having a low property tax base. Named as defendants were the State Board of Education, the Commissioner of Education, the State Attorney General, and the Bexar County (San Antonio) Board of Trustees. The complaint was filed in the summer of 1968 and a three-judge court was impaneled in January 1969. In December 1971 the panel rendered its judgment in a per curiam opinion holding the Texas school finance system unconstitutional under the Equal Protection Clause of the Fourteenth Amendment. The State appealed, and we noted probable jurisdiction to consider the far-reaching constitutional questions presented. 406 U.S. 966 (1972). For the reasons stated in this opinion we reverse the decision of the District Court. . . .

Recognizing the need for increased state funding to help offset disparities in local spending and to meet Texas' changing educational requirements, the state legislature in the late 1940's undertook a thorough evaluation of public education with an eye toward major reform. In 1947 an 18-member committee, composed of educators and legislators, was appointed to explore alternative systems in other States and to propose a funding scheme that would guarantee a minimum or basic educational offering to each child and that would help overcome interdistrict disparities in taxable resources. The Committee's efforts led to the passage of the Gilmer-Aiken bills, named for the Committee's co-chairmen, establishing the Texas Minimum Foundation School Program. Today this Program accounts for approximately half of the total educational expenditures in Texas.

The Program calls for state and local contributions to a fund earmarked specifically for teacher salaries, operating expenses, and transportation costs. The State, supplying funds from its general revenues, finances approximately 80% of the Program, and the school districts are responsible — as a unit — for providing the remaining 20%. The districts' share, known as the Local Fund Assignment, is apportioned among the school districts under a formula designed to reflect each district's relative taxpaying ability. The Assignment is first divided among Texas' 254 counties pursuant to a complicated economic index that takes into account the relative value of each county's contribution to the State's total income from manufacturing, mining, and agricultural activities. It also considers each county's relative share of all payrolls paid within the State and, to a lesser extent, considers each county's share of all property in the State. Each county's assignment is then divided among its school districts on the basis of each district's share of assessable property within the county. The district, in turn, finances its share of the Assignment out of revenues from local property taxation.

The design of this complex system was two-fold. First, it was an attempt to assure that the Foundation Program would have an equalizing influence on expenditure levels between school districts by placing the heaviest burden on the school districts most capable of paying. Second, the Program's architects sought to establish a Local Fund Assignment that would force every school district to contribute to the education of its children but that would not by itself exhaust any district's resources. Today every school district does impose a property tax from which it derives locally expendable funds in excess of the amount necessary to satisfy its Local Fund Assignment under the Foundation Program.

In the years since this program went into operation in 1949, expenditures for education — from State as well as local sources — have increased steadily. Between 1949 and 1967 expenditures increased by approximately 500%. In the last decade alone the total public school budget rose from $750 million to $2.1 billion and these increases have been reflected in consistently rising per pupil expenditures throughout the State. Teacher salaries, by far the largest item in any school's budget, have increased dramatically — the state-supported minimum teacher salary has risen from $2,400 to $6,000 over the last 20 years.

The school district in which appellees reside, the Edgewood Independent School District, has been compared throughout this litigation with the Alamo Heights Independent School District. This comparison between the least and the most affluent districts in the San Antonio area serves to illustrate the manner in which the dual system of finance operates and to indicate the extent to which substantial disparities exist despite the State's impressive progress in recent years. Edgewood is one of seven public school districts in the metropolitan area. Approximately 22,000 students are enrolled in its 25 elementary and secondary schools. The district is situated in the core-city sector of San Antonio in a residential neighborhood that has little commercial or industrial property. The residents are predominantly of Mexican-American descent: approximately 90% of the student population is Mexican-American and over 6% is Negro. The average assessed property value per pupil is $5,960 — the lowest in the metropolitan area — and the median family income ($4,686) is also the lowest. At an equalized tax rate of $1.05 per $100 of assessed property — the highest in the metropolitan area — the district contributed $26 to the education of each child for the 1967-1968 school year above its Local Fund Assignment for the Minimum Foundation Program. The Foundation Program contributed $222 per pupil for a state-local total of $248. Federal funds added another $108 for a total of $356 per pupil.

Alamo Heights is the most affluent school district in San Antonio. Its six schools, housing approximately 5,000 students, are situated in a residential community quite unlike the Edgewood District. The school population is predominantly Anglo, having only 18% Mexican-Americans and less than 1% Negroes. The assessed property value per pupil exceeds $49,001 and the median family income is $8,001. In 1967-1968 the local tax rate of $.85 per $100 of valuation yielded $333 per pupil over and above its contribution to the Foundation Program. Coupled with the $225 provided from that Program, the district was able to supply $558 per student. Supplemented by a $36 per pupil grant from federal sources, Alamo Heights spent $594 per pupil.

Although the 1967-1968 school year figures provide the only complete statistical breakdown for each category of aid, more recent partial statistics indicate that the previously noted trend of increasing state aid has been significant. For the 1970-1971 school year, the Foundation School Program allotment for Edgewood was $356 per pupil, a 62% increase over the 1967-68 school year. Indeed, state aid alone in 1970-1971 equaled Edgewood's entire 1967-1968 school budget from local, state, and federal sources. Alamo Heights enjoyed a similar increase under the Foundation Program, netting $491 per pupil in 1970-1971. These recent figures also reveal the extent to which these two districts' allotments were funded from their own required contributions to the local Fund Assignment. Alamo Heights, because of its relative wealth, was required to contribute out of its local property tax collections approximately $100 per pupil, or about 20% of its Foundation grant. Edgewood, on the other hand, paid only $8.46 per pupil, which is about 2.4% of its grant. It does appear then that, at least as to these two districts, the Local Fund Assignment does reflect a rough approximation of the relative taxpaying potential of each.

Despite these recent increases, substantial interdistrict disparities in school expenditures found by the District Court to prevail in San Antonio and in varying degrees throughout the State still exist. And it was these disparities, largely attributable to differences in the amounts of money collected through local property taxation, that led the District Court to conclude that Texas' dual system of public school finance violated the Equal Protection Clause. The District Court held that the Texas system discriminates on the basis of wealth in the manner in which education is provided for its people. 337 F. Supp., at 282. Finding that wealth is a "suspect" classification and that education is a "fundamental" interest, the District Court held that the Texas system could be sustained only if the State could show that it was premised upon some compelling state interest. Id., at 282-284. On this issue the court concluded that "[n]ot only are defendants unable to demonstrate compelling state interests . . . they fail even to establish a reasonable basis for these classifications." Id., at 284.

Texas virtually concedes that its historically rooted dual system of financing education could not withstand the strict judicial scrutiny that this Court has found appropriate in reviewing legislative judgments that interfere with fundamental constitutional rights or that involve suspect classifications.

[The Court held that the statute made no "suspect classification." All pupils received an adequate minimum education. And expenditures per pupil, varying with the taxable property values in counties or districts, bore no necessary correlation to the income of families, since poor families are found concentrated in districts having property of relatively high value, and vice versa.]

[Appellees] also assert that the State's system impermissibly interferes with the exercise of a "fundamental" right and that accordingly the prior decisions of this Court require the application of the strict standard of judicial review. . . . It is not the province of this Court to create substantive constitutional rights in the name of guaranteeing equal protection of the laws. [The Court concluded that in a constitutional sense education, at least beyond a minimal level, is not a fundamental right, either explicitly or as an implicit corollary of the right of speech, voting, and political participation. If it were, a similar claim could be made, for example, with respect to improved housing and nutrition.]

In addition to matters of fiscal policy, this case also involves the most persistent and difficult questions of educational policy, another area in which this Court's lack of specialized knowledge and experience counsels against premature interference with the informed judgments made at the state and local levels. Education, perhaps even more than welfare assistance, presents a myriad of "intractable economic, social, and even philosophical problems." Dandridge v. Williams, 397 U.S., at 487. The very complexity of the problems of financing and managing a statewide public school system suggest that "there will be more than one constitutionally permissible method of solving them," and that, within the limits of rationality, "the legislature's efforts to tackle the problems" should be entitled to respect. Jefferson v. Hackney, 406 U.S. 535, 546-547 (1972). On even the most basic questions in this area the scholars and educational experts are divided. Indeed, one of the hottest sources of controversy concerns the extent to which there is a demonstrable correlation between educational expenditures and the quality of education — an assumed correlation underlying virtually every legal conclusion drawn by the District Court in this case. Related to the questioned relationship between cost and quality is the equally unsettled controversy as to the proper goals of a system of public education. And the question regarding the most effective relationship between state boards of education and local school boards, in terms of their respective responsibilities and degrees of control, is now undergoing searching re-examination. The ultimate wisdom as to these and related problems of education is not likely to be divined for all time even by the scholars who now so earnestly debate the issues. In such circumstances the judiciary is well advised to refrain from interposing on the States inflexible constitutional restraints that could circumscribe or handicap the continued research and experimentation so vital to finding even partial solutions to educational problems and to keeping abreast of ever changing conditions. . . .

MR. JUSTICE MARSHALL, with whom MR. JUSTICE DOUGLAS concurs, dissenting.

To avoid having the Texas financing scheme struck down because of the interdistrict variations in taxable property wealth, the District Court determined that it was insufficient for appellants to show merely that the State's scheme was rationally related to some legitimate state purpose; rather, the discrimination inherent in the scheme had to be shown necessary to promote a "compelling state interest" in order to withstand constitutional scrutiny. The basis for this determination was twofold: first, the financing scheme divides citizens on a wealth basis, a classification which the District Court viewed as highly suspect; and second, the discriminatory scheme directly affects what it considered to be a "fundamental interest," namely, education.

This Court has repeatedly held that state discrimination which either adversely affects a "fundamental interest," see, e.g., Dunn v. Blumstein, 405 U.S. 330, 336-342 (1972); Shapiro v. Thompson, 394 U.S. 618, 629-631 (1969), or is based on a distinction of a suspect character, see, e.g., Graham v. Richardson, 403 U.S. 365, 372 (1971); McLaughlin v. Florida, 379 U.S. 184, 191-192 (1964), must be carefully scrutinized to ensure that the scheme is necessary to promote a substantial, legitimate state interest. See, e.g., Dunn v. Blumstein, supra, at 342-343; Shapiro v. Thompson, supra, at 634. The majority today concludes, however, that the Texas scheme is not subject to such a strict standard of review under the Equal Protection Clause. . . . By so doing, the Court avoids the telling task of searching for a substantial state interest which the Texas financing scheme, with its variations in taxable district property wealth, is necessary to further. I cannot accept such an emasculation of the Equal Protection Clause in the context of this case.

A

To begin, I must once more voice my disagreement with the Court's rigidified approach to equal protection analysis. See Dandridge v. Williams, 397 U.S. 471, 519-521

(1970) (dissenting opinion); Richardson v. Belcher, 404 U.S. 78, 90 (1971) (dissenting opinion). The Court apparently seeks to establish today that equal protection cases fall into one of two neat categories which dictate the appropriate standard of review — strict scrutiny or mere rationality. But this Court's decisions in the field of equal protection defy such easy categorization. A principled reading of what this Court has done reveals that it has applied a spectrum of standards in reviewing discrimination allegedly violative of the Equal Protection Clause. This spectrum clearly comprehends variations in the degree of care with which the Court will scrutinize particular classifications, depending, I believe, on the constitutional and societal importance of the interest adversely affected and the recognized invidiousness of the basis upon which the particular classification is drawn. I find in fact that many of the Court's recent decisions embody the very sort of reasoned approach to equal protection analysis for which I previously argued — that is, an approach in which "concentration [is] placed upon the character of the classification in question, the relative importance to individuals in the class discriminated against of the governmental benefits that they do not receive, and the asserted state interests in support of the classification." Dandridge v. Williams, supra, at 520-521 (dissenting opinion).

I therefore cannot accept the majority's labored efforts to demonstrate that fundamental interests, which call for strict scrutiny of the challenged classification, encompass only established rights which we are somehow bound to recognize from the text of the Constitution itself. To be sure, some interests which the Court has deemed to be fundamental for purposes of equal protection analysis are themselves constitutionally protected rights. Thus, discrimination against the guaranteed right of freedom of speech has called for strict judicial scrutiny. See Police Dept. of Chicago v. Mosley, 408 U.S. 92 (1972). Further, every citizen's right to travel interstate, although nowhere expressly mentioned in the Constitution, has long been recognized as implicit in the premises underlying that document: the right "was conceived from the beginning to be a necessary concomitant of the stronger Union the Constitution created." United States v. Guest, 383 U.S. 745, 758 (1966). See also Crandall v. Nevada, 6 Wall. 35, 48 (1868). Consequently, the Court has required that a state classification affecting the constitutionally protected right to travel must be "shown to be necessary to promote a *compelling* governmental interest." Shapiro v. Thompson, 394 U.S., at 634. But it will not do to suggest that the "answer" to whether an interest is fundamental for purposes of equal protection analysis is *always* determined by whether that interest "is a right . . . explicitly or implicitly guaranteed by the Constitution," ante, at 33-34.

I would like to know where the Constitution guarantees the right to procreate, Skinner v. Oklahoma, 316 U.S. 535, 541 (1942), or the right to vote in state elections, e.g., Reynolds v. Sims, 377 U.S. 533 (1964), or the right to an appeal from a criminal conviction, e.g., Griffin v. Illinois, 351 U.S. 12 (1956). These are instances in which, due to the importance of the interests at stake, the Court has displayed a strong concern with the existence of discriminatory state treatment. But the Court has never said or indicated that these are interests which independently enjoy full-blown constitutional protection. . . .

The majority is, of course, correct when it suggests that the process of determining which interests are fundamental is a difficult one. But I do not think the problem is insurmountable. And I certainly do not accept the view that the process need necessarily degenerate into an unprincipled, subjective "picking-and-choosing" between various interests or that it must involve this Court in creating "substantive constitutional rights in the name of guaranteeing equal protection of the laws," ante, at 33. Although not all fundamental interests are constitutionally guaranteed, the determination of which interests are fundamental should be firmly rooted in the text of the Constitution. The task in every case should be to determine the extent to which constitutionally guaranteed rights are dependent on interests not mentioned in the Constitution. As the nexus between the specific constitutional guarantee and the nonconstitutional interest draws closer, the nonconstitutional interest becomes more fundamental and the degree of judicial scrutiny applied when the interest is infringed on a discriminatory basis must be adjusted accordingly. Thus, it cannot be denied that interests such as procreation, the exercise of the state franchise, and access to criminal appellate processes are not fully guaranteed to the citizen by our Constitution. But these interests have nonetheless been afforded special judicial consideration in the face of discrimination because they are, to some extent, interrelated with constitutional guarantees. Procreation is now understood to be important because of its interaction with the established constitutional right of privacy. The exercise of the state franchise is closely tied to basic civil and political rights inherent in the First Amendment. And access to criminal appellate processes enhances the integrity of the range of rights implicit in the Fourteenth Amendment guarantee of due process of law. Only if we closely protect the related interests from state discrimination do we ultimately ensure the integrity of the constitutional guarantee itself. This is the real lesson that must be taken from our previous decisions involving interests deemed to be fundamental. . . .

A similar process of analysis with respect to the invidiousness of the basis on which a particular classification is drawn has also influenced the Court as to the appropriate degree of scrutiny to be accorded any particular case. The highly suspect character of classifications based on race, nationality, or alienage is well established. The reasons why such classifications call for close judicial scrutiny are manifold. Certain racial and ethnic groups have frequently been recognized as "discrete and insular minorities" who are relatively powerless to protect their interests in the political process. See Graham v. Richardson, 403 U.S., at 372; cf. United States v. Carolene Products Co., 304 U.S. 144, 152-153, n.4 (1938). Moreover, race, nationality, or alienage is " 'in most circumstances irrelevant' to any constitutionally acceptable legislative purpose, Hirabayashi v. United States, 320 U.S. 81, 100." McLaughlin v. Florida, 379 U.S., at 192. Instead, lines drawn on such bases are frequently the reflection of historic prejudices rather than legislative rationality. It may be that all of these considerations, which make for particular judicial solicitude in the face of discrimination on the basis of race, nationality, or alienage, do not coalesce — or at least not to the same degree — in other forms of discrimination. Nevertheless, these considerations have undoubtedly influenced the care with which the Court has scrutinized other forms of discrimination.

In James v. Strange, 407 U.S. 128 (1972), the Court held unconstitutional a state statute which provided for recoupment from indigent convicts of legal defense fees paid by the State. The Court found that the statute impermissibly differentiated between indigent criminals in debt to the State and civil judgment debtors, since criminal debtors were denied various protective exemptions afforded civil judgment debtors. . . .

Similarly, in Reed v. Reed, 404 U.S. 71 (1971), the Court, in striking down a state statute which gave men preference over women when persons of equal entitlement apply for assignment as an administrator of a particular estate, resorted to a more stringent standard of equal protection review than that employed in cases involving commercial matters. . . .

James and Reed can only be understood as instances in which the particularly invidious character of the classification caused the Court to pause and scrutinize with more than traditional care the rationality of state discrimination. Discrimination on the basis of past criminality and on the basis of sex posed for the Court the specter of forms of discrimination which it implicitly recognized to have deep social and legal roots without necessarily having any basis in actual differences. Still, the Court's sensitivity to the invidiousness of the basis for discrimination is perhaps most apparent in its decisions protecting the interests of children born out of wedlock from discriminatory state action. See Weber v. Aetna Casualty & Surety Co., 406 U.S. 164 (1972); Levy v. Louisiana, 391 U.S. 68 (1968). . . .

. . . Status of birth, like the color of one's skin, is something which the individual cannot control, and should generally be irrelevant in legislative considerations. Yet illegitimacy has long been stigmatized by our society. Hence, discrimination on the basis of birth — particularly when it affects innocent children — warrants special judicial consideration.

In summary, it seems to me inescapably clear that this Court has consistently adjusted the care with which it will review state discrimination in light of the constitutional significance of the interests affected and the invidiousness of the particular classification. In the context of economic interests, we find that discriminatory state action is almost always sustained, for such interests are generally far removed from constitutional guarantees. Moreover, "[t]he extremes to which the Court has gone in dreaming up rational bases for state regulation in that area may in many instances be ascribed to a healthy revulsion from the Court's earlier excesses in using the Constitution to protect interests that have more than enough power to protect themselves in the legislative halls." Dandridge v. Williams, 397 U.S., at 520 (dissenting opinion). But the situation differs markedly when discrimination against important individual interests with constitutional implications and against particularly disadvantaged or powerless classes is involved. The majority suggests, however, that a variable standard of review would give this Court the appearance of a "superlegislature." Ante, at 31. I cannot agree. Such an approach seems to me a part of the guarantees of our Constitution and of the historic experiences with oppression of and discrimination against discrete, powerless minorities which underlie that document. In truth, the Court itself will be open to the criticism raised by the majority so long as it continues on its present course of effectively selecting in private which cases will be afforded special consideration without acknowledging the true basis of its action. Opinions such as those in Reed and James seem drawn more as efforts to shield rather than to reveal the true basis of the Courts decisions. Such obfuscated action may be appropriate to a political body such as a legislature, but it is not appropriate to this Court. Open debate of the bases for the Court's action is essential to the rationality and consistency of our decisionmaking process. Only in this way can we avoid the label of legislature and ensure the integrity of the judicial process.

Nevertheless, the majority today attempts to force this case into the same category for purposes of equal protection analysis as decisions involving discrimination affecting commercial interests. By so doing, the majority singles this case out for analytic treatment at odds with what seems to me to be the clear trend of recent decisions in this Court, and thereby ignores the constitutional importance of the interest at stake and the invidiousness of the particular classification, factors that call for far more than the lenient scrutiny of the Texas financing scheme which the majority pursues. Yet if the discrimination inherent in the Texas scheme is scrutinized with the care demanded by the interest and classification present in this case, the unconstitutionality of that scheme is unmistakable. . . . [x]

NOTE Municipal Services and Equal Protection

Compare Hawkins v. Town of Shaw, 437 F.2d 1286 (5th Cir. 1971), adhered to on rehearing en banc, 461 F.2d 1171 (1972), holding that "clear overtones of racial discrimination" in the distribution of municipal services justified issuance of an injunction ordering the town to eliminate the disparity in provision of services such as street paving, water mains and sewer systems; Serrano v. Priest, 5 Cal. 3d 584, 487 P.2d 1241, 96 Cal. Rptr. 601 (1971) (en banc), holding that California's district-based public school financing system involved both a fundamental interest in education and suspect classification on the basis of wealth and violated the equal protection provisions of both the state and federal constitutions. A financing plan subsequently adopted by the state legislature which decreased the disparity between local districts while still permitting higher expenditures by

[x] A concurring opinion by Justice Stewart, a dissenting opinion by Justice Brennan, and a dissenting opinion by Justice White, joined by Justices Douglas and Brennan, are omitted. — ED.

wealthier districts was declared unconstitutional in Serrano v. Priest, 45 U.S.L.W. 2340 (Cal. Sup. Ct. 1976). The court based its decision on the state constitution, declining to follow Rodriguez.

On equal protection and public education, see Coons, Clure & Sugarman, Educational Opportunity: A Workable Constitutional Test of State Financial Structures, 57 Calif. L. Rev. 305 (1969); Goldstein, Interdistrict Inequalities in School Financing: A Critical Analysis of Serrano v. Priest and Its Progeny, 120 U. Pa. L. Rev. 504 (1972); Areen & Ross, The Rodriguez Case: Judicial Oversight of School Finance, 1973 Sup. Ct. Rev. 33 (1974); Note, A Statistical Analysis of the School Finance Decisions: On Winning Battles and Losing Wars, 81 Yale L.J. 1303 (1972); Note, The Supreme Court, 1972 Term, 87 Harv. L. Rev. 1, 105-116 (1973).

On the right to municipal services, see Abascal, Municipal Services and Equal Protection: Variations on a Theme by Griffin v. Illinois, 20 Hastings L.J. 1367 (1967); Fessler & Haar, Beyond the Wrong Side of the Tracks: Municipal Services in the Interstices of Procedure, 6 Harv. Civ. Rights-Civ. Lib. L. Rev. 441 (1971).

See generally Karst, Serrano v. Priest: A State Court's Responsibilities and Opportunities in the Development of Federal Constitutional Law, 60 Calif. L. Rev. 720 (1972); Michelman, The Supreme Court, 1968 Term — Foreword: On Protecting the Poor Through the Fourteenth Amendment, 83 Harv. L. Rev. 7 (1969); Note, The Evolution of Equal Protection: Education, Municipal Services, and Wealth, 7 Harv. Civ. Rights-Civ. Lib. L. Rev. 103 (1972).

Regarding Justice Marshall's comments on the two-tier test, compare the standard propounded in his opinion for the Court in Chicago Police Department v. Mosley, 408 U.S. 92, 95 (1972) (invalidating a city ordinance banning all picketing within 150 feet of city school buildings, except if school is involved in a labor dispute): ". . . the crucial question is whether there is an appropriate governmental interest furthered by the differential treatment."

In re Griffiths *413 U.S. 717, 93 S. Ct. 2851, 37 L. Ed. 2d 910 (1973)*

MR. JUSTICE POWELL delivered the opinion of the Court.

This case presents a novel question as to the constraints imposed by the Equal Protection Clause of the Fourteenth Amendment on the qualifications which a State may require for admission to the bar. Appellant, Fre Le Poole Griffiths, is a citizen of the Netherlands who came to the United States in 1965, originally as a visitor. In 1967 she married a citizen of the United States and became a resident of Connecticut.[1] After her graduation from law school, she applied in 1970 for permission to take the Connecticut bar examination. The County Bar Association found her qualified in all respects save that she was not a citizen of the United States as required by Rule 8(1) of the Connecticut Practice Book (1963), and on that account refused to allow her to take the examination. She then sought judicial relief, asserting that the regulation was unconstitutional but her claim was rejected, first by the Superior Court and ultimately by the Connecticut Supreme Court. 162 Conn. 249, 294 A.2d 281 (1972). We noted probable jurisdiction, 406 U.S. 966 (1972), and now hold that the rule unconstitutionally discriminates against resident aliens.

---

[1] Appellant is eligible for naturalization by reason of her marriage to a citizen of the United States and residence in the United States for more than three years, 8 U.S.C. § 1430(a). She has not filed a declaration of intention to become a citizen of the United States, 8 U.S.C. § 1445(f), and has no present intention of doing so. Brief for Appellant 4. In order to become a citizen, appellant would be required to renounce her citizenship of the Netherlands. 8 U.S.C. § 1448(a).

I

We begin by sketching the background against which the State Bar Examining Committee attempts to justify the total exclusion of aliens from the practice of law. From its inception, our Nation welcomed and drew strength from the immigration of aliens. Their contributions to the social and economic life of the country were self-evident, especially during the periods when the demand for human resources greatly exceeded the native supply. This demand was by no means limited to the unskilled or the uneducated. In 1873, this Court noted that admission to the practice of law in the courts of a State "in no sense depends on citizenship of the United States. It has not, as far as we know, ever been made in any State, or in any case, to depend on citizenship at all. Certainly many prominent and distinguished lawyers have been admitted to practice, both in the State and Federal courts, who were not citizens of the United States or of any State." Bradwell v. State, 16 Wall. 130, 139. But shortly thereafter, in 1879, Connecticut established the predecessor to its present rule totally excluding aliens from the practice of law. 162 Conn., at 253, 294 A.2d, at 283. In subsequent decades, wide-ranging restrictions for the first time began to impair significantly the efforts of aliens to earn a livelihood in their chosen occupations.

In the face of this trend, the Court nonetheless held in 1886 that a lawfully admitted resident alien is a "person" within the meaning of the Fourteenth Amendment's directive that a State must not "deny to any person within its jurisdiction the equal protection of the laws." Yick Wo v. Hopkins, 118 U.S. 356, 369. The decision in Yick Wo invalidated a municipal ordinance regulating the operation of laundries on the ground that the ordinance was discriminatorily enforced against Chinese operators. Some years later, the Court struck down an Arizona statute requiring employers of more than five persons to employ at least 80% "qualified electors or native-born citizens of the United States or some subdivision thereof." Truax v. Raich, 239 U.S. 33, 35 (1915). As stated for the Court by Mr. Justice Hughes: "It requires no argument to show that the right to work for a living in the common occupations of the community is of the very essence of the personal freedom and opportunity that it was the purpose of the [Fourteenth] Amendment to secure. [Citations omitted.] If this could be refused solely upon the ground of race or nationality, the prohibition of the denial to any person of the equal protection of the laws would be a barren form of words." Id., at 41.

To be sure, the course of decisions protecting the employment rights of resident aliens has not been an unswerving one. In Clarke v. Deckebach, 274 U.S. 392 (1927), the Court was faced with a challenge to a city ordinance prohibiting the issuance to aliens of licenses to operate pool and billiard rooms. Characterizing the business as one having "harmful and vicious tendencies," the Court found no constitutional infirmity in the ordinance: "It was competent for the city to make such a choice, not shown to be irrational, by excluding from the conduct of a dubious business an entire class rather than its objectionable members selected by more empirical methods." Id., at 397. This easily expandable proposition supported discrimination against resident aliens in a wide range of occupations.

But the doctrinal foundations of Clarke were undermined in Takahashi v. Fish & Game Comm'n, 334 U.S. 410 (1948), where, in ruling unconstitutional a California statute barring issuance of fishing licenses to persons "ineligible to citizenship," the Court stated that "the power of a state to apply its laws exclusively to its alien inhabitants as a class is confined within narrow limits." Id., at 420. Indeed, with the issue squarely before it in Graham v. Richardson, 403 U.S. 365 (1971), the Court concluded: "[C]lassifications based on alienage, like those based on nationality or race, are inherently suspect and subject to close judicial scrutiny. Aliens as a class are a prime example of a 'discrete and insular' minority (see United States v. Carolene Products Co., 304 U.S. 144, 152-153, n.4 (1938)) for whom such heightened judicial solicitude is appropriate." Id., at 372. (Footnotes omitted.)

The Court has consistently emphasized that a State which adopts a suspect classification "bears a heavy burden of justification," McLaughlin v. Florida, 379 U.S. 184, 196 (1964), a burden which, though variously formulated, requires the State to meet certain standards of proof. In order to justify the use of a suspect classification, a State must show that its purpose or interest is both constitutionally permissible and substantial, and that its use of the classification is "necessary . . . to the accomplishment" of its purpose or the safeguarding of its interest.

Resident aliens, like citizens, pay taxes, support the economy, serve in the Armed Forces, and contribute in myriad other ways to our society. It is appropriate that a State bear a heavy burden when it deprives them of employment opportunities.

II

We hold that the Committee, acting on behalf of the State, has not carried its burden. . . .

The Committee defends Rule 8(1)'s requirement that applicants for admission to the bar be citizens of the United States on the ground that the special role of the lawyer justifies excluding aliens from the practice of law. In Connecticut, the Committee points out, the maxim that a lawyer is an "officer of the court" is given concrete meaning by a statute which makes every lawyer a "commissioner of the Superior Court." As such, a lawyer has authority to "sign writs and subpoenas, take recognizances, administer oaths and take depositions and acknowledgements of deeds." Conn. Gen. Stat. Rev. §51-85. . . . In order to establish a link between citizenship and the powers and responsibilities of the lawyer in Connecticut, the Committee contrasts a citizen's undivided allegiance to this country with a resident alien's possible conflict of loyalties. From this, the Committee concludes that a resident alien lawyer might in the exercise of his functions ignore his responsibilities to the courts or even his clients in favor of the interest of a foreign power.

We find these arguments unconvincing. It in no way denigrates a lawyer's high responsibilities to observe that the powers "to sign writs and subpoenas, take recognizances, [and] administer oaths" hardly involve matters of state policy or acts of such unique responsibility as to entrust them only to citizens. Nor do we think that the practice of law offers meaningful opportunities adversely to affect the interest of the United States. Certainly the Committee has failed to show the relevance of citizenship to any likelihood that a lawyer will fail to protect faithfully the interest of his clients.

Nor would the possibility that some resident aliens are unsuited to the practice of law be a justification for a wholesale ban. . . .

Connecticut has wide freedom to gauge on a case-by-case basis the fitness of an applicant to practice law. Connecticut can, and does, require appropriate training and familiarity with Connecticut law. Apart from such tests of competence, it requires a new lawyer to take both an "attorney's oath" to perform his functions faithfully and honestly and a "commissioner's oath" to "support the constitution of the United States, and the constitution of the state of Connecticut." . . . Moreover, once admitted to the bar, lawyers are subject to continuing scrutiny by the organized bar and the courts. In addition to discipline for unprofessional conduct, the range of post-admission sanctions extends from judgments for contempt to criminal prosecutions and disbarment. In sum, the Committee simply has not established that it must exclude all aliens from the practice of law in order to vindicate its undoubted interest in high professional standards. . . .

NOTE Aliens and Equal Protection

In a case decided the same day as In re Griffiths, the Court struck down a section of a New York law that provided that only U.S. citizens could hold permanent positions in the competitive class of the state civil service. Sugarman v. Dougall, 413 U.S. 634 (1973). As in Griffiths, the Court found that the restriction swept too "indiscriminately" to survive strict scrutiny. The ban applied, wrote Justice Blackmun, "to the office worker . . . as well as to the person who directly participates in the formulation and execution of important state policy." Citizenship limits on this latter class, he noted, may well be justified by the state's interest in "preserv[ing] . . . political community." Compare the treatment of overbreadth here with the analysis in the Hatch Act cases, United Public Workers v. Mitchell, 330 U.S. 75 (1947), and U.S. Civil Service Commn. v. National Assn. of Letter Carriers, 413 U.S. 548 (1973).

Writing in dissent in both Griffiths and Sugarman, Justice Rehnquist objected to the invocation of strict scrutiny in Graham, which first considered alienage suspect, and in these cases: "Our society, consisting of over 200 million individuals of multitudinous origins, customs, tongues, beliefs, and cultures is, to say the least, diverse. It would hardly take extraordinary ingenuity for a lawyer to find 'insular and discrete' minorities at every turn in the road. Yet, unless the Court can precisely define and constitutionally justify both the terms and the analysis it uses, these decisions today stand for the proposition that the Court can choose a 'minority' it 'feels' deserves 'solicitude' and thereafter prohibit the States from classifying that 'minority' differently from the 'majority.' I cannot find, and the Court does not cite, any constitutional authority for such a 'ward of the Court' approach to equal protection."

In the training for and the experience of citizenship, Justice Rehnquist would find the rational basis for the distinction: "An alien who grew up in a country in which political mores do not reject bribery or self-dealing to the same extent that our culture does . . . could rationally be thought not to be able to deal with the public and with citizen civil servants with the same rapport that one familiar with our political and social mores would. . . ."

See generally Comment, The Constitutional Status of State and Federal Government Discrimination against Resident Aliens, 16 Harv. Intl. L.J. 113 (1975).

NOTE Other Suspect Classifications: Illegitimacy

In Levy v. Louisiana, 391 U.S. 68 (1968), and Glona v. American Guarantee & Liability Ins. Co., 391 U.S. 73 (1968), the Supreme Court upheld equal protection challenges to a Louisiana wrongful death statute which denied recovery to illegitimate children on the death of the mother and to the mother on the death of an illegitimate child. Writing for the Court, Justice Douglas rejected the proffered justification that the exclusions served to discourage parenthood out of wedlock. On the denial of recovery to illegitimate children, he stated:

"Legitimacy or illegitimacy of birth has no relation to the nature of the wrong allegedly inflicted on the mother. These children, though illegitimate, were dependent on her; she cared for them and nurtured them; they were indeed hers in the biological and in the spiritual sense; in her death they suffered wrong in the sense that any dependent would.

"We conclude that it is invidious to discriminate against them when no action, conduct, or demeanor of theirs is possibly relevant to the harm that was done the mother."

On the ban on recovery by the mother of an illegitimate decedent, Justice Douglas wrote: "[W]e see no possible rational basis (Morey v. Doud, 354 U.S. 457, 465-466) for assuming that if the natural mother is allowed recovery for the wrongful death of her illegitimate child, the cause of illegitimacy will be served. It would, indeed, be farfetched to assume that women have illegitimate children so that they can be compensated in damages for their death."

Justice Harlan dissented, joined by Justices Stewart and White, in both Levy and Glona:

"These decisions can only be classed as constitutional curiosities.

"At common law, no person had a legally cognizable interest in the wrongful death of another person, and no person could inherit the personal right of another to recover for tortious injuries to his body. By statute, Louisiana has created both rights in favor of certain classes of persons. The question in these cases is whether the way in which Louisiana has defined the classes of persons who may recover is constitutionally permissible. The Court has reached a negative answer to this question by a process that can only be described as brute force.

"One important reason why recovery for wrongful death had everywhere to await statutory delineation is that the interest one person has in the life of another is inherently intractable. Rather than hear offers of proof of love and affection and economic dependence from every person who might think or claim that the bell had tolled for him, the courts stayed their hands pending legislative action. Legislatures, responding to the same diffuseness of interests, generally defined classes of proper plaintiffs by highly arbitrary lines based on family relationships, excluding issues concerning the actual effect of the death on the plaintiff.

"Louisiana has followed the traditional pattern. . . . According to this scheme, a grown man may sue for the wrongful death of parents he did not love, even if the death relieves him of a great economic burden or entitles him to a large inheritance. But an employee who loses a job because of the death of his employer has no cause of action, and a minor child cared for by neighbors or relatives 'as if he were their own son' does not therefore have a right to sue for their death. Perhaps most dramatic, a surviving parent, for example, of a Louisiana deceased may sue if and only if there is no surviving spouse or child: it does not matter who loved or depended on whom, or what the economic situation of any survivor may be, or even whether the spouse or child elects to sue.[3] In short, the whole scheme of the Louisiana wrongful death statute, which is similar in this respect to that of most other States, makes everything the Court says about affection and nurture and dependence altogether irrelevant. . . .

". . . The rights at issue here stem from the existence of a family relationship, and the State has decided only that it will not recognize the family relationship unless the formalities of marriage, or of the acknowledgment of children by the parent in question, have been complied with.

"There is obvious justification for this decision. If it be conceded, as I assume it is, that the State has power to provide that people who choose to live together should go through the formalities of marriage and, in default, that people who bear children should acknowledge them, it is logical to enforce these requirements by declaring that the general class of rights that are dependent upon family relationships shall be accorded only when the formalities as well as the biology of these relationships are present. Moreover, and for many of the same reasons why a State is empowered to require formalities in the first place, a State may choose to simplify a particular proceeding by reliance on formal papers rather than a contest of proof. That suits for wrongful death, actions to determine the heirs of intestates, and the like, must as a constitutional matter deal with every claim of biological paternity on its merits is an exceedingly odd proposition.

[3] ". . . Under the Court's opinion, the right of legitimate and perhaps dependent parents to sue will henceforth be cut off by the mere existence of an illegitimate child, though the child be a self-supporting adult, and though the child elect not to sue. Incidentally, the burden of proving the nonexistence of such a child will be on the plaintiff parent. Trahan v. Southern Pacific Co., 209 F. Supp. 334."

"The Equal Protection Clause states a complex and difficult principle. Certain classifications are 'inherently suspect,' which I take to mean that any reliance upon them in differentiating legal rights requires very strong affirmative justification. The difference between a child who has been formally acknowledged and one who has not is hardly one of these. Other classifications are impermissible because they bear no intelligible proper relation to the consequences that are made to flow from them. This does not mean that any classification this Court thinks could be better drawn is unconstitutional. But even if the power of this Court to improve the lines that Congress and the States have drawn were very much broader than I consider it to be, I could not understand why a State which bases the right to recover for wrongful death strictly on family relationships could not demand that those relationships be formalized. . . ."

Levy and Glona were distinguished, however, in Labine v. Vincent, 401 U.S. 532 (1971). There, the Court sustained, 5 to 4, a provision of Louisiana law excluding from intestate succession an illegitimate or acknowledged but not legitimated child, where the parent is survived by direct or collateral kin. Writing for the Court, Justice Black pointed to the state's interest in "promoting family life and of directing the disposition of property left within the State" and to the decedent's ability to include the child in his estate either by legitimating her or by executing a will in her favor. Justices Brennan, Douglas, White, and Marshall dissented.

In Weber v. Aetna Casualty & Surety Co., 406 U.S. 164 (1972), the Court invalidated provisions of the Louisiana workmen's compensation laws which discriminated between unacknowledged, illegitimate children and other children regarding recovery of benefits on the death of the natural father. Under these provisions, legitimate and acknowledged illegitimate children were entitled to full recovery; unacknowledged illegitimate children, however, were classed as "other dependents," who could recover only if there were not enough fully entitled children to exhaust the maximum allowable benefits. Writing for the Court, Justice Powell distinguished Labine v. Vincent on the grounds that that case had involved state regulation of real property, traditionally the special province of the states, and that, unlike Labine, the decedent in this case could not have made provision for his illegitimate offspring: Louisiana law barred acknowledgement where the parents could not have been legally married at the time of conception, and the decedent in this case was thus disqualified because he was already married to someone else. The Court then struck down the classification as "bear[ing], in this instance, no reasonable relationship to those recognized purposes of recovery which workmen's compensation statutes commendably serve." Justice Blackmun, concurring in the result, stated that he would have limited the holding to instances where the decedent was ineligible to acknowledge an illegitimate child. Justice Rehnquist dissented.

Should it have made any difference in the result that the classification in Weber was between classes of illegitimates rather than between legitimate and illegitimate offspring?

In Gomez v. Perez, 409 U.S. 535 (1973) (per curiam), the Supreme Court held it a violation of the equal protection clause for a state not to recognize a natural father's support obligation to illegitimate children while recognizing such obligation to legitimate offspring.

Various provisions of social welfare legislation discriminating against illegitimates have been declared unconstitutional. See Davis v. Richardson, 432 F. Supp. 588 (D. Conn.) (three-judge court), aff'd mem., 409 U.S. 1069 (1972), and Griffin v. Richardson, 346 F. Supp. 1226 (D. Md.) (three-judge court), aff'd mem., 409 U.S. 1069 (1972) (invalidating discrimination in rights of children to payment on death of wage earner parent under the Social Security Act, 42 U.S.C. §403 (a)); New Jersey Welfare Rights Organization v. Cahill, 411 U.S. 619 (1973) (per curiam) (invalidating state statute limiting benefits of assistance program to households in which parents are ceremonially married and have at least one legitimate child).

In Jimenez v. Weinberger, 417 U.S. 628 (1974), the Court held invalid a section of the

Social Security Act, 42 U.S.C. §416(h)(3), which provided that illegitimate children of a disabled wage earner parent who did not become dependents of that parent until after he had been disabled were eligible for benefits only if: (1) they were entitled under applicable state law to inherit the parent's personal property; (2) they were legitimated; or (3) their illegitimacy resulted from nonobvious defects in their parents' ceremonial marriage. The district court had upheld the provision as "rationally related to the legitimate governmental interest in avoiding spurious claims." Jimenez v. Richardson, 353 F. Supp. 1356 (N.D. Ill. 1973).

Writing for the Court, Chief Justice Burger first ruled that it would be unnecessary to reach appellants' argument that the provision was "based on the so-called 'suspect classification' of illegitimacy" because the provision would fit within the language of Weber that "'the Equal Protection Clause does enable us to strike down discriminatory laws relating to status of birth where . . . the classification is justified by no legitimate state interest, compelling or otherwise.'" Second, the Chief Justice distinguished Dandridge v. Williams, 397 U.S. 471 (1970), on the ground that judicial interference with the legislative judgments underlying the challenged provision would not, in contrast to the situation in Dandridge, "significantly impair the federal Social Security trust fund and necessitate a reduction in the scope of persons benefited by the Act."

The Chief Justice described the provision as dividing illegitimate children born after the onset of the parent's disability into two classes: those who qualify for benefits under any of the three categories set out above and those who don't. He contested the government's argument that this classification was justified by the relative likelihood of actual dependency on the disabled parent or by its interest in discouraging spurious claims: "Assuming that the appellants are in fact dependent on the claimant, it would not serve the purposes of the Act to conclusively deny them an opportunity to establish their dependency and their right to insurance benefits, and it would discriminate between the two subclasses of afterborn illegitimates without any basis for the distinction since the potential for spurious claims is exactly the same as to both subclasses.

". . . Even if children might rationally be classified on the basis of whether they are dependent upon their disabled parent, the Act's definition of these two subclasses of illegitimates is 'over-inclusive' in that it benefits some children who are legitimated, or entitled to inherit, or illegitimate solely because of a defect in the marriage of their parents, but who are not dependent on their disabled parent. Conversely, the Act is 'under-inclusive' in that it conclusively excludes some illegitimates in appellants' subclass who are, in fact, dependent upon their disabled parent. Thus, for all that is shown in the record, the two subclasses of illegitimates stand on equal footing, and the potential for spurious claims is the same as to both; hence to conclusively deny one subclass benefits presumptively available to the other denies the former the equal protection of the law guaranteed by the due process provisions of the Fifth Amendment."

In dissent Justice Rehnquist began:

"I frankly find the Court's opinion in this case a perplexing three-legged stool. The holding is clearly founded in notions of equal protection, . . . and the Court speaks specifically of improper 'discrimination.' Yet the opinion has strong due process overtones as well, at times appearing to pay homage to the still novel, and I think unsupportable, theory that 'irrebuttable presumptions' violate due process. At other times the opinion seems to suggest that the real problem in this case is the Government's failure to build an adequate evidentiary record in support of the challenged legislation. The result is a rather impressionistic determination that Congress' efforts to cope with spurious claims of entitlement, while preserving maximum benefits for those persons most likely to be deserving, are simply not satisfactory to the members of this Court. I agree with neither the Court's approach nor its decision."

In Mathews v. Lucas, 427 U.S. 495 (1976), the Court upheld a provision of the Social Security Act denying the benefit of a conclusive presumption of dependency to an illegitimate child who is unable to inherit under state intestacy laws, who is not illegitimate merely by reason of some technical defect in his parents' marriage, and whose father has neither acknowledged paternity nor been adjudicated to be his father nor been ordered by a court to support him. The six-member majority denied that illegitimacy was a suspect classification, and applied "less than strictest scrutiny," citing Labine v. Vincent, supra.

Frontiero v. Richardson 411 U.S. 677, 93 S. Ct. 1764, 36 L. Ed. 2d 583 (1973)

MR. JUSTICE BRENNAN announced the judgment of the Court and an opinion in which MR. JUSTICE DOUGLAS, MR. JUSTICE WHITE, and MR. JUSTICE MARSHALL join.

The question before us concerns the right of a female member of the uniformed services to claim her spouse as a "dependent" for the purposes of obtaining increased quarters allowances and medical and dental benefits under 37 U.S.C. §§401, 403 and 10 U.S.C. §§1072, 1076 on an equal footing with male members. Under these statutes, a serviceman may claim his wife as a "dependent" without regard to whether she is in fact dependent upon him for any part of her support. . . . A servicewoman, on the other hand, may not claim her husband as a "dependent" under these programs unless he is in fact dependent upon her for over one-half of his support. . . . Thus, the question for decision is whether this difference in treatment constitutes an unconstitutional discrimination against servicewomen in violation of the Due Process Clause of the Fifth Amendment. A three-judge District Court for the Middle District of Alabama, one judge dissenting, rejected this contention and sustained the constitutionality of the provisions of the statutes making this distinction. 341 F. Supp. 201 (1972). We noted probable jurisdiction. 409 U.S. 840. We reverse.

I

In an effort to attract career personnel through re-enlistment, Congress established . . . a scheme for the provision of fringe benefits to members of the uniformed services on a competitive basis with business and industry. Thus, under 37 U.S.C. §403, a member of the uniformed services with dependents is entitled to an increased "basic allowance for quarters" and, under 10 U.S.C §1076, a member's dependents are provided comprehensive medical and dental care.

Appellant Sharron Frontiero, a lieutenant in the United States Air Force, sought increased quarters allowances, and housing and medical benefits for her husband, appellant Joseph Frontiero, on the ground that he was her "dependent." Although such benefits would automatically have been granted with respect to the wife of a male member of the uniformed services, appellant's application was denied because she failed to demonstrate that her husband was dependent on her for more than one-half of his support. Appellants then commenced this suit, contending that, by making this distinction, the statutes unreasonably discriminate on the basis of sex in violation of the Due Process Clause of the Fifth Amendment. In essence, appellants asserted that the discriminatory impact of the statutes is twofold: first, as a procedural matter, a female member is required to demonstrate her spouse's dependency, while no such burden is imposed upon male members; and, second, as a substantive matter, a male member who does not provide more than one-half of his wife's support receives benefits, while a similarly situated female member is denied such benefits. Appellants therefore sought a permanent injunction against the continued enforcement of these statutes and an order directing the appellees to provide Lieutenant Frontiero with the same housing and medical benefits that a similarly situated male member would receive.

Although the legislative history of these statutes sheds virtually no light on the purposes underlying the differential treatment accorded male and female members, a majority of the three-judge District Court surmised that Congress might reasonably have concluded that, since the husband in our society is generally the "breadwinner" in the family — and the wife typically the "dependent" partner — "it would be more economical to require married female members claiming husbands to prove actual dependency than to extend the presumption of dependency to such members." 341 F. Supp., at 207. Indeed, given the fact that approximately 99% of all members of the uniformed services are male, the District Court speculated that such differential treatment might conceivably lead to a "considerable saving of administrative expense and manpower." Ibid.

II

At the outset, appellants contend that classifications based upon sex, like classifications based upon race, alienage, and national origin, are inherently suspect and must therefore be subjected to close judicial scrutiny. We agree and, indeed, find at least implicit support for such an approach in our unanimous decision only last Term in Reed v. Reed, 404 U.S. 71 (1971). [In Reed, the appellant challenged a provision of the Idaho probate code requiring automatic preference of men over women when persons of the same entitlement class apply for appointment as administrator of a decedent's estate.] [A]ppellee contended that the statutory scheme was a reasonable measure designed to reduce the workload on probate courts by eliminating one class of contests. Moreover, appellee argued that the mandatory preference for male applicants was in itself reasonable since "men [are] as a rule more conversant with business affairs than . . . women." Indeed, appellee maintained that "it is a matter of common knowledge, that women still are not engaged in politics, the professions, business or industry to the extent that men are." And the Idaho Supreme Court, in upholding the constitutionality of this statute, suggested that the Idaho Legislature might reasonably have "concluded that in general men are better qualified to act as an administrator than are women."

Despite these contentions, however, the Court held the statutory preference for male applicants unconstitutional. In reaching this result, the Court implicitly rejected appellee's apparently rational explanation of the statutory scheme, and concluded that, by ignoring the individual qualifications of particular applicants, the challenged statute provided "dissimilar treatment for men and women who are . . . similarly situated." Reed v. Reed, supra, at 77. The Court therefore held that, even though the State's interest in achieving administrative efficiency "is not without some legitimacy," "[t]o give a mandatory preference to members of either sex over members of the other, merely to accomplish the elimination of hearings on the merits, is to make the very kind of arbitrary legislative choice forbidden by the [Constitution]. . . ." Id., at 76. This departure from "traditional" rational-basis analysis with respect to sex-based classifications is clearly justified.

There can be no doubt that our Nation has had a long and unfortunate history of sex discrimination.[13] Traditionally, such discrimination was rationalized by an attitude of "romantic paternalism" which, in practical effect, put women, not on a pedestal, but in a cage. Indeed, this paternalistic attitude became so firmly rooted in our national consciousness that, 100 years ago, a distinguished Member of this Court was able to proclaim:

"Man is, or should be, woman's protector and defender. The natural and proper timidity and delicacy which belongs to the female sex evidently unfits it for many of the

---

[13] Indeed, the position of women in this country at its inception is reflected in the view expressed by Thomas Jefferson that women should be neither seen nor heard in society's decisionmaking councils. See M. Gruberg, Women in American Politics 4 (1968). See also 2 A. de Tocqueville, Democracy in America (Reeves Trans. 1948).

occupations of civil life. The constitution of the family organization, which is founded in the divine ordinance, as well as in the nature of things, indicates the domestic sphere as that which properly belongs to the domain and functions of womanhood. The harmony, not to say identity, of interests and views which belong, or should belong, to the family institution is repugnant to the idea of a woman adopting a distinct and independent career from that of her husband. . . .

". . . The paramount destiny and mission of woman are to fulfil the noble and benign offices of wife and mother. This is the law of the Creator." Bradwell v. Illinois, 16 Wall 141, 21 L. Ed. 442 (1873) (Bradley, J., concurring).

As a result of notions such as these, our statute books gradually became laden with gross, stereotyped distinctions between the sexes and, indeed, throughout much of the 19th century the position of women in our society was, in many respects, comparable to that of blacks under the pre-Civil War slave codes. Neither slaves nor women could hold office, serve on juries, or bring suit in their own names, and married women traditionally were denied the legal capacity to hold or convey property or to serve as legal guardians of their own children. See generally L. Kanowitz, Women and the Law: The Unfinished Revolution 5-6 (1969); G. Myrdal, An American Dilemma 1073 (20th anniversary ed. 1962). And although blacks were guaranteed the right to vote in 1870, women were denied even that right — which is itself "preservative of other basic civil and political rights" — until adoption of the Nineteenth Amendment half a century later.

It is true, of course, that the position of women in America has improved markedly in recent decades. Nevertheless, it can hardly be doubted that, in part because of the high visibility of the sex characteristic, women still face pervasive, although at times more subtle, discrimination in our educational institutions, in the job market and, perhaps most conspicuously, in the political arena. See generally K. Amundsen, The Silenced Majority: Women and American Democracy (1971); The President's Task Force on Women's Rights and Responsibilities, A Matter of Simple Justice (1970).

Moreover, since sex, like race and national origin, is an immutable characteristic determined solely by the accident of birth, the imposition of special disabilities upon the members of a particular sex because of their sex would seem to violate "the basic concept of our system that legal burdens should bear some relationship to individual responsibility. . . ." Weber v. Aetna Casualty & Surety Co., 406 U.S. 164 (1972). And what differentiates sex from such nonsuspect statuses as intelligence or physical disability, and aligns it with the recognized suspect criteria, is that the sex characteristic frequently bears no relation to ability to perform or contribute to society. As a result, statutory distinctions between the sexes often have the effect of invidiously relegating the entire class of females to inferior legal status without regard to the actual capabilities of its individual members.

We might also note that, over the past decade, Congress has itself manifested an increasing sensitivity to sex-based classifications. In Title VII of the Civil Rights Act of 1964, for example, Congress expressly declared that no employer, labor union, or other organization subject to the provisions of the Act shall discriminate against any individual on the basis of "race, color, religion, *sex*, or national origin." Similarly, the Equal Pay Act of 1963 provides that no employer covered by the Act "shall discriminate . . . between employees on the basis of *sex*." And § 1 of the Equal Rights Amendment, passed by Congress on March 22, 1972, and submitted to the legislatures of the States for ratification, declares that "[e]quality of rights under the law shall not be denied or abridged by the United States or by any State on account of sex." Thus, Congress itself has concluded that classifications based upon sex are inherently invidious, and this conclusion of a coequal branch of Government is not without significance to the question presently under consideration. Cf. Oregon v. Mitchell, 400 U.S. 112, 240, 248-249 (1970) (opinion of Brennan, White, and Marshall, JJ.); Katzenbach v. Morgan, 384 U.S. 641, 648-649 (1966).

With these considerations in mind, we can only conclude that classifications based upon sex, like classifications based upon race, alienage, or national origin, are inherently suspect, and must therefore be subjected to strict judicial scrutiny. Applying the analysis mandated by that stricter standard of review, it is clear that the statutory scheme now before us is constitutionally invalid.

III

The sole basis of the classification established in the challenged statutes is the sex of the individuals involved. Thus, under 37 U.S.C. §§ 401, 403 and 10 U.S.C. §§ 1072, 1076 a female member of the uniformed services seeking to obtain housing and medical benefits for her spouse must prove his dependency in fact, whereas no such burden is imposed upon male members. In addition, the statutes operate so as to deny benefits to a female member, such as appellant Sharron Frontiero, who provides less than one-half of her spouse's support, while at the same time granting such benefits to a male member who likewise provides less than one-half of his spouse's support. Thus, to this extent at least, it may fairly be said that these statutes command "dissimilar treatment for men and women who are . . . similarly situated." Reed v. Reed, 404 U.S., at 77.

Moreover, the Government concedes that the differential treatment accorded men and women under these statutes serves no purpose other than mere "administrative convenience." In essence, the Government maintains that, as an empirical matter, wives in our society frequently are dependent upon their husbands, while husbands rarely are dependent upon their wives. Thus, the Government argues that Congress might reasonably have concluded that it would be both cheaper and easier simply conclusively to presume that wives of male members are financially dependent upon their husbands, while burdening female members with the task of establishing dependency in fact.

The Government offers no concrete evidence, however, tending to support its view that such differential treatment in fact saves the Government any money. In order to satisfy the demands of strict judicial scrutiny, the Government must demonstrate, for example, that it is actually cheaper to grant increased benefits with respect to *all* male members, than it is to determine which male members are in fact entitled to such benefits and to grant increased benefits only to those members whose wives actually meet the dependency requirement. Here, however, there is substantial evidence that, if put to the test, many of the wives of male members would fail to qualify for benefits.[23] And in light of the fact that the dependency determination with respect to the husbands of female members is presently made solely on the basis of affidavits, rather than through the more costly hearing process, the Government's explanation of the statutory scheme is, to say the least, questionable.

In any case, our prior decisions make clear that, although efficacious administration of governmental programs is not without some importance, "the Constitution recognizes higher values than speed and efficiency." Stanley v. Illinois, 405 U.S. 645, 656 (1972). And when we enter the realm of "strict judicial scrutiny," there can be no doubt that "administrative convenience" is not a shibboleth, the mere recitation of which dictates constitutionality. See Shapiro v. Thompson, 394 U.S. 618 (1969); Carrington v. Rash, 380 U.S. 89 (1965). . . . We therefore conclude that, by according differential treatment to male and female members of the uniformed services for the sole purpose of achieving administrative convenience, the challenged statutes violate the Due Process Clause of the Fifth Amendment insofar as they require a female member to prove the dependency of her husband.

[23] In 1971, 43% of all women over the age of 16 were in the labor force, and 18% of all women worked full time 12 months per year. See U.S. Women's Bureau, Dept. of Labor, Highlights of Women's Employment & Education 1 (W. B. Pub. No. 72-191, Mar. 1972). Moreover, 41.5% of all married women are employed. See U.S. Bureau of Labor Statistics, Dept. of Labor, Work Experience of the Population in 1971, p. 4 (Summary Special Labor Force Report, Aug. 1972). . . .

Reversed.

Mr. Justice Stewart concurs in the judgment, agreeing that the statutes before us work an invidious discrimination in violation of the Constitution. Reed v. Reed, 404 U.S. 71.

Mr. Justice Powell, with whom The Chief Justice and Mr. Justice Blackmun join, concurring in the judgment.

I agree that the challenged statutes constitute an unconstitutional discrimination against servicewomen in violation of the Due Process Clause of the Fifth Amendment, but I cannot join the opinion of Mr. Justice Brennan, which would hold that all classifications based upon sex, "like classifications based upon race, alienage, and national origin," are "inherently suspect and must therefore be subjected to close judicial scrutiny." Ante, at 682. It is unnecessary for the Court in this case to characterize sex as a suspect classification, with all of the far-reaching implications of such a holding. Reed v. Reed, 404 U.S. 71, which abundantly supports our decision today, did not add sex to the narrowly limited group of classifications which are inherently suspect. In my view, we can and should decide this case on the authority of Reed and reserve for the future any expansion of its rationale.

There is another, and I find compelling, reason for deferring a general categorizing of sex classifications as invoking the strictest test of judicial scrutiny. The Equal Rights Amendment, which if adopted will resolve the substance of this precise question, has been approved by the Congress and submitted for ratification by the States. If this Amendment is duly adopted, it will represent the will of the people accomplished in the manner prescribed by the Constitution. By acting prematurely and unnecessarily, as I view it, the Court has assumed a decisional responsibility at the very time when state legislatures, functioning within the traditional democratic process, are debating the proposed Amendment. It seems to me that this reaching out to pre-empt by judicial action a major political decision which is currently in process of resolution does not reflect appropriate respect for duly prescribed legislative processes.

There are times when this Court, under our system, cannot avoid a constitutional decision on issues which normally should be resolved by the elected representatives of the people. But democratic institutions are weakened, and confidence in the restraint of the Court is impaired, when we appear unnecessarily to decide sensitive issues of broad social and political importance at the very time they are under consideration within the prescribed constitutional processes.[y]

NOTE Classification Based on Sex

1. Should sex be considered a "suspect" classification? See Sail'er Inn, Inc. v. Kirby, 5 Cal. 3d 1, 485 P.2d 529 (1971) (no compelling state interest in prohibition of women as bartenders). See also Ely, Judicial Review of Suspicious Classifications: Why Is Classification by Race Suspect and Should Classification by Sex Similarly Be Subjected to Extraordinary Scrutiny? (1971) (unpublished manuscript on file with the Yale Law Journal), summarized in Note, Mental Illness: A Suspect Classification?, 83 Yale L.J. 1237, 1245-1250, 1251-1252 (1974).

On March 22, 1972, Congress passed and sent to the States for ratification the following Constitutional Amendment:

"Section 1. Equality of rights under the law shall not be denied or abridged by the United States or by any State on account of sex.

"Section 2. The Congress shall have the power to enforce, by appropriate legislation, the provisions of this article.

"Section 3. This amendment shall take effect two years after the date of ratification."

---

[y] A dissenting opinion of Justice Rehnquist is omitted. — Ed.

Would adoption of this amendment change the results in some cases? How? Would courts retain any scope for sustaining laws that embody gender classifications? Would a separate-but-equal standard be as impermissible as in the case of race? See Brown, Emerson, Falk & Freedman, The Equal Rights Amendment: A Constitutional Basis for Equal Rights for Women, 80 Yale L.J. 871 (1971); Equal Rights for Women: A Symposium on the Proposed Constitutional Amendment, 6 Harv. Civ. Rights-Civ. Lib. L. Rev. 215 (1971).

2. Discrimination according to sexual characteristics. Reed and Frontiero were distinguished in Geduldig v. Aiello, 417 U.S. 484 (1974). There, respondent challenged a provision of a California state disability insurance system paying benefits to persons in private employment temporarily out of work because of disabilities not covered by workmen's compensation. The system was a self-supporting insurance scheme funded by mandatory payments of up to one percent of annual salary. The challenged provision stated that disability arising in connection with a "normal" pregnancy was not compensable under the scheme. Writing for the Court, Justice Stewart upheld the provision. The Court noted that in setting up the disability fund the state had to make measured judgments regarding the level of mandatory payments and of benefits, which would have to be greatly revised if the state were required to extend coverage to all pregnancies. Citing Dandridge v. Williams, 397 U.S. 471 (1970), the Court stated, "Particularly with respect to social welfare programs, so long as the line drawn by the State is rationally supportable, the courts will not interpose their judgment as to the appropriate stopping point."

To the argument that the provision worked an invidious discrimination according to sex, the Court answered: "The dissenting opinion to the contrary, this case is a far cry from cases like Reed and Frontiero, involving discrimination based upon gender as such. The California insurance program does not exclude anyone from benefit eligibility because of gender but merely removes one physical condition — pregnancy — from the list of compensable disabilities. While it is true that only women can become pregnant, it does not follow that every legislative classification concerning pregnancy is a sex-based classification like those considered in Reed and Frontiero. Normal pregnancy is an objectively identifiable physical condition with unique characteristics. Absent a showing that distinctions involving pregnancy are mere pretexts designed to effect an invidious discrimination against the members of one sex or the other, lawmakers are constitutionally free to include or exclude pregnancy from the coverage of legislation such as this on any reasonable basis, just as with respect to any other physical condition."

The Court concluded: "There is no evidence in the record that the selection of the risks insured by the program worked to discriminate against any definable group or class from the program. There is no risk from which men are protected and women are not. Likewise, there is no risk from which women are protected and men are not."

In dissent Justice Brennan, joined by Justices Douglas and Marshall, pointed out the similarity of need resulting from pregnancy and from disabilities covered under the plan. He continued: "In my view, by singling out for less favorable treatment a gender-linked disability peculiar to women, the State has created a double standard for disability compensation: a limitation is imposed upon the disabilities for which women workers may recover, while men receive full compensation for all disabilities suffered, including those that affect only or primarily their sex, such as prostatectomies, circumcision, hemophilia and gout. In effect, one set of rules is applied to females and another to males. Such dissimilar treatment of men and women, on the basis of physical characteristics inextricably linked to one sex, inevitably constitutes sex discrimination." Justice Brennan went on to argue that the discriminatory statute must fall, for the state had failed to show a compelling justification.

See also General Electric Co. v. Gilbert, 97 S. Ct. 401 (1976), reaching the same conclusion under Title VII of the Civil Rights Act of 1964, with respect to a private disability plan excluding pregnancy.

Compare Phillips v. Martin Marietta Corp., 400 U.S. 542 (1971) (per curiam), holding it a violation of §703 of the Civil Rights Act of 1964, 42 U.S.C. §2000e, for an employer to refuse to hire women with pre-school-age children while hiring men with such children. The Court remanded, however, stating: "The existence of . . . conflicting family obligations, if demonstrably more relevant to job performance for a woman than for a man, could arguably be a basis for distinction under §703(e) of the Act. But that is a matter of evidence tending to show that the condition in question [in the words of §703(e)] 'is a bona fide occupational qualification reasonably necessary to the normal operation of that particular business or enterprise.' The record before us, however, is not adequate for resolution of these important issues."

See also Equal Employment Opportunity Commission, Guidelines on Discrimination Because of Sex, 29 C.F.R. §§1604.1 to 1604.10 (1973); Developments in the Law — Employment Discrimination and Title VII of the Civil Rights Act of 1964, 84 Harv. L. Rev. 1109, 1166-1195 (1971); Comment, Geduldig v. Aiello: Pregnancy Classifications and the Definition of Sex Discrimination, 75 Colum. L. Rev. 441 (1975); Note, Pregnancy Discharges in the Military: The Air Force Experience, 86 Harv. L. Rev. 568 (1973).

3. Discrimination against men or in favor of women. Certain statutory schemes benefiting women but not men have been upheld against equal protection challenges. In Kahn v. Shevin, 416 U.S. 351 (1974), the Court refused to invalidate a Florida statute granting a $500 property tax exemption to widows but not to widowers. Writing for the Court, Justice Douglas upheld the tax as "reasonably designed to further the state policy of cushioning the financial impact of spousal loss upon the sex for whom that loss imposes a disproportionately heavy burden." He pointed to traditional judicial respect for state tax systems. In dissent Justice White argued that the exemption fell under the Reed standard of equal protection as bearing no substantial relation to the actual financial condition of those benefited, aiding wealthy and poor widows alike but not needy widowers. Justice Brennan, joined by Justice Marshall, also dissented. He stated that "as an affirmative step toward alleviating the effects of past economic discrimination against women," a classification by sex might satisfy the compelling interest test, but that in this case the overinclusiveness of the exemption was fatal. Justice Brennan wrote: "By providing a property tax exemption for widows, [the statute] assists in reducing that economic disparity for a class of women particularly disadvantaged by the legacy of economic discrimination. In that circumstance, the purpose and effect of the suspect classification is ameliorative: the statute neither stigmatizes nor denigrates widowers not also benefited by the legislation." See The Supreme Court, 1973 Term, 88 Harv. L. Rev. 41, 129-139 (1974).

In Schlesinger v. Ballard, 419 U.S. 498 (1975), the Court divided along similar lines with respect to the constitutionality of separate standards for men and women officers in the Navy's mandatory attrition statutes. The appellee, a Navy lieutenant, became subject to mandatory discharge for failure to make the grade of lieutenant commander within 9 years of his commission. Women officers, however, had 13 years to make the same grade. Writing for the Court, Justice Stewart distinguished Frontiero and Reed on the ground that the classification at issue here "reflects, not archaic and overbroad generalizations, but, instead, the demonstrable fact that male and female line officers in the Navy are *not* similarly situated with respect to opportunities for professional service." He pointed to restrictions on women officers' participation in combat or service on naval vessels, which were not also challenged by the plaintiff. "Congress may thus quite rationally have believed that women line officers had less opportunity for promotion than did their male counterparts, and that a longer period of tenure for women officers would, therefore, be consistent with the goal to provide women officers with 'fair and equitable career advancement programs.'"

In dissent Justice Brennan, joined by Justices Douglas and Marshall, took issue with the majority's determination of Congress' purpose in setting different limits for male and female officers. He concluded that the compensatory purpose cited by the majority could in fact "be shown conclusively *not* to have underlain the classification in any way" and that "the Government has advanced no governmental interest fairly to be gleaned from [the statutes] or their legislative history which can justify this gender-based classification." In a footnote, Justice Brennan indicated dissatisfaction with the majority's equal protection analysis, aside from their reading of the legislative history: "I find quite troublesome the notion that a gender-based difference in treatment can be justified by another, broader, gender-based difference in treatment imposed directly and currently by the Navy itself. While it is true that the restrictions upon women officers' opportunities for professional service are not here directly under attack, they are obviously implicated on the Court's chosen ground for decision, and the Court ought at least to consider whether they *may* be valid before sustaining a provision it conceives to be based upon them." Justice White also dissented, noting that he agreed "for the most part" with Justice Brennan's opinion.

However, in Weinberger v. Wiesenfeld, 420 U.S. 636 (1975), the Court held, 8 to 0, that a provision of the Social Security Act, 42 U.S.C. §402(g), granting benefits to widows with minor children but not to widowers violated the equal protection component of the Fifth Amendment. Writing for the Court, Justice Brennan stated that the statute was "indistinguishable from that invalidated in Frontiero": "A virtually identical 'archaic and overbroad' generalization, . . . 'not . . . tolerated under the Constitution' underlies the distinction drawn by §402(g), namely, that male workers' earnings are vital to the support of their families, while the earnings of female wage-earners do not significantly contribute to their families' support." The Court rejected the government's arguments that Kahn and Schlesinger barred a finding of unconstitutionality: "the mere recitation of a benign, compensatory purpose is not an automatic shield which protects against any inquiry into the actual purposes underlying a statutory scheme. Here, it is apparent both from the statutory scheme itself and from the legislative history of §402(g) that Congress' purpose in providing benefits to young widows with children was not to provide an income to women who were, because of economic discrimination, unable to provide for themselves. Rather, §402(g), linked as it is directly to responsibility for minor children, was intended to permit women to elect not to work and to devote themselves to the care of children. Since this purpose in no way is premised upon any special disadvantages of women, it cannot serve to justify a gender-based distinction which diminishes the protection afforded to women who do work."

In Craig v. Boren, 97 S. Ct. 451 (1976), the Court declared unconstitutional an Oklahoma statute permitting the sale of 3.2 percent beer to females but not males between 18 and 21 years of age.

4. Sex equality and other constitutional policies. A collision between equal rights and freedom of the press was thought to be presented in Pittsburgh Press Co. v. Pittsburgh Commission on Human Relations, 413 U.S. 376 (1973). An ordinance prohibiting newspapers from carrying "help-wanted" advertisements in sex-designated columns as an adjunct to provisions forbidding sex discrimination in employment was sustained. Chief Justice Burger and Justices Douglas, Stewart and Blackmun dissented. Justice Stewart declared: "Those who think the First Amendment can and should be subordinated to other socially desirable interests will hail today's decision. But I find it frightening. For I believe the constitutional guaranty of a free press is more than precatory. I believe it is a clear command that the Government must never be allowed to lay its heavy hand on any newspaper in this country."

5. Sex discrimination and due process. In several cases the Court has held that statutes discriminating by sex violate due process rights. In Stanley v. Illinois, 405 U.S. 645 (1971), an unmarried father challenged a state statute under which he was automatically deprived of custody of his children on the death of their mother. Under Illinois law, the state did not assume custody of the children of married or divorced parents or unwed mothers until after a hearing on parental fitness. The Court held first that the unmarried

father was entitled to such a hearing as a matter of procedural due process and second that the state's failure to extend the hearing rule to him was a denial of equal protection.

In Cleveland Board of Education v. LaFleur, 414 U.S. 632 (1974), the Court struck down school board regulations requiring pregnant teachers to take unpaid leaves of absence for a set period beginning four or five months before birth was due. Writing for the Court, Justice Stewart bypassed the equal protection arguments on which lower courts had invalidated the regulations and placed his decision on due process grounds. Noting that the due process clause protects "freedom of personal choice in matters of marriage and family life," including the decision whether to have children, the Court held that the school boards had failed to justify their automatic regulations. The rules bore only a passing relationship to a pregnant teacher's continuing ability to teach as the time of delivery neared, and an "individualized determination" in each case should be required. And administrative convenience did not, given the importance of the teacher's interest in working and the wide range of individual situations, justify use of an "irrebuttable presumption" of inability to teach after a certain stage of pregnancy. Justice Powell, concurring in the result, would have placed the holding on equal protection grounds. Justice Rehnquist dissented, joined by Chief Justice Burger.

6. In Taylor v. Louisiana, 419 U.S. 522 (1975), the Court overturned appellant's conviction on the ground that his right to trial by a jury selected from a representative cross-section of his community, guaranteed by the Sixth and Fourteenth Amendments, was denied by jury selection procedures which limited the number of prospective women jurors. Under Louisiana law, a woman would not be subject to call for jury duty unless she had first filed a written statement with the local court clerk stating her willingness to serve. The result was a "grossly disproportionate" representation of women on local juries. The Court rejected the state's contention that its exemption of all women but volunteers was justified by the need to protect "the state's own idea of family life." Compare Hoyt v. Florida, 368 U.S. 57 (1961), upholding similar selection procedures against challenge under the due process and equal protection clauses of the Fourteenth Amendment.

In Stanton v. Stanton, 421 U.S. 7 (1975), the Court struck down as violative of equal protection a Utah statute setting the age of majority, for purposes of determining the support obligation of a divorced father, at 21 for males and 18 for females. The Court held, in an opinion by Justice Blackmun, that it was unnecessary to rule on whether the statute was subject to strict scrutiny, as it was plainly unconstitutional under Reed. Justice Rehnquist dissented.

NOTE Discrimination by Age and by Social Grouping

The Age Discrimination in Employment Act of 1967, Pub. L. No. 90-202, 81 Stat. 603, 29 U.S.C. §§621 et seq. (1975), prohibits private employers, employment agencies, and labor organizations from discriminating solely on the basis of age between employees or job applicants who are between the ages of 40 and 65 with regard to compensation, conditions, or other terms of employment. As amended in 1974, Pub. L. No. 93-259, 88 Stat. 74, the act now extends its coverage to employees of the federal, state, and local governments. Is there any question about the power of Congress to regulate this type of discrimination under §5 of the Fourteenth Amendment? See Katzenbach v. Morgan, page 902 supra, but see also Oregon v. Mitchell, page 987 infra.

Age discrimination is allowed, however, where "age is a bona fide occupational qualification reasonably necessary to the normal operations of a particular business." 29 U.S.C. §623(f)(1). Should this standard be considered the codification of equal protection review? In Murgia v. Commonwealth, 376 F. Supp. 753 (D. Mass. 1974), a three-judge district court ruled unconstitutional a state's mandatory retirement age of 50 for state police officers. It declined to use strict scrutiny because it found that the state failed to show even a rational basis for the mandatory age, particularly since the state already used annual physical examinations to evaluate the fitness of the officers. The Supreme Court reversed sub nom. Massachusetts Bd. of Retirement v. Murgia, 427 U.S. 307 (1976).

Should age of entry be scrutinized differently? See United States v. Duncan, 456 F.2d 1401 (9th Cir. 1972) (age requirement of 21 for jury selection not arbitrary), and Manson v. Edwards, 482 F.2d 1076 (6th Cir. 1973) (age requirement of 25 for elective office to be tested by rational basis).

Discrimination against households of unrelated individuals. In United States Department of Agriculture v. Moreno, 413 U.S. 528 (1973), the Court invalidated a provision of the Food Stamp Act of 1964 which excluded from participation in that program any household containing an individual who is unrelated to any other member of the household. Writing for the Court, Justice Brennan found that the exclusion was not rationally related either to the stated purposes of the act — providing for nutritional needs and stimulating agricultural economy — or to the government objective of guarding against fraudulent claims for benefits. The purpose, demonstrated in the legislative history of the exclusion, of discriminating against "so-called 'hippies' " was held to be an impermissible objective. The exclusion was thus held to be an irrational classification violative of equal protection. Justice Douglas, concurring, argued that the exclusion violated the First Amendment guarantee of freedom of association. Chief Justice Burger and Justice Rehnquist dissented.

Moreno was distinguished in Village of Belle Terre v. Boraas, 416 U.S. 1 (1974). There the Court upheld against an equal protection attack a zoning ordinance restricting use of the Village's land to one-family dwellings and defining family to mean any number of related persons but no more than two unrelated persons. Writing for the Court, Justice Douglas cited prior decisions deferring to the judgment of local authorities on land use legislation and classified the ordinance with "economic and social legislation where legislatures have historically drawn lines which we respect against the charge of violation of the Equal Protection Clause if the law be 'reasonable, not arbitrary' (quoting F. S. Royster Guano Co. v. Virginia, 253 U.S. 412, 415) and bears 'a rational relationship to a [permissible] state objective.' Reed v. Reed, 404 U.S. 71."

Justice Douglas rejected respondents' arguments that the ordinance infringed on specially protected fundamental interests, such as the rights of association or travel, and held it rationally related to permissible land use planning objectives, such as minimizing traffic, noise and crowding. In dissent Justice Marshall argued that the ordinance violated equal protection as it burdened First Amendment rights of privacy and association without a compelling justification for so doing. See The Supreme Court, 1973 Term, 88 Harv. L. Rev. 41, 119-129 (1974); Comment, All in the "Family": Legal Problems of Communes, 7 Harv. Civ. Rights-Civ. Lib. L. Rev. 393 (1972).

5. Alternative Approaches: "Irrebuttable Presumptions"

United States Dept. of Agriculture v. Murry *413 U.S. 508,*
93 S. Ct. 2832, 37 L. Ed. 2d 767 (1973)

MR. JUSTICE DOUGLAS delivered the opinion of the Court.

The Food Stamp Act of 1964, 7 U.S.C. §2011 et seq., as amended in 1971, has been applied to these appellees so as to lead the three-judge District Court to hold one provision of it unconstitutional. 348 F. Supp. 242. We noted probable jurisdiction.

[The provision states that any household which includes a member who has reached his eighteenth birthday and who is claimed as a dependent child for federal income tax purposes by a taxpayer who is not a member of an eligible household, shall be ineligible to participate in any food stamp program during the tax period such dependency is claimed and for a period of one year thereafter. The cases before the Court involved families where an estranged husband claimed a child of 18 or over as a dependent.]

. . . We have difficulty in concluding that it is rational to assume that a child is not indigent this year because the parent declared the child as a dependent in his tax return for the prior year. But even on that assumption our problem is not at an end. Under the Act the issue is not the indigency of the child but the indigency of a different household with which the child happens to be living. Members of that different household are denied food stamps if one of its present members was used as a tax deduction in the past year by his parents even though the remaining members have no relation to the parent who used the tax deduction, even though they are completely destitute, and even though they are one, or 10 or 20 in number. We conclude that the deduction taken for the benefit of the parent in the prior year is not a rational measure of the need of a different household with which the child of the tax-deducting parent lives and rests on an irrebuttable presumption often contrary to fact. It therefore lacks critical ingredients of due process found wanting in Vlandis v. Kline, 412 U.S. 441; Stanley v. Illinois, [405 U.S. 645]; and Bell v. Burson, 402 U.S. 535.

Affirmed.

MR. JUSTICE STEWART, concurring. . . .

Rather than requiring an individualized determination that a particular household linked to a relatively more affluent household by a claimed tax dependency was not in fact needy, Congress chose instead to utilize a conclusive presumption. The simple fact that a *household member* has been claimed as a tax dependent by a non-indigent taxpayer results in the complete termination of benefits for that *entire household* in relevant tax period and in the subsequent 12 months as well. 7 U.S.C. §2014(b). It matters not whether that dependency claim was fraudulent, what the amount of support from the non-indigent taxpayer actually was, whether that support was still available at the time the welfare officials learned of it, or even whether the claimed dependent was still living in the household. . . .

Similarly, I think, the conclusive presumption that led to the termination of the appellees' benefits without any opportunity for them to prove present need denied them due process of law. Accordingly, I concur in the opinion and judgment of the Court.

MR. JUSTICE MARSHALL, concurring.

I join the opinion of the Court. I wish to state briefly what I believe are the analytic underpinnings of that opinion. One aspect of fundamental fairness, guaranteed by the Due Process Clause of the Fifth Amendment, is that individuals similarly situated must receive the same treatment by the Government. As Mr. Justice Jackson put it, the Government "must exercise [its] powers so as not to discriminate between [its] inhabitants except upon some reasonable differentiation fairly related to the object of the regulation." Railway Express Agency v. New York, 336 U.S. 106, 112 (1949) (concurring opinion). It is a corollary of this requirement that, in order to determine whether persons are indeed similarly situated, "such procedural protections as the particular situation demands" must be provided. Morrissey v. Brewer, 408 U.S. 471, 481 (1972). Specifically, we must decide whether, considering the private interest affected and the governmental interest sought to be advanced, a hearing must be provided to one who claims that the application of some general provision of the law aimed at certain abuses will not in fact lower the incidence of those abuses but will instead needlessly harm him. Cf. Reed v. Reed, 404 U.S. 71 (1971); Vlandis v. Kline, 412 U.S. 441 (1973). In short, where the private interests affected are very important and the governmental interest can be promoted without much difficulty by a well-designed hearing procedure, the Due Process Clause requires the Government to act on an individualized basis, with general propositions serving only as rebuttable presumptions or other burden-shifting devices. That, I think, is the import of Stanley v. Illinois, 405 U.S. 645 (1972). . . .

It is, of course, quite simple for Congress to provide an administrative mechanism to guarantee that abusers of the program were eliminated from it. All that is needed is some way for a person whose household would otherwise be ineligible for food stamps because of this statute to show that the support presently available from the person claiming a member of the household as a tax dependent does not in fact offset the loss of benefits. Reasonable rules stating what a claimant must show before receiving a hearing on the question could easily be devised. We deal here with a general rule that may seriously affect the ability of persons genuinely in need to provide an adequate diet for their households. In the face of readily available alternatives that might prevent abuse of the program, Congress did not choose a method of reducing abuses that was "fairly related to the object of the regulation," by enacting the statute challenged in this case.

This analysis, of course, combines elements traditionally invoked in what are usually treated as distinct classes of cases, involving due process and equal protection. But the elements of fairness should not be so rigidly cabined. Sometimes fairness will require a hearing to determine whether a statutory classification will advance the legislature's purposes in a particular case so that the classification can properly be used only as a burden-shifting device, while at other times the fact that a litigant falls within the classification will be enough to justify its application. There is no reason, I believe, to categorize inflexibly the rudiments of fairness. Instead, I believe that we must assess the public and private interests affected by a statutory classification and then decide in each instance whether individualized determination is required or categorical treatment is permitted by the Constitution.

Mr. Justice Rehnquist, with whom The Chief Justice and Mr. Justice Powell concur, dissenting.

. . . [I]n order to disqualify a household for food stamps, the taxpayer claiming one of its members as a dependent must both provide over half of the dependent's support and must himself be a member of a household with an income large enough to disqualify that household for food stamps. These characteristics indicate that the taxpayer is both willing and able to provide his dependent with a significant amount of support. To be sure, there may be no perfect correlation between the fact that the taxpayer is part of a household which has income exceeding food stamp eligibility standards and his provision of enough support to raise his dependent's household above such standards. But there is some correlation, and the provision is, therefore, not irrational. Dandridge v. Williams, supra.

Nor is § 5(b) deprived of a rational basis because disqualification of the household extends one year beyond the year in which the dependency deduction is claimed. Since income tax returns are not filed until after the termination of the tax year, the carryover provision is the only practical means of enforcing the congressional purpose unless Congress were to establish an administrative adjudication procedure wholly independent of the existing tax collection structure. Such an alternative system would doubtless have its own delays, inefficiencies, and inequities. Under these circumstances we cannot say that Congress acted irrationally in judging a person's need in one year by whether he was claimed as a tax dependent in the previous year. . . .[z]

NOTE Questioning the "Irrebuttable Presumption" Doctrine

Compare United States Department of Agriculture v. Moreno, 413 U.S. 528 (1973). In Moreno, decided the same day as Murry, the Court invalidated § 3(e) of the Food Stamp Act, under which households of unrelated persons were made ineligible for benefits under the act. The Court stated the traditional test of permissive equal protection analysis, that "a legislative classification must be sustained, if the classification itself is rationally related to a legitimate government interest," and went on to hold § 3(e) "wholly

---

[z] A dissenting opinion by Justice Blackmun is omitted. — Ed.

without any rational basis." Would the analysis applied in Moreno apply equally well to Murry? See Note, The Irrebuttable Presumption Doctrine in the Supreme Court, 87 Harv. L. Rev. 1534 (1974).

See also Justice Powell's comments on the irrebuttable presumption doctrine in his concurring opinion to Cleveland Board of Education v. LaFleur, 414 U.S. 632 (1974), noted page 938 supra: "I concur in the Court's result, but I am unable to join its opinion. In my view these cases should not be decided on the ground that the mandatory maternity leave regulations impair any right to bear children or create an 'irrebuttable presumption.' It seems to me that equal protection analysis is the appropriate frame of reference. . . .

"I am . . . troubled by the Court's return to the 'irrebuttable presumption' line of analysis of Stanley v. Illinois, 405 U.S. 645 (1972) (Powell, J., not participating), and Vlandis v. Kline, 412 U.S. 441 (1973). Although I joined the opinion of the Court in Vlandis and continue fully to support the result reached there, the present cases have caused me to reexamine the 'irrebuttable presumption' rationale. This has led me to the conclusion that the Court should approach that doctrine with extreme care. There is much to what Mr. Justice Rehnquist says in his dissenting opinion . . . about the implications of the doctrine for the traditional legislative power to operate by classification. As a matter of logic, it is difficult to see the terminus of the road upon which the Court has embarked under the banner of 'irrebuttable presumptions.' If the Court nevertheless uses 'irrebuttable presumption' reasoning selectively, the concept at root often will be something else masquerading as a due process doctrine. That something else, of course, is the Equal Protection Clause.

"These cases present precisely the kind of problem susceptible to treatment by classification. Most school teachers are women, a certain percentage of them are pregnant at any given time, and pregnancy is a normal biological function possessing, in the great majority of cases, a fairly well defined term. The constitutional difficulty is not that the boards attempted to deal with this problem by classification. Rather, it is that the boards chose irrational classifications. . . .

". . . I believe the linkage between the boards' legitimate ends and their chosen means is too attenuated to support those portions of the regulations overturned by the Court. . . .

". . . School boards, confronted with sensitive and widely variable problems of public education, must be accorded latitude in the operation of school systems and in the adoption of rules and regulations of general application, E.g., San Antonio Independent School District v. Rodriguez, 411 U.S. 1, 42-43 (1973). A large measure of discretion is essential to the effective discharge of the duties vested in these local, often elective, governmental units. My concern with the Court's opinion is that, if carried to logical extremes, the emphasis on individualized treatment is at war with this need for discretion. Indeed, stringent insistence on individualized treatment may be quite impractical in a large school district with thousands of teachers. . . ."

See also Note, Irrebuttable Presumptions: An Illusory Analysis, 27 Stan. L. Rev. 449 (1975). A sympathetic treatment is Tribe, Structural Due Process, 10 Harv. Civ. Rights-Civ. Lib. L. Rev. 269 (1975). If the doctrine serves any useful function, how should it be applied?

WEINBERGER v. SALFI, 422 U.S. 749, 95 S. Ct. 2457, 45 L. Ed. 2d 522 (1975). Rehnquist, J.: "Appellee Salfi married the deceased wage earner, Londo L. Salfi, on May 27, 1972. Despite his alleged apparent good health at the time of the marriage, he suffered a heart attack less than a month later, and died on November 21, 1972, less than six months after the marriage. Appellee filed applications for mother's insurance benefits for herself and child's insurance benefits for her daughter by a previous marriage, Doreen Kalnins. These applications were denied by the Social Security Administration, both initially and on reconsideration at the regional level, solely on the basis of the duration-of-relationship requirements of [42 U.S.C.] §416(c)(5) and (e)(2), which define "widow" and "child." The definitions exclude surviving wives and stepchildren who had their respective relationships to a deceased wage earner for less than nine months prior to his death. . . .

"The District Court relied on congressional history for the proposition that the duration-of-relationship requirement was intended to prevent the use of sham marriages to secure Social Security payments. As such, concluded the court, "the requirement constitutes a presumption that marriages like Mrs. Salfi's, which did not precede the wage earner's death by at least nine months, were entered into for the purpose of securing Social Security benefits." 373 F. Supp., at 965. The presumption was moreover, conclusive, because applicants were not afforded an opportunity to disprove the presence of the illicit purpose. The court held that . . . the requirement was unconstitutional, because it presumed a fact which was not necessarily or universally true."

What decision? Why?

Section H. THE SUFFRAGE

Ex parte Yarbrough 110 U.S. 651, 4 S. Ct. 152, 28 L. Ed. 274 (1884)

[Petitioners in the circuit court had been denied habeas corpus following their conviction under §5508 of the Revised Statutes, supra page 760, and under §5520, a section making it a crime for two or more persons to conspire "to prevent by force, intimidation, or threat, any citizen who is lawfully entitled to vote, from giving his support or advocacy, in a legal manner, toward or in favor of the election of any qualified person as an elector for President or Vice President, or as a member of the Congress of the United States; or to injure any citizen in person or property on account of such support or advocacy." After making it clear that the writ of habeas corpus could not issue for mere error but only if the court which had tried the offense had no jurisdiction, denial of the petition was affirmed in the Supreme Court.]

MR. JUSTICE MILLER delivered the opinion of the court. . . .

Stripped of its technical verbiage, the offence charged in this indictment is that the defendants conspired to intimidate Barry Saunders, a citizen of African descent, in the exercise of his right to vote for a member of the Congress of the United States, and in the execution of that conspiracy they beat, bruised, wounded and otherwise maltreated him; and in the second count that they did this on account of his race, color, and previous condition of servitude, by going in disguise and assaulting him on the public highway and on his own premises. . . .

That a government whose essential character is republican, whose executive head and legislative body are both elective, whose most numerous and powerful branch of the legislature is elected by the people directly, has no power by appropriate laws to secure this election from the influence of violence, or corruption and of fraud, is a proposition so startling as to arrest attention and demand the gravest consideration. . . .

The proposition that it has no such power is supported by the old argument often heard, often repeated, and in this court never assented to, that when a question of the power of Congress arises the advocate of the power must be able to place his finger on words which expressly grant it. [The Court here reviewed Congressional statutes of varying sorts in which federal officers and federal property were secured against injury.]

So, also, has the Congress been slow to exercise the powers expressly conferred upon it in relation to elections by the fourth section of the first article of the Constitution.

This section declares that:

"The times, places, and manner of holding elections for senators and representatives shall be prescribed in each State by the Legislature thereof; but the Congress may at any time make or alter such regulations, except as to the place of choosing senators."

It was not until 1842 that Congress took any action under the power here conferred, when, conceiving that the system of electing all the members of the House of Representatives from a State by general ticket, as it was called, that is, every elector voting for as many names as the State was entitled to representatives in that house, worked injustice to other States which did not adopt that system, and gave an undue preponderance of power to the political party which had a majority of votes in the State, however small, enacted that each member should be elected by a separate district, composed of contiguous territory. 5 Stat. 491. [Mr. Justice Miller then summarized other Congressional statutes with respect to federal elections.]

It is said that the parties assaulted in these cases are not officers of the United States, and their protection in exercising the right to vote by Congress does not stand on the same ground.

But the distinction is not well taken. The power in either case arises out of the circumstance that the function in which the party is engaged or the right which he is about to exercise is dependent on the laws of the United States.

In both cases it is the duty of that government to see that he may exercise this right freely, and to protect him from violence, while so doing, or on account of so doing. This duty does not arise solely from the interest of the party concerned, but from the necessity of the government itself, that its service shall be free from the adverse influence of force and fraud practised on its agents, and that the votes by which its members of Congress and its President are elected shall be the *free* votes of the electors, and the officers thus chosen the free and uncorrupted choice of those who have the right to take part in that choice.

This proposition answers also another objection to the constitutionality of the laws under consideration, namely, that the right to vote for a member of Congress is not dependent upon the Constitution or laws of the United States, but is governed by the law of each State respectively. . . .

But it is not correct to say that the right to vote for a member of Congress does not depend on the Constitution of the United States.

That office, if it be properly called an office, is created by that Constitution and by that alone. It also declares how it shall be filled, namely, by election.

Its language is: "The House of Representatives shall be composed of members chosen every second year by the people of the several States, and the electors in each State shall have the qualifications requisite for electors of the most numerous branch of the State legislature." Article I., section 2.

The States in prescribing the qualifications for voters for the most numerous branch of their own legislatures, do not do this with reference to the election of members of Congress. Nor can they prescribe the qualification for voters for those eo nomine. They define who are to vote for the popular branch of their own legislature, and the Constitution of the United States says the same persons shall vote for members of Congress in that State. It adopts the qualification thus furnished as the qualification of its own electors for members of Congress.

It is not true, therefore, that electors for members of Congress owe their right to vote to the State law in any sense which makes the exercise of the right to depend exclusively on the law of the State.

Counsel for petitioners, seizing upon the expression found in the opinion of the court in the case of Minor v. Happersett, 21 Wall. 162, that "the Constitution of the United States does not confer the right of suffrage upon any one," without reference to the connection in which it is used, insists that the voters in this case do not owe their right to vote in any sense to that instrument.

But the court was combating the argument that this right was conferred on all citizens, and therefore upon women as well as men.

In opposition to that idea, it was said that the Constitution adopts as the qualification for voters of members of Congress that which prevails in the State where the voting is to be done; therefore, said the opinion, the right is not definitely conferred on any person or class of persons by the Constitution alone, because you have to look to the law of the State for the description of the class. But the court did not intend to say that when the class or the person is thus ascertained, his right to vote for a member of Congress was not fundamentally based upon the Constitution, which created the office of member of Congress, and declared it should be elective, and pointed to the means of ascertaining who should be electors. . . .

The rule is discharged, and the writ of habeas corpus is denied.[aa]

United States v. Classic 313 U.S. 299, 61 S. Ct. 1031, 85 L. Ed. 1368 (1941)

MR. JUSTICE STONE delivered the opinion of the Court:

Two counts of an indictment found in a federal district court charged that appellees, Commissioners of Elections, conducting a primary election under Louisiana law, to nominate a candidate of the Democratic Party for representative in Congress, willfully altered and falsely counted and certified the ballots of voters cast in the primary election. The questions for decision are whether the right of qualified voters to vote in the Louisiana primary and to have their ballots counted is a right "secured by the Constitution" within the meaning of §§ 19 and 20 of the Criminal Code, and whether the acts of appellees charged in the indictment violate those sections.

On September 25, 1940, appellees were indicted in the District Court for Eastern Louisiana for violations of §§ 19 and 20 of the Criminal Code, 18 U.S.C. §§ 51, 52. The first count of the indictment alleged that a primary election was held on September 10, 1940, for the purpose of nominating a candidate of the Democratic Party for the office of Representative in Congress for the Second Congressional District of Louisiana, to be chosen at an election to be held on November 10th; that in that district nomination as a candidate of the Democratic Party is and always has been equivalent to an election; that appellees were Commissioners of Election, selected in accordance with the Louisiana law to conduct the primary in the Second Precinct of the Tenth Ward of New Orleans, in which there were five hundred and thirty-seven citizens and qualified voters.

The charge, based on these allegations, was that the appellees conspired with each other and with others unknown, to injure and oppress citizens in the free exercise and enjoyment of rights and privileges secured to them by the Constitution and Laws of the United States, namely, (1) the right of qualified voters who cast their ballots in the primary election to have their ballots counted as cast for the candidate of their choice, and (2) the right of the candidates to run for the office of Congressman and to have the votes in favor of their nomination counted as cast. The overt acts alleged were that the appellees altered eighty-three ballots cast for one candidate and fourteen cast for another, marking and counting them as votes for a third candidate, and that they falsely certified the number of votes cast for the respective candidates to the chairman of the Second Congressional District Committee.

The second count, repeating the allegations of fact already detailed, charged that the appellees, as Commissioners of Election willfully and under color of law subjected registered voters at the primary who were inhabitants of Louisiana to the deprivation of rights,

---

[aa] In Burroughs and Cannon v. United States, 290 U.S. 534 (1934), it was held that the Federal Corrupt Practices Act was applicable to conduct designed to influence the election of presidential and vice-presidential electors, despite the constitutional grant of power to the states to regulate the manner of choosing such electors. — ED.

privileges and immunities secured and protected by the Constitution and Laws of the United States, namely their right to cast their votes for the candidates of their choice and to have their votes counted as cast. It further charged that this deprivation was effected by the willful failure and refusal of defendants to count the votes as cast, by their alteration of the ballots, and by their false certification of the number of votes cast for the respective candidates in the manner already indicated.

The District Court sustained a demurrer to counts 1 and 2 on the ground that §§ 19 and 20 of the Criminal Code under which the indictment was drawn do not apply to the state of facts disclosed by the indictment and that, if applied to those facts, §§ 19 and 20 are without constitutional sanction, citing United States v. Gradwell, 243 U.S. 476, 488, 489; Newberry v. United States, 256 U.S. 232. The case comes here on direct appeal from the District Court under the provisions of the Criminal Appeals Act, Judicial Code, § 238, 18 U.S.C. § 682; 28 U.S.C. § 345, which authorize an appeal by the United States from a decision or judgment sustaining a demurrer to an indictment where the decision or judgment is "based upon the invalidity or construction of the statute upon which the indictment is founded." . . .

Section 19 of the Criminal Code condemns as a criminal offense any conspiracy to injure a citizen in the exercise "of any right or privilege secured to him by the Constitution or laws of the United States." Section 20 makes it a penal offense for anyone who, "acting under color of any law" "willfully subjects, or causes to be subjected, any inhabitant of any State . . . to the deprivation of any rights, privileges and immunities secured and protected by the Constitution and laws of the United States." The Government argues that the right of a qualified voter in a Louisiana congressional primary election to have his vote counted as cast is a right secured by Article 1, §§ 2 and 4 of the Constitution, and that a conspiracy to deprive the citizen of that right is a violation of § 19, and also that the willful action of appellees as state officials, in falsely counting the ballots at the primary election and in falsely certifying the count, deprived qualified voters of that right and of the equal protection of the laws guaranteed by the Fourteenth Amendment, all in violation of § 20 of the Criminal Code. . . .

The right to vote for a representative in Congress at the general election is, as a matter of law, . . . restricted to the successful party candidate at the primary, to those not candidates at the primary who file nomination papers, and those whose names may be lawfully written into the ballot by the electors. Even if, as appellees argue, contrary to the decision in Serpas v. Trebucq, supra, voters may lawfully write into their ballots, cast at the general election, the name of a candidate rejected at the primary and have their ballots counted, the practical operation of the primary law in otherwise excluding from the ballot on the general election the names of candidates rejected at the primary is such as to impose serious restrictions upon the choice of candidates by the voters save by voting at the primary election. In fact, as alleged in the indictment, the practical operation of the primary in Louisiana, is and has been since the primary election was established in 1900 to secure the election of the Democratic primary nominee for the Second Congressional District of Louisiana.[2]

Interference with the right to vote in the congressional primary in the Second Congressional District for the choice of Democratic candidate for Congress is thus as a matter of law and in fact an interference with the effective choice of the voters at the only stage of the election procedure when their choice is of significance, since it is at the only stage when such interference could have any practical effect on the ultimate result, the choice of the Congressman to represent the district. The primary in Louisiana is an integral part

---

[2] For a discussion of the practical effect of the primary in controlling or restricting election of candidates at general elections, see Hasbrouck, Party Government in the House of Representatives 1927, 172, 176, 177; Merriam and Overpacker, Primary Elections 1928, 267-269; Stoney, Suffrage in the South; 29 Survey Graphic, 163, 164.

of the procedure for the popular choice of Congressmen. The right of qualified voters to vote at the congressional primary in Louisiana and to have their ballots counted is thus the right to participate in that choice.

We come then to the question whether that right is one secured by the Constitution. Section 2 of Article 1 commands that Congressmen shall be chosen by the people of the several states by electors, the qualifications of which it prescribes. The right of the people to choose, whatever its appropriate constitutional limitations, where in other respects it is defined, and the mode of its exercise is prescribed by state action in conformity to the Constitution, is a right established and guaranteed by the Constitution and hence is one secured by it to those citizens and inhabitants of the state entitled to exercise the right. Ex parte Yarbrough, 110 U.S. 651; United States v. Mosley, 238 U.S. 383. . . . While, in a loose sense, the right to vote for representatives in Congress is sometimes spoken of as a right derived from the states, see Minor v. Happersett, 21 Wall. 162, 170; United States v. Reese, 92 U.S. 214, 217, 218; McPherson v. Blacker, 146 U.S. 1, 38, 39; Breedlove v. Suttles, 302 U.S. 277, 283; this statement is true only in the sense that the states are authorized by the Constitution, to legislate on the subject as provided by §2 of Art. 1, to the extent that Congress has not restricted state action by the exercise of its powers to regulate elections under §4 and its more general power under Article 1, §8, clause 18 of the Constitution "to make all laws which shall be necessary and proper for carrying into execution the foregoing powers." See Ex parte Siebold, 100 U.S. 371. . . .

Obviously included within the right to choose, secured by the Constitution, is the right of qualified voters within a state to cast their ballots and have them counted at congressional elections. And since the constitutional command is without restriction or limitation, the right, unlike those guaranteed by the Fourteenth and Fifteenth Amendments, is secured against the action of individuals as well as of states. Ex parte Yarbrough, 110 U.S. 651, and Logan v. United States [144 U.S. 263]. . . .

. . . Where the state law has made the primary an integral part of the procedure of choice, or where in fact the primary effectively controls the choice, the right of the elector to have his ballot counted at the primary, is likewise included in the right protected by Article 1, §2. And this right of participation is protected just as is the right to vote at the election, where the primary is by law made an integral part of the election machinery, whether the voter exercises his right in a party primary which invariably, sometimes or never determines the ultimate choice of the representative. Here, even apart from the circumstance that the Louisiana primary is made by law an integral part of the procedure of choice, the right to choose a representative is in fact controlled by the primary because, as is alleged in the indictment, the choice of candidates at the Democratic primary determines the choice of the elected representative. . . .

The suggestion that §19, concededly applicable to conspiracies to deprive electors of their votes at congressional elections, is not sufficiently specific to be deemed applicable to primary elections, will hardly bear examination. Section 19 speaks neither of elections nor of primaries. In unambiguous language it protects "any right or privilege secured by the Constitution," a phrase which as we have seen extends to the right of the voter to have his vote counted in both the general election and in the primary election, where the latter is a part of the election machinery, as well as to numerous other constitutional rights which are wholly unrelated to the choice of a representative in Congress. . . .

The right of the voters at the primary to have their votes counted is, as we have stated, a right or privilege secured by the Constitution, and to this §20 also gives protection. The alleged acts of appellees were committed in the course of their performance of duties under the Louisiana statute requiring them to count the ballots, to record the result of the count, and to certify the result of the election. Misuse of power, possessed by virtue of state law and made possible only because the wrongdoer is clothed with the authority of state law, is action taken "under color of" state law. Ex parte Virginia, 100 U.S. 339, 346; Home Teleph. & Teleg. Co. v. Los Angeles, 227 U.S. 278, 287, et seq.; Hague v. Committee for Industrial Organization, 307 U.S. 496, 507, 519; cf. (C.C.A. 3d) 101 F.2d 774, 790. Here the acts of appellees infringed the constitutional right and deprived the voters of the benefit of it within the meaning of §20, unless by its terms its application is restricted to deprivations "on account of such inhabitant being an alien or by reason of his color or race."...

We do not discuss the application of §20 to deprivations of the right to equal protection of the laws guaranteed by the Fourteenth Amendment, a point apparently raised and discussed for the first time in the Government's brief in this Court. The point was not specially considered or decided by the court below, and has not been assigned as error by the Government. Since the indictment on its face does not purport to charge a deprivation of equal protection to voters or candidates, we are not called upon to construe the indictment in order to raise a question of statutory validity or construction which we are alone authorized to review upon this appeal.

Reversed.

THE CHIEF JUSTICE took no part in the consideration or decision of this case.[bb]

UNITED STATES v. SAYLOR, 322 U.S. 385, 64 S. Ct. 1101, 88 L. Ed. 1341 (1944). Roberts, J.: "The District Court sustained demurrers to indictments for conspiracies forbidden by Sec. 19 of the Criminal Code.... The indictment charged that a general election was held November 3, 1942, in Harlan County, Kentucky, for the purpose of electing a Senator of the United States, at which election the defendants served as the duly qualified officers of election; that they conspired to injure and oppress divers citizens of the United States who were legally entitled to vote at the polling places where the defendants officiated, in the free exercise and enjoyment of the rights and privileges guaranteed to the citizens by the Constitution and laws of the United States, namely, the right and privilege to express by their votes their choice of a candidate for Senator and their right to have their expressions of choice given full value and effect by not having their votes impaired, lessened, diminished, diluted and destroyed by fictitious ballots fraudulently cast and counted, recorded, returned, and certified. The indictment charged that the defendants pursuant to their plan, tore from the official ballot book and stub book furnished them, blank unvoted ballots and marked, forged, and voted the same for the candidate of a given party, opposing the candidate for whom the injured voters had voted, in order to deprive the latter of their rights to have their votes cast, counted, certified and recorded and given full value and effect; that the defendants inserted the false ballots they had so prepared into the ballot box, and returned them, together with the other ballots lawfully cast, so as to create a false and fictitious return respecting the votes lawfully cast.

"... The District Court decided only that the indictment charged no offense against the laws of the United States. This ruling presents the question for decision."

What decision? Why?

Smith v. Allwright 321 U.S. 649, 64 S. Ct. 757, 88 L. Ed. 987 (1944)

MR. JUSTICE REED delivered the opinion of the Court:

This writ of certiorari brings here for review a claim for damages in the sum of $5,000 on the part of petitioner, a Negro citizen of the 48th precinct of Harris County, Texas, for the refusal of respondents, election and associate election judges respectively of that precinct, to give petitioner a ballot or to permit him to cast a ballot in the primary election

---

[bb] The dissenting opinion of Douglas, J., in which Black and Murphy, JJ., concurred, is omitted. It was based on the conviction that the Congress had not intended to reach primary elections in its civil rights legislation. — ED.

of July 27, 1940, for the nomination of Democratic candidates for the United States Senate and House of Representatives, and Governor and other state officers. The refusal is alleged to have been solely because of the race and color of the proposed voter.

The actions of respondents are said to violate §§31 and 43 of title 8[1] of the United States Code in that petitioner was deprived of rights secured by §§2 and 4 of Article I and the Fourteenth, Fifteenth and Seventeenth Amendments to the United States Constitution. The suit was filed in the District Court of the United States for the Southern District of Texas, which had jurisdiction under Judicial Code §24, subsection 14, 28 U.S.C. §41(14).

The District Court denied the relief sought and the Circuit Court of Appeals quite properly affirmed its action on the authority of Grovey v. Townsend, 295 U.S. 45.[5] We granted the petition for certiorari to resolve a claimed inconsistency between the decision in the Grovey Case and that of United States v. Classic, 313 U.S. 299, 319 U.S. 738.

The State of Texas by its Constitution and statutes provides that every person, if certain other requirements are met which are not here in issue, qualified by residence in the district or county "shall be deemed a qualified elector." Constitution of Texas, Article 6, §2; Vernon's Civil Statutes (1939 ed.) Article 2955. Primary elections for United States Senators, Congressmen and state officers are provided for by Chapters Twelve and Thirteen of the statutes. Under these chapters, the Democratic Party was required to hold the primary which was the occasion of the alleged wrong to petitioner. . . . These nominations are to be made by the qualified voters of the party. Art. 3101.

The Democratic Party of Texas is held by the Supreme Court of that state to be a "voluntary association," Bell v. Hill, 123 Tex. 531, 534, protected by §27 of the Bill of Rights, Art. 1, Constitution of Texas, from interference by the state except that:

"In the interest of fair methods and a fair expression by their members of their preferences in the selection of their nominees, the State may regulate such elections by proper laws." P. 545.

That court stated further:

"Since the right to organize and maintain a political party is one guaranteed by the Bill of Rights of this State, it necessarily follows that every privilege essential or reasonably appropriate to the exercise of that right is likewise guaranteed, — including, of course, the privilege of determining the policies of the party and its membership. Without the privilege of determining the policy of a political association and its membership, the right to organize such an association would be a mere mockery. We think these rights, — that is, the right to determine the membership of a political party and to determine its policies, of necessity are to be exercised by the State Convention of such party, and cannot, under any circumstances, be conferred upon a State or governmental agency." P. 546. Cf. Waples v. Marrast, 108 Tex. 5.

The Democratic party on May 24, 1932, in a State Convention adopted the following resolution, which has not since been "amended, abrogated, annulled or avoided":

"Be it resolved that all white citizens of the State of Texas who are qualified to vote under the Constitution and laws of the State shall be eligible to membership in the Democratic party and, as such, entitled to participate in its deliberations."

[1] 8 U.S.C. §31:
"All citizens of the United States who are otherwise qualified by law to vote at any election by the people in any State, Territory, district, county, city, parish, township, school district, municipality, or other territorial subdivision, shall be entitled and allowed to vote at all such elections, without distinction of race, color, or previous condition of servitude; any constitution, law, custom, usage, or regulation of any State or Territory, or by or under its authority, to the contrary notwithstanding."

§43: "Every person who, under color of any statute, ordinance, regulation, custom, or usage, of any State or Territory, subjects, or causes to be subjected, any citizen of the United States or other person within the jurisdiction thereof to the deprivation of any rights, privileges, or immunities secured by the Constitution and laws, shall be liable to the party injured in an action at law, suit in equity, or other proper proceeding for redress."

[5] Smith v. Allwright, 131 F.2d 593.

It was by virtue of this resolution that the respondents refused to permit the petitioner to vote.

Texas is free to conduct her elections and limit her electorate as she may deem wise, save only as her action may be affected by the prohibitions of the United States Constitution or in conflict with powers delegated to and exercised by the National Government. The Fourteenth Amendment forbids a state from making or enforcing any law which abridges the privileges or immunities of citizens of the United States and the Fifteenth Amendment specifically interdicts any denial or abridgement by a state of the right of citizens to vote on account of color. Respondents appeared in the District Court and the Circuit Court of Appeals and defended on the ground that the Democratic party of Texas is a voluntary organization with members banded together for the purpose of selecting individuals of the group representing the common political beliefs as candidates in the general election. As such a voluntary organization, it was claimed, the Democratic party is free to select its own membership and limit to whites participation in the party primary. Such action, the answer asserted, does not violate the Fourteenth, Fifteenth or Seventeenth Amendment as officers of government cannot be chosen at primaries and the Amendments are applicable only to general elections where governmental officers are actually elected. Primaries, it is said, are political party affairs, handled by party not governmental officers. No appearance for respondents is made in this Court. Arguments presented here by the Attorney General of Texas and the Chairman of the State Democratic Executive Committee of Texas, as amici curiae, urged substantially the same grounds as those advanced by the respondents.

The right of a Negro to vote in the Texas primary has been considered heretofore by this Court. The first case was Nixon v. Herndon, 273 U.S. 536. At that time, 1924, the Texas statute, Art. 3093a, afterwards numbered Art. 3107 (Rev. Stat. 1925) declared "in no event shall a Negro be eligible to participate in a Democratic Party primary election in the State of Texas." Nixon was refused the right to vote in a Democratic primary and brought a suit for damages against the election officers under Rev. Stat. §§ 1979 and 2004, the present §§ 43 and 31 of 8 U.S.C. It was urged to this Court that the denial of the franchise to Nixon violated his Constitutional rights under the Fourteenth and Fifteenth Amendments. Without consideration of the Fifteenth, this Court held that the action of Texas in denying the ballot to Negroes by statute was in violation of the equal protection clause of the Fourteenth Amendment and reversed the dismissal of the suit.

The legislature of Texas reenacted the article but gave the State Executive Committee of a party the power to prescribe the qualifications of its members for voting or other participation. This article remains in the statutes. The State Executive Committee of the Democratic party adopted a resolution that white Democrats and none other might participate in the primaries of that party. Nixon was refused again the privilege of voting in a primary and again brought suit for damages by virtue of § 31, 8 U.S.C. This Court again reversed the dismissal of the suit for the reason that the Committee action was deemed to be State action and invalid as discriminatory under the Fourteenth Amendment. The test was said to be whether the Committee operated as representative of the State in the discharge of the State's authority. Nixon v. Condon, 286 U.S. 73. The question of the inherent power of a political party in Texas "without restraint by any law to determine its own membership" was left open. Id. 286 U.S. 84, 85.

In Grovey v. Townsend, 295 U.S. 45, this Court had before it another suit for damages for the refusal in a primary of a county clerk, a Texas officer with only public functions to perform, to furnish petitioner, a Negro, an absentee ballot. The refusal was solely on the ground of race. This case differed from Nixon v. Condon, supra, in that a state convention of the Democratic party had passed the resolution of May 24, 1932, hereinbefore quoted. It was decided that the determination by the state convention of the membership of the Democratic party made a significant change from a determination by the Executive Committee. The former was party action, voluntary in character. The latter, as had been held in the Condon Case, was action by authority of the State. The managers of the primary election were therefore declared not to be state officials in such sense that their action was state action. A state convention of a party was said not to be an organ of the state. This Court went on to announce that to deny a vote in a primary was a mere refusal of party membership with which "the State need have no concern," loc. cit. 295 U.S. at 55, while for a State to deny a vote in a general election on the ground of race or color violated the Constitution. Consequently, there was found no ground for holding that the county clerk's refusal of a ballot because of racial ineligibility for party membership denied the petitioner any right under the Fourteenth or Fifteenth Amendments.

Since Grovey v. Townsend and prior to the present suit, no case from Texas involving primary elections has been before this Court. We did decide, however, United States v. Classic, 313 U.S. 299. We there held that §4 of Article 1 of the Constitution authorized Congress to regulate primary as well as general elections, 313 U.S. at 316, 317, "where the primary is by law made an integral part of the election machinery." 313 U.S. at 318. Consequently, in the Classic Case, we upheld the applicability to frauds in a Louisiana primary of §§19 and 20 of the Criminal Code, 18 U.S.C. §§51, 52. Thereby corrupt acts of election officers were subjected to Congressional sanctions because that body had power to protect rights of Federal suffrage secured by the Constitution in primary as in general elections. 313 U.S. at 323. This decision depended, too, on the determination that under the Louisiana statutes the primary was a part of the procedure for choice of Federal officials. By this decision the doubt as to whether or not such primaries were a part of "elections" subject to Federal control, which had remained unanswered since Newberry v. United States, 256 U.S. 232, was erased. The Nixon Cases were decided under the equal protection clause of the Fourteenth Amendment without a determination of the status of the primary as a part of the electoral process. The exclusion of Negroes from the primaries by action of the State was held invalid under that Amendment. The fusing by the Classic Case of the primary and general elections into a single instrumentality for choice of officers has a definite bearing on the permissibility under the Constitution of excluding Negroes from primaries. This is not to say that the Classic Case cuts directly into the rationale of Grovey v. Townsend. This latter case was not mentioned in the opinion. Classic bears upon Grovey v. Townsend not because exclusion of Negroes from primaries is any more or less state action by reason of the unitary character of the electoral process but because the recognition of the place of the primary in the electoral scheme makes clear that state delegation to a party of the power to fix the qualifications of primary elections is delegation of a state function that may make the party's action the action of the State. When Grovey v. Townsend was written, the Court looked upon the denial of a vote in a primary, as a mere refusal by a party of party membership. 295 U.S. at 55. As the Louisiana statutes for holding primaries are similar to those of Texas, our ruling in Classic as to the unitary character of the electoral process calls for a reexamination as to whether or not the exclusion of Negroes from a Texas party primary was state action.

The statutes of Texas relating to primaries and the resolution of the Democratic party of Texas extending the privileges of membership to white citizens only are the same in substance and effect today as they were when Grovey v. Townsend was decided by a unanimous Court. The question as to whether the exclusionary action of the party was the action of the State persists as the determinative factor. In again entering upon consideration of the inference to be drawn as to state action from a substantially similar factual situation, it should be noted that Grovey v. Townsend upheld exclusion of Negroes from primaries through the denial of party membership by a party convention. A few years before this Court refused approval of exclusion by the State Executive Committee of the party. A different result was reached on the theory that the Committee action was state authorized and the Convention action was unfettered by statutory control. Such a variation in the result from so slight a change in form influences us to consider anew the legal validity of the distinction which has resulted in barring Negroes from participating in the nominations of candidates of the Democratic party in Texas. . . .

It may now be taken as a postulate that the right to vote in such a primary for the nomination of candidates without discrimination by the State, like the right to vote in a general election, is a right secured by the Constitution. . . . Under our Constitution the great privilege of the ballot may not be denied a man by the State because of his color.

We are thus brought to an examination of the qualifications for Democratic primary electors in Texas, to determine whether state action or private action has excluded Negroes from participation. Despite Texas' decision that the exclusion is produced by private or party action, Bell v. Hill, 123 Tex. 531, supra, Federal courts must for themselves appraise the facts leading to that conclusion. It is only by the performance of this obligation that a final and uniform interpretation can be given to the Constitution, the "Supreme Law of the Land." Nixon v. Condon, 286 U.S. 73, 88; Standard Oil Co. v. Johnson, 316 U.S. 481, 483; Bridges v. California, 314 U.S. 252; Lisenba v. California, 314 U.S. 219, 238; Union P.R. Co. v. United States, 313 U.S. 450, 467; Milk Wagon Drivers Union v. Meadowmoor Dairies, 312 U.S. 287, 294; Chambers v. Florida, 309 U.S. 227, 228. Texas requires electors in a primary to pay a poll tax. Every person who does so pay and who has the qualifications of age and residence is an acceptable voter for the primary. Art. 2955. . . . Texas requires by the law the election of the county officers of a party. These compose the county executive committee. The county chairmen so selected are members of the district executive committee and choose the chairman for the district. Precinct primary election officers are named by the county executive committee. Statutes provide for the election by the voters of precinct delegates to the county convention of a party and the selection of delegates to the district and state conventions by the county convention. The state convention selects the state executive committee. No convention may place in platform or resolution any demand for specific legislation without endorsement of such legislation by the voters in a primary. Texas thus directs the selection of all party officers. . . .

The state courts are given exclusive original jurisdiction of contested elections and of mandamus proceedings to compel party officers to perform their statutory duties.

We think that this statutory system for the selection of party nominees for inclusion on the general election ballot makes the party which is required to follow these legislative directions an agency of the state in so far as it determines the participants in a primary election. The party takes its character as a state agency from the duties imposed upon it by state statutes; the duties do not become matters of private law because they are performed by a political party. The plan of the Texas primary follows substantially that of Louisiana, with the exception that in Louisiana the state pays the cost of the primary while Texas assesses the cost against candidates. In numerous instances, the Texas statutes fix or limit the fees to be charged. Whether paid directly by the state or through state requirements, it is state action which compels. When primaries become a part of the machinery for choosing officials, state and national, as they have here, the same tests to determine the character of discrimination or abridgement should be applied to the primary as are applied to the general election. If the state requires a certain electoral procedure, prescribes a general election ballot made up of party nominees so chosen and limits the choice of the electorate in general elections for state offices, practically speaking, to those whose names appear on such a ballot, it endorses, adopts and enforces the discrimination against Negroes, practiced by a party entrusted by Texas law with the determination of the qualifications of participants in the primary. This is state action within the meaning of the Fifteenth Amendment. Guinn v. United States, 238 U.S. 347, 362.

The United States is a constitutional democracy. Its organic law grants to all citizens a right to participate in the choice of elected officials without restriction by any state because of race. This grant to the people of the opportunity for choice is not to be nullified by a state through casting its electoral process in a form which permits a private organization to practice racial discrimination in the election. Constitutional rights would be of little value if they could be thus indirectly denied. Lane v. Wilson, 307 U.S. 268, 275.

The privilege of membership in a party may be, as this Court said in Grovey v. Townsend, 295 U.S. 45, 55, no concern of a state. But when, as here, that privilege is also the essential qualification for voting in a primary to select nominees for a general election, the state makes the action of the party the action of the state. In reaching this conclusion we are not unmindful of the desirability of continuity of decision in constitutional questions. However, when convinced of former error, this Court has never felt constrained to follow precedent. In constitutional questions, where correction depends upon amendment and not upon legislative action this Court throughout its history has freely exercised its power to reexamine the basis of its constitutional decisions. This has long been accepted practice, and this practice has continued to this day. This is particularly true when the decision believed erroneous is the application of a constitutional principle rather than an interpretation of the Constitution to extract the principle itself. Here we are applying, contrary to the recent decision in Grovey v. Townsend, the well established principle of the Fifteenth Amendment, forbidding the abridgement by a state of a citizen's right to vote. Grovey v. Townsend is overruled.

Judgment reversed.

MR. JUSTICE FRANKFURTER concurs in the result.[cc]

NOTE

Should Smith v. Allwright be extended to political organizations that endorse candidates in primary races? In Terry v. Adams, 345 U.S. 461 (1953), the Court considered the preprimary activities of the Jaybird Democratic Association in Texas, which excluded blacks from membership. The white voters on the official county list, on the other hand, were automatically members and entitled to vote in the Jaybird primary. The successful Jaybird candidates would then "with few exceptions . . . run and [win] without opposition in the Democratic primaries and the general elections that followed." In applying the Fifteenth Amendment, Justice Black, writing for a plurality of the Court, found that "The Jaybird primary has become an integral part, indeed the only effective part, of the elective process that determines who shall rule and govern in the county."

On representation at party nominating conventions, see page 85 supra.

Under the decisions in Smith and Terry, are religious parties outlawed from the American scene? See Wechsler, Toward Neutral Principles of Constitutional Law, 73 Harv. L. Rev. 1, 28-29 (1959), reprinted in Principles, Politics, and Fundamental Law 3, 39-40 (1961); Lewis, The Meaning of State Action, 60 Colum. L. Rev. 1083, 1095-1096 (1960).

Gomillion v. Lightfoot 364 U.S. 339, 81 S. Ct. 125, 5 L. Ed. 2d 110 (1960)

MR. JUSTICE FRANKFURTER delivered the opinion of the Court.

This litigation challenges the validity, under the United States Constitution, of Local Act No. 140, passed by the Legislature of Alabama in 1957, redefining the boundaries of the City of Tuskegee. Petitioners, Negro citizens of Alabama who were, at the time of this redistricting measure, residents of the City of Tuskegee, brought an action in the United States District Court for the Middle District of Alabama for a declaratory judgment that

---

[cc] The dissenting opinion of Mr. Justice Roberts is omitted. His dissent was based on the conviction that the Court was too hastily overruling Grovey v. Townsend. "The reason for my concern," he said, "is that the instant decision, overruling that announced about nine years ago, tends to bring adjudications of this tribunal into the same class as a restricted railroad ticket, good for this day and train only." 321 U.S. at 666. — ED.

954 Chapter Fourteen. Privileges & Immunities; Equality; Civil Rights

Act 140 is unconstitutional, and for an injunction to restrain the Mayor and officers of Tuskegee and the officials of Macon County, Alabama, from enforcing the Act against them and other Negroes similarly situated. Petitioners' claim is that enforcement of the statute, which alters the shape of Tuskegee from a square to an uncouth twenty-eight-sided figure, will constitute a discrimination against them in violation of the Due Process and Equal Protection Clauses of the Fourteenth Amendment to the Constitution and will deny them the right to vote in defiance of the Fifteenth Amendment.

The respondents moved for dismissal of the action for failure to state a claim upon which relief could be granted and for lack of jurisdiction of the District Court. The Court granted the motion, stating, "This Court has no control over, no supervision over, and no power to change any boundaries of municipal corporations fixed by a duly convened and elected legislative body, acting for the people in the State of Alabama." 167 F. Supp. 405, 410. On appeal, the Court of Appeals for the Fifth Circuit, affirmed the judgment, one judge dissenting. 270 F.2d 594. We brought the case here since serious questions were raised concerning the power of a State over its municipalities in relation to the Fourteenth and Fifteenth Amendments. 362 U.S. 916.

At this stage of the litigation we are not concerned with the truth of the allegations, that is, the ability of petitioners to sustain their allegations by proof. The sole question is whether the allegations entitle them to make good on their claim that they are being denied rights under the United States Constitution. The complaint, charging that Act 140 is a device to disenfranchise Negro citizens, alleges the following facts: Prior to Act 140 the City of Tuskegee was square in shape; the Act transformed it into a strangely irregular twenty-eight-sided figure as indicated in the diagram appended to this opinion. The essential inevitable effect of this redefinition of Tuskegee's boundaries is to remove from the city all save only four or five of its 400 Negro voters while not removing a single white voter or resident. The result of the Act is to deprive the Negro petitioners discriminatorily of the benefits of residence in Tuskegee, including inter alia, the right to vote in municipal elections.

These allegations, if proven, would abundantly establish that Act 140 was not an ordinary geographic redistricting measure even within familiar abuses of gerrymandering. If these allegations upon a trial remained uncontradicted or unqualified, the conclusion would be irresistible, tantamount for all practical purposes to a mathematical demonstration, that the legislation is solely concerned with segregating white and colored voters by fencing Negro citizens out of town so as to deprive them of their pre-existing municipal vote. . . .

The respondents find [a] barrier to the trial of this case in Colegrove v. Green, 328 U.S. 549. In that case the Court passed on an Illinois law governing the arrangement of congressional districts within that State. The complaint rested upon the disparity of population between the different districts which rendered the effectiveness of each individual's vote in some districts far less than in others. This disparity came to pass solely through shifts in population between 1901, when Illinois organized its congressional districts, and 1946, when the complaint was lodged. During this entire period elections were held under the districting scheme devised in 1901. The Court affirmed the dismissal of the complaint on the ground that it presented a subject not meet for adjudication. The decisive facts in this case, which at this stage must be taken as proved, are wholly different from the considerations found controlling in Colegrove.

That case involved a complaint of discriminatory apportionment of congressional districts. The appellants in Colegrove complained only of a dilution of the strength of their votes as a result of legislative inaction over a course of many years. The petitioners here complain that affirmative legislative action deprives them of their votes and the consequent advantages that the ballot affords. When a legislature thus singles out a readily isolated segment of a racial minority for special discriminatory treatment, it violates the

Fifteenth Amendment. In no case involving unequal weight in voting distribution that has come before the Court did the decision sanction a differentiation on racial lines whereby approval was given to unequivocal withdrawal of the vote solely from colored citizens. Apart from all else, these considerations lift this controversy out of the so-called "political" arena and into the conventional sphere of constitutional litigation.

In sum, as Mr. Justice Holmes remarked, when dealing with a related situation, in Nixon v. Herndon, 273 U.S. 536, 540, "Of course the petition concerns political action," but "The objection that the subject matter of the suit is political is little more than a play upon words." A statute which is alleged to have worked unconstitutional deprivations of petitioners' rights is not immune to attack simply because the mechanism employed by the legislature is a redefinition of municipal boundaries. According to the allegations here made, the Alabama Legislature has not merely redrawn the Tuskegee city limits with incidental inconvenience to the petitioners; it is more accurate to say that it has deprived the petitioners of the municipal franchise and consequent rights and to that end it has incidentally changed the city's boundaries. While in form this is merely an act redefining metes and bounds, if the allegations are established, the inescapable human effect of this essay in geometry and geography is to despoil colored citizens, and only colored citizens, of their theretofore enjoyed voting rights. That was not Colegrove v. Green.

When a State exercises power wholly within the domain of state interest, it is insulated from federal judicial review. But such insulation is not carried over when state power is used as an instrument for circumventing a federally protected right. This principle has had many applications. It has long been recognized in cases which have prohibited a State from exploiting a power acknowledged to be absolute in an isolated context to justify the imposition of an "unconstitutional condition." What the Court has said in those cases is equally applicable here, viz., that "Acts generally lawful may become unlawful when done to accomplish an unlawful end, United States v. Reading Co., 226 U.S. 324, 357, and a constitutional power cannot be used by way of condition to attain an unconstitutional result." Western Union Telegraph Co. v. Foster, 247 U.S. 105, 114. The petitioners are entitled to prove their allegations at trial.

For these reasons, the principal conclusions of the District Court and the Court of Appeals are clearly erroneous and the decision below must be

Reversed.

MR. JUSTICE DOUGLAS, while joining the opinion of the Court, adheres to the dissents in Colegrove v. Green, 328 U.S. 549, and South v. Peters, 339 U.S. 276.

MR. JUSTICE WHITTAKER, concurring.

I concur in the Court's judgment, but not in the whole of its opinion. It seems to me that the decision should be rested not on the Fifteenth Amendment, but rather on the Equal Protection Clause of the Fourteenth Amendment to the Constitution. I am doubtful that the averments of the complaint, taken for present purposes to be true, show a purpose by Act 140 to abridge petitioner's "right . . . to vote," in the Fifteenth Amendment sense. It seems to me that the "right . . . to vote" that is guaranteed by the Fifteenth Amendment is but the same right to vote as is enjoyed by all others within the same election precinct, ward or other political division. And, inasmuch as no one has the right to vote in a political division, or in a local election concerning only an area in which he does not reside, it would seem to follow that one's right to vote in Division A is not abridged by a redistricting that places his residence in Division B *if* he there enjoys the same voting privileges as all others in that Division, even though the redistricting was done by the State for the purpose of placing a racial group of citizens in Division B rather than A.

But it does seem clear to me that accomplishment of a State's purpose — to use the Court's phrase — of "fencing Negro citizens out of" Division A and into Division B is an unlawful segregation of races of citizens, in violation of the Equal Protection Clause of the Fourteenth Amendment, Brown v. Board of Education, 347 U.S. 483; Cooper v.

956   Chapter Fourteen.   **Privileges & Immunities; Equality; Civil Rights**

Aaron, 358 U.S. 1; and, as stated, I would think the decision should be rested on that ground — which, incidentally, clearly would not involve, just as the cited cases did not involve, the Colegrove problem.

Baker v. Carr *369 U.S. 186, 86 S. Ct. 691, 7 L. Ed. 2d 633 (1962)*

[For the opinion in this case see page 56 supra.]

The Cases of the State Legislatures

In June 1964 the Court held that in six states the systems of apportionment of one or both houses of the legislatures were unconstitutional. The cases came from Alabama, Colorado, Delaware, Maryland, New York, and Virginia. Excerpts from the Chief Justice's opinions for a majority of the Court in the Alabama and Colorado cases, from Justice Stewart's dissent in the Colorado and New York cases, and from Justice Harlan's dissent in all cases follow.

Alabama: Reynolds v. Sims *377 U.S. 533, 84 S. Ct. 1362, 12 L. Ed. 2d 506 (1964)*

[The State Constitution of 1901 prescribed the number of members in the two branches of the state legislature and the methods which should, periodically, be followed in apportioning the seats among the state's sixty-seven counties. Though the prescribed method of apportionment required that representation in both houses should be based upon population, no significant changes in district and county representation in either house had been effected since 1900.]

MR. CHIEF JUSTICE WARREN delivered the opinion of the Court. . . .

II

Undeniably the Constitution of the United States protects the right of all qualified citizens to vote, in state as well as in federal elections. A consistent line of decisions by this Court in cases involving attempts to deny or restrict the right of suffrage has made this indelibly clear. It has been repeatedly recognized that all qualified voters have a constitutionally protected right to vote, Ex parte Yarbrough, 110 U.S. 651, and to have their votes counted, United States v. Mosley, 238 U.S. 383. In Mosley the Court stated that it is "as equally unquestionable that the right to have one's vote counted is as open to protection . . . as the right to put a ballot in a box." 238 U.S., at 386. The right to vote can neither be denied outright, Guinn v. United States, 238 U.S. 347, Lane v. Wilson, 307 U.S. 268, nor can it be destroyed by alteration of ballots, see United States v. Classic, 313 U.S. 299, 315, nor diluted by ballot-box stuffing, Ex parte Siebold, 100 U.S. 371, United States v. Saylor, 322 U.S. 385. As the Court stated in Classic, "Obviously included within the right to choose, secured by the Constitution, is the right of qualified voters within a State to cast their ballots and have them counted. . . ." 313 U.S., at 315. Racially based gerrymandering, Gomillion v. Lightfoot, 364 U.S. 339, and the conducting of white primaries, Nixon v. Herndon, 273 U.S. 536. Nixon v. Condon, 286 U.S. 73, Smith v. Allwright, 321 U.S. 649, Terry v. Adams, 345 U.S. 461, both of which result in denying to some citizens their right to vote, have been held to be constitutionally impermissible. And history has seen a continuing expansion of the scope of the right of suffrage in this country. The right to vote freely for the candidate of one's choice is of the essence of a democratic society, and any restrictions on that right strike at the heart of representative government. And the right of suffrage can be denied by a debasement or dilution of the weight of a citizen's vote just as effectively as by wholly prohibiting the free exercise of the franchise. . . .

In Gray v. Sanders, 372 U.S. 368, we held that the Georgia county unit system, applicable in statewide primary elections, was unconstitutional since it resulted in a dilution of the weight of the votes of certain Georgia voters merely because of where they resided. After indicating that the Fifteenth and Nineteenth Amendments prohibit a State from overweighting or diluting votes on the basis of race or sex, we stated:

"How then can one person be given twice or ten times the voting power of another person in a state-wide election merely because he lives in a rural area or because he lives in the smallest rural county? Once the geographical unit for which a representative is to be chosen is designated, all who participate in the election are to have an equal vote — whatever their race, whatever their sex, whatever their occupation, whatever their income, and wherever their home may be in that geographical unit. This is required by the Equal Protection Clause of the Fourteenth Amendment. The concept of 'we the people' under the Constitution visualizes no preferred class of voters but equality among those who meet the basic qualifications. The idea that every voter is equal to every other voter in his State, when he casts his ballot in favor of one of several competing candidates, underlies many of our decisions.". . .

In Wesberry v. Sanders, 376 U.S. 1, decided earlier this Term, we held that attacks on the constitutionality of congressional districting plans enacted by state legislatures do not present nonjusticiable questions and should not be dismissed generally for "want of equity." We determined that the constitutional test for the validity of congressional districting schemes was one of substantial equality of population among the various districts established by a state legislature for the election of members of the Federal House of Representatives.

In that case we decided that an apportionment of congressional seats which "contracts the value of some votes and expands that of others" is unconstitutional, since "the Federal Constitution intends that when qualified voters elect members of Congress each vote be given as much weight as any other vote. . . ." We concluded that the constitutional prescription for election of members of the House of Representatives "by the People," construed in its historical context, "means that as nearly as is practicable one man's vote in a congressional election is to be worth as much as another's." We further stated:

"It would defeat the principle solemnly embodied in the Great Compromise — equal representation in the House for equal numbers of people — for us to hold that, within the States, legislatures may draw the lines of congressional districts in such a way as to give some voters a greater voice in choosing a Congressman than others." . . .

Gray and Wesberry are of course not dispositive of or directly controlling on our decision in these cases involving state legislative apportionment controversies. Admittedly, those decisions, in which we held that, in statewide and in congressional elections, one person's vote must be counted equally with those of all other voters in a State, were based on different constitutional considerations and were addressed to rather distinct problems. But neither are they wholly inapposite. Gray, though not determinative here since involving the weighting of votes in statewide elections, established the basic principle of equality among voters within a State, and held that voters cannot be classified, constitutionally, on the basis of where they live, at least with respect to voting in statewide elections. And our decision in Wesberry was of course grounded on that language of the Constitution which prescribes that members of the Federal House of Representatives are to be chosen "by the People," while attacks on state legislative apportionment schemes, such as that involved in the instant cases, are principally based on the Equal Protection Clause of the Fourteenth Amendment. Nevertheless, Wesberry clearly established that the fundamental principle of representative government in this country is one of equal representation for equal numbers of people, without regard to race, sex, economic status, or place of residence within a State. Our problem, then, is to ascertain, in the instant cases, whether there are any constitutionally cognizable principles which would justify departures from the basic standard of equality among voters in the apportionment of seats in state legislatures.

III

A predominant consideration in determining whether a State's legislative apportionment scheme constitutes an invidious discrimination violative of rights asserted under the Equal Protection Clause is that the rights allegedly impaired are individual and personal in nature. As stated by the Court in United States v. Bathgate, 246 U.S. 220, 227, "the right to vote is personal. . . ." While the result of a court decision in a state legislative apportionment controversy may be to require the restructuring of the geographical distribution of seats in a state legislature, the judicial focus must be concentrated upon ascertaining whether there has been any discrimination against certain of the State's citizens which constitutes an impermissible impairment of their constitutionally protected right to vote. . . .

Legislators represent people, not trees or acres. Legislators are elected by voters, not farms or cities or economic interests. As long as ours is a representative form of government, and our legislatures are those instruments of government elected directly by and directly representative of the people, the right to elect legislators in a free and unimpaired fashion is a bedrock of our political system. It could hardly be gainsaid that a constitutional claim had been asserted by an allegation that certain otherwise qualified voters had been entirely prohibited from voting for members of their state legislature. And, if a State should provide that the votes of citizens in one part of the State should be given two times, or five times, or 10 times the weight of votes of citizens in another part of the State, it could hardly be contended that the right to vote of those residing in the disfavored areas had not been effectively diluted. It would appear extraordinary to suggest that a state could be constitutionally permitted to enact a law providing that certain of the state's voters could vote two, five, or 10 times for their legislative representatives, while voters living elsewhere could vote only once. And it is inconceivable that a state law to the effect that, in counting votes for legislators, the votes of citizens in one part of the State would be multiplied by two, five, or 10, while the votes of persons in another area would be counted only at face value, could be constitutionally sustainable. Of course, the effect of state legislative districting schemes which give the same number of representatives to unequal numbers of constituents is identical. Overweighting and overvaluation of the votes of those living here has the certain effect of dilution and undervaluation of the votes of those living there. The resulting discrimination against those individual voters living in disfavored areas is easily demonstrable mathematically. Their right to vote is simply not the same right to vote as that of those living in a favored part of the State. Two, five, or 10 of them must vote before the effect of their voting is equivalent to that of their favored neighbor. Weighting the votes of citizens differently, by any method or means, merely because of where they happen to reside, hardly seems justifiable. One must be ever aware that the Constitution forbids "sophisticated as well as simple-minded modes of discrimination." Lane v. Wilson, 307 U.S. 268, 275; Gomillion v. Lightfoot, 364 U.S. 339, 342. . . .

We are told that the matter of apportioning representation in a state legislature is a complex and many-faceted one. We are advised that States can rationally consider factors other than population in apportioning legislative representation. We are admonished not to restrict the power of the States to impose differing views as to political philosophy on their citizens. We are cautioned about the dangers of entering into political thickets and mathematical quagmires. Our answer is this: a denial of constitutionally protected rights demands judicial protection; our oath and our office require no less of us. . . . To the extent that a citizen's right to vote is debased, he is that much less a citizen. The fact that an individual lives here or there is not a legitimate reason for overweighting or diluting the efficacy of his vote. The complexions of societies and civilizations change, often with amazing rapidity. A nation once primarily rural in character becomes predominantly urban. Representation schemes once fair and equitable become archaic and outdated. But the basic principle of representative government remains, and must remain, unchanged — the weight of a citizen's vote cannot be made to depend on where he lives. Population is, of necessity, the starting point for consideration and the controlling criterion for judgment in legislative apportionment controversies. A citizen, a qualified voter, is no more nor no less so because he lives in the city or on the farm. This is the clear and strong command of our Constitution's Equal Protection Clause. This is an essential part of the concept of a government of laws and not men. This is at the heart of Lincoln's vision of "government of the people, by the people, [and] for the people." The Equal Protection Clause demands no less than substantially equal state legislative representation for all citizens, of all places as well as of all races.

IV

We hold that, as a basic constitutional standard, the Equal Protection Clause requires that the seats in both houses of a bicameral state legislature must be apportioned on a population basis. Simply stated, an individual's right to vote for state legislators is unconstitutionally impaired when its weight is in a substantial fashion diluted when compared with votes of citizens living on other parts of the State. Since, under neither the existing apportionment provisions nor under either of the proposed plans was either of the houses of the Alabama Legislature apportioned on a population basis, the District Court correctly held that all three of these schemes were constitutionally invalid. . . .

Legislative apportionment in Alabama is signally illustrative and symptomatic of the seriousness of this problem in a number of the States. At the time this litigation was commenced, there had been no reapportionment of seats in the Alabama Legislature for over 60 years. Legislative inaction, coupled with the unavailability of any political or judicial remedy, had resulted, with the passage of years, in the perpetuated scheme becoming little more than an irrational anachronism. Consistent failure by the Alabama Legislature to comply with state constitutional requirements as to the frequency of reapportionment and the bases of legislative representation resulted in a minority strangle hold on the State Legislature. Inequality of representation in one house added to the inequality in the other. . . .

V

Since neither of the houses of the Alabama Legislature, under any of the three plans considered by the District Court, was apportioned on a population basis, we would be justified in proceeding no further. However, one of the proposed plans, that contained in the so-called 67-Senator Amendment, at least superficially resembles the scheme of legislative representation followed in the Federal Congress. . . .

Much has been written since our decision in Baker v. Carr about the applicability of the so-called federal analogy to state legislative apportionment arrangements. After considering the matter, the court below concluded that no conceivable analogy could be drawn between the federal scheme and the apportionment of seats in the Alabama Legislature under the proposed constitutional amendment. We agree with the District Court, and find the federal analogy inapposite and irrelevant to state legislative districting schemes. . . .

The system of representation in the two Houses of the Federal Congress is one ingrained in our Constitution, as part of the law of the land. It is one conceived out of compromise and concession indispensable to the establishment of our federal republic. Arising from unique historical circumstances, it is based on the consideration that in establishing our type of federalism a group of formerly independent States bound themselves together under one national government. Admittedly, the original 13 States surrendered some of their sovereignty in agreeing to join together "to form a more perfect Union." But at the heart of our constitutional system remains the concept of separate and distinct governmental entities which have delegated some, but not all, of their formerly held powers to the single national government. The fact that almost three-fourths of our present States were never in fact independently sovereign does not detract from our view that the so-called federal analogy is inapplicable as a sustaining precedent for state legislative apportionments. The developing history and growth of our republic cannot cloud the fact that, at the time of the inception of the system of representation in the Federal Congress, a compromise between the larger and smaller States on this matter averted a deadlock in the constitutional convention which had threatened to abort the birth of our Nation. . . .

Since we find the so-called federal analogy inapposite to a consideration of the constitutional validity of state legislative apportionment schemes, we necessarily hold that the Equal Protection Clause requires both houses of a state legislature to be apportioned on a population basis. The right of a citizen to equal representation and to have his vote weighted equally with those of all other citizens in the election of members of one house of a bicameral state legislature would amount to little if States could effectively submerge the equal-population principle in the apportionment of seats in the other house. If such a scheme were permissible, an individual citizen's ability to exercise an effective voice in the only instrument of state government directly representative of the people might be almost as effectively thwarted as if neither house were apportioned on a population basis. . . .

We do not believe that the concept of bicameralism is rendered anachronistic and meaningless when the predominant basis of representation in the two state legislative bodies is required to be the same — population. A prime reason for bicameralism, modernly considered, is to insure mature and deliberate consideration of, and to prevent precipitate action on, proposed legislative measures. Simply because the controlling criterion for apportioning representation is required to be the same in both houses does not mean that there will be no differences in the composition and complexion of the two bodies. Different constituencies can be represented in the two houses. One body could be composed of single-member districts while the other could have at least some multimember districts. The length of terms of the legislators in the separate bodies could differ. The numerical size of the two bodies could be made to differ, even significantly, and the geographical size of districts from which legislators are elected could also be made to differ. And apportionment in one house could be arranged so as to balance off minor inequities in the representation of certain areas in the other house. In summary, these and other factors could be, and are presently in many States, utilized to engender differing complexions and collective attitudes in the two bodies of a state legislature, although both are apportioned substantially on a population basis.

VI

By holding that as a federal constitutional requisite both houses of a state legislature must be apportioned on a population basis, we mean that the Equal Protection Clause requires that a State make an honest and good faith effort to construct districts, in both houses of its legislature, as nearly of equal population as is practicable. We realize that it is a practical impossibility to arrange legislative districts so that each one has an identical number of residents, or citizens, or voters. Mathematical exactness or precision is hardly a workable constitutional requirement. . . .

A State may legitimately desire to maintain the integrity of various political subdivisions, insofar as possible, and provide for compact districts of contiguous territory in designing a legislative apportionment scheme. Valid considerations may underlie such aims. Indiscriminate districting, without any regard for political subdivision or natural or historical boundary lines, may be little more than an open invitation to partisan gerrymandering. Single-member districts may be the rule in one State, while another State might desire to achieve some flexibility by creating multimember or floterial districts. Whatever the means of accomplishment, the overriding objective must be substantial equality of population among the various districts, so that the vote of any citizen is approximately equal in weight to that of any other citizen in the State.

History indicates, however, that many States have deviated, to a greater or lesser degree, from the equal-population principle in the apportionment of seats in at least one house of their legislatures. So long as the divergences from a strict population standard are based on legitimate considerations incident to the effectuation of a rational state policy, some deviations from the equal-population principle are constitutionally permissible with respect to the apportionment of seats in either or both of the two houses of a bicameral state legislature. But neither history alone, nor economic or other sorts of group interests, are permissible factors in attempting to justify disparities from population-based representation. Citizens, not history or economic interests, cast votes. Considerations of area alone provide an insufficient justification for deviations from the equal-population principle. Again, people, not land or trees or pastures, vote. Modern developments and improvements in transportation and communications make rather hollow, in the mid-1960's, most claims that deviations from population-based representation can validly be based solely on geographical considerations. Arguments for allowing such deviations in order to insure effective representation for sparsely settled areas and to prevent legislative districts from becoming so large that the availability of access of citizens to their representatives is impaired are today, for the most part, unconvincing.

A consideration that appears to be of more substance in justifying some deviations from population-based representation in state legislatures is that of insuring some voice to political subdivisions, as political subdivisions. Several factors make more than insubstantial claims that a State can rationally consider according political subdivisions some independent representation in at least one body of the state legislature, as long as the basic standard of equality of population among districts is maintained. Local governmental entities are frequently charged with various responsibilities incident to the operation of state government. In many States much of the legislature's activity involves the enactment of socalled local legislation, directed only to the concerns of particular political subdivisions. And a State may legitimately desire to construct districts along political subdivision lines to deter the possibilities of gerrymandering. However, permitting deviations from population-based representation does not mean that each local governmental unit or political subdivision can be given separate representation, regardless of population. Carried too far, a scheme of giving at least one seat in one house to each political subdivision (for example, to each county) could easily result, in many States, in a total subversion of the equal-population principle in that legislative body. This would be especially true in a State where the number of counties is large and many of them are sparsely populated, and the number of seats in the legislative body being apportioned does not significantly exceed the number of counties. Such a result, we conclude, would be constitutionally impermissible. And careful judicial scrutiny must of course be given, in evaluating state apportionment schemes, to the character as well as the degree of deviations from a strict population basis. But if, even as a result of a clearly rational state policy of according some legislative representation to political subdivisions, population is submerged as the controlling consideration in the apportionment of seats in the particular legislative body, then the right of all of the State's citizens to cast an effective and adequately weighted vote would be unconstitutionally impaired. . . .

X

We do not consider here the difficult question of the proper remedial devices which federal courts should utilize in state legislative apportionment cases. Remedial techniques in this new and developing area of the law will probably often differ with the circumstances of the challenged apportionment and a variety of local conditions. It is enough to say now that, once a State's legislative apportionment scheme has been found to be unconstitutional, it would be the unusual case in which a court would be justified in not taking appropriate action to insure that no further elections are conducted under the invalid plan. However, under certain circumstances, such as where an impending election is imminent and a State's election machinery is already in progress, equitable considerations might justify a court in withholding the granting of immediately effective relief in a legislative apportionment case, even though the existing apportionment scheme was found invalid. In awarding or withholding immediate relief, a court is entitled to and should consider the proximity of a forthcoming election and the mechanics and complexities of state election laws, and should act and rely upon general equitable principles. With respect to the timing of relief, a court can reasonably endeavor to avoid a disruption of the election process which might result from requiring precipitate changes that could make unreasonable or embarrassing demands on a State in adjusting to the requirements of the court's decree. . . .

We find, therefore, that the action taken by the District Court in this case, in ordering into effect a reapportionment of both houses of the Alabama Legislature for purposes of the 1962 primary and general elections, by using the best parts of the two proposed plans which it had found, as a whole, to be invalid, was an appropriate and well-considered exercise of judicial power. Admittedly, the lower court's ordered plan was intended only as a temporary and provisional measure and the District Court correctly indicated that the plan was invalid as a permanent apportionment. In retaining jurisdiction while deferring a hearing on the issuance of a final injunction in order to give the provisionally reapportioned legislature an opportunity to act effectively, the court below proceeded in a proper fashion. Since the District Court evinced its realization that its ordered reapportionment could not be sustained as the basis for conducting the 1966 election of Alabama legislators, and avowedly intends to take some further action should the reapportioned Alabama Legislature fail to enact a constitutionally valid, permanent apportionment scheme in the interim, we affirm the judgment below and remand the cases for further proceedings consistent with the views stated in this opinion.

It is so ordered.[dd]

Colorado: Lucas v. Forty-fourth General Assembly 377 U.S. 713, 84 S. Ct. 351, 12 L. Ed. 2d 632 (1964)

[In this case taxpaying residents of Denver, Colorado, challenged the constitutionality of the apportionment of seats in both houses of the legislature. In 1962 the people of the state had approved amendments to the Constitution of the state — those amendments includ-

---

[dd] Concurring opinions by Clark and Stewart, JJ., are omitted. — Ed.

ing "Amendment No. 7" — an enactment providing for the apportionment of the House of Representatives on the basis of population, but also maintaining, in the state Senate, an earlier formula for representation which gave appreciable weight to considerations other than population.]

MR. CHIEF JUSTICE WARREN delivered the opinion of the Court. . . .

III

Several aspects of this case serve to distinguish it from the other cases involving state legislative apportionment also decided this date. Initially, one house of the Colorado Legislature is at least arguably apportioned substantially on a population basis under Amendment No. 7 and the implementing statutory provisions. Under the apportionment schemes challenged in the other cases, on the other hand, clearly neither of the houses in any of the state legislatures is apportioned sufficiently on a population basis so as to be constitutionally sustainable. Additionally, the Colorado scheme of legislative apportionment here attacked is one adopted by a majority vote of the Colorado electorate almost contemporaneously with the District Court's decision on the merits in this litigation. Thus, the plan at issue did not result from prolonged legislative inaction. However, the Colorado General Assembly, in spite of the state constitutional mandate for periodic reapportionment, has enacted only one effective legislative apportionment measure in the past 50 years.

As appellees have correctly pointed out, a majority of the voters in every county of the State voted in favor of the apportionment scheme embodied in Amendment No. 7's provisions, in preference to that contained in proposed Amendment No. 8, which, subject to minor deviations, would have based the apportionment of seats in both houses on a population basis. However, the choice presented to the Colorado electorate, in voting on these two proposed constitutional amendments, was hardly as clear-cut as the court below regarded it. One of the most undesirable features of the existing apportionment scheme was the requirement that, in counties given more than one seat in either or both of the houses of the General Assembly, all legislators must be elected at large from the county as a whole. Thus, under the existing plan, each Denver voter was required to vote for eight senators and 17 representatives. Ballots were long and cumbersome, and an intelligent choice among candidates for seats in the legislature was made quite difficult. No identifiable constituencies *within* the populous counties resulted, and the residents of those areas had no single member of the Senate or House elected specifically to represent them. Rather, each legislator elected from a multimember county represented the county as a whole. Amendment No. 8, as distinguished from Amendment No. 7, while purportedly basing the apportionment of seats in both houses on a population basis, would have perpetuated, for all practical purposes, this debatable feature of the existing scheme. Under Amendment No. 8, senators were to be elected at large in those counties given more than one Senate seat, and no provision was made for subdistricting within such counties for the purpose of electing senators. Representatives were also to be elected at large in multimember counties pursuant to the provisions of Amendment No. 8, at least initially, although subdistricting for the purpose of electing House members was permitted if the voters of a multimember county specifically approved a representative subdistricting plan for that county. Thus, neither of the proposed plans was, in all probability, wholly acceptable to the voters in the populous counties, and the assumption of the court below that the Colorado voters made a definitive choice between two contrasting alternatives and indicated that "minority process in the Senate is what they want" does not appear to be factually justifiable.

Finally, this case differs from the others decided this date in that the initiative device provides a practicable political remedy to obtain relief against alleged legislative malapportionment in Colorado. An initiated measure proposing a constitutional amendment or a statutory enactment is entitled to be placed on the ballot if the signatures of 8% of those voting for the Secretary of State in the last election are obtained. No geographical distribution of petition signers is required. Initiative and referendum has been frequently utilized throughout Colorado's history. Additionally, Colorado courts have traditionally not been hesitant about adjudicating controversies relating to legislative apportionment. However, the Colorado Supreme Court, in its 1962 decision discussed previously in this opinion, refused to consider or pass upon the federal constitutional questions, but instead held only that the Colorado General Assembly was not required to enact a reapportionment statute until the following legislative session. . . .

IV

. . . Except as an interim remedial procedure justifying a court in staying its hand temporarily, we find no significance in the fact that a nonjudicial, political remedy may be available for the effectuation of asserted rights to equal representation in a state legislature. Courts sit to adjudicate controversies involving alleged denials of constitutional rights. While a court sitting as a court of equity might be justified in temporarily refraining from the issuance of injunctive relief in an apportionment case in order to allow for resort to an available political remedy, such as initiative and referendum, individual constitutional rights cannot be deprived, or denied judicial effectuation, because of the existence of a nonjudicial remedy through which relief against the alleged malapportionment, which the individual voters seek, might be achieved. An individual's constitutionally protected right to cast an equally weighted vote cannot be denied even by a vote of a majority of a State's electorate, if the apportionment scheme adopted by the voters fails to measure up to the requirements of the Equal Protection Clause. Manifestly, the fact that an apportionment plan is adopted in a popular referendum is insufficient to sustain its constitutionality or to induce a court of equity to refuse to act. As stated by this Court in West Virginia State Bd. of Educ. v. Barnette, 319 U.S. 624, 638, "One's right to life, liberty, and property . . . and other fundamental rights may not be submitted to vote; they depend on the outcome of no elections." A citizen's constitutional rights can hardly be infringed simply because a majority of the people choose to do so. We hold that the fact that a challenged legislative apportionment plan was approved by the electorate is without federal constitutional significance, if the scheme adopted fails to satisfy the basic requirements of the Equal Protection Clause, as delineated in our opinion in Reynolds v. Sims. And we conclude that the fact that a practicably available political remedy, such as initiative and referendum, exists under state law provides justification only for a court of equity to stay its hand temporarily while recourse to such a remedial device is attempted or while proposed initiated measures relating to legislative apportionment are pending and will be submitted to the State's voters at the next election.

[The dissenting opinion of MR. JUSTICE STEWART was applicable to both the New York and the Colorado cases:]

MR. JUSTICE STEWART, whom MR. JUSTICE CLARK joins, dissenting.

It is important to make clear at the outset what these cases are not about. They have nothing to do with the denial or impairment of any person's right to vote. Nobody's right to vote has been denied. Nobody's right to vote has been restricted. Nobody has been deprived of the right to have his vote counted. The voting right cases which the Court cites are, therefore, completely wide of the mark. Secondly, these cases have nothing to do with the "weighting" or "diluting" of votes cast within any electoral unit. The rule of Gray v. Sanders, 372 U.S. 368, is, therefore, completely without relevance here. Thirdly, these cases are not concerned with the election of members of the Congress of the United States, governed by Article I of the Constitution. Consequently, the Court's decision in Wesberry v. Sanders, 376 U.S. 1, throws no light at all on the basic issue now before us.

The question involved in these cases is quite a different one. Simply stated, the question is to what degree, if at all, the Equal Protection Clause of the Fourteenth Amendment limits each sovereign State's freedom to establish appropriate electoral constituencies from which representatives to the State's bicameral legislative assembly are to be chosen. The Court's answer is a blunt one, and, I think, woefully wrong. The Equal Protection Clause, says the Court, "requires that the seats in both houses of a bicameral state legislature must be apportioned on a population basis."

After searching carefully through the Court's opinions in these and their companion cases, I have been able to find but two reasons offered in support of this rule. First, says the Court, it is "established that the fundamental principle of representative government in this country is one of equal representation for equal numbers of people. . . ." With all respect, I think that this is not correct, simply as a matter of fact. It has been unanswerably demonstrated before now that this "was not the colonial system, it was not the system chosen for the national government by the Constitution, it was not the system exclusively or even predominantly practiced by the States at the time of adoption of the Fourteenth Amendment, it is not predominantly practiced by the States today." Secondly, says the Court, unless legislative districts are equal in population, voters in the more populous districts will suffer a "debasement" amounting to a constitutional injury. As the Court explains it, "To the extent that a citizen's right to vote is debased, he is that much less a citizen." We are not told how or why the vote of a person in a more populated legislative district is "debased," or how or why he is less a citizen, nor is the proposition self-evident. I find it impossible to understand how or why a voter in California, for instance, either feels or is less a citizen than a voter in Nevada, simply because, despite their population disparities, each of those States is represented by two United States Senators.

To put the matter plainly, there is nothing in all the history of this Court's decisions which supports this constitutional rule. The Court's draconian pronouncement, which makes unconstitutional the legislatures of most of the 50 States, finds no support in the words of the Constitution, in any prior decision of this Court, or in the 175-year political history of our Federal Union. With all respect, I am convinced these decisions mark a long step backward into that unhappy era when a majority of the members of this Court were thought by many to have convinced themselves and each other that the demands of the Constitution were to be measured not by what it says, but by their own notions of wise political theory. The rule announced today is at odds with long-established principles of constitutional adjudication under the Equal Protection Clause, and it stifles values of local individuality and initiative vital to the character of the Federal Union which it was the genius of our Constitution to create.

I

What the Court has done is to convert a particular political philosophy into a constitutional rule, binding upon each of the 50 States, from Maine to Hawaii, from Alaska to Texas, without regard and without respect for the many individualized and differentiated characteristics of each State, characteristics stemming from each State's distinct history, distinct geography, distinct distribution of population, and distinct political heritage. My own understanding of the various theories of representative government is that no one theory has ever commanded unanimous assent among political scientists, historians, or others who have considered the problem. But even if it were thought that the rule announced today by the Court is, as a matter of political theory, the most desirable general rule which can be devised as a basis for the make-up of the representative assembly of a typical State, I could not join in the fabrication of a constitutional mandate which imports and forever freezes one theory of political thought into our Constitution, and forever denies to every State any opportunity for enlightened and progressive innovation in the design of its democratic institutions, so as to accommodate within a system of representative government the interests and aspirations of diverse groups of people, without subjecting any group or class to absolute domination by a geographically concentrated or highly organized majority. . . .

I do not pretend to any specialized knowledge of the myriad of individual characteristics of the several States, beyond the records in the cases before us today. But I do know enough to be aware that a system of legislative apportionment which might be best for South Dakota, might be unwise for Hawaii with its many islands, or Michigan with its Northern Peninsula. I do know enough to realize that Montana with its vast distances is not Rhode Island with its heavy concentrations of people. I do know enough to be aware of the great variations among the several States in their historic manner of distributing legislative power — of the Governors' Councils in New England, of the broad powers of initiative and referendum retained in some States by the people, of the legislative power which some States give to their Governors, by the right of veto or otherwise, of the widely autonomous home rule which many States give to their cities. The Court today declines to give any recognition to these considerations and countless others, tangible and intangible, in holding unconstitutional the particular systems of legislative apportionment which these States have chosen. Instead, the Court says that the requirements of the Equal Protection Clause can be met in any State only by the uncritical, simplistic, and heavy-handed application of sixth-grade arithmetic.

But legislators do not represent faceless numbers. They represent people, or, more accurately, a majority of the voters in their districts — people with identifiable needs and interests which require legislative representation, and which can often be related to the geographical areas in which these people live. The very fact of geographic districting, the constitutional validity of which the Court does not question, carries with it an acceptance of the idea of legislative representation of regional needs and interests. Yet if geographical residence is irrelevant, as the Court suggests, and the goal is solely that of equally "weighted" votes, I do not understand why the Court's constitutional rule does not require the abolition of districts and the holding of all elections at large. . . .

II

This brings me to what I consider to be the proper constitutional standards to be applied in these cases. Quite simply, I think the cases should be decided by application of accepted principles of constitutional adjudication under the Equal Protection Clause. . . . These principles reflect an understanding respect for the unique values inherent in the Federal Union of States established by our Constitution. They reflect, too, a wise perception of this Court's role in that constitutional system. . . .

Moving from the general to the specific, I think that the Equal Protection Clause demands but two basic attributes of any plan of state legislative apportionment. First, it demands that, in the light of the State's own characteristics and needs, the plan must be a rational one. Secondly, it demands that the plan must be such as not to permit the systematic frustration of the will of a majority of the electorate of the State. I think it is apparent that any plan of legislative apportionment which could be shown to reflect no policy, but simply arbitrary and capricious action or inaction, and that any plan which could be shown systematically to prevent ultimate effective majority rule, would be invalid under accepted Equal Protection Clause standards. But, beyond this, I think there is nothing in the Federal Constitution to prevent a State from choosing any electoral legislative structure it thinks best suited to the interests, temper, and customs of its people. In the light of these standards, I turn to the Colorado and New York plans of legislative apportionment.

III

COLORADO

[Justice Stewart found that the departures from a population basis in the Colorado Senate could be justified under equal protection review. Because of the distinct interests and characteristics of the state's various regions, he thought that smaller population districts might be necessary in some instances, as in the sparsely populated areas of the mountainous west, for example, in order for senators "to maintain close contact with . . . constituents," or as in the agricultural areas of the Great Plains, in order for this portion of the electorate not to be grouped "in districts with larger numbers of voters with wholly different interests." Moreover, Justice Stewart argued, because of the strength of the metropolitan areas, "no possible combination of Colorado senators from rural districts . . . could control the Senate."]

IV

NEW YORK

[Because counties in New York carry out many of the governmental programs that citizens may wish to effect in the legislative process, Justice Stewart contended that the apportionment formula was justified which provided that "each county shall have at least one representative in the Assembly." The formula also assured smaller counties greater representation than would be warranted under a population basis and limited representation in the largest counties. This was also justified, Justice Stewart argued, as a counterweight to New York City's "concentration of population, homogeneity of interest, and political cohesiveness."]

V

In the allocation of representation in their State Legislatures, Colorado and New York have adopted completely rational plans which reflect an informed response to their particularized characteristics and needs. The plans are quite different, just as Colorado and New York are quite different. But each State, while clearly ensuring that in its legislative councils the will of the majority of the electorate shall rule, has sought to provide that no identifiable minority shall be completely silenced or engulfed. The Court today holds unconstitutional the considered governmental choices of these two Sovereign States. By contrast, I believe that what each State has achieved fully comports with the letter and the spirit of our constitutional traditions.

I would affirm the judgments in both cases.[ee]

MR. JUSTICE HARLAN dissenting. . . .

PRELIMINARY STATEMENT

Today's holding is that the Equal Protection Clause of the Fourteenth Amendment requires every State to structure its legislature so that all the members of each house represent substantially the same number of people; other factors may be given play only to the extent that they do not significantly encroach on this basic "population" principle. What-

---

[ee] A dissenting opinion of Mr. Justice Clark, applicable to the New York and Colorado cases, is omitted. — ED.

ever may be thought of this holding as a piece of political ideology — and even on that score the political history and practices of this country from its earliest beginnings leave wide room for debate (see the dissenting opinion of Frankfurter, J., in Baker v. Carr, 369 U.S. 186, 266, 301-323) — I think it demonstrable that the Fourteenth Amendment does not impose this political tenet on the States or authorize this Court to do so.

The Court's constitutional discussion, found in its opinion in the Alabama cases . . . is remarkable (as, indeed, is that found in the separate opinions of my Brothers Stewart and Clark, ante, pp. 588, 587) for its failure to address itself at all to the Fourteenth Amendment as a whole or to the legislative history of the Amendment pertinent to the matter at hand. Stripped of aphorisms, the Court's argument boils down to the assertion that petitioners' right to vote has been invidiously "debased" or "diluted" by systems of apportionment which entitle them to vote for fewer legislators than other voters, an assertion which is tied to the Equal Protection Clause only by the constitutionally frail tautology that "equal" means "equal." . . .

The Court relies exclusively on that portion of §1 of the Fourteenth Amendment which provides that no State shall "deny to any person within its jurisdiction the equal protection of the laws," and disregards entirely the significance of §2, which reads:

"Representatives shall be apportioned among the several States according to their respective numbers, counting the whole number of persons in each State, excluding Indians not taxed. But when the right to vote at any election for the choice of electors for President and Vice President of the United States, Representatives in Congress, the Executive and Judicial officers of a State, or the members of the Legislature thereof, is denied to any of the male inhabitants of such State, being twenty-one years of age, and citizens of the United States, or in any way abridged, except for participation in rebellion, or other crime, the basis of representation therein shall be reduced in the proportion which the number of such male citizens shall bear to the whole number of male citizens twenty-one years of age in such State."

. . . Whatever one might take to be the application to these cases of the Equal Protection Clause if it stood alone, I am unable to understand the Court's utter disregard of the second section which expressly recognizes the States' power to deny "or in any way" abridge the right of their inhabitants to vote for "the members of the [State] Legislature," and its express provision of a remedy for such denial or abridgment. The comprehensive scope of the second section and its particular reference to the state legislatures precludes the suggestion that the first section was intended to have the result reached by the Court today. . . .

[Mr. Justice Harlan then extensively reviewed the history of the proposal and ratification of the Fourteenth Amendment. An element in that history which received special emphasis was the fact that the ratifying states very commonly were governed by legislatures of which either one house or both houses were constituted on principles not dominated by a principle of numerical representation. "Can it be seriously contended that the legislatures of these States, or almost two-thirds of those concerned, would have ratified an amendment which might render their own State constitutions unconstitutional?" Mr. Justice Harlan also emphasized the fact that the constitutions of many Southern states, as they were readmitted to the Union after the adoption of the Fourteenth Amendment, "contained provisions departing substantially from the method of apportionment now held to be required by the Amendment."]

It should by now be obvious that these cases do not mark the end of reapportionment problems in the courts. Predictions once made that the courts would never have to face the problem of actually working out an apportionment have proved false. This Court, however, continues to avoid the consequences of its decisions, simply assuring us that the lower courts "can and . . . will work out more concrete and specific standards," . . . . Deeming it "expedient" not to spell out "precise constitutional tests," the Court contents itself with stating "only a few rather general considerations." . . .

Generalities cannot obscure the cold truth that cases of this type are not amenable to the development of judicial standards. No set of standards can guide a court which has to decide how many legislative districts a State shall have, or what the shape of the districts shall be, or where to draw a particular district line. No judicially manageable standard can determine whether a State should have single-member districts or multimember districts or some combination of both. No such standard can control the balance between keeping up with population shifts and having stable districts. In all these respects, the courts will be called upon to make particular decisions with respect to which a principle of equally populated districts will be of no assistance whatsoever. Quite obviously, there are limitless possibilities for districting consistent with such a principle. Nor can these problems be avoided by judicial reliance on legislative judgments so far as possible. Reshaping or combining one or two districts, or modifying just a few district lines, is no less a matter of choosing among many possible solutions, with varying political consequences, than reapportionment broadside. . . .

Although the Court — necessarily, as I believe — provides only generalities in elaboration of its main thesis, its opinion nevertheless fully demonstrates how far removed these problems are from fields of judicial competence. Recognizing that "indiscriminate districting" is an invitation to "partisan gerrymandering," . . . the Court nevertheless excludes virtually every basis for the formation of electoral districts other than "indiscriminate districting." In one or another of today's opinions, the Court declares it unconstitutional for a State to give effective consideration to any of the following in establishing legislative districts:

(1) history;
(2) "economic or other sorts of group interests";
(3) area;
(4) geographical considerations;
(5) a desire "to insure effective representation for sparsely settled areas";
(6) "availability of access of citizens to their representatives";
(7) theories of bicameralism (except those approved by the Court);
(8) occupation;
(9) "an attempt to balance urban and rural power";
(10) the preference of a majority of voters in the State.

So far as presently appears, the only factor which a State may consider, apart from numbers, is political subdivisions. But even "a clearly rational state policy" recognizing this factor is unconstitutional if "population is submerged as the controlling consideration. . . ."

I know of no principle of logic or practical or theoretical politics, still less any constitutional principle, which establishes all or any of these exclusions. Certain it is that the Court's opinion does not establish them. So far as the Court says anything at all on this score, it says only that "legislators represent people, not trees or acres," . . . that "citizens, not history or economic interests, cast votes," . . . that "people, not land or trees or pastures, vote," . . . . All this may be conceded. But it is surely equally obvious, and, in the context of elections, more meaningful to note that people are not ciphers and that legislators can represent their electors only by speaking for their interests — economic, social, political — many of which do reflect the place where the electors live. The Court does not establish, or indeed even attempt to make a case for the proposition that conflicting interests within a State can only be adjusted by disregarding them when voters are grouped for purposes of representation.

CONCLUSION

With these cases the Court approaches the end of the third round set in motion by the complaint filed in Baker v. Carr. What is done today deepens my conviction that judicial entry into this realm is profoundly ill-advised and constitutionally impermissible. As I have said before, Wesberry v. Sanders [376 U.S. 1], at 48, I believe that the vitality of our political system, on which in the last analysis all else depends, is weakened by reliance on the judiciary for political reform; in time a complacent body politic may result.

These decisions also cut deeply into the fabric of our federalism. What must follow from them may eventually appear to be the product of State Legislatures. Nevertheless, no thinking person can fail to recognize that the aftermath of these cases, however desirable it may be thought in itself, will have been achieved at the cost of a radical alteration in the relationship between the States and the Federal Government, more particularly the Federal Judiciary. Only one who has an overbearing impatience with the federal system and its political processes will believe that that cost was not too high or was inevitable.

Finally, these decisions give support to a current mistaken view of the Constitution and the constitutional function of this Court. This view, in a nutshell, is that every major social ill in this country can find its cure in some constitutional "principle," and that this Court should "take the lead" in promoting reform when other branches of government fail to act. The Constitution is not a panacea for every blot upon the public welfare, nor should this Court, ordained as a judicial body, be thought of as a general haven for reform movements. The Constitution is an instrument of government, fundamental to which is the premise that in a diffusion of governmental authority lies the greatest promise that this Nation will realize liberty for all its citizens. This Court, limited in function in accordance with that premise, does not serve its high purpose when it exceeds its authority, even to satisfy justified impatience with the slow workings of the political process. For when, in the name of constitutional interpretation, the Court adds something to the Constitution that was deliberately excluded from it, the Court in reality substitutes its view of what should be so for the amending process. . . .[ff]

NOTE The Unit Count and Contingency Elections

May a state adopt a system, comparable to the federal electoral college, which provides for the election of a state officer, not by direct, popular vote, but by the vote of political subdivisions within the state? In Gray v. Sanders, 372 U.S. 368 (1963), the Court struck down the Georgia county-unit system by which candidates in the Democratic primary were elected by a majority of counties voting as units instead of by a majority of individual voters. Writing for the Court, Justice Douglas concluded: "The conception of political equality from the Declaration of Independence, to Lincoln's Gettysburg Address, to the Fifteenth, Seventeenth, and Nineteenth Amendments can mean only one thing — one person, one vote."

Would a state system also be unconstitutional which provided that if no candidate for Governor received a majority of votes then the state legislature would select the Governor from the two persons with the highest totals? As in Gray v. Sanders, the result might be that the candidate with the highest popular total would not be the winner. In Fortson v. Morris, 385 U.S. 231 (1966), however, the Court sustained such a system, even though, in addition, the Georgia General Assembly that would elect the Governor was itself malapportioned. Justice Black, writing for the Court, said: "Statewide elections cost time and money and it is not strange that Georgia's people decided to avoid repeated elections. The method they chose for this purpose was not unique, but well known and frequently utilized before and since the Revolutionary War." The particular provision in Georgia's case, Justice Black emphasized, "has remained in its constitution for 142 years." Finally,

---

[ff] See Note, Reapportionment, 79 Harv. L. Rev. 1226 (1966); Shapiro, Law and Politics in the Supreme Court, c. 5 (1964); McKay, Reapportionment: The Law and Politics of Equal Representation (1965); Comment, Reapportionment and the Problem of Remedy, 13 U.C.L.A.L. Rev. 1345 (1966); Auerbach, the Reapportionment Cases: One Person, One Vote — One Vote, One Value, 1964 Sup. Ct. Rev. 1. — Ed.

although the legislature was malapportioned, with respect to this duty, it "could continue to function." See Toombs v. Fortson, 384 U.S. 210, aff'g 241 F. Supp. 65 (1966).

In Fortson v. Morris, Justice Douglas wrote a dissent, concurred in by Chief Justice Warren and Justices Brennan and Fortas. In a separate dissent, joined by Justice Douglas, Justice Fortas argued that Gray v. Sanders controlled this case: "No less than the county unit system, this means that the vote cast by a citizen is subject to nullification by the legislature. The integrity of the vote is undermined and destroyed by any scheme which can result in the selection of a person as Governor who receives the lesser number of popular votes." As for the long tradition here, Justice Fortas wrote: "Certainly the antiquity of the practice did not cause this Court to refrain from invalidating malapportionment under the Equal Protection Clause." Moreover, he said, to allow this legislature to select the Governor would be "to perpetuate the electoral vices" of malapportionment.

NOTE Developments in Reapportionment

1. The use of statistics in reapportionment cases. The courts have come to look at a number of statistical indices to measure how an apportionment plan varies from the strict ideal of one person, one vote. A prominent index is the "maximum percentage deviation." See, e.g., Mahan v. Howell, 410 U.S. 315, 320 (1973). This is computed by averaging the number of representatives to be elected into the total population to determine the population of an ideal district. The maximum percentage deviation equals the sum of the differences between the population of the ideal district and those of the largest and smallest districts in the apportionment plan. Thus, if a state with a population of 10 million is allotted 10 congressmen, the ideal district will have a population of one million. If the largest district has a population of 1.1 million (10 percent over the ideal) and the smallest has 0.9 million (10 percent below), the maximum percentage deviation would equal 20 percent.

2. Congressional districts. In Wesberry v. Sanders, 376 U.S. 1 (1964), the Court held that the provision of Article I, §2, that United States representatives "be chosen 'by the People of the several States' means that as nearly as is practicable one man's vote in a congressional election is to be worth as much as another's." The Court thus struck down a Georgia congressional districting plan with a maximum percentage deviation — although the Court didn't compute it — of more than 140 percent. Justices Harlan and Stewart dissented, arguing that neither the text nor the intentions of the Framers gave support to the majority's reading of Article I, §2.

The Court has relied on Wesberry to invalidate congressional districting plans with much smaller deviations. See White v. Weiser, 412 U.S. 783 (1973) (4.13 percent); Wells v. Rockefeller, 394 U.S. 542 (1969) (13.1 percent); Kirkpatrick v. Preisler, 394 U.S. 526 (1969) (5.97 percent). In Kirkpatrick the Court refused to recognize any particular amount of deviation as low enough to be de minimis and thus automatically within the "as nearly as practicable standard." Rather, the states were required to make "a good-faith effort to achieve precise mathematical equality" and to be able to justify each deviation from the ideal. The Court rejected state arguments that its variations were justified by the desire to keep areas intact that are geographically compact or have distinct economic and social interests, by the practical political problems in getting a districting scheme through the state legislature, or by the desire to have congressional districts congruent with other political subdivisions such as towns or counties. The Court further held that the state had not brought forth sufficient evidence to show that the variations were justified by differences in the proportion of eligible voters to total population or by projected population shifts.

3. Malapportionment in state and local districting plans. Under the equal protection clause of the Fourteenth Amendment, the standard of review of state and local districting

plans has become less strict. In Mahan v. Howell, 410 U.S. 315 (1973), the Court reversed a three-judge district court decision invalidating a Virginia legislative districting plan with a maximum percentage deviation of 16.4 percent and prescribing a plan with a deviation of 10 percent. Writing for the Court, Justice Rehnquist ruled that the court below had erred in applying the standards laid down in Wesberry and Kirkpatrick. The goal, stated in Reynolds v. Sims, of "substantial equality of population" was held to allow "broader latitude" to state legislative districting schemes. The variations in the Virginia plan were held to be justified by "the State's policy of maintaining the integrity of political subdivision lines." The Court pointed to Virginia's traditional adherence to this policy and to its usefulness in the formulation and passage of legislation affecting local interests.

Later the same term, in Gaffney v. Cummings, 412 U.S. 735 (1973), and White v. Regester, 412 U.S. 755 (1973), the Court further reduced the vulnerability of state districting plans to judicial review. In opinions by Justice White, the Court reversed three-judge district court decisions which had struck down Texas and Connecticut legislative districting plans with maximum percentage deviations of 9.9 and 7.83. These deviations, said the Court, "fail in size and quality to amount to an invidious discrimination under the Fourteenth Amendment which would entitle appellees to relief, absent some countervailing showing by the State." Thus, "absent further proof of invidiousness," these plans were not subject to challenge under the equal protection clause. Justice White noted Reynolds v. Sims's mandate of "substantial equality," the inevitable inaccuracies of census data, and the unseemliness of "repeated displacement [by the courts] of otherwise appropriate state decisionmaking in the name of essentially minor deviations." The Court further held that the Connecticut legislature's observation of a "political fairness principle" intended to assure that the "statewide political strengths" of the Democratic and Republican parties would be reflected in the new districting scheme did not indicate invidious discrimination. Justices Douglas, Brennan, and Marshall dissented in Mahan, Gaffney, and White.

Compare Chapman v. Meier, 420 U.S. 1 (1975). There, the Court unanimously invalidated a reapportionment plan for North Dakota with a maximum deviation of 20.14 percent which had been developed by the court below. So large a deviation was held impermissible in a court-ordered plan "in the absence of significant state policies or other acceptable considerations that require [its] adoption." The proffered justifications, including an absence of "electorally victimized minorities," sparseness of population, and observation of geographical and political subdivisions, were rejected. The opinion, by Justice Blackmun, further suggested that court-ordered districting plans are subject to more rigorous scrutiny than those designed by legislatures.

The rule of Reynolds v. Sims was extended to subunits of state government in Avery v. Midland County, 390 U.S. 474 (1968), invalidating an apportionment scheme for the election of county commissioners. Of the five commissioners, one was elected at large and the others from four districts, one of which contained 95 percent of the county's human population. Writing for the Court, Justice White emphasized the wide authority exercised by local governments, whose "responsible and responsive operation is today of increasing importance to the quality of life of more and more of our citizens." He further rejected the argument that the commissioners' responsibilities were "insufficiently 'legislative' " to subject their election to the principle of one person, one vote. Although the commissioners exercised a variety of functions that might properly be classified as administrative or judicial, their jurisdiction over tax rates and adoption of the county budget was held to constitute a considerable legislative role.

In Abate v. Mundt, 403 U.S. 182 (1971), a reapportionment plan for the legislature of a county containing five towns, which provided for representatives from five corresponding districts, was upheld despite a maximum percentage deviation of 11.9.

In a separate opinion in Whitcomb v. Chavis, 403 U.S. 124 (1971), decided the same day as Abate, Justice Harlan made the following statements:

Section H. **The Suffrage** 973

"Past decisions have held that districting in local governmental units must approach equality of voter population 'as far as is practicable,' Hadley v. Junior College District, 397 U.S. 50, 56 (1970), and that the 'as nearly as is practicable' standard of Wesberry v. Sanders, 376 U.S. 1, 7-8 (1964), for congressional districting forbade a maximum variation of 6%. Kirkpatrick v. Preisler, 394 U.S. 526 (1969). Today the Court sustains a local governmental apportionment scheme with a 12% variation. . . .

"Other past decisions have suggested that multi-member constituencies would be unconstitutional if they could be shown 'under the circumstances of a particular case, . . . to minimize or cancel out the voting strength of racial or political elements of the voting population.' Fortson v. Dorsey, 379 U.S. 433, 439 (1965); Burns v. Richardson, 384 U.S. 73, 88 (1966). Today the Court holds that a three-judge District Court, which struck down an apportionment scheme for just this reason, 'misconceived the Equal Protection Clause.' Whitcomb v. Chavis. . . .

"Prior opinions stated that 'once the class of voters is chosen and their qualifications specified, we see no constitutional way by which equality of voting power may be evaded.' Gray v. Sanders, 372 U.S. 368, 381 (1963); Hadley v. Junior College District, 397 U.S. 50, 59 (1970). Today the Court sustains a provision that gives opponents of school bond issues half again the voting power of proponents. Gordon v. Lance, 403 U.S. 1.

"II. The Court justifies the wondrous results in these cases by relying on different combinations of factors . . . .

"To my mind the relevance of such considerations . . . is undeniable and their cumulative effect is unanswerable. I can only marvel, therefore, that they were dismissed, singly and in combination, in a line of cases which began with Gray v. Sanders, 372 U.S. 368 (1963), and ended with Hadley v. Junior College District, 397 U.S. 50 (1970).

"That line of cases can best be understood, I think, as reflections of deep *personal* commitments by some members of the Court to the principles of pure majoritarian democracy. This majoritarian strain and its nonconstitutional sources are most clearly revealed in Gray v. Sanders, 372 U.S. 368, 381 (1963), where my Brother Douglas, speaking for the Court, said: '[t]he conception of political equality from the Declaration of Independence, to Lincoln's Gettysburg Address, to the Fifteenth, Seventeenth, and Nineteenth Amendments can mean only one thing — one person, one vote.' If this philosophy of majoritarianism had been given its head, it would have led to different results in each of the cases decided today, for it is in the very nature of the principle that it regards majority-rule as an imperative of social organization, not subject to compromise in furtherance of merely political ends. It is a philosophy which ignores or overcomes the fact that the scheme of the Constitution is one not of majoritarian democracy, but of federal republics, with equality of representation a value subordinate to many others, as both the body of the Constitution and the Fourteenth Amendment itself show on their face. See generally Baker v. Carr, 369 U.S. 186, 297-324 (1962) (Frankfurter, J., dissenting). . . .

"This case is nothing short of a complete vindication of Mr. Justice Frankfurter's warning 10 years ago 'of the mathematical quagmire (apart from divers judicially inappropriate and elusive determinants) into which this Court today catapults the lower courts of the country.' Baker v. Carr, 369 U.S. 186, 268 (1962) (dissenting opinion). With all respect, it also bears witness to the morass into which the Court has gotten itself by departing from sound constitutional principle in the electoral field. See the dissenting opinion of Mr. Justice Frankfurter in Baker v. Carr, supra, and the separate opinions of this writer in Reynolds v. Sims, 377 U.S. 533, 589 (1964), and in Oregon v. Mitchell, 400 U.S. 112, 152 (1970). Hopefully, the day will come when the Court will frankly recognize the error of its ways in ever having undertaken to restructure state electoral processes."

4. On the analogy of the reapportionment cases, with their standard of one person, one vote, citizens of Roane County, West Virginia, challenged a state law requiring approval in a referendum of 60 percent of county voters to increase tax rates or incur bonded indebtedness beyond the limits set in the state constitution. The state supreme court held

the requirement invalid under such decisions as Gray v. Sanders, 372 U.S. 368 (1963), invalidating Georgia's county-unit system under which Democratic primary elections were determined by county-unit rather than popular majority. The Supreme Court reversed, holding that since the extraordinary majority requirement did not discriminate against any definable group on geographic or racial lines it was not forbidden by the principles of the apportionment cases. Gordon v. Lance, 403 U.S. 1 (1971). Justices Brennan and Marshall dissented.

5. Multimember districts. In Whitcomb v. Chavis, 403 U.S. 124 (1971), a three-judge district court had ruled that an Indiana legislative apportionment plan making one multimember district of Marion County caused the underrepresentation of a black ghetto area within the county. This area had 17.8 percent of the county's population but from 1960 to 1968 had been the residence of only 4.75 percent of the county's senators and 5.97 percent of its representatives. The district court ordered redistricting into single-member units, requiring as a consequence redistricting throughout the state. On appeal, the Supreme Court reversed. The Court observed that the multimember plan had not been adopted for purposes of racial discrimination, that there were multimember districts elsewhere in the state, and that it would be an impossible task to subject to judicial scrutiny the responsiveness of representatives to various segments of their constituencies. Justices Douglas, Brennan and Marshall dissented.

However, in White v. Regester, supra, the Court unanimously upheld the disestablishment of two multimember districts in a Texas legislative districting plan. The Court held that plaintiffs had met the test of showing not merely that a racial group within the multimember district had not received legislative seats in proportion to its population but "the political processes leading to nomination and election were not equally open to participation by the group in question." Regarding a multimember district in Dallas County alleged to discriminate against black voters, the Court pointed to the use of electoral rules which enhanced the ability of a simple majority to control all seats, the history of official racial discrimination in Texas, the very low proportion of blacks among county officeholders since Reconstruction, and the recent use of "racial campaign tactics" by Democratic candidates. Regarding a multimember district in Bexar County alleged to discriminate against Mexican-American voters, the Court noted a pattern of pervasive and continuing social and economic discrimination against Mexican-Americans, the cultural and language barriers to Mexican-American participation in politics, and the history of official discrimination against them.

Imposition of multimember districts by federal courts fashioning relief in reapportionment cases has been strongly disfavored by the Supreme Court, in distinction to multimember districting initiated by state legislatures. See Chapman v. Meier, supra; Connor v. Johnson, 402 U.S. 690 (1971). Compare Mahan v. Howell, supra, upholding imposition of multimember district as an interim measure.

South Carolina v. Katzenbach 383 U.S. 301, 86 S. Ct. 803, 15 L. Ed. 2d 769 (1966)

MR. CHIEF JUSTICE WARREN delivered the opinion of the Court.

By leave of the Court, 382 U.S. 898, South Carolina has filed a bill of complaint, seeking a declaration that selected provisions of the Voting Rights Act of 1965 violate the Federal Constitution, and asking for an injunction against enforcement of these provisions by the Attorney General. Original jurisdiction is founded on the presence of a controversy between a state and a citizen of another State under Art. III, §2, of the Constitution. . . .

The Voting Rights Act of 1965 reflects Congress' firm intention to rid the country of racial discrimination in voting. The heart of the Act is a complex scheme of stringent remedies aimed at areas where voting discrimination has been most flagrant. Section 4(a)-(d) lays down a formula defining the States and political subdivisions to which these new remedies apply. The first of the remedies, contained in §4(a), is the suspension of literacy tests and similar voting qualifications for a period of five years from the last occurrence of substantial voting discrimination. Section 5 prescribes a second remedy, the suspension of all new voting regulations pending review by federal authorities to determine whether their use would perpetuate voting discrimination. The third remedy, covered in §§6(b), 7, 9, and 13(a), is the assignment of federal examiners by the Attorney General to list qualified applicants who are thereafter entitled to vote in all elections.

Other provisions of the Act prescribe subsidiary cures for persistent voting discrimination. Section 8 authorizes the appointment of federal poll-watchers in places to which federal examiners have already been assigned. Section 10(d) excuses those made eligible to vote in sections of the country covered by §4(b) of the Act from paying accumulated past poll taxes for state and local elections. Section 12(e) provides for balloting by persons denied access to the polls in areas where federal examiners have been appointed.

The remaining remedial portions of the Act are aimed at voting discrimination in any area of the country where it may occur. Section 2 broadly prohibits the use of voting rules to abridge exercise of the franchise on racial grounds. Sections 3, 6(a), and 13(b) strengthen existing procedures for attacking voting discrimination by means of litigation. Section 4(e) excuses citizens educated in American schools conducted in a foreign language from passing English-language literacy tests. Section 10(a)-(c) facilitates constitutional litigation challenging the imposition of all poll taxes for state and local elections. Sections 11 and 12(a)-(d) authorize civil and criminal sanctions against interference with the exercise of rights guaranteed by the Act. . . .

These provisions of the Voting Rights Act of 1965 are challenged on the fundamental ground that they exceed the powers of Congress and encroach on an area reserved to the States by the Constitution. South Carolina and certain of the amici curiae also attack specific sections of the Act for more particular reasons. They argue that the coverage formula prescribed in §4(a)-(d) violates the principle of the equality of States, denies due process by employing an invalid presumption and by barring judicial review of administrative findings, constitutes a forbidden bill of attainder, and impairs the separation of powers by adjudicating guilt through legislation. They claim that the review of new voting rules required in §5 infringes Article III by directing the District Court to issue advisory opinions. They contend that the assignment of federal examiners authorized in §6(b) abridges due process by precluding judicial review of administrative findings and impairs the separation of powers by giving the Attorney General judicial functions; also that the challenge procedure prescribed in §9 denies due process on account of its speed. Finally, South Carolina and certain of the amici curiae maintain that §§4(a) and 5, buttressed by §14(b) of the Act, abridge due process by limiting litigation to a distant forum.

Some of these contentions may be dismissed at the outset. The word "person" in the context of the Due Process Clause of the Fifth Amendment cannot, by any reasonable mode of interpretation, be expanded to encompass the States of the Union, and to our knowledge no court has ever done so. See International Shoe Co. v. Cocreham, 246 La. 244, 266, n.5; cf. United States v. City of Jackson, 318 F.2d 1, 8 (C.A. 5th Cir.). Likewise, courts have consistently regarded the Bill of Attainder Clause of Article I and the principle of the separation of powers only as protections for individual persons and private groups, those who are peculiarly vulnerable to non-judicial determinations of guilt. . . . Nor does a State have standing as the parent of its citizens to invoke these constitutional provisions against the Federal Government, the ultimate parens patriae of every American citizen. Com. of Massachusetts v. Mellon, 262 U.S. 447, 485-486; State of Florida v. Mellon, 273 U.S. 12, 18. The objections to the Act which are raised under these provisions may therefore be considered only as additional aspects of the basic question presented by the case: Has Congress exercised its powers under the Fifteenth Amendment in an appropriate manner with relation to the States?

The ground rules for resolving this question are clear. The language and purpose of the Fifteenth Amendment, the prior decisions construing its several provisions, and the general doctrines of constitutional interpretation, all point to one fundamental principle. As against the reserved powers of the States, Congress may use any rational means to effectuate the constitutional prohibition of racial discrimination in voting. . . .

Section 1 of the Fifteenth Amendment declares that "the right of citizens of the United States to vote shall not be denied or abridged by the United States or by any State on account of race, color, or previous condition of servitude." This declaration has always been treated as self-executing and has repeatedly been construed, without further legislative specification, to invalidate state voting qualifications or procedures which are discriminatory on their face or in practice. . . .

South Carolina contends that the cases cited above are precedents only for the authority of the judiciary to strike down state statutes and procedures — that to allow an exercise of this authority by Congress would be to rob the courts of their rightful constitutional role. On the contrary, §2 of the Fifteenth Amendment expressly declares that "Congress shall have the power to enforce this article by appropriate legislation." By adding this authorization, the Framers indicated that Congress was to be chiefly responsible for implementing the rights created in §1. "It is the power of Congress which has been enlarged. Congress is authorized to *enforce* the prohibitions by appropriate legislation. Some legislation is contemplated to make the [Civil War] amendments fully effective." Ex parte Virginia, 100 U.S. 339, 345. Accordingly, in addition to the courts, Congress has full remedial powers to effectuate the constitutional prohibition against racial discrimination in voting. . . .

The basic test to be applied in a case involving §2 of the Fifteenth Amendment is the same as in all cases concerning the express powers of Congress with relation to the reserved powers of the States. Chief Justice Marshall laid down the classic formulation, 50 years before the Fifteenth Amendment was ratified: "Let the end be legitimate, let it be within the scope of the constitution, and all means which are appropriate, which are plainly adapted to that end, which are not prohibited, but consist with the letter and spirit of the constitution, are constitutional." McCulloch v. Maryland, 4 Wheat. 316, 421. . . .

COVERAGE FORMULA

We now consider the related question of whether the specific States and political subdivisions within §4(b) of the Act were an appropriate target for the new remedies. South Carolina contends that the coverage formula is awkwardly designed in a number of respects and that it disregards various local conditions which have nothing to do with racial discrimination. These arguments, however, are largely beside the point. Congress began work with reliable evidence of actual voting discrimination in a great majority of the States and political subdivisions affected by the new remedies of the Act. The formula eventually evolved to describe these areas was relevant to the problem of voting discrimination, and Congress was therefore entitled to infer a significant danger of the evil in the few remaining States and political subdivisions covered by §4(b) of the Act. No more was required to justify the application to these areas of Congress' express powers under the Fifteenth Amendment. . . .

To be specific, the new remedies of the Act are imposed on three States — Alabama, Louisiana, and Mississippi — in which federal courts have repeatedly found substantial voting discrimination. Section 4(b) of the Act also embraces two other States — Georgia and South Carolina — plus large portions of a third State — North Carolina — for which there was more fragmentary evidence of recent voting discrimination mainly adduced by the Justice Department and the Civil Rights Commission. All of these areas were appropriately subjected to the new remedies. In identifying past evils, Congress obviously may avail itself of information from any probative source. . . .

The areas listed above, for which there was evidence of actual voting discrimination, share two characteristics incorporated by Congress into the coverage formula: the use of tests and devices for voter registration, and a voting rate in the 1964 presidential election at least 12 points below the national average. Tests and devices are relevant to voting discrimination because of their long history as a tool for perpetuating the evil; a low voting rate is pertinent for the obvious reason that widespread disenfranchisement must inevitably affect the number of actual voters. Accordingly, the coverage formula is rational in both practice and theory. It was therefore permissible to impose the new remedies on the few remaining States and political subdivisions covered by the formula, at least in the absence of proof that they have been free of substantial voting discrimination in recent years. Congress is clearly not bound by the rules relating to statutory presumptions in criminal cases when it prescribes civil remedies against other organs of government under §2 of the Fifteenth Amendment. . . .

It is irrelevant that the coverage formula excludes certain localities which do not employ voting tests and devices but for which there is evidence of voting discrimination by other means. Congress had learned that widespread and persistent discrimination in voting during recent years has typically entailed the misuse of tests and devices, and this was the evil for which the new remedies were specifically designed. At the same time, through §§3, 6(a), and 13(b) of the Act, Congress strengthened existing remedies for voting discrimination in other areas of the country. Legislation need not deal with all phases of a problem in the same way, so long as the distinctions drawn have some basis in practical experience. See Williamson v. Lee Optical Co., 348 U.S. 483, 488-489; Railway Express Agency v. People of State of New York, 336 U.S. 106. There are no States or political subdivisions exempted from coverage under §4(b) in which the record reveals recent racial discrimination involving tests and devices. This fact confirms the rationality of the formula.

Acknowledging the possibility of overbreadth, the Act provides for termination of special statutory coverage at the behest of States and political subdivisions in which the danger of substantial voting discrimination has not materialized during the preceding five years. Despite South Carolina's argument to the contrary, Congress might appropriately limit litigation under this provision to a single court in the District of Columbia, pursuant to its constitutional power under Art. III, §1, to "ordain and establish" inferior federal tribunals. . . . At the present time, contractual claims against the United States for more than $10,000 must be brought in the Court of Claims, and until 1962, the District of Columbia was the sole venue of suits against federal officers officially residing in the Nation's capital. We have discovered no suggestion that Congress exceeded constitutional bounds in imposing these limitations on litigation against the Federal Government, and the Act is no less reasonable in this respect. . . .

SUSPENSION OF TESTS

We now arrive at consideration of the specific remedies prescribed by the Act for areas included within the coverage formula. South Carolina assails the temporary suspension of existing voting qualifications, reciting the rule laid down by Lassiter v. Northampton County Bd. of Elections, 360 U.S. 45, that literacy tests and related devices are not in themselves contrary to the Fifteenth Amendment. In that very case, however, the Court went on to say, "Of course a literacy test, fair on its face, may be employed to perpetuate that discrimination which the Fifteenth Amendment was designed to uproot." Id., at 53. The record shows that in most of the States covered by the Act, including South Carolina, various tests and devices have been instituted with the purpose of disenfranchising Ne-

978   Chapter Fourteen. Privileges & Immunities; Equality; Civil Rights

groes, have been framed in such a way as to facilitate this aim, and have been administered in a discriminatory fashion for many years. Under these circumstances, the Fifteenth Amendment has clearly been violated. . . .

REVIEW OF NEW RULES

The Act suspends new voting regulations pending scrutiny by federal authorities to determine whether their use would violate the Fifteenth Amendment. This may have been an uncommon exercise of congressional power, as South Carolina contends, but the Court has recognized that exceptional conditions can justify legislative measures not otherwise appropriate. See Home Bldg. & Loan Ass'n v. Blaisdell, 290 U.S. 398; Wilson v. New, 243 U.S. 332. Congress knew that some of the States covered by §4(b) of the Act had resorted to the extraordinary stratagem of contriving new rules of various kinds for the sole purpose of perpetuating voting discrimination in the face of adverse federal decrees. Congress had reason to suppose that these States might try similar maneuvers in the future, in order to evade the remedies for voting discrimination contained in the Act itself. Under the compulsion of these unique circumstances, Congress responded in a permissibly decisive manner. . . .

For reasons already stated, there was nothing inappropriate about limiting litigation under this provision to the District Court for the District of Columbia, and in putting the burden of proof on the areas seeking relief. Nor has Congress authorized the District Court to issue advisory opinions, in violation of the principles of Article III invoked by Georgia as amicus curiae. The Act automatically suspends the operation of voting regulations enacted after November 1, 1964, and furnishes mechanisms for enforcing the suspension. A State or political subdivision wishing to make use of a recent amendment to its voting laws therefore has a concrete and immediate "controversy" with the Federal Government. . . . An appropriate remedy is a judicial determination that continued suspension of the new rule is unnecessary to vindicate rights guaranteed by the Fifteenth Amendment.

FEDERAL EXAMINERS

The Act authorizes the appointment of federal examiners to list qualified applicants who are thereafter entitled to vote, subject to an expeditious challenge procedure. This was clearly an appropriate response to the problem, closely related to remedies authorized in prior cases. See Alabama v. United States, supra; United States v. Thomas, 362 U.S. 58. In many of the political subdivisions covered by §4(b) of the Act, voting officials have persistently employed a variety of procedural tactics to deny Negroes the franchise, often in direct defiance or evasion of federal decrees. Congress realized that merely to suspend voting rules which have been misused or are subject to misuse might leave this localized evil undisturbed. As for the briskness of the challenge procedure, Congress knew that in some of the areas affected, challenges had been persistently employed to harass registered Negroes. It chose to forestall this abuse, at the same time providing alternative ways for removing persons listed through error or fraud. In addition to the judicial challenge procedure, §7(d) allows for the removal of names by the examiner himself, and §11(c) makes it a crime to obtain a listing through fraud. . . .

After enduring nearly a century of widespread resistance to the Fifteenth Amendment, Congress has marshalled an array of potent weapons against the evil, with authority in the Attorney General to employ them effectively. Many of the areas directly affected by this development have indicated their willingness to abide by any restraints legitimately imposed upon them. We here hold that the portions of the Voting Rights Act properly before us are a valid means for carrying out the commands of the Fifteenth Amendment. Hopefully, millions of non-white Americans will now be able to participate for the first time on an equal basis in the government under which they live. We may finally look forward to the day when truly "the right of citizens of the United States to vote shall not be denied or abridged by the United States or by any State on account of race, color, or previous condition of servitude."

The bill of complaint is dismissed.

Bill dismissed.

MR. JUSTICE BLACK, concurring and dissenting.

I agree with substantially all of the Court's opinion sustaining the power of Congress under §2 of the Fifteenth Amendment to suspend state literacy tests and similar voting qualifications and to authorize the Attorney General to appoint federal examiners to register qualified voters in various sections of the country. . . .

Though, as I have said, I agree with most of the Court's conclusions, I dissent from its holding that every part of §5 of the Act is constitutional. Section 4(a), to which §5 is linked, suspends for five years all literacy tests and similar devices in those States coming within the formula of §4(b). Section 5 goes on to provide that a State covered by §4(b) can in no way amend its constitution or laws relating to voting without first trying to persuade the Attorney General of the United States or the Federal District Court for the District of Columbia that the new proposed laws do not have the purpose and will not have the effect of denying the right to vote to citizens on account of their race or color. I think this section is unconstitutional on at least two grounds.

(a) The Constitution gives federal courts jurisdiction over cases and controversies only. If it can be said that any case or controversy arises under this section which gives the District Court for the District of Columbia jurisdiction to approve or reject state laws or constitutional amendments, then the case or controversy must be between a State and the United States Government. But it is hard for me to believe that a justiciable controversy can arise in the constitutional sense from a desire by the United States Government or some of its officials to determine in advance what legislative provisions a State may enact or what constitutional amendments it may adopt. If this dispute between the Federal Government and the States amounts to a case or controversy it is a far cry from the traditional constitutional notion of a case or controversy as a dispute over the meaning of enforceable laws or the manner in which they are applied. And if by this section Congress has created a case or controversy, and I do not believe it has, then it seems to me that the most appropriate judicial forum for settling these important questions is this Court acting under its original Art. III, §2, jurisdiction to try cases in which a State is a party. At least a trial in this Court would treat the States with dignity to which they should be entitled as constituent members of our Federal Union.

(b) My second and more basic objection to §5 is that Congress has here exercised its power under §2 of the Fifteenth Amendment through the adoption of means that conflict with the most basic principles of the Constitution. . . . Certainly if all the provisions of our Constitution which limit the power of the Federal Government and reserve other power to the States are to mean anything, they mean at least that the States have power to pass laws and amend their constitutions without first sending their officials hundreds of miles away to beg federal authorities to approve them. . . .

I see no reason to read into the Constitution meanings it did not have when it was adopted and which have not been put into it since. The proceedings of the original Constitutional Convention show beyond all doubt that the power to veto or negative state laws was denied Congress. On several occasions proposals were submitted to the convention to grant this power to Congress. These proposals were debated extensively and on every occasion when submitted for vote they were overwhelmingly rejected. The refusal to give Congress this extraordinary power to veto state laws was based on the belief that if such power resided in Congress the States would be helpless to function as effective governments. Since that time neither the Fifteenth Amendment nor any other Amendment to the Constitution has given the slightest indication of a purpose to grant Congress the power to veto state laws either by itself or its agents. Nor does any provision in the Constitution endow the federal courts with power to participate with state legislative bodies in determining what state policies shall be enacted into law. The judicial power to invalidate a law in a case or controversy after the law has become effective is a long way from the power to prevent a State from passing a law. I cannot agree with the Court that Congress — denied a power in itself to veto a state law — can delegate this same power to the Attorney General or the District Court for the District of Columbia. For the effect on the States is the same in both cases — they cannot pass their laws without sending their agents to the City of Washington to plead to federal officials for their advance approval. . . .

NOTE Section 5 of the Voting Rights Act

Section 5 of the Voting Rights Act, 79 Stat. 439, 42 U.S.C. §1973c (1964 ed. Supp. V), provides that whenever a state or political subdivision covered by the act seeks to change "any voting qualification or prerequisite to voting, or standard, practice, or procedure with respect to voting . . . no person shall be denied the right to vote for failure to comply with such qualification, prerequisite, standard, practice, or procedure" unless the state or political subdivision obtains prior approval from the Attorney General or the district court in Washington. The district court is to grant its approval if the state or political subdivision shows that the change "does not have the purpose and will not have the effect of denying or abridging the right to vote on account of race or color."

The Supreme Court has read § 5 to cover such new actions as a change from district to at-large elections, Allen v. State Board of Elections, 393 U.S. 544 (1969), or as a change in boundary lines through annexation, Perkins v. Matthews, 400 U.S. 379 (1971). Underpinning this construction of § 5 is the Court's understanding that "[t]he right to vote can be affected by a dilution of voting power as well as by an absolute prohibition on casting a ballot. See Reynolds v. Sims, 377 U.S. 533, 555 (1964)." Allen v. State Board of Elections, supra, at 569. See also, it might have added, Gomillion v. Lightfoot, page 953 supra.

One can readily imagine, however, how a court would be reluctant to prevent cities from annexing surrounding suburbs since the results are usually quite benevolent: a sounder tax base for the city, the possibility of greater integration in the schools, and so on. But if the annexed area has a higher percentage of white voters than the city, as is often true for suburban additions, and if there is a history of racial bloc voting in the region, as may also be true in the states covered by the act, the effect of the annexation may often be to dilute and thus abridge the voting power of the black city residents. The Voting Rights Act, as quoted above, requires that any change have neither the purpose nor the effect of abridging the right to vote on account of race. Thus, even if annexation is undertaken for racially neutral reasons, the statute might seem to bar such annexations that dilute the voting power of black city residents.

In 1970 the city of Richmond annexed an adjacent area in Chesterfield County, which reduced the proportion of blacks in the city from 52 percent to 42 percent. Furthermore, the district court concluded, the annexation was prompted by an invidious racial purpose with no "legitimate purpose" for the change otherwise. On direct review, City of Richmond v. United States, 422 U.S. 358 (1975), the Court refused to prevent the annexation. Instead, by a vote of 5 to 3, with Justice Powell not participating, the Court remanded for further proceedings on whether there "are now demonstrable reasons in support of the annexation." In doubting that the record below was fully complete, Justice White, for the Court, quoted from the special state annexation court that had earlier approved the annexation: " 'Obviously cities must in some manner be permitted to grow in territory and population or they will face disastrous economic and social problems.' "

Justice White acknowledged that "[i]t is true that the black community, if there is bloc racial voting, will command fewer seats on the city council." But, the Court held, as long as the city electoral system "fairly reflects the strength of the Negro community as it exists after the annexation," then their voting rights are not "undervalued" and hence not abridged. For to forbid all such annexations, he argued, could not have been the consequence Congress intended. Justice Brennan dissented, joined by Justices Douglas and Marshall. The majority's reliance on "postelection fairness," he charged, was "inconsistent with what I take to be the fundamental objective of §5, namely, the protection of *present* levels of voting effectiveness for the black population." If there should be a "municipal hardship" exception for some annexations, he said, Congress should fashion it, not the courts.

Should it make a difference that the "dilution" of black voting power here took away majority control? Should it make a difference that the Attorney General, without the limit of standards under the act, may grant §5 approval to annexations? Is the substantive review of an annexation in the district court now any different under §5 than it would be under the Fifteenth Amendment?

Harper v. Virginia Board of Elections 383 U.S. 663, 86 S. Ct. 1079, 16 L. Ed. 2d 169 (1966)

MR. JUSTICE DOUGLAS delivered the opinion of the Court.

These are suits by Virginia residents to have declared unconstitutional Virginia's poll tax.[1] The three-judge District Court, feeling bound by our decision in Breedlove v. Suttles, 302 U.S. 277, dismissed the complaint. See 240 F. Supp. 270. The cases came here on appeal and we noted probable jurisdiction. 380 U.S. 930.

While the right to vote in federal elections is conferred by Art. I, §2, of the Constitution (United States v. Classic, 313 U.S. 299, 314-315), the right to vote in state elections is nowhere expressly mentioned. It is argued that the right to vote in state elections is implicit, particularly by reason of the First Amendment and that it may not constitutionally be conditioned upon the payment of a tax or fee. Cf. Murdock v. Commonwealth of Pennsylvania, 319 U.S. 105, 113. We do not stop to canvass the relation between voting and political expression. For it is enough to say that once the franchise is granted to the electorate, lines may not be drawn which are inconsistent with the Equal Protection Clause of the Fourteenth Amendment. That is to say, the right of suffrage "is subject to the imposition of state standards which are not discriminatory and which do not contravene any restriction that Congress, acting pursuant to its constitutional powers, has imposed." Lassiter v. Northampton County Board of Elections, 360 U.S. 45, 51. We were speaking there of a state literacy test which we sustained, warning that the result would be different if a literacy test, fair on its face, were used to discriminate against a class. Id., at 53. But the Lassiter case does not govern the result here, because, unlike a poll tax, the

---

[1] Section 173 of Virginia's Constitution directs the General Assembly to levy an annual poll tax not exceeding $1.50 on every resident of the State 21 years of age and over (with exceptions not relevant here). One dollar of the tax is to be used by state officials "exclusively in aid of the public free schools" and the remainder is to be returned to the counties for general purposes. Section 18 of the Constitution includes payment of poll taxes as a precondition for voting. Section 20 provides that a person must "personally" pay all state poll taxes for the three years preceding the year in which he applies for registration. By §21 the poll tax must be paid at least six months prior to the election in which the voter seeks to vote. Since the time for election of state officials varies (24 Va. Code §§136, 160-168; id., at §22), the six months' deadline will vary, election from election. The poll tax is often assessed along with the personal property tax. Those who do not pay a personal property tax are not assessed for a poll tax, it being their responsibility to take the initiative and request to be assessed. 58 Va. Code §1163. Enforcement of poll taxes takes the form of disenfranchisement of those who do not pay, §22 of the Virginia Constitution providing that collection of delinquent poll taxes for a particular year may not be enforced by legal proceedings until the tax for that year has become three years delinquent.

"ability to read and write . . . has some relation to standards designed to promote intelligent use of the ballot." Id., at 51.

We conclude that a State violates the Equal Protection Clause of the Fourteenth Amendment whenever it makes the affluence of the voter or payment of any fee an electoral standard. Voter qualifications have no relation to wealth nor to paying or not paying this or any other tax. Our cases demonstrate that the Equal Protection Clause of the Fourteenth Amendment restrains the States from fixing voter qualifications which invidiously discriminate. . . .

Long ago in Yick Wo v. Hopkins, 118 U.S. 356, 370, the Court referred to "the political franchise of voting" as a "fundamental political right, because preservative of all rights." Recently in Reynolds v. Sims, 377 U.S. 533, 561-562, we said, "Undoubtedly, the right of suffrage is a fundamental matter in a free and democratic society. Especially since the right to exercise the franchise in a free and unimpaired manner is preservative of other basic civil and political rights, any alleged infringement of the right of citizens to vote must be carefully and meticulously scrutinized." There we were considering charges that voters in one part of the State had greater representation per person in the State Legislature than voters in another part of the State. . . .

We say the same whether the citizen, otherwise qualified to vote, has $1.50 in his pocket or nothing at all, pays the fee or fails to pay it. The principle that denies the State the right to dilute a citizen's vote on account of his economic status or other such factors by analogy bars a system which excludes those unable to pay a fee to vote or who fail to pay.

It is argued that a State may exact fees from citizens for many different kinds of licenses; that if it can demand from all an equal fee for a driver's license, it can demand from all an equal poll tax by voting. But we must remember that the interest of the State, when it comes to voting, is limited to the power to fix qualifications. Wealth, like race, creed, or color, is not germane to one's ability to participate intelligently in the electoral process. Lines drawn on the basis of wealth or property, like those of race (Korematsu v. United States, 323 U.S. 214, 216), are traditionally disfavored. See Edwards v. People of State of California, 314 U.S. 160, 184-185 (Jackson, J., concurring); Griffin v. People of State of Illinois, 351 U.S. 12, Douglas v. People of State of California, 372 U.S. 353. To introduce wealth or payment of a fee as a measure of a voter's qualifications is to introduce a capricious or irrelevant factor. The degree of the discrimination is irrelevant. . . .

We agree, of course, with Mr. Justice Holmes that the Due Process Clause of the Fourteenth Amendment "does not enact Mr. Herbert Spencer's Social Statics" (Lochner v. People of State of New York, 198 U.S. 45, 75). Likewise, the Equal Protection Clause is not shackled to the political theory of a particular era. In determining what lines are unconstitutionally discriminatory, we have never been confined to historic notions of equality, any more than we have restricted due process to a fixed catalogue of what was at a given time deemed to be the limits of fundamental rights. See Malloy v. Hogan, 378 U.S. 1, 5-6. Notions of what constitutes equal treatment for purposes of the Equal Protection Clause *do* change. This Court in 1896 held that laws providing for separate public facilities for white and Negro citizens did not deprive the latter of the equal protection and treatment that the Fourteenth Amendment commands. Plessy v. Ferguson, 163 U.S. 537. Seven of the eight Justices then sitting subscribed to the Court's opinion, thus joining in expressions of what constituted unequal and discriminatory treatment that sound strange to a contemporary ear. When, in 1954 — more than a half-century later — we repudiated the "separate-but-equal doctrine" of Plessy as respects public education we stated, "In approaching this problem, we cannot turn the clock back to 1868 when the Amendment was adopted or even to 1896 when Plessy v. Ferguson was written." Brown v. Board of Education, 347 U.S. 483, 492.

In a recent searching re-examination of the Equal Protection Clause, we held, as already noted, that "the opportunity for equal participation by all voters in the election of state legislators" is required. Reynolds v. Sims, supra, 377 U.S. at 566. We decline to qualify that principle by sustaining this poll tax. Our conclusion, like that in Reynolds v. Sims, is founded not on what we think governmental policy should be, but on what the Equal Protection Clause requires. . . .

Those principles apply here. For to repeat, wealth or fee paying has, in our view, no relation to voting qualifications; the right to vote is too precious, too fundamental to be so burdened or conditioned.

Reversed.

MR. JUSTICE BLACK, dissenting.

In Breedlove v. Suttles, 302 U.S. 277, decided December 6, 1937, a few weeks after I took my seat as a member of this Court, we unanimously upheld the right of the State of Georgia to make payment of its poll tax a prerequisite to voting in state elections. We rejected at that time contentions that the state law violated the Equal Protection Clause of the Fourteenth Amendment because it put an unequal burden on different groups of people according to their age, sex, and ability to pay. . . .

(1) I think the interpretation that this Court gave the Equal Protection Clause in Breedlove was correct. The mere fact that a law results in treating some groups differently from others does not, of course, automatically amount to a violation of the Equal Protection Clause. To bar a State from drawing any distinctions in the application of its laws would practically paralyze the regulatory power of legislative bodies. . . . Voting laws are no exception to this principle. All voting laws treat some persons differently from others in some respects. Some bar a person from voting who is under 21 years of age; others bar those under 18. Some bar convicted felons or the insane, and some have attached a freehold or other property qualification for voting. The Breedlove case upheld a poll tax which was imposed on men but not equally imposed on women and minors, and the Court today does not overrule that part of Breedlove which approved those discriminatory provisions. And in Lassiter v. Northampton Election Board, 360 U.S. 45, this court held that state laws which disqualified the illiterate from voting did not violate the Equal Protection Clause. From these cases and all the others decided by this Court interpreting the Equal Protection Clause it is clear that some discriminatory voting qualifications can be imposed without violating the Equal Protection Clause. . . .

(2) Another reason for my dissent from the Court's judgment and opinion is that it seems to be using the old "natural-law-due-process formula" to justify striking down state laws as violations of the Equal Protection Clause. I have heretofore had many occasions to express my strong belief that there is no constitutional support whatever for this Court to use the Due Process Clause as though it provided a blank check to alter the meaning of the Constitution as written so as to add to it substantive constitutional changes which a majority of the Court at any given time believes are needed to meet present-day problems. Nor is there in my opinion any more constitutional support for this Court to use the Equal Protection Clause, as it has today, to write into the Constitution its notions of what it thinks is good governmental policy. If basic changes as to the respective powers of the state and national governments are needed, I prefer to let those changes be made by amendment as Article V of the Constitution provides. For a majority of this Court to undertake that task, whether purporting to do so under the Due Process or the Equal Protection Clause amounts, in my judgment, to an exercise of power the Constitution makers with foresight and wisdom refused to give the Judicial Branch of the Government. I have in no way departed from the view I expressed in Adamson v. People of State of California [332 U.S. 46,] 90, decided June 23, 1947, that the "natural-law-due-process formula" under which courts make the Constitution mean what they think it should at a given time "has been used in the past, and can be used in the future, to license this Court, in considering regulatory legislation, to roam at large in the broad expanses of policy and morals and to trespass, all too freely, on the legislative domain of the States as well as the Federal Government."

The Court denies that it is using the "natural-law-due-process formula." It says that its invalidation of the Virginia law "is founded not on what we think governmental policy should be, but on what the Equal Protection Clause requires." I find no statement in the Court's opinion, however, which advances even a plausible argument as to why the alleged discriminations which might possibly be affected by Virginia's poll tax law are "irrational," "unreasonable," "arbitrary," or "invidious" or have no relevance to a legitimate policy which the State wishes to adopt. The Court gives no reason at all to discredit the long-standing beliefs that making the payment of a tax a prerequisite to voting is an effective way of collecting revenue and that people who pay their taxes are likely to have a far greater interest in their government. The Court's failure to give any reasons to show that these purposes of the poll tax are "irrational," "unreasonable," "arbitrary," or "invidious" is a pretty clear indication to me that none exist. I can only conclude that the primary, controlling, predominant, if not the exclusive reason for declaring the Virginia law unconstitutional is the Court's deep-seated hostility and antagonism, which I share, to making payment of a tax a prerequisite to voting. . . .[gg]

NOTE Property Qualifications for Voting in Special-Purpose Units of Government

In Avery v. Midland County, 390 U.S. 474 (1968), the Court reserved the question whether preferential voting schemes might be allowed in connection with "a special-purpose unit of government assigned the performance of functions affecting definable groups of constituents more than other constituents." A New York statute limiting the franchise in certain school board elections to owners or lessees of taxable realty and parents or guardians of children enrolled in the public schools was held invalid in Kramer v. Union Free School District No. 15, 395 U.S. 621 (1969). Writing for the Court, Chief Justice Warren ruled that the classification, as measured by "exacting scrutiny," did not achieve its stated purpose of limiting school board elections solely to those "primarily concerned" with school matters. Justices Stewart, Black, and Harlan dissented. Similarly, in Cipriano v. Houma, 395 U.S. 701 (1969), and Phoenix v. Kolodziejski, 399 U.S. 204 (1970), the Court invalidated Louisiana and Arizona statutes which permitted only real property taxpayers to vote in referenda approving the issuance of municipal bonds.

However, in Salyer Land Co. v. Tulare Lake Basin Water Storage District, 410 U.S. 719 (1973), the Court upheld, 6 to 3, a preferential voting scheme for the election of the board of directors of a California water storage district. The board was responsible for acquiring, storing, and distributing water for irrigation in the district, with incidental powers to engage in flood control activities. In elections to the board, only landowners could vote, and votes were distributed according to the assessed value of the land, one for each $100 valuation. Writing for the Court, Justice Rehnquist held that this election scheme involved the sort of "special-purpose unit" referred to in Avery. Reasoning that the popular election requirements of Reynolds v. Sims were inapplicable to such a unit, the Court evaluated the scheme under the test of minimum rationality. It found that the election plan was reasonably aimed at securing landowner cooperation with the district and that the apportionment of votes according to land value reasonably reflected the assessment of district project costs against landowners. In Associated Enterprises, Inc. v. Toltec Watershed Improvement District, 410 U.S. 743 (1973), decided the same day, the Court upheld a Wyoming statute which provided that only landowners could vote in referenda on the establishment of watershed districts. For comment on the Salyer case, see The Supreme Court, 1972 Term, 87 Harv. L. Rev. 1, 94-105 (1973).

May a state require a person to list some item of property, real or personal, even though

---

[gg] A dissenting opinion by Harlan, J., in which Stewart, J., concurred is omitted. — ED.

of only nominal worth, on the tax rolls prior to voting in city bond elections? Relying on Phoenix v. Kolodziejski, supra, the Court in Hill v. Stone, 421 U.S. 289 (1975), considered a city election on bonds for library construction not to be "of special interest to a particular, well-defined portion of the electorate" and held that the listing or "rendering" requirement served no compelling state interest. Justice Rehnquist, in dissent, joined by the Chief Justice and Justice Stewart, argued that strict scrutiny was inappropriate because "The burden imposed by the qualification was de minimis and compliance was universally easy." Writing for the Court, Justice Marshall said "If anyone can become eligible to vote by rendering property of even negligible value, the rendering requirement can hardly be said to select voters according to the magnitude of their prospective liability for the city's indebtedness."

NOTE Restrictions on Ballot Access

1. Access requirements for third parties and independent candidates. In Williams v. Rhodes, 393 U.S. 23 (1968), the Supreme Court struck down as violative of equal protection the Ohio election laws which "made it virtually impossible for a new political party, even though it has hundreds of thousands of members, or an old party, which has a very small number of members, to be placed on the State ballots to choose [Presidential] electors." The Ohio laws required that a new party establish an elaborate organization and present petitions signed by qualified voters totaling 15 percent of the number of ballots cast in the last preceding gubernatorial election. Recognized parties automatically retained their position on the ballot if they had obtained at least 10 percent of the votes in the last gubernatorial election. In addition, Ohio law did not provide space on the ballot for independent or write-in candidates. For the Court, Justice Black first rejected the state's contention that Article II, §1, which provides that "Each State shall appoint, in such Manner as the Legislature thereof may direct, a Number of Electors . . . ," insulated the Ohio laws from Fourteenth Amendment attack. The Court then held that the burden placed on the rights of political association and voting was not justified by any compelling state interest. Among proffered justifications, the Court rejected arguments that the election laws were necessary to preserve a compelling interest in the two-party system or to prevent ballots from becoming so intricate that they would confuse voters. Chief Justice Warren and Justices Stewart and White dissented.

Williams v. Rhodes has been distinguished, however, in several decisions. In Jenness v. Fortson, 403 U.S. 431 (1971), the Court unanimously upheld Georgia election laws requiring an independent candidate who wished a place on the ballot to submit nominating petitions signed by not less than 5 percent of those eligible to vote at the last election for the office he is seeking. Georgia law allowed 180 days for the collection of these signatures and provided space for write-in voting. Noting that in recent elections a candidate for Governor and a candidate for President had gained ballot designation by nominating petitions, the Court ruled that the Georgia law, unlike the Ohio laws considered in Williams v. Rhodes, "in no way freezes the status quo, but implicitly recognizes the potential fluidity of American political life." Writing for the Court, Justice Stewart concluded: "There is surely an important state interest in requiring some preliminary showing of a significant modicum of support before printing the name of a political organization's candidate on the ballot — the interest, if no other, in avoiding confusion, deception, and even frustration of the democratic process at the general election." In American Party of Texas v. White, 415 U.S. 767 (1974), the Court rejected challenges brought by third parties and independent candidates against the Texas ballot access laws. These provided that a party which had failed to receive more than 2 percent of the votes for governor in the last general election could receive a place on the ballot by nominating candidates through a series of precinct conventions attended by persons numbering at least 1 percent of the votes cast for governor in the last preceding general election. If the number attending were less than that (approximately 22,000 would have been required at the time suit was brought), the third party could make up the difference by presenting signature nominating petitions. The law allowed a 55-day period for circulation of such petitions and required that persons attending the conventions or signing the petitions not have voted in that year's primary elections. In the case of independent candidates, Texas election laws required that within 30 days after the primaries candidates submit nominating petitions signed by a number of persons not less than a certain percentage of the votes cast in the relevant electoral district in the general gubernatorial election. The percentages ranged up to 5 percent, but in any event no more than 500 signatures were required. Again, to be valid, a person signing a petition could not have voted in that year's primaries. In Storer v. Brown, 415 U.S. 724 (1974), decided the same day as American Party, the Court vacated and remanded a three-judge district court decision upholding California ballot access procedures for independent candidates for presidential elector. California law allowed a 24-day period for collection of nominating petitions signed by 5 percent of the vote cast in the last preceding general election and disqualified from signing any voter who had participated in that year's primary. The Court held that it was impossible, without analysis of the actual figures involved, to determine how much of a burden these requirements placed on independent candidates. The relevant questions were how many signatures were needed to meet the 5 percent standard and how large was the pool of voters who had not participated in the primary.

2. Restrictions based on prior or conflicting party membership. In Storer v. Brown, supra, the Court upheld a California law denying ballot position to an independent candidate who voted in the immediately preceding primary election or was a registered member of an established political party at any time within the year prior to the last preceding primary. The Court held such disqualification a justified means of protecting the direct party primary method of nominating candidates for office. Similar reasoning has been held to sustain election laws disqualifying participants in primary elections from signing nominating petitions for independents. See American Party of Texas v. White, supra.

In Rosario v. Rockefeller, 410 U.S. 752 (1973), the Court upheld a New York statute requiring a voter to enroll in a party at least 30 days before a general election in order to vote in the next following primary elections, that is, 8 to 11 months prior to the date of the primary itself. The statute was held to be reasonably related to the goal of discouraging interparty raiding. Justices Powell, Douglas, Brennan, and Marshall dissented. The next term, in Kusper v. Pontikes, 414 U.S. 51 (1973), the Court overturned an Illinois statute prohibiting a person from voting in the primary election of a political party if he has voted in the primary of any other party within the preceding 23 months. The Court distinguished Rosario on the ground that the New York statute did not foreclose the possibility that a voter might vote in a different primary each year but merely set time limits according to which the voter would have to change his party affiliation. The Illinois statute, however, completely barred voters from voting in different party primaries in consecutive years.

3. Distribution of nominating signatures. In Moore v. Ogilvie, 394 U.S. 814 (1969), the Court struck down as a violation of the equal protection clause an Illinois law requiring independent candidates for presidential elector to submit petitions signed by 25,000 qualified voters, including 200 from each of 50 counties. Illinois has 102 counties, and it was alleged that 93.4 percent of the registered voters resided in the 49 most populous counties.

4. Filing fees. In Bullock v. Carter, 405 U.S. 134 (1972), the Court invalidated Texas primary filing fees amounting in some cases to as much as $8000. Although the Court distinguished the direct burden on the right to vote posed by poll taxes, see Harper v. Virginia Board of Elections, supra, and stated that candidates' filing fees were not neces-

sarily subject to strict scrutiny, it held that the Texas system was invalid as being of "patently exclusionary character." In Lubin v. Panish, 415 U.S. 709 (1974), the Court upheld a challenge brought by an indigent candidate to a California provision requiring a filing fee equal to 2 percent of the salary of the office sought. The Court held that the state's interest in assuring the integrity of elections by limiting ballot access and discouraging frivolous candidacies could be attained by less restrictive alternative means, such as submission of nominating petitions. The Court further stated that allowance of write-in votes on the ballot would not afford an acceptable alternative to having the candidate's name placed on the ballot.

5. See also Note: State Durational Residency Requirements After Shapiro v. Thompson, page 351 supra. See generally Note, Developments in the Law — Elections, 88 Harv. L. Rev. 1111 (1975).

Oregon v. Mitchell 400 U.S. 112, 91 S. Ct. 260, 27 L. Ed. 2d 272 (1970)

MR. JUSTICE BLACK, announcing the judgments of the Court in an opinion expressing his own view of the cases.

In these suits the States resist compliance with the Voting Rights Act Amendments of 1970, Pub. L. 91-285, 84 Stat. 314, because they believe that the Act takes away from them powers reserved to the States by the Constitution to control their own elections. By its terms the Act does three things. First: It lowers the minimum age of voters in both state and federal elections from 21 to 18. Second: Based upon a finding by Congress that literacy tests have been used to discriminate against voters on account of their color, the Act enforces the Fourteenth and Fifteenth Amendments by barring the use of such tests in all elections, state and national. Third: The Act forbids States from disqualifying voters in national elections for presidential and vice presidential electors because they have not met state residency requirements.

For the reasons set out in Part I of this opinion, I believe Congress can fix the age of voters in national elections, such as congressional, senatorial, Vice-Presidential and Presidential elections, but cannot set the voting age in state and local elections. For reasons expressed in separate opinions, my Brothers Douglas, Brennan, White, and Marshall join me in concluding that Congress can enfranchise 18-year-old citizens in national elections, but dissent from the judgment that Congress cannot extend the franchise to 18-year-old citizens in state and local elections. For reasons expressed in separate opinions, my Brothers The Chief Justice, Harlan, Stewart, and Blackmun join me in concluding that Congress cannot interfere with the age for voters set by the States for state and local elections. They, however, dissent from the judgment that Congress can control voter qualifications in federal elections. In summary, it is the judgment of the Court that the 18-year-old vote provisions of the Voting Rights Act Amendments of 1970 are constitutional and enforceable insofar as they pertain to federal elections and unconstitutional and unenforceable insofar as they pertain to state and local elections.

For the reasons set out in Part II of this opinion, I believe that Congress, in the exercise of its power to enforce the Fourteenth and Fifteenth Amendments, can prohibit the use of literacy tests or other devices used to discriminate against voters on account of their race in both state and federal elections. For reasons expressed in separate opinions, all of my Brethren join me in this judgment. Therefore the literacy test provisions of the Act are upheld.

For the reasons set out in Part III of this opinion, I believe Congress can set residency requirements and provide for absentee balloting in elections for presidential and vice presidential electors. For reasons expressed in separate opinions, my Brothers The Chief Justice, Douglas, Brennan, Stewart, White, Marshall, and Blackmun concur in this judgment. My Brother Harlan, for the reasons stated in his separate opinion, considers that the residency provisions of the statute are unconstitutional. Therefore the residency and absentee balloting provisions of the Act are upheld.

I

The Framers of our Constitution provided in Art. I, §2, that members of the House of Representatives should be elected by the people and that the voters for Representatives should have "the Qualifications requisite for Electors of the most numerous Branch of the State Legislature." Senators were originally to be elected by the state legislatures, but under the Seventeenth Amendment Senators are also elected by the people, and voters for Senators have the same qualifications as voters for Representatives. In the very beginning the responsibility of the States for setting the qualifications of voters in congressional elections was made subject to the power of Congress to make or alter such regulations if it deemed advisable. This was done in Art. I, §4, of the Constitution which provides: "The Times, Places and Manner of holding Elections for Senators and Representatives, shall be prescribed in each state by the legislature thereof; *but the Congress may at any time by Law make or alter such Regulations*, except as to the Place of Chusing Senators." (Emphasis supplied.)

Moreover, the power of Congress to make election regulations in national elections is augmented by the Necessary and Proper Clause. See McCulloch v. Maryland, 4 Wheat. 316 (1819). In United States v. Classic, 313 U.S. 299 (1941), where the Court upheld congressional power to regulate party primaries, Mr. Justice Stone speaking for the Court construed the interrelation of these clauses of the Constitution, stating: "While, in a loose sense, the right to vote for representatives in Congress is sometimes spoken of as a right derived from the states, . . . this statement is true only in the sense that the states are authorized by the Constitution, to legislate on the subject as provided by §2 of Art. I, to the extent that Congress has not restricted state action by the exercise of its powers to regulate elections under §4 and its more general power under Article I, §8, clause 18 of the Constitution 'to make all laws which shall be necessary and proper for carrying into execution the foregoing powers' " 313 U.S., at 315. . . .

The breadth of power granted to Congress to make or alter election regulations in national elections, including the qualifications of voters, is demonstrated by the fact that the framers of the Constitution and the state legislatures which ratified it intended to grant to Congress the power to lay out or alter the boundaries of the congressional districts. In the ratifying conventions speakers "argued that the power given Congress in Art. 1, §4, was meant to be used to vindicate the people's right to equality of representation in the House." Wesberry v. Sanders, 376 U.S. 1, 16 (1964), and that Congress would "most probably . . . lay the state off into districts." And in Colegrove v. Green, 328 U.S. 549 (1946), no Justice of this Court doubted Congress' power to rearrange the congressional districts according to population; the fight in that case revolved about the judicial power to compel redistricting.

Surely no voter *qualification* was more important to the Framers than the *geographical qualification* embodied in the concept of congressional districts. The Framers expected Congress to use this power to eradicate "rotten boroughs," and Congress has in fact used its power to prevent States from electing all Congressmen at large. There can be no doubt that the power to alter congressional district lines is vastly more significant in its effect than the power to permit 18-year-old citizens to go to the polls and vote in all federal elections.

Any doubt about the powers of Congress to regulate congressional elections, including the age and other qualifications of the voters should be dispelled by the opinion of this Court in Smiley v. Holm, 285 U.S. 355 (1932). There, Chief Justice Hughes writing for a unanimous Court discussed the scope of congressional power under §4 at some length. He said:

"The subject matter is the 'times, places and manner of holding elections for Senators and Representatives.' It cannot be doubted that these comprehensive words embrace authority to provide a complete code for congressional elections, not only as to times and places, but in relation to notices, registration, supervision of voting, protection of voters, prevention of fraud and corrupt practices, counting of votes, duties of inspectors and canvassers, and making and publication of election returns; in short, to enact the numerous requirements as to procedure and safeguards which experience shows are necessary in order to enforce the fundamental right involved. . . ."

In short, the Constitution allotted to the States the power to make laws regarding national elections, but provided that if Congress became dissatisfied with the state laws, Congress could alter them.[5] . . . It cannot be seriously contended that Congress has less power over the conduct of presidential elections than it has over congressional elections.

On the other hand, the Constitution was also intended to preserve to the States the power that even the Colonies had to establish and maintain their own separate and independent governments, except insofar as the Constitution itself commands otherwise. . . . And the Equal Protection Clause of the Fourteenth Amendment was never intended to destroy the States' power to govern themselves, making the Nineteenth and Twenty-Fourth Amendments superfluous. My Brother Brennan's opinion, if carried to its logical conclusion, would, under the guise of insuring equal protection, blot out all state power, leaving the 50 States little more than impotent figureheads. In interpreting what the Fourteenth Amendment means, the Equal Protection Clause should not be stretched to nullify the States' powers over elections which they had before the Constitution was adopted and which they have retained throughout our history.

Of course, the original design of the Founding Fathers was altered by the Civil War Amendments and various other amendments to the Constitution. The Thirteenth, Fourteenth, Fifteenth, and Nineteenth Amendments have expressly authorized Congress to "enforce" the limited prohibitions of those amendments by "appropriate legislation." The Solicitor General contends in these cases that Congress can set the age qualifications for voters in state elections under its power to enforce the Equal Protection Clause of the Fourteenth Amendment. . . .

As broad as the congressional enforcement power is, it is not unlimited. Specifically, there are at least three limitations upon Congress' power to enforce the guarantees of the Civil War Amendments. First, Congress may not by legislation repeal other provisions of the Constitution. Second, the power granted to Congress was not intended to strip the States of their power to govern themselves or to convert our national government of enumerated powers into a central government of unrestrained authority over every inch of the whole Nation. Third, Congress may only "enforce" the provisions of the amendments and may do so only by "appropriate legislation." Congress has no power under the enforcement sections to undercut the Amendments' guarantees of personal equality and freedom from discrimination, see Katzenbach v. Morgan, 384 U.S. 641, 651 n.10 (1966), or to undermine those protections of the Bill of Rights which we have held the Fourteenth Amendment made applicable to the States.

Of course, we have upheld congressional legislation under the Enforcement Clauses in

[5] My Brother Stewart has cited the debates of the Constitutional Convention to show that Oliver Ellsworth, George Mason, Madison, and Franklin successfully opposed granting Congress the power to regulate federal elections, including the qualifications of voters, in the original Constitution. I read the history of our Constitution differently. Mr. Madison, for example, explained Art. I, §4, to the Virginia ratifying convention as follows:

"[I]t was thought that the regulation of the time, place and manner, of electing Representatives, should be uniform throughout the continent. Some States might regulate the elections on the principles of equality, and others might regulate them otherwise. This diversity would be obviously unjust. . . . Should the people of any State by any means be deprived of the right of suffrage, it was judged proper that it should be remedied by the general government." 3 Elliot's Debates on the Federal Constitution 367 (1876).

And Mr. Mason, who was supposedly successful in opposing a broad grant of power to Congress to regulate federal elections, still found it necessary to support an unsuccessful Virginia proposal to curb the power of Congress under Art. I, §4. Id., at 403.

some cases where Congress has interfered with state regulation of the local electoral process. In Katzenbach v. Morgan, supra, the Court upheld a statute which outlawed New York's requirement of literacy in English as a prerequisite for voting as this requirement was applied to Puerto Ricans with certain educational qualifications. The New York statute overridden by Congress applied to all elections. And in South Carolina v. Katzenbach,[383 U.S. 301] (Mr. Justice Black dissenting on other grounds), the Court upheld the literacy test ban of the Voting Rights Act of 1965. That Act proscribed the use of the literacy test in all elections in certain areas. But division of power between state and national governments, like every provision of the Constitution, was expressly qualified by the Civil War Amendments' ban on racial discrimination. Where Congress attempts to remedy racial discrimination under its enforcement powers, its authority is enhanced by the avowed intention of the Framers of the Thirteenth, Fourteenth and Fifteenth Amendments. Cf. Harper v. Virginia Board of Elections, 383 U.S. 663, 670 (1966) (dissenting opinion of Mr. Justice Black).

In enacting the 18-year-old vote provisions of the Act now before the Court, Congress made no legislative findings that 21-year-old vote requirements were used by the States to disenfranchise voters on account of race. I seriously doubt that such a finding, if made, could be supported by substantial evidence. Since Congress has attempted to invade an area preserved to the States by the Constitution without a foundation for enforcing the Civil War Amendments' ban on racial discrimination, I would hold that Congress has exceeded its powers in attempting to lower the voting age in state and local elections. On the other hand, where Congress legislates in a domain not exclusively reserved by the Constitution to the States, its enforcement power need not be tied so closely to the goal of eliminating discrimination on account of race.

To invalidate part of the Voting Rights Act Amendments of 1970, however, does not mean that the entire Act must fall or that the constitutional part of the 18-year-old vote provision cannot be given effect. . . .

. . . In this case, it is the judgment of the Court that Title III, lowering the voting age to 18, is invalid as applied to voters in state and local elections. It is also the judgment of the Court that Title III is valid with respect to national elections. We would fail to follow the express will of Congress in interpreting its own statute if we refuse to sever these two distinct aspects of Title III. . . .

II

In Title I of the Voting Rights Act Amendments of 1970 Congress extended the provisions of the Voting Rights Act of 1965 which ban the use of literacy tests in certain States upon the finding of certain conditions by the United States Attorney General. The Court upheld the provisions of the 1965 Act over my partial dissent in South Carolina v. Katzenbach, supra, and Gaston County v. United States, 395 U.S. 285 (1969). The constitutionality of Title I is not raised by any of the parties to these suits.

In Title II of the Amendments Congress prohibited the use of any test or device resembling a literacy test in any national, state, or local election in any area of the United States where such a test is not already proscribed by the Voting Rights Act of 1965. The State of Arizona maintains that Title II cannot be enforced to the extent that it is inconsistent with Arizona's literacy test requirement. Ariz. Rev. Stat. Ann. §§ 16-101.A.4, 16-101.A.5 (1956). I would hold that the literacy test ban of the 1970 Amendments is constitutional under the Enforcement Clause of the Fifteenth Amendment and that it supersedes Arizona's conflicting statutes under the Supremacy Clause of the Federal Constitution.

In enacting the literacy test ban of Title II Congress had before it a long history of the discriminatory use of literacy tests to disfranchise voters on account of their race. Congress could have found that as late as the summer of 1968, the percentage registration of nonwhite voters in seven Southern States was substantially below the percentage registration of white voters. Moreover, Congress had before it striking evidence to show that the provisions of the 1965 Act had in the span of four years had a remarkable impact on minority group voter registration. . . .

. . . And as to the Nation as a whole, Congress had before it statistics which demonstrate that voter registration and voter participation are consistently greater in States without literacy tests.

Congress also had before it this country's history of discriminatory educational opportunities in both the North and the South. The children who were denied an equivalent education by the "separate but equal" rule of Plessy v. Ferguson, 163 U.S. 537 (1896), overruled in Brown v. Board of Education, 347 U.S. 483 (1954), are now old enough to vote. There is substantial, if not overwhelming, evidence from which Congress could have concluded that it is a denial of equal protection to condition the political participation of children educated in a dual school system upon their educational achievement. Moreover, the history of this legislation suggests that concern with educational inequality was perhaps uppermost in the minds of the congressmen who sponsored the Act. The hearings are filled with references to educational inequality. Faced with this and other evidence that literacy tests reduce voter participation in a discriminatory manner not only in the South but throughout the Nation, Congress was supported by substantial evidence in concluding that a nationwide ban on literacy tests was appropriate to enforce the Civil War Amendments.

Finally, there is yet another reason for upholding the literacy test provisions of this Act. In imposing a nationwide ban on literacy tests, Congress has recognized a national problem for what it is — a serious national dilemma that touches every corner of our Land. In this legislation Congress has recognized that discrimination on account of color and racial origin is not confined to the South, but exists in various parts of the country. Congress has decided that the way to solve the problems of racial discrimination is to deal with nationwide discrimination with nationwide legislation. . . .

III

In Title II of the Voting Rights Act Amendments Congress also provided that in presidential and vice presidential elections, no voter could be denied his right to cast a ballot because he had not lived in the jurisdiction long enough to meet its residency requirements. Furthermore, Congress provided uniform national rules for absentee voting in presidential and vice presidential elections. In enacting these regulations for national elections Congress was attempting to insure a fully effective voice to all citizens in national elections. What I said in Part I of this opinion applies with equal force here. Acting under its broad authority to create and maintain a national government, Congress unquestionably has power under the Constitution to regulate federal elections. The Framers of our Constitution were vitally concerned with setting up a national government that could survive. Essential to the survival and to the growth of our national government is its power to fill its elective offices and to insure that the officials who fill those offices are as responsive as possible to the will of the people whom they represent.

Our judgment today gives the Federal Government the powers the Framers conferred upon it, that is, the final control of the elections of its own officers. Our judgment also saves for the States the power to control state and local elections which the Constitution originally reserved to them and which no subsequent amendment has taken from them. The generalities of the Equal Protection Clause of the Fourteenth Amendment were not designed or adopted to render the States impotent to set voter qualifications in elections for their own local officials and agents in the absence of some specific constitutional limitations.

[MR. JUSTICE HARLAN alone took the position, on the basis of his examination of the legislative history of the adoption of the equal protection clause, that it does not apply to political interests, such as the suffrage. His opinion concludes:

"In conclusion I add the following. The consideration that has troubled me most in deciding that the 18-year-old and residency provisions of this legislation should be held unconstitutional is whether I ought to regard the doctrine of stare decisis as preventing me from arriving at that result. For as I indicated at the outset of this opinion, were I to continue to consider myself constricted by recent past decisions holding that the Equal Protection Clause of the Fourteenth Amendment reaches state electoral processes, I would . . . be led to cast my vote with those of my Brethren who are of the opinion that the lowering of the voting age and the abolition of state residency requirements in presidential elections are within the ordinary legislative power of Congress.

"After much reflection I have reached the conclusion that I ought not to allow stare decisis to stand in the way of casting my vote in accordance with what I am deeply convinced the Constitution demands. In the annals of this Court few developments in the march of events have so imperatively called upon us to take a fresh hard look at past decisions, which could well be mustered in support of such developments, than do the legislative lowering of the voting age and, albeit to a lesser extent, the elimination of state residential requirements in presidential elections. Concluding, as I have, that such decisions cannot withstand constitutional scrutiny, I think it is my duty to depart from them, rather than to lend my support to perpetuating their constitutional error in the name of stare decisis.

"In taking this position, I feel fortified by the evident malaise among the members of the Court with those decisions. Despite them, a majority of the Court holds that this congressional attempt to lower the voting age by simple legislation is unconstitutional, insofar as it relates to state elections. Despite them, four members of the Court take the same view of this legislation with respect to federal elections as well; and the fifth member of the Court who considers the legislation constitutionally infirm as regards state elections relies not at all on any of those decisions in reaching the opposite conclusion in federal elections. And of the eight members of the Court who vote to uphold the residential provision of the statute, only four appear to rely upon any of those decisions in reaching that result.

"In these circumstances I am satisfied that I am free to decide these cases unshackled from a line of decisions which I have felt from the start entailed a basic departure from sound constitutional principle."]

Chapter Fifteen Constitutional Requirements of Fair Procedure

Section A. THE BILL OF RIGHTS AND THE MEANING OF PROCEDURAL DUE PROCESS

"The history of liberty has largely been the history of observance of procedural safeguards."[a]

"If . . . it were possible to define what it is for a State to deprive a person of life, liberty or property without due process of law, in terms which would cover every exercise of power thus forbidden to the State, and exclude those which are not, no more useful construction could be furnished by this or any other court to any part of the fundamental law.

"But, apart from the imminent risk of a failure to give any definition which would be at once perspicuous, comprehensive and satisfactory, there is wisdom, we think, in the ascertaining of the intent and application of such an important phrase in the Federal Constitution, by the gradual process of judicial inclusion and exclusion, as the cases presented for decision shall require, with the reasoning on which such decisions may be founded. This court is, after an experience of nearly a century, still engaged in defining the obligation of contracts, the regulation of commerce, and other powers conferred on the Federal Government, or limitations imposed upon the States."[b]

NOTE Due Process in Substance and Procedure (Adamson v. California)

Judges continually seek a verbal formula, a definition of due process, which will help in making a just choice between conflicting claims in society. This search is never very successful. The variety and complexity of inconsistent human aspirations make a resolving formula which may serve in one conflict of interests almost certainly unserviceable in various others. Different elements are present in new balances of interests, and an un-

---

[a] Mr. Justice Frankfurter in McNabb v. United States, 318 U.S. 332, 347 (1943). — ED.
[b] Mr. Justice Miller in Davidson v. New Orleans, 96 U.S. 97, 104 (1877). — ED.

994   Chapter Fifteen.   Fair Procedure

deviating formula could there dictate a decision leaving the arbiter with a "sense of injustice."[c]

Such conflicting aspirations occur both in matters of procedure and in matters of substance; the difference between these two is sometimes difficult to perceive. Procedure could be described as the system arranged by government to ensure to the governed a reasonable opportunity to protest before the power of organized society is applied to the protester. Substantive decisions and rules are harder to characterize. Examples of the substantive are easy: a speed limit on a street; a statute forbidding "obscene" publications; a judgment fixing the compensation to be paid on eminent domain. Each of these involves choice between the inconsistent desires of different people. But choice of policy is similarly involved in a decision that confessions obtained during undue police detention are inadmissible in evidence. Perhaps one can most usefully characterize substance as that which is not procedural.

The quality of detachment, of disinterest, in decisional arrangements has been suggested as a cardinal element in due process. Mr. Justice Frankfurter wrote for the Supreme Court in 1959:

"Decisions under the Due Process Clause require close and perceptive inquiry into fundamental principles of our society. The Anglo-American system of law is based not upon transcendental revelation but upon the conscience of society ascertained as best it may be by a tribunal disciplined for the task and environed by the best safeguards for disinterestedness and detachment."[d]

And Professor Herbert Wechsler, in his 1959 Holmes Lecture at Harvard, said:

"I put it to you that the main constituent of the judicial process is precisely that it must be genuinely principled, resting with respect to every step that is involved in reaching judgment on analysis and reasons quite transcending the immediate result that is achieved. To be sure, the courts decide, or should decide, only the case they have before them. But must they not decide on grounds of adequate neutrality and generality, tested not only by the instant application but by others that the principles imply? Is it not the very essence of judicial method to insist upon attending to such other cases, preferably those involving an opposing interest, in evaluating any principle avowed?"[e]

Procedural due process aspires to neutrality and generality of decision. And while "due process" in substantive matters is impossible to define, still in a system with neutral and general procedure, substantive results are less likely to leave a "sense of injustice."

Certainly the two due process clauses, in the Fifth and the Fourteenth Amendments, do bar the national and state governments from some activity which is substantive, not merely procedural. In 1954 the Supreme Court held, in Bolling v. Sharpe,[f] that the due process clause of the Fifth Amendment invalidated an act of Congress providing for segregation by race in the public schools of the District of Columbia. In 1931 in Near v. Minnesota[g] the Supreme Court held unconstitutional a Minnesota state court injunction against publication of a newspaper. Chief Justice Hughes wrote for the majority, "It is no longer open to doubt that the liberty of the press and speech is within the liberty safeguarded by the due process clause of the Fourteenth Amendment from invasion by state action."

Trouble with substantive due process arose, however, from its indefinite meaning, which is not clarified by its distinguished descent. The due process formula is traceable to Chapter 3 of 28 Edward III (1354), which rendered as "par due process de ley" the Latin

[c] See Professor Edmond M. Cahn's book of that title; and Felix S. Cohen's review, 63 Harv. L. Rev. 1481 (1950). — ED.
[d] Bartkus v. Illinois, 359 U.S. 121, 128 (1959). — ED.
[e] Wechsler, Toward Neutral Principles of Constitutional Law, 73 Harv. L. Rev. 1, 15 (1959). — ED.
[f] 347 U.S. 497. — ED.
[g] 283 U.S. 697. — ED.

Section A. The Bill of Rights and Procedural Due Process

phrase "per legem terre"[h] in the thirty-ninth chapter of Magna Carta. Coke's Second Institute, published in 1642 eight years after Coke died, emphasized the protection guaranteed to the subject by the thirty-ninth chapter of the Charter, and by Edward III's restatement of it. In the eighteenth century every law student was weaned on Coke: Madison included "due process of law" in the fourth proposal for amending the new Constitution, which on June 8, 1789, he introduced in the House of Representatives,[i] and thus the due process clause became part of the Fifth Amendment, which took effect on December 5, 1791. When the Joint Congressional Committee on Reconstruction was drafting the Fourteenth Amendment in 1866, Representative Bingham of Ohio proposed inclusion of the due process clause in language indistinguishable from that of the Fifth Amendment.[j] Magna Carta, Edward III, Coke, Madison, the Bill of Rights — with such distinguished ancestry for due process of law, few senators or congressmen in 1866 could doubt that due process would be useful to protect the newly enfranchised Negroes against the lately Confederate States, and was indeed a wholesome guarantee for everybody against all states. But no one who discussed due process in the Senate or the House in 1866 expressed any definite idea of its content.

During the years since adoption of the Fourteenth Amendment, the due process clause has had intense scrutiny by historians, politicians, political theorists, judges, and comparative jurists, but no consensus as to its intended substance has emerged in legislative debates, judicial opinions, or the writings of political philosophers. The practical operation of the federal and state due process clauses has, however, been observable: these clauses have delegated to the judicial branches of the national and state governments, and ultimately to the Supreme Court of the United States, a power to review both procedures and substance of governmental measures; the grounds are essentially grounds of policy. What Holmes said of judicial lawmaking generally is particularly true of adjudication under the due process clauses:

"[I]n substance the growth of the law is legislative. . . . It is legislative in its grounds. The very considerations which judges most rarely mention, and always with an apology, are the secret root from which the law draws all the juices of life."[k]

Between 1890[l] and 1937 the Supreme Court of the United States from time to time held that various pieces of federal and state legislation which undertook to regulate the economy did so in such a drastic and untraditional manner that the regulation was invalid under the relevant due process clause. Conspicuous examples were Lochner v. New York[m] in 1905, which struck down a ten-hour workday law for bakers, and Adkins v. Children's Hospital,[n] which in 1923 held unconstitutional a federal minimum wage statute for the District of Columbia. "Economic due process" came under its heaviest fire during the period of New Deal legislation in 1935 and 1936.[o] Since the Supreme Court's change of attitude in 1937, however, the Fifth and Fourteenth Amendment due process clauses have ceased to be obstacles to economic reform, though they continue effective in protecting substantive interests of personality and in guaranteeing fair governmental procedures by nation and states.

Mr. Justice Black, as a senator, and Mr. Justice Douglas, as a member of President

---

[h] "Terre," a medieval Latin form of the classical genitive singular "terrae." — ED.

[i] See I Annals of Congress 433 et seq. — ED.

[j] Charles Fairman has carefully traced these Congressional origins in his essay "Does the Fourteenth Amendment Incorporate the Bill of Rights? The Original Understanding," 2 Stan. L. Rev. 5 (1949). — ED.

[k] The Common Law 35 (1881). — ED.

[l] The year of the Minnesota Rate Case, 134 U.S. 418. In 1918 Judge Hough, in his witty essay, Due Process of Law Today, 32 Harv. L. Rev. 218, 228, wrote, "It is from that decision that I date the flood." — ED.

[m] 198 U.S. 45. See page 1083 infra. — ED.

[n] 261 U.S. 525. See page 1089 infra. — ED.

[o] See page 260 supra. — ED.

Roosevelt's administration, during the Supreme Court crisis of 1935 and 1936 were particularly struck by what seemed to them, and to many others, the potential dangers to desirable economic change implicit in the undefined scope of the due process clauses. They have advanced the theory that the first section of the Fourteenth Amendment was intended to, and should be held to, apply against the states precisely the provisions of the federal Bill of Rights, neither more nor less. In Adamson v. California a majority of the Supreme Court in 1947 upheld a state statute permitting the prosecutor in a criminal case to comment on the defendant's failure to take the stand.[p] Justices Black, Douglas, Murphy, and Rutledge dissented. Mr. Justice Black wrote:

"This decision reasserts a constitutional theory spelled out in Twining v. New Jersey, 211 U.S. 78, that this Court is endowed by the Constitution with boundless power under 'natural law' periodically to expand and contract constitutional standards to conform to the Court's conception of what at a particular time constitutes 'civilized decency' and 'fundamental liberty and justice.'[1] Invoking this Twining rule, the Court concludes that although comment upon testimony in a federal court would violate the Fifth Amendment, identical comment in a state court does not violate today's fashion in civilized decency and fundamentals and is therefore not prohibited by the Federal Constitution as amended.

"The Twining Case was the first, as it is the only, decision of this Court, which has squarely held that states were free, notwithstanding the Fifth and Fourteenth Amendments, to extort evidence from one accused of crime.[2] I agree that if Twining be reaffirmed, the result reached might appropriately follow. But I would not reaffirm the Twining decision. I think that decision and the 'natural law' theory of the Constitution upon which it relies degrade the constitutional safeguards of the Bill of Rights and simultaneously appropriate for this Court a broad power which we are not authorized by the Constitution to exercise. Furthermore, the Twining decision rested on previous cases and broad hypotheses which have been undercut by intervening decisions of this Court. See Corwin, The Supreme Court's Construction of the Self-Incrimination Clause, 29 Mich. L. Rev. 1, 191, 202. My reasons for believing that the Twining decision should not be revitalized can best be understood by reference to the constitutional, judicial, and general history that preceded and followed the case. That reference must be abbreviated far more than is justified but for the necessary limitations of opinion-writing.

"The first ten amendments were proposed and adopted largely because of fear that Government might unduly interfere with prized individual liberties. The people wanted and demanded a Bill of Rights written into their Constitution. The amendments embodying the Bill of Rights were intended to curb all branches of the Federal Government in the fields touched by the amendments — Legislative, Executive, and Judicial. The Fifth, Sixth, and Eighth Amendments were pointedly aimed at confining exercise of power by courts and judges within precise boundaries, particularly in the procedure used for the trial of criminal cases.[3] Past history provided strong reasons for the apprehensions which brought these procedural amendments into being and attest the wisdom of their adoption. For the fears of arbitrary court action sprang largely from the past use of courts in the imposition of criminal punishments to suppress speech, press, and religion. Hence the constitutional limitations of courts' powers were, in the view of the Founders, essential supplements to the First Amendment, which was itself designed to protect the widest scope

---

[p] 332 U.S. 46. — ED.

[1] The cases on which the Court relies seem to adopt these standards. Malinski v. New York, 324 U.S. 401, concurring opinion, 412-417; Buchalter v. New York, 319 U.S. 427, 429; Hebert v. Louisiana, 272 U.S. 312, 316.

[2] "The question in the case at bar has been twice before us, and been left undecided, as the cases were disposed of on other grounds." Twining v. New Jersey, supra (211 U.S. 92). In Palko v. Connecticut, 302 U.S. 319, relied on by the Court, the issue was double jeopardy and not enforced self-incrimination.

[3] [Mr. Justice Black here summarized the Fifth, Sixth, and Eighth Amendments. — ED.]

Section A. The Bill of Rights and Procedural Due Process

for all people to believe and to express the most divergent political, religious, and other views.

"But these limitations were not expressly imposed upon state court action. In 1833, Barron v. Baltimore, 7 Pet. 243, . . . was decided by this Court. It specifically held inapplicable to the states that provision of the Fifth Amendment which declares: 'nor shall private property be taken for public use, without just compensation.' In deciding the particular point raised, the Court there said that it could not hold that the first eight amendments applied to the states. This was the controlling constitutional rule when the Fourteenth Amendment was proposed in 1866.

"My study of the historical events that culminated in the Fourteenth Amendment, and the expressions of those who sponsored and favored, as well as those who opposed its submission and passage, persuades me that one of the chief objects that the provisions of the Amendment's first section, separately, and as a whole, were intended to accomplish was to make the Bill of Rights, applicable to the states.[5] With full knowledge of the import of the Barron decision, the framers and backers of the Fourteenth Amendment proclaimed its purpose to be to overturn the constitutional rule that case had announced. This historical purpose has never received full consideration or exposition in my opinion of this Court interpreting the Amendment.

"In construing other constitutional provisions, this Court has almost uniformly followed the precept of Ex parte Bain, 121 U.S. 1, 12, that 'It is never to be forgotten that in the construction of the language of the Constitution . . . as indeed in all other instances where construction becomes necessary, we are to place ourselves as nearly as possible in the condition of the men who framed that instrument.' . . .

"Investigation of the cases relied upon in Twining v. New Jersey to support the conclusion there reached that neither the Fifth Amendment's prohibition of compelled testimony, nor any of the Bill of Rights, applies to the States, reveals an unexplained departure from this salutary practice. Neither the briefs nor opinions in any of these cases, except Maxwell v. Dow, 176 U.S. 581, make reference to the legislative and contemporary history for the purpose of demonstrating that those who conceived, shaped, and brought about the adoption of the Fourteenth Amendment intended it to nullify this Court's decision in Barron v. Baltimore, 7 Pet. 243, supra, and thereby to make the Bill of Rights applicable to the States. . . . [In Twining v. New Jersey, 211 U.S. 92 (1908)] the Court declined and again today declines, to appraise the relevant historical evidence of the intended scope of the first section of the Amendment. Instead it relied upon previous cases, none of which had analyzed the evidence showing that one purpose of those who framed, advocated, and adopted the Amendment had been to make the Bill of Rights applicable to the States. None of the cases relied upon by the Court today made such an analysis.

"For this reason, I am attaching to this dissent an appendix which contains a résumé, by no means complete, of the Amendment's history. In my judgment that history conclusively demonstrates that the language of the first section of the Fourteenth Amendment, taken as a whole, was thought by those responsible for its submission to the people, and by those who opposed its submission, sufficiently explicit to guarantee that thereafter no state could deprive its citizens of the privileges and protections of the Bill of Rights. Whether

---

[5] Another prime purpose was to make colored people citizens entitled to full equal rights as citizens despite what this Court decided in the Dred Scott case. Scott v. Sandford, 19 How. 393.

A comprehensive analysis of the historical origins of the Fourteenth Amendment, Flack, The Adoption of the Fourteenth Amendment (1908) 94, concludes that "Congress, the House and the Senate, had the following objects and motives in view for submitting the first section of the Fourteenth Amendment to the States for ratification:

"1. To make the Bill of Rights (the first eight Amendments) binding upon, or applicable to, the States.
"2. To give validity to the Civil Rights Bill.
"3. To declare who were citizens of the United States."

this Court ever will, or whether it now should, in the light of past decisions, give full effect to what the Amendment was intended to accomplish is not necessarily essential to a decision here. However that may be, our prior decisions, including Twining, do not prevent our carrying out that purpose, at least to the extent of making applicable to the states, not a mere part, as the Court has, but the full protection of the Fifth Amendment's provision against compelling evidence from an accused to convict him of crime. And I further contend that the 'natural law' formula which the Court uses to reach its conclusion in this case should be abandoned as an incongruous excrescence on our Constitution. I believe that formula to be itself a violation of our Constitution, in that it subtly conveys to courts, at the expense of legislatures, ultimate power over public policies in fields where no specific provision of the Constitution limits legislative power. . . .

"I cannot consider the Bill of Rights to be an outworn 18th Century 'strait jacket' as the Twining opinion did. Its provisions may be thought outdated abstractions by some. And it is true that they were designed to meet ancient evils. But they are the same kind of human evils that have emerged from century to century wherever excessive power is sought by the few at the expense of the many. In my judgment the people of no nation can lose their liberty so long as a Bill of Rights like ours survives and its basic purposes are conscientiously interpreted, enforced and respected so as to afford continuous protection against old, as well as new, devices and practices which might thwart those purposes. I fear to see the consequences of the Court's practice of substituting its own concepts of decency and fundamental justice for the language of the Bill of Rights as its point of departure in interpreting and enforcing that Bill of Rights. If the choice must be between the selective process of the Palko decision applying some of the Bill of Rights to the States, or the Twining rule applying none of them, I would choose the Palko selective process. But rather than accept either of these choices, I would follow what I believe was the original purpose of the Fourteenth Amendment — to extend to all the people of the nation the complete protection of the Bill of Rights. To hold that this Court can determine what, if any, provisions of the Bill of Rights will be enforced, and if so to what degree, is to frustrate the great design of a written Constitution.

"Conceding the possibility that this Court is now wise enough to improve on the Bill of Rights by substituting natural law concepts for the Bill of Rights, I think the possibility is entirely too speculative to agree to take that course. I would therefore hold in this case that the full protection of the Fifth Amendment's proscription against compelled testimony must be afforded by California. This I would do because of reliance upon the original purpose of the Fourteenth Amendment.

"It is an illusory apprehension that literal application of some or all of the provisions of the Bill of Rights to the States would unwisely increase the sum total of the powers of this Court to invalidate state legislation. The Federal Government has not been harmfully burdened by the requirement that enforcement of federal laws affecting civil liberty conform literally to the Bill of Rights. Who would advocate its repeal? It must be conceded, of course, that the natural-law-due-process formula, which the Court today reaffirms, has been interpreted to limit substantially this Court's power to prevent state violations of the individual civil liberties guaranteed by the Bill of Rights.[16] But this formula also has been used in the past, and can be used in the future, to license this Court, in considering regulatory legislation, to roam at large in the broad expanses of policy and morals and to trespass, all too freely, on the legislative domain of the States as well as the Federal Government.

"Since Marbury v. Madison, 1 Cranch 137, was decided, the practice has been firmly established, for better or worse, that courts can strike down legislative enactments which violate the Constitution. This process, of course, involves interpretation, and since words can have many meanings, interpretation obviously may result in contraction or extension

---

[16] See e.g., Betts v. Brady 316 U.S. 455; Feldman v. United States, 322 U.S. 487.

of the original purpose of a constitutional provision thereby affecting policy. But to pass upon the constitutionality of statutes by looking to the particular standards enumerated in the Bill of Rights and other parts of the Constitution is one thing; to invalidate statutes because of application of 'natural law' deemed to be above and undefined by the Constitution is another.[18] 'In the one instance, courts proceeding within clearly marked constitutional boundaries seek to execute policies written into the Constitution; in the other, they roam at will in the limitless area of their own beliefs as to reasonableness and actually select policies, a responsibility which the Constitution entrusts to the legislative representatives of the people.' Federal Power Commission v. Natural Gas Pipeline Co., 315 U.S. 575, 599, 601, note 4.

"Mr. Justice Douglas joins in this opinion."

Mr. Justice Murphy, with whom Mr. Justice Rutledge concurred, dissented:

"While in substantial agreement with the views of Mr. Justice Black, I have one reservation and one addition to make.

"I agree that the specific guarantees of the Bill of Rights should be carried over intact into the first section of the Fourteenth Amendment. But I am not prepared to say that the latter is entirely and necessarily limited by the Bill of Rights. Occasions may arise where a proceeding falls so far short of conforming to fundamental standards of procedure as to warrant constitutional condemnation in terms of a lack of due process despite the absence of a specific provision in the Bill of Rights.

"That point, however, need not be pursued here inasmuch as the Fifth Amendment is explicit in its provision that no person shall be compelled in any criminal case to be a witness against himself. That provision, as Mr. Justice Black demonstrates, is a constituent part of the Fourteenth Amendment.

"Moreover, it is my belief that this guarantee against self-incrimination has been violated in this case. . . ."

The Appendix to Mr. Justice Black's opinion, discussing the legislative origin of the Fourteenth Amendment, is omitted. See, for a discussion, Fairman and Morrison, Does the Fourteenth Amendment Incorporate the Bill of Rights? 2 Stan. L. Rev. 5 (1949). For other material on self-incrimination see pages 1012 et seq. infra.[q]

Rochin v. California *342 U.S. 165, 72 S. Ct. 205, 96 L. Ed. 183 (1952)*

MR. JUSTICE FRANKFURTER delivered the opinion of the Court.

Having "some information that [the petitioner here] was selling narcotics," three deputy sheriffs of the County of Los Angeles, on the morning of July 1, 1949, made for the

---

[18] An early and prescient exposé of the inconsistency of the natural law formula with our constitutional form of government appears in the concurring opinion of Mr. Justice Iredell in Calder v. Bull, 3 Dall. 386, 398, 399: "If any act of Congress, or of the Legislature of a state, violates . . . constitutional provisions, it is unquestionably void; though, I admit, that as the authority to declare it void is of a delicate and awful nature, the Court will never resort to that authority, but in a clear and urgent case. If, on the other hand, the Legislature of the Union, or the Legislature of any member of the Union, shall pass a law, within the general scope of their constitutional power, the Court cannot pronounce it to be void, merely because it is, in their judgment, contrary to the principles of natural justice. The ideas of natural justice are regulated by no fixed standard: the ablest and the purest men have differed upon the subject; and all that the Court could properly say, in such an event, would be, that the Legislature (possessed of an equal right of opinion) had passed an act which, in the opinion of the judges, was inconsistent with the abstract principles of natural justice."

See also Haines, The Law of Nature in State and Federal Decisions, 25 Yale L.J. 617 (1916); Judicial Review of Legislation in the United States and the Doctrines of Vested Rights and of Implied Limitations on Legislatures, 2 Tex. L. Rev. 257 (1924), 3 Tex. L. Rev. 1 (1924); The Revival of Natural Law Concepts (1930); The American Doctrine of Judicial Supremacy (1932); The Role of the Supreme Court in American Government and Politics (1944).

[q] The Supreme Court overruled Adamson in Malloy v. Hogan, 378 U.S. 1 (1964). See page 1012 infra. — ED.

1000   Chapter Fifteen. **Fair Procedure**

two-story dwelling house in which Rochin lived with his mother, his common-law wife, brothers and sisters. Finding the outside door open, they entered and then forced open the door to Rochin's room on the second floor. Inside they found petitioner sitting partly dressed on the side of the bed, upon which his wife was lying. On a "night stand" beside the bed the deputies spied two capsules. When asked "Whose stuff is this?" Rochin seized the capsules and put them in his mouth. A struggle ensued, in the course of which the three officers "jumped upon him" and attempted to extract the capsules. The force they applied proved unavailing against Rochin's resistance. He was handcuffed and taken to a hospital. At the direction of one of the officers a doctor forced an emetic solution through a tube into Rochin's stomach against his will. This "stomach pumping" produced vomiting. In the vomited matter were found two capsules which proved to contain morphine.

Rochin was brought to trial before a California Superior Court, sitting without a jury, on the charge of possessing "a preparation of morphine" in violation of the California Health and Safety Code, 1947, § 11, 500. Rochin was convicted and sentenced to sixty days' imprisonment. The chief evidence against him was the two capsules. They were admitted over petitioner's objection, although the means of obtaining them was frankly set forth in the testimony by one of the deputies, substantially as here narrated.

On appeal, the District Court of Appeal affirmed the conviction, despite the finding that the officers "were guilty of unlawfully breaking into and entering defendant's room and were guilty of unlawfully assaulting and battering defendant while in the room," and "were guilty of unlawfully assaulting, battering, torturing and falsely imprisoning the defendant at the alleged hospital." 101 Cal. App. 2d 140, 143. One of the three judges, while finding that "the record in this case reveals a shocking series of violations of constitutional rights," concurred only because he felt bound by decisions of his Supreme Court. These, he asserted, "have been looked upon by law enforcement officers as an encouragement, if not an invitation, to the commission of such lawless acts." Ibid. The Supreme Court of California denied without opinion Rochin's petition for a hearing. Two justices dissented from this denial, and in doing so expressed themselves thus: ". . . a conviction which rests upon evidence of incriminating objects obtained from the body of the accused by physical abuse is as invalid as a conviction which rests upon a verbal confession extracted from him by such abuse. . . . Had the evidence forced from the defendant's lips consisted of an oral confession that he illegally possessed a drug . . . he would have the protection of the rule of law which excludes coerced confessions from evidence. But because the evidence forced from his lips consisted of real objects the People of this state are permitted to base a conviction upon it. [We] find no valid ground of distinction between a verbal confession extracted by physical abuse and a confession wrested from defendant's body by physical abuse." 101 Cal. App. 2d 143, 149, 150.

This Court granted certiorari, 341 U.S. 939, because a serious question is raised as to the limitations which the Due Process Clause of the Fourteenth Amendment imposes on the conduct of criminal proceedings by the States.

In our federal system the administration of criminal justice is predominantly committed to the care of the States. The power to define crimes belongs to Congress only as an appropriate means of carrying into execution its limited grant of legislative powers. U.S. Const. Art. 1, § 8, cl. 18. Broadly speaking, crimes in the United States are what the laws of the individual States make them, subject to the limitations of Art. 1, § 10[1], in the orginal Constitution, prohibiting bills of attainder and ex post facto laws, and of the Thirteenth and Fourteenth Amendments.

These limitations, in the main, concern not restrictions upon the power of the States to define crime, except in the restricted area where federal authority has preempted the field, but restrictions upon the manner in which the States may enforce their penal code. Accordingly, in reviewing a State criminal conviction under a claim of right guaranteed by the Due Process Clause of the Fourteenth Amendment, from which is derived the most far-reaching and most frequent federal basis of challenging State criminal justice, "we must be deeply mindful of the responsibilities of the States for the enforcement of criminal laws, and exercise with due humility our merely negative function in subjecting convictions from state courts to the very narrow scrutiny which the Due Process Clause of the Fourteenth Amendment authorizes." Malinski v. New York, 324 U.S. 401, 412, 418. Due process of law, "itself a historical product," Jackman v. Rosenbaum Co., 260 U.S. 22, 31, is not to be turned into a destructive dogma against the States in the administration of their systems of criminal justice.

However, this Court too has its responsibility. Regard for the requirements of the Due Process Clause "inescapably imposes upon this Court an exercise of judgment upon the whole course of the proceedings [resulting in a conviction] in order to ascertain whether they offend those canons of decency and fairness which express the notions of justice of English-speaking peoples even toward those charged with the most heinous offenses." Malinski v. New York, supra (342 U.S. at 416). These standards of justice are not authoritatively formulated anywhere as though they were specifics. Due process of law is a summarized constitutional guarantee of respect for those personal immunities which, as Mr. Justice Cardozo twice wrote for the Court, are "so rooted in the traditions and conscience of our people as to be ranked as fundamental," Snyder v. Massachusetts, 291 U.S. 97, 105, or are "implicit in the concept of ordered liberty." Palko v. Connecticut, 302 U.S. 319, 325.[2]

The Court's function in the observance of this settled conception of the Due Process Clause does not leave us without adequate guides in subjecting State criminal procedures to constitutional judgment. In dealing not with the machinery of government but with human rights, the absence of formal exactitude, or want of fixity of meaning, is not an unusual or even regrettable attribute of constitutional provisions. Words being symbols do not speak without a gloss. On the one hand the gloss may be the deposit of history, whereby a term gains technical content. Thus the requirements of the Sixth and Seventh Amendments for trial by jury in the Federal courts have a rigid meaning. No changes or chances can alter the content of the verbal symbol of "jury" — a body of twelve men who must reach a unanimous conclusion if the verdict is to go against the defendant.[3] On the other hand, the gloss of some of the verbal symbols of the Constitution does not give them a fixed technical content. It exacts a continuing process of application.

When the gloss has thus not been fixed but is a function of the process of judgment, the judgment is bound to fall differently at different times and differently at the same time through different judges. Thus it is that even more specific provisions, such as the guaranty of freedom of speech and the detailed protection against unreasonable searches and seizures, have inevitably evoked as sharp divisions in this Court as the least specific and most comprehensive protection of liberties, the Due Process Clause.

The vague contours of the Due Process Clause do not leave judges at large.[4] We may not draw on our merely personal and private notions and disregard the limits that bind

---

[2] What is here summarized was deemed by a majority of the Court, in Malinski v. New York, 324 U.S. 401, 412 and 438, to be "the controlling principles upon which this Court reviews on constitutional grounds a state court conviction for crime." They have been applied by this Court many times, long before and since the Malinski Case.

[3] This is the federal jury required constitutionally although both in England and in at least half of the States a jury may be composed of less than twelve or a verdict may be less than unanimous. Arizona State Legislative Bureau, Legislative Briefs No. 4, Grand and Petit Juries in the United States v-vi (Feb. 15, 1940); Council of State Governments, The Book of the States 1950-1951, 515.

[4] Burke's observations on the method of ascertaining law by judges are pertinent:

"Your committee do not find any positive law which binds the judges of the courts in Westminister-hall publicly to give a reasoned opinion from the bench, in support of their judgment upon matters that are stated before them. But the course hath prevailed from the oldest times. It hath been so general and so uniform, that it must be considered as the law of the land." Report of the Committee of Managers on the Causes of the Duration of Mr. Hasting's Trial, 4 Speeches of Edmund Burke (1816), 200-201.

And Burke had an answer for those who argue that the liberty of the citizen cannot be adequately protected by the flexible conception of due process of law: ". . . the English jurisprudence has not any other sure foundation, nor consequently the lives and properties of the subject any sure hold, but in the maxims, rules, and principles, and juridical traditionary line of decisions. . . ." Id., at 201.

judges in their judicial function. Even though the concept of due process of law is not final and fixed, these limits are derived from considerations that are fused in the whole nature of our judicial process. See Cardozo, The Nature of the Judicial Process; The Growth of the Law; The Paradoxes of Legal Science. These are considerations deeply rooted in reason and in the compelling traditions of the legal profession. The Due Process Clause places upon this Court the duty of exercising a judgment, within the narrow confines of judicial power in reviewing State convictions, upon interests of society pushing in opposite directions.

Due process of law thus conceived is not to be derided as resort to a revival of "natural law."[5] To believe that this judicial exercise of judgment could be avoided by freezing "due process of law" at some fixed stage of time or thought is to suggest that the most important aspect of constitutional adjudication is a function for inanimate machines and not for judges, for whom the independence safeguarded by Article 3 of the Constitution was designed and who are presumably guided by established standards of judicial behavior. Even cybernetics has not yet made that haughty claim. To practice the requisite detachment and to achieve sufficient objectivity no doubt demands of judges the habit of self-discipline and self-criticism, incertitude that one's own views are incontestable and alert tolerance toward views not shared. But these are precisely the presuppositions of our judicial process. They are precisely the qualities society has a right to expect from those entrusted with ultimate judicial power.

Restraints on our jurisdiction are self-imposed only in the sense that there is from our decisions no immediate appeal short of impeachment or constitutional amendment. But that does not make due process of law a matter of judicial caprice. The faculties of the Due Process Clause may be indefinite and vague, but the mode of their ascertainment is not self-willed. In each case "due process of law" requires an evaluation based on a disinterested inquiry pursued in the spirit of science, on a balanced order of facts exactly and fairly stated, on the detached consideration of conflicting claims, see Hudson County Water Co. v. McCarter, 209 U.S. 349, 355, on a judgment not ad hoc and episodic but duly mindful of reconciling the needs both of continuity and of change in any progressive society.

Applying these general considerations to the circumstances of the present case, we are compelled to conclude that the proceedings by which this conviction was obtained do more than offend some fastidious squeamishness or private sentimentalism about combatting crime too energetically. It is conduct that shocks the conscience. Illegally breaking into the privacy of the petitioner, the struggle to open his mouth and remove what was there, the forcible extraction of his stomach's contents — this course of proceeding by agents of government to obtain evidence is bound to offend even hardened sensibilities. They are methods too close to the rack and the screw to permit of constitutional differentiation.

It has long since ceased to be true that due process of law is heedless of the means by which otherwise relevant and credible evidence is obtained. Even before the series of recent cases enforced the constitutional principle the States could not base convictions upon confessions, however much verified, but obtained by coercion. These decisions are not arbitrary exceptions to the comprehensive right of States to fashion their own rules of evidence for criminal trials. They are not sports in our constitutional law but applications of a general principle. They are only instances of the general requirement that States in their prosecutions respect certain decencies of civilized conduct. Due process of law, as a historic and generative principle, precludes defining, and thereby confining, these standards of conduct more precisely than to say that convictions cannot be brought about by

---

[5] Morris R. Cohen, "Jus Naturale Redivivum," 25 Philosophical Review 761 (1916), and "Natural Rights and Positive Law," Reason and Nature 401-426 (1931); F. Pollock, "The History of the Law of Nature," Essays in the Law 31-79 (1922).

methods that offend "a sense of justice." See Mr. Chief Justice Hughes, speaking for a unanimous Court in Brown v. Mississippi, 297 U.S. 278, 285, 286. It would be a stultification of the responsibility which the course of constitutional history has cast upon this Court to hold that in order to convict a man the police cannot extract by force what is in his mind but can extract what is in his stomach.[6]

To attempt in this case to distinguish what lawyers call "real evidence" from verbal evidence is to ignore the reasons for excluding coerced confessions. Use of involuntary verbal confessions in State criminal trials is constitutionally obnoxious not only because of their unreliability. They are inadmissible under the Due Process Clause even though statements contained in them may be independently established as true. Coerced confessions offend the community's sense of fair play and decency. So here, to sanction the brutal conduct which naturally enough was condemned by the court whose judgment is before us, would be to afford brutality the cloak of law. Nothing would be more calculated to discredit law and thereby to brutalize the temper of a society. . . .

On the facts of this case the conviction of the petitioner has been obtained by methods that offend the Due Process Clause. The judgment below must be

Reversed.

MR. JUSTICE MINTON took no part in the consideration or decision of this case.

MR. JUSTICE BLACK, concurring.

Adamson v. California, 332 U.S. 46, 68-123, sets out reasons for my belief that state as well as federal courts and law enforcement officers must obey the Fifth Amendment's command that "No person . . . shall be compelled in any criminal case to be a witness against himself." I think a person is compelled to be a witness against himself not only when he is compelled to testify, but also when as here, incriminating evidence is forcibly taken from him by a contrivance of modern science. Cf. Boyd v. United States, 116 U.S. 616; Counselman v. Hitchcock, 142 U.S. 547, 562; Bram v. United States, 168 U.S. 532; Chambers v. Florida, 309 U.S. 227. California convicted this petitioner by using against him evidence obtained in this manner, and I agree with Mr. Justice Douglas that the case should be reversed on this ground.

In the view of a majority of the Court, however, the Fifth Amendment imposes no restraint of any kind on the states. They nevertheless hold that California's use of this evidence violated the Due Process Clause of the Fourteenth Amendment. Since they hold as I do in this case, I regret my inability to accept their interpretation without protest. But I believe that faithful adherence to the specific guarantees in the Bill of Rights insures a more permanent protection of individual liberty than that which can be afforded by the nebulous standards stated by the majority.

What the majority hold is that the Due Process Clause empowers this Court to nullify any state law if its application "shocks the conscience," offends "a sense of justice" or runs counter to the "decencies of civilized conduct." The majority emphasize that these statements do not refer to their own consciences or to their senses of justice and decency. For we are told that "we may not draw on our merely personal and private notions"; our judgment must be grounded on "considerations deeply rooted in reason, and in the compelling traditions of the legal profession." We are further admonished to measure the validity of state practices, not by our reason, or by the traditions of the legal profession, but by "the community's sense of fair play and decency"; by the "traditions and consciences of our people"; or by "those canons of decency and fairness which express the notions of justice of English-speaking peoples." These canons are made necessary it is said, because of "interests of society pushing in opposite directions."

If the Due Process Clause does vest this Court with such unlimited power to invalidate

---

[6] As to the difference between the privilege against self-crimination protected, in federal prosecutions, under the Fifth Amendment, and the limitations which the Due Process Clause of the Fourteenth Amendment imposes upon the states against the use of coerced confessions, see Brown v. Mississippi, 297 U.S. 278, 285.

laws, I am still in doubt as to why we should consider only the notions of English-speaking peoples to determine what are immutable and fundamental principles of justice. Moreover, one may well ask what avenues of investigation are open to discover "canons" of conduct so universally favored that this Court should write them into the Constitution? All we are told is that the discovery must be made by an "evaluation based on a disinterested inquiry pursued in the spirit of science on a balanced order of facts."

. . . What paralyzing role this same philosophy will play in the future economic affairs of this country is impossible to predict. Of even graver concern, however, is the use of the philosophy to nullify the Bill of Rights. I long ago concluded that the accordion-like qualities of this philosophy must inevitably imperil all the individual liberty safeguards specifically enumerated in the Bill of Rights.[2] Reflection and recent decisions[3] of this Court sanctioning abridgment of the freedom of speech and press have strengthened this conclusion.[r]

NOTE Poe v. Ullman

In Poe v. Ullman, 367 U.S. 497 (1961), the Supreme Court was asked to rule on the constitutionality of a Connecticut statute which prohibited the use of contraceptive devices and the giving of medical advice about their use. The Court dismissed these appeals for declaratory judgments as not presenting a case or controversy within the meaning of Article III of the Constitution. Because the long history of nonenforcement of the statute suggested a "tacit agreement" not to prosecute this case either, Mr. Justice Frankfurter wrote for a plurality, this controversy was deprived of "the immediacy which is an indispensable condition of constitutional adjudication." Justices Black, Douglas, Harlan, and Stewart dissented. In a separate dissent, Justice Harlan gave his reasons why the case was justiciable and also why the statute violated due process. His discussion of the nature of due process follows:

"In reviewing state legislation, whether considered to be in the exercise of the State's police powers, or in provision for the health, safety, morals or welfare of its people, it is clear that what is concerned are 'the powers of government inherent in every sovereignty.' The License Cases, 5 How. 504, 583. Only to the extent that the Constitution so requires may this Court interfere with the exercise of this plenary power of government. Barron v. Mayor of Baltimore, 7 Pet. 243. But precisely because it is the Constitution alone which warrants judicial interference in sovereign operations of the State, the basis of judgment as to the Constitutionality of state action must be a rational one, approaching the text which is the only commission for our power not in a literalistic way, as if we had a tax statute before us, but as the basic charter of our society, setting out in spare but meaningful terms the principles of government. McCulloch v. Maryland, 4 Wheat, 316. But as inescapable as is the rational process in Constitutional adjudication in general, nowhere is it more so than in giving meaning to the prohibitions of the Fourteenth Amendment and, where the Federal Government is involved, the Fifth Amendment, against the deprivation of life, liberty or property without due process of law.

"It is but a truism to say that this provision of both Amendments is not self-explanatory. As to the Fourteenth, which is involved here, the history of the Amendment also sheds little light on the meaning of the provision. Fairman, Does the Fourteenth Amendment Incorporate the Bill of Rights, 2 Stan. L. Rev. 15. It is important to note, however, that two views of the Amendment have not been accepted by this Court as delineating its scope. One view, which was ably and insistently argued in response to what were felt to be

---

[2] E.g., Adamson v. California, supra, and cases cited in the dissent.
[3] American Communications Assn. C.I.O. v. Douds, 339 U.S. 382; Feiner v. New York, 340 U.S. 315; Dennis v. United States, 341 U.S. 494.
[r] A concurring opinion of Mr. Justice Douglas is omitted. — Ed.

Section A. The Bill of Rights and Procedural Due Process

abuses by this Court of its reviewing power, sought to limit the provision to a guarantee of procedural fairness. See Davidson v. New Orleans, 96 U.S. 97, 105; Brandeis, J., in Whitney v. California, 274 U.S. 357, at 373; Warren, The New 'Liberty' under the 14th Amendment, 39 Harv. L. Rev. 431; Reeder, The Due Process Clauses and 'The Substance of Individual Rights,' 58 U. Pa. L. Rev. 191; Shattuck, The True Meaning of The Term 'Liberty' in Those Clauses in the Federal and State Constitutions Which Protect 'Life, Liberty, and Property,' 4 Harv. L. Rev. 365. The other view which has been rejected would have it that the Fourteenth Amendment, whether by way of the Privileges and Immunities Clause or the Due Process Clause, applied against the States only and precisely those restraints which had prior to the Amendment been applicable merely to federal action. However, 'due process' in the consistent view of this Court has ever been a broader concept than the first view and more flexible than the second. . . .

"Due process has not been reduced to any formula; its content cannot be determined by reference to any code. The best that can be said is that through the course of this Court's decisions it has represented the balance which our Nation, built upon postulates of respect for the liberty of the individual, has struck between that liberty and the demands of organized society. If the supplying of content to this Constitutional concept has of necessity been a rational process, it certainly has not been one where judges have felt free to roam where unguided speculation might take them. The balance of which I speak is the balance struck by this country, having regard to what history teaches are the traditions from which it developed as well as the traditions from which it broke. That tradition is a living thing. A decision of this Court which radically departs from it could not long survive, while a decision which builds on what has survived is likely to be sound. No formula could serve as a substitute, in this area, for judgment and restraint.

"It is this outlook which has led the Court continuingly to perceive distinctions in the imperative character of Constitutional provisions, since that character must be discerned from a particular provision's larger context. And inasmuch as this context is one not of words, but of history and purposes, the full scope of the liberty guaranteed by the Due Process Clause cannot be found in or limited by the precise terms of the specific guarantees elsewhere provided in the Constitution. This 'liberty' is not a series of isolated points pricked out in terms of the taking of property; the freedom of speech, press, and religion; the right to keep and bear arms; the freedom from unreasonable searches and seizures; and so on. It is a rational continuum which, broadly speaking, includes a freedom from all substantial arbitrary impositions and purposeless restraints, see Allgeyer v. Louisiana, 165 U.S. 578; Holden v. Hardy, 169 U.S. 366; Booth v. Illinois, 184 U.S. 425; Nebbia v. New York, 291 U.S. 502; Skinner v. Oklahoma, 316 U.S. 535, 544 (concurring opinion); Schware v. Board of Bar Examiners, 353 U.S. 232, and which also recognizes, what a reasonable and sensitive judgment must, that certain interests require particularly careful scrutiny of the state needs asserted to justify their abridgment. Cf. Skinner v. Oklahoma, supra; Bolling v. Sharpe, supra.

"As was said in Meyer v. Nebraska, 262 U.S. 390, 399, 'this Court has not attempted to define with exactness the liberty thus guaranteed. . . . Without doubt, it denotes not merely freedom from bodily restraint. . . .' Thus, for instance, when in that case and in Pierce v. Society of Sisters, 268 U.S. 510, the Court struck down laws which sought not to require what children must learn in schools, but to prescribe, in the first case, what they must *not* learn, and in the second, *where* they must acquire their learning, I do not think it was wrong to put those decisions on 'the right of the individual to . . . establish a home and bring up children,' Meyer v. Nebraska, ibid., or on the basis that 'The fundamental theory of liberty upon which all governments in this Union repose excludes any general power of the State to standardize its children by forcing them to accept instruction from public teachers only,' Pierce v. Society of Sisters, at 535. I consider this so, even though today those decisions would probably have gone by reference to the concepts of freedom of expression and conscience assured against state action by the Fourteenth

Amendment, concepts that are derived from the explicit guarantees of the First Amendment against federal encroachment upon freedom of speech and belief. See West Virginia State Board of Education v. Barnette, 319 U.S. 624, and 656 (dissenting opinion); Prince v. Massachusetts, 321 U.S. 158, 166. For it is the purposes of those guarantees and not their text, the reasons for their statement by the Framers and not the statement itself, see Palko v. Connecticut, 302 U.S. 319, 324-327; United States v. Carolene Prods., 304 U.S. 144, 152-153, which have led to their present status in the compendious notion of "liberty" embraced in the Fourteenth Amendment.

"Each new claim to Constitutional protection must be considered against a background of Constitutional purposes, as they have been rationally perceived and historically developed. Though we exercise limited and sharply restrained judgment, yet there is no 'mechanical yardstick,' no 'mechanical answer.' The decision of an apparently novel claim must depend on grounds which follow closely on well-accepted principles and criteria. The new decision must take 'its place in relation to what went before and further [cut] a channel for what is to come.' Irvine v. California, 347 U.S. 128, 147 (dissenting opinion). . . ."

Because this ban on the use of contraceptives allowed for "the intrusion of the machinery of the criminal law into the very heart of marital privacy, requiring husband and wife to render account before a criminal tribunal of their uses of that intimacy," it impaired a fundamental aspect of "liberty," the privacy of the home, and of the marital relationship. Hence Justice Harlan called for a "stronger justification" for this measure than he would have for other measures, such as direct regulation of sales of contraceptive devices, which also served the state interest of preventing what it considered an "immoral" practice but which would not invade so deeply our basic notions of privacy. Justice Harlan found that the state had not even "remotely suggest[ed] a justification" for the means it had chosen. Moreover, and "conclusive[ly]," he found that "no nation, including several which quite evidently share Connecticut's moral policy, [footnote omitted] has seen fit to effectuate that policy by the means presented here."[s]

Section B. APPLICATIONS OF DUE PROCESS IN A FEDERAL SYSTEM

1. Freedom from Unreasonable Searches and Seizures

Wolf v. Colorado 338 U.S. 25, 69 S. Ct. 1359, 93 L. Ed. 1782 (1949)

MR. JUSTICE FRANKFURTER delivered the opinion of the Court.

The precise question for consideration is this: Does a conviction by a State court for a State offense deny the "due process of law" required by the Fourteenth Amendment, solely because evidence that was admitted at the trial was obtained under circumstances which would have rendered it inadmissible in a prosecution for violation of a federal law in a court of the United States because there deemed to be an infraction of the Fourth Amendment as applied in Weeks v. United States, 232 U.S. 383? The Supreme Court of Colorado has sustained convictions in which such evidence was admitted, 117 Col. 279,

---

[s] The Supreme Court later struck down the Connecticut statute in Griswold v. Connecticut, 381 U.S. 479 (1965). See page 1112 infra. — ED.

Section B. Applications of Due Process in a Federal System

187 P.2d 926; 117 Col. 321, 187 P.2d 928, and we brought the cases here. 333 U.S. 879. . . .

The security of one's privacy against arbitrary intrusion by the police — which is at the core of the Fourth Amendment — is basic to a free society. It is therefore implicit in "the concept of ordered liberty" and as such enforceable against the States through the Due Process Clause. The knock at the door, whether by day or by night, as a prelude to a search, without authority of law but solely on the authority of the police, did not need the commentary of recent history to be condemned as inconsistent with the conception of human rights enshrined in the history and the basic constitutional documents of English-speaking peoples.

Accordingly, we have no hesitation in saying that were a State affirmatively to sanction such police incursion into privacy it would run counter to the guaranty of the Fourteenth Amendment. But the ways of enforcing such a basic right raise questions of a different order. How such arbitrary conduct should be checked, what remedies against it should be afforded, the means by which the right should be made effective, are all questions that are not to be so dogmatically answered as to preclude the varying solutions which spring from an allowable range of judgment on issues not susceptible of quantitative solution.

In Weeks v. United States, supra, this Court held that in a federal prosecution the Fourth Amendment barred the use of evidence secured through an illegal search and seizure. This ruling was made for the first time in 1914. It was not derived from the explicit requirements of the Fourth Amendment; it was not based on legislation expressing Congressional policy in the enforcement of the Constitution. The decision was a matter of judicial implication. Since then it has been frequently applied and we stoutly adhere to it. But the immediate question is whether the basic right to protection against arbitrary intrusion by the police demands the exclusion of logically relevant evidence obtained by an unreasonable search and seizure because, in a federal prosecution for a federal crime, it would be excluded. As a matter of inherent reason, one would suppose this to be an issue as to which men with complete devotion to the protection of the right of privacy might give different answers. When we find that in fact most of the English-speaking world does not regard as vital to such protection the exclusion of evidence thus obtained, we must hesitate to treat this remedy as an essential ingredient of the right. The contrariety of views of the States is particularly impressive in view of the careful reconsideration which they have given the problem in the light of the Weeks decision. . . .

. . . As of today 31 States reject the Weeks doctrine, 16 States are in agreement with it (Table I.) . . .[t] Of 10 jurisdictions within the United Kingdom and the British Commonwealth of Nations which have passed on the question, none has held evidence obtained by illegal search and seizure inadmissible. (Table J.)

The jurisdictions which have rejected the Weeks doctrine have not left the right to privacy without other means of protection. Indeed, the exclusion of evidence is a remedy which directly serves only to protect those upon whose person or premises something incriminating has been found. We cannot, therefore, regard it as a departure from basic standards to remand such persons, together with those who emerge scatheless from a search, to the remedies of private action and such protection as the internal discipline of the police, under the eyes of an alert public opinion, may afford. Granting that in practice the exclusion of evidence may be an effective way of deterring unreasonable searches, it is not for this Court to condemn as falling below the minimal standards assured by the Due Process Clause a State's reliance upon other methods which, if consistently enforced, would be equally effective. . . . There are, moreover, reasons for excluding evidence unreasonably obtained by the federal police which are less compelling in the case of police under State or local authority. The public opinion of a community can far more effectively be exerted against oppressive conduct on the part of police directly responsible to the

[t] Tables A through J of the Appendix are omitted. — ED.

community itself than can local opinion, sporadically aroused, be brought to bear upon remote authority pervasively exerted throughout the country.

We hold, therefore, that in a prosecution in a State court for a State crime the Fourteenth Amendment does not forbid the admission of evidence obtained by an unreasonable search and seizure. . . .

Affirmed.

MR. JUSTICE BLACK, concurring.

. . . I should be for reversal of this case if I thought the Fourth Amendment not only prohibited "unreasonable searches and seizures," but also, of itself, barred the use of evidence so unlawfully obtained. But I agree with what appears to be a plain implication of the Court's opinion that the federal exclusionary rule is not a command of the Fourth Amendment but is a judicially created rule of evidence which Congress might negate. See McNabb v. United States, 318 U.S. 332.

MR. JUSTICE MURPHY, with whom MR. JUSTICE RUTLEDGE joins, dissenting.

. . . [B]ut one remedy exists to deter violations of the search and seizure clause. That is the rule which excludes illegally obtained evidence. Only by exclusion can we impress upon the zealous prosecutor that violation of the Constitution will do him no good. And only when that point is driven home can the prosecutor be expected to emphasize the importance of observing constitutional demands in his instructions to the police. . . .

I cannot believe that we should decide due process questions by simply taking a poll of the rules in various jurisdictions, even if we follow the Palko "test." Today's decision will do inestimable harm to the cause of fair police methods in our cities and states. Even more important, perhaps, it must have tragic effect upon public respect for our judiciary. For the Court now allows what is indeed shabby business: lawlessness by officers of the law. . . .[u]

Mapp v. Ohio 367 U.S. 643, 81 S. Ct. 1684, 6 L. Ed. 2d 1081 (1961)

MR. JUSTICE CLARK delivered the opinion of the Court.

Appellant stands convicted of knowingly having had in her possession and under her control certain lewd and lascivious books, pictures, and photographs. . . . [T]he Supreme Court of Ohio found that her conviction was valid though "based primarily upon the introduction in evidence of lewd and lascivious books and pictures unlawfully seized during an unlawful search of defendant's home. . . ." 170 Ohio St. 427, 428.

On May 23, 1957, three Cleveland police officers arrived at appellant's residence in that city pursuant to information that "a person [was] hiding out in the home, who was wanted for questioning in connection with a recent bombing, and that there was a large amount of policy paraphernalia being hidden in the home." Miss Mapp and her daughter by a former marriage lived on the top floor of the two-family dwelling. Upon their arrival at that house, the officers knocked on the door and demanded entrance but appellant, after telephoning her attorney, refused to admit them without a search warrant. They advised their headquarters of the situation and undertook a surveillance of the house.

The officers again sought entrance some three hours later when four or more additional officers arrived on the scene. When Miss Mapp did not come to the door immediately, at least one of the several doors to the house was forcibly opened and the policemen gained admittance. Meanwhile Miss Mapp's attorney arrived, but the officers, having secured their own entry, and continuing in their defiance of the law, would permit him neither to see Miss Mapp nor to enter the house. It appears that Miss Mapp was halfway down the stairs from the upper floor to the front when the officers, in this highhanded manner, broke into the hall. She demanded to see the search warrant. A paper, claimed to be a

---

[u] Dissenting opinions of Justices Douglas and Rutledge are omitted. — ED.

Section B. Applications of Due Process in a Federal System 1009

warrant, was held up by one of the officers. She grabbed the "warrant" and placed it in her bosom. A struggle ensued in which the officers recovered the piece of paper and as a result of which they handcuffed appellant because she had been "belligerent" in resisting their official rescue of the "warrant" from her person. Running roughshod over appellant, a policeman "grabbed" her, "twisted [her] hand," and she "yelled [and] pleaded with him" because "it was hurting." Appellant, in handcuffs, was then forcibly taken upstairs to her bedroom where the officers searched a dresser, a chest of drawers, a closet and some suitcases. They also looked into a photo album and through personal papers belonging to the appellant. The search spread to the rest of the second floor including the child's bedroom, the living room, the kitchen and a dinette. The basement of the building and a trunk found therein were also searched. The obscene materials for possession of which she was ultimately convicted were discovered in the course of that widespread search.

At the trial no search warrant was produced by the prosecution, nor was the failure to produce one explained or accounted for. At best, "There is, in the record, considerable doubt as to whether there ever was any warrant for the search of defendant's home." 170 Ohio St., at 430. The Ohio Supreme Court believed a "reasonable argument" could be made that the conviction should be reversed "because the 'methods' employed to obtain the [evidence] . . . were such as to 'offend "a sense of justice," ' " but the court found determinative the fact that the evidence had not been taken "from defendant's person by the use of brutal or offensive physical force against defendant." 170 Ohio St., at 431.

The State says that even if the search were made without authority, or otherwise unreasonably, it is not prevented from using the unconstitutionally seized evidence at trial, citing Wolf v. Colorado, 338 U.S. 25, in which this Court did indeed hold "that in a prosecution in a State court for a State crime the Fourteenth Amendment does not forbid the admission of evidence obtained by an unreasonable search and seizure." At p. 33. On this appeal, of which we have noted probable jurisdiction, 364 U.S. 868, it is urged once again that we review that holding.

. . . [I]n the year 1914, in the Weeks Case, this Court "for the first time" held that "in a federal prosecution the Fourth Amendment barred the use of evidence secured through an illegal search and seizure." Wolf v. Colorado, supra (338 U.S. at 28). This Court has ever since required of federal law officers a strict adherence to that command which this Court has held to be a clear, specific, and constitutionally required — even if judicially implied — deterrent safeguard without insistence upon which the Fourth Amendment would have been reduced to "a form of words." Holmes, J., Silverthorne Lumber Co. v. United States, 251 U.S. 385, 392 (1920). It meant, quite simply, that "conviction by means of unlawful seizures and enforced confessions . . . should find no sanction in the judgments of the courts. . . ." Weeks v. United States, supra (232 U.S. at 392), and that such evidence "shall not be used at all." Silverthorne Lumber Co. v. United States, supra (251 U.S., at 392). . . .

In 1949, 35 years after Weeks was announced this Court, in Wolf v. Colorado (U.S.), supra, again for the first time, discussed the effect of the Fourth Amendment upon the States through the operation of the Due Process Clause of the Fourteenth Amendment. . . .

. . . The Court's reasons for not considering essential to the right to privacy, as a curb imposed upon the States by the Due Process Clause, that which decades before had been posited as part and parcel of the Fourth Amendment's limitation upon federal encroachment of individual privacy, were bottomed on factual considerations. . . .

While in 1949, prior to the Wolf Case, almost two-thirds of the States were opposed to the use of the exclusionary rule, now, despite the Wolf Case, more than half of those since passing upon it, by their own legislative or judicial decision, have wholly or partly adopted or adhered to the Weeks rule. See Elkins v. United States, 364 U.S. 206, Appx., pp. 224-232 (1960). Significantly, among those now following the rule is California, which, according to its highest court, was "compelled to reach that conclusion because other remedies have completely failed to secure compliance with the constitutional provisions...." People v. Cahan, 44 Cal. 2d 434, 445 (1955).... The experience of California that such other remedies have been worthless and futile is buttressed by the experience of other States. The obvious futility of relegating the Fourth Amendment to the protection of other remedies has, moreover, been recognized by this Court since Wolf. See Irvine v. California, 347 U.S. 128, 137 (1954)....

It, therefore, plainly appears that the factual considerations supporting the failure of the Wolf Court to include the Weeks exclusionary rule when it recognized the enforceability of the right to privacy against the States in 1949, while not basically relevant to the constitutional consideration, could not, in any analysis, now be deemed controlling....

... Today we once again examine Wolf's constitutional documentation of the right to privacy free from unreasonable state intrusion, and, after its dozen years on our books, are led by it to close the only courtroom door remaining open to evidence secured by official lawlessness in flagrant abuse of that basic right, reserved to all persons as a specific guarantee against that very same unlawful conduct. We hold that all evidence obtained by searches and seizures in violation of the Constitution is, by that same authority, inadmissible in a state court....

... [T]he admission of the new constitutional right by Wolf could not consistently tolerate denial of its most important constitutional privilege, namely, the exclusion of the evidence which an accused had been forced to give by reason of the unlawful seizure. To hold otherwise is to grant the right but in reality to withhold its privilege and enjoyment. Only last year the Court itself recognized that the purpose of the exclusionary rule "is to deter — to compel respect for the constitutional guaranty in the only effectively available way — by removing the incentive to disregard it." Elkins v. United States, supra (364 U.S. at 217)....

... Nor can it lightly be assumed that, as a practical matter, adoption of the exclusionary rule fetters law enforcement. Only last year this Court expressly considered that contention and found that "pragmatic evidence of a sort" to the contrary was not wanting. Elkins v. United States, supra (364 U.S. at 218). The Court noted that "The federal courts themselves have operated under the exclusionary rule of Weeks for almost half a century; yet it has not been suggested either that the Federal Bureau of Investigation [10] has thereby been rendered ineffective, or that the administration of criminal justice in the federal courts has thereby been disrupted. Moreover, the experience of the states is impressive.... The movement towards the rule of exclusion has been halting but seemingly inexorable." Id. 364 U.S. at 218, 219.

The ignoble shortcut to conviction left open to the State tends to destroy the entire system of constitutional restraints on which the liberties of the people rest. Having once recognized that the right to privacy embodied in the Fourth Amendment is enforceable against the States, and that the right to be secure against rude invasions of privacy by state officers is, therefore, constitutional in origin, we can no longer permit that right to remain an empty promise....

The judgment of the Supreme Court of Ohio is reversed and the cause remanded for further proceedings not inconsistent with this opinion.

Reversed and remanded.[v]

UNITED STATES v. CALANDRA, 414 U.S. 338, 94 S. Ct. 613, 38 L. Ed. 2d 561 (1974). Powell, J.: "This case presents the question whether a witness summoned to ap-

---

[10] See the remarks of Mr. Hoover, Director of the Federal Bureau of Investigation. FBI Law Enforcement Bulletin, September, 1952, pp. 1-2, quoted in Elkins v. United States, 364 U.S. 206, 218, 219, note.

[v] Justices Black and Douglas wrote separate concurring opinions. Mr. Justice Harlan, with whom Justices Frankfurter and Whittaker joined, wrote a dissenting opinion. Mr. Justice Stewart joined in the judgment of reversal on the ground that the Ohio statute "making criminal the mere knowing possession of obscene material," violates the Fourteenth Amendment's assurance of free thought and expression. — ED.

Section B. Applications of Due Process in a Federal System

pear and testify before a grand jury may refuse to answer questions on the ground that they are based on evidence obtained from an unlawful search and seizure. The issue is of considerable importance to the administration of criminal justice. . . .

"On March 1, 1971, a special grand jury was convened in the Northern District of Ohio to investigate possible loansharking activities in violation of federal laws. The grand jury subpoenaed Calandra in order to ask him questions based on the evidence seized during the search of his place of business on December 15, 1970. . . .

". . . On August 27, the District Court held a hearing at which Calandra stipulated that he would refuse to answer questions based on the seized materials. On October 1, the District Court entered its judgment ordering the evidence suppressed and returned to Calandra and further ordering that Calandra need not answer any of the grand jury's questions based on the suppressed evidence. 332 F. Supp. 737 (1971). The court held that 'due process . . . allows a witness to litigate the question of whether the evidence which constitutes the basis for the questions asked of him before the grand jury has been obtained in a way which violates the constitutional protection against unlawful search and seizure.' Id., at 742. The court found that the search warrant had been issued without probable cause and that the search had exceeded the scope of the warrant.

"The Court of Appeals for the Sixth Circuit affirmed. . . . 465 F.2d 1218 (1972). . . .

"We granted the Government's petition for certiorari, 410 U.S. 925 (1973). We now reverse.

"The institution of the grand jury is deeply rooted in Anglo-American history. . . . Its responsibilities continue to include both the determination whether there is probable cause to believe a crime has been committed and the protection of citizens against unfounded criminal prosecutions. Branzburg v. Hayes, 408 U.S. 665, 686-687 (1972).

"Traditionally the grand jury has been accorded wide latitude to inquire into violations of criminal law. No judge presides to monitor its proceedings. It deliberates in secret and may determine alone the course of its inquiry. The grand jury may compel the production of evidence or the testimony of witnesses as it considers appropriate, and its operation generally is unrestrained by the technical procedural and evidentiary rules governing the conduct of criminal trials. . . .

"In the instant case, the Court of Appeals held that the exclusionary rule of the Fourth Amendment limits the grand jury's power to compel a witness to answer questions based on evidence obtained from a prior unlawful search and seizure. . . .

"The purpose of the exclusionary rule is not to redress the injury to the privacy of the search victim. . . . Instead, the rule's prime purpose is to deter future unlawful police conduct and thereby effectuate the guarantee of the Fourth Amendment against unreasonable searches and seizures. . . .

"In deciding whether to extend the exclusionary rule to grand jury proceedings, we must weigh the potential injury to the historic role and functions of the grand jury against the potential benefits of the rule as applied in this context. It is evident that this extension of the exclusionary rule would seriously impede the grand jury. . . . Permitting witnesses to invoke the exclusionary rule before a grand jury would precipitate adjudication of issues hitherto reserved for the trial on the merits and would delay and disrupt grand jury proceedings. . . .

"Against this potential damage to the role and functions of the grand jury, we must weigh the benefits to be derived from this proposed extension of the exclusionary rule. . . .

". . . The incentive to disregard the requirement of the Fourth Amendment solely to obtain an indictment from a grand jury is substantially negated by the inadmissibility of the illegally seized evidence in a subsequent criminal prosecution of the search victim. For the most part, a prosecutor would be unlikely to request an indictment where a conviction could not be obtained. We therefore decline to embrace a view that would achieve

1012   Chapter Fifteen.   Fair Procedure

a speculative and undoubtedly minimal advance in the deterrence of police misconduct at the expense of substantially impeding the role of the grand jury. . . .

"Mr. Justice Brennan, with whom Mr. Justice Douglas and Mr. Justice Marshall join, dissenting.

". . . [T]he Court seriously errs in describing the exclusionary rule as merely 'a judicially created remedy designed to safeguard Fourth Amendment rights generally through its deterrent effect. . . .' Ante, at 348. . . .

". . . For the first time, the Court today discounts to the point of extinction the vital function of the rule to insure that the judiciary avoid even the slightest appearance of sanctioning illegal government conduct. This rejection of 'the imperative of judicial integrity,' Elkins v. United States, 364 U.S. 206, 222 (1960), openly invites '[t]he conviction that all government is staffed by . . . hypocrites[, a conviction] easy to instill and difficult to erase.' Paulsen, The Exclusionary Rule and Misconduct by the Police, 52 J. Crim. L.C. & P.S. 255, 258 (1961). . . .

"[T]o allow Calandra to be subjected to questions derived from the illegal search of his office and seizure of his files is 'to thwart the [Fourth and Fourteenth Amendments' protection] of . . . individual privacy . . . and to entangle the courts in the illegal acts of Government agents.' Ibid. . . .

". . . Respondent is told that he must look to damages to redress the concededly unconstitutional invasion of his privacy. In other words, officialdom may profit from its lawlessness if it is willing to pay a price. . . .

". . . I . . . fear that when next we confront a case of conviction rested on illegally seized evidence, today's decision will be invoked to sustain the conclusion in that case also, that 'it is unrealistic to assume' that application of the rule at trial would 'significantly further' the goal of deterrence — though, if the police are presently undeterred, it is difficult to see how removal of the sanction of exclusion will induce more lawful official conduct. . . ."

2. Freedom from Compulsory Self-Incrimination

Malloy v. Hogan   378 U.S. 1, 84 S. Ct. 1489, 12 L. Ed. 2d 653 (1964)

Mr. Justice Brennan delivered the opinion of the Court.

In this case we are asked to reconsider prior decisions holding that the privilege against self-incrimination is not safeguarded against state action by the Fourteenth Amendment. Twining v. New Jersey, 211 U.S. 78; Adamson v. California, 332 U.S. 46.[1]

The petitioner was arrested during a gambling raid in 1959 by Hartford, Connecticut, police. He pleaded guilty to the crime of pool-selling, a misdemeanor, and was sentenced to one year in jail and fined $500. The sentence was ordered to be suspended after 90 days, at which time he was to be placed on probation for two years. About 16 months after his guilty plea, petitioner was ordered to testify before a referee appointed by the Superior Court of Hartford County to conduct an inquiry into alleged gambling and other criminal activities in the county. The petitioner was asked a number of questions related to events surrounding his arrest and conviction. He refused to answer any question "on the grounds

---

[1] In both cases the question was whether comment upon the failure of an accused to take the stand in his own defense in a state prosecution violated the privilege. It was assumed, but not decided, in both cases that such comment in a federal prosecution for a federal offense would infringe the provision of the Fifth Amendment that "no person . . . shall be compelled in any criminal case to be a witness against himself." For other statements by the Court that the Fourteenth Amendment does not apply the federal privilege in state proceedings, see Cohen v. Hurley, 366 U.S. 117, 127-129; Snyder v. Massachusetts, 291 U.S. 97, 105.

Section B. Applications of Due Process in a Federal System 1013

it may tend to incriminate me." The Superior Court adjudged him in contempt, and committed him to prison until he was willing to answer the questions. Petitioner's application for a writ of habeas corpus was denied by the Superior Court, and the Connecticut Supreme Court of Errors affirmed. 150 Conn. 220; 187 A.2d 744. The latter court held that the Fifth Amendment's privilege against self-incrimination was not available to a witness in a state proceeding, that the Fourteenth Amendment extended no privilege to him, and that the petitioner had not properly invoked the privilege available under the Connecticut Constitution. We granted certiorari. 373 U.S. 948. We reverse. We hold that the Fourteenth Amendment guaranteed the petitioner the protection of the Fifth Amendment's privilege against self-incrimination, and that under the applicable federal standard, the Connecticut Supreme Court of Errors erred in holding that the privilege was not properly invoked.

The extent to which the Fourteenth Amendment prevents state invasion of rights enumerated in the first eight Amendments has been considered in numerous cases in this Court since the Amendment's adoption in 1868. Although many Justices have deemed the Amendment to incorporate all eight of the Amendments,[2] the view which has thus far prevailed dates from the decision in 1897 in Chicago, B. & O. R. Co. v. Chicago, 166 U.S. 226, which held that the Due Process Clause requires the States to pay just compensation for private property taken for public use.[3] It was on the authority of that decision that the Court said in 1908 in Twining v. New Jersey, supra, that "it is possible that some of the personal rights safeguarded by the first eight Amendments against National action may also be safeguarded against state action, because a denial of them would be a denial of due process of law." 211 U.S., at 99.

The Court has not hesitated to re-examine past decisions according the Fourteenth Amendment a less central role in the preservation of basic liberties than that which was contemplated by its Framers when they added the Amendment to our constitutional scheme. Thus, although the Court as late as 1922 said that "neither the Fourteenth Amendment nor any other provision of the Constitution of the United States imposes upon the States any restrictions about 'freedom of speech' . . . ," Prudential Ins. Co. v. Cheek, 259 U.S. 530, 543, three years later Gitlow v. New York, 268 U.S. 652, initiated a series of decisions which today holds immune from state invasion every First Amendment protection for the cherished rights of mind and spirit — the freedoms of speech, press, religion, assembly, association, and petition for redress of grievances.[4]

Similarly, Palko v. Connecticut, 302 U.S. 319, decided in 1938, suggested that the

---

[2] Ten Justices have supported this view. See Gideon v. Wainwright, 372 U.S. 335, 346 (opinion of Mr. Justice Douglas). The Court expressed itself as unpersuaded to this view in In re Kemmler, 136 U.S. 436, 448-449; McElvaine v. Brush, 142 U.S. 155, 158-159; Maxwell v. Dow, 176 U.S. 581, 597-598; Twining v. New Jersey, supra, p. 96. See Spies v. Illinois, 123 U.S. 131. Decisions that particular guarantees were not safeguarded against state action by the Privileges and Immunities Clause or other provisions of the Fourteenth Amendment are: United States v. Cruikshank, 92 U.S. 542, 551; Prudential Ins. Co. v. Cheek, 259 U.S. 530, 543 (First Amendment); Presser v. Illinois, 116 U.S. 252, 265 (Second Amendment); Weeks v. United States, 232 U.S. 383, 398 (Fourth Amendment); Hurtado v. California, 110 U.S. 516, 538 (Fifth Amendment requirement of grand jury indictments); Palko v. Connecticut, 302 U.S. 319, 328 (Fifth Amendment double jeopardy); Maxwell v. Dow, 176 U.S. 581, 595 (Sixth Amendment jury trial); Walker v. Sauvinet, 92 U.S. 90, 92 (Seventh Amendment jury trial); In re Kemmler, supra; McElvaine v. Brush, supra; O'Neil v. Vermont, 144 U.S. 323, 332 (Eighth Amendment prohibition against cruel and unusual punishment).

[3] In Barron v. Baltimore, 7 Pet. 243, decided before the adoption of the Fourteenth Amendment, Chief Justice Marshall, speaking for the Court, held that this right was not secured against state action by the Fifth Amendment's provision: "Nor shall private property be taken for public use, without just compensation."

[4] E.g., Gitlow v. New York, 268 U.S. 652, 666 (speech and press); Lovell v. City of Griffin, 303 U.S. 444, 450 (speech and press); Sullivan v. New York Times Co., 376 U.S. 264 (speech and press); Staub v. City of Baxley, 355 U.S. 313 (speech); Grosjean v. American Press Co., 297 U.S. 233, 244 (press); Cantwell v. Connecticut, 210 U.S. 296, 303 (religion); De Jonge v. Oregon, 200 U.S. 353, 364 (assembly); Shelton v. Tucker 364 U.S. 479, 486 (association); Louisiana ex rel. Gremillion v. NAACP, 366 U.S. 293, 296 (association); NAACP v. Button, 371 U.S. 415 (association and speech); Brotherhood of Railroad Trainmen v. Virginia ex rel. Virginia State Bar, 377 U.S. 1 (association).

rights secured by the Fourth Amendment, were not protected against state action, citing at 302 U.S. 324, the statement of the Court in 1914 in Weeks v. United States, 232 U.S. 383, 398, that "the Fourth Amendment is not directed to individual misconduct of [state] officials." In 1961, however, the Court held that in the light of later decisions,[5] it was taken as settled that ". . . the Fourth Amendment's right of privacy has been declared enforceable against the States through the Due Process Clause of the Fourteenth. . . ." Mapp v. Ohio, 367 U.S. 643, 655. Again, although the Court held in 1942 that in a state prosecution for a noncapital offense, "appointment of counsel is not a fundamental right," Betts v. Brady, 316 U.S. 455, 471; cf. Powell v. Alabama, 287 U.S. 45, only last Term this decision was reexamined and it was held that provision of counsel in all criminal cases was "a fundamental right essential to a fair trial," and thus was made obligatory on the States by the Fourteenth Amendment. Gideon v. Wainwright, 372 U.S. 335, 344-345.[6]

We hold today that the Fifth Amendment's exception from compulsory self-incrimination is also protected by the Fourteenth Amendment against abridgment by the States. Decisions of the Court since Twining and Adamson have departed from the contrary view expressed in those cases. We discuss first the decisions which forbid the use of coerced confessions in state criminal prosecutions. . . .

[Mr. Justice Brennan here summarized a number of Supreme Court opinions in which confessions were held inadmissible in state court trials where not truly voluntary. He added:] The Fourteenth Amendment secures against state invasion the same privilege that the Fifth Amendment guarantees against federal infringement — the right of a person to remain silent unless he chooses to speak in the unfettered exercise of his own will, and to suffer no penalty, as held in Twining, for such silence.

This conclusion is fortified by our recent decision in Mapp v. Ohio, 367 U.S. 643, overruling Wolf v. Colorado, supra, which had held "that in a prosecution in a state court for a state crime the Fourteenth Amendment does not forbid the admission of evidence obtained by an unreasonable search and seizure". . . . In thus returning to the Boyd view that the privilege is one of the "principles of a free government," 116 U.S., at 632,[7] Mapp necessarily repudiated the Twining concept of the privilege as a mere rule of evidence "best defended not as an unchangeable principle of universal justice but as a law proved by experience to be expedient." 211 U.S., at 113.

The respondent State of Connecticut concedes in its brief that under our decisions, particularly those involving coerced confessions, "the accusatorial system has become a fundamental part of the fabric of our society and, hence, is enforceable against the States." The State urges, however, that the availability of the federal privilege to a witness in a state inquiry is to be determined according to a less stringent standard than is applicable in a federal proceeding. We disagree. We have held that the guarantees of the First Amendment, Gitlow v. New York, supra; Cantwell v. Connecticut, supra; Louisiana ex rel. Gremillion v. NAACP, supra, the prohibition of unreasonable searches and seizures of the Fourth Amendment, Ker v. California, 374 U.S. 23, and the right to counsel guaranteed by the Sixth Amendment, Gideon v. Wainwright, supra, are all to be enforced against the States under the Fourteenth Amendment according to the same standards that

[5] See Wolf v. Colorado, 338 U.S. 25, 27-28; Elkins v. United States, 364 U.S. 206, 213.

[6] See also Robinson v. California, 370 U.S. 660, 666, which, despite In re Kemmler, supra; McElvaine v. Brush, supra; O'Neil v. Vermont, supra, made applicable to the States the Eighth Amendment's ban on cruel and unusual punishments.

[7] Boyd had said of the privilege, ". . . any compulsory discovery by extorting the party's oath . . . to convict him of crime . . . is contrary to the principles of a free government. It is abhorrent to the instincts of an Englishman; it is abhorrent to the instincts of an American. It may suit the purposes of despotic power; but it cannot abide the pure atmosphere of political liberty and personal freedom." 116 U.S. 631-632.

Dean Griswold has said: "I believe the Fifth Amendment is, and has been through this period of crisis, an expression of the moral striving of the community. It has been a reflection of our common conscience, a symbol of the America which stirs our hearts." The Fifth Amendment Today 73 (1955).

Section B. Applications of Due Process in a Federal System 1015

protect those personal rights against federal encroachment. In the coerced confession cases, involving the policies of the privilege itself, there has been no suggestion that a confession might be considered coerced if used in a federal but not a state tribunal. The Court thus has rejected the notion that the Fourteenth Amendment applies to the states only a "watered-down, subjective version of the Bill of Rights." Ohio ex rel. Eaton v. Price, 364 U.S. 263, 275 (dissenting opinion). If Cohen v. Hurley, 366 U.S. 117, and Adamson v. California, supra, suggest such an application of the privilege against self-incrimination, that suggestion cannot survive recognition of the degree to which the Twining view of the privilege has been eroded.[w] What is accorded is a privilege of refusing to incriminate one's self, and the feared prosecution may be by either federal or state authorities. Murphy v. Waterfront Comm'n, 378 U.S. 52. It would be incongruous to have different standards determine the validity of a claim of privilege based on the same feared prosecution, depending on whether the claim was asserted in a state or federal court. Therefore, the same standards must determine whether an accused's silence in either a federal or state proceeding is justified.

We turn to the petitioner's claim that the State of Connecticut denied him the protection of his federal privilege. It must be considered irrelevant that the petitioner was a witness in a statutory inquiry and not a defendant in a criminal prosecution, for it has long been settled that the privilege protects witnesses in similar federal inquiries. Counselman v. Hitchcock, 142 U.S. 547; McCarthy v. Arndstein, 266 U.S. 34; Hoffman v. United States, 341 U.S. 479. . . .

We conclude, therefore, that as to each of the questions, it was "evident from the implication of the question, in the setting in which it [was] asked, that a responsive answer to the question or an explanation of why it [could not] be answered might be dangerous because injurious disclosure could result," Hoffman v. United States, supra, 341 U.S. 486-487; see Singleton v. United States, 343 U.S. 944.

Reversed.

While MR. JUSTICE DOUGLAS joins the opinion of the Court, he also adheres to his concurrence in Gideon v. Wainwright, 372 U.S. 335, 345.[x]

LEFKOWITZ v. TURLEY, 414 U.S. 70, 94 S. Ct. 316, 38 L. Ed. 2d 274 (1973). White, J.: "New York [laws] . . . require public contracts to provide that if a contractor refuses to waive immunity or to answer questions when called to testify concerning his contracts with the State or any of its subdivisions, his existing contracts may be canceled and he shall be disqualified from further transactions with the State for five years. In addition to specifying these contract terms, the statutes require disqualification from contracting with public authorities upon failure of any person to waive immunity or to answer questions with respect to his transactions with the State or its subdivisions. The issue in this case is whether these sections are consistent with the Fourteenth Amendment insofar as it makes applicable to the States the Fifth Amendment privilege against compelled self-incrimination.

"[Two licensed architects who were called before a grand jury refused to waive their right not to be compelled in a criminal case to be a witness against themselves.] [T]he District Attorney, as directed by law, notified various contracting authorities of appellees' conduct and called attention to the applicable disqualification statutes. [Upon appellees' action,] a three-judge District Court was convened and declared the four statutory provi-

---

[w] In Griffin v. California, 380 U.S. 609 (1965), the Court reversed a California state court conviction of murder. The trial judge had instructed the jury that it could consider the defendant's failure to testify on the trial of the issue of guilt as tending to indicate the truth of evidence adverse to him as to matters within his knowledge; the prosecutor had made much of the defendant's failure to testify. — ED.

[x] Mr. Justice Harlan wrote a dissenting opinion, in which Mr. Justice Clark joined. Mr. Justice White wrote a dissenting opinion in which Mr. Justice Stewart joined. — ED.

sions at issue unconstitutional under the Fourteenth and Fifth Amendments, 342 F. Supp. 544 (WDNY 1972). . . .

"[T]here is no room for urging that the Fifth Amendment privilege is inapplicable simply because the issue arises, as it does here, in the context of official inquiries into the job performance of a public contractor. Surely, the ordinary rule is that the privilege is available to witnesses called before grand juries as these appellee architects were. Hale v. Henkel, 201 U.S. 43, 66 (1906).

"It is true that the State has a strong, legitimate interest in maintaining the integrity of its civil service and of its transactions with independent contractors furnishing a wide range of goods and services; and New York would have it that this interest is sufficiently strong to override the privilege. . . . But claims of overriding interests are not unusual in Fifth Amendment litigation and they have not fared well. . . .

"The issue in Gardner v. Broderick [392 U.S. 273 (1968)] was whether the State might discharge a police officer who, after he was summoned before a grand jury to testify about the performance of his official duties and was advised of his right against compulsory self-incrimination, then refused to waive that right as requested by the State. Conceding that appellant could be discharged for refusing to answer questions about the performance of his official duties, if not required to waive immunity, the Court held that the officer could not be terminated, as he was, for refusing to waive his constitutional privilege. Although . . . any waiver executed may have been invalid and any answers elicited inadmissible in evidence, the State did not purport to recognize as much and instead attempted to coerce a waiver on the penalty of loss of employment. The 'testimony was demanded before the grand jury in part so that it might be used to prosecute him, and not solely for the purpose of securing an accounting of his performance of his public trust.' 392 U.S., at 279. Hence, the State's statutory provision requiring his dismissal for his refusal to waive immunity could not stand. . . .

"The State nevertheless asserts that whatever may be true of state employees, a different rule is applicable to public contractors such as architects. Because independent contractors may not depend entirely on transactions with the State for their livelihood, it is suggested that disqualification from contracting with official agencies for a period of five years is [not] a forbidden penalty for refusing to answer questions put to them about their job performance. . . .

". . . In some sense the plight of the architect may be worse, for under the New York statutes it may be that any firm that employs him thereafter will also be subject to contract cancellation and disqualification. A significant infringement of constitutional rights cannot be justified by the speculative ability of those affected to cover the damage.

"We should make clear, however, what we have said before. Although due regard for the Fifth Amendment forbids the State to compel incriminating answers from its employees and contractors that may be used against them in criminal proceedings, the Constitution permits that very testimony to be compelled if neither it nor its fruits are available for such use. Kastigar v. United States, [406 U.S. 446 (1972).] . . . Also, given adequate immunity, the State may plainly insist that employees either answer questions under oath about the performance of their job or suffer the loss of employment. By like token, the State may insist that the architects involved in this case either respond to relevant inquiries about the performance of their contracts or suffer cancellation of current relationships and disqualification from contracting with public agencies for an appropriate time in the future. . . . Hence, if answers are to be required in such circumstances States must offer to the witness whatever immunity is required to supplant the privilege and may not insist that the employee or contractor waive such immunity.

"Affirmed.

"Mr. Justice Brennan, with whom Mr. Justice Douglas and Mr. Justice Marshall join.

"I join the Court's opinion in all respects but one. It is my view that immunity which permits testimony to be compelled 'if neither it nor its fruits are available for . . . use' in criminal proceedings does not satisfy the privilege against self-incrimination. 'I believe that the Fifth Amendment's privilege against self-incrimination requires that any jurisdiction that compels a man to incriminate himself grant him absolute immunity under its laws from prosecution for any transaction revealed in that testimony.' Piccirillo v. New York, 400 U.S. 548, 562 (1971) (Brennan, J., dissenting.)"

NOTE Compelled Testimony and the Fifth Amendment

Note in Turley that the Court recites the settled rule that the state may compel incriminating answers from a witness, provided that the state offers to the witness "whatever immunity is required to supplant the privilege." The Court differs, however, on what the scope of that immunity must be. The majority relies on Kastigar, supra, for the current rule that "use and fruits" immunity is sufficient, while the concurring Justices repeat their earlier insistence on "transactional" immunity.

The genesis of this dispute traces back to the 1892 case of Counselman v. Hitchcock, 142 U.S. 547. In this first consideration of an immunity statute, the Court found insufficient a grant of immunity from future use in court of compelled testimony because the statute would not also prevent the use of the compelled testimony to search out other evidence to be used against the witness. The Counselman Court also stated, in dictum: "[A] statutory enactment, to be valid, must afford absolute immunity against future prosecution for the offense to which the question relates." 142 U.S. at 586. Congress responded by assuring full transactional immunity in subsequent legislation. See, e.g., the Compulsory Testimony Act of 1893, 27 Stat. 443, repealed by the Organized Crime Control Act of 1970, 84 Stat. 931.

When the Court held the privilege applicable to the states in Malloy, it also held, in a case decided the same day, Murphy v. Waterfront Commission of New York Harbor, 378 U.S. 52 (1964), that a state must grant a "use and fruits" immunity to a witness with regard to future federal prosecution. Congress construed this case as a revision of the Counselman rule and replaced the "transactional" immunity law, supra, with a "use and fruits" immunity, supra, now codified at 18 U.S.C. §6002 (1970). The Supreme Court then found the "use and fruits" immunity adequate to supplant the Fifth Amendment privilege, both in federal courts, Kastigar v. United States, supra, and in state courts, Zicarelli v. New Jersey State Commission of Investigation, 406 U.S. 472 (1972), provided, as the Court had said in Murphy, that the government is charged with the burden of showing in any later case that its evidence is derived from a source "wholly independent" of the compelled testimony. With such an immunity, Justice Powell wrote for the Court in Kastigar, a witness can be compelled to testify because the effect of the protection is the same as if he had claimed the privilege itself.

Justices Brennan and Douglas, who joined in the Court's opinion in Murphy, however, have argued that intrajurisdictional immunity must provide more extensive protection to the witness. Dissenting from a dismissal of a writ of certiorari, Justice Brennan wrote in Piccirillo v. New York, 400 U.S. 548, 568, that "in dealing with a single jurisdiction," the Court should recognize the "enormous difficulty" of determining whether a prosecution derives from a separate source or from compelled testimony. "Men working in the same office or department exchange information without recording carefully how they obtained certain information; it is often impossible to remember in retrospect how or when or from whom information was obtained." "Use and fruits" immunity may be a more realistic rule, Justice Brennan continued, between jurisdictions because the exchange of information is less "informal and undetected."

What are some rules that might lessen the minority's apprehensions about the "use and fruits" immunity in an intrajurisdictional setting? See Note, Standards for Exclusion in Immunity Cases after Kastigar and Zicarelli, 82 Yale L.J. 171, 182 (1972), e.g.: "In prosecuting an individual for a matter concerning which he has previously been compelled to testify under a grant of immunity, the government will be confined to evidence which was certified by the court before the testimony was compelled." Should a breach or abuse of a grant of immunity by the government support an action for damages? Cf. Bivens v. Six Unknown Named Agents of the Federal Bureau of Narcotics, supra page 867. To what extent should the work product of the prosecution be available to complainants or the courts in order to monitor compliance with immunity grants? Cf. Note: Equal Protection as a Limit on Administrative Discretion, supra page 872. These questions suggest that the "use and fruits" immunity may often entail sensitive inquiries by federal courts, in habeas actions for example, into the inside operations and decisions of state prosecuting offices. "Transactional" immunity, on the other hand, involves the simpler question whether the subsequent prosecution is related to the substance of the compelled testimony. As Justice Brennan noted, "No question arises of tracing the use or non-use of information gleaned from the witness' compelled testimony." Piccirillo, supra, at 569. Which immunity might be expected to promote a smoother working of the federal system?

3. Right to the Assistance of Counsel

Gideon v. Wainwright 372 U.S. 355, 83 S. Ct. 792, 9 L. Ed. 2d 799 (1963)

MR. JUSTICE BLACK delivered the opinion of the Court.

Petitioner was charged in a Florida state court with having broken and entered a poolroom with intent to commit a misdemeanor. This offense is a felony under Florida law. Appearing in court without funds and without a lawyer, petitioner asked the court to appoint counsel for him, whereupon the following colloquy took place:

"The COURT: Mr. Gideon, I am sorry, but I cannot appoint Counsel to represent you in this case. Under the laws of the State of Florida, the only time the Court can appoint Counsel to represent a Defendant is when that person is charged with a capital offense. I am sorry, but I will have to deny your request to appoint Counsel to defend you in this case.

"The DEFENDANT: The United States Supreme Court says I am entitled to be represented by Counsel."

Put to trial before a jury, Gideon conducted his defense about as well as could be expected from a layman. He made an opening statement to the jury, cross-examined the State's witnesses, presented witnesses in his own defense, declined to testify himself, and made a short argument "emphasizing his innocence to the charge contained in the Information filed in this case." The jury returned a verdict of guilty, and petitioner was sentenced to serve five years in the state prison. Later, petitioner filed in the Florida Supreme Court this habeas corpus petition attacking his conviction and sentence on the ground that the trial court's refusal to appoint counsel for him denied him rights "guaranteed by the Constitution and the Bill of Rights by the United States Government." Treating the petition for habeas corpus as properly before it, the State Supreme Court, "upon consideration thereof" but without an opinion, denied all relief. Since 1942, when Betts v. Brady, 316 U.S. 455, was decided by a divided Court, the problem of a defendant's federal constitutional right to counsel in a state court has been a continuing source of controversy and litigation in both state and federal courts. To give this problem another review here, we granted certiorari. 370 U.S. 908. Since Gideon was proceeding in forma pauperis, we appointed counsel to represent him and requested both sides to discuss in their briefs and oral arguments the following: "Should this Court's holding in Betts v. Brady, 316 U.S. 455, be reconsidered?"

Section B. Applications of Due Process in a Federal System

The facts upon which Betts claimed that he had been unconstitutionally denied the right to have counsel appointed to assist him are strikingly like the facts upon which Gideon here bases his federal constitutional claim. Betts was indicted for robbery in a Maryland state court. On arraignment, he told the trial judge of his lack of funds to hire a lawyer and asked the court to appoint one for him. Betts was advised that it was not the practice in that county to appoint counsel for indigent defendants except in murder and rape cases. He then pleaded not guilty, had witnesses summoned, cross-examined the State's witnesses, examined his own, and chose not to testify himself. He was found guilty by the judge, sitting without a jury, and sentenced to eight years in prison. Like Gideon, Betts sought release by habeas corpus, alleging that he had been denied the right to assistance of counsel in violation of the Fourteenth Amendment. Betts was denied any relief, and on review this Court affirmed. It was held that a refusal to appoint counsel for an indigent defendant charged with a felony did not necessarily violate the Due Process Clause of the Fourteenth Amendment, which for reasons given the Court deemed to be the only applicable federal constitutional provision. The Court said: "Asserted denial [of due process] is to be tested by an appraisal of the totality of facts in a given case. That which may, in one setting, constitute a denial of fundamental fairness, shocking to the universal sense of justice, may, in other circumstances, and in the light of other considerations, fall short of such denial." 316 U.S., at 462.

. . . Since the facts and circumstances of the two cases are so nearly indistinguishable, we think the Betts v. Brady holding if left standing would require us to reject Gideon's claim that the Constitution guarantees him the assistance of counsel. Upon full reconsideration we conclude that Betts v. Brady should be overruled.

The Sixth Amendment provides, "In all criminal prosecutions, the accused shall enjoy the right . . . to have the Assistance of Counsel for his defence." We have construed this to mean that in federal courts counsel must be provided for defendants unable to employ counsel unless the right is competently and intelligently waived.[3] . . .

We accept Betts v. Brady's assumption, based as it was on our prior cases, that a provision of the Bill of Rights which is "fundamental and essential to a fair trial" is made obligatory upon the States by the Fourteenth Amendment. We think the Court in Betts was wrong, however, in concluding that the Sixth Amendment's guarantee of counsel is not one of these fundamental rights. Ten years before Betts v. Brady, this Court, after full consideration of all the historical data examined in Betts, had unequivocally declared that "the right to the aid of counsel is of this fundamental character." Powell v. Alabama, 287 U.S. 45, 68 (1932). While the Court at the close of its Powell opinion did by its language, as this Court frequently does, limit its holding to the particular facts and circumstances of that case, its conclusions about the fundamental nature of the right to counsel are unmistakable. . . .

. . . A defendant's need for a lawyer is nowhere better stated than in the moving words of Mr. Justice Sutherland in Powell v. Alabama: "The right to be heard would be, in many cases, of little avail if it did not comprehend the right to be heard by counsel. Even the intelligent and educated layman has small and sometimes no skill in the science of law. If charged with crime, he is incapable, generally, of determining for himself whether the indictment is good or bad. He is unfamiliar with the rules of evidence. Left without the aid of counsel he may be put on trial without a proper charge, and convicted upon incompetent evidence, or evidence irrelevant to the issue or otherwise inadmissible. He lacks both the skill and knowledge adequately to prepare his defense, even though he have a perfect one. He requires the guiding hand of counsel at every step in the proceedings against him. Without it, though he be not guilty, he faces the danger of conviction because he does not know how to establish his innocence." 287 U.S., at 68-69.

The Court in Betts v. Brady departed from the sound wisdom upon which the Court's holding in Powell v. Alabama rested. Florida, supported by two other States, has asked

---

[3] Johnson v. Zerbst, 304 U.S. 458 (1938).

1020   Chapter Fifteen. Fair Procedure

that Betts v. Brady be left intact. Twenty-two States, as friends of the Court, argue that Betts was "an anachronism when handed down" and that it should now be overruled. We agree.

The judgment is reversed and the cause is remanded to the Supreme Court of Florida for further action not inconsistent with this opinion.

Reversed.[y]

Mr. Justice Harlan, concurring.

I agree that Betts v. Brady should be overruled, but consider it entitled to a more respectful burial than has been accorded, at least on the part of those of us who were not on the Court when that case was decided.

I cannot subscribe to the view that Betts v. Brady represented "an abrupt break with its own well-considered precedents." Ante, p. 344. In 1932, in Powell v. Alabama, 287 U.S. 45, a capital case, this Court declared that under the particular facts there presented — "the ignorance and illiteracy of the defendants, their youth, the circumstances of public hostility . . . and above all that they stood in deadly peril of their lives" (287 U.S., at 71) — the state court had a duty to assign counsel for the trial as a necessary requisite of due process of law. It is evident that these limiting facts were not added to the opinion as an afterthought; they were repeatedly emphasized, see 287 U.S., at 52, 57-58, 71, and were clearly regarded as important to the result.

Thus when this Court, a decade later, decided Betts v. Brady, it did no more than to admit of the possible existence of special circumstances in noncapital as well as capital trials, while at the same time insisting that such circumstances be shown in order to establish a denial of due process. The right to appointed counsel had been recognized as being considerably broader in federal prosecutions, see Johnson v. Zerbst, 304 U.S. 458, but to have imposed these requirements on the States would indeed have been "an abrupt break" with the almost immediate past. The declaration that the right to appointed counsel in state prosecutions, as established in Powell v. Alabama, was not limited to capital cases was in truth not a departure from, but an extension of, existing precedent. . . .

In noncapital cases, the "special circumstances" rule has continued to exist in form while its substance has been substantially and steadily eroded. In the first decade after Betts, there were cases in which the Court found special circumstances to be lacking, but usually by a sharply divided vote. However, no such decision has been cited to us, and I have found none, after Quicksall v. Michigan, 339 U.S. 660, decided in 1950. At the same time, there have been not a few cases in which special circumstances were found in little or nothing more than the "complexity" of the legal questions presented, although those questions were often of only routine difficulty. The Court has come to recognize, in other words, that the mere existence of a serious criminal charge constituted in itself special circumstances requiring the services of counsel at trial. In truth the Betts v. Brady rule is no longer a reality.[z]

NOTE Right to Counsel

Gideon v. Wainwright, supra, did not delimit the scope of the right to assigned counsel in criminal prosecution. Was the right applicable only to felonies? Serious misdemeanors? Misdemeanors? In the per curiam decision in Patterson v. Warden, 372 U.S. 776 (1963), the Court indicated that Gideon applied at least to misdemeanors punishable by felony-

---

[y] Following the remand, a Florida court retried Gideon, after assigning to him experienced counsel of his own choice. The jury acquitted Gideon. Anthony Lewis tells Gideon's story in his book, Gideon's Trumpet (1964). — Ed.

[z] Separate concurring opinions of Justices Clark and Douglas are omitted. For a discussion of the contrasting techniques of Black and Harlan in overruling Betts, see Israel, Gideon v. Wainwright: The "Art" of Overruling, 1963 Sup. Ct. Rev. 211. — Ed.

length sentences in addition to felonies, and recently, in Argersinger v. Hamlin, 407 U.S. 25 (1972), a unanimous Court extended this right by prohibiting imprisonment for any offense where the defendant was not provided counsel. In a separate opinion, Justice Brennan added that, thanks to clinical programs and student practice rules, "I think it plain that law students can be expected to make a significant contribution, quantitatively and qualitatively, to the representation of the poor in many areas, including cases reached by today's decision." See Junker, The Right to Counsel in Misdemeanor Cases, 43 Wash. L. Rev. 685 (1965); and on the impact of Argersinger, see Symposium, The Right to Counsel and the Indigent Defendant, 12 Am. Crim. L. Rev. 587 (1975).

United States v. Wade, 388 U.S. 218 (1967), and Gilbert v. California, 388 U.S. 263 (1967), held that a person accused of a crime is entitled under the Sixth and Fourteenth Amendments to have an attorney present at pretrial lineups conducted for identification purposes. Wade precluded any in-court identification preceded by a defective lineup absent a showing of no taint, and Gilbert required exclusion of all testimony concerning impermissible lineups. In Kirby v. Illinois, 406 U.S. 682 (1972), these principles were held inapplicable to the period prior to the start of formal prosecutorial proceedings. Instead the Court adopted a balancing test based on the "totality of the circumstances" of each confrontation. See Stovall v. Denno, 388 U.S. 293 (1967), which, in refusing to apply Wade and Gilbert retroactively, confirmed the standard that previous lineups were violative of due process if "unnecessarily suggestive and conducive to mistaken identification." And Neal v. Biggers, 409 U.S. 188 (1972), applied a similar balancing test to a stationhouse show-up identification, finding no fault with police conduct in that case.

Does the Sixth Amendment entitle a defendant to have counsel present at a postindictment "lineup" by photographic display? The Court refused to apply Wade here because this was not a "critical stage" of the prosecution. United States v. Ash, 413 U.S. 300 (1973). As Justice Stewart said in concurrence, "there are substantially fewer possibilities of impermissible suggestion when photographs are used, and those unfair influences can be readily reconstructed at trial." See Grano, *Kirby*, *Biggers* and *Ash*: Do Any Constitutional Safeguards Remain Against the Danger of Convicting the Innocent?, 72 Mich. L. Rev. 717 (1974). To what extent does the experience of judicial review under a test of "totality of the circumstances" contribute to the later adoption of rules that are both more realistic and more acceptable? Compare Mapp and Gideon with Miranda, infra.

Escobedo v. Illinois 378 U.S. 478, 84 S. Ct. 1758, 12 L. Ed. 2d 977 (1964)

MR. JUSTICE GOLDBERG delivered the opinion of the Court.

The critical question in this case is whether, under the circumstances, the refusal by the police to honor petitioner's request to consult with his lawyer during the course of an interrogation constitutes a denial of "the Assistance of Counsel" in violation of the Sixth Amendment to the Constitution as "made obligatory upon the States by the Fourteenth Amendment," Gideon v. Wainwright, 372 U.S. 335, 342, and thereby renders inadmissible in a state criminal trial any incriminating statement elicited by the police during the interrogation.

On the night of January 19, 1960, petitioner's brother-in-law was fatally shot. At 2:30 A.M. that morning, petitioner was arrested without a warrant and interrogated. Petitioner made no statement to the police and was released at 5 P.M. that afternoon pursuant to a state court writ of habeas corpus obtained by Mr. Warren Wolfson, a lawyer who had been retained by petitioner.

On January 30, Benedict DiGerlando, who was then in police custody and who was later indicted for the murder along with petitioner, told the police that petitioner had fired the fatal shots. Between 8 and 9 P.M. that evening, petitioner and his sister, the widow of the deceased, were arrested and taken to police headquarters. En route to the police station, the police "had handcuffed the defendant behind his back," and "one of the arresting officers, told defendant that DiGerlando had named him as the one who shot" the deceased. Petitioner testified, without contradiction, that the "detectives said they had us pretty well, up pretty tight, and we might as well admit to this crime," and that he replied, "I am sorry but I would like to have advice from my lawyer." A police officer testified that although petitioner was not formally charged "he was in custody" and "couldn't walk out the door."

Shortly after petitioner reached police headquarters, his retained lawyer arrived. The lawyer described the ensuing events in the following terms:

"On that day I received a phone call [from 'the mother of another defendant'] and pursuant to that phone call I went to the Detective Bureau at 11th and State. The first person I talked to was the Sergeant on duty at the Bureau Desk, Sergeant Pidgeon. I asked Sergeant Pidgeon for permission to speak to my client, Danny Escobedo. . . . Sergeant Pidgeon made a call to the Bureau lockup and informed me that the boy had been taken from the lockup to the Homicide Bureau. This was between 9:30 and 10:00 in the evening. Before I went anywhere, he called the Homicide Bureau and told them there was an attorney waiting to see Escobedo. He told me I could not see him. Then I went upstairs to the Homicide Bureau. There were several Homicide Detectives around and I talked to them. I identified myself as Escobedo's attorney and asked permission to see him. They said I could not. . . . The police officer told me to see Chief Flynn who was on duty. I identified myself to Chief Flynn and asked permission to see my client. He said I could not. . . . I think it was approximately 11:00 o'clock. He said I couldn't see him because they hadn't completed questioning. . . . [F]or a second or two I spotted him in an office in the Homicide Bureau. The door was open and I could see through the office. . . . I waved to him and he waved back and then the door was closed, by one of the officers at Homicide.[1] There were four or five officers milling around the Homicide Detail that night. As to whether I talked to Captain Flynn any later that day, I waited around for another hour or two and went back again and renewed by [sic] request to see my client. He again told me I could not. . . . I filed an official complaint with Commissioner Phelan of the Chicago Police Department. I had a conversation with every police officer I could find. I was told at Homicide that I couldn't see him and I would have to get a writ of habeas corpus. I left the Homicide Bureau and from the Detective Bureau at 11th and State at approximately 1:00 A.M. [Sunday morning] I had no opportunity to talk to my client that night. I quoted to Captain Flynn the Section of the Criminal Code which allows an attorney the right to see his client."

Petitioner testified that during the course of the interrogation he repeatedly asked to speak to his lawyer and that the police said that his lawyer "didn't want to see" him. The testimony of the police officers confirmed these accounts in substantial detail. . . .

There is testimony by the police that during the interrogation, petitioner, a 22-year-old of Mexican extraction with no record of previous experience with the police, "was handcuffed" in a standing position and that he "was nervous, he had circles under his eyes and he was upset" and was "agitated" because "he had not slept well in over a week."

It is undisputed that during the course of the interrogation Officer Montejano, who "grew up" in petitioner's neighborhood, who knew his family, and who uses "Spanish language in [his] police work," conferred alone with petitioner "for about a quarter of an hour. . . ." Petitioner testified that the officer said to him "in Spanish that my sister and I could go home if I pinned it on Benedict DiGerlando," that "he would see to it that we

---

[1] Petitioner testified that this ambiguous gesture "could have meant most anything," but that he "took it upon [his] own to think that [the lawyer was telling him] not to say anything," and that the lawyer "wanted to talk" to him.

would go home and be held only as witnesses, if anything, if we had made a statement against DiGerlando . . . , that we would be able to go home that night." Petitioner testified that he made the statement in issue because of this assurance. Officer Montejano denied offering any such assurance.

A police officer testified that during the interrogation the following occurred:

"I informed him of what DiGerlando told me and when I did, he told me that DiGerlando was [lying] and I said, 'Would you care to tell DiGerlando that?' And he said, 'yes, I will.' So, I brought . . . Escobedo in and he confronted DiGerlando and he told him that he was lying and said, 'I didn't shoot Manuel, you did it.' "

In this way, petitioner, for the first time, admitted to some knowledge of the crime. After that he made additional statements further implicating himself in the murder plot. At this point an Assistant State's Attorney, Theodore J. Cooper, was summoned "to take" a statement. Mr. Cooper, an experienced lawyer who was assigned to the Homicide Division to take "statements from some defendants and some prisoners that they had in custody," "took" petitioner's statement by asking carefully framed questions apparently designed to assure the admissibility into evidence of the resulting answers. Mr. Cooper testified that he did not advise petitioner of his constitutional rights, and it is undisputed that no one during the course of the interrogation so advised him.

Petitioner moved both before and during trial to suppress the incriminating statement, but the motions were denied. Petitioner was convicted of murder and he appealed the conviction. . . .

We granted a writ of certiorari to consider whether the petitioner's statement was constitutionally admissible at his trial. 375 U.S. 902. We conclude, for the reasons stated below, that it was not and, accordingly, we reverse the judgment of conviction. . . .

The interrogation here was conducted before petitioner was formally indicted. But in the context of this case, that fact should make no difference. When petitioner requested, and was denied, an opportunity to consult with his lawyer, the investigation had ceased to be a general investigation of "an unsolved crime." Spano v. New York, 360 U.S. 315, 327 (Stewart, J., concurring). Petitioner had become the accused, and the purpose of the interrogation was to "get him" to confess his guilt despite his constitutional right not to do so. At the time of his arrest and throughout the course of the interrogation, the police told petitioner that they had convincing evidence that he had fired the fatal shots. Without informing him of his absolute right to remain silent in the face of this accusation, the police urged him to make a statement. . . .

Petitioner, a layman, was undoubtedly unaware that under Illinois law an admission of "mere" complicity in the murder plot was legally as damaging as an admission of firing of the fatal shots. Escobedo v. Illinois, 28 Ill. 2d 41. The "guiding hand of counsel" was essential to advise petitioner of his rights in this delicate situation. Powell v. Alabama, 287 U.S. 45, 69. This was the "stage when legal aid and advice" were most critical to petitioner. Massiah v. United States, [377 U.S. 201] at 204. It was a stage surely as critical as was the arraignment in Hamilton v. Alabama, 368 U.S. 52, and the preliminary hearing in White v. Maryland, 373 U.S. 59. What happened at this interrogation could certainly "affect the whole trial," Hamilton v. Alabama, supra, at 54, since rights "may be as irretrievably lost, if not then and there asserted, as they are when an accused represented by counsel waives a right for strategic purposes." Ibid. It would exalt form over substance to make the right to counsel, under these circumstances, depend on whether at the time of the interrogation, the authorities had secured a formal indictment. Petitioner had, for all practical purposes, already been charged with murder. . . .

In Gideon v. Wainwright, 372 U.S. 335, we held that every person accused of a crime, whether state or federal, is entitled to a lawyer at trial. The rule sought by the State here, however, would make the trial no more than an appeal from the interrogation; and the "right to use counsel at the formal trial [would be] a very hollow thing [if], for all practical purposes, the conviction is already assured by pretrial examination." In re Groban, 352 U.S. 330, 344 (Black, J., dissenting).[8] "One can imagine a cynical prosecutor saying: 'Let them have the most illustrious counsel, now. They can't escape the noose. There is nothing that counsel can do for them at trial.' " Ex parte Sullivan, 107 F. Supp. 514, 517-518.

It is argued that if the right to counsel is afforded prior to indictment, the number of confessions obtained by the police will diminish significantly, because most confessions are obtained during the period between arrest and indictment, and "any lawyer worth his salt will tell the suspect in no uncertain terms to make no statement to police under any circumstances." Watts v. Indiana, 338 U.S. 49, 59 (Jackson, J., concurring in part and dissenting in part). This argument, of course, cuts two ways. The fact that many confessions are obtained during this period points up its critical nature as a "stage when legal aid and advice" are surely needed. Massiah v. United States, supra, at 204; Hamilton v. Alabama, supra; White v. Maryland, supra. The right to counsel would indeed be hollow if it began at a period when few confessions were obtained. There is necessarily a direct relationship between the importance of a stage to the police in their quest for a confession and the criticalness of that stage to the accused in his need for legal advice. Our Constitution, unlike some others, strikes the balance in favor of the right of the accused to be advised by his lawyer of his privilege against self-incrimination.

We have learned the lesson of history, ancient and modern, that a system of criminal law enforcement which comes to depend on the "confession" will, in the long run, be less reliable [10] and more subject to abuses [11] than a system which depends on extrinsic evidence independently secured through skillful investigation. . . .

Nothing we have said today affects the powers of the police to investigate "an unsolved crime," Spano v. New York, 360 U.S. 315, 327 (Stewart, J., concurring), by gathering information from witnesses and by other "proper investigative efforts." Haynes v. Washington, 373 U.S. 503, 519. We hold only that when the process shifts from investigatory to accusatory — when its focus is on the accused and its purpose is to elicit a confession — our adversary system begins to operate, and, under the circumstances here, the accused must be permitted to consult with his lawyer.

The judgment of the Illinois Supreme Court is reversed and the case remanded for proceedings not inconsistent with this opinion.

Reversed and remanded.[aa]

Miranda v. Arizona[*] 384 U.S. 436, 86 S. Ct. 1602, 16 L. Ed. 2d 694 (1966)

MR. CHIEF JUSTICE WARREN delivered the opinion of the Court.

The cases before us raise questions which go to the roots of our concepts of American

---

[8] The Soviet criminal code does not permit a lawyer to be present during the investigation. The Soviet trial has thus been aptly described as "an appeal from the pretrial investigation." Feifer, Justice in Moscow (1964), 86.

[10] See Committee Print, Subcommittee to Investigate Administration of the Internal Security Act, Senate Committee on the Judiciary, 85th Cong., 1st Sess., reporting and analyzing the proceedings at the XXth Party, Congress of the Communist Party of the Soviet Union, February 25, 1956, exposing the false confessions obtained during the Stalin purges of the 1930's. See also Miller v. United States, 320 F.2d 767, 772-773 (opinion of Chief Judge Bazelon); Lifton, Thought Reform and the Psychology of Totalism (1963); Rogge, Why Men Confess (1959); Schein, Coercive Persuasion (1961).

[11] See Stephen, History of the Criminal Law, quoted in 8 Wigmore, Evidence (3d ed. 1940), 312 (emphasis in original); Report and Recommendations of the Commissioners' Committee on Police Arrest for Investigation, District of Columbia (1962).

[aa] Mr. Justice Harlan and Mr. Justice Stewart wrote dissenting opinions. Mr. Justice White wrote a dissenting opinion in which Justices Clark and Stewart joined. — ED.

[*] Together with No. 760, Vignera v. New York . . . and No. 761, Westover v. United States . . . and No. 584, California v. Stewart. . . .

Section B. Applications of Due Process in a Federal System

criminal jurisprudence: the restraints society must observe consistent with the Federal Constitution in prosecuting individuals for crime. More specifically, we deal with the admissibility of statements obtained from an individual who is subjected to custodial police interrogation and the necessity for procedures which assure that the individual is accorded his privilege under the Fifth Amendment to the Constitution not to be compelled to incriminate himself. . . .

We start here, as we did in Escobedo, with the premise that our holding is not an innovation in our jurisprudence, but is an application of principles long recognized and applied in other settings. We have undertaken a thorough re-examination of the Escobedo decision and the principles it announced, and we reaffirm it. That case was but an explication of basic rights that are enshrined in our Constitution — that "No person . . . shall be compelled in any criminal case to be a witness against himself," and that "the accused shall . . . have the Assistance of Counsel" — rights which were put in jeopardy in that case through official overbearing. . . .

The constitutional issue we decide in each of these cases is the admissibility of statements obtained from a defendant questioned while in custody and deprived of his freedom of action. In each, the defendant was questioned by police officers, detectives, or a prosecuting attorney in a room in which he was cut off from the outside world. In none of these cases was the defendant given a full and effective warning of his rights at the outset of the interrogation process. In all the cases, the questioning elicited oral admissions, and in three of them, signed statements as well which were admitted at their trials. . . .

An understanding of the nature and setting of this in-custody interrogation is essential to our decisions today. The difficulty in depicting what transpires at such interrogations stems from the fact that in this country they have largely taken place incommunicado. From extensive factual studies undertaken in the early 1930's, including the famous Wickersham Report to Congress by a Presidential Commission, it is clear that police violence and the "third degree" flourished at that time. In a series of cases decided by the Court long after these studies, the police resorted to physical brutality — beatings, hanging, whipping — and to sustained and protracted questioning incommunicado in order to extort confessions.[6] The 1961 Commission on Civil Rights found much evidence to indicate that "some policemen still resort to physical force to obtain confessions." 1961 Comm'n on Civil Rights Rep. Justice, pt. 5, 17. . . .

. . . [T]he modern practice of in-custody interrogation is psychologically rather than physically oriented. As we have stated before, "Since Chambers v. Florida, 309 U.S. 227, this Court has recognized that coercion can be mental as well as physical, and that the blood of the accused is not the only hallmark of an unconstitutional inquisition." Blackburn v. Alabama, 361 U.S. 199, 206 (1960). Interrogation still takes place in privacy. Privacy results in secrecy and this in turn results in a gap in our knowledge as to what in fact goes on in the interrogation rooms. A valuable source of information about present police practices, however, may be found in various police manuals and texts which document procedures employed with success in the past, and which recommend various other effective tactics. These texts are used by law enforcement agencies themselves as guides.[9]

---

[6] Brown v. Mississippi, 297 U.S. 278 (1936); Chambers v. Florida, 309 U.S. 227 (1940); Canty v. Alabama, 309 U.S. 629 (1940); White v. Texas, 310 U.S. 530 (1940); Vernon v. Alabama, 313 U.S. 547 (1941); Ward v. Texas, 316 U.S. 547 (1942); Ashcraft v. Tennessee, 322 U.S. 143 (1944); Molinski v. New York, 324 U.S. 301 (1945); Leyra v. Denno, 347 U.S. 556 (1954). See also Williams v. United States, 341 U.S. 97 (1951).

[9] The methods described in Inbau and Reid, Criminal Interrogation and Confessions (1962), are a revision and enlargement of material presented in three prior editions of a predecessor text, Lie Detection and Criminal Interrogation (3d ed. 1953). The authors and their associates are officers of the Chicago Police Scientific Crime Detection Laboratory and have had extensive experience in writing, lecturing and speaking to law enforcement authorities over a 20-year period. They say that the techniques portrayed in their manuals reflect their experiences and are the most effective psychological stratagems to employ during interrogations. Similarly, the techniques described in O'Hara, Fundamentals of Criminal Investigation (1959), were gleaned from long service as observer, lecturer in police science, and work as a federal criminal investigator. All these texts have had rather

1026   Chapter Fifteen.   Fair Procedure

It should be noted that these texts professedly present the most enlightened and effective means presently used to obtain statements through custodial interrogation. By considering these texts and other data, it is possible to describe procedures observed and noted around the country. . . .

The texts thus stress that the major qualities an interrogator should possess are patience and perseverance. One writer describes the efficacy of these characteristics in this manner: "In the preceding paragraphs emphasis has been placed on kindness and stratagems. The investigator will, however, encounter many situations where the sheer weight of his personality will be the deciding factor. Where emotional appeals and tricks are employed to no avail, he must rely on an oppressive atmosphere of dogged persistence. He must interrogate steadily and without relent, leaving the subject no prospect of surcease. He must dominate his subject and overwhelm him with his inexorable will to obtain the truth. He should interrogate for a spell of several hours pausing only for the subject's necessities in acknowledgment of the need to avoid a charge of duress that can be technically substantiated. In a serious case, the interrogation may continue for days, with the required intervals for food and sleep, but with no respite from the atmosphere of domination. It is possible in this way to induce the subject to talk without resorting to duress or coercion. This method should be used only when the guilt of the subject appears highly probable."[14] . . .

When the techniques described above prove unavailing, the texts recommend they be alternated with a show of some hostility. One ploy often used has been termed the "friendly-unfriendly" or the "Mutt and Jeff" act: ". . . In this technique, two agents are employed, Mutt, the relentless investigator, who knows the subject is guilty and is not going to waste any time. He's sent a dozen men away for this crime and he's going to send the subject away for the full term. Jeff, on the other hand, is obviously a kindhearted man. He has a family himself. He has a brother who was involved in a little scrape like this. He disapproves of Mutt and his tactics and will arrange to get him off the case if the subject will cooperate. He can't hold Mutt off for very long. The subject would be wise to make a quick decision. The technique is applied by having both investigators present while Mutt acts out his role. Jeff may stand by quietly and demur at some of Mutt's tactics. When Jeff makes his plea for cooperation, Mutt is not present in the room." . . .[17]

In the cases before us today, given this background, we concern ourselves primarily with this interrogation atmosphere and the evils it can bring. In No. 759, Miranda v. Arizona, the police arrested the defendant and took him to a special interrogation room where they secured a confession. In No. 760, Vignera v. New York, the defendant made oral admissions to the police after interrogation in the afternoon, and then signed an inculpatory statement upon being questioned by an assistant district attorney later the same evening. In No. 761, Westover v. United States, the defendant was handed over to the Federal Bureau of Investigation by local authorities after they had detained and interrogated him for a lengthy period, both at night and the following morning. After some two hours of questioning, the federal officers had obtained signed statements from the defendant. Lastly, in No. 584, California v. Stewart, the local police held the defendant five days in the station and interrogated him on nine separate occasions before they secured his inculpatory statement.

In these cases, we might not find the defendant's statements to have been involuntary in

---

extensive use among law enforcement agencies and among students of police science, with total sales and circulation of over 44,000.

[14] O'Hara, supra, at 112.

[17] O'Hara, supra, at 104, Inbau and Reid, supra, at 58-59. See Spano v. New York, 360 U.S. 315 (1950). A variant on the technique of creating hostility is one of engendering fear. This is perhaps best described by the prosecuting attorney in Malinski v. New York, 324 U.S. 401, 407 (1945): "Why all this talk about being undressed? Of course, they had a right to undress him to look for bullet scars, and keep the clothes off him. That was quite proper police procedure. That is some more psychology — let him sit around with a blanket on him, humiliate him there for a while; let him sit in the corner, let him think he is going to get a shellacking."

Section B. Applications of Due Process in a Federal System

traditional terms. Our concern for adequate safeguards to protect precious Fifth Amendment rights is, of course, not lessened in the slightest. In each of the cases, the defendant was thrust into an unfamiliar atmosphere and run through menacing police interrogation procedures. The potentiality for compulsion is forcefully apparent, for example, in Miranda, where the indigent Mexican defendant was a seriously disturbed individual with pronounced sexual fantasies, and in Stewart, in which the defendant was an indigent Los Angeles Negro who had dropped out of school in the sixth grade. To be sure, the records do not evince overt physical coercion or patented psychological ploys. The fact remains that in none of these cases did the officers undertake to afford appropriate safeguards at the outset of the interrogation to insure that the statements were truly the product of free choice.

It is obvious that such an interrogation environment is created for no purpose other than to subjugate the individual to the will of his examiner. This atmosphere carries its own badge of intimidation. To be sure, this is not physical intimidation, but it is equally destructive of human dignity. The current practice of incommunicado interrogation is at odds with one of our Nation's most cherished principles — that the individual may not be compelled to incriminate himself. Unless adequate protective devices are employed to dispel the compulsion inherent in custodial surroundings, no statement obtained from the defendant can truly be the product of his free choice. . . .

It is impossible for us to foresee the potential alternatives for protecting the privilege which might be devised by Congress or the States in the exercise of their creative rule-making capacities. Therefore we cannot say that the Constitution necessarily requires adherence to any particular solution for the inherent compulsions of the interrogation process as it is presently conducted. Our decision in no way creates a constitutional straitjacket which will handicap sound efforts at reform, nor is it intended to have this effect. We encourage Congress and the States to continue their laudable search for increasingly effective ways of protecting the rights of the individual while promoting efficient enforcement of our criminal laws. However, unless we are shown other procedures which are at least as effective in apprising accused persons of their right of silence and in assuring a continuous opportunity to exercise it, the following safeguards must be observed.

At the outset, if a person in custody is to be subjected to interrogation, he must first be informed in clear and unequivocal terms that he has the right to remain silent. For those unaware of the privilege, the warning is needed simply to make them aware of it — the threshold requirement for an intelligent decision as to its exercise. . . .

The warning of the right to remain silent must be accomplished by the explanation that anything said can and will be used against the individual in court. This warning is needed in order to make him aware not only of the privilege, but also of the consequences of forgoing it. . . .

The circumstances surrounding in-custody interrogation can operate very quickly to overbear the will of one merely made aware of his privilege by his interrogators. Therefore, the right to have counsel present at the interrogation is indispensable to the protection of the Fifth Amendment privilege under the system we delineate today. Our aim is to assure that the individual's right to choose between silence and speech remains unfettered throughout the interrogation process. . . .

The presence of counsel at the interrogation may serve several significant subsidiary functions as well. If the accused decides to talk to his interrogators, the assistance of counsel can mitigate the dangers of untrustworthiness. With a lawyer present the likelihood that the police will practice coercion is reduced, and if coercion is nevertheless exercised the lawyer can testify to it in court. The presence of a lawyer can also help to guarantee that the accused gives a fully accurate statement to the police and that the statement is rightly reported by the prosecution at trial. . . .

Accordingly we hold that an individual held for interrogation must be clearly informed that he has the right to consult with a lawyer and to have the lawyer with him during interrogation under the system for protecting the privilege we delineate today. As with the warnings of the right to remain silent and that anything stated can be used in evidence against him, this warning is an absolute prerequisite to interrogation. No amount of circumstantial evidence that the person may have been aware of this right will suffice to stand in its stead. Only through such a warning is there ascertainable assurance that the accused was aware of this right. . . .

In order fully to apprise a person interrogated of the extent of his rights under this system then, it is necessary to warn him not only that he has the right to consult with an attorney, but also that if he is indigent a lawyer will be appointed to represent him. Without this additional warning, the admonition of the right to consult with counsel would often be understood as meaning only that he can consult with a lawyer if he has one or has the funds to obtain one. The warning of a right to counsel would be hollow if not couched in terms that would convey to the indigent — the person most often subjected to interrogation — the knowledge that he too has a right to have counsel present. . . .

Once warnings have been given, the subsequent procedure is clear. If the individual indicates in any manner, at any time prior to or during questioning, that he wishes to remain silent, the interrogation must cease. . . . If the individual states that he wants an attorney, the interrogation must cease until an attorney is present. . . .

If the interrogation continues without the presence of an attorney and a statement is taken, a heavy burden rests on the Government to demonstrate that the defendant knowingly and intelligently waived his privilege against self-incrimination and his right to retained or appointed counsel. Escobedo v. Illinois, 378 U.S. 478, 490, n.14. This Court has always set high standards of proof for the waiver of constitutional rights, Johnson v. Zerbst, 304 U.S. 458 (1938), and we re-assert these standards as applied to in-custody interrogation. Since the State is responsible for establishing the isolated circumstances under which the interrogation takes place and has the only means of making available corroborated evidence of warnings given during incommunicado interrogation, the burden is rightly on its shoulders. . . .

In dealing with statements obtained through interrogation, we do not purport to find all confessions inadmissible. Confessions remain a proper element in law enforcement. Any statement given freely and voluntarily without any compelling influences is, of course, admissible in evidence. The fundamental import of the privilege while an individual is in custody is not whether he is allowed to talk to the police without the benefit of warnings and counsel, but whether he can be interrogated. There is no requirement that police stop a person who enters a police station and states that he wishes to confess to a crime, or a person who calls the police to offer a confession or any other statement he desires to make. Volunteered statements of any kind are not barred by the Fifth Amendment and their admissibility is not affected by our holding today.

. . . The limits we have placed on the interrogation process should not constitute an undue interference with a proper system of law enforcement. As we have noted, our decision does not in any way preclude police from carrying out their traditional investigatory functions. Although confessions may play an important role in some convictions, the cases before us present graphic examples of the overstatement of the "need" for confessions. In each case authorities conducted interrogations ranging up to five days in duration despite the presence, through standard investigating practices, of considerable evidence against each defendant.[51] Further examples are chronicled in our prior cases. See, e.g., Haynes v. Washington 373 U.S. 503, 518-519 (1963); Rogers v. Richmond, 365 U.S. 534, 541 (1961); Malinski v. New York, 324 U.S. 401, 402 (1945). . . .[52]

[51] Miranda, Vignera, and Westover were identified by eyewitnesses. Marked bills from the bank robbed were found in Westover's car. Articles stolen from the victim as well as from several other robbery victims were found in Stewart's home at the outset of the investigation.

[52] Dealing as we do here with constitutional standards in relation to statements made, the existence of independent corroborating evidence produced at trial is, of course, irrelevant to our decisions. Haynes v. Wash-

Section B. **Applications of Due Process in a Federal System** 1029

Because of the nature of the problem and because of its recurrent significance in numerous cases, we have to this point discussed the relationship of the Fifth Amendment privilege to police interrogation without specific concentration on the facts to consider the application to these cases of the constitutional principles discussed above. In each instance, we have concluded that statements were obtained from the defendant under circumstances that did not meet constitutional standards for protection of the privilege.

NO. 759. MIRANDA V. ARIZONA

On March 13, 1963, petitioner, Ernesto Miranda, was arrested at his home and taken in custody to a Phoenix police station. He was there identified by the complaining witness. The police then took him to "Interrogation Room No. 2" of the detective bureau. There he was questioned by two police officers. The officers admitted at trial that Miranda was not advised that he had a right to have an attorney present. Two hours later, the officers emerged from the interrogation room with a written confession signed by Miranda. At the top of the statement was a typed paragraph stating that the confession was made voluntarily, without threats or promises of immunity and "with full knowledge of my legal rights, understanding any statement I make may be used against me."[67]

At his trial before a jury, the written confession was admitted into evidence over the objection of defense counsel, and the officers testified to the prior oral confession made by Miranda during the interrogation. Miranda was found guilty of kidnapping and rape. He was sentenced to 20 to 30 years' imprisonment on each count, the sentence to run concurrently. On appeal, the Supreme Court of Arizona held that Miranda's constitutional rights were not violated in obtaining the confession and affirmed the conviction. 98 Ariz. 18, 401 P.2d 721. In reaching its decision, the court emphasized heavily the fact that Miranda did not specifically request counsel.

We reverse. From the testimony of the officers and by the admission of respondent, it is clear that Miranda was not in any way apprised of his right to consult with an attorney and to have one present during the interrogation, nor was his right not to be compelled to incriminate himself effectively protected in any other manner. Without these warnings the statements were inadmissible. The mere fact that he signed a statement which contained a typed-in clause stating that he had "full knowledge" of his "legal rights" does not approach the knowing and intelligent waiver required to relinquish constitutional rights. Cf. Haynes v. Washington, 373 U.S. 503, 512-513 (1963); Haley v. Ohio, 332 U.S. 596, 601 (1948) (opinion of Mr. Justice Douglas. . . .[bb]

NO. 584. CALIFORNIA V. STEWART

In the course of investigating a series of purse-snatch robberies in which one of the victims had died of injuries inflicted by her assailant, repondent, Roy Allen Stewart, was pointed out to Los Angeles police as the endorser of dividend checks taken in one of the robberies. At about 7:15 P.M., January 31, 1963, police officers went to Stewart's house and arrested him. One of the officers asked Stewart if they could search the house, to which he replied, "Go ahead." The search turned up various items taken from the five robbery victims. At the time of Stewart's arrest, police also arrested Stewart's wife and three other persons who were visiting him. These four were jailed along with Stewart and

---

ington, 373 U.S. 503, 518-519 (1963); Lynumn v. Illinois, 372 U.S. 528, 537-538 (1963); Rogers v. Richmond, 365 U.S. 534, 541 (1961); Blackburn v. Alabama, 361 U.S. 199, 206 (1960).

[67] One of the officers testified that he read this paragraph to Miranda. Apparently, however, he did not do so until after Miranda had confessed orally.

[bb] The statement of facts in No. 760, Vignera v. New York, and in No. 761, Westover v. United States, is omitted. The Court found that before interrogation by New York police in Vignera, and by local police and FBI agents in Westover, the defendants had not been adequately warned of their rights. In both cases the Court reversed convictions for robbery. — ED.

were interrogated. Stewart was taken to the University Station of the Los Angeles Police Department where he was placed in a cell. During the next five days, police interrogated Stewart on nine different occasions. Except during the first interrogation session, when he was confronted with an accusing witness, Stewart was isolated with his interrogators.

During the ninth interrogation session, Stewart admitted that he had robbed the deceased and stated that he had not meant to hurt her. Police then brought Stewart before a magistrate for the first time. Since there was no evidence to connect them with any crime, the police then released the other four persons arrested with him.

Nothing in the record specifically indicates whether Stewart was or was not advised of his right to remain silent or his right to counsel. In a number of instances, however, the interrogating officers were asked to recount everything that was said during the interrogations. None indicated that Stewart was ever advised of his rights.

Stewart was charged with kidnapping to commit robbery, rape, and murder. At his trial, transcripts of the first interrogation and the confession at the last interrogation were introduced in evidence. The jury found Stewart guilty of robbery and first degree murder and fixed the penalty as death. On appeal, the Supreme Court of California reversed. 62 Cal. 2d 571, 400 P.2d 97, 43 Cal. Rptr. 201. It held that under this Court's decision in Escobedo, Stewart should have been advised of his right to remain silent and of his right to counsel and that it would not presume in the face of a silent record that the police advised Stewart of his rights.

We affirm.[71] In dealing with custodial interrogation, we will not presume that a defendant has been effectively apprised of his rights and that his privilege against self-incrimination has been adequately safeguarded on a record that does not show that any warnings have been given or that any effective alternative, has been employed. Nor can a knowing and intelligent waiver of these rights be assumed on a silent record. Furthermore, Stewart's steadfast denial of the alleged offenses through eight of the nine interrogations over a period of five days is subject to no other construction than that he was compelled by persistent interrogation to forgo his Fifth Amendment privilege.

Therefore, in accordance with the foregoing, the judgments of the Supreme Court of Arizona in No. 759, of the New York Court of Appeals in No. 760, and of the Court of Appeals for the Ninth Circuit in No. 761 are reversed. The judgment of the Supreme Court of California in No. 584 is affirmed.

It is so ordered.

Mr. JUSTICE CLARK, dissenting in Nos. 759, 760, and 761, and concurring in result in No. 584.

It is with regret that I find it necessary to write in these cases. However, I am unable to join the majority because its opinion goes too far on too little, while my dissenting brethren do not go quite far enough. Nor can I agree with the Court's characterization of the present practices of police and investigatory agencies as to custodial interrogation. The materials referred to as "police manuals"[1] are not shown by the record here to be the official manuals of any police department, much less in universal use in crime detection. Moreover, the examples of police brutality mentioned by the Court are rare exceptions to the thousands of cases that appear every year in the law reports. . . .

MR. JUSTICE HARLAN, whom MR. JUSTICE STEWART and MR. JUSTICE WHITE join, dissenting.

I believe the decision of the Court represents poor constitutional law and entails harm-

---

[71] After certiorari was granted in this case, respondent moved to dismiss on the ground that there was no final judgment from which the State could appeal since the judgment below directed that he be retried. In the event respondent was successful in obtaining an acquittal on retrial, however, under California law the State would have no appeal. Satisfied that in these circumstances the decision below constituted a final judgment under 28 U.S.C. §1257(3) (1964 ed.), we denied the motion. 383 U.S. 903.

[1] E.g., Inbau and Reid, Criminal Interrogation and Confessions (1962); O'Hara, Fundamentals of Criminal Interrogation (1956); Dienstein, Technics for the Crime Investigator (1952); Mulbar, Interrogation (1951); Kidd, Police Interrogation (1940).

ful consequences for the country at large. How serious these consequences may prove to be only time can tell. . . .

. . . The new rules are not designed to guard against police brutality or other unmistakably banned forms of coercion. Those who use third-degree tactics and deny them in court are equally able and destined to lie as skillfully about warnings and waivers. Rather, the thrust of the new rules is to negate all pressures, to reinforce the nervous or ignorant suspect, and ultimately to discourage any confession at all. The aim in short is toward "voluntariness" in a utopian sense, or to view it from a different angle, voluntariness with a vengeance. . . .

MR. JUSTICE WHITE, with whom MR. JUSTICE HARLAN and MR. JUSTICE STEWART join, dissenting.

The proposition that the privilege against self-incrimination forbids in-custody interrogation without the warning specified in the majority opinion and without a clear waiver of counsel has no significant support in the history of the privilege or in the language of the Fifth Amendment. As for the English authorities and the common-law history, the privilege, firmly established in the second half of the seventeenth century, was never applied except to prohibit compelled judicial interrogations. The rule excluding coerced confessions matured about 100 years later, "[b]ut there is nothing in the reports to suggest that the theory has its roots in the privilege against self-incrimination. And so far as the cases reveal, the privilege, as such, seems to have been given effect only in judicial proceedings, including the preliminary examinations by authorized magistrates." Morgan, The Privilege Against Self-Incrimination, 34 Minn. L. Rev. 1, 18 (1949). . . .

Nor can this decision do other than have a corrosive effect on the criminal law as an effective device to prevent crime. A major component in its effectiveness in this regard is its swift and sure enforcement. The easier it is to get away with rape and murder, the less the deterrent effect on those who are inclined to attempt it. This is still good common sense. If it were not, we should posthaste liquidate the whole law enforcement establishment as a useless, misguided effort to control human conduct.

And what about the accused who has confessed or would confess in response to simple, noncoercive questioning, and whose guilt could not otherwise be proved? Is it so clear that release is the best thing for him in every case? Has it so unquestionably been resolved that in each and every case it would be better for him not to confess and to return to his environment with no attempt whatsoever to help him? I think not. It may well be that in many cases it will be no less than a callous disregard for his own welfare as well as for the interests of his next victim.

There is another aspect to the effect of the Court's rule on the person whom the police have arrested on probable cause. The fact is that he may not be guilty at all and may be able to extricate himself quickly and simply if he were told the circumstances of his arrest and were asked to explain. This effort, and his release, must now await the hiring of a lawyer or his appointment by the court, consultation with counsel and then a session with the police or the prosecutor. Similarly, where probable cause exists to arrest several suspects, as where the body of the victim is discovered in a house having several residents, see Johnson v. State, 238 Md. 140, 207 A.2d 643 (1965), pet. for cert. pending No. 274 Misc. O.T. 1965, it will often be true that a suspect may be cleared only through the results of interrogation of other suspects. Here too the release of the innocent may be delayed by the Court's rule. . . .

For all these reasons, if further restriction on police interrogation are desirable at this time, a more flexible approach, makes much more sense than the Court's constitutional straitjacket which forecloses more discriminating treatment by legislative or rule-making pronouncements.

Applying the traditional standards to the cases before the Court, I would hold these confessions voluntary. I would therefore affirm in Nos. 759, 760, and 761 and reverse in No. 584.

Johnson and Cassidy v. New Jersey 384 U.S. 719, 86 S. Ct. 1772, 16 L. Ed. 2d 882 (1966)

Mr. Chief Justice Warren delivered the opinion of the Court.

In this case we are called upon to determine whether Escobedo v. Illinois, 378 U.S. 478 (1964), and Miranda v. Arizona, 384 U.S. 436 (1966) should be applied retroactively. We hold that Escobedo affects only those cases in which the trial began after June 22, 1964, the date of that decision. We hold further that Miranda applies only to cases in which the trial began after the date of our decision one week ago. The convictions assailed here were obtained at trials completed long before Escobedo and Miranda were rendered, and the rulings in these cases are therefore inapplicable to the present proceeding. Petitioners have also asked us to overturn their convictions on a number of other grounds, but we find these contentions to be without merit, and consequently we affirm the decision below. . . .

In the past year we have twice dealt with the problem of retroactivity in connection with other constitutional rules of criminal procedure. Linkletter v. Walker, 381 U.S. 618 (1965); Tehan v. Shott, 382 U.S. 406 (1966). These cases establish the principle that in criminal litigation concerning constitutional claims, "the Court may in the interest of justice make the rule prospective . . . where the exigencies of the situation require such an application." 381 U.S., at 628; 382 U.S., at 410. These cases also delineate criteria by which such an issue may be resolved. We must look to the purpose of our new standards governing police interrogation, the reliance which may have been placed upon prior decisions on the subject, and the effect on the administration of justice of a retroactive application of Escobedo and Miranda. See 381 U.S., at 626; 382 U.S., at 413.

In Linkletter we declined to apply retroactively the rule laid down in Mapp v. Ohio, 367 U.S. 643 (1961), by which evidence obtained through an unreasonable search and seizure was excluded from state criminal proceedings. In so holding, we relied in part on the fact that the rule affected evidence "the reliability and relevancy of which is not questioned." 381 U.S., at 639. Likewise in Tehan we declined to give retroactive effect to Griffin v. California, 380 U.S. 609 (1965), which forbade prosecutors and judges to comment adversely on the failure of a defendant to testify in a state criminal trial. In reaching this result, we noted that the basic purpose of the rule was to discourage courts from penalizing use of the privilege against self-incrimination. 382 U.S., at 414.

As Linkletter and Tehan acknowledged, however, we have given retroactive effect to other constitutional rules of criminal procedure laid down in recent years, where different guarantees were involved. For example, in Gideon v. Wainwright, 372 U.S. 335 (1963), which concerned the right of an indigent to the advice of counsel at trial, we reviewed a denial of habeas corpus. Similarly, Jackson v. Denno, 378 U.S. 368 (1964), which involved the right of an accused to effective exclusion of an involuntary confession from trial, was itself a collateral attack. In each instance we concluded that retroactive application was justified because the rule affected "the very integrity of the fact-finding process" and averted "the clear danger of convicting the innocent." Linkletter v. Walker, 381 U.S., at 639; Tehan v. Shott, 382 U.S., at 416.

We here stress that the choice between retroactivity and nonretroactivity in no way turns on the value of the constitutional guarantee involved. The right to be represented by counsel at trial, applied retroactively in Gideon v. Wainwright, supra, has been described by Justice Schaefer of the Illinois Supreme Court as "by far the most pervasive . . . of all of the rights that an accused person has."[7] Yet Justice Brandeis even more boldly characterized the immunity from unjustifiable intrusions upon privacy, which was denied retroactive enforcement in Linkletter, as "the most comprehensive of rights and the right most

---

[7] Federalism and State Criminal Procedure, 70 Harv. L. Rev. 1, 8 (1965).

Section B. Applications of Due Process in a Federal System 1033

valued by civilized men."[8] To reiterate what was said in Linkletter, we do not disparage a constitutional guarantee in any manner by declining to apply it retroactively. See 381 U.S., at 629. . . .

. . . [T]he question whether a constitutional rule of criminal procedure does or does not enhance the reliability of the fact-finding process at trial is necessarily a matter of degree. We gave retroactive effect to Jackson v. Denno, supra, because confessions are likely to be highly persuasive with a jury, and if coerced they may well be untrustworthy by their very nature. On the other hand, we denied retroactive application to Griffin v. California, supra, despite the fact that comment on the failure to testify may sometimes mislead the jury concerning the reasons why the defendant has refused to take the witness stand. We are thus concerned with a question of probabilities and must take account, among other factors, of the extent to which other safeguards are available to protect the integrity of the truth-determining process at trial.

Having in mind the course of the prior cases, we turn now to the problem presented here: whether Escobedo and Miranda should be applied retroactively.[10] Our opinion in Miranda makes it clear that the prime purpose of these rulings is to guarantee full effectuation of the privilege against self-incrimination, the mainstay of our adversary system of criminal justice. See, ante, pp. 20-29. They are designed in part to assure that the person who responds to interrogation while in custody does so with intelligent understanding of his right to remain silent and of the consequences which may flow from relinquishing it. In this respect the rulings secure scrupulous observance of the traditional principle, often quoted but rarely heeded to the full degree, that "the law will not suffer a prisoner to be made the deluded instrument of his own conviction."[11] Thus while Escobedo and Miranda guard against the possibility of unreliable statements in every instance of in-custody interrogation, they encompass situations in which the danger is not necessarily as great as when the accused is subjected to overt and obvious coercion. . . .

As for the standards laid down one week ago in Miranda, if we were persuaded that they had been fully anticipated by the holding in Escobedo, we would measure their prospectivity from the same date. Defendants still to be tried at that time would be entitled to strict observance of constitutional doctrines already clearly foreshadowed. The disagreements among other courts concerning the implications of Escobedo, however, have impelled us to lay down additional guidelines for situations not presented by that case. This we have done in Miranda, and these guidelines are therefore available only to persons whose trials had not begun as of June 13, 1966. See Tehan v. Shott, 382 U.S., at 409, n. 3, with reference to Malloy v. Hogan, 378 U.S. 1 (1964), and Griffin v. California, supra. . . .

The judgment of the Supreme Court of New Jersey is
Affirmed.

MR. JUSTICE CLARK concurs in the opinion and judgment of the Court. He adheres, however, to the views stated in his separate opinion in Miranda v. Arizona [384 U.S. 436].

MR. JUSTICE HARLAN, MR. JUSTICE STEWART, and MR. JUSTICE WHITE concur in the opinion and judgment of the Court. They continue to believe, however, for the reasons stated in the dissenting opinions of Mr. Justice Harlan and Mr. Justice White in Miranda

---

[8] Olmstead v. United States, 277 U.S. 438, 478 (1928) (dissenting opinion).

[10] It appears that every state supreme court and federal court of appeals which has discussed the question has declined to apply the tenets of Escobedo retroactively. For example, see In re Lopez, 62 Cal. 2d 368, 42 Cal. Rptr. 188, 398 P.2d 380 (1965); Ruark v. People, — Colo. —, 405 P.2d 751 (1965); Commonwealth v. Negri, 419 Pa. 117, 213 A.2d 670 (1965); United States ex rel. Walden v. Pate, 350 F.2d 240 (C.A. 7th Cir. 1965). The commentators, however, are divided on this issue. Compare Mishkin, Forward: The High Court, The Great Writ, and the Due Process of Time and Law, 79 Harv. L. Rev. 56 (1965), which opposes retroactive application, with Comment, Linkletter, Shott, and the Retroactivity Problem in Escobedo, 64 Mich. L. Rev. 832 (1966).

[11] 2 Hawkins, Pleas of the Crown 595 (8th ed. 1824).

1034   Chapter Fifteen.   Fair Procedure

v. Arizona and its companion cases, 384 U.S. 436, that the new constitutional rules promulgated in those cases are both unjustified and unwise.

MR. JUSTICE BLACK, with whom MR. JUSTICE DOUGLAS joins, dissents from the Court's holding that the petitioners here are not entitled to the full protections of the Fifth and Sixth Amendments as this Court has construed them in Escobedo v. Illinois, 378 U.S. 478, and Miranda v. Arizona, [384 U.S. 436] for substantially the same reasons stated in their dissenting opinion in Linkletter v. Walker, 381 U.S. 618, at 640.

NOTE Retreat from Miranda

In enacting the Omnibus Crime Control and Safe Streets Act of 1968, Pub. L. No. 90-351, its sponsors in Congress believed that "crime will not be effectively abated so long as criminals who have voluntarily confessed their crimes are released on mere technicalities." S. Rep. No. 1097, 90th Cong., 2d Sess. (1968), 1968 U.S. Code Cong. & Adm. News 2123. Title II of this act, now codified at 18 U.S.C. §§3501-3502 (1969), therefore instructs federal courts to admit into evidence confessions which are "voluntarily given." 18 U.S.C. §3501(a). In determining voluntariness, "the presence or absence" of Miranda warnings "need not be conclusive." 18 U.S.C. §3501(b).

Could this statute be construed to continue to require the Miranda warnings for admissibility? See Recent Statute, 82 Harv. L. Rev. 1392 (1969). Assuming that it purports to reinstate the "totality of the circumstances" test that preceded Miranda, is it unconstitutional without more? Consider the question of the sponsors: "But if, *in fact*, custodial interrogation is not inherently coercive, how does the constitutional basis of the decision fare?" (italics in original). S. Rep., supra, 1968 U.S. Code Cong. & Adm. News 2147. This legislation reaches only the federal courts, under the general supervisory power of Congress. Should the constitutional outcome be any different if Congress sought to apply these standards to the states through its power to enforce the due process guarantee under §5 of the Fourteenth Amendment? Compare the opinion of Justice Brennan in Katzenbach v. Morgan, supra page 904 n.10. The constitutionality of 18 U.S.C. §3501(a)-(b) has yet to be decided. See also Wright, Federal Practice §76 at 120-122 (1969).

On the usefulness of the Miranda warnings, see Note, Interrogations in New Haven: The Impact of Miranda, 76 Yale L.J. 1519 (1967).

The Miranda case was distinguished in Harris v. New York, 401 U.S. 222 (1971), holding that a confession inadmissible under Miranda as evidence in chief could be introduced by the prosecution to impeach the credibility of a defendant who has taken the stand. Otherwise, said the Court, per Burger, C.J., the defendant would have a license to commit perjury, free from the risk of confrontation with prior inconsistent statements. Justices Brennan, Douglas, and Marshall dissented. It had been held in Walder v. United States, 347 U.S. 62 (1954), that physical evidence, illegally obtained, could be used for impeachment; but in the case the impeachment was on a collateral matter, not the central issue of guilt. For a criticism of the Court's opinion in Harris, see Dershowitz and Ely, Harris v. New York: Some Anxious Observations on the Candor and Logic of the Emerging Nixon Majority, 80 Yale L.J. 1198 (1971).

In Oregon v. Hass, 420 U.S. 714 (1975), the Court held that a statement given the police after the defendant had requested his lawyer and had been told he would have to wait was admissible for impeachment purposes.

In Lego v. Twomey, 404 U.S. 477 (1972), the Court held that the standard for determining the voluntariness of a confession is preponderance of the evidence rather than beyond a reasonable doubt. The case clarifies Jackson v. Denno, 378 (1964), a pre-Miranda decision which held that a hearing on the voluntariness of a confession is constitutionally required.

See also Michigan v. Tucker, 417 U.S. 433 (1974), holding that evidence obtained as a result of an interrogation conducted before Miranda was decided and without full Miranda warnings could be used by the prosecution in a post-Miranda trial.

In Michigan v. Mosley, 423 U.S. 96 (1975), the Court found admissible a confession that was given after full Miranda warnings, although the suspect had refused questioning two hours earlier, again after full Miranda warnings, on an unrelated offense. Justice Brennan, in a dissenting opinion joined by Justice Marshall, argued that the resumption of questioning in this case should, at least, have "await[ed] appointment and arrival of counsel for the suspect."

In Williams v. Brewer, 509 F.2d 227 (8th Cir.), cert. granted, 423 U.S. 1031 (1975), the incriminating statements of a murder suspect and the discovery of the victim's body obtained through his statements were excluded from evidence because the police interrogation was undertaken despite the suspect's indications that he did not want to talk about the case and despite his counsel's advice earlier that he should stay silent. Among the questions presented in the petition for certiorari is, "(3) Should more flexible police interrogation standard be adopted to replace requirements of Miranda . . . ?" 44 U.S.L.W. 3023 (1975).

4. Right to Jury Trial

Duncan v. Louisiana 391 U.S. 145, 88 S. Ct. 1444, 20 L. Ed. 2d 491 (1968)

MR. JUSTICE WHITE delivered the opinion of the Court.

Appellant, Gary Duncan, was convicted of simple battery in the Twenty-fifth Judicial District Court of Louisiana. Under Louisiana law simple battery is a misdemeanor, punishable by a maximum of two years' imprisonment and a $300 fine. Appellant sought trial by jury, but because the Louisiana Constitution grants jury trials only in cases in which capital punishment or imprisonment at hard labor may be imposed, the trial judge denied the request. Appellant was convicted and sentenced to serve 60 days in the parish prison and pay a fine of $150. Appellant sought review in the Supreme Court of Louisiana, asserting that the denial of jury trial violated rights guaranteed to him by the United States Constitution. The Supreme Court, finding "[n]o error of law in the ruling complained of," denied appellant a writ of certiorari. Pursuant to 28 U.S.C. §1257 (2) appellant sought review in this Court, alleging that the Sixth and Fourteenth Amendments to the United States Constitution secure the right to jury trial in state criminal prosecutions where a sentence as long as two years may be imposed. . . .

. . . Because we believe that trial by jury in criminal cases is fundamental to the American scheme of justice, we hold that the Fourteenth Amendment guarantees a right of jury trial in all criminal cases which — were they to be tried in a federal court — would come within the Sixth Amendment's guarantee.[14] Since we consider the appeal before us

[14] In one sense recent cases applying provisions of the first eight Amendments to the States represent a new approach to the "incorporation" debate. Earlier the Court can be seen as having asked, when inquiring into whether some particular procedural safeguard was required of a State, if a civilized system could be imagined that would not accord the particular protection. . . . The recent cases, on the other hand, have proceeded upon the valid assumption that state criminal processes are not imaginary and theoretical schemes but actual systems bearing virtually every characteristic of the common-law system that has been developing contemporaneously in England and in this country. The question thus is whether given this kind of system a particular procedure is fundamental — whether, that is, a procedure is necessary to an Anglo-American regime of ordered liberty. . . .

When the inquiry is approached in this way the question whether the States can impose criminal punishment without granting a jury trial appears quite different from the way it appeared in the older cases opining that States might abolish jury trial. See, e.g., Maxwell v. Dow, 176 U.S. 581 (1900). A criminal process which was fair and equitable but used no juries is easy to imagine. It would make use of alternative guarantees and protections which would serve the purposes that the jury serves in the English and American systems. Yet no American

to be such a case, we hold that the Constitution was violated when appellant's demand for jury trial was refused.

[A "skeletal" history of the jury trial in England and America is omitted.]

The guarantees of jury trial in the Federal and State Constitutions reflect a profound judgment about the way in which law should be enforced and justice administered. A right to jury trial is granted to criminal defendants in order to prevent oppression by the Government. Those who wrote our constitutions knew from history and experience that it was necessary to protect against unfounded criminal charges brought to eliminate enemies and against judges too responsive to the voice of higher authority. The framers of the constitutions strove to create an independent judiciary but insisted upon further protection against arbitrary action. Providing an accused with the right to be tried by a jury of his peers gave him an inestimable safeguard against the corrupt or overzealous prosecutor and against the compliant, biased, or eccentric judge. If the defendant preferred the commonsense judgment of a jury to the more tutored but perhaps less sympathetic reaction of the single judge, he was to have it. Beyond this, the jury trial provisions in the Federal and State Constitutions reflect a fundamental decision about the exercise of official power — a reluctance to entrust plenary powers over the life and liberty of the citizen to one judge or to a group of judges. Fear of unchecked power, so typical of our State and Federal Governments in other respects, found expression in the criminal law in this insistence upon community participation in the determination of guilt or innocence. The deep commitment of the Nation to the right of jury trial in serious criminal cases as a defense against arbitrary law enforcement qualifies for protection under the Due Process Clause of the Fourteenth Amendment, and must therefore be respected by the States.

Of course jury trial has "its weaknesses and the potential for misuses," Singer v. United States, 380 U.S. 24, 35 (1965). We are aware of the long debate, especially in this century, among those who write about the administration of justice, as to the wisdom of permitting untrained laymen to determine the facts in civil and criminal proceedings.[24] Although the debate has been intense, with powerful voices on either side, most of the controversy has centered on the jury in civil cases. Indeed, some of the severest critics of civil juries acknowledge that the arguments for criminal juries are much stronger. In addition, at the heart of the dispute have been express or implicit assertions that juries are incapable of adequately understanding evidence or determining issues of fact, and that they are unpredictable, quixotic, and little better than a roll of dice. Yet, the most recent and exhaustive study of the jury in criminal cases concluded that juries do understand the evidence and come to sound conclusions in most of the cases presented to them and that when juries differ with the result at which the judge would have arrived, it is usually because they are serving some of the very purposes for which they were created and for which they are now employed.[26]

The State of Louisiana urges that holding that the Fourteenth Amendment assures a right to jury trial will cast doubt on the integrity of every trial conducted without a jury. Plainly, this is not the import of our holding. Our conclusion is that in the American States, as in the federal judicial system, a general grant of jury trial for serious offenses is a fundamental right, essential for preventing miscarriages of justice and for assuring that fair

---

State has undertaken to construct such a system. Instead, every American State, including Louisiana, uses the jury extensively, and imposes very serious punishments only after a trial at which the defendant has a right to a jury's verdict. In every State, including Louisiana, the structure and style of the criminal process — the supporting framework and the subsidiary procedures — are of the sort that naturally complement jury trial, and have developed in connection with and in reliance upon jury trial.

[24] A thorough summary of the arguments that have been made for and against jury trial and an extensive bibliography of the relevant literature is available at Hearings on Recording of Jury Deliberations before the Subcommittee to Investigate the Administration of the Internal Security Act of the Senate Committee on the Judiciary, 84th Cong., 1st Sess., 63-81 (1955). A more selective bibliography appears at H. Kalven, Jr. & H. Zeisel, The American Jury 4, n.2 (1966).

[26] Kalven & Zeisel, n.24, supra.

trials are provided for all defendants. We would not assert, however, that every criminal trial — or any particular trial — held before a judge alone is unfair or that a defendant may never be as fairly treated by a judge as he would be by a jury. . . .

. . . So-called petty offenses were tried without juries both in England and in the Colonies and have always been held to be exempt from the otherwise comprehensive language of the Sixth Amendment's jury trial provisions. There is no substantial evidence that the Framers intended to depart from this established common-law practice, and the possible consequences to defendants from convictions for petty offenses have been thought insufficient to outweigh the benefits to efficient law enforcement and simplified judicial administration resulting from the availability of speedy and inexpensive nonjury adjudications. These same considerations compel the same result under the Fourteenth Amendment. . . .

. . . We need not, however, settle in this case the exact location of the line between petty offenses and serious crimes. It is sufficient for our purposes to hold that a crime punishable by two years in prison is, based on past and contemporary standards in this country, a serious crime and not a petty offense. Consequently, appellant was entitled to a jury trial and it was error to deny it. . . .[cc]

MR. JUSTICE HARLAN, whom MR. JUSTICE STEWART joins, dissenting. . . .

It can hardly be gainsaid . . . that the principal original virtue of the jury trial — the limitations a jury imposes on a tyrannous judiciary — has largely disappeared. We no longer live in a medieval or colonial society. Judges enforce laws enacted by democratic decision, not by regal fiat. They are elected by the people or appointed by the people's elected officials, and are responsible not to a distant monarch alone but to reviewing courts, including this one.

The jury system can also be said to have some inherent defects, which are multiplied by the emergence of the criminal law from the relative simplicity that existed when the jury system was devised. It is a cumbersome process, not only imposing great cost in time and money on both the State and the jurors themselves, but also contributing to delay in the machinery of justice. Untrained jurors are presumably less adept at reaching accurate conclusions of fact than judges, particularly if the issues are many or complex. And it is argued by some that trial by jury, far from increasing public respect for law, impairs it: the average man, it is said, reacts favorably neither to the notion that matters he knows to be complex are being decided by other average men,[38] nor to the way the jury system distorts the process of adjudication.[39]

That trial by jury is not the only fair way of adjudicating criminal guilt is well attested by the fact that it is not the prevailing way, either in England or in this country. For England, one expert makes the following estimates. Parliament generally provides that new statutory offenses, unless they are of "considerable gravity" shall be tried to judges; consequently, summary offenses now outnumber offenses for which jury trial is afforded by more than six to one. Then, within the latter category, 84% of all cases are in fact tried to the court. Over all, "the ratio of defendants actually tried by jury becomes in some years little more than 1 per cent."

In the United States, where it has not been as generally assumed that jury waiver is permissible, the statistics are only slightly less revealing. Two experts have estimated that, of

---

[cc] Concurring opinions of Justice Fortas and Justice Black, joined by Justice Douglas, are omitted. In Baldwin v. New York, 399 U.S. 66 (1970), any crime where imprisonment for longer than six months is authorized was held to be a "serious" offense. — ED.

[38] E.g., Boston, Some Practical Remedies for Existing Defects in the Administration of Justice, 61 U. Pa. L. Rev. 1, 16: "There is not one important personal or property interest, outside of a Court of justice, which any of us would willingly commit to the first twelve men that come along the street. . . ."

[39] E.g., McWhorter, [Abolish the Jury, 57 Am. L. Rev. 42,] 46: "It is the jury system that consumes time at the public expense in gallery playing and sensational and theatrical exhibitions before the jury, whereby the public interest and the dignity of the law are swallowed up in a morbid, partisan or emotional personal interest in the parties immediately concerned."

all prosecutions for crimes triable to a jury, 75% are settled by guilty plea and 40% of the remainder are tried to the court.[42] In one State, Maryland, which has always provided for waiver, the rate of court trial appears in some years to have reached 90%.[43] . . . I . . . see no reason why this Court should reverse the conviction of appellant, absent any suggestion that his particular trial was in fact unfair, or compel the State of Louisiana to afford jury trial in an as yet unbounded category of cases that can, without unfairness, be tried to a court. . . .

Apodaca v. Oregon 406 U.S. 404, 92 S. Ct. 1628, 32 L. Ed. 2d 184 (1972)

MR. JUSTICE WHITE announced the judgment of the Court and an opinion in which THE CHIEF JUSTICE, MR. JUSTICE BLACKMUN, and MR. JUSTICE REHNQUIST joined.

Robert Apodaca, Henry Morgan Cooper, Jr., and James Arnold Madden were convicted respectively of assault with a deadly weapon, burglary in a dwelling, and grand larceny before separate Oregon juries, all of which returned less-than-unanimous verdicts. The vote in the cases of Apodaca and Madden was 11[to]1, while the vote in the case of Cooper was 10[to]2, the minimum requisite vote under Oregon law for sustaining a conviction. After their convictions had been affirmed by the Oregon Court of Appeals, 1 Ore. App. 483, 462 P.2d 691 (1969), and review had been denied by the Supreme Court of Oregon, all three sought review in this Court upon a claim that conviction of crime by a less-than-unanimous jury violates the right to trial by jury in criminal cases specified by the Sixth Amendment and made applicable to the States by the Fourteenth. See Duncan v. Louisiana, 391 U.S. 145 (1968). We granted certiorari to consider this claim, 400 U.S. 901 (1970), which we now find to be without merit.

In Williams v. Florida, 399 U.S. 78 (1970), we had occasion to consider a related issue: whether the Sixth Amendment's right to trial by jury requires that all juries consist of 12 men. After considering the history of the 12-man requirement and the functions it performs in contemporary society, we concluded that it was not of constitutional stature. We reach the same conclusion today with regard to the requirement of unanimity.

[The Court reviewed the relevant history of the Sixth Amendment and could not "divine" the intent of the Framers on the issue of unanimity.]

Our inquiry must focus upon the function served by the jury in contemporary society. Cf. Williams v. Florida, supra, at 99-100. As we said in Duncan, the purpose of trial by jury is to prevent oppression by the Government by providing a "safeguard against the corrupt or overzealous prosecutor and against the compliant, biased, or eccentric judge." Duncan v. Louisiana, 391 U.S., at 156. "Given this purpose, the essential feature of a jury obviously lies in the interposition between the accused and his accuser of the commonsense judgment of a group of laymen. . . ." Williams v. Florida, supra, at 100. A requirement of unanimity, however, does not materially contribute to the exercise of this commonsense judgment. As we said in Williams, a jury will come to such a judgment as long as it consists of a group of laymen representative of a cross section of the community who have the duty and the opportunity to deliberate, free from outside attempts at intimidation, on the question of a defendant's guilt. In terms of this function we perceive no difference between juries required to act unanimously and those permitted to convict or acquit by votes of 10 to two or 11 to one. Requiring unanimity would obviously produce hung juries in some situations where nonunanimous juries will convict or acquit. But in either case, the interest of the defendant in having the judgment of his peers interposed between himself and the officers of the State who prosecute and judge him is equally well served.

---

[42] Kalven & Zeisel, supra, at 12-32.
[43] See Oppenheim, Waiver of Trial by Jury in Criminal Cases, 25 Mich. L. Rev. 695, 728.

[The Court rejected the argument that the unanimity requirement was necessary to implement the reasonable-doubt standard which had been mandated in criminal cases under the due process clause. The Court also rejected the argument that unanimity was necessary to implement the requirement that the jury panel represent a cross section of the community, a requirement stemming from the equal protection clause.]

We accordingly affirm the judgment of the Court of Appeals of Oregon.

MR. JUSTICE POWELL, concurring in the judgment, printed at Johnson v. Louisiana, 406 U.S. 356, 366.

. . . I concur in the plurality opinion in this case insofar as it concludes that a defendant in a state court may constitutionally be convicted by less than a unanimous verdict, but I am not in accord with a major premise upon which that judgment is based. Its premise is that the concept of jury trial, as applicable to the States under the Fourteenth Amendment, must be identical in every detail to the concept required in federal courts by the Sixth Amendment. I do not think that all of the elements of jury trial within the meaning of the Sixth Amendment are necessarily embodied in or incorporated into the Due Process Clause of the Fourteenth Amendment. . . .

In an unbroken line of cases reaching back into the late 1800's, the Justices of this Court have recognized, virtually without dissent, that unanimity is one of the indispensable features of *federal* jury trial. Andres v. United States, 333 U.S. 740, 748-749 (1948); Patton v. United States, 281 U.S. 276, 288-290 (1930); Hawaii v. Mankichi, 190 U.S. 197, 211-212 (1903) (see also Mr. Justice Harlan's dissenting opinion); Maxwell v. Dow, 176 U.S. 581, 586 (1900) (see also Mr. Justice Harlan's dissenting opinion); Thompson v. Utah, 170 U.S. 343, 355 (1898). In these cases, the Court has presumed that unanimous verdicts are essential in federal jury trials, not because unanimity is necessarily fundamental to the function performed by the jury, but because that result is mandated by history. The reasoning that runs throughout this Court's Sixth Amendment precedents is that, in amending the Constitution to guarantee the right to jury trial, the framers desired to preserve the jury safeguard as it was known to them at common law.[7] At the time the Bill of Rights was adopted, unanimity had long been established as one of the attributes of a jury conviction at common law.[8] It therefore seems to me, in accord both with history and precedent, that the Sixth Amendment requires a unanimous jury verdict to convict in a federal criminal trial. . . .

The question . . . that should be addressed in this case is whether unanimity is in fact so fundamental to the essentials of jury trial that this particular requirement of the Sixth Amendment is necessarily binding on the States under the Due Process Clause of the Fourteenth Amendment. . . .

The importance that our system attaches to trial by jury derives from the special confidence we repose in a "body of one's peers to determine guilt or innocence as a safeguard against arbitrary law enforcement." Williams v. Florida, 399 U.S. 78, 87 (1970). It is this safeguarding function, preferring the commonsense judgment of a jury as a bulwark "against the corrupt or overzealous prosecutor and against the compliant, biased, or eccentric judge," that lies at the core of our dedication to the principles of jury determination of guilt or innocence. This is the fundamental of jury trial that brings it within the mandate of due process. It seems to me that this fundamental is adequately preserved by the jury-verdict provision of the Oregon Constitution. There is no reason to believe, on the basis of experience in Oregon or elsewhere, that a unanimous decision of 12 jurors is more likely to serve the high purpose of jury trial, or is entitled to greater respect in the community, than the same decision joined in by 10 members of a jury of 12. . . .

While the Civil War Amendments altered substantially the balance of federalism, it

---

[7] See, e.g., R. Perry, Sources of Our Liberties 270, 281-282, 288, 429 (1959); 3 J. Story, Commentaries on the Constitution 652-653 (1st ed. 1833).

[8] See, e.g., 4 W. Blackstone, Commentaries *376; W. Forsyth, History of Trial By Jury 238-258 (1852); M. Hale, Analysis of the Law of England 119 (1716).

strains credulity to believe that they were intended to deprive the States of all freedom to experiment with variations in jury-trial procedure. In an age in which empirical study is increasingly relied upon as a foundation for decisionmaking, one of the more obvious merits of our federal system is the opportunity it affords each State, if its people so choose, to become a "laboratory" and to experiment with a range of trial and procedural alternatives. Although the need for the innovations that grow out of diversity has always been great, imagination unimpeded by unwarranted demands for national uniformity is of special importance at a time when serious doubt exists as to the adequacy of our criminal justice system. The same diversity of local legislative responsiveness that marked the development of economic and social reforms in this country,[16] if not barred by an unduly restrictive application of the Due Process Clause, might well lead to valuable innovations with respect to determining — fairly and more expeditiously — the guilt or innocence of the accused. . . .

MR. JUSTICE DOUGLAS, with whom MR. JUSTICE BRENNAN and MR. JUSTICE MARSHALL concur, dissenting, printed at Johnson v. Louisiana, 406 U.S. 356, 380.

[C]ivil rights — whether they concern speech, searches and seizures, self-incrimination, criminal prosecutions, bail, or cruel and unusual punishments extend, of course, to everyone, but in cold reality touch mostly the lower castes in our society. I refer, of course, to the blacks, the Chicanos, the one-mule farmers, the agricultural workers, the offbeat students, the victims of the ghetto. Are we giving the States the power to experiment in diluting their civil rights? It has long been thought that the "thou shalt nots" in the Constitution and Bill of Rights protect everyone against governmental intrusion or overreaching. The idea has been obnoxious that there are some who can be relegated to second-class citizenship. But if we construe the Bill of Rights and the Fourteenth Amendment to permit States to "experiment" with the basic rights of people, we open a veritable Pandora's box. For hate and prejudice are versatile forces that can degrade the constitutional scheme.[dd]

NOTE Identity of State and Federal Rights

In 1969, the Court applied the double jeopardy prohibition to the states, Benton v. Maryland, 395 U.S. 784, thereby overruling Palko. Duncan and Benton were the last major cases to decide which of the provisions in the first eight amendments were incorporated into the due process clause of the Fourteenth Amendment. The following are some of the other major incorporation cases not covered in this chapter: Gitlow v. New York, 268 U.S. 652 (1925) (freedom of speech and press); Cantwell v. Connecticut, 310 U.S. 296 (1940) (free exercise of religion); Everson v. Board of Education, 330 U.S. 1 (1947) (establishment of religion); DeJonge v. Oregon, 299 U.S. 353 (1937) (right of assembly); NAACP v. Alabama, 357 U.S. 449 (1958) (freedom of association); Chicago, B. & Q.R. Co. v. Chicago, 166 U.S. 226 (1897) (just compensation); In re Oliver, 333 U.S. 257 (1948) (public trial); Klopfer v. North Carolina, 386 U.S. 213 (1967) (speedy trial); Pointer v. Texas, 380 U.S. 400 (1965) (confrontation with witness); Washington v. Texas, 388 U.S. 14 (1967) (compulsory process for obtaining witness); and Robinson v. California, 370 U.S. 660 (1962) (cruel and unusual punishment). In addition, Schilb v. Kuebel, 404 U.S. 357 (1971), intimates that the proscription of excessive bail is to be applied against the states.

The current debate, as Apodaca exemplifies, centers upon the content of the incorporated guarantees. Justice Powell's position in Apodaca, that some provisions need not be

---

[16] See Mr. Justice Brandeis' oft-quoted dissent in New State Ice Co. v. Liebmann, 285 U.S. 262, 280, 309-311 (1932), in which he details the stultifying potential of the substantive due process doctrine.

[dd] A concurring opinion of Justice Blackmun and dissenting opinions of Justices Brennan, Stewart, and Marshall are omitted. — ED.

applied identically against the federal and state governments, however, is neither novel nor untried. Justice Harlan in Roth v. United States, infra page 1285, argued that the First Amendment imposed fewer limits on state regulation of obscenity than it did on federal regulation because the interests sought to be protected are "primarily entrusted to the care" of the states. Justice Jackson, before him, had likewise contended in Beauharnais v. Illinois, infra page 1210, that state control over criminal libel ought to be more expansive under the First Amendment than would federal power. Justice Jackson, in turn, had relied upon the dictum of Justice Holmes in dissent in Gitlow v. New York, infra page 1134, that the First Amendment might be construed more loosely against the states than against the federal government (although Justice Holmes then proceeded to apply the same "clear and present danger" test that had been formulated in Schenck v. United States, 249 U.S. 47 (1919)).

Does the above line of dissents provide support for Justice Powell's position in Apodaca? Is it his argument that there is a stronger state interest and, hence, more state power behind a less-than-unanimous jury system than the federal government could be said to have? Or is his position instead that while the federal and state interest in jury verdicts is the same, a federalist system ought to allow the states some room to experiment to determine which mechanisms best serve those interests? As to the latter view, Justice Douglas in his dissent, supra, at 384-385, warns Justice Powell that the only departure from the coextensive coverage of the incorporated guarantees was Wolf v. Colorado, supra page 1006. By what measure should Wolf be judged a "success" or a "failure"? Did the steady acceptance of the exclusionary rule by many individual states prior to Mapp make for a more confident and acceptable extension of that rule to all the states? How valuable will the pre-Mapp experience be if and when the Court reconsiders the necessity for an exclusionary rule at all, e.g. in light of an alternative tort remedy established by statute?

Justice Douglas also warns in his dissent that Justice Powell's view could open a "Pandora's box." What should be the standards for delimiting state experimentation with the details of incorporated guarantees? Would it be sufficient that there be substantial disagreement about the necessity of the detail in question in implementing the underlying right? But consider that at the time of Apodaca, "[o]nly four states other than Louisiana and Oregon allow[ed] non-unanimous jury verdicts in criminal cases." Recent Developments, Non-Unanimous Jury Verdicts, 61 Geo. L.J. 223, 235 n. 53 (1972). Compare Justice Powell's reliance upon Kalven & Zeisel's The American Jury (1971): "The available empirical research indicates that the jury-trial protection is not substantially affected by less-than-unanimous verdict requirements." Supra, at 374 n. 12. Or should state experimentation be allowed with any detail that is involved with the implementation of a constitutional command? See Friendly, The Bill of Rights as a Code of Criminal Procedure, 53 Calif. L. Rev. 929 (1965); see also Monaghan, The Supreme Court, 1974 Term — Foreword: Constitutional Common Law, 89 Harv. L. Rev. 1 (1975).

Section C. PROCEDURAL DUE PROCESS IN NONCRIMINAL SETTINGS

Board of Regents v. Roth 408 U.S. 564, 92 S. Ct. 2701, 33 L. Ed. 2d 548 (1972)

MR. JUSTICE STEWART delivered the opinion of the Court.

In 1968 the respondent, David Roth, was hired for his first teaching job as assistant professor of political science at Wisconsin State University-Oshkosh. He was hired for a fixed term of one academic year. . . . The respondent completed that term. But he was informed that he would not be rehired for the next academic year.

[He brought suit claiming that the due process clause of the Fourteenth Amendment entitled him to a statement of reasons why his contract was not renewed and a hearing at which he might contest the university's decision. The rules of the Board of Regents did not provide such protection for nontenured teachers.]

The District Court decided that procedural due process guarantees apply in this case by assessing and balancing the weights of the particular interests involved. It concluded that the respondent's interest in re-employment at Wisconsin State University-Oshkosh outweighed the University's interest in denying him re-employment summarily. . . . Undeniably, the respondent's re-employment prospects were of major concern to him — concern that we surely cannot say was insignificant. And a weighing process has long been a part of any determination of the *form* of hearing required in particular situations by procedural due process. But, to determine whether due process requirements apply in the first place, we must look not to the "weight" but to the *nature* of the interest at stake. See Morrissey v. Brewer, [408 U.S. 471, 481 (1972)]. We must look to see if the interest is within the Fourteenth Amendment's protection of liberty and property.

"Liberty" and "property" are broad and majestic terms. They are among the "[g]reat [constitutional] concepts . . . purposely left to gather meaning from experience. . . . [T]hey relate to the whole domain of social and economic fact, and the statesmen who founded this Nation knew too well that only a stagnant society remains unchanged." National Ins. Co. v. Tidewater Co., 337 U.S. 582, 646 (Frankfurter, J., dissenting). For that reason, the Court has fully and finally rejected the wooden distinction between "rights" and "privileges" that once seemed to govern the applicability of procedural due process rights.[9] The Court has also made clear that the property interests protected by procedural due process extend well beyond actual ownership of real estate, chattels, or money. By the same token, the Court has required due process protection for deprivations of liberty beyond the sort of formal constraints imposed by the criminal process.

Yet, while the Court has eschewed rigid or formalistic limitations on the protection of procedural due process, it has at the same time observed certain boundaries. For the words "liberty" and "property" in the Due Process Clause of the Fourteenth Amendment must be given some meaning.

"While this Court has not attempted to define with exactness the liberty . . . guaranteed [by the Fourteenth Amendment], the term has received much consideration and some of the included things have been definitely stated. Without doubt, it denotes not merely freedom from bodily restraint but also the right of the individual to contract, to engage in any of the common occupations of life, to acquire useful knowledge, to marry, establish a home and bring up children, to worship God according to the dictates of his own conscience, and generally to enjoy those privileges long recognized . . . as essential to the orderly pursuit of happiness by free men." Meyer v. Nebraska, 262 U.S. 390, 399. In a Constitution for a free people, there can be no doubt that the meaning of "liberty" must be broad indeed. See, e.g., Bolling v. Sharpe, 347 U.S. 497, 499-500; Stanley v. Illinois, 405 U.S. 645.

The State, in declining to rehire the respondent, did not make any charge against him that might seriously damage his standing and associations in his community. It did not base the nonrenewal of his contract on a charge, for example, that he had been guilty of dishonesty, or immorality. Had it done so, this would be a different case. For "[w]here a person's good name, reputation, honor, or integrity is at stake because of what the government is doing to him, notice and an opportunity to be heard are essential." Wisconsin v.

---

[9] In a leading case decided many years ago, the Court of Appeals for the District of Columbia Circuit held that public employment in general was a "privilege," not a "right," and that procedural due process guarantees therefore were inapplicable. Bailey v. Richardson, 86 U.S. App. D.C. 248, 182 F.2d 46, aff'd by an equally divided Court, 341 U.S. 918. The basis of this holding has been thoroughly undermined in the ensuing years. . . . [See, e.g.,] Graham v. Richardson, 403 U.S. 365, 374. . . .

Constantineau, 400 U.S. 433, 437 [requiring notice and a hearing before "posting" of notices in retail liquor outlets forbidding sales or gifts of liquor to a named individual]. . . . In such a case, due process would accord an opportunity to refute the charge before University officials. In the present case, however, there is no suggestion whatever that the respondent's "good name, reputation, honor, or integrity" is at stake.

Similarly, there is no suggestion that the State, in declining to reemploy the respondent, imposed on him a stigma or other disability that foreclosed his freedom to take advantage of other employment opportunities. . . . Had it done so, this, again, would be a different case. . . .

The Fourteenth Amendment's procedural protection of property is a safeguard of the security of interests that a person has already acquired in specific benefits. These interests — property interests — may take many forms.

Thus, the Court has held that a person receiving welfare benefits under statutory and administrative standards defining eligibility for them has an interest in continued receipt of those benefits that is safeguarded by procedural due process. Goldberg v. Kelly, 397 U.S. 254. See Flemming v. Nestor, 363 U.S. 603, 611. Similarly, in the area of public employment, the Court has held that a public college professor dismissed from an office held under tenure provisions, Slochower v. Board of Education, 350 U.S. 551, and college professors and staff members dismissed during the terms of their contracts, Wieman v. Updegraff, 344 U.S. 183, have interests in continued employment that are safeguarded by due process. Only last year, the Court held that this principle "proscribing summary dismissal from public employment without hearing or inquiry required by due process" also applied to a teacher recently hired without tenure or a formal contract, but nonetheless with a clearly implied promise of continued employment. Connell v. Higginbotham, 403 U.S. 207, 208.

Certain attributes of "property" interests protected by procedural due process emerge from these decisions. To have a property interest in a benefit, a person clearly must have more than an abstract need or desire for it. He must have more than a unilateral expectation of it. He must, instead, have a legitimate claim of entitlement to it. It is a purpose of the ancient institution of property to protect those claims upon which people rely in their daily lives, reliance that must not be arbitrarily undermined. It is a purpose of the constitutional right to a hearing to provide an opportunity for a person to vindicate those claims.

Property interests, of course, are not created by the Constitution. Rather, they are created and their dimensions are defined by existing rules or understandings that stem from an independent source such as state law — rules or understandings that secure certain benefits and that support claims of entitlement to those benefits. Thus, the welfare recipients in Goldberg v. Kelly, supra, had a claim of entitlement to welfare payments that was grounded in the statute defining eligibility for them. The recipients had not yet shown that they were, in fact, within the statutory terms of eligibility. But we held that they had a right to a hearing at which they might attempt to do so.

Just as the welfare recipients' "property" interest in welfare payments was created and defined by statutory terms, so the respondent's "property" interest in employment at Wisconsin State University-Oshkosh was created and defined by the terms of his appointment. Those terms secured his interest in employment up to June 30, 1969. But the important fact in this case is that they specifically provided that the respondent's employment was to terminate on June 30. They did not provide for contract renewal absent "sufficient cause." Indeed, they made no provision for renewal whatsoever.

. . . In these circumstances, the respondent surely had an abstract concern in being rehired, but he did not have a *property* interest sufficient to require the University authorities to give him a hearing when they declined to renew his contract of employment.[ee] . . .

[ee] A concurring opinion of Chief Justice Burger and dissenting opinions by Justices Douglas, Marshall, and Brennan are omitted. — ED.

NOTE "Liberty" and "Property" under Due Process

Compare Perry v. Sindermann, 408 U.S. 593 (1972), decided the same day as Roth. There, the Court held that a public university professor who was not tenured but had been hired under a series of one-year contracts could establish a property interest entitling him to a statement of reasons and a hearing on the state's decision not to renew his contract if he could show that he had tenure "de facto . . . in light of the policies and practices of the institution." The Court further held that respondent's claim that he had been denied renewal in retaliation for expressions of opinion by him and therefore in violation of his First and Fourth Amendment rights was cognizable regardless of the status of his interest in continued employment.

For other decisions finding interests to be "liberty" or "property" within the meaning of the due process clauses, see, e.g., Morrissey v. Brewer, 408 U.S. 471 (1972) (revocation of parole); Gagnon v. Scarpelli, 411 U.S. 778 (1973) (revocation of probation); Bell v. Burson, 402 U.S. 535 (1971) (suspension of driver's license); Wolff v. McDonnell, 418 U.S. 539 (1974) (cancellation of prisoner's good-time credits); Goss v. Lopez, 419 U.S. 565 (1975) (suspension of students from public high school).

Is it satisfactory to set up as a threshold inquiry in these cases the question whether the plaintiff possesses a "liberty" or "property," and to reject his or her Fifth or Fourteenth Amendment claim if the answer is negative? Suppose that the teacher in the Roth case had been refused reappointment because of race or color. Or suppose that a mere applicant for a teaching position in the District of Columbia claims he was denied appointment on that ground. Is he outside the protection of the "property" clause of the Fifth Amendment?

More recently, the Court has refused recognition of procedural due process claims in a number of cases. See Paul v. Davis, 424 U.S. 693 (1976) (circulation by police to local merchants of plaintiff's picture as active shoplifter); Bishop v. Wood, 426 U.S. 341 (1976) (discharge of police officers); Meachum v. Fano, 427 U.S. 215 (1974) (transfer of prisoners to another prison). In the Paul and Bishop cases, the Court suggested that only specific state-created rights are interests protected by the due process clause. See Note, The Supreme Court, 1975 Term, 90 Harv. L. Rev. 59, 86-104 (1976).

A closely debated question of the scope of the due process clause's protection of "property" has arisen with regard to summary prejudgment remedies for creditors. In Sniadach v. Family Finance Corp., 395 U.S. 337 (1969), the Court invalidated, 7 to 1, a Wisconsin statute authorizing summary prejudgment garnishment of wages. The statute provided that even before a creditor had filed suit, a court clerk would, on the request of the creditor's lawyer, issue a summons compelling the debtor's employer to pay the employee only a small "subsistence allowance" and withhold the rest of her wages pending further order by the court. The Court held that the due process clause of the Fourteenth Amendment required that the debtor be afforded notice and a hearing prior to garnishment. Writing for the Court, Justice Douglas emphasized the hardship imposed by such deprivation of wages, which he described as "a specialized type of property presenting distinct problems in our economic system." Justice Harlan, concurring, argued that the application of due process protection did not turn on the special importance of the property interest involved. He wrote: "The 'property' of which petitioner has been deprived is the *use* of the garnished portion of her wages during the interim period between the garnishment and the culmination of the main suit. Since this deprivation cannot be characterized as de minimis, she must be accorded the usual requisites of procedural due process. . . ."

The implications of Justice Harlan's view were fully realized in Fuentes v. Shevin, 407 U.S. 67 (1972), where the Court held, 4 to 3,[ff] that the summary prejudgment replevin

---

[ff] Two new Justices, Powell and Rehnquist, had not heard the argument and did not participate. Compare the statement of Chief Justice Marshall in New York v. Miln, 8 Pet. 118 (1834): "The practice of this court is, not

Section C. **Procedural Due Process in Noncriminal Settings**

provisions of Florida and Pennsylvania law violated procedural due process. The cases involved ex parte issuance of writs of replevin against household goods, including for example a gas stove and a stereo. In each state a debtor could regain possession of the chattels, pending final judgment, by posting a counterbond. Holding that Fourteenth Amendment due process requires that the debtor be afforded notice and a hearing before seizure of his goods, Justice Stewart held that replevin procedures affected protected "property" interests even though the deprivation were only temporary and the debtors lacked full legal title to the chattels: "the[ir] interest in continued possession and use of the goods" was sufficient. The Court further rejected the district courts' conclusion that due process was required only where the interest involved could be characterized as a "necessity." The Court noted, however, that "[t]he relative weight of liberty or property interests is relevant, of course, to the form of notice and hearing required by due process." The Court left open the possibility that in a limited class of "extraordinary situations," as where immediate seizure is necessary to establish a state court's jurisdiction or to protect the public after a bank failure, postponement of due process safeguards would be justified.

The pendulum swung back, however, in Mitchell v. W. T. Grant Co., 416 U.S. 600 (1974). There, the Supreme Court upheld, 5 to 4, Louisiana statutes authorizing summary prejudgment issuance of writs of sequestration ordering the sheriff to seize and hold chattels. Writing for the Court, Justice White distinguished Fuentes on several grounds: that the Louisiana writ is issued by a judge rather than by a court clerk, that the party seeking the writ must more clearly establish his interest in the chattel, that Louisiana law requires full damages and attorneys' fees to be awarded the debtor should the creditor not prevail at trial, and that Louisiana requires a hearing immediately following the execution of the writ. Justice White emphasized that the lien creditor, as well as the debtor, has a property interest in the chattel and that surprise might be necessary to ensure that the debtor would not waste or dispose of the goods. While framing the question as one of the sufficiency of particular procedures, the Court appears to have held that interest-balancing may in fact be taken into account even in situations that are not "extraordinary" to determine whether due process requires any sort of notice or hearing at all prior to a taking. See Note, The Supreme Court, 1973 Term, 88 Harv. L. Rev. 41, 71-83 (1974). Compare the standards set out in Board of Regents v. Roth, supra.

In North Georgia Finishing, Inc. v. Di-Chem, Inc., 419 U.S. 601 (1975), the Court followed Fuentes to invalidate a Georgia law authorizing summary prejudgment garnishment of a bank account where the writ was issued by a court clerk on a creditor's affidavit that "need contain only conclusory allegations," where the defendant was required to post bond in order to dissolve the writ, and where there was no provision for an early hearing.

On the "constitutionalization" of creditors' remedies, see Clark & Landers, Sniadach, Fuentes, and Beyond: The Creditor Meets the Constitution, 59 Va. L. Rev. 355 (1973); Countryman, The Bill of Rights and the Bill Collector, 15 Ariz. L. Rev. 521 (1973); Kripke, Gesture and Reality in Consumer Credit Reform, 44 N.Y.U.L. Rev. 1 (1969); Wallace, The Logic of Consumer Credit Reform, 82 Yale L.J. 461 (1973). On the scope of due process protections of "liberty" and "property," see Reich, The New Property, 73 Yale L.J. 733 (1964); Van Alstyne, The Demise of the Right-Privilege Distinction in Constitutional Law, 81 Harv. L. Rev. 1439 (1968); Comment, Entitlement, Enjoyment, and Due Process of Law, 1974 Duke L.J. 89.

(except in cases of absolute necessity) to deliver any judgment in cases where constitutional questions are involved, unless four judges concur in opinion, thus making the decision that of a majority of the whole court. In the present cases, four judges do not concur in opinion as to the constitutional questions which have been argued. The court therefore directs these cases to be reargued at the next term, under the expectation that a larger number of the judges may be present." See also Roofing Wholesale Co. v. Palmer, 502 P.2d 1327 (Ariz. 1972), holding that since it was a 4 to 3 decision Fuentes was not binding on the state court. Roofing Wholesale is noted at 86 Harv. L. Rev. 1307 (1973). — ED.

1046   Chapter Fifteen. **Fair Procedure**

NOTE What Process Is Due?

"Once it is determined that due process applies, the question remains what process is due. . . . [D]ue process is flexible and calls for such procedural protection as the particular situation demands." Morrissey v. Brewer, 408 U.S. 471, 481 (1972). As Justice Stewart indicated in Fuentes, supra, determination of the form of notice and hearing required in a particular setting may vary with the importance of the interest at stake, the nature of the inquiry being undertaken, and the administrative costs associated with various procedural safeguards. In Goldberg v. Kelly, 397 U.S. 354 (1970), holding that a welfare recipient is entitled to a hearing before termination of benefits, the Court discussed in some detail the nature of the hearing and individual procedural safeguards that must be accorded the recipient: "[T]he pre-termination hearing need not take the form of a judicial or quasi-judicial trial. We bear in mind that the statutory [post-termination] 'fair hearing' will provide the recipient with a full administrative review. Accordingly, the pre-termination hearing has one function only: to produce an initial determination of the validity of the welfare department's grounds for discontinuance of payments in order to protect a recipient against an erroneous termination of his benefits. Cf. Sniadach v. Family Finance Corp., 395 U.S. 337, 343 (Harlan, J., concurring). Thus, a complete record and a comprehensive opinion, which would serve primarily to facilitate judicial review and to guide future decisions, need not be provided at the pre-termination stage. . . .

" 'The fundamental requisite of due process of law is the opportunity to be heard.' Grannis v. Ordean, 234 U.S. 385, 394 (1914). The hearing must be 'at a meaningful time and in a meaningful manner.' Armstrong v. Manzo, 380 U.S. 545, 552 (1965). In the present context these principles require that a recipient have timely and adequate notice detailing the reasons for a proposed termination, and an effective opportunity to defend by confronting any adverse witnesses and by presenting his own arguments and witnesses orally. These rights are important in cases such as those before us, where recipients have challenged proposed terminations as resting on incorrect or misleading factual information or on misapplication of rules or policies to the facts of particular cases. . . .

"In almost every setting where important decisions turn on questions of fact, due process requires an opportunity to confront and cross-examine adverse witnesses. . . . Welfare recipients must . . . be given an opportunity to confront and cross-examine the witnesses relied on by the department.

" 'The right to be heard would be, in many cases, of little avail if it did not comprehend the right to be heard by counsel.' Powell v. Alabama, 287 U.S. 45, 68-69 (1932). We do not say that counsel must be provided at the pre-termination hearing but only that the recipient must be allowed to retain an attorney if he so desires. . . .

"Finally, the decisionmaker's conclusion as to a recipient's eligibility must rest solely on the legal rules and evidence adduced at the hearing. . . ."

For discussions of the procedural safeguards that may be required in other contexts, see Gerstein v. Pugh, 419 U.S. 815 (1975) (probable cause hearing for person detained pending trial); Morrissey v. Brewer, 408 U.S. 471 (1972) (revocation of parole); Richardson v. Perales, 402 U.S. 389 (1972) (social security disability benefits); Goss v. Lopez, 419 U.S. 565 (1975) (suspension of public high school students); Baker v. Owen, 423 U.S. 907, aff'g 395 F. Supp. 294 (M.D.N.C. 1975) (corporal punishment in public schools); Meyerhoff & Mishkin, Application of Goldberg v. Kelly Hearing Requirements to Termination of Social Security Benefits, 26 Stan. L. Rev. 549 (1974); Tobriner & Cohen, How Much Process Is "Due"?: Parolees and Prisoners, 25 Hastings L.J. 801 (1974); Note, Procedural Due Process in Government-Subsidized Housing, 86 Harv. L. Rev. 880 (1973); Note, Fourteenth Amendment Due Process in Terminations of Utility Services for Nonpayment, 86 Harv. L. Rev. 1477 (1973). Compare the procedures upheld in Mitchell v. W. T. Grant Co., 416 U.S. 600 (1974), with those held insufficient in North Georgia

Section C. Procedural Due Process in Noncriminal Settings 1047

Finishing, Inc. v. Di-Chem, Inc., 419 U.S. 601 (1975). See also Note, Specifying the Procedures Required by Due Process: Toward Limits on the Use of Interest Balancing, 88 Harv. L. Rev. 1510 (1975).

The capacities of the parties to be afforded procedural rights constitute still another determinative element in the fashioning of due process. In re Gault, 387 U.S. 1 (1967), extended rights such as assistance of counsel and confrontation with witnesses to proceedings in juvenile court. In also assuring the privilege against self-incrimination to young defendants, Justice Fortas wrote for the Court that: "[A]uthoritative opinion has cast formidable doubt upon the reliability and trustworthiness of 'confessions' by children." Id. at 52. See Paulsen, Juvenile Court and the Legacy of '67, 43 Ind. L.J. 527 (1968), and also Canon and Kolson, Rural Compliance with Gault: Kentucky, A Case Study, 10 J. Fam. L. 300 (1971).

The Court has also begun to protect mental patients against the continuation of groundless civil commitment. O'Connor v. Donaldson, 422 U.S. 563 (1975). See generally Developments in the Law — Civil Commitment of the Mentally Ill, 87 Harv. L. Rev. 1190 (1974).

May the government, in setting the substantive limits of a statutory entitlement, determine as well the procedural safeguards applicable to its termination? In Arnett v. Kennedy, 416 U.S. 134 (1974), three Justices argued that it could. Kennedy, a discharged employee of the Office of Economic Opportunity, brought suit challenging the sufficiency of the procedures under which his employment had been terminated. Under the Lloyd-LaFollette Act, 5 U.S.C. §7501 (1970), Kennedy could be "removed . . . only for such cause as will promote the efficiency of the service." The act further prescribed removal procedures to which Kennedy was entitled. These included notice, a statement of charges, opportunity to file a written answer, and a written decision. A trial-type hearing was not required but left to the discretion of the decisionmaker. If a hearing were not afforded, however, an employee could obtain one, following discharge, on appeal to higher authorities in OEO or to the Civil Service Commission. If his appeal were successful, the employee would be entitled to reinstatement and full back pay. The Court held, 5 to 4, that the Lloyd-LaFollette Act met the requirements of due process under the Fifth Amendment.

Writing for himself, the Chief Justice, and Justice Stewart, Justice Rehnquist argued that the substantive right in which Kennedy was asserting a property interest was itself limited by the procedural provisions of the Act. He wrote: ". . . appellee did have a statutory expectancy that he not be removed other than for 'such cause as will promote the efficiency of the service.' But the very section of the statute which granted him that right, a right which had previously existed only by virtue of administrative regulation, expressly provided also for the procedure by which 'cause' was to be determined, and expressly omitted the procedural guarantees which appellee insists are mandated by the Constitution. . . . Congress was obviously intent on according a measure of statutory job security to governmental employees which they had not previously enjoyed, but was likewise intent on excluding more elaborate procedural requirements which it felt would make the operation of the new scheme unnecessarily burdensome in practice. Where the focus of legislation was this strongly on the procedural mechanism for enforcing the substantive right which was simultaneously conferred, we decline to conclude that the substantive right may be viewed wholly apart from the procedure provided for its enforcement. The employee's statutorily defined right is not a guarantee against removal without cause in the abstract, but such a guarantee as enforced by the procedures which Congress has designated for the determination of cause."

Justice Powell, with whom Justice Blackmun joined, concurred in the plurality's conclusion that Kennedy's discharge did not violate Fifth Amendment due process but took the ground that the procedures afforded under the Lloyd-LaFollette Act met due process standards. He rejected the plurality's argument that the act conclusively defined the procedural safeguards available to the employee. He wrote: "While the legislature may elect not to confer a property interest in federal employment, it may not constitutionally authorize the deprivation of such an interest, once conferred, without appropriate procedural safeguards. . . ."

The four dissenting Justices also rejected Justice Rehnquist's view on this issue. For comment on Arnett v. Kennedy, see Note, The Supreme Court, 1973 Term, 88 Harv. L. Rev. 41, 83-90 (1974).

Section D. THE CONSTITUTION AND MILITARY TRIBUNALS

For additional material on this subject, see Chapter 13, "The Constitution Overseas."

Ex parte MERRYMAN, 17 F. Cas. 144, No. 9,487 (C.C.D. Md. 1861). On May 26, 1861, a petition for habeas corpus was presented to Chief Justice Taney of the Supreme Court of the United States on behalf of one John Merryman of Baltimore. The petition stated that at two o'clock in the morning of the preceding day Merryman had been taken from his bed by an armed force, and that he was confined in Fort McHenry near Baltimore. Chief Justice Taney thereupon issued a writ of habeas corpus directed to Brevet Major General Cadwalader, commanding at Fort McHenry, directing him to bring the body of John Merryman before the Chief Justice in the United States courtroom at Baltimore on May 27, at eleven in the morning. A United States marshal served the writ on General Cadwalader, who sent an officer with a return stating that Merryman was charged with various acts of treason, and with holding a commission as a lieutenant in a company possessing arms belonging to the government, avowing a purpose of armed hostility against the United States. General Cadwalader also stated in his return that he was duly authorized by the President of the United States to suspend the writ of habeas corpus; he requested that Chief Justice Taney would postpone further action until the General could obtain further instructions from the President of the United States.

The Chief Justice thereupon directed that an attachment issue against General Cadwalader, returnable the following day.

"At twelve o'clock, on the 28th May 1861, the chief justice again took his seat on the bench, and called for the marshal's return to the writ of attachment. It was as follows:

" 'I hereby certify to the Honorable Roger B. Taney, chief justice of the supreme court of the United States, that by virtue of the within writ of attachment, to me directed, on the 27th day of May 1861, I proceeded, on the 28th day of May 1861, to Fort McHenry, for the purpose of serving the said writ. I sent in my name at the outer gate; the messenger returned with the reply, "that there was no answer to my card," and therefore, I could not serve the writ, as I was commanded. I was not permitted to enter the gate. So answers Washington Bonifant, U.S. Marshal for the District of Maryland.'

"After it was read, the chief justice said, that the marshal had the power to summon the posse comitatus to aid him in seizing and bringing before the court, the party named in the attachment, who would, when so brought in, be liable to punishment by fine and imprisonment; but where, as in this case, the power refusing obedience was so notoriously superior to any the marshal could command, he held that officer excused from doing anything more than he had done. The chief justice then proceeded as follows:

" 'I ordered this attachment yesterday, because, upon the face of the return, the detention of the prisoner was unlawful, upon the grounds: 1. That the president, under the constitution of the United States, cannot suspend the privilege of the writ of habeas cor-

Section D. The Constitution and Military Tribunals

pus, nor authorize a military officer to do it. 2. A military officer has no right to arrest and detain a person not subject to the rules and articles of war, for an offence against the laws of the United States, except in aid of the judicial authority, and subject to its control; and if the party be arrested by the military, it is the duty of the officer to deliver him over immediately to the civil authority, to be dealt with according to law. It is, therefore, very clear that John Merryman, the petitioner, is entitled to be set at liberty and discharged immediately from imprisonment. I forbore yesterday to state orally the provisions of the constitution of the United States, which make those principles the fundamental law of the Union, because an oral statement might be misunderstood in some portions of it, and I shall therefore put my opinion in writing, and file it in the office of the clerk of the circuit court, in the course of this week.'

"He concluded by saying, that he should cause his opinion, when filed, and all the proceedings, to be laid before the president, in order that he might perform his constitutional duty, to enforce the laws, by securing obedience to the process of the United States."

[Chief Justice Taney's opinion included the following statement.]

"As the case comes before me, therefore, I understand that the president not only claims the right to suspend the writ of habeas corpus himself, at his discretion, but to delegate that discretionary power to a military officer, and to leave it to him to determine whether he will or will not obey judicial process that may be served upon him. No official notice has been given to the courts of justice, or to the public, by proclamation or otherwise, that the president claimed this power, and had exercised it in the manner stated in the return. And I certainly listened to it with some surprise, for I had supposed it to be one of those points of constitutional law upon which there was no difference of opinion, and that it was admitted on all hands, that the privilege of the writ could not be suspended, except by act of Congress. . . .

"The constitution provides, as I have before said, that 'no person shall be deprived of life, liberty or property, without due process of law.' It declares that 'the right of the people to be secure in their persons, houses, papers and effects, against unreasonable searches and seizures, shall not be violated; and no warrant shall issue, but upon probable cause, supported by oath or affirmation, and particularly describing the place to be searched, and the persons or things to be seized.' It provides that the party accused shall be entitled to a speedy trial in a court of justice.

"These great and fundamental laws, which congress itself could not suspend, have been disregarded and suspended, like the writ of habeas corpus, by a military order, supported by force of arms. Such is the case now before me, and I can only say that if the authority which the constitution has confided to the judiciary department and judicial officers, may thus, upon any pretext or under any circumstances, be usurped by the military power, at its discretion, the people of the United States are no longer living under a government of laws, but every citizen holds life, liberty and property at the will and pleasure of the army officer in whose military district he may happen to be found.

". . . It is possible that the officer who has incurred this grave responsibility may have misunderstood his instructions, and exceeded that authority intended to be given him; I shall, therefore, order all the proceedings in this case, with my opinion, to be filed and recorded in the circuit court of the United States for the district of Maryland, and direct the clerk to transmit a copy, under seal, to the president of the United States. It will then remain for that high officer, in fullfilment of his constitutional obligation to 'take care that the laws be faithfully executed,' to determine what measures he will take to cause the civil process of the United States to be respected and enforced."

Shortly after the delivery of Chief Justice Taney's opinion, Merryman was released from Fort McHenry and transferred to civil custody. He was indicted for treason in the United States District Court of Baltimore, and posted a recognizance for $20,000 to appear in the Circuit Court of the United States for the District of Maryland. After some continuance by the order of the court, the case against Merryman was finally dropped.

The circumstances are described in Randall, Constitutional Problems Under Lincoln, 162 (rev. ed. 1951); Swisher, The Taney Period (5 Holmes Devise History of the Supreme Court) c. 33 (1974).[gg]

Ex parte Milligan 4 Wall. 2, 18 L. Ed. 281 (1866)

MR. JUSTICE DAVIS delivered the opinion of the court:

On the 10th day of May, 1865, Lambdin P. Milligan presented a petition to the circuit court of the United States for the district of Indiana, to be discharged from an alleged unlawful imprisonment. The case made by the petition is this: Milligan is a citizen of the United States; has lived for twenty years in Indiana; and at the time of the grievances complained of, was not and never had been in the military service of the United States. On the 5th day of October, 1864, while at home, he was arrested by order of Gen. Alvin P. Hovey, commanding the military district of Indiana; and has ever since been kept in close confinement.

On the 21st day of October, 1864, he was brought before a Military Commission, convened at Indianapolis, by order of Gen. Hovey, tried on certain charges and specifications, found guilty, and sentenced to be hanged, and the sentence ordered to be executed on Friday, the 19th day of May, 1865.

On the 2d day of January, 1865, after the proceedings of the Military Commission were at an end, the circuit court of the United States for Indiana met at Indianapolis and impaneled a grand jury, who were charged to inquire whether the laws of the United States had been violated, and if so, to make presentments. The court adjourned on the 27th day of January, having prior thereto discharged from further service the grand jury, who did not find any bill of indictment or make any presentment against Milligan for any offense whatever, and, in fact, since his imprisonment, no bill of indictment has been found or presentment made against him by any grand jury of the United States.

Milligan insists that said Military Commission had no jurisdiction to try him upon the charges preferred, or upon any charge whatever, because he was a citizen of the United States and the state of Indiana, and had not been, since the commencement of the late Rebellion, a resident of any of the states whose citizens were arrayed against the government, and that the right of trial by jury was guaranteed to him by the Constitution of the United States. . . .

[gg] On April 13, 1863, Major General Burnside, commanding the Military Department of Ohio, issued General Order No. 38, declaring, for the information of all concerned, that thereafter all persons found within his lines who should "commit acts for the benefit of the enemies of the country" should be tried as spies or traitors, and if convicted should suffer death; among other acts prohibited, was "the habit of declaring sympathy for the enemy"; "it must be distinctly understood that treason, expressed or implied, will not be tolerated."

On May 5, 1863, Vallandigham, a resident of the state of Ohio, and a citizen of the United States, was arrested at his residence and taken to Cincinnati, and there imprisoned. On the following day, he was arraigned before a military commission, on a charge of having expressed sympathies for those in arms against the government of the United States, and for having uttered, in a speech at a public meeting, disloyal sentiments and opinions, with the object and purpose of weakening the power of the government in its efforts for the suppression of an unlawful rebellion. The commission found Vallandigham guilty and sentenced him to confinement for the remainder of the war. A judge of the United States Circuit Court in Cincinnati refused habeas corpus. President Lincoln, in commutation of the sentence, ordered Vallandigham put beyond the Union lines, and he was thereupon sent South into the hands of the Confederates. He made his way to Canada, ran unsuccessfully for governor of Ohio on the Democratic ticket, and while he was thus absent, attorneys on his behalf petitioned the United States Supreme Court for a writ of certiorari to the Judge Advocate General. In Ex parte Vallandigham, 1 Wall. 243 (1864), the Supreme Court held that it had no original jurisdiction under Article III of the Constitution to grant certiorari to a military commission; and as the authority exercised by such a commission is not judicial, the Supreme Court could not exercise appellate jurisdiction. In June 1864, Vallandigham slipped back into Ohio and continued his agitation during the rest of the war. See 3 Sandburg, Abraham Lincoln: The War Years 109 (1939); Randall, Constitutional Problems Under Lincoln 176 (rev. ed. 1951); Rossiter, The Supreme Court and the Commander in Chief 28 (1951). — ED.

Section D. The Constitution and Military Tribunals

With the petition were filed the order for the commission, the charges and specifications, the findings of the court, with the order of the War Department reciting that the sentence was approved by the President of the United States, and directing that it be carried into execution without delay. The petition was presented and filed in open court by the counsel for Milligan; at the same time the district attorney of the United States for Indiana appeared, and, by the agreement of counsel, the application was submitted to the court. The opinions of the judges of the circuit court were opposed on three questions, which are certified to the Supreme Court:

1st. "On the facts stated in said petition and exhibits, ought a writ of habeas corpus to be issued?"

2d. "On the facts stated in said petition and exhibits, ought the said Lambdin P. Milligan to be discharged from custody as in said petition prayed?"

3d. "Whether, upon the facts stated in said petition and exhibits, the Military Commission mentioned therein had jurisdiction legally to try and sentence said Milligan in manner and form as in said petition and exhibits is stated."

The importance of the main question presented by this record cannot be overstated, for it involves the very framework of the government and the fundamental principles of American liberty.

During the late wicked Rebellion the temper of the times did not allow that calmness in deliberation and discussion so necessary to a correct conclusion of a purely judicial question. Then, considerations of safety were mingled with the exercise of power, and feelings and interests prevailed which are happily terminated. . . .

No graver question was ever considered by this court, nor one which more nearly concerns the rights of the whole people; for it is the birthright of every American citizen when charged with crime, to be tried and punished according to law. . . .

. . . The Constitution of the United States is a law for rulers and people, equally in war and in peace, and covers with the shield of its protection all classes of men, at all times, and under all circumstances. No doctrine, involving more pernicious consequences, was ever invented by the wit of man than that any of its provisions can be suspended during any of the great exigencies of government. Such a doctrine leads directly to anarchy or despotism, but the theory of necessity on which it is based is false: for the government, within the Constitution, has all the powers granted to it which are necessary to preserve its existence, as has been happily proved by the result of the great effort to throw off its just authority.

Have any of the rights guaranteed by the Constitution been violated in the case of Milligan? and if so, what are they? . . .

[I]t is said that the jurisdiction is complete under the "laws and usages of war."

It can serve no useful purpose to inquire what those laws and usages are, whence they originated, where found, and on whom they operate; they can never be applied to citizens in states which have upheld the authority of the government, and where the courts are open and their process unobstructed. This court has judicial knowledge that in Indiana the Federal authority was always unopposed, and its courts always open to hear criminal accusations and redress grievances; and no usage of war could sanction a military trial there for any offense whatever of a citizen in civil life, in nowise connected with the military service. . . .

Another guarantee of freedom was broken when Milligan was denied a trial by jury. . . .

The discipline necessary to the efficiency of the army and navy, required other and swifter modes of trial than are furnished by the common law courts; and, in pursuance of the power conferred by the Constitution, Congress has declared the kinds of trial and the manner in which they shall be conducted, for offenses committed while the party is in the military or naval service. Every one connected with these branches of public service is amenable to the jurisdiction which Congress has created for their government, and, while thus serving, surrenders his right to be tried by the civil courts. All other persons, citizens of states where the courts are open, if charged with crime, are guaranteed the inestimable privilege of trial by jury. This privilege is a vital principle, underlying the whole administration of criminal justice; it is not held by sufferance, and cannot be frittered away on any plea of state or political necessity. When peace prevails, and the authority of the government is undisputed, there is no difficulty in preserving the safeguards of liberty; for the ordinary modes of trial are never neglected, and no one wishes it otherwise; but if society is disturbed by civil commotion — if the passions of men are aroused and the restraints of law weakened, if not disregarded — these safeguards need, and should receive, the watchful care of those intrusted with the guardianship of the Constitution and laws. In no other way can we transmit to posterity unimpaired the blessings of liberty, consecrated by the sacrifices of the Revolution. . . .

It is essential to the safety of every government that, in a great crisis, like the one we have just passed through, there should be a power somewhere of suspending the writ of habeas corpus. . . . The Constitution goes no further. It does not say after a writ of habeas corpus is denied a citizen, that he shall be tried otherwise than by the course of common law. If it had intended this result, it was easy by the use of direct words to have accomplished it. . . .

It will be borne in mind that this is not a question of the power to proclaim martial law, when war exists in a community and the courts and civil authorities are overthrown. Nor is it a question what rule a military commander, at the head of his army, can impose on states in rebellion to cripple their resources and quell the insurrection. The jurisdiction claimed is much more extensive. The necessities of the service, during the late Rebellion, required that the loyal states should be placed within the limits of certain military districts and commanders appointed in them; and, it is urged, that this, in a military sense, constituted them the theater of military operations; and, as in this case, Indiana had been and was again threatened with invasion by the enemy, the occasion was furnished to establish martial law. The conclusion does not follow from the premises. If armies were collected in Indiana, they were to be employed in another locality, where the laws were obstructed and the national authority disputed. On her soil there was no hostile foot; if once invaded, that invasion was at an end, and with it all pretext for martial law. Martial law cannot arise from a threatened invasion. The necessity must be actual and present; the invasion real, such as effectually closes the courts and deposes the civil administration. . . .

. . . As necessity creates the rule, so it limits its duration; for, if this government is continued after the courts are reinstated, it is a gross usurpation of power. Martial rule can never exist where the courts are open, and in the proper and unobstructed exercise of their jurisdiction. It is also confined to the locality of actual war. Because, during the late Rebellion it could have been enforced in Virginia, where the national authority was overturned and the courts driven out, it does not follow that it should obtain in Indiana, where that authority was never disputed, and justice was always administered. And so in the case of a foreign invasion, martial rule may become a necessity, in one state, when, in another, it would be "mere lawless violence." . . .

To the third question, then, on which the judges below were opposed in opinion, an answer in the negative must be returned.

It is proper to say, although Milligan's trial and conviction by a military commission was illegal, yet, if guilty of the crimes imputed to him, and his guilt had been ascertained by an established court and impartial jury, he deserved severe punishment. . . .

The two remaining questions in this case must be answered in the affirmative. . . .

THE CHIEF JUSTICE delivered the following opinion:

Four members of the court, concurring with their brethren, in the order heretofore made in this cause, but unable to concur in some important particulars with the opinion which has just been read, think it their duty to make a separate statement of their views of the whole case.

Section D. The Constitution and Military Tribunals   1053

We do not doubt that the circuit court for the district of Indiana had jurisdiction of the petition of Milligan for the writ of habeas corpus. . . .

The first question, therefore, — Ought the writ to issue? — must be answered in the affirmative. And it is equally clear that he was entitled to the discharge prayed for.

It must be borne in mind that the prayer of the petition was not for an absolute discharge, but to be delivered from military custody and imprisonment, and if found probably guilty of any offense, to be turned over to the proper tribunal for inquiry and punishment; or, if not found thus probably guilty, to be discharged altogether. . . .

An affirmative answer must, therefore, be given to the second question, namely: Ought Milligan to be discharged according to the prayer of the petition?

That the third question, namely: Had the Military Commission in Indiana, under the facts stated, jurisdiction to try and sentence Milligan? must be answered negatively as an unavoidable inference from affirmative answers to the other two. . . .

But the opinion which has just been read goes further; and as we understand it, asserts not only that the military commission held in Indiana was not authorized by Congress, but that it was not in the power of Congress to authorize it; from which it may be thought to follow, that Congress had no power to indemnify the officers who composed the commission against liability in civil courts for acting as members of it.

We cannot agree to this.

We agree in the proposition that no department of the government of the United States — neither President, nor Congress, nor the courts — possesses any power not given by the Constitution.

We assent fully to all that is said, in the opinion, of the inestimable value of the trial by jury, and of the other constitutional safeguards of civil liberty. And we concur, also, in what is said of the writ of habeas corpus, and of its suspension, with two reservations: (1) That, in our judgment, when the writ is suspended, the Executive is authorized to arrest as well as to detain; and (2) that there are cases in which, the privilege of the writ being suspended, trial and punishment by military commission, in states where civil courts are open, may be authorized by Congress, as well as arrest and detention.

We think that Congress had power, though not exercised, to authorize the military commission which was held in Indiana. . . .

We think, therefore, that the power of Congress in the government of the land and naval forces and the militia, is not at all affected by the fifth or any other amendment. It is not necessary to attempt any precise definition of the boundaries of this power. But may it not be said that government includes protection and defense as well as the regulation of internal administration? And is it impossible to imagine cases in which citizens conspiring or attempting the destruction or great injury of the national forces may be subjected by Congress to military trial and punishment in the just exercise of this undoubted constitutional power? . . .

We by no means assert that Congress can establish and apply the laws of war where no war has been declared or exists.

Where peace exists the laws of peace must prevail. What we do maintain is that when the nation is involved in war, and some portions of the country are invaded, and all are exposed to invasion, it is within the power of Congress to determine to what states or districts such great and imminent public danger exists as justifies the authorization of military tribunals for the trial of crimes and offenses against the discipline or security of the army or against the public safety. . . .

There are under the Constitution three kinds of military jurisdictions: one to be exercised both in peace and war; another to be exercised in time of foreign war without the boundaries of the United States, or in time of rebellion and civil war within states or districts occupied by rebels treated as belligerents; and a third to be exercised in time of invasion or insurrection within the limits of the United States, or during rebellion within the limits of states maintaining adhesion to the national government, when the public

1054   Chapter Fifteen.   Fair Procedure

danger requires its exercise. The first of these may be called jurisdiction under military law, and is found in acts of Congress prescribing rules and articles of war, or otherwise providing for the government of the national forces; the second may be distinguished as military government, superseding, as far as may be deemed expedient, the local law, and exercised by the military commander, under the direction of the President, with the express or implied sanction of Congress; while the third may be denominated martial law proper, and is called into action by Congress, or temporarily, when the action of Congress cannot be invited, and in the case of justifying or excusing peril, by the President, in times of insurrection or invasion, or of civil or foreign war, within districts or localities where ordinary law no longer adequately secures public safety and private rights.

We think that the power of Congress, in such times and in such localities, to authorize trials for crimes against the security and safety of the national forces, may be derived from its constitutional authority to raise and support armies and to declare war, if not from its constitutional authority to provide for governing the national forces.

We have no apprehension that this power, under our American system of government, in which all official authority is derived from the people, and exercised under direct responsibility to the people, is more likely to be abused than the power to regulate commerce or the power to borrow money. And we are unwilling to give our assent by silence to expressions of opinion which seem to us calculated, though not intended, to cripple the constitutional powers of the government, and to augment the public dangers in times of invasion and rebellion.

MR. JUSTICE WAYNE, MR. JUSTICE SWAYNE and MR. JUSTICE MILLER, concur with me in these views.[hh]

Ex parte Quirin   317 U.S. 1, 63 S. Ct. 1, 87 L. Ed. 3 (1942)

MR. CHIEF JUSTICE STONE delivered the opinion of the Court:

These cases are brought here by petitioners' several applications for leave to file petitions for habeas corpus in this Court, and by their petitions for certiorari to review orders of the District Court for the District of Columbia, which denied their applications for leave to file petitions for habeas corpus in that court.

The question for decision is whether the detention of petitioners by respondent for trial by Military Commission, appointed by Order of the President of July 2, 1942, on charges preferred against them purporting to set out their violations of the law of war and of the Articles of War, is in conformity to the laws and Constitution of the United States.

After denial of their applications by the District Court, 47 F. Supp. 431, petitioners asked leave to file petitions for habeas corpus in this Court. In view of the public importance of the questions raised by their petitions and of the duty which rests on the courts, in time of war as well as in time of peace, to preserve unimpaired the constitutional safeguards of civil liberty, and because in our opinion the public interest required that we consider and decide those questions without any avoidable delay, we directed that petitioners' applications be set down for full oral argument at a special term of this Court, convened on July 29, 1942. The applications for leave to file the petitions were presented in open court on that day and were heard on the petitions, the answers to them of respon-

---

[hh] Milligan was released after the Supreme Court's decision, and in March 1868 he recovered a judgment against General Hovey for nominal damages; claims arising out of all but a few days of his imprisonment were barred by a two-year statute of limitations.

For an account of the litigation see Fairman, Reconstruction and Reunion (6 Holmes Devise History of the Supreme Court) c. 5 (1971). Randall, Constitutional Problems Under Lincoln 82 et seq. (rev. ed. 1951), tells of the numerous organizations in parts of the North active in the Confederate interest during the war. For the effect of federal legislation relieving federal officers of liability for their official acts, see Randall, id., c. 9. See also Klaus, The Milligan Case (1929). — ED.

Section D. The Constitution and Military Tribunals 1055

dent, a stipulation of facts by counsel, and the record of the testimony given before the Commission.

While the argument was proceeding before us, petitioners perfected their appeals from the orders of the District Court to the United States Court of Appeals for the District of Columbia and thereupon filed with this Court petitions for certiorari to the Court of Appeals before judgment, pursuant to §240(a) of the Judicial Code, 28 U.S.C. §347(a). We granted certiorari before judgment for the reasons which moved us to convene the special term of Court. In accordance with the stipulation of counsel we treat the record, briefs and arguments upon the writs of certiorari.

On July 31, 1942, after hearing argument of counsel[ii] and after full consideration of all questions raised, this Court affirmed the orders of the District Court and denied petitioners' applications for leave to file petitions for habeas corpus. By per curiam opinion we announced the decision of the Court,[*] and that the full opinion in the causes would be prepared and filed with the Clerk.

The following facts appear from the petitions or are stipulated. Except as noted they are undisputed.

All the petitioners were born in Germany; all have lived in the United States. All returned to Germany between 1933 and 1941. All except petitioner Haupt are admittedly citizens of the German Reich, with which the United States is at War. Haupt came to this country with his parents when he was five years old; it is contended that he became a citizen of the United States by virtue of the naturalization of his parents during his minority and that he has not since lost his citizenship. The Government, however, takes the position that on attaining his majority he elected to maintain German allegiance and citizenship or in any case that he has by his conduct renounced or abandoned his United States citizenship. See Perkins v. Elg, 307 U.S. 325, 334; United States ex rel. Rojak v. Marshall, 34 F.(2d) 219; United States ex rel. Scimeca v. Husband (C.C.A. 2d) 6 F.(2d) 957, 958; 8 U.S.C. §801, and compare 8 U.S.C. §808. For reasons presently to be stated we do not find it necessary to resolve these contentions.

After the declaration of war between the United States and the German Reich, petitioners received training at a sabotage school near Berlin, Germany, where they were instructed in the use of explosives and in methods of secret writing. Thereafter petitioners, with a German citizen, Dasch, proceeded from Germany to a seaport in Occupied France, where petitioners Burger, Heinck and Quirin, together with Dasch, boarded a German submarine which proceeded across the Atlantic to Amagansett Beach on Long Island, New York. The four were there landed from the submarine in the hours of darkness, on or about June 13, 1942, carrying with them a supply of explosives, fuses, and in-

---

[ii] Colonel Kenneth C. Royall of the United States Army, assigned as counsel for the prisoners, argued the cause, and with Colonel Cassius M. Dowell presented a brief urging Ex parte Milligan, 4 Wall. 2, page 1050 supra, as a precedent for denial of jurisdiction in the Commission. — ED.

[*] . . . [F]iled July 31, 1942:
PER CURIAM: . . .

The Court has fully considered the questions raised in these cases and thoroughly argued at the Bar, and has reached its conclusion upon them. It now announces its decision and enters its judgment in each case in advance of the preparation of a full opinion which necessarily will require a considerable period of time for its preparation and which, when prepared, will be filed with the Clerk.

The Court holds:

(1) That the charges preferred against petitioners on which they are being tried by military commission appointed by the order of the President of July 2, 1942, allege an offense or offenses which the President is authorized to order tried before a military commission.

(2) That the military commission was lawfully constituted.

(3) That petitioners are held in lawful custody, for trial before the military commission, and have not shown cause for being discharged by writ of habeas corpus.

The motions for leave to file petitions for writs of habeas corpus are denied.

The orders of the District Court are affirmed. The mandates are directed to issue forthwith.

Mr. Justice Murphy took no part in the consideration or decision of these cases.

cendiary and timing devices. While landing they wore German Marine Infantry uniforms or parts of uniforms. Immediately after landing they buried their uniforms and the other articles mentioned, and proceeded in civilian dress to New York City.

The remaining four petitioners at the same French port boarded another German submarine, which carried them across the Atlantic to Ponte Vedra Beach, Florida. On or about June 17, 1942, they came ashore during the hours of darkness wearing caps of the German Marine Infantry and carrying with them a supply of explosives, fuses, and incendiary and timing devices. They immediately buried their caps and the other articles mentioned, and proceeded in civilian dress to Jacksonville, Florida, and thence to various points in the United States. All were taken into custody in New York or Chicago by agents of the Federal Bureau of Investigation. All had received instructions in Germany from an officer of the German High Command to destroy war industries and war facilities in the United States, for which they or their relatives in Germany were to receive salary payments from the German Government. They also had been paid by the German Government during their course of training at the sabotage school and had received substantial sums in United States currency, which were in their possession when arrested. The currency had been handed to them by an officer of the German High Command, who had instructed them to wear their German uniforms while landing in the United States.

The President, as President and Commander in Chief of the Army and Navy, by Order of July 2, 1942, appointed a Military Commission and directed it to try petitioners for offenses against the law of war and the Articles of War, and prescribed regulations for the procedure on the trial and for review of the record of the trial and of any judgment or sentence of the Commission. On the same day, by Proclamation, the President declared that "all persons who are subjects, citizens or residents of any nation at war with the United States or who give obedience to or act under the direction of any such nation, and who during time of war enter or attempt to enter the United States . . . through coastal or boundary defenses, and are charged with committing or attempting or preparing to commit sabotage, espionage, hostile or warlike acts, or violations of the law of war, shall be subject to the law of war and to the jurisdiction of military tribunals."

The Proclamation also stated in terms that all such persons were denied access to the courts.

Pursuant to direction of the Attorney General, the Federal Bureau of Investigation surrendered custody of petitioners to respondent, Provost Marshal of the Military District of Washington, who was directed by the Secretary of War to receive and keep them in custody, and who thereafter held petitioners for trial before the Commission.

On July 3, 1942, the Judge Advocate General's Department of the Army prepared and lodged with the Commission the following charges against petitioners, supported by specifications:
1. Violation of the law of war.
2. Violation of Article 81 of the Articles of War, defining the offense of relieving or attempting to relieve, or corresponding with or giving intelligence to, the enemy.
3. Violation of Article 82, defining the offense of spying.
4. Conspiracy to commit the offenses alleged in charges 1, 2 and 3.

The Commission met on July 8, 1942, and proceeded with the trial, which continued in progress while the causes were pending in this Court. On July 27th, before petitioners' applications to the District Court, all the evidence for the prosecution and the defense had been taken by the Commission and the case had been closed except for arguments of counsel. It is conceded that ever since petitioners' arrest the state and federal courts in Florida, New York, and the District of Columbia, and in the States in which each of the petitioners was arrested or detained, have been open and functioning normally.

While it is the usual procedure on an application for a writ of habeas corpus in the federal courts for the court to issue the writ and on the return to hear and dispose of the case, it may without issuing the writ consider and determine whether the facts alleged by the pe-

Section D. The Constitution and Military Tribunals

tition, if proved, would warrant discharge of the prisoner. Walker v. Johnston, 312 U.S. 275, 284. Presentation of the petition for judicial action is the institution of a suit. Hence denial by the district court of leave to file the petitions in these causes was the judicial determination of a case or controversy, reviewable on appeal to the Court of Appeals and reviewable here by certiorari. See Ex parte Milligan, 4 Wall. 2, 110-113; Betts v. Brady, decided June 1, 1942 [316 U.S. 455, 457-461].

Petitioners' main contention is that the President is without any statutory or constitutional authority to order the petitioners to be tried by military tribunal for offenses with which they are charged; that in consequence they are entitled to be tried in the civil courts with the safeguards, including trial by jury, which the Fifth and Sixth Amendments guarantee to all persons charged in such courts with criminal offenses. In any case it is urged that the President's Order, in prescribing the procedure of the Commission and the method for review of its findings and sentence, and the proceedings of the Commission under the Order, conflict with Articles of War adopted by Congress — particularly Articles 38, 43, 46, 50½ and 70 — and are illegal and void.

The Government challenges each of these propositions. But regardless of their merits, it also insists that petitioners must be denied access to the courts, both because they are enemy aliens or have entered our territory as enemy belligerents, and because the President's Proclamation undertakes in terms to deny such access to the class of persons defined by the Proclamation, which aptly describes the character and conduct of petitioners. It is urged that if they are enemy aliens or if the Proclamation has force no court may afford the petitioners a hearing. But there is certainly nothing in the Proclamation to preclude access to the courts for determining its applicability to the particular case. And neither the Proclamation nor the fact that they are enemy aliens forecloses consideration by the courts of petitioners' contentions that the Constitution and laws of the United States constitutionally enacted forbid their trial by military commission. As announced in our per curiam opinion, we have resolved those questions by our conclusion that the Commission has jurisdiction to try the charge preferred against petitioners. There is therefore no occasion to decide contentions of the parties unrelated to this issue. We pass at once to the consideration of the basis of the Commission's authority.

We are not here concerned with any question of the guilt or innocence of petitioners. Constitutional safeguards for the protection of all who are charged with offenses are not to be disregarded in order to inflict merited punishment on some who are guilty. Ex parte Milligan, supra (4 Wall. 119, 132); Tumey v. Ohio, 273 U.S. 510, 535; Hill v. Texas, decided June 1, 1942 [316 U.S. 400, 406]. But the detention and trial of petitioners — ordered by the President in the declared exercise of his powers as Commander in Chief of the Army in time of war and of grave public danger — are not to be set aside by the courts without the clear conviction that they are in conflict with the Constitution or laws of Congress constitutionally enacted.

Congress and the President, like the courts, possess no power not derived from the Constitution. But one of the objects of the Constitution, as declared by its preamble, is to "provide for the common defense." As a means to that end the Constitution gives to Congress the power to "provide for the common Defense," Art. 1, §8, cl. 1; "To raise and support Armies," "To provide and maintain a Navy," Art. 1, §8, cl. 12, 13; and "To make Rules for the Government and Regulation of the land and naval Forces," Art. 1, §8, cl. 14. Congress is given authority "To declare War, grant Letters of Marque and Reprisal, and make Rules concerning Captures on Land and Water," Art. 1, §8, cl. 11; and "To define and punish Piracies and Felonies committed on the high Seas, and Offences against the Law of Nations," Art. 1, §8, cl. 10. And finally the Constitution authorizes Congress "To make all Laws which shall be necessary and proper for carrying into Execution the foregoing Powers, and all other Powers vested by this Constitution in the Government of the United States, or in any Department or Officer thereof." Art. 1, §8, cl. 18.

The Constitution confers on the President the "executive Power," Art. 2, §1, cl. 1, and imposes on him the duty to "take Care that the Laws be faithfully executed." Art. 2, §3. It makes him the Commander in Chief of the Army and Navy, Art. 2, §2, cl. 1, and empowers him to appoint and commission officers of the United States. Art. 2, §3, cl. 1.

The Constitution thus invests the President as Commander in Chief with the power to wage war which Congress has declared, and to carry into effect all laws passed by Congress for the conduct of war and for the government and regulation of the Armed Forces, and all laws defining and punishing offenses against the law of nations, including those which pertain to the conduct of war. . . .

From the very beginning of its history this Court has recognized and applied the law of war as including that part of the law of nations which prescribes, for the conduct of war, the status, rights and duties of enemy nations as well as of enemy individuals. By the Articles of War, and especially Article 15, Congress has explicitly provided, so far as it may constitutionally do so, that military tribunals shall have jurisdiction to try offenders or offenses against the law of war in appropriate cases. Congress, in addition to making rules for the government of our Armed Forces, has thus exercised its authority to define and punish offenses against the law of nations by sanctioning, within constitutional limitations, the jurisdiction of military commissions to try persons for offenses which, according to the rules and precepts of the law of nations, and more particularly the law of war, are cognizable by such tribunals. And the President, as Commander in Chief, by his Proclamation in time of war has invoked that law. By his Order creating the present Commission he has undertaken to exercise the authority conferred upon him by Congress, and also such authority as the Constitution itself gives the Commander in Chief, to direct the performance of those functions which may constitutionally be performed by the military arm of the nation in time of war.

An important incident to the conduct of war is the adoption of measures by the military command not only to repel and defeat the enemy, but to seize and subject to disciplinary measures those enemies who in their attempt to thwart or impede our military effort have violated the law of war. It is unnecessary for present purposes to determine to what extent the President as Commander in Chief has constitutional power to create military commissions without the support of Congressional legislation. For here Congress has authorized trial of offenses against the law of war before such commissions. We are concerned only with the question whether it is within the constitutional power of the national government to place petitioners upon trial before a military commission for the offenses with which they are charged. We must therefore first inquire whether any of the acts charged is an offense against the law of war cognizable before a military tribunal, and if so whether the Constitution prohibits the trial. We may assume that there are acts regarded in other countries, or by some writers on international law, as offenses against the law of war which would not be triable by military tribunal here, either because they are not recognized by our courts as violations of the law of war or because they are of that class of offenses constitutionally triable only by a jury. It was upon such grounds that the Court denied the right to proceed by military tribunal in Ex parte Milligan, 4 Wall. 2, supra. But as we shall show, these petitioners were charged with an offense against the law of war which the Constitution does not require to be tried by jury.

It is no objection that Congress in providing for the trial of such offenses has not itself undertaken to codify that branch of international law or to mark its precise boundaries, or to enumerate or define by statute all the acts which that law condemns. An act of Congress punishing "the crime of piracy, as defined by the law of nations" is an appropriate exercise of its constitutional authority, Art. 1, §8, cl. 10, "to define and punish" the offense since it has adopted by reference the sufficiently precise definition of international law. United States v. Smith, 5 Wheat. 153; see The Marianna Flora, 11 Wheat. 1, 40, 41; United States v. The Malek Adhel, 2 How. 210, 232; The Ambrose Light, 25 F. 408, 423-428; 18 U.S.C. §481. Similarly by the reference in the 15th Article of War to "of-

Section D. The Constitution and Military Tribunals

fenders or offenses that . . . by the law of war may be triable by such military commissions," Congress has incorporated by reference, as within the jurisdiction of military commissions, all offenses which are defined as such by the law of war (compare Dynes v. Hoover, 20 How. 65, 82), and which may constitutionally be included within that jurisdiction. Congress had the choice of crystallizing in permanent form and in minute detail every offense against the law of war, or of adopting the system of common law applied by military tribunals so far as it should be recognized and deemed applicable by the courts. It chose the latter course.

By universal agreement and practice the law of war draws a distinction between the armed forces and the peaceful populations of belligerent nations and also between those who are lawful and unlawful combatants. Lawful combatants are subject to capture and detention as prisoners of war by opposing military forces. Unlawful combatants are likewise subject to capture and detention, but in addition they are subject to trial and punishment by military tribunals for acts which render their belligerency unlawful. The spy who secretly and without uniform passes the military lines of a belligerent in time of war, seeking to gather military information and communicate it to the enemy, or an enemy combatant who without uniform comes secretly through the lines for the purpose of waging war by destruction of life or property, are familiar examples of belligerents who are generally deemed not to be entitled to the status of prisoners of war, but to be offenders against the law of war subject to trial and punishment by military tribunals. . . .

Such was the practice of our own military authorities before the adoption of the Constitution, and during the Mexican and Civil Wars. . . .

Citizenship in the United States of an enemy belligerent does not relieve him from the consequences of a belligerency which is unlawful because in violation of the law of war. Citizens who associate themselves with the military arm of the enemy government, and with its aid, guidance and direction enter this country bent on hostile acts are enemy belligerents within the meaning of the Hague Convention and the law of war. Cf. Gates v. Goodloe, 101 U.S. 612, 615, 617, 618. It is as an enemy belligerent that petitioner Haupt is charged with entering the United States, and unlawful belligerency is the gravamen of the offense of which he is accused. . . .

But petitioners insist that even if the offenses with which they are charged are offenses against the law of war, their trial is subject to the requirement of the Fifth Amendment that no person shall be held to answer for a capital or otherwise infamous crime unless on a presentment or indictment of a grand jury, and that such trials by Article 3, §2, and the Sixth Amendment must be by jury in a civil court. Before the Amendments, §2 of Article 3, the Judiciary Article, had provided: "The Trial of all crimes, except in Cases of Impeachment, shall be by Jury," and had directed that "such Trial shall be held in the State where the said Crimes shall have been committed." . . .

The Fifth and Sixth Amendments, while guaranteeing the continuance of certain incidents of trial by jury which Article 3, §2 had left unmentioned, did not enlarge the right to jury trial as it had been established by that Article. Callan v. Wilson, 127 U.S. 540, 549. . . .

. . . In the light of this long-continued and consistent interpretation we must conclude that §2 of Article 3 and the Fifth and Sixth Amendments cannot be taken to have extended the right to demand a jury to trials by military commission, or to have required that offenses against the law of war not triable by jury at common law be tried only in the civil courts.

The fact that "cases arising in the land or naval forces" are excepted from the operation of the Amendments does not militate against this conclusion. Such cases are expressly excepted from the Fifth Amendment, and are deemed excepted by implication from the Sixth. Ex parte Milligan, supra (4 Wall. 123, 138, 139). It is argued that the exception, which excludes from the Amendment cases arising in the armed forces, has also by implication extended its guaranty to all other cases; that since petitioners, not being members of the Armed Forces of the United States, are not within the exception, the Amendment operates to give to them the right to a jury trial. But we think this argument misconceives both the scope of the Amendment and the purpose of the exception.

We may assume, without deciding, that a trial prosecuted before a military commission created by military authority is not one "arising in the land . . . forces," when the accused is not a member of or associated with those forces. But even so, the exception cannot be taken to affect those trials before military commissions which are neither within the exception nor within the provisions of Article 3, §2, whose guaranty the Amendments did not enlarge. No exception is necessary to exclude from the operation of these provisions cases never deemed to be within their terms. An express exception from Article 3, §2, and from the Fifth and Sixth Amendments, of trials of petty offenses and of criminal contempts has not been found necessary in order to preserve the traditional practice of trying those offenses without a jury. It is no more so in order to continue the practice of trying, before military tribunals without a jury, offenses committed by enemy belligerents against the law of war. . . .

. . . We conclude that the Fifth and Sixth Amendments did not restrict whatever authority was conferred by the Constitution to try offenses against the law of war by military commission, and that petitioners, charged with such an offense not required to be tried by jury at common law, were lawfully placed on trial by the Commission without a jury.

Petitioners, and especially petitioner Haupt, stress the pronouncement of this Court in the Milligan Case, [4 Wall.] supra, p. 121, that the law of war "can never be applied to citizens in states which have upheld the authority of the government, and where the courts are open and their process unobstructed." Elsewhere in its opinion, at pp. 118, 121, 122 and 131, the Court was at pains to point out that Milligan, a citizen twenty years resident in Indiana, who had never been a resident of any of the states in rebellion, was not an enemy belligerent either entitled to the status of a prisoner of war or subject to the penalties imposed upon unlawful belligerents. We construe the Court's statement as to the inapplicability of the law of war to Milligan's Case as having particular reference to the facts before it. From them the Court concluded that Milligan, not being a part of or associated with the armed forces of the enemy, was a non-belligerent, not subject to the law of war save as — in circumstances found not there to be present and not involved here — martial law might be constitutionally established.

The Court's opinion is inapplicable to the case presented by the present record. We have no occasion now to define with meticulous care the ultimate boundaries of the jurisdiction of military tribunals to try persons according to the law of war. It is enough that petitioners here, upon the conceded facts, were plainly within those boundaries. . . .

Accordingly, we conclude that Charge I, on which petitioners were detained for trial by the Military Commission, alleged an offense which the President is authorized to order tried by military commission; that his Order convening the Commission was a lawful order and that the Commission was lawfully constituted; that the petitioners were held in lawful custody and did not show cause for their discharge. It follows that the orders of the District Court should be affirmed, and that leave to file petitions for habeas corpus in this Court should be denied.

MR. JUSTICE MURPHY took no part in the consideration or decision of these cases.

For a discussion of the treason clause of the Constitution, Article III, §3, and the Quirin case, see Hurst, Treason in the United States, 58 Harv. L. Rev. 226, 395, at 421 (1944-1945). For a discussion of Chief Justice Stone's activity in the formulation of the Quirin opinion, see Mason, Inter Arma Silent Leges; Chief Justice Stone's Views, 69 id. 808 (1956).

Section D. **The Constitution and Military Tribunals** 1061

Duncan v. Kahanamoku 327 U.S. 304, 66 S. Ct. 606, 90 L. Ed. 688 (1946)

MR. JUSTICE BLACK delivered the opinion of the Court.

The petitioners in these cases were sentenced to prison by military tribunals in Hawaii. Both are civilians. The question before us is whether the military tribunals had power to do this. The United States District Court for Hawaii in habeas corpus proceedings held that the military tribunals had no such power and ordered that they be set free. The Circuit Court of Appeals reversed, and ordered that the petitioners be returned to prison. 146 F.2d 576. Both cases thus involve the rights of individuals charged with crime and not connected with the armed forces to have their guilt or innocence determined in courts of law which provide established procedural safeguards, rather than by military tribunals which fail to afford many of these safeguards. Since these judicial safeguards are prized privileges of our system of government we granted certiorari.

The following events led to the military tribunals' exercise of jurisdiction over the petitioners. On December 7, 1941, immediately following the surprise air attack by the Japanese on Pearl Harbor, the Governor of Hawaii by proclamation undertook to suspend the privilege of the writ of habeas corpus and to place the Territory under "martial law." Section 67 of the Hawaiian Organic Act [April 30, 1900] 31 Stat. 141, c. 339, 48 U.S.C. § 532, authorizes the Territorial Governor to take this action "in case of rebellion or invasion, or imminent danger thereof, when the public safety requires it." His action was to remain in effect only "until communication can be had with the President and his decision thereon made known." The President approved the Governor's action on December 9th. The Governor's proclamation also authorized and requested the Commanding General, "during the . . . emergency and until danger of invasion is removed, to exercise all the powers normally exercised" by the Governor and by the "judicial officers and employees of this Territory."

Pursuant to this authorization the commanding general immediately proclaimed himself Military Governor and undertook the defense of the Territory and the maintenance of order. On December 8th, both civil and criminal courts were forbidden to summon jurors and witnesses and to try cases. The commanding general established military tribunals to take the place of the courts. These were to try civilians charged with violating the laws of the United States and of the Territory, and rules, regulations, orders or policies of the Military Government. Rules of evidence and procedure of courts of law were not to control the military trials. In imposing penalties the military tribunals were to be "guided by, but not limited to the penalties authorized by the courts martial manual, the laws of the United States, the Territory of Hawaii, the District of Columbia, and the customs of war in like cases." The rule announced was simply that punishment was to be "commensurate with the offense committed" and that the death penalty might be imposed "in appropriate cases." Thus the military authorities took over the government of Hawaii. They could and did, by simply promulgating orders, govern the day-to-day activities of civilians who lived, worked, or were merely passing through there. The military tribunals interpreted the very orders promulgated by the military authorities and proceeded to punish violators. The sentences imposed were not subject to direct appellate court review, since it had long been established that military tribunals are not part of our judicial system. Ex parte Vallandigham, 1 Wall. 243. The military undoubtedly assumed that its rule was not subject to any judicial control whatever, for by orders issued on August 25, 1943, it prohibited even accepting of a petition for writ of habeas corpus by a judge or judicial employee or the filing of such a petition by a prisoner or his attorney. Military tribunals could punish violators of these orders by fine, imprisonment or death.

White, the petitioner in No. 15, was a stockbroker in Honolulu. Neither he nor his business was connected with the armed forces. On August 20, 1942, more than eight months after the Pearl Harbor attack, the military police arrested him. The charge against

1062   Chapter Fifteen. **Fair Procedure**

him was embezzling stock belonging to another civilian in violation of chapter 183 of the Revised Laws of Hawaii. Though by the time of White's arrest the courts were permitted "as agents of the Military Governor" to dispose of some nonjury civil cases, they were still forbidden to summon jurors and to exercise criminal jurisdiction. On August 22d, White was brought before a military tribunal designated as a "Provost Court." The "Court" orally informed him of the charge. He objected to the tribunal's jurisdiction but the objection was overruled. He demanded to be tried by a jury. This request was denied. His attorney asked for additional time to prepare the case. This was refused. On August 25th he was tried and convicted. The tribunal sentenced him to five years imprisonment. Later the sentence was reduced to four years.

Duncan, the petitioner in No. 14, was a civilian shipfitter employed in the Navy Yard at Honolulu. On February 24th, 1944, more than two years and two months after the Pearl Harbor attack, he engaged in a brawl with two armed Marine sentries at the yard. He was arrested by the military authorities. By the time of his arrest the military had to some extent eased the stringency of military rule. Schools, bars and motion picture theatres had been reopened. Courts had been authorized to "exercise their normal jurisdiction." They were once more summoning jurors and witnesses and conducting criminal trials. There were important exceptions, however. One of these was that only military tribunals were to try "Criminal Prosecutions for violations of military orders." As the record shows, these military orders still covered a wide range of day to day civilian conduct. Duncan was charged with violating one of these orders, paragraph 8.01, Title 8, of General Order No. 2, which prohibited assault on military or naval personnel with intent to resist or hinder them in the discharge of their duty. He was, therefore, tried by a military tribunal rather than the Territorial Court, although the general laws of Hawaii made assault a crime. Revised L.H. 1935, c. 166. A conviction followed and Duncan was sentenced to six months imprisonment.

Both White and Duncan challenged the power of the military tribunals to try them by petitions for writs of habeas corpus filed in the District Court for Hawaii on March 14 and April 14, 1944, respectively. Their petitions urged both statutory and Constitutional grounds. The court issued orders to show cause. Returns to these orders contended that Hawaii had become part of an active theatre of war constantly threatened by invasion from without; that the writ of habeas corpus had therefore properly been suspended and martial law had validly been established in accordance with the provisions of the Organic Act; that consequently the District Court did not have jurisdiction to issue the writ; and that the trials of petitioners by military tribunals pursuant to orders by the Military Governor issued because of military necessity were valid. Each petitioner filed a traverse to the returns, which traverse challenged among other things the suspension of habeas corpus, the establishment of martial law and the validity of the Military Governor's orders, asserting that such action could not be taken except when required by military necessity due to actual or threatened invasion, which even if it did exist on December 7, 1941, did not exist when the petitioners were tried; and that, whatever the necessity for martial law, there was no justification for trying them in military tribunals rather than the regular courts of law. The District Court, after separate trials, found in each case, among other things, that the courts had always been able to function but for the military orders closing them, and that consequently there was no military necessity for the trial of petitioners by military tribunals rather than regular courts. It accordingly held the trials void and ordered the release of the petitioners.

The Circuit Court of Appeals, assuming without deciding that the District Court had jurisdiction to entertain the petitions, held the military trials valid and reversed the ruling of the District Court. 146 F.2d 576. It held that the military orders providing for military trials were fully authorized by §67 of the Organic Act and the Governor's actions taken under it. The Court relied on that part of the section which as we have indicated authorizes the Governor with the approval of the President to proclaim "martial law," whenever the public safety requires it. The Circuit Court thought that the term "martial law" as used in the Act denotes among other things the establishment of a "total military government" completely displacing or subordinating the regular courts, that the decision of the executive as to what the public safety requires must be sustained so long as that decision is based on reasonable grounds and that such reasonable grounds did exist.

In presenting its argument before this Court the government for reasons set out in the margin [5] abandons its contention as to the suspension of the writ of habeas corpus and advances the argument employed by the circuit court for sustaining the trials and convictions of the petitioners by military tribunals. The petitioners contend that "martial law" as provided for by §67 did not authorize the military to try and punish civilians such as petitioners and urge further that if such authority should be inferred from the Organic Act, it would be unconstitutional. We need decide the Constitutional question only if we agree with the government that Congress did authorize what was done here.

Did the Organic Act during the period of martial law give the armed forces power to supplant all civilian laws and to substitute military for judicial trials under the conditions that existed in Hawaii at the time these petitioners were tried? The relevant conditions, for our purposes, were the same when both petitioners were tried. The answer to the question depends on a correct interpretation of the Act. But we need not construe the Act, insofar as the power of the military might be used to meet other and different conditions and situations. The boundaries of the situation with reference to which we do interpret the scope of the Act can be more sharply defined by stating at this point some different conditions which either would or might conceivably have affected to a greater or lesser extent the scope of the authorized military power. We note first that at the time the alleged offenses were committed the dangers apprehended by the military were not sufficiently imminent to cause them to require civilians to evacuate the area or even to evacuate any of the buildings necessary to carry on the business of the courts. In fact, the buildings had long been open and actually in use for certain kinds of trials. Our question does not involve the well-established power of the military to exercise jurisdiction over members of the armed forces, those directly connected with such forces, or enemy belligerents, prisoners of war, or others charged with violating the laws of war. We are not concerned with the recognized power of the military to try civilians in tribunals established as part of a temporary military government over occupied enemy territory or territory regained from an enemy where civilian government cannot and does not function. For Hawaii since annexation has been held by and loyal to the United States. Nor need we here consider the power of the military simply to arrest and detain civilians interfering with a necessary military function at a time of turbulence and danger from insurrection or war. And finally, there was no specialized effort of the military, here, to enforce orders which related only to military functions, such as, for illustration, curfew rules or blackouts. For these petitioners were tried before tribunals set up under a military program which took over all government and superseded all civil laws and courts. If the Organic Act, properly interpreted, did not give the armed forces this awesome power, both petitioners are entitled to their freedom.

I

In interpreting the Act we must first look to its language. Section 67 makes it plain that Congress did intend the Governor of Hawaii, with the approval of the President, to invoke military aid under certain circumstances. But Congress did not specifically state to what

---

[5] The Government points out that since the privilege of the writ was restored and martial law terminated by Presidential Proclamation on October 24, 1944, petitioners are entitled to their liberty if the military tribunals were without jurisdiction to try them. We therefore do not pass upon the validity of the order suspending the privilege of habeas corpus or the power of the military to detain persons under other circumstances and conditions.

extent the army could be used or what power it could exercise. It certainly did not explicitly declare that the Governor in conjunction with the military could for days, months or years close all the courts and supplant them with military tribunals. Cf. Coleman v. Tennessee, 97 U.S. 509, 514. If a power thus to obliterate the judicial system of Hawaii can be found at all in the Organic Act, it must be inferred from §67's provision for placing the Territory under "martial law." But the term "martial law" carries no precise meaning. The Constitution does not refer to "martial law" at all and no Act of Congress has defined the term. It has been employed in various ways by different people and at different times. By some it has been identified as "military law" limited to members of, and those connected with, the armed forces. Others have said that the term does not imply a system of established rules but denotes simply some kind of day-to-day expression of a General's will dictated by what he considers the imperious necessity of the moment. See United States v. Diekelman, 92 U.S. 520, 526. In 1857 the confusion as to the meaning of the phrase was so great that the Attorney General in an official opinion had this to say about it: "The Common Law authorities and commentators afford no clue to what martial law as understood in England really is. . . . In this country it is still worse." 8 Ops. Atty. Gen. 365, 367, 368. What was true in 1857 remains true today. The language of §67 thus fails to define adequately the scope of the power given to the military and to show whether the Organic Act provides that courts of law be supplanted by military tribunals.

II

Since the Act's language does not provide a satisfactory answer, we look to the legislative history for possible further aid in interpreting the term "martial law" as used in the statute. The government contends that the legislative history shows that Congress intended to give the armed forces extraordinarily broad powers to try civilians before military tribunals. Its argument is as follows: That portion of the language of §67 which prescribes the prerequisites to declaring martial law is identical with a part of the language of the original Constitution of Hawaii. Before Congress enacted the Organic Act the Supreme Court of Hawaii had construed that language as giving the Hawaiian President power to authorize military tribunals to try civilians charged with crime whenever the public safety required it. Re Kalanianaole, 10 Haw. 29. When Congress passed the Organic Act it simply enacted the applicable language of the Hawaiian Constitution and with it the interpretation of that language by the Hawaiian Supreme Court.

In disposing of this argument we wish to point out at the outset that even had Congress intended the decision in the Kalanianaole Case to become part of the Organic Act, that case did not go so far as to authorize military trials of the petitioners for these reasons. There the defendants were insurrectionists taking part in the very uprising which the military were to suppress, while here the petitioners had no connection with any organized resistance to the armed forces or the established government. If, on the other hand, we should take the Kalanianaole Case to authorize the complete supplanting of courts by military tribunals, we are certain that Congress did not wish to make that case part of the Organic Act. . . .

. . . Along with §67 Congress enacted §5 of the Organic Act which provides "that the Constitution . . . shall have the same force and effect within the said Territory as elsewhere in the United States." 31 Stat. 141, c. 339, 48 U.S.C. §495. Even when Hawaii was first annexed Congress had provided that the Territory's existing laws should remain in effect unless contrary to the Constitution. [July 7, 1898] 30 Stat. 750. And the House Committee Report in explaining §5 of the Organic Act stated: "Probably the same result would obtain without this provision under §1891, c. 1, Title XXIII, of the Revised Statutes, *but to prevent possible question*, the section is inserted in the bill." (Italics supplied.)

It follows that civilians in Hawaii are entitled to the Constitutional guarantee of a fair

Section D. The Constitution and Military Tribunals

trial to the same extent as those who live in any other part of our country. . . . Whatever power the Organic Act gave the Hawaiian military authorities, such power must therefore be construed in the same way as a grant of power to troops stationed in any one of the states.

III

Since both the language of the Organic Act and its legislative history fail to indicate that the scope of "martial law" in Hawaii includes the supplanting of courts by military tribunals, we must look to other sources in order to interpret that term. We think the answer may be found in the birth, development and growth of our governmental institutions up to the time Congress passed the Organic Act. Have the principles and practices developed during the birth and growth of our political institutions been such as to persuade us that Congress intended that loyal civilians in loyal territory should have their daily conduct governed by military orders substituted for criminal laws, and that such civilians should be tried and punished by military tribunals? Let us examine what those principles and practices have been, with respect to the position of civilian government and the courts and compare that with the standing of military tribunals throughout our history.

People of many ages and countries have feared and unflinchingly opposed the kind of subordination of executive, legislative and judicial authorities to complete military rule which according to the government Congress has authorized here. In this country that fear has become part of our cultural and political institutions. The story of that development is well known and we see no need to retell it all. But we might mention a few pertinent incidents. As early as the 17th Century our British ancestors took political action against aggressive military rule. When James I and Charles I authorized martial law for purposes of speedily punishing all types of crimes committed by civilians the protest led to the historic Petition of Right which in uncompromising terms objected to this arbitrary procedure and prayed that it be stopped and never repeated. When later the American colonies declared their independence one of the grievances listed by Jefferson was that the King had endeavored to render the military superior to the civil power. The executive and military officials who later found it necessary to utilize the armed forces to keep order in a young and turbulent nation, did not lose sight of the philosophy embodied in the Petition of Right and the Declaration of Independence, that existing civilian government and especially the courts were not to be interfered with by the exercise of military power. In 1787, the year in which the Constitution was formulated, the Governor of Massachusetts colony used the militia to cope with Shay's Rebellion. In his instructions to the Commander of the troops the Governor listed the "great objects" of the mission. The troops were to "protect the judicial courts . . . ," "to assist the civil magistrates in executing the laws . . . ," and to "aid them in apprehending the disturbers of the public peace. . . ." The Commander was to consider himself "constantly as under the direction of the civil officer, saving where any armed force shall appear and oppose . . . [his] . . . marching to execute these orders." President Washington's instructions to the Commander of the troops sent into Pennsylvania to suppress the Whiskey Rebellion of 1794 were to the same effect. The troops were to see to it that the laws were enforced and were to deliver the leaders of armed insurgents to the regular courts for trial. The President admonished the Commanding General "that the judge can not be controlled in his functions." In the many instances of the use of troops to control the activities of civilians that followed, the troops were generally again employed merely to aid and not to supplant the civilian authorities. The last noteworthy incident before the enactment of the Organic Act was the rioting that occurred in the Spring of 1899 at the Coeur-d'Alene mines of Shoshone County, Idaho. The President ordered the regular troops to report to the Governor for instructions and to support the civil authorities in preserving the peace. Later the State

Auditor as agent of the Governor, and not the Commanding General, ordered the troops to detain citizens without trial and to aid the Auditor in doing all he thought necessary to stop the riot. Once more, the military authorities did not undertake to supplant the courts and to establish military tribunals to try and punish ordinary civilian offenders.

. . . Legislatures and courts are not merely cherished American institutions; they are indispensable to our government.

Military tribunals have no such standing. For as this Court has said before: ". . . the military should always be kept in subjection to the laws of the country to which it belongs, and that he is no friend to the Republic who advocates the contrary. The established principle of every free people is, that the law shall alone govern; and to it the military must always yield." Dow v. Johnson, 100 U.S. 158, 169. Congress prior to the time of the enactment of the Organic Act had only once authorized the supplanting of the courts by military tribunals. Legislation to that effect was enacted immediately after the South's unsuccessful attempt to secede from the Union. Insofar as that legislation applied to the Southern States after the war was at an end it was challenged by a series of Presidential vetoes as vigorous as any in the country's history. And in order to prevent this Court from passing on the constitutionality of this legislation Congress found it necessary to curtail our appellate jurisdiction. Indeed, prior to the Organic Act, the only time this Court had ever discussed the supplanting of courts by military tribunals in a situation other than that involving the establishment of a military government over recently occupied enemy territory, it had emphatically declared that "civil liberty and this kind of martial law cannot endure together; the antagonism is irreconcilable; and, in the conflict, one or the other must perish." Ex parte Milligan, 4 Wall. 2, 124, 125.

We believe that when Congress passed the Hawaiian Organic Act and authorized the establishment of "martial law" it had in mind and did not wish to exceed the boundaries between military and civilian power, in which our people have always believed, which responsible military and executive officers had heeded, and which had become part of our political philosophy and institutions prior to the time Congress passed the Organic Act. The phrase "martial law" as employed in that Act, therefore, while intended to authorize the military to act vigorously for the maintenance of an orderly civil government and for the defense of the Islands against actual or threatened rebellion or invasion, was not intended to authorize the supplanting of courts by military tribunals. Yet the government seeks to justify the punishment of both White and Duncan on the ground of such supposed Congressional authorization. We hold that both petitioners are now entitled to be released from custody.

Reversed.

MR. JUSTICE JACKSON took no part in the consideration or decision of these cases.

MR. JUSTICE MURPHY, concurring.

The Court's opinion, in which I join, makes clear that the military trials in these cases were unjustified by the martial law provisions of the Hawaiian Organic Act. Equally obvious, as I see it, is the fact that these trials were forbidden by the Bill of Rights of the Constitution of the United States, which applies in both spirit and letter to Hawaii. . . .

The so-called "open court" rule of the Milligan Case, to be sure, has been the subject of severe criticism, especially by military commentators. That criticism is repeated by the Government in these cases. It is said that the fact that courts are open is but one of many factors relevant to determining the necessity and hence the constitutionality of military trials of civilians. The argument is made that however adequate the "open court" rule may have been in 1628 or 1864 it is distinctly unsuited to modern warfare conditions where all of the territories of a warring nation may be in combat zones or imminently threatened with long-range attack even while civil courts are operating. Hence if a military commander, on the basis of his conception of military necessity, requires all civilians accused of crime to be tried summarily before martial law tribunals, the Bill of Rights

Section D. **The Constitution and Military Tribunals** 1067

must bow humbly to his judgment despite the unquestioned ability of the civil courts to exercise their criminal jurisdiction.

The argument thus advanced is as untenable today as it was when cast in the language of the Plantagenets, the Tudors and the Stuarts. . . .

The reasons here advanced for abandoning the "open court" rule of the Milligan Case are without substance. . . .

MR. CHIEF JUSTICE STONE, concurring.

I concur in the result.

I do not think that "martial law," as used in §67 of the Hawaiian Organic Act, is devoid of meaning. This Court has had occasion to consider its scope and has pointed out that martial law is the exercise of the power which resides in the executive branch of the government to preserve order and insure the public safety in times of emergency, when other branches of the government are unable to function, or their functioning would itself threaten the public safety. Luther v. Borden, 7 How. 1, 45. It is a law of necessity to be prescribed and administered by the executive power. Its object, the preservation of the public safety and good order, defines its scope, which will vary with the circumstances and necessities of the case. The exercise of the power may not extend beyond what is required by the exigency which calls it forth. Mitchell v. Harmony, 13 How. 115, 133; United States v. Russell, 13 Wall. 623, 628; Raymond v. Thomas, 91 U.S. 712, 716; Sterling v. Constantin, 287 U.S. 378, 400, 401. Any doubts that might be entertained that such is the true limit of martial law in this case are put at rest by §67 of the Hawaiian Organic Act, which, "in case of rebellion or invasion, or imminent danger thereof," authorizes martial law only "when the public safety requires it."

The Executive has broad discretion in determining when the public emergency is such as to give rise to the necessity of martial law, and in adapting it to the need. Cf. Hirabayashi v. United States, 320 U.S. 81. But executive action is not proof of its own necessity, and the military's judgment here is not conclusive. . . .

The full record in this case shows the conditions prevailing in Hawaii throughout 1942 and 1943. It demonstrates that from February, 1942 on, the civil courts were capable of functioning, and that trials of petitioners in the civil courts no more endangered the public safety than the gathering of the populace in saloons and places of amusement, which was authorized by military order. . . . I can only conclude that the trials and the convictions upon which petitioners are now detained, were unauthorized by the statute, and without lawful authority. . . .

MR. JUSTICE BURTON, with whom MR. JUSTICE FRANKFURTER concurs, dissenting:

With the rest of this Court I subscribe unreservedly to the Bill of Rights. I recognize the importance of the civil courts in protecting individual rights guaranteed by the Constitution. I prefer civil to military control of civilian life and I agree that in war our Constitution contemplates the preservation of the individual rights of all of our people in accordance with a plan of constitutional procedure fitted to the needs of a self-governing republic at war.

Our Constitution expressly provides for waging war, and it is with the constitutional instruments for the successful conduct of war that I am concerned. I recognize here, as elsewhere, the constitutional direction that our respective branches of the Government do not exceed their allotted shares of authority. The courts, as well as our other agencies of the Government, accordingly owe a constitutional obligation not to invade the fields reserved either to the people, the states, or the other coordinate branches of the Government. . . .

It is in the application of these views to the cases before us that I am obliged to dissent from the majority of this Court and to sound a note of warning against the dangers of overexpansion of judicial control into the fields allotted by the Constitution to agencies of legislative and executive action.

The controlling facts in the cases before us are the extraordinary conditions created by the surprise Japanese invasion by air of Pearl Harbor on December 7, 1941. . . . . The attack demonstrated that it was part of a carefully planned major military operation against not only Hawaii but the United States. Presumably it would be pressed further. It might well be followed by a land invasion of the Islands and by aerial attacks upon their centers of population. . . .

The conduct of war under the Constitution is largely an executive function. Within the field of military action in time of war, the executive is allowed wide discretion. While, even in the conduct of war, there are many lines of jurisdiction to draw between the proper spheres of legislative, executive and judicial action, it seems clear that at least on an active battle field, the executive discretion to determine policy is there intended by the Constitution to be supreme. The question then arises: What is a battle field and how long does it remain one after the first barrage?

It is well that the outer limits of the jurisdiction of our military authorities is subject to review by our courts even under such extreme circumstances as those of the battle field. This, however, requires the courts to put themselves as nearly as possible in the place of those who had the constitutional responsibility for immediate executive action. . . .

It is all too easy in this postwar period to assume that the success which our forces attained was inevitable and that military control should have been relaxed on a schedule based upon such actual developments. . . . Those were critical days when the United States could afford no military mistakes and when the safety and control of the Hawaiian key to the Pacific was essential. It was the responsibility of our military commanders not only to do the right thing in the interests of safety but to take no chances of error or surprise. It was the obligation of our military commanders to insure safety rather than to risk it. Acting as they were in the "fog of war," they were entitled to a wide range of discretion if they were to meet the obligations imposed upon them. . . .

One way to test the soundness of a decision today that the trial of petitioner White on August 25, 1942, before a provost court on a charge of embezzlement and the trial of petitioner Duncan on March 2, 1944, before a similar court on a charge of maliciously assaulting marine sentries were unconstitutional procedures, is to ask ourselves whether or not on those dates, with the war against Japan in full swing, this Court would have, or should have, granted a writ of habeas corpus, an injunction or a writ of prohibition to release the petitioners or otherwise to oust the provost courts of their claimed jurisdiction. Such a test emphasizes the issue. I believe that this Court would not have been justified in granting the relief suggested at such times. Also I believe that this Court might well have found itself embarrassed had it ordered such relief and then had attempted to enforce its order in the theater of military operations, at a time when the area was under martial law and the writ of habeas corpus was still suspended, all in accordance with the orders of the President of the United States and the Governor of Hawaii issued under their interpretation of the discretion and responsibility vested in them by the Constitution of the United States and by the Organic Act of Hawaii enacted by Congress.

In order to recognize the full strength of our Constitution, both in time of peace and in time of war, it is necessary to protect the authority of our legislative and executive officials, as well as that of our courts, in the performance of their respective obligations to help to "establish Justice, insure domestic Tranquility, provide for the common defence, promote the general Welfare and secure the Blessings of Liberty to ourselves and our Posterity."[jj]

[jj] For additional facts concerning the Hawaiian situation in 1941-1944, see Fairman, The Supreme Court on Military Jurisdiction: Martial Rule in Hawaii and the Yamashita Case, 59 Harv. L. Rev. 883 (1946), and Rossiter, The Supreme Court and the Commander in Chief, 54 (1951). Both authors give many references. — ED.

Section D. The Constitution and Military Tribunals 1069

Reid v. Covert 354 U.S. 1, 77 S. Ct. 1222, 1 L. Ed. 2d 1148 (1957)

Mr. Justice Black announced the judgment of the Court and delivered an opinion in which the Chief Justice, Mr. Justice Douglas, and Mr. Justice Brennan join.

These cases raise basic constitutional issues of the utmost concern. They call into question the role of the military under our system of government. They involve the power of Congress to expose civilians to trial by military tribunals, under military regulations and procedures, for offenses against the United States thereby depriving them of trial in civilian courts, under civilian laws and procedures and with all the safeguards of the Bill of Rights. These cases are particularly significant because for the first time since the adoption of the Constitution wives of soldiers have been denied trial by jury in a court of law and forced to trial before courts-martial.

In No. 701 Mrs. Clarice Covert killed her husband, a sergeant in the United States Air Force, at an airbase in England. Mrs. Covert, who was not a member of the armed services, was residing on the base with her husband at the time. She was tried by a court-martial for murder under Article 118 of the Uniform Code of Military Justice [U.C.M.J.]. The trial was on charges preferred by Air Force personnel and the court-martial was composed of Air Force officers. The court-martial asserted jurisdiction over Mrs. Covert under Article 2(11) of the U.C.M.J., which provides:

"The following persons are subject to this code: . . .

"(11) Subject to the provisions of any treaty or agreement to which the United States is or may be a party or to any accepted rule of international law, all persons serving with, employed by, or accompanying the armed forces without the continental limits of the United States. . . ."

Counsel for Mrs. Covert contended that she was insane at the time she killed her husband, but the military tribunal found her guilty of murder and sentenced her to life imprisonment. The judgment was affirmed by the Air Force Board of Review, 16 C.M.R. 465, but was reversed by the Court of Military Appeals, 6 U.S.C.M.A. 48, because of prejudicial errors concerning the defense of insanity. While Mrs. Covert was being held in this country pending a proposed retrial by court-martial in the District of Columbia, her counsel petitioned the District Court for a writ of habeas corpus to set her free on the ground that the Constitution forbade her trial by military authorities. Construing this Court's decision in United States ex rel. Toth v. Quarles, 350 U.S. 11, as holding that "a civilian is entitled to a civilian trial" the District Court held that Mrs. Covert could not be tried by court-martial and ordered her released from custody. The Government appealed directly to this Court under 28 U.S.C. § 1252. See 350 U.S. 985.

In No. 713 Mrs. Dorothy Smith killed her husband, an Army officer, at a post in Japan where she was living with him. She was tried for murder by a court-martial and despite considerable evidence that she was insane was found guilty and sentenced to life imprisonment. The judgment was approved by the Army Board of Review, 10 C.M.R. 350, 13 C.M.R. 307, and the Court of Military Appeals, 5 U.S.C.M.A. 314. Mrs. Smith was then confined in a federal penitentiary in West Virginia. Her father, respondent here filed a petition for habeas corpus in a District Court for West Virginia. The petition charged that the court-martial was without jurisdiction because Article 2(11) of the U.C.M.J. was unconstitutional insofar as it authorized the trial of civilian dependents accompanying servicemen overseas. The District Court refused to issue the writ, 137 F. Supp. 806, and while an appeal was pending in the Court of Appeals for the Fourth Circuit we granted certiorari at the request of the Government, 350 U.S. 986.

The two cases were consolidated and argued last Term and a majority of the Court, with three Justices dissenting and one reserving opinion, held that military trial of Mrs. Smith and Mrs. Covert for their alleged offenses was constitutional. 351 U.S. 470, 487. The majority held that the provisions of Article III and the Fifth and Sixth Amendments which require that crimes be tried by a jury after indictment by a grand jury did not protect an American citizen when he was tried by the American Government in foreign lands for offenses committed there and that Congress could provide for the trial of such offenses in any manner it saw fit so long as the procedures established were reasonable and consonant with due process. The opinion then went on to express the view that military trials, as now practiced, were not unreasonable or arbitrary when applied to dependents accompanying members of the armed forces overseas. In reaching their conclusion the majority found it unnecessary to consider the power of Congress "To make Rules for the Government and Regulation of the land and naval Forces" under Article I of the Constitution.

Subsequently, the Court granted a petition for rehearing, 352 U.S. 901. Now, after further argument and consideration, we conclude that the previous decisions cannot be permitted to stand. We hold that Mrs. Smith and Mrs. Covert could not constitutionally be tried by military authorities.

I

At the beginning we reject the idea that when the United States acts against citizens abroad it can do so free of the Bill of Rights. The United States is entirely a creature of the Constitution. Its power and authority have no other source. It can only act in accordance with all the limitations imposed by the Constitution. When the Government reaches out to punish a citizen who is abroad, the shield which the Bill of Rights and other parts of the Constitution provide to protect his life and liberty should not be stripped away just because he happens to be in another land. This is not a novel concept. To the contrary, it is as old as government. It was recognized long before Paul successfully invoked his right as a Roman citizen to be tried in strict accordance with Roman law. And many centuries later an English historian wrote:

"In a settled Colony the inhabitants have all the rights of Englishmen. They take with them, in the first place, that which no Englishman can by expatriation put off, namely, allegiance to the Crown, the duty of obedience to the lawful commands of the Sovereign, and obedience to the Laws which Parliament may think proper to make with reference to such a Colony. But, on the other hand, they take with them all the rights and liberties of British Subjects; all the rights and liberties as against the Prerogative of the Crown, which they would enjoy in this country."

The rights and liberties which citizens of our country enjoy are not protected by custom and tradition alone, they have been jealously preserved from the encroachments of Government by express provisions of our written Constitution.

Among those provisions, Art. 3, §2 and the Fifth and Sixth Amendments are directly relevant to these cases. . . .

The language of Art. 3, §2 manifests that constitutional protections for the individual were designed to restrict the United States Government when it acts outside of this country, as well as here at home. After declaring that all criminal trials must be by jury, the section states that when a crime is "not committed within any State, the Trial shall be at such Place or Places as the Congress may by Law have directed." If this language is permitted to have its obvious meaning, §2 is applicable to criminal trials outside of the States as a group without regard to where the offense is committed or the trial held. From the very first Congress, federal statutes have implemented the provisions of §2 by providing for trial of murder and other crimes committed outside the jurisdiction of any State "in the district where the offender is apprehended, or into which he may first be brought." The Fifth and Sixth Amendments, like Art. 3, §2, are also all inclusive with their sweeping references to "no person" and to "all criminal prosecutions."

This Court and other federal courts have held or asserted that various constitutional limitations apply to the Government when it acts outside the continental United States.

Section D. The Constitution and Military Tribunals

While it has been suggested that only those constitutional rights which are "fundamental" protect Americans abroad, we can find no warrant, in logic or otherwise, for picking and choosing among the remarkable collection of "Thou shalt nots" which were explicitly fastened on all departments and agencies of the Federal Government by the Constitution and its Amendments. Moreover, in view of our heritage and the history of the adoption of the Constitution and the Bill of Rights, it seems peculiarly anomalous to say that trial before a civilian judge and by an independent jury picked from the common citizenry are not fundamental rights. . . .

The keystone of supporting authorities mustered by the Court's opinion last June to justify its holding that Art. 3, §2 and the Fifth and Sixth Amendments did not apply abroad was Re Ross, 140 U.S. 453. The Ross Case is one of those cases that cannot be understood except in its peculiar setting; even then, it seems highly unlikely that a similar result would be reached today. Ross was serving as a seaman on an American ship in Japanese waters. He killed a ship's officer, was seized and tried before a consular "court" in Japan. At that time, statutes authorized American consuls to try American citizens charged with committing crimes in Japan and certain other "non-Christian" countries. These statutes provided that the laws of the United States were to govern the trial except:

". . . where such laws are not adapted to the object, or are deficient in the provisions necessary to furnish suitable remedies, the common law and the law of equity and admiralty shall be extended in like manner over such citizens and others in those countries; and if neither the common law, nor the law of equity or admiralty, nor the statutes of the United States, furnish appropriate and sufficient remedies, the ministers in those countries, respectively, shall, by decrees and regulations which shall have the force of law, supply such defects and deficiencies."

The consular power approved in the Ross Case was about as extreme and absolute as that of the potentates of the "non-Christian" countries to which the statutes applied. Under these statutes consuls could and did make the criminal laws, initiate charges, arrest alleged offenders, try them, and after conviction take away their liberty or their life — sometimes at the American consulate. Such a blending of executive, legislative, and judicial powers in one person or even in one branch of the government is ordinarily regarded as the very acme of absolutism. Nevertheless, the Court sustained Ross' conviction by the consul. It stated that constitutional protections applied "only to citizens and others within the United States, or who are brought there for trial for alleged offences committed elsewhere, and not to residents or temporary sojourners abroad." Despite the fact that it upheld Ross' conviction under United States laws passed pursuant to asserted constitutional authority, the Court went on to make a sweeping declaration that "[t]he Constitution can have no operation in another country."

The Ross approach that the Constitution has no applicability abroad has long since been directly repudiated by numerous cases. That approach is obviously erroneous if the United States Government, which has no power except that granted by the Constitution, can and does try citizens for crimes committed abroad. Thus the Ross Case rested, at least in substantial part, on a fundamental misconception and the most that can be said in support of the result reached there is that the consular court jurisdiction had a long history antedating the adoption of the Constitution. The Congress has recently buried the consular system of trying Americans. We are not willing to jeopardize the lives and liberties of Americans by disinterring it. At best, the Ross Case should be left as a relic from a different era.

The Court's opinion last Term also relied on the "Insular Cases" to support its conclusion that Article III and the Fifth and Sixth Amendments were not applicable to the trial of Mrs. Smith and Mrs. Covert. We believe that reliance was misplaced. The "Insular Cases," which arose at the turn of the century, involved territories which had only recently been conquered or acquired by the United States. These territories, governed and regulated by Congress under Art. IV, §3, had entirely different cultures and customs from those of this country. This Court, although closely divided, ruled that certain constitutional safeguards were not applicable to these territories since they had not been "expressly or impliedly incorporated" into the Union by Congress. While conceding that "fundamental" constitutional rights applied everywhere, the majority found that it would disrupt long-established practices and would be inexpedient to require a jury trial after an indictment by a grand jury in the insular possessions.

The "Insular Cases" can be distinguished from the present cases in that they involved the power of Congress to provide rules and regulations to govern temporarily territories with wholly dissimilar traditions and institutions whereas here the basis for governmental power is American citizenship. None of these cases had anything to do with military trials and they cannot properly be used as vehicles to support an extension of military jurisdiction to civilians. Moreover, it is our judgment that neither the cases nor their reasoning should be given any further expansion. The concept that the Bill of Rights and other constitutional protections against arbitrary government are inoperative when they become inconvenient or when expediency dictates otherwise is a very dangerous doctrine and if allowed to flourish would destroy the benefit of a written Constitution and undermine the basis of our Government. If our foreign commitments become of such nature that the Government can no longer satisfactorily operate within the bounds laid down by the Constitution, that instrument can be amended by the method which it prescribes. But we have no authority, or inclination, to read exceptions into it which are not there.

II

At the time of Mrs. Covert's alleged offense, an executive agreement was in effect between the United States and Great Britain which permitted United States' military courts to exercise exclusive jurisdiction over offenses committed in Great Britain by American servicemen or their dependents. For its part, the United States agreed that these military courts would be willing and able to try and to punish all offenses against the laws of Great Britain by such persons. In all material respects, the same situation existed in Japan when Mrs. Smith killed her husband. Even though a court-martial does not give an accused trial by jury and other Bill of Rights protections, the Government contends that Art. 2(11) of the U.C.M.J., insofar as it provides for the military trial of dependents accompanying the armed forces in Great Britain and Japan, can be sustained as legislation which is necessary and proper to carry out the United States' obligations under the international agreements made with those countries. The obvious and decisive answer to this, of course, is that no agreement with a foreign nation can confer power on the Congress, or on any other branch of Government, which is free from the restraints of the Constitution. . . .

. . . Nor is there anything in the debates which accompanied the drafting and ratification of the Constitution which even suggests such a result. These debates as well as the history that surrounds the adoption of the treaty provision in Article VI make it clear that the reason treaties were not limited to those made in "pursuance" of the Constitution was so that agreements made by the United States under the Articles of Confederation, including the important peace treaties which concluded the Revolutionary War, would remain in effect. . . .

III

[The opinion of Mr. Justice Black rejects the argument that Article I, §8, Cl. 14, empowering Congress "To make rules for the Government and Regulation of the land and naval Forces," taken together with the necessary and proper clause, authorized the Congress to subject Mrs. Smith or Mrs. Covert to a military trial.]

In No. 701, Reid v. Covert, the judgment of the District Court directing that Mrs. Covert be released from custody is

Affirmed.

In No. 713, Kinsella v. Krueger, the judgment of the District Court is reversed and the case is remanded with instructions to order Mrs. Smith released from custody.

Reversed and remanded.

MR. JUSTICE WHITTAKER took no part . . .

[The opinion of Mr. Justice Frankfurter concurring in the result emphasized ". . . that it is only the trial of civilian dependents in a capital case in time of peace that is in question." Mr. Justice Harlan wrote a concurring opinion, "on the narrow ground that where the offense is capital, Article 2(11) cannot constitutionally be applied to the trial of civilian dependents of members of the armed forces overseas in times of peace." Mr. Justice Clark, joined by Mr. Justice Burton, wrote a dissenting opinion.

See infra for a discussion of cases involving noncapital trials of dependents, and trials of civilian employees of the armed forces, in military courts.]

NOTE Trials of Servicemen in the Courts of the Nation Overseas in Which They Are Stationed

Girard, an American soldier stationed in Japan, fatally wounded a Japanese woman while he was on guard in a military area. An administrative agreement, authorized by a treaty, gave primary jurisdiction to the United States over members of the United States forces for offenses arising from official duties, but provided that this jurisdiction might be waived. The Japanese authorities requested waiver, and the American authorities turned Girard over to the Japanese civil authorities for civil trial. The Supreme Court of the United States found no constitutional or statutory barrier to carrying out the arrangement so made. Wilson v. Girard, 354 U.S. 524 (1957). See Snee and Pye, Status of Forces Agreements and Criminal Jurisdiction (1957).

NOTE Military Trials of Dependents of Servicemen Stationed Overseas for Noncapital Crimes, and Military Trials of Civil Employees of the Armed Forces Stationed Overseas in Peacetime

In Reid v. Covert, 354 U.S. 1 (1957), the Supreme Court held it unconstitutional to try in a military court on a capital charge the wife of a serviceman with whom the wife was stationed abroad. Mr. Justice Black, with the concurrence of Chief Justice Warren and Justices Douglas and Brennan, distinguished Madsen v. Kinsella, 343 U.S. 341 (1952), on the ground that it "concerned trials in enemy territory which had been conquered and held by force of arms and which was being governed at the time by our military forces. In such areas the Army commander can establish military or civilian commissions as an arm of the occupation to try everyone in the occupied area whether they are connected with the Army or not." No five Justices agreed on an opinion in that case, and two questions remained open. What was the liability of such civilian dependents to military trial for noncapital crimes? And what was the extent of military jurisdiction over military employees serving with the armed forces in time of peace? On January 18, 1960, the Supreme Court held that a soldier's dependent wife accompanying the armed forces overseas in peacetime could not constitutionally be convicted by court-martial of a noncapital crime. Kinsella v. United States ex rel. Singleton, 361 U.S. 234. The Supreme Court on the same day further held that overseas civilian employees of the armed forces could not in peacetime constitutionally be tried by court-martial even for comparatively small offenses. McElroy v. Guagliardo, Wilson v. Bohlender, 361 U.S. 281; and see Grisham v. Hagan, 361 U.S. 278 (1960).

The Guagliardo and Wilson cases presented the narrowest question, and the Court, understandably, divided 5 to 4. Dissenting Justices pointed out that during the Revolutionary War, and during the military operation in the West during the immediate post-Civil War days, and on naval vessels, civilian employees had been tried by military courts and the jurisdiction for these trials had in some cases not been questioned, in others had been upheld by opinion of the Attorney General, and in some instances had been sustained by the Supreme Court of the United States.

For a discussion of the "law of war" as a "system of military common law," part of the "law of nations" recognized by Article I, §8, cl. 10 of the United States Constitution, see In re Yamashita, 327 U.S. 1, 7 (1946), page 715 supra. Trial of offenses against the law of war by military commissions is recognized by Article 21 of the Uniform Code of Military Justice, Act of May 5, 1950, 64 Stat. 108, 115, 50 U.S.C. §581. See also Ex parte Quirin, 317 U.S. 1 (1942), page 1054 supra; Madsen v. Kinsella, 343 U.S. 341, 354 (1952).

O'Callahan v. Parker, 395 U.S. 258 (1969), held that a member of the United States Army could not be tried by court martial for a non-service-connected crime, i.e., on charges of attempted rape, housebreaking, and assault with intent to rape while on a pass and not on a military post.

In Relford v. Commandant, 401 U.S. 355 (1971), court-martial jurisdiction was upheld for the offense of kidnapping and rape committed by a soldier on a military reservation. O'Callahan v. Parker was distinguished.

In William v. Froehlke, 490 F.2d 998 (2d Cir. 1974), the court upheld court-martial jurisdiction over a soldier stationed in West Germany who was accused of a non-service-connected crime (robbery) against a German citizen on German soil. The court distinguished O'Callahan, noting that unless military jurisdiction were upheld the United States would have no jurisdiction at all over the offense and that the government had a substantial interest in being able to discipline servicemen whom it had stationed abroad.

NOTE The Function of Civilian Courts in Review of Military Convictions

"It is well settled that 'by habeas corpus the civil courts exercise no supervisory or correcting power over the proceedings of a court-martial. . . . The single inquiry, the test, is jurisdiction.' Re Grimley (United States v. Grimley) 137 U.S. 147, 150 (1890). In this case the court-martial had jurisdiction of the person accused and the offense charged, and acted within its lawful powers. The correction of any errors it may have committed is for the military authorities which are alone authorized to review its decision. In re Yamashita, 327 U.S. 1, 8, 9 (1946); Swaim v. United States, supra, 165 U.S. at 562." Hiatt v. Brown, 339 U.S. 103, 111 (1950).

See also In re Yamashita, 327 U.S. 1 (1946), page 715 supra; Burns v. Wilson, 346 U.S. 137, 346 U.S. 844 (1953), discussed in 67 Harv. L. Rev. 160 (1953). The meaning of "jurisdiction" as used in this connection is not clear, as may be seen from the prevailing and dissenting opinions in Burns v. Wilson.

NOTE "Miranda Rules" and Military Justice

The United States Court of Military Appeals has held that the constitutional protections of the accused, announced in Miranda v. Arizona, 384 U.S. 436 (1966), applied to an accused serviceman on trial before a court-martial. See United States v. Tempia, 16 U.S. Court of Military Appeals Reports 629 (1967).

Chapter Sixteen Constitutional Safeguards of Substantive Rights

Section A. PROPERTY: ITS REGULATION AND ITS TAKING

1. Regulations of Business Activity

INTRODUCTORY NOTE

In a series of discerning essays, later summarized in a volume of lectures, Professor Corwin told of the process by which the American courts, before the Civil War, transformed political theory into constitutional law and thus provided substantive safeguards for interests of property. See Corwin, The Doctrine of Due Process before the Civil War, 24 Harv. L. Rev. 366, 460 (1911); Corwin, The Basic Doctrine of American Constitutional Law, 12 Mich. L. Rev. 247 (1914); Corwin, The "Higher Law" Background of American Constitutional Law, 42 Harv. L. Rev. 149, 365 (1928-1929); Corwin, Liberty Against Government (1948). On one unhappy occasion, Chief Justice Taney found that the due process clause of the Fifth Amendment did something more than assure procedural safeguards to persons — he suggested that it put certain interests of property beyond the reach of federal authority. Dred Scott v. Sandford, 19 How. 393, 450 (1857). Cf. Wynehamer v. The People, 13 N.Y. 358 (1856). These intermittent intimations of things to come did not, however, explicitly involve repudiation of the prevailing doctrine that the due process clause of the Fifth Amendment contained no broader assurance than that accepted procedures would be observed by the federal government when it sought to control the lives, liberties, and properties of the American people. See Den ex dem. Murray v. Hoboken Land & Improvement Co., 18 How. 272 (1855).

After the Civil War the due process clauses of the Fourteenth and Fifth Amendments became the constitutional provisions which served most effectively to secure business enterprise from extensive governmental control. Whether other clauses might have been utilized for similar purposes cannot, of course, be stated with certainty. It is well to remember, however, that in so far as state power was concerned the clause prohibiting the impairment of the obligations of contracts had set limits to state power and had proved advantageous to private energy and initiative. See Maine, Popular Government, 186 (1885).

Due process review over the substance of state regulation became recognized only gradually as a judicial prerogative primarily through dissents and extrajudicial influences. See, e.g., the dissents of Justice Field in the Slaughter-House cases, supra page 763, and in Munn v. Illinois, infra; see also, e.g., Cooley's Constitutional Limitations (1868). Eventually too, decisions sustaining state power admitted and warned of "limits beyond which legislation cannot rightfully go" in the regulation of business. Mugler v. Kansas, 123 U.S. 623, 661 (1887). "By the 1880's the development signalized by such pronouncements had run its course, and the concept of due process as a judicially enforced bar to arbitrary economic legislation was ready for action." McCloskey, The American Supreme Court 131 (1960).

NOTE Corporations as "Persons"

Not until comparatively recent years did any Justice of the Court question the holdings of 1886 and 1889 that corporations may claim the benefit of the equal protection clause (Santa Clara County v. Southern Pacific R.R., 118 U.S. 394) and the due process clause (Minneapolis & St. Louis R.R. v. Beckwith, 129 U.S. 26) of the Fourteenth Amendment. In 1938, Mr. Justice Black, dissenting in Connecticut General Life Ins. Co. v. Johnson, 303 U.S. 77, 85-90, stated that he did not believe "the word 'person' in the Fourteenth Amendment includes corporations." He urged, therefore, that the Court "should now overrule previous decisions which interpreted the Fourteenth Amendment to include corporations." Mr. Justice Douglas, with Black, J., concurring, developed the same thesis in his dissent in Wheeling Steel Corp. v. Glander, 337 U.S. 562, 576 (1949). Mr. Justice Jackson commented on these dissenting opinions in a special opinion in the Glander case. Id. at 574-576.

In argument before the Supreme Court in 1882 a former member of the Joint Congressional Committee that drafted the Fourteenth Amendment in 1866 relied upon the manuscript journal of the committee, previously secret, to show its intention to include corporations within "person." Graham, The "Conspiracy Theory" of the Fourteenth Amendment, 47 Yale L.J. 371 (1938). The Court accepted this view four years later in Santa Clara County, supra. "Thus, E. S. Bates, in his Story of Congress, declares that Bingham and Conkling members of the Joint Committee in inserting the due process phraseology, 'smuggled' into the Fourteenth Amendment 'a capitalist joker.' " Graham, supra. Justice Black's answer is that, even if the "conspiracy" theory is true, "[t]he history of the Amendment proves that the people were told that its purpose was to protect weak and helpless human beings and were not told that it was intended to remove corporations in any fashion from the control of state governments." Connecticut General Life Ins. Co., supra, at 87. See also Freund, The Supreme Court of the United States 46-49 (1961); Mendelson, Mr. Justice Black and the Rule of Law, 4 Midwest J. Pol. Sci. 250, 251 (1960).

Munn v. Illinois 94 U.S. 113, 24 L. Ed. 77 (1877)

MR. CHIEF JUSTICE WAITE delivered the opinion of the court:

The question to be determined in this case is whether the General Assembly of Illinois can, under the limitations upon the legislative power of the States imposed by the Constitution of the United States, fix by law the maximum of charges for the storage of grain in warehouses at Chicago and other places in the State having not less than one hundred thousand inhabitants, "in which grain is stored in bulk, and in which the grain of different owners is mixed together, or in which grain is stored in such a manner that the identity of different lots or parcels cannot be accurately preserved."

It is claimed that such a law is repugnant: . . .

3. To that part of Amendment XIV. which ordains that no State shall "Deprive any person of life, liberty or property, without due process of law, nor deny to any person within its jurisdiction the equal protection of the laws." . . .

Every statute is presumed to be constitutional. The courts ought not to declare one to be unconstitutional, unless it is clearly so. If there is doubt, the expressed will of the Legislature should be sustained.

The Constitution contains no definition of the word "deprive," as used in the 14th Amendment. To determine its signification, therefore, it is necessary to ascertain the effect which usage has given it, when employed in the same or a like connection.

While this provision of the Amendment is new in the Constitution of the United States as a limitation upon the powers of the States, it is old as a principle of civilized government. It is found in Magna Charta, and, in substance if not in form, in nearly or quite all the constitutions that have been from time to time adopted by the several States of the Union. By the 5th Amendment, it was introduced into the Constitution of the United States as a limitation upon the powers of the National Government, and by the 14th, as a guaranty against any encroachment upon an acknowledged right of citizenship by the Legislatures of the States. . . . With the 5th Amendment in force, Congress, in 1820, conferred power upon the City of Washington "to regulate . . . the rates of wharfage at private wharves, . . . the sweeping of chimneys, and to fix the rates of fees therefor, . . . and the weight and quality of bread," 3 Stat. at L., 587, sec. 7; and in 1848, "to make all necessary regulations respecting hackney carriages and the rates of fare of the same, and the rates of hauling by cartmen, wagoners, carmen and draymen, and the rates of commission of auctioneers," 9 Stat. at L., 224, sec. 2.

From this it is apparent that, down to the time of the adoption of the 14th Amendment, it was not supposed that statutes regulating the use, or even the price of the use, of private property necessarily deprived an owner of his property without due process of law. Under some circumstances they may, but not under all. The Amendment does not change the law in this particular; it simply prevents the States from doing that which will operate as such a deprivation.

This brings us to inquire as to the principles upon which this power of regulation rests, in order that we may determine what is within and what without its operative effect. Looking, then, to the common law, from whence came the right which the Constitution protects, we find that when private property is "affected with a public interest, it ceases to be juris privati only." This was said by Lord Chief Justice Hale more than two hundred years ago, in his treatise De Portibus Maris, 1 Harg. L. Tr., 78, and has been accepted without objection as an essential element in the law of property ever since. Property does become clothed with a public interest when used in a manner to make it of public consequence, and affect the community at large. When, therefore, one devotes his property to a use in which the public has an interest, he, in effect, grants to the public an interest in that use, and must submit to be controlled by the public for the common good, to the extent of the interest he has thus created. He may withdraw his grant by discontinuing the use; but, so long as he maintains the use, he must submit to the control.

[Lord Hale includes ferries and wharves as businesses "affected with public interest."]

Common carriers [as well] exercise a sort of public office, and have duties to perform in which the public is interested. N.J. Nav. Co. v. Merch. Bk., 6 How., 382.

Their business is, therefore, "affected with a public interest," within the meaning of the doctrine which Lord Hale has so forcibly stated.

But we need not go further. Enough has already been said to show that, when private

Chapter Sixteen. Substantive Rights

property is devoted to a public use, it is subject to public regulation. It remains only to ascertain whether the warehouses of these plaintiffs in error, and the business which is carried on there, come within the operation of this principle.

For this purpose we accept as true the statements of fact contained in the elaborate brief of one of the counsel of the plaintiffs in error. From these it appears that "The great producing region of the West and Northwest sends its grain by water and rail to Chicago, where the greater part of it is shipped by vessel for transportation to the sea-board by the Great Lakes, and some of it is forwarded by railway to the Eastern ports. . . . Vessels, to some extent, are loaded in the Chicago harbor, and sailed through the St. Lawrence directly to Europe. . . . The quantity (of grain) received in Chicago has made it the greatest grain market in the world. This business has created a demand for means by which the immense quantity of grain can be handled or stored, and these have been found in grain warehouses. . . . The grain warehouses or elevators in Chicago are immense structures, holding from 300,000 to 1,000,000 bushels at one time, according to size. They are divided into bins of large capacity and great strength. . . . They are located with the river harbor on one side and the railway tracks on the other; and the grain is run through them from car to vessel, or boat to car, as may be demanded in the course of business. . . .

. . . Certainly, if any business can be clothed "with a public interest, and cease to be juris privati only," this has been. It may not be made so by the operation of the Constitution of Illinois or this statute, but it is by the facts. . . .

It is insisted, however, that the owner of property is entitled to a reasonable compensation for its use, even though it be clothed with a public interest, and that what is reasonable is a judicial and not a legislative question.

As has already been shown, the practice has been otherwise. In countries where the common law prevails, it has been customary from time immemorial for the Legislature to declare what shall be a reasonable compensation under such circumstances, or perhaps more properly speaking, to fix a maximum beyond which any charge made would be unreasonable. Undoubtedly, in mere private contracts, relating to matters in which the public has no interest, what is reasonable must be ascertained judicially. But this is because the Legislature has no control over such a contract. So, too, in matters which do affect the public interest, and as to which legislative control may be exercised, if there are no statutory regulations upon the subject, the courts must determine what is reasonable. The controlling fact is the power to regulate at all. If that exists, the right to establish the maximum of charge, as one of the means of regulation, is implied. In fact, the common law rule, which requires the charge to be reasonable, is itself a regulation as to price. Without it the owner could make his rates at will, and compel the public to yield to his terms, or forego the use.

But a mere common law regulation of trade or business may be changed by statute. A person has no property, no vested interest, in any rule of the common law. That is only one of the forms of municipal law, and is no more sacred than any other. Rights of property which have been created by the common law cannot be taken away without due process; but the law itself, as a rule of conduct, may be changed at the will, or even at the whim, of the Legislature, unless prevented by constitutional limitations. Indeed, the great office of statutes is to remedy defects in the common law as they are developed, and to adapt it to the changes of time and circumstances. To limit the rate of charge for services rendered in a public employment, or for the use of property in which the public has an interest, is only changing a regulation which existed before. It establishes no new principle in the law, but only gives a new effect to an old one.

We know that this is a power which may be abused; but that is no argument against its existence. For protection against abuses by Legislatures the people must resort to the polls, not to the courts. . . .

We conclude, therefore, that the statute in question is not repugnant to the Constitution of the United States, and that there is no error in the judgment. In passing upon this

Section A. Property: Its Regulation and Its Taking 1081

case we have not been unmindful of the vast importance of the questions involved. This and cases of a kindred character were argued before us more than a year ago by the most eminent counsel, and in a manner worthy of their well earned reputations. We have kept the cases long under advisement, in order that their decision might be the result of our mature deliberations.

The judgment is affirmed.[a]

MR. JUSTICE FIELD, dissenting:

I am compelled to dissent from the decision of the court in this case, and from the reasons upon which that decision is founded. The principle upon which the opinion of the majority proceeds is, in my judgment, subversive of the rights of private property, heretofore believed to be protected by constitutional guaranties against legislative interference, and is in conflict with the authorities cited in its support. . . .

[I]t would seem from its opinion that the court holds that property loses something of its private character when employed in such a way as to be generally useful. . . . The building used by the defendants was for the storage of grain; in such storage, says the court, the public has an interest; therefore, the defendants, by devoting the building to that storage, have granted the public an interest in that use, and must submit to have their compensation regulated by the Legislature.

If this be sound law, if there be no protection, either in the principles upon which our republican government is founded, or in the prohibitions of the Constitution against such invasion of private rights, all property and all business in the State are held at the mercy of a majority of its Legislature. The public has no greater interest in the use of buildings for the storage of grain than it has in the use of buildings for the residences of families, nor, indeed, anything like so great an interest; and, according to the doctrine announced, the Legislature may fix the rent of all tenements used for residences, without reference to the cost of their erection. If the owner does not like the rates prescribed, he may cease renting his houses. He has granted to the public, says the court, an interest in the use of the buildings, and "He may withdraw his grant by discontinuing the use; but, so long as he maintains the use, he must submit to the control." The public is interested in the manufacture of cotton, woolen and silken fabrics; in the construction of machinery; in the printing and publication of books and periodicals, and in the making of utensils of every variety, useful and ornamental; indeed, there is hardly an enterprise or business engaging the attention and labor of any considerable portion of the community, in which the public has not an interest in the sense in which that term is used by the court in its opinion; and the doctrine which allows the Legislature to interfere with and regulate the charges which the owners of property thus employed shall make for its use, that is, the rates at which all these different kinds of business shall be carried on, has never before been asserted, so far as I am aware, by any judicial tribunal in the United States.

The doctrine of the state court, that no one is deprived of his property, within the meaning of the constitutional inhibition, so long as he retains its title and possession, and the doctrine of this court, that, whenever one's property is used in such a manner as to affect the community at large, it becomes by that fact clothed with a public interest, and ceases to be juris privati only, appear to me to destroy, for all useful purposes, the efficacy of the constitutional guaranty. All that is beneficial in property arises from its use, and the fruits of that use; and whatever deprives a person of them deprives him of all that is desirable or valuable in the title and possession. If the constitutional guaranty extends no further than to prevent a deprivation of title and possession, and allows a deprivation of use and the fruits of that use, it does not merit the encomiums it has received. Unless I have misread the history of the provision now incorporated into all our State Constitutions, and by the 5th and 14th Amendments into our Federal Constitution, and have misunderstood

---

[a] The extent to which Mr. Justice Bradley contributed to the Chief Justice's opinion is discussed in Fairman, The So-called Granger Cases, Lord Hale, and Justice Bradley, 5 Stan. L. Rev. 587 (1953). — ED.

the interpretation it has received, it is not thus limited in its scope, and thus impotent for good. It has a much more extended operation than either court, State or Federal, has given to it. The provision, it is to be observed, places property under the same protection as life and liberty. Except by due process of law, no State can deprive any person of either. The provision has been supposed to secure to every individual the essential conditions for the pursuit of happiness; and for that reason has not been heretofore, and should never be, construed in any narrow or restricted sense.[b] . . .

MR. JUSTICE STRONG, also dissenting:

When the judgment in this case was announced by direction of a majority of the court, it was well known by all my brethren that I did not concur in it. It had been my purpose to prepare a dissenting opinion, but I found no time for the preparation, and I was reluctant to dissent in such a case without stating my reasons. MR. JUSTICE FIELD has now stated them as fully as I can, and I concur in what he has said.

NOTE

In the Minnesota Rate Case (Chicago, Milwaukee and St. Paul Ry. v. Minnesota), 134 U.S. 418 (1890), the Court condemned a state statute making rates as established by a commission final and conclusive. Mr. Justice Blatchford wrote as follows for a majority of the Court: "The question of the reasonableness of a rate of charge for transportation by a railroad company, involving as it does the element of reasonableness both as regards the company and as regards the public is eminently a question for judicial investigation, requiring due process of law for its determination. If the company is deprived of the power of charging reasonable rates for the use of its property, and such deprivation takes place in the absence of investigation by judicial machinery, it is deprived of the lawful use of its property, and thus, in substance and effect, of the property itself, without due process of law. . . ." Id. at 458. In dissent, Mr. Justice Bradley (Gray and Lamar, JJ., concurring) said that the decision of the majority practically overruled Munn v. Illinois. In 1918, Judge Hough, speaking of the Minnesota Rate Case, said: "It is from that decision that I date the flood." Hough, Due Process of Law — Today, 32 Harv. L. Rev. 218, 228 (1919).

Out of the Minnesota Rate Case there developed the rule of Smyth v. Ames, 169 U.S. 466 (1898), that rates must yield a fair return upon a fair present value. In determining fair value it came to be accepted that the most important criterion was replacement cost of the physical assets. McCardle v. Indianapolis Water Co., 272 U.S. 400 (1926). The complexities, not to say absurdities, in the application of these principles were never satisfactorily justified, and it was not until 1942 that a majority of the Court were willing to agree that "the Constitution does not bind rate-making bodies to the service of a single formula." Stone, J., in Federal Power Commission v. Natural Gas Pipe Line Co., 315 U.S. 575, 586. At length, in Federal Power Commission v. Hope Natural Gas Co., 320 U.S. 591 (1944), a majority repudiated the rule of Smyth v. Ames, agreeing, apparently, that a "rate cannot be made to depend upon 'fair value' when the value of the going enterprise depends on earnings." Douglas, J., at 601.

In Allgeyer v. Louisiana, 165 U.S. 578 (1897), Mr. Justice Peckham, writing for a unanimous Court, construed the "liberty" of the Fourteenth Amendment to include "the right of the citizen . . . to earn his livelihood by any lawful calling . . . and for that purpose to enter into any contract which may be proper [and] necessary." The Court then struck down a state statute which prohibited any person from effecting insurance on property in the state with companies that had not been admitted to do business in the state.

[b] The relationship between Locke's conception of property and the phrase "pursuit of happiness" in the Declaration of Independence is discussed in Cahn, Madison and the Pursuit of Happiness, 27 N.Y.U.L. Rev. 265 (1952). See also Howard Mumford Jones, The Pursuit of Happiness (1953). — ED.

Section A. Property: Its Regulation and Its Taking   1083

HOLDEN v. HARDY, 169 U.S. 366, 18 S. Ct. 383, 42 L. Ed. 780 (1898). State law set a maximum day of eight hours for workers in underground mines and smelters, "except in cases of emergency where life or property is in imminent danger." Convicted of having employed workmen in violation of the statute, Holden challenged the law on Fourteenth Amendment grounds. Justice Brown delivered the opinion of the court:
. . . "[The] right of contract . . . is itself subject to certain limitations which the state may lawfully impose in the exercise of its police powers. While this power is inherent in all governments, it has doubtless been greatly expanded in its application during the past century, owing to an enormous increase in the number of occupations which are dangerous, or so far detrimental to the health of employees as to demand special precaution for their well-being and protection, or the safety of adjacent property. . . .
"While the business of mining coal and manufacturing iron began in Pennsylvania as early as 1716, and in Virginia, North Carolina and Massachusetts even earlier than this, both mining and manufacturing were carried on in such a limited way and by such primitive methods that no special laws were considered necessary, prior to the adoption of the Constitution, for the protection of the operatives, but, in the vast proportions which these industries have since assumed, it has been found that they can no longer be carried on with the due regard to the safety and health of those engaged in them, without special protection against the dangers necessarily incident to these employments. . . .
"[W]e think the act in question may be sustained as a valid exercise of the police power of the state. The enactment does not profess to limit the hours of all workmen, but merely those who are employed in underground mines, or in the smelting, reduction, or refining of ores or metals. These employments when too long pursued the legislature has judged to be detrimental to the health of the employees, and, so long as there are reasonable grounds for believing that this is so, its decision upon this subject cannot be reviewed by the Federal courts. . . .
"[A]lthough the prosecution in this case was against the employer of labor, who apparently under the statute is the only one liable, his defense is not so much that his right to contract has been infringed upon, but that the act works a peculiar hardship to his employees, whose right to labor as long as they please is alleged to be thereby violated. The argument would certainly come with better grace and greater cogency from the latter class. But the fact that both parties are of full age and competent to contract does not necessarily deprive the state of the power to interfere where the parties do not stand upon an equality, or where the public health demands that one party to the contract shall be protected against himself. "The state still retains an interest in his welfare, however reckless he may be. The whole is no greater than the sum of all the parts, and when the individual health, safety, and welfare are sacrificed or neglected, the state must suffer." . . .
Justices Brewer and Peckham dissented.

Lochner v. New York *198 U.S. 45, 25 S. Ct. 539, 49 L. Ed. 937 (1905)*

Mr. Justice Peckham . . . delivered the opinion of the court:
The indictment . . . charges that the plaintiff in error violated the 110th section of article 8, chapter 415, of the Laws of 1897, known as the labor law of the state of New York, in that he wrongfully and unlawfully required and permitted an employee working for him to work more than sixty hours in one week. . . . The mandate of the statute, that "no employee shall be required or permitted to work," is the substantial equivalent of an enactment that "no employee shall contract or agree to work," more than ten hours per day; and, as there is no provision for special emergencies, the statute is mandatory in all cases. It is not an act merely fixing the number of hours which shall constitute a legal day's work, but an absolute prohibition upon the employer permitting, under any circumstances, more than ten hours' work to be done in his establishment. The employee may

desire to earn the extra money which would arise from his working more than the prescribed time, but this statute forbids the employer from permitting the employee to earn it.

The statute necessarily interferes with the right of contract between the employer and employees, concerning the number of hours in which the latter may labor in the bakery of the employer. The general right to make a contract in relation to his business is part of the liberty of the individual protected by the 14th Amendment of the Federal Constitution. Allgeyer v. Louisiana, 165 U.S. 578. Under that provision no state can deprive any person of life, liberty, or property without due process of law. The right to purchase or to sell labor is part of the liberty protected by this amendment, unless there are circumstances which exclude the right. There are, however, certain powers, existing in the sovereignty of each state in the Union, somewhat vaguely termed police powers, the exact description and limitation of which have not been attempted by the courts. Those powers, broadly stated, and without, at present, any attempt at a more specific limitation, relate to the safety, health, morals, and general welfare of the public. Both property and liberty are held on such reasonable conditions as may be imposed by the governing power of the state in the exercise of those powers, and with such conditions the 14th Amendment was not designed to interfere. Mugler v. Kansas, 123 U.S. 623. . . .

The state, therefore, has power to prevent the individual from making certain kinds of contracts, and in regard to them the Federal Constitution offers no protection. If the contract be one which the state, in the legitimate exercise of its police power, has the right to prohibit, it is not prevented from prohibiting it by the 14th Amendment. . . .

This court has recognized the existence and upheld the exercise of the police powers of the states in many cases which might fairly be considered as border ones, and it has, in the course of its determination of questions regarding the asserted invalidity of such statutes, on the ground of their violation of the rights secured by the Federal Constitution, been guided by rules of a very liberal nature, the application of which has resulted, in numerous instances, in upholding the validity of state statutes thus assailed. Among the later cases where the state law has been upheld by this court is that of Holden v. Hardy. . . .

The Utah statute (in Holden v. Hardy) provided for cases of emergency wherein the provisions of the statute would not apply. The statute now before this court has no emergency clause in it, and, if the statute is valid, there are no circumstances and no emergencies under which the slightest violation of the provisions of the act would be innocent. There is nothing in Holden v. Hardy which covers the case now before us. . . .

It must, of course, be conceded that there is a limit to the valid exercise of the police power by the state. There is no dispute concerning this general proposition. Otherwise the 14th Amendment would have no efficacy and the legislatures of the states would have unbounded power, and it would be enough to say that any piece of legislation was enacted to conserve the morals, the health, or the safety of the people; such legislation would be valid, no matter how absolutely without foundation the claim might be. The claim of the police power would be a mere pretext, — become another and delusive name for the supreme sovereignty of the state to be exercised free from constitutional restraint. . . .

This is not a question of substituting the judgment of the court for that of the legislature. If the act be within the power of the state it is valid, although the judgment of the court might be totally opposed to the enactment of such a law. But the question would still remain: Is it within the police power of the state? and that question must be answered by the court. . . .

We think the limit of the police power has been reached and passed in this case. There is, in our judgment, no reasonable foundation for holding this to be necessary or appropriate as a health law to safeguard the public health, or the health of the individuals who are following the trade of a baker. If this statute be valid, and if, therefore, a proper case is made out in which to deny the right of an individual, sui juris, as employer or employee, to make contracts for the labor of the latter under the protection of the provisions of the

Federal Constitution, there would seem to be no length to which legislation of this nature might not go. . . .

We think that there can be no fair doubt that the trade of a baker, in and of itself, is not an unhealthy one to that degree which would authorize the legislature to interfere with the right to labor, and with the right of free contract on the part of the individual, either as employer or employee. In looking through statistics regarding all trades and occupations, it may be true that the trade of a baker does not appear to be as healthy as some other trades, and is also vastly more healthy than still others. To the common understanding the trade of a baker has never been regarded as an unhealthy one. Very likely physicians would not recommend the exercise of that or of any other trade as a remedy for ill health. Some occupations are more healthy than others, but we think there are none which might not come under the power of the legislature to supervise and control the hours of working therein, if the mere fact that the occupation is not absolutely and perfectly healthy is to confer that right upon the legislative department of the government. It might be safely affirmed that almost all occupations more or less affect the health. There must be more than the mere fact of the possible existence of some small amount of unhealthiness to warrant legislative interference with liberty. It is unfortunately true that labor, even in any department, may possibly carry with it the seeds of unhealthiness. But are we all, on that account, at the mercy of legislative majorities? A printer, a tinsmith, a locksmith, a carpenter, a cabinetmaker, a dry goods clerk, a bank's, a lawyer's, or a physician's clerk, or a clerk in almost any kind of business, would all come under the power of the legislature, on this assumption. No trade, no occupation, no mode of earning one's living, could escape this all-pervading power, and the acts of the legislature in limiting the hours of labor in all employments would be valid, although such limitation might seriously cripple the ability of the laborer to support himself and his family. In our large cities there are many buildings into which the sun penetrates for but a short time in each day, and these buildings are occupied by people carrying on the business of bankers, brokers, lawyers, real estate, and many other kinds of business, aided by many clerks, messengers, and other employees. Upon the assumption of the validity of this act under review, it is not possible to say that an act, prohibiting lawyers, or bank clerks, or others, from contracting to labor for their employers more than eight hours a day would be invalid. It might be said that it is unhealthy to work more than that number of hours in an apartment lighted by artificial light during the working hours of the day; that the occupation of the bank clerk, the lawyer's clerk, the real-estate clerk, or the broker's clerk, in such offices is therefore unhealthy, and the legislature, in its paternal wisdom, must, therefore, have the right to legislate on the subject of, and to limit, the hours for such labor; and, if it exercises that power, and its validity be questioned, it is sufficient to say, it has reference to the public health; it has reference to the health of the employees condemned to labor day after day in buildings where the sun never shines; it is a health law, and therefore it is valid, and cannot be questioned by the courts.

. . . Statutes of the nature of that under review, limiting the hours in which grown and intelligent men may labor to earn their living, are mere meddlesome interferences with the rights of the individual, and they are not saved from condemnation by the claim that they are passed in the exercise of the police power and upon the subject of the health of the individual whose rights are interfered with, unless there be some fair ground, reasonable in and of itself, to say that there is material danger to the public health, or to the health of the employees, if the hours of labor are not curtailed. If this be not clearly the case, the individuals whose rights are thus made the subject of legislative interference, are under the protection of the Federal Constitution regarding their liberty of contract as well as of person; and the legislature of the state has no power to limit their right as proposed in this statute. . . .

It was further urged on the argument that restricting the hours of labor in the case of bakers was valid because it tended to cleanliness on the part of the workers, as a man was

1086   Chapter Sixteen.   **Substantive Rights**

more apt to be cleanly when not overworked, and if cleanly then his "output" was also more likely to be so. What has already been said applies with equal force to this contention. We do not admit the reasoning to be sufficient to justify the claimed right of such interference. The state in that case would assume the position of a supervisor, or pater familias, over every act of the individual, and its right of governmental interference with his hours of labor, his hours of exercise, the character thereof, and the extent to which it shall be carried would be recognized and upheld. In our judgment it is not possible in fact to discover the connection between the number of hours a baker may work in the bakery and the healthful quality of the bread made by the workman. The connection, if any exist, is too shadowy and thin to build any argument for the interference of the legislature. . . .

It is manifest to us that the limitation of the hours of labor as provided for in this section of the statute under which the indictment was found, and the plaintiff in error convicted, has no such direct relation to, and no such substantial effect upon, the health of the employee, as to justify us in regarding the section as really a health law. It seems to us that the real object and purpose were simply to regulate the hours of labor between the master and his employees (all being men, sui juris), in a private business, not dangerous in any degree to morals, or in any real and substantial degree to the health of the employees. Under such circumstances the freedom of master and employee to contract with each other in relation to their employment, and in defining the same, cannot be prohibited or interfered with, without violating the Federal Constitution.

The judgment of the Court of Appeals of New York, as well as that of the Supreme Court and of the County Court of Oneida County, must be reversed and the case remanded to the County Court for further proceedings not inconsistent with this opinion. Reversed.

MR. JUSTICE HARLAN (with whom MR. JUSTICE WHITE and MR. JUSTICE DAY concurred) dissenting:

While this court has not attempted to mark the precise boundaries of what is called the police power of the state, the existence of the power has been uniformly recognized, equally by the Federal and State courts. . . .

It is plain that this statute was enacted in order to protect the physical well-being of those who work in bakery and confectionery establishments. It may be that the statute had its origin, in part, in the belief that employers and employees in such establishments were not upon an equal footing, and that the necessities of the latter often compelled them to submit to such exactions as unduly taxed their strength. Be this as it may, the statute must be taken as expressing the belief of the people of New York that, as a general rule, and in the case of the average man, labor in excess of sixty hours during a week in such establishments may endanger the health of those who thus labor. Whether or not this be wise legislation it is not the province of the court to inquire. Under our systems of government the courts are not concerned with the wisdom or policy of legislation. So that, in determining the question of power to interfere with liberty of contract, the court may inquire whether the means devised by the state are germane to an end which may be lawfully accomplished and have a real or substantial relation to the protection of health, as involved in the daily work of the persons, male and female, engaged in bakery and confectionery establishments. . . .

Professor Hirt in his treatise on the "Diseases of the Workers" has said: "The labor of the bakers is among the hardest and most laborious imaginable, because it has to be performed under conditions injurious to the health of those engaged in it. It is hard, very hard, work, not only because it requires a great deal of physical exertion in an over-heated workshop and during unreasonably long hours, but more so because of the erratic demands of the public, compelling the baker to perform the greater part of his work at night, thus depriving him of an opportunity to enjoy the necessary rest and sleep, — a fact which is highly injurious to his health." Another writer says: "The constant inhaling of flour dust causes inflammation of the lungs and of the bronchial tubes. The eyes also suffer through this dust, which is responsible for the many cases of running eyes among the bakers. The long hours of toil to which all bakers are subjected produce rheumatism, cramps, and swollen legs. The intense heat in the workshops induces the workers to resort to cooling drinks, which, together with their habit of exposing the greater part of their bodies to the change in the atmosphere, is another source of a number of diseases of various organs. Nearly all bakers are palefaced and of more delicate health than the workers of other crafts, which is chiefly due to their hard work and their irregular and unnatural mode of living, whereby the power of resistance against disease is greatly diminished. The average age of a baker is below that of other workmen; they seldom live over their fiftieth year, most of them dying between the ages of forty and fifty. During periods of epidemic diseases the bakers are generally the first to succumb to the disease, and the number swept away during such periods far exceeds the number of other crafts in comparison to the men employed in the respective industries. When, in 1720, the plague visited the city of Marseilles, France, every baker in the city succumbed to the epidemic, which caused considerable excitement in the neighboring cities and resulted in measures for the sanitary protection of the bakers." . . .

. . . There are many reasons of a weighty, substantial character, based upon the experience of mankind, in support of the theory that, all things considered, more than ten hours' steady work each day, from week to week, in a bakery or confectionery establishment, may endanger the health and shorten the lives of the workmen, thereby diminishing their physical and mental capacity to serve the state and to provide for those dependent upon them. . . .

I take leave to say that the New York statute, in the particulars here involved, cannot be held to be in conflict with the 14th Amendment, without enlarging the scope of the amendment far beyond its original purpose, and without bringing under the supervision of this court matters which have been supposed to belong exclusively to the legislative departments of the several states when exerting their conceded power to guard the health and safety of their citizens by such regulations as they in their wisdom deem best. Health laws of every description constitute, said Chief Justice Marshall, a part of that mass of legislation which "embraces everything within the territory of a state, not surrendered to the general government; all which can be most advantageously exercised by the states themselves." Gibbons v. Ogden, 9 Wheat. 1, 203. A decision that the New York statute is void under the 14th Amendment will, in my opinion, involve consequences of a far-reaching and mischievous character; for such a decision would seriously cripple the inherent power of the states to care for the lives, health, and well-being of their citizens. Those are matters which can be best controlled by the states. The preservation of the just powers of the states is quite as vital as the preservation of the powers of the general government. . . .

The judgment, in my opinion, should be affirmed.

MR. JUSTICE HOLMES dissenting:

I regret sincerely that I am unable to agree with the judgment in this case, and that I think it my duty to express my dissent.

This case is decided upon an economic theory which a large part of the country does not entertain. If it were a question whether I agreed with that theory, I should desire to study it further and long before making up my mind. But I do not conceive that to be my duty, because I strongly believe that my agreement or disagreement has nothing to do with the right of a majority to embody their opinions in law. It is settled by various decisions of this court that state constitutions and state laws may regulate life in many ways which we as legislators might think as injudicious, or if you like as tyrannical, as this, and which, equally with this, interfere with the liberty to contract. Sunday laws and usury laws are ancient examples. A more modern one is the prohibition of lotteries. The liberty of the citizen to do as he likes so long as he does not interfere with the liberty of others to do the same, which has been a shibboleth for some well-known writers, is interfered with by school laws, by the Postoffice, by every state or municipal institution which takes his money for purposes thought desirable, whether he likes it or not. The 14th Amendment does not enact Mr. Herbert Spencer's Social Statics. The other day we sustained the Massachusetts vaccination law. Jacobson v. Massachusetts, 197 U.S. 11. United States and state statutes and decisions cutting down the liberty to contract by way of combination are familiar to this court. Northern Securities Co. v. United States, 193 U.S. 197. Two years ago we upheld the prohibition of sales of stock on margins, or for future delivery, in the Constitution of California. Otis v. Parker, 187 U.S. 606. The decision sustaining an eight-hour law for miners is still recent. Holden v. Hardy, 169 U.S. 366. Some of these laws embody convictions or prejudices which judges are likely to share. Some may not. But a Constitution is not intended to embody a particular economic theory, whether of paternalism and the organic relation of the citizen to the state or of laissez faire. It is made for people of fundamentally differing views, and the accident of our finding certain opinions natural and familiar, or novel, and even shocking, ought not to conclude our judgment upon the question whether statutes embodying them conflict with the Constitution of the United States.

General propositions do not decide concrete cases. The decision will depend on a judgment or intuition more subtle than any articulate major premise. But I think that the proposition just stated, if it is accepted, will carry us far toward the end. Every opinion tends to become a law. I think that the word "liberty," in the 14th Amendment, is perverted when it is held to prevent the natural outcome of a dominant opinion, unless it can be said that a rational and fair man necessarily would admit that the statute proposed would infringe fundamental principles as they have been understood by the traditions of our people and our law. It does not need research to show that no such sweeping condemnation can be passed upon the statute before us. A reasonable man might think it a proper measure on the score of health. Men whom I certainly could not pronounce unreasonable would uphold it as a first instalment of a general regulation of the hours of work. Whether in the latter aspect it would be open to the charge of inequality I think it unnecessary to discuss.

NOTE

The principles of Holden v. Hardy were so applied in Muller v. Oregon, 208 U.S. 412 (1908), as to sustain against due process challenge an Oregon statute forbidding the employment of women "in any mechanical establishment, or factory, or laundry" for more than ten hours in any one day. The Lochner case was not considered to be controlling, for the evidence marshaled by Louis D. Brandeis in his "factual" brief persuaded the Court that there was ample justification for the "widespread belief that woman's physical structure, and the functions she performs in consequence thereof, justify special legislation restricting or qualifying the conditions under which she should be permitted to toil." 208 U.S. at 420.

In Coppage v. Kansas, 236 U.S. 1 (1915), over the dissent of Holmes, Day, and Hughes, JJ., the Court held that a Kansas statute making it a misdemeanor for an employer to require that his employees execute a "yellow-dog contract" (a promise not to join a labor union) as a condition of employment was in violation of the due process clause of the Fourteenth Amendment. For the majority, Mr. Justice Pitney stated that the statute involved in Holden v. Hardy had been sustained because it was designed to protect "the public health, safety, morals, or general welfare" but that "an interference with the normal exercise of personal liberty and property rights is the primary object of the [Kansas] statute, and not an incident to the advancement of the general welfare." 236 U.S. at 18.

Fluctuation between the poles of state power (Holden v. Hardy) and personal liberty (Lochner v. New York) marked the course of judicial decision throughout the 1920s. For an earlier consideration of the problem with many references to state decisions see Pound, Liberty of Contract, 18 Yale L.J. 454 (1909), reprinted in 2 Selected Essays on Constitutional Law 208 (1938). Although there was good reason to believe that the Lochner case had been overruled sub silentio in 1916 (Bunting v. Oregon, 243 U.S. 426), the constitutional theory on which it was based was accepted by many lawyers and energetically enforced by many courts. Liberty of contract approached, if it did not reach, its high water mark in Adkins v. Children's Hospital, 261 U.S. 525 (1923), when a majority of five invalidated under the Fifth Amendment a congressional statute establishing minimum wages for women employed in the District of Columbia. See Powell, The Judiciality of Minimum Wage Legislation, 37 Harv. L. Rev. 545 (1924). The leading cases are considered historically in Jacobson, Federalism and Property Rights, 15 N.Y.U.L.Q. Rev. 319 (1938).

In the line of cases after Munn, supra page 1078, the Court initially defined businesses "affected with a public interest" loosely enough to sustain state regulation of prices in fire insurance, German Alliance Ins. Co. v. Lewis, 233 U.S. 389 (1914), and in rental housing, Block v. Hirsh, 256 U.S. 135 (1921). But then with an increasingly narrow definition the Court invalidated regulatory schemes with regard to the meat packing industry, Wolff v. Industrial Court, 262 U.S. 522 (1923), employment agencies, Ribnik v. McBride, 277 U.S. 350 (1928), gasoline prices, Williams v. Standard Oil Co., 278 U.S. 235 (1929), and the ice business, New State Ice Co. v. Liebmann, 285 U.S. 262 (1932). In a dissent from the holding that New York could not control the resale prices of theatre tickets, Tyson v. Banton, 273 U.S. 418, 447 (1927), Justice Holmes wrote: "[I]t seems to me that theatres are as much devoted to public use as anything well can be. We have not that respect for art that is one of the glories of France. But to many people the superfluous is the necessary, and it seems to me that Government does not go beyond its sphere in attempting to make life livable for them."

Nebbia v. New York 291 U.S. 502, 54 S. Ct. 505, 78 L. Ed., 940 (1934)

MR. JUSTICE ROBERTS delivered the opinion of the Court.

The Legislature of New York established by Chapter 158 of the Laws of 1933, a Milk Control Board with power, among other things, to "fix minimum and maximum . . . retail prices to be charged by . . . stores to consumers for consumption off the premises where sold." The Board fixed nine cents as the price to be charged by a store for a quart of milk. Nebbia, the proprietor of a grocery store in Rochester, sold two quarts and a five cent loaf of bread for eighteen cents; and was convicted for violating the Board's order. At his trial he asserted the statute and order contravene the equal protection clause and the due process clause of the Fourteenth Amendment, and renewed the contention in successive appeals to the county court and the Court of Appeals. Both overruled his claim and affirmed the conviction.

The question for decision is whether the Federal Constitution prohibits a state from so fixing the selling price of milk. We first inquire as to the occasion for the legislation and its history.

[The legislation was based upon conclusions contained in a "conscientious . . . and thorough" report of a legislative committee.]

In part those conclusions are:

Milk is an essential item of diet. It cannot long be stored. It is an excellent medium for growth of bacteria. These facts necessitate safeguards in its production and handling for human consumption which greatly increase the cost of the business. Failure of producers to receive a reasonable return for their labor and investment over an extended period threatens a relaxation of vigilance against contamination.

The production and distribution of milk is a paramount industry of the state, and largely affects the health and prosperity of its people. Dairying yields fully one-half of the total income from all farm products. Dairy farm investment amounts to approximately $1,000,000,000. Curtailment or destruction of the dairy industry would cause a serious economic loss to the people of the state. . . .

The Fifth Amendment, in the field of federal activity, and the Fourteenth, as respects State action, do not prohibit governmental regulation for the public welfare. They merely condition the exertion of the admitted power, by securing that the end shall be accomplished by methods consistent with due process. And the guaranty of due process, as has often been held, demands only that the law shall not be unreasonable, arbitrary or capricious, and that the means selected shall have a real and substantial relation to the object sought to be attained. It results that a regulation valid for one sort of business, or in given circumstances, may be invalid for another sort, or for the same business under other circumstances, because the reasonableness of each regulation depends upon the relevant facts. . . .

The milk industry in New York has been the subject of long-standing and drastic regulation in the public interest. The legislative investigation of 1932 was persuasive of the fact that for this and other reasons unrestricted competition aggravated existing evils and the normal law of supply and demand was insufficient to correct maladjustments detrimental to the community. The inquiry disclosed destructive and demoralizing competitive conditions and unfair trade practices which resulted in retail price cutting and reduced the income of the farmer below the cost of production. We do not understand the appellant to deny that in these circumstances the legislature might reasonably consider further regulation and control desirable for protection of the industry and the consuming public. That body believed conditions could be improved by preventing destructive price-cutting by stores which, due to the flood of surplus milk, were able to buy at much lower prices than the larger distributors and to sell without incurring the delivery costs of the latter. In the order of which complaint is made the Milk Control Board fixed a price of ten cents per quart for sales by a distributor to a consumer, and nine cents by a store to a consumer, thus recognizing the lower costs of the store, and endeavoring to establish a differential which would be just to both. In the light of the facts the order appears not to be unreasonable or arbitrary, or without relation to the purpose to prevent ruthless competition from destroying the wholesale price structure on which the farmer depends for his livelihood, and the community for an assured supply of milk. . . .

We may as well say at once that the dairy industry is not, in the accepted sense of the phrase, a public utility. We think the appellant is also right in asserting that there is in this case no suggestion of any monopoly or monopolistic practice. It goes without saying that those engaged in the business are in no way dependent upon public grants or franchises for the privilege of conducting their activities. But if, as must be conceded, the industry is subject to regulation in the public interest, what constitutional principle bars the state from correcting existing maladjustments by legislation touching prices? We think there is no such principle. The due process clause makes no mention of sales or of prices any more than it speaks of business or contracts or buildings or other incidents of property. The thought seems nevertheless to have persisted that there is something peculiarly sacrosanct about the price one may charge for what he makes or sells, and that, however able to regulate other elements of manufacture or trade, with incidental effect upon price, the state is incapable of directly controlling the price itself. This view was negatived many years ago. Munn v. Illinois, 94 U.S. 113. . . .

It is clear that there is no closed class or category of businesses affected with a public interest, and the function of courts in the application of the Fifth and Fourteenth Amendments is to determine in each case whether circumstances vindicate the challenged regulation as a reasonable exertion of governmental authority or condemn it as arbitrary or discriminatory. Chas. Wolff Packing Co. v. Court of Industrial Relations, 262 U.S. 522, 535. The phrase "affected with a public interest" can, in the nature of things, mean no more than that an industry, for adequate reason, is subject to control for the public good. In several of the decisions of this court wherein the expressions "affected with a public interest," and "clothed with a public use," have been brought forward as the criteria of the validity of price control, it has been admitted that they are not susceptible of definition and form an unsatisfactory test of the constitutionality of legislation directed at business practices or prices. These decisions must rest, finally, upon the basis that the requirements of due process were not met because the laws were found arbitrary in their operation and effect. But there can be no doubt that upon proper occasion and by appropriate measures the state may regulate a business in any of its aspects, including the prices to be charged for the products or commodities it sells.

So far as the requirement of due process is concerned, and in the absence of other constitutional restriction, a state is free to adopt whatever economic policy may reasonably be deemed to promote public welfare, and to enforce that policy by legislation adapted to its purpose. The courts are without authority either to declare such policy, or, when it is declared by the legislature, to override it. If the laws passed are seen to have a reasonable relation to a proper legislative purpose, and are neither arbitrary nor discriminatory, the requirements of due process are satisfied, and judicial determination to that effect renders a court functus officio. . . . The Constitution does not secure to any one liberty to conduct his business in such fashion as to inflict injury upon the public at large, or upon any substantial group of the people. Price control, like any other form of regulation, is unconstitutional only if arbitrary, discriminatory, or demonstrably irrelevant to the policy the legislature is free to adopt, and hence an unnecessary and unwarranted interference with individual liberty.

Tested by these considerations we find no basis in the due process clause of the Fourteenth Amendment for condemning the provisions of the Agriculture and Markets Law here drawn into question.

The judgment is affirmed.[c]

West Coast Hotel Co. v. Parrish 300 U.S. 379, 57 S. Ct. 578, 81 L. Ed. 703 (1937)

Mr. Chief Justice Hughes delivered the opinion of the court.

This case presents the question of the constitutional validity of the minimum wage law of the State of Washington.

The appellant conducts a hotel. The appellee Elsie Parrish was employed as a chambermaid and (with her husband) brought this suit to recover the difference between the wages paid her and the minimum wage fixed pursuant to the state law. The minimum wage was $14.50 per week of 48 hours. The appellant challenged the act as repugnant to the due process clause of the Fourteenth Amendment of the Constitution of the United States. The Supreme Court of the State, reversing the trial court, sustained the statute and directed judgment for the plaintiffs. Parrish v. West Coast Hotel Co., 185 Wash. 581. The case is here on appeal.

The appellant relies upon the decision of this Court in Adkins v. Children's Hospital, 261 U.S. 525, which held invalid the District of Columbia Minimum Wage Act which was attacked under the due process clause of the Fifth Amendment. On the argument at bar, counsel for the appellees attempted to distinguish the Adkins Case upon the ground that the appellee was employed in a hotel and that the business of an innkeeper was affected with a public interest. That effort at distinction is obviously futile, as it appears that in one of the cases ruled by the Adkins opinion the employee was a woman employed as

---

[c] A dissenting separate opinion by McReynolds, J., is omitted. It was concurred in by Van Devanter, Sutherland, and Butler, JJ. — Ed.

an elevator operator in a hotel. Adkins v. Children's Hospital, 261 U.S. 525, at p. 542.

The recent case of Morehead v. New York, 298 U.S. 587, came here on certiorari to the New York court which had held the New York minimum wage act for women to be invalid. A minority of this Court thought that the New York statute was distinguishable in a material feature from that involved in the Adkins Case and that for that and other reasons the New York statute should be sustained. But the Court of Appeals of New York had said that it found no material difference between the two statutes and this Court held that the "meaning of the statute" as fixed by the decision of the state court "must be accepted here as if the meaning had been specifically expressed in the enactment." Id., p. 609. That view led to the affirmance by this Court of the judgment in the Morehead Case, as the Court considered that the only question before it was whether the Adkins Case was distinguishable and that reconsideration of that decision had not been sought. Upon that point the Court said: "The petition for the writ sought review upon the ground that this case [Morehead] is distinguishable from that one [Adkins]. No application has been made for reconsideration of the constitutional question there decided. The validity of the principles upon which that decision rests is not challenged. This court confines itself to the ground upon which the writ was asked or granted. . . . Here the review granted was no broader than that sought by the petitioner. . . . He is not entitled and does not ask to be heard upon the question whether the Adkins Case should be overruled. He maintains that it may be distinguished on the ground that the statutes are vitally dissimilar." Id., pp. 604, 605.

We think that the question which was not deemed to be open in the Morehead Case is open and is necessarily presented here. The Supreme Court of Washington has upheld the minimum wage statute of that State. It has decided that the statute is a reasonable exercise of the police power of the State. In reaching that conclusion the state court has invoked principles long established by this Court in the application of the Fourteenth Amendment. The state court has refused to regard the decision in the Adkins Case as determinative and has pointed to our decisions both before and since that case as justifying its position. We are of the opinion that this ruling of the state court demands on our part a reexamination of the Adkins Case. The importance of the question, in which many States having similar laws are concerned, the close division by which the decision in the Adkins Case was reached, and the economic conditions which have supervened, and in the light of which the reasonableness of the exercise of the protective power of the State must be considered, make it not only appropriate, but we think imperative, that in deciding the present case the subject should receive fresh consideration. . . .

The principle which must control our decision is not in doubt. The constitutional provision invoked is the due process clause of the Fourteenth Amendment governing the States, as the due process clause invoked in the Adkins Case governed Congress. In each case the violation alleged by those attacking minimum wage regulation for women is deprivation of freedom of contract. What is this freedom? The Constitution does not speak of freedom of contract. It speaks of liberty and prohibits the deprivation of liberty without due process of law. In prohibiting that deprivation the Constitution does not recognize an absolute and uncontrollable liberty. Liberty in each of its phases has its history and connotation. But the liberty safeguarded is liberty in a social organization which requires the protection of law against the evils which menace the health, safety, morals and welfare of the people. Liberty under the Constitution is thus necessarily subject to the restraints of due process, and regulation which is reasonable in relation to its subject and is adopted in the interests of the community is due process. . . .

It is manifest that this established principle is peculiarly applicable in relation to the employment of women in whose protection the State has a special interest. That phase of the subject received elaborate consideration in Muller v. Oregon (1908) 208 U.S. 412, where the constitutional authority of the State to limit the working hours of women was sustained. . . . Again, in Quong Wing v. Kirkendall, 223 U.S. 59, 63, in referring to a differentiation with respect to the employment of women, we said that the Fourteenth Amendment did not interfere with state power by creating a "fictitious equality." We referred to recognized classifications on the basis of sex with regard to hours of work and in other matters, and we observed that the particular points at which that difference shall be enforced by legislation were largely in the power of the State. In later rulings this Court sustained the regulation of hours of work of women employees in Riley v. Massachusetts, 232 U.S. 671 (factories); Miller v. Wilson, 236 U.S. 373 (hotels); and Bosley v. McLaughlin, 236 U.S. 385 (hospitals).

There is an additional and compelling consideration which recent economic experience has brought into a strong light. The exploitation of a class of workers who are in an unequal position with respect to bargaining power and are thus relatively defenceless against the denial of a living wage is not only detrimental to their health and well-being but casts a direct burden for their support upon the community. What these workers lose in wages the taxpayers are called upon to pay. The bare cost of living must be met. We may take judicial notice of the unparalleled demands for relief which arose during the recent period of depression and still continue to an alarming extent despite the degree of economic recovery which has been achieved. It is unnecessary to cite official statistics to establish what is of common knowledge through the length and breadth of the land. While in the instant case no factual brief has been presented, there is no reason to doubt that the State of Washington has encountered the same social problem that is present elsewhere. The community is not bound to provide what is in effect a subsidy for unconscionable employers. The community may direct its law-making power to correct the abuse which springs from their selfish disregard of the public interest. The argument that the legislation in question constitutes an arbitrary discrimination, because it does not extend to men, is unavailing. This Court has frequently held that the legislative authority, acting within its proper field, is not bound to extend its regulation to all cases which it might possibly reach. The legislature "is free to recognize degrees of harm and it may confine its restrictions to those classes of cases where the need is deemed to be clearest." If "the law presumably hits the evil where it is most felt, it is not to be overthrown because there are other instances to which it might have been applied." There is no "doctrinaire requirement" that the legislation should be couched in all embracing terms. Carroll v. Greenwich Ins. Co., 199 U.S. 401, 411. . . .

Our conclusion is that the case of Adkins v. Children's Hospital, 261 U.S. 525, supra, should be and it is, overruled. The judgment of the Supreme Court of the State of Washington is affirmed.

Mr. Justice Sutherland, dissenting:

Mr. Justice Van Devanter, Mr. Justice McReynolds, Mr. Justice Butler and I think the judgment of the court below should be reversed.

The principles and authorities relied upon to sustain the judgment, were considered in Adkins v. Children's Hospital, 261 U.S. 525, and Morehead v. New York, 298 U.S. 587; and their lack of application to cases like the one in hand was pointed out. A sufficient answer to all that is now said will be found in the opinions of the court in those cases. Nevertheless, in the circumstances, it seems well to restate our reasons and conclusions.

Under our form of government, where the written Constitution, by its own terms, is the supreme law, some agency, of necessity, must have the power to say the final word as to the validity of a statute assailed as unconstitutional. The Constitution makes it clear that the power has been intrusted to this court when the question arises in a controversy within its jurisdiction; and so long as the power remains there, its exercise cannot be avoided without betrayal of the trust.

It has been pointed out many times, as in the Adkins Case, that this judicial duty is one of gravity and delicacy, and that rational doubts must be resolved in favor of the constitutionality of the statute. But whose doubts, and by whom resolved? Undoubtedly it is the duty of a member of the court, in the process of reaching a right conclusion, to give due weight to the opposing views of his associates; but in the end, the question which he must answer is not whether such views seem sound to those who entertain them, but whether they convince him that the statute is constitutional or engender in his mind a rational doubt upon that issue. The oath which he takes as a judge is not a composite oath, but an individual one. And in passing upon the validity of a statute, he discharges a duty imposed upon *him*, which cannot be consummated justly by an automatic acceptance of the views of others which have neither convinced, nor created a reasonable doubt in, his mind. If upon a question so important he thus surrender his deliberate judgment, he stands forsworn. He cannot subordinate his convictions to that extent and keep faith with his oath or retain his judicial and moral independence.

The suggestion that the only check upon the exercise of the judicial power, when properly invoked, to declare a constitutional right superior to an unconstitutional statute is the judge's own faculty of self-restraint, is both ill considered and mischievous.[d] Self-restraint belongs in the domain of will and not of judgment. The check upon the judge is that imposed by his oath of office, by the Constitution and by his own conscientious and informed convictions; and since he has the duty to make up his own mind and adjudge accordingly, it is hard to see how there could be any other restraint. This court acts as a unit. It cannot act in any other way; and the majority (whether a bare majority or a majority of all but one of its members), therefore, establishes the controlling rule as the decision of the court, binding, so long as it remains unchanged, equally upon those who disagree and upon those who subscribe to it. Otherwise, orderly administration of justice would cease. But it is the right of those in the minority to disagree, and sometimes, in matters of grave importance, their imperative duty to voice their disagreement at such length as the occasion demands — always, of course, in terms which, however forceful, do not offend the proprieties or impugn the good faith of those who think otherwise. . . .

The judicial function is that of interpretation; it does not include the power of amendment under the guise of interpretation. To miss the point of difference between the two is to miss all that the phrase "supreme law of the land" stands for and to convert what was intended as inescapable and enduring mandates into mere moral reflections.

If the Constitution, intelligently and reasonably construed in the light of these principles, stands in the way of desirable legislation, the blame must rest upon that instrument, and not upon the court for enforcing it according to its terms. The remedy in that situation — and the only true remedy — is to amend the Constitution. . . .

NOTE

Mr. Justice Roberts prepared a contemporaneous memorandum concerning his "vote" in the Parrish case. It is to be found in Frankfurter, Mr. Justice Roberts, 104 U. Pa. L. Rev. 311, 314-315 (1955).

In 1941 the Court held, unanimously, that a state might limit the fees charged by private employment agencies. Olsen v. Nebraska, 313 U.S. 236, overruling Ribnik v. McBride, 277 U.S. 350 (1928).

Since 1937 the Court's abandonment of "substantive due process" review over economic regulation has been constant and unequivocal. Lincoln Union v. Northwestern Co., 335 U.S. 525 (1949); Ferguson v. Skrupa, 372 U.S. 726 (1963). See, e.g., Day-Brite Lighting, Inc. v. Missouri, 342 U.S. 421, 425 (1952): "[I]f our recent cases mean anything, they leave debatable issues as respects business, economic, and social affairs to legislative decision." Should the Court instead have "establish[ed] a halfway house between the extremes, retaining a measure of control over economic legislation but exercising that control with discrimination and self-restraint"? McCloskey, Economic Due Pro-

---

[d] See Stone, J., dissenting in United States v. Butler, 297 U.S. 1, 78-79 (1936). — ED.

Section A. Property: Its Regulation and Its Taking 1095

cess and the Supreme Court: An Exhumation and Reburial, 1962 Sup. Ct. Rev. 34, 41. See also Freund, The Supreme Court of the United States 31-39 (1961).

Due process review has persisted with some vitality in state adjudication. See Paulsen, The Persistence of Substantive Due Process in the States, 34 Minn. L. Rev. 92 (1950); Note, Substantive Due Process in the States Revisited, 18 Ohio St. L.J. 384 (1957); cf. Struve, The Less-Restrictive-Alternative Theory and Economic Due Process, 80 Harv. L. Rev. 1463 (1967).

2. "Taking" and Compensation

INTRODUCTORY NOTE

In Jackman v. Rosenbaum Co., 260 U.S. 22 (1922), the Court sustained against due process objections a Pennsylvania statute adopting a rule of the state's common law by which the person reconstructing a party wall was immunized from liability to his neighbor. In the original draft of his opinion for the Court, Mr. Justice Holmes had stated that a statute which embodies the community's understanding of the reciprocal rights and duties of neighboring landowners "does not need to invoke the petty larceny of the police power" in its justification. Holmes' brethren, correcting his taste, persuaded him to amend the passage so that it spoke only of invoking the police power. See 1 Holmes-Laski Letters 457 (1953).

"We fear to grant power and are unwilling to recognize it when it exists. . . . [W]hen legislatures are held to be authorized to do anything considerably affecting public welfare it is covered by apologetic phrases like the police power, or the statement that the business concerned has been dedicated to a public use. The former expression is convenient, to be sure, to conciliate the mind to something that needs explanation: the fact that the constitutional requirement of compensation when property is taken cannot be pressed to its grammatical extreme; that property rights may be taken for public purposes without pay if you do not take too much; that some play must be allowed to the joints if the machine is to work. But police power is often used in a wide sense to cover and, as I said, to apologize for the general power of the legislature to make a part of the community uncomfortable by a change." Holmes, J., dissenting in Tyson and Brother v. Banton, 273 U.S. 418, 445-446 (1927).

Miller v. Schoene 276 U.S. 272, 48 S. Ct. 246, 72 L. Ed. 568 (1928)

MR. JUSTICE STONE delivered the opinion of the court:

Acting under the Cedar Rust Act of Virginia, Va. Acts 1914, chap. 36, as amended by Va. Acts 1920, chap. 260, now embodied in Va. Code (1924) as §§ 885 to 893, defendant in error, the state entomologist, ordered the plaintiffs in error to cut down a large number of ornamental red cedar trees growing on their property, as a means of preventing the communication of a rust or plant disease with which they were infected to the apple orchards in the vicinity. The plaintiffs in error appealed from the order to the circuit court of Shenandoah county, which, after a hearing and a consideration of evidence, affirmed the order and allowed to plaintiffs in error $100 to cover the expense of removal of the cedars. Neither the judgment of the court nor the statute as interpreted allows compensation for the value of the standing cedars or the decrease in the market value of the realty caused by their destruction whether considered as ornamental trees or otherwise. But they save to plaintiffs in error the privilege of using the trees when felled. On appeal the supreme court of appeals of Virginia affirmed the judgment. Miller v. State Entomologist, 146 Va. 175. Both in the circuit court and the supreme court of appeals plaintiffs in error challenged the constitutionality of the statute under the due process clause of the 14th Amendment, and the case is properly here on writ of error. Judicial Code, §237(a).

The Virginia statute presents a comprehensive scheme for the condemnation and destruction of red cedar trees infected by cedar rust. By §1 it is declared to be unlawful for any person to "own, plant, or keep alive and standing" on his premises any red cedar tree which is or may be the source or "host plant" of the communicable plant disease known as cedar rust, and any such tree growing within a certain radius of any apple orchard is declared to be a public nuisance, subject to destruction. Section 2 makes it the duty of the state entomologist, "upon the request in writing of ten or more reputable freeholders of any county or magisterial district, to make a preliminary investigation of the locality . . . to ascertain if any cedar tree or trees . . . are the source of or constitute the host plant for the said disease . . . and constitute a menace to the health of any apple orchard in said locality, and that said cedar tree or trees exist within a radius of two miles of an apple orchard in said locality." If affirmative findings are so made, he is required to direct the owner in writing to destroy the trees and, in his notice, to furnish a statement of the "fact found to exist whereby it is deemed necessary or proper to destroy" the trees and to call attention to the law under which it is proposed to destroy them. Section 5 authorizes the state entomologist to destroy the trees if the owner, after being notified, fails to do so. Section 7 furnishes a mode of appealing from the order of the entomologist to the circuit court of the county, which is authorized to "hear the objections" and "pass upon all questions involved," the procedure followed in the present case. . . .

. . . [C]edar rust is an infectious plant disease in the form of a fungoid organism which is destructive of the fruit and foliage of the apple, but without effect on the value of the cedar. Its life cycle has two phases which are passed alternately as a growth on red cedar and on apple trees. It is communicated by spores from one to the other over a radius of at least 2 miles. It appears not to be communicable between trees of the same species, but only from one species to the other, and other plants seem not to be appreciably affected by it. The only practicable method of controlling the disease and protecting apple trees from its ravages is the destruction of all red cedar trees, subject to the infection, located within 2 miles of apple orchards.

The red cedar, aside from its ornamental use, has occasional use and value as lumber. It is indigenous to Virginia, is not cultivated or dealt in commercially on any substantial scale, and its value throughout the state is shown to be small as compared with that of the apple orchards of the state. Apple growing is one of the principal agricultural pursuits in Virginia. The apple is used there and exported in large quantities. Many millions of dollars are invested in the orchards, which furnish employment for a large portion of the population, and have induced the development of attendant railroad and cold storage facilities.

On the evidence we may accept the conclusion of the supreme court of appeals that the state was under the necessity of making a choice between the preservation of one class of property and that of the other, wherever both existed in dangerous proximity. It would have been none the less a choice if, instead of enacting the present statute, the state, by doing nothing, had permitted serious injury to the apple orchards within its border to go on unchecked. When forced to such a choice the state does not exceed its constitutional powers by deciding upon the destruction of one class of property in order to save another which, in the judgment of the legislature, is of greater value to the public. It will not do to say that the case is merely one of a conflict of two private interests and that the misfortune of apple growers may not be shifted to cedar owners by ordering the destruction of their property; for it is obvious that there may be, and that here there is, a preponderant public concern in the preservation of the one interest over the other. Compare Bacon v. Walker,

204 U.S. 311. . . . And where the public interest is involved preferment of that interest over the property interest of the individual, to the extent even of its destruction, is one of the distinguishing characteristics of every exercise of the police power which affects property. Mugler v. Kansas, 123 U.S. 623; Hadacheck v. Los Angeles, 239 U.S. 394; Euclid v. Ambler Realty Co., 272 U.S. 365. . . .

We need not weigh with nicety the question whether the infected cedars constitute a nuisance according to the common law; or whether they may be so declared by statute. See Hadacheck v. Los Angeles, supra, 411. For where, as here, the choice is unavoidable, we cannot say that its exercise, controlled by considerations of social policy which are not unreasonable, involves any denial of due process. The injury to property here is no more serious, nor the public interest less, than in Hadacheck v. Los Angeles, supra; . . . or Sligh v. Kirkwood, 237 U.S. 52. . . .

The objection of plaintiffs in error to the vagueness of the statute is without weight. The state court has held it to be applicable and that is enough when, by the statute, no penalty can be incurred or disadvantage suffered in advance of the judicial ascertainment of its applicability. Compare Connally v. General Constr. Co., 269 U.S. 385.

Affirmed.

United States v. Causby 328 U.S. 256, 66 S. Ct. 1062, 90 L. Ed. 1206 (1946)

MR. JUSTICE DOUGLAS delivered the opinion of the Court.

This is a case of first impression. The problem presented is whether respondents' property was taken, within the meaning of the Fifth Amendment, by frequent and regular flights of army and navy aircraft over respondents' land at low altitudes. The Court of Claims held that there was a taking and entered judgment for respondents, one judge dissenting. 104 Ct. Cls. 342, 60 F. Supp. 751. The case is here on a petition for a writ of certiorari which we granted because of the importance of the question presented.

Respondents own 2.8 acres near an airport outside Greensboro, North Carolina. It has on it a dwelling house, and also various outbuildings which were mainly used for raising chickens. The end of the airport's northwest-southwest runway is 2,220 feet from respondents' barn and 2,275 feet from their house. The path of glide to this runway passes directly over the property — which is 100 feet wide and 1,200 feet long. The 30 to 1 safe glide angle [1] approved by the Civil Aeronautics Authority [2] passes over this property at 83 feet, which is 67 feet above the house, 63 feet above the barn and 18 feet above the highest tree.[3] The use by the United States of this airport is pursuant to a lease executed in May, 1942, for a term commencing June 1, 1942 and ending June 30, 1942, with a provision for renewals until June 30, 1967, or six months after the end of the national emergency, whichever is the earlier.

Various aircraft of the United States use this airport — bombers, transports and fighters. The direction of the prevailing wind determines when a particular runway is used. The northwest-southeast runway in question is used about four per cent of the time in taking off and about seven per cent of the time in landing. Since the United States began operations in May, 1942, its four-motored heavy bombers, other planes of the heavier type, and its fighter planes have frequently passed over respondents' land and buildings in considerable numbers and rather close together. They come close enough at times to appear barely to miss the tops of the trees and at times so close to the tops of the trees as to blow the old leaves off. The noise is startling. And at night the glare from the planes brightly lights up the place. As a result of the noise, respondents had to give up their chicken business. As

[1] A 30 to 1 glide angle means one foot of elevation or descent for every 30 feet of horizontal distance.
[2] Military planes are subject to the rules of the Civil Aeronautics Board where, as in the present case, there are no Army or Navy regulations to the contrary. Cameron v. Civil Aeronautics Board, 140 F.2d 482.
[3] The house is approximately 16 feet high, the barn 20 feet, and the tallest tree 65 feet.

many as six to ten of their chickens were killed in one day by flying into the walls from fright. The total chickens lost in that manner was about 150. Production also fell off. The result was the destruction of the use of the property as a commercial chicken farm. Respondents are frequently deprived of their sleep and the family has become nervous and frightened. Although there have been no airplane accidents on respondents' property, there have been several accidents near the airport and close to respondents' place. These are the essential facts found by the Court of Claims. On the basis of these facts, it found that respondents' property had depreciated in value. It held that the United States had taken an easement over the property on June 1, 1942, and that the value of the property destroyed and the easement taken was $2,000.

I. The United States relies on the Air Commerce Act of 1926, 44 Stat. 568, 49 U.S.C. §171, as amended by the Civil Aeronautics Act of 1938, 52 Stat. 973, 49 U.S.C. §401. Under those statutes the United States has "complete and exclusive national sovereignty in the air space" over this country. 49 U.S.C. §176(a). They grant any citizen of the United States "a public right of freedom of transit in air commerce through the navigable air space of the United States." 49 U.S.C. §403. And "navigable air space" is defined as "airspace above the mimimum safe altitudes of flight prescribed by the Civil Aeronautics Authority." 49 U.S.C. §180. And it is provided that "such navigable airspace shall be subject to a public right of freedom of interstate and foreign air navigation." Id. It is, therefore, argued that since these flights were within the minimum safe altitudes of flight which had been prescribed, they were an exercise of the declared right of travel through the airspace. The United States concludes that when flights are made within the navigable airspace without any physical invasion of the property of the landowners, there has been no taking of property. It says that at most there was merely incidental damage occurring as a consequence of authorized air navigation. It also argues that the landowner does not own superadjacent airspace which he has not subjected to possession by the erection of structures or other occupancy. Moreover, it is argued that even if the United States took airspace owned by respondents, no compensable damage was shown. Any damages are said to be merely consequential for which no compensation may be obtained under the Fifth Amendment.

It is ancient doctrine that at common law ownership of the land extended to the periphery of the universe — *Cujus est solum ejus est usque ad coelum.* But that doctrine has no place in the modern world. The air is a public highway, as Congress has declared. Were that not true, every transcontinental flight would subject the operator to countless trespass suits. Common sense revolts at the idea. To recognize such private claims to the airspace would clog these highways, seriously interfere with their control and development in the public interest, and transfer into private ownership that to which only the public has a just claim.

But that general principle does not control the present case. For the United States conceded on oral argument that if the flights over respondents' property rendered it uninhabitable, there would be a taking compensable under the Fifth Amendment. It is the owner's loss, not the taker's gain, which is the measure of the value of the property taken. United States v. Miller, 317 U.S. 369. Market value fairly determined is the normal measure of the recovery. Id. And that value may reflect the use to which the land could readily be converted, as well as the existing use. United States v. Powelson, 319 U.S. 266, 275, and cases cited. If, by reason of the frequency and altitude of the flights, respondents could not use this land for any purpose, their loss would be complete. It would be as complete as if the United States had entered upon the surface of the land and taken exclusive possession of it.

We agree that in those circumstances there would be a taking. Though it would be only an easement of flight which was taken, that easement, if permanent and not merely temporary, normally would be the equivalent of a fee interest. It would be a definite exercise of complete dominion and control over the surface of the land. The fact that the planes never touched the surface would be as irrelevant as the absence in this day of the feudal livery of seisin on the transfer of real estate. The owner's right to possess and exploit the land — that is to say, his beneficial ownership of it — would be destroyed. . . .

There is no material difference between the supposed case and the present one, except that here enjoyment and use of the land are not completely destroyed. But that does not seem to us to be controlling. The path of glide for airplanes might reduce a valuable factory site to grazing land, an orchard to a vegetable patch, a residential section to a wheat field. Some value would remain. But the use of the airspace immediately above the land would limit the utility of the land and cause a diminution in its value. That was the philosophy of Portsmouth Co. v. United States, 260 U.S. 327. In that case the petition alleged that the United States erected a fort on nearby land, established a battery and a fire control station there, and fired guns over petitioner's land. The Court, speaking through Mr. Justice Holmes, reversed the Court of Claims, which dismissed the petition on a demurrer, holding that "the specific facts set forth would warrant a finding that a servitude has been imposed." 260 U.S. p. 330. . . .

We have said that the airspace is a public highway. Yet it is obvious that if the landowner is to have full enjoyment of the land, he must have exclusive control of the immediate reaches of the enveloping atmosphere. Otherwise buildings could not be erected, trees could not be planted, and even fences could not be run. . . . The fact that he does not occupy it in a physical sense — by the erection of buildings and the like — is not material. As we have said, the flight of airplanes, which skim the surface but do not touch it, is as much an appropriation of the use of the land as a more conventional entry upon it. We would not doubt that, if the United States erected an elevated railway over respondents' land at the precise altitude where its planes now fly, there would be a partial taking, even though none of the supports of the structure rested on the land. The reason is that there would be an intrusion so immediate and direct as to subtract from the owner's full enjoyment of the property and to limit his exploitation of it. While the owner does not in any physical manner occupy that stratum of airspace or make use of it in the conventional sense, he does use it in somewhat the same sense that space left between buildings for the purpose of light and air is used. The superadjacent airspace at this low altitude is so close to the land that continuous invasions of it affect the use of the surface of the land itself. We think that the landowner, as an incident to his ownership, has a claim to it and that invasions of it are in the same category as invasions of the surface.

In this case, as in Portsmouth Co. v. United States, supra, the damages were not merely consequential. They were the product of a direct invasion of respondents' domain. As stated in United States v. Cress, 243 U.S. 316, 328, ". . . it is the character of the invasion, not the amount of damage resulting from it, so long as the damage is substantial, that determines the question whether it is a taking." . . .

The airplane is part of the modern environment of life, and the inconveniences which it causes are normally not compensable under the Fifth Amendment. The airspace apart from the immediate reaches above the land, is part of the public domain. We need not determine at this time what those precise limits are. Flights over private land are not a taking, unless they are so low and so frequent as to be a direct and immediate interference with the enjoyment and use of the land. We need not speculate on that phase of the present case. For the findings of the Court of Claims plainly establish that there was a diminution in value of the property and that the frequent, low-level flights were the direct and immediate cause. We agree with the Court of Claims that a servitude has been imposed upon the land. . . .

Since on this record it is not clear whether the easement taken is a permanent or a temporary one, it would be premature for us to consider whether the amount of the award made by the Court of Claims was proper.

The judgment is reversed and the cause is remanded to the Court of Claims so that it may make the necessary findings in conformity with this opinion.

Reversed.

MR. JUSTICE JACKSON took no part in the consideration or decision of this case.

MR. JUSTICE BLACK dissenting.

The Fifth Amendment provides that "private property" shall not "be taken for public use without just compensation." The Court holds today that the Government has "taken" respondents' property by repeatedly flying Army bombers directly above respondents' land at a height of eighty-three feet where the light and noise from these planes caused respondents to lose sleep and their chickens to be killed. . . .

. . . The concept of taking property as used in the Constitution has heretofore never been given so sweeping a meaning. The Court's opinion presents no case where a man who makes noise or shines light onto his neighbor's property has been ejected from that property for wrongfully taking possession of it. Nor would anyone take seriously a claim that noisy automobiles passing on a highway are taking wrongful possession of the homes located thereon, or that a city elevated train which greatly interferes with the sleep of those who live next to it wrongfully takes their property. Even the one case in this Court which in considering the sufficiency of a complaint gave the most elastic meaning to the phrase "private property be taken" as used in the Fifth Amendment, did not go so far. Portsmouth Co. V. United States, 260 U.S. 327. I am not willing, nor do I think the Constitution and the decisions authorize me, to extend that phrase so as to guarantee an absolute constitutional right to relief not subject to legislative change, which is based on averments that at best show mere torts committed by government agents while flying over land. The future adjustment of the rights and remedies of property owners, which might be found necessary because of the flight of planes at safe altitudes, should, especially in view of the imminent expansion of air navigation, be left where I think the Constitution left it, with Congress. . . .

MR. JUSTICE BURTON joins in this dissent.

United States v. Central Eureka Mining Co. 357 U.S. 155,
78 S. Ct. 1097, 2 L. Ed. 2d 1228 (1958)

MR. JUSTICE BURTON delivered the opinion of the Court. . . .

Early in 1941, it became apparent to those in charge of the Nation's defense mobilization that we faced a critical shortage of nonferrous metals, notably copper, and a comparable shortage of machinery and supplies to produce them. Responsive to this situation, the Office of Production Management (OPM) and its successor, the War Production Board (WPB), issued a series of Preference Orders. These gave the producers of mining machinery and supplies relatively high priorities for the acquisition of needed materials. They also gave to those mines, which were deemed important from the standpoint of defense or essential civilian needs, a high priority in the acquisition of such machinery. Gold mines were classified as nonessential and eventually were relegated to the lowest priority rating. These orders prevented the mines operated by respondents from acquiring new machinery or supplies so that, by March of 1942, respondents were reduced to using only the machinery and supplies which they had on hand.

Soon thereafter, a severe shortage of skilled labor developed in the nonferrous metal mines. This was due in part to the expanding need for nonferrous metals, and in part to a depletion of mining manpower as a result of the military draft and the attraction of higher wages paid by other industries. It became apparent that the only reservoir of skilled mining labor was that which remained in the gold mines. Pressure was brought to bear on the WPB to close down the gold mines with the expectation that many gold miners would thus be attracted to the nonferrous mines.

As a part of this conservation program, WPB, on October 8, 1942, issued Limitation Order L-208 now before us. That order was addressed exclusively to the gold mining industry which it classified as nonessential. It directed each operator of a gold mine to take steps immediately to close down its operations and, after seven days, not to acquire, use or consume any material or equipment in development work. The order directed that, within 60 days, all operations should cease, excepting only the minimum activity necessary to maintain mine buildings, machinery and equipment, and to keep the workings safe and accessible. . . . The WPB did not take physical possession of the gold mines. It did not require the mine owners to dispose of any of their machinery or equipment. . . . The order, thus amended, remained in effect until revoked on June 30, 1945.

[I]t is clear from the record that the Government did not occupy, use, or in any manner take physical possession of the gold mines or of the equipment connected with them. Cf. United States v. Pewee Coal Co., 341 U.S. 114. [The United States "took" coal mines by actually assuming possession and operation of the facilities to avert a strike.] All that the Government sought was the cessation of the consumption of mining equipment and manpower in the gold mines and the conservation of such equipment and manpower for more essential war uses. The Government had no need for the gold or the gold mines. The mere fact that L-208 was in the form of an express prohibition of the *operation* of the mines, rather than a prohibition of the use of the scarce equipment in the mines, did not convert the order into a "taking" of a right to operate the mines. Obviously, if the use of equipment were prohibited, the mines would close and it did not make that order a "taking" merely because the order was, in form, a direction to close down the mines. The record shows that the WPB expected that L-208 would release substantial amounts of scarce mining equipment for use in essential industries, and also that experienced gold miners would transfer to other mines whose product was in gravely short supply. The purpose of L-208 was to encourage voluntary reallocation of scarce resources from the unessential to the essential.

[T]he WPB made a reasoned decision that, under existing circumstances, the Nation's need was such that the unrestricted use of mining equipment and manpower in gold mines was so wasteful of wartime resources that it must be temporarily suspended. Traditionally, we have treated the issue as to whether a particular governmental restriction amounted to a constitutional taking as being a question properly turning upon the particular circumstances of each case. See Pennsylvania Coal Co. v. Mahon, 260 U.S. 393, 416. In doing so, we have recognized that action in the form of regulation can so diminish the value of property as to constitute a taking. E.g., United States v. Kansas City Ins. Co., 339 U.S. 799; United States v. Causby, 328 U.S. 256. However, the mere fact that the regulation deprives the property owner of the most profitable use of his property is not necessarily enough to establish the owner's right to compensation. See Mugler v. Kansas, 123 U.S. 623, 664, 668, 669. In the context of war, we have been reluctant to find that degree of regulation which, without saying so, requires compensation to be paid for resulting losses of income. E.g., Hamilton v. Kentucky Distilleries Co., 251 U.S. 146; Jacob Ruppert v. Caffey, 251 U.S. 264; Bowles v. Willingham, 321 U.S. 503; and see United States v. Caltex, Inc., 344 U.S. 149. The reasons are plain. War, particularly in modern times, demands the strict regulation of nearly all resources. It makes demands which otherwise would be insufferable. But wartime economic restrictions, temporary in character, are insignificant when compared to the widespread uncompensated loss of life and freedom of action which war traditionally demands.

We do not find in the temporary restrictions here placed on the operation of gold mines a taking of private property that would justify a departure from the trend of the above decisions. . . .

Mr. Justice Harlan, dissenting.

. . . I cannot agree with the Court's conclusion that the Order was simply a "regulation" incident to which respondents happened to suffer financial loss. Instead, I believe that L-208 effected a temporary "taking" of the respondents' right to mine gold which is compensable under the Fifth amendment.

L-208 was the only order promulgated during World War II which by its terms required a lawful and productive industry to shut down at a severe economic cost. See S. Rep. No. 1605, 82d Cong., 2d Sess. 3. As a result of the Order the respondents were totally deprived of the beneficial use of their property. Any suggestion that the mines could have been used in such a way (that is, other than to mine gold) so as to remove them from the scope of the Order would be chimerical. Not only were the respondents completely prevented from making profitable use of their property, but the Government acquired all that it wanted from the mines — their complete immobilization and the resulting discharge of the hardrock miners. It is plain that as a practical matter the Order led to consequences no different from those that would have followed the temporary acquisition of physical possession of these mines by the United States.

In these circumstances making the respondents' right to compensation turn on whether the Government took the ceremonial step of planting the American flag on the mining premises, cf. United States v. Pewee Coal Co., 341 U.S. 114, 116, is surely to permit technicalities of form to dictate consequences of substance. In my judgment the present case should be viewed precisely as if the United States, in order to accomplish its purpose of freeing gold miners for essential work, had taken possession of the gold mines and allowed them to lie fallow for the duration of the war. Had the Government adopted the latter course it is hardly debatable that respondents would have been entitled to compensation. See United States v. Pewee Coal Co., supra.

As the Court recognizes, governmental action in the form of regulation which severely diminishes the value of property may constitute a "taking." See United States v. Kansas City Life Ins. Co., 339 U.S. 799; United States v. Causby, 328 U.S. 256; Richards v. Washington Terminal Co., 233 U.S. 546. "The general rule at least is, that while property may be regulated to a certain extent, if regulation goes too far it will be recognized as a taking." Pennsylvania Coal Co. v. Mahon, 260 U.S. 393, 415. In my opinion application of this principle calls here for the conclusion that there was a "taking," for it is difficult to conceive of a greater impairment of the use of property by a regulatory measure than that suffered by the respondents as a result of L-208.[e] . . .

NOTE

See generally Sax, Takings and the Police Power, 74 Yale L.J. 36 (1964); and also Michelman, Property, Utility and Fairness: Comments on the Ethical Foundations of "Just Compensation" Law, 80 Harv. L. Rev. 1165 (1967). For a debate on how to read Miller v. Schoene, supra, in economic terms, see Samuels, Interrelations between Legal and Economic Processes, 14 J. Law & Econ. 435 (1971), and Buchanan, Politics, Property, and the Law: An Alternative Interpretation of Miller et al. v. Schoene, 15 J. Law & Econ. 439 (1972). See Griggs v. Allegheny County, 369 U.S. 84 (1962) for a sequel to United States v. Causby, supra. When a municipality constructs and maintains an airport, and commercial planes departing and landing fly over adjoining private property at low levels, within glide paths prescribed by the Civil Aeronautics Board, against whom, and on what basis, may the property owners recover compensation?

The measure of just compensation when property is taken for public use presents many complex problems. See generally McCormick, The Measure of Compensation in Eminent Domain, 17 Minn. L. Rev. 461 (1933). The elementary principle is that market value at the time of the taking is the proper measure and that "the question is what has the owner lost, not what has the taker gained." Boston Chamber of Commerce v. Boston, 217 U.S. 189, 195 (1910), per Holmes, J. Cf. Hale, Value to the Taker in Condemnation Cases, 31 Colum L. Rev. 1 (1931).

---

[e] A dissenting opinion of Mr. Justice Frankfurter is omitted. — ED.

Section A. Property: Its Regulation and Its Taking   1103

This formula is hardly adequate to solve a number of special questions arising out of the contemporary exercise of the eminent domain power.

1. What is the effect of market controls by the government, including the fixing of ceiling prices, on the measure of just compensation for a taking? See United States v. Commodities Trading Corp., 339 U.S. 121 (1950); Safeway Stores, Inc. v. United States, 93 F. Supp. 900 (Ct. Cl. 1950), cert. denied, 341 U.S. 953 (1951); Braucher, Requisition at a Ceiling Price, 64 Harv. L. Rev. 1103 (1951).

2. To what extent does the measure of just compensation in the case of a temporary taking (e.g., a leasehold interest) differ from that in the case of a permanent taking, with respect to such items as moving expenses and loss of business good will? See United States v. Westinghouse Electric and Mfg. Co., 339 U.S. 261 (1950); Kimball Laundry Co. v. United States, 338 U.S. 1 (1949), noted in 63 Harv. L. Rev. 352 (1949); Dolan, Consequential Damages in Federal Condemnation, 35 Va. L. Rev. 1059 (1949). See also Note, Eminent Domain Valuations in an Age of Redevelopment: Incidental Losses, 67 Yale L.J. 61 (1957).

3. To what extent, if at all, may Congress provide a measure of just compensation differing from that which the courts would independently prescribe? Is there an analogy in the effect of congressional action in the fields of intergovernmental immunities and state power over interstate commerce? Cf. Note, Change in Constitutional Doctrine Through Legislation, 63 Harv. L. Rev. 861 (1950).

4. To what extent, if at all, may there be excluded from just compensation an enhancement in market value of the property caused by the needs of the government which have occasioned the taking? See United States v. Cors, 337 U.S. 325 (1949).

United States v. Fuller 409 U.S. 488, 93 S. Ct. 801, 35 L. Ed. 2d 16 (1973)

MR. JUSTICE REHNQUIST delivered the opinion of the Court.

Respondents operated a large-scale "cow-calf" ranch near the confluence of the Big Sandy and Bill Williams Rivers in western Arizona. Their activities were conducted on lands consisting of 1,280 acres that they owned in fee simple (fee lands), 12,027 acres leased from the State of Arizona, and 31,461 acres of federal domain held under Taylor Grazing Act permits issued in accordance with §3 of the Act, 48 Stat. 1270, as amended, 43 U.S.C. §315b. The Taylor Grazing Act authorizes the Secretary of the Interior to issue permits to livestock owners for grazing their stock on Federal Government lands. These permits are revocable by the Government. The Act provides, moreover, that its provisions "shall not create any right, title, interest, or estate in or to the lands." Ibid.

The United States, petitioner here, condemned 920 acres of respondents' fee lands. . . . [At the trial the respondents contended] that if on the open market the value of their fee lands was enhanced because of their actual or potential use in conjunction with permit lands, that element of value of the fee lands could be testified to by appraisers and considered by the jury. The District Court substantially adopted respondents' position, first in a pretrial order and then in its charge to the jury over appropriate objection by the Government.

On the Government's appeal, the Court of Appeals for the Ninth Circuit affirmed the judgment and approved the charge of the District Court. . . .

Our prior decisions have variously defined the "just compensation" that the Fifth Amendment requires to be made when the Government exercises its power of eminent domain. The owner is entitled to fair market value, United States v. Miller, 317 U.S. 369, 374 (1943), but that term is "not an absolute standard nor an exclusive method of valuation." United States v. Virginia Electric & Power Co., 365 U.S. 624, 633 (1961). The constitutional requirement of just compensation derives as much content from the basic equitable principles of fairness, United States v. Commodities Trading Corp., 339 U.S. 121, 124 (1950), as it does from technical concepts of property law. . . .

United States v. Cors, 337 U.S. 325 (1949), held that the just compensation required to be paid to the owner of a tug requisitioned by the Government in October 1942, during the Second World War, could not include the appreciation in market value for tugs created by the Government's own increased wartime need for such vessels. The Court said: "That is a value which the government itself created and hence in fairness should not be required to pay." Id., at 334. A long line of cases decided by this Court dealing with the Government's navigational servitude with respect to navigable waters evidences a continuing refusal to include, as an element of value in compensating for fast lands that are taken, any benefits conferred by access to such benefits as a potential portsite or a potential hydro-electric site. United States v. Rands, [389 U.S. 121 (1967)]; United States v. Twin City Power Co., 350 U.S. 222 (1956); United States v. Commodore Park, 324 U.S. 386 (1945).

These cases go far toward establishing the general principle that the Government as condemnor may not be required to compensate a condemnee for elements of value that the Government has created, or that it might have destroyed under the exercise of governmental authority other than the power of eminent domain. If, as in Rands, the Government need not pay for value that it could have acquired by exercise of a servitude arising under the commerce power, it would seem a fortiori that it need not compensate for value that it could remove by revocation of a permit for the use of lands that it owned outright.

We do not suggest that such a general principle can be pushed to its ultimate logical conclusion. In United States v. Miller, supra, the Court held that "just compensation" did include the increment of value resulting from the completed project to neighboring lands originally outside the project limits, but later brought within them. Nor may the United States "be excused from paying just compensation measured by the value of the property at the time of the taking" because the State in which the property is located might, through the exercise of its lease power, have diminished that value without paying compensation. United States ex rel. TVA v. Powelson, 319 U.S. 266, 284 (1943).

"Courts have had to adopt working rules in order to do substantial justice in eminent domain proceedings." United States v. Miller, supra, at 375. Seeking as best we may to extrapolate from these prior decisions such a "working rule," we believe that there is a significant difference between the value added to property by a completed public works project, for which the Government must pay, and the value added to fee lands by a revocable permit authorizing the use of neighboring lands that the Government owns. . . . We hold that the Fifth Amendment does not require the Government to pay for that element of value based on the use of respondents' fee lands in combination with the Government's permit lands. . . .

Reversed.

MR. JUSTICE POWELL, with whom MR. JUSTICE DOUGLAS, MR. JUSTICE BRENNAN, and MR. JUSTICE MARSHALL join, dissenting.

I dissent from a decision which, in my view, dilutes the meaning of the just compensation required by the Fifth Amendment when property is condemned by the Government.

. . . If the Government need not pay location value in this case, what are the limits upon the principle today announced? Will the Government be relieved from paying location value whenever it condemns private property adjacent to or favorably located with respect to Government property? [5] Does the principle apply, for example, to the taking of a gasoline station at an interchange of a federal highway, or to the taking of a farm which in private hands could continue to be irrigated with water from a federal reservoir? The ma-

---

[5] If so, the contrast between condemnation proceedings and other transactions would be stark: the enhancement of value stemming from public highways, parks, buildings, and recreational facilities is commonly recognized for purposes of taxation, mortgaging, and private sales.

jority proposes to distinguish such cases with the "working rule" that "there is a significant difference between the value added to property by a completed public works project, for which the Government must pay, and the value added to fee lands by a revocable permit authorizing the use of neighboring lands which the Government owns." Ante, at 492.

The Court can hardly be drawing a distinction between Government-owned "completed public works" and Government-owned parks and grazing lands in their natural state. The "working rule" as articulated can, therefore, only mean that the respondents' revocable permit to use the neighboring lands is regarded by the Court as the distinguishing element. This is an acceptance of the Government's argument that the added value derives from the permit and not from the favorable location with respect to the grazing land. The answer to this, not addressed either by the Government or the Court, is that the favorable location is the central fact. Even if no permit had been issued to these respondents, their three tracts of land — largely surrounded by the grazing land — were strategically located and logical beneficiaries of the Taylor Grazing Act. In determining the market value of respondents' land, surely this location — whether or not a permit had been issued would enter into any rational estimate of value. This is precisely the rationale of the District Court's jury instruction, which carefully distinguished between the revocable permits "not compensable as such" and the "availability and accessibility" of the grazing land. It is this distinction which the Court's opinion simply ignores.

Finally, I do not think the Court's deviation from the market-value rule can be justified by invocation of long-established "basic equitable principles of fairness." Ante, at 490. It hardly serves the principles of fairness as they have been understood in the law of just compensation to disregard what respondents could have obtained for their land on the open market in favor of its value artificially denuded of its surroundings.

I would affirm the judgment of the Court of Appeals.

3. Zoning

Village of Euclid v. Ambler Realty Co. 272 U.S. 365, 47 S. Ct. 114, 71 L. Ed. 303 (1926)

MR. JUSTICE SUTHERLAND delivered the opinion of the Court.

The Village of Euclid is an Ohio municipal corporation. It adjoins and practically is a suburb of the City of Cleveland. Its estimated population is between 5,000 and 10,000 and its area from twelve to fourteen square miles, the greater part of which is farm lands or unimproved acreage. . . .

Appellee is the owner of a tract of land containing 68 acres, situated in the westerly end of the village, abutting on Euclid Avenue to the south and the Nickel Plate railroad to the north. Adjoining this tract, both on the east and on the west, there have been laid out restricted residential plats upon which residences have been erected.

On November 13, 1922, an ordinance was adopted by the Village Council, establishing a comprehensive zoning plan for regulating and restricting the location of trades, industries, apartment houses, two-family houses, single family houses, etc., the lot area to be built upon, the size and height of buildings, etc.

The entire area of the village is divided by the ordinance into six classes of use districts, denominated U-1 to U-6, inclusive; three classes of height districts, denominated H-1 to H-3 inclusive; and four classes of area districts, denominated A-1 to A-4, inclusive. The use districts are classified in respect of the buildings which may be erected within their respective limits, as follows: U-1 is restricted to single family dwellings, public parks, water towers and reservoirs, suburban and interurban electric railway passenger stations and

1106 Chapter Sixteen. **Substantive Rights**

rights of way, and farming, noncommercial greenhouse nurseries and truck gardening; U-2 is extended to include two-family dwellings; U-3 is further extended to include apartment houses, hotels, churches, schools, public libraries, museums, private clubs, community center buildings, hospitals, sanitariums, public playgrounds and recreation buildings, and a city hall and courthouse; U-4 is further extended to include banks, offices, studios, telephone exchanges, fire and police stations, restaurants, theatres and moving picture shows, retail stores and shops, sales offices, sample rooms, wholesale stores for hardware, drugs and groceries, stations for gasoline and oil (not exceeding 1,000 gallons' storage) and for ice delivery, skating rinks and dance halls, electric substations, job and newspaper printing, public garages for motor vehicles, stables and wagon sheds (not exceeding five horses, wagons or motor trucks) and distributing stations for central store and commercial enterprises; U-5 is further extended to include billboards and advertising signs (if permitted), warehouses, ice and ice cream manufacturing and cold storage plants, bottling works, milk bottling and central distribution stations, laundries, carpet cleaning, dry cleaning and dyeing establishments, blacksmith, horseshoeing, wagon and motor vehicle repair shops, freight stations, streetcar barns, stables and wagon sheds (for more than five horses, wagons or motor trucks), and wholesale produce markets and salesrooms; U-6 is further extended to include plants for sewage disposal and for producing gas, garbage and refuse incineration, scrap iron, junk, scrap paper and rag storage, aviation fields, cemeteries, crematories, penal and correctional institutions, insane and feeble minded institutions, storage of oil and gasoline (not to exceed 25,000 gallons), and manufacturing and industrial operations of any kind other than, and any public utility not included in, a class U-1, U-2, U-3, U-4, or U-5 use. There is a seventh class of uses which is prohibited altogether.

Class U-1 is the only district in which buildings are restricted to those enumerated. In the other classes the uses are cumulative; that is to say, uses in class U-2 include those enumerated in the preceding class, U-1; class U-3 includes uses enumerated in the preceding classes, U-2 and U-1; and so on. In addition to the enumerated uses, the ordinance provides for accessory uses, that is, for uses customarily incident to the principal use, such as private garages. Many regulations are provided in respect of such accessory uses.

Appellee's tract of land comes under U-2, U-3 and U-6. The first strip of 620 feet immediately north of Euclid Avenue falls in class U-2, the next 130 feet to the north, in U-3 and the remainder in U-6. The uses of the first 620 feet, therefore, do not include apartment houses, hotels, churches, schools, or other public and semi-public buildings, or other uses enumerated in respect of U-3 to U-6, inclusive. The uses of the next 130 feet include all of these, but exclude industries, theatres, banks, shops, and the various other uses set forth in respect of U-4 to U-6, inclusive. [Appellee's bill in the District Court complained that its land was much more valuable for industrial use, and the ordinance prevented sale of much of the land for that purpose.]

The enforcement of the ordinance is entrusted to the inspector of buildings, under rules and regulations of the board of zoning appeals. Meetings of the board are public, and minutes of its proceedings are kept. It is authorized to adopt rules and regulations to carry into effect provisions of the ordinance. Decisions of the inspector of buildings may be appealed to the board by any person claiming to be adversely affected by any such decision. The board is given power in specific cases of practical difficulty or unnecessary hardship to interpret the ordinance in harmony with its general purpose and intent, so that the public health, safety and general welfare may be secure and substantial justice done. Penalties are prescribed for violations, and it is provided that the various provisions are to be regarded as independent and the holding of any provision to be unconstitutional, void or ineffective shall not affect any of the others.

The ordinance is assailed on the grounds that it is in derogation of § 1 of the Fourteenth Amendment to the Federal Constitution in that it deprives appellee of liberty and property

Section A. Property: Its Regulation and Its Taking 1107

without due process of law and denies it the equal protection of the law, and that it offends against certain provisions of the Constitution of the State of Ohio. The prayer of the bill is for an injunction restraining the enforcement of the ordinance and all attempts to impose or maintain as to appellee's property any of the restrictions, limitations or conditions. The court below held the ordinance to be unconstitutional and void, and enjoined its enforcement. 297 Fed. 307. . . .

It is not necessary to set forth the provisions of the Ohio Constitution which are thought to be infringed. The question is the same under both Constitutions, namely, as stated by appellee: Is the ordinance invalid in that it violates the constitutional protection "to the right of property in the appellee by attempted regulations under the guise of the police power, which are unreasonable and confiscatory"?

Building zone laws are of modern origin. They began in this country about twenty-five years ago. Until recent years, urban life was comparatively simple; but with the great increase and concentration of population, problems have developed, and constantly are developing, which require, and will continue to require, additional restrictions in respect of the use and occupation of private lands in urban communities. Regulations, the wisdom, necessity and validity of which, as applied to existing conditions, are so apparent that they are now uniformly sustained, a century ago, or even half a century ago, probably would have been rejected as arbitrary and oppressive. Such regulations are sustained, under the complex conditions of our day, for reasons analogous to those which justify traffic regulations, which, before the advent of automobiles and rapid transit street railways, would have been condemned as fatally arbitrary and unreasonable. And in this there is no inconsistency, for while the meaning of constitutional guaranties never varies, the scope of their application must expand or contract to meet the new and different conditions which are constantly coming within the field of their operation. In a changing world, it is impossible that it should be otherwise. But although a degree of elasticity is thus imparted, not to the *meaning*, but to the *application* of constitutional principles, statutes and ordinances, which, after giving due weight to the new conditions, are found clearly not to conform to the Constitution, of course, must fall.

The ordinance now under review, and all similar laws and regulations, must find their justification in some aspect of the police power, asserted for the public welfare. The line which in this field separates the legitimate from the illegitimate assumption of power is not capable of precise delimitation. It varies with circumstances and conditions. A regulatory zoning ordinance, which would be clearly valid as applied to the great cities, might be clearly invalid as applied to rural communities. In solving doubts, the maxim *sic utere tuo ut alienum non laedas*, which lies at the foundation of so much of the common law of nuisances, ordinarily will furnish a fairly helpful clew. And the law of nuisances, likewise, may be consulted, not for the purpose of controlling, but for the helpful aid of its analogies in the process of ascertaining the scope of, the power. Thus the question whether the power exists to forbid the erection of a building of a particular kind or for a particular use, like the question whether a particular thing is a nuisance, is to be determined, not by an abstract consideration of the building or of the thing considered apart, but by considering it in connection with the circumstances and the locality. Sturgis v. Bridgeman, L.R. 11 Ch. 852, 865. A nuisance may be merely a right thing in the wrong place, — like a pig in the parlor instead of the barnyard. If the validity of the legislative classification for zoning purposes be fairly debatable, the legislative judgment must be allowed to control. Radice v. New York, 264 U.S. 292, 294.

There is no serious difference of opinion in respect of the validity of laws and regulations fixing the height of buildings within reasonable limits, the character of materials and methods of construction, and the adjoining area which must be left open, in order to minimize the danger of fire or collapse, the evils of over-crowding, and the like, and excluding from residential sections offensive trades, industries and structures likely to create nuisances. See Welch v. Swasey, 214 U.S. 91; Hadacheck v. Los Angeles, 239

U.S. 394; Reinman v. Little Rock, 237 U.S. 171; Cusack Co. v. City of Chicago, 242 U.S. 526, 529-530.

Here, however, the exclusion is in general terms of all industrial establishments, and it may thereby happen that not only offensive or dangerous industries will be excluded, but those which are neither offensive nor dangerous will share the same fate. But this is no more than happens in respect of many practice-forbidding laws which this Court has upheld although drawn in general terms so as to include individual cases that may turn out to be innocuous in themselves. Hebe Co. v. Shaw, 248 U.S. 297, 303; Pierce Oil Corp. v. City of Hope, 248 U.S. 498, 500. The inclusion of a reasonable margin to insure effective enforcement, will not put upon a law, otherwise valid, the stamp of invalidity. . . .

We find no difficulty in sustaining restrictions of the kind thus far reviewed. The serious question in the case arises over the provisions of the ordinance excluding from residential districts, apartment houses, business houses, retail stores and shops, and other like establishments. This question involves the validity of what is really the crux of the more recent zoning legislation, namely the creation and maintenance of residential districts from which business and trade of every sort, incuding hotels and apartment houses, are excluded. Upon that question this Court has not thus far spoken. The decisions of the state courts are numerous and conflicting; but those which broadly sustain the power greatly outnumber those which deny altogether or narrowly limit it; and it is very apparent that there is a constantly increasing tendency in the direction of the broader view. We shall not attempt to review these decisions at length, but content ourselves with citing a few as illustrative of all. [Citations omitted.]

The decisions enumerated . . . agree that the exclusion of buildings devoted to business, trade, etc., from residential districts, bears a rational relation to the health and safety of the community. Some of the grounds for this conclusion are — promotion of the health and security from injury of children and others by separating dwelling houses from territory devoted to trade and industry; suppression and prevention of disorder; facilitating the extinguishment of fires, and the enforcement of street traffic regulations and other general welfare ordinances; aiding the health and safety of the community by excluding from residential areas the confusion and danger of fire, contagion and disorder which in greater or less degree attach to the location of stores, shops and factories. Another ground is that the construction and repair of streets may be rendered easier and less expensive by confining the greater part of the heavy traffic to the streets where business is carried on. . . .

If these reasons, thus summarized, do not demonstrate the wisdom or sound policy in all respects of those restrictions which we have indicated as pertinent to the inquiry, at least, the reasons are sufficiently cogent to preclude us from saying, as it must be said before the ordinance can be declared unconstitutional, that such provisions are clearly arbitrary and unreasonable, having no substantial relation to the public health, safety, morals, or general welfare. Cusack Co. v. City of Chicago, supra, pp. 530-531; Jacobson v. Massachusetts, 197 U.S. 11, 30-31.

[I]t is enough for us to determine, as we do, that the ordinance in its general scope and dominant features, so far as its provisions are here involved, is a valid exercise of authority, leaving other provisions to be dealt with as cases arise directly involving them.

And this is in accordance with the traditional policy of this Court. In the realm of constitutional law, especially, this Court has perceived the embarrassment which is likely to result from an attempt to formulate rules or decide questions beyond the necessities of the immediate issue. It has preferred to follow the method of a gradual approach to the general by a systematically guarded application and extension of constitutional principles to particular cases as they arise, rather than by out of hand attempts to establish general rules to which future cases must be fitted. This process applies with peculiar force to the solution of questions arising under the due process clause of the Constitution as applied to the exercise of the flexible powers of police, with which we are here concerned.

Decree reversed.

MR. JUSTICE VAN DEVANTER, MR. JUSTICE MCREYNOLDS and MR. JUSTICE BUTLER, dissent.

Village of Belle Terre v. Boraas 416 U.S. 1, 94 S. Ct. 1536, 39 L. Ed. 2d 797 (1974)

MR. JUSTICE DOUGLAS delivered the opinion of the Court.

Belle Terre is a village on Long Island's north shore of about 220 homes inhabited by 700 people. Its total land area is less than one square mile. It has restricted land use to one-family dwellings excluding lodging houses, boarding houses, fraternity houses, or multiple-dwelling houses. The word "family" as used in the ordinance means, "[o]ne or more persons related by blood, adoption, or marriage, living and cooking together as a single housekeeping unit, exclusive of household servants. A number of persons but not exceeding two (2) living and cooking together as a single housekeeping unit though not related by blood, adoption, or marriage shall be deemed to constitute a family."

Appellees the Dickmans are owners of a house in the village and leased it in December 1971 for a term of 18 months to Michael Truman. Later Bruce Boraas became a colessee. Then Anne Parish moved into the house along with three others. These six are students at nearby State University at Stony Brook and none is related to the other by blood, adoption, or marriage. When the village served the Dickmans with an "Order to Remedy Violations" of the ordinance, the owners plus three tenants thereupon brought this action under 42 U.S.C. §1983 for an injunction declaring the ordinance unconstitutional. The District Court held the ordinance constitutional, 367 F. Supp. 136, and the Court of Appeals reversed, one judge dissenting, 476 F.2d 806. The case is here by appeal, 28 U.S.C. §1254(2); and we noted probable jurisdiction, 414 U.S. 907.

This case brings to this Court a different phase of local zoning regulations than we have previously reviewed. [The Court summarized Euclid v. Ambler Realty Co., supra page 1105, and Berman v. Parker, 348 U.S. 26 (1954). The latter case had held that the legislative police power, as exercised in a land-use project in the District of Columbia, could be directed at making a community "beautiful as well as healthy, spacious as well as clean."]

The present ordinance is challenged on several grounds: that it interferes with a person's right to travel; that it interferes with the right to migrate to and settle within a State; that it bars people who are uncongenial to the present residents; that it expresses the social preferences of the residents for groups that will be congenial to them; that social homogeneity is not a legitimate interest of government; that the restriction of those whom the neighbors do not like trenches on the newcomers' rights of privacy; that it is of no rightful concern to villagers whether the residents are married or unmarried; that the ordinance is antithetical to the Nation's experience, ideology, and self-perception as an open, egalitarian, and integrated society.

We find none of these reasons in the record before us. It is not aimed at transients. Cf. Shapiro v. Thompson, 394 U.S. 618. It involves no procedural disparity inflicted on some but not on others such as was presented by Griffin v. Illinois, 351 U.S. 12. It involves no "fundamental" right guaranteed by the Constitution, such as voting, Harper v. Virginia Board, 383 U.S. 663; the right of association, NAACP v. Alabama, 357 U.S. 449; the right of access to the courts, NAACP v. Button, 371 U.S. 415; or any rights of privacy, cf. Griswold v. Connecticut, 381 U.S. 479; Eisenstadt v. Baird, 405 U.S. 438, 453-454. We deal with economic and social legislation where legislatures have historically drawn lines which we respect against the charge of violation of the Equal Protection Clause if the law be " 'reasonable, not arbitrary' " (quoting Royster Guano Co. v. Virginia, 253 U.S. 412, 415) and bears "a rational relationship to a [permissible] state objective." Reed v. Reed, 404 U.S. 71, 76.

It is said, however, that if two unmarried people can constitute a "family," there is no reason why three or four may not. But every line drawn by a legislature leaves some out that might well have been included. That exercise of discretion, however, is a legislative, not a judicial, function.

It is said that the Belle Terre ordinance reeks with an animosity to unmarried couples who live together. There is no evidence to support it; and the provision of the ordinance bringing within the definition of a "family" two unmarried people belies the charge.

The ordinance places no ban on other forms of association, for a "family" may, so far as the ordinance is concerned, entertain whomever it likes.

The regimes of boarding houses, fraternity houses, and the like present urban problems. More people occupy a given space; more cars rather continuously pass by; more cars are parked; noise travels with crowds.

A quiet place where yards are wide, people few, and motor vehicles restricted are legitimate guidelines in a land-use project addressed to family needs. This goal is a permissible one within Berman v. Parker, supra. The police power is not confined to elimination of filth, stench, and unhealthy places. It is ample to lay out zones where family values, youth values, and the blessings of quiet seclusion and clean air make the area a sanctuary for people. . . .[f]

MR. JUSTICE MARSHALL, dissenting.

. . . Zoning officials properly concern themselves with the uses of land — with, for example, the number and kind of dwellings to be constructed in a certain neighborhood or the number of persons who can reside in those dwellings. But zoning authorities cannot validly consider who those persons are, what they believe, or how they choose to live, whether they are Negro or white, Catholic of Jew, Republican or Democrat, married or unmarried.

My disagreement with the Court today is based upon my view that the ordinance in this case unnecessarily burdens appellees' First Amendment freedom of association and their constitutionally guaranteed right to privacy. Our decisions establish that the First and Fourteenth Amendments protect the freedom to choose one's associates. NAACP v. Button, 371 U.S. 415, 430 (1963). Constitutional protection is extended, not only to modes of association that are political in the usual sense, but also to those that pertain to the social and economic benefit of the members. [Citations omitted.] The selection of one's living companions involves similar choices as to the emotional, social, or economic benefits to be derived from alternative living arrangements.

The freedom of association is often inextricably entwined with the constitutionally guaranteed right of privacy. The right to "establish a home" is an essential part of the liberty guaranteed by the Fourteenth Amendment. Meyer v. Nebraska, 262 U.S. 390, 399 (1923); Griswold v. Connecticut, 381 U.S. 479, 495 (1965) (Goldberg, J., concurring). And the Constitution secures to an individual a freedom "to satisfy his intellectual and emotional needs in the privacy of his own home." Stanley v. Georgia, 394 U.S. 557, 565 (1969); see Paris Adult Theatre I v. Slaton, 413 U.S. 49, 66-67 (1973). Constitutionally protected privacy is, in Mr. Justice Brandeis' words, "as against the Government, the right to be let alone . . . the right most valued by civilized man." Olmstead v. United States, 277 U.S. 438, 478 (1928) (dissenting opinion). The choice of household companions — of whether a person's "intellectual and emotional needs" are best met by living with family, friends, professional associates or others — involves deeply personal considerations as

---

[f] A separate opinion of Mr. Justice Brennan, dissenting on standard grounds, is omitted. — ED.

to the kind and quality of intimate relationships within the home. That decision surely falls within the ambit of the right to privacy protected by the Constitution. . . .

[Applying close scrutiny to the zoning ordinance, Justice Marshall concluded that the governmental interest in population density, noise level, and the like could be adequately served by means "less intrusive" on constitutional rights.]

NOTE Developments in Zoning

Does Belle Terre suggest that with regard to zoning an even more lenient rational relation test applies than in other equal protection and due process cases? See Note, The Supreme Court, 1973 Term, 88 Harv. L. Rev. 41, 128 (1974). But compare those "zoning" cases that have involved racial classifications, e.g., Jones v. Mayer, 392 U.S. 409 (1968), and Shelley v. Kraemer, 334 U.S. 1 (1948). What, then, should be the standard of review for facially "neutral" classifications that have the effect, if not the purpose, of excluding minorities and the poor from certain residential areas? Many communities, especially in suburban areas, not only deny entry to low-income, multifamily housing but also make single-family housing unavailable by means of high requirements for minimum lot size and minimum floor space. See generally Sager, Tight Little Islands: Exclusionary Zoning, Equal Protection, and the Indigent, 21 Stan. L. Rev. 767 (1969); Davidoff and Gold, Exclusionary Zoning, 1 Yale Rev. L. & Soc. Act. 2&3:56 (1970); Note, Exclusionary Zoning and Equal Protection, 84 Harv. L. Rev. 1645 (1971).

Some state legislation has empowered state authorities to override local zoning decisions. See Legislative Development, Snob Zoning: Developments in Massachusetts and New Jersey, 7 Harv. J. Legis. 246 (1970). Some state courts have also determined that local exclusionary zoning does not promote the goal of "general welfare" that animates the police power. See, e.g., Southern Burlington County NAACP v. Township of Mount Laurel, 67 N.J. 151, 336 A.2d 713 (1975). Warth v. Seldin, 422 U.S. 490 (1975), denied standing to low-income nonresidents to challenge the zoning practices of a Rochester suburb. Speaking for the Court in a 5 to 4 decision, Justice Powell found that the facts alleged did not show a "substantial probability" that the plaintiffs could obtain housing in the suburban area even without the restrictive zoning. Also over the dissents of Douglas, Brennan, White, and Marshall, the Court denied standing to groups of Rochester taxpayers, residents of the suburb seeking integration, and housing contractors. The Warth Court, supra, at 507, n.17, did suggest, however, which plaintiffs could properly raise the merits: "See, e.g., Park View Heights Corporation v. City of Black Jack, 467 F.2d 1208 (CA8 1972) [sponsor of actual project blocked by zoning ordinance] . . ." See Note, The Supreme Court, 1974 Term, 89 Harv. L. Rev. 47, 189 (1975).

Also under challenge in the federal courts are zoning plans that seek to limit the growth of communities, even though the plans may allow for low-income and multifamily housing. Finding that one such scheme abridged the right to travel, the trial court wrote that "a municipality capable of supporting a natural population expansion [may not] limit growth simply because it does not prefer to grow at the rate which would be dictated by prevailing market demand." Construction Ind. Assn. of Sonoma City v. City of Petaluma, 375 F. Supp. 574 (N.D. Cal. 1974), rev'd on other grounds, 522 F.2d 897 (9th Cir.), cert. denied, 424 U.S. 934 (1975). See Note, Freedom of Travel and Exclusionary Land Use Regulations, 84 Yale L.J. 1564 (1975). If a zoning plan for limited growth does provide real access to persons of all incomes and races, should there be strict judicial review, cf. Shapiro v. Thompson, supra page 346, of the state interests that are advanced to justify an attempt to keep the population below the "natural" capacity of the area?

Does a disproportionate racial impact of a zoning order trigger a presumption of unconstitutionality, rebuttable only by proof of a compelling justification? The Court of Appeals for the Seventh Circuit so held, in a decision reached before Washington v. Davis, supra page 901. The Supreme Court reversed, in Village of Arlington Heights v. Metropolitan Housing Development, 97 S. Ct. 555 (1977). The Village had refused to grant a zoning variance in favor of a low- and moderate-income multiple-family housing development. Reviewing the findings of the courts below and the evidence, the Court accepted the conclusion that the refusal was due to a desire "to protect property values and the integrity of the Village's zoning plan," a proper objective of the zoning board. Since there was not a finding of discriminatory intent, the Fourteenth Amendment was not violated. The case was remanded for consideration of the applicability of the Fair Housing Act. Justices Brennan, White, and Marshall would have remanded also for reconsideration of the evidence under the standards of Washington v. Davis. Compare also the application of that case in the area of school desegregation, supra page 902.

The plaintiffs in the Arlington Heights case were, inter alia, a nonprofit developer, which was held to have standing by virtue of its expenditures on planning and its "interest in making suitable low-cost housing available in areas where such housing is scarce," and a black worker who had standing by virtue of his eligibility for and interest in living in the proposed project.

Section B. THE NEW "LIBERTY"

Griswold v. Connecticut 381 U.S. 479, 85 S. Ct. 1678, 14 L. Ed. 2d 510 (1965)

MR. JUSTICE DOUGLAS delivered the opinion of the Court.

Appellant Griswold is Executive Director of the Planned Parenthood League of Connecticut. Appellant Buxton is a licensed physician and a professor at the Yale Medical School who served as Medical Director for the League at its Center in New Haven — a center open and operating from November 1 to November 10, 1961, when appellants were arrested.

They gave information, instruction, and medical advice to *married persons* as to the means of preventing conception. They examined the wife and prescribed the best contraceptive device or material for her use. Fees were usually charged, although some couples were serviced free.

The statutes whose constitutionality is involved in this appeal are §§ 53-32 and 54-196 of the General Statutes of Connecticut (1938). The former provides:

"Any person who uses any drug, medicinal article or instrument for the purpose of preventing conception shall be fined not less than fifty dollars or imprisoned not less than sixty days nor more than one year or be both fined and imprisoned."

Section 54-196 provides:

"Any person who assists, abets, counsels, causes, hires, or commands another to commit any offense may be prosecuted and punished as if he were the principal offender."

The appellants were found guilty as accessories and fined $100 each, against the claim that the accessory statute as so applied violated the Fourteenth Amendment. The Appellate Division of the Circuit Court affirmed. The Court of Errors affirmed that judgment. 151 Conn. 544, 200 A.2d 479. We noted probable jurisdiction. 379 U.S. 926.

We think that appellants have standing to raise the constitutional rights of the married people with whom they had a professional relationship. Tileston v. Ullman, 318 U.S. 44, is different, for there the plaintiff seeking to represent others asked for a declaratory judgment. In that situation we thought that the requirements of standing should be strict, lest the standards of "case or controversy" in Article III of the Constitution become blurred. Here those doubts are removed by reason of a criminal conviction for serving married couples in violation of an aiding-and-abetting statute. Certainly the accessory should have standing to assert that the offense which he is charged with assisting is not, or cannot constitutionally be, a crime.

This case is more akin to Truax v. Raich, 239 U.S. 33, where an employee was permitted to assert the rights of his employer; to Pierce v. Society of Sisters, 268 U.S. 510, where the owners of private schools were entitled to assert the rights of potential pupils and their parents; and to Barrows v. Jackson, 346 U.S. 249, where a white defendant, party to a racially restrictive covenant, who was being sued for damages by the covenantors because she had conveyed her property to Negroes, was allowed to raise the issue that enforcement of the covenant violated the rights of prospective Negro purchasers to equal protection, although no Negro was a party to the suit. . . . The rights of husband and wife, pressed here, are likely to be diluted or adversely affected unless those rights are considered in a suit involving those who have this kind of confidential relation to them.

Coming to the merits, we are met with a wide range of questions that implicate the Due Process Clause of the Fourteenth Amendment. Overtones of some arguments suggest that Lochner v. New York, 198 U.S. 45, should be our guide. But we decline that invitation as we did in West Coast Hotel Co. v. Parrish, 300 U.S. 379; Olsen v. Nebraska, 313 U.S. 236; Lincoln Union v. Northwestern Co., 335 U.S. 525; Williamson v. Lee Optical Co., 348 U.S. 483; Giboney v. Empire Storage Co., 336 U.S. 490. We do not sit as a super-legislature to determine the wisdom, need, and propriety of laws that touch economic problems, business affairs, or social conditions. This law, however, operates directly on an intimate relation of husband and wife and their physician's role in one aspect of that relation.

The association of people is not mentioned in the Constitution nor in the Bill of Rights. The right to educate a child in a school of the parents' choice — whether public or private or parochial — is also not mentioned. Nor is the right to study any particular subject or any foreign language. Yet the First Amendment has been construed to include certain of those rights. . . .

In NAACP v. Alabama, 357 U.S. 449, 462, we protected the "freedom to associate and privacy in one's associations," noting that freedom of association was a peripheral First Amendment right. Disclosure of membership lists of a constitutionally valid association, we held, was invalid "as entailing the likelihood of a substantial restraint upon the exercise by petitioner's members of their right to freedom of association." Ibid. In other words, the First Amendment has a penumbra where privacy is protected from governmental intrusion. In like context, we have protected forms of "association" that are not political in the customary sense but pertain to the social, legal, and economic benefit of the members. NAACP v. Button, 371 U.S. 415, 430-431. . . .

The foregoing cases suggest that specific guarantees in the Bill of Rights have penumbras, formed by emanations from those guarantees that help give them life and substance. See Poe v. Ullman, 367 U.S. 497, 516-522 (dissenting opinion). Various guarantees create zones of privacy. The right of association contained in the penumbra of the First Amendment is one, as we have seen. The Third Amendment in its prohibition against the quartering of soldiers "in any house" in time of peace without the consent of the owner is another facet of that privacy. The Fourth Amendment explicitly affirms the "right of the people to be secure in their persons, houses, papers, and effects against unreasonable searches and seizures." The Fifth Amendment in its Self-Incrimination Clause enables the citizen to create a zone of privacy which government may not force him to surrender to his detriment. The Ninth Amendment provides: "The enumeration in the Constitution, of certain rights, shall not be construed to deny or disparage others retained by the people." . . .

The present case, then, concerns a relationship lying within the zone of privacy created by several fundamental constitutional guarantees. And it concerns a law which, in forbidding the *use* of contraceptives rather than regulating their manufacture or sale, seeks to achieve its goals by means having a maximum destructive impact upon that relationship. Such a law cannot stand in light of the familiar principle, so often applied by this Court, that a "governmental purpose to control or prevent activities constitutionally subject to state regulation may not be achieved by means which sweep unnecessarily broadly and thereby invade the area of protected freedom." NAACP v. Alabama, 377 U.S. 288, 307. Would we allow the police to search the sacred precincts of marital bedrooms for telltale signs of the use of contraceptives? The very idea is repulsive to the notions of privacy surrounding the marriage relationship.

We deal with a right of privacy older than the Bill of Rights — older than our political parties, older than our school system. Marriage is a coming together for better or for worse, hopefully enduring, and intimate to the degree of being sacred. It is an association that promotes a way of life, not causes; a harmony in living, not political faiths; a bilateral loyalty, not commercial or social projects. Yet it is an association for as noble a purpose as any involved in our prior decisions.

Reversed.[g]

MR. JUSTICE GOLDBERG, whom THE CHIEF JUSTICE and MR. JUSTICE BRENNAN join, concurring.

I agree with the Court that Connecticut's birth control law unconstitutionally intrudes upon the right of marital privacy, and I join in its opinion and judgment. Although I have not accepted the view that " 'due process' as used in the Fourteenth Amendment incorporates all of the first eight Amendments," . . . I do agree that the concept of liberty protects those personal rights that are fundamental, and is not confined to the specific terms of the Bill of Rights. My conclusion that the concept of liberty is not so restricted and that it embraces the right of marital privacy though that right is not mentioned explicitly in the Constitution is supported both by numerous decisions of this Court, referred to in the Court's opinion, and by the language and history of the Ninth Amendment. In reaching the conclusion that the right of marital privacy is protected, as being within the protected penumbra of specific guarantees of the Bill of Rights, the Court refers to the Ninth Amendment, ... I add these words to emphasize the relevance of that Amendment to the Court's holding. . . .

The Ninth Amendment reads, "The enumeration in the Constitution, of certain rights, shall not be construed to deny or disparage others retained by the people." The Amendment is almost entirely the work of James Madison. It was introduced in Congress by him and passed the House and Senate with little or no debate and virtually no change in language. It was proffered to quiet expressed fears that a bill of specifically enumerated rights could not be sufficiently broad to cover all essential rights and that the specific mention of certain rights would be interpreted as a denial that others were protected. . . .

A dissenting opinion suggests that my interpretation of the Ninth Amendment somehow "broaden[s] the powers of this Court." . . . With all due respect, I believe that it misses the import of what I am saying. I do not take the position of my Brother Black in his dissent in Adamson v. California, 332 U.S. 46, 68, that the entire Bill of Rights is incorporated in the Fourteenth Amendment, and I do not mean to imply that the Ninth Amendment is applied against the States by the Fourteenth. Nor do I mean to state that the Ninth Amendment constitutes an independent source of rights protected from infringement by either the State or Federal Government. Rather, the Ninth Amendment shows a belief of the Constitution's authors that fundamental rights exist that are not expressly enumerated in the first eight amendments and an intent that the list of rights included there not be exhaustive. As any student of this Court's opinions knows, this Court

---

[g] A concurring opinion by Mr. Justice White is omitted. — ED.

has held, often unanimously, that the Fifth and Fourteenth Amendments protect certain fundamental personal liberties from abridgment by the Federal Government or the States. . . . The Ninth Amendment simply shows the intent of the Constitution's authors that other fundamental personal rights should not be denied such protection or disparaged in any other way simply because they are not specifically listed in the first eight constitutional amendments. I do not see how this broadens the authority of the court; rather it serves to support what this Court has been doing in protecting fundamental rights.

Nor am I turning somersaults with history in arguing that the Ninth Amendment is relevant in a case dealing with a State's infringement of a fundamental right. While the Ninth Amendment — and indeed the entire Bill of Rights — originally concerned restrictions upon *federal* power, the subsequently enacted Fourteenth Amendment prohibits the States as well from abridging fundamental personal liberties. And, the Ninth Amendment, in indicating that not all such liberties are specifically mentioned in the first eight amendments, is surely relevant in showing the existence of other fundamental personal rights, now protected from state, as well as federal, infringement. In sum, the Ninth Amendment simply lends strong support to the view that the "liberty" protected by the Fifth and Fourteenth Amendments from infringement by the Federal Government or the States is not restricted to rights specifically mentioned in the first eight amendments. Cf. United Public Workers v. Mitchell, 330 U.S. 75, 94-95. . . .

Although the Connecticut birth-control law obviously encroaches upon a fundamental personal liberty, the State does not show that the law serves any "subordinating [state] interest which is compelling" or that it is "necessary . . . to the accomplishment of a permissible state policy." The State, at most, argues that there is some rational relation between this statute and what is admittedly a legitimate subject of state concern — the discouraging of extra-marital relations. It says that preventing the use of birth control devices by married persons helps prevent the indulgence by some in such extra-marital relations. The rationality of this justification is dubious, particularly in light of the admitted widespread availability to all persons in the State of Connecticut, unmarried as well as married, of birth control devices for the prevention of disease, as distinguished from the prevention of conception, see Tileston v. Ullman, 129 Conn. 84, 26 A.2d 582. But, in any event, it is clear that the State interest in safeguarding marital fidelity can be served by a more discriminately tailored statute, which does not, like the present one, sweep unnecessarily broadly, reaching far beyond the evil sought to be dealt with and intruding upon the privacy of all married couples. . . .

Finally, it should be said of the Court's holding today that it in no way interferes with a State's proper regulation of sexual promiscuity or misconduct. As my Brother Harlan so well stated in his dissenting opinion in Poe v. Ullman, supra, at 553:

"Adultery, homosexuality and the like are sexual intimacies which the State forbids . . . but the intimacy of husband and wife is necessarily an essential and accepted feature of the institution of marriage, an institution which the State not only must allow, but which always and in every age it has fostered and protected. It is one thing when the State exerts its power either to forbid extra-marital sexuality . . . or to say who may marry, but it is quite another when, having acknowledged a marriage and the intimacies inherent in it, it undertakes to regulate by means of the criminal law the details of that intimacy."

In sum, I believe that the right of privacy in the marital relation is fundamental and basic — a personal right "retained by the people" within the meaning of the Ninth Amendment. Connecticut cannot constitutionally abridge this fundamental right, which is protected by the Fourteenth Amendment from infringement by the States. I agree with the Court that petitioners' convictions must therefore be reversed.

MR. JUSTICE HARLAN, concurring in the judgment.

I fully agree with the judgment of reversal, but find myself unable to join the Court's opinion. The reason is that it seems to me to evince an approach to this case very much like that taken by my Brothers Black and Stewart in dissent, namely: the Due Process Clause of the Fourteenth Amendment does not touch this Connecticut statute unless the enactment is found to violate some right assured by the letter or penumbra of the Bill of Rights. . . .

In my view, the proper constitutional inquiry in this case is whether this Connecticut statute infringes the Due Process Clause of the Fourteenth Amendment because the enactment violates basic values "implicit in the concept of ordered liberty," Palko v. Connecticut, 302 U.S. 319, 325. For reasons stated at length in my dissenting opinion in Poe v. Ullman, supra, I believe that it does. While the relevant inquiry may be aided by resort to one or more of the provisions of the Bill of Rights, it is not dependent on them or any of their radiations. The Due Process Clause of the Fourteenth Amendment stands, in my opinion, on its own bottom.

A further observation seems in order respecting the justification of my Brothers Black and Stewart for their "incorporation" approach to this case. Their approach does not rest on historical reasons, which are of course wholly lacking (see Fairman, Does the Fourteenth Amendment Incorporate the Bill of Rights? The Original Understanding, 2 Stan. L. Rev. 5 (1949)), but on the thesis that by limiting the content of the Due Process Clause of the Fourteenth Amendment to the protection of rights which can be found elsewhere in the Constitution, in this instance in the Bill of Rights, judges will thus be confined to "interpretation" of specific constitutional provisions, and will thereby be restrained from introducing their own notions of constitutional right and wrong into the "vague contours of the Due Process Clause." Rochin v. California, 342 U.S. 165, 170.

While I could not more heartily agree that judicial "self restraint" is an indispensable ingredient of sound constitutional adjudication, I do submit that the formula suggested for achieving it is more hollow than real. "Specific" provisions of the Constitution, no less than "due process," lend themselves as readily to "personal" interpretations by judges whose constitutional outlook is simply to keep the Constitution in supposed "tune with the times" . . . . Need one go further than to call up last Term's reapportionment cases, Wesberry v. Sanders, 376 U.S. 1, and Reynolds v. Sims, 377 U.S. 533, where a majority of the Court "interpreted" "by the People" (Art. I, §2) and "equal protection" (Amd. 14) to command "one person, one vote," an interpretation that was made in the face of irrefutable and still unanswered history to the contrary? See my dissenting opinions in those cases, 376 U.S., at 20; 377 U.S., at 589.

Judicial self-restraint will not, I suggest, be brought about in the "due process" area by the historically unfounded incorporation formula long advanced by my Brother Black, and now in part espoused by my Brother Stewart. It will be achieved in this area, as in other constitutional areas, only by continual insistence upon respect for the teachings of history, solid recognition of the basic values that underlie our society, and wise appreciation of the great roles that the doctrines of federalism and separation of powers have played in establishing and preserving American freedoms. . . . Adherence to these principles will not, of course, obviate all constitutional differences of opinion among judges, nor should it. Their continued recognition will however, go farther toward keeping most judges from roaming at large in the constitutional field than will the interpolation into the Constitution of an artificial and largely illusory restriction on the content of the Due Process Clause.

Mr. Justice Stewart, whom Mr. Justice Black joins dissenting.

Since 1879 Connecticut has had on its books a law which forbids the use of contraceptives by anyone. I think this is an uncommonly silly law. As a practical matter, the law is obviously unenforceable, except in the oblique context of the present case. As a philosophical matter, I believe the use of contraceptives in the relationship of marriage should be left to personal and private choice, based upon each individual's moral, ethical, and religious beliefs. As a matter of social policy, I think professional counsel about methods of birth control should be available to all, so that each individual's choice can be meaningfully made. But we are not asked in this case to say whether we think this law is unwise, or even asinine. We are asked to hold that it violates the United States Constitution. And that I cannot do.

In the course of its opinion the Court refers to no less than six Amendments to the Constitution: the First, the Third, the Fourth, the Fifth, the Ninth, and the Fourteenth. But the Court does not say which of these Amendments, if any, it thinks is infringed by this Connecticut law.

We *are* told that the Due Process Clause of the Fourteenth Amendment is not, as such, the "guide" in this case. With that much I agree. There is no claim that this law, duly enacted by the Connecticut Legislature, is unconstitutionally vague. There is no claim that the appellants were denied any of the elements of procedural due process at their trial, so as to make their convictions constitutionally invalid. And, as the Court says, the day has long passed since the Due Process Clause was regarded as a proper instrument for determining "the wisdom, need, and propriety" of state laws. Compare Lochner v. New York, 198 U.S. 45, with Ferguson v. Skrupa, 372 U.S. 726. . . .

As to the First, Third, Fourth, and Fifth Amendments, I can find nothing in any of them to invalidate this Connecticut law, even assuming that all those Amendments are fully applicable against the States. It has not even been argued that this is a law "respecting an establishment of religion, or prohibiting the free exercise thereof." And surely, unless the solemn process of constitutional adjudication is to descend to the level of a play on words, there is not involved here any abridgment of "the freedom of speech, or of the press; or of the right of the people peaceably to assemble, and to petition the Government for a redress of grievances." No soldier has been quartered in any house. There has been no search, and no seizure. Nobody has been compelled to be a witness against himself.

The Court also quotes the Ninth Amendment, and my brother Goldberg's concurring opinion relies heavily upon it. But to say that the Ninth Amendment has anything to do with this case is to turn somersaults with history. The Ninth Amendment, like its companion the Tenth, which this Court held "states but a truism that all is retained which has not been surrendered," United States v. Darby, 312 U.S. 100, 124, was framed by James Madison and adopted by the States simply to make clear that the adoption of the Bill of Rights did not alter the plan that the Federal Government was to be a government of express and limited powers, and that all rights and powers not delegated to it were retained by the people and the individual States. Until today no member of this Court has ever suggested that the Ninth Amendment meant anything else, and the idea that a federal court could ever use the Ninth Amendment to annul a law passed by the elected representatives of the people of the State of Connecticut would have caused James Madison no little wonder.

What provision of the Constitution, then, does make this state law invalid? The Court says it is the right of privacy "created by several fundamental constitutional guarantees." With all deference, I can find no such general right of privacy in the Bill of Rights, in any other part of the Constitution, or in any case ever before decided by this Court. . . .

Mr. Justice Black, with whom Mr. Justice Stewart joins dissenting.

I agree with my Brother Stewart's dissenting opinion. And like him I do not to any extent whatever base my view that this Connecticut law is constitutional on a belief that the law is wise or that its policy is a good one. In order that there may be no room at all to doubt why I vote as I do, I feel constrained to add that the law is every bit as offensive to me as it is to my Brethren of the majority and my Brothers Harlan, White and Goldberg, who, reciting reasons why it is offensive to them, hold it unconstitutional. There is no single one of the graphic and eloquent strictures and criticisms fired at the policy of this Connecticut law either by the Court's opinion or by those of my concurring Brethren to which I cannot subscribe — except their conclusion that the evil qualities they see in the law make it unconstitutional. . . .

The Court talks about a constitutional "right of privacy" as though there is some constitutional provision or provisions forbidding any law ever to be passed which might abridge the "privacy" of individuals. But there is not. There are, of course, guarantees in certain specific constitutional provisions which are designed in part to protect privacy at certain times and places with respect to certain activities. Such, for example, is the Fourth Amendment's guarantee against "unreasonable searches and seizures." But I think it belittles that Amendment to talk about it as though it protects nothing but "privacy." To treat it that way is to give it a niggardly interpretation, not the kind of liberal reading I think any Bill of Rights provision should be given. The average man would very likely not have his feelings soothed any more by having his property seized openly than by having it seized privately and by stealth. He simply wants his property left alone. And a person can be just as much, if not more, irritated, annoyed and injured by an unceremonious public arrest by a policeman as he is by a seizure in the privacy of his office or home.

One of the most effective ways of diluting or expanding a constitutionally guaranteed right is to substitute for the crucial word or words of a constitutional guarantee another word, more or less flexible and more or less restricted in its meaning. This fact is well illustrated by the use of the term "right of privacy" as a comprehensive substitute for the Fourth Amendment's guarantee against "unreasonable searches and seizures." "Privacy" is a broad, abstract and ambiguous concept which can easily be shrunken in meaning but which can also, on the other hand, easily be interpreted as a constitutional ban against many things other than searches and seizures. . . . I like my privacy as well as the next one, but I am nevertheless compelled to admit that government has a right to invade it unless prohibited by some constitutional provision. For these reasons I cannot agree with the Court's judgment and the reasons it gives for holding this Connecticut law unconstitutional. . . .

The due process argument which my Brothers Harlan and White adopt here is based, as their opinions indicate, on the premise that this Court is vested with power to invalidate all state laws that it considers to be arbitrary, capricious, unreasonable, or oppressive, or because of this Court's belief that a particular state law under scrutiny has no "rational or justifying purpose," or is offensive to a "sense of fairness and justice." If these formulas based on "natural justice," or others which mean the same thing, are to prevail, they require judges to determine what is or is not constitutional on the basis of their own appraisal of what laws are unwise or unnecessary. The power to make such decisions is of course that of a legislative body. Surely it has to be admitted that no provision of the Constitution specifically gives such blanket power to courts to exercise such a supervisory veto over the wisdom and value of legislative policies and to hold unconstitutional those laws which they believe unwise or dangerous. . . .

My Brother Goldberg has adopted the recent discovery that the Ninth Amendment as well as the Due Process Clause can be used by this Court as authority to strike down all state legislation which this Court thinks violates "fundamental principles of liberty and justice," or is contrary to the "traditions and collective conscience of our people." He also states, without proof satisfactory to me, that in making decisions on this basis judges will not consider "their personal and private notions." One may ask how they can avoid considering them. Our Court certainly has no machinery with which to take a Gallup Poll. And the scientific miracles of this age have not yet produced a gadget which the Court can use to determine what traditions are rooted in the "collective conscience of our people." Moreover, one would certainly have to look far beyond the language of the Ninth Amendment to find that the Framers vested in this Court any such awesome veto powers over lawmaking, either by the States or by the Congress. Nor does anything in the history of the Amendment offer any support for such a shocking doctrine. The whole history of the adoption of the Constitution and Bill of Rights points the other way, and the very material quoted by my Brother Goldberg shows that the Ninth Amendment was intended to protect against the idea that "by enumerating particular exceptions to the grant of power" to the Federal Government, "those rights which were not singled out, were intended to be assigned into the hands of the General Government [the United States], and were consequently insecure." That Amendment was passed, not to broaden the powers of this Court or any other department of "the General Government," but, as every student of history knows, to assure the people that the Constitution in all its provisions was intended to limit the Federal Government to the powers granted expressly or by necessary implication. If any broad, unlimited power to hold laws unconstitutional because they offend what this Court conceives to be "the collective conscience of our people" is vested in this Court by the Ninth Amendment, the Fourteenth Amendment, or any other provision of the Constitution, it was not given by the Framers, but rather has been bestowed on the Court by the Court. This fact is perhaps responsible for the peculiar phenomenon that for a period of a century and a half no serious suggestion was ever made that the Ninth Amendment, enacted to protect State powers against federal invasion, could be used as a weapon of federal power to prevent state legislatures from passing laws they consider appropriate to govern local affairs. Use of any such broad, unbounded judicial authority would make of this Court's members a day-to-day constitutional convention. . . .

The late Judge Learned Hand, after emphasizing his view that judges should not use the due process formula suggested in the concurring opinions today or any other formula like it to invalidate legislation offensive to their "personal preferences," made the statement, with which I fully agree, that: "For myself it would be most irksome to be ruled by a bevy of Platonic Guardians, even if I knew how to choose them, which I assuredly do not."[23] So far as I am concerned, Connecticut's law as applied here is not forbidden by any provision of the Federal Constitution as that Constitution was written, and I would therefore affirm.

NOTE

A Massachusetts statute prohibited all distribution of contraceptives to unmarried persons but allowed married persons to obtain them from doctors and pharmacists. In a review of a conviction under the statute, the Court in Eisenstadt v. Baird, 405 U.S. 438 (1972), did not hold that Griswold extended to include the right of unmarried persons to access to contraceptive materials but relied instead upon equal protection analysis. The Court rejected the state's contention that the purpose of the statute was either to deter fornication or to protect the health of the community. Deciding rather that the purpose of the statute was to prohibit the use of contraception itself, the Court could find no rational basis for the distinction between married and unmarried persons: "In each case the evil, as perceived by the State, would be identical, and the underinclusiveness would be invidious." Id. at 454. Speaking for a four-man majority in this 6 to 1 decision, Justice Brennan added, nonetheless, about the reach of Griswold that: "If the right of privacy means anything, it is the right of the *individual*, married or single, to be free from unwarranted governmental intrusion into matters so fundamentally affecting a person as the decision whether to bear or beget a child." Id. at 453.

Roe v. Wade 410 U.S. 113, 93 S. Ct. 705, 35 L. Ed. 2d 147 (1973)

MR. JUSTICE BLACKMUN delivered the opinion of the Court. This Texas federal appeal and its Georgia companion, Doe v. Bolton, [410 U.S. 179], present constitutional challenges

---

[23] [The Bill of Rights (1958)], at 73. While Judge Hand condemned as unjustified the invalidation of state laws under the natural law due process formula, see id., at 35-45, he also expressed the view that this Court in a number of cases had gone too far in holding legislation to be in violation of specific guarantees of the Bill of Rights. Although I agree with his criticism of use of the due process formula, I do not agree with all the views he expressed about construing the specific guarantees of the Bill of Rights.

to state criminal abortion legislation. The Texas statutes under attack here are typical of those that have been in effect in many States for approximately a century. . . .

We forthwith acknowledge our awareness of the sensitive and emotional nature of the abortion controversy, of the vigorous opposing views, even among physicians, and of the deep and seemingly absolute convictions that the subject inspires. One's philosophy, one's experiences, one's exposure to the raw edges of human existence, one's religious training, one's attitudes toward life and family and their values, and the moral standards one establishes and seeks to observe, are all likely to influence and to color one's thinking and conclusions about abortion.

In addition, population growth, pollution, poverty, and racial overtones tend to complicate and not to simplify the problem.

Our task, of course, is to resolve the issue by constitutional measurement free of emotion and of predilection. We seek earnestly to do this, and, because we do, we have inquired into, and in this opinion place some emphasis upon, medical and medical-legal history and what that history reveals about man's attitudes toward the abortive procedure over the centuries. We bear in mind, too, Mr. Justice Holmes' admonition in his now vindicated dissent in Lochner v. New York, 198 U.S. 45, 76 (1905): "It [the Constitution] is made for people of fundamentally differing views, and the accident of our finding certain opinions natural and familiar or novel and even shocking ought not to conclude our judgment upon the question whether statutes embodying them conflict with the Constitution of the United States."

I

The Texas statutes that concern us here are Arts. 1191-1194 and 1196 of the State's Penal Code. These make it a crime to "procure an abortion," as therein defined, or to attempt one, except with respect to "an abortion procured or attempted by medical advice for the purpose of saving the life of the mother." Similar statutes are in existence in a majority of the States. . . .

II

Jane Roe, a single woman who was residing in Dallas County, Texas, instituted this federal action in March 1970 against the District Attorney of the county. She sought a declaratory judgment that the Texas criminal abortion statutes were unconstitutional on their face, and an injunction restraining the defendant from enforcing the statutes.

Roe alleged that she was unmarried and pregnant; that she wished to terminate her pregnancy by an abortion "performed by a competent, licensed physician, under safe, clinical conditions"; that she was unable to get a "legal" abortion in Texas because her life did not appear to be threatened by the continuation of her pregnancy; and that she could not afford to travel to another jurisdiction in order to secure a legal abortion under safe conditions. She claimed that the Texas statutes were unconstitutionally vague and that they abridged her right of personal privacy, protected by the First, Fourth, Fifth, Ninth, and Fourteenth Amendments. By an amendment to her complaint Roe purported to sue "on behalf of herself and all other women" similarly situated.

[Since Roe's pregnancy had long since terminated, the Court considered whether the case was not moot. Holding that it was not, the court said: "Pregnancy provides a classic case of nonmootness. It truly could be 'capable of repetition, yet evading review.' " Two additional parties sought to intervene or to bring suit. A physician, against whom a prosecution was pending in a state court, sought injunctive and declaratory relief; his standing was rejected, under the principle that only where bad faith or harassment is shown will a federal court interfere with state criminal proceedings. A married woman sought injunctive and declaratory relief on the ground that she must avoid pregnancy for medical reasons, and that if she were to become pregnant she would want to procure an abortion; her complaint was held to be too conjectural and contingent to give standing.]

V

The principal thrust of appellant's attack on the Texas statutes is that they improperly invade a right, said to be possessed by the pregnant woman, to choose to terminate her pregnancy. Appellant would discover this right in the concept of personal "liberty" embodied in the Fourteenth Amendment's Due Process Clause; or in personal, marital, familial, and sexual privacy said to be protected by the Bill of Rights or its penumbras, see Griswold v. Connecticut, 381 U.S. 479 (1965); Eisenstadt v. Baird, 405 U.S. 438 (1972); id., at 460 (White, J., concurring); or among those rights reserved to the people by the Ninth Amendment, Griswold v. Connecticut, 381 U.S., at 486 (Goldberg, J., concurring). Before addressing this claim, we feel it desirable briefly to survey, in several aspects, the history of abortion, for such insight as that history may afford us, and then to examine the state purposes and interests behind the criminal abortion laws.

VI

[The Court surveyed ancient attitudes toward abortion in Greece and Rome and traced the common and statutory law on the subject in England and America. Early English law, probably influenced by canon law concepts of "ensoulment" or "animation," distinguished between abortion before "quickening" (from the 16th to the 18th week of pregnancy) and after. Only the latter was a crime, according to Bracton and Coke. Whether even this degree of criminality was actually recognized in the courts is a matter of some dispute. Statutory law in England dates from 1803, preserving a line at quickening, but making abortion a crime, though of lesser magnitude, before quickening. American statutory law, from the early and mid-19th century, generally followed this model. Beginning in the late 19th century, abortion was generally punishable without regard to the fetal stage.]

VII

Three reasons have been advanced to explain historically the enactment of criminal abortion laws in the 19th century and to justify their continued existence.

It has been argued occasionally that these laws were the product of a Victorian social concern to discourage illicit sexual conduct. Texas, however, does not advance this justification in the present case, and it appears that no court or commentator has taken the argument seriously. The appellants and amici contend, moreover, that this is not a proper state purpose at all and suggest that, if it were, the Texas statutes are overboard in protecting it since the law fails to distinguish between married and unwed mothers.

A second reason is concerned with abortion as a medical procedure. When most criminal abortion laws were first enacted, the procedure was a hazardous one for the woman. This was particularly true prior to the development of antisepsis.

Modern medical techniques have altered this situation. Appellants and various amici refer to medical data indicating that abortion in early pregnancy, that is, prior to the end of first trimester, although not without its risk, is now relatively safe. Mortality rates for women undergoing early abortions, where the procedure is legal, appear to be as low as or lower than the rates for normal childbirth. Consequently, any interest of the State in protecting the woman from an inherently hazardous procedure, except when it would be equally dangerous for her to forgo it, has largely disappeared. Of course, important state interests in the area of health and medical standards do remain. The State has a legitimate interest in seeing to it that abortion, like any other medical procedure, is performed under circumstances that insure maximum safety for the patient. This interest obviously extends at least to the performing physician and his staff, to the facilities involved, to the availability of after-care, and to adequate provision for any complication or emergency that might arise. The prevalence of high mortality rates at illegal "abortion mills" strengthens, rather than weakens, the State's interest in regulating the conditions under which abortions are performed. Moreover, the risk to the woman increases as her pregnancy continues. Thus the State retains a definite interest in protecting the woman's own health and safety when an abortion is proposed at a late stage of pregnancy.

The third reason is the State's interest — some phrase it in terms of duty — in protecting prenatal life. Some of the argument for this justification rests on the theory that a new human life is present from the moment of conception. The State's interest and general obligation to protect life then extends, it is argued, to prenatal life. Only when the life of the pregnant mother herself is at stake, balanced against the life she carries within her, should the interest of the embryo or fetus not prevail. Logically, of course, a legitimate state interest in this area need not stand or fall on acceptance of the belief that life begins at conception or at some other point prior to live birth. In assessing the State's interest, recognition may be given to the less rigid claim that as long as at least *potential life* is involved, the State may assert interests beyond the protection of the pregnant woman alone. . . .

It is with these interests, and the weight to be attached to them, that this case is concerned.

VIII

The Constitution does not explicitly mention any right of privacy. In a line of decisions, however, going back perhaps as far as Union Pacific R. Co. v. Botsford, 141 U.S. 250, 251 (1891), the Court has recognized that a right of personal privacy, or a guarantee of certain areas or zones of privacy, does exist under the Constitution. In varying contexts the Court or individual Justices have indeed found at least the roots of that right in the First Amendment, Stanley v. Georgia, 394 U.S. 557, 564 (1969); in the Fourth and Fifth Amendments, Terry v. Ohio, 392 U.S. 1, 8-9 (1968), Katz v. United States, 389 U.S. 347, 350 (1967), Boyd v. United States, 116 U.S. 616 (1886), see Olmstead v. United States, 277 U.S. 438, 478 (1928) (Brandeis, J., dissenting); in the penumbras of the Bill of Rights, Griswold v. Connecticut, 381 U.S. 479, 484-485 (1965); in the Ninth Amendment, id., at 486 (Goldberg, J., concurring); or in the concept of liberty guaranteed by the first section of the Fourteenth Amendment, see Meyer v. Nebraska, 262 U.S. 390, 399 (1923). These decisions make it clear that only personal rights that can be deemed "fundamental" or "implicit in the concept of ordered liberty," Palko v. Connecticut, 302 U.S. 319, 325 (1937), are included in this guarantee of personal privacy. They also make it clear that the right has some extension to activities relating to marriage, Loving v. Virginia, 388 U.S. 1, 12 (1967), procreation, Skinner v. Oklahoma, 316 U.S. 535, 541-542 (1942), contraception, Eisenstadt v. Baird, 405 U.S. 438, 453-454 (1972); id., at 460, 463-65 (White, J., concurring), family relationships, Prince v. Massachusetts, 321 U.S. 158, 166 (1944), and child rearing and education, Pierce v. Society of Sisters, 268 U.S. 510, 535 (1925), Meyer v. Nebraska, supra.

This right of privacy, whether it be founded in the Fourteenth Amendment's concept of personal liberty and restrictions upon state action, as we feel it is, or, as the District Court determined, in the Ninth Amendment's reservation of rights to the people, is broad enough to encompass a woman's decision whether or not to terminate her pregnancy. . . . The Court's decisions recognizing a right of privacy also acknowledge that some state regulation in areas protected by that right is appropriate. As noted above, a state may properly assert important interests in safeguarding health, in maintaining medical standards, and in protecting potential life. At some point in pregnancy, these respective interests become sufficiently compelling to sustain regulation of the factors that govern the abortion decision. The privacy right involved, therefore, cannot be said to be absolute. In fact, it is not clear to us that the claim asserted by some amici that one has an unlimited right to do with one's body as one pleases bears a close relationship to the right of privacy previously articulated in the Court's decisions. The Court has refused to recognize an unlimited right of this kind in the past. Jacobson v. Massachusetts, 197 U.S. 11 (1905) (vaccination); Buck v. Bell, 274 U.S. 200 (1927) (sterilization).

We therefore conclude that the right of personal privacy includes the abortion decision, but that this right is not unqualified and must be considered against important state interests in regulation. . . .

Where certain "fundamental rights" are involved, the Court has held that regulation limiting these rights may be justified only by a "compelling state interest," . . . and that legislative enactments must be narrowly drawn to express only the legitimate state interests at stake. . . .

IX

. . . Appellant, as has been indicated, claims an absolute right that bars any state imposition of criminal penalties in the area. Appellee argues that the State's determination to recognize and protect prenatal life from and after conception constitutes a compelling state interest. As noted above, we do not agree fully with either formulation.

A. The appellee and certain amici argue that the fetus is a "person" within the language and meaning of the Fourteenth Amendment. In support of this they outline at length and in detail the well-known facts of fetal development. If this suggestion of personhood is established, the appellant's case, of course, collapses, for the fetus' right to life is then guaranteed specifically by the Amendment. The appellant conceded as much on reargument. On the other hand, the appellee conceded on reargument that no case could be cited that holds that a fetus is a person within the meaning of the Fourth Amendment. . . .

[We are persuaded] that the word "person," as used in the Fourteenth Amendment, does not include the unborn. This is in accord with the results reached in those few cases where the issue has been squarely presented.

This conclusion, however, does not of itself fully answer the contentions raised by Texas, and we pass on to other considerations.

B. The pregnant woman cannot be isolated in her privacy. She carries an embryo and, later, a fetus, if one accepts the medical definitions of the developing young in the human uterus. See Dorland's Illustrated Medical Dictionary, 478-479, 547 (24th ed. 1965). The situation therefore is inherently different from marital intimacy, or bedroom possession of obscene material, or marriage, or procreation, or education, with which Eisenstadt, Griswold, Stanley, Loving, Skinner, Pierce, and Meyer were respectively concerned. As we have intimated above, it is reasonable and appropriate for a State to decide that at some point in time another interest, that of health of the mother or that of potential human life, becomes significantly involved. The woman's privacy is no longer sole and any right of privacy she possesses must be measured accordingly. . . .

We need not resolve the difficult question of when life begins. When those trained in the respective disciplines of medicine, philosophy, and theology are unable to arrive at any consensus, the judiciary, at this point in the development of man's knowledge, is not in a position to speculate as to the answer.

It should be sufficient to note briefly the wide divergency of thinking on this most sensitive and difficult question. There has always been strong support for the view that life does not begin until live birth. . . . As we have noted, the common law found greater significance in quickening. Physicians and their scientific colleagues have regarded that event with less interest and have tended to focus either upon conception or upon live birth or upon the interim point at which the fetus becomes "viable," that is, potentially able to live outside the mother's womb, albeit with artificial aid. Viability is usually placed at about seven months (28 weeks) but may occur earlier, even at 24 weeks. The Aristotelian theory of "mediate animation," that held sway throughout the Middle Ages and the Renaissance in Europe, continued to be official Roman Catholic dogma until the 19th century, despite opposition to this "ensoulment" theory from those in the Church who would recognize the existence of life from the moment of conception. The latter is now, of course, the official belief of the Catholic Church. As one of the briefs amicus discloses, this is a view strongly held by many non-Catholics as well, and by many physicians. Substantial problems for precise definition of this view are posed, however, by new embryological data that purport to indicate that conception is a "process" over time, rather than an event, and by new medical techniques such as menstrual extraction, the "morning after" pill, implantation of embryos, artificial insemination, and even artificial wombs. . . .

X

. . . In view of all this, we do not agree that, by adopting one theory of life, Texas may override the rights of the pregnant woman that are at stake. We repeat, however, that the State does have an important and legitimate interest in preserving and protecting the health of the pregnant woman, whether she be a resident of the State or a nonresident who seeks medical consultation and treatment there, and that it has still *another* important and legitimate interest in protecting the potentiality of human life. These interests are separate and distinct. Each grows in substantiality as the woman approaches term and, at a point during pregnancy, each becomes "compelling."

With respect to the State's important and legitimate interest in the health of the mother, the "compelling" point, in the light of present medical knowledge, is at approximately the end of the first trimester. This is so because of the now established medical fact, . . . that until the end of the first trimester mortality in abortion is less than mortality in normal childbirth. It follows that, from and after this point, a State may regulate the abortion procedure to the extent that the regulation reasonably relates to the preservation and protection of maternal health. Examples of permissible state regulation in this area are requirements as to the qualifications of the person who is to perform the abortion; as to the licensure of that person; as to the facility in which the procedure is to be performed, that is, whether it must be a hospital or may be a clinic or some other place of less-than-hospital status; as to the licensing of the facility; and the like.

This means, on the other hand, that, for the period of pregnancy prior to this "compelling" point, the attending physician, in consultation with his patient, is free to determine, without regulation by the State, that in his medical judgment the patient's pregnancy should be terminated. If that decision is reached, the judgment may be effectuated by an abortion free of interference by the State.

With respect to the State's important and legitimate interest in potential life, the "compelling" point is at viability. This is so because the fetus then presumably has the capability of meaningful life outside the mother's womb. State regulation protective of fetal life after viability thus has both logical and biological justifications. If the State is interested in protecting fetal life after viability, it may go so far as to proscribe abortion during that period except when it is necessary to preserve the life or health of the mother.

Measured against these standards, Art. 1196 of the Texas Penal Code, in restricting legal abortions to those "procured or attempted by medical advice for the purpose of saving the life of the mother," sweeps too broadly. The statute makes no distinction between abortions performed early in pregnancy and those performed later, and it limits to a single reason, "saving" the mother's life, the legal justification of the procedure. The statute, therefore, cannot survive the constitutional attack made upon it here.

This conclusion makes it unnecessary for us to consider the additional challenge to the Texas statute asserted on grounds of vagueness. See United States v. Vuitch, 402 U.S. 62, 67-72 (1971). . . .[h]

NOTE Reaction to Roe

Roe v. Wade has been criticized as an instance of judicial legislation no more justifiable than the substantive due process holdings of the Lochner era. Witness the following selection from Ely, The Wages of Crying Wolf: A Comment on Roe v. Wade, 82 Yale L.J. 920, 935-936 (1973): "What is frightening about Roe is that this super-protected right [of a woman to choose an abortion as an aspect of her right of "privacy"] is not inferable from the language of the Constitution, the framers' thinking respecting the specific problem in issue, any general value derivable from the provisions they included, or the nation's governmental structure. Nor is it explainable in terms of the unusual political impotence of the group judicially protected vis-à-vis the interest that legislatively prevailed over it. And that, I believe . . . is a charge that can responsibly be leveled at no other decision of the past twenty years." See also Epstein, Substantive Due Process by Any Other Name: The Abortion Cases, 1973 Sup. Ct. Rev. 159. For arguments defending the decision against the Lochner analogy, see Heymann & Barzelay, The Forest and the Trees: Roe v. Wade and Its Critics, 53 B.U.L. Rev. 765 (1973); Tribe, The Supreme Court, 1972 Term — Foreword: Toward a Model of Roles in the Due Process of Life and Law, 87 Harv. L. Rev. 1 (1973).

Consider the application of the following words of Justice Holmes in a speech made in 1913: ". . . It cannot be helped, it is as it should be, that the law is behind the times. . . . As law embodies beliefs that have triumphed in the battle of ideas and then have translated themselves into action, while there still is doubt, while opposite convictions still keep a battle front against each other, the time for law has not come; the notion destined to prevail is not yet entitled to the field. It is a misfortune if a judge reads his conscious or unconscious sympathy with one side or the other prematurely into the law, and forgets that what seem to him to be first principles are believed by half his fellow men to be wrong. . . . Judges are apt to be naif, simple-minded men, and they need something of Mephistopheles. We too need education in the obvious — to learn to transcend our own convictions and to leave room for much that we hold dear to be done away with short of revolution by the orderly change of law.

"I have no belief in panaceas and almost none in sudden ruin. I believe with Montesquieu that if the chance of a battle — I may add, the passage of a law — has ruined a state, there was a general cause at work that made the state ready to perish by a single battle or law. Hence I am not much interested one way or the other in the nostrums now so strenuously urged. . . . For most of the things that properly can be called evils in the present state of law I think the main remedy, as for the evils of public opinion, is for us to

---

[h] Concurring opinions of Chief Justice Burger and Justices Douglas and Stewart as well as dissenting opinions of Justices White and Rehnquist are omitted. — ED.

grow more civilized." The Occasional Speeches of Justice Oliver Wendell Holmes 171-73 (M. Howe ed. 1962).

Is judicial review more consonant with democratic political theory when it is addressed to old laws than when it is directed to contemporary laws? Are there two questions here: whether a law does indeed reflect prevailing social or moral norms; and if so, whether the law nevertheless violates a constitutional guarantee?

NOTE **The Developing Right of Privacy**

The disagreement among the Justices on the textual locus of the constitutional right of privacy recognized in Griswold and Roe — whether in the "penumbras" of the Bill of Rights, the "saving clause" of the Ninth Amendment, or the Fifth and Fourteenth Amendment guarantees of due process — reflects not only their discomfort that their decisions might resemble too much the "subjective" substantive due process decisions of the late nineteenth and early twentieth centuries but also uncertainty as to the scope and purposes of a right "to be let alone." Recent opinions have expounded a right of privacy that is variously linked to a citizen's right to be free of state intrusion in certain activities, relationships, and places; yet it is uncertain which of these factors is determinant and, therefore, which the right of privacy is designed to protect.

In Roe and the companion case of Doe v. Bolton, 410 U.S. 179 (1973), the Court made clear that a woman's right to decide without state interference whether to bear a child forbade the state from restricting except in carefully described and limited respects the woman's ability to obtain an abortion. Contrast the decisions limiting Stanley v. Georgia, 394 U.S. 557 (1969). There, the Court struck down as violative of a constitutional right of privacy a Georgia statute making criminal the "mere private possession of obscene matter." The constitutional right was founded in the First Amendment, as applied to the states by the Fourteenth. Writing for the Court, Justice Marshall said:

"[Appellant] is asserting the right to read or observe what he pleases — the right to satisfy his intellectual and emotional needs in the privacy of his own home. He is asserting the right to be free from state inquiry into the contents of his library. Georgia contends that appellant does not have these rights, that there are certain types of materials that the individual may not read or even possess. Georgia justifies this assertion by arguing that the films in the present case are obscene. But we think that mere categorization of these films as "obscene" is insufficient justification for such a drastic invasion of personal liberties guaranteed by the First and Fourteenth Amendments. Whatever may be the justifications for other statutes regulating obscenity, we do not think they reach into the privacy of one's own home. If the First Amendment means anything, it means that a State has no business telling a man, sitting alone in his own house, what books he may read or what films he may watch. Our whole constitutional heritage rebels at the thought of giving government the power to control men's minds."

Decisions since Stanley have indicated that it was the location of the appellant's activities, a consideration more appropriate to a Fourth Amendment analysis than to a First, rather than simply the nature of appellant's activities, that entitled him to assert a right of privacy. And the Court has made clear that the right to read whatever one wants in the privacy of one's home does not carry with it protection of the means by which one might obtain reading materials. Thus, in United States v. Reidel, 402 U.S. 351 (1971), the Court upheld a federal statute making it a criminal offense to transport obscene materials. The Court rejected the argument, based on Stanley, that "if a person has a right to receive and possess this material, then someone must have the right to deliver it to him."

Reidel was carried further, however, in the 1972 Term. In United States v. Orito, 413 U.S. 139 (1973), the Court held that Stanley does not prohibit prosecution for transportation of obscene matter in interstate commerce, even in a private vehicle and even if the matter is intended for the private use of the transporter. Justices Douglas, Brennan, Stewart, and Marshall dissented, citing Stanley. Compare United States v. 12 200-ft. Reels of Super 8mm. Film, 413 U.S. 123 (1973), and United States v. Thirty-seven Photographs, 402 U.S. 363 (1971), which reached the same result regarding obscene matter being imported into the United States.

In Paris Adult Theatre I v. Slaton, 413 U.S. 49 (1973), the Court rejected a claim based on both Stanley and Roe that the constitutional right of privacy extended to protect the exhibition of obscene films to consenting adults. Writing for the Court, Chief Justice Burger discussed the sources and extent of the privacy right:

"Even assuming that petitioners have vicarious standing to assert potential customers' rights, it is unavailing to compare a theatre, open to the public for a fee, with the private home of Stanley v. Georgia . . . and the marital bedroom of Griswold v. Connecticut. . . .

"Our prior decisions recognizing a right to privacy guaranteed by the Fourteenth Amendment included 'only those personal rights that can be deemed "fundamental" or "implicit in the concept of ordered liberty." Palko v. Connecticut. . . .' . . . This privacy right encompasses and protects the personal intimacies of the home, the family, marriage, motherhood, procreation, and child rearing. . . . Nothing, however, in this Court's decisions intimates that there is any 'fundamental' privacy right 'implicit in the concept of ordered liberty' to watch obscene movies in places of public accommodation.

"If obscene material unprotected by the First Amendment in itself carried with it a 'penumbra' of constitutionally protected privacy, this Court would not have found it necessary to decide Stanley on the narrow basis of the 'privacy of the home,' which was hardly more than a reaffirmation that 'a man's home is his castle.'[13] . . . Moreover, we have declined to equate the privacy of the home relied on in Stanley with a 'zone' of 'privacy' that follows a distributor or a consumer of obscene materials wherever he goes. . . . The idea of a 'privacy' right and a place of public accommodation are, in this context, mutually exclusive. Conduct or depictions of conduct that the state police power can prohibit on a public street does not become automatically protected by the Constitution merely because the conduct is moved to a bar or a 'live' theatre stage, any more than a 'live' performance of a man and woman locked in a sexual embrace at high noon in Times Square is protected by the Constitution because they simultaneously engage in a valid political dialogue.

"It is also argued that the State has no legitimate interest in 'control [of] the moral content of a person's thoughts,' Stanley v. Georgia, . . . and we need not quarrel with this. But we reject the claim that the State of Georgia is here attempting to control the minds or thoughts of those who patronize theatres. Preventing unlimited display or distribution of obscene material, which by definition lacks any serious literary, artistic, political, or scientific value as communication . . . is distinct from a control of reason and the intellect. . . . Where communication of ideas, protected by the First Amendment, is not involved, nor the particular privacy of the home protected by Stanley, nor any of the other 'areas or zones' of constitutionally protected privacy, the mere fact that, as a consequence, some human 'utterances' or 'thoughts' may be incidentally affected does not bar the State from acting to protect legitimate state interests. . . . The fantasies of a drug addict are his own and beyond the reach of government, but government regulation of drug sales is not prohibited by the Constitution. . . .

---

[13] "The protection afforded by Stanley v. Georgia, supra, is restricted to a place, the home. In contrast, the constitutionally protected privacy of family, marriage, motherhood, procreation, and child rearing is not just concerned with a particular place, but with a protected intimate relationship. Such protected privacy extends to the doctor's office, the hospital, the hotel room, or as otherwise required to safeguard the right to intimacy involved. Cf. Roe v. Wade, supra, . . . ; Griswold v. Connecticut, supra. . . . Obviously, there is no necessary or legitimate expectation of privacy which would extend to marital intercourse on a street corner or a theatre stage.

1128 Chapter Sixteen. Substantive Rights

"Finally, petitioners argue that conduct which directly involves 'consenting adults' only has, for that sole reason, a special claim to constitutional protection. Our Constitution established a broad range of conditions on the exercise of power by the States, but for us to say that our Constitution incorporates the proposition that conduct involving consenting adults only is always beyond state regulations, that is a step we are unable to take."

Compare the dissenting opinion of Justice Brennan, joined by Justices Stewart and Marshall, citing both Stanley and Roe:

"[S]ince the attempt to curtail unprotected speech necessarily spills over into the area of protected speech, the effort to serve this speculative interest through the suppression of obscene material must tread heavily on rights protected by the First Amendment.

". . . Like the proscription of abortions, the effort to suppress obscenity is predicated on unprovable, although strongly held, assumptions about human behavior, morality, sex, and religion. The existence of these assumptions cannot validate a statute that substantially undermines the guarantees of the First Amendment, any more than the existence of similar assumptions on the issue of abortion can validate a statute that infringes the constitutionally protected privacy interests of a pregnant woman.

"If, as the Court today assumes, 'a state legislature may . . . act on the . . . assumption that . . . commerce in obscene books, or public exhibitions focused on obscene conduct, have a tendency to exert a corrupting and debasing impact leading to antisocial behavior,' . . . then it is hard to see how state-ordered regimentation of our minds can ever be forestalled. For if a State may, in an effort to maintain or create a particular moral tone, prescribe what its citizens cannot read or cannot see, then it would seem to follow that in pursuit of that same objective a State could decree that its citizens must read certain books or must view certain films. . . ."

(Justice Douglas dissented in a separate opinion.)

For commentary on the implications of the privacy right recognized in Stanley v. Georgia, see Katz, Privacy and Pornography: Stanley v. Georgia, 1969 Sup. Ct. Rev. 203; Note, Still More Ado About Dirty Books (and Pictures): Stanley, Reidel, and Thirty-seven Photographs, 81 Yale L.J. 309 (1971); Comment, Stanley v. Georgia: New Directions in Obscenity Regulation?, 48 Texas L. Rev. 646 (1970).

But if Stanley, and for that matter Griswold v. Connecticut, may be restricted to the proposition that the state may not, without a compelling justification, invade the privacy of certain places, the home or the marital bedroom, they may be brought with little difficulty into relatively traditional constitutional rubrics. Compare, e.g., Katz v. United States, 389 U.S. 347 (1967), holding that electronic monitoring of petitioner's telephone conversation from a pay phone booth violated his "justifiable expectation of privacy" under the Fourth Amendment. Other recent holdings, particularly Roe v. Wade, appear to strike out in new directions that may not be so confined.

Although the right of privacy has not yet made great inroads on the government's authority to control obscenity, the constitutional right recognized in Griswold and Roe has a potentially broad and various impact. In the hands of challengers to government action, and in the courts, it has emerged as a protean doctrine, capable of changing shape to challenge a variety of forms of governmental regulation. See Hufstedler, Directions and Misdirections of a Constitutional Right of Privacy, 26 Record of N.Y.C.B.A. 546 (1971); Note, On Privacy: Constitutional Protection for Personal Liberty, 48 N.Y.U.L. Rev. 670 (1973) Note, Roe and Paris: Does Privacy Have a Principle?, 26 Stan. L. Rev. 1161 (1974). First, Roe and Griswold have led to greater concern with claims that governmental action interferes with a certain (or uncertain) sphere of autonomy or personal liberty — the ability to make a decision or behave in a certain way without interference by the state. This has been recognized as implicit in Roe in decisions holding that husbands or parents of pregnant women may not be required to give permission before an abortion may legally be performed and may not maintain an action to enjoin an abortion despite their interest in the life of the fetus. See, e.g., Bellotti v. Baird, 393 F. Supp. 847 (D.

Mass. 1975), vacated and remanded, 96 S. Ct. 2857 (1976) (parental consent); Doe v. Doe, 314 N.E.2d 128 (Mass. 1974); Tribe, The Supreme Court, 1972 Term — Foreword: Toward a Model of Roles in the Due Process of Life and Law, 87 Harv. L. Rev. 1 (1973). Courts have further discussed whether the privacy right may reach to private consensual sexual acts, such as sodomy and homosexuality. See Cotner v. Henry, 394 F.2d 873 (7th Cir. 1968) (invalidating Indiana sodomy statute as applied to private consensual acts between married people); Note, The Constitutionality of Laws Forbidding Homosexual Conduct, 72 Mich. L. Rev. 1613 (1974). But see Doe v. Commonwealth's Attorney, 425 U.S. 901 (1976), aff'g 403 F. Supp. 1199 (E.D. Va.) (sustaining a state law against sodomy between consenting adult homosexuals in private). Claimants have also argued, but with varied success, that the right of privacy protects private use and possession of marijuana. See Louisiana Affiliate of the Natl. Org. for the Reform of Marijuana Laws (NORML) v. Guste, 380 F.2d 404 (E.D. La. 1974) (motion for three-judge court denied for lack of substantial federal question); United States v. Drotar, 416 F.2d 914 (5th Cir. 1969), vacated on other grounds, 402 U.S. 939 (1971); Commonwealth v. Leis, 355 Mass. 189, 243 N.E.2d 898 (1969). But see the unanimous decision of the Alaska Supreme Court, Ravin v. State, 537 P.2d 494 (1975), that the federal (and the state) right of privacy protected the possession of marijuana by an adult for personal consumption in the home. And see Village of Belle Terre v. Boraas, 416 U.S. 1 (1974) (Marshall, J., dissenting) (exclusionary zoning and right of association of unmarried adults wishing to live together). Consider finally in this aspect of privacy the right of a mental patient to refuse treatment which might constitute an "impermissible tinkering with the mental processes," Mackey v. Procunier, 477 F.2d 877 (9th Cir. 1973) (reversing dismissal of complaint); Developments in the Law — Civil Commitment of the Mentally Ill, 87 Harv. L. Rev. 1190, 1194-1195 & n.12 (1974).

Second, the right to privacy announced in Griswold and Roe may bar some forms of governmental regulation which only indirectly affect a protected personal relationship. See Berch v. Stahl, 373 F. Supp. 412 (W.D.N.C. 1974) (interference with mail between state prisoner and wife may be an unconstitutional infringement of rights attached to the marital state); Hess v. Schlesinger, 486 F.2d 1311 (D.C. cir. 1973) (reversal of dismissal of complaint; lower court declined to inquire whether a 60-day limit on visits of Marine dependents to soldiers stationed in the Western Pacific violates the right to marital privacy).

Third, the concern with personal privacy shown in Griswold and Roe may account for greater regard being shown for the protection of individuals from governmental collection or publication of information regarding their private lives. In Doe v. McMillan, 412 U.S. 306 (1973), parents of District of Columbia school children sought to enjoin further distribution of a House committee report on the D.C. schools which reproduced the disciplinary records of named students. Writing for the Court, Mr. Justice White decided only the issue of immunity asserted by various defendants, and the case was remanded to proceed against the nonlegislative defendants, liability to be determined according to whether the publication served a legitimate legislative interest. Justice Douglas, concurring in an opinion joined by Justices Brennan and Marshall, stated his view that the naming of individual students was clearly outside any legitimate purpose and would entitle plaintiffs to injunctive relief, if otherwise appropriate. Compare Tarlton v. Saxbe, 507 F.2d 1116 (D.C. Cir. 1974), and Menard v. Saxbe, 498 F.2d 1017 (D.C. Cir. 1974), on the responsibility of the Federal Bureau of Investigation for the accuracy of the criminal records it maintains. Considering the doctor-patient relationship as an aspect of the right to privacy, Roe v. Ingraham, 403 F. Supp. 931 (S.D.N.Y. 1975), rev'd sub nom. Whalen v. Roe, 97 S. Ct. 869 (1977), found privacy impermissibly invaded by a N.Y. law that required that the names and addresses of patients receiving certain prescribed drugs be filed with the state. For cases upholding reporting requirements against right-of-privacy challenge, see Illinois State Employees Assn. v. Walker, 57 Ill. 2d 512, 315 N.E. 2d 9

(1974) (Governor's order that state employees file financial disclosure statements); Schulman v. New York City Dept. of Health and Hospitals, 44 A.D. 2d 482, 355 N.Y.S. 2d 781 (1974) (reporting name of mother on fetal death certificate filed after abortion). More case law, albeit nonconstitutional, about the privacy that is to be protected from public disclosure can be found in connection with the provision of the Freedom of Information Act that exempts from public access those files "the disclosure of which would constitute a clearly unwarranted invasion of personal privacy." 5 U.S.C. §552(b)(6) (1970). See Note, The Freedom of Information Act, page 1259 infra.

See also California Bankers Assn. v. Shultz, 416 U.S. 21 (1974), where the Court rejected, 6 to 3, First, Fourth, and Fifth Amendment challenges to recordkeeping and reporting requirements imposed by the Bank Secrecy Act of 1970. The Court's decision turned, however, largely on questions of standing and prematurity. Justices Powell and Blackmun, concurring, stated that should the regulations promulgated under the act be amended to effect a "significant extension" of the reporting requirements, "substantial and difficult constitutional questions" would arise. "In their full reach, the reports apparently authorized by the open-ended language of the Act touch upon intimate areas of an individual's personal affairs. Financial transactions can reveal much about a person's activities, associations, and beliefs. At some point governmental intrusion upon these areas would implicate legitimate expectations of privacy. Moreover, the potential for abuse is particularly acute where, as here, the legislative scheme permits access to this information without invocation of the judicial process. . . ." See Note, The Supreme Court, 1973 Term, 88 Harv. L. Rev. 41, 188-196 (1974).

Section C. FREEDOM OF SPEECH AND ASSOCIATION

1. The Search for Standards

INTRODUCTORY NOTE

It is a striking fact that before the adoption of the Fourteenth Amendment, and in truth long after its enactment, questions concerning the meaning and scope of the guarantees of free speech and a free press in the First Amendment and equivalent clauses in state constitutions did not fall to the judiciary for determination with any frequency. The efforts of the Federalists through the Alien and Sedition Acts to control political opinion were so fruitlessly unhappy that it became something close to a constitutional tradition that such federal legislation, if it were ever enacted again, would be unconstitutional.

The Sedition Act of 1798 expired by its own terms in 1801. Those of its provisions which dealt with speech were as follows:

"SEC. 2. . . . [I]f any person shall write, print, utter or publish . . . any false, scandalous and malicious writings against the government of the United States, or either house of the Congress of the United States, or the President of the United States, with intent to defame the said government, or either house of the said Congress, or the said President, or to bring them or either of them, into contempt or disrepute; or to excite against them or either or any of them, the hatred of the good people of the United States, or to stir up sedition within the United States, or to excite any unlawful combinations therein, for opposing or resisting any law of the United States, or any act of the President of the United States, done in pursuance of any such law, or of the powers in him vested by the Constitution of the United States, or to resist, oppose or defeat any such law or act, or to aid, encourage or abet any hostile designs of any foreign nation against the United States, their people or government, then such person, being thereof convicted before any court of the United States having jurisdiction thereof, shall be punished by a fine not exceeding two thousand dollars, and by imprisonment not exceeding two years.

"SEC. 3. . . . . [I]f any person shall be prosecuted under this act, for the writing or publishing any libel aforesaid, it shall be lawful for the defendant . . . to give in evidence in his defence, the truth of the matter contained in the publication charged as a libel. And the jury who shall try the cause, shall have a right to determine the law and the fact, under the direction of the court, as in other cases." I Stat. 596.

Significant cases under the Sedition Act are printed, with discerning comment, in Wharton, State Trials (1849). The story of the enforcement of the Alien and Sedition Acts is told briefly and with liveliness in Miller, Crisis in Freedom (1951). A more detailed account of the statutes and their enforcement is given in James Morton Smith's Freedom's Fetters (1956). Problems of federalism, sometimes overlooked in discussions of the Sedition Act, are emphasized in a review of Miller's book in 66 Harv. L. Rev. 189 (1952).

The law of seditious libel as it was enforced by British authority in India and as it was affected by traditions of freedom is discussed in Niharendu Dutt Majumdar v. The King Emperor, [1942] F.C.R. 38.

The condition of freedom in the years of controversy concerning slavery is described with detailed learning in Nye, Fettered Freedom (1949). See also Savage, Controversy over Distribution of Abolitionist Literature (1938). During the Civil War, when it might have been expected that repressive legislation would be enacted by Congress to control seditious publications and disloyal speeches, the matter was handled by the executive and by military tribunals established by Lincoln's authority. Thus it came about that the issues of free speech were subordinated to problems of the scope of executive power in wartime and never, as such, received careful judicial consideration. See Randall, Constitutional Problems Under Lincoln 176-179, 525-529 (rev. ed. 1951). The extraordinary liberties of the press in the Confederacy are described in Coulter, The Confederate States of America, 1861-1865 (1950). The libertarian reflections of Mr. Justice Field in Ex parte Jackson, 96 U.S. 727, 733 (1877), did not make a great mark on constitutional doctrine.

It was not until the Congress adopted a series of statutes during World War I that the courts of the United States were called upon to consider the effect which the First Amendment had on that legislation, and, later, the effect which the due process clause of the Fourteenth Amendment had on state legislation dealing with speech, advocacy, and the press.

Schenck v. United States 249 U.S. 47, 39 S. Ct. 247, 63 L. Ed. 470 (1919)

MR. JUSTICE HOLMES delivered the opinion of the court:

This is an indictment in three counts. The first charges a conspiracy to violate the Espionage Act of June 15, 1917, chap. 30, §3, 40 Stat. at L. 217, 219, by causing and attempting to cause insubordination, etc., in the military and naval forces of the United States, and to obstruct the recruiting and enlistment service of the United States, when the United States was at war with the German Empire; to wit, that the defendant wilfully conspired to have printed and circulated to men who had been called and accepted for military service under the Act of May 18, 1917, a document set forth and alleged to be calculated to cause such insubordination and obstruction. The count alleges overt acts in pursuance of the conspiracy, ending in the distribution of the document set forth. The second count alleges a conspiracy to commit an offense against the United States; to wit, to use the mails for the transmission of matter declared to be nonmailable by title 12, §2, of the Act of June 15, 1917, to wit, the above-mentioned document, with an averment of the same overt acts. The third count charges an unlawful use of the mails for the transmission of the same matter and otherwise as above. The defendants were found guilty on all the counts. They set up the First Amendment to the Constitution, forbidding Congress to make any law abridging the freedom of speech or of the press, and, bringing the case here on that ground, have argued some other points also of which we must dispose.

The document in question, upon its first printed side, recited the 1st section of the Thirteenth Amendment, said that the idea embodied in it was violated by the Conscription Act, and that a conscript is little better than a convict. In impassioned language it intimated that conscription was despotism in its worst form and a monstrous wrong against humanity, in the interest of Wall Street's chosen few. It said: "Do not submit to intimidation"; but in form at least confined itself to peaceful measures, such as a petition for the repeal of the act. The other and later printed side of the sheet was headed, "Assert Your Rights." It stated reasons for alleging that anyone violated the Constitution when he refused to recognize "your right to assert your opposition to the draft," and went on: "If you do not assert and support your rights, you are helping to deny or disparage rights which it is the solemn duty of all citizens and residents of the United States to retain." It described the arguments on the other side as coming from cunning politicians and a mercenary capitalist press, and even silent consent to the Conscription Law as helping to support an infamous conspiracy. It denied the power to send our citizens away to foreign shores to shoot up the people of other lands, and added that words could not express the condemnation such cold-blooded ruthlessness deserves, etc., etc., winding up, "You must do your share to maintain, support, and uphold the rights of the people of this country." Of course the document would not have been sent unless it had been intended to have some effect, and we do not see what effect it could be expected to have upon persons subject to the draft except to influence them to obstruct the carrying of it out. The defendants do not deny that the jury might find against them on this point.

But it is said, suppose that that was the tendency of this circular, it is protected by the First Amendment to the Constitution. Two of the strongest expressions are said to be quoted respectively from well-known public men. It well may be that the prohibition of laws abridging the freedom of speech is not confined to previous restraints, although to prevent them may have been the main purpose, as intimated in Patterson v. Colorado, 205 U.S. 454, 462. We admit that in many places and in ordinary times the defendants, in saying all that was said in the circular, would have been within their constitutional rights. But the character of every act depends upon the circumstances in which it is done. Aikens v. Wisconsin, 195 U.S. 194, 205, 206. The most stringent protection of free speech would not protect a man in falsely shouting fire in a theater, and causing a panic. It does not even protect a man from an injunction against uttering words that may have all the effect of force. Gompers v. Buck's Stove & Range Co., 221 U.S. 418, 439. The question in every case is whether the words used are used in such circumstances and are of such a nature as to create a clear and present danger that they will bring about the substantive evils that Congress has a right to prevent. It is a question of proximity and degree. When a nation is at war many things that might be said in time of peace are such a hindrance to its effort that their utterance will not be endured so long as men fight, and that no Court could regard them as protected by any constitutional right. It seems to be admitted that if an actual obstruction of the recruiting service were proved, liability for words that produced that effect might be enforced. The Statute of 1917, in §4, punishes conspiracies to obstruct as well as actual obstruction. If the act, (speaking, or circulating a paper,) its tendency and the intent with which it is done, are the same, we perceive no ground for saying that success alone warrants making the act a crime. Goldman v. United States, 245 U.S. 474, 477. Indeed, that case might be said to dispose of the present contention if the precedent covers all media concludendi. But as the right to free speech was not referred to specially we have thought fit to add a few words. . . .

Judgments affirmed.

Section C. **Freedom of Speech and Association** 1133

Abrams v. United States 250 U.S. 616, 40 S. Ct. 17, 63 L. Ed. 1173 (1919)

[The five defendant-appellants had been convicted of conspiring to violate the Federal Espionage Act of 1917, as amended in 1918 (see Schenck case, supra), and had been sentenced to twenty years' imprisonment. A majority of the Supreme Court, in an opinion by Mr. Justice Clarke, sustained the conviction.]

MR. JUSTICE HOLMES dissenting.

This indictment is founded wholly upon the publication of two leaflets which I shall describe in a moment. The first count charges a conspiracy pending the war with Germany to publish abusive language about the form of government of the United States, laying the preparation and publishing of the first leaflet as overt acts. The second count charges a conspiracy pending the war to publish language intended to bring the form of government into contempt, laying the preparation and publishing of the two leaflets as overt acts. The third count alleges a conspiracy to encourage resistance to the United States in the same war and to attempt to effectuate the purpose by publishing the same leaflets. The fourth count lays a conspiracy to incite curtailment of production of things necessary to the prosecution of the war and to attempt to accomplish it by publishing the second leaflet to which I have referred.

The first of these leaflets says that the President's cowardly silence about the intervention in Russia reveals the hypocrisy of the plutocratic gang in Washington. It intimates that "German militarism combined with allied capitalism to crush the Russian revolution" — goes on that the tyrants of the world fight each other until they see a common enemy — working class enlightenment, when they combine to crush it; and that now militarism and capitalism combined, though not openly, to crush the Russian revolution. It says that there is only one enemy of the workers of the world and that is capitalism; that it is a crime for workers of America, &c., to fight the workers' republic of Russia, and ends "Awake! Awake, you Workers of the World! Revolutionists." A note adds "It is absurd to call us pro-German. We hate and despise German militarism more than do you hypocritical tyrants. We have more reasons for denouncing German militarism than has the coward of the White House."

The other leaflet, headed "Workers — Wake Up," with abusive language says that America together with the Allies will march for Russia to help the Czecho-Slovaks in their struggle against the Bolsheviki, and that this time the hypocrites shall not fool the Russian emigrants and friends of Russia in America. It tells the Russian emigrants that they now must spit in the face of the false military propaganda by which their sympathy and help to the prosecution of the war have been called forth and says that with the money they have lent or are going to lend "they will make bullets not only for the Germans but also for the Workers Soviets of Russia," and further, "Workers in the ammunition factories, you are producing bullets, bayonets, cannon, to murder not only the Germans, but also your dearest, best, who are in Russia and are fighting for freedom." It then appeals to the same Russian emigrants at some length not to consent to the "inquisitionary expedition to Russia," and says that the destruction of the Russian revolution is "the politics of the march to Russia." The leaflet winds up by saying "Workers, our reply to this barbarous intervention has to be a general strike!," and after a few words on the spirit of revolution, exhortations not to be afraid, and some usual tall talk ends "Woe unto those who will be in the way of progress. Let solidarity live! The Rebels."

In this case sentences of twenty years imprisonment have been imposed for the publishing of two leaflets that I believe the defendants had as much right to publish as the Government has to publish the Constitution of the United States now vainly invoked by them. Even if I am technically wrong and enough can be squeezed from these poor and puny anonymities to turn the color of legal litmus paper; I will add, even if what I think the necessary intent were shown; the most nominal punishment seems to me all that possibly could be inflicted, unless the defendants are to be made to suffer not for what the indictment alleges but for the creed that they avow — a creed that I believe to be the creed of ignorance and immaturity when honestly held, as I see no reason to doubt that it was held here, but which, although made the subject of examination at the trial, no one has a right even to consider in dealing with the charges before the Court.

Persecution for the expression of opinions seems to me perfectly logical. If you have no doubt of your premises or your power and want a certain result with all your heart you naturally express your wishes in law and sweep away all opposition. To allow opposition by speech seems to indicate that you think the speech impotent, as when a man says that he has squared the circle, or that you do not care whole-heartedly for the result, or that you doubt either your power or your premises. But when men have realized that time has upset many fighting faiths, they may come to believe even more than they believe the very foundations of their own conduct that the ultimate good desired is better reached by free trade in ideas — that the best test of truth is the power of the thought to get itself accepted in the competition of the market, and that truth is the only ground upon which their wishes safely can be carried out. That at any rate is the theory of our Constitution. It is an experiment, as all life is an experiment. Every year if not every day we have to wager our salvation upon some prophecy based upon imperfect knowledge. While that experiment is part of our system I think that we should be eternally vigilant against attempts to check the expression of opinions that we loathe and believe to be fraught with death, unless they so imminently threaten immediate interference with the lawful and pressing purposes of the law that an immediate check is required to save the country. I wholly disagree with the argument of the Government that the First Amendment left the common law as to seditious libel in force. History seems to me against the notion. I had conceived that the United States through many years had shown its repentance for the Sedition Act of 1798, by repaying fines that it imposed. Only the emergency that makes it immediately dangerous to leave the correction of evil counsels to time warrants making any exception to the sweeping command, "Congress shall make no law . . . abridging the freedom of speech." Of course I am speaking only of expressions of opinion and exhortations, which were all that were uttered here, but I regret that I cannot put into more impressive words my belief that in their conviction upon this indictment the defendants were deprived of their rights under the Constitution of the United States.

Mr. Justice Brandeis concurs with the foregoing opinion.

Gitlow v. New York 268 U.S. 652, 45 S. Ct. 625, 69 L. Ed. 1138 (1925)

Mr. Justice Sanford delivered the opinion of the court:

Benjamin Gitlow was indicted in the supreme court of New York, with three others, for the statutory crime of criminal anarchy. New York Penal Laws, §§ 160, 161. He was separately tried, convicted, and sentenced to imprisonment. The judgment was affirmed by the appellate division and by the court of appeals. 195 App. Div. 773, 234 N.Y. 132 and 539. The case is here on writ of error to the supreme court, to which the record was remitted. 260 U.S. 703.

The contention here is that the statute, by its terms and as applied in this case, is repugnant to the due process clause of the 14th Amendment. Its material provisions are:

"§ 160. Criminal anarchy defined. — Criminal anarchy is the doctrine that organized government should be overthrown by force or violence, or by assassination of the executive head or of any of the executive officials of government, or by any unlawful means. The advocacy of such doctrine either by word of mouth or writing is a felony.

"§ 161. Advocacy of criminal anarchy. — Any person who:

"1. By word of mouth or writing advocates, advises or teaches the duty, necessity or propriety of overthrowing or overturning organized government by force or violence, or by assassination of the executive head or of any of the executive officials of government, or by any unlawful means; or,

"2. Prints, publishes, edits, issues or knowingly circulates, sells, distributes or publicly displays any book, paper, document, or written or printed matter in any form, containing or advocating, advising or teaching the doctrine that organized government should be overthrown by force, violence or any unlawful means. . . .

"Is guilty of a felony and punishable" by imprisonment or fine, or both.

The indictment was in two counts. The first charged that the defendant had advocated, advised and taught the duty, necessity, and propriety of overthrowing and overturning organized government by force, violence, and unlawful means, by certain writings therein set forth, entitled, "The Left Wing Manifesto"; the second, that he had printed, published, and knowingly circulated and distributed a certain paper called "The Revolutionary Age," containing the writings set forth in the first count, advocating, advising, and teaching the doctrine that organized government should be overthrown by force, violence, and unlawful means.

There was no evidence of any effect resulting from the publication and circulation of the Manifesto. . . .

The statute does not penalize the utterance or publication of abstract "doctrine" or academic discussion having no quality of incitement to any concrete action. It is not aimed against mere historical or philosophical essays. It does not restrain the advocacy of changes in the form of government by constitutional and lawful means. What it prohibits is language advocating, advising, or teaching the overthrow of organized government by unlawful means. These words imply urging to action. . . .

The Manifesto, plainly, is neither the statement of abstract doctrine nor, as suggested by counsel, mere prediction that industrial disturbances and revolutionary mass strikes will result spontaneously in an inevitable process of evolution in the economic system. It advocates and urges in fervent language mass action which shall progressively foment industrial disturbances, and, through political mass strikes and revolutionary mass action, overthrow and destroy organized parliamentary government. It concludes with a call to action in these words: "The proletariat revolution and the Communist reconstruction of society — *the struggle for these* — is now indispensable. . . . The Communist International calls the proletariat of the world to the final struggle!" This is not the expression of philosophical abstraction, the mere prediction of future events: it is the language of direct incitement. . . .

For present purposes we may and do assume that freedom of speech and of the press — which are protected by the First Amendment from abridgment by Congress — are among the fundamental personal rights and "liberties" protected by the due process clause of the Fourteenth Amendment from impairment by the States. We do not regard the incidental statement in Prudential Ins. Co. v. Cheek, 259 U.S. 530, 543, that the Fourteenth Amendment imposes no restrictions on the States concerning freedom of speech, as determinative of this question. . . .

By enacting the present statute the state has determined, through its legislative body, that utterances advocating the overthrow of organized government by force, violence, and unlawful means, are so inimical to the general welfare, and involve such danger of substantive evil, that they may be penalized in the exercise of its police power. That determination must be given great weight. Every presumption is to be indulged in favor of the validity of the statute. Mugler v. Kansas, 123 U.S. 623, 661. . . . That utterances inciting to the overthrow of organized government by unlawful means present a sufficient danger of substantive evil to bring their punishment within the range of legislative discretion is clear. Such utterances, by their very nature, involve danger to the public peace and to the security of the state. They threaten breaches of the peace and ultimate revolution. And the immediate danger is none the less real and substantial because the effect of a given utterance cannot be accurately foreseen. The state cannot reasonably be required to measure the danger from every such utterance in the nice balance of a jeweler's scale. A single revolutionary spark may kindle a fire that, smoldering for a time, may burst into a sweeping and destructive conflagration. It cannot be said that the state is acting arbitrarily or unreasonably when, in the exercise of its judgment as to the measures necessary to protect the public peace and safety, it seeks to extinguish the spark without waiting until it has enkindled the flame or blazed into the conflagration. It cannot reasonably be required to defer the adoption of measures for its own peace and safety until the revolutionary utterances lead to actual disturbances of the public peace or imminent and immediate danger of its own destruction; but it may, in the exercise of its judgment, suppress the threatened danger in its incipiency. . . .

We cannot hold that the present statute is an arbitrary or unreasonable exercise of the police power of the state, unwarrantably infringing the freedom of speech or press; and we must and do sustain its constitutionality.

This being so it may be applied to every utterance — not too trivial to be beneath the notice of the law — which is of such a character and used with such intent and purpose as to bring it within the prohibition of the statute. This principle is illustrated in Fox v. Washington, 236 U.S. 277; Abrams v. United States, 250 U.S. 616, 624; Schaefer v. United States, 251 U.S. 479, 480; Pierce v. United States, 252 U.S. 239, 250, 251, and Gilbert v. Minnesota, 254 U.S. p. 333. In other words, when the legislative body has determined generally, in the constitutional exercise of its discretion, that utterances of a certain kind involve such danger of substantive evil that they may be punished, the question whether any specific utterance coming within the prohibited class is likely, in and of itself, to bring about the substantive evil, is not open to consideration. It is sufficient that the statute itself be constitutional, and that the use of the language comes within its prohibition.

And finding, for the reasons stated, that the statute is not in itself unconstitutional, and that it has not been applied in the present case in derogation of any constitutional right, the judgment of the Court of Appeals is affirmed.

Mr. Justice Holmes dissenting:

Mr. Justice Brandeis and I are of opinion that this judgment should be reversed. The general principle of free speech, it seems to me, must be taken to be included in the Fourteenth Amendment, in view of the scope that has been given to the word "liberty" as there used, although perhaps it may be accepted with a somewhat larger latitude of interpretation than is allowed to Congress by the sweeping language that governs, or ought to govern, the laws of the United States. If I am right, then I think that the criterion sanctioned by the full court in Schenck v. United States, 249 U.S. 47, 52, applies: "The question in every case is whether the words used are used in such circumstances and are of such a nature as to create a clear and present danger that they will bring about the substantive evils that [the state] has a right to prevent." It is true that in my opinion this criterion was departed from in Abrams v. United States, 250 U.S. 616, but the convictions that I expressed in that case are too deep for it to be possible for me as yet to believe that it and Schaefer v. United States, 251 U.S. 466, have settled the law. If what I think the correct test is applied, it is manifest that there was no present danger of an attempt to overthrow the government by force on the part of the admittedly small minority who shared the defendant's views. It is said that this Manifesto was more than a theory, that it was an incitement. Every idea is an incitement. It offers itself for belief, and, if believed, it is acted on unless some other belief outweighs it, or some failure of energy stifles the movement at its birth. The only difference between the expression of an opinion and an incitement in the narrower sense is the speaker's enthusiasm for the result. Eloquence may set fire to reason. But whatever may be thought of the redundant discourse before us, it had no chance of starting a present conflagration. If, in the long run, the beliefs expressed in proletarian dictatorship are destined to be accepted by the dominant forces of the community, the only meaning of free speech is that they should be given their chance and have their way.

If the publication of this document had been laid as an attempt to induce an uprising against government at once, and not at some indefinite time in the future, it would have presented a different question. The object would have been one with which the law might deal, subject to the doubt whether there was any danger that the publication could produce any result; or, in other words, whether it was not futile and too remote from possible consequences. But the indictment alleges the publication and nothing more.

NOTE The Learned Hand Alternative to the Clear and Present Danger Test

What other tests, besides the clear and present danger test, might Holmes and the Court have considered in these various prosecutions of "subversive" advocacy? Should the Court, in particular, have used a test that focused less on the circumstances of the speech and more on its characteristics? Consider the following opinion of Judge Learned Hand in a case under the Espionage Act of 1917, decided two years before Schenck. In construing the act to allow punishment of speech only if it constituted "direct incitement" to illegal action, Hand held that the act did not mean to reach "hostile criticism" which might do damage to the war effort due to the circumstances of the speech.

Recent disclosures about the correspondence between Holmes and Hand have confirmed that Holmes was fully aware of the Hand formula but was "impervious" to it as an alternative. See Gunther, Learned Hand and the Origins of Modern First Amendment Doctrine: Some Fragments of History, 27 Stan. L. Rev. 719 (1975). For a critical view of Justice Holmes in this period, see Ragan, Justice Oliver Wendell Holmes, Jr., Zechariah Chafee, Jr., and the Clear and Present Danger Test for Free Speech: The First Year, 1919, 58 J. Am. Hist. 24 (1971).

Judge Hand's decision was reversed on appeal. Masses Publishing Co. v. Patten, 246 F.24 (2d Circ. 1917). Flatly disagreeing with Hand's construction, the Court of Appeals said: "If the natural and reasonable effect of what is said is to encourage resistance to a law, and the words are used in an endeavor to persuade to resistance, it is immaterial that the duty to resist is not mentioned, or the interest of the persons addressed in resistance is not suggested." Nor were other reactions to Hand's opinion very supportive: Zechariah Chafee, Jr. wrote to Hand, "Your test is surely easier to apply although our old friend Marc Anthony's speech is continually thrown at me in discussion." Gunther, supra, at 773.

Would the early Hand formula have yielded a different result in such cases as Dennis, infra page 1162? Has the formula reappeared in contemporary tests of "subversive" advocacy, as in Brandenburg, infra page 1173?

Masses Pub. Co. v. Patten 244 F. 535 (S.D.N.Y 1917)

The plaintiff applies for a preliminary injunction against the postmaster of New York to forbid his refusal to accept its magazine in the mails under the following circumstances: The plaintiff is a publishing company in the city of New York engaged in the production of a monthly revolutionary journal called "The Masses," containing both text and cartoons, each issue of which is ready for the mails during the first ten days of the preceding month. In July, 1917, the postmaster of New York, acting upon the direction of the Postmaster General, advised the plaintiff that the August number to which he had had access would be denied the mails under the Espionage Act of June 15, 1917. . . .

The second cartoon shows a cannon to the mouth of which is bound the naked figure of a youth, to the wheel that of a woman, marked "Democracy," and upon the carriage that of a man, marked "Labor." On the ground kneels a draped woman marked "Motherhood" in a posture of desperation, while her infant lies on the ground. The import of this cartoon is obviously that conscription is the destruction of youth, democracy, and labor, and the desolation of the family. No one can dispute that it was intended to rouse detestation for the draft law. . . .

The four pieces of text are annexed to the end of this report as addenda, A, B, C and D. After that part of B so set forth, the article continues, showing the hardships and maltreatment of a number of English conscientious objectors, partly from excerpts out of their letters, partly from reports of what they endured. These statements show much brutality in the treatment of these persons. . . .

LEARNED HAND, DISTRICT JUDGE (after stating the facts as above). . . .

It must be remembered at the outset, and the distinction is of critical consequence throughout, that no question arises touching the war powers of Congress. It may be that Congress may forbid the mails to any matter which tends to discourage the successful prosecution of the war. It may be that the fundamental personal rights of the individual must stand in abeyance, even including the right of the freedom of the press, though that is not here in question. . . .

The next phrase [of §3 of the act] relied upon is that which forbids any one from willfully causing insubordination, disloyalty, mutiny, or refusal of duty in the military or naval forces of the United States. The defendant's position is that to arouse discontent and disaffection among the people with the prosecution of the war and with the draft tends to promote a mutinous and insubordinate temper among the troops. This, too, is true; men who become satisfied that they are engaged in an enterprise dictated by the unconscionable selfishness of the rich, and effectuated by a tyrannous disregard for the will of those who must suffer and die, will be more prone to insubordination than those who have faith in the cause and acquiesce in the means. Yet to interpret the word "cause" so broadly would, as before, involve necessarily as a consequence the suppression of all hostile criticism, and of all opinion except what encouraged and supported the existing policies, or which fell within the range of temperate argument. It would contradict the normal assumption of democratic government that the suppression of hostile criticism does not turn upon the justice of its substance or the decency and propriety of its temper. Assuming that the power to repress such opinion may rest in Congress in the throes of a struggle for the very existence of the state, its exercise is so contrary to the use and wont of our people that only the clearest expression of such a power justifies the conclusion that it was intended.

The defendant's position, therefore, in so far as it involves the suppression of the free utterance of abuse and criticism of the existing law, or of the policies of the war, is not, in my judgment, supported by the language of the statute. Yet there has always been a recognized limit to such expressions, incident indeed to the existence of any compulsive power of the state itself. One may not counsel or advise others to violate the law as it stands. Words are not only the keys of persuasion, but the triggers of action, and those which have no purport but to counsel the violation of law cannot by any latitude of interpretation be a part of that public opinion which is the final source of government in a democratic state. The defendant asserts not only that the magazine indirectly through its propaganda leads to a disintegration of loyalty and a disobedience of law, but that in addition it counsels and advises resistance to existing law, especially to the draft. The consideration of this aspect of the case more properly arises under the third phrase of section 3, which forbids any willful obstruction of the recruiting or enlistment service of the United States, but, as the defendant urges that the magazine falls within each phrase, it is as well to take it up now. To counsel or advise a man to an act is to urge upon him either that it is his interest or his duty to do it. While, of course, this may be accomplished as well by indirection as expressly, since words carry the meaning that they impart, the definition is exhaustive, I think, and I shall use it. Political agitation, by the passions it arouses or the convictions it engenders, may in fact stimulate men to the violation of law. Detestation of existing policies is easily transformed into forcible resistance of the authority which puts them in execution, and it would be folly to disregard the causal relation between the two. Yet to assimilate agitation, legitimate as such, with direct incitement to violent resistance, is to disregard the tolerance of all methods of political agitation which in normal times is a safeguard of free government. The distinction is not a scholastic subterfuge, but a hard-bought acquisition in the fight for freedom, and the purpose to disregard it must be evident when the power exists. If one stops short of urging upon others that it is their duty or their interest to resist the law, it seems to me one should not be held to have attempted to cause its violation. If that be not the test, I can see no escape from the conclusion that under this section every political agitation which can be shown to be apt to create a seditious temper is illegal. I am confident that by such language Congress had no such revolutionary purpose in view.

It seems to me, however, quite plain that none of the language and none of the cartoons in this paper can be thought directly to counsel or advise insubordination or mutiny, without a violation of their meaning quite beyond any tolerable understanding. I come, therefore, to the third phrase of the section, which forbids any one from willfully obstructing the recruiting or enlistment service of the United States. I am not prepared to assent to the plaintiff's position that this only refers to acts other than words, nor that the act thus defined must be shown to have been successful. One may obstruct without preventing, and the mere obstruction is an injury to the service; for it throws impediments in its way. Here again, however, since the question is of the expression of opinion, I construe the sentence, so far as it restrains public utterance, as I have construed the other two, and as therefore limited to the direct advocacy of resistance to the recruiting and enlistment service. If so, the inquiry is narrowed to the question whether any of the challenged matter may be said to advocate resistance to the draft, taking the meaning of the words with the utmost latitude which they can bear.

As to the cartoons it seems to me quite clear that they do not fall within such a test. Certainly the nearest is that entitled "Conscription," and the most that can be said of that is that it may breed such animosity to the draft as will promote resistance and strengthen the determination of those disposed to be recalcitrant. There is no intimation that, however hateful the draft may be, one is in duty bound to resist it, certainly none that such resistance is to one's interest. I cannot, therefore, even with the limitations which surround the power of the court, assent to the assertion that any of the cartoons violate the act.

The text offers more embarrassment. The poem to Emma Goldman and Alexander Berkman, at most, goes no further than to say that they are martyrs in the cause of love among nations. Such a sentiment holds them up to admiration, and hence their conduct to possible emulation. The paragraph in which the editor offers to receive funds for their appeal also expresses admiration for them, but goes no further. The paragraphs upon conscientious objectors are of the same kind. They go no further than to express high admiration for those who have held and are holding out for their convictions even to the extent of resisting the law. . . .

The defendant's action was based, as I understand it, not so much upon the narrow question whether these . . . passages actually advocated resistance, though that point was distinctly raised, as upon the doctrine that the general tenor and animus of the paper as a whole were subversive to authority and seditious in effect. I cannot accept this test under the law as it stands at present. The tradition of English-speaking freedom has depended in no small part upon the merely procedural requirement that the state point with exactness to just that conduct which violates the law. It is difficult and often impossible to meet the charge that one's general ethos is treasonable; such a latitude for construction implies a personal latitude in administration which contradicts the normal assumption that law shall be embodied in general propositions capable of some measure of definition. The whole crux of this case turns indeed upon this thesis. I make no question of the power of Congress to establish a personal censorship of the press under the war power; that question, as I have already said, does not arise. I am quite satisfied that it has not as yet chosen to create one, and with the greatest deference it does not seem to me that anything here challenged can be illegal upon any other assumption.

It follows that the plaintiff is entitled to the usual preliminary injunction.

Whitney v. California 274 U.S. 357, 47 Ct. 641, 71 L. Ed. 1095 (1927)

MR. JUSTICE SANFORD delivered the opinion of the court:

By a criminal information filed in the superior court of Alameda county, California, the plaintiff in error was charged, in five counts, with violations of the Criminal Syndicalism Act of that state. Statutes 1919, chap. 188, p. 281. She was tried, convicted on the first count, and sentenced to imprisonment. The judgment was affirmed by the District Court of Appeal. 57 Cal. App. 449. Her petition to have the case heard by the Supreme Court was denied. Id. 453. And the case was brought here on a writ of error which was allowed by the Presiding Justice of the Court of Appeal, the highest court of the state in which a decision could be had. Judicial Code, §237.

On the first hearing in this Court, the writ of error was dismissed for want of jurisdiction, 269 U.S. 530. Thereafter, a petition for rehearing was granted (269 U.S. 538), and the case was again heard and reargued both as to the jurisdiction and the merits.

The pertinent provisions of the Criminal Syndicalism Act are:

"Section 1. The term 'criminal syndicalism' as used in this act is hereby defined as any doctrine or precept advocating, teaching or aiding and abetting the commission of crime, sabotage (which word is hereby defined as meaning wilful and malicious physical damage or injury to physical property), or unlawful acts of force and violence or unlawful methods of terrorism as a means of accomplishing a change in industrial ownership or control, or effecting any political change.

"Sec. 2. Any person who: . . . (4) Organizes or assists in organizing, or is or knowingly becomes a member of, any organization, society, group or assemblage of persons organized or assembled to advocate, teach or aid and abet criminal syndicalism. . . .

"Is guilty of a felony and punishable by imprisonment."

The first count of the information, on which the conviction was had, charged that on or about November 28, 1919, in Alameda county, the defendant, in violation of the Criminal Syndicalism Act, "did then and there unlawfully, wilfully, wrongfully, deliberately and feloniously organize and assist in organizing, and was, is, and knowingly became a member of an organization, society, group and assemblage of persons organized and assembled to advocate, teach, aid and abet criminal syndicalism." . . .

By enacting the provisions of the Syndicalism Act the state has declared, through its legislative body, that to knowingly be or become a member of or assist in organizing an association to advocate, teach or aid and abet the commission of crimes or unlawful acts of force, violence or terrorism as a means of accomplishing industrial or political changes, involves such danger to the public peace and the security of the state, that these acts should be penalized in the exercise of its police power. That determination must be given great weight. Every presumption is to be indulged in favor of the validity of the statute (Mugler v. Kansas, 123 U.S. 623, 661), and it may not be declared unconstitutional unless it is an arbitrary or unreasonable attempt to exercise the authority vested in the state in the public interest (Great Northern R. Co. v. Clara City, 246 U.S. 434, 439).

The essence of the offense denounced by the act is the combining with others in an association for the accomplishment of the desired ends through the advocacy and use of criminal and unlawful methods. It partakes of the nature of a criminal conspiracy. See People v. Steelik, 187 Cal 376. That such united and joint action involves even greater danger to the public peace and security than the isolated utterances and acts of individuals, is clear. We cannot hold that, as here applied, the act is an unreasonable or arbitrary exercise of the police power of the state, unwarrantably infringing any right of free speech, assembly or association, or that those persons are protected from punishment by the due process clause who abuse such rights by joining and furthering an organization thus menacing the peace and welfare of the state.

We find no repugnancy in the Syndicalism Act as applied in this case to either the due process or equal protection clause of the Fourteenth Amendment, on any of the grounds upon which its validity has been here challenged.

The order dismissing the writ of error will be vacated and set aside, and the judgment of the Court of Appeal affirmed.

MR. JUSTICE BRANDEIS, concurring:

Miss Whitney was convicted of the felony of assisting in organizing, in the year 1919, the Communist Labor Party of California, of being a member of it, and of assembling with it. These acts are held to constitute a crime, because the party was formed to teach criminal syndicalism. The statute which made these acts a crime restricted the right of free speech and of assembly theretofore existing. The claim is that the statute, as applied, denied to Miss Whitney the liberty guaranteed by the Fourteenth Amendment.

Despite arguments to the contrary which had seemed to me persuasive, it is settled that the due process clause of the Fourteenth Amendment applies to matters of substantive law as well as to matters of procedure. Thus all fundamental rights comprised within the term "liberty" are protected by the Federal Constitution from invasion by the states. The right of free speech, the right to teach, and the right of assembly are, of course, fundamental rights. [Citations omitted.] These may not be denied or abridged. But, although the rights of free speech and assembly are fundamental, they are not in their nature absolute. Their exercise is subject to restriction, if the particular restriction proposed is required in order to protect the state from destruction or from serious injury, political, economic or moral. That the necessity which is essential to a valid restriction does not exist unless speech would produce, or is intended to produce, a clear and imminent danger of some substantive evil which the state constitutionally may seek to prevent has been settled. See Schenck v. United States, 249 U.S. 47, 52.

It is said to be the function of the legislature to determine whether at a particular time and under the particular circumstances the formation of, or assembly with, a society organized to advocate criminal syndicalism constitutes a clear and present danger of substantive evil; and that by enacting the law here in question the legislature of California determined that question in the affirmative. Compare Gitlow v. New York, 268 U.S. 652, 668-671. The legislature must obviously decide, in the first instance, whether a danger exists which calls for a particular protective measure. But where a statute is valid only in case certain conditions exist, the enactment of the statute cannot alone establish the facts which are essential to its validity. Prohibitory legislation has repeatedly been held invalid, because unnecessary, where the denial of liberty involved was that of engaging in a particular business. The power of the courts to strike down an offending law is no less when the interests involved are not property rights, but the fundamental personal rights of free speech and assembly.

This court has not yet fixed the standard by which to determine when a danger shall be deemed clear; how remote the danger may be and yet be deemed present; and what degree of evil shall be deemed sufficiently substantial to justify resort to abridgment of free speech and assembly as the means of protection. To reach sound conclusions on these matters, we must bear in mind why a state is, ordinarily, denied the power to prohibit dissemination of social, economic and political doctrine which a vast majority of its citizens believes to be false and fraught with evil consequence.

Those who won our independence believed that the final end of the state was to make men free to develop their faculties; and that in its government the deliberative forces should prevail over the arbitrary. They valued liberty both as an end and as a means. They believed liberty to be the secret of happiness and courage to be the secret of liberty. They believed that freedom to think as you will and to speak as you think are means indispensable to the discovery and spread of political truth; that without free speech and assembly discussion would be futile; that with them, discussion affords ordinarily adequate protection against the dissemination of noxious doctrine; that the greatest menace to freedom is an inert people; that public discussion is a political duty; and that this should be a fundamental principle of the American government. They recognized the risks to which all human institutions are subject. But they knew that order cannot be secured merely through fear of punishment for its infraction; that it is hazardous to discourage thought, hope and imagination; that fear breeds repression; that repression breeds hate; that hate menaces stable government; that the path of safety lies in the opportunity to discuss freely supposed grievances and proposed remedies; and that the fitting remedy for evil counsels is good ones. Believing in the power of reason as applied through public discussion, they eschewed silence coerced by law — the argument of force in its worst form. Recognizing the occasional tyrannies of governing majorities, they amended the Constitution so that free speech and assembly should be guaranteed.

Fear of serious injury cannot alone justify suppression of free speech and assembly. Men feared witches and burned women. It is the function of speech to free men from the bondage of irrational fears. To justify suppression of free speech there must be reasonable ground to fear that serious evil will result if free speech is practiced. There must be reasonable ground to believe that the danger apprehended is imminent. There must be reasonable ground to believe that the evil to be prevented is a serious one. Every denunciation of existing law tends in some measure to increase the probability that there will be violation of it. Condonation of a breach enhances the probability. Expressions of approval add to the probability. Propagation of the criminal state of mind by teaching syndicalism increases it. Advocacy of lawbreaking heightens it still further. But even advocacy of violation, however reprehensible morally, is not a justification for denying free speech where the advocacy falls short of incitement and there is nothing to indicate that the advocacy would be immediately acted on. The wide difference between advocacy and incitement, between preparation and attempt, between assembling and conspiracy, must be borne in mind. In order to support a finding of clear and present danger it must be shown either that immediate serious violence was to be expected or was advocated, or that the past conduct furnished reason to believe that such advocacy was then contemplated.

Those who won our independence by revolution were not cowards. They did not fear political change. They did not exalt order at the cost of liberty. To courageous, self-reliant men, with confidence in the power of free and fearless reasoning applied through the processes of popular government, no danger flowing from speech can be deemed clear and present, unless the incidence of the evil apprehended is so imminent that it may befall before there is opportunity for full discussion. If there be time to expose through discussion the falsehood and fallacies, to avert the evil by the processes of education, the remedy to be applied is more speech, not enforced silence. Only an emergency can justify repression. Such must be the rule if authority is to be reconciled with freedom. Such, in my opinion, is the command of the Constitution. It is, therefore, always open to Americans to challenge a law abridging free speech and assembly by showing that there was no emergency justifying it.

Moreover, even imminent danger cannot justify resort to prohibition of these functions essential to effective democracy, unless the evil apprehended is relatively serious. Prohibition of free speech and assembly is a measure so stringent that it would be inappropriate as the means for averting a relatively trivial harm to society. A police measure may be unconstitutional merely because the remedy, although effective as means of protection, is unduly harsh or oppressive. Thus, a state might, in the exercise of its police power, make any trespass upon the land of another a crime, regardless of the results or of the intent or purpose of the trespasser. It might, also, punish an attempt, a conspiracy, or an incitement to commit the trespass. But it is hardly conceivable that this court would hold constitutional a statute which punished as a felony the mere voluntary assembly with a society formed to teach that pedestrians had the moral right to cross unenclosed, unposted, waste

Section C. Freedom of Speech and Association

lands and to advocate their doing so, even if there was imminent danger that advocacy would lead to a trespass. The fact that speech is likely to result in some violence or in destruction of property is not enough to justify its suppression. There must be the probability of serious injury to the state. Among freemen, the deterrents ordinarily to be applied to prevent crime are education and punishment for violations of the law, not abridgment of the rights of free speech and assembly.

The California Syndicalism Act recites, in §4:

"Inasmuch as this act concerns and is necessary to the immediate preservation of the public peace and safety, for the reason that at the present time large numbers of persons are going from place to place in this state advocating, teaching and practicing criminal syndicalism, this act shall take effect upon approval by the Governor."

This legislative declaration satisfies the requirement of the Constitution of the state concerning emergency legislation. Re McDermott, 180 Cal. 783. But it does not preclude inquiry into the question whether, at the time and under the circumstances, the conditions existed which are essential to validity under the Federal Constitution. As a statute, even if not void on its face, may be challenged because invalid as applied (Dahnke-Walker Mill. Co. v. Bondurant, 257 U.S. 282), the result of such an inquiry may depend upon the specific facts of the particular case. Whenever the fundamental rights of free speech and assembly are alleged to have been invaded, it must remain open to a defendant to present the issue whether there actually did exist at the time a clear danger; whether the danger, if any, was imminent; and whether the evil apprehended was one so substantial as to justify the stringent restriction interposed by the legislature. The legislative declaration, like the fact that the statute was passed and was sustained by the highest court of the state, creates merely a rebuttable presumption that these conditions have been satisfied.

Whether, in 1919, when Miss Whitney did the things complained of, there was in California such clear and present danger of serious evil, might have been made the important issue in the case. She might have required that the issue be determined either by the court or the jury. She claimed below that the statute as applied to her violated the Federal Constitution; but she did not claim that it was void because there was no clear and present danger of serious evil, nor did she request that the existence of these conditions of a valid measure thus restricting the rights of free speech and assembly be passed upon by the court or a jury. On the other hand, there was evidence on which the court or jury might have found that such danger existed. I am unable to assent to the suggestion in the opinion of the court that assembling with a political party, formed to advocate the desirability of a proletarian revolution by mass action at some date necessarily far in the future, is not a right within the protection of the Fourteenth Amendment. In the present case, however, there was other testimony which tended to establish the existence of a conspiracy, on the part of members of the International Workers of the World, to commit present serious crimes; and likewise to show that such a conspiracy would be furthered by the activity of the society of which Miss Whitney was a member. Under these circumstances the judgment of the state court cannot be disturbed.

Our power of review in this case is limited not only to the question whether a right guaranteed by the Federal Constitution was denied (Murdock v. Memphis, 20 Wall. 590; Montana ex rel. Haire v. Rice, 204 U.S. 291, 301); but to the particular claims duly made below, and denied (Seaboard Air Line R. Co. v. Duvall, 225 U.S. 477, 485-488). We lack here the power occasionally exercised on review of judgments of lower federal courts to correct in criminal cases vital errors, although the objection was not taken in the trial court. Wiborg v. United States, 163 U.S. 632, 658-660; Clyatt v. United States, 197 U.S. 207, 221, 222. This is a writ of error to a state court. Because we may not inquire into the errors now alleged, I concur in affirming the judgment of the state court.

MR. JUSTICE HOLMES joins in this opinion.[1]

---

[1] A statute similar to the California Criminal Syndicalism Act was held unconstitutional in Brandenburg v. Ohio, 395 U.S. 444 (1969), infra page 1163. — ED.

Freund, The Great Disorder of Speech (1975) *

. . . Liberty and community, freedom of expression and its limits, were notably addressed by the great English secular trinity of Johns: Milton, Locke, and Mill. "Give me liberty to know, to utter, and to argue freely according to conscience, above all liberties." Milton's attack on licensing of printing was passionate, but it was prudently circumscribed in two, and possibly three, respects. This exalted liberty was for the exalted in belief:

"I mean not tolerated popery, and open superstition, which as it extirpates all religious and civil supremacies, so itself should be extirpate, provided first that all charitable and compassionate means be used to win and regain the weak and the misled; that also which is impious or evil absolutely either against faith or manners no law can possibly permit, that intends not to unlaw itself."

What was to be fostered in the quest for truth were "those neighboring differences, or rather indifferences," that marked the disputations among Protestant sects.

Milton's argument was circumscribed, not only doctrinally, but procedurally as well. The attack was directed against licensing, prior restraint, censorship in its most literal form. The criminal law, in its seventeenth-century mercies, remained. For those publications that, coming forth unlicensed, were "found mischievous and libellous, the fire and the executioner will be the timeliest and the most effectual remedy that man's prevention can use." Precisely why, from the point of view of either the publisher or the victim of a criminal libel, it is more obnoxious to ban the publication than to inflict condign punishment thereafter was not made clear. This is not to be critical or condescending toward the most magisterial pronouncement on the pursuit of truth, any more than it is in derogation of Democritus that his vision did not dissect the atom in the terms of Niels Bohr. The case against prior restraint remained to be elaborated by history. A third limitation in the *Areopagitica* is problematic. The fact that Milton himself subsequently served for a year as a censor of newssheets suggests, at least, that the omission in his great tract of explicit reference to that form of publication may have been deliberate.

A generation after the *Areopagitica*, John Locke extended the scope of toleration, as befits one who objected to the doctrine of innate ideas, but still with caution in the name of the social compact: ". . . those are not at all to be tolerated who deny the being of God. Promises, covenants, and oaths, which are the bonds of human society, can have no hold upon an atheist."

More than a century later, when John Stuart Mill took up the theme of liberty, the religious-political complex had receded as a threat, but there was a residual apprehension of the mob, the great unwashed. "Liberty as a principle," Mill wrote, "has no application to any state of things anterior to the time when mankind have become capable of being improved by free and equal discussion. Until then, there is nothing for them but implicit obedience to an Akbar or a Charlemagne, if they are so fortunate as to find one."

In his well-known reply to Mill, Sir James Stephen thrust at the chink in the armor. "Why then," asked Stephen, "may not educated men coerce the ignorant? What is there in the character of a very commonplace ignorant peasant or petty shopkeeper in these days which makes him a less fit subject for coercion on Mr. Mill's principle than the Hindoo nobles and princes who were coerced by Akbar?" As it might be put today, the descent from the tutelary state to the totalitarian is easy.

Each of these philosophers saw liberty of expression as an instrumental value, an aid to the apprehension of something identified as the true or the good; accordingly the limits of

---

* A selection from the fourth Jefferson Lecture in the Humanities, reprinted at 44 Am. Scholar 541, 542-545 (1975). — ED.

expression were to be drawn in light of its serviceability. What warrant then could be found for freedom of expression in the philosophy of a skeptic, or in a skeptical age? For an answer we would do well to turn to the thought of Mr. Justice Holmes, for whom "truth" was "the power of the thought to get itself accepted in the competition of the market." Freedom of expression was not instrumental in a quest; it created its own object, its Holy Grail. The principle of freedom of speech from repression was not, however, subject to the same relaxed skepticism. In Holmes's existentialism the activity of speech was of a different order from its particular content, and so the issue of freedom versus restraint was salvaged from the class of issues to be left to the competition of the market. The process, unlike any of its content, was intrinsically good; and Holmes was able to escape from his own skepticism by a hierarchy of categories akin to Bertrand Russell's theory of types.

Skepticism in a jurist is matched by humility in a theologian. Holmes, the believing unbeliever, and Reinhold Niebuhr, the unbelieving believer, reached a point of convergence. Dr. Niebuhr was speaking of moral truths and their inevitable historical corruptions and misappropriations and fragmentary formulations.

"This alone [he submitted] would justify the ultimate freedom of a democratic society, in which not even the moral presuppositions upon which the society rests are withdrawn from constant scrutiny and reexamination. Only through such freedom can the premature arrest of new vitalities in history be prevented. . . . A society which exempts ultimate principles from criticism will find difficulty in dealing with the historical forces which have appropriated these truths as their special possession."

Once a principle is established, a jurist has a special obligation to delineate its limits. Not for him the exhilaration of dangling in the void from a lofty premise; he must find his footing on the hard rung of a middle axiom. Justice Holmes found the limiting principle in the test of clear and present danger, which he appropriated from the criminal law, where it served to mark the line at which innocuous preparation for a crime passed over into a punishable attempt. Speech, then, would be privileged if, and only if, it did not create a clear and present danger of a result that society could properly forbid. The celebrated example is falsely crying "Fire!" in a crowded theater — an example, it has always seemed to me, that is singularly unhelpful. For the cry of "Fire!" is a peculiar kind of speech, not the sort that gives rise to the troublesome problems in this field. The cry is not the ordinary communication of information, or argument, or exhortation, or entertainment. It is in the nature of a preset signal to action, which could have been conveyed by lanterns in a belfry. More to the point would have been a discussion of what may be said on the stage, not in the pit.

There are difficulties with the clear-and-present-danger test apart from the illustration. For one thing, it does not analyze the causal link between the speech and the danger: although the speech may be moderate and rational, the audience may be hostile and emotional. A clear and present danger of violence is created, but in which direction should the strong arm of the law be pointed? Another difficulty is that no account is taken of the relative seriousness of the danger (it might be simply a trespass on barren land) compared with the importance of the speech. Moreover, the test of certainty and imminence is subject to loose construction by an apprehensive jury, and even to manipulation by judges, as when the Smith Act, directed against the teaching of communism, was sustained by use of a sliding scale, weighing the gravity of the danger discounted by its improbability, thus countenancing speculation in historical futures, the most dangerous form of gambling with the liberty of speech. And finally, the clear-and-present-danger test, although it has its uses in the area of seditious speech where it arose, is not a broad-spectrum sovereign remedy for such other complaints as defamation, obscenity, and invasions of privacy, where the complex of interests at stake requires closer diagnosis and more refined treatment.

Near v. Minnesota 283 U.S. 697, 51 S. Ct. 625, 75 L. Ed. 1357 (1931)

MR. CHIEF JUSTICE HUGHES delivered the opinion of the court:

Chapter 285 of the Session Laws of Minnesota for the year 1925 provides for the abatement, as a public nuisance, of a "malicious, scandalous and defamatory newspaper, magazine or other periodical." Section one of the act is as follows:

"Section 1: Any person who, as an individual, or as a member or employee of a firm, or association or organization, or as an officer, director, member or employee of a corporation, shall be engaged in the business of regularly or customarily producing, publishing or circulating, having in possession, selling or giving away,

"(a) an obscene, lewd and lascivious newspaper, magazine, or other periodical, or

"(b) a malicious, scandalous and defamatory newspaper, magazine or other periodical, is guilty of a nuisance, and all persons guilty of such nuisance may be enjoined, as hereinafter provided.

"Participation in such business shall constitute a commission of such nuisance and render the participant liable and subject to the proceedings, orders and judgments provided for in this act. Ownership, in whole or in part, directly or indirectly, of any such periodical, or of any stock or interest in any corporation or organization which owns the same in whole or in part, or which publishes the same, shall constitute such participation.

"In actions brought under (b) above, there shall be available the defense that the truth was published with good motives and for justifiable ends and in such actions of periodicals taking place more than three months before the commencement of the action."

Section two provides that whenever any such nuisance is committed or exists, the county attorney of any county where any such periodical is published or circulated, or, in case of his failure or refusal to proceed upon written request in good faith of a reputable citizen, the attorney general, or upon like failure or refusal of the latter, any citizen of the county, may maintain an action in the district court of the county in the name of the state to enjoin perpetually the persons committing or maintaining any such nuisance from further committing or maintaining it. Upon such evidence as the court shall deem sufficient, a temporary injunction may be granted. The defendants have the right to plead by demurrer or answer, and the plaintiff may demur or reply as in other cases.

The action, by section three, is to be "governed by the practice and procedure applicable to civil actions for injunctions," and after trial the court may enter judgment permanently enjoining the defendants found guilty of violating the act from continuing the violation and, "in and by such judgment, such nuisance may be wholly abated." The court is empowered, as in other cases of contempt, to punish disobedience to a temporary or permanent injunction by fine of not more than $1,000 or by imprisonment in the county jail for not more than twelve months.

Under this statute, clause (b), the County Attorney of Hennepin County brought this action to enjoin the publication of what was described as a "malicious, scandalous and defamatory newspaper, magazine and periodical," known as "The Saturday Press," published by the defendants in the city of Minneapolis. The complaint alleged that the defendants, on September 24, 1927, and on eight subsequent dates in October and November, 1927, published and circulated editions of that periodical which were "largely devoted to malicious, scandalous and defamatory articles." . . .

Without attempting to summarize the contents of the voluminous exhibits attached to the complaint, we deem it sufficient to say that the articles charged in substance that a Jewish gangster was in control of gambling, bootlegging and racketeering in Minneapolis, and that law enforcing officers and agencies were not energetically performing their duties. Most of the charges were directed against the Chief of Police; he was charged with gross neglect of duty, illicit relations with gangsters, and with participation in graft. The County Attorney was charged with knowing the existing conditions and with failure to take adequate measures to remedy them. The Mayor was accused of inefficiency and dereliction. One member of the grand jury was stated to be in sympathy with the gangsters. A special grand jury and a special prosecutor were demanded to deal with the situation in general, and, in particular, to investigate an attempt to assassinate one Guilford, one of the original defendants, who, it appears from the articles was shot by gangsters after the first issue of the periodical had been published. There is no question but that the articles made serious accusations against the public officers named and others in connection with the prevalence of crimes and the failure to expose and punish them.

[Upon a demurrer by the defendant publisher, the Supreme Court of the state found the statute constitutional. The trial court then found that the publication did constitute a public nuisance as defined by the statute and perpetually enjoined the defendant from publishing any further "malicious, scandalous or defamatory newspaper, as defined by law." From the affirmance of this order by the state supreme court, Near appealed.]

This statute, for the suppression as a public nuisance of a newspaper or periodical, is unusual, if not unique, and raises questions of grave importance transcending the local interests involved in the particular action. It is no longer open to doubt that the liberty of the press and of speech is within the liberty safeguarded by the due process clause of the Fourteenth Amendment from invasion by state action. It was found impossible to conclude that this essential personal liberty of the citizen was left unprotected by the general guaranty of fundamental rights of person and property. . . .

First. The statute is not aimed at the redress of individual or private wrongs. Remedies for libel remain available and unaffected. . . .

Second. The statute is directed not simply at the circulation of scandalous and defamatory statements with regard to private citizens, but at the continued publication by newspapers and periodicals of charges against public officers of corruption, malfeasance in office, or serious neglect of duty. . . .

Third. The object of the statute is not punishment, in the ordinary sense, but suppression of the offending newspaper or periodical. . . .

Fourth. The statute not only operates to supress the ofending newspaper or periodical but to put the publisher under an effective censorship. When a newspaper or periodical is found to be "malicious, scandalous and defamatory," and is suppressed as such, resumption of publication is punishable as a contempt of court by fine or imprisonment. Thus, where a newspaper or periodical has been suppressed because of the circulation of charges against public officers of official misconduct, it would seem to be clear that the renewal of the publication of such charges would constitute a contempt and that the judgment would lay a permanent restraint upon the publisher, to escape which he must satisfy the court as to the character of a new publication. . . .

The question is whether a statute authorizing such proceedings in restraint of publication is consistent with the conception of the liberty of the press as historically conceived and guaranteed. In determining the extent of the constitutional protection, it has been generally, if not universally, considered that it is the chief purpose of the guaranty to prevent previous restraints upon publication. The struggle in England, directed against the legislative power of the licenser, resulted in renunciation of the censorship of the press. . . . The distinction was early pointed out between the extent of the freedom with respect to censorship under our constitutional system and that enjoyed in England. Here, as Madison said, "The great and essential rights of the people are secured against legislative as well as against executive ambition. They are secured, not by laws paramount to prerogative, but by constitutions paramount to laws. This security of the freedom of the press requires that it should be exempt not only from previous restraint by the executive, as in Great Britain, but from legislative restraint also." Report on the Virginia Resolutions, Madison's Works, vol. 4, p. 543. . . . In the present case, we have no occasion to inquire as to the permissible scope of subsequent punishment. For whatever wrong the appellant has committed or may commit, by his publications, the state appropriately affords both public and private redress by its libel laws. As has been noted, the statute in question does not deal with punishments; it provides for no punishment, except in case of contempt for violation of the court's order, but for suppression and injunction, that is, for restraint upon publication.

The objection has also been made that the principle as to immunity from previous restraint is stated too broadly, if every such restraint is deemed to be prohibited. That is undoubtedly true; the protection even as to previous restraint is not absolutely unlimited. But the limitation has been recognized only in exceptional cases. "When a nation is at war many things that might be said in time of peace are such a hindrance to its effort that their utterance will not be endured so long as men fight and that no court could regard them as protected by any constitutional right." Schenck v. United States, 249 U.S. 47, 52. No one would question but that a government might prevent actual obstruction to its recruiting service or the publication of the sailing dates of transports or the number and location of troops. On similar grounds, the primary requirements of decency may be enforced against obscene publications. The security of the community life may be protected against incitements to acts of violence and the overthrow by force of orderly government. The constitutional guaranty of free speech does not "protect a man from an injunction against uttering words that may have all the effect of force. Gompers v. Bucks Stove & Range Co., 221 U.S. 418, 439." Schenck v. United States, supra. These limitations are not applicable here. Nor are we now concerned with questions as to the extent of authority to prevent publications in order to protect private rights according to the principles governing the exercise of the jurisdiction of courts of equity.

The exceptional nature of its limitations places in a strong light the general conception that liberty of the press, historically considered and taken up by the Federal Constitution, has meant, principally, although not exclusively, immunity from previous restraints or censorship. The conception of the liberty of the press in this country had broadened with the exigencies of the colonial period and with the efforts to secure freedom from oppressive administration. That liberty was especially cherished for the immunity it afforded from previous restraint of the publication of censure of public officers and charges of official misconduct. . . .

The statute in question cannot be justified by reason of the fact that the publisher is permitted to show, before injunction issues, that the matter published is true and is published with good motives and for justifiable ends. If such a statute, authorizing suppression and injunction on such a basis, is constitutionally valid, it would be equally permissible for the legislature to provide that at any time the publisher of any newspaper could be brought before a court, or even an administrative officer (as the constitutional protection may not be regarded as resting on mere procedural details) and required to produce proof of the truth of his publication, or of what he intended to publish, and of his motives, or stand enjoined. If this can be done, the legislature may provide machinery for determining in the complete exercise of its discretion what are justifiable ends and restrain publication accordingly. And it would be but a step to a complete system of censorship. The recognition of authority to impose previous restraint upon publication in order to protect the community against the circulation of charges of misconduct, and especially of official misconduct, necessarily would carry with it the admission of the authority of the censor against which the constitutional barrier was erected. . . .

Equally unavailing is the insistence that the statute is designed to prevent the circulation of scandal which tends to disturb the public peace and to provoke assaults and the commission of crime. Charges of reprehensible conduct, and in particular of official malfeasance, unquestionably create a public scandal, but the theory of the constitutional guaranty is that even a more serious public evil would be caused by authority to prevent publication. . . .

For these reasons we hold the statute, so far as it authorized the proceedings in this action under clause (b) of section one, to be an infringement of the liberty of the press guaranteed by the Fourteenth Amendment. We should add that this decision rests upon the operation and effect of the statute, without regard to the question of the truth of the charges contained in the particular periodical. The fact that the public officers named in this case, and those associated with the charges of official dereliction, may be deemed to be impeccable, cannot affect the conclusion that the statute imposes an unconstitutional restraint upon publication.

Judgment reversed.

MR. JUSTICE BUTLER, dissenting: . . .

The Minnesota statute does not operate as a *previous* restraint on publication within the proper meaning of that phrase. It does not authorize administrative control in advance such as was formerly exercised by the licensers and censors but prescribes a remedy to be enforced by a suit in equity. In this case there was previous publication made in the course of the business of regularly producing malicious, scandalous and defamatory periodicals. . . . The doctrine that measures such as the one before us are invalid because they operate as previous restraints to infringe freedom of press, exposes the peace and good order of every community and the business and private affairs of every individual to the constant and protracted false and malicious assaults of any insolvent publisher who may have purpose and sufficient capacity to contrive and put into effect a scheme or program for oppression, blackmail or extortion.

The judgment should be affirmed.

MR. JUSTICE VAN DEVANTER, MR. JUSTICE MCREYNOLDS, and MR. JUSTICE SUTHERLAND, concur in this opinion.

New York Times Co. v. United States; United States v. Washington Post Co. 403 U.S. 713, 91 S. Ct. 2140, 29 L. Ed. 2d 822 (1971)

PER CURIAM. We granted certiorari in these cases in which the United States seeks to enjoin the New York Times and the Washington Post from publishing the contents of a classified study entitled "History of U.S. Decision-Making Process on Viet Nam Policy."

"Any system of prior restraints of expression comes to this Court bearing a heavy presumption against its constitutional validity." Bantam Books, Inc. v. Sullivan, 372 U.S. 58, 70 (1963); see also Near v. Minnesota, 283 U.S. 697 (1931). The Government "thus carries a heavy burden of showing justification for the enforcement of such a restraint." Organization for a Better Austin v. Keefe, 412 U.S. 415, 419 (1971). The District Court for the Southern District of New York in the New York Times case and the District Court for the District of Columbia and the Court of Appeals for the District of Columbia Circuit in the Washington Post case held that the Government had not met that burden. We agree.

The judgment of the Court of Appeals for the District of Columbia Circuit is therefore affirmed. The order of the Court of Appeals for the Second Circuit is reversed and the case is remanded with directions to enter a judgment affirming the judgment of the District Court for the Southern District of New York. The stays entered June 25, 1971, by the Court are vacated. The judgments shall issue forthwith.

So ordered.

MR. JUSTICE BLACK, with whom MR. JUSTICE DOUGLAS joins, concurring. I adhere to the view that the Government's case against the Washington Post should have been dismissed and that the injunction against the New York Times should have been vacated without oral argument when the cases were first presented to this Court. I believe that every moment's continuance of the injunctions against these newspapers amounts to a flagrant, indefensible, and continuing violation of the First Amendment. Furthermore, after oral arguments, I agree completely that we must affirm the judgment of the Court of Appeals for the District of Columbia and reverse the judgment of the Court of Appeals for the Second Circuit for the reasons stated by my Brothers Douglas and Brennan. In my view it is unfortunate that some of my Brethren are apparently willing to hold that the publication of news may sometimes be enjoined. Such a holding would make a shambles of the First Amendment.

Our Government was launched in 1789 with the adoption of the Constitution. The Bill of Rights, including the First Amendment, followed in 1791. Now, for the first time in the 182 years since the founding of the Republic, the federal courts are asked to hold that the First Amendment does not mean what it says, but rather means that the Government can halt the publication of current news of vital importance to the people of this country.

In seeking injunctions against these newspapers and in its presentation to the Court, the Executive Branch seems to have forgotten the essential purpose and history of the First Amendment. . . .

In the First Amendment the Founding Fathers gave the free press the protection it must have to fulfill its essential role in our democracy. The press was to serve the governed, not the governors. The Government's power to censor the press was abolished so that the press would remain forever free to censure the Government. The press was protected so that it could bare the secrets of government and inform the people. Only a free and unrestrained press can effectively expose deception in government. And paramount among the responsibilities of a free press is the duty to prevent any part of the government from deceiving the people and sending them off to distant lands to die of foreign fevers and foreign shot and shell. In my view, far from deserving condemnation for their courageous reporting, the New York Times, the Washington Post, and other newspapers should be commended for serving the purpose that the Founding Fathers saw so clearly. In revealing the workings of government that led to the Viet Nam war, the newspapers nobly did precisely that which the Founders hoped and trusted they would do. . . .

The word "security" is a broad, vague generality whose contours should not be invoked to abrogate the fundamental law embodied in the First Amendment. The guarding of military and diplomatic secrets at the expense of informed representative government provides no real security for our Republic. . . .

Mr. Justice Douglas, with whom Mr. Justice Black joins, concurring. While I join the opinion of the Court I believe it necessary to express my views more fully.

It should be noted at the outset that the First Amendment provides that "Congress shall make no law . . . abridging the freedom of speech or of the press." That leaves, in my view, no room for governmental restraint on the press.

There is, moreover, no statute barring the publication by the press of the material which the Times and Post seek to use. [A review of the pertinent statutes is omitted.] Thus Congress has been faithful to the command of the First Amendment in this area.

So any power that the Government possesses must come from its "inherent power."

The power to wage war is "the power to wage war successfully." See Hirabayashi v. United States, 320 U.S. 81, 93. But the war power stems from a declaration of war. The Constitution by Article I, §8, gives Congress, not the President, power "to declare war." Nowhere are presidential wars authorized. We need not decide therefore what leveling effect the war power of Congress might have.

These disclosures may have a serious impact. But that is no basis for sanctioning a previous restraint on the press. . . .

The Government says that it has inherent powers to go into court and obtain an injunction to protect that national interest, which in this case is alleged to be national security.

Near v. Minnesota, 283 U.S. 697, repudiated that expansive doctrine in no uncertain terms.

The dominant purpose of the First Amendment was to prohibit the widespread practice of governmental suppression of embarrassing information. It is common knowledge that

Section C. Freedom of Speech and Association

the First Amendment was adopted against the widespread use of the common law of seditious libel to punish the dissemination of material that is embarrassing to the powers-that-be. See Emerson, The System of Free Expressions, c. V (1970); Chafee, Free Speech in the United States, c. XIII (1941). The present cases will, I think, go down in history as the most dramatic illustration of that principle. A debate of large proportions goes on in the Nation over our posture in Vietnam. That debate antedated the disclosure of the contents of the present documents. The latter are highly relevant to the debate in progress.

Secrecy in government is fundamentally anti-democratic, perpetuating bureaucratic errors. Open debate and discussion of public issues are vital to our national health. On public questions there should be "open and robust debate." New York Times, Inc. v. Sullivan, 376 U.S. 254, 269-270.

MR. JUSTICE BRENNAN concurring.

I write separately in these cases only to emphasize what should be apparent: that our judgment in the present cases may not be taken to indicate the propriety, in the future, of issuing temporary stays and restraining orders to block the publication of material sought to be suppressed by the Government. So far as I can determine, never before has the United States sought to enjoin a newspaper from publishing information in its possession. . . . Our cases, it is true, have indicated that there is a single, extremely narrow class of cases in which the First Amendment's ban on prior judicial restraint may be overridden. Our cases have thus far indicated that such cases may arise only when the Nation "is at war," Schenck v. United States, 249 U.S. 47, 52 (1919), during which times "no one would question but that a Government might prevent actual obstruction to its recruiting service or the publication of the sailing dates of transports or the number and location of troops." Near v. Minnesota, 283 U.S. 697, 716 (1931). Even if the present world situation were assumed to be tantamount to a time of war, or if the power of presently available armaments would justify even in peacetime the suppression of information that would set in motion a nuclear holocaust, in neither of these actions has the Government presented or even alleged that publication of items from or based upon the material at issue would cause the happening of an event of that nature. "The chief purpose of [the First Amendment's] guarantee [is] to prevent previous restraints upon publication." Near v. Minnesota, supra, at 713. Thus, only governmental allegation and proof that publication must inevitably, directly and immediately cause the occurrence of an event kindred to imperiling the safety of a transport already at sea can support even the issuance of an interim restraining order. . . .

MR. JUSTICE STEWART, with whom MR. JUSTICE WHITE joins, concurring. In the governmental structure created by our Constitution, the Executive is endowed with enormous power in the two related areas of national defense and international relations. This power, largely unchecked by the Legislative and Judicial branches, has been pressed to the very hilt since the advent of the nuclear missile age. For better or for worse, the simple fact is that a President of the United States possesses vastly greater constitutional independence in these two vital areas of power than does, say, a prime minister of a country with a parliamentary form of government.

In the absence of the governmental checks and balances present in other areas of our national life, the only effective restraint upon executive policy and power in the areas of national defense and international affairs may lie in an enlightened citizenry — in an informed and critical public opinion which alone can here protect the values of democratic government. For this reason, it is perhaps here that a press that is alert, aware, and free most vitally serves the basic purpose of the First Amendment. For without an informed and free press there cannot be an enlightened people.

Yet it is elementary that the successful conduct of international diplomacy and the maintenance of an effective national defense require both confidentiality and secrecy. Other nations can hardly deal with this Nation in an atmosphere of mutual trust unless they can be assured that their confidences will be kept. And within our own executive departments, the development of considered and intelligent international policies would be impossible if those charged with their formulation could not communicate with each other freely, frankly, and in confidence. In the area of basic national defense the frequent need for absolute secrecy is, of course, self-evident.

I think there can be but one answer to this dilemma, if dilemma it be. The responsibility must be where the power is. If the Constitution gives the Executive a large degree of unshared power in the conduct of foreign affairs and the maintenance of our national defense, then under the Constitution the Executive must have the largely unshared duty to determine and preserve the degree of internal security necessary to exercise that power successfully. It is an awesome responsibility, requiring judgment and wisdom of a high order. I should suppose that moral, political, and practical considerations would indicate that a very first principle of that wisdom would be an insistence upon avoiding secrecy for its own sake. For when everything is classified, then nothing is classified, and the system becomes one to be disregarded by the cynical or the careless, and to be manipulated by those intent on self-protection or self-promotion. . . .

This is not to say that Congress and the courts have no role to play. Undoubtedly Congress has the power to enact specific and appropriate criminal laws to protect government property and preserve government secrets. Congress has passed such laws, and several of them are of very colorable relevance to the apparent circumstances of these cases. And if a criminal prosecution is instituted, it will be the responsibility of the courts to decide the applicability of the criminal law under which the charge is brought. Moreover, if Congress should pass a specific law authorizing civil proceedings in this field, the courts would likewise have the duty to decide the constitutionality of such a law as well as its applicability to the facts proved.

But in the cases before us we are asked neither to construe specific regulations nor to apply specific laws. We are asked, instead, to perform a function that the Constitution gave to the Executive, not the Judiciary. We are asked, quite simply, to prevent the publication by two newspapers of material that the Executive Branch insists should not, in the national interest, be published. I am convinced that the Executive is correct with respect to some of the documents involved. But I cannot say that disclosure of any of them will surely result in direct, immediate, and irreparable damage to our Nation or its people. That being so, there can under the First Amendment be but one judicial resolution of the issues before us. I join the judgments of the Court.

Mr. Justice White, with whom Mr. Justice Stewart joins, concurring. I concur in today's judgments, but only because of the concededly extraordinary protection against prior restraints enjoyed by the press under our constitutional system. I do not say that in no circumstances would the First Amendment permit an injunction against publishing information about government plans or operations. Nor, after examining the materials the Government characterizes as the most sensitive and destructive, can I deny that revelation of these documents will do substantial damage to public interests. Indeed, I am confident that their disclosure will have that result. But I nevertheless agree that the United States has not satisfied the very heavy burden which it must meet to warrant an injunction against publication in these cases, at least in the absence of express and appropriately limited congressional authorization for prior restraints in circumstances such as these.

At least in the absence of legislation by Congress, based on its own investigations and findings, I am quite unable to agree that the inherent powers of the Executive and the courts reach so far as to authorize remedies having such sweeping potential for inhibiting publications by the press. Much of the difficulty inheres in the "grave and irreparable danger" standard suggested by the United States. If the United States were to have judgment under such a standard in these cases, our decision would be of little guidance to other courts in other cases, for the material at issue here would not be available from the Court's opinion or from public records, nor would it be published by the press. Indeed, even today where we hold that the United States has not met its burden, the material remains sealed in court records and it is properly not discussed in today's opinions. Moreover, because the material poses substantial dangers to national interests and because of the hazards of criminal sanctions, a responsible press may choose never to publish the more sensitive materials. To sustain the Government in these cases would start the courts down a long and hazardous road that I am not willing to travel at least without congressional guidance and direction. . . .

The criminal code contains numerous provisions potentially relevant to these cases. Section 797 makes it a crime to publish certain photographs or drawings of military installations. Section 798, also in precise language, proscribes knowing and willful publications of any classified information concerning the cryptographic systems or communication intelligence activities of the United States as well as any information obtained from communication intelligence operations. If any of the material here at issue is of this nature, the newspapers are presumably now on full notice of the position of the United States and must face the consequences if they publish. I would have no difficulty in sustaining convictions under these sections on facts that would not justify the intervention of equity and the imposition of a prior restraint.

The same would be true under those sections of the criminal code casting a wider net to protect the national defense. Section 793(e) makes it a criminal act for any unauthorized possessor of a document "relating to national defense" either (1) willfully to communicate or cause to be communicated that document to any person not entitled to receive it or (2) willfully to retain the document and fail to deliver it to an officer of the United States entitled to receive it. The subsection was added in 1950 because pre-existing law provided no penalty for the unauthorized possessor unless demand for the documents was made. . . .

It is thus clear that Congress has . . . apparently been satisfied to rely on criminal sanctions and their deterrent effect on the responsible as well as the irresponsible press. I am not, of course, saying that either of these newspapers has yet committed a crime or that either would commit a crime if they published all the material now in their possession. That matter must await resolution in the context of a criminal proceeding if one is instituted by the United States. In that event, the issue of guilt or innocence would be determined by procedures and standards quite different from those that have purported to govern these injunctive proceedings.

MR. JUSTICE MARSHALL, concurring. . . . The issue is whether this Court or the Congress has the power to make law.

In this case there is no problem concerning the President's power to classify information as "secret" or "top secret." Congress has specifically recognized Presidential authority, which has been formally exercised in Executive Order 10501, to classify documents and information. See, e.g., 18 U.S.C. §798, 50 U.S.C. §783. Nor is there any issue here regarding the President's power as Chief Executive and Commander-in-Chief to protect national security by disciplining employees who disclose information and by taking precautions to prevent leaks.

The problem here is whether in this particular case the Executive Branch has authority to invoke the equity jurisdiction of the courts to protect what it believes to be the national interest. See In re Debs, 158 U.S. 564, 584 (1895). . . .

It would, however, be utterly inconsistent with the concept of separation of power for this Court to use its power of contempt to prevent behavior that Congress has specifically declined to prohibit. . . .

On at least two occasions Congress has refused to enact legislation that would have made the conduct engaged in here unlawful and given the President the power that he seeks in this case. In 1917 during the debate over the original Espionage Act, still the basic provisions of §793, Congress rejected a proposal to give the President in time of war or threat of war authority to directly prohibit by proclamation the publication of information relating to national defense that might be useful to the enemy. . . . Congress rejected this proposal after war against Germany had been declared even though many believed that there was a grave national emergency and that the threat of security leaks and espionage were serious. The Executive has not gone to Congress and requested that the decision to provide such power be reconsidered. Instead, the Executive comes to this Court and asks that it be granted the power Congress refused to give.

In 1957 the United States Commission on Government Security found that "[a]irplane journals, scientific periodicals, and even the daily newspaper have featured articles containing information and other data which should have been deleted in whole or in part for security reasons." In response to this problem the Commission, which was chaired by Senator Cotton, proposed that "Congress enact legislation making it a crime for any person willfully to disclose without proper authorization, for any purpose whatever, information classified 'secret' or 'top secret', knowing, or having reasonable grounds to believe, such information to have been so classified." Report of Commission on Government Security 619-620 (1957). After substantial floor discussion on the proposal, it was rejected. See 103 Cong. Rec. 10447-10450. If the proposal that Senator Cotton championed on the floor had been enacted, the publication of the documents involved here would certainly have been a crime. Congress refused, however, to make it a crime. The Government is here asking this Court to remake that decision. This Court has no such power.

Mr. Chief Justice Burger, dissenting. . . . Only those who view the First Amendment as an absolute in all circumstances — a view I respect, but reject — can find such a case as this to be simple or easy.

This case is not simple for another and more immediate reason. We do not know the facts of the case. No District Judge knew all the facts. No Court of Appeals judge knew all the facts. No member of this Court knows all the facts.

Why are we in this posture, in which only those judges to whom the First Amendment is absolute and permits of no restraint in any circumstances or for any reason, are really in a position to act?

I suggest we are in this posture because these cases have been conducted in unseemly haste. . . .

Here, moreover, the frenetic haste is due in large part to the manner in which the Times proceeded from the date it obtained the purloined documents. It seems reasonably clear now that the haste precluded reasonable and deliberate judicial treatment of these cases and was not warranted. The precipitous action of this Court aborting a trial not yet completed is not the kind of judicial conduct which ought to attend the disposition of a great issue. . . .

Would it have been unreasonable, since the newspaper could anticipate the government's objections to release of secret material, to give the government an opportunity to review the entire collection and determine whether agreement could be reached on publication? Stolen or not, if security was not in fact jeopardized, much of the material could no doubt have been declassified, since it spans a period ending in 1968. With such an approach — one that great newspapers have in the past practiced and stated editorially to be the duty of an honorable press — the newspapers and government might well have narrowed the area of disagreement as to what was and was not publishable, leaving the remainder to be resolved in orderly litigation if necessary. To me it is hardly believable that a newspaper long regarded as a great institution in American life would fail to perform one of the basic and simple duties of every citizen with respect to the discovery or possession of stolen property or secret government documents. That duty, I had thought — perhaps naively — was to report forthwith, to responsible public officers. This duty rests on taxi drivers, Justices and the New York Times. The course followed by the Times, whether so calculated or not, removed any possibility of orderly litigation of the issues. If the action of the judges up to now has been correct, that result is sheer happenstance.[1] . . .

---

[1] Interestingly the Times explained its refusal to allow the government to examine its own purloined documents by saying in substance this might compromise *their* sources and informants! The Times thus asserts a right to guard the secrecy of its sources while denying that the Government of the United States has that power.

Section C. Freedom of Speech and Association

The consequence of all this melancholy series of events is that we literally do not know what we are acting on. . . .

I would affirm the Court of Appeals for the Second Circuit and allow the District Court to complete the trial aborted by our grant of certiorari, meanwhile preserving the status quo in the Post case. I would direct that the District Court on remand give priority to the Times case to the exclusion of all other business of that court but I would not set arbitrary deadlines.

I should add that I am in general agreement with much of what Mr. Justice White has expressed with respect to penal sanctions concerning communication or retention of documents or information relating to the national defense.

We all crave speedier judicial processes but when judges are pressured as in these cases the result is a parody of the judicial process.

Mr. Justice Harlan, with whom The Chief Justice and Mr. Justice Blackmun join, dissenting. . . . With all respect, I consider that the Court has been almost irresponsibly feverish in dealing with these cases. . . .

This frenzied train of events took place in the name of the presumption against prior restraints created by the First Amendment. Due regard for the extraordinarily important and difficult questions involved in these litigations should have led the Court to shun such a precipitate timetable. In order to decide the merits of these cases properly, some or all of the following questions should have been faced:

1. Whether the Attorney General is authorized to bring these suits in the name of the United States. Compare In re Debs, 158 U.S. 564 (1895), with Youngstown Sheet & Tube Co. v. Sawyer, 343 U.S. 579 (1952). This question involves as well the construction and validity of a singularly opaque statute — the Espionage Act, 18 U.S.C. §793(e).

2. Whether the First Amendment permits the federal courts to enjoin publication of stories which would present a serious threat to national security. See Near v. Minnesota, 283 U.S. 697, 716 (1931) (dictum).

3. Whether the threat to publish highly secret documents is of itself a sufficient implication of national security to justify an injunction on the theory that regardless of the contents of the documents harm enough results simply from the demonstration of such a breach of secrecy.

4. Whether the unauthorized disclosure of any of these particular documents would seriously impair the national security.

5. What weight should be given to the opinion of high officers in the Executive Branch of the Government with respect to questions 3 and 4.

6. Whether the newspapers are entitled to retain and use the documents notwithstanding the seemingly uncontested facts that the documents, or the originals of which they are duplicates, were purloined from the Government's possession and that the newspapers received them with knowledge that they had been feloniously acquired. Cf. Liberty Lobby, Inc. v. Pearson, 390 F.2d 489 (CADC 1968).

7. Whether the threatened harm to the national security or the Government's possessory interest in the documents justifies the issuance of an injunction against publication in light of —
   a. The strong First Amendment policy against prior restraints on publication;
   b. The doctrine against enjoining conduct in violation of criminal statutes; and
   c. The extent to which the materials at issue have apparently already been otherwise disseminated.

These are difficult questions of fact, of law, and of judgment; the potential consequences of erroneous decision are enormous. The time which has been available to us, to the lower courts, and to the parties has been wholly inadequate for giving these cases the kind of consideration they deserve. It is a reflection on the stability of the judicial process that these great issues — as important as any that have arisen during my time on the Court — should have been decided under the pressures engendered by the torrent of publicity that has attended these litigations from their inception.

1156   Chapter Sixteen. Substantive Rights

Forced as I am to reach the merits of these cases, I dissent from the opinion and judgments of the Court. . . . It is plain to me that the scope of the judicial function in passing upon the activities of the Executive Branch of the Government in the field of foreign affairs is very narrowly restricted. This view is, I think, dictated by the concept of separation of powers upon which our constitutional system rests. . . .

The power to evaluate the "pernicious influence" of premature disclosure is not, however, lodged in the Executive alone. I agree that, in performance of its duty to protect the values of the First Amendment against political pressures, the judiciary must review the initial Executive determination to the point of satisfying itself that the subject matter of the dispute does lie within the proper compass of the President's foreign relations power. Constitutional considerations forbid "a complete abandonment of judicial control." Cf. United States v. Reynolds, 345 U.S. 1, 8 (1953). Moreover, the judiciary may properly insist that the determination that disclosure of the subject matter would irreparably impair the national security be made by the head of the Executive Department concerned — here the Secretary of State or the Secretary of Defense — after actual personal consideration by that officer. This safeguard is required in the analogous area of executive claims of privilege for secrets of state. See United States v. Reynolds, supra, at 8 and n. 20; Duncan v. Cammell, Laird & Co., [1942] A.C. 624, 638 (House of Lords).

But in my judgment the judiciary may not properly go beyond these two inquiries and redetermine for itself the probable impact of disclosure on the national security. . . .

Even if there is some room for the judiciary to override the executive determination, it is plain that the scope of review must be exceedingly narrow. I can see no indication in the opinions of either the District Court or the Court of Appeals in the Post litigation that the conclusions of the Executive were given even the deference owing to an administrative agency, much less that owing to a co-equal branch of the Government operating within the field of its constitutional prerogative.

Accordingly, I would vacate the judgment of the Court of Appeals for the District of Columbia Circuit on this ground and remand the case for further proceedings in the District Court. . . .

MR. JUSTICE BLACKMUN. I join Mr. Justice Harlan in his dissent. I also am in substantial accord with much that Mr. Justice White says, by way of admonition, in the latter part of his opinion.

At this point the focus is on *only* the comparatively few documents specified by the Government as critical. So far as the other material — vast in amount — is concerned, let it be published and published forthwith if the newspapers, once the strain is gone and the sensationalism is eased, still feel the urge so to do. . . .

The First Amendment, after all, is only one part of an entire Constitution. Article II of the great document vests in the Executive Branch primary power over the conduct of foreign affairs and places in that branch the responsibility for the Nation's safety. . . . What is needed here is a weighing, upon properly developed standards, of the broad right of the press to print and of the very narrow right of the Government to prevent. Such standards are not yet developed. The parties here are in disagreement as to what those standards should be. But even the newspapers concede that there are situations where restraint is in order and is constitutional. . . .

I therefore would remand these cases to be developed expeditiously, of course, but on a schedule permitting the orderly presentation of evidence from both sides, with the use of discovery, if necessary, as authorized by the rules, and with the preparation of briefs, oral argument and court opinions of a quality better than has been seen to this point. In making this last statement, I criticize no lawyer or judge. I know from past personal experience the agony of time pressure in the preparation of litigation. But these cases and the issues involved and the courts, including this one, deserve better than has been produced thus far. . . .

The Court, however, decides the cases today the other way. I therefore add one final comment.

I strongly urge, and sincerely hope, that these two newspapers will be fully aware of their ultimate responsibilities to the United States of America. Judge Wilkey, dissenting in the District of Columbia case, after a review of only the affidavits before his court (the basic papers had not then been made available by either party), concluded that there were a number of examples of documents that, if in the possession of the Post, and if published, "could clearly result in great harm to the nation," and he defined "harm" to mean "the death of soldiers, the destruction of alliances, the greatly increased difficulty of negotiation with our enemies, the inability of our diplomats to negotiate. . . ." I, for one, have now been able to give at least some cursory study not only to the affidavits, but to the material itself. I regret to say that from this examination I fear that Judge Wilkey's statements have possible foundation. I therefore share his concern. I hope that damage already has not been done. If, however, damage has been done, and if, with the Court's action today, these newspapers proceed to publish the critical documents and there results therefrom "the death of soldiers, the destruction of alliances, the greatly increased difficulty of negotiation with our enemies, the inability of our diplomats to negotiate," to which list I might add the factors of prolongation of the war and further delay in the freeing of United States prisoners, then the Nation's people will know where the responsibility for these sad consequences rests.

NOTE Marchetti v. United States

Compare Marchetti v. United States, 466 F.2d 1309 (4th Cir.), cert. denied, 409 U.S. 1063 (1972). While employed by the Central Intelligence Agency, Marchetti had signed agreements not to disclose any information received in his employment and to submit to the agency any future writing relating to his employment, "fictional or non-fictional," for approval before publication. As Marchetti was preparing to publish an article reporting some of his experiences as a CIA agent, the government brought suit to enjoin publication and to enforce the agreements. The court framed the question as that of "the enforceability of a secrecy agreement exacted by the government, in its capacity as employer, from an employee of the Central Intelligence Agency." It held the agreement enforceable, but only to the extent of allowing the agency to keep Marchetti from disclosing information that was classified under applicable Executive Orders and that had not previously been publicly disclosed. Writing for the court, Judge Haynsworth based the decision on a balancing of the government's need to protect state secrets against Marchetti's First Amendment claim:
". . . Marchetti by accepting employment with the CIA and by signing a secrecy agreement did not surrender his First Amendment right of free speech. The agreement is enforceable only because it is not a violation of those rights. We would decline enforcement of the secrecy oath signed when he left the employment of the CIA to the extent that it purports to prevent disclosure of unclassified information, for, to that extent, the oath would be in contravention of his First Amendment rights."
Judge Haynsworth also instructed the trial court on remand not to consider the propriety of the classifications in ordering their deletions from the Marchetti manuscript: "If in the conduct of [CIA] operations the need for secrecy requires a system of classification of documents and information, the process of classification is part of the executive function beyond the scope of judicial review. [Citations omitted.]" Id. at 1317. In a later review of the proceeding before the trial court, sub nom. Knopf v. Colby, 509 F.2d 1362 (4th Cir. 1975), Judge Haynsworth instructed the trial court on remand again that it could and should consider whether the material sought to be deleted had, in fact, been properly classified; an intervening amendment to the Freedom of Information Act had authorized judicial review of the classification decisions. See Note: Freedom of Information Act, infra page 1259. What about Judge Haynsworth's earlier objection to judicial review, with its implicit constitutional dimension? See also the scope of review that Justice Harlan

found permissible in New York Times Co. v. United States, supra page 1155. How should the First Amendment interests here be accommodated with the separation of powers between the executive and the judiciary in foreign affairs? Does de novo review by the courts under the Freedom of Information Act of classification decisions — where the standard for "Confidential," for instance, is whether disclosure "could reasonably be expected to cause serious damage to the national security" — appear to be a satisfactory resolution?

2. "Outdoors" Speech

a. "Subversive" Advocacy

Chafee, Free Speech in the United States 388-398 (1941)

Herndon v. Lowry[40] was another sedition case of the same year, the first to come to the Court from the South.

Angelo Herndon was a Communist Negro, who had gone as a paid organizer to Atlanta where he enrolled at least five members and held three meetings. When arrested he carried under his arm a box of membership blanks and pamphlets, and the police found bundles of more in his room. The authorities were especially concerned over a booklet named The Communist Position on the Negro Question. On its cover was a map of the United States, with a dark belt across several Southern states and the phrase "Self-Determination for the Black Belt." Its author urged that the Black Belt should be made one governmental unit, ruled by the Negro majority. This interstate domain was to be freed from class rule and from American imperialism, even to the point of deciding its foreign relations with other nations and with the government of the United States. Lands of whites were to be confiscated for the benefit of Negro farmers. It also advocated strikes, boycotts, and a revolutionary struggle for power against the white bourgeoisie, "even if the situation does not yet warrant the raising of the question of uprising." There was no evidence that he had distributed any of this material except membership blanks and two innocuous circulars about county relief.

Georgia has the distinction of being one of the few states that did not enact a sedition statute after the World War. However, the authorities dug up an old law which might serve to incarcerate such unwelcome visitors. Before the Civil War Georgia had a statute punishing with death anybody who attempted, by speech or writing, to excite an insurrection of slaves. An accompanying provision imposed the same penalty on anybody who brought in printed matter calculated to excite a slave insurrection; this was to take care of Garrison's Liberator and other Abolitionist publications. After Appomattox, the legislature dropped out the references to slaves; but these laws stayed on the statute book, never enforced so far as reported cases show until the following section was invoked against Herndon and his fellow Communists:

"Any attempt, by persuasion or otherwise, to induce others to join in any combined resistance to the lawful authority of the State shall constitute an attempt to incite insurrection."

The penalty is still death; but if the jury recommends mercy, then imprisonment for five to twenty years.

So a statute inspired by Nat Turner's Rebellion in 1832 was first used against Communist organizers in 1932. Herndon was indicted for attempting to incite an insurrection,

---

[40] 301 U.S. 242 (1937) revg. 182 Ga. 582 (1936). See 34 Columbia Law Review 1357; 50 Harvard Law Review 1313; 35 Michigan Law Review 1373.

with intent to overthrow the government of Georgia by open force. The evidence at the trial was as already indicated. The judge charged the jury that, in order to convict the defendant, "it must appear clearly by the evidence that *immediate violence* against the state of Georgia was to be expected or advocated." Herndon was convicted. The jury could have let him be hanged, but it recommended mercy and only sent him to prison for eighteen or twenty years.

Herndon claimed a new trial, for want of any evidence of his advocating the *immediate* violence required by the trial judge. The highest court in Georgia held that lack of this evidence was immaterial; the trial judge had construed the statute too narrowly; it really made him guilty if he intended insurrection "to happen *at any time,* as a result of his influence." On rehearing, the court said "at any time" meant *a reasonable time.* So the conviction was affirmed, inasmuch as the court found in the Black Belt booklets sufficient intention of a real revolution some day or other. It felt sure Herndon expected to distribute these booklets, else why did he have them around. This unexpected broad interpretation of the law led Herndon to invoke the Fourteenth Amendment for the first time and try to get to the United States Supreme Court. His lateness made the task very difficult,[45] but at last a writ of habeas corpus was directed to Lowry, the sheriff.

Then the Supreme Court, by a bare majority, released Herndon. The Court's opinion was delivered by Justice Roberts, with the support of the Chief Justice and Justices Brandeis, Stone, and Cardozo.

Justice Roberts concentrated his attention on the two worst groups of evidence: (1) The membership blanks vaguely declared the Communist Party to be the party of the working class, personifying "proletarian revolutionary action." This, he concluded, "falls short of an attempt to bring about insurrection either immediately or within a reasonable time." More specific aims like unemployment insurance, emergency relief for poor farmers, their exemption from taxes and debts, opposition to wage-cuts, and equal rights for Negroes, were not criminal upon their face. (2) The prosecution asserted that the demand for equal racial rights was rendered criminal by extrinsic facts like the Black Belt booklets in Herndon's possession, which showed the Communist Party aiming at forcible subversion of the lawful authority of Georgia. But Justice Roberts did not consider these booklets an attempt to cause insurrection. First, no evidence showed that Herndon distributed or even approved of them. Secondly, "the fantastic programme they envisaged" was no more than "an ultimate ideal." Nothing indicated that Herndon wanted to establish the Black Belt Free State at once or made it one of his principal aims. All he talked about, according to the state's proof, was relief.

To interject my own views for a moment, this old statute is valid in itself. A real attempt to cause a real insurrection in Georgia could of course be punished severely. But that does not mean that anything the community dislikes can be called an attempt. The word has a well-established meaning in our common law. A criminal attempt requires more than a bad intention or even a slight overt act in pursuance thereof. The defendant must do enough to bring his unlawful intention reasonably near to a successfully completed crime. The attempt test, as Holmes's opinions show, is related to his free speech test of "clear and present danger." The evil-minded man must get well down the path toward his destination before he is guilty of an attempt as defined by the common law.[47] No matter how much Herndon intended to circulate his material, this was just looking along the path. It takes a good deal more than a war-map to make a victory.

---

[45] The Supreme Court at first refused to consider the case at all. Herndon v. Georgia, 295 U.S. 441 (1935), affg. 179 Ga. 597 (1934). See 35 Columbia Law Review 1145; 49 Harvard Law Review 150; 30 Illinois Law Review 530; 20 Minnesota Law Review 216; 84 University of Pennsylvania Law Review 256.

[47] The legislature can, if it desires, expressly enlarge the common law scope of attempt and push the critical point back nearer the beginning of the path. — Commonwealth v. Mehales, 284 Mass. 412 (1933). But the Georgia statute merely used the word "attempt," with no qualifications, so it should be regarded as an expression of the common law of criminal attempts, especially when occurring in such an old statute.

1160   Chapter Sixteen. Substantive Rights

Visualize a slave insurrection such as this statute was originally enacted to prevent, and then think of what Herndon did. It is hard to believe that anybody in Atlanta actually saw any resemblance. My guess is that the men concerned in this prosecution were not worried in the slightest about any plotted insurrection or the possibility of a new Liberia between the Tennessee Valley Authority and the Gulf of Mexico. But they were worried, I suspect, about something else that Herndon really wanted — his demand for equal rights for Negroes. If he got going with that, there was a clear and present danger of racial friction and isolated acts of violence by individuals on both sides. They were afraid, not that the United States Constitution would be overthrown, but that it might be enforced. Yet you cannot indict a man for seeking to put the Fifteenth Amendment into wider effect. And the advocacy of other kinds of racial equality, even of intermarriage, is not, I assume, a serious crime in Georgia, if it be a crime at all. So the best way to remove the dangers of colored assertiveness and racial friction created by this outspoken Negro who would not let sleeping dogs lie, was to seize on the Black Belt pamphlet and stretch the old drastic statute to cover it. This the state court made possible by saying that Herndon's documents had a "dangerous tendency" to cause an insurrection. It was the fringe thus annexed to the statute that the United States Supreme Court held bad, not the statute itself. . . .

Herndon had the constitutional right to address meetings and organize parties unless he actually attempted to incite insurrection by violence. Since the evidence failed to show that he did so incite, then the application of this statute to him unreasonably limited freedom of speech and freedom of assembly.

Justice Roberts brings out better than anybody hitherto the importance of the procedure in a sedition prosecution. He says the statute, as construed by the Georgia court, is so vague and indefinite as to be bad under the Stromberg case. It does not furnish "a sufficiently ascertainable standard of guilt." It does not, like the Espionage Act, pin the issue down to one particular activity of the government, and oblige the jury to decide whether the prisoner was urging interference with that single activity. It does not give the judge and jury any standard for appraising the circumstances and character of the defendant's utterances and conduct, so as to see whether they create "a clear and present danger of forcible obstruction of a particular state function." Nor does it make any specified conduct or utterance an offense.

Finally, he condemns the Georgia court's view that the accused was properly found guilty if he intended an insurrection to happen "at any time within which he might reasonably expect his influence to continue to be directly operative in causing such action by those whom he sought to induce." The consequences of such a view are so wide as to be fatal to open discussion. It raises the same procedural objection, that the jurymen are given no standard of guilt that they know how to apply. They are merely left free to punish the defendant terrifically if they happen to dislike his opinions.

Justices Van Devanter, McReynolds, Sutherland, and Butler once more dissented, the last time that they were all together in a free speech case, for within a few months Justice Van Devanter, who wrote the opinion, retired and was succeeded by Justice Black. To give only a few of his points, Justice Van Devanter felt sure that Herndon was planning to distribute the Black Belt booklets. Although there was no direct testimony to that effect, he never denied it; he was an active member of the party, sent to Atlanta as a paid organizer, and the literature was shipped to him for use in soliciting new members. Furthermore, he was not convicted just for urging reforms by lawful means. He approved of the party program and apparently brought it to the attention of others. He was a Negro getting Southern Negroes into the party, with a booklet in his hands which described measures that particularly appealed to such Negroes, like the establishment of an independent state for their benefit and the adoption of a fighting alliance with the revolutionary white proletariat. "Proposing these measures was nothing short of advising a resort to force and violence, for all know that such measures could not be effected otherwise."

There is a good deal of force in what Justice Van Devanter says. Why did Herndon have all this literature if he was not planning to distribute it? That is what he was sent South for. Some of it was explosive stuff and he sounds like the kind of man to cause trouble. Perhaps a conviction would have been sustained if he had been specially charged with possessing such printed material for distribution, under a statute with a light maximum penalty. But it is quite another thing to let printed words be called an attempt at insurrection like Dorr's Rebellion, the kind of crime that necessarily carries a heavy maximum punishment. Just as the Constitution will not allow the capital crime of "treason" to be stretched to cover mere words however violent, a similar stretch of the capital crime of "insurrection" is equally repugnant to American traditions. Speech and writing that amounts at most to a breach of the peace ought not to be transformed into a major crime by the process of calling them big names. . . .

Furthermore, it was impossible to ignore the severity of Herndon's sentence, or the fact that if he was validly imprisoned the next Negro Communist to enter Georgia could be validly put to death under the same statute without having done a bit more than Herndon. Logically perhaps, the degree of the punishment ought not to influence an upper court's determination of errors of law below; but just the same it is bound to affect kindly men. In the Herndon case the Supreme Court was faced for the first time with the possibility that American citizens might be hanged or electrocuted for nothing except expressing objectionable opinions or owning objectionable books. They might not be burned at the stake as Giordano Bruno and Servetus were for equivalent crimes, but they would be just as dead. Something had to be done to prevent such disasters from occurring within these United States. It must be remembered, as I have insisted elsewhere, that the Supreme Court (and usually a state appellate court) has no control over the severity of a sentence. Of that, the trial judge (or the jury as in this case) is complete master. So unless the Supreme Court held that no sentence could be imposed for what Herndon did, it would be obliged to approve whatever punishment a Georgia jury saw fit to impose upon Communists, including death. It was a case of all or nothing, and the Supreme Court chose nothing.

I have let my mind run over all the chief sedition defendants discussed in this book, from Debs down to date — Abrams, Berger, Gilbert, Gitlow, Miss Whitney, and the rest — and tried to decide which of them I myself honestly think did create a "clear and present danger" of unlawful acts under the circumstances surrounding his words. The upshot is, all but one seem to me fairly harmless. The one exception is Herndon. Not that there was clear and present danger of the insurrection for which he was indicted. Not that the Black Free State could have suddenly emerged into being. But, given the unrest of Negroes, share croppers, mill-workers, his demands for equal racial rights, lavish relief, and the virtual abolition of debts might have produced some sort of disorder in the near future. Smoking is all right, but not in a powder magazine.

Yet that raises the question — if agitation which would be just blowing off steam in the rest of the country is going to be forbidden in the South because of its peculiar kinds of unrest among the underprivileged, what legitimate hopeful alternatives are available to the unrestful and those that want to remove the causes of their unrest? Elsewhere one can urge the discontented classes to drop all thought of violence and try to remedy their grievances by the ballot. But how can you tell a Southern Negro to go and vote at state elections for the reforms he desires? The right so to vote is one of the main things a Negro agitator demands. The whites' fear of the consequences of success — and an outsider cannot call that fear unreasonable in view of Reconstruction experiences — is a big cause why men of Herndon's stamp are likely to bring about real trouble. In short, the very conditions that cause the grievances render agitation to remove the grievances dangerous.

When the possibility of reaching natural political objectives by peaceful political methods is considerably impaired, this encourages men like Herndon to use tactics close to the danger-line. There ought to be a wider middle ground between speech that is liable to cause outbreaks, and the helpless submission of the under-privileged to their lot. And sedition prosecutions are only likely to make matters worse.

Dennis v. United States *341 U.S. 494, 71 S. Ct. 857, 95 L. Ed. 1137 (1951)*

MR. CHIEF JUSTICE VINSON announced the judgment of the Court and an opinion in which MR. JUSTICE REED, MR. JUSTICE BURTON and MR. JUSTICE MINTON join.

Petitioners were indicted in July, 1948, for violation of the conspiracy provisions of the Smith Act, 54 Stat. 670, 671, ch. 439, 18 U.S.C. (1946 ed.) §11, during the period of April 1945, to July, 1948. The pretrial motion to quash the indictment on the grounds, inter alia, that the statute was unconstitutional was denied, United States v. Foster, 80 F. Supp. 479, and the case was set for trial on January 17, 1949. A verdict of guilty as to all the petitioners was returned by the jury on October 14, 1949. The Court of Appeals affirmed the convictions. 183 F.2d 201. We granted certiorari, 340 U.S. 863, limited to the following two questions: (1) Whether either §2 or §3 of the Smith Act, inherently or as construed and applied in the instant case, violates the First Amendment and other provisions of the Bill of Rights; (2) whether either §2 or §3 of the Act, inherently or as construed and applied in the instant case, violates the First and Fifth Amendments because of indefiniteness.

Sections 2 and 3 of the Smith Act, 54 Stat. 670, 671, ch. 439, 18 U.S.C. (1946 ed.) §§10, 11 (see present 18 U.S.C. §2385), provide as follows:

"Sec. 2.

"(a) It shall be unlawful for any person —

"(1) to knowingly or willfully advocate, abet, advise, or teach the duty, necessity, desirability, or propriety of overthrowing or destroying any government in the United States by force or violence, or by the assassination of any officer of such government;

"(2) with the intent to cause the overthrow or destruction of any government in the United States, to print, publish, edit, issue, circulate, sell, distribute, or publicly display any written or printed matter advocating, advising, or teaching the duty, necessity, desirability, or propriety of overthrowing or destroying any government in the United States by force or violence;

"(3) to organize or help to organize any society, group, or assembly of persons who teach, advocate, or encourage the overthrow or destruction of any government in the United States by force or violence; or to be or become a member of, or affiliate with, any such society, group or assembly of persons, knowing the purposes thereof.

"Sec. 3. It shall be unlawful for any person to attempt to commit, or to conspire to commit, any of the acts prohibited by the provisions of . . . this title."

The indictment charged the petitioners with willfully and knowingly conspiring (1) to organize as the Communist Party of the United States of America a society, group and assembly of persons who teach and advocate the overthrow and destruction of the Government of the United States by force and violence, and (2) knowingly and willfully to advocate and teach the duty and necessity of overthrowing and destroying the Government of the United States by force and violence. The indictment further alleged that §2 of the Smith Act proscribes these acts and that any conspiracy to take such action is a violation of §3 of the Act.

The trial of the case extended over nine months, six of which were devoted to the taking of evidence, resulting in a record of 16,000 pages. Our limited grant of the writ of certiorari has removed from our consideration any question as to the sufficiency of the evidence to support the jury's determination that petitioners are guilty of the offense charged. Whether on this record petitioners did in fact advocate the overthrow of the Government by force and violence is not before us, and we must base any discussion of this point upon

Section C. Freedom of Speech and Association

the conclusion stated in the opinion of the Court of Appeals, which treated the issue in great detail. That court held that the record in this case amply supports the necessary finding of the jury that petitioners, the leaders of the Communist Party in this country, were unwilling to work within our framework of democracy, but intended to initiate a violent revolution whenever the propitious occasion appeared. Petitioners dispute the meaning to be drawn from the evidence, contending that the Marxist-Leninist doctrine they advocated taught that force and violence to achieve a Communist form of government in an existing democratic state would be necessary only because the ruling classes of that state would never permit the transformation to be accomplished peacefully, but would use force and violence to defeat any peaceful political and economic gain the Communists could achieve. But the Court of Appeals held that the record supports the following broad conclusions: By virtue of their control over the political apparatus of the Communist Political Association, petitioners were able to transform that organization into the Communist Party; that the policies of the Association were changed from peaceful cooperation with the United States and its economic and political structure to a policy which had existed before the United States and the Soviet Union were fighting a common enemy, namely, a policy which worked for the overthrow of the Government by force and violence; that the Communist Party is a highly disciplined organization, adept at infiltration into strategic positions, use of aliases, and double-meaning language; that the Party is rigidly controlled; that Communists, unlike other political parties, tolerate no dissension from the policy laid down by the guiding forces, but that the approved program is slavishly followed by the members of the Party; that the literature of the Party and the statements and activities of its leaders, petitioners here, advocate, and the general goal of the Party was, during the period in question, to achieve a successful overthrow of the existing order by force and violence. . . .

The obvious purpose of the statute is to protect existing Government, not from change by peaceable, lawful and constitutional means, but from change by violence, revolution and terrorism. That it is within the *power* of the Congress to protect the Government of the United States from armed rebellion is a proposition which requires little discussion. Whatever theoretical merit there may be to the argument that there is a "right" to rebellion against dictatorial governments is without force where the existing structure of the government provides for peaceful and orderly change. We reject any principle of governmental helplessness in the face of preparation for revolution, which principle, carried to its logical conclusion, must lead to anarchy. No one could conceive that it is not within the power of Congress to prohibit acts intended to overthrow the Government by force and violence. The question with which we are concerned here is not whether Congress has such *power*, but whether the *means* which it has employed conflict with the First and Fifth Amendments to the Constitution.

One of the bases for the contention that the means which Congress has employed are invalid takes the form of an attack on the face of the statute on the grounds that by its terms it prohibits academic discussion of the merits of Marxism-Leninism, that it stifles ideas and is contrary to all concepts of a free speech and a free press. Although we do not agree that the language itself has that significance, we must bear in mind that it is the duty of the federal courts to interpret federal legislation in a manner not inconsistent with the demands of the Constitution. American Communications Asso. v. Douds, 339 U.S. 382, 407. . . .

The very language of the Smith Act negates the interpretation which petitioners would have us impose on that Act. It is directed at advocacy, not discussion. Thus, the trial judge properly charged the jury that they could not convict if they found that petitioners did "no more than pursue peaceful studies and discussions or teaching and advocacy in the realm of ideas." He further charged that it was not unlawful "to conduct in an American college and university a course explaining the philosophical theories set forth in the books which have been placed in evidence." Such a charge is in strict accord with the stat-

1164   Chapter Sixteen.   Substantive Rights

utory language, and illustrates the meaning to be placed on those words. Congress did not intend to eradicate the free discussion of political theories, to destroy the traditional rights of Americans to discuss and evaluate ideas without fear of governmental sanction. . . .

But although the statute is not directed at the hypothetical cases which petitioners have conjured, its application in this case has resulted in convictions for the teaching and advocacy of the overthrow of the Government by force and violence, which, even though coupled with the intent to accomplish that overthrow, contains an element of speech. For this reason, we must pay special heed to the demands of the First Amendment marking out the boundaries of speech. . . .

No important case involving free speech was decided by this Court prior to Schenck v. United States, 249 U.S. 47. . . . It was not until the classic dictum of Justice Holmes in the Schenck Case that speech per se received that emphasis in a majority opinion. . . . Writing for a unanimous Court, Justice Holmes stated that the "question in every case is whether the words used are used in such circumstances and are of such a nature as to create a clear and present danger that they will bring about the substantive evils that Congress has a right to prevent." 249 U.S. at 52. But the force of even this expression is considerably weakened by the reference at the end of the opinion to Goldman v. United States, 245 U.S. 474, a prosecution under the same statute. Said Justice Holmes, "Indeed [Goldman] might be said to dispose of the present contention if the precedent covers all media concludendi. But as the right to free speech was not referred to specially, we have thought fit to add a few words." 249 U.S. at 52. The fact is inescapable, too, that the phrase bore no connotation that the danger was to be any threat to the safety of the Republic. The charge was causing and attempting to cause insubordination in the military forces and obstruct recruiting. The objectionable document denounced conscription and its most inciting sentence was, "You must do your share to maintain, support and uphold the rights of the people of this country." 249 U.S. at 51. Fifteen thousand copies were printed and some circulated. This insubstantial gesture toward insubordination in 1917 during war was held to be a clear and present danger of bringing about the evil of military insubordination. [The Chief Justice then summarized other cases under the Federal Espionage Act.]

The rule we deduce from these cases is that where an offense is specified by a statute in nonspeech or nonpress terms, a conviction relying upon speech or press as evidence of violation may be sustained only when the speech or publication created a "clear and present danger" of attempting or accomplishing the prohibited crime, e.g., interference with enlistment. The dissents, we repeat, in emphasizing the value of speech, were addressed to the argument of the sufficiency of the evidence.

[The Chief Justice reviewed the path of the "clear and present danger" test in Whitney and Gitlow, supra pages 1140 and 1134.]

Although no case subsequent to Whitney and Gitlow has expressly over-ruled the majority opinions in those cases, there is little doubt that subsequent opinions have inclined toward the Holmes-Brandeis rationale. . . .

In this case we are squarely presented with the application of the "clear and present danger" test, and must decide what that phrase imports. We first note that many of the cases in which this Court has reversed convictions by use of this or similar tests have been based on the fact that the interest which the State was attempting to protect was itself too insubstantial to warrant restriction of speech. [Citations omitted.] Overthrow of the Government by force and violence is certainly a substantial enough interest for the Government to limit speech. Indeed, this is the ultimate value of any society, for if a society cannot protect its very structure from armed internal attack, it must follow that no subordinate value can be protected. If, then, this interest may be protected, the literal problem which is presented is what has been meant by the use of the phrase "clear and present danger" of the utterances bringing about the evil within the power of Congress to punish.

Obviously, the words cannot mean that before the Government may act, it must wait until the putsch is about to be executed, the plans have been laid and the signal is awaited. If Government is aware that a group aiming at its overthrow is attempting to indoctrinate its members and to commit them to a course whereby they will strike when the leaders feel the circumstances permit, action by the Government is required. The argument that there is no need for Government to concern itself, for Government is strong, it possesses ample powers to put down a rebellion, it may defeat the revolution with ease needs no answer. For that is not the question. Certainly an attempt to overthrow the Government by force, even though doomed from the outset because of inadequate numbers or power of the revolutionists, is a sufficient evil for Congress to prevent. The damage which such attempts create both physically and politically to a nation makes it impossible to measure the validity in terms of the probability of success, or the immediacy of a successful attempt. In the instant case the trial judge charged the jury that they could not convict unless they found that petitioners intended to overthrow the Government "as speedily as circumstances would permit." This does not mean, and could not properly mean, that they would not strike until there was certainty of success. What was meant was that the revolutionists would strike when they thought the time was ripe. We must therefore reject the contention that success or probability of success is the criterion.

The situation with which Justices Holmes and Brandeis were concerned in Gitlow was a comparatively isolated event, bearing little relation in their minds to any substantial threat to the safety of the community. . . . They were not confronted with any situation comparable to the instant one — the development of an apparatus designed and dedicated to the overthrow of the Government, in the context of world crisis after crisis.

Chief Judge Learned Hand, writing for the majority below, interpreted the phrase as follows: "In each case [courts] must ask whether the gravity of the 'evil,' discounted by its improbability, justifies such invasion of free speech as is necessary to avoid the danger." 183 F.2d at 212. We adopt this statement of the rule. As articulated by Chief Judge Hand, it is as succinct and inclusive as any other we might devise at this time. It takes into consideration those factors which we deem relevant, and relates their significances. More we cannot expect from words.

Likewise, we are in accord with the court below, which affirmed the trial court's finding that the requisite danger existed. The mere fact that from the period 1945 to 1948 petitioners' activities did not result in an attempt to overthrow the Government by force and violence is of course no answer to the fact that there was a group that was ready to make the attempt. The formation by petitioners of such a highly organized conspiracy, with rigidly disciplined members subject to call when the leaders, these petitioners, felt that the time had come for action, coupled with the inflammable nature of world conditions, similar uprisings in other countries, and the touch-and-go nature of our relations with countries with whom petitioners were in the very least ideologically attuned, convince us that their convictions were justified on this score. And this analysis disposes of the contention that a conspiracy to advocate, as distinguished from the advocacy itself, cannot be constitutionally restrained, because it comprises only the preparation. It is the existence of the conspiracy which creates the danger. Cf. Pinkerton v. United States, 328 U.S. 640; Goldman v. United States, 245 U.S. 474; United States v. Rabinowich, 238 U.S. 78. If the ingredients of the reaction are present, we cannot bind the Government to wait until the catalyst is added.

There remains to be discussed the question of vagueness — whether the statute as we have interpreted it is too vague, not sufficiently advising those who would speak of the limitations upon their activity. It is urged that such vagueness contravenes the First and Fifth Amendments. This argument is particularly nonpersuasive when presented by petitioners, who, the jury found, intended to overthrow the Government as speedily as circumstances would permit. See Abrams v. United States, 250 U.S. 616, 627-629. . . . A claim of guilelessness ill becomes those with evil intent. Williams v. United States, 341 U.S. 97, 101, 102, ...

We agree that the standard as defined is not a neat, mathematical formulary. Like all verbalizations it is subject to criticism on the score of indefiniteness. But petitioners themselves contend that the verbalization, "clear and present danger" is the proper standard. We see no difference from the standpoint of vagueness, whether the standard of "clear and present danger" is one contained in haec verba within the statute, or whether it is the judicial measure of constitutional applicability. We have shown the indeterminate standard the phrase necessarily connotes. We do not think we have rendered that standard any more indefinite by our attempt to sum up the factors which are included within its scope. We think it well serves to indicate to those who would advocate constitutionally prohibited conduct that there is a line beyond which they may not go — a line which they, in full knowledge of what they intend and the circumstances in which their activity takes place, will well appreciate and understand. . . . Where there is doubt as to the intent of the defendants, the nature of their activities, or their power to bring about the evil, this Court will review the convictions with the scrupulous care demanded by our Constitution. But we are not convinced that because there may be borderline cases at some time in the future, these convictions should be reversed because of the argument that these petitioners could not know that their activities were constitutionally proscribed by the statute. . . .

We hold that §§2(a)(1), (2)(a)(3) and 3 of the Smith Act, do not inherently, or as construed or applied in the instant case, violate the First Amendment and other provisions of the Bill of Rights, or the First and Fifth Amendments because of indefiniteness. Petitioners intended to overthrow the Government of the United States as speedily as the circumstances would permit. Their conspiracy to organize the Communist Party and to teach and advocate the overthrow of the Government of the United States by force and violence created a "clear and present danger" of an attempt to overthrow the Government by force and violence. They were properly and constitutionally convicted for violation of the Smith Act. The judgments of conviction are affirmed.

MR. JUSTICE CLARK took no part in the consideration or decision of this case.

MR. JUSTICE FRANKFURTER, concurring. . . .

. . . The demands of free speech in a democratic society as well as the interest in national security are better served by candid and informed weighing of the competing interests, within the confines of the judicial process, than by announcing dogmas too inflexible for the non-Euclidian problems to be solved.

But how are competing interests to be assessed? Since they are not subject to quantitative ascertainment, the issue necessarily resolves itself into asking, who is to make the adjustment? — who is to balance the relevant factors and ascertain which interest is in the circumstances to prevail? Full responsibility for the choice cannot be given to the courts. Courts are not representative bodies. They are not designed to be a good reflex of a democratic society. Their judgment is best informed, and therefore most dependable, within narrow limits. Their essential quality is detachment, founded on independence. History teaches that the independence of the judiciary is jeopardized when courts become embroiled in the passions of the day and assume primary responsibility in choosing between competing political, economic and social pressures.

Primary responsibility for adjusting the interests which compete in the situation before us of necessity belongs to the Congress. The nature of the power to be exercised by this Court has been delineated in decisions not charged with the emotional appeal of situations such as that now before us. We are to set aside the judgment of those whose duty it is to legislate only if there is no reasonable basis for it. . . .

On the one hand is the interest in security. The Communist Party was not designed by these defendants as an ordinary political party. For the circumstances of its organization, its aims and methods, and the relation of the defendants to its organization and aims we are concluded by the jury's verdict. . . .

. . . But in determining whether application of the statute to the defendants is within the constitutional powers of Congress, we are not limited to the facts found by the jury.

We must view such a question in the light of whatever is relevant to a legislative judgment. We may take judicial notice that the Communist doctrines which these defendants have conspired to advocate are in the ascendancy in powerful nations who cannot be acquitted of unfriendliness to the institutions of this country. We may take account of evidence brought forward at this trial and elsewhere, much of which has long been common knowledge. In sum, it would amply justify a legislature in concluding that recruitment of additional members for the Party would create a substantial danger to national security.

On the other hand is the interest in free speech. The right to exert all governmental powers in aid of maintaining our institutions and resisting their physical overthrow does not include intolerance of opinions and speech that cannot do harm although opposed and perhaps alien to dominant, traditional opinion. The treatment of its minorities, especially their legal position, is among the most searching tests of the level of civilization attained by a society. It is better for those who have almost unlimited power of government in their hands to err on the side of freedom. We have enjoyed so much freedom for so long that we are perhaps in danger of forgetting how much blood it cost to establish the Bill of Rights.

It is not for us to decide how we would adjust the clash of interests which this case presents were the primary responsibility for reconciling it ours. Congress has determined that the danger created by advocacy of overthrow justifies the ensuing restriction on freedom of speech. The determination was made after due deliberation, and the seriousness of the congressional purpose is attested by the volume of legislation passed to effectuate the same ends.

To make validity of legislation depend on judicial reading of events still in the womb of time — a forecast, that is, of the outcome of forces at best appreciated only with knowledge of the topmost secrets of nations — is to charge the judiciary with duties beyond its equipment. . . .

Civil liberties draw at best only limited strength from legal guarantees. Preoccupation by our people with the constitutionality, instead of with the wisdom, of legislation or of executive action is preoccupation with a false value. . . . Focusing attention on constitutionality tends to make constitutionality synonymous with wisdom. When legislation touches freedom of thought and freedom of speech, such a tendency is a formidable enemy of the free spirit. Much that should be rejected as illiberal, because repressive and envenoming, may well be not unconstitutional. The ultimate reliance for the deepest needs of civilization must be found outside their vindication in courts of law; apart from all else, judges, howsoever they may conscientiously seek to discipline themselves against it, unconsciously are too apt to be moved by the deep undercurrents of public feeling. A persistent, positive translation of the liberating faith into the feelings and thoughts and actions of men and women is the real protection against attempts to strait-jacket the human mind. . . .[j]

MR. JUSTICE BLACK, dissenting.

Here again, as in Breard v. Alexandria, decided this day [341 U.S. 622] my basic disagreement with the Court is not as to how we should explain or reconcile what was said in prior decisions but springs from a fundamental difference in constitutional approach. Consequently, it would serve no useful purpose to state my position at length.

At the outset I want to emphasize what the crime involved in this case is, and what it is not. These petitioners were not charged with an attempt to overthrow the Government. They were not charged with overt acts of any kind designed to overthrow the Government. They were not even charged with saying anything or writing anything designed to overthrow the Government. The charge was that they agreed to assemble and to talk and publish certain ideas at a later date: The indictment is that they conspired to organize the Communist Party and to use speech or newspapers and other publications in the future to

---

[j] A concurring opinion of Mr. Justice Jackson is omitted. — ED.

teach and advocate the forcible overthrow of the Government. No matter how it is worded, this is a virulent form of prior censorship of speech and press, which I believe the First Amendment forbids. I would hold §3 of the Smith Act authorizing this prior restraint unconstitutional on its face and as applied.

But let us assume, contrary to all constitutional ideas of fair criminal procedure that the petitioners although not indicted for the crime of actual advocacy, may be punished for it. Even on this radical assumption, the other opinions in this case show that the only way to affirm these convictions is to repudiate directly or indirectly the established "clear and present danger" rule. This the Court does in a way which greatly restricts the protections afforded by the First Amendment. The opinions for affirmance indicate that the chief reason for jettisoning the rule is the expressed fear that advocacy of Communist doctrine endangers the safety of the Republic. Undoubtedly, a governmental policy of unfettered communication of ideas does entail dangers. To the Founders of this Nation, however, the benefits derived from free expression were worth the risk. They embodied this philosophy in the First Amendment's command that Congress "shall make no law abridging . . . the freedom of speech, or of the press. . . ." I have always believed that the First Amendment is the keystone of our Government, that the freedoms it guarantees provide the best insurance against destruction of all freedom. At least as to speech in the realm of public matters, I believe that the "clear and present danger" test does not "mark the furthermost constitutional boundaries of protected expression" but does "no more than recognize a minimum compulsion of the Bill of Rights." Bridges v. California, 341 U.S. 252, 263.

So long as this Court exercises the power of judicial review of legislation, I cannot agree that the First Amendment permits us to sustain laws suppressing freedom of speech and press on the basis of Congress' or our own notions of mere "reasonableness." Such a doctrine waters down the First Amendment so that it amounts to little more than an admonition to Congress. The Amendment as so construed is not likely to protect any but those "safe" or orthodox views which rarely need its protection. . . .

Public opinion being what it now is, few will protest the conviction of these Communist petitioners. There is hope, however, that in calmer times, when present pressures, passions and fears subside, this or some later Court will restore the First Amendment liberties to the high preferred place where they belong in a free society.

MR. JUSTICE DOUGLAS, dissenting.

If this were a case where those who claimed protection under the First Amendment were teaching the techniques of sabotage, the assassination of the President, the filching of documents from public files, the planting of bombs, the art of street warfare, and the like, I would have no doubts. The freedom to speak is not absolute; the teaching of methods of terror and other seditious conduct should be beyond the pale along with obscenity and immorality. This case was argued as if those were the facts. The argument imported much seditious conduct into the record. That is easy and it has popular appeal, for the activities of Communists in plotting and scheming against the free world are common knowledge. But the fact is that no such evidence was introduced at the trial. There is a statute which makes a seditious conspiracy unlawful.[1] Petitioners, however, were not charged with a "conspiracy to overthrow" the Government. They were charged with a conspiracy to form a party and groups and assemblies of people who teach and advocate the overthrow of our Government by force or violence and with a conspiracy to advocate and teach its overthrow by force and violence. It may well be that indoctrination in the

---

[1] 18 U.S.C. §2384 provides: "If two or more persons in any State or Territory, or in any place subject to the jurisdiction of the United States, conspire to overthrow, put down, or destroy by force the Government of the United States, or to levy war against them, or to oppose by force the authority thereof, or by force to prevent, hinder, or delay the execution of any law of the United States, or by force to seize, take, or possess any property of the United States contrary to the authority thereof, they shall each be fined not more than $5,000 or imprisoned not more than six years, or both."

techniques of terror to destroy the Government would be indictable under either statute. But the teaching which is condemned here is of a different character.

So far as the present record is concerned, what petitioners did was to organize people to teach and themselves teach the Marxist-Leninist doctrine contained chiefly in four books: Foundations of Leninism, by Stalin (1924), The Communist Manifesto, by Marx and Engels (1848), State and Revolution, by Lenin (1917), History of the Communist Party of the Soviet Union (B.) (1939). . . .

The opinion of the Court does not outlaw these texts nor condemn them to the fire, as the Communists do literature offensive to their creed. But if the books themselves are not outlawed, if they can lawfully remain on library shelves, by what reasoning does their use in a classroom become a crime? It would not be a crime under the Act to introduce these books to a class, though that would be teaching what the creed of violent overthrow of the government is. The Act, as construed, requires the element of intent — that those who teach the creed believe in it. The crime then depends not on what it taught but on who the teacher is. That is to make freedom of speech turn not on *what is said*, but on the intent with which it is said. Once we start down that road we enter territory dangerous to the liberties of every citizen. . . .

The nature of Communism as a force on the world scene would, of course, be relevant to the issue of clear and present danger of petitioners' advocacy within the United States. But the primary consideration is the strength and tactical position of petitioners and their converts in this country. On that there is no evidence in the record. If we are to take judicial notice of the threat of Communists within the nation, it should not be difficult to conclude that *as a political party* they are of little consequence. Communists in this country have never made a respectable or serious showing in any election. I would doubt that there is a village, let alone a city or county or state, which the Communists could carry. Communism in the world scene is no bogey-man; but Communism as a political faction or party in this country plainly is. Communism has been so thoroughly exposed in this country that it has been crippled as a political force. Free speech has destroyed it as an effective political party. It is inconceivable that those who went up and down this country preaching the doctrine of revolution which petitioners espouse would have any success. In days of trouble and confusion when bread lines were long, when the unemployed walked the streets, when people were starving, the advocates of a short-cut by revolution might have had a chance to gain adherents. But today there are no such conditions. The country is not in despair; the people know Soviet Communism; the doctrine of Soviet revolution is exposed in all of its ugliness and the American people want none of it.

How it can be said that there is a clear and present danger that this advocacy will succeed is, therefore, a mystery. Some nations less resilient than the United States, where illiteracy is high and where democratic traditions are only budding, might have to take drastic steps and jail these men for merely speaking their creed. But in America they are miserable merchants of unwanted ideas; their wares remain unsold. The fact that their ideas are abhorrent does not make them powerful.

The political impotence of the Communists in this country does not, of course, dispose of the problem. Their numbers; their positions in industry and government; the extent to which they have in fact infiltrated the police, the armed services, transportation, stevedoring, power plants, munitions works, and other critical places — these facts all bear on the likelihood that their advocacy of the Soviet theory of revolution will endanger the Republic. But the record is silent on these facts. If we are to proceed on the basis of judicial notice, it is impossible for me to say that the Communists in this country are so potent or so strategically deployed that they must be suppressed in their speech. I could not so hold unless I were willing to conclude that the activities in recent years of committees of Congress, of the Attorney General, of labor unions, of state legislatures, and of Loyalty Boards were so futile as to leave the country on the edge of grave peril. To believe that petitioners and their following are placed in such critical positions as to endanger the Nation is to believe the incredible. It is safe to say that the followers of the creed of Soviet Communism are known to the F.B.I.; that in case of war with Russia they will be picked up overnight as were all prospective saboteurs at the commencement of World War II; that the invisible army of petitioners is the best known, the most beset, and the least thriving of any fifth column in history. Only those held by fear and panic could think otherwise. . . .

Yates v. United States 354 U.S. 298, 77 S. Ct. 1064, 1 L. Ed. 2d 1356 (1957)

MR. JUSTICE HARLAN delivered the opinion of the Court.

We brought these cases here to consider certain questions arising under the Smith Act which have not heretofore been passed upon by this Court, and otherwise to review the convictions of these petitioners for conspiracy to violate that Act. Among other things, the convictions are claimed to rest upon an application of the Smith Act which is hostile to the principles upon which its constitutionality was upheld in Dennis v. United States, 341 U.S. 494.

These 14 petitioners stand convicted, after a jury trial in the United States District Court for the Southern District of California, upon a single count indictment charging them with conspiring (1) to advocate and teach the duty and necessity of overthrowing the Government of the United States by force and violence, and (2) to organize, as the Communist Party of the United States, a society of persons who so advocate and teach, all with the intent of causing the overthrow of the Government by force and violence as speedily as circumstances would permit. Act of June 28, 1940, §2(a)(1) and (3), 54 Stat. 670, 671, 18 U.S.C. §§371, 2385. The conspiracy is alleged to have originated in 1940 and continued down to the date of the indictment in 1951. The indictment charged that in carrying out the conspiracy the defendants and their co-conspirators would (a) become members and officers of the Communist Party, with knowledge of its unlawful purposes, and assume leadership in carrying out its policies and activities; (b) cause to be organized units of the Party in California and elsewhere; (c) write and publish, in the "Daily Worker" and other Party organs, articles on the proscribed advocacy and teaching; (d) conduct schools for the indoctrination of Party members in such advocacy and teaching, and (e) recruit new Party members, particularly from among persons employed in the key industries of the nation. Twenty-three overt acts in furtherance of the conspiracy were alleged.

Upon conviction each of the petitioners was sentenced to five years' imprisonment and a fine of $10,000. The Court of Appeals affirmed. 225 F.2d 146. We granted certiorari for the reasons already indicated. 350 U.S. 860.

In the view we take of this case, it is necessary for us to consider only the following of petitioners' contentions: (1) that the term "organize" as used in the Smith Act was erroneously construed by the two lower courts; (2) that the trial court's instructions to the jury erroneously excluded from the case the issue of "incitement to action"; (3) that the evidence was so insufficient as to require this Court to direct the acquittal of these petitioners and (4) that petitioner Schneiderman's conviction was precluded by this Court's judgment in Schneiderman v. United States, 320 U.S. 118, under the doctrine of collateral estoppel. For reasons given hereafter, we conclude that these convictions must be reversed and the case remanded to the District Court with instructions to enter judgments of acquittal as to certain of the petitioners, and to grant a new trial as to the rest.

I. THE TERM "ORGANIZE"

[The discussion of this point is here omitted. The Court held that "organize" in the statute meant creation of a new organization, not maintenance of an old one; the Com-

Section C. Freedom of Speech and Association

munist Party was organized in 1945; the present indictment was returned in 1951; the charge of "organization" was barred by the three-year statute of limitations.]

II. INSTRUCTIONS TO THE JURY

Petitioners contend that the instructions to the jury were fatally defective in that the trial court refused to charge that, in order to convict, the jury must find that the advocacy which the defendants conspired to promote was of a kind calculated to "incite" persons to action for the forcible overthrow of the Government. . . . The Government, which at the trial also requested the court to charge in terms of "incitement," now takes the position, however, that the true constitutional dividing line is not between inciting and abstract advocacy of forcible overthrow, but rather between advocacy as such, irrespective of its inciting qualities, and the mere discussion or exposition of violent overthrow as an abstract theory.

. . . After telling the jury that it could not convict the defendants for holding or expressing mere opinions, beliefs, or predictions relating to violent overthrow, the trial court defined the content of the proscribed advocacy or teaching in the following terms, which are crucial here:

"Any advocacy or teaching which does not include the urging of force and violence as the means of overthrowing and destroying the Government of the United States is not within the issue of the indictment here and can constitute no basis for any finding against the defendants.

"The kind of advocacy and teaching which is charged and upon which your verdict must be reached is not merely a desirability but a necessity that the Government of the United States be overthrown and destroyed by force and violence and not merely a propriety but a duty to overthrow and destroy the Government of the United States by force and violence."

There can be no doubt from the record that in so instructing the jury the court regarded as immaterial, and intended to withdraw from the jury's consideration, any issue as to the character of the advocacy in terms of its capacity to stir listeners to forcible action. Both the petitioners and the Government submitted proposed instructions which would have required the jury to find that the proscribed advocacy was not of a mere abstract doctrine of forcible overthrow, but of action to that end, by the use of language reasonably and ordinarily calculated to incite persons to such action. The trial court rejected these proposed instructions on the ground that any necessity for giving them which may have existed at the time the Dennis case was tried was removed by this Court's subsequent decision in that case. The court made it clear in colloquy with counsel that in its view the illegal advocacy was made out simply by showing that what was said dealt with forcible overthrow and that it was uttered with a specific intent to accomplish that purpose, insisting that all such advocacy was punishable "whether it is language of incitement or not." The Court of Appeals affirmed on a different theory, as we shall see later on.

We are thus faced with the question whether the Smith Act prohibits advocacy and teaching of forcible overthrow as an abstract principle, divorced from any effort to instigate action to that end, so long as such advocacy or teaching is engaged in with evil intent. We hold that it does not.

The distinction between advocacy of abstract doctrine and advocacy directed at promoting unlawful action is one that has been consistently recognized in the opinions of this Court, beginning with Fox v. Washington, 236 U.S. 273, and Schenck v. United States, 249 U.S. 47. This distinction was heavily underscored in Gitlow v. New York, 268 U.S. 652, in which the statute involved was nearly identical with the one now before us. . . .

We need not, however, decide the issue before us in terms of constitutional compulsion, for our first duty is to construe this statute. In doing so we should not assume that Congress chose to disregard a constitutional danger zone so clearly marked, or that it used the words "advocate" and "teach" in their ordinary dictionary meanings when they had already been construed as terms of art carrying a special and limited connotation. . . . The legislative history of the Smith Act and related bills shows beyond all question that Congress was aware of the distinction between the advocacy or teaching of abstract doctrine and the advocacy or teaching of action, and that it did not intend to disregard it. The statute was aimed at the advocacy and teaching of concrete action for the forcible overthrow of the Government, and not of principles divorced from action.

The Government's reliance on this Court's decision in Dennis is misplaced. The jury's instructions which were refused here were given there, and were referred to by this Court as requiring "the jury to find the facts *essential* to establish the substantive crime." 341 U.S., at 512 (emphasis added). It is true that at one point in the late Chief Justice's opinion it is stated that the Smith Act "is directed at advocacy, not discussion," id., at 502, but it is clear that the reference was to advocacy of action, not ideas, for in the very next sentence the opinion emphasizes that the jury was properly instructed that there could be no conviction for "advocacy in the realm of ideas." The two concurring opinions in that case likewise emphasize the distinction with which we are concerned. . . .

. . . The essence of the Dennis holding was that indoctrination of a group in preparation for future violent action, as well as exhortation to immediate action, by advocacy found to be directed to "action for the accomplishment" of forcible overthrow, to violence as "a rule or principle of action," and employing "language of incitement," id., at 511-512, is not constitutionally protected when the group is of sufficient size and cohesiveness, is sufficiently oriented towards action, and other circumstances are such as reasonably to justify apprehension that action will occur. This is quite a different thing from the view of the District Court here that mere doctrinal justification of forcible overthrow, if engaged in with the intent to accomplish overthrow, is punishable per se under the Smith Act. That sort of advocacy, even though uttered with the hope that it may ultimately lead to violent revolution, is too remote from concrete action to be regarded as the kind of indoctrination preparatory to action which was condemned in Dennis. As one of the concurring opinions in Dennis put it: "Throughout our decisions there has recurred a distinction between the statement of an idea which may prompt its hearers to take unlawful action, and advocacy that such action be taken." Id., at 545. There is nothing in Dennis which makes that historic distinction obsolete. . . .[k]

NOTE

Discerning comment on the Dennis case is found in the following articles: Richardson, Freedom of Expression and the Function of Courts, 65 Harv. L. Rev. 1 (1951); Gorfinkel and Mack, Dennis v. United States and the Clear and Present Danger Rule, 39 Calif. L. Rev. 476 (1951); Mendelson, Clear and Present Danger — From Schenck to Dennis, 52 Colum. L. Rev. 313 (1952). See also Wyzanski, The Communist Party and the Law, 187 Atlantic Monthly 27 (May 1951); Ernst and Katz, Speech: Public and Private, 53 Colum. L. Rev. 620 (1953).

Alexander Meikeljohn has urged a new interpretation of the First Amendment — an interpretation which would almost wholly immunize political discussion from governmental penalty, while permitting reasonable restrictions on nonpolitical speech and writing. See his Free Speech and Its Relation to Self-government (1948), and his essay, What Does the First Amendment Mean, 20 U. Chi. L. Rev. 461 (1953). For critical comment on the Meikeljohn thesis see Chafee, Review, 62 Harv. L. Rev. 891 (1941), and Mendelson, The Clear and Present Danger Test — A Reply to Mr. Meikeljohn, 5 Vand. L. Rev.

---

[k] Concurring opinions of Burton and Black, JJ., and a dissent by Mr. Justice Clark are omitted. Mr. Justice Brennan and Mr. Justice Whittaker took no part in the consideration or decision of the case. — ED.

Section C. **Freedom of Speech and Association** 1173

792 (1952). See also Brennan, The Supreme Court and the Meikeljohn Interpretation of the First Amendment, 79 Harv. L. Rev. 1 (1965).

A radical and learned reinterpretation of English and American backgrounds of the First Amendment is presented in Levy, Legacy of Suppression (1960).

Mr. Justice Black has discussed his reading of the First Amendment in his lecture, The Bill of Rights, 35 N.Y.U.L. Rev. 865 (1960). Another exposition of his views is set forth by Black & Cahn, Justice Black and First Amendment "Absolutes": A Public Interview, 37 N.Y.U.L. Rev. 549 (1962). See generally Hugo Black, A Constitutional Faith (1969).

On remand in Yates, the government requested dismissal of the indictments. In another round of cases under the Smith Act, Justice Harlan again construed the statute strictly to conform it with the First Amendment: Scales v. United States, 367 U.S. 203 (1961), and Noto v. United States, 367 U.S. 290 (1961). In Scales, the Court sustained the provision of the Smith Act that prohibited the acquisition or holding of membership in any organization which advocated the overthrow of the government of the United States by force or violence. But, Justice Harlan held, the prohibition reached only "active" members of the Communist party who knew and approved of its illegal advocacy. Under that construction the Court affirmed the conviction of Scales but reversed the conviction of Noto for insufficiency of evidence. Although the Smith Act is still law, 18 U.S.C. §2385 (1970), no one has been convicted under its provisions since Scales.

Brandenburg v. Ohio 395 U.S. 444, 89 S. Ct. 1827, 23 L. Ed. 2d 430 (1969)

PER CURIAM. The appellant, a leader of a Ku Klux Klan group, was convicted under the Ohio Criminal Syndicalism statute of "advocat[ing] . . . the duty, necessity, or propriety of crime, sabotage, violence, or unlawful methods of terrorism as a means of accomplishing industrial or political reform" and of "voluntarily assembl[ing] with any society, group or assemblage of persons formed to teach or advocate the doctrines of criminal syndicalism." Ohio Rev. Code §2923.13. He was fined $1,000 and sentenced to one to 10 years' imprisonment. The appellant challenged the constitutionality of the criminal syndicalism statute under the First and Fourteenth Amendments to the United States Constitution, but the intermediate appellate court of Ohio affirmed his conviction without opinion. The Supreme Court of Ohio dismissed his appeal, sua sponte, "for the reason that no substantial constitutional question exists herein." It did not file an opinion or explain its conclusions. Appeal was taken to this Court, and we noted probable jurisdiction. 393 U.S. 948 (1968). We reverse.

The record shows that a man, identified at trial as the appellant, telephoned an announcer-reporter on the staff of a Cincinnati television station and invited him to come to a Ku Klux Klan "rally" to be held at a farm in Hamilton County. With the cooperation of the organizers, the reporter and a cameraman attended the meeting and filmed the events. Portions of the films were later broadcast on the local station and on a national network.

The prosecution's case rested on the films and on testimony identifying the appellant as the person who communicated with the reporter and who spoke at the rally. The State also introduced into evidence several articles appearing in the film, including a pistol, a rifle, a shotgun, ammunition, a Bible, and a red hood worn by the speaker in the films.

One film showed 12 hooded figures, some of whom carried firearms. They were gathered around a large wooden cross, which they burned. No one was present other than the participants and the newsman who made the film. Most of the words uttered during the scene were incomprehensible when the film was projected, but scattered phrases could be understood that were derogatory of Negroes and, in one instance, of Jews. Another scene on the same film showed the appellant, in Klan regalia, making a speech. The speech, in full, was as follows:

"This is an organizers' meeting. We have had quite a few members here today which are — we have hundreds, hundreds of members throughout the State of Ohio. I can quote from a newspaper clipping from the Columbus Ohio Dispatch, five weeks ago Sunday morning. The Klan has more members in the State of Ohio than does any other organization. We're not a revengent organization, but if our President, our Congress, our Supreme Court, continues to suppress the white, Caucasian race, it's possible that there might have to be some revengence taken.

"We are marching on Congress July the Fourth, four hundred thousand strong. From there we are dividing into two groups, one group to march on St. Augustine, Florida, the other group to march into Mississippi. Thank you."

The second film showed six hooded figures one of whom, later identified as the appellant, repeated a speech very similar to that recorded on the first film. The reference to the possibility of "revengence" was omitted, and one sentence was added: "Personally, I believe the nigger should be returned to Africa, the Jew returned to Israel." Though some of the figures in the films carried weapons, the speaker did not.

The Ohio Criminal Syndicalism Statute was enacted in 1919. From 1917 to 1920, identical or quite similar laws were adopted by 20 States and two territories. E. Dowell, A History of Criminal Syndicalism Legislation in the United States 21 (1939). In 1927, this Court sustained the constitutionality of California's Criminal Syndicalism Act . . . , the text of which is quite similar to that of the laws of Ohio. Whitney v. California, 274 U.S. 357 (1927). The Court upheld the statute on the ground that, without more, "advocating" violent means to effect political and economic change involves such danger to the security of the State that the State may outlaw it. Cf. Fiske v. Kansas, 274 U.S. 380 (1927). But Whitney has been thoroughly discredited by later decisions. See Dennis v. United States, 341 U.S. 494, at 507 (1951). These later decisions have fashioned the principle that the constitutional guarantees of free speech and free press do not permit a State to forbid or proscribe advocacy of the use of force or of law violation except where such advocacy is directed to inciting or producing imminent lawless action and is likely to incite or produce such action.[1] As we said in Noto v. United States, 367 U.S. 290, 297-298 (1961), "the mere abstract teaching . . . of the moral propriety or even moral necessity for a resort to force and violence, is not the same as preparing a group for violent action and steeling it to such action." See also Herndon v. Lowry, 301 U.S. 242, 259-261 (1937); Bond v. Floyd, 385 U.S. 116, 134 (1966). A statute which fails to draw this distinction impermissibly intrudes upon the freedoms guaranteed by the First and Fourteenth Amendments. It sweeps within its condemnation speech which our Constitution has immunized from governmental control. Cf. Yates v. United States, 354 U.S. 298 (1957); DeJonge v. Oregon, 299 U.S. 353 (1937); Stromberg v. California, 283 U.S. 359 (1931). See also United States v. Robel, 389 U.S. 258 (1967); Keyishian v. Board of Regents, 385 U.S. 589 (1967); Elfbrandt v. Russell, 384 U.S. 11 (1966); Aptheker v. Secretary of State, 378 U.S. 500 (1964); Baggett v. Bullitt, 377 U.S. 360 (1964).

Measured by this test, Ohio's Criminal Syndicalism Act cannot be sustained. . . . Neither the indictment nor the trial judge's instructions to the jury in any way refined the statute's bald definition of the crime in terms of mere advocacy not distinguished from incitement to imminent lawless action.

Accordingly, we are here confronted with a statute which, by its own words and as applied, purports to punish mere advocacy and to forbid, on pain of criminal punishment, assembly with others merely to advocate the described type of action. Such a statute

---

[1] It was on the theory that the Smith Act, 54 Stat. 670, 18 U.S.C. §2385, embodied such a principle and that it had been applied only in conformity with it that this Court sustained the Act's constitutionality. Dennis v. United States, 341 U.S. 494 (1951). That this was the basis for Dennis was emphasized in Yates v. United States, 354 U.S. 298, 320-324 (1957), in which the Court overturned convictions for advocacy of the forcible overthrow of the Government under the Smith Act, because the trial judge's instructions had allowed conviction for mere advocacy, unrelated to its tendency to produce forcible action.

falls within the condemnation of the First and Fourteenth Amendments. The contrary teaching of Whitney v. California, supra, cannot be supported, and that decision is therefore overruled.

Reversed.

MR. JUSTICE BLACK, concurring. I agree with the views expressed by Mr. Justice Douglas in his concurring opinion in this case that the "clear and present danger" doctrine should have no place in the interpretation of the First Amendment. I join the Court's opinion, which, as I understand it, simply cites Dennis v. United States, 341 U.S. 494 (1951), but does not indicate any agreement on the Court's part with the "clear and present danger" doctrine on which Dennis purported to rely.[1]

NOTE Developments under the Brandenburg Test

The stringency of the Brandenburg test was further demonstrated in Hess v. Indiana, 414 U.S. 105 (1973), where the Court reversed the conviction for disorderly conduct of a person who had shouted, "We'll take the fucking street later (or again)," during an antiwar demonstration. In applying Brandenburg, the per curiam opinion of the Court noted that the words were not "intended to produce, and likely to produce, *imminent* disorder." (Emphasis in original.) Id. at 109. The Chief Justice and Justice Blackmun joined in a dissent by Justice Rehnquist. The Court also relied upon Brandenburg in Communist Party of Indiana v. Whitcomb, 414 U.S. 441 (1974), invalidating a state statute which denied a place on the ballot to any new party which failed to file "an affidavit, by its officers, under oath, that it does not advocate the overthrow of local, state or national government by force or violence. . . ."

Should a standard less strict than Brandenburg be applied where noncriminal sanctions are imposed? May a lesser standard be more appropriate for special institutional settings? See, for example, Healy v. James, 408 U.S. 169 (1972) (refusal of state college to recognize chapter of SDS overturned), but compare Parker v. Levy, 417 U.S. 133 (1974) (court-martial conviction for urging refusal to go to Viet Nam affirmed). See Comment, Brandenburg v. Ohio, A Speech Test For All Seasons?, 43 U. Chi. L. Rev. 151 (1975).

b. The Public Forum

Thornhill v. Alabama 310 U.S. 88, 60 S. Ct. 736, 84 L. Ed. 109 (1940)

MR. JUSTICE MURPHY delivered the opinion of the Court.

Petitioner, Byron Thornhill, was convicted in the Circuit Court of Tuscaloosa County, Alabama, of the violation of § 3448 of the State Code of 1923. The Code section reads as follows:

"Section 3448. Loitering or picketing forbidden. — Any person or persons, who, without a just cause or legal excuse therefor, go near to or loiter about the premises or place of business of any other person, firm, corporation, or association of people, engaged in a lawful business, for the purpose, or with the intent of influencing, or inducing other persons not to trade with, buy from, sell to, have business dealings with, or be employed by such persons, firm, corporation, or association, or who picket the works or place of business of such other persons, firms, corporations, or associations of persons, for the purpose of hindering, delaying, or interfering with or injuring any lawful business or enterprise of another, shall be guilty of a misdemeanor; but nothing herein shall prevent any person from soliciting trade or business for a competitive business."

---

[1] A concurring opinion of Mr. Justice Douglas is omitted. — ED.

1176   Chapter Sixteen. **Substantive Rights**

    The complaint against petitioner . . . is phrased substantially in the very words of the statute. The first and second counts charge that petitioner, without just cause or legal excuse, did "go near to or loiter about the premises" of the Brown Wood Preserving Company with the intent or purpose of influencing others to adopt one of enumerated courses of conduct. In the third count, the charge is that petitioner "did picket" the works of the Company "for the purpose of hindering, delaying or interfering with or injuring [its] lawful business." Petitioner demurred to the complaint on the grounds, among others, that § 3448 was repugnant to the Constitution of the United States in that it deprived him of "the right of peaceful assemblage," "the right of freedom of speech," and "the right to petition for redress." The demurrer, so far as the record shows, was not ruled upon, and petitioner pleaded not guilty. The Circuit Court then proceeded to try the case without a jury, one not being asked for or demanded. At the close of the case for the State, petitioner moved to exclude all the testimony taken at the trial on the ground that § 3448 was violative of the Constitution of the United States. The Circuit Court overruled the motion, found petitioner "guilty of Loitering and Picketing as charged in the complaint," and entered judgment accordingly. The judgment was affirmed by the Court of Appeals, which considered the constitutional question and sustained the section on the authority of two previous decisions in the Alabama courts. . . . A petition for certiorari was denied by the Supreme Court of the State. The case is here on certiorari granted because of the questions presented. . . .

    The proofs consist of the testimony of two witnesses for the prosecution. It appears that petitioner on the morning of his arrest was seen "in company with six or eight other men" "on the picket line" at the plant of the Brown Wood Preserving Company. Some weeks previously a strike order had been issued by a Union, apparently affiliated with the American Federation of Labor, which had as members all but four of the approximately one hundred employees of the plant. Since that time a picket line with two picket posts of six to eight men each had been maintained around the plant twenty-four hours a day. The picket posts appear to have been on Company property, "on a private entrance for employees, and not on any public road." One witness explained that practically all of the employees live on Company property and get their mail from a post office on Company property and that the Union holds its meetings on Company property. No demand was ever made upon the men not to come on the property. There is no testimony indicating the nature of the dispute between the Union and the Preserving Company, or the course of events which led to the issuance of the strike order, or the nature of the efforts for conciliation.

    The Company scheduled a day for the plant to resume operations. One of the witnesses, Clarence Simpson, who was not a member of the Union, on reporting to the plant on the day indicated, was approached by petitioner who told him that "they were on strike and did not want anybody to go up there to work." None of the other employees said anything to Simpson, who testified: "Neither Mr. Thornhill nor any other employee threatened me on the occasion testified to. Mr. Thornhill approached me in a peaceful manner, and did not put me in fear; he did not appear to be mad." "I then turned and went back to the house, and did not go to work." The other witness, J. M. Walden, testified: "At the time Mr. Thornhill and Clarence Simpson were talking to each other, there was no one else present, and I heard no harsh words and saw nothing threatening in the manner of either man." For engaging in some or all of these activities, petitioner was arrested, charged, and convicted as described.

    First. The freedom of speech and of the press, which are secured by the First Amendment against abridgment by the United States, are among the fundamental personal rights and liberties which are secured to all persons by the Fourteenth Amendment against abridgment by a State.

    . . . It is imperative that, when the effective exercise of these rights is claimed to be abridged, the courts should "weigh the circumstances" and "appraise the substantiality of the reasons advanced" in support of the challenged regulations. Schneider v. State, 308 U.S. 147, 161, 162.

Second. The section in question must be judged upon its face.

The finding against petitioner was a general one. It did not specify the testimony upon which it rested. The charges were framed in the words of the statute and so must be given a like construction. The courts below expressed no intention of narrowing the construction put upon the statute by prior state decisions. In these circumstances, there is no occasion to go behind the face of the statute or of the complaint for the purpose of determining whether the evidence together with the permissible inferences to be drawn from it, could ever support a conviction founded upon different and more precise charges. . . .

There is a further reason for testing the section on its face. Proof of an abuse of power in the particular case has never been deemed a requisite for attack on the constitutionality of a statute purporting to license the dissemination of ideas. Schneider v. State, 308 U.S. 147, 162-165; Hague v. C.I.O., 307 U.S. 496, 516; Lovell v. Griffin, 303 U.S. 444, 451. The cases when interpreted in the light of their facts indicate that the rule is not based upon any assumption that application for the license would be refused or would result in the imposition of other unlawful regulations. Rather it derives from an appreciation of the character of the evil inherent in a licensing system. . . . A like threat is inherent in a penal statute, like that in question here, which does not aim specifically at evils within the allowable area of state control but, on the contrary, sweeps within its ambit other activities that in ordinary circumstances constitute an exercise of freedom of speech or of the press. The existence of such a statute, which readily lends itself to harsh and discriminatory enforcement by local prosecuting officials, against particular groups deemed to merit their displeasure, results in a continuous and pervasive restraint on all freedom of discussion that might reasonably be regarded as within its purview.[11] It is not any less effective or, if the restraint is not permissible, less pernicious than the restraint on freedom of discussion imposed by the threat of censorship. An accused, after arrest and conviction under such a statute, does not have to sustain the burden of demonstrating that the State could not constitutionally have written a different and specific statute covering his activities as disclosed by the charge and the evidence introduced against him. . . .

Third. Section 3448 has been applied by the state courts so as to prohibit a single individual from walking slowly and peacefully back and forth on the public sidewalk in front of the premises of an employer, without speaking to anyone, carrying a sign or placard on a staff above his head stating only the fact that the employer did not employ union men affiliated with the American Federation of Labor; the purpose of the described activity was concededly to advise customers and prospective customers of the relationship existing between the employer and its employees and thereby to induce such customers not to patronize the employer. O'Rourke v. Birmingham, 27 Ala. App. 133, cert. denied, 232 Ala. 355. The statute as thus authoritatively construed and applied leaves room for no exceptions based upon either the number of persons engaged in the proscribed activity, the peaceful character of their demeanor, the nature of their dispute with an employer, or the restrained character and the accurateness of the terminology used in notifying the public of the facts of the dispute.

Fourth. We think that §3448 is invalid on its face.

The freedom of speech and of the press guaranteed by the Constitution embraces at the least the liberty to discuss publicly and truthfully all matters of public concern without previous restraint or fear of subsequent punishment. . . .

In the circumstances of our times the dissemination of information concerning the facts

---

[11] The record in the case at bar permits the inference that, while picketing had been carried on for several weeks, with six to eight men at each of two picket posts, §3448 was not enforced against anyone other than petitioner, the Union President, and then only after his conversation with Simpson who thereupon returned home rather than report for work.

of a labor dispute must be regarded as within that area of free discussion that is guaranteed by the Constitution. . . .

The range of activities proscribed by §3448, whether characterized as picketing or loitering or otherwise, embraces nearly every practicable, effective means whereby those interested — including the employees directly affected — may enlighten the public on the nature and causes of a labor dispute. The safeguarding of these means is essential to the securing of an informed and educated public opinion with respect to a matter which is of public concern. It may be that effective exercise of the means of advancing public knowledge may persuade some of those reached to refrain from entering into advantageous relations with the business establishment which is the scene of the dispute. Every expression of opinion on matters that are important has the potentiality of inducing action in the interests of one rather than another group in society. But the group in power at any moment may not impose penal sanctions on peaceful and truthful discussion of matters of public interest merely on a showing that others may thereby be persuaded to take action inconsistent with its interests. Abridgment of the liberty of such discussion can be justified only where the clear danger of substantive evils arises under circumstances affording no opportunity to test the merits of ideas by competition for acceptance in the market of public opinion. We hold that the danger of injury to an industrial concern is neither so serious nor so imminent as to justify the sweeping proscription of freedom of discussion embodied in §3448.

The State urges that the purpose of the challenged statute is the protection of the community from the violence and breaches of the peace, which, it asserts, are the concomitants of picketing. The power and the duty of the State to take adequate steps to preserve the peace and to protect the privacy, the lives, and the property of its residents cannot be doubted. But no clear and present danger of destruction of life or property, or invasion of the right of privacy, or breach of the peace can be thought to be inherent in the activities of every person who approaches the premises of an employer and publicizes the facts of a labor dispute involving the latter. We are not now concerned with picketing en masse or otherwise conducted which might occasion such imminent and aggravated danger to these interests as to justify a statute narrowly drawn to cover the precise situation giving rise to the danger. . . . Section 3448 in question here does not aim specifically at serious encroachments on these interests and does not evidence any such care in balancing these interests against the interest of the community and that of the individual in freedom of discussion on matters of public concern.

It is not enough to say that §3448 is limited or restricted in its application to such activity as takes place at the scene of the labor dispute. "[The] streets are natural and proper places for the dissemination of information and opinion; and one is not to have the exercise of his liberty of expression in appropriate places abridged on the plea that it may be exercised in some other place." Schneider v. State, 308 U.S. 147, 161, 163; Hague v. C.I.O., 307 U.S. 496, 515-16.[23] The danger of breach of the peace or serious invasion of rights of property or privacy at the scene of a labor dispute is not sufficiently imminent in all cases to warrant the legislature in determining that such place is not appropriate for the range of activities outlawed by §3448.

Reversed.

MR. JUSTICE MCREYNOLDS is of opinion that the judgment below should be affirmed.

---

[23] The fact that the activities for which petitioner was arrested and convicted took place on the private property of the Preserving Company is without significance. Petitioner and the other employees were never treated as trespassers, assuming that they could be where the Company owns such a substantial part of the town. . . . And §3448, in any event, must be tested upon its face.

NOTE

Note the following restatement of the "Thornhill Standing Doctrine": "Where a statute by its terms prohibits the exercise of expression the Court will pass on the validity of the statute without reference to the quality of the conduct of the assailant." Sedler, Standing to Assert Constitutional Jus Tertii in the Supreme Court, 71 Yale L.J. 599, 613 (1962). Is this doctrine consistent with the principles enunciated by Mr. Justice Brandeis in the Ashwander case, supra page 95? How sound are the rationales for allowing a defendant to challenge a statute "on its face"? See United States v. Raines, 362 U.S. 19 (1960), and Gooding v. Wilson, 405 U.S. 518 (1972). See generally Note, The First Amendment Overbreadth Doctrine, 83 Harv. L. Rev. 844 (1970). But, with regard to expressive activity that is deemed to be "conduct" rather than "speech," see Broadrick v. Oklahoma, 413 U.S. 601 (1973). See also Comment, The Hatch Act Reaffirmed: The Demise of Overbreadth Review?, 42 Ford. L. Rev. 161 (1973).

Insofar as the Thornhill case established doctrine with respect to picketing by labor unions as protected speech, later decisions significantly refined — some might say vaporized — the principle. The Court reviewed the course of decisions in International Brotherhood of Teamsters v. Vogt, 354 U.S. 284 (1957). In that case the defendant union had attempted unsuccessfully to persuade Vogt's employees to join the union. It then peacefully picketed the entrance to Vogt's gravel pit. The Supreme Court of Wisconsin upheld an injunction against this picketing on the ground that the inducing of the employer to interfere with its employees' freedom to join or not to join the union was an unfair labor practice. On certiorari the Supreme Court affirmed. Mr. Justice Douglas, with whom the Chief Justice and Mr. Justice Black concurred, dissented.

The issues of preemption which have played such a significant part in the development of doctrine with respect to picketing are discussed in the following articles: Cox, Federalism in the Law of Labor Relations, 67 Harv. L. Rev. 1297 (1954); Wellington, Labor and the Federal System, 26 U. Chi. L. Rev. 542 (1959); Aaron, The Labor-Management Reporting and Disclosure Act of 1959, 73 Harv. L. Rev. 1086 (1960).

Cantwell v. Connecticut 310 U.S. 296, 60 S. Ct. 900, 84 L. Ed. 1213 (1940)

MR. JUSTICE ROBERTS delivered the opinion of the Court.

Newton Cantwell and his two sons, Jesse and Russell, members of a group known as Jehovah's Witnesses, and claiming to be ordained ministers, were arrested in New Haven, Connecticut, and each was charged by information in five counts, with statutory and common law offenses. After trial in the Court of Common Pleas of New Haven County each of them was convicted on the third count, which charged a violation of §6294 of the General Statutes of Connecticut, and on the fifth count, which charged commission of the common law offense of inciting a breach of the peace. On appeal to the Supreme Court the conviction of all three on the third count was affirmed. The conviction of Jesse Cantwell, on the fifth count, was also affirmed, but the conviction of Newton and Russell on that count was reversed and a new trial ordered as to them.

The facts adduced to sustain the convictions on the third count follow. On the day of their arrest the appellants were engaged in going singly from house to house on Cassius Street in New Haven. They were individually equipped with a bag containing books and pamphlets on religious subjects, a portable phonograph and a set of records, each of which, when played, introduced, and was a description of, one of the books. Each appellant asked the person who responded to his call for permission to play one of the records. If permission was granted he asked the person to buy the book described and, upon refusal, he solicited such contribution towards the publication of the pamphlets as the listener was willing to make. If a contribution was received a pamphlet was delivered upon condition that it would be read.

Cassius Street is in a thickly populated neighborhood, where about ninety per cent of the residents are Roman Catholics. A phonograph record, describing a book entitled "Enemies," included an attack on the Catholic religion. None of the persons interviewed were members of Jehovah's Witnesses.

The statute under which the appellants were charged provides:

"No person shall solicit money, services, subscriptions or any valuable thing for any alleged religious, charitable or philanthropic cause, from other than a member of the organization for whose benefit such person is soliciting or within the county in which such person or organization is located unless such cause shall have been approved by the secretary of the public welfare council. Upon application of any person in behalf of such cause, the secretary shall determine whether such cause is a religious one or is a bona fide object of charity or philanthropy and conforms to reasonable standards of efficiency and integrity, and, if he shall so find, shall approve the same and issue to the authority in charge a certificate to that effect. Such certificate may be revoked at any time. Any person violating any provision of this section shall be fined not more than one hundred dollars or imprisoned not more than thirty days or both."

The appellants claimed that their activities were not within the statute but consisted only of distribution of books, pamphlets, and periodicals. The State Supreme Court construed the finding of the trial court to be that "in addition to the sale of books and the distribution of the pamphlets the defendants were also soliciting contributions or donations of money for an alleged religious cause, and thereby came within the purview of the statute." It overruled the contention that the Act, as applied to the appellants, offends the due process clause of the Fourteenth Amendment, because it abridges or denies religious freedom and liberty of speech and press. The court stated that it was the solicitation that brought the appellants within the sweep of the Act and not their other activities in the dissemination of literature. It declared the legislation constitutional as an effort by the State to protect the public against fraud and imposition in the solicitation of funds for what purported to be religious, charitable, or philanthropic causes.

The facts which were held to support the conviction of Jesse Cantwell on the fifth count were that he stopped two men in the street, asked, and received, permission to play a phonograph record, and played the record "Enemies," which attacked the religion and church of the two men, who were Catholics. Both were incensed by the contents of the record and were tempted to strike Cantwell unless he went away. On being told to be on his way he left their presence. There was no evidence that he was personally offensive or entered into any argument with those he interviewed.

The court held that the charge was not assault or breach of the peace or threats on Cantwell's part, but invoking or inciting others to breach of the peace, and that the facts supported the conviction of that offense.

First. We hold that the statute, as construed and applied to the appellants, deprives them of their liberty without due process of law in contravention of the Fourteenth Amendment. The fundamental concept of liberty embodied in that Amendment embraces the liberties guaranteed by the First Amendment. . . . No one would contest the proposition that a State may not, by statute, wholly deny the right to preach or to disseminate religious views. Plainly such a previous and absolute restraint would violate the terms of the guarantee. It is equally clear that a State may by general and non-discriminatory legislation regulate the times, the places, and the manner of soliciting upon its streets, and of holding meetings, thereon; and may in other respects safeguard the peace, good order and comfort of the community, without unconstitutionally invading the liberties protected by the Fourteenth Amendment. The appellants are right in their insistence that the Act in question is not such a regulation. If a certificate is procured, solicitation is permit-

Section C. Freedom of Speech and Association

ted without restraint but, in the absence of a certificate, solicitation is altogether prohibited.

The appellants urge that to require them to obtain a certificate as a condition of soliciting support for their views amounts to a prior restraint on the exercise of their religion within the meaning of the Constitution. The State insists that the Act, as construed by the Supreme Court of Connecticut, imposes no previous restraint upon the dissemination of religious views or teaching but merely safeguards against the perpetration of frauds under the cloak of religion. Conceding that this is so, the question remains whether the method adopted by Connecticut to that end transgresses the liberty safeguarded by the Constitution.

The general regulation, in the public interest, of solicitation, which does not involve any religious test and does not unreasonably obstruct or delay the collection of funds, is not open to any constitutional objection, even though the collection be for a religious purpose. Such regulation would not constitute a prohibited previous restraint on the free exercise of religion or interpose an inadmissible obstacle to its exercise.

It will be noted, however, that the Act requires an application to the secretary of the public welfare council of the State; that he is empowered to determine whether the cause is a religious one, and that the issue of a certificate depends upon his affirmative action. If he finds that the cause is not that of religion, to solicit for it becomes a crime. He is not to issue a certificate as a matter of course. His decision to issue or refuse it involves appraisal of facts, the exercise of judgment, and the formation of an opinion. He is authorized to withhold his approval if he determines that the cause is not a religious one. Such a censorship of religion as the means of determining its right to survive is a denial of liberty protected by the First Amendment and included in the liberty which is within the protection of the Fourteenth.

Nothing we have said is intended even remotely to imply that, under the cloak of religion, persons may, with impunity, commit frauds upon the public. Certainly penal laws are available to punish such conduct. Even the exercise of religion may be at some slight inconvenience in order that the State may protect its citizens from injury. Without doubt a State may protect its citizens from fraudulent solicitation by requiring a stranger in the community, before permitting him publicly to solicit funds for any purpose, to establish his identity and his authority to act for the cause which he purports to represent. The State is likewise free to regulate the time and manner of solicitation generally, in the interest of public safety, peace, comfort or convenience. But to condition the solicitation of aid for the perpetuation of religious views or systems upon a license, the grant of which rests in the exercise of a determination by state authority as to what is a religious cause, is to lay a forbidden burden upon the exercise of liberty protected by the Constitution.

Second. We hold that, in the circumstances disclosed, the conviction of Jesse Cantwell on the fifth count must be set aside. Decision as to the lawfulness of the conviction demands the weighing of two conflicting interests. The fundamental law declares the interest of the United States that the free exercise of religion be not prohibited and that freedom to communicate information and opinion be not abridged. The State of Connecticut has an obvious interest in the preservation and protection of peace and good order within her borders. We must determine whether the alleged protection of the State's interest, means to which end would, in the absence of limitation by the Federal Constitution, lie wholly within the State's discretion, has been pressed, in this instance, to a point where it has come into fatal collision with the overriding interest protected by the federal compact.

Conviction on the fifth count was not pursuant to a statute evincing a legislative judgment that street discussion of religious affairs, because of its tendency to provoke disorder, should be regulated, or a judgment that the playing of a phonograph on the streets should in the interest of comfort or privacy be limited or prevented. Violation of an Act exhibiting such a legislative judgment and narrowly drawn to prevent the supposed evil, would pose a question differing from that we must here answer. Such a declaration of the State's policy would weigh heavily in any challenge of the law as infringing constitutional limitations. Here, however, the judgment is based on a common law concept of the most general and undefined nature. The court below has held that the petitioner's conduct constituted the commission of an offense under the state law, and we accept its decision as binding upon us to that extent.

The offense known as breach of the peace embraces a great variety of conduct destroying or menacing public order and tranquillity. It includes not only violent acts but acts and words likely to produce violence in others. No one would have the hardihood to suggest that the principle of freedom of speech sanctions incitement to riot or that religious liberty connotes the privilege to exhort others to physical attack upon those belonging to another sect. When clear and present danger of riot, disorder, interference with traffic upon the public streets, or other immediate threat to public safety, peace, or order, appears, the power of the State to prevent or punish is obvious. Equally obvious is it that a State may not unduly suppress free communication of views, religious or other, under the guise of conserving desirable conditions. Here we have a situation analogous to a conviction under a statute sweeping in a great variety of conduct under a general and indefinite characterization, and leaving to the executive and judicial branches too wide a discretion in its application.

Having these considerations in mind, we note that Jesse Cantwell, on April 26, 1938, was upon a public street, where he had a right to be, and where he had a right peacefully to impart his views to others. There is no showing that his deportment was noisy, truculent, overbearing or offensive. He requested of two pedestrians permission to play to them a phonograph record. The permission was granted. It is not claimed that he intended to insult or affront the hearers by playing the record. It is plain that he wished only to interest them in his propaganda. The sound of the phonograph is not shown to have disturbed residents of the street, to have drawn a crowd, or to have impeded traffic. Thus far he had invaded no right or interest of the public or of the men accosted.

The record played by Cantwell embodies a general attack on all organized religious systems as instruments of Satan and injurious to man; it then singles out the Roman Catholic Church for strictures couched in terms which naturally would offend not only persons of that persuasion, but all others who respect the honestly held religious faith of their fellows. The hearers were in fact highly offended. One of them said he felt like hitting Cantwell and the other that he was tempted to throw Cantwell off the street. The one who testified he felt like hitting Cantwell said, in answer to the question "Did you do anything else or have any other reaction?" "No, sir, because he said he would take the victrola and he went." The other witness testified that he told Cantwell he had better get off the street before something happened to him and that was the end of the matter as Cantwell picked up his books and walked up the street.

Cantwell's conduct, in the view of the court below, considered apart from the effect of his communication upon his hearers, did not amount to a breach of the peace. One may, however, be guilty of the offense if he commit acts or make statements likely to provoke violence and disturbance of good order, even though no such eventuality be intended. Decisions to this effect are many, but examination discloses that, in practically all, the provocative language which was held to amount to a breach of the peace consisted of profane, indecent, or abusive remarks directed to the person of the hearer. Resort to epithets or personal abuse is not in any proper sense communication of information or opinion safeguarded by the Constitution, and its punishment as a criminal act would raise no question under that instrument.

We find in the instant case no assault or threatening of bodily harm, no truculent bearing, no intentional discourtesy, no personal abuse. On the contrary, we find only an effort to persuade a willing listener to buy a book or to contribute money in the interest of what Cantwell, however misguided others may think him, conceived to be true religion.

In the realm of religious faith, and in that of political belief, sharp differences arise. In both fields the tenets of one man may seem the rankest error to his neighbor. To persuade others to his own point of view, the pleader, as we know, at times, resorts to exaggeration, to vilification of men who have been, or are, prominent in church or state, and even to false statement. But the people of this nation have ordained in the light of history, that, in spite of the probability of excesses and abuses, these liberties are, in the long view, essential to enlightened opinion and right conduct on the part of the citizens of a democracy.

Although the contents of the record not unnaturally aroused animosity, we think that, in the absence of a statute narrowly drawn to define and punish specific conduct as constituting a clear and present danger to a substantial interest of the State, the petitioner's communication, considered in the light of the constitutional guarantees, raised no such clear and present menace to public peace and order as to render him liable to conviction of the common law offense in question.

The judgment affirming the convictions on the third and fifth counts is reversed and the cause is remanded for further proceedings not inconsistent with this opinion.

Reversed.

NOTE The Licensing of the Use of the Public Forum

The Court's treatment of licensing requirements for the use of the public forum, as in Cantwell, has tracked the Court's very careful scrutiny of prior restraints on the press, as in Near and New York Times, supra pages 1146 and 1149. Indeed, in Lovell v. Griffin, 303 U.S. 444 (1938), voiding a standardless ordinance which required written permission for any leafletting, Chief Justice Hughes wrote of the ordinance, "Whatever the motive which induced its adoption, its character is such that it strikes at the very foundation of the freedom of the press by subjecting it to license and censorship." Id. at 451. Yet, as the Court conceded in Cantwell, the prior restraints of "time, place and manner" rules could be acceptable conditions on the use of the public forum. Thus, in Cox v. Louisiana, 312 U.S. 569 (1941), a unanimous Court, per Hughes, C.J., sustained a permit system that meant to give the authorities notice for planning purposes provided, however, that permits be issued with "uniformity" and without "discrimination."

Would Cantwell and Cox allow a state law that required a labor union organizer to obtain a card identifying his name and affiliation before being able to solicit members? Could such a law be constitutionally applied to someone simply seeking to make a public speech to enlist support for a union? See Thomas v. Collins, 323 U.S. 516 (1945).

A permit for the Jehovah's Witnesses to use a public park for a meeting, the Court held in Niemotko v. Maryland, 340 U.S. 268 (1951), could not be denied where the city had regularly allowed permits for similar purposes, including religious gatherings. Cf. Police Dept. v. Mosley, infra page 1203. In Niemotko, the city had denied the permit to the Jehovah's Witnesses because of its evident "disagreement . . . with their views," id. at 272; could a city refuse a permit to a speaker where his past performance suggested that future speeches might lead to disorder or violence? In Kunz v. New York, 340 U.S. 290 (1951), the police commissioner had revoked the permit of a speaker after his determination that the speaker had "ridiculed and denounced other religious beliefs," as prohibited by city law. The police commissioner then refused the speaker's subsequent applications for a permit. In addition to noting that the licensing law contained no grounds for the denial of a permit, the Court said in reversing, "There are appropriate public remedies to protect the peace and order of the community if appellant's speeches should result in disorder or violence." Id. at 294. In dissent, Justice Jackson asked: "And so the matter eventually comes down to the question whether the 'words used are used in such circumstances and are of such a nature' that we can say a reasonable man would anticipate the evil result. In this case the Court does not justify, excuse, or deny the inciting and provocative character of the language, and it does not, and on this record could not, deny that when Kunz speaks he poses a 'clear and present' danger to peace and order. Why, then, does New York have to put up with it?" Id. at 302.

Compare Freedman v. Maryland, 380 U.S. 51 (1965), for the Court's specification of what procedural safeguards would constitutionally allow the "State Board of Censors" to license motion pictures. See Note: Developments in Obscenity, infra page 1298. Does Freedman suggest that with greater procedural fairness Kunz could be decided differently?

Because a statute for parade permits had, in fact, been administered in an arbitrary and discriminatory manner, the Court reversed the convictions of civil rights demonstrators who had marched without a permit, Shuttlesworth v. Birmingham, 394 U.S. 147 (1969). Compare Cox v. New Hampshire, supra. Should the Court require expedited treatment of applications for permits by local authorities and state courts? See the concurring opinion of Justice Harlan in Shuttlesworth, supra. Consider also the 5 to 4 affirmance of contempt convictions in Walker v. City of Birmingham, 388 U.S. 307 (1967), against demonstrators who had marched without permits in violation of a court injunction. Even though the statute that was the basis for the temporary injunction was later found to be unconstitutionally administered, see Shuttlesworth, supra, the Court in Walker held that the demonstrators should have sought to challenge the injunction through the judicial process. See generally Blasi, Prior Restraints on Demonstrations, 68 Mich. L. Rev. 1481 (1970).

Kovacs v. Cooper 336 U.S. 77, 69 S. Ct. 448, 93 L. Ed. 513 (1949)

MR. JUSTICE REED announced the judgment of the Court and an opinion in which the CHIEF JUSTICE and MR. JUSTICE BURTON join.

This appeal involves the validity of a provision of Ordinance No. 430 of the City of Trenton, New Jersey. It reads as follows:

"4. That it shall be unlawful for any person, firm or corporation, either as principal, agent or employee, to play, use or operate for advertising purposes, or for any other purpose whatsoever, on or upon the public streets, alleys or thoroughfares in the City of Trenton, any device known as a sound truck, loud speaker or sound amplifier, or radio or phonograph with a loud speaker or sound amplifier, or any other instrument known as a calliope or any instrument of any kind or character which emits therefrom loud and raucous noises and is attached to and upon any vehicle operated or standing upon said streets or public places aforementioned."

The appellant was found guilty of violating this ordinance by the appellee, a police judge of the City of Trenton. His conviction was upheld by the New Jersey Supreme Court, Kovacs v. Cooper, 135 N.J.L. 64, and the judgment was affirmed without a majority opinion by the New Jersey Court of Errors and Appeals in an equally divided court. The dissents are printed. 135 N.J.L. 584.

We took jurisdiction to consider the challenge made to the constitutionality of the section on its face and as applied on the ground that §1 of the Fourteenth Amendment of the United States Constitution was violated because the section and the conviction are in contravention of rights of freedom of speech, freedom of assemblage and freedom to communicate information and opinions to others. The ordinance is also challenged as violative of the Due Process Clause of the Fourteenth Amendment on the ground that it is so obscure, vague, and indefinite as to be impossible of reasonably accurate interpretation. No question was raised as to the sufficiency of the complaint.

At the trial in the Trenton police court, a city patrolman testified that while on his post

Section C. Freedom of Speech and Association

he heard a sound truck broadcasting music. Upon going in the direction of said sound, he located the truck on a public street near the municipal building. As he approached the truck, the music stopped and he heard a man's voice broadcasting from the truck. The appellant admitted that he operated the mechanism for the music and spoke into the amplifier. The record from the police court does not show the purpose of the broadcasting but the opinion in the Supreme Court suggests that the appellant was using the sound apparatus to comment on a labor dispute then in progress in Trenton.

The contention that the section is so vague, obscure and indefinite as to be unenforceable merits only a passing reference. This objection centers around the use of the words "loud and raucous." While these are abstract words, they have through daily use acquired a content that conveys to any interested person a sufficiently accurate concept of what is forbidden. . . .

The use of sound trucks and other peripatetic or stationary broadcasting devices for advertising, for religious exercises and for discussion of issues or controversies has brought forth numerous municipal ordinances. The avowed and obvious purpose of these ordinances is to prohibit or minimize such sounds on or near the streets since some citizens find the noise objectionable and to some degree an interference with the business or social activities in which they are engaged or the quiet that they would like to enjoy. A satisfactory adjustment of the conflicting interests is difficult as those who desire to broadcast can hardly acquiesce in a requirement to modulate their sounds to a pitch that would not rise above other street noises nor would they deem a restriction to sparsely used localities or to hours after work and before sleep — say 6 to 9 P.M. — sufficient for the exercise of their claimed privilege. Municipalities are seeking actively a solution. National Institute of Municipal Law Officers, Report No. 123, 1948. Unrestrained use throughout a municipality of all sound amplifying devices would be intolerable. Absolute prohibition within municipal limits of all sound amplification, even though reasonably regulated in place, time and volume, is undesirable and probably unconstitutional as an unreasonable interference with normal activities.

We have had recently before us an ordinance of the City of Lockport, New York, prohibiting sound amplification whereby the sound was cast on public places so as to attract the attention of the passing public to the annoyance of those within the radius of the sounds. The ordinance contained this exception:

"Section 3. Exception. — Public dissemination, through radio loudspeakers, of items of news and matters of public concern and athletic activities shall not be deemed a violation of this section provided that the same be done under permission obtained from the Chief of Police."

This Court held the ordinance "unconstitutional on its face," Saia v. New York, 334 U.S. 558, because the quoted section established a "previous restraint" on the free speech with "no standards prescribed for the exercise" of discretion by the Chief of Police.[m] When ordinances undertake censorship of speech or religious practices before permitting their exercise, the Constitution forbids their enforcement. . . .

This ordinance is not of that character. It contains nothing comparable to the above quoted §3 of the ordinance in the Saia Case. It is an exercise of the authority granted to the city by New Jersey "to prevent disturbing noises," N.J. Stat. Anno. title 40, §48-1(8), nuisances well within the municipality's power to control. The police power of a state extends beyond health, morals and safety, and comprehends the duty, within constitutional limitations, to protect the well-being and tranquility of a community. A state or city may prohibit acts or things reasonably thought to bring evil or harm to its people.

In this case, New Jersey necessarily has construed this very ordinance as applied to sound amplification. The Supreme Court said, 135 N.J.L. 64, 66:

---

[m] In the Saia case the opinion of the Court was delivered by Douglas, J. Frankfurter, Reed, Burton, and Jackson, JJ., dissented. — ED.

"The relevant provisions of the ordinance apply only to (1) vehicles (2) containing an instrument in the nature of a sound amplifier or any other instrument emitting loud and raucous noises and (3) such vehicles operated or standing upon the public streets, alleys or thoroughfares of the city."

If that means that only amplifiers that emit, in the language of the ordinance, "loud and raucous noises" are barred from the streets, we have a problem of regulation. The dissents accept that view. So did the appellant in his Statement as to Jurisdiction and his brief. Although this Court must decide for itself whether federal questions are presented and decided, we must accept the state courts' conclusion as to the scope of the ordinance. We accept the determination of New Jersey that §4 applies only to vehicles with sound amplifiers emitting loud and raucous noises. Courts are inclined to adopt that reasonable interpretation of a statute which removes it farthest from possible constitutional infirmity. . . . We need not determine whether this ordinance so construed is regulatory or prohibitory. All regulatory enactments are prohibitory so far as their restrictions are concerned, and the prohibition of this ordinance as to a use of streets is merely regulatory. Sound trucks may be utilized in places such as parks or other open spaces off the streets. The constitutionality of the challenged ordinance as violative of appellant's right of free speech does not depend upon so narrow an issue as to whether its provisions are cast in the words of prohibition or regulation. The question is whether or not there is a real abridgment of the rights of free speech. . . .

While this Court, in enforcing the broad protection the Constitution gives to the dissemination of ideas, has invalidated an ordinance forbidding a distributor of pamphlets or handbills from summoning householders to their doors to receive the distributor's writings, this was on the ground that the home owner could protect himself from such intrusion by an appropriate sign "that he is unwilling to be disturbed." The Court never intimated that the visitor could insert a foot in the door and insist on a hearing. Martin v. Struthers, 319 U.S. 141, 143, 148. We do not think that the Struthers Case requires us to expand this interdiction of legislation to include ordinances against obtaining an audience for the broadcaster's ideas by way of sound trucks with loud and raucous noises on city streets. The unwilling listener is not like the passer-by who may be offered a pamphlet in the street but cannot be made to take it. In his home or on the streets he is practically helpless to escape this interference with his privacy by loud speakers except through the protection of the municipality.

City streets are recognized as a normal place for the exchange of ideas by speech or paper. But this does not mean the freedom is beyond all control. We think it is a permissible exercise of legislative discretion to bar sound trucks with broadcasts of public interest, amplified to a loud and raucous volume, from the public ways of municipalities. On the business streets of cities like Trenton, with its more than 125,000 people, such distractions would be dangerous to traffic at all hours useful for the dissemination of information, and in the residential thoroughfares the quiet and tranquility so desirable for city dwellers would likewise be at the mercy of advocates of particular religious, social or political persuasions. We cannot believe that rights of free speech compel a municipality to allow such mechanical voice amplification on any of its streets.

The right of free speech is guaranteed every citizen that he may reach the minds of willing listeners and to do so there must be opportunity to win their attention. This is the phase of freedom of speech that is involved here. We do not think the Trenton ordinance abridges that freedom. It is an extravagant extension of due process to say that because of it a city cannot forbid talking on the streets through a loud speaker in a loud and raucous tone. Surely such an ordinance does not violate our people's "concept of ordered liberty" so as to require federal intervention to protect a citizen from the action of his own local government. Cf. Palko v. Connecticut, 302 U.S. 319, 325. Opportunity to gain the public's ears by objectionably amplified sound on the streets is no more assured by the right of free speech than is the unlimited opportunity to address gatherings on the streets.

Section C. Freedom of Speech and Association

The preferred position [14] of freedom of speech in a society that cherishes liberty for all does not require legislators to be insensible to claims by citizens to comfort and convenience. To enforce freedom of speech in disregard of the rights of others would be harsh and arbitrary in itself. That more people may be more easily and cheaply reached by sound trucks, perhaps borrowed without cost from some zealous supporter, is not enough to call forth constitutional protection for what those charged with public welfare reasonably think is a nuisance when easy means of publicity are open. Section 4 of the ordinance bars sound trucks from broadcasting in a loud and raucous manner on the streets. There is no restriction upon the communication of ideas or discussion of issues by the human voice, by newspapers, by pamphlets, by dodgers. We think that the need for reasonable protection in the homes or business houses from the distracting noises of vehicles equipped with such sound amplifying devices justifies the ordinance.

Affirmed.[n]

MR. JUSTICE FRANKFURTER, concurring. . . .

. . . My brother Reed speaks of "the preferred position of freedom of speech," though, to be sure, he finds that the Trenton ordinance does not disregard it. This is a phrase that has uncritically crept into some recent opinions of this Court. I deem it a mischievous phrase, if it carries the thought, which it may subtly imply, that any law touching communication is infected with presumptive invalidity. It is not the first time in the history of constitutional adjudication that such a doctrinaire attitude has disregarded the admonition most to be observed in exercising the Court's reviewing power over legislation, "that it is *a constitution* we are expounding," M'Culloch v. Maryland, 4 Wheat. 316, 407. I say the phrase is mischievous because it radiates a constitutional doctrine without avowing it. . . .

Behind the notion sought to be expressed by the formula as to "the preferred position of freedom of speech" lies a relevant consideration in determining whether an enactment relating to the liberties protected by the Due Process Clause of the Fourteenth Amendment is violative of it. In law also, doctrine is illuminated by history. The ideas now governing the constitutional protection of freedom of speech derive essentially from the opinions of Mr. Justice Holmes.

The philosophy of his opinions on that subject arose from a deep awareness of the extent to which sociological conclusions are conditioned by time and circumstance. Because of this awareness Mr. Justice Holmes seldom felt justified in opposing his own opinion to economic views which the legislature embodied in law. But since he also realized that the progress of civilization is to a considerable extent the displacement of error which once held sway as official truth by beliefs which in turn have yielded to other beliefs, for him the right to search for truth was of a different order than some transient economic dogma. And without freedom of expression, thought becomes checked and atrophied. Therefore, in considering what interests are so fundamental as to be enshrined in the Due Process Clause, those liberties of the individual which history has attested as the indispensable conditions of an open as against a closed society come to this Court with a momentum for respect lacking when appeal is made to liberties which derive merely from shifting economic arrangements. Accordingly, Mr. Justice Holmes was far more ready to find legislative invasion where free inquiry was involved than in the debatable area of economics. See my Mr. Justice Holmes and the Supreme Court, 58 et seq.

The objection to summarizing this line of thought by the phrase "the preferred position of freedom of speech" is that it expresses a complicated process of constitutional adjudication by a deceptive formula. And it was Mr. Justice Holmes who admonished us that "To rest upon a formula is a slumber that, prolonged, means death." Collected Legal Papers, 306. Such a formula makes for mechanical jurisprudence. . . .

[14] Thomas v. Collins, 323 U.S. 516, 527, note 12, 530; Murdock v. Pennsylvania, 319 U.S. 105.

[n] A concurring opinion of Mr. Justice Jackson is omitted, as is a dissenting opinion by Mr. Justice Rutledge. Murphy, J., dissented without opinion. — ED.

Only a disregard of vital differences between natural speech, even of the loudest spellbinders, and the noise of sound trucks would give sound trucks the constitutional rights accorded to the unaided human voice. Nor is it for this Court to devise the terms on which sound trucks should be allowed to operate, if at all. These are matters for the legislative judgment controlled by public opinion. So long as a legislature does not prescribe what ideas may be noisily expressed and what may not be, nor discriminate among those who would make inroads upon the public peace, it is not for us to supervise the limits the legislature may impose in safeguarding the steadily narrowing opportunities for serenity and reflection. Without such opportunities freedom of thought becomes a mocking phrase, and without freedom of thought there can be no free society.

MR. JUSTICE BLACK, with whom MR. JUSTICE DOUGLAS, and MR. JUSTICE RUTLEDGE concur, dissenting.

The question in this case is not whether appellant may constitutionally be convicted of operating a sound truck that emits "loud and raucous noises." The appellant was neither charged with nor convicted of operating a sound truck that emitted "loud and raucous noises." The charge against him in the police court was that he violated the city ordinance "in that he did, on South Stockton Street, in said City, play, use and operate a device known as a sound truck." The record reflects not even a shadow of evidence to prove that the noise was either "loud or raucous," unless these words of the ordinance refer to any noise coming from an amplifier, whatever its volume or tone.

After appellant's conviction in the police court, the case was taken to the Supreme Court of New Jersey for review. That court, composed of three judges, stated with reference to the ordinance and charge: "In simple, unambiguous language it prohibits the use upon the public streets of any device known as a sound truck, loud speaker or sound amplifier. This is the only charge made against the defendant in the complaint." Kovacs v. Cooper, 135 N.J.L. 63, 69. That this court construed the ordinance as an absolute prohibition of all amplifiers on any public street at any time and without regard to volume of sound is emphasized by its further statement that "the ordinance leaves untouched the right of the prosecutor to express his views *orally without the aid of an amplifier.*" 135 N.J.L. Id. at 66. (Emphasis supplied.) Thus the New Jersey Supreme Court affirmed the conviction on the ground that the appellant was shown guilty of the only offense of which he was charged — speaking through an amplifier on a public street. If as some members of this Court now assume, he was actually convicted for operating a machine that emitted "loud and raucous noises," then he was convicted on a charge for which he was never tried. "It is as much a violation of due process to send an accused to prison following conviction of a charge on which he was never tried as it would be to convict him upon a charge that was never made." Cole v. Arkansas, 333 U.S. 196, 201.

In this case the Court denies speech amplifiers the constitutional shelter recognized by our decisions and holding in the Saia Case. This is true because the Trenton, New Jersey, ordinance here sustained goes beyond a mere prior censorship of all loud speakers with authority in the censor to prohibit some of them. This Trenton ordinance wholly bars the use of all loud speakers mounted upon any vehicle in any of the city's public streets.

In my view this repudiation of the prior Saia opinion makes a dangerous and unjustifiable breach in the constitutional barriers designed to insure freedom of expression. Ideas and beliefs are today chiefly disseminated to the masses of people through the press, radio, moving pictures, and public address systems. To some extent at least there is competition of ideas between and within these groups. The basic premise of the First Amendment is that all present instruments of communication, as well as others that inventive genius may bring into being, shall be free from governmental censorship or prohibition. Laws which hamper the free use of some instruments of communication thereby favor competing channels. Thus, unless constitutionally prohibited, laws like this Trenton ordinance can give an overpowering influence to views of owners of legally favored instruments of communication. This favoritism, it seems to me, is the inevitable result of today's decision.

For the result of today's opinion in upholding this statutory prohibition of amplifiers would surely not be reached by this Court if such channels of communication as the press, radio, or moving pictures were similarly attacked. . . .

I would reverse the judgment.

PUBLIC UTILITIES COMMISSION v. POLLAK, 343 U.S. 451, 72 S. Ct. 813, 96 L. Ed. 2d 1068 (1952). The Capital Transit Company, enjoying "a substantial monopoly of street railway and bus transportation in the District of Columbia," installed radio receivers for the reception of commercial and other programs on its buses and streetcars. The Public Utilities Commission of the District, responding to protests from passengers that their constitutional rights were being infringed, conducted an investigation, determined that the practice was consistent with public convenience, and dismissed its investigation. All Justices participating in the case[°] agreed that "the action of Capital Transit in installing and operating the radio receivers, coupled with the action of the Public Utilities Commission in dismissing its own investigation of the practice, sufficiently involved the Federal Government in responsibility for the radio programs to make the First and Fifth Amendments to the Constitution of the United States applicable to this radio service." Id. at 461. Programing broadcast on the buses generally consisted of 90 percent music, 5 percent news and announcements, and 5 percent commercial advertising. As a rider, Pollak claimed that the programs interfered with his rights of free speech and privacy.

What decision? Why?

Feiner v. New York 340 U.S. 315, 71 S. Ct. 303, 95 L. Ed. 295 (1951)

MR. CHIEF JUSTICE VINSON delivered the opinion of the Court.

Petitioner was convicted of the offense of disorderly conduct, a misdemeanor under the New York penal laws. . . . The case is here on certiorari, 339 U.S. 962, petitioner having claimed that the conviction is in violation of his right of free speech under the Fourteenth Amendment.

In the review of state decisions where First Amendment rights are drawn in question, we of course make an examination of the evidence to ascertain independently whether the right has been violated. Here, the trial judge who heard the case without a jury rendered an oral decision at the end of the trial setting forth his determination of the facts upon which he found the petitioner guilty. His decision indicated generally that he believed the state's witnesses, and his summation of the testimony was used by the two New York courts on review in stating the facts. Our appraisal of the facts is, therefore, based upon the uncontroverted facts and, where controversy exists, upon that testimony which the trial judge did reasonably conclude to be true.

On the evening of March 8, 1949, petitioner Irving Feiner was addressing an open-air meeting at the corner of South McBride and Harrison Streets in the City of Syracuse. At approximately 6:30 P.M., the police received a telephone complaint concerning the meeting, and two officers were detailed to investigate. One of these officers went to the scene immediately, the other arriving some twelve minutes later. They found a crowd of about seventy-five or eighty people, both Negro and white, filling the sidewalk and spreading out into the street. Petitioner, standing on a large wooden box on the sidewalk, was addressing the crowd through a loud-speaker system attached to an automobile. Although the purpose of his speech was to urge his listeners to attend a meeting to be held that night in the Syracuse Hotel, in its course he was making derogatory remarks concerning President

[°] Justice Frankfurter recused himself from the case, saying, "My feelings are so strongly engaged as a victim of the practice in controversy that I had better not participate in judicial judgment upon it." Id. at 467. — ED.

Truman, the American Legion, the Mayor of Syracuse, and other local political officials.

The police officers made no effort to interfere with petitioner's speech, but were first concerned with the effect of the crowd on both pedestrian and vehicular traffic. They observed the situation from the opposite side of the street, noting that some pedestrians were forced to walk in the street to avoid the crowd. Since traffic was passing at the time, the officers attempted to get the people listening to petitioner back on the sidewalk. The crowd was restless and there was some pushing, shoving and milling around. One of the officers telephoned the police station from a nearby store, and then both policemen crossed the street and mingled with the crowd without any intention of arresting the speaker.

At this time, petitioner was speaking in a "loud, high-pitched voice." He gave the impression that he was endeavoring to arouse the Negro people against the whites, urging that they rise up in arms and fight for equal rights. The statements before such a mixed audience "stirred up a little excitement." Some of the onlookers made remarks to the police about their inability to handle the crowd and at least one threatened violence if the police did not act. There were others who appeared to be favoring petitioner's arguments. Because of the feeling that existed in the crowd both for and against the speaker, the officers finally "stepped in to prevent it from resulting in a fight." One of the officers approached the petitioner, not for the purpose of arresting him, but to get him to break up the crowd. He asked petitioner to get down off the box, but the latter refused to accede to his request and continued talking. The officer waited for a minute and then demanded that he cease talking. Although the officer had thus twice requested petitioner to stop over the course of several minutes, petitioner not only ignored him but continued talking. During all this time, the crowd was pressing closer around petitioner and the officer. Finally, the officer told petitioner he was under arrest and ordered him to get down from the box, reaching up to grab him. Petitioner stepped down, announcing over the microphone that "the law has arrived, and I suppose they will take over now." In all, the officer had asked petitioner to get down off the box three times over a space of four or five minutes. Petitioner had been speaking for over a half hour.

On these facts, petitioner was specifically charged with violation of §722 of the Penal Law of New York, the pertinent part of which is set out in the margin.[1] The bill of particulars, demanded by petitioner and furnished by the state, gave in detail the facts upon which the prosecution relied to support the charge of disorderly conduct. Paragraph C is particularly pertinent here: "By ignoring and refusing to heed and obey reasonable police orders issued at the time and place mentioned in the information to regulate and control said crowd and to prevent a breach or breaches of the peace and to prevent injury to pedestrians attempting to use said walk, and being forced into the highway adjacent to the place in question, and prevent injury to the public generally."

We are not faced here with blind condonation by a state court of arbitrary police action. Petitioner was accorded a full, fair trial. The trial judge heard testimony supporting and contradicting the judgment of the police officers that a clear danger of disorder was threatened. After weighing this contradictory evidence, the trial judge reached the conclusion that the police officers were justified in taking action to prevent a breach of the peace. The exercise of the police officers' proper discretionary power to prevent a breach of the peace was thus approved by the trial court and later by two courts on review. The courts below recognized petitioners' right to hold a street meeting at this locality, to make use of loud-speaking equipment in giving his speech, and to make derogatory remarks concerning public officials and the American Legion. They found that the officers in making the ar-

---

[1] "Section 722. Any person who with intent to provoke a breach of the peace, or whereby a breach of the peace may be occasioned, commits any of the following acts shall be deemed to have committed the offense of disorderly conduct:

"1. Uses offensive, disorderly, threatening, abusive or insulting language, conduct or behavior;

"2. Acts in such a manner as to annoy, disturb, interfere with, obstruct, or be offensive to others:

"3. Congregates with others on a public street and refuses to move on when ordered by the police; . . ."

rest were motivated solely by a proper concern for the preservation of order and protection of the general welfare, and that there was no evidence which could lend color to a claim that the acts of the police were a cover for suppression of petitioner's views and opinions. Petitioner was thus neither arrested nor convicted for the making or the content of his speech. Rather, it was the reaction which it actually engendered. . . .

We are well aware that the ordinary murmurings and objections of a hostile audience cannot be allowed to silence a speaker, and also mindful of the possible danger of giving overzealous police officials complete discretion to break up otherwise lawful public meetings. . . . But we are not faced here with such a situation. It is one thing to say that the police cannot be used as an instrument for the suppression of unpopular views, and another to say that, when as here the speaker passes the bounds of argument or persuasion and undertakes incitement to riot, they are powerless to prevent a breach of the peace. Nor in this case can we condemn the considered judgment of three New York courts approving the means which the police, faced with a crisis, used in the exercise of their power and duty to preserve peace and order. The findings of the state courts as to the existing situation and the imminence of greater disorder coupled with petitioner's deliberate defiance of the police officers convince us that we should not reverse this conviction in the name of free speech.

Affirmed.[p]

MR. JUSTICE BLACK, dissenting.

The record before us convinces me that petitioner, a young college student, has been sentenced to the penitentiary for the unpopular views he expressed on matters of public interest while lawfully making a street-corner speech in Syracuse, New York. Today's decision, however, indicates that we must blind ourselves to this fact because the trial judge fully accepted the testimony of the prosecution witnesses on all important points. Many times in the past this Court has said that despite findings below, we will examine the evidence for ourselves to ascertain whether federally protected rights have been denied; otherwise review here would fail of its purpose in safeguarding constitutional guaranties. Even a partial abandonment of this rule marks a dark day for civil liberties in our Nation.

But still more has been lost today. Even accepting every "finding of fact" below, I think this conviction makes a mockery of the free speech guarantees of the First and Fourteenth Amendments. The end result of the affirmance here is to approve a simple and readily available technique by which cities and states can with impunity subject all speeches, political or otherwise, on streets or elsewhere, to the supervision and censorship of the local police. I will have no part or parcel in this holding which I view as a long step toward totalitarian authority.

The Court's opinion apparently rests on this reasoning: The policeman, under the circumstances detailed, could reasonably conclude that serious fighting or even riot was imminent; therefore he could stop petitioner's speech to prevent a breach of peace; accordingly, it was "disorderly conduct" for petitioner to continue speaking in disobedience of the officer's request. As to the existence of a dangerous situation on the street corner, it seems far-fetched to suggest that the "facts" show any imminent threat of riot or uncontrollable disorder. It is neither unusual nor unexpected that some people at public street meetings mutter, mill about, push, shove, or disagree, even violently, with the speaker. Indeed, it is rare where controversial topics are discussed that an outdoor crowd does not do some or all of these things. Nor does one isolated threat to assault the speaker forebode disorder. Especially should the danger be discounted where, as here, the person threatening was a man whose wife and two small children accompanied him and who, so far as the record shows, was never close enough to petitioner to carry out the threat.

[p] A concurring opinion of Mr. Justice Frankfurter and a dissenting opinion of Mr. Justice Douglas, in which Minton, J., concurred, are omitted. — ED.

Moreover, assuming that the "facts" did indicate a critical situation, I reject the implication of the Court's opinion that the police had no obligation to protect petitioner's constitutional right to talk. The police of course have power to prevent breaches of the peace. But if, in the name of preserving order, they ever can interfere with a lawful public speaker, they first must make all reasonable efforts to protect him. Here the policeman did not even pretend to try to protect petitioner. According to the officers' testimony, the crowd was restless but there is no showing of any attempt to quiet it; pedestrians were forced to walk into the street, but there was no effort to clear a path on the sidewalk; one person threatened to assault petitioner but the officers did nothing to discourage this when even a word might have sufficed. Their duty was to protect petitioner's right to talk, even to the extent of arresting the man who threatened to interfere. Instead, they shirked that duty and acted only to suppress the right to speak.

Finally, I cannot agree with the Court's statement that petitioner's disregard of the policeman's unexplained request amounted to such "deliberate defiance" as would justify an arrest or conviction for disorderly conduct. On the contrary, I think that the policeman's action was a "deliberate defiance" of ordinary official duty as well as of the constitutional right of free speech. For at least where time allows, courtesy and explanation of commands are basic elements of good official conduct in a democratic society. Here petitioner was "asked" then "told" then "commanded" [sic] to stop speaking, but a man making a lawful address is certainly not required to be silent merely because an officer directs it. Petitioner was entitled to know why he should cease doing a lawful act. Not once was he told. I understand that people in authoritarian countries must obey arbitrary orders. I had hoped that there was no such duty in the United States.

NOTE

Compare Terminiello v. Chicago, 337 U.S. 1 (1949), where the Court reversed a conviction for disorderly conduct arising out of a speech delivered under the following circumstances: "The auditorium was filled to capacity with over eight hundred persons present. Others were turned away. Outside of the auditorium a crowd of about one thousand persons gathered to protest against the meeting. A cordon of policemen was assigned to the meeting to maintain order; but they were not able to prevent several disturbances. The crowd outside was angry and turbulent." In its vicious condemnation of various political and racial groups, Terminiello's speech, Justice Jackson said in dissent, "followed, with fidelity that is more than coincidental, the pattern of European fascist leaders."

The jury was instructed that the charge against him included speech which "stirs the public to anger, invites dispute, brings about a condition of unrest, or creates a disturbance. . . ." Such a charge, wrote Justice Douglas for the Court, violated the First Amendment because "A function of free speech under our system of government is to invite dispute. . . . Speech is often provocative and challenging. It may strike at prejudices and preconceptions and have profound unsettling effects as it presses for acceptance of an idea."

Cox v. Louisiana 379 U.S. 536, 85 S. Ct. 453, 13 L. Ed. 2d 471 (1965)

MR. JUSTICE GOLDBERG delivered the opinion of the Court.

Appellant, the Reverend Mr. B. Elton Cox, the leader of a civil rights demonstration, was arrested and charged with four offenses under Louisiana law — criminal conspiracy, disturbing the peace, obstructing public passages and picketing before a courthouse. In a consolidated trial before a judge without a jury, and on the same set of facts, he was acquitted of criminal conspiracy but convicted of the other three offenses. He was sentenced to serve four months in jail and pay a $200 fine for disturbing the peace, to serve five months in jail and pay a $500 fine for obstructing public passages, and to serve one year in jail and pay a $5,000 fine for picketing before a courthouse. The sentences were cumulative. . . .

. . . This case, No. 24, involves the convictions for disturbing the peace and obstructing public passages, and No. 49 concerns the conviction for picketing before a courthouse.

I. THE FACTS

On December 14, 1961, 23 students from Southern University, a Negro college, were arrested in downtown Baton Rouge, Louisiana, for picketing stores that maintained segregated lunch counters. This picketing, urging a boycott of those stores, was part of a general protest movement against racial segregation, directed by the local chapter of the Congress of Racial Equality, a civil rights organization. The appellant, an ordained Congregational minister, the Reverend Mr. B. Elton Cox, a Field Secretary of CORE, was an advisor to this movement. On the evening of December 14, appellant and Ronnie Moore, student president of the local CORE chapter, spoke at a mass meeting at the college. The students resolved to demonstrate the next day in front of the courthouse in protest of segregation and the arrest and imprisonment of the picketers who were being held in the parish jail located on the upper floor of the courthouse building.

The next morning about 2,000 students left the campus, which was located approximately five miles from downtown Baton Rouge. Most of them had to walk into the city since the drivers of their busses were arrested. Moore was also arrested at the entrance to the campus while parked in a car equipped with a loudspeaker, and charged with violation of an antinoise statute. Because Moore was immediately taken off to jail and the vice president of the CORE chapter was already in jail for picketing, Cox felt it his duty to take over the demonstration and see that it was carried out as planned. He quickly drove to the city "to pick up this leadership and keep things orderly."

When Cox arrived, 1,500 of the 2,000 students were assembling at the site of the Old State Capitol Building, two and one-half blocks from the courthouse. Cox walked up and down cautioning the students to keep to one side of the sidewalk while getting ready for their march to the courthouse. The students circled the block in a file two or three abreast occupying about half of the sidewalk. The police had learned of the proposed demonstration the night before from news media and other sources. Captain Font of the City Police Department and Chief Kling of the Sheriff's office, two high-ranking subordinate officials, approached the group and spoke to Cox at the northeast corner of the capitol grounds. Cox identified himself as the group's leader, and, according to Font and Kling, he explained that the students were demonstrating to protest "the illegal arrest of some of their people who were being held in jail." The version of Cox and his witnesses throughout was that they came not "to protest just the arrest but . . . [also] to protest the evil of discrimination." Kling asked Cox to disband the group and "take them back from whence they came." Cox did not acquiesce in this request but told the officers that they would march by the courthouse, say prayers, sing hymns, and conduct a peaceful program of protest. The officer repeated his request to disband, and Cox again refused. Kling and Font then returned to their car in order to report by radio to the Sheriff and Chief of Police who were in the immediate vicinity; while this was going on, the students, led by Cox, began their walk toward the courthouse.

They walked in an orderly and peaceful file, two or three abreast, one block east, stopping on the way for a red traffic light. In the center of this block they were joined by another group of students. The augmented group now totaling about 2,000 turned the corner and proceeded south, coming to a halt in the next block opposite the courthouse.

As Cox, still at the head of the group, approached the vicinity of the courthouse, he was stopped by Captain Font and Inspector Trigg and brought to Police Chief Wingate White, who was standing in the middle of St. Louis Street. The Chief then inquired as to the purpose of the demonstration. Cox, reading from a prepared paper, outlined his program to White, stating that it would include a singing of the Star Spangled Banner and a "freedom song," recitation of the Lord's Prayer and the Pledge of Allegiance, and a short speech. White testified that he told Cox that "he must confine" the demonstration "to the west side of the street." White added, "This, of course, was not — I didn't mean it in the import that I was giving him any permission to do it, but I was presented with a situation that was accomplished, and I had to make a decision." Cox testified that the officials agreed to permit the meeting. James Erwin, news director of radio station WIBR, a witness for the State, was present and overheard the conversation. He testified that "My understanding was that they would be allowed to demonstrate if they stayed on the west side of the street and stayed within the recognized time," and that this was "agreed to" by White.

The students were then directed by Cox to the west sidewalk, across the street from the courthouse, 101 feet from its steps. They were lined up on this sidewalk about five deep and spread almost the entire length of the block. The group did not obstruct the street. It was close to noon and, being lunch time, a small crowd of 100 to 300 curious white people, mostly courthouse personnel, gathered on the east sidewalk and courthouse steps, about 100 feet from the demonstrators. Seventy-five to eighty policemen, including city and state patrolmen and members of the Sheriff's staff, as well as members of the fire department and a fire truck were stationed in the street between the two groups. Rain fell throughout the demonstration.

Several of the students took from beneath their coats picket signs similar to those which had been used the day before. These signs bore legends such as "Don't buy discrimination for Christmas," "Sacrifice for Christ, don't buy," and named stores which were proclaimed "unfair." They then sang "God Bless America," pledged allegiance to the flag, prayed briefly, and sang one or two hymns including "We Shall Overcome." The 23 students, who were locked in jail cells in the courthouse building out of the sight of the demonstrators, responded by themselves singing; this in turn was greeted with cheers and applause by the demonstrators. Appellant gave a speech, described by a State's witness as follows:

"He said that in effect that it was a protest against the illegal arrest of some of their members and that other people were allowed to picket and he said that they were not going to commit any violence, that if anyone spit on them, they would not spit back on the person that did it."

Cox then said:

"All right. It's lunch time. Let's go eat. There are twelve stores we are protesting. A number of these stores have twenty counters; they accept your money from nineteen. They won't accept it from the twentieth counter. This is an act of racial discrimination. These stores are open to the public. You are members of the public. We pay taxes to the Federal Government and you who live here pay taxes to the state."

In apparent reaction to these last remarks, there was what state witnesses described as "muttering" and "grumbling" by the white onlookers.

The Sheriff, deeming, as he testified, Cox's appeal to the students to sit in at the lunch counters to be "inflammatory," then took a power microphone and said, "Now, you have been allowed to demonstrate. Up until now your demonstration has been more or less peaceful, but what you are doing now is a direct violation of the law, a disturbance of the peace, and it has to be broken up immediately." The testimony as to what then happened is disputed. Some of the State's witnesses testified that Cox said, "don't move"; others stated that he made a "gesture of defiance." It is clear from the record, however, that Cox and the demonstrators did not then and there break up the demonstration. Two of the Sheriff's deputies immediately started across the street and told the group, "You have heard what the Sheriff said, now, do what he said." A state witness testified that they put

Section C. **Freedom of Speech and Association** 1195

their hands on the shoulders of some of the students "as though to shove them away."

Almost immediately thereafter — within a time estimated variously at two to five minutes — one of the policemen exploded a tear gas shell at the crowd. This was followed by several other shells. The demonstrators quickly dispersed, running back towards the State Capitol and the downtown area; Cox tried to calm them as they ran and was himself one of the last to leave.

No Negroes participating in the demonstration were arrested on that day. The only person then arrested was a young white man, not a part of the demonstration, who was arrested "because he was causing a disturbance." The next day appellant was arrested and charged with the four offenses above described.

II. THE BREACH OF THE PEACE CONVICTION

Appellant was convicted of violating a Louisiana "disturbing the peace" statute, which provides:

"Whoever with intent to provoke a breach of the peace, or under circumstances such that a breach of the peace may be occasioned thereby . . . crowds or congregates with others . . . in or upon . . . a public street or public highway, or upon a public sidewalk, or any other public place or building . . . and who fails or refuses to disperse and move on . . . when ordered so to do by any law enforcement officer of any municipality, or parish, in which such act or acts are committed, or by any law enforcement officer of the state of Louisiana, or any other authorized person . . . shall be guilty of disturbing the peace." LSA-Rev. Stat. 14:103.1 (Cum. Supp. 1962).

It is clear to us that on the facts of this case, which are strikingly similar to those present in Edwards v. South Carolina, 372 U.S. 229, and Fields v. South Carolina, 375 U.S. 44, Louisiana infringed appellant's rights of free speech and free assembly by convicting him under this statute. As in Edwards, we do not find it necessary to pass upon appellant's contention that there was a complete absence of evidence so that his conviction deprived him of liberty without due process of law. Cf. Thompson v. City of Louisville, 362 U.S. 199. We hold that Louisiana may not constitutionally punish appellant under this statute for engaging in the type of conduct which this record reveals, and also that the statute as authoritatively interpreted by the Louisiana Supreme Court is unconstitutionally broad in scope. . . .

The State argues, . . . that while the demonstrators started out to be orderly, the loud cheering and clapping by the students in response to the singing from the jail converted the peaceful assembly into a riotous one. The record, however, does not support this assertion. It is true that the sudents, in response to the singing of their fellows who were in custody, cheered and applauded. However, the meeting was an outdoor meeting and a key state witness testified that while the singing was loud, it was not disorderly. There is moreover, no indication that the mood of the students was ever hostile, aggressive, or unfriendly. Our conclusion that the entire meeting from the beginning until its dispersal by tear gas was orderly and not riotous is confirmed by a film of the events taken by a television news photographer, which was offered in evidence as a state exhibit. We have viewed the film, and it reveals that the students, though they undoubtedly cheered and clapped, were well-behaved throughout. . . .

Finally, the State contends that the conviction should be sustained because of fear expressed by some of the state witnesses that "violence was about to erupt" because of the demonstration. It is virtually undisputed, however, that the students themselves were not violent and threatened no violence. The fear of violence seems to have been based upon the reaction of the group of white citizens looking on from across the street. One state witness testified that "he felt the situation was getting out of hand" as on the courthouse side of St. Louis Street "were small knots or groups of white citizens who were muttering words, who seemed a little bit agitated." A police officer stated that the reaction of the white crowd was not violent, but "was rumblings." Others felt the atmosphere became "tense" because of "mutterings," "grumbling," and "jeering" from the white group. There is no indication, however, that any member of the white group threatened violence. And this small crowd estimated at between 100 and 300 was separated from the students by "seventy-five to eighty" armed policemen, including "every available shift of the City Police," the "Sheriff's Office in full complement," and "additional help from the State Police," along with a "fire truck and the Fire Department." As Inspector Trigg testified, they could have handled the crowd.

This situation, like that in Edwards, is "a far cry from the situation in Feiner v. New York, 340 U.S. 315." See Edwards v. South Carolina, supra, at 236. Nor is there any evidence here of "fighting words." See Chaplinsky v. New Hampshire, 315 U.S. 568. Here again, as in Edwards, this evidence "showed no more than that the opinions which . . . [the students] were peaceably expressing were sufficiently opposed to the views of the majority of the community to attract a crowd and necessitate police protection." Edwards v. South Carolina, supra, at 237. Conceding this was so, the "compelling answer . . . is that constitutional rights may not be denied simply because of hostility to their assertion or exercise." Watson v. Memphis, 373 U.S. 526, 535.

There is an additional reason why this conviction cannot be sustained. The statute at issue in this case, as authoritatively interpreted by the Louisiana Supreme Court, is unconstitutionally vague in its overly broad scope. The statutory crime consists of two elements: (1) congregating with others "with intent to provoke a breach of the peace, or under circumstances such that a breach of the peace may be occasioned," and (2) a refusal to move on after having been ordered to do so by a law enforcement officer. While the second part of this offense is narrow and specific, the first element is not. The Louisiana Supreme Court in this case defined the term "breach of the peace" as "to agitate, to arouse from a state of repose, to molest, to interrupt, to hinder, to disquiet." 244 La., at 1105, 156 So. 2d, at 455. In Edwards, defendants had been convicted of a common-law crime similarly defined by the South Carolina Supreme Court. Both definitions would allow persons to be punished merely for peacefully expressing unpopular views. Yet, a "function of free speech under our system of government is to invite dispute. It may indeed best serve its high purpose when it induces a condition of unrest, creates dissatisfaction with conditions as they are, or even stirs people to anger. . . ." Terminiello v. City of Chicago, 337 U.S. 1, 4-5. . . .

For all these reasons we hold that appellant's freedom of speech and assembly, secured to him by the First Amendment, as applied to the States by the Fourteenth Amendment, were denied by his conviction for disturbing the peace. The conviction on this charge cannot stand.

III. THE OBSTRUCTING PUBLIC PASSAGES CONVICTION

We now turn to the issue of the validity of appellant's conviction for violating the Louisiana statute, LSA-Rev. Stat. 14:100.1 (Cum. Supp. 1962), which provides:

"*Obstructing Public Passages*

"No person shall willfully obstruct the free, convenient and normal use of any public sidewalk, street, highway, bridge, alley, road, or other passageway, or the entrance, corridor or passage of any public building, structure, water craft or ferry, by impeding, hindering, stifling, retarding or restraining traffic or passage thereon or therein.

"Providing however nothing herein contained shall apply to a bona fide legitimate labor organization or to any of its legal activities such as picketing, lawful assembly or concerted activity in the interest of its members for the purpose of accomplishing or securing more favorable wage standards, hours of employment and working conditions."

Appellant was convicted under this statute, not for leading the march to the vicinity of the courthouse, which the Louisiana Supreme Court stated to have been "orderly," 244

La., at 1096, 156 So. 2d, at 451, but for leading the meeting on the sidewalk across the street from the courthouse. Id., at 1094, 1106-1107, 156 So. 2d, at 451, 455. In upholding appellant's conviction under this statute, the Louisiana Supreme Court thus construed the statute so as to apply to public assemblies which do not have as their specific purpose the obstruction of traffic. There is no doubt from the record in this case that this far sidewalk was obstructed, and thus, as so construed, appellant violated the statute.

Appellant, however, contends that as so construed and applied in this case, the statute is an unconstitutional infringement on freedom of speech and assembly. This contention on the facts here presented raises an issue with which this Court has dealt in many decisions. That is, the right of a State or municipality to regulate the use of city streets and other facilities to assure the safety and convenience of the people in their use and the concomitant right of the people of free speech and assembly. . . .

From these decisions certain clear principles emerge. The rights of free speech and assembly, while fundamental in our democratic society, still do not mean that everyone with opinions or beliefs to express may address a group at any public place and at any time. The constitutional guarantee of liberty implies the existence of an organized society maintaining the public order, without which liberty would be lost in the excesses of anarchy. The control of travel on the streets is a clear example of governmental responsibility to insure this necessary order. A restriction in that relation, designed to promote the public convenience in the interest of all, and not susceptible to abuses of discriminatory application, cannot be disregarded by the attempted exercise of some civil right which, in other circumstances, would be entitled to protection. . . .

We have no occasion in this case to consider the constitutionality of the uniform, consistent, and nondiscriminatory application of a statute forbidding all access to streets and other public facilities for parades and meetings. Although the statute here involved on its face precludes all street assemblies and parades, it has not been so applied and enforced by the Baton Rouge authorities. City officials who testified for the State clearly indicated that certain meetings and parades are permitted in Baton Rouge, even though they have the effect of obstructing traffic, provided prior approval is obtained. This was confirmed in oral argument before this Court by counsel for the State. He stated that parades and meetings are permitted, based on "arrangements . . . made with officials." The statute itself provides no standards for the determination of local officials as to which assemblies to permit or which to prohibit. Nor are there any administrative regulations on this subject which have been called to our attention. From all the evidence before us it appears that the authorities in Baton Rouge permit or prohibit parades or street meetings in their completely uncontrolled discretion.

The situation is thus the same as if the statute itself expressly provided that there could only be peaceful parades or demonstrations in the unbridled discretion of the local officials. The pervasive restraint on freedom of discussion by the practice of the authorities under the statute is not any less effective than a statute expressly permitting such selective enforcement. . . .

For the reasons discussed above the judgment of the Supreme Court of Louisiana is reversed.

Reversed.[q]

MR. JUSTICE BLACK, concurring in No. 24 and dissenting in No. 49. . . .

---

[q] In No. 49, Cox v. Louisiana, 379 U.S. 559 (1965), the Court also reversed the appellant's conviction for picketing near a courthouse. While admitting the legitimacy of such a statutory ban as a safeguard "to assure that the administration of justice at all stages is free from outside control and influence," the Court nonetheless held that a conviction here would constitute an "entrapment" violative of due process since the police had, in effect, "told the demonstrators that they could meet where they did." — ED.

I. THE BREACH-OF-PEACE CONVICTION

I agree with that part of the Court's opinion holding that the Louisiana breach-of-the-peace statute on its face and as construed by the State Supreme Court is so broad as to be unconstitutionally vague under the First and Fourteenth Amendments. . . . The statute does not itself define the conditions upon which people who want to express views may be allowed to use the public streets and highways, but leaves this to be defined by law enforcement officers. The statute therefore neither forbids all crowds to congregate and picket on streets, nor is it narrowly drawn to prohibit congregating or patrolling under certain clearly defined conditions while preserving the freedom to speak of those who are using the streets as streets in the ordinary way that the State permits. A state statute of either of the two types just mentioned, regulating *conduct* — patrolling and marching — as distinguished from *speech*, would in my judgment be constitutional, subject only to the condition that if such a law had the effect of indirectly impinging on freedom of speech, press, or religion, it would be unconstitutional if under the circumstances it appeared that the State's interest in suppressing the conduct was not sufficient to outweigh the individual's interest in engaging in conduct closely involving his First Amendment freedoms. . . .

The First and Fourteenth Amendments, I think, take away from government, state and federal, all power to restrict freedom of speech, press, and assembly *where people have a right to be for such purposes*. This does not mean however, that these amendments also grant a constitutional right to engage in the conduct of picketing or patrolling, whether on publicly owned streets or on privately owned property. . . . Were the law otherwise, people on the streets, in their homes and anywhere else could be compelled to listen against their will to speakers they did not want to hear. Picketing, though it may be utilized to communicate ideas, is not speech, and therefore is not of itself protected by the First Amendment. Hughes v. Superior Court, 339 U.S. 460, 464-466; Giboney v. Empire Storage & Ice Co., 336 U.S. 490; Bakery and Pastry Drivers and Helpers Local 802, etc. v. Wohl, 315 U.S. 769, 775-777 (Douglas, J. concurring).

However, because Louisiana's breach-of-peace statute is not narrowly drawn to assure nondiscriminatory application, I think it is constitutionally invalid under our holding in Edwards v. South Carolina, 372 U.S. 229 . . . In the case before us Louisiana has by a broad, vague statute given policemen an unlimited power to order people off the streets, not to enforce a specific, nondiscriminatory state statute forbidding patrolling and picketing, but rather whenever a policeman makes a decision on his own personal judgment that views being expressed on the street are provoking or might provoke a breach of the peace. Such a statute does not provide for government by clearly defined laws, but rather for government by the moment-to-moment opinions of a policeman on his beat. . . .

II. THE OBSTRUCTING-PUBLIC-PASSAGES CONVICTION

The Louisiana law against obstructing the streets and sidewalks, while applied here so as to convict Negroes for assembling and picketing on streets and sidewalks for the purpose of publicly protesting racial discrimination, expressly provides that the statute shall not bar picketing and assembly by labor unions protesting unfair treatment of union members. I believe that the First and Fourteenth Amendments require that if the streets of a town are open to some views, they must be open to all. . . . As I said above, I have no doubt about the general power of Louisiana to bar all picketing on its streets and highways. Standing, patrolling, or marching back and forth on streets is conduct, not speech, and as conduct can be regulated or prohibited. But by specifically permitting picketing for the publication of labor union views, Louisiana is attempting to pick and choose among the views it is willing to have discussed on its streets. It thus is trying to prescribe by law what matters of public interest people whom it allows to assemble on its streets may or may not discuss.

Section C. Freedom of Speech and Association

This seems to me to be censorship in a most odious form, unconstitutional under the First and Fourteenth Amendments. And to deny this appellant and his group use of the streets because of their views against racial discrimination, while allowing other groups to use the streets to voice opinions on other subjects, also amounts, I think, to an invidious discrimination forbidden by the Equal Protection Clause of the Fourteenth Amendment. Moreover, as the Court points out, city officials despite this statute apparently have permitted favored groups other than labor unions to block the streets with their gatherings. For these reasons I concur in reversing the conviction based on this law.[r]

Adderly v. Florida 385 U.S. 39, 87 S. Ct. 242, 17 L. Ed. 2d 149 (1966)

MR. JUSTICE BLACK delivered the opinion of the Court.

Petitioners, Harriett Louise Adderley and 31 other persons, were convicted by a jury in a joint trial in the County Judge's Court of Leon County, Florida, on a charge of "trespass with a malicious and mischievous intent" upon the premises of the county jail contrary to §821.18 of the Florida statutes set out below.[1] Petitioners, apparently all students of the Florida A. & M. University in Tallahassee, had gone from the school to the jail about a mile away, along with many other students, to "demonstrate" at the jail their protests because of arrests of other protesting students the day before, and perhaps to protest more generally against state and local policies and practices of racial segregation, including segregation of the jail. The county sheriff, legal custodian of the jail and jail grounds, tried to persuade the students to leave the jail grounds. When this did not work, he notified them that they must leave, or he would arrest them for trespassing, and notified them further that if they resisted arrest he would arrest them for resisting arrest as well. Some of the students left but others, including petitioners, remained and they were arrested. On appeal the convictions were affirmed by the Florida Circuit Court and then by the Florida District Court of Appeals, 175 So. 2d 249. That being the highest state court to which they could appeal, petitioners applied to us for certiorari contending that, in view of petitioners' purpose to protest against jail and other segregation policies, their conviction denied them "rights of free speech, assembly, petition, due process of law and equal protection of the laws as guaranteed by the Fourteenth Amendment to the Constitution of the United States."

I

Petitioners have insisted from the beginning of these cases that they are controlled and must be reversed because of our prior cases of Edwards v. South Carolina, 372 U.S. 229, and Cox v. Louisiana, 379 U.S. 536, 559. We cannot agree.

The Edwards case, like this one, did come up when a number of persons demonstrated on public property against their State's segregation policies. They also sang hymns and danced, as did the demonstrators in this case. But here the analogies to this case end. In Edwards, the demonstrators went to the South Carolina State Capitol grounds to protest. In this case they went to the jail. Traditionally, state capitol grounds are open to the public. Jails, built for security purposes, are not. The demonstrators at the South Carolina Capitol went in through a public driveway and as they entered they were told by state officials there that they had a right as citizens to go through the State House grounds as long

---

[r] Mr. Justice White, with Harlan, J., concurring, dissented from the majority's reversal of the conviction for the obstruction of public passages. — ED.

[1] "[E]very trespass upon the property of another, committed with a malicious and mischievous intent, the punishment of which is not specially provided for, shall be punished by imprisonment not exceeding three months, or by fine not exceeding one hundred dollars." Fla. Stat. §821.18 (1965).

as they were peaceful. Here the demonstrators entered the jail grounds through a driveway used only for jail purposes and without warning to or permission from the sheriff. More importantly, South Carolina sought to prosecute its State Capitol demonstrators by charging them with the common-law crime of breach of the peace. This Court in Edwards took pains to point out at length the indefinite, loose, and broad nature of this charge; indeed, this Court pointed out at p. 237, that the South Carolina Supreme Court had itself declared that the "breach of the peace charge" is "not susceptible of exact definition." South Carolina's power to prosecute, it was emphasized at p. 236, would have been different had it proceeded under a "precise and narrowly drawn regulatory statute evincing a legislative judgment that certain specific conduct be limited or proscribed" such as, for example, "limiting the periods during which the State House grounds were open to the public. . . ." The South Carolina breach-of-the-peace statute was thus struck down as being so broad and all-embracing as to jeopardize speech, press, assembly and petition, under the constitutional doctrine enunciated in Cantwell v. Connecticut, 310 U.S. 296, 307-308, and followed in many subsequent cases. And it was on this same ground of vagueness that in Cox v. Louisiana, supra, at 551-552, the Louisiana breach-of-the-peace law used to prosecute Cox was invalidated.

The Florida trespass statute under which these petitioners were charged cannot be challenged on this ground. It is aimed at conduct of one limited kind, that is for one person or persons to trespass upon the property of another with a malicious and mischievous intent. There is no lack of notice in this law, nothing to entrap or fool the unwary.

Petitioners seem to argue that the Florida trespass law is void for vagueness because it requires a trespass to be "with a malicious and mischievous intent. . . ." But these words do not broaden the scope of trespass so as to make it cover a multitude of types of conduct as does the common-law breach-of-the-peace charge. On the contrary, these words narrow the scope of the offense. The trial court charged the jury as to their meaning and petitioners have not argued that this definition, set out below,[2] is not a reasonable and clear definition of the terms. The use of these terms in the statute, instead of contributing to uncertainty and misunderstanding, actually makes its meaning more understandable and clear. . . .

IV

Petitioners here contend that "Petitioners' convictions are based on a total lack of relevant evidence." If true, this would be a denial of due process under Garner v. Louisiana, 368 U.S. 157, and Thompson v. City of Louisville, 362 U.S. 199. Both in the petition for certiorari and in the brief on the merits petitioners state that their summary of the evidence "does not conflict with the facts contained in the Circuit Court's opinion" which was in effect affirmed by the District Court of Appeals. 175 So. 2d 249. That statement is correct and petitioners' summary of facts, as well as that of the Circuit Court, shows an abundance of facts to support the jury's verdict of guilty in these cases.

In summary both these statements show testimony ample to prove this: Disturbed and upset by the arrest of their schoolmates the day before, a large number of Florida A. & M. students assembled on the school grounds and decided to march down to the county jail.

[2] " 'Malicious' means wrongful, you remember back in the original charge, the State has to prove beyond a reasonable doubt there was malicious and mischievous intent. The word 'malicious' means that the wrongful act shall be done voluntarily, unlawfully, and without excuse or justification. The word 'malicious' that is used in these affidavits does not necessarily allege nor require the State to prove that the defendant had actual malice in his mind at the time of the alleged trespass. Another way of stating the definition of 'malicious' is by 'malicious' is meant the act was done knowingly and willfully and without any legal justification.

" 'Mischievous,' which is also required, means that the alleged trespass shall be inclined to cause petty and trivial trouble, annoyance and vexation to others in order for you to find that the alleged trespass was committed with mischievous intent." R. 74.

Section C. Freedom of Speech and Association

Some apparently wanted to get themselves put in jail too, along with the students already there. A group of around 200 marched from the school and arrived at the jail singing and clapping. They went directly to the jail door entrance where they were met by a deputy sheriff, evidently surprised by their arrival. He asked them to move back, claiming they were blocking the entrance to the jail and fearing that they might attempt to enter the jail. They moved back part of the way, where they stood or sat, singing, clapping and dancing, on the jail driveway and on an adjacent grassy area upon the jail premises. This particular jail entrance and driveway were not normally used by the public, but by the sheriff's department for transporting prisoners to and from the courts several blocks away and by commercial concerns for servicing the jail. Even after their partial retreat, the demonstrators continued to block vehicular passage over this driveway up to the entrance of the jail. Someone called the sheriff who was at the moment apparently conferring with one of the state court judges about incidents connected with prior arrests for demonstrations. When the sheriff returned to the jail, he immediately inquired if all was safe inside the jail and was told it was. He then engaged in a conversation with two of the leaders. He told them that they were trespassing upon jail property and that he would give them 10 minutes to leave or he would arrest them. Neither of the leaders did anything to disperse the crowd, and one of them told the sheriff that they wanted to get arrested. A local minister talked with some of the demonstrators and told them not to enter the jail, because they could not arrest themselves, but just to remain where they were. After about 10 minutes, the sheriff, in a voice loud enough to be heard by all, told the demonstrators that he was the legal custodian of the jail and its premises, that they were trespassing on county property in violation of the law, that they should all leave forthwith or he would arrest them, and that if they attempted to resist arrest, he would charge them with that as a separate offense. Some of the group then left. Others, including all petitioners, did not leave. Some of them sat down. In a few minutes, realizing that the remaining demonstrators had no intention of leaving, the sheriff ordered his deputies to surround those remaining on jail premises and placed them, 107 demonstrators, under arrest. The sheriff unequivocally testified that he did not arrest any person other than those who were on the jail premises. Of the three petitioners testifying, two insisted that they were arrested before they had a chance to leave, had they wanted to, and one testified that she did not intend to leave. The sheriff again explicitly testified that he did not arrest any person who was attempting to leave.

Under the foregoing testimony the jury was authorized to find that the State had proven every essential element of the crime, as it was defined by the state court. That interpretation is, of course, binding on us, leaving only the question of whether conviction of the state offense, thus defined, unconstitutionally deprives petitioners of their rights to freedom of speech, press, assembly or petition. We hold it does not. The sheriff, as jail custodian, had power, as the state courts have here held, to direct that this large crowd of people get off the grounds. There is not a shred of evidence in this record that this power was exercised, or that its exercise was sanctioned by the lower courts, because the sheriff objected to what was being sung or said by the demonstrators or because he disagreed with the objectives of the protest. The record reveals that he objected only to their presence on that part of the jail grounds reserved for jail uses. There is no evidence at all that on any other occasion had similarly large groups of the public been permitted to gather on this portion of the jail grounds for any purpose. Nothing in the Constitution of the United States prevents Florida from even-handed enforcement of its general trespass statute against those refusing to obey the sheriff's order to remove themselves from what amounted to the curtilage of the jailhouse. The State, no less than a private owner of property, has power to preserve the property under its control for the use to which it is lawfully dedicated. For this reason there is no merit to the petitioners' argument that they had a constitutional right to stay on the property, over the jail custodian's objections, because this "area chosen for the peaceful civil rights demonstration was not only 'reasonable' but also particularly appropriate. . . ." Such an argument has as its major unarticulated premise the assumption that people who want to propagandize protests or views have a constitutional right to do so whenever and however and wherever they please. That concept of constitutional law was vigorously and forthrightly rejected in two of the cases petitioners rely on, Cox v. Louisiana, supra, at 554-555 and 563-564. We reject it again. The United States Constitution does not forbid a State to control the use of its own property for its own lawful nondiscriminatory purpose.

These judgments are affirmed.

MR. JUSTICE DOUGLAS, with whom THE CHIEF JUSTICE, MR. JUSTICE BRENNAN, and MR. JUSTICE FORTAS concur, dissenting.

The First Amendment, applicable to the States by reason of the Fourteenth (Edwards v. South Carolina, 372 U.S. 229, 235), provides that "Congress shall make no law respecting . . . the right of the people peaceably to assemble, and to petition the government for a redress of grievances." These rights, along with religion, speech, and press, are preferred rights of the Constitution, made so by reason of that explicit guarantee and what Edmond Cahn in Confronting Injustice (1966) referred to as "The Firstness of the First Amendment." With all respect, therefore, the Court errs in treating the case as if it were an ordinary trespass case or an ordinary picketing case.

The jailhouse, like an executive mansion, a legislative chamber, a courthouse, or the statehouse itself (Edwards v. South Carolina, supra) is one of the seats of government whether it be the Tower of London, the Bastille, or a small county jail. And when it houses political prisoners or those whom many think are unjustly held, it is an obvious center for protest. The right to petition for the redress of grievances has an ancient history and is not limited to writing a letter or sending a telegram to a congressman; it is not confined to appearing before the local city council, or writing letters to the President or Governor or Mayor. See NAACP v. Button, 371 U.S. 415, 429-431. Conventional methods of petitioning may be, and often have been, shut off to large groups of our citizens. Legislators may turn deaf ears; formal complaints may be routed endlessly through a bureaucratic maze; courts may let the wheels of justice grind very slowly. Those who do not control television and radio, those who cannot afford to advertise in newspapers or circulate elaborate pamphlets may have only a more limited type of access to public officials. Their methods should not be condemned as tactics of obstruction and harassment as long as the assembly and petition are peaceable, as these were. . . .

We do violence to the First Amendment when we permit this "petition for redress of grievances" to be turned into a trespass action. It does not help to analogize this problem to the problem of picketing. Picketing is a form of protest usually directed against private interests. I do not see how rules governing picketing in general are relevant to this express constitutional right to assembly and to petition for redress of grievances. In the first place the jailhouse grounds were not marked with "NO TRESPASSING!" signs, nor does respondent claim that the public was generally excluded from the grounds. Only the sheriff's fiat transformed lawful conduct into an unlawful trespass. To say that a private owner could have done the same if the rally had taken place on private property is to speak of a different case, as an assembly and a petition for redress of grievances run to government not to private proprietors. . . .

There may be some public places which are so clearly committed to other purposes that their use for the airing of grievances is anomalous. There may be some instances in which assemblies and petitions for redress of grievances are not consistent with other necessary purposes of public property. A noisy meeting may be out of keeping with the serenity of the statehouse or the quiet of the courthouse. No one, for example, would suggest that the Senate gallery is the proper place for a vociferous protest rally. And, in other cases it may be necessary to adjust the right to petition for redress of grievances to the other interests inhering in the uses to which the public property is normally put. See Cox v. New

Hampshire, supra; Poulos v. New Hampshire, 345 U.S. 395. But this is quite different than saying that all public places are off-limits to people with grievances. . . .

Today a trespass law is used to penalize people for exercising a constitutional right. Tomorrow a disorderly conduct statute, a breach of the peace statute, a vagrancy statute will be put to the same end. It is said that the sheriff did not make the arrests because of the views which petitioners espoused. That excuse is usually given, as we know from the many cases involving arrests of minority groups for breaches of the peace, unlawful assemblies, and parading without a permit. The charge against William Penn, who preached a nonconformist doctrine in a street in London, was that he caused "a great concourse and tumult of people" in contempt of the King and "to the great disturbance of the peace." 6 St. Tr. 951, 955. That was in 1670. In modern times also such arrests are usually sought to be justified by some legitimate function of government. Yet by allowing these orderly and civilized protests against injustice to be suppressed, we only increase the forces of frustration which the conditions of second-class citizenship are generating amongst us.

NOTE The "Public Forum"

See Kalven, The Concept of the Public Forum: Cox v. Louisiana, 1965 Sup. Ct. Rev. 1, for a classic discussion of Cox and its predecessors. Some recent articles include Stone, Fora Americana: Speech in Public Places, 1974 Sup. Ct. Rev. 233, and Note, The Public Forum: Minimum Access, Equal Access, and the First Amendment, 28 Stan. L. Rev. 117 (1975).

In Brown v. Louisiana, 383 U.S. 131 (1966), the Court reviewed a set of convictions based on the same breach of the peace statute that it had considered in Cox. Justice Fortas, for the Chief Justice and Justice Douglas, found that there was not "the slightest evidence" that the peaceful demonstration by five blacks in a public library either provoked a breach of the peace or was done with such an intent. Justice Brennan deemed the statute overbroad and Justice White believed their arrest was a violation of equal protection. Justices Clark, Harlan, and Stewart joined in a dissenting opinion of Justice Black.

Police Dept. of Chicago v. Mosley 408 U.S. 92, 92 S. Ct. 2286, 33 L. Ed. 2d 212 (1972)

MR. JUSTICE MARSHALL delivered the opinion of the Court.

At issue in this case is the constitutionality of the following Chicago ordinance:

"A person commits disorderly conduct when he knowingly: . . .

"(i) Pickets or demonstrates on a public way within 150 feet of any primary or secondary school building while the school is in session and one-half hour before the school is in session and one-half hour after the school session has been concluded, provided that this subsection does not prohibit the peaceful picketing of any school involved in a labor dispute. . . ." Municipal Code, c. 193-1 (i).

The suit was brought by Earl Mosley, a federal postal employee, who for seven months prior to the enactment of the ordinance had frequently picketed Jones Commercial High School in Chicago. During school hours and usually by himself, Mosley would walk the public sidewalk adjoining the school, carrying a sign that read: "Jones High School practices black discrimination. Jones High School has a black quota." His lonely crusade was always peaceful, orderly, and quiet, and was conceded to be so by the city of Chicago.

[Mosley sought declaratory and injunctive relief against the ordinance, which was granted by the district court and affirmed by the Seventh Circuit.]

The central problem with Chicago's ordinance is that it describes permissible picketing in terms of its subject matter. Peaceful picketing on the subject of a school's labor-management dispute is permitted, but all other peaceful picketing is prohibited. The operative distinction is the message on a picket sign. But, above all else, the First Amendment means that government has no power to restrict expression because of its message, its ideas, its subject matter, or its content. [Citations omitted.]

To permit the continued building of our politics and culture, and to assure self-fulfillment for each individual, our people are guaranteed the right to express any thought, free from government censorship. The essence of this forbidden censorship is content control. Any restriction on expressive activity because of its content would completely undercut the "profound national commitment to the principle that debate on public issues should be uninhibited, robust, and wide-open." New York Times Co. v. Sullivan, [376 U.S. 254 (1964)] at 270.

Necessarily, then, under the Equal Protection Clause, not to mention the First Amendment itself, government may not grant the use of a forum to people whose views it finds acceptable, but deny use to those wishing to express less favored or more controversial views. And it may not select which issues are worth discussing or debating in public facilities. There is an "equality of status in the field of ideas,"[4] and government must afford all points of view an equal opportunity to be heard. Once a forum is opened up to assembly or speaking by some groups, government may not prohibit others from assembling or speaking on the basis of what they intend to say. Selective exclusions from a public forum may not be based on content alone, and may not be justified by reference to content alone.

The late Mr. Justice Black, who thought that picketing was not only a method of expressing an idea but also conduct subject to broad state regulation, nevertheless recognized the deficiencies of laws like Chicago's ordinance. This was the thrust of his opinion concurring in Cox v. Louisiana, 379 U.S. 536 (1965). . . .

This is not to say that all picketing must always be allowed. We have continually recognized that reasonable "time, place and manner" regulations of picketing may be necessary to further significant governmental interests. Cox v. New Hampshire, 312 U.S. 569, 575-576 (1941); Poulos v. New Hampshire, 345 U.S. 395, 398 (1953); Cox v. Louisiana, 379 U.S., at 554-555; Cox v. Louisiana, 379 U.S. 559 (1965); Adderley v. Florida, 385 U.S. 39, 46-48 (1966). Similarly, under an equal protection analysis, there may be sufficient regulatory interests justifying selective exclusions or distinctions among pickets. Conflicting demands on the same place may compel the State to make choices among potential users and uses. And the State may have a legitimate interest in prohibiting some picketing to protect public order. . . .

Although preventing school disruption is a city's legitimate concern, Chicago itself has determined that peaceful labor picketing during school hours is not an undue interference with school. Therefore, under the Equal Protection Clause, Chicago may not maintain that other picketing disrupts the school unless that picketing is clearly more disruptive than the picketing Chicago already permits. Cf. Tinker v. Des Moines School District, 393 U.S. 503, 511 (1969); Wirta v. Alameda-Contra Costa Transit District, 68 Cal. 2d 51, 434 P.2d 982 (1967). If peaceful labor picketing is permitted, there is no justification for prohibiting all nonlabor picketing, both peaceful and nonpeaceful. "Peaceful" nonlabor picketing, however the term "peaceful" is defined, is obviously no more disruptive than "peaceful" labor picketing. . . .

. . . Predictions about imminent disruption from picketing involve judgments appropriately made on an individualized basis, not by means of broad classifications, especially those based on subject matter. . . . No labor picketing could be more peaceful or less prone to violence than Mosley's solitary vigil. In seeking to restrict nonlabor picketing that

---

[4] A. Meikeljohn, Political Freedom: The Constitutional Powers of The People 27 (1948).

Section C. Freedom of Speech and Association   1205

is clearly more disruptive than peaceful labor picketing, Chicago may not prohibit all nonlabor picketing at the school forum. . . .

The judgment is

Affirmed.[s]

NOTE

How, if at all, does the equal protection analysis of Mosley change the traditional approaches of the First Amendment to issues of the public forum? obscenity? commercial advertising? See Karst, Equality as a Central Principle in the First Amendment, 43 U. Chi. L. Rev. 20 (1975). If Mosley portended no change in doctrinal approach, why did the Court use equal-protection analysis? See Comment, Equal But Inadequate Protection: A Look at Mosley and Grayned, 8 Harv. Civ. Rights-Civ. Lib. L. Rev. 469 (1973).

What would be the constitutionality after Mosley of a city policy of refusing available advertising space on the vehicles of its transit system to political advertising? See Lehman v. City of Shaker Heights, 418 U.S. 298 (1974), for a 5 to 4 decision of the Court sustaining the policy just described.

In addition to the difficulties of applying Mosley, see Lehman, supra, its "equality principle" still leaves other problems entirely unresolved. Suppose, for example, that the city of Chicago after Mosley simply banned all picketing near schools; what "minimum access" to public places does the First Amendment require the city to afford to demonstrators? Consider the following reaction to the neutrality of flat prohibitions: "We would do well to avoid the occasion for any new epigrams about the majestic equality of the law prohibiting the rich man, too, from distributing leaflets or picketing.". Kalven, The Concept of the Public Forum: Cox v. Louisiana, 1965 Sup. Ct. Rev. 1, 30. Thus, the persistent question, as Justice Douglas highlighted in his dissenting opinion in Adderly, supra, is what places ought to be public forums, regardless of even-handed prohibitions on their use? What should be the standards for the Court's decision, for example, in Greer v. Spock, 424 U.S. 828 (1976), that all leafleting can be banned on quasi-public thoroughfares in military bases? Compare Tinker v. Des Moines Indep. Community School Dist., infra page 1207.

See also Madison v. Wisconsin Employment Relations Commn., 97 S. Ct. 421 (1976), holding that the state may not enjoin a dissident member of a teacher's union from speaking at a public meeting of the board of education while permitting the unit representative to speak. Justices Brennan and Marshall, concurring, distinguished a meeting where "negotiation" was being conducted.

c. Symbolic Speech

United States v. O'Brien 391 U.S. 367, 88 S. Ct. 1673,
20 L. Ed. 2d 672 (1968)

Mr. Chief Justice Warren delivered the opinion of the Court.

On the morning of March 31, 1966, David Paul O'Brien and three companions burned their Selective Service registration certificates on the steps of the South Boston Courthouse. . . .

For this act, O'Brien was indicted, tried, convicted, and sentenced in the United States District Court for the District of Massachusetts. He did not contest the fact that he had

---

[s] Justices Blackmun and Rehnquist concurred in the result. The Chief Justice concurred in a separate opinion. — Ed.

1206 Chapter Sixteen. Substantive Rights

burned the certificate. He stated in argument to the jury that he burned the certificate publicly to influence others to adopt his antiwar beliefs. . . .

The indictment upon which he was tried charged that he "willfully and knowingly did mutilate, destroy, and change by burning . . . [his] Registration Certificate (Selective Service System Form No. 2); in violation of Title 50, App., United States Code, Section 462(b)." Section 462(b) is part of the Universal Military Training and Service Act of 1948. Section 462(b)(3), one of six numbered subdivisions of §462(b), was amended by Congress in 1965, 79 Stat. 586 (adding the words italicized below), so that at the time O'Brien burned his certificate an offense was committed by any person, "who forges, alters, *knowingly destroys, knowingly mutilates*, or in any manner changes any such certificate. . . ." (Italics supplied.)

On appeal, the Court of Appeals for the First Circuit held the 1965 Amendment unconstitutional as a law abridging freedom of speech.[4] . . .

O'Brien first argues that the 1965 Amendment is unconstitutional as applied to him because his act of burning his registration certificate was protected "symbolic speech" within the First Amendment. His argument is that the freedom of expression which the First Amendment guarantees includes all modes of "communication of ideas by conduct," and that his conduct is within this definition because he did it in "demonstration against the war and against the draft."

We cannot accept the view that an apparently limitless variety of conduct can be labeled "speech" whenever the person engaging in the conduct intends thereby to express an idea. However, even on the assumption that the alleged communicative element in O'Brien's conduct is sufficient to bring into play the First Amendment, it does not necessarily follow that the destruction of a registration certificate is constitutionally protected activity. This Court has held that when "speech" and "nonspeech" elements are combined in the same course of conduct, a sufficiently important governmental interest in regulating the nonspeech element can justify incidental limitations on First Amendment freedoms. To characterize the quality of the governmental interest which must appear, the Court has employed a variety of descriptive terms: compelling; substantial; subordinating; paramount; cogent; strong. Whatever imprecision inheres in these terms, we think it clear that a government regulation is sufficiently justified if it is within the constitutional power of the Government; if it furthers an important or substantial governmental interest; if the governmental interest is unrelated to the suppression of free expression; and if the incidental restriction on alleged First Amendment freedoms is no greater than is essential to the furtherance of that interest. We find that the 1965 Amendment to §12(b)(3) of the Universal Military Training and Service Act meets all of these requirements, and consequently that O'Brien can be constitutionally convicted for violating it.

The constitutional power of Congress to raise and support armies and to make all laws necessary and proper to that end is broad and sweeping. Lichter v. United States, 334 U.S. 742, 755-758 (1948); Selective Draft Law Cases, 245 U.S. 366 (1918); see also Ex parte Quirin, 317 U.S. 1, 25-26 (1942). The power of Congress to classify and conscript manpower for military service is "beyond question." Lichter v. United States, supra, at 756; Selective Draft Law Cases, supra. Pursuant to this power, Congress may establish a system of registration for individuals liable for training and service, and may require such individuals within reason to cooperate in the registration system. . . .

The registration certificate serves as proof that the individual described thereon has registered for the draft. The classification certificate shows the eligibility classification of a named but undescribed individual. Voluntarily displaying the two certificates is an easy and painless way for a young man to dispel a question as to whether he might be delinquent in his Selective Service obligations. . . . Additionally, in a time of national crisis, reasonable availability to each registrant of the two small cards assures a rapid and un-

---

[4] O'Brien v. United States, 376 F.2d 538 (C.A. 1st Cir. 1967).

complicated means for determining his fitness for immediate induction, no matter how distant in our mobile society he may be from his local board.

The many functions performed by Selective Service certificates establish beyond doubt that Congress has a legitimate and substantial interest in preventing their wanton and unrestrained destruction and assuring their continuing availability by punishing people who knowingly and wilfully destroy or mutilate them. . . .

It is equally clear that the 1965 Amendment specifically protects this substantial governmental interest. We perceive no alternative means that would more precisely and narrowly assure the continuing availability of issued Selective Service certificates than a law which prohibits their wilful mutilation or destruction. Compare Sherbert v. Verner, 374 U.S. 398, 407-408 (1963), and the cases cited therein. The 1965 Amendment prohibits such conduct and does nothing more. . . .

The case at bar is therefore unlike one where the alleged governmental interest in regulating conduct arises in some measure because the communication allegedly integral to the conduct is itself thought to be harmful. In Stromberg v. California, 283 U.S. 359 (1931), for example, this Court struck down a statutory phrase which punished people who expressed their "opposition to organized government" by displaying "any flag, badge, banner, or device." Since the statute there was aimed at suppressing communication it could not be sustained as a regulation of noncommunicative conduct. See also, NLRB v. Fruit & Vegetable Packers Union, 377 U.S. 58, 79 (1964) (concurring opinion).

In conclusion, we find that because of the Government's substantial interest in assuring the continuing availability of issued Selective Service certificates, because amended §462(b) is an appropriately narrow means of protecting this interest and condemns only the independent noncommunicative impact of conduct within its reach, and because the noncommunicative impact of O'Brien's act of burning his registration certificate frustrated the Government's interest, a sufficient governmental interest has been shown to justify O'Brien's conviction.

O'Brien finally argues that the 1965 Amendment is unconstitutional as enacted because what he calls the "purpose" of Congress was "to suppress freedom of speech." We reject this argument because under settled principles the purpose of Congress, as O'Brien uses that term, is not a basis for declaring this legislation unconstitutional. . . .

Since the 1965 Amendment to § 12(b)(3) of the Universal Military Training and Service Act is constitutional as enacted and as applied, the Court of Appeals should have affirmed the judgment of conviction entered by the District Court. Accordingly, we vacate the judgment of the Court of Appeals, and reinstate the judgment and sentence of the District Court. . . .[t]

Tinker v. Des Moines Indep. Community School Dist.
393 U.S. 503, 89 S. Ct. 733, 21 L. Ed. 2d 731 (1969)

MR. JUSTICE FORTAS delivered the opinion of the Court.

Petitioner John F. Tinker, 15 years old, and petitioner Christopher Eckhardt, 16 years old, attended high schools in Des Moines, Iowa. Petitioner Mary Beth Tinker, John's sister, was a 13-year-old student in junior high school.

In December 1965, a group of adults and students in Des Moines held a meeting at the Eckhardt home. The group determined to publicize their objections to the hostilities in Vietnam and their support for a truce by wearing black armbands during the holiday season and by fasting on December 16 and New Year's Eve. Petitioners and their parents

---

[t] Mr. Justice Marshall took no part in the consideration or decision of these cases. A concurring opinion of Justice Harlan is omitted. Justice Douglas, in dissent, urged reargument on the question of "whether conscription is permissible in the absence of a declaration of war." — ED.

had previously engaged in similar activities, and they decided to participate in the program.

The principals of the Des Moines schools became aware of the plan to wear armbands. On December 14, 1965, they met and adopted a policy that any student wearing an armband to school would be asked to remove it, and if he refused he would be suspended until he returned without the armband. Petitioners were aware of the regulation that the school authorities adopted.

On December 16, Mary Beth and Christopher wore black armbands to their schools. John Tinker wore his armband the next day. They were all sent home and suspended from school until they would come back without their armbands. They did not return to school until after the planned period for wearing armbands had expired — that is, until after New Year's Day.

[The District Court denied an injunction sought against the school officials, and the court of appeals affirmed.]

First Amendment rights, applied in light of the special characteristics of the school environment, are available to teachers and students. It can hardly be argued that either students or teachers shed their constitutional rights to freedom of speech or expression at the schoolhouse gate. . . .

The problem posed by the present case does not relate to regulation of the length of skirts or the type of clothing, to hair style, or deportment. . . . It does not concern aggressive, disruptive action or even group demonstrations. Our problem involves direct, primary First Amendment rights akin to "pure speech."

The school officials banned and sought to punish petitioners for a silent, passive expression of opinion, unaccompanied by any disorder or disturbance on the part of petitioners. . . .

In order for the State in the person of school officials to justify prohibition of a particular expression of opinion, it must be able to show that its action was caused by something more than a mere desire to avoid the discomfort and unpleasantness that always accompany an unpopular viewpoint. Certainly where there is no finding and no showing that engaging in the forbidden conduct would "materially and substantially interfere with the requirements of appropriate discipline in the operation of the school," the prohibition cannot be sustained. Burnside v. Byars, [363 F.2d 744, 749 (5th Cir. 1966)].

In the present case, the District Court made no such finding, and our independent examination of the record fails to yield evidence that the school authorities had reason to anticipate that the wearing of the armbands would substantially interfere with the work of the school or impinge upon the rights of other students. Even an official memorandum prepared after the suspension that listed the reasons for the ban on wearing the armbands made no reference to the anticipation of such disruption.

On the contrary, the action of the school authorities appears to have been based upon an urgent wish to avoid the controversy which might result from the expression, even by the silent symbol of armbands, of opposition to this Nation's part in the conflagration in Vietnam. . . .

It is also relevant that the school authorities did not purport to prohibit the wearing of all symbols of political or controversial significance. The record shows that students in some of the schools wore buttons relating to national political campaigns, and some even wore the Iron Cross, traditionally a symbol of Nazism. The order prohibiting the wearing of armbands did not extend to these. Instead, a particular symbol — black armbands worn to exhibit opposition to this Nation's involvement in Vietnam — was singled out for prohibition. Clearly, the prohibition of expression of one particular opinion, at least without evidence that it is necessary to avoid material and substantial interference with schoolwork or discipline, is not constitutionally permissible.

If a regulation were adopted by school officials forbidding discussion of the Vietnam conflict, or the expression by any student of opposition to it anywhere on school property except as part of a prescribed classroom exercise, it would be obvious that the regulation would violate the constitutional rights of students, at least if it could not be justified by a showing that the students' activities would materially and substantially disrupt the work and discipline of the school. . . . In the circumstances of the present case, the prohibition of the silent, passive "witness of the armbands," as one of the children called it, is no less offensive to the Constitution's guarantees.

We express no opinion as to the form of relief which should be granted, this being a matter for the lower courts to determine. We reverse and remand for further proceedings consistent with this opinion.

Reversed and remanded.[u]

MR. JUSTICE BLACK, dissenting.

. . . While I have always believed that under the First and Fourteenth Amendments neither the State nor the Federal Government has any authority to regulate or censor the content of speech, I have never believed that any person has a right to give speeches or engage in demonstrations where he pleases when he pleases. This Court has already rejected such a notion. In Cox v. Louisiana, 379 U.S. 536, 554 (1965), for example, the Court clearly stated that the rights of free speech and assembly "do not mean that everyone with opinions or beliefs to express may address a group at any public place and at any time."

While the record does not show that any of these armband students shouted, used profane language, or were violent in any manner, detailed testimony by some of them shows their armbands caused comments, warnings by other students, the poking of fun at them, and a warning by an older football player that other, nonprotesting students had better let them alone. There is also evidence that a teacher of mathematics had his lesson period practically "wrecked" chiefly by disputes with Mary Beth Tinker, who wore her armband for her "demonstration." Even a casual reading of the record shows that this armband did divert students' minds from their regular lessons, and that talk, comments, etc., made John Tinker "self-conscious" in attending school with his armband. While the absence of obscene remarks or boisterous and loud disorder perhaps justifies the Court's statement that the few armband students did not actually "disrupt" the classwork, I think the record overwhelmingly shows that the armbands did exactly what the elected school officials and principals foresaw they would, that is, took the student's minds off their classwork and diverted them to thoughts about the highly emotional subject of the Vietnam war. And I repeat that if the time has come when pupils of state-supported schools, kindergartens, grammar schools, or high schools, can defy and flout orders of school officials to keep their minds on their own schoolwork, it is the beginning of a new revolutionary era of permissiveness in this country fostered by the judiciary. . . .

NOTE Flag Desecration

In People v. Street, 20 N.Y.2d 231, 229 N.E.2d 187 (1967), the New York Court of Appeals upheld a conviction for violating § 1425(16)(d) of the New York Penal Law, which makes it a misdemeanor "publicly [to] mutilate" the flag of the United States. Evidence indicated that the defendant had burned an American flag at the corner of a street intersection in New York City and had made certain comments to persons gathered nearby. In Street v. New York, 394 U.S. 576 (1969), the Supreme Court reversed the judgment below on the ground that the conviction may have rested upon the utterance of the words he spoke.

See Note, Symbolic Conduct, 68 Colum. L. Rev. 1091 (1968). See also People v. Radich, 26 N.Y.2d 114, 257 N.E.2d 30, aff'd by an equally divided court, 401 U.S. 531

---

[u] Concurring opinions of Justices Stewart and White are omitted, as well as a dissenting opinion by Justice Harlan. — ED.

(1970), for a conviction under the same New York Penal Statute of an art dealer who displayed the flag in the form of a male sexual organ in order to protest the nation's "aggressive acts" in Viet Nam. For a useful survey, see Rosenblatt, Flag Desecration Statutes: History and Analysis, 1972 Wash. U.L.Q. 193.

Two convictions under state flag desecration statutes were overturned by the Supreme Court in 1974. In Spence v. Washington, 418 U.S. 405 (1974) (per curiam), the appellant had in May 1970, in protest against the invasion of Cambodia and the killings at Kent State University, taped peace symbols to the surfaces of an American flag and hung it out his window. He was arrested and convicted under a statute forbidding the exhibition of a United States flag to which there is attached or superimposed any figure or design. The Court held, 6 to 3, that as applied to the appellant the statute impermissibly infringed his right to freedom of expression. In Smith v. Goguen, 415 U.S. 566 (1974), the Court invalidated, 6 to 3, a Massachusetts statute making it a criminal offense to "publicly . . . treat contemptuously the flag of the United States" as impermissibly vague under the due process clause of the Fourteenth Amendment. See Ely, Flag Desecration: A Case Study in the Roles of Categorization and Balancing in First Amendment Analysis, 88 Harv. L. Rev. 1482 (1975).

3. Defamation and Invasion of Privacy

Beauharnais v. Illinois 343 U.S. 250, 72 S. Ct. 725, 96 L. Ed. 919 (1952)

MR. JUSTICE FRANKFURTER delivered the opinion of the Court.

The petitioner was convicted upon information in the Municipal Court of Chicago of violating §224a of Division 1 of the Illinois Penal Code, Ill. Rev. Stat. 1949, c. 38, §471. He was fined $200. The section provides:

"It shall be unlawful for any person, firm or corporation to manufacture, sell, or offer for sale, advertise or publish, present or exhibit in any public place in this state any lithograph, moving picture, play, drama or sketch, which publication or exhibition portrays depravity, criminality, unchastity, or lack of virtue to a class of citizens, of any race, color, creed or religion which said publication or exhibition exposes the citizens of any race, color, creed or religion to contempt, derision, or obloquy or which is productive of breach of the peace or riots. . . ."

Beauharnais challenged the statute as violating the liberty of speech and of the press guaranteed as against the States by the Due Process Clause of the Fourteenth Amendment, and as too vague, under the restrictions implicit in the same Clause, to support conviction for crime. The Illinois courts rejected these contentions and sustained defendant's conviction. 408 Ill. 512. We granted certiorari in view of the serious questions raised concerning the limitations imposed by the Fourteenth Amendment on the power of a State to punish utterances promoting friction among racial and religious groups. 342 U.S. 809.

The information, cast generally in the terms of the statute, charged that Beauharnais "did unlawfully . . . exhibit in public places lithographs, which publications portray depravity, criminality, unchastity or lack of virtue to citizens of Negro race and color and which exposes [sic] citizens of Illinois of the Negro race and color to contempt, derision, or obloquy. . . ." The lithograph complained of was a leaflet setting forth a petition calling on the Mayor and City Council of Chicago "to halt the further encroachment, harassment and invasion of white people, their property, neighborhoods and persons, by the Negro. . . ." Below was a call for "One million self-respecting white people in Chicago to unite . . ." with the statement added that "If persuasion and the need to prevent the white race from becoming mongrelized by the negro will not unite us, then

Section C. **Freedom of Speech and Association** 1211

the aggressions . . . rapes, robberies, knives, guns and marijuana of the negro, surely will." This, with more language, similar if not so violent, concluded with an attached application for membership in the White Circle League of America, Inc.

The testimony at the trial was substantially undisputed. From it the jury could find that Beauharnais was president of the White Circle League; that, at a meeting on January 6, 1950, he passed out bundles of the lithographs in question, together with other literature, to volunteers for distribution on downtown Chicago street corners the following day; that he carefully organized that distribution, giving detailed instructions for it; and that the leaflets were in fact distributed on January 7 in accordance with his plan and instructions. The court, together with other charges on burden of proof and the like, told the jury "if you find . . . that the defendant, Joseph Beauharnais, did . . . manufacture, sell, or offer for sale, advertise or publish, present or exhibit in any public place the lithograph . . . then you are to find the defendant guilty. . . ." He refused to charge the jury, as requested by the defendant, that in order to convict they must find "that the article complained of was likely to produce a clear and present danger of a serious substantive evil that rises far above public inconvenience, annoyance or unrest." Upon this evidence and these instructions, the jury brought in the conviction here for review.

The statute before us is not a catchall enactment left at large by the State court which applied it. . . . It is a law specifically directed at a defined evil, its language drawing from history and practice in Illinois and in more than a score of other jurisdictions a meaning confirmed by the Supreme Court of that State in upholding this conviction. We do not, therefore, parse the statute as grammarians or treat it as an abstract exercise in lexicography. . . .

The Illinois Supreme Court tells us that § 224a "is a form of criminal libel law." 408 Ill. 512, 517. The defendant, the trial court and the Supreme Court consistently treated it as such. The defendant offered evidence tending to prove the truth of parts of the utterance, and the courts below considered and disposed of this offer in terms of ordinary criminal libel precedents. Section 224a does not deal with the defense of truth, but by the Illinois Constitution, Art. II, §4, S.H.A., "in all trials for libel, both civil and criminal, the truth, when published with good motives and for justifiable ends, shall be a sufficient defense." See also Ill. Rev. Stat. 1949, c. 38, §404. Similarly, the action of the trial court in deciding as a matter of law the libelous character of the utterance, leaving to the jury only the question of publication, follows the settled rule in prosecutions for libel in Illinois and other States. Moreover, the Supreme Court's characterization of the words prohibited by the statute as those "liable to cause violence and disorder" paraphrases the traditional justification for punishing libels criminally, namely their "tendency to cause breach of the peace."

Libel of an individual was a common-law crime, and thus criminal in the colonies. Indeed, at common law, truth or good motives was no defense. In the first decades after the adoption of the Constitution, this was changed by judicial decision, statute or constitution in most States, but nowhere was there any suggestion that the crime of libel be abolished. Today, every American jurisdiction — the forty-eight States, the District of Columbia, Alaska, Hawaii and Puerto Rico — punish libels directed at individuals. "There are certain well-defined and narrowly limited classes of speech, the prevention and punishment of which has never been thought to raise any Constitutional problem. These include the lewd and obscene, the profane, the libelous, and the insulting or 'fighting' words — those which by their very utterance inflict injury or tend to incite an immediate breach of the peace. It has been well observed that such utterances are no essential part of any exposition of ideas, and are of such slight social value as a step to truth that any benefit that may be derived from them is clearly outweighed by the social interest in order and morality. 'Resort to epithets or personal abuse is not in any proper sense communication of information or opinion safeguarded by the Constitution, and its punishment as a criminal act would raise no question under that instrument.' Cantwell v. State of Connecticut, 310

U.S. 296, 309, 310." Such were the views of a unanimous Court in Chaplinsky v. State of New Hampshire, 315 U.S. at pages 571-572.

No one will gainsay that it is libelous falsely to charge another with being a rapist, robber, carrier of knives and guns, and user of marijuana. The precise question before us, then, is whether the protection of "liberty" in the Due Process Clause of the Fourteenth Amendment prevents a State from punishing such libels — as criminal libel has been defined, limited and constitutionally recognized time out of mind — directed at designated collectivities and flagrantly disseminated. There is even authority, however dubious, that such utterances were also crimes at common law. It is certainly clear that some American jurisdictions have sanctioned their punishment under ordinary criminal libel statutes. We cannot say, however, that the question is concluded by history and practice. But if an utterance directed at an individual may be the object of criminal sanctions, we cannot deny to a State power to punish the same utterance directed at a defined group, unless we can say that this is a willful and purposeless restriction unrelated to the peace and well-being of the State.

Illinois did not have to look beyond her own borders or await the tragic experience of the last three decades to conclude that wilful purveyors of falsehood concerning racial and religious groups promote strife and tend powerfully to obstruct the manifold adjustments required for free, ordered life in a metropolitan, polyglot community. From the murder of the abolitionist Lovejoy in 1837 to the Cicero riots of 1951, Illinois has been the scene of exacerbated tension between races, often flaring into violence and destruction. In many of these outbreaks, utterances of the character here in question, so the Illinois legislature could conclude, played a significant part. The law was passed on June 29, 1917, at a time when the State was struggling to assimilate vast numbers of new inhabitants, as yet concentrated in discrete racial or national or religious groups — foreign-born brought to it by the crest of the great wave of immigration, and Negroes attracted by jobs in war plants and the allurements of northern claims. Nine years earlier, in the very city where the legislature sat, what is said to be the first northern race riot had cost the lives of six people, left hundreds of Negroes homeless and shocked citizens into action far beyond the borders of the State. Less than a month before the bill was enacted, East St. Louis had seen a day's rioting, prelude to an outbreak, only four days after the bill became law, so bloody that it led to Congressional investigation. A series of bombings had begun which was to culminate two years later in the awful race riot which held Chicago in its grip for seven days in the summer of 1919. Nor has tension and violence between the groups defined in the statute been limited in Illinois to clashes between whites and Negroes.

In the face of this history and its frequent obligato of extreme racial and religious propaganda, we would deny experience to say that the Illinois legislature was without reason in seeking ways to curb false or malicious defamation of racial and religious groups, made in public places and by means calculated to have a powerful emotional impact on those to whom it was presented. . . .

It may be argued, and weightily, that this legislation will not help matters; that tension and on occasion violence between racial and religious groups must be traced to causes more deeply embedded in our society than the rantings of modern Know-nothings. Only those lacking responsible humility will have a confident solution for problems as intractable as the frictions attributable to differences of race, color or religion. This being so, it would be out of bounds for the judiciary to deny the legislature a choice of policy, provided it is not unrelated to the problem and not forbidden by some explicit limitation on the State's power. That the legislative remedy might not in practice mitigate the evil, or might itself raise new problems, would only manifest once more the paradox of reform. It is the price to be paid for the trial-and-error inherent in legislative efforts to deal with obstinate social issues. . . .

The scope of the statute before us, as construed by the Illinois court, disposes of the contention that the conduct prohibited by the law is so ill-defined that judges and juries in applying the statute and men in acting cannot draw from it adequate standards to guide them. The clarifying construction and fixed usage which govern the meaning of the enactment before us were not present, so the Court found, in the New York law held invalid in Winters v. People of State of New York, 333 U.S. 507. Nor, thus construed and limited, is the act so broad that the general verdict of guilty on an indictment drawn in the statutory language might have been predicated on constitutionally protected conduct. On this score, the conviction here reviewed differs from those upset in Stromberg v. People of State of California, 283 U.S. 359; Thornhill v. State of Alabama, supra, and Terminiello v. City of Chicago, 337 U.S. 1. Even the latter case did not hold that the unconstitutionality of a statute is established *because* the speech prohibited by it raises a ruckus. . . .

As to the defense of truth, Illinois in common with many States requires a showing not only that the utterance state the facts, but also that the publication be made "with good motives and for justifiable ends." Ill. Const., Art. II, §4. Both elements are necessary if the defense is to prevail. What has been called "the common sense of American criminal law," as formulated, with regard to necessary safeguards in criminal libel prosecutions, in the New York Constitution of 1821, Art. VII, §8, has been adopted in terms by Illinois. The teaching of a century and a half of criminal libel prosecutions in this country would go by the board if we were to hold that Illinois was not within her rights in making this combined requirement. Assuming that defendant's offer of proof directed to a part of the defense was adequate,[21] it did not satisfy the entire requirement which Illinois could exact.[22]

Libelous utterances, not being within the area of constitutionally protected speech, it is unnecessary, either for us or for the State courts, to consider the issues behind the phrase "clear and present danger." Certainly no one would contend that obscene speech, for example, may be punished only upon a showing of such circumstances. Libel, as we have seen, is in the same class.

We find no warrant in the Constitution for denying to Illinois the power to pass the law here under attack. But it bears repeating — although it should not — that our finding that the law is not constitutionally objectionable carries no implication of approval of the wisdom of the legislation or of its efficacy. These questions may raise doubts in our minds as well as in others. It is not for us, however, to make the legislative judgment. We are not at liberty to erect those doubts into fundamental law.

Affirmed.[v]

MR. JUSTICE BLACK, with whom MR. JUSTICE DOUGLAS concurs, dissenting. . . .

The Court condones this expansive state censorship by painstakingly analogizing it to the law of criminal libel. As a result of this refined analysis, the Illinois statute emerges labeled a "group libel law." This label may make the Court's holding more palatable for those who sustain it, but the sugar-coating does not make the censorship less deadly. However tagged, the Illinois law is not that criminal libel which has been "defined, limited and constitutionally recognized time out of mind." For as "constitutionally recog-

---

[21] Defendant offered to show (1) that crimes were more frequent in districts heavily populated by Negroes than in those where whites predominated; (2) three specific crimes allegedly committed by Negroes; and (3) that property values declined when Negroes moved into a neighborhood. It is doubtful whether such a showing is as extensive as the defamatory allegations in the lithograph circulated by the defendant.

[22] The defense attorney put a few questions to the defendant on the witness stand which tended toward elaborating his motives in circulating the lithograph complained of. When objections to these questions were sustained, no offer of proof was made, in contrast to the rather elaborate offer which followed the refusal to permit questioning tending to show the truth of the matter. Indeed, in that offer itself, despite its considerable detail, no mention was made of the necessary element of good motive or justifiable ends. In any event, the question of exclusion of this testimony going to motive was not raised by motion in the trial court, on appeal in Illinois, or before us.

[v] Dissenting opinions by Justices Reed, Douglas, and Jackson are omitted. — ED.

nized" that crime has provided for punishment of false, malicious, scurrilous charges against individuals, not against huge groups. This limited scope of the law of criminal libel is of no small importance. It has confined state punishment of speech and expression to the narrowest of areas involving nothing more than purely private feuds. Every expansion of the law of criminal libel so as to punish discussions of matters of public concern means a corresponding invasion of the area dedicated to free expression by the First Amendment.

Prior efforts to expand the scope of criminal libel beyond its traditional boundaries have not usually met with widespread popular acclaim. "Seditious libel" was such an expansion and it did have its day, particularly in the English Court of Star Chamber. But the First Amendment repudiated seditious libel for this country. And one need only glance through the parliamentary discussion of Fox's Libel Law passed in England in 1792, to sense the bad odor of criminal libel in that country even when confined to charges against individuals only. . . .

Unless I misread history the majority is giving libel a more expansive scope and more respectable status than it was accorded even in the Star Chamber. For here it is held to be punishable to give publicity to any picture, moving picture, play, drama or sketch, or any printed matter which a judge may find unduly offensive to any race, color, creed or religion. In other words, in arguing for or against the enactment of laws that may differently affect huge groups, it is now very dangerous indeed to say something critical of one of the groups. And any "person, firm or corporation" can be tried for this crime. "Person, firm or corporation" certainly includes a book publisher, newspaper, radio or television station, candidate or even a preacher.

It is easy enough to say that none of this latter group have been proceeded against under the Illinois Act. And they have not — yet. But emotions bubble and tempers flare in racial and religious controversies, the kind here involved. It would not be easy for any court, in good conscience, to narrow this Act so as to exclude from it any of those I have mentioned. Furthermore, persons tried under the Act could not even get a jury trial except as to the bare fact of publication. Here, the court simply charged the jury that Beauharnais was guilty if he had caused distribution of the leaflet. Such trial by judge rather than by jury was outlawed in England in 1792 by Fox's Libel Law. . . .

We are told that freedom of petition and discussion are in no danger "while this Court sits." This case raises considerable doubt. Since those who peacefully petition for changes in the law are not to be protected "while this Court sits," who is? I do not agree that the Constitution leaves freedom of petition, assembly, speech, press or worship at the mercy of a case-by-case, day-by-day majority of this Court. I had supposed that our people could rely for their freedom on the Constitution's commands, rather than on the grace of this Court on an individual case basis. To say that a legislative body can, with this Court's approval, make it a crime to petition for and publicly discuss proposed legislation seems as farfetched to me as it would be to say that a valid law could be enacted to punish a candidate for President for telling the people his views. I think the First Amendment, with the Fourteenth, "absolutely" forbids such laws without any "ifs" or "buts" or "whereases." Whatever the danger, if any, in such public discussions, it is a danger the Founders deemed outweighed by the danger incident to the stifling of thought and speech. The Court does not act on this view of the Founders. It calculates what it deems to be the danger of public discussion, holds the scales are tipped on the side of state suppression, and upholds state censorship. This method of decision offers little protection to First Amendment liberties "while this Court sits."

If there be minority groups who hail this holding as their victory, they might consider the possible relevancy of this ancient remark:

"Another such victory and I am undone."

Section C. **Freedom of Speech and Association** 1215

NOTE

To what extent does Beauharnais survive New York Times Co. v. Sullivan, infra? To what extent may group libel laws still be desirable? Compare Arkes, Civility and the Restriction of Speech: Rediscovering the Defamation of Groups, 1974 Sup. Ct. Rev. 281, with Pemberton, Can the Law Provide a Remedy for Race Defamation in the United States?, 14 N.Y.L. Forum 33 (1968).

New York Times Co. v. Sullivan 376 U.S. 254, 84 S. Ct. 710, 11 L. Ed. 2d 686 (1964)

MR. JUSTICE BRENNAN delivered the opinion of the Court.

We are required for the first time in this case to determine the extent to which the constitutional protections for speech and press limit a State's power to award damages in a libel action brought by a public official against critics of his official conduct.

Respondent L. B. Sullivan is one of the three elected Commissioners of the City of Montgomery, Alabama. He testified that he was "Commissioner of Public Affairs and the duties are supervision of the Police Department, Fire Department, Department of Cemetery and Department of Scales." He brought this civil libel action against the four individual petitioners, who are Negroes and Alabama clergymen, and against petitioner the New York Times Company, a New York corporation which publishes the New York Times, a daily newspaper. A jury in the Circuit Court of Montgomery County awarded him damages of $500,000, the full amount claimed, against all the petitioners, and the Supreme Court of Alabama affirmed. 273 Ala. 656, 144 So. 2d 25.

Respondent's complaint alleged that he had been libeled by statements in a full-page advertisement that was carried in the New York Times on March 29, 1960. Entitled "Heed Their Rising Voices," the advertisement began by stating that "As the whole world knows by now, thousands of Southern Negro students are engaged in widespread nonviolent demonstrations in positive affirmation of the right to live in human dignity as guaranteed by the U.S. Constitution and the Bill of Rights." It went on to charge that "in their efforts to uphold these guarantees, they are being met by an unprecedented wave of terror by those who would deny and negate that document which the whole world looks upon as setting the pattern for modern freedom. . . ." Succeeding paragraphs purported to illustrate the "wave of terror" by describing certain alleged events. The text concluded with an appeal for funds for three purposes: support of the student movement, "the struggle for the right-to-vote," and the legal defense of Dr. Martin Luther King, Jr., leader of the movement, against a perjury indictment then pending in Montgomery.

The text appeared over the names of 64 persons, many widely known for their activities in public affairs, religion, trade unions, and the performing arts. Below these names, and under a line reading "We in the south who are struggling daily for dignity and freedom warmly endorse this appeal," appeared the names of the four individual petitioners and of 16 other persons, all but two of whom were identified as clergymen in various Southern cities. The advertisement was signed at the bottom of the page by the "Committee to Defend Martin Luther King and the Struggle for Freedom in the South," and the officers of the Committee were listed.

Of the 10 paragraphs of text in the advertisement, the third and a portion of the sixth were the basis of respondent's claim of libel. They read as follows:

Third paragraph:

"In Montgomery, Alabama, after students sang 'My Country, 'Tis of Thee' on the State Capitol steps, their leaders were expelled from school, and truckloads of police armed with shotguns and tear-gas ringed the Alabama State College Campus. When the entire

1216   Chapter Sixteen.   Substantive Rights

student body protested to state authorities by refusing to re-register, their dining hall was padlocked in an attempt to starve them into submission."

Sixth paragraph:

"Again and again the Southern violators have answered Dr. King's peaceful protests with intimidation and violence. They have bombed his home almost killing his wife and child. They have assaulted his person. They have arrested him seven times — for 'speeding,' 'loitering' and similar 'offenses.' And now they have charged him with 'perjury' — a *felony* under which they would imprison him for *ten years*. . . ."

Although neither of these statements mentions respondent by name, he contended that the word "police" in the third paragraph referred to him as the Montgomery Commissioner who supervised the Police Department, so that he was being accused of "ringing" the campus with police. He further claimed that the paragraph would be read as imputing to the police, and hence to him, the padlocking of the dining hall in order to starve the students into submission. As to the sixth paragraph, he contended that since arrests are ordinarily made by the police, the statement "They have arrested [Dr. King] seven times" would be read as referring to him; he further contended that the "They" who did the arresting would be equated with the "They" who committed the other described acts and with the "Southern violators." Thus, he argued, the paragraph would be read as accusing the Montgomery police, and hence him, of answering Dr. King's protests with "intimidation and violence," bombing his home, assaulting his person, and charging him with perjury. Respondent and six other Montgomery residents testified that they read some or all of the statements as referring to him in his capacity as Commissioner.

It is uncontroverted that some of the statements contained in the two paragraphs were not accurate descriptions of events which occurred in Montgomery. Although Negro students staged a demonstration on the State Capitol steps, they sang the National Anthem and not "My Country, 'Tis of Thee." Although nine students were expelled by the State Board of Education, this was not for leading the demonstration at the Capitol, but for demanding service at a lunch counter in the Montgomery County Courthouse on another day. Not the entire student body, but most of it, had protested the expulsion, not by refusing to register, but by boycotting classes on a single day; virtually all the students did register for the ensuing semester. The campus dining hall was not padlocked on any occasion, and the only students who may have been barred from eating there were the few who had neither signed a preregistration application nor requested temporary meal tickets. Although the police were deployed near the campus in large numbers on three occasions, they did not at any time "ring" the campus, and they were not called to the campus in connection with the demonstration on the State Capitol steps, as the third paragraph implied. Dr. King had not been arrested seven times, but only four; and although he claimed to have been assaulted some years earlier in connection with his arrest for loitering outside a courtroom, one of the officers who made the arrest denied that there was such an assault.

On the premise that the charges in the sixth paragraph could be read as referring to him, respondent was allowed to prove that he had not participated in the events described. Although Dr. King's home had in fact been bombed twice when his wife and child were there, both of these occasions antedated respondent's tenure as Commissioner, and the police were not only not implicated in the bombing, but had made every effort to apprehend those who were. Three of Dr. King's four arrests took place before respondent became Commissioner. Although Dr. King had in fact been indicted (he was subsequently acquitted) on two counts of perjury, each of which carried a possible five-year sentence, respondent had nothing to do with procuring the indictment.

Respondent made no effort to prove that he suffered actual pecuniary loss as a result of the alleged libel. One of his witnesses, a former employer, testified that if he had believed the statements, he doubted whether he "would want to be associated with anybody who would be a party to such things as are stated in that ad," and that he would not re-employ

Section C. Freedom of Speech and Association

respondent if he believed "that he allowed the Police Department to do the things that the paper says he did." But neither this witness nor any of the others testified that he had actually believed the statements in their supposed reference to respondent.

The cost of the advertisement was approximately $4800, and it was published by the Times upon an order from a New York advertising agency acting for the signatory Committee. The agency submitted the advertisement with a letter from A. Philip Randolph, Chairman of the Committee, certifying that the persons whose names appeared on the advertisement had given their permission. Mr. Randolph was known to the Times' Advertising Acceptability Department as a responsible person, and in accepting the letter as sufficient proof of authorization it followed its established practice. There was testimony that the copy of the advertisement which accompanied the letter listed only the sixty-four names appearing under the text, and that the statement, "We in the south . . . warmly endorse this appeal" and the list of names thereunder, which included those of the individual petitioners, were subsequently added when the first proof of the advertisement was received. Each of the individual petitioners testified that he had not authorized the use of his name, and that he had been unaware of its use until receipt of respondent's demand for a retraction. The manager of the Advertising Acceptability Department testified that he had approved the advertisement for publication because he knew nothing to cause him to believe that anything in it was false, and because it bore the endorsement of "a number of people who are well known and whose reputation" he "had no reason to question." Neither he nor anyone else at the Times made an effort to confirm the accuracy of the advertisement, either by checking it against recent Times news stories relating to some of the described events or by some other means.

Alabama law denies a public officer recovery of punitive damages in a libel action brought on account of a publication concerning his offical conduct unless he first makes a written demand for a public retraction and the defendant fails or refuses to comply. Alabama Code, Tit. 7, §914. Respondent served such a demand upon each of the petitioners. None of the individual petitioners responded to the demand, primarily because each took the position that he had not authorized the use of his name on the advertisement and therefore had not published the statements that respondent alleged to have libeled him. The Times did not publish a retraction in response to the demand, but wrote respondent a letter stating, among other things, that "we . . . are somewhat puzzled as to how you think the statements in any way reflect on you," and "you might, if you desire, let us know in what respect you claim that the statements in the advertisement reflect on you." Respondent filed this suit a few days later without answering the letter. The Times did, however, subsequently publish a retraction of the advertisement upon the demand of Governor John Patterson of Alabama, who asserted that the publication charged him with "grave misconduct and . . . improper actions and omissions as Governor of Alabama and Ex-Officio Chairman of the State Board of Education of Alabama." When asked to explain why there had been a retraction for the Governor but not for respondent, the Secretary of the Times testified: "We did that because we didn't want anything that was published by The Times to be a reflection on the State of Alabama and the Governor was, as far as we could see, the embodiment of the State of Alabama and the proper representative of the State and furthermore, we had by that time learned more of the actual facts which the ad purported to recite and, finally, the ad did refer to the action of the State authorities and the Board of Education presumably of which the Governor is ex-officio chairman. . . ." On the other hand, he testified that he did not think that "any of the language in there referred to Mr. Sullivan."

The trial judge submitted the case to the jury under instructions that the statements in the advertisement were "libelous per se" and were not privileged, so that petitioners might be held liable if the jury found that they had published the advertisement and that the statements were made "of and concerning" respondent. The jury was instructed that, because the statements were libelous per se, "the law . . . implies legal injury from the bare fact of publication itself," "falsity and malice are presumed," general damages need not be alleged or proved but are presumed," and "punitive damages may be awarded by the jury even though the amount of actual damages is neither found nor shown." An award of punitive damages — as distinguished from "general" damages, which are compensatory in nature — apparently requires proof of actual malice under Alabama law, and the judge charged that "mere negligence or carelessness is not evidence of actual malice or malice in fact, and does not justify an award of exemplary or punitive damages." He refused to charge, however, that the jury must be "convinced" of malice, in the sense of "actual intent" to harm or "gross negligence and recklessness," to make such an award, and he also refused to require that a verdict for respondent differentiate between compensatory and punitive damages. The judge rejected petitioners' contention that his rulings abridged the freedoms of speech and of the press that are guaranteed by the First and Fourteenth Amendments.

In affirming the judgment, the Supreme Court of Alabama sustained the trial judge's rulings and instructions in all respects. 273 Ala. 656, 144 So. 2d 25. . . .

Because of the importance of the constitutional issues involved, we granted the separate petitions for certiorari of the individual petitioners and of the Times. 371 U.S. 946. We reverse the judgment. We hold that the rule of law applied by the Alabama courts is constitutionally deficient for failure to provide the safeguards for freedom of speech and of the press that are required by the First and Fourteenth Amendments in a libel action brought by a public official against critics of his official conduct. We further hold that under the proper safeguards the evidence presented in this case is constitutionally insufficient to support the judgment for respondent.

I

We may dispose at the outset of two grounds asserted to insulate the judgment of the Alabama courts from constitutional scrutiny. The first is the proposition relied on by the State Supreme Court — that "The Fourteenth Amendment is directed against State action and not private action." That proposition has no application to this case. Although this is a civil lawsuit between private parties, the Alabama courts have applied a state rule of law which petitioners claim to impose invalid restrictions on their constitutional freedoms of speech and press. It matters not that that law has been applied in a civil action and that it is common law only, though supplemented by statute. See, e.g., Alabama Code, Tit. 7, §§ 908-917. The test is not the form in which state power has been applied but, whatever the form, whether such power has in fact been exercised. See Ex parte Virginia, 100 U.S. 339, 346-347; American Federation of Labor v. Swing, 312 U.S. 321.

The second contention is that the constitutional guarantees of freedom of speech and of the press are inapplicable here, at least so far as the Times is concerned, because the allegedly libelous statements were published as part of a paid, "commercial" advertisement. The argument relies on Valentine v. Chrestensen, 316 U.S. 52, where the Court held that a city ordinance forbidding street distribution of commercial and business advertising matter did not abridge the First Amendment freedoms, even as applied to a handbill having a commercial message on one side but a protest against certain official action on the other. The reliance is wholly misplaced. The Court in Chrestensen reaffirmed the constitutional protection for "the freedom of communicating information and disseminating opinion"; its holding was based upon the factual conclusions that the handbill was "purely commercial advertising" and that the protest against official action had been added only to evade the ordinance.

The publication here was not a "commercial" advertisement in the sense in which the word was used in Chrestensen. It communicated information, expressed opinion, recited grievances, protested claimed abuses, and sought financial support on behalf of a movement whose existence and objectives are matters of the highest public interest and concern. See NAACP v. Button, 371 U.S. 415, 435. That the Times was paid for publishing the advertisement is as immaterial in this connection as is the fact that newspapers and books are sold. Smith v. California, 361 U.S. 147, 150; cf. Bantam Books, Inc. v. Sullivan, 372 U.S. 58, 64, n.6. Any other conclusion would discourage newspapers from carrying "editorial advertisements" of this type, and might shut off an important outlet for the promulgation of information and ideas by persons who do not themselves have access to publishing facilities — who wish to exercise their freedom of speech even though they are not members of the press. Cf. Lovell v. Griffin, 303 U.S. 444, 452; Schneider v. State, 308 U.S. 147, 164. The effect would be to shackle the First Amendment in its attempt to secure "the widest possible dissemination of information from diverse and antagonistic sources." Associated Press v. United States, 326 U.S. 1, 20. To avoid placing such a handicap upon the freedoms of expression, we hold that if the allegedly libelous statements would otherwise be constitutionally protected from the present judgment, they do not forfeit that protection because they were published in the form of a paid advertisement.

II

Under Alabama law as applied in this case, a publication is "libelous per se" if the words "tend to injure a person . . . in his reputation" or to "bring [him] into public contempt"; the trial court stated that the standard was met if the words are such as to "injure him in his public office, or impute misconduct to him in his office, or want of official integrity, or want of fidelity to a public trust. . . ." The jury must find that the words were published "of and concerning" the plaintiff, but where the plaintiff is a public official his place in the governmental hierarchy is sufficient evidence to support a finding that his reputation has been affected by statements that reflect upon the agency of which he is in charge. Once "libel per se" has been established, the defendant has no defense as to stated facts unless he can persuade the jury that they were true in all their particulars. . . . His privilege of "fair comment" for expressions of opinion depends on the truth of the facts upon which the comment is based. . . . Unless he can discharge the burden of proving truth, general damages are presumed, and may be awarded without proof of pecuniary injury. A showing of actual malice is apparently a prerequisite to recovery of punitive damages, and the defendant may in any event forestall these by a retraction meeting the statutory requirements. Good motives and belief in truth do not negate an inference of malice, but are relevant only in mitigation of punitive damages if the jury chooses to accord them weight. . . .

The question before us is whether this rule of liability, as applied to an action brought by a public official against critics of his official conduct, abridges the freedom of speech and of the press that is guaranteed by the First and Fourteenth Amendments. . . .

[W]e consider this case against the background of a profound national commitment to the principle that debate on public issues should be uninhibited, robust, and wide-open, and that it may well include vehement, caustic, and sometimes unpleasantly sharp attacks on government and public officials. See Terminiello v. Chicago, 337 U.S. 1, 4; De Jonge v. Oregon, 299 U.S. 353, 365. The present advertisement, as an expression of grievance and protest on one of the major public issues of our time, would seem clearly to qualify for the constitutional protection. The question is whether it forfeits that protection by the falsity of some of its factual statements and by its alleged defamation of respondent.

Authoritative interpretations of the First Amendment guarantees have consistently refused to recognize an exception for any test of truth, whether administered by judges, juries, or administrative officials — and especially not one that puts the burden of proving truth on the speaker. Cf. Speiser v. Randall, 357 U.S. 513, 525-526. The constitutional protection does not turn upon "the truth, popularity, or social utility of the ideas and beliefs which are offered." NAACP v. Button, 371 U.S. 415, 445. As Madison said, "Some degree of abuse is inseparable from the proper use of every thing; and in no instance is this more true than in that of the press." 4 Elliot's Debates on the Federal Constitution (1876), p. 571. . . .

Just as factual error affords no warrant for repressing speech that would otherwise be free, the same is true of injury to official reputation. Where judicial officers are involved, this Court has held that concern for the dignity and reputation of the courts does not justify the punishment as criminal contempt of criticism of the judge or his decision. Bridges v. California, 314 U.S. 252. This is true even though the utterance contains "half-truths" and "misinformation." Pennekamp v. Florida, 328 U.S. 331, 342, 343, n.5, 345; such repression can be justified, if at all, only by a clear and present danger of the obstruction of justice. . . .

If neither factual error nor defamatory content suffices to remove the constitutional shield from criticism of official conduct, the combination of the two elements is no less inadequate. This is the lesson to be drawn from the great controversy over the Sedition Act of 1798, 1 Stat. 596, which first crystallized a national awareness of the central meaning of the First Amendment. See Levy, Legacy of Suppression (1960), at 258 et seq.; Smith, Freedom's Fetters (1956), at 426, 431, and passim. That statute made it a crime, punishable by a $5,000 fine and five years in prison, "if any person shall write, print, utter or publish . . . any false, scandalous and malicious writing or writings against the government of the United States, or either house of the Congress . . . or the President . . . with the intent to defame . . . or to bring them or either of them, into contempt or disrepute; or to excite against them, or either or any of them, the hatred of the good people of the United States." The Act allowed the defendant the defense of truth, and provided that the jury were to be judges both of the law and the facts. Despite these qualifications, the Act was vigorously condemned as unconstitutional in an attack joined in by Jefferson and Madison. . . .

Although the Sedition Act was never tested in this Court, the attack upon its validity has carried the day in the court of history. Fines levied in its prosecution were repaid by Act of Congress on the ground that it was unconstitutional. See, e.g., Act of July 4, 1840, c. 45, 6 Stat. 802, accompanied by H.R. Rep. No. 86, 26th Cong., 1st Sess. (1840). Calhoun, reporting to the Senate on February 4, 1836, assumed that its invalidity was a matter "which no one now doubts." Report with Senate bill No. 122, 24th Cong., 1st Sess., p. 3. Jefferson, as President, pardoned those who had been convicted and sentenced under the Act and remitted their fines, stating: "I discharged every person under punishment or prosecution under the Sedition Law because I considered, and now consider, that law to be a nullity, as absolute and as palpable as if Congress had ordered us to fall down and worship a golden image." Letter to Mrs. Adams, July 22, 1804, 4 Jefferson's Works (Washington ed.) pp. 555-556. The invalidity of the Act has also been assumed by Justices of this Court. Holmes, J., dissenting and joined by Brandeis, J., in Abrams v. United States, 250 U.S. 616, 630; Jackson, J., dissenting in Beauharnais v. Illinois, 343 U.S. 250, 288-289; Douglas, The Right of the People (1958), p. 47. . . .

What a State may not constitutionally bring about by means of a criminal statute is likewise beyond the reach of its civil law of libel. The fear of damage awards under a rule such as that invoked by the Alabama courts here may be markedly more inhibiting than the fear of prosecution under a criminal statute. See City of Chicago v. Tribune Co., 307 Ill. 596, 607, 139 N.E. 86, 90 (1923). Alabama, for example, has a criminal libel law which subjects to prosecution "any person who speaks, writes, or prints of and concerning another any accusation falsely and maliciously importing the commission by such person of a felony, or any other indictable offense involving moral turpitude," and which allows as punishment upon conviction a fine not exceeding $500 and a prison sentence of six months. Alabama Code, Tit. 14, §350. Presumably a person charged with violation of this statute enjoys ordinary criminal-law safeguards such as the requirements of an indictment and of proof beyond a reasonable doubt. These safeguards are not available to the defendant in a civil action. The judgment awarded in this case — without the need for any proof of actual pecuniary loss — was one thousand times greater than the maximum fine provided by the Alabama criminal statute, and one hundred times greater than that provided by the Sedition Act. And since there is no double-jeopardy limitation applicable to civil lawsuits, this is not the only judgment that may be awarded against petitioners for the same publication. Whether or not a newspaper can survive a succession of such judgments, the pall of fear and timidity imposed upon those who would give voice to public criticism is an atmosphere in which the First Amendment freedoms cannot survive. Plainly the Alabama law of civil libel is "a form of regulation that creates hazards to protected freedoms markedly greater than those that attend reliance upon the criminal law." Bantam Books, Inc. v. Sullivan, 372 U.S. 58, 70.

A rule compelling the critic of official conduct to guarantee the truth of all his factual assertions — and to do so on pain of libel judgments virtually unlimited in amount — leads to a . . . "self-censorship." Allowance of the defense of truth, with the burden of proving it on the defendant, does not mean that only false speech will be deterred. Even courts accepting this defense as an adequate safeguard have recognized the difficulties of adducing legal proofs that the alleged libel was true in all its factual particulars. . . . Under such a rule, would-be critics of official conduct may be deterred from voicing their criticism, even though it is believed to be true and even though it is in fact true, because of doubt whether it can be proved in court or fear of the expense of having to do so. They tend to make only statements which "steer far wider of the unlawful zone." Speiser v. Randall, supra, 357 U.S., at 526. The rule thus dampens the vigor and limits the variety of public debate. It is inconsistent with the First and Fourteenth Amendments.

The constitutional guarantees require, we think, a federal rule that prohibits a public official from recovering damages for a defamatory falsehood relating to his official conduct unless he proves that the statement was made with "actual malice" — that is, with knowledge that it was false or with reckless disregard of whether it was false or not. . . .

Such a privilege for criticism of official conduct is appropriately analogous to the protection accorded a public official when *he* is sued for libel by a private citizen. In Barr v. Matteo, 360 U.S. 564, 575, this Court held the utterance of a federal official to be absolutely privileged if made "within the outer perimeter" of his duties. The States accord the same immunity to statements of their highest officers, although some differentiate their lesser officials and qualify the privilege they enjoy. But all hold that all officials are protected unless actual malice can be proved. The reason for the official privilege is said to be that the threat of damage suits would otherwise "inhibit the fearless, vigorous, and effective administration of policies of government" and "dampen the ardor of all but the most resolute, or the most irresponsible, in the unflinching discharge of their duties." Barr v. Matteo, supra, 360 U.S., at 571. Analogous considerations support the privilege for the citizen-critic of government. It is as much his duty to criticize as it is the official's duty to administer. . . .

We conclude that such a privilege is required by the First and Fourteenth Amendments. . . .

III

We hold today that the Constitution delimits a State's power to award damages for libel in actions brought by public officials against critics of their official conduct. Since this is such an action, the rule requiring proof of actual malice is applicable. While Alabama law apparently requires proof of actual malice for an award of punitive damages, where general damages are concerned malice is "presumed." Such a presumption is inconsistent with the federal rule. "The power to create presumptions is not a means of escape from constitutional restrictions," Bailey v. Alabama, 219 U.S. 219, 239; "the showing of malice required for the forfeiture of the privilege is not presumed but is a matter for proof by the plaintiff . . ." Lawrence v. Fix, 357 Mich. 134, 146, 97 N.W.2d 719, 725 (1959). Since the trial judge did not instruct the jury to differentiate between general and punitive damages, it may be that the verdict was wholly an award of one or the other. But it is impossible to know, in view of the general verdict returned. Because of this uncertainty, the judgment must be reversed and the case remanded. . . .

Since respondent may seek a new trial, we deem that considerations of effective judicial administration require us to review the evidence in the present record to determine whether it could constitutionally support a judgment for respondent. . . .

[The Court concluded that the evidence would not support a finding of malice — of willful or reckless misrepresentation; and that it could not support a finding that the allegedly libelous statements were made "of and concerning" the plaintiff, as distinguished from governmental operations generally.][w]

NOTE Developments in Defamation

In Garrison v. Louisiana, 379 U.S. 64 (1964), arising as a result of public accusations made at a press conference against state court judges, the rule of New York Times was applied to a statute making malicious defamation criminal. Mr. Justice Douglas, with Justice Black concurring, protested that the majority in making malice relevant in cases of seditious libel was permitting the circumvention of the First Amendment guarantee of freedom of speech.

In Rosenblatt v. Baer, 383 U.S. 75, 85 (1966), the Court held that the "public official" designation of New York Times reached "at the very least to those among the hierarchy of government employees who have, or appear to the public to have, substantial responsibility for or control over the conduct of government affairs." Subsequent cases also imposed a more stringent libel standard on persons considered to be "public figures": Curtis Publishing Co. v. Butts, 388 U.S. 130 (1967) (famous athletic director); Monitor Patriot Co. v. Roy, 401 U.S. 265 (1971) (candidate for public office). But see Time, Inc. v. Firestone, 424 U.S. 448 (1976) (wife of notable industrialist not a "public figure").

For a further explication of what constitutes "reckless disregard" see St. Amant v. Thompson, 390 U.S. 727 (1968). In Time, Inc. v. Pape, 401 U.S. 279 (1971), the Court found that a magazine had acted without "reckless disregard" for the truth in its report of a somewhat ambiguous document of the Civil Rights Commission which omitted the term "alleged" in describing complaints of police misconduct set forth in that document.

The rule of the New York Times case was held to extend to a letter to a local newspaper by a public school teacher critical of the local board of education and superintendent of schools. The Court held that the teacher could not be dismissed for false statements unless these were shown to have been made knowingly or recklessly. Pickering v. Board of Education, 391 U.S. 563 (1968). The Court's holding was limited, however, to the facts of the case before it: ". . . It cannot be gainsaid that the State has interests as an employer in regulating the speech of its employees that differ significantly from those it possesses in connection with regulation of the speech of the citizenry in general. The problem in any case is to arrive at a balance between the interests of the teacher, as a citizen, in commenting upon matters of public concern and the interest of the State, as an employer, in

---

[w] Justices Black, Douglas, and Goldberg, concurring specially, urged that the First Amendment confers an absolute immunity on press and citizens to say what they please in criticism of the conduct of public affairs. — ED.

promoting the efficiency of the public services it performs through its employees." Noting that the teacher's statements had not been shown "to have in any way either impeded the teacher's proper performance of his daily duties in the classroom or to have interfered with the regular operation of the schools generally," the Court concluded that "in a case such as the present one, in which the fact of employment is only tangentially and insubstantially involved in the subject matter of the public communication made by a teacher, . . . it is necessary to regard the teacher as the member of the general public he seeks to be [and thus as under the protection of the rule of New York Times v. Sullivan]."

Gertz v. Robert Welch, Inc. *418 U.S. 323, 94 S. Ct. 2997, 41 L. Ed. 2d 789 (1974)*

[Plaintiff was an attorney who represented the family of a man killed by a Chicago policeman. The latter was convicted of murder. Defendant published a magazine which stated that plaintiff was a Communist-fronter and had arranged a frame-up of the policeman, and implied that plaintiff had a criminal record; all these assertions were untrue. In a libel action in the district court the judge instructed the jury that there was strict liability, and the jury returned a verdict for $50,000. The judge then granted a motion for judgment notwithstanding the verdict, on the ground that the standard in New York Times v. Sullivan applied, even though plaintiff was not a public officer or public figure, since the libel occurred in a discussion of a public issue and "malice" was not proved. The court of appeals affirmed.]

MR. JUSTICE POWELL delivered the opinion of the Court.

This Court has struggled for nearly a decade to define the proper accommodation between the law of defamation and the freedoms of speech and press protected by the First Amendment. With this decision we return to that effort. We granted certiorari to reconsider the extent of a publisher's constitutional privilege against liability for defamation of a private citizen. 410 U.S. 925 (1973). . . .

II

The principal issue in this case is whether a newspaper or broadcaster that publishes defamatory falsehoods about an individual who is neither a public official nor a public figure may claim a constitutional privilege against liability for the injury inflicted by those statements. The Court considered this question on the rather different set of facts presented in Rosenbloom v. Metromedia, Inc., 403 U.S. 29 (1971). Rosenbloom, a distributor of nudist magazines, was arrested for selling allegedly obscene material while making a delivery to a retail dealer. The police obtained a warrant and seized his entire inventory of 3,000 books and magazines. He sought and obtained an injunction prohibiting further police interference with his business. He then sued a local radio station for failing to note in two of its newscasts that the 3,000 items seized were only "reportedly" or "allegedly" obscene and for broadcasting references to "the smut literature racket" and to "girlie-book peddlers" in its coverage of the court proceeding for injunctive relief. He obtained a judgment against the radio station, but the Court of Appeals for the Third Circuit held the New York Times privilege applicable to the broadcast and reversed. 415 F.2d 892 (1969).

This Court affirmed the decision below, but no majority could agree on a controlling rationale. The eight Justices who participated in Rosenbloom announced their views in five separate opinions, none of which commanded more than three votes. The several statements not only reveal disagreement about the appropriate result in that case; they also reflect divergent traditions of thought about the general problem of reconciling the law of defamation with the First Amendment. One approach has been to extend the New York Times test to an expanding variety of situations. Another has been to vary the level of constitutional privilege for defamatory falsehood with the status of the person defamed. And a third view would grant to the press and broadcast media absolute immunity from liability for defamation. To place our holding in the proper context, we preface our discussion of this case with a review of the several Rosenbloom opinions and their antecedents. . . .

In his opinion for the plurality in Rosenbloom v. Metromedia, Inc., 403 U.S. 29 (1971), Mr. Justice Brennan took the New York Times privilege one step further. He concluded that its protection should extend to defamatory falsehoods relating to private persons if the statements concerned matters of general or public interest. He abjured the suggested distinction between public officials and public figures on the one hand and private individuals on the other. He focused instead on society's interest in learning about certain issues: 'If a matter is a subject of public or general interest, it cannot suddenly become less so merely because a private individual is involved, or because in some sense the individual did not 'voluntarily' choose to become involved." Id., at 43. Thus, under the plurality opinion, a private citizen involuntarily associated with a matter of general interest has no recourse for injury to his reputation unless he can satisfy the demanding requirements of the New York Times test.

Two Members of the Court concurred in the result in Rosenbloom but departed from the reasoning of the plurality. Mr. Justice Black restated his view, long shared by Mr. Justice Douglas, that the First Amendment cloaks the news media with an absolute and indefeasible immunity from liability for defamation. Id., at 57. Mr. Justice White concurred on a narrower ground. Ibid. He concluded that "the First Amendment gives the press and the broadcast media a privilege to report and comment upon the official actions of public servants in full detail, with no requirement that the reputation or the privacy of an individual involved in or affected by the official action be spared from public view." Id., at 62. He therefore declined to reach the broader questions addressed by the other Justices.

Mr. Justice Harlan dissented. . . .

He acquiesced in the application of the privilege to defamation of public figures but argued that a different rule should obtain where defamatory falsehood harmed a private individual. He noted that a private person has less likelihood "of securing access to channels of communication sufficient to rebut falsehoods concerning him" than do public officials and public figures, 403 U.S., at 70, and has not voluntarily placed himself in the public spotlight. Mr. Justice Harlan concluded that the States could constitutionally allow private individuals to recover damages for defamation on the basis of any standard of care except liability without fault.

Mr. Justice Marshall dissented in Rosenbloom in an opinion joined by Mr. Justice Stewart. Id., at 78. He thought that the plurality's "public or general interest" test for determining the applicability of the New York Times privilege would involve the courts in the dangerous business of deciding "what information is relevant to self-government." Id., at 79. He also contended that the plurality's position inadequately served "society's interest in protecting private individuals from being thrust into the public eye by the distorting light of defamation." Ibid. Mr. Justice Marshall therefore reached the conclusion, also reached by Mr. Justice Harlan, that the States should be "essentially free to continue the evolution of the common law of defamation and to articulate whatever fault standard best suits the State's need," so long as the States did not impose liability without fault. Id., at 86. The principal point of disagreement among the three dissenters concerned punitive damages. Whereas Mr. Justice Harlan thought that the States could allow punitive damages in amounts bearing "a reasonable and purposeful relationship to the actual harm done . . . ," id., at 75, Mr. Justice Marshall concluded that the size and unpredictability of jury awards of exemplary damages unnecessarily exacerbated the problems of media self-censorship and that such damages should therefore be forbidden.

III

We begin with the common ground. Under the First Amendment there is no such thing as a false idea. However pernicious an opinion may seem, we depend for its correction not on the conscience of judges and juries but on the competition of other ideas. But there is no constitutional value in false statements of fact. Neither the intentional lie nor the careless error materially advances society's interest in "uninhibited, robust, and wide-open" debate on public issues. New York Times Co. v. Sullivan, 376 U.S., at 270. They belong to that category of utterances which "are no essential part of any exposition of ideas, and are of such slight social value as a step to truth that any benefit that may be derived from them is clearly outweighed by the social interest in order and morality." Chaplinsky v. New Hampshire, 315 U.S. 568, 572 (1942).

Although the erroneous statement of fact is not worthy of constitutional protection, it is nevertheless inevitable in free debate. . . . And punishment of error runs the risk of inducing a cautious and restrictive exercise of the constitutionally guaranteed freedoms of speech and press. . . .

The need to avoid self-censorship by the news media is, however, not the only societal value at issue. If it were, this Court would have embraced long ago the view that publishers and broadcasters enjoy an unconditional and indefeasible immunity from liability for defamation. See New York Times Co. v. Sullivan, supra, at 293 (Black, J., concurring); Garrison v. Louisiana, 379 U.S., at 80 (Douglas, J., concurring); Curtis Publishing Co. v. Butts, 388 U.S., at 170 (opinion of Black, J.). Such a rule would, indeed, obviate the fear that the prospect of civil liability for injurious falsehood might dissuade a timorous press from the effective exercise of First Amendment freedoms. Yet absolute protection for the communications media requires a total sacrifice of the competing value served by the law of defamation. . . .

The New York Times standard defines the level of constitutional protection appropriate to the context of defamation of a public person. . . . For the reasons stated below, we conclude that the state interest in compensating injury to the reputation of private individuals requires that a different rule should obtain with respect to them. . . .

More important than the likelihood that private individuals will lack effective opportunities for rebuttal, there is a compelling normative consideration underlying the distinction between public and private defamation plaintiffs. An individual who decides to seek governmental office must accept certain necessary consequences of that involvement in public affairs. He runs the risk of closer public scrutiny than might otherwise be the case. And society's interest in the officers of government is not strictly limited to the formal discharge of official duties. As the Court pointed out in Garrison v. Louisiana, 379 U.S., at 77, the public's interest extends to "anything which might touch on an official's fitness for office. . . . Few personal attributes are more germane to fitness for office than dishonesty, malfeasance, or improper motivation, even though these characteristics may also affect the official's private character."

Those classed as public figures stand in a similar position. . . . Some occupy positions of such persuasive power and influence that they are deemed public figures for all purposes. More commonly, those classed as public figures have thrust themselves to the forefront of particular public controversies in order to influence the resolution of the issues involved. In either event, they invite attention and comment.

Even if the foregoing generalities do not obtain in every instance, the communications media are entitled to act on the assumption that public officials and public figures have voluntarily exposed themselves to increased risk of injury from defamatory falsehood concerning them. No such assumption is justified with respect to a private individual. He has not accepted public office or assumed an "influential role in ordering society." Curtis Publishing Co. v. Butts, supra, at 164 (Warren, C.J., concurring in result). He has relinquished no part of his interest in the protection of his own good name, and consequently he has a more compelling call on the courts for redress of injury inflicted by defamatory falsehood. Thus, private individuals are not only more vulnerable to injury than public officials and public figures; they are also more deserving of recovery.

For these reasons we conclude that the States should retain substantial latitude in their efforts to enforce a legal remedy for defamatory falsehood injurious to the reputation of a private individual. The extension of the New York Times test proposed by the Rosenbloom plurality would abridge this legitimate state interest to a degree that we find unacceptable. And it would occasion the additional difficulty of forcing state and federal judges to decide on an ad hoc basis which publications address issues of "general or public interest" and which do not — to determine, in the words of Mr. Justice Marshall, "what information is relevant to self-government." Rosenbloom v. Metromedia, Inc., 403 U.S., at 79. We doubt the wisdom of committing this task to the conscience of judges. Nor does the Constitution require us to draw so thin a line between the drastic alternatives of the New York Times privilege and the common law of strict liability for defamatory error. . . .

We hold that, so long as they do not impose liability without fault, the States may define for themselves the appropriate standard of liability for a publisher or broadcaster of defamatory falsehood injurious to a private individual.[10] . . .

IV

. . . The common law of defamation is an oddity of tort law, for it allows recovery of purportedly compensatory damages without evidence of actual loss. Under the traditional rules pertaining to actions for libel, the existence of injury is presumed from the fact of publication. Juries may award substantial sums as compensation for supposed damage to reputation without any proof that such harm actually occurred. The largely uncontrolled discretion of juries to award damages where there is no loss unnecessarily compounds the potential of any system of liability for defamatory falsehood to inhibit the vigorous exercise of First Amendment freedoms. Additionally, the doctrine of presumed damages invites juries to punish unpopular opinion rather than to compensate individuals for injury sustained by the publication of a false fact. More to the point, the States have no substantial interest in securing for plaintiffs such as this petitioner gratuitous awards of money damages far in excess of any actual injury.

. . . It is necessary to restrict defamation plaintiffs who do not prove knowledge of falsity or reckless disregard for the truth to compensation for actual injury. We need not define "actual injury," as trial courts have wide experience in framing appropriate jury instructions in tort actions. Suffice it to say that actual injury is not limited to out-of-pocket loss. Indeed, the more customary types of actual harm inflicted by defamatory falsehood include impairment of reputation and standing in the community, personal humiliation, and mental anguish and suffering. Of course, juries must be limited by appropriate instructions, and all awards must be supported by competent evidence concerning the injury, although there need be no evidence which assigns an actual dollar value to the injury.

[10] . . . Mr. Justice White asserts that our decision today "trivializes and denigrates the interest in reputation," Miami Herald Publishing Co. v. Tornillo, ante, at 262 (concurring opinion), that it "scuttle[s] the libel laws of the States in . . . wholesale fashion" and renders ordinary citizens "powerless to protect themselves." Post, at 370. In light of the progressive extension of the knowing-or-reckless-falsity requirement detailed in the preceding paragraph, one might have viewed today's decision allowing recovery under any standard save strict liability as a more generous accommodation of the state interest in comprehensive reputational injury to private individuals than the law presently affords.

Section C. Freedom of Speech and Association

We also find no justification for allowing awards of punitive damages against publishers and broadcasters held liable under state-defined standards of liability for defamation. In most jurisdictions jury discretion over the amounts awarded is limited only by the gentle rule that they not be excessive. Consequently, juries assess punitive damages in wholly unpredictable amounts bearing no necessary relation to the actual harm caused. And they remain free to use their discretion electively to punish expressions of unpopular views. Like the doctrine of presumed damages, jury discretion to award punitive damages unnecessarily exacerbates the danger of media self-censorship, but, unlike the former rule, punitive damages are wholly irrelevant to the state interest that justifies a negligence standard for private defamation actions. They are not compensation for injury. Instead, they are private fines levied by civil juries to punish reprehensible conduct and to deter its future occurrence. In short, the private defamation plaintiff who establishes liability under a less demanding standard than that stated by New York Times may recover only such damages as are sufficient to compensate him for actual injury.

V

Notwithstanding our refusal to extend the New York Times privilege to defamation of private individuals, respondent contends that we should affirm the judgment below on the ground that petitioner is either a public official or a public figure. There is little basis for the former assertion. . . .

Respondent's characterization of petitioner as a public figure raises a different question. That designation may rest on either of two alternative bases. In some instances an individual may achieve such pervasive fame or notoriety that he becomes a public figure for all purposes and in all contexts. More commonly, an individual voluntarily injects himself or is drawn into a particular public controversy and thereby becomes a public figure for a limited range of issues. In either case such persons assume special prominence in the resolution of public questions.

Petitioner has long been active in community and professional affairs. He has served as an officer of local civic groups and of various professional organizations, and he has published several books and articles on legal subjects. Although petitioner was consequently well known in some circles, he had achieved no general fame or notoriety in the community. None of the prospective jurors called at the trial had ever heard of petitioner prior to this litigation, and respondent offered no proof that this response was atypical of the local population. We would not lightly assume that a citizen's participation in community and professional affairs rendered him a public figure for all purposes. Absent clear evidence of general fame or notoriety in the community, and pervasive involvement in the affairs of society, an individual should not be deemed a public personality for all aspects of his life. It is preferable to reduce the public figure question to a more meaningful context by looking to the nature and extent of an individual's participation in the particular controversy giving rise to the defamation.

In this context it is plain that petitioner was not a public figure. He played a minimal role at the coroner's inquest, and his participation related solely to his representation of a private client. He took no part in the criminal prosecution of Officer Nuccio. Moreover, he never discussed either the criminal or civil litigation with the press and was never quoted as having done so. He plainly did not thrust himself into the vortex of this public issue, nor did he engage the public's attention in an attempt to influence its outcome. We are persuaded that the trial court did not err in refusing to characterize petitioner as a public figure for the purpose of this litigation.

We therefore conclude that the New York Times standard is inapplicable to this case and that the trial court erred in entering judgment for respondent. Because the jury was allowed to impose liability without fault and was permitted to presume damages without proof of injury a new trial is necessary. We reverse and remand for further proceedings in accord with this opinion.

It is so ordered.[x]

NOTE

May a state apply the Sullivan standard in a case like Gertz?

May a state apply a strict-liability standard if the plaintiff seeks a declaratory judgment, without damages?

May a court ask a jury for a special verdict on separate issues of truth, defendant's fault, and damages, so that plaintiff's reputation might be vindicated even though he cannot recover?

May a state apply a strict-liability standard to libel actions in a commercial setting, e.g., credit-rating reports or advertising?

Is the requirement of negligence applicable in a case based on a right of privacy rather than libel? If not, is it thus easier to secure redress for a true statement than for a false one?

Would a defamation of a private citizen by a state official be an abridgement of any rights of "liberty" or "property" secured by Fourteenth Amendment due process? See Paul v. Davis, 424 U.S. 693 (1976).

NOTE Invasion of Privacy and the First Amendment

A New York "privacy" law prohibited any person from publishing "for the purposes of trade" the "name, portrait or picture of any living person" without prior permission and further provided an action for injunction and damages for its violation. In Time, Inc. v. Hill, 385 U.S. 374 (1967), the Court considered a claim for damages under the New York law brought by Hill for an article in Life magazine which falsely reported that a Broadway play, "The Desperate Hours," portrayed an experience suffered by Hill and his family when they were held as hostages in the Hill house by escaped convicts. The New York Court of Appeals affirmed a verdict of compensatory damages. 15 N.Y.2d 986, 207 N.E.2d 604. In a 6 to 3 decision, the Supreme Court, per Justice Brennan, held that "The constitutional protections for speech and press preclude the application of the New York statute to redress false reports of matters of public interest in the absence of proof that the defendant published the report with knowledge of its falsity or in reckless disregard of the truth." Since the verdict below had not been based upon the New York Times standard, the Court reversed and remanded.

A jury verdict and award of compensatory damages in a "false light" action for invasion of privacy was upheld in Cantrell v. Forest City Publishing Co., 419 U.S. 245 (1974). The district court had instructed the jury that a verdict for plaintiff required a finding that

---

[x] A concurring opinion of Justice Blackmun is omitted. Chief Justice Burger dissented on the ground that plaintiff, as an attorney, was a private citizen who should be allowed to recover whether or not the defendant was negligent. Justice Douglas dissented on the ground that, at least in the realm of public affairs, a publisher enjoys absolute freedom; there is no room-for "accommodation" of interests, since the Framers made the controlling judgment in the First Amendment. Justice Brennan dissented, on the ground that the rule in the Sullivan case should be applicable to the discussion of matters of public interest or concern. Justice White delivered an extensive dissent on both the issue of necessary fault and the issue of permitted damages, taking the position that the states should be at liberty to follow their own law of defamation, except in the cases of public officers and public figures: "From all that I have seen, the Court has miscalculated and denigrates that interest [in redressing attacks on reputation] at a time when escalating assaults on individuality and personal dignity counsel otherwise. At the very least, the issue is debatable, and the Court has not carried its heavy burden of proof to justify tampering with state libel laws." — ED.

Section C. Freedom of Speech and Association

the defendant had made the false statements knowingly or recklessly. In affirming, the Supreme Court noted "this case presents no occasion to consider whether a State may constitutionally apply a more relaxed standard of liability for a publisher or broadcaster of false statements injurious to a private individual under a false-light theory of invasion of privacy, or whether the constitutional standard announced in Time, Inc. v. Hill applies to all false-light cases. Cf. Gertz v. Welch, Inc., supra page 1223.

A tort claim for invasion of privacy was rejected, however, in Cox Broadcasting Co. v. Cohn, 420 U.S. 469 (1975). There, the Court reversed, 8 to 1, a decision of the Georgia Supreme Court holding that the father of a rape-murder victim whose name was broadcast in a report of the prosecution of her alleged attackers had an action against the broadcaster for invasion of privacy. The state court had further upheld the constitutionality of a criminal statute relied on by the plaintiff, which made it a misdemeanor to publish or broadcast the identity of a rape victim. Writing for the Court, Justice White stated: "[There] are impressive credentials for a right of privacy, but we should recognize that we do not have at issue here an action for the invasion of privacy involving the appropriation of one's name or photograph, a physical or other tangible intrusion into a private area, or a publication of otherwise private information that is also false although perhaps not defamatory. The version of the privacy tort now before us — termed in Georgia 'the tort of public disclosure' . . . — is that in which the plaintiff claims the right to be free from unwanted publicity about his private affairs, which, although wholly true, would be offensive to a person of ordinary sensibilities. Because the gravamen of the claimed injury is the publication of information, whether true or not, the dissemination of which is embarrassing or otherwise painful to an individual, it is here that claims of privacy must directly confront the constitutional freedoms of speech and press. . . .

". . . Time v. Hill, supra, expressly saved the question whether truthful publication of very private matters unrelated to public affairs could be constitutionally proscribed. . . .

". . . In this sphere of collision between claims of privacy and those of the free press, the interests on both sides are plainly rooted in the traditions and significant concerns of our society. Rather than address the broader question whether truthful publications may ever be subjected to civil or criminal liability consistently with the First and Fourteenth Amendments, or to put it another way, whether the State may ever define and protect an area of privacy free from unwanted publicity in the press, it is appropriate to focus on the narrower interface between press and privacy that this case presents, namely, whether the State may impose sanctions on the accurate publication of the name of a rape victim obtained from public records — more specifically, from judicial records which are maintained in connection with a public prosecution and which themselves are open to public inspection. We are convinced that the State may not do so."

See generally Bloustein, The First Amendment and Privacy: The Supreme Court Justice and the Philosopher, 28 Rutgers L. Rev. 41 (1974), and see also Nimmer, The Right to Speak from Time to Time: First Amendment Theory Applied to Libel and Misapplied to Privacy, 56 Calif. L. Rev. 935 (1968). Compare the decisions enjoining publication of a book or distribution of a film alleged to violate complainant's right to privacy. See Doe v. Roe, 345 N.Y.S.2d 560, 42 A.D.2d 559 (1973) (per curiam) (preliminary injunction granted former patient to restrain publication of analyst's book discussing patient's case history); Commonwealth v. Wiseman, 356 Mass. 251, 249 N.E.2d 610, cert. denied, 398 U.S. 960 (1970) (enjoining showing of film containing identifiable pictures of inmates of state mental facility, but allowing showing of film to scientific community and to general audiences if film were edited to mask identities). (A similar request regarding the Wiseman film was denied in Cullen v. Grove Press, Inc., 276 F. Supp. 727 (S.D.N.Y. 1967).)

Organization for a Better Austin v. Keefe, 402 U.S. 415 (1971), pitted the right to privacy against the right peacefully to distribute informational literature. The petitioner was a community organization committed to stabilizing the racial mix in the Austin neighborhood of Chicago. The respondent was a realtor accused by the community organization of "blockbusting." The realtor lived in Winchester, Illinois, a suburb seven miles away from Austin. Members of the organization distributed leaflets in Winchester alleging that the respondent was a "panic peddler" and quoting a newspaper article describing his real estate practices in Austin. The Court, per Chief Justice Burger, held in favor of the organization and ordered vacated as a prior restraint on publication an injunction issued by the Illinois courts against the organization's distribution of leaflets.

4. Freedom of Association

New York ex rel. Bryant v. Zimmerman 278 U.S. 63, 49 S. Ct. 61, 73 L. Ed. 184 (1928)

MR. JUSTICE VAN DEVANTER delivered the opinion of the Court.

The relator, Bryant, who was held in custody to answer a charge of violating a statute of New York, brought a proceeding in habeas corpus in a court of that State to obtain his discharge on the ground, as was stated in the petition, that the warrant under which he was arrested and detained was issued without any jurisdiction, in that the statute which he was charged with violating was unconstitutional.

The court sustained the validity of the statute and refused to discharge him, 123 Misc. 859; and that judgment was affirmed by the Appellate Division, 213 App. Div. 414, and by the Court of Appeals, 241 N.Y. 405. He then sued out the present writ of error under §237(a) of the Judicial Code — his assignment of errors presented in obtaining the writ being to the effect that the Court of Appeals erroneously had held the statute valid against a contention made by him that it was invalid because repugnant to . . . the Fourteenth Amendment. . . .

The material parts of the state statute (Art. V-A Civil Rights Law; c. 664, Laws 1923, 1110) are as follows:

"Sec. 53. Every existing membership corporation, and every existing unincorporated association having a membership of twenty or more persons, which corporation or association requires an oath as a prerequisite or condition of membership, other than a labor union or a benevolent order mentioned in the benevolent orders law, within thirty days after this article takes effect, and every such corporation or association hereafter organized, within ten days after the adoption thereof, shall file with the secretary of state a sworn copy of its constitution, by-laws, rules, regulations and oath of membership, together with a roster of its membership and a list of its officers for the current year. . . ."

"Sec. 56. . . . Any person who becomes a member of any such corporation or association, or remains a member thereof, or attends a meeting thereof, with knowledge that such corporation or association has failed to comply with any provision of this article, shall be guilty of a misdemeanor." . . .

The offense charged against the relator is that he attended meetings and remained a member of the Buffalo Provisional Klan of the Knights of the Ku Klux Klan, an unincorporated association — but neither a labor union nor a benevolent order mentioned in the benevolent orders law — having a membership of more than twenty persons and requiring an oath as a prerequisite or condition of membership, he then having knowledge that such association had wholly failed to comply with the requirement in §53. . . .

The relator's contention under the due process clause is that the statute deprives him of liberty in that it prevents him from exercising his right of membership in the association. But his liberty in this regard, like most other personal rights, must yield to the rightful exertion of the police power. There can be no doubt that under that power the State may prescribe and apply to associations having an oath-bound membership any reasonable regulation calculated to confine their purposes and activities within limits which are consistent with the rights of others and the public welfare. The requirement in § 53 that each association shall file with the secretary of state a sworn copy of its constitution, oath of membership, etc., with a list of members and officers is such a regulation. It proceeds on the two-fold theory that the State within whose territory and under whose protection the association exists is entitled to be informed of its nature and purpose, of whom it is composed and by whom its activities are conducted, and that requiring this information to be supplied for the public files will operate as an effective or substantial deterrent from violations of public and private right to which the association might be tempted if such a disclosure were not required. The requirement is not arbitrary or oppressive, but reasonable and likely to be of real effect. Of course, power to require the disclosure includes authority to prevent individual members of an association which has failed to comply from attending meetings or retaining membership with knowledge of its default. We conclude that the due process clause is not violated.

The main contention made under the equal protection clause is that the statute discriminates against the Knights of the Ku Klux Klan and other associations in that it excepts from its requirements several associations having oath-bound membership, such as labor unions, the Masonic fraternity, the Independent Order of Odd Fellows, the Grand Army of the Republic and the Knights of Columbus — all named in another statute which provides for their incorporation and requires the names of their officers as elected from time to time to be reported to the secretary of state. . . .

The courts below . . . reached the conclusion that the classification was justified by a difference between the two classes of associations shown by experience, and that the difference consisted (a) in a manifest tendency on the part of one class to make the secrecy surrounding its purposes and membership a cloak for acts and conduct inimical to personal rights and public welfare, and (b) in the absence of such a tendency on the part of the other class. In pointing out this difference one of the courts said of the Ku Klux Klan, the principal association in the included class: "It is a matter of common knowledge that this organization functions largely at night, its members disguised by hoods and gowns and doing things calculated to strike terror into the minds of the people"; and later said of the other class: "These organizations and their purposes are well known, many of them having been in existence for many years. Many of them are oath-bound and secret. But we hear no complaints against them regarding violation of the peace or interfering with the rights of others." Another of the courts said: "It is a matter of common knowledge that the association or organization of which the relator is concededly a member exercises activities tending to the prejudice and intimidation of sundry classes of our citizens. But the legislation is not confined to this society"; and later said of the other class, "Labor unions have a recognized lawful purpose. The benevolent orders mentioned in the Benevolent Orders Law have already received legislative scrutiny and been granted special privileges so that the legislature may well consider them beneficial rather than harmful agencies." The third court after recognizing "the potentialities of evil in secret societies" and observing that "the danger of certain organizations has been judicially demonstrated" — meaning in that State, — said: "Benevolent orders, labor unions and college fraternities have existed for many years, and, while not immune from hostile criticism, have on the whole justified their existence."

We assume that the legislature had before it such information as was readily available, including the published report of a hearing before a committee of the House of Representatives of the 57th Congress relating to the formation, purposes and activities of the Ku Klux Klan. If so, it was advised — putting aside controverted evidence — that the order was a revival of the Ku Klux Klan of an earlier time with additional features borrowed from the Know Nothing and the A.P.A. orders of other periods; that its membership was limited to native born, gentile, protestant whites; that in part of its constitution and printed creed it proclaimed the widest freedom for all and full adherence to the Constitution of the United States, in another exacted of its members an oath to shield and preserve "white supremacy," and in still another declared any person actively opposing its principles to be "a dangerous ingredient in the body politic of our country and an enemy to the weal of our national commonwealth"; that it was conducting a crusade against Catholics, Jews and Negroes and stimulating hurtful religious and race prejudices; that it was striving for political power and assuming a sort of guardianship over the administration of local, state and national affairs; and that at times it was taking into its own hands the punishment of what some of its members conceived to be crimes.

We think it plain that the action of the courts below in holding that there was a real and substantial basis for the distinction made between the two sets of associations or orders was right and should not be disturbed.

Criticism is made of the classification on the further ground that the regulation is confined to associations having a membership of twenty or more persons. Classification based on numbers is not necessarily unreasonable. There are many instances in which it has been sustained. We think it not unreasonable in this instance. With good reason the legislature may have thought that an association of less than twenty persons would have only a negligible influence and be without the capacity for harm that would make regulation needful.

We conclude that all the objections urged against the statute are untenable as held by the courts below.

Judgment affirmed.[y]

De Jonge v. Oregon 299 U.S. 353, 57 S. Ct. 255, 81 L. Ed. 278 (1937)

MR. CHIEF JUSTICE HUGHES delivered the opinion of the Court.

Appellant, Dirk De Jonge, was indicted in Multnomah County, Oregon, for violation of the Criminal Syndicalism Law of that State. The Act . . . defines "criminal syndicalism" as "the doctrine which advocates crime, physical violence, sabotage or any unlawful acts or methods as a means of accomplishing or effecting industrial or political change or revolution." With this preliminary definition the Act proceeds to describe a number of offenses, embracing the teaching of criminal syndicalism, the printing or distribution of books, pamphlets, etc., advocating that doctrine, the organization of a society or assemblage which advocates it, and presiding at or assisting in conducting a meeting of such an organization, society or group. The prohibited acts are made felonies, punishable by imprisonment for not less than one year nor more than ten years, or by a fine of not more than $1,000, or by both.

We are concerned with but one of the described offenses and with the validity of the statute in this particular application. The charge is that appellant assisted in the conduct of a meeting which was called under the auspices of the Communist Party, an organization advocating criminal syndicalism. The defense was that the meeting was public and orderly and was held for a lawful purpose; that while it was held under the auspices of the Communist Party, neither criminal syndicalism nor any unlawful conduct was taught or advocated at the meeting either by appellant or by others. Appellant moved for a direction of acquittal, contending that the statute as applied to him, for merely assisting at a meeting called by the Communist Party at which nothing unlawful was done or advocated, violated the due process clause of the Fourteenth Amendment of the Constitution of the United States.

This contention was overruled. Appellant was found guilty as charged and was sentenced to imprisonment for seven years. The judgment was affirmed by the Supreme

---

[y] A dissenting opinion of McReynolds, J., based on jurisdictional grounds, is omitted. — ED.

Section C. Freedom of Speech and Association

Court of the State which considered the constitutional question and sustained the statute as thus applied. 152 Ore. 315. The case comes here on appeal.

The record does not present the evidence adduced at the trial. The parties have substituted a stipulation of facts, which was made and filed after the decision of the Supreme Court of the State and after the Chief Justice of that court had allowed the appeal and had directed transmission here of a certified transcript of the record. We do not approve of that practice, where it does not appear that the stipulation has received the approval of the court, as we think that adherence to our rule as to the preparation of records is important for the protection of the court whose decision is under review as well as of this Court. See Rule 10. But as the question presented in this instance does not turn upon an appreciation of the facts on any disputed point, we turn to the merits.

The stipulation, after setting forth the charging part of the indictment, recites in substance the following: That on July 27, 1934, there was held in Portland, a meeting which had been advertised by handbills issued by the Portland section of the Communist Party; that the number of persons in attendance was variously estimated at from 150 to 300; that some of those present, who were members of the Communist Party, estimated that not to exceed ten to fifteen per cent of those in attendance were such members; that the meeting was open to the public without charge and no questions were asked of those entering, with respect to their relation to the Communist Party; that the notice of the meeting advertised it as a protest against illegal raids on workers' halls and homes and against the shooting of striking longshoremen by Portland police; that the chairman stated that it was a meeting held by the Communist Party; that the first speaker dwelt on the activities of the Young Communist League; that the defendant De Jonge, the second speaker, was a member of the Communist Party and went to the meeting to speak in its name; that in his talk he protested against conditions in the county jail, the action of city police in relation to the maritime strike then in progress in Portland and numerous other matters; that he discussed the reason for the raids on the Communist headquarters and workers' halls and offices; that he told the workers that these attacks were due to efforts on the part of the steamship companies and stevedoring companies to break the maritime longshoremen's and seamen's strike; that they hoped to break the strike by pitting the longshoremen and seamen against the Communist movement; that there was also testimony to the effect that defendant asked those present to do more work in obtaining members for the Communist Party and requested all to be at the meeting of the party to be held in Portland on the following evening and to bring their friends to show their defiance to local police authority and to assist them in their revolutionary tactics; that there was also testimony that defendant urged the purchase of certain communist literature which was sold at the meeting; that while the meeting was still in progress it was raided by the police; that the meeting was conducted in an orderly manner; that defendant and several others who were actively conducting the meeting were arrested by the police and that on searching the hall the police found a quantity of communist literature.

The stipulation then set forth various extracts from the literature of the Communist Party to show its advocacy of criminal syndicalism. The stipulation does not disclose any activity by the defendant as a basis for his prosecution other than his participation in the meeting in question. Nor does the stipulation show that the communist literature distributed at the meeting contained any advocacy of criminal syndicalism or of any unlawful conduct. It was admitted by the Attorney General of the State in his argument at the bar of this Court that the literature distributed in the meeting was not of that sort and that the extracts contained in the stipulation were taken from communist literature found elsewhere. Its introduction in evidence was for the purpose of showing that the Communist Party as such did advocate the doctrine of criminal syndicalism, a fact which is not disputed on this appeal.

The broad reach of the statute as . . . applied is plain. While defendant was a member of the Communist Party, that membership was not necessary to conviction on such a charge. A like fate might have attended any speaker, although not a member, who "assisted in the conduct" of the meeting. However innocuous the object of the meeting, however lawful the subjects and tenor of the addresses, however reasonable and timely the discussion, all those assisting in the conduct of the meeting would be subject to imprisonment as felons if the meeting were held by the Communist Party. This manifest result was brought out sharply at this bar by the concessions which the Attorney General made, and could not avoid, in the light of the decision of the state court. Thus if the Communist Party had called a public meeting in Portland to discuss the tariff, or the foreign policy of the Government, or taxation, or relief, or candidacies for the offices of President, members of Congress, Governor, or state legislators, every speaker who assisted in the conduct of the meeting would be equally guilty with the defendant in this case, upon the charge as here defined and sustained. The list of illustrations might be indefinitely extended to every variety of meetings under the auspices of the Communist Party although held for the discussion of political issues or to adopt protests and pass resolutions of an entirely innocent and proper character.

While the States are entitled to protect themselves from the abuse of the privileges of our institutions through an attempted substitution of force and violence in the place of peaceful political action in order to effect revolutionary changes in government, none of our decisions go to the length of sustaining such a curtailment of the right of free speech and assembly as the Oregon statute demands in its present application. In Gitlow v. New York, 268 U.S. 652, under the New York statute defining criminal anarchy, the defendant was found to be responsible for a "manifesto" advocating the overthrow of the government by violence and unlawful means. Id., pp. 656, 662, 663. In Whitney v. California, 274 U.S. 357, under the California statute relating to criminal syndicalism, the defendant was found guilty of wilfully and deliberately assisting in the forming of an organization for the purpose of carrying on a revolutionary class struggle by criminal methods. The defendant was convicted of participation in what amounted to a conspiracy to commit serious crimes. Id., pp. 363, 364, 367, 369. . . .

Freedom of speech and of the press are fundamental rights which are safeguarded by the due process clause of the Fourteenth Amendment of the Federal Constitution. . . . The right of peaceable assembly is a right cognate to those of free speech and free press and is equally fundamental. As this Court said in United States v. Cruikshank, 92 U.S. 542, 552: "The very idea of a government, republican in form, implies a right on the part of its citizens to meet peaceably for consultation in respect to public affairs and to petition for a redress of grievances." The First Amendment of the Federal Constitution expressly guarantees that right against abridgment by Congress. But explicit mention there does not argue exclusion elsewhere. For the right is one that cannot be denied without violating those fundamental principles of liberty and justice which lie at the base of all civil and political institutions, — principles which the Fourteenth Amendment embodies in the general terms of its due process clause. . . .

These rights may be abused by using speech or press or assembly in order to incite to violence and crime. The people through their legislatures may protect themselves against that abuse. But the legislative intervention can find constitutional justification only by dealing with the abuse. The rights themselves must not be curtailed. The greater the importance of safeguarding the community from incitements to the overthrow of our institutions by force and violence, the more imperative is the need to preserve inviolate the constitutional rights of free speech, free press and free assembly in order to maintain the opportunity for free political discussion, to the end that government may be responsive to the will of the people and that changes, if desired, may be obtained by peaceful means. Therein lies the security of the Republic, the very foundation of constitutional government.

It follows from these considerations that, consistently with the Federal Constitution, peaceable assembly for lawful discussion cannot be made a crime. The holding of meetings for peaceable political action cannot be proscribed. Those who assist in the conduct of such meetings cannot be branded as criminals on that score. The question, if the rights of free speech and peaceable assembly are to be preserved, is not as to the auspices under which the meeting is held but as to its purpose; not as to the relations of the speakers, but whether their utterances transcend the bounds of the freedom of speech which the Constitution protects. If the persons assembling have committed crimes elsewhere, if they have formed or are engaged in a conspiracy against the public peace and order, they may be prosecuted for their conspiracy or other violation of valid laws. But it is a different matter when the State, instead of prosecuting them for such offenses, seizes upon mere participation in a peaceable assembly and a lawful public discussion as the basis for a criminal charge. . . .

We hold that the Oregon statute as applied to the particular charge as defined by the state court is repugnant to the due process clause of the Fourteenth Amendment. The judgment of conviction is reversed and the cause is remanded for further proceedings not inconsistent with this opinion.

Reversed.

Mr. Justice Stone took no part in the consideration or decision of this case.

NAACP v. Alabama 357 U.S. 449, 78 S. Ct. 1163, 2 L. Ed. 2d 1488 (1958)

Mr. Justice Harlan delivered the opinion of the Court.

We review from the standpoint of its validity under the Federal Constitution a judgment of civil contempt entered against petitioner, the National Association for the Advancement of Colored People, in the courts of Alabama. The question presented is whether Alabama, consistently with the Due Process Clause of the Fourteenth Amendment, can compel petitioner to reveal to the State's Attorney General the names and addresses of all its Alabama members and agents, without regard to their positions or functions in the Association. The judgment of contempt was based upon petitioner's refusal to comply fully with a court order requiring in part the production of membership lists. Petitioner's claim is that the order, in the circumstances shown by this record, violated rights assured to petitioner and its members under the Constitution.

Alabama has a statute similar to those of many other States which requires a foreign corporation, except as exempted, to qualify before doing business by filing its corporate charter with the Secretary of State and designating a place of business and an agent to receive service of process. The statute imposes a fine on a corporation transacting intrastate business before qualifying and provides for criminal prosecution of officers of such a corporation. Ala. Code, 1940, Tit. 10, §§ 192-198. The National Association for the Advancement of Colored People is a nonprofit membership corporation organized under the laws of New York. Its purposes, fostered on a nationwide basis, are those indicated by its name,[1] and it operates through chartered affiliates which are independent unincorporated associations, with membership therein equivalent to membership in petitioner. The first Alabama affiliates were chartered in 1918. Since that time the aims of the Association have been advanced through activities of its affiliates, and in 1951 the Association itself opened a regional office in Alabama, at which it employed two supervisory persons and one clerical worker. The Association has never complied with the qualification statute, from which it considered itself exempt.

---

[1] The Certificate of Incorporation of the Association provides that its ". . . principal objects . . . are voluntarily to promote equality of rights and eradicate caste or race prejudice among the citizens of the United States; to advance the interest of colored citizens; to secure for them impartial suffrage; and to increase their opportunities for securing justice in the courts, education for their children, employment according to their ability, and complete equality before the law."

1236   *Chapter Sixteen.*   **Substantive Rights**

In 1956 the Attorney General of Alabama brought an equity suit in the State Circuit Court, Montgomery County, to enjoin the Association from conducting further activities within, and to oust it from, the State. Among other things the bill in equity alleged that the Association had opened a regional office and had organized various affiliates in Alabama; had recruited members and solicited contributions within the State; had given financial support and furnished legal assistance to Negro students seeking admission to the state university; and had supported a Negro boycott of the bus lines in Montgomery to compel the seating of passengers without regard to race. The bill recited that the Association, by continuing to do business in Alabama without complying with the qualification statute, was ". . . causing irreparable injury to the property and civil rights of the residents and citizens of the State of Alabama for which criminal prosecution and civil actions at law afford no adequate relief . . ." On the day the complaint was filed, the Circuit Court issued ex parte an order restraining the Association, pendente lite, from engaging in further activities within the State and forbidding it to take any steps to qualify itself to do business therein.

Petitioner demurred to the allegations of the bill and moved to dissolve the restraining order. It contended that its activities did not subject it to the qualification requirements of the statute and that in any event what the State sought to accomplish by its suit would violate rights to freedom of speech and assembly guaranteed under the Fourteenth Amendment to the Constitution of the United States. Before the date set for a hearing of this motion, the State moved for the production of a large number of the Association's records and papers, including bank statements, leases, deeds, and records containing the names and addresses of all Alabama "members" and "agents" of the Association. It alleged that all such documents were necessary for adequate preparation for the hearing, in view of petitioner's denial of the conduct of intrastate business within the meaning of the qualification statute. Over petitioner's objections, the court ordered the production of a substantial part of the requested records, including the membership lists, and postponed the hearing on the restraining order to a date later than the time ordered for production.

Thereafter petitioner filed its answer to the bill in equity. It admitted its Alabama activities substantially as alleged in the complaint and that it had not qualified to do business in the State. Although still disclaiming the statute's application to it, petitioner offered to qualify if the bar from qualification made part of the restraining order were lifted, and it submitted with the answer an executed set of the forms required by the Statute. However petitioner did not comply with the production order, and for this failure was adjudged in civil contempt and fined $10,000. The contempt judgment provided that the fine would be subject to reduction or remission if compliance were forthcoming within five days but otherwise would be increased to $100,000.

At the end of the five-day period petitioner produced substantially all the data called for by the production order except its membership lists, as to which it contended that Alabama could not constitutionally compel disclosure, and moved to modify or vacate the contempt judgment, or stay its execution pending appellate review. This motion was denied. While a similar stay application, which was later denied, was pending before the Supreme Court of Alabama, the Circuit Court made a further order adjudging petitioner in continuing contempt and increasing the fine already imposed to $100,000. Under Alabama law, see Jacoby v. Goetter, Weil & Co., 74 Ala. 427, the effect of the contempt adjudication was to foreclose petitioner from obtaining a hearing on the merits of the underlying ouster action, or from taking any steps to dissolve the temporary restraining order which had been issued ex parte, until it purged itself of contempt. But cf. Harrison v. St. Louis & S.F.R. Co., 232 U.S. 318; Hovey v. Elliott, 167 U.S. 409.

The State Supreme Court thereafter twice dismissed petitions for certiorari to review this final contempt judgment, the first time, 265 Ala. 699, for insufficiency of the petition's allegations and the second time on procedural grounds. 265 Ala. 349. We granted certiorari because of the importance of the constitutional questions presented. 353 U.S. 972.

II

The Association both urges that it is constitutionally entitled to resist official inquiry into its membership lists, and that it may assert, on behalf of its members, a right personal to them to be protected from compelled disclosure by the State of their affiliation with the Association as revealed by the membership lists. We think that petitioner argues more appropriately the rights of its members, and that its nexus with them is sufficient to permit that it act as their representative before this Court. In so concluding, we reject respondent's argument that the Association lacks standing to assert here constitutional rights pertaining to the members, who are not of course parties to the litigation.

To limit the breadth of issues which must be dealt with in particular litigation, this Court has generally insisted that parties rely only on constitutional rights which are personal to themselves. Tileston v. Ullman, 318 U.S. 44; Robertson and Kirkham, Jurisdiction of the Supreme Court (1951 ed.), § 298. This rule is related to the broader doctrine that constitutional adjudication should where possible be avoided. See Ashwander v. Tennessee Valley Authority, 297 U.S. 288, 346-348 (concurring opinion). The principle is not disrespected where constitutional rights of persons who are not immediately before the Court could not be effectively vindicated except through an appropriate representative before the Court. See Barrows v. Jackson, 346 U.S. 249, 255-259; Joint Anti Fascist Refugee Committee v. McGrath, 341 U.S. 123, 183-187 (concurring opinion).

If petitioner's rank-and-file members are constitutionally entitled to withhold their connection with the Association despite the production order, it is manifest that this right is properly assertable by the Association. To require that it be claimed by the members themselves would result in nullification of the right at the very moment of its assertion. Petitioner is the appropriate party to assert these rights, because it and its members are in every practical sense identical. The Association which provides in its constitution that "[a]ny person who is in accordance with [its] principles and policies . . ." may become a member, is but the medium through which its individual members seek to make more effective the expression of their own views. The reasonable likelihood that the Association itself through diminished financial support and membership may be adversely affected if production is compelled is a further factor pointing towards our holding that petitioner has standing to complain of the production order on behalf of its members. Cf. Pierce v. Society of Sisters, 268 U.S. 510.

III

We thus reach petitioner's claim that the production order in the state litigation trespasses upon fundamental freedoms protected by the Due Process Clause of the Fourteenth Amendment. Petitioner argues that in view of the facts and circumstances shown in the record, the effect of compelled disclosure of the membership lists will be to abridge the rights of its rank-and-file members to engage in lawful association in support of their common beliefs. It contends that governmental action which, although not directly suppressing association, nevertheless carries this consequence, can be justified only upon some overriding valid interest of the State.

Effective advocacy of both public and private points of view, particularly controversial ones, is undeniably enhanced by group association, as this Court has more than once recognized by remarking upon the close nexus between the freedoms of speech and assembly. De Jonge v. Oregon, 299 U.S. 353, 364; Thomas v. Collins, 323 U.S. 516, 530. It is beyond debate that freedom to engage in association for the advancement of beliefs and ideas is an inseparable aspect of the "liberty" assured by the Due Process Clause of the Fourteenth Amendment, which embraces freedom of speech. See Gitlow v. New York, 268 U.S. 652; Palko v. Connecticut, 302 U.S. 319, 324; Cantwell v. Connecticut, 310 U.S. 296, 303; Staub v. Baxley, 355 U.S. 313, 321. Of course, it is immaterial whether the beliefs sought to be advanced by association pertain to political, economic, religious or cultural matters, and state action which may have the effect of curtailing the freedom to associate is subject to the closest scrutiny.

We think that the production order, in the respects here drawn in question, must be regarded as entailing the likelihood of a substantial restraint upon the exercise by petitioner's members of their right to freedom of association. Petitioner has made an uncontroverted showing that on past occasions revelation of the identity of its rank-and-file members has exposed these members to economic reprisal, loss of employment, threat of physical coercion, and other manifestations of public hostility. Under these circumstances, we think it apparent that compelled disclosure of petitioner's Alabama membership is likely to affect adversely the ability of petitioner and its members to pursue their collective efforts to foster beliefs which they admittedly have the right to advocate, in that it may induce members to withdraw from the Association and dissuade others from joining it because of fear of exposure of their beliefs shown through their associations and of the consequences of this exposure.

It is not sufficient to answer, as the State does here, that whatever repressive effect compulsory disclosure of names of petitioner's members may have upon participation by Alabama citizens in petitioner's activities follows not from *state* action but from *private* community pressures. The crucial factor is the interplay of governmental and private action, for it is only after the initial exertion of state power represented by the production order that private action takes hold.

We turn to the final question whether Alabama has demonstrated an interest in obtaining the disclosures it seeks from petitioner which is sufficient to justify the deterrent effect which we have concluded these disclosures may well have on the free exercise by petitioner's members of their constitutionally protected right of association. See American Communications Asso. v. Douds, supra; Schneider v. Irvington, 308 U.S. 147, 161. Such a ". . . subordinating interest of the state must be compelling," Sweezy v. New Hampshire, 354 U.S. 234, 265 (concurring opinion). It is not of moment that the State has here acted solely through its judicial branch, for whether legislative or judicial, it is still the application of state power which we are asked to scrutinize.

Whether there was "justification" in this instance turns solely on the substantiality of Alabama's interest in obtaining the membership lists. During the course of a hearing before the Alabama Circuit Court on a motion of petitioner to set aside the production order, the State Attorney General presented at length, under examination by petitioner, the State's reason for requesting the membership lists. The exclusive purpose was to determine whether petitioner was conducting intrastate business in violation of the Alabama foreign corporation registration statute, and the membership lists were expected to help resolve this question. The issues in the litigation commenced by Alabama by its bill in equity were whether the character of petitioner and its activities in Alabama had been such as to make petitioner subject to the registration statute, and whether the extent of petitioner's activities without qualifying suggested its permanent ouster from the State. Without intimating the slightest view upon the merits of these issues, we are unable to perceive that the disclosure of the names of petitioner's rank-and-file members has a substantial bearing on either of them. As matters stand in the state court, petitioner (1) has admitted its presence and conduct of activities in Alabama since 1918; (2) has offered to comply in all respects with the state qualification statute, although preserving its contention that the statute does not apply to it; and (3) has apparently complied satisfactorily with the production order, except for the membership lists, by furnishing the Attorney General with varied business records, its charter and statement of purposes, the names of all of its directors and officers, and with the total number of its Alabama members and the amount of their dues. These last items would not on this record appear subject to constitutional challenge and have been furnished, but whatever interest the State may have in obtaining names of ordinary members has not been shown to be sufficient to overcome petitioner's constitutional objections to the production order.

From what has already been said, we think it apparent that New York ex rel. Bryant v. Zimmerman, 278 U.S. 63, cannot be relied on in support of the State's position, for that case involved markedly different considerations in terms of the interest of the State in obtaining disclosure. There, this Court upheld as applied to a member of a local chapter of the Ku Klux Klan, a New York statute requiring any unincorporated association which demanded an oath as a condition to membership to file with state officials copies of its ". . . constitution, by-laws, rules, regulations and oath of membership, together with a roster of its membership and a list of its officers for the current year." N.Y. Laws 1923, ch. 664, §§ 53, 56. In its opinion, the Court took care to emphasize the nature of the organization which New York sought to regulate. The decision was based on the particular character of the Klan's activities, involving acts of unlawful intimidation and violence, which the Court assumed was before the state legislature when it enacted the statute, and of which the Court itself took judicial notice. Furthermore, the situation before us is significantly different from that in Bryant, because the organization there had made no effort to comply with any of the requirements of New York's statute but rather had refused to furnish the State with any information as to its local activities.

We hold that the immunity from state scrutiny of membership lists which the Association claims on behalf of its members is here so related to the right of the members to pursue their lawful private interests privately and to associate freely with others in so doing as to come within the protection of the Fourteenth Amendment. As we conclude that Alabama has fallen short of showing a controlling justification for the deterrent effect on the free enjoyment of the right to associate which disclosure of membership lists is likely to have. Accordingly, the judgment of civil contempt and the $100,000 fine which resulted from petitioner's refusal to comply with the production order in this respect must fall.

NOTE

For a later development in the preceding case see NAACP v. Alabama, 360 U.S. 240 (1959). See also Bates v. Little Rock, 361 U.S. 516 (1960) (demand for names of members for purposes of a "license tax").

On the fourth occasion when NAACP v. Alabama came before the Supreme Court, it was requested that the Court should, as in Martin v. Hunter's Lessee, page 20 supra, formulate a decree for entry in the state courts which would assure "the Association's right to conduct activities in Alabama without further delay." Mr. Justice Harlan, speaking for a unanimous Court, conceded the existence of power to enter such an order but said that the Court preferred to follow its usual course. It, accordingly, remanded the case to the Supreme Court of Alabama "for further proceedings not inconsistent with this opinion." The concluding reflection in the opinion was as follows: "Should we unhappily be mistaken in our belief that the Supreme Court of Alabama will promptly implement this disposition, leave is given the Association to apply to this Court for further appropriate relief." 377 U.S. 288, 310 (1964).

INTERNATIONAL ASSN. OF MACHINISTS v. STREET, 367 U.S. 740, 81 S. Ct. 1784, 6 L. Ed. 2d 1141 (1961). In Railway Employes' Dept. v. Hanson, 351 U.S. 225, the Court held that §2 of the Railway Labor Act authorizing union shop agreements between interstate railways and unions of their employees was a constitutional regulation of commerce. The Court left undecided, however, the question whether a railroad employee, forced against his will to become a dues paying member of the union if he wanted to retain his job, had valid due process or First Amendment objections to political expenditures by the union for objectives that he did not approve. On June 19, 1961, a majority of five found that it was possible to give an interpretation to §2 of the Railway Labor Act which would deny authority to a union, over the employee's objection, to spend his money for political causes which he opposes. The majority of the Court thus avoided a resolution of the constitutional question whether First Amendment rights are infringed by the enforcement of an agreement which would enable compulsorily collected funds to be used for political purposes. The majority of the Court, speaking through Brennan, J., was satisfied that the legislative history of the act "contemplated compulsory unionism to force employees to share the cost of negotiation and administering collective agreements, and the costs of the adjustment and settlement of disputes. One looks in vain for any suggestion that Congress also meant . . . to provide the unions with a means for forcing employees, over their objection, to support political causes which they oppose." Justices Black, Douglas, Frankfurter, and Harlan believed it inappropriate to avoid the constitutional issue by means of a straining of legislative history and statutory language. In opinions by Black and Douglas, JJ., it was asserted that the freedom of speech of union members was violated by the spending of union funds for political purposes opposed by those members. Mr. Justice Black stated that "there can be no doubt that the federally sanctioned union-shop contract here, as it actually works, takes a part of the earnings of some men and turns it over to others, who spend a substantial part of the funds so received in efforts to thwart the political, economic and ideological hopes of those whose money has been forced from them under authority of law. This injects federal compulsion into the political and ideological processes, a result which I have supposed everyone would agree the First Amendment was particularly intended to prevent." Mr. Justice Frankfurter, with Harlan, J., concurring, denied that group disposition of union funds for political purposes not shared by all of its members infringed the constitutional rights of dissenters. "It is a commonplace of all organizations that a minority of a legally recognized group may at times see an organization's funds used for promotion of ideas opposed by the minority. . . . To come closer to the heart of the immediate matter, is the union's choice of when to picket or to go out on strike unconstitutional? Picketing is still deemed also a form of speech, but surely the union's decision to strike under its statutory aegis as a bargaining unit is not an unconstitutional compulsion forced upon members who strongly oppose a strike, as minorities not infrequently do. . . . The notion that economic and political concerns are separable is pre-Victorian. . . . It is not true in life that political protection is irrelevant to, and insulated from economic interests. . . . Is it respectful of the modes of thought of Madison and Jefferson projected into our day to attribute to them the view that the First Amendment must be construed to bar unions from concluding, by due procedural steps, that civil-rights legislation conduces to their interest, thereby prohibiting union funds to be expended to promote the passage of such measures?"

Given the majority reading of §2, what should be the nature of the relief afforded in Street? A restitution to dissenting members of that portion of the dues spent on objectionable political activity? A ban on those political activities objectionable to any members? What others?

On the same day on which the Street case was decided, the Court disposed of Lathrop v. Donohue, 367 U.S. 820 (1961). The issue there presented concerned the question whether a lawyer can constitutionally be compelled to pay dues to an "integrated" bar when that organization may take political positions with which the lawyer is not in agreement. Mr. Justice Brennan, with the concurrence of the Chief Justice and of Clark and Stewart, JJ., was persuaded that "on this record we have no sound basis for deciding appellant's constitutional claim insofar as it rests on the assertion that his rights of free speech are violated by the use of his money for causes which he opposes." The record, in their judgment, was inadequate for the presentation of this issue, since it nowhere apprised the Court "as to the views of the appellant on any particular legislative issues on which the State bar has taken a position, or as to the way in which and the degree to which funds compulsorily exacted from its members are used to support the organization's political activities." Mr. Justice Harlan, with Frankfurter, J., concurring, believed that the constitutional issues avoided by the plurality of their brethren, were clearly presented and were ripe for adjudication, and, on grounds substantially like those stated in his opinion in the Street case, expressed their view that the appellant's constitutional claim had no merit. Mr. Justice Whittaker wrote a brief opinion on the merits, asserting that state compulsion on members of the bar to pay an annual fee "as a condition of its grant, or of continuing its grant, to him of the *special privilege* (which is what it is) of practicing law in the State . . . does not violate any provision of the United States Constitution." Mr. Justice Black and Mr. Justice Douglas delivered dissenting opinions in which they condemned compulsory membership in a bar association which would engage in political activities. Mr. Justice Black saw the opinion of Harlan, J., as another unhappy instance of that "balancing" argument "which has recently produced a long line of liberty-stifling decisions in the name of 'self-preservation.'" Mr. Justice Douglas suggested that to tolerate the integrated bar is "practically to give carte blanche to any legislature to put at least professional people into goose-step brigades."

On the Railway Labor Act problem, see further Brotherhood of Railway Clerks v. Allen, 373 U.S. 113 (1963). See also Wellington, The Constitution, The Labor Union, and "Governmental Action," 70 Yale L.J. 345 (1961); Wellington, Machinists v. Street, Statutory Interpretation and the Avoidance of Constitutional Issues, 1961 Sup. Ct. Rev. 49.

NAACP v. Button 371 U.S. 415, 83 S. Ct. 328, 9 L. Ed. 2d 405 (1963)

MR. JUSTICE BRENNAN delivered the opinion of the Court.

[This case originated in suits by the NAACP and the NAACP Legal Defense Fund in both state and federal courts. The suits resulted in the invalidation as unconstitutional of Chapters 31, 32, 35, and 36 of the Virginia Acts of Assembly, 1956 Extra Session. At issue on review by the Supreme Court was the constitutionality of Chapter 33 as applied to the activities of the NAACP.]

The NAACP was formed in 1909 and incorporated under New York law as a nonprofit membership corporation in 1911. It maintains its headquarters in New York and presently has some 1,000 active unincorporated branches throughout the Nation. The corporation is licensed to do business in Virginia, and has 89 branches there. The Virginia branches are organized into the Virginia State Conference of NAACP Branches (the Conference), an unincorporated association, which in 1957 had some 13,500 members. The activities of the Conference are financed jointly by the national organization and the local branches from contributions and membership dues. NAACP policy, binding upon local branches and conferences, is set by the annual national convention.

The basic aims and purposes of NAACP are to secure the elimination of all racial barriers which deprive Negro citizens of the privileges and burdens of equal citizenship rights in the United States. To this end the Association engages in extensive educational and lobbying activities. It also devotes much of its funds and energies to an extensive program of assisting certain kinds of litigation on behalf of its declared purposes. For more than 10 years, the Virginia Conference has concentrated upon financing litigation aimed at ending racial segregation in the public schools of the Commonwealth.

The Conference ordinarily will finance only cases in which the assisted litigant retains an NAACP staff lawyer to represent him. The Conference maintains a legal staff of 15 attorneys, all of whom are Negroes and members of the NAACP. The staff is elected at the Conference's annual convention. Each legal staff member must agree to abide by the policies of the NAACP, which, insofar as they pertain to professional services, limit the kinds of litigation which the NAACP will assist. Thus the NAACP will not underwrite ordinary damages actions, criminal actions in which defendant raises no question of possible racial discrimination, or suits in which the plaintiff seeks separate but equal rather than fully desegregated public school facilities. The staff decides whether a litigant, who may or may not be an NAACP member, is entitled to NAACP assistance. The Conference defrays all expenses of litigation in an assisted case, and usually, although not always, pays each lawyer on the case a per diem fee not to exceed $60, plus out-of-pocket expenses. The assisted litigant receives no money from the Conference or the staff lawyers. The staff member may not accept, from the litigant or any other source, any other compensation for his services in an NAACP-assisted case. None of the staff receives a salary or retainer from NAACP; the per diem fee paid only for professional services in a particular case. This per diem payment is smaller than the compensation ordinarily received for equivalent private professional work. The actual conduct of assisted litigation is under the control of the attorney, although the NAACP continues to be concerned that the outcome of the lawsuit should be consistent with NAACP's policies already described. A client is free at any time to withdraw from an action.

The members of the legal staff of the Virginia Conference and other NAACP or Defense Fund lawyers called in by the staff to assist are drawn into litigation in various ways. One is for an aggrieved Negro to apply directly to the Conference or the legal staff for assistance. His application is referred to the Chairman of the legal staff. The Chairman, with the concurrence of the President of the Conference, is authorized to agree to give legal assistance in an appropriate case. In litigation involving public school segregation, the procedure tends to be different. Typically, a local NAACP branch will invite a member of the legal staff to explain to a meeting of parents and children the legal steps necessary to achieve desegregation. The staff member will bring printed forms to the meeting authorizing him, and other NAACP or Defense Fund attorneys of his designation, to represent the signers in legal proceedings to achieve desegregation. On occasion, blank forms have been signed by litigants, upon the understanding that a member or members of the legal staff, with or without assistance from other NAACP lawyers, or from the Defense Fund, would handle the case. It is usual, after obtaining authorizations, for the staff lawyer to bring into the case the other staff members in the area where suit is to be brought, and sometimes to bring in lawyers from the national organization or the Defense Fund. In effect, then, the prospective litigant retains not so much a particular attorney as the "firm" of NAACP and Defense Fund lawyers, which has a corporate reputation for expertness in presenting and arguing the difficult questions of law that frequently arise in civil rights litigation.

These meetings are sometimes prompted by letters and bulletins from the Conference urging active steps to fight segregation. The Conference has on occasion distributed to the local branches petitions for desegregation to be signed by parents and filed with local school boards, and advised branch officials to obtain, as petitioner, persons willing to "go all the way" in any possible litigation that may ensue. While the Conference in these ways encourages the bringing of lawsuits, the plaintiffs in particular actions, so far as appears, make their own decisions to become such.

Statutory regulation of unethical and nonprofessional conduct by attorneys has been in force in Virginia since 1849. These provisions outlaw, inter alia, solicitation of legal business in the form of "running" or "capping." Prior to 1956, however, no attempt was made to proscribe under such regulations the activities of the NAACP, which had been carried on openly for many years in subtantially the manner described. In 1956, however, the legislature amended, by the addition of Chapter 33, the provisions of the Virginia Code forbidding solicitation of legal business by a "runner" or "capper" to include in the definition of "runner" or "capper," any agent for an individual or organization which retains a lawyer in connection with an action to which it is not a party and in which it has no pecuniary right or liability. The Virginia Supreme Court of Appeals held that the chapter's purpose "was to strengthen the existing statutes to further control the evils of solicitation of legal business. . . ." 202 Va., at 154, 116 S.E.2d, at 65. The court held that the activities of NAACP, the Virginia Conference, the Defense Fund, and the lawyers furnished by them, fell within, and could constitutionally be proscribed by the chapter's expanded definition of improper solicitation of legal business, and also violated Canons 35 and 47 of the American Bar Association's Canons of Professional Ethics, which the court had adopted in 1938. Specifically the court held that, under the expanded definition, such activities on the part of NAACP, the Virginia Conference, and the Defense Fund constituted "fomenting and soliciting legal business in which they are not parties and have no pecuniary right or liability, and which they channel to the enrichment of certain lawyers employed by them, at no cost to the litigants and over which the litigants have no control." 202 Va., at 155; 116 S.E.2d, at 66. . . .

Petitioner challenges the decision of the Supreme Court of Appeals on many grounds. But we reach only one: that Chapter 33 as construed and applied abridges the freedoms of the First Amendment, protected against state action by the Fourteenth. More specifically, petitioner claims that the chapter infringes the right of the NAACP and its members and lawyers to associate for the purpose of assisting persons who seek legal redress for infringements of their constitutionally guaranteed and other rights. We think petitioner may assert this right on its own behalf, because, though a corporation, it is directly engaged in those activities, claimed to be constitutionally protected, which the statute would curtail. Cf. Grosjean v. American Press Co., 297 U.S. 233. We also think petitioner has standing to assert the corresponding rights of its members. See NAACP v. Alabama ex rel. Patterson, 357 U.S. 449, 458-460; Bates v. City of Little Rock, 361 U.S. 516, 523, n. 9; Louisiana ex rel. Gremillion v. NAACP, 366 U.S. 293, 296.

We reverse the judgment of the Virginia Supreme Court of Appeals. We hold that the activities of the NAACP, its affiliates and legal staff shown on this record are modes of expression and association protected by the First and Fourteenth Amendments which Virginia may not prohibit, under its power to regulate the legal profession, as improper solicitation of legal business violative of Chapter 33 and the Canons of Professional Ethics.

A

We meet at the outset the contention that "solicitation" is wholly outside the area of freedoms protected by the First Amendment. To this contention there are two answers. The first is that a State cannot foreclose the exercise of constitutional rights by mere labels. The second is that abstract discussion is not the only species of communication which the Constitution protects; the First Amendment also protects vigorous advocacy, certainly of lawful ends, against governmental intrusion. . . . In the context of NAACP objectives, litigation is not a technique of resolving private differences; it is a means for achieving the lawful objectives of equality of treatment by all government, federal, state and local for the members of the Negro community in this country. It is thus a form of political expression. Groups which find themselves unable to achieve their objectives through the ballot frequently turn to the courts. Just as it was true of the opponents of New Deal legislation during the 1930's, for example, no less is it true of the Negro minority today. And under the conditions of modern government, litigation may well be the sole practicable avenue open to a minority to petition for redress of grievances. . . .

B

Our concern is with the impact of enforcement of Chapter 33 upon First Amendment freedoms. We start, of course, from the decree of the Supreme Court of Appeals. Although the action before it was one basically for declaratory relief, that court not only expounded the purpose and reach of the chapter but held concretely that certain of petitioner's activities had, and certain others had not violated the chapter. These activities had been explored in detail at the trial and were spread out plainly on the record. We have no doubt that the opinion of the Supreme Court of Appeals in the instant case was intended as a full and authoritative construction of Chapter 33 as applied in a detailed factual context. That construction binds us. . . .

But it does not follow that this Court now has only a clear-cut task to decide whether the activities of the petitioner deemed unlawful by the Supreme Court of Appeals are constitutionally privileged. If the line drawn by the decree between the permitted and prohibited activities of the NAACP, its members and lawyers is an ambiguous one, we will not presume that the statute curtails constitutionally protected activity as little as possible. For standards of permissible statutory vagueness are strict in the area of free expression. . . . Furthermore, the instant decree may be invalid if it prohibits privileged exercises of First Amendment rights whether or not the record discloses that the petitioner had engaged in privileged conduct. For in appraising a statute's inhibitory effect upon such rights, this Court has not hesitated to take into account possible applications of the statute in other factual contexts besides that at bar. Thornhill v. Alabama, 310 U.S. 88, 97-98; Winters v. New York, [333 U.S. 507], at 518-520. Cf. Staub v. City of Baxley, 355 U.S. 313. It makes no difference that the instant case was not a criminal prosecution and not based on a refusal to comply with a licensing requirement. The objectionable quality of vagueness and overbreadth does not depend upon absence of fair notice to a criminally accused or upon unchanneled delegation of legislative powers, but upon the danger of tolerating, in the area of First Amendment freedoms, the existence of a penal statute susceptible of sweeping and improper application. . . .

We conclude that under Chapter 33, as authoritatively construed by the Supreme Court of Appeals, a person who advises another that his legal rights have been infringed and refers him to a particular attorney or group of attorneys (for example, to the Virginia Conference's legal staff) for assistance has committed a crime, as has the attorney who knowingly renders assistance under such circumstances. There thus inheres in the statute the gravest danger of smothering all discussion looking to the eventual institution of litigation on behalf of the rights of members of an unpopular minority. Lawyers on the legal staff or even mere NAACP members or sympathizers would understandably hesitate, at an NAACP meeting or on any other occasion, to do what the decree purports to allow, namely, acquaint "persons with what they believe to be their legal rights and . . . [advise] them to assert their rights by commencing or further prosecuting a suit. . . ." For if the lawyers, members or sympathizers also appeared in or had any connection with any litigation supported with NAACP funds contributed under the provision of the decree by which the NAACP is not prohibited "from contributing money to persons to assist them in commencing or further prosecuting such suits," they plainly would risk (if lawyers) disbarment proceedings and, lawyers and non-lawyers alike, criminal prosecution for the offense of "solicitation," to which the Virginia court gave so broad and uncertain a meaning. It makes no difference whether such prosecutions or proceedings would actually be commenced. It is enough that a vague and broad statute lends itself to selective enforcement against unpopular causes. We cannot close our eyes to the fact that the militant Negro civil rights movement has engendered the intense resentment and opposition of the politically dominant white community of Virginia; litigation assisted by the NAACP has been

Section C. **Freedom of Speech and Association** 1245

bitterly fought. In such circumstances, a statute broadly curtailing group activity leading to litigation may easily become a weapon of oppression, however evenhanded its terms appear. Its mere existence could well freeze out of existence all such activity on behalf of the civil rights of Negro citizens. . . .

C

The second contention is that Virginia has a subordinating interest in the regulation of the legal profession, embodied in Chapter 33, which justified limiting petitioner's First Amendment rights. Specifically, Virginia contends that the NAACP's activities in furtherance of litigation, being "improper solicitation" under the state statute, fall within the traditional purview of state regulation of professional conduct. However, the State's attempt to equate the activities of the NAACP and its lawyers with common-law barratry, maintenance and champerty, and to outlaw them accordingly, cannot obscure the serious encroachment worked by Chapter 33 upon protected freedoms of expression. The decisions of this Court have consistently held that only a compelling state interest in the regulation of a subject within the State's constitutional power to regulate can justify limiting First Amendment freedoms. . . .

However valid may be Virginia's interest in regulating the traditionally illegal practices of barratry, maintenance and champerty, that interest does not justify the prohibition of the NAACP activities disclosed by this record. . . .

Resort to the courts to seek vindication of constitutional rights is a different matter from the oppressive, malicious, or avaricious use of the legal process for purely private gain. Lawsuits attacking racial discrimination, at least in Virginia, are neither very profitable nor very popular. They are not an object of general competition among Virginia lawyers; the problem is rather one of an apparent dearth of lawyers who are willing to undertake such litigation. There has been neither claim nor proof that any assisted Negro litigants have desired, but have been prevented from retaining, the services of other counsel. We realize that an NAACP lawyer must derive personal satisfaction from participation in litigation on behalf of Negro rights, else he would hardly be inclined to participate at the risk of financial sacrifice. But this would not seem to be the kind of interest or motive which induces criminal conduct.

We conclude that although the petitioner has amply shown that its activities fall within the First Amendment's protections, the State has failed to advance any substantial regulatory interest, in the form of substantive evils flowing from petitioner's activities, which can justify the broad prohibitions which it has imposed. Nothing that this record shows as to the nature and purpose of NAACP activities permits an inference of any injurious intervention in or control of litigation which would constitutionally authorize the application of Chapter 33 to those activities. A fortiori, nothing in this record justifies the breadth and vagueness of the Virginia Supreme Court of Appeals' decree.

A final observation is in order. Because our disposition is rested on the First Amendment as absorbed in the Fourteenth, we do not reach the considerations of race or racial discrimination which are the predicate of petitioner's challenge to the statute under the Equal Protection Clause. That the petitioner happens to be engaged in activities of expression and association on behalf of the rights of Negro children to equal opportunity is constitutionally irrelevant to the ground of our decision. The course of our decisions in the First Amendment area makes plain that its protections would apply as fully to those who would arouse our society against the objectives of the petitioner. See e.g., Near v. Minnesota, 283 U.S. 697; Terminiello v. Chicago, 337 U.S. 1; Kuntz v. New York, 340 U.S. 290. For the Constitution protects expression and association without regard to the race, creed, or political or religious affiliation of the members of the group which invokes its shield, or to the truth, popularity, or social utility of the ideas and beliefs which are offered.

Reversed.[z]

NOTE Constitutional Status of Certain Associations

1. *Legal aid by labor unions.* In Brotherhood of Railroad Trainmen v. Virginia, 377 U.S. 1 (1964), a majority of the Court, speaking through Mr. Justice Black, held that the Brotherhood could not be enjoined from carrying out a plan by which its Legal Aid Department selected local lawyers to represent members of the Brotherhood and their families in enforcing personal injury claims. "We hold that the First and Fourteenth Amendments protect the right of the members through their Brotherhood to maintain and carry out their plan for advising workers who are injured to obtain legal advice and for recommending specific lawyers." Mr. Justice Clark delivered a dissenting opinion, in which Harlan, J., concurred.

See also United Mine Workers v. State Bar Assn., 389 U.S. 217 (1967), and United Transportation Union v. Michigan Bar, 401 U.S. 576 (1971).

2. *Compulsory disclosure of membership.* In Communist Party v. Subversive Activities Control Board, 367 U.S. 1 (1961), the Court considered the meaning and constitutionality of certain sections of the Subversive Activities Control Act of 1950. A majority of the Court, speaking through Justice Frankfurter, rejected the contention that the statute's requirement that "Communist-action" organizations should register and list their members with the Control Board violated the freedoms of speech and association guaranteed by the First Amendment. Passages from Mr. Justice Frankfurter's opinion follow.

"No doubt, a governmental regulation which requires registration as a condition upon the exercise of speech may in some circumstances affront the constitutional guarantee of free expression. Thomas v. Collins, 323 U.S. 516. In that case . . . the decision was a narrow one, striking down the registration requirement only as applied to the particular circumstances of the case . . . that is, to an individual who . . . had come into the State 'for one purpose and one only — to make the speech in question.' . . . The present statute does not, of course, attach the registration requirement to the incident of speech, but to the incidents of foreign domination and of operation to advance the objectives of the world Communist movement — operation which, the Board has found here, includes extensive, long-continuing organizational, as well as 'speech' activity. . . .

"Similarly, we agree that compulsory disclosure of the names of an organization's members may in certain instances infringe constitutionally protected rights of association. NAACP v. Alabama, 357 U.S. 449; Bates v. Little Rock, 361 U.S. 516; Shelton v. Tucker, 364 U.S. 479. But to say this much is only to recognize one of the points of reference from which analysis must begin. To state that individual liberties may be affected is to establish the condition for, not to arrive at the conclusion of, constitutional decision. Against the impediments which particular governmental regulation causes to entire freedom of individual action, here must be weighed the value to the public of the ends which the regulation may achieve. . . .

"The present case differs from Thomas v. Collins, and from NAACP, Bates, and Shelton in the magnitude of the public interests which registration and disclosure provisions are designed to protect and in the pertinence which registration and disclosure bear to the

---

[z] Separate opinions by Justices Douglas (concurring) and White (concurring in part and dissenting in part) are omitted, as is a dissent by Justice Harlan, in which Clark and Stewart, JJ., joined. — ED.

protection of those interests. Congress itself has expressed in Sec. 2 of the Act both what those interests are and what, in its view, threatens them. On the basis of its detailed investigations Congress has found that there exists a world Communist movement, foreign-controlled, whose purpose it is by whatever means necessary to establish Communist totalitarian dictatorship in the countries throughout the world, and which has already succeeded in supplanting governments in other countries. . . . The purpose of the Subversive Activities Control Act is said to be to prevent the world-wide Communist conspiracy from accomplishing its purpose in this country.

"It is not for the courts to re-examine the validity of these legislative findings and reject them. . . . They are the product of extensive investigation by Committees of Congress over more than a decade and a half. Cf. Nebbia v. New York, 291 U.S. 502, 516, 530. We certainly cannot dismiss them as unfounded or irrational imaginings. . . .

"[S]ecrecy of associations and organizations, even among groups concerned exclusively with political processes, may under some circumstances constitute a danger which legislatures do not lack constitutional power to curb. . . . It was the nature of the organization regulated, and hence the danger involved in its covert operation, which justified the [New York statute which we sustained in New York ex rel. Bryant v. Zimmerman, 278 U.S. 63] and caused us to distinguish the Bryant case in NAACP v. Alabama, supra."

3. *Status of Communist-front organizations.* On the status of "Communist-front organizations" under the Subversive Activities Control Act, see American Committee for Protection of Foreign Born v. Subversive Activities Control Board, 380 U.S. 503 (1965); Veterans of the Abraham Lincoln Brigade v. SACB, 380 U.S. 513 (1965). On registration of individuals, see Albertson v. SACB, 382 U.S. 70 (1965); and Mansfield, The Albertson Case, 1966 Sup. Ct. Rev. 103.

5. Access to and by the Media

a. Access to the Media

Red Lion Broadcasting Co. v. FCC *395 U.S. 367, 89 Sup. Ct. 1794, 23 L. Ed. 2d 371 (1969)*

MR. JUSTICE WHITE delivered the opinion of the Court. The Federal Communications Commission has for many years imposed on radio and television broadcasters the requirement that discussion of public issues be presented on broadcast stations, and that each side of those issues must be given fair coverage. This is known as the fairness doctrine, which originated very early in the history of broadcasting and has maintained its present outlines for some time. It is an obligation whose content has been defined in a long series of FCC rulings in particular cases, and which is distinct from the statutory requirement of §315 of the Communications Act that equal time be allotted all qualified candidates for public office. Two aspects of the fairness doctrine, relating to personal attacks in the context of controversial public issues and to political editorializing, were codified more precisely in the form of FCC regulations in 1967. The two cases before us now, which were decided separately below, challenge the constitutional and statutory bases of the doctrine and component rules. Red Lion involves the applications of the fairness doctrine to a particular broadcast, and RTNDA arises as an action to review the FCC's 1967 promulgation of the personal attack and political editorializing regulations, which were laid down after the Red Lion litigation had begun.

1248   Chapter Sixteen. Substantive Rights

I

A

The Red Lion Broadcasting Company is licensed to operate a Pennsylvania radio station, WGCB. On November 27, 1964, WGCB carried a 15-minute broadcast by Reverend Billy James Hargis as part of a "Christian Crusade" series. A book by Fred J. Cook entitled "Goldwater — Extremist on the Right" was discussed by Hargis, who said that Cook had been fired by a newspaper for fabricating false charges against city officials; that Cook had then worked for a Communist-affiliated publication; that he had defended Alger Hiss and attacked J. Edgar Hoover and the Central Intelligence Agency; and that he had now written a "book to smear and destroy Barry Goldwater." When Cook heard of the broadcast he concluded that he had been personally attacked and demanded free reply time, which the station refused. After an exchange of letters among Cook, Red Lion, and the FCC, the FCC declared that the Hargis broadcast constituted a personal attack on Cook; that Red Lion had failed to meet its obligation under the fairness doctrine as expressed in Times-Mirror Broadcasting Co., 24 P & F Radio Reg. 404 (1962), to send a tape, transcript or summary of the broadcast to Cook and offer him reply time; and that the station must provide reply time whether or not Cook would pay for it. On review in the Court of Appeals for the District of Columbia, the FCC's position was upheld as constitutional and otherwise proper. 318 F.2d 908 (1967).

B

Not long after the Red Lion litigation was begun, the FCC issued a Notice of Proposed Rule Making, 31 Fed. Reg. 5710, with an eye to making the personal attack aspect of the fairness doctrine more precise and more readily enforceable, and also to specify its rules relating to political editorials. After considering written comments supporting and opposing the rules, the FCC adopted them substantially as proposed, 32 Fed. Reg. 10303. Twice amended, 32 Fed. Reg. 11531, 33 Fed. Reg. 5362, the rules were held unconstitutional in the RTNDA litigation by the Court of Appeals for the Seventh Circuit on review of the rule-making proceeding as abridging the freedoms of speech and press. 400 F.2d 1002 (1968).

As they now stand amended, the regulations read as follows:

"Personal attacks; political editorials.

"(a) When, during the presentation of views on a controversial issue of public importance, an attack is made upon the honesty, character, integrity or like personal qualities of an identified person or group, the licensee shall, within a reasonable time and in no event later than one week after the attack, transmit to the person or group attacked (1) notification of the date, time and identification of the broadcast; (2) a script or tape (or an accurate summary if a script or tape is not available) of the attack; and (3) an offer of a reasonable opportunity to respond over the licensee's facilities.

"(b) The provisions of paragraph (a) of this section shall not be applicable (i) to attacks on foreign groups or foreign public figures; (ii) to personal attacks which are made by legally qualified candidates, their authorized spokesmen, or those associated with them in the campaign, on other such candidates, their authorized spokesmen, or persons associated with the candidates in the campaign; and (iii) to bona fide newscasts, bona fide news interviews, and on-the-spot coverage of a bona fide news event (including commentary or analysis contained in the foregoing programs, but the provisions of paragraph (a) shall be applicable to editorials of the licensee).

"NOTE: The fairness doctrine is applicable to situations coming within (iii), above, and, in a specific factual situation, may be applicable in the general area of political broadcasts (ii), above. See Section 315(a) of the Act, 47 U.S.C. 315(a); Public Notice: *Applicability of the Fairness Doctrine in the Handling of Controversial Issues of Public Importance,* 29 Fed. Reg. 10415. The categories listed in (iii) are the same as those specified in Section 315(a) of the Act.

"(c) Where a licensee, in an editorial, (i) endorses or (ii) opposes a legally qualified candidate or candidates, the licensee shall, within 24 hours after the editorial, transmit to respectively (i) the other qualified candidate or candidates for the same office or (ii) the candidate opposed in the editorial (1) notification of the date and the time of the editorial; (2) a script or tape of the editorial; and (3) an offer of a reasonable opportunity for a candidate or spokesman of the candidate to respond over the licensee's facilities: *Provided, however,* That where such editorials are broadcast within 72 hours prior to the day of the election, the licensee shall comply with the provisions of this subsection sufficiently far in advance of the broadcast to enable the candidate or candidates to have a reasonable opportunity to prepare a response and to present it in a timely fashion." 47 CFR §§73.123, 73.300, 73.598, 73.679 (all identical).

C

Believing that the specific application of the fairness doctrine in Red Lion, and the promulgation of the regulations in RTNDA, are both authorized by Congress and enhance rather than abridge the freedoms of speech and press protected by the First Amendment, we hold them valid and constitutional, reversing the judgment below in RTNDA and affirming the judgment below in Red Lion. . . .

III

The broadcasters challenge the fairness doctrine and its specific manifestations in the personal attack and political editorials rules on conventional First Amendment grounds, alleging that the rules abridge their freedom of speech and press. Their contention is that the First Amendment protects their desire to use their allotted frequencies continuously to broadcast whatever they choose, and to exclude whomever they choose from ever using that frequency. No man may be prevented from saying or publishing what he thinks, or from refusing in his speech or other utterances to give equal weight to the views of his opponents. This right, they say, applies equally to broadcasters.

A

Although broadcasting is clearly a medium affected by a First Amendment interest, United States v. Paramount Pictures, Inc., 334 U.S. 131, 166 (1948), differences in the characteristics of new media justify differences in the First Amendment standards applied to them. Joseph Burstyn, Inc. v. Wilson, 343 U.S. 495, 503 (1952). For example, the ability of new technology to produce sounds more raucous than those of the human voice justifies restrictions on the sound level, and on the hours and places of use, of sound trucks so long as the restrictions are reasonable and applied without discrimination. Kovacs v. Cooper, 336 U.S. 77 (1949).

Just as the Government may limit the use of sound amplifying equipment potentially so noisy that it drowns out civilized private speech, so may the Government limit the use of broadcast equipment. The right of free speech of a broadcaster, the user of a sound truck, or any other individual does not embrace a right to snuff out the free speech of others. Associated Press v. United States, 326 U.S. 1, 20 (1945). . . .

Where there are substantially more individuals who want to broadcast than there are frequencies to allocate, it is idle to posit an unabridgeable First Amendment right to broadcast comparable to the right of every individual to speak, write, or publish. . . .

By the same token, as far as the First Amendment is concerned those who are licensed stand no better than those to whom licenses are refused. . . .

This is not to say that the First Amendment is irrelevant to public broadcasting. . . . It is the right of the viewers and listeners, not the right of the broadcasters, which is paramount. See FCC v. Sanders Bros. Radio Station, 309 U.S. 470, 475 (1940); FCC v. Allentown Broadcasting Corp., 349 U.S. 358, 361-362 (1955); Z. Chafee, Government and Mass Communications 546 (1947). It is the purpose of the First Amendment to preserve an uninhibited market-place of ideas in which truth will ultimately prevail, rather than to countenance monopolization of that market, whether it be by the Government itself or a private licensee. Associated Press v. United States, 326 U.S. 1, 20 (1945); New York Times Co. v. Sullivan, 376 U.S. 254, 270 (1964); Abrams v. United States, 250 U.S. 616, 630 (1919) (Holmes, J., dissenting). "[S]peech concerning public affairs is more than self-expression; it is the essence of self-government." Garrison v. Louisiana, 379 U.S. 64, 74-75 (1964). See Brennan, The Supreme Court and the Meiklejohn Interpretation of the First Amendment, 79 Harv. L. Rev. 1 (1965). It is the right of the public to receive suitable access to social, political, esthetic, moral, and other ideas and experiences which is crucial here. That right may not constitutionally be abridged either by Congress or by the FCC.

B

. . . In terms of constitutional principle, and as enforced sharing of a scarce resource, the personal attack and political editorials rules are indistinguishable from the equal-time provision of §315, a specific enactment of Congress requiring stations to set aside reply time under specified circumstances and to which the fairness doctrine and these constituent regulations are important complements. That provision, which has been part of the law since 1927, . . . has been held valid by this Court as an obligation of the licensee relieving him of any power in any way to prevent or censor the broadcast, and thus insulating him from liability for defamation. The constitutionality of the statute under the First Amendment was unquestioned. Farmers Educ. & Coop. Union v. WDAY, 360 U.S. 525 (1959).

Nor can we say that it is inconsistent with the First Amendment goal of producing an informed public capable of conducting its own affairs to require a broadcaster to permit answers to personal attacks occurring in the course of discussing controversial issues, or to require that the political opponents of those endorsed by the station be given a chance to communicate with the public. Otherwise, station owners and a few networks would have unfettered power to make time available only to the highest bidders, to communicate only their own views on public issues, people and candidates, and to permit on the air only those with whom they agreed. There is no sanctuary in the First Amendment for unlimited private censorship operating in a medium not open to all. "Freedom of the press from governmental interference under the First Amendment does not sanction repression of that freedom by private interests." Associated Press v. U.S., 326 U.S. 1, 20 (1944).

C

It is strenuously argued, however, that if political editorials or personal attacks will trigger an obligation in broadcasters to afford the opportunity for expression to speakers who need not pay for time and whose views are unpalatable to the licensees, then broadcasters will be irresistibly forced to self-censorship and their coverage of controversial public issues will be eliminated or at least rendered wholly ineffective. Such a result would indeed be a serious matter, for should licensees actually eliminate their coverage of controversial issues, the purposes of the doctrine would be stifled.

At this point, however, as the Federal Communications Commission has indicated, that possibility is at best speculative. . . . And if experience with the administration of these doctrines indicates that they have the net effect of reducing rather than enhancing the volume and quality of coverage, there will be time enough to reconsider the constitutional implications. The fairness doctrine in the past has had no such overall effect.

That this will occur now seems unlikely, however, since if present licensees should suddenly prove timorous, the Commission is not powerless to insist that they give adequate and fair attention to public issues. It does not violate the First Amendment to treat licensees given the privilege of using scarce radio frequencies as proxies for the entire community, obligated to give suitable time and attention to matters of great public concern. . . .

D

It is argued that even if at one time the lack of available frequencies for all who wished to use them justified the Government's choice of those who would best serve the public interest by acting as proxy for those who would present differing views, or by giving the latter access directly to broadcast facilities, this condition no longer prevails so that continuing control is not justified. To this there are several answers.

Scarcity is not entirely a thing of the past. Advances in technology, such as microwave transmission, have led to more efficient utilization of the frequency spectrum, but uses for that spectrum have also grown apace. . . . Some present possibility for new entry by competing stations is not enough, in itself, to render unconstitutional the Government's effort to assure that a broadcaster's programming ranges widely enough to serve the public interest.

In view of the prevalence of scarcity of broadcast frequencies, the Government's role in allocating those frequencies, and the legitimate claims of those unable without governmental assistance to gain access to those frequencies for expression of their views, we hold the regulations and ruling at issue here are both authorized by statute and constitutional.[1] The judgment of the Court of Appeals in Red Lion is affirmed and that in RTNDA reversed and the causes remanded for proceedings consistent with this opinion.

It is so ordered.[aa]

NOTE The Newspaper Analogy?

Media-access advocates were rebuffed in Miami Herald Publishing Co. v. Tornillo, 418 U.S. 241 (1974), where the Court unanimously invalidated a Florida statute requiring

---

[1] We need not deal with the argument that even if there is no longer a technological scarcity of frequencies limiting the number of broadcasters, there nevertheless is an economic scarcity in the sense that the Commission could or does limit entry to the broadcasting market on economic grounds and licenses no more stations than the market will support. Hence, it is said, the fairness doctrine or its equivalent is essential to satisfy the claims of those excluded and of the public generally. A related argument, which we also put aside, is that quite apart from scarcity of frequencies, technological or economic, Congress does not abridge freedom of speech or press by legislation directly or indirectly multiplying the voices and views presented to the public through time sharing, fairness doctrines, or other devices which limit or dissipate the power of those who sit astride the channels of communication with the general public. Cf. Citizens Publishing Co. v. United States, 394 U.S. 131 (1969).

[aa] Not having heard oral argument in these cases, Justice Douglas took no part in the Court's decision. — ED.

newspapers to print a political candidate's reply to an adverse editorial. Although the statute appeared to suffer in several respects from impermissible vagueness, Chief Justice Burger placed the Court's holding on broad ground: "The appellee and supporting advocates of an enforceable right of access to the press vigorously argue that government has an obligation to ensure that a wide variety of views reach the public. . . .

"However much validity may be found in these arguments, at each point the implementation of a remedy such as an enforceable right of access necessarily calls for some mechanism, either governmental or consensual. If it is governmental coercion, this at once brings about a confrontation with the express provisions of the First Amendment and the judicial gloss on that Amendment developed over the years. . . .

"Even if a newspaper would face no additional costs to comply with a compulsory access law and would not be forced to forgo publication of news or opinion by the inclusion of a reply, the Florida statute fails to clear the barriers of the First Amendment because of its intrusion into the function of editors. A newspaper is more than a passive receptacle or conduit for news, comment, and advertising. The choice of materials to go into a newspaper, and the decisions made as to limitations on the size and content of the paper, and treatment of public issues and public officials — whether fair or unfair — constitute the exercise of editorial control and judgment. It has yet to be demonstrated how governmental regulation of this crucial process can be exercised consistent with First Amendment guarantees of a free press as they have evolved to this time."

Justice Brennan, concurring, stated: "I join the Court's opinion which, as I understand it, addresses only 'right of reply' statutes and implies no view upon the constitutionality of 'retraction' statutes affording plaintiffs able to prove defamatory falsehoods a statutory action to require retraction. See generally Note, Vindication of the Reputation of a Public Official, 80 Harv. L. Rev. 1730, 1739-1747 (1967)."

Are Red Lion and Tornillo at odds? Why should government "intrusion" upon the editorial discretion of the print and broadcasting media be regarded differently under the First Amendment? Consider the following comment upon Tornillo from Freund, The Great Disorder of Speech, 44 Amer. Scholar 541, 557-558 (1975): "While the outcome was disappointing to those who saw in the electronic field a model for the press in a time of scarcity, the differences are significant. The distinctive impact of television, in particular, and its potential for powerful partisanship make some mild form of balance appropriate. Journals of news and opinion have more counterparts in the printed media: the daily press is supplemented and to some extent offset by weekly magazines, neighborhood newssheets, trade and religious periodicals, and more. And although a right of reply to an attack on one's character is a very limited inroad on editorial autonomy — particularly given the very circumscribed right of public officers and public figures to recover damages for defamation — the principle of resisting the government's entering wedge is probably a salutary one in the context of journals of opinion, where factual and judgmental attacks on the editorial page may be hard to distinguish." See also Note, Reconciling Red Lion and Tornillo: A Consistent Theory of Media Regulation, 28 Stan. L. Rev. 563 (1976).

b. Political and Commercial Advertising

NOTE Political Advertising

In Columbia Broadcasting System v. Democratic National Committee, Inc., 412 U.S. 94 (1973), the Court affirmed an FCC decision that a broadcaster presenting full and fair coverage of controversial issues in satisfaction of the fairness doctrine could maintain a policy of refusing to accept paid editorial advertisements on public issues. In response to suits brought by the Democratic National Committee and the Business Executives' Movement for Vietnam Peace, the FCC ruled that a broadcaster who meets his public obligation to provide full and fair coverage of public issues is not required to accept editorial advertisements by either the Communications Act of 1934 or the First Amendment, but the court of appeals reversed and remanded the cases to the commission for development of procedures and guidelines for administering a First Amendment right of access.

Writing for the Supreme Court, Chief Justice Burger reaffirmed the familiar proposition that the fundamental criterion governing the use of broadcast frequencies is the public's right to be informed, and elaborated the character of the regulatory scheme which has evolved over half a century. That scheme historically placed broad journalistic discretion in the hands of the licensees. Congress has repeatedly rejected attempts to impose a "common carrier" right of access to broadcasters for all persons wishing to comment on public issues, in favor of reposing in the FCC authority by which the fairness doctrine evolved to insure the fair and complete coverage of public issues. For himself and Justices Stewart and Rehnquist, Chief Justice Burger added that a broadcast licensee's refusal to accept paid editorial advertisements did not constitute governmental action within the scope of the First Amendment. The decision to decline such advertisements is an exercise of the journalistic discretion expressly conferred upon broadcasters by Congress rather than action undertaken with governmental partnership or benefit. To hold otherwise would force the FCC into an even more intimate and threatening relationship in the regulation of broadcast material. But in any event, the opinion added, there was no First Amendment duty to furnish access to political advertisers.

Finally, the Court found that the FCC was justified in concluding that the "public interest" standard of the Communications Act would not be served by compelling broadcasters to accept paid public advertising. Such a system would be prejudiced in favor of the affluent, could undermine the effective operation of the fairness doctrine, and would dilute the public accountability which now resides in broadcasters. Further, it would inevitably enmesh the FCC in an undesirable case-by-case determination of broadcasting material.

On the First Amendment issue there was sharp disagreement. Justices Douglas and Stewart, concurring, insisted that not only was there no constitutional duty to provide access, but it would be an unconstitutional infringement of the liberty of the broadcaster to impose such a duty. The fairness doctrine, in their view, went to the verge, if not beyond. Justices Brennan and Marshall, dissenting, approved the view of the court of appeals that the broadcasters who accept commercial advertising are obligated under the First Amendment to make time available for political messages as well. Justice Stewart's opinion closes with these words: "If we must choose whether editorial decisions are to be made in the free judgment of individual broadcasters, or imposed by bureaucratic fiat, the choice must be for freedom." The cleavage on the Court illustrates the ambiguities of liberty and the liberal philosophy.

Should the CBS decision apply in the realm of cable television, where broadcast frequencies are much more numerous? See Pemberton, The Right of Access to Mass Media, in The Right of Americans 177 (N. Dorsen ed. 1971).

Compare Lehman v. City of Shaker Heights, 418 U.S. 298 (1974), upholding the refusal of a public mass transportation system to accept political advertising, although it accepted commercial advertisements. See Note, The Supreme Court, 1973 Term, 88 Harv. L. Rev. 41, 149-156 (1974).

Are the same considerations applicable to newspapers? See Barron, Access to the Press — A New First Amendment Right, 80 Harv. L. Rev. 1641 (1967); Note, Resolving the Free Speech-Free Press Dichotomy: Access to the Press Through Advertising, 32 U. Fla. L. Rev. 293 (1969).

Bigelow v. Virginia 421 U.S. 809, 95 S. Ct. 2222, 44 L. Ed. 2d 600 (1975)

MR. JUSTICE BLACKMUN delivered the opinion of the Court. . . .

The Virginia Weekly was a newspaper published by the Virginia Weekly Associates of Charlottesville. It was issued in that city and circulated in Albemarle County, with particular focus on the campus of the University of Virginia. Appellant, Jeffrey C. Bigelow, was a director and the managing editor and responsible officer of the newspaper.

On February 8, 1971, the Weekly's Vol. V, N. 6, was published and circulated under the direct responsibility of the appellant. On page 2 of that issue was the following advertisement:

> "UNWANTED PREGNANCY
> LET US HELP YOU
> Abortions are now legal in New York.
> FOR IMMEDIATE PLACEMENT IN ACCREDITED
> HOSPITALS AND CLINICS AT LOW COST
> Contact
> WOMEN'S PAVILION
> 515 Madison Avenue
> New York, N. Y. 10022
> or call any time
> (212) 371-6670 or (212) 371-6650
> AVAILABLE 7 DAYS A WEEK
> STRICTLY CONFIDENTIAL. We will make
> all arrangements for you and help you
> with information and counseling."

On May 13 Bigelow was charged with violating Va. Code Ann. § 18.1-63 (1960). The statute at that time read: "If any person, by publication, lecture, advertisement, or by the sale or circulation of any publication, or in any other manner, encourage or prompt the procuring of abortion or miscarriage, he shall be guilty of a misdemeanor."[2]

[Bigelow's conviction, affirmed by the Supreme Court of Virginia, was vacated by the Supreme Court and remanded for further consideration in the light of Roe v. Wade and Doe v. Bolton, page 1119 supra. The Supreme Court of Virginia affirmed again, finding nothing in Roe or Doe "which in any way affects our earlier view," 214 Va. 341, 342, 200 S.E.2d 680, and Bigelow appealed.

The Court declined to consider an overbreadth challenge to the statute which was the basis for the conviction of Bigelow. An amendment to the statute, passed after Bigelow published the advertisement, prohibited the solicitation or encouragement only of illegal abortions. Since the new statute would not have the effect of "chill[ing] the rights of others," the Court concluded that the overbreadth issue "had become moot for the future."]

The central assumption made by the Supreme Court of Virginia was that the First Amendment guarantees of speech and press are inapplicable to paid commercial advertisements. Our cases, however, clearly establish that speech is not stripped of First Amendment protection merely because it appears in that form. Pittsburgh Press Co. v. Human Rel. Comm'n, 413 U.S. 376, 384 (1973); New York Times Co. v. Sullivan, 376 U.S. 254, 266 (1964).

The appellee, as did the Supreme Court of Virginia, relies on Valentine v. Chresten-

---

[2] We were advised by the State at oral argument that the statute dated back to 1878, and that Bigelow's was the first prosecution under the statute "in modern times," and perhaps the only prosecution under it "at any time." Tr. of Oral Arg. 40. The statute appears to have its origin in Va. Acts of Assembly 1877-1878, p. 281, c. 2, §8.

sen, 316 U.S. 52 (1942), where a unanimous Court, in a brief opinion, sustained an ordinance which had been interpreted to ban the distribution of a handbill advertising the exhibition of a submarine. The handbill solicited customers to tour the ship for a fee. The promoter-advertiser had first attempted to distribute a single-faced handbill consisting only of the advertisement, and was denied permission to do so. He then had printed, on the reverse side of the handbill, a protest against official conduct refusing him the use of wharfage facilities. The Court found that the message of asserted "public interest" was appended solely for the purpose of evading the ordinance and therefore did not constitute an "exercise of the freedom of communicating information and disseminating opinion." Id., at 54. . . .

The principle that commercial advertising enjoys a degree of First Amendment protection was reaffirmed [after New York Times Co. v. Sullivan] in Pittsburgh Press Co. v. Human Rel. Comm'n, 413 U.S. 376 (1973). There, the Court, although divided, sustained an ordinance that had been construed to forbid newspapers to carry help-wanted advertisements in sex-designated columns except where based upon a bona fide occupational exemption. The Court did describe the advertisements at issue as "classic examples of commercial speech," for each was "no more than a proposal of possible employment." Id., at 385. But the Court indicated that the advertisements would have received some degree of First Amendment protection if the commercial proposal had been legal. The illegality of the advertised activity was particularly stressed. . . .

The legitimacy of appellant's First Amendment claim in the present case is demonstrated by the important differences between the advertisement presently at issue and those involved in Chrestensen and in Pittsburgh Press. The advertisement published in appellant's newspaper did more than simply propose a commercial transaction. It contained factual material of clear "public interest." Portions of its message, most prominently the lines, "Abortions are now legal in New York. There are no residency requirements," involve the exercise of the freedom of communicating information and disseminating opinion.

Viewed in its entirety, the advertisement conveyed information of potential interest and value to a diverse audience — not only to readers possibly in need of the services offered, but also to those with a general curiosity about, or genuine interest in, the subject matter or the law of another State and its development, and to readers seeking reform in Virginia. The mere existence of the Women's Pavilion in New York City, with the possibility of its being typical of other organizations there, and the availability of the services offered, were not unnewsworthy. Also, the activity advertised pertained to constitutional interests. See Roe v. Wade, 410 U.S. 113 (1973), and Doe v. Bolton, 410 U.S. 179 (1973). Thus, in this case, appellant's First Amendment interests coincided with the constitutional interests of the general public.

Moreover, the placement services advertised in appellant's newspaper were legally provided in New York at that time. The Virginia Legislature could not have regulated the advertiser's activity in New York, and obviously could not have proscribed the activity in that State. Huntington v. Attrill, 146 U.S. 657, 669 (1892).

We conclude, therefore, that the Virginia courts erred in their assumptions that advertising, as such, was entitled to no First Amendment protection and that appellant Bigelow had no legitimate First Amendment interest. We need not decide in this case the precise extent to which the First Amendment permits regulation of advertising that is related to activities the State may legitimately regulate or even prohibit.[10]

[10] Nor need we comment here on the First Amendment ramifications of legislative prohibitions of certain kinds of advertising in the electronic media, where the "unique characteristics" of this form of communication "make it especially subject to regulation in the public interest." Capital Broadcasting Co. v. Mitchell, 333 F. Supp. 582, 584 (DC 1971), aff'd, 405 U.S. 1000 (1972). See also Banzhaf v. FCC, 132 U.S. App. D.C. 14, 405 F.2d 1082 (1968), cert. denied sub nom. Tobacco Institute, Inc. v. FCC, 396 U.S. 842 (1969); Columbia Broadcasting System, Inc. v. Democratic National Committee, 412 U.S. 94 (1973).

Advertising, like all public expression, may be subject to reasonable regulation that serves a legitimate public interest. See Pittsburgh Press Co. v. Human Rel. Comm'n, supra; Lehman v. City of Shaker Heights, 418 U.S. 298 (1974). To the extent that commercial activity is subject to regulation, the relationship of speech to that activity may be one factor, among others, to be considered in weighing the First Amendment interest against the governmental interest alleged. . . .

The task of balancing the interests at stake here was one that should have been undertaken by the Virginia courts before they reached their decision. We need not remand for that purpose, however, because the outcome is readily apparent from what has been said above.

In support of the statute, the appellee contends that the commercial operations of abortion referral agencies are associated with practices, such as fee splitting, that tend to diminish, or at least adversely affect, the quality of medical care, and that advertising of these operations will lead women to seek services from those who are interested only or mainly in financial gain apart from professional integrity and responsibility.

The State, of course, has a legitimate interest in maintaining the quality of medical care provided within its borders. Barsky v. Board of Regents, 347 U.S. 442, 451 (1954). No claim has been made, however, that this particular advertisement in any way affected the quality of medical services within Virginia. As applied to Bigelow's case, the statute was directed at the publishing of informative material relating to services offered in another State and was not directed at advertising by a referral agency or a practitioner whose activity Virginia had authority or power to regulate.

To be sure, the agency-advertiser's practices, although not then illegal, may later have proved to be at least "inimical to the public interest" in New York. S.P.S. Consultants, Inc. v. Lefkowitz, 333 F. Supp. 1373, 1378 (S.D.N.Y. 1971). But this development would not justify a Virginia statute that forbids Virginians from using in New York the then legal services of a local New York agency. Here, Virginia is really asserting an interest in regulating what Virginians may *hear* or *read* about the New York services. It is, in effect, advancing an interest in shielding its citizens from information about activities outside Virginia's borders, activities that Virginia's police powers do not reach. This asserted interest, even if understandable, was entitled to little, if any, weight under the circumstances.

No claim has been made, nor could any be supported on this record, that the advertisement was deceptive or fraudulent, or that it related to a commodity or service that was then illegal in either Virginia or in New York, or that it otherwise furthered a criminal scheme in Virginia. There was no possibility that appellant's activity would invade the privacy of other citizens, Breard v. Alexandria, supra, or infringe on other rights. Observers would not have the advertiser's message thrust upon them as a captive audience. Lehman v. City of Shaker Heights, supra; Packer Corp. v. Utah, 285 U.S. 105, 110 (1932).

The strength of appellant's interest was augmented by the fact that the statute was applied against him as publisher and editor of a newspaper, not against the advertiser or a referral agency or a practitioner. The prosecution thus incurred more serious First Amendment overtones.

If application of this statute were upheld under these circumstances, Virginia might exert the power sought here over a wide variety of national publications or interstate newspapers carrying advertisements similar to the one that appeared in Bigelow's newspaper or containing articles on the general subject matter to which the advertisement referred.

Our decision also is in no way inconsistent with our holdings in the Fourteenth Amendment cases that concern the regulation of professional activity. See North Dakota Pharmacy Bd. v. Snyder's Stores, 414 U.S. 156 (1973); Head v. New Mexico Board, 374 U.S. 424 (1963); Williamson v. Lee Optical Co., 348 U.S. 483 (1955); Barsky v. Board of Regents, 347 U.S. 442 (1954); Semler v. Dental Examiners, 294 U.S. 608 (1935).

Other States might do the same. The burdens thereby imposed on publications would impair, perhaps severely, their proper functioning. See Miami Herald Publishing Co. v. Tornillo, 418 U.S. 241, 257-258 (1974). . . .

We conclude that Virginia could not apply Va. Code Ann. § 18.1-63 (1960), as it read in 1971, to appellant's publication of the advertisement in question without unconstitutionally infringing upon his First Amendment rights. The judgment of the Supreme Court of Virginia is therefore reversed.[bb]

It is so ordered.

NOTE Commercial Advertising

What would be the constitutionality of a state ban on the advertising by pharmacists of the retail prices of prescription drugs? Should it make any difference whether the parties seeking relief consist of consumers, pharmacists, or newspapers? See Virginia Citizens Consumer Council, Inc. v. State Bd. of Pharmacy, 425 U.S. 748 (1976).

How should the First Amendment accommodate the claims for advertising by attorneys? See 62 A.B.A.J. 470 (1976) for amendments to the Code of Professional Responsibility to allow fee advertising in telephone directories. See also Note, Bar Restrictions on Dissemination of Information about Legal Services, 22 U.C.L.A.L. Rev. 483 (1974). See generally Redish, The First Amendment in the Marketplace: Commercial Speech and the Values of Free Expression, 39 Geo. Wash. L. Rev. 429 (1971); Developments in the Law — Deceptive Advertising, 80 Harv. L. Rev. 1005 (1967).

c. Access by the Media

NOTE A Claimed Right of Access to Information

Consider the following selection from Lewis, Cantankerous, Obstinate, Ubiquitous: The Press, 1975 Utah L. Rev. 75, 92: "[W]e must recognize that the battleground for freedom of expression has shifted. The traditional issue was really freedom of *opinion;* that was the Holmesian marketplace for 'free trade in ideas.' Now the demand is for freedom to publish *facts* — a right that has become crucially important as the Government has cloaked more and more of its vital business in secrecy, denying the public the basis for political judgment. The trial judge in the Pentagon Papers case, Murray I. Gurfein, well understood the point. Reflecting the argument made to him by Alexander M. Bickel, counsel for The Times, Judge Gurfein wrote: 'In this case there has been no attempt by the Government . . . to stifle criticism. Yet in the last analysis it is not merely the opinion of the editorial writer or of the columnist which is protected by the First Amendment. It is the free flow of information so that the public will be informed about the Government and its action.' [328 F. Supp. 324, 331]."

In Pell v. Procunier, 417 U.S. 817 (1974), and Saxbe v. Washington Post Co., 417 U.S. 843 (1974), the Supreme Court upheld, 5 to 4, California and federal prison regulations banning press interviews with specific individual inmates. In Pell, the Court turned aside prisoner claims of a First Amendment right to meet individually with members of the press on the grounds that prisoners had alternative channels of communication with the outside world through the mails and authorized visitors, such as family members, friends, and clergy, and that the regulations were a proper exercise of the state's power to regulate the "time, place, and manner" of expression. The media plaintiffs argued that the regulations violated their First Amendment "right to gather news without govern-

---

[bb] A dissenting opinion of Justice Rehnquist, joined by Justice White, is omitted. — ED.

mental interference, . . . includ[ing] a right of access to the sources of what is regarded as newsworthy information." With regard to these claims, Justice Stewart, writing for the Court, first noted that members of the press were allowed access to the prisons to examine general prison conditions and to interview randomly selected prisoners and that the ban on interviews with specific prisoners served the goal of reducing disciplinary problems that arose when individual prisoners gain notoriety and influence within a prison. The Court concluded: "[N]ewsmen have no constitutional right of access to prisons or their inmates beyond that afforded the general public.

"The First and Fourteenth Amendments bar government from interfering in any way with a free press. The Constitution does not, however, require government to accord the press special access to information not shared by members of the public generally. It is one thing to say that a journalist is free to seek out sources of information not available to members of the general public, that he is entitled to some constitutional protection of such sources, cf. Branzburg v. Hayes, supra, and that government cannot restrain the publication of news emanating from such sources. Cf. New York Times Co. v. United States, [403 U.S. 713 (1971)]. It is quite another thing to suggest that the Constitution imposes upon government the affirmative duty to make available to journalists sources of information not available to members of the public generally. . . ."

In dissent Justice Powell stated: "I agree, of course, that neither any news organization nor reporters as individuals have constitutional rights superior to those enjoyed by ordinary citizens. The guarantees of the First Amendment broadly secure the rights of every citizen; they do not create special privileges for particular groups or individuals. . . . But I cannot follow the Court in concluding that *any* governmental restriction on press access to information, so long as it is nondiscriminatory, falls outside the purview of First Amendment concern.

". . . It goes too far to suggest that the government must justify under the stringent standards of First Amendment review every regulation that might affect in some tangential way the availability of information to the news media. But to my mind it is equally impermissible to conclude that no governmental inhibition of press access to newsworthy information warrants constitutional scrutiny. At some point official restraints on access to news sources, even though not directed solely at the press, may so undermine the function of the First Amendment that it is both appropriate and necessary to require the government to justify such regulations in terms more compelling than discretionary authority and administrative convenience. . . .

"What is at stake here is the societal function of the First Amendment in preserving free public discussion of governmental affairs. No aspect of that constitutional guarantee is more rightly treasured than its protection of the ability of our people through free and open debate to consider and resolve their own destiny. . . . And public debate must not only be unfettered; it must also be informed. For that reason this Court has repeatedly stated that First Amendment concerns encompass the receipt of information and ideas as well as the right of free expression. Kleindienst v. Mandel, 408 U.S. 753, 762 (1972); Red Lion Broadcasting Co. v. FCC, 395 U.S. 367, 390 (1969); Lamont v. Postmaster General, 381 U.S. 301 (1965); Martin v. City of Struthers, 319 U.S. 141, 143 (1943).

". . . No individual can obtain for himself the information needed for the intelligent discharge of his political responsibilities. . . . In seeking out the news the press therefore acts as an agent of the public at large. . . . By enabling the public to assert meaningful control over the political process, the press performs a crucial function in effecting the societal purposes of the First Amendment. . . .

"The constitutionally established role of the news media is directly implicated here. For good reasons, unrestrained public access is not permitted. The people must therefore depend on the press for information concerning public institutions. The Bureau [of Prison]'s absolute prohibition of prisoner-press interviews negatives the ability of the press to discharge that function and thereby substantially impairs the right of the people to a free flow of information and ideas on the conduct of their Government. The underlying right is the right of the public generally. The press is the necessary representative of the public's interest in this context and the instrumentality which effects the public's right. I therefore conclude that the Bureau's ban against personal interviews must be put to the test of First Amendment review."

See Note, Rights of the Public and the Press to Gather Information, 87 Harv. L. Rev. 1505 (1974).

Consider also the implications of the following excerpt from Justice Stewart's "Or of the Press," Address to the Yale Law School Sesquicentennial, 1974, printed at 26 Hastings L.J. 631, 633 (1975): "[T]he Free Press guarantee is, in essence, a *structural* provision of the Constitution. Most of the other provisions in the Bill of Rights protect specific liberties or specific rights of individuals: freedom of speech, freedom of worship, the right to counsel, the privilege against compulsory self-incrimination, to name a few. In contrast, the Free Press Clause extends protection to an institution. The publishing business is, in short, the only organized private business that is given explicit constitutional protection."[cc]

On the cognate problem of a journalist's privilege of confidentiality, see Branzburg v. Hayes, infra page 1310.

NOTE The Freedom of Information Act

Under the Freedom of Information Act of 1967, as amended in 1974, Pub. L. No. 93-502, 88 Stat. 1561, 5 U.S.C. §552 (Supp. IV 1974), federal agencies must respond promptly to requests for government records and documents made by anyone, including of course members of the press, and must furnish the information requested unless it falls within a category expressly excluded from the provisions of the act. All agencies and units of the federal government, except the President's immediate advisory staff, are subject to the act. Persons seeking information need provide only a "reasonable description" of the records desired. An agency must respond within 10 days, barring specific "unusual circumstances," and if the request is refused, state the reasons justifying its decision. A disappointed information-seeker may take the agency to court; and the act provides for accelerated judicial proceedings, places the burden of justification on the agency, and authorizes awards of attorney fees. Should the court find that an agency may have acted "arbitrarily or capriciously" in withholding information, the Civil Service Commission is required to investigate whether the personnel responsible for the withholding should be disciplined. The act further requires each federal agency to report annually to Congress on its response to Freedom of Information Act requests.

The records excluded from the disclosure requirements of the Act, as amended, are the following:

"matters that are —

"(1) (A) specifically authorized under criteria established by an Executive order to be kept secret in the interest of national defense or foreign policy and (B) are in fact properly classified pursuant to such Executive order;

"(2) related solely to the internal personnel rules and practices of an agency;

"(3) specifically exempted from disclosure by statute;

[cc] Cf. Grosjean v. American Press Co., 297 U.S. 233 (1936). Under the influence of Governor Huey Long, the Louisiana legislature enacted "a tax of two per cent on the gross receipts derived from advertisements carried in . . . newspapers when, and only when, the newspapers . . . enjoy a circulation of more than 20,000 copies per week." Id. at 244. The Court struck it down as "a deliberate and calculated device in the guise of a tax to limit the circulation of information to which the public is entitled in virtue of the constitutional guaranties." Id. at 250. Writing for the Court, Justice Sutherland concluded, "To allow [the press] to be fettered is to fetter ourselves." — ED.

1260   Chapter Sixteen. Substantive Rights

"(4) trade secrets and commercial or financial information obtained from a person and privileged or confidential;

"(5) inter-agency or intra-agency memorandums or letters which would not be available by law to a party other than an agency in litigation with the agency;

"(6) personnel and medical files and similar files the disclosure of which would constitute a clearly unwarranted invasion of personal privacy;

"(7) investigatory records compiled for law enforcement purposes, but only to the extent that the production of such records would (A) interfere with enforcement proceedings, (B) deprive a person of a right to a fair trial on an impartial adjudication, (C) constitute an unwarranted invasion of personal privacy, (D) disclose the identity of a confidential source and, in the case of a record compiled by a criminal law enforcement authority in the course of a criminal investigation, or by an agency conducting a lawful national security intelligence investigation, confidential information furnished only by the confidential source, (E) disclose investigative techniques and procedures, or (F) endanger the life or physical safety of law enforcement personnel;

"(8) contained in or relating to examination, operating, or condition reports prepared by, on behalf of, or for the use of an agency responsible for the regulation or supervision of financial institutions; or

"(9) geological and geophysical information and data, including maps, concerning wells.

"Any reasonably segregable portion of a record shall be provided to any person requesting such record after deletion of the portions which are exempt under this subsection."

See Association of the Bar of New York City, Amendments to the Freedom of Information Act (April 22, 1974); Clark, Holding Government Accountable: The Amended Freedom of Information Act: An Article in Honor of Fred Rodell, 84 Yale L.J. 741 (1975); Note, The Freedom of Information Act: A Seven-Year Assessment, 74 Colum. L. Rev. 895 (1974).

6. Political Campaigns

United Public Workers v. Mitchell 330 U.S. 75, 67 S. Ct. 556, 91 L. Ed. 754 (1947)

MR. JUSTICE REED delivered the opinion of the Court.

The Hatch Act, enacted in 1940, declares unlawful certain specified political activities of federal employees. Section 9 forbids officers and employees in the executive branch of the Federal Government, with exceptions, from taking "any active part in political management or in political campaigns." Section 15 declares that the activities theretofore determined by the United States Civil Service Commission to be prohibited to employees in the classified civil service of the United States by the Civil Service Rules shall be deemed to be prohibited to federal employees covered by the Hatch Act. These sections of the Act cover all federal officers and employees whether in the classified civil service or not and a penalty of dismissal from employment is imposed for violation. There is no designation of a single governmental agency for its enforcement.

For many years before the Hatch Act the Congress had authorized the exclusion of federal employees in the competitive classified service from active participation in political management and political campaigns. In June, 1938, the congressional authorization for exclusion had been made more effective by a Civil Service Commission disciplinary rule. That power to discipline members of the competitive classified civil service continues in the Commission under the Hatch Act by virtue of the present applicability of the Execu-

Section C. Freedom of Speech and Association

tive Order No. 8705, March 5, 1941. The applicable Civil Service Commission rules are printed in the margin.[6] . . .

The present appellants sought an injunction before a statutory three-judge district court of the District of Columbia against appellees, members of the United States Civil Service Commission, to prohibit them from enforcing against appellants the provisions of the second sentence of §9(a) of the Hatch Act for the reason that the sentence is repugnant to the Constitution of the United States. A declaratory judgment of the unconstitutionality of the sentence was also sought. The sentence referred to reads, "No officer or employee in the executive branch of the Federal Government . . . shall take any active part in political management or in political campaigns."

Various individual employees of the federal executive civil service and the United Public Workers of America, a labor union with these and other executive employees as members, as a representative of all its members, joined in the suit. It is alleged that the individuals desire to engage in acts of political management and in political campaigns. . . .

None of the appellants, except George P. Poole, has violated the provisions of the Hatch Act. They wish to act contrary to its provisions and those of §1 of the Civil Service Rules and desire a declaration of the legally permissible limits of regulation. Defendants moved to dismiss the complaint for lack of a justiciable case or controversy. The District Court determined that each of these individual appellants had an interest in their claimed privilege of engaging in political activities, sufficient to give them a right to maintain this suit. United Federal Workers of America (C.I.O.) v. Mitchell, 56 F. Supp. 621, 624. The District Court further determined that the questioned provision of the Hatch Act was valid and that the complaint therefore failed to state a cause of action. It accordingly dismissed the complaint and granted summary judgment to defendants. . . .

[The Court dismissed the complaints of all the appellants, except Poole, for lack of a justiciable case or controversy. Noting that "[n]o threat of interference by the Commission with rights of these appellants appears beyond that implied by the existence of the law and the regulations," the Court considered that the appellants with only "a hypothetical threat" of harm seemed to be seeking advisory opinions.]

. . . The appellant Poole does present by the complaint and affidavit matters appropriate for judicial determination.[23] The affidavits filed by appellees confirm that Poole has been charged by the Commission with political activity and a proposed order for his removal from his position adopted subject to his right under Commission procedure to reply to the charges and to present further evidence in refutation. We proceed to consider the

---

[6] 5 C.F.R., Cum. Supp., §1.1: "No interference with elections. No person in the executive civil service shall use his official authority or influence for the purpose of interfering with an election or affecting the results thereof. Persons who by the provisions of the rules in this chapter are in the competitive classified service, while retaining the right to vote as they please and to express their opinion on all political subjects, shall take no active part in political management or in political campaigns."

[23] "I have for a long time been interested in political activities. Both before and since my employment in the United States Mint, I have taken an active part in political campaigns and political management. In the 28th Ward, 7th Division in the City of Philadelphia I am and have been a Ward Executive Committeeman. In that position I have on many occasions taken an active part in political management and political campaigns. I have visited the residents of my Ward and solicited them to support my party and its candidates; I have acted as a watcher at the polls; I have contributed money to help pay for its expenses; I have circulated literature, placed banners and posters in public places, distributed leaflets, assisted in organizing political rallies and assemblies, and have done any and all acts which were asked of me in my capacity as a Ward Executive Committeeman. I have engaged in these activities both before and after my employment in the United States Mint. I intend to continue to engage in these activities on my own time as a private citizen, openly, freely, and without concealment.

"However, I have been served with a proposed order of the United States Civil Service Commission, dated January 12, 1944, which advises me that because of the political activities mentioned above, and for no other reason, 'it is . . . the opinion of this Commission that George P. Poole, an employee of the United States Mint at Philadelphia, Pennsylvania, has been guilty of political activity in violation of Section 1, Civil Service Rule I' and that unless I can refute the charges that I have engaged in political activity, I will be dismissed from my position as a Roller in the United States Mint at Philadelphia, Pennsylvania."

controversy over constitutional power at issue between Poole and the Commission as defined by the charge and preliminary finding upon one side and the admissions of Poole's affidavit upon the other. Our determination is limited to those facts. This proceeding so limited meets the requirements of defined rights and a definite threat to interfere with a possessor of the menaced rights by a penalty for an act done in violation of the claimed restraint. . . .

. . . This brings us to consider the narrow but important point involved in Poole's situation. Poole's stated offense is taking an "active part in political management or in political campaigns." He was a ward executive committeeman of a political party and was politically active on election day as a worker at the polls and a paymaster for the services of other party workers. The issue for decision and the only one we decide is whether such a breach of the Hatch Act and Rule 1 of the Commission can, without violating the Constitution, be made the basis for disciplinary action.

When the issue is thus narrowed, the interference with free expression is seen in better proportion as compared with the requirements of orderly management of administrative personnel. Only while the employee is politically active, in the sense of Rule 1, must he withhold expression of opinion on public subjects. See note 6. We assume that Mr. Poole would be expected to comment publicly as committeeman on political matters, so that indirectly there is an attenuated interference. . . .

As pointed out hereinbefore in this opinion, the practice of excluding classified employees from party offices and personal political activity at the polls has been in effect for several decades. Some incidents similar to those that are under examination here have been before this Court and the prohibition against certain types of political activity by officeholders has been upheld. The leading case was decided in 1882. Ex parte Curtis, 106 U.S. 371. There a subordinate United States employee was indicted for violation of an act that forbade employees who were not appointed by the President and confirmed by the Senate from giving money for political purposes from or to other employees of the government on penalty of discharge and criminal punishment. Curtis urged that the statute was unconstitutional. This Court upheld the right of Congress to punish the infraction of this law. The decisive principle was the power of Congress, within reasonable limits, to regulate, so far as it might deem necessary, the political conduct of its employees. . . .

The provisions of §9 of the Hatch Act and the Civil Service Rule 1 are not dissimilar in purpose from the statutes against political contributions of money. The prohibitions now under discussion are directed at political contributions of energy by government employees. These contributions, too, have a long background of disapproval. Congress and the President are responsible for an efficient public service. If, in their judgment, efficiency may be best obtained by prohibiting active participation by classified employees in politics as party officers or workers, we see no constitutional objection.

Another Congress may determine that, on the whole, limitations on active political management by federal personnel are unwise. The teaching of experience has evidently led Congress to enact the Hatch Act provisions. To declare that the present supposed evils of political activity are beyond the power of Congress to redress would leave the nation impotent to deal with what many sincere men believe is a material threat to the democratic system. Congress is not politically naive or regardless of public welfare or that of the employees. It leaves untouched full participation by employees in political decisions at the ballot box and forbids only the partisan activity of federal personnel deemed offensive to efficiency. With that limitation only, employees may make their contributions to public affairs to protect their own interests, as before the passage of the Act. . . .

Appellants urge that federal employees are protected by the Bill of Rights and that Congress may not "enact a regulation providing that no Republican, Jew or Negro shall be appointed to federal office, or that no federal employee shall attend Mass or take any active part in missionary work." None would deny such limitations on congressional power but, because there are some limitations, it does not follow that a prohibition against

Section C. **Freedom of Speech and Association** 1263

acting as ward leader or worker at the polls is invalid. A reading of the Act and Rule 1, notes 2 and 6, supra, together with the Commission's determination shows the wide range of public activities with which there is no interference by the legislation. It is only partisan political activity that is interdicted. It is active participation in political management and political campaigns. Expressions, public or private, on public affairs, personalities and matters of public interest, not an objective of party action, are unrestricted by law so long as the government employee does not direct his activities toward party success.

It is urged, however, that Congress has gone further than necessary in prohibiting political activity to all types of classified employees. It is pointed out by appellants "that the impartiality of many of these is a matter of complete indifference to the effective performance" of their duties. Mr. Poole would appear to be a good illustration for appellants' argument. The complaint states that he is a roller in the mint. We take it this is a job calling for the qualities of a skilled mechanic and that it does not involve contact with the public. Nevertheless, if in free time he is engaged in political activity, Congress may have concluded that the activity may promote or retard his advancement or preferment with his superiors. Congress may have thought that government employees are handy elements for leaders in political policy to use in building a political machine. For regulation of employees it is not necessary that the act regulated be anything more than an act reasonably deemed by Congress to interfere with the efficiency of the public service. There are hundreds of thousands of United States employees with positions no more influential upon policy determination than that of Mr. Poole. Evidently what Congress feared was the cumulative effect on employee morale of political activity by all employees who could be induced to participate actively. It does not seem to us an unconstitutional basis for legislation. . . .

The judgment of the District Court is accordingly affirmed.[dd]

Mr. Justice Murphy and Mr. Justice Jackson took no part in the consideration or decision of this case.

Mr. Justice Rutledge dissents as to Poole for the reasons stated by Mr. Justice Black. He does not pass upon the constitutional questions presented by the other appellants for the reason that he feels the controversy as to them is not yet appropriate for the discretionary exercise of declaratory judgment jurisdiction.

Mr. Justice Douglas, dissenting in part.

I disagree with the Court on two of the four matters decided.

First. There are twelve individual appellants here asking for an adjudication of their rights. The Court passes on the claim of only one of them, Poole. It declines to pass on the claims of the other eleven on the ground that they do not present justiciable cases or controversies. With this conclusion I cannot agree.

What these appellants propose to do is plain enough. If they do what they propose to do, it is clear that they will be discharged from their positions. . . .

On a discharge these employees would lose their jobs, their seniority, and other civil service benefits. They could, of course, sue in the Court of Claims. United States v. Lovett, 328 U.S. 303. But the remedy there is a money judgment, not a restoration to the office formerly held. Of course, there might be other remedies available in these situations to determine their rights to the offices from which they are discharged. See White v. Berry, 171 U.S. 366, 377. But to require these employees first to suffer the hardship of a discharge is not only to make them incur a penalty; it makes inadequate, if not wholly illusory, any legal remedy which they may have. . . .

Second. Poole is not in the administrative category of civil service. He is an industrial worker — a roller in the mint, a skilled laborer or artisan whose work or functions in no way affect the policy of the agency nor involve relationships with the public. . . .

. . . Poole, being an industrial worker, is as remote from contact with the public or

---

[dd] A concurring opinion of Mr. Justice Frankfurter is omitted, as is a dissent of Mr. Justice Black. — Ed.

from policy making or from the functioning of the administrative process as a charwoman. The fact that he is in the classified civil service is not, I think, relevant to the question of the degree to which his political activities may be curtailed. He is in a position not essentially different from one who works in the machine shop of a railroad or steamship which the Government runs, or who rolls aluminum in a manufacturing plant which the Government owns and operates. Can all of those categories of industrial employees constitutionally be insulated from American political life? If at some future time it should come to pass in this country, as it has in England, that a broad policy of state ownership of basic industries is inaugurated, does this decision mean that all of the hundreds of thousands of industrial workers affected could be debarred from the normal political activity which is one of our valued traditions?

The evils of the "spoils" system do not, of course, end with the administrative group of civil servants. History shows that the political regimentation of government industrial workers produces its own crop of abuses. Those in top policy posts or others in supervisory positions might seek to knit the industrial workers in civil service into a political machine. As a weapon they might seek to make the advancement of industrial workers dependent on political loyalty, on financial contributions, or on other partisan efforts. Or political activities of these workers might take place on government premises, on government time, or otherwise at government expense. These are special evils which would require a special treatment. . . .

The question is whether a permissible remedy is complete or partial political sterilization of the industrial group. . . . In other situations where the balance was between constitutional rights of individuals and a community interest which sought to qualify those rights, we have insisted that the statute be "narrowly drawn to define and punish specific conduct as constituting a clear and present danger to a substantial interest" of government. . . .

. . . It seems plain to me that that evil has its roots in the coercive activity of those in the hierarchy who have the power to regiment the industrial group or who undertake to do so. To sacrifice the political rights of the industrial workers goes far beyond any demonstrated or demonstrable need. Those rights are too basic and fundamental in our democratic political society to be sacrificed or qualified for anything short of a clear and present danger to the civil service system. No such showing has been made in the case of these industrial workers which justifies their political sterilization as distinguished from selective measures aimed at the coercive practices on which the spoils system feeds.

NOTE

United Public Workers v. Mitchell was reaffirmed in United States Civil Service Commn. v. National Assn. of Letter Carriers, 413 U.S. 548 (1973). See also Broadrick v. Oklahoma, 413 U.S. 601 (1973), upholding similar provisions of a state "Hatch Act." See Note, The Supreme Court, 1972 Term, 87 Harv. L. Rev. 1, 149-153 (1973).

The Code of Judicial Conduct, adopted by the American Bar Association in August 1972, provides as follows: "Canon 7B(1). A candidate, including an incumbent judge, for a judicial office that is filled either by public election between competing candidates or on the basis of a merit system election: (c) should not make pledges or promises of conduct in office other than the faithful and impartial performance of the duties of the office; announce his views on disputed legal or political issues; or misrepresent his identity, qualifications, present position, or other fact." Is the prohibition on the "announce[ment] of views on disputed legal or political issues" an overly broad remedy for whatever government interests are involved in elections for judicial office? See Kaufman, Problems in Professional Responsibility, c. 12 (1975).

Section C. **Freedom of Speech and Association**

Buckley v. Valeo 424 U.S. 1, 96 S. Ct. 612, 46 L. Ed. 2d 659 (1976)

PER CURIAM.*

These appeals present constitutional challenges to the key provisions of the Federal Election Campaign Act of 1971, as amended in 1974.[1]

The Court of Appeals, in sustaining the Act in large part against various constitutional challenges, viewed it as "by far the most comprehensive reform legislation [ever] passed by Congress concerning the election of the President, Vice-President, and members of Congress." 519 F.2d, at 831. The Act, summarized in broad terms, contains the following provisions: (a) individual political contributions are limited to $1,000 to any single candidate per election, with an overall annual limitation of $25,000 by any contributor; independent expenditures by individuals and groups "relative to a clearly identified candidate" are limited to $1,000 a year; campaign spending by candidates for various federal offices and spending for national conventions by political parties are subject to prescribed limits; (b) contributions and expenditures above certain threshold levels must be reported and publicly disclosed; (c) a system for public funding of Presidential campaign activities is established by Subtitle H of the Internal Revenue Code;[3] and (d) a Federal Election Commission is established to administer and enforce the Act.

This suit was originally filed by appellants in the United States District Court for the District of Columbia. Plaintiffs included a candidate for the Presidency of the United States, a United States Senator who is a candidate for re-election, a potential contributor, the Committee for a Constitutional Presidency — McCarthy '76, the Conservative Party of the State of New York, the Mississippi Republican Party, the Libertarian Party, the New York Civil Liberties Union, Inc., the American Conservative Union, the Conservative Victory Fund, and Human Events, Inc. The defendants included the Secretary of the United States Senate and the Clerk of the United States House of Representatives, both in their official capacities and as ex officio members of the Federal Election Commission. The Commission itself was named as a defendant. Also named were the Attorney General of the United States and the Comptroller General of the United States.

. . . [T]he District Judge entered a memorandum order adopting extensive findings of fact and transmitting the augmented record back to the Court of Appeals.

On plenary review, a majority of the Court of Appeals rejected, for the most part, appellants' constitutional attacks. [519 F.2d 821 (D.C. Cir. 1975).]

In this Court, appellants argue that the Court of Appeals failed to give this legislation the critical scrutiny demanded under accepted First Amendment and equal protection principles. . . .

I. CONTRIBUTION AND EXPENDITURE LIMITATIONS

The intricate statutory scheme adopted by Congress to regulate federal election campaigns includes restrictions on political contributions and expenditures that apply broadly to all phases of and all participants in the election process. The major contribution and expenditure limitations in the Act prohibit individuals from contributing more than

---

* The Court issued a per curiam opinion, in which Brennan, Stewart, and Powell, JJ., joined; in all but Part I-C-2 of which Marshall, J., joined; in all but Part I-B of which Blackmun, J., joined; in all but Part III-B-1 of which Rehnquist, J., joined; in Parts I-C and IV (except insofar as it accords de facto validity for past acts of the Commission) of which Burger, C.J., joined; and in Part III of which White, J., joined. Burger, C.J., and White, Marshall, Blackmun, and Rehnquist, JJ., filed opinions concurring in part and dissenting in part. Stevens, J., took no part in the consideration or decision of these cases. [From headnote.]

[1] Federal Election Campaign Act of 1971, Pub. L. No. 92-225, 86 Stat. 3, as amended, Federal Election Campaign Act Amendments of 1974, Pub. L. No. 93-443, 83 Stat. 1263. . . .

[3] The Revenue Act of 1971, Pub. L. No. 92-178, 85 Stat. 562, as amended, Pub. L. No. 93-53, 87 Stat. 138, as amended, Federal Election Campaign Act Amendments of 1974, Pub. L. No. 93-443, 88 Stat. 1291. This Subtitle consists of two parts: Chapter 95 deals with funding national party conventions and general election campaigns for President, and Chapter 96 deals with matching funds for Presidential primary campaigns.

$25,000 in a single year or more than $1,000 to any single candidate for an election campaign and from spending more than $1,000 a year "relative to a clearly identified candidate." Other provisions restrict a candidate's use of personal and family resources in his campaign and limit the overall amount that can be spent by a candidate in campaigning for federal office.

The constitutional power of Congress to regulate federal elections is well established and is not questioned by any of the parties in this case. Thus, the critical constitutional questions presented here go not to the basic power of Congress to legislate in this area, but to whether the specific legislation that Congress has enacted interferes with First Amendment freedoms or invidiously discriminates against nonincumbent candidates and minor parties in contravention of the Fifth Amendment.

A. *General Principles*

The Act's contribution and expenditure limitations operate in an area of the most fundamental First Amendment activities. Discussion of public issues and debate on the qualifications of candidates are integral to the operation of the system of government established by our Constitution. The First Amendment affords the broadest protection to such political expression in order "to assure the unfettered interchange of ideas for the bringing about of political and social changes desired by the people." Roth v. United States, 354 U.S. 476, 484 (1957). . . .

The First Amendment protects political association as well as political expression. The constitutional right of association explicated in NAACP v. Alabama, 357 U.S. 449, 460 (1958), stemmed from the Court's recognition that "[e]ffective advocacy of both public and private points of view, particularly controversial ones, is undeniably enhanced by group association." . . .

It is with these principles in mind that we consider the primary contentions of the parties with respect to the Act's limitations upon the giving and spending of money in political campaigns. Those conflicting contentions could not more sharply define the basic issues before us. Appellees contend that what the Act regulates is conduct, and that its effect on speech and association is incidental at most. Appellants respond that contributions and expenditures are at the very core of political speech, and that the Act's limitations thus constitute restraints on First Amendment liberty that are both gross and direct.

In upholding the constitutional validity of the Act's contribution and expenditure provisions on the ground that those provisions should be viewed as regulating conduct not speech, the Court of Appeals relied upon United States v. O'Brien, 391 U.S. 367 (1968). See 519 F.2d, at 840. The O'Brien case involved a defendant's claim that the First Amendment prohibited his prosecution for burning his draft card because his act was "symbolic speech" engaged in as a " 'demonstration against the war and against the draft.' " 391 U.S., at 376. On the assumption that "the alleged communicative element in O'Brien's conduct [was] sufficient to bring into play the First Amendment," the Court sustained the conviction because it found "a sufficiently important governmental interest in regulating the nonspeech element" that was "unrelated to the suppression of free expression" and that had an "incidental restriction on alleged First Amendment freedoms . . . no greater than [was] essential to the furtherance of that interest." Id., at 376-377. The Court expressly emphasized that O'Brien was not a case "where the alleged governmental interest in regulating conduct arises in some measure because the communication allegedly integral to the conduct is itself thought to be harmful." Id., at 382.

We cannot share the view that the present Act's contribution and expenditure limitations are comparable to the restrictions on conduct upheld in O'Brien. The expenditure of money simply cannot be equated with such conduct as destruction of a draft card. Some forms of communication made possible by the giving and spending of money involve speech alone, some involve conduct primarily, and some involve a combination of the two. Yet this Court has never suggested that the dependence of a communication on the expenditure of money operates itself to introduce a nonspeech element or to reduce the exacting scrutiny required by the First Amendment. See Bigelow v. Virginia, 421 U.S. 809, 820 (1975); New York Times Co. v. Sullivan, 376 U.S., at 266. . . .

Even if the categorization of the expenditure of money as conduct were accepted, the limitations challenged here would not meet the O'Brien test because the governmental interests advanced in support of the Act involve "suppressing communication." The interests served by the Act include restricting the voices of people and interest groups who have money to spend and reducing the overall scope of federal election campaigns. Although the Act does not focus on the ideas expressed by persons or groups subjected to its regulations, it is aimed in part at equalizing the relative ability of all voters to affect electoral outcomes by placing a ceiling on expenditures for political expression by citizens and groups. Unlike O'Brien, where the Selective Service System's administrative interest in the preservation of draft cards was wholly unrelated to their use as a means of communication, it is beyond dispute that the interest in regulating the alleged "conduct" of giving or spending money "arises in some measure because the communication allegedly integral to the conduct is itself thought to be harmful." 391 U.S., at 382.

Nor can the Act's contribution and expenditure limitations be sustained, as some of the parties suggest, by reference to the constitutional principles reflected in such decisions as Cox v. Louisiana, supra, Adderley v. Florida, 385 U.S. 39 (1966), and Kovacs v. Cooper, 336 U.S. 77 (1949). Those cases stand for the proposition that the government may adopt reasonable time, place, and manner regulations, which do not discriminate between speakers or ideas, in order to further an important governmental interest unrelated to the restriction of communication. See Erznoznik v. City of Jacksonville, 422 U.S. 205, 209 (1975). In contrast to O'Brien, where the method of expression was held to be subject to prohibition, Cox, Adderley, and Kovacs involved place or manner restrictions on legitimate modes of expression — picketing, parading, demonstrating, and using a soundtruck. The critical difference between this case and those time, place and manner cases is that the present Act's contribution and expenditure limitations impose direct quantity restrictions on political communication and association by persons, groups, candidates and political parties in addition to any reasonable time, place, and manner regulations otherwise imposed.[17]

A restriction on the amount of money a person or group can spend on political communication during a campaign necessarily reduces the quantity of expression by restricting the number of issues discussed, the depth of their exploration, and the size of the audience reached. This is because virtually every means of communicating ideas in today's mass society requires the expenditure of money. The distribution of the humblest handbill or leaflet entails printing, paper, and circulation costs. Speeches and rallies generally necessitate hiring a hall and publicizing the event. The electorate's increasing dependence on television, radio, and other mass media for news and information has made these expensive modes of communication indispensable instruments of effective political speech.

The expenditure limitations contained in the Act represent substantial rather than merely theoretical restraints on the quantity and diversity of political speech. The $1,000

---

[17] The nongovernmental appellees argue that just as the decibels emitted by a sound truck can be regulated consistent with the First Amendment, Kovacs, supra, the Act may restrict the volume of dollars in political campaigns without impermissibly restricting freedom of speech. See Freund, Commentary in A. Rosenthal, Federal Regulation of Campaign Finance: Some Constitutional Questions 72 (1971). This comparison underscores a fundamental misconception. The decibel restriction upheld in Kovacs limited the *manner* of operating a sound truck but not the *extent* of its proper use. By contrast, the Act's dollar ceilings restrict the extent of the reasonable use of virtually every means of communicating information. As the Kovacs Court emphasized, the nuisance ordinance only barred sound trucks from broadcasting "in a loud and raucous manner on the streets," 336 U.S., at 89, and imposed "no restriction upon the communication of ideas or discussion of issues by the human voice, by newspapers, by pamphlets, by dodgers" or by sound trucks operating at a reasonable volume. Ibid. See Saia v. New York, 334 U.S. 558, 561-562 (1948).

ceiling on spending "relative to a clearly identified candidate," 18 U.S.C. §608(e)(1), would appear to exclude all citizens and groups except candidates, political parties and the institutional press from any significant use of the most effective modes of communication.[20] Although the Act's limitations on expenditures by campaign organizations and political parties provide substantially greater room for discussion and debate, they would have required restrictions in the scope of a number of past congressional and Presidential campaigns and would operate to constrain campaigning by candidates who raise sums in excess of the spending ceiling.

By contrast with a limitation upon expenditures for political expression, a limitation upon the amount that any one person or group may contribute to a candidate or political committee entails only a marginal restriction upon the contributor's ability to engage in free communication. A contribution serves as a general expression of support for the candidate and his views, but does not communicate the underlying basis for the support. The quantity of communication by the contributor does not increase perceptibly with the size of his contribution, since the expression rests solely on the undifferentiated, symbolic act of contributing. At most, the size of the contribution provides a very rough index of the intensity of the contributor's support for the candidate. A limitation on the amount of money a person may give to a candidate or campaign organization thus involves little direct restraint on his political communication, for it permits the symbolic expression of support evidenced by a contribution but does not in any way infringe the contributor's freedom to discuss candidates and issues. While contributions may result in political expression if spent by a candidate or an association to present views to the voters, the transformation of contributions into political debate involves speech by someone other than the contributor.

In sum, although the Act's contribution and expenditure limitations both implicate fundamental First Amendment interests, its expenditure ceilings impose significantly more severe restrictions on protected freedoms of political expression and association than do its limitations on financial contributions.

B. Contribution Limitations

1. The $1,000 Limitation on Contributions by Individuals and Groups to Candidates and Authorized Campaign Committees. Section 608(b) provides, with certain limited exceptions, that "no person shall make contributions to any candidate with respect to any election for Federal office which, in the aggregate, exceeds $1,000." . . .

Appellants contend that the $1,000 contribution ceiling unjustifiably burdens First Amendment freedoms, employs overbroad dollar limits, and discriminates against candidates opposing incumbent officeholders and against minor-party candidates in violation of the Fifth Amendment. We address each of these claims of invalidity in turn.

. . . In view of the fundamental nature of the right to associate, governmental "action which may have the effect of curtailing the freedom to associate is subject to the closest scrutiny." NAACP v. Alabama, supra, at 460-461. Yet, it is clear that "[n]either the right to associate nor the right to participate in political activities is absolute." Civil Service Comm'n v. Letter Carriers, 413 U.S. 548, 567 (1973). Even a " 'significant interference' with protected rights of political association" may be sustained if the State demonstrates a sufficiently important interest and employs means closely drawn to avoid unnecessary abridgment of associational freedoms. Cousins v. Wigoda, 419 U.S., at 488; NAACP v. Button, supra, at 438; Shelton v. Tucker, supra, at 488.

Appellees argue that the Act's restrictions on large campaign contributions are justified

---

[20] The record indicates that, as of January 1, 1975, one full-page advertisement in a daily edition of a certain metropolitan newspaper cost $6,971.04 — almost seven times the annual limit on expenditures "relative to" a particular candidate imposed on the vast majority of individual citizens and associations by §608(e)(1).

by three governmental interests. According to the parties and amici, the primary interest served by the limitations and, indeed, by the Act as a whole, is the prevention of corruption and the appearance of corruption spawned by the real or imagined coercive influence of large financial contributions on candidates' positions and on their actions if elected to office. Two "ancillary" interests underlying the Act are also allegedly furthered by the $1,000 limits on contributions. First, the limits serve to mute the voices of affluent persons and groups in the election process and thereby to equalize the relative ability of all citizens to affect the outcome of elections. Second, it is argued, the ceilings may to some extent act as a brake on the skyrocketing cost of political campaigns and thereby serve to open the political system more widely to candidates without access to sources of large amounts of money.

It is unnecessary to look beyond the Act's primary purpose — to limit the actuality and appearance of corruption resulting from large individual financial contributions — in order to find a constitutionally sufficient justification for the $1,000 contribution limitation. . . . To the extent that large contributions are given to secure political quid pro quos from current and potential office holders, the integrity of our system of representative democracy is undermined. Although the scope of such pernicious practices can never be reliably ascertained, the deeply disturbing examples surfacing after the 1972 election demonstrate that the problem is not an illusory one.[28]

Of almost equal concern as the danger of actual quid pro quo arrangements is the impact of the appearance of corruption stemming from public awareness of the opportunities for abuse inherent in a regime of large individual financial contributions. In Civil Service Comm'n v. Letter Carriers, supra, the Court found that the danger to "fair and effective government" posed by partisan political conduct on the part of federal employees charged with administering the law was a sufficiently important concern to justify broad restrictions on the employees' right of partisan political association. Here, as there, Congress could legitimately conclude that the avoidance of the appearance of improper influence "is also critical . . . if confidence in the system of representative Government is not to be eroded to a disastrous extent." Id., at 565.

Appellants contend that the contribution limitations must be invalidated because bribery laws and narrowly-drawn disclosure requirements constitute a less restrictive means of dealing with "proven and suspected quid pro quo arrangements." But laws making criminal the giving and taking of bribes deal with only the most blatant and specific attempts of those with money to influence governmental action. And while disclosure requirements serve the many salutary purposes discussed elsewhere in this opinion, Congress was surely entitled to conclude that disclosure was only a partial measure, and that contribution ceilings were a necessary legislative concomitant to deal with the reality or appearance of corruption inherent in a system permitting unlimited financial contributions, even when the identities of the contributors and the amounts of their contributions are fully disclosed.

[The Court also did not accept contentions that the contribution ceiling of $1000 was an overbroad remedy for the problems of improper influence.]

Apart from these First Amendment concerns, appellants argue that the contribution limitations work such an invidious discrimination between incumbents and challengers that the statutory provisions must be declared unconstitutional on their face. In considering this contention, it is important at the outset to note that the Act applies the same limitations on contributions to all candidates regardless of their present occupations, ideological views, or party affiliations. Absent record evidence of invidious discrimination against challengers as a class, a court should generally be hesitant to invalidate legislation which on its face imposes evenhanded restrictions. Cf. James v. Valtierra, 402 U.S. 137 (1971).

---

[28] The Court of Appeals' opinion in this case discussed a number of the abuses uncovered after the 1972 elections. See 519 F.2d, at 839-840 & nn. 36-38.

There is no such evidence to support the claim that the contribution limitations in themselves discriminate against major-party challengers to incumbents. . . .

The charge of discrimination against minor-party and independent candidates is more troubling, but the record provides no basis for concluding that the Act invidiously disadvantages such candidates. . . .

2. *The $5,000 Limitation on Contributions by Political Committees.* Section 608(b)(2) of Title 18 permits certain committees, designated as "political committees" to contribute up to $5,000 to any candidate with respect to any election for federal office. In order to qualify for the higher contribution ceiling, a group must have been registered with the Commission as a political committee under 2 U.S.C. §433 for not less than 6 months, have received contributions from more than 50 persons and, except for state political party organizations, have contributed to five or more candidates for federal office. Appellants argue that these qualifications unconstitutionally discriminate against ad hoc organizations in favor of established interest groups and impermissibly burden free association. The argument is without merit. Rather than undermining freedom of association, the basic provision enhances the opportunity of bona fide groups to participate in the election process, and the registration, contribution, and candidate conditions serve the permissible purpose of preventing individuals from evading the applicable contribution limitations by labeling themselves committees.

3. *Limitations on Volunteers' Incidental Expenses.* The Act excludes from the definition of contribution "the value of services provided without compensation by individuals who volunteer a portion or all of their time on behalf of a candidate or political committee." §591(e)(5)(A). Certain expenses incurred by persons in providing volunteer services to a candidate are exempt from the $1,000 ceiling only to the extent that they do not exceed $500. . . .

If, as we have held, the basic contribution limitations are constitutionally valid, then surely these provisions are a constitutionally acceptable accommodation of Congress' valid interest in encouraging citizen participation in political campaigns while continuing to guard against the corrupting potential of large financial contributions to candidates. . . .

4. *The $25,000 Limitation on Total Contributions During any Calendar Year.* In addition to the $1,000 limitation on the nonexempt contributions that an individual may make to a particular candidate for any single election, the Act contains an overall $25,000 limitation on total contributions by an individual during any calendar year. §608(b)(3). . . . [T]his quite modest restraint upon protected political activity serves to prevent evasion of the $1,000 contribution limitation by a person who might otherwise contribute massive amounts of money to a particular candidate through the use of unearmarked contributions to political committees likely to contribute to that candidate, or huge contributions to the candidate's political party. . . .

C. *Expenditure Limitations*

The Act's expenditure ceilings impose direct and substantial restraints on the quantity of political speech. . . . It is clear that a primary effect of these expenditure limitations is to restrict the quantity of campaign speech by individuals, groups, and candidates. The restrictions, while neutral as to the ideas expressed, limit political expression "at the core of our electoral process and of First Amendment freedoms." Williams v. Rhodes, 393 U.S. 23, 32 (1968).

1. *The $1,000 Limitation on Expenditures "Relative to a Clearly Identified Candidate."* Section 608(e)(1) provides that "[n]o person may make any expenditure . . . relative to a clearly identified candidate during a calendar year which, when added to all other expenditures made by such person during the year advocating the election or defeat of such candidate, exceeds $1,000." . . . The provision, for example, would make it a federal criminal offense for a person or association to place a single one-quarter page ad-

vertisement "relative to a clearly identified candidate" in a major metropolitan newspaper.[46] . . .

. . . [I]n order to preserve the provision against invalidation on vagueness grounds, §608(e)(1) must be construed to apply only to expenditures for communications that in express terms advocate the election or defeat of a clearly identified candidate for federal office.

We turn then to the basic First Amendment question — whether §608(e)(1), even as thus narrowly and explicitly construed, impermissibly burdens the constitutional right of free expression. The Court of Appeals summarily held the provision constitutionally valid on the ground that "section 608(e) is a loophole-closing provision only" that is necessary to prevent circumvention of the contribution limitations. 519 F.2d, at 853. We cannot agree.

The discussion in Subpart I-A, supra, explains why the Act's expenditure limitations impose far greater restraints on the freedom of speech and association than do its contribution limitations. The markedly greater burden on basic freedoms caused by §608(e)(1) thus cannot be sustained simply by invoking the interest in maximizing the effectiveness of the less intrusive contribution limitations. Rather, the constitutionality of §608(e)(1) turns on whether the governmental interests advanced in its support satisfy the exacting scrutiny applicable to limitations on core First Amendment rights of political expression.

. . . [T]he independent advocacy restricted by the provision does not presently appear to pose dangers of real or apparent corruption comparable to those identified with large campaign contributions. The parties defending §608(e)(1) contend that it is necessary to prevent would-be contributors from avoiding the contribution limitations by the simple expedient of paying directly for media advertisements or for other portions of the candidate's campaign activities. They argue that expenditures controlled by or coordinated with the candidate and his campaign might well have virtually the same value to the candidate as a contribution and would pose similar dangers of abuse. Yet such controlled or coordinated expenditures are treated as contributions rather than expenditures under the Act. Section 608(b)'s contribution ceilings rather than §608(e)(1)'s independent expenditure limitation prevent attempts to circumvent the Act through prearranged or coordinated expenditures amounting to disguised contributions. By contrast, §608(e)(1) limits expenditures for express advocacy of candidates made totally independently of the candidate and his campaign. Unlike contributions, such independent expenditures may well provide little assistance to the candidate's campaign and indeed may prove counterproductive. The absence of prearrangement and coordination of an expenditure with the candidate or his agent not only undermines the value of the expenditure to the candidate, but also alleviates the danger that expenditures will be given as a quid pro quo for improper commitments from the candidate. Rather than preventing circumvention of the contribution limitations, §608(e)(1) severely restricts all independent advocacy despite its substantially diminished potential for abuse.

While the independent expenditure ceiling thus fails to serve any substantial governmental interest in stemming the reality or appearance of corruption in the electoral process, it heavily burdens core First Amendment expression. . . . Advocacy of the election or defeat of candidates for federal office is no less entitled to protection under the First Amendment than the discussion of political policy generally or advocacy of the passage or defeat of legislation.

It is argued, however, that the ancillary governmental interest in equalizing the relative ability of individuals and groups to influence the outcome of elections serves to justify the limitation on express advocacy of the election or defeat of candidates imposed by §608(e)(1)'s expenditure ceiling. But the concept that government may restrict the speech

---

[46] Section 608(i) provides that any person convicted of exceeding any of the contribution or expenditure limitations "shall be fined not more than $25,000 or imprisoned not more than 1 year, or both."

of some elements of our society in order to enhance the relative voice of others is wholly foreign to the First Amendment, which was designed "to secure 'the widest possible dissemination of information from diverse and antagonistic sources,' " and " 'to assure unfettered interchange of ideas for the bringing about of political and social changes desired by the people.' " New York Times Co. v. Sullivan, supra, at 266, 269, quoting Associated Press v. United States, 326 U.S. 1, 20 (1945), and Roth v. United States, 354 U.S., at 484. The First Amendment's protection against governmental abridgement of free expression cannot properly be made to depend on a person's financial ability to engage in public discussion. Cf. Eastern R. Conf. v. Noerr Motors, 365 U.S. 127, 139 (1961).[55]

For the reasons stated, we conclude that §608(e)(1)'s independent expenditure limitation is unconstitutional under the First Amendment.

2. *Limitation on Expenditures by Candidates from Personal or Family Resources.* The Act also sets limits on expenditures by a candidate "from his personal funds, or the personal funds of his immediate family, in connection with his campaigns during any calendar year." §608(a)(1). These ceilings vary from $50,000 for Presidential or Vice Presidential candidates to $35,000 for Senate candidates, and $25,000 for most candidates for the House of Representatives.

The primary governmental interest served by the Act — the prevention of actual and apparent corruption of the political process — does not support the limitation on the candidate's expenditure of his own personal funds. As the Court of Appeals concluded, "[m]anifestly, the core problem of avoiding undisclosed and undue influence on candidates from outside interests has lesser application when the monies involved come from the candidate himself or from his immediate family." 519 F.2d, at 855. Indeed, the use of personal funds reduces the candidate's dependence on outside contributions and thereby counteracts the coercive pressures and attendant risks of abuse to which the Act's contribution limitations are directed.

The ancillary interest in equalizing the relative financial resources of candidates competing for elective office, therefore, provides the sole relevant rationale for Section 608(a)'s expenditure ceiling. That interest is clearly not sufficient to justify the provision's infringement of fundamental First Amendment rights. First, the limitation may fail to promote financial equality among candidates. A candidate who spends less of his personal resources on his campaign may nonetheless outspend his rival as a result of more successful fundraising efforts. Indeed, a candidate's personal wealth may impede his efforts to persuade others that he needs their financial contributions or volunteer efforts to conduct an effective campaign. Second, and more fundamentally, the First Amendment simply cannot

---

[55] Neither the voting rights cases nor the Court's decision upholding the FCC's fairness doctrine lends support to appellees' position that the First Amendment permits Congress to abridge the rights of some persons to engage in political expression in order to enhance the relative voice of other segments of our society.

Cases invalidating governmentally imposed wealth restrictions on the right to vote or file as a candidate for public office rest on the conclusion that wealth "is not germane to one's ability to participate intelligently in the electoral process" and is therefore an insufficient basis on which to restrict a citizen's fundamental right to vote. Harper v. Virginia Bd. of Elections, 383 U.S. 663, 668 (1966). . . . [T]he principles that underlie invalidation of governmentally imposed restrictions on the franchise do not justify governmentally imposed restrictions on political expression. Democracy depends on a well-informed electorate, not a citizenry legislatively limited in its ability to discuss and debate candidates and issues.

In Red Lion Broadcasting Co. v. FCC, 395 U.S. 367 (1969), the Court upheld the political editorial and personal attack portions of the Communication Commission's fairness doctrine. That doctrine requires broadcast licensees to devote programming time to the discussion of controversial issues of public importance and to present both sides of such issues. Red Lion "makes clear that the broadcast media pose unique and special problems not present in the traditional free speech case," by demonstrating that " 'it is idle to posit an unabridgeable First Amendment right to broadcast comparable to the right of every individual to speak, write, or publish.' " Columbia Broadcasting System v. Democratic National Committee, 412 U.S. 94, 101 (1973), quoting Red Lion Broadcasting Co., supra, at 388. Red Lion therefore undercuts appellees' claim that §608(e)(1)'s limitations may permissibly restrict the First Amendment rights of individuals in this "traditional free speech case." Moreover, in contrast to the undeniable effect of §608(e)(1), the presumed effect of the fairness doctrine is one of "enhancing the volume and quality of coverage" of public issues. 395 U.S., at 393.

tolerate §608(a)'s restriction upon the freedom of a candidate to speak without legislative limit on behalf of his own candidacy. We therefore hold that §608(a)'s restrictions on a candidate's personal expenditures is unconstitutional.

3. *Limitations on Campaign Expenditures.* Section 608(c) of the Act places limitations on overall campaign expenditures by candidates seeking nomination for election and election to federal office. . . .

No governmental interest that has been suggested is sufficient to justify the restriction on the quantity of political expression imposed by §608(c)'s campaign expenditure limitations. The major evil associated with rapidly increasing campaign expenditures is the danger of candidate dependence on large contributions. The interest in alleviating the corrupting influence of large contributions is served by the Act's contribution limitations and disclosure provisions rather than by §608(c)'s campaign expenditure ceilings. The Court of Appeal's assertion that the expenditure restrictions are necessary to reduce the incentive to circumvent direct contribution limits is not persuasive. See 519 F.2d, at 859. There is no indication that the substantial criminal penalties for violating the contribution ceilings combined with the political repercussion of such violations will be insufficient to police the contribution provisions. Extensive reporting, auditing, and disclosure requirements applicable to both contributions and expenditures by political campaigns are designed to facilitate the detection of illegal contributions. Moreover, as the Court of Appeals noted, the Act permits an officeholder or successful candidate to retain contributions in excess of the expenditure ceiling and to use these funds for "any other lawful purpose." 2 U.S.C. §439a. This provision undercuts whatever marginal role the expenditure limitations might otherwise play in enforcing the contribution ceilings.

The interest in equalizing the financial resources of candidates competing for federal office is no more convincing a justification for restricting the scope of federal election campaigns. Given the limitation on the size of outside contributions, the financial resources available to a candidate's campaign, like the number of volunteers recruited, will normally vary with the size and intensity of the candidate's support. There is nothing invidious, improper, or unhealthy in permitting such funds to be spent to carry the candidate's message to the electorate. . . .

The campaign expenditure ceilings appear to be designed primarily to serve the governmental interests in reducing the allegedly skyrocketing costs of political campaigns. . . . The First Amendment denies government the power to determine that spending to promote one's political views is wasteful, excessive, or unwise. In the free society ordained by our Constitution it is not the government but the people — individually as citizens and candidates and collectively as associations and political committees — who must retain control over the quantity and range of debate on public issues in a political campaign.

For these reasons we hold that §608(c) is constitutionally invalid.

In sum, the provisions of the Act that impose a $1,000 limitation on contributions to a single candidate, §608(b)(1), a $5,000 limitation on contributions by a political committee to a single candidate, §608(b)(2), and a $25,000 limitation on total contributions by an individual during any calendar year, §608(b)(3), are constitutionally valid. These limitations along with the disclosure provisions, constitute the Act's primary weapons against the reality or appearance of improper influence stemming from the dependence of candidates on large campaign contributions. The contribution ceilings thus serve the basic governmental interest in safeguarding the integrity of the electoral process without directly impinging upon the rights of individual citizens and candidates to engage in political debate and discussion. By contrast, the First Amendment requires the invalidation of the Act's independent expenditure ceiling, §608(e)(1), its limitation on a candidate's expenditures from his own personal funds, §608(a), and its ceilings on overall campaign expenditures, §608(c). These provisions place substantial and direct restrictions on the ability of candidates, citizens, and associations to engage in protected political expression, restrictions that the First Amendment cannot tolerate.

II. REPORTING AND DISCLOSURE REQUIREMENTS

Unlike the limitations on contributions and expenditures imposed by 18 U.S.C. §608, the disclosure requirements of the Act, 2 U.S.C. §431 et seq., are not challenged by appellants as per se unconstitutional restrictions on the exercise of First Amendment freedoms of speech and association. Indeed, appellants argue that "narrowly drawn disclosure requirements are the proper solution to virtually all of the evils Congress sought to remedy." The particular requirements embodied in the Act are attacked as overbroad — both in their application to minor-party and independent candidates and in their extension to contributions as small as $10 or $100. Appellants also challenge the provision for disclosure by those who make independent contributions and expenditures, §434(e). The Court of Appeals found no constitutional infirmities in the provisions challenged here. We affirm the determination on overbreadth and hold that §434(e), if narrowly construed, also is within constitutional bounds.

The Act presently under review replaced all prior disclosure laws. Its primary disclosure provisions impose reporting obligations on "political committees" and candidates. . . .

Each political committee is required to register with the Commission, §433, and to keep detailed records of both contributions and expenditures, §§432(c), (d). These records are required to include the name and address of everyone making a contribution in excess of $10, along with the date and amount of the contribution. If a person's contributions aggregate more than $100, his occupation and principal place of business are also to be included. §432(c)(2). These files are subject to periodic audits and field investigations by the Commission. §438(a)(8).

Each committee and each candidate also is required to file quarterly reports. §434(a). The reports are to contain detailed financial information, including the full name, mailing address, occupation, and principal place of business of each person who has contributed over $100 in a calendar year, as well as the amount and date of the contributions. §434(b). They are to be made available by the Commission "for public inspection and copying." §438(a)(4). Every candidate for Federal office is required to designate a "principal campaign committee," which is to receive reports of contributions and expenditures made on the candidate's behalf from other political committees and to compile and file these reports, together with its own statements, with the Commission. §432(f).

Every individual or group, other than a political committee or candidate, who makes "contributions" or "expenditures" of over $100 in a calendar year "other than by contribution to a political committee or a candidate" is required to file a statement with the Commission. §434(e). Any violation of these record-keeping and reporting provisions is punishable by a fine of not more than $1,000 or a prison term of not more than a year, or both. §441(a).

A. *General Principles*

Unlike the overall limitations on contributions and expenditures, the disclosure requirements impose no ceiling on campaign-related activities. But we have repeatedly found that compelled disclosure, in itself, can seriously infringe on privacy of association and belief guaranteed by the First Amendment. E.g., Gibson v. Florida Legislative Investigation Comm., 372 U.S. 539 (1963); NAACP v. Button, 371 U.S. 415 (1963); Shelton v. Tucker, 364 U.S. 479 (1960); Bates v. Little Rock, 361 U.S. 516 (1960); NAACP v. Alabama, 357 U.S. 449 (1958).

We long have recognized that significant encroachments on First Amendment rights of the sort that compelled disclosure imposes cannot be justified by a mere showing of some legitimate governmental interest. Since Alabama we have required that the subordinating interests of the State must survive exacting scrutiny. We also have insisted that there be a "relevant correlation" or "substantial relation" between the governmental interest and the information required to be disclosed. . . .

Section C. Freedom of Speech and Association

The strict test established by Alabama is necessary because compelled disclosure has the potential for substantially infringing the exercise of First Amendment rights. But we have acknowledged that there are governmental interests sufficiently important to outweigh the possibility of infringement, particularly when the "free functioning of our national institutions" is involved. Communist Party v. Subversive Activities Control Bd., 367 U.S. 1, 97 (1961).

The governmental interests sought to be vindicated by the disclosure requirements are of this magnitude. They fall into three categories. First, disclosure provides the electorate with information "as to where political campaign money comes from and how it is spent by the candidate" in order to aid the voters in evaluating those who seek Federal office. . . .

Second, disclosure requirements deter actual corruption and avoid the appearance of corruption by exposing large contributions and expenditures to the light of publicity. . . .

Third, and not least significant, record-keeping, reporting and disclosure requirements are an essential means of gathering the data necessary to detect violations of the contribution limitations described above.

The disclosure requirements, as a general matter, directly serve substantial governmental interests. In determining whether these interests are sufficient to justify the requirements we must look to the extent of the burden that they place on individual rights.

It is undoubtedly true that public disclosure of contributions to candidates and political parties will deter some individuals who otherwise might contribute. In some instances, disclosure may even expose contributors to harassment or retaliation. These are not insignificant burdens on individual rights, and they must be weighed carefully against the interests which Congress has sought to promote by this legislation. . . .

B. Application to Minor Parties and Independents

Appellants contend that the Act's requirements are overbroad insofar as they apply to contributions to minor parties and independent candidates because the governmental interest in this information is minimal and the danger of significant infringement on First Amendment rights is greatly increased.

1. *Requisite Factual Showing.* In Alabama the organization had "made an uncontroverted showing that on past occasions revelation of the identity of its rank-and-file members [had] exposed these members to economic reprisal, loss of employment, threat of physical coercion, and other manifestations of public hostility," 357 U.S. at 462, and the State was unable to show that the disclosure it sought had a "substantial bearing" on the issues it sought to clarify, id., at 464. Under those circumstances, the Court held that "whatever interest the State may have in [disclosure] has not been shown to be sufficient to overcome petitioner's constitutional objections." Id., at 465.

The Court of Appeals rejected appellants' suggestion that this case fits into the Alabama mold. It concluded that substantial governmental interests in "informing the electorate and preventing the corruption of the political process" were furthered by requiring disclosure of minor parties and independent candidates, 519 F.2d, at 867, and therefore found no "tenable rationale for assuming that the public interest in minority party disclosure of contributions above a reasonable cut-off point is uniformly outweighed by potential contributors' associational rights," id., at 868. The court left open the question of the application of the disclosure requirements to candidates and parties who could demonstrate injury of the sort at stake in Alabama. No record of harassment on a similar scale was found in this case. We agree with the Court of Appeals' conclusion that Alabama is inapposite where, as here, any serious infringement on First Amendment rights brought about by the compelled disclosure of contributors is highly speculative.

2. *Blanket Exemption.* Appellants agree that "the record here does not reflect the kind of focused and insistent harassment of contributors and members that existed in the

NAACP cases." They argue, however, that a blanket exemption for minor parties is necessary lest irreparable injury be done before the required evidence can be gathered.

Where it exists the type of chill and harassment identified in Alabama can be shown. We cannot assume that courts will be insensitive to similar showings when made in future cases. We therefore conclude that a blanket exemption is not required.

C. Section 434(e)

Section 434(e) requires "[e]very person (other than a political committee or candidate) who makes contributions or expenditures" aggregating over $100 in a calendar year "other than by contribution to a political committee or candidate" to file a statement with the Commission. Unlike the other disclosure provisions, this section does not seek the contribution list of any association. Instead, it requires direct disclosure of what an individual or group contributes or spends.

. . . [Section] 434(e) as construed [to avoid vagueness] imposes independent reporting requirements on individuals and groups that are not candidates or political committees only in the following circumstances: (1) when they make contributions earmarked for political purposes or authorized or requested by a candidate or his agent, to some person other than a candidate or political committee, and (2) when they make an expenditure for a communication that expressly advocates the election or defeat of a clearly identified candidate.

. . . The burden imposed by §434(e) is no prior restraint, but a reasonable and minimally restrictive method of furthering First Amendment values by opening the basic processes of our federal election system to public view.

D. Thresholds

Appellants' third contention, based on alleged overbreadth, is that the monetary thresholds in the record-keeping and reporting provisions lack a substantial nexus with the claimed governmental interests, for the amounts involved are too low even to attract the attention of the candidate, much less have a corrupting influence.

The $10 and $100 [for recording and reporting] thresholds are indeed low. Contributors of relatively small amounts are likely to be especially sensitive to recording or disclosure of their political preferences. These strict requirements may well discourage participation by some citizens in the political process, a result that Congress hardly could have intended. Indeed, there is little in the legislative history to indicate that Congress focused carefully on the appropriate level at which to require recording and disclosure. Rather, it seems merely to have adopted the thresholds existing in similar disclosure laws since 1910. But we cannot require Congress to establish that it has chosen the highest reasonable threshold. The line is necessarily a judgmental decision, best left in the context of this complex legislation to congressional discretion. We cannot say, on this bare record, that the limits designated are wholly without rationality.[111] . . .

In summary, we find no constitutional infirmities in the record-keeping, reporting, and disclosure provisions of the Act.

III. PUBLIC FINANCING OF PRESIDENTIAL ELECTION CAMPAIGNS

A. Summary of Subtitle H

Section 9006 establishes a Presidential Election Campaign Fund, financed from general revenues in the aggregate amount designated by individual taxpayers, under §6096,

---

[111] "Looked at by itself without regard to the necessity behind it the line or point seems arbitrary. It might as well or nearly as well be a little more to one side or the other. But when it is seen that a line or point there must be, and that there is no mathematical or logical way of fixing it precisely, the decision of the legislature must be accepted unless we can say that it is very wide of any reasonable mark." Louisville Gas & Electric Co. v. Coleman, 277 U.S. 32, 41 (1928) (Holmes, J., dissenting).

who on their income tax returns may authorize payment to the Fund of one dollar of their tax liability in the case of an individual return or two dollars in the case of a joint return. The Fund consists of three separate accounts to finance (1) party nominating conventions, §9008(a), (2) general election campaigns, §9006(a), and (3) primary campaigns, §9037(a).

Chapter 95 of Title 26, which concerns financing of party nominating conventions and general election campaigns, distinguishes among "major," "minor," and "new" parties. A major party is defined as a party whose candidate for President in the most recent election received 25% or more of the popular vote. §9002(6). A minor party is defined as a party whose candidate received at least 5% but less than 25% of the vote at the most recent election. §9002(7). All other parties are new parties, §9002(8), including both newly created parties and those receiving less than 5% of the vote in the last election.

Major parties are entitled to $2,000,000 to defray their national committee Presidential nominating convention expenses, must limit total expenditures to that amount, §9008(d), and they may not use any of this money to benefit a particular candidate or delegate, §9008(c). A minor party receives a portion of the major-party entitlement determined by the ratio of the votes received by the party's candidate in the last election to the average of the votes received by the major-parties' candidates. §9008(b)(2). The amounts given to the parties and the expenditure limit are adjusted for inflation, using 1974 as the base year. §9008(b)(5). No financing is provided for new parties, nor is there any express provision for financing independent candidates or parties not holding a convention.

For expenses in the general election campaign, §9004(a)(1) entitles each major-party candidate to $20,000,000. This amount is also adjusted for inflation. See §9004(a)(1). To be eligible for funds the candidate must pledge not to incur expenses in excess of the entitlement under §9004(a)(1) and not to accept private contributions except to the extent that the fund is insufficient to provide the full entitlement. §9003(b). Minor-party candidates are also entitled to funding, again based on the ratio of the vote received by the party's candidate in the preceding election to the average of the major-party candidates. §9004(a)(2)(A). Minor-party candidates must certify that they will not incur campaign expenses in excess of the major-party entitlement and that they will accept private contributions only to the extent needed to make up the difference between that amount and the public funding grant. §9003(c). New-party candidates receive no money prior to the general election, but any candidate receiving 5% or more of the popular vote in the election is entitled to post-election payments according to the formula applicable to minor-party candidates. §9004(a)(3). Similarly, minor-party candidates are entitled to post-election funds if they receive a greater percentage of the average major-party vote than their party's candidate did in the preceding election; the amount of such payments is the difference between the entitlement based on the preceding election and that based on the actual vote in the current election. §9004(a)(3). A further eligibility requirement for minor- and new-party candidates is that the candidate's name must appear on the ballot, or electors pledged to the candidate must be on the ballot, in at least 10 States. §9002(2)(B).

Chapter 96 establishes a third account in the Fund, the Presidential Primary Matching Payment Account. §9037(a). This funding is intended to aid campaigns by candidates seeking Presidential nomination "by a political party," §9033(b)(2), in "primary elections," §9032(7). The threshold eligibility requirement is that the candidate raise at least $5,000 in each of 20 States, counting only the first $250 from each person contributing to the candidate. §§9033(b)(3), (4). In addition, the candidate must agree to abide by the spending limits in §9035. See §9033(b)(1). Funding is provided according to a matching formula: each qualified candidate is entitled to a sum equal to the total private contributions received, disregarding contributions from any person to the extent that total contributions to the candidate by that person exceed $250. §9034(a). Payments to any candidate under Chapter 96 may not exceed 50% of the overall expenditure ceiling accepted by the candidate. §9034(b).

B. Constitutionality of Subtitle H

Appellants argue that Subtitle H is invalid (1) as "contrary to the 'general welfare,'" Art. I, §8, (2) because any scheme of public financing of election campaigns is inconsistent with the First Amendment, and (3) because Subtitle H invidiously discriminates against certain interests in violation of the Due Process Clause of the Fifth Amendment. We find no merit in these contentions.

Appellants' "general welfare" contention erroneously treats the General Welfare Clause as a limitation upon congressional power. It is rather a grant of power, the scope of which is quite expansive, particularly in view of the enlargement of power by the Necessary and Proper Clause. McCulloch v. Maryland, 4 Wheat. 316, 420 (1819). Congress has power to regulate Presidential elections and primaries, United States v. Classic, 313 U.S. 299 (1941); Burroughs v. United States, 290 U.S. 534 (1934); and public financing of Presidential elections as a means to reform the electoral process was clearly a choice within the granted power. It is for Congress to decide which expenditures will promote the general welfare. . . . Any limitations upon the exercise of that granted power must be found elsewhere in the Constitution. . . .

[The Court also rejected the contention that the Free Speech Clause, by analogy to the command of "neutrality" of the Religion Clauses, itself constituted a limit to spending in this area.]

1. General Election Campaign Financing. Appellants insist that Chapter 95 falls short of the constitutional requirement in that the provisions provide larger, and equal, sums to candidates of major parties, use prior vote levels as the sole criterion for pre-election funding, limit new-party candidates to post-election funds, and deny any funds to candidates of parties receiving less than 5% of the vote. These provisions, it is argued, are fatal to the validity of the scheme, because they work invidious discrimination against minor and new parties in violation of the Fifth Amendment. We disagree.

. . . [A]ppellants have made no showing that the election funding plan disadvantages nonmajor parties by operating to reduce their strength below that attained without any public financing. First, such parties are free to raise money from private sources, and by our holding today new parties are freed from any expenditure limits, although admittedly those limits may be a largely academic matter to them. But since any major-party candidate accepting public financing of a campaign voluntarily assents to a spending ceiling, other candidates will be able to spend more in relation to the major-party candidates. The relative position of minor parties that do qualify to receive some public funds because they received 5% of the vote in the previous Presidential election is also enhanced. Public funding for candidates of major parties is intended as a substitute for private contributions; but for minor-party candidates such assistance may be viewed as a supplement to private contributions since these candidates may continue to solicit private funds up to the applicable spending limit. Thus, we conclude that the general election funding system does not work an invidious discrimination against candidates of nonmajor parties.

Appellants challenge reliance on the vote in past elections as the basis for determining eligibility. That challenge is foreclosed, however, by our holding in Jenness v. Fortson, 403 U.S., at 439-440, that popular vote totals in the last election are a proper measure of public support. And Congress was not obliged to select instead from among appellants' suggested alternatives. Congress could properly regard the means chosen as preferable, since the alternative of petition drives presents cost and administrative problems in validating signatures, and the alternative of opinion polls might be thought inappropriate since it would involve a government agency in the business of certifying polls or conducting its own investigation of support for various candidates, in addition to serious problems with reliability.

[With further findings of "reasonableness," the Court sustained the provisions for financing nominating conventions and primary election campaigns. Subtitle H, the Court also concluded, was severable from the expenditure limits held unconstitutional.]

Section C. Freedom of Speech and Association

IV. THE FEDERAL ELECTION COMMISSION

The 1974 Amendments to the Act create an eight-member Federal Election Commission, and vest in it primary and substantial responsibility for administering and enforcing the Act. The question that we address in this portion of the opinion is whether, in view of the manner in which a majority of its members are appointed, the Commission may under the Constitution exercise the powers conferred upon it. . . .

[Among the many provisions in its authority, the FEC is empowered and directed to receive the various reports required to be filed, to prescribe rules and regulations to carry out the Act, to issue advisory opinions, to disburse the various monies paid under the Act, and to institute civil actions for injunctive relief against activities violative of the Act. The FEC consists of eight members, with six having the right to vote. Two of these are selected by the President, two by the Speaker of the House, and two by the President pro tempore of the Senate. All must be confirmed by both Houses of Congress. The Court held that this method of selection violated the mandate of Art. II, §2, cl. 2 that "[The President] shall nominate . . . Ambassadors . . . Judges . . . and all other Officers of the United States." The Court found that in their enforcement and administrative powers the FEC members fell into the definition of "Officers" as "appointee[s] exercising significant authority pursuant to the laws of the United States." The Court, however, did accord de facto validity to the past acts of the FEC and stayed its judgment for 30 days.]

CONCLUSION

In summary, we sustain the individual contribution limits, the disclosure and reporting provisions, and the public financing scheme. We conclude, however, that the limitations on campaign expenditures, on independent expenditures by individuals and groups, and on expenditures by a candidate from his personal funds are constitutionally infirm. Finally, we hold that most of the powers conferred by the Act upon the Federal Election Commission can be exercised only by "Officers of the United States," appointed in conformity with Art. II, §2, cl. 2, of the Constitution, and therefore cannot be exercised by the Commission as presently constituted.

MR. CHIEF JUSTICE BURGER, concurring in part and dissenting in part.

For reasons set forth more fully later, I dissent from those parts of the Court's holding sustaining the Act's provisions (a) for disclosure of small contributions, (b) for limitations on contributions, and (c) for public financing of Presidential campaigns. In my view, the Act's disclosure scheme is impermissibly broad and violative of the First Amendment as it relates to reporting $10 and $100 contributions. The contribution limitations infringe on First Amendment liberties and suffer from the same infirmities that the Court correctly sees in the expenditure ceilings. The Act's system for public financing of Presidential campaigns is, in my judgment, an impermissible intrusion by the Government into the traditionally private political process.

More broadly, the Court's result does violence to the intent of Congress in this comprehensive scheme of campaign finance. By dissecting the Act bit by bit, and casting off vital parts, the Court fails to recognize that the whole of this Act is greater than the sum of its parts. Congress intended to regulate all aspects of federal campaign finances, but what remains after today's holding leaves no more than a shadow of what Congress contemplated. I question whether the residue leaves a workable program.

DISCLOSURE PROVISIONS

Disclosure is, in principle, the salutary and constitutional remedy for most of the ills Congress was seeking to alleviate. I therefore agree fully with the broad proposition that public disclosure of contributions by individuals and by entities — particularly corporations and labor unions — is an effective means of revealing the type of political support that is sometimes coupled with expectations of special favors or rewards. That disclosure impinges on First Amendment rights is conceded by the Court, ante, at 58-60, but given the objectives to which disclosure is directed, I agree that the need for disclosure outweighs individual constitutional claims.

Disclosure is, however, subject to First Amendment limitations which are to be defined by looking to the relevant public interests. The legitimate public interest is the elimination of the appearance and reality of corrupting influences. Serious dangers to the very processes of government justify disclosure of contributions of such dimensions reasonably thought likely to purchase special favors. . . .

[I]t seems to me that the threshold limits fixed at $10 and $100 for anonymous contributions are constitutionally impermissible on their face. As the Court's opinion notes, ante, at 77, Congress gave little or no thought, one way or the other, to these limits, but rather lifted figures out of a 65-year-old statute. As we are all painfully aware, the 1976 dollar is not what it used to be and is surely not the dollar of 1910. Ten dollars in 1976 will, for example, purchase only what $1.68 would buy in 1910. Handbook of Labor Statistics — 1975, Reference Ed., at 313. To argue that a 1976 contribution of $10 or $100 entails a risk of corruption or its appearance is simply too extravagant to be maintained. No public right-to-know justifies the compelled disclosure of such contributions, at the risk of discouraging them. There is, in short, no relation whatever between the means used and the legitimate goal of ventilating possible undue influence. Congress has used a shotgun to kill wrens as well as hawks.

CONTRIBUTION AND EXPENDITURE LIMITS

. . . [W]hen it approves similarly stringent limitations on contributions, the Court ignores the reasons it finds so persuasive in the context of expenditures. For me contributions and expenditures are two sides of the same First Amendment coin.

The Court's attempt to distinguish the communication inherent in political *contributions* from the speech aspects of political *expenditures* simply will not wash. We do little but engage in word games unless we recognize that people — candidates and contributors — spend money on political activity because they wish to communicate ideas, and their constitutional interest in doing so is precisely the same whether they or someone else utter the words.

. . . In striking down the limitations on campaign expenditures, the Court relies in part on its conclusion that other means — namely, disclosure and contribution ceilings — will adequately serve the statute's aim. It is not clear why the same analysis is not also appropriate in weighing the need for contribution ceilings in addition to disclosure requirements. Congress may well be entitled to conclude that disclosure was a "partial measure," but I had not thought until today that Congress could enact its conclusions in the First Amendment area into laws immune from the most searching review by this Court.

PUBLIC FINANCING

. . . [I]n my view, the inappropriateness of subsidizing, from general revenues, the actual political dialog of the people — the process which begets the Government itself — is as basic to our national tradition as the separation of church and state also deriving from the First Amendment, see Lemon v. Kurtzman, 403 U.S. 602, 612 (1971); Waltz v. Tax Commission, 397 U.S. 664, 668-669 (1970), or the separation of civilian and military authority, see Orloff v. Willoughby, 395 U.S. 83, 93-94 (1953), neither of which is explicit in the Constitution but which have developed through case by case adjudication of express provisions of the Constitution. . . . [O]nce the Government finances these national conventions by the expenditure of millions of dollars from the public treasury, we may be providing a springboard for later attempts to impose a whole range of requirements

Section C. Freedom of Speech and Association

on delegate selection and convention activities. Does this foreshadow judicial decisions allowing the federal courts to "monitor" these conventions to assure compliance with court orders or regulations? . . .

MR. JUSTICE WHITE, concurring in part and dissenting in part.

. . . I dissent . . . from the Court's view that the expenditure limitations of 18 U.S.C. §§ 608(c) and (e) violate the First Amendment.

It would make little sense to me, and apparently made none to Congress, to limit the amounts an individual may give to a candidate or spend with his approval but fail to limit the amounts that could be spent on his behalf. Yet the Court permits the former while striking down the latter limitation. No more than $1,000 may be given to a candidate or spent at his request or with his approval or cooperation; but otherwise, apparently, a contributor is to be constitutionally protected in spending unlimited amounts of money in support of his chosen candidate or candidates.

Let us suppose that each of two brothers spends one million dollars on TV spot announcements that he has individually prepared and in which he appears, urging the election of the same named candidate in identical words. One brother has sought and obtained the approval of the candidate; the other has not. The former may validly be prosecuted under § 608(e); under the Court's view, the latter may not, even though the candidate could scarcely help knowing about and appreciating the expensive favor. For constitutional purposes it is difficult to see the difference between the two situations. I would take the word of those who know — that limiting independent expenditures is essential to prevent transparent and widespread evasion of the contribution limits.

In sustaining the contribution limits, the Court recognizes the importance of avoiding public misapprehension about a candidate's reliance on large contributions. It ignores that consideration in invalidating § 608(e). In like fashion, it says that Congress was entitled to determine that the criminal provisions against bribery and corruption, together with the disclosure provisions, would not in themselves be adequate to combat the evil and that limits on contributions should be provided. Here, the Court rejects the identical kind of judgment made by Congress as to the need for and utility of expenditure limits. I would not do so.

The Court also rejects Congress' judgment manifested in § 608(c) that the federal interest in limiting total campaign expenditures by individual candidates justifies the incidental effect on their opportunity for effective political speech. I disagree both with the Court's assessment of the impact on speech and with its narrow view of the values the limitations will serve.

. . . The record before us no more supports the conclusion that the communicative efforts of congressional and Presidential candidates will be crippled by the expenditure limitations than it supports the contrary. The judgment of Congress was that reasonably effective campaigns could be conducted within the limits established by the Act and that the communicative efforts of these campaigns would not seriously suffer. In this posture of the case, there is no sound basis for invalidating the expenditure limitations, so long as the purposes they serve are legitimate and sufficiently substantial, which in my view they are.

In the first place, expenditure ceilings reinforce the contribution limits and help eradicate the hazard of corruption. . . . Without limits on total expenditures, campaign costs will inevitably and endlessly escalate. Pressure to raise funds will constantly build and with it the temptation to resort in "emergencies" to those sources of large sums, who, history shows, are sufficiently confident of not being caught to risk flouting contribution limits. Congress would save the candidate from this predicament by establishing a reasonable ceiling on all candidates. . . .

. . . [T]he corrupt use of money by candidates is as much to be feared as the corrosive influence of large contributions. There are many illegal ways of spending money to influence elections. One would be blind to history to deny that unlimited money tempts people to spend it on *whatever* money can buy to influence an election. On the assumption that financing illegal activities is low on the campaign organization's priority list, the expenditure limits could play a substantial role in preventing unethical practices. There just wouldn't be enough of "that kind of money" to go around.

The ceiling on candidate expenditures represents the considered judgment of Congress that elections are to be decided among candidates none of whom has overpowering advantage by reason of a huge campaign war chest. At least so long as the ceiling placed upon the candidates is not plainly too low, elections are not to turn on the difference in the amounts of money that candidates have to spend. This seems an acceptable purpose and the means chosen a common sense way to achieve it. The Court nevertheless holds that a candidate has a constitutional right to spend unlimited amounts of money, mostly that of other people, in order to be elected. The holding perhaps is not that federal candidates have the constitutional right to purchase their election, but many will so interpret the Court's conclusion in this case. I cannot join the Court in this respect.

I also disagree with the Court's judgment that §608(a), which limits the amount of money that a candidate or his family may spend on his campaign, violates the Constitution. Although it is true that this provision does not promote any interest in preventing the corruption of candidates, the provision does, nevertheless, serve salutary purposes related to the integrity of federal campaigns. By limiting the importance of personal wealth, §608(a) helps to assure that only individuals with a modicum of support from others will be viable candidates. This in turn would tend to discourage any notion that the outcome of elections is primarily a function of money. . . .

MR. JUSTICE MARSHALL, concurring in part and dissenting in part.

I join in all of the Court's opinion except Part I-C-2, which deals with §608(a) of the Act. That section limits the amount a candidate can spend from his personal funds, or family funds under his control, in connection with his campaigns during any calendar year. See ante, at 46 n.57. The Court invalidates §608(a) as violative of the candidate's First Amendment rights. "[T]he First Amendment," the Court explains, "simply cannot tolerate §608(a)'s restriction upon the freedom of a candidate to speak without legislative limit on behalf of his own candidacy." Ante, at 48. I disagree.

The Court views "[t]he ancillary interest in equalizing the relative financial resources of candidates" as the relevant rationale for §608(a), and deems that interest insufficient to justify §608(a). Ante, at 48. In my view the interest is more precisely the interest in promoting the reality and appearance of equal access to the political arena. Our ballot-access decisions serve as a reminder of the importance of the general interest in promoting equal access among potential candidates. See, e.g., Lubin v. Panish, 415 U.S. 709 (1974); Bullock v. Carter, 405 U.S. 134 (1972). While admittedly those cases dealt with barriers to entry different from those we consider here, the barriers to which §608(a) is directed are formidable ones, and the interest in removing them substantial.

One of the points on which all Members of the Court agree is that money is essential for effective communication in a political campaign. It would appear to follow that the candidate with a substantial personal fortune at his disposal is off to a significant "head start." Of course, the less wealthy candidate can potentially overcome the disparity in resources through contributions from others. But ability to generate contributions may itself depend upon a showing of a financial base for the campaign or some demonstration of pre-existing support, which in turn is facilitated by expenditures of substantial personal sums. Thus the wealthy candidate's immediate access to a substantial personal fortune may give him an initial advantage that his less wealthy opponent can never overcome. And even if the advantage can be overcome, the perception that personal wealth wins elections may not only discourage potential candidates without significant personal wealth from entering the political arena, but also undermine public confidence in the integrity of the electoral process.[1]

[1] "In the Nation's seven largest States in 1970, 11 of the 15 major senatorial candidates were millionaires. The four who were not millionaires lost their bid for election." 117 Cong. Rec. 42065 (1971) (remarks of Rep. MacDonald).

Section C. **Freedom of Speech and Association**

MR. JUSTICE REHNQUIST, concurring in part and dissenting in part. . . .

Congress, of course, does have an interest in not "funding hopeless candidacies with large sums of public money," ante, at 90, and may for that purpose legitimately require " 'some preliminary showing of a significant modicum of support,' Jenness v. Fortson, supra, at 442, as an eligibility requirement for public funds." Ante, at 90. But Congress in this legislation has done a good deal more than that. It has enshrined the Republican and Democratic Parties in a permanently preferred position, and has established requirements for funding minor party and independent candidates to which the two major parties are not subject. Congress would undoubtedly be justified in treating the Presidential candidates of the two major parties differently from minor party or independent Presidential candidates, in view of the long demonstrated public support of the former. But because of the First Amendment overtones of the appellants' Fifth Amendment equal protection claim, something more than a merely rational basis for the difference in treatment must be shown, as the Court apparently recognizes. I find it impossible to subscribe to the Court's reasoning that because no third party has posed a credible threat to the two major parties in Presidential elections since 1860, Congress may by law attempt to assure that this pattern will endure forever.

I would hold that, as to general election financing, Congress has not merely treated the two major parties differently from minor parties and independents, but has discriminated in favor of the former in such a way as to run afoul of the Fifth and First Amendments to the United States Constitution.[ee]

NOTE

See Cutler & Johnson, Regulation and the Political Process, 84 Yale L.J. 1395 (1975); Developments in the Law — Elections, 88 Harv. L. Rev. 1111, 1233-98 (1975).

On May 11, 1976 President Ford signed Pub. L. No. 94-283 to reconstitute the Federal Election Commission. It provided that its six members would be appointed by the President and made some additional changes, such as allowing either House of Congress to veto regulations promulgated by the commission and limiting the amount of money a wealthy candidate may invest in his own presidential campaign if he accepts federal subsidies.

7. Obscenity

JOSEPH BURSTYN, INC. v. WILSON, 343 U.S. 495, 72 S. Ct. 777, 96 L. Ed. 1098 (1952). Clark, J.: "The issue here is the constitutionality, under the First and Fourteenth Amendments, of a New York statute which permits the banning of motion picture films on the ground that they are 'sacrilegious.' . . .

". . . On February 16, 1951, the [Board of] Regents, after viewing 'The Miracle,' determined that it was 'sacrilegious' and for that reason ordered the Commissioner of Education to rescind appellant's license to exhibit the picture. The Commissioner did so.

"It is urged that motion pictures do not fall within the First Amendment's aegis because their production, distribution, and exhibition is a large-scale business conducted for private profit. We cannot agree. That books, newspapers, and magazines are published and sold for profit does not prevent them from being a form of expression whose liberty is safeguarded by the First Amendment. We fail to see why operation for profit should have any different effect in the case of motion pictures.

[ee] A separate opinion of Justice Blackmun, concurring in part and dissenting in part, is omitted. — ED.

"New York's highest court says there is 'nothing mysterious' about the statutory provision applied in this case: 'It is simply this: that no religion, as that word is understood by the ordinary, reasonable person, shall be treated with contempt, mockery, scorn and ridicule. . . .'" This is far from the kind of narrow exception to freedom of expression which a state may carve out to satisfy the adverse demands of other interests of society. In seeking to apply the broad and all-inclusive definition of 'sacrilegious' given by the New York courts, the censor is set adrift upon a boundless sea amid a myriad of conflicting currents of religious views, with no charts but those provided by the most vocal and powerful orthodoxies. New York cannot vest such unlimited restraining control over motion pictures in a censor. . . . Under such a standard the most careful and tolerant censor would find it virtually impossible to avoid favoring one religion over another, and he would be subject to an inevitable tendency to ban the expression of unpopular sentiments sacred to a religious minority. Application of the 'sacrilegious' test, in these or other respects, might raise substantial questions under the First Amendment's guaranty of separate church and state with freedom of worship for all. However, from the standpoint of freedom of speech and the press, it is enough to point out that the state has no legitimate interest in protecting any or all religions from views distasteful to them which is sufficient to justify prior restraints upon the expression of those views. It is not the business of government in our nation to suppress real or imagined attacks upon a particular religious doctrine, whether they appear in publications, speeches, or motion pictures."

Kingsley International Pictures Corp. v. Regents of New York
360 U.S. 684, 79 S. Ct. 1362, 3 L. Ed. 2d 1512 (1959)

Mr. Justice Stewart delivered the opinion of the Court.

Once again the Court is required to consider the impact of New York's motion picture licensing law upon First Amendment liberties, protected by the Fourteenth Amendment from infringement by the States. Cf. Joseph Burstyn, Inc. v. Wilson, 343 U.S. 495.

The New York Statute makes it unlawful "to exhibit, or to sell, lease or lend for exhibition at any place of amusement for pay or in connection with any business in the state of New York, any motion picture film or reel [with certain exceptions not relevant here], unless there is at the time in full force and effect a valid license or permit therefor of the education department. . . ." The law provides that a license shall issue "unless such film or a part thereof is obscene, indecent, immoral, inhuman, sacrilegious, or is of such a character that its exhibition would tend to corrupt morals or incite to crime. . . ." A recent statutory amendment provides that, "the term 'immoral' and the phrase 'of such a character that its exhibition would tend to corrupt morals' shall denote a motion picture film or part thereof, the dominant purpose or effect of which is erotic or pornographic; or which portrays acts of sexual immorality, perversion, or lewdness, or which expressly or impliedly presents such acts as desirable, acceptable or proper patterns of behavior."

As the distributor of a motion picture entitled "Lady Chatterley's Lover," the appellant Kingsley submitted that film to the Motion Picture Division of the New York Education Department for a license. Finding three isolated scenes in the film " 'immoral' within the intent of our Law," the Division refused to issue a license until the scenes in question were deleted. The distributor petitioned the Regents of the State of New York for a review of that ruling. The Regents upheld the denial of a license, but on the broader ground that "the whole theme of this motion picture is immoral under said law, for that theme is the presentation of adultery as a desirable, acceptable and proper pattern of behavior."

Kingsley sought judicial review of the Regents' determination. The Appellate Division unanimously annulled the action of the Regents and directed that a license be issued. 4 App. Div. 2d 348, 165 N.Y.S.2d 681. A sharply divided Court of Appeals, however, reversed the Appellate Division and upheld the Regents' refusal to license the film for exhibition. 4 N.Y.2d 349, 175 N.Y.S.2d 39, 151 N.E.2d 197.

The Court of Appeals unanimously and explicitly rejected any notion that the film is obscene. . . . Rather, the court found that the picture as a whole "alluringly portrays adultery as proper behavior." As Chief Judge Conway's prevailing opinion emphasized, therefore, the only portion of the statute involved in this case is that part of §§ 122 and 122(a) of the Education Law requiring the denial of a license to motion pictures "which are immoral in that they portray 'acts of sexual immorality . . . as desirable, acceptable, or proper patterns of behavior.' " . . . A majority of the Court of Appeals ascribed to that language a precise purpose of the New York Legislature to require the denial of a license to a motion picture "because its subject matter is adultery presented as being right and desirable for certain people under certain circumstances." . . .

What New York has done, therefore, is to prevent the exhibition of a motion picture because that picture advocates an idea — that adultery under certain circumstances may be proper behavior. Yet the First Amendment's basic guarantee is of freedom to advocate ideas. The State, quite simply, has thus struck at the very heart of constitutionally protected liberty. . . .

Advocacy of conduct proscribed by law is not, as Mr. Justice Brandeis long ago pointed out, "a justification for denying free speech where the advocacy falls short of incitement and there is nothing to indicate that the advocacy would be immediately acted on." Whitney v. California, 274 U.S. 357, at 376. . . .

The inflexible command which the New York Court of Appeals has attributed to the State Legislature thus cuts so close to the core of constitutional freedom as to make it quite needless in this case to examine the periphery. Specifically, there is no occasion to consider the appellant's contention that the State is entirely without power to require films of any kind to be licensed prior to their exhibition. Nor need we here determine whether, despite problems peculiar to motion pictures, the controls which a State may impose upon this medium of expression are precisely coextensive with those allowable for newspapers, books, or individual speech. It is enough for the present case to reaffirm that motion pictures are within the First and Fourteenth Amendments' basic protection. Joseph Burstyn, Inc. v. Wilson, 343 U.S. 495.

Reversed.[ff]

Roth v. United States; Alberts v. California 354 U.S. 476, 77 S. Ct. 1304, 1 L. Ed. 2d 1498 (1957)

MR. JUSTICE BRENNAN delivered the opinion of the Court.

The constitutionality of a criminal obscenity statute is the question in each of these cases. In Roth, the primary constitutional question is whether the federal obscenity statute[1] violates the provision of the First Amendment that "Congress shall make no law . . .

[ff] Concurring opinions of Frankfurter, Douglas, Black, Harlan, and Clark, JJ., are omitted. — ED.

[1] The federal obscenity statute provided, in pertinent part:

"Every obscene, lewd, lascivious, or filthy book, pamphlet, picture, paper, letter, writing, print, or other publication of an indecent character; and — . . .

"Every written or printed card, letter, circular, book, pamphlet, advertisement, or notice of any kind giving information, directly or indirectly, where, or how, or from whom, or by what means any of such mentioned matters, articles, or things may be obtained or made, . . . whether sealed or unsealed . . . .

"Is declared to be nonmailable matter and shall not be conveyed in the mails or delivered from any post office or by any letter carrier.

"Whoever knowingly deposits for mailing or delivery, anything declared by this section to be nonmailable, or knowingly takes the same from the mails for the purpose of circulating or disposing thereof, or of aiding in the circulation or disposition thereof, shall be fined not more than $5,000 or imprisoned not more than five years, or both." 18 U.S.C. § 1461.

The 1955 amendment of this statute, 69 Stat. 183, is not applicable to this case.

abridging the freedom of speech, or of the press. . . ." In Alberts, the primary constitutional question is whether the obscenity provisions of the California Penal Code[2] invade the freedoms of speech and press as they may be incorporated in the liberty protected from state action by the Due Process Clause of the Fourteenth Amendment.

Roth conducted a business in New York in the publication and sale of books, photographs and magazines. He used circulars and advertising matter to solicit sales. He was convicted by a jury in the District Court for the Southern District of New York upon 4 counts of a 26-count indictment charging him with mailing obscene circulars and advertising, and an obscene book, in violation of the federal obscenity statute. His conviction was affirmed by the Court of Appeals for the Second Circuit. We granted certiorari.

Alberts conducted a mail-order business from Los Angeles. He was convicted by the Judge of the Municipal Court of the Beverly Hills Judicial District (having waived a jury trial) under a misdemeanor complaint which charged him with lewdly keeping for sale obscene and indecent books, and with writing, composing and publishing an obscene advertisement of them, in violation of the California Penal Code. The conviction was affirmed by the Appellate Department of the Superior Court of the State of California in and for the County of Los Angeles. We noted probable jurisdiction.

The dispositive question is whether obscenity is utterance within the area of protected speech and press. Although this is the first time the question has been squarely presented to this Court, either under the First Amendment or under the Fourteenth Amendment, expressions found in numerous opinions indicate that this Court has always assumed that obscenity is not protected by the freedoms of speech and press. . . .

In light of . . . history, it is apparent that the unconditional phrasing of the First Amendment was not intended to protect every utterance. This phrasing did not prevent this Court from concluding that libelous utterances are not within the area of constitutionally protected speech. Beauharnais v. Illinois, 343 U.S. 250, 266. At the time of the adoption of the First Amendment, obscenity law was not as fully developed as libel law, but there is sufficiently contemporaneous evidence to show that obscenity, too, was outside the protection intended for speech and press.

All ideas having even the slightest redeeming social importance — unorthodox ideas, controversial ideas, even ideas hateful to the prevailing climate of opinion — have the full protection of the guaranties, unless excludable because they encroach upon the limited area of more important interests. But implicit in the history of the First Amendment is the rejection of obscenity as utterly without redeeming social importance. This rejection for that reason is mirrored in the universal judgment that obscenity should be restrained, reflected in the international agreement of over 50 nations, in the obscenity laws of all of the 48 States, and in the 20 obscenity laws enacted by the Congress from 1842 to 1956. . . .

We hold that obscenity is not within the area of constitutionally protected speech or press.

It is strenuously urged that these obscenity statutes offend the constitutional guaranties because they punish incitation to impure sexual *thoughts*, not shown to be related to any overt antisocial conduct which is or may be incited in the persons stimulated to such *thoughts*. In Roth, the trial judge instructed the jury: "The words 'obscene, lewd and lascivious' as used in the law, signify that form of immorality which has relation to sexual

---

[2] The California Penal Code provides, in pertinent part:

"Every person who wilfully and lewdly, either: . . .

"3. Writes, composes, stereotypes, prints, publishes, sells, distributes, keeps for sale, or exhibits any obscene or indecent writing, paper, or book; or designs, copies, draws, engraves, paints, or otherwise prepares any obscene or indecent picture or print; or molds, cuts, casts, or otherwise makes any obscene or indecent figure; or,

"4. Writes, composes, or publishes any notice advertisement of any such writing, paper, book, picture, print or figure; . . .

"6. . . . is guilty of a misdemeanor. . . ." West's Cal. Penal Code Ann., 1955, §311.

impurity and has a tendency to excite lustful *thoughts.*" (Emphasis added.) In Alberts, the trial judge applied the test laid down in People v. Wepplo, 78 Cal. App. 2d Supp. 959, 178 P.2d 853, namely, whether the material has "a substantial tendency to deprave or corrupt its readers by inciting lascivious *thoughts* or arousing lustful desires." (Emphasis added.) It is insisted that the constitutional guaranties are violated because convictions may be had without proof either that obscene material will perceptibly create a clear and present danger to anti-social conduct, or will probably induce its recipients to such conduct. But, in light of our holding that obscenity is not protected speech, the complete answer to this argument is in the holding of this Court in Beauharnais v. Illinois, supra. . . .

However, sex and obscenity are not synonymous. Obscene material is material which deals with sex in a manner appealing to prurient interest.[20] The portrayal of sex, e.g., in art, literature and scientific words, is not itself sufficient reason to deny material the constitutional protection of freedom of speech and press. Sex, a great and mysterious motive force in human life, has indisputably been a subject of absorbing interest to mankind through the ages; it is one of the vital problems of human interest and public concern. . . .

The early leading standard of obscenity allowed material to be judged merely by the effect of an isolated excerpt upon particularly susceptible persons. Regina v. Hicklin, [1868] L.R. 3 Q.B. 360. Some American courts adopted this standard but later decisions have rejected it and substituted this test: whether to the average person, applying contemporary community standards, the dominant theme of the material taken as a whole appeals to prurient interest. The Hicklin test, judging obscenity by the effect of isolated passages upon the most susceptible persons, might well encompass material legitimately treating with sex, and so it must be rejected as unconstitutionally restrictive of the freedoms of speech and press. On the other hand, the substituted standard provides safeguards adequate to withstand the charge of constitutional infirmity.

Both trial courts below sufficiently followed the proper standard. Both courts used the proper definition of obscenity. . . .

It is argued that the statutes do not provide reasonably ascertainable standards of guilt and therefore violate the constitutional requirements of due process. Winters v. New York, 333 U.S. 507. The federal obscenity statute makes punishable the mailing of material that is "obscene, lewd, lascivious, or filthy . . . or other publication of an indecent character." The California statute makes punishable, inter alia, the keeping for sale or advertising material that is "obscene or indecent." The thrust of the argument is that these words are not sufficiently precise because they do not mean the same thing to all people, all the time, everywhere.

Many decisions have recognized that these terms of obscenity statutes are not precise. This Court, however, has consistently held that lack of precision is not itself offensive to the requirements of due process. ". . . [T]he Constitution does not require impossible standards"; all that is required is that the language "conveys sufficiently definite warning as to the proscribed conduct when measured by common understanding and practices. . . ." United States v. Petrillo, 332 U.S. 1, 7-8. These words, applied according to the proper standard for judging obscenity, already discussed, give adequate warning of the conduct proscribed and mark ". . . boundaries sufficiently distinct for judges and juries fairly to administer the law. . . . That there may be marginal cases in which it is difficult to determine the side of the line on which a particular fact situation falls is no sufficient reason to hold the language too ambiguous to define a criminal offense. . . ." Id., at 7. . . .

---

[20] I.e., material having a tendency to excite lustful thoughts. Webster's New International Dictionary (Unabridged, 2d ed., 1949) defines prurient, in pertinent part, as follows:

". . . Itching; longing; uneasy with desire or longing; of persons, having itching, morbid, or lascivious longings; of desire, curiosity, or propensity, lewd. . . ."

In summary, then we hold that these statutes, applied according to the proper standard for judging obscenity, do not offend constitutional safeguards against convictions based upon protected material, or fail to give men in acting adequate notice of what is prohibited. . . .

The judgments are affirmed.[gg]

MR. JUSTICE HARLAN, concurring in the result in No. 61, and dissenting in No. 582.

I regret not to be able to join the Court's opinion. I cannot do so because I find lurking beneath its disarming generalizations a number of problems which not only leave me with serious misgivings as to the future effect of today's decisions, but which also, in my view, call for different results in these two cases.

. . . Every communication has an individuality and "value" of its own. The suppression of a particular writing or other tangible form of expression is, therefore, an individual matter, and in the nature of things every such suppression raises an individual constitutional problem, in which a reviewing court must determine for itself whether the attacked expression is suppressible within constitutional standards. Since those standards do not readily lend themselves to generalized definitions, the constitutional problem in the last analysis becomes one of particularized judgments which appellate courts must make for themselves.

I do not think that reviewing courts can escape this responsibility by saying that the trier of the facts, be it a jury or a judge, has labeled the questioned matter as "obscene," for, if "obscenity" is to be suppressed, the question whether a particular work is of that character involves not really an issue of fact but a question of constitutional judgment of the most sensitive and delicate kind. Many juries might find that Joyce's "Ulysses" or Boccaccio's "Decameron" was obscene, and yet the conviction of a defendant for selling either book would raise, for me, the gravest constitutional problems, for no such verdict could convince me, without more, that these books are "utterly without redeeming social importance." In short, I do not understand how the Court can resolve the constitutional problems now before it without making its own independent judgment upon the character of the material upon which these convictions were based. . . .

I concur in the judgment of the Court in No. 61, Alberts v. California.

In judging the constitutionality of this conviction, we should remember that our function in reviewing state judgments under the Fourteenth Amendment is a narrow one. We do not decide whether the policy of the State is wise, or whether it is based on assumptions scientifically substantiated. We can inquire only whether the state action so subverts the fundamental liberties implicit in the Due Process Clause that it cannot be sustained as a rational exercise of power. . . .

What, then, is the purpose of this California statute? Clearly the state legislature has made the judgment that printed words can "deprave or corrupt" the reader — that words can incite to anti-social or immoral action. The assumption seems to be that the distribution of certain types of literature will induce criminal or immoral sexual conduct. It is well known, of course, that the validity of this assumption is a matter of dispute among critics, sociologists, psychiatrists, and penologists. There is a large school of thought, particularly in the scientific community, which denies any causal connection between the reading of pornography and immorality, crime, or delinquency. Others disagree. Clearly it is not our function to decide this question. That function belongs to the state legislature. Nothing in the Constitution requires California to accept as truth the most advanced and sophisticated psychiatric opinion. It seems to me clear that it is not irrational, in our present state of knowledge, to consider that pornography can induce a type of sexual conduct which a State may deem obnoxious to the moral fabric of society. In fact the very division of opinion on the subject counsels us to respect the choice made by the State.

Furthermore, even assuming that pornography cannot be deemed ever to cause, in an

---

[gg] A concurring opinion of Warren, C.J., is omitted. — ED.

immediate sense, criminal sexual conduct, other interests within the proper cognizance of the States may be protected by the prohibition placed on such materials. The State can reasonably draw the inference that over a long period of time the indiscriminate dissemination of materials, the essential character of which is to degrade sex, will have an eroding effect on moral standards. And the State has a legitimate interest in protecting the privacy of the home against invasion of unsolicited obscenity.

What has been said, however, does not dispose of the case. It still remains for us to decide whether the state courts' determination that this material should be suppressed is consistent with the Fourteenth Amendment; and that, of course, presents a federal question as to which we, and not the state court, have the ultimate responsibility. And so, in the final analysis, I concur in the judgment because, upon an independent perusal of the material involved, and in light of the considerations discussed above, I cannot say that its suppression would so interfere with the communication of "ideas" in any proper sense of that term that it would offend the Due Process Clause. I therefore agree with the Court that appellant's conviction must be affirmed.

I dissent in No. 582, Roth v. United States.

We are faced here with the question whether the federal obscenity statute, as construed and applied in this case, violates the First Amendment to the Constitution. To me, this question is of quite a different order than one where we are dealing with state legislation under the Fourteenth Amendment. I do not think it follows that state and federal powers in this area are the same, and that just because the State may suppress a particular utterance, it is automatically permissible for the Federal Government to do the same. I agree with Mr. Justice Jackson that the historical evidence does not bear out the claim that the Fourteenth Amendment "incorporates" the First in any literal sense. See Beauharnais v. Illinois, supra. . . .

. . . What Mr. Justice Jackson said in Beauharnais, supra, 343 U.S., at 294-295, about criminal libel is equally true of obscenity:

"The inappropriateness of a single standard for restricting State and Nation is indicated by the disparity between their functions and duties in relation to those freedoms. Criminality of defamation is predicated upon power either to protect the private right to enjoy integrity of reputation or the public right to tranquillity. Neither of these are objects of federal cognizance except when necessary to the accomplishment of some delegated power. . . . When the Federal Government puts liberty of press in one scale, it has a very limited duty to personal reputation or local tranquillity to weigh against it in the other. But state action affecting speech or press can and should be weighed against and reconciled with these conflicting social interests."

Not only is the federal interest in protecting the Nation against pornography attenuated, but the dangers of federal censorship in this field are far greater than anything the State may do. It has often been said that one of the great strengths of our federal system is that we have, in the forty-eight States, forty-eight experimental social laboratories. "State statutory law reflects predominantly this capacity of a legislature to introduce novel techniques of social control. The federal system has the immense advantage of providing forty-eight separate centers for such experimentation." Different States will have different attitudes toward the same work of literature. The same book which is freely read in one State might be classed as obscene in another. And it seems to me that no overwhelming danger to our freedom to experiment and to gratify our tastes in literature is likely to result from the suppression of a borderline book in one of the States, so long as there is no uniform nation-wide suppression of the book, and so long as other States are free to experiment with the same or bolder books.

Quite a different situation is presented, however, where the Federal Government imposes the ban. The danger is perhaps not great if the people of one State, through their legislature, decide that "Lady Chatterley's Lover" goes so far beyond the acceptable standards of candor that it will be deemed offensive and non-sellable, for the State next door is still free to make its own choice. At least we do not have one uniform standard. But the dangers to free thought and expression are truly great if the Federal Government imposes a blanket ban over the Nation on such a book. The prerogative of the States to differ on their ideas of morality will be destroyed, the ability of States to experiment will be stunted. The fact that the people of one State cannot read some of the works of D. H. Lawrence seems to me, if not wise or desirable, at least acceptable. But that no person in the United States should be allowed to do so seems to me to be intolerable, and violative of both the letter and spirit of the First Amendment.

MR. JUSTICE DOUGLAS, with whom MR. JUSTICE BLACK concurs, dissenting.

When we sustain these convictions, we make the legality of a publication turn on the purity of thought which a book or tract instills in the mind of the reader. I do not think we can approve that standard and be faithful to the command of the First Amendment, which by its terms is a restraint on Congress and which by the Fourteenth is a restraint on the States.

By these standards punishment is inflicted for thoughts provoked, not for overt acts nor antisocial conduct. This test cannot be squared with our decisions under the First Amendment. Even the ill-starred Dennis case conceded that speech to be punishable must have some relation to action which could be penalized by government. Dennis v. United States, 341 U.S. 494, 502-511. Cf. Chafee, The Blessings of Liberty (1956), p. 69. This issue cannot be avoided by saying that obscenity is not protected by the First Amendment. The question remains what is the constitutional test of obscenity?

The tests by which these convictions were obtained require only the arousing of sexual thoughts. Yet the arousing of sexual thoughts and desires happens every day in normal life in dozens of ways. Nearly 30 years ago a questionnaire sent to college and normal school women graduates asked what things were most stimulating sexually. Of 409 replies, 9 said "music"; 18 said "pictures"; 29 said "dancing"; 40 said "drama"; 95 said "books"; and 218 said "man." Alpert, Judicial Censorship of Obscene Literature, 52 Harv. L. Rev. 40, 73.

The test of obscenity the Court endorses today gives the censor free range over a vast domain. To allow the State to step in and punish mere speech or publication that the judge or the jury thinks has an undesirable impact on thoughts but that is now shown to be a part of unlawful action is drastically to curtail the First Amendment. . . .

I do not think that the problem can be resolved by the Court's statement that "obscenity is not expression protected by the First Amendment." With the exception of Beauharnais v. Illinois, 343 U.S. 250, none of our cases has resolved problems of free speech and free press by placing any form of expression beyond the pale of the absolute prohibition of the First Amendment. Unlike the law of libel, wrongfully relied on in Beauharnais, there is no special historical evidence that literature dealing with sex was intended to be treated in a special manner by those who drafted the First Amendment. In fact, the first reported court decision in this country involving obscene literature was in 1821. Lockhart & McClure, op. cit. supra, at 324, n.200. I reject too the implication that problems of freedom of speech and of the press are to be resolved by weighing against the values of free expression, the judgment of the Court that a particular form of that expression has "no redeeming social importance." The First Amendment, its prohibition in terms absolute, was designed to preclude courts as well as legislatures from weighing the values of speech against silence. The First Amendment puts free speech in the preferred position.

NOTE

See Kalven, The Metaphysics of the Law of Obscenity, 1960 Sup. Ct. Rev. 1. See also Lockhart & McClure, Censorship of Obscenity: The Developing Constitutional Standards, 45 Minn. L. Rev. 5 (1960).

Section C. **Freedom of Speech and Association** 1291

Alternative methods of censorship, both public and private, are discussed at length in a Note, Entertainment: Public Pressures and the Law, 71 Harv. L. Rev. 326 (1957). Consider the licensing scheme set out in Freedman v. Maryland, which follows.

FREEDMAN v. MARYLAND, 380 U.S. 51, 85 S. Ct. 734, 13 L. Ed. 2d 649 (1965). Brennan, J.: "[W]e hold that a noncriminal process which requires the prior submission of a film to a censor avoids constitutional infirmity only if it takes place under procedural safeguards designed to obviate the dangers of a censorship system. First, the burden of proving that the film is unprotected expression must rest on the censor. . . . [T]he exhibitor must be assured, by statute or authoritative judicial construction, that the censor will, within a specified brief period, either issue a license or go to court to restrain showing the film. . . . [T]he procedure must also assure a prompt final judicial decision, to minimize the deterrent effect of an interim and possibly erroneous denial of a license."

"Memoirs" v. Massachusetts 383 U.S. 413, 86 S. Ct. 975, 16 L. Ed. 2d 1 (1966)

MR. JUSTICE BRENNAN announced the judgment of the Court and delivered an opinion in which THE CHIEF JUSTICE and MR. JUSTICE FORTAS join.

This is an obscenity case in which "Memoirs of a Woman of Pleasure" (commonly known as "Fanny Hill"), written by John Cleland in about 1750, was adjudged obscene in a proceeding that put on trial the book itself, and not its publisher or distributor. The proceeding was a civil equity suit brought by the Attorney General of Massachusetts, pursuant to General Laws of Massachusetts, Chapter 272, §§28C-28H, to have the book declared obscene. Section 28C requires that the petition commencing the suit be "directed against [the] book by name" and that an order to show cause "why said book should not be judicially determined to be obscene" be published in a daily newspaper and sent by registered mail "to all persons interested in the publication." Publication of the order in this case occurred in a Boston daily newspaper, and a copy of the order was sent by registered mail to G. P. Putnam's Sons, alleged to be the publisher and copyright holder of the book.

As authorized by §28D, G. P. Putnam's Sons intervened in the proceedings in behalf of the book, but it did not claim the right provided by that section to have the issue of obscenity tried by a jury. At the hearing before a justice of the Superior Court, which was conducted, under §28F, "in accordance with the usual course of proceedings in equity," the court received the book in evidence and also, as allowed by the section, heard the testimony of experts and accepted other evidence such as book reviews, in order to assess the literary, cultural or educational character of the book. This constituted the entire evidence, as neither side availed itself of the opportunity provided by the section to introduce evidence "as to the manner and form of its publication, advertisement, and distribution." The trial justice entered a final decree, which adjudged "Memoirs" obscene and declared that the book "is not entitled to the protection of the First and Fourteenth Amendments to the Constitution of the United States against action by the Attorney General or other law enforcement officers pursuant to the provisions of . . . §28B, or otherwise." The Massachusetts Supreme Judicial Court affirmed the decree. 349 Mass. 69, 206 N.E.2d 403 (1965). We noted probable jurisdiction. 382 U.S. 900. We reverse.

The term "obscene" appearing in the Massachusetts statute has been interpreted by the Supreme Judicial Court to be as expansive as the Constitution permits: the "statute covers all material that is obscene in the constitutional sense." Attorney General v. A Book Named "Tropic of Cancer," 345 Mass. 11, 13, 184 N.E.2d 328, 330 (1962). Indeed, the final decree before us equates the finding that "Memoirs" is obscene within the meaning of the statute with the declaration that the book is not entitled to the protection of the First Amendment. Thus the sole question before the state courts was whether "Memoirs" satisfies the test of obscenity established in Roth v. United States, 354 U.S. 476.

We defined obscenity in Roth in the following terms: "Whether to the average persons, applying contemporary community standards, the dominant theme of the material taken as a whole appeals to prurient interest." 354 U.S., at 489. Under this definition, as elaborated in subsequent cases, three elements must coalesce: it must be established that (a) the dominant theme of the material taken as a whole appeals to a prurient interest in sex; (b) the material is patently offensive because it affronts contemporary community standards relating to the description or representation of sexual matters; and (c) the material is utterly without redeeming social value.

The Supreme Judicial Court purported to apply the Roth definition of obscenity and held all three criteria satisfied. We need not consider the claim that the court erred in concluding that "Memoirs" satisfied the prurient appeal and patent offensiveness criteria; for reversal is required because the court misinterpreted the social value criterion. The court applied the criterion in this passage: "It remains to consider whether the book can be said to be 'utterly without social importance.' We are mindful that there was expert testimony, much of which was strained, to the effect that "Memoirs" is a structural novel with literary merit; that the book displays a skill in characterization and a gift for comedy; that it plays a part in the history of the development of the English novel; and that it contains a moral, namely, that sex with love is superior to sex in a brothel. But the fact that the testimony may indicate this book has some minimal literary value does not mean it is of any social importance. We do not interpret the 'social importance' test as requiring that a book which appeals to prurient interest and is patently offensive must be unqualifiedly worthless before it can be deemed obscene." 349 Mass., at 73, 206 N.E.2d, at 406.

The Supreme Judicial Court erred in holding that a book need not be "unqualifiedly worthless before it can be deemed obscene." A book can not be proscribed unless it is found to be *utterly* without redeeming social value. This is so even though the book is found to possess the requisite prurient appeal and to be patently offensive. Each of the three federal constitutional criteria is to be applied independently; the social value of the book can neither be weighed against nor canceled by its prurient appeal or patent offensiveness. Hence, even on the view of the court below that "Memoirs" possessed only a modicum of social value, its judgment must be reversed as being founded on an erroneous interpretation of a federal constitutional standard.

MR. JUSTICE HARLAN, dissenting.

The central development that emerges from the aftermath of Roth v. United States, 354 U.S. 476, is that no stable approach to the obscenity problem has yet been devised by this Court. Two Justices believe that the First and Fourteenth Amendments absolutely protect obscene and nonobscene material alike. Another Justice believes that neither the States nor the Federal Government may suppress any material save for "hard-core pornography." Roth in 1957 stressed prurience and utter lack of redeeming social importance; as Roth has been expounded in this case, in Ginzburg v. United States [383 U.S. 463 (1966)], and in Mishkin v. New York, 383 U.S. 502, it has undergone significant transformation. The concept of "pandering," emphasized by the separate opinion of The Chief Justice in Roth, now emerges as an uncertain gloss of interpretive aid, and the further requisite of "patent offensiveness" has been made explicit as a result of intervening decisions. Given this tangled state of affairs, I feel free to adhere to the principles first set forth in my separate opinion in Roth, 354 U.S., at 496, which I continue to believe represent the soundest constitutional solution to this intractable problem.

My premise is that in the area of obscenity the Constitution does not bind the States and the Federal Government in precisely the same fashion. This approach is plainly consistent with the language of the First and Fourteenth Amendments and, in my opinion, more responsive to the proper functioning of a federal system of government in this area. See my opinion in Roth, 354 U.S., at 505-506. . . .

Federal suppression of allegedly obscene matter should, in my view, be constitutionally limited to that often described as "hard-core pornography." To be sure, that rubric is not a self-executing standard, but it does describe something that most judges and others will "know . . . when [they] see it" (Stewart, J., in Jacobellis v. Ohio, 378 U.S. 184, 197) and that leaves the smallest room for disagreement between those of varying tastes. To me it is plain, for instance, that "Fanny Hill" does not fall within this class and could not be barred from the federal mails. . . .

State obscenity laws present problems of quite a different order. The varying conditions across the country, the range of views on the need and reasons for curbing obscenity, and the traditions of local self-government in matters of public welfare all favor a more flexible attitude in defining the bounds for the States. From my standpoint, the Fourteenth Amendment requires of a State only that it apply criteria rationally related to the accepted notion of obscenity and that it reach results not wholly out of step with current American standards. As to criteria, it should be adequate if the court or jury considers such elements as offensiveness, pruriency, social value, and the like. The latitude which I believe the States deserve cautions against any federally imposed formula listing the exclusive ingredients of obscenity and fi⟩ ⟩ their proportions. . . .[hh]

Ginzburg v. United States 383 U.S. 463, 86 S. Ct. 942, 16 L. Ed. 2d 31 (1966)

MR. JUSTICE BRENNAN delivered the opinion of the Court.

A judge sitting without a jury in the District Court for the Eastern District of Pennsylvania convicted petitioner Ginzburg and three corporations controlled by him upon all 28 counts of an indictment charging violation of the federal obscenity statute, 18 U.S.C. §1461.[2] 224 F. Supp. 129. Each count alleged that a resident of the Eastern District received mailed matt̶̶̶ ̶̶̶̶̶̶her one of three publications challenged as obscene, or advertising telling how ar̶̶̶ ̶̶̶̶̶̶the publications might be obtained. The Court of Appeals for the Third Circuit ̶̶̶ ̶̶̶̶̶̶338 F.2d 12. We granted certiorari, 380 U.S. 961. We affirm. Since petitio̶̶̶ ̶̶̶̶̶̶argue that the trial judge misconceived or failed to apply the standards we first ̶̶̶ ̶̶̶̶̶̶in Roth v. United States, 354 U.S. 476, the only serious question is wheth̶̶̶ ̶̶̶̶̶̶dards were correctly applied.

In the cases in ̶̶̶ ̶̶̶̶̶̶Court has decided obscenity questions since Roth, it has regarded the mater̶̶̶ ̶̶̶̶̶̶cient in themselves for the determination of the question. In the present case, ho̶̶̶ ̶̶̶̶̶̶e prosecution charged the offense in the context that, standing alone, the public̶̶̶ ̶̶̶̶̶̶themselves might not be obscene. We agree that the question of obscenity may include consideration of the setting in which the publications were presented as an aid to determining the question of obscenity, and assume without deciding that the prosecution could not have succeeded otherwise. As in Mishkin v. New York, 383 U.S. 502 (1966), and as did the courts below, 224 F. Supp., at 134, 338 F.2d, at 14-15, we view the publications against a background of commercial exploitation of erotica

---

[hh] Concurring opinions of Justices Black, Stewart, and Douglas are omitted, as are dissenting opinions of Justices White and Clark. — ED.

[2] The federal obscenity statute, 18 U.S.C. §1461, provides in pertinent part:

"Every obscene, lewd, lascivious, indecent, filthy or vile article, matter, thing, device, or substance; and — . . .

"Every written or printed card, letter, circular, book, pamphlet, advertisement, or notice of any kind giving information, directly or indirectly, where, or how, or from whom, or by what means any of such mentioned matters . . . may be obtained. . . .

"It is declared to be nonmailable matter and shall not be conveyed in the mails or delivered from any post office or by any letter carrier.

"Whoever knowingly uses the mails for the mailing, carriage in the mails, or delivery of anything declared by this section to be nonmailable . . . shall be fined not more than $5,000 or imprisoned not more than five years, or both, for the first such offense. . . ."

solely for the sake of their prurient appeal. The record in that regard amply supports the decision of the trial judge that the mailing of all three publications offended the statute.[6]

The three publications were "Eros," a hard-cover magazine of expensive format; "Liaison," a bi-weekly newsletter; and "The Housewife's Handbook on Selective Promiscuity" (hereinafter the "Handbook"), a short book. The issue of "Eros" specified in the indictment, Vol. 1, No. 4, contains 15 articles and photo-essays on the subject of love, sex, and sexual relations. The specified issue of "Liaison," Vol. 1, No. 1, contains a prefatory "Letter from the Editors" announcing its dedication to "keeping sex an art and preventing it from becoming a science." The remainder of the issue consists of digests of two articles concerning sex and sexual relations which had earlier appeared in professional journals and a report of an interview with a psychotherapist who favors the broadest license in sexual relationships. As the trial judge noted, "[w]hile the treatment is largely superficial, it is presented entirely without restraint of any kind. According to defendants' own expert, it is entirely without literary merit." 224 F. Supp., at 134. The "Handbook" purports to be a sexual autobiography detailing with complete candor the author's sexual experiences from age 3 to age 36. The text includes, and prefatory and concluding sections of the book elaborate, her views on such subjects as sex education of children, laws regulating private consensual sexual practices, and the equality of women in sexual relationships. It was claimed at trial that women would find the book valuable, for example as a marriage manual or as an aid to the sex education of their children.

Besides testimony as to the merit of the material, there was abundant evidence to show that each of the accused publications was originated or sold as stock in trade of the sordid business of pandering — "the business of purveying textual or graphic matter openly advertised to appeal to the erotic interest of their customers." "Eros" early sought mailing privileges from the postmasters of Intercourse and Blue Ball, Pennsylvania. The trial court found the obvious, that these hamlets were chosen only for the value their names would have in furthering petitioners' efforts to sell their publications on the basis of salacious appeal; the facilities of the post offices were inadequate to handle the anticipated volume of mail, and the privileges were denied. Mailing privileges were then obtained from the postmaster of Middlesex, New Jersey. "Eros" and "Liaison" thereafter mailed several million circulars soliciting subscriptions from that post office; over 5,500 copies of the "Handbook" were mailed.

The "leer of the sensualist" also permeates the advertising for the three publications. The circulars sent for "Eros" and "Liaison" stressed the sexual candor of the respective publications, and openly boasted that the publishers would take full advantage of what they regarded as unrestricted license allowed by law in the expression of sex and sexual matters. The advertising for the "Handbook," apparently mailed from New York, consisted almost entirely of a reproduction of the introduction of the book, written by one Dr. Albert Ellis. Although he alludes to the book's informational value and its putative therapeutic usefulness, his remarks are preoccupied with the book's sexual imagery. The solicitation was indiscriminate, not limited to those, such as physicians or psychiatrists, who might independently discern the book's therapeutic worth. Inserted in each advertisement was a slip labeled "GUARANTEE" and reading, "Documentary Books, Inc., unconditionally guarantees full refund of the price of 'The Housewife's Handbook on Selective Promiscuity' if the book fails to reach you because of U.S. Post Office censorship interference." Similar slips appeared in the advertising of "Eros" and "Liaison"; they highlighted the gloss petitioners put on the publications, eliminating any doubt what the purchaser was being asked to buy.

[6] It is suggested in dissent that petitioners were unaware that the record being established could be used in support of such an approach, and that petitioners should be afforded the opportunity of a new trial. However, the trial transcript clearly reveals that at several points the Government announced its theory that made the mode of distribution relevant to the determination of obscenity, and the trial court admitted evidence, otherwise irrelevant, toward that end.

This evidence, in our view, was relevant in determining the ultimate question of "obscenity" and, in the context of this record, serves to resolve all ambiguity and doubt. The deliberate representation of petitioners' publications as erotically arousing, for example, stimulated the reader to accept them as prurient; he looks for titillation, not for saving intellectual content. Similarly, such representation would tend to force public confrontation with the potentially offensive aspects of the work; the brazenness of such an appeal heightens the offensiveness of the publications to those who are offended by such material. And the circumstances of presentation and dissemination of material are equally relevant to determining whether social importance claimed for material in the courtroom was, in the circumstances, pretense or reality — whether it was the basis upon which it was traded in the market-place or a spurious claim for litigation purposes. Where the purveyor's sole emphasis is on the sexually provocative aspects of his publications, that fact may be decisive in the determination of obscenity. Certainly in a prosecution which, as here, does not necessarily imply suppression of the materials involved, the fact that they originate or are used as a subject of pandering is relevant to the application of the Roth test. . . .

We perceive no threat to First Amendment guarantees in thus holding that in close cases evidence of pandering may be probative with respect to the nature of the material in question and thus satisfy the Roth test. . . . A conviction for mailing obscene publications, but explained in part by the presence of this element, does not necessarily suppress the materials in question, nor chill their proper distribution for a proper use. Nor should it inhibit the enterprise of others seeking through serious endeavor to advance human knowledge or understanding in science, literature, or art. . . .

MR. JUSTICE STEWART, dissenting.

Ralph Ginzburg has been sentenced to five years in prison for sending through the mail copies of a magazine, a pamphlet, and a book. There was testimony at his trial that these publications possess artistic and social merit. Personally, I have a hard time discerning any. Most of the material strikes me as both vulgar and unedifying. But if the First Amendment means anything, it means that a man cannot be sent to prison merely for distributing publications which offend a judge's esthetic sensibilities, mine or any other's. . . .

The Court today appears to concede that the materials Ginzburg mailed were themselves protected by the First Amendment. But, the Court says, Ginzburg can still be sentenced to five years in prison for mailing them. Why? Because, says the Court, he was guilty of "commercial exploitation," of "pandering," and of "titillation." But Ginzburg was not charged with "commercial exploitation"; he was not charged with "pandering"; he was not charged with "titillation." Therefore, to affirm his conviction now on any of those grounds, even if otherwise valid, is to deny him due process of law. Cole v. Arkansas, 333 U.S. 196. But those grounds are *not*, of course, otherwise valid. Neither the statute under which Ginzburg was convicted nor any other federal statute I know of makes "commercial exploitation" or "pandering" or "titillation" a criminal offense. And any criminal law that sought to do so in the terms so elusively defined by the Court would, of course, be unconstitutionally vague and therefore void. All of these matters are developed in the dissenting opinions of my Brethren, and I simply note here that I fully agree with them.[ii]

Ginsberg v. New York *390 U.S. 629, 88 S. Ct. 1274, 20 L. Ed. 2d 195 (1968)*

MR. JUSTICE BRENNAN delivered the opinion of the Court. This case presents the question of the constitutionality on its face of a New York criminal obscenity statute which pro-

---

[ii] Dissenting opinions by Black, Harlan, and Douglas, JJ., are omitted. — ED.

hibits the sale to minors under 17 years of age of material defined to be obscene on the basis of its appeal to them whether or not it would be obscene to adults.

Appellant and his wife operate "Sam's Stationery and Luncheonette" in Bellmore, Long Island. They have a lunch counter, and, among other things, also sell magazines including some so-called "girlie" magazines. Appellant was prosecuted under two informations, each in two courts, which charged that he personally sold a 16-year-old boy two "girlie" magazines on each of two dates in October 1965, in violation of §484-h of the New York Penal Law. . . . [The court] held that both sales to the 16-year-old boy therefore constituted the violation under §484-h of "knowingly to sell . . . to a minor" under 17 of "(a) any picture . . . which depicts nudity . . . and which is harmful to minors," and "(b) any . . . magazine . . . which contains . . . [such pictures] . . . and which, taken as a whole, is harmful to minors." The conviction was affirmed without opinion by the Appellate Term, Second Department, of the Supreme Court. Appellant was denied leave to appeal to the New York Court of Appeals and then appealed to this Court. We noted probable jurisdiction. 388 U.S. 904. We affirm.

The "girlie" picture magazines involved in the sales here are not obscene for adults, Redrup v. New York, 386 U.S. 767. But §484-h does not bar the appellant from stocking the magazines and selling them to persons 17 years of age or older, and therefore the conviction is not invalid under our decision in Butler v. Michigan, 352 U.S. 380.

Obscenity is not within the area of protected speech or press. Roth v. United States, 354 U.S. 476, 485. The three-pronged test of subsection 1(f) for judging the obscenity of material sold to minors under 17 is a variable from the formulation for determining obscenity under Roth stated in the plurality opinion in Memoirs v. Massachusetts, 383 U.S. 413, 418. Appellant's primary attack upon §484-h is leveled at the power of the State to adapt this Memoirs formulation to define the material's obscenity on the basis of its appeal to minors, and thus exclude material so defined from the area of protected expression. He makes no argument that the magazines are not "harmful to minors" within the definition in subsection 1(f). Thus "[n]o issue is presented . . . concerning the obscenity of the material involved." Roth, supra, at 481, n.8. . . .

Appellant's attack is not that New York was without power to draw the line at age 17. Rather, his contention is the broad proposition that the scope of the constitutional freedom of expression secured to a citizen to read or see material concerned with sex cannot be made to depend upon whether the citizen is an adult or a minor.

Appellant argues that there is an invasion of protected rights under §484-h constitutionally indistinguishable from the invasions under the Nebraska statute forbidding children to study German, which was struck down in Meyer v. Nebraska, 262 U.S. 290; the Oregon statute interfering with children's attendance at private and parochial schools, which was struck down in Pierce v. Society of Sisters, 268 U.S. 510; and the statute compelling children against their religious scruples to give the flag salute, which was struck down in West Virginia State Board of Education v. Barnette, 319 U.S. 624. We reject that argument. We do not regard New York's regulation in defining obscenity on the basis of its appeal to minors under 17 as involving an invasion of such minors' constitutionally protected freedoms. Rather §484-h simply adjusts the definition of obscenity "to social realities by permitting the appeal of this type of material to be assessed in terms of the sexual interests . . ." of such minors. Mishkin v. New York, 383 U.S. 502, 509; Bookcase, Inc. v. Broderick, supra, at 75, 218 N.E.2d at 671. That the State has power to make that adjustment seems clear, for we have recognized that even where there is an invasion of protected freedoms "the power of the state to control the conduct of children reaches beyond the scope of its authority over adults. . . ." Prince v. Massachusetts, 321 U.S. 158, 170. In Prince we sustained the conviction of the guardian of a nine-year-old girl, both members of the sect of Jehovah's Witnesses, for violating the Massachusetts Child Labor Law by permitting the girl to sell the sect's religious tracts on the streets of Boston.

The well-being of its children is of course a subject within the State's constitutional power to regulate, and, in our view, two interests justify the limitations in §484-h upon the availability of sex material to minors under 17, at least if it was rational for the legislature to find that the minors' exposure to such material might be harmful. First of all, constitutional interpretation has consistently recognized that the parents' claim to authority in their own household to direct the rearing of their children is basic in the structure of our society. "It is cardinal with us that the custody, care and nurture of the child reside first in the parents, whose primary function and freedom include preparation for obligations the state can neither supply nor hinder." Prince v. Massachusetts, supra, at 166. The legislature could properly conclude that parents and others, teachers for example, who have this primary responsibility for children's well-being are entitled to the support of laws designed to aid discharge of that responsibility. . . . Moreover, the prohibition against sales to minors does not bar parents who so desire from purchasing the magazines for their children.

The State also has an independent interest in the well-being of its youth. . . .

In Prince v. Massachusetts, supra, at 165, this Court, too, recognized that the State has an interest "to protect the welfare of children" and to see that they are "safeguarded from abuses" which might prevent their "growth into free and independent well-developed men and citizens." The only question remaining, therefore, is whether the New York Legislature might rationally conclude, as it has, that exposure to the materials proscribed by §484-h constitutes such an "abuse."

Section 484-3 of the law states a legislative finding that the material condemned by §484-h is "a basic factor in impairing the ethical and moral development of our youth and a clear and present danger to the people of the state." It is very doubtful that this finding expresses an accepted scientific fact. But obscenity is not protected expression and may be suppressed without a showing of the circumstances which lie behind the phrase "clear and present danger" in its application to protected speech. Roth v. United States, supra, at 486-487. To sustain state power to exclude material defined as obscenity by §484-h requires only that we be able to say that it was not irrational for the legislature to find that exposure to material condemned by the statute is harmful to minors. . . . To be sure, there is no lack of "studies" which purport to demonstrate that obscenity is or is not "a basic factor in impairing the ethical and moral development of . . . youth and a clear and present danger to the people of the state." But the growing consensus of commentators is that "while these studies all agree that a causal link has not been demonstrated, they are equally agreed that a causal link has not been disproved either." We do not demand of legislatures "scientifically certain criteria of legislation." Noble State Bank v. Haskell, 219 U.S. 104, 110. We therefore cannot say that §484-h, in defining the obscenity of material on the basis of its appeal to minors under 17, has no rational relation to the objective of safeguarding such minors from harm.

II

Appellant challenges subsections (f) and (g) of §484-h as in any event void for vagueness. The attack on subsection (f) is that the definition of obscenity "harmful to minors" is so vague that an honest distributor of publications cannot know when he might be held to have violated §484-h. But the New York Court of Appeals construed this definition to be "virtually identical to the Supreme Court's most recent statement of the elements of obscenity. [Memoirs v. Massachusetts, 383 U.S. 413, 418]," Bookcase, Inc. v. Broderick, supra, at 76, 218 N.E.2d, at 672. The definition therefore gives "men in acting adequate notice of what is prohibited" and does not offend the requirements of due process. Roth v. United States, supra, at 492; see also Winters v. New York, 333 U.S. 507, 520.

As is required by Smith v. California, 361 U.S. 147, §484-h prohibits only those sales made "knowingly." . . .

... The constitutional requirement of scienter, in the sense of knowledge of the contents of material, rests on the necessity "to avoid the hazard of self-censorship of constitutionally protected material and to compensate for the ambiguities inherent in the definition of obscenity," Mishkin v. New York, supra, at 511. The Court of Appeals in Finkelstein interpreted §1141 to require "the vital element of scienter" and defined that requirement in these terms: "A reading of the statute [§1141] as a whole clearly indicates that only those who are *in some manner aware of the character of the material* they attempt to distribute should be punished. It is not innocent but *calculated* purveyance of filth which is exorcised. . . ." 9 N.Y. 2d, at 344-345, 174 N.E.2d, at 471. (Emphasis supplied.) In Mishkin v. New York, supra, at 510-511, we held that a challenge to the validity of §1141 founded on Smith v. California, supra, was foreclosed in light of this construction. . . . In that circumstance Mishkin requires rejection of appellant's challenge to provision (i) and makes it unnecessary for us to define further today "what sort of mental element is requisite to a constitutionally permissible prosecution," Smith v. California, supra, at 154. . . .

Affirmed.

MR. JUSTICE STEWART, concurring in the result. A doctrinaire, kneejerk application of the First Amendment would, of course, dictate the nullification of this New York Statute. But that result is not required, I think, if we bear in mind what it is that the First Amendment protects.

The First Amendment guarantees liberty of human expression in order to preserve in our Nation what Mr. Justice Holmes called a "free trade in ideas." To that end, the Constitution protects more than just a man's freedom to say or write or publish what he wants. It secures as well the liberty of each man to decide for himself what he will read and to what he will listen. The Constitution guarantees, in short, a society of free choice. Such a society presupposes the capacity of its members to choose. . . .

I think a State may permissibly determine that, at least in some precisely delineated areas, a child — like someone in a captive audience — is not possessed of that full capacity for individual choice which is the presupposition of First Amendment guarantees. It is only upon such a premise, I should suppose, that a State may deprive children of other rights — the right to marry, for example, or the right to vote — deprivations that would be constitutionally intolerable for adults.

I cannot hold that this state law, on its face, violates the First and Fourteenth Amendments.[jj]

NOTE Developments in Obscenity

1. The city of Dallas enacted an ordinance establishing a Motion Picture Classification Board to classify films as suitable or not suitable for young persons under 16 years of age, with standards for classification set forth in the ordinance. A "not suitable" classification required notices in advertising, restrictions upon attendance, etc. If a classification was not accepted by an exhibitor, a suit to enjoin showing, and de novo review were provided. On the same day that it decided the Ginsberg case, the Supreme Court reversed a judgment enjoining the showing of a film entitled "Viva Maria" on the ground that the standards set forth in the ordinance were too vague, and that the evil of vagueness was not cured because the ordinance was adopted for the salutary purpose of protecting children. Interstate Circuit, Inc. v. City of Dallas, 390 U.S. 676 (1968).

2. Officers searching Stanley's home under authority of a warrant found some films in his bedroom. He was charged and convicted of violating Ga. Code Ann. §26-6301 by vir-

---

[jj] Appendices A and B to the opinion of the Court are omitted, as are dissenting opinions of Justice Fortas and Justice Douglas, joined by Justice Black. A concurring opinion of Justice Harlan is also omitted. — ED.

Section C. Freedom of Speech and Association 1299

tue of "knowingly hav[ing] possession of . . . obscene matter." The conviction was reversed on the ground that the Fourteenth Amendment prohibited a state from punishing private possession of obscene material. Stanley v. Georgia, 394 U.S. 557 (1969).

Conversely, in Rowan v. United States Post Office Dept., 397 U.S. 728 (1970), the Court upheld Title III of the Postal Revenue and Federal Salary Act of 1967 allowing any person receiving in the mail "a pandering advertisement which offers for sale matter which the addressee in his sole discretion believes to be erotically arousing or sexually provocative" to request the post office to send an enforcible order to the sender barring further mailings.

3. United States v. Reidel, 402 U.S. 351 (1971), involved an indictment for knowing use of the mails for the delivery of obscene matter to willing recipients who state that they are adults. Seven justices joined in upholding the indictment. Justices Douglas and Black dissented. The majority interpreted Stanley v. Georgia to immunize only a person's interest in possessing and reading obscene material in his home, not an interest in making the material commercially available to him. The Court rejected the argument that, as a constitutional limitation, government may control obscene matter only where children are involved or where it is imposed on unwilling recipients. "This may prove to be the desirable and eventual legislative course," but the choice was held not for the courts to make. Justice Marshall, the author of the Stanley opinion, concurred in the result on the ground that mail order distribution without more stringent safeguards than the distributor imposed presents a danger that the material will be sent to children. In Justice Marshall's view, only the protection of children and unwilling adults is a legitimate governmental interest in the control of obscenity.

4. On a showing that, under the Chicago Motion Picture Censorship Ordinance, 50 to 57 days were provided to complete the administrative process if a permit was not issued upon application, and that there was no provision for a prompt judicial decision by a trial court, the Supreme Court reversed a judgment enjoining the appellants from showing certain motion pictures publicly in Chicago. Teitel Film Corp. v. Cusack, 390 U.S. 139 (1968).

Seizure of obscene materials by customs officers was considered in United States v. Thirty-seven Photographs, 402 U.S. 463 (1971). The Court upheld the procedures involved as conforming to the standards in Freedman v. Maryland, 380 U.S. 51. On the substantive issue four justices (White, Brennan, and Blackmun, JJ., and Burger, C.J.) were prepared to support the seizure whether the material imported was intended for commercial or for private use, since it could be treated as contraband. Harlan and Stewart, JJ., concurred in the result on the ground that commercial use was in fact contemplated by the importer. Black, Douglas, and Marshall, JJ., dissented.

The procedural requirements for motion picture censorship were held applicable to the denial of the mails to commercial distributors of obscene literature. Blount v. Rizzi, 400 U.S. 410 (1971).

The procedural requirements for imposition of a prior restraint laid down in Freedman v. Maryland, supra, were held to apply to a city's decision not to allow presentation of the musical "Hair" at a municipal theater, where that decision was based solely on the city's judgment as to whether the musical was obscene and whether its production would be "in the best interest of the community." Southeastern Promotions, Ltd. v. Conrad, 420 U.S. 546 (1975).

Alabama law precluded a defendant from litigating the obscenity of a publication which had already been judicially declared obscene in an earlier civil proceeding. The Court found this procedure unconstitutional in McKinney v. Alabama, 424 U.S. 669 (1976), because the defendant had received no prior notice of the earlier proceeding and because there was no indication that the party in the earlier proceeding had sufficiently identical interests to protect the defendant's First Amendment rights.

5. By 1967, the views of the Justices had become so "divergent" that "the Court began

1300   Chapter Sixteen.   Substantive Rights

the practice in Redrup v. New York, 386 U.S. 767 (1967), the per curiam reversals of convictions for the dissemination of materials that at least five members of the Court, applying their separate tests, deemed not to be obscene. . . . No fewer than 31 cases have been disposed of in this fashion. . . ." Paris Adult Theatre I v. Slaton, 413 U.S. 49, 82 and n.8 (1973) (Brennan, J., dissenting). In a comprehensive reexamination of the subject, the impasse was broken in the cases which follow.

Miller v. California   413 U.S. 15, 93 S. Ct. 2607, 37 L. Ed. 2d 419 (1973)

MR. CHIEF JUSTICE BURGER delivered the opinion of the Court.

This is one of a group of "obscenity-pornography" cases being reviewed by the Court in a re-examination of standards enunciated in earlier cases involving what Mr. Justice Harlan called "the intractable obscenity problem." Interstate Circuit, Inc. v. Dallas, 390 U.S. 676, 704 (1968) (concurring and dissenting).

Appellant conducted a mass mailing campaign to advertise the sale of illustrated books, euphemistically called "adult" material. After a jury trial, he was convicted of violating California Penal Code §311.2(a), a misdemeanor, by knowingly distributing obscene matter, and the Appellate Department, Superior Court of California, County of Orange, summarily affirmed the judgment without opinion. Appellant's conviction was specifically based on his conduct in causing five unsolicited advertising brochures to be sent through the mail in an envelope addressed to a restaurant in Newport Beach, California. The envelope was opened by the manager of the restaurant and his mother. They had not requested the brochures; they complained to the police.

Apart from the initial formulation in the Roth case, no majority of the Court has at any given time been able to agree on a standard to determine what constitutes obscene, pornographic material subject to regulation under the States' police power. See, e.g., Redrup v. New York, 386 U.S., at 770-771. We have seen "a variety of views among the members of the Court unmatched in any other course of constitutional adjudication." Interstate Circuit, Inc. v. Dallas, 390 U.S., at 704-705 (Harlan, J., concurring and dissenting) (footnote omitted). . . .

This much has been categorically settled by the Court, that obscene material is unprotected by the First Amendment. Kois v. Wisconsin, 408 U.S. 229 (1972); United States v. Reidel, 402 U.S., at 354; Roth v. United States, supra, at 485. "The First and Fourteenth Amendments have never been treated as absolutes [footnote omitted]." Breard v. Alexandria, 341 U.S., at 642, and cases cited. See Times Film Corp. v. Chicago, 365 U.S. 43, 47-50 (1961); Joseph Burstyn, Inc. v. Wilson, 343 U.S., at 502. We acknowledge, however, the inherent dangers of undertaking to regulate any form of expression. State statutes designed to regulate obscene materials must be carefully limited. . . .

The basic guidelines for the trier of fact must be: (a) whether "the average person, applying contemporary community standards" would find that the work, taken as a whole, appeals to the prurient interest, Kois v. Wisconsin, supra, at 230, quoting Roth v. United States, supra, at 489; (b) whether the work depicts or describes, in a patently offensive way, sexual conduct specifically defined by the applicable state law; and (c) whether the work, taken as a whole, lacks serious literary, artistic, political, or scientific value. We do not adopt as a constitutional standard the *"utterly* without redeeming social value" test of Memoirs v. Massachusetts, 383 U.S., at 419; that concept has never commanded the adherence of more than three Justices at one time. See supra, at 21. If a state law that regulates obscene material is thus limited, as written or construed, the First Amendment values applicable to the States through the Fourteenth Amendment are adequately protected by the ultimate power of appellate courts to conduct an independent review of constitutional claims when necessary. . . .

We emphasize that it is not our function to propose regulatory schemes for the States.

That must await their concrete legislative efforts. It is possible, however, to give a few plain examples of what a state statute could define for regulation under part (b) of the standard announced in this opinion, supra:

(a) Patently offensive representations or descriptions of ultimate sexual acts, normal or perverted, actual or simulated.

(b) Patently offensive representations or descriptions of masturbation, excretory functions, and lewd exhibition of the genitals.

Sex and nudity may not be exploited without limit by films or pictures exhibited or sold in places of public accommodation any more than live sex and nudity can be exhibited or sold without limit in such public places. At a minimum, prurient, patently offensive depiction or description of sexual conduct must have serious literary, artistic, political, or scientific value to merit First Amendment protection. . . .

Mr. Justice Brennan, author of the opinions of the Court, or the plurality opinions, in Roth v. United States, supra; Jacobellis v. Ohio, supra; Ginzburg v. United States, 383 U.S. 463 (1966), Mishkin v. New York, 383 U.S. 502 (1966); and Memoirs v. Massachusetts, supra, has abandoned his former position and now maintains that no formulation of this Court, the Congress, or the States can adequately distinguish obscene material unprotected by the First Amendment from protected expression, Paris Adult Theatre I v. Slaton, post, p. 73 (Brennan, J., dissenting). Paradoxically, Mr. Justice Brennan indicates that suppression of unprotected obscene material is permissible to avoid exposure to unconsenting adults, as in this case, and to juveniles, although he gives no indication of how the division between protected and nonprotected materials may be drawn with greater precision for these purposes than for regulation of commercial exposure to consenting adults only. Nor does he indicate where in the Constitution he finds the authority to distinguish between a willing "adult" one month past the state law age of majority and a willing "juvenile" one month younger.

Under the holdings announced today, no one will be subject to prosecution for the sale or exposure of obscene materials unless these materials depict or describe patently offensive "hard core" sexual conduct specifically defined by the regulating state law, as written or construed. We are satisfied that these specific prerequisites will provide fair notice to a dealer in such materials that his public and commercial activities may bring prosecution. . . .

Under a National Constitution, fundamental First Amendment limitations on the powers of the States do not vary from community to community, but this does not mean that there are, or should or can be, fixed, uniform national standards of precisely what appeals to the "prurient interest" or is "patently offensive." These are essentially questions of fact, and our Nation is simply too big and too diverse for this Court to reasonably expect that such standards could be articulated for all 50 States in a single formulation, even assuming the prerequisite consensus exists. When triers of fact are asked to decide whether "the average person, applying contemporary community standards" would consider certain materials "prurient," it would be unrealistic to require that the answer be based on some abstract formulation. The adversary system, with lay jurors as the usual ultimate fact finders in criminal prosecutions, has historically permitted triers of fact to draw on the standards of their community, guided always by limiting instructions on the law. To require a State to structure obscenity proceedings around evidence of a *national* "community standard" would be an exercise in futility.

It is neither realistic nor constitutionally sound to read the First Amendment as requiring that the people of Maine or Mississippi accept public depiction of conduct found tolerable in Las Vegas, or New York City. . . .

The dissenting Justices sound the alarm of repression. But, in our view, to equate the free and robust exchange of ideas and political debate with commercial exploitation of obscene material demeans the grand conception of the First Amendment and its high purposes in the historic struggle for freedom. . . .

There is no evidence, empirical or historical, that the stern 19th century American censorship of public distribution and display of material relating to sex, see Roth v. United States, supra, at 482-485, in any way limited or affected expression of serious literary, artistic, political, or scientific ideas. On the contrary, it is beyond any question that the era following Thomas Jefferson to Theodore Roosevelt was an "extraordinarily vigorous period," not just in economics and politics, but in *belles lettres* and in "the outlying fields of social and political philosophies." We do not see the harsh hand of censorship of ideas — good or bad, sound or unsound — and "repression" of political liberty lurking in every state regulation of commercial exploitation of human interest in sex.

. . . The judgment of the Appellate Department of the Superior Court, Orange County, California, is vacated and the case remanded to that court for further proceedings not inconsistent with the First Amendment standards established by this opinion. . . .[kk]

Paris Adult Theatre I v. Slaton 413 U.S. 49, 93 S. Ct. 2628, 37 L. Ed. 2d 446 (1973)

MR. CHIEF JUSTICE BURGER delivered the opinion of the Court.

Petitioners are two Atlanta, Georgia, movie theaters and their owners and managers, operating in the style of "adult" theaters. On December 28, 1970, respondents, the local state district attorney and the solicitor for the local state trial court, filed civil complaints in that court alleging that petitioners were exhibiting to the public for paid admission two allegedly obscene films. . . .

. . . Certain photographs, also produced at trial, were stipulated to portray the single entrance to both Paris Adult Theatre I and Paris Adult Theatre II as it appeared at the time of the complaints. These photographs show a conventional, inoffensive theater entrance, without any pictures, but with signs indicating that the theaters exhibit "Atlanta's Finest Mature Feature Films." On the door itself is a sign saying: "Adult Theatre — You must be 21 and able to prove it. If viewing the nude body offends you, Please Do Not Enter."

. . . [T]he trail judge dismissed respondents' complaints. He assumed "that obscenity is established," but stated: "It appears to the Court that the display of these films in a commercial theatre, when surrounded by requisite notice to the public of their nature and by reasonable protection against the exposure of these films to minors, is constitutionally permissible."

On appeal, the Georgia Supreme Court unanimously reversed. . . . Citing the opinion of this Court in United States v. Reidel, 402 U.S. 351 (1971), the Georgia court stated that "the sale and delivery of obscene material to willing adults is not protected under the first amendment." . . .

We categorically disapprove the theory, apparently adopted by the trial judge, that obscene, pornographic films acquire constitutional immunity from state regulation simply because they are exhibited for consenting adults only. This holding was properly rejected by the Georgia Supreme Court. Although we have often pointedly recognized the high importance of the state interest in regulating the exposure of obscene materials to juveniles and unconsenting adults, see Miller v. California, ante, at 18-20; Stanley v. Georgia, 394 U.S., at 567; Redrup v. New York, 386 U.S. 767, 769 (1967), this Court has never declared these to be the only legitimate state interests permitting regulation of obscene material. . . .

In particular, we hold that there are legitimate state interests at stake in stemming the tide of commercialized obscenity, even assuming it is feasible to enforce effective safeguards against exposure to juveniles and to passersby. Rights and interests "other than

---

[kk] Dissenting opinions of Justice Douglas and Justice Brennan, joined by Justices Stewart and Marshall, are omitted. — ED.

those of the advocates are involved." Breard v. Alexandria, 341 U.S. 622, 642 (1951). These include the interest of the public in the quality of life and the total community environment, the tone of commerce in the great city centers, and, possibly, the public safety itself. The Hill-Link Minority Report of the Commission on Obscenity and Pornography indicates that there is at least an arguable correlation between obscene material and crime. . . .

[An extensive discussion of the various state interests served by the regulation of obscenity is omitted.]

. . . The judgment is vacated and the case remanded to the Georgia Supreme Court for further proceedings not inconsistent with this opinion and Miller v. California, supra. . . .[11]

MR. JUSTICE BRENNAN, with whom MR. JUSTICE STEWART and MR. JUSTICE MARSHALL join, dissenting. . . .

. . . The essence of our problem in the obscenity area is that we have been unable to provide "sensitive tools" to separate obscenity from other sexually oriented but constitutionally protected speech, so that efforts to suppress the former do not spill over into the suppression of the latter. . . .

Our experience since Roth requires us not only to abandon the effort to pick out obscene materials on a case-by-case basis, but also to reconsider a fundamental postulate of Roth: that there exists a definable class of sexually oriented expression that may be totally suppressed by the Federal and State Governments. Assuming that such a class of expression does in fact exist, I am forced to conclude that the concept of "obscenity" cannot be defined with sufficient specificity and clarity to provide fair notice to persons who create and distribute sexually oriented materials, to prevent substantial erosion of protected speech as a byproduct of the attempt to suppress unprotected speech, and to avoid very costly institutional harms. Given these inevitable side effects of state efforts to suppress what is assumed to be unprotected speech, we must scrutinize with care the state interest that is asserted to justify the suppression. . . .

The opinions in Redrup and Stanley reflected our emerging view that the state interests in protecting children and in protecting unconsenting adults may stand on a different footing from the other asserted state interests. It may well be, as one commentator has argued, that "exposure to [erotic material] is for some persons an intense emotional experience. A communication of this nature, imposed upon a person contrary to his wishes, has all the characteristics of a physical assault. . . . [And it] constitutes an invasion of his privacy. . . ."[24] But cf. Cohen v. California, 403 U.S., at 21-22. Similarly, if children are "not possessed of that full capacity for individual choice which is the presupposition of the First Amendment guarantees," Ginsberg v. New York, 390 U.S., at 649-650 (Stewart, J., concurring), then the State may have a substantial interest in precluding the flow of obscene materials even to consenting juveniles. But cf. id., at 673-674 (Fortas, J., dissenting).

But, whatever the strength of the state interests in protecting juveniles and unconsenting adults from exposure to sexually oriented materials, those interests cannot be asserted in defense of the holding of the Georgia Supreme Court in this case. . . .

In Stanley we pointed out that "[t]here appears to be little empirical basis for" the assertion that "exposure to obscene materials may lead to deviant sexual behavior or crimes of sexual violence." Id., at 566 and n.9. In any event, we added that "if the State is only concerned about printed or filmed materials inducing antisocial conduct, we believe that in the context of private consumption of ideas and information we should adhere to the view that '[a]mong free men, the deterrents ordinarily to be applied to prevent crime are education and punishment for violations of the law. . . .' Whitney v. California, 274 U.S. 357, 378 (1927) (Brandeis, J., concurring)." Id., at 566-567.

---

[11] A dissenting opinion of Justice Douglas is omitted. — ED.
[24] T. Emerson, The System of Freedom of Expression 496 (1970).

Moreover, in Stanley we rejected as "wholly inconsistent with the philosophy of the First Amendment," id., at 566, the notion that there is a legitimate state concern in the "control [of] the moral content of a person's thoughts," id., at 565, and we held that a State "cannot constitutionally premise legislation on the desirability of controlling a person's private thoughts." Id., at 566. That is not to say, of course, that a State must remain utterly indifferent to — and take no action bearing on — the morality of the community. The traditional description of state police power does embrace the regulation of morals as well as the health, safety, and general welfare of the citizenry. See e.g., Village of Euclid v. Ambler Realty Co., 272 U.S. 365, 395 (1926). And much legislation — compulsory public education laws, civil rights laws, even the abolition of capital punishment — is grounded, at least in part, on a concern with the morality of the community. But the State's interest in regulating morality by suppressing obscenity, while often asserted, remains essentially unfocused and ill defined. And, since the attempt to curtail unprotected speech necessarily spills over into the area of protected speech, the effort to serve this speculative interest through the suppression of obscene material must tread heavily on rights protected by the First Amendment.

. . . I would hold, therefore, that at least in the absence of distribution to juveniles or obtrusive exposure to unconsenting adults, the First and Fourteenth Amendments prohibit the State and Federal Governments from attempting wholly to suppress sexually oriented materials on the basis of their allegedly "obscene" contents. Nothing in this approach precludes those governments from taking action to serve what may be strong and legitimate interests through regulation of the manner of distribution of sexually oriented material. . . .

NOTE Developments under Miller

In recent cases the Court has discussed the proper application of the Miller tests. In Jenkins v. Georgia, 418 U.S. 153 (1974), the Court overturned a verdict based on the jury's finding that the film "Carnal Knowledge" was obscene. On its own viewing of the film, the Court concluded that its depiction of sexual conduct was not "patently offensive." Although acknowledging that application of the Miller tests involved "essentially questions of fact" properly within the province of a jury, the Court justified its rejection of the jury's finding in this case on two grounds. First, the Court noted its power of independent review of constitutional claims. Second, the Court argued that Miller had been intended "to fix substantive constitutional limitations, deriving from the First Amendment, on the type of material subject to [a jury obscenity] determination. It would be wholly at odds with this aspect of Miller to uphold an obscenity conviction based upon a defendant's depiction of a woman with a bare midriff, even though a properly charged jury unanimously agreed on a verdict of guilty." Similarly, "Carnal Knowledge" was held to be outside the category of arguably obscene materials and should never have been submitted to a jury.

In Hamling v. United States, 418 U.S. 87 (1974), the Court considered the meaning of the "community standards" test set out in Miller. Petitioner had been convicted of mailing obscene matter in violation of 18 U.S.C. §1461. The judge had charged the jury to apply the standards of "the nation as a whole" and had refused to admit testimony regarding a poll of attitudes towards the materials in question in Southern California, where the case was tried. The Court noted that Miller had rejected as "hypothetical and unascertainable" the notion of uniform national standards on obscenity. In a federal obscenity prosecution, jurors may draw on local understandings in determining whether a hypothetical "average person, applying contemporary community standards" would consider the materials obscene. The Court acknowledged that one effect of the refusal to pursue national standards in federal cases would be that "distributors of allegedly obscene materials may be subjected to varying community standards in the various federal judicial districts into which they transmit the materials" and indicated that in a federal trial the court would be free to allow introduction of evidence of attitudes regarding obscenity in other parts of the nation. Nonetheless, the variation in local standards, like the variation in substantive state laws, was regarded not to be in violation of a distributor's due process or other constitutional rights. The Court then held that, although the trial court's instructions on national standards may have been based on notions rejected in Miller, they had nonetheless met the underlying purpose of enjoining the jury to make a relatively objective determination of "community standards." As excision of the court's references to a "national standard" would probably not have affected the verdict, the Supreme Court refused to overturn the convictions on that ground. As to the district court's refusal to admit evidence on obscenity standards in Southern California, the Court held that the exclusion was a permissible exercise of the trial court's discretion in the admission of expert testimony.

See Note, Community Standards, Class Actions, and Obscenity Under Miller v. California, 88 Harv. L. Rev. 1838 (1975).

Where the conduct occurred before the Miller decision, what standards should the trial court apply? See Marks v. United States, 97 S. Ct. 990 (1977).

May a city zoning ordinance prohibit the establishment of "adult" book stores and theatres within 500 feet of residential units or within 1000 feet of each other? See Young v. American Mini Theatres, Inc., 427 U.S. 50 (1976). May a city zoning ordinance require instead that all "adult" facilities be located in specified, contiguous areas?

8. Freedom of the Press and Criminal Justice

Sheppard v. Maxwell *384 U.S. 333, 86 S. Ct. 1507, 16 L. Ed. 2d 600 (1966)*

[The following statement is that of the headnote in 384 U.S.

Petitioner's wife was bludgeoned to death July 4, 1954. From the outset officials focused suspicion on petitioner, who was arrested on a murder charge July 30 and indicted August 17. His trial began October 18 and terminated with his conviction December 21, 1954. During the entire pretrial period virulent and incriminating publicity about petitioner and the murder made the case notorious, and the news media frequently aired charges and countercharges besides those for which petitioner was tried. Three months before trial he was examined for more than five hours without counsel in a televised three-day inquest conducted before an audience of several hundred spectators in a gymnasium. Over three weeks before trial the newspapers published the names and addresses of prospective jurors causing them to receive letters and telephone calls about the case. The trial began two weeks before a hotly contested election at which the chief prosecutor and the trial judge were candidates for judgeships. Newsmen were allowed to take over almost the entire small courtroom, hounding petitioner and most of the participants. Twenty reporters were assigned seats by the court within the bar and in close proximity to the jury and counsel, precluding privacy between petitioner and his counsel. The movement of the reporters in the courtroom caused frequent confusion and disrupted the trial; and in the corridors and elsewhere in and around the courthouse they were allowed free rein by the trial judge. A broadcasting station was assigned space next to the jury room. Before the jurors began deliberations they were not sequestered and had access to all news media though the court made "suggestions" and "requests" that the jurors not expose themselves to comment about the case. Though they were sequestered during the five days and four nights of their deliberations, the jurors were allowed to make inadequately supervised telephone calls during that period. Pervasive publicity was given to the case throughout the trial, much of it involving incriminating matter not introduced at the trial, and the jurors were thrust into the role of celebrities. At least some of the publicity deluge reached the jurors. At the very inception of the proceedings and later, the trial judge announced that neither he nor anyone else could restrict the prejudicial news accounts. Despite his awareness of the excessive pretrial publicity, the trial judge failed to take effective measures against the massive publicity which continued throughout the trial or to take adequate steps to control the conduct of the trial.]

MR. JUSTICE CLARK delivered the opinion of the Court.

This federal habeas corpus application involves the question whether Sheppard was deprived of a fair trial in his state conviction for the second-degree murder of his wife because of the trial judge's failure to protect Sheppard sufficiently from the massive, pervasive and prejudicial publicity that attended his prosecution.[1] The United States District Court held that he was not afforded a fair trial and granted the writ subject to the State's right to put Sheppard to trial again, 231 F. Supp. 37 (D.C.S.D. Ohio 1964). The Court of Appeals for the Sixth Circuit reversed by a divided vote, 346 F.2d 707 (1965). We granted certiorari, 382 U.S. 916 (1965). We have concluded that Sheppard did not receive a fair trial consistent with the Due Process Clause of the Fourteenth Amendment and, therefore, reverse the judgment. . . .

The court's fundamental error is compounded by the holding that it lacked power to control the publicity about the trial. From the very inception of the proceedings the judge announced that neither he nor anyone else could restrict prejudicial news accounts. And he reiterated this view on numerous occasions. Since he viewed the news media as his target, the judge never considered other means that are often utilized to reduce the appearance of prejudicial material and to protect the jury from outside influence. We conclude that these procedures would have been sufficient to guarantee Sheppard a fair trial and so do not consider what sanctions might be available against a recalcitrant press nor the charges of bias now made against the state trial judge.

The carnival atmosphere at trial could easily have been avoided since the courtroom and courthouse premises are subject to the control of the court. As we stressed in Estes, the presence of the press at judicial proceedings must be limited when it is apparent that the accused might otherwise be prejudiced or disadvantaged.[12] Bearing in mind the massive pretrial publicity, the judge should have adopted stricter rules governing the use of the courtroom by newsmen, as Sheppard's counsel requested. The number of reporters in the courtroom itself could have been limited at the first sign that their presence would disrupt the trial. They certainly should not have been placed inside the bar. Furthermore, the judge should have more closely regulated the conduct of newsmen in the courtroom. For instance, the judge belatedly asked them not to handle and photograph trial exhibits lying on the counsel table during recesses.

Secondly, the court should have insulated the witnesses. All of the newspapers and radio stations apparently interviewed prospective witnesses at will, and in many instances disclosed their testimony. A typical example was the publication of numerous statements by Susan Hayes, before her appearance in court, regarding her love affair with Sheppard. Although the witnesses were barred from the courtroom during the trial the full vebatim testimony was available to them in the press. This completely nullified the judge's imposition of the rule. See Estes v. Texas [381 U.S. 532 (1965)] at 547.

Thirdly, the court should have made some effort to control the release of leads, infor-

---

[1] Sheppard was convicted in 1954 in the Court of Common Pleas of Cuyahoga County, Ohio. His conviction was affirmed by the Court of Appeals for Cuyahoga County, 100 Ohio App. 345, 128 N.E.2d 471 (1955), and the Ohio Supreme Court, 165 Ohio St. 293, 135 N.E.2d 340 (1956). We denied certiorari on the original appeal. 352 U.S. 910 (1956).

[12] The judge's awareness of his power in this respect is manifest from his assignment of seats to the press.

mation, and gossip to the press by police officers, witnesses, and the counsel for both sides. Much of the information thus disclosed was inaccurate, leading to groundless rumors and confusion.[13] That the judge was aware of his responsibility in this respect may be seen from his warning to Steve Sheppard, the accused's brother, who had apparently made public statements in an attempt to discredit testimony for the prosecution. The judge made this statement in the presence of the jury:

"Now, the Court wants to say a word. That he was told — he has not read anything about it at all — but he was informed that Dr. Steve Sheppard, who has been granted the privilege of remaining in the court room during the trial, has been trying the case in the newspapers and making rather uncomplimentary comments about the testimony of the witnesses for the State.

"Let it be now understood that if Dr. Steve Sheppard wishes to use the newspapers to try his case while we are trying it here, he will be barred from remaining in the court room during the progress of the trial if he is to be a witness in the case.

"The Court appreciates he cannot deny Steve Sheppard the right of free speech, but he can deny him the . . . privilege of being in the court room, if he wants to avail himself of that method during the progress of the trial."

Defense counsel immediately brought to the court's attention the tremendous amount of publicity in the Cleveland press that "misrepresented entirely the testimony" in the case. Under such circumstances, the judge should have at least warned the newspapers to check the accuracy of their accounts. And it is obvious that the judge should have further sought to alleviate this problem by imposing control over the statements made to the news media by counsel, witnesses, and especially the Coroner and police officers. The prosecution repeatedly made evidence available to the news media which was never offered in the trial. Much of the "evidence" disseminated in this fashion was clearly inadmissible. The exclusion of such evidence in court is rendered meaningless when news media make it available to the public. For example, the publicity about Sheppard's refusal to take a lie detector test came directly from police officers and the Coroner. The story that Sheppard had been called a "Jekyll-Hyde" personality by his wife was attributed to a prosecution witness. No such testimony was given. The further report that there was "a 'bombshell witness' on tap" who would testify as to Sheppard's "fiery temper" could only have emanated from the prosecution. Moreover, the newspapers described in detail clues that had been found by the police, but not put into the record.[15]

The fact that many of the prejudicial news items can be traced to the prosecution, as well as the defense, aggravates the judge's failure to take any action. See Stroble v. California, 343 U.S. 181, 201 (1952) (Frankfurter, J., dissenting). Effective control of these sources — concededly within the court's power — might well have prevented the divulgence of inaccurate information, rumors, and accusations that made up much of the inflammatory publicity, at least after Sheppard's indictment.

More specifically, the trial court might well have proscribed extrajudicial statements by any lawyer, party, witness, or court official which divulged prejudicial matters. . . . Being advised of the great public interest in the case, the mass coverage of the press, and

---

[13] The problem here was further complicated by the independent action of the newspapers in reporting "evidence" and gossip which they uncovered. The press not only inferred that Sheppard was guilty because he "stalled" the investigation, hid behind his family, and hired a prominent criminal lawyer, but denounced as "mass jury tempering" his efforts to gather evidence of community prejudice caused by such publications. Sheppard's counterattacks added some fuel but, in these circumstances, cannot preclude him from asserting his right to a fair trial. Putting to one side news stories attributed to police officials, prospective witnesses, the Sheppards, and the lawyers, it is possible that the other publicity "would itself have had a prejudicial effect." See Report of the President's Commission on the Assassination of President Kennedy, at 239.

[15] Such "premature disclosure and weighing of the evidence" may seriously jeopardize a defendant's right to an impartial jury. "[N]either the press nor the public had a right to be contemporaneously informed by the police or prosecuting authorities of the details of the evidence being accumulated against [Sheppard]." Report of the President's Commission, supra, at 239-240.

the potential prejudicial impact of publicity, the court could also have requested the appropriate city and county officials to promulgate a regulation with respect to dissemination of information about the case by their employees.[16] In addition, reporters who wrote or broadcast prejudicial stories, could have been warned as to the impropriety of publishing material not introduced in the proceedings. The judge was put on notice of such events by defense counsel's complaint about the WHK broadcast on the second day of trial. See p. 346, supra. In this manner, Sheppard's right to a trial free from outside interference would have been given added protection without corresponding curtailment of the news media. Had the judge, the other officers of the court, and the police placed the interest of justice first, the news media would have soon learned to be content with the task of reporting the case as it unfolded in the courtroom — not pieced together from extrajudicial statements.

From the cases coming here we note that unfair and prejudicial news comment on pending trials has become increasingly prevalent. Due process requires that the accused receive a trial by an impartial jury free from outside influences. Given the pervasiveness of modern communications and the difficulty of effacing prejudicial publicity from the minds of the jurors, the trial courts must take strong measures to ensure that the balance is never weighed against the accused. And appellate tribunals have the duty to make an independent evaluation of the circumstances. Of course, there is nothing that proscribes the press from reporting events that transpire in the courtroom. But where there is a reasonable likelihood that prejudicial news prior to trial will prevent a fair trial, the judge should continue the case until the threat abates, or transfer it to another county not so permeated with publicity. In addition, sequestration of the jury was something the judge should have raised sua sponte with counsel. If publicity during the proceedings threatens the fairness of the trial, a new trial should be ordered. But we must remember that reversals are but palliatives; the cure lies in those remedial measures that will prevent the prejudice at its inception. The courts must take such steps by rule and regulation that will protect their processes from prejudicial outside interferences. Neither prosecutors, counsel for defense, the accused, witnesses, court staff nor enforcement officers coming under the jurisdiction of the court should be permitted to frustrate its function. Collaboration between counsel and the press as to information affecting the fairness of a criminal trial is not only subject to regulation, but is highly censurable and worthy of disciplinary measures.

Since the state trial judge did not fulfill his duty to protect Sheppard from the inherently prejudicial publicity which saturated the community and to control disruptive influences in the court room, we must reverse the denial of the habeas petition. The case is remanded to the District Court with instructions to issue the writ and order that Sheppard be released from custody unless the State puts him to its charges again within a reasonable time.

It is so ordered.[mm]

MR. JUSTICE BLACK dissents.

NOTE Free Press and Fair Trial

The Sheppard case prompted various studies and recommendations. See American Bar Association Project on Minimum Standards for Criminal Justice, Standards Relating to Fair Trial and Free Press (1966) (Justice Paul C. Reardon, Chairman; David L. Shapiro, Reporter), reprinted at 54 A.B.A.J. 343 (1968). See also Judicial Conference of the

---

[16] The Department of Justice, the City of New York, and other governmental agencies have issued such regulations. E.g., 28 CFR §50.2 (1966). For general information on this topic see periodic publications (e.g., Nos. 71, 124, and 158) by the Freedom of Information Center, School of Journalism, University of Missouri.

[mm] On retrial in November 1966, a jury in the Ohio trial court acquitted Dr. Sheppard. See. N.Y. Times, Nov. 17, 1966, at 1, col. 7. — ED.

Section C. Freedom of Speech and Association 1309

United States, Report of the Committee on the Operation of the Jury System on the "Free Press-Fair Trial" Issue (1968) (Judge Irving R. Kaufman, Chairman), 45 F.R.D. 391 and 51 F.R.D. 135.

See also Pennekamp v. Florida, 328 U.S. 331 (1946); Craig v. Harney, 331 U.S. 367 (1947); Sheppard v. Florida, 341 U.S. 50 (1951). Illustrations of judicial overreaction to critical comment from outside the courtroom can be found at Bridges v. California, 314 U.S. 252 (1941). To what extent can judges limit broadcasts before trial to assure the selection of an impartial jury? See the statement of facts by Justice Frankfurter in Maryland v. Baltimore Radio Show, 338 U.S. 912 (1950) (opinion respecting the denial of the petition for writ of certiorari). See generally Warren and Abell, Free Press-Fair Trial: The "Gag Order," A California Aberration, 45 S. Cal. L. Rev. 51 (1972); Comment, the Gag Order, Exclusion and the Press's Right to Information, 39 Albany L. Rev. 317 (1975).

The question whether a trial court can enjoin the press from publication of pretrial confessions in an attempt to minimize jury bias came before the Court in Nebraska Press Assn. v. Stuart, 427 U.S. 539 (1976). The Nebraska court, prior to a trial for multiple murders, enjoined the news media from publishing or broadcasting accounts of confessions or admissions of the defendant as well as other facts "strongly implicative" of the defendant. There was no evidence or finding "that alternative measures would not have protected [defendant's] rights." (Id. at 565.) Moreover, the order applied to certain statements made at an open preliminary hearing, and was thus in contravention of Cox Broadcasting Co. v. Cohn. The plurality opinion reversing the order was delivered by Burger, C.J. Concurring opinions, suggesting with varying emphasis that prior restraint of the media could almost never be justified, were delivered by White, J., Powell, J., Brennan, J. (with whom Stewart and Marshall, JJ., joined), and Stevens, J. Justice Brennan added: "Of course, even if the press cannot be enjoined. . . , that does not necessarily immunize it from civil liability for libel or invasion of privacy or from criminal liability for transgressions of general criminal law during the course of obtaining that information." (Id. at 588 n.15.) Would the result of the case have been different if the trial judge had ordered the preliminary hearing to be closed? May a judge invoke the contempt power for publishing grand jury testimony?

What alternatives are open to a reporter who is enjoined from publishing information concerning an ongoing trial? In United States v. Dickinson, 465 F.2d 496 (1972), a VISTA worker who had been indicted in Louisiana for conspiracy to murder the mayor of Baton Rouge brought suit to enjoin the prosecution. In the course of evidentiary hearings on petitioner's claim that the prosecution was groundless and had been initiated simply to harass the accused, the district court ordered reporters not to report the evidence. Two local newspaper reporters nonetheless wrote stories detailing the day's testimony. They were found guilty of criminal contempt and fined. On appeal, the court held that the district court's order had been beyond the scope of the "Free-Press — Fair-Trial" Rules adopted by the Judicial Conference, see 45 F.R.D. 391 (1968), and an unconstitutional infringement of the freedom of the press. Nonetheless, the court further held that under the rule that "[i]nvalidity is no defense to criminal contempt," see Walker v. City of Birmingham, 388 U.S. 307 (1967), the reporters were not entitled to relief. The court rejected the argument that timely reporting required the newsmen to violate the order rather than moving to have it vacated. "Timeliness of publication is the hallmark of 'news' and the difference between 'news' and 'history' is merely a matter of hours. Thus, where the publishing of news is sought to be restrained, the incontestable inviolability of the order may depend on the immediate accessibility of orderly review. But in the absence of strong indications that the appellate process was being deliberately stalled — certainly not so in this record — violation with impunity does not occur simply because immediate decision is not forthcoming, even though the communication enjoined is 'news.' . . . [Newsmen] are not yet wrapped in an immunity or given the absolute right to decide with impunity whether a Judge's order is to be obeyed or whether an appellate court is acting promptly enough."

Branzburg v. Hayes 408 U.S. 665, 92 S. Ct. 2646, 33 L. Ed. 2d 626 (1972)

Opinion of the Court by MR. JUSTICE WHITE, announced by the Chief Justice. The issue in these cases is whether requiring newsmen to appear and testify before state or federal grand juries abridges the freedom of speech and press guaranteed by the First Amendment. We hold that it does not.

I

[Three cases were argued and decided together. In Branzburg, petitioner had published newspaper stories describing his observations of hashish-making and interviews with drug users in Frankfort, Kentucky, and stating that he had promised not to reveal the identity of the hashish-makers. Subpoenaed to appear before a grand jury, he invoked the First Amendment and the Kentucky statute conferring a newsman's privilege. The state court ruled that the statute protected only the identity of informants, not personal observation of events and people, and rejected also the constitutional claim.

In In re Pappas, a news photographer was given access to Black Panther headquarters in New Bedford, Massachusetts, in anticipation of a police raid in connection with fires and street disorders. He agreed not to disclose anything he saw or heard except the expected raid, which, however, never materialized. Summoned later before a grand jury, he refused to reveal anything that had taken place at the headquarters. The Massachusetts Supreme Judicial Court, presuming that the grand jury investigation concerned civil disorders, refused to quash the summons, rejecting First Amendment claims.

In U.S. v. Caldwell, respondent refused to appear before a grand jury to testify concerning interviews given him by officers of the Black Panther party regarding the purposes and activities of the organization. The grand jury was investigating possible violations of federal laws, among others, relating to threats against the President, and respondent had published articles referring to the advocacy of violence against the government and possession of guns for that purpose. Respondent refused to appear before the grand jury, on the ground that to do so would destroy his working relationship with the party. The district court was prepared to protect respondent from disclosure of information received in confidence, but ordered him to disclose information given for publication. On his appeal, the court of appeals ruled that he need not appear before the grand jury in the absence of compelling reasons for requiring his testimony.]

II

Petitioners Branzburg and Pappas and respondent Caldwell press First Amendment claims that may be simply put: that to gather news it is often necessary to agree either not to identify the source of information published or to publish only part of the facts revealed, or both; that if the reporter is nevertheless forced to reveal these confidences to a grand jury, the source so identified and other confidential sources of other reporters will be measurably deterred from furnishing publishable information, all to the detriment of the free flow of information protected by the First Amendment. Although the newsmen in these cases do not claim an absolute privilege against official interrogation in all circumstances, they assert that the reporter should not be forced either to appear or to testify

Section C. Freedom of Speech and Association

before a grand jury or at trial until and unless sufficient grounds are shown for believing that the reporter possesses information relevant to a crime the grand jury is investigating, that the information the reporter has is unavailable from other sources, and that the need for the information is sufficiently compelling to override the claimed invasion of First Amendment interests occasioned by the disclosure. . . .

It has generally been held that the First Amendment does not guarantee the press a constitutional right of special access to information not available to the public generally. Zemel v. Rusk, 381 U.S. 1, 16-17 (1965). . . . In Zemel v. Rusk, supra, for example, the Court sustained the Government's refusal to validate passports to Cuba even though that restriction "render[ed] less than wholly free the flow of information concerning that country." Id., at 16. The ban on travel was held constitutional, for "[t]he right to speak and publish does not carry with it the unrestrained right to gather information." Id., at 17.

Despite the fact that news gathering may be hampered, the press is regularly excluded from grand jury proceedings, our own conferences, the meetings of other official bodies gathered in executive session, and the meetings of private organizations. Newsmen have no constitutional right of access to the scenes of crime or disaster when the general public is excluded, and they may be prohibited from attending or publishing information about trials if such restrictions are necessary to assure a defendant a fair trial before an impartial tribunal. In Sheppard v. Maxwell, 384 U.S. 333 (1966), for example, the Court reversed a state court conviction where the trial court failed to adopt "stricter rules governing the use of the courtroom by newsmen, as Sheppard's counsel requested," neglected to insulate witnesses from the press, and made no "effort to control the release of leads, information, and gossip to the press by police officers, witnesses, and the counsel for both sides." Id., at 358, 359. "[T]he trial court might well have proscribed extrajudicial statements by any lawyer, party, witness, or court official which divulged prejudicial matters." Id., at 361. See also Estes v. Texas, 381 U.S. 532, 539-540 (1965); Rideau v. Louisiana, 373 U.S. 723, 726 (1963).

It is thus not surprising that the great weight of authority is that newsmen are not exempt from the normal duty of appearing before a grand jury and answering questions relevant to a criminal investigation. At common law, courts consistently refused to recognize the existence of any privilege authorizing a newsman to refuse to reveal confidential information to a grand jury. . . . In 1958, a news gatherer asserted for the first time that the First Amendment exempted confidential information from public disclosure pursuant to a subpoena issued in a civil suit, Garland v. Torre, 259 F.2d 545 (CA2), cert. denied, 358 U.S. 910 (1958), but the claim was denied, and this argument has been almost uniformly rejected since then, although there are occasional dicta that, in circumstances not presented here, a newsman might be excused. . . .

The prevailing constitutional view of the newsman's privilege is very much rooted in the ancient role of the grand jury that has the dual function of determining if there is probable cause to believe that a crime has been committed and of protecting citizens against unfounded criminal prosecutions. Grand jury proceedings are constitutionally mandated for the institution of federal criminal prosecutions for capital or other serious crimes, and "its constitutional prerogatives are rooted in long centuries of Anglo-American history." Hannah v. Larche, 363 U.S. 420, 489-490 (1960) (Frankfurter, J., concurring in result). . . . Because its task is to inquire into the existence of possible criminal conduct and to return only well-founded indictments, its investigative powers are necessarily broad. "It is a grand inquest, a body with powers of investigation and inquisition, the scope of whose inquiries is not to be limited narrowly by questions of propriety or forecasts of the probable result of the investigation, or by doubts whether any particular individual will be found properly subject to an accusation of crime." Blair v. United States, 250 U.S. 273, 282 (1919). Hence, the grand jury's authority to subpoena witnesses is not only historic, id., at 279-281, but essential to its task. Although the powers of the grand jury are not unlimited and are subject to the supervision of a judge, the longstanding principle that "the public . . . has a right to every man's evidence," except for those persons protected by a constitutional, common-law, or statutory privilege . . . is particularly applicable to grand jury proceedings.

A number of States have provided newsmen a statutory privilege of varying breadth, but the majority have not done so, and none has been provided by federal statute. Until now the only testimonial privilege for unofficial witnesses that is rooted in the Federal Constitution is the Fifth Amendment privilege against compelled self-incrimination. We are asked to create another by interpreting the First Amendment to grant newsmen a testimonial privilege that other citizens do not enjoy. This we decline to do. . . .

Grand juries address themselves to the issues of whether crimes have been committed and who committed them. Only where news sources themselves are implicated in crime or possess information relevant to the grand jury's task need they or the reporter be concerned about grand jury subpoenas. Nothing before us indicates that a large number or percentage of *all* confidential news sources fall into either category and would in any way be deterred by our holding that the Constitution does not, as it never has, exempt the newsman from performing the citizen's normal duty of appearing and furnishing information relevant to the grand jury's task. . . .

[W]e cannot seriously entertain the notion that the First Amendment protects a newsman's agreement to conceal the criminal conduct of his source, or evidence thereof, on the theory that it is better to write about crime than to do something about it. Insofar as any reporter in these cases undertook not to reveal or testify about the crime he witnessed, his claim of privilege under the First Amendment presents no substantial question. The crimes of news sources are no less reprehensible and threatening to the public interest when witnessed by a reporter than when they are not.

There remain those situations where a source is not engaged in criminal conduct but has information suggesting illegal conduct by others. Newsmen frequently receive information from such sources pursuant to a tacit or express agreement to withhold the source's name and suppress any information that the source wishes not published. Such informants presumably desire anonymity in order to avoid being entangled as a witness in a criminal trial or grand jury investigation. They may fear that disclosure will threaten their job security or personal safety or that it will simply result in dishonor or embarrassment.

The argument that the flow of news will be diminished by compelling reporters to aid the grand jury in a criminal investigation is not irrational, nor are the records before us silent on the matter. But we remain unclear how often and to what extent informers are actually deterred from furnishing information when newsmen are forced to testify before a grand jury. The available data indicate that some newsmen rely a great deal on confidential sources and that some informants are particularly sensitive to the threat of exposure and may be silenced if it is held by this Court that, ordinarily, newsmen must testify pursuant to subpoenas, but the evidence fails to demonstrate that there would be a significant constriction of the flow of news to the public if this Court reaffirms the prior common-law and constitutional rule regarding the testimonial obligations of newsmen. Estimates of the inhibiting effect of such subpoenas on the willingness of informants to make disclosures to newsmen are widely divergent and to a great extent speculative. . . .

Accepting the fact, however, that an undetermined number of informants not themselves implicated in crime will nevertheless, for whatever reason, refuse to talk to newsmen if they fear identification by a reporter in an official investigation, we cannot accept the argument that the public interest in possible future news about crime from undisclosed, unverified sources must take precedence over the public interest in pursuing and prosecuting those crimes reported to the press by informants and in thus deterring the commission of such crimes in the future. . . .

The argument for such a constitutional privilege rests heavily on those cases holding that the infringement of protected First Amendment rights must be no broader than necessary to achieve a permissible governmental purpose. . . . We do not deal, however, with a governmental institution that has abused its proper function, as a legislative committee does when it "expose[s] for the sake of exposure." Watkins v. United States, 354 U.S. 178, 200 (1957). Nothing in the record indicates that these grand juries were "prob[ing] at will and without relation to existing need." DeGregory v. Attorney General of New Hampshire, 383 U.S. 825, 829 (1966). Nor did the grand juries attempt to invade protected First Amendment rights by forcing wholesale disclosure of names and organizational affiliations for a purpose that was not germane to the determination of whether crime has been committed, cf. NAACP v. Alabama, 357 U.S. 449 (1958); NAACP v. Button, 371 U.S. 415 (1963); Bates v. Little Rock, 361 U.S. 516 (1960), and the characteristic secrecy of grand jury proceedings is a further protection against the undue invasion of such rights. . . .

The requirements of those cases . . . which hold that a State's interest must be "compelling" or "paramount" to justify even an indirect burden on First Amendment rights, are also met here. . . . If the test is that the government "convincingly show a substantial relation between the information sought and a subject of overriding and compelling state interest," Gibson v. Florida Legislative Investigation Committee, 372 U.S. 539, 546 (1963), it is quite apparent (1) that the State has the necessary interest in extirpating the traffic in illegal drugs, in forestalling assassination attempts on the President, and in preventing the community from being disrupted by violent disorders endangering both persons and property; and (2) that, based on the stories Branzburg and Caldwell wrote and Pappas' admitted conduct, the grand jury called these reporters as they would others — because it was likely that they could supply information to help the government determine whether illegal conduct had occurred and, if it had, whether there was sufficient evidence to return an indictment.

Similar considerations dispose of the reporters' claims that preliminary to requiring their grand jury appearance, the State must show that a crime has been committed and that they possess relevant information not available from other sources, for only the grand jury itself can make this determination. . . .

The privilege claimed here is conditional, not absolute; given the suggested preliminary showings and compelling need, the reporter would be required to testify. . . . If newsmen's confidential sources are as sensitive as they are claimed to be, the prospect of being unmasked whenever a judge determines the situation justifies it is hardly a satisfactory solution to the problem. For them, it would appear that only an absolute privilege would suffice.

We are unwilling to embark the judiciary on a long and difficult journey to such an uncertain destination. The administration of a constitutional newsman's privilege would present practical and conceptual difficulties of a high order. Sooner or later, it would be necessary to define those categories of newsmen who qualified for the privilege. . . . The informative function asserted by representatives of the organized press in the present cases is also performed by lecturers, political pollsters, novelists, academic researchers, and dramatists. Almost any author may quite accurately assert that he is contributing to the flow of information to the public, that he relies on confidential sources of information, and that these sources will be silenced if he is forced to make disclosures before a grand jury.

In each instance where a reporter is subpoenaed to testify, the courts would also be embroiled in preliminary factual and legal determinations with respect to whether the proper predicate had been laid for the reporter's appearance: Is there probable cause to believe a crime has been committed? Is it likely that the reporter has useful information gained in confidence? Could the grand jury obtain the information elsewhere? Is the official interest sufficient to outweigh the claimed privilege? . . .

At the federal level, Congress has freedom to determine whether a statutory newsman's privilege is necessary and desirable and to fashion standards and rules as narrow or broad as deemed necessary to deal with the evil discerned and, equally important, to refashion those rules as experience from time to time may dictate. There is also merit in leaving state legislatures free, within First Amendment limits, to fashion their own standards in light of the conditions and problems with respect to the relations between law enforcement officials and press in their own areas. It goes without saying, of course, that we are powerless to bar state courts from responding in their own way and construing their own constitutions so as to recognize a newsman's privilege, either qualified or absolute. . . .

Finally, as we have earlier indicated, news gathering is not without its First Amendment protections, and grand jury investigations if instituted or conducted other than in good faith, would pose wholly different issues for resolution under the First Amendment. Official harassment of the press undertaken not for purposes of law enforcement but to disrupt a reporter's relationship with his news sources would have no justification. Grand juries are subject to judicial control and subpoenas to motions to quash. We do not expect courts will forget that grand juries must operate within the limits of the First Amendment as well as the Fifth. . . .

Mr. Justice Powell, concurring. I add this brief statement to emphasize what seems to me to be the limited nature of the Court's holding. The Court does not hold that newsmen, subpoenaed to testify before a grand jury, are without constitutional rights with respect to the gathering of news or in safeguarding their sources. . . .

As indicated in the concluding portion of the opinion, the Court states that no harassment of newsmen will be tolerated. If a newsman believes that the grand jury investigation is not being conducted in good faith he is not without remedy. Indeed, if the newsman is called upon to give information bearing only a remote and tenuous relationship to the subject of the investigation, or if he has some other reason to believe that his testimony implicates confidential source relationships without a legitimate need of law enforcement, he will have access to the Court on a motion to quash and an appropriate protective order may be entered. The asserted claim to privilege should be judged on its facts by the striking of a proper balance between freedom of the press and the obligation of all citizens to give relevant testimony with respect to criminal conduct. The balance of these vital constitutional and societal interests on a case-by-case basis accords with the tried and traditional way of adjudicating such questions.

In short, the courts will be available to newsmen under circumstances where legitimate First Amendment interests require protection.[nn]

NOTE

On the impact of Branzburg, see generally Murasky, The Journalist's Privilege: Branzburg and Its Aftermath, 52 Texas L. Rev. 829 (1974). The story of Congress' decision not to enact a shield law in the wake of Branzburg is told by Senator Ervin, In Pursuit of a Press Privilege, 11 Harv. J. Legis. 233, 274 (1974), e.g.: "Senator Alan Cranston (D.-Cal.), one of the Senate's leading proponents of the privilege, conceded: 'Watergate, I think, improved the general attitude toward the press, but, on the other hand, it was all done without a shield law, so why do we need one?' "

[nn] A dissenting opinion was delivered by Douglas, J., and one by Stewart, J., in which Justices Brennan and Marshall joined. — Ed.

Section C. **Freedom of Speech and Association** 1315

9. Requirements of Disclosure and Disclaimer

a. Legislative Investigation

HISTORICAL NOTE

Article I, §5 of the United States Constitution confers on each House of Congress power to punish contempts committed by its own members. On many occasions in the early history of the nation both the Senate and the House of Representatives took action against contemptuous nonmembers, thus indicating that congressional opinion did not consider that the affirmative grant of power over members implied a lack of power over nonmembers. (See 2 Hinds' Precedents of the House of Representatives 1046 et seq. (1907).) In 1800, for instance, William Duane, editor of the anti-Federalist newspaper, the Aurora, was summoned to the bar of the Senate, as was then the custom in all such matters, and charged with a breach of its privileges in having published a libel on the Senate. Thomas Jefferson in his Manual of Parliamentary Practice (1873 ed.), p. 18, wrote of the constitutional issue thus presented as follows:

"The editor of the Aurora having, in his paper of February 19, 1800, inserted some paragraphs defamatory of the Senate, and failed in his appearance was ordered to be committed. In debating the legality of this order it was insisted in support of it that every man, by the law of nature, and every body of men, possess the right of self-defense; that all public functionaries are essentially invested with the powers of self-preservation; that they have an inherent right to do all acts necessary to keep themselves in a condition to discharge the trusts confided to them; that whenever authorities are given, the means of carrying them into execution are given by necessary implication; that thus we see the British Parliament exercise the right of punishing contempts; all the state legislatures exercise the same power, and every court does the same; that if we have it not, we sit at the mercy of every intruder who may enter our doors or gallery, and, by noise and tumult, render proceedings in business impracticable; that if our tranquility is to be perpetually disturbed by newspaper defamation, it will not be possible to exercise our functions with the requisite coolness and deliberation; and that we must therefore have a power to punish these disturbers of our peace and proceedings. To this it was answered that the Parliament and courts of England have cognizance of contempts by the express provisions of their law; that the State legislatures have equal authority because their powers are plenary; they represent their constituents completely; and possess all their powers, except such as their constitutions have expressly denied them; that the courts of the several states have the same powers by the laws of their States, and those of the Federal Government by the same State laws adopted in each State, by a law of Congress; that none of these bodies, therefore, derive those powers from natural or necessary right, but from express law; that Congress have no such natural or necessary power, nor any powers but such as are given them by the Constitution; that that has given them directly exemption from personal arrest, exemption from any question elsewhere for what is said in their House, and power over their own Members and proceedings; for these no further law is necessary, the Constitution being the law; that, moreover, by that article of the Constitution which authorizes them 'to make all laws necessary and proper for carrying into execution the powers vested by the Constitution in them,' they may provide by law for an undisturbed exercise of their functions, e.g., for the punishment of contempts, of affrays or tumult in their presence, etc., but, till the law be made, it does not exist, and does not exist from their own neglect; that, in the meantime, however, they are not unprotected, the ordinary magistrates and courts of law being open and competent to punish all unjustifiable disturbances or defamations, and even their own sergeant, who may appoint deputies ad libitum to aid him (3 Grey,

59, 147, 255), is equal to small disturbances; that in requiring a previous law, the Constitution had regard to the inviolability of the citizen, as well as of the Member; as, should one House, in the regular form of a bill, aim at too broad privileges without control, it may do it on the spur of the occasion, conceal the law in its own breast, and, after the fact committed, make its sentence both the law and the judgment on that fact; if the offense is to be kept undefined and to be declared only ex re nata, and according to the passions of the moment, and there be no limitation either in the manner or measure of the punishment, the condition of the citizen will be perilous indeed. Which of these doctrines will prevail time will decide."

Time, as Jefferson predicted, has made its decision, but not with perfect clarity. In Anderson v. Dunn, 6 Wheat. 204 (1821), the Supreme Court sustained the contention that each House possesses an inherent power to imprison nonmembers for the obstructive contempt of refusing to respond to its summons or to give testimony. Both Houses of Congress continued to assert that those persons who interfered with the orderly conduct of congressional business, as by physical assaults on members of the Congress or by bribery, were punishable by the offended House for their contempt. In 1857 the procedure for handling certain of these charges was altered, however, when the Congress provided by statute that on the refusal of a witness to testify, his recalcitrance was to be reported to the offended House, which would certify the fact of contempt to the District Attorney for the District of Columbia, who would then prosecute the witness for a misdemeanor. That procedure still prevails (2 U.S.C. §§192, 194), though punishment by the offended House itself is still, apparently, an alternative. See McGrain v. Daugherty, 273 U.S. 135 (1927); Jurney v. MacCracken, 294 U.S. 125 (1935).

The issue presented in the matter of William Duane's alleged contempt was not considered by the Court until 1917. In Marshall v. Gordon, 243 U.S. 521, it was held that neither House possessed an inherent power to punish as for a contempt conduct which did not tend to obstruct or prevent the discharge of legislative duties. Accordingly, it was held that the publication of offensive and vexatious charges against the Congress could not be labeled contempt, when the only effect of assertions would be to arouse public opinion and to stir the indignation of members of the Congress. This limitation on the congressional power did not, however, qualify the holding of Anderson v. Dunn, supra.

The decisions in the Anderson and Marshall cases did not directly concern the scope of congressional powers of investigation, nor indicate what substantive or procedural limits, if any, the Court might put upon those powers. In Kilbourn v. Thompson, 103 U.S. 168 (1880), Mr. Justice Miller included in an opinion for the Court passages which suggested that congressional powers of investigation were to be controlled by the judiciary in the fulfillment of its responsibility to maintain a separation between the legislative and judicial powers. In 1927 the Court significantly qualified these earlier intimations that investigatory powers were to be narrowly confined, and formulated basic principles which have since that time prevailed without serious challenge. In McGrain v. Daugherty, 273 U.S. 135, 173-175 (1927), Mr. Justice Van Devanter summarized two propositions which the Court considered settled: "One, that the two houses of Congress, in their separate relations, possess not only such powers as are expressly granted to them by the Constitution, but such auxiliary powers as are necessary and appropriate to make the express powers effective; and, the other, that neither house is invested with 'general' power to inquire into private affairs and compel disclosures, but only with such limited power of inquiry as is shown to exist when the rule of constitutional interpretation just stated is rightly applied." It was later indicated, in Sinclair v. United States, 279 U.S. 263, 291-292 (1929), that the only significant limitations on the congressional power of investigation under the principles of the McGrain case were that the power "must be exerted with due regard for the right of witnesses, and that a witness rightfully may refuse to answer where the bounds of the power are exceeded or where the questions asked are not pertinent to the matter under inquiry." Subsequent cases reaffirmed the limiting principles of McGrain: United States

v. Rumely, 345 U.S. 41 (1953) (authorization); Watkins v. United States, 354 U.S. 178 (1957) (pertinency).

Important articles on the problems of congressional investigations are to be found in a symposium, 18 U. Chi. L. Rev. 421 (1951). See also Carr, The House Committee on Un-American Activities, 1945-1950 (1952); Taylor, Grand Inquest: The Story of Congressional Investigations (1955); Nutting, Freedom of Silence: Constitutional Protection Against Governmental Intrusions in Political Affairs, 47 Mich. L. Rev. 181 (1948).

Barenblatt v. United States 360 U.S. 109, 79 S. Ct. 1081, 3 L. Ed. 2d 1115 (1959)

MR. JUSTICE HARLAN delivered the opinion of the Court. . . .

We here review petitioner's conviction under 2 U.S.C. § 192 for contempt of Congress, arising from his refusal to answer certain questions put to him by a Subcommittee of the House Committee on Un-American Activities during the course of an inquiry concerning alleged Communist infiltration in the field of education. . . .

Pursuant to a subpoena, and accompanied by counsel, petitioner on June 28, 1954, appeared as a witness before this congressional Subcommittee. After answering a few preliminary questions and testifying that he had been a graduate student and teaching fellow at the University of Michigan from 1947 to 1950 and an instructor in psychology at Vassar College from 1950 to shortly before his appearance before the Subcommittee, petitioner objected generally to the right of the Subcommittee to inquire into his "political" and "religious" beliefs or any "other personal and private affairs" or "associational activities," upon grounds set forth in a previously prepared memorandum which he was allowed to file with the Subcommittee. Thereafter petitioner specifically declined to answer each of the following five questions:

"Are you now a member of the Communist Party? (Count One.)

"Have you ever been a member of the Communist Party? (Count Two).

"Now you have stated that you knew Francis Crowley. Did you know Francis Crowley as a member of the Communist Party? (Count Three.)

"Were you ever a member of the Haldane Club of the Communist Party while at the University of Michigan? (Count Four.)

"Were you a member while a student of the University of Michigan Council of Arts, Sciences, and Professions?" (Count Five.)

In each instance the grounds of refusal were those set forth in the prepared statement. Petitioner expressly disclaimed reliance upon "the Fifth Amendment."[3]

Following receipt of the Subcommittee's report of these occurrences the House duly certified the matter to the District of Columbia United States Attorney for contempt proceedings. An indictment in five Counts, each embracing one of petitioner's several refusals to answer, ensued. With the consent of both sides the case was tried to the court without a jury, and upon conviction under all Counts a general sentence of six months' imprisonment and a fine of $250 was imposed.

Since this sentence was less than the maximum punishment authorized by the statute for conviction under any one Count, the judgment below must be upheld if the conviction upon any of the Counts is sustainable. . . . As we conceive the ultimate issue in this case to be whether petitioner could properly be convicted of contempt for refusing to answer questions relating to his participation in or knowledge of alleged Communist Party activities at educational institutions in this country, we find it unnecessary to consider the validity of his conviction under the Third and Fifth Counts, the only ones involving questions which on their face do not directly relate to such participation or knowledge.

[3] We take this to mean the privilege against self-incrimination.

Petitioner's various contentions resolve themselves into three propositions: First, the compelling of testimony by the Subcommittee was neither legislatively authorized nor constitutionally permissible because of the vagueness of Rule XI of the House of Representatives, Eighty-third Congress, the charter of authority of the parent Committee. Second, petitioner was not adequately apprised of the pertinency of the Subcommittee's questions to the subject matter of the inquiry. Third, the questions petitioner refused to answer infringed rights protected by the First Amendment.

SUBCOMMITTEE'S AUTHORITY TO COMPEL TESTIMONY

At the outset it should be noted that Rule XI authorized this Subcommittee to compel testimony within the framework of the investigative authority conferred on the Un-American Activities Committee.[6] Petitioner contends that Watkins v. United States, 354 U.S. 178, . . . nevertheless held the grant of this power in all circumstances ineffective because of the vagueness of Rule XI in delineating the Committee jurisdiction to which its exercise was to be appurtenant. This view of Watkins was accepted by two of the dissenting judges below. 252 F.2d at 136.

The Watkins Case cannot properly be read as standing for such a proposition. A principal contention in Watkins was that the refusals to answer were justified because the requirement of 2 U.S.C. §192 that the questions asked be "pertinent to the question under inquiry" had not been satisfied. 354 U.S. at 208, 209. This Court reversed the conviction solely on that ground, holding that Watkins had not been adequately apprised of the subject matter of the Subcommittee's investigation or the pertinency thereto of the questions he refused to answer. . . . In short, while Watkins was critical of Rule XI, it did not involve the broad and inflexible holding petitioner now attributes to it.

Petitioner also contends, independently of Watkins, that the vagueness of Rule XI deprived the Subcommittee of the right to compel testimony in this investigation into Communist activity. We cannot agree with this contention, which in its furthest reach would mean that the House Un-American Activities Committee under its existing authority has no right to compel testimony in any circumstances. Granting the vagueness of the Rule, we may not read it in isolation from its long history in the House of Representatives. Just as legislation is often given meaning by the gloss of legislative reports, administrative interpretation, and long usage, so the proper meaning of an authorization to a congressional committee is not to be derived alone from its abstract terms unrelated to the definite content furnished them by the course of congressional actions. The Rule comes to us with a "persuasive gloss of legislative history," United States v. Witkovich, 353 U.S. 194, 199, which shows beyond doubt that in pursuance of its legislative concerns in the domain of "national security" the House has clothed the Un-American Activities Committee with pervasive authority to investigate Communist activities in this country.

The essence of that history can be briefly stated. The Un-American Activities Committee, originally known as the Dies Committee, was first established by the House in 1938. The Committee was principally a consequence of concern over the activities of the German-American Bund, whose members were suspected of allegiance to Hitler Germany, and of the Communist Party, supposed by many to be under the domination of the Soviet Union. From the beginning, without interruption to the present time, and with the undoubted knowledge and approval of the House, the Committee has devoted a major part of its energies to the investigation of Communist activities. More particularly, in

---

[6] "The Committee on Un-American Activities, as a whole or by subcommittee, is authorized to make from time to time investigations of (1) the extent, character, and objects of un-American propaganda activities in the United States, (2) the diffusion within the United States of subversive and un-American propaganda that is instigated from foreign countries or of a domestic origin and attacks the principle of the form of government as guaranteed by our Constitution, and (3) all other questions in relation thereto that would aid Congress in any necessary remedial legislation."

1947 the Committee announced a wide-range program in this field, pursuant to which during the years 1948 to 1952 it conducted diverse inquiries into such alleged Communist activities as espionage; efforts to learn atom bomb secrets; infiltration into labor, farmer, veteran, professional, youth, and motion picture groups; and in addition held a number of hearings upon various legislative proposals to curb Communist activities.

In the context of these unremitting pursuits, the House has steadily continued the life of the Committee at the commencement of each new Congress; it has never narrowed the powers of the Committee, whose authority has remained throughout identical with that contained in Rule XI; and it has continuingly supported the Committee's activities with substantial appropriations. Beyond this, the Committee was raised to the level of a standing committee of the House in 1945, it having been but a special committee prior to that time.

In light of this long and illuminating history it can hardly be seriously argued that the investigation of Communist activities generally, and the attendant use of compulsory process, was beyond the purview of the Committee's intended authority under Rule XI.

We are urged, however, to construe Rule XI so as at least to exclude the field of education from the Committee's compulsory authority. Two of the four dissenting judges below relied entirely, the other two alternatively, on this ground. 252 F.2d at 136, 138. The contention is premised on the course we took in United States v. Rumely, 345 U.S. 41, where in order to avoid constitutional issues we construed narrowly the authority of the congressional committee here involved. We cannot follow that route here for this is not a case where Rule XI has to "speak for itself, since Congress put no gloss upon it at the time of its passage," nor one where the subsequent history of the Rule has the "infirmity of post litem motam, self serving declarations." See United States v. Rumely, supra.

To the contrary, the legislative gloss on Rule XI is again compelling. Not only is there no indication that the House ever viewed the field of education as being outside the Committee's authority under Rule XI, but the legislative history affirmatively evinces House approval of this phase of the Committee's work. . . .

In this framework of the Committee's history we must conclude that its legislative authority to conduct the inquiry presently under consideration is unassailable, and that independently of whatever bearing the broad scope of Rule XI may have on the issue of "pertinency" in a given investigation into Communist activities, as in Watkins, the Rule cannot be said to be constitutionally infirm on the score of vagueness. The constitutional permissibility of that authority otherwise is a matter to be discussed later.

PERTINENCY CLAIM

Undeniably a conviction for contempt under 2 U.S.C. §192 cannot stand unless the questions asked are pertinent to the subject matter of the investigation. Watkins v. United States, supra. But the factors which led us to rest decision on this ground in Watkins were very different from those involved here.

In Watkins the petitioner had made specific objection to the Subcommittee's questions on the ground of pertinency; the question under inquiry had not been disclosed in any illuminating manner; and the questions asked the petitioner were not only amorphous on their face, but in some instances clearly foreign to the alleged subject matter of the investigation — "Communism in labor." Id. 354 U.S. at 185, 209-215.

In contrast, petitioner in the case before us raised no objections on the ground of pertinency at the time any of the questions were put to him. . . .

We need not, however, rest decision on petitioner's failure to object on this score, for here "pertinency" was made to appear "with undisputable clarity." Id. at 214. First of all, it goes without saying that the scope of the Committee's authority was for the House, not a witness, to determine, subject to the ultimate reviewing responsibility of this Court. What we deal with here is whether petitioner was sufficiently apprised of "the topic under inquiry" thus authorized "and the connective reasoning whereby the precise questions asked relate[d] to it." Id. at 215. In light of his prepared memorandum of constitutional objections there can be no doubt that this petitioner was well aware of the Subcommittee's authority and purpose to question him as it did. See p. 13, supra. In addition the other sources of this information which we recognized in Watkins, supra, leave no room for a "pertinency" objection on this record. The subject matter of the inquiry had been identified at the commencement of the investigation as Communist infiltration into the field of education. . . .

Petitioner's contentions on this aspect of the case cannot be sustained.

CONSTITUTIONAL CONTENTIONS

Our function, at this point, is purely one of constitutional adjudication in the particular case and upon the particular record before us, not to pass judgment upon the general wisdom or efficacy of the activities of this Committee in a vexing and complicated field.

The precise constitutional issue confronting us is whether the Subcommittee's inquiry into petitioner's past or present membership in the Communist Party transgressed the provisions of the First Amendment, which of course reach and limit congressional investigations. Watkins, supra. . . .

The first question is whether this investigation was related to a valid legislative purpose, for Congress may not constitutionally require an individual to disclose his political relationships or other private affairs except in relation to such a purpose. See Watkins v. United States, supra.

That Congress has wide power to legislate in the field of Communist activity in this Country, and to conduct appropriate investigations in aid thereof, is hardly debatable. The existence of such power has never been questioned by this Court, and it is sufficient to say, without particularization, that Congress has enacted or considered in this field a wide range of legislative measures, not a few of which have stemmed from recommendations of the very Committee whose actions have been drawn in question here. In the last analysis this power rests on the right of self-preservation, "the ultimate value of any society," Dennis v. United States, 341 U.S. 494, 509. Justification for its exercise in turn rests on the long and widely accepted view that tenets of the Communist Party include the ultimate overthrow of the Government of the United States by force and violence, a view which has been given formal expression by the Congress. . . .

We think that investigatory power in this domain is not to be denied Congress solely because the field of education is involved. . . . Indeed we do not understand petitioner here to suggest that Congress in no circumstances may inquire into Communist activity in the field of education. Rather, his position is in effect that this particular investigation was aimed not at the revolutionary aspects but at the theoretical classroom discussion of communism.

In our opinion this position rests on a too constricted view of the nature of the investigatory process, and is not supported by a fair assessment of the record before us. An investigation of advocacy of or preparation for overthrow certainly embraces the right to identify a witness as a member of the Communist Party, see Barsky v. United States, 83 App. D.C. 127, 167 F.2d 241, and to inquire into the various manifestations of the Party's tenets. The strict requirements of a prosecution under the Smith Act, see Dennis v. United States, 341 U.S. 494, supra, and Yates v. United States, 354 U.S. 298, are not the measure of the permissible scope of a congressional investigation into "overthrow," for of necessity the investigatory process must proceed step by step. Nor can it fairly be concluded that this investigation was directed at controlling what is being taught at our universities rather than at overthrow. The statement of the Subcommittee Chairman at the opening of the investigation evinces no such intention, and so far as this record reveals nothing thereafter transpired which would justify our holding that the thrust of the investigation later changed. The record discloses considerable testimony concerning the foreign domination and revolutionary purpose and efforts of the Communist Party. That there was also testimony on the abstract philosophical level does not detract from the dominant theme of this investigation — Communist infiltration furthering the alleged ultimate purpose of overthrow. And certainly the conclusion would not be justified that the questioning of petitioner would have exceeded permissible bounds had he not shut off the Subcommittee at the threshold.

Nor can we accept the further contention that this investigation should not be deemed to have been in furtherance of a legislative purpose because the true objective of the Committee and of the Congress was purely "exposure." So long as Congress acts in pursuance of its constitutional power, the judiciary lacks authority to intervene on the basis of the motives which spurred the exercise of that power. . . .

Finally, the record is barren of other factors which in themselves might sometimes lead to the conclusion that the individual interests at stake were not subordinate to those of the state. There is no indication in this record that the Subcommittee was attempting to pillory witnesses. Nor did petitioner's appearance as a witness follow from indiscriminate dragnet procedures, lacking in probable cause for belief that he possessed information which might be helpful to the Subcommittee. And the relevancy of the questions put to him by the Subcommittee is not open to doubt.

We conclude that the balance between the individual and the governmental interests here at stake must be struck in favor of the latter, and that therefore the provisions of the First Amendment have not been offended.

We hold that petitioner's conviction for contempt of Congress discloses no infirmity, and that the judgment of the Court of Appeals must be

Affirmed.

MR. JUSTICE BLACK, with whom THE CHIEF JUSTICE, and MR. JUSTICE DOUGLAS concur, dissenting. . . .

The Court today affirms, and thereby sanctions the use of the contempt power to enforce questioning by congressional committees in the realm of speech and association. I cannot agree with this disposition of the case for I believe that the resolution establishing the House Un-American Activities Committee and the questions that Committee asked Barenblatt violate the Constitution in several respects. (1) Rule XI creating the Committee authorizes such a sweeping, unlimited, all-inclusive and undiscriminating compulsory examination of witnesses in the field of speech, press, petition and assembly that it violates the procedural requirements of the Due Process Clause of the Fifth Amendment. (2) Compelling an answer to the questions asked Barenblatt abridges freedom of speech and association in contravention of the First Amendment. (3) The Committee proceedings were part of a legislative program to stigmatize and punish by public identification and exposure all witnesses considered by the Committee to be guilty of Communist affiliations, as well as all witnesses who refused to answer Committee questions on constitutional grounds; the Committee was thus improperly seeking to try, convict, and punish suspects, a task which the Constitution expressly denies to Congress and grants exclusively to the courts, to be exercised by them only after indictment and in full compliance with all the safeguards provided by the Bill of Rights. . . .

MR. JUSTICE BRENNAN, dissenting.

I would reverse this conviction. It is sufficient that I state my complete agreement with my Brother Black that no purpose for the investigation of Barenblatt is revealed by the record except exposure purely for the sake of exposure. This is not a purpose to which Barenblatt's rights under the First Amendment can validly be subordinated. An investigation in which the process of law-making and law-evaluating are submerged entirely in exposure of individual behavior — in adjudication, of a sort, through the exposure process — is outside the constitutional pale of congressional inquiry. . . .

1322   Chapter Sixteen.   Substantive Rights

Gibson v. Florida Legislative Investigation Committee
372 U.S. 539, 83 S. Ct. 889, 9 L. Ed. 2d 929 (1963)

Mr. Justice Goldberg delivered the opinion of the Court.

This case is the culmination of protracted litigation involving legislative investigating committees of the State of Florida and the Miami branch of the National Association for the Advancement of Colored People.

The origins of the controversy date from 1956, when a committee of the Florida Legislature commenced an investigation of the NAACP. Upon expiration of this committee's authority, a new committee was established to pursue the inquiry. The new committee, created in 1957, held hearings and sought by subpoena to obtain the entire membership list of the Miami branch of the NAACP; production was refused and the committee obtained a court order requiring that the list be submitted. On appeal, the Florida Supreme Court held that the committee could not require production and disclosure of the entire membership list of the organization, but that it could compel the custodian of the records to bring them to the hearings and to refer to them to determine whether specific individuals, otherwise identified as, or "suspected of being," Communists, were NAACP members. 108 So. 2d 729, cert. denied, 360 U.S. 919.

Because of the impending expiration of the authority of the 1957 committee, the Florida Legislature in 1959 established the respondent Legislative Investigation Committee to resume the investigation of the NAACP. The authorizing statute, c. 59-207, Fla. Laws 1959, defining the purpose and operations of the respondent, declared: "It shall be the duty of the committee to make as complete an investigation as time permits of all organizations whose principles or activities include a course of conduct on the part of any person or group which would constitute violence, or a violation of the laws of the state, or would be inimical to the well-being and orderly pursuit of their personal and business activities by the majority of the citizens of this state. . . ."

The petitioner, then president of the Miami branch of the NAACP, was ordered to appear before the respondent Committee on November 4, 1959, and, in accordance with the prior decision of the Florida Supreme Court, to bring with him records of the association which were in his possession or custody and which pertained to the identity of members of, and contributors to, the Miami and state NAACP organizations. Prior to interrogation of any witnesses the Committee chairman read the text of the statute creating the Committee and declared that the hearings would be "concerned with the activities of various organizations which have been or are presently operating in this State in the fields of, first, race relations; second, the coercive reform of social and educational practices and mores by litigation and pressured administrative action; third, of labor; fourth, of education; fifth, and other vital phases of life in this State." The chairman also stated that the inquiry would be directed to Communists and Communist activities, including infiltration of Communists into organizations operating in the described fields.

Upon being called to the stand, the petitioner admitted that he was custodian of his organization's membership records and testified that the local group had about 1,000 members, that individual membership was renewed annually, and that the only membership lists maintained were those for the then current year.

The petitioner told the Committee that he had not brought these records with him to the hearing and announced that he would not produce them for the purpose of answering questions concerning membership in the NAACP. He did, however, volunteer to answer such questions on the basis of his own personal knowledge; when given the names and shown photographs of 14 persons previously identified as Communists or members of Communist front or affiliated organizations, the petitioner said that he could associate none of them with the NAACP.

The petitioner's refusal to produce his organization's membership lists was based on the

Section C. **Freedom of Speech and Association** 1323

ground that to bring the lists to the hearing and to utilize them as the basis of his testimony would interfere with the free exercise of Fourteenth Amendment associational rights of members and prospective members of the NAACP.

In accordance with Florida procedure, the petitioner was brought before a state court and, after a hearing, was adjudged in contempt, and sentenced to six months' imprisonment and fined $1,200, or, in default in payment thereof, sentenced to an additional six months' imprisonment. The Florida Supreme Court sustained the judgment below, 126 So. 2d 129, and this Court granted certiorari, 366 U.S. 917. . . .

The First and Fourteenth Amendment rights of free speech and free association are fundamental and highly prized, and "need breathing space to survive." NAACP v. Button, 371 U.S. 415, 433. "Freedoms such as these are protected not only against heavy-handed frontal attack, but also from being stifled by more subtle governmental interference." Bates v. Little Rock, supra, 361 U.S., at 523. And, as declared in NAACP v. Alabama, supra, 357 U.S., at 462, "It is hardly a novel perception that compelled disclosure of affiliation with groups engaged in advocacy may constitute [an] . . . effective . . . restraint on freedom of association. . . . This Court has recognized the vital relationship between freedom to associate and privacy in one's associations. . . . Inviolability of privacy in group association may in many circumstances be indispensable to preservation of freedom of association, particularly where a group espouses dissident beliefs." So it is here.

At the same time, however, this Court's prior holdings demonstrate that there can be no question that the State has power adequately to inform itself — through legislative investigation, if it so desires — in order to act and protect its legitimate and vital interests. . . . "The scope of the power of inquiry, in short, is as penetrating and far-reaching as the potential power to enact and appropriate under the Constitution." Barenblatt v. United States, 360 U.S. 109, 111. It is no less obvious, however, that the legislative power to investigate, broad as it may be, is not without limit. The fact that the general scope of the inquiry is authorized and permissible does not compel the conclusion that the investigatory body is free to inquire into or demand all forms of information. . . . When, as in this case, the claim is made that particular legislative inquiries and demands infringe substantially upon First and Fourteenth Amendment associational rights of individuals, the courts are called upon to, and must, determine the permissibility of the challenged actions. . . .

Significantly, the parties are in substantial agreement as to the proper test to be applied to reconcile the competing claims of government and individual and to determine the propriety of the Committee's demands. As declared by the respondent Committee in its brief to this Court, "Basically, this case hinges entirely on the question of whether the evidence before the Committee [was] . . . sufficient to show probable cause or nexus between the NAACP Miami Branch, and Communist activities." We understand this to mean — regardless of the label applied, be it "nexus," "foundation," or whatever — that it is an essential prerequisite to the validity of an investigation which intrudes into the area of constitutionally protected rights of speech, press, association and petition that the State convincingly show a substantial relation between the information sought and a subject of overriding and compelling state interest. Absent such a relation between the NAACP and conduct in which the State may have a compelling regulatory concern, the Committee has not "demonstrated so cogent an interest in obtaining and making public" the membership information sought to be obtained as to "justify the substantial abridgment of associational freedom which such disclosures will effect." Bates v. Little Rock, supra, 361 U.S., at 524. "Where there is a significant encroachment upon personal liberty, the State may prevail only upon showing a subordinating interest which is compelling." Ibid.

Applying these principles to the facts of this case, the respondent Committee contends that the prior decisions of this Court in Uphaus v. Wyman, 360 U.S. 72; Barenblatt v. United States, 360 U.S. 109; Wilkinson v. United States, 365 U.S. 399; and Braden v.

United States, 365 U.S. 431, compel a result here upholding the legislative right of inquiry. In Barenblatt, Wilkinson, and Braden, however, it was a refusal to answer a question or questions concerning the witness' *own* past or present membership *in the Communist Party* which supported his conviction. It is apparent that the necessary preponderating governmental interest and, in fact, the very result in those cases were founded on the holding that the Communist Party is not an ordinary or legitimate political party, as known in this country, and that, because of its particular nature, membership therein is *itself* a permissible subject of regulation and legislative scrutiny. Assuming the correctness of the premises on which those cases were decided, no further demonstration of compelling governmental interest was deemed necessary, since the direct object of the challenged questions there was discovery of membership in the Communist Party, a matter held pertinent to a proper subject then under inquiry.

Here, however, it is not alleged Communists who are the witnesses before the Committee and it is not discovery of their membership in that party which is the object of the challenged inquiries. Rather, it is the NAACP itself which is the subject of the investigation, and it is its local president, the petitioner, who was called before the Committee and held in contempt because he refused to divulge the contents of its membership records. There is no suggestion that the Miami branch of the NAACP or the national organization with which it is affiliated was, or is, itself a subversive organization. Nor is there any indication that the activities or policies of the NAACP were either Communist dominated or influenced. . . .

. . . Compelling such an organization, engaged in the exercise of First and Fourteenth Amendment rights, to disclose its membership presents, under our cases, a question wholly different from compelling the Communist Party to disclose its own membership. Moreover, even to say, as in Barenblatt, supra, 360 U.S., at 129, that it is permissible to inquire into the subject of Communist infiltration of educational or other organizations does not mean that it is permissible to demand or require from such other groups disclosure of their membership by inquiry into their records when such disclosure will seriously inhibit or impair the exercise of constitutional rights and has not itself been demonstrated to bear a crucial relation to a proper governmental interest or to be essential to fulfillment of a proper governmental purpose. . . .

In the absence of directly determinative authority, we turn, then, to consideration of the facts now before us. . . .

[A] summary of the evidence discloses the utter failure to demonstrate the existence of any substantial relationship between the NAACP and subversive or Communist activities. In essence, there is here merely indirect, less than unequivocal, and mostly hearsay testimony that in years past some 14 people who were asserted to be, or to have been, Communists or members of Communist front or "affiliated organizations" attended occasional meetings of the Miami branch of the NAACP "and/or" were members of that branch, which had a total membership of about 1,000.

On the other hand, there was no claim made at the hearings, or since, that the NAACP or its Miami branch was engaged in any subversive activities or that its legitimate activities have been dominated or influenced by Communists. . . . The respondent Committee has laid no adequate foundation for its direct demands upon the officers and records of a wholly legitimate organization for disclosure of its membership. . . .

Nothing we say here impairs or denies the existence of the underlying legislative right to investigate or legislate with respect to subversive activities by Communists or anyone else; our decision today deals only with the manner in which such power may be exercised and we hold simply that groups which themselves are neither engaged in subversive or other illegal or improper activities nor demonstrated to have any substantial connections with such activities are to be protected in their rights of free and private association. . . .

To permit legislative inquiry to proceed on less than an adequate foundation would be to sanction unjustified and unwarranted intrusions into the very heart of the constitutional privilege to be secure in associations in legitimate organizations engaged in the exercise of First and Fourteenth Amendment rights; to impose a lesser standard than we here do would be inconsistent with the maintenance of those essential conditions basic to the preservation of our democracy.

The judgment below must be and is

Reversed.[oo]

MR. JUSTICE HARLAN, whom MR. JUSTICE CLARK, MR. JUSTICE STEWART, and MR. JUSTICE WHITE join, dissenting. . . .

This Court rests reversal on its finding that the Committee did not have sufficient justification for including the Miami Branch of the NAACP within the ambit of its investigation — that, in the language of our cases (Uphaus v. Wyman, 360 U.S. 72, 79), an adequate "nexus" was lacking between the NAACP and the subject matter of the Committee's inquiry.

. . . [U]nless "nexus" requires an investigating agency to prove in advance the very things it is trying to find out, I do not understand how it can be said that the information preliminarily developed by the Committee's investigator was not sufficient to satisfy, under any reasonable test, the requirement of "nexus."

I also find it difficult to see how this case really presents any serious question as to interference with freedom of association. Given the willingness of the petitioner to testify from recollection as to individual memberships in the local branch of the NAACP, the germaneness of the membership records to the subject matter of the Committee's investigation, and the limited purpose for which their use was sought — as an aid to refreshing the witness' recollection, involving their divulgence only to the petitioner himself (supra, pp. 577-578) — this case of course bears no resemblance whatever to NAACP v. Alabama, 357 U.S. 449, or Bates v. Little Rock, 361 U.S. 516. In both of those cases the State had sought general divulgence of local NAACP membership lists without any showing of a justifying state interest. In effect what we are asked to hold here is that the petitioner had a constitutional right to give only partial or inaccurate testimony, and that indeed seems to me the true effect of the Court's holding today.

Tenney v. Brandhove 341 U.S. 367, 71 S. Ct. 783, 95 L. Ed. 1019 (1951)

MR. JUSTICE FRANKFURTER delivered the opinion of the Court.

William Brandhove brought this action in the United States District Court for the Northern District of California, alleging that he had been deprived of rights guaranteed by the Federal Constitution. The defendants are Jack B. Tenney and other members of a committee of the California Legislature, the Senate Fact-Finding Committee on Un-American Activities, colloquially known as the Tenney Committee. Also named as defendants are the Committee and Elmer E. Robinson, Mayor of San Francisco.

The action is based on §§43 and 47(3) of Title 8 of the United States Code, U.S.C. §§43, 47(3). These sections derive from one of the statutes, passed in 1871, aimed at enforcing the Fourteenth Amendment. Act of April 20, 1871, c. 22, §§1, 2, 17 Stat. 13. Section 43 provides:

"Every person who, under color of any statute, ordinance, regulation, custom, or usage, of any State or Territory, subjects, or causes to be subjected, any citizen of the United States or other person within the jurisdiction thereof to the deprivation of any rights, privileges, or immunities secured by the Constitution and laws, shall be liable to the party injured in an action at law, suit in equity, or other proper proceeding for redress." R.S. §1979.

[oo] Concurring opinions of Justices Black and Douglas are omitted, as well as a dissenting opinion of Justice White — ED.

1326   *Chapter Sixteen.*   **Substantive Rights**

Section 47(3) provides a civil remedy against "two or more persons" who may conspire to deprive another of constitutional rights, as therein defined.

Reduced to its legal essentials, the complaint shows these facts. The Tenney Committee was constituted by a resolution of the California Senate on June 20, 1947. On January 28, 1949, Brandhove circulated a petition among members of the State Legislature. He alleges that it was circulated in order to persuade the Legislature not to appropriate further funds for the Committee. The petition charged that the Committee had used Brandhove as a tool in order "to smear Congressman Franck R. Havenner as a 'Red' when he was a candidate for Mayor of San Francisco in 1947, and that the Republican machine in San Francisco and the campaign management of Elmer E. Robinson, Franck Havenner's opponent, conspired with the Tenney Committee to this end." In view of the conflict between this petition and evidence previously given by Brandhove, the Committee asked local prosecuting officials to institute criminal proceedings against him. The Committee also summoned Brandhove to appear before them at a hearing held on January 29. Testimony was there taken from the Mayor of San Francisco, allegedly a member of the conspiracy. The plaintiff appeared with counsel, but refused to give testimony. For this, he was prosecuted for contempt in the State courts. Upon the jury's failure to return a verdict this prosecution was dropped. After Brandhove refused to testify, the Chairman quoted testimony given by Brandhove at prior hearings. The Chairman also read into the record a statement concerning an alleged criminal record of Brandhove, a newspaper article denying the truth of his charges, and a denial by the Committee's counsel — who was absent — that Brandhove's charges were true.

Brandhove alleges that the January 29 hearing "was not held for a legislative purpose," but was designed "to intimidate and silence plaintiff and deter and prevent him from effectively exercising his constitutional rights of free speech and to petition the Legislature for redress of grievances, and also to deprive him of the equal protection of the laws, due process of law, and of the enjoyment of equal privileges and immunities as a citizen of the United States under the law, and so did intimidate, silence, deter, and prevent and deprive plaintiff." Damages of $10,000 were asked for "legal counsel, traveling, hotel accommodations, and other matters pertaining and necessary to his defense" in the contempt proceeding arising out of the Committee hearings. The plaintiff also asked for punitive damages.

The action was dismissed without opinion by the District Judge. The Court of Appeals for the Ninth Circuit held, however, that the complaint stated a cause of action against the Committee and its members. 183 F. 2d 121. We brought the case here because important issues are raised concerning the rights of individuals and the power of State legislatures. 340 U.S. 903.

We are again faced with the Reconstruction legislation which caused the Court such concern in Screws v. United States, 325 U.S. 91, and in the Williams cases decided this term. Williams v. U.S., 341 U.S. 97, id. 70. But this time we do not have to wrestle with far-reaching questions of constitutionality or even of construction. We think it is clear that the legislation on which this action is founded does not impose liability on the facts before us, once they are related to the presuppositions of our political history.

The privilege of legislators to be free from arrest or civil process for what they do or say in legislative proceedings has taproots in the Parliamentary struggles of the Sixteenth and Seventeenth Centuries. As Parliament achieved increasing independence from the Crown, its statement of the privilege grew stronger. In 1523, Sir Thomas More could make only a tentative claim. Roper, Life of Sir Thomas More, in More's Utopia (Adams ed.) 10. In 1668, after a long and bitter struggle, Parliament finally laid the ghost of Charles I, who had prosecuted Sir John Elliot and others for "seditious" speeches in Parliament. Proceedings against Sir John Elliot, 3 How. St. Tr., 294, 332. In 1689, the Bill of Rights declared in unequivocal language: "That the Freedom of Speech, and Debates

Section C. **Freedom of Speech and Association** 1327

or Proceedings in Parliament, ought not to be impeached or questioned in any Court or Place out of Parliament," 1 Wm. & Mary, Sess. 2, cap. 2.

Freedom of speech and action in the legislature was taken as a matter of course by those who severed the Colonies from the Crown and founded our Nation. It was deemed so essential for representatives of the people that it was written into the Articles of Confederation and later into the Constitution. Article 5 of the Articles of Confederation is quite close to the English Bill of Rights: "Freedom of speech and debate in Congress shall not be impeached or questioned in any court, or place out of Congress. . . ." Article I, §6, of the Constitution provides: ". . . for any Speech or Debate in either House, [the Senators and Representatives] shall not be questioned in any other Place."

The reason for the privilege is clear. It was well summarized by James Wilson, an influential member of the Committee of Detail which was responsible for the provision in the Federal Constitution. "In order to enable and encourage a representative of the public to discharge his public trust with firmness and success, it is indispensably necessary, that he should enjoy the fullest liberty of speech, and that he should be protected from the resentment of every one, however powerful, to whom the exercise of that liberty may occasion offence." II Works of James Wilson (Andrews ed. 1896) 38. See the statement of the reason for the privilege in the Report from the Select Committee on the Official Secrets Act (House of Commons, 1939) xiv.

The provision in the United States Constitution was a reflection of political principles already firmly established in the States. Three State Constitutions adopted before the Federal Constitution specifically protected the privilege. The Maryland Constitution of 1776 provided: "That freedom of speech and debates, or proceedings in the Legislature, ought not to be impeached in any other court of judicature." Part I, Art. VIII. The Massachusetts Constitution of 1780 provided: "The freedom of deliberation, speech, and debate, in either house of the legislature, is so essential to the rights of the people, that it cannot be the foundation of any accusation or prosecution, action or complaint, in any other court or place whatsoever." Part. I, Art. XXI. . . .

The New Hampshire Constitution of 1784 provided: "The freedom of deliberation, speech, and debate, in either house of the legislature, is so essential to the rights of the people, that it cannot be the foundation of any action, complaint, or prosecution, in any other court or place whatsoever." Part I, Art. 30.

It is significant that legislative freedom was so carefully protected by constitutional framers at a time when even Jefferson expressed fear of legislative excess.[4] For the loyalist executive and judiciary had been deposed, and the legislature was supreme in most States during and after the Revolution. "The legislative department is everywhere extending the sphere of its activity, and drawing all power into its impetuous vortex." Madison, The Federalist Papers, No. XLVIII.

As other States joined the Union or revised their Constitutions, they took great care to preserve the principle that the legislature must be free to speak and act without fear of criminal and civil liability. Forty-one of the forty-eight States now have specific provisions in their Constitutions protecting the privilege.

Did Congress by the general language of its 1871 statute mean to overturn the tradition of legislative freedom achieved in England by Civil War and carefully preserved in the formation of State and National Governments here? Did it mean to subject legislators to civil liability for acts done within the sphere of legislative activity? Let us assume, merely for the moment, that Congress has constitutional power to limit the freedom of State legislators acting within their traditional sphere. That would be a big assumption. But we would have to make an even rasher assumption to find that Congress through it had exercised the power. These are difficulties we cannot handle. The limits of §§1 and 2 of the

[4] See Jefferson, Notes on the State of Virginia (3d Am. ed. 1801) 174-175. . . .

1328   Chapter Sixteen.   **Substantive Rights**

1871 statute now §§43 and 47(3) of Title 8 — were not spelled out in debate. We cannot believe that Congress — itself a staunch advocate of legislative freedom — would impinge on a tradition so well grounded in history and reason by covert inclusion in the general language before us.

We come then to the question whether from the pleadings it appears that the defendants were acting in the sphere of legitimate legislative activity. Legislatures may not of course acquire power by an unwarranted extension of privilege. The House of Commons' claim of power to establish the limits of its privilege has been little more than a pretense since Ashby v. White, 2 Ld. Raym. 938, 3 Id. 320. This Court has not hesitated to sustain the rights of private individuals when it found Congress was acting outside its legislative role. Kilbourn v. Thompson, 103 U.S. 168; Marshall v. Gordon, 243 U.S. 521; compare McGrain v. Daugherty, 273 U.S. 135, 176.

The claim of an unworthy purpose does not destroy the privilege. Legislators are immune from deterrents to the uninhibited discharge of their legislative duty, not for their private indulgence but for the public good. One must not expect uncommon courage even in legislators. The privilege would be of little value if they could be subjected to the cost and inconvenience and distractions of a trial upon a conclusion of the pleader, or to the hazard of a judgment against them based upon a jury's speculation as to motives. The holding of this Court in Fletcher v. Peck, 6 Cranch 87, 130, that it was not consonant with our scheme of government for a court to inquire into the motives of legislators, has remained unquestioned. See cases cited in State of Arizona v. State of California, 283 U.S. 423, 455.

Investigations, whether by standing or special committees, are an established part of representative government. Legislative committees have been charged with losing sight of their duty of disinterestedness. In times of political passion, dishonest or vindictive motives are readily attributed to legislative conduct and as readily believed. Courts are not the place for such controversies. Self-discipline and the voters must be the ultimate reliance for discouraging or correcting such abuses. The courts should not go beyond the narrow confines of determining that a committee's inquiry may fairly be deemed within its province. To find that a committee's investigation has exceeded the bounds of legislative power it must be obvious that there was a usurpation of functions exclusively vested in the Judiciary or the Executive. The present case does not present such a situation. Brandhove indicated that evidence previously given by him to the committee was false, and he raised serious charges concerning the work of a committee investigating a problem within legislative concern. The Committee was entitled to assert a right to call the plaintiff before it and examine him.

It should be noted that this is a case in which the defendants are members of a legislature. Legislative privilege in such a case deserves greater respect than where an official acting on behalf of the legislature is sued or the legislature seeks the affirmative aid of the courts to assert a privilege. In Kilbourn v. Thompson, supra, this Court allowed a judgment against the Sergeant-at-Arms, but found that one could not be entered against the defendant members of the House.

We have only considered the scope of the privilege as applied to the facts of the present case. As Mr. Justice Miller said in the Kilbourn case: "It is not necessary to decide here that there may not be things done, in the one House or the other, of an extraordinary character, for which the members who take part in the act may be held legally responsible." 103 U.S. at page 204. We conclude only that here the individual defendants and the legislative committee were acting in a field where legislators traditionally have power to act, and that the statute of 1871 does not create civil liability for such conduct.

The judgment of the Court of Appeals is reversed and that of the District Court affirmed.

Reversed.

Section C. Freedom of Speech and Association

Mr. Justice Black, concurring.

The Court holds that the Civil Rights statutes were not intended to make legislators personally liable for damages to a witness injured by a committee exercising legislative power. This result is reached by reference to the long-standing and wise tradition that legislators are immune from legal responsibility for their legislative statements and activities. The Court's opinion also points out that Kilbourn v. Thompson, 103 U.S. 168, 26 L. Ed. 377, held legislative immunity to have some limits. And today's decision indicates that there is a point at which a legislator's conduct so far exceeds the bounds of legislative power that he may be held personally liable in a suit brought under the Civil Rights Act. I substantially agree with the Court's reasoning and its conclusion. But since I have a great deal of difficulty with this case, I think it important to emphasize what we do *not* decide here.

It is not held that the validity of legislative action is coextensive with the personal immunity of the legislators. That is to say, the holding that the chairman and the other members of his Committee cannot be sued in this case is not a holding that their alleged persecution of Brandhove is legal conduct. Indeed, as I understand the decision, there is still much room for challenge to the Committee action. Thus for example, in any proceeding instituted by the Tenney Committee to fine or imprison Brandhove on perjury, contempt or other charges, he would certainly be able to defend himself on the ground that the resolution creating the Committee or the Committee's actions under it were unconstitutional and void.

Mr. Justice Douglas, dissenting.

I agree with the opinion of the Court as a statement of general principles governing the liability of legislative committees and members of the legislatures. But I do not agree that all abuses of legislative committees are solely for the legislative body to police.

We are dealing here with a right protected by the Constitution — the right of free speech. The charge seems strained and difficult to sustain; but it is that a legislative committee brought the weight of its authority down on respondent for exercising his right of free speech. Reprisal for speaking is as much an abridgment as a prior restraint. If a committee departs so far from its domain to deprive a citizen of a right protected by the Constitution, I can think of no reason why it should be immune. Yet that is the extent of the liability sought to be imposed on petitioners under 8 U.S.C. §43.

It is speech and debate in the legislative department which our constitutional scheme makes privileged. Included, of course, are the actions of legislative committees that are authorized to conduct hearings or make investigations so as to lay the foundation for legislative action. But we are apparently holding today that the actions of those committees have no limits in the eyes of the law. May they depart with impunity from their legislative functions, sit as kangaroo courts, and try men for their loyalty and their political beliefs? May they substitute trial before committees for trial before juries? May they sit as a board of censors over industry, prepare their blacklists of citizens, and issue pronouncements as devastating as any bill of attainder?

No other public official has complete immunity for his actions. Even a policeman who exacts a confession by force and violence can be held criminally liable under the Civil Rights Act, as we ruled only the other day in Williams v. United States, 341 U.S. 97. Yet now we hold that no matter the extremes to which a legislative committee may go it is not answerable to an injured party under the civil rights legislation. That result is the necessary consequence of our ruling since the test of the statute, so far as material here, is whether a constitutional right has been impaired, not whether the domain of the committee was traditional. It is one thing to give great leeway to the legislative right of speech, debate, and investigation. But when a committee perverts its power, brings down on an individual the whole weight of government for an illegal or corrupt purpose, the reason for the immunity ends. It was indeed the purpose of this civil rights legislation to secure federal rights against invasion by officers and agents of the states. I see no reason why any officer of government should be higher than the Constitution from which all rights and privileges of an office obtain.

NOTE Developments in Legislative Immunity

Drawn upon by Justice Frankfurter for support in Tenney v. Brandhove, supra, Article I, §6 of the Constitution provides: "... for any Speech or Debate in either House, [the Senators and Representatives] shall not be questioned in any other Place." Recent cases under this clause have reaffirmed the doctrine that congressmen are immune from judicial interference in the "sphere of legitimate legislative activity." Eastland v. United States Servicemen's Fund, 421 U.S. 491, 501 (1975). These cases have "read the Speech or Debate Clause broadly . . . [in order] to insure that the legislative function the Constitution allocates to Congress may be performed independently." Id. at 501-502. Judicial interference has been stayed with regard to members of Congress in a wide variety of areas: Eastland v. United States Servicemen's Fund, supra (subpoena of financial records of antiwar service organization); Doe v. McMillan, 412 U.S. 306 (1973) (dissemination of congressional report on D.C. schools that identified named students in a derogatory context); Gravel v. United States, 408 U.S. 606 (1972) (the reading of classified documents — the Pentagon Papers — into the public record).

Citing Kilbourn v. Thompson, supra, where a judgment was allowed against the Sergeant at Arms of the House, Justice Frankfurter in Tenney also suggested that legislative privilege may be overborne "where an official acting on behalf of the legislative is sued." Recent cases have followed Kilbourn and the Tenney dictum in allowing suits against "functionaries" while holding members of Congress immune: Doe v. McMillan, supra (suit allowed against Public Printer and Superintendent of Documents); Powell v. McCormack, 395 U.S. 486 (1969) (suit allowed against House Clerk, Sergeant at Arms, and Doorkeeper).

Is the clause to be read literally, however, to extend protection only to senators and representatives? No, the Court held in Gravel v. United States, supra, as it immunized the aide of Senator Gravel because it deemed that protection of these "alter egos" of the congressmen was necessary to prevent the "intimidation" of legislators. Compare Dombrowski v. Eastland, 387 U.S. 82 (1967), where suit was allowed against a subcommittee counsel charged with conspiracy in an illegal search and seizure of records sought by the committee. "Unlawful conduct of this kind [in Dombrowski] the Speech or Debate Clause simply did not immunize." Gravel, supra, at 620.

For an analysis of United States Servicemen's Fund, see Note, The Supreme Court, 1972 Term, 89 Harv. L. Rev. 47, 131 (1975). See generally Reinstein & Silvergate, Legislative Privilege and the Separation of Powers, 86 Harv. L. Rev. 1113 (1973).

b. Loyalty Oaths and Related Tests

United States v. Lovett 328 U.S. 303, 66 S. Ct. 1073, 90 L. Ed. 1252 (1946)

MR. JUSTICE BLACK delivered the opinion of the Court.

In 1943 the respondents, Lovett, Watson, and Dodd, were and had been for several years working for the Government. The Government agencies which had lawfully employed them were fully satisfied with the quality of their work and wished to keep them employed on their jobs. Over the protest of those employing agencies, Congress provided in §304 of the Urgent Deficiency Appropriation Act of 1943, by way of an amendment attached to the House bill, that after November 15, 1943, no salary or compensation should

Section C. **Freedom of Speech and Association** 1331

be paid respondents out of any monies then or thereafter appropriated except for services as jurors or members of the armed forces, unless they were prior to November 15, 1943, again appointed to jobs by the President with the advice and consent of the Senate. 57 Stat. 431, 450, c. 218. Notwithstanding the Congressional enactment, and the failure of the President to reappoint respondents, the agencies kept all the respondents at work on their jobs for varying periods after November 15, 1943; but their compensation was discontinued after that date. To secure compensation for this post-November 15th work, respondents brought these actions in the Court of Claims. They urged that §304 is unconstitutional and void on the grounds that: (1) The Section, properly interpreted, shows a Congressional purpose to exercise the power to remove executive employees, a power not entrusted to Congress but to the Executive Branch of Government under Article 2, §§1, 2, 3, and 4 of the Constitution; (2) the section violates Article 1, §9, and Clause 3, of the Constitution which provides that "no bill of attainder or ex post facto law shall be passed"; (3) the Section violates the Fifth Amendment, in that it singles out these three respondents and deprives them of their liberty and property without due process of law. The Solicitor General, appearing for the Government, joined in the first two of respondents' contentions but took no position on the third. House Resolution 386, 89 Cong. Rec. 10,882, and Public Law 249, 78th Congress, authorized a special counsel to appear on behalf of the Congress.[pp] This counsel denied all three of respondents' contentions. . . . Counsel for Congress also urged that §304 did not purport to terminate respondents' employment. According to him, it merely cut off respondents' pay and deprived governmental agencies of any power to make enforceable contracts with respondents for any further compensation. The contention was that this involved simply an exercise of Congressional powers over appropriations, which according to the argument, are plenary and not subject to judicial review. On this premise counsel for Congress urged that the challenge of the constitutionality of §304 raised no justiciable controversy. The Court of Claims entered judgments in favor of respondents. . . . 104 Ct. Cl. 557, 66 F. Supp. 142. We granted certiorari because of the manifest importance of the questions involved.

In this Court the parties and counsel for Congress have urged the same points as they did in the Court of Claims. According to the view we take we need not decide whether §304 is an unconstitutional encroachment on executive power or a denial of due process of law, and the section is not challenged on the ground that it violates the First Amendment. Our inquiry is thus confined to whether the actions in the light of a proper construction of the Act present justiciable controversies and if so whether §304 is a bill of attainder against these respondents involving a use of power which the Constitution unequivocally declares Congress can never exercise. These questions require an interpretation of the meaning and purpose of the section, which in turn requires an understanding of the circumstances leading to its passage. We, consequently, find it necessary to set out these circumstances somewhat in detail.

In the background of the statute here challenged lies the House of Representatives' feeling in the late thirties that many "subversives" were occupying influential positions in the Government and elsewhere and that their influence must not remain unchallenged. As part of its program against "subversive" activities the House in May 1938 created a Committee on Un-American Activities, which became known as the Dies Committee after its Chairman, Congressman Martin Dies. . . . This Committee conducted a series of investigations and made lists of people and organizations it thought "subversive." . . . The creation of the Dies Committee was followed by provisions such as §9A of the Hatch Act, 53 Stat. 1147, 1148, 1149, c. 410, 18 U.S.C. §61i, 7 F.C.A. title 18, §61i, and §§15 (f) and 17 (b) of the Emergency Relief Appropriation Act of 1941, 54 Stat. 611, c. 432, which forbade the holding of a federal job by anyone who was a member of a political

---

[pp] A full development of the strategy and of the arguments in this case is set out in Ely, United States v. Lovett: Litigating the Separation of Powers, 10 Harv. Civ. Rights-Civ. Lib. L. Rev. 1 (1975). — Ed.

1332   Chapter Sixteen.   **Substantive Rights**

party or organization that advocated the overthrow of our Constitutional form of Government in the United States. It became the practice to include a similar prohibition in all appropriations acts, together with criminal penalties for its violation. Under these provisions the Federal Bureau of Investigation began wholesale investigations of federal employees, which investigations were financed by special Congressional appropriations. 55 Stat. 265, 292, c. 258, 56 Stat. 468, 482, c. 472. Thousands were investigated.

While all this was happening Mr. Dies on February 1, 1943, in a long speech on the floor of the House attacked thirty-nine named Government employees as "irresponsible, unrepresentative, crackpot, radical bureaucrats" and affiliates of "communist front organizations." Among these named individuals were the three respondents. Congressman Dies told the House that respondents, as well as the other thirty-six individuals he named were because of their beliefs and past associations unfit to "hold a government position" and urged Congress to refuse "to appropriate money for their salaries." In this connection he proposed that the Committee on Appropriations "take immediate and vigorous steps to eliminate these people from public office." 89 Cong. Rec. 474, 479, 486. Four days later an amendment was offered to the Treasury-Post Office Appropriation Bill which provided that "no part of any appropriation contained in this Act shall be used to pay the compensation of" the thirty-nine individuals Dies had attacked. 89 Cong. Rec. 645. The Congressional Record shows that this amendment precipitated a debate that continued for several days. Id. 645-742. All of those participating agreed that the "charges" against the thirty-nine individuals were serious. Some wanted to accept Congressman Dies' statements as sufficient proof of "guilt," while others referred to such proposed action as "legislative lynching," Id. at 651, smacking "of the procedure in the French Chamber of Deputies, during the Reign of Terror." Id. at 659. The Dies charges were referred to as "indictments," and many claimed this made it necessary that the named federal employees be given a hearing and a chance to prove themselves innocent. Id. at 771. Congressman Dies then suggested that the Appropriations Committee "weigh the evidence and . . . take immediate steps to dismiss these people from the federal service." Id. at 651. Eventually a resolution was proposed to defer action until the Appropriations Committee could investigate, so that accused federal employees would get a chance to prove themselves "innocent" of communism or disloyalty, and so that each "man would have his day in court," and "There would be no star chamber proceedings." Id. at 711 and 713; but see id. at 715. The resolution which was finally passed authorized the Appropriations Committee acting through a special subcommittee ". . . to examine into any and all allegations or charges that certain persons in the employ of the several executive departments and other executive agencies are unfit to continue in such employment by reason of their present association or membership or past association or membership in or with organizations whose aims or purposes are or have been subversive to the Government of the United States." Id. at 734, 742. The Committee was to have full plenary powers, including the right to summon witnesses and papers, and was to report its "findings and determination" to the House. . . .

After the resolution was passed a special subcommittee of the Appropriations Committee held hearings in secret executive session. Those charged with "subversive" beliefs and "subversive" associations were permitted to testify, but lawyers including those representing the agencies by which the accused were employed were not permitted to be present. At the hearings, committee members, the committee staff, and whatever witness was under examination were the only ones present. The evidence, aside from that given by the accused employees, appears to have been largely that of reports made by the Dies Committee, its investigators, and Federal Bureau of Investigation reports, the latter being treated as too confidential to be made public.

After this hearing the subcommittee's reports and recommendations were submitted to the House as part of the Appropriation Committee's report. The subcommittee stated that it had regarded the investigations "as in the nature of an inquest of office" with the ultimate purpose of purging the public service of anyone found guilty of "subversive activity." The committee, stating that "subversive activity" had not before been defined by Congress or by the courts formulated its own definition of "subversive activity" which we set out in the margin.[3] Respondents Watson, Dodd, and Lovett were, according to the subcommittee guilty of having engaged in "subversive activity within the definition adopted by the Committee." H. Rep. No. 448, 78th Cong. 1st Sess. 5-7, 9. . . .

Section 304 was submitted to the House along with the Committee Report. . . .

. . . Finally §304 was passed by the House.

The Senate Appropriation Committee eliminated Section 304 and its action was sustained by the Senate. . . .

. . . Finally after the fifth conference report showed that the House would not yield the Senate adopted §304. When the President signed the bill he stated: "The Senate yielded, as I have been forced to yield, to avoid delaying our conduct of the war. But I cannot yield without placing on record my view that this provision is not only unwise and discriminatory, but unconstitutional." H. Doc. 264, 78th Cong. 1st Sess.

I

In view of the facts just set out we cannot agree with the two judges of the Court of Claims who held that §304 required "a mere stoppage of disbursing routine, nothing more," and left the employer governmental agencies free to continue employing respondents and to incur contractual obligations by virtue of such continued work which respondents could enforce in the Court of Claims. Nor can we agree with counsel for Congress that the Section did not provide for the dismissal of respondents but merely forbade governmental agencies to compensate respondents for their work or to incur obligations for such compensation at any and all times. We therefore cannot conclude, as he urges, that §304 is a mere appropriation measure, and that since Congress under the Constitution has complete control over appropriations, a challenge to the measure's constitutionality does not present a justiciable question in the courts, but is merely a political issue over which Congress has final say.

We hold that the purpose of §304 was not merely to cut off respondents' compensation through regular disbursing channels but permanently to bar them from government service, and that the issue of whether it is constitutional is justiciable. . . . Any other interpretation of the Section would completely frustrate the purpose of all who sponsored §304, which clearly was to "purge" the then existing and all future lists of Government employees of those whom Congress deemed guilty of "subversive activities" and therefore "unfit" to hold a federal job. What was challenged, therefore, is a statute which, because of what Congress thought to be their political beliefs, prohibited respondents from ever engaging in any government work, except as jurors or soldiers. . . . Were this case to be not justiciable, Congressional action, aimed at three named individuals, which stigmatized their reputation and seriously impaired their chance to earn a living, could never be challenged in any court. Our Constitution did not contemplate such a result. . . .

---

[3] "Subversive activity in this country derives from conduct intentionally destructive of or inimical to the Government of the United States — that which seeks to undermine its institutions, or to distort its functions, or to impede its projects, or to lessen its efforts, the ultimate end being to overturn it all. Such activity may be open and direct as by effort to overthrow, or subtle and indirect as by sabotage." H. Rep. No. 448, 78th Cong. 1st Sess. p. 5.

II

We hold that § 304 falls precisely within the category of congressional actions which the Constitution barred by providing that "No Bill of Attainder or ex post facto Law shall be passed." In Cummings v. Missouri, 4 Wall. 277, 323, this Court said, "A bill of attainder is a legislative act which inflicts punishment without a judicial trial. If the punishment be less than death, the act is termed a bill of pains and penalties. Within the meaning of the Constitution, bills of attainder include bills of pains and penalties." The Cummings decision involved a provision of the Missouri Reconstruction Constitution which required persons to take an Oath of Loyalty as a prerequisite to practicing a profession. Cummings, a Catholic Priest, was convicted for teaching and preaching as a minister without taking the oath. The oath required an applicant to affirm that he had never given aid or comfort to persons engaged in hostility to the United States and had never "been a member of, or connected with, any order, society, or organization, inimical to the government of the United States . . ." In an illuminating opinion which gave the historical background of the Constitutional prohibition against bills of attainder, this Court invalidated the Missouri Constitutional provision both because it constituted a bill of attainder and because it had an ex post facto operation. On the same day the Cummings Case was decided, the Court, in Ex parte Garland, 4 Wall. 333, also held invalid on the same grounds an Act of Congress which required attorneys practicing before this Court to take a similar oath.[qq] Neither of these cases has ever been overruled. They stand for the proposition that legislative acts, no matter what their form, that apply either to named individuals or to easily ascertainable members of a group in such a way as to inflict punishment on them without a judicial trial are bills of attainder prohibited by the Constitution. Adherence to this principle requires invalidation of § 304. We do adhere to it. . . .

Section 304, thus, clearly accomplishes the punishment of named individuals without a judicial trial. The fact that the punishment is inflicted through the instrumentality of an Act specifically cutting off the pay of certain named individuals found guilty of disloyalty, makes it no less galling or effective than if it had been done by an Act which designated the conduct as criminal. No one would think that Congress could have passed a valid law, stating that after investigation it had found Lovett, Dodd, and Watson "guilty" of the crime of engaging in "subversive activities," defined that term for the first time, and sentenced them to perpetual exclusion from any government employment. Section 304, while it does not use that language, accomplishes that result. The effect was to inflict punishment without the safeguards of a judicial trial and "determined by no previous law or fixed rule." The Constitution declares that that cannot be done either by a state or by the United States. . . .

Section 304 therefore does not stand as an obstacle to payment of compensation to Lovett, Watson, and Dodd. The judgment in their favor is affirmed.[rr]

Mr. Justice Jackson took no part in the consideration or decision of these cases.

Garner v. Board of Public Works 341 U.S. 716, 71 S. Ct. 909, 95 L. Ed. 1317 (1951)

Mr. Justice Clark delivered the opinion of the Court. . . .

Pursuant to the authority . . . conferred [by the City Charter], the City of Los Angeles

[qq] The political background of the Cummings and Garland cases is described in Hyman, Era of the Oath: Northern Loyalty Tests During the Civil War and Reconstruction (1954). The reaction to the Test Oath cases, including "defiant" resistance in some instances, is chronicled in Fairman, Reconstruction and Reunion, 1864-88, Part One, 240-248 (1971) (Volume Six of The Oliver Wendell Holmes Devise History of the Supreme Court of the United States). — Ed.

[rr] A concurring opinion of Justice Frankfurter, joined by Justice Reed, is omitted. — Ed.

Section C. **Freedom of Speech and Association** 1335

in 1948 passed Ordinance No. 94,004, requiring every person who held an office or position in the service of the city to take an oath prior to January 6, 1949. In relevant part the oath was as follows:

"I further swear (or affirm) that I do not advise, advocate or teach, and have not within the period beginning five (5) years prior to the effective date of the ordinance requiring the making of this oath or affirmation, advised, advocated or taught, the overthrow by force, violence or other unlawful means, of the Government of the United States of America or of the State of California and that I am not now and have not, within said period, been or become a member of or affiliated with any group, society, association, organization or party which advises, advocates or teaches, or has, within said period, advised, advocated or taught, the overthrow by force, violence or other unlawful means of the Government of the United States of America, or of the State of California. I further swear (or affirm) that I will not, while I am in the service of the City of Los Angeles, advise, advocate or teach, or be or become a member of or affiliated with any group, association, society, organization or party which advises, advocates or teaches, or has within said period, advised, advocated or taught, the overthrow by force, violence or other unlawful means, of the Government of the United States of America or of the State of California . . . ."

The ordinance also required every employee to execute an affidavit "stating whether or not he is or ever was a member of the Communist Party of the United States of America or of the Communist Political Association, and if he is or was such a member, stating the dates when he became, and the periods during which he was, such a member . . ."

On the final date for filing of the oath and affidavit petitioners were civil service employees of the City of Los Angeles. Petitioners Pacifico and Schwartz took the oath but refused to execute the affidavit. The remaining fifteen petitioners refused to do either. All were discharged for such cause, after administrative hearing, as of January 6, 1949. In this action they sue for reinstatement and unpaid salaries. The District Court of Appeal denied relief. 98 Cal. App. 2d 493 (1950). We granted certiorari, 340 U.S. 941 (1951).

Petitioners attack the ordinance as violative of the provision of Art. I, § 10 of the Federal Constitution that "No State shall . . . pass any Bill of Attainder, [or] ex post facto Law . . . ." They also contend that the ordinance deprives them of freedom of speech and assembly and of the right to petition for redress of grievances.

Petitioners have assumed that the oath and affidavit provisions of the ordinance present similar constitutional considerations and stand or fall together. We think, however, that separate disposition is indicated.

1. The affidavit raises the issue whether the City of Los Angeles is constitutionally forbidden to require that its employees disclose their past or present membership in the Communist Party or the Communist Political Association. Not before us is the question whether the city may determine that an employee's disclosure of such political affiliation justifies his discharge.

We think that a municipal employer is not disabled because it is an agency of the State from inquiring of its employees as to matters that may prove relevant to their fitness and suitability for the public service. Past conduct may well relate to present fitness; past loyalty may have a reasonable relationship to present and future trust. Both are commonly inquired into in determining fitness for both high and low positions in private industry and are not less relevant in public employment. The affidavit requirement is valid.

2. In our view the validity of the oath turns upon the nature of the Charter amendment (1941) and the relation of the ordinance (1948) to this amendment. Immaterial here is any opinion we might have as to the Charter provision insofar as it purported to apply retrospectively for a five-year period prior to its effective date. We assume that under the Federal Constitution the Charter amendment is valid to the extent that it bars from the city's public service persons who, subsequent to its adoption in 1941, advise, advocate, or teach the violent overthrow of the Government or who are or become affiliated with any group doing so. The provisions operating thus prospectively were a reasonable regulation to pro-

tect the municipal service by establishing an employment qualification of loyalty to the State and the United States. Cf. Gerende v. Board of Supervisors of Elections, 341 U.S. 56. Likewise, as a regulation of political activity of municipal employees, the amendment was reasonably designed to protect the integrity and competency of the service. This court has held that Congress may reasonably restrict the political activity of federal civil service employees for such a purpose, United Public Workers v. Mitchell, 330 U.S. 75, 102-103, and a State is not without power to do as much.

The Charter amendment defined standards of eligibility for employees and specifically denied city employment to those persons who thereafter should not comply with these standards. While the amendment deprived no one of employment with or without trial, yet from its effective date it terminated any privilege to work for the city in the case of persons who thereafter engaged in the activity proscribed.

The ordinance provided for administrative implementation of the provisions of the Charter amendment. The oath imposed by the ordinance proscribed to employees activity which had been denied them in identical terms and with identical sanctions in the Charter provision effective in 1941. The five-year period provided by the oath extended back only to 1943.

The ordinance would be ex post facto if it imposed punishment for past conduct lawful at the time it was engaged in. Passing for the moment the question whether separation of petitioners from their employment must be considered as punishment, the ordinance clearly is not ex post facto. The activity covered by the oath had been proscribed by the Charter in the same terms, for the same purpose, and to the same effect over seven years before, and two years prior to the period embraced in the oath. Not the law but the fact was posterior. . . .

Petitioners rely heavily upon United States v. Lovett, 328 U.S. 303, in which a legislative act effectively separating certain public servants from their positions was held to be a bill of attainder. Unlike the provisions of the Charter and ordinance under which petitioners were removed, the statute in the Lovett case did not declare general and prospectively operative standards of qualification and eligibility for public employment. Rather, by its terms it prohibited any further payment of compensation to named individual employees. Under these circumstances, viewed against the legislative background, the statute was held to have imposed penalties without judicial trial.

Nor are we impressed by the contention that the oath denies due process because its negation is not limited to affiliations with organizations known to the employee to be in the proscribed class. We have no reason to suppose that the oath is or will be construed by the City of Los Angeles or by California courts as affecting adversely those persons who during their affiliation with a proscribed organization were innocent of its purpose, or those who severed their relations with any such organization when its character became apparent, or those who were affiliated with organizations which at one time or another during the period covered by the ordinance were engaged in proscribed activity but not at the time of affiant's affiliation. We assume that scienter is implicit in each clause of the oath. As the city has done nothing to negative this interpretation, we take for granted that the ordinance will be so read to avoid raising difficult constitutional problems which any other application would present. Fox v. Washington, 236 U.S. 273, 277 (1915). It appears from correspondence of record between the city and petitioners that although the city welcomed inquiry as to its construction of the oath, the interpretation upon which we have proceeded may not have been explicitly called to the attention of petitioners before their refusal. We assume that, if our interpretation of the oath is correct, the City of Los Angeles will give those petitioners who heretofore refused to take the oath an opportunity to take it as interpreted and resume their employment.

The judgment as to Pacifico and Schwartz is affirmed. The judgment as to the remaining petitioners is affirmed on the basis of the interpretation of the ordinance which we have felt justified in assuming.

Section C. **Freedom of Speech and Association** 1337

Affirmed.[ss]

MR. JUSTICE DOUGLAS, with whom MR. JUSTICE BLACK joins, dissenting. . . .

The case is governed by Cummings v. Missouri, 4 Wall. 277, and Ex parte Garland, 4 Wall. 333, which struck down test oaths adopted at the close of the Civil War. . . .

. . . Bills of attainder usually declared the guilt; here they assumed the guilt and adjudged the punishment conditionally, i.e., they deprived the parties of their right to preach and to practice law unless the presumption were removed by the expurgatory oath. That was held to be as much a bill of attainder as if the guilt had been irrevocably pronounced. The laws were also held to be ex post facto since they imposed a penalty for an act not so punishable at the time it was committed.

There are, of course, differences between the present case and the Cummings and Garland cases. Those condemned by the Los Angeles ordinance are municipal employees; those condemned in the others were professional people. Here the past conduct for which punishment is exacted is single — advocacy within the past five years of the overthrow of the Government by force and violence. In the other cases the acts for which Cummings and Garland stood condemned covered a wider range and involved some conduct which might be vague and uncertain. But those differences, seized on here in hostility to the constitutional provisions, are wholly irrelevant. Deprivation of a man's means of livelihood by reason of past conduct, not subject to this penalty when committed, is punishment whether he is a professional man, a day laborer who works for private industry, or a government employee. The deprivation is nonetheless unconstitutional whether it be for one single past act or a series of past acts. The degree of particularity with which the past act is defined is not the criterion. We are not dealing here with the problem of vagueness in criminal statutes. No amount of certainty would have cured the laws in the Cummings and Garland cases. They were stricken down because of the mode in which punishment was inflicted.

Petitioners were disqualified from office not for what they are today, not because of any program they currently espouse (cf. Gerende v. Board of Supervisors, 341 U.S. 56), not because of standards related to fitness for the office (cf. Dent v. West Virginia, 129 U.S. 114; Hawker v. New York, 170 U.S. 189), but for what they once advocated. They are deprived of their livelihood by legislative act, not by judicial processes. We put the case in the aspect most invidious to petitioners. Whether they actually advocated the violent overthrow of Government does not appear. But here, as in the Cummings case, the vice is in the presumption of guilt which can only be removed by the expurgatory oath. That punishment, albeit conditional, violates here as it did in the Cummings case the constitutional prohibition against bills of attainder. Whether the ordinance also amounts to an ex post facto law is a question we do not reach.

FLEMMING v. NESTOR, 363 U.S. 603, 80 S. Ct. 1367, 4 L. Ed. 2d 1435 (1960): "[Section 202(n) of the Social Security Act] provides for the termination of old-age, survivor, and disability insurance benefits payable to, or in certain cases in respect of, an alien individual who, after September 1, 1954 (the date of enactment of the section), is deported under §241(a) of the Immigration and Nationality Act (8 U.S.C. §1251a) on any one of certain grounds specified in §202(n).

"Appellee, an alien, immigrated to this country from Bulgaria in 1913, and became eligible for old-age benefits in November 1955. In July 1956 he was deported pursuant to §241(a)(6)(C)(i) of the Immigration and Nationality Act for having been a member of the Communist Party from 1933 to 1939. This being one of the benefit-termination deportation grounds specified in §202(n), appellee's benefits were terminated soon thereafter, and notice of the termination was given to his wife, who had remained in this country. Upon

---

[ss] Opinions by Frankfurter, J., and Burton, J., each concurring in part and dissenting in part, are omitted. A dissenting opinion by Black, J., is also omitted. — ED.

his failure to obtain administrative reversal of the decision, appellee commenced this action in the District Court, pursuant to §205(g) of the Social Security Act (53 Stat. 1370, as amended, 42 U.S.C. §405(g)), to secure judicial review. On cross-motions for summary judgment, the District Court ruled for appellee, holding §202(n) unconstitutional under the Due Process Clause of the Fifth Amendment in that it deprived appellee of an accrued property right. 169 F. Supp. 922. The Secretary prosecuted an appeal to this Court, and, subject to a jurisdictional question hereinafter discussed, we set the case down for plenary hearing. 360 U.S. 915. . . ."

What result? Why?

UNITED STATES v. BROWN, 381 U.S. 437, 85 S. Ct. 1707, 14 L. Ed. 2d 484 (1966). Warren, C.J.: "[Section] 504 of the Labor-Management Reporting and Disclosure Act of 1959 . . . makes it a crime for a member of the Communist Party to serve as an officer or . . . as an employee of a labor union. . . .

"Respondent has been a working longshoreman on the San Francisco docks, and an open and avowed Communist, for more than a quarter of a century. He was elected to the Executive Board of Local 10 of the International Longshoremen's and Warehousemen's Union for consecutive one-year terms in 1959, 1960 and 1961. [Respondent was convicted of a violation of Section 504.] The Court of Appeals for the Ninth Circuit, sitting en banc, reversed and remanded with instructions to set aside the convictions and dismiss the indictment, holding that § 504 violates the First and Fifth Amendments to the Constitution. We granted certiorari, 379 U.S. 899.

"Respondent urges — in addition to the grounds relied on by the court below — that the statute under which he was convicted is a bill of attainder, and therefore violates Art. I, §9, of the Constitution. We agree that §504 is void as a bill of attainder and affirm the decision of the Court of Appeals on that basis. We therefore find it unnecessary to consider the First and Fifth Amendment arguments.

". . . [T]he Bill of Attainder Clause was intended not as a narrow, technical (and therefore soon to be outmoded) prohibition, but rather as an implementation of the separation of powers, a general safeguard against legislative exercise of the judicial function, or more simply — trial by legislature.

". . . In §504, however, Congress has exceeded the authority granted it by the Constitution. The statute does not set forth a generally applicable rule decreeing that any person who commits certain acts or possesses certain characteristics (acts and characteristics which, in Congress' view, make them likely to initiate political strikes) shall not hold union office, and leave to courts and juries the job of deciding what persons have committed the specified acts or possess the specified characteristics. Instead, it designates in no uncertain terms the persons who possess the feared characteristics and therefore cannot hold union office without incurring criminal liability — members of the Communist Party.

"We do not hold today that Congress cannot weed dangerous persons out of the labor movement, any more than the Court held in Lovett that subversives must be permitted to hold sensitive government positions. Rather, we make again the point made in Lovett: that Congress must accomplish such results by rules of general applicability. It cannot specify the people upon whom the sanction it prescribes is to be levied. Under our Constitution, Congress possesses full legislative authority, but the task of adjudication must be left to other tribunals.

"The judgment of the Court of Appeals is affirmed.

"Affirmed.

"Mr. Justice White, with whom Mr. Justice Clark, Mr. Justice Harlan, and Mr. Justice Stewart join dissenting. . . .

". . . [T]he Court implies that legislation is sufficiently general if it specifies a characteristic that makes it *likely* that individuals falling within the group designated will engage in conduct Congress may prohibit. But the Court then goes on to reject the argument that Communist Party membership is in itself a characteristic raising such a likelihood. The Court declares that "[e]ven assuming that Congress had reason to conclude that *some* Communists would use union positions to bring about political strikes, . . . it cannot automatically be inferred that *all* members shar[e] their evil purposes or participat[e] in their illegal conduct." . . . (Emphasis added.) . . .

"But how does one prove that a person would be disloyal? The Communist Party's illegal purpose and its domination by foreign power have already been adjudicated, both administratively and judicially. If this does not in itself provide a sufficient probability with respect to the individual who persists in remaining a member of the Party, or if a probability is in any event insufficient, what evidence with regard to the individual will be sufficient to disqualify him? If he must be apprehended in the act of calling one political strike or in one act of disloyalty before steps can be taken to exclude him from office, there is little or nothing left of the preventive or prophylactic function of § 504. . . ."

NOTE United States v. Robel

After the Communist party had been ordered to register as a Communist-action organization under the Subversive Activities Control Act, Robel, a member of that party, remained an employee at a shipyard that had been designated a "defense facility" by the Secretary of Defense under that act. His continued employment constituted a violation of § 5(a)(1)(D) of the Subversive Activities Control Act, and he was indicted therefor. In affirming an order dismissing the indictment, the Supreme Court held that § 5(a)(1)(D)'s overbreadth unconstitutionally abridged the right of association protected by the First Amendment. United States v. Robel, 389 U.S. 258 (1967).

Keyishian v. Board of Regents 385 U.S. 589, 87 S. Ct. 675, 17 L. Ed. 2d 629 (1967)

Mr. Justice Brennan delivered the opinion of the Court.

Appellants were members of the faculty of the privately owned and operated University of Buffalo, and became state employees when the University was merged in 1962 into the State University of New York, an institution of higher education owned and operated by the State of New York. As faculty members of the State University their continued employment was conditioned upon their compliance with a New York plan, formulated partly in statutes and partly in administrative regulations, which the State utilizes to prevent the appointment or retention of "subversive" persons in state employment.

Appellants Hochfield and Maud were Assistant Professors of English, appellant Keyishian an instructor in English, and appellant Garver, a lecturer in philosophy. Each of them refused to sign, as regulations then in effect required, a certificate that he was not a Communist, and that if he had ever been a Communist, he had communicated that fact to the President of the State University of New York. Each was notified that his failure to sign the certificate would require his dismissal. Keyishian's one-year-term contract was not renewed because of his failure to sign the certificate. Hochfield and Garver, whose contracts still had time to run, continue to teach, but subject to proceedings for their dismissal if the constitutionality of the New York plan is sustained. Maud has voluntarily resigned and therefore no longer has standing in this suit.

Appellant Starbuck was a nonfaculty library employee and part-time lecturer in English. Personnel in that classification were not required to sign a certificate but to answer in writing under oath the question, "Have you ever advised or taught or were you ever a member of any society or group of people which taught or advocated the doctrine that the Government of the United States or of any political subdivisions thereof should be overthrown or overturned by force, violence or any unlawful means?" Starbuck refused to answer the question and as a result was dismissed.

Appellants brought this action for declaratory and injunctive relief alleging that the state program violated the Federal Constitution in various respects. A three-judge federal court held that the program was constitutional. 255 F. Supp. 981. We noted probable jurisdiction of appellant's appeal. 384 U.S. 998. We reverse.

I

[The Court found that the issues at bar were not settled by reference to Adler v. Board of Education, 342 U.S. 485 (1952), which had sustained elements of the New York "Feinberg Law." Adler had not considered the question of vagueness in the Feinberg Law, and had rested some of its conclusions about substantive challenges on "constitutional doctrines . . . since rejected."]

II

A 1953 amendment extended the application of the Feinberg Law to personnel of any college or other institution of higher education owned and operated by the State or its subdivisions. In the same year, the Board of Regents, after notice and hearing, listed the Communist Party of the United States and of the State of New York as "subversive organizations." In 1956 each applicant for an appointment or the renewal of an appointment was required to sign the so-called "Feinberg Certificate" declaring that he had read the Regents Rules and understood that the Rules and the statutes constituted terms of employment, and declaring further that he was not a member of the Communist Party, and that if he had ever been a member he had communicated that fact to the President of the State University. This was the certificate that appellants Hochfield, Maud, Keyishian, and Garver refused to sign.

In June 1965, shortly before the trial of this case, the Feinberg Certificate was rescinded and it was announced that no person then employed would be deemed ineligible for continued employment "solely" because he refused to sign the certificate. In lieu of the certificate, it was provided that each applicant be informed before assuming his duties that the statutes, §§ 3021 and 3022 of the Education Law and § 105 of the Civil Service Law, constituted part of his contract. He was particularly to be informed of the disqualification which flowed from membership in a listed "subversive" organization. The 1965 announcement further provides: "Should any question arise in the course of such inquiry such candidate may request . . . a personal interview. Refusal of a candidate to answer any question relevant to such inquiry by such officer shall be sufficient ground to refuse to make or recommend appointment." A brochure is also given new applicants. It outlines and explains briefly the legal effect of the statutes and invites any applicant who may have any question about possible disqualification to request an interview. The covering announcement concludes that "a prospective appointee who does not believe himself disqualified need take no affirmative action. No disclaimer oath is required."

The change in procedure in no wise moots appellants' constitutional questions raised in the context of their refusal to sign the now abandoned Feinberg Certificate. The substance of the statutory and regulatory complex remains and from the outset appellants' basic claim has been that they are aggrieved by its application.

Section C. **Freedom of Speech and Association** 1341

III

Section 3021 requires removal for "treasonable or seditious" utterances or acts. The 1958 amendment to § 105 of the Civil Service Law, now subdivision 3 of that section, added such utterances or acts as a ground for removal under that law also. . . .

[After review of the further statutory definition and coverage of these two provisions, the Court voided the "regulatory maze" of these prohibitions because "[v]agueness of wording is aggravated by prolixity and profusion of statutes, regulations, and administrative machinery, and by manifold cross-references to interrelated enactments and rules."]

IV

Appellants have also challenged the constitutionality of the discrete provisions of subdivision (1)(c) of § 105 and subdivision (2) of the Feinberg Law, which make Communist Party membership, as such, prima facie evidence of disqualification. The provision was added to subdivision (1)(c) of § 105 in 1958 after the Board of Regents, following notice and hearing, listed the Communist Party of the United States and the Communist Party of the State of New York as "subversive" organizations. Subdivision (2) of the Feinberg Law was, however, before the Court in Adler and its constitutionality was sustained. But constitutional doctrine which has emerged since that decision has rejected its major premise. That premise was that public employment, including academic employment, may be conditioned upon the surrender of constitutional rights which could not be abridged by direct government action. . . .

We proceed then to the question of the validity of the provisions of subdivision (c) of § 105 and subdivision (2) of § 3022, barring employment to members of listed organizations. Here again constitutional doctrine has developed since Adler. Mere knowing membership without a specific intent to further the unlawful aims of an organization is not a constitutionally adequate basis for exclusion from such positions as those held by appellants.

In Elfbrandt v. Russell, 384 U.S. 11, we said, "Those who join an organization but do not share its unlawful purposes and who do not participate in its unlawful activities surely pose no threat, either as citizens or as public employees." We there struck down a statutorily required oath binding the state employee not to become a member of the Communist Party with knowledge of its unlawful purpose, on threat of discharge and perjury prosecution if the oath were violated. We found that "any lingering doubt that proscription of mere knowing membership, without any showing of 'specific intent,' would run afoul of the Constitution was set at rest by our decision in Aptheker v. Secretary of State, 378 U.S. 500." Elfbrandt v. Russell, supra, at 16. In Aptheker we held that Party membership, without knowledge of the Party's unlawful purposes *and* specific intent to further its unlawful aims, could not constitutionally warrant deprivation of the right to travel abroad. . . .

These limitations clearly apply to a provision, like § 105(1)(c), which blankets all state employees, regardless of the "sensitivity" of their positions. But even the Feinberg Law provision, applicable primarily to activities of teachers, who have captive audiences of young minds, are subject to these limitations in favor of freedom of expression and association; the stifling effect on the academic mind from curtailing freedom of association in such manner is manifest, and has been documented in recent studies. Elfbrandt and Aptheker state the governing standard: legislation which sanctions membership unaccompanied by specific intent to further the unlawful goals of the organization or which is not active membership violates constitutional limitations.

Measured against this standard, both Civil Service Law § 105(1)(c) and Education Law

1342   Chapter Sixteen.   **Substantive Rights**

§3022(2) sweep overbroadly into association which may not be proscribed. The presumption of disqualification arising from proof of mere membership may be rebutted, but only by (a) a denial of membership, (b) a denial that the organization advocates the overthrow of government by force, or (c) a denial that the teacher has knowledge of such advocacy. Lederman v. Board of Education, 276 App. Div. 527, 96 N.Y.S.2d 466, aff'd 301 N.Y. 476. Thus proof of nonactive membership or a showing of the absence of intent to further unlawful aims will not rebut the presumption and defeat dismissal. . . .

Thus §105(1)(c) and §3022(2) suffer from impermissible "overbreadth." Elfbrandt v. Russell, supra, at 19; Aptheker v. Secretary of State, supra; N.A.A.C.P. v. Button [371 U.S. 415]; Saia v. New York, 334 U.S. 558; Schneider v. State, 308 U.S. 147; Lovell v. Griffin, 303 U.S. 444; cf. Hague v. C.I.O., 307 U.S. 496, 515-516; see generally Dombrowski v. Pfister, 380 U.S. 479, 486. They seek to bar employment both for association which legitimately may be proscribed and for association which may not be proscribed consistently with First Amendment rights. Where statutes have an overbroad sweep, just as where they are vague, "the hazard of loss or substantial impairment of those precious rights may be critical," Dombrowski v. Pfister, supra, at 486, since those covered by the statute are bound to limit their behavior to that which is unquestionably safe. As we said in Shelton v. Tucker, supra, at 488, "The breadth of legislative abridgment must be viewed in the light of less drastic means for achieving the same basic purpose."

We therefore hold that Civil Service Law §105(1)(c) and Education Law §3022(2) are invalid insofar as they proscribe mere knowing membership without any showing of specific intent to further the unlawful aims of the Communist Party of the United States or of the State of New York.

The judgment of the District Court is reversed and the case is remanded for further proceedings consistent with this opinion.

Reversed and remanded.

MR. JUSTICE CLARK, with whom MR. JUSTICE HARLAN, MR. JUSTICE STEWART and MR. JUSTICE WHITE join, dissenting.

The blunderbuss fashion in which the majority couches "its artillery of words" together with the morass of cases it cites as authority and the obscurity of their application to the question at hand makes it difficult to grasp the true thrust of its decision. At the outset, it is therefore necessary to focus on its basis.

This is a declaratory judgment action testing the *application* of the Feinberg Law to appellants. The certificate and statement once required by the Board and upon which appellants base their attack were, before the case was tried, abandoned by the Board and are no longer required to be made. Despite this fact the majority proceeds to its decision striking down New York's Feinberg Law and other statutes as applied to appellants on the basis of the old certificate and statement. It does not explain how the statute can be applied to appellants under procedures which have been for almost two years a dead letter. The issues posed are, therefore, purely abstract and entirely speculative in character. The Court under such circumstances has in the past refused to pass upon constitutional questions. In addition, the appellants have neither exhausted their administrative remedies, nor pursued the remedy of judicial review of agency action as provided earlier by subdivision (d) of §12-a of the Civil Service Law. Finally, one of the sections stricken, §105(3), has been amended and under its terms will not become effective until September 1, 1967. (L. 1965, Ch. 1030.) . . .

This Court has again and again, since at least 1951, approved procedures either identical or at least similar to the ones the Court condemns today. In Garner v. Board of Works of Los Angeles [341 U.S. 716], we held that a public employer was not precluded, simply because it was an agency of the State, "from inquiring of its employees as to matters that may prove relevant to their fitness and suitability for the public service." 341 U.S., at p. 720. The oath there used practically the same language as the Starbuck statement here and the affidavit reflects the same type of inquiry as was made in the old certificate condemned here. Then in 1952, in Adler v. Board of Education, supra, this Court passed upon the identical statute condemned here. It, too, was a declaratory judgment action — as in this case. However, there the issues were not so abstractly framed. Our late Brother Minton wrote for the Court: "A teacher works in a sensitive area in a schoolroom. There he shapes the attitude of young minds toward the society in which they live. In this, the state has a vital concern. It must preserve the integrity of the schools. That the school authorities have the right and the duty to screen the officials, teachers, and employees as to their fitness to maintain the integrity of the schools as a part of ordered society, cannot be doubted." . . .

In view of [the] long list of decisions covering over 15 years of this Court's history, in which no opinion of this Court even questioned the validity of the Adler line of cases, it is strange to me that the Court now finds that the "constitutional doctrine which has emerged since . . . has rejected [Adler's] major premise." With due respect, as I read them, our cases have done no such thing.

IV

. . . The majority says that the Feinberg Law is bad because it has an "overbroad sweep." I regret to say — and I do so with deference — that the majority has by its broadside swept away one of our most precious rights, namely, the right of self-preservation. Our public educational system is the genius of our democracy. The minds of our youth are developed there and the character of that development will determine the future of our land. Indeed, our very existence depends upon it. The issue here is a very narrow one. It is not freedom of speech, freedom of thought, freedom of press, freedom of assembly, or of association, even in the Communist Party. It is simply this: May the State provide that one who, after a hearing with full judicial review, is found to wilfully and deliberately advocate, advise, or teach that our Government should be overthrown by force or violence or other unlawful means; or who wilfully and deliberately prints, publishes, etc., any book or paper that so advocates *and who personally* advocates such doctrine himself; or who wilfully and deliberately becomes a member of an organization that advocates such doctrine, is prima facie disqualified from teaching in its university? My answer, in keeping with all of our cases up until today, is "Yes"!

I dissent.

NOTE Loyalty Oaths and Inquiries

In re George Anastaplo, 366 U.S. 82, 81 S. Ct. 978, 6 L. Ed. 2d 135 (1961). For a majority of five, Mr. Justice Harlan sustained the decision of the Illinois court that an application for admission to the bar might be denied because the applicant, against whom no suspicion of membership in subversive organizations existed, had refused on grounds of the First and Fourteenth Amendments to state whether or not he was a member of the Communist party. "Where, as with membership in the bar, the State may withhold a privilege available only to those possessing the requisite qualifications, it is of no constitutional significance whether the State's interrogation of an applicant on matters relevant to these qualifications — in this case Communist Party membership — is prompted by information which it already has about him from other sources, or arises merely from a good faith belief in the need for exploratory or testing questioning of the applicant. Were it otherwise, a bar examining committee such as this, having no resources of its own for independent investigation, might be placed in the untenable position of having to certify an applicant without assurance as to a significant aspect of his qualifications which the applicant himself is best circumstanced to supply. The Constitution does not so unreasonably fetter the States." See also Konigsberg v. State Bar of California, 353 U.S. 252 (1957), 366 U.S. 36 (1961).

A series of cases in 1971 again presented questions concerning requirements of disclosure for admission to the bar. Refusal of the applicant to answer the question whether he had ever belonged to an organization that advocates overthrow of the government by force or violence was held not to warrant the rejection of the applicant. Chief Justice Burger and Justices Blackmun, Harlan, and White dissented. Baird v. State Bar, 401 U.S. 1 (1971); In re Stolar, 401 U.S. 23 (1971). But in Law Students Research Council v. Wadmond, 401 U.S. 154 (1971), the Court upheld the New York admission requirements that were challenged on a broad front because of their "chilling effect" on beliefs and associations. A question concerning membership was phrased in terms of the applicant's knowledge of the organization's purposes and his intent to further them, and an oath to support the Constitution was required. Justices Black, Douglas, Brennan, and Marshall dissented.

In Connell v. Higgenbotham, 403 U.S. 207 (1971), the Court held that a state may not require, upon pain of dismissal without further inquiry, an oath from its employees that they do not believe in the violent overthrow of the government.

See also Cole v. Richardson, 405 U.S. 676 (1972), in which a loyalty oath to "oppose the overthrow" of the government, which Massachusetts administers to its state employees, was interpreted as not requiring any action of those who took the oath, and was then upheld.

See also Communist Party of Indiana v. Whitcomb, 414 U.S. 441 (1974), invalidating a state statute which denied a place on the ballot to any new party which failed to file "an affidavit, by its officers, under oath, that it does not advocate the overthrow of local, state or national government by force or violence. . . ."

Section D. RELIGION

Men of ardent faith have often assumed that a man's conscience immunizes his conduct from state control. The Mormon followers of Joseph Smith learned, however, that their religious liberty did not safeguard them from the law's condemnation of polygamy (Reynolds v. United States, 98 U.S. 145 (1878)). Compare, however, People v. Woody, 61 Cal. 2d 716, 394 P.2d 813, 40 Cal. Rptr. 69 (1964). Students in a state university discovered that they could not demand exemption from a required course of military training because their faith wholly condemned war and training for war (Hamilton v. Regents of the University of California, 293 U.S. 245 (1934); see also United States v. Henderson, 180 F.2d 711 (7th Cir. 1950)). In the nineteenth century many a Roman Catholic parent learned that his children attending public schools could be compelled to participate in exercises and ceremonies colored by Protestant tradition (Spiller v. Woburn, 12 Allen 127 (1866); Donahoe v. Richards, 38 Me. 376 (1854)). They also discovered that the prudential committee of a public school district could expel those children who obeyed their priests' instructions to cut classes on holy days in order that they might attend religious exercises (Ferriter v. Tyler, 48 Vt. 444 (1876)). Yet it has also been held that children could not be removed from public schools for refusing, on religious grounds, to dance the waltz, polka, or two-step (Hardwick v. Board of School Trustees, 54 Cal. App. 696 (1921)).

During the 1930s and 1940s the Supreme Court, in a series of cases, vigorously applied the Fourteenth Amendment to secure religious liberty against state action. The cases characteristically involved speech, and though there were occasional indications that speech motivated by religious conviction was entitled to greater constitutional protection than utterances unrelated to faith (see, e.g., Jackson, J., dissenting in United States v. Ballard, 322 U.S. 78, 92 (1944)), it may be taken as generally true that the measure of freedom secured to religious speaking is no different from that by which speech concerned with other themes and prompted by other impulses is secured. Most of the recent cases in which religious speech has been considered have already been presented or referred to in earlier sections of this chapter.

CANTWELL v. CONNECTICUT, 310 U.S. 296, 303-304, 60 S. Ct. 900, 903, 84 L. Ed. 1213, 1218 (1940). Roberts, J.: "The First Amendment declares that Congress shall make no law respecting an establishment of religion or prohibiting the free exercise thereof. The Fourteenth Amendment has rendered the legislatures of the states as incompetent as Congress to enact such laws. The constitutional inhibition of legislation on the subject of religion has a double aspect. On the one hand, it forestalls compulsion by law of the acceptance of any creed or the practice of any form of worship. Freedom of conscience and freedom to adhere to such religious organization or form of worship as the individual may choose cannot be restricted by law. On the other hand, it safeguards the free exercise of the chosen form of religion. Thus the amendment embraces two concepts, — freedom to believe and freedom to act. The first is absolute but, in the nature of things, the second cannot be."

West Virginia State Board of Education v. Barnette 319 U.S. 624, 63 S. Ct. 1178, 87 L. Ed. 1628 (1943)

MR. JUSTICE JACKSON delivered the opinion of the Court:

Following the decision by this Court on June 3, 1940, in Minersville School Dist. v. Gobitis, 310 U.S. 586, the West Virginia legislature amended its statutes to require all schools therein to conduct courses of instruction in history, civics, and in the Constitutions of the United States and of the State "for the purpose of teaching, fostering and perpetuating the ideals, principles and spirit of Americanism, and increasing the knowledge of the organization and machinery of the government." . . .[tt]

The Board of Education on January 9, 1942, adopted a resolution containing recitals taken largely from the Court's Gobitis opinion and ordering that the salute to the flag become "a regular part of the program of activities in the public schools," that all teachers and pupils "shall be required to participate in the salute honoring the Nation represented by the Flag; provided, however, that refusal to salute the Flag be regarded as an Act of insubordination, and shall be dealt with accordingly."

The resolution originally required the "commonly accepted salute to the Flag" which it defined. Objections to the salute as "being too much like Hitler's" were raised by the Parent and Teachers Association, the Boy and Girl Scouts, the Red Cross, and the Federation of Women's Clubs. Some modification appears to have been made in deference to these objections, but no concession was made to Jehovah's Witnesses. What is now required is the "stiff-arm" salute, the saluter to keep the right hand raised with palm turned up while the following is repeated: "I pledge allegiance to the Flag of the United States of America and to the Republic for which it stands; one Nation, indivisible, with liberty and justice for all."

Failure to conform is "insubordination" dealt with by expulsion. Readmission is denied by statute until compliance. Meanwhile the expelled child is "unlawfully absent" and may be proceeded against as a delinquent. His parents or guardians are liable to prosecu-

---

[tt] In the Gobitis case the Supreme Court, in an opinion of Mr. Justice Frankfurter, with Stone, C.J., dissenting, had sustained the constitutionality of a compulsory flag salute in public schools, despite the religious protestations of Jehovah's Witnesses. — ED.

tion, and if convicted are subject to fine not exceeding $50 and jail term not exceeding thirty days.

Appellees, citizens of the United States and of West Virginia, brought suit in the United States District Court for themselves and others similarly situated asking its injunction to restrain enforcement of these laws and regulations against Jehovah's Witnesses. The Witnesses are an unincorporated body teaching that the obligation imposed by law of God is superior to that of laws enacted by temporal government. Their religious beliefs include a literal version of Exodus, Chapter 20, verses 4 and 5, which says: "Thou shalt not make unto thee any graven image, or any likeness of anything that is in heaven above, or that is in the earth beneath, or that is in the water under the earth; thou shalt not bow down thyself to them, nor serve them." They consider that the flag is an "image" within this command. For this reason they refuse to salute it.

. . . The cause was submitted on the pleadings to a District Court of three judges. It restrained enforcement as to the plaintiffs and those of that class. The Board of Education brought the case here by direct appeal.

This case calls upon us to reconsider a precedent decision, as the Court throughout its history often has been required to do.[10] Before turning to the Gobitis Case, however, it is desirable to notice certain characteristics by which this controversy is distinguished.

The freedom asserted by these appellees does not bring them into collision with rights asserted by any other individual. It is such conflicts which most frequently require intervention of the State to determine where the rights of one end and those of another begin. But the refusal of these persons to participate in the ceremony does not interfere with or deny rights of others to do so. Nor is there any question in this case that their behavior is peaceable and orderly. The sole conflict is between authority and rights of the individual. The State asserts power to condition access to public education on making a prescribed sign and profession and at the same time to coerce attendance by punishing both parent and child. The latter stand on a right of self-determination in matters that touch individual opinion and personal attitude.

As the present Chief Justice said in dissent in the Gobitis Case, the State may "require teaching by instruction and study of all in our history and in the structure and organization of our government, including the guaranties of civil liberty, which tend to inspire patriotism and love of country." 310 U.S. at 604. Here, however, we are dealing with a compulsion of students to declare a belief. They are not merely made acquainted with the flag salute so that they may be informed as to what it is or even what it means. The issue here is whether this slow and easily neglected route to aroused loyalties constitutionally may be short-cut by substituting a compulsory salute and slogan. This issue is not prejudiced by the Court's previous holding that where a State, without compelling attendance, extends college facilities to pupils who voluntarily enroll, it may prescribe military training as part of the course without offense to the Constitution. It was held that those who take advantage of its opportunities may not on ground of conscience refuse compliance with such conditions. Hamilton v. University of California, 293 U.S. 245. In the present case attendance is not optional. That case is also to be distinguished from the present one because, independently of college privileges or requirements, the State has power to raise militia and impose the duties of service therein upon its citizens.

There is no doubt that, in connection with the pledges, the flag salute is a form of utterance. Symbolism is a primitive but effective way of communicating ideas. The use of an emblem or flag to symbolize some system, idea, institution, or personality, is a short cut from mind to mind. Causes and nations, political parties, lodges and ecclesiastical groups seek to knit the loyalty of their followings to a flag or banner, a color or design. The State announces rank, function, and authority through crowns and maces, uniforms and black robes; the church speaks through the Cross, the Crucifix, the altar and shrine and clerical

---

[10] See authorities cited in Helvering v. Griffiths, 318 U.S. 371, 401.

raiment. Symbols of State often convey political ideas just as religious symbols come to convey theological ones. Associated with many of these symbols are appropriate gestures of acceptance or respect: a salute, a bowed or bared head, a bended knee. A person gets from a symbol the meaning he puts into it, and what is one man's comfort and inspiration is another's jest and scorn. . . .

Nor does the issue as we see it turn on one's possession of particular religious views or the sincerity with which they are held. While religion supplies appellees' motive for enduring the discomforts of making the issue in this case, many citizens, who do not share these religious views hold such a compulsory rite to infringe constitutional liberty of the individual. It is not necessary to inquire whether nonconformist beliefs will exempt from the duty to salute unless we first find power to make the salute a legal duty.

The Gobitis decision, however, *assumed*, as did the argument in that case and in this, that power exists in the State to impose the flag salute discipline upon school children in general. The Court only examined and rejected a claim based on religious beliefs of immunity from an unquestioned general rule. The question which underlies the flag salute controversy is whether such a ceremony so touching matters of opinion and political attitude may be imposed upon the individual by official authority under powers committed to any political organization under our Constitution. We examine rather than assume existence of this power and, against this broader definition of issues in this case, re-examine specific grounds assigned for the Gobitis decision.

1. It was said that the flag-salute controversy confronted the Court with "the problem which Lincoln cast in memorable dilemma: 'Must a government of necessity be too *strong* for the liberties of its people, or too *weak* to maintain its own existence?' " and that the answer must be in favor of strength. Minersville School Dist. v. Gobitis, supra, 310 U.S. at 596.

We think these issues may be examined free of pressure or restraint growing out of such considerations.

It may be doubted whether Mr. Lincoln would have thought that the strength of government to maintain itself would be impressively vindicated by our confirming power of the state to expel a handful of children from school. Such oversimplification, so handy in political debate, often lacks the precision necessary to postulates of judicial reasoning. If validly applied to this problem, the utterance cited would resolve every issue of power in favor of those in authority and would require us to override every liberty thought to weaken or delay execution of their policies.

Government of limited power need not be anemic government. Assurance that rights are secure tends to diminish fear and jealousy of strong government, and by making us feel safe to live under it makes for its better support. Without promise of a limiting Bill of Rights it is doubtful if our Constitution could have mustered enough strength to enable its ratification. To enforce those rights today is not to choose weak government over strong government. It is only to adhere as a means of strength to individual freedom of mind in preference to officially disciplined uniformity for which history indicates a disappointing and disastrous end.

2. It was also considered in the Gobitis Case that functions of educational officers in states, counties and school districts were such that to interfere with their authority "would in effect make us the school board for the country." Id. at 598.

The Fourteenth Amendment, as now applied to the States, protects the citizen against the State itself and all of its creatures — Boards of Education not excepted. These have, of course, important, delicate, and highly discretionary functions, but none that they may not perform within the limits of the Bill of Rights. That they are educating the young for citizenship is reason for scrupulous protection of Constitutional freedoms of the individual, if we are not to strangle the free mind at its source and teach youth to discount important principles of our government as mere platitudes.

Such Boards are numerous and their territorial jurisdiction often small. But small and local authority may feel less sense of responsibility to the Constitution, and agencies of publicity may be less vigilant in calling it to account. . . . There are village tyrants as well as village Hampdens, but none who acts under color of law is beyond reach of the Constitution.

3. The Gobitis opinion reasoned that this is a field "where courts possess no marked and certainly no controlling competence," that it is committed to the legislatures as well as the courts to guard cherished liberties and that it is constitutionally appropriate to "fight out the wise use of legislative authority in the forum of public opinion and before legislative assemblies rather than to transfer such a contest to the judicial arena," since all the "effective means of inducing political changes are left free." Id. 310 U.S. at 597, 598, 600.

The very purpose of a Bill of Rights was to withdraw certain subjects from the vicissitudes of political controversy, to place them beyond the reach of majorities and officials and to establish them as legal principles to be applied by the courts. One's right to life, liberty, and property, to free speech, a free press, freedom of worship and assembly, and other fundamental rights may not be submitted to vote; they depend on the outcome of no elections.

In weighing arguments of the parties it is important to distinguish between the due process clause of the Fourteenth Amendment as an instrument for transmitting the principles of the First Amendment and those cases in which it is applied for its own sake. The test of legislation which collides with the Fourteenth Amendment, because it also collides with the principles of the First, is much more definite than the test when only the Fourteenth is involved. . . .

. . . We cannot, because of modest estimates of our competence in such specialties as public education, withhold the judgment that history authenticates as the function of this Court when liberty is infringed.

4. Lastly, and this is the very heart of the Gobitis opinion, it reasons that "national unity is the basis of national security," that the authorities have "the right to select appropriate means for its attainment," and hence reaches the conclusion that such compulsory measures toward "national unity" are constitutional. Id. at 595. Upon the verity of this assumption depends our answer in this case.

National unity as an end which officials may foster by persuasion and example is not in question. The problem is whether under our Constitution compulsion as here employed is a permissible means for its achievement.

The case is made difficult not because the principles of its decision are obscure but because the flag involved is our own. Nevertheless, we apply the limitations of the Constitution with no fear that freedom to be intellectually and spiritually diverse or even contrary will disintegrate the social organization. To believe that patriotism will not flourish if patriotic ceremonies are voluntary and spontaneous instead of a compulsory routine is to make an unflattering estimate of the appeal of our institutions to free minds. We can have intellectual individualism and the rich cultural diversities that we owe to exceptional minds only at the price of occasional eccentricity and abnormal attitudes. When they are so harmless to others or to the State as those we deal with here, the price is not too great. But freedom to differ is not limited to things that do not matter much. That would be a mere shadow of freedom. The test of its substance is the right to differ as to things that touch the heart of the existing order.

If there is any fixed star in our constitutional constellation, it is that no official, high or petty, can prescribe what shall be orthodox in politics, nationalism, religion, or other matters of opinion or force citizens to confess by word or act their faith therein. If there are any circumstances which permit an exception, they do not now occur to us.

We think the action of the local authorities in compelling the flag salute and pledge transcends constitutional limitations on their power and invades the sphere of intellect and spirit which it is the purpose of the First Amendment to our Constitution to reserve from all official control.

The decision of this Court in Minersville School Dist. v. Gobitis and the holdings of those few per curiam decisions which preceded and foreshadowed it are overruled, and the judgment enjoining enforcement of the West Virginia Regulation is affirmed.[uu]

Mr. Justice Roberts and Mr. Justice Reed adhere to the views expressed by the Court in Minersville School Dist. v. Gobitis, 310 U.S. 586, and are of the opinion that the judgment below should be reversed.

Mr. Justice Frankfurter, dissenting:

One who belongs to the most vilified and persecuted minority in history is not likely to be insensible to the freedoms guaranteed by our Constitution. Were my purely personal attitude relevant I should wholeheartedly associate myself with the general libertarian views in the Court's opinion, representing as they do the thought and action of a lifetime. But as judges we are neither Jew nor Gentile, neither Catholic nor agnostic. We owe equal attachment to the Constitution and are equally bound by our judicial obligations whether we derive our citizenship from the earliest or the latest immigrants to these shores. As a member of this Court I am not justified in writing my private notions of policy into the Constitution, no matter how deeply I may cherish them or how mischievous I may deem their disregard. The duty of a judge who must decide which of two claims before the Court shall prevail, that of a State to enact and enforce laws within its general competence or that of an individual to refuse obedience because of the demands of his conscience, is not that of the ordinary person. It can never be emphasized too much that one's own opinion about the wisdom or evil of a law should be excluded altogether when one is doing one's duty on the bench. The only opinion of our own even looking in that direction that is material is our opinion whether legislators could in reason have enacted such a law. In the light of all the circumstances, including the history of this question in this Court, it would require more daring than I possess to deny that reasonable legislators could have taken the action which is before us for review. Most unwillingly, therefore, I must differ from my brethren with regard to legislation like this. I cannot bring my mind to believe that the "liberty" secured by the Due Process Clause gives this Court authority to deny to the State of West Virginia the attainment of that which we all recognize as a legitimate legislative end, namely, the promotion of good citizenship, by employment of the means here chosen. . . .

The constitutional protection of religious freedom terminated disabilities, it did not create new privileges. It gave religious equality, not civil immunity. Its essence is freedom from conformity to religious dogma, not freedom from conformity to law because of religious dogma. Religious loyalties may be exercised without hindrance from the state, not the state may not exercise that which except by leave of religious loyalties is within the domain of temporal power. Otherwise each individual could set up his own censor against obedience to laws conscientiously deemed for the public good by those whose business it is to make laws.

The prohibition against any religious establishment by the government placed denominations on an equal footing — it assured freedom from support by the government to any mode of worship and the freedom of individuals to support any mode of worship. Any person may therefore believe or disbelieve what he pleases. He may practice what he will in his own house of worship or publicly within the limits of public order. But the lawmaking authority is not circumscribed by the variety of religious beliefs, otherwise the constitutional guaranty would be not a protection of the free exercise of religion but a denial of the exercise of legislation.

One's conception of the Constitution cannot be severed from one's conception of a judge's function in applying it. The Court has no reason for existence if it merely reflects

---

[uu] Concurring opinions by Mr. Justice Black (concurred in by Douglas, J.) and Mr. Justice Murphy are omitted. In 1942 those three Justices, in a dissenting opinion, had announced that though they had joined the majority opinion in the Gobitis case, they had come to believe that it was wrongly decided. See Jones v. Opelika, 316 U.S. 584, 623-624 (1942). — Ed.

the pressures of the day. Our system is built on the faith that men set apart for this special function, freed from the influences of immediacy and from the deflections of worldly ambition, will become able to take a view of longer range than the period of responsibility entrusted to Congress and legislatures. We are dealing with matters as to which legislators and voters have conflicting views. Are we as judges to impose our strong convictions on where wisdom lies? That which three years ago had seemed to five successive Courts to lie within permissible areas of legislation is now outlawed by the deciding shift of opinion of two Justices. What reason is there to believe that they or their successors may not have another view a few years hence? Is that which was deemed to be of so fundamental a nature as to be written into the Constitution to endure for all times to be the sport of shifting winds of doctrine? Of course, judicial opinions, even as to questions of constitutionality, are not immutable. As has been true in the past, the Court will from time to time reverse its position. But I believe that never before these Jehovah's Witnesses cases (except for minor deviations subsequently retraced) has this Court overruled decisions so as to restrict the powers of democratic government. Always heretofore, it has withdrawn narrow views of legislative authority so as to authorize what formerly it had denied.

Of course patriotism cannot be enforced by the flag salute. But neither can the liberal spirit be enforced by judicial invalidation of illiberal legislation. Our constant preoccupation with the constitutionality of legislation rather than with its wisdom tends to preoccupation of the American mind with a false value. The tendency of focussing attention on constitutionality is to make constitutionality synonymous with wisdom, to regard a law as all right if it is constitutional. Such an attitude is a great enemy of liberalism. Particularly in legislation affecting freedom of thought and freedom of speech much which should offend a free-spirited society is constitutional. Reliance for the most precious interests of civilization, therefore, must be found outside of their vindication in courts of law. Only a persistent positive translation of the faith of a free society into the convictions and habits and actions of a community is the ultimate reliance against unabated temptations to fetter the human spirit.

Everson v. Board of Education *330 U.S. 1, 67 S. Ct. 504, 91 L. Ed. 711 (1947)*

MR. JUSTICE BLACK delivered the opinion of the Court.

A New Jersey statute authorizes its local school districts to make rules and contracts for the transportation of children to and from schools.[1] The appellee, a township board of education, acting pursuant to this statute, authorized reimbursement to parents of money expended by them for the bus transportation of their children on regular busses operated by the public transportation system. Part of this money was for the payment of transportation of some children in the community to Catholic parochial schools. These church schools give their students, in addition to secular education, regular religious instruction conforming to the religious tenets and modes of worship of the Catholic Faith. The superintendent of these schools is a Catholic priest.

The appellant, in his capacity as a district taxpayer, filed suit in a State court challeng-

---

[1] "Whenever in any district there are children living remote from any schoolhouse, the board of education of the district may make rules and contracts for the transportation of such children to and from school, including the transportation of school children to and from school other than a public school, except such school as is operated for profit in whole or in part.

"When any school district provides any transportation for public school children to and from school, transportation from any point in such established school route to any other point in such established school route shall be supplied to school children residing in such school district in going to and from school other than a public school, except such school as is operated for profit in whole or in part." New Jersey Laws, 1941, c. 191, p. 581; N.J. Rev. Stat. 18:14-8.

ing the right of the Board to reimburse parents of parochial school students. He contended that the statute and the resolution passed pursuant to it violated both the State and the Federal Constitutions. That court held that the legislature was without power to authorize such payment under the State constitution. 132 N.J.L. 98. The New Jersey Court of Errors and Appeals reversed, holding that neither the statute nor the resolution passed pursuant to it was in conflict with the State constitution or the provisions of the Federal Constitution in issue. 133 N.J.L. 350. The case is here on appeal under 28 U.S.C. §344(a).

Since there has been no attack on the statute on the ground that a part of its language excludes children attending private schools operated for profit from enjoying State payment for their transportation, we need not consider this exclusionary language; it has no relevancy to any constitutional question here presented. Furthermore, if the exclusion clause had been properly challenged, we do not know whether New Jersey's highest court would construe its statutes as precluding payment of the school transportation of any group of pupils, even those of a private school run for profit. Consequently, we put to one side the question as to the validity of the statute against the claim that it does not authorize payment for the transportation generally of school children in New Jersey.

. . . The New Jersey statute is challenged as a "law respecting the establishment of religion." The First Amendment, as made applicable to the states by the Fourteenth, Murdock v. Pennsylvania, 319 U.S. 105, commands that a state "shall make no law respecting an establishment of religion, or prohibiting the free exercise thereof." . . . These words of the First Amendment reflected in the minds of early Americans a vivid mental picture of conditions and practices which they fervently wished to stamp out in order to preserve liberty for themselves and for their posterity. Doubtless their goal has not been entirely reached; but so far has the Nation moved toward it that the expression "law respecting the establishment of religion," probably does not so vividly remind present-day Americans of the evils, fears, and political problems that caused that expression to be written into our Bill of Rights. Whether this New Jersey law is one respecting an "establishment of religion" requires an understanding of the meaning of that language, particularly with respect to the imposition of taxes. [The review of historical events is omitted.]

The "establishment of religion" clause of the First Amendment means at least this: Neither a state nor the Federal Government can set up a church. Neither can pass laws which aid one religion, aid all religions, or prefer one religion over another. Neither can force nor influence a person to go to or to remain away from church against his will or force him to profess a belief or disbelief in any religion. No person can be punished for entertaining or professing religious beliefs or disbeliefs, for church attendance or non-attendance. No tax in any amount, large or small, can be levied to support any religious activities or institutions, whatever they may be called, or whatever form they may adopt to teach or practice religion. Neither a state nor the Federal Government can, openly or secretly, participate in the affairs of any religious organizations or groups and vice versa. In the words of Jefferson, the clause against establishment of religion by law was intended to erect "a wall of separation between Church and State." Reynolds v. United States, 98 U.S. 145, at 164.

We must consider the New Jersey statute in accordance with the foregoing limitations imposed by the First Amendment. But we must not strike that state statute down if it is within the State's constitutional power even though it approaches the verge of that power.

. . . New Jersey cannot consistently with the "establishment of religion" clause of the First Amendment contribute tax-raised funds to the support of an institution which teaches the tenets and faith of any church. On the other hand, other language of the amendment commands that New Jersey cannot hamper its citizens in the free exercise of their own religion. Consequently, it cannot exclude individual Catholics, Lutherans, Mohammedans, Baptists, Jews, Methodists, Non-believers, Presbyterians, or the members of any other faith, *because of their faith, or lack of it*, from receiving the benefits of public welfare legislation. While we do not mean to intimate that a state could not provide transportation only to children attending public schools, we must be careful in protecting the citizens of New Jersey against state-established churches, to be sure that we do not inadvertently prohibit New Jersey from extending its general state law benefits to all its citizens without regard to their religious belief.

Measured by these standards, we cannot say that the First Amendment prohibits New Jersey from spending tax-raised funds to pay the bus fares of parochial school pupils as a part of a general program under which it pays the fares of pupils attending public and other schools. It is undoubtedly true that children are helped to get to church schools. There is even a possibility that some of the children might not be sent to the church schools if the parents were compelled to pay their children's bus fares out of their own pockets when transportation to a public school would have been paid for by the State. The same possibility exists where the state requires a local transit company to provide reduced fares to school children including those attending parochial schools, or where a municipally owned transportation system undertakes to carry all school children free of charge. Moreover, state-paid policemen, detailed to protect children going to and from church schools from the very real hazards of traffic, would serve much the same purpose and accomplish much the same result as state provisions intended to guarantee free transportation of a kind which the state deems to be best for the school children's welfare. And parents might refuse to risk their children to the serious danger of traffic accidents going to and from parochial schools, the approaches to which were not protected by policemen. Similarly, parents might be reluctant to permit their children to attend schools which the state had cut off from such general government services as ordinary police and fire protection, connections for sewage disposal, public highways and sidewalks. Of course, cutting off church schools from these services, so separate and so indisputably marked off from the religious function, would make it far more difficult for the schools to operate. But such is obviously not the purpose of the First Amendment. That Amendment requires the state to be a neutral in its relations with groups of religious believers and non-believers; it does not require the state to be their adversary. State power is no more to be used so as to handicap religions than it is to favor them.

This Court has said that parents may, in the discharge of their duty under state compulsory education laws, send their children to a religious rather than a public school if the school meets the secular educational requirements which the state has power to impose. See Pierce v. Society of Sisters, 268 U.S. 510. It appears that these parochial schools meet New Jersey's requirements. The State contributes no money to the schools. It does not support them. Its legislation, as applied, does no more than provide a general program to help parents get their children, regardless of their religion, safely and expeditiously to and from accredited schools.

The First Amendment has erected a wall between church and state. That wall must be kept high and impregnable. We could not approve the slightest breach. New Jersey has not breached it here.

Affirmed.

Mr. Justice Jackson, dissenting. . . .

The Court sustains this legislation by assuming two deviations from the facts of this particular case; first, it assumes a state of facts the record does not support, and secondly, it refuses to consider facts which are inescapable on the record.

The Court concludes that this "legislation, as applied, does no more than provide a general program to help parents get their children, regardless of their religion, safely and expeditiously to and from accredited schools," and it draws a comparison between "state provisions intended to guarantee free transportation" for school children with services such as police and fire protection, and implies that we are here dealing with "laws authorizing new types of public services. . . ." This hypothesis permeates the opinion. The facts will not bear that construction.

The Township of Ewing is not furnishing transportation to the children in any form; it is not operating school busses itself or contracting for their operation; and it is not performing any public service of any kind with this taxpayer's money. All school children are left to ride as ordinary paying passengers on the regular busses operated by the public transportation system. What the Township does, and what the taxpayer complains of, is at stated intervals to reimburse parents for the fares paid, provided the children attend either public schools or Catholic Church schools. This expenditure of tax funds has no possible effect on the child's safety or expedition in transit. As passengers on the public busses they travel as fast and no faster, and are as safe and no safer, since their parents are reimbursed as before.

In addition to thus assuming a type of service that does not exist, the Court also insists that we must close our eyes to a discrimination which does exist. The resolution which authorizes disbursement of this taxpayer's money limits reimbursement to those who attend public schools and Catholic schools. That is the way the Act is applied to this taxpayer.

The New Jersey Act in question makes the character of the school, not the needs of the children, determine the eligibility of parents to reimbursement. The Act permits payment for transportation to parochial schools or public schools but prohibits it to private schools operated in whole or in part for profit. Children often are sent to private schools because their parents feel that they require more individual instruction than public schools can provide, or because they are backward or defective and need special attention. If all children of the state were objects of impartial solicitude, no reason is obvious for denying transportation reimbursement to students of this class, for these often are as needy and as worthy as those who go to public or parochial schools. Refusal to reimburse those who attend such schools is understandable only in the light of a purpose to aid the schools, because the state might well abstain from aiding a profit-making private enterprise. Thus, under the Act and resolution brought to us by this case, children are classified according to the schools they attend and are to be aided if they attend the public schools or private Catholic schools, and they are not allowed to be aided if they attend private secular schools or private religious schools of other faiths. . . .

If we are to decide this case on the facts before us, our question is simply this: Is it constitutional to tax this complainant to pay the cost of carrying pupils to Church schools of one specified denomination? . . .

It seems to me that the basic fallacy in the Court's reasoning, which accounts for its failure to apply the principles it avows, is in ignoring the essentially religious test by which beneficiaries of this expenditure are selected. A policeman protects a Catholic, of course — but not because he is a Catholic; it is because he is a man and a member of our society. The fireman protects the Church school — but not because it is a Church school; it is because it is property, part of the assets of our society. Neither the fireman nor the policeman has to ask before he renders aid "Is this man or building identified with the Catholic Church?" But before these school authorities draw a check to reimburse for a student's fare they must ask just that question, and if the school is a Catholic one they may render aid because it is such, while if it is of any other faith or is run for profit, the help must be withheld. . . .

MR. JUSTICE FRANKFURTER joins in this opinion.

MR. JUSTICE RUTLEDGE, with whom MR. JUSTICE FRANKFURTER, MR. JUSTICE JACKSON and MR. JUSTICE BURTON agree, dissenting.

"Congress shall make no law respecting an establishment of religion, or prohibiting the free exercise thereof. . . ." U.S. Const., Amend. 1.

"Well aware that Almighty God hath created the mind free; . . . that to compel a man to furnish contributions of money for the propagation of opinions which he disbelieves, is sinful and tyrannical; . . .

"*We, the General Assembly, do enact,* That no man shall be compelled to frequent or support any religious worship, place, or ministry whatsoever, nor shall be enforced, restrained, molested, or burthened in his body or goods, nor shall otherwise suffer, on account of his religious opinions or belief. . . ."[1]

I cannot believe that the great author of those words, or the men who made them law, could have joined in this decision. Neither so high nor so impregnable today as yesterday is the wall raised between church and state by Virginia's great statute of religious freedom and the First Amendment, now made applicable to all the states by the Fourteenth. . . .

This case forces us to determine squarely for the first time what was "an establishment of religion" in the First Amendment's conception; and by that measure to decide whether New Jersey's action violates its command. . . .

I

Not simply an established church, but any law respecting an establishment of religion is forbidden. The Amendment was broadly but not loosely phrased. It is the compact and exact summation of its author's views formed during his long struggle for religious freedom. In Madison's own words characterizing Jefferson's Bill for Establishing Religious Freedom, the guaranty he put in our national charter, like the bill he piloted through the Virginia Assembly, was "a Model of technical precision, and perspicuous brevity."[8] Madison could not have confused "church" and "religion," or "an established church" and "an establishment of religion."

The Amendment's purpose was not to strike merely at the official establishment of a single sect, creed or religion, outlawing only a formal relation such as had prevailed in England and some of the colonies. Necessarily it was to uproot all such relationships. But the object was broader than separating church and state in this narrow sense. It was to create a complete and permanent separation of the spheres of religious activity and civil authority by comprehensively forbidding every form of public aid or support for religion. In proof the Amendment's wording and history unite with this Court's consistent utterances whenever attention has been fixed directly upon the question. . . .

II

No provision of the Constitution is more closely tied to or given content by its generating history than the religious clause of the First Amendment. It is at once the refined product and the terse summation of that history. The history includes not only Madison's authorship and the proceedings before the First Congress, but also the long and intensive struggle for religious freedom in America, more especially in Virginia,[11] of which the Amendment was the direct culmination. In the documents of the times, particularly of Madison, who was leader in the Virginia struggle before he became the Amendment's

---

[1] "A Bill for Establishing Religious Freedom," enacted by the General Assembly of Virginia, January 19, 1786. See 1 Randall, The Life of Thomas Jefferson (1858) 219-220; XII Hening's Statutes of Virginia (1823) 84.

[8] IX Writings of James Madison (ed. by Hunt, 1904) 288; Padover, Jefferson (1942) 74. Madison's characterization related to Jefferson's entire revision of the Virginia Code, of which the Bill for Establishing Religious Freedom was part. . . .

[11] Conflicts in other states, and earlier in the colonies, contributed much to generation of the Amendment, but none so directly as that in Virginia or with such formative influence on the Amendment's content and wording. See Cobb, Rise of Religious Liberty in America (1902); Sweet, The Story of Religion in America (1939). The Charter of Rhode Island of 1663, II Poore, Constitutions (1878) 1595, was the first colonial charter to provide for religious freedom.

The climactic period of the Virginia struggle covers the decade 1776-1786, from adoption of the Declaration of Rights to enactment of the Statute for Religious Freedom. For short accounts see Padover, Jefferson (1942) c. V; Brant, James Madison, The Virginia Revolutionist (1941) cc. XII, XV; James, The Struggle for Religious Liberty in Virginia (1900) cc. X, XI; Eckenrode, Separation of Church and State in Virginia (1919). . . .

sponsor, but also in the writings of Jefferson and others and in the issues which engendered them is to be found irrefutable confirmation of the Amendment's sweeping content.

For Madison, as also for Jefferson, religious freedom was the crux of the struggle for freedom in general. . . . Madison was coauthor with George Mason of the religious clause in Virginia's great Declaration of Rights of 1776. He is credited with changing it from a mere statement of the principle of tolerance to the first official legislative pronouncement that freedom of conscience and religion are inherent rights of the individual. He sought also to have the Declaration expressly condemn the existing Virginia establishment. But the forces supporting it were then too strong.

Accordingly Madison yielded on this phase but not for long. At once he resumed the fight, continuing it before succeeding legislative sessions. As a member of the General Assembly in 1779 he threw his full weight behind Jefferson's historic Bill for Establishing Religious Freedom. That bill was a prime phase of Jefferson's broad program of democratic reform undertaken on his return from the Continental Congress in 1776 and submitted for the General Assembly's consideration in 1779 as his proposed revised Virginia code. With Jefferson's departure for Europe in 1784, Madison became the Bill's prime sponsor. Enactment failed in successive legislatures from its introduction in June, 1779, until its adoption in January, 1786. But during all this time the fight for religious freedom moved forward in Virginia on various fronts with growing intensity. Madison led throughout, against Patrick Henry's powerful opposing leadership, until Henry was elected governor in November, 1784.

The climax came in the legislative struggle of 1784-1785 over the Assessment Bill. . . . This was nothing more nor less than a taxing measure for the support of religion, designed to revive the payment of tithes suspended since 1777. So long as it singled out a particular sect for preference it incurred the active and general hostility of dissentient groups. It was broadened to include them, with the result that some subsided temporarily in their opposition. As altered, the bill gave to each taxpayer the privilege of designating which church should receive his share of the tax. In default of designation the legislature applied it to pious uses. But what is of the utmost significance here, "in its final form the bill left the taxpayer the option of giving his tax to education."

Madison was unyielding at all times, opposing with all his vigor the general and non-discriminatory as he had the earlier particular discriminatory assessments proposed. The modified Assessment Bill passed second reading in December, 1784, and was all but enacted. Madison and his followers, however, maneuvered deferment of final consideration until November, 1785. And before the Assembly reconvened in the fall he issued his historic Memorial and Remonstrance.

This is Madison's complete, though not his only, interpretation of religious liberty. It is a broadside attack upon all forms of "establishment" of religion, both general and particular, nondiscriminatory or selective. Reflecting not only the many legislative conflicts over the Assessment Bill and the Bill for Establishing Religious Freedom but also, for example, the struggles for religious incorporations and the continued maintenance of the glebes, the Remonstrance is at once the most concise and the most accurate statement of the views of the First Amendment's author concerning what is "an establishment of religion." . . .

The Remonstrance, stirring up a storm of popular protest, killed the Assessment Bill. It collapsed in committee shortly before Christmas, 1785. With this, the way was cleared at last for enactment of Jefferson's Bill for Establishing Religious Freedom. Madison promptly drove it through in January of 1786, seven years from the time it was first introduced. This dual victory substantially ended the fight over establishments, settling the issue against them. . . .

The next year Madison became a member of the Constitutional Convention. Its work done, he fought valiantly to secure the ratification of its great product in Virginia as elsewhere, and nowhere else more effectively. Madison was certain in his own mind that

1356 Chapter Sixteen. **Substantive Rights**

under the Constitution "there is not a shadow of right in the general government to intermeddle with religion" and that "this subject is, for the honor of America, perfectly free and unshackled. The government has no jurisdiction over it. . . ." Nevertheless he pledged that he would work for a Bill of Rights, including a specific guaranty of religious freedom, and Virginia, with other states, ratified the Constitution on this assurance.

Ratification thus accomplished, Madison was sent to the first Congress. There he went at once about performing his pledge to establish freedom for the nation as he had done in Virginia. Within a little more than three years from his legislative victory at home he had proposed and secured the submission and ratification of the First Amendment as the first article of our Bill of Rights.[27]

All the great instruments of the Virginia struggle for religious liberty thus became warp and woof of our constitutional tradition, not simply by the course of history, but by the common unifying force of Madison's life, thought and sponsorship. He epitomized the whole of that tradition in the Amendment's compact, but nonetheless comprehensive, phrasing.

As the Remonstrance discloses throughout, Madison opposed every form and degree of official relation between religion and civil authority. For him religion was a wholly private matter beyond the scope of civil power either to restrain or to support. Denial or abridgment of religious freedom was a violation of rights both of conscience and of natural equality. State aid was no less obnoxious or destructive to freedom and to religion itself than other forms of state interference. "Establishment" and "free exercise" were correlative and coextensive ideas, representing only different facets of the single great and fundamental freedom. The Remonstrance, following the Virginia statute's example, referred to the history of religious conflicts and the effects of all sorts of establishments, current and historical to suppress religion's free exercise. With Jefferson, Madison believed that to tolerate any fragment of establishment would be by so much to perpetuate restraint upon that freedom. Hence he sought to tear out the institution not partially but root and branch, and to bar its return forever.

In no phase was he more unrelentingly absolute than in opposing state support or aid by taxation. Not even "three pence" contribution was thus to be exacted from any citizen for such a purpose. . . . Tithes had been the lifeblood of establishment before and after other compulsions disappeared. Madison and his coworkers made no exceptions or abridgments to the complete separation they created. Their objection was not to small tithes. It was to any tithes whatsoever. "If it were lawful to impose a small tax for religion, the admission would pave the way for oppressive levies." Not the amount but "the principle of assessment was wrong." And the principle was as much to prevent "the interference of law in religion" as to restrain religious intervention in political matters. In this field the authors of our freedom would not tolerate "the first experiment on our liberties" or "wait till usurped power had strengthened itself by exercise, and entangled the question in precedents." . . . Nor should we.

In view of this history no further proof is needed that the Amendment forbids any appropriation, large or small, from public funds to aid or support any and all religious exercises. But if more were called for, the debates in the First Congress and this Court's consistent expressions, whenever it has touched on the matter directly, supply it.

By contrast with the Virginia history, the congressional debates on consideration of the Amendment reveal only sparse discussion, reflecting the fact that the essential issues had been settled. Indeed the matter had become so well understood as to have been taken for granted in all but formal phrasing. Hence, the only enlightening reference shows con-

---

[27] The amendment with respect to religious liberties read, as Madison introduced it: "The civil rights of none shall be abridged on account of religious belief or worship, nor shall any national religion be established, nor shall the full and equal rights of conscience be in any manner, or on any pretext, infringed." 1 Annals of Congress 434. In the process of debate this was modified to its present form. See especially 1 Annals of Congress 729-731, 765. . . .

Section D. Religion

cern, not to preserve any power to use public funds in aid of religion, but to prevent the Amendment from outlawing private gifts inadvertently by virtue of the breadth of its wording. . . .

III

Compulsory attendance upon religious exercises went out early in the process of separating church and state, together with forced observance of religious forms and ceremonies. Test oaths and religious qualification for office followed later. These things none devoted to our great tradition of religious liberty would think of bringing back. Hence today, apart from efforts to inject religious training or exercises and sectarian issues into the public schools, the only serious surviving threat to maintaining that complete and permanent separation of religion and civil power which the First Amendment commands is through use of the taxing power to support religion, religious establishments, or establishments having a religious foundation whatever their form or special religious function.

Does New Jersey's action furnish support for religion by use of the taxing power? Certainly it does, if the test remains undiluted as Jefferson and Madison made it, that money taken by taxation from one is not to be used or given to support another's religious training or belief, or indeed one's own. Today as then the furnishing of "contributions of money for the propagation of opinions which he disbelieves" is the forbidden exaction; and the prohibition is absolute for whatever measure brings that consequence and whatever amount may be sought or given to that end.

The funds used here were raised by taxation. The Court does not dispute, nor could it, that their use does in fact give aid and encouragement to religious instruction. It only concludes that this aid is not "support" in law. But Madison and Jefferson were concerned with aid and support in fact, not as a legal conclusion "entangled in precedents." . . . Here parents pay money to send their children to parochial schools and funds raised by taxation are used to reimburse them. This not only helps the children to get to school and the parents to send them. It aids them in a substantial way to get the very thing which they are sent to the particular school to secure, namely, religious training and teaching. . . .

New Jersey's action therefore exactly fits the type of exaction and the kind of evil at which Madison and Jefferson struck. Under the test they framed it cannot be said that the cost of transportation is no part of the cost of education or of the religious instruction given. That it is a substantial and a necessary element is shown most plainly by the continuing and increasing demand for the state to assume it. Nor is there pretense that it relates only to the secular instruction given in religious schools or that any attempt is or could be made toward allocating proportional shares as between the secular and the religious instruction. It is precisely because the instruction is religious and relates to a particular faith, whether one or another, that parents send their children to religious schools under the Pierce doctrine. And the very purpose of the state's contribution is to defray the cost of conveying the pupil to the place where he will receive not simply secular, but also and primarily religious, teaching and guidance. . . .

V

No one conscious of religious values can be unsympathetic toward the burden which our constitutional separation puts on parents who desire religious instruction mixed with secular for their children. They pay taxes for others' children's education, at the same time the added cost of instruction for their own. Nor can one happily see benefits denied to children which others receive, because in conscience they or their parents for them desire a different kind of training others do not demand.

But if those feelings should prevail, there would be an end to our historic constitutional policy and command. No more unjust or discriminatory in fact is it to deny attendants at religious schools the cost of their transportation than it is to deny them tuitions, sustenance for their teachers, or any other educational expense which others receive at public cost. Hardship in fact there is which none can blink. But, for assuring to those who undergo it the greater, the most comprehensive freedom, it is one written by design and firm intent into our basic law.

Of course discrimination in the legal sense does not exist. The child attending the religious school has the same right as any other to attend the public school. But he foregoes exercising it because the same guaranty which assures this freedom forbids the public school or any agency of the state to give or aid him in securing the religious instruction he seeks. . . .

VI

Two great drives are constantly in motion to abridge, in the name of education, the complete division of religion and civil authority which our forefathers made. One is to introduce religious education and observances into the public schools. The other, to obtain public funds for the aid and support of various private religious schools. See Johnson, The Legal Status of Church-State Relationships in the United States (1934); Thayer, Religion in Public Education (1957); Note (1941) 50 Yale L.J. 917. In my opinion both avenues were closed by the Constitution. Neither should be opened by this Court. The matter is not one of quantity, to be measured by the amount of money expended. Now as in Madison's day it is one of principle, to keep separate the separate spheres as the First Amendment drew them; to prevent the first experiment upon our liberties; and to keep the question from becoming entangled in corrosive precedents. We should not be less strict to keep strong and untarnished the one side of the shield of religious freedom than we have been of the other.

The judgment should be reversed.

NOTE

The accuracy and sufficiency of Mr. Justice Rutledge's examination of the history which produced the First Amendment have been questioned by scholars, theologians, polemicists, and judges. See e.g., Corwin, The Supreme Court as National School Board, 14 Law & Contemp. Prob. 3 (1949); Parsons, The First Freedom: Considerations on Church and State in the United States (1948); O'Neill, Religion and Education under the Constitution (1949); Desmond, J., in Zorach v. Clauson, 303 N.Y. 161, 181 (1951). It has also been defended. See, e.g., Konvitz, Separation of Church and State: The First Freedom, 14 Law & Contemp. Prob. 44 (1949); Pfeffer, Church, State, and Freedom 118-159 (1953).

A suburban community adopted a zoning ordinance which permitted the building of public schools and private elementary schools in Zone A. Representatives of the Lutheran Church requested a permit to erect a parochial high school in Zone A. May the permit constitutionally be denied? See State ex rel. Wisconsin Lutheran High School Conference v. Sinar, 267 Wis. 87, 65 N.W.2d 43 (1954); State ex rel. Lake Drive Baptist Church v. Barside Village Board, 12 Wis. 2d 585, 108 N.W.2d 288 (1960). Cf. Roman Catholic Welfare Corp. v. City of Piedmont, 278 P.2d 943 (Cal. App. 1955); Diocese of Rochester v. Planning Board, 1 N.Y.2d 508, 136 N.E.2d 827 (1956); Congregation Temple Israel v. City of Creve Coeur, 320 S.W.2d 451 (Mo. 1959). See Note, 70 Harv. L. Rev. 1428 (1957).

In England the established Church has paid the price of establishment, for the ecclesiastical decisions of its highest tribunals have been reversed by secular judges. See Figgis, Churches in the Modern State (1913); Cockshut, Anglican Attitudes: A Study of Victorian Religious Controversies (1959). While English judges were forcing the established Church to a greater liberalism in theology than its hierarchy considered fitting, American courts so interpreted the policy of nonestablishment as to prohibit the state from preventing orthodoxy from having its way. Compare Williams v. Bishop of Salisbury, 2 Moore (N.S.) 375 (1863), with Chase v. Cheney, 58 Ill. 509 (1871). In Watson v. Jones, 13 Wall. 679 (1871), the Supreme Court defined the circumstances in which the federal courts are bound to accept church adjudications as conclusive on interests of property. In recent years the doctrine of Watson v. Jones has been given constitutional status, so that it now seems that the states and nation are compelled to respect not merely the religious liberty of natural persons but to secure the liberty of churches, domestic and foreign, to govern themselves without interference by American secular authority, whether legislative or judicial. See Kedroff v. Saint Nicholas Cathedral, 344 U.S. 94 (1952); Kreshik v. Saint Nicholas Cathedral, 363 U.S. 190 (1960). See also Presbyterian Church v. Mary Elizabeth Blue Hull Memorial Presbyterian Church, 393 U.S. 440 (1969); Serbian Eastern Orthodox Diocese v. Milivojevich, 426 U.S. 696 (1976).

Zorach v. Clauson 343 U.S. 306, 72 S. Ct. 679, 96 L. Ed. 954 (1952)

MR. JUSTICE DOUGLAS delivered the opinion of the Court.

New York City has a program which permits its public schools to release students during the school day so that they may leave the school buildings and school grounds and go to religious centers for religious instruction or devotional exercises. A student is released on written request of his parents. Those not released stay in the classrooms. The churches make weekly reports to the schools, sending a list of children who have been released from public school but who have not reported for religious instruction.

This "released time" program involves neither religious instruction in public school classrooms nor the expenditure of public funds. All costs, including the application blanks, are paid by the religious organizations. The case is therefore unlike McCollum v. Board of Education, 333 U.S. 203, which involved a "released time" program for Illinois. In that case the classrooms were turned over to religious instructors. We accordingly held that the program violated the First Amendment which (by reason of the Fourteenth Amendment) prohibits the states from establishing religion or prohibiting its free exercise.

Appellants, who are taxpayers and residents of New York City and whose children attend its public schools, challenge the present law, contending it is in essence not different from the one involved in the McCollum case. Their argument, stated elaborately in various ways, reduces itself to this: the weight and influence of the school is put behind a program for religious instruction; public school teachers police it, keeping tab on students who are released; the classroom activities come to a halt while the students who are released for religious instruction are on leave; the school is a crutch on which the churches are leaning for support in their religious training; without the cooperation of the schools this "released time" program, like the one in the McCollum case, would be futile and ineffective. The New York Court of Appeals sustained the law against this claim of unconstitutionality. 303 N.Y. 161. The case is here on appeal. 28 U.S.C. § 1257(2).

The briefs and arguments are replete with data bearing on the merits of this type of "released time" program. Views pro and con are expressed, based on practical experience with these programs and with their implications. We do not stop to summarize these materials nor to burden the opinion with an analysis of them. For they involve considerations not germane to the narrow constitutional issue presented. They largely concern the wisdom of the system, its efficiency from an educational point of view, and the political considerations which have motivated its adoption or rejection in some communities. Those matters are of no concern here, since our problem reduces itself to whether New York by this system has either prohibited the "free exercise" of religion or has made a law "respecting an establishment of religion" within the meaning of the First Amendment.

It takes obtuse reasoning to inject any issue of the "free exercise" of religion into the present case. No one is forced to go to the religious classroom and no religious exercise or instruction is brought to the classrooms of the public schools. A student need not take religious instruction. He is left to his own devices as to the manner or time of his religious devotions, if any.

There is a suggestion that the system involves the use of coercion to get public school students into religious classrooms. There is no evidence in the record before us that supports that conclusion.[6] The present record indeed tells us that the school authorities are neutral in this regard and do no more than release students whose parents so request. If in fact coercion were used, if it were established that any one or more teachers were using their office to persuade or force students to take the religious instruction, a wholly different case would be presented.[7] Hence we put aside that claim of coercion both as respects the "free exercise" of religion and "an establishment of religion" within the meaning of the First Amendment.

Moreover, apart from that claim of coercion, we do not see how New York by this type of "released time" program has made a law respecting an establishment of religion within the meaning of the First Amendment. There is much talk of the separation of Church and State in the history of the Bill of Rights and in the decisions clustering around the First Amendment. See Everson v. Board of Education, 330 U.S. 1; McCollum v. Board of Education, supra. There cannot be the slightest doubt that the First Amendment reflects the philosophy that Church and State should be separated. And so far as interference with the "free exercise" of religion and an "establishment" of religion are concerned, the separation must be complete and unequivocal. The First Amendment within the scope of its coverage permits no exception; the prohibition is absolute. The First Amendment, however, does not say that in every and all respects there shall be a separation of Church and State. Rather, it studiously defines the manner, the specific ways, in which there shall be no concert or union or dependency one on the other. That is the common sense of the matter. Otherwise the state and religion would be aliens to each other — hostile, suspicious, and even unfriendly. Churches could not be required to pay even property taxes. Municipalities would not be permitted to render police or fire protection to religious groups. Policemen who helped parishioners into their places of worship would violate the Constitution. Prayers in our legislative halls, the appeals to the Almighty in the messages of the Chief Executive; the proclamations making Thanksgiving Day a holiday; "so help me God" in our courtroom oaths — these and all other references to the Almighty that run through our laws, our public rituals, our ceremonies would be flouting the First

---

[6] Nor is there any indication that the public schools enforce attendance at religious schools by punishing absentees from the released time programs for truancy.

[7] Appellants contend that they should have been allowed to prove that the system is in fact administered in a coercive manner. The New York Court of Appeals declined to grant a trial on this issue, noting, inter alia, that appellants had not properly raised their claim in the manner required by state practice. 303 N.Y. 161, 174. This independent state ground for decision precludes appellants from raising the issue of maladministration in this proceeding. See Louisville & Nashville R. Co. v. Woodford, 234 U.S. 46, 51; Atlantic Coast Line R. Co. v. Mims, 242 U.S. 532, 535; American Surety Co. v. Baldwin, 287 U.S. 156, 169.

The only allegation in the complaint that bears on the issue is that the operation of the program "has resulted and inevitably results in the exercise of pressure and coercion upon parents and children to secure attendance by the children for religious instruction." But this charge does not even implicate the school authorities. The New York Court of Appeals was therefore generous in labeling it a "conclusory" allegation. 303 N.Y., at 174. Since the allegation did not implicate the school authorities in the use of coercion, there is no basis for holding that the New York Court of Appeals under the guise of local practice defeated a federal right in the manner condemned by Brown v. Western R. of Alabama, 338 U.S. 294, and related cases.

Amendment. A fastidious atheist or agnostic could even object to the supplication with which the Court opens each session: "God save the United States and this Honorable Court."

We are a religious people whose institutions presuppose a Supreme Being. We guarantee the freedom to worship as one chooses. We make room for as wide a variety of beliefs and creeds as the spiritual needs of man deem necessary. We sponsor an attitude on the part of government that shows no partiality to any one group and that lets each flourish according to the zeal of its adherents and the appeal of its dogma. When the state encourages religious instruction or cooperates with religious authorities by adjusting the schedule of public events to sectarian needs, it follows the best of our traditions. For it then respects the religious nature of our people and accommodates the public service to their spiritual needs. To hold that it may not would be to find in the Constitution a requirement that the government show a callous indifference to religious groups. That would be preferring those who believe in no religion over those who do believe. . . .

This program may be unwise and improvident from an educational or a community viewpoint. That appeal is made to us on a theory, previously advanced, that each case must be decided on the basis of "our own prepossessions." See McCollum v. Board of Education, supra, p. 238. Our individual preferences, however, are not the constitutional standard. The constitutional standard is the separation of Church and State. The problem, like many problems in constitutional law, is one of degree. See McCollum v. Board of Education, supra, p. 231.

In the McCollum case the classrooms were used for religious instruction and the force of the public school was used to promote that instruction. Here, as we have said, the public schools do no more than accommodate their schedules to a program of outside religious instruction. We follow the McCollum case. But we cannot expand it to cover the present released time program unless separation of Church and State means that public institutions can make no adjustments of their schedules to accommodate the religious needs of the people. We cannot read into the Bill of Rights such a philosophy of hostility to religion.

Affirmed.[vv]

MR. JUSTICE FRANKFURTER, dissenting. . . .

The pith of the case is that formalized religious instruction is substituted for other school activity which those who do not participate in the released time program are compelled to attend. The school system is very much in operation during this kind of released time. If its doors are closed, they are closed upon those students who do not attend the religious instruction, in order to keep them within the school. That is the very thing which raises the constitutional issue. It is not met by disregarding it. Failure to discuss this issue does not take it out of the case.

Again, the Court relies upon the absence from the record of evidence of coercion in the operation of the system. "If in fact coercion were used," according to the Court, "if it were established that any one or more teachers were using their office to persuade or force students to take the religious instruction, a wholly different case would be presented." Thus, "coercion" in the abstract is acknowledged to be fatal. But the Court disregards the fact that as the case comes to us, there could be no proof of coercion, for the appellants were not allowed to make proof of it. Appellants alleged that "The operation of the released time program has resulted and inevitably results in the exercise of pressure and coercion upon parents and children to secure attendance by the children for religious instruction." This allegation — that coercion was in fact present and is inherent in the system, no matter what disavowals might be made in the operating regulations — was denied by appellees. Thus were drawn issues of fact which cannot be determined, on any conceivable view of judicial notice, by judges out of their own knowledge or experience.

[vv] A dissenting opinion of Mr. Justice Black is omitted. — ED.

Appellants sought an opportunity to adduce evidence in support of these allegations at an appropriate trial. And though the courts below cited the concurring opinion in McCollum v. Board of Education, 333 U.S. 203, 226, to "emphasize the importance of detailed analysis of the facts to which the Constitutional test of Separation is to be applied," they denied that opportunity on the ground that such proof was irrelevant to the issue of constitutionality. See 198 Misc. 631, 641; 303 N.Y. 161, 174-175.[1]

When constitutional issues turn on facts, it is a strange procedure indeed not to permit the facts to be established. When such is the case, there are weighty considerations for us to require the State court to make its determination only after a thorough canvass of all the circumstances and not to bar them from consideration. . . .

The deeply divisive controversy aroused by the attempts to secure public school pupils for sectarian instruction would promptly end if the advocates of such instruction were content to have the school "close its door or suspend its operations" — that is, dismiss classes in their entirety, without discrimination — instead of seeking to use the public schools as the instrument for security of attendance at denominational classes. The unwillingness of the promoters of this movement to dispense with such use of the public schools betrays a surprising want of confidence in the inherent power of the various faiths to draw children to outside sectarian classes — an attitude that hardly reflects the faith of the greatest religious spirits.

MR. JUSTICE JACKSON, dissenting.

This released time program is founded upon a use of the State's power of coercion, which, for me, determines its unconstitutionality. . . .

The greater effectiveness of this system over voluntary attendance after school hours is due to the truant officer who, if the youngster fails to go to the Church school, dogs him back to the public schoolroom. Here schooling is more or less suspended during the "released time" so the nonreligious attendants will not forge ahead of the churchgoing absentees. But it serves as a temporary jail for a pupil who will not go to Church. It takes more subtlety of mind than I possess to deny that this is governmental constraint in support of religion. It is as unconstitutional, in my view, when exerted by indirection as when exercised forthrightly.

As one whose children, as a matter of free choice, have been sent to privately supported Church schools, I may challenge the Court's suggestion that opposition to this plan can only be antireligious, atheistic, or agnostic. My evangelistic brethren confuse an objection to compulsion with an objection to religion. It is possible to hold a faith with enough confidence to believe that what should be rendered to God does not need to be decided and collected by Caesar.

The day that this country ceases to be free for irreligion it will cease to be free for religion — except for the sect that can win political power. The same epithetical jurisprudence used by the Court today to beat down those who oppose pressuring children into some religion can devise as good epithets tomorrow against those who object to pressuring them into a favored religion. And, after all, if we concede to the State power and wisdom to single out "duly constituted religious" bodies as exclusive alternatives for compulsory secular instruction, it would be logical to also uphold the power and wisdom to choose the true faith among those "duly constituted." We start down a rough road when we begin to mix compulsory public education with compulsory godliness.

A number of Justices just short of a majority of the majority that promulgates today's passionate dialectics joined in answering them in Illinois ex rel. McCollum v. Board of Education, 333 U.S. 203. The distinction attempted between that case and this is trivial, almost to the point of cynicism, magnifying its nonessential details and disparaging com-

---

[1] Issues that raise federal claims cannot be foreclosed by the State court treating the allegations as "conclusory in character." 303 N.Y. 161, 174. This is so even when a federal statute is involved. Brown v. Western R. of Alabama, 338 U.S. 294. A fortiori when the appeal is to the Constitution of the United States.

pulsion which was the underlying reason for invalidity. A reading of the Court's opinion in that case along with its opinion in this case will show such difference of overtones and undertones as to make clear that the McCollum case has passed like a storm in a teacup. The wall which the Court was professing to erect between Church and State has become even move warped and twisted than I expected. Today's judgment will be more interesting to students of psychology and of the judicial processes than to students of constitutional law.

NOTE

Private and official responses to the McCollum and Zorach cases are discussed and analyzed in Sorauf, Zorach v. Clauson: The Impact of a Supreme Court Decision, 53 Am. Pol. Sci. Rev. 777 (1959).

Concerning the developing possibility of "shared time," see Powell, Shared Time, 1964: A Turning Point? 1964 Religion and the Public Order 62.

NOTE Sunday Closing Laws

On May 29, 1961, the Supreme Court of the United States decided four cases, upholding as there applied the "Sunday closing laws" of Maryland, Pennsylvania, and Massachusetts. In McGowan v. Maryland, 366 U.S. 420 (1961), the Maryland courts had convicted the employees of a large discount store of selling merchandise on Sunday in violation of the Maryland statute. In Two Guys From Harrison-Allentown, Inc. v. McGinley, 366 U.S. 582 (1961), a corporation operating a discount department store had unsuccessfully sought an injunction against enforcement of Pennsylvania Sunday closing laws in a three-judge federal district court. In neither of these two cases was any problem presented of a person refraining from business on Saturday for religious scruples and by operation of the Sunday law kept from business on a second of the days of the week. The unsuccessful parties in both these cases appealed to the Supreme Court of the United States, contending that the state statutes in question constituted "establishments of religion" in violation of the First Amendment as "incorporated in the Fourteenth," and also contending that because of numerous exceptions in the Maryland and Pennsylvania Sunday closing statutes, the application of the statutes to the appellants denied to them the equal protection of the laws guaranteed by the Fourteenth Amendment.

In a third case, Gallagher v. Crown Kosher Super Market of Mass., Inc., 366 U.S. 617 (1961), a Massachusetts corporation operating a supermarket brought suit in a three-judge federal district court and successfully enjoined the chief of police of Springfield, Massachusetts, and other officials from enforcing the Sunday closing statutes. The four stockholders, the officers and the directors of the plaintiff corporation were all Orthodox Jews who refrained from business on Saturday for conscientious reasons. Other plaintiffs in the Crown Kosher case were three customers of the plaintiff's market and the rabbi of a Jewish congregation in that area. The unsuccessful defendants below appealed to the Supreme Court from the judgment enjoining them. In Braunfeld v. Brown, 366 U.S. 599 (1961), the unsuccessful plaintiffs who had sought in a three-judge federal court to enjoin the operation of the Pennsylvania Sunday laws appealed to the Supreme Court of the United States. These plaintiffs were Orthodox Jewish merchants whose religion required them to remain closed on Saturday, and who contended that compulsory Sunday closing deprived them of religious freedom. In addition to their contentions concerning religious freedom, the plaintiffs in Crown Kosher and Braunfeld urged the same grounds urged in McGowan and Two Guys.

In McGowan and Two Guys, Chief Justice Warren delivered the opinion of the Court.

1364   Chapter Sixteen.   **Substantive Rights**

In Gallagher v. Crown Kosher, and Braunfeld, no opinion spoke for "the Court." Chief Justice Warren announced the Court's judgment reversing Crown Kosher and affirming Braunfeld; he delivered an opinion in which Justices Black, Clark, and Whittaker concurred. Mr. Justice Frankfurter, joined by Mr. Justice Harlan, wrote a separate opinion upholding the statutes as applied in all four cases. (Mr. Justice Frankfurter believed, however, that in Braunfeld the plaintiff should have been permitted to offer proof on the issues of inequality.) Justices Brennan and Stewart dissented in Crown Kosher and Braunfeld on the ground that the Massachusetts and Pennsylvania statutes, as applied to Orthodox Jewish persons who for conscientious reasons did no business on Saturday, unconstitutionally interfered with the free exercise of their religion. Mr. Justice Douglas dissented in all four cases.

Chief Justice Warren's opinion for the Court in McGowan and Two Guys found no merit in the contention that the classification of vendors, permitting some categories to do business on Sunday and forbidding others, unreasonably discriminated against those inhibited and so violated the equal protection clause of the Fourteenth Amendment. He held that a legislature could reasonably find that "the Sunday sale of the exempted commodities was necessary either for the health of the populace or for the enhancement of the recreational atmosphere of the day." He rejected the contention that Sunday legislation constituted an unconstitutional establishment of religion, by reasoning that although originally Sunday closing laws reflected religious ideas they have now become lay statutes providing a day off from work. "These provisions, along with those which permit various sports and entertainments on Sunday, seem clearly to be fashioned for the purpose of providing a Sunday atmosphere of recreation, cheerfulness, repose and enjoyment. Coupled with the general proscription against other types of work, we believe that the air of the day is one of relaxation rather than one of religion. . . ." Chief Justice Warren's opinion in Two Guys found that case "essentially the same as McGowan v. Maryland."

The Chief Justice's opinions in Crown Kosher and Braunfeld found no merit in the claim of unconstitutionality in either case on the ground of establishment of religion or denial of religious freedom. In Crown Kosher he wrote:

". . . The relevant factors having been most carefully considered, we do not find that the present statutes' purpose or effect is religious. Although the three-judge court found that Massachusetts had no legitimate secular interest in maintaining Sunday closing, we have held differently in McGowan v. Maryland, 366 U.S. 420. And, for the reasons stated in that case, we reject appellees' request to hold these statutes invalid on the ground that the State may accomplish its secular purpose by alternative means that would not even remotely or incidentally aid religion. . . .

"*Secondly*, appellees contend that the application to them of the Sunday Closing Laws prohibits the free exercise of their religion. Crown alleges that if it is required by law to abstain from business on Sunday, then, because its owners' religion demands closing from sundown Friday to sundown Saturday, Crown will be open only four and one-half days a week, thereby suffering extreme economic disadvantage. Crown's Orthodox Jewish customers allege that because their religious beliefs forbid their shopping on the Jewish Sabbath, the statute's effect is to deprive them, from Friday afternoon until Monday of each week, of the opportunity to purchase the kosher food sanctioned by their faith. The orthodox rabbis allege that the statutes' effect greatly complicates their task of supervising the condition of kosher meat because the meat delivered on Friday would have to be kept until Monday. Furthermore, appellees contend that, because of all this, the statute discriminates against their religion.

"These allegations are similar, although not as grave, as those made by appellants in Braunfeld v. Brown, 366 U.S. 599. Since the decision in that case rejects the contentions presented by these appellees on the merits, we need not decide whether appellees have standing to raise these questions.

"Mr. Justice Frankfurter and Mr. Justice Harlan concur in a separate opinion.

"Accordingly, the decision below is reversed."

In Braunfeld, Chief Justice Warren wrote (for himself and Justices Black, Clark, and Whittaker):

"Concededly, appellants and all other persons who wish to work on Sunday will be burdened economically by the State's day of rest mandate; and appellants point out that their religion requires them to refrain from work on Saturday as well. Our inquiry then is whether, in these circumstances, the First and Fourteenth Amendments forbid application of the Sunday Closing Law to appellants.

"Certain aspects of religious exercise cannot, in any way, be restricted or burdened by either federal or state legislation. Compulsion by law of the acceptance of any creed or the practice of any form of worship is strictly forbidden. The freedom to hold religious beliefs and opinions is absolute. Cantwell v. Connecticut, 310 U.S. 296, 303; Reynolds v. United States, 98 U.S. 145, 166. Thus, in West Virginia State Board of Education v. Barnette, 319 U.S. 624, this Court held that state action compelling school children to salute the flag, on pain of expulsion from public school, was contrary to the First and Fourteenth Amendments when applied to those students whose religious beliefs forbade saluting a flag. But, this is not the case at bar; the statute before us does not make criminal the holding of any religious belief or opinion, nor does it force anyone to embrace any religious belief or to say or believe anything in conflict with his religious tenets.

"However, the freedom to act, even when the action is in accord with one's religious convictions, is not totally free from legislative restrictions. Cantwell v. Connecticut, supra, at pp. 303-304, 306. As pointed out in Reynolds v. United States, supra, at p. 164, lesislative power over mere opinion is forbidden but it may reach people's actions when they are found to be in violation of important social duties or subversive of good order, even when the actions are demanded by one's religion. . . . And, in the Barnette case, the Court was careful to point out that 'the freedom asserted by these appellees does not bring them into collision with rights asserted by any other individual. It is such conflicts which most frequently require intervention of the State to determine where the rights of one end and those of another begin. . . . It is . . . to be noted that the compulsory flag, salute and pledge requires *affirmation of a belief* and an *attitude of mind*.' 319 U.S., at 630, 633. (Emphasis added.)

"Thus, in Reynolds v. United States, this Court upheld the polygamy conviction of a member of the Mormon faith despite the fact that an accepted doctrine of his church then imposed upon its male members the *duty* to practice polygamy. And, in Prince v. Massachusetts, 321 U.S. 158, this Court upheld a statute making it a crime for a girl under eighteen years of age to sell any newspapers, periodicals or merchandise in public places despite the fact that a child of the Jehovah's Witnesses faith believed that it was her religious *duty* to perform this work.

"It is to be noted that, in the two cases just mentioned, the religious practices themselves conflicted with the public interest. In such cases, to make accommodation between the religious action and an exercise of state authority is a particularly delicate task, id., at 165, because resolution in favor of the State results in the choice to the individual of either abandoning his religious principles or facing criminal prosecution.

"But, again, this is not the case before us because the statute at bar does not make unlawful any religious practices of appellants; the Sunday law simply regulates a secular activity and, as applied to appellants, operates so as to make the practice of their religious beliefs more expensive. Furthermore, the law's effect does not inconvenience all members of the Orthodox Jewish faith but only those who believe it necessary to work on Sunday. And even these are not faced with as serious a choice as forsaking their religious practices or subjecting themselves to criminal prosecution. Fully recognizing that the alternatives open to appellants and others similarly situated — retaining their present occupations and incurring economic disadvantage or engaging in some other commercial activity which does not call for either Saturday or Sunday labor — may well result in some financial sacrifice in order to observe their religious beliefs, still the option is wholly different than when the legislation attempts to make a religious practice itself unlawful.

"To strike down, without the most critical scrutiny, legislation which imposes only an inherent burden on the exercise of religion, i.e., legislation which does not make unlawful the religious practice itself, would radically restrict the operating latitude of the legislature. Statutes which tax income and limit the amount which may be deducted for religious contributions impose an indirect economic burden on the observance of the religion of the citizen whose religion requires him to donate a greater amount to his church; statutes which require the courts to be closed on Saturday and Sunday impose a similar indirect burden on the observance of the religion of the trial lawyer whose religion requires him to rest on a weekday. The list of legislation of this nature is nearly limitless.

"Of course, to hold unassailable all legislation regulating conduct which imposes solely an indirect burden on the observance of religion would be a gross oversimplification. If the purpose or effect of a law is to impede the observance of one or all religions or is to discriminate invidiously between religions, that law is constitutionally invalid even though the burden may be characterized as being only indirect. But if the State regulates conduct by enacting a general law within its power, the purpose and effect of which is to advance the State's secular goals, the statute is valid despite its indirect burden on religious observance unless the State may accomplish its purpose by means which do not impose such a burden. See Cantwell v. Connecticut, supra, at pp. 304-305.

"As we pointed out in McGowan v. Maryland . . . we cannot find a State without power to provide a weekly respite from all labor and, at the same time, to set one day of the week apart from the others as a day of rest, repose, recreation and tranquility — a day when the hectic tempo of everyday existence ceases and a more pleasant atmosphere is created, a day which all members of the family and community have the opportunity to spend and enjoy together, a day in which people may visit friends and relatives who are not available during working days, a day when the weekly laborer may best regenerate himself. This is particularly true in this day and age of increasing state concern with public welfare legislation. . . .

"However, appellants advance yet another means at the State's disposal which they would find unobjectionable. They contend that the State should cut an exception from the Sunday labor proscription for those people who, because of religious conviction, observe a day of rest other than Sunday. By such regulation, appellants contend, the economic disadvantages imposed by the present system would be removed and the State's interest in having all people rest one day would be satisfied.

"A number of States provide such an exemption, and this may well be the wiser solution to the problem. But our concern is not with the wisdom of legislation but with its constitutional limitation. Thus, reason and experience teach that to permit the exemption might well undermine the State's goal of providing a day that, as best possible, eliminate the atmosphere of commercial noise and activity. Although not dispositive of the issue, enforcement problems would be more difficult since there would be two or more days to police rather than one and it would be more difficult to observe whether violations were occurring.

"Additional problems might also be presented by a regulation of this sort. To allow only people who rest on a day other than Sunday to keep their businesses open on that day might well provide these people with an economic advantage over their competitors who must remain closed on that day; this might cause the Sunday-observers to complain that their religions are being discriminated against. With this competitive advantage existing, there could well be the temptation for some, in order to keep their businesses open on Sunday, to assert that they have religious convictions which compel them to close their businesses on what had formerly been their least profitable day. This might make necessary a state-conducted inquiry into the sincerity of the individual's religious beliefs, a practice which a State might believe would itself run afoul of the spirit of constitutionally protected religious guarantees. . . ."

Mr. Justice Brennan, while concurring with the Chief Justice in the view that there was neither an unconstitutional establishment nor a denial of equal protection, urged that Pennsylvania had prohibited the free exercise of religion. In his judgment, constitutionality could be secured only by granting an exemption for those who in good faith observe a day of rest other than Sunday. "It is true," he said, "that the granting of such an exemption would make Sundays a little noisier, and the task of police and prosecutor a little more difficult. It is also true that a majority — 21 — of the 34 States which have general Sunday regulations have exemptions of this kind. We are not told that those States are significantly noisier, or that their police are significantly more burdened, than Pennsylvania's." Mr. Justice Stewart delivered a brief opinion concurring in that of Brennan, J. "Pennsylvania," he said, "has passed a law which compels an Orthodox Jew to choose between his religious faith and his economic survival. This is a cruel choice. It is a choice which I think no State can constitutionally demand. For me this is not something that can be swept under the rug and forgotten in the interest of enforced Sunday togetherness. I think the impact of this law upon these appellants grossly violates their constitutional right to the free exercise of their religion."

Mr. Justice Frankfurter wrote an elaborate separate opinion concurring in the result reached by the majority of the Court in all four cases. Mr. Justice Harlan joined in this opinion. These two Justices set forth a history of Sunday closing legislation, and emphasized the widespread acceptance of such statutes in the United States and elsewhere. They examined the efforts of labor groups to free themselves from the compulsion of employment on a common day of the week so that all members of a family, including schoolchildren, may be free to do as they please on the same day. The first appendix to this opinion sets forth the history of Sunday legislation in the thirteen colonies and the states through the eighteenth century. A second appendix gives a diagrammatic analysis of Sunday legislation in all States of the Union, in Puerto Rico, and in the District of Columbia.

Mr. Justice Douglas dissented from the judgment in all four cases. He wrote:

". . . The reverse side of an 'establishment' is a burden on the 'free exercise' of religion. Receipt of funds from the state benefits the established church directly; laying an extra tax on non-members benefits the established church indirectly. Certainly the present Sunday laws place Orthodox Jews and Sabbatarians under extra burdens because of their religious opinions or beliefs. Requiring them to abstain from their trade or business on Sunday reduces their work-week to five days, unless they violate their religious scruples. This places them at a competitive disadvantage and penalizes them for adhering to their religious beliefs.

"The sanction imposed by the state for observing a day other than Sunday as holy time is certainly more serious economically than the imposition of a license tax for preaching, which we struck down in Murdock v. Pennsylvania 319 U.S. 105, and in Follett v. McCormick 321 U.S. 573. The special protection which Sunday laws give the dominant religious groups and the penalty they place on minorities whose holy day is Saturday constitute in my view state interference with the 'free exercise' of religion.

"I dissent from applying criminal sanctions against any of these complainants since to do so implicates the States in religious matters contrary to the constitutional mandate . . ."

Sherbert v. Verner *374 U.S. 398, 83 S. Ct. 1790, 10 L. Ed. 2d 965 (1963)*

MR. JUSTICE BRENNAN delivered the opinion of the Court.

Appellant, a member of the Seventh-day Adventist Church, was discharged by her South Carolina employer because she would not work on Saturday, the Sabbath Day of her faith. When she was unable to obtain other employment because from conscientious scruples she would not take Saturday work, she filed a claim for unemployment compensation benefits under the South Carolina Unemployment Compensation Act. That law provides that, to be eligible for benefits, a claimant must be "able to work and . . . available for work"; and, further, that a claimant is ineligible for benefits "[i] f . . . he has failed, without good cause . . . to accept available suitable work when offered him by the employment office or the employer. . . ." [The State Commission denied benefits to appellant; the State Supreme Court affirmed.]

. . . If . . . the decision of the South Carolina Supreme Court is to withstand appellant's constitutional challenge, it must be either because her disqualification as a beneficiary represents no infringement by the State of her constitutional rights of free exercise, or because any incidental burden on the free exercise of appellant's religion may be justified by a "compelling state interest in the regulation of a subject within the State's constitutional power to regulate. . . ." NAACP v. Button, 371 U.S. 415, 438.

We turn first to the question whether the disqualification for benefits imposes any burden on the free exercise of appellant's religion. We think it is clear that it does. In a sense the consequences of such a disqualification to religious principles and practices may be only an indirect result of welfare legislation within the State's general competence to enact; it is true that no criminal sanctions directly compel appellant to work a six-day week. But this is only the beginning, not the end, of our inquiry. For "[i]f the purpose or effect of a law is to impede the observance of one or all religions or is to discriminate invidiously between religions, that law is constitutionally invalid even though the burden may be characterized as being only indirect." Braunfeld v. Brown, [366 U.S.], at 607. Here not only is it apparent that appellant's declared ineligibility for benefits derives solely from the practice of her religion, but the pressure upon her to forego that practice is unmistakable. The ruling forces her to choose between following the precepts of her religion and forfeiting benefits, on the one hand, and abandoning one of the precepts of her religion in order to accept work, on the other hand. Governmental imposition of such a choice puts the same kind of burden upon the free exercise of religion as would a fine imposed against appellant for her Saturday worship.

Nor may the South Carolina court's construction of the statute be saved from constitutional infirmity on the ground that unemployment compensation benefits are not appellant's "right" but merely a "privilege." It is too late in the day to doubt that the liberties of religion and expression may be infringed by the denial of or placing of conditions upon a benefit or privilege. . . .

Significantly South Carolina expressly saves the Sunday worshipper from having to make the kind of choice which we here hold infringes the Sabbatarian's religious liberty. When in times of "national emergency" the textile plants are authorized by the State Commissioner of Labor to operate on Sunday, "no employee shall be required to work on Sunday . . . who is conscientiously opposed to Sunday work; and if any employee should refuse to work on Sunday on account of conscientious . . . objections he or she shall not jeopardize his or her seniority by such refusal or be discriminated against in any other manner." S.C. Code, §64-4. No question of the disqualification of a Sunday worshipper for benefits is likely to arise, since we cannot suppose that an employer will discharge him in violation of this statute. The unconstitutionality of the disqualification of the Sabbatarian is thus compounded by the religious discrimination which South Carolina's general statutory scheme necessarily effects.

We must next consider whether some compelling state interest enforced in the eligibility provisions of the South Carolina statute justifies the substantial infringement of appellant's First Amendment right. It is basic that no showing merely of a rational relationship to some colorable state interest would suffice; in this highly sensitive constitutional area, "[o]nly the gravest abuses, endangering paramount interests, give occasion for permissible limitation," Thomas v. Collins, 323 U.S. 516, 530. No such abuse or danger has been advanced in the present case. The appellees suggest no more than a possibility that the filing of fraudulent claims by unscrupulous claimants feigning religious objections to Saturday work might not only dilute the unemployment compensation fund but also hinder the scheduling by employers of necessary Saturday work. But that possibility is not apposite here because no such objection appears to have been made before the South Carolina Supreme Court, and we are unwilling to assess the importance of an asserted state interest without the views of the state court. Nor, if the contention had been made below, would the record appear to sustain it; there is no proof whatever to warrant such fears of malingering or deceit as those which the respondents now advance. Even if consideration of such evidence is not foreclosed by the prohibition against judicial inquiry into the truth or falsity of religious beliefs, United States v. Ballard, 322 U.S. 78 — a question as to which we intimate no view since it is not before us — it is highly doubtful whether such evidence would be sufficient to warrant a substantial infringement of religious liberties. For even if the possibility of spurious claims did threaten to dilute the fund and disrupt the scheduling of work, it would plainly be incumbent upon the appellees to demonstrate that no alternative forms of regulation would combat such abuses without infringing First Amendment rights.[7] Cf. Shelton v. Tucker, 364 U.S. 479, 487-490; Talley v. California, 362 U.S. 60, 64; Schneider v. State, 308 U.S. 147, 161; Martin v. Struthers, 319 U.S. 141, 144-149.

In these respects, then, the state interest asserted in the present case is wholly dissimilar to the interests which were found to justify the less direct burden upon religious practices in Braunfeld v. Brown, supra. The Court recognized that the Sunday closing law which that decision sustained undoubtedly served "to make the practice of [the Orthodox Jewish merchants'] . . . religious beliefs more expensive," 366 U.S., at 605. But the statute was nevertheless saved by a countervailing factor which finds no equivalent in the instant case — a strong state interest in providing one uniform day of rest for all workers. That secular objective could be achieved, the Court found, only by declaring Sunday to be that day of rest. Requiring exemptions for Sabbatarians, while theoretically possible, appeared to present an administrative problem of such magnitude, or to afford the exempted class so great a competitive advantage, that such a requirement would have rendered the entire statutory scheme unworkable. In the present case no such justifications underlie the determination of the state court that appellant's religion makes her ineligible to receive benefits.

. . . Our holding today is only that South Carolina may not constitutionally apply the eligibility provisions so as to constrain a worker to abandon his religious convictions respecting the day of rest. This holding but reaffirms a principle that we announced a decade and a half ago, namely that no State may "exclude individual Catholics, Lutherans, Mohammedans, Baptists, Jews, Methodists, Non-believers, Presbyterians, or the members of any other faith, *because of their faith, or lack of it*, from receiving the benefits of public welfare legislation." Everson v. Board of Education, 330 U.S. 1, 16.

In view of the result we have reached under the First and Fourteenth Amendments' guarantee of free exercise of religion, we have no occasion to consider appellant's claim that the denial of benefits also deprived her of the equal protection of the laws in violation of the Fourteenth Amendment.

The judgment of the South Carolina Supreme Court is reversed and the case is remanded for further proceedings not inconsistent with this opinion.[ww]

---

[7] We note that before the instant decision, state supreme courts had, without exception, granted benefits to persons who were physically available for work but unable to find suitable employment solely because of a religious prohibition against Saturday work. [Citations omitted.]

[ww] Concurring opinions of Justices Douglas and Stewart are omitted, as is a dissenting opinion of Justice Harlan, joined in by Justice White. — Ed.

NOTE Developments in Religious Exemptions

May a court authorize a blood transfusion for a person whose religious beliefs prohibit such a medical practice? See In Re Estate of Bernice Brooks, 32 Ill. 2d 361, 205 N.E. 2d 435 (1965), where the patient had "previously refused [a transfusion] with full knowledge of the consequences." See also Application of President and Directors of Georgetown College, 331 F.2d 1000 (D.C. Cir. 1964), and comment in 1964 Religion and the Public Order 209. Compare Pack v. Tennessee 527 S.W.2d 99 (Tenn. Sup. Ct.), cert. denied, 424 U.S. 954 (1976) (public handling of snakes and drinking of poison as parts of religious ritual are enjoinable as public nuisance).

May conscientious objection be available only to those opposed to war on religious grounds, not to those opposed on moral grounds? Would such a preference violate the establishment clause? The Supreme Court skirted this issue in United States v. Seeger, 380 U.S. 163 (1965), by including as religion "belief that is sincere and meaningful [and that] occupies a place in the life of its possessor parallel to that filled by the orthodox belief in God of one who clearly qualifies for the exemption."

In Gillette v. United States, 401 U.S. 437 (1971), the Court held that neither the Selective Service Act nor the First Amendment entitled a conscientious objector, a Roman Catholic, to an exemption, where his objection was based on religious objection to participation in the Vietnam conflict, not to war in general. Marshall, J., for the Court, concluded that the statute did not prefer one religious group over another or abridge the free exercise of religion. Douglas, J., dissented, stressing the Catholic doctrine of just and unjust wars.

In Wisconsin v. Yoder, 406 U.S. 205 (1972), the Court held that the free exercise clause of the First Amendment granted to the Amish the right not to send their children to public school after the eighth grade. Justice Douglas dissented in part, expressing his fear that not enough protection was given to the child's right to be prepared for the modern world if he later chose to leave the Amish community.

When should a religious exemption be held to violate the establishment clause? "If Jehovah's Witnesses are entitled to exemption from the flag salute because for them it is a religious exercise, why must it not be banned in the public schools as an establishment of religion? The answer is that for purposes of free exercise, religion is defined by the nonconformist, but for purposes of establishment it is defined by the dominant consensus." Freund, The First Amendment: Freedom of Religion (speech of Feb. 27, 1976). Compare Kurland, Of Church and State and the Supreme Court, 29 U. Chi. L. Rev. 1 (1961).

Title VII of the Civil Rights Act of 1964, 42 U.S.C. §2000e, makes unlawful the discharge of an employee because of his religion. Pursuant to that statute, the EEOC adopted a rule requiring employers "to make reasonable accommodations to the religious needs of employees and prospective employees. . . ." 29 C.F.R. §1605.1 (1974). Does such a rule violate the establishment clause? Compare Cummius v. Parker Seal Co., 516 F.2d 544 (6th Cir. 1975), aff'd by an equally divided Court, 97 S. Ct. 342 n. (1976) (mem.) (holding that it does not), with Yolt v. North American Rockwell Corp., 45 U.S.L.W. 2367 (C.D. Cal., Jan. 10, 1977) (holding that it does).

School District of Abington v. Schempp; Murray v. Curlett
374 U.S. 203, 83 S. Ct. 1560, 10 L. Ed. 2d 844 (1963)

MR. JUSTICE CLARK delivered the opinion of the Court.

Once again we are called upon to consider the scope of the provision of the First Amendment to the United States Constitution which declares that "Congress shall make

Section D. Religion

no law respecting an establishment of religion or prohibiting the free exercise thereof. . . ." These companion cases present the issues in the context of state action requiring that schools begin each day with readings from the Bible. While raising the basic questions under slightly different factual situations, the cases permit of joint treatment. In light of the history of the First Amendment and of our cases interpreting and applying its requirements, we hold that the practices at issue and the laws requiring them are unconstitutional under the Establishment Clause, as applied to the states through the Fourteenth Amendment.

I

The Facts in Each Case: No. 142. The Commonwealth of Pennsylvania by law, 24 Pa. Stat. §15-1516, as amended, Pub. Law 1928 (Supp. 1960) Dec. 17, 1959, requires that "At least ten verses from the Holy Bible shall be read, without comment, at the opening of each public school on each school day. Any child shall be excused from such Bible reading, or attending such Bible reading, upon the written request of his parent or guardian." The Schempp family, husband and wife and two of their children, brought suit to enjoin enforcement of the statute. . . . A three-judge statutory District Court for the Eastern District of Pennsylvania held that the statute is violative of the Establishment Clause of the First Amendment as applied to the States by the Due Process Clause of the Fourteenth Amendment and directed that appropriate injunctive relief issue. . . .

No. 119. In 1905 the Board of School Commissioners of Baltimore City adopted a rule pursuant to Art. 77, §202 of the Annotated Code of Maryland. The rule provided for the holding of opening exercises in the Schools of the City consisting primarily of the "reading, without comment, of a chapter in the Holy Bible and/or the use of the Lord's Prayer." The petitioners, Mrs. Madalyn Murray and her son, William J. Murray, III, are both professed atheists. Following unsuccessful attempts to have the respondent school board rescind the rule this suit was filed for mandamus to compel its rescission and cancellation. . . .

The respondents demurred and the trial court, recognizing that the demurrer admitted all facts well pleaded, sustained it without leave to amend. The Maryland Court of Appeals affirmed, the majority of four justices holding the exercise not in violation of the First and Fourteenth Amendments, with three justices dissenting. . . .

II

It is true that religion has been closely identified with our history and government. As we said in Engel v. Vitale, 370 U.S. 421, 434 (1962), "The history of man is inseparable from the history of religion. And . . . since the beginning of that history many people have devoutly believed that 'More things are wrought by prayer than this world dreams of.'" In Zorach v. Clauson, 343 U.S. 306, 313 (1952), we gave specific recognition to the proposition that "[w]e are a religious people whose institutions presuppose a Supreme Being." The fact that the Founding Fathers believed devoutly that there was a God and that the unalienable rights of man were rooted in Him is clearly evidenced in their writings, from the Mayflower Compact to the Constitution itself. . . .

This is not to say, however, that religion has been so identified with our history and government that religious freedom is not likewise as strongly imbedded in our public and private life. Nothing but the most telling of personal experiences in religious persecution suffered by our forebears, see Everson v. Board of Education, supra, at 8-11, could have planted our belief in liberty of religious opinion any more deeply in our heritage. . . .

1372   Chapter Sixteen. **Substantive Rights**

IV

[A discussion of the Cantwell, Everson, McCollum, Zorach, Torcaso, and Engel cases is omitted.]

V

The wholesome "neutrality" of which this Court's cases speak thus stems from a recognition of the teachings of history that powerful sects or groups might bring about a fusion of governmental and religious functions or a concert or dependency of one upon the other to the end that official support of the State or Federal Government would be placed behind the tenets of one or of all orthodoxies. This the Establishment Clause prohibits. And a further reason for neutrality is found in the Free Exercise Clause, which recognizes the value of religious training, teaching and observance and, more particularly, the right of every person to freely choose his own course with reference thereto, free of any compulsion from the state. This the Free Exercise Clause guarantees. Thus, as we have seen, the two clauses may overlap. As we have indicated, the Establishment Clause has been directly considered by this Court eight times in the past score of years and, with only one Justice dissenting on the point, it has consistently held that the clause withdrew all legislative power respecting religious belief or the expression thereof. The test may be stated as follows: what are the purpose and primary effect of the enactment? If either is the advancement or inhibition of religion then the enactment exceeds the scope of legislative power as circumscribed by the Constitution. That is to say that to withstand the strictures of the Establishment Clause there must be a secular legislative purpose and a primary effect that neither advances nor inhibits religion. Everson v. Board of Education, supra; McGowan v. Maryland [365 U.S. 420,] 442 [(1961)]. The Free Exercise Clause, likewise considered many times here, withdraws from legislative power, state and federal, the exertion of any restraint on the free exercise of religion. Its purpose is to secure religious liberty in the individual by prohibiting any invasions thereof by civil authority. Hence it is necessary in a free exercise case for one to show the coercive effect of the enactment as it operates against him in the practice of his religion. The distinction between the two clauses is apparent — a violation of the Free Exercise Clause is predicated on coercion while the Establishment Clause violation need not be so attended.

Applying the Establishment Clause principles to the cases at bar we find that the States are requiring the selection and reading at the opening of the school day of verses from the Holy Bible and the recitation of the Lord's Prayer by the students in unison. These exercises are prescribed as part of the curricular activities of students who are required by law to attend school. They are held in the school buildings under the supervision and with the participation of teachers employed in those schools. None of these factors, other than compulsory school attendance, was present in the program upheld in Zorach v. Clauson. The trial court in No. 142 has found that such an opening exercise is a religious ceremony and was intended by the State to be so. We agree with the trial court's finding as to the religious character of the exercises. Given that finding the exercises and the law requiring them are in violation of the Establishment Clause.

There is no such specific finding as to the religious character of the exercises in No. 119, and the State contends (as does the State in No. 142) that the program is an effort to extend its benefits to all public school children without regard to their religious belief. Included within its secular purposes, it says, are the promotion of moral values, the contradiction to the materialistic trends of our times, the perpetuation of our institutions and the teaching of literature. The case came up on demurrer, of course, to a petition which alleged that the uniform practice under the rule had been to read from the King James version of the Bible and that the exercise was sectarian. The short answer, therefore, is that the religious character of the exercise was admitted by the State. But even if its purpose is not strictly religious, it is sought to be accomplished through readings, without comment, from the Bible. Surely the place of the Bible as an instrument of religion cannot be gainsaid, and the State's recognition of the pervading religious character of the ceremony is evident from the rule's specific permission of the alternative use of the Catholic Douay version as well as the recent amendment permitting nonattendance at the exercises. None of these factors is consistent with the contention that the Bible is here used either as an instrument for nonreligious moral inspiration or as a reference for the teaching of secular subjects.

The conclusion follows that in both cases the laws require religious exercises and such exercises are being conducted in direct violation of the rights of the appellees and petitioners. Nor are these required exercises mitigated by the fact that individual students may absent themselves upon parental request, for that fact furnishes no defense to a claim of unconstitutionality under the Establishment Clause. See Engel v. Vitale, supra, at 430. Further, it is no defense to urge that the religious practices here may be relatively minor encroachments on the First Amendment. The breach of neutrality that is today a trickling stream may all too soon become a raging torrent and, in the words of Madison, "it is proper to take alarm at the first experiment on our liberties." Memorial and Remonstrance Against Religious Assessments, quoted in Everson, supra at 65.

It is insisted that unless these religious exercises are permitted a "religion of secularism" is established in the schools. We agree of course that the State may not establish a "religion of secularism" in the sense of affirmatively opposing or showing hostility to religion, thus "preferring those who believe in no religion over those who do believe." Zorach v. Clauson, supra, at 314. We do not agree, however, that this decision in any sense has that effect. In addition, it might well be said that one's education is not complete without a study of comparative religion or the history of religion and its relationship to the advancement of civilization. It certainly may be said that the Bible is worthy of study for its literary and historic qualities. Nothing we have said here indicates that such study of the Bible or of religion, when presented objectively as part of a secular program of education, may not be effected consistent with the First Amendment. But the exercises here do not fall into those categories. They are religious exercises, required by the States in violation of the command of the First Amendment that the Government maintain strict neutrality, neither aiding nor opposing religion.

Finally, we cannot accept that the concept of neutrality, which does not permit a State to require a religious exercise even with the consent of the majority of those affected, collides with the majority's right to free exercise of religion.[10] While the Free Exercise Clause clearly prohibits the use of state action to deny the rights of free exercise to *anyone*, it has never meant that a majority could use the machinery of the State to practice its beliefs. . . .

The place of religion in our society is an exalted one, achieved through a long tradition of reliance on the home, the church and the inviolable citadel of the individual heart and mind. We have come to recognize through bitter experience that it is not within the power of government to invade that citadel, whether its purpose or effect be to aid or oppose, to advance or retard. In the relationship between man and religion, the State is firmly committed to a position of neutrality. Though the application of that rule requires interpretation of a delicate sort, the rule itself is clearly and concisely stated in the words of the First Amendment. Applying that rule to the facts of these cases, we affirm the judgment in No. 142. In No. 119, the judgment is reversed and the cause remanded to the Maryland Court of Appeals for further proceedings consistent with this opinion.

[10] We are not of course presented with and therefore do not pass upon a situation such as military service, where the Government regulates the temporal and geographic environment of individuals to a point that, unless it permits voluntary religious services to be conducted with the use of government facilities, military personnel would be unable to engage in the practice of their faiths.

1374   Chapter Sixteen.   Substantive Rights

It is so ordered.

MR. JUSTICE BRENNAN, concurring. . . .

I join fully in the opinion and the judgment of the Court. I see no escape from the conclusion that the exercises called in question in these two cases violate the constitutional mandate. The reasons we gave only last Term in Engel v. Vitale, 370 U.S. 421, for finding in the New York Regents' prayer an impermissible establishment of religion, compel the same judgment of the practices at bar. The involvement of the secular with the religious is no less intimate here; and it is constitutionally irrelevant that the State has not composed the material for the inspirational exercises presently involved. It should be unnecessary to observe that our holding does not declare that the First Amendment manifests hostility to the practice or teaching of religion, but only applies prohibitions incorporated in the Bill of Rights in recognition of historic need shared by Church and State alike. While it is my view that not every involvement of religion in public life is unconstitutional, I consider the exercises at bar a form of involvement which clearly violates the Establishment Clause.

[After a brief examination of the intention of those who framed the First Amendment, Mr. Justice Brennan proceeded as follows:]

A too literal quest for the advice of the Founding Fathers upon the issues of these cases seems to me futile and misdirected for several reasons: First, on our precise problem the historical record is at best ambiguous, and statements can readily be found to support either side of the proposition. The ambiguity of history is understandable if we recall the nature of the problems uppermost in the thinking of the statesmen who fashioned the religious guarantees; they were concerned with far more flagrant intrusions of government into the realm of religion than any that our century has witnessed. While it is clear to me that the Framers meant the Establishment Clause to prohibit more than the creation of an established federal church such as existed in England, I have no doubt that, in their preoccupation with the imminent question of established churches, they gave no distinct consideration to the particular question whether the clause also forbade devotional exercises in public institutions.

Second, the structure of American education has greatly changed since the First Amendment was adopted. In the context of our modern emphasis upon public education available to all citizens, any views of the eighteenth century as to whether the exercises at bar are an "establishment" offer little aid to decision. Education, as the Framers knew it, was in the main confined to private schools more often than not under strictly sectarian supervision. Only gradually did control of education pass largely to public officials. It would, therefore, hardly be significant if the fact was that the nearly universal devotional exercises in the schools of the young Republic did not provoke criticism; even today religious ceremonies in church-supported private schools are constitutionally unobjectionable.

Third, our religious composition makes us a vastly more diverse people than were our forefathers. They knew differences chiefly among Protestant sects. Today the Nation is far more heterogeneous religiously, including as it does substantial minorities not only of Catholics and Jews but as well of those who worship according to no version of the Bible and those who worship no God at all. See Torcaso v. Watkins, 367 U.S. 488, 495. In the face of such profound changes, practices which may have been objectionable to no one in the time of Jefferson and Madison may today be highly offensive to many persons, the deeply devout and the nonbelievers alike.

Whatever Jefferson or Madison would have thought of Bible reading or the recital of the Lord's Prayer in what few public schools existed in their day, our use of the history of their time must limit itself to broad purposes, not specific practices. By such a standard, I am persuaded, as is the Court, that the devotional exercises carried on in the Baltimore and Abington schools offend the First Amendment because they sufficiently threaten in our day those substantive evils the fear of which called forth the Establishment Clause of the First Amendment. It is "*a constitution* we are expounding," and our interpretation of the First Amendment must necessarily be responsive to the much more highly charged nature of religious questions in contemporary society.

Fourth, The American experiment in free public education available to all children has been guided in large measure by the dramatic evolution of the religious diversity among the population which our public schools serve. The interaction of these two important forces in our national life has placed in bold relief certain positive values in the consistent application to public institutions generally, and public schools particularly, of the constitutional decree against official involvements of religion which might produce the evils the Framers meant the Establishment Clause to forestall. The public schools are supported entirely, in most communities, by public funds — funds exacted not only from parents, nor alone from those who hold particular religious views, nor indeed from those who subscribe to any creed at all. It is implicit in the history and character of American public education that the public schools serve a uniquely *public* function: the training of American citizens in an atmosphere free of parochial, divisive, or separatist influences of any sort — an atmosphere in which children may assimilate a heritage common to all American groups and religions. See Illinois ex rel. McCollum v. Board of Education, 333 U.S. 203. This is a heritage neither theistic nor atheistic, but simply civic and patriotic. See Meyer v. Nebraska, 262 U.S. 390, 400-403.[xx]

NOTE Reactions and References

On the prayer cases, including Engel v. Vitale, 370 U.S. 421 (1962), see Sutherland, Establishment According to Engel, 76 Harv. L. Rev. 25 (1962); Brown, Quis Custodiet Ipsos Custodes? — The School-Prayer Cases, 1963 Sup. Ct. Rev. 1 (1963).

National and congressional reactions, particularly the effort to secure a school prayer amendment, are described in Beaney and Beiser, Prayer and Politics: the Impact of Engel and Schempp on the Political Process, 13 J. Pub. L. 475 (1964). How did the prayer decisions affect the attitudes of public school teachers and administrators towards the worth of school prayer and the power of the Supreme Court? At what point does an involuntary change in behavior, such as the termination of devotional Bible reading in the classroom, prompt an adjustment of attitudes in support of the change? At what point does it prompt resistance? Works of political science that consider these issues include, e.g., Muir, Prayer in the Public Schools: Law and Attitude Change (1967).

DeSPAIN v. DeKALB COUNTY COMMUNITY SCHOOL DISTRICT, 255 F. Supp. 655 (N.D. Ill. 1966). "Plaintiffs seek an injunction against the alleged violation of their constitutional rights by virtue of the recital in the kindergarten class which their child, Laura I. DeSpain attends, of the following verse, which they deem to be a prayer:

> We thank you for the flowers so sweet;
> We thank you for the food we eat;
> We thank you for the birds that sing;
> We thank you for everything.

"The complaint . . . alleges that from the commencement of the 1965-1966 school year until the present date Mrs. Watne has conducted the 'prayer' and has required all of her students, including Laura, to fold their hands in their laps, close their eyes and assume a traditional devotional and prayerful attitude immediately prior to its recitation."

What decision? Why? See also Stein v. Oshinsky, 348 F.2d 999 (2d Cir. 1965).

[xx] A concurring opinion of Justice Douglas and a concurring opinion of Justice Goldberg, joined by Justice Harlan, are omitted, as is a dissenting opinion of Justice Stewart. — ED.

Epperson v. Arkansas 393 U.S. 97, 89 S. Ct. 266, 21 L. Ed. 2d 228 (1968)

MR. JUSTICE FORTAS delivered the opinion of the Court.

I

This appeal challenges the constitutionality of the "anti-evolution" statute which the State of Arkansas adopted in 1928 to prohibit the teaching in its public schools and universities of the theory that man evolved from other species of life. The statute was a product of the upsurge of "fundamentalist" religious fervor of the twenties. The Arkansas statute was an adaptation of the famous Tennessee "monkey law" which that State adopted in 1925. The constitutionality of the Tennessee law was upheld by the Tennessee Supreme Court in the celebrated Scopes case in 1927.

The Arkansas law makes it unlawful for a teacher in any state-supported school or university "to teach the theory or doctrine that mankind ascended or descended from a lower order of animals," or "to adopt or use in any such institution a textbook that teaches" this theory. Violation is a misdemeanor and subjects the violator to dismissal from his position.

The present case concerns the teaching of biology in a high school in Little Rock. According to the testimony, until the events here in litigation, the official textbook furnished for the high school biology course did not have a section on the Darwinian Theory. Then, for the academic year 1965-1966, the school administration, on recommendation of the teachers of biology in the school system, adopted and prescribed a textbook which contained a chapter setting forth "the theory about the origin . . . of man from a lower form of animal."

Susan Epperson, a young woman who graduated from Arkansas' school system and then obtained her master's degree in zoology at the University of Illinois, was employed by the Little Rock school system in the fall of 1964 to teach 10th grade biology at Central High School. At the start of the next academic year, 1965, she was confronted by the new textbook (which one surmises from the record was not unwelcome to her). She faced at least a literal dilemma because she was supposed to use the new textbook for classroom instruction and presumably to teach the statutorily condemned chapter; but to do so would be a criminal offense and subject her to dismissal.

She instituted the present action in the Chancery Court of the State, seeking a declaration that the Arkansas statute is void and enjoining the State and the defendant officials of the Little Rock school system from dismissing her for violation of the statute's provisions. H. H. Blanchard, a parent of children attending the public schools, intervened in support of the action.

The Chancery Court, in an action by Chancellor Murray O. Reed, held that the statute violated the Fourteenth Amendment to the United States Constitution. The court noted that this Amendment encompasses the prohibitions upon state interference with freedom of speech and thought which are contained in the First Amendment. Accordingly, it held that the challenged statute is unconstitutional because, in violation of the First Amendment, it "tends to hinder the quest for knowledge, restrict the freedom to learn, and restrain the freedom to teach." In this perspective, the Act, it held, was an unconstitutional and void restraint upon the freedom of speech guaranteed by the Constitution.

On appeal, the Supreme Court of Arkansas reversed.[1] Its two-sentence opinion is set forth in the margin.[2] It sustained the statute as an exercise of the State's power to specify

---

[1] 242 Ark. 922, 416 S.W.2d 322 (1967).

[2] "Per Curiam. Upon the principal issue, that of constitutionality, the court holds that Initiated Measure No. 1 of 1928, Ark. Stat. Ann. §80-1627 and §80-1628 (Repl. 1960), is a valid exercise of the state's power to specify

the curriculum in public schools. It did not address itself to the competing constitutional considerations.

Appeal was duly prosecuted to this Court under 28 U.S.C. § 1257 (2). Only Arkansas and Mississippi have such "anti-evolution" or "monkey" laws on their books. There is no record of any prosecutions in Arkansas under its statute. It is possible that the statute is presently more of a curiosity than a vital fact of life in these States. Nevertheless, the present case was brought, the appeal as of right is properly here, and it is our duty to decide the issues presented.

II

At the outset, it is urged upon us that the challenged statute is vague and uncertain and therefore within the condemnation of the Due Process Clause of the Fourteenth Amendment. The contention that the Act is vague and uncertain is supported by language in the brief opinion of Arkansas' Supreme Court. . . . Regardless of this uncertainty, the court held that the statute is constitutional. . . .

On the other hand, counsel for the State, in oral argument in this Court, candidly stated that, despite the State Supreme Court's equivocation, Arkansas would interpret the statute "to mean that to make a student aware of the theory . . . just to teach that there was such a theory" would be grounds for dismissal and for prosecution under the statute; and he said "that the Supreme Court of Arkansas' opinion should be interpreted in that manner." He said "If Mrs. Epperson would tell her students that 'Here is Darwin's theory, that man ascended or descended from a lower form of being,' then I think she would be under this statute liable for prosecution."

In any event, we do not rest our decision upon the asserted vagueness of the statute. On either interpretation of its language, Arkansas' statute cannot stand. It is of no moment whether the law is deemed to prohibit mention of Darwin's theory, or to forbid any or all of the infinite varieties of communication embraced within the term "teaching." Under either interpretation, the law must be stricken because of its conflict with the constitutional prohibition of state laws respecting an establishment of religion or prohibiting the free exercise thereof. The overriding fact is that Arkansas' law selects from the body of knowledge a particular segment which it proscribes for the sole reason that it is deemed to conflict with a particular religious doctrine; that is, with a particular interpretation of the Book of Genesis by a particular religious group.

III

The antecedents of today's decision are many and unmistakable. They are rooted in the foundation soil of our Nation. They are fundamental to freedom.

Government in our democracy, state and national, must be neutral in matters of religious theory, doctrine, and practice. It may not be hostile to any religion or to the advocacy of no-religion; and it may not aid, foster, or promote one religion or religious theory against another or even against the militant opposite. The First Amendment mandates governmental neutrality between religion and religion, and between religion and nonreligion.

---

the curriculum in its public schools. The court expresses no opinion on the question whether the Act prohibits any explanation of the theory of evolution or merely prohibits teaching that the theory is true; the answer not being necessary to a decision in the case, and the issue not having been raised.

"The decree is reversed and the cause dismissed.

"Ward, J., concurs. Brown, J., dissents.

"Paul Ward, Justice, concurring. I agree with the first sentence in the majority opinion.

"To my mind, the rest of the opinion beclouds the clear announcement made in the first sentence."

1378   Chapter Sixteen.   **Substantive Rights**

As early as 1872, this Court said: "The law knows no heresy, and is committed to the support of no dogma, the establishment of no sect." Watson v. Jones, 13 Wall. 679, 728. . . .

There is and can be no doubt that the First Amendment does not permit the State to require that teaching and learning must be tailored to the principles or prohibitions of any religious sect or dogma. . . .

. . . While study of religions and of the Bible from a literary and historic viewpoint, presented objectively as part of a secular program of education, need not collide with the First Amendment's prohibition, the State may not adopt programs or practices in its public schools or colleges which "aid or oppose" any religion. Abington School District, 374 U.S., at 225. This prohibition is absolute. It forbids alike the preference of a religious doctrine or the prohibition of theory which is deemed antagonistic to a particular dogma. As Mr. Justice Clark stated in Joseph Burstyn, Inc. v. Wilson, "the state has no legitimate interest in protecting any or all religions from views distasteful to them. . . ." 343 U.S. 495, 505 (1952). . . .

. . . No suggestion has been made that Arkansas' law may be justified by considerations of state policy other than the religious views of some of its citizens. It is clear that fundamentalist sectarian conviction was and is the law's reason for existence. Its antecedent, Tennessee's "monkey law," candidly stated its purpose: to make it unlawful "to teach any theory that denies the story of the Divine Creation of man as taught in the Bible, and to teach instead that man has descended from a lower order of animals." Perhaps the sensational publicity attendant upon the Scopes trial induced Arkansas to adopt less explicit language. It eliminated Tennessee's reference to "the story of the Divine Creation of man" as taught in the Bible, but there is no doubt that the motivation for the law was the same: to suppress the teaching of a theory which, it was thought, "denied" the divine creation of man.

Arkansas' law cannot be defended as an act of religious neutrality. Arkansas did not seek to excise from the curricula of its schools and universities all discussion of the origin of man. The law's effort was confined to an attempt to blot out a particular theory because of its supposed conflict with the Biblical account, literally read. Plainly, the law is contrary to the mandate of the First, and in violation of the Fourteenth, Amendment to the Constitution.

The judgment of the Supreme Court of Arkansas is
Reversed.

Mr. Justice Black, concurring. I am by no means sure that this case presents a genuinely justiciable case or controversy. Although Arkansas Initiated Act No. 1, the statute alleged to be unconstitutional, was passed by the voters of Arkansas in 1928, we are informed that there has never been even a single attempt by the State to enforce it. And the pallid, unenthusiastic, even apologetic defense of the Act presented by the State in this Court indicates that the State would make no attempt to enforce the law should it remain on the books for the next century. Now, nearly 40 years after the law has slumbered on the books as though dead, a teacher alleging fear that the State might arouse from its lethargy and try to punish her has asked for a declaratory judgment holding the law unconstitutional. She was subsequently joined by a parent who alleged his interest in seeing that his two then school-age sons "be informed of all scientific theories and hypotheses. . . ." But whether this Arkansas teacher is still a teacher, fearful of punishment under the Act, we do not know. It may be, as has been published in the daily press, that she has long since given up her job as a teacher and moved to a distant city, thereby escaping the dangers she had imagined might befall her under this lifeless Arkansas Act. And there is not one iota of concrete evidence to show that the parent-intervenor's sons have not been or will not be taught about evolution. The textbook adopted for use in biology classes in Little Rock includes an entire chapter dealing with evolution. There is no evidence that this chapter is not being freely taught in the schools that use the textbook and no evidence of the intervenor's sons, who were 15 and 17 years old when this suit was brought three years ago, are still in high school or yet to take biology. Unfortunately, however, the State's languid interest in the case has not prompted it to keep this Court informed concerning facts that might easily justify dismissal of this alleged lawsuit as moot or as lacking the qualities of a genuine case or controversy.

Notwithstanding my own doubts as to whether the case presents a justiciable controversy, the Court brushes aside these doubts and leaps headlong into the middle of the very broad problems involved in federal intrusion into state powers to decide what subjects and schoolbooks it may wish to use in teaching state pupils. While I hesitate to enter into the consideration and decision of such sensitive state-federal relationships, I reluctantly acquiesce. . . .

It is plain that a state law prohibiting all teaching of human development or biology is constitutionally quite different from a law that compels a teacher to teach as true only one theory of a given doctrine. It would be difficult to make a First Amendment case out of a state law eliminating the subject of higher mathematics, or astronomy, or biology from its curriculum. And for all the Supreme Court of Arkansas has said, this particular Act may prohibit that and nothing else. . . .

It seems to me that in this situation the statute is too vague for us to strike it down on any ground but that: vagueness. Under this statute as construed by the Arkansas Supreme Court, a teacher cannot know whether he is forbidden to mention Darwin's theory at all or only free to discuss it as long as he refrains from contending that it is true. . . .

The Court, not content to strike down this Arkansas Act on the unchallengeable ground of its plain vagueness, chooses rather to invalidate it as a violation of the Establishment of Religion Clause of the First Amendment. I would not decide this case on such a sweeping ground for the following reasons, among others.

1. In the first place I find it difficult to agree with the Court's statement that "there can be no doubt that Arkansas has sought to prevent its teachers from discussing the theory of evolution because it is contrary to the belief of some that the Book of Genesis must be the exclusive source of doctrine as to the origin of man." It may be instead that the people's motive was merely that it would be best to remove this controversial subject from its schools; there is no reason I can imagine why a State is without power to withdraw from its curriculum any subject deemed too emotional and controversial for its public schools. . . .

2. A second question that arises for me is whether this Court's decision forbidding a State to exclude the subject of evolution from its schools infringes the religious freedom of those who consider evolution an anti-religious doctrine. If the theory is considered antireligious, as the Court indicates, how can the State be bound by the Federal Constitution to permit its teachers to advocate such an "anti-religious" doctrine to schoolchildren? . . . Unless this Court is prepared simply to write off as pure nonsense the views of those who consider evolution an anti-religious doctrine, then this issue presents problems under the Establishment Clause far more troublesome than are discussed in the Court's opinion.

3. I am also not ready to hold that a person hired to teach school children takes with him into the classroom a constitutional right to teach sociological, economic, political, or religious subjects that the school's managers do not want discussed. This Court has said that the rights of free speech, "while fundamental in our democratic society, still do not mean that everyone with opinions or beliefs to express may address a group at any public place and at any time." Cox v. Louisiana, 379 U.S. 536, 554; Cox v. Louisiana, 379 U.S. 559, 574. I question whether it is absolutely certain, as the Court's opinion indicates that "academic freedom" permits a teacher to breach his contractual agreement to teach only the subjects designated by the school authorities who hired him.

Certainly the Darwinian theory, precisely like the Genesis story of the creation of man, is not above challenge. In fact the Darwinian theory has not merely been criticized by religionists but by scientists, and perhaps no scientist would be willing to take an oath and swear that everything announced in the Darwinian theory is unquestionably true. . . .

I would either strike down the Arkansas Act as too vague to enforce, or remand to the State Supreme Court for clarification of its holding and opinion.[yy]

NOTE

Could the principles of Epperson adequately provide a rationale for the result in Roe v. Wade, supra page 1119? See Tribe, Foreword: Toward a Model of Roles in the Due Process of Life and Law, 87 Harv. L. Rev. 1, 18–25 (1973).

Lemon v. Kurtzman; Early v. DiCenso 403 U.S. 602, 91 S. Ct. 2105, 29 L. Ed. 2d 45 (1971)

MR. CHIEF JUSTICE BURGER delivered the opinion of the Court. These two appeals raise questions as to Pennsylvania and Rhode Island statutes providing state aid to church-related elementary and secondary schools. Both statutes are challenged as violative of the Establishment and Free Exercise Clauses of the First Amendment and the Due Process Clause of the Fourteenth Amendment.

Pennsylvania has adopted a statutory program that provides financial support to nonpublic elementary and secondary schools by way of reimbursement for the cost of teachers' salaries, textbooks, and instructional materials in specified secular subjects. Rhode Island has adopted a statute under which the State pays directly to teachers in nonpublic elementary schools a supplement of 15% of their annual salary. Under each statute state aid has been given to church-related educational institutions as well as to other private schools. We hold that both statutes are unconstitutional.

I

THE RHODE ISLAND STATUTE

. . . In order to be eligible for the Rhode Island salary supplement, the recipient must teach in a nonpublic school at which the average per-pupil expenditure on secular education is less than the average in the State's public schools during a specified period. Appellant state Commissioner of Education also requires eligible schools to submit financial data. If this information indicates a per-pupil expenditure in excess of the statutory limitation, the records of the school in question must be examined in order to assess how much of the expenditure is attributable to secular education and how much to religious activity.

The Act also requires that teachers eligible for salary supplement must teach only those subjects that are offered in the State's public schools. They must use "only teaching materials which are used in the public schools." Finally, any teacher applying for a salary supplement must first agree in writing "not to teach a course in religion for so long as or during such time as he or she receives any salary supplements" under the Act.

Appellees are citizens and taxpayers of Rhode Island. They brought this suit to declare the Rhode Island Salary Supplement Act unconstitutional and to enjoin its operation on the grounds that it violates the Establishment and Free Exercise Clauses of the First Amendment. Appellants are state officials charged with administration of the Act, teachers eligible for salary supplements under the Act, and parents of children in church-related elementary schools whose teachers would receive state salary assistance.

[yy] Concurring opinions by Justices Harlan and Stewart are omitted — ED.

A three-judge federal court was convened pursuant to 28 U.S.C. §§2281, 2284. It found that Rhode Island's nonpublic elementary schools accommodated approximately 25% of the state's pupils. About 95% of these pupils attended schools affiliated with the Roman Catholic church. To date some 250 teachers have applied for benefits under the Act. All of them are employed by Roman Catholic schools.

The court held a hearing at which extensive evidence was introduced concerning the nature of the secular instruction offered in the Roman Catholic schools whose teachers would be eligible for salary assistance under the Act. Although the court found that concern for religious values does not necessarily affect the content of secular subjects, it also found that the parochial school system was "an integral part of the religious mission of the Catholic Church."

The District Court concluded that the Act violated the Establishment Clause, holding that it fostered "excessive entanglement" between government and religion. In addition two judges thought that the Act had the impermissible effect of giving "significant aid to a religious enterprise." 316 F. Supp. 112. We affirm.

THE PENNSYLVANIA STATUTE

Pennsylvania has adopted a program which has some but not all of the features of the Rhode Island program. . . .

The statute authorizes appellee state Superintendent of Public Instruction to "purchase" specified "secular educational services" from nonpublic schools. Under the "contracts" authorized by the statute, the State directly reimburses nonpublic schools solely for their actual expenditures for teachers' salaries, textbooks, and instructional materials. A school seeking reimbursement must maintain prescribed accounting procedures that identify the "separate" cost of the "secular educational service." These accounts are subject to state audit. The funds for this program were originally derived from a new tax on horse and harness racing, but the Act is now financed by a portion of the state tax on cigarettes.

There are several significant statutory restrictions on state aid. Reimbursement is limited to courses "presented in the curricula of the public schools." It is further limited "solely" to courses in the following "secular" subjects: mathematics, modern foreign languages, physical science, and physical education. Textbooks and instructional materials included in the program must be approved by the state Superintendent of Public Instruction. Finally, the statute prohibits reimbursement for any course that contains "any subject matter expressing religious teaching, or the morals or forms of worship of any sect." . . .

Appellants brought this action in the District Court to challenge the constitutionality of the Pennsylvania statute. The organizational plaintiffs-appellants are associations of persons resident in Pennsylvania declaring belief in the separation of church and state; individual plaintiffs-appellants are citizens and taxpayers of Pennsylvania. Plaintiff Lemon, in addition to being a citizen and a taxpayer, is a parent of a child attending public school in Pennsylvania. In addition, Lemon alleges that he purchased a ticket at a race track and thus had paid the specific tax which supports the expenditures under the Act. Appellees are state officials who have the responsibility for administering the Act. In addition, seven church-related schools are defendants-appellees.

A three-judge federal court was convened pursuant to 28 U.S.C. §§2281, 2284. The District Court held that Lemon alone had standing to challenge the Act since he alone had paid the tax that financed the statutory scheme. The organizational plaintiffs-appellant were denied standing under Flast v. Cohen, 382 U.S. 83, 99, 101 (1967).

The court granted Pennsylvania's motion to dismiss the complaint for failure to state a claim for relief. 310 F. Supp. 35. It held that the Act violated neither the Establishment nor the Free Exercise Clauses, Chief Judge Hastie dissenting. We reverse.

II

... In the absence of precisely stated constitutional prohibitions, we must draw lines with reference to the three main evils against which the Establishment Clause was intended to afford protection: "sponsorship, financial support, and active involvement of the sovereign in religious activity." Walz v. Tax Commission, 397 U.S. 664, 668 (1970).

Every analysis in this area must begin with consideration of the cumulative criteria developed by the Court over many years. Three such tests may be gleaned from our cases. First, the statute must have a secular legislative purpose; second, its principal or primary effect must be one that neither advances nor inhibits religion, Board of Education v. Allen, 392 U.S. 236, 243 (1968); finally, the statute must not foster "an excessive government entanglement with religion." Walz, supra, at 674.

Inquiry into the legislative purposes of the Pennsylvania and Rhode Island statutes affords no basis for a conclusion that the legislative intent was to advance religion. . . . A State always has a legitimate concern for maintaining minimum standards in all schools it allows to operate. As in Allen, we find nothing here that undermines the stated legislative intent; it must therefore be accorded appropriate deference. . . .

The two legislatures, however, have also recognized that church-related elementary and secondary schools have a significant religious mission and that a substantial portion of their activities are religiously oriented. They have therefore sought to create statutory restrictions designed to guarantee the separation between secular and religious educational functions and to ensure that state financial aid supports only the former. All these provisions are precautions taken in candid recognition that these programs approached, even if they did not intrude upon, the forbidden areas under the Religion Clauses. We need not decide whether these legislative precautions restrict the principal or primary effect of the programs to the point where they do not offend the Religion Clauses, for we conclude that the cumulative impact of the entire relationship arising under the statutes in each State involves excessive entanglement between government and religion.

III

. . . Our prior holdings do not call for total separation between church and state; total separation is not possible in an absolute sense. Some relationship between government and religious organizations is inevitable. . . . Judicial caveats against entanglement must recognize that the line of separation, far from being a "wall," is a blurred, indistinct, and variable barrier depending on all the circumstances of a particular relationship.

This is not to suggest, however, that we are to engage in a legalistic minuet in which precise rules and forms must govern. A true minuet is a matter of pure form and style, the observance of which is itself the substantive end. Here we examine the form of the relationship for the light that it casts on the substance.

In order to determine whether the government entanglement with religion is excessive, we must examine the character and purposes of the institutions which are benefited, the nature of the aid that the State provides, and the resulting relationship between the government and the religious authority. . . . Here we find that both statutes foster an impermissible degree of entanglement.

(A) RHODE ISLAND PROGRAM

The District Court made extensive findings on the grave potential for excessive entanglement that inheres in the religious character and purpose of the Roman Catholic elementary schools of Rhode Island, to date the sole beneficiaries of the Rhode Island Salary Supplement Act.

The church schools involved in the program are located close to parish churches. . . . The school buildings contain identifying religious symbols such as crosses on the exterior and crucifixes, religious paintings and statues either in the classrooms or hallways. . . . Approximately two-thirds of the teachers in the schools are nuns of various religious orders. . . .

On the basis of these findings the District Court concluded that parochial schools constituted "an integral part of the religious mission of the Catholic Church." . . .

Our decisions from Everson to Allen have permitted the States to provide church-related schools with secular, neutral, or nonideological services, facilities, or materials. Bus transportation, school lunches, public health services, and secular textbooks supplied in common to all students were not thought to offend the Establishment Clause. We note that the dissenters in Allen seemed chiefly concerned with the pragmatic difficulties involved in ensuring the truly secular content of the textbooks provided at State expense.

In Allen the Court refused to make assumptions, on a meager record, about the religious content of the textbooks that the State would be asked to provide. We cannot, however, refuse here to recognize that teachers have a substantially different ideological character than books. . . .

We do not assume, however, that parochial school teachers will be unsuccessful in their attempts to segregate their religious beliefs from their secular educational responsibilities. But the potential for impermissible fostering of religion is present. The Rhode Island Legislature has not, and could not, provide state aid on the basis of a mere assumption that secular teachers under religious discipline can avoid conflicts. The State must be certain, given the Religion Clauses, that subsidized teachers do not inculcate religion — indeed the State here has undertaken to do so. To ensure that no trespass occurs, the State has therefore carefully conditioned its aid with pervasive restrictions. An eligible recipient must teach only those courses that are offered in the public schools and use only those texts and materials that are found in the public schools. In addition the teacher must not engage in teaching any course in religion.

A comprehensive, discriminating, and continuing state surveillance will inevitably be required to ensure that these restrictions are obeyed and the First Amendment otherwise respected. . . .

(B) PENNSYLVANIA PROGRAM

The Pennsylvania statute also provides state aid to church-related schools for teachers' salaries. The complaint describes an educational system that is very similar to the one existing in Rhode Island. According to the allegations, the church-related elementary and secondary schools are controlled by religious organizations, have the purpose of propagating and promoting a particular religious faith, and conduct their operations to fulfill that purpose. Since this complaint was dismissed for failure to state a claim for relief, we must accept these allegations as true for purposes of our review.

As we noted earlier, the very restrictions and surveillance necessary to ensure that teachers play a strictly nonideological role give rise to entanglements between church and state. . . .

The Pennsylvania statute, moreover, has the further defect of providing state financial aid directly to the church-related school. This factor distinguishes both Everson and Allen, for in both those cases the Court was careful to point out that state aid was provided to the student and his parents — not to the church-related school. . . . The history of government grants of a continuing cash subsidy indicates that such programs have almost always been accompanied by varying measures of control and surveillance. The Government cash grants before us now provide no basis for predicting that comprehensive measures of surveillance and controls will not follow. In particular the government's post-audit power to inspect and evaluate a church-related school's financial records and to determine which expenditures are religious and which are secular creates an intimate and continuing relationship between church and state.

IV

A broader base of entanglement of yet a different character is presented by the divisive political potential of these state programs. In a community where such a large number of pupils are served by church-related schools, it can be assumed that state assistance will entail considerable political activity. Partisans of parochial schools, understandably concerned with rising costs and sincerely dedicated to both the religious and secular educational missions of their schools, will inevitably champion this cause and promote political action to achieve their goals. Those who oppose state aid, whether for constitutional, religious, or fiscal reasons, will inevitably respond and employ all of the usual political campaign techniques to prevail. Candidates will be forced to declare and voters to choose. It would be unrealistic to ignore the fact that many people confronted with issues of this kind will find their votes aligned with their faith.

Ordinarily political debate and division, however vigorous or even partisan, are normal and healthy manifestations of our democratic system of government, but political division along religious lines was one of the principal evils against which the First Amendment was intended to protect. Freund, Comment: Public Aid to Parochial Schools, 82 Harv. L. Rev. 1680, 1692 (1969). The potential divisiveness of such conflict is a threat to the normal political process. . . . It conflicts with our whole history and tradition to permit questions of the Religion Clauses to assume such importance in our legislatures and in our elections that they could divert attention from the myriad issues and problems which confront every level of government. The highways of church and state relationships are not likely to be one-way streets, and the Constitution's authors sought to protect religious worship from the pervasive power of government. The history of many countries attests to the hazards of religion's intruding into the political arena or of political power intruding into the legitimate and free exercise of religious belief.

Of course, as the Court noted in Walz, "adherents of particular faiths and individual churches frequently take strong positions on public issues." Walz v. Tax Commission, supra, at 670. We could not expect otherwise, for religious values pervade the fabric of our national life. But in Walz we dealt with a status under state tax laws for the benefit of all religious groups. Here we are confronted with successive and very likely permanent annual appropriations which benefit relatively few religious groups. Political fragmentation and divisiveness on religious lines is thus likely to be intensified.

The potential for political divisiveness related to religious belief and practice is aggravated in these two statutory programs by the need for continuing annual appropriations and the likelihood of larger and larger demands as costs and populations grow. . . .

V

In Walz it was argued that a tax exemption for places of religious worship would prove to be the first step in an inevitable progression leading to the establishment of state churches and state religion. That claim could not stand up against more than 200 years of virtually universal practice imbedded in our colonial experience and continuing into the present.

The progression argument, however, is more persuasive here. We have no long history of state aid to church-related educational institutions comparable to 200 years of tax exemption for churches. Indeed, the state programs before us today represent something of an innovation. We have already noted that modern governmental programs have self-perpetuating and self-expanding propensities. These internal pressures are only enhanced when the schemes involve institutions whose interests have substantial political support. Nor can we fail to see that in constitutional adjudication some steps, which when taken were thought to approach "the verge," have become the platform for yet further steps. . . .

Finally, nothing we have said can be construed to disparage the role of church-related elementary and secondary schools in our national life. Their contribution has been and is enormous. Nor do we ignore their economic plight in a period of rising costs and expanding need. Taxpayers generally have been spared vast sums by the maintenance of these educational institutions by religious organizations, largely by the gifts of faithful adherents.

The merit and benefits of these schools, however, are not the issue before us in these cases. The sole question is whether state aid to these schools can be squared with the dictates of the Religion Clauses. Under our system the choice has been made that government is to be entirely excluded from the area of religious instruction and churches excluded from the affairs of government. The Constitution decrees that religion must be a private matter for the individual, the family, and the institutions of private choice, and that while some involvement and entanglement is inevitable, lines must be drawn. . . .[zz]

NOTE Further Issues in Public Aid to Church-Related Schools

In a 5 to 4 decision the Court differentiated the issues in the Rhode Island and Pennsylvania cases from that of federal construction grants to church-related institutions of higher learning. Tilton v. Richardson, 403 U.S. 672 (1971). The distinguishing factors were the absence of religious indoctrination; the pluralistic nature of the faculty and student body; the single occasion for making the grant; the nonideological character of the buildings, specifically not to be used for a theological program. Justices Douglas, Black, Brennan, and Marshall dissented.

In a series of cases at the 1972 Term, the Court applied Lemon v. Kurtzman to various state programs of aid to nonpublic schools or to parents of school children attending them. A New York statute in 1972 provided (a) direct grants to qualifying nonpublic schools for maintenance and repair "to ensure the health, welfare and safety of enrolled pupils"; (b) tuition reimbursement, not to exceed $50 per elementary school child and $100 per high school child, to parents having taxable income less than $5,000; (c) for those not qualifying under (b), a deduction from adjusted gross income of amounts in respect of tuition payments, scaled inversely to income. Each provision was held invalid as having the effect of advancing religion. Powell, J., delivered the opinion of the Court. White, J., dissented. Burger, C.J., and Rehnquist, J., dissented with respect to (b) and (c), on the ground that such payments or deductions to individuals are general welfare benefits, which the donees may use as they wish. Committee for Public Education v. Nyquist, 413 U.S. 756 (1973). See also Sloan v. Lemon, 413 U.S. 825 (1973) (Pennsylvania Parent Reimbursement Act).

A New York statute granted funds to nonpublic schools to pay the cost of testing pupils, on both internally prepared tests and those formulated by state authorities. The giving of the tests was mandatory under state law. The grants were held invalid, Justice White dissenting, as applied to tests prepared in church-related schools. Levitt v. Committee for Public Education, 413 U.S. 472 (1973).

In contrast, the Court sustained a South Carolina law providing for revenue bonds to assist nonpublic institutions of higher learning to finance construction. Justices Brennan, Douglas, and Marshall dissented. Hunt v. McNair, 413 U.S. 734 (1973).

[zz] Justices Douglas, Brennan and Marshall concurred specially. Justice White dissented. — ED.

Application of the three-part test of Kurtzman and Nyquist was held to invalidate a Pennsylvania law authorizing the loan of instructional material and equipment directly to qualifying nonpublic schools in Meek v. Pittinger, 422 U.S. 1049 (1975). For the Court, Justice Stewart distinguished state aid in the form of "secular and nonideological services unrelated to the primary, religious-oriented educational function of the sectarian school," from the "[s]ubstantial aid to the educational function" of sectarian schools involved here. This aid "inescapably results in the direct and substantial advancement of religious activity, . . . and thus constitutes an impermissible establishment of religion." Relying on Board of Education v. Allen, the Court, however, upheld a Pennsylvania provision authorizing textbook loans to students in public and nonpublic schools. For comment see Note, The Supreme Court, 1974 Term, 89 Harv. L. Rev. 47, 104 (1975).

In 1971, Maryland enacted a statute making lump-sum grants to private colleges and universities. In 1972, the statute was amended to provide that these grants could not be used for sectarian purposes. In Roemer v. Maryland Public Works Bd., 426 U.S. 736 (1976), the Court sustained the act against a challenge that it violated the establishment clause. Justice Blackmun, with whom Chief Justice Burger and Justice Powell concurred, found that none of the five sectarian colleges which had received aid was "pervasively sectarian" under Tilton, supra, and Hunt, supra; refused to consider possible sectarian use of the grants where the statute prohibited such use; concluded that the oversight of the use of the grants would not involve "excessive entanglements," stressing that the recipients were only secondarily sectarian; and found no substantial danger of political divisiveness, again because of the character of the institutions. Justice White, joined by Justice Rehnquist, concurred on the basis of his dissent in Lemon, supra. Justice Brennan, with whom Justice Marshall joined, Justice Stewart, and Justice Stevens each filed dissenting opinions. See Note, The Supreme Court, 1975 Term, 90 Harv. L. Rev. 56, 133-142 (1976).

Chapter Seventeen Retroactivity

INTRODUCTORY NOTE

In 1829 Mr. Justice Washington stated that "retrospective laws which do not impair the obligation of contracts, or partake of the character of ex post facto laws, are not condemned or forbidden" by the Constitution. Satterlee v. Matthewson, 2 Pet. 380, 413. Other sections of this volume have indicated that the reach of the ex post facto clauses has been so limited, and the grasp of the contracts clause has been so weakened, that other clauses have been called into unexpected service. This brief chapter does not purport to present in fullness the totality of doctrine with respect to retroactivity. What it seeks principally to do is to show some of the major efforts, successful and unsuccessful, to find other constitutional barriers to retroactivity of governmental action and legal doctrine than those mentioned by Mr. Justice Washington. The topic is helpfully analyzed in Smith, Retroactive Laws and Vested Rights, 5 Texas L. Rev. 231 (1927), 6 id. 409 (1928), reprinted in 1 Selected Essays on Constitutional Law 266 (1938); Hochman, The Supreme Court and the Constitutionality of Retroactive Legislation, 73 Harv. L. Rev. 692 (1960); Slawson, Constitutional and Legislative Considerations in Retroactive Lawmaking, 48 Calif. L. Rev. 216 (1960).

The opinions in the Blaisdell case, reflecting classic and conflicting views of the contracts clause, also bespeak principles of broader relevance.

Home Building & Loan Assn. v. Blaisdell 290 U.S. 398, 54 S. Ct. 231, 78 L. Ed. 413 (1934)

MR. CHIEF JUSTICE HUGHES delivered the opinion of the Court.

Appellant contests the validity of Chapter 339 of the Laws of Minnesota of 1933, p. 514, approved April 18, 1933, called the Minnesota Mortgage Moratorium Law, as being repugnant to the contract clause (Art. I, §10) and the due process and equal protection clauses of the Fourteenth Amendment, of the Federal Constitution. The statute was sustained by the Supreme Court of Minnesota, 189 Minn. 422, 448; 249 N.W. 334, 893, and the case comes here on appeal.

The Act provides that, during the emergency declared to exist, relief may be had through authorized judicial proceedings with respect to foreclosures of mortgages, and execution sales, of real estate; that sales may be postponed and periods of redemption may be extended. The Act does not apply to mortgages subsequently made nor to those made previously which shall be extended for a period ending more than a year after the passage of the Act (Part One, §8). There are separate provisions in Part Two relating to homesteads, but these are to apply "only to cases not entitled to relief under some valid provision of Part One." The Act is to remain in effect "only during the continuance of the emergency and in no event beyond May 1, 1935." No extension of the period for redemption and no postponement of sale is to be allowed which would have the effect of extending the period of redemption beyond that date. Part Two, §8.

The Act declares that the various provisions for relief are severable; that each is to stand on its own footing with respect to validity. Part One, §9. We are here concerned with the provisions of Part One, §4, authorizing the District Court of the county to extend the period of redemption from foreclosure sales "for such additional time as the court may deem just and equitable," subject to the above described limitation. . . .

Invoking the relevant provision of the statute, appellees applied to the District Court of Hennepin County for an order extending the period of redemption from a foreclosure sale. . . .

The court entered its judgment extending the period of redemption to May 1, 1935, [provided that appellees make monthly payments equal to the reasonable rental value of the property to appellant.] It is this judgment, sustained by the Supreme Court of the State on the authority of its former opinion, which is here under review. 189 Minn. 448.

The state court upheld the statute as an emergency measure. Although conceding that the obligations of the mortgage contract were impaired, the court decided that what it thus described as an impairment was, notwithstanding the contract clause of the Federal Constitution, within the police power of the State as that power was called into exercise by the public economic emergency which the legislature had found to exist. Attention is thus directed to the preamble and first section of the statute, which described the existing emergency in terms that were deemed to justify the temporary relief which the statute affords. The state court, declaring that it could not say that this legislative finding was without basis, supplemented that finding by its own statement of conditions of which it took judicial notice. . . .

In determining whether the provision for this temporary and conditional relief exceeds the power of the State by reason of the clause in the Federal Constitution prohibiting impairment of the obligations of contracts, we must consider the relation of emergency to constitutional power, the historical setting of the contract clause, the development of the jurisprudence of this Court in the construction of that clause, and the principles of construction which we may consider to be established.

Emergency does not create power. Emergency does not increase granted power or remove or diminish the restrictions imposed upon power granted or reserved. The Constitution was adopted in a period of grave emergency. Its grants of power to the Federal Government and its limitations of the power of the States were determined in the light of emergency and they are not altered by emergency. What power was thus granted and what limitations were thus imposed are questions which have always been, and always will be, the subject of close examination under our constitutional system. . . .

. . . The occasion and general purpose of the contract clause are summed up in the terse statement of Chief Justice Marshall in Ogden v. Saunders, 12 Wheat. pp. 213, 354, 355: "The power of changing the relative situation of debtor and creditor, of interfering with contracts, a power which comes home to every man, touches the interest of all, and controls the conduct of every individual in those things which he supposes to be proper for his own exclusive management, had been used to such an excess by the state legislatures, as to break in upon the ordinary intercourse of society, and destroy all confidence between man and man. This mischief had become so great, so alarming, as not only to impair commercial intercourse, and threaten the existence of credit, but to sap the morals of the people, and destroy the sanctity of private faith. To guard against the continuance of the evil was an object of deep interest with all the truly wise, as well as the virtuous, of this great community, and was one of the important benefits expected from a reform of the government."

. . . To ascertain the scope of the constitutional prohibition we examine the course of judicial decisions in its application. These put it beyond question that the prohibition is not an absolute one and is not to be read with literal exactness like a mathematical formula. . . .

The obligation of a contract is "the law which binds the parties to perform their agreement." Sturges v. Crowninshield, 4 Wheat. 122, 197; Story, On the Constitution, §1378. This Court has said that "the laws which subsist at the time and place of the making of a contract, and where it is to be performed, enter into and form a part of it, as if they were expressly referred to or incorporated in its terms. This principle embraces alike those which affect its validity, construction, discharge and enforcement. . . . Nothing can be more material to the obligation than the means of enforcement. . . . The ideas of validity and remedy are inseparable, and both are parts of the obligation, which is guaranteed by the Constitution against invasion." Von Hoffman v. City of Quincy, 4 Wall. 535, 550, 552. See, also, Walker v. Whitehead, 16 Wall. 314, 317. But this broad language cannot be taken without qualification. Chief Justice Marshall pointed out the distinction between obligation and remedy. Sturges v. Crowninshield, supra, p. 200. Said he: "The distinction between the obligation of a contract, and the remedy given by the legislature to enforce that obligation, has been taken at the bar, and exists in the nature of things. Without impairing the obligation of the contract, the remedy may certainly be modified as the wisdom of the nation shall direct." . . .

The obligations of a contract are impaired by a law which renders them invalid, or releases or extinguishes them (Sturges v. Crowninshield, supra, pp. 197, 198) and impairment, as above noted, has been predicated of laws which without destroying contracts derogate from substantial contractual rights. In Sturges v. Crowninshield, supra, a state insolvent law, which discharged the debtor from liability was held to be invalid as applied to contracts in existence when the law was passed. [The Court reviewed various early cases finding a violation of the contract clause.]

None of these cases, and we have cited those upon which appellant chiefly relies, is directly applicable to the question now before us in view of the condition with which the Minnesota statute seeks to safeguard the interests of the mortgagee-purchaser during the extended period. . . .

Not only is the constitutional provision qualified by the measure of control which the State retains over remedial processes, but the State also continues to possess authority to safeguard the vital interests of its people. It does not matter that legislation appropriate to that end "has the result of modifying or abrogating contracts already in effect." Stephenson v. Binford, 287 U.S. 251, 276. Not only are existing laws read into contracts in order to fix obligations as between the parties, but the reservation of essential attributes of sovereign power is also read into contracts as a postulate of the legal order. The policy of protecting contracts against impairment pre-supposes the maintenance of a government by virtue of which contractual relations are worth while, — a government which retains adequate authority to secure the peace and good order of society. This principle of harmonizing the constitutional prohibition with the necessary residuum of state power has had progressive recognition in the decisions of this Court.

[The Court reviewed various cases sustaining state power against contract clause challenges, e.g., Charles River Bridge v. Warren Bridge, 11 Pet. 420 (1837).]

The argument is pressed that in the cases we have cited the obligation of contracts was affected only incidentally. This argument proceeds upon a misconception. The question is not whether the legislative action affects contracts incidentally, or directly or indirectly, but whether the legislation is addressed to a legitimate end and the measures taken are reasonable and appropriate to that end. Another argument, which comes more closely to the point, is that the state power may be addressed directly to the prevention of the enforcement of contracts only when these are of a sort which the legislature in its discretion may denounce as being in themselves hostile to public morals, or public health, safety or welfare, or where the prohibition is merely of injurious practices; that interference with the enforcement of other and valid contracts according to appropriate legal procedure, although the interference is temporary and for a public purpose, is not permissible. This is but to contend that in the latter case the end is not legitimate in the view that it cannot be reconciled with a fair interpretation of the constitutional provision.

Undoubtedly, whatever is reserved of state power must be consistent with the fair intent of the constitutional limitation of that power. The reserved power cannot be construed so as to destroy the limitation, nor is the limitation to be construed to destroy the reserved power in its essential aspects. They must be contrued in harmony with each other. This principle precludes a construction which would permit the State to adopt as its policy the repudiation of debts or the destruction of contracts or the denial of means to enforce them. But it does not follow that conditions may not arise in which a temporary restraint of enforcement may be consistent with the spirit and purpose of the constitutional provision and thus be found to be within the range of the reserved power of the State to protect the vital interests of the community. It cannot be maintained that the constitutional prohibition should be so construed as to prevent limited and temporary interpositions with respect to the enforcement of contracts if made necessary by a great public calamity such as fire, flood, or earthquake. See American Land Co. v. Zeiss, 219 U.S. 47. The reservation of state power appropriate to such extraordinary conditions may be deemed to be as much a part of all contracts, as is the reservation of state power to protect the public interest in the other situations to which we have referred. And if state power exists to give temporary relief from the enforcement of contracts in the presence of disasters due to physical causes such as fire, flood or earthquake, that power cannot be said to be non-existent when the urgent public need demanding such relief is produced by other and economic causes.

Whatever doubt there may have been that the protective power of the State, its police power, may be exercised — without violating the true intent of the provision of the Federal Constitution — in directly preventing the immediate and literal enforcement of contractual obligations, by a temporary and conditional restraint, where vital public interests would otherwise suffer, was removed by our decisions relating to the enforcement of provisions of leases during a period of scarcity of housing. Block v. Hirsh, 256 U.S. 135. . . .

It is manifest from this review of our decisions that there has been a growing appreciation of public needs and of the necessity of finding ground for a rational compromise between individual rights and public welfare. The settlement and consequent contraction of the public domain, the pressure of a constantly increasing density of population, the interrelation of the activities of our people and the complexity of our economic interests, have inevitably led to an increased use of the organization of society in order to protect the very bases of individual opportunity. Where, in earlier days, it was thought that only the concerns of individuals or of classes were involved and that those of the State itself were touched only remotely, it has later been found that the fundamental interests of the State are directly affected; and that the question is no longer merely that of one party to a contract as against another, but of the use of reasonable means to safeguard the economic structure upon which the good of all depends.

It is no answer to say that this public need was not apprehended a century ago, or to insist that what the provision of the Constitution meant to the vision of that day it must mean to the vision of our time. If by the statement that what the Constitution meant at the time of its adoption it means to-day, it is intended to say that the great clauses of the Constitution must be confined to the interpretation which the framers, with the conditions and outlook of their time, would have placed upon them, the statement carries its own refutation. It was to guard against such a narrow conception that Chief Justice Marshall uttered the memorable warning — "We must never forget that it is a *constitution* we are expounding" (McCulloch v. Maryland, 4 Wheat. 316, 407) — "a constitution intended to endure for ages to come, and consequently, to be adapted to the various *crises* of human affairs." Id., p. 415. . . .

. . . With a growing recognition of public needs and the relation of individual right to public security, the court has sought to prevent the perversion of the clause through its use as an instrument to throttle the capacity of the States to protect their fundamental interests. This development is a growth from the seeds which the fathers planted. . . .

Applying the criteria established by our decisions we conclude:

1. An emergency existed in Minnesota which furnished a proper occasion for the exercise of the reserved power of the State to protect the vital interests of the community. . . .

2. The legislation was addressed to a legitimate end, that is, the legislation was not for the mere advantage of particular individuals but for the protection of a basic interest of society.

3. In view of the nature of the contracts in question — mortgages of unquestionable validity — the relief afforded and justified by the emergency, in order not to contravene the constitutional provision, could only be of a character appropriate to that emergency and could be granted only upon reasonable conditions.

4. The conditions upon which the period of redemption is extended do not appear to be unreasonable. The initial extension of the time of redemption for thirty days from the approval of the Act was obviously to give a reasonable opportunity for the authorized application to the court. As already noted, the integrity of the mortgage indebtedness is not impaired. . . .

5. The legislation is temporary in operation. It is limited to the exigency which called it forth. While the postponement of the period of redemption from the foreclosure sales is to May 1, 1935, that period may be reduced by the order of the court under the statute, in a case of a change in circumstances, and the operation of the statute itself could not validly outlast the emergency or be so extended as virtually to destroy the contracts.

We are of the opinion that the Minnesota statute as here applied does not violate the contract clause of the Federal Constitution. Whether the legislation is wise or unwise as a matter of policy is a question with which we are not concerned.

What has been said on that point is also applicable to the contention presented under the due process clause. Block v. Hirsh, supra.

Nor do we think that the statute denies to the appellant the equal protection of the laws. The classification which the statute makes cannot be said to be an arbitrary one. Magoun v. Illinois Trust & Savings Bank, 170 U.S. 283; Clark v. Titusville, 184 U.S. 329; Quong Wing v. Kirkendall, 223 U.S. 59; Ohio Oil Co. v. Conway, 281 U.S. 146; Sproles v. Binford, 286 U.S. 374.

The judgment of the Supreme Court of Minnesota is affirmed.

Mr. Justice Sutherland, dissenting. . . .

A provision of the Constitution, it is hardly necessary to say, does not admit of two distinctly opposite interpretations. It does not mean one thing at one time and an entirely different thing at another time. If the contract impairment clause, when framed and adopted, meant that the terms of a contract for the payment of money could not be altered in invitum by a state statute enacted for the relief of hardly pressed debtors to the end and with the effect of postponing payment or enforcement during and because of an economic or financial emergency, it is but to state the obvious to say that it means the same now. This view, at once so rational in its application to the written word, and so necessary to the stability of constitutional principles, though from time to time challenged, has never, unless recently, been put within the realm of doubt by the decisions of this court. . . .

The whole aim of construction, as applied to a provision of the Constitution, is to discover the meaning, to ascertain and give effect to the intent, of its framers and the people who adopted it. . . .

The present exigency is nothing new. From the beginning of our existence as a nation, periods of depression, of industrial failure, of financial distress, of unpaid and unpayable indebtedness, have alternated with years of plenty. The vital lesson that expenditure beyond income begets poverty, that public or private extravagance, financed by promises to pay, either must end in complete or partial repudiation or the promises be fulfilled by self-denial and painful effort, though constantly taught by bitter experience, seems never to be learned; and the attempt by legislative devices to shift the misfortune of the debtor to the shoulders of the creditor without coming into conflict with the contract impairment clause has been persistent and oft-repeated.

The defense of the Minnesota law is made upon grounds which were discountenanced by the makers of the Constitution and have many times been rejected by this court. That defense should not now succeed, because it constitutes an effort to overthrow the constitutional provision by an appeal to facts and circumstances identical with those which brought it into existence. With due regard for the processes of logical thinking, it legitimately cannot be urged that conditions which produced the rule may now be invoked to destroy it. . . .

The Minnesota statute either impairs the obligation of contracts or it does not. If it does not, the occasion to which it relates becomes immaterial, since then the passage of the statute is the exercise of a normal, unrestricted, state power and requires no special occasion to render it effective. If it does, the emergency no more furnishes a proper occasion for its exercise than if the emergency were non-existent. And so, while, in form, the suggested distinction seems to put us forward in a straight line, in reality it simply carries us back in a circle, like bewildered travelers lost in a wood, to the point where we parted company with the view of the state court.

If what has now been said is sound, as I think it is, we come to what really is the vital question in the case: Does the Minnesota statute constitute an impairment of the obligation of the contract now under review?

It is quite true also that "the reservation of essential attributes of sovereign power is also read into contracts"; and that the legislature cannot "bargain away the public health or the public morals." General statutes to put an end to lotteries, the sale or manufacture of intoxicating liquors, the maintenance of nuisances, to protect the public safety, etc., although they have the indirect effect of absolutely destroying private contracts previously made in contemplation of a continuance of the state of affairs then in existence but subsequently prohibited, have been uniformly upheld as not violating the contract impairment clause. The distinction between legislation of that character and the Minnesota statute, however, is readily observable. . . .

The rent cases — Block v. Hirsh, 256 U.S. 135; Marcus Brown Co. v. Feldman, 256 U.S. 170; Levy Leasing Co. v. Siegel, 258 U.S. 242 — which are here relied upon, dealt with an exigent situation due to a period of scarcity of housing caused by the war. I do not stop to consider the distinctions between them and the present case or to do more than point out that the question of contract impairment received little, if any, more than casual consideration. The writer of the opinions in the first two cases, speaking for this court in a later case, Pennsylvania Coal Co. v. Mahon, 250 U.S. 393, 416, characterized all of them as having gone "to the verge of the law." . . .

We come back, then, directly, to the question of impairment. As to that, the conclusion reached by the court here seems to be that the relief afforded by the statute does not contravene the constitutional provision because it is of a character appropriate to the emergency and allowed upon what are said to be reasonable conditions. . . .

... Assuming for the moment, that a statute extending the period of redemption may be upheld if something of commensurate value be given the creditor by way of compensation, a conclusion that payment of the rental value during the two years' period of postponement is even the approximate equivalent of immediate ownership and possessions is purely gratuitous. How can such payment be regarded, in any sense, as compensation for the postponement of the contract right? The ownership of the property to which petitioner was entitled carried with it not only the right to occupy or sell it, but, ownership being retained, the right to the rental value as well. So that in the last analysis petitioner simply is allowed to retain a part of what is its own as compensation for surrendering the remainder. Moreover, it cannot be foreseen what will happen to the property during that long period of time. The buildings may deteriorate in quality; the value of the property may fall to a sum far below the purchase price; the financial needs of appellant may become so pressing as to render it urgently necessary that the property shall be sold for whatever it may bring.

However these or other supposable contingencies may be, the statute denies appellant for a period of two years the ownership and possession of the property — an asset which, in any event, is of substantial character, and which possibly may turn out to be of great value. The statute, therefore, is not merely a modification of the remedy; it effects a material and injurious change in the obligation. . . .

I am authorized to say that MR. JUSTICE VAN DEVANTER, MR. JUSTICE MCREYNOLDS and MR. JUSTICE BUTLER concur in this opinion.

NOTE Results of Blaisdell

"Chief Justice Hughes, the author of Blaisdell, later reiterated and emphasized that that case had upheld only a temporary restraint which provided for compensation, when four months later he spoke for the Court in striking down a law which did not. W. B. Worthen Co. v. Thomas, 292 U.S. 426. Other state laws which did not meet the constitutional standard applied in Blaisdell were subsequently struck down. See, e.g., W. B. Worthen Co. v. Kavanaugh, 295 U.S. 56; Treigle v. Acme Homestead Assn., 297 U.S. 189; Wood v. Lovett, 313 U.S. 362." Black, J., dissenting in El Paso v. Simmons, 379 U.S. 497, 526 (1965). In the Simmons case, public land in Texas was sold under a law which entitled a purchaser in default on interest payments to reinstate his claim, after forfeiture, by payment of accrued interest, provided no rights of third parties had intervened. Thereafter the law was amended to limit reinstatement rights to five years after forfeiture. The Supreme Court sustained the statute, over the sole dissent of Mr. Justice Black, who would have applied the obligation of contracts clause more literally. But compare his dissent in Wood v. Lovett, supra. Is his position in the Simmons case consistent with his constitutional philosophy in other fields? See Freund, Mr. Justice Black and the Judicial Function, 14 U.C.L.A.L. Rev. 407 (1967).

Norman v. Baltimore & Ohio R.R. 294 U.S. 240, 55 S. Ct. 407, 79 L. Ed. 885 (1935)

[For the opinion in this case see page 310 supra.]

Perry v. United States 294 U.S. 330, 55 S. Ct. 432, 79 L. Ed. 912 (1935)

[For the opinion in this case see page 317 supra.]

FAITOUTE IRON & STEEL CO. v. CITY OF ASBURY PARK, 316 U.S. 502, 62 S. Ct. 1129, 86 L. Ed. 1629 (1942). Frankfurter, J.: "A New Jersey statute, adopted in 1931, authorized state control over insolvent municipalities. By a supplementary law, enacted in 1933, a plan for adjustment of the claims of creditors of such an insolvent municipality could be made binding upon all creditors. The question is whether an adjustment so authorized by a state impairs rights in violation of the Constitution of the United States.

"The City of Asbury Park is a seashore resort with a resident population of 15,000. It presents a familiar picture of optimistic and extravagant municipal expansion caught in the destructive grip of general economic depression: elaborate beachfront improvements, costs in excess of estimates, deficits not annually met by taxation, declining real-estate values, inability to refinance a disproportionately heavy load of short-term obligations, and, inevitably, default. Accordingly, in January, 1935, availing themselves of the New Jersey Municipal Finance Act, creditors applied to the Supreme Court of New Jersey to place the state Municipal Finance Commission in control of the city's finances.

[After approval was secured from the New Jersey Court, the commission, and the creditors, the plan for refunding the city's obligations was put into operation in 1938.]

"The appellants were holders of defaulted bonds and interest coupons issued by the City of Asbury Park in 1929 and 1930 — prior, therefore, to the legislation which authorized the proceedings resulting in the challenged refunding scheme. The bonds of the appellants were part of the $10,750,000 of refunded bonds which, under the adjustment decreed by the court, could only be converted into new bonds maturing in 1966 and bearing a lower rate of interest than the original bonds. Deeming the arrangement authorized under the New Jersey statute to be violative of the Constitution of the United States, the appellants brought this suit for the face value of the old bonds and coupons. . . .

"The real constitutional question is whether the Contract Clause of the Constitution bars the only proven way for assuring payment of unsecured municipal obligations. For, in the light of history, and more particularly on the basis of the recommendations of its expert advisers, the New Jersey legislature was entitled to find that in order to keep its insolvent municipalities going, and at the same time fructify their languishing sources of revenue and thus avoid repudiation, fair and just arrangements by way of compositions, scrutinized and authorized by a court, might be necessary, and that to be efficacious such a composition must bind all, after 85 per cent of the creditors assent, in order to prevent unreasonable minority obstruction. As the court below pointed out, in view of the slump of the credit of the City of Asbury Park before the adoption of the plan now assailed, appellants' bonds had little value; the new bonds issued under the plan, however, are not in default and there is a very substantial market for them. The refunding scheme, as part of a comprehensive plan for salvaging Asbury Park, both governmentally and financially, was so successful that the refunding bonds were selling at around 69 at the time of refunding, while at about the time the present suit was brought commanded a market at better than 90. See Second Annual Report of the New Jersey Local Government Board, 1940, p. 39.

". . . To call a law so beneficent in its consequences on behalf of the creditor who, having had so much restored to him, now insists on standing on the paper rights that were merely paper before this resuscitating scheme, an impairment of the obligation of contract is indeed to make of the Constitution a code of lifeless forms instead of an enduring framework of government for a dynamic society. . . ."

See also East New York Savings Bank v. Hahn, 326 U.S. 230 (1945). See generally Hale, The Supreme Court and the Contract Clause, 57 Harv. L. Rev. 512 (1944).

In Flushing Natl. Bank v. Municipal Assistance Corp., 40 N.Y.2d 731, 358 N.E.2d 848 (1976), a 3-year statutory moratorium on payment of the principal of New York City short-term notes was held invalid under the state constitutional provision requiring a pledge of the city's "faith and credit." A dissenting opinion, finding this ground unpersuasive, would have sustained the statute as a crisis measure under the federal decisions interpreting the obligation of contract clause.

Addison v. Huron Stevedoring Corp. 204 F.2d 88 (2d Cir.), cert. denied, 346 U.S. 877 (1953)

[Swan, Chief Judge, thus stated the matters in issue: "The plaintiffs were employed under a collective bargaining contract between their employers and a longshoremen's union which provided 'straight time hourly rates' for work done within prescribed hours and 'overtime hourly rates' for work done outside the straight time hours, with no differential for work in excess of 40 hours per week. The longshoremen worked a varying and irregular number of hours throughout a given workweek, and the same man's workweek might consist of work done partly at 'straight time hourly rates' and partly at 'overtime hourly rates.' The problem of determining the 'regular rate' of pay upon which the excess statutory compensation required by section 7(a) of the Fair Labor Standards Act of 1938 is based was settled by the Supreme Court in the Bay Ridge Case [Bay Ridge Operating Co. v. Aaron, 334 U.S. 446]. It was there held that what the collective bargaining contract called 'overtime hourly rates,' was really a 'shift differential'; and that the 'regular rate' was to be found by dividing the weekly compensation by the hours worked, unless compensation paid contains some amount that represents an 'overtime premium' which was defined as 'extra pay for work *because* of previous work for a specified number of hours in the workweek or workday' (italics added); in that event any overtime premium paid may be credited against the obligation to pay statutory excess compensation. The trial now before us for review was had under the mandate of the Supreme Court permitting the District Court to consider any defense which the employers may have under the Portal to Portal Act and to allow any amendments to the complaint or answer or any further evidence that the court may consider just. During the course of the trial defenses based on further amendment of the Fair Labor Standards Act were allowed to be pleaded."[a] Chief Judge Swan then delivered an opinion for the Court sustaining the decision of Judge Leibell that the Portal to Portal Act and the "Overtime on Overtime" statute could validly be given effect to bar the claims founded on the Bay Ridge interpretation of the contract. The following concurring and dissenting opinions were delivered in the court of appeals.]

L. HAND, Circuit Judge (concurring).

I concur in Judge Swan's opinion, but I am not entirely satisfied with the grounds on which we rested the constitutionality of the Portal to Portal Act in Battaglia v. General Motors Company [169 F.2d 254]. It is true that there is language in some of the cases that appears to hold that in exercising its power to regulate interstate commerce Congress is more free of the Fifth Amendment than it is as to others of its powers; but I do not believe that in the end this will prove a tenable distinction; and, although I should have felt bound to accept our decision, even if I had not agreed with it, I think it not improper to give my reasons for independently reaching the same result. Several times before 1947 the Supreme Court[3] had so interpreted the Fair Labor Standards Act that Congress in that year declared the result to be a "disregard of long-established customs, practices, and contracts between employers and employees, thereby creating wholly unexpected liabilities, immense in amount and retroactive in operation, upon employers with the results that, if said Act, as so interpreted or claims arising under such interpretations, were permitted to stand," inconveniences, and indeed public disasters, would ensue that were described in the ten specific items that followed. This declaration was a preamble of the kind that has reappeared in recent times; its function now is to justify constitutionally a statute that without it might lack adequate support. When made after adequate hearings and upon

---

[a] These amendments (29 U.S.C.A. §207(d)(5), (d)(6), (d)(7), and (g)) redefined words used in the Fair Labor Standards Act so as to excuse all employers who in good faith had not supposed that the collective agreement required the payment of overtime on overtime from making such payments under existing contracts. — ED.

[3] Tennessee Coal, Iron & Railroad Co. v. Muscoda Local, 321 U.S. 590; Jewell Ridge Coal Corp. v. Local 6167, 325 U.S. 161; Anderson v. Mt. Clemens Pottery Co., 328 U.S. 680.

timely notice to all who might choose to appear, such "a declaration by a legislature concerning public conditions that by necessity and duty it must know, is entitled at least to great respect";[4] though apparently it is not conclusive, for any party to an action may challenge it. The curious consequences of such a challenge Taney, C.J., set forth at length in Luther v. Borden, 7 How. 1, 41, 42, though he found it unnecessary to decide the point, because the controversy was within that nebulous field, called "political," which courts will not enter. The embarrassments that would necessarily attend a judicial trial of the facts in the declaration at bar — particularly if the trial were to a jury, as Taney, C.J. supposed — would be no less than those in Luther v. Borden; and indeed they might be greater, if we consider the scope of the inquiry and the kind of evidence that Congress accepts and must needs accept, if it is to proceed at all. Happily, in the case at bar we are not faced with that difficulty, and may accept the declaration as it reads, for the plaintiffs put in no evidence to disprove it. If the facts declared be taken as data, the validity of the Act and its later amendments depends upon whether the occasion permitted Congress to release the defendants from a part, though only a small part, of the performance to which their contracts bound them.

The plaintiffs performed all their services between October 15, 1943, and September 30, 1945, at a time when the Supreme Court had not answered the precise question now before us: i.e. whether "overtime" in the Act meant something different from "overtime" as the parties understood it. It is quite true that in March, 1944, the Court had declared in another connection that the customary and accepted construction of the parties should not prevail; but this did not appear to everyone to be conclusive as to "overtime"; and before October 15, 1943, a conflict had arisen between the rulings of governmental "agencies," so that an employer who wished to proceed had to choose at his peril which ruling to follow. It does not appear how far the plaintiffs at bar were aware of these divergent interpretations, although the longshoremen's union was fully advised of them; but certainly we should have no warrant for supposing that, as individuals, they relied upon the interpretations that finally prevailed. The existence of these doubts about pay for "overtime," did not, of course, affect the plaintiffs' right to all that was eventually determined to be due, and I agree that that right was "vested" in every sense of that word. However, it is another matter whether the uncertainty that had prevailed and the unexpectedness of the new liabilities were irrelevant upon whether the Act was constitutional.

As I view it, two questions arise: (1) whether it was unconstitutional because it took the plaintiffs' "property for public use without just compensation"; and (2) whether it "deprived" them of property "without due process of law." I agree that a contract is "property" within the meaning of both clauses;[6] and I shall assume arguendo that the first command is unconditional, so that the Act would have been invalid, if it had attempted to release the defendants from any payment whatever for the plaintiffs' work.[7] In short, I shall assume — though I should hesitate before so holding — that no "public use" can be so urgent as to justify "taking" property without "just compensation." On that hypothesis the first of the two questions I have raised, comes down to whether the Act "took" the plaintiffs' contracts. It has been several times declared that to constitute a "taking" something must be "transferred" to the "taker";[8] and it could be argued that even completely to release the employers from their obligations would not "transfer" anything from their employees to them. That appears to me an extremely narrow view, and I shall assume that the situation was the same as though the payments, from which the employers were released, were "transferred" to them. What I rest on is that a release from a part of their

---

[4] Block v. Hirsh, 256 U.S. 135, 154.
[6] Omnia Commercial Co., Inc. v. United States, 261 U.S. 502, 508.
[7] Cities Service Co. v. McGrath, 342 U.S. 330, 334, 335, 336.
[8] Mitchell v. United States, 267 U.S. 341; United States ex rel. Tennessee Valley Authority v. Powelson, 319 U.S. 266; United States v. Petty Motor Company, 327 U.S. 372; Kimball Laundry Co. v. United States, 338 U.S. 1, 5.

obligations, unlike a release from all of it, was not a "taking" at all. If we were dealing in verbal dialectics, I agree that it would be hard to defend such a distinction, but we are not; we are dealing with a constitutional limitation, and there is no surer way to misapprehend its scope than to ignore its history, and treat it as inspired text. This clause in its origin forbade the seizure of tangible property — land or chattels — by which the owner lost the whole enjoyment of what he had possessed; and it was later extended to intangible property by analogy, for otherwise the fundamental purpose of the original would not have been fully realized. On the other hand it has never been extended to every diminution of an owner's enjoyment of his property. True, the law protects all the uses to which "property" can be put; the word is, indeed, a compendium: the sum of them. But to deprive the owner of a part of these uses is not to "take" his property; it is a question of degree, like so much else in law. If this were not so, no enforced compromise between the claims of two groups of persons would ever be valid without "compensating" whoever suffered any impairment of the enjoyment of his property; and that would mean that a right, once "vested," could never be circumscribed, no matter how much it might stand in the path of the public interest. The Supreme Court has many times declared the contrary. The Portal to Portal Act was of their kind; it did not "take" from the plaintiffs all that they had earned for statutory overtime, though it did take a part. So much for the first point.

The second is vaguer in its outlines, since it concerns the validity of Congress's preference of the public interest — including the employers' — over the employees'. Frequently — usually indeed — when a court seeks for some reason to defend such a legislative choice, it says that the statute will stand, unless the choice was "arbitrary," "oppressive," "capricious," or "unreasonable." That obviously conceals what the court is doing, although, so far as I can see, uncertainty is inherent in the situation. . . .

In the case at bar I am not aware of any disinterested opinion in this country that would find the choice made abhorrent to prevailing standards of "justice." On the one hand the plaintiffs do of course lose a part of what was theirs; but as to any who knew nothing about the contradictory interpretations and who were working under the old terms, to deprive them of their windfall would not, I believe, be deemed a serious grievance. As to those who knew of the contradictory interpretations of "overtime," so far as they were working for more than they were getting it was on a chance, and they have no more ground for complaint than any other loser on a chance, deliberately accepted. Moreover all were getting what had sufficed to keep them on their jobs throughout the period. Against their disappointment Congress had to weigh the loss of the employers who had in good faith relied upon a ruling favorable to them. True, they too had taken a chance, and, like the last class of employees, they had no greater complaint; but at least their interest matched that of the employees. With the opposed interests so nearly in balance, it seems to me, not only that Congress was free to make controlling the indirect effects of the new and unexpected reading of the Fair Labor Standards Act, but that it would have been most recreant in its responsibilities, if it had not done so. I trust I do not undervalue the importance of not disturbing "vested" rights; but the pith and kernel of our well-founded reluctance to do so is because otherwise the hopes of their possessors will be disappointed and they will be unable pro tanto to plan their future. I do not believe that that is so imperious an interest as of itself to justify sacrifices of the general interest, no matter how grave; and, in the case of an assurance so contingent and doubtful as was any that these plaintiffs could have had, it would have been shocking to allow the retention of their bonanzas to bring about the evils described in the declaration. For these reasons I think the Act was constitutional.

FRANK, Circuit Judge (dissenting in part).

I agree with my colleagues that the retroactive features of the 1947 Portal-to-Portal Act are valid. I disagree, however, as to the constitutionality of the retroactive aspects of the 1949 and 1950 statutes. . . .

The constitutional question, as to the 1949 and 1950 statutes, is this: Can the United States, after the Supreme Court has decided that it owes large sums to some of its citizens, resort to retroactive legislation to destroy the right to those sums, in the absence of some justifying major social need: Is the doctrine of Lynch v. United States, 292 U.S. 571, extinct?

That the destruction of such a right against the United States was the purpose of these statutes can scarcely be doubted. For everyone agrees that anything which the titular defendants here seemingly owed plaintiffs was, for all practical purposes, actually owed by the United States, under its cost-plus contracts with those defendants. In everything but form, then, the United States is the actual defendant. For that reason, the Attorney General of the United States has conducted the defense of this litigation from its inception. That there was no paramount social need to justify the 1949 and 1950 statutes I shall try to show.

1. After the Supreme Court in Bay Ridge Operating Co., Inc. v. Aaron, 1948, 334 U.S. 446, had held that these plaintiffs, under the Fair Labor Standards Act, were entitled to so-called "clock overtime" for work done during the years 1943-1945, Congress — as a result of urging primarily from the Attorney General — enacted the 1949 and 1950 amendments, which were avowedly designed to wipe out those rights (as well as similar rights of other employees not parties to these suits). Relative to retroactivity, those amendatory statutes were significantly different from the Portal-to-Portal Act, enacted in 1947. In 1948, in litigation not involving these plaintiffs, this court, in two decisions, held constitutional the retroactive features of the Portal-to-Portal Act.[2] That Act cancelled rights that had already accrued to employees under the Fair Labor Standards Act — as construed in Anderson v. Mt. Clemens Pottery Co., 328 U.S. 680 — for overtime compensation and liquidated damages, due for time spent upon an employer's premises preliminary to, or after engagement in, the principal activities of the employees. Stating that, thanks to decisions like Ettor v. City of Tacoma, 228 U.S. 148, such retroactive legislation, cutting off consummated statutory rights, would have been invalid if enacted by a State, this court sustained this Act (1) because Congress had enacted it "in the exercise of its commerce power," and (2) because of the grave nationwide emergency (as recited in the preamble of that Act) created by the Mt. Clemens decision. Those decisions I think correct. Judicial notice supports the legislative recitals as to that emergency: The Supreme Court's interpretation did give rise to liabilities which were "wholly unexpected," and "immense in amount," and which therefore, on a nation-wide scale, might well "bring about financial ruin of many employers and seriously impair the capital resources of many others." For doubtless thousands of employers, not on any notice that the Fair Labor Standards Act would be so interpreted, had set aside no reserves and had not otherwise so conducted themselves as to be able to meet these unanticipated liabilities.

2. Vastly different is the background (nowhere mentioned by my colleagues) of the 1949 and 1950 amendatory statutes which are deliberately intended to expunge the Supreme Court's Bay Ridge ruling. Neither of these statutes contains a recital or legislative declaration of any emergency. True, the Senate Committee Report on the 1949 legislation does purport to describe a financial emergency affecting some employers. . . .

But I think the Senate Committee Report, with its recital of a financial emergency, cannot be considered as a substitute for a Congressional declaration in the face of the fact that the House Committee Report (1) is utterly silent as to any financial difficulties of employers due to liabilities under the Supreme Court's Bay Ridge interpretation of the Fair Labor Standards Act, and (2) states merely the following as occasioning the need for the amendatory statute: "The Committee has heard testimony of representatives of labor, management, and the Department of Labor, all of whom are in agreement that the present law, in circumstances such as those considered by the Supreme Court in the Bay Ridge case, is creating serious difficulty in maintenance of desirable labor standards arrived at through collective bargaining in the longshore, stevedoring, building and con-

---

[2] Battaglia v. General Motors Corp., 2 Cir., 169 F.2d 254; Darr v. Mutual Life Insurance Co., 2 Cir., 169 F.2d 262.

struction industries, and that the amendment of the Act to correct this situation is urgently necessary in order to prevent labor disputes which would seriously burden and obstruct commerce. The potential effects of the present overtime requirements on these types of agreements were demonstrated in the negotiations of a new contract for the east coast longshore industry in the fall of 1948. The inability of the parties to agree on a substitute for their traditional work pattern was an obstacle to settling a crippling strike. The anticipation of prompt legislative action to remedy this situation was one of the factors inducing settlement." So the House Committee gave as explanation nothing but factors looking to the future; it said nothing to support retroactivity. In these circumstances, I think this retroactive legislation finds no support in any emergency.

3. I assume that the concept of substantive due process still has some vitality, and that the doctrine of Ettor v. Tacoma, 228 U.S. 148,[13] applies to the federal legislature, so that the 1949 and 1950 statutes were invalid in confiscating "vested rights" unless justified by a sufficiently grave social crisis. But what constitutes a sufficiently grave social crisis to meet this test presents a difficult problem. In the last analysis, the courts must give the answer, but always with marked respect to the legislature. A decision, however, like that of this court in this case — refusing to nullify a confiscatory statute when no real crisis exists — justifies future legislation that will endanger the sort of society which the great majority of our people cherish. It puts in jeopardy all so-called "vested rights." . . .

. . . Whether, outside the field of major civil rights, there are fundamentals which, short of constitutional amendments, remain legally unalterable no matter what the alterations in basic social attitudes, need not here be considered. For I am satisfied that today the overwhelming majority of our citizens, if they clearly comprehended the significance for the future of the decision here, would be deeply disturbed. Business men, if well advised, will not shrug it off as one affecting wage-earners only; for the rationale of this decision is far broader. A mere declaration of emergency in a Committee Report becomes by this decision virtually the only necessary basis for a drastic attack on "property" rights. And debts owing (directly or indirectly) from the government can thus neatly be expunged by the government itself.

I grant that no clear-cut rules of constitutionality are possible. But the 1949 and 1950 statutes represent too gross an incursion on what I think the most modest notions of substantive constitutional limitations.

4. Absent an emergency, the sole asserted justification of this retroactive legislation is that it cut out rights which were but a "windfall." As constitutionality is made to hang on that word, its definition becomes important. The dictionary defines it as an "unexpected acquisition or advantage" or "an unexpected legacy or other gain." Judge Learned Hand, in his concurring opinion here, used it as meaning a right which one obtains either without being aware of it or when acting without reliance upon obtaining it. I take it, then, that we are to understand that if money comes due to a person without his knowledge, the mere fact of that ignorance converts his right to that money into a "windfall," with the consequence that the legislature may validly pass a statute eliminating that right.

Surely it cannot be sound doctrine that "vested rights" are thus vulnerable (i.e., if only the rightholders did not know of their rights when they "vested"), that due process insulates from legislative onslaughts only one's known rights. If that were true, our legislatures would not be restrained by the due process clause from rubbing out rights in any of the following illustrative instances: An heir is ignorant of a legacy; the beneficiary of a trust has not heard of the trust; a party to a contract thinks the other party owes him $1000 but,

---

[13] There the Court said, 228 U.S. at page 156: "The necessary effect of the repealing act, as construed and applied by the court below, was to deprive the plaintiffs in error of any remedy to enforce the fixed liability of the city to make compensation. This was to deprive the plaintiffs in error of a right which had vested before the repealing act — a right which was in every sense a property right. Nothing remained to be done to complete the plaintiffs' right to compensation except the ascertainment of the amount of damage to their property. The right of the plaintiffs in error was fixed by the law in force when their property was damaged for public purposes, and the right so vested cannot be defeated by subsequent legislation."

under judicial decisions of which he has not yet learned, the correct amount is $15,000. . . . Any such doctrine, if thoroughly understood, will shock most Americans. Particularly will it shock them when, as here, it is used by the United States to welsh on its own monetary obligations. . . .

NOTE Retroactive and Prospective Judicial Decisions

Where a change in judicial doctrine results in an abridgment of contractual rights as previously understood, the judicial change is not deemed to violate the terms of the obligation of contracts clause. Tidal Oil Co. v. Flanagan, 263 U.S. 444 (1924), explaining the celebrated case of Gelpcke v. Dubuque, 1 Wall. 175 (1864). But due process of law may be denied by a decision that so reinterprets procedural law as to take away all opportunity of the litigant to raise a constitutional claim. Brinkerhoff-Faris Trust & Savings Co. v. Hill, 281 U.S. 673 (1930); see also NAACP v. Alabama, 357 U.S. 449 (1958). Similarly, due process precludes the application of newly established standards of free expression, more restrictive of speech, to conduct occurring prior to the new judicial standards. Marks v. United States, 97 S. Ct. 990 (1977). The same case held that where new standards of protected speech are more favorable to the criminal defendant they must be applied retroactively in his trial.

The latter problem has engaged the Court in several recent cases. Where a constitutional right is recognized for the first time, the question is whether the courts *must* give retrospective effect to the decision, or may apply it in some sense "prospectively" only: to conduct occurring after the date of the new decision, or in trials so occurring; or in all cases on direct review, but in collateral attack on final judgments only where the trial occurred after the date of the new decision. The last course has been followed in several instances. "Considerations of fundamental fairness have led to the opening of final judgments in criminal cases when it has appeared that a conviction was achieved in violation of basic constitutional standards. Thus, in the decisions which have been applied retroactively, Gideon v. Wainwright, 372 U.S. 335, Douglas v. California, 372 U.S. 353, Griffin v. Illinois, 351 U.S. 12, and Jackson v. Denno, 378 U.S. 368, the Court concluded that the constitutional error perceived undermined 'the very integrity of the fact-finding process,' Linkletter v. Walker, 381 U.S. 618, 639, and the fundamental fairness of the resulting conviction. On the other hand, our decisions in Linkletter and Tehan v. United States ex rel. Shott, 382 U.S. 406, demonstrate that practices found to violate the Due Process Clause of the Fourteenth Amendment need not necessarily be applied to final convictions. The factors adverted to in those cases for determining whether a constitutional decision should be applied to final cases were the State's reliance on the conduct newly found unconstitutional, whether the purpose of the new rule would be served by fully retroactive effect, and the effect of retroactivity on the administration of justice." Warren, C.J., dissenting, in Spencer v. Texas, 385 U.S. 554 (1967). Compare Mishkin, The High Court, the Great Writ, and the Due Process of Time and Law, 79 Harv. L. Rev. 56 (1965). On "prospective" overruling in state courts see Leach, Divorce by Plane-Ticket in the Affluent Society — With a Side-Order of Jurisprudence, 14 Kan. L. Rev. 549 (1966).

Consider the form of "prospective" application adopted in Johnson v. New Jersey, 384 U.S. 719 (1966). The Court granted certiorari in five cases out of about a hundred on its docket, raising similar questions concerning pretrial interrogation and resulting confessions. In four of the five, the Court laid down new standards under the self-incrimination guarantee and reversed the convictions for failure to meet these standards. Miranda v. Arizona, 384 U.S. 436 (1966). A week later, in the fifth case (Johnson v. New Jersey), the Court ruled that the Miranda decision would not be applied in other cases on direct review, and would be enforced only in respect of trials occurring after the date of that decision. Accordingly the other petitions for certiorari in the group were denied. Does this disposition raise constitutional objections of its own? Could the Court have adopted a different course to obviate those objections and still have made an accommodation through "prospective" applications? See Note, 80 Harv. L. Rev. 91, 136-141 (1966). See also page 133 supra.

Post-Linkletter developments are described by Justice Harlan, dissenting in Desist v. United States, 394 U.S. 244, at 256 (1969), as follows:

"In the four short years since we embraced the notion that our constitutional decisions in criminal cases need not be retroactively applied, Linkletter v. Walker, 381 U.S. 618 (1965),[1] we have created an extraordinary collection of rules to govern the application of that principle. We have held that certain 'new' rules are to be applied to all cases then subject to direct review, Linkletter v. Walker, supra; Tehan v. Shott, 382 U.S. 406 (1966); certain others are to be applied to all those cases in which trials have not yet commenced, Johnson v. New Jersey, 384 U.S. 719 (1966); certain others are to be applied to all those cases in which the tainted evidence has not yet been introduced at trial, Fuller v. Alaska, 393 U.S. 80 (1968); and still others are to be applied only to the party involved in the case in which the new rule is announced and to all future cases in which the proscribed official conduct has not yet occurred. Stovall v. Denno, 388 U.S. 293 (1967); DeStefano v. Woods, 392 U.S. 631 (1968).

"Although it has more than once been said that 'new' rules affecting 'the very integrity of the fact-finding process,' are to be retroactively applied, Linkletter v. Walker, 381 U.S., 618, 639; see also Tehan v. Shott, 382 U.S., 406, 416; Fuller v. Alaska, 393 U.S., 80, 81, this requirement was eroded to some extent in Johnson v. New Jersey, 384 U.S., 719, 728-729, and yet further in Stovall v. Denno, 388 U.S., 293, 299; see also DeStefano v. Woods, supra. Again, although it has been said that a decision will be retroactively applied when it has been 'clearly foreshadowed' in our prior case law, Johnson v. New Jersey, supra, 731; Berger v. California, 393 U.S. 314 (1969), the Court today rejects such a contention. . . . Indeed, the Court now also departs from pre-existing doctrine in refusing retroactive application within the federal system of the 'new' rule ultimately laid down in Katz v. United States, 389 U.S. 347 (1967), despite its concession that 'relatively few' federal cases would have to be reconsidered. . . .

"I have in the past joined in some of those opinions which have, in so short a time, generated so many incompatible rules and inconsistent principles. I did so because I thought it important to limit the impact of constitutional decisions which seemed to me profoundly unsound in principle. I can no longer, however, remain content with the doctrinal confusion that has characterized our efforts to apply the basic Linkletter principle. 'Retroactivity' must be rethought."

Recent decisions holding earlier decisions retroactive are: Roberts v. Russell, 392 U.S. 293 (1968) (re Bruton v. United States, 391 U.S. 123); McConnell v. Rhay, 393 U.S. 2 (1968) (re Mempha v. Rhay, 389 U.S. 128); Arsenault v. Massachusetts, 393 U.S. 5 (1968) (re White v. Maryland, 373 U.S. 59); Berger v. California, 393 U.S. 314 (1969) (re Barber v. Page, 390 U.S. 719).

Recent decisions holding earlier decisions nonretroactive are: Stovall v. Denno, 388 U.S. 293 (1967) (re United States v. Wade, 388 U.S. 218, and Gilbert v. California, 388 U.S. 263); but cf. Foster v. California, 394 U.S. 440 (1969); DeStefano v. Woods, 392 U.S. 631 (1968) (re Duncan v. Louisiana, 391 U.S. 145, and Bloom v. Illinois, 391 U.S. 194); Fuller v. Alaska, 393 U.S. 80 (1968) (re Lee v. Florida, 392 U.S. 378); Desist v. United States, 394 U.S. 244 (1969) (re Katz v. United States, 389 U.S. 347); Hill v. California, 401 U.S. 797 (1971) (re Chimel v. California, 395 U.S. 752).

Compare United States v. United States Coin & Currency, 401 U.S. 715 (1971), holding Grosso v. United States, 390 U.S. 62, and Marchetti v. United States, 390 U.S. 394, retroactive in forfeiture proceedings, with Mackey v. United States, 401 U.S. 667 (1971), holding those decisions not retroactive in income tax evasion cases.

[1] In one instance this doctrine has been applied to a nonconstitutional decision. See Lee v. Florida, 392 U.S. 378 (1968), and its aftermath in Fuller v. Alaska, 393 U.S. 80 (1968).

Table of Cases

Italics indicate principal cases.

Abate v. Mundt, 972
Abington v. Schempp, 1370
Abrams v. United States, 1133
Action v. Gannon, 867
Adams v. Engley, 840
Adams v. Southern California First Natl. Bank, 841
Adams, J. D., Mfg. Co. v. Storen, 569
Adamson v. California, 996
Adderly v. Florida, 1199
Addison v. Huron Stevedoring Corp., 1395
Addyston Pipe & Steel Co. v. United States, 227
Adickes v. Kress & Co., 860
Adkins v. Children's Hospital, 132, 1089
Adler v. Board of Education, 122
Afroyim v. Rusk, 19, 741
Ahrens v. Clark, 717
Alabama v. King & Boozer, 629
Alberts v. California, 1285
Albertson v. SACB, 19
Alejandrin v. Quezon, 74, 86
Allen v. Pullman Palace Car Co., 488
Allgeyer v. Louisiana, 444, 1082
Amalgamated Food Employees Union v. Logan Valley Plaza, 802
Amalgamated Meat Cutters v. Connally, 657
American Party of Texas v. White, 985
American Refrigerator Transit Co. v. Hall, 504
Ames v. Kansas, 10
Anastaplo, In re, 1343
Anderson v. Dunn, 1316
Apodaca v. Oregon, 1038
Aptheker v. Secretary of State, 19, 750
Argersinger v. Hamlin, 1021
Arizona v. California, 210, 332

Arnett v. Kennedy, 1048
Ashwander v. Tennessee Valley Authority, 91, 326
Askew v. American Waterways Operators, Inc., 479
Association of Data Processing Service Organizations v. Camp, 118
Atlantic Coast Line R.R. v. Daughton, 548
Atlantic Refining Co. v. Virginia, 497
Austin v. New Hampshire, 345
Austin v. Tennessee, 200
Austin Indep. School Dist. v. United States, 902
Avery v. Midland County, 984

Bailey v. Drexel Furniture Co., 237
Baird v. State Bar, 1344
Baker v. Carr, 56, 956
Baldwin v. G.A.F. Seelig, Inc., 293, 381
Banker Brothers Co. v. Pennsylvania, 564
Barenblatt v. United States, 1317
Barr v. Matteo, 673
Barron v. Baltimore, 753
Barrows v. Jackson, 120
Battaglia v. General Motors Corp., 138
Baumgartner v. United States, 744
Bayside Fish Flour Co. v. Gentry, 400
Beauharnais v. Illinois, 1210
Benton v. Maryland, 1040
Best v. United States, 714
Best & Co. v. Maxwell, 358
Betts v. Brady, 1018
Bibb v. Navajo Freight Lines, 426
Bigelow v. Virginia, 1254
Bishop v. Wood, 1044

Table of Cases

Bivens v. Six Unknown Named Agents of Federal Bureau of Narcotics, 867
Black v. Cutter Laboratories, 813
Block v. Hirsh, 335
Blount v. Rizzi, 13, 1299
Board of Regents v. Roth, 1041
Bob-Lo Excursion Co. v. Michigan, 432
Boddie v. Connecticut, 911
Bode v. Barrett, 489
Bolling v. Sharpe, 18, 290
Bonham's Case, 17
Bors v. Preston, 10
Bradley v. Public Utilities Commn., 408
Brandenburg v. Ohio, 1173
Braniff Airways, Inc. v. Nebraska State Board, 508
Branzburg v. Hayes, 1310
Braunfeld v. Brown, 1363
Breard v. Alexandria, 373
Breedlove v. Suttles, 983
Brewer v. Hoxie School District No. 46, 793
Briggs v. Elliott, 887
Brimmer v. Rebman, 365
Brinkerhoff-Faris Co. v. Hill, 1400
Britt v. North Carolina, 910
Broadrick v. Oklahoma, 120
Brooks, In re Estate of, 1370
Brooks v. Dewar, 648
Brotherhood of Locomotive Firemen & Enginemen v. Chicago, R.I. & P.R. Co., 426
Brotherhood of Railroad Trainmen v. Virginia, 1246
Brown v. Board of Education, 887, 891
Brown v. Houston, 191
Brown v. Louisiana, 1203
Brown v. Maryland, 185
Brown v. Walker, 668
Browning v. Waycross, 482
Buchanan v. Warley, 121
Buck v. Bell, 874
Buck v. Kuykendall, 407
Buckley v. Valeo, 20, 659, 1265
Bullock v. Carter, 986
Burco v. Whitworth, 102
Burnet v. Coronado Oil & Gas Co., 134
Burstyn, Inc. v. Wilson, 1283
Burton v. Wilmington Parking Authority, 823
Buttfield v. Stranahan, 654

California Bankers Assn. v. Shultz, 1130
Caminetti v. United States, 234
Cantrell v. Forest City Publishing Co., 1228
Cantwell v. Connecticut, 1179, 1345
Capitol Greyhound Lines v. Brice, 489, 519
Cardinale v. Louisiana, 47
Carroll v. President & Commissioners, 86
Carson v. Roane-Anderson Co., 630
Carter v. Carter Coal Co., 243, 657

Case v. Bowles, 290
Castle v. Hayes Freight Lines, Inc., 467
Central R.R. Co. v. Pennsylvania, 531
Chambers v. Mississippi, 47
Champion v. Ames, 230
Chapman v. Meier, 972
Chastleton Corp. v. Sinclair, 335
Chicago v. Willett Co., 489
Chicago Police Department v. Mosley, 923
Chicago & Southern Air Lines v. Waterman SS. Corp., 84
Chicot County Drainage District v. Baxter State Bank, 133
Child Labor Tax Case, 237
Chinese Exclusion Case, 694
Cities Service Gas Co. v. Peerless Oil & Gas Co., 412
City of Atlanta v. Ickes, 118
City of Burbank v. Lockheed Air Terminal, Inc., 479
City of Detroit v. Murray Corp., 635
City of Kenosha v. Bruno, 860
City of Madison v. Wisconsin Employ. Relations Commn., 1205
City of Richmond v. United States, 980
Civil Rights Cases, 302, 777
Clark v. Gabriel, 141
Clark v. Poor, 489
Clark Distilling Co. v. Western Maryland Ry., 603
Clason v. Indiana, 400
Cleveland Board of Education v. La Fleur, 938, 942
Coe v. Erroll, 226
Cohens v. Virginia, 26
Cole v. Richardson, 1344
Colegrove v. Green, 954
Coleman v. Miller, 84
Colgate v. Harvey, 401
Collector v. Day, 621
Collins v. Hardyman, 864
Collins v. New Hampshire, 200
Colonial Pipeline Co. v. Traigle, 555
Colorado v. United States, 217
Columbia Broadcasting System, Inc. v. Democratic National Committee, 830, 1252
Committee for Public Education v. Nyquist, 1385
Communist Party v. Subversive Activities Control Board, 1246
Communist Party of Indiana v. Whitcomb, 1344
Connecticut Mutual Life Ins. Co. v. Moore, 448
Connell v. Higgenbotham, 1344
Construction Ind. Assn. of Sonoma City v. City of Petaluma, 1111
Contractors Assn. of Eastern Pennsylvania v. Secretary of Labor, 906
Cook v. Tait, 738

Table of Cases 1405

Cooley v. Board of Wardens of the Port of Philadelphia, 175
Cooper v. Aaron, 13, 893
Coppage v. Kansas, 1088
Corfield v. Coryell, 754
Coronado Coal Co. v. United Mine Workers, 229, 246
Counselman v. Hitchcock, 1017
Cousins v. Wigoda, 85
Cox v. Louisiana, 1183, 1192
Cox Broadcasting Co. v. Cohn, 1229
Craig v. Boren, 916, 937
Crandall v. Nevada, 339, 757
Crew Levick Co. v. Pennsylvania, 544
Cummins v. Parker Seal Co., 1370

Dahnke-Walder Milling Co. v. Bondurant, 390
Dandridge v. Williams, 912
Daniel v. Paul, 308
Daniel Ball, The, 207
Daniels v. Allen, 43
Davis v. County School Board, 887
Dayton–Goose Creek Ry. v. United States, 217
Dean Milk Co. v. City of Madison, 367
Debs, In re, 220
DeFunis v. Odegaard, 87, 906
De Jonge v. Oregon, 1232
DeLovio v. Boit, 334
Denman v. Slayton, 643
Dennis v. United States, 1162
Department of Agriculture v. Moreno, 20
Department of Revenue v. James B. Beam Distilling Co., 380
Desist v. United States, 1401
DeSpain v. DeKalb County School District, 1375
Doe v. McMillan, 1129
Dombrowski v. Eastland, 74
Doremus v. Board of Education, 108
Downes v. Bidwell, 712
Dred Scott v. Sandford, 729, 760
Duckworth v. Arkansas, 438
Dunbar-Stanley Studios, Inc. v. Alabama, 362, 487
Duncan v. Kahanamoku, 1061
Duncan v. Louisiana, 1035
Dunn v. Blumstein, 86, 351

Eakin v. Raub, 10
Early v. DiCenso, 1380
Edelman v. Boeing Air Transport, Inc., 531
Edelman v. Jordan, 131, 863
Edwards v. California, 341
Eisenstadt v. Baird, 121, 1119
Electric Bond & Share Co. v. SEC, 103
El Paso v. Simmons, 1393
Empresa Siderurgica v. County of Merced, 522
Endo, Ex parte, 718

Engel v. Vitale, 1375
Epperson v. Arkansas, 1376
Erie R.R. v. Tompkins, 33
Erznoznik v. City of Jacksonville, 807
Escobedo v. Illinois, 1021
Estep v. United States, 140
Evans v. Abney, 835
Evans v. Newton, 832
Evansville-Vanderburgh Airport Authority District v. Delta Airlines, Inc., 341
Everson v. Board of Education, 1350

Faitoute Iron & Steel Co. v. City of Asbury Park, 1394
Falbo v. United States, 139
Fay v. Noia, 43
Federal Baseball Club v. National League, 229
Federal Power Commission v. Hope Natural Gas Co., 616, 1082
Feiner v. New York, 1189
Ficklen v. Shelby County Taxing District, 354
Field v. Clark, 84, 654
First Agricultural Natl. Bank v. State Tax Commission, 621
First National Bank v. Fellows, 162
First National Bank v. United Air Lines, 615
Fiswick v. United States, 86
Flast v. Cohen, 111
Flemming v. Nestor, 1337
Fletcher v. Peck, 28
Flood v. Kuhn, 230
Florida v. Mellon, 267
Florida ex rel. Hawkins v. Board of Control, 48
Ford Motor Co. v. Beauchamp, 497
Foster-Fountain Packing Co. v. Haydel, 398
Francis v. Henderson, 44
Freedman v. Maryland, 1291
Freeman v. Hewit, 583
Frontiero v. Richardson, 20, 930
Frothingham v. Mellon, 103
Fry v. United States, 289
Fuentes v. Shevin, 1044
Fujii v. California, 692
Fuller v. Oregon, 910

Gaffney v. Cummings, 972
Gallagher v. Crown Kosher Super Market, 1363
Gallagher v. Lynn, 372
Gardella v. Chandler, 229
Gardner v. Broderick, 1016
Gardner v. California, 910
Garland, Ex parte, 668
Garner v. Board of Public Works, 1334
Garrison v. Louisiana, 1222
Gebhart v. Belton, 887
Geduldig v. Aiello, 935
Geer v. Connecticut, 396
Gelpcke v. Dubuque, 1400

Table of Cases

General Electric Co. v. Gilbert, 935
General Motors Corp. v. Washington, 593
General Railway Signal Co. v. Virginia, 487
General Trading Co. v. State Tax Commission, 576
Genesee Chief v. Fitzhugh, 334
Georgia v. Pennsylvania R. Co., 108
Georgia v. Rachel, 616
Georgia v. Stanton, 105
Gertz v. Robert Welch, Inc., 1223
Gibbons v. Ogden, 164
Gibson v. Florida Legislative Investigation Committee, 1322
Gideon v. Wainwright, 1018
Gilbert v. California, 1021
Gillette v. United States, 1370
Gilmore v. City of Montgomery, 836
Ginsberg v. New York, 86, 1295
Ginzburg v. United States, 1293
Girouard v. United States, 739
Gitlow v. New York, 1134
Glidden v. Zdanok, 54
Glona v. American Guarantee & Liability Ins. Co., 926
Goesaert v. Cleary, 877
Gomez v. Perez, 928
Gomillion v. Lightfoot, 953
Gordon v. Lance, 974
Graves v. O'Keefe, 635
Gray v. Sanders, 974
Green v. County School Board, 897
Greenwood v. Peacock, 616
Greer v. Spock, 1205
Griffin v. Breckenridge, 864
Griffin v. Illinois, 907
Griffin v. Prince Edward School Board, 894
Griffiths, In re, 923
Grisham v. Hagan, 18, 1074
Griswold v. Connecticut, 121, 1112
Groppi v. Leslie, 679
Grosjean v. American Press Co., 1259
Grosso v. United States, 19, 241
Gulf Oil Corp. v. Copp Paving Co., 299

Hague v. CIO, 857
Hall v. De Cuir, 427
Hamilton v. Regents of the University of California, 1344
Hamling v. United States, 1304
Hammer v. Dagenhart, 233
Hammerstein v. Lyne, 738
Hampton & Co. v. United States, 654
Harisiades v. Shaughnessy, 746
Harper v. Virginia Board of Elections, 981
Harris v. New York, 1034
Hawkins v. Town of Shaw, 862, 922
Hayburn's Case, 18
Hayes v. United States, 867

Haynes v. United States, 19
Hays v. Pacific Mail Steamship Co., 505
Heart of Atlanta Motel v. United States, 300
Heisler v. Thomas Colliery, 538
Helson v. Kentucky, 531
Helvering v. Davis, 272
Helvering v. Gerhardt, 630
Hendrick v. Maryland, 489
Henneford v. Silas Mason Co., 385, 565
Henry v. Mississippi, 44
Herndon v. Lowry, 1158
Hess v. Indiana, 1175
Hill v. Stone, 985
Hill v. Wallace, 241
Hinderlider v. La Plata River & C. Creek Ditch Co., 611
Hirota v. MacArthur, 716
Holden v. Hardy, 1083
Holtzman v. Schlesinger, 707
Home Building & Loan Assn. v. Blaisdell, 1388
Hood & Sons, Inc. v. Du Mond, 401
Hopkins Federal Savings & Loan Assn. v. Cleary, 324
Horn Silver Mining Co. v. New York, 492
Houston, East & West Texas Ry. v. United States, 214
Hudgens v. NLRB, 808
Hudson Water Co. v. McCarter, 397
Hughes v. Fetter, 615
Humphrey's Executor v. United States, 9, 242, 670
Hunter v. Erickson, 841
Hurd v. Hodge, 815
Huron Portland Cement Co. v. Detroit, 468

Illinois Central R.R. v. Minnesota, 528
Imbler v. Pachtman, 862
International Assn. of Machinists v. Street, 841, 1239
International Brotherhood of Teamsters v. Vogt, 1179
International Harvester Co. v. Department of Treasury, 578
Interstate Circuit, Inc. v. City of Dallas, 1298
Ives v. South Buffalo Ry., 40

Jackman v. Rosenbaum Co., 1095
Jackson v. Metropolitan Edison Co., 830
James v. Dravo Contracting Co., 623
James v. Pinnix, 841
James v. Valtierra, 841
James Stewart & Co. v. Sadrakula, 645
Jenkins v. Georgia, 1304
Jenness v. Fortson, 985
Jimenez v. Weinberger, 20, 928
J. D. Adams Mfg. Co. v. Storen, 569
Johnson v. Eisentrager, 719
Johnson v. Maryland, 644

Johnson v. New Jersey, 1400
Johnson and Cassidy v. New Jersey, 134, 1032
Johnson Oil Co. v. Oklahoma, 505
Jones v. Alfred H. Mayer Co., 814
Joseph v. Carter & Weeks Stevedoring Co., 531
Joseph Burstyn, Inc. v. Wilson, 1283
Joy Oil Co., Ltd. v. State Tax Commission, 522

Kahn v. Shevin, 936
Kastigar v. United States, 1016
Katzenbach v. McClung, 304
Katzenbach v. Morgan, 902
Kawakita v. United States, 740
Keane v. National Democratic Party, 85
Kendall v. United States, 10
Kennedy v. Mendoza-Martinez, 18
Kentucky v. Dennison, 760
Kern-Limerick v. Schurlock, 630
Keyes v. School District No. 1, Denver, 899
Keyishian v. Board of Regents, 1339
Kidd v. Pearson, 226
Kilbourn v. Thompson, 74, 679, 1316
Kingsley Intl. Pictures Corp. v. Regents of New York, 1284
Kinsella v. Kreuger, 18
Kinsella v. United States, 18, 1074
Kirby v. Illinois, 1021
Kirkpatrick v. Preisler, 971
Kleindienst v. Mandel, 751
Knauer v. United States, 745
Knauff v. Shanghnessy, 750
Knickerbocker Ice Co. v. Stewart, 606
Knote v. United States, 669
Korematsu v. United States, 914
Kotch v. Board of River Port Pilot Commissioners, 876
Kovacs v. Cooper, 1184
Kramer v. Union Free School District No. 15, 984
Kunz v. New York, 1183
Kusper v. Pontikes, 986

Labine v. Vincent, 928
Lamont v. Postmaster General, 19
Landis v. North American Co., 102
Lathrop v. Donahue, 1240
Lauf v. E. G. Shinner & Co., 137
Lawrence v. State Tax Commission, 562
Law Students Research Council v. Wadmond, 1344
Leary v. United States, 19
Lefkowitz v. Turley, 1015
Legal Tender Cases, 309
Lego v. Twomey, 1034
Leisy v. Hardin, 197
Leloup v. Port of Mobile, 488
Lemke v. Farmers' Grain Co., 390
Lemon v. Kurtzman, 1380

Lenrich Associates v. Heyda, 807
Levitt v. Committee for Public Education, 1385
Levy v. Louisiana, 926
License Cases, 175
Lindsey v. Normet, 911
Linkletter v. Walker, 133, 1032, 1400
Livingston v. Van Ingen, 163
Lloyd Corp. v. Tanner, 801
Lochner v. New York, 1083
Lockerty v. Phillips, 139
Loewe v. Lawlor, 229
Logan v. United States, 788
Lottery Case, 230
Louisville Joint Stock Land Bank v. Radford, 242
Louisville & Nashville R.R. Co. v. Mottley, 40
Lovell v. Griffin, 1183
Low v. Austin, 192
Lubin v. Panish, 987
Lucas v. Forty-Fourth General Assembly, 962
Luther v. Borden, 67
Lynch v. Clark, 755
Lynch v. Household Finance Corp., 859

McAllister v. United States, 10
McCardle, Ex parte, 141
McCarroll v. Dixie Greyhound Lines, 434
McCray v. United States, 240
McCulloch v. Maryland, 621
McDermott v. Wisconsin, 202
McDonald v. Santa Fe Transp. Co., 822
McElroy v. United States, 18
McGoldrick v. Berwind-White Coal Mining Co., 565
McGowan v. Maryland, 1363
McGrain v. Daugherty, 1316
Mackenzie v. Hare, 741
McKinney v. Alabama, 1299
McLaurin v. Oklahoma State Regents, 886
McLeod v. Dilworth Co., 574
McNally v. Hill, 134
Madison v. Kinsella, 1073
Magill v. Brown, 753
Maguire v. Trefry, 562
Mahan v. Howell, 971
Maine v. Grand Trunk Ry., 489
Malloy v. Hogan, 1012
Mapp v. Ohio, 1008
Marbury v. Madison, 3
Marchetti v. United States, 19, 241, 1157
Marks v. United States, 1305, 1400
Marsh v. Alabama, 797
Marshall v. Gordon, 679, 1316
Martin v. Hunter's Lessee, 20
Maryland v. Wirtz, 287
Massachusetts v. Mellon, 103
Massachusetts v. Missouri, 10
Massachusetts Bd. of Retirement v. Murgia, 939
Masses Pub. Co. v. Patten, 1137

Mathews v. Lucas, 929
Maurer v. Hamilton, 465
Maxwell v. Bugbee, 642
Mayer v. City of Chicago, 909
Mayor of New York v. Miln, 175
Mayor of Vidalia v. McNeely, 410
Meachum v. Fano, 1044
Meek v. Pittinger, 1386
"Memoirs" v. Massachusetts, 1291
Memorial Hospital v. Maricopa County, 351
Memphis Steam Laundry Cleaner, Inc. v. Stone, 359
Merryman, Ex parte, 667, 1048
Miami Herald Publishing Co. v. Torrillo, 1251
Michelin Tire Corp. v. Wages, 192
Michigan v. Mosley, 1035
Michigan v. Tucker, 1034
Michigan-Wisconsin Pipe Line Co. v. Calvert, 540
Milk Control Board v. Eisenberg Farm Products, 388
Miller v. California, 1300
Miller v. Milwaukee, 642
Miller v. Schoene, 1095
Miller Bros. Co. v. Maryland, 591
Milligan, Ex parte, 1050
Milliken v. Bradley, 899
Minersville School Dist. v. Gobitis, 1345
Minnesota v. Barber, 362
Minnesota v. Blasius, 519
Minnesota Rate Cases, 213, 1082
Mintz v. Baldwin, 366
Miranda v. Arizona, 1024
Missouri v. Holland, 134, 695
Missouri ex rel. Gaines v. Canada, 884
Missouri Life Ins. Co. v. Gehner, 643
Mitchell v. Laird, 84, 706
Mitchell v. W. T. Grant Co., 1045
Monger v. Florida, 47
Monroe v. Board of Commissioners, 898
Monroe v. Pape, 861
Montgomery Ward & Co. v. United States, 86
Moore v. Ogilvie, 986
Moose Lodge No. 107 v. Irvis, 828
Morey v. Doud, 915
Morgan v. Virginia, 429
Mulford v. Smith, 658
Muller v. Oregon, 1088
Munn v. Illinois, 213, 1078
Murgia v. Commonwealth, 938
Murphy v. Waterfront Commission, 1017
Murray v. Curlett, 1370
Muskrat v. United States, 49
Myers v. United States, 9, 653, 669

NAACP v. Alabama, 121, 1235
NAACP v. Button, 1241

Nader v. Bork, 670
National Bellas Hess, Inc. v. Department of Revenue, 601
National League of Cities v. Usery, 20, 286
National Life Ins. Co. v. United States, 601
Neagle, In re, 616
Near v. Minnesota, 1146
Nebbia v. New York, 293, 1089
Nebraska v. Wyoming, 333
Nebraska Press Assn. v. Stuart, 1309
Nelson v. Sears, Roebuck & Co., 572
New Orleans v. Dukes, 915
New York v. United States, 290, 637
New York ex rel. Bryant v. Zimmerman, 1230
New York ex rel. Cohn v. Graves, 562
New York ex rel. Whitney v. Graves, 562
New York Central R. R. v. Miller, 505
New York Central R. R. v. Winfield, 457
New York Times Co. v. Sullivan, 1215
New York Times Co. v. United States, 1149
Niemotko v. Maryland, 1183
Nippert v. Richmond, 358
Nixon v. Condon, 950
Nixon v. Herndon, 950
NLRB v. Jones & Laughlin Steel Corp., 273
Norfolk & Western Ry. v. State Tax Commission, 505
Norman v. Baltimore & Ohio R.R., 310, 1393
Norman v. Consolidated Edison Co., 121
North Carolina State Board of Education v. Swann, 899
Northern Securities Co. v. United States, 227
North Georgia Finishing, Inc. v. Di-Chem, Inc., 1045
Northwest Airlines, Inc. v. Minnesota, 505
Northwestern States Portland Cement Co. v. Minnesota, 555
Norton Co. v. Department of Revenue, 588
Norwood v. Harrison, 835
Noto v. United States, 1173

O'Brien v. Brown, 85
O'Callahan v. Parker, 19, 1074
Oestereich v. Selective Service System Local Board No. 11, 140
Ohio v. Thomas, 643
Ohio v. Wyandotte Chemicals Corp., 10, 107
Okanogon Indian Tribe v. United States, 673
Oklahoma v. United States Civil Service Commission, 107
Oklahoma Press Publishing Co. v. Walling, 286
Olsen v. Nebraska, 1094
Oregon v. Mitchell, 19, 987
Organization for a Better Austin v. Keefe, 1229
Orlando v. Laird, 706
Ortwein v. Schwab, 911
Osborn v. Ozlin, 441

Table of Cases

Pacific States Tel. Co. v. Oregon, 84
Pacific Tel. & Tel. Co. v. State Tax Commn., 488
Pack v. Tennessee, 1370
Palko v. Connecticut, 996
Palmer v. Thompson, 835, 872
Panama Refining Co. v. Ryan, 655
Paris Adult Theatre I v. Slaton, 1127, 1302
Parker v. Brown, 401
Parker v. Levy, 120
Parsons v. United States, 9
Passenger Cases, 134, 175
Patterson v. Alabama, 42
Patterson v. Warden, 1020
Paul v. Davis, 1044, 1228
Paul v. Virginia, 230
Pell v. Procunier, 1257
Pennsylvania v. Nelson, 473
Pennsylvania v. West Virginia, 390
Pennsylvania v. Wheeling & Belmont Bridge Co., 145, 178, 184
Perez v. Brownell, 741
Perez v. United States, 309
Perry v. Sindermann, 1044
Perry v. United States, 317, 1393
Peru, Ex parte, 84
Philadelphia & Southern Steamship Co. v. Pennsylvania, 528
Phillips v. Martin Marietta Corp., 935
Phillips Petroleum Co. v. Wisconsin, 412
Pickering v. Board of Education, 1222
Pierce v. Society of Sisters, 85, 121
Pierson v. Ray, 862
Pittsburgh Press Co. v. Pittsburgh Commn. of Human Relations, 937
Plessy v. Ferguson, 881
Pocket Veto Cases, 673
Poe v. Ullman, 1004
Police Dept. of Chicago v. Mosley, 1203
Pollock v. Farmers' Loan & Trust Co., 97
Pope v. United States, 19
Powe v. Miles, 829
Powell v. Alabama, 1019
Powell v. McCormack, 71
Preiser v. Rodriguez, 860
Prigg v. Pennsylvania, 757
Prince v. Massachussetts, 1297
Prize Cases, 706
Public Utilities Commission v. Pollak, 1189
Pullman's Palace Car Co. v. Pennsylvania, 499

Quirin, Ex parte, 1054

Radio Station WOW v. Johnson, 616
Rahrer, In re, 200
Railroad Co. v. Maryland, 209

Railroad Commission of Wisconsin v. Chicago, B. & Q. R.R., 217
Railroad Retirement Bd. v. Alton R.R., 241
Railway Express Agency v. New York, 879
Railway Express Agency v. Virginia, 534
Railway Express Agency, Inc. v. Virginia, 497
Real Silk Hosiery Mills v. Portland, 358
Red Lion Broadcasting Co. v. FCC, 1247, 1272
Reid v. Covert, 18, 1069
Reitman v. Mulkey, 837
Relford v. Commandant, 1074
Reymann Brewing Co. v. Brister, 365
Reynolds v. Sims, 34, 956
Rice v. Sioux City Memorial Park Cemetery, Inc., 813
Rickert Rice Mills v. Fontenot, 259
Robbins v. Shelby County Taxing District, 354, 482
Rochin v. California, 999
Roe v. Wade, 86, 1119
Roemer v. Maryland Public Works Bd., 1386
Rogers v. Bellei, 742
Rosario v. Rockefeller, 986
Rosenblatt v. Baer, 1222
Rosenbloom v. Metromedia, Inc., 1224
Ross, In re, 709
Roth v. United States, 1285
Rowan v. United States Post Office Dept., 1299
Runyon v. McCrary, 822

Saia v. New York, 1185
St. Pierre v. United States, 86
Salyer Land Co. v. Tulare Lake Basin Water Storage Dist., 984
San Antonio Indep. School Dist. v. Rodriguez, 916
Saxbe v. Washington Post Co., 1257
Scales v. United States, 1173
Schacht v. United States, 19
Schechter Poultry Corp. v. United States, 242, 656
Schenck v. United States, 1131
Scheuer v. Rhodes, 129, 862
Schick v. Reed, 669
Schlib v. Kuebel, 910
Schlesinger v. Ballard, 936
Schlesinger v. Reservists Committee to Stop the War, 119
Schneider v. Rusk, 18, 746
Schneiderman v. United States, 745
Schollenberger v. Pennsylvania, 200
School District of Abington v. Schempp, 1370
Screws v. United States, 841
Scripto, Inc. v. Carson, 591
Second Employers' Liability Cases, 217
Senate Select Committee on Presidential Campaign Activities v. Nixon, 690

Table of Cases

Serrano v. Priest, 922
Shaffer v. Carter, 562
Shapiro v. Thompson, 13, 346, 912
Shaughnessy v. Pedreiro, 750
Sheldon v. Sill, 136
Shelley v. Kraemer, 808
Sheppard v. Maxwell, 1305
Sherbert v. Verner, 1367
Shirley v. State National Bank of Connecticut, 841
Shreveport Case, 214
Shuttlesworth v. Birmingham, 1184
Sibron v. New York, 86
Sierra Club v. Morton, 118
Simon v. Eastern Kentucky Welfare Rights Org., 119
Sinclair v. United States, 1316
Skinner v. Oklahoma, 872
Slaughter-House Cases, 763
Sligh v. Kirkwood, 397
Smith v. Allwright, 134, 948
Smith v. Goguen, 1210
Smith v. Kansas City Title Co., 93
Smyth v. Ames, 1082
Sniadach v. Family Finance Corp., 1044
Sonzinsky v. United States, 240
South Carolina v. Katzenbach, 974
South Carolina State Highway Dept. v. Barnwell Bros., 412
Southeastern Promotions, Ltd. v. Conrad, 1299
Southern Pac. Co. v. Arizona, 418
Southern Pac. Co. v. Jensen, 606
Southern Pacific Terminal Co. v. ICC, 86
Spector Motor Service, Inc. v. O'Connor, 552
Spence v. Washington, 1210
Springer v. Philippine Islands, 658
Sprout v. South Bend, 488
Stafford v. Wallace, 228
Standard Oil Co. v. New Jersey, 451
Standard Oil Co. v. Peck, 506
Stanley v. Georgia, 1126, 1299
Stanley v. Illinois, 937
Stanton v. Stanton, 938
State Board v. Young's Market Co., 378
State Board of Insurance v. Todd Shipyards Corp., 444
State Freight Tax, Case of the, 523
State Tax on Railway Gross Receipts, 525
Steel Seizure Case, 34, 659, 668
Stein v. Oshinsky, 1375
Steward Machine Co. v. Davis, 262, 607
Stewart, James, & Co. v. Sadrakula, 645
Stolar, In re, 1344
Storer v. Brown, 986
Street v. New York, 1209
Sugarman v. Dongall, 926
Sullivan v. Little Hunting Park, Inc., 43
Sunshine Anthracite Coal Co. v. Adkins, 252

Super Tire Engineering Co. v. McCorkle, 86
Swann v. Board of Education, 898
Sweatt v. Painter, 885
Swift v. Tyson, 33
Swift & Co. v. United States, 228, 246
Swift & Co. v. Wickham, 479

Tapes Case, The, 671
Tate v. Short, 910
Taylor v. Louisiana, 938
Tehan v. Shott, 133, 1032, 1400
Teitel Film Corp. v. Cusack, 1299
Tennessee Electric Power Co. v. TVA, 118, 331
Tenney v. Brandhove, 75, 1325
Terminiello v. Chicago, 1192
Terral v. Burke Constr. Co., 497
Terry v. Adams, 953
Testa v. Katt, 613
Texas v. Florida, 453
Texas v. New Jersey, 455
Thornhill v. Alabama, 120, 1175
Thornton v. United States, 174
Tidal Oil Co. v. Flanagan, 1400
Tilton v. Richardson, 19, 1385
Time, Inc. v. Hill, 1228
Time, Inc. v. Pape, 1222
Tinker v. Des Moines Indep. Community School Dist., 1207
Toolson v. New York Yankees, 229
Tot v. United States, 18
Toth v. Quarles, 18, 725
Train v. City of New York, 671
Trevett v. Weeden, 17
Trop v. Dulles, 18, 741
Truax v. Corrigan, 137, 121
Truax v. Raich, 121
Turner v. Bank of North America, 136
TVA v. Lenoir City, 332
Two Guys from Harrison-Allentown, Inc. v. McGinley, 1363
Tyler v. Magwire, 48
Tyson & Brother v. Banton, 1095

Underwood Typewriter Co. v. Chamberlain, 549
Union Brokerage Co. v. Jensen, 487
Union Refrigerator Transit Co. v. Kentucky, 505
Union Tank Line Co. v. Wright, 503
United Air Lines, Inc. v. Mahin, 531
United Farmworkers of Florida Housing Project, Inc., v. City of Delray, 860
United Mine Workers v. Coronado Coal Co., 229
United Public Workers v. Mitchell, 1260
United States v. Ash, 1021
United States v. Ballard, 1345
United States v. Bass, 309
United States v. Brown, 19, 1338

Table of Cases

United States v. Butler, 34, 253
United States v. Calandra, 1010
United States v. California, 291, 333, 647
United States v. Cardiff, 18
United States v. Carolene Products Co., 914
United States v. Causby, 1097
United States v. Central Eureka Mining Co., 1100
United States v. Classic, 945
United States v. Constantine, 240
United States v. Coolidge, 26
United States v. Cruikshank, 772
United States v. Curtiss-Wright Export Corp., 697
United States v. Darby, 281
United States v. Dickinson, 1309
United States v. E. C. Knight Co., 225
United States v. Enmons, 309
United States v. Falk, 872
United States v. Ferger, 174
United States v. Five Gambling Devices, 286
United States v. Fuller, 1103
United States v. Gerlach Live Stock Co., 332
United States v. Grimaud, 654
United States v. Guest, 851
United States v. Guy W. Capps, Inc., 705
United States v. Hall, 771
United States v. Hill, 174
United States v. Hudson, 259
United States v. Jackson, 19
United States v. Johnson (390 U.S. 563), 857
United States v. Johnson (383 U.S. 169), 74
United States v. Johnson (319 U.S. 302), 54
United States v. Kahriger, 241
United States v. Klein, 145, 668
United States v. Kras, 911
United States v. Le Baron, 9
United States v. Louisiana, 333
United States v. Lovett, 18, 1330
United States v. MacIntosh, 739
United States v. Maine, 333
United States v. Nixon, 671, 679
United States v. O'Brien, 1205
United States v. Orito, 1126
United States v. Phillips, 81
United States v. Pink, 700
United States v. Reidel, 1126, 1299
United States v. Richardson, 120
United States v. Robel, 13, 1339
United States v. Rock Royal Co-op, Inc., 657
United States v. Romano, 19
United States v. Sanchez, 240
United States v. Saylor, 948
United States v. Schwimmer, 739
United States v. SCRAP, 119
United States v. Seeger, 1370
United States v. Sisson, 80
United States v. Smith, 9
United States v. South-Eastern Underwriters, 299
United States v. Texas, 333
United States v. Thirty-seven Photographs, 1299
United States v. Wade, 1021
United States v. Washington Post Co., 1149
United States v. Willow River Power Co., 332
United States v. Witkovich, 750
United States v. Wong Kim Ark, 734
United States Dept. of Agriculture v. Moreno, 20, 939, 941
United States Dept. of Agriculture v. Murray, 20, 939
United States Glue Co. v. Town of Oak Creek, 545

Veazie Bank v. Fenno, 240
Village of Arlington Heights v. Metropolitan Housing Dev. Corp., 1112
Village of Belle Terre v. Boraas, 939, 1109
Village of Euclid v. Ambler Realty Co., 1105
Virginia, Ex parte, 774
Vlandis v. Kline, 351

Wabash, St. Louis & Pacific Ry. v. Illinois, 210, 411
Wagner v. City of Covington, 357
Walker v. City of Birmingham, 1184
Warth v. Seldin, 1111
Washington v. Davis, 901, 1112
Washington v. Dawson & Co., 606
Washington v. Legrant, 19
Watkins v. United States, 679, 1318
Watson v. Jones, 1359
Weber v. Aetna Casualty & Surety Co., 928
Weinberger v. Salfi, 942
Weinberger v. Wiesenfeld, 937
Welton v. Missouri, 352
Wesberry v. Sanders, 971
Westberry v. Fisher, 860
West Coast Hotel Co. v. Parrish, 132, 1091
Western Live Stock v. Bureau of Revenue, 540
Western Union Tel. Co. v. Kansas, 493
Western Union Tel. Co. v. Pennsylvania, 451
West Point Wholesale Grocery Co. v. Opelika, 362
West Pub. Co. v. McColgan, 558
West Virginia v. Sims, 608
West Virginia State Board of Education v. Barnette, 1345
Whalen v. Roe, 1129
Whitcomb v. Chavis, 972, 974
White v. Regester, 972, 974
Whitney v. California, 1140
Wickard v. Filburn, 293
Wiener v. United States, 10, 670

Table of Cases

William v. Froehlke, 1074
Williams v. Brewer, 1035
Williams v. Georgia, 42
Williams v. Illinois, 910
Williams v. Rhodes, 985
Williams v. United States, 850
Willing v. Chicago Auditorium Assn., 121
Willson v. Black Bird Creek Marsh Co., 174
Wilson v. Bohlender, 18, 1074
Wilson v. Girard, 1073
Wisconsin v. FPC, 412
Wisconsin v. J. C. Penney Co., 552
Wisconsin v. Yoder, 1370
Wolf v. Colorado, 1006
Wolff v. Selective Service Board No. 16, 140
Wood v. Strickland, 862
Woodruff v. Parham, 188
Woods v. Miller Co., 336

Yakus v. United States, 139, 300, 657
Yale Todd's Case, 18
Yamashita, In re, 715
Yarbrough, Ex parte, 943
Yates v. United States, 1170
Yick Wo v. Hopkins, 869
York Manufacturing Co. v. Colley, 485
Yott v. North American Rockwell Corp., 1370
Young, Ex parte, 129, 648
Young v. American Mini Theatres, Inc., 1305
Youngstown Sheet & Tube Co. v. Sawyer, 34, 659

Zemel v. Rusk, 750
Ziccarelli v. New Jersey State Commn. of Investigation, 1017
Zorach v. Clauson, 1359

Index

Abortion, 1119, 1125, 1126, 1254
Academic freedom, 122, 1317, 1339
Admiralty. *See* Maritime law; Navigable waters
Advertising
   gross receipts, tax on, 540
   political and commercial, 1246, 1251, 1252, 1254, 1257
   on Railway Express trucks, 879
Advisory opinions, 49, 1260
Age discrimination, 938
Agriculture, control of production, 253, 293
Airlines, equipment, property tax on, 505-506, 508
Air space, control of, 1097
Alien and Sedition Acts, 13, 1134
Alien Registration Act (federal), 766
Aliens
   congressional powers over, 746
   constitutional rights as "persons," 869
   deportation of. *See* Deportation
   inheritance, rights of, 729, 755
"Anti-evolution" statute, Arkansas, 1376
Antitrust laws
   baseball, 229-230
   labor, 212-213, 218, 229
   manufacturing, 225
   newspapers, 298-299
   railroad holding companies, 227-228
   stockyards, 228
Appeal, right to, and due process, 907
Apportionment. *See* Reapportionment
Articles of Confederation, 239
Assembly, right of, as privilege of citizenship, 857. *See also* Association
Assimilative Crimes Act, 607
Association, 1140, 1162, 1170, 1230, 1232, 1235, 1241. *See also* Assembly, right of
Atomic Energy Act, 629

Attachment and garnishment, 1044
Attainder. *See* Bills of attainder
Australia, legislation in
   agriculture, 296
   fiscal policy, 607-608
   motives of, 240
   social security, 273
Autonomy, executive and legislative branches, 673-690

Bail, right to, 1040
Bakers, 1083
Ballot access, restrictions on, 985
Barges, property taxes on, 506
Baseball, 229-230
Belief. *See also* Freedom of religious belief; Freedom of speech
   compulsion to declare, 1345
   punishment of, 1162
Bible reading, 108, 1370
Bill of Rights
   adoption, reasons for, 753
   federal judiciary as limited by, 753
   Fourteenth Amendment as incorporating, 994, 995-998, 1008, 1018
   treaties as affecting, 692
Bills of attainder, character of, 1330, 1338
Bingham, John A., 1078
Birth control, 1004, 1112, 1119
Bisbee deportations, 790
Bituminous Coal Act, 243
Bridges, 178
Busses. *See* Carriers, motor

Canada, legislation in
   fiscal policy, 608
   social security, 273

Carriers, motor
  licensing of, by state, 407, 488
  routing of, by state, 408
  segregation by, 427, 429, 432, 777, 881
  size, weight, 412
Cattle
  slaughtering of, 763
  state restrictions on import, 362, 366
Censorship. See Freedom of speech, prior restraint
Chafee, Zechariah, Jr., on Herndon case, 1158
Child Labor Amendment, 84
Child Labor Laws, 233, 281
Chinese
  citizenship, eligibility for, 739
  discriminations against, 869, 872
Churches. See also Freedom of religious belief; Religion, prohibition of establishment of
  self-government of, 1359
  zoning against, 1358
Citizenship. See State citizenship; United States citizenship
Civil liberty. See Assembly, right of; Constitutionality, presumption of; Freedom of religious belief; Freedom of speech
Civil Rights Acts
  judges, applicability to, 774, 1325
  scope of, 841-869
  section 1983, 859
  state legislators, applicability to, 1325
Civil War Amendments. See also Bill of Rights, Fourteenth Amendment as incorporating
  abolition of slavery and its incidents, 781, 881
  adoption of, 760
  congressional powers under, 777
Coal, processing tax on, 538
Coke, Sir Edward, opinion in Bonham's Case, 17
Collusive suits, 54
Color of Law, 859. See also State action
Common law. See Federal common law
Compacts between states, 608
Company towns, 797
Compelled testimony, 1012, 1015, 1017, 1318-1319. See also Disclosure and disclaimer
Compensation. See Eminent domain; Private use, taking for
Confessions, forced, 1021, 1024, 1034
Conflict of laws, constitutional aspects of, 455
  See also Jurisdiction
Confrontation, 1040
Congressional districting, 977. See also Elections
Congressional investigations, un-American activities, 1315, 1317, 1320, 1325
Conscientious objectors, 739

Conservation. See Fish; Game; Gas; Oysters
Constitution, overseas, 709-726
Constitutionality, presumption of, 136
Consular courts, Fifth and Sixth Amendments as applied to, 1018
Contempts, congressional power to punish, 677, 1315
Contract, liberty of, 1083, 1091
Contract Renegotiation Act, 1395
Contracts clause
  contract, obligation of, 28, 317, 1077, 1387
  due process clauses, relationship to, 1395
  remedies, applicability to, 1387
Conventions, nominating, 85
Cooperative federalism
  federal legislation validating or adopting state laws, 200, 603, 606
  federal tax with credit, 262
  judicial cooperation, 612
Corporation
  as "persons" within Fourteenth Amendment, 857
  foreign, state power to exclude, 497
Counsel, right of accused to
  cases in state courts, 1018
  federal courts, 1020
  self-incrimination, relationship to privilege against, 1008
Court of Claims, 49, 54, 131
Court Reorganization Plan of 1937, 260
Courts. See also Federal courts.
  action of, as state action, 772, 808, 1179
Courts-martial and military commissions. See also Martial law; Military powers
  congressional powers to establish and govern, 1050, 1054
  habeas corpus, civil courts, powers as to, 1048, 1054, 1073
  international authority, 715, 716, 719
Cruel and unusual punishment, 1040

Dairy industry. See Agriculture; Milk
Debate, freedom of, 1325
Declaratory judgments, 9
Defamation, 1146, 1210-1228
Delegation of power
  general doctrine, 653-658
  maximum hours of labor, fixing of, by private groups, 243
  prices of trademarked articles, contract between producer and dealers as to, 252
Denaturalization. See also Deportation; Expatriation
  fraud as ground for, 745-746
  statutory provisions concerning, 743
Deportation. See also Denaturalization
  civil or criminal procedure, 746
  refusal of other nations to receive, 750

Dicey, A. V., on federalism, 148
Disclosure and disclaimer
  history, 1315-1317
  requirements of, 1315-1330
Dividends, escheat of, 451
Doing business, license taxes on, 482
Drummers. *See* Salesmen, drummers, or peddlers
Due process of law
  "liberty" and "property" under, 1044
  in noncriminal settings, 1041
  procedure and substance, 993, 1046

Education. *See* Schools and colleges
Elections
  federal powers over, 943, 945, 974
  political parties and state action, 948
  unit count and, 970
Electric power, sale of, by TVA, 91, 326
Emergency. *See also* Military powers
  constitutional powers, as affected by, 1387
Emergency Price Control Act, 139, 290
Eminent domain
  navigable waters, losses from development of, 331
  police power distinguished, 1095
  property of another sovereign, 648
  what constitutes a taking, 1097, 1100
Employment agencies, 1094
Equal footing clause, 333
Equal protection of the laws
  administration of laws as denying, 869
  aliens and, 923, 926
  due process, compared with, 880
  historical themes, 869-881
  illegitimacy and, 926
  "last resort of constitutional arguments," 874
  as limit on administrative discretion, 872
  municipal services and, 922
  poverty and equality, 907, 912
  racial discrimination, 881-901
  racial exclusion of jurors, 772
  restrictive covenants, 808
  "separate but equal" doctrine, 881, 887
  standard of review, 914
  suspect classifications, 907-937
Escheat
  deposits, 451
  dividends, 451
  insurance policies, 448
Estoppel to raise constitutional questions, 93, 98
European Coal-Steel Community, tax problems of, 587-588
Executive agreements. *See also* Treaties
  congressional power to abrogate, 694
  scope of power to conclude, 695
  state power as affected by, 700

Executive personnel, control of, 669
Executive privilege, 679
Expatriation. *See also* Denaturalization; Deportation
  voluntary, 739, 740
Exports
  property tax on, 522
  sales tax on, 544
  stevedoring, tax on gross receipts, 531
Ex post facto laws, 746, 1330
Expropriation by foreign government, 700

Fair Labor Standards Act, 281, 286, 293
Fair trial. *See* Judges; Newspaper, trial by
Fairness doctrine, 1247, 1251
Federal common law, 33, 179, 849
Federal Communications Act, 616
Federal courts
  congressional power over, 136-146
  jurisdiction, 37-41
Federal Employers' Liability Act
  enactment and constitutionality, 218
  workmen's compensation as affected by, 457
Federalism, basic issues of, 148-153. *See also* Bill of Rights, Fourteenth Amendment as incorporating
Ferries
  establishment, state regulation of, 410, 411, 432
  public interest in, 1080
Firearms Act, 240
Fish. *See also* Game; Oysters
  catching, state regulation of, 398, 754
  use, state regulation of, 400
Flag salute, 1210, 1345
Food and Drug Act, 203, 234, 236, 298
Food Stamp Act of 1964, 939, 941
Foreign commerce, 185, 192, 380, 432, 522, 531, 544
Foreign countries. *See* Constitution, overseas
Fourteenth Amendment. *See* Civil War Amendments: Due Process; Equal Protection
Franchise taxes, state or local
  entrance fee distinguished, 497
  gross receipts as measure of, 489, 497, 534
  income as measure of, 549, 551
  interstate business, exclusively, 482, 534, 552
  property as measure of, 492, 493, 497
  railroads, 489
  telegraph companies, 493, 497
Freedom of Information Act of 1967, 1259
Freedom of religious belief. *See also* Conscientious objectors; Religion, prohibition of establishment of
  Bible reading in schools, 108, 1370
  character of, 1345, 1350, 1367, 1370, 1376

1416 Index

Freedom of religious belief (cont.)
"Fourteenth Amendment, incorporation in, 1179, 1354, 1370
nonestablishment, relationship to, 1354
Freedom of speech and press
advertising, political and commercial, 1247-1257
business, persons engaged in, 1293
"captive audience," 1189
"clear and present danger" test for, 1137
common-law restrictions on, 1179
federal and state restrictions of, contrasted, 1289
Freedom of Information Act of 1967, 1259
history, 1144
hostile audience, 1179, 1189
investigation of lobbying as denial of, 1325
libel, 1146, 1210-1228
literature, licensing distribution of, 797, 801, 1180-1181
media, access to and by, 1247-1260
moving pictures, 1173, 1283, 1284, 1291
obscenity, control of, 1284, 1285, 1290, 1291, 1293
picketing, 1203
"preferred position," 34, 800, 1187
press and, 1137, 1149, 1157, 1158, 1305-1310
prior restraint, 1146, 1149, 1157, 1283, 1284, 1291
privacy, invasion of, 1210, 1228
privilege of citizenship, 858-859
public places, 797, 1179, 1183, 1189, 1192, 1199, 1203, 1205, 1207, 1209
rationale of, 1175, 1187, 1286
sound trucks and amplifiers, control of, 1184
symbolic speech, 1205, 1207, 1209
Freight, tax on, 523, 525, 528
Fruit
citrus, unripe, 397
marketing regulation of, 401, 478
Full faith and credit clause, 456, 615
Funds, impoundment of, 671

Gambling, 230, 241, 286
Game. See also Fish; Oysters
migratory birds, state and national power over, 397, 695
removal from state, 397
Gas
federal regulation of, 411
gathering of, excise tax on, 540
sales and service, state regulation of, 390, 411
wellhead, price of, 412
Gasoline taxes, state and local, 434
Gold clauses, 310, 317, 322, 324
Grain elevators, state regulations of, 1078
Grain Futures Act, 241

Granger cases, 213, 1078
Grants-in-aid, 263, 607
Gross receipts taxes, state or local. See also Franchise taxes, state or local
advertising, 540
income taxes distinguished, 545
property taxes, in lieu of, 528
railroads, 523, 525
steamships, 528
stevedoring, 531
Group libel. See Libel
Guilt by association. See Assembly, right of; Association; Test oaths

Habeas corpus. See also Remedies
courts-martial, power of civil courts to review, 1048, 1054, 1073
federal officers, 616
federal prisoners, power of state court to discharge, 647
military tribunals abroad, 716, 718-725
American, 719
international, 716
suspension of writ of, 1048, 1054, 1061
Happiness, pursuit of, 770, 1082
Hawaii, martial law in, after Pearl Harbor, 1061
Hearing, right to, 1041, 1044
Highways, use of
charge for, 434, 488
state regulation of, 407, 408, 412, 426, 465, 467
History, English, uses of, in constitutional decision, 16, 134, 1065, 1079, 1326-1327
Home Owners' Loan Act, 324-325
Hours of work, 1082, 1083, 1088. See also Labor relations
Housing, racial restrictions in, 808, 814, 822, 1111-1112

Immunity from liability, executive and legislative branches, 673-679, 862-864, 1330
Imports
definition of, 185, 189
state taxation of, 185, 189, 192, 380
Impoundment of funds, president and, 671
Income taxes, net, state, or local. See also Franchise taxes, state or local
apportionment, 545, 549, 551
congressional legislation concerning (1959), 560
gross receipts taxes distinguished, 545, 548
interstate business, 555, 560
jurisdiction, 562
Incorporation, federal power of, 155, 162
Incorporation of Bill of Rights. See Bill of Rights
Indians, American, citizenship of, 736-737
Indigence, 341, 907, 912
Informers, 1230, 1235, 1322

Inheritance or estate taxes, state or local, jurisdiction, 562
Injunctions
   federal courts, limitations on issuance in, 39
   matters subject to federal statutes, enforcement, 39, 648
   state statutes, enforcement, 38-39, 648
   taxes, collection of, 259
   United States, suit by, 220, 225, 300
In lieu taxes, state or local, 528
Inns, exclusion of Negroes from, 300, 539
Inspection laws, 206, 362, 365, 366, 367, 372, 438
Insurance
   benefits, 942
   as commerce, 299
   cooperative regulation of, 606
   escheat of policy proceeds, 448
   state regulation of, 441, 444, 455
Intergovernmental immunities
   eminent domain, 647
   federal agencies, state regulation affecting, 643, 645
   federal agencies, contractors, and employees, state taxation of, 563, 574, 623, 624, 630, 634, 641
   government bonds, taxation of, 641
   habeas corpus, 647
   mandamus, 647
   state agencies, federal regulation affecting, 647
   state agencies, contractors, and employees, federal taxation of, 621, 623, 630, 634, 641
Interstate commerce. *See also* State or local regulation; Taxes, state or local
   federal regulation of, 225-309
Interstate Commerce Act, 213
Interstate compact, 608, 612
Interstate sales
   sales or gross receipts taxes on, 564, 565, 572, 574, 578, 588
   use taxes on, 572, 576, 591, 601
Intoxicating liquor
   congressional prohibition of, in wartime, 336
   federal regulation of, 174, 200, 603
   state regulation of, 197, 603
   Twenty-first Amendment, 378, 380, 438
"Irrebuttable presumptions," 939-943

Japanese, relocation of, 345
Jehovah's Witnesses, 797, 1345
Johnson, John G., 229
Joint Resolution of Congress (1934), 697
Judges, liabilities of, 774
Judicial Code (Title 28, U.S.C.), 37
Judicial review, 3, 13-18, 33, 132-135

Judiciary Act of 1789
   Section 13, 6
   Section 25, 21, 26
Judiciary Act of 1937, 261
Jurisdiction
   due process, 441-456, 479
   federal courts, 37, 40, 136-146
Jurors, Negroes, exclusion of, 774
Jury, trial by *See also* Jurors
   consular courts, 709
   federal courts, 1050
   Fourteenth Amendment and, 1035
   occupation Cuba, 712
   unanimity, 1038
Justiciability, 71-87

Kentucky Resolutions, 27
Kidnaping, federal powers over, 345, 790

Labor relations. *See also* Hours of work; Mining
   antitrust laws, 218, 229
   coal mining, 243
   Fair Labor Standards Act, 281, 286
   National Labor Relations Act, 273
   steel strike and seizure, 659, 667
   strike by railroad employees, 220
   wages, regulation of, 242
Labor unions, 273, 1239
Laski, Harold, on federalism, 149
Laundries
   Chinese, controls discriminating against, 869
   license tax on, 359
Law of nature. *See* Natural law
Lawyers
   character and fitness, 1343, 1344
   self-incrimination by, 1343
   test oath for, 1343
Leaflets. *See* Literature, licensing distribution of
Legal Tender Acts, 135, 309
Legislative branch, 673-679
Legislative investigations, 1315, 1322. *See also* Congressional investigations
Legislators
   Civil Rights Acts as applicable to, 1325
   debate, freedom of, 1325
   motives of, 29, 1320-1321, 1328
Libel, 1146, 1210-1228
License taxes, state or local. *See also* Freedom of speech, prior restraint as denial of
   broker or commission merchant, 487
   doing business, 482, 485, 487
   drummers, 354, 358
   fixed-fee license taxes, 482
   hotel rooms, sales from, 358
   laundry business and trucks, 359
   lightning rod agents, 482
   liquor, sale of, 365, 378

1418 Index

License taxes, state or local (*cont.*)
   literature, distribution of, 797, 802
   motor vehicles, 489
   peddlers, 352
   Pullman Company, 488
   telegraph companies, 487
Liquor. *See* Intoxicating liquor
Literature, licensing distribution of, 797, 802, 1179
Local option laws, 202
Lotteries, 230
Loyalty. *See* Test oaths

Mandamus
   federal officers, 3, 647
   state officers, 647
Mann Act, 233, 345
Maritime law, 206, 333, 606
Martial law. *See also* Courts-martial and military commissions; Military powers
   meaning of, 1050, 1067
   proclamations of, 1050, 1061
Meat, state or local regulation of sale of, 362, 365
Migration, interstate. *See* Movement of persons
Migratory Bird Treaty, 695
Military commissions. *See* Courts-martial and military commissions
Military powers. *See also* Courts-martial and military commissions; War powers
   compulsory military service, 80
   habeas corpus, president's power to suspend writ of, 1048
   Japanese-Americans, exclusion of, from West Coast, 345
   judicial control of military authorities, 1054
Military Selective Service Act of 1967, 80
Milk
   marketing of, 293, 401
   pasteurization of, 367
   price, regulation of, 381, 388, 1089
   sale, local regulation of, 367, 372, 381, 388, 401
Mining
   miscellaneous regulations concerning, 243, 1083
   regulation of hours in, 1083
Mootness, 73-75, 85-87, 108, 750, 1120
Mortgages, moratoria on foreclosure of, 1387
Motive, legislative. *See* Legislators
Motor Carrier Act (federal), 465, 466
Movement of persons, 339-352
   federal regulation of, 300, 345
   state regulation and taxation of, 339, 341, 345, 427, 429, 432
Moving pictures. *See* Freedom of speech, moving pictures

Narcotic drugs, 239-240, 867
National Association for the Advancement of Colored People, 1235, 1241, 1322
National banks, 155, 162, 326
National Industrial Recovery Act, 242
Nationality. *See* United States citizenship
National Labor Relations Act, 273
Nationals, distinguished from citizens, 738
Natural gas. *See* Gas
Natural Gas Act (federal), 411
Naturalization
   Constitution as affecting, 739
   pacifists as entitled to, 739
   pre-Constitution powers as to, 739
Natural law, due process as, 754, 995-996, 1002, 1077
Natural resources. *See* Fish; Game; Gas; Oysters
Navigable waters, 206, 209, 326, 332, 334-335. *See also* Navigation
Navigation
   federal power over, 164, 178, 184, 206
   state laws regulating or affecting, 163, 165, 174, 175, 178
Negroes. *See* Racial discrimination
New Deal cases, 260
Newspaper, trial by, 1305. *See also* Contempt of court; Freedom of speech and press
Ninth Amendment, 1112
Nominating conventions. *See* Conventions
Noncitizen nationals, 738
Norris-La Guardia Act, 137-138

Obscenity, 1283-1305. *See also* Freedom of speech, obscenity, control of
"Occupation of the field." *See* Preemption
Offshore resources, 333
Oil, 333
Old-age pensions. *See* Social security legislation
Oleomargarine, 200, 239, 298, 643
Olney, Richard, memorandum concerning Pullman strike, 218
Original package doctrine, 185, 188, 192, 197, 200, 380
Overbreadth, 1342
Overruling decisions
   constitutional problems presented by, 1400
   prospective overruling, 133, 634
Oysters, state power to control taking of, 754. *See also* Fish

Pacifists. *See* Conscientious objectors; Naturalization, pacifists as entitled to
Packers and Stockyards Act, 228
Pardoning Power, president and, 667
Parks. *See* Freedom of speech, public places
Peddlers. *See* Salesmen, drummers, or peddlers

Petitions to redress grievances
   free speech, relationship to, 1202
   privilege of citizenship, 857
Philippine Organic Act, 658
Picketing, 1203
Pilotage, 876
Pocket veto, president and, 672
Police power
   contracts, existing, as affecting, 1387
   eminent domain compared, 1095, 1097
   "petty larceny" of, 1095
Political activities and contributions, 1239, 1260-1283
Political Questions, 71, 80, 84, 700, 716, 746, 953
Poll taxes, 981
Portal-to-Portal Act, 1395
Portal-to-portal litigation, 138
Pound, Roscoe, on federalism, 151
Preemption, 164, 174, 178, 456-478
President
   appointing and removal power, 3, 243, 669
   executive privilege, 679
   impoundment of funds, 671
   pardoning power, 667
   pocket veto, 672
   power to commit military forces to action, 706
   relation to courts in determining constitutionality of laws, 13-14, 15, 252
   war powers of, 336, 659
Press. See Freedom of speech and press
Price control. See also Rates; Rent control
   coal industry, 243, 252
   milk industry, 381, 388, 1089
   wartime legislation, 139, 300, 613
Primaries. See Elections, federal powers over
Prior restraint. See Freedom of speech and press
Privacy, invasion of, 1210, 1228
Privacy, right of, 1126. See also Congressional investigations, as limitation on; Privacy, invasion of; Searches and seizures; Self-incrimination, privilege against
Private use, taking for, 1095. See also Eminent domain
Privileges and immunities of citizens. See also Bill of Rights; State citizenship; United States citizenship
   character and scope of, 339, 341, 754, 785, 867
   movement, interstate, 339, 341
Procedure, history of, as history of liberty, 993
Property. See Public interest, business and property affected by
Property of the United States
   jurisdiction over reservations, 624
   power of disposal, 326
Property taxes, state or local. See also Franchise taxes, state or local

   airline equipment, 505-506, 508
   cattle at market, 519
   Minnesota airline equipment tax, 505-506
   moving goods, 519-523
   railroad rolling stock, 499-506, 513
   ships, barges, 505, 506
   uniform airline equipment tax,
Prosecution, interstate movement to avoid, 345
Prospective overruling, 133, 634, 1400
Prostitution, transportation for, 345
Public employment, 121, 621, 630, 635, 1339
Public interest, business and property affected by, 1078, 1089
Public schools. See Schools and colleges
Public utilities. See Public interest, business and property affected by
Public Utility Holding Company Act, 101-102
Pullman Company
   license tax, per car, 488
   property taxes on cars, 499
Pullman strike, 218, 220
Punishment, severity of as affecting constitutionality, 871

Racial discriminations. See Chinese; Japanese
   carriers, segregation by, 427, 429, 432, 777, 881
   citizenship, 729, 755
   housing discriminations, 814, 822, 841, 902, 1111-1112
   inns, exclusion from, 300, 777
   interstate travel, 864
   juries, exclusion from, 774
   libels, 1210
   political segregation, 953
   poll taxes, 981
   private discrimination, 864, 866
   recreational facilities, exclusion from, 308
   restaurants, exclusion from, 304, 823
   restrictive covenants, 808, 813
   sedition and, 1158
   separate schools, 884-902
   suffrage, right of, 943, 948, 974, 981
   theatres, discrimination in, 300, 777
Railroad Retirement Act, 241
Railroads
   franchise taxes, 489
   gross receipts taxes, 525, 528
   holding companies, 227-228
   property taxes, 481
   rates, regulation of, 210-219
   rolling stock, property taxes on, 504, 513
   strike by employees, 220
   train length, 418
   workmen's compensation, liability for, 457
Raisins, marketing of, state regulation, 401
Rates, states' legislative power to fix, 1078, 1082, 1089. See also Price control; Rent control

1420 Index

Real estate, property taxes and valuation, 481
Reapportionment, 956-974
Reconstruction, 141, 760
Religion, prohibition of establishment of. *See also* Bible reading; Freedom of religious belief; Schools and colleges; Sunday laws
  history of, 1354-1357, 1358
  meaning of, 1351-1352
  religious freedom, relationship to, 1354-1357
Remedies
  alterations in, 1387, 1395
  exhaustion of, in state, 860
Removal of causes, 616
Rent control, 54, 336
Requisitions. *See* Eminent domain
Restaurants, exclusion of Negroes from, 300, 304, 823
Restrictive covenants, 808, 813
Retroactivity. *See also* Contracts clause; Ex post facto laws; Remedies
  generally, 1387
  overruling decision as constituting, 1400
"Reverse discrimination," 906

Safety Appliance Acts, 217
Salesmen, drummers, or peddlers
  licenses, state or local, 352, 354, 358
  regulation, state or local, 373
Sales taxes, state or local. *See also* Use taxes
  automobiles manufactured extrastate, 564
  exports, 531, 544
  interstate sales, 565, 574, 578, 583, 588
Schools and colleges. *See also* Equal protection of the laws; Teachers
  Bible reading, 108, 1370
  flag salutes, 1345
  nonpublic, state aid to, 1350, 1380, 1385
  parochial, 1350
  release time programs, 1359
  teachers, rights of, 1041
Searches and seizures
  Fourteenth Amendment, applicability of, 1008
  unreasonable
    evidence secured by, 1006, 1008, 1010
    prevention of, 1008
Seditious libel, 13, 1134, 1146
Segregated institution, private, government assistance to, 835
Selective Service cases, 139-141
Self-incrimination, privilege against
  compulsory testimony as violation of, 1012
  due process of Fourteenth Amendment, relationship to, 1012
  stomach pump, extraction of evidence by, 999
Separability, 243, 872, 876
Separation of powers, 649-673

Sex discrimination, 930, 934
Shanghaiing sailors, 345
Ships, property taxes on, 505-506
Shrimp, *See also* Fish catching 398, state regulation of, 398
Sidewalks, distribution of literature on, 1179
Sit-ins, 813
Slavery, 521, 523. *See also* Civil War Amendments
Social security legislation, 262, 272
Sound trucks and amplifiers, control of, 1184
Sovereign immunity
  congressional waiver of, 130
  generally, 128, 862
  withdrawal of consent to sue United States on existing contracts, 318-319
Spending power, 103, 253, 262
Standing to sue
  advisory opinions, 13, 49, 96, 1261
  declaratory judgments, 94, 108, 121, 1339
  estoppel to raise constitutional questions, 91
  injury affecting complainant, 103, 111, 118
  standing to raise constitutional issues, 87, 91, 793, 1083, 1112, 1119, 1175, 1179, 1235, 1370
  states, 103, 107, 178, 262, 390
  taxpayers
    federal, 103, 111, 118, 253, 262
    local, 108, 122, 1350, 1359, 1370
Stare decisis, scope of in constitutional law, 134, 891, 893, 948, 1012, 1091, 1184, 1345, 1359, 1400
State action, 178, 220, 771, 773, 788, 793, 797, 808, 813, 823, 828, 832, 840, 1376. *See also* Courts, action of, as state action
State citizenship. *See also* Privileges and immunities of citizens; United States citizenship
  privileges of, 753, 763, 777
State or local regulation
  animals, dead, 400
  carriers, motor, 407, 408, 412, 465
  cattle, importation of, 362, 366
  citrus fruit, unripe, 397
  ferries
    establishment of, 410
    rates, 411
  fish, use of, 400
  game, removal of, 397
  gas
    rates, 411
    sales and service, 390, 411
  highways, use of, 407, 408, 412, 465
  indigent persons, transportation of, 341, 345
  insurance, 441, 444, 448, 455
  liquor
    sale of, 197, 200, 378
    transportation of, 438

Index 1421

meat, sale of, 362, 365
milk
   prices of, 381, 388, 1089
   sale of, 367, 372, 381, 401
railroads, liability to employees of, 457
raisins, marketing of, 401
salesmen, house-to-house, 358, 373
segregation by carriers, 427, 429, 432, 881
shrimp, packing, of, 398
trains, length of, 418
trucks, size and weight of, 412, 465, 467
water, removal of, 397
wheat, marketing of, 390
State or local taxation. See Taxes, state or local
States, litigation
   suits against, 128
   suits by, 103, 178, 390
Statutory coverage of commerce, 297
Steel seizure case, 659, 667
Sterilization, 872
Stevedoring, state or local tax on, 531
Stockholders' suits, 87, 91, 243
Stockyards, 228
Stomach pump, 999
Strikebreakers, transportation of, 345
Strike by railroad employees, 220
Submerged Lands Act, 333
Subversive organizations. See Guilt by association; Test oaths
Suffrage. See also Reapportionment
   citizenship, relation to, 756
   denial of on racial grounds, 756, 943, 948, 974, 981
   elections, federal powers over, 943, 945, 974
   generally, 943-992
Sunday laws, 1363
Switzerland, judicial review in, 17
Symbolic speech, 1205, 1207, 1209

Tapes Case, 671, 679
Tariff Act of 1890, 654
Taxation. See also Intergovernmental immunities
   collateral motives, effect of, 237, 240
   federal power of, 237, 240, 243, 253, 262
   public vs. private purposes of, 1350
   uniformity of, in Puerto Rico, 712
Taxes, state or local. See Franchise taxes; Gasoline taxes; Gross receipts taxes; Income taxes; Inheritance or estate taxes; In lieu taxes; License taxes; Property taxes; Sales taxes; Transportation taxes; Use taxes
Taxpayers' suit. See Standing to sue, taxpayers
Teachers
   right to hearing, 1041
   test oath for, 122, 1339

Telegraph companies
   franchise taxes, 493, 497
   license tax, fixed-fee, 487-488
Tennessee Valley Authority, validity, suits attacking, 87, 91, 99, 326
Terrorism, 1173
Testifying, interstate movement to avoid, 345
Test oaths, 1330-1344
Theatres, discrimination against Blacks in, 304, 777
Third degree. See Confessions, forced
Three-judge courts, 37, 99, 262, 478, 479
Tidelands. See Offshore resources
Tobacco
   cigarette taxes, 606
   marketing control, federal, 297
Tort Claims Act, 131
Trademarks, 299
Transportation taxes, state or local
   freight, 523
   gross receipts, 525, 528, 531, 534
   stevedoring, 531
Treason
   citizens overseas, 492
   elements of, 1061
Treaty power. See also Executive agreements; Treaties
   citizenship provision of Fourteenth Amendment, as affected by, 734
   history of, 690
   possible limits on, 693, 695
   proposed constitutional amendments with respect to, 705
Trucks. See Carriers, motor
Twenty-first Amendment, 378, 380, 438

Unconstitutional conditions, 493, 497
Unconstitutional federal action, liability for, 869
Unconstitutional statute, effects of, 133
Unemployment compensation. See Social security legislation
Uniform Transfer of Dependents Act, 345
United Nations Charter, as law in the United States, 692
United States citizenship. See also Nationals; Privileges and immunities of citizens
   acquisition by birth, 734
   after the Fourteenth Amendment, 741, 743, 762
   American Indians, 736-737
   before the Fourteenth Amendment, 729, 734, 755, 760
   free speech as privilege of, 858-859
   jurisdiction to tax, 738
   loss of. See Expatriation
   privileges of, 339, 341, 858-859
   voluntary renunciation of, 740

United States government, judicial and congressional powers to protect, 220, 349, 473, 943. *See also* Intergovernmental immunities
Urban renewal, 1105
Use taxes, state and local
  collection of, 572, 576, 591, 601
  sales taxes, compensating for, 385, 572, 576, 591, 601

Vagueness
  act establishing Un-American Activities Committee, 1317, 1325
  free speech cases, 1162, 1317, 1322, 1339
Valuation. *See* Rates
Vietnam, U.S. military involvement in, 80, 84
Virginia Resolutions, 14
Voting, property qualifications for, 984. *See also* Suffrage
Voting Rights Act of 1965, 902
  amendments (1970), 987

Wagering, tax on, 241
Wages and hours, regulation of *See* Labor relations; Hours of work
War, declaration of, 54
War, law of, 1054

War powers. *See also* Military powers; control; Rent control
  dangers of, 336
  delegation of powers, 336
  manufacturing and sale of liquor, 336
  presidential, 336
  prices, 613
  rents, 335
War Powers Resolution, 54
Warehouses. *See* Grain elevators
Water, removal from state, 397. *See also* Navigable waters
Webb-Kenyon Act, 603
Wheat, marketing, state or local regulation of, 390
Windfall tax, 259
Women
  equality of, 877, 1091
  regulation of employment
    hours of work, 1088
    in bars, 877
    wages, 1091
Workmen's compensation, applicability to railroads, 457

Zoning, 1105, 1109, 1111